W9-CTW-227

Contemporary Authors

Contemporary Authors

A Bio-Bibliographical Guide to
Current Writers in Fiction, General Nonfiction,
Poetry, Journalism, Drama, Motion Pictures,
Television, and Other Fields

FRANCES C. LOCHER
Editor

volumes 89-92

GALE RESEARCH COMPANY • THE BOOK TOWER • DETROIT, MICHIGAN 48226

CONTEMPORARY AUTHORS

Published by
Gale Research Company, Book Tower, Detroit, Michigan 48226
Each Year's Volumes Are Revised About Five Years Later

Frederick G. Ruffner, *Publisher*   James M. Ethridge, *Editorial Director*

Christine Nasso, *General Editor, Contemporary Authors*

Frances C. Locher, *Editor, Original Volumes*

Ann F. Ponikvar, *Associate Editor*
Anne M. Guerrini, Victoria France Hutchinson, B. Hal May,
Kathleen Ceton Newman, Nancy M. Rusin, Les Stone,
David Versical, Barbara A. Welch,
and Martha G. Winkel, *Assistant Editors*
Kim Jakubiak, Juanita M. Krygier, Norma Sawaya,
Shirley Seip, and Laurie M. Serwatowski, *Editorial Assistants*

Alan E. Abrams and Adele Sarkissian, *Contributing Editors*
Martha J. Abele, Andrea Geffner, Arlene True,
and Benjamin True, *Sketchwriters*
John F. Baker, Al Purdy, Jean W. Ross,
and Richard E. Ziegfeld, *Interviewers*

Eunice Bergin, *Copy Editor*
Michaeline Nowinski, *Production Director*

Special recognition is given to the staffs of
Journalist Biographies Master Index
and
Young People's Literature Department

ISBN 0-8103-0048-6

Preface

The more than 1,500 entries in *Contemporary Authors,* Volumes 89-92, bring to nearly 59,000 the number of authors, either living or deceased since 1960, now represented in the *Contemporary Authors* series. *CA* includes nontechnical writers in all genres—fiction, nonfiction, poetry, drama, etc.—whose books are issued by commercial, risk publishers or by university presses. Authors of books published only by known vanity or author-subsidized firms are ordinarily not included. Since native language and nationality have no bearing on inclusion in *CA,* authors who write in languages other than English are included in *CA* if their works have been published in the United States or translated into English.

Although *CA* focuses primarily on authors of published books, the series also encompasses prominent persons in communications: newspaper and television reporters and correspondents, columnists, newspaper and periodical editors, photojournalists, syndicated cartoonists, screenwriters, television scriptwriters, and other media people.

No charge or obligation is attached to a *CA* listing. Authors are included in the series solely on the basis of the above criteria and their interest to *CA* users.

Compilation Methods

The editors make every effort to secure information directly from the authors through questionnaires and personal correspondence. If authors of special interest to *CA* users are deceased or fail to reply to requests for information, material is gathered from other reliable sources. Biographical dictionaries are checked (a task made easier through the use of Gale's *Biographical Dictionaries Master Index, Author Biographies Master Index,* and other volumes in the "Gale Biographical Index Series"), as are bibliographical sources, such as *Cumulative Book Index* and *The National Union Catalog.* Published interviews, feature stories, and book reviews are examined, and often material is supplied by the authors' publishers. All sketches, whether prepared from questionnaires or through extensive research, are sent to the authors for review prior to publication.

The value of such cooperation by the individual authors listed in *CA* is very great. Not only do most authors check manuscripts of their entries, but some often work even more closely with *CA*'s editors, both to ensure the completeness of their listings and to provide incisive sidelights—comments on their lives and writings, personal philosophies, etc. Among the authors in this volume who have amplified their sketches with lengthy sidelights are Nicholas de Lange, who talks about his approach to doing translations; Pavel Litvinov, a physics lecturer and human rights activist expelled from the U.S.S.R., who speaks of his experiences resulting from his activism; and Janet McFadden Patterson, who comments about some medical and moral issues of particular importance to women.

If an author of special importance is difficult to reach, the editors sometimes engage an expert's assistance to ensure that the sketch is as complete and accurate as possible. Film critic and screenwriter Joseph McBride, for example, very generously reviewed Billy Wilder's entry and supplied his own comments for incorporation into assistant editor B. Hal May's adroitly written sidelights.

Similar efforts go into the compilation of full-length entries on deceased authors of current interest to *CA* readers. This volume contains listings on, among others, Albert Camus, Robert Frost, Golda Meir, Sean O'Casey, Norman Rockwell, Richard Rodgers, and William Carlos Williams.

In addition to the individuals mentioned above, numerous other authors and media people of particular interest are sketched in this volume, such as Theodor W. Adorno, Edwin E. Aldrin, Jr., Stewart Alsop, Jose Maria Arguedas, Rudolf Bing, Jim Bouton, Lenny Bruce, Whitey Ford, Zbigniew Herbert, Michael Herr, Werner Herzog, Heinar Kipphardt, Ann Landers, Frank Mankiewicz, Claude Mauriac, Ed McMahon, David Rudkin, Claude Simon, Lucian K. Truscott IV, Arnold Vieth von Golssenau, and Andrei Voznesensky.

New Feature: Exclusive Interviews

Beginning with this volume, *Contemporary Authors* includes exclusive new primary information. The new section of the sketch headed *CA INTERVIEWS THE AUTHORS* presents a never-before-published conversation with the author, prepared specifically for *CA*. Previously, authors' remarks to *CA*'s editors were reserved for the sidelights section of their sketches. While no limitations are placed on the length of such material, the editors believed that readers might want even more comment from some of *CA*'s authors.

The new interview feature, with its give-and-take format, provides such additional commentary. Through *CA*'s interviewers, the user is given the opportunity to learn the authors' thoughts, in depth, about their craft. Subjects chosen for interviews are authors who the editors feel hold special interest for *CA*'s readers, and their remarks are a further source of useful primary material.

Authors in this volume whose sketches include interviews are George Birimisa, Michael French, Shirley Ann Grau, James Herndon, Joshua Lockwood Logan, John Patrick, Thomas Hunton Rogers, Anne Richardson Roiphe, Joseph Rosenblatt, Mary Lee Settle, Charles Simmons, Isaiah Elezer Trunk, and Hugh Wheeler.

Obituary Notices Make *CA* Timely and Comprehensive

To be as timely and comprehensive as possible, *CA* publishes obituary notices on deceased authors within the scope of the series. These notices provide date and place of birth and death, highlight the author's career and writings, and list other sources where additional biographical information and obituaries may be found. To distinguish them from full-length sketches, obituaries are identified with the heading *OBITUARY NOTICE.*

CA includes obituary notices both for authors who already have full-length sketches in earlier *CA* volumes, thus effectively completing the sketches, and for authors not yet sketched in the series. Twenty percent of the obituary notices contained in this volume are for authors with listings already in *CA*. Deceased authors of special interest presently represented in the series only by obituary notices are scheduled for full-length sketch treatment in forthcoming *CA* volumes.

Cumulative Index Should Always Be Consulted

Since *CA* is a multi-volume series that does not repeat author entries from volume to volume, the cumulative index published in alternate new volumes of *CA* should always be consulted to locate an individual author's listing. Each new volume contains authors not previously included in the series and is revised approximately five years after its original publication. The cumulative index indicates the original or revised volume in which an author appears. Authors removed from the revision cycle and placed in the *CA Permanent Series* are listed in the index as having appeared in specific original volumes of *CA* (for the benefit of those who do not hold *Permanent Series* volumes), and as having their finally revised sketches in a specific *Permanent Series* volume.

For the convenience of *CA* users, the *CA* cumulative index also includes references to all entries in three related Gale series—*Contemporary Literary Criticism,* which is devoted entirely to current criticism of major authors, poets, and playwrights, *Something About the Author,* a series of heavily illustrated sketches on juvenile authors and illustrators, and *Authors in the News,* a compilation of news stories and feature articles from American newspapers and magazines covering writers and other members of the communications media.

As always, suggestions from users about any aspect of *CA* will be welcomed.

CONTEMPORARY AUTHORS

**Indicates that a listing has been compiled from secondary sources believed to be reliable, but has not been personally verified for this edition by the author sketched.*

A

ABBOTT, Claude Colleer 1889-1971

OBITUARY NOTICE—See index for *CA* sketch: Born April 17, 1889, in Broomfield, Chelmsford, Essex, England; died September 17, 1971, in England. Educator, poet, and author of scholarly works. Abbott, who served on the faculty of the University of Durham from 1932 until his death, was best known for his discovery of a valuable collection of James Boswell's papers. Obituaries and other sources: *The Author's and Writer's Who's Who,* 6th edition, Burke's Peerage, 1971; *AB Bookman's Weekly,* November 8, 1971.

* * *

ABRAHAM, Gerald Ernest Heal 1904-

PERSONAL: Born March 9, 1904, in Newport, Isle of Wight, England; son of Ernest and Dorothy Mary Abraham; married Isobel Patsie Robinson, May 2, 1936; children: one daughter. *Home:* Old School House, Ebernoe, near Petworth, Sussex, England.

CAREER: Radio Times, London, England, assistant editor, 1935-39; *Listener,* London, deputy editor, 1939-42; British Broadcasting Corp. (BBC), London, director of gramophone department, 1942-47; University of Liverpool, Liverpool, England, James and Constance Alsop Professor of Music, 1947-62; British Broadcasting Corp., assistant controller of music, 1962-67; *Daily Telegraph,* London, music critic, 1967-68; University of California, Berkeley, Ernest Bloch Professor of Music, 1968-69. Chairman of music section of *Critics' Circle,* 1944-46; deputy chairman of Haydn Institute (Cologne), 1961-68; governor of Dolmetsch Foundation, 1970-75. *Member:* International Society for Music Education (president, 1958-61), British Academy (fellow), Royal Musical Association (president, 1970-74), Royal Society of Arts (fellow), Royal Academy of Music, Early English Church Music Committee (chairman, 1970). *Awards, honors:* D.Mus. from University of Durham, 1961, University of Liverpool, 1978, and University of Southampton, 1979; D.F.A. from University of California, Berkeley, 1969.

WRITINGS: Borodin: The Composer and His Music, W. Reeves, 1927, A.M.S. Press, 1976; *Nietzsche,* Macmillan, 1933, Haskell House, 1974; *This Modern Stuff: A Fairly "Plaine and Easie" Introduction to Contemporary Music,* Archer Press, 1933, 2nd revised edition, Duckworth, 1939, published as *This Modern Music,* Norton, 1952; *Tolstoy,* Duckworth, 1935, Haskell House, 1974; *Studies in Russian Music: Critical Essays,* W. Reeves, 1935, Scribner's, 1936, reprinted, Books for Libraries, 1968; (With Michel D. Calvocoressi) *Masters of Russian Music,* Duckworth, 1936, Johnson Reprint, 1971; *Dostoevsky,* Duckworth, 1936, Haskell House, 1974; *A Hundred Years of Music,* Knopf, 1938, 3rd edition, Aldine, 1964; *On Russian Music: Critical and Historical Studies,* W. Reeves, 1939, Johnson Reprint, 1970; *Chopin's Musical Style,* Oxford University Press, 1939, reprinted, 1960.

Beethoven's Second-Period Quartets, Oxford University Press, 1942, Scholarly Press, 1978; *Eight Soviet Composers,* Oxford University Press, 1943, Greenwood Press, 1970; *Rimsky-Korsakov: A Short Biography,* Duckworth, 1945, A.M.S. Press, 1976; (editor) *Tchaikovsky: A Symposium,* Lindsay Drummond, 1945, published as *The Music of Tchaikovsky,* Norton, 1946, reprinted, 1974; (with Calvocoressi) *Masters of Russian Music,* Duckworth, 1945; (editor) Calvocoressi, *Mussorgsky: The Master Musicians,* Dutton, 1946, Collier Books, 1962; (editor) *Schubert: A Symposium,* Lindsay Drummond, 1946; (editor) *The Music of Schubert,* Norton, 1947, Kennikat, 1969; (editor) *The Music of Sibelius,* Norton, 1947, Da Capo Press, 1975; (editor) *Sibelius: A Symposium,* Lindsay Drummond, 1948; *Mussorgsky: Boris Godunov, Rimsky-Korsakov Version,* Boosey & Hawkes, 1948; (editor) *Grieg: A Symposium,* Lindsay Drummond, 1948, University of Oklahoma Press, 1950, Greenwood Press, 1971; *Design in Music,* Oxford University Press, 1949; *Tchaikovsky: A Short Biography,* Duckworth, 1949.

(Editor) *Schumann: A Symposium,* Oxford University Press, 1952; (editor) *Handel: A Symposium,* Oxford University Press, 1954; *The Mozart Companion,* edited by Howard Chandler Robbins Landon and Donald Mitchell, Rockliff, 1956, corrected edition, Norton, 1969; (editor with Calvocoressi) *Modest Mussorgsky: His Life and Works,* Essential Books, 1956.

(Editor with Anselm Hughes) *Ars Nova and the Renaissance,* Oxford University Press, 1960; *Slavonic and Romantic Music: Essays and Studies,* St. Martin's, 1968; (editor) *The Age of Humanism,* Oxford University Press, 1968; (translator from the German) Werner Menke, *History of the Trumpet of Bach and Handel,* Brass Press, 1972; *The Tradition of Western Music,* University of California Press, 1974; *The Concise Oxford History of Music,* Oxford University Press, 1979.

General editor of "The History of Music in Sound," Oxford

University Press, 1953; chairman of editorial board of *Grove's Dictionary of Music and Musicians.* Editor of *Monthly Musical Record,* 1945-60. Member of editorial committee of *Musica Britannica.*

SIDELIGHTS: An eminent British musicologist, Abraham has produced studies of Western music ranging from the Medieval origins of Russian music to the electronic experiments of computerized music. His *Studies in Russian Music* and the supplemental *On Russian Music* "form a most valuable repository of first-rate criticism," according to Desmond Shawe-Taylor. The books consider the same period of history, beginning with the operas of Glinka and closing with the Balakirev group.

Another book, *Slavonic and Romantic Music,* studies the relationship of Slavonic music to the Western world. Among chapters devoted to Chopin, Dvorak, Rubinstein, and Tchaikovsky is an account of Fibich's "erotic diary" for piano in which are recorded the secrets of his love affair with Anezka Schulzova. The essays are written in "a delightfully readable style" and provide "valuable insights into compositional techniques and personalities as well," wrote a *Choice* critic. The *Times Literary Supplement* also noted that operatic issues "inspire Professor Abraham to some of his most stimulating and perceptive writing."

In *This Modern Music,* a book directed toward the layman, Abraham explains such modern techniques as polytonality, atonality, and the twelve-tone system. A *New Yorker* reviewer found the style "wonderfully affable and unpretentious," while Rudolph Reti regarded the book as "one of the most transparently written, most persuasively formulated, and, indeed, most elucidating discourses on modern music."

AVOCATIONAL INTERESTS: Walking, languages, military history.

BIOGRAPHICAL/CRITICAL SOURCES: New Statesman, May 20, 1939; *New York Times,* October 1, 1939; *New Yorker,* March 22, 1952; *Saturday Review,* April 26, 1952; *Times Literary Supplement,* August 1, 1968, September 12, 1968; *Choice,* October, 1968.

* * *

ABRAMOV, Emil
See DRAITSER, Emil

* * *

ABRAMS, Alan E(dwin) 1941-

PERSONAL: Born February 19, 1941, in Detroit, Mich.; son of Harry J. (a wholesaler) and Mildred (Volod) Abrams; divorced twice. *Education:* Educated in Detroit, Mich. *Politics:* "Conservative Republican." *Religion:* Jewish. *Address:* P.O. Box 35295, Detroit, Mich. 48235. *Office:* Gale Research Co., Book Tower, Detroit, Mich. 48226.

CAREER: Motown Record Corp., Detroit, Mich., 1959-66, became publicity director; Al Abrams Associates (public relations), Detroit, founder and coordinator of activities, 1967-69; Invictus Record Corp., Detroit, publicity director, 1969-70; Al Abrams Associates, Detroit, coordinator of activities, 1970-73; PR Communications, Detroit, in public relations and publicity, 1973-74; Gale Research Co., Detroit, public relations director, 1974-76, editor of journalism-related reference books, 1976—, contributing editor to *Contemporary Authors.* Founder of Noisy Minority, Inc., 1970. Owner and publisher of W-Hollow Books; co-owner and co-publisher with Al Purdy of Dalloway Press Ltd. Appraiser of books and manuscripts for Internal Revenue Service, 1978—. *Member:* Publishers Publicity Association, Detroit Press Club. *Awards, honors:* Award of merit from U.S. Department of Labor, 1969, for work on "Stay in School" program.

WRITINGS: (Editor) *Journalist Biographies Master Index,* Gale, 1979; (editor) *Media Personnel Directory,* Gale, 1979. Author of forewords to numerous reference books, including *Legends of Le Detroit,* Gale, 1977, and *Who Was Who in Journalism,* Gale, 1978. Contributor of articles to *AB Bookman's Weekly.*

SIDELIGHTS: Abrams told *CA:* "As publicity director of Motown, I was solely responsible for the successful publicity campaign which led Motown to its position of dominance of the international music industry for most of the decade. Through my efforts, the Supremes and the interchangeable 'Motown Sound' and 'Detroit Sound' in popular music became household words. I created and implemented the publicity campaigns for all of the Motown recording artists: Diana Ross and the Supremes, Stevie Wonder, Smokey Robinson and the Miracles, the Temptations, the Four Tops, etc. In addition, I was in charge of all publicity for Berry Gordy, Jr., the founder and president of Motown, as well as for the corporation itself. I was, in fact, Motown's first employee."

Abrams also told *CA* that during his years with Al Abrams Associates, he listed Stax/Volt Record Co. among his key clients. "For Stax/Volt, I established the identity of the 'Memphis Sound,'" he wrote, "and implemented publicity for such artists as the late Otis Redding, Sam and Dave, Booker T. and the M.G.'s, Carla Thomas, etc. The *Detroit Free Press* has, on several occasions, credited me with the publicity success of both the 'Detroit Sound' and the 'Memphis Sound.'

"Through my efforts, Stax/Volt became actively involved in public service campaigns which resulted in my 'ghosting' record liner notes for the late Hubert H. Humphrey, then vice-president of the United States, and Senator Howard H. Baker, Jr., of Tennessee. I coordinated the participation of Stax/Volt in the U.S. Department of Labor's 1968 'Stay in School' campaign.

"In addition to my work with Stax/Volt, I represented a wide range of clients, including *Detroit Scope* magazine and pop artist and film director Andy Warhol. I introduced Mr. Warhol to Detroit audiences through the medium of the 'Mod Wedding,' which I conceived and staged at the Michigan State Fairgrounds. This event made front pages around the world, including those of such diverse publications as the *New York Times, Stars and Stripes,* and *Jewish Daily Forward.*

"As an independent publicist, I created a 'First on the Moon, First on the Mall' shopping center opening promotion for Neil Armstrong. I also introduced Flair pens to the People's Republic of China in 1971, for which I received the thanks of Madame Soong Ching Ling, vice-chairman of the Communist Party. . . . I created the Spiro Agnew Golf Ball ('guaranteed to go right') for Noisy Minority, Inc., in 1970. With Berry Gordy, Jr., I co-wrote 'I Love the Way You Love,' as recorded by Marv Johnson, which became one of 1960's top popular songs."

AVOCATIONAL INTERESTS: "Collection, preservation, and research with primary resource materials on the history of journalism, i.e. newspapers, letters, books, periodicals; collecting historical documents, letters, manuscripts; collecting books, especially association and presentation copies."

BIOGRAPHICAL/CRITICAL SOURCES: Detroit Magazine, March 21, 1965, January 30, 1966; *Los Angeles Herald-Examiner,* July 11, 1965; *Toledo Blade,* August 22, 1965; *Washington Star,* September 18, 1965, November 27, 1965; *R'n'B World,* June 13, 1968; *Ottawa Journal,* July 5, 1968; *Detroit Free Press,* August 27, 1970; Peter Benjaminson, *The Story of Motown,* Grove, 1979.

* * *

ABRAMSON, Jesse P. 1904-1979

OBITUARY NOTICE: Born March 10, 1904, in Mountaindale, N.Y.; died of cancer, June 11, 1979, in Mount Vernon, N.Y. Sportswriter widely recognized as the nation's leading authority on track and field. Abramson, who possessed a profound knowledge of the sport and a phenomenal memory for facts, was nicknamed "The Book" by Dan Parker of the *New York Daily Mirror,* and Stan Saplin, a colleague, once wrote, "the fact is that Jesse Abramson has never lost an argument." He was a reporter for the *New York Herald Tribune* until its demise in 1966, and a writer known for his accuracy and blend of color, background, and news. His many honors included the Grantland Rice Award and the James J. Walker Award. The annual award given by track writers to the outstanding male athlete of the indoor season was named after Abramson. Obituaries and other sources: *New York Times,* June 12, 1979.

* * *

ACHENBAUM, W(ilbert) Andrew 1947-

PERSONAL: Born March 2, 1947, in Philadelphia, Pa.; son of Wilbert A. (in business) and Muriel (a volunteer worker; maiden name, Maine) Achenbaum; married Mary A. Schieve (in historic preservation), April 17, 1971; children: Emily Schieve. *Education:* Amherst College, B.A., 1968; University of Pennsylvania, M.A., 1970; University of Michigan, M.A., 1971, Ph.D., 1976. *Politics:* Liberal. *Religion:* Episcopalian. *Home:* 175 Roycroft Blvd., Snyder, N.Y. 14226. *Office:* Department of History, Canisius College, Buffalo, N.Y. 14208.

CAREER: Canisius College, Buffalo, N.Y., assistant professor of history, 1976—. Assistant research scientist at University of Michigan's Institute of Gerontology, 1977—. *Military service:* U.S. Army, 1970-72. *Member:* American Historical Association Organization of American Historians, Gerontological Society, Social Science History Association, Phi Beta Kappa.

WRITINGS: Old Age in the New Land: The American Experience Since 1790, Johns Hopkins Press, 1978; (with Peggy Ann Kusnerz) *Images of Old Age in America: 1790 to the Present,* Institute of Gerontology, University of Michigan, 1978.

WORK IN PROGRESS: Research on the history of social welfare in America and on the relationships between old age, human values, and social policies, particularly in the twentieth century.

SIDELIGHTS: Achenbaum teaches history, but his research centers on society's traditional historians, the elderly. He is concerned not only with their history but with contemporary society's conceptions of old age. He feels that, so far, these conceptions have been neither accurate nor up to date, and one of his goals is to change the current notion that elderly Americans are problems into a concentration on the problems that these people have.

He writes: "When I began my research in 1972, very few scholars had done any systematic inquiries into the history of old age. Most of the work dealt with twentieth-century issues such as the development of the Social Security Act. I consider myself, therefore, very fortunate to have entered a new historical frontier in its formative stages. Many kind people have helped me over the years: professors at the University of Michigan and elsewhere helped me to broaden my horizons with their hunches, hypotheses, and barbs; friends and students in various seminars I offered between 1975 and 1978 provided a patient and perceptive audience; my wife provided critical support throughout. But in the end, I felt responsible for what I was producing. Since I knew that I was blazing new ground, I considered it imperative to be judicious, exacting, and tentative when I simply did not know the answers; on the other hand, I tried to be provocative enough to stimulate others to do work in the field.

"At the moment there are few professional historians who study aging. I hope the situation changes, and it may well as the continuing decline in teaching positions forces graduate students to apply their expertise to matters of national policy and international concern in efforts to enhance their employment prospects. In this context, I believe that historians have an unprecedented opportunity to play three crucial roles in writing the next chapter in the history of old age in the United States. They can work with other social scientists and humanists to formulate interpretations of that past that facilitate rather than complicate our ability to assess the elderly's current conditions and future prospects. Secondly, historians ought to apply their expertise in trend analysis and actively engage in establishing, monitoring, and evaluating old-age policies and priorities as they affect the elderly and the aging. At the same time, however, they dare not forget that history is both an art and a science. Accordingly, they must continually sensitize themselves, other gerontologists, and concerned citizens, as well as the public at large, to the dynamic ways that implicit and explicit values shape our thoughts and influence our actions about old age.

"It is difficult to scrutinize our assumptions about old age. It is harder still to discard ones that we discover are wrong, stereotypic, or obsolete. It is very painful, or at least quite inconvenient, to acknowledge that the values and the society in which we live are constantly changing, thereby forcing us to challenge prevailing verities and to rethink continually the ways we perceive and deal with growing old in America. Yet it can be done if we hope to address the elderly's real needs and desires rather that our own perceptions and wishes. And it must be done if elderly Americans— and hence ultimately ourselves—are to play roles that ensure their lives meaning and dignity."

AVOCATIONAL INTERESTS: Travel.

BIOGRAPHICAL/CRITICAL SOURCES: Modern Maturity, June, 1979.

* * *

ACKER, Robert Flint 1920-

PERSONAL: Born August 24, 1920; children: four. *Education:* Indiana University, B.A., 1942, M.A., 1948; Rutgers University, Ph.D., 1953. *Religion:* Presbyterian. *Home:* 4 East Lenox St., Chevy Chase, Md. 20015. *Office:* American Society for Microbiology, 1913 I St. N.W., Washington, D.C. 20006.

CAREER: Iowa State University, Ames, assistant professor of bacteriology, 1954-59; Microbiological Associates, Inc., Bethesda, Md., assistant chief of cancer chemotherapy department, became chief of quality control department, 1960-

62, chief of cell and media production department, 1961-62; Department of the Navy, Office of Naval Research, Washington, D.C., director of microbiology program, 1962-69; Northwestern University, Evanston, Ill., professor of biological sciences, director of federal program development, and assistant dean of faculties for research, 1969-74; American Society for Microbiology, Washington, D.C., executive director, 1974—. Diplomate of American Board of Clinical Microbiology. Member of faculty at Georgetown University, 1963-69; guest lecturer at Portsmouth College of Technology, 1969. Head of urban ministry committee of national Presbyterian Church, 1978; vice-president of board of directors of Iona House Center for the Elderly, 1978—. U.S. representative to Organization for Economic Cooperation and Development, 1965-69.

MEMBER: American Society for Microbiology (fellow), Society for Industrial Microbiology (member of board of directors, 1970-73; vice-president, 1973-74), American Institute of Biological Sciences, Council of Engineering and Scientific Society Executives, American Society of Association Executives, Inter-Society Council for Biology and Medicine, Society for General Microbiology (England), Sigma Xi. *Awards, honors:* Outstanding service award from Office of Naval Research, 1969.

WRITINGS: (With Robert K. Jennings) *The Protistan Kingdom,* Van Nostrand, 1970; (co-editor) *Proceedings of the Third International Congress on Marine Corrosion and Fouling,* Northwestern University Press, 1973. Member of editorial board of *Applied Microbiology,* 1962-73.

* * *

ACKERLEY, J(oe) R(andolph) 1896-1967

OBITUARY NOTICE: Born 1896 in London, England; died June 4, 1967, in Herne Hill, Kent, England. Dramatist, novelist, poet, editor, and author of "The Prisoners of War," considered to be one of the best plays inspired by the war. For more than twenty years, Ackerley was the literary editor of the *Listener,* a weekly magazine put out by the British Broadcasting Corp. (BBC). He also served in India as the private secretary and tutor to the ruler of a small state. Obituaries and other sources: J. R. Ackerley *My Father and Myself,* Bodley Head, 1968, Coward, 1969; *Longman Companion to Twentieth Century Literature,* Longman, 1970; *World Authors, 1950-1970,* Wilson, 1975.

* * *

ADAMS, Cedric M. 1902-1961

OBITUARY NOTICE: Born May 27, 1902, in Adrian, Minn.; died February 18, 1961. Radio and television news commentator, and popular columnist for the *Minneapolis Star.* Adams contributed to many magazines, including *Reader's Digest, Esquire,* and *Holiday,* in addition to writing two books, *The Country Plumber* and *Poor Cedric's Almanac.* Obituaries and other sources: *Minnesota Writers,* Denison, 1961; *Who Was Who in America,* 4th edition, Marquis, 1968.

* * *

ADAMS, Howard (Joseph) 1928-

PERSONAL: Born September 8, 1928, in St. Louis, Saskatchewan, Canada: married wife, Margaret (a librarian), February 9, 1957. *Education:* University of British Columbia, B.A., 1950; University of California, Berkeley, M.A., 1963, Ph.D., 1966. *Home:* 517 K St., Davis, Calif. 95616. *Office:* Department of Native American Studies, University of California, Davis, Calif. 95616.

CAREER: Served in Royal Canadian Mounted Police; teacher in Vancouver, British Columbia, 1950-56; teacher in public schools in Coquitlam and New Westminster, British Columbia, 1957-62; University of Saskatchewan, Saskatoon, community development specialist, 1966-68, associate professor of education, 1966-74; University of California, Davis, professor of native American studies, 1975—. Professor at Sir George Williams University, summers, 1970 and 1971. Lecturer. *Member:* Writers' Union of Canada, Saskatchewan Metis Association (president, 1968-70), California Indian Education Association, University of California Faculty Association.

WRITINGS: The Education of Canadians, 1800-1867, Harvest Press, 1968; *Prison of Grass: Canada From a Native Point of View,* General Publishers, 1975; *A History of the Metis of the Northwest,* New Star Books, 1977. Contributor to education journals.

WORK IN PROGRESS: Indian Reservations as Internal Colonies; Colonization: A Psychohistory Process, a monograph.

BIOGRAPHICAL/CRITICAL SOURCES: A History of the Metis and Non-Status Indian in Saskatchewan, Human Rights Commission (Regina, Saskatchewan), 1976.

* * *

ADAMS, Michael C(harles) C(orringham) 1945-

PERSONAL: Born July 26, 1945, in Chesterfield, Derbyshire, England; came to the United States in 1972; son of Albert Edward and Mabel (Clarke) Adams; married Joan Gregory (a writer), August 26, 1969; children: David Owen Edward, Kathleen Saxton Francis. *Education:* University of Wales, B.A. (magna cum laude), 1966; attended University of Kentucky, 1967-69; University of Sussex, D.Phil., 1973. *Home:* 261 Military Parkway, Fort Thomas, Ky. 41075. *Office:* Department of Graduate Studies, Northern Kentucky University, Highland Heights, Ky. 41076.

CAREER: North Nottinghamshire College of Further Education, Worksop, England, lecturer in English and general studies, 1970-71; Northern Kentucky University, Highland Heights, assistant professor, 1972-77, associate professor of history, 1977—, assistant to the president, 1976-77, director of Graduate Center, 1977-78, associate provost for graduate studies, 1978—. *Member:* Phi Alpha Theta, Phi Delta Kappa. *Awards, honors:* Jefferson Davis Award from Museum of the Confederacy, 1979.

WRITINGS: Our Masters the Rebels: A Speculation on Union Military Failure in the East, 1861-1865, Harvard University Press, 1978. Contributor to *Journal of the History of Ideas.*

WORK IN PROGRESS: A novel about American university life; a book on U.S. and British military culture, 1860-1914, with wife, Joan Adams; research for a book on stereotypes of the South.

SIDELIGHTS: Adams comments: "I am a committed educator with a deep belief that Western civilization faces its worst crisis in the test of whether it can restrain its exploitative instincts sufficiently to survive. Education should play a role which it has yet barely recognized, let alone assumed. As a writer, teacher, and graduate dean, I try to look at issues in new ways and adapt present tools to future needs."

* * *

ADAMS, Rolland Leroy 1905(?)-1979

OBITUARY NOTICE: Born c. 1905 in Huntington, Pa.; died

September 1, 1979, in Bethlehem, Pa. Publisher. Adams bought the *Globe-Times* of Bethlehem, Pa., in 1942, after managing the newspaper's financial affairs for twelve years. He also owned several other newspapers, all of which he subsequently sold, including the *Atlantic City Press, Evening Union, Daily World, Bethlehem Times-Herald, Levittown Press, Bucks County News,* and *Easton Free Press.* Obituaries and other sources: *New York Times,* September 3, 1979.

* * *

ADLER, C(arole) S(chwerdtfeger) 1932-

PERSONAL: Born February 23, 1932, in Long Island, N.Y.; daughter of Oscar Edward and Clarice (Landsberg) Schwerdtfeger; married Arnold R. Adler (an engineer), June, 1952; children: Steven and Clifford (twins), Kenneth. *Education:* Hunter College (now of the City University of New York), B.A. (cum laude), 1952; Russell Sage College, M.S., 1964. *Home:* 1350 Ruffner Rd., Schenectady, N.Y. 12309.

CAREER: Worthington Corp., Harrison, N.J., advertising assistant, 1952-54; Niskayuna Middle Schools, Niskayuna, N.Y., English teacher, 1967-77; writer, 1977—. Volunteer worker in child abuse and protection program at local children's shelter, and as tutor of foster children. *Member:* Society of Children's Book Writers, Phi Beta Kappa.

WRITINGS—For children: *The Magic of the Glits,* Macmillan, 1979; *The Silver Coach* (Junior Literary Guild selection), Coward, 1979; *Scott Is My Brother,* Macmillan, 1980. Contributor of articles to adult magazines and stories to *American Girl, Co-Ed,* and *Ingenue.*

WORK IN PROGRESS: Down by the River, publication by Coward expected in 1982; a book about a girl's involvement with a dog at an animal shelter.

SIDELIGHTS: Carole Adler told *CA:* "I loved reading, and at the age of seven decided nothing could be better than to write some of those books myself. My interest in writing for children came from my teaching experience. I learned what complex emotional creatures children are and was touched by their frequently helpless situations in life and their difficulty in communicating with the adults who wield power over them. Children, I discovered, are both more marvelous and much less simple than I had supposed, and well worth writing about and for."

* * *

ADLER, Elmer 1884-1962

OBITUARY NOTICE: Born July 22, 1884, in Rochester, N.Y.; died January 11, 1962. Publisher, editor, educator, and author. Adler was the founder and director for over fifteen years of Pynson Printers, the founder and editor of the *Colophon* for ten years, and one of the founders and first vice-president of Random House. He was affiliated with Princeton University as a research associate of graphic arts, later becoming a member of the faculty. He is the author of *Breaking Into Print* and *On Books, Etc.,* and was a contributor of articles and reviews to various publications. Obituaries and other sources: *Who Was Who in America,* 4th edition, Marquis, 1968.

* * *

ADORNO, Theodor W(iesengrund) 1903-1969

PERSONAL: Born September 11, 1903, in Frankfurt, Germany (now West Germany); died August 6, 1969; son of Oscar Wiesengrund (a wine merchant) and Maria (a singer; maiden name, Calvelli) Adorno; married Gretel Karplus, 1937. *Education:* University of Frankfurt, Ph.D., 1924, postdoctoral study, 1928-31. *Religion:* None. *Politics:* Marxist.

CAREER: Musicologist, sociologist, literary and cultural critic, and philosopher. Institut fuer Sozialforschung (Institute for Social Research), 1928-69, informally associated with Institute in Frankfurt, Germany (now West Germany), in Vienna, Austria, and in New York, N.Y., 1928-38, head of music study in Institute's Office of Radio Research, Princeton, N.J., 1938-41, involved in various Institute projects in California, 1941-49, assistant director in Frankfurt, 1950-55, co-director, 1955-58, director, 1958-69; University of Frankfurt, Frankfurt, professor of philosophy and sociology, 1958-69. *Awards, honors:* Arnold Schoenberg Medal, 1954; Critics' Prize for Literature, 1959; Goethe Medal of the City of Frankfurt, 1963.

WRITINGS—In English: *Memorandum: Music in Radio,* Princeton Radio Research Project, 1938; (with Max Horkheimer) *Philosophische fragmente,* Institute for Social Research (New York), 1944, revised edition published as *Dialektik der Aufklarung: philosophische fragmente,* Querido (Amsterdam), 1947, translation by John Cumming published as *Dialectic of Enlightenment,* Seabury, 1972; *Philosophie der neuen Musik,* Mohr, 1949, translation by Anna G. Mitchell and Wesley V. Blomster published as *Philosophy of Modern Music,* Seabury, 1973; (with others) *The Authoritarian Personality,* Harper, 1950; *Minima Moralia: Reflexionen aus dem beschaedigten Leben,* Suhrkamp, 1951, translation by E.F.N. Jephcott published as *Minima Moralia: Reflections From Damaged Life,* New Left Books, 1974; *Prismen: Kulturkritik und Gesellschaft,* Suhrkamp, 1955, translation by Samuel Weber and Shierry Weber published as *Prisms,* Spearman, 1967.

Einleitung in die Musiksoziologie, Suhrkamp, 1962, translation by E. B. Ashton published as *Introduction to the Sociology of Music,* Seabury, 1976; *Jargon der Eigentlichkeit: zur deutschen Ideologie,* Suhrkamp, 1965, translation by Knut Tarnowski and Frederick Will published as *The Jargon of Authenticity,* Northwestern University Press, 1973; *Negative Dialektik,* Suhrkamp, 1966, translation by Ashton published as *Negative Dialectics,* Seabury, 1973; (with Hanns Eisler) *Komposition fuer den Film,* Rogner & Bernhard, 1969, translation published as *Composing for the Films,* Books for Libraries Press, 1971; (contributor) *The Positivist Dispute in German Sociology,* Harper, 1976.

Other works: *Kierkegaard: Konstruktion des aesthetischen* (title means "Kierkegaard: Construction of the Aesthetics"), Mohr, 1933; *Versuch ueber Wagner* (title means "Essay on Wagner"), Suhrkamp, 1952; *Die gegaengelte Musik: Bemerkungen ueber die Musikpolitik der Ostblockstaaten* (title means "Fettered Music: Observations on the Musical Politics of the Eastern Bloc"), Eremiten Presse, 1954; *Dissonanzen: Musik in der verwalteten Welt* (title means "Dissonances: Music in the World of the Administered Life"), Vandenhoeck & Ruprecht, 1956; *Zur Metakritik der Erkenntnistheorie: Studien ueber Husserl and die phaenomenologischen Antinomien* (title means "Towards a Metacriticism of the Theory of Knowledge: Studies in Husserl and the Phenomenalist Antimonies"), Kohlhammer, 1956; *Aspekte der Hegelschen Philosophie* (title means "Aspects of Hegelian Philosophy"), Suhrkamp, 1957; *Die Funktion des Kontrapunkts in der neuen Musik* (title means "The Function of Counterpoint in the New Music"), Akademie der Kuenste (Berlin), 1957; *Noten zur Literatur* (title means "Notes on Literature"), four volumes, Suhrkamp, 1958-74;

Klangfiguren: Musikalische Schriften I (title means "Acoustic Figures: Writings on Music I"), Suhrkamp, 1959.

Mahler: Eine Musikalische Physiognomik (title means "Mahler: A Musical Physiognomy"), Suhrkamp, 1960; *Eingriffe: neun kritische Modelle* (title means "Interventions: Nine Critical Models"), Suhrkamp, 1963; *Der getreue Korrepetitor: Lehrschriften zur musikalischen Praxis* (title means "The Loyal Co-Reviser: Instructional Writings on Musical Practice"), Fischer, 1963; *Quasi una fantasia: Musikalische Schriften II* (title means "Almost a Fantasia: Writings on Music II"), Suhrkamp, 1963; *Moments musicaux: Neu gedruckte Aufsaetze 1928-1962* (title means "Musical Moments: Newly Published Essays, 1928-1962"), Suhrkamp, 1964; *Drei Studien zu Hegel* (title means "Three Studies on Hegel"), Suhrkamp, 1966; *Ohne Leitbild: Parva Aesthetics* (title means "Without a Guiding Image: Minor Aesthetics"), Suhrkamp, 1967; *Ueber einige Relationen zwischen Musik und Malerei: Die Kunst und die Kuenste* (title means "On Some Relationships Between Music and Painting: Art and the Arts"), Akademie der Kuenste, 1967; *Berg: Der Meister des kleinsten Uebergangs* (title means "Berg: The Master of the Smallest Transition"), Oesterreichischer Bundesverlag, 1968; *Ueber Walter Benjamin* (title means "On Walter Benjamin"), Suhrkamp, 1968; *Impromptus: Zweite Folge neu gedruckter musicalischer Aufsaetze* (title means "Impromptus: A Second Collection of Newly Published Essays on Music"), Suhrkamp, 1968; *Stichworte: Kritische Modelle 2* (title means "Catchwords: Critical Models 2"), Suhrkamp, 1969.

Aesthetische Theorie (title means "Theory of Aesthetics"), edited by wife, Gretcl Adorno, and Rolf Tiedemann, Suhrkamp, 1970; *Aufsaetze zur Gesellschaftstheorie und Methodology* (title means "Essays on Social Theory and Methodology"), Suhrkamp, 1970; *Erziehung zur Muendigkeit: Vortraege und Gespraeche mit Helmut Becker* (title means "Education for Maturity: Lectures and Conversations With Helmut Becker"), edited by Gerd Kadelbach, Suhrkamp, 1970; *Gesammelte Schriften* (title means "Collected Writings"), Suhrkamp, 1970; *Vorlesungen zur Aesthetik* (title means "Lectures on Aesthetics"), edited and postscript by Christof Subik, Schindel, 1970; *Theodor W. Adorno: Eine Auswahl* (title means "Theodor W. Adorno: A Selection"), edited by Tiedemann, Buechergilde Gutenberg, 1971; *Kritik: kleine Schriften zur Gesellschaft* (title means "Criticism: Minor Writings on Society"), edited by Tiedemann, Suhrkamp, 1971; *Versuch, das Endspiel zu verstehen: Aufsaetze zur Literatur des 20. Jahrhunderts 1*, Suhrkamp, 1973; *Zur Dialektik des Engagements: Aufsaetze zur Literatur des 20. Jahrhunderts 2* (title means "Towards a Dialectic of Engagement: Essays on Twentieth Century Literature 2"), Suhrkamp, 1973; *Vorlesungen zur Aesthetik 1967-1968* (title means "Lectures on Aesthetics, 1967-1968"), H. Mayer Nachfolger, 1973; *Vorlesung zur Einleitung in die Soziologie* (title means "Introductory Lecture on Sociology"), Junius-Drucke, 1973; *Vorlesung zur Einleitung in die Erkenntnistheorie* (title means "Introductory Lecture on the Theory of Knowledge"), Junius-Drucke, 1973; *Philosophische Terminologie: Zur Einleitung* (title means "Philosophical Terminology: An Introduction"), edited by Rudolf zur Lippe, Suhrkamp, 1973; (with Ernst Krenek) *Briefwechsel: Theodor W. Adorno und Ernst Krenek* (title means "Correspondence: Theodor W. Adorno and Ernst Krenek"), edited by Wolfgang Rogge, Suhrkamp, 1974; *Gesellschaftstheorie und Kulturkritik* (title means "Social Theory and Cultural Criticism"), Suhrkamp, 1975.

SIDELIGHTS: Adorno was the son of a wealthy Jewish wine merchant and a non-Jewish mother. Maria Calvelli-Adorno was a well-known professional singer, daughter of a German woman, also a singer, and of a French Corsican army officer of Genoese descent (hence the Italianate name, which Adorno adopted as his own). Adorno, shy and intensely intellectual, grew up in Frankfurt in a household which was always full of music and musicians. He conceived an ambition to become a composer.

Music was by no means Adorno's only interest: his studies at the University of Frankfurt included philosophy, psychology, and sociology as well as musicology. However, in 1925, having earned his doctorate in philosophy, Adorno went to Vienna to study composition with Alban Berg, one of the pioneers of twelve-tone music. The most bitter disappointment of his life was his discovery that he was without talent as a composer. Nevertheless, Adorno's excursion into the Viennese musical world brought him other rewards. He began to contribute essays and reviews to various Viennese journals, and soon established himself as a profoundly knowledgeable, original, and perceptive critic and philosopher of music, as well as a redoubtable champion of such avant-garde composers as Berg, Schoenberg, and Webern. The range of his critical writings soon widened to include literature, aesthetic theory, and culture in general, while his approach to the arts, under the influence of his friend Walter Benjamin, became increasingly sociological and political.

Returning in 1928 to Frankfurt, Adorno maintained his connections in Vienna as editor of the influential Viennese musical journal *Anbruch*. He resumed his studies at the University of Frankfurt and wrote a thesis (later published) on the aesthetic theories of philosopher Soren Kierkegaard. In 1931 he received his *Habilitation* (right to lecture). At about the same time he began his long friendship and collaboration with the sociologist Max Horkheimer, director from 1930 to 1958 of the Frankfurt Institut fuer Sozialforschung (Institute for Social Research). The Institute, privately endowed as a center for Marxist studies, concentrated under Horkheimer on the study of Marxist theory itself and on investigations into the nature and development of authority and into the role of popular culture in mass societies. The "Frankfurt School" of sociologists, psychologists, and others formally or loosely associated with the Institute included such major figures as Erich Fromm, Herbert Marcuse, Walter Benjamin, and Franz Neumann.

Adorno did not at first become a member of the Institute, but through his friendship with Horkheimer he greatly influenced its work and the development of the Frankfurt School's "Critical Theory." This is not so much a philosophical system as "a gadfly of other systems," drawing on Marxist dialectics, on the thought of Hegel and Kant, and on the methods and insights of psychoanalysis and modern sociology. Its purpose was to provide a technique for the analysis and criticism of philosophies and ideologies, so that the critical theorist may move towards an objective and creative view of society, unblinkered by false theories and inherited assumptions. Critical Theory has played an important part in the postwar revitalization of Western European Marxism and in the development of the New Left in the United States. It is to some extent an expression of Adorno's and Horkheimer's own temperaments, which were remarkably similar. As Martin Jay has written, the two men shared an instinctive distrust of rigid philosophical systems and ideologies: Adorno's thought, like Horkheimer's, "was always rooted in a kind of cosmic irony, a refusal to rest somewhere and say finally, Here is where truth lies."

The Institute, being mainly Jewish as well as Marxist in its personnel, left Frankfurt when Hitler came to power in 1933. In 1934, after a brief spell in Geneva, it reestablished itself in the United States, where it was at first associated with Columbia University in New York. Adorno himself, still not formally affiliated with the Institute, went to Merton College, Oxford, where he worked on a critical study of the philosophy of Husserl, published many years later as *Zur Metakritik der Erkenntnistheorie*. He joined the Institute at last in 1938, initially as head of music studies at the Institute's Office of Radio Research at Princeton. In 1941, when ill-health prompted Horkheimer to move to California, Adorno joined him at Pacific Palisades, becoming part of a brilliant expatriate community that included Thomas and Heinrich Mann, Bertolt Brecht, and Alfred Doeblin.

From 1942 until 1944 Adorno and Horkheimer collaborated in writing the "philosophical fragments" published under that title in 1944 and later as *Dialectic of Enlightenment*. It showed that the Nazi years had turned its authors into critics not merely of capitalism but of the whole history of Western civilization. They argued that the European masses had allowed themselves to be exploited by their leaders, who had substituted the pursuit of power for the pursuit of happiness. Driven by their hunger for domination, these leaders had deliberately abased and mortified their own instincts, and had sought to impose their wills not only upon the societies they created but on the natural world around them. The history of civilization was a "history of renunciation" which had ushered in "a new kind of barbarism."

Adorno served as co-director and theoretician of the most famous of the Institute's American projects, the Research Project on Social Discrimination, from 1944 until 1949. The study's approach was basically Freudian, but it benefited a great deal from the empirical skills of the Berkeley psychologists who collaborated with Institute personnel. They interviewed some two thousand American citizens, seeking to establish which personality traits and family backgrounds characterized those who developed racist and anti-democratic views. The results of the study were published in 1950 as *The Authoritarian Personality*.

The Institute for Social Research returned to Frankfurt in 1949, and nine years later Adorno succeeded Horkheimer as director. At the same time he became professor of philosophy and sociology at the University of Frankfurt, into which the Institute was incorporated. The Frankfurt School had by now shed its connections with orthodox Marxism, and was disillusioned both with the Soviet Union and the industrial working class. In the postwar years it functioned primarily as a center of academic sociology, where Adorno and Horkheimer passed on to their students what they had learned of empirical social science in the United States.

Adorno published many books on many subjects in the postwar years. *The Philosophy of Modern Music* presents Schoenberg and Stravinsky as the positive and negative poles of the new music, praising the former for reflecting in his music the dissonance of contemporary society, condemning the latter for his "objectivism" and "schizophrenia." Richard Middleton, writing in *Music and Letters*, called it "by far the best, the most profound, the most intelligent discussion of modern music we have." *Versuch ueber Wagner*, without underestimating Wagner's genius, suggests that his music helped to nurture the seeds of National Sociolism. Other essays on music (which fill eight volumes in Adorno's collected works) have been translated in *Prisms* and *Introduction to the Sociology of Music*. Adorno was hostile to jazz and to popular music in general, regarding it as a drug employed by the establishment to pacify the exploited masses. Even critics who reject this and other aspects of his approach to music acknowledge that his criticism is full of "marvellous insights." His friend Thomas Mann made extensive use of Adorno's perceptions in his novel *Doktor Faustus*.

Minima Moralia, a collection of aphorisms composed between 1944 and 1947, is subtitled *Reflections from Damaged Life*. What has damaged life, Adorno maintains, is the "technological rationality," the materialism and power-hunger of modern industrial civilization: even "the body movements that machines" demanded "of those who served them," he wrote, prefigured all that was violent and unrelenting in "fascist abuse." This is a more personal book than *Dialectic of Enlightenment* but expresses similar views, concluding (long before the ecological movement became fashionable) that man's arrogant denial of his oneness with nature is the original sin of our society. Jeremy Shapiro wrote in the *Times Literary Supplement* that *Dialectic of Enlightenment* and *Minima Moralia* already "rank as classics of twentieth-century thought."

During the 1950's and 1960's, Adorno also published books and articles on literature, various aspects of popular culture and superstition, Hegel, and Heidegger (whom Adorno attacked in *The Jargon of Authenticity*). Adorno was an opponent of logical positivism, and his 1961 debate on this subject with Karl Popper provoked a prolonged and widespread debate, the principal documents in which have been published as *The Positivist Dispute in German Sociology*. Adorno's aesthetics, published incomplete as volume seven of his collected works, seemed to most reviewers uninspired. According to Jeremy Shapiro, the most discussed of Adorno's later works, *Negative Dialectics*, proposed a manner of critical thought "so conceived that it cannot be co-opted into the apparatus of domination."

Adorno's writings are abstruse, dense, and difficult, characterized by "a sometimes dazzling, sometimes bewildering juxtaposition of highly abstract statements with seemingly trivial observations." H. Stuart Hughes says that Adorno consciously chose "a style refined and formalized to the point of complete artificiality," and George Lichtheim suggested that this deliberate obscurity was intended as a warning to the reader of the price that must be paid for genuine thinking. Perhaps Adorno's most famous saying was that there should be no poetry after Auschwitz—that after such horrors, self-conscious art would seem barbarous.

H. Stuart Hughes said of Adorno that, "enclosed by the devotion of his great friend [Horkheimer] and his utterly loyal wife, [he] managed to live a rare and uncompromisingly intellectual existence right up to the bizarre tragedy with which his life ended." Though few had done more to lay the intellectual foundations of revolutionary thought in postwar Europe, Adorno's fastidious refusal to involve himself in any kind of practical political action was incomprehensible to his Maoist and anarchist students. Their growing hostility was no doubt exacerbated by Adorno's role during his last years as a sort of public oracle, "the most prestigious intellectual on the German scene." In the heady atmosphere of the late 1960's, the Institute was repeatedly invaded and occupied by students. One day in April, 1969, according to Hughes, "the young militants invaded Arno's classroom; three girl students bared their breasts and mockingly overwhelmed him with flowers and kisses. Thereupon, with characteristic cruelty, they declared him dead 'as an institution.'" It was an upsurge of the irrationality which had always horrified and fascinated Adorno. He never recovered from this assault upon his sensibilities and five months later he died of a heart attack.

BIOGRAPHICAL/CRITICAL SOURCES: Commentary, June 1950, March 1951; Richard Christie and Marie Jahoda, editors, *Studies in the Scope and Method of "The Authoritarian Personality,"* Free Press of Glencoe, 1954; *Zeugnisse: Theodor W. Adorno zum sechzigsten Geburtstag,* 1963; *Times Literary Supplement,* September 28, 1967, March 9, 1973, October 4, 1974; Kirt Oppens and others, *Ueber Theodor W. Adorno,* Suhrkamp, 1968; *London Times,* August 7, 1969; *New York Times,* August 7, 1969; *Encounter,* September, 1969, October, 1976; Donald Fleming and Bernard Bailyn, editors, *The Intellectual Migration,* Belknap Press, 1969.

Books Abroad, spring, 1970; George Lichtheim, *From Marx to Hegel,* Orbach & Chambers, 1971; *Music and Letters,* July, 1971, April, 1974; John Crowe Ransom, *Beating the Bushes,* New Directions, 1972; Robert Boyers, editor, *The Legacy of the German Refugee Intellectuals,* Schocken, 1972; Martin Jay, *The Dialectical Imagination,* Heinemann, 1973; Gerhard Kaiser, *Benjamin; Adorno: zwei Studien,* Athenaeum-Fischer-Taschenbuch Verlag, 1974; Bernd Braeutigam, *Reflexion des Schoenen–Schoene Reflexion,* Bouvier, 1975; Henry Stuart Hughes, *The Sea Change,* Harper, 1975; Karol Sauerland, *Adornos Aesthetik des Nichtidentischen,* University of Warsaw, 1975; Manfred Jablinski, *Theodor W. Adorno,* Bouvier, 1976; John O'Neill, editor, *On Critical Theory,* Seabury, 1976; *Political Studies,* March, 1976; Susan Buck-Morss, *The Origin of Negative Dialectics,* Free Press, 1977; Phil Slater, *Origin and Significance of the Frankfurt School,* Routledge & Kegan Paul, 1977; Zoltan Tar, *The Frankfurt School,* Wiley, 1977.*

* * *

AEBI, Ormond 1916-

PERSONAL: Surname is pronounced "abbey"; born February 10, 1916, in Suver, Ore.; son of Harry J. (a beekeeper) and Mathilda (Willwock) Aebi. *Education:* Oregon College of Education, teaching diploma, 1938. *Politics:* Republican. *Religion:* Advent Christian. *Home:* 710 17th Ave., Santa Cruz, Calif. 95062. *Agent:* Randy Nauert, 3525 Encinal Canyon Rd., Malibu, Calif. 90265.

CAREER: Farmer and beekeeper, 1930-37; teacher at rural elementary school in Dallas, Ore., 1938-41; beekeeper and carpenter, 1945-50; beekeeper in Santa Cruz, Calif., 1950—. *Military service:* U.S. Army Air Forces, 1941-45; became sergeant.

WRITINGS: (With father, Harry Aebi) *The Art and Adventure of Beekeeping,* Unity Press, 1975; (with H. Aebi) *Mastering the Art of Beekeeping,* Unity Press, 1979.

WORK IN PROGRESS: That Big Sheep Minnie, for suburban farmers who want to keep a few sheep or goats; *Bonnie the Honeybee,* a children's book.

SIDELIGHTS: Aebi writes: "We are not all born equal, with the same gifts of strength, speech, and ability. I had a twin sister. We were each given but one-half of the vitality of life. My people came from central Europe, where we would have been called 'half-life' children, because in the old days we would have died somewhere in our twenties. By the grace of God and modern medicine we both lived many more years than was our normal expectation.

"Ever since I was a boy it has been my goal to set a new world's record of wild flower honey production from one queen bee, in one hive, in one season. On August 29, 1974, we set a new record of 404 pounds of wild flower honey from one hive, breaking the old record of 300 pounds, set in 1895. Many books tell how to keep bees. My books tell how to keep bees and *get honey* in abundance."

BIOGRAPHICAL/CRITICAL SOURCES: Santa Cruz Sentinel, September 5, 1975; *Palo Alto Times,* October 3, 1975; *Grit,* January, 1976; *Healthways Magazine Digest,* March, 1976; *Organic Gardening,* January, 1979; *Santa Cruz* magazine, Volume II, number 1, 1979.

* * *

AGNEW, James Barron 1930-

PERSONAL: Born September 10, 1930, in Charlotte, N.C.; son of Joseph Barron (a druggist) and Anne (an executive secretary; maiden name, Adams) Agnew; married Harriet Dotterer (a physician's secretary), November 8, 1952; children: Virginia Gray, Harriet Adams Agnew Kastner, Sarah Victoria. *Education:* The Citadel, A.B., 1952; Princeton University, M.P.A., 1966; U.S. Army War College, diploma, 1971. *Religion:* Protestant. *Home:* 6602 Rosecroft Place, Falls Church, Va. 22043. *Office:* D. D. Eisenhower Institute, NMH&T, Smithsonian Institution, Washington, D.C. 20560.

CAREER: U.S. Army, career officer, 1952-77, with assignments and staff assignments with Department of the Army Headquarters and Office of the Secretary of Defense; overseas assignments in Germany, Korea, and Vietnam; served in Field Artillery Command; appointed assistant professor of history at U.S. Military Academy, West Point, N.Y., 1972; director of Army Military History Institute, Carlisle, Pa., 1974-77, retiring as colonel. D. D. Eisenhower fellow at Institute of Historic Research, Smithsonian Institution, Washington, D.C., 1978-80. Vice-president of Omar N. Bradley Foundation; associate of Strategy Corp., Arlington, Va.; consultant to U.S. Arms Control/Disarmament Agency, Washington, D.C. *Member:* International Commission on Military History, Council on Abandoned Military Posts, Association of the U.S. Army, Retired Officers Association, Civil War Round Table (Washington, D.C.), Military Classics Seminar (Washington, D.C.), Gettysburg National Military Park, Association of Licensed Guides, Association of Citadel Men. *Awards, honors*—Military: Three Legions of Merit; Bronze Star; three Air Medals; Vietnamese campaign medal with five battle stars; U.S. and Vietnamese Parachutists Badges; Department of the Army staff badge, 1952-77; military research award from U.S. Army Military History Institute, 1979.

WRITINGS: (With W. R. Griffith) *The Great War,* U.S. Military Academy, 1978; *Eggnog Riot: Christmas Mutiny at West Point,* Presidio Press, 1979. Contributor to military and civilian journals.

WORK IN PROGRESS: A book, *Encyclopedia and Source Book of the Gettysburg Campaign,* a novel, *Enemies, Foreign and Domestic,* and a study of coalition warfare, for U.S. Department of Defense, publication for all expected in 1980.

SIDELIGHTS: Agnew comments: "I write for fun and profit (not much to date) because I do that better than anything else I've ever attempted. I have become increasingly frustrated because the officer corps of the armed forces *will not* read, so our military leaders continue to make mistakes as occurred in Vietnam because they were ignorant of the lessons of the Seminole Wars, the Philippine insurrection, and others. But I'm afraid I'm preaching to deaf ears, and unless the war colleges and the chiefs of the services force-feed the lessons of the past to the rising leadership groups, U.S. national security will be in jeopardy in another decade."

AVOCATIONAL INTERESTS: The Gettysburg Campaign, woodworking.

* * *

AGRESS, Hyman 1931-

PERSONAL: Born July 6, 1931, in Brooklyn, N.Y.; son of Joshua (a rabbi) and Ida (Kirson) Agress; married Frances Newmark, November 2, 1958; children: Michael, Stephen, Alexandra. *Education:* Yeshiva University, B.A., 1953; Hunter College (now of the City University of New York), M.A., 1956; Northern Illinois University, M.S., 1979. *Politics:* Independent. *Home:* 91 North Rosedale, Aurora, Ill. 60506. *Office:* Temple B'nai Israel, 400 North Edgelawn, Aurora, Ill. 60506.

CAREER: Worked as rabbi of Congregation Beth Moses, Detroit, Mich., 1957-61, Northeast Jewish Center, Yonkers, N.Y., 1961-64, and Temple B'nai Israel, Aurora, Ill., 1964—. Professor at Aurora College, 1971—. President of Aurora Family Counseling, 1974-76; member of advisory board of Mercy Medical Center, 1976—.

WRITINGS: Why Me?, Creation House, 1974; *A Thanksgiving Celebration,* Abbey Press, 1976; (with wife, Frances Agress) *The Firing of Rabbi Levi* (novel), Manor, 1978.

WORK IN PROGRESS: A sequel to *The Firing of Rabbi Levi,* with Frances Agress; a study of the effects of a retarded child on a marriage.

SIDELIGHTS: Agress writes: "I began my first book at the age of forty with the hope that my personal experiences would help other parents of retarded children. This book was most difficult to write because of its emotional intensity. After every day's writing, my wife and I would relive the experiences of our first few years with our brain-damaged son Mike. The many phone calls and letters from parents of handicapped children, including one from a parent who had contemplated suicide, made the effort worthwhile. At present, negotiations are going on with television and movie production companies for the purpose of turning the book into a movie."

BIOGRAPHICAL/CRITICAL SOURCES: Conservative Judaism, spring, 1974.

* * *

ALBAUGH, Edwin (Doll, Jr.) 1935-

PERSONAL: Born June 9, 1935, in Frederick, Md.; son of Edwin Doll (an accountant) and Helen (Rosenberry) Albaugh; married Annemarie Schautes (a library researcher), April 9, 1960; children: Strawinski, Kirstin. *Education:* Attended Western Maryland College, 1955-56, University of Miami, 1957, and Johns Hopkins University, 1957. *Home:* 6401 Cardinal Lane, Columbia, Md. 21044. *Office: Washington Star,* 225 Virginia Ave. S.E., Washington, D.C. 20061.

CAREER/WRITINGS: Sunpapers, Baltimore, Md., reporter, 1961-62; WJZ-TV, Baltimore, news editor, 1963-64; Sunpapers, Baltimore, editor, 1965-70; *Washington Star,* Washington, D.C., editor, reporter and chess columnist, 1970—. Notable assignments include coverage of such chess tournaments as the 1974 Solingen International Tournament, the 1975 U.S. Championship, the 1976 U.S. Open, and the 1979 Statham Masters-Plus, as well as interviews with composers George Crumb and Steve Reich, and football quarterbacks Johnny Unitas and Bert Jones. Writer of "Area Chess" column in *Washington Star,* 1972—; contributor of articles to *Chess Life and Review, Washingtonian,* and *Baltimore Sun;* contributor of poems to *Voices. Military service:* U.S. Army, 1957-59. *Member:* International Association of Chess Journalists, United States Chess Federation. *Awards, honors:* Merit awards, 1976, 1977, from United States Association of Chess Journalists.

WORK IN PROGRESS: Research of World War I and Lafayette Escadrille fighter pilot Raoul Lufbery.

SIDELIGHTS: Albaugh wrote: "I got into chess writing when Bobby Fischer was en route to the world championship and a strong demand existed for information about him and the game. I have the greatest respect for good chess players (not being one myself), who, it seems to me, are mental athletes. The best games of chess come close to being works of art."

* * *

ALDRIN, Edwin E(ugene), Jr. 1930-

PERSONAL: Born January 20, 1930, in Montclair, N.J.; son of Edwin E. (an oil executive and aviator) and Marion (Moon) Aldrin; married Joan A. Archer, December 29, 1954 (divorced); married Beverly Van Zile, in 1975 (divorced); children: James Michael, Janice Ross, Andrew John. *Education:* United States Military Academy, B.S., 1951; Massachusetts Institute of Technology, Sc.D. in Astronautics, 1963; also attended Air University, Maxwell Air Force Base, Ala. *Residence:* Los Angeles, Calif. *Office:* Research and Engineering Consultants, Inc., 1801 Federal Ave., Apt. 106, Los Angeles, Calif. 90025.

CAREER: U.S. Air Force, career officer, 1951-72, retiring as colonel; Research and Engineering Consultants, Inc., Los Angeles, Calif., president, 1972—. Received wings, 1951; served as fighter pilot in Korea; aerial gunnery instructor, Nellis Air Force Base, Nev.; flight commander with 36th Tactical Fighter Wing, Bitburg, Germany; worked with experiments in Gemini-Titan rocket flights at Gemini Target Office, Air Force Space Systems Division, Los Angeles, and at Air Force Field Office, Manned Spacecraft Center, Houston, Tex.; selected for 3rd group of astronauts by National Aeronautics and Space Administration (NASA), 1963; pilot for orbital rendezvous space flight, *Gemini XII* mission, 1966; lunar module pilot, *Apollo XI* moon mission, first lunar landing with Neil Armstrong, 1969; Aerospace Research Pilots School, Edwards Air Force Base, Calif., 1971-72. Member of board of directors of National Association for Mental Health (national chairman, 1974); member of board of visitors of Department of Earth and Planetary Sciences, Massachusetts Institute of Technology; member of board of directors of Mutual of Omaha Insurance Co.

MEMBER: International Academy of Astronautics (corresponding member), International Association of Machinists and Aerospace Workers (honorary member), American Institute of Aeronautics and Astronautics (fellow), American Society for Oceanography (director), National Collegiate Athletic Association (NCAA), Royal Aeronautics Society (honorary member), Society of Experimental Test Pilots, Sea Space Symposium (charter member), Theodore Roosevelt Award Jury, Aerospace Medical Association (honorary member), Masons, Sigma Xi, Sigma Gamma Tau, Tau Beta Pi. *Awards, honors:* Decorated with Distinguished Service Medal, Distinguished Flying Cross with oak-leaf cluster, and Air Medal with two oak-leaf clusters; received honorary doctorate degrees from Gustavus Adolphus College, 1967, Clark University and Montclair State College, 1969, and

University of Portland, St. Peter's College, and Seton Hall University, 1970; awards from NASA include Distinguished Service Medal, Exceptional Service Medal, and group achievement award; received numerous other awards, including Presidential Medal of Freedom, Kitty Hawk Memorial award, Robert J. Collier trophy, and Pere Marquette Medal, all 1969, and Hubbard Medal, Robert H. Goddard Memorial trophy, and Iven C. Kincheloe award, all 1970.

WRITINGS: (With Neil Armstrong, Michael Collins, Gene Farmer, and Dora Jane Hamblin) *First on the Moon,* Little, Brown, 1970; (with Armstrong and Collins) *The First Lunar Landing as Told by the Astronauts Armstrong, Aldrin, and Collins in a Post-Flight Press Conference* (booklet), National Aeronautics and Space Administration, 1970; (with Wayne Warga) *Return to Earth* (autobiography), Random House, 1973.

SIDELIGHTS: On July 20, 1969, Edwin "Buzz" Aldrin and co-pilot Neil Armstrong landed on the moon. It was the first achievement of its kind, a historic event televised around the world and viewed by an estimated half-billion people. Along with Michael Collins, Armstrong and Aldrin became instant celebrities, and a heroes' welcome awaited their return to earth. But as Aldrin has observed, he was better prepared for the unknown lunar surface than his return to the known and familiar earth. His encounter with fame brought the dissolution of his marriage, recurring bouts of depression and mental breakdowns, and the end of his military career. Ironically, success, and this his greatest success, seemed a thing for which he had rehearsed all his life.

"Very early in my life," Aldrin once remarked, "I had a tremendous competitive spirit. I had to be the best." Even before his birth a family standard of achievement had been established; his father was an oil executive and a distinguished aviator in the 1920's and 1930's whose friends included Orville Wright, Charles Lindbergh, and rocket pioneer Robert Goddard. Although Aldrin's sister can recall when he was "more inclined to buckle down to neighborhood football games than to his homework—his report cards were mostly C's and D's," his later performance dramatically improved. He produced A's and B's at Montclair High School, played center on the school's championship football team, and won admittance to West Point. He was graduated third in his class from the academy in 1951.

After a year spent learning how to fly, Aldrin was sent to Korea as a fighter pilot, where he completed sixty-six fighter missions, destroyed two MIG's and damaged another, and won the Distinguished Flying Cross. When he returned home he resumed a pre-war acquaintance with Joan Archer. But because she resided in New Jersey and he was then an Air Force instructor stationed in Nevada, he conducted his courtship largely by mail. When they eventually married it was only the fifth time they had been out together.

Aldrin decided in 1959 that he needed a new challenge. As Gene Farmer observed: "'Challenge' is a word Buzz Aldrin uses frequently. 'What is a challenge?' he asked once. 'What determines excellence? In grade school it's the grades you get, what you do on the athletic field. At West Point the name of the game is, "Do what people tell you to do, keep your nose clean and work out your academic progress." I fitted into that pretty well. I'm sort of a mechanical man—or I was.'" The U.S. space program became his new objective. At Massachusetts Institute of Technology Aldrin developed a doctoral thesis that dealt with the piloting and rendezvous of two spacecraft in orbit. "That, and not being a crew member, was my best contribution to the program," he thinks. Though Aldrin was turned down for the 1962 class of astronauts, his expertise in orbital rendezvous suited him perfectly for the Gemini program. In 1966, he piloted the *Gemini XII* mission and established a new record for extravehicular activity (the "space walk").

In January, 1969, NASA announced that Aldrin would journey to the moon aboard *Apollo XI.* As he prepared for the mission, Joan Aldrin wondered if her husband would return the same man. She had expected, after *Gemini XII,* that "our marriage wouldn't be the same, that it would be so much more magical and meaningful and magnificent because he'd done this wonderful thing." But she eventually realized that their marriage was unaffected. "At first I was disappointed, and then it was comforting to think that it hadn't changed him. I really do believe that after all this is over, and if it is a lunar landing, that he will be the same person."

"I began to be depressed immediately after the flight," Aldrin reminisced in 1974. "It had nothing to do with the technical part of operating the mission. It was merely having a tremendous change of life come about—and not having an objective." During the months of celebrity following the moon flight, Aldrin was overwhelmed by the public adulation, an exhausting forty-five-day world tour, endless speaking engagements, and a growing sense of isolation and worthlessness. "I was so enmeshed in this [the moon mission] that I didn't give any thought to what would happen afterward," Aldrin remarked. "That's what caught me—I wasn't prepared. Up till then, I had always been in control of my life. . . . All [the touring, press meetings, and speeches were] interfering with my efforts to figure out what I was going to do next. Some people take to these situations easier than others. I couldn't."

Over time, an estrangement developed between Aldrin and his wife, and his psychological condition worsened. He became romantically involved with a New York divorcee and considered ending his marriage of seventeen years. As he recalled in *Return to Earth,* "Playing off my life styles one against the other had started me on my way to a collision within myself. I had used my two life styles in the most extreme way to establish a maze through which I could travel no more. I finally became helplessly lost within myself."

In 1971, Aldrin entered a San Antonio hospital and underwent treatment for a mental breakdown. At the time, he noted, "I was not only incapable of making a decision, I could not even complete a coherent sentence. . . . I yearned for a bright oblivion—wept for it." With the aid of tranquilizers, antidepressants, and analysis, Aldrin began to sort out his life and set some priorities. "I was able to say that what I really wanted was to live my life on my own. My entire adult life had been spent either in the Air Force or with NASA. . . . I decided to leave the nest I had occupied for so many years." He retired from the Air Force in 1972 ("My chances for promotion ended when I asked for psychiatric help"), settled in Los Angeles, and began a new career as a consultant to technical firms. "I'm trying to replace one big objective," he told *Newsweek,* "with several smaller ones."

Aldrin has since made periodic reentries into the news. In 1974, he acted as chairman of the National Association for Mental Health. He made public appearances around the country and discussed his illness openly, disclosing that he had experienced many relapses of depression and that he continues with drug and psychiatric therapies. He later appeared with other celebrities at a news conference sponsored by the National Council on Alcoholism. Before hospitalization, he announced, he had been drinking quite heavily, as much as a quart of liquor a day. "My excessive use of alcohol was brought about by my depression, which was brought about by alcohol," he said. It has also been a time when his first marriage ended in divorce, as did a second, and the loss of old friendships has followed. "He lives by himself now in a modest apartment in Los Angeles near the VA hospital," reported *Look* magazine.

In *Return to Earth,* Aldrin recounts "the most significant voyage of my life." As Joseph McElroy observed, "it is a story of lost bearings" and Aldrin's particular need "to lay bare his feelings." The account of his life "is admirable for its basic dedication to truth: unvarnished, cruel, yet liberating," wrote E. J. Linehan. "One is left at book's end with a sincere prayer that his life is today more rewarding than all the attention of parades, gifts, notoriety which followed upon that historic visit to the moon."

BIOGRAPHICAL/CRITICAL SOURCES: Life, July 4, 1969, July 17, 1970; *New York Times Biographical Edition,* January 14, 1971; Colonel Edwin E. "Buzz" Aldrin, Jr., with Wayne Warga, *Return to Earth,* Random House, 1973; *Village Voice,* September 13, 1973; *New York Times Book Review,* October 21, 1973; *Best Sellers,* November 15, 1973; *Saturday Evening Post,* April, 1974; *Newsweek,* April 1, 1974, May 17, 1976; *Detroit News,* September 15, 1974; *Biography News,* Gale, November, 1974; *Look,* July, 1979.*

—Sketch by B. Hal May

* * *

ALEXEEV, Wassilij 1906-

PERSONAL: Born October 6, 1906, in Vladimir, Russia; U.S. citizen; son of Ivan and Vera (Iljinsky) Alexeev; married Ludmila Levitsky (a librarian), November 23, 1948; children: Sergei Schachowskoj (stepson). *Education:* Moscow University, graduated, 1930; University of Minnesota, Ph.D., 1967. *Religion:* Eastern Orthodox. *Home:* 318 West 25th St., Minneapolis, Minn. 55404.

CAREER: Inmate of Soviet concentration camp, accused of belonging to Russian Orthodox underground movement, 1930-34; part-time researcher and member of editoral staff of various scholarly and literary institutions, Moscow, Russia, 1934-41; teacher of history in Russian secondary school, Munich, Germany, 1941-51; University of Minnesota, Minneapolis, visiting lecturer, 1955-62, assistant professor, 1964-67, associate professor of Russian studies, 1967-75, professor emeritus, 1975—. *Military service:* Served in World War II. *Member:* American Association of Teachers of Slavic and East European Languages. *Awards, honors:* Research grants from East Europe Fund, Inc., 1951-55.

WRITINGS: Nevidimaya Rossiya (title means "The Hidden Russia"), Chekhov Publishing, 1952; *Rossiya Soldatskaya* (title means "The Soldier's Russia"), Chekhov Publishing, 1954; *Russian Orthodox Bishops in the Soviet Union, 1941-1953,* Research Program on the U.S.S.R., 1954; *The Foreign Policy of the Moscow Patriarchate, 1939-1953,* Research Program on the U.S.S.R., 1955; (with Theofanis G. Stavrou) *The Great Revival: The Russian Church Under German Occupation,* Burgess, 1976. Also author of *The Two Russian Revolutions of 1917,* General Extension Division, University of Minnesota. Contributor to Russian and European studies journals. Co-editor of *Russkoe Vozrozhdenie.*

WORK IN PROGRESS: Rossiya Okkupirovannaya, a novel (title means "Russia Under Occupation"); continuing research on the history of the Russian Orthodox Church.

SIDELIGHTS: Alexeev told *CA* that his novels are "fictional accounts of an underground religious organization in the Soviet Union, 1917-45." *Avocational interests:* Music, art, visiting art galleries.

* * *

ALLEN, Anita
See SCHENCK, Anita A(llen)

* * *

ALLEN, Henry Wilson 1912-
(Clay Fisher, Will Henry)

PERSONAL: Born September 29, 1912, in Kansas City, Mo.; son of H. Wilson (an oral surgeon) and Ella E. P. (a commercial artist; maiden name, Jensen) Allen; married Amy Geneva Watson, November, 1937; children: Valerie Hope, Christopher Bruce. *Education:* Attended Kansas City Junior College (now University of Kansas City), 1929-30. *Politics:* "Neanderthal." *Religion:* None. *Residence:* Encino, Calif. *Agent:* August Lenniger, Lenniger Literary Agency, Inc., 437 Fifth Ave., New York, N.Y. 10016; and Evarts Ziegler, Ziegler/Diskant, 9255 Sunset Blvd., Los Angeles, Calif. 90069.

CAREER: Novelist, 1950—.

WRITINGS: Genesis Five, Morrow, 1968; *Tayopa!,* Pocket Books, 1970; *See How They Run,* Pocket Books, 1970.

Under pseudonym Clay Fisher: *Red Blizzard,* Simon & Schuster, 1951; *Santa Fe Passage,* Houghton, 1952; *War Bonnet,* Houghton, 1953; *Yellow Hair,* Houghton, 1953; *The Tall Men,* Houghton, 1954; *The Brass Command,* Houghton, 1955; *The Big Pasture,* Houghton, 1955; *The Blue Mustang,* Houghton, 1956; *Yellowstone Kelly,* Houghton, 1957; *The Crossing,* Houghton, 1958; *Nino: The Life and Legend of Apache Kid,* Houghton, 1961; *The Return of the Tall Man,* Pocket Books, 1961; *The Pitchfork Patrol,* Macmillan, 1962; *The Oldest Maiden Lady in New Mexico,* Macmillan, 1962; *Valley of the Bear,* Houghton, 1964; *Outcasts of Canyon Creek,* Bantam, 1972; *Apache Ransom,* Bantam, 1974; *Black Apache,* Bantam, 1976; *Nine Lives West,* Bantam, 1978.

Under pseudonym Will Henry: *No Survivors,* Random House, 1950; *Wolf-Eye, the Bad One,* Messner, 1951; *To Follow a Flag,* Random House, 1952; *Death of a Legend,* Random House, 1954; *The Fourth Horseman,* Random House, 1954; *Who Rides With Wyatt,* Random House, 1954; *The North Star,* Random House, 1956; *The Texas Rangers,* Random House, 1957; *Orphans of the North,* Random House, 1958; *Reckoning at Yankee Flat,* Random House, 1958; *The Seven Men at Mimbres Springs,* Random House, 1958; *From Where the Sun Now Stands,* Random House, 1960; *Journey to Shiloh,* Random House, 1960; *San Juan Hill,* Random House, 1962; *The Feleen Brand,* Bantam, 1962; *The Gates of the Mountains,* Random House, 1963; *Mackenna's Gold,* Random House, 1963; *In the Land of the Mandans,* Houghton, 1965; *Sons of the Western Frontier,* Chilton, 1966; *The Last Warpath,* Random House, 1966; *Custer's Last Stand,* Chilton, 1966; *One More River to Cross,* Random House, 1967; *Alias Butch Cassidy,* Random House, 1967; *Maheo's Children,* Chilton, 1968; *The Day Fort Larking Fell,* Chilton, 1969; *Chiricahua,* Lippincott, 1972; *The Bear Paw Horses,* Lippincott, 1973; *I, Tom Horn,* Lippincott, 1975; *Summer of the Gun,* Lippincott, 1978.

WORK IN PROGRESS: The Winter of Mrs. Dorion, "a serious novel about a little known American woman who should be remembered, particularly in these days of the loss of heroes both in life and in literature"; *Dark River,* "a novel in the sweeping style of the family saga depicting one man's indomitable rise and spectacular fall in the thirty years that he set aside to build an empire and put his name on the land so that it would be there not in thirty but three hundred years."

SIDELIGHTS: Allen told *CA:* "I believe writers are born to write. It remains only for them to arrive at what to write about. For myself, I was submitting short stories to the old *Liberty* and *Collier's* magazines when I was twelve years old. Since no one bothered to tell me this was an exercise in artless despair, I continued to write and be rejected until I discovered girls. That took up the whole of high school and so to college, where I discovered knowledge. Now I could both write and know something to write about. So naturally I left school and went 'out West' to learn about cattle and horses and sheep and grass and water and shelter and survival as a boy among men. I was almost eighteen years old and continuing to write—letters home pleading for money to ease my pains of existence as a journeyman cowhand/sheepherder/horse wrangler/hard rock miner. These pleas went unanswered, my father believing I had disinherited myself by refusing to obey his orders to report to the University of Missouri School of Journalism and learn to be a newsman. Father had influence with the *Kansas City Star* and had the past summer secured a summer stint for me on the sports desk answering the telephones from drunks in bars on the 9:00 P.M. to 5:00 A.M. shift. He figured a good son ought to be able to take it from there, but where his figuring fell all apart was that he didn't have a good son. He had a drifter and a vagrant by career choice. He never understood that and, although he lived several books into my writings of the American West, he never read a line of any of them and always believed that there was still time to get that good job on the *Star* back and so amount to something.

"Well, likely he was right. I've still never amounted to anything by my own estimate. But I have wandered the far mesas, whistled up the racing sheepdog, ridden 'round the bedding herd of whitefaced cattle, been 'throwed' a mile and twenty minutes by the salty bronco that did not care for the bite of the frosty saddle at four o'clock in the morning, worked nine hundred feet down in the deepshaft Colorado gold mines, flunkied for the post store on Indian reservations, tended rodeo stock, stick-and-balled strings of green polo ponies, pitched sweet prairie hay and likewise sour stall-strod straw-manure and, well, just about done what had to be done wherever I was at whatever particular moment of my growing years, boy to man, out in the still-wonderful American West of the early 1930's. And *that* was my motivating factor to write the books I have written. I was there: God couldn't have sent me to wander in a better wilderness, nor enrolled me in a fitter school, to teach me what it was I must write about that others might learn to love the land and its people, and to honor them and their remarkable history, as they really were and not as fabricated on Hollywood celluloid or in the sulphured world of penny-a-word pulpsters.

"My principal fascination with the West, early and late, became the story of the high plains horseback Indian. I began with the Indian history of the Little Big Horn in my first book, *No Survivors,* and ended with that of Chief Joseph and the Nez Perce in their tragic retreat to the Bear Paws. In between were books on Geronimo, Apache Kid, Loco, Mangas Coloradas, Roman Nose, Chato, Crazy Horse, Red Cloud, Black Kettle, Peaches, Watangoa, Sacajawea, Yellow Wolf, Sitting Bull, Little Wolf, Dullknife—all the old warriors of the last grand troops of magnificent wild red cavalry to ride against the White Eyes, to die rather than surrender to dishonor and the double tongue.

"The thrust of this accent on the horseback Indian, the wildest of the wild, the freest of the free, has been a journey of thirty winters for me. If, in this search back through the ponytracks of time, I could stir the heart and memory of only one Indian, returning him his pride and his heritage of honor, then the long ride will have found its proper ending, will have found what it set out to seek: justice.

"The fighting Indian of the American West is forgotten neither at home nor around the world. (More than fifty percent of my reader mail comes from overseas.) There is something magic in the cry of 'Indians—!' I write to keep that magic alive. Thanks to Maheo and to Hunyewat and to mighty Wakan Tonka, the spirits are yet good to us."

Allen's Will Henry and Clay Fisher Indian books have been printed in numerous foreign languages. More than a dozen of his books have been purchased for motion picture production. Others, including *The Tall Men, Pillars of the Sky, Yellowstone Kelly,* and *Santa Fe Passage,* have been made into movies that appear often on late-night television.

* * *

ALLEN, Herman R. 1913(?)-1979

OBITUARY NOTICE: Born c. 1913 in Hurley, S.D.; died of cancer June 28, 1979, in Washington, D.C. Editor and author. Allen was director of editorial services for the Department of Health, Education and Welfare's Office of Education. He had earlier been an education editor for *Newsweek* and Washington chief of Associated Press Newsfeatures. He supervised the publications program at the Office of Education and the production of its magazine, *American Education.* Obituaries and other sources: *Washington Post,* June 29, 1979.

* * *

ALLEN, Sarah (Pearson) Sawyer 1920-

PERSONAL: Born February 15, 1920, in Windsor, N.C.; daughter of Charles J. (a physician) and Foy (Allen) Sawyer; married Asa B. Phelps, Jr., October 30, 1943 (died January 24, 1945); married William A. Allen, Jr. (an attorney), September 7, 1946; children: William A. III, Foy Allen Best, Reynold S. *Education:* Attended St. Mary's Junior College, Raleigh, N.C., 1937-39; University of North Carolina, A.B., 1941. *Religion:* Episcopalian. *Home:* 2106 Greenbriar Rd., Kinston, N.C. 28501.

CAREER: Bank teller in Windsor, N.C., 1941-43; high school teacher of French in Weldon, N.C., 1944-45; accountant in New York, N.Y., 1945-46; writer, 1973—. *Military service:* U.S. Army, Signal Corps, cryptographer, 1943. *Member:* Phi Beta Kappa.

WRITINGS: Ginger Hill (novel), Blair, 1973.

WORK IN PROGRESS: Another novel.

SIDELIGHTS: Sarah Allen writes: "I always had the impulse to write, but was a slow starter. I began by writing short stories, but none was ever published, so I tried a novel. I do not regard writing as a profession, but as a hobby and private joy. I also like to compose children's music."

* * *

ALLOTT, Kenneth 1912-1973

OBITUARY NOTICE: Born 1912; died May 23, 1973. Poet, playwright, editor, writer of fiction, and educator at Liverpool University for more than twenty years. Allott was very concerned with the future of European civilization. His poetry, in particular, characterizes his anger and forboding uncertainty over the fate of humanity. Obituaries and other sources: *Contemporary Poets,* St. Martin's, 1970.

* * *

ALPERT, Richard 1931- (Ram Dass)

PERSONAL: Born April 6, 1931, in Boston, Mass.; son of George (a lawyer) and Gertrude (Levin) Alpert. *Education:* Tufts University, A.B., 1952; Wesleyan University, Middletown, Conn., M.A., 1954; Stanford University, Ph.D., 1957. *Politics:* Democrat. *Religion:* "All." *Home and office:* P.O. Box 928, Soquel, Calif. 95073.

CAREER: Harvard University, Cambridge, Mass., assistant professor of psychology, 1958-63; writer, lecturer, and yogi, 1963—.

WRITINGS: (With Robert Sears and Lucy Rau) *Identification and Child Rearing,* Stanford University Press, 1960; (with Timothy Leary and Ralph Metzner) *The Psychedelic Experience,* Morrow, 1964; (with Sydney Cohen and Laurence Schiller) *L.S.D.,* New American Library, 1966.

Under pseudonym Ram Dass: *Be Here Now,* Lama Foundation, 1970; *The Only Dance There Is,* Doubleday, 1974; (with Stephen Levine) *Grist for the Mill,* Unity Press, 1977; *Journey of Awakening,* Bantam, 1978; *Miracle of Love,* Dutton, 1979.

WORK IN PROGRESS: A book concerning spiritual awakening through dying, perhaps in novel form.

SIDELIGHTS: Alpert became popular in the early 1960's as a user of LSD and other psychedelics. Together with Timothy Leary, Alpert helped popularize hallucinogens. The two met at Harvard University, where Leary was involved in a research project on the effects of hallucinogens. Alpert's first experience with psylocybin was so powerful that he became convinced that psychedelic drugs could illuminate the subconscious. Leary and Alpert intensified their experiments with the drugs at the expense of their academic careers. Leary was released from Harvard in 1963 after refusing to grade his students. Shortly afterwards, Alpert was dismissed for dispensing drugs to a student.

From 1963 to 1967, Alpert and Leary encouraged the rest of society to use LSD. They were most influential with students and musicians, and the increasing use of the drug contributed to the drastic changes in American culture during the sixties. The two became underground celebrities, especially Leary, who coined the phrase, "Tune in, turn on, drop out." Alpert eventually dropped out of the radical environment after suffering from depression brought on by using hallucinogens more than three hundred times.

To escape the drug culture, Alpert agreed to accompany a friend on an excursion to India to meet religious leaders. In India, Alpert underwent a spiritual rebirth. After meeting a maharaji, Alpert became a disciple and changed his name to Ram Dass. He returned to the United States in 1968 and began preaching his new beliefs. Although some members of the press dubbed him "Rum Dum," Dass enjoyed new popularity on college campuses, where his lectures sometimes ran for more than six hours. Upon publication of *Be Here Now,* Dass found himself the center of attention from thousands of followers who flocked to his farm in New Hampshire. His religious philosophy, which relied primarily on Eastern religions but also embraced Moslem and Christian concepts, was accepted by many of the same people who'd earlier attached themselves to the psychedelic culture. And as he'd earlier become disillusioned with the drug culture, so did he also become depressed about his religious followers.

In 1974, Dass was preparing to return to India when he decided instead to visit Joya, a popular spiritual leader in New York City. After establishing rapport with her, Dass became her willing disciple and instructed his followers to do the same. In turn, Joya informed Dass that he was destined to become an important teacher and she encouraged him to behave as one.

The association between Dass and Joya dissolved in 1976, after Dass, who insisted on celibacy from his followers, disclosed that he'd been intimate with Joya. Joya denied it, and the friendship ended bitterly.

Since leaving Joya, Dass has done extensive traveling and returned to the lecture circuit. "I don't know," he confessed, "if I'm going to be enlightened this lifetime or in 60 billion lifetimes or if I've fallen off the path. . . . Was I just a fad? Is it over? Is it just beginning? I don't know."

He writes: "I do not consider myself a writer. Most of my books have just happened along the way. Primarily I'm a spiritual seeker sharing with others the maps and pitfalls of the spiritual path. The toughest book to complete has been *Miracle of Love*. It collates material from over two thousand stories about my Indian teacher, Neem Karoli Baba. His existence stretched my model of the human possibility and I wanted to share these stories with others. But it is hard to write a biography about a person who isn't like other people. Every book has forced my own growth, thus I see these books as work on myself."

BIOGRAPHICAL/CRITICAL SOURCES: Ramparts, February, 1973; *New York Times Magazine,* December 4, 1977; *New Times,* September 4, 1978.

* * *

ALSCHULER, Rose Haas 1887-1979

OBITUARY NOTICE—See index for *CA* sketch: Born December 17, 1887, in Chicago, Ill.; died July 4, 1979, in Highland Park, Ill. Educator, administrator, and author of several nonfiction books on children. Considered a pioneer in the field of elementary education, Alschuler was the organizer and director of the first public nursery school in the United States. For more than forty years, she was affiliated, both as director and consultant, with several nursery schools and kindergartens in Illinois. She also served on numerous national and local committees for the upgrading of children's education and the safe construction of nursery schools. Her books include *Children's Centers* and *Play: The Child's Response to Life*. Obituaries and other sources: *Who's Who in World Jewry,* Pitman, 1972; *Chicago Tribune,* July 8, 1979.

* * *

ALSOP, Stewart (Johonnot Oliver) 1914-1974

PERSONAL: Surname is pronounced *All*-sop; born May 17, 1914, in Avon, Conn.; died May 26, 1974, in Bethesda, Md.; son of Joseph Wright (an insurance executive) and Corinne Douglas (a state legislator; maiden name, Robinson) Alsop; married Patricia Hankey, October, 1944; children: Joseph Wright, Ian Alexander, Elizabeth Winthrop (Mrs. Walter Butler Mahony III), Stewart Johonnot Oliver, Richard Nicholas, Andrew Christian. *Education:* Yale University, A.B., 1936. *Home:* 3520 Springland Lane, Washington, D.C.

20008. *Office:* 1750 Pennsylvania Ave., Washington, D.C. 20006.

CAREER: Doubleday Doran & Co., New York City, editor, beginning 1936; teamed with brother, Joseph, to write column, "Matter of Fact," for New York Herald Tribune syndicate, 1945-58; *Saturday Evening Post,* Philadelphia, Pa., national affairs contributing editor, 1958-62, Washington editor, 1962-68; *Newsweek,* New York City, columnist, 1968-74. Author. *Military service:* British Army, King's Rifle Corps, 1942-44. U.S. Army, Office of Strategic Services, 1944-45; became commander; received Croix de Guerre with palm, mentioned in dispatches. *Member:* River Club (New York City), Metropolitan Club (Washington, D.C.). *Awards, honors:* Overseas Press Club awards, 1950 and 1952, for best interpretation of foreign news; Authors Guild annual prize for contributing to civil liberties, 1955, for article "We Accuse."

WRITINGS: (With Thomas Braden) *Sub Rosa: The O.S.S. and American Espionage,* Reynal & Hitchcock, 1946; (with brother, Joseph Alsop) *We Accuse! The Story of the Miscarriage of American Justice in the Case of J. Robert Oppenheimer,* Simon & Schuster, 1954; (with J. Alsop) *The Reporter's Trade,* Reynal, 1958; *Nixon and Rockefeller: A Double Portrait,* Doubleday, 1960; *The Center: People and Power in Political Washington,* Harper, 1968 (published in England as *The Center: The Anatomy of Power in Washington,* Hodder & Stoughton, 1968); *Stay of Execution: A Sort of Memoir,* Lippincott, 1973.

SIDELIGHTS: Columnist Stewart Alsop spent his career observing the center of American life: Washington, D.C. His focus suddenly turned inward, however, one day in 1971. While emptying some trash outside his home he felt a sudden pain and began "gasping like a fish on a beach." Doctors first diagnosed an acute myeloblastic leukemia—and gave Alsop a year to live. He lived nearly three, in many ways as productively as ever. In addition to continuing his work with *Newsweek,* he became the center of his own poignant story in his *Stay of Execution.*

World War II gave Alsop an inadvertant push towards a career in writing. After graduating from Yale and working for a time at Doubleday, Alsop volunteered for service in the U.S. Army. Rejected for medical reasons, he headed for England, where he joined the King's Rifle Corps. Later he transferred to the U.S. Army as a parachutist with the Office of Strategic Services. His experience there provided him with the material for his first book, *Sub Rosa: The O.S.S. and American Espionage.* "The most remarkable fact about *Sub Rosa,*" said David Dempsey of the *New York Times,* "is that it is one of the very few books about the war in which the authors have been dazzled by the war without being blinded. In no sense a criticism of the O.S.S., it still reveals many of its faults."

The end of the war provided Stewart with another writing opportunity. His brother Joseph, having just returned from service, was ready to resume the column he had previously co-authored with Robert Kintner. Searching for a new collaborator, he chose Stewart, leading the younger Alsop to remark, "The best way to become a columnist is to have a brother who is one already." Under their shared by-line one brother would typically travel and report news from around the world while the other guarded news in Washington. By 1950, their pungent, informative, and often speculative column had found its way into nearly one hundred forty newspapers.

Reviews of the brothers' book, *The Reporter's Trade,* indicate the wide respect the columnists earned. Containing their views of journalism as well as reprints of some of their columns, *The Reporter's Trade* declared war on government secrecy. S. R. Davis thanked the authors for waging "a heroic two-man battle against one of the biggest Goliaths of our time—Official Secrecy. . . . For anyone who values public information and the right of a people honestly to be taken into the confidence of its government and told of crucial decisions to be made, this is one of the notable achievements of our time." Another reviewer, Patrick O'Donovan, while admitting "this is a tendentious book," valued it for implying: "'We like a fight.' That is a proper attitude for a journalist who must always be at war with government, but God forbid they should ever totally win this unending war."

Though the brothers themselves were never known to battle over writing policy, their shared by-line betrayed a uniform personality and political outlook which they never knew. "Joe was the brilliant polemicist; Stewart the steady fellow and, among other things, a more conscientious legman than his brother," wrote *Time.* When their partnership ended in 1958, they parted amicably, with Stewart moving to the *Saturday Evening Post* and then, finally, to *Newsweek.* Their political differences didn't end with their broken partnership, however, as the Vietnam war had become a major source of disagreement between the two. "It is not practical to continue to fight a war that has no popular support at all," Stewart once said. Joe, on the other hand, was a "hawk with the sharpest of beaks," declared Courtney R. Sheldon. Nevertheless, they remained close brothers. During Stewart's illness, Joe provided him with over forty platelet transfusions, each taking three hours. At that time Stewart quipped that he had become more conservative after "getting so many of Joe's elderly platelets."

Alsop reflected on the community that had fascinated him for more than twenty years in his 1968 book, *The Center.* In it, he spared few capital institutions his scrutiny. "Alsop penetrates the Pentagon, State Department and CIA headquarters at a depth impossible for journalists working against deadlines," noted Kenneth Crawford. But, as William V. Shannon pointed out, "this is not a muckraker's book. Alsop's Washington has little in common with Ralph Nader's and Drew Pearson's." Alsop himself admitted in his preface that "there are just too many Washingtons to get inside of. And a good many of these Washingtons are interesting only to the people who inhabit them, or are in some way involved in them. This book turned out to be only about the Washington that is inhabited by political journalists they write about."

Presidents, naturally, received much of Alsop's attention. His assessment of Lyndon B. Johnson revealed a highly intelligent man who would have been much more popular had it not been for the Vietnam war. That tragedy, Alsop contended, was due largely to John F. Kennedy's presidential policies. After the Bay of Pigs incident and a diplomatic loss with Laos, Kennedy, according to Alsop, committed troops to Southeast Asia in order to preserve the U.S. reputation as protector of world peace. One of the lessons of the era, Alsop regretfully admitted, was that the U.S. era as a superpower had ended. "It is Vietnam that is tearing Washington apart. . . . Above all, it is Vietnam that has ended the basic self-confidence of the Washington political community." Understandably, then, Alsop wrote with a touch of nostalgia in *The Center,* but as Arthur Scheslinger, Jr., pointed out in his review, "The understanding that 'there cannot be an American solution to every problem' may be the end of glory, but it is the beginning of wisdom. As this essential truth begins to permeate the Center, we may hope for a renunciation of messianic illusions and a new definition of the American role in a world of diversity."

When doctors diagnosed Alsop's leukemia in 1971, Alsop faced the terrifying prospect of finding a new definition of himself. He had no illusions of living long: typically, the disease claims the untreated victim within a few weeks of detection; doctors gave Alsop a year to live. But the disease proved temperamental. A series of remissions followed by a sudden rise in malignant cells led baffled doctors to describe the condition as "smoldering leukemia."

Shocked by the realization that his life was coming to an end, but not quite sure when, Alsop began to put his life into perspective, first by thinking, then by writing. The result, *Stay of Execution,* is the moving, insightful, sometimes funny, though never bitter story of "the process of adjustment whereby one comes to terms with death." "This is a most interesting experience, although one wishes one were not so personally involved," Alsop wrote at the beginning of this "medical detective story." Other observations are often far more chilling: One day he and his wife were discussing roses while driving to the National Institute of Health when Alsop suddenly remembered the purpose of the drive. "There was a moment's silence," he recalled. "And then I knew that I wouldn't see the roses next year. . . . I reached out my hand for Tish's. 'I have just now run out of my small store of courage,' I said. She squeezed my hand and said nothing." Yet, when Alsop sees pale leukemic children in the hospital wearing wigs and reading comic books, he is satisfied that he "has lived a full life and is grateful for it," commented E. S. Turner.

At the end of *Stay of Execution,* Alsop admitted the inevitability of his own death: "A dying man needs to die, as a sleepy man needs to sleep, and there comes a time when it is wrong, as well as useless, to resist." Alsop died a year later. Newton Koltz praised Alsop's book for confronting death directly, not later, as we normally do. "For him," stated Koltz, "there is no such luxury. He can't trick fear away as we do. Because he can't, the story of his fear becomes, more than anything else, his real story. In telling it he shows, once again, how possible it is for even a desperate and dying man to grow."

Alsop built a legacy through the courage he displayed in living in face of death and through the book that traced it. Aside from writing his book, he continued to write his *Newsweek* column, the last appearing less than a month before his death. To Mel Elfin, "there seemed, for so long, no limit to Stewart Alsop's will to resist. All through a debilitating, wasting illness, Stew lived so gracefully, so courageously and so productively that sometimes it was hard to believe him a man under sentence of early death. . . . As he vowed he would, Stewart Alsop did not go gentle into the night. The way he died kept faith with the way he had lived—proudly, fully, wisely, lovingly."

BIOGRAPHICAL/CRITICAL SOURCES: New York Times, February 24, 1946, December 14, 1958, May 27, 1974; *Saturday Review,* March 16, 1946, November 22, 1958; *Nation,* March 23, 1946; *Christian Science Monitor,* November 20, 1958, June 4, 1968; *New York Herald Tribune Book Review,* November 23, 1958, January 24, 1960; *New Yorker,* December 20, 1958, February 11, 1974; *New Republic,* December 29, 1958; *New York Times Book Review,* January 24, 1960, December 30, 1973; Stewart Alsop, *The Center: People and Power in Political Washington,* Harper, 1968; *Book World,* April 28, 1968; *Washington Post,* May 2, 1968; *Best Sellers,* May 15, 1968; *Newsweek,* June 10, 1968, December 31, 1973, June 3, 1974; *New Leader,* June 11, 1968; *Punch,* October 30, 1968; *Times Literary Supplement,* October 31, 1968, May 3, 1974; *New Statesman,* February 21, 1969; Alsop, *Stay of Execution: A Sort of Memoir,* Lippincott, 1973; *Washington Post Book World,* December 16, 1973; *Atlantic,* February, 1974; *Commentary,* February, 1974; *National Review,* February 15, 1974; *Economist,* April 13, 1974; *Time,* June 10, 1974; *Listener,* August 11, 1974; *Commonweal,* September 20, 1974.*

—*Sketch by David Versical*

* * *

ALTMAN, Thomas
See BLACK, Campbell

* * *

AMFITHEATROF, Erik 1931-

PERSONAL: Born June 29, 1931, in Milan, Italy; son of Daniele (a composer) and May (Semenza) Amfitheatrof; married Elvira Pauer, May 15, 1965; children: Stefania, Francesca. *Education:* Harvard University, B.A., 1954. *Home:* 44 Thurloe Sq., London S.W.7, England. *Agent:* John Hawkins, Paul R. Reynolds, Inc., 12 East 41st St., New York, N.Y. 10017. *Office: Time,* Time & Life Building, 153 New Bond St., London W.1, England.

CAREER: Time-Life Books, New York City, correspondent from Rome, Italy, 1966, and Tokyo, Japan, 1966-69, staff writer in New York City, 1969-73; *Time,* New York City, correspondent from Rome, 1975-77, and London, England, 1977—. *Military service:* Served in Air Force, 1955-57. *Member:* American Correspondents Club, Writers Guild.

WRITINGS: The Children of Columbus: An Informal History of the Italians in the New World, Little, Brown, 1973.

WORK IN PROGRESS: Enchanted Ground, publication expected by Little, Brown.

* * *

AMIN, Samir 1931-

PERSONAL: Born September 4, 1931, in Cairo, Egypt; son of Farid and Odette (Boeringer) Amin; married Isabelle Eynard, August 20, 1957. *Education:* University of Paris, Ph.D., 1957. *Office:* African Institute for Economic Development and Planning, BP 3186, Dakar, Senegal.

CAREER: Economic Development Organization, Cairo, Egypt, senior economist, 1957-60; Government of Mali, Bamako, technical adviser for planning, 1960-63; University of Poitiers, Poitiers, France, professor of economics, 1966-68; University of Paris, Paris, France, and University of Dakar, Dakar, Senegal, professor of economics, 1968-70; United Nations African Institute for Economic Development and Planning, Dakar, director, 1970—. *Member:* Association of Third World Economists.

WRITINGS—In English: *Le Maghreb moderne,* Minuit, 1970, translation by Michael Perl published as *The Maghreb in the Modern World: Algeria, Tunisia, Morocco,* Penguin, 1970; *L'Accumulation a l'echelle mondiale: critique de la theorie du sous-developpement,* two volumes, Institut fondamental d'Afrique noire, 1970, 2nd edition, 1971, translation by Brian Pearce published as *Accumulation on a World Scale: A Critique of the Theory of Underdevelopment,* Monthly Review Press, 1974; *L'Afrique de l'Ouest bloquee: l'economie politique de la colonisation, 1880-1970,* Minuit, 1971, translation by Francis McDonagh published as *Neo-*

Colonialism in West Africa, Penguin, 1973; *Le Developpement inegal: essai sur les formations sociales du capitalisme peripherique,* Minuit, 1973, translation by Pearce published as *Unequal Development: An Essay on the Social Formations of Peripheral Capitalism,* Monthly Review Press, 1976; *L'Echange inegal et la loi de la valeur,* Institut africain de developpement economique et de planification (IDEP), 1973, translation published as Part IV of *Imperialism and Unequal Development,* Monthly Review Press, 1977 (also see below), published as *The Law of Value and Historical Materialism,* Monthly Review Press, 1978; (editor) *Les Migrations contemporaines en Afrique de l'Ouest* [or] *Modern Migrations in Western Africa* (text in English and in French), Oxford University Press, 1974; *L'Imperialisme et le developpement inegal,* Minuit, 1976, translation by Alfred Ehrenfeld and Joan Pinkham published as *Imperialism and Unequal Development,* Monthly Review Press, 1977; *La Nation arabe: nationalisme et luttes de classes,* Minuit, 1976, translation by Michael Pallis published as *The Arab Nation,* Zed, 1978; *La Loi de la valeur et le materialisme historique,* Minuit, 1977, translation by Pearce published as *The Law of Value and Historical Materialism,* Monthly Review Press, 1978; *Classes, nations, etat, questions du materialisme historique,* Minuit, 1979, translation published as *Classes, Nations, and States in Historical Materialism,* Monthly Review Press, 1979.

Other: *Dirasa fil tayarat al naydia wal malia fi Micr am 1957* (title means "A Study of Financial and Monetary Flows in Egypt, 1957"), Centre des Hautes Etudes Arabes, 1959; *Comptes economiques de la Republique du Mali en 1959* (title means "National Accounts of the Republic of Mali for 1959"), Ministere de la Cooperation, 1961, revised edition, 1962; *Hassan Riad, l'Egypte nasserienne* (title means "Nasserian Egypt"), Minuit, 1964; *Trois experiences africaines de developpement: le Mali, la Guinee, et le Ghana* (title means "Three African Experiences in Development and Planning: Mali, Guinea, and Ghana"), Presses Universitaires de France, 1965; *L'Economie du Maghreb,* Volume I: *La Colonisation et la decolonisation,* Volume II: *Les Perspectives d'avenir* (title means "The Economy of Maghreb," Volume I: "Colonization and Decolonization," Volume II: "Future Projects") Minuit, 1966; *Le Developpement du capitalisme en Cote d'Ivoire* (title means "The Development of Capitalism in Ivory Coast"), Minuit, 1967; *Le Monde des affaires senegalais* (title means "The World of Senegalese Affairs"), Minuit, 1969; (with Catherine Coquery-Vidrovitch) *Du Congo francais a l' U.D.E.A.C.: histoire economique de l'Afrique Equatoriale, 1880-1968* (title means, "From the French Congo to the Economic and Customs Union of Central Africa: An Economic History of Equatorial Africa, 1880-1968"), Institut Fondamental d'Afrique Noire, 1969.

(With Kostas Vergopoulos) *La Question paysanne et le capitalisme* (title means "The Peasant Question and Capitalism"), Anthropos, 1974; (contributor) Dieter Senghaas, editor, *Peripherer Kapitalismus: Analysen ueber Abhaengigkeit und Unterentwicklung* (title means "Peripheral Capitalism: Analyses of Dependency and Underdevelopment"), Suhrkamp, 1974; (with others) *Domination et sous-developpement* (title means "Domination and Underdevelopment"), Presses Universitaires de Montreal, 1974; (editor) *L'Agriculture africaine et le capitalisme* (title means "African Agriculture and Capitalism"), Anthropos, 1975; (with Alexandre Faire, Mahmoud Hussein, and Gustave Massiah) *La Crise de l'imperialisme* (title means "The Crisis of Imperialism"), Minuit, 1975; (with Andre Frank and Hosea Jaffe) *Quale 1984: Relazioni e discussione al Convegno di studi ISTRA sulla crisi attuale del capitalismo* (title means "Which 1984?: Reports and Discussions at the ISTRA Convention on the Present Crisis of Capitalism"), ISTRA (Milan), 1975; (with Mark Franco and Samba Sow) *La Planification du sous-developpement: critique de l'analyse de projets* (title means "The Planning of Underdevelopment: Critique of Project Analysis"), Anthropos, 1975; *Imperialisme et sous-developpement en Afrique* (title means "Imperialism and Underdevelopment in Africa"), Anthropos, 1976; *Eloge du socialisme: lithographies de Paul Rebeyrolle* (title means "In Praise of Socialism"), Editions Maeght, 1976; (with others) *Le Marxisme* (title means, "Marxism"), Larousse, 1977; (editor with Frank, and contributor) *L'Accumulation dependante* (title means "Dependant Accumulation"), Anthropos, 1978.

SIDELIGHTS: Amin told *CA* that his work "deals primarily with the problems of unequal developments of capitalism on a world scale, i.e., the gradual rise of captialist developed and dominated countries versus the gradual formation of underdeveloped and dominated countries."

Amin's books have been translated into Spanish, Yugoslav, Polish, Italian, Arabic, Greek, German, Portugese, Danish, Japanese, and Swedish.

BIOGRAPHICAL/CRITICAL SOURCES: Times Literary Supplement, April 25, 1975; *Science and Society,* summer, 1978.

* * *

ANATOL, A.
See KUZNETSOV, Anatoli

* * *

ANDELIN, Helen B. 1920-

PERSONAL: Born May 22, 1920, in Mesa, Ariz.; daughter of Herbert A. and Anna May (Whiting) Berry; married Aubrey P. Andelin (in business promotion), July 23, 1942; children: Lane B., Brian B., Dixie Andelin Forsyth, Kristine Andelin Hales, John B., Virginia Andelin Leavitt, Paul B., Merilee. *Education:* Attended Brigham Young University, 1938, and University of Utah, 1940. *Religion:* Church of Jesus Christ of Latter-day Saints (Mormons). *Home address:* P.O. Box 219, Pierce City, Mo. 65723.

CAREER: Writer.

WRITINGS: Fascinating Womanhood, Pacific Press Publishing Association, 1965, revised edition, 1974; *The Fascinating Girl,* Pacific Press Publishing Association, 1970. Contributing editor of *Fascinating Womanhood Newsletter.*

WORK IN PROGRESS: The Family, with Robert R. Forsyth.

SIDELIGHTS: In her newsletter, Helen Andelin wrote: "When I married I had my heart set on achieving 'the ideal marriage'.... I strived earnestly for this ..., doing all I knew to measure up to my part by trying to become the ideal wife. However, after several years of marriage, it was distressing to me to realize that my husband did not seem fully pleased with me. I felt loved but not cherished, taken care of but not treasured. Instead of my marriage reaching the idealistic state I had planned, I had to admit that it was quite mediocre....

"I did, however, view this situation as my own fault. The teachings of my youth led me to believe that we make our own happiness and if we are unhappy we are to blame.... I observed many other women in the same situation as myself—unhappy or disillusioned with their marriages. Some were in real trouble. . . .

"It was then I began my search for knowledge. . . . Books on marriage dealt only with sex. . . . I searched the scriptures. They were profound in wisdom but I felt applied mostly to men's problems. . . . In faith I turned to God. . . .

"As my search for knowledge continued I began to discover fragments of information here and there, new insights, and gradually a greater understanding. . . . I caught a glimpse of a new world—a world of exquisite happiness that could be experienced between husband and wife—a devoted love that could continue throughout a lifetime of marriage.

"The impact of this new knowledge on my own marriage was tremendous. . . . I organized a class and invited a few women to attend. This class grew in a short time from eight to a hundred-seventy. Enthusiasm was high as the women applied the teachings and met with the same success I was having. . . . It was then I first conceived the idea of writing my book."

Andelin added: "There has been a great deal of controversy, and considerable opposition, to the teachings of Fascinating Womanhood. Its opponents have been the Women's Liberation movement and those who favor abortion. It has had much support from church groups and homemakers, the medical profession, and many psychologists."

BIOGRAPHICAL/CRITICAL SOURCES: Fascinating Womanhood Newsletter, September, 1975, December, 1977.

* * *

ANDERSON, Dave
See ANDERSON, David Poole

* * *

ANDERSON, David Poole 1929-
(Dave Anderson)

PERSONAL: Born May 6, 1929, in Troy, N.Y.; son of Robert P. (an advertising executive) and Josephine (an insurance broker; maiden name, David); married Maureen Ann Young, October 24, 1953; children: Stephen, Mark, Mary Jo, Jean Marie. *Education:* Holy Cross College, B.A., 1951. *Home:* 8 Inness Rd., Tenafly, N.J. 07670. *Office: New York Times,* 229 West 43rd St., New York, N.Y. 10036.

CAREER: Brooklyn Eagle, Brooklyn, N.Y., sports writer, 1951-55; *New York Journal-American,* New York City, sports writer, 1955-66; *New York Times,* New York City, sports writer, 1966—, author of column "Sports of The Times," 1971—. *Awards, honors:* Best Sports Stories award, 1965, for "The Longest Day of Sugar Ray," and 1972, for "Beaufort, S.C. Loves Joe Frazier . . . Now"; Page One Award from New York Newspaper Guild, 1972, for "Beaufort, S.C. Loves Joe Frazier . . . Now"; Pro Football Writers Story of the Year award, 1972; Nat Fleischer Award, 1974, for distinguished boxing journalism.

WRITINGS—All under name Dave Anderson: *Great Quarterbacks of the NFL* (juvenile), Random House, 1965; *Great Pass Receivers of the NFL* (juvenile), Random House, 1966; *Great Defensive Players of the NFL* (juvenile), Random House, 1967; *Countdown to Super Bowl,* Random House, 1969; (with Sugar Ray Robinson) *Sugar Ray,* Viking, 1970; (with Larry Csonka and Jim Kiick) *Always on the Run,* Random House, 1973; *Pancho Gonzalez: The Golden Year,* Prentice-Hall, 1974; (with Frank Robinson) *Frank: The First Year,* Holt, 1976; *The Yankees,* Random House, 1979; *Sports of Our Times,* Random House, 1979. Contributor of more than two hundred articles to magazines, including *Reader's Digest* and *Sports Illustrated.*

SIDELIGHTS: After the New York Jets' 1969 victory over the Baltimore Colts in Super Bowl III, quarterback Joe Namath announced that he would be interviewed only by New York reporters, and among them, Dave Anderson. Anderson had covered the Jets when they were first known as the Titans and was an admirer of Namath's skill, in addition to harboring the idea that the Jets could beat Baltimore. *Countdown to Super Bowl,* Anderson's chronicle of the days prior to football's most prestigious event, was praised for its clear, concise, and unbiased sports presentation. Arthur Cooper of *Newsweek* noted that Anderson "has written a day-by-day account in an understated style that is mercifully free of sport cliches."

Pete Axthelm, in his review of *Countdown,* called Anderson "a fine reporter with a spare, straightforward style, remarkably free of cliches of the all-out rooting for the home team that afflicts most football writers." It is "the controlled narrative," noted Axthelm, "that only increases the emotional impact of what the Jets were accomplishing. In addition to being great entertainment for football fans, the crisp and original account of the game should be a textbook for future sportswriters, as well as many of Anderson's present colleagues."

In an interview with *Editor & Publisher,* Anderson was asked about sportswriting. "I'd say it's generally good and sometimes excellent in the major cities and in many of the smaller cities," he said. "There are more realists than romantics now. The best way to improve sportswriting is to hire the best writers and reporters available. Don't let them dismiss journalism as a profession because of its comparatively low pay scale. The better the pay, the better writers and reporters it will attract."

Jim Scott praised Anderson for his professional attitude and noted that he "has long been in demand by magazine editors for he always turns out a masterful job."

AVOCATIONAL INTERESTS: Golf.

BIOGRAPHICAL/CRITICAL SOURCES: Newsweek, August 4, 1969; *New York,* September 29, 1969; *New York Times,* February 25, 1970; *Editor & Publisher,* April 6, 1974; *Authors in the News,* Volume 2, Gale, 1976; *New York Times Book Review,* April 15, 1979.

* * *

ANDERSON, Doris (Hilda) 1925-

PERSONAL: Born November 10, 1925, in Calgary, Alberta; daughter of Thomas (a miner) and Rebecca (Laycock) McCubbin; married David Anderson (a lawyer), May 24, 1957 (divorced in 1972); children: Peter David, Stephan Robert, Mitchell Richard. *Education:* University of Alberta, B.A., 1945. *Religion:* Anglican. *Home:* 174 Dufferin Rd., #11, Ottawa, Ontario, Canada. *Office:* 151 Sparks St., Ottawa, Ontario, Canada.

CAREER: Star Weekly, Toronto, Ontario, editorial assistant, 1946; T. Eaton Co., Ltd, Toronto, copywriter, 1948-51; Maclean-Hunter Publishing Co., Ltd., Toronto, *Chatelaine* magazine, assistant editor, 1951-52, associate editor, 1952-55, managing editor, 1955-57, editor, 1958-77, director, 1972-77. Member of national planning committee of National Centennial Confederation, 1965-67. Member of board of directors of Metropolitan Children's Aid of Toronto, 1966-69, York University, 1971—, Trilateral Commission, and Institute of Research on Public Policy. *Awards, honors:* Centennial medal, Canadian Government, 1967; L.L.D. from University of Alberta, 1974; member of Order of Canada, 1975.

WRITINGS: Two Women, Macmillan, 1978.

WORK IN PROGRESS: Another novel.

SIDELIGHTS: Doris Anderson began writing at the age of sixteen when she contributed articles to various magazines. She wrote that her aim in writing is "to influence and entertain the public," and noted that she began her first novel because she was "frustrated with the heroines in the current crop of fiction." *Avocational interests:* Reading, travel, antique collecting, entertaining.

* * *

ANGLO, Sydney 1934-

PERSONAL: Born March 1, 1934, in London, England; son of Harry and Ray (Pelter) Anglo; married Margaret M. McGowen, December, 1964. *Education:* University of London, B.A. (with honors), 1955, Ph.D., 1959. *Home:* 6 Mill Rise, Brighton, England. *Office:* Department of History, University College of Swansea, Singleton Park, Swansea SA2 8PP, Wales.

CAREER: University of Reading, Reading, England, fellow, 1958-61; University College of Swansea, Swansea, Wales, lecturer, 1961-69, senior lecturer, 1969-75, reader in the history of ideas, 1975—. Senior fellow at Warburg Institute, University of London, 1971-72. *Member:* Society of Antiquaries (fellow), Royal Historical Society (fellow), Society for Renaissance Studies (secretary, 1967-70).

WRITINGS: (Editor and author of introduction) *The Great Tournament Roll of Westminster,* two volumes, Clarendon Press, 1968; *Spectacle, Pageantry, and Early Tudor Policy,* Clarendon Press, 1969; *Machiavelli: A Dissection,* Gollancz, 1969, Harcourt, 1970; *L'Entree de Charles V: Bruges 1515,* Theatrum Orbis Terrarum, 1974; *The Damned Art: Essays in the Literature of Witchcraft,* Routledge & Kegan Paul, 1977; *Studies in the Early Reception of Machiavelli,* Routledge & Kegan Paul, 1980. Contributor to academic journals, including *Il Politico, Guildhall Miscellany, Antiquaries Journal,* and *Journal of the Society of Archivists.*

WORK IN PROGRESS: History of the Tournament and Duel, publication by Routledge & Kegan Paul expected in 1981.

SIDELIGHTS: Anglo included a collotype reproduction of the fifty-nine-foot roll of Westminster in Volume 2 of *The Great Tournament Role of Westminster.* N. Denholm-Young revealed that the roll "was made to commemorate the tournament held at Westminster to celebrate the birth of a prince to Katherine of Aragon and Henry VIII on New Year's Day 1511" and "has long been esteemed the greatest treasure of the College of Arms." Denholm-Young continued: "Mr. Anglo has produced an exceptional book. It is exhaustive, well written, and every statement is backed up with a wealth of historical fact. The book is much more than an introduction to the Tournament of 1511. It comprises an analysis of all the relevant Tudor revels at which lance-play was used, . . . and a prefatory section on the history of the tournament in England." *English Historical Review* critic M. Maclagan also praised Anglo's work. "The author is to be congratulated," Maclagan said, "on the skill and learning with which he has brought this great function to life in a truly splendid production, worthy of the lavish Tudor ruler who inspired the original."

Anglo's next book, *Spectacle, Pageantry, and Early Tudor Policy,* analyzed the political and social significance of early Tudor pageantry. "Anglo dwells at length with descriptions of royal progresses and banquets, London's celebrations for Tudor weddings and for visiting foreign dignitaries," noted *Choice.* L. B. Smith called the book "an engrossing, if heavy-going iconographic study. . . . As a scholarly portrayal of a vital and colorful aspect of Tudor life, [it] is splendid."

Machiavelli: A Dissection was praised by Gabriel Gersh as "a work of genuine scholarship and readability." He noted that "what emerges is neither a monster, nor a patriotic hero, nor the superintellect and universal genius lauded by modern scholars, but someone who is a 'good deal more credible and just as well worth reading.'" The *Times Literary Supplement* observed that "Dr. Anglo's admiration for Machiavelli is well this side of idolatry, and it is not until the last chapter that one can be sure he admires Machiavelli at all."

The collection of ten essays in *The Damned Art* "are, for the most part, informative introductions to significant witchcraft tracts," stated B. P. Copenhaver. Copenhaver also contended, "Had the individual essays appeared as preliminary material in editions of primary works, most might have gone unnoticed, but collected they become a chorus of insistent questions about our understanding of early modern witchcraft." Norman Cohn was also surprised that the essays were so illuminating and that Anglo had succeeded in establishing "a far more differentiated and accurate picture [of witchcraft] than has hitherto been possible."

Anglo told *CA:* "Academic research and writing—despite a large admixture of sheer drudgery—is usually a very enjoyable (and not infrequently exciting) activity. Its purpose, however, is unclear: and I have come to think that, on the whole, its principal value is to the scholar engaged in it rather than to his readers. Indeed, I often wonder whether readers find in books anything other than they wish. This is less the problem when you write on materials which have been largely unworked. But if you venture into one of the big academic industries, then beware! One Machiavelli-mogul, for example, was so vexed by my *Machiavelli* that he seemed quite unable to quote a single phrase accurately; and he even attacked me for not being conversant with research which had not been published until a year after my own book. Still, I must admit that there are some perceptive readers—those, for instance, who considered that book to be the best English language study of its subject. Yes, occasionally you do encounter sensitive and just criticism."

AVOCATIONAL INTERESTS: Piano virtuosity.

BIOGRAPHICAL/CRITICAL SOURCES: London Times, March 5, 1969; *London Sunday Telegraph,* May 4, 1969; *Times Literary Supplement,* May 29, 1969, November 18, 1977; *New Statesman,* June 20, 1969; *Medium Aevum,* Volume 38, No. 3, 1969; *Renaissance Quarterly,* winter, 1970; *Choice,* April, 1970; *Saturday Review,* April 18, 1970; *English Historical Review,* July, 1970; *American History Review,* December, 1970, April, 1978; *Nation,* January 4, 1971.

* * *

ANGUS, Fay 1929-

PERSONAL: Born May 25, 1929, in Brisbane, Australia; came to the United States in 1957, naturalized citizen, 1967; daughter of Ernest William and Amy Beatrice Westwood; married John S. Angus (a civil engineer), September 3, 1957; children: Anne, Ian. *Education:* Attended convent school in

Shanghai, China. *Religion:* Christian. *Home:* 405 North Canon Dr., Sierra Madre, Calif. 91024.

CAREER: Writer, 1974—. Founder of "outreach houses" in Sierra Madre Canyon. Public speaker. *Member:* International P.E.N., International Platform Association, National League of American Pen Women, Church Women United, Evangelical Women's Caucus, California Federation of Chaparral Poets.

WRITINGS: Between Your Status and Your Quo, Regal Books (Glendale), 1975; *Up to Heaven and Down to Earth,* Regal Books (Glendale), 1977; *The White Pagoda,* Tyndale, 1978; *The Catalyst,* Tyndale, 1979; *Signature of Faith,* Tyndale, 1980.

WORK IN PROGRESS: Attitudes and Alternatives: A Dictionary of Moral Character; Running Around in Evangelical Circles; a novel set in China.

SIDELIGHTS: Fay Angus's first two books are inspirational humor. She calls *Up to Heaven and Down to Earth* "a primer of practical Christianity, designed to help you over the hurdles of daily life and on to productive living."

Angus adds: "One just can't grow up in China and be interned for two and a half years during the war without writing about it, so I knew that at some time I'd write my autobiography. I'm glad I waited and let the experience incubate and mature a bit, as it gave me a better perspective. *The White Pagoda* is the China story, the story of a young girl growing up in metropolitan Shanghai and the impressions of her teenage years in a prisoner-of-war camp in Yangchow. *The Catalyst* is a sequel, a romantic story of my quest for faith.

"With a background in China, naturally I'll return. I've done a lot of interviews on the China situation and the exciting potential of their Great Leap Outward. My novel in progress has a China base and I hope to spend several months over there.

"Undoubtedly my sense of humor got me through the trauma of the concentration camp. When given the alternative to laugh or to cry, I found at a very impressionable age that it's far easier to laugh. It definitely eases the agony! Inspirational humor is my forte and I have several other books planned along this line."

* * *

ANSBACHER, Max G. 1935-

PERSONAL: Born December 16, 1935, in New York, N.Y.; son of Heinz L. (a professor) and Rowena (a psychologist; maiden name, Ripin) Ansbacher. *Education:* University of Vermont, B.A., 1957; Yale University, LL.B., 1960. *Home:* 20 Park Ave., New York, N.Y. 10016. *Office:* Bear, Stearns, 55 Water St., New York, N.Y. 10041.

CAREER: Bear, Stearns (investment firm), New York, N.Y., vice-president, 1955—. Professor at New York University.

WRITINGS: The New Options Market, Walker & Co., 1975, revised edition, 1979.

SIDELIGHTS: Ansbacher writes: "I am interested in applying logic to the investment process, particularly utilizing stock options as a means of increasing investments."

* * *

ANTHONY, Susan B(rownell) 1916-

PERSONAL: Born July 26, 1916, in Easton, Pa.; daughter of Luther Burt (a play doctor) and Charlotte (a writer; maiden name, Sutherland) Anthony. *Education:* University of Rochester, B.A., 1938; American University, M.A., 1941; Saint Mary's College, Notre Dame, Ind., M.A., 1963, Ph.D., 1965. *Politics:* Democrat. *Religion:* Roman Catholic. *Home:* 1963 North East Sixth St., Deerfield Beach, Fla. 33441. *Agent:* Ellen Levine, Curtis Brown Ltd., 575 Madison Ave., New York, N.Y. 10022.

CAREER: Writer, lecturer, and theologian. Worked as reporter for *Washington Star* in Washington, D.C., 1942-43, *Key West Citizen* in Key West, Fla., 1950-53, and *Jamaica/Gleaner* in Jamaica, West Indies, 1956-60; Saint Mary's College, Notre Dame, Ind., assistant professor of theology, 1965-66; Marymount College, Boca Raton, Fla., assistant professor of theology, 1965-69; South County Mental Health Center, Delray Beach, Fla., substance abuse coordinator, 1974-75. Stringer for Associated Press, 1942-43, 1950-53, and 1956-60; commentator with WMCA-Radio, 1946; co-founder of national prayer group movement of Roman Catholic Church and chairman of conference, "Prayer Unites," 1965-68; co-founder and honorary chairman of the board of Wayside House, 1975—; lecturer with National Council on Alcoholism, 1976—; delegate from Florida to National Women's Conference, 1977; sponsor of Women's Ordination Conference, 1978-79; women's representative of National Institute on Alcohol Abuse and Alcoholism National Plan of Action Steering Group, 1978-79. *Awards, honors:* Honoree at reception by United States Senate, 1976, for work in alcoholism; Pioneer Award from National Council on Alcoholism, 1977; co-honoree at reception by U.S. House of Representatives, 1978; co-honoree with sister Charlotte Anthony at White House, 1979, for Susan B. Anthony dollar coin issue.

WRITINGS: Out of the Kitchen–Into the War; Women's Winning Role in the Nation's Drama, Stephen Daye Press, 1943; (with Ann Shyne) *Women During the War and After,* Curtis Publishing, 1945; *The Prayer-Supported Apostle,* Catholic Action, 1965; *The Ghost in My Life* (autobiography), Chosen Books, 1971; *Survival Kit,* New American Library, 1972; *Sobriety of the Heart,* privately printed, 1978. Contributor to periodicals, including *Christian Science Monitor, New York Times Magazine, Saturday Evening Post, Spiritual Life,* and *U.S. Catholic.*

WORK IN PROGRESS: Volume II of her autobiography; writing upcoming lectures and editing those from 1976-79 for future book.

SIDELIGHTS: Anthony is a great-niece of Susan B. Anthony, pioneer suffragist, author of the Nineteenth Amendment to the U.S. Constitution giving women the right to vote, and the first American woman to be engraved on a U.S. coin. The second Susan, a feminist since her youth, not only helped found women's organizations and the first women's studies course in the United States (1966), but is a leading state and national proponent of the Equal Rights Amendment.

A recovered alcoholic since 1946, Anthony has lectured in the United States, Africa, and Jamaica, combining her feminism with temperance in her talks and her counseling. In addition to temperance and feminism, mysticism is her third discipline. "My works past and present show these converging interests," she told *CA.*

A convert to Roman Catholicism in 1961, Anthony became one of the first fifteen Catholic laywomen to obtain a doctorate in theology. In 1973 she took private vows of poverty, chastity, and obedience, and serves as a eucharistic minister at her parish, St. Ambrose Church, in Deerfield Beach.

"In the time that is left," she told *CA*, "I hope to extract from my rather full life what will be most useful for readers and listeners. My personal goal reflects the convergence of what I have learned in prayer, in helping others and myself recover from alcoholism, and in my work for justice, especially for women. That goal is a society that renders contemplation possible for its members."

BIOGRAPHICAL/CRITICAL SOURCES: New York Times, September 21, 1971; Susan B. Anthony, *The Ghost in My Life* (autobiography), Chosen Books, 1971.

* * *

APPEL, Kenneth Ellmaker 1896-1979

OBITUARY NOTICE: Born May 15, 1896, in Lancaster, Pa.; died August 27, 1979, in Ardmore, Pa. Psychiatrist and author. A psychiatrist and former head of the psychiatry department at the University of Pennsylvania, Appel was responsible for the establishment of the U.S. Joint Commission of Mental Illness and Health. His writings included *Psychiatry in Modern Warfare* and *Living Wisely and Well*. Obituaries and other sources: *Who's Who in America*, 38th edition, Marquis, 1974; *Chicago Tribune*, September 2, 1979.

* * *

APPLE, R(aymond) W(alter), Jr. 1934-

PERSONAL: Born November 20, 1934, in Akron, Ohio; son of R.W. (a business executive) and Julia (Albrecht) Apple; married Edith Smith, October 1, 1966 (divorced). *Education:* Attended Princeton University, 1952-56; Columbia University, A.B., 1961. *Home:* 24 Eaton Pl., London S.W.1, England. *Office: New York Times*, 76 Shoe Lane, London EC4, England.

CAREER: Wall Street Journal, New York City, reporter, 1956-57, 1959-61; NBC News, New York City, correspondent, 1961-63; *New York Times*, New York City, bureau chief in Albany, N.Y., 1964-65, bureau chief in Saigon, South Vietnam, 1965-68, chief African correspondent, 1969, national political correspondent in Washington, D.C., 1970-76, London bureau chief, 1977—. Visiting lecturer in politics at several universities, including Yale University. *Military service:* U.S. Army, 1957-59. *Member:* American Newspaper Guild. *Awards, honors:* Award from Academy of Television Arts and Sciences, 1962, for "The Huntley-Brinkley Report"; Overseas Press Club Award and George Polk Memorial Award, both 1967, both for Vietnam reporting.

WRITINGS: (Contributor) John Arthur Garraty, editor, *Quarrels That Have Shaped the Constitution*, Harper, 1964. Contributor to several books on Watergate. Also contributor of articles to *Esquire, Saturday Review, Reporter, Harper's, New Statesman*, and other periodicals.

SIDELIGHTS: Apple has covered the Vietnam War, the civil rights movement in Oxford, Birmingham, and Selma, the Biafra War, Watergate, the Iranian revolution, and presidential campaigns since 1964.

BIOGRAPHICAL/CRITICAL SOURCES: More, July-August, 1976.

* * *

APPLEWHITE, Cynthia

PERSONAL: Born in St. Louis, Mo.; daughter of Eric Leon (in sales) and Julia Marie (Hoffman) Applewhite; married Louis Zamperini (an evangelist); children: Cynthia, Luke. *Education:* Attended Bennett Junior College, 1947-48, and American Academy of Dramatic Arts, 1949-50. *Religion:* Society of Friends (Quakers). *Home:* 2338 Hollyridge Dr., Hollywood, Calif. 90068. *Agent:* Barbara Lowenstein, 250 West 57th St., New York, N.Y. 10019.

CAREER: Painter, 1964—, with solo shows in California. Formerly active with American Friends Service Committee and United Farm Workers Crusade.

WRITINGS: Sundays (novel), Avon, 1979.

WORK IN PROGRESS: Summer, Dreams, and the Klieg Light Gas Company, a novel, publication expected in 1981.

SIDELIGHTS: Cynthia Applewhite writes: "*Sundays* is my first published work, but the book began many years before in the form of poetry, descriptive paragraphs, and short stories. How all this gradually flowered into a novel seems to be a matter of persistent images finally becoming energized enough to coalesce and become a world of their own.

"In writing, I try to reach to my deepest level, seeking images which I hope exist in the unconscious of everyone. Once glimpsed, I place these images on paper, sometimes with words, sometimes in the form of sketches. In brooding upon these images time after time, I find they become more inclusive, taking on aspects of everyday conversation and everyday thought. It is then a book begins."

AVOCATIONAL INTERESTS: Skin diving, music, "long, solitary expeditions in Africa, Asia, Oceania, and Europe."

* * *

APPLEWHITE, E(dgar) J(arratt, Jr.) 1919-

PERSONAL: Born April 24, 1919, in Newport News, Va.; son of Edgar Jarratt (a dentist) and Mabel Agnes (Metzler); married Joyce Knowlton Zinsser, May 21, 1941; children: Jarratt, Ashton (daughter), Maria Joyce, Anthony Zinsser. *Education:* Yale University, B.A., 1941; attended Harvard University, 1967. *Politics:* Democrat. *Religion:* Episcopalian. *Home and office:* 3200 Idaho Ave. N.W., Washington, D.C. 20016. *Agent:* Gerald Dickler, Esq., Hall, Dickler, Lawler, Kent & Howley, 460 Park Ave., New York, N.Y. 10022.

CAREER: Writer. U.S. Government, Central Intelligence Agency (CIA), Washington, D.C., deputy inspector general and chief of inspection staff, 1963-66, intelligence assistant to secretary of defense, 1966-67. *Military service:* U.S. Navy, 1940-46; became lieutenant commander; received six service citations and presidential unit citation. *Awards, honors:* Intelligence medal of merit, CIA, 1970.

WRITINGS: (With R. Buckminster Fuller) *Synergetics: Explorations in the Geometry of Thinking*, Macmillan, 1975; *Cosmic Fishing: An Account of Writing Synergetics With Buckminster Fuller*, Macmillan, 1977; (with Fuller) *Synergetics Two*, Macmillan, 1979.

WORK IN PROGRESS: "A study of the ambivalence of the intelligence function in government, under the working title of *Plausible Denial;* an informal social and artistic critique of the city of Washington; a popular explication of R. B. Fuller's synergetics mathematics and philosophy—particularly in terms of the impact of quantum mechanics on contemporary thought."

SIDELIGHTS: Applewhite told *CA:* "Sometimes people say to me, 'Isn't it too bad you didn't begin to write until you were fifty? I don't feel any deprivation. I like the detachment of the writer's life, but for that I would not want to have given up a happy career in the mainstream."

The former intelligence officer collaborated with R. Buckminster Fuller, noted author and inventor of the geodesic dome, in writing *Synergetics*. The book combines Fuller's theories on philosophy, mathematics, and design, deftly organized and edited by Applewhite. Applewhite's contribution in this effort makes "Maxwell Perkins's famous labors with Thomas Wolfe seem modest by comparison," declared O. B. Hardison. This tour de force "will be debated, acclaimed, questioned, and, in some cases, attacked for years to come."

Synergetics emerged from piles of disorganized notes collected by Fuller over the years. In the semi-autobiographical *Cosmic Fishing,* Applewhite relates with wit how he managed to "keep the project rolling, translating (as no one else could) the Fuller scrawls into understandable paragraphs," wrote Alexander C. Brown. Maintaining communications with the globe-trotting Fuller was another challenge Applewhite faced in preparing the manuscript for publication: much of their collaboration took place via long distance telephone calls. *Cosmic Fishing* "radiates the heat of hard work," concluded William Marlin, and the result, added Brown, is "delightful."

BIOGRAPHICAL/CRITICAL SOURCES: Wall Street Journal, April 8, 1975; *New York Times Book Review,* June 29, 1975; *Washington Star,* April 27, 1977; *Newport News Daily Press,* May 1, 1977; E. J. Applewhite, *Cosmic Fishing,* Macmillan, 1977; *Christian Science Monitor,* May 19, 1978.

* * *

ARATA, Esther S(pring) 1918-

PERSONAL: Born February 5, 1918, in Newark, Ohio; daughter of Herman M. (a pattern maker) and Lillian (Mullen) Spring; married John J. Arata (an instructor, photographer, and artist). *Education:* College of St. Francis, Joliet, Ill., B.A., 1942; St. Louis University, M.Ed., 1958, M.A., 1967. *Politics:* "Depends . . . " *Religion:* Roman Catholic. *Residence:* Eau Claire, Wis. *Office:* Department of English, University of Wisconsin, Eau Claire, Wis. 54701.

CAREER: College of St. Francis, Joliet, Ill., head of home economics department, 1943-51; English teacher at private school in Maumee, Ohio, 1951-59, and high schools in Columbus, Ohio, 1961-63, and East St. Louis, Mo., 1963-66; St. Louis University, St. Louis, Mo., instructor of English, 1966-67; Mercy Junior College, St. Louis, Mo., instructor of English, 1967-68; University of Wisconsin, Eau Claire, assistant professor of English, 1968—. Member of faculty at McKendree Junior College, 1964-66. *Member:* American Association of University Women, National Writers Club, College English Association, Midwest Modern Language Association, Friends of Channel 28. *Awards, honors: Black American Writers Past and Present* was cited by American Library Association as one of the outstanding reference books of 1975.

WRITINGS: Black American Writers Past and Present: A Biographical and Bibliographical Dictionary, two volumes, Scarecrow, 1975; *Black American Playwrights, 1800 to the Present,* Scarecrow, 1976; *More Black American Playwrights,* Scarecrow, 1978.

WORK IN PROGRESS: A historical novel about three women who lived during the time of Louis XIV, publication expected in 1981.

SIDELIGHTS: Esther Arata told *CA:* "While spending seven years researching, publishing, and teaching the works of Black American writers, I believe that the women writers are exceptional innovators to be reckoned with in the kaleidoscope of American literature.

"The writings of Mary Renault and Francois Mauriac have quickened my desire to tell a story. Consequently, I have spent two-and-a-half years researching and traveling in search of certain facts to unravel the mystery surrounding the life of a young French woman who lived during the reign of Louis XIV, the Sun King. Her birthright was deliberately, cleverly denied her so that she lived as a prisoner all her life. Many people hold dearly to the right and freedom of a person to grow and develop into a unique individual. For anyone, under any circumstance, to be denied this right and freedom is very sad. Thus, there is this desire to tell a story about such an individual, and pay, posthumously, a tribute to a unique woman forced to re-structure her life by the decree of a king."

AVOCATIONAL INTERESTS: Travel, photography, Little Theatre activities, art, history.

* * *

ARBOGAST, William F. 1908-1979

OBITUARY NOTICE: Born June 12, 1908, in Bellevue, Ky.; died of cancer, November 13, 1979, in Fairfax, Va. Journalist and assistant staff director of the House Committee on Standards of Official Conduct. Arbogast covered the U.S. House of Representatives for the Associated Press from 1941 until his retirement in 1973, an assignment he called "the best beat in town." A close associate of Representative and Speaker of the House Sam Rayburn, Arbogast regularly attended Rayburn's so-called "board of education" sessions, when congressional leaders met over a glass of bourbon to gossip and plan strategy. One of his most notable assignments occurred March 1, 1954, the day a group of Puerto Rican extremists shot five members of the House. From a crouched position behind the press gallery, Arbogast phoned in a running account of the gun attack. He also covered the Alger Hiss hearings of the House Committee on Un-American Activities. Obituaries and other sources: *Washington Post,* November 15, 1979.

* * *

ARCHER, H(orace) Richard 1911-1978

OBITUARY NOTICE—See index for *CA* sketch: Born September 13, 1911, in Albuquerque, N.M.; died January 19, 1978, in Boston, Mass. Librarian, rare book collector, and author of books in his field. In addition to his job as Chapin Librarian at Williams College, Archer operated his own printing press, the Hippogryph Press. A noted book collector, Archer was especially proud of his Faulkner collection, which contained a number of first editions. Obituaries and other sources: *A Biographical Directory of Librarians in the United States and Canada,* 5th edition, American Library Association, 1970; *AB Bookman's Weekly,* February 20, 1978.

* * *

ARDIZZONE, Edward (Jeffrey Irving) 1900-1979

OBITUARY NOTICE—See index for *CA* sketch: Born October 16, 1900, in Haiphong, French Indochina (now Vietnam); died November 8, 1979, in London, England. Painter, illustrator, and author of children's books. Although he is best known for his illustrations of children's books, Ardizzone also painted combat scenes during World War II. An official war artist, he often accompanied Allied troops into battle in

France, North Africa, Sicily, Italy, and Germany, and among his works exhibited in the Imperial War Museum are paintings of the fall of France, the bombing of London, and the Normandy and Anzio offensives. Ardizzone illustrated more than one hundred books, but his most famous work, "Magic Carpet," is a painting of several turbanned Indian children on a flying carpet. Possessed with a love for the sea, he created a series about a young boy's adventures at sea, "Little Tim." His work is exhibited at the Tate Gallery, Liverpool Gallery, and in private collections. Obituaries and other sources: *Current Biography,* Wilson, 1964; *Who's Who in the World,* 4th edition, Marquis, 1978; *International Who's Who,* Europa, 1979; *Who's Who,* 131st edition, St. Martin's, 1979; *New York Times,* November 9, 1979; *Time,* November 19, 1979.

* * *

AREM, Joel E(dward) 1943-

PERSONAL: Born December 28, 1943, in Brooklyn, N.Y.; son of Milton (a consultant) and Sylvia (a hospital administrator; maiden name, Cagan) Arem; married Deborah Meiselman, September 28, 1979. *Education:* Brooklyn College of the City University of New York, B.S. (magna cum laude), 1964; Harvard University, M.A., 1967, Ph.D., 1970. *Residence:* Laytonsville, Md. *Office:* Multifacet, Inc., P.O. Box 996, Laytonsville, Md. 20760.

CAREER: Brooklyn Children's Museum, Brooklyn, N.Y., director of geology program, 1963-64; Smithsonian Institution, Washington, D.C., staff crystallographer and founder and curator of National Synthetics Collection, 1970-74; Multifacet, Inc. (gem dealers and appraisers), Laytonsville, Md., president, 1974—. Public speaker; consultant to Eastman Kodak Co., National Geographic Society, and U.S. Atomic Energy Commission. *Member:* American Association for Crystal Growth (charter member), Mineralogical Society of America, Accredited Gemologists Association (president), Friends of Mineralogy (founder), Gemmological Association of Great Britain (fellow), Phi Beta Kappa, Sigma Xi. *Awards, honors:* Tully Memorial Medal from Gemmological Association of Great Britain, 1976.

WRITINGS: Rocks and Minerals, Bantam, 1973; (also photographer) *Man-Made Crystals,* Smithsonian Institution Press, 1973; (also photographer) *Gems and Jewelry,* Bantam, 1975; (also photographer) *Color Encyclopedia of Gemstones,* Van Nostrand, 1977; *Precious Stones Buyers Guide,* PreciouStones Newsletter, in press; *Topics in Gemology,* Van Nostrand, in press. Contributor of articles and photographs to gem magazines and popular periodicals, including *Saturday Review of Science, Smithsonian,* and *Omni.* Editor of *PreciouStones Newsletter;* member of editorial board of *Rocks and Minerals.*

SIDELIGHTS: Arem, an expert on investment gems as well as rare and exotic gemstones, has other interests in mineral and gem synthesis and crystal growth. At the Smithsonian Institution, he had the opportunity to photograph and examine some of the world's finest stones. Later he developed a technique for photographing gems that illuminates nearly all the facets of the stone, without the harsh white reflections that characterize many gem photographs.

He writes: "Considering the importance of technology to modern society, communication in this area is vital. My main concern is communication of technical information in a way that is relevant and easy to understand. I travel extensively in connection with my business, and this provides an excellent perspective for putting American viewpoints and problems in a larger context and reaching better conclusions."

* * *

ARENS, William 1940-

PERSONAL: Born August 31, 1940, in New York, N.Y.; son of Nicholas (a proprietor) and Sarah (Woods) Arens; married Diana Antos (a sociologist), September 1, 1963; children: Geoffrey W. *Education:* Long Island University, B.A., 1963; University of New Mexico, M.A., 1965; University of Virginia, Ph.D., 1970; research student at Oxford University, 1970. *Home:* 12 North Rd., Stony Brook, N.Y. 11790. *Office:* Department of Anthropology, State University of New York at Stony Brook, Stony Brook, N.Y. 11790.

CAREER: Brooklyn College of the City University of New York, Brooklyn, N.Y., lecturer in student services, 1965-66; State University of New York at Stony Brook, assistant professor, 1970-75, associate professor of anthropology, 1975—. Research associate at University of Khartoum and University of Dar es Salaam; conducted field research in the Sudan and Tanzania. Organizer and director of symposia. *Awards, honors:* Social Science Research Council grant, 1978.

WRITINGS: (Contributor) Angela Molnos, editor, *Cultural Source Materials for Population Planning in East Africa,* Volume II and III, East African Publishing House, 1972; (editor and contributor) *A Century of Change in Eastern Africa,* Mouton, 1976; (editor with Susan Montague) *The American Dimension,* Alfred Publishing, 1976; *The Man-Eating Myth: Anthropology and Anthropophagy,* Oxford University Press, 1979; *On the Frontier of Change,* University of Michigan Press, 1979; (contributor) Ivan Karp, editor, *Explorations in African Systems of Thought,* Indiana University Press, 1980. Contributor of about thirty-five articles and reviews to anthropology and sociology journals. Member of editorial board of *Anthropology.*

WORK IN PROGRESS: Incest: A Cross-Cultural Analysis of the Taboo and Its Violation, publication by Oxford University Press expected in 1982.

SIDELIGHTS: Arens writes: "*The Man Eating Myth* and *The American Dimension,* in contrast to *A Century of Change in Eastern Africa* and *On the Frontier of Change,* indicate an interest to communicate with both colleagues and a more general audience. Future publications concerned with the topic of incest and the history and culture of the Shilluk people of the southern Sudan will maintain the dual emphases since they provide the opportunity to pursue the general interests which brought me into anthropology as well as those which emerged during the past ten years as a professional practitioner."

BIOGRAPHICAL/CRITICAL SOURCES: New York Times Book Review, July 29, 1979.

* * *

ARGUEDAS, Jose Maria 1911-1969

PERSONAL: Born January 18, 1911, in Andahuaylas, Peru; committed suicide November 28, 1969, in Lima, Peru; son of Victor Manuel (a provincial traveling judge) and Dona Victoria (Altamirano) Arguedas; married Celia Bustamente Vernal, 1939. *Education:* Received doctorate from University of San Marcos, Lima. *Address:* Apartado Postal 43, Lima, Peru.

CAREER: Post office employee in Lima, Peru, 1932-37; arrested and imprisoned for organizing a demonstration against an Italian Fascist general at University of San Marcos, 1937; National University, Sicuani, Peru, teacher of Spanish, 1939-41; head of department of folklore and popular arts at Ministry of Public Education, beginning 1945; director of Institute of Ethnological Studies at Peruvian Museum of Culture, beginning 1951; University of San Marcos, Lima, professor of regional cultures of Peru, 1959-69. Member of a commission to reform secondary education in Peru, 1940. Director of the Casa de la Cultura, 1963-64, and of the National Museum of History, 1964-69. Professor of Quechua at Universidad Nacional Agraria, 1963-69. Lecturer. *Awards, honors:* Inca Garcilaso Prize, 1968.

WRITINGS—In English: *Canciones y cuentos del pueblo quechua,* Editorial Huascaran (Lima), 1949, translation by Ruth Walgreen Stephan published as *The Singing Mountaineers: Songs and Tales of the Quechua People,* University of Texas Press, 1957; *Los rios profundos* (novel), Editorial Losada (Buenos Aires), 1958, translation by Frances H. Barraclough published as *Deep Rivers,* University of Texas Press, 1978.

Other: *Agua* (short stories; title means "Water"), [Peru], 1935; (translator from the Quechua) *Canto kechwa* (title means "Quechua Song"), Ediciones Club del libro peruano, 1938; *Runa yupay,* Comision central del censo, 1939; *Yawar fiesta* (novel; title means "Blood Feast"), CIP (Lima), 1941, reprinted, Editorial Universitaria (Santiago), 1968; *Cusco,* Corporacion Nacional de Turismo (Lima), 1947; (editor with Francisco Izquierdo Rios) *Mitos, leyendas y cuentos Peruanos,* Ediciones de la Direccion de Educacion Artistica y Extension Cultural (Lima), 1947, second edition, 1970.

Cuentos magico-realistas y canciones de fiestas tradicionales: Folklore del valle del Mantaro, provincias de Jauja y Concepcion, Editora Medica Peruana (Lima), 1953; *Diamantes y pedernales* (short stories; title means "Diamonds and Gems"), J. Mejia Baca & P. L. Villaneuva (Lima), 1954; *Las comunidades de Espana y del Peru* (title means "The Communities of Spain and Peru"), University of San Marcos, 1954; *Evolucion de las comunidades indigenas,* [Lima], 1957; *El arte popular religioso y la cultura mestiza,* Revista del Museo Nacional (Lima), 1958.

(Author of introduction) *Bibliografia del folklore Peruano,* Institute Panamericano de Geografia e Historia (Mexico City), 1960; *El sexto* (novel; title means "The Sixth One"), Libreria-Editorial J. Mejia Baca, 1961; *La agonia de Rasu Niti* (novel), Populibros Peruanos (Lima), c. 1964; *Todas las sangres* (novel; title means "All the Races"), Editorial Losada, 1964; (translator from the Quechua) *Poesia quechua* (title means "Quechua Poetry"), Editorial Universitaria de Buenos Aires, 1966; (translator from the Quechua) Francisco de Avila, *Dioses y hombres de Huarochiri* (title means "Gods and Men of Huarochiri"), Museo Nacional de Historia ye el Instituto de Estudios Peruanos, 1966; *Amor mundo y otros relatos* (short stories), Arca (Montevideo), 1967.

El zorro de arriba y el zorro de abajo (novel; title means "The Fox From Above and the Fox From Below"), Editorial Losada, 1971; *Temblar/Katatay,* INC, 1972; *El forastero y otros cuentos* (short stories), Sandino (Montevideo), 1972; *Paginas escogidas* (selected works), Editorial Universo, 1972; *Cuentos olvidades,* Ediciones Imagenes ye Letras, 1973; (contributor) Mario Vargas Llosa, *La novela,* America Nueva, 1974; *Relatos completos* (complete short stories), Editorial Losada, 1974; *Formacion de una cultura nacional indoamericana* (addresses, essays, and lectures), compiled by Angel Rama, Siglo Veintiuno Editores (Mexico), 1975; *Senores e indios: Acerca de la cultura quechua* (essays, addresses, and lectures), Arca, 1976.

Editor of *Palabra,* a literary review.

SIDELIGHTS: Ever since Pizarro conquered the Incas in 1533, Peru has had two cultures, Indian and Hispanic. For centuries the Indian civilization had been forgotten, ignored, or misunderstood by scholars and writers. In the 1920's, however, a new literary wave which emphasized native rather than European culture swept Latin America. Called the indigenous movement, it attracted a number of Peruvian authors, among whom the most famous was Jose Arguedas.

Arguedas championed the cause of the Quechua Indians, who were descendants of the Incas. Born in a city where the vast majority of people spoke Quechua, Arguedas learned to speak Quechua before he spoke Spanish. Because his mother died when he was only three, he was often cared for by his family's Quechua servants, for whom he developed a deep affection and respect. When Arguedas was a teenager, he began to accompany his father, a traveling lawyer, on his journeys. As the two men traveled through many remote regions in Peru, they became acquainted with some of the Indian serfs who were working for large landowners. For a time the young Arguedas worked on one of the haciendas, where he befriended the serfs and came to sympathize with their oppression.

Having gained such an intimate look at Quechua life and culture, Arguedas was shocked when he first began reading Peruvian fiction. In most of the literature written at that time, the Andean Indians were mere cardboard characters, depicted either as noble savages or as violent people whose ways could never be understood by white men. Even those writings which were sympathetic to the Indians' plight disturbed Arguedas, for they presented a stereotyped image of landowners as cruel and inhuman. In his own writing, Arguedas sought to show the complexity of both peoples.

Agua, Arguedas's first book, is a collection of three stories. The narratives, which are semi-autobiographical, are all told from the point of view of a child who sympathizes with the Indians whom he describes. The most notable feature of *Agua* is its style. In this book, Arguedas began to develop a language that would show the interrelationship between the Indian and Hispanic cultures of Peru. Although the book is written in Spanish, it is liberally sprinkled with Quechua expressions. The Quechua syntax is applied to the Spanish language to further emphasize the connection between the two cultures.

Arguedas's style was to become more skilled with time. Commenting on the development of his style, Phyllis Rodriguez-Peralta wrote: "For the bilingual Arguedas it was impossible to convey the essence of the Indian in either traditional Spanish or in a dialect concocted for picturesque effects. Indeed his laborious search for a valid style of speech inserts a unique tone in his writing. . . . By the time Arguedas reaches his major novels, the intertwining of Quechua and Spanish is handled so magnificently that the reader himself is aware of the psychological and artistic distinctions of language."

Among Arguedas's major novels are *Yawar fiesta* and *Todas las sangres.* In *Yawar fiesta,*, the authorities prohibit their Indian subjects from practicing a primitive version of bullfighting at the Yawar fiesta. Instead the magistrates hire a professional bullfighter, who panics and flees from the ring. The courageous Indian who carries on the bullfight is killed. The novel points out that the so-called civilized element of society can be even more savage than the Indians whom it scorns. *Todas las sangres* deals with the rivalry between two brothers, a farmer and a mine owner, but the book extends far beyond their personal struggles. Rodriguez-Peralta termed *Todas las sangres* "a vast sociological document which focuses on the latent unrest in all social strata of Peruvian society."

Although Arguedas's work is highly regarded in his own country, only one of his novels, *Los rios profundos (Deep Rivers),* has been translated into English. The plot of *Deep Rivers* bears many similarities to Arguedas's own life: Ernesto, the protagonist, is the son of an itinerant lawyer. Raised by Indian servants and appreciative of their folkways, the boy undergoes an identity crisis when he attends a Catholic boarding school where most of the students have nothing but disdain for the Indians. "The book movingly dramatizes the difference between the worlds of the Indian and the Spaniard, and so is an essential part of the canon of the new Latin-American literature," noted a critic for *New Yorker.* "The violation of the Indians' dignity by the harsh imposition of Spanish order is made both tangible and inevitable." A commentator for the *Virginia Quarterly Review* also lauded *Deep Rivers:* "Arguedas is dramatic rather than dogmatic in his portrayal of social forces, and his use of Quechua songs and his vivid descriptions of landscape and wildlife give the novel charm and power. Notable is his evocation of Ernesto's magical perception of things, the 'deep river' of Indian consciousness that underlies the whole novel."

Arguedas's scholarly work went hand-in-hand with his literary ventures. An anthropologist, his dissertation compared the Andean Indians of Puquio with the residents of some isolated communities in Spain. He published a number of works on Peruvian folklore and translated Quechua songs and folk tales into Spanish. As director of several museums in Peru, he had access to a wealth of information about Indian culture. In 1950 and 1951 he delivered a series of lectures, "The Problems of Peruvian Culture," which provoked much commentary. The reforms that Arguedas advocated in these lectures and in his writings were slow in coming, and as his final book reveals, he gradually began to lose hope that change would ever be effected.

Arguedas's last novel, *El zorro de arriba y el zorro de abajo* ("The Fox From Above and the Fox From Below"), was published posthumously. As Wolfgang A. Luchting explained, the "above" in the title refers to the Sierra, where the Indians have lived for centuries; "below" refers to Chimbote, a boom town on the coast to which the Indians flock to get jobs. The novel, which is incomplete, consists of narrative sections interspersed with segments from Arguedas's diary. The despair evinced in this novel over the continued exploitation of the Indians is perhaps what drove Arguedas to take his own life in 1969. Luchting wrote of *El zorro* and its creator: "Julio Ortega has made the best observation: this is a novel written to defeat death; but death won. All in all, a novel replete with defects, as is all Arguedas's fiction, but defects one feels ashamed to point out, for one feels that by criticizing one again destroys life, that of the author's memory and perhaps of a vital myth. *El zorro* is in parts deeply moving and disturbing: it proves that writing can be living, or even death. Arguedas was a very great man, and this book proves it."

BIOGRAPHICAL/CRITICAL SOURCES: Times Literary Supplement, March 17, 1966; *Hispania,* May, 1972, March, 1978; *Books Abroad,* autumn, 1972; *World Literature Today,* winter, 1977, winter, 1978; *Washington Post Book World,* July 9, 1978; *New Yorker,* October 16, 1978; *Virginia Quarterly Review,* autumn, 1978; *Best Sellers,* November, 1978; *Contemporary Literary Criticism,* Volume 10, Gale, 1979.*

—Sketch by Ann F. Ponikvar

ARIES, Philippe 1914-

PERSONAL: Born July 21, 1914, in Blois, France. *Education:* University of Paris, Sorbonne, licence, diplome d'etudes superieures. *Home:* 94 rue Jean Mermoz, Maisons Lafitte 78, Yvelines, France.

CAREER: Information specialist. Institut francais de recherches fruitieres Outre Mer, France, director of publications and of documentation center, 1943—. *Awards, honors:* Prix Gabriel Monod, for *Histoire des populations francaises et leurs attitudes durant la vie depuis le XVIIIe siecle,* Prix Choix d'Est-Ange, for *Le Temps de l'histoire,* and Prix Le Dissez de Penanrum, for *L'Enfant et la vie familiale sous l'ancien regime,* all from Academie des Sciences Morales et Politiques; Prix Rocheron from l'Academie Francaise, for *L'Enfant et la vie familiale sous l'ancien regime.*

WRITINGS—In English: *L'Enfant et la vie sous l'ancien regime,* Plon, 1960, translation by Robert Baldick published as *Centuries of Childhood: A Social History of Family Life,* Knopf, 1962; *Western Attitudes Toward Death: From the Middle Ages to the Present,* translated from the original French by Patricia M. Ranum, Johns Hopkins University Press, 1974; (contributor) David E. Stannard, editor, *Death in America,* University of Pennsylvania Press, 1974.

Other: *Les Traditions sociales dans les pays de France* (title means "Social Traditions in the Regions of France"), Editions de la nouvelle France, 1943; *Histoire des populations francaises et de leurs attitudes devant la vie depuis le XVIIIe siecle* (title means "History of French Populations and Their Attitudes Towards Life Since the Eighteenth Century"), SELF, 1948; *Le Temps de l'histoire* (title means "The Time of History"), Rocher, 1954; (contributor) *Cinquante Ans de pensee catholique francaise* (title means "Fifty Years of French Catholic Thought"), Fayard, 1955; (author of preface) Helene Derreal, *Un Missionaire de la contre-reforme, saint Pierre Fourier* (title means "A Missionary of the Counter-Reformation, Saint Pierre Fourier"), Plon, 1965.

(Contributor) *Le Marriage: Engagement pour la vie?* (title means "Marriage: Engagement for Life?"), Desclee, 1972; (with others) *Religion populaire et reforme liturgique* (title means "Popular Religion and Liturgical Reform"), Cerf, 1975; *Essais sur l'histoire de la mort en occident du moyen-age a nos jours* (title means "Essays on the History of Death in the West from the Middle Ages to the Present"), Seuil, 1975.

Director of the collection "Civilisations d'hier d'aujourd'hui" at Librarie Plon. Contributor to Encyclopedie "La Pleiade," and to *Populations, Cahier de l'Institut national d'etudes demographiques,* and *Foi et vie.*

SIDELIGHTS: A writer for *Newsweek* described Aries as "a maverick social historian whose pioneering studies of non-events . . . have helped to create a new kind of history." He has explored "those elusive dimensions of social consciousness that once were considered static and too inaccessible for historical investigation."

One of those dimensions studied by Aries is the changing social viewpoint toward death during various periods in history. With the publication of *Western Attitudes Toward Death* he "has enriched history with a supply of hypotheses that will reorient research," Robert Darnton pointed out, "even if many of them prove to be false."

Another area in which Aries has done research is the way in which children have been looked upon through the ages. His book *Centuries of Childhood,* "which has never been surpassed," stated *Newsweek,* has held appeal not only for historians and history buffs, but also for militant feminists in the United States. The latter are attracted to the book, *Newsweek* said, as "an ideological weapon against the idea of cohesive family." Aries's own comment was, "each generation asks something new of history."

BIOGRAPHICAL/CRITICAL SOURCES: Times Literary Supplement, September 14, 1962; *New Yorker,* December 1, 1962; *Time,* December 28, 1962; *Saturday Review,* March 23, 1963; *Scientific American,* April, 1963; *New York Review of Books,* June 13, 1974; *Newsweek,* July 8, 1974; *New York Times Book Review,* July 21, 1974; *New Republic,* August 23, 1974; *Psychology Today,* August, 1975.

* * *

ARIMOND, Carroll 1909-1979

OBITUARY NOTICE: Born December 25, 1909, in Milwaukee, Wis.; died July 14, 1979, in Sarasota, Fla. Journalist. For three decades the city editor of the Chicago bureau of the Associated Press, Arimond's most notable assignments included coverage of the 1946 La Salle Hotel fire and the 1968 Democratic National Convention riots. His story about a priest who worked with ex-convicts became the basis for the film "The Hoodlum Priest." Obituaries and other sources: *Chicago Tribune,* July 16, 1979.

* * *

ARIYOSHI, Shoichiro 1939(?)-1979

OBITUARY NOTICE: Born c. 1939; died of cancer November 13, 1979, in Tokyo, Japan. Journalist and New York correspondent for the Japanese newspaper *Asahi Shimbun,* and author. During his five years in the United States, Ariyoshi became known for the affectionate stories he wrote about New York City. He was the author of *New York: Day and Night of the Big Apple.* Obituaries and other sources: *New York Times,* November 14, 1979.

* * *

ARMBRISTER, Trevor 1933-

PERSONAL: Born December 4, 1933, in Norwalk, Conn.; son of Geoffrey C. (a stockbroker) and Mary K. (Minor) Armbrister; married Frances Dubos Middeton, September 12, 1958 (separated, 1976); children: Robertson, Alec. *Education:* Washington and Lee University, B.A., 1956. *Politics:* Independent. *Religion:* Episcopalean. *Home:* 3720 Macomb St. N.W., Washington, D.C. 20007. *Agent:* William Morris Agency, 1350 Avenue of the Americas, New York, N.Y. 10019. *Office: Reader's Digest,* 1730 Rhode Island Ave. N.W., Washington, D.C. 20036.

CAREER: J. Walter Thompson Co., New York City, public relations assistant, 1958-62; *Saturday Evening Post,* New York City, contributing editor, 1962-69; *Reader's Digest,* Washington, D.C., senior editor, 1970—. *Military service:* U.S. Army, 1956-60; became captain. *Member:* Federal City Club.

WRITINGS: A Matter of Accountability: The True Story of the Pueblo Affair, Coward, 1970; (with Donald Riegle) *O Congress* (memoirs of Riegle), Doubleday, 1972; *Act of Vengeance: The Yablonski Murders and Their Solution,* Dutton, 1975; (with Gerald Ford) *A Time to Heal* (autobiography of Ford), Harper, 1979. Contributor to periodicals, including *Saturday Evening Post, Parade, Skeptic,* and *Pageant.*

SIDELIGHTS: Aside from his collaborative efforts with political figures Donald Riegle and Gerald Ford, Armbrister has recounted a pair of disturbing events. His first book, *A Matter of Accountability,* delves into life aboard the Pueblo, an American ship which was siezed by North Koreans in 1968. Richard Halloran called the book "an objective, dispassionate and graphic piece of reportage about perhaps the most controversial incident in modern American naval history." A. R. Dodd deemed it "an extensively detailed volume in the now familiar 'The day that . . .' style. Armbrister records everything recordable."

Armbrister's *Act of Vengeance* details the murder of Joseph Yablonski and his family after his failed attempt to usurp the presidency of the United Mine Workers Union from Tony Boyle. Max Egremont claimed that Armbrister tended to "sentimentalize Yablonski." He added, "Another tiresome feature is the direct reporting of conversations particularly between the killers which Mr. Armbrister cannot possibly have overheard. . . . Gaps also exist in the political side of the story." But B. A. Franklin stated that the book reports "with the authority of the best journalism." He noted, "Armbrister has vacuum cleaned this incredible tale. . . . This is one of the better books . . . about a horrifying and fascinating criminal conspiracy."

BIOGRAPHICAL/CRITICAL SOURCES: New York Times Book Review, July 26, 1970, November 9, 1975; *Saturday Review,* August 15, 1970; *Times Literary Supplement,* July 30, 1976.

* * *

ARMSTRONG, (Grace) April (Oursler) 1926-

PERSONAL: Born October 15, 1926, in New York, N.Y.; daughter of Fulton (a writer and editor) and Grace (a writer and editor; maiden name, Perkins) Oursler; married Martin Armstrong II (a writer; marriage ended); children: Martin III, Michael, Catherine Armstrong King, Fulton, Kevin, Clare, Paul. *Education:* Bryn Mawr College, A.B., 1946; Fordham University, M.A., 1965, Ph.D., 1972. *Religion:* Roman Catholic. *Home:* 13 Ameridge Dr., Bridgeport, Conn. 06606.

CAREER: Sacred Heart University, Bridgeport, Conn., associate professor of theology, 1965-78; Mount Sacred Heart College, Hamden, Conn., lecturer in theology, 1979—. Member of Secular Franciscan Order. *Awards, honors:* Christopher Award, 1954; Georgetown Award, 1970, for work in the church.

WRITINGS: (With mother, Grace Oursler) *When Sorrow Comes,* Doubleday, 1950; (with father, Fulton Oursler) *The Greatest Faith Ever Known,* Doubleday, 1953; (with husband, Martin F. Armstrong, Jr.) *Fatima: Pilgrimage to Peace,* Doubleday, 1954; *Stories From the Life of Jesus* (juvenile), Garden City Books, 1955; *Bible Stories for Young Readers,* Garden City Books, 1956; *Ben and the Green Corduroy Angel* (juvenile), Bruce Books, 1957; *The Book of God: Adventures From the Old Testament* (juvenile), two volumes, Compton, 1957; *The Tales Christ Told,* Doubleday, 1959.

The Conversion of St. Paul, Doubleday, 1963; *Water in the Wine,* McGraw, 1963; *House With a Hundred Gates* (autobiography), McGraw, 1965; *St. Francis of Assisi: A Concise Biography,* American R.D.M. Corp., 1966; *What's Happening to the Catholic Church?,* Doubleday, 1966; *Cry Babel,* Doubleday, 1979. Translator of religious works. Contributor of nearly six hundred articles to newspapers and periodicals, including *Readers Digest* and *Saturday Evening Post.*

WORK IN PROGRESS: Arc of the Covenant: Mary, Mother of the Church.

SIDELIGHTS: Armstrong told *CA:* "My profession is to be a Secular Order of St. Francis. Whatever talents God has given to me I offer Him. I am a translator of the handicapped at all ages and volunteer at the Easter Seal Hospitals, convalescent homes, and families. I am a translator of religious studies, deeply involved in ecumenical work. I read more than write. I listen more than talk. *Cry Babel* is not only about aphasia, or physical therapy, but the need to learn that God is Love. Writing is not to me a job, but part of breathing. So too is marvelling at life."

* * *

ARMSTRONG, Marjorie Moore 1912-

PERSONAL: Born September 12, 1912, in Athens, Ga.; daughter of Henry Walter (a realtor) and Kate (a boarding house operator; maiden name, Johns) Moore; married Orland Kay Armstrong (a journalist), December 11, 1949; children: five stepchildren. *Education:* Converse College, B.A., 1933; Woman's Missionary Union Training School, M.R.E., 1935; Northwestern University, M.S.J., 1950. *Politics:* Republican. *Religion:* Baptist. *Home and office:* The Highlands, Route 2, Republic, Mo. 65738.

CAREER: Baptist Student, Nashville, Tenn., assistant editor, 1935-42; *Commission,* Richmond, Va., managing editor, 1942-49; *Baptist World,* Washington, D.C., co-editor, 1954-56; free-lance writer, 1950—. Summer teacher at Carver School of Missions and Social Work, 1969-71. *Member:* Missouri Writers Guild (past president), Springfield International Relations Club, Springfield Republican Women's Club, Kappa Tau Alpha.

WRITINGS: Face Today's World, Convention Press, 1963; (with husband, O. K. Armstrong) *Religion Can Conquer Communism,* Thomas Nelson, 1964; (with O. K. Armstrong) *The Indomitable Baptists,* Doubleday, 1967; *School Someday,* Convention Press, 1976; (with O. K. Armstrong) *Baptists Who Shaped a Nation,* Broadman, 1976; (with O. K. Armstrong) *The Baptists in America,* Doubleday-Galilee, 1979. Past editor of *Guild News* of Missouri Writers Guild.

SIDELIGHTS: Marjorie Armstrong told *CA:* "My career in feature article writing began with letter-writing. Producing vivid accounts of experiences for parents, brother and sister who welcomed these handwritten, often embellished descriptions of my life after graduation from college encouraged me to write.

"An encounter with a journalist-lecturer at the time when I was a stenographer with ambition to get a promotion to youth leadership among the churches changed my direction. He led me to appreciate the written word as a message to a larger audience than the oral message could reach, and I began to concentrate on professional journalism. My meeting with a professor from Northwestern University and his wife also was a major influence. Both Roland E. Wolseley and his wife, Bernice, respected my ambition to improve the quality of my work as an editor of a missions journal. They expressed admiration for my goals and appreciated the quality of my work. Most of all, they urged me to cultivate originality, sincerity, and pride in the spiritual message I wished to proclaim."

* * *

ASHBY, Lloyd W. 1905-

PERSONAL: Born May 16, 1905, in Guide Rock, Neb.; son of Earnest Winfield (a farmer) and Virginia (Walsh) Ashby; married wife, Lois I., August 21, 1926; children: Carolyn (Mrs. William C. Hughes), Elaine (Mrs. Kenneth P. Goodrich). *Education:* Hastings College, B.A., 1926; Columbia University, M.A., 1935, Ed.D., 1950. *Religion:* Protestant. *Home and office:* 3321 Village Green Dr., Sarasota, Fla. 33579.

CAREER: Superintendent of schools in Cheltenham Township, Pa., 1950-58, and in Ridgewood, N.J., 1958-66; Lehigh University, Bethlehem, Pa., professor, 1966-71, professor emeritus, 1971—; writer, 1971—. President of Sarasota's Community Mobile Meals. *Member:* American Association of School Administrators (emeritus member).

WRITINGS: The Effective School Board Member, Interstate, 1968; *Man in the Middle: Superintendent of Schools,* Interstate, 1968; *Student Activism,* Interstate, 1970; *Common Sense in Negotiations,* Interstate, 1972. Contributor to education and administration journals.

WORK IN PROGRESS: A book of essays for school administrators.

* * *

ASHBY, Neal 1924-

PERSONAL: Born October 28, 1924, in Des Moines, Iowa; son of Ted (a writer) and Eva (Meyer) Ashby; married Joan Millhaem (died); married Babette Brimberg (an editor), October 22, 1971; children: Laurel Ashby Dann, Lucianne Ashby Wickline, Lawrence T. *Education:* Attended State University of Iowa, 1942, and Drake University, 1943. *Home:* 17 Leeds Dr., Port Washington, N.Y. 11050.

CAREER: Kansas City Star, Kansas City, Mo., reporter, 1944; *Des Moines Register,* Des Moines, Iowa, reporter, 1944-45; *New York Mirror,* New York City, writer and editor, 1945-63; *Parade,* New York City, writer and editor, 1963-69; *Family Week,* New York City, managing editor, 1970; free-lance writer, 1970—. President of board of trustees of New York Public Library, Williston Park branch, 1962-67. *Member:* American Society of Journalists and Authors. *Awards, honors:* School Bell Award from National Education Association, 1965, for distinguished service in the interpretation of education.

WRITINGS: (Contributor) Susan E. Mayer, editor, *20 Oil Painters and How They Work,* Watson-Guptill, 1978; *Joe Papp's Fabulous Play Factory,* Putnam, 1980. Contributor to periodicals, including *Good Housekeeping, Catholic Digest, Seventeen, Sports Illustrated, Working Woman,* and *New York Times.*

WORK IN PROGRESS: "Articles are always in progress."

SIDELIGHTS: Ashby noted that he finds writing on a "wide variety of subjects, ranging from sports through medicine and archaeology invigorating."

* * *

AUBURN, Mark Stuart 1945-

PERSONAL: Born December 9, 1945, in Cincinnati, Ohio; married Sandra Korman (a speech pathologist), January 25, 1969; children: David, Benjamin. *Education:* University of Akron, B.S. and B.A., 1967; University of Chicago, M.A., 1968, Ph.D., 1971. *Religion:* Unitarian-Universalist. *Office:* Department of English, Ohio State University, Columbus, Ohio 43210.

CAREER: Ohio State University, Columbus, assistant professor, 1971-77, associate professor of English, 1977—. *Member:* Modern Language Association of America, American Society for Eighteenth-Century Studies, American Society for Theatre Research, American Association of University Professors. *Awards, honors:* American Philosophical Society grant, 1972.

WRITINGS: Sheridan's Comedies: Their Contexts and Achievements, University of Nebraska Press, 1977; (with K. H. Burkman) *Drama Through Performance,* Houghton, 1977; (editor) John Dryden, *Marriage A-la-Mode,* University of Nebraska Press, 1980.

WORK IN PROGRESS: Research on eighteenth-century drama, fiction, and society.

* * *

AUERBACH, Stuart C(harles) 1935-

PERSONAL: Born October 28, 1935, in New York, N.Y.; son of Jack S. (a businessman) and Betty (Segnes) Auerbach; married Carol A. Honsa. *Education:* Williams College, B.A., 1957. *Home:* 4624 Asbury Pl. N.W., Washington, D.C., 20016. *Office: Washington Post,* 1150 15th St. N.W., Washington, D.C., 20071.

CAREER/WRITINGS: Berkshire Evening Eagle, Pittsfield, Mass., reporter, 1957-60; *Miami Herald,* Miami, Fla., reporter, 1960-66; *Washington Post,* Washington, D.C., medical and science writer, 1968-76, Middle East correspondent, 1976-77, legal affairs correspondent and columnist, 1977-78, South Asia correspondent, 1979—. Notable assignments include coverage of moon landing, civil rights, Nixon's resignation and subsequent illness, the civil war in Lebanon, and genetic engineering. *Member:* National Press Club, National Association of Science Writers, Overseas Press Club, Washington Press Club, Federal City Club. *Awards, honors:* Award from National Association of Science Writers, 1976, for "And Man Created Risks," an article on the future of genetic engineering.

* * *

AUSTIN, (John) Norman 1937-

PERSONAL: Born May 20, 1937, in Anshun, China; came to the United States in 1958, naturalized citizen, 1972; son of John Alfred (a missionary) and Lillian Maud (a missionary; maiden name, Reeks) Austin. *Education:* University of Toronto, B.A. (with honors), 1958; University of California, Berkeley, M.A., 1960, Ph.D., 1965. *Office:* Department of Classics, University of Massachusetts, Amherst, Mass. 01003.

CAREER: University of California, Los Angeles, assistant professor, 1966-72, associate professor of classics, 1972-76; Boston University, Boston, Mass., Aurelio Professor of Classics, 1976-78; University of Massachusetts, Amherst, professor of classics, 1978—. Visiting lecturer at Yale University, 1972. *Member:* American Philological Association. *Awards, honors:* Fellow of Center for Hellenic Studies, Washington, D.C., 1968-69; Guggenheim fellowship, 1974.

WRITINGS: The Greek Historians: Selections, Van Nostrand, 1970; *Archery at the Dark of the Moon: Poetic Problems in Homer's "Odyssey,"* University of California Press, 1976. Associate editor of "Works of John Dryden," Volume III, University of California Press. Contributor to classical journals and literary magazines, including *Shenandoah.* Senior co-editor of *California Studies in Classical Antiquity,* 1973-74.

WORK IN PROGRESS: Research on Homer, myth, optometry, and dance.

SIDELIGHTS: Austin writes: "I spent my early years in China and India, as the son of missionaries. My education was in China, England, Canada, and the United States. My interest is in mythology and its relation to psychology and modern science.

"*Archery at the Dark of the Moon* is a first attempt to perceive the unified world view of the poem. I continue research and writing in this direction, now more particularly trying to define what the Homer of the *Odyssey* understood as mind. My interests in early Greek poetry center on cosmology, psychology, and structures of thought. In connecting ancient cosmologies with modern science, I look for those archetypes that Heisenberg believed physics shared with psychology. In an article on Martha Graham's 'Clytemnestra,' I studied the significance of the ancient classical world on the creative imagination of the twentieth-century artists, in this case an American artist working in, indeed creating, the American idiom, while drawing on a fountain of energy from ancient Greece."

AVOCATIONAL INTERESTS: Classical dance.

* * *

AUSTIN, (Stewart) Reid 1931-

PERSONAL: Born March 11, 1931, in Norwich, Conn.; son of Herman William (an electrician) and Adelaide (a nurse; maiden name, Christman) Austin. *Education:* Attended Cartoonists and Illustrators School, New York City, 1949-50, and Art Career School, New York City, 1950-51. *Politics:* "Across the board." *Religion:* Protestant. *Home:* 1634 Seabreeze Blvd., Fort Lauderdale, Fla. 33316. *Office:* Michael Reid, Inc., 1018 East Las Olas Blvd., Fort Lauderdale, Fla. 33301.

CAREER: Fawcett World Library, New York City, art assistant, 1950-55; Bantam Books, Inc., New York City, art associate, 1956-59; *Playboy,* Chicago, Ill., associate art director, 1959-66; Michael Reid, Inc. (retail shop), Fort Lauderdale, Fla., co-owner, 1966—. *Awards, honors:* Graphic arts awards include awards from Art Directors Club of Chicago and New York Art Directors Club.

WRITINGS: Vargas (semi-biographical), Crown, 1978.

WORK IN PROGRESS: A novel based on the life of a small boy in a small New England town in the 1940's.

SIDELIGHTS: Austin comments: "*Playboy* was the best job I ever had, but I really got tired of looking at buttocks and breasts. What attracted me to Vargas and his work was his sincerity as an artist. He respects women to begin with and at his best that respect comes through. Vargas is to the American girl what Norman Rockwell was to the family. Aside from writing some headlines and an occasional record review, I had never aspired to write. With the advent of *Vargas* the challenge was thrown, and I am determined not to let the effort and experience go to waste.

"I want very much to see if I can go beyond *Vargas,* to dig below the surface of my own personal experience and present a story, or stories, that will have meaning for others. Meanwhile, I 'build our house and chop our wood and make our garden grow' and look forward to living on a mountain top, miles from the nearest moped or motorcycle."

* * *

AVEY, Ruby 1927-
(Vicki Page)

PERSONAL: Born January 29, 1927, in Hove, Sussex, England; daughter of Albert Ernest (a compositor) and Dora

(Bidwell) Avey. *Education:* Attended secretarial school in Hove, England. *Home:* 53 Norway St., Portslade, Brighton, Sussex BN4 1AE, England. *Agent:* J. F. Gibson's Literary Agency, P.O. Box 173, London S.W.3, England.

CAREER: Secretary for printing company in Hove, England, 1942-78; writer, 1978—. Broadcaster (under pseudonym Vicki Page) for BBC-Radio, 1968—. Tutor at prison in Ford, England, 1974-76, and at Portland Further Education Centre for Adults, 1971—. *Member:* Romantic Novelists Association.

WRITINGS—All novels under pseudonym Vicki Page; all published by R. Hale: *Holiday Hostess,* 1971; *A Rose by Moonlight,* 1973; *Doctor in Bangkok,* 1973; *Adam's Woman,* 1975; *Partnership of Hearts,* 1975; *Night of Lammas,* 1976; *Bride for Beltane,* 1976; *The House of Harron,* 1977; *Shadows on the Snow,* 1978; *A Wedding in Winter,* 1978; *Love Is for Tomorrow,* 1979; *Lord of the Watchtower,* 1979; *Call for Nurse Hope,* 1980; *Bracelet for a Bride,* 1980; *Portrait of a Woman,* 1980. Contributor of stories to women's magazines.

WORK IN PROGRESS: A book on hospital romance and life; a romantic suspense novel set in Bruges.

SIDELIGHTS: Most of Ruby Avey's books have been published in France, Germany, and the Netherlands, and one was serialized and broadcast.

She writes: "Since childhood I have been drawn intensely to the craft of writing and communication through the printed word. Fiction writing opens doors to fresh worlds and to life in general. It is the one craft which uses each minutest degree of experience the writer assimilates and, consequently, is enriched rather than impoverished by the passing of time.

"I always feel an urge to write 'happy endings' because I believe it is the writer's duty to entertain, rather than to pose problems to a public which only has to view the general situation of the world today to be confronted with sufficient questions to disturb even the most quiescent of consciences. This is not to say that I do not hold in the greatest respect those writers who try to alter the course of events through their work. I do, however, become extremely angry when it is presumed that, because a writer carries the tag 'popular,' his or her work is of little intrinsic worth. It is a false and snobbish attitude to assume that what is popular is necessarily bad writing but that is, unhappily, too often the case.

"I spent many years writing short stories and articles before I came to the world of novels—and then it was more by chance than design, since my first book was written solely as an escape from a bad attack of influenza in the middle of a drear winter. I am old fashioned enough to consider that all books should contain plots with a beginning, a middle, and an end, and dislike the modern tendency to substitute lack of clarity for lack of plot and stark writing for an absence of style.

"I have travelled extensively throughout the main European countries: France, Italy, Germany, Switzerland, and Portugal, and enjoy using these backgrounds for books. As I was fortunate enough to have been born in Sussex, which I consider one of England's loveliest counties, I am also interested in research on local history, and have used that subject for a considerable number of radio talks."

AVOCATIONAL INTERESTS: Driving, walking, reading.

* * *

AXINN, June 1923-

PERSONAL: Born December 30, 1923, in New York, N.Y.; daughter of Arthur (an attorney) and Sylvia (a personnel manager; maiden name, Jedel) Morris; married Sidney Axinn (a professor), June 21, 1947; children: Constance (Mrs. Peter Johnson), David. *Education:* Queens College (now of the City University of New York), B.A. (with honors), 1945; graduate study at New School for Social Research, 1946-47; University of Pennsylvania, Ph.D., 1964. *Office:* School of Social Work, University of Pennsylvania, 3701 Locust Walk, Philadelphia, Pa. 19104.

CAREER: Philadelphia Evening Bulletin, Philadelphia, Pa., research analyst, 1948-50; University of Pennsylvania, Philadelphia, lecturer in economics, 1964-65, assistant professor, 1965-68, associate professor, 1969-74, professor of social welfare, 1975—. Participant in scholarly meetings. Lecturer and consultant. *Member:* American Economic Association, American Public Welfare Association, Association for Social Economics, Council on Social Work Education, History of Economics Society, National Conference on Social Welfare, Social Welfare History Group, Eastern Economic Association.

WRITINGS: (Editor with Michael Cenci and others, and contributor) *The Century of the Child,* School of Social Work, University of Pennsylvania, 1973; (contributor) Mary Howard, editor, *The Family in Industrial and Post-Industrial Society: A Radical Analysis,* Addison-Wesley, 1974; (with Herman Levin) *Social Welfare: A History of the American Response to Need,* Harper, 1975. Contributor of more than a dozen articles and reviews to social work, economic, and history journals, and *Congressional Record.* Book review editor of *Review of Social Economy,* 1975—, *Administration in Social Work,* 1977—, and *Humboldt Journal of Social Relations, 1979–.*

WORK IN PROGRESS: A book, *Family Policy,* with Levin; an article, "Some Social Uses of Social Security Reserves," for *The Forum.*

SIDELIGHTS: Axinn told *CA:* "I have a broad interest in social welfare policy—especially policy for the aged. Currently I am doing research on Family policy and income maintenance programs."

* * *

AYME, Marcel (Andre) 1902-1967

PERSONAL: Born March 28, 1902, in Joigny, France; died of pneumonia, October 14, 1967, in Paris, France; son of a blacksmith; married Marie-Antoinette Arnaud, 1932. *Education:* Studied medicine for one year. *Residence:* Paris, France.

CAREER: Novelist; author of short stories; playwright. Worked as bank clerk, insurance broker, movie extra, bricklayer, crime reporter, salesman, export firm employee, and accountant in the Paris bourse. *Military service:* Served in French Army. *Awards, honors:* Theophraste Renaudot prize, 1929, for *La Table-aux-creves.*

WRITINGS—In English; novels: *La Table-aux-creves* (also see below), Gallimard, 1929, reprinted, 1972, translation by Helen Waddell published as *The Hollow Field,* Dodd, 1933; *La Jument verte* (also see below), Gallimard, 1933, reprinted, 1972, translation by Norman Denny published as *The Green Mare,* Harper, 1955; *Le Moulin de la Sourdine* (also see below), Gallimard, 1936, reprinted, 1973, translation by Denny published as *The Secret Stream,* Harper, 1953; *La Belle Image,* Gallimard, 1941, reprinted, 1972, translation by Denny published as *The Second Face,* Bodley Head, 1951, Harper, 1952; *Travelingue,* Gallimard, 1943, reprinted, 1973, translation by Sutton published as *The Miraculous Barber,* Bodley Head, 1950, Harper, 1951; *La Vouivre* (also see below), 1943, reprinted, 1972, translation by Sutton published as *The Fable and the Flesh,* Mayflower Books, 1965; *Le Chemin des ecoliers,* Gallimard, 1946, reprinted, 1972, translation by Eric Sutton published as *The Transient Hour,* A. A. Wyn, 1948; *Uranus* (also see below), Gallimard, 1948, reprinted, 1972, translation by Denny published as *The Bar Keep of Blemont,* Harper, 1950; *Les Tiroirs de l'inconnu,* [France], 1960, translation by Denny published as *The Conscience of Love,* Atheneum, 1962.

Short stories: *Le Passe-Muraille* (contains "Le Passe-Muraille," "Les Sabines," "Le Carte," "Le Decret," "Le Proverbe," "Legende poideve," "Le Precepteur d'epouses," "Les Bottes de sept lieues," "L'Huissier," and "En attendant"), Gallimard, 1943, reprinted, 1968, translation by Denny published as *The Walker Through Walls, and Other Stories* (contains "The Walker Through Walls," "The Retreat From Moscow," "A Roll of Daughters," "Rue dell'Evangele" [also published in *Derriere Chez Martin;* see below] "The State of Grace," "The Proverb," "Legend of Poldevia," "The Walking Stick," "Couldn't Care Less," "The Wine of Paris," "Martin the Novelist," "The Seven League Books," "Josse" [also published in *Enamere: nouvelles;* see below] "The Life-Ration," and "The Last"), Bodley Head, 1972. Also author of *Across Paris, and Other Stories,* translated by Denny, 1961.

Plays: *Clerambard* (four-act), B. Grasset, 1950, translation by Denny published as *Clerambard: A Comedy in Four Acts* (first produced in Paris at Comedie des Champs-Elysees, 1950, produced Off-Broadway, 1957), prepared for stage by Leo Kerz and Alvin Sapinskley, Samuel French, 1958; *Les Oiseaux de la lune* (four-act), Gallimard, 1956, translation by John Parker published as *Moonbirds,* Hart Stenographic Bureau, 1959.

For children: *The Wonderful Farm,* translated by Denny, illustrations by Maurice Sendak, Harper, 1951; *The Magic Pictures, More About the Wonderful Farm,* translated by Denny, pictures by Sendak, Harper, 1954.

Other: (With Patrice Moulard) *The Paris I Love,* Tudor, 1956.

In French; novels; all published by Gallimard, except as noted: *Brulebois* (also see below), Poitiers, 1926, reprinted, 1975; *Aller retour,* 1927; *La Rue sans nom,* 1930; *Le Vaurien,* 1931; *Le Mauvais Jars,* 1935; *L'Elephant,* 1935; *Maison basse,* 1935; *Gustalin* (also see below,), 1937; *Silhouette du scandale,* Editions du Sagittaire, 1938; *Le Boeuf clandestin,* 1939, reprinted, 1973; *Le Confort intellectuel,* Flammarion, 1949; *L'Hopital,* illustrations by Rio, Amio-Dumont, 1951; *Romans de la province* (contains "Brulebois" [also see above], "La Table-aux creves" [also see above], "La Jument Verte" [also see above], "Le Moulin de la Sourdine" [also see above], "Gustalin" [also see above], and "La Vouivre" [also see above]), illustrations by Pierre Berger, 1956; *Image de l'amour,* G. Guillot, 1957; *Romans parisiens, suivi d'Uranus* (also see *Uranus* above), watercolors by Gen Paul, 1959; *Lucienne et le boucher,* Le Club francais du livre, 1959; *Oscar et Erik* (also see below), illustrations by Jacques Carelman, Gautier-Languereau, 1961; *Les Maxibules,* 1962; James H. Baltzell, editor, *Les Meilleures Nouvelles de Marcel Ayme,* Scribner, 1964; *Enjambes,* illustrations by Giani Esposito, 1967; *Istres historique dans son cadre provencal, Istres touristique, son folklore,* illustrations by P. Fievet and E. Aquaron, Imprimerie Mistral, 1968.

Short stories: *Le Puit sux images* (contains "Le Puits aux images," "La Retraite de rurale," "Les Mauvaises Flevres," "Noblesse," "A et B," "Pastorale," "Les Clochards," "L'individu," "Au clair de la lune," "La Lanterne," and "Enfants perdus"), Gallimard, 1932; *Le Nain,* Gallimard, 1934; *Derriere chez Martin* (contains "Le Romancier Martin," "Je suis renboye," "L'Eleve Martin," "Le Temps mort," "Le Cour nombreaux," "L'Ame de Martin," "Rue de l'Evangile" [also published in *The Walker Through Walls, and Other Stories;* see above], "Conte de Noel," and "La Statue"), Livre de poche, 1938, reprinted, 1969; *Le Vin de Paris,* Gallimard, 1947; *Les Chiens,* illustrations by Nathalie Parain, Gallimard, 1948; *Soties de la ville et des champs,* Club des librairies de France, 1958; *Contes choisis,* original copper plates by Gaston Barret, Cercle Grolier, 1961.

Plays: *Vogue la galere* (title means "Here Goes"), B. Grasset, 1944; *Les Quatres Verites* (title means "Home Truths"), B. Grasset, 1954; *Les Sorcieres de Salem* (adapted from "The Crucible" by Arthur Miller), [Paris], 1955; *La Mouche bleue* (four-act; title means "The Blue Fly"), 1957; *Louisiane* (four-act), Gallimard, 1961; *Les Maxibules,* Gallimard, 1962; *Meilleures Nouvelles de Marcel Ayme,* Scribner, 1965; *Le Minotaure, precede de La Convention Belzebir and Consummation* ("La Convention Belzebir" first produced in Paris at Theatre de l'Athenee, November 20, 1966), Gallimard, 1967.

For children; all published by Gallimard: *Les Contes du chat perche,* illustrations by N. Altman, 1934; *Autres contes du chat perche,* illustrations by Nathalie Parain, 1950; *Derniers contes du chat perche,* illustrations by Lesly Queneau, 1958; *Les Contes bleus du chat perche,* 1975.

Other: *Silhouette du scandale,* Editions du Sagittarie, 1938; *Le Confort intellectuel,* Flammarion, 1949; *En arriere: nouvelles* (selected works; contains "Oscar et Erik" [also see above] "Financailles," "Rechute," "Avenue Junot," "Les Chiens de notre vie," "Conte du milieu," "Josse" [also published in *The Walker Through Walls, and Other Stories;* see above] "La Vamp et le normalien," "Le Mendiant," and "En arriere"), 1950; *L'Epuration et le delit d'opinion* (booklet), preface by Lucien Rebalet, Editions dynamo, 1968; *Marcel Leprin . . . Exhibition,* Vestart, 1970.

Screenplays: "Papa, Mama, the Maid and Me"; "La Jumente Verte" (adaptation of original novel); "Les Sorcieres de Salem" (adaptation of play "The Crucible" by Arthur Miller); "Desert Vivant", 1957 (adaptation of "Living Desert," released by Walt Disney Productions).

SIDELIGHTS: Orville Prescott once described Ayme as "one of the most prolific of modern French novelists and quite probably the best." But as a man who sincerely enjoyed his vocation and life in general, the unpretentious Ayme shunned public recognition for his writings, deeming such accolades unnecessary. Members of the prestigious Academie Francaise sought to rank Ayme among them, but he refused even that highly coveted honor.

As he was growing up Ayme detested formal education. "I had a horror of school," he once admitted, "and even today in my most horrible nightmares, I dream that I am in the classroom." As a result, Ayme learned much on his own. At sixteen he discovered the earthy poetry of Francois Villon and the realistic novels of Honore de Balzac, both of which later influenced his own writing. He eventually enrolled in medical school, but, after a year, dropped out.

Subsequently Ayme worked at a variety of jobs in Paris before finding his metier as an author, writing in what has been called a "lean, spare style." His colorful early stories take place in the country, reflecting his own provincial Franche-Comte background. Later Ayme wrote more ascerbic satires of the Parisian bourgeoisie.

Whether writing about the bucolic life or about living in the city, Ayme was "more interested in people than ideas," noted a writer in *Atlantic*. An astute observer of human foibles, Ayme often spoke through the mouths of children or animals, as in his popular novel *The Green Mare*. Moreover, while Ayme introduced supernatural elements in his work (the green mare, for example), he did so in a realistic manner.

Because of his affection for life as it really is, Ayme applauded those who follow their natural inclinations. He deplored hypocrisy and any form of escapism using these and other human vices as targets for his satire. It was in his allegorical short stories, written for children as well as adults, that Ayme lampooned social "stratification, preconceived ideas, cliches, and pomposity of men engaged in the posture of social relations," wrote Dorothy Brodin.

Henri Peyre declared that Ayme "is totally unequaled in France as a writer of racy and humorous short stories." Bree and Guiton further noted that he had a talent for making "his reader laugh out loud." But, added Peyre, "these pungent, entertaining stories a la Maupassant leave an aftertaste of bitterness."

For the latter part of his career, Ayme focused most of his creative energies on writing plays. He became recognized as a playwright in 1950 when *Clerambard* became the biggest success of the year in Paris. Described by Francois Mauriac as "an extraordinarily amusing satire," the play is about a worldly aristocrat, Clerambard, who is suffering from financial problems. To help defray his family's living expenses, the protagonist forces each member to make and peddle woven goods. When St. Francis appears to Clerambard, the latter forgets such secular pursuits as money making and soon after devotes himself to converting the villagers to Christianity. He has just managed to convert some stubborn neighbors when St. Francis again appears, this time to everyone in the village except the local priest. Clerambard and his family then take to the road as evangelists.

For humor and irony displayed in his plays and short stories alike, Ayme has been compared to Voltaire, Anatole France, and Moliere. But he was an individualist who did not really fall into any particular school of writing. Ayme "wrote in absolute freedom exactly what he wished to write," remarked Brodin. He "appeals to readers of all kinds because of his vivid and unusual style, his extraordinary ability to put words through their paces, and especially because of the fresh and unexpected quality of his vision."

BIOGRAPHICAL/CRITICAL SOURCES: Times Literary Supplement, February 16, 1933, December 18, 1948, October 26, 1951, March 6, 1953; *New Statesman & Nation,* February 18, 1933, June 4, 1955; *New York Times,* April 9, 1933, March 28, 1948, May 15, 1950, April 22, 1951, November 11, 1951, April 13, 1952, February 7, 1954, April 1, 1956, January 25, 1959, April 30, 1961; *Books,* April 9, 1933; *New Yorker,* April 3, 1948, June 17, 1950, December 1, 1951, January 30, 1954, March 31, 1956, April 29, 1961; *Saturday Review of Literature,* April 17, 1948, May 15, 1950, April 21, 1951, February 6, 1954, January 24, 1959; *New Republic,* June 26, 1950, August 20, 1951; *Time,* April 23, 1951, April 14, 1952, February 8, 1954, February 2, 1959, April 21, 1961, May 4, 1962; *Atlantic,* April 23, 1951, April 14, 1952, February 8, 1954, February 2, 1959, April 21, 1961, May 4, 1962; *New York Herald Book Review,* May 6, 1951, February 7, 1954, July 8, 1955, April 1, 1956, January 25, 1959; *Saturday Review,* April 19, 1952, July 22, 1961, April 7, 1962; *Nation,* April 28, 1956; *Commonweal,* May 11, 1956; *New York Times Book Review,* April 30, 1961, March 25, 1962; Dorothy R. Brodin, *The Comic World of Marcel Ayme,* Debresse, 1964; Brodin, *Marcel Ayme,* Columbia University Press, 1968; *Contemporary Literary Criticism,* Volume 11, Gale, 1979.

OBITUARIES: New York Times, October 15, 1967; *Newsweek,* October 30, 1967.*

B

BABSON, Roger W(ard) 1875-1967

OBITUARY NOTICE: Born July 6, 1875, in Gloucester, Mass.; died March 5, 1967. Statistician, economist, and author. Babson founded the Babson Statistical Organization with his wife in 1902 to assess the stock market and predict future trends in order to help guide investors into safe and lucrative ventures. He later founded the Babson Institute (a business school), Webber College (a women's school for business), and Babson's Reports, Inc. (a statistical service). He is the author of more than forty books on different subjects, ranging from *How to Increase Church Attendance* to *Business and Investing Fundamentals,* in addition to the column "Be Right With Babson." Obituaries and other sources: Roger W. Babson, *Actions and Reactions: Autobiography of Roger W. Babson,* Harper, 1935; *Current Biography,* Wilson, 1945, May, 1967; *New York Times,* March 6, 1967.

* * *

BACHELARD, Gaston 1884-1962

OBITUARY NOTICE: Born June 27, 1884, in Bar-sur-Aube, France; died October 16, 1962, in Paris, France. Philosopher, critic, educator, and author. Bachelard is considered to have been one of the greatest psychoanalysts since Sigmund Freud. Like Freud, he worked from the basic assumption of the half-conscious mind as a door to revelation. Bachelard believed, however, that reverie or day-dreaming was not a private sensation but rather a collective experience. He is the author of *The Psychoanalysis of Fire, The Philosophy of No, The Poetics of Reverie,* and others. Bachelard was a member of the faculty at the Sorbonne in Paris, and received the French Grand Prix for literature shortly before his death. Obituaries and other sources: *The Penguin Companion to European Literature,* McGraw, 1969; *Cassell's Encyclopaedia of World Literature,* revised edition, Morrow, 1973; *World Authors, 1950-1970,* Wilson, 1975; *Who's Who in Twentieth Century Literature,* Holt, 1976.

* * *

BACON, Joan Chase
See BOWDEN, Joan Chase

* * *

BADE, Jane (Ruth) 1932-

PERSONAL: Born October 29, 1932, in Chicago, Ill.; daughter of Kenneth George (a lawyer) and Ruth (in newspaper sales; maiden name, Parish) Meyer; married Thomas A. Bade, June 16, 1952 (divorced, 1972); children: Carol Bade Ferguson, Sasha, Amy, Donna. *Education:* Attended Wheaton College, Wheaton, Ill., 1950-52, and Pasadena City College, 1965—. *Home:* 5575 Terrace Dr., La Crescenta, Calif. 91214. *Office:* Jet Propulsion Laboratory, 4800 Oak Grove Dr., Pasadena, Calif. 91103.

CAREER: Free-lance writer, 1952-71; Bowmar Publishing Co., Glendale, Calif., editor of textbook series, "Happy Holidays," 1971-73; Adcom-West (advertising agency), Glendale, Calif., copywriter and publicity writer, 1973; Jet Propulsion Laboratory, Pasadena, Calif., associate editor of *Universe,* 1976—. Free-lance interior designer and consultant; buyer for model home design firm; operator of antique shops.

WRITINGS: Nine on a String (elementary school reader), Ginn, 1972. Contributor of about forty articles and stories to magazines and newspapers, including *Motor Trend, Children's Friend, Highlights for Children, Moody Monthly, Cycle World, American Home, American Girl, NASA Activities,* and *Los Angeles Times.*

WORK IN PROGRESS: Picture books for pre-schoolers; grade school books on space; magazine articles on interior decorating the "single state."

SIDELIGHTS: Jane Bade writes: "Writing has been a natural means of expression for me since childhood. My creativity usually takes a practical bent—thus the article is more comfortable for me than fiction. I sold my first piece to *Motor Trend* when I was twenty and also wrote a monthly column for *Moody Monthly.* However, I didn't find time to write seriously until 1965, when I joined a workshop of productive writers in Pasadena. My reading book for Ginn has been adapted as a playlet for educational TV in Australia. Although science and engineering are not my forte, I find relaying technical data to the lay reader challenging. The Jet Propulsion Laboratory is a gold mine of information about fascinating subjects. While here as an editor I hope to complete some children's books on space exploration. Meanwhile, my growing interior design business is competing strongly for my attention."

* * *

BADE, Patrick 1951-

PERSONAL: Born August 31, 1951, in Leatherhead, Surrey, England. *Education:* University College, London, B.A., 1972; Courtauld Institute of Art, London, M.A., 1974. *Home:* 2 Crossley St., London N.7, England.

CAREER: Nonington College, Kent, England, lecturer in art history, 1975-78; Central College for Education Abroad, London, England, lecturer in art history, 1977—. Lecturer for Extra-Mural Department of University of London, 1977—.

WRITINGS: Femme Fatale: Images of Evil and Fascinating Women, Mayflower, 1979. Contributor of articles to *Sunday Telegraph.*

WORK IN PROGRESS: A book on self-portraits, publication expected in 1981; research on European art magazines, 1890-1905.

SIDELIGHTS: Bade writes: "Although I am trained as an art historian, I am less interested in pure art historical research than in investigating links between the arts and in looking at the arts in their social and historical contexts. I aim to write books which have a serious content of ideas, but which will be comprehensible and interesting to a wide public.

My father's family emigrated from Germany earlier in this century, and I feel a special affinity for German history and culture. Munich has become a second home to me. I have a passionate interest in opera and particularly in historical recordings. These are things about which I would like to write in the future."

* * *

BAILEY, F(rancis) Lee 1933-

PERSONAL: Born June 10, 1933, in Waltham, Mass.; son of Grace Bailey Mitchell (a teacher and nursery school director); married Florence Gott (divorced, 1961); married Froma Victoria (divorced, 1972); married Lynda Hart, August 26, 1972; children: (first marriage) Ben, Brian; (second marriage) Scott Frederick. *Education:* Attended Harvard University; Boston University, LL.B., 1960; attended Keeler Polygraph Institute, Chicago. *Residence:* Marshfield, Mass. *Office:* 1 Center Plaza, Boston, Mass. 02108.

CAREER: Founder of private detective agency; admitted to the Bar of Massachusetts, 1960; partner in Bailey, Alch & Gillis (law firm), Boston, Mass. Host of weekly program, "Good Company," American Broadcasting Companies, Inc. (ABC-TV), 1967. Publisher of *Gallery* magazine, 1972—; president of Enstrom Helicopter Corp., 1972—. Lecturer. *Military service:* U.S. Marine Corps; became second lieutenant. *Member:* American Bar Association.

WRITINGS—Nonfiction, except as noted: (Author of foreword) Samuel H. Sheppard, *Endure and Conquer,* World Publishing, 1966; (with Harvey Aronson) *The Defense Never Rests: The Art of Cross-Examination,* Stein & Day, 1971; (with John Greenya) *For the Defense,* Atheneum, 1975; (with Greenya) *Cleared for Approach: F. Lee Bailey in Defense of Flying,* Prentice-Hall, c.1977; *Secrets* (novel), Stein & Day, 1978.

With Henry P. Rothblatt; all nonfiction; all published by Lawyers' Cooperative Publishing Co. (Phillipines): *Complete Manual of Criminal Forms: Federal and State,* 1968, 2nd edition, 1974; *Defending Business and White Collar Crimes: Federal and State* , 1969; *Investigation and Preparation of Criminal Cases: Federal and State,* 1970; *Successful Techniques for Criminal Trials,* 1971; *Handling Narcotic and Drug Cases,* 1972; *Crimes of Violence,* 1973; *Fundamentals of Criminal Advocacy,* 1974; *Handling Misdemeanor Cases,* 1976.

WORK IN PROGRESS: A book about the Hearst case for Putnam.

SIDELIGHTS: Reminiscent of Clarence Darrow, Lloyd Paul Stryker, and Percy Foreman before him, F. Lee Bailey is perhaps the best known criminal lawyer in the United States today. To date he has represented over one hundred indicted criminals, only a handful of whom were finally convicted of their alleged crimes.

A penchant for exhaustive pretrial investigation and a talent for analyzing the facts are Bailey's hallmarks. Another quality that sets him apart from other lawyers, Bailey himself has said, is a respect for the jurors rather than a desire to manipulate them. His reasoning is that if good evidence is brought forth in a clear-cut manner, the jury can be counted on to reach the proper conclusion.

As a student at the University of Boston's law school, the indefatigable Bailey scored the highest grade point average in its history. At the same time, he was an avid hockey player and ran a detective agency he himself founded.

When newly graduated from law school, Bailey became involved in the highly publicized case of George Elderly. Elderly was accused of murdering his wife and dumping her dismembered body into a river. When the original defense lawyer suffered a heart attack, Bailey, who had been called in as a polygraph (lie detector) specialist, replaced him. Bailey won his client an acquittal.

The Elderly trial helped launch the young Bailey on a brilliant career. He went on to represent some of the most notorious defendants of the past two decades, including Dr. Samuel H. Sheppard, the Boston Strangler (Albert De Salvo), Captain Ernest Medina, and Patty Hearst. As a *Time* reporter put it, Bailey has represented and "won victories for sure losers."

Shortly after the Elderly acquittal, Bailey represented convicted murderer Samuel H. Sheppard in an appeal. Sheppard, an osteopath, had allegedly killed his wife. By scrupulously researching the case, Bailey discovered that the judge had allowed some of the jurors to go home in the evenings without screening them from adverse publicity. Through Bailey's efforts, the original verdict was reversed and Sheppard was set free.

Albert De Salvo was an inmate of the Bridgewater hospital for the criminally insane when he decided to confess that he was the Boston Strangler, the killer of thirteen women. Bailey took up the case. Certain that De Salvo was insane when he committed the killings, Bailey fought to have him acquitted by the state of Massachusetts. Bailey lost, claiming that "Massachusetts just burned another witch," and vowed to fight what he considered to be an outdated insanity law in an appeal.

Then in 1971 Bailey defended Captain Ernest L. Medina, who was being court-martialed for his involvement in the Mai Lai massacre in Vietnam. Medina had been charged specifically with killing a Vietnamese woman and young boy, and for being responsible for the deaths of over one hundred other Mai Lai villagers killed by his men. Before Bailey was through, however, the charges were shaved down to the direct killing of the woman and involuntary manslaughter of the others. Bailey had put nearly thirty defense witnesses on the stand and "turned his client into his own best witness," noted a *Newsweek* reporter. In little more than an hour the five-member military jury reached a decision of not guilty, resulting in what Bailey termed Medina's "thumping acquittal."

The most recent case involving Bailey to make newspaper headlines was the thirty-nine day trial of newspaper fortune heiress Patty Hearst. Hearst, who had been kidnapped by members of the Symbionese Liberation Army (SLA), was indicted for participating in the armed robbery of a branch of the Hibernia Bank in San Francisco. Lawrence Friedman called the ordeal "the most sensational trial of the television era."

The main question raised in the trial was: Did Hearst ultimately join up with the SLA of her own accord or was she coerced into remaining with the revolutionary group? Bailey's primary objective was to convince the court that Hearst's criminal actions were brought about by brainwashing, or "induced insanity," which was defined in *Newsweek* as "behavioral changes induced by somebody or something." In support of this stance, Bailey called UCLA psychiatry department chairman Dr. Louis West to the witness stand. West concluded that Hearst suffered from "a traumatic neurosis, acute and chronic, with dissociative features."

With Bailey's prompting, Hearst herself often testified during the trial. She told the court the SLA had given her the ultimatum to "either fight or die . . . stay with them and join up with them or . . . be killed." To explain the ease with which she appeared to be handling a semi-automatic carbine in a bank film of the robbery, Hearst further stated that she was forcibly taught by SLA members Emily and Bill Harris to maintain and shoot the firearm. When asked if she had considered actually firing the weapon while in the bank, "under any circumstances," Hearst replied, "No." Seventy-one witnesses in all were called to the stand, and from most indications, the trial seemed to be leaning in Hearst's favor.

For this reason the actual verdict came as a surprise to many: the jury concluded that Hearst was guilty as charged. "It was kind of like the hare and the tortoise," remarked Judge Carter in reference to Bailey and the less flamboyant prosecuting attorney, James L. Browning, Jr. Hearst had been forced to take the Fifth Amendment forty-two times when cross-examined by Browning, who, according to *Newsweek*, "correctly deduced that Patty's credibility as a witness was the weakest link in Bailey's defense."

As can be expected, reactions to the verdict conflicted. One government official remarked: "The Hearst case stands for the proposition that if you rob a bank, you've got to pay the piper—no matter how bizarre the circumstances, no matter how you can pay for your defense, no matter how brilliant the counsel you can afford." Others strongly supported Bailey's decision to appeal. Bailey's own response to the verdict was to note that the SLA's prophecy that Hearst would be severely punished if she returned to society was fulfilled.

Bailey has also weathered more personal encounters with the courts. He was criticized by the Massachusetts Bar Association for "talking too much out of court," noted *Newsweek*. Then in 1971, the supreme court of New Jersey barred him from practicing law in that state for a year on the same grounds. Bailey's retort was: "When there's a barrage of publicity coming out and suggesting that your client is every kind of s.o.b., then there is some kind of responsibility to balance the record and at least keep the presumption of innocence alive." Two years later Bailey was arraigned for conspiring with entrepreneur Glenn W. Turner in various dealings, but that case was eventually thrown out of court.

In his best-selling book, *The Defense Never Rests*, Bailey discusses some of the cases in which he has been involved, including the trials of Samuel H. Sheppard and the Boston Strangler. He also expresses his views on the present legal system, suggesting "better training of criminal lawyers through an extra year of criminal law courses followed by a year as clerk to a trial judge, a year as an assistant prosecutor, and a year as an aide to a defense lawyer," wrote a *Library Journal* reviewer. Arthur Cooper described the book in *Newsweek* as "breezy, blunt and immensely readable." In *For the Defense*, Bailey goes on to write about the court-martial of Ernest L. Medina and the trial involving Glenn W. Turner.

Bailey has also tried his hand at other types of writing. *Secrets* is a novel that concerns an eminent lawyer who finds he must retain a defense attorney for himself. "The courtroom stuff in the novel is nice and crisp," wrote a critic in the *New York Times Book Review*, "especially the cross-examinations intended to discredit witnesses. And the seamy background of the case—a web of corrupt witnesses, old grudges and criminal mischief—has a gamy reek of the real thing." *Cleared for the Approach* is about one of Bailey's hobbies: flying. Since it is Bailey's belief that ignorance of the facts is often behind any fear, he tackles the fear of flying by supplying detailed information on the subject.

Bailey lectures on law throughout the United States and has appeared on numerous television programs.

AVOCATIONAL INTERESTS: Flying planes, sailing, playing hockey, driving cars and motorcycles.

BIOGRAPHICAL/CRITICAL SOURCES: Saturday Evening Post, November 5, 1966; *Time*, December 9, 1966, October 4, 1971, July 9, 1973, October 24, 1975, February 9, 1976, February 16, 1976, March 15, 1976, March 22, 1976, March 29, 1976; *Newsweek*, December 19, 1966, October 6, 1969, September 27, 1971, December 20, 1971, January 3, 1972, October 20, 1975, March 1, 1976, March 8, 1976, March 15, 1976, March 29, 1976, January 2, 1978; *New York Times Magazine*, September 20, 1970, October 18, 1970; *Washington Post Book World*, December 26, 1971, May 1, 1977; *Library Journal*, January 1, 1972; *Best Sellers*, January 15, 1972, July, 1975; *New York Times Book Review*, January 23, 1972, February 4, 1979; *America*, May 20, 1972; *Spectator*, July 29, 1972; *Times Literary Supplement*, August 11, 1972; *Life*, November 17, 1972; *Christian Science Monitor*, June 17, 1977; *People*, September 4, 1978; *Rolling Stone*, December, 1978.*

—Sketch by Victoria France Hutchinson

* * *

BAILLIE, Hugh 1890-1966

OBITUARY NOTICE: Born October 23, 1890, in Brooklyn, N.Y.; died March 1, 1966. Journalist and newspaper executive. Baillie was affiliated with the United Press (now United Press International) as president and board chairman for over forty years. After World War II, Baillie launched a one-man campaign dedicated to the assurance of freedom of the press around the world. Within a year he was able to obtain affirmative agreements from ten governments, the United States Congress passing a resolution to the effect. During his career, Baillie interviewed such notables as Joseph Stalin, Douglas MacArthur, Emperor Hirohito, Chiang Kai-shek, Adolf Hitler, and Benito Mussolini. He is the author of *Two Battlefronts*, *Men at Crisis*, and *High Tension*. Obituaries and other sources: *Current Biography*, Wilson, 1946, March, 1966; *New York Times*, March 2, 1966.

BAIRD, Nancy Disher 1935-

PERSONAL: Born April 30, 1935, in Cincinnati, Ohio; daughter of I. Clinton (a consulting engineer) and Whitlock (a professor of home economics; maiden name, Fennell) Disher; married Thomas H. Baird (a physician), June 21, 1958; children: Alice Whitlock, Mary Nell. *Education:* University of Kentucky, B.A., 1957; Western Kentucky University, M.A., 1972, Ed.S., 1975. *Religion:* Episcopalian. *Home:* 1913 Nashville Rd., Bowling Green, Ky. 42101. *Office:* Kentucky Library, Western Kentucky University, Bowling Green, Ky. 42101.

CAREER: High school history teacher in Cincinnati, Ohio, 1957-58; history teacher at preparatory school in New Orleans, La., 1958-59; Western Kentucky University, Bowling Green, part-time instructor in history, 1974-75, special collections librarian at Kentucky Library, 1975—. *Member:* Kentucky Historical Society, Phi Alpha Theta, Filson Club.

WRITINGS: David Wendel Yandell: Physician of Old Louisville, University Press of Kentucky, 1978; *Luke Pryor Blackburn: Physician, Governor, Reformer,* University Press of Kentucky, 1979. Contributor to history journals.

WORK IN PROGRESS: A history of Cincinnati's oldest masonry construction company, publication expected in 1980; editing letters of Elizabeth Cox Underwood to her husband, U.S. Senator Joseph R. Underwood, 1848-53.

* * *

BALANCY, Pierre Guy Girald 1924-1979

OBITUARY NOTICE: Born April 8, 1924, in Port Louis, Mauritius; died after abdominal surgery, September 22, 1979, in Washington, D.C. Journalist, politician, diplomat who served as ambassador of Mauritius to the United States and as permanent representative to the United Nations, and author. Balancy was elected to the Mauritius Parliament in 1959 and later became a cabinet minister. A strong spokesman on behalf of African nations at the U.S. State Department, he was also his country's chief diplomatic representative to Argentina, Brazil, Mexico, Canada, and several Caribbean states. A well-known journalist and writer in Mauritius, Balancy was founder and editor-in-chief of an important daily newspaper, *L'Express,* editor of the literary review *Escales,* and author of a book, *Human Brotherhood in a Multi-Racial Society.* Obituaries and other sources: *Who's Who in Government,* Marquis, 1972; *The International Who's Who,* Europa, 1974; *Washington Post,* September 23, 1979.

* * *

BALDICK, Robert 1927-1972

OBITUARY NOTICE: Born November 9, 1927, in Huddersfield, Yorkshire, England; died April 24, 1972. Educator, editor, translator, and author. Produced from his doctoral thesis on the French author Huysmans, Baldick's first book met with wide acclaim, launching him into a highly successful literary career. He was the editor of the Oxford Library of French Classics and joint-editor of the Penguin Classics. Baldick was made a fellow of Oxford University in 1958, a post he held until his death. He is the author of many books, including *The Life and Times of Frederic Lemaitre* and *The Life of Henry Murger.* Obituaries and other sources: *The Author's and Writer's Who's Who,* 6th edition, Burke's Peerage, 1971; *London Times,* April 25, 1972.

BALL, Marion J(okl) 1940-

PERSONAL: Born August 25, 1940, in Johannesburg, South Africa; came to United States in 1953, naturalized citizen, 1959; daughter of Ernst (a physician and professor) and Erica (a physical education teacher; maiden name, Lestman) Jokl; married John C. Ball in 1959; children: Charles, Elizabeth. *Education:* Attended Northwestern University, 1957-58; University of Kentucky, B.A. (with distinction), 1961, M.A., 1965; Temple University, Ed.D., 1978. *Office:* Computer Systems and Management Information Group, Temple University, 3333 North Broad St., Room 331, Philadelphia, Pa. 19140.

CAREER: High school mathematics teacher in Lexington, Ky., 1961-62; University of Kentucky, Lexington, instructor in behavioral science, 1965-68, and computer science, 1967-68, computer program analyst, 1965-67; Temple University, Medical School, Philadelphia, Pa., assistant professor, 1968-72, associate professor of medical physics and biometrics, 1973—, director of Computer Systems and Management Information Group, 1972—. Participant in national and international meetings on computers in medicine.

MEMBER: Association of American Medical Colleges, Association for Computing Machinery, American Association of University Women, American Medical Record Association, American Society for Testing Materials, COMMON, Montessori Society, Society for Advanced Medical Systems, Society for Computer Medicine (member of board of directors, 1972-78), American Hospital Association (member of advisory council, 1972-74), College of Physicians of Philadelphia (fellow), Kappa Delta Phi, Delta Phi Alpha, Kappa Delta Pi, Pi Mu Epsilon. *Awards, honors:* Travel grant for international meeting in Sweden from National Research Council, 1974.

WRITINGS: (Contributor) Erich Goode, editor, *Marihuana,* Atherton Press, 1969; *Selecting a Computer System for the Clinical Laboratory,* C. C Thomas, 1971; *What Is a Computer?,* Houghton, 1972; (contributor) G. A. Schwartz Bekey, editor, *Hospital Information Systems,* Dekker, 1972; (contributor) E. R. Gabrielli, editor, *Clinical-Oriented Documentation of Laboratory Data,* Academic Press, 1972; *How to Select a Computerized Hospital Information System,* S. Karger, 1973; (with S. Charp) *Be a Computer Literate!,* Creative Computing, 1978.

Author of "What Is a Computer?," a filmed interview and lecture broadcast on television in 1977. Contributor of about twenty-five articles to medical, health care, and computer science journals.

WORK IN PROGRESS: Two papers, one on the "state of the art and future of hospital information systems," and one on "the current status of clinical laboratory systems," to be published by the *Journal of Hospital Financial Management.*

SIDELIGHTS: Marion Ball's research interests include utilization of computers in medicine, computerization of clinical pathology laboratories, comparative systems analysis in hospital information systems development, use of computers in medical and health sciences education and in continuing medical education.

* * *

BALTES, Paul B. 1939-

PERSONAL: Born June 18, 1939, in Saarlouis, Germany (now West Germany); came to the United States in 1968; son of Johann (in business) and Katharina (in business; maiden name, Haser) Baltes; married wife, Margret M. (a professor), 1963; children: Boris B., Anushka M. *Education:* University of Saar, B.A., 1961, M.A., 1963, Ph.D. (magna cum laude), 1967; graduate study at University of Nebraska, 1963-64. *Home:* 1845 Woodledge Dr., State College, Pa. 16801. *Office:* Division of Individual and Family Studies, College of Human Development, Pennsylvania State University, University Park, Pa. 16802.

CAREER: West Virginia University, Morgantown, assistant professor, 1968-70, associate professor of psychology, 1970-72; Pennsylvania State University, University Park, associate professor, 1972-74, professor of human development, 1974—, director of Division of Individual and Family Studies, 1972-78. Visiting professor at University of Southern California, summer, 1971, and University of Trier, summer, 1972. Fellow of Center for Advanced Study in the Behavioral Sciences, 1978-79. Member of Social Science Research Council committees and National Institutes of Health study sections. *Member:* International Society for the Study of Behavioral Development (member of executive board, 1977—), American Psychological Association (fellow; Division 20 president, 1976-77), Gerontological Society (fellow; head of research committee, 1975-76), Society for Research in Child Development, Society for Multivariate Experimental Psychology. *Awards, honors:* Grants from U.S. Office of Education, 1969-70, 1971-73, Administration on Aging, 1973-77, National Institute on Education, 1974-76, National Institute of Mental Health, 1976-81, and from National Institute on Aging, 1976-80; R. B. Cattell Award for distinguished research from Society for Multivariate Experimental Psychology, 1975; Stanford Center for Advanced Study fellowship, 1978-79.

WRITINGS: (Editor with L. R. Goulet, and contributor) *Life-Span Developmental Psychology: Research and Theory,* Academic Press, 1970; (editor with K. W. Schaie, and contributor) *Life-Span Developmental Psychology: Personality and Socialization,* Academic Press, 1973; (with J. R. Nesselroade) *Adolescent Personality Development and Historical Change* (monograph), Society for Research in Child Development, 1974; (with Nesselroade and H. W. Reese) *Life-Span Developmental Psychology: An Introduction to Research Methods,* Brooks/Cole, 1977; (editor) *Life-Span Development and Behavior: Advances in Research and Theory,* Academic Press, Volume I, 1978, Volume II (with O .G. Brim, and contributor), 1979, Volume III (with Brim), 1980; (editor with Nesselroade, and contributor) *Longitudinal Research in the Behavioral Sciences: Design and Analysis,* Academic Press, 1979; (editor with Lutz Eckensberger) *Entwicklungspsychologie und Lebensspanne* (tittle means "Life-Span Developmental Psychology"), Klett Verlag, 1979.

Contributor: Nesselroade and Reese, editors, *Life-Span Developmental Psychology: Methodological Issues,* Academic Press, 1973; C. Eisdorfer and P. Lawton, editors, *The Psychology of Adult Development and Aging,* American Psychological Association, 1973; Reese, editor, *Advances in Child Development and Behavior,* Academic Press, 1976; Reese and Nancy Datan, editors, *Life-Span Developmental Psychology: Dialectical Perspectives,* Academic Press, 1977; M .W. Riley, editor, *Aging From Birth to Death,* American Association for the Advancement of Science, 1978; F. Hoffmeister, editor, *The Evaluation of Old-Related Changes and Disorders of Brain Functions,* Springer (Heldelberg, Germany), 1979.

Contributor to *International Encyclopedia of Neurology, Psychiatry, Psychoanalysis, and Psychology* and *Handbook of the Psychology of Aging.* Contributor of more than fifty articles and reviews to journals in the behavioral sciences. Member of editorial board of *Developmental Psychology,* 1969-76, *Human Development,* 1974—, *Experimental Aging,* 1975—, and *Multivariate Behavioral Research,* 1975-78 (head of editorial board, 1978-79).

WORK IN PROGRESS: Editing, with L. P. Lipsitt and Reese, a textbook on lifespan developmental psychology, for Scott, Foresman.

SIDELIGHTS: Baltes is a developmental psychologist and gerontologist. His research interests include longitudinal and sequential methodology, intervention in adult development and aging, simulation and modification (control) of developmental processes, development of ability and personality structure, cultural change and adolescent and adult personality, and inter-generational and inter-age relationships.

* * *

BANKS, Harlan Parker 1913-

PERSONAL: Born September 1, 1913, in Cambridge, Mass.; son of Carl T. and Hazel (Cummings) Banks; married Rosamond L. Shurtleff, December 23, 1939; children: Jane Ann, Susan Elizabeth. *Education:* Dartmouth University, A.B., 1934; Cornell University, Ph.D., 1940. *Home:* 1005 Highland Rd., Ithaca, N.Y. 14850.

CAREER: Botanist and writer. University of Minnesota, Minneapolis, assistant professor of botany, 1947-49; Cornell University, Ithaca, N.Y., associate professor, 1949-50, professor of botany, 1950—, head of department, 1952-61. Also worked as instructor of biology at Acadia University; director of Summer Institute of Botany at Cornell University. *Member:* International Association of Plant Taxonomists, International Organization of Paleobotany (vice-president, 1964-69; president, 1969—), International Society of Plant Morphology, Botany Society of America (treasurer, 1964-67, president, 1969), Torrey Botany Club, Phi Kappa Phi, Sigma Xi.

WRITINGS: (With James D. Grierson) *Lycopods of the Devonian of New York State,* Paleontological Research Institution, 1963; *Evolution and Plants of the Past,* Wadsworth, 1970; (contributor) *Symposium on Major Evolutionary Events,* Cambridge University Press, 1970; (with Suzanne Leclercq and F. M. Hueber) *Anatomy and Morphology of Psilophyton Dawsonnii,* Paleontological Research Institution, 1975. Member of editorial board of *Plant Science Bulletin,* 1953—, and *Review of Paleobotany and Palynology,* 1968—.*

* * *

BANKS, James Houston 1925-
(Jimmy Banks)

PERSONAL: Born November 3, 1925, in Waco, Tex.; son of Elijah Halbert and Evelyn Virginia (Haralson) Banks; married Mary Virginia Bussey, June 15, 1947; children: Virginia Anne, Janet Lynn (Mrs. Dean Tate). *Education:* Attended University of Texas, 1943, 1946-47. *Religion:* Methodist. *Home:* 6113 Rickey Dr., Austin, Tex. 78731. *Office:* Texas Railroad Association, 212 Vaughn Building, Austin, Tex. 78701.

CAREER: Sports editor for *Austin American-Statesman,* Austin, Tex.; *Dallas Morning News,* Dallas, Tex., reporter, 1950-53; press secretary to Governor Allan Shivers in Austin, Tex., 1954-57; *Dallas Morning News,* capitol correspondent in Austin, 1957-70; *Texas Star* (weekly magazine), Austin, founding editor, 1970-72; executive assistant to U.S. Senator John Tower in Austin, Tex., 1972-74; Texas Railroad Association, Austin, public relations director and founding editor of *Texas Railways,* 1975—. Member of Austin Group (public relations organization). *Military service:* U.S. Army Air Forces, bombardier-navigator, 1943-45. U.S. Air Force, 1951-52; became first lieutenant. *Member:* International Association of Business Communicators, Railroad Public Relations Association (regional vice-president), Association of Railroad Editors (member of executive committee), Texas Public Relations Association, Headliners Club of Austin (president, 1976), Sigma Delta Chi (president, 1962). *Awards, honors:* Journalism awards include three awards from Association of Railroad Editors for *Texas Railways.*

WRITINGS—All under name Jimmy Banks: *Money, Marbles, and Chalk: The Wondrous World of Texas Politics,* Texas Publishing, 1971; *The Darrell Royal Story,* Shoal Creek Publishers, 1973. Also editor of *Allan Shivers: The Pied Piper of Texas Politics* and *Blackie Sherrod Scattershooting.* Austin correspondent for *Sports Illustrated,* 1958—. Contributor of more than one hundred articles to magazines. Past editor of magazines for Texas State Teachers Association and Texas Society of Architects.

SIDELIGHTS: Banks comments: "I have a wide variety of interests, having covered politics, sports, and general assignments during my twenty-one-year newspaper career. I love to travel and I take photographs to illustrate many of my magazine articles."

* * *

BANKS, Jimmy
See BANKS, James Houston

* * *

BANNING, Lance (Gilbert) 1942-

PERSONAL: Born January 24, 1942, in Kansas City, Mo.; son of E. Willis (a painter) and Marie (Gilbert) Banning; married Lana June Sampson, July 11, 1964; children: Clinton Edward. *Education:* University of Missouri, Kansas City, B.A., 1964; Washington University, St. Louis, Mo., Ph.D., 1971. *Home:* 604 Cromwell Way, Lexington, Ky. 40503. *Office:* Department of History, University of Kentucky, Lexington, Ky. 40506.

CAREER: Brown University, Providence, R.I., lecturer in American civilization, 1971-73; University of Kentucky, Lexington, assistant professor, 1973-78, associate professor of history, 1978—. *Member:* American Historical Association, Organization of American Historians. *Awards, honors:* National Endowment for the Humanities younger humanist fellowship, 1974-75; Guggenheim fellowship, 1979-80.

WRITINGS: The Jeffersonian Persuasion: Evolution of a Party Ideology, Cornell University Press, 1978. Contributor of articles and reviews to history journals.

WORK IN PROGRESS: James Madison and the Evolution of American Republicanism.

* * *

BARBOUR, Ruth P(eeling) 1924-

PERSONAL: Born October 24, 1924, in York, Pa.; daughter of Lucien C. (in sales) and Hilda (a teacher; maiden name, Leckey) Peeling; married J. O. Barbour, Jr. (a company president), September 26, 1970. *Education:* Syracuse University, B.A., 1946; Florida State University, M.A., 1953. *Religion:* Lutheran. *Home address:* P.O. Box 35, Beaufort, N.C. 28516. *Office: Carteret County News-Times,* P.O. Box 1679, Morehead City, N.C. 28557.

CAREER: Carteret County News-Times, Morehead City, N.C., editor, 1946-75, author of weekly column, 1952—. Past president of local amateur theater group; volunteer teacher of slow readers in public schools. *Member:* Phi Beta Kappa. *Awards, honors:* First place award in statewide contest sponsored by Greensboro Writers Club, 1959, for children's story, "In the Valley of the Rainbow."

WRITINGS: Cruise of the Snap Dragon (historical novel), Blair, 1976.

Plays: "Bonnie Blue Sweetheart" (three-act), first produced in Morehead City, N.C., at Morehead City elementary school auditorium, June 12, 1959; "Blackbeard, Raider of the Carolina Seas" (three-act), first produced in Beaufort, N.C., July 23, 1964; "Otway Burns, Firebrand of 1812" (three-act), first produced in Beaufort, N.C., June 27, 1969; "It Happened Here" (nine episodes), first produced in Morehead City, N.C., at Morehead City elementary school auditorium, June 24, 1976; "The Best of All" (ten scenes), first produced in Beaufort, N.C., June 23, 1976.

WORK IN PROGRESS: A sequel to *Cruise of the Snap Dragon,* publication by John F. Blair.

SIDELIGHTS: Ruth Barbour writes: "My first love is writing plays, but it was not until 1958-59 that my first historical play was written. It was about a woman Confederate spy in Carteret County, N.C. All the plays deal with local history. *Cruise of the Snap Dragon* evolved after the production of 'Otway Burns, Firebrand of 1812,' using much of the research done for that play.

"Writing plays and novels is stimulating. I enjoy doing the plays, novels not so much. The major satisfaction from 'writing a book' is the achievement—merely having done it! I have also dabbled in poetry and writing for children, but neither interests me as much as historical prose."

AVOCATIONAL INTERESTS: Travel (including Europe and Mexico).

BIOGRAPHICAL/CRITICAL SOURCES: Raleigh News and Observer, March 31, 1968.

* * *

BARFORD, Carol 1931-

PERSONAL: Born May 12, 1931, in Milwaukee, Wis.; daughter of Jerry (a contractor) and Anna (Blaha) Murray; married Roger Barford (a social science teacher), October 24, 1953; children: Stephen John, Dana Leigh Barford Jamerson, David Grant. *Education:* Sacred Heart School of Nursing (now Alverno College), R.N., 1951; attended College of the Desert, 1966-72; University of Redlands, B.A., 1974, graduate study, 1974, 1977. *Politics:* Democrat. *Religion:* Roman Catholic. *Home address:* Star Route 1, Box 1180-D, Yucca Valley, Calif. 92284.

CAREER: Registered nurse at hospitals in Wisconsin and California, 1951-67; San Bernardino County Health Department, Yucca Valley, Calif., assistant public health nurse, 1968-69; Visiting Nurses Association, Palm Desert, Calif., visiting nurse, 1972-73; San Bernardino County Health Department, assistant public health nurse, 1974-75; substitute teacher at public schools in Yucca Valley and Twenty-Nine Palms, Calif., 1975-76; free-lance writer, 1976—. Teacher of creative writing at College of the Desert. *Member:* Society of Children's Book Writers.

WRITINGS: Let Me Hear the Music (juvenile novel), Seabury, 1979. Contributor of poems, articles, and stories to national magazines.

WORK IN PROGRESS: The Orchid Willow, a young adult novel about a public health nurse in the Mojave Desert.

SIDELIGHTS: Carol Barford comments: "As a registered nurse I learned to observe the human condition and to empathize with it. Now, as a writer, I want to comment on that, and tell a good story."

Let Me Hear the Music has been optioned for television by producer Martin Tahse.

* * *

BARKER, Elliott S(peer) 1886-

PERSONAL: Born December 25, 1886, in Moran, Tex.; son of Squire L. (a farmer) and Pricilla J. (McGuire) Barker; married Ethel M. Arnold, 1911; children: Roy E., Florence Barker Giers, Dorothy Barker Elmore. *Education:* Attended high school in Las Vegas, N.M. *Politics:* "Democrat, but I often split the ticket." *Religion:* Methodist. *Home and office:* 343 Palace Ave., Santa Fe, N.M. 87501.

CAREER: Professional guide and hunter near Las Vegas, N.M., 1907-08; U.S. Forest Service, Washington, D.C., forest ranger in Cuba, N.M., 1909, Pecos, N.M., 1909-12, and Tres Piedras, N.M., 1913-14, forest supervisor in Taos, N.M., 1915-19; rancher near Las Vegas, 1919-30; game manager and predator controller at Vermejo Park, N.M., 1930-31; New Mexico Department of Game and Fish, Santa Fe, state game warden and director of department, 1931-53; conservationist and writer, 1953—. Past member of New Mexico State Personnel Board.

MEMBER: International Association of Game, Fish, and Conservation Commissioners (president, 1936-37), Western Writers of America, National Wildlife Federation (past member of board of directors; past state representative), Western Association of Game and Fish Commissioners (honorary life member; president, 1934-36, 1946-47), New Mexico Wildlife Federation (life member; life member of board of directors; past executive director; president emeritus), Santa Fe Wildlife and Conservation Association, Santa Fe Camera Club, Masons (Scottish Rite), Shriners. *Awards, honors:* Dozens of awards for conservation work include meritorious service citation from New Mexico Wildlife Conservation Association, 1953; conservation awards from KOB-Radio and Television and American Motors Co., 1964; conservationist of the year award from National Wildlife Federation, 1965, communication award, 1966; Golden Spur Award from Western Writers of America, 1972, for *Western Life and Adventures, 1889-1970;* LL.D. from New Mexico State University, 1976.

WRITINGS: When the Dogs Barked "Treed": A Year on the Trail of the Longtails, University of New Mexico Press, 1946, third edition, Bishop Printing, 1975; *Beatty's Cabin: Adventures in the Pecos High Country,* University of New Mexico Press, 1953, reprinted, Gannon, 1977; *A Medley of Wilderness and Other Poems,* Vergara Printing, 1962; *Outdoors, Faith, Fun, and Other Poems,* Rydal Press, 1968; *Western Life and Adventures, 1889 to 1970,* Calvin Horn, 1970, reprinted as *Western Life and Adventures in the Great Southwest,* Lowell Press, 1974; *Ramblings in the Field of Conservation,* Sunstone Press, 1976; *Eighty Years With Rod and Rifle,* Bishop Printing, 1976; *101 Smiles, Chuckles, and Hearty Laughs,* Bishop Printing, 1979. Contributor of articles and stories to national magazines.

SIDELIGHTS: A conservationist for most of his life, Barker donated Smokey the Bear to the U.S. Forest Service in 1950, specifying that his life was to be devoted to forest fire prevention and wildlife conservation. In 1966, the U.S. Game Commission dedicated to Barker a five-thousand-acre wildlife area which was named for him in recognition of the assistance he had given to the regional Girl Scout Council.

Barker writes: "My books are all authentic. I was inspired to write them because I had information and experiences and adventures which I thought should be recorded for posterity, particularly activities from my earlier days. I've known too many men who had a lot of good information stored up in their heads who were indiscreet enough to die without recording a word of it. In recording my own experiences and adventures I have made it good, entertaining reading."

Barker's first book described his work on Vermejo Park Ranch. *Beatty's Cabin* is about some of his earlier activities and adventures in what is now the Pecos Wilderness in the Sangre de Cristo Mountains. *Ramblings in the Field of Conservation* recounts such events as the birth of the National Wildlife Federation, the Wilderness Bill battle, and the rescue and dedication of Smokey the Bear.

Barker was the only man ever to have the honor of being president of the International Association of Games, Fish, and Conservation Commissioners and of the Western Association of Game and Fish Commissioners at the same time.

* * *

BARNES, Harry Elmer 1889-1968

PERSONAL: Born June 15, 1889, in Auburn, N.Y.; died August 25, 1968; son of William Henry, Jr. (a school superintendent) and Lulu C. (Short) Barnes; married L. Grace Stone, June 8, 1910 (divorced); married Jean Hutchison; children: (first marriage) one son. *Education:* Syracuse University, A.B., 1913, M.A., 1914; Harvard University, postgraduate study, 1917; Columbia University, Ph.D., 1918. *Home address:* R.F.D. 5, Auburn, N.Y. 13021. *Office:* 230 Park Ave., New York, N.Y. 10017.

CAREER: Historian; sociologist; writer. Worked as bridge engineer; Clark University, Worcester, Mass., professor of history, beginning in 1920; Amherst College, Amherst, Mass., professor of economics and sociology, 1923-25; Smith College, Northampton, Mass., professor of historical sociology, 1923-29; member of editorial staff, Scripps-Howard Newspapers, 1929-40; U.S. Government, member of staff, 1941-43, historian and consultant to Prison Industries Branch of War Production Board, 1943-44; historian and consultant to Smaller War Plants Corp., 1945-46; visiting professor of sociology at Temple University, 1946, University of Colorado, 1948-49, and University of Indiana, 1951. Affiliated with New School for Social Research. Director of study tours abroad, summers, 1950, 1951. *Member:* P.E.N., American Association for the Advancement of Science, Authors Club of London, Phi Beta Kappa, Beta Epsilon, Alpha Pi Zeta, Pi Gamma Mu, Kappa Beta Phi.

WRITINGS: A History of the Penal, Reformatory and Correctional Institutions of the State of New Jersey, MacCrellish, 1918; *History, Its Rise and Development: A Survey of the Progress of Historical Writing From its Origins to the Present Day,* Encyclopedia Americana Corp., 1919, first published in 1919 edition of *Encyclopedia Americana; The Social History of the Western World,* Appleton, 1921; *Sociology and Political Theory: A Consideration of the Sociological Basis of Politics,* Knopf, 1924; *Psychology and History,* Century, 1925; *The New History and the Social Studies,* Century, 1925, reprinted, Revisionist Press, 1972; (author with others, and editor) *The History and Prospects of the Social Sciences,* Knopf, 1925.

The Repression of Crime: Studies in Historical Penology, Patterson Smith, c.1926, reprinted, 1969; *History and Social Intelligence,* Knopf, 1926; *The Genesis of the World War: An Introduction to the Problem of War Guilt,* Knopf, 1926, revised edition, 1929, reprinted, 1970; *The Evolution of Penology in Pennsylvania: A Study in American Social History,* Bobbs-Merrill, c.1927, reprinted, Patterson Smith, 1968; *Living in the Twentieth Century: A Consideration of How We Got This Way,* Bobbs-Merrill, c.1928; *In Quest of Truth and Justice: De-Bunking the War Guilt Myth,* National Historical Society, 1928, reprinted, Arno, 1972; (with Elisabeth A. Dexter and Mabel Walker) *The Making of a Nation,* Knopf, 1929.

The Story of Punishment: A Record of Man's Inhumanity to Man, Stratford C., c.1930, 2nd edition, 1972; *World Politics in Modern Civilization: The Contributions of Nationalism, Capitalism, Imperialism and Militarism to Human Culture and International Anarchy,* Knopf, 1930; *Battling the Crime Wave: Applying Sense and Science to the Repression of Crime,* Stratford Co., c.1931; *Prohibition Versus Civilization: Analyzing the Dry Psychosis,* Viking, 1932; *Can Man Be Civilized?,* Brentano's, c.1932; *Money Changers vs. the New Deal: A Candid Analysis of the Inflation Controversy,* R. Long & R. R. Smith, 1934; *The History of Western Civilization,* two volumes, Harcourt, 1935; *A History of Historical Writing,* University of Oklahoma Press, 1937, 2nd edition, 1962; *An Intellectual and Cultural History of the Western World,* Harcourt, 1937; (with Howard Beck and others) *Social Thought From Lore to Science,* two volumes, Heath, c.1938, 3rd edition published in three volumes, Dover, 1961; *Society in Transition: Problems of Changing Age,* Prentice-Hall, 1939, 2nd edition, 1968.

(Editor with H. Becker and Frances B. Becker) *Contemporary Social Theory,* Appleton-Century-Crofts, c.1940, reprinted, Russell, 1971; *An Intellectual and Cultural History of the Western World,* Reynal & Hitchcock, c.1941, 3rd edition published in three volumes, Dover, 1965; *Social Institutions in an Era of World Upheaval,* Prentice-Hall, 1942, reprinted, 1977; (with others) *The American Way of Life: An Introduction to the Study of Society and Social Problems,* Prentice-Hall, c.1942, 2nd edition, 1950; (with Negley K. Teeters) *New Horizons in Criminology: The American Crime Problem,* foreword by Frank Tannenbaum, Prentice-Hall, 1943, 2nd edition, 1951; *Pennsylvania Penology: 1944,* Pennsylvania Municipal Publications Service, 1944; *A Survey of Western Civilization,* Crowell, 1947; (editor) *An Introduction to the History of Sociology,* University of Chicago Press, 1948, abridged edition, c.1948; *Historical Sociology: Its Origins and Development,* Philosophical Library, 1948.

(Editor with others) *Perpetual War for Perpetual Peace: A Critical Examination of the Foreign Policy of Franklin Delano Roosevelt and Its Aftermath,* Greenwood Press, 1953; (editor) *An Introduction to the History of Sociology,* Chicago University Press, 1958; (with Nathan F. Leopold, Jr. and others) *The Future of Imprisonment in a Free Society,* St. Leonard's House, 1965; *Pearl Harbor After a Quarter of a Century,* Arno, 1972; *Sociology and Political Theory: A Consideration of the Sociological Basis of Politics,* Revisionist Press, 1972; *Selected Revisionist Pamphlets,* Arno, 1972. Also author of *The Struggle Against the Historical Blackout,* 1949, 9th edition, 1952. Author of booklets in his field.

SIDELIGHTS: Barnes has been viewed as an irreverent historian whose knowledge of facts was phenomenal. His numerous writings are geared toward the general public as well as toward his professional colleagues. *Genesis of the World War* was well-received by the Germans: in it Barnes contended that Germany should not shoulder all the blame for World War I after all. But after subsequently criticizing Hitler's actions during World War II, Barnes was no longer welcome in that country.

Although Barnes did become involved in the war effort, he initially stood firmly against the United States' proposal to enter World War II. He espoused the liberal, peace-oriented views prevalent before 1937 and several of his writings sought to revive this Revisionist way of thinking.

"Twilight of Christianity," a speech delivered by Barnes at the 1928 Meeting of the American Association for the Advancement of Science, was accorded numerous accolades.

BIOGRAPHICAL/CRITICAL SOURCES: New York Times, January 31, 1926, June 27, 1926, May 11, 1930, September 15, 1935; *New Republic,* August 18, 1926, November 20, 1935; *Times Literary Supplement,* September 30, 1926; *Saturday Review of Literature,* November 20, 1926; *World Tomorrow,* February, 1930; *Current History,* March, 1930; *Boston Transcript,* September 11, 1935; *Nation,* December 19, 1953.

OBITUARIES: New York Times, August 28, 1968; *Washington Post,* August 29, 1968; *Time,* September 6, 1968; *Antiquarian Bookman,* September 16, 1968.*

* * *

BARNES, Jack 1920-

PERSONAL: Born November 9, 1920, in New York, N.Y. *Home and office:* 17-89 166th St., Whitestone, N.Y. 11357.

CAREER/WRITINGS: Journalist. Associated Press, New York City, correspondent, 1954-79. Editor, Barnes International Syndicate, 1956—; political editor, *El Tiempo,* New York City, 1963-75; associate editor, *Diplomatic World Bulletin,* 1971-72, 1978-79; editor, *Protection Industry Times,* New York City, 1973—; editor, *Aviation News,* New York City, 1973—; editor, *Freight Shipper,* New York City, 1975—. Author of syndicated newspaper column entitled "Crime Science," 1972—. *Military service:* Served in U.S. Army Air Forces. *Member:* Aviation Space Writers, United Nations Correspondents Association, Veterans of Foreign Wars of the United States of America, New York Press Club.

* * *

BARNETT, Lincoln (Kinnear) 1909-1979

OBITUARY NOTICE: Born February 12, 1909, in New York, N.Y.; died September 8, 1979, in Plattsburgh, N.Y. Journalist and author. Named after President Abraham Lincoln, Barnett won special attention in 1948 for his book, *The Universe and Dr. Einstein.* The book sold more than one million copies, won a National Book Award special citation in 1949, and was translated into twenty-eight languages. Previously, Barnett had worked as a reporter for the *New York Herald Tribune* and a writer and editor for *Life* magazine, where many of his profiles of Hollywood and Broadway celebrities were first published. His other writings included *Writing on Life: Sixteen Close-ups* and *The Treasure of Our Tongue: The Story of English From Its Obscure Beginnings to Its Present Eminence as the Most Widely Spoken Language.* Obituaries and other sources: *World Authors, 1950-1970,* Wilson, 1975; *New York Times,* September 10, 1979.

BARRELL, Sarah Webb 1946(?)-1979

OBITUARY NOTICE: Born c. 1946 in Connecticut; died June 13, 1979, in Salisbury, Rhodesia. Free-lance journalist who specialized in feature photo essays. A former fashion model, Barrell was a self-taught photographer and writer who covered fighting in Lebanon and Indochina, and was one of the last Americans to leave Vietnam in 1975. After an acclaimed photo series on Appalachian miners, she traveled to Rhodesia in 1978, vowing that the conflict there "would be her last war." Her death, an apparent suicide, came two days after the funeral of her close friend, Major Andre Dennison, a Rhodesian war hero killed in combat. Obituaries and other sources: *New York Times,* June 14, 1979.

* * *

BARRY, Scott 1952-

PERSONAL: Born December 1, 1952, in Flushing, N.Y.; son of Martin and Elayne (Rosenbaum) Barry. *Education:* Attended Hunter College of the City University of New York, 1970-74. *Home:* 79-43 210th St., Oakland Gardens, N.Y. 11364. *Agent:* Bertha Klausner, International Literary Agency, Inc., 71 Park Ave., New York, N.Y. 10016.

CAREER: Photographer of dog shows, 1972-74; free-lance photographer, lecturer, and writer, 1974—. Photographs exhibited at Smithsonian Institution, Carnegie Hall, and on television programs, including "Today Show."

WRITINGS: The Kingdom of Wolves (with own photographs), Putnam, 1979. Contributor of articles and photographs to magazines and newspapers, including *Pet News, Nature Canada,* and *National Wildlife.*

WORK IN PROGRESS: Diary of a Wolf Pack, with own photographs, based on his own observations, publication expected in 1980; *The Faces of Life,* a photo essay comparing all forms of life through dramatic shots.

SIDELIGHTS: Barry worked with and studied thirty-five wolves over the past seven years, and has observed over one-hundred others. Since then, he has traveled throughout the United States and Canada, lecturing and showing his photographs to countless groups of school children, to conservation and research groups and government agencies, and at universities and museums.

He writes: "I am doing exactly what I would like to do most: teaching the public about the things that are closest to my heart—wildlife, wilderness, a healthy natural world, and a healthy human society. I have the greatest love and respect for wolves, after having worked and lived with them."

BIOGRAPHICAL/CRITICAL SOURCES: St. Louis Post Dispatch, October 8, 1975, May 7, 1979; *St. Louis Globe Democrat,* October 20, 1975; *Toronto Star,* November 13, 1975; *Chicago Tribune,* November 3, 1976; *Waukegan New Sun,* December 17, 1977; *National Star,* June 16, 1978.

* * *

BART, Andre Schwarz
See SCHWARZ-BART, Andre

* * *

BARTLETT, Bruce R(eeves) 1951-

PERSONAL: Born October 11, 1951, in Ann Arbor, Mich.; son of Frank and Marjorie (Stern) Bartlett. *Education:* Rutgers University, B.A., 1973; Georgetown University, M.A., 1976. *Politics:* Republican. *Home:* 4201 South 31st St., Apt. 825, Arlington, Va. 22206. *Office:* Office of Senator Roger Jepsen, U.S. Senate, Washington, D.C. 20510.

CAREER: Office of Congressman Ron Paul, Washington, D.C., economist, 1976; Office of Congressman Jack Kemp, Washington, D.C., economist, 1977-78; Office of Senator Roger Jepsen, Washington, D.C., legislative assistant, 1979—. *Member:* American Economic Association, Committee for Monetary Research and Education.

WRITINGS: Coverup: The Politics of Pearl Harbor, 1941-1946, Arlington House, 1979. Contributor to magazines, including *National Review, Human Events, Conservative Digest,* and *Modern Age,* and newspapers. Contributing editor of *Libertarian Review.*

WORK IN PROGRESS: Research on government economic policy, especially fiscal and monetary policy.

SIDELIGHTS: Bartlett told *CA:* "One of the greatest things about writing is that it can be learned; one does not need to be born with the talent to do it well. Moreover, it is something which can be learned without going to schools or classes. All you have to do is write, and keep writing until it sounds good.

"When first starting I found it very useful to try and copy the style of a writer I greatly admire, Albert J. Nock, an early twentieth-century essayist. I soon discovered that the key to his style was to basically write as though he were talking. With this insight I soon learned that one of the best things I can do to improve the quality of something I have written is to read it out loud to myself. It is really invaluable for punctuation and catching small stylistic errors, such as using the same word too often to say the same thing. It also helps eliminate redundancy and verbosity.

"It may seem odd that as a writer my profession is that of an economist. Actually it is not odd at all. My writing skills, as evidenced by my published work, have been instrumental in getting employment. Moreover, writing is a much more integral part of almost all non-manual labor than people realize. Very frequently I see people in both government and business with sharp minds and good ideas who simply cannot express themselves on paper. Eventually it catches up with them and they lose advancement opportunities. For this reason I always advise people to write and get published anywhere they can, even if it is a trade journal or local newspaper, as a means of advancement. It may not seem like much but it shows evidence of ambition and an ability to express oneself which is very important to employers in all businesses.

"This brings me to a final point which has always bothered me: the way writing is taught in this country. I think it is a total waste of time to go to college and major in English or journalism. Instead, one should study anything substantive which one finds interesting: history, economics, anthropoligy, whatever. The purpose is simply to learn something worth writing about. It seems to me that the tragedy of writing in America is that there are loads of people around who have the technical ability to write but who have absolutely nothing to say. I think that this is putting the cart before the horse."

* * *

BARTLETT, Kim 1941-

PERSONAL: Born January 25, 1941, in Syracuse, N.Y.; son of Donald L. and Emeroy (a librarian; maiden name, Burton) Bartlett; married Judy Stephens (a psychologist and social worker), July 22, 1967; children: Dirk, Jake. *Education:* Attended Boston University, 1963-67. *Home and office:* 255 Concord St., Gloucester, Mass. 01930. *Agent:* Carl A. Brandt, 101 Park Ave., New York, N.Y. 10017.

CAREER: Writer. Buckingham, Browne, & Nichols, Cambridge, Mass., teacher of English, 1967-69; Institute of Contemporary Art, Boston, Mass., teacher of English, 1969-70; *Gloucester Daily Times,* Gloucester, Mass., reporter, 1971-74. *Awards, honors:* Awards from United Press International, 1971.

WRITINGS: The Finest Kind, Norton, 1977; *Gulf Star 45,* Norton, 1979.

WORK IN PROGRESS: "A novel concerning confrontation between fishermen and oil men in area known as Georges Bank."

* * *

BARTON, Bruce Walter 1935-

PERSONAL: Born September 2, 1935, in Ottumwa, Iowa; son of Harold H. and Edith (a nurse; maiden name, Nye) Barton; married Beverly Ann Manassero, January 17, 1959; children: Bric, Peter Bret Charles. *Education:* San Francisco Art Institute, B.F.A., 1962; San Diego State College (now University), M.A., 1963. *Religion:* Roman Catholic. *Home:* 108 Crestline Dr., Missoula, Mont. 59801. *Office:* Department of Art, University of Montana, Missoula, Mont. 59812.

CAREER: NAS Miramar, San Diego, Calif., photography teacher, 1955-58; Convair/Astronautics Atlas Missile Project, San Diego, photographer, 1958-59; Community Educational Resources, San Diego, illustrator and photographer, 1963-64; Boeing Co., Seattle, Wash., art director, 1964-65; East Texas State University, Commerce, instructor in art, 1965-66; University of Manitoba, Winnipeg, lecturer in art, 1966-67; Ohio State University, Columbus, professor of art and head of department, 1967-69; University of Montana, Missoula, professor of art, 1969—, head of department, 1969-72. Professional artist, with group and solo shows in the United States and Canada. Director of seminars. *Military service:* U.S. Navy, reconnaissance photographer, 1954-58; served in Pacific theater. *Member:* International Society for Sociolinguistics, American Academy of Religion, American Anthropological Association, Society for Anthropology of Visual Communication, American Catholic Historical Association, Erasmus Society. *Awards, honors:* Grants from National Endowment for the Humanities, 1971, Bureau of Indian Affairs, 1972, U.S. Office of Economic Opportunity, 1972, and from U.S. Office of Education, 1972.

WRITINGS: The Tree at the Center of the World, Ross-Erikson Publishing, 1979. Contributor to *CAS Forum.* Publisher of *Chapter Ten* (journal of Erasmus Society) and *The Medicine Child News.*

WORK IN PROGRESS: Research in hermetic arts.

SIDELIGHTS: Barton writes: "My interests are the interface of religious traditions, particularly those of Native Americans and Roman Catholics, religion and the arts, art criticism, the American experience, and contemporary American art." *Avocational interests:* Beekeeping.

* * *

BASH, Harry H(arvey) 1926-

PERSONAL: Born January 25, 1926, in Berlin, Germany; came to the United States in 1938, naturalized citizen, 1945; son of Eric A. (a physician) and Margaret (a photographer) Bash; married Carrie E. Street (an Urban League research director), September, 1958. *Education:* University of Chicago, A.B., 1951; Indiana University, M.A., 1958; University of Pennsylvania, Ph.D., 1969. *Office:* Department of Sociology, University of Missouri, St. Louis, Mo. 63121.

CAREER: Temple University, Philadelphia, Pa., instructor in sociology, 1964-66; University of Missouri, St. Louis, assistant professor, 1966-78, associate professor of sociology, 1978—, head of department, 1974—. *Military service:* U.S. Air Force, 1945-48; became sergeant. *Member:* American Sociological Association, Society for the Study of Social Problems.

WRITINGS: Sociology, Race, and Ethnicity: A Critique of American Ideological Intrusions Upon Sociological Theory, Gordon & Breach, 1979. Contributor to philosophy and sociology journals.

WORK IN PROGRESS: A book discussing "the relationship between socio-political ideology and value-neutral sociological theory to the sociology of social problems and social movements, especially the American and German approaches."

SIDELIGHTS: Bash writes: "My specialized interests center on sociological theory, sociology of dominant/minority relations, sociology of knowledge, and problems of concepts and conceptualization in sociology."

* * *

BASHSHUR, Rashid L. 1933-

PERSONAL: Born May 8, 1933, in Safita, Syria; came to the United States in 1956, naturalized citizen, 1970; son of Lutfallah (a landlord) and Yamna Bashshur; married Naziha Simon; children: Ramona, Noura. *Education:* American University of Beirut, B.A., 1954, M.A., 1956; University of Michigan, Ph.D., 1962. *Home:* 1383 Esch Court, Ann Arbor, Mich. 48104. *Office:* Department of Medical Care Organization, School of Public Health, University of Michigan, Ann Arbor, Mich. 48104.

CAREER: American University of Beirut, Beirut, Lebanon, assistant instructor, 1954, instructor in sociology, 1956; Institute for Social Research, Ann Arbor, Mich., statistical assistant, 1957-59; Eastern Michigan University, Ypsilanti, visiting lecturer, 1961, assistant professor of sociology, 1962, director of special research projects, 1962; University of Michigan, Ann Arbor, research associate with Middle Eastern language research project, 1962, and with Bureau of Public Health Economics, 1963-70, associate professor, 1968-77, professor of medical care organization, 1977—, acting chairman of department, 1978—. Visiting lecturer at University of Alberta, summers, 1965, 1968. Staff associate of National Academy of Sciences Institute of Medicine, 1970-72; study director for U.S. Information Center in Beirut, 1955; consultant to National Science Foundation and National Center for Health Services Research.

WRITINGS: (With Ernest McCarus and Adil Yacoub) *Contemporary Arabic Readers,* Volume II: *Arabic Essays,* University of Michigan Press, 1963; (with Ralph V. Smith, Stanley Flory, and Gary Shannon) *Community Support for the Public Schools in a Large Metropolitan Area,* Office of Education, U.S. Department of Health, Education & Welfare, 1968; (with David Kessner and Carolyn Kalk) *Development of Methodology for Evaluation of Neighborhood Health Centers,* Institute for Medicine, National Academy of Sciences, 1972; (editor with Patricia A. Armstrong and Zakhour I. Youssef) *Telemedicine: Explorations in the Use of Telecommunication in Health Care,* C. C Thomas, 1975. Contributor to *A Companion to the Life Sciences.* Contributor of about twenty articles and reviews to health care journals.

WORK IN PROGRESS: Technology Serves the People, for Government Printing Office.

SIDELIGHTS: Bashshur writes: "I am working with several native American tribes and urban groups to determine their health care needs."

* * *

BASON, Fred
See BASON, Frederick (Thomas)

* * *

BASON, Frederick (Thomas) 1907-1973
(Fred Bason; The Gallerite)

OBITUARY NOTICE—See index for *CA* sketch: Born August 29, 1907, in Southwark, London, England; died in 1973. Bookseller, lecturer, broadcaster, and author. Bason worked as a bookseller in London for forty-one years. His best-known writings are his diaries, in which he reminisces about writers and the buying and selling of books. Obituaries and other sources: *Longman Companion to Twentieth Century Literature,* Longman, 1970; *The Author's and Writer's Who's Who,* 6th edition, Burke's Peerage, 1971; *AB Bookman's Weekly,* October 1, 1973.

* * *

BASSO, (Joseph) Hamilton 1904-1964

PERSONAL: Born September 5, 1904, in New Orleans, La.; died May 13, 1964; married Etolia Moore Simmons in 1930; children: one son. *Education:* Attended Tulane University, 1922-26. *Residence:* Weston, Conn.

CAREER: Worked in New York City in print shop, in department store, and trucking freight; reporter in New Orleans for *Tribune* (now defunct) and *Item; Times-Picayune,* New Orleans, began as reporter, became night city editor, then advertising copy-writer; associate editor of *New Republic,* 1935-37; *Time* magazine, New York City, contributing editor, 1942-43; *New Yorker,* New York City, associate editor, 1943-64; literary critic; writer. *Awards, honors:* Southern Authors award, 1940, for *Days Before Lent.*

WRITINGS—Novels: *Relics and Angels,* Macaulay, 1929; *Cinnamon Seed,* Scribner, 1934; *In Their Own Image,* Scribner, 1935; *Court-House Square,* Scribner, 1936; *Days Before Lent,* Scribner, 1939; *Wine of the Country,* Scribner, 1941; *Sun in Capricorn,* Scribner, 1942; *The Greenroom,* Doubleday, 1949; *The View From Pompey's Head,* Doubleday, 1954; *The Light From Infantry Ball,* Doubleday, 1959; *A Touch of the Dragon,* Viking, 1964.

Other: *Beauregard, the Great Creole,* Scribner, 1933, *Mainstream* (essays; contains "Cotton Mather and John Smith," "Farewell and Hail to Thomas Jefferson," "John Calhoun of Fort Hill," "Let Us Kneel to Good Abe Lincoln," "Andrew Carnegie, or From Rags to Riches," "P. T. Barnum Sits for a Portrait," "Henry Adams and William Jennings Bryan," "Theodore Roosevelt Feels Fit as a Bull Moose," "Huey P. Long: Kingfish," and "Franklin Delano Roosevelt"), Reynal & Hitchcock, 1943, reprinted, Books for Libraries Press, 1970; (editor) William Henry Herndon, *Exploration of the Valley of the Amazon,* McGrant, 1956; (not associated with earlier editions) *A Quota of Seaweed: Persons and Places in Brazil, Spain, Honduras, Jamaica, Tahiti, and Samoa* (travel sketches), Doubleday, 1960. Also editor, with wife, Etolia Basso, of *The World From Jackson Square,* 1948. Works published in anthologies. Contributor to *New Yorker.*

SIDELIGHTS: With his first novel behind him, Basso moved from New York to the mountains of North Carolina. He resided there between jaunts to various parts of the United States, Europe, and the Caribbean. For a year, Basso made a village in southern France his home. Throughout his travels Basso gathered material for the novels he would write, but it is chiefly his impressions of life in his native South that permeate his works. In *The View From Pompey's Head,* for instance, a native Southerner is called back to his hometown from New York City to solve a legal problem. He becomes wrapped up again in the town's complicated social structure, discovering a part of himself in the process. John Brooks observed that the theme of the story is "characteristically American. . . . And there have been few writers, since Thomas Wolfe opened it up in his vital, intense and wordy way, who have handled it so deftly and entertainingly as Hamilton Basso." *Light Infantry* deals with the Civil War's influence on the same town.

In another novel, *Days Before Lent,* the protagonist is a New Orleans bacteriologist who must choose one career path from three alternatives. It is "a curiously healthy novel, and the secret of its health is Jason Kent, who is one of the most charming characters in American fiction," commented Alfred Kazin. William Soskin remarked that "in spite of the platform manners and soapbox orations that dominate its pages, 'Days Before Lent' breathes a fiery and vitalizing spirit."

But Basso is perhaps best known for *Sun in Capricorn.* In this novel, a Yale University graduate clashes with a ruthless politician, said to be modeled after Huey Long, who attempts to destroy anyone who bars his way to success. "It is a swift little narrative, stripped to its essential elements, written with a kind of casual hardness and accuracy more effective than any amount of heroics," wrote Margaret Wallace. Isaac Rosenfeld concluded that Basso's "depiction of the South is singularly lucid."

Basso also successfully tried his hand at writing nonfiction. In his biography of Civil War General Pierre Beauregard, Basso exhibits "insight and a fine sense of balance," noted Grenville Vernon.

Days Before Lent and *The View From Pompey's Head* have been adapted as screenplays.

BIOGRAPHICAL/CRITICAL SOURCES: New Republic, October 23, 1929, May 31, 1933, May 29, 1935, November 25, 1936, December 15, 1941, October 19, 1942, November 15, 1943; *New York Times,* March 3, 1933, February 25, 1934, October 25, 1936, August 6, 1939, October 12, 1941, September 13, 1942, November 28, 1943, September 18, 1949, October 24, 1954, June 7, 1959; *Commonweal,* May 12, 1933; *Saturday Review of Literature,* April 13, 1935, November 7, 1936, November 1, 1941, September 24, 1949; *Books,* August 6, 1939; *New Yorker,* September 24, 1942; *Atlantic,* November, 1949, November 1, 1954, April, 1964; *Saturday Review,* June 6, 1959; *New York Times Book Review,* October 9, 1960; *New Statesman,* August 18, 1961, March 22, 1964, February 19, 1965; *Times Literary Supplement,* February 18, 1965.*

* * *

BATAILLE, Georges 1897-1962

OBITUARY NOTICE: Born September 10, 1897, in Puy-de-Dome, France; died July 8, 1962, in Puy-de-Dome, France. Philosopher, editor, essayist, poet, and novelist. In 1946, Bataille founded *Critique,* one of the most significant intellectual journals in France, and remained its editor until his death. Many of Bataille's works deal with atheism and mysticism. He believed that through excess rather than deprivation, one could obtain a freedom of the spirit. His books include *Lascaux; or, The Birth of Art, Death and Sensuality: A Study of Eroticism and the Taboo,* and *The Hatred of Poetry.* Obituaries and other sources: *Encyclopedia of World Literature in the Twentieth Century,* updated edition, Ungar, 1967; *Cassell's Encyclopaedia of World Literature,* revised edition, Morrow, 1973; *World Authors, 1950-1970,* Wilson, 1975.

* * *

BATRA, Raveendra N(ath) 1943-

PERSONAL: Born June 27, 1943, in Punjab, India; came to the United States in 1966, naturalized citizen, 1976; son of Harish C. (a professor) and Kusum (Thakur) Batra; married Diane J. Spiegel (in business), February 21, 1970; children: Marlo Sheila. *Education:* Punjab University, B.A., 1963; Delhi School of Economics, M.A., 1965; Southern Illinois University, Carbondale, Ph.D., 1969. *Home:* 6423 Mercedes, Dallas, Tex. 75214. *Office:* Department of Economics, Southern Methodist University, Dallas, Tex. 75275.

CAREER: Hindu College, Delhi, India, assistant lecturer in economics, 1965-66; Southern Illinois University, Carbondale, assistant professor of economics, 1969-70; University of Western Ontario, London, assistant professor of economics, 1970-72; Southern Methodist University, Dallas, Tex., associate professor, 1972-73, professor of economics and head of department, 1973—. *Member:* American Economic Association. *Awards, honors:* Canada Council fellowship, 1971-72.

WRITINGS: Studies in the Pure Theory of International Trade, St. Martin's, 1973; *The Pure Theory of International Trade Under Uncertainty,* Wiley, 1975; *The Downfall of Capitalism and Communism: A New Study of History,* Humanities, 1979. Also author of *Alternatives to Capitalism and Communism,* 1980. Contributor of more than thirty articles to economic journals.

WORK IN PROGRESS: Multinational Corporations, publication expected in 1981.

SIDELIGHTS: Batra told *CA:* "At first I wrote articles and books to build my own career. Now I write them to build a new society. I believe that every society was first ruled by warriors, then by intellectuals (or priests), and finally by acquisitors, whose rule ended in a social revolution of physical workers. After this revolution, the warriors took over again, followed by the intellectuals and so on. Russia today is in the era of warriors and will soon move into the era of intellectuals. India and the West are today governed by the acquisitors. They both are heading towards revolutions, which will occur by the year 2000. The time will then be ripe to build a new, just, and humane society."

AVOCATIONAL INTERESTS: Meditation, studying yoga, philosophy, and religion.

* * *

BAUCHART
See CAMUS, Albert

* * *

BAUMANN, Charly 1928-

PERSONAL: Born September 14, 1928, in Berlin, Germany; son of Erich and Margaretta (Georgi) Baumann; married Araceli Rodriguez, May 7, 1944. *Education:* Attended high school in Germany. *Religion:* Lutheran. *Home:* 4562 Woodside Rd., Sarasota, Fla. 33581. *Office:* Ringling Brothers Barnum & Bailey Circus, 1015 18th St. N.W., Washington, D.C. 20036.

CAREER: Ringling Brothers Barnum & Bailey Circus, Washington, D.C., tiger trainer and performers' director, 1964—. *Member:* American Guild of Variety Artists, Show Folks of Sarasota.

WRITINGS: (With Leonard A. Stevens) *Tiger, Tiger: My Twenty-Five Years With the Big Cats,* Playboy Press, 1975.

* * *

BAXTER, William F(rancis) 1929-

PERSONAL: Born July 13, 1929, in New York, N.Y.; son of William Francis and Ruth (Cummings) Baxter; children: William Francis III, Marcia, Stuart. *Education:* Stanford University, B.A., 1951, J.D., 1956. *Home:* 294 Oak Grove Ave., Atherton, Calif. 94025. *Office:* School of Law, Stanford University, Stanford, Calif. 94305.

CAREER: Admitted to California bar, 1956; Stanford University, Stanford, Calif., assistant professor of law, 1956-58; Covington & Burling, Washington, D.C., law associate, 1958-60; Stanford University, associate professor, 1960-64, professor of law, 1964—. Antitrust counsel to Levi-Strauss & Co., 1977—. Visiting professor at Yale University, 1964-65. Fellow of Center for Advanced Studies in the Behavioral Sciences, 1972-73. Member of White House task forces on communications policy, 1968-69, and antitrust policy, 1969; consultant to Federal Aviation Agency, Federal Reserve Board, and Brookings Institution. *Military service:* U.S. Navy, navigation officer, 1951-54. *Member:* Phi Beta Kappa.

WRITINGS: People or Penguins: An Optimum Level of Pollution, Columbia University Press, 1974; (with K. E. Scott and P. H. Cootner) *Retail Banking in the Electronic Age: The Law and Economics of Electronic Funds Transfer,* Allanheld, Osmun, 1977. Contributor to law journals.

* * *

BEARDWOOD, Roger 1932-

PERSONAL: Born April 10, 1932, in Chester, England; came to the United States in 1967; son of Kenneth J. (an executive) and Elsie (a writer; maiden name, Martin) Beardwood; married Beverly Russell, August, 1972 (divorced, 1972); married Francoise Catelain (a journalist), November, 1972; children: (first marriage) Benjamin; (second marriage) Alexandra. *Education:* Attended secondary schools in England and Scotland. *Politics:* Independent. *Religion:* Church of England. *Residence:* Portugal. *Agent:* Harold Ober Associates, Inc., 40 East 49th St., New York, N.Y. 10017.

CAREER: Reporter for provincial newspapers in England, 1946-53; *Western Daily Press,* Bristol, England, reporter, 1953-54; United Press, London, England, at rewrite desk, 1954-56; Press Association, London, sub-editor, 1956-58; *Daily Herald,* London, assistant night foreign editor, 1958-59; *Evening Standard,* London, editor of column, "In London Last Night," 1959-62; City Business Properties, London, business executive, 1962-64; *Financial Times,* London, author of column, "Men and Matters," 1964-66; *Fortune,* New York City, associate editor, 1967-69; *Time,* New York City, U.S. business correspondent, 1969-71, European economic correspondent in Brussels, Belgium, 1971-73, bureau chief in Paris, France, 1973-75, senior correspondent in Bonn, West Germany, 1975-76; free-lance writer, 1976—. *Military service:* British Army, Educational Corps, 1950-52; became staff sergeant. *Member:* Institute of Journalists, Eccentric Club, Naval and Military Club.

WRITINGS: (Contributor) *The Negro and the City,* Time-Life, 1968; (editor and contributor) Milton Spencer, *Contemporary Economics,* Worth Publishers, 1971; (editor) George Taber, *Patterns and Prospects of Common Market Trade,* P. Owen, 1974; *Innocent Employments* (novel), Doubleday, 1978; *The Winner's Share* (novel), Doubleday, 1979; *Backtrack* (novel), Doubleday, 1980; *Black March* (novel), Rawson, Wade, 1980. Contributor to magazines and newspapers, including *Telegraph Sunday Magazine, Arab Month,* and *Profile.*

WORK IN PROGRESS: Houston Stewart Chamberlain and the Wagner Circle, a biography.

SIDELIGHTS: Roger Beardwood writes: "My earliest memories include books and writing. When I was three, my parents launched a successful popular magazine about birds, later selling it to a large British publishing house. My mother then free-lanced, writing stories, articles, and poetry for British magazines, and during World War II became a reporter for a weekly newspaper in Tenby, South Wales. From that time—I was nine—there was never any doubt in my mind that I'd become a journalist. I did, at the age of fourteen, working first for a weekly newspaper in Ayrshire, Scotland, and moving on to papers in Ireland and England. Perhaps because a newspaperman's life is busy, perhaps because I lacked confidence, I did not think of writing a book until quite late on, when the group journalism practised at *Time* began to pall. But when I did start to write fiction, in 1977, it emerged from my typewriter at a speed that surprised me: three novels in eighteen months. The first, *Innocent Employments,* has been bought so far by eight publishers around the world.

"I find most of my themes in business and finance: to a greater degree than most people realize, we live in a world created and influenced by the decisions of businessmen and bankers. What I hope to do is to explain the reasons for those decisions. The prospect of profit is important, to be sure; but it is only part of the equation. In the future I want to write a novel that is set at the nexus between business and government. One of its purposes will be to show that politicians and civil servants are equipped poorly to intervene in business. This novel will probably be international in scope, since I am deeply interested in multinational corporations and their managers. My experience as an international financial journalist and economics commentator has been an important influence, and I continue as a free-lance to visit corporate offices in the United States and Europe. Another influence has been the Victorian novel, which tells a story, and tells it well. Most Victorian novels, however, treat of the characters' private and personal lives. Mine try to show men and women at work; and business executives, who populate most of my fiction, tend to work sixty or more hours a week, and then to take the job home with them. I do not commiserate with them: that is their choice, or perhaps their compulsion.

"What do I rate most highly in a writer? Artistry and skill, of course; but also honesty. Honesty with the publisher, honesty with the reader. For that reason I am pleased to have been one of the team at *Time* that unmasked Clifford Irving as the faker of the Howard Hughes autobiography that he was (I was the correspondent who learned from Credit Suisse that the McGraw-Hill money purportedly being paid to Hughes was in reality going to Irving's wife). I don't describe myself as an artist or even a novelist, but as a journeyman wordsmith who works hard at trying to provide publisher and reader with a story that always entertains and occasionally illuminates."

AVOCATIONAL INTERESTS: Travel, reading, "finding good restaurants before they are listed in tourist guides," sampling wines, talking ("preferably while sampling wines"), cooking ("preferably while sampling wines and talking"), photography, collecting vintage cameras.

* * *

BEAVERBROOK, William Maxwell Aitken 1879-1964

OBITUARY NOTICE: Born May 25, 1879, in Maple, Ontario, Canada; died June 9, 1964. Publisher. Beaverbrook bought the failing *London Daily Express* in 1917, and although it had lost over one million dollars in the first years of production, he turned it into one of the largest newspapers in the world. Beaverbrook was knighted in 1911, made a baronet in 1916, and a baron in 1917. He was chiefly a political writer of books such as *Politicians and the Press, Men and Power, Politicians and the War,* and an autobiography entitled *Headlines All My Life.* Obituaries and other sources: *Current Biography,* Wilson, 1940, September 1964; *Longman Companion to Twentieth Century Literature,* Longman, 1970; Linton Andrews and H. A. Taylor, *Lords and Laborers of the Press: Men Who Fashioned the Modern British Newspaper,* Southern Illinois University Press, 1970.

* * *

BEE, Helen L. 1939-
(Helen Bee Douglas)

PERSONAL: Born April 27, 1939, in Tacoma, Wash.; daughter of Austin Edward (in business) and Susan (Emmons) Bee; married George C. Douglas, March 19, 1972; children: Rex, Arwen. *Education:* Radcliffe College, B.A., 1960; Stanford University, Ph.D., 1964. *Office:* School of Nursing, University of Washington, Seattle, Wash. 98195.

CAREER: Clark University, Worcester, Mass., assistant professor of psychology, 1964-65; University of Washington, Seattle, 1965-72, began as assistant professor, became associate professor of psychology; free-lance writer and consultant, 1972—. Senior research associate at University of Washington, Seattle, 1977-79. Member of board of trustees of Orcas Island Foundation, 1972-78. Consultant to RAND Corp., Danforth Foundation, and Aspen Institute for Humanistic Studies. *Member:* Society for Research in Child Development.

WRITINGS: Social Issues in Developmental Psychology, Harper, 1974, 2nd edition, 1978; (under name Helen Bee Douglas) *Child Health Assessment,* U.S. Department of Health, Education and Welfare, 1974; *The Developing Child,* Harper, 1975, 3rd edition, in press; *Invitation to Psychology,* Academic Press, 1979; *The Developing Person,* Harper, 1980. Contributor to psychology journals.

SIDELIGHTS: Helen Bee writes: "For seven years, aside from consulting positions, I have written full-time, but now I plan to combine writing with teaching again."

AVOCATIONAL INTERESTS: Marathon running, music (playing guitar), international travel.

* * *

BEEBE, Frank L(yman) 1914-

PERSONAL: Born May 25, 1914, in Lacombe, Alberta, Canada; son of Oscar Oren (a farmer) and Eva May (Parker) Beebe; married Vera Betsy Hynes (a practical nurse), September 11, 1940; children: Kerry Don, Ervine Ray, Merle, Marilynn Beebe Cadell. *Education:* Attended high school in

Peers, Alberta, Canada. *Politics:* Progressive Conservative. *Home:* 1093 Laurel Rd., North Saanich, British Columbia, Canada.

CAREER: British Columbia Department of Health, British Columbia, field worker on sylvatic plague surveys, 1939-45; City of Vancouver, British Columbia, curator of city zoo, 1945-42; Provincial Museum, Victoria, British Columbia, illustrator and diorama artist, 1952-74; artist and sculptor, 1974—.

WRITINGS: (With Harold Melvin Webster) *North American Falconry and Hunting Hawks,* North American Falconry and Hunting Hawks, 1964, 4th edition (with J. H. Enderson), 1976; *Field Studies of the Falconiformes of British Columbia,* Provincial Museum (Vancouver), 1974; *Hawks, Falcons, and Falconry,* Hancock House, 1976.

WORK IN PROGRESS: Small Potatoes, "a series of semibiographical essays and observations, primarily ecological and zoologically-oriented, based on notes dating back to 1933."

SIDELIGHTS: Beebe writes: "My primary avocation remains that of the artist. Since retirement I have moved from painting to stonecarving, including work with gemstones.

"Raptorial birds have not been an avocation, but a lifelong interest. My books appear to have been a primary force in establishing recreational falconry in most states and provinces on this continent.

"The books on raptorial birds were intended to counter a hostility toward the recreational use of these birds, a hostility that I cannot understand, but one which persists and is not confined to the ignorant or uneducated.

"Despite the programming of the American-Canadian public (by television) to the point where everyone knows that peregrine falcons are almost extinct due to DDT, which causes their eggshells to break, I remain convinced that this whole thing was a hoax. There are not merely thousands, there are *hundreds* of thousands of perfectly healthy peregrine falcons breeding all across the Alaska-Canadian-Greenland Arctic that are not endangered and never have been. The best things that can be said for the hoax are that it led, or helped, in that phasing out of some of the more lethal pesticides, and that the artificial scarcity of falcons caused by the official endangering of the species (in the United States) acted as a stimulus to private breeders.

"Nothing good can be said of the institutional breeders; they have done their best to keep access to wild breeding stock entirely to themselves, both in Canada and the United States, and if they have not succeeded, it has not been for any lack of greed. I know of no instance where any of these federally funded raptor (falcon) breeding projects have made breeding stock available to private breeders. Instead, they embark on highly publicized 're-introduction' projects, and release all surplus 'back into the wild.' "

* * *

BEGGS, Edward Larry 1933-

PERSONAL: Born April 9, 1933, in Los Angeles, Calif.; son of Edward Latchford and Lois Lee (Dabney) Beggs; married Nina Florence Ellington, June, 1959 (marriage ended); married Nan Ullrike Koehler (a midwife), December, 1971 (marriage ended); children: Breean, Kevin, Joshua, Jubilee. *Education:* Compton Community College, A.A., 1952; California State College (now University), Fresno, B.A., 1954; Pacific School of Religion, M.Div., 1957; Boston University, M.A., 1959. *Home:* 1682 Indian Valley Rd., Novato, Calif. 94947.

CAREER: Ordained minister of United Church of Christ, 1959; pastor of Congregational churches in Long Beach, Calif., 1959-62, Lewiston, Calif., 1962-64, and San Mateo, Calif., 1964-67; Huckleberry's for Runaways, San Francisco, Calif., founder and director, 1967-70; Marin Open House, San Rafael, Calif., family and drug abuse counselor, 1970-72; Rites of Passage (drug prevention agency), San Rafael, founder and director, 1972-75; soymilk and tofu maker at large religious commune in Tennessee, 1976; San Francisco Study Center, San Francisco, interviewer and writer for local oral history project, 1977-78; free-lance writer and manual laborer, 1978—. Consultant to centers for runaway children.

WRITINGS: Huckleberry's for Runaways, Ballantine, 1969; *Open House: A Successful New Community Treatment Approach for Young Suburban Addicts,* Ballantine, 1973; *San Francisco Neighborhoods,* San Francisco Study Center, 1980. Contributor to *Youth* and *California Living.*

WORK IN PROGRESS: History of Eagle Scouts; Rites of Passage USA: A Manual of Initiation Experiences; Huckleberry Runaways 12 Years Later.

SIDELIGHTS: Beggs told *CA:* "My writing emerges from my activity in the world. So far the activities I've written about are social change agencies I've created or helped to create. I write as a participating observer of the things happening around me and the things I'm helping to make happen. The material is usually so strong that it just needs someone to translate it into verbal symbols.

"There are also interesting threads in the diversity of my experience. The book about runaways and the book about addicts in suburbia have strong connective cords to two other books I'm working on: *The History of Eagle Scouting* and *Rites of Passage USA.* All of these books have a focus that pertains to the transitional processes between childhood and young adulthood. In the Eagle Scout book I want to look at those aspects of Boy Scout training which encourage self-reliance and to see what kind of carry-over adult Eagle Scouts experience from their prior training as a youth in the scouting movement. In *Rites of Passage USA,* I'm trying to put together a manual of those rather intimate experiences people have which give them knowledge and power to live their lives. Adolescents experience a lot of isolation and non-communication regarding their sexual experiences and sometimes think their experience is abnormal when actually it is typical. If they had a manual of experiences to read, those self-accusatory feelings could never haunt them. In addition, they could pick up skills and other information from this manual."

* * *

BEIMILLER, Carl 1913(?)-1979

OBITUARY NOTICE: Born c. 1913 in Haddonfield, N.J.; died October 2, 1979, in Monmouth, N.J. Editor and writer. Beimiller was a founding editor of *Holiday* magazine and served as its executive editor from 1945 to 1957. He had previously been an assistant publisher of the *Philadelphia Daily News.* He wrote more than one thousand articles for newspapers and magazines, three novels for adults, and ten others for teenagers. All of his books were concerned with environmental subjects. Obituaries and other sources: *New York Times,* October 3, 1979.

* * *

BELL, (Arthur) Clive (Howard) 1881-1964

OBITUARY NOTICE: Born September 16, 1881, in East

Shefford, Bedfordshire, England; died 1964. Critic of politics, literature, and art. Bell believed in the existence of a purely aesthetic quality in art not related to the physical beauty, but rather the beauty of ideas as expressed by the artist. In his first book, *Art,* he coined the term "significant form" as a rule for judging the aesthetic value of a work of art. Bell's books include *Since Cezanne, Landmarks in Nineteenth-Century Painting,* and *An Account of French Painting,* and he was a regular contributor to *New Statesman* and *Nation.* Bell was made a Chevalier of the Legion of Honor in 1936. Obituaries and other sources: *The Reader's Encyclopedia,* 2nd edition, Crowell, 1965; *The New Century Encyclopedia,* 2nd edition, Crowell, 1965; *The New Century Handbook of English Literature,* revised edition, Appleton, 1967; *The Oxford Companion to English Literature,* 4th edition, Oxford University Press, 1967; *Longman Companion to Twentieth Century Literature,* Longman, 1970; *The Penguin Companion to English Literature,* McGraw, 1971.

* * *

BELL, Irene Wood 1944-

PERSONAL: Born January 31, 1944, in New York, N.Y.; daughter of Robert Ellis (a contractor) and Ann Hedvig (Swanson) Bell. *Education:* State University of New York College at Potsdam, B.A., 1965; University of Massachusetts, M.A. (American history), 1968; University of Denver, M.A. (librarianship), 1975. *Home:* 7900 West Layton Ave., Littleton, Colo. 80123. *Office:* Moore Elementary School, 846 Corona, Denver, Colo. 80218.

CAREER: Ipswich Junior High School, Ipswich, Mass., history teacher, 1969-74; Littleton Public Library, Littleton, Colo., part-time children's librarian, 1975-78; Moore Elementary School, Denver, Colo., media specialist, 1976—. *Member:* American Library Association, Colorado Educational Media Association, Beta Phi Mu.

WRITINGS: (With Jeanne E. Wieckert) *Basic Media Skills Through Games,* Libraries Unlimited, 1979; (with Wieckert) *Related Media Skills Through Games,* Libraries Unlimited, 1979.

SIDELIGHTS: Bell writes: "The games and activities in *Basic Media Skills Through Games* evolved as a result of a change in philosophy. Children had changed, had become more verbal and critical about their treatment and education. They were less willing to participate in learning just because a teacher said that it would be good for them. In a search for a better way, one of the outcomes included these new approaches to teaching library skills and basic educational skills.

"As an educator, you can never offer students too many learning opportunities. The more a student is exposed to interesting materials of all kinds, the more he/she learns, and the greater is the motivation for learning. When a student arrives in the Instructional Materials Center (IMC) with the spoken or unspoken question, 'What are we going to do today?' you know he/she is interested in and receptive to new ideas.

"An IMC is an exciting place, not only to media specialists but also to any students who will seek out information on their special interests, for there is something for each student in an IMC. The main objective of a media specialist is to aid each student in satisfying his or her needs and interests in the IMC. While satisfying these needs and interests, the media specialist can share the excitement of media with students by conveying a supportive attitude, providing them orientation to the IMC, and imparting some basic library skills. These basic skills can be acquired through various modes of learning; however, students prefer learning such basic skills through playing educational games and they retain information acquired in this manner.

"*Basic Media Skills Through Games* presents seventy-four games that can be used in a variety of combinations to teach the progression of skills necessary for elementary school students to effectively use the IMC. This progression involves introducing students to the IMC, explaining the logic and use of the card catalog, teaching the structure and application of the Dewey Decimal Classification, identifying reference books and their uses, and demonstrating the functions and applications of basic audiovisual hardware and software."

* * *

BENARY, Margot
See BENARY-ISBERT, Margot

* * *

BENARY-ISBERT, Margot 1889-1979
(Margot Benary)

OBITUARY NOTICE—See index for *CA* sketch: Born December 2, 1889, in Saarbruecken, Germany; died in Santa Barbara, Calif. Translator and author of books for young people. Benary-Isbert wrote more than ten novels for young people in German, and translated English works of Julia Cunningham into German. Obituaries and other sources: *Authors of Books for Young People,* 2nd edition, Scarecrow, 1971; *Publishers Weekly,* June 25, 1979.

* * *

BENET, Sula 1906-

PERSONAL: Born September 24, 1906, in Warsaw, Poland; daughter of Moris and Sophia (Epsztein) Benet; married Waldermar Syrkus, 1950. *Education:* University of Warsaw, diploma, 1935; Columbia University, Ph.D., 1944. *Home:* 315 Central Park West, New York, N.Y. 10025. *Office:* Research Institute for the Study of Man, 162 East 78th St., New York, N.Y. 10021.

CAREER: Hunter College of the City University of New York, New York, N.Y., professor of anthropology, 1944—. Columbia University, instructor, 1950-51, professor of anthropology, 1958 and 1959; lecturer at Fairleigh Dickinson University, 1951-54, Pratt Institute, 1955-60, and Quaker Conference and Seminar (Hungary), 1964. *Member:* American Anthropological Association, American Ethnological Society, Polish Institute of Science, New York Academy of Science. *Awards, honors:* Buell Quain Fund and Institute of Intercultural Studies travel grant, 1949; City University of New York faculty research award, summers, 1971 and 1972.

WRITINGS: Konopie w wierzeniach i zwyczajach ludowych (title means "Hemp [Hashish] in Folk Customs and Beliefs"), Warsaw Society of Science, 1936; *Song, Dance, and Customs of Peasant Poland,* Roy, 1951, reprinted, AMS Press, 1977; *Patterns of Thought and Behavior in the Culture of Poland,* Columbia University Press, 1952; (compiler with Carl Withers) *The American Riddle Book* (juvenile), Abelard, 1954; (compiler with Withers) *Riddles of Many Lands* (juvenile; Junior Literary Guild selection), Abelard, 1956; *Festival Menus 'Round the World,* Abelard, 1957, reprinted as *Festive Recipes and Festival Menus,* Abelard, 1970.

(Editor and translator) *The Village of Viriatino: An Ethnographic Study of a Russian Village From Before the Revolu-*

tion to the Present, Doubleday-Anchor, 1970; *Abkhasians: The Long-Living People of the Caucasus,* Holt, 1974; *How to Live to Be 100: The Life-Style of the People of the Caucasus,* Dial, 1976. Contributor of articles to journals in her field.

SIDELIGHTS: The long-lived people of the Soviet Caucasus have interested scientists for some time. In an effort to determine why the people of the Caucasus often reach their one-hundredth birthdays feeling happy and healthy, Sula Benet spent four years living among them and studying their culture. The results of her research are set forth in *How to Live to Be 100.* Benet first summarizes the work of researchers who went before her. Previous researchers had cited a number of factors that contributed to the longevity of these mountain folk, including diet, folk medicine, climate, recreation, attitudes toward life, and family and sexual relations. Benet argues in her book that the single most important factor contributing to the longevity of the people of the Caucasus is their culture, which stresses consistency and continuity in behavior and relationships as well as respect for the aged.

There has been a growing interest in the United States in the rights of older people, and Gloria Levitas noted that *How to Live to Be 100* might shed some light on the way Americans treat the aged. Levitas maintained that although Benet's book "may be faulted on numerous grounds—for its unquestioning assumption that the golden mean is the road to salvation, for its dependence upon impressions rather than upon clearly defined and measurable attributes—it does imply that neither Band-Aid programs for 'senior citizens' nor better information about nutrition will go far in altering either the aging process or our attitudes towards it. Only by understanding that the role of the aged cannot be torn from context, that consignment of the elderly to homes or isolated housing seems to run counter to human needs for meaningful work and a role in society, can we begin to work out, within the special framework afforded by our own economic and political imperatives, a way of life that offers the potential of meaning and belonging to the aged."

BIOGRAPHICAL/CRITICAL SOURCES: Saturday Review, August 21, 1954, February 7, 1976; *Booklist,* May 15, 1956; *New York Times Book Review,* April 4, 1976; *Best Sellers,* June, 1976.

* * *

BENEVOLO, Leonardo 1923-

PERSONAL: Born September 25, 1923, in Orta, Italy; son of Oreste and Bianca (Angiolini) Benevolo; married Renza Giorgini, February 8, 1962; children: Alessandro, Luigi. *Education:* University of Rome, laurea in architettura, 1946. *Home:* 78 Via Gramsci, Cellatica, Italy 25060.

CAREER: University of Rome, Rome, Italy, professor of history of architecture, 1955-60; University of Florence, Florence, Italy, professor of history of architecture, 1960-63; University of Venice, Venice, Italy, professor of history of architecture, 1963-72; University of Palermo, Palermo, Italy; professor of history of architecture, 1972-74; University of Rome, Rome, professor of history of architecture, 1974-77; consultant of civic administration, Brescia, Italy, 1977—. Visiting lecturer at Yale University, 1969-70.

WRITINGS: Storia dell, architettura moderna, two volumes, Laterza, 1960, 7th edition, 1977, translation by H. J. Landry published as *History of Modern Architecture,* Volume I: *The Tradition of Modern Architecture,* Volume II: *The Modern Movement,* M.I.T. Press, 1971; *Le Origini dell'urbanistica moderna,* Laterza, 1963, translation by Judith Landry published as *The Origins of Modern Town Planning,* M.I.T. Press, 1967; *Storia dell'architettura del Rinascimento,* two volumes, Laterza, 1968, 2nd edition, 1973, translation by Landry published as *The Architecture of the Renaissance,* 1973.

In Italian: *Ascoli Piceno* (with own photographs), Editoriale Domus, 1957; *Una introduzione all'architetture* (title means "An Introduction to Architecture"), Laterza, 1960, 3rd edition, 1966; (with Giancarlo de Carlo) *La Pianificazione territoriale urbanistica nell'area Bolognese* (title means "Country Planning in the Area Near Bologna, Italy"), Marsilio, 1965; *L'architettura delle citta nell'Italia comtemporanea* (title means "The Architecture of Towns in Contemporary Italy"), Laterza, 1968, 2nd edition, 1970; *La citta italiana nel Rinascimento* (title means "The Italian Renaissance Town"), Il polifilo, 1969; Robert Mainardi, editor, *Le grandi citta italiene* (title means "The Great Italian Towns"), F. Angeli, 1971; *Roma da ieri a domani* (title means "Rome From Yesterday to Tomorrow"), Laterza, 1971; (with Tommaso Giura Longo and Carlo Melograni) *I modelli di progettazione della citta moderna: Tre lezioni* (title means "The Patterns of the Modern Town"), Cluva, 1972; *Le avventure della citta* (title means "The Adventures of Towns"), Laterza, 1973; *Storia della citta* (title means "A History of Towns"), Laterza, 1975, 2nd edition, 1976; (with Giura Longo and Melograni) *Le progettazione della citta moderna,* Laterza, 1977; *Roma oggi* (title means "Rome Today"), Laterza, 1977; *Citta in discunione: Venezia e Roma* (title means "Cities in Discussion: Venice and Rome"), Laterza, 1979. Contributor to *Corriere della Sera.*

* * *

BENFORD, Harry (Bell) 1917-

PERSONAL: Born August 7, 1917, in Schenectady, N.Y.; son of Frank Albert (a physicist) and Georgia (a teacher; maiden name, Rattray) Benford; married Elizabeth Smallman (a librarian), April 26, 1941; children: Howard, Frank, Robert. *Education:* University of Michigan, B.S.E., 1940. *Politics:* Conservative. *Religion:* Protestant. *Home:* 1710 Shadford, Ann Arbor, Mich. 48104. *Office:* Naval Architecture and Marine Engineering Building, University of Michigan, North Campus, Ann Arbor, Mich. 48109.

CAREER: Newport News Shipbuilding Co., Newport News, Va., worked variously as engineer, staff supervisor, and ship repair cost estimator, 1940-48; University of Michigan, Ann Arbor, assistant professor, 1948-55, associate professor, 1955-59, professor of naval architecture and marine engineering, 1959—, chairman of department, 1967—. Executive director of National Academy of Sciences/National Research Council maritime research advisory committee, 1959-60. *Member:* Society of Naval Architects and Marine Engineers (fellow; vice-president, 1975—), Royal Institution of Naval Architects (fellow), Tau Beta Pi. *Awards, honors:* Taylor Medal from Society of Naval Architects and Marine Engineers; Linnard Prize from Society of Naval Architects and Marine Engineers, 1963.

WRITINGS: (With John C. Mathes) *Your Future in Naval Architecture,* Richards Rosen, 1968; *The Gilbert and Sullivan Lexicon,* Richards Rosen, 1978. Contributor to journals.

* * *

BENSON, Eugene 1928-

PERSONAL: Born July 6, 1928, in Larne, Ireland; son of John Joseph (a police officer) and Isabel (a nurse; maiden name, Greene) Benson; married Renate Niklaus (a professor), April 30, 1968; children: Ormonde, Shaun. *Education:* National University of Ireland, B.A. (with honors), 1950; University of Western Ontario, M.A., 1958; University of Toronto, Ph.D., 1966. *Home:* 55 Palmer St., Guelph, Ontario, Canada N1E 2P9. *Agent:* L. Hoffman, 51 Spruce St., Toronto, Ontario, Canada. *Office:* Department of English, University of Guelph, Guelph, Ontario, Canada N1G 2W1.

CAREER: Royal Military College of Canada, Kingston, Ontario, lecturer in English, 1960-61; Laurentian University, Sudbury, Ontario, assistant professor of English, 1961-64; University of Guelph, Guelph, Ontario, assistant professor, 1965-67, associate professor, 1967-71, professor of English, 1971—. Language teacher for North Atlantic Treaty Organization; researcher for British Broadcasting Corp. Member of board of directors of Edward Johnson Music Foundation (president, 1971-72). *Member:* Writers Union of Canada. *Awards, honors:* Canada Council grant S, 1970, 1971, 1978.

WRITINGS: *Joan of Arc's Violin* (one-act play; broadcast by Canadian Broadcasting Corp. [CBC], 1970; first produced in Toronto, Ontario, at Backdoor Theatre, 1972), Playwrights Co-Op, 1972; *The Gunner's Rope* (one-act play; broadcast by CBC, 1970; first produced at Backdoor Theatre, 1972), Playwrights Co-Op, 1973; "The Doctor's Wife" (one-act play), first broadcast by CBC, December, 1973; *Heloise and Abelard* (libretto for opera; first produced in Toronto, Ontario, at O'Keefe Centre, September, 1973), Canadian Opera Company, 1973; *Encounter: Canadian Drama in Four Media,* Methuen, 1973; *The Bulls of Ronda* (novel), Methuen, 1976; *The Making of a Prime Minister,* N.C. Press, 1979.

Unpublished librettos: "Everyman," produced in Halifax, Nova Scotia, at Dalhousie University, April, 1973; "Psycho Red," produced in Guelph, Ontario, at Guelph Spring Festival, Ross Hall, May, 1978.

WORK IN PROGRESS: "Shock Treatment," a three-act play.

SIDELIGHTS: Benson commented: "In many of my plays, libretti, and novels I have been concerned with death—whether actual death or psychic death. Although I do a great deal of research before I begin writing, I am primarily interested in entertaining my reader. By that I mean that I try to disguise my art in the belief that the best style is the least obtrusive style."

* * *

BERELSON, Bernard R(euben) 1912-1979

OBITUARY NOTICE—See index for *CA* sketch: Born June 2, 1912, in Spokane, Wash.; died September 25, 1979, in North Tarrytown, N.Y. Sociologist, educator, foundation executive, and author of books on the behavioral and social sciences. Berelson was affiliated with the University of Chicago and Columbia University as a professor of sociology and behavioral sciences. He was director of the behavioral sciences program of the Ford Foundation from 1951 to 1957, and was vice-president of the Population Council. Throughout his professional career, Berelson was concerned with the causes in the shifts of public opinion, the social effects of reading, and the improvement of education. His books include *What Reading Does to People, Reader in Public Opinion and Communication, Content Analysis,* and *Human Behavior: An Inventory of Scientific Findings.* Obituaries and other sources: *Current Biography,* Wilson, 1961, November, 1979; *Who's Who in World Jewry,* Pitman, 1972; *American Men and Women of Science: The Social and Behavioral Sciences,* 12th edition, Bowker, 1973; *The Writers Directory, 1980-82,* St. Martin's, 1979; *AB Bookman's Weekly,* October 22, 1979.

* * *

BERG, Friedrich Kantor
See KANTOR-BERG, Friedrich

* * *

BERGERON, Victor (Jules, Jr.) 1902-
(Trader Vic)

PERSONAL: Born December 10, 1902, in San Francisco, Calif.; son of Victor Jules (a waiter and grocery store operator) and Marie (Camount) Bergeron; married Helen Harwood; children: Victor Jules III, Lyn, Jeanne Bergeron Hittell, Yvonne Bergeron Seely, Helen Ann DeWerd (stepdaughter). *Education:* Received degree from Heald's Business College. *Home:* 20 Cosmo Pl., San Francisco, Calif. 94109.

CAREER: Restaurateur; artist; writer. Worked as cable office boy for Pacific Telephone Co., and as assistant bookkeeper for Athenian-Nile Club, Oakland, Calif.; former owner of service station in Calif.; former independent salesman of tire tube patching sets, eventually opened store; owner of Hinky Dinks restaurant, 1934-38, changed name of restaurant to Trader Vic's, 1938—; owner of Senor Pico's restaurant. Owner of Trader Vic's Food Products, Trader Vic's Wholesale Division, and Trader Vic's Art Company. General food consultant to United Airlines.

WRITINGS—All published by Doubleday: *Trader Vic's Book of Food and Drink,* 1946; *Original Trader Vic's Bartender's Guide,* 1947, revised edition published as *Revised Trader Vic's Bartender Guide,* 1972; *Trader Vic's Kitchen Kibitzer,* 1952; *Trader Vic's Pacific Island Cookbook: With Side Trips to Hong Kong, Southeast Asia, Mexico and Texas,* 1968; *The Menehune Story,* 1972; *Frankly Speaking: Trader Vic's Own Story,* introduction by Herb Caen, 1973; *Trader Vic's Book of Mexican Cooking,* 1973; *Trader Vic's Rum Cookery and Drinkery,* 1974; *Trader Vic's Helluva Man's Cookbook: With Side Trips to Hong Kong, Southeast Asia, Mexico and Texas,* 1976.

SIDELIGHTS: "When I started the restaurant business, I did everything to keep customers. I sang and even let them stick an ice pick in my wooden leg," Victor Bergeron, popularly known as Trader Vic, told interviewer Leigh Fenley. Through his persistance he was able to parlay one restaurant into a highly successful international chain that now grosses thirty-three million dollars annually.

Bergeron's first restaurant was actually a beer parlor named Hinky Dinks. After four years of business he decided to make over the entire establishment, adopting a South Pacific theme to provide an ambience of "complete escape and relaxation." He chose the name Trader Vic both for the new restaurant and for himself.

The one eating place eventually grew to be twenty, with locations throughout the United States, in England, Canada, Japan, and Germany. Trader Vic's restaurants now purvey Polynesian, Oriental, Japanese, Chinese, and French cuisine, and specialize in exotic rum concoctions. It was Trader Vic himself who created the world-famous Mai Tai drink.

Trader Vic has further expanded his enterprises to include two Senor Pico's Mexican restaurants. In addition, he has established two companies that market unusual food products.

Besides being a renowned restaurateur and businessman, Trader Vic is an artist. He retails his paintings, jewelry, and sculptures through Trader Vic's Art Company. His sculpture of the Smiloden saber-toothed tiger found in the La Brea Tar Pits is housed in the museum of paleontology at the University of California, Berkeley.

When Trader Vic was six years old his left leg was amputated to prevent the tuberculosis in his knee from spreading. He remained undaunted, however, and credits his parents for not pampering him. As a result, he has a casual attitude toward his loss. "Let's say I'm inconvenienced and let it go at that," he stated. His book, *Frankly Speaking,* is dedicated to "any young person who is having a tough life because he is handicapped."

BIOGRAPHICAL/CRITICAL SOURCES: Victor Bergeron, *Frankly Speaking,* Doubleday, 1973; L. Fenly, *Trader Vic Talks Straight About Food, Texans, Life,* Doubleday, 1973; *Newsweek,* March 31, 1975; *Business People in the News,* Volume 1, Gale, 1976.

* * *

BERMAN, Harold Joseph 1918-

PERSONAL: Born February 13, 1918, in Hartford, Conn.; son of Saul and Emma Rose (Kaplan) Berman; married Ruth Carol Harlow, June 10, 1941; children: Stephen Harlow, Jean Carol, Susanna, John Kingsley. *Education:* Dartmouth College, B.A., 1938; London School of Economics and Political Science, London, certificate, 1939; Yale University, M.A., 1942, LL.B., 1947. *Home:* 7 Chauncy Lane, Cambridge, Mass. 02138. *Office:* Law School, Harvard University, Cambridge, Mass. 02138.

CAREER: Stanford University, Stanford, Calif., assistant professor of law, 1947-48; Harvard University, Cambridge, Mass., assistant professor, 1949-52, professor, 1952-73, Joseph Story professor of law, 1973—, research associate at Russian Research Center, 1948—, member of center's executive committee, 1952—. Visiting professor at Harvard University, 1948-49. Lecturer at Institut des Hautes Etudes International, 1956-57, and Moscow State University, 1961-62. *Military service:* U.S. Army, 1942-45; became sergeant; received Bronze Star. *Member:* International Law Society, International Academy of Comparative Law (associate), American Society of International Law, American Society for Legal History, Foreign Law Association, Phi Beta Kappa, Coif.

WRITINGS: Justice in Russia: An Interpretation of Soviet Law, Harvard University Press, 1950, revised edition published as *Justice in the U.S.S.R.: An Interpretation of Soviet Law,* 1963; (with Boris Konstantinovsky) *Soviet Law in Action: The Recollected Case of a Soviet Lawyer,* Harvard University Press, 1953; *The Russians in Focus,* Little, Brown, 1953; (with Miroslav Kerner) *Soviet Military Law and Administration,* Harvard University Press, 1955; (editor and translator, with Kerner) *Documents on Soviet Military Law and Administration,* Harvard University Press, 1955; *On the Teaching of Law in the Liberal Arts Curriculum,* Foundation Press, 1956; *The Nature and Functions of Law: An Introduction for Students of the Arts and Sciences,* Foundation Press, 1958, 3rd edition (with William R. Greiner), 1972.

(Editor) *Talks on American Law,* Random House, 1961, revised edition, 1971; (translator, with James W. Spindler, and author of introduction), *Soviet Criminal Law and Procedure: The RSFSR Codes,* Cambridge University Press, 1966, 2nd edition, Harvard University Press, 1972; (with Peter B. Maggs) *Disarmament Inspection Under Soviet Law,* Oceana, 1967; (with John B. Quigley, Jr.) *Basic Laws on the Structure of the Soviet State,* Harvard University Press, 1969; *The Interaction of Law and Religion,* Abingdon, 1974.

Contributor of more than two hundred articles to scholarly journals. Editor of *Denver Journal of International Law and Policy,* 1975. Member of editorial advisory board of *Law and Policy in International Business.*

WORK IN PROGRESS: The Western Legal Tradition and Its Relation to the Great Revolutions of Western History.

SIDELIGHTS: Berman's books have been published in Japanese, Portuguese, Arabic, French, Spanish, Vietnamese, and Chinese.

* * *

BERNARD, Paul Peter 1929-

PERSONAL: Born July 5, 1929, in Antwerp, Belgium; came to the United States in 1939, naturalized citizen, 1945; son of Oscar Arthur (an industrialist) and Margaret (Fuchs) Bernard; married Edna Mary Jones (a home economist), March 24, 1949; children: Steven Leon, James Peter, Alison Rose. *Education:* Attended New York University, 1945-46; University of Denver, A.B., 1948; University of Colorado, M.A., 1952, Ph.D., 1955. *Home:* 312 West Cheyenne Mountain Blvd., Colorado Springs, Colo. 80906. *Office:* Department of History, University of Illinois, Urbana, Ill. 61801.

CAREER: University of Colorado, Boulder, instructor in French, 1955; Colorado College, Colorado Springs, instructor, 1955-57, assistant professor, 1957-62, associate professor of history, 1962-68; University of Illinois, Urbana-Champaign, professor of history, 1968—, associate of Center for Advanced Study, 1970-71, 1979-80. *Member:* American Historical Association, Conference Group on Central European History. *Awards, honors:* Fulbright fellow, 1953-54; Ford Foundation fellow in Austria, 1960-61; National Endowment for the Humanities senior fellow, 1975-76.

WRITINGS: Joseph II and Bavaria, Nijhoff, 1965; *Joseph II,* Twayne, 1968; *Jesuits and Jacobins,* University of Illinois Press, 1971; *Rush to the Alps,* Columbia University Press, 1978; *The Limits of Enlightenment,* University of Illinois Press, 1979. Contributor to *Austrian History Yearbook.* Contributor to history journals.

WORK IN PROGRESS: "A prosopographical study of the year 1785 in Austria, Germany, and Switzerland"; research on Prince Kaunitz and the internal administration of the Austrian monarchy.

SIDELIGHTS: Bernard's languages include French, German, Italian, Flemish, Czech, Swedish, and Latin. He has traveled in western and central Europe and western Asia.

* * *

BERNDT, Walter 1900(?)-1979

OBITUARY NOTICE: Born c. 1900; died August 13, 1979, in Port Jefferson, N.Y. Cartoonist best known for his comic strip, "Smitty." The strip, syndicated by the Chicago Tribune-New York Daily News Syndicate, appeared in hundreds of newspapers for more than fifty years. Based on Berndt's own experiences as an office boy at the *New York Journal,* the cartoon featured a moon-faced youth in a bow tie and cap whose attempts to impress his boss were constantly upset by misadventures. In 1970, the National Cartoonist Society named Berndt the "outstanding cartoonist of the year" and awarded him the Reuben Statuette. Obituaries and other sources: *New York Times,* August 15, 1979.

BERNER, Jeff 1940-

PERSONAL: Born December 10, 1940, in Troy, N.Y.; son of A. Bill and Jeannette C. Berner. *Education:* San Francisco State University, B.A., 1965. *Home address:* P.O. Box 503, Mill Valley, Calif. 94941. *Agent:* John Brockman Associates, Inc., 200 West 57th St., New York, N.Y. 10019.

CAREER: San Francisco State University, Downtown Center, San Francisco, Calif., instructor in avante-garde art history, 1966-69; writer, 1969—. Instructor at University of California extensions in Berkeley and San Francisco, 1965-69, and San Francisco Art Institute, 1968. *Awards, honors:* Honorable mentions from *Life* photography contests, 1970, 1971; first citation for photography in design from Desi: Graphics, U.S.A., 1978.

WRITINGS: Aktual Art International: Stanford Art Book, Number Eight, Stanford University Press, 1967; *The Innerspace Project,* World Publishing, 1972; *The Photographic Experience,* Doubleday, 1975; (photographer) Alan Watts, *Uncarved Block, Unbleached Silk,* A & W Visual Library, 1978; *The Holography Book,* Avon, 1980; *How to Tell Your Camera What to Do in Plain English,* Bantam, 1980. Author of "Astronauts of Inner Space," a weekly column in *San Francisco Examiner & Chronicle.* Editor of *Stolen Paper Review,* 1963-65.

WORK IN PROGRESS: Finding Things: An Art Awareness Handbook for Young People; "a picaresque novel of California and points west."

SIDELIGHTS: Berner told *CA:* "I believe that developing a broad aesthetic interest in life is a healing path. My interests are primarily centered on the visual experience, visual education, visual meditation, and human and environmental ecology. Frankly, I often feel like a Martian anthropologist visiting earth with pen and camera, having an affectionate curiosity about this garden planet."

BIOGRAPHICAL/CRITICAL SOURCES: San Francisco Chronicle, January 31, 1979; *San Francisco Examiner,* February 1, 1979.

* * *

BERNSTEIN, Alvin H(owell) 1939-

PERSONAL: Born August 4, 1939, in New York, N.Y.; son of Elias (in business) and Celia (Gurr) Bernstein; married Sandra Catherine Kidson, August 18, 1964; children: Aaron Alexander, Robin David. *Education:* Cornell University, A.B., 1961, Ph.D., 1968; Oxford University, B.A., 1964, M.A., 1969. *Home:* 3 Sunny Knoll, Ithaca, N.Y. 14850. *Office:* Department of History, Cornell University, Ithaca, N.Y. 14853.

CAREER: University of Missouri, Columbia, assistant professor of ancient history, 1968-69; Cornell University, Ithaca, N.Y., assistant professor, 1969-75, associate professor of ancient history, 1975—, head of department of Near Eastern studies, 1979—. Visiting associate professor at Yale University, 1974-75.

WRITINGS: Tiberius Sempronius Gracchus: Tradition and Apostasy, Cornell University Press, 1978; *Polybius on Roman Imperialism,* Gateway Editions, 1979.

WORK IN PROGRESS: The Rise and Fall of Classical Antiquity, publication by Knopf expected in 1982.

* * *

BEROFSKY, Bernard 1935-

PERSONAL: Born July 5, 1935, in Jersey City, N.J.; son of Charles (a compositor) and Etta (Obolsky) Berofsky; married Barbara Sailer (a music teacher), August 12, 1962; children: Adrienne, Aaron. *Education:* New York University, B.A., 1956; Columbia University, M.A., 1959, Ph.D., 1963. *Home:* 119 Lily Pond Lane, Katonah, N.Y. 10536. *Office:* Columbia University, Philosophy Hall, New York, N.Y. 10027.

CAREER: Vassar College, Poughkeepsie, N.Y., instructor in philosophy, 1963-64; University of Michigan, Ann Arbor, assistant professor of philosophy, 1964-67; Columbia University, New York, N.Y., associate professor, 1967-70, professor of philosophy, 1970—. *Member:* American Philosophical Association, Society of American Magicians (member of parent assembly). *Awards, honors:* American Council of Learned Societies fellowship, 1972-73.

WRITINGS: (Editor) *Free Will and Determinism,* Harper, 1966; (co-editor) *Introductory Philosophy,* Harper, 1967, 2nd edition, 1971; *Determinism,* Princeton University Press, 1971. Contributor to philosophy journals. Member of editorial board of *Journal of Philosophy.*

WORK IN PROGRESS: A book on freedom of will.

* * *

BERRY, James Gomer 1883-1968 (Viscount Kemsley)

OBITUARY NOTICE: Born May 7, 1883 in Gwaeldoygarth, Merthyr Tydfil, Wales; died February 6, 1968. Newspaper executive. Along with his brother, Berry (Viscount Kemsley) collaborated in the purchase of a number of newspapers, most notably the *London Sunday Times* in 1915 and the *London Daily Telegraph* in 1927. The brothers helped found Allied Newspapers Ltd., which became Kemsley Newspapers in 1943. Kemsley served as editor-in-chief of the *London Sunday Times* from 1937 until 1959. Obituaries and other sources: *Current Biography,* Wilson, 1951, March, 1968; *New York Times,* February 7, 1968; *Time,* February 16, 1968; *Newsweek,* February 19, 1968; *Who Was Who in America,* 5th edition, Marquis, 1973.

* * *

BERTONASCO, Marc F(rancis) 1934-

PERSONAL: Born February 26, 1934, in Valperga, Italy; came to the United States in 1937, naturalized citizen, 1945; son of Thomas E. (a bacteriologist) and Lydia (Castigliano) Bertonasco. *Education:* St. Paul Seminary, St. Paul, Minn., B.A., 1958; University of Michigan, M.A., 1959; University of Wisconsin—Madison, Ph.D., 1964. *Politics:* Democrat. *Home:* 9 El Limon, #4, Sacramento, Calif. 95823. *Office:* Department of English, California State University, 6000 Jay St., Sacramento, Calif. 95819.

CAREER: High school English teacher in Garden Grove, Calif., 1959-62; California State University, Sacramento, instructor, 1964-65, assistant professor, 1966-68, associate professor, 1968-72, professor of English, 1972—.

WRITINGS: Crashaw and the Baroque, University of Alabama Press, 1971; (with Robert Miles) *Prose Style for the Modern Writer,* Prentice-Hall, 1977. Contributor of articles and reviews to scholarly journals.

WORK IN PROGRESS: A textbook on argumentation; a book on American mythology; research on rhetorical theory and Jungian psychology.

SIDELIGHTS: Bertonasco told *CA:* "Although an ardent supporter of the humanistic revolution of the late sixties, I believe this movement has fostered a weakening and depreciation of the basic intellectual virtues. The cultural tradition of the West is in danger of being lost. My main professional concern is to encourage a movement on my own campus which seeks to reaffirm the traditional intellectual virtues and to prevent the further erosion of standards. My main interests include: applying principles of classical rhetoric to the teaching of college composition; stylistic theory; Jungian psychology, as applied to American culture (American mythology); and mythopoeic criticism (especially its application to metaphysical poetry)."

AVOCATIONAL INTERESTS: Travel (Europe, the Far East, Latin America).

* * *

BEYNON, John
See HARRIS, John (Wyndham Parkes Lucas) Beynon

See HARRIS, John (Wyndham Parkes Lucas) Beynon

* * *

BING, Rudolf 1902-

PERSONAL: Born January 9, 1902, in Vienna, Austria; son of Ernst (an industrial executive) and Stefanie (Hoenigsvald) Bing; married Nina Schelesmskaya-Schelesnaya, 1929; *Education:* Privately educated in Vienna, Austria. *Home and office:* Essex House, 160 Central Park S., New York, N.Y. 10019.

CAREER: Hessian State Theatre, Darmstadt, Germany, manager, 1928-30; Civic Opera, Berlin, Germany, 1930-33; Glyndebourne Opera, Glyndebourne, England, general manager, 1935-49; Edinburgh International Festival, Edinburgh, Scotland, artistic director, 1947-50; Metropolitan Opera, New York, N.Y., general manager, 1950-72; Brooklyn College of the City University of New York, Brooklyn, N.Y., distinguished visiting professor of music, 1972-75; Columbia Artists Management, Inc., consultant, 1974—. *Awards, honors:* Knight of the British Empire, 1971; D. Mus. from Lafayette College; D. Litt. from Dickinson College; D.H.L. from New York University, Temple University, and Wagner College; LL.D. from Jacksonville University; Chevalier Legion d'Honneur; Grand Officer Order of Merit of Republic of Italy, Grand Silver Medal of Honour of Republic of Austria, Commander's Cross of Order of Merit of Federal Republic of Germany.

WRITINGS: Five Thousand Nights at the Opera (memoirs), Doubleday, 1972.

SIDELIGHTS: Rudolf Bing was the general manager of the Metropolitan Opera for twenty-two years. His tenure was often controversial and was frequently troubled by a variety of financial and personnel-related crises. Bing's autobiography is, according to a *New York Times* critic, "a serious . . . and valuable defense of his administration at the Met and an always absorbing account of how a great house is run." Donal Henahan commented: "As a strongly personal account of what an opera manager faces in his daily work, Sir Rudolf's book is as valuable as it is readable. It is also a trifle mythic at times, as apologias usually are. What one carries away is a sense of continual battle, with Sir Rudolf cast as Leonidas, surrounded and outnumbered but hacking away at his foes with swordlike tongue."

The first half of the book concerns Bing's positions at various opera houses in Germany, England, and Scotland. It has a "very pleasing objectivity and mellowness," Louis Snyder wrote. Particularly fascinating is Bing's experience as the general manager of the Glyndebourne Opera in England. A wealthy Englishman, Sir John Christie, had, in the mid-1930's, transformed his country estate into an opera theatre. There, operas by Mozart and Verdi were standard fare, and Christie's wife, a soprano, was featured in many performances. The festival's great success was in large part due to Bing's managerial effectiveness.

"All my life up to 1949 could be seen as the proper preparation for being manager of the Metropolitan," Bing wrote in *Five Thousand Nights at the Opera.* Although Bing was well-known in European music circles, the announcement that he had been chosen to be the general manager of the Metropolitan Opera in 1949 surprised the American musical establishment. As general manager, Bing was responsible for all of the company's artistic decisions, which included hiring and firing singers, conductors, and other personnel, as well as scheduling operas (which had to be done several seasons in advance). He stated that the opera was organized as "a militant democracy, in which one man ruled." Faye Levine wrote that "in his two decades at the Metropolitan he exerted a significant artistic influence and combined the two different kinds of power, artistic and financial, more than any other contemporary figure in the fields of music and dance."

When Bing arrived in New York, he related in his memoirs, he found the Metropolitan to be in disarray. The chorus was superannuated and underpaid, the stage was cramped and in bad condition, budgeting was a practice virtually unknown, and relationships between various members of the administrattive staff were strained. Bing immediately set to alleviate these problems. His improvements in stage management were especially prompt and wide-ranging and Bing counts these as among his most important accomplishments.

Most critical, when Bing assumed control of the Metropolitan, was the absence of a principal conductor. The Metropolitan had been getting along with several good conductors, but arrangements with them were always tenuous, and Bing realized that one strong artistic leader was needed. Unfortunately the conductors he suggested were either unavailable or were unacceptable to the Metropolitan's board of directors. Bing spent several seasons trying to convince the board to hire Wilhelm Furtwangler, but the German conductor was suspected of sympathizing with the Nazis. Bing was convinced of Furtwangler's innocence, but by the time he convinced the board, Furtwangler was in ill-health. He died before he could be approached about the position.

Bing never rectified the conductor situation to his satisfaction, but thought that the criticism he received was unfounded. He also noted in his memoirs that "the usual criticism that the Metropolitan has not had great conductors in my time is both unfair and uninformed." Bing worked with many of the most important conductors of the century, including Karl Boehm, Georg Solti, Leonard Bernstein, Herbert von Karajan, Erich Leinsdorf, Thomas Schippers, and Pierre Monteux.

Bing also faced opposition in hiring singers. The appointment of Kirsten Flagstad was at first resisted because of her suspected Nazi sympathies, but she was later hired and went on to a long and successful career with the Metropolitan. One of Bing's proudest accomplishments, he wrote, was the appointment of Marian Anderson, the first black singer to appear with the company.

The hiring of the soprano Maria Callas was one of Bing's greatest coups. Callas's performances in *Norma, Traviata, Lucia,* and *Tosca* were some of the finest moments of Bing's tenure, he commented. From the beginning the relationship between Callas and Bing was stormy, although Bing made unprecedented concessions to the temperamental singer and her demanding husband. Finally, during the 1958-59 season when Callas broke her contract, Bing fired her in a headline-making story. Several years later, however, Callas was again invited to perform at the Metropolitan.

Bing's outstanding ability to manage artists was noted by a reviewer who called his memoirs "a shrewd study of the genus artist." The reviewer wrote that "the author shows an insightful sympathy and understanding of their nature and psychological bent. He understood their prickliness, their sense of insecurity, their jealousies. 'It is much worse to be a mediocre artist,' he says at one point, 'than to be a mediocre post-office clerk'—a remark that is almost painfully acute." However tactful Bing was with artists, he was perceived by the public as somewhat arrogant and tactless. His mordant wit is much in evidence in *Five Thousand Nights at the Opera*. Irving Kolodin commented: "Those who don't know [Bing] must wonder why they have heard so many unpleasant stories about him. Many of the answers are contained in this outspoken and nearly candid recollection. Needless to say, he doesn't tell all—who does?—but he tells enough to make the reading as absorbing, and sometimes as incredible, as the man himself."

Critics have also bemoaned the scarcity of Metropolitan productions of modern operas. Bing is opposed to their production on artistic and financial grounds: in his opinion there is only a small repertoire of artistically valid modern works and he has found that they don't sell tickets. He judged Benjamin Britten's *Peter Grimes* to be the only thoroughly successful modern opera to be performed during his association with the Metropolitan. Bing remarked: "I am always being told that opera will die unless the new works are performed. It seems to be that these days a better case can be made for the proposition that opera will *never* die *unless* the new works are performed."

After Bing left the Metropolitan he spent several years as a popular professor at Brooklyn College and is currently a consultant for Columbia Artists Management, Inc., where he arranges concerts by opera singers. Recently, a *Newsweek* writer reported that since Bing's retirement, "he refuses to go to the opera in Europe or in America ('I've had enough'), never listens to opera at home ('I don't have a record player'), and has very little contact with his former colleagues. . . . Still, Bing admits he misses the Met. 'I'm glad I'm out of it,' he says, 'but after 22 years—a third of my life—I just can't shrug it off."

BIOGRAPHICAL/CRITICAL SOURCES: Rudolph Bing, *Five Thousand Nights at the Opera* (memoirs), Doubleday, 1972; *New York Times Book Review*, October 22, 1972; *Times Literary Supplement*, October 27, 1972; *New York Times*, November 3, 1972; *Saturday Review*, November 4, 1972; *New Statesmen*, November 24, 1972; *Chrisitan Science Monitor*, December 6, 1972; *Newsweek*, November 11, 1974; Faye Levine, *The Culture Barons*, Crowell, 1976.

—*Sketch by Barbara A. Welch*

* * *

BINZEN, Bill
See BINZEN, William

BINZEN, William
(Bill Binzen)

PERSONAL: Born in New Jersey. *Education:* Attended University of Virginia, and Art Students League in New York City. *Residence:* Salisbury, Conn.

CAREER: Author and illustrator. Former art director for advertising agency in New York, N.Y.

WRITINGS—Under name Bill Binzen; juveniles; all self-illustrated: *Little Will, the Bugle Boy*, Abelard, 1963; *Tenth Street*, Paragraphic Books, 1968; *Miguel's Mountain*, Coward, 1968; *Punch and Jonathan*, Pantheon, 1969; *Alfred, the Little Bear*, Doubleday, 1970; *Carmen*, Coward, 1970; *Doubletake*, Grossman, 1972; *First Day in School*, Doubleday, 1972; *Rooftop Hogi*, Doubleday, 1972; *The Walk*, Coward, 1972; *Alfred Goes House Hunting*, Doubleday, 1974; *The Rory Story*, Doubleday, 1974; *Alfred Goes Flying*, Doubleday, 1976; *Year After Year*, Coward, 1976.

Illustrator: William Wise, *All on a Summer's Day*, Pantheon, 1971; Philip Ressner, *The Park in the City*, Dutton, 1971.

SIDELIGHTS: Binzen illustrates his children's books with photographs rather than drawings or pictures. His 1969 book, *Punch and Jonathan*, was adapted as a motion picture by Connecticut Films in 1972.*

* * *

BIRCHAM, Deric Neale 1934-

PERSONAL: Born December 16, 1934, in Wellington, New Zealand; son of Stanley Ernest (a painter) and Rita Muriel (Sanvig) Bircham; married Patricia Frances Simkin, April 18, 1960; children: Venessa Frances, Melanie Elenor. *Education:* Attended Victoria University of Wellington. *Religion:* Roman Catholic. *Home:* 139 Eglington Rd., Mornington, Dunedin, New Zealand. *Office:* Department of Photography, University of Otago, Box 913, Dunedin, New Zealand.

CAREER: Ministry of Works and Development, Wellington, New Zealand, photographer, 1954-68, senior photographer, 1968-78, chief photographer, 1976-78; free-lance photographer, 1978-79; Victoria University of Wellington, Wellington, visual communicator, 1979; University of Otago, Dunedin, New Zealand, head of department of photography, 1980—. Lecturer; judge of visual communication competitions; consultant. *Military service:* New Zealand Army, Territorial Force, 1952-62.

MEMBER: International Institute of Professional Photographers (honorary fellow), International Institute of Community Service (fellow), New Zealand Professional Photographers Association (fellow; chairperson of national scientific and technical group, 1967-71, and qualifications board, 1974-76; member of national executive council, 1967-71, 1974-76), Royal Photographic Society of Great Britain (fellow; national chairperson of professional convention, 1976), Royal Society of Arts (fellow), Institute of Incorporated Photographers (fellow), Professional Photographers of America (international member). *Awards, honors:* Honorary doctorate from International Institute of Photographers, 1974; international visual communication awards include merit award for distinguished achievement, 1973; merit award for distinguished service in International Photographic Expertise, 1974; Internationale de l'Industrie Photographique, 1976.

WRITINGS: *Seeing New Zealand*, A. H. & A. W. Reed, 1971, 4th edition, 1975, Tuttle, 1972; *Towards a More Just World*, Government Printing, 1973; *Waitomo Tourist Caves*, A. H. & A. W. Reed, 1975; *Table Tennis*, A. H. & A. W.

Reed, 1976; *Old St. Paul's,* A. H. & A. W. Reed, 1980; *New Zealanders of Destiny,* A. H. & A. W. Reed, 1980; *The Life and Complete Works of Lindauer,* A. H. & A. W. Reed, in press. Contributor to *Australian Photography.*

WORK IN PROGRESS: Stained Glass Windows of St. Mary's; The Stations; Spirits Within; Illustrated Poems.

SIDELIGHTS: Bircham is internationally known for his visual exhibitions as well as his books. He has portrayed onto canvas Queen Elizabeth II, Prince Philip, governors general, prime ministers, and other dignitaries. His "New Zealanders of Destiny" exhibition is on permanent display at Auckland City Art Gallery.

"I am a person who likes to do things all the time, so writing and illustrating books started, and continues," Bircham told *CA*. "My books began when a publishing house approached me and asked if I would like to do a book for them. *Seeing New Zealand* was the result, and it became a best-seller. Other books followed naturally. What I hope to achieve through my books is pleasure for others. When working I require pleasant surroundings and peace of mind.

"I am still looking for the opportunity to really move myself into the true creative career I am seeking. Any success I've had to date has come about through my love of people and humanity."

AVOCATIONAL INTERESTS: Playing classical piano.

* * *

BIRIMISA, George 1924-

PERSONAL: Born February 21, 1924, in Santa Cruz, Calif.; son of Charles and Anna (Gjurovich) Birimisa; married Nancy Linden, 1952 (divorced, 1961). *Education:* Attended schools through ninth grade; studied with Uta Hagen at Herbert Berghof Studios, New York, 1965-66; attended New School for Social Research. *Home:* 1148½ Seward St., Hollywood, Calif. 90038.

CAREER: Actor, director, and playwright. Worked in a factory, as a disc jockey, health studio manager, clerk, salesman, bartender, bellhop, page for National Broadcasting Co.; Howard Johnson's, New York City, counterman, 1952-56; Laurie Girls, New York, typist, 1969-70; Theatre of All Nations, New York City, artistic director, 1974-76; full-time writer, 1966—. *Military service:* U.S. Naval Reserve, 1942-43. *Awards, honors:* Received Rockefeller grant, 1969; award from *Drama Logue,* 1978, for "A Rainbow in the Night."

WRITINGS—Plays: *Degrees* (one-act; first produced Off-Off-Broadway at Theatre Genesis, St. Marks in the Bouwerie, February, 1966), [New York], 1966; *17 Loves and 17 Kisses* (one-act; first produced Off-Off-Broadway at Playwright's Workshop Club, September, 1966), [New York], 1966; *Daddy Violet* (one-act; first produced in New York City at Caffe Cino, June, 1967), [New York], 1967, published in *Prism International,* [Vancouver], 1968; *How Come You Don't Dig Chicks?* (one-act; first produced Off-Off-Broadway at Troupe Theatre Club, June 1, 1967), [New York], 1967; "Mister Jello" (two-act), first produced in New York City at Playbox, 1968, revised version produced Off-Off-Broadway at La Mama ETC, April, 1974; "Georgie Porgie" (two-act; first produced in New York City at Eugenia's Cooper Square Theatre, November 20, 1968, produced Off-Broadway at Village Arena Theatre, August 10, 1971), published in *More Plays From Off-Off Broadway,* edited by Michael Smith, Bobbs-Merrill, 1973.

"Adrian" (one act), first produced in New York City at New York Theatre Ensemble, 1974; "Will the Real Yoganga Please Stand Up?" (one-act), first produced in New York City at New York Theatre Ensemble, 1974; "A Dress Made of Diamonds" (two-act), first produced in Los Angeles at Matrix Theatre, April, 1976; "Pogey Bait!" (two-act), first produced in Los Angeles at Las Palmas Theatre, September, 1976, produced Off-Off-Broadway at 13th Street Theatre, November, 1977; "A Rainbow in the Night" (two-act), first produced in Los Angeles at Matrix Theatre, March 13, 1978.

WORK IN PROGRESS: "Georgie," an autobiography of his first seventeen years.

SIDELIGHTS: Birimisa's plays feature themes of human isolation, frustrated idealism, and rage against needless suffering, usually centered around homosexual characters. His most popular play, "Georgie Porgie," for example, contains nine scenes dealing with homosexual encounters. According to *Variety,* the play is an advance in its field, and "unlike many of its stage predecessors, ('Boys In the Band' and 'Foreplay,' to pick two), Birimisa's play minces few images or words in describing the plight of its characters." The coarse language and nudity are used for psychological effect as the characters face melodramatic situations, continued *Variety,* while Birimisa "permits the action to develop to logical and sometimes surprising conclusions."

A collection of George Birimisa's manuscripts is housed at Joe Cino Memorial Library, Lincoln Center Library of the Performing Arts, in New York.

CA INTERVIEWS THE AUTHOR

George Birimisa was interviewed during a morning's work at home in Hollywood on April 16, 1979.

CA: You dropped out of school in the ninth grade, and you've worked at a variety of jobs—disc jockey, bartender, factory worker, sales. Were you working toward a career in theatre, or did you just drift into it?

BIRIMISA: I was always writing and always getting rejected. But I was scared to death to write a play. I didn't know how to attack it, how to go about it.

CA: What other kinds of writing were you doing?

BIRIMISA: I was writing one bad novel after the other. I had four novels rejected. Short stories, and on and on and on.

CA: Were they bad, or were they just rejected?

BIRIMISA: I think they were bad. You see, I had to find something inside of myself. I had to face the pain, face what was really going on inside of me. It just happened that two things came together. Just as I was going through that life-and-death crisis, I began to write plays; I was able to express it in plays.

CA: Had you done any acting?

BIRIMISA: Oh, yes. I'd done acting. And shortly before, I had a personal crisis in my life. I'd been away from New York, and I went back to New York. I was very crazy at this period in my life I said, "I'm either going to make it in the theatre or kill myself." I studied with Uta Hagen for a year with the express purpose of learning how to write a play through studying acting, learning what it was all about from the viewpoint of a great artist. That was when I wrote my first play, in '65.

CA: This was about the time Off-Off-Broadway was beginning to go well, wasn't it?

BIRIMISA: Yes. I came to New York, and I remember seeing in the Sunday supplement an article on the Caffe Cino. And I got all excited and thought it would be the greatest fantasy in the world to write a play and have it done at the Caffe Cino, which I did. A dream that came true.

CA: Did you go to New York because of Off-Off-Broadway?

BIRIMISA: No, I didn't know it existed until I got there.

CA: Did a number of playwrights go to New York for different reasons and just happen into Off-Off-Broadway?

BIRIMISA: I think so. It was a very heavy, personal, painful thing for me. Then, when I found Off-Off-Broadway opened up to me, I found this marvelous way of being able to express myself. There it was in the mid-sixties—the magical access to say truly how I really felt. I did it *all* in the sixties; I said it loud and clear and I'm still alive and kicking. Yes, they were miracle times. I'm an innocent and an optimist. Especially in those early years. I'd walk down the street, and someone would walk up to me and say, "Hey, George, someone canceled out. Do you have a play you could get together in a week or ten days?" I'd say, "Hell, if I don't, I'll write one." And I'd put it on, direct it, do the lead—whatever had to be done. I did one play on fifteen cents. It was like that. And then the same thing happened to Off-Off-Broadway. The goddamned Establishment moved in, with all the grants, and almost all the theatres turned commercial. One of the reasons I left, when I finally left New York, was that I'd have to submit a play to a board to get it done. It's like any rebellion in the United States—gobbled up by the Establishment, not fighting it, but embracing it.

CA: Are there grants now for experimental theatre?

BIRIMISA: If I'm not mistaken, Mobil Oil is now giving grants to Off-Off-Broadway. There are grants all over the place, but I don't go after them anymore. Like the grant I got at the Rockefeller Foundation [1969]. The man who got it for me, in fact, left. I don't know exactly why he left, but I have my suspicions. Word goes out that this time you have to play down homosexuality, that the Rockefellers are down on gays for now, or this or that. Anyone who's "crazy" or "nuts," but also a good writer, is out. Don't misunderstand. I don't think of myself as a great writer. I feel I've searched for the truth and I try to tell it. That's all. It's up to other people to decide where I'm coming from. I don't think I've come anywhere near where I want to go as a writer. I think I'm just beginning to find out what it's all about.

CA: In retrospect, do you think Off-Off-Broadway has had any lasting effect on theatre?

BIRIMISA: All I know is that it had a lasting effect on me. All I can say is that the intensity of the experience, to me, was mind-boggling. It opened up a whole world to me. When all is said and done, it gave me my dignity as a person. It gave me certain stature as a playwright and a little faith in myself—not much, but a little bit.

CA: What kind of audiences are there?

BIRIMISA: I've had everything from seven people to audiences who were standing up on their chairs screaming for more. By the way, I was one of the few Off-Off-Broadway playwrights to take a play from Off-Off-Broadway on a tour of colleges. It was "Daddy Violet" [1967].

CA: That was an anti-Vietnam play, wasn't it?

BIRIMISA: It was that and more. I wrote it before My Lai, and it's about three violets overlooking the Mekong Delta. There's a fog over the valley, and when the fog lifts, they see all the women and children being napalmed. The play was also sexually very outrageous. It was using the whole theatre, running into the audience, jumping over them, pools of improvisation, one scene where the lead actor goes up to a guy in the audience and puts the make on him—asks him what he's doing after the show. One time the actor almost got killed; he almost got beaten up by a macho stud. It was insane. I don't know how I even got away with it without being lynched. We did 107 performances of "Daddy Violet." We even did it at Actors Studio in New York, but they were so old-fashioned—like a kettle of wet fish!

CA: Maybe it was more audience involvement than your audience was ready for.

BIRIMISA: It was. I'd always considered myself a very liberal person, and the far Left called me a turd. They wanted a certain orthodoxy. What was also interesting was the reaction of American college students as compared to Canadian college students. The American students were passive. They are such victims of the school system. The Americans were frightened, whereas the Canadians tore the place down—just loved it, went out of their minds. A play has to be significant; that is, the playwright must somehow be superior. He's a truly great playwright if he deliberately does not communicate.

CA: Was that surprising to you?

BIRIMISA: Yeah. And the thing that surprised me was that the Canadians knew more about Off-Off-Broadway at the University of British Columbia, Vancouver, and also Simon Fraser. They knew all the playwrights, and they had a sexual sophistication, whereas the Americans were just naive. Oh, the American students *liked* it, but the Canadians were really tearing down the theatre. Then I did it in San Francisco, for the Establishment, people in their forties—you know, great San Francisco—and it freaked 'em out. Couldn't handle it. They sat and stared; they didn't believe it was happening to them. They sat on their hands in stony silence from beginning to end.

CA: Is California a better place for a playwright right now than New York?

BIRIMISA: No. I've been out here since 1976, and I've done three plays. After my last one, which I did last year [1978], called "A Rainbow in the Night"—it won an award from *Drama Logue*—I'm leaving the theatre for a while. It's just so totally commercial out here. I've reached the point where if I hear another actor talk about his agent and another producer talk about who's interested. . . . What happened was that Allan Carr agreed to put up some of the money to produce my last play, and it turned into one of these insane things when it looked like he was going to take it to New York; everyone was fighting over everything—percentages, this and that—even my producer, to the point that I said, "I don't need this." So I just pulled out. What I'm doing now is writing a prose piece; I'm writing my autobiography.

CA: Do you enjoy the change of pace?

BIRIMISA: Oh, boy! After fifteen years of contention, of going from one crisis to another every week—that's what theatre is, no doubt about it. As far as I know, for a couple of years I'm going to be working on my autobiography. It's wonderful, but it's scary to do it. It comes right down to the question, can I do prose? But now I think I can. It's going well. I'm feeling so good doing it, that's almost enough.

CA: You've directed and acted in your own plays a lot, haven't you?

BIRIMISA: Quite a bit, yes. Bite into it—eat it up—do it!

CA: Do you find it more difficult to direct or to act in other writers' plays than in your own?

BIRIMISA: Oh, it's much easier in other people's work. I guess it's because of my own ego. You see, usually when I act in my own plays—like in New York when I did "Daddy Violet," I played Daddy Violet—the only reason is I can't get anyone else. They thought Daddy Violet was so crazy they said, "You're nuts! You think I'm going to get up and do *That*? Hell, no!" No one would do it. You see, most of my plays never get a second production. . . . Give them another twenty years—after the revolution!

CA: Did Off-Off-Broadway influence Broadway?

BIRIMISA: No, I think when all is said and done, most of us were just dying to get on Broadway. To be honest about it, I had a really ambivalent thing going then; it's taken me analysis and all kinds of things to figure it out and understand what I was up to. I wanted it my way, but I wanted my stuff on Broadway. I still haven't figured the whole thing out, but I do know I was not a knight in shining armor in any sense of the word. I was pretty corrupt. Writing my autobiography is helping me understand my motivations in a lot of things that I wasn't able to understand before.

CA: What do you think of theatre now?

BIRIMISA: What the theatre needs is passion—blood and guts. Down with the intellectual stuff and the "Oh I'm so weary with life and above it all" theatre. Theatre now is a manifestation of the middle class, of a racist society; it's bourgeois. Anything that has any true revolutionary concept is automatically naive. I've got to think like the silly critics. Anything that goes against the Establishment is down the tube. They're clever and well trained. They use words like "boring." They're the artistic assassins for the U.S.A., and they are the ones who have the nerve to say, "Where are the great American playwrights?" They killed them off. One touch of talent and "Off with their heads. Kill! Kill! Kill!" You can't expect the *New York Times* to advocate cutting its own throat. So I can't expect a good review from the *New York Times*.

CA: Are there any playwrights today that you admire?

BIRIMISA: Well, I've got to say that I have a lot of ignorance about that. I have seen flashes from Sam Shepard, but I think generally he's naive and just silly. But he does certain scenes that I think are just marvelous. There is one favorite—Jeff Weiss. He's won five "Obies." I think he's the greatest. In Off-Off-Broadway, everyone bows to Jeff Weiss. He is the exception that proves the rule.

CA: Do you write every day?

BIRIMISA: Yeah. I went through a period of four years when I couldn't write anything. At one time I was writing, drinking martinis, and taking uppers. But the last two or three years I get up at seven or eight o'clock in the morning, sit down at my typewriter every day, seven days a week. I stopped drinking; I don't smoke. It's wonderful. I was in group therapy for a couple of years, and it's really helped me. I feel good about myself now. I even have that middle class affliction: I jog every day. And I have my Writers Workshop. I've been running it in my apartment for over two years now. There are some wonderful young people in it, especially a young man of sixteen who might one day be a great writer. I try in the workshop to pass on the passion and the searing anger. We must search for the truth, find it, spend a lifetime learning how to be true. That is what I give; that is my children.

BIOGRAPHICAL/CRITICAL SOURCES: Village Voice, September 4, 1969; *New York Times,* August 11, 1971; *Variety,* September 1, 1971.

—Interview by Jean W. Ross

* * *

BISCHOFF, F(rederick) A(lexander) 1928-

PERSONAL: Born May 18, 1928, in Vienna, Austria. *Education:* Ecole des Langues orientales vivantes, diploma (Chinese), 1950; Institut des Hautes Etudes indiennes, certificate (Sanskrit), 1952; Ecole pratique des Hautes Etudes, diploma (Tibetan), 1956; University of Paris, Ph.D., 1959. *Home:* 1018 University Ave., Bloomington, Ind. 47401. *Office:* Department of East Asian Languages and Literatures, Indiana University, Bloomington, Ind. 47401.

CAREER: University of Bonn, Bonn, West Germany, lecturer in Tibetan, 1961-62, member of exchange faculty at Waseda University, 1962-63; Indiana University, Bloomington, assistant professor of Chinese and Tibetan, 1964-67, associate professor of Uralic and Altaic studies and East Asian languages, 1967—. *Member:* Societe Asiatique, Societas Uralo-Altaica. *Awards, honors:* Fellowships from Committee of Sciences of the Mongolian People's Republic, summers, 1956-57, and Peking University, 1956-57; grant from Deutscher Forschungsgemeinschaft, 1959-63.

WRITINGS: Contribution a l'etude des divinites mineures du buddhisme tantrique: Arya Mahabala-Nama-Mahayansutra, tibetain et chinois, Buddhica, 1956; *La Foret des Pinceaux: etude sur l'Academie du Han'lin sous la Dynastie des T'ang et traduction du Han lin tche,* Bibliotheque de l'Institut des Hautes Etudes Chinoises, 1963; *Der Kanjur und seine Kolophone,* two volumes, Selbstverlag Press, 1968; (contributor) *Studies in South, East, and Central Asia Presented as a Memorial Volume to the Late Professor Raghu Vira,* International Academy of Indian Culture, 1968; (editor with Marianne Macdonal, and contributor) *Etudes tibetaines dediees a la memoire de Marcelle Lalou,* [Paris], 1971; (editor with Wu-chi, Jerome P. Seaton, and Kenneth Yasuda) *K'uei Hsing: A Repository of Asian Literature in Translation,* Indiana University Press, 1974; *Interpreting the Fu: A Study in Chinese Literary Rhetoric,* Muenchener Ostasiatische Studien, 1976. Contributor of more than twenty-five articles and reviews to asian studies journals and to newspapers. Editor of *Tea Leaves,* 1965-69.

WORK IN PROGRESS: Interpreting Landscape Symbolism: A Study in Chinese Literary Rhetoric; Interpreting the Li Sao: A Study in Chinese Literary Rhetoric.

* * *

BISHOP, Elizabeth 1911-1979

OBITUARY NOTICE—See index for *CA* sketch: Born February 8, 1911, in Worcester, Mass.; died October 6, 1979, in Boston, Mass. Poet known for her stark, tightly structured verse that contrasted sharply with the confessional mode popular during her lifetime. Bishop published only five collections in her more than thirty years as a poet. Among her best known volumes are *Poems: North and South* and *A Cold Spring,* two collections for which she received the Pulitzer Prize for poetry in 1955. Many of her poems were also featured in *New Yorker.* Obituaries and other sources: *The Oxford Companion to American Literature,* 4th edition, Oxford University Press, 1965; *Encyclopedia of World Literature in the Twentieth Century,* updated edition, Ungar, 1967; *The Penguin Companion to English Literature,* McGraw, 1971; *Celebrity Register,* 3rd edition, Simon & Schuster, 1973; *Who's Who in America,* 40th edition, Marquis, 1978; *The Writers Directory, 1980-82,* St. Martin's, 1979; *New York Times,* October 8, 1979; *Time,* October 22, 1979; *Newsweek,* October 22, 1979.

* * *

BLACK, Campbell 1944-
(Thomas Altman; Jeffrey Campbell, a joint pseudonym)

PERSONAL: Born February, 1944, in Glasgow, Scotland; son of Thomas and Mary (Campbell) Black; married Eileen Altman, December, 1964; children: Iain, Stephen, Keiron. *Education:* University of Sussex, B.A. (with honors), 1967. *Politics:* None. *Religion:* None. *Home and office:* 411 East Cornell, Tempe, Ariz. 85283. *Agent:* International Creative Management, 40 West 57th St., New York, N.Y. 10019.

CAREER: Granada Publishing, London, England, editor, 1967-71; State University of New York at Oswego, instructor in creative writing, 1971-75; Arizona State University, Tempe, instructor in creative writing, 1975-78; full-time writer, 1978—. *Awards, honors:* Scottish Arts Council Award, 1970, for *The Punctual Rape.*

WRITINGS—All novels, except as noted: *Assassins and Victims,* Harper Magazine Press, 1969; *The Punctual Rape,* Lippincott, 1970; *Death's Head,* Lippincott, 1972; "And They Used to Star in Movies" (one-act play), first produced in London at Soho Poly Theatre, October, 1975; *Asterisk Destiny,* Morrow, 1978; *Brainfire,* Morrow, 1979; (with Jeffrey Caine under joint pseudonym Jeffrey Campbell) *The Homing,* Putnam, 1980; (under pseudonym Thomas Altman) *Kiss Daddy Goodbye,* Bantam, 1980.

WORK IN PROGRESS: A novel based on a screenplay by Brian de Palma entitled *Dressed to Kill.*

SIDELIGHTS: Black told *CA:* "I write in the hope of entertaining, to tell a story. If there are other merits—literary, stylistic, etc.—they seem like accidental by-products of the entertainment. In a review of my last book, *Brainfire,* the *New York Times* critic mentioned that I had a 'gift for understanding character.' It's good when reviewers or readers notice such stylistic subtleties as might exist, but they do seem to me secondary to the unfolding of the story, which is my main interest. I don't deliberately set out to write stylishly. Like most other writers, I rely heavily on that magic we commonly call intuition; I let that faculty do the writing for me. I don't understand it, and I don't think I even want to, but it does exist. And without it writing would be impossible."

* * *

BLACK, Roe C(oddington) 1926-

PERSONAL: Born January 15, 1926, in Milwaukee, Wis.; son of Roe R. (in business) and Avis (Coddington) Black; married Carolyn Lapp (a university assistant dean), January 9, 1947; children: Donna Black Watt, Avis E., Thomas C., Phillip R. *Education:* Dartmouth College, B.A., 1949. *Home:* 233 Kent Rd., Warminster, Pa. 18974. *Office: Farm Journal,* 230 West Washington Sq., Philadelphia, Pa. 19105.

CAREER: Black Ranches, Inc., ranch manager in San Antonio, Tex., and Aurora, Neb., 1949-53; Corn Belt Farm dailies, Aurora, Neb., field editor, 1953-64; *Farm Journal,* Philadelphia, Pa., field editor, 1964-69; *Top Operator,* Philadelphia, editor, 1969-74; *Farm Journal,* executive editor, 1974—. *Military service:* U.S. Army, 1944-46. *Member:* Agricultural History Society, Phi Beta Kappa, Dartmouth Club of Philadelphia.

WRITINGS: (Editor) *One Hundred Years of Farm Journal,* Farm Journal, 1976. Contributor of more than five hundred articles to farm journals. Field editor for *Beef Extra* and *Hog Extra,* 1964-69. Editor of *Outlook for Agribusiness,* 1974—.

SIDELIGHTS: Black comments: "History was an early interest and is ongoing. Farm and ranch experience after college and the service qualified me to write on farm and livestock subjects.

"Writing for farmers is especially challenging and rewarding because of the fundamental importance of food production and the nature of those who produce it. American farmers and their families, who comprise less than four percent of the nation's population, provide the nation with one of the best national diets in the world for a proportion of personal income that is the lowest in the world. They also produce an exportable surplus that amounts to the production of one out of three planted acres. This exportable surplus permits nations like the Soviet Union to maintain a continually improving diet for its people in spite of devastating crop disasters that occur from time to time. It also permits Third World countries to initiate and maintain programs of improved nutrition.

"Farmers need all the help they can get to do this big job, and one of the major sources of this help is the farm press. Farm families have always been isolated to some extent and they still are. Farm magazines that come directly to their homes have for over one hundred years been a prime source of information on production, management, and marketing for farmers. These journals are even more important today as the business of farming is increasingly complicated by new discoveries, government regulations and taxes, electronic record-keeping and decision-making processes, and all the complexities of modern life. They undoubtedly will be just as necessary in the future, since ninety-five percent of the farms in this country are still owned and operated by individual farm families."

* * *

BLAIR, J(oseph) Allen 1913-

PERSONAL: Born August 10, 1913, in Atlantic City, N.J.; son of George (a contractor) and Rena Ridgeway (Allen) Blair; married Elva Erma Butcher (an office worker), August 10, 1938; children: Sherril Sandra (Mrs. C. H. Harrill), Judith Anne (Mrs. Gary Janes), Cynthia Faye (Mrs. Harry Adams). *Education:* Moody Bible Institute, graduated, 1938; Bradley University, B.A., 1942; University of Dubuque, M.Th., 1943. *Office:* Glad Tidings, Inc., 2131 Eastway Dr., Charlotte, N.C. 28205.

CAREER: Ordained Presbyterian minister, 1943; pastor of Presbyterian churches in LeRoy, Minn., 1943-47, Flushing, N.Y., 1947-52, and St. Louis, Mo., 1952-56; employed by Itinerant Bible Conference Ministry, 1956-59; pastor of Presbyterian church in Charlotte, N.C., 1959-66; Glad Tidings,

Inc., Charlotte, N.C., director and radio broadcaster, 1966—. Missionary conference speaker. Director of Bible Conferences. *Awards, honors:* D.D. from Wheaton College, Wheaton, Ill., 1953.

WRITINGS: *Living Reliantly: The Twenty-Third Psalm,* Loizeaux Brothers, 1958; *Living Peacefully: First Peter,* Loizeaux Brothers, 1959; *Living Faithfully: Second Peter,* Loizeaux Brothers, 1961; *Living Victoriously: Philippians,* Loizeaux Brothers, 1962; *Living Obediently: Jonah,* Loizeaux Brothers, 1963; *Living Patiently: Job,* Loizeaux Brothers, 1966; *Living Wisely: First Corinthians,* Loizeaux Brothers, 1969; *Living Courageously: Daniel,* Loizeaux Brothers, 1971; *Profile of a Christian,* Good News Publishers, 1972; *Living Eternally: John,* Loizeaux Brothers, 1978. Author of tracts and booklets. Contributor to *Seek.* Editor of *Glad Tidings.*

WORK IN PROGRESS: A verse-by-verse exposition of John's first epistle, publication expected by Loizeaux Brothers.

SIDELIGHTS: While serving as a pastor for twenty-six years, Blair had a responsibility to communicate with the "man on the street." This responsibility prompted him to begin a radio ministry which expanded to such proportions that it was necessary for him to leave the pastorate and give full time to the radio. He told *CA:* "Since founding Glad Tidings I have been the regular speaker on its broadcast. Aired on over sixty stations throughout the United States, the program is also heard in Panama, South America, and the Caribbean area." He has also made about fifteen records and tapes on religious subjects.

Blair's books are scriptural expositions of the Bible. He aims for a practical and contemporary style in his writing. "I really had no desire to write," he commented. "In fact, I did not like to write. But after giving a message some years ago, several people encouraged me to put it in print. It was sent to the Moody Press and they put it in booklet form. This publication inspired me to write other articles, and these were followed by books. The realization came that here was another opportunity to communicate God's wonderful message of salvation through Jesus Christ."

* * *

BLANCHARD, J. Richard 1912-

PERSONAL: Born March 3, 1912, in Delphos, Kan.; son of J. Richard (in business) and Cecelia Glendora (Campbell) Blanchard; married Christine Hayward Johnson (a social worker), June 3, 1939; children: Richard Campbell, Christine H. (Mrs. Edward Ramm), Mary E. Blanchard Leonard. *Education:* University of Oklahoma, A.B., 1933; George Washington University, A.B., 1935; University of Illinois, M.S., 1953. *Politics:* Democrat. *Religion:* Unitarian-Universalist. *Home:* 441 West Eighth St., Davis, Calif. 95616. *Office:* University Library, University of California, Davis, Calif. 95616.

CAREER: Library of Congress, Washington, D.C., reference assistant, 1933-46; U.S. Department of Agriculture Library, Washington, D.C., chief of reference section, 1947-49; University of Nebraska, Lincoln, librarian at College of Agriculture and divisional librarian in science and technology, 1949-51; University of California, Davis, university librarian and member of faculty, 1951-74, university librarian emeritus, researcher, and consultant, 1974—. Instructor at Catholic University of America, 1943-44, 1946-47; member of faculty at Keio University, 1964. Adviser to governments of Chile, Argentina, and Iran, and to World Bank and United Nations Educational, Scientific and Cultural Organization. Delegate to international meetings. *Military service:* U.S. Navy, 1943-46; became lieutenant, senior grade.

MEMBER: American Library Association (member of council, 1954-56, 1960-63; head of university libraries section, 1973-74), Sierra Club, Audubon Society, California Library Association (president of college, university, and research libraries section, 1953; president of Golden Empire district, 1954), Book Club of California, Roxborough Club. *Awards, honors:* Oberly Award from American Library Association, 1959, for *The Literature of Agricultural Research.*

WRITINGS: (With Harald Ostvald) *The Literature of Agricultural Research,* University of California Press, 1958. Contributor to *Encyclopedia of Library and Information Science.* Contributor of articles and reviews to library journals.

WORK IN PROGRESS: *Guide to Sources for Agricultural and Biological Research,* publication by University of California Press expected in 1979 or 1980.

SIDELIGHTS: Blanchard writes: "I have had several assignments abroad with international organizations in connection with the development of library resources for science in other countries. One of my major interests has been providing library resources for scientists and preparing bibliographical guides to important reference works in biology and agriculture."

* * *

BLASING, Mutlu Konuk 1944-

PERSONAL: Born June 27, 1944, in Istanbul, Turkey; married Randy Blasing (a poet), August 21, 1965. *Education:* Attended Carleton College, 1963-65; College of William and Mary, B.A., 1969; Brown University, Ph.D., 1974. *Office:* Department of English, Brown University, Providence, R.I. 02912.

CAREER: Pomona College, Claremont, Calif., assistant professor of English, 1977-79; Brown University, Providence, R.I., assistant professor of American literature, 1979—.

WRITINGS: (Translator with husband, Randy Blasing) Nazim Hikmet, *Things I Didn't Know I Loved,* Persea, 1975; (translator with R. Blasing) Hikmet, *The Epic of Sheik Bedreddin and Other Poems,* Persea, 1977; *The Art of Life: Studies in American Autobiographical Literature,* University of Texas Press, 1977.

* * *

BLEEKER, Mordecia

See MORGAN, Fred Troy

* * *

BLOCK, Joel D(avid) 1943-

PERSONAL: Born July 10, 1943, in New York, N.Y.; son of Abraham and Rose (Priemazon) Block; married Gail Jaeger (a clinical social worker), June 20, 1965; children: Abbey, Fred. *Education:* State University of New York College at Oswego, B.S., 1966, M.S., 1968; Syracuse University, Ph.D., 1970; postdoctoral study at Institute for Advanced Study in Rational Psychotherapy. *Home and office:* 11 Lucille Lane, Dix Hills, N.Y. 11746. *Agent:* Lisa Collier, Collier Associates, 280 Madison Ave., New York, N.Y. 10016.

CAREER: Rikers Island Reformatory, New York City, psychologist in charge of mental health unit, 1970-71; Bureau of Child Guidance, New York City, consulting psychologist,

1971-74; clinical psychologist with private practice on Long Island, 1974—. Adjunct clinical supervisor at Institute for Advanced Study in Rational Psychotherapy. *Member:* American Association of Marriage and Family Therapists (clinical member), American Psychological Association, American Academy of Psychotherapists, Association for the Advancement of Behavior Therapy.

WRITINGS: The Other Man, the Other Woman: Understanding and Coping With Extramarital Affairs, Grosset, 1978; *To Marry Again,* Grosset, 1979; *The Friendship Experience* (working title), Macmillan, in press. Contributor to psychology journals.

WORK IN PROGRESS: "A short book of commentary on a range of psycho/social subjects—marriage, family, sex, parenting, psychotherapy, death, and so on."

SIDELIGHTS: Block practices marital and individual psychotherapy on Long Island. His consulting and research activities range from weight control to delinquent behavior. Most of Block's work as a therapist is concerned with couples. "There is a myth in this country that you only have to work on your relationship in the first few months of your marriage," he told an interviewer. "It implies that people and relationships are static. And that's the beginning of disaster."

To help people cope with marital disasters, Block wrote *The Other Man, the Other Woman.* He described the book as "an honest guide to the risks, the consequences, the emotional joys, traumas and traps generated by marriage and its most enticing complication—the extramarital affair. I think that the temptation to have an affair is a dilemma that most married people face. I try to look at it in a compassionate, nonmoralistic way."

AVOCATIONAL INTERESTS: Jui Jitsu, running.

BIOGRAPHICAL/CRITICAL SOURCES: New York Times, August 6, 1978.

* * *

BLOCK, Seymour Stanton 1918-

PERSONAL: Born May 16, 1918, in New York, N.Y.; son of Mark and Frances (Mantell) Block; married Gertrude H. Hecht, September 29, 1942; children: Sara Block Morton, Judith Block McLaughlin. *Education:* Pennsylvania State University, B.S., 1939, M.S., 1941, Ph.D., 1942. *Home:* 2906 Southwest Second Ave., Gainesville, Fla. 32607. *Office:* 217 Chemical Engineering Building, University of Florida, Gainesville, Fla. 32611.

CAREER: Joseph Seagram & Sons, Louisville, Ky., research chemist, 1942-44; University of Florida, Gainesville, assistant professor, 1944-50, associate professor, 1950-66, professor of chemical engineering, 1966—. President of Citizens Committee on Planning and Zoning, 1965-70. Member of National Research Council committee for the approval of U.S. Army research, 1976—; consultant to government and industry. *Member:* American Chemical Society (state president, 1950; member of national council, 1951), Society for Industrial Microbiology (charter member), American Association of University Professors (state president, 1960), Zero Population Growth (member of board of directors, 1970), Sierra Club, Defenders of the Environment, Planned Parenthood, and World Population, Civic Action Association (Gainesville; member of board of directors, 1958-62), Phi Beta Kappa. *Awards, honors:* Seymour S. Block Award created in his honor by Alpha Epsilon Pi, 1967.

WRITINGS: (Editor) *Disinfection, Sterilization, and Preservation,* Lea & Febiger, 1968, 2nd edition, 1977; *Benjamin Franklin: His Wit, Wisdom, and Women,* Hastings House, 1975. Editor of "Hazardous and Toxic Substances," series published by Dekker. Contributor to scientific journals.

WORK IN PROGRESS: Toxic and Hazardous Wastes, publication by Dekker expected in 1980 or 1981; a book of essays on Benjamin Franklin, publication expected in 1982 or 1983.

SIDELIGHTS: Block told *CA:* "My patents are related to improving fermentation or chemicals for use as pesticides. An interesting invention of mine, not patented, involves an electronic method for shaping cigars which reduced the time from 24 hours to 2.4 seconds. Another 'invention' was a process for growing a wild mushroom (Pleurotus ostreatus—the oyster mushroom) commercially. This was the first wild mushroom in modern times to be cultivated commercially, and is now produced in many countries in Europe and Asia.

My book, *Disinfection, Sterilization, and Preservation,* is the leading book (in sales and in size) in its field. My Benjamin Franklin book is the first book to attempt to present two sides of Franklin's nature that were his trademarks, his humor and his wisdom."

* * *

BLOS, Peter 1904-

PERSONAL: Born February 2, 1904, in Germany; married Merta Groene, 1929 (deceased); children: Peter, Jr., Lillemor. *Education:* Attended University of Munich and University of Freiburg; University of Vienna, Ph.D., 1934. *Agent:* Raines & Raines, 475 Fifth Ave., New York, N.Y. 10017. *Office:* 56 West 91st St., New York, N.Y. 10024.

CAREER: Private practice of psychoanalysis (including child analysis) in New York, N.Y., 1934—. Member of faculty at New York Psychoanalytic Institute, 1967—, and Columbia University Center for Psychoanalytic Training and Research, 1973—. Consultant to Child Guidance Institute and Court Clinic of Jewish Board of Guardians. *Member:* International Psycho-Analytic Association, American Psychoanalytic Association, Association for Child Psychoanalysis, American Orthopsychiatric Association, American Psychological Association, Society for Adolescent Psychiatry, New York Psychoanalytic Society.

WRITINGS: The Adolescent Personality, Appleton, 1941; *On Adolescence: A Psychoanalytic Interpretation,* Free Press, 1962; *The Young Adolescent: Clinical Studies,* Free Press, 1970; *The Adolescent Passage: Developmental Issues,* International Universities Press, 1979.

* * *

BOATRIGHT, Mody Coggin 1896-1970

OBITUARY NOTICE—See index for *CA* sketch: Born October 16, 1896, in Colorado City, Tex.; died August 20, 1970, in Abilene, Tex. Educator, folklorist, and author. Among Boatright's books were *Tall Tales From Texas* and *Folklore of the Oil Industry.* Obituaries and other sources: *AB Bookman's Weekly,* September 21, 1970; *Journal of American Folklore,* April, 1971.

* * *

BOGEN, James Benjamin 1935-

PERSONAL: Born August 17, 1935, in Los Angeles, Calif.; son of David and Edith (Rapaport) Bogen; married Amy Goldman (a teacher), August 30, 1959; children: Elizabeth

Alexandra Bogen Aubrey, Carlota Amelia Anne Bogen Hobbes. *Education:* Pomona College, B.A., 1957; University of California, Berkeley, M.A., Ph.D., also studied at Oxford University, 1963-64. *Office:* Pitzer College, Mills Ave., Claremont, Calif. 91711.

CAREER: Oberlin College, Oberlin, Ohio, instructor in philosophy, 1964-67; Pitzer College, Claremont, Calif., assistant professor, 1967-72, associate professor of philosophy, 1972—. Visiting professor at Indiana University, Ohio State University, Queen's University, Kingston, Ontario, and University of Utah. *Awards, honors:* Woodrow Wilson fellowship, 1962-63; James Sutton traveling fellowship, 1963-64, for Oxford University; grant from CSF, summer, 1970.

WRITINGS: (Contributor) Norman S. Care and Charles Landesman, editors, *Readings in the Theory of Action,* Indiana University Press, 1968; *Wittgenstein's Philosophy of Language,* Routledge & Kegan Paul, 1973; (contributor) J.M.E. Moravcsik, editor, *Patterns in Plato's Thought,* Dordrecht, Reidel, 1973. Contributor to philosophy journals.

WORK IN PROGRESS: Research on theory of pictorial representation (aesthetics), theory of perception, ancient philosophy, and philosophical psychology.

SIDELIGHTS: Bogen writes: "I'm presently trying to learn neuro-anatomy as a background to work I'm now doing on the mind-body problem, and plan to begin studying neurophysiology next year."

AVOCATIONAL INTERESTS: "Music. Last year I toured Poland for two weeks with Cottonmouth D'arcy's Jazz Vipers, a traditional band for which I play clarinet. The tour ended with a concert at Congress Hall in the Palace of Culture in Warsaw."

* * *

BOHI, Charles W(esley) 1940-

PERSONAL: Born November 14, 1940, in Estherville, Iowa; son of William G. (a minister) and Esther (a teacher; maiden name, Michiner) Bohi; married Lynnette Leverett (a test technician), November 27, 1970. *Education:* Simpson College, Indianola, Iowa, B.A., 1963; Case Western Reserve University, M.A., 1969. *Religion:* Methodist. *Home:* 6 Manning Dr., White River Junction, Vt. 05001. *Office:* Hanover High School, Hanover, N.H. 03755.

CAREER: Hanover High School, Hanover, N.H., history teacher, 1971—, coordinator of social studies department, 1978—. *Member:* National Education Association, Lexington Group of Transportation History.

WRITINGS: Canadian National's Western Depots, Railfare Enterprises, 1978; (with H. Roger Grant) *The Country Railroad Station in America,* Pruett, 1978. Contributor to history journals.

WORK IN PROGRESS: A study of rail abandonment in western Canada; a study of Canadian Pacific stations in western Canada.

SIDELIGHTS: Bohi writes: "When I started a hobby of photographing railroad stations, I never thought it would lead to the opportunities that it has. Because of the encouragement of my family, I was able to pursue an interesting hobby to the point of publication. Preserving a small bit of history in print has been very rewarding."

* * *

BOLSTER, John

PERSONAL: Born in London, England; son of Richard (a major in the British Army Royal Horse Artillery) and Vary Cargill (Finlay) Bolster; married Barbara Katherine Skinner (deceased); married Georgina Elizabeth Dunnell (divorced); married Rosemary Alison Pringle (an antique china restorer), January 6, 1970; children: Annabelle Bolster Swain, Marilyn Bolster Walsh, William. *Education:* Attended public school in Tonbridge, Kent, England. *Politics:* Conservative. *Religion:* Church of Scotland. *Home:* Medhurst Row Farm, Four Elms, Edenbridge, Kent TN8 6LX, England.

CAREER: Farmer, 1930-57; race car driver, 1932-49; British Broadcasting Corp. (BBC), London, England, radio and television commentator, 1951—; *Autosport,* London, contributor, technical editor, and road test driver, 1951—. *Member:* British Racing Drivers' Club, Veteran Car Club of Great Britain, Rolls-Royce Enthusiasts Club, Guild of Motoring Writers, Vintage Sports Car Club.

WRITINGS: Specials, Foulis, 1950; *Motoring Is My Business,* Autosport, 1958; *French Vintage Cars,* Autosport, 1964; *The Upper Crust,* Follett, 1976; (translator) Pierre Dumont, *French Cars, 1920-1925,* Warne, 1978; *The Rolls-Royce Silver Shadow,* Osprey, 1979; *Rolls-Royce* (in French), Lariviere, 1979; (translator) Serge Bellu, *Blue Blood,* Warne, 1979; *Lotus: The Elan and the Europa—A Collector's Guide,* Motor Racing Publications, in press.

WORK IN PROGRESS: Collaborating on a book about veteran car road tests, publication by National Motor Museum expected in 1980.

SIDELIGHTS: Bolster writes: "I have always been extremely interested in cars and engines, especially from a technical and historical point of view. I raced cars for many years, some of which I designed and built myself. In 1949 I had an enormous accident in the British *Grand Prix* and broke my neck, so I started writing and broadcasting instead.

"I still write about the technical side of racing and I also cover it historically, but I am less involved with racing nowadays as I dislike the commercial atmosphere and find advertising on cars distasteful. In any case, there are now so many new production cars to test that I have less time to attend competitive events. To keep abreast of progress I must fly all over Europe, but this is interesting and exciting work."

* * *

BOLTON, Guy (Reginald) 1884-1979

OBITUARY NOTICE—See index for *CA* sketch: Born November 23, 1884, in Brozbourne, Hertfordshire, England; died in September, 1979, in Goring-on-Thames, England. Playwright and screenwriter. Bolton, who often collaborated with P. G. Wodehouse and Oscar Hammerstein, was the author of more than fifty plays and musicals. Numbered among his best-loved works are "Lady Be Good," "Anything Goes," and "Anastasia." He also wrote the screenplays for such films as "Transatlantic" and "Weekend at the Waldorf." Obituaries and other sources: *The ASCAP Biographical Dictionary of Composers, Authors, and Publishers,* American Society of Composers, Authors and Publishers, 1966; *Longman Companion to Twentieth Century Literature,* Longman, 1970; *Modern World Drama: An Encyclopedia,* Dutton, 1972; *Who's Who in the Theatre,* 15th edition, Pitman, 1972; *New Yorker,* January 30, 1978; *New York,* February 20, 1978; *Who's Who,* 131st edition, St. Martin's, 1979; *Chicago Tribune,* September 8, 1979.

BOODY, Shirley Bright 1919-

PERSONAL: Born December 12, 1919, in Winnipeg, Manitoba, Canada; daughter of William John (a merchant) and Mae (Berrisford) Bright; married David E. Boody (a physician), September 16, 1944 (divorced, 1967); married Philip H. Dustrud (a company vice-president), November 27, 1976; children: (first marriage) Diana Boody McGinity, Pamela J. *Education:* University of California, Los Angeles, B.S., 1942. *Religion:* Episcopalian. *Home:* 7135 Hollywood Blvd., Los Angeles, Calif. 90046. *Office:* Eat Yourself Slim, Inc., 9301 Wilshire Blvd., Beverly Hills, Calif. 90210.

CAREER: Highland Alameda County Hospital, Oakland, Calif., intern in dietetics, 1943-44; St. Francis Hospital, San Francisco, Calif., staff dietitian, 1944-45; Stanford University, Stanford, Calif., instructor in diet therapy, 1945-48; private practice of diet therapy in San Francisco, 1948-66, and Beverly Hills, Calif., 1966—; Eat Yourself Slim, Inc., Beverly Hills, Calif., founder and president, 1966—; University of California, Experimental College, Los Angeles, instructor in diet therapy, 1973—. Public speaker; guest on television and radio programs. *Member:* American Dietetic Association (life member), California Dietetic Association (life member), Los Angeles Athletic Club, Sunrise Country Club. *Awards, honors:* Professional achievement award from Los Angeles Athletic Club, 1978.

WRITINGS: Eat Yourself Slim, A. S. Barnes, 1968; *One Hundred Delicious Ways to Stay Slim,* Award Books, 1969; (with Marvin O. Clausen) *The High Energy Low Budget Weight Loss Diet,* Ritchie, 1974, revised edition, 1976. Author of "Eat Yourself Slim," a national column syndicated by Copley News Service, 1974—.

WORK IN PROGRESS: Men, Money, and Marriage, publication expected in 1979; *How to Be Thin and Rich,* publication expected in 1980.

SIDELIGHTS: Shirley Boody writes: "After a divorce in 1967, I was faced with raising two teen-age daughters with no money. I opened an office for overweight people, wrote my first book, and developed my own company. Now we are planning for nation-wide expansion—a very exciting career. I have also invested in California real estate. I believe women can be highly successful in business, and will cover that subject in my next two books.

"Public interest in diet and nutrition is at an all-time high and writing about it is as natural to me as breathing. The thrill of seeing miserable obese people change into vibrant, healthy, and even richer human beings is phenomenal. I can't think of a more rewarding job. I love it."

BIOGRAPHICAL/CRITICAL SOURCES: Harper's Bazaar, February, 1975.

* * *

BORIS, Martin 1930-

PERSONAL: Born August 7, 1930, in New York, N.Y.; son of David and Jean (Enden) Boris: married Gloria Sharf (a teacher), June 13, 1952; children: Elizabeth, Adam, Haryn. *Education:* New York University, B.A., 1951, M.A., 1953; Long Island University, B.S., 1957. *Politics:* None. *Religion:* Jewish. *Home:* 1019 Northfield Rd., Woodmere, N.Y. 11598. *Agent:* Arthur Pine Associates, Inc., 1780 Broadway, New York, N.Y. 10019.

CAREER: Jewelry contractor, New York City, 1954-57; president of Madison Drug, 1957-79; Drug Masters of Hicksville, Hicksville, N.Y., president, 1969-79; Drug Masters of Hempstead, Hempstead, N.Y., president, 1971-79. Registered pharmacist. Instructor at Long Island University, 1958.

WRITINGS: Two & Two (novel), Times Books, 1979; *The Early Risers,* Crown, 1980.

WORK IN PROGRESS: Artificial Respiration, a novel, completion expected in 1982.

SIDELIGHTS: Boris writes: "Middle age and its problems currently generate my creativity. During that period in life all the errors—a past of skating on thin ice, the misjudgments, unwarranted cockiness, and abuse of nature—come home to roost. What could be more interesting than a soul in torment?"

* * *

BORKIN, Joseph 1911-1979

OBITUARY NOTICE: Born November 12, 1911, in New York, N.Y.; died of a heart attack, July 5, 1979, in Chevy Chase, Md. Lawyer, economist, and writer whose 1978 book, *The Crime and Punishment of I. G. Farben,* revealed how the huge German chemical cartel enabled Germany to wage war while cut off from supplies of raw materials. He began his career as a congressional staff assistant, moved to the antitrust division of the Justice Department in 1938, and went into the private practice of law in 1946. At the Justice Department, Borkin led an antitrust investigation that resulted in indictments against some of this country's largest corporations. A teacher of professional ethics at Catholic University's Columbia School of Law, Borkin's other writings included *Germany's Master Plan, The Corrupt Judge, Robert R. Young: The Populist of Wall Street,* and an unfinished work, *The Lawyers of Watergate*. Obituaries and other sources: *Washington Post,* July 6, 1979; *New York Times,* July 6, 1979; *Time,* July 16, 1979; *AB Bookman's Weekly,* August 6, 1979.

* * *

BORNHEIMER, Deane G(ordon) 1935-

PERSONAL: Born August 29, 1935, in Yarmouth, Maine; son of Millard G. (in business) and Gertrude (Kinney) Bornheimer; married Thelma Ernst (a guidance counselor), August 17, 1957; children: David Brian, Jeffrey Deane. *Education:* Gettysburg College, A.B., 1957; graduate study at Boston College, 1959-60; University of Maine, M.Ed., 1960; Rutgers University, Ed.D., 1967. *Home:* 34 Nassau Place, Princeton Junction, N.J. 08550. *Office:* Department of Organizational and Administrative Studies, School of Education, Health, Nursing, and Arts Professions, New York University, Washington Sq., New York, N.Y. 10003.

CAREER: High school teacher of mathematics in Falmouth, Maine, 1957-59; Gettysburg College, Gettysburg, Pa., admissions counselor, 1960-62, assistant dean of admissions, 1963-65; Princeton University, Princeton, N.J., assistant dean of Graduate School, 1965-68; New York University, New York, N.Y., assistant professor, 1968-71, associate professor of higher education, 1968—, director of higher education program, 1972—, chairman of department of interdisciplinary studies, 1973-76. *Member:* American Association for Higher Education, Association for the Study of Higher Education, American Educational Research Association, American Association of University Professors; Eastern Education Research Association.

WRITINGS: (With Gerald P. Burns and Glenn S. Dumke) *The Faculty in Higher Education,* Interstate, 1973.

WORK IN PROGRESS: Obstacles to Faculty Unionization (tentative title).

BORNTRAGER, Karl A. 1892-

PERSONAL: Born January 2, 1892, in Toinnville, Pa.; son of Adam (a farmer) and Mary (Prather) Borntrager; married Mary Casey, November 28, 1968; children: Mary Jo Borntrager Ray, Louise Borntrager Weigel. *Education:* Ohio State University, B.C.E. *Politics:* Independent. *Religion:* Protestant. *Home:* 2 Legget Rd., Bronxville, N.Y. 10708.

CAREER: Employed by New York Central Railroad, 1917-57, began as civil engineer, became division superintendent, manager of freight train operation, general manager, and vice-president. Consultant on labor matters and interstate commerce hearings, 1957-64. *Military service:* U.S. Navy, 1918-19. *Member:* Association of American Railroads (past president).

WRITINGS: *Keeping the Railroads Running,* Hastings House, 1974.

SIDELIGHTS: Borntrager writes: "Through much of my career I have been concerned with the deteriorating condition of American railroads. Following the failure of Penn-Central, I decided to write a book that would point out the reasons for its failure and the steps necessary to remedy such a situation."

* * *

BOSTICK, William A(llison) 1913-

PERSONAL: Born February 21, 1913, in Marengo, Ill.; son of William Frederick (a minister) and Alice (a teacher and historian; maiden name, Johnson) Bostick; married Mary Jane Barbey (a university professor), June 14, 1942; children: Beatrice Annette Barbey, Christopher Barbey. *Education:* Carnegie Institute of Technology (now Carnegie-Mellon University), B.S., 1934; Wayne State University, M.A., 1954; also studied at Art School of Detroit Society of Arts and Crafts and Cranbrook Academy of Art. *Politics:* Republican. *Religion:* Congregational. *Home:* 9340 West Outer Dr., Detroit, Mich. 48219.

CAREER: City of Detroit, Mich., supervisor of printing, 1940-42, 1946; Detroit Institute of Arts, Detroit, administrator and secretary, 1946-76, executive secretary of Founders Society, 1946-59; writer and calligrapher, 1976—. Instructor at Wayne State University and Detroit Society of Arts and Crafts. Past regional vice-president of American Institute of Graphic Arts. Has exhibited painting and calligraphy in solo and group shows since 1938; work represented in private and public collections, including Museum of Cranbrook Academy of Art, Detroit Institute of Arts, Detroit Public Library, and Evansville (Ind.) Museum of Arts and Sciences. *Military service:* U.S. Naval Reserve, active duty, 1942-45; designed and supervised production of maps for invasions of Sicily and Normandy; became lieutenant.

MEMBER: International Council of Museums, International Committee on Museum Security, American Association of Museums (member of accreditation committee), Midwest Museums Conference (president, 1956-57), Michigan Water Color Society (co-founder; past chairperson), Michigan Museums Association, Detroit Council of the Arts, Alliance Francaise of Detroit (vice-president), Scarab Club of Detroit (president, 1962-63), Torch Club of Detroit (president, 1956-57), Book Club of Detroit (past president). *Awards, honors:* Knight of Order of Italian Solidarity; chevalier of French Order of Arts and Letters; American Institute of Graphic Arts named *The Mysteries of Blair House* one of the best fifty books of the year in 1948 and named *Flanders in the Fifteenth Century* in 1960; fellow of Belgian Art Seminar, 1956; exhibition awards include board of directors prizes from Scarab Gold Medal Exhibitions, 1960, 1963, and Garelick's Gallery purchase prize and museum collection purchase prize from Detroit Institute of Arts, both 1963; alumni award, Wayne State University, 1976.

WRITINGS: *An Amphibious Sketch,* Hydrographic Office, U.S. Navy, 1945; (self-illustrated) *England Under G.I's Reign*, Conjure House, 1946; *A Guide to the Guarding of Cultural Property* (bilingual French-English edition), United Nations Educational, Scientific, and Cultural Organization, 1977; (self-illustrated) *A Manual on the Acquiring of a Beautiful and Legible Handwriting,* La Stampa Calligrafica, 1977, revised edition, 1980; *Applied Calligraphy,* La Stampa Calligrafica, 1980.

Illustrator: John Mason Brown, *To All Hands,* McGraw, 1943; *Many a Watchful Night,* McGraw, 1944; Aimee Crane, *Art in Armed Forces,* Hyperion Press, 1944; Roy Eastman, *Mysteries of Blair House,* Conjure House, 1948.

SIDELIGHTS: Bostick writes: "During my career at the Detroit Institute of Arts my interests were twofold: museum administration with particular emphasis on museum security and design of museum publications. I designed virtually all of the museum's catalogues and other publications from 1946 until 1971, when a publications department was established. I have been involved in international conferences on museum security and have visited Europe and the Near East numerous times.

"Since my retirement in 1976 I have been actively engaged in teaching calligraphy and art history at suburban adult education centers. I have developed my calligraphy manual for use in my classes and have calligraphed the entire text—there is not one word of *typesetting* in the whole book. I believe devoutly in Thomas Carlyle's enduring dictum: 'Certainly the Art of Writing is the most miraculous of all things man has devised.'"

* * *

BOTTOMS, Lawrence W(endell) 1908-

PERSONAL: Born April 9, 1908, in Selma, Ala.; son of William M. and Gussie (a teacher) Bottoms; married Elizabeth Stallworth (a teacher), September 9, 1933; children: Lawrence W., Jr., Jean Bottoms Perry, Leticia Bottoms Alfred, Janice Bottoms Batts. *Education:* Geneva College, A.B., 1944; graduate study at Reformed Presbyterian Seminary of Pittsburgh and at Atlanta University. *Home:* 381 Peyton Rd. S.W., Atlanta, Ga. 30311.

CAREER: Ordained Presbyterian minister, 1936; pastor of Presbyterian churches in Selma, Ala., 1935-38, Louisville, Ky., 1938-49, Miami, Fla., 1961-64, and Decatur, Ga., 1973-74; Presbyterian Church of the United States of America, regional director of Christian education, 1949-53, secretary of department of Negro work for the Assembly, 1953-64, assistant secretary of Division of Home Mission, Board of Church Extension, 1964-66, associate secretary of Division of Education and Research, 1966-69, coordinator of support services for Board of National Ministries, 1969—. Settles Lecturer at Austin Presbyterian Theological Seminary, 1960. Moderator of Presbyterian Synod of Kentucky, 1963-64, and national general assembly, 1974-75; Presbyterian member of Commission on Missionary Education, of National Council of Churches. Member of board of directors of Metropolitan Atlanta Council of Churches (president-elect), Trinity Day Care Center, Rabun Gap-Nacoochee School, and North Central Georgia Health Systems Agency. Member of international programs, including World Conference on Christian

Education, 1972. *Member:* Mental Health Association of Metropolitan Atlanta (president, 1978). *Awards, honors:* D.D. from Davis and Elkins College, 1966, from Stillman College and Oglethorpe University, both 1975, and from St. Andrews Presbyterian College, 1978; D.H.L. from Tarkio College, and LL.D. from Geneva College, both 1975.

WRITINGS: Ecclesiastes Speaks to Us Today, John Knox, 1979. Also author of *Through Conflict to Victory,* 1958. Associate editor of *Presbyterian Outlook,* 1963-64.

WORK IN PROGRESS: Daniel Speaks to Us Today.

SIDELIGHTS: Bottoms's work for the church has taken him to Brazil, Africa, Portugal, Peru, England, and Germany. He writes: "In my travels and speaking for the church, and now through writing, I try to make clear that the origin and purpose of the world cannot be found in the world—we have to look beyond the world because 'man is not lord of his own being.' Man is dependent not only on the visible world but also on the invisible and mysterious powers which influence him. Man can be delivered from those powers through the creator who is Lord of his being. I want to make clear that there needs to be a renewal of the mind. Reason is not the only reality; there is also love and faith and hope. Man is called to transcend the world by becoming a new creature."

* * *

BOUTON, James Alan 1939-
(Jim Bouton)

PERSONAL: Born March 8, 1939, in Newark, N.J.; son of George Hempstead (an executive) and Gertrude (Vischer) Bouton; married Barbara Ann Heister, December 23, 1962 (separated, 1978); children: Michael George, David Kyong Jo, Laurie Collette. *Education:* Western Michigan University, graduated, 1961; postgraduate study at Fairleigh Dickinson University, 1964-66. *Office:* c/o CBS-TV, 51 West 52nd St., New York, N.Y. 11104.

CAREER: Worked as pitcher for baseball teams, including New York Yankees, 1962-68, Seattle Pilots, 1969, Houston Astros, 1969-70, and Atlanta Braves, 1978; writer, 1970—; sportscaster for American Broadcasting Co. (ABC-TV), 1970-73, and Columbia Broadcasting System (CBS-TV), 1978—; lecturer. Actor in motion picture "The Long Goodbye," 1973, and television series "Ball Four," 1976. Delegate to Democratic National Convention, 1972. Member of National Peace Action Coalition and of board of directors of National Organization for Non-Parents; chairman of Friends of Children of Vietnam. *Awards, honors:* Named to American League All-Star Team, 1963; "hustlingest player" in Southern League, 1978.

WRITINGS—Sports: *Ball Four: My Life and Hard Times Throwing the Knuckleball in the Big Leagues* (journal), edited by Leonard Schecter, World Publishing, 1970; *I'm Glad You Didn't Take It Personally* (nonfiction), edited by Schecter, Morrow, 1971; (contributor and editor) *"I Managed Good But Boy Did They Play Bad"* (anecdotes), Playboy Press, 1973. Scriptwriter for television series "Ball Four," 1976. Contributor to periodicals, including *Esquire* and *Sports Illustrated.*

SIDELIGHTS: In 1963 and 1964 Bouton was considered one of the premier pitchers in the American League. Renowned for his competitive spirit (his teammates nicknamed him "Bulldog") and cap-twirling delivery, he twice helped pitch the New York Yankees into the World Series. In 1963, he won twenty-one games; the following year he won eighteen during the regular season and two more in the World Series. He seemed bound for baseball stardom.

But in 1965 a painful arm injury resulted in a complete turnabout of Bouton's success. He managed only four victories in nineteen decisions that year and in 1966 compiled a disappointing 3-8 record. Despite his potential, the Yankees were forced to relegate him to the minor leagues in 1967. He played briefly for the parent club in 1968 before his contract was sold to a minor league franchise in Seattle.

The move worked to Bouton's advantage, though, for that year Seattle was granted major league status. That spring, Bouton realized that he would have little chance of making the squad as the hard-thrower he had been with the Yankees. His arm was not strong enough. Instead, Bouton decided to tackle the knuckleball: a pitch as difficult to throw as it is to hit.

With guidance from pitching expert Johnny Sain, Bouton concentrated on his knuckleball and made the team as a reliever. That year he played in fifty-seven games for the Pilots and was among their most often used pitchers. Late in the season his contract was purchased by the pennant-contending Houston Astros of the National League. He pitched in several key games for the Astros, and although they finished out of the race, the team ended the season with their best record ever.

In 1970, Bouton was still with the Astros. However, his knuckleball became unmanageable and he was sent to the minor league team in Oklahoma City. His first two appearances there resulted in defeats for his team and finally, in early August, he retired. "You see," Bouton wrote earlier, "you spend a good piece of your life gripping a baseball and in the end it turns out that it was the other way around."

But 1970 saw the beginning of a new career for Bouton. Throughout the 1969 season Bouton had kept a daily journal of his activities as a ballplayer. When the journal was published as *Ball Four,* it shook the sports world as an exposé of life in the "big leagues." Bouton portrayed his teammates as men not above "peeping toms," as men who not only like to play baseball but to drink, carouse, and play practical jokes. Because of accurate but unflattering depictions in the book, Bouton was roundly condemned by the baseball hierarchy. Commissioner Bowie Kuhn reprimanded him for his actions, ballplayers indignantly called him a "traitor" and a "liar," sportswriter Dick Young called him a "social leper," and one team actually burned the book in their locker room.

The critics, however, had praise for the candid work. Roger Angell wrote that Bouton "should be celebrated as the author of the most intelligent and entertaining participant's account of the national pastime yet published." He added: "His book never settles into sportswriting cliches of debunking and anecdotage. What he has given us, rather, is a rare view of a highly complex public profession seen from the innermost inside along with an even more rewarding inside view of an ironic and courageous mind." Angell summed up *Ball Four* as "very likely, the funniest book of the year." Rex Lardner bestowed similar praise, declaring that *Ball Four* "is a gem of honest, goodnaturedly biased reporting."

Bouton's new career landed him still another one as a sportscaster in New York alongside Howard Cosell. Their needling repartee served to boost that station's ratings. Bouton also followed the success of *Ball Four* with another book, *I'm Glad You Didn't Take It Personally,* which chronicled not only peer reaction to *Ball Four* but his dealings with publishers, the press, and his new co-workers, including Cosell.

After appearances in Robert Altman's film "The Long Goodbye" and the television series "Ball Four," Bouton decided to return to baseball. His comeback began inauspiciously enough when he was refused a tryout by every major league team. A team in Knoxville, Tennessee, finally took a chance with him, but he ended up losing six games without a victory. Undaunted, Bouton turned to pitching for a team in Mexico before finishing the year with another team in Portland.

That winter Bouton became interested in Ted Turner, owner of the Atlanta Braves, through an article he had read. He arranged a meeting and afterwards Turner found a place for him with a minor league team. Once he began pitching again, he became the best pitcher in the Braves' system. "I threw a one-hitter and a two-hitter and a 13-inning shutout," he recalled, "pitching in 100 degree heat after all-night bus rides and with two days' rest. . . . The Atlanta Braves had to call me up."

Bouton's big opportunity came when he was handed the starting assignment in a game between the Braves and their minor league players. With Turner umpiring at third base and an overflow crowd, Bouton responded by striking out seven Atlanta hitters and allowing only one run. The Braves' management was impressed, and Bouton was reassigned to another minor league team. Again Bouton pitched well and towards the end of the season he was called to the Atlanta Braves.

The Braves' schedule involved games against three teams competing for a playoff position, the Dodgers, Reds, and Giants. Starting his first game in eight years against a major league team, the Dodgers, Bouton performed brilliantly in the early innings. Nursing a no-hitter, his timing was disrupted in the fourth inning when an argument broke out between an opposing batter and the umpire. When the game recommenced, Bouton surrendered the lead and was replaced. Afterwards Dodger players fumed about facing Bouton. Dave Lopes, who had struck out his first time against Bouton but later hit a home run, stated: "I mean, I don't have anything against Jim Bouton personally, but you . . . don't know what it's like to go up against somebody like that. It's *rough*. He doesn't have it anymore."

In his next start, Bouton defeated the San Francisco Giants 4-1, but again the opposition failed to be impressed. Mike Ivie, who went hitless against him, called Bouton "terrible." Bouton's last decision was a defeat against Cincinnati, 2-1, despite surrendering only five hits. After the game, Reds' manager Sparky Anderson declared, "We didn't even hit a ball hard off him. We got two runs we shouldn't have gotten."

Bouton retired after the 1978 season and resumed his career as a writer and sportscaster. When he picked up a baseball later, he noted that the grip felt unfamiliar. "In the past I would have panicked," he wrote. "Now I was different. This time I simply smiled. Now I could release my grip on the baseball. It didn't matter anymore. Baseball had released its grip on me. And it was O.K."

BIOGRAPHICAL/CRITICAL SOURCES: Jim Bouton, *Ball Four: My Life and Hard Times Throwing the Knuckleball in the Big Leagues,* World Publishing, 1970; *New Yorker,* July 25, 1970; *New York Times Book Review,* July 26, 1970, July 11, 1971; Bouton, *I'm Glad You Didn't Take It Personally,* Morrow, 1971; *Newsweek,* June 5, 1978; *New Times,* June 12, 1978, October 2, 1978; *Sports Illustrated,* September 18, 1978, April 9, 1979.

—Sketch by Les Stone

BOUTON, Jim
See BOUTON, James Alan

* * *

BOWDEN, Joan Chase 1925-
(Joan Chase Bacon; Jane Godfrey, Charlotte Graham, Kathryn Kenny, pseudonyms)

PERSONAL: Born May 1, 1925, in London, England; came to the United States in 1953, naturalized citizen, 1960; daughter of Charles William Chase (an accountant) and Adelaide M. F. (Godfrey) Bacon; married Archie N. Bowden, November 11, 1948; children: Frances, Andrew, Pamela. *Education:* Attended school in London, England. *Religion:* Episcopal. *Residence:* San Diego, Calif. *Address:* c/o Macmillan Publishing Co., 866 Third Ave., New York, N.Y. 10022.

CAREER: Stenographer in London, England, 1943-47, private secretary, 1947-49; London Films Association, London, England, executive secretary, 1949-50; Minneapolis-Honeywell Corp., Toronto, Ontario, executive secretary, 1951-53; writer for children, 1969—. Instructor at Institute of Children's Literature; guest lecturer at college writing conferences. *Member:* Authors League of America, Society of Children's Book Writers, National League of American Pen Women.

WRITINGS—All juveniles; under name Joan Chase Bowden: *A New Home for Snowball,* Golden Press, 1974; *Who Took the Top Hat Trick?,* Golden Press, 1974; *Bear's Surprise Party,* Golden Press, 1975; *Elizabeth and the Magic Lamp,* Golden Press, 1975; *The Waltons and the Birthday Present,* Golden Press, 1975; *The Ice Cream Parade,* Golden Press, 1976; *The Backward Picnic,* Golden Press, 1976; *The Island Adventure,* Golden Press, 1976; *The Bouncy Baby Bunny Finds His Bed,* Golden Press, 1976; *Something Wonderful Happened,* Concordia, 1977; *Little Gray Rabbit,* Golden Press, 1979; *The Bean Boy,* Macmillan, 1979; *Why the Tides Ebb and Flow,* Houghton, 1979; *Strong John,* Macmillan, 1980.

Under name Joan Chase Bacon: *Thin Arnold,* Western, 1970; *The Pussycat Tiger,* Golden Press, 1972; *A Hat for the Queen,* Golden Press, 1974; *Boo and the Flying Flews,* Golden Press, 1974.

Under pseudonym Jane Godfrey: *The Dinosaur Adventure,* Golden Press, 1975.

Under pseudonym Charlotte Graham: *Elizabeth and the Magic Lamp,* Western, 1975.

Under pseudonym Kathryn Kenny: *The Mystery of the Headless Horseman,* Golden Press, 1979; *The Mystery of the Ghostly Galleon,* Golden Press, 1979.

Also author of *Mystery of the Midnight Marauder* (juvenile), Golden Press, 1980; *Mystery of the Whispering Bride* (juvenile), Golden Press, 1980; *The Prince and the Dairymaid* (juvenile), Western, 1980; and *My Measuring Book* (juvenile), Golden Press, 1980. Contributor to adult and children's magazines, including *Humpty Dumpty's, Happy Times, Wonder Time,* and *The Friend.*

SIDELIGHTS: Joan Bowden writes: "I am a transplanted American citizen who was born in London on May 1, 1925. On this date in England, most schoolchildren dance around the maypole fa-la to celebrate May Day. Being more enchanted with maypole-dancing than with writing of any kind, my progress through school was unremarkable—if you discount the fact that World War II broke out in Europe just as I was about to begin my senior year in high school.

"In spite of Hitler's shenanigans, I received a thorough grounding in the use of the English language.

"My children have, I think, inspired most of my writing. Their trials and tribulations, their triumphs and defeats, their likes and dislikes in reading, have always been watched closely.

"I began writing professionally in 1968 and sold the first children's book I ever wrote. It took me another two years to discover what I had done right! I learned, at last, by applying the old adage—seat of the pants to the seat of the chair.

"Some of my books were written for the beginning reader, a favorite audience of mine. If a child can't read, I feel he is handicapped for the rest of his life. My books are usually entertaining and have the appearance of having been rushed through my typewriter in two minutes flat, which, of course, they are not. Throughout my story, I'm trying to beckon and encourage the child to read on to discover for himself what happens next. For some children reading is difficult. These youngsters need the special encouragement which comes from reading a story entirely on their own."

* * *

BOWDITCH, James L(owell) 1939-

PERSONAL: Born January 30, 1939, in Boston, Mass.; son of Richard Lyon (in business) and Mabel Lowell (Rantoul) Bowditch; married Felicity Joan Sexton (a teacher), April 4, 1964; children: Matthew and Andrew (twins), Sarah. *Education:* Yale University, B.A., 1961; Western Michigan University, M.A., 1965; Purdue University, Ph.D., 1969. *Politics:* Democrat. *Religion:* Episcopalian. *Home:* 103 Loring Rd., Weston, Mass. 02193. *Office:* School of Management, Boston College, Chestnut Hill, Mass. 02167.

CAREER: Boston College, Chestnut Hill, Mass., assistant professor, 1969-72, associate professor of management, 1972—. Chairperson of board of trustees of Meadowbrook School of Weston and campus ministry committee of Episcopal Diocese of Massachusetts. *Military service:* U.S. Army, 1961-64; became first lieutenant. *Member:* American Psychological Association, Academy of Management, Sigma Xi, Beta Gamma Sigma. *Awards, honors:* Grant from Carnegie-Mellon Foundation, 1975.

WRITINGS: (With E. F. Huse) *Behavior in Organizations: A Systems Approach to Managing,* Addison-Wesley, 1973, 2nd edition, 1977; (with Huse and Dalmar Fisher) *Readings on Behavior in Organizations,* Addison-Wesley, 1975.

WORK IN PROGRESS: Primer in Organizational Behavior.

SIDELIGHTS: Bowditch writes: "In writing a textbook you have to strike the delicate balance between being interesting to the student and rigorous enough for the professor."

* * *

BOWER, Eli M(ichael) 1917-

PERSONAL: Born October 6, 1917, in New York, N.Y. *Education:* New York University, B.S., 1937; Columbia University, M.A., 1947; Stanford University, Ed.D., 1954. *Home:* 23 Norwood Ave., Kensington, Calif. 94707. *Office:* School of Education, University of California, Berkeley, Calif. 94720.

CAREER: Teacher of biology and chemistry in Hawthorne, N.Y., 1939-40; U.S. Coast and Geodetic Survey, Tampa, Fla., photogrammetric engineer, 1942-43; high school teacher of biology and chemistry, and counselor in Tuckahoe, N.Y., 1946-47; Coalinga High School and Junior College, Coalinga, Calif., teacher of biology and health, and counselor, 1947-48; consulting psychologist for public schools in Visalia, Calif., 1948-50; California State Department of Education, Sacramento, consultant, 1950-57, research coordinator, 1957-60; California State Department of Mental Hygiene, Sacramento, deputy director, 1960-62; National Institute of Mental Health, Bethesda, Md., consultant on mental health in education, 1962-68; University of California, Berkeley, professor of educational psychology, 1968—, associate dean of Graduate Division and director of health and medical sciences, 1974-76. *Military service:* U.S. Navy, in photographic intelligence, 1943-46; became lieutenant senior grade.

MEMBER: American Orthopsychiatric Association (president, 1971-72), American Association on Mental Deficiency (fellow), American Psychological Association (fellow), Council for Exceptional Children. *Awards, honors:* Fulbright fellowship for Bogazici University, 1976-77.

WRITINGS: A Process for Early Identification of Emotionally Disturbed Children, California State Department of Education, 1958; *Early Identification of Emotionally Handicapped Children in School,* C. C Thomas, 1960, 2nd edition, 1969; *Fostering Maximum Growth in Children,* National Education Association, 1965; (with W. G. Hollister) *Behavioral Science Frontiers in Education,* Wiley, 1967; (editor and contributor) *Orthopsychiatry and Education,* Wayne State University Press, 1971; (editor with L. S. Blackman, Gerald Caplan, and S. R. Roen) J. Fassler, *One Little Girl* (juvenile), Behavioral Publications, 1971; (editor with Blackman, Caplan, and Roen) Fassler, *My Grandpa Died Today* (juvenile), Behavioral Publications, 1971; (editor with Blackman, Caplan, and Roen) Fassler, *I Have Feelings* (juvenile), Behavioral Publications, 1971; *Teachers Talk About Their Feelings,* National Institute of Mental Health, 1973; (with Kendra Bersamin, Amy Fine, and Joy Carlson) *Learning to Play, Playing to Learn,* School of Education, University of California, Berkeley, 1974; (editor with Loyda Shears) *Games in Education and Development,* C. C Thomas, 1974; *Games in Turkey,* Redhouse Press, 1977.

Contributor: James Magary and John R. Eichorn, editors, *The Exceptional Child: A Book of Readings,* Holt, 1960; Gerald Caplan, editor, *Prevention of Mental Disorders in Children,* Basic Books, 1960; E. Phillips Trapp and Philip Himelstein, editors, *Readings on the Exceptional Child: Research and Theory,* Appleton, 1961; Magary, editor, *School Psychology,* Prentice-Hall, 1962; *Mental Health and Learning,* Association for Supervision and Curriculum Development, 1966; Pearl Berkowitz and Esther Rothman, editors, *Public Education for Disturbed Children in New York City,* C. C Thomas, 1966; *Social Deviancy,* National Society for the Study of Education, 1966; H. F. Clarizio, editor, *Mental Health and the Educative Process: Selected Readings,* Rand McNally, 1969.

L. A. Faas, editor, *The Emotionally Disturbed Child: A Book of Readings,* C. C Thomas, 1970; F. D. Holt and R. H. Kicklighter, editors, *Psychological Services in the Schools,* W. C. Brown, 1971; G. D. Mills, editor, *Elementary School Guidance and Counseling,* Random House, 1971; R. L. Jones, editor, *Problems and Issues in the Education of Exceptional Children,* Houghton, 1971; N. J. Long, W. C. Morse, and R. G. Newman, editors, *Conflict in the Classroom: The Education of Children With Problems,* Wadsworth, 2nd edition (Bower was not included in 1st edition), 1971; Morse and C. M. Wingo, editors, *Classroom Psychology: Readings in Educational Psychology,* Scott, Foresman, 3rd edition (Bower was not included in earlier editions),

1971; Forest B. Tyler, editor, *Community Trends in Community Psychology,* University of Maryland Press, 1972; William L. Claiborn and Robert Cohen, editors, *School Intervention,* Behavioral Publications, 1973; Sol Gordon and G. J. Williams, editors, *Clinical Child Psychology,* Behavioral Publications, 1974; George Albee, editor, *Promoting Social Competence and Coping in Children,* New England Press, 1977. Also contributor to *Mainstreaming,* edited by Keith Beery, and to *Prevention of Emotional Problems in Children,* edited by S. C. Smith.

Contributor to *Handbook of Community Mental Health* and *Handbook of School Psychological Services.* Contributor of about fifty articles and reviews to psychology, education, and mental health journals. Editor of *American Journal of Orthopsychiatry,* 1973-78; associate editor of *Community Mental Health Journal, Professional Psychology, Psychology in the Schools,* and *People Watching.*

SIDELIGHTS: Bower's special areas of interest are emotionally disturbed children, mental retardation, sensory defects, mental health programs, and affective training (including games, role playing, sensitivity training, and play therapy).

* * *

BOWMAN, Raymond Albert 1903-1979

OBITUARY NOTICE: Born April 14, 1903, in Chicago, Ill.; died October 29, 1979, in Harvard, Ill. Educator, international scholar of Near Eastern studies, and author. A professor at the University of Chicago, Bowman served as chairman of the university's department of Near Eastern languages and civilizations from 1962 to 1968. He was an authority on the Semitic language of Aramaic and the author of *Aramaic Ritual Texts From Persepolis.* Obituaries and other sources: *Who's Who in America,* 38th edition, Marquis, 1974; *Directory of American Scholars,* Volume III: *Foreign Languages, Linguistics, and Philology,* 6th edition, Bowker, 1974; *Chicago Tribune,* October 31, 1979.

* * *

BOYLE, Hal
See BOYLE, Harold V(incent)

* * *

BOYLE, Harold V(incent) 1911-1974
(Hal Boyle)

OBITUARY NOTICE: Born February 21, 1911, in Kansas City, Mo.; died April 1, 1974. Journalist. Boyle was affiliated with the Associated Press for over forty-five years. He was a foreign correspondent during World War II in Europe and the Pacific, and later in Korea and Vietnam. His column written during World War II, "Leaves From a War Correspondent's Notebook," appeared in more than four hundred Associated Press newspapers. Boyle won a Pulitzer Prize for Distinguished Correspondence in 1945. Obituaries and other sources: *Current Biography,* 1945, May, 1974; *New York Times,* April 2, 1974.

* * *

BRADFORD, Barbara Taylor 1933-

PERSONAL: Born in 1933, in Leeds, Yorkshire, England; came to the United States in 1964; daughter of Winston and Freda (Walker) Taylor; married Robert Bradford. *Home:* 2 East 86th St., New York, N.Y. 10028.

CAREER: Yorkshire Evening Post, Yorkshire, England, reporter, 1949-51, women's editor, 1951-53; *Woman's Own,* London, England, fashion editor, 1953-54; *London Evening News,* London, columnist, 1955-57; executive editor for a publication in London, 1959-62; *Woman,* London, features editor, 1962-64; editor for National Design Center, 1964-65; Newsday Specials, Garden City, Long Island, N.Y., syndicated columnist, 1966—; writer.

WRITINGS: (Editor) *Children's Stories of the Bible From the Old Testament,* Lion Press, c. 1966; (editor) *Children's Stories of Jesus From the New Testament,* Lion Press, c. 1966; (editor) Samuel Nisenson, *The Dictionary of One Thousand and One Famous People,* Lion Press, 1966; *A Garland of Children's Verse,* Lion Press, 1968; *The Complete Encyclopedia of Homemaking Ideas,* Meredith Press, 1968; *How to Be the Perfect Wife: Etiquette to Please Him,* Essandess, 1969; *How to Be the Perfect Wife: Entertaining to Please Him,* Essandess, 1969; *How to Be the Perfect Wife: Fashions That Please Him,* Essandess, c. 1970; *Easy Steps to Successful Decorating,* Simon & Schuster, 1971; *How to Solve Your Decorating Problems,* Simon & Schuster, 1976; *Decorating Ideas for Casual Living,* Simon & Schuster, c. 1977; *Making Space Grow,* Simon & Schuster, 1979; *A Woman of Substance* (novel; alternate selection of Doubleday Book Club and Literary Guild), Doubleday, 1979. Editor-in-chief of "Guide to Home Decorating Ideas," 1966—.

WORK IN PROGRESS: A novel.

SIDELIGHTS: Although Bradford was only twelve years old when she sold her first short story, she went on to publish many nonfiction books before turning to novels. Describing her first lengthy work of fiction—her latest book to date—Bradford wrote: "What I set out to do in 'A Woman of Substance' was tell the story of a strong woman, Emma Harte, who overcomes all the obstacles of her lowly birth, lack of education, the prejudices and conventions of her time, and countless adversities, to rise to triumph over all. Through her iron will, her passionate determination, her brains and her audacity she forges a business empire out of nothing and founds a dynasty as unconventional as she is herself. The novel is the saga of Emma Harte's life, from her impoverished youth as a servant, through marriages, love affairs, children and her dramatic and rapid ascension in the business world." The story takes place in Yorkshire, the English county of Bradford's childhood.

As author of what Jan Frazer called "a wonderfully romantic novel," Bradford has been hailed as the British counterpart to Helen Van Slyke. In a review of *A Woman of Substance,* Jo Modert commented that "though less than profound, this first novel is substantial," adding that, overall, Bradford "writes well and vividly." Maude McDaniel, on the other hand, found in the story "no growth . . . and no depth, and still worse, no originality." But the book is obviously a result of "meticulous historical research," as Georgia Zeedick pointed out. "Early 20th century Leeds literally marches in front of the reader's chair. The descriptions are excellent."

BIOGRAPHICAL/CRITICAL SOURCES: Atlanta Journal, June 8, 1979; *Daily Messenger,* June 11, 1979; *Washington Post,* June 12, 1979; *St. Louis Post-Dispatch,* June 24, 1979; *Columbus Dispatch,* July 8, 1979; *Naples Daily News,* July 29, 1979; *New York Times Book Review,* September 9, 1979.*

* * *

BRADFORD, Richard H(eadlee) 1938-

PERSONAL: Born April 14, 1938, in Waynesburg, Pa.; son

of Charles Ward (an auditor) and Bertha (a teacher; maiden name, Headlee) Bradford; married Mary Elizabeth Heffernen (a librarian), August 27, 1966. *Education:* Pennsylvania State University, B.A., 1962; Indiana University, M.A., 1964, Ph.D., 1973. *Politics:* Independent. *Home:* 1410 Linden Lane, Oak Hill, W.Va. 25901. *Office:* Department of History, West Virginia Institute of Technology, Montgomery, W.Va. 25136.

CAREER: Meramec Community College, St. Louis, Mo., instructor in history, 1964-66; West Virginia Institute of Technology, Montgomery, assistant professor, 1968-73, associate professor, 1973-78, professor of history, 1978—. *Military service:* U.S. Marine Corps, 1956-68. *Member:* American Historical Association, Organization of American Historians, Society for Historians of American Foreign Relations.

WRITINGS: The "Virginius" Affair, Colorado Associated University Press, 1979. Author of "Petticoats" (three-act play). Contributor to history journals.

WORK IN PROGRESS: A novel dealing with Sir William Johnson and the Mohawk Indians during the eighteenth century; research on twentieth-century American diplomacy.

SIDELIGHTS: Bradford writes: "The study of history is both vocation and avocation with me. I hope to write history both in fictional and factual form in the future. Regardless of whether I am writing fiction or fact, I prefer stories that deal with strong individuals in conflict with each other, with their environment, and with their times."

AVOCATIONAL INTERESTS: Travel (to spots of historical interest), swimming, baking bread, theatre (actor in amateur productions), films.

* * *

BRADLEY, (Edward) Sculley 1897-

PERSONAL: Born January 4, 1897, in Philadelphia, Pa.; son of Stephen Edward (in sales) and Annette Evelyn (Palmer) Bradley; married Anna Marguerite Cashner, June 11, 1921; children: Deborah Bradley Oberholtzer, Alison Bradley Wilhelm. *Education:* University of Pennsylvania, B.A., 1919, M.A., 1920, Ph.D., 1925. *Religion:* Society of Friends (Quakers). *Home address:* Kendal at Longwood, Kennett Square, Pa. 19348.

CAREER: University of Pennsylvania, Philadelphia, instructor, 1919-26, assistant professor, 1926-37, associate professor, 1937-40, professor of English, 1940-67, vice-provost, 1956-63, moderator of Radio Forum on Public Opinion, 1943-49; writer, 1967-73. Visiting professor at Duke University, 1932, 1937, 1941, Northwestern University, 1938, and University of Southern California, 1940; lecturer at Ogontz School, 1926-32, Rosemont College, 1930-33, and Upton School of Drama, 1930-34. Past member of board of directors of Friends Hospital, Philadelphia, Pa.; member of board of trustees of Walt Whitman Foundation. *Military service:* U.S. Navy, 1918-19. *Member:* Modern Language Association of America, Society for American Studies (fellow), American Association of University Professors, Phi Beta Kappa, Alpha Chi Rho, Delta Sigma Rho, Lenape Club. *Awards, honors:* LL.D. from Baylor University, 1950.

WRITINGS: George Henry Boker: Poet and Patriot, University of Pennsylania Press, 1927, reprinted, AMS Press, 1969; *Henry Charles Lea,* University of Pennsylvania Press, 1931.

Editor: George Henry Boker, *The Sonnets: A Sequence on Profane Love,* University of Pennsylvania Press, 1929; Boker, *Nydia: A Tragic Play,* University of Pennsylvania Press, 1929, reprinted, 1974; Boker, *Glaucus and Other Plays,* Princeton University Press, 1940, reprinted, 1972; (with John Stevenson) *Walt Whitman's Backward Glances: A Backward Glance O'er Travel'd Roads,* University of Pennsylvania Press, 1947, reprinted, Books for Libraries, 1968; Walt Whitman, *Leaves of Grass and Selected Prose,* Rinehart, 1949; (with Richmond Croom Beatty and E. Hudson Long) *The American Tradition in Literature,* two volumes, Norton, 1956, 4th edition, Grosset, 1974, abridged edition, 1956, 4th abridged edition, Grosset, 1974; Horace Traubel, *With Walt Whitman in Camden, January 21-April 7, 1889,* Southern Illinois University Press, 1959; Nathaniel Hawthorne, *The Scarlet Letter: An Authoritative Text, Backgrounds and Sources, Criticism,* Norton, 1962, 2nd edition, 1978; Stephen Crane, *The Red Badge of Courage,* Norton, 1962, 2nd edition, 1976; (with Long) Samuel Langhorne Clemens, *The Adventures of Huckleberry Finn,* Norton, 1962, 2nd edition, 1977; (with Harold W. Blodgett) *Walt Whitman: Comprehensive Reader's Edition,* New York University Press, 1965; (with Blodgett) Whitman, *Leaves of Grass,* Norton, 1973. General editor of *Collected Writings of Walt Whitman,* fourteen volumes.

Contributor to *Literary History of the United States,* 1948, *Revolt in the Arts: Benjamin Franklin Lectures,* 1950, and to *A Time of Harvest: American Literature, 1910-60,* 1962. Contributor to *Collier's Encyclopedia* and *Chambers's Encyclopedia.* Contributor to literature journals. Assistant literary editor of *Philadelphia Record,* 1930-31; member of advisory editorial board of *American Literature,* 1932-34, 1939-43.

* * *

BRADY, Peter
See DANIELS, Norman

* * *

BRAMBLE, Forbes 1939-

PERSONAL: Born April 11, 1939, in Hornchurch, England; son of Stanley T. (a town planner) and Eleanor (Jackson) Bramble; married Anna Owen, September 19, 1964; children: Matthew, Blane, James. *Education:* University of London, B.A. (with honors), 1963. *Home:* 59 Mercers Rd., London N.19, England. *Agent:* Curtis Brown Ltd., 1 Craven Hill, London W.2, England. *Office:* Forbes Bramble Associates, 39 Bedford Sq., London W.C.1, England.

CAREER: Chamberlin, Powell & Bon (architects), London, England, project architect, 1963-69; Madame Tussaud's, London, company architect, 1969-72; Bickerdike, Allen, Bramble—Architects, London, partner, 1972-78; Forbes Bramble Associates, (architects, planners, and building consultants) London, partner and principal, 1978—. *Member:* Royal Institute of British Architects. *Awards, honors:* Writing award from Scottish Arts Council, 1973, for *Stone.*

WRITINGS: The Dice (one-act play; first produced at Edinburgh Festival Fringe, 1960), Samuel French, 1962, Harrap, 1963; *Stone* (novel), Wildwood House, 1973; *The Strange Case of Deacon Brodie* (historical novel), Hamish Hamilton, 1975, Coward, 1976; *Regent Square* (novel), Coward, 1977; *King's Bench* (novel; sequel to *Regent Square),* Hamish Hamilton, 1979.

Unpublished plays: "When Silver Drinks" (three-act), first aired by Granada TV, Manchester, England, 1962; "The Two-Timers" (three-act), first produced in Kassel, Germany at Staats Theater, 1963.

Work represented in anthologies, including *Essays on Local Government Enterprise,* 1964, and *Mehr Gespenster,* Diogenes Verlag, 1978. Theater architecture critic for *Theatre Quarterly,* 1971-73.

WORK IN PROGRESS: A book about the people of Scotland, publication by Hamish Hamilton expected in 1980.

SIDELIGHTS: Bramble writes: "I am an architect and writer, enjoying the variety of both careers, and unwilling to give up either for the other."

BIOGRAPHICAL/CRITICAL SOURCES: John Russell Taylor, *Anger and After,* Pelican, 1963.

* * *

BRANNER, Hans Christian 1903-1966

OBITUARY NOTICE: Born June 23, 1903, in Ordrup, Denmark; died April 24, 1966, in Copenhagen, Denmark. Novelist, short story writer, and playwright. Branner studied the psychological motivations and actions of the human condition in his writings. His works often deal with everyday people and everyday situations at a single moment of pain or pleasure. Branner is the author of *No Man Knows the Night, The Riding Master,* and *Two Minutes of Silence.* Obituaries and other sources: *Encyclopedia of World Literature in the Twentieth Century,* updated edition, Ungar, 1967; *Everyman's Dictionary of European Writers,* Dent & Sons, 1968; *The Penguin Companion to European Literature,* McGraw, 1969; *Twentieth Century Writing: A Reader's Guide to Contemporary Literature,* Transatlantic, 1969; *Cassell's Encyclopaedia of World Literature,* revised edition, Morrow, 1973; *World Authors, 1950-1970,* Wilson, 1975.

* * *

BRAVERMAN, Kate 1950-

PERSONAL: Born February 5, 1950, in Philadelphia, Pa.; daughter of Irving D. and Millicent (an executive) Braverman. *Education:* University of California, Berkeley, B.A., 1971. *Politics:* "Radical." *Religion:* Jewish. *Agent:* George Discant, 9255 Sunset Blvd., Los Angeles, Calif. 90069. *Office:* 9255 Sunset Blvd., #308, Los Angeles, Calif. 90069.

CAREER: Free-lance writer, 1971—. Gives poetry readings; conducts creative writing workshops.

WRITINGS: *Milk Run* (poems), Momentum Press, 1977; (editor) *Cameos* (poetry anthology), Crossing Press, 1978; (editor) *Ten Los Angeles Poets* (anthology), Momentum Press, 1978; *Lithium for Medea* (novel), Harper, 1979; *Poems,* Harper, 1979. Contributor of poems and reviews to literary magazines and newspapers.

WORK IN PROGRESS: Poems.

SIDELIGHTS: Braverman's first novel, *Lithium for Medea,* is the story of Rose, a woman trying to cope with a parasitic relationship and parents (one of whom is afflicted with cancer) who constantly battle. Katha Pollitt declares that Braverman writes with "energy to burn" and with "passion and a sense of urgency." Pollitt complains that Braverman's attributes sometimes lead to overwriting. "Rose," notes Pollitt, "when elated or high, is prone to remarks like, 'I am windsong.'"

Pollitt reserves most of the praise for Braverman's knack for characterization. "The vigor with which Miss Braverman has endowed Rose's parents undermines what little sympathy one might otherwise have felt for Rose's attempts to indict them," Pollitt writes. "While that may not have been the effect Miss Braverman was seeking, it suggests a latent gift for naturalism that I hope she won't neglect. Angst is easy. Only a novelist of real perception and wide sympathies could have invented this pair."

BIOGRAPHICAL/CRITICAL SOURCES: *New York Times Book Review,* August 5, 1979.

* * *

BRENNAN, Richard O(liver) 1916-

PERSONAL: Born in 1916, in Maplehill, Kan.; son of William Michael and Cora (Alzora) Brennan. *Education:* Missouri College of Pharmacy, Ph.G., 1932; attended Kansas City Junior College, 1933; Kansas City College of Osteopathic Medicine, D.O., 1936; Kansas City University of Physicians and Surgeons, M.D., D.P.H., 1939. *Agent:* Richard Curtis Literary Agency, 156 East 52nd St., New York, N.Y. 10022.

CAREER: Bush Hospital, Harper, Kan., intern, 1937; Lakeside Hospital, Kansas City, Mo., intern, 1937; Urological Clinic, Philadelphia, Pa., resident, 1938; Presbyterian Hospital, Philadelphia, resident, 1938; Warren Urological Clinic, Kansas City, preceptee, 1939; Houston Osteopathic Medical Hospital, Houston, Tex., chief of staff, 1950; Doctors Hospital, Houston, member of staff, 1952-79; Bellevue Metabolic Clinic, director, 1979—. Instructor at Kansas City College of Osteopathic Medicine, 1937, and Kansas City University of Physicians and Surgeons, 1939; visiting professor at Oklahoma College of Osteopathic Medicine, 1978. Founder and president of International Preventive Medicine Foundation; co-founder and past president of National Child Health Conference. Lecturer to professional and lay audiences; guest on several hundred television and radio programs, including "Today Show." Testified before U.S. Congress.

MEMBER: International College of Applied Nutrition (fellow), International Academy of Preventive Medicine (fellow; founder and chairman emeritus of board of directors), International Metabolic Society (founding member; member of board of directors), International Academy of Applied Nutrition, World Medical Association, American College of General Practitioners in Osteopathic Medicine and Surgery (fellow; past national president), American College of General Practitioners (honorary life member), American Osteopathic Association (life member), American Osteopathic College of Preventive Medicine (past president), American Osteopathic Society of Rheumatic Diseases (past vice-president), American Public Health Association, American Geriatric Society, American Clinical Society of Arthritis, American Osteopathic College of Proctology, American Medical Writers Association, American Medical Society of Vienna, Authors Guild, Authors League of America, Orthomolecular Psychiatric Society, Texas Association of Osteopathic Medicine, Texas Society of General Practitioners (founder; past president), Texas Society of Osteopathic Radiologists (founder; past president), Jackson County Society of Osteopathic Medicine (past president), Harris County Society of Osteopathic Medicine (past president), Psi Sigma Alpha, Alumni of Kansas City College of Osteopathic Medicine (founder; past president), Central Lions Club (past member of board of directors), Houston Rotary Club, Arabian Shrine. *Awards, honors:* Founders award from International Academy of Preventive Medicine, 1971; appreciation award from International Preventive Medicine Foundation, 1973; Miller Biomedical Award, 1974; commendation from city of Los Angeles, Calif., 1975.

WRITINGS: (With Virginia Simpson) *Help for the Loser: The Doctor's Special Five-Hundred Calorie Diet Menu-Plan*

Recipe Cookbook, Educational Editions, 1970; (with William C. Mulligan) *Nutrigenetics: New Concepts for Relieving Hypoglycemia,* M. Evans, 1975; *Dr. Brennan's Treasury of Diet Menus,* Educational Editions, 1979; (with Helen Hosier) *Coronary? Cancer? God's Answer,* Harvest House, 1979. Also author of *Become Nutrition-Wise,* 1968, *Dr. Brennan's Handbook for Diabetes and Hypoglycemia,* 1979, *Complete Cottage Cheese Cookbook,* 1979.

Contributor to medical journals. Member of editorial board of *Journal of the International Academy of Preventive Medicine* and *Journal of the Midwest Academy of Preventive Medicine.*

WORK IN PROGRESS: Dr. Brennan's Handbook of Nutrient Therapy: Healing Hypoglycemia.

* * *

BRINDLE, Reginald Smith
See SMITH BRINDLE, Reginald

* * *

BRINK, T(erry) L(ee) 1949-

PERSONAL: Born August 16, 1949, in San Jose, Calif.; son of L. L. (a technician) and Marceline (an office manager; maiden name, Benech) Brink; married Gloria Solis (a model), August 16, 1975. *Education:* Claremont Men's College, B.A. (summa cum laude), 1971; attended San Jose State University, 1972; University of Chicago, Ph.D., 1976; University of Santa Clara, M.B.A., 1980. *Religion:* Roman Catholic. *Home:* 1044 Sylvan, San Carlos, Calif. 94070.

CAREER: Notre Dame High School, Chicago, Ill., teacher of religion, 1975-76; consulting psychologist in the United States and Mexico, 1976—. Member of faculty at Palo Alto School of Professional Psychology and College of Notre Dame, Belmont, Calif. Member of Roman Catholic Archdiocese Commission on Social Justice. *Awards, honors:* Won Siddons Club dramatic writing contest, 1971, with "No Room in Hell" and "Viva Nada."

WRITINGS: Geriatric Psychotherapy, Human Sciences Press, 1979.

Plays: "Viva Nada" (one-act), first produced in Claremont, Calif., at Balch Theatre, 1971; "No Room in Hell" (one-act), first produced at Balch Theatre, 1971.

Unproduced plays: "Let Reason Prevail" (three-act), 1969; "Justice Is Served" (one-act), 1970; "A Hero's Eulogy" (one-act), 1970; "A Man for All Pleasings" (one-act), 1972. Contributor to education, psychology, medical, and religious journals.

WORK IN PROGRESS: Adolescent Psychology for Religious Educators, completion expected in 1980; *Statistics for Psychology,* a simple and relevant approach, completion expected in 1980; *No More Nonsense!,* completion expected in 1981.

SIDELIGHTS: Brink wrote: "For the past five years I have placed my literary and theological interests on a back burner and have devoted all of my time and talent to the topic of geriatric psychometry and psychotherapy. I selected this field because I sensed a need to establish my reputation as a competent clinician and researcher and deduced that this relatively new field offered me more opportunity to make a name for myself in a brief time. My thinking proved to be correct, and the field has been fascinating and rewarding, except for the frustration of having to deal with governmental and health care bureaucracy. Other clinical interests include dreams (especially their therapeutic application) and adolescents. Within the next two or three years I hope to return to more religious and philosophical topics, devise a theory of the human personality, and write the grand synthesis of psychology, philosophy and religion. This has been my desire since I was nineteen."

* * *

BRISTOL, Lee Hastings, Jr. 1923-1979

OBITUARY NOTICE—See index for *CA* sketch: Born April 9, 1923; died August 11, 1979, in Syracuse, N.Y. Executive, administrator, composer, and author of *Developing the Corporate Image.* Bristol was a grandson of the founder of the Bristol-Meyers Co. and was a director of public relations for the firm. He wrote numerous choral and organ compositions and was president of the Westminster Choir College from 1962 to 1969. Obituaries and other sources: *Current Biography,* Wilson, 1962; *Who's Who in Public Relations (International),* 4th edition, PR Publishing, 1972; *Who's Who in America,* 40th edition, Marquis, 1978; *New York Times,* August 12, 1979.

* * *

BRITTAN, Gordon G(oodhue), Jr. 1939-

PERSONAL: Born August 29, 1939, in Chicago, Ill.; son of Gordon Goodhue (in business) and Thelma (Scott) Brittan; married Vanessa Jonquiere (a singer and rancher), August 1, 1962; children: Philip, Lorna. *Education:* University of Lausanne, diplome, 1960; Amherst College, B.A., 1962; Stanford University, Ph.D., 1966. *Home address:* P.O. Box 1360, Livingston, Mont. 59047. *Office:* Department of History and Philosophy, Montana State University, Bozeman, Mont. 59715.

CAREER: University of California, Irvine, assistant professor, 1966-71, associate professor of philosophy, 1971-73; Montana State University, Bozeman, associate professor, 1973-78, professor of philosophy, 1978—. Rancher. Member of Montana Committee for the Humanities; member of board of directors of Institute of the Rockies. *Awards, honors:* National Endowment for the Humanities fellow, 1972-73.

WRITINGS: (With Karel Lambert) *An Introduction to the Philosophy of Science,* Prentice-Hall, 1970, revised edition, Ridgeview, 1979; *Kant's Theory of Science,* Princeton University Press, 1978.

WORK IN PROGRESS: Research on philosophy and Nobel Prize-winning physicist, P. W. Bridgman.

SIDELIGHTS: Brittan comments: "My interests are in the history and philosophy of science, in part as a way of understanding the outline of our own culture. As a rancher my ontological commitments are to water and grass. My ethical ideals involve the raising of good children and fast horses."

* * *

BROAD, C(harlie) D(unbar) 1887-1971

OBITUARY NOTICE: Born December 30, 1887, in Harlesden, Middlesex, England; died March 11, 1971. Educator and philosopher. Broad was concerned with the importance of the senses and the ultimate reality of the objects in our perceptions. His first two books, *Perception, Physics, and Reality* and *Scientific Thought,* discuss this concept in depth. Broad became both a Knightbridge Professor and a professor emeritus at Cambridge University. Obituaries and other sources: *The Author's and Writer's Who's Who,* 6th edition, Burke's Peerage, 1971; *World Authors, 1950-1970,* Wilson, 1975.

BROADFOOT, Barry 1926-

PERSONAL: Born January 21, 1926, in Winnipeg, Manitoba, Canada; son of Samuel James (an accountant) and Sylvia Marie (Scoular) Broadfoot; married Anne Cornelia Muelenbroek (a publicity director); children: Susan Broadfoot-Hodgson. *Education:* University of Manitoba, B.A., 1949. *Politics:* "I vote for the man, not the party." *Religion:* "United." *Residence:* Bowen Island, British Columbia, Canada.

CAREER: Journalist for thirty years for several Canadian daily newspapers. *Military service:* Canadian Army, Infantry, during World War II. *Member:* Vancouver Newsmen's Club.

WRITINGS: Ten Lost Years, 1929-1939: Memories of Canadians Who Survived the Depression, Doubleday, 1973; *Six War Years, 1939-1945: Memories of Canadians at Home and Abroad,* Doubleday, 1974; *The Pioneer Years, 1895-1914: Memories of Settlers Who Opened the West,* Doubleday, 1976; *Years of Sorrow, Years of Shame,* Doubleday, 1977. Ghostwriter. Contributor of several dozen articles and poems to scholarly journals and popular magazines.

WORK IN PROGRESS: Broadfoot's Canada; Anatomy of an Island, a study of Bowen Island, British Columbia; a book about the long friendship between a white Arctic trader and an Eskimo hunter.

SIDELIGHTS: Broadfoot comments: "My four books, all best-sellers in Canada, used the so-called oral history technique which I call 'living history.' They were my contribution to Canadian history, a process of filling in the flesh and blood and the smiles and frowns and hopes and dreams of Canadians who lived through the years of the opening of the West, the Great Depression, World War II, and the forced evacuation of Canada's West Coast Japanese during World War II."

BIOGRAPHICAL/CRITICAL SOURCES: New York Review of Books, March 21, 1974; *Canadian Forum,* August, 1974, November/December, 1974.

* * *

BRONK, William 1918-

PERSONAL: Born February 17, 1918, in Fort Edward, N.J.; son of William M. and Ethel (Funston) Bronk. *Home:* 57 Pearl St., Hudson Falls, N.Y. 12839.

CAREER: Poet and essayist. *Military service:* U.S. Army, 1941-45; became lieutenant.

WRITINGS—All poetry, except as noted: *Light and Dark,* Origin Press, 1956, 2nd edition, Elizabeth Press, 1975; *The World, the Worldless,* New Directions, 1964; *The Empty Hands,* Elizabeth Press, 1969; *That Tantalus,* Elizabeth Press, 1971; *Utterances: The Loss of Grass, Trees, Water: The Unbecoming of Wanted and Wanter,* Burning Deck, 1972; *To Praise the Music,* Elizabeth Press, 1972; *Looking at It,* Sceptre Press, 1973; *The New World* (essays), Elizabeth Press, 1974; *A Partial Glossary: Two Essays,* Elizabeth Press, 1974; *The Stance,* Graywolf Press, 1975; *Silence and Metaphor,* Elizabeth Press, 1975; *Finding Losses,* Elizabeth Press, 1976; *The Meantime,* Elizabeth Press, 1976; *My Father Photographed With Friends and Other Pictures,* Elizabeth Press, 1976; *Twelve Losses Found,* Grosseteste, 1976; *That Beauty Still,* Burning Deck, 1978; *The Brother in Elysium* (essays), Elizabeth Press, 1980; *Collected Poems,* Elizabeth Press, 1981.

SIDELIGHTS: In poems that have often been compared to those of Wallace Stevens, Bronk investigates the nature of consciousness, time and space, and the poetic fictions that will suffice in an age of disbelief and uncertainty. As Michael Heller remarked, Bronk's poetry "offers another way of looking at our common humanity, not in some imagined concurrence of shared knowledge, but in our need to construct and reconstruct worlds, in our attempts to appease a common metaphysical hunger." Many critics also note that his meditative and experimental poems use a language stripped of ornament, imagery, and metaphor. "His poetry of statement," commented Robert D. Spector, "impresses with its clarity and precision of language; it manages to make metaphysics a subject of human emotion rather than a grand abstraction."

Both Felix Stefanile and Richard Elman have called Bronk one of the best, if uncelebrated, of America's poets. In his discussion of Bronk's approach to time and human history, Stefanile observed: "[For] Bronk ancient mountains and modern cities coexist in the flux of time in which man is trapped. That is why his startling connections are always so utterly contemporary, and personally relevant. Man is not man-in-history, or man-as-savage, but *man.* No other poet in the United States is quite like this." And though his poetry describes the anguish and uncertainty of modern life, it does not succumb to despair. Instead, as Spector pointed out, "it recognizes our need 'to make / a world for survival . . . ,' since 'One is nothing with no world.'" His poems instruct us, Heller remarked, "that the worlds we seem to share are created worlds; 'like pieces of music, they are composed, oh wholly and well composed.'"

Bronk's poetry considers the limits of human knowledge. "The natural world, Bronk would insist, is a world we can never know," explained Heller. Consequently, Heller noted, Bronk's work suggests that the recognition of this basic estrangement between man and nature "illuminates and clarifies the human situation." To address this understanding and the need for "well-composed" worlds, Bronk searches for the appropriate form, style, and language. Elman declared: "Every new volume of his poems is engraved with terse statement, a high seriousness and strong uncluttered feeling. With each new volume he seems to be determined to make his utterance all the more specific, determined and quiet, as if he wrote his poems in the voice and with the mind in which we all truly sometimes think, beautifully and sublimely, through our perceptions." Heller also applauded Bronk's attempt to find a suitable language for describing human perception and its limits; he noted that Bronk seeks to discover "the exacting and naked process of realization."

BIOGRAPHICAL/CRITICAL SOURCES: Saturday Review, February 13, 1965, July 8, 1978; *Grosseteste Review,* Volume V, number 1, spring, 1972; *New York Times Book Review,* March 9, 1975, September 18, 1977; *Hudson Review,* winter, 1976-77; *Parnassus: Poetry in Review,* spring-summer, 1977; *Contemporary Literary Criticism,* Volume 10, Gale, 1979.

* * *

BROOKS, Charlotte K.

PERSONAL: Born in Washington, D.C.; married Walter H. Brooks; children: Joseph. *Education:* Howard University, A.B.; New York University, M.A., 1951.

CAREER: Teacher, assistant director of English department, and supervising director with Washington, D.C., Public Schools; English and social studies supervisor at Princeton Institute for Teachers of the Disadvantaged, Princeton,

N.J. Fulbright professor in England, 1960-61; consultant to U.S. Office of Education. *Member:* National Council of Teachers of English (professional relations representative), International Reading Association. *Awards, honors:* Meyer Travel Award; Winifred Cullis lecture fellowship.

WRITINGS—Editor, except as noted; juvenile: *The Outnumbered: Stories, Essays and Poems About Minority Groups by America's Leading Writers,* Dell, 1967; (with Lawana Trout) *I've Got a Name,* Holt, 1968; *Search for America,* with teacher's guide, Holt, 1970.

Other: (With Edith G. Stull) *Larger Than Life,* Holt, 1968; (author) *They Can Learn English,* Wadsworth, 1973; *African Rhythms: Selected Stories and Poems,* photographs by husband, Walter H. Brooks, Pocket Books, 1974.

SIDELIGHTS: Reviewing Charlotte Brooks's first work as an editor, a *Young Readers Review* critic praised her competence: "Each selection presents a different aspect of what it means to be a member of a minority group. Every group, at one time or another, has suffered many or all of the injustices or difficulties presented here. The book as a whole is an unforgettable experience. . . . Chances are, after reading this book, young people will want other material by these writers, and other material on the subject. The editor has done a fine job. It's a high quality, far-ranging, well-balanced book and deserves wide circulation."

BIOGRAPHICAL/CRITICAL SOURCES: Young Readers Review, May, 1969.*

* * *

BROWN, Anthony Eugene 1937-

PERSONAL: Born July 22, 1937, in Rocky Mount, N.C.; son of Allan Eugene and Ruth (a librarian; maiden name, Scott) Brown; married second wife, Theresa Marie Fiore (a kindergarten teacher), July 22, 1973; children: (first marriage) Anthony Eugene, Jr., Carleton Robert, David Byrd; (second marriage; stepchildren) Joseph Francis, Mary Monica, Miriam Agnes, Peter Anthony, Paul Gerard, Thomas Cornelius. *Education:* University of South Carolina, B.A., 1960, M.A., 1961; Vanderbilt University, Ph.D., 1963. *Home address:* P.O. Drawer A-B, Cullowhee, N.C. 28723. *Office:* Department of English, Western Carolina University, Cullowhee, N.C. 28723.

CAREER: Western Carolina University, Cullowhee, assistant professor, 1964-71, associate professor of English, 1971—. *Member:* South Atlantic Modern Language Association. *Awards, honors:* American Philosophical Society grant, 1971; American Council of Learned Societies grant, 1972; National Endowment for the Humanities grant, 1979.

WRITINGS: Boswellian Studies: A Bibliography, Shoe String, 1972.

WORK IN PROGRESS: Toward the Dawn, a book of essays; *The Literary and Personal Reputation of James Boswell,* publication by Shoe String expected in 1981.

SIDELIGHTS: Brown writes: "In a seminar at Vanderbilt in 1962, a student made a wrong remark about James Boswell's appearance at the Shakespeare Jubilee of 1769. I called attention to the error, and the professor ordered me to prove the point. This led to my continuing interest in Boswell." *Avocational interests:* Acting, photography, natural science.

* * *

BROWN, Kevin V. 1922-

PERSONAL: Born June 19, 1922, in Chicago, Ill.; son of William (a railway clerk) and Mary Jane (Vizzard) Brown. *Education:* Loyola University, Ph.B., 1950; graduate study at Northwestern University, 1950-51. *Politics:* Independent. *Religion:* Roman Catholic. *Home and office:* 2710 West Lunt Ave., Chicago, Ill. 60645.

CAREER: Milwaukee Journal, Milwaukee, Wis., reporter, 1953-56; *Chicago Tribune,* Chicago, Ill., copy editor, 1956-57; *Family Weekly,* Chicago, associate editor, 1957-60; *Popular Mechanics,* Chicago and New York City, aviation editor, 1960-69; writer. *Military service:* U.S. Army Air Forces, 1943-46, fighter pilot; became captain; received Distinguished Flying Cross. *Member:* American Society of Journalists and Authors, Aviation/Space Writers Association, Midwest Writers Group.

WRITINGS: (With Kenneth Cooper) *Aerobics,* M. Evans, 1968. Also author, with Francis Gabreski, of *Gabreski.* Contributor of articles to *Family Weekly, Mechanix Illustrated, Popular Mechanics, Popular Science,* and *Chicago Tribune Magazine.*

WORK IN PROGRESS: A biography; a travel book.

AVOCATIONAL INTERESTS: Aviation, exercise, food, travel, wine.

* * *

BROWN, Mac Alister 1924-

PERSONAL: Born July 7, 1924, in Newton, Mass.; son of Clifford K. (an executive) and Marion (McAllister) Brown; married Adriana Millenaar (a teacher), September 3, 1967; children: Laura M., John S., Andrew M. *Education:* Wesleyan University, Middletown, Conn., B.A., 1947; Harvard University, Ph.D., 1953; also studied at Institut des Hautes Etudes Internationales. *Home:* 41 School St., Williamstown, Mass. 01267. *Office:* Department of Political Science, Williams College, Williamstown, Mass. 01267.

CAREER: Williams College, Williamstown, Mass., professor of political science, 1956—.

WRITINGS: (Editor with Joseph J. Zasloff) *Communism in Indochina: New Perspectives,* Heath, 1975; (with Zasloff) *Communist Indochina and U.S. Foreign Policy: Postwar Realities,* Westview Press, 1978; (with Zasloff) *History of the Lao People's Revolutionary Party,* Hoover Institution Press, 1980.

SIDELIGHTS: "Events in Indochina since the American departure have been turbulent and confusing for a now inattentive American public," Brown wrote. "I plan to continue with my co-author to seek out the underlying explanatory factors, so as to provide a basis for better public understanding."

* * *

BRUCE, Lenny
See SCHNEIDER, Leonard Alfred

* * *

BRUCE, Leo
See CROFT-COOKE, Rupert

* * *

BRUCE, R(aymon) R(ene) 1934-

PERSONAL: Born September 18, 1934, in Denver, Colo.; son of William R. and Eugenia Alice Bruce; married Sharon E. Dudley (an account executive), June 27, 1976; children: Esther, Joshua, Jessie. *Education:* Attended University of

Heidelberg, 1958-59; University of Montana, B.A. (with honors), 1962, M.A., 1965; Pepperdine University, M.S., 1979. *Home:* 691 Dolores St., San Francisco, Calif. 94110. *Agent:* Bertha Klausner, International Literary Agency, Inc., 71 Park Ave., New York, N.Y. 10016.

CAREER: Metro-Goldwyn-Mayer, Los Angeles, Calif., assistant producer, 1965-66; New Playwrights Theatre, Los Angeles, theatre producer and artistic director, 1967-68; San Francisco Repertory Theatre, San Francisco, Calif., theatre producer and artistic director, 1968-72; Universe Survey, Inc. (management consultants), San Francisco, president, 1972—. Member of National Training and Development Service seminar renewal group.

MEMBER: Dramatists Guild, Corporate Planners Association. *Awards, honors:* German Consul Award from German consul, Seattle, Wash., 1962, for outstanding scholarship in German literature; best play awards from University of Montana, 1962, for "The Grand Inquisitor," and 1965, for *Crime and Punishment;* first prize from Immaculate Heart College, Los Angeles, 1964, for one-act play, "Across Between."

WRITINGS: Crime and Punishment (three-act play; adaptation of novel by Dostoevsky; first produced in Missoula, Mont., at University of Montana, 1965), Hohokam Press, 1965; *Revolucion* (three-act play; first produced in San Francisco at New World Theatre, 1972), New World Theatre Press, 1972; *What Are My Words Inside* (poetry), New Albion Press, 1976; *Ray's Cafe* (poetry), New Albion Press, 1977; *City Sandwich* (poetry), New Albion Press, 1978. Also author of *Arizona Gold* (novel), 1976.

Unpublished plays: "Jim Nation" (two-act), first produced in Missoula, Mont., at University of Montana, 1964; "Journey of a Modern Hero" (two-act verse play), first produced in Missoula, Mont., at Golden Horn Theatre, 1965; "Daddy Battlebucks" (three-act musical), first produced in San Francisco at San Francisco Repertory Theatre, 1968; "Alice's Wonderland" (three-act), first produced in San Francisco at San Francisco Repertory Theatre, 1973. Also author of "The Grand Inquisitor" (one-act) and "Across Between."

Unproduced plays: "Theseus and Oedipus" (three-act), 1963; "Land Destroyer" (screenplay), 1966; "Molly Crisp" (two-act), 1971; "Wunder Woman" (three-act), 1973; "Poe: The Fractured Eye" (three-act), 1974; "Messiah From the Madhouse" (three-act), 1975.

Contributor to literary, technical, and business journals. Editor of New Albion Press.

WORK IN PROGRESS: The Acceptance/Rejection Syndrome of New Technology in Work Units; Network Development in Managing Change.

SIDELIGHTS: Bruce wrote: "I have been looking into what it is to be a human. My plays and poetry are vehicles for me to adventure into the dimly chartered areas of human relations. They have carried me away from the procenium arch into a field called organization development. I apply Stanislawski system principles to managing change in organizations.

"I have found that poetry and drama have a key role to play in changing our modern organizations. The situation at work is not unlike a play in rehearsal. I am presently doing research in the relationship between work and human identity, including the nature of worker alienation."

BRUHN, John Glyndon 1934-

PERSONAL: Born April 27, 1934, in Norfolk, Neb.; son of John Franz and Margaret Constance (Treiber) Bruhn. *Education:* University of Nebraska, B.A., 1956, M.A., 1958; Yale University, Ph.D., 1961. *Home:* 416 First St., Galveston, Tex. 77550. *Office:* University of Texas, Medical Branch, Galveston, Tex. 77550.

CAREER: Connecticut Department of Mental Health, New Haven, researcher, 1958-59; Southern Connecticut College, New Haven, instructor in sociology, 1960-61; Grace-New Haven Community Hospital, Psychiatric Out-Patient Clinic, New Haven, research sociologist, 1960-61; University of Edinburgh, Edinburgh, Scotland, research sociologist in psychological medicine, 1961-62; University of Oklahoma, Oklahoma City, instructor, 1962-63, assistant professor, 1963-67, associate professor, 1967-69, professor of human ecology and head of department, 1969-72 (also taught medical sociology, preventive medicine, and public health), research sociologist, 1964-67, Clinical investigator for Oklahoma Medical Research Foundation, 1965-67, co-director of National Drug Education Center, 1970-71, director of research and evaluation, 1970-73, also associate professor of sociology at University of Oklahoma, Norman, 1967-72; University of Texas, Medical Branch, Galveston, professor of preventive medicine and community health, 1972—, associate dean for community affairs, 1972—, director of planning and evaluation for Area Health Education Center, 1972-75, also professor at University of Texas, Houston, 1975—. President and director of Totts Gap Institute of Human Ecology, 1975-77; member of board of advisers of Foundation of Thanatology, 1979—. Member of Oklahoma governor's mental health planning committee, 1963-65. Member of board of directors of St. Vincent's House, 1974-75, Galveston County Cultural Arts Council, 1974-75, William Temple Community House, 1974-78, Galveston Alternative School Program, 1976-77, and Galveston County Coordinated Community Clinics, 1977— (head of board of directors, 1979—); head of Houston Health Systems Agency technical advisory committee on health promotion, 1978. *Military service:* U.S. Army, 1957-58; U.S. Army Reserve, 1958-63.

MEMBER: American Sociological Association, American Public Health Association (fellow), American Heart Association (fellow), American Association for the Advancement of Science, Association of American Medical Colleges, American Psychosomatic Society, American Association of University Professors, Association of Teachers of Preventive Medicine, Royal Society of Health (fellow), Southwestern Sociological Association, New York Academy of Science, Galveston County Cancer Society (member of board of directors, 1979—), Sigma Xi, Alpha Kappa Delta, Kappa Sigma. *Awards, honors:* Fulbright fellow, 1961-62; career development award from National Heart Institute, 1968-69; Danforth associate, 1973—.

WRITINGS: (With Ramiro Caballero and others) *A Doctor in the House?: Information for Parents and Spouses of Premedical and Medical Students,* Medical Branch, University of Texas, Galveston, 1978; (with P. R. Nader and others) *Options for School Health,* Aspen Publishing, 1978; (with Stewart Wolf and Helen Goodell) *Occupational Health as Human Ecology,* C. C Thomas, 1978; (with Wolf) *The Roseto Story: An Anatomy of Health,* University of Oklahoma Press, 1979.

Contributor: Maurice B. Visscher, editor, *Humanistic Perspectives in Medical Ethics,* Prometheus Books, 1972; John Naughton and Herman Hellerstein, editors, *Exercise*

Testing and Exercise Training in Coronary Heart Disease, Academic Press, 1973; William McKee, editor, *Environmental Problems in Medicine,* C. C Thomas, 1974; G. S. Parcel, editor, *First Aid in Emergency Care,* Mosby, 1977; John P. Foreyt, editor, *Cognitive Behavior Therapy: Research and Application,* Plenum, 1978; Jeanette Lancaster, editor, *An Ecological Perspective in Community Mental Health Nursing,* Mosby, 1979. Contributor of about one hundred articles and reviews to journals in the social sciences and medicine. Member of editorial board of *Health Values: Achieving High Level Wellness,* 1979—; member of editorial board of *Wellness,* 1979—.

WORK IN PROGRESS: Research on health education among preschool children.

SIDELIGHTS: Bruhn writes: "Presently several colleagues and I are developing a health curriculum for three- and four-year-olds and their parents. It is our view that health as a positive value should be learned at the earliest possible age, at the time when children are forming their self-concepts. Health should be taught beginning in preschool to all children and they should actively participate in this learning. The health curriculum should then be age-graded and taught throughout kindergarten through twelfth grade; then we would begin to turn around our present view of health as something to be regained by a 'fix-it' health technology."

* * *

BRUNDAGE, Percival F(lack) 1892-1979

OBITUARY NOTICE: Born April 2, 1892, in Amsterdam, N.Y.; died July 16, 1979, in Ridgewood, N.J. Businessman and author. A former senior partner with the accounting firm of Price Waterhouse & Co., Burndage served as director of the old Bureau of the Budget, now the Office of Management and Budget. He first joined the bureau in 1954 as deputy director and became its director in 1956, a post he held for two years. His 1970 book, *The Bureau of the Budget,* recommended that the bureau be restructured along the lines of the present Office of Management and Budget. Brundage was active in several health and international organizations, including Project Hope, and was a member of the Accounting Hall of Fame. Obituaries and other sources: *Current Biography,* Wilson, 1957; *Who's Who in America,* 38th edition, Marquis, 1974; *Washington Post,* July 18, 1979.

* * *

BRUNETTI, Mendor Thomas 1894-1979

OBITUARY NOTICE: Born June 22, 1894, in Alfedena, Italy; died October 20, 1979, in New York, N.Y. Educator, translator, and author. A teacher of Romance languages at New York University for fifty four years, Brunetti founded the foreign language program of the school's General Education Division in 1930 as well as the American Language Institute of the School of Continuing Education in 1945. In 1961 he was a recipient of the university's Great Teacher Awards. He was author of several language textbooks. Obituaries and other sources: *Who's Who in the East,* 14th edition, Marquis, 1973; *Directory of American Scholars,* Volume III: *Foreign Languages, Linguistics, and Philology,* 6th edition, Bowker, 1974; *New York Times,* October 25, 1979.

* * *

BUDENZ, Louis F(rancis) 1891-1972

OBITUARY NOTICE: Born July 17, 1891, in Indianapolis, Ind.; died April 27, 1972. Editor, educator, and writer. Budenz was a member of the Communist party in the United States for ten years, serving as director and editor of several publications, including the *Daily Worker.* After leaving the party, Budenz acted as government witness and informer on Communism. He has written numerous books on both Communism and Catholicism, his original faith. He was a frequent lecturer and contributor to periodicals, including *Collier's* and *Nation.* Obituaries and other sources: Louis Francis Budenz, *This Is My Story,* Whittlesey House, 1947; *Current Biography,* Wilson, 1951, June, 1972; *New York Times,* April 29, 1972.

* * *

BUIST, Vincent 1919(?)-1979

OBITUARY NOTICE: Born c. 1919; died September 18, 1979, in London, England. Journalist. Buist was a correspondent for the Reuters news agency after World War II and an authority on Communist affairs. A reporter in Eastern Europe for twenty-five years, his most notable assignments included coverage of the East Berlin uprising in 1953 and the launch of *Sputnik* in 1957. Obituaries and other sources: *Chicago Tribune,* September 21, 1979.

* * *

BULLITT, Orville H(orwitz) 1894-1979

OBITUARY NOTICE—See index for *CA* sketch: Born July 30, 1894, in Cape May, N.J.; died July 31, 1979, in Fort Washington, Pa. Philanthropist, banker, and author. Bullitt was the president of numerous Pennsylvania companies and the trustee of several universities and museums, including the University of Pennsylvania. In 1938, he co-founded the Pennyslvania Blue Cross and became chairman of the board of the Philadelphia Orchestra Association. Bullitt financed the archaeological expedition which uncovered the lost city of Sybaris in 1964. He was the author of *Search for Sybaris.* Obituaries and other sources: *Who's Who in America,* 40th edition, Marquis, 1978; *The Writers Directory, 1980-82,* St. Martin's, 1979; *New York Times,* August 3, 1979.

* * *

BULLITT, William C(hristian) 1891-1967

OBITUARY NOTICE: Born January 25, 1891, in Philadelphia, Pa.; died February, 1967. Diplomat, foreign correspondent, and author. Bullitt was the first U.S. ambassador to Russia, the ambassador to France, and ambassador-at-large. He was also involved in the preparation of the peace treaties at Versailles. He is the author of *The Great Glove Itself* and *It's Not Done.* Obituaries and other sources: *Current Biography,* Wilson, 1940, April, 1967; *The Reader's Encyclopedia,* 2nd edition, Crowell, 1965.

* * *

BULLOCK, Alice 1904-

PERSONAL: Born July 12, 1904, in Buck, Ind.; daughter of Richard (a steam engineer) and Jeannette (Nichols) Lowe; married Dale Bullock (a printer and publisher), 1924; children: Patricia (Mrs. Walter Kiesow), Mrs. Tom Chumbley. *Education:* Attended New Mexico Normal University (now New Mexico Highlands University) and University of Southern California. *Home:* 812 Gildersleeve, Santa Fe, N.M. 87501.

CAREER: Worked as a merchant, waitress, and women's coat and suit designer; former teacher in New Mexico; book review editor for the *New Mexican* and *El Palacio;* free-lance writer. *Member:* Western Writers of America, New Mexico Press Association. *Awards, honors:* Member of New Mexico Folklore Society Hall of Fame, 1979.

WRITINGS: *What's New in Parties?,* Reader Mail, Inc., 1938; *Living Legends of the Santa Fe Country,* Green Mountain Press, 1970, revised edition, Sunstone Press, 1972; *Mountain Villages,* Sunstone Press, 1973; *The Squaw Tree: Ghosts, Miracles, and Mysteries of New Mexico,* Lightning Tree, 1978; *Loretto and the Miraculous Staircase,* Sunstone Press, in press. Also author of *Discover Santa Fe,* Rydal. Contributor of more than two hundred articles, stories, poems, and reviews to magazines.

WORK IN PROGRESS: Four books for Sunstone Press.

SIDELIGHTS: Alice Bullock writes: "I've played all over the field—fiction, history, poetry, biographies, religious material, etc., but I don't keep track, because it means slighting work in progress. The things ahead are so much more important."

* * *

BULLOCK, C(larence) Hassell 1939-

PERSONAL: Born April 20, 1939, in Bessemer, Ala.; son of Erbie Laurie (a barber) and Agnes (Farr) Bullock; married Rhonda Nichols, July 2, 1965; children: Scott, Rebecca. *Education:* Samford University, B.A., 1961; Columbia Theological Seminary, Decatur, Ga., B.D., 1964; Hebrew Union College-Jewish Institute of Religion, Ph.D., 1970. *Home:* 1111 North Washington St., Wheaton, Ill. 60187. *Office:* Department of Bible, Religion, and Archaeology, Wheaton College, Wheaton, Ill. 60187.

CAREER: Ordained United Presbyterian minister, 1972; Lee College, Cleveland, Tenn., assistant professor of Old Testament, 1968-72; pastor of Presbyterian church in Trussville, Ala., 1972-73; Wheaton College, Wheaton, Ill., associate professor of biblical studies, 1973—. *Member:* Society of Biblical Literature, Evangelical Theological Society.

WRITINGS: (Contributor) S. J. Schultz and Morris A. Inch, editors, *Interpreting the Word of God,* Moody, 1975; (with Elmer Johnson) *Studies in the Bible,* Chicago Sunday Evening Club, 1976; *Introduction to the Poetic Books of the Old Testament,* Moody, 1979.

WORK IN PROGRESS: *The Biblical Process: Creation and Redemption, a Comprehensive Theme;* "The Songs of Israel," to be included in *The Interpretation and Meaning of Scripture,* edited by Morris A. Inch and C. Hassell Bullock, for Baker Book.

SIDELIGHTS: Bullock writes: "My interest in biblical wisdom literature began with my teaching of the Book of Job. It began to grow on me and now I see it to have profound relevance for our uneasy, skeptical world. A literary genre presenting a biblical humanism, it leads directly to biblical theism and stands in stark contrast to modern humanism that begins and ends with man."

* * *

BUMAGIN, Victoria E. 1923-

PERSONAL: Surname is pronounced Beau-*may*-jin; born June 20, 1923, in Danzig, Poland; daughter of Isaac A. (a lawyer) and Zinaida (Towbin) Werosub; married Victor I. Bumagin (a management consultant), March 16, 1946; children: Louise Bumagin Hellegers, Susan, Elizabeth, Deborah Bumagin Millman, Jennifer. *Education:* Brooklyn College (now of the City University of New York), B.A., 1945; Columbia University, M.S.S.W., 1969; doctoral study at University of Chicago, 1974—. *Home:* 435 Lake Ave., Wilmette, Ill. 60091. *Agent:* Oliver Swan, Collier Associates, 280 Madison Ave., New York, N.Y. 10016. *Office:* Council for the Jewish Elderly, 1015 West Howard St., Evanston, Ill. 60202.

CAREER: Department of Welfare, New York, N.Y., caseworker, 1946-48; New Jersey Bureau of Children's Services, Trenton, caseworker, intake supervisor, and case supervisor, 1962-69; Department of Social Services, Reading, England, senior social worker, 1970-73; Council for the Jewish Elderly, Chicago, Ill., director of social services in Chicago and Evanston, 1974—. Lecturer at University of Reading, 1972-73; field instructor at Oxford University, 1971-73, University of Illinois, 1975—, and Northwestern University, 1978—; instructor at University of Chicago, summers, 1974— (senior clinical associate, 1977), and at Loyola University, Chicago, summers, 1977—; instructor at Berkshire College of Further Education, 1971-73. Member of faculty at Chicago's Urban Center for Research, Training, and Service in Aging, 1978—. Speaker at professional and community meetings; workshop director; guest on radio programs. Member of Chicago's technical advisory committee on protective services to the aged and Task Force on Age Discrimination, Metropolitan Forum on Aging, both 1977—. *Member:* Academy of Certified Social Workers, National Association of Social Workers, Gerontological Society, Society for Life Cycle Psychology and Aging, British Association of Social Workers, Columbia University School of Social Work Alumni Association (member of board of directors).

WRITINGS: *The Appliance Cookbook,* Macmillan, 1971; (with Kathryn Hirn) *Aging Is a Family Affair,* Crowell, 1979. Contributor to social work journals and *Woman's Day.*

WORK IN PROGRESS: *Gerontological Social Work; Clinical Practice With the Aged.*

SIDELIGHTS: Victoria Bumagin comments: "My most recent work stems from a deep concern for the aging population, its problems, losses, and still-available gains; this is particularly pertinent in view of the growing numbers of elderly in our society. My professional efforts are directed toward improving the quality of life of the older generation and encouraging independent, productive living; this is also the subject of my teaching and public lecturing." *Avocational interests:* Travel (England and Europe), gourmet cooking, miniatures.

BIOGRAPHICAL/CRITICAL SOURCES: *Bergen Record,* March, 1969; *Chicago Sun-Times,* January 17, 1979; *Washington Post Book World,* August 26, 1979.

* * *

BURCHAM, Nancy A(nn) 1942-

PERSONAL: Born October 24, 1942, in Decatur, Ill.; daughter of J. Dale (a farmer) and Wilma (Hogue) Lane; married Richard Burcham (a banker), August 7, 1960; children: Jill, Doug, Brad. *Education:* Attended high school in Sullivan, Ill. *Religion:* Disciples of Christ. *Home address:* R.R.2, Sullivan, Ill. 61951.

CAREER: Writer, 1968—. *Member:* National Writers Club, Christian Women's Fellowship.

WRITINGS: *Everything Happens With Kids,* United Church Press, 1973; *Country Girl* (nonfiction humor), Wallace-Homestead, 1977. Contributor to adult and juvenile magazines, including *Family Digest, Stitch 'n' Sew, Household Plants, Jack and Jill,* and *Explore.*

WORK IN PROGRESS: Laughter With the Pastor, nonfiction; *Cornfield Carousel of Stars,* a history of Sullivan's Little Theater; *Those Tantalizing Teens.*

SIDELIGHTS: Nancy Burcham writes: "I like to write about life from a down-to-earth humorous point of view. In our hurry-scurry society we sometimes forget to look at the funny side and end up 'tied in knots.' My philosophy is 'Live for others, laugh with others, and love the life you're living.'"

* * *

BURCHARDT, Bill
See BURCHARDT, William Robert

* * *

BURCHARDT, William Robert 1917-
(Bill Burchardt)

PERSONAL: Born August 16, 1917, in Guthrie, Okla.; son of Gustav Oscar and Jessie Muriel (Daniels) Burchardt; married Clara Chaves (a foreign language consultant). *Education:* Central State University, Edmond, Okla., B.A., 1938; University of Oklahoma, M.Mus.Ed., 1947. *Office:* Will Rogers Memorial Building, Oklahoma City, Okla. 73105.

CAREER: High school music director in Seminole, Okla., and Oklahoma City, Okla., 1938-42; high school teacher of music and journalism in Grove, Okla., and Duncan, Okla.; instructor in music and journalism at Northern Oklahoma Junior College, Tonkawa; *Oklahoma Today,* Oklahoma City, associate editor, 1957-60, editor, 1960—. Writer-in-residence at Central State University, Edmond, Okla., 1955-60, 1972-75. Member of historical committee of Oklahoma Petroleum Council and Western Heritage Committee of National Cowboy Hall of Fame. *Military service:* U.S. Navy, 1942-45; became lieutenant. *Member:* Authors Guild, Western Writers of America (national president, 1960), Society of American Travel Writers, Oklahoma Writers Federation, Oklahoma Westerners (Indian Territory posse), Central State University Alumni Association (president, 1972-73). *Awards, honors:* Award from Oklahoma Writers' Federation, 1959, for short story; Oklahoma Writing Award from University of Oklahoma, 1965; Wrangler Western Heritage Award from National Cowboy Hall of Fame and Tepee Award, both 1975; award from Oklahoma Writers' Federation for best novel of the year, 1979, for *Buck.*

WRITINGS—Novels; all under name Bill Burchardt: *The Wildcatters,* Ace Books, 1963; *Yankee Longstraw,* Doubleday, 1965; *Shotgun Bottom,* Doubleday, 1966; *The Birth of Logan Station,* Doubleday, 1974; *The Mexican,* Doubleday, 1977; *Buck,* Doubleday, 1978.

Work represented in anthologies, including *The Pick of the Roundup,* Avon, 1963; *Great Western Stories,* Berkley, 1965; *Water Trails West,* Doubleday, 1978. Contributor of articles and stories to religion, education, and travel magazines, men's magazines, and popular journals, including *Texas Western, Cavalier, True West,* and *Undiscovered America.*

WORK IN PROGRESS: Medicine Man, a novel, publication by Doubleday.

SIDELIGHTS: Burchardt's books have been published in Sweden, England, and Germany. In 1959, he was made an adopted grandson of Kiowa elder Henry Tenandoah and given the Indian name Padl'ta'-de'kih.

BURRELL, Berkeley G(raham) 1919-1979

OBITUARY NOTICE—See index for *CA* sketch: Born June 12, 1919, in Washington, D.C.; died August 31, 1979, in Washington, D.C. Businessman, association executive, and author. Burrell, who was the founder and owner of his own dry cleaning service, was the president of the National Business League and a board member of the Council for Financial Aid to Education and Corporation for Blacks in Public Broadcasting. In addition to his syndicated column in black-owned newspapers, Burrell was also the author of *Getting It Together: Black Businessmen in America.* Obituaries and other sources: *Who's Who in America,* 40th edition, Marquis, 1978; *New York Times,* September 2, 1979.

* * *

BURROS, Marian (Fox)

PERSONAL: Born in Waterbury, Conn.; daughter of Myron and Dorothy (Derby) Fox; married Donald Burros (an executive), 1959; children: Michael, Ann. *Education:* Wellesley College, B.A., 1954. *Home:* 7215 Helmsdale Rd., Bethesda, Md. 20034. *Office: Washington Post,* 1150 15th St. N.W., Washington, D.C. 20071.

CAREER: Teacher of cooking, 1961-64; *Maryland News* (weekly), Montgomery County, food columnist, 1962-63; *Maryland Monitor* (weekly), Montgomery County, food columnist, 1963-64; *Washington Daily News,* Washington, D.C., food editor, 1964-68; *Washington Evening Star,* Washington, D.C., food editor, 1968-74; *Washington Post,* Washington, D.C., food editor, 1974—. Consumer affairs reporter for National Broadcasting Co. (NBC-TV), 1973—. Notable assignments include coverage of addition of powdered wood pulp to a brand of bread, ban of red dye #2, and occurrence of asbestos in talcum powder. *Member:* American Newspaper Women's Club, Women's Press Club. *Awards, honors:* Emmy Award from National Academy of Television Arts and Sciences, 1974, for consumer affairs reporting; won Vesta award twice, for best newspaper food pages; Association of Federal Investigators award for consumer reporting; won American Association of University Women Mass Media award twice, for consumer reporting and nutrition education; Tastemaker award for *The Summertime Cookbook.*

WRITINGS—Cookbooks: (With Lois Levine) *Elegant but Easy: A Cookbook for Hostesses,* Collier Books, 1962; (with Levine) *Freeze With Ease,* Macmillan, 1965; (with Levine) *The Elegant but Easy Cookbook,* Macmillan, 1967, revised edition, Collier Books, 1968; (with Levine) *Come for Cocktails, Stay for Supper,* Macmillan, 1970; (with Levine) *The Summertime Cookbook: Elegant but Easy Dining In-Doors and Out,* Macmillan, 1972; *Pure and Simple: Delicious Recipes for Additive-Free Cooking,* Morrow, 1978.

WORK IN PROGRESS: A book on consumer affairs; a cookbook.

SIDELIGHTS: Burros is known for her ability to devise tasty, yet relatively inexpensive meals. Her latest book to date, *Pure and Simple,* made the *New York Times* bestseller list. In the book, Burros provides the reader with recipes that are international in scope, "blessedly brief though complete, and delicious sounding," noted Mimi Sheraton. Moreover, Burros provides the reader with tips on how to prepare one's own "convenience food" without the use of additives. Judith Huxley calls Burros "one tough-minded reporter who is a master exposer of the ersatz and debunker of the super-hype behind and in the food we feed ourselves and our families."

BIOGRAPHICAL/CRITICAL SOURCES: New York Times Book Review, June 4, 1967, December 6, 1970; *New York Times,* May 31, 1978; *Washington Post Book World,* June 25, 1978.

* * *

BUTH, Lenore 1932-

PERSONAL: Born October 22, 1932, in Wadena, Minn.; daughter of William L. (a Lutheran minister) and Golda (Brandes) Stellwagen; married Robert A. Buth (an insurance counselor), February 4, 1951; children: Beverly (Mrs. Thomas R. Mundt), Donna (Mrs. Michael R. Deems), Roberta, Janet. *Education:* Student at Los Angeles Pierce College, 1975—. *Politics:* "Uncommitted." *Religion:* Lutheran. *Home:* 29431 Quail Run Dr., Agoura, Calif. 91301.

CAREER: Free-lance writer, 1970—. Member of Village Voices Chorale, 1973—, and Arts Council of Conejo Valley, 1979—. *Member:* Christian Writers Guild.

WRITINGS: Empty Nest Parents, Concordia, 1979; *Sexuality: God's Precious Gift,* Concordia, 1980. Author of *IAA Record* columns "Woman's View," 1971-77, and "Bicentennial Diary," 1975-76, and *Family* columns "Consumer View" and "Family Pastimes," both 1977—(all publications of Illinois Agricultural Association). Contributor to magazines, including *Lutheran Women, Lutheran Witness, Reporter,* and *Farm Wife News.*

WORK IN PROGRESS: I Can't Make It Alone, Lord, "a book of honest prayers for women."

SIDELIGHTS: Lenore Buth writes: "In everything I write, I aim to speak to people where they are. Usually that takes the form of practical information on improving the quality of life. Happily, in my books I have been able to couple that with Christian principles. But whatever form it takes, I hope my writing will make a positive difference—however small—in the lives of my readers."

* * *

BUTLER, Stefan Congrat
See CONGRAT-BUTLER, Stefan

* * *

BUTT, (Dorcas) Susan 1938-

PERSONAL: Born March 19, 1938, in Vancouver, British Columbia, Canada; daughter of Kenneth John (an investment counsellor) and Molly (a teacher; maiden name, Edwards) Butt; children: (from previous marriage) Tara Susan Finn, Donal Lee Finn. *Education:* University of British Columbia, B.A., 1960, M.A., 1963; University of Chicago, Ph.D., 1967. *Office:* Department of Psychology, University of British Columbia, Vancouver, British Columbia, Canada.

CAREER: Crease Clinic of Psychological Medicine, Essondale, British Columbia, clinical psychologist, 1962; Burnaby Mental Health Center, Burnaby, British Columbia, clinical psychologist, 1963-64; University of British Columbia, Vancouver, assistant professor, 1967-72, associate professor of psychology, 1973—. Research associate with Canadian Welfare Council, 1968. Tennis player; captain of Canadian Federation Cup team, 1970-72. *Member:* Canadian Lawn Tennis Association (vice-president, 1971-72). *Awards, honors:* Tennis championships include first prizes in Canadian women's tennis matches, 1960-61, 1967; Canada Council fellow, 1973-74.

WRITINGS: (Contributor) G. H. McGlynn, editor, *Issues in Physical Education and Sports,* National Press, 1974; (contributor) H.T.A. Whiting, editor, *Readings in the Psychology of Sport II,* Kimpton, 1975; *Psychology of Sport: The Behavior, Motivation, Personality, and Performance of Athletes,* Van Nostrand, 1976; (contributor) C. S. Adamec, editor, *Sex Roles: Origins, Influences, and Implications for Women,* Eden Press, 1979; (contributor) R. M. Suinn, editor, *Psychology in Sports: Methods and Applications,* Burgess, 1980. Contributor to *Mental Measurements Yearbook.* Contributor to sport journals.

WORK IN PROGRESS: Research on the theory and measurement of sport motivations.

SIDELIGHTS: Butt commented: "I am concerned with the negative relationship between constructive personal and social development and the competitive ethic."

* * *

BUTTON, Daniel E(van) 1917-

PERSONAL: Born November 1, 1917, in Dunkirk, N.Y.; son of Roy and Alice (Root) Button; married Rebecca Pool, 1945 (divorced, 1969); married Rena Pritsker (an administrator), August 16, 1969; children: Nancy Button Nathan, Sarah, Daniel, Jefferson, Mary. *Education:* University of Delaware, A.B., 1938; Columbia University, M.S., 1939. *Residence:* South Egremont, Mass. *Office:* Hearst Magazines, 250 West 57th St., New York, N.Y. 10019.

CAREER: Wilmington News-Journal, Wilmington, Del., reporter and editor, 1939-43; Associated Press, New York City, reporter and editor, 1943-46; University of Delaware, Newark, director of public relations, 1947-52; State University of New York at Albany, assistant to president, 1952-58; *Albany Times-Union,* Albany, N.Y., executive editor, 1959-66; U.S. House of Representatives, Washington, D.C., Republican member representing 29th District in New York, 1967-71; Arthritis Foundation, New York City, president, 1971-75; Hearst Magazines, New York City, editor of *Science Digest,* 1976—.

WRITINGS: Lindsay: Man for Tomorrow, Random House, 1965.

WORK IN PROGRESS: Two books.

SIDELIGHTS: Button's main interests are public affairs, political affairs, government, and popularization of scientific subjects.

C

CALABRESE, Anthony 1938-

PERSONAL: Born April 14, 1938, in Brooklyn, N.Y.; son of Samuel (an antiques dealer) and Viola (an antiques dealer; maiden name, Ziccardi) Calabrese; married Rosalie Hochman, June 15, 1960 (divorced November 3, 1972); married Rosemary LaPlaca Peters (an actress), October 15, 1977; children: (first marriage) Christopher. *Education:* City College (now of the City University of New York), B.A., 1959; RCA Institutes, diploma, 1968. *Religion:* Roman Catholic. *Home and office:* 33 West 63rd St., New York, N.Y. 10023. *Agent:* Charles Hunt, 19 West 44th St., New York, N.Y. 10023.

CAREER: Writer. Dean of Television Studio School, 1975-77; writer and producer, Hal Roach Studios, New York, N.Y., 1975-78. *Member:* Dramatists Guild.

WRITINGS: (With Maurice Waller) *Fats Waller,* Macmillan, 1977. Also author of television and film scripts, including "Six Plus One," NBC-TV, "Those Darn Kids," Hal Roach Studios, and "Those Dizzy Dames," Hal Roach Studios. Writer and director of "Holiday Storybook," a television series. Contributor to newspapers.

WORK IN PROGRESS: Hal Roach, Clown Prince of Hollywood, with publication by Prentice-Hall; *We Have the Pope;* "Just One More Spring," a musical play.

SIDELIGHTS: Calabrese writes: "I believe life itself is the greatest inspiration to a writer. Biographies are fascinating to write, but that might be because I really enjoy research. It's like working on a giant puzzle; even *you* don't know it will turn out." *Avocational interests:* Gardening.

* * *

CALHOUN, Thomas 1940-

PERSONAL: Born March 1, 1940, in Pittsburgh, Pa.; son of Robert B. (in business) and Mary Elizabeth (an educator) Calhoun; divorced; children: Kristin, Corinna. *Education:* Princeton University, A.B., 1962; University of Pittsburgh, M.A., 1964; University of Michigan, Ph.D., 1967. *Office:* Department of English, University of Delaware, Newark, Del. 19711.

CAREER: University of Michigan, Ann Arbor, instructor in English, 1964-67; University of Delaware, Newark, assistant professor, 1967-73, associate professor of English, 1973—. Participant in international seminars. *Member:* Modern Language Association of America, Renaissance Society of America, Milton Society.

WRITINGS: (Editor with J. M. Potter) *Andrew Marvell: The Garden,* C. E. Merrill, 1970; *Henry Vaughan: The Achievement of Silex Scintillans,* University of Delaware Press, 1980.

WORK IN PROGRESS: Poems; research on Petrarch's *Canzoniere,* Renaissance lyric and sonnet sequences, and contemporary fiction.

* * *

CAMERON, George Glenn 1905-1979

OBITUARY NOTICE: Born July 30, 1905, in Washington, Pa.; died September 15, 1979, in Ann Arbor, Mich. Educator and writer who founded the University of Michigan's department of Near Eastern studies. A professor of Near Eastern culture, Cameron was an expert on ancient Persia and the author of numerous articles and books on the subject, including *History of Early Iran* and *Persepolis Treasury Tablets.* Obituaries and other sources: *Directory of American Scholars,* Volume I: *History,* 6th edition, Bowker, 1974; *Who's Who in America,* 38th edition, Marquis, 1974; *New York Times,* September 17, 1979.

* * *

CAMPBELL, Jeffrey
See BLACK, Campbell

* * *

CAMUS, Albert 1913-1960
(Bauchart, Albert Mathe; Saetone, a joint pseudonym)

PERSONAL: Name pronounced Al-*bair* Kah-*mu;* born November 7, 1913, in Mondovi, Algeria; died January 4, 1960, in an automobile accident; son of Lucien (a farm laborer) and Catherine (a charwoman; maiden name, Sintes) Camus; married Simone Hie, 1933 (divorced); married Francine Faure, 1940; children: (second marriage) Jean (son) and Catherine (twins). *Education:* University of Algiers, diplome d'etudes superieures, 1936. *Religion:* "Atheistic humanist." *Home:* 29 rue Madame, Paris 6eme, France.

CAREER: Novelist, essayist, and playwright. Worked as meteorologist, stockbroker's agent, and civil servant; actor, writer, and producer of stage productions with Theatre du travail (later named Theatre de l'equipe), 1935-38; journalist with *Alger-Republican,* 1938-40; teacher in Oran, Algeria, 1940-42; journalist in Paris, France, 1942-45; Editions Gallimard, reader, 1943-60, director of Espoir collection; *Combat* (daily newspaper), co-founder, 1945, editor, 1945-47. Staff member of *Paris Soir,* 1938. Founder of Committee to Aid the Victims of Totalitarian States. *Wartime service:* Member of the French resistance movement. *Awards, honors:* Awarded Medal of the Liberation; Prix de la critique, 1947, for *La Peste;* Nobel Prize for Literature, 1957, for *L'Exil et le royaume;* awarded Prix algerian du roman.

WRITINGS—Novels: *L'Etranger,* Gallimard, 1942, translation by Stuart Gilbert published as *The Stranger,* Knopf, 1946 (published in England as *The Outsider,* Hamish Hamilton, 1946), reprinted U.S. edition, Vintage Books, 1972; *La Peste,* Gallimard, 1947, translation by Gilbert published as *The Plague,* Knopf, 1948, reprinted, Vintage Books, 1972; *La Chute,* Gallimard, 1956, translation by Justin O'Brien published as *The Fall,* Knopf, 1957.

Plays: *Le Malentendu* [and] *Caligula* (former, three-act, first produced at Theatre des Mathurins, May, 1944; latter, four-act, first produced at Theatre Hebertot in 1945), Gallimard, 1944, translation by Gilbert published as *Caligula* [and] *Cross Purpose* (former produced in New York City, February 10, 1960), New Directions, 1947 (also see below); *L'Etat de siege* (first produced in 1948), Gallimard, 1948, translation published as "State of Siege" in *Caligula and Three Other Plays* (also see below); *Les Justes* (first produced at Theatre Hebertot, December, 1949), Gallimard, 1950, translation by Elizabeth Sprigge and Philip Warner published as *The Just Assassins,* Microfilm, 1957, published in *Caligula and Three Other Plays* (also see below).

La Devotion a la croix (title means "Devotion to the Cross"; adaptation of the work by Calderon de la Barca), Gallimard, 1953; *Les Esprits* (title means "The Wits"; adaptation of the work by Pierre de Larivey), Gallimard, 1953; *Un Cas interessant* (title means "An Interesting Case"; adaptation of the work by Dino Buzatti; first produced at Theatre La Bruyere, May, 1955), L'Avant-scene, 1955; *Requiem pour une nonne* (adaptation of the novel *Requiem for a Nun,* by William Faulkner; first produced at Theatre des Mathurins, October, 1956), Gallimard, 1956; *Caligula and Three Other Plays* (also contains "State of Siege," "Cross Purpose," and "The Just Assassins"), Knopf, 1958; *Les Possedes* (adaptation of the novel *The Possessed,* by Fyodor Dostoyevsky; first produced at Theatre Antoine, February, 1955), Gallimard, 1959, translation published as *The Possessed,* Knopf, 1960.

Essays: *L'Envers et l'endroit* (title means "Inside and Out"), Charlot Alger, 1937; *Le Mythe de Sisyphe,* Gallimard, 1942, translation by O'Brien published as *The Myth of Sisyphus and Other Essays,* Knopf, 1955; *Lettres a un ami allemand,* Gallimard, 1945; *Noces* (title means "Nuptials"), Charlot Alger, 1945; *L'Existence,* Gallimard, 1945; *Le Minotaur; ou, La Halte d'Oran* (title means "The Minotaur; or, Stopping at Oran"), Charlot Alger, 1950; *Actuelles I: Chroniques, 1944-1948* (title means "Now I: Chronicles, 1944-1948"), Gallimard, 1950; *L'Homme revolte,* Gallimard, 1951, translation by Anthony Bower published as *The Rebel: An Essay on Man in Revolt,* Knopf, 1954, revised edition, 1956; *Actuelles II: Chroniques, 1948-1953* (title means "Now II: Chronicles, 1948-1953"), Gallimard, 1953; *L'Ete* (title means "Summer"), Gallimard, 1954.

(With Arthur Koestler) *Reflexions sur la peine capitale* (contains "Reflexions sur la potence," by Koestler, and "Reflexions sur la guillotine," by Camus; translation of latter published separately as *Reflections on the Guillotine;* see below), Calman-Levy, 1957; *Actuelles III: Chronique algerienne, 1939-1958* (title means "Now III: Algerian Chronicle, 1939-1958"), Gallimard, 1958; *Discours de suede,* Gallimard, 1958, translation by O'Brien published as *Speech of Acceptance Upon the Award of the Nobel Prize for Literature, Delivered in Stockholm on the Tenth of December, 1957,* Knopf, 1958.

Reflections on the Guillotine: An Essay on Capital Punishment, translation by Richard Howard of "Reflections sur la guillotine" (see above), Fridtjof-Karla Publications, 1960; *Neither Victims nor Executioners,* translated from the French by Dwight Macdonald, Liberation, 1960; *Resistance, Rebellion, and Death,* translated from the French by O'Brien, Knopf, 1961; *Meditations sur le theatre et la vie,* P. Alberts, 1961; *Essais,* Gallimard, 1965; *Lyrical and Critical Essays,* edited by Philip Thody, translated from the French by Ellen Conroy Kennedy, Knopf, 1968.

Other: *L'Exile et le royaume* (short stories; contains "Le Renegat," "Jonas," "La Femme adultere," "Les Muets," "L'Hote," and "La Pierre qui pousse"), Gallimard, 1957, translation by O'Brien published as *Exile and the Kingdom,* Hamish Hamilton, 1960; *Lettre a Bernanos,* Minard, 1963; *Carnets: Janvier 1942-mars 1951,* Gallimard, 1964, translation by O'Brien published as *Notebooks: 1942-1951,* Modern Library, 1970; *La Mort heureuse,* Gallimard, 1971, translation by Jean Sarocchi published as *A Happy Death,* Vintage Books, 1973; *Youthful Writings,* translated from the French by Kennedy, Vintage Books, 1977.

Author of prefaces to many works. Contributor to *Combat* (under pseudonyms Bauchart and Albert Mathe, and under joint pseudonym Saetone), to *Alger-Republican, Soir-Republican, L'Express,* and many other newspapers and magazines.

WORK IN PROGRESS: Le Premier Homme (title means "The First Man"), a novel; "Don Juan," a play.

SIDELIGHTS: "Above all his contemporaries," declared *Time* magazine, Camus "was the authentic voice of France's war generation." It was he who elucidated the unique problems that troubled his generation, noted Francois Mauriac. Camus, typically pictured in a rumpled trenchcoat with a cigarette dangling from his mouth, his brow furrowed, was also deeply admired by the generation following his own. "He was a moral conscience for thousands of young people in Europe and the United States, as he is still today," William Barnett observed. In response to the international acclaim that seemed to greet him overnight, Camus asks in *L'Ete* simply, "What else have I done but meditate on an idea I found in the streets of my time?"

Camus did indeed capture in his writings the moral climate of the mid-twentieth century. In the 1940's, values were being challenged as no longer relevant. With the atrocities and feelings of hopelessness brought about by World War II, many people concluded there is no reason for human existence. But while Camus did most certainly perceive life's absurdity, he did not adopt this point of view. "In the darkest depths of our nihilism," he wrote, "I have sought only for the means to transcend nihilism." *Time* observed that "because Camus articulated despair so eloquently, a generation bred in depression, surrender and occupation chose him its leader in its quest for something to believe in."

In his search to break through the pervading sense of meaninglessness to discover happiness, Camus charted a plan of writing that would eventually encompass at least three cycles. He named each cycle after a figure in mythology, calling the first Sisyphus, the second Prometheus, and the third Nemesis. The novel *The Stranger,* the play *Caligula,* and the essay *The Myth of Sisyphus* together form cycle one which is concerned with a certain duality in man's nature: the love of life vs. the hatred of death.

In *The Stranger,* perhaps Camus's most famous work, the protagonist Meursault takes life for granted until he finds himself awaiting the death penalty for having killed an Arab in a bizarre sequence of events. Meursault is a stranger in life because he does not parrot conventional cant—neither at his mother's funeral nor as the defendant in the courtroom. When his mother dies, for example, he feels little emotion and does not pretend otherwise. Then when his lawyer tries to induce him to respond to judicial questions in the socially acceptable way, Meursault refuses to do so. Those around him are threatened by his candor. He is subsequently sentenced, shunning last of all the chaplain's offer of God. As Maurois put it, "Meursault is saved by that which destroys him," that is, by death.

When *The Stranger* first appeared in print, Jean-Paul Sartre predicted it would become a classic. Often required reading for literature classes, *The Stranger* has been viewed as Camus's only nihilist novel. John Weightman wrote that it is "one of the first modern books—perhaps the very first—in which the Absurdist awareness of the absence of any settled moral truth is worked into all the details of the story." To Henri Peyre, "the romantic condemnation of a bourgeois society whose judges sentence a murder too harshly is a little facile. But the young Camus had thus to begin by setting himself against the world as he found it; before he could discover how to change it or how to rethink it, he had to depict it as unsatisfactory."

In *Caligula,* the concept of the absurd is taken further than in *The Stranger*. The character Caligula is based on Caius Caesare Augustus Germanicus, called Caligula, who became emperor of Rome at the age of twenty-five. A gentle man at the onset of his reign, Caligula gradually evolved into a cruel and heartless ruler who was assassinated several years later. In Camus's portrayal of Caligula, the latter is transformed into a tyrant after the death of his sister-lover Drusilla. It becomes clear to the emperor that "men die and they are unhappy." Like Meursault, Caligula rebels, but his revolt takes a far more extreme form.

Since life is absurd, Caligula reasons, every act is equally senseless. He then proceeds to prove his point by destroying accepted conventions. For instance, he seduces a man's wife, with the man himself as witness, causes a famine, and tortures his subjects indiscriminately. His aim is to educate the self-deluding patricians, noted Germaine Bree. A segment of the oppressed people revolt, which culminates in the assassination of the emperor. Before the end, Caligula laments, "I didn't take the right road, I came out nowhere. My freedom is not the right kind." Robert Jay Lifton called *Caligula* Camus's "most vivid rendition of the absurd survivor, and one of the most important plays ever written about the aberrations of the survivor state."

Sisyphus is another survivor. According to the legend, he is eternally condemned to push a boulder the full height of a mountain only for it to roll back down to the starting point. Sisyphus "is the absurd hero," explains Camus in the essay "The Myth of Sisyphus." "He *is,* as much through his passions as through his torture. His scorn of the gods, his hatred of death, and his passion for life won him that unspeakable penalty in which the whole being is exerted toward accomplishing nothing. This is the price that must be paid for the passions of this world." For Camus, Sisyphus represents all men.

The Fall links the idea of the absurd to Camus's second cycle of writing, Bree pointed out. Written in the first person, as are all of Camus's novels, this particular work can be grouped with the *roman personnels,* observed Rima Drell Reck, as can *The Nephew of Rameau* and *The Rhyme of the Ancient Mariner. The Fall* is a monologue delivered by Jean-Baptiste Clemence over a period of five days. Clemence, a one-time lawyer, had abandoned a lucrative practice in Paris. He could no longer in good conscience judge other people without viewing himself as a hypocrite: "Who is to say he is not equally guilty?" he asks himself. Clemence ends up relating his transgressions to all who will listen in a Dutch bar frequented by sailors. "In short," he confesses, "I never bothered with larger concerns except in the intervals between my little flings." His frankness evokes similar disclosures from his listeners, and to Clemence this proves that all men are inherently wicked. Camus describes him as "an empty prophet for a mediocre era." Reck wrote that *The Fall* is "a brilliant representation of the problems of justice and guilt which were Camus's consistent themes."

Revolt is the theme of Prometheus, the mythological hero who represents Camus's second cycle. Camus's version of the parable is against traditional revolution. Prometheus loves man and leads him to battle against the gods, whom Prometheus despises. Eventually, man begins to question his mission, but Prometheus avows his belief in their actions. "Those who doubt will be thrown out into the desert, nailed on a rock, offered as prey to cruel birds. All others shall walk in the dark behind the pensive and solitary master." As Camus puts it, Prometheus has thus become Caesar.

In the novel *The Plague,* the plays *The Just Assassins* and *The State of Siege,* and the essay *The Rebel,* Camus "examines the notion of revolt, as he had already taken and deduced the practical consequences of such a position," observed Bree. Camus's is a metaphysical kind of revolt, referring to "the vision, the questioning, the *protest* which man finds in himself," explained David Anderson. Similarly, Camus writes in *Notebooks* that "the revolutionary spirit lies in man's protest against the human condition."

The Plague is Camus's "most complex and probably his most satisfying work," Philip Thody commented. Moreover, Bree observed that *The Plague* is "within its limits, a great novel, the most disturbing, most moving novel yet to have come out of the chaos of the mid-century." On the other hand, Reck wrote that while the book met with popular acclaim in 1947, she considered it for the contemporary public "a novel whose message is too obvious and whose means are scant."

The story takes place in the Algerian town of Oran where life is very routine. As the tale progresses, one rat dies, more rats, then one human, and before long a pestilence has almost imperceptibly ravaged the city. The pain that the plague causes, Maurois pointed out, has at least elicited real feeling from the normally sedate townspeople. The actions of the characters illustrate that the complacent can be moved to take heroic action when faced with an emergency situation. Therefore, there is hope for the human condition, as long as the transition is not forgotten when life returns to normal.

The events are related in the third person by Dr. Rieux, who is not revealed as the narrator until the end of the book. Throughout the story Dr. Rieux fervently strives to aid the plague victims. For him, wrote Bree, "the plague is, in essence, the clear inner awareness of man's accidental and transitory presence on the earth, an awareness that is the source of all metaphysical torment, a torment which in Camus's eyes is one of the characteristics of our time."

The artist Tarrou also combats the disease, alongside his friend Rieux. A sensitive intellectual, Tarrou chronicles in his diary the events taking place in Oran. In one entry he states, "I know with a certain knowledge that each man carries a plague within." The principal difference between Rieux and Tarrou, noted Bree, is that the latter "is trying to purge himself of all evil, trying to transcend his human condition."

The Plague has been viewed as Camus's "most anti-Christian" novel. To Reck, Camus "suggests that faith is questionable, that man's torments are unjustifiable, that religion offers no answers to the travail of quotidian existence." It thus becomes apparent in the narrative that whether there is a God or not, man must take the responsibility for his life into his own hands.

But, to Camus, the plague itself served also as a metaphor for "Fascism, the Nazi era, [and] the occupation of France," wrote Lottman. Irene Finel-Honigman similarly called the story an allegory "of the concentration camps and the prisoner-of-war camps. Oran in this interpretation transcends its definition as a city and becomes a microcosm of a war-torn state."

Although the personification of evil in the symbolic play *The State of Siege* is named "King Plague," and though there are surface similarities to the novel, Camus averred that the play is not an adaptation of *The Plague*. As Bree pointed out, it is instead redolent of *Ubu roi* by Alfred Jarry. When compared to Camus's own works, *The State of Siege* is most similar to *Caligula*, also a "play with death," Bree wrote. "This time, however, death alone does not hold sway, for *L'Etat de siege* also concerns love and life." Diego, the rebel in the play, "stirs up the latent forces of energy and freedom among the inhabitants of Cadiz, awakening the citizens from their lethargy, calling them back to life."

The State of Siege was one of Camus's favorite works, but at its Paris opening the play was a flop. Lottman noted: "With an all-star cast and contributions from ... notable artists nothing should have gone wrong. But everything did." French author Rene Barjavel's reaction to the production was, "Since I have been going to the theatre, I believe that I have never suffered as much." Camus remarked in the introduction to the English translation of the play that *The State of Siege* "had without effort achieved critical unanimity" and "a complete cutting up."

The Just Assassins (Les Justes) was greeted with more opposing reactions. The Communist newspaper *L'Humanite* found the characters unrealistic and the play itself "worse than cold—icy." But *Le Populaire*, a Socialist party publication, reviewed it as "powerful and moving." *The Just Assassins* deals with Russian terrorism in the early 1900's. The plot involves a Socialist group that makes plans to assassinate the Grand Duke. A young poet, Kaliayev, who is totally committed to the cause of the organization, is chosen to throw the bomb that will kill the Duke. Seeing himself as "the avenger of the people," as Bree noted, Kaliayev dies for his actions without regret. But his death raises the question, Is the sacrifice of one person worth the promise of a better future for mankind? Chiarmonte concluded in the *Partisan Review* that "after all is said about the weakness of *Les Justes* as a play, it remains a piece of literary work that commands respect."

Writing *The Rebel, (L'Homme revolte)*, the last volume in the cycle of Prometheus, was not an easy task for Camus. But he felt it was his responsibility: afterward he could freely devote his time to creating more literature. In his *Notebooks* he states: "For my own part, I should not have written *L'Homme revolte* if in the forties I had not found myself face to face with men whose acts I did not understand. To put it briefly, I did not understand that men could torture others without ever ceasing to look at them."

In *The Rebel*, Camus defines revolt as the "impulse that drives an individual to the defense of a dignity common to all men." He takes the phrase by Descartes, "I think, therefore I am," and turns it into "I revolt, therefore we are." Citing paths of rebellion chosen by numerous figures throughout history, Camus illustrates how each was unsuccessful according to his own definition of revolt. The Marquis de Sade's actions were too calculated, too intellectual; Rimbaud's too individualized. But Camus criticized Hegel's method of rebellion above all, stating that "any revolt which does not recognize that it should transcend nihilism and establish [a] limit is doomed to justify murder and lead to dictatorship," noted Thody.

The Rebel's "structural and rational flaws are glaring," Reck contended, but even so, it sparked more controversy than any other writing by Camus. It is "the only thing written by Camus resembling a political philosophy," said Reck. Probably one of the major conflicts was fostered by Camus's condemnation of Marxism: "End satisfies the means? Is this possible? But what will justify the ends?" Camus further asserted that the Left should oppose Stalinism. This tenet led to an attack of *The Rebel* in *Le Temps moderne* by Francis Jeanson. Camus's friend from Paris's Left Bank, existentialist Jean-Paul Sartre, suggested that Camus respond to the article. Camus did indeed reply, criticizing Sartre's belief that Stalinism should be accepted by the leftists because the majority of the working class had already adopted that philosophy. The result was a much publicized rift between Camus and Sartre. "The break between these two leading French writers touched off literary pyrotechnics vivid even for Paris," wrote the *New York Times*.

Camus never completed the third cycle of his writing to be called Nemesis, concerning measure. At the time of his death, plans for a play entitled "Don Juan" were on the drawing board. Camus had also written about one hundred pages of the rough draft of his epic novel, *The First Man*. Based on the first French settlers in Algeria, the book was to be Camus's *War and Peace*. In addition, Bree gathered from Camus's *Notebooks* that the author was planning on a fourth cycle, dealing with compassion and "a certain kind of love."

Not all of Camus's writings fall specifically into the aforementioned categories. Although less open to critical dispute than *The Stranger, The Fall*, and *The Plague*, it was the collection of short stories, *Exile and the Kingdom*, that won Camus the Nobel Prize for Literature in 1957. In these six stories, Camus emphasizes "the kingdom of man" in which each hero reaches a new awareness of life, Bree pointed out. Camus also successfully adapted plays, staged others of his own, and wrote a variety of other essays.

The publication of any work by Camus was "eagerly anticipated and greeted in Paris itself," noted Bree. "Discussed, attacked, and defended, it was promptly translated into many languages, and as it crossed national frontiers it was once again attacked, praised, or refuted." But as literature, Rima Drell Reck remarked, Camus's fiction is "conceptionally thin." His novels, for instance, are all essays in fictional form, she said. Camus deliberately chose this medium of expression, though, explained Henri Peyre, to keep his ideas from appearing overly "dry." Reck concluded that "Camus' originality as a novelist lay in his ability to state his insights ambiguously, that is, with the density and complexity of human existence."

The first major writer to emerge from North Africa, Camus was imbued with a "Mediterranean sensibility," wrote Reck, a sensibility that profoundly influenced his writings. Camus saw the Algeria of his youth as a place of perpetual summer. "The sun, the sea, the flowers, the desert, and in contrast, the teeming cities composed his inner, passionately cherished landscape," noted Bree. "At the heart of Camus's sensitivity, imagination and thought, and at the heart of his work, are the beauty of the African coast and the glory of an 'inexhaustible sun.'"

Camus spent the first twenty-seven years of his life in Algiers, Algeria's capital. His family was poor, but because of the sunny Algerian climate, he never felt destitute. He was raised in a second floor apartment—three rooms and a kitchen—in a working-class section of the city. (Later, Camus was to say that he belonged only to the class of mankind). Besides Camus, the household was made up of his mother, brother, maternal grandmother, and two uncles.

Camus's father, a native Algerian of Alsacian descent, had been killed at the first battle of the Marne when Camus was just a year old. Catherine Sintes Camus, Camus's mother, was of Spanish heritage. Although, unlike her husband, Catherine was illiterate, it has been said that Camus acquired from her a certain Castilian air of nobility, or *pudeur,* as Lottman described it. Because she was partially deaf, and much affected by her husband Lucien's death, Catherine left the rearing of her sons to her own strong-willed mother. That Camus still focused his love on his mother later becomes evident in some of his writings. But, "without general availability of Camus's unfinished novel, *Le Premier Homme* [The First Man], readers will not know the full story of Camus's feelings for this silent, submissive figure who became a more marvelous woman to her son as he grew older," Lottman observed.

Despite the lack of an intellectual atmosphere at home, Camus was nonetheless a superior student at school. An instructor, Louis Germain, recognized potential in the young Camus and encouraged him to excel. Germain lent him books to read, spent extra time with him, and persuaded Camus's autocratic grandmother to permit him to remain in school rather than go to work. He also urged Camus to vie for the scholarship that allowed him to attend high school. In 1957, Camus dedicated his Nobel Prize acceptance speech to this first mentor.

While in his early teens, Camus was an active sports enthusiast. He swam often and was an avid soccer player, serving as goalie for the Racing Universitaire Algerois (RUA). As an adult, he wrote of this experience, "After many years during which I saw many things, what I know most surely about morality and the duty of man I owe to sport and learned in the RUA."

Camus's sports activities came to a halt when, at seventeen, he contracted tuberculosis in his right lung. The disease eventually spread to his left lung as well. With no method yet discovered of removing the tubercle bacilli, Camus was to be afflicted for the remainder of his life, making him a target for depression and flu. At his doctor's recommendation, the seventeen-year-old Camus convalesced at the home of his more affluent Aunt Antoinette and Uncle Acault, a man of "extreme republican and Voltairian persuasion," wrote Philip Thody.

Undaunted by his illness, Camus entered the University of Algiers. There, with Jean Grenier as his new mentor, Camus studied Greek literature, poetry, and philosophy, and discovered the works of Pascal, St. Augustine, Kierkegaard, and Plato. He also belonged to a young intellectual group known as the "North Africa Literary School," which would meet in cafes in the Kasbah to talk, over cups of mint tea. Even then Camus had a unique quality about him. Jacques Huergon, a University of Algiers Latin professor, recalled, "He simply loomed up among us as someone whose life was going to be important, who was going to begin, starting at zero and without complacency, the great enterprise of being a man."

In 1936, Camus earned his diplome d'etudes superieures in philosophy, but, because he could not pass the required physical, Camus was prevented from receiving his agregation, the degree that would allow him to teach. He subsequently began a career in journalism, writing first for the *Alger-Republican.* Meanwhile, Camus became involved in politics and joined up with the Communist party. As was typical of other leftist students, Camus was "anti-Mussolini, anti-Hitler, anti-Franco, rather vague on facts and enthusiastically in favor of social reform in France," Bree pointed out. Eventually, though, he became disillusioned with the party and broke all ties with it in 1937.

By 1942, Camus had moved to Paris where he became a part of the French resistance movement against German occupation. He was writing *The Plague* and *The Rebel,* while simultaneously working as a reader at the Gallimard publishing company during the day and writing for the underground newspaper *Combat* at night. Jean-Paul Sartre and Simone de Beauvoir were also on the *Combat* staff. So were Andre Malraux and Michel Gallimard (a relative of the publisher), both of whom became Camus's friends. At *Combat,* Camus wrote clandestinely under the names Albert Mathe, Bauchart, and the joint pseudonym Saetone. Despite his precautions, Camus barely escaped being caught by the Nazi gestapo at least once.

The day before Paris's liberation, *Combat* became a full-fledged daily newspaper, with Camus as editor. It had become "one of the best-written newspapers of the French press since the beginning of its existence," contended Jean Daniel. Sartre commented that Camus's editorship of *Combat* was "the admirable coming together of a person, an action, and a work." "He couldn't have known it," observed Lottman, "but the mission he had undertaken was designed to catapult him into instant postwar stardom, he more than anyone else connected with *Combat.*" In 1944, Camus left journalism for good to focus entirely on other forms of writing.

Camus became known as an existentialist and a philosopher, but he himself adamantly rejected both labels. In *Actuelles I* he wrote, "I have little liking for the too famous existential philosophy, and to speak frankly, I think its conclusions are false." He further asserted in *Actuelles II,* "I am not a philosopher and never claimed to be one." Instead, he viewed himself as a moralist, by his own definition, "a man with a passion for the human heart."

But even above being a moralist, Camus perceived himself as an artist with a responsibility to mankind. In his Nobel Prize acceptance speech, Camus said: "In my eyes, art is not a solitary pleasure. It is a means of moving the greatest number of men by offering them a privileged image of common sufferings and common joys. Thus art forces the artist to isolate himself." Furthermore, the responsibility of the artist is to be aware of and even active in political affairs. Yet this concept is in conflict with the solitude demanded by the actual act of creating art. In Bernard Malamud's opinion, some of Camus's "best writing deals with the relationship between . . . political action and artistic creation."

Camus had just emerged from a long-lived writer's block, full of ideas for future writings, when he died suddenly. On January 4, 1960, Camus was apparently planning on riding the train to Paris from his farmhouse in Loumarin when his friend, Michel Gallimard, traveling with his wife and daughter, offered him a ride. Camus accepted, taking with him the beginnings of *The First Man*. According to *Time* magazine, the Gallimards and Camus were eighty miles outside of Paris when the left rear tire of the Facel Vega blew out. The car spun out of control, hitting one tree, then smashing into another, Camus died upon impact. He was forty-six years old. "News of the death stunned the French literary world of which M. Camus was one of the brightest lights," wrote the *New York Times*. In Francois Mauriac's words, Camus's death was "one of the greatest losses that could have affected French letters at the present time." In general, newspapers commented that it was the absurd death of a man who recognized life as absurd.

BIOGRAPHICAL/CRITICAL SOURCES—Selected books: Jean-Paul Sartre, *Situations I,* Gallimard, 1947; Thomas Hanna, *The Thought and Art of Albert Camus,* Regnery, 1958; Claude Mauriac, *The New Literature,* translated from the French by Samuel I. Stone, Braziller, 1959; John Cruickshank, *Albert Camus and the Literature of Revolt,* Galaxy, 1960; Philip Thody, *Albert Camus, 1913-1960,* Macmillan, 1962; Alfred Kazin, *Contemporaries,* Little, Brown, 1962; *Camus: A Collection of Critical Essays,* edited by Germaine Bree, Prentice-Hall, 1962; Philip H. Rhein, *The Urge to Live: A Comparative Study of Franz Kafka's Der Prozess and Albert Camus' L'Etranger,* University of North Carolina Press, 1964; Bree, *Camus,* Rutgers University Press, revised edition, 1964; Norman Podhoretz, *Doings and Undoings,* Farrar, Straus, 1964.

Forms of Extremity in the Modern Novel, edited by Nathan A. Scott, Jr., John Knox, 1965; Emmett Parker, *Albert Camus: The Artist in the Arena,* University of Wisconsin Press, 1966; Henri Peyre, *French Novelists of Today,* Oxford University Press, 1967; Maurice Nadeau, *The French Novel Since the War,* translated from the French by A. M. Sheridan-Smith, Methuen, 1967; Bree and Margaret Otis Guiton, *An Age of Fiction: The French Novel From Gide to Camus,* Rutgers University Press, 1968; David Anderson, *The Tragic Protest,* John Knox, 1969; Rhein, *Albert Camus,* Twayne, 1969; Rima Drell Reck, *Literature and Responsibility: The French Novelist in the Twentieth Century,* Louisiana State University Press, 1969.

Conor Cruise O'Brien, *Albert Camus of Europe and Africa,* Viking, 1970; Leo Pollman, *Sartre and Camus: Literature of Existence,* Ungar, 1970; *The Politics of Twentieth-Century Novelists,* edited by George A. Panichas, Hawthorne, 1971; Morvan Lebesque, *Portrait of Camus,* Herder, 1971; Bree, *Camus and Sartre: Crisis and Commitment,* Delacorte, 1972; Albert Maquet, *Albert Camus: The Invincible Summer,* Humanities Press, 1972; Donald Lazere, *The Unique Creation of Albert Camus,* Yale University Press, 1973; *Contemporary Literary Criticism,* Gale, Volume 1, 1973, Volume 2, 1974, Volume 4, 1975, Volume 9, 1978, Volume 11, 1979; Jean Defrees Kellogg, *Dark Prophets of Hope: Dostoevsky, Sartre, Camus, Faulkner,* Loyola University Press, 1975; Paul Viallaneix, *The First Camus: An Introductory Essay and Youthful Writings by Albert Camus,* translated from the French by Ellen Conroy Kennedy, Knopf, 1976; Herbert R. Lottman, *Albert Camus: A Biography,* Doubleday, 1979.

Books by the author: *The Stranger,* Knopf, 1946; *The Plague,* Knopf, 1948; *Actuelles I: Chroniques, 1944-48,* Gallimard, 1950; *Actuelles II: Chroniques, 1948-53,* Gallimard, 1953; *The Rebel,* Knopf, 1954; *The Myth of Sisyphus and Other Essays,* Vintage Books, 1955; *The Fall,* Knopf, 1957; *Exile and the Kingdom,* Knopf, 1958; *Caligula and Three Other Plays,* Knopf, 1958; *Actuelles III: Chronique algerienne, 1939-1958,* Gallimard, 1958; *Notebooks: 1942-1951,* Modern Library, 1970.

Selected articles: *New York Review of Books,* June 15, 1972; *American Poetry Review,* January-February, 1973; *Modern Fiction Studies,* summer, 1973, spring, 1978; *Renascence,* winter, 1976; *Scandinavian Studies,* summer, 1976; *Time,* March 19, 1979.

OBITUARIES: New York Times, January 5, 1960; *France-Observateur,* January 7, 1960; *New Statesman,* January 9, 1960; *New Yorker,* January 16, 1960; *Time,* January 18, 1960; *Newsweek,* January 18, 1960; *New Republic,* January 18, 1960; *Commonweal,* February 12, 1960.*

—Sketch by Victoria France Hutchinson

* * *

CANBY, Henry Seidel 1878-1961

OBITUARY NOTICE: Born September 6, 1878, Wilmington, Del.; died April 5, 1961. Educator, editor, literary critic, and biographer. Canby was the co-founder and first editor of *Saturday Review of Literature* (now *Saturday Review*), and chairman of the editorial board of the Book-of-the Month Club for over twenty-eight years. He was an educator at Yale University for more than twenty years. Canby is the author of *Walt Whitman: An American* and *Turn West, Turn East: Mark Twain and Henry James,* in addition to numerous English textbooks. Obituaries and other sources: Henry Seidel Canby, *The Age of Confidence: Life in the Nineties,* Farrar & Rinehart, c. 1934; *Current Biography,* Wilson, 1942, June, 1961; *The Reader's Encyclopedia,* 2nd edition, Crowell, 1965; *The Oxford Companion to American Literature,* 4th edition, Oxford University Press, 1965; *Longman Companion to Twentieth Century Literature,* Longman, 1970.

* * *

CANN, Marjorie Mitchell 1924-

PERSONAL: Born August 26, 1924, in Moncton, New Brunswick, Canada; came to the United States in 1961; daughter of Douglas Robert and Maude (Dunham) Mitchell; married Donald Bruce Cann (a federal agronomist; divorced). *Education:* Nova Scotia Teachers College, professional certificate, 1934; Acadia University, B.Sc., 1940; Michigan State University, M.A., 1953, Ph.D., 1957. *Religion:* Christian. *Home:* 4740 Peacock Dr., Pensacola, Fla. 32504.

CAREER: Teacher and administrator of schools in Ontario, Nova Scotia, and Quebec, 1934-56; Acadia University, Wolfville, Nova Scotia, professor of mathematics, 1957-61; Delta College, University Center, Mich., director of mathematics programs, 1961-63; Greater Cleveland Mathematics Program, Cleveland, Ohio, research director, 1963-64; University of Akron, Akron, Ohio, professor of mathematics,

1964-67; Pensacola Junior College, Pensacola Fla., professor of education and psychology, 1967-79, administrator, 1975-79; writer, 1964—. Consultant. *Awards, honors:* Certificate of meritorious service from Northwest Florida Cerebral Palsy Association; distinguished service award from Florida's United Cerebral Palsy Association.

WRITINGS: Synthesis of Teaching Methods, McGraw (Canada), 1964, 3rd edition, 1972; (editor and contributor) *An Introduction to Education,* Crowell, 1972. Contributor to education journals.

WORK IN PROGRESS: A book on leadership qualities and personal characteristics in teachers; a collection of seminars on personnel management.

SIDELIGHTS: Marjorie Cann writes: "Important throughout my entire career has been my desire to 'light some candles' among my students so that their pathways may be lit with greater understanding and appreciation of the dedication characteristic of teachers who have made worthwhile contributions to their fields."

* * *

CANNING, John 1920-

PERSONAL: Original name, John Shushtary; name legally changed in 1948; born July 28, 1920, in Streatham, London, England; son of Mohammed Jaffah (a merchant and ship owner) and Aileen Norah (Gannon) Shushtary. *Education:* London School of Economics and Political Science, B.Sc., 1940. *Residence:* London, England. *Agent:* John Farquharson Ltd., Bell House, Bell Yard, London WC2A 2TU, England.

CAREER: Vawser & Wiles, London, England, editorial assistant, 1947-48; Odhams Press, London, editor of general books, 1948-67; Hamlyn Group, Feltham, England, managing editor, 1967-71; free-lance editor, 1971—. *Military service:* Royal Air Force, 1941-46; became squadron leader; mentioned in dispatches. *Member:* Press Club (London).

WRITINGS—Editor: *100 Great Events That Changed the World,* Odhams, 1966; *Living History: 1914,* Odhams, 1967; *50 Great Journeys,* Odhams, 1968; *50 Great Ghost Stories,* Souvenir Press, 1971; *50 Great Horror Stories,* Souvenir Press, 1971; *50 True Tales of Terror,* Souvenir Press, 1972; *100 Great Modern Lives,* Souvenir Press, 1972; *100 Great Adventures,* Souvenir Press, 1973; *100 Great Kings, Queens, and Rulers of the World,* Souvenir Press, 1973; *Great Europeans,* Souvenir Press, 1973; *100 Great Books,* Souvenir Press, 1974; *50 Strange Stories of the Supernatural,* Souvenir Press, 1974; *100 Great Lives,* Souvenir Press, 1975; *Great Disasters,* Octopus Books, 1976; *Adventure Stories for Boys,* Octopus Books, 1978; *Adventure Stories for Girls,* Octopus Books, 1978; *50 Strange Mysteries of the Sea,* Souvenir Press, 1979.

WORK IN PROGRESS: A compilation of short stories; an audio-cassette series on the occult.

SIDELIGHTS: Canning told *CA:* "It may be somewhat unusual to find a books editor in a reference volume on authors. However, the processes of each type of activity are not so very different from one another: the conception of a selling idea; the development of that idea into the structured framework; the effort to ensure that the result is an organic whole. The editor also has a number of responsibilities which are not normally the concern of the authors, namely, supervision of jacket design, prelims design, part titles and typography; compilation of glossary, index, notes on contributing authors, etc.; and writing of introductory matter and blurbs. In short, without taking anything away from the writers, the editor of a multi-authored compilation has to be both prime mover and orchestrator.

"I first started to produce lists of titles conceived and commissioned within the house whilst a staff editor at Odhams. I found that this mode of operation gave one greater freedom and commercial viability; one could deliberately choose the area and subject(s) for a book and commission the author(s) oneself without having to wait for random submissions by agents. It was like taking a hand in one's own evolution. But this type of operation does presuppose a nonfiction list."

Canning gave this advice to commissioning editors: "Know your market and build in relation to it, not to placate your own interests or hobby-horses (unless, of course, they happen to coincide)."

He continued: "Without, I hope, seeming to sound priggish, I believe that creativity of any sort has to be harnessed to a disciplined regimen to be properly exploited. I start work at 8:45 a.m. and carry on through the day as if still a staff editor."

Canning's books have been published in Scandinavian, Dutch, Greek, Spanish, Portuguese, and Italian. Selections from *100 Great Adventures* were broadcast on South African radio.

AVOCATIONAL INTERESTS: Philosophy, reading, walking, talking.

* * *

CANTOR, Paul A(rthur) 1945-

PERSONAL: Born October 25, 1945, in Brooklyn, N.Y.; son of Harry (in sales) and Helen (a teacher; maiden name, Katz) Cantor. *Education:* Harvard University, A.B., 1966, Ph.D., 1971. *Home:* 820-L Cabell Ave., Charlottesville, Va. 22903. *Office:* Department of English, University of Virginia, Charlottesville, Va. 22903.

CAREER: Harvard University, Cambridge, Mass., assistant professor of English, 1971-77; University of Virginia, Charlottesville, associate professor of English, 1977—. *Member:* Modern Language Association of America, Shakespeare Association of America.

WRITINGS: Shakespeare's Rome: Republic and Empire, Cornell University Press, 1976.

WORK IN PROGRESS: Romantic Man: The Creature and the Creator; studying Romantic creation myths, including Blake's *Book of Urizen.*

* * *

CANTOR, Paul David 1916-1979

OBITUARY NOTICE: Born March 7, 1916, in Fairmont, W.Va.; died of a stroke, October 21, 1979, in Bethesda, Md. Physician and lawyer who was a leading consultant on medical jurisprudence. Cantor was in private medical practice from 1942 until 1975 and had served as a medico-legal consultant to the Department of Justice. He was the editor-in-chief of the ten-volume *Traumatic Medicine and Surgery for Attorneys* and the executive editor of *Trauma.* Obituaries and other sources; *Who's Who in the East,* 14th edition, Marquis, 1973; *Washington Post,* October 24, 1979.

* * *

CAPLIN, Alfred Gerald 1909-1979 (Al Capp)

OBITUARY NOTICE—See index for *CA* sketch: Born September 28, 1909, in New Haven, Conn.; died November 5, 1979, in Cambridge, Mass. Columnist, television commentator, lecturer, and cartoonist best known for his comic strip "Li'l Abner," which featured a naive, nineteen-year-old Southerner living in the fictitious town of Dogpatch, Lower Slobbovia. The comic strip enjoyed a great deal of success from its beginning in the mid-1930's until the 1960's, when Capp's own political views, made obvious within the strip, changed from liberal to conservative. Because of the nature of "Li'l Abner," Capp is often compared to Mark Twain. Capp's strips have also been published in separate volumes, including *The Life and Times of the Shmoo, Fearless Fosdick,* and *The World of Li'l Abner.* Obituaries and other sources: *Current Biography,* Wilson, 1947; *Celebrity Register,* 3rd edition, Simon & Schuster, 1973; *Time,* October 17, 1977; *Newsweek,* October 17, 1977; *Who's Who in America,* 40th edition, Marquis, 1978; *New York Times,* November 6, 1979.

* * *

CAPP, Al
See CAPLIN, Alfred Gerald

* * *

CAPRON, Walter Clark 1904-1979

OBITUARY NOTICE—See index for *CA* sketch: Born September 25, 1904, in Elmira, N.Y.; died October 17, 1979, in Raynham, Mass. Career officer and author of several books on the U.S. Coast Guard. Capron was associated with the U.S. Coast Guard for thirty-five years before his retirement as captain in 1963. He spent about twenty years on sea duty and was deputy chief of staff from 1957 to 1962. Obituaries and other sources: *Washington Post,* October 20, 1979.

* * *

CARDIFF, Gray Emerson 1949-

PERSONAL: Born November 29, 1949, in Woodstock, Ill.; son of Edward Wesley Cardiff (in sales) and Nancy Jane (an art historian; maiden name, Gray) Cardiff Troyer. *Education:* Milwaukee School of Engineering, B.S. *Home:* 320 North Civic Dr., #302, Walnut Creek, Calif. 94596. *Office:* Shearson, Hayden, Stone, 1990 California Blvd., Walnut Creek, Calif. 94596.

CAREER: Electrical engineering consultant and construction cost estimator in Milwaukee, Wis., 1970-73; Bechtel Corp., San Francisco, Calif., cost engineer for nuclear plants, 1973-74; Merrill Lynch, Pierce, Fenner & Smith, San Francisco, stockbroker, 1974-78; Shearson, Hayden, Stone, Walnut Creek, Calif., investment advisor, 1978—.

WRITINGS: (With J. W. English) *The Coming Real Estate Crash,* Arlington House, 1979.

SIDELIGHTS: Cardiff writes: "The emotional state of people currently investing in real estate is intriguing. Their optimism is without foundation. People by the millions are aggressive speculators who don't perceive any risk whatsoever. These observations were the prime motivation for writing *The Coming Real Estate Crash.*"

* * *

CARMOY, Guy de 1907-

PERSONAL: Born February 20, 1907, in Paris, France; son of Pierre and Marguerite (Perquer) de Carmoy; married Marie de Gourcuff, 1934; children: Helene de Carmoy de Vogue, Herve, Beatrice de Carmoy Terray, Isabelle de Carmoy Matheus. *Education:* Paris Law School, licence en droit, 1928, additional diplomas in political economics and public law, 1929; Paris School of Arts, licence es lettres, 1928; Ecole Libre des Sciences Politiques, diploma, 1928. *Home:* 22 avenue de Suffren, Paris 15, France.

CAREER: Government of France, inspector of finances, beginning 1930, affiliated with general information commisariat, 1939, head of film department of Ministry of Information, 1940-41, budgetary controller, 1941-43; deported to Germany, 1943-45; International Bank for Reconstruction and Development, Washington, D.C., alternative executive director, 1946-48; Organization for European Economic Cooperation, director of administration and conferences, 1948-52; Institut d'Etudes Politiques, Paris, professor, 1950—. Associated with Institut Europeen d'Administration des Affaires, Fontainebleau, France, 1961—. Member of French delegation to meeting of European Economic Cooperation, 1948. *Awards, honors:* Decorated officer of Legion of Honor.

WRITINGS—In English: *Les Politiques etrangeres de la France, 1944-1966,* Table, 1967, translation by Elaine P. Halperin published as *The Foreign Policies of France, 1944-1968,* University of Chicago Press, 1970; *Energy for Europe: Economic and Political Implications,* American Enterprise, 1977.

Other works: *Les Organisations economiques internationales,* Les Cours de droit, 1950; *L'Economie internationale contemporaine,* Les Cours de droit, 1951, 3rd edition, 1958; *Fortune de l'Europe,* Editions Domat, 1953; *L'Economie francaise devant le march commun,* L'Organisation Francaise du Mouvement Europeen, 1957; *L'Adaptation de l'economie francaise au marche commun,* Sirey, 1958; *Professions et regions devant le march commun,* [Paris], 1959; *L'Economie europeene contemporaine,* Les Cours de droit, 1959-60, 5th edition, 1968; *L'Alliance Atlantique disloquee,* Association francais pour la Communaute Atlantique, 1966; *Le Dossier europeen de l'energie: les marches, les industries, les politiques,* Editions d'organisation, 1971.

SIDELIGHTS: Reviewing *The Foreign Policies of France, 1944-1968,* a *Times Literary Supplement* critic commented, "It is clear and well-documented and, although some will complain that it is too traditional in its approach, it is a book which many will like to read and consult."

BIOGRAPHICAL/CRITICAL SOURCES: Times Literary Supplement, September 18, 1970; *American Political Science Review,* December, 1970, December, 1978.*

* * *

CARON, Roger 1938-

PERSONAL: Born April 12, 1938, in Cornwall, Ontario, Canada; son of Donat and Yvonne (Carriere) Caron. *Education:* "True schooling at the Ontario Reformatory Guelph (ORG), 1954; graduated with honours to the BIG HOUSE (Kingston Penitentiary), January, 1956." *Politics:* "None other than proud to be a Canadian." *Religion:* "Lost that notion in solitary." *Home:* 285 Laurier St., Apt. 905, Hull, Quebec, Canada. *Agent:* Marilyn Gray, c/o McGraw-Hill Ryerson, 330 Progress Ave., Scarborough, Ontario, Canada M1P 2Z5.

CAREER: Writer. Incarcerated in institutions of the Canadian Penal System, 1954-78. *Member:* Ottawa Skydiving Center. *Awards, honors:* Governor General Award for best nonfiction, 1978, for *Go-Boy!*

WRITINGS: Go-Boy! Memoirs of a Life Behind Bars (autobiography), McGraw, 1978; *Bingo!* (nonfiction), McGraw, 1980.

SIDELIGHTS: John Faustmann described *Go-Boy!* as "one of the best prison books likely to emerge during this century." Noting Caron's descriptions of killing rats, communicating through plumbing, and receiving electro-shock therapy, Faustmann insisted that Caron "takes us closer to the heart of prison than most of us would ever like to go."

Caron earned his reputation as a dangerous criminal by exhibiting violent behavior and staging a number of daring bank robberies. He explained his criminal behavior by relating, "When I was young I had done a few bad things and people were always predicting my future. They said that I would die in prison or that I would be killed in a hail of police bullets. Well I said to myself, if these people think I'm bad now wait until I'm older. This terrific drive just kept me going and going until I ended up in prison."

Caron told *CA:* "Writing *Go-Boy!* was a voyage of self-discovery for me. Some people find out about themselves stretched out on a shrink's couch; my inner-therapy came from writing my own story, a compulsion that was greater and more compelling than the act of breathing. Because of my original caveman education it took fifteen years of daily writing and correcting myself with a dictionary to write well enough to be published."

Caron's second book, *Bingo,* centers around the 1971 uprising at Kingston Penitentiary.

AVOCATIONAL INTERESTS: Parachuting, jogging, tennis, roller skating, weightlifting, chess, horseback riding, gliding, "being called an 'escape artist' (thirteen jailbreaks)."

BIOGRAPHICAL/CRITICAL SOURCES: MacLeans, April 30, 1979; *Vancouver Free Press,* June 6, 1979; *Montreal Star,* September 1, 1979.

* * *

CAROUSSO, Georges 1909-

PERSONAL: Born February 28, 1909, in Alexandria, Egypt; came to the United States in 1919, naturalized citizen, 1924; son of Aristide S. (an inventor) and Corinne (a countess; maiden name, Castagna) Carousso; married Dorothee Hughes (a writer and genealogist), December 30, 1930; children: Dorothee Nowell Carousso McKinnon. *Education:* Attended Victoria College, Alexandria, Egypt, 1927, and Columbia University, 1929. *Religion:* Episcopalian. *Home:* 64 Cygnet Dr., Smithtown, N.Y. 11787. *Agent:* McIntosh & Otis, Inc., 475 Fifth Ave., New York, N.Y. 10017. *Office:* Georges Carousso & Associates, 220-D Blair Mill Village E., Horsham, Pa. 19044.

CAREER: City of New York, N.Y., engineering inspector, 1933-50; associated with Carl Boyir & Associates, in public relations, 1950-56; Gray & Rogers, Philadelphia, Pa., in public relations, 1956-60; C. Schmidt & Sons, Philadelphia, public relations director, 1960-67; Georges Carousso & Associates, Horsham, Pa., president, 1967—. Head of Philadelphia Safety Council. *Member:* International Institute of Arts and Letters (fellow), American Society of Journalists and Authors, Public Relations Society of America (local president), Pennsylvania Paraplegics Association (chairman), Metropolitan Rod and Gun Club (president), Bucks County Writers Guild. *Awards, honors:* Silver Anvil Award from Public Relations Society of America, 1960.

WRITINGS: I Wonder Why, Putnam, 1958. Work represented in anthologies, including *Alfred Hitchcock Stories of Suspense* and *Hilton Bedside Reader: Adventure for Americans.* Contributor of articles and stories to professional journals and popular magazines, including *Reader's Digest, Saturday Evening Post, Life, Cosmopolitan,* and *New Republic,* and newspapers.

WORK IN PROGRESS: A biography of Sir Richard Francis Burton; research on photovoltaic batteries.

SIDELIGHTS: Georges Carousso comments: "All subjects are vital. It's what you bring to them that counts. I write because I have always wanted to write, just as I hunt and fish because I want to hunt and fish. I don't always kill game, nor do I keep all the fish I catch. I left engineering because too much of it is 'two plus two equals four.' I'm still trying to prove that it may equal five—or that there is no such thing as a straight line. But engineering teaches structure. I hope I have incorporated *that* in my writings."

* * *

CARPENTER, Humphrey (William Bouverie) 1946-

PERSONAL: Born April 29, 1946, in Oxford, England. *Education:* Keble College, Oxford, B.A. and diploma in education.

CAREER: British Broadcasting Corp., London, England, radio producer, 1968-74; writer, 1974—.

WRITINGS: (With Mari Prichard) *A Thames Companion,* Oxford Illustrated Press, 1975; *The Joshers* (juvenile), Allen & Unwin, 1977; *J.R.R. Tolkien* (biography), Houghton, 1977; *The Inklings: C. S. Lewis, J.R.R. Tolkien, Charles Williams, and Their Friends,* Houghton, 1979; *The Captain Hook Affair* (juvenile), Allen & Unwin, 1979.

SIDELIGHTS: Carpenter's *The Inklings,* an examination of the literary group that counted J.R.R. Tolkien and C. S. Lewis among its membership, was deemed a "splendid entry" by Paul Piazza. Carpenter focuses on Lewis as the center of the group, although this may be due, in part, to the fact that he had already written a biography of Tolkien, and the other well-known member of the group, Charles Williams, had little impact on literature outside the group. Still, Piazza notes, "Tolkien and Williams were not significantly altered by the group, but Lewis was changed profoundly."

Concerning Lewis, Carpenter delves into his personal as well as literary life. He documents Lewis's thirty years of cohabitation with Janie Moore, mother of one of Lewis's friends, a woman described as "peevish and perverse," but Piazza notes that her relationship with Lewis was probably neither romantic or sexual. Carpenter also details Lewis's tragic relationship with Joy Davidman, an American Jew whom he married so that she could live in England. Lewis eventually fell in love with Davidman and they renewed their vows in a more elaborate ritual than their previous civil ceremony. Unfortunately, Joy Lewis died of cancer three years later. Carpenter reveals that the marriage may never have been consumated.

Carpenter's attention to Tolkien is largely centered around the latter's relationship with Lewis. Although the two men had opposing backgrounds, they enjoyed an immediate friendship and often read aloud to each other when the Inklings convened. Carpenter attributes their eventual split to Lewis's enthusiasm for Charles Williams, whom Tolkien once called a "witch doctor". Lewis, in return, was dismayed by Tolkien's dismissal of the former's "Narnia" series.

For all the emotional intrigue and complexity of the principal characters, Carpenter does not deal offensively with his subject. As Christopher Ricks writes, "The book exercises curiosity, not nosiness. No punches are pulled—or pushed; the pugnacious yet unviolent Lewis would have approved."

BIOGRAPHICAL/CRITICAL SOURCES: Washington Post, March 26, 1979; *New York Times,* March 29, 1979; *New York Times Book Review,* April 8, 1979.

* * *

CARR, Jay Phillip 1936-

PERSONAL: Born August 19, 1936, in New York, N.Y.; son of Andrew Joseph and Florence (Glassman) Carr; married Nancy Lou Hutchison, October 27, 1962; children: Diane Elizabeth, Richard Joseph, Julia Veronica. *Education:* City College (now of the City University of New York), B.S., 1958. *Home:* 781 East Snell Rd., Rochester, Mich. 48063. *Office: Detroit News,* 615 West Lafayette, Detroit, Mich. 48231.

CAREER/WRITINGS: Drama, music, and film critic. *Jersey City Journal,* Jersey City, N.J., reporter, 1957; *New York Post,* New York City, editorial assistant, amusement department staff writer, 1957-64; *Detroit News,* Detroit, Mich., drama and music critic, 1964—. Part-time instructor in journalism, Wayne State University. *Military service:* U.S. Army, 1960-62. *Awards, honors:* George Jean Nathan Award for dramatic criticism, 1971-72.

* * *

CARSTAIRS, Kathleen
See PENDOWER, Jacques

* * *

CARTER, Burnham 1901(?)-1979

OBITUARY NOTICE: Born C. 1901 in New York, N.Y.; died July 6, 1979, in Orford, N.H. Businessman and writer who served two terms in the New Hampshire House of Representatives. He was a former partner in the Ivy Lee Public Relations firm and a contributor of short stories to *Saturday Evening Post, Collier's, Redbook,* and *Atlantic Monthly.* Obituaries and other sources: *New York Times,* July 7, 1979.

* * *

CARTER, Elliott Cook 1908-

PERSONAL: Born December 11, 1908, in New York, N.Y.; son of Elliott Cook and Florence (Chambers) Carter; married Helen Frost-Jones, 1939; children: David Chambers. *Education:* Harvard University, M.A., 1932; Ecole Normale, Paris, France, D.Mus., 1935. *Home address:* Mead St., Waccabuc, N.Y. 10597.

CAREER: Musical composer, 1942—. Professor at St. John's College, Annapolis, Md., 1940-42, Columbia University, 1948-50, Yale University, 1960-61, and Juilliard School of Music, 1972-79; Andrew P. White Professor-at-Large at Cornell University, 1970-74. Member of board of directors of American Academy in Rome and Naunberg Music Foundation. *Member:* National Institute of Arts and Letters, American Academy of Arts and Letters, American Academy of Arts and Sciences, Akademie der Kunste. *Awards, honors:* Award from New York Critics' Circle, Pulitzer Prize, and first prize from UNESCO, all 1960, for composition, "Second String Quartet"; award from New York Critics' Circle, 1961, for "Double Concerto for Harpsichord and Piano"; Sibelius Medal from Harriet Cohen Foundation, 1961; Premio delle Muse from City of Florence, Italy, 1969; Pulitzer Prize, 1971, for "Third String Quartet"; gold medal for music from National Institute of Arts and Letters, 1971; Handel Medallion from City of New York, 1978; honorary degrees.

WRITINGS: The Writings of Elliott Carter: An American Composer Looks at Modern Music, edited by Else Stone and Kurt Stone, Indiana University Press, 1977. Compositions include "Pastoral for Piano and Viola, English Horn or Clarinet," 1945; *Piano Sonata, 1945-46,* Music Press, 1948; *Musicians Wrestle Everywhere* (vocal score), Music Press, 1948.

BIOGRAPHICAL/CRITICAL SOURCES: Allen Edwards, *Flawed Words and Stubborn Sounds,* Norton, 1971.

* * *

CARTWRIGHT, Desmond S(pencer) 1924-

PERSONAL: Born October 27, 1924, in London, England; came to United States in 1952, naturalized citizen, 1953; son of Alfred Spencer (a jeweler) and Margaret Mary (Bounds) Cartwright; married Carol Irene Hawkins, December 19, 1961; children: Jacqueline, Christine, Carolyn. *Education:* University of London, B.A., 1951, graduate study, 1951-52; University of Chicago, Ph.D., 1954. *Religion:* Christian. *Office:* Department of Psychology, CLIPR, University of Colorado, Campus Box 346, Boulder, Colo. 80309.

CAREER: School teacher in London, England, 1951-52; University of Chicago, Chicago, Ill., instructor, 1954-55, assistant professor of psychology, 1955-60, director of Psychological Assessment Laboratory, 1959-61; University of Colorado, Boulder, associate professor, 1960-65, professor of psychology, 1966—, director of Regional Delinquency Information System, 1970-72, fellow of Bureau of Sociological Research, 1971-74. Member of Colorado governor's advisory board on juvenile delinquency prevention and control, 1970-73.

MEMBER: American Psychological Association (fellow), Society of Multivariate Experimental Psychology (president, 1972-73), Psychometric Society. *Awards, honors:* Award from American Personnel and Guidance Association, 1955, for research on psychotherapy and personality change; certificate of commendation from American Psychological Association, 1964, for research on method factors in changes associated with psychotherapy.

WRITINGS: (With Goodrich Walton, Nicholas Reuterman, and others) *Child and Youth Services Planning: Statewide Survey, Forecasts to 1980, and Recommendations,* Youth Services Division, Department of Institutions, State of Colorado, 1968; (with wife, Carol I. Cartwright) *Psychological Adjustment,* Rand McNally, 1971; *Introduction to Personality,* Rand McNally, 1974; (editor with Barbara Tomson and Hershey Schwartz, and contributor) *Gang Delinquency,* Brooks/Cole, 1975; (with Kurt Schlesinger, Philip Groves, and others) *Psychology: A Dynamic Science,* W. C. Brown, 1976; (with Michael Toglia, W. F. Battig, and others) *Handbook of Semantic Word Norms,* Erlbaum Associates, 1978; *Theories and Models of Personality,* W. C. Brown, 1979.

Contributor: C. R. Rogers and Rosalind F. Dymond, editors, *Psychotherapy and Personality Change,* University of Chicago Press, 1954; Charles Wrigley, editor, *Symposium on Research and Teaching Methods in Multivariate Experimental Design,* Educational Testing Service, 1962; J. L. Short and F. L. Strodtbeck, editors, *Group Process and Gang Delinquency,* University of Chicago Press, 1965; E. F. Borgatta and G. Bohrnstedt, editors, *Sociological Methodology,* Jossey-Bass, 1969; J. R. Royce, editor, *Multivariate Analysis and Psychological Theory,* Academic Press, 1973; Irene

Waskow and M. B. Parloff, editors, *Psychotherapy Change Measures,* U.S. Government Printing Office, 1975.

Contributor to *Britannica Yearbook* and *International Encyclopedia of Neurology, Psychiatry, Psychoanalysis, and Psychology.* Contributor of more than forty articles and reviews to journals in the behavioral sciences. Editor of *Multivariate Behavioral Research,* 1966-71.

WORK IN PROGRESS: Research on imagery and identity.

SIDELIGHTS: Cartwright commented: "Writing is very hard work, a fact that few non-writers realize."

* * *

CARTWRIGHT, Gary 1934-

PERSONAL: Born August 10, 1934, in Dallas, Tex.; son of Roy Allen (a cost-price estimator) and Vera Lee (Self) Cartwright; married three times; children: Mark, Lea, Shea. *Education:* Texas Christian University, B.A., 1957; attended University of Texas at Arlington and Austin. *Politics:* "Semi-moderate Anarchist." *Religion:* "God." *Home and office:* 809 West Ave., Austin, Tex. 78701.

CAREER: Fort Worth Star-Telegram, Fort Worth, Tex., reporter, 1956-58; *Fort Worth Press,* Fort Worth, sports reporter, 1958-60; *Dallas Times Herald,* Dallas, Tex., sports reporter, 1960-63; *Dallas Morning News,* Dallas, sports columnist 1963-67; free-lance writer, 1967—. *Military service:* U.S. Army, 1954-56. *Awards, honors:* Stanley Walker Award for journalism, Texas Institute of Letters, 1977, for "The Endless Odyssey of Patrick Henry Polk," published in *Texas Monthly,* 1977.

WRITINGS: The Hundred Yard War (novel), Doubleday, 1968; *Thin Ice* (novel), Gold Medal, 1975; *Blood Will Tell,* (nonfiction) Harcourt, 1979.

Co-author of screenplay, "J. W. Coup," released by Columbia, 1973. Contributor to popular magazines, including *Esquire, Life, Harper's, Saturday Review,* and *Rolling Stone.*

WORK IN PROGRESS: A screenplay for United Artists, tentatively entitled "The Sugar Man."

SIDELIGHTS: Cartwright comments: "I love writing. I can't do anything else. My motive is fear, my circumstances as good as I can make them. My style is involvement—getting personally involved, then writing about it. I know how to make it work. It's not a new or orginal approach. The second Tom Wolfe wrote about it—speedrap, spin-it-hard journalism, but in novel form.

"I like to think of myself as an across-the-board writer, though some may interpret this as meaning a pen-for-hire. Basically I write whatever interests me at the moment and holds the prospect of good financial reward. For example, *Blood Will Tell* was a book about high society in Fort Worth, Texas, as well as murder and the workings of the judicial system. These elements plus the commercial potential attracted me to the project."

Blood Will Tell is a documented account of the Cullen and Priscilla Davis affair. In this Fort Worth murder trial, millionaire Cullen Davis was charged with the 1976 murder of his twelve-year-old daughter and his estranged wife's fiance, Stan Farr. In addition to the two deaths, Priscilla Davis and a family friend were also wounded in the attack.

In his review of *Blood Will Tell,* Robert Sherrill wrote: "In [this book] you get . . . a splendid portrayal of Texas life and lore. Like a masterly archeologist sinking his shovel into a midden heap, Mr. Cartwright delicately uncovers one layer of trash only to lay bare the mysteries of a second layer of trash, which, being uncovered, reveals still a third layer of trash, and so on. Sometimes amiable, sometimes bloodthirsty, sometimes raunchy, sometimes pious, but trashy through and through: here is a society whose various strata are delineated only by differences in income."

BIOGRAPHICAL/CRITICAL SOURCES: Dallas Morning News, May 25, 1979; *New York Times Book Review,* June 17, 1979; *People,* July 2, 1979.

* * *

CASEY, Robert J(oseph) 1890-1962

OBITUARY NOTICE: Born March 14, 1890, in Beresford, S.D.; died December 4, 1962. Editor and writer. Casey was a journalist with the *Chicago Daily News* for over twenty-five years. His notable assignments during World War II include the collapse of the French Army, the battle of London, and the invasion of Normandy. He is the author of over thirty books, including *The Cannoneers Have Hairy Ears* and *I Can't Forget,* two volumes that deal with his wartime experiences. Obituaries and other sources: *Current Biography,* Wilson, 1943, January, 1963; *New York Times,* December 5, 1962.

* * *

CASSIDY, John R(ufus) 1922-

PERSONAL: Born August 4, 1922, in Brookfield, Mo.; son of Clyde D. and Gladys (Booth) Cassidy; married Gloria A. Bonacossa, January 20, 1945; children: Catherine A. Jaspers, Ray R., Alice Ellen. *Education:* University of Missouri, A.B., 1948. *Religion:* Presbyterian. *Residence:* Clifton, Va. *Agent:* Howard Moorepark, 444 East 82nd St., New York, N.Y. 10028.

CAREER: Teacher at high school in Brookfield, Mo., 1949; Office of Naval Intelligence, Washington, D.C., civilian analyst, 1949-51; Central Intelligence Agency, Washington, D.C., operations officer and associate in Latin America, Vietnam, and Spain, 1951-73; writer. *Member:* Phi Beta Kappa. *Awards, honors:* Studies in Intelligence Award from Central Intelligence Agency, 1973, for "contribution to the literature of intelligence"; Career Intelligence Medal from Central Intelligence Agency, 1974.

WRITINGS: A Station in the Delta (novel), Scribner, 1979. Contributor to *Saturday Evening Post.*

WORK IN PROGRESS: Another novel.

SIDELIGHTS: Cassidy told *CA:* "Before my employment with the CIA, I had sold two articles to the old *Saturday Evening Post,* but the necessary secrecy requirements made further writing for publication so complicated as to be totally discouraging. I had always thought that nonfiction was the only thing I could write, although I thought I was pretty good at the nonfiction. When I retired from the CIA, I considered it a heaven-sent opportunity to write without financial worries. Nonfiction now turned out by now to be such a different and difficult market, that I was almost in despair of ever selling again. And then I turned my hand to fiction, in a novel about the Vietnam War, and it seems that I can write fiction well enough to sell.

"How were people misinformed about the Vietnam War? It would take a big book to answer that question. There is such a book—Peter Braestrup's *The Big Story* (Westview Press, 1977). There is also an excellent film series called 'The Vietnam War on TV,' put together by Professor Lawrence Lichty. . . . Both of these exhaustive investigations led the authors to conclude that the U.S. press had misreported the war badly. . . .

"These are the authorities who confirmed to me my own observations, based obviously on a much narrower viewpoint than theirs, that the press bears a heavy responsibility for the outcome of the Vietnam War, culminating in such a bad job of reporting the Tet Offensive that what was in reality a military victory was presented to the American public as a disastrous defeat.

"I have read other books about Vietnam, but not many. Of those written by soldiers, I think the best is James Webb's *Fields of Fire*. It is hard for me to judge this kind of book, because I can claim no expertise or special knowledge or understanding whatsoever of the *soldier's* side of the war. The soldiers I associated with in Vietnam were engaged, with me, in counter-insurgency operations, and that is another thing altogether.

"As to my motives, circumstances, reasons and hopes for a writing career, these are so varied and ill-defined that I can't really pick out simple elements among them. I think conceit must be a major factor in any writer—the immodest assessment of himself as being good with words, and the conviction that others are certain to admire and enjoy his writing enough to want to pay for the privilege. All my life I have dreamed of money and fame, but the dream has been tempered considerably by half a century of living with modest amounts of one, and none of the other."

BIOGRAPHICAL/CRITICAL SOURCES: St. Louis Post-Dispatch, July 8, 1979; *Waterbury Republican,* July 8, 1979; *Boston Globe,* July 13, 1979; *Washington Post,* July 21, 1979; *Philadelphia Bulletin,* August 12, 1979.

* * *

CASSILL, Kay

PERSONAL: Born in Des Moines, Iowa; daughter of Everett V. (a brickmason) and Vivian (Jorgensen) Adams; married R. V. Cassill (a writer and professor of English); children: Orin, Erica, Jesse. *Education:* University of Iowa, B.A. (with honors), 1953, graduate study, 1960-65; graduate study at Academie de la Grande Chaumier, 1956, New School for Social Research, 1957-60, and Brown University. *Religion:* Protestant. *Home and office:* 22 Boylston Ave., Providence, R.I. 02906. *Agent:* Charles Taylor, 45 Brook St., Manchester, Mass. 01944.

CAREER: Mademoiselle, New York City, guest editor-in-chief of college edition, 1951; CSM Publications, New York City, secretary to general editor, 1952; Pegasus International Corp., New York City, secretary and executive assistant, 1953; Ford Foundation, Division of Education and Arts, New York City, research assistant, 1953-56; Fram Corp., Paris, France, assistant to vice-president, 1956; B. Rosenthal Rare Books, Inc., New York City, executive assistant, 1957; artist (printmaker and painter), 1957-66; Associated Writing Programs, Providence, R.I., and Norfolk, Va., founding executive secretary and member of board of directors, 1967-70; free-lance writer, 1970—. Lecturer at Providence College and University of Rhode Island, 1975—. Art work represented in galleries, solo exhibitions, and public collections, including Metropolitan Museum of Art. Also worked as book and television series agent and professional swimmer; judge for poetry contests; consultant.

MEMBER: International Association of Business Communicators, American Society of Journalists and Authors, Authors Guild of Authors League of America, Overseas Press Club of America, Associated Writing Programs, Women in Communications, New England Woman's Press Association, Connecticut Academy of Artists, Silvermine Guild of Artists, Hunterdon Art Guild, Provincetown Art Association. *Awards, honors:* Art awards for graphics, paintings, and dress design; Iowa Poetry Day award from Iowa Poetry Day Association, 1950, for poem, "The Writer's Dilemma"; Penney-Missouri Award from University of Missouri journalism school, 1975, for article, "The Tomboy in Your Office."

WRITINGS: The Freelance Writer's Handbook, Crowell, 1980.

Work represented in anthologies, including *Quixote Anthology,* edited by Jean Rikhoff, Grosset, 1961; *Prize Winning Graphics,* Allied Publications, 1965; *The Best American Short Stories, 1976,* edited by Martha Foley, Houghton, 1976. Television and radio scriptwriter; publicity writer. Author of "Travel Addict," a column syndicated by TransWorld News Service, 1976—. Stringer for magazines and newspapers, including *People* and New York Times Syndicate. Contributor of articles, stories, poems, and art work to magazines, including *Cosmopolitan, Saturday Review,* and *Viva,* and newspapers. Contributing editor of *Foxy Lady,* 1970—; articles editor of *National Enquirer,* 1977—.

WORK IN PROGRESS: The Single Woman's Guide to Business and Pleasure Travel; Comeback: Ten Stories of Survival, nonfiction; *Re-Enactments,* a novel, publication expected in 1981.

SIDELIGHTS: Cassill commented on her recent writings: "*Comeback: Ten Stories of Survival* is based on intensive interviews with ten survivors of trauma and their eventual return to everyday life. *Re-Enactments* is a novel of twentieth-century American problems, focusing on the interwoven experiences of two primary characters whose lives are entangled though they are lived on two seemingly totally different stages."

AVOCATIONAL INTERESTS: Art, photography, travel.

* * *

CAYROL, Jean 1911-

PERSONAL: Born June 6, 1911, in Bordeaux, France; son of Antoine and Marie (Berrogain) Cayrol. *Education:* Faculte de droit et des lettres, Bordeaux, France, received licence es lettres. *Residence:* France. *Address:* c/o Editions du Seuil, 27, rue Jacob, F-75261, Paris, France.

CAREER: Poet, novelist, author of filmscripts, and song composer. Founder of *Abeilles et Pensees,* 1929; librarian in Bordeaux, France, 1936-42; director of *Ecrire,* 1956—; director of "Le Coup de grace" (original screenplay), 1965. Member of selection committee, Editions de Seuil. *Awards, honors:* Commandeur des Arts et des Lettres; Prix Renaudot for *Je vivrai l'amour des autres,* Volume I and II; Grand Prix de Monaco; Prix americain.

WRITINGS—Novels: *Je vivrai l'amour des autres* (trilogy; title means "I Will Live the Love of Others"), Baconniere, includes *On vous parle* (title means "Someone Is Speaking to You"), 1946, *Les Premiers Jours* (title means "The First Days"), 1947, and *Le Feu qui prend* (title means "The Fire That Seizes"), 1947; *La Noire* (title means "The Dark Water"), Baconniere, 1949; *Le Vent de la memoire* (title means "The Wind of Memory"), Baconniere, 1952; *L'Espace d'une nuit,* Baconniere, 1954, translation by Gerard Hopkins published as *All in a Night,* Faber, 1957; *Le Demenagement* (title means "The Removal"), Seuil, 1956; *La Gaffe* (title means "The Mistake"), Seuil, 1957; *Les Corps etrangers,* Seuil, 1959, translation by Richard Howard published as *Foreign Bodies,* Putnam, 1960.

Les Pleins et les delies (title means "The Full and the Delirious"), Seuil, 1960; *Le Froid du soleil* (title means "The Chill of the Sun"), Seuil, 1963; *Midi-Minuit* (title means "Midday-Midnight"), Seuil, 1966; *Je l'entends encore* (title means "I Still Hear It"), Seuil, 1968; *Histoire d'un prairie* (title means "History of a Prairie"), Seuil, 1969; *N'oubliez pas que nous nous aimons* (title means "Do Not Forget That We Love Each Other"), Seuil, 1971; *Histoire d'un desert* (title means "History of a Desert"), Seuil, 1972; *Histoire de la mer* (title means "History of the Sea"), Seuil, 1973; *Kakemono hotel,* Seuil, 1974; *Histoire de la foret* (title means "History of the Forest"), Seuil, 1975; *Histoire d'une maison* (title means "History of a House"), Seuil, 1976.

Poetry: *Le Hollandais volant* (title means "The Flying Dutchman"), Cahiers du Sud, 1936; *Les Phenomenes celestes* (title means "Celestial Phenomena"), Cahiers du sud, 1939; *Miroir de la redemption* [and] *Et nunc* (titles mean "The Mirror of Redemption" [and] "And Now"), Baconniere, 1944; *Poemes de la nuit et du brouillard* (title means "Poems of the Night and the Fog"), P. Seghers, 1946; *Passe-temps de l'homme et des oiseaux* (title means "Pastimes of Man and Birds"), Baconniere, 1947; *Les Mots sont aussi des demeures* (title means "The Words Also Live"), Baconniere, 1952; *Pour tous les temps* (title means "For All of Time"), Seuil, 1955; *Poesie-Journal* (title means "Poetry Journal"), Seuil, 1969.

Essays: *Lazare parmi nous* (title means "Lazare Among Us"), Baconniere, 1950; (with Claude Durand) *Le Droit du regard* (title means "The Right to Look"), Seuil, 1963; *De l'espace humain* (title means "On Human Space"), Seuil, 1968; *Lectures; essais* (title means "Lectures; Essays"), Seuil, 1973.

Screenplays: *Muriel,* Seuil, 1963; (with Claude Durand) *Le Coup de grace* (title means "The Final Blow"), Seuil, 1965.

SIDELIGHTS: As a member of the Resistance during World War II, Cayrol was captured by the Gestapo, detained in Fresnes prison, then deported to the concentration camp at Mauthausen, Austria. Since that time, the experience of camp survivors has been a primary concern for him, the fragmentation and dislocation translating into a surrealist's approach to fiction. His central character is usually, to use the *Times Literary Supplement*'s term, a "compulsive creator" who is "unable to manage the present or the future because of the void where his past ought to be." And the major theme of Cayrol's fiction, Robert Hagspiel noted, "is the reconstruction of man in the destruction of history."

Although he was an established writer before the "new novel" emerged, Cayrol has been associated with the French New Novelists, for whom a work of fiction exists as an autonomous universe, operating according to its own laws without necessarily referring to the outside world. Laurent LeSage observed that a Cayrol hero "moves blindly along in the adventure of his life, neither knowing where he is going nor ever really arriving. He is seeking something, his salvation perhaps, but all we can be sure of is that he will discover the world." Thus, like younger French writers, Cayrol writes novels of "duration," and again like them, LeSage further pointed out, he uses such devices as monologues and restricted point of view.

Cayrol's only book to see American publication was *Foreign Bodies,* and it baffled American critics. William Dunlea called it "one of those uncommon novels that cannot be read cursorily the first time, and one of those still rarer novels that compel, if through sheer annoyance, an immediate second reading." Dorothy Nyren considered it "a complex, highly sophisticated. . . . difficult novel, but noteworthy for its originality." On the other hand, Martin Levin focused on two aspects of the novel—its unique lyricism and sequential framework—on the basis of which he concluded that *Foreign Bodies* is "a novel which enlarges the reader's sympathies and his view of the world."

BIOGRAPHICAL/CRITICAL SOURCES: Yale French Studies, summer, 1959; *Library Journal,* February 15, 1960; *New York Times Book Review,* March 20, 1960; *New York Herald Tribune Book Review,* May 15, 1960; *Commonweal,* June 17, 1960; Laurent LeSage, *The French New Novel,* Pennsylvania State University Press, 1962; John Cruickshank, editor, *The Novelist as Philosopher,* Oxford University Press, 1962; *Times Literary Supplement,* February 29, 1968; *Books Abroad,* autumn, 1968, winter, 1971; *Contemporary Literary Criticism,* Volume 11, Gale, 1979.

* * *

CERNUDA (y BIDON), Luis 1902-1963

OBITUARY NOTICE: Born September 21, 1902, in Seville, Spain; died November 6, 1963, in Mexico. Poet, literary critic, and educator. Cernuda wrote of the mortality of man and the desire to transcend these boundaries. His early works reveal the influence of surrealism, while his later works show a stong leaning toward the poetry of England, particularly John Donne and Shakespeare. His principal works in English translation include *The Poetry of Cernuda.* Obituaries and other sources: *The Reader's Encyclopedia,* 2nd edition, Crowell, 1965; *Encyclopedia of World Literature in the Twentieth Century,* updated edition, Ungar, 1967; *The Penguin Companion to European Literature,* McGraw, 1969; *Twentieth Century Writing: A Reader's Guide to Contemporary Literature,* Transatlantic, 1969; *Cassell's Encyclopaedia of World Literature,* revised edition, Morrow, 1973; *World Authors, 1950-1970,* Wilson, 1975.

* * *

CERRI, Lawrence J. 1923-
(Lawrence Cortesi)

PERSONAL: Born August 6, 1923, in Troy, N.Y.; son of Vincent (a locomotive engineer) and Assunta (Cortesi) Cerri; married Frances Barringer (a registered nurse), January 17, 1953; children: David, Diane, Richard, Catherine, Elizabeth. *Education:* Siena College, B.A., 1950; State University of New York at Albany, M.A., 1951. *Politics:* Independent. *Religion:* Roman Catholic. *Home:* 79 Boght Rd., Watervliet, N.Y. 12189.

CAREER: Equifax, Inc., Atlanta, Ga., claim director and investigator, 1942-43, 1950-57; *Albany Times Union,* Albany, N.Y., reporter, 1957-58; Waterford-Halfmoon High School, Waterford, N.Y., teacher of English, 1958-76; freelance writer, 1976—. *Military service:* U.S. Army Air Forces, aerial gunner, 1943-45; served in Pacific theatre; received Air Medal.

WRITINGS—All under pseudonym Lawrence Cortesi: *Mission Incredible* (fiction), Tower, 1967; *Battle of the Bismarck Sea* (fiction), Tower, 1968; *The Magnificent Bastards* (fiction), Tower, 1969; *Jim Beckwourth: Explorer Patriot of the Rockies* (juvenile nonfiction), Criterion, 1973; *Jean duSable: Father of Chicago* (juvenile nonfiction), Chilton, 1974; *Operation Bismarck Sea* (nonfiction), Major Books, 1977; *Escape From Mindanao* (fiction), Tower, 1978; *Rogue Sergeant* (fiction), Tower, 1979; *Target: Daimler-Benz* (nonfiction), Tower, 1979; *Operation Friday the Thirteenth* (nonfiction), Major Books, 1980.

Plays: *Adorable Imp* (three-act juvenile; first produced in Trafalgar, Ind., at Indian Creek High School, 1970), Arts Craft Publishers, c. 1970; *For Services Due* (three-act juvenile; first produced in Claremont, S.D., at Claremont High School, 1972), Arts Craft Publishers, c. 1972. Author of educational filmscripts. Contributor of stories to magazines, including *True Detective, Fate,* and *Wild West.*

WORK IN PROGRESS: Research for a series of educational mystery story controlled reading filmstrips for A/V Concepts; an educational series on writing skills for Contemporary Drama Service, 1981; research for nonfiction western, *Bill Doolin: Last of Horseback Outlaws,* for Tower Books.

SIDELIGHTS: Cerri writes: "I have had a love for storytelling since I was seven or eight years old. My motivation is generally an interest in a subject that starts me researching. I have often taken one of my magazine stories and researched the story further for a book. I do not consider myself a social mover, but merely a writer who likes to entertain and who likes to write about people and events that have had little coverage in books or other media."

AVOCATIONAL INTERESTS: Travel, fishing, bowling, model railroading.

* * *

CERTNER, Simon 1909(?)-1979

OBITUARY NOTICE: Born c. 1909; died October 7, 1979, in Queens. N.Y. An English teacher in New York City schools for forty-two years, Certner edited *Short Stories for Our Times* and *101 Jewish Stories.* Obituaries and other sources: *New York Times,* October 9, 1979.

* * *

CHALHOUB, Michael 1932-
(Omar Sharif)

PERSONAL: Born April 10, 1932, in Alexandria, Egypt; son of Joseph and Claire (Saada) Chalhoub; married Faten Hamama, 1955 (separated, 1966); children: one son. *Education:* Attended Victoria College, Cairo, Egypt. *Religion:* Moslem. *Residence:* Paris, France. *Agent:* William Morris Agency, 1350 Avenue of the Americas, New York, N.Y. 10019.

CAREER: Actor. Made film debut in "The Blazing Sun," c. 1953; subsequently appeared in other Egyptian and French productions, including "Goha," winner of the Best Picture Award at the Cannes Film Festival in 1959; made British film debut in "Lawrence of Arabia," 1962; has appeared in such films as "Genghis Khan," 1965, "The Yellow Rolls-Royce," 1965, "Doctor Zhivago," 1966, "The Night of the Generals," 1967, "Funny Girl," 1968, "Mayerling," 1968, "Che!," 1969, "The Tamarind Seed," 1974, "Funny Lady," 1975, and "Bloodline," 1979. *Awards, honors:* "Best Supporting Actor" nomination from the Academy of Motion Picture Arts and Sciences, 1963, for "Lawrence of Arabia"; Golden Globe Award as "Best Actor" from Hollywood Foreign Press Association, 1966, for performance in "Doctor Zhivago."

WRITINGS—Under professional name Omar Sharif: *How to Play the Blue Team Club* (bridge manual), Stancraft Products, 1970; (with Marie-Therese Guinchard) *L'Eternel Masculin,* Stock, 1976, translation by Martin Sokolinsky published as *The Eternal Male,* Doubleday, 1977. Also author of a syndicated column on bridge.

SIDELIGHTS: Omar Sharif first made a name for himself through his appearances in numerous low-budget Egyptian films as a leading man opposite his then-future wife, Faten Hamama. But in the eyes of American audiences, it was "Lawrence of Arabia" that launched Sharif's acting career. His role as the Arab shiek who supported Lawrence through all his exploits won for Sharif the praise of numerous critics and a nomination for best supporting actor from the Academy of Motion Picture Arts and Sciences.

Sharif followed this stunning performance with roles in "The Fall of the Roman Empire," "Behold a Pale Horse," "The Yellow Rolls-Royce," and "Genghis Khan." Then, in 1965, the film "Doctor Zhivago" was released, and Sharif's portrayal of the idealistic and sensitive doctor-poet established him as a romantic lead for future pictures. The exquisite scenery and the love scenes with two beautiful leading ladies also contributed to the Sharif magic on the screen. For his performance as Zhivago, Sharif won a Golden Globe Award.

Sharif was reunited with former co-star Peter O'Toole in "The Night of the Generals," where his role of the German intelligence officer was enthusiastically received. Then he starred opposite Barbara Streisand in William Wyler's screen adaptation of the Broadway musical "Funny Girl." As Fanny Brice's gambler husband, Nick Arnstein, Sharif received mixed reviews, but the film was immensely popular and Sharif continued to wow female audiences with his "bedroom eyes" and sophisticated manners and charm. He followed this role with another romantic lead: Crown Prince Rudolf in the film "Mayerling."

In 1969, Sharif played the title role in "Che!," a film based on the life of Fidel Castro's compatriot, Che Guevara. This was his only political movie role, and Sharif now says that he regrets doing it: "It occurred to me that the cinema was becoming less and less an entertainment business and more and more dedicated to propaganda. So I decided to become a swinger with the rest of the now actors and signed to play Che Guevara. It was a disaster. Here I was, Omar Sharif, the great lover, playing a Communist hero. . . . I have nothing in common with Che, except that Hollywood makeup artists made me up to look like his photographs. It was a stupid thing for me to have done."

But Sharif's performance in "Che!" did not alter his popularity as a matinee idol. He subsequently appeared in "The Tamarind Seed," where he played a Russian spy who falls in love with a soulful and sophisticated Julie Andrews, in "Funny Lady," and his most recent film, "Bloodline."

In addition to his popularity as an actor, Sharif has also gained recognition as a championship bridge player. He was a member of the Egyptian team at the second Bridge Olympiad in 1964 and took second place at the London Invitational Bridge Tournament in 1967.

Recently a guest on "The Phil Donahue Show," Sharif told an aghast female audience that now it is his son who is the great lover in the family; he prefers to spend a quiet evening at home reading or playing bridge.

BIOGRAPHICAL/CRITICAL SOURCES: Cleveland Plain Dealer, December 16, 1973; *Biography News,* Gale, January, 1974; Omar Sharif and Marie-Therese Guinchard, *The Eternal Male,* translated by Martin Sokolinsky, Doubleday, 1977.*

* * *

CHAMBERS, (David) Whittaker 1901-1961

OBITUARY NOTICE: Born April 1, 1901, in Philadelphia, Pa.; died July 9, 1961. Editor. Chambers began working for *Time* in 1939, first as a book reviewer and later as a writer of editorial articles and cover stories. He reached the position of senior editor before retiring. Chambers was also active as a translator of French and German books. Obituaries and other sources: Whittaker Chambers, *Witness,* Random House, 1952; *World Authors, 1950-70,* Wilson, 1975.

* * *

CHANDLER, Norman 1899-1973

OBITUARY NOTICE: Born September 14, 1899, in Los Angeles, Calif.; died October 20, 1973. Publisher and business executive. Chandler was affiliated with the Times Mirror Co., which includes the *Los Angeles Times, Los Angeles Mirror News,* and television station KTTV, for more than fifty years. Third-generation publisher of the *Times,* he rocketed the organization to phenomenal success and was considered by many as one of the most influential and powerful men in California. Chandler expanded the parent company's scope to include book publishing and the procurement of other newspapers. Obituaries and other sources: *Current Biography,* Wilson, 1957, December, 1973; *New York Times,* October 21, 1973.

* * *

CHANDRASEKHAR, Sripati 1918-

PERSONAL: Born November 22, 1918, in Rajahmundry, Andhra Pradesh, India; son of Sripati (a professor) and Rajamma Sarangapanni; married Dorothy Anne Downes, 1947; children: Radha, Prema, Sheila. *Education:* Madras Presidency College, graduated with honors in economics, 1938; University of Madras, M.A., 1939, M.Litt., 1940; New York University, Ph.D. (demography and sociology), 1944; attended Columbia University, 1941-42.

CAREER: University of Pennsylvania, Philadelphia, lecturer in Indian economics, 1944-45; Office of Strategic Services, Washington, D.C., demographer, 1945-46; Annamalai University, Chidambaram, India, professor of economics and chairman of economics department, 1947-50; Maharaja Sayajirao University of Baroda, Baroda, India, professor of economics and head of economics department, 1950-53; University of London, London School of Economics and Political Science, London, England, Nuffield Fellow in Demography, 1953-55; Indian Institute for Population Studies, Madras, director, 1955-64; member of Indian Parliament, 1964-70, minister of health and family planning, 1967-71; Battelle Research Centre, Seattle, Wash., fellow, 1971-72; California State University, San Diego, distinguished professor of sociology, 1973-74; University of California, Los Angeles, professor of demography and public health, 1974-75; Annamalai University, vice-chancellor, 1975-78; Mills College, Oakland, Calif., Lucie Stern Trustee Professor of Sociology, 1979. Director of demographic research, UNESCO, Paris, France, 1948-50; delegate representing either the government of India or the United Nations to over thirty international conferences, including: World Population Conference, Geneva, Switzerland, 1949; International Conference on Planned Parenthood, Stockholm, Sweden, 1953; International Economic Association Seminar on Migration, Kitzbuehl, Austria, 1955; International Conference of Humanists, Paris, 1957; Pacific Sciences Congress, Honolulu, Hawaii, 1962; United Nations World Population Conference, Belgrade, Yugoslavia, 1965; International Red Cross Round Table Conference on Red Cross and World Peace, Geneva, 1968; First (British) Commonwealth Ecological Conference, Malta, 1970; Conference of Executive Heads of the Association of Commonwealth Universities, Wellington, New Zealand, 1976; Twelfth Commonwealth Universities Congress, Vancouver, B.C., 1978. Visiting professor at University of Missouri, Columbia, 1957-58, University of Pittsburgh, Pittsburgh, Pa., 1962, and University of California, Riverside, 1964-65; honorary visiting professor of demography at New Delhi School of Economics, University of Delhi, 1967-70; Regents Professor, University of California, Santa Barbara, 1975. Has lectured at more than fifty international universities and symposia, including Tokyo University, University of Hong Kong, University of Sydney, and Soviet Academy of Medical Sciences. *Member:* British Eugenics Society (life fellow). *Awards, honors:* D.H.L. from University of Redlands, 1965; M.D. from Hungarian Academy of Medicine, 1968; D.Litt. from University of Kurukshetra, 1969; D.Sc. from University of the Pacific, 1970; LL.D. from Punjabi University, 1976. Watumull Award, 1964, for excellence in Indian demography; Kaufman Award (Canada), 1969, for distinguished work in family planning at the highest level; Margaret Sanger Gold Medal, 1971; India League of America Honour Award, 1975, for contributions to the promotion of Indo-American goodwill; U.S. Bicentennial Gold Medal from Population Dynamics and the Sunnen Foundation, 1977.

WRITINGS: India and the War, Newsindia, 1941; *Indian Emigration to America,* Oxford University Press, 1945; *India's Population: Fact and Policy,* John Day, 1946, 2nd edition, 1950; *Census and Statistics in India,* Annamalai University Press, 1948, 2nd edition, 1976; *Hungry People and Empty Lands,* Maharaja Sayajirao University of Baroda, 1953, 3rd edition, Macmillan, 1955; *Population and Planned Parenthood in India,* foreword by Jawaharlal Nehru and Julian Huxley, Allen & Unwin, 1955, 3rd edition, Macmillan, 1956; *Indians in South Africa: A Survey,* Indian Institute for Population Studies, 1957; *Report on a Survey of Attitudes of Married Couples Toward Family Planning in the City of Madras,* Government of Madras Press, 1958; *China's Population Problems,* Hong Kong University, 1959, revised edition published as *China's Population: Census and Vital Statistics,* 1960, 2nd edition, Oxford University Press, 1962.

A Report of South Indian Reading Habits, Ford Foundation, 1960; *Communist China Today,* Asia Publishing House, 1961, 3rd edition, 1964; (editor) *A Decade of Mao's China,* Perennial Press, 1962; *Red China: An Asian View,* Praeger, 1964; *American Aid and India's Economic Development,* Pall Mall, 1966; (editor) *Problems in Economic Development,* Heath, 1967; *Asia's Population Problems,* Praeger, 1967; *India's Population: Facts, Problems, and Policies,* Meenakshi Prakashan, 1967, 2nd edition, 1970; *Infant Mortality, Population Growth, and Family Planning in India,* Allen & Unwin, 1972, 2nd edition, University of North Carolina Press, 1975; *Abortion in a Crowded World: The Problem of Abortion With Special Reference to India,* University of Washington Press, 1974; *Ananda K. Coomaraswamy, 1877-1947,* Blackie & Son, 1977; *Population and Law in India,* 2nd edition, Macmillan, 1978.

Contributor: Manilal B. Nanavati, editor, *India Speaking,* Vora & Co. (Bombay), 1945; *Essays on Food and People,* Bureau of Current Affairs (London), 1950; Lyle W. Shannon, editor, *Under-developed Areas,* Harper, 1957; *A Decade Under Mao Tse-Tung,* Green Pagoda Press (Hong Kong), 1959; Kimball Young and Raymond W. Mack, editors, *Principles of Sociology: A Reader in Theory and Research,* American Book Co., 1960; Morris L. Haimowitz and Natalie R. Haimowitz, editors, *Human Development: Selected Readings,* Crowell, 1960; Guy Wint, editor, *Asia–A Handbook,* Praeger, 1966, published as *Asia Handbook,* Penguin, 1969; Edward T. Tyler, editor, *Birth Control: A*

Continuing Controversy, C. C Thomas, 1967. Also contributor of more than two hundred articles to scientific journals and popular magazines. Founder and editor of *Population Review,* 1956—.

WORK IN PROGRESS: Hindu View of Population; Women, Law and Population in India.

SIDELIGHTS: Sripati Chandrasekhar's books have been translated into fifteen foreign languages.

BIOGRAPHICAL/CRITICAL SOURCES: Ashish Bose and others, editors, *Studies in Demography: Essays in Honour of S. Chandrasekhar,* Allen & Unwin, 1971, University of North Carolina Press, 1974.

* * *

CHANIN, Abraham (Solomon) 1921-

PERSONAL: Born September 19, 1921, in New York, N.Y.; son of Isadore (in insurance sales) and Anna (in real estate; maiden name, Jaffe) Chanin; married Mildred Maxine Perelman (an editor), August 4, 1946; children: Beth Ann Chanin Rudolph. *Education:* University of Arizona, B.A., 1949. *Religion:* Jewish. *Home:* 5536 North Via Entrada, Tucson, Ariz. 85719. *Office:* Department of Journalism, University of Arizona, Tucson, Ariz. 85721.

CAREER: Arizona Daily Star, Tucson, sports editor, 1940-71, public affairs editor, 1971, editorial director, 1971-76, president of Sportsmen's Fund, 1947-76; University of Arizona, Tucson, instructor, 1976-77, assistant professor, 1977-78, professor of journalism, 1978—. Vice-president of Jewish Community Center, 1958-60; member of board of directors of Jewish Community Council, 1956-60, U.S. Baseball Federation, and U.S. Olympic Baseball Committee. *Military service:* U.S. Army, 1943-45.

MEMBER: National Collegiate Baseball Writers Association (president, 1961-62), American Association of College Baseball Coaches (chairperson of public relations, 1958-68). *Awards, honors:* Writing awards from American Association of College Baseball Coaches, 1950, for best sports story on college baseball in the nation, 1951, 1954, and 1955, for best baseball stories in the nation, and from Arizona Newspapers Association, 1959, 1961, for best sports story; Carnegie Human Relations Award from Carnegie Foundation, 1961; Silver Baseball Award from American Association of College Baseball Coaches, 1962; service award from Rockney Club of America, 1963, and Tucson Jewish Community Council, 1969; distinguished citizen award from city of Tucson, 1968.

WRITINGS: This Land, These Voices (nonfiction), Northland Press, 1977; *They Fought Like Wildcats* (nonfiction), Midbar Press, 1979. Editor and publisher of *Arizona Post,* 1955-68, and *Collegiate Baseball,* 1959-70.

WORK IN PROGRESS: The Flames of Freedom, publication expected in 1981; *This Land, These Voices,* an oral history of Arizona; *They Fought Like Wildcats,* a history of eighty years of college athletics at the University of Arizona.

* * *

CHANT, Ken(neth David) 1933-

PERSONAL: Born June 6, 1933, in Adelaide, Australia; son of James Oswald (a teacher) and Vera (Penno) Chant; married Alison McIntyre (in accounting), March 6, 1953; children: Dale Morris, Sharon Elizabeth, Eric David, Baden Matthew. *Education:* Berean Christian College, B. Min., 1974, M.Th., 1978. *Politics:* "An inclination toward socialism, but definitely not communism!" *Home and office:* 1 Dick St., Randwick, New South Wales, Australia 2031.

CAREER: Ordained minister of Christian Revival Crusade, 1953; pastor of churches in Ballarat and Dandenong, Victoria, 1953-57, Adelaide, South Australia, 1958-62, and Launceston, Tasmania, Australia, 1963-78; Crusade Bible College, Adelaide, founding member, 1958, senior visiting lecturer, 1958—. Member of Commonwealth Council of Christian Revival Crusade, 1958-78, national vice-chairperson of crusade, 1975-76, chairperson of Tasmanian State Council, 1970-78. Established Launceston College of Theology, 1975, merged it with Vision College, Sydney, Australia, 1978, principal, 1979—. Member of board of directors of Vision Ministries; member of Berean Christian Fellowship.

WRITINGS: This We Believe, Crusader Publications, 1962; *Asked and Answered: Secrets of Prayer,* Crusader Publications, 1963; *Sitting on Top of the World,* Bethany Fellowship, 1972. Also author of textbook series, *Diploma Correspondence Course,* published by Vision College. Author of pamphlets and college course material. Contributor of about two hundred articles to magazines.

WORK IN PROGRESS: Diploma Correspondence Course series.

SIDELIGHTS: Chant writes: "The hardest thing in writing is to begin. There are few things more discouraging than a pile of blank paper hungry to consume 50,000 words, especially when the author is obliged to write every one of them in longhand, three or four times over. This is my problem. I write best when I write by hand, and even then I have to recast each sentence several times before it reads smoothly. I never seem to get it right the first time! I early proved for myself the truth of Sheridan's dictum, 'Easy writing's curst hard reading!'

"Faced by this kind of toil, I would never have stuck to writing if three things had not happened: I was encouraged by the surprising discovery that there are not enough books in the world and that there is still room for another writer; I learned that even the inspired P. G. Wodehouse, whose Jeeves' stories have such a casual and easy air, often had to recast his sentences a score of times before he achieved the effect he was looking for; and I heard that a famous writer had given the secret of his success in three words: 'Write! Write! Write!'

"So I learned that writing is craft more than art, perspiration more than inspiration, grit more than genius. If an author has something to say, and enough patient discipline to struggle until he has said it well, then he may hope that the world will want to read his book. This discovery provided me with enough incentive to start writing, writing, writing. I churned out hundreds of pages before my first book was published. But gradually I gained a measure of competence, and now more people every year are pleased to read what I have written.

"My ambition is to achieve a style that combines the whimsy of Pelham Wodehouse (who I regret has only one quotation in Bartlett) with the sublimity of Winston Churchill (who has many). An unlikely combination, perhaps; but my inability to equal either man obliges me to aim for a congenial compromise. I also greatly admire Oscar Wilde; but it would be a wild fancy to think that I could approach his wit.

"All of my writings have a didactic purpose, which might be thought to be an awesome responsibility. It is not a light thing to take authority over the faith, morals, and life-style of other people. But I confess that the burden does not sit too heavily. Despite its drudgery, I enjoy writing, and I remain excited about the great ideas I am privileged to share with my readers.

"My particular gift seems to be a facility for taking hold of abstract or complex ideas and expressing them in a way that lay people find appealing and practical. At least, this is what readers all over Australia, and abroad, have told me.

"My basic motivation is a desire to collect the incredible ideas that fill the Bible, and to put them together in a manner that will achieve two things: to help people to find happiness and to create a uniquely Australian theology. This latter quest has been called the search for a 'gum-leaf' theology, and it must be admitted that I am still a long way from finding this Aussie Grail. But perhaps the eventual production will become as ubiquitous as the Australian gum-tree itself. The kind of cheerful, affirmative life-style represented by this eucalyptus-flavored faith is certainly proving to have universal appeal.

"Those are my goals as a teacher. But as a writer I have a different goal. I dislike the abbreviated outline style of many modern teaching programs, which presuppose that no one today is interested in reading beautiful prose. I also dislike that style which prefers asking questions to giving answers, as though there are no more students eager to beat a path to the door of a wise man. For myself, I am sure there are still people who look for poetry and melody in the words they read, people who thirst for knowledge, and who are doubly delighted when learning comes to them through "words fitly spoken, like apples of gold in a setting of silver" (Proverbs 25:11). It is a crime to possess the most marvelous expressive tool ever invented by man, the English language, yet not strive to master its infinite potential for beauty.

"Though I have not yet realized my dream, even now no one can give me a higher accolade than to say that what I have written was worth writing, and that it was written well."

* * *

CHAPMAN, Guy (Patterson) 1889-1972

OBITUARY NOTICE: Born September 11, 1889, in Cookham Dean, Berkshire, England; died June 30, 1972. Editor, historian, and biographer. Chapman worked as an editor with such publishing firms as Eyre & Spottiswoode for over thirty-five years. During that time he wrote a number of books of history and biography, including *The Dreyfuss Case: A Reassessment* and *The Third Republic of France: The First Phase*. Obituaries and other sources: Guy Chapman, *A Passionate Prodigality: Fragments of Autobiography,* [London], 1933, Holt, 1966; *The Author's and Writer's Who's Who,* 6th edition, Burke's Peerage, 1971; *World Authors, 1950-1970,* Wilson, 1975.

* * *

CHAPPEL, Bernice M(arie) 1910-

PERSONAL: Born June 4, 1910, in Fowlerville, Mich.; daughter of George L. (a farmer) and Gertrude (Avery) Klein; married Kenneth F. Chappel, December 24, 1929; children: Kenneth F., Jr. *Education:* Eastern Michigan University, B.S., 1956; University of Michigan, M.A., 1961. *Religion:* Methodist. *Home and office:* 205 North Fifth St., Brighton, Mich. 48116.

CAREER: Rural school teacher in Perry, Mich., 1929-32; elementary school teacher in Brighton, Mich., 1944-60; Farmington Public Schools, Farmington, Mich., school social worker, 1960-70; writer, 1970—. *Member:* National Writers Club.

WRITINGS: Harvey Hopper (juvenile), Denison, 1966; *Language Arts Seatwork,* Fearon, 1967; *Rudolph, the Rooster* (juvenile), Bethany Press, 1969; *Mathematics Seatwork for Primary Grades,* Fearon, 1970; *Independent Language Arts Activities,* Fearon, 1973; *Listening and Learning,* Fearon, 1973; *A Time for Learning,* Ann Arbor Publishers, 1974.

WORK IN PROGRESS: A collection of stories, *Living Today;* a juvenile novel, *Kabloona,* title means "White Boy"; *Once Within a Mitten,* juvenile nonfiction, a nostalgic account of life in the early 1900's, seen through the eyes of a child.

SIDELIGHTS: Bernice Chappel writes: "In my career, first as a classroom teacher and later as a school social worker, I was impressed with the number of unhappy children in our society. Many of these children had academic learning problems. Some were merely slow 'starters,' rather than slow learners. By the time their maturity was adequate they were far behind their age mates.

"Because of my interest in these children of adequate intelligence I could see the need for usable teacher-aid material. I knew there was not time for the average teacher to meet the needs of these children in a regular classroom. It was for this reason that I wrote several of my books.

"I endeavor to tie learning to interesting child-centered stories or activities. For example, *Listening and Learning* and *Living Today* consist of stories, poems, and games which are followed by correlated pupil learning activities.

"*A Time for Learning* is a self-instruction handbook for parents and teachers of young children. It is intended to help guide the youngsters toward an enjoyment of learning and a satisfactory social life.

"*Living Today* is a series of juvenile stories and poems dealing with life in various parts of today's world. Topics include fantasy, courage, compassion for unfortunate individuals, inner city pollution and vandalism, the joys and hardships of an Alaskan pioneer family, the ways of life of a Navajo Indian family, life on the island of Jamaica, and several poems dealing with nature and natural science."

AVOCATIONAL INTERESTS: Travel (Mexico, Central and South America, the Orient, India, Nepal).

* * *

CHARTERIS, Hugo (Francis Guy) 1922-1970

OBITUARY NOTICE: Born December 11, 1922, in London, England; died December 20, 1970. Novelist and author of television plays. Charteris's writings are sometimes compared to the hard stone that is hewn into a rough and craggy, yet disturbingly realistic, sculpture. He was critical of contemporary society, his works bearing the weight of his anger and frustrations. His later works, however, were more direct and subdued. Obituaries and other sources: *World Authors, 1950-1970,* Wilson, 1975.

* * *

CHENEY, Lynne 1941-

PERSONAL: Born August 14, 1941, in Casper, Wyo.; daughter of Wayne E. (an engineer) and Edna (a deputy sheriff; maiden name, Lybyer) Vincent; married Richard Cheney (in U.S. Congress), August 29, 1964; children: Elizabeth, Mary. *Education:* Colorado College, B.A., 1963; University of Colorado, M.A., 1964; University of Wisconsin, Madison, Ph.D., 1970. *Politics:* Republican. *Religion:* Methodist. *Home:* 902 South Beech, Casper, Wyo. 82601; and

7434 Hallcrest Dr., McLean, Va. 22101. *Agent:* Bill Adler, 1230 Avenue of the Americas, New York, N.Y. 10020.

CAREER: George Washington University, Washington, D.C., lecturer in English, 1974-76; University of Wyoming, Casper, lecturer in English, 1977-78; writer, 1978—. *Member:* Phi Beta Kappa.

WRITINGS: Executive Privilege (novel), Simon & Schuster, 1979; *Sisters* (novel), Simon & Schuster, in press. Contributor to magazines and newspapers, including *Smithsonian* and *American Heritage*.

SIDELIGHTS: "In *Executive Privilege,*" Cheney reported, "two investigative reporters uncover a story so explosive, that simply by revealing it, they will determine our country's policy. They, rather than the President or our other elected officials, will be deciding the nation's course. Should they be the ones to do this? Do they have the right? Or, looked at from another perspective, do they have the right not to? Is it proper for them—or for anyone—to set limits on freedom of the press?

"In *Executive Privilege,* I wanted to show responsible people trying to deal with these difficult issues, as well as trying to handle the more personal pressures which go along with life at the center of power."

BIOGRAPHICAL/CRITICAL SOURCES: Library Journal, June 15, 1979; *New York Times,* June 19, 1979; *Washington Post,* July 2, 1979.

* * *

CHINAS, Beverly N(ewbold) 1924-

PERSONAL: Surname rhymes with "genius"; born September 1, 1924, in Minden, Neb.; daughter of Lewis Francis (a farmer) and Glennie Athel (Shoemaker) Newbold; married Carlos Chinas, 1969; children: Lewis Lee Litzler, Barbara Marie Litzler Zgonc. *Education:* Fresno State College (now California State University, Fresno), B.A., 1963; University of California, Los Angeles, M.A., 1965, Ph.D., 1968. *Office:* Department of Anthropology, California State University, Chico, Calif. 95929.

CAREER: California State University, Chico, assistant professor, 1968-70, associate professor of anthropology, 1970—.

WRITINGS: The Isthmus Zapotecs, Holt, 1973; *Las Mujeres de San Juan,* SepSetenta, 1975.

WORK IN PROGRESS: Research on women's economic roles, gender role socialization, and Isthmus Zapotecs.

* * *

CHITRABHANU, Gurudev Shree 1922-

PERSONAL: Born July 26, 1922, in Tumkur, India; came to the United States in 1971; married Pramoda Shah (a teacher); children: Rajeev, Darshan. *Education:* St. Joseph University, Bangalore, India, B.A., 1941. *Office:* Jain Meditation International Center, 120 East 86th St., New York, N.Y. 10028.

CAREER: Jain monk in India, 1942-70; State University of New York College at Purchase, adjunct associate professor, 1970-72, professor of comparative philosophy, 1972-74; Jain Meditation International Center, New York, N.Y., founder and president, 1975—. Speaker at Princeton University, Sarah Lawrence College, Cornell University, the United Nations, and Koinonia Foundation; participant in international spiritual conferences.

WRITINGS: Ten Days Journey Into the Self, Vakils, 1975; *The Philosophy of Soul and Matter,* Vakils, 1976; *Realize What You Are: The Dynamics of Jain Meditation,* Dodd, 1977; *The Psychology of Enlightenment: Meditations on the Seven Centers of Energy,* Dodd, 1979; *Twelve Steps to Awareness,* Dodd, 1980. Also author of about twenty-five books in various Indian languages.

SIDELIGHTS: Chitrabhanu spent nearly thirty years as a Jain monk, walking from Indian village to village, meditating and spreading his teachings on compassion and reverence for life to villagers of many different faiths. He founded volunteer social welfare organizations. Then he attended international conferences and began lecturing throughout Europe and Africa. His decision to leave the monastic life was based on his observation that Western civilization wanted and needed his non-sectarian message of ahimsa. He has since conferred with world leaders and heads of state, and spoken to large public gatherings.

Chitrabhanu has written: "Something in us knows that what we have is not permanent. Knowing this inside, we are never satisfied. What we want is beyond. Deep in us there is a longing, a quest. It is not an ephemeral desire. For that we have to go beyond the mind. The mind is limited. What do we find when we go beyond mental barriers? Experience. We surrender to experience. It is not surrendering to anybody, but your own self. And who is the teacher? He or she who takes you to yourself. That awareness which is at the center of your being is always there, waiting to be your best friend, your highest self."

* * *

CHRISTMAN, Elizabeth 1914-

PERSONAL: Born January 18, 1914, in St. Louis, Mo.; daughter of Edwin Roy (in business) and Genevieve (Templeman) Christman. *Education:* Webster College, Webster Groves, Mo., A.B., 1935; New York University, M.A., 1966, Ph.D., 1972. *Religion:* Roman Catholic. *Residence:* South Bend, Ind. *Agent:* Harold Ober Associates, Inc., 40 East 49th St., New York, N.Y. 10017. *Office:* Department of American Studies, University of Notre Dame, Notre Dame, Ind. 46556.

CAREER: Harold Ober Associates, New York, N.Y., literary agent, 1946-69; DePauw University, Greencastle, Ind., assistant professor, 1969-74, associate professor of English, 1974-76; University of Notre Dame, Notre Dame, Ind., associate professor of American studies, 1976—. *Military service:* U.S. Navy Women's Reserve, Women Accepted for Volunteer Emergency Service (WAVES), 1944-46; became lieutenant junior grade.

WRITINGS: A Nice Italian Girl (novel), Dodd, 1976; *Flesh and Spirit* (novel; *Reader's Digest* Condensed Books selection), Morrow, 1979. Contributor of stories and poems to magazines, including *Saturday Evening Post, Critic, Colorado Quarterly, Southern Humanities Review,* and *Reporter*.

WORK IN PROGRESS: Another novel.

SIDELIGHTS: Elizabeth Christman writes: "After working for half a lifetime in a literary agency, I decided to become a college teacher. I was interested in young writers, and wanted to put my experience to work in helping talented young people to write well and to get their work published. Teaching writing helped me to improve my own writing. I had more success with my own stories after I began to teach.

"Have I been influenced by other writers? Yes. Henry James. I admire and believe in The Master's theory and practice on 'point of view.' He said that telling a story through a single point of view increases the intensity. Both my novels are restricted to a single point of view. I did this consciously and with conviction. I consider Henry James the novelist from whom any novelist can learn much. Most of them have, whether they acknowledge it or not.

"To me, the single most interesting element in novel-reading as in novel writing is *character*. That's why I admire Henry James and George Eliot and Jane Austen and Anthony Trollope and Saul Bellow and Bernard Malamud and Flannery O'Connor."

A Nice Italian Girl was adapted for television and released by ABC-TV as "Black Market Baby," October, 1977.

BIOGRAPHICAL/CRITICAL SOURCES: Notre Dame, February, 1977.

* * *

CHRISTMAN, R(aymond) J(ohn) 1919-

PERSONAL: Born May 6, 1919, in Stark County, Ohio; son of John J. (a mill worker) and Effie (Steiner) Christman; married Dorothy Critchfield, June, 1943; children: Steven, Raymond J., Jr., Karl, Thomas, Patricia. *Education:* Ohio State University, B.A., 1947, M.A., 1948, Ph.D., 1952. *Politics:* Conservative. *Religion:* None. *Home address:* R.D.1, Marcy, N.Y. 13403. *Office:* Behavioral Studies Divison, Utica College, Syracuse University, Burrstone Rd., Utica, N.Y. 13502.

CAREER: West Virginia University, Morgantown, instructor in psychology, 1950-52; Rome Air Development Center, Griffiss Air Force Base, N.Y., research psychologist, 1952-68; Syracuse University, Utica College, Utica, N.Y., associate professor of psychology, 1968—. *Military service:* U.S. Army, 1942-44. *Member:* American Association for the Advancement of Science.

WRITINGS: Sensory Experience, International Textbook Co., 1971, 2nd edition, Harper, 1979. Contributor to psychology and human engineering journals.

WORK IN PROGRESS: A book on vision; a book on hearing.

SIDELIGHTS: Christman told *CA:* "My present book, *Sensory Experience,* was the result of my recognizing a need for a general, intermediate level textbook that would summarize the basic knowledge of the senses: their anatomy and physiology, how they are studied, and their significance for psychology. I tried to make the book easy to read and interesting without sacrificing too much detail and complexity. The fact that the book sold over twenty thousand copies and is now in its second edition seems to me to be evidence that I was successful.

"The second pair of books that I am working on are not textbooks. Rather, they will be short unpretentious paperbacks, aimed at the general public. One will be on vision; the other, hearing. They will have much of the same material I included in my textbook, but written in an even chummier, less pedagogic manner."

* * *

CHURCHILL, Randolph (Frederick Edward Spencer) 1911-1968

OBITUARY NOTICE: Born May 28, 1911, in London, England; died June 6, 1968. Lecturer and journalist. Churchill, son of former British Prime Minister Winston Churchill, was himself a member of parliament for five years. He wrote for many London newspapers, including the *London Daily Mail* and the *London Daily Express,* and interviewed Adolf Hitler, ex-Kaiser Wilhelm, and Mohandas Gandhi. He wrote a column on international affairs, "Today in Europe," for United Feature Syndicate. Churchill compiled two collections of his father's speeches, and was working on a five-volume biography of Sir Winston when he died, leaving only two volumes completed. Obituaries and other sources: *Current Biography,* Wilson, 1947, 1968; *New York Times,* June 7, 1968; *Longman Companion to Twentieth Century Literature,* Longman, 1970.

* * *

CIENCIALA, Anna M(aria) 1929-

PERSONAL: Born November 8, 1929, in Gdansk, Poland; came to United States in 1965, naturalized citizen, 1970; daughter of Andrew M. (in shipping) and Wanda (a beautician; maiden name, Waissmann) Cienciala. *Education:* University of Liverpool, B.A. (with honors), 1952; graduate study at Columbia University, 1952-53; McGill University, M.A., 1955; Indiana University, Ph.D., 1962. *Office:* Department of History, University of Kansas, Lawrence, Kan. 66045.

CAREER: University of Ottawa, Ottawa, Ontario, lecturer in history, 1960-61; University of Toronto, Toronto, Ontario, lecturer in history, 1961-65; University of Kansas, Lawrence, assistant professor, then associate professor, 1965-71, professor of history, 1971—. Adviser on translations for Kosciuszko Foundation. Gives public history lectures; participant in professional meetings; consultant to Canada Council. *Member:* American Historical Association (member of Conference for Russian and East European History, 1977-79), American Association for the Advancement of Slavic Studies, Polish Institute of Arts and Sciences, Polish-American Historical Association (member of advisory council, 1978-80). *Awards, honors:* Grants from Canada Council, 1963, Fulbright-Hays National Defense Education Act Center, 1968-69, Social Science Research Council and American Council of Learned Societies, 1970, and Jurzykowski Foundation, 1975, 1979-80; prize from Pilsudski Institute of America, 1968, for *Poland and the Western Powers, 1938-1939.*

WRITINGS: Poland and the Western Powers, 1938-1939: A Study in the Interdependence of Eastern and Western Europe, University of Toronto Press, 1969; (editor with Agnes Headlam-Morley, Russell Bryant, and James W. Headlam-Morley) *A Memoir of the Paris Peace Conference, 1919,* Methuen, 1972; (editor) *American Contributions to the Seventh International Congress of Slavists, Warsaw, August 21-27, 1973,* Volume III: *History,* Mouton, 1973. Contributor of more than thirty articles and reviews to professional journals in the United States and abroad.

WORK IN PROGRESS: The Free City of Danzig as a Reflection of the German Problem, 1919-1939; with Titus Komarnicki, *Poland and Europe: From Versailles to Locarno, 1919-1935; The Polish Communists: The Evolution of Their Concept of a Postwar Poland, 1943-45.*

SIDELIGHTS: Anna Cienciala writes: "My interest in history originated with a desire to understand the reasons for the outbreak of World War II. I then witnessed the German campaign in Poland and became a refugee. I traveled across Europe to France and, when the Germans entered Paris, fled to Spain, Portugal, and England. I arrived in London just in time for the Blitz and Battle of Britain. My research has, therefore, been mainly concerned with the foreign policies of Poland, Germany, the U.S.S.R., France, and Britain, 1919-39. I am interested in the psychology, traditions, values, and goals of the leading statesmen of those countries at that time.

This interest carries over into the period of World War II, where my particular concern is the 'Polish question' in British and U.S.-Soviet relations, as well as the thinking and goals of the Polish Government in London on the one hand, and of the Polish Communists in the U.S.S.R. and occupied Poland on the other."

* * *

CLARK, Gregory 1892-1977

OBITUARY NOTICE: Born September 25, 1892, in Toronto, Ontario, Canada; died in 1977. Journalist and editor. Clark was a member of the editorial staff of the *Toronto Star* for more than thirty years. As a feature writer, he covered such events as the royal and papal coronations, and served as a war correspondent in Italy and Normandy. He later became the associate editor of *Weekend Magazine*. Clark is the author of *The Best of Gregory Clark* and *Greg's Choice*. Obituaries and other sources: *The Canadian Who's Who*, Volume 12, Who's Who Canadian Publications, 1972.

* * *

CLARK, Samuel 1945-

PERSONAL: Born November 14, 1945, in Toronto, Ontario, Canada; son of Samuel Delbert (a professor) and Rosemary (a returning officer; maiden name, Landry) Clark; married Claudia Searle (a social worker), March 29, 1969; children: Claude Robert, Rosemary Josephine, Laura Frances. *Education:* Carleton University, B.A., 1967; University of Toronto, M.A., 1968; Harvard University, Ph.D., 1973. *Home:* 941 Wellington St., London, Ontario, Canada N6A 3T1. *Office:* Department of Sociology, University of Western Ontario, London, Ontario, Canada N6A 5C2.

CAREER: University of Western Ontario, London, lecturer, 1972-73, assistant professor, 1973-79, associate professor of sociology, 1979—. Visiting assistant professor at McGill University, 1978. *Member:* Canadian Sociology and Anthropology Association, Canadian Ethnic Studies Association, American Sociological Association, American Committee for Irish Studies, Economic and Social History Society of Ireland, Social Science History Association.

WRITINGS: (Editor with J. P. Grayson and L. M. Grayson) *Prophecy and Protest: Social Movements in Twentieth-Century Canada*, Gage, 1975; *Social Origins of the Irish Land War*, Princeton University Press, 1979. Contributor to history, sociology, and anthropology journals.

WORK IN PROGRESS: Research on the effect of the industrial revolution on class structure in western Europe, focusing on Ulster and Belgium.

SIDELIGHTS: Clark writes: "I am generally interested in the evolution of modern Europe and my work is interdisciplinary. I am trying to answer sociological questions, but the methods I employ are primarily historical."

* * *

CLARKE, Basil F(ulford) L(owther) 1908-1978

OBITUARY NOTICE—See index for *CA* sketch: Born March 6, 1908, in Harlton, Cambridgeshire, England; died January 27, 1978, in England. Anglican priest and writer on church architecture and religion. Clarke's books include *Church Builders of the Nineteenth Century, My Parish Church,* and *English Churches*. Obituaries and other sources: *The Writers Directory, 1976-78,* St. Martin's, 1976; *The Author's and Writer's Who's Who,* 8th edition, Burke's Peerage, 1977; *AB Bookman's Weekly,* March 20, 1978.

CLAYTON, John 1892-1979

OBITUARY NOTICE—See index for *CA* sketch: Born December 1, 1892, in Fosten, Mont.; died July 4, 1979, in Chicago, Ill. Journalist, public relations and advertising executive, and author. From 1919 to 1928, Clayton acted as foreign correspondent in the Middle East for the *Chicago Tribune*. For more than twenty years he served as advertising executive and writer for Edward H. Weiss & Co. He was also manager of the public relations department of the Civic Opera Company. Clayton was the compiler of *Illinois Fact Book and Historical Almanac, 1763-1968*. Obituaries and other sources: *Chicago Tribune,* July 8, 1979, July 11, 1979.

* * *

CLEMENTS, Barbara Evans 1945-

PERSONAL: Born May 26, 1945, in Richmond, Va.; daughter of Lorenzo Silbert, Jr. (an army officer) and Champe (a clerk; maiden name, Winston) Evans. *Education:* University of Richmond, B.A., 1967; Duke University, M.A., 1969, Ph.D., 1971. *Office:* Department of History, University of Akron, 302 East Buchtel Ave., Akron, Ohio 44304.

CAREER: University of Akron, Akron, Ohio, assistant professor, 1971-78, associate professor of history, 1978—. *Member:* American Historical Association, American Association for the Advancement of Slavic Studies, Coordinating Committee for Women in the Historical Profession, Ohio Academy of History (member of executive committee, 1977-80), Phi Beta Kappa. *Awards, honors:* Grant from American Council of Learned Societies and Social Science Research Council, 1972-73.

WRITINGS: *Bolshevik Feminist,* Indiana University Press, 1979.

WORK IN PROGRESS: A collective biography of women in the Bolshevik party before 1930.

* * *

CLISTIER, Adeline
See DENNY, Alma

* * *

CLOSE, Upton
See HALL, Josef Washington

* * *

CLOWER, Robert W(ayne) 1926-

PERSONAL: Born February 13, 1926, in Pullman, Wash.; son of Fay Walter (a professor of economics) and Mary (Gilchrist) Clower; married Frances Hepburn, January 7, 1946 (divorced, July, 1975); married Georgene Thousendfriend, January 30, 1976; children: (first marriage) Ailsa Clower Chick, Leslie Clower Richardson, Stephanie Clower Callari, Robert Ian, Valerie; (second marriage) Anastasia. *Education:* Washington State University, B.A. (with distinction), 1948, M.A., 1949; Oxford University, B.Litt., 1952, D.Litt., 1978. *Residence:* Los Angeles, Calif. *Office:* Department of Economics, University of California, Los Angeles, Calif. 90024.

CAREER: Washington State University, Pullman, instructor, 1948-49, assistant professor of economics, 1952-57; Northwestern University, Evanston, Ill., associate professor, 1957-62, professor of economics, 1963-71, head of department, 1958-64, director of economic survey of Liberia, 1961-62; University of California, Los Angeles, professor of economics, 1971—. Visiting professor at University of the Punjab, 1954-56, Makcrere College, summer, 1965, Monash University, summer, 1972, and University of Western Ontario, autumns, 1974, 1977; faculty visitor at Cambridge University, spring, 1962; John Maynard Keynes Visiting Professor of Economics at University of Essex, 1965-66, professor and dean of School of Social Studies, 1968-69; adjunct professor at Washington State University, 1978—. Head of Oxford-London-Cambridge Joint Economic Seminars, 1950-52. *Military service:* U.S. Army, 1943-46; became warrant officer junior grade.

MEMBER: American Economic Association (member of executive committee, 1978-81), American Association of Rhodes Scholars, Econometric Society (fellow), Royal Economic Society, Phi Beta Kappa, Phi Kappa Phi. *Awards, honors:* Rhodes scholar at Oxford University, 1949-52; Guggenheim fellow, 1965-66; fellow of Brasenose College, Oxford, 1978—.

WRITINGS: (With D. W. Bushaw) *Introduction to Mathematical Economics,* Irwin, 1957; (with J. F. Due) *Intermediate Economic Analysis,* 4th edition (Clower was not associated with earlier editions), Irwin, 1961, 5th edition, 1966; (with G. Dalton, A. Walters, and M. Harwitz) *Growth Without Development: An Economic Survey of Liberia,* Northwestern University Press, 1966; (editor) *Monetary Theory,* Penguin, 1969; (with Due) *Microeconomics,* Irwin, 1972; *Thinking Economically,* Basic Books, 1981.

Contributor: F. H. Hahn and F.P.R. Brechling, editors, *The Theory of Interest Rates,* Macmillan (England), 1965; *Essays in Honour of Sir John Hicks,* Edinburgh University Press, 1968; George Clayton and other editors, *Monetary Theory and Monetary Policy in the 1970's,* Oxford University Press, 1971; L. P. Cain and P. J. Uselding, editors, *Business Enterprise and Economic Change,* Kent State University Press, 1973; (author of foreword) John Hicks, *The Crisis in Keynesian Economics,* Basic Books, 1974; M. Allingham and M. L. Burstein, editors, *Resource Allocation and Economic Policy,* Macmillan (England), 1976.

Contributor to *International Encyclopedia of the Social Sciences.* Contributor of more than fifty articles and reviews to scholarly journals, including *Annals of the American Academy of Political and Social Science.* Editor of *American Economic Review,* 1963-66, and *Economic Inquiry,* 1973—.

* * *

COBURN, D(onald) L(ee) 1938-

PERSONAL: Born August 4, 1938, in East Baltimore, Md.; son of Guy Dabney (a salesman) and Ruth Margaret (Somers) Coburn; married Nazle Joyce French in 1964 (divorced, 1971); married Marsha Woodruff Maher in 1975; children: Donn, Kimberly. *Education:* High school graduate, 1957. *Residence:* Dallas, Tex.

CAREER: Coburn and Associates Advertising Agency, Baltimore, Md., owner and operator, 1965-68; Stanford Advertising Agency, Dallas, Tex., writer, 1968-71; Donald L. Colburn, Dallas, creative and marketing consultant, 1973-76; playwright, 1976—. *Military service:* U.S. Navy, 1958-60. *Member:* Soaring Society of America. *Awards, honors:* Pulitzer Prize in Drama, 1978, for *The Gin Game.*

WRITINGS: The Gin Game (two-act; first produced in Los Angeles at American Theatre Arts, September 24, 1976; produced on Broadway at John Golden Theatre, October 6, 1977), Drama Book Specialists, 1978.

WORK IN PROGRESS: A play.

SIDELIGHTS: While writing short stories for his own amusement, Coburn discovered a talent for dialogue and decided "that regardless of the lack of evidence, I was a serious writer." Shortly thereafter he began work on "The Gin Game," but set it aside after writing eight pages. Two years later, he resumed work on the manuscript and completed it in four months. The play became an overnight success story. Soon after its Los Angeles production in a small forty-nine-seat theatre, and a subsequent production at the Actors Theatre of Louisville, Mike Nichols and Hume Cronyn decided to take the play to Broadway.

Set in a home for the aged, "The Gin Game" focuses on two elderly people who engage in a series of gin rummy games. Weller, who isolates himself from the other residents, is the embodiment of cantakerousness. Fonsia is a prudish, apologetic woman who quietly needles and torments her opponent as she wins hand after hand. The card games become "a fine and deadly mechanism of destruction," remarked Richard Eder. "[Weller and Fonsia] act out, as if trapped into it, the impoverishment and self-impoverishment that has marked all their lives." Commented Coburn: "It deals with people who at a very late age confront many areas of their lives which have remained unexamined. This coming to a greater knowledge of self is a painful experience—at any age. But, when nearing the end of life, to have revelations about your entire life and all the choices you've made, that's a cataclysmic experience—I would imagine."

Richard Eder found the play "extremely intelligent" and "written with remarkable shrewdness. . . . As the characters' deadly and inevitable frustrations build up—it is the playwright's as well as the actors' skill to make them seem inevitable: after all, an old age home is for dying and Weller and Fonsia are simply living a demonstration of how life kills itself—the language and recriminations occasionally come near a melodramatic obviousness. But it is not a fatal defect, and it does not prevent 'Gin Game' from being a notable and moving play." In another review, Brendan Gill wrote: "The last notes struck in the play are unalleviatedly despairing, and it is one of the most precious mysteries of the theatre that, having heard these notes struck, we should go up the aisle and out onto Broadway with happy hearts."

BIOGRAPHICAL/CRITICAL SOURCES: New York Times, October 8, 1977, October 11, 1977; *New Yorker,* October 17, 1977; *Nation,* October 29, 1977; *New Republic,* November 12, 1977; *America,* November 12, 1977; *Contemporary Literary Criticism,* Volume 10, Gale, 1979; *Baltimore Sun,* April 3, 1979.

* * *

COHEN, Bruce J. 1938-

PERSONAL: Born January 17, 1938, in Glen Cove, N.Y.; son of Frederick (in real estate) and Beatrice (Siegel) Cohen. *Education:* Michigan State University, B.A., 1959, M.A., 1960, Ph.D., 1964. *Home:* 189 Lodge Ave., Huntington Station, N.Y. 11746. *Office:* Department of Criminal Justice, C. W. Post Center, Long Island University, Greenvale, N.Y. 11548.

CAREER: Michigan State University, East Lansing, associate professor of criminal justice, 1966-70; Long Island University, C. W. Post Center, Greenvale, N.Y., professor of criminal justice, 1970—, head of department. Member of Nassau County Criminal Justice Coordinating Committee, 1975—. *Member:* American Academy of Criminal Justice Sciences, New York State Criminal Justice Educators Association, Nassau County Legal Aid Society (vice-president and member of board of directors, 1979).

WRITINGS: Study Guide and Source Book for Sociology, McGraw, 1964, 4th edition, 1977; *Crime in America,* F. E. Peacock, 1970, 2nd edition, 1977; *Introduction to Sociology,* McGraw, 1979.

* * *

COHN, Theodore 1923-

PERSONAL: Born June 15, 1923, in Newark, N.J.; son of Julius H. (a certified public accountant) and Bessie (Einson) Cohn; married Dina Berkson, November 26, 1946; children: Don Jonathan, Jordan Ellis, Karen Jane. *Education:* Harvard University, A.B., 1943; Columbia University, M.A., 1951. *Home and office:* 57 Winding Way, West Orange, N.J. 07052.

CAREER: J. H. Cohn & Co. (certified public accountants), Newark, N.J., partner, 1951-74; management consultant in West Orange, N.J., 1975—. Member of board of directors of Dynatech Corp., Jabel, and Auric Corp. *Military service:* U.S. Army, Office of Strategic Services, 1943-46; served in Europe; became sergeant major. *Member:* American Psychological Association, American Management Association, Institute of British Management, New Jersey and New York Societies of Certified Public Accountants.

WRITINGS: (With Roy A. Lindberg) *How Management Is Different in Small Companies,* American Management Association, 1971; (with Lindberg) *Operations Auditing,* American Management Association, 1972; (with Lindberg) *Survival and Growth,* American Management Association, 1974; *How to Grow,* National Business Forms Association, 1977; (with Lindberg) *Compensating Key Executives in the Smaller Company,* American Management Association, 1979; *How to Take a Management Physical,* privately printed, 1980; *How to Value the Closely-Held Company,* privately printed, 1980. Contributor of more than one hundred articles to professional journals.

WORK IN PROGRESS: Marketing for the Smaller Company, publication expected in 1980.

AVOCATIONAL INTERESTS: Tennis, sailing, collecting musical manuscripts, running.

* * *

COLBERT, Anthony 1934-

PERSONAL: Born July 17, 1934, in Isle of Wight, England; son of William Edward (a chemist) and Nita (Roberts) Colbert; married Angela Trollope (a secretary), 1964; children: Amanda, Gemma, Laurence. *Education:* West Sussex College of Art & Crafts, M.S.I.A., 1953. *Religion:* Catholic. *Home:* 42 Burton Rd., Kingston-on-Thames, Surrey, England. *Agent:* B. L. Kearley, Ltd., 33 Chiltern St., London, England.

CAREER: Illustrator for books, periodicals, and television; writer. Has held exhibitions at AIA Gallery, "The Workshop,' and Claud Gallery, all in London, England.

WRITINGS—All self-illustrated: *Amanda Has a Surprise,* Macmillan, 1971; *Amanda Goes Dancing,* Macmillan, 1972.

BIOGRAPHICAL/CRITICAL SOURCES: Arts Review, August 19, 1967.

* * *

COLE, Doris 1938-

PERSONAL: Born March 9, 1938, in Chicago, Ill.; daughter of Louis and Helen (Moore) Cole; married Sergio Berizzi, May 17, 1970 (died April 12, 1976); married Harold Goyette (an architect), January 21, 1979. *Education:* Radcliffe College, A.B. (cum laude), 1959; Harvard University, M.Arch., 1963. *Residence:* Concord, Mass. *Office:* Physical Plant, Massachusetts Institute of Technology, Cambridge, Mass. 02139.

CAREER: Boston Redevelopment Authority, Boston, Mass., junior planner, 1962-63; Atelier d'Architecture, Mount Rouge, France, architect, 1964; Pan Design, Cambridge, Mass., architect, 1965; J. Timothy Anderson & Associates, Boston, architect, 1965-67; Drummey Rosanne Anderson, Wellesley, Mass., architect and project captain, 1967-72; Earl Flansburgh & Associates, Cambridge, architect, 1972-73; Massachusetts Institute of Technology, Cambridge, administrative staff architect, 1973—. Private practice as architect, 1972—. Visiting critic at Rhode Island School of Design, 1965-66; lecturer at universities and architectural centers. *Member:* American Institute of Architects, Boston Preservation Alliance, Boston Society of Architects.

WRITINGS: From Tipi to Skyscraper: A History of Women in Architecture, i press, 1973; (contributor) Susanna Torres, editor, *Women in American Architecture: A Historic and Contemporary Perspective,* Watson-Guptill, 1977. Contributor to architecture and other technical journals.

WORK IN PROGRESS: Eleanor Raymond, Architect.

SIDELIGHTS: Cole has designed exhibitions, a vacation village in Southern France, facilities for children, housing, and an art museum.

BIOGRAPHICAL/CRITICAL SOURCES: Bay State Architect, April, 1969; *Architectural Record,* June, 1969, July, 1972; *Architecture d'Aujourd'hui,* 1972.

* * *

COLECCHIA, Francesca Maria

PERSONAL: Born in Pittsburgh, Pa.; daughter of Albert and Ambrosina (Donatelli) Colecchia. *Education:* Duquesne University, B.E., 1947; University of Pittsburgh, M.Litt., 1949, and Ph.D., 1954; postdoctoral study at Universidad Autonoma de Mexico and Universidad Central del Ecuador, 1962. *Office:* Department of Modern Languages, Duquesne University, Pittsburgh, Pa. 15219.

CAREER: Duquesne University, Pittsburgh, Pa., 1947—, currently professor of modern languages, director of language laboratory program, 1960-72, head of department, 1977—. Fulbright lecturer in Colombia, 1965; visiting professor at Mt. Mercy College, Pittsburgh, Pa., spring, 1968; lecturer at East Carolina University, 1969. Member of board of directors of Female Offenders Program of Western Pannsylvania; past member of board of directors and regional vice-president of Pennsylvania Program for Women and Girl Offenders, Inc. *Member:* Zonta International (member of board of directors), Instituto Internacional de Literatura Iberoamericana, Asociacion Internacional de Hispanistas, American Association of University Women (member of board of directors, 1961—; local first vice-president, 1965-67; president, 1968-70), Modern Language Association of America (local vice-president), National Association of Language Laboratory Directors, Administrative Women in Education, American Association of Teachers of Spanish and Portuguese, Latin American Studies Association, Delta Kappa Gamma (member of board of directors), Sigma Kappa Phi, Sigma Tau Delta, Phi Sigma Iota. *Awards, honors:* Commendation from Asociacion Colombiana de Profesores de Ingles, 1964; national award from Amita, 1969; grant from U.S. Office of Education Institute, 1971.

WRITINGS: (Editor) *Las tradiciones de Ricardo Palma,* Duquesne University, 1960; *Paisajes y personajes latinoamericanos* (cultural essays) Van Nostrand, 1971; (editor and translator, with Julio Matas) *Selected Latin American One-Act Plays,* University of Pittsburgh Press, 1973; *Garcia Lorca: An Annotated Bibliography,* Volume I, Garland Publishing, in press. Contributor to language journals. Associate editor of *Duquesne Historical Review,* 1961—, and *Estudios;* co-editor of *Garcia Lorca Review.*

* * *

COLETTE, Jacques 1929-

PERSONAL: Born June 5, 1929, in Wellin, Belgium; son of Louis (a forester and engineer) and Odile (Lavis) Colette; married Marie-Noelle Pattyn, April 4, 1973; children: Elise, Augustin. *Education:* Faculte du Saulchoir, D.Th., 1958; University of Paris, D.Phil., 1972. *Religion:* Roman Catholic. *Home:* 12 rue des Wallons, Paris 75013, France. *Office:* Centre National de la Recherche Scientifique, 15 Quai Anatole France, Paris 75007, France.

CAREER: Faculte du Saulchoir, Paris, France, professor of philosophy, 1967-72; Centre National de la Recherche Scientifique, Paris, researcher, 1974—. Professor at Facultes Saint-Louis, Brussels, Belgium, 1968-72. *Member:* Kierkegaard Selskab, Societe Philosophique de Louvain.

WRITINGS: Kierkegaard: discours e'defiants, Desclee de Brouwer, 1962; *Kierkegaard: le difficulte d'etre Chretien,* Editions du Cerf, 1964, translation published as *Kierkegaard: The Difficulty of Being Christian,* University of Notre Dame Press, 1968; *Kierkegaard: Chretien incognito,* Editions du Cerf, 1968; *Histoire et absolu,* Desclee de Brouwer, 1972. Contributor to philosophy journals.

WORK IN PROGRESS: Three books, *Harmonia et Kierkegaard, Le Langage et l'immediat,* and *Chroniques de phenomenologie.*

SIDELIGHTS: Colette's research interests include nineteenth-century German and Scandinavian philosophy and German phenomenologists Husserl and Heidegger.

* * *

COLLIER, Margaret
See TAYLOR, Margaret Stewart

* * *

COLLIGNON, Joseph 1930-

PERSONAL: Surname is accented on first syllable; born March 26, 1930, in St. Cloud, Minn.; son of Philip H. (in real estate) and Irene (Kinsella) Collignon; married Joan Lantz (a teacher), June 23, 1956; children: Kay Collignon Moncayo, Lantz, Ann. *Education:* St. John's University, Collegeville, Minn., B.A., 1952; University of Arizona, M.Ed., 1956; Arizona State University, M.A., 1964. *Residence:* Irvine, Calif. *Office:* Department of English, Fullerton College, 321 East Chapman, Fullerton, Calif. 92632.

CAREER: Fullerton College, Fullerton, Calif., instructor in English, 1964—. *Military service:* U.S. Army, 1952-54; became corporal.

WRITINGS: Figures of Speech (workbook), Coronet Films, 1961; *Patterns for Composition,* Glencoe Press, 1969; *The Sound of Prose,* Glencoe Press, 1971; *Sentence Sounds,* Soundwrite Publishing, 1978, revised edition, 1979. Contributor of articles and reviews to magazines, including *Saturday Review, Christian Century,* and *Reason,* and newspapers.

SIDELIGHTS: Collignon wrote in a *College English* article, "Why Leroy Can't Write": "The reason Leroy writes poorly is that he can't hear the sound of his voice on paper. . . . He has the voice for it, he can even get excited about it, but he doesn't have the training to put that voice on paper. So what's the solution? . . .

". . . Most teachers don't ask students to hear anything. It's still a sight game; it's still mental gymnastics apart from the act of writing. *Look* at the word to see how it's spelled. *Think* about a good thesis statement. *Study* those rules for organizing an essay. . . .

"The sound method is an effective means of solving traditional 'English' problems, like comma faults and run-on sentences. The sound method eliminates spelling problems far more quickly than any list of 100-most-misspelled words. The sound method brings rhythm and sentence variety into the students' papers. . . .

"Once Leroy hears the variety and rhythm of his native tongue, he may just write his own book. He'll probably call it, *Why Johnny Can't Write.* I hope he makes a million."

Collignon told *CA:* "The revised *Sentence Sounds* will include more exercises in basic sentence sounds and more reading-aloud materials, including a section using student essays, library papers, and literary criticism. These are from students who learned to write by sound, and the results are quite apparent."

* * *

COLLINS, Charles William 1880-1964

OBITUARY NOTICE: Born November 19, 1880, in Madison, Ind.; died March 3, 1964. Journalist and drama critic. Collins was a drama critic for over a quarter of a century, serving the *Chicago Evening Post* and several other newspapers. He was affiliated with the *Chicago Tribune* as drama critic, editor of the column "A Line o'Type or Two," and author of a daily feature appearing on the editorial page, "100 Years Ago." Collins is the author of *Great Love Stories of the Theatre* and *The Sins of St. Anthony: Tales of the Theatre.* Obituaries and other sources: *American Authors and Books: 1640 to the Present Day,* 3rd revised edition, Crown, 1972; *Who Was Who in America,* 4th edition, Marquis, 1978.

* * *

COLLINS, Margaret (Brandon James) 1909-
(Susan Welsh)

PERSONAL: Born June 1, 1909, in Pittsburgh, Pa.; daughter of Robert Leroy (in business) and Elora (Brandon) James; married Fletcher Collins, Jr. (a scholar and dramatic producer), 1932; children: Christopher, Brandon, Fletcher III, Francis. *Education:* Wells College, B.A. (magna cum laude), 1930; Yale University, M.A., 1931. *Home:* 437 East Beverley, Staunton, Va. 24401. *Office:* Theater Wagon, East Beverley, Staunton, Va. 24401.

CAREER: National Park Service, Washington, D.C., teacher, 1931-32; school teacher in Greenwich, Conn., 1932; Mary Baldwin College, Staunton, Va., instructor in English, 1953-55; Oak Grove Theater, Staunton, co-founder and resident playwright, 1954—. Co-producer for Theater Wagon, 1968—. *Awards, honors:* Grant from National Endowment for the Humanities, 1979, for the Theater Wagon.

WRITINGS: (Editor) *Theater Wagon Plays of Place and Any Place,* University Press of Virginia, 1973.

Author of plays; all two-act: "Love Is a Daisy," first produced in Staunton, Va., at Oak Grove Theater, 1955; "Do You Daydream?," first produced in Staunton at Oak Grove Theatre, 1959; "The Terrace," first produced in Chapel Hill, N.C., 1960; "Two Sisters," first produced in Monterey, Mass., 1962; "Take Away the Lady," first produced in Covington, Va., 1963; "Three Filosofers in a Firetower," first produced Off-Broadway at Greenwich Mews Playhouse, 1963; "The Motel and the Chickenhouse," first produced at the Wayside Theater, 1964; "The Lady and the Unicorn," first produced in Lorton, Va., at Gunston Hall, 1967; "Yaqui," first produced at the Theater Wagon Festival, 1970; "The Hub," first produced at the Theater Wagon Festival, 1972; "Bliss Towers," first produced in Richmond, Va., at Stage Center, 1973; "The Pond," first produced in Staunton at Oak Grove Theater, 1976. Also author of "Rebellion."

Contributor to magazines, including *Mademoiselle* (under pseudonym Susan Welsh), *This Week*, and *Newsday*.

WORK IN PROGRESS: The Quilt, "a philosophical patchwork, a narrative of other voices, other rooms."

SIDELIGHTS: Margaret Collins writes: "As a playwright I'm interested in an audience of the Many (rather than the Mass) who think ideas are fun, language exciting, and art challenging. Alienation and despair are not their thing. They are involved. So my plays are upbeat comedies, a natural form for a writer who believes in the worth of each human being. Comedy never gives up on the human condition. It celebrates hope.

"Yesterday's playwrights had a national audience. Today television makes it, theater is in search of its audience. Television is global, theater a handcraft in a machine society, and more people prefer machine productions. But the more machines there are, the more some of us need to work with our hands. The more we are enveloped by numbers, the more essential is the intimacy of person to person. The greater the crowds, the more necessary our humanity. In an age of electricity we still like candlelight, fireplaces, and sailboats.

"As to how I got hooked on playwriting—pleasures in acting, singing, and writing led naturally to starting a theater on our own farm in the Shenandoah Valley. And of course creating celebrations for the usual family holidays led naturally to Twelfth Night revels and summer festivals featuring our plays, folk music, square-dancing, or whatever. And when we wrote too many plays to be realized for a local audience at our Oak Grove Theater, we naturally established Theater Wagon to tour our plays in the Berkshires and Pennsylvania, the Edinburgh Festival Fringe, and a French abbey."

* * *

COLLINS, Robert 1924-

PERSONAL: Born September 10, 1924, in Shamrock, Saskatchewan, Canada; son of John Douglas (a farmer) and Floy Leona (a teacher; maiden name, Hartzell) Collins; married twice (divorced); children: Lesley Anne, Catherine Mary. *Education:* University of Western Ontario, B.A., 1950. *Residence:* Toronto, Ontario, Canada. *Office: Reader's Digest* (Canada), 215 Redfern Ave., Montreal, Quebec, Canada H3Z 2V9.

CAREER: Maclean's, Toronto, Ontario, western editor, 1953-58; *Imperial Oil Review*, Toronto, editor, 1959-65; *Reader's Digest* (Canada), Montreal, Quebec, associate editor, 1966; free-lance writer, 1966-70; *Toronto Life*, Toronto, editor, 1970-72; *Reader's Digest* (Canada), contributing editor, 1973-76, roving editor, 1976—. *Military service:* Royal Canadian Air Force, 1943-46; became leading aircraftsman. *Member:* Writers' Union of Canada. *Awards, honors:* President's medal from University of Western Ontario, 1978, for magazine article, "Kosmos 954: The Spy That Fell From the Sky."

WRITINGS—All nonfiction, except as noted: *Legend of the Devil's Lode* (juvenile fiction), Little, Brown, 1962; *Rory's Wildcat* (juvenile fiction), McClelland & Stewart, 1965; *East to Cathay*, McGraw, 1968; *A Great Way to Go*, Ryerson, 1969; *The Medes and the Persians*, McGraw, 1972; *The Age of Innocence, 1870-1880*, Natural Science Press, 1977; *A Voice From Afar*, McGraw, 1977.

Work represented in anthologies, including *Canada: This Land, These People*, Reader's Digest Press (Canada), 1968; *The Formative Years: Canada, 1812-1871*, Ryerson Press, 1968; *Canada: The Treasure and the Challenge*, Reader's Digest Press (Canada), 1978.

WORK IN PROGRESS: Two nonfiction books.

BIOGRAPHICAL/CRITICAL SOURCES: Maclean's, September 15, 1951; *Reader's Digest* (Canada), June, 1977, August, 1978; *North Toronto Free Press*, November 17, 1977.

* * *

COLLIS, Maurice 1889-1973

OBITUARY NOTICE—See index for *CA* sketch: Born January 10, 1889, in Dublin, Ireland; died January 12, 1973. Civil servant, painter, art critic, and writer on the Orient. After a career as a civil servant in Burma, Collis devoted himself to writing and painting. In addition to his autobiographical accounts of life in the Far East, he wrote biographies of Marco Polo and Fernao Mendes Pinto, a study of Confucianism, and a history of the opium wars in China. Collis also turned out several books of art criticism. Obituaries and other sources: Maurice Collis, *Trials in Burma*, Faber, 1938; Collis, *The Journey Outward*, Faber, 1952; Collis, *Into Hidden Burma*, Faber, 1953; Collis, *Journey Up: Reminiscences*, Faber, 1970; *Longman Companion to Twentieth Century Literature*, Longman, 1970; *The Author's and Writer's Who's Who*, 6th edition, Burke's Peerage, 1971; *AB Bookman's Weekly*, March 19, 1973.

* * *

COLQUHOUN, Archibald 1912-1964

OBITUARY NOTICE: Born November 16, 1912, in Yorkshire, England; died March 22, 1964. Translator and critic. Colquhoun chose modern works for his translations, works that echoed his own disillusionments in contemporary society. He is the author of *Manzoni and His Times*. Obituaries and other sources: *World Authors, 1950-1970*, Wilson, 1975.

* * *

COLWIN, Laurie 1945(?)-

CAREER: Writer.

WRITINGS: Passion and Affect (short stories), Viking, 1974 (published in England as *Dangerous French Mistress, and Other Stories*, Chatto & Windus, 1975); *Shine on, Bright and Dangerous Object* (novel), Viking, 1975; *Happy All the Time* (novel), Knopf, 1978. Contributor of short stories and reviews to periodicals, including *New Yorker, New York Times Book Review, Mademoiselle*, and *Redbook*.

SIDELIGHTS: "The surprising thing about Laurie Colwin's first book of short stories, *Passion and Affect*, is that it's so good," John Agar wrote. "The stories have a quality of grace and understatement which takes one by surprise. Partly this is the result of Colwin's style, which is often so bare and unadorned as to seem pinched. Yet the style is eminently suited for her subjects. And it can perform wonders."

Peter Wolfe was impressed by Colwin's "bright, figured prose" and "her short, terse paragraphs [which] transmit sharp-cut images and bright little rips of meaning." Her characterizations are particularly praiseworthy and, as Wolfe commented, "the main currents of *Passion and Affect* are psychological, not satiric. Personality neither flattens nor falls into patterns. Rather, the reverse applies: the more Colwin says about her groping, decent people, the more she prods our imaginations." Similarly, Agar declared: "Colwin's great strength is not that she has a theme, but that she has a particularly fertile way of seeing her characters. She obviously believes that life is exciting when people are emotionally alive, and that the quirks and inconsistencies are what the story is all about."

The humor of Colwin's stories was appealing to Judith Roscoe. She explained: "Her comedy is the comedy of manners, and it succeeds by its style and observation. The stories aren't anecdotal—I can't give you plot summaries that you can retell at your next party. But when you've read her stories, your next party may seem to you as if Laurie Colwin had written it."

Shine on, Bright and Dangerous Object also charmed reviewers. Dorothy Rabinowitz called it a "bright and elegant novel [which] has been accomplished without a jot of fashionable cant." Although Gabriele Annan described the novel as the long-awaited "Daughter of 'Love Story'," she found the work to be "thoughtful" and "probing." According to Helen Chasin, the book "has the style, wit, and intuitions of intelligent writing. . . . Laurie Colwin has a keen ear and a talent for rendering individual and particular ways of speaking."

Of Colwin's latest novel, *Happy All the Time,* Ross Feld wrote: "It's bright, it's funny, and it's very very willful; Colwin is out to invent not only a Seventies comedy of manners but the manners themselves. What makes the book special fun are the tartly endearing reversals: The girls are close-to-the-vest and tentative, while the slightly boobish boys roll with the punches, secure in their eagerness to love, attend, and do their full duty. Colwin writes effervescently—if the book has a flaw, it's that there is a sludgy build-up of adorableness." Lucinda Franks found that flaw to be more detractive. "The truth is that Colwin's flippant style does not allow her to do justice to her complex themes of male-female relationships and role reversal," Franks commented. "Happiness happens to be serious business, and it comes unbelievably easy here to people who are not quite believable. When one closes the covers of *Happy All the Time,* one feels vaguely unhappy—like waking up after having downed a magnum of cheap wine that tasted fine the night before."

"It's a lovely book," John Roman declared. "I mean it. The people in it are nice and better than nice. Laurie Colwin writes a sentence of porcelain-like clarity, to use an adjective she favors. Her book has the elegance called Mozartian—pretty themes, memorable melodies. The four people in it are a kind of quartet, a counterpoint of character-types, and their effect is harmony. If I found myself hoping, halfway through, that a busload of underprivileged kids with tommy-guns would disembark in the novel's sunny landscape, this should perhaps be chalked up to some morbid restlessness of my own."

BIOGRAPHICAL/CRITICAL SOURCES: *Rolling Stone,* March 28, 1974; *New Republic,* April 27, 1974; *Carolina Quarterly,* spring, 1974; *Saturday Review,* June 14, 1975, October 14, 1978; *Village Voice,* August 4, 1975; *Times Literary Supplement,* June 11, 1976; *Contemporary Literary Criticism,* Volume 5, Gale, 1976; *Ms.,* October, 1978; *Washington Post,* November 3, 1978; *New York Times,* November 7, 1978; *New York Times Book Review,* November 19, 1978.*

* * *

COMSTOCK, Helen 1893-1970

OBITUARY NOTICE—See index for *CA* sketch: Born October 17, 1893, in Kansas City, Mo.; died on July 1, 1970, in South Peacham, Vt. Editor and writer on antiques. Comstock wrote a number of standard reference books on antiques, including *American Lithographs, Concise Encyclopedia of American Antiques,* and *American Furniture.* Obituaries and other sources: *AB Bookman's Weekly,* July 20, 1970.

* * *

CONGRAT-BUTLER, Stefan 1914(?)-1979

OBITUARY NOTICE: Born c. 1914 in Chicago, Ill.; died of leukemia, October 27, 1979, in New York, N.Y. Linguist, editor, and scholar of Russian culture who compiled and edited the landmark directory, *Translation and Translators: An International Directory and Guide.* The first comprehensive work of its kind, the book was published by R. R. Bowker in 1979 and provided a register of translators and interpreters, lists of associations and centers of translation, and information about related awards and fellowships. Congrat-Butler was also the author of the first Russian-English dictionary based on American usage, *Russian Vest Pocket Dictionary,* and co-editor of *Anthology of Old Russian Literature.* He spent most of his career working as a consultant to numerous institutions and publishers, but at one time had been a reporter for the *Chicago Daily News* and a writer of radio commercials. A serious photographer, his many exhibits featured photographs of writers at work and scenes of New York City. Obituaries and other sources: *New York Times,* October 30, 1979; *Publishers Weekly,* November 5, 1979.

* * *

CONNOR, Lawrence S(tanton) 1925-

PERSONAL: Born August 31, 1925, in Indianapolis, Ind.; son of Nicholas John (a secretary for a manufacturing firm) and Agnes (Peelle) Connor; married Patricia Jean Alandt (a nurse), November 3, 1956; children: Carolyn, Julia, Lawrence Stanton, Maureen, Janet, Michael. *Education:* Attended Butler University, summers, 1943-47, University of Kentucky, 1943, and Mississippi State University, 1944; University of Notre Dame, A.B., 1949; postgraduate study at Fordham University, summer, 1949. *Religion:* Roman Catholic. *Home:* 9102 Colgate St., Indianapolis, Ind. 46268. *Office: Indianapolis Star,* 307 North Pennsylvania St., Indianapolis, Ind. 46206.

CAREER/WRITINGS: *Indianapolis Star,* Indianapolis, Ind., 1949—, reporter, 1949-63, city editor, 1963-79, editor, 1979. Indiana correspondent for *National Observer,* 1963-78. Past president of board of Catholic Communications Center; past vice-president of United Way; member of board of Catholic Social Services. Contributor of articles to magazines, including *Holiday, Saturday Evening Post,* and many detective magazines. *Military service:* U.S. Army Air Corps,

1943-46. *Member:* American Society of Newspaper Editors, Associated Press Managing Editors, Indianapolis Press Club.

WORK IN PROGRESS: A book on dealing with the daily newspaper.

* * *

CONOVER, Carole 1941-

PERSONAL: Born January 28, 1941, in New York; daughter of Harry Sayles (a model agent) and Gloria Belle (Daton) Conover; married Henry Meursinge Duys, Jr. (a florist), May 30, 1964; children: Henry Meursinge III, Lizabeth Conover, Noah Ogden. *Education:* Attended Smith College. *Religion:* Christian. *Home and office:* 1230 Park Ave., New York, N.Y. 10028. *Agent:* Gloria Safier, Inc., 667 Madison Ave., New York, N.Y. 10028.

CAREER: Advertising and publicity writer in New York City, 1960-64; Carole Conover, Inc. (public relations firm), New York City, president, 1972—. President of C. C. SportsKids, 1979—, and C. C. Skiers, Inc.; director of Winter's Sports Clubs, 1972-78, and American Flag Institute, 1978—. Member of local Animal Medical Center. *Member:* Humane Society of the United States.

WRITINGS: *Cover Girls* (biography of father, Harry Conover), Prentice-Hall, 1978.

WORK IN PROGRESS: *Another Other Woman,* a satirical novel.

SIDELIGHTS: Carole Conover writes: "I can write on all sports, beauty, grooming, cooking, children—and animals especially."

* * *

CONSTABLE, Trevor James 1925-
(Trevor James)

PERSONAL: Born September 17, 1925, in Wellington, New Zealand; came to United States in 1952, naturalized citizen, 1957; son of David James (an executive) and Maude Melba (in business; maiden Name, Ball) Constable; married Irene T. Knight, May 1950 (marriage ended); married Linda Christine Mladsi, August 19, 1975 (died October 2, 1975); children: (first marriage) Diana Ruth. *Education:* Attended McKenzie Engineering Academy, 1942-44. *Residence:* San Pedro, Calif. *Office:* P.O. Box 891, Reno, Nev. 89504.

CAREER: New Zealand Merchant Navy, radio officer and chief radio officer, 1944-46; British Merchant Navy, radio officer and chief radio officer on various ships, including "R.M.S. Queen Mary," 1946-50; International Broadcasting Co., Vancouver, B.C., writer and announcer, 1950-52; affiliated with various businesses; consultant in business aviation electronics in North Hollywood, 1955-62; Marketing Engineer, Santa Ana, Calif., account executive, 1963-66; U.S. Merchant Marine, radio electronics officer, 1966—, on container ship "S.S.Maui," 1978—, also participated in Vietnam Sealift. Founder of TJC-Atmos, Inc. (weather engineering consultants), 1978. Member of Borderland Sciences Research Foundation. *Member:* American Radio Association. *Awards, honors:* Nonfiction book of the year award from Aviation and Aerospace Writers of America, 1977, for *Fighter Aces of the Luftwaffe.*

WRITNGS: (Under name Trevor James) *They Live in the Sky,* New Age Press, 1958; (with Ray Toliver) *Fighter Aces,* Macmillan, 1966; (with Toliver) *Horrido,* Macmillan, 1968; (with Toliver) *Blond Knight of Germany,* Doubleday, 1970; *Hidden Heroes,* Arthur Barker, 1971; *Orgone Energy Weather Engineering: The Law and the Environmental Crisis* (monograph), U.S. Government, 1973; *The Cosmic Pulse of Life,* Merlin Press, 1976; (with Toliver) *Fighter Aces of the Luftwaffe,* Aero, 1977; *The Sycamore Canyon Fire and Primary Energy Weather Engineering* (monograph), Merlin Weather Engineering, 1977; *Sky Creatures: Living UFOs,* Pocket Books, 1978; (with Toliver) *Fighter Aces of the U.S.A.,* Aero, 1979. Contributor to men's magazines and *Journal of Borderland Research.*

WORK IN PROGRESS: *The Test Pilots: From the Wrights to the Moon,* with Ray Toliver; *Sex, Muscles, and Diamonds,* a biography of athlete Mildred Burke; *You'll Be Back,* a "modern Western look at reincarnation."

SIDELIGHTS: Constable's military history books have been published in German, French, Japanese, Swedish, and Afrikaans.

He writes: "My writing partnership with Colonel Ray Toliver has been a classic example of flawless literary cooperation, and we are happy that our books are artistic as well as nonfictional factual successes. This labor in the service of history has underpinned my main life's work in the highly unorthodox area of UFOs, spiritual science, and weather engineering, the latter now the main focus of my activities.

"My main statement for this incarnation is *The Cosmis Pulse of Life,* which I am told will be a great classic after I am dead, but not before. The crucial message of that book is the absolute necessity for humanity to conquer the mechanistic world concept, transmute mechanistic science, and create a New Technology, life-positive and life-giving.

"I hate writing as I do no other activity on this earth, but forced myself to acquire its skills in order to pass on my hard-won experience to others. Our battered, poisoned, polluted planet can still be a beautiful place for humanity to evolve into godhood, but the hour is late. Perceiving this, I became a writer, much against my own wishes for an easier life."

AVOCATIONAL INTERESTS: "My avocation is the technological control of the primary natural forces underlying weather formation. From the fundamental discoveries of Wilhelm Reich, and thirteen years of field experiments, I have been able to bring weather engineering, in the true sense of the word, within human reach. Fortunately, arrogant ignorance protects the world from military misuse of these discoveries but, so far as I am concerned, they will be used solely to generate funding for education along the lines demonstrated by the late Dr. Rudolf Steiner. The "Old Education' cannot cultivate the 'New Humanity,' and has become the major single impasse on the road to the new civilization we must create out of the best in the old."

* * *

COOK, Luther T(ownsend) 1901-

PERSONAL: Born April 22, 1901, in Baltimore, Md.; son of Emory Charles (a chamber of commerce secretary) and Jessie (Parks) Cook; married Irene Pearson (a home missionary), March 11, 1956; children: Mona Rae Cook Abel, Clark D. Wooten. *Education:* Attended military academy in Culver, Ind. *Politics:* "Patriotic American." *Religion:* "Undenominational Christian." *Home and office:* 3733 Clyde Park Ave. S.W., Grand Rapids, Mich. 49509.

CAREER: Private secretary in New York, N.Y., 1921-42; Indianapolis Symphony, Indianapolis, Ind., timpanist, 1945-50; home missionary in Grand Rapids, Mich., 1950—. *Mili-*

tary service: U.S. Army Air Forces, with Air Force Band, 1942-45; became staff sergeant.

WRITINGS: Calling for Christ, Moody, 1974.

SIDELIGHTS: Cook writes: "I became interested in music as a young teenager, especially percussion instruments, and I was self-taught. During the summer of 1918 I played drums in the orchestra of a vaudeville summer theater in an amusement park in Erie, Pa. In the summer of 1919 I played for the symphony orchestra at the chautauqua in Lake Chautauqua, N.Y. While working as a private secretary in New York, I played club dates with dance bands and shows, and did symphonic, operatic, and recording dates as a substitute timpanist and drummer. In the Air Force marching and concert band, I was appointed chief drummer.

"After re-entering civilian life, I determined to devote the rest of my life to a musical career. But, although I attained a modest measure of success as a professional musician, I gradually drifted far away from the Godly life and Christian upbringing. I had become addicted to many bad habits, including the excessive use of alcohol and tobacco. It was a fearful shock to me to find that alcohol held me in its awful bondage.

"In 1949 I planned to blow out my brains with a Colt automatic pistol. I went to a restaurant to drink some strong black coffee as a bracer. A youngster placed her food tray on my table and seated herself in a vacant chair, bowed her head, and closed her eyes. It started a chain of thoughts in my mind of things I had not thought of for years. That same night, instead of blowing out my brains, I cried aloud to God to forgive all my sins and save me."

Cook has been a home missionary ever since. He founded The Just Shall Live by Faith Mission, Inc. and has taken his message all over the United States and to Canada.

* * *

COOPER, John O(wen) 1938-

PERSONAL: Born May 8, 1938, in Princeton, Ind.; son of Carroll F. and Vera L. (Ross) Cooper; married Bernice J. Manseault, August 1, 1964; children: Christopher, Sharon, Gregory, Brian. *Education:* Attended St. Petersburg Junior College, 1962; Florida State University, B.Mus., 1965; University of Kansas, M.Mus. Ed., 1968, D.Ed., 1970. *Home:* 783 Oxford St., Worthington, Ohio. *Office:* Faculty for Exceptional Children, Ohio State University, 375-B Arps Hall, 1945 North High St., Columbus, Ohio 43210.

CAREER: Milledgeville State Hospital, Milledgeville, Ga., music teacher, 1964-66; Parsons State Hospital and Training Center, Parsons, Kan., research assistant at Parsons Research Center, 1967-68; City of Kansas City, Kan., psychologist and researcher for Head Start Program, 1969-70; Ohio State University, Columbus, assistant professor, 1970-73, associate professor, 1973-79, professor of education, 1979—, director of Education Clinic, 1971-73, assistant chairperson of programs for the mildly handicapped, 1976—. Member of advisory board of Camp Nuhop, 1978—. Workshop director; participant in professional meetings. *Member:* American Educational Research Association, Council for Children With Behavioral Disorders, Council for Exceptional Children, Association for Behavior Analysis.

WRITINGS: (Contributor) R. T. Fulton and L. L. Lloyd, editors, *Audiometry for the Retarded,* Williams & Wilkins, 1969; (with W. J. Cegelka, T. E. Jordan, and others) *Policy Statements on the Education of Mentally Retarded Children,* National Association for Retarded Children, 1971; (with T. M. Stephens) *Procedures for Designing Training Programs for Directive Teaching,* School Management Institute, 1971; (with H. A. Norman, J. M. Johnson, and D. E. Lema) *Ohio State Education Plan for Institution Schools: Mentally Handicapped,* Ohio Department of Mental Health and Mental Retardation, 1972; (contributor) J. S. Payne, C. D. Mercer, and other editors, *Head Start: A Tragicomedy With Epilogue,* Behavioral Publications, 1973; *Measurement and Analysis for Behavioral Techniques,* C. E. Merrill, 1974, 2nd edition, 1980; (editor with Joseph E. Fisher and Helen Jorgensen, and contributor) *Skill Development: Practicum Training Modules for Teachers,* AVICOM, 1974; (with Denzil Edge) *Parenting: Strategies and Educational Methods,* C. E. Merrill, 1978; (contributor) Edge, B. J. Strenecky, and S. I. Mour, editors, *Parenting Learning-Problem Children,* Ohio State University Press, 1979.

Contributor of more than a dozen articles to education and psychology journals. Field editor for *Behavior Modification Technology,* 1973; research editor of *Directive Teaching Newsletter,* 1977—; associate editor of *Exceptional Children,* 1977—.

SIDELIGHTS: Cooper's current work involves experimental analysis of learning and behavioral handicaps of children, including application of directive teaching principles to special education classrooms.

* * *

COOPER, Kent 1880-1965

OBITUARY NOTICE: Born March 22, 1880, in Columbus, Ind.; died January 31, 1965. Journalist and publisher. Cooper joined the Associated Press in 1910, rising to the post of executive director in 1943, and remained there until the time of his death. He originated the idea of using the telephone service to relay stories instead of the telegraph, and was the first to adopt Wirephoto, a device capable of sending photographs across the country in a matter of minutes to accompany a news article. Cooper revamped the customary and tedious presentation of the news into reports that were entertaining as well as factual; he included comic strips, crossword puzzles, and women's page activities, in addition to amusing or unusual stories. When world freedom of the press was threatened in the 1940's, Cooper was instrumental in breaking the strong-hold and ensuring international presses the freedom they had been denied. Cooper authored *Barriers Down* and *The Right to Know,* in addition to several musical compositions. Obituaries and other sources: *Current Biography,* Wilson, 1944, 1965; *New York Times,* January 31, 1965; *The ASCAP Biographical Dictionary of Composers, Authors, and Publishers,* American Society of Composers, Authors and Publishers, 1966.

* * *

COPANI, Peter 1942-

PERSONAL: Born September 2, 1942, in Syracuse, N.Y.; son of Michael and Lucy (Fiumara) Copani. *Education:* Attended Syracuse University, 1961, and The New School, 1972-76. *Home:* 59 Carmine St., New York, N.Y. 10014.

CAREER: Writer, director, and producer of stage productions; songwriter. Founder and administrative director of People's Performing Co., 1971-76; head of Theatre Arts Department of Massive Economic Neighborhood Development, 1973-74. *Awards, honors:* Grants from Creative Artist Public Service Program, 1971, 1973, and Cultural Affairs Department, 1972; City of New York Certificate of Appreciation, 1975; award from American Society of Composers, Authors, and Publishers, 1976, for "Fire of Flowers,"

WRITINGS—Plays: "Where People Gather" (two-act), first produced in New York City at Playbox Studio, September 20, 1967, produced Off-Broadway at Gramercy Arts Theater, October 25, 1967; "Bliss or a Psycho-Bedellic Attack" (two-act), produced in New York City by Extension Theater Club, April 10, 1968; "Puppy Love" (one-act), produced in New York City at Playbox Studio, May 15, 1968; "The Star Is Always Loved and Loved" (one-act), produced in New York City at Playbox Studio, May 15, 1968; "What's the Game Now?" (two-act), produced in New York City at Playbox Studio, March 13, 1969; "The Land I Love" (two-act), produced in New York City at Playbox Studio, July 22, 1969; "Scream Revolution" (one-act), produced in New York City at New York Theater Ensemble, December 26, 1969; "When the Bough Breaks" (one-act), produced in New York City at New York Theatre Ensemble, December 26, 1969.

"The First Day of Us" (two-act), produced in Binghamton, N.Y., at Twin Rivers Theatre, July 14, 1970; "The Blind Junkie" (one-act), produced in New York City at Lincoln Center Festival, August 23, 1971; "Choices" (one-act musical), produced in New York City at Lincoln Center Festival, August 23, 1972; "Blind Junkie Choices" (one-act musical), produced in New York City by People's Performing Co., February 15, 1973; "The Opposite Side of Sonny" (two-act musical-drama), produced in New York City by People's Performing Co., June 29, 1973; "Power" (one-act musical), produced in New York City by People's Performing Co., June 7, 1973, produced at Lincoln Center Community Street Theater Festival, August 30, 1973; "Street Jesus" (one-act musical), produced in New York City by Union Betterment People's Performing Co., July, 1973; "America and Its People" (one-act musical), produced in New York City at Lincoln Center Outdoor Theatre Festival, August, 1974; "The Great American Soccer Family" (one-act musical), produced Off-Off-Broadway at Provincetown Playhouse, summer, 1975; "The New York City Street Show" (two-act musical), produced in New York City at Greenwich House, January 21, 1977.

Also author of poems and songs.

WORK IN PROGRESS: "Feast on Dream Street."

SIDELIGHTS: Copani told *CA:* "My goal is to make changes in the structure of our educational approach and to re-educate people, especially the young. Through my writing I have been able to know and understand myself better and have been able to get in touch with my own true feelings. According to a study made by the O'Neill Foundation, theater is the best way to educate. Since my work deals with the present day problems, I will be participating in a program . . . of media experience for high school people. This will help me to get a fuller background for the book I will write.

"I believe that we have raped the minds of young people and have cheated them of their feelings by not putting them in touch with their *own* true feelings. We have progressively cut off their feelings by passing down slogans like 'Men don't cry' and in doing so have distorted their ideas concerning the value of life. There are reasons why we attack people instead of problems.

"My studies deal with the human mind through books by Karl Menninger and philosophy from such contemporary thinkers as Dr. Arthur Janov and Robert S. DeRopp but most of all through my own experiences. I will be in England . . . to study acupuncture and the philosophy behind it. Most of my theories have come from my life experiences working with people and especially in street theater where there is an untapped source of information vital to us all. My work is to grow and understand myself more fully so that I will be able to understand others with compassion and to teach through my writing.

"My working procedure involves going into a community, working with the people to discover their feelings, anxieties and aspirations, and then writing a musical dealing with those people in a way that articulates and expresses their emotions. This process contributes to their level of consciousness, to their understanding of their own lives. It takes me one year to do the research of working with the people of a given community, to write up the musical, to do a neighborhood production, and then to formulate a final draft of the show."

Copani was hailed by a writer for the *New York Times* as the "leading playwright of the streets."

BIOGRAPHICAL/CRITICAL SOURCES: Village Voice, September 2, 1971; *Newsweek,* September 6, 1971; *New York Daily News,* July 28, 1974; *New York Times,* August 20, 1972, August 21, 1972, August 24, 1972, September 2, 1972, August 19, 1973, August 27, 1974; *Greenwich Village Television News,* August 24, 1974; *After Dark,* October, 1974; *Wisdom's Child,* January 10, 1977; *New Yorker,* May 9, 1977.

*   *   *

CORBITT, Helen Lucy 1906-1978

OBITUARY NOTICE—See index for *CA* sketch: Born January 25, 1906, in Benson Mines, N.Y.; died January 16, 1978, in Dallas, Tex. Dietitian and author of cookbooks. Corbitt worked as the food service operator at Nieman-Marcus department store in Dallas. In 1961 she became the first woman to receive the food industry's prestigious Golden Plate Award. Among her books are *Helen Corbitt's Cookbook* and *Helen Corbitt's Greenhouse Cookbook.* Obituaries and other sources: *Foremost Women in Communications,* Bowker, 1970; *Publishers Weekly,* September 20, 1978.

*   *   *

CORDWELL, Miriam 1908-

PERSONAL: Born January 6, 1908, in Brooklyn, N.Y.; daughter of Thomas Joseph (an accountant) and Sarah (Lynch) Bradley; married Richard Cordwell, April 17, 1926; children: Miriam Ann (Mrs. Richard Kurisko), Lorraine (Mrs. Robert Yarsinsky). *Education:* Attended St. Joseph's Business School, Brooklyn, N.Y., and Baurs Beauty Academy. *Politics:* Republican. *Religion:* Roman Catholic. *Home address:* P.O. Box 31, Wilmington, N.Y. 12997. *Office:* Miriam Cordwell, Inc., 254 North Main St., New City, N.Y. 10956.

CAREER: Owner and operator of beauty salon in New City, N.Y., 1934-72; writer. Member of faculty at University of Maryland, summers, 1950-59, Ohio State University, summers, 1960-62, State University of New York Agricultural and Technical Institutes at Alfred, summers, 1962-64, and University of Arkansas, 1964. Teacher of hair design and fashion and coordinator of speech and platform development for New York Hairdressers Board of Trade, 1940-48, head of styles committee, 1949-50. Guest on television and radio programs. Member of New City Fireman's Auxiliary, 1928—. *Member:* National Hairdressers and Cosmetologists Association (chairwoman of hair fashion committee, 1953-54), Mental Hygiene Association of Essex County (member of board of directors, 1976-79), Business and Professional Women's Club, Soroptimist International (charter member of local chapter; member of board of directors, 1959-61). *Awards, honors:* Charles Award from National Hairdressers and Cosmetologists Association, 1963, member of Hairstyling Hall of Renown, 1975—.

WRITINGS—All with Marion Rudoy: *Hair Design and Fashion,* Crown, 1956, 6th edition, 1977; *The Complete Book of Hair Styling, Beauty, and Fashion,* Crown, 1971; *The Complete Book of Men's Hairstyles and Haircare,* Crown, 1974. Contributor to trade journals and newspapers.

SIDELIGHTS: Miriam Cordwell writes: "In the late 1940's, accelerated summer courses in advanced cosmetology became available to licensed cosmetologists. They were offered by colleges throughout the United States and proved very worthwhile. Cosmetologists who wished to progress, develop their ideals and goals, and expand their horizons enrolled. At the University of Maryland and other state colleges, I taught the relation of art and design principles to hair design and I integrated physical structure, personality types, and fashion. Platform development, speech, and related technology were also included.

"Research showed that there were no ready reference books for any of these studies. Consequently *Hair Design and Fashion* needed to be written. Recent revisions have incorporated information and guides for men's grooming. It has become a factual reference book and is widely used for many ladies magazines. It has also been included in the curriculum of some cosmetology schools in Canada."

* * *

CORNELL, Francis Griffith 1906-1979

OBITUARY NOTICE: Born October 10, 1906, in Red Springs, N.C.; died of a heart attack, June 30, in North Tarrytown, N.Y. Author and educator who helped rebuild West Germany's postwar educational system. A specialist in educational statistics and consultation, Cornell had earlier worked at the U.S. Office of Education, where he drew up plans for the education of returning World War II veterans. Subsequently, in 1948, the U.S. Army engaged him in the reconstruction of West Germany's educational system. He was the head of his own educational consulting firm, Educational Research Services, and the author of numerous articles and books, including *Essentials of Educational Statistics.* Obituaries and other sources: *American Men and Women of Science: The Social and Behavorial Sciences,* 12th edition, Bowker, 1973; *Leaders in Education,* 5th edition, Bowker, 1974; *New York Times,* July 3, 1979.

* * *

CORONEL, Jorge Icaza
See ICAZA CORONEL, Jorge

* * *

CORSI, Jerome R(obert) 1946-

PERSONAL: Born August 31, 1946, in East Cleveland, Ohio; son of Louis E. (a union public relations director) and Alice (Hanlon) Corsi: married Joy Dugan, May 8, 1970. *Education:* Case Western Reserve University, B.A. (magna cum laude), 1968; Harvard University, Ph.D., 1972. *Home:* 1221 Elizabeth St., Denver, Colo. 80206. *Agent:* Bertha Klausner, International Literary Agency, Inc., 71 Park Ave., New York, N.Y. 10016. *Office:* Department of Political Science, University of Denver, Denver, Colo. 80208.

CAREER: Edward Howard & Co. (public relations firm), Cleveland, Ohio, staff writer and research associate, 1964-68; Franconia College, Franconia, N.H., professor of politics and philosophy, 1972-76; University of New Mexico, Albuquerque, visiting associate professor of political science, 1976-77, research associate professor of public administration, 1977-79; University of Denver, Denver, Colo., associate research professor of political science, 1979—. Research associate at Lemberg Center for the Study of Violence, Brandeis University, 1968-73; participant in scholarly meetings. Professional photographer, with solo show in Colorado.

MEMBER: International Society for Research on Aggression, American Political Science Association, American Philosophical Association, Law and Society Association, Western Social Science Association, Phi Beta Kappa. *Awards, honors:* Grants from National Science Foundation, 1977, 1979.

WRITINGS: (With Louis Masotti, Jeffrey Hadden, and Kenneth Seminatore) *A Time to Burn?,* Rand McNally, 1971; *The King, the Dragon, the Witch* (juvenile), Ginn, 1972; (with Masotti) *Shoot-Out in Cleveland,* Praeger, 1979; *Judicial Politics: An Introduction,* Prentice-Hall, in press.

Musical plays: "Leonis" (three-act for children), first produced in South Yarmouth, Mass., at Camp Kirkland, August, 1972; "The Magic Harp" (three-act for children), first produced in South Yarmouth, Mass., at Camp Kirkland, August, 1973; "The Secret of the Christmas Crystal-Flower" (three-act for children), first produced in Franconia, N.H., at Franconia Town Hall, December, 1975; "Three by Five" (one-act), first produced in Catskills, N.Y., at Grossinger's, October 27, 1975.

Contributor to political science, law and sociology journals. Editor of *Journal of Urban Law,* summer, 1978.

WORK IN PROGRESS: Research on the use of teleconferencing in administrative fair hearings.

SIDELIGHTS: Corsi told *CA:* "I have tried to combine my academic career with fictional writing and photography because I need several different avenues of expression. In my academic writing I have explored several different topics. I have written some limited pieces on philosophic issues. My first academic love for both teaching and writing is political philosophy. I pursue this whenever I get this opportunity. In both my graduate work at Harvard and teaching at Franconia College my primary interest was political philosophy.

"In the modern academic world, there is little room (unfortunately) for philosophy. Most of the rewards go to those who do empirical work, often with a behaviorial emphasis. This for me is both a problem and an opportunity. The situation draws me farther from philosophy but it gives me an opportunity to pursue other interests. I have researched and written extensively on racial violence and the political protest of the late 1960's and early 1970's. My doctoral thesis at Harvard looked at the question of free speech and political dissent. I have done several case studies, including *Shoot-Out in Cleveland* on the gun battle between police and black militants in the summer of 1968. Currently I am developing a theoretical piece on terrorism.

"My other current academic interests have focused on directing a large-scale grant funded by the National Science Foundation to examine the use of the telephone to conduct administrative appeals hearings. This research utilizes an applied experimental design (rare in the social sciences) to examine a practical question. Here I am able to explore my curiosity with communications technology and the logic of empirical inquiry. While technology exists and can do wondrous things, we still must attempt to use it intelligently, to rule the technology rather than being ruled by it."

About his other interests, Corsi commented: "I like writing for children. Children appreciate a simplicity and humor which I often find adults have left behind while they complicate the world in a humorless fashion. Also, I have learned never to 'write down' to children. All too often children see far more than we do.

"In 1975 I began to pursue photography professionally. So much of my work has been with words; photography on the other hand gives me an opportunity for a totally different form of communication, and I have enjoyed exploring this dimension of expression."

* * *

CORTESI, Lawrence
See CERRI, Lawrence J.

* * *

COULSON, William D(onald) E(dward) 1942-

PERSONAL: Born September 17, 1942, in London, England; came to the United States in 1956; married Mary Lee King, 1965; children: Anne, Edward. *Education:* Trinity College, Hartford, Conn., B.A. (with honors), 1964; graduate study at American School of Classical Studies in Athens, 1966-67; Princeton University, Ph.D., 1968. *Office:* Department of Classics, University of Minnesota, 310 Folwell Hall, 9 Pleasant St. S.E., Minneapolis, Minn. 55455.

CAREER: University of Minnesota, Minneapolis, assistant professor of classics and classical archaeology, 1968—. Staff member of Corinth excavations, 1967; senior staff member of Nichoria excavations, 1970-76; supervisor of excavations at Tel Mikhal, Israel, 1977-78; co-director of Naukratis project in Egypt, 1977—. Participant in conferences and professional meetings. *Member:* American Philological Association, Archaeological Institute of America, Association for Field Archaeology, Society of Professional Archaeologists, Phi Beta Kappa, Pi Gamma Mu, Delta Phi Alpha. *Awards, honors:* John Williams White fellow of American School of Classical Studies in Athens, 1966-67; National Endowment for the Humanities fellow, 1973-74; travel grant from University of Minnesota, 1973-74, and Macmillan Fund, 1977-78, both for Greece; American Council of Learned Societies fellow, 1977-78; grants from Control Data Corp., 1977, for Israel, Smithsonian Institution, 1977, for Egypt, University of Minnesota, 1978, for England, and from American Philosophical Society, 1979, for Crete.

WRITINGS: An Annotated Bibliography of Greek and Roman Art, Architecture, and Archaeology, Garland Publishing, 1975; (with John Rosser) *Nichoria III: Dark Age and Byzantine Periods,* University of Minnesota Press, 1979. Contributor to *Princeton Encyclopaedia of Classical Sites.* Contributor of about twenty articles and reviews to classical studies journals. Editor of newsletter of Minnesota Society of Archaeological Institute of America, 1974-75.

SIDELIGHTS: Coulson's special interest is classical archaeology, especially Greek Dark Ages archaeology and Hellenistic sculpture.

* * *

COUSER, G(riffith) Thomas 1946-

PERSONAL: Born September 22, 1946, in Melrose, Mass.; son of William Griffith (a teacher) and Ann (a teacher; maiden name, Van Stelten) Couser; married Margaret Jackson, August 10, 1974. *Education:* Dartmouth College, B.A. (summa cum laude), 1968; graduate study at Magdalen College, Oxford, 1968-69; Brown University, Ph.D., 1977. *Home:* 7 Northwood Rd., Quaker Hill, Conn. 06375. *Office:* Box 1412, Connecticut College, New London, Conn. 06320.

CAREER: English teacher at private secondary school in Meriden, N.H., 1969-72; Connecticut College, New London, assistant professor of English, 1976—. Lecturer to adult education classes.

WRITINGS: American Autobiography: The Prophetic Mode, University of Massachusetts Press, 1979. Contributor to literature journals.

WORK IN PROGRESS: Research on developments in literature and architecture in Chicago at the turn of the century.

SIDELIGHTS: Couser told *CA:* "In my book I tried to determine what was distinctly American about our classic, or major, autobiographies: those by Jonathan Edwards, Ben Franklin, Frederick Douglass, Henry Thoreau, Walt Whitman, Henry Adams, Louis Sullivan, Frank Lloyd Wright, Malcolm X, and others. The most striking feature shared by these books is their tendency to venture prophetic interpretations of American history. The shape of the author's life is often compared to the course of American history, either actual or ideal; as a result, the tradition becomes a dialogue on what it means to be American.

"My research on Chicago is impelled by my sense that modern American civilization has been decisively shaped by many developments that took place in that city around the turn of the century: the skyscraper, the slaughterhouses, the settlement houses, the World's Fair of 1893 and Burnham's city plan of 1909. This 'vast and sudden municipality' (in Henry B. Fuller's apt phrase) quickly outgrew traditional ways of perceiving the city and approaching its problems and genteel ways of portraying urban life. This lack of tradition is evident in the functionalism of Sullivan and Wright and naturalism of Dreiser."

* * *

COUSTEAU, Philippe Pierre 1940-1979

OBITUARY NOTICE—See index for *CA* sketch: Born December 30, 1940, in Toulon, Var, France; died in a seaplane accident, June 28, 1979, near Alverca, Portugal. Oceanographer, photographer, filmmaker, and author. Cousteau, who made his first aqualung dive at the age of four, was best known for his filming of the television series "The Undersea World of Jacques Cousteau." Cousteau was the younger son of French oceanographer Jacques-Yves Cousteau and made his first trip on his father's ship, *Calypso,* when he was eleven years old. Cousteau was also director of Les Requins Associes, his father's film production company, and vice-president of the Cousteau Society. He was the co-author of *The Shark: Splendid Savage of the Sea.* Obituaries and other sources: *New York Times,* June 29, 1979; *Washington Post,* June 30, 1979.

* * *

COUTO, Richard A. 1941-

PERSONAL: Born December 31, 1941, in Lawrence, Mass.; son of Anthony (a welder) and Beatrice (a factory worker; maiden name, Silva) Couto; married Patricia Rutherford (an office manager), December 21, 1972; children: Nathan Craddock, Jason Craddock, Barbara. *Education:* Marist College, B.A., 1964; Boston College, M.A., 1969; University of Kentucky, Ph.D., 1973. *Home:* 303 Greenway Ave., Nashville,

Tenn. 37205. *Office:* Department of Political Science, Vanderbilt University, Nashville, Tenn. 37240.

CAREER: High school teacher in New York, N.Y., and Lawrence, Mass., 1964-69; teacher at Northern Kentucky State College, 1972-75; associated with Vanderbilt University Center for Health Services and department of political science, 1975—.

WRITINGS: Poverty, Politics, and Health Care: An Appalachian Experience, Praeger, 1975. Author of scripts for "If You Lie You Can't Be President" (a film), and videotapes.

* * *

COWIE, Margaret 1903-1975 (Lesley Storm)

OBITUARY NOTICE: Born in 1903 in Maud, Aberdeenshire, Scotland; died October 19, 1975. Playwright and screenwriter. Under the pseudonym Lesley Storm, she wrote several plays of which two, "Black Chiffon" and "Roar Like a Dove," had long, successful runs in London's West End. Her screenwriting credits include "The Spanish Gardener," "The Heart of the Matter," and the much-praised "The Fallen Idol." Obituaries and other sources: *Who's Who in the Theatre,* 15th edition, Pitman, 1972; *Who's Who,* 126th edition, St. Martin's, 1974.

* * *

COX, James Middleton, Jr. 1903-1974

OBITUARY NOTICE: Born June 27, 1903, in Dayton, Ohio; died 1974. Publisher. Cox was affiliated with Dayton Newspapers, Inc. since 1929. He was concurrently the president and director of both the *Dayton Daily News* and *Dayton Journal-Herald* for many years. Cox was the founder of the Cox Broadcasting Corp. and Cox Enterprises, Inc. Obituaries and other sources: *Who Was Who in America,* 6th edition, Marquis, 1976.

* * *

COXHEAD, Elizabeth 1909(?)-1979

OBITUARY NOTICE: Author of eight novels, her *One Green Bottle* demonstrated the kind of social realism that would later be found in the work of Alan Sillitoe. Published in 1951, the book was condemned for its explicitness by the Bishop of Chester. Coxhead's other writings included a biography of Lady Gregory and a collection of profiles of prominent Irishwomen called *Daughters of Erin.* Obituaries and other sources: *AB Bookman's Weekly,* November 5, 1979.

* * *

CRAIG, (Elizabeth) May 1889(?)-1975

OBITUARY NOTICE: Born c. 1889 in Coosaw Island, S.C.; died July 15, 1975, in Silver Springs, Md. Journalist. Craig was Washington correspondent and author of the column "Inside Washington" for the *Portland Press Herald* and several other newspapers owned by Guy Gannett in Maine. She was active in the battles for women's rights, becoming the first woman correspondent to cover official presidential trips abroad, the first woman to be allowed on board a naval air carrier to report on sea operations, and numerous other "firsts." Craig was a frequent participant on both the radio and television broadcasts of "Meet the Press." Obituaries and other sources: *Current Biography,* Wilson, 1949, September, 1975; *New York Times,* July 16, 1975.

CRAIN, John 1926(?)-1979

OBITUARY NOTICE: Born c. 1926; died June 6, 1979. College accounting editor with John Wiley & Sons, Inc., who had worked many years for other publishers before joining the company in 1971. Crain won Wiley's 1978 College Editor of the Year Award for outstanding editorial achievement. Obituaries and other sources: *Publishers Weekly,* June 18, 1979.

* * *

CRANE, Diana 1933-

PERSONAL: Born April 5, 1933, in Toronto, Ontario, Canada; came to the United States in 1949, naturalized citizen, 1960; daughter of J. Halliday and Lorna (Somerville) Crane; married Michel Herve (an economist), September 13, 1965; children: Adrienne. *Education:* Radcliffe College, A.B. (cum laude), 1953; Columbia University, M.A., 1961, Ph.D., 1964. *Home:* 13 rue Cassette, 75006 Paris, France. *Office:* Department of Sociology, University of Pennsylvania, Philadelphia, Pa. 19104.

CAREER: Yale University, New Haven, Conn., assistant professor of sociology, 1964-68; Johns Hopkins University, Baltimore, Md., assistant professor, 1968-69, associate professor of sociology, 1970-72; University of Pennsylvania, Philadelphia, associate professor of sociology, 1973—. Member of Institute for Advanced Study, Princeton, N.J., 1976-77. Participant in scholarly meetings; consultant to Organization for Economic Cooperation and Development. *Member:* International Sociological Association, American Sociological Association, Society for Social Studies of Science, American Association for the Advancement of Science. *Awards, honors:* National Science Foundation grants, 1966-68, 1968-69, 1975-78; Russell Sage Foundation grant, 1969-72; Ford Foundation travel grant, 1974; Guggenheim fellow, 1974-75.

WRITINGS: Invisible College: Diffusion of Knowledge in Scientific Communities, University of Chicago Press, 1972; *The Sanctity of Social Life: Physicians' Treatment of Critically Ill Patients,* Russell Sage Foundation, 1975.

Contributor: Morris Philipson, editor, *Automation: Implications for the Future,* Vintage Books, 1962; James E. Curtis and John W. Petras, editor, *The Sociology of Knowledge: A Reader,* Praeger, 1970; Larry T. Reynolds and Janice M. Reynolds, editors, *The Sociology of Sociology,* McKay, 1970; Ronald M. Pavalko, editor, *Readings in the Sociology of Occupations,* F. E. Peacock, 1971; Bernice Eiduson and Laura Beckwith, editors, *Sourcebook on Career Choice and Development in Science,* Russell Sage Foundation, 1972; Robert O. Keohane and Joseph S. Nye, editors, *Transnational Relations and World Politics,* Harvard University Press, 1972; Sissela Bok and J. A. Behnke, editors, *The Dilemmas of Euthanasia,* Doubleday, 1975; Richard A. Peterson, editor, *The Production of Culture,* Sage Publications, 1976; Walter P. Metzger, editor, *Reader on the Sociology of the Academic Profession,* Arno, 1977; Paul Durban, editor, *A Guide to Science, Technology, and Medicine,* Free Press, 1979. Contributor to *Britannica Yearbook of Science and the Future.* Contributor of about thirty articles and reviews to academic journals, including *Annals of the American Academy of Political and Social Science.*

WORK IN PROGRESS: The Sociology of Culture: Essays on Art, Science, and Religion; From Cult to Corporation: A Theory of Religious Growth and Change; editing and writing a chapter for *Technology and Society: An Introduction to the Sociology and Political Science of Technology.*

SIDELIGHTS: Crane told *CA:* "Throughout my career, I have been interested in the environmental factors affecting creativity in all fields. Under what circumstances does innovation occur and under what conditions does it have an impact? Innovation is rarely an individual phenomenon. It is more often the product of a group of individuals who explore different aspects of the same problem. I am currently concerned with understanding the similarities and differences in the process of innovation in different cultural institutions (art, science and religion)."

* * *

CRANE, Frank H. 1912-

PERSONAL: Born February 8, 1912, in Des Moines, Iowa; son of Stephen Alexander (a construction worker) and Minnie (a teacher; maiden name, Harrison); married Eleanor May Woods, October 5, 1937; children: Carol L. Crane Engledow, Stephen W. *Education:* Attended Drake University, 1930, 1932. *Politics:* Republican. *Religion:* Methodist. *Home:* 8260 Windcombe Blvd., Indianapolis, Ind. 46240.

CAREER: International News Service, Des Moines, Iowa, reporter, 1930-31; *Des Moines Tribune,* Des Moines, reporter, 1933-35; *Ireton Ledger,* Ireton, Iowa, editor, 1935-37; *News-Chronicle,* Shippensburg, Pa., city editor, 1937-43, managing editor, 1946-47; *Alburn Bureau,* Cleveland, Ohio, editor, 1948-52; *Cleveland News,* Cleveland, copy editor, 1952-53; *Idaho Daily Statesman,* Boise, Idaho, managing editor, 1953-54; *Indianapolis Star,* Indianapolis, Ind., editorial writer, 1954-61, chief editorial writer, 1961-69, editor, 1969-79. Member of advisory board, Indiana University—Purdue University at Indianapolis. *Military:* U.S. Army, Signal Corps, 1943-46; became lieutenant. U.S. Army Reserve, 1946-58; became captain.

MEMBER: National Conference of Editorial Writers, American Society of Newspaper Editors, Indianapolis Press Club (president, 1969), Sigma Delta Chi (president of Indiana chapter, 1964). *Awards, honors:* Freedoms Foundation George Washington Medal, 1955, 1972; Indianapolis Press Club best editorial award, 1968, 1970, 1973.

SIDELIGHTS: Crane's "driving motivation," he told *CA,* "is the preservation of a free political and economic system." He has traveled throughout the United States, and in Canada, Europe, the Middle East, the Far East, and South Africa.

* * *

CRANE, M. A.
See WARTSKI, Maureen (Ann Crane)

* * *

CRANE, Royston Campbell 1901-1977

OBITUARY NOTICE: Born November 22, 1901, in Abilene, Tex.; died in 1977. Cartoonist. Crane was the illustrator and writer of the newspaper comic strip, "Wash Tubbs—Captain Easy," for more than fifteen years. He authored the "Buz Sawyer" cartoon for King Features Syndicate from 1943 until his death. Obituaries and other sources: *Who's Who in the World,* 2nd edition, Marquis, 1973.

* * *

CRAWFORD, James M. 1925-

PERSONAL: Born September 18, 1925, in Commerce, Ga.; son of James M. (a farmer) and Bessie (Ingram) Crawford; married Judith Gail Hummell (a fabric designer and weaver), March 25, 1969; children: Elisabeth. *Education:* University of Georgia, B.S., 1949; University of California, Berkeley, Ph.D., 1966. *Home:* 165 Gaines Court, Athens, Ga. 30605. *Office:* Department of Anthropology, University of Georgia, Athens, Ga. 30602.

CAREER: Georgia Forestry Commission, Butler, county ranger, 1949-50; California Forest and Range Experiments Station, Berkeley, reserach forester, 1956-59; Idaho State University, Pocatello, assistant professor, 1966-68; University of Georgia, Athens, associate professor of anthropology, 1968—. *Military service:* U.S. Army, 1943-46. *Member:* American Anthropological Association, Linguistic Society of America. *Awards, honors:* National Science Foundation grant, 1970-73.

WRITINGS: (Editor) *Studies in Southeastern Indian Languages,* University of Georgia Press, 1975; *The Mobilian Trade Language,* University of Tennessee Press, 1978. Contributor to linguistic and anthropology journals.

WORK IN PROGRESS: Writing entries for *Cocopa Dictionary: Texts and Grammar,* and *Yuchi Dictionary: Texts and Grammar.*

SIDELIGHTS: Crawford comments: "Three interests have stayed with me since the age of twelve: music, trees, and languages. Neither music nor languages seemed a practical career, so I chose forestry. After a year of forestry work in Georgia and a year of graduate study in forestry I dropped out and held a miscellany of jobs in the west, including lumber grader, surveyor, and soils analyst. I discovered linguistics and American Indian languages at Berkeley in 1957, and two years later decided to change careers."

AVOCATIONAL INTERESTS: "Music still remains an avocation and trees have now become one."

* * *

CRICHTON, Kyle Samuel 1896-1960
(Robert Forsythe)

OBITUARY NOTICE: Born November 5, 1896, in Peale, Pa.; died November 24, 1960. Author and associate editor of *Scribner's* and *Collier's Weekly.* Under the pseudonym Robert Forsythe, Crichton wrote critiques of the American capitalist society. He contributed articles to the Communist *Daily Worker* and *New Masses,* and wrote *Reading From Left to Right* and *Redder Than the Rose,* a sharp commentary on American celebrities. Crichton also wrote biographies, including *The Marx Brothers,* and novels under his real name. Obituaries and other sources: *Who Was Who in America,* 4th edition, Marquis, 1968; *The Author's and Writer's Who's Who,* 6th edition, Burke's Peerage, 1971.

* * *

CRILE, Barney
See CRILE, George, Jr.

* * *

CRILE, George, Jr. 1907-
(Barney Crile)

PERSONAL: Born November 3, 1907, in Cleveland, Ohio; son of George Washington (a surgeon) and Grace (McBride) Crile; married Jane Halle, December 5, 1935 (deceased); married Helga Sandburg (a writer), November 9, 1963; children: Ann Esselstyn, Joan Foster, Susan, George. *Education:* Yale University, Ph.B., 1929; Harvard University, M.D., 1933. *Home:* 2060 Kent Rd., Cleveland, Ohio 44106.

Agent: Don Congdon, 22 East 40th St., New York, N.Y. 10016. *Office:* Cleveland Clinic, 9500 Euclid Ave., Cleveland, Ohio 44106.

CAREER: Surgeon; writer. Barnes Hospital, St. Louis, Mo., intern, 1933-34; Cleveland Clinic, Cleveland, Ohio, resident surgeon, 1934-37, member of surgical staff, 1937—, head of department of general surgery, 1956-69, senior consultant of department of surgery, 1969-72, emeritus consultant, 1972—. Honorary civilian consultant to surgeon general. *Military service:* U.S. Navy, 1942-46. *Member:* American College of Surgeons, American Surgical Association, Central Surgical Association, Southern Surgical Association. *Awards, honors:* Royal College of Surgeons honorary fellowship, 1978.

WRITINGS—All nonfiction: (With Franklin L. Shively, Jr.) *The Hospital Care of the Surgical Patient: A Surgeon's Handbook,* foreword by Evarts A. Graham, C. C Thomas, 1943, 2nd edition, 1946; *Practical Aspects of Thyroid Disease,* Saunders, 1949; (with Jane Crile), *Treasure-Diving Holidays,* Viking, 1954; *Cancer and Common Sense,* Viking, 1955; (with Jane Crile, under pseudonym Barney Crile) *More Than Booty,* McGraw, 1965; *A Biological Consideration of Treatment of Breast Cancer,* C. C Thomas, 1967; *A Naturalistic View of Man: The Importance of Early Training in Learning, Living, and the Organization of Society,* World Publishing, 1969; (with Helga Sandburg) *Above and Below: A Journey Through Our National Underwater Parks,* McGraw, 1969; *What Women Should Know About the Breast Cancer Controversy,* Macmillan, 1973; *Surgery, Your Choices, Your Alternatives,* Delacorte, 1978.

WORK IN PROGRESS: Reflections on a Misspent Youth.

SIDELIGHTS: "I have always written because I had something to say," Crile told *CA*. A surgeon and specialist in cancer research, he has not only covered medical topics in his writing, but has written adventure books as well.

Anthony Storr described one of Crile's professional books, *A Naturalistic View of Man,* as a "stimulating, rewarding, enlivening . . . surgeon's conspectus of his own species." Here Crile contends that "there is a critical time in the life of each cell, each organ, each animal, each society and perhaps even in the ecology of the world, at which the organism in question is particularly sensitive to its environment and best able to make an adaptive change." In regard to human beings in particular, and in accord with many of today's psychoanalysts, Crile holds that early childhood experiences are crucial in shaping the adult life. "The mood of a lifetime is set in the forgotten events of childhood," he wrote. While Storr observed that Crile "may have fallen into the utopian trap of believing that all man's ills can be cured by proper infantile handling," Storr applauded Crile's concept of combining the study of human behavior with that of the physiology of the brain.

Representative of Crile's books on adventure is *Treasure Diving Holidays,* co-authored with Jane Halle Crile. The authors relate their experiences as skin divers in Lake Erie, in the waters around the West Indies, and in the Mediterranean Sea. They describe what an underwater explorer in these areas may expect to observe in the way of aquatic animals, marine plantlife, and scenic beauty. The book takes the reader "on a delightful, informative, unusual voyage of discovery in a fascinating new marine world," commented Al Chase.

BIOGRAPHICAL/CRITICAL SOURCES: Chicago Sunday Tribune, May 7, 1954; *Book World,* January 26, 1969; *Natural History,* June, 1969; *Yale Review,* Volume 48, number 4, summer, 1969; *Washington Post,* May 10, 1970; *Choice,* July, 1970.

* * *

CROCKETT, Albert Stevens 1873-1969

OBITUARY NOTICE: Born June 19, 1873, in Solomons, Md.; died November, 1969. Writer, reporter, publicist, and editor. Crockett was a reporter for many newspapers, including the *Philadelphia Inquirer,* the *London Daily Telegraph,* and the *New York Herald.* He was also a special correspondent for the *New York Times,* where he surveyed the Orient, and wrote a study on the ability of the Philippine Islands to successfully implement self-rule. Crockett had a flair for big publicity and once chartered a steam yacht to cover the finish of the International Yacht Race for the German Kaiser's Cup in 1905. He was the author of many books, including *Ditties From a Ditty Bag, When James Gordon Bennett Was Caliph of Bagdad,* and *Old Waldorf Bar Days.* Crockett was editor of *World Traveler* and president of World Traveler Publishing Co. Obituaries and other sources: *Who Was Who in America,* 5th edition, Marquis, 1973.

* * *

CROCKETT, James Underwood 1915-1979

OBITUARY NOTICE—See index for *CA* sketch: Born October 9, 1915, in Haverhill, Mass.; died of cancer, July 11, 1979, in Jamaica. Horticulturalist, television host, and author of more than fifteen books on gardening. Crockett, who was reputed to possess a green thumb even at the age of three, opened his own flower shop shortly after World War II. In 1947 he began writing a monthly newsletter, *Flowery Talks,* to help his customers care for their plants and flowers. His newsletter was so successful that Crockett began to write books on gardening; his first was *Windowsill Gardening.* He became the host of a television program, "Crockett's Victory Garden," in 1973, and received an Emmy nomination for the series in 1978. His books include *Crockett's Victory Garden* and *Crockett's Indoor Garden.* Obituaries and other sources: *Who's Who in the East,* 14th edition, Marquis, 1973; *Washington Post,* July 14, 1979; *Chicago Tribune,* July 15, 1979; *Newsweek,* July 23, 1979; *Publishers Weekly,* August 20, 1979.

* * *

CROFT-COOKE, Rupert 1903-1979
(Leo Bruce)

OBITUARY NOTICE—See index for *CA* sketch: Born June 20, 1903, in Edenbridge, Kent, England; died in 1979 in Bournemouth, England. Writer best known for producing more than twenty autobiographical volumes. Croft-Cooke wrote more than thirty novels, including several thrillers under the pseudonym Leo Bruce. He was also the author of a controversial biography of Lord Alfred Douglas. Obituaries and other sources: *The New Century Handbook of English Literature,* revised edition, Appleton, 1967; *Longman Companion to Twentieth Century Literature,* Longman, 1970; *The Author's and Writer's Who's Who,* 6th edition, Burke's Peerage, 1971; *The Writers Directory, 1980-82,* St. Martin's, 1979; *Who's Who,* 131st edition, St. Martin's, 1979; *AB Bookman's Weekly,* August 6, 1979.

* * *

CROMMELYNCK, Fernand 1885-1970

OBITUARY NOTICE: Born November 19, 1885, in Brussels, Belgium; died March 17, 1970. Playwright and author of the famous play, "The Magnificent Cuckold." When first produced in Paris in 1920, "The Magnificent Cuckold" became an instant success. The play was praised by critics as the best in Belgian literature and its author was ranked among the greatest playwrights alive. The movie versions of the play appeared in French in 1946, and in English in 1965. Crommelynck's style is characterized by the use of biting language and grotesque imagery. His plays are a mixture of cynicism, comedy, and tragedy, and often deal with the difference between reality and fantasy. His other works include "Le Sculpteur de Masques," "Le Marchand de Regrets," and "Le Triomphe de Don Juan." Obituaries and other sources: *The Reader's Encyclopedia,* 2nd edition, Crowell, 1965; *Encyclopedia of World Literature in the Twentieth Century,* updated edition, Ungar, 1967; *Everyman's Dictionary of European Writers,* Dent & Sons, 1968; *The Reader's Encyclopedia of World Drama,* Crowell, 1969; *Cassell's Encyclopaedia of World Literature,* revised edition, Morrow, 1973; *World Authors, 1950-1970,* Wilson, 1975.

* * *

CROMWELL, Chester R. 1925-

PERSONAL: Born April 14, 1925, in Michigan; son of Chester Mix (an artist) and Helen (Glancy) Cromwell; married Annabelle Flohr (a college instructor), November 27, 1948; children: Kristi Lynn Cromwell Cain, Charles Chase. *Education:* Attended Canisius College, 1943-44; Manchester College, B.S., 1949; University of Denver, M.A., 1953; also attended University of Utah and University of Colorado. *Religion:* Unitarian-Universalist. *Home:* 6802 Kipling St., Arvada, Colo. 80004. *Office:* North Arvada Junior High School, 7285 Pierce St., Arvada, Colo. 80003.

CAREER: Elementary school teacher and principal in Lowell, Ind., 1949-52, and Wheat Ridge, Colo., 1952-53; Douglas Aircraft Corp., El Segundo, Calif., technical writer, 1953-54; elementary school teacher in Lakewood, Colo., dean of boys, counselor, and acting principal, 1954-78; currently associated with North Arvada Junior High School, Arvada, Colo. Member of State Commission on Teacher Training and Certification. Coordinator of summer training programs for teachers. *Member:* National Education Association, Colorado Education Association, Jefferson County Education Association, Jefferson County Counselors Association.

WRITINGS: (With William Ohs, Albert E. Roark, and Gene Stanford) *Becoming: A Course in Human Relations,* Lippincott, 1975.

* * *

CROMWELL, John 1887-1979

OBITUARY NOTICE: Born December 23, 1887, in Toledo, Ohio; died of a pulmonary embolism, September 26, 1979, in Santa Barbara, Calif. Actor, director, and producer of stage productions and motion picitures. In the theatre, Cromwell distinguished himself primarily as an actor, appearing in such productions as "Hamlet," "Death of a Salesman," and "Richard III." He began his career in motion pictures as an actor but quickly turned to direction. His films include "Close Harmony" and "Of Human Bondage." Obituaries and other sources: *Who's Who in the Theatre,* 16th edition, Pitman, 1977; *New York Times,* September 28, 1979.

* * *

CROMWELL, John 1914(?)-1979

OBITUARY NOTICE: Born c. 1914; died September 1, 1979, in London, England. Actor, novelist, and playwright. Cromwell quit his studies at Harvard University to pursue an acting career, making his Broadway debut in the Pulitzer Prize-winning play, "The Old Maids," in 1935. He subsequently appeared in stage productions of "Romeo and Juliet," "Bright Rebel," "Candida," "Outward Bound," "Macbeth," and "Pygmalion." Cromwell was the author of two novels, *Egan Rendy* and *A Grain of Sand,* and several plays, including "Opening Night," "Banquet for the Moon," and "Jardie's Roommate," all produced Off Broadway. Obituaries and other sources: *New York Times,* September 5, 1979.

* * *

CRONIN, Sylvia 1929-

PERSONAL: Born January 17, 1929, in Newark, N.J.; daughter of Jack (a jeweler) and Esther (a nurse; maiden name, Warner) Ash; married Ronald Dresner, January 8, 1954 (died); married Henry C. Cronin (in communications engineering), August 29, 1976; children: Edward Dresner. *Education:* Attended New York University, 1946, and University of Miami, 1958. *Religion:* "Half Jewish and half Gentile." *Home and office:* 8418 South West 103rd Ave., Miami, Fla. 33173.

CAREER/WRITINGS: Miami Herald, Miami, Fla., co-author of column "Jacqueline," 1958-65; WIOD-Radio, Miami, writer and broadcaster of poetic advice show, "Advice Is Nice," 1965-70; Sylvia Ash Productions, Miami, president, 1970-76; author of syndicated column "Tip Off . . . The Rip Off," 1976—. Notable assignments include research trips to Turks, Caicos, and Bahama Islands for travel column, 1976-78. Free-lance lecturer. Editor of *Who's in Town,* 1960-62; consumer writer for Panex Newspapers, 1977—; associate editor of *Campus,* 1979—; consumer editor of *Kendall Gazette,* 1979. Member of board of directors of Sales and Marketing Executive Club, 1970-73. *Member:* Economic Society of Southern Florida. *Awards, honors:* Dale Carnegie Human Relations Award, 1969; commendation from U.S. Patent Office, 1973, for industrial trade show; Congressional recognition from Claude Pepper, 1976, for consumer assistance.

WORK IN PROGRESS: "I am in constant research for my column 'Tip Off . . . The Rip Off.'"

SIDELIGHTS: Cronin told *CA:* "I strongly believe if consumers are tipped off with information their chances of being ripped off are limited." She also insisted that "the writer has got to practice the three T's: Tenacity, Tolerance, and Time. The writer MUST have the tenacity to persevere, the tolerance to condone those who procrastinate in giving decisions, and the time to devote to the dedication required.

"After four years of total dedication my columns are now catching on both in print and on broadcasts."

* * *

CROSBY, James O('Hea) 1924-

PERSONAL: Born December 5, 1924, in New York, N.Y.; son of Laurence A. (an attorney and business executive) and Aileen (O'Hea) Crosby; married, 1950 (divorced, 1972); children: Elizabeth Anne, Laurence A., Caroline L. *Education:* Yale University, B.A., 1947, M.A., 1952, Ph.D., 1954. *Office:* Department of Modern Languages, Florida International University, Tamiami Campus, Miami, Fla. 33199.

CAREER: University of Illinois, Urbana, instructor, 1955-57, assistant professor, 1957-59, associate professor, 1959-

62, professor of Spanish, 1962-68; Dartmouth College, Hanover, N.H., professor of Spanish, 1968-72; Florida International University, Miami, professor of Spanish, 1972—. Lecturer at University of Barcelona, University of Zaragosa, University of Cologne, Bochum University, Smith College, Western Reserve University (now Case Western Reserve University), Johns Hopkins University, University of Minnesota, and Duke University, 1961-77. *Military service:* U.S. Navy, 1943-46, served in India and Japan; became ensign. *Member:* Modern Language Association of America, Hispanic Society of America. *Awards, honors:* Guggenheim fellowship, 1962-63; research fellowship at Center for Advanced Study, University of Illinois, 1966-67; National Endowment for the Humanities grant, 1978-79.

WRITINGS: The Text Tradition of the Memorial "Catolica, sacra, real Magestad," University of Kansas, 1958; *The Sources of the Text of Quevedo's "Politica de Dios,"* Modern Language Association of America, 1959; (editor of critical edition) Francisco de Quevedo, *Politica de Dios* (title means "The Policies of God"), University of Illinois, 1966; *En torno a la poesia de Quevedo* (title means "On Quevedo's Poetry"), Castalia, 1967; *Guia bibliografica para el estudio critico de Quevedo* (title means "Bibliographical Guide for Critical Studies on Quevedo"), Grant & Cutler, 1976. Contributor of book reviews and twenty scholarly articles on the poetry, manuscript sources, and biography of Francisco de Quevedo to journals, including *Hispanic Review, Modern Language Notes, Publications of the Modern Language Association* and *Nueva Revista de Filologia Hispanica.*

WORK IN PROGRESS: A full-length critical edition of Quevedo's *Suenos* (title means "Visions of Hell"), containing five major satires "and a comprehensive line-by-line commentary on the sources and the meaning of these satires," publication expected in 1982; a book on *Don Quixote;* "popular editions and translations of the *Suenos,* of Quevedo's poetry, and of other satires in both Spanish and English."

SIDELIGHTS: Crosby's consistent professional aim has been to provide readers with access to true and accurate versions of the works of Spain's greatest Baroque satirist, Francisco de Quevedo. This complex life-long project has involved the description and classification of large masses of original materials, the discovery of unknown texts, the introduction of theories of analysis to untried areas, and the application of such theories to the solution of practical problems. It is a comprehensive effort to correct the three centuries of scholarly neglect of Quevedo's work.

In his 1958 book, *The Text Tradition,* Crosby applied biblical, classical, and medieval French theories of textual analysis to some twenty different manuscripts of a Baroque poem attributed to Quevedo. He demonstrated in practical terms the successive steps in the history of how this poem was copied and recopied, and included a critical edition of it. Crosby's book was widely reviewed in Europe and America, and prompted other scholars to undertake similar editions of some of Quevedo's works (F. Lazaro Carreter, 1965; L. Lopez Grigera, 1969; F.C.R. Maldonado, 1972). Although reviewers found "minor technical errors" and said that "a few details need correction," they praised Crosby's "most precise, patient and persevering form of investigation," "as successful as it was humanly possible to be," and "an example of procedure and method which should certainly be emulated." "He has shown great patience and skill, and great patience and skill will be required to follow his example"; "the text is a delight"; " as nearly definitive a text as we are likely to have"; "anyone who brings such names as Greg and Bowers to the notice of Hispanists performs a public service."

Crosby's next book, *The Sources,* proposed to do for printed editions what *The Text Tradition* had done for the study of Spanish manuscripts, and was based on the principles of Shakespearean textual analysis. Critics commended the author: "With resourcefulness commensurate with his demanding task, he has set a brilliant example for others to follow," and "has achieved a scrupulous, detailed and exhaustive study, for which he had almost no precedents in the field of seventeenth-century Spanish research." "Of considerable practical use to many who are not specifically interested in Quevedo."

In 1966 Crosby published the practical and tangible results of his earlier study, in what the *Times Literary Supplement* called "a magnificent edition of Quevedo's *Politica de Dios,* with full and scrupulous scholarly apparatus and a definitive text which is a pleasure to read." Professional reviewers in America wrote that "Professor Crosby's model edition of the *Politica de Dios* manifests the care, precision and thoroughness with which its editor approaches all scholarly problems. . . . It is typical of the soundness and completeness of his scholarship." In a different vein, Raimundo Lida and Andree Collard remarked that "Crosby's way of putting the cards on the table invites future scholars to look at the material and follow a method the soundness of which is attested by this edition. . . . His thorough approach . . . is sensitive to the 'linguistic flexibility of the time,' and mindful of divergent critical points of view. . . . The alert scholar knows that his efforts are provisional. But there is a hierarchy of provisionalities: Crosby leaves the field open precisely because he is aware that to present a classical author is far from being a mechanical and superstitious routine. . . . This edition . . . is not only a pleasure for the eyes and the mind; it offers the additional perfection of not claiming conclusiveness."

A year after the edition of the *Politica,* Crosby published a book on Quevedo's poetry which was described as follows in the *Times Literary Supplement:* "Professor Crosby's work as a student and editor of Quevedo is well known on both sides of the Atlantic, and in *En torno a la poesia de Quevedo* he turns his attention to a number of textual and bibliographical subjects. . . . His studies are enlightening to the general student of Quevedo's work, and will be invaluable to future editors of his poetry." Other reviewers called this book "An outstanding study . . . : here is an abundance of new material, . . . inaccessible for many years. Hispanists owe an immense debt to Professor Crosby for this information."

In 1976 Crosby published the first comprehensive bibliographical guide to everything that has been written about Quevedo since 1700. One reviewer called the *Guia bibliograpfica* "an invaluable aid to scholars, who once again owe the author a debt of gratitude," and another said that "the name of the compiler is the best possible guarantee for the quality of this most useful guide."

In 1969 and 1970, a few reviewers looked back on Crosby's works and said that "in recent years he has led the way in applying to Quevedo the methods of modern textual criticism," and that in America he was "already well known as the Quevedo textual authority." In the *Hispanic Review,* Edwin S. Morby wrote: "As for our conception of Quevedo ten or fifteen years from now, American Hispanists can already foresee that it will owe much to James O. Crosby. This was evident from his monographs, models of their kind, . . . [and from] the edition of the *Politica de Dios,* a masterly structure fully confirming the earlier indication.... His treatment of his materials is flexible, varying according to the nature of the problem. But there is never the slightest uncertainty about the procedures being applied, their consistency, or the reasons for their adoption. By now, taking together all Quevedo texts prepared by him, we have a substantial corpus; which ... accounts in large measure for the sense of increasing mastery that I have spoken of.... Accustomed to looking to Crosby for diligence, thoroughness, painstaking accuracy and scrupulous method, we may not have realized the extent of his aesthetic sensibility and imagination. These qualities are a welcome enhancement."

BIOGRAPHICAL/CRITICAL SOURCES: Modern Language Notes, March, 1960, March, 1970; *Symposium,* April, 1960; *Hispanic Review,* October, 1960, July, 1961, January, 1970; *Filologia,* April, 1961; *Bulletin of Hispanic Studies,* April, 1961, April, 1969, April, 1978; *Modern Language Review,* January, 1962; *Times Literary Supplement,* August 24, 1967, February 26, 1970; *Hispania,* September, 1968; *Hispanofila,* January, 1971; *Year's Work in Modern Language Studies,* Volume 35, 1973; *Journal of Hispanic Philology,* April, 1977.

* * *

CROSS, Leslie (Frank) 1909-1977

OBITUARY NOTICE—See index for *CA* sketch: Born May 12, 1909, in Milwaukee, Wis.; died of a heart attack, July 3, 1977. Journalist and author of *Written in Wisconsin.* While working as a book editor and columnist for the *Milwaukee Journal,* Cross established a reputation as one of the finest book reviewers in the Midwest. Obituaries and other sources: *Who's Who in America,* 39th edition, Marquis, 1976; *Publishers Weekly,* July 18, 1977.

* * *

CROUCH, Harold (Arthur) 1940-

PERSONAL: Born July 18, 1940, in Melbourne, Australia; son of Harold (a businessman) and Marjorie (Morris) Crouch; married Khasnor Johan (a lecturer), June 14, 1973; children: Zamir, Azlan, Nurida. *Education:* University of Melbourne, B.A., 1963; University of Bombay, M.A., 1966; Monash University, Ph.D., 1975. *Home:* G35 Taman Bukit, Kajang, Selangor, Malaysia. *Office:* Department of Political Science, National University of Malaysia, Bangi, Selangor, Malaysia.

CAREER: Australian Government, Department of Labour and National Service, research officer, 1962-63 and 1966; Monash University, Melbourne, Australia, senior teaching fellow in department of politics, 1967; University of Indonesia, Jakarta, lecturer in department of political science, 1968-71; National University of Malaysia, Bangi, lecturer in department of political science, 1976—. *Member:* Australian Institute of International Affairs, Asian Studies Association of Australia, Malaysian Economics Association.

WRITINGS: Trade Unions and Politics in India, Manaktales, 1966; *The Army and Politics in Indonesia,* Cornell University Press, 1978; (editor with Michael Ong and Lee Kam Hing) *Malaysian Politics and the 1978 Elections,* Oxford University Press, 1980. Contributor to *Dyason House Papers, Pacific Affairs, World Politics,* and *Indonesia.*

WORK IN PROGRESS: Political development in Southeast Asia.

CROUCH, W(illiam) George (Alfred) 1903-1970

OBITUARY NOTICE—See index for *CA* sketch: Born January 16, 1903, in London, England; died April 13, 1970, in Pittsburgh, Pa. Educator, business consultant, and author of books on writing, including *A Guide to Technical Writing* and *Successful Communication in Science and Industry.* A professor of English at the University of Pittsburgh, Crouch was considered an expert on Charles Dickens. Obituaries and other sources: *AB Bookman's Weekly,* May 4, 1970.

* * *

CROY, Homer 1883-1965

OBITUARY NOTICE: Born March 11, 1883, near Maryville, Mo.; died May, 1965. Humorist, reporter, and author of *They Had to See Paris,* a novel which became Will Rogers's first talking motion picture. Croy's stories were used for Rogers's movies more than any other author's. After attending the country's first school of journalism at Missouri University, Croy became a reporter with Missouri's *St. Joseph Gazette.* He soon moved to New York where he wrote humorous pieces for Theodore Dreiser, editor of three Butterick magazines. Croy wrote many novels, including *West of the Water Tower* and *Mr. Meek Marches On.* He also wrote nonfiction works such as *How Motion Pictures Are Made.* Croy was the first person to tour the world shooting motion pictures. Obituaries and other sources: *Twentieth Century Authors: A Biographical Dictionary of Modern Literature,* Wilson, 1942; *Who Was Who in America,* 5th edition, Marquis, 1973.

* * *

CRUICKSHANK, William M(ellon) 1915-

PERSONAL: Born March 25, 1915, in Detroit, Mich.; son of Ward and Alice (Shanor) Cruickshank; married Dorothy Jane Wager, December 26, 1940; children: Alice Ann (Mrs. Roger Johanson), Dorothy Patricia (Mrs. David Crosson), Carol Jean. *Education:* Eastern Michigan University, A.B., 1937; University of Chicago, M.A., 1938; further graduate study at Cite Universitaire, Paris, France, 1944; University of Michigan, Ph.D., 1945. *Home:* 2855 Whippoorwill Lane, Ann Arbor, Mich. 48103. *Office:* Institute for the Study of Mental Retardation and Related Disabilities, University of Michigan, 130 South First St., Ann Arbor, Mich. 48109.

CAREER: Eastern Michigan University, Ypsilanti, instructor in special education, 1939-41; Boys' Vocational School, Lansing, Mich., special education executive, 1945-46; Syracuse University, Syracuse, N.Y., Margaret O. Slocum Distinguished Professor of Education and Psychology and director of Division of Special Education and Rehabilitation, 1946-67, dean of summer sessions, 1953-66; University of Michigan, Ann Arbor, professor of psychology, maternal and child health, and education, 1966—, director of Institute for the Study of Mental Retardation and Related Disabilities, 1966—, head of special education, speech, and hearing sciences program, 1977—. Visiting professor at Texas Women's University, Florida State University, State University of New York at Buffalo, University of Oregon, and Ohio State University; Fulbright lecturer and associate director of Institute San Gabriel Archangel, 1962-63, 1968; visiting lecturer at Northwestern University, Yeshiva University, University of Uppsala, University of San Marcos, University of Trujillo, Kumamato University, and University of Birmingham. Member of Michigan Developmental Disabilities Council, 1971—; vice-chairman of technical research advisory committee of Michigan Department of Mental Health,

1975—; head of professional advisory board of Detroit Orthopaedic Center, 1976—; member of board of trustees of Detroit League for the Handicapped, 1978—. Past member of educational advisory committee of Federal Epilepsy Foundation; past adviser to Educational Policies Commission. Member of state advisory committee on education for Government of American Samoa, 1969-72. Founder and past chairman of New York State Planning Council for Exceptional Children; past member of New York State Board of Regents Council on the Physically Handicapped. Consultant to federal government agencies. *Military service:* U.S. Army, clinical psychologist, 1941-43, instructor at American Army University, Shriveham, England, 1943-44.

MEMBER: International Council for Exceptional Children (past president), International Neuropsychology Society, American Psychological Association (fellow; member of National Council on the Psychological Aspects of Physical Disability), American Association on Mental Deficiency (fellow; life member), American Academy of Mental Deficiency (charter member), American Academy of Cerebral Palsy and Developmental Medicine, Council for Exceptional Children (life member; past division president), National Society for Crippled Children and Adults (past member of professional advisory council). *Awards, honors:* Leadership award from National Epilepsy League, 1959; Sc.D. from Eastern Michigan University, 1962; catedratico honorario from Universidad Nacional Mayor de San Marcos, 1962; merit award from Centro Peruano de Audicion y Languaje, 1962; medical writing award from Pratt Library, 1962, for *A Teaching Method for Brain-Injured and Hyperactive Children;* J. E. Wallace Wallin Award from Council for Exceptional Children, 1965; distinguished professional service award from Association for Children with Learning Disabilities, 1970; merit award from city of New Orleans, La., 1974; education award from American Association on Mental Deficiency, 1975; distinguished service award from Louisiana Division for Children with Learning Disabilities, 1976; award of honor from International Federation of Learning Disabilities, 1976; Newell C. Kephart Award from Purdue University, 1977.

WRITINGS: (Editor with G. M. Raus, and contributor) *Cerebral Palsy: Its Individual and Community Problems,* Syracuse University Press, 1955, 3rd edition published as *Cerebral Palsy: A Developmental Disability,* 1976; (editor and contributor) *The Psychology of Exceptional Children and Youth,* Prentice-Hall, 1955, 3rd edition, 1971; *Frontiers in the Education of Exceptional Children,* Syracuse University Press, 1956; (with H. V. Bice and N. E. Wallen) *Perception and Cerebral Palsy: A Study of the Figure-Background Relationship,* Syracuse University Press, 1957, 2nd edition (with Bice, Wallen, and K. S. Lynch), 1965; *Two Stars Take Their Place* (poems), privately printed, 1957; (with N. J. Haring and G. G. Stern) *Attitudes of Educators Toward Exceptional Children* (monograph), Syracuse University Press, 1958; (editor with G. O. Johnson, and contributor) *The Education of Exceptional Children and Youth,* Prentice-Hall, 1958, 3rd edition, 1975; (with M. J. Trippe) *Services to Blind Children in New York State,* Syracuse University Press, 1959.

(With F. Bentzen, F. Ratzeberg, and N. Tanhauser) *A Teaching Method for Brain-Injured and Hyperactive Children,* Syracuse University Press, 1961; *The Brain-Injured Child in Home, School, and Community,* Syracuse University Press, 1967, 2nd edition published as *Learning Disabilities in Home, School, and Community,* 1977; (with J. B. Junkala and J. L. Paul) *The Preparation of Teachers of Brain-Injured Children,* Syracuse University Press, 1968; (with Junkala and Paul) *Misfits in the Public Schools,* Syracuse University Press, 1969; (with E. D. Marshall and M. A. Hurley) *Foundations for Mathematics,* with teachers' guides, Volume I: *Concepts for Sets and Curves,* Volume II: *Exploring Sets,* Volume III: *Motor Development: Lines and Planes,* Volume IV: *Comparing Sets and Numbers,* Teaching Resources Corp., 1971; (with D. P. Hallahan) *Psychoeducational Foundations of Learning gdisabilities,* Prentice-Hall, 1973; (editor with Hallahan, and contributor) *Perceptual and Learning Disabilities in Children,* Volume I: *Psychoeducational Procedures,* Volume II: *Research and Theory,* Syracuse University Press, 1975; (with Paul and A. P. Turnbull) *Mainstreaming: A Practical Guide,* Syracuse University Press, 1977.

Contributor: *The Education of Exceptional Children,* National Society for the Study of Education, 1950; *Freeing Capacity to Learn,* Association for Supervision and Curriculum Development, 1960; Alexander Ewing, editor, *The Modern Educational Treatment of Deafness,* Manchester University Press, 1960; P. Knoblock and J. L. Johnson, editors, *The Teaching-Learning Process in Educating Emotionally Disturbed Children,* Division of Special Education and Rehabilitation, Syracuse University, 1967; *Educational Implications of Psychopathology for Brain-Injured Children,* Graduate School of Education, Leslie College, 1967; J. Wolf and R. Anderson, editors, *The Multiply Handicapped Child,* C. C Thomas, 1969; (author of foreword) S. R. Rappaport, *Public Education for Children With Brain Dysfunction,* Syracuse University Press, 1969.

The Challenge of Mental Retardation in the Community, Institute for the Study of Mental Retardation and Related Disabilities, University of Michigan, 1970; D. P. Hallahan, editor, *Guidelines for the Preparation of Support Personnel,* Institute for the Study of Mental Retardation and Related Disabilities, University of Michigan, 1971; N. Hobbs, editor, *Issues in the Classification of Children,* Volume I, Jossey-Bass, 1974; S. A. Kirk and J. McCarthy, editors, *Learning Disabilities: Selected ACLD Papers,* Houghton, 1975; Hallahan and J. Kauffman, editors, *Teaching Children With Learning Disabilities: Personal Perspectives,* C. E. Merrill, 1976; (author of foreword) J. L. Paul, G. R. Neufel, and J. W. Pelosi, editors, *Child Advocacy Within the System,* Syracuse University Press, 1977; E. Polak, editor, *Learning Disabilities: Information Please,* Quebec Association for Children with Learning Disabilities, 1978. Also contributor to *Special Education: Instrument of Change in Education for the Seventies,* edited by D. L. Walker and D. P. Howard, 1971.

Contributor of more than one hundred articles and reviews to psychology and education journals. Special education editor for Syracuse University Press, 1960—, and Prentice-Hall, 1960-78; member of editorial advisory board of *Journal of Learning Disabilities,* 1970-78; member of editorial board of *Exceptional Child,* 1976—.

SIDELIGHTS: Cruickshank's books have been published in Dutch, Spanish, German, and Japanese, as well as in editions for the blind.

* * *

CRUMP, J(ames) Irving 1887-1979

OBITUARY NOTICE—See index for *CA* sketch: Born December 7, 1887, in Saugerties, N.Y.; died July 3, 1979, in Hackensack, N.J. Editor and author. For nearly twenty-five years Crump was editor of *Boy's Life,* the official magazine of the Boy Scouts of America. He was also the author of more than forty books for young people, including *The Pilot of the Cloud Patrol, Og: Son of Og, Our G-Men, Our Oil Hunters,* and *Our United States Coast Guard Academy.* Obituaries and other sources: *Junior Book of Authors,* 2nd edition, Wilson, 1951; *Authors of Books for Young People,* 2nd edition, Scarecrow, 1971; *New York Times,* July 4, 1979; *AB Bookman's Weekly,* July 30, 1979.

* * *

CUMBLER, John T(aylor) 1946-

PERSONAL: Born January 11, 1946, in Doylestown, Pa.; son of John and Jean (a teacher; maiden name, Maddock) Cumbler; married Judith Kwiat (a social worker), June 8, 1967; children: Ethan U., Kazia E. *Education:* University of Wisconsin, Madison, B.A. (with distinction), 1969; University of Michigan, M.A., 1970, Ph.D., 1974. *Home:* 1947 Roanoke, Louisville, Ky. 40205. *Office:* Department of History, University of Louisville, Louisville, Ky. 40208.

CAREER: San Diego State University, San Diego, Calif., assistant professor of history, 1974-75; University of Louisville, Louisville, Ky., assistant professor of history, 1975-79, assistant professor of American studies, 1976—. *Member:* Organization of American Historians, Social Science History Association.

WRITINGS: Working Class Community in Industrial America: Work, Leisure, and Struggle in Two Industrial Cities, 1880-1930, Greenwood Press, 1979. Contributor to history journals and *Adena.*

WORK IN PROGRESS: Up From Kentucky, a monograph on Appalachian migration, completion expected in 1980.

SIDELIGHTS: Cumbler told *CA:* "My research involves looking at working class communities from the perspective of both urban history and labor history. I am interested in how the work process, the geographic and economic structure of an industrial city, and the nature of social institutions interact and affect working class activity and community. My interest in these questions comes from my commitment to working to create an environment that is healthy, livable, and positively creative for its inhabitants. I believe we can create that environment only through the creative efforts of the ordinary citizens who live, work, and struggle in our cities, towns, and farms. Understanding how workers in the nineteenth and early twentieth century struggled to maintain their dignity and community will give us a guide to the future."

* * *

CUMMINGS, Arthur J. 1920(?)-1979

OBITUARY NOTICE: Born c. 1920; died June 27, 1979, in Venice, Italy. Cummings was a former editor of the *American People's Encyclopedia* and author of a novel about ballet life called *Charade for Happiness.* Obituaries and other sources: *Chicago Tribune,* July 3, 1979.

* * *

CURRAN, Bob
See CURRAN, Robert

* * *

CURRAN, Robert 1923-
(Bob Curran)

PERSONAL: Born October 4, 1923, in Boston, Mass.; married Mary Sullivan (an executive secretary), June 14, 1952; children: Robert, Jr., Mark S., John F. *Education:* Cornell University, B.A., 1949. *Politics:* Republican. *Religion:* Roman Catholic. *Office: Buffalo Evening News,* 1 News Plaza, Buffalo, N.Y. 14240.

CAREER: Fawcett World Library, New York City, publicity editor, 1951-61; NBC-TV, New York City, sports director, 1964-65; Hall Syndicate, New York City, author of column, "Bob Curran on Sports," 1965-67; presently author of column, "Curran's Corner," for *Buffalo Evening News,* Buffalo, N.Y. *Military service:* U.S. Army, 1942-45; served in Germany; became staff sergeant; received Silver Star, Bronze Star, two Purple Hearts, and Combat Infantryman's Badge. *Member:* American Society of Journalists and Authors, Overseas Press Club of America, Sigma Delta Chi. *Awards, honors:* Best column awards from New York State Associated Press, 1970, and Freedoms Foundation, 1971; ten Page One Awards.

WRITINGS—All under name Bob Curran: *Kennedy Women,* Lancer Books, 1963; *Pro Football in the Rag Days,* Prentice-Hall, 1964; *$400,000 Quarterback; or, The League That Came In From the Cold,* Macmillan, 1965; *The Violence Game,* Macmillan, 1966; *$4,100,000 Quarterback,* New American Library, 1967. Also author of *Now a Word From the Sponsor.* Editor of "Ask Them Yourself," a column in *Family Weekly,* 1966-77. Contributor to magazines, including *Saturday Evening Post, Sports Illustrated, Pageant, Reader's Digest,* and *TV Guide.*

SIDELIGHTS: Curran's interest in football began early (he played on the college team at Cornell University) and culminated in his writing career. *The Violence Game* is the diary of one season of a professional football team.

It was Curran who located the Australian coast watcher who saved the crew of "P.T. 109" in World War II and brought him to the United States to meet President John F. Kennedy. Curran was also the man who started the fund to pay the back taxes of World War I hero Sergeant Alvin York.

BIOGRAPHICAL/CRITICAL SOURCES: Editor and Publisher, September 24, 1966.

* * *

CURTIS, Paul
See CZURA, R(oman) P(eter)

* * *

CURTIS, Tom
See PENDOWER, Jacques

* * *

CURTLER, Hugh Mercer 1937-

PERSONAL: Born December 31, 1937, in Charlottesville, Va.; son of Hugh Mercer and Nancy Daingerfield (Elsroad) Curtler; married Linda Edith Lockwood, June 15, 1962; children: Hugh Mercer III, Rudolph Hirsch. *Education:* St. John's College, Annapolis, Md., B.A., 1959; Northwestern University, M.A., 1962, Ph.D., 1964. *Home:* 134 Cottonwood St., Cottonwood, Minn. 56229. *Office:* Department of Literature, Language, and Philosophy, Southwest State University, Marshall, Minn. 56258.

CAREER: University of Rhode Island, Kingston, instructor, 1964-65, assistant professor of philosophy, 1965-66; Midwestern College, Denison, Iowa, assistant professor of humanities and philosophy and head of department, 1966-68; Southwest State University, Marshall, Minn., assistant professor, 1968-70, associate professor, 1970-78, professor of philosophy, 1978—, head of department of philosophy, 1968-76, department of philosophy and foreign languages, 1976-77, and department of literature, language, and philosophy, 1977—. Visiting fellow at the Center for the Study of Democratic Institutions, 1972. *Member:* American Philosophical Association, American Society for Value Inquiry, Society for Political and Legal Philosophy, Delta Tau Kappa. *Awards, honors:* Northwestern fellowship, 1961-64; Younger humanist fellowship from National Endowment for the Humanities, 1971-72.

WRITINGS: *Prologue to Philosophy,* University Press of America, 1976; *Persons and Values: The Philosophy of Eliseo Vivas,* Haven Publishing, 1980. Contributor of about thirty articles and reviews to philosophy and literature journals.

WORK IN PROGRESS: A bibliography on Eliseo Vivas, publication by Garland Publishing expected in 1982.

SIDELIGHTS: Curtler writes: "Recently my work has focused on the writings of Eliseo Vivas, one of the most important philosophers this country has produced, though his work has been largely ignored in the preoccupation of current philosophers with analytic philosophy. Following Vivas, I am interested in the relationship between literature and philosophy and in questions of value generally.

"I write because I see writing as a part of, and not antithetical to, my teaching. But primarily I write because I enjoy it."

* * *

CZURA, R(oman) P(eter) 1913-
(Paul Curtis, Roman Dale)

PERSONAL: Surname is pronounced with a silent "C"; born September 28, 1913, in Hammond, Ind.; son of Walter (a cooper) and Stella (Pupsiewicz) Czura; married Patricia A. Bartley (a buyer for a department store), February 14, 1955; children: Sandra Cullinane, Judy Mercer. *Education:* Attended University of Arizona, 1933-36. *Home:* 3781 Washington St., Lincoln, Neb. 68506.

CAREER: Herald Newspapers, Gary, Ind., outdoor recreation editor, 1950-57; *Nebraskaland* (magazine), Lincoln, Neb., associate editor, 1957-59; free-lance magazine writer and photographer, 1959-79; *Argosy* (magazine), New York, N.Y., field editor, 1971-75; executive editor of *Today's Jogger,* 1975—. Lecturer on outdoor recreation, travel, and photography at Ohio State University, 1978, University of Nebraska, 1978-79, and University of Wisconsin, 1979. *Military service:* U.S. Navy, 1943-46; became chief. *Member:* Outdoor Writers Association of America (president, 1978-79), Midwest Travel Writers Association, Association of Great Lakes Outdoor Writers (past president), Sigma Delta Chi. *Awards, honors:* Award from Nebraska Council of Sportsmen's Clubs, 1960, for outstanding writing about wildlife conservation and outdoor recreation; national press awards from Recreational Vehicle Institute, 1966-69, for radio and television coverage of camping; national awards from Alcan, 1967, Thermos, 1968, and Garcia, 1970-71, for outstanding photography; Peabody Award for outstanding wildlife and nature photography, 1975; "best of show" photography award from Outdoor Writers Association of America, 1979.

WRITINGS: *Sportfishing,* Peterson, 1974; (contributor) Norman Strung, editor, *Communicating the Outdoor Experience,* Outdoor Writers Association of America, 1975. Contributor to *The Ford Four Seasons Library,* 1970. Contributor of more than seven hundred fifty articles, some under pseudonyms Paul Curtis and Roman Dale, to nearly one hundred magazines, including *Field & Stream, Life, Sports Afield, True, Argosy, Boys Life, Travel, Ford Times, Outdoor Life, Vista, National Wildlife,* and *Reader's Digest.*

WORK IN PROGRESS: A pictorial essay on America's vanishing ghost towns, for Doubleday; pictorial and editorial projects for numerous magazines; shooting color photographs for the covers of *Field & Stream* and *Sports Afield;* "Poetry of Photography" lectures for the Nebraska Arts Council.

SIDELIGHTS: Working "strictly on assignment only," Czura travels fifty thousand miles a year "in pursuit of material and photos for a variety of publications, using planes, camels, dugout canoes, horseback, and on foot. I am a specialist covering all aspects of outdoor recreation activities, travel, and adventure. My work has taken me to Kenya, Uganda, Tanzania, South Africa, Rhodesia, Botswana, Japan, France, Italy, England, Scotland, Argentina, Brazil, Chile, Peru, Colombia, Ecuador, and all parts of the United States and Canada."

D

DAILEY, Charles A(lvin) 1923-

PERSONAL: Born June 28, 1923, in Dallas, Tex.; son of Lawson O. (an accountant) and Madge (a teacher; maiden name, Roberts) Dailey; married Ann Madsen, September 3, 1949 (divorced, 1977); married Marguerite McCauley, November 5, 1977; children: Thomas. *Education:* Southern Methodist University, B.A., 1946; University of Michigan, Ph.D., 1950. *Politics:* Democrat. *Religion:* Protestant. *Office:* Bio-Data, Inc., P.O. Box 82, Sudbury, Mass. 01776.

CAREER: Veterans Administration Medical and Surgical Hospital, St. Louis, Mo., chief psychologist, 1950-57; Interstate Brands Corp., Kansas City, Mo., director of management development, 1957-64; American University, Washington, D.C., associate professor of industrial relations, 1964-68; Dartmouth College, Hanover, N.H., adjunct professor of psychology and director of institutional research, 1968-72; McBer Co., Boston, Mass., senior associate, 1972-74; Bio-Data, Inc., Sudbury, Mass., president, 1974—. Diplomate of American Board of Examiners in Psychology. Faculty member at Pepsi Cola Management Institute. Research associate at Harvard University, 1972-73; senior associate of McBer & Co., 1972—. Member of board of directors of Church Executive Development Corp., 1971—. *Military service:* U.S. Naval Reserve, active duty, 1943-46; became lieutenant, senior grade. *Member:* American Psychological Association, American Sociological Association, Academy of Management.

WRITINGS: Assessment of Lives, Jossey-Bass, 1971; *Entrepreneurial Management,* McGraw, 1972; (with Ann Madsen) *Evaluating People,* McGraw, 1979; *Job Stress: Logs, Journals, and Dialogues,* Prentice-Hall, 1980. Contributor of about twenty-five articles to psychology journals.

SIDELIGHTS: Dailey comments: "My major interest is industrial and public leadership and my major concern is integration between scientific method and humanistic insight. Much of my writing has been on the nature and use of biographical and other historical material. In the future, as our population gets older, we will value 'youth' less and 'experience' more. As biography and history *are* the study of experience, they will provide more and more of our insights into human nature.

"Curiously, the greatest interest in my work has been in Japan, where there seems to be more leadership energy available. (*Entrepreneurial Management* was translated into Japanese and sold through a book club there.)

"While my writing is technical, my ideas relate to literature (to biography, at least). My opinions of current literature are that it provides strong support to the idea that the normal human condition is trivial and banal, whereas my own belief is that exaltation and creativity are normal. No one is a fit leader who resembles the hero of the modern novel."

* * *

DAILEY, Janet 1944-

PERSONAL: Born May 21, 1944, in Storm Lake, Iowa; married William Dailey; stepchildren: two. *Religion:* Methodist. *Home address:* P.O. Box 420, Leon, Iowa 50144.

CAREER: Worked as a secretary in Nebraska and Iowa, 1962-74; writer, 1974—.

WRITINGS—Novels; all published by Harlequin: *Savage Land,* 1976; *Something Extra,* 1978; *To Tell the Truth,* 1978; *Sonora Sundown,* 1978; *The Matchmakers,* 1978; *The Master Fiddler,* 1978; *Giant of Mesabi,* 1978; *Beware the Stranger,* 1978; *For Bitter or Worse,* 1979; *Low Country Liar,* 1979; *Green Mountain Man,* 1979; *Tidewater Lover,* 1979; *The Bride of the Delta Queen,* 1979; *Strange Bedfellow,* 1979; *Touch the Wind,* 1979; *For Mike's Sake,* 1979; *Sentimental Journey,* 1979; *Sweet Promise,* 1979.

Other novels; all published by Mills & Boon, 1976: *The Homeplace; Dangerous Masquerade; Show Me; Valley of the Vapors; The Night of the Cotillion; Six White Horses.* Also author of Harlequin novels *No Quarter Asked, Darling Jenny, Fire and Ice, Bossman From Ogallala, After the Storm, Land of Enchantment, Bluegrass King, Sweet Promise, A Lyon's Share, Fiesta San Antonio, The Widow and the Wastrel, The Ivory Cane, Big Sky Country, The Indy Man, Reilly's Woman, A Tradition of Pride,* and *Summer Mahogany.*

SIDELIGHTS: When working on a book, Dailey wakes up at 4:00 a.m. every day and writes until she completes exactly eleven pages of manuscript. *Avocational interests:* Travel (Canada, Mexico, England, Holland, France, the Bahamas).

BIOGRAPHICAL/CRITICAL SOURCES: Forbes, March 6, 1978.*

* * *

DALE, Roman
See CZURA, R(oman) P(eter)

DALGLIESH, Alice 1893-1979

OBITUARY NOTICE—See index for *CA* sketch: Born October 7, 1893, in Trinidad, British West Indies; died June 11, 1979, in Woodbury, Conn. Educator, editor, book reviewer, and author. Dalgliesh was an elementary school teacher for nearly seventeen years, and later taught a course in children's literature at Columbia University. From 1934 to 1960 she served as children's book editor for Charles Scribner's Sons. In addition to her book reviews for such magazines as *Saturday Review of Literature* and *Parents' Magazine*, Dalgliesh wrote more than forty books for children and about children's literature. Obituaries and other sources: *Junior Book of Authors*, 2nd edition, Wilson, 1951; *Authors of Books for Young People*, 2nd edition, Scarecrow, 1971; *New York Times*, June 13, 1979; *Publishers Weekly*, July 2, 1979; *AB Bookman's Weekly*, August 13, 1979.

* * *

DALY, Herman E. 1938-

PERSONAL: Born July 21, 1938, in Houston, Tex.; married in 1963; children: two. *Education:* Rice University, B.A., 1960; Vanderbilt University, Ph.D., 1967. *Office:* Department of Economics, Louisiana State University, Baton Rouge, La. 70803.

CAREER: Vanderbilt University, Nashville, Tenn., instructor in economics, 1964; Louisiana State University, Baton Rouge, assistant professor, 1964-67, professor of economics, 1968—. Ford Foundation visiting professor in Ceara, Brazil, 1967-68; resident associate at Yale University, 1969-70. *Member:* American Economic Association.

WRITINGS: (Editor and contributor) *Toward a Steady-State Economy*, W. H. Freeman, 1973; *Steady-State Economics*, W. H. Freeman, 1977. Contributor to journals.

* * *

DANAN, Alexis 1889(?)-1979

OBITUARY NOTICE: Born c. 1889; died November 14, 1979, in Paris, France. Journalist whose 1936 series of articles about conditions at Devil's Island prison in French Guyana led to the prison's closing eleven years later. Obituaries and other sources: *Chicago Tribune*, November 18, 1979.

* * *

DANE, Les(lie A.) 1925-

PERSONAL: Born March 3, 1925, in Niagara Falls, N.Y.; son of Leslie A. and Ruth (Bolton) Dane; married Lois Bentz (a legal secretary), November 25, 1948; children: Lois Dane Richter, Leslie A., Jr., Carol Dane Sellers, Elizabeth Dane Bee, John B. *Education:* Attended high school in Niagara Falls, N.Y. *Politics:* Democrat. *Religion:* Episcopalian. *Home address:* Route 1, Box 232, Wadmalaw Island, S.C. 29487. *Office:* c/o Mendel J. Davis, M.C., Federal Building, Charleston, S.C. 29403.

CAREER: Author, 1971—. Reporter with *Charleston Evening Post*, Charleston, S.C.; also worked as an automobile dealership owner, bartender, machinist, shrimper and fisherman, Congressional aide, junk dealer, and fruit picker. *Military service:* U.S. Coast Guard. *Member:* Sigma Delta Chi. *Awards, honors:* Seven awards from Associated Press for work appearing in the *Charleston Evening Post*.

WRITINGS: Big League Sales Closing Techniques, Parker Publishing, 1971; *Strike-It-Rich Sales Prospecting*, Parker Publishing, 1972; *Amateurs Don't Make a Dime Selling Hardgoods: Fourteen Steps to Big Money Success*, Parker Publishing, 1974; *Les Dane's Master Sales Guide*, Parker Publishing, 1978. Contributor of more than one hundred articles to magazines, including *House Beautiful*, *American Salesman*, *Bassmaster*, *National Fisherman*, and *Outdoors*.

WORK IN PROGRESS: Research for a consumer sales book.

SIDELIGHTS: Dane writes: "Any person who says 'I have no education' as an alibi for failure is a fool. Education comes from living, reading everything from cereal boxtops to the classics, and paying attention to what is going on. I wish to live only so long as my interest in the printed word remains acute." *Avocational interest:* "I love to fish, work in my shop, fish, read (Shakespeare is a favorite), fish, and write. And laugh."

* * *

DANIELE, Joseph William 1927-

PERSONAL: Born April 3, 1927, in Springfield, Mass.; son of Joseph and Jane (Dynan) Daniele; married Jean Marie Hegarty (a secretary), July 31, 1948; children: Sharon Daniele Kida, Lanore, Daria Daniele Deshais. *Education:* American International College, B.A., 1965; Westfield State College, M.Ed., 1970; further graduate study at Springfield College, 1975, and Fitchburg State College. *Home and office:* 282 Maple St., East Longmeadow, Mass. 01028.

CAREER: Carpenter and general contractor (including work for California film studios), 1947-55; cabinet maker, 1955-65; Ludlow High School, Ludlow, Mass., teacher of industrial education and head of department, 1965—. *Military service:* U.S. Navy, on destroyers, 1944-46. *Member:* National Education Association, New England Industrial Arts Association, Massachusetts Education Association.

WRITINGS: Early American Metal Projects, McKnight, 1971; *Building Early American Furniture*, Stackpole, 1974; *Building Colonial Furnishings, Miniatures, and Folk Art*, Stackpole, 1976; *Building Masterpiece Miniatures*, Stackpole, 1979. Contributor of more than thirty-five articles to *Early American Society*. Crafts editor of *Early American Life*.

WORK IN PROGRESS: A book on period furnishing, publication by Stackpole expected in 1981; a book on metalworking, including work in wrought iron and sheet stock, Stackpole, 1983; a book on miniature furnishing.

SIDELIGHTS: Daniele writes: "I was a late bloomer; so there is still hope for those in their late thirties who are still undecided about their futures. My first book was completed when I was forty-four.

"When I started to teach 'shop' classes I could not find suitable books with projects for my students to make. I wanted something of value to come out of their efforts. I did not want to teach just soldering, or bending, or isolated procedures; the students' work had to produce something they could look back on with some degree of pride.

"This led to a search-and-sketch mission through several New England museums and restoration settlements. I found many stories on the background and development of colonial and early American crafts work. The combination of these factors seemed an excellent way to teach students the art of making hand-crafted reproductions and contribute to their knowledge of American history as well, a way to make our history more personal and down to earth.

"I like what I do, and woodworking is my second best love. I love the smell, the feel, the workability, the grain and texture, and the feeling of satisfaction from building something with my own hands and mind from a rough board.

"I think part of the reason I went into teaching the crafts was that I found the construction industry moving more and more toward mechanized, mechanical manufactured work. Everything was being done by machines; carpenters and cabinetmakers became 'installers' rather than craftsmen. In the classroom each project and student is an individual undertaking, and no two days or reproductions are ever exactly alike.

"Some people say I am an anachronism, that I was born two hundred years too late, and very often I think they are right. I would have liked to live and work in colonial times, but without a time machine to transport me back, I do the next best thing: draw, illustrate, and make the work of that era."

* * *

DANIELLS, Lorna M(cLean) 1918-

PERSONAL: Born July 13, 1918, in Toledo, Ohio; daughter of John E. (a lawyer) and Mary (McLean) Daniells. *Education:* Miami University, Oxford, Ohio, A.B., 1940; Columbia University, B.S., 1941. *Home:* 26 Concord Ave., Apt. 511, Cambridge, Mass. 02138. *Office:* Baker Library, Business School, Harvard University, Soldiers Field, Boston, Mass. 02163.

CAREER: Vassar College, Poughkeepsie, N.Y., assistant in library catalog department, 1941-43, serials cataloger, 1943-46; Harvard University, Business School, Baker Library, Boston, Mass., cataloger, 1946-49, reference assistant, 1949-57, reference librarian, 1958-69, head of reference department, 1970—. *Member:* North American Society of Corporate Planners, Special Libraries Association (head of business-finance division, 1958-59, 1973-75, and publication committee, 1978—; head of advisory council, 1964-65; local president, 1968-69; member of board of directors, 1969-70), Associated Information Managers. *Awards, honors:* Professional award from Special Libraries Association, 1978.

WRITINGS: Studies in Enterprise: A Selected Bibliography of American and Canadian Company Histories and Biographies of Businessmen, Baker Library, Harvard University, 1957; *Business Information Sources,* University of California Press, 1976. Compiler of annual reference lists and bibliographies for Baker Library, Business School, Harvard University. Contributor to business and library journals. Editor of *Business Division Bulletin* (of Special Libraries Association), 1957-58.

WORK IN PROGRESS: Bibliographies on strategic and corporate planning and on business forecasting; a revised edition of *Business Information Sources,* publication expected in 1981.

* * *

DANIELS, Dorothy 1915-
(Danielle Dorsett, Angela Gray, Cynthia Kavanaugh, Helaine Ross, Suzanne Somers, Geraldine Thayer, Helen Gray Weston)

PERSONAL: Born July 1, 1915, in Connecticut; daughter of Judson R. (a traffic manager) and Mary (Guilfoile) Smith; married Norman A. Daniels (a writer). *Education:* Normal School, New Britain, Conn. (now Central Connecticut State College), earned diploma. *Home:* 6107 Village 6, Camarillo, Calif. 93010. *Agent:* Robert P. Mills Ltd., 156 East 52nd St., New York, N.Y. 10022.

CAREER: Professional actress; elementary school teacher in New Britain, Conn.; writer. Member of citizens advisory committee and volunteer worker at Ventura School (correctional institution). *Member:* Authors Guild, Authors League of America, Ventura County Writers Club.

WRITINGS—All gothic novels: *The Leland Legacy,* Pyramid Publications, 1965; *Shadow Glen,* Paperback Library, c. 1965; *Marriott Hall,* Paperback, c. 1965; *Dockhaven,* Paperback Library, c. 1965; *The Unguarded,* Lancer Books, c. 1965; *Mistress of Falcon Hill,* Pyramid Publications, c. 1965; *Dance in Darkness,* Lancer Books, c. 1965; *Cliffside Castle,* Lancer Books, c. 1965; *Lily Pond,* Paperback Library, c. 1965; *Marble Leaf,* Lancer Books, c. 1966; *Midday Moon,* Lancer Books, c. 1966; *Knight in Red Armor,* Lancer Books, 1966; *Nurse at Danger Mansion,* Lancer Books, c. 1966; *Mansion of Lost Memories,* Lancer Books, 1967; *Sevier Secrets,* Lancer Books, 1967; *Dark Villa,* Lancer Books, 1967; *Affair in Marrakesh,* Pyramid Publications, 1968; *Duet,* Lancer Books, 1968.

The Man From Yesterday, Paperback Library, 1970; *House of Many Doors,* Paperback Library, 1971; *The Bell,* Paperback Library, 1971; *Diablo Manor,* Paperback Library, 1971; *Witch's Castle,* Paperback Library, 1971; *Conover's Folly,* Paperback Library, 1971; *House of Broken Dolls,* Paperback Library, 1972; *The Lanier Riddle,* Paperback Library, 1972; *Castle Morvant,* Paperback Library, 1972; *Maya Temple,* Paperback Library, 1972; *The Larrabee Heiress,* Paperback Library, 1972; *Stone House,* Paperback Library, 1973; *The Duncan Dynasty,* Paperback Library, 1973; *Silent Halls of Ashendon,* Paperback Library, 1973; *The Possession of Tracy Corbin,* Paperback Library, 1973; *Dark Haven,* Paperback Library, 1974; *The Apollo Fountain,* Warner Paperback Library, 1974; *Voice on the Wind,* Paperback Library, 1974; *Dark Stage,* Paperback Library, 1974; *Island of Bitter Memories,* Warner Paperback, 1974; *Child of Darkness,* Pocket Books, 1974; *Ghost Song,* Pocket Books, 1974; *The Two Worlds of Peggy Scott,* Pocket Books, 1974; *The Exorcism of Jenny Slade,* Pocket Books, 1974.

The Carson Inheritance, Paperback Library, 1975; *Shadows From the Past,* Paperback Library, 1975; *The House on Circus Hill,* Paperback Library, 1975; *Emerald Hill,* Paperback Library, 1975; *Prisoner of Malville Hall,* Paperback Library, 1975; *Hills of Fire,* Warner Paperback, 1975; *Illusion at Haven's Edge,* Pocket Books, 1975; *The Possessed,* Pocket Books, 1975; *The Guardian of Willow House,* Pocket Books, 1975; *The Unlamented,* Pocket Books, 1975; *Marble Hills,* Warner Paperback, 1975.

The Tormented, Paperback Library, 1976; *The Beaumont Tradition,* Paperback Library, 1976; *Dark Island,* Paperback Library, 1976; *Jade Green,* Warner Paperback, 1976; *Whistle in the Wind,* Pocket Books, 1976; *The Apollo Fountain,* Warner Paperback, 1976; *Nightshade,* Pocket Books, 1976; *Vineyard Chapel,* Pocket Books, 1976; *Circle of Guilt,* Pocket Books, 1976; *Juniper Hill,* Pocket Books, 1976; *Portrait of a Witch,* Pocket Books, 1976; *Summer House,* Warner Paperback, 1976; *Blue Devil Suite,* Belmont Productions, 1977; *Spanish Chapel,* Tower, 1977; *Poison Flower,* Pocket Books, 1977; *Nightfall,* Pocket Books, 1977; *Wines of Cyprien,* Pyramid Publications, 1977; *Mirror of Shadows,* Warner Paperback, 1977; *In the Shadows,* New American Library, 1978; *The Lonely Place,* New American Library, 1978; *Hermitage Hill,* New American Library, 1978; *Perrine,* Warner Paperback, 1978; *The Magic Ring,* Warner Paperback, 1978; *Meg,* New American Library, 1979.

Also author of: *The Caduceus Tree,* Avalon; *A Nurse for*

Doctor Keith, Paperback Library; *The Dark Rider,* Avalon; *No Tears Tomorrow,* Avalon; *Eve Originals,* Lancer Books; *Cruise Ship Nurse,* Paperback Library; *Country Nurse,* Berkeley Publishing; *Island Nurse,* Paperback Library; *Tower Room,* Lancer Books; *World's Fair Nurse,* Paperback Library; *Mostly by Moonlight,* Lancer Books; *Mists of Mourning,* Tower; *The Templeton Memoirs,* Lancer Books; *Screentest for Laurel,* Avon; *Ancient Evil,* Lancer Books; *Bride of Lenore,* Pyramid Publications; *Survivor of Darkness,* Lancer Books; *Last of the Mansions,* Lancer Books; *Traitor's Road,* Lancer Books; *Stolen Mansions,* Lancer Books; *House of Seven Courts,* Lancer Books; *Eagle's Nest,* Lancer Books; *Affair in Hong Kong,* Pyramid Publications; *Candle in the Sun,* Lancer Books.

Lady of the Shadows, Paperback Library; *Web of Peril,* Pyramid Publications; *Curse of Mallory Hall,* Gold Medal; *Willow Weep,* Pyramid Publications; *Strange Paradise,* Paperback Library; *Island of Evil,* Paperback Library; *Voodoo Princess,* Paperback Library; *Raging Waters,* Pyramid Publications; *Attic Rope,* Lancer Books; *Marble Angel,* Paperback Library; *Romany Curse,* Belmont-Tower; *The Unearthly,* Lancer Books; *The Latimer Legend,* Lancer Books; *Ashes of Falconwyke,* Lancer Books; *Ghost Dancer,* Lancer Books; *Warlock's Daughter,* Lancer Books; *Golden Packet,* Lancer Books; *The Caldwell Shadow,* Warner Paperback; *Shadows of Tomorrow,* Paperback Library; *Image of a Ghost,* Warner Paperback; *Blackthorn,* Pocket Books; *Terror of the Twins,* Berkeley Publishing; *Dark Heritage,* New American Library; *Woman in Silk and Shadows,* New American Library; *Twilight at the Elms,* New American Library; *The Cormac Legend,* New American Library; *The Purple and the Gold,* New American Library; *Yesterday's Evil,* New American Library; *Legend of Death,* New American Library.

Under pseudonym Danielle Dorsett: *Dueling Oaks,* Pinnacle Books.

Under pseudonym Angela Gray: *Watcher in the Dark,* Ballantine, 1973. Also author of: *Blackwell's Ghost,* Lancer Books; *Nightmare at Riverview,* Lancer Books; *Island of Fear,* Lancer Books; *Ravenswood Hall,* Lancer Books.

Under pseudonym Cynthia Kavanaugh: *The Deception,* Pyramid Publications.

Under pseudonym Suzanne Somers: *House of Eve,* Avalon; *Image of Truth,* Avalon; *Until Death,* Popular Library; *Thunder Hill,* Popular Library; *Tidemill,* Popular Library; *Shadow of a Man,* Popular Publications.

Under pseudonym Helen Gray Weston: *House of False Faces,* Paperback Library, 1974. Also author of *Mystic Manor,* Paperback Library. Also author of novels under pseudonyms Helaine Ross and Geraldine Thayer.

Contributor of about thirty-five stories to magazines.

WORK IN PROGRESS: Gothic novels.

SIDELIGHTS: Dorothy Daniels wrote short stories for magazines during the early 1940's, then stopped writing until she moved to the West Coast in the late 1950's. Her husband urged her to try her hand at full-length books. For a while they collaborated on gothic novels, but in order to keep up with the public demand for their books they had to return to writing separately. They use a standard formula for their novels, creating variety through characterization, and their books have a wide appeal.

Daniels told *CA:* "I have one motive for writing—that is to entertain. To me, receiving a letter from a reader stating that one of my books has given a few hours of entertainment is like receiving a beautiful gift. I can think of no higher tribute which can be paid to a writer. If, in reading one of my books, a reader gets something more out of it, that too is highly rewarding."

* * *

DANIELS, Norman
(Peter Brady, Harrison Judd)

PERSONAL: Born in Connecticut; married Dorothy Smith (a writer). *Education:* Attended Columbia University and Northwestern University. *Home:* 6107 Village 6, Camarillo, Calif. 93010. *Agent:* Robert P. Mills Ltd., 156 East 52nd St., New York, N.Y. 10022.

CAREER: Writer. Vice-president of citizens advisory committee of Ventura School (correctional institution).

WRITINGS: The Mausoleum Key, Gateway Books, 1942; *Colt Law,* Lancer Books, 1956; *Back Trails,* Avalon, 1962; *Showdown,* Avalon, 1963; *Gun Empire,* Avalon, 1963; *Dr. Kildare's Secret Romance,* Lancer Books, 1964; *Dr. Kildare's Finest Hour,* Lancer Books, 1965; *The Deadly Ride,* Lancer Books, 1968; *Slave Rebellion,* Paperback Library, 1970; *Wyndward Passion,* Warner Paperback, 1978.

Also author of: *Spy Hunt,* Pyramid Publications; *Suddenly by Shotgun,* Gold Medal Books; *Something Burning,* Gold Medal Books; *Jennifer James, R.N.,* Gold Medal Books; *Killing in the Market,* Lancer Books; *The Surgeon,* Lancer Books; *County Hospital,* Gold Medal Books; *A Rage for Justice,* Lancer Books; *Disciplinary Board,* Lancer Books; *Dark Desire,* Lancer Books; *The Fire Within,* Lancer Books; *The Strong Also Cry,* Lancer Books; *Arrest and Trial,* Lancer Books; *The Missing Witness,* Lancer Books; *Walk the Evil Street,* Gallimard; *Overkill,* Pyramid Publications; *The Deadly Game,* Falcon Press; *When Love Must Hide,* Lancer Books; *The Hunt Club,* Pyramid Publications; *Moments of Glory,* Paperback Library; *Strike Force,* Lancer Books; *Battalion,* Pyramid Publications; *Spy Ghost,* Pyramid Publications; *Operation N,* Pyramid Publications.

Operation K, Pyramid Publications; *Operation VC,* Pyramid Publications; *Operation T,* Pyramid Publications; *Rat Patrol,* Paperback Library; *Baron of Hong Kong,* Lancer Books; *Operation SL,* Pyramid Publications; *Duet,* Lancer Books; *The Baron's Mission to Peking,* Lancer Books; *The Forbidden City,* Berkley Publishing; *Tarnished Scalpel,* Lancer Books; *Stanton Bishop, M.D.,* Lancer Books; *The Kono Diamond,* Berkley Publishing; *The Savage Heart,* Lancer Books; *The Magnetic Man,* Berkley Publishing; *Moon Express,* Berkley Publishing; *Campus Rebels,* Belmont Productions; *Law of the Lash,* Lancer Books; *Master Wyndward,* Lancer Books; *The Plunderers,* Ace Books; *Jubal,* Paperback Library.

Rape of a Town, Pyramid Publications; *One Angry Man,* Pyramid Publications; *Waco,* Lancer Books; *License to Kill,* Pyramid Publications; *The Smith Family,* Berkley Publishing; *Chase #1,* Berkley Publishing; *Chase #2,* Berkley Publishing; *Chase #3,* Berkley Publishing; *Wyndward Fury,* Warner Paperback; *Wyndward Scandals,* Warner Paperback; and *Robert Taylor's Detective Series.*

Under pseudonym Peter Brady: *Two Trails to Bannock,* Avalon; *Marshal of Winter Gap,* Avalon.

Under pseudonym Harrison Judd: *Shadow of a Doubt,* Gold Medal Books; *Experiment in Fear,* Gallimard.

Author of about four hundred radio and television scripts, including scripts for "Ben Casey," "The Avengers," "Dr. Kildare," "Ellery Queen," and "General Electric Theatre."

WORK IN PROGRESS: Research in the South for five novels about slavery.

SIDELIGHTS: Daniels has been a writer since the 1930's. Earlier jobs in a police station and as an ambulance attendant and insurance claims investigator provided his first story ideas. He wrote for radio in New York, then moved to Los Angeles and began writing for television, then switched to full-length novels. He and his wife collaborated on gothic novels for a while, then Daniels returned to writing on his own. His gothic novels follow a standard formula, but his books provide more adventure than the standard fare, without the violence that accompanies many of today's popular novels.

Daniels's lectures to other writers emphasize that book publishing is a healthy business, especially paperback publishing. He recommends literary agents, but not writing courses, adding that writing is hard lonely work that the writer ultimately must do by himself.

* * *

DARLING, Louis, Jr. 1916-1970

OBITUARY NOTICE—See index for *CA* sketch: Born April 26, 1916, in Stamford, Conn.; died of cancer, January 21, 1970, in Norwich, Conn. Artist, illustrator, and author of children's books. Darling illustrated more than sixty books, including Rachel Carson's *Silent Spring* and Beverly Cleary's "Henry Huggins" series. Many of his books were written in collaboration with his wife, Lois Darling. Among them are *Before and After Dinosaurs* and *A Place in the Sun*. In 1966 he received the John Burroughs Medal for *The Gull's Way*. Obituaries and other sources: *New York Times,* January 24, 1970; *AB Bookman's Weekly,* February 16, 1970; *Publishers Weekly,* February 23, 1970; *Authors of Books for Young People,* 2nd edition, Scarecrow, 1971.

* * *

DARLINGTON, Joy 1947-

PERSONAL: Born December 23, 1947, in New Jersey; daughter of John Vincent and Esther (Nocero) Aumente. *Education:* New York University, A.B., 1968. *Religion:* Roman Catholic. *Residence:* New York, N.Y. *Agent:* William Morris Agency, 1350 Avenue of the Americas, New York, N.Y. 10019.

CAREER: Professional actress (stage and television), 1968-76; writer, 1976—.

WRITINGS: *Those Van Der Meer Women* (novel), Putnam, 1979; *Fast Friends* (novel), Doubleday, 1979.

SIDELIGHTS: Joy Darlington writes: "When I graduated from college, I went into acting. After awhile it became apparent to me that I had a considerable amount of free time and I decided I could, perhaps, write a television script—at least as good as the ones I'd been looking at for the past few years. I wrote a ninety-minute 'Colombo' script, and sent it to an agent. He liked it but suggested (perhaps because of all the characters?) I should try my hand at writing a novel. The result was *Those Van Der Meer Women.* It was a long first draft, which was revised and finally published. It was a learning process for me. My second book was written very briskly.

"I love writing—much more than acting, possibly because I am more in control. I consider myself privileged to be able to make a living this way."

DARROCH, Sandra Jobson 1942- (Sandra Jobson)

PERSONAL: Born April 5, 1942, in Sydney, Australia; daughter of Philip Latham (an anesthesiologist) and Barbara (Ure) Jobson; married Robert Darroch (a writer), January 29, 1965. *Education:* Attended Julian Ashton Art School, 1958-64; University of Sydney, B.A., 1964, graduate study, 1967-68; attended London International Film School, 1979—. *Politics:* "Asquithian liberal." *Religion:* None. *Home and office:* 214 Kensington Park Rd., London W.11, England. *Agent:* Curtis Brown Ltd., 1 Craven Hill, London W.2, England.

CAREER: *Daily Telegraph,* Australia, reporter, 1964; *Woman's Day,* Australia, feature writer, 1965; *Sydney Morning Herald,* Sydney, Australia, book reviewer, 1965, correspondent in London, England, 1966, reporter and columnist, 1967-70; *Woman's Own,* England, sub-editor, 1965-66; ATN7-TV, Sydney, Australia, producer of "Sidney Tonight," 1967-69; returned to London, England, 1971, and wrote book, *Ottoline: The Life of Lady Ottoline Morrell,* 1971-75; *The Australian,* Australia, feature writer, 1976-77; *Woman's Day,* Australia, features editor, 1977-78; TCN9-TV, Sydney, Australia, associate producer of "60 Minutes," 1978-79; returned to London, England, 1979—; free-lance writer, 1979—. *Member:* National Union of Journalists, Australian Journalist Association, Australian Writers Guild, Society of Authors.

WRITINGS: (Self-illustrated) *Once Upon a Vase* (juvenile), Macmillan, 1970; (editor) *Frank Hutchens,* Wentworth Press, 1971; *Ottoline: The Life of Lady Ottoline Morrell,* Coward, 1975; (contributor; under name Sandra Jobson) Geoffrey Dutton, editor, *Republican Australia?,* Sun Books, 1977. Contributor to Australian newspapers, sometimes under name Sandra Jobson.

WORK IN PROGRESS: Two children's books, *Catnapped!* and *Trilby and the Mice From Mars.*

SIDELIGHTS: Sandra Darroch told *CA:* "Although I was born and educated in Australia, I now live most of the time in London. Many people were interested that an Australian should have written the biography of Lady Ottoline Morrell. When I approached Ottoline's daughter to ask permission to write the book, she agreed, saying she had turned down a long list of others because she feared that, because they were English, they couldn't view the class situation objectively. An Australian, or an American, she believed, could do a fairer job.

"My other interests are many and varied. I took part in the debate in Australia about the forming of an Australian republic, and though I feel the monarchy is fine for Britain, where it developed naturally over many centuries, I think Australia should cut her ties with the British monarchy and establish a republic.

"Other things I feel strongly about include the still-oppressed role of women in Australia, where a paternalistic form of male chauvinism makes rebellion particularly difficult.

"A specific concern of mine is about the publication of material from hitherto unpublished sources. The biographer is greatly handicapped by the present law of copyright which insists that *unpublished* material such as letters cannot be quoted—even briefly—without the permission of descendants or executors of the original writer. An independent body should at least be set up to arbitrate such matters of copyright. The alternative is far worse: descendents of great men and women often act with cupidity or false motives which are not in the interest of public knowledge or good scholarship.

"I am currently studying film at the London International Film School because I want to gain a firm grasp of the technical side of filmmaking with the eventual aim of making good documentary films and, perhaps, dramas for television."

AVOCATIONAL INTERESTS: Horseback riding.

* * *

DASHIELL, Alfred Sheppard 1901-1970

OBITUARY NOTICE: Born April 29, 1901, in Snow Hill, Md.; died October 3, 1970. Author, editor, and journalist. Dashiell worked for such newspapers as the *Baltimore Evening Sun, New York World, Boston Transcript,* and the *New York Evening Post.* He was an editor of *Scribner's* and *Reader's Digest,* where he worked for over thirty years. Dashiell's works include *How Not to Write Short Stories* and *Editor's Choice.* Obituaries and other sources: *Who Was Who in America,* 5th edition, Marquis, 1973; *Who Was Who Among North American Authors, 1921-1939,* reprinted edition, Gale, 1976.

* * *

DASS, Ram
See ALPERT, Richard

* * *

DAUER, Manning J(ulian) 1909-

PERSONAL: Born August 12, 1909, in Wilmington, N.C.; son of Manning J., Sr. (a railway employee) and Martha Eddins (a Latin and English teacher; maiden name, Fitts) Dauer. *Education:* University of Florida, B.A.E., 1930, M.A., 1931; University of Illinois, Ph.D., 1933. *Politics:* Democrat. *Religion:* Episcopal. *Home:* 2255 Northwest Fifth Place, Gainesville, Fla. 32603. *Office:* Department of Political Science, University of Florida, GPA-3326-B, Gainesville, Fla. 32611.

CAREER: University of Florida, Gainesville, instructor, 1933-34, assistant professor, 1934-35, associate professor, 1941-46, professor of political science, 1946—, distinguished service professor, 1972—, head of department, 1950-75, director of Division of Social Sciences, 1964-75, director of Civics Institute, summer, 1966. Visiting professor at University of Alabama, 1953, and New York University, summer, 1957; lecturer at Johns Hopkins University, 1953, University of Massachusetts, 1968, and Stetson University, 1969. Managing editor of *Journal of Politics,* 1938-42, 1946—. Expert witness in federal district court; consultant to state government. *Military service:* U.S. Army Air Forces, 1942-46; served in Pacific theater; became lieutenant colonel; received four battle stars. U.S. Air Force Reserve, 1946-67.

MEMBER: American Political Science Association (member of council, 1953-55; vice-president, 1965-66), American Historical Association, Southern Political Science Association (president, 1954-55), Florida Political Science Association (president, 1972-73), Phi Beta Kappa (local president, 1947-48; historian, 1964—). *Awards, honors:* Litt.D. from University of West Florida, 1973; bicentennial award from governor of Florida, 1976.

WRITINGS: (Editor) *Proceedings of the Southern Political Science Association,* Southern Political Science Association, 1937; *The Constitution of Florida,* Public Administration Service, University of Florida, 1950; *Political Science Scope and Method: An Introductory Manual,* Public Administration Clearing Service, University of Florida, 1953, 3rd edition, 1965; *Adams Federalists,* Johns Hopkins Press, 1953; (with G. J. Miller) *Municipal Charters in Florida: Law and Drafting* (monograph), Public Administration Clearing Service, University of Florida, 1953; (with W. C. Havard) *The Florida Constitution,* Public Administration Clearing Service, University of Florida, 1955; (with J. E. Dovell and D. G. Temple) *Constitutional Amendments, 1956,* Public Administration Clearing Service, University of Florida, 1956; *The Proposed New Constitution: An Analysis,* Public Administration Clearing Service, University of Florida, 1958; (with Morris W. H. Collins, Jr., Paul T. David, and others) *Evolving Issues and Patterns of State Legislative Redistricting in Large Metropolitan Areas,* Institute of Metropolitan Studies, Division of Public Administration, Oklahoma City University, 1966; (with Clement H. Donovan and Gladys M. Kammerer) *Florida Constitutional Amendments, 1970: An Analysis,* Public Administration Clearing Service, University of Florida, 1970; (editor and contributor) *Your Florida Government,* University of Florida Press, 1979.

Contributor: Paul T. David, editor, *Presidential Nominating Politics in 1952,* Volume III, Johns Hopkins Press, 1954; Howard P. Hamilton, editor, *Legislative Apportionment: Key to Power,* Harper, 1964; Norman Risjord, editor, *The Early American Party System,* Harper, 1969; George A. Billias, editor, *The Federalists, Realists, or Ideologues,* Heath, 1970; Arthur F. Schlesinger and Fred Israel, editors, *Presidential Elections,* three volumes, Chelsea House, 1971; W. C. Havard, editor, *The Changing Politics of the South,* Louisiana State University Press, 1972; Havard, editor, *Two Hundred Years of the Republic,* University Press of Virginia, 1976. Contributor to *Compendium on Legislative Apportionment.* Contributor of about thirty articles and reviews to political science, law, and economic journals, and *Congressional Record.*

WORK IN PROGRESS: The Political Theory of Thomas Jefferson; research on multi-member political districts and apportionment.

AVOCATIONAL INTERESTS: Travel (Europe, Australia, Asia, South America).

* * *

DAVIS, Harold Lenoir 1896-1960

OBITUARY NOTICE: Born October 18, 1896, in Yoncalla, Ore.; died October 31, 1960. Poet and author of the novel, *Honey in the Horn,* for which he won the Pulitzer and Harper Prizes. As a hesitant writer, Davis was encouraged by the famous writer H. L. Mencken to pursue a writing career. Davis began writing stories and sketches for the *American Mercury,* in addition to contributing short stories, articles, and poetry to *Collier's Weekly, Holiday, Poetry,* and the *Saturday Evening Post.* He also received a Guggenheim fellowship to Mexico. Davis's works include *Proud Riders* (a book of poetry), *Beulah Land,* and *Kettle of Fire.* Obituaries and other sources: *Twentieth Century Authors: A Biographical Dictionary of Modern Literature,* Wilson, 1942; *Who Was Who in America,* 4th edition, Marquis, 1968.

* * *

DAVIS, James H. 1932-

PERSONAL: Born August 6, 1932, in Effingham, Ill.; son of Kenneth and Forest Davis; married Elisabeth Bachman (a biology librarian), June 27, 1954; children: Stephen, Kristin, Leah. *Education:* University of Illinois, B.S., 1954; Michigan State University, M.A., 1958, Ph.D., 1961. *Residence:* Champaign, Ill. *Office:* Department of Psychology, University of Illinois, Champaign, Ill. 61820.

CAREER: Miami University, Oxford, Ohio, instructor, 1960-61, assistant professor, 1961-65, associate professor of psychology, 1965-66; Yale University, New Haven, Conn., associate professor of psychology, 1966-67; University of Illinois, Champaign, associate professor, 1967-70, professor of psychology, 1970—. *Military service:* U.S. Army, 1954-56. *Member:* American Psychological Association (fellow), Psychonomic Society, American Association for the Advancement of Science, Society of Experimental Social Psychologists, Public Choice Society, American Psychology and Law Society, Midwestern Psychological Association, Sigma Xi. *Awards, honors:* National Science Foundation grant, 1973-81.

WRITINGS: Group Performance, Addison-Wesley, 1969; (contributor) J. Tapp and F. Levine, editors, *Law, Justice, and the Individual in Society,* Holt, 1977; (editor with H. Brandstaetter and H. Schuler) *Dynamics of Group Decisions,* Sage Publications, 1978; (contributor) M. Fishbein, editor, *Progress in Social Psychology,* Erlbaum Associates, 1979. Contributor to psychology journals. Co-editor of series, "Progress in Applied Social Psychology," Wiley. Member of editorial board of *Journal of Experimental Social Psychology* and *Journal of Personality and Social Psychology.*

WORK IN PROGRESS: A revision of *Group Performance;* a book on theories of collective behavior.

* * *

DAVIS, Jerome 1891-1979

OBITUARY NOTICE—See index for *CA* sketch: Born December 2, 1891, in Kyoto, Japan; died October 19, 1979, in Olney, Md. Sociologist, educator, organization executive, and author. During World War I, Davis visited prison camps in Russia and, as a result, became interested in the necessity for world peace. Later he made more than fifteen trips to the Soviet Union and interviewed Jozef Stalin in 1926, Nikita Khrushchev in 1957, and Aleksei Kosygin in 1970. Davis was also a personal friend of Nikolai Lenin and often dined with him at the Kremlin. From 1924 to 1937, Davis held the Gilbert L. Stark Chair of Practical Philanthropy at Yale Divinity School. For more than fifteen years he was executive director of the Promoting Enduring Peace organization. His books include *World Leaders I Have Known, Citizens of One World,* and *Behind Soviet Power.* Obituaries and other sources: *American Men and Women of Science: The Social and Behavioral Sciences,* 12th edition, Bowker, 1973; *The Writers Directory, 1976-78,* St. Martin's, 1976; *Who's Who in America,* 40th edition, Marquis, 1978; *The International Who's Who,* Europa, 1979; *AB Bookman's Weekly,* November 26, 1979.

* * *

DAWSON, Howard A. 1895(?)-1979

OBITUARY NOTICE: Born c. 1895 in Arkansas; died of congestive heart failure, September 25, 1979, in Chevy Chase, Md. Educator and official of the National Educational Association who was recognized as an expert on the reorganization of public school districts. An authority on state and federal financing of public schools, Dawson helped draft the first legislation providing federal assistance to education. He was the author of several books on educational administration. Obituaries and other sources: *Washington Post,* September 27, 1979.

DAYAN, Yael 1939-

PERSONAL: Born February 12, 1939, in Nahalal, Palestine (now Israel); daughter of Moshe (a former foreign minister of Israel) and Ruth (Schwartz) Dayan; married Tat-Aluf Dov Sion (a colonel in the Israeli Army), July 22, 1967; children: two. *Education:* Studied political science at Hebrew University of Jerusalem. *Home:* 16 Oppenheimer St., Ramat-Aviv, Israel.

CAREER: Journalist and novelist. Public relations worker for the Israeli Government Tourist Office; assistant to Greek film director Michael Cacoyannes, 1964; correspondent in the Sinai during Six-Day War, 1967, and in Vietnam. *Military service:* Israeli Army, 1956-58; became lieutenant. Israeli Army Reserves, 1967; morale officer during Six-Day War.

WRITINGS: New Face in the Mirror (autobiographical novel), World Publishing, 1959; *Envy the Frightened* (novel), World Publishing, 1961; *Dust* (novel), World Publishing, 1963; *Death Had Two Sons* (novel), McGraw, 1967; *Israel Journal: June, 1967* (diary), McGraw, 1967 (published in England as *A Soldier's Diary: Sinai, 1967,* Weidenfeld & Nicolson, 1967); *Three Weeks in October* (autobiographical novel), Delacorte, 1979. Also author of a travel book. Contributor of articles to Israeli and to international newspapers.

SIDELIGHTS: At the age of twenty, Yael Dayan was a world famous author whose first novel, *New Face in the Mirror,* had been published in fourteen languages. Written during her compulsory two years in the military service, *New Face* is autobiographical, tracing the life of a young Israeli woman who often reveals herself to be an "arrogant, able, independent Israeli woman soldier." Her next three books were all written in Greece, the country Dayan considers her second home. Of the three, *Death Had Two Sons* is perhaps her most successful. Printed during the summer of 1967 and before the Six-Day War, the novel, according to Charles Poore, "gives a superbly balanced view of everyday life among the old families and the new pioneers, the ancient fortitudes and the young love affairs."

Critics reviewing *Death Had Two Sons* were reminded of the Bible story of Abraham, who was asked by God to sacrifice his son Isaac. In her novel, however, Dayan has replaced Abraham with Haim Kalinsky, a Polish Jew who is forced by the Nazis to choose between his two sons for the sacrifice. Ironically, Daniel, the son who was chosen for death, survives and grows up on an Israeli kibbutz. Father and son are finally reunited through the efforts of an Israeli social agency which has traced Haim Kalinsky to a Beer-Sheba hospital where he lays dying of lung cancer.

"Dayan writes," a *Harper's* critic observed, "with involvement and a passion for life, of death and guilt and the tragedy inherent in human choices. And she writes with riveting and beautiful intensity of the geography and physical feel of the country. . . . If she keeps on writing we shall all soon know well the long roads, the deserts, the fertile valleys, the star-filled nights of her country in a context of human drama told with such vitality and simplicity that nobody can ignore it."

Not all critics, however, agreed with Poore and the *Harper's* reviewer. A critic from *Books and Bookmen,* for example, found the story to be "too one-sided . . . and its picture of life in Israel with its differing ideologies, overheated emotional climate and casual sex encounters is clearer than its view of life outside, which is sketched too hazily, like the faintest childhood memory." Although Dayan "creates a drama of considerable potential," wrote a *Times Literary Supplement* critic, "its effect is dispersed in unnecessary peripheral events. And Miss Dayan's style is far too prone to rhetoric." For Saul Maloff, Dayan's novel was "full of verbal and syntactic inaccuracies and false tonaltities."

Published in 1967, but some months after *Death Had Two Sons, Israel Journal* is Dayan's personal account of the Six-Day War from her position in the Sinai. Assigned to General Ariel Sharon's division for one month, Dayan was both war correspondent and army officer, whose duties often included cooking. Although the book is a record of how "Sharon, outmanned and outranked, swept out of the Negev, cracked the Egyptian main line of resistance at Um-Katef, and opened the route to the Suez Canal for Israeli armor," a *New York Times Book Review* critic declared that Dayan had somehow failed "to reproduce the full excitement of those momentous days."

According to Chaim Bermant, *Israel Journal* is "a taut, dry, almost callous account of the 1967 Sinai campaign, and I know of few books which bring out so completely the rigour, bravery, pathos and, above all, the confusion of war." But Bermant also pointed out that Dayan "starts badly. Her drawn-out description of the prelude to war, which occupies a third of the book, conveys much of the ennui of the long, long wait, but little of the tension. Her book comes to life once the guns begin to roar, and gathers pace with the advance towards Suez. There are moments of Hemingway in her stark, sinewy prose."

After twelve years of silence, Dayan has written another novel, *Three Weeks in October*. Like *New Face in the Mirror* it is also autobiographical, and like *Israel Journal* it deals with another Arab-Israeli war—the Yom Kippur War in 1973. *Three Weeks in October* tells the story of Amalia and her disintegrating marriage which is somehow revived during the war. For Amalia the war is particularly painful for she is forced to remember her lover who died in battle in a previous war. She longs to be young again and free.

"Dayan has written her heroine," Adrianne Blue observed, "to the point of insight, to the point of escape from what Friedan, who was certainly no radical, long ago named 'the comfortable concentration camp.' But Amalia stays put. The logic of the novel is meant to convince us, its heroine, and quite possibly the author, that Amalia's acquiescence to this strained and straining marriage signifies 'maturity.' Well, in this, it fails. But if Amalia is dull, the book is not. It skitters across a lot of ground. Cosmic issues: war, death, duty, the impropriety of a small nation's having an unknown soldier."

Benjamin DeMott wrote: "'Three Weeks in October' accomodates truth of a sort hard to come by in news dispatches and color sidebars. At the simplest level, Yael Dayan dramatizes the 'fury and boredom and utter frustration' of noncombatants—housewives alone in their apartments listening to the sounds of a nearby battle, struggling to invent distractions. She establishes, furthermore, the degree to which expectations of violent surprise do and don't control the daily experience of those for whom beleaguerment becomes a norm." A *New Yorker* critic commented, "The power of personal and national devotion, and the ways in which one may inspire or undermine the other, are Yael Dayan's concern, and she describes with luminous precision the charged atmosphere bending these impassioned people."

Yael Dayan often visits the United States and tours as a speaker for such causes as the United Jewish Appeal. While in Florida in 1975 she spoke about Israel's future: "We have already accomplished the most difficult tasks. We have absorbed people from backward countries, one million Jews from Arab areas who came to us with nothing. Now we will spend the next 10-15 years homogenizing our culture." She also pointed out that there "is no generation gap in Israel. The only difference between the old and the young is they have different tasks." Now Dayan believes that the building of industry is important; but it's "simply not as heroic" as the settling of the marshlands by the early pioneers.

In a *McCall's* article Dayan talked about what the "Good Life" meant for Israelis. In a country scarred by war and ever on guard for terrorist attacks, "the Good Life is simply *life itself*. It is not having to pay the top price of one's life for the most elementary rights—the right to have a home and to bring up children without wondering whether they will reach their twentieth birthday."

Dayan speaks French, Hebrew, Greek, and English, and writes all her novels in English. She has traveled in Europe, South America, Africa, and the Far East.

BIOGRAPHICAL/CRITICAL SOURCES: Books and Bookmen, May,1967; *Times Literary Supplement,* May 25, 1967; *New York Times,* November 2, 1967; *Time,* November 17, 1967; *National Observer,* November 20, 1967; *Best Sellers,* December 1, 1967; *Observer Review,* December 10, 1967; *New York Times Book Review,* December 17, 1967, December 31, 1967, March 11, 1979; *Jewish Quarterly,* winter, 1967/1968; *Harper's,* January, 1968; *McCall's,* January, 1970; *Authors in the News,* Volume I, Gale, 1976; *Washington Post,* March 5, 1979; *New Yorker,* April 23, 1979.

—Sketch by Nancy M. Rusin

* * *

DEACON, William Arthur 1890-1964

OBITUARY NOTICE: Born April 6, 1890, in Pembroke, Ontario, Canada; died in 1964. Journalist, author, and editor. Deacon was literary editor of the *Toronto Mail and Empire,* the *Toronto Globe and Mail,* and Toronto's *Saturday Night,* where he created its supplement "The Bookshelf." Deacon wrote for many journals and reviews, such as the *Canadian Annual Review,* the *New York Times Book Review,* and the *Canadian Geographical Journal.* He also worked for Ontario's *London Advertiser* and the *Montreal Daily Herald.* In addition, Deacon was the Canadian correspondent for *Argus,* of Melbourne, Australia. Deacon's books include *Pens and Pirates, My Vision of Canada,* and *SH-H-H . . . Here Comes the Censor.* Obituaries and other sources: *Canadian Writers: A Biographical Dictionary,* revised edition, Ryerson Press, 1966; *The Oxford Companion to Canadian History and Literature,* Oxford University Press, 1967.

* * *

DEAN, Ida
See GRAE, Ida

* * *

DEANE, James G(arner) 1923-

PERSONAL: Born April 5, 1923, in Hartford, Conn.; son of Julian Lowrie (an advertising executive) and Miriam (Grover) Deane. *Education:* Swarthmore College, B.A., 1943. *Home:* 4200 Cathedral Ave., N.W., Washington, D.C. 20016. *Office:* The Wilderness Society, 1901 Pennsylvania Ave. N.W., Washington, D.C. 20006.

CAREER/WRITINGS: Journalist. *Musical Courier,* Washington, D.C., correspondent, 1945-55; *Washington Star,* Washington, D.C., staff writer, 1946-60, education editor, 1952-57, record critic, 1952-60; *The Living Wilderness,* assistant editor, 1969-71, executive editor, 1971-75, editor,

1975—; The Wilderness Society, Washington, D.C., director of information and publications, 1975-77. Contributing editor of *High Fidelity,* 1953-55; contributor to *Compton's Yearbook* and *Atlantic Naturalist.* Chairman of Potomac Valley Conservation and Recreation Council, 1967; co-chairman of Canada-United States Environmental Council, 1975—. Member of Committee of 100 on the Federal City, 1963—, vice-chairman, 1967-69, trustee, 1967—; member of committee on the transportation environmental review process, transportation research board of the National Academy of Sciences-National Research Council, 1974-77. Member of steering committee, Citizens Committee on a Clean Potomac, 1966-74. *Military service:* U.S. Army, 1946-47; served in Signal Corps. *Member:* The Wilderness Society, National Audubon Society, Defenders of Wildlife, Audubon Naturalist Society of the Central Atlantic States, American Forestry Association, City Tavern Club (Washington, D.C.). *Awards, honors:* Award from Education Writers Association, 1956, for outstanding general coverage; public service award from Washington Newspaper Guild, 1956; honorable mention in public service from Washington Newspaper Guild, 1957; Charles Carroll Glover award from National Park Service, 1967, for conservation leadership in the Washington, D.C., area.

SIDELIGHTS: Deane told *CA:* "I have been interested in nature, writing, and journalism since my early years. I first learned to love wild places on childhood vacations in Vermont and in regular visits to Forest Park in Springfield, Mass., and Rock Creek Park in Washington, D.C. My journalistic career began with editing a high school literary magazine and college paper. Sixteen years on the *Washington Star* began as copy boy fresh out of college. I was education editor during desegregation of the nation's public schools and the first major move toward federal aid to education. Later I covered Congress, acquiring a deep interest in the processes of government.

"I became interested in environmental issues at a time when there was no environment beat on the *Washington Star* (a decade before Earth Day), quit to investigate the impacts of interstate highway development, eventually was drawn into an activist role in environmental controversies (especially involving encroachment on parks), and finally accepted an invitation to become an editor of *National Parks,* a long-established journal in the conservation field. From there I moved to *The Living Wilderness,* the flagship of the wilderness preservation movement that has been growing steadily since the 1930's."

AVOCATIONAL INTERESTS: Bird watching, listening to classical music.

* * *

DEARDORFF, Tom 1940-

PERSONAL: Born July 27, 1940, in Lafayette, Ind.; son of Thomas Jackson (an engineer) and Mildred (Mauch) Deardorff; married Linda Jann Smith (a publisher), September 1, 1962; children: Jeffrey, Kristina, Kerry, Julie. *Education:* Attended Ball State University, 1959-62; Indiana University, A.B., 1964. *Religion:* "Have no religion; have great faith." *Home:* 726 South Candler St., Decatur, Ga. 30030.

CAREER: Retail Corporate Management, Cincinnati, Ohio, researcher, 1964-71; free-lance writer, 1971-76; WRNG-Radio, Atlanta, Ga., production manager and performer, 1976-77; free-lance writer, 1978—. Public relations director for Friendship Force International Exchange, 1978-79.

WRITINGS: (With Jack Niles) *Taxpayers' Coloring Book,* Fulcourte Press, 1978. Contributor to magazines, including *Family Digest, Playgirl,* and *Harper's Weekly.*

WORK IN PROGRESS: Taxpayers' Coloring Book #2, with Niles, publication expected in 1980; *I.R.S. Coloring Book,* with Niles, publication expected in 1980; *A Taxing Fable; His and Hers,* with wife, Linda Deardorff.

SIDELIGHTS: Deardorff writes: "The world is a funny place. The people in it are funny. There is a plethora of writers who are experts at warning us of impending doom. I am called to spend my time trying to make sure that the world around me does not take itself too seriously.

"*Taxpayers' Coloring Book,* featuring the Golden Fleece Awards of Senator William Proxmire, is a humorously written and illustrated book which points out, through satire, how the United States Government and its various agencies squander the money paid by its citizens in taxes.

"I have written articles on what it is like to be a full-time househusband, charged with the care and feeding of four young children, the maintenance of a semblance of order in a twelve-room house, and society's view of this bizarre behavior. My wife and I are presently writing a lighthearted book recounting the three-year period during which our traditional roles were switched.

"The *I.R.S. Coloring Book* is a humorous, detailed explanation of various federal tax forms which most Americans are required to fill out. The emphasis will be on a satirical, line-by-line explanation of the notorious 1040 form.

"I am motivated to write by my sense of humor. I am able to see humor in everything around me, and I love to observe the human comedy. I have traveled extensively in Latin America. I do not have a prison record. I like to swim in the nude. I do not do windows."

* * *

de CHIRICO, Giorgio 1888-1978

PERSONAL: Born July 10, 1888, in Volos, Greece; died November 20, 1978, in Rome, Italy; son of Evaristo (an engineer) and Gemma (Cervetto) de Chirico; married Isabella Far (a writer), 1931. *Education:* Graduated from Polytechnic Institute, Athens, 1906; attended Academy of Fine Arts, Munich. *Home:* 31 Piazza di Spagna, Rome, Italy.

CAREER: Painter, sculptor, set and costume designer, and writer. Paintings include "The Enigma of an Autumn Afternoon," 1910, "Melancholy," 1912, "Delights of the Poet," 1913, "Lassitude of the Infinite," 1913, "Joys and Enigmas of a Strange Hour," 1913, "Anxious Journey," 1913, "The Square," 1913, "Turin, Spring," 1914, "Portrait of Guillaume Apollinaire," 1914; "Inconsistencies of the Thinker," 1915, "Hector and Andromache," 1916, "Evangelical Still Life," 1917, "Metaphysical Interior with Waterfall," 1918, "Roman Villa and Knights," 1922, and "Autoritratto," 1924. *Military service:* Italian Army, 1915-19. *Member:* Royal Society of British Artists (honorary member).

WRITINGS: Hebdomeros (novel), Editions du Carrefour (Paris), 1929, translation by Margaret Crosland published as *Hebdomeros,* Owen (London), 1968; *1918-1925: Riccordi di Roma* (correspondence and reminiscences), Editrice Cultura moderna, 1945; *Une aventure de m. Dudron,* Fontaine (Paris), 1945; *Memorie della mia vita* (autobiography), Astrolabio (Rome), 1945, translation by Crosland published as *The Memoirs of Giorgio de Chirico,* University of Miami Press, 1971. Also author of *Gustave Courbet,* 1925; *Piccolo trattato di technica pittorica,* 1928; *Commedia dell'arte moderna,* 1945.

Catalogs: *De Chirico,* text by wife, Isabella Far, translated from the French by Joseph M. Bernstein, Abrams, 1968; *194 Drawings,* selected by Ezio Gribaudo, introduction by Luigi Carluccio, Abrams, c. 1969; *De Chirico by de Chirico,* New York Cultural Center, 1972; *Giorgio de Chirico,* Wildenstein (London), 1976. Art work also collected in numerous catalogs published in Italian and French. Also illustrator of numerous works.

SIDELIGHTS: De Chirico was known as a father of surrealism, the artistic school that took images from the unconscious. Although he later repudiated modern art and even some of his own work, the paintings de Chirico did from 1910 to 1919 are regarded by art critic James Thrall Soby to have had "a more profound effect on European art in the first half of this century than those of any contemporary artist except Picasso."

De Chirico was born of Italian parents in Greece and moved with them to Florence in 1910. Previously, he had studied art in Athens and in Munich, where he was influenced by the German artists Arnold Boecklin and Max Klinger. In Italy he began a series of paintings known as "the Italian squares" or "the memories of Italy," which feature city squares devoid of people. At that time, de Chirico sought to create an "art of dreamed sensation," and, to that end, in 1917 he established the *scuolo metafisica*—the "metaphysical school"—with artist Carlo Carra.

In 1919, while standing in front of a painting by Titian, de Chirico was seized by a revelation of "what great painting was." He abandoned his previous style and began copying paintings by Raphael and Michelangelo, embracing a style that critics have termed "romantic neoclassicism." He became a vocal critic of modernism. Although de Chirico had a brief neo-metaphysical period from 1924 to 1928, he broke with the surrealists for good in 1928. For the remainder of his long career he was largely influenced by the French painters Delacroix, Gericault, Renoir, and Chardin.

In 1972 the New York Cultural Center held a retrospective show comprised of 182 pieces, including paintings, sculptures, drawings, and lithographs. The show, "de Chirico by de Chirico," was called the "only completely authentic de Chirico exhibition ever held" by the painter. At one time de Chirico estimated that at least 3,000 paintings, attributed to him were counterfeits. In 1947 he said that a painting owned by an Italian art dealer was a fraud. The dealer took de Chirico to court and won a judgment against him. De Chirico was involved in another suit in 1968 in a dispute over the reproduction rights of his sculptures: he had given exclusive rights to several galleries.

De Chirico's autobiographical novel, *Hebdomeros,* is known as an important surrealist literary work.

BIOGRAPHICAL/CRITICAL SOURCES: Giorgio de Chirico, *1918-1925: Riccordi di Roma* (correspondence and reminiscences), Editrice Cultura moderna, 1945; de Chirico, *Memorie della mia vita* (autobiography), Astrolabio, 1945, translation by Margaret Crosland published as *The Memoirs of Giorgio de Chirico,* University of Miami Press, 1971; *Newsweek,* October 3, 1955; *Washington Post,* November 22, 1978.*

* * *

DeFANTI, Charles 1942-

PERSONAL: Born September 14, 1942, in New York, N.Y.; son of Charles, Sr. and Madeline (Kaiser) DeFanti. *Education:* Queens College of the City University of New York, B.A., 1963; New York University, M.A., 1964, Ph.D., 1974. *Home:* 393 West Broadway, New York, N.Y. 10012. *Office:* Department of English, Kean College of New Jersey, Union, N.J. 07083.

CAREER: Kean College of New Jersey, Union, assistant professor, 1966-76, associate professor of English, 1976—. Adviser to Rahway State Prison Prisoners' Forum; speaker on ecology and conservation. *Member:* College English Association, New York University Graduate English Association. *Awards, honors:* New York State Regents College Teaching fellowship, 1963-66; research grants from the state of New Jersey, 1977 and 1979; National Book Award nomination, 1979, for *The Wages of Expectation.*

WRITINGS: The Wages of Expectation (biography), New York University Press, 1978. Editor of *Fiction,* 1973-75.

WORK IN PROGRESS: The Beat Legacy (tentative title), a literary evaluation, based partly on interviews, of the older members of the "Beat Generation," publication by New York University Press expected in 1981.

SIDELIGHTS: DeFanti writes: "My book, which came from interviews with my subject and with people who surrounded him and knew him throughout his lifetime, follows a trend which has been developing in the craft of biography for some time now: the documenting of the circumstances of an author's life while he is still living. It was my privilege to know Edward Dahlberg and to be able to leaven his recollections with those of his family and friends.

"I have always been fascinated by complex and violent personalities, so the opportunity to write the biography of Dahlberg, a writer whose work had always awed me, was one that I siezed immediately. Dahlberg possessed charm (which he could turn on and off with alarming speed and intensity) and, more important, genius, which was too often overlooked thanks to his even greater genius of alienating people. I believe he had one of the most complex and chaotic lives in history. The bastard son of two itinerant barbers (though he didn't learn the identity of his father until he was grown), Dahlberg spent his early childhood in the Midwest and in a Catholic orphanage, his adolescence in a Jewish orphanage, and his early youth as a hobo. He graduated from college, became an expatriate in London and Paris, then a Communist, then a recluse, and finally an ultra-conservative. During this time, his writing style evolved from the most colloquial to the most baroque and stylized of this century."

DeFanti also alluded to a review of the biography in *Village Voice.* Critic William O'Rourke wrote: "I found myself laughing out loud at every other page at the marvelous human comedy DeFanti captures. It sounds like low praise, but Dahlberg never lost his sense of humor, even though it could entirely disappear. Dahlberg's moods were medieval, more like humors, and one would take over from the other completely.

"He was a hard man, but, unlike many, he did apply his own severe standards to himself. And DeFanti has finally unlocked the stuff of Dahlberg's life from the oppressive rococo cage, fit only for solitude . . . that he fashioned for himself. Truly Dahlberg was paid the wages of his own expectations: rejection, isolation, and the curse of superfluity."

DeFanti stated: "Out of this raw material, Dahlberg fashioned one of the world's most beautiful (if mythologized) autobiographies. I hope my book will help rescue him from his undeserved obscurity and add a rather bizarre chapter to American literary history.

"I find that I have an appetite for literary detective work. Furthermore, I feel there is great value in providing biographical backdrops for the more colorful writers of the twentieth century, especially if their work is of a 'confessional mode'"

BIOGRAPHICAL/CRITICAL SOURCES: Village Voice, April 16, 1979.

* * *

de GUINGAND, Francis Wilfred 1900-1979

OBITUARY NOTICE: Born February 28, 1900, in London, England; died June 29, 1979, in Cannes, France. Soldier and industrialist who became a major general in the British Army during World War II and served as chief of staff to Field Marshall Montgomery. A major architect of the Allied victory, de Guingand also served as a mediator of the frequent disagreements between Montgomery and General Dwight D. Eisenhower. After the war, de Guingand tried farming in Rhodesia for a brief time before joining the board of the Alpha Cement Co. in Johannesburg, South Africa. He later held industrial posts with the Rothmans tobacco group and Carreras, another tobacco company. De Guingand was a defender of apartheid and supported the South Africa Foundation's efforts "to present the positive South African story to the world." He received the Knight Commander of the Order of the British Empire in 1944 and was the author of *African Assignment, Operation Victory,* and *Generals at War.* Obituaries and other sources: *The Author's and Writer's Who's Who,* 6th edition, Burke's Peerage, 1971; *Who's Who in the World,* 2nd edition, Marquis, 1973; *The International Who's Who,* Europa, 1974; *Who's Who,* 126th edition, St. Martin's, 1974; *New York Times,* June 30, 1979.

* * *

de HARTMANN, Olga 1883(?)-1979

OBITUARY NOTICE: Born c. 1883 in St. Petersburg (now Leningrad), Russia; died September 12, 1979, in Santa Fe, N.M. Widow of Russian pianist and composer Thomas de Hartmann, and author. In recent years, she worked diligently with American conductors wanting to perform her husband's music. She and her husband joined the cult founded by G. I. Gurdjieff, which sought calm through exercises, and wrote *Our Life With Gurdjieff.* Obituaries and other sources: *New York Times,* September 15, 1979.

* * *

DEHN, Paul (Edward) 1912-1976

PERSONAL: Born November 5, 1912, in Manchester, England; died September 30, 1976; son of Frederick Edward and Helen (Susman) Dehn. *Education:* Brasenose College, Oxford, B.A. *Home:* 19 Bramerton St., Chelsea S.W.3, England.

CAREER: Poet, critic, lyricist, and free-lance writer. *Sunday Referee,* London, England, film critic and columnist, 1936-39; film critic in London for the *Sunday Chronicle,* 1945-53, *News Chronicle,* 1954-60, and *Daily Herald,* 1960-63. *Military service:* Her Majesty's Forces, with Special Operations Executive, 1939-45; became major. *Member:* London Critics' Circle (president, 1956), Royal Society for the Protection of Birds (former councillor). *Awards, honors:* Co-recipient of Academy Award for best original story from Academy of Motion Picture Arts and Sciences, 1962, for "Seven Days to Noon"; Venice award, 1952, for commentary on documentary "Waters of Time"; Cheltenham Festival poetry prize, 1957; British Film Academy Award for best British screenplay, 1958, for "Orders to Kill."

WRITINGS—Poetry: *The Day's Alarm: Poems,* Hamish Hamilton, 1949; *Romantic Landscape,* Hamish Hamilton, 1952, Simon & Schuster, 1960; *Quake, Quake, Quake: A Leaden Treasury of English Verse,* Simon & Schuster, 1961; *The Fern on the Rock: Collected Poems, 1935-65,* Hamish Hamilton, 1965.

Other: *For Love and Money* (prose and verse), Reinhardt, 1956, Vanguard, 1957; (author of text) Ronald Spillman and Jack Ramsay, *Cat's Cradle* (photographic essay), Doubleday, 1959; (author of text) Spillman and Ramsay, *Kittens on the Keys* (photographic essay), Doubleday, 1961; (author of text) Spillman, *Cat's Whiskers* (photographic essay), Doubleday, 1963.

Adaptations: (Author of libretto) Lennox Berkeley, "A Dinner Engagement" (one-act opera), first produced at the Aldeburgh Festival, 1954; (author of adaptation) Oscar F. Wilde, *A Woman of No Importance* (first produced on the West End at the Savoy Theatre, 1953), Evans Brothers, 1954; (author of book and lyrics) "Virtue in Danger," adapted from Sir John Vanbrugh's "The Relapse," first produced on the West End at the Strand Theatre, 1963; (author of libretto with William Walton) Walton, *The Bear: An Extravaganza in One Act,* Oxford University Press, 1967; (author of libretto) Berkeley, *Castaway: A One-Act Opera Designed as a Companion Piece to "A Dinner Engagement,"* J. & W. Chester, 1968.

Film scripts: (Author of screen story with James Bernard) "Seven Days to Noon," Mayer-Kingsley, 1952; "Waters of Time," 1952; "Orders to Kill," Independent, 1959; "A Place for Gold," 1960; (with Richard Maibaum) "Goldfinger" (adapted from the novel by Ian Fleming), United Artists, 1964; "The Deadly Affair" (adapted from the novel, *Call for the Dead,* by John LeCarre), Columbia, 1965; (with Guy Trosper) "The Spy Who Came in From the Cold" (adapted from the novel by LeCarre), Paramount, 1965; (with Suso Cecchi D'Amico and Franco Zeffirelli) "The Taming of the Shrew" (adapted from the comedy by William Shakespeare), Columbia, 1967; (with Joseph Kessel) "The Night of the Generals" (adapted from the novel, *Die Nacht der Generale,* by Hans Hellmut Kirst and the novel, *The Wary Transgressor,* by James Hadley Chase), Columbia, 1967; "Beneath the Planet of the Apes," Twentieth Century-Fox, 1970; "A Fragment of Fear" (adapted from the novel by John Bingham), Columbia, 1970; "Escape From the Planet of the Apes," Twentieth Century-Fox, 1971; "Conquest of the Planet of the Apes," Twentieth Century-Fox, 1972; (author of screen story) "Battle for the Planet of the Apes," Twentieth Century-Fox, 1974; "Murder on the Orient Express" (adapted from the novel by Agatha Christie), Brabourne/Goodwin-EMI, 1975.

(Author of lyrics) Terence Rattigan, "Joie de Vivre" (musical comedy), first produced on the West End at Queen's Theatre, 1960. Author of lyrics and sketches for revues, all produced in London: "The Lyric Revue," 1951; "Penny Plain," 1952; "The Globe Revue," 1952; "At the Lyric," 1953; "Going to Town," 1954; "The Punch Revue," 1955.

Work represented in numerous anthologies, including *20th Century Parody: American and British,* edited by Buling Lowrey, Harcourt, 1960; *Poetry of War, 1939-1945,* edited by Ian Hamilton and Alan Ross, 1965; *Modern Love Poems,* edited by John Smith, Studio Vista, 1966; *Poetry of the Forties,* Penguin (Harmondsworth, Middlesex), 1968. Regular contributor to British Broadcasting Corp. program, "The Critics," 1936-63, and to *Punch.*

SIDELIGHTS: Though Paul Dehn considered himself primarily a poet, his best-known works were the screenplays for "The Deadly Affair," "The Spy Who Came in From the Cold," "Murder on the Orient Express," and the sequels to "Planet of the Apes."

Judith Crist praised "The Deadly Affair," saying it "demonstrates the conversion of a run-of-the-mill mystery story into a topical top-notch thriller by means of a literate script. . . . What might have been a routine unraveling of a mystery down to a corpse-strewn conclusion is transformed by suspense-ridden subtleties, intriguing characters and authenticity of locale into a first-rate entertainment."

Dehn's "Planet of the Apes" sequels were extremely successful. When "Escape From the Planet of the Apes" opened in New York, Roger Greenspun remarked, "Nobody is going to believe it, but I must say anyway that . . . [This] is one of the better movies in town." And though he felt "the film is much stronger in fiction than in science," he praised the credibility of the characters and the amount of thought put into the plot. Louise Sweeney declared that "Beneath the Planet of the Apes" "entertains without insulting the intelligence. This sequel to 'Planet of the Apes' is billed as science fiction but there's so much about it that borders on satire or camp you're bound to laugh."

Dehn traveled extensively in western Europe, eastern Canada, eastern Africa, the United States, Mexico, and Jamaica. He was the associate producer of the film "A Fragment of Fear," which he wrote in 1971.

AVOCATIONAL INTERESTS: Ornithology.

BIOGRAPHICAL/CRITICAL SOURCES: TV Guide, March 28, 1970; *Christian Science Monitor,* June 3, 1970; *New York Times,* May 29, 1971.*

* * *

DEIBLER, William E. 1932-

PERSONAL: Born April 18, 1932, in Altoona, Pa.; son of Edwin H. (a railroader) and Elizabeth (Sheehan) Deibler; married Phyllis Gates, January 17, 1953; children: Gail, Eric. *Education:* Pennsylvania State University, B.A., 1958. *Home:* 1233 Satellite Circle, Pittsburgh, Pa. 15241. *Office: Pittsburgh Post-Gazette,* 50 Blvd. of the Allies, Pittsburgh, Pa. 15222.

CAREER/WRITINGS: Centre Daily Times, State College, Pa., reporter, 1958-60; *Daily Messenger,* Homestead, Pa., editor, 1960-63; *The Patriot,* Harrisburg, Pa., city editor, 1964-66; Associated Press, Harrisburg, legislative correspondent, 1966-68; *Pittsburgh Post-Gazette,* Pittsburgh, Pa., 1968—, began as legislative correspondent, then city editor and assistant managing editor, currently managing editor. Faculty adviser for *Daily Collegian,* Pennsylvania State University, 1963. Notable assignments include coverage of the Pennsylvania Constitutional Convention, 1967-68, the Nixon-Humphrey campaign, 1968, Democratic and Republican national conventions in Chicago and Miami, 1968, and Jimmy Hoffa's arrival at Lewisburg Federal Prison, 1968. *Military service:* U.S. Air Force, 1951-54; became staff sergeant. *Member:* Society of Professional Journalists, Sigma Delta Chi, Kappa Tau Alpha. *Awards, honors:* Commendation medal and Department of Defense citation for military journalism; American Political Science Association Award for distinguished reporting of public affairs, 1971; several Keystone Press awards for news writing, editorial writing, layout and design, and public affairs reporting.

DELANEY, Marshall
See FULFORD, Robert

* * *

de LANGE, Nicholas (Robert Michael) 1944-

PERSONAL: Born August 7, 1944, in Nottingham, England; son of George David and Elaine (Jacobus) de Lange. *Education:* Christ Church, Oxford, B.A., 1966, M.A., 1969, D.Phil., 1970. *Office:* Faculty of Oriental Studies, Cambridge University, Sidgwick Ave., Cambridge CB3 9DA, England.

CAREER: University of Southampton, Southampton, England, Parkes Library fellow, 1969-71; Cambridge University, Cambridge, England, lecturer in Rabbinics, 1971—.

WRITINGS: A Woman in Israel, Ecumenical Society of the Blessed Virgin Mary, 1975; *Origen and the Jews: Studies in Jewish-Christian Relations in Third-Century Palestine,* Cambridge University Press, 1976; *Apocrypha: Jewish Literature of the Hellenistic Age,* Viking, 1978.

Translator: Amos Oz, *My Michael,* Knopf, 1972; Oz, *Elsewhere, Perhaps,* Harcourt, 1973; Oz, *Touch the Water Touch the Wind,* Harcourt, 1974; Oz, *Unto Death,* Harcourt, 1975; Oz, *The Hill of Evil Counsel,* Harcourt, 1978.

Contributor: J. A. Michener, editor, *Firstfruits,* Jewish Publication Society, 1973; Jacob Sonntag, editor, *New Writing From Israel,* Corgi, 1976; (author of introduction) Peter Levy, translator, *The Psalms,* Penguin, 1976; Elliott Anderson, editor, *Contemporary Israeli Literature,* Jewish Publication Society, 1977; P.D.A. Garnsey and C. R. Whittaker, editors, *Imperialism in the Ancient World,* Cambridge University Press, 1978; Emanuel Litvinoff, editor, *Jewish Short Stories,* Penguin, 1979; (translator and author of introduction and notes, with Marguerite Harl) *Origene: Philscalie 1-20 et Lettre a Africanus,* Editions du Cerf (Paris), in press.

Contributor to *Encyclopaedia Judaica* and *Dictionary of Philosophy.* Contributor of more than twenty-five articles, translations, and reviews to theology journals and other periodicals, including *Commentary* and *Harper's.*

SIDELIGHTS: "I am interested in texts and translations, texts as translations, translations as texts," de Lange told *CA.* "The most influential translation of all time was the translation of the Bible from Hebrew into Greek. I have written about this event in *Apocrypha.* But the Hebrew Bible was also in a sense a translation; a translation into words of the experiences and yearnings of an amazing people, and of their deepest reflections on the nature of human life. This text, through its translations into other languages, has become the foundation of Western thought. I am fascinated by the Bible and its influence. In my work on Origen, the first great Christian interpreter of the Bible, I have concentrated on his relationship to this text. Each generation needs to relate to the past in its own way—to make its own translations. We live in an age which is not particularly religious, but which is obsessed with history. We are constantly reinterpreting the texts which make up our history, translating them into our own language. All writing, perhaps all thought, is translation. Reading is an act of translation, too.

"Most readers are unaware of this question of translation and the problems it raises. Even in the narrowest sense of the word—translation of a text from one language into another—the meaning of translation is too little understood. People think they have read an author if they have read his works in translation. What they have read is the work of a translator—a reader who is also a writer. Because of the barriers of language, readers need translators. But they do not appreciate them. The translator is noticed only when he manifestly fails, when he intrudes between reader and author. There are many fine translators: their writings are read, but their names are hardly known.

"I first took up the challenge of translation seriously in 1970, when I started translating the writings of Amos Oz. We met in Oxford and became friends. All our translations are produced in collaboration. He reads, I listen and write; I read, he listens and comments. I believe this process is the most satisfactory way of translating. When translating dead authors, I have often longed to hear their voices, to ask them questions. I do not know if my translations of Amos Oz are good translations, but at least I know that they are faithful to the author's intentions. I used to think, as many people think, that translation consists of exchanging one word for another, like changing money. I have learned through experience that a faithful translation is not necessarily a literal one. A translator's loyalty is not to words. He has to be faithful to his author, to himself, to his readers. He has to interpret ideas, longings, moods. He has to absorb them, make them his own, and pass them on. The words help, but sometimes they get in the way.

"Amos Oz is a skillful writer (to my mind he is the best living writer of Hebrew prose). Although there is a great deal of local color in his books, their themes are universal themes, and I think he has important things to say to English readers. These factors help me as a translator. But I believe that Oz and I also have a common philosophy, a philosophy of translation in its widest sense. His characters struggle to express themselves in words; they are aware of the inadequacy of language and of its magic. They quote the Hebrew Bible and interpret it in their own way. They wrestle with the burden of their past and try to find its meaning for the present.

"This is the way I see my own task, too."

* * *

de la TORRE, Victor Raul Haya
See HAYA de la TORRE, Victor Raul

* * *

DELL, Floyd 1887-1969

OBITUARY NOTICE: Born June 28, 1887, in Barry, Ill.; died in 1969. Dell became the literary editor of the *Chicago Evening Post* where he developed its "Literary Review" into a major newspaper supplement. While in Chicago, he became one of the group of midwestern authors who formed the famous "Chicago School," which included such notable writers as Carl Sandburg, Ben Hecht, and Charles MacArthur. Dell, a socialist, also was editor of the radical *Masses* and later the *Liberator*. During the Depression, he became associated with the Works Progress Administration (WPA) doing editorial work. Dell wrote many one-act plays, including "The Angel Intrudes" and "Sweet-and-Twenty." His numerous novels include such works as *Moon-Calf, The Briary Bush,* and *The Golden Spike*. Dell contributed stories to *Harper's, Cosmopolitan, Vanity Fair,* and *Nation*. Obituaries and other sources: *The Oxford Companion to American Literature,* 4th edition, Oxford University Press, 1965; *The Reader's Encyclopedia,* 2nd edition, Crowell, 1965; *Longman Companion to Twentieth Century Literature,* Longman, 1970; *The Penguin Companion to American Literature,* McGraw, 1971.

de MEDICI, Marino 1933-

PERSONAL: Surname pronounced de Me-*dee*-chee; born May 16, 1933, in Rome, Italy; son of Pompeo (a navy officer) and Maria (Turchi) de Medici; married Marianne Bengtsson, April 6, 1960. *Education:* University of Rome, Rome, Italy, degree in political science; University of Washington, Seattle, Wash., B.A.; University of California, Berkeley, M.A. *Office:* 856 National Press Building, Washington, D.C. 20045.

CAREER/WRITINGS: Il Giornale della Sera, Rome, Italy, staff member, 1952; *Il Messaggero,* Rome, staff member, 1953-54; foreign desk editor and Washington, D.C. correspondent for A.N.S.A. (Italian national news agency), 1957-64; *Il Tempo* (daily newspaper), Rome, U.S. correspondent, 1964—. Lecturer, North Atlantic Treaty Organization (NATO) defense college, International Affairs Association, Catholic University, Washington, D.C., Pennsylvania State University, and other organizations. Notable assignments include interview with President Gerald Ford, May, 1975; interviews with President Sukarno of Indonesia and President Marcos of the Philippines as special correspondent in the Far East; interviews with other prominent figures as special correspondent in South America, Central America, and South Africa. Contributor to various Italian and American publications.

* * *

DEMPSEY, Jack
See DEMPSEY, William Harrison

* * *

DEMPSEY, William Harrison 1895-
(Jack Dempsey)

PERSONAL: Born June 24, 1895, in Manassa, Colo.; married fourth wife, Deanna; children: two daughters. *Residence:* New York N.Y. *Office:* 1619 Broadway, New York, N.Y. 10019.

CAREER: Professional boxer, 1917-32; restaurateur. Worked in shipyards during World War I; boxing referee during 1920's and '30's. *Military service:* U.S. Coast Guard, 1942-45; became commander.

WRITINGS—Under name Jack Dempsey: (With Myron M. Stearns) *Round by Round* (autobiography), Whittlesey House, 1940; (with Frank G. Menke) *How to Fight Tough,* Hillman Periodicals, 1942; *Championship Fighting: Explosive Punching and Aggressive Defense,* edited by Jack Cuddy, Prentice-Hall, 1950; (with Bob Considine and Bill Slocum) *Dempsey, by the Man Himself* (autobiography), Simon & Schuster, 1960; (with stepdaughter Barbara Piattelli Dempsey) *Dempsey* (autobiography), Harper, 1977.

SIDELIGHTS: Although Dempsey had knocked out numerous opponents in 1915 and 1916, he was virtually unknown as a boxer in the United States. Then in 1917 he met boxing manager Jack Kearns who helped guide Dempsey to fame and the heavyweight championship of the world. The soon-to-be champ fought hard for the next two years, defeating larger fighters such as Carl Morris and Fred Fulton easily. With only one defeat on his record, Dempsey was finally given a fight with champion Jess Willard.

At six and one-half feet, Willard stood much taller than the six foot Dempsey. Willard also outweighed him by seventy pounds. Nonetheless, in his first chance for the heavyweight crown, Dempsey knocked down Willard seven times in four rounds. The fight appeared over as early as the third round when Willard failed to rise at a count of ten. However, the timekeeper declared that the round had ended before the referee was able to complete his count. The fourth round was Willard's last though, for his cheek bone was already broken, as Dempsey pounded him enough times to end the fight.

Defending the championship was not an easy task for Dempsey during his seven-year reign. The "Manassa Mauler" went twelve rounds with challenger Bill Brennan before knocking him out. Then, after knocking out Georges Carpentier in the fourth round of their fight, Dempsey won a fifteen-round decision against Tommy Gibbons. Next came one of the most famous fights in boxing history.

In 1923, more than 85,000 fans packed into the Polo Grounds in Brooklyn to witness Dempsey's fight with Luis Firpo, an Argentinian who outweighed him by twenty-five pounds. In the first round Dempsey was knocked down twice but countered by flooring Firpo ten times. Then, towards the end of the round, Firpo delivered a smashing right that sent Dempsey completely out of the ring. As Dempsey remembered, "I was knocked out of the ring in the first round and got back in just in time to be saved by the bell. I was pretty groggy, but my head cleared at the start of the second round." He charged back out to meet Firpo and then stunned the crowd by knocking him out before one minute had passed.

Aside from the battle with Firpo, Dempsey's most famous fight was probably against Gene Tunney in 1926. He had not fought much after the Firpo fight and was faced with legal action from Kearns. The fight went ten rounds before Tunney was declared the new champion by decision. "Jack the Giant Killer" had been dethroned.

But the two fought again the following year in another famous and highly controversial bout. In the seventh round of the rematch, Dempsey slammed Tunney to the canvas but stood over his fallen opponent instead of retreating to a neutral corner. When he finally did move away from Tunney, the referee began counting. But by then Tunney had revived sufficiently and was able to continue. He finally defeated Dempsey in ten hard fought rounds.

After his fight with Tunney, Dempsey stayed in boxing as an advisor and referee before the Depression forced him back into the ring. In 1931 he fought fifty-six exhibition matches before influenza slowed his pace. Finally, in 1932 Dempsey retired following his bout with King Levinsky. Of his sixty-nine fights as a professional, Dempsey won fifty-four, including forty-seven by knockout.

Since retiring, Dempsey has written three autobiographies. Writing about *Round by Round,* Caswell Adams noted, "It's well written, in a manner to be devoted to a mighty politician or a bishop, but surely not in the style for the bruising, mauling, rollicking and moneyed Dempsey." In the *New York Times,* a critic wrote, "An absence of boastfulness is conspicuous throughout the book, and the ex-champion is sparing in his use of alibis for his defeat."

Dempsey's second autobiography was called "the best of the Dempsey books" by W. C. Heinz. D. B. Bagg declared that Dempsey's "heaviest blows are aimed at himself, with only an occasional jab or hook at somebody else." And the third autobiography, *Dempsey,* was praised by a *Newsweek* reviewer as a "sunny, likable account of his career." Peter Andrews commented, "The great champion of the 1920's has fashioned a memoir that is mellow and gracious with a kind word for just about everybody."

BIOGRAPHICAL/CRITICAL SOURCES: Jack Dempsey and Myron Stearns, *Round by Round,* Whittlesey House, 1940; *Books,* September 29, 1940; *New York Times,* October 13, 1940, September 14, 1973; Dempsey, Bob Considine, and Bill Slocum, *Dempsey, by the Man Himself,* Simon & Schuster, 1960; *New York Times Book Review,* April 15, 1960, May 29, 1977; *Springfield Republican,* May 29, 1960; Dempsey and Barbara Piattelli Dempsey, *Dempsey,* Harper, 1977; *Newsweek,* April 14, 1977.*

* * *

DENNY, Alma 1912-
(Adeline Clistier)

PERSONAL: Birth-given name, Alma Denenholz; born December 27, 1912, in New York, N.Y.; daughter of Jacob Henry (an attorney) and Pauline (a secretary; maiden name, Freed) Denenholz; married Theodore Kaplan (a doctor), July 1, 1932 (died September, 1964); children: Laura K. Popenoe, Elizabeth K. Secor. *Education:* Hunter College (now of the City University of New York), B.A. (cum laude), 1927; Columbia University, M.A., 1937. *Home:* 127 Maple St., Brooklyn, N.Y. 11225.

CAREER: Teacher of French, English, and speech in New York City, 1927-29; R. H. Macy & Co., New York City, section manager, 1929-30; Simmons-Boardman Publishing Co., New York City, editorial assistant, 1946-49; assistant editor with Sex Information and Education Council of the United States (SIECUS), 1958-68; syndicated columnist, General Features Corp., 1960-65; free-lance writer. Consultant to Peace Corps, 1952. *Member:* American Society of Journalists and Authors, Association for Humanistic Psychology.

WRITINGS: (Contributor) Thomas Earl Sullenger, editor, *Neglected Areas in Family Living,* Christopher, 1960. Work anthologized in *The Fiction of the Forties,* edited by Whit Burnet, Dutton, 1949. Contributor to *Forum,* under pseudonym Adeline Clistier, and to periodicals, including *Canadian Home Journal, Saturday Evening Post, Ms., Parents' Magazine, Wall Street Journal, New York Times Magazine,* and *Playbill.*

WORK IN PROGRESS: A novel.

SIDELIGHTS: Denny told *CA:* "Writing is my joy, but I am not a 'dedicated' writer. I have a large family, hence I work at my writing sporadically and fitfully."

When asked to give advice to aspiring writers, Denny replied: "Learn the business end of writing. Unless you get printed, what's the point? You're talking to yourself. As for the current literary scene, it scares me. It seems *everybody* is writing and *nobody* is reading, except the 'book people,' of course. The professionals read each other. Oh, they carry around all the 'in' books, and maybe they flip through them. But writing should be communication, not just entertainment. And how many writers really reach anyone in a substantive way, making them think, changing people in some way? Who is really listening?

"Escape is the name of the game for writing that sells. Help people get away and forget and they will love you. Self-help books? People buy them, but they give them to somebody *else* who, they are sure, needs help."

* * *

DESMOND, Shaw 1877-1960

OBITUARY NOTICE: Born January 19, 1877, in Dungarran, Ireland; died December 23, 1960, in London, England. Poet, lecturer, journalist, and author. Desmond founded the short-lived International Institute for Psychical Research in his fervor to learn more about psychic phenomena, his all-pervading interest. Many of his more than sixty books reflect this interest, including *We Do Not Die, Reincarnation for Everyman, After Sudden Death,* and *Healing: Psychic and Divine*. Desmond traveled widely, visiting the Arctic, sailing around Cape Horn, and trekking through Africa. He also lectured in the United States, Britain, and Scandinavia. Obituaries and other sources: *The New Century Handbook of English Literature,* revised edition, Appleton, 1967.

* * *

DESTLER, I(rving) M(cArthur) 1939-

PERSONAL: Born August 21, 1939, in Statesboro, Ga.; son of Chester M. (a historian) and Katharine (a Red Cross executive; maiden name, Hardesty) Destler; married Harriett Parsons (a consultant), July 27, 1968; children; Mark Dodson, Katharine Elizabeth. *Education:* Harvard University, B.A. (magna cum laude), 1961; Princeton University, M.P.A., 1965, Ph.D., 1971. *Politics:* Democrat. *Home:* 1478 Waggaman Circle, McLean, Va. 22101. *Office:* Carnegie Endowment for International Peace, 11 Dupont Circle N.W., Washington, D.C. 20036.

CAREER: U.S. Peace Corps, volunteer assistant lecturer at University of Nigeria, 1961-63; assistant to U.S. Senator Walter F. Mondale, 1965-67; U.S. Department of Agriculture, International Agricultural Development Service, Washington, D.C., program analyst and acting regional coordinator for Asia, 1967-69; Council on Foreign Relations, New York, N.Y., fellow, 1969-70, member; Princeton University, Princeton, N.J., visiting lecturer in public and international affairs, 1971-72; Brookings Institution, Washington, D.C., research associate, 1972-76, senior fellow in foreign policy studies, 1976-77, member of associated staff; Carnegie Endowment for International Peace, Washington, D.C., senior associate and director of project on executive-congressional relations in foreign policy, 1977—. Lecturer at Johns Hopkins University, 1976-77. Staff associate of President's Task Force on Government Organization, 1967; fellow of Council on Foreign Relations, 1969-70; consultant to Office of Management and Budget and U.S. Department of State. *Member:* American Political Science Association, Arms Control Association, National Academy of Public Administration, Panel on Effectiveness of Organizational Change in Foreign Policy, Phi Beta Kappa. *Awards, honors:* Woodrow Wilson fellow, 1963-64; McConnell fellow in international affairs, 1964-65.

WRITINGS: Presidents, Bureaucrats, and Foreign Policy: The Politics of Organizational Reform, Princeton University Press, 1972, revised edition, 1974; (with Hideo Sato, Priscilla Clapp, and Haruhiro Fukui) *Managing an Alliance: The Politics of U.S.-Japanese Relations,* Brookings Institution, 1976; (with Sato and Fukui) *The Textile Wrangle: Conflict in Japanese-American Relations, 1969-71,* Cornell University Press, 1979; *Making Foreign Economic Policy,* Brookings Institution, 1980. Contributor to politics and international affairs journals.

WORK IN PROGRESS: Research on executive-congressional conflict and its impact on foreign policy.

SIDELIGHTS: Destler writes: "The central goal of my writing is to shed light on how the United States government deals, in practice, with important foreign policy issues. This concern has colored all of my writing: on foreign policy organization and bureaucratic politics, on American dealings (and mis-dealings) with Japan, on making foreign economic policy, and on Congress and its foreign policy role."

DEUTSCH, Herbert A(rnold) 1932-

PERSONAL: Born February 9, 1932, in Baldwin, N.Y.; son of Barnet B. (a mail carrier) and Miriam (Meyersburg) Deutsch; married Margaret Carbray (a social worker), April 10, 1955; children: Lisbeth Ann, Edmund Barnet. *Education:* Hofstra University, B.S., 1956; Manhattan School of Music, B.Mus., 1960, M.Mus., 1961; doctoral study at New York University. *Home:* 19 Crossman Place, Huntington, N.Y. 11743. *Office:* Department of Music, Hofstra University, Hempstead, N.Y. 11550.

CAREER: Hofstra University, Hempstead, N.Y., instructor, 1963-68, assistant professor, 1968-73, associate professor of music, 1973—, head of department, 1973—, director of Institute of Arts, 1977—. Member of board of directors of Long Island Symphony Orchestra, 1973-76, and Family Service League of Suffolk County, 1974—. Consultant to Moog Music, Norlin Industries. *Military service:* U.S. Army, 1956-58. *Member:* American Society of Composers, Authors, and Publishers, American Federation of Musicians, American Association of University Professors, Music Educators' National Conference, American Music Center, New York State Council of Administrators of Music Education, Long Island Composers Alliance (founding co-director, 1973-78; now director).

WRITINGS: Synthesis: An Introduction to Electronic Music, Alfred Publishing, 1976; *The Complete Synthesist,* Alfred Publishing, 1980. Contributor to orchestra and audio engineering journals.

WORK IN PROGRESS: "Music and the Electron," a television documentary film script.

SIDELIGHTS: Deutsch comments: "As a student, I had hoped to become either a composer, a jazz musician, or a college professor. By good fortune I have achieved all of those to some degree, and have managed to write a bit and become a business consultant. Electronic music, my foremost activity, satisfies many needs—musical, manual-manipulative, and emotional. I run a couple of miles each day to set my psyche up to sustain a good deal of activity and am a 'comfortable workaholic.'"

* * *

De VALERA, Eamon 1882-1975

OBITUARY NOTICE: Born October 14, 1882, in New York, N.Y.; died August 30, 1975. Teacher, author, former prime minister and president of the Irish Republic. A determined fighter for Ireland's complete independence from English rule, De Valera began his career as a teacher of mathematics, physics, Latin, and French. Soon, though, he joined the Gaelic League, the fountainhead of the Irish nationalist political and literary movement, and the Irish Volunteers, of which he was president for several years. De Valera participated in the Easter Week Rebellion of 1916, was captured, and sentenced to death. Unlike his compatriots, though, De Valera's sentence was commuted to life imprisonment and he was later freed in the general amnesty of 1917. As one of the survivors of the Easter Week Rebellion, De Valera became a hero. He was elected president of the nationalist group Sinn Fein and was a representative of the Dial Eireann, the lower house of the first parliament to meet in Ireland in over one hundred years. In 1919, De Valera was elected president of the Irish Republic by the Dial. In his official capacity, he traveled to the United States and raised more than $6 million to aid Ireland in its fight with England in the Civil War of 1919. When peace was declared in 1921, De Valera strongly denounced the treaty creating the Irish Free

State as it did not incorporate the six counties of Northern Ireland. Civil was broke out again and De Valera became the leader of the Irish Republican Army (IRA). He was arrested and imprisoned for the third time in his revolutionary career. When released, he formed his own political party, Fianna Fail. In 1932, De Valera's party obtained a majority in the Dial, bringing him into power as the president of the executive council and minister of external affairs. In 1938, De Valera became Taoiseach (prime minister) of Ireland and held the office off and on until 1959. In 1959, he again became president of Ireland and served as such until 1973. This tireless fighter for independence wrote many books on Ireland's plight, including *Ireland's Case Against Conscription, The Foundation of the Republic of Ireland in the Vote of the People,* and *Ireland's Stand, 1939-1945.* Obituaries and other sources: *Current Biography,* Wilson, 1940, 1951; *The Reader's Encyclopedia,* 2nd edition, Crowell, 1965; *Who's Who in Government,* Marquis, 1972; *International Who's Who,* Europa, 1974.

* * *

DEWSBURY, Donald A(llen) 1939-

PERSONAL: Born August 11, 1939, in Brooklyn, N.Y.; son of Edwin L. (in banking) and Carol (Neil) Dewsbury; married Joyce R. Kraekel, June 8, 1963; children: Bryan, Laura. *Education:* Bucknell University, A.B., 1961; University of Michigan, Ph.D., 1965; postdoctoral study at University of California, Berkeley, 1965-66. *Home:* 840 Northwest 20th St., Gainesville, Fla. 32603. *Office:* Department of Psychology, University of Florida, Gainesville, Fla. 32611.

CAREER: University of Florida, Gainesville, assistant professor, 1966-70, associate professor, 1970-73, professor of psychology, 1973—. Member of Center for Neurobiological Sciences. *Member:* American Psychological Association (fellow), Animal Behavior Society (president, 1978-79), American Society of Zoologists (member of executive committee, 1978-79), Psychonomic Society, American Association for the Advancement of Science, American Society of Mammalogists, Phi Beta Kappa, Sigma Xi.

WRITINGS: (With D. A. Rethlingshafer) *Comparative Psychology: A Modern Survey,* McGraw, 1973; *Comparative Animal Behavior,* McGraw, 1978; (with T. E. McGill and B. D. Sachs) *Sex and Behavior: Status and Prospectus,* Plenum, 1978. Advisory editor of *Contemporary Psychology.*

WORK IN PROGRESS: Research on animal behavior.

SIDELIGHTS: Dewsbury told *CA:* "The study of animal behavior has fascinated a considerable range of people. Scientists trained in psychology, zoology, anthropology, psychiatry, animal science, and other disciplines all have contributed. I think it very important that each appreciate the approach and contributions of the others. Animal behavior is in a dynamic state of growth. The individual who would understand the full range of research on animal behavior needs a balanced presentation and may then come to view this fascinating field in all of its complexity."

* * *

DIAMOND, Milton 1934-

PERSONAL: Born March 6, 1934, in New York, N.Y.; son of Aaron (a grocer) and Jennie (Arber) Diamond; married Grace Hope Whitney (a psychologist), December 18, 1955; children: Hinda Louise, Irene Wanda, Sara Elizabeth, Leah Naiomi. *Education:* City College (now of the City University of New York), B.S., 1955; University of Kansas, Ph.D., 1962; postdoctoral study at University of Louisville, 1962-66. *Politics:* Independent. *Religion:* Jewish. *Agent:* Lynn Nesbit, International Creative Management, 40 West 57th St., New York, N.Y. 10019. *Office:* John A. Burns School of Medicine, University of Hawaii, Honolulu, Hawaii 96822.

CAREER: University of Louisville, Louisville, Ky., instructor, 1962-63, assistant professor of anatomy, 1963-67; University of Hawaii, Honolulu, associate professor, 1967-71, professor of anatomy and reproductive biology, 1971—. Research professor of psychiatry at State University of New York at Stony Brook, 1976-78; lecturer at colleges and universities in the United States and abroad. Presented human sexuality series on KHET-TV, 1973; producer of television programs for State of Hawaii Department of Education. Member of board of directors of Honolulu's Sexual Identity Center, 1976—. Organizer of national and international workshops and symposia; consultant to Center for Advanced Study in Developmental Sciences, National Science Foundation, and Merrel National Laboratories.

MEMBER: International Academy for Sex Research (charter member), American Association for the Advancement of Science, American Associations of Anatomists, American Association of Sex Educators, Counselors, and Therapists, Animal Behavior Society (charter member), Society for Developmental Psychobiology, Society for the Scientific Study of Sex (fellow), Society for the Study of Fertility, Society for the Study of Reproduction (charter member), Sigma Xi. *Awards, honors:* Lederle Medical Faculty Award from Lederle Foundation, American Cyanamid Co., 1968-71; citation for creative programming excellence from National University Extension Association's Arts and Humanities Division, 1973, for human sexuality series on KHET-TV; research awards include grants from National Institutes of Health, Ford Foundation, Population Council of America, and Program for Applied Reproduction and Fertility Research.

WRITINGS: (Editor and contributor) *Perspectives in Reproduction and Sexual Behavior,* Indiana University Press, 1968; (contributor) Richard Green, editor, *Human Sexuality: Health Practitioner's Text,* Williams & Wilkins, 1975, 2nd edition, 1978; (contributor) F. A. Beach, editor, *Human Sexuality in Four Perspectives,* Johns Hopkins Press, 1976; (with P. G. Steinhoff) *Abortion Politics,* University Press of Hawaii, 1977; *Sexuality and the Handicapped* (audio series with bibliography), Jeffrey Norton, 1979; (contributor) Vern Bullough, editor, *Sex Research Today,* Prometheus Books, 1979; (with Arno Karlen) *Sexual Decisions,* Little, Brown, 1980.

Contributor to *American Medical Association Handbook on Human Sexuality.* Contributor of more than thirty-five articles to scholarly journals. Member of editorial and review staff of *Journal of Human Reproduction, Biology of Reproduction, Sexology, Developmental Psychobiology, Animal Behavior, Medical Aspects of Human Sexuality, Journals of Sex Education,* and *Alternative Lifestyles.*

SIDELIGHTS: Diamond comments: "I regret not being able to write more quickly and for many different audiences. I find writing extremely difficult and painful. Nevertheless, it is rewarding in that I feel some crucial ideas are put forth for discussion and consideration.

"I know much of what I write is popular, but some of my ideas are unpopular. In the area of sex and sexuality, agreement is not always my goal; sometimes just understanding is enough, and at other times discussion or even rejection is worthwhile. The field of sexology has been left too long to popularists and advocates of one cause or another. My writings, I hope, can generate light, even if they generate heat. My cause is allowing a reader the ability to make informed, rational, and satisfying decisions on highly sensitive and personal matters."

AVOCATIONAL INTERESTS: Flying, scuba diving, fishing, photography.

* * *

DIAMOND, Stephen A(rthur) 1946-

PERSONAL: Born December 7, 1946, in Panama; came to the United States in 1962; son of W. W. and Hindi Diamond; married Judith Rubenstein (an attorney), May 1, 1974; children: Crescent Alexandra. *Education:* Attended Columbia University, 1964-68. *Politics:* "Cosmic Christian Communalism." *Religion:* "Judeao-Hindu." *Home address:* P.O. Box 177, Montague, Mass. 01351. *Agent:* Ron Bernstein, Inc., 200 West 58th St., New York, N.Y. 10022.

CAREER: *New York Times,* New York City, copyboy, summer, 1965; Columbia University, American Press Institute, New York City, copyboy, 1966; *Medical Opinion and Review,* New York City, assistant to publisher, 1967; *Liberation News Service,* New York City, reporter, 1967, editor, 1968; *Dock of the Bay,* San Francisco, Calif., co-founder and co-editor, 1969; free-lance writer, 1969—. Co-founder and producer for Green Mountain Post Films. Executive secretary of Bloom Institute of Media Studies. *Member:* International Owls Club. *Awards, honors:* Best film award from New York-Montreal Psychic Film Festival, 1975, for "Voices of the Spirit"; grant from Massachusetts Arts and Humanities Foundation, 1977.

WRITINGS: *What the Trees Said: Life on a New Age Farm* (nonfiction), Delacorte, 1971; *Panama Red: The Adventures of Jacob Light* (novel), Avon, 1979; *Anatomy of a Rose* (novel), Avon, in press.

Author of "Voices of the Spirit" (documentary film script), released by Green Mountain Post Films, 1972.

Work represented in anthologies, including *Current Thinking and Writing,* Series 7, Prentice-Hall, 1975. Contributor to magazines and newspapers in the United States and abroad, including *Atlantic Monthly, New Republic, New Age Journal,* and *High Times.* Associate editor of *Industria Turistica.* Editor of *Art/Works, Green Mountain Post, Valley Advocate,* and *Cambridge Phoenix.*

WORK IN PROGRESS: Research on materials concerning the unity of all religious systems.

SIDELIGHTS: In 1967 and 1968 Diamond was working for an anti-war movement news agency which syndicated his articles to more than five hundred subscribers, most of them members of the underground press. In 1974 he was news director for Radio Caroline, an unlicensed "pirate" radio station floating in the North Sea. Since 1976, his articles have been syndicated to daily newspapers all over the world by New York Times Syndication Service.

Diamond writes: "My aim is to entertain and, when the energy is right, to educate. I call this system the Double E."

* * *

DILLON, George 1906-1968

OBITUARY NOTICE: Born November 12, 1906, in Jacksonville, Fla.; died in 1968. Poet and editor, Dillon won the Pulitzer Prize for his collection of poems, *The Flowering Stone.* He was the editor of *Poetry* and also translated a number of poems by Baudelaire with Edna St. Vincent Millay in *Flowers of Evil.* Dillon's other book of poetry is *Boy in the Wind.* Obituaries and other sources: *The Oxford Companion to American Literature,* 4th edition, Oxford University Press, 1965; *The Reader's Encyclopedia,* 2nd edition, Crowell, 1965.

* * *

DINGWALL, E(ric) J(ohn)

PERSONAL: Born in Ceylon; son of Alexander Harvey Dingwall. *Education:* Pembroke College, Cambridge, M.A., 1912; University of London, earned D.Sc. and Ph.D. *Home:* 171 Marine Court, St. Leonards-on-Sea, East Sussex, England.

CAREER: Anthropologist; parapsychologist. Former staff member of Cambridge University Library, Cambridge, England; American Society for Psychical Research, New York, N.Y., director of department of physical phenomena, 1921; Society for Psychical Research, England, research officer, 1922-27; investigated many mediums in New York City, Boston, Paris, Copenhagen, Warsaw, Munich, and Gratz, Austria; researched social and religious conditions relating to abnormal mental phenomena in Spain, 1935, and in West Indies, 1936. Honorary assistant keeper of printed books at British Library, London. *Wartime service:* Ministry of Information and British Foreign Office, 1941-45. *Member:* Magic Circle (honorary vice-president; founding member of Occult Committee), Society for Psychical Research.

WRITINGS: (Editor with Harry Price) *Revelations of a Spirit Medium,* Kegan Paul Trench, Trubner, 1922, reprinted, Arno, 1975; *Studies in the Sexual Life of Ancient and Mediaeval Peoples,* John Bale, Sons & Danielsson, 1925; *How to Go to a Medium,* Kegan Paul Trench, Trubner, 1927; *Ghosts and Spirits in the Ancient World,* Kegan Paul Trench, Trubner, 1930; *The Girdle of Chastity,* Routledge & Sons, 1931; *Artificial Cranial Deformation,* John Bale, Sons & Danielsson, 1931; *How to Use a Large Library,* Bowes & Bowes, 1933; (editor) Hermann Heinrich Ploss and others, *Woman: An Historical, Gynecological and Anthropological Compendium* (author associated with British edition only), Medical Press, 1935; *Racial Pride and Prejudice,* C. A. Watts, 1946; *Some Human Oddities,* Home & Van Thal, 1947, University Books, 1962; *Very Peculiar People,* Rider, 1950, University Books, 1962; (with K. M. Goldney and T. H. Hall) *The Haunting of Borley Rectory,* Duckworth, 1956; (with J. Langdon-Davies) *The Unknown: Is It Nearer?,* New American Library, 1956; *The American Woman,* Duckworth, 1956, reprinted, Octagon Books, 1976; (with Hall) *Four Modern Ghosts,* Duckworth, 1958; *The Critics' Dilemma,* privately printed, 1966; (editor with others, and contributor) *Abnormal Hypnotic Phenomena,* 4 volumes, Churchill, 1967-68. Contributor to British and foreign journals.

SIDELIGHTS: E. J. Dingwall has established an international reputation as one of the most experienced psychical investigators of modern times, having studied the phenomena of such famous mediums as "Eva C.," Rudi and Willi Schneider, Stephan Ossowiecki, and "Margery" (Crandon). He is also noted for his comprehensive knowledge of the history and literature of psychic phenomena and parapsychology, as well as some of the more bizarre and out-of-the-way aspects of the human personality.

AVOCATIONAL INTERESTS: Traveling by car, bibliography.

BIOGRAPHICAL/CRITICAL SOURCES: *Times Literary Supplement,* February 8, 1957; *New York Times,* March 10, 1957; *New York Herald Tribune Book Review,* May 26, 1957.

DIRKSEN, Louella Carver 1899-1979

OBITUARY NOTICE: Born in 1899 in Pekin, Ill.; died of cancer, July 18, 1979, in Washington, D.C. Widow of the late Senator Everett M. Dirksen, she was an important part of her husband's political campaigns and held several civic and charitable posts. President Richard Nixon appointed her to the President's Commission on Aging, and in recent years she worked as a fund raiser for the Everett McKinley Dirksen Memorial Library in Pekin, Ill. She wrote, with N. L. Browning, *The Honorable Mr. Marigold: My Life With Everett Dirksen.* Obituaries and other sources: Louella Dirksen and N. L. Browning, *The Honorable Mr. Marigold: My Life With Everett Dirksen,* Doubleday, 1972; *Washington Post,* July 19, 1979.

* * *

DITTMER, Lowell 1941-

PERSONAL: Born October 12, 1941, in Greenville, N.C.; son of Alma L. (a professor) and Veda Faye (a teacher; maiden name, Kartchner) Dittmer; married Helen Roth Bergman (a history teacher); children: Mark Jason. *Education:* Utah State University, B.A., 1965; University of Chicago, M.A., 1967, Ph.D., 1971. *Home:* 5743 Snake Rd., Oakland, Calif. 94611. *Office:* Center for Chinese Studies, University of California, 210 Barrows, Berkeley, Calif. 94720.

CAREER: State University of New York at Buffalo, assistant professor of political science, 1972-78; University of California, Berkeley, associate professor of political science, 1978—, co-director of Center for Chinese Studies, 1978—. Visiting assistant professor at University of Michigan, 1977-78. *Military service:* U.S. Army, 1970-71; became captain.

WRITINGS: Lin Shao-ch'i and the Chinese Cultural Revolution, University of California Press, 1974; *Governments and Leaders,* Houghton, 1977. Contributor to political science and Chinese studies journals.

* * *

DIXON, Stephen 1936-

PERSONAL: Born June 6, 1936, in New York, N.Y. *Education:* City College of New York (now of the City University of New York), B.A., 1958. *Residence:* New York, N.Y. *Agent:* Felicia Eth, Writers House, Inc., 21 West 26th St., New York, N.Y. 10010.

CAREER: Writer. Also worked as fiction consultant. *Awards, honors:* O. Henry Award for "Mac in Love" and Pushcart Prize, both 1977.

WRITINGS: No Relief (stories) Street Fiction Press, 1976; *Work* (novel), Street Fiction Press, 1977; *Too Late* (novel), Harper, 1978; *Quite Contrary* (interrelated stories), Harper, 1979. Work anthologized in *Making a Break,* Latitudes Press, 1975. Contributor of stories to periodicals, including *Harper's, Viva, Playboy, Paris Review, American Review, Atlantic,* and *Pequod.*

SIDELIGHTS: Dixon's story collections, *No Relief* and *Quite Contrary,* deal specifically with man-woman themes. Jon Etra praised the stories in *No Relief* as "supremely powerful" demonstrations of Dixon's "understanding of the will-o'-the-wisp forces driving man to and from woman, woman to and from man." In the story "Last May," for example, "need and loss tangle into desire" when a dying man's son and a dying woman's daughter begin a relationship during their waits at the hospital. The romance between the two fades, however, when their visits to the hospital are no longer necessary. The "soil" of their affair "was death," argued Thomas A. Stumpf of the *South Carolina Review.* "The apparent motivelessness of the characters in this story is a feature of all the other stories [in *No Relief*], all of which are about love. Love begins and ends mysteriously. It has its own, unknown, cycle and laws, and the characters are as puzzled by it as the readers. No one in the stories falls in or out of love willingly. It happens, as death happens, and they adjust to it as best they can. It is the characters more than the author who refuse, or are unable, to provide a structure."

Dixon's later book, *Quite Contrary,* is a collection of eleven interrelated stories on the "turbulent" relationship between Newt and Mary. Continually arguing, separating, and getting back together, Newt and Mary in the meantime tell their own stories. The paradox of the relationship is expressed by Mary, who at one point says, "if only we could see each other when we wanted to and have fun without getting so gripping and glum." As the stories progress, a *Kirkus Reviews* critic pointed out, "Dixon's theme becomes clear: love affairs are like fiction—stories that are added to, rubbed out, obsessively charged, matters of chosen order and nuance and correction."

In his second novel, *Too Late,* Dixon takes the story of a separated couple and turns it into an indictment of American cities. The novel begins when Donna leaves a movie theatre because she feels the picture is too violent. Art, the man she lives with, decides to stay for the remainder of the picture, expecting to see Donna when he returns home. He doesn't. While others believe she has simply skipped town, Art is convinced she is the victim of foul play. He spends the rest of the novel looking for her, but finds the city indifferent, if not hostile, to his efforts. In the process, he becomes entangled in some comically bizarre situations which only a city could foster. Alan Cheuse cited a few such instances, as when Art "finds himself in the middle of a brawl between an irate customer and a harassed counterman in the bus-terminal at Walgreens, or another in which he attempts to bargain for his valuables with the thief who has just burgled his apartment and become stuck inside the building's dumbwaiter." Jerome Klinkowitz, too, appreciated this "mad spectacle," and saw *Too Late* as evidence that Dixon "is fast becoming the foremost chronicler of life in our cities, especially on the deeper level of our souls. He is to present-day New York and Chicago as Franz Kafka was to turn-of-the-century Vienna and Prague."

BIOGRAPHICAL/CRITICAL SOURCES: Soho Weekly News, December 2, 1976; *New York Times Book Review,* August 31, 1977, May 7, 1978; *Chicago Sun Times,* June 4, 1978; *The South Carolina Review,* November, 1978; *Kirkus Reviews,* May 1, 1979; *New York Times,* June 9, 1979; *Chicago Tribune Book World,* July 15, 1979.

* * *

DODGE, Marshall 1935-

PERSONAL: Born December 17, 1935, in New York, N.Y.; son of Marshall J., Jr. (a fund raiser) and Mary (a painter; maiden name, Reed) Dodge. *Education:* Yale University, B.A., 1957, M.A., 1959. *Home:* 56 Clifford St., Portland, Maine 04102.

CAREER: Bert and I Corp., Ipswich, Mass., vice-president, 1959-75; writer. Founder of Maine Festival. *Member:* Yale Club.

WRITINGS: Frost, You Say (photo essay), Chatham Press, 1972; *Bert and I and Other Stories From Down East,* Bert and I Corp., 1980.

WORK IN PROGRESS: The Architecture of Philosophy.

SIDELIGHTS: Dodge writes: "My first love in philosophy. I have been working on *The Architecture of Philosophy* for twenty years. It is intended to show the person who couldn't care less about philosophy the usefulness and beauty of philosophy."

* * *

DOEBLER, John (Willard) 1932-

PERSONAL: Born February 9, 1932, in New York, N.Y.; son of Belden Prior (a banker) and Margaret (Dressler) Doebler; married Bettie Anne Young (a professor), September 1, 1954; children: Ruthanne, Mark Belden. *Education:* Duke University, B.A., 1954; University of Wisconsin, M.A., 1955, Ph.D., 1961. *Religion:* Episcopalian. *Home:* 6102 East Calle Del Norte, Scottsdale, Ariz. 85251. *Office:* Department of English, Arizona State University, Tempe, Ariz. 85281.

CAREER: Northwestern University, Evanston, Ill., instructor, 1959-61; Dickinson College, Carlisle, Pa., assistant professor, 1961-65, associate professor of English, 1965-70; Arizona State University, Tempe, Arizona, associate professor, 1970-72, professor of English, 1972—. *Member:* Modern Language Association, Renaissance Society of America, Friends of the Folger Library. *Awards, honors:* Fellowships from Folger Shakespeare Library, 1966, Southeastern Institute of Medieval and Renaissance Studies, 1975, and National Endowment for the Humanities, 1978.

WRITINGS: (Editor) Francis Beaumont, *The Knight of the Burning Pestle* (comedy), University of Nebraska Press, 1967; *Shakespeare's Speaking Pictures* (scholarly), University of New Mexico Press, 1974. Contributor to journals, including *Shakespeare Survey, Shakespeare Quarterly,* and *Journal of European Studies.*

WORK IN PROGRESS: The Court of Venus: Neoplatonic Iconography in the Poems of Shakespeare.

SIDELIGHTS: Doebler told *CA:* "My major contribution to the field of Shakespearean studies is my book on iconography in the plays: *Shakespeare's Speaking Pictures.* Since its appearance in 1974 it has been reviewed by all the major Shakespeare journals and yearbooks and in a number of other journals devoted to scholarship in the general field of English. The importance of the book is well summarized in a review written for *Shakespeare Studies:* 'One comes to John Doebler's book aware that a comprehensive analysis of Shakespeare's relationship to the visual is long overdue. . . . John Doebler argues articulately and persuasively for the validity of iconographic studies of the plays. "Shakespeare lived," he writes, "in a world saturated with visual tropes conveyed by paintings, stained-glass windows, tapestries, household objects, and even armor, as well as by widely distributed books and graphics. Thread, printer's ink, and paint were the media for an enormously rich storehouse of conventional motifs, emblems, and impresas. . . ." Doebler's excellent bibliography, comprising more than three hundred entries, reveals the extensiveness of recent critical interest in the relationship between Shakespeare's works and the visual arts, as well as the rich reserve of primary materials available to scholars who believe, with Doebler, that "Art can clearly draw us back into the frame of Renaissance culture, and in a way at least as closely related to Shakespeare's genius as political theory or natural history."'

"Not all evaluation of the book has been this favorable. In a way, the book was published both ten years too late and ten years too early. Shakespearean studies are inclined to go through twenty year phases alternating scholarship and criticism, and this scholarly book was published directly in the middle of a critical phase. Some critics have, therefore, complained about the abundance of its documentation. The reviewer for the *Shakespeare Quarterly,* for instance, objected to the amount of evidence used to support the introductory chapter as 'forty-eight notes running to nearly six pages of reduced type. A good deal of this annotation is unfocused . . . , with strict accounts of scholarly debt packed in alongside of brief discussions of recent trends in scholarship and surveys of the material available to interested students of the subject.' The way in which this scholarly technique makes the introduction itself all the more accessible to the less specialized reader is ignored by the reviewer.

"*Shakespeare's Speaking Pictures* will probably survive the intellectual warfare. . . . Most readers seem to feel that the book, while less than perfect, partly because of its ambition, has a reasonable number of genuine contributions to make to its field. The influential *Goldentree Bibliography for Shakespeare* (1978) has cited the book as 'nearly indispensable.'"

BIOGRAPHICAL/CRITICAL SOURCES: Shakespeare Studies, Volume 10, 1977; *Shakespeare Quarterly,* summer, 1977.

* * *

DONAHUE, Roy L(uther) 1908-

PERSONAL: Born November 3, 1908, in Ringgold, Tex.; son of Peter Jerome and Nellie Grace (Boicourt) Donahue. *Education:* Michigan State University, B.S., 1932; Cornell University, Ph.D., 1939. *Home and office address:* Lookout Acres, Route 1, Box 169, Forsyth, Mo. 65653.

CAREER: Michigan Department of Conservation, forest mapper and control chief, summers, 1927-33; Michigan State University, East Lansing, instructor in soil science, 1934-35; Mississippi State University, Mississippi State, research professor of forest soils and head of department of forestry, 1935-37; Texas A & M University, College Station, associate professor of agronomy, 1939-44, extension agronomist, 1945-52; University of New Hampshire, Durham, head of department of agronomy, 1952-56; Kansas State University, Manhattan, visiting professor of agronomy in Hyderabad, India, 1956-61; Ford Foundation, New Delhi, India, consultant on soils and fertilizers, 1961-66; Michigan State University, professor of soil science, 1966-72, professor emeritus, 1972—. Senior forester for U.S. Department of Commerce in Brazil, 1943; agronomy consultant for Koppers Co. in Greece, 1955; visiting professor at University of the Ryukyus, 1966-67; agronomist for Institute of Agricultural Research, Addis Ababa, Ethiopia, 1967-69; staff associate of Midwest Research Institute, 1973-75. Member of Ozark Trail Council; secretary of Taney County Clean Water Commission and Taney County Planning Commission; chairman of Community Services Committee.

MEMBER: International Society of Soil Science (life member), American Association for the Advancement of Science, American Association of Teacher Educators in Agriculture (honorary member), American Hiking Society, American Society of Agronomy, American Society for Horticultural Science, Society of American Foresters (senior member), Soil Science Society of America, Explorers Club, Indian Society of Agronomy (life member), Indian Society of Soil Science (life member), Soil Conservation Society of India (life member), Ozark Society, Texas Academy of Science (fellow), Sigma Xi, Alpha Zeta, Phi Kappa Phi, Xi Sigma Pi.

WRITINGS: The Story of the Soil, Extension Service, Texas A & M University, 1947; *Farm and Home Planning,* Extension Service, Texas A&M University, 1947; (with E. F. Evans) *Our South: Its Resources and Their Use* (juvenile), Steck, 1949; (with Lloyd E. Garland and Henry F. Adams) *Soils and Their Crop Adaptations in New Hampshire,* Agriculture Experiment Station, University of New Hampshire, 1956; *Our Soils and Their Management: An Introduction to Soil and Water Conservation,* Interstate Printers & Publishers, 1955, 4th edition (with Hunter Follett and Rodney Tulloch), 1977; (with Evans and L. I. Jones) *The Range and Pasture Book,* Prentice-Hall, 1956; (with Evans) *Exploring Agriculture,* Prentice-Hall, 1957, 5th edition (with Evans and James Christiansen), 1979; *Soils: An Introduction to Soils and Plant Growth,* Prentice-Hall, 1958, 4th edition (with Raymond W. Miller and John C. Shickluna), 1977; (with H. R. Arakeri, G. V. Chalam, and P. Satyanarayana) *Soil Management in India,* Asia Publishing House, 1959, 2nd edition, 1962.

(With L.S.S. Kumar, A. C. Aggarwala, and others) *Agriculture in India,* Volume I: *General,* Volume II: *Crops,* Volume III: *Animals,* Asia Publishing House, 1963; (with Gilbert R. Muhr, N. P. Datta, and others) *Soil Testing in India,* U.S. Agency for International Development, 1963, 2nd edition, 1965; (with R. V. Tamhane, D. P. Motiramani, and Y. P. Bali) *Soils: Their Chemistry and Fertility in Tropical Asia,* Prentice-Hall of India, 1964; *Estimates of Fertilizer Consumption in India, 1970-71,* Fertilizer Association of India, 1966; (with T. Chinzei, Kazuhiro Oya, and others) *Soil and Land-Use in the Ryukyu Islands* (bilingual English-Japanese edition), University of the Ryukyus, 1967; (with C. K. Kline, D.A.G. Green, and B. A. Stout) *Agricultural Mechanization in Equatorial Africa,* Lithocrafter, 1969; *Soils of Equatorial Africa and Their Relevance to Rational Agricultural Development,* Institute of International Agriculture, Michigan State University, 1970; *Ethiopia: Taxonomy, Cartography, and Ecology of Soils,* African Studies Center, Michigan State University, 1972; (with Hunter Follett and Larry Murphy) *Fertilizers, Soil Amendments, and Plant Nutrition,* Prentice-Hall, 1980; (with Frederick Troeh and Arthur Hobbs) *Soil and Water Conservation,* Prentice-Hall, 1980. Also author of *Soils of Texas,* 1948. Editor of *Farm Unit Demonstration News* and *Farm Unit Demonstration Notes,* 1945-52.

WORK IN PROGRESS: A book on soil and water management in India, with H. R. Arakeri, publication by Prentice-Hall of India expected in 1981.

SIDELIGHTS: Donahue's books have been published in Spanish, French, Hindi, and eleven other official languages of India, Turkish, and Japanese. "Until now my writings have been factual," Donahue commented. "However, at age seventy I feel bolder and am considering a book for everyone on 'If This Is Sunday, I'm Going to Church,' a characterization of the aging."

AVOCATIONAL INTERESTS: "Gardening, walking, backpacking, camping, leading wilderness walks, helping to build a permanent multipurpose community center and library, helping to restore Lake Taneycomo, helping to elect to office like-minded persons, and helping the garden club and the local town to beautify the area."

* * *

DONALD, Maxwell 1897-1978

OBITUARY NOTICE: Born July 20, 1897; died January 6, 1978. Educator, chemist, and writer. Donald was a professor of chemical engineering at the University of London. He worked at various jobs in the chemical field and won the Moulton and Osborne Reynolds Medals. His works include two books on the history of metallurgy, *Elizabethan Monopolies* and *Elizabethan Copper.* Obituaries and other sources: *Who's Who,* 126th edition, St. Martin's, 1974; *The Writer's Directory, 1976-78,* St. Martin's, 1976.

* * *

DONALDSON, Stephen R. 1947-
(Reed Stephens)

PERSONAL: Born May 13, 1947, in Cleveland, Ohio; son of James R. (a medical missionary) and Mary Ruth (a prosthetist; maiden name, Reeder) Donaldson; divorced. *Education:* College of Wooster, B.A., 1968; Kent State University, M.A., 1971. *Residence:* Albuquerque, N.M.

CAREER: Writer. *Awards, honors:* British Fantasy Society first prize for 1977-78, for *The Chronicles of Thomas Covenant the Unbeliever;* John W. Campbell Award for best new science fiction writer, 1978.

WRITINGS: The Chronicles of Thomas Covenant the Unbeliever (trilogy), Holt, 1977, Volume I: *Lord Foul's Bane,* Volume II: *The Illearth War,* Volume III: *The Power That Preserves;* (contributor) Judy-Lynn del Rey, editor, *Stellar #4,* Del Rey, 1978; (contributor) Terry Carr, editor, *Year's Finest Fantasy,* Berkley Books, 1979. Contributor to science fiction magazines.

WORK IN PROGRESS: The Second Chronicles of Thomas Covenant, Volume I: *The Wounded Land,* Volume II: *The One Tree,* for Del Rey; *The Man Who Killed His Brother,* under pseudonym Reed Stephens, for Ballantine.

SIDELIGHTS: Writing full time, Donaldson created *The Chronicles of Thomas Covenant the Unbeliever* in almost five years. The trilogy recalls other well-known fantasy and science fiction tales, as Ray Walters pointed out: the "Narnia" series by C. S. Lewis, Frank Herbert's "Dune" trilogy, and the currently popular "Middle-Earth" stories by J.R.R. Tolkien. Like these, Donaldson's chronicle "will certainly find a place on the small list of true classics in its specialized field," Joseph McLellan commented. In England, Donaldson has already been received as the next Tolkien.

Donaldson's protagonist, Thomas Convenant, is a writer who has contracted leprosy. Because of certain attributes possessed by Covenant, he is chosen by the Powers That Be to rescue another world, "The Land," from the clutches of the evil Lord Foul Bane. John Calvin Batchelor called Covenant "Donaldson's genius." McLellan wrote that the character is "believable not only because he shares our background and outlook but because he is such a flawed, diffident hero."

Although Batchelor reacted favorably to most of the trilogy, he found the ending unsatisfactory. As he put it, Covenant is offered a dubious reward for prevailing over evil: he must choose "either life as a leper on the real Earth, where [he] is a believer in himself; or life as an immortal hero in the seemingly unreal land, where [he] was always an unbeliever in everything."

Donaldson responded to such criticism: "Endings should not be taken out of context. Since Covenant's inner journey revolves around his leprosy, any ending which ignored the problems of a leper in the real world would be trivial. But Covenant's self-recognition as he returns to reality is squarely based on the resolution of his Unbelief in the Land. Confronting the Despiser, Covenant finds his answer in between the impossibility of believing the Land true and the impossibility of believing it false. In context, I consider this to be a valid and satisfying ending. Of course, it should go without saying that any serious moral resolution of an important human dilemma is open-ended (therefore unsatisfactory?) in some of its implications."

BIOGRAPHICAL/CRITICAL SOURCES: San Francisco Examiner, October 5, 1977; *Village Voice,* October 10, 1977; *Washington Post Book World,* November 25, 1977; *Montreal Star,* December 13, 1977; *Los Angeles Times,* January 29, 1978; *New York Times Book Review,* February 18, 1979.

* * *

DONOHUE, Mark 1937-1975

OBITUARY NOTICE—See index for *CA* sketch: Born March 18, 1937, in Orange, N.J.; died August 19, 1975, in Graz, Austria. Racing car driver and author of an autobiography, *The Unfair Advantage.* Winner of the Indianapolis 500 Race in 1972, Donohue died at the age of thirty-eight after crashing at the Austrian Grand Prix. Obituaries and other sources: *Publishers Weekly,* September 15, 1975; Mark Donohue, *The Unfair Advantage,* Dodd, 1975.

* * *

DONOVAN, James Britt 1916-1970

OBITUARY NOTICE—See index for *CA* sketch: Born February 29, 1916, in New York, N.Y.; died of a heart attack, January 19, 1970, in New York, N.Y. Lawyer, educator, and author. From 1945 to 1946 Donovan served as associate prosecutor at the principal Nuremberg trial. His most famous case, however, began in 1957, when he was appointed by the government to defend accused Soviet spy Rudolf Abel. Although his client was highly unpopular, Donovan launched a vigorous defense that earned the respect of many legal experts. Abel was found guilty, a conviction that was upheld by the Supreme Court. Later Donovan arranged the trade of Abel for U-2 pilot Francis Gary Powers. He also successfully negotiated with the Castro regime for the release of the Bay of Pigs prisoners and their families. Obituaries and other sources: *Current Biography,* Wilson, 1961, March, 1970; James Britt Donovan, *Strangers on a Bridge: The Case of Colonel Abel,* Atheneum, 1964; Donovan, *Challenges: Reflections of a Lawyer-at-Large,* Atheneum, 1967; *New York Times,* January 20, 1970; *Newsweek,* February 2, 1970; *Time,* February 2, 1970; *AB Bookman's Weekly,* February 2, 1970.

* * *

DORE, Ronald Philip 1925-

PERSONAL: Born February 1, 1925, in Bournemouth, England; son of Philip Brine and Elsie Constance Dore; married Nancy Macdonald, 1957; children: Sally, Jonathan. *Education:* School of Oriental and African Studies, London, B.A., 1947. *Home:* 157 Surrenden Rd., Brighton, East Sussex, England. *Office:* Institute of Development Studies, University of Sussex, Falmer, Brighton, Sussex BN1 9QX, England.

CAREER: University of London, School of Oriental and African Studies, London, England, lecturer in Japanese institutions, 1951-56; University of British Columbia, Vancouver, professor of Asian studies, 1956-60; University of London, School of Economics and Political Science, reader, 1961-65, professor of sociology, 1965-69; University of Sussex, Brighton, England, fellow of Institute of Development Studies, 1969—. *Member:* British Academy (fellow).

WRITINGS: City Life in Japan: A Study of a Tokyo Ward, Routledge & Kegan Paul, 1958, University of California Press, 1967; *Land Reform in Japan,* Oxford University Press, 1959; *Education in Tokugawa, Japan,* University of California Press, 1965; (editor) *Aspects of Social Change in Modern Japan,* Princeton University Press, 1967; *British Factory, Japanese Factory: The Origins of National Diversity in Industrial Relations,* University of California Press, 1973; *The Diploma Disease: Education, Qualification, and Development,* University of California Press, 1976; *Shinohata: A Portrait of a Japanese Village,* Pantheon, 1978.

WORK IN PROGRESS: Books on development theory, community development, and industrial relations in Mexico, Senegal, and Sri Lanka.

SIDELIGHTS: Dore writes: "My career has developed by a process of natural evolution. I learned Japanese during World War II and subsequently took a degree in Japanese language and literature. Through doctoral research on education in traditional Japan and its sociological aspects, I gradually drifted into sociology and study of the social changes in Japan in the last century." *Avocational interests:* Daydreaming.

* * *

DORO, Marion Elizabeth 1928-

PERSONAL: Born October 9, 1928, in Miami, Fla.; daughter of George and Alma (Carram) Doro. *Education:* Florida State University, B.A., 1951, M.A., 1952; University of Pennsylvania, Ph.D., 1959. *Office:* Department of Government, Connecticut College, New London, Conn. 06320.

CAREER: Johns Hopkins School of Advanced International Studies, Washington, D.C., research assistant, 1955-56; Wheaton College, Norton, Mass., instructor in political science, 1958-60; Connecticut College, New London, assistant professor, 1962-66, associate professor, 1966-71, professor of political science, 1971—, director of graduate studies, 1975—. Visiting lecturer at Makerere University, 1963-64, senior associate, 1971-72; senior associate at St. Antony's College, Oxford, 1977-78. *Member:* African Studies Association, American Political Science Association, American Association of University Professors, American Association of University Women, Society of Fellows of Radcliffe Institute, Northeastern Political Science Association (member of executive council, 1974-77), New England Political Science Association (member of executive council, 1973-76; head of status of women committee, 1972-75), Phi Beta Kappa, Phi Kappa Phi, Pi Sigma Alpha. *Awards, honors:* Ford Foundation fellow in Kenya and at Institute of Commonwealth Studies, London, 1960-62; grant from University of Chicago committee on international exchange of persons, 1963-64, for Uganda; Radcliffe scholar at Radcliffe Institute, 1968-69; American Philosophical Society grant, 1971-72, for East Africa; American Association of University Women founder's fellow, 1977-78, in England and Kenya.

WRITINGS: (Editor with Newell M. Stultz) *Governing in Black Africa: Perspectives on New States,* Prentice-Hall, 1970; (contributor) *Constitutions of the Countries of the World,* Oceana, 1973; *Rhodesia: A Bibliographic Essay, Themes, and Resources,* Connecticut College, 1973; (contributor) Y. Tandon and D. Chandarana, editors, *Horizons of African Diplomacy,* East African Literature Bureau, 1974. Contributor to *Collier's Yearbook.* Contributor of about fifty articles and reviews to African studies and law journals.

DORSETT, Danielle
See DANIELS, Dorothy

* * *

DOUGLAS, Helen Bee
See BEE, Helen L.

* * *

DOUGLAS, Mike 1925-

PERSONAL: Birth-given name, Michael Delaney Dowd, Jr.; born August 11, 1925, in Chicago, Ill.; son of Michael Delaney (a railway freight agent) and Gertrude (Smith) Dowd; married Genevieve Purnell, 1943; children: Michele and Christine (twins), Kelly Anne. *Education:* Attended Oklahoma City University. *Office:* Television City, 7800 Beverly Blvd., Los Angeles, Calif. 90036.

CAREER: WLS-Radio, Chicago, Ill., singer on "The Irish Hour" amateur program in the 1930's; *Seeandbee* Great Lakes cruise ship, based in Chicago, singer and master of ceremonies in the 1940's; WKY-Radio, Oklahoma City, Okla., singer in the 1940's; singer at supper clubs and on radio programs, Hollywood, Calif., 1945-52; made appearances on Kay Kyser's "Kollege of Musical Knowledge," Hollywood, 1950-52; WGN-Radio, Chicago, host of "Hi, Ladies" radio show and host of radio bingo show, in the 1950's; made appearances on National Broadcasting Co. (NBC-TV) television variety show, "Club 60," Chicago; singer in a piano bar in Calif.; Westinghouse Broadcasting Co., KYW-TV, Cleveland, Ohio, host of "The Mike Douglas Show," afternoon television program, 1961-65, show moved to Philadelphia, Pa., 1965-78, show moved to Hollywood, 1978—. Recording artist; guest personality on television programs. *Military service:* U.S. Navy, 1943-45, V-12 program at University of Wisconsin. *Awards, honors:* Received Emmy award for daytime programming from National Academy of Television Arts and Sciences, 1967, for "The Mike Douglas Show."

WRITINGS: (With Dan Morris) *The Mike Douglas Cookbook,* Funk, 1969; *Mike Douglas: My Story,* Putnam, 1978. Contributor to *Today's Health.*

SIDELIGHTS: "The Mike Douglas Show" is the longest running series on television, and in 1967 became the first syndicated production ever to win a Emmy. The ninety-minute afternoon variety show began in 1961 in Cleveland, Ohio, where it was shown locally. Guests were difficult to obtain since Cleveland is some distance from the usual show business centers and the program's budget allowed for only a minimal guest fee. In order to attract more guests, Douglas developed a co-host format where a well-known celebrity would stay on the show for one week. This was so successful that it has been retained for the past eighteen years.

As the show's following grew, Westinghouse Broadcasting Company began to air it on other stations it owned, and later the show was syndicated. With a move to Philadelphia in 1965 the program gained access to a variety of talents from the New York area. Guests were happy to appear on the show because of the widespread publicity it provided, even though the pay was still low for each appearance.

To facilitate Douglas's guest appearances throughout the country, the five weekly shows are taped in three days. Approximately forty copies of each are made and sent to stations which run them and pass them on to other subscribers. The show is now sold to nearly 130 stations in the United States and fifteen in Canada. This is three times the number of stations that subscribe to other successfully syndicated shows.

While the celebrities and co-hosts help to attract the audience, it is Mike Douglas who holds the show together. His simple charm, openness, and spontaneity are the mainstay of the show. He has engaged in pie-throwing, exercise sessions, cooking, singing, and playing polo in the streets, as well as entertaining serious questions with such notables as Malcolm X, Ralph Nader, and Governor Ronald Reagan.

The afternoon time slot for "The Mike Douglas Show" results in a largely female audience. Mike seems to have a special rapport with women, possibly because he is the only male in a family with his wife and three daughters. Men also enjoy the program, but usually admit to watching it only if they have been home sick from work. Douglas told Susan Forrest, "I must have the sickest male audience in television."

The same sensitivity and warmth that attracts audiences helps Douglas to produce good television interviews. His guests include everyone from actors and singers to authors, sociologists, and politicians. Mike claims his secret for an effective interview lies in finding the proper timing for each person and adapting to it.

Mike Douglas calls himself a "square." He does not smoke or drink and is a dedicated family man. Though the television audience has never seen Mike's wife, he and Gen have been happily married for thirty-six years, a remarkable feat in the show business industry. Douglas attributes their long marriage to the fact that the family has stayed together. Even when the girls were young, the whole family accompanied him on his appearances across the country. Gen uses their legal surname, Dowd, and insists on remaining a private person, refusing to appear on "The Mike Douglas Show." She supports Mike's career in other ways, by traveling with him and helping with his business and creative needs.

The Mike Douglas Cookbook contains various ethnic recipes prepared by Douglas and his guests on "The Mike Douglas Show." Friede Gruenrock declared, "So many of these recipes are well known elsewhere that to pass them off as the invention of the various celebrities, male or female, might be considered plagiaristic."

Douglas's autobiography, *My Story,* describes his adventures in show business and contains anecdotes about personalities he has known. "His numerous stories . . . are extremely funny in the vitality of their telling," assessed Tony Bednarczyk. "I recommend it highly to anyone who likes to smile from the heart and who enjoys reading about a true hometown boy who made good."

Mike Douglas has produced four full-length record albums. His most popular song was "The Men in My Little Girl's Life," which was released as a single.

BIOGRAPHICAL/CRITICAL SOURCES: Look, August 9, 1966; *Newsweek,* June 19, 1967; *Business Week,* July 22, 1967; *Time,* October 6, 1967; *Ladies' Home Journal,* March, 1968, September, 1978; *Good Housekeeping,* September, 1969, May, 1973, March, 1975, July, 1978; *Best Sellers,* November 15, 1969, September, 1978; *Saturday Evening Post,* March, 1974; *Ft. Lauderdale News,* December 18, 1974; *Biography News,* Gale, January/February, 1975; Harry Harris, *Mike Douglas,* Award Books, 1976.*

* * *

DOWDEY, Landon Gerald 1923-

PERSONAL: Born August 2, 1923, in Washington, D.C.;

son of Landon Ashton and Dorothy (Fogarty) Dowdey; married Mary Shinners, June 6, 1947; children: Patrick Francis, Martin Joseph, Kathleen. *Education:* University of Pennsylvania, B.S., 1946; Georgetown University, J.D., 1948. *Home:* 3731 Warren St. N.W., Washington, D.C. 20016. *Office:* 1629 K St. N.W., Washington, D.C. 20006.

CAREER: Lawyer in private practice, 1948-59; head of law firms, Dowdey & Bartow, 1960-67, Dowdey, Levy & Cohen, 1968-73, and Dowdey & Urbina, Washington, D.C., 1973—. *Member:* American Civil Liberties Union, American Bar Association, National Lawyers Guild, Bar Association of the District of Columbia.

WRITINGS Religion Against Poverty, Citizens for Educational Freedom, 1964; (compiler) *Journey to Freedom: A Casebook With Music,* Swallow, 1969; (with Julius Hobson) *The Damned Information,* Washington Institute for Quality Education, 1970; (with Ramsey Clark, Harry Kalvin, Jr., and editors of Swallow Press) *Contempt,* Swallow, 1970.

AVOCATIONAL INTERESTS: Painting, writing, poetry, and playing music.*

* * *

DOWER, Penn
See PENDOWER, Jacques

* * *

DRAGNICH, Alex N. 1912-

PERSONAL: Born February 22, 1912, in Republic, Wash.; son of Nick D. (a farmer) and Stella (Knezevich) Dragnich; married Adele Jonas (a nurse), March 25, 1937; children: Alix Sandra Dragnich Liebman, Paul Nicholas, George Stephen. *Education:* Attended Linfield College, 1933-35; University of Washington, Seattle, B.A., 1938; University of California, M.A., 1939, Ph.D., 1945. *Politics:* Democrat. *Religion:* Protestant. *Residence:* Nashville, Tenn. *Office:* Department of Political Science, Vanderbilt University, Nashville, Tenn. 37235.

CAREER: U.S. Department of Justice, Washington, D.C., senior propaganda analyst, 1942-44; Office of Strategic Services, Washington, D.C., research analyst, 1944-45; Western Reserve University (now Case Western Reserve University), Cleveland, Ohio, assistant professor of political science, 1945-47; American Embassy, Belgrade, Yugoslavia, cultural attache and public affairs officer, 1947-50; Vanderbilt University, Nashville, Tenn., associate professor, 1950-52, professor of political science, 1952-78, professor emeritus, 1978—, head of department, 1965-69. Chester W. Nimitz Professor of Social and Political Philosophy at Naval War College, 1959-60. Consultant to U.S. Department of Defense.

MEMBER: American Political Science Association (member of council, 1971-73), American Association for the Advancement of Slavic Studies, American Association of University Professors, Southern Political Science Association (vice-president, 1972-73; president, 1973-74), Phi Beta Kappa. *Awards, honors:* Social Science Research Council fellow, 1952-53; Ford Foundation fellow at Harvard University, 1955-56.

WRITINGS: (With Robert J. Kerner and others) *Yugoslavia,* University of California Press, 1949; *Tito's Promised Land,* Rutgers University Press, 1954; (with Stephen Kertesz and others) *The Fate of East Central Europe,* University of Notre Dame Press, 1956; *Major European Governments,* Dorsey, 1961, 5th edition, 1978; (with John C. Wahlke and others) *Government and Politics,* Random House, 1966, revised edition, 1971; (contributor) Tinsley E. Yarbrough, John P. East, and Sandra Hough, editors, *Politics '73: Minorities in Politics,* East Carolina University Publications, 1973; *Serbia, Nikola Pasic, and Yugoslavia,* Rutgers University Press, 1974; *The Development of Parliamentary Government in Serbia,* Columbia University Press, 1978. Contributor of about fifteen articles to history and political science journals, and *New Leader.*

WORK IN PROGRESS: The First Yugoslavia: Search for a Viable Political System.

SIDELIGHTS: Dragnich told *CA:* "My writing has been closely related to my teaching. I discovered that one never learns a subject as well as when he is forced to put it on paper, to organize it into chapters, sections, paragraphs, and even sentences. Consequently, I am convinced that my writing improved my teaching. I hope that my textbooks have helped students who read them.

"My principal advice to aspiring writers: write in clear and understandable prose. Avoid vagueness and excess verbiage that does not tell the reader much.

"My first book, *Tito's Promised Land,* was motivated by my desire to spell out how a communist system actually functions. When I returned from my service in the American Embassy in Belgrade, having observed the system in operation, my fondest hope was that somehow I could get those students together whom I had taught at Western Reserve in my first two years of teaching, and to tell them what a lot of nonsense I had taught them about communist systems.

"A writer, while striving to be objective, need not be ashamed of his convictions. For example, I have been a supporter of a free society and against dictatorships of every type. My one time faith in government intervention to redress various injustices has waned considerably. Democracy is a fragile system, and there is a danger that we will demand too much of it. This is especially true now when so many groups are demanding compensation for past or present injustices and even favors for themselves, which serve to undermine our common purposes and goals.

"So many of our common domestic problems—crime, drugs, pornography, etc.—demand attention. If our democratic institutions are unable to deal with them, there will be voices raised in favor of a temporary dictatorship of one type or another, which may result in an end to our way of life as we have known it. The challenge is there; we ignore it at our peril."

* * *

DRAGO, Harry Sinclair 1888-1979
(Will Ermine, Bliss Lomax)

OBITUARY NOTICE: Born March 20, 1888, in Toledo, Ohio; died October 25, 1979, in White Plains, N.Y. Author of more than one hundred western novels, some under the pseudonyms Will Ermine and Bliss Lomax, and historian of the Old West. Drago began his writing career as a Sunday columnist for the *Toledo Bee,* but quit journalism after the publication of his first book, *Out of the Silent North.* After five years as a scriptwriter in Hollywood, where he worked for silent screen stars Tom Mix, Buck Jones, and Ken Maynard, Drago moved to New York in 1933. He became a prolific writer in the following years, turning out one thousand words a day, an average of three books a year, and in one case, wrote a sixty thousand-word novel, *Oh, Susannah,* in just eleven days. He once told a reporter that he used the

Ermine and Lomax pen names because he did not want so many books signed Drago. His fiction included *Whispering Sage, Buckskin Affair, Fenced Off,* and *Decision at Broken Butte.* Among his histories of the Old West are *The Great American Cattle Trails, Road Agents and Train Robbers,* and *The Great Range Wars,* for which he received the Western Heritage Award for the most outstanding western nonfiction book of 1970. Obituaries and other sources: *New York Times,* October 27, 1979; *Publishers Weekly,* November 12, 1979.

* * *

DRAITSER, Emil 1937-
(Emil Abramov)

PERSONAL: Born December 18, 1937, in Odessa, Soviet Union; came to United States in 1974, naturalized citizen, 1979; son of Abram (a painter) and Soybel (Benderskaya) Draitser; married Natasha Meliushkina (an electronic technician), January 7, 1972; children: Maxim. *Education:* Odessa Polytechnic Institute, B.S., 1960; attended Moscow Publishing Institute, 1966-78; Moscow Institute of Journalism, M.A. (journalism), 1974; University of California, Los Angeles, M.A. (Russian literature), 1978. *Residence:* Los Angeles, Calif. *Office:* Department of Slavic Languages and Literatures, University of California, 405 Hilgard Ave., Los Angeles, Calif. 90024.

CAREER: Electrical Assembling Management, Kiev, Soviet Union, electrical engineer, 1960-66; Nedra (publishing house), Moscow, Soviet Union, editor, 1966-74; University of California, Los Angeles, lecturer in Russian, 1976—. Russian-language translator; conductor of lecture tours. *Member:* American Association of Teachers of Slavic and East European Languages (local vice-president), Book Publicists of Southern California. *Awards, honors:* Prize from *The Star* (youth newspaper), 1972, for humor stories on the All-Union Contest in Odessa.

WRITINGS: Contemporary Soviet Satire, University of California, 1976; (editor) *Forbidden Laughter,* Almanac, 1978, Russian edition published as *Nedozvolennyj Smech,* 1978, bilingual edition, 1978, revised edition, 1979; *Satire in a Totalitarian Country,* Rand Corporation, 1980. Writer for Russian television and radio programs; script writer for Mosfilm Studios, Moscow. Contributor of articles and stories to Russian magazines and newspapers, all under pseudonym Emil Abramov, and to American newspapers.

WORK IN PROGRESS: The Tradition of Russian Satire, on Saltykov-Shehedrin, publication by University of California expected in 1981; a collection of satirical stories for Almanac Press.

SIDELIGHTS: Draitser told *CA:* "I started my writing career in Russia being pretty naive. I thought that, besides receiving pleasure from seeing your work in print, you can really improve the quality of life by attacking the vices of society. It took me some time to realize that I had been used by authorities. Since the Soviet press is strictly guided, as well as severely controlled, there was no chance to express your *own* opinion or even use an artistic method you prefer. I faced the option of either ceasing my writing or emigrating: I chose the latter.

"It is my strong belief that humor is the most powerful communication tool and that humor will help the American public better understand Russia and Russians. This was the motivation for *Forbidden Laughter.*"

Draitser's travels include Austria and Italy.

AVOCATIONAL INTERESTS: Chess.

BIOGRAPHICAL/CRITICAL SOURCES: Sun-Telegram, November 24, 1975; *Daily Bruin,* January 12, 1979.

* * *

DRAKE, Kimbal
See GALLAGHER, Rachel

* * *

DRAPER, James T(homas), Jr. 1935-

PERSONAL: Born October 10, 1935, in Hartford, Ark.; son of James T. (a minister) and Lois (Keeling) Draper; married Carol Ann Floyd, July 14, 1956; children: Randy, Bailey, Terri. *Education:* Baylor University, B.A., 1958; Southwestern Baptist Theological Seminary, B.D., 1961, M.Div., 1973. *Office:* First Baptist Church, Euless, Tex. 76039.

CAREER: Ordained Southern Baptist minister, 1956; pastor of Baptist churches in Bryan, Tex., 1956-58, Iredell, Tex., 1959-61, Tyler, Tex., 1961-62, San Antonio, Tex., 1961-65, Kansas City, Mo., 1965-70, and Del City, Okla., 1970-73; associate pastor of Baptist church in Dallas, Tex., 1973-75; First Baptist Church, Euless, Tex., pastor, 1975—. Speaker at conventions and lay assemblies. Member of board of trustees of Baylor University and Baylor Medical Center. *Member:* Fellowship of Christian Athletes. *Awards, honors:* D.D. from Howard Payne University, 1975.

WRITINGS: The Church Christ Approves, Broadman, 1974; *Say, Neighbor, Your House Is on Fire,* Crescendo Book, 1975; *Hebrews: The Life That Pleases God,* Tyndale, 1976; *Proverbs: The Secret of Beautiful Living,* Tyndale, 1977; *Titus: Patterns for Church Living,* Tyndale, 1978; *I and II Thessalonians: The Hope of a Waiting Church,* Tyndale, 1979; *Foundations of Biblical Faith,* Broadman, 1979.

WORK IN PROGRESS: Books on Philippians, Jonah, James, and Ecclesiastes for Tyndale.

AVOCATIONAL INTERESTS: Basketball, golf, racquetball.

* * *

DREBINGER, John 1891(?)-1979

OBITUARY NOTICE: Born c. 1891; died October 22, 1979, in Greensboro, N.C. Journalist who, after forty years with the *New York Times,* was regarded as the dean of the nation's baseball writers. "He could give a completely accurate report of a game without making it sound like Armageddon," according to *Times* sports columnist Red Smith. By Drebinger's own estimate, he traveled 1.23 million miles covering the Yankees, Giants, and Dodgers, saw about six thousand baseball games, and "ate tons of hot dogs." The sports writer, though, might have been a concert pianist but for a thumb wound he suffered as a youngster while sharpening ice skates. And though he was friends with players like Babe Ruth and Casey Stengel, Drebinger considered his most exciting experience to have been an ill-fated, cross-country, covered-wagon trip he made while a reporter for the *Staten Island Advance.* Upon his death, a colleague remarked, "I think in his time he wrote the purest and most intelligent baseball stories in the country." Obituaries and other sources: *New York Times,* October 24, 1979.

* * *

DREUX, William B(ehan) 1911-

PERSONAL: Born March 18, 1911, in Paris, France; came to the United States in 1919, naturalized citizen, 1928; son of

Andre A. (an archivist) and Catherine (Behan) Dreux; married Nancy Reeves, October 29, 1936. *Education:* University of Notre Dame, B.A., 1929; graduate study at Northwestern University, 1933-35; Tulane University, LL.B., 1936. *Politics:* Democrat. *Religion:* Roman Catholic. *Home:* 529 Woodvine, Metairie, La. 70005. *Office:* 505 Hibernia Bank Building, New Orleans, La. 70112.

CAREER: Attorney in New Orleans, La., 1937—. President of Bureau of Governmental Research, 1958-59; chairperson of Arts and Letters Council at University of Notre Dame, 1965-66. *Military service:* U.S. Army, Infantry, paratrooper, 1942-46; became captain; received Legion of Honor, Croix de Guerre, Bronze Star, mentioned in dispatches. *Member:* Special Forces Club (England).

WRITINGS: *No Bridges Blown* (memoirs), University of Notre Dame Press, 1971.

WORK IN PROGRESS: A novel about agents in Austria, publication expected in 1981.

SIDELIGHTS: Dreux comments: "I speak French fluently and have traveled there numerous times. I jumped into France as a member of a three-man 'jedburgh' team during World War II and what I experienced then gave me the idea for my book. Before jumping, I had been a lumberjack and a hobo in the summer of 1929, and I feel that those experiences helped me to escape the Gestapo at times when it was 'third down and long yardage.'"

* * *

DROWATZKY, John N(elson) 1936-

PERSONAL: Born April 11, 1936, in Wichita, Kan.; son of Mark Leonard (a florist) and Minnie (a teacher; maiden name, Nelson) Drowatzky; married Linnea Swanson, May 27, 1962; children: Kara, Katrina. *Education:* University of Kansas, B.S., 1957; graduate study at University of Wichita and Texas Western College (now University of Texas, El Paso); University of Oregon, M.S., 1962, D.Ed., 1965; University of Toledo, J.D., 1979. *Religion:* Lutheran. *Home:* 3332 Brantford Rd., Toledo, Ohio 43606. *Office:* Department of Exercise Science and Physical Education, University of Toledo, Toledo, Ohio 43606.

CAREER: Junior high school teacher and athletic coach in Wichita, Kan., 1961-62; Institute of Logopedics, Wichita, director of physical education for brain-injured children, 1962-63; University of Toledo, Toledo, Ohio, assistant professor, 1965-68, associate professor, 1968-71, professor of exercise science and physical education, 1971—, head of department, 1972-76, director of Combined Exercise Physiology and Motor Learning Research Laboratories, 1965-70, and Motor Learning Research Laboratory, 1970-73. Adjunct professor at University of Oregon, 1976. Conductor of workshops; lecturer and consultant. *Military service:* U.S. Army, missile systems instructor, 1958-60; became first lieutenant.

MEMBER: International Society of Sports Psychology, North American Society for the Psychology of Sport and Physical Activity (charter member), American Association for Health, Physical Education and Recreation (member of research council; chairperson of research section, 1970-71), National College Physical Education Association for Men, American Bar Association, Ohio Association for Health, Physical Education and Recreation, American Trauma Association of Northwest Ohio, Lucas County Association for Mentally Retarded Children, Phi Epsilon Kappa, Phi Delta Kappa. *Awards, honors:* Certificate of recognition from Lucas County Association for Mentally Retarded Children, 1970; Corpus Juris Secundum Award for significant legal scholarship.

WRITINGS: (contributor) Charles A. Bucher and Myra Goldman, editors, *Dimensions of Physical Education*, Mosby, 1969; (editor) *Abstracts of Research Papers, 1970: AAHPER Convention*, American Association for Health, Physical Education and Recreation, 1970; *Physical Education for the Mentally Retarded*, Lea & Febiger, 1971; *Motor Learning: Theory and Principles*, Burgess, 1975, 2nd edition, 1980. Contributor to *Encyclopedia of Sports Medicine*. Contributor of about thirty articles to law and education journals.

WORK IN PROGRESS: Research on education and law.

SIDELIGHTS: Drowatzky told *CA:* "Down deep inside I am a perpetual student; my writing, professional life and academic pursuits are simply the overt expression of this state. My interest in law was one of those unfulfilled 'childhood' dreams until recently. Since beginning my studies in law I have become more and more aware of its value and impact on all professions. It is my plan to use my legal training, as well as my other training, to teach others how to prevent and solve problems rather than become adversaries. The new law relating to education for the handicapped is an attempt to provide this opportunity for all. Today all of us, educators and parents alike, must guard against overreaction and strive to make sure the purpose of the law is achieved. I feel my next book will deal with some aspect of law and education and be written for the educator's use."

* * *

DRYDEN, Edgar A. 1937-

PERSONAL: Born June 28, 1937, in Salisbury, Md.; married wife, Mary N. (a field director for Girl Scouts of America), August 22, 1959; children: Jonathan, Stephanie, Nathan. *Education:* Washington College, Chestertown, Md., B.A., 1959; University of Rhode Island, M.A., 1961; Johns Hopkins University, Ph.D., 1965. *Residence:* Tucson, Ariz. *Office:* Department of English, University of Arizona, Tucson, Ariz. 85721.

CAREER: Johns Hopkins University, Baltimore, Md., assistant professor of English, 1965-67; State University of New York at Buffalo, 1967-78, began as assistant professor, became professor of English; University of Arizona, Tucson, professor of English and head of department, 1978—. *Member:* Modern Language Association of America.

WRITINGS: *Melville's Thematics of Form*, Johns Hopkins Press, 1968; *Nathaniel Hawthorne: The Poetics of Enchantment*, Cornell University Press, 1977.

WORK IN PROGRESS: A book on the thematics of reading in the American novel.

* * *

DRYSDALE, Frank R(eiff) 1943-

PERSONAL: Born August 16, 1943, in Long Beach, Calif.; son of Myron William (an electrician) and Sylvia (Williams) Drysdale. *Education:* California State Polytechnic University, B.S., 1965; Utah State University, M.S., 1968; University of California, Davis, Ph.D., 1971. *Residence:* Martinez, Calif.

CAREER: Foundation for the Junior Blind, Los Angeles, Calif., nature study instructor, 1963-64; Crippled Children's Society of Los Angeles, Los Angeles, nature study instructor, 1964; Los Angeles State and County Arboretum, Arcadia, Calif., research assistant in genetics, 1965-66; Ohio University, Athens, visiting assistant professor of botany, 1971-73; Brookhaven National Laboratory, National Center for the Analysis of Energy Systems, Upton, N.Y., environmental scientist in Biomedical and Environmental Assessment Division, 1974-76; California Energy Resources Conservation and Development Commission, Sacramento, staff energy resources specialist, 1976-78; independent consulting ecologist in Martinez, Calif., 1978—. Consultant to National Academy of Sciences. *Member:* American Association for the Advancement of Science, Ecological Society of America, Sigma Xi.

WRITINGS: (With M. G. Barbour, R. B. Craig, and M. Ghiselin) *Coastal Ecology: Bodega Head,* University of California Press, 1973; (with C. E. Calef) *The Energetics of the United States of America: An Atlas,* Brookhaven National Laboratory, 1976, 2nd edition, 1977. Contributor to botany journals.

WORK IN PROGRESS: Research on the impact of the U.S. energy system on the environment and human health; a history of industrialization along the Carquinez Straits.

SIDELIGHTS: Drysdale writes: "The past year has been filled with travel, especially an extended overland trip throughout South America, and several excursions along the Pacific coast of North America."

* * *

DUBOV, Paul ?-1979

OBITUARY NOTICE: Died of cancer, September 20, 1979, in Encino, Calif. Author who with his wife, Gwen Bagni, collaborated on the novel *With Six You Get Eggroll,* based on the story of their marriage and adoption of each other's children. The couple later adapted their novel for motion pictures, released by National General Pictures in 1968 under the same title. In 1979, NBC-TV aired the Dubov-Bagni screenplay "Backstairs at the White House," an eight-hour dramatic series based on the lives of White House maids Lillian Rogers Parks and her mother, Maggie Rogers. Obituaries and other sources: *New York Times,* September 22, 1979.

* * *

DUNAWAY, John M(arson) 1945-

PERSONAL: Born June 24, 1945, in Washington, Ga.; son of Marson Gale, Jr. (an attorney) and Katey Frances (Matteson) Dunaway; married Patricia Annette Tompkins (a teacher), August 7, 1966; children: Michael John, Jennifer Brooks. *Education:* Emory University, B.A., 1967; Duke University, M.A., 1971, Ph.D., 1972. *Religion:* Methodist. *Home:* 2411 Old Holton Rd., Macon, Ga. 31204. *Office:* Department of Modern Foreign Languages, Mercer University, Box G, Macon, Ga. 31207.

CAREER: Mercer University, Macon, Ga., assistant professor, 1972-77, associate professor of French, 1977—, head of department, 1977-79. *Military service:* Georgia and North Carolina National Guard, 1968-74. *Member:* American Association of Teachers of French (state vice-president, 1974-75; president, 1975-77), South Atlantic Modern Language Association, Foreign Language Association of Georgia. *Awards, honors:* Don Quixote Award from Valdosta State College, 1976.

WRITINGS: Jacques Maritain, Twayne, 1978; *The Metamorphoses of the Self: The Mystic, the Sensualist, and the Artist in the Works of Julien Green,* University Press of Kentucky, 1978.

WORK IN PROGRESS: Simone Weil, publication by Twayne expected in 1982.

SIDELIGHTS: Dunaway writes: "As a Christian, I have a sense of vocation that informs my understanding of my roles of writer and teacher. My experiences of reading, study, and intellectual exchange have had a deeply felt impact on my personal spiritual development, and my scholarly interests are thus focused largely on writers whose quest for the proper relationship of art, faith, and reason may serve as models. I believe that the struggle to express one's self is an adventure in self-discovery that is not easily equalled by other means."

* * *

DUNNELL, Robert C(hester) 1942-

PERSONAL: Born December 4, 1942, in Wheeling, W.Va.; son of Arthur R. and Kathryn (McCarter) Dunnell; married Mary Davidson, 1966. *Education:* University of Kentucky, B.A., 1964; Yale University, Ph.D., 1967. *Office:* Department of Anthropology, University of Washington, Seattle, Wash. 98195.

CAREER: Yale University, New Haven, Conn., curatorial assistant at Peabody Museum, 1966-67; University of Washington, Seattle, assistant professor, 1967-71, associate professor, 1971-74, professor of anthropology, 1974—, head of department, 1973—. Adjunct curator of North American archaeology at Burke Memorial Washington State Museum, 1971—; member of scientific committee of Washington Archaeological Research Center, 1975—. Visiting lecturer at Universidad Nacional Autonoma de Mexico, 1974; adjunct professor, research associate, and member of advisory council of Quaternary Research Center, 1976—. Conducted and supervised archaeological field work in Kentucky, Wyoming, West Virginia, Missouri, and Washington. Speaker at scholarly meetings.

MEMBER: American Anthropological Association (fellow), Current Anthropology (associate), Classification Society, Society for American Archaeology, American Association for the Advancement of Science, American Society for Conservation Archaeology, New York Academy of Science (fellow). *Awards, honors:* More than thirty grants and fellowships, including Woodrow Wilson fellow, 1964-65; grants from U.S. Army Corps of Engineers, National Park Service, Wenner-Gren Foundation for Anthropological Research, U.S. Forest Service, National Science Foundation, U.S. Environmental Protection Agency, U.S. Soil Conservation Service, and U.S. Department of the Army.

WRITINGS: Systematics in Prehistory, Free Press, 1971; *Prehistory of Fishtrap, Kentucky,* Yale University Publications in Anthropology, 1972; (editor with E. S. Hall, and contributor) *Archaeological Essays in Honor of Irving B. Rouse,* Mouton, 1978. Author of monographs. Contributor of articles and reviews to archaeology, anthropology, and civil engineering journals. Member of editorial board of *Advances in Archaeological Theory and Method,* 1977—.

WORK IN PROGRESS: Monographs, articles, and an "introductory text."

SIDELIGHTS: Dunnell counts among his interests a formal theory of prehistory, the development of stable nucleated settlements and seasonal sound settlement systems, and the archaeology of North America, especially the forested East.

* * *

DURAC, Jack
See RACHMAN, Stanley Jack

DURRELL, Zoe C(ompton) 1910-

PERSONAL: Born July 26, 1910, in Boston, Mass.; daughter of William B. (a publisher) and Sibyl (Moore) Warner; married Oliver H. Durrell (a publisher), November 14, 1931; children: David, William, Oliver H. III, Zoe Durrell Bruner. *Education:* Goddard College, B.A., 1971. *Politics:* Independent. *Religion:* Protestant. *Home:* 4 Mast Cove Lane, Kennebunkport, Maine 04046.

CAREER: Durrell Publications, Kennebunkport, Maine, editor, 1965—.

WRITINGS: (With husband, Oliver Durrell) *Motorists Journal,* Durrell, 1960; *Innocent Island: Abaco in the Bahamas,* Stephen Greene Press, 1972.

SIDELIGHTS: Zoe Durrell writes: "My one shot at authorship was the result of acquiring a home in Abaco, and being extremely curious about the island, at that time relatively unknown. There wasn't a book about the lovely place. I knew practically nothing about botany or ornithology, and studied a lot to prepare those sections of the book, but the history and economics of the island were more familiar territory. I doubt very much that I'll ever give birth to another book, but writing this one was a great experience."

* * *

DUSSEL, Enrique D. 1934-

PERSONAL: Born December 24, 1934, in Argentina; son of Enrique (a physician) and Elsa Rosa Dussel; married Johanna Peters (a language professor), October 22, 1964; children: Enrique S., Susanne C. *Education:* Universidad Nacional de Cuyo, masters degree in philosophy, 1957; Universidad Central Madrid, Dr.Phil., 1959; Institut Catholique, Paris, France, masters degree in theology, 1965; Sorbonne, University of Paris, Dr.Hist., 1967. *Religion:* Roman Catholic. *Office:* Apartado Postal 11-671, Mexico City 11, D.F., Mexico.

CAREER: Universidad Nacional de Cuyo, Mendoza, Argentina, titular professor of philosophical ethics, 1968-75; Universidad Nacional Autonoma de Mexico, Mexico City, professor of ethics, 1976—. Professor at Universidad Autonoma Metropolitana, 1975—, at Centro Intercultural de Documentation, Instituto Pastoral Latinoamericano, and Lumen Vitae, and MACC in Texas. Founder and president of Studies Commission for Latin American Church History; participant in international conferences.

WRITINGS—In English: *Teologia de la liberacion y etica,* Latinoamerica Libros, 1964, translation published as *Ethics and Theology of Liberation,* Orbis, 1978; *Interpretacion historicoteologica de nuestro continente latinoamericano,* Latinoamerica Libros, 1972, third edition, 1975, translation published as *History and the Theology of Liberation,* Orbis, 1976; *Ethics and Theology of Liberation,* Orbis, 1978; *Historia de la inglesia en America Latin: colonizaje y liberacion (1492-1973),* Nova Terra, 1972, translation published as *History of the Church in Latin America,* Eerdmans, 1979.

In Spanish: *Hipotesis para una historia de la iglesia en America Latina,* Editora Estela, 1967; *El humanismos semita: estructuras intencionales radicales del pueblo de Israel y otros semitas,* Editora Endeba, 1969; *America Latina y conciencia cristiana,* Instituto Pastoral Latinoamerican IPLA, 1970; *Historia del catolicismo popular en Argentina,* Editora Bonum, 1970; *Para una destruccion de la historia de la etica,* Ser y Tiempo, 1972; *La dialectica hegeliana: supuestos y supracim o del inicio originario del filosofar,* Ser y Tiempo, 1972; *America Latina: dependencia y liberacion,* Editora Fernando Garcia Cambeiro, 1973; *Para una etica de la liberacion latinoamericana,* Volume I: *Siglo XXI,* [Buenos Aires], 1973, Volume II: *Siglo XXI,* 1973, Volume III, two parts, [Mexico], 1978.

Ed dualismo en la antropologia de la cristiandad: desde los origenes hasta antes de la conquista de America, Editora Guadalupe, 1974; *Metodo para una filosofia de la liberacion: superacion analectica de la dialectica hegeliana* (title means "Method for a Liberation Philosophy"), Sigueme, 1974; *Liberacion latinoamericana y Emmanual Levinal,* Editora Bonum, 1975; *Introduccion a una filosofia de la liberacion latinoamericana,* Editores Extemporaneos, 1977; *Filosofia de la liberacion,* Editora Edicol, 1977; *Religion,* Editora Edicol, 1977; *Desintegracion de la cristiandad colonial y liberacion: perspectiva latinoamericana,* Editora Sigueme, 1978.

SIDELIGHTS: Dussel is a well-known member of the "liberation philosophers" group.

* * *

DUUS, Masayo 1938-

PERSONAL: Born September 12, 1938, in Hokkaido, Japan; came to the United States in 1963; daughter of Kiichi and Hana Umezawa; married Peter Duus (a professor of history), November 25, 1964; children: Erik. *Education:* Waseda University, B.A., 1961. *Home:* 818 Esplanada Way, Stanford, Calif. 94305.

CAREER: Writer. *Awards, honors:* First Kodansha Cultural Award for nonfiction from Kodansha Publishing Co., 1977, for *Tokyo Rose.*

WRITINGS: *Tokyo Rose,* Simul Press, 1976; *Tokyo Rose: Orphan of the Pacific,* Kodansha International, 1979; *Haisha no okurimono* (title means "Gift From a Loser"), Kodansha Publishing Co., 1979; *Duus Masayo no Amerika dayori* (title means "Life in America"), Bungeishunju, 1979. Contributor to Japanese periodicals.

WORK IN PROGRESS: *Nisei butai,* about Japanese-American troops in World War II, publication by Bungeishunju expected in 1981.

SIDELIGHTS: Masayo Duus writes: "I am interested in U.S.-Japanese relations, especially during the occupation period, 1945-51, and in the history of Japanese-Americans during World War II."

BIOGRAPHICAL/CRITICAL SOURCES: *Pacific Citizen,* February 13, 1979; *Houston Chronicle,* April 15, 1979; *El Paso Herald Post,* April 21, 1979; *Kirkus Review,* May 1, 1979; *Library Journal,* May 21, 1979; *Hokubei Mainichi,* June 27, 1979; *Peninsula Times Tribune,* June 27, 1979; *West Coast Review of Books,* July, 1979.

* * *

DWOSKIN, Stephen 1939-

PERSONAL: Born January 15, 1939, in New York, N.Y.; married wife, Suzanne, 1960 (divorced, 1965). *Home:* 208 Ladbroke Grove, London W.10, England. *Office:* Film School, Royal College of Art, Queensgate, London S.W.7, England.

CAREER: London College of Printing, London, England, lecturer in graphic design, drawing, film, and video, 1964-73; Royal College of Art, London, England, lecturer and tutor in film and television, 1973—. Graphic designer in the United States and England, 1959-76, film director, 1960-76; assistant director for Columbia Broadcasting System and Whitney

Publications. Lecturer at Parsons School of Design. *Member:* American Institute of Graphic Arts. *Awards, honors:* Fulbright fellow; fellow of Deutscher Akademischer Austauschdienst in West Germany.

WRITINGS: (With Harry Smith) *Rainscent,* Caput Press, 1962; (contributor) Joseph Berke, editor, *Counter Culture,* P. Owen, 1969; *Film Is: The International Free Cinema,* Overlook Press, 1975. Also author of filmscripts.

WORK IN PROGRESS: "Silent Scream," a filmscript.

* * *

DYCK, Cornelius J(ohn) 1921-

PERSONAL: Born August 20, 1921, in Lysanderhoeh, U.S.S.R.; naturalized U.S. citizen, 1961; son of John J. (a farmer) and Renate (Mathies) Dyck; married Wilma Louise Regier (an elementary school teacher), August 12, 1952; children: Mary Johanna, Jennifer Louise, Suzanne Renee. *Education:* Attended Rosthern Junior College, 1940; Bethel College, North Newton, Kan., B.A., 1953; University of Wichita, M.A., 1955; University of Chicago, B.D., 1959, Ph.D., 1962. *Home:* 57694 CR 107 S., Elkhart, Ind. 46514. *Office:* Associated Mennonite Seminaries, 3003 Benham Ave., Elkhart, Ind. 46514.

CAREER: Fulfilled alternative service as conscientious objector to military duty, 1940-45; served in Europe and South America with Mennonite Central Committee, 1945-51; ordained Mennonite minister, 1952; pastor of Mennonite church in Elbing, Kan., 1951-55; Associated Mennonite Seminaries, Elkhart, Ind., part-time business manager, 1957-59, professor of historical theology, 1959—, acting dean, 1973-74. Fellow of Ecumenical Institute, Collegeville, Minn., 1972-73; director of Institute of Mennonite Studies, 1958—; honorary member of faculty at Chicago Theological Seminary, Garrett Theological Seminary, McCormick Theological Seminary, and Seabury Western Theological Seminary. Executive secretary of Mennonite World Conference, 1962-73; member of Mennonite Central Committee, 1968-74 (vice-president, 1972-74); head of Mennonite board of business administration, 1956-63; consultant to Foundation for Reformation Research. *Member:* American Society of Church History, American Society for Reformation Research, Religious Research Association, Mennonite Historical Society (vice-president), National Association for the Advancement of Colored People, Elkhart Urban League (vice-president, 1964-68).

WRITINGS: (Editor and contributor) *A Legacy of Faith: The Heritage of Menno Simons,* Faith & Life, 1962; (editor, translator, and contributor) *The Lordship of Christ,* Mennonite World Conference, 1962; *They Gave Themselves: Lessons in Christian Stewardship,* Faith & Life, 1964; (editor, translator, and contributor) *The Witness of the Holy Spirit,* Mennonite World Conference, 1967; (editor and contributor) *An Introduction to Mennonite History,* Herald Press, 1967; (editor, translator, and contributor) *Jesus Christ Reconciles,* Mennonite World Conference, 1972; *Twelve Becoming: Biographies of Mennonite Disciples From the Sixteenth to the Twentieth Centuries,* Faith & Life, 1973.

Contributor: M. Shelly, editor, *Studies in Church Discipline,* Mennonite Publishing, 1958; Paul Toews, editor, *Pilgrims and Strangers: Essays in Mennonite Brethren History,* Center for Mennonite Brethren Studies, 1977; I. B. Horst and others, editors, *De geest in het geding,* H. D. Tjeenk Willink, 1978. Also contributor to *The Impact of the Church Upon Its Culture,* edited by Jerald C. Brauer, 1968. Contributor to *Encyclopaedia Britannica, Mennonite Encyclopedia,* and *Mennonite World Handbook.* Contributor of articles and reviews to church history and theology journals. Member of board of editors of *Mennonite Quarterly Review*'s "Studies in Anabaptist and Mennonite History" (editor-in-chief, 1974—).

WORK IN PROGRESS: Anabaptism and Sixteenth-Century Studies.

SIDELIGHTS: Dyck has written: "The study of history is not an antiquarian obsession but the search for understanding of a meaningful past and present and future. It is a search for self-understanding as individuals and as a people. In this search we are not called to master the past, but to enter into dialog with it, to hear the questions it asks of us, and to let it speak to us. The past is a teacher to those who hear it and, in the church, a servant facilitating the theological task of defining, testing, and communicating the faith delivered to the saints in Jesus Christ, the Lord of history."

AVOCATIONAL INTERESTS: Photography, swimming, tennis, interracial dialogue.

* * *

DYSON, Freeman John 1923-

PERSONAL: Born December 15, 1923, in Crowthorne, England; came to the United States in 1947, naturalized citizen, 1957; son of George (a musician) and Mildred (a lawyer: maiden name, Atkey) Dyson: married Verena Esther Huber, 1950 (divorced, 1958); married Imme Jung, November 21, 1958; children: (first marriage) Esther, George; (second marriage) Dorothy, Emily, Miriam, Rebecca. *Education:* Cambridge University, B.A., 1945; graduate study at Cornell University, 1947-48. *Home:* 105 Battle Road Circle, Princeton, N.J. 08540. *Office:* School of Natural Sciences, Institute for Advanced Study, Princeton, N.J. 08540.

CAREER: Cambridge University, Cambridge, England, fellow of Trinity College, 1946-50; Cornell University, Ithaca, N.Y., professor of physics, 1951-53; Institute for Advanced Study, Princeton, N.J., professor of physics, 1953—. Warren research fellow at University of Birmingham, 1949; member of Institute for Advanced Study, Princeton, N.J., 1948-49. Chairman of Federation of American Scientists, 1962-63. *Wartime service:* Royal Air Force, civilian researcher for Bomber Command, 1943-45. *Member:* National Academy of Sciences, Royal Society (fellow), Athenaeum Club. *Awards, honors:* Lorentz Medal from Royal Netherlands Academy of Sciences, 1966; Hughes Medal from Royal Society, 1968; Max Planck Medal from German Physical Society, 1969; Harvey Prize from Israel Institute of Technology, 1977.

WRITINGS: Disturbing the Universe, Harper, 1979. Contributor to mathematics and physics journals and popular magazines, including *Scientific American* and *New Yorker.*

SIDELIGHTS: Nina King found *Disturbing the Universe* to confirm "a truth many of us prefer not to contemplate: Contemporary scientists, who deal with forces of awe-inspiring power, are mere human beings, frequently as shortsighted and as selfish as the rest of us. It is reassuring because Dyson himself . . . emerges as a responsible and thoughtful person who is willing to learn from his mistakes and to face the moral and philosophical implications of his work. He is also a fine writer." Though describing himself as a problem solver rather than a creator of ideas, King applauded Dyson's "invaluable ability to make connections—to bring together ideas from widely disparate disciplines so that they complement and illuminate one another." Christopher Lehmann-

Haupt agreed, noting that Dyson "certainly impresses us with the breadth of his imagination."

BIOGRAPHICAL/CRITICAL SOURCES: Kenneth Brower, *The Starship and the Canoe,* Holt, 1978; *New York Times Book Review,* August 19, 1979; *New York Times,* August 21, 1979; *Detroit News,* September 16, 1979.

E

EATOCK, Marjorie 1927-

PERSONAL: Born May 30, 1927, in Centerville, Iowa; daughter of Lloyd George (owner and operator of an ambulance service) and Mabel (a teacher; maiden name, Mishler) Curl; married Samuel Eatock (in sales), December 20, 1952; children: Jim, Ann. *Education:* Centerville Community College, degree in education, 1948; also attended Drake University, 1949-51. *Religion:* Episcopalian. *Home:* 330 East Washington, Pittsfield, Ill. 62363.

CAREER: Washington Junior High School, Centerville, Iowa, teacher of history and physical education, 1948-55; writer, 1954—. "Home-Bound" librarian for senior citizens' program at Pittsfield Public Library.

WRITINGS: *The Ivory Tower* (gothic mystery), Curtis Books, 1972; *The Haunted Heirloom* (mystery), Popular Library, 1975; *Too Many Candles* (mystery), Fawcett, 1979; *The Wedding Journey* (historical suspense), Dell, 1980. Contributor to magazines, including *American Girl*.

WORK IN PROGRESS: Research on the Illinois River area, 1800-1850.

SIDELIGHTS: Marjorie Eatock writes: "After some years of writing teen-age material, I became fascinated with local history in the early 1800's. I have intentions of writing a novel dealing with antique aircraft, as that is our family's recreation. I am also working on a police-type mystery novel. My aim is purely to entertain."

AVOCATIONAL INTERESTS: Flying (1930 Spartan biplane, J-3 Cub).

* * *

EBEL, Robert L(ouis) 1910-

PERSONAL: Born November 14, 1910, in Waterloo, Iowa; son of Louis August (a teacher) and Lillian (a teacher; maiden name, Stubbs) Ebel; married Hazel June Frank, June 5, 1933; children: David Robert, Mary Ellen Ebel Wheeler, Margaret Louise Ebel Breece. *Education:* University of Northern Iowa, B.A., 1932; University of Iowa, M.A., 1936, Ph.D., 1947. *Religion:* Presbyterian. *Home:* 2594 Lake Lansing Rd., East Lansing, Mich. 48823. *Office:* Department of Counseling, Personnel Services and Educational Psychology, Michigan State University, 449 Erickson Hall, East Lansing, Mich. 48824.

CAREER: High school teacher of science and mathematics in Webster City, Iowa, 1932-34, Cedar Rapids, Iowa, 1934-37, and Dearborn, Mich., 1937-41; high school principal in Dearborn, 1941-44; University of Iowa, Iowa City, assistant professor, 1947-50, associate professor, 1950-53, professor of education, 1953-57, director of University Examinations Service, 1945-57, and Bureau of Educational Research and Service, 1955-57; Educational Testing Service, Princeton, N.J., vice-president, 1957-63; Michigan State University, East Lansing, professor of education and psychology, 1963—. Visiting professor at University of Wisconsin—Madison, summer, 1959, University of Southern California, summer, 1960, and Michigan State University, summer, 1961. Member of American Council on Education, 1958-61, Secondary School Admission Test Board, 1964-67, College Entrance Examination Board, 1965-68, 1971—, National Board of Medical Examiners, 1967—, and Great Lakes Assessment Council, 1972-73; head of Invitational Conference on Testing Problems, 1965; consultant to American Institutes for Research, Educational Records Bureau, and U.S. Office of Education.

MEMBER: American Association for the Advancement of Science, American Educational Research Association (president, 1972-73), American Psychological Association (division president, 1971-72), National Council on Measurement in Education (head of test standard committee, 1953-55; president, 1957), National Society for the Study of Education, Psychometric Society, Sigma Xi, Phi Delta Kappa, University Club.

WRITINGS: *Measuring Educational Achievement,* Prentice-Hall, 1965; *Principles of Educational and Psychological Measurement,* Rand McNally, 1967; (editor) *Encyclopedia of Education Research,* Macmillan, 1969; *Essentials of Educational Measurement,* Prentice-Hall, 1972, 2nd edition, 1979; *Practical Problems of Educational Measurement,* Heath, 1980. Contributor to education and psychology journals. Editor of American Educational Research Association newsletter, 1956-59; member of editorial board of Michigan State University Press, 1970-73.

SIDELIGHTS: Ebel's teaching and consulting commitments have resulted in travel to Germany, Brazil, Japan, Sweden, England, South Africa, Saudi Arabia, Greece, and Singapore.

EDELBERG, Cynthia Dubin 1940-

PERSONAL: Born July 24, 1940, in New York, N.Y.; daughter of Jacob (in business) and Bertha (a teacher; maiden name, Tarin) Dubin; married Stuart Edelberg (a physician), June 21, 1959; children: Jay, Jacqueline, Wendy. *Education:* Attended Cornell University, 1957-59; City University of New York, B.A., 1961; New York University, M.A., 1963, Ph.D., 1977. *Home:* 3248 Via Palos Verdes, Tucson, Ariz. 85716. *Office:* Department of English, University of Arizona, Tucson, Ariz. 85721.

CAREER: University of Arizona, Tucson, adjunct assistant professor of American literature, 1979—. *Member:* Modern Language Association of America, Rocky Mountain Modern Language Association.

WRITINGS: Robert Creeley's Poetry: A Critical Introduction, University of New Mexico Press, 1978.

WORK IN PROGRESS: American War Poetry: From the Revolution to Vietnam, publication expected in 1982.

SIDELIGHTS: Cynthia Edelberg wrote: "Several conclusions have already emerged from my research on American war poetry. Although one would not want to discuss war poems as a group completely apart from the mainstream of American poetry, the fact is that war poetry has a recurrent rhythm of its own: the confidently justified call to arms or to non-intervention, the confused response to the slaughter itself, the plea for reconciliation, and the search for solace spawned by shared suffering. A careful reading of American war poetry reveals the fact that we have neglected whole collections of war poems, such as Loyalist poetry and nineteenth-century Indian prose poems, and the fact that we have failed to focus sufficient attention on specific poems: Cummings's 'listen' and Twain's 'The War Prayer,' to name but two.

"War poetry reflects, shapes, and informs moral assumptions and social attitudes. Implications abound and it is necessary to probe them: the significance of the religious convictions which stand behind both the battle cry and the elegy, the persistent fascination with violence, the on-going controversy which surrounds the government subsidy, beginning with Trumbull's *M'Fingal,* and the realization that the veteran often becomes an alien in the society he served, noted early in our literature by Freneau in 'The American Soldier.' There are always ideas in the air about poetic form. A study of American war poetry suggests that innovations occur on the battlefield, crystallize in the trenches.

"In sum, I want to produce a literary history of our response to war: to analyze the substance and style of poems of literary merit, to recover for the canon of American literature ignored poems which deserve place, and to explore those cultural attitudes our poets tell us we must explore."

* * *

EINZIG, Paul 1897-1973

OBITUARY NOTICE—See index for *CA* sketch: Born August 25, 1897, in Brasov, Transylvania, Hungary (now Romania); died in 1973, in London, England. Journalist, writer on politics and finance, and author of an autobiography. Einzig worked as a correspondent for the *Financial News, Financial Times,* and *Commercial and Financial Chronicle.* His books include *The Destiny of the Dollar* and *A Textbook on Monetary Policy.* Obituaries and other sources: Paul Einzig, *In the Centre of Things,* Hutchinson, 1960; *The Author's and Writer's Who's Who,* 6th edition, Burke's Peerage, 1971; *AB Bookman's Weekly,* July 30, 1973; *Who's Who in the World,* 2nd edition, Marquis, 1973.

EISENSTEIN, Elizabeth L(ewisohn) 1923-

PERSONAL: Born October 11, 1923, in New York, N.Y.; daughter of Sam A. and Margaret (Seligman) Lewisohn; married Julian C. Eisenstein (a physicist), May 30, 1948; children: Margaret Eisenstein DeLacy, John (deceased), Edward. *Education:* Vassar College, B.A., 1944; Radcliffe College, M.A., 1947, Ph.D., 1953. *Office:* Department of History, University of Michigan, Ann Arbor, Mich. 48109.

CAREER: Time-Life, Inc., New York City, foreign policy researcher, 1945; American University, Washington, D.C., served as lecturer and then adjunct professor, 1959-70, associate professor of history, 1970-75; University of Michigan, Ann Arbor, Alice Freeman Palmer Professor of History, 1975—. Matthew Vassar Lecturer at Vassar College, 1973; Engelhardt Lecturer at Library of Congress, 1977; scholar-in-residence at Rockefeller Foundation Study and Conference Center, Bellagio, Italy, 1977; resident-consultant for Center for the Book, Library of Congress, 1979. *Member:* American Historical Association, Renaissance Society of America, Society for French Historical Studies (vice-president, 1970), Society for Eighteenth Century Studies (vice-president, 1975). *Awards, honors:* National Endowment for the Humanities fellow, 1977; D.Litt. from Mount Holyoke College, 1979.

WRITINGS: The First Professional Revolutionist: F. M. Buonarroti, Harvard University Press, 1959; *The Printing Press as an Agent of Change: Communications and Cultural Transformations in Early Modern Europe,* two volumes, Cambridge University Press, 1979. Contributor to history journals. Member of board of editors of *Journal of Modern History,* 1973-76.

BIOGRAPHICAL/CRITICAL SOURCES: New York Times Book Review, March 25, 1979.

* * *

EITINGER, Leo 1912-

PERSONAL: Born December 12, 1912; immigrated to Norway in 1939; naturalized Norwegian citizen; son of Shlomo and Helene (Kurtz) Eitinger; married Lisl Kohn, July 1, 1946. *Education:* Masaryk University, Brno, Czechoslovakia, medical degree, 1937; University of Oslo, Doctor of Medicine, 1958. *Home:* Ovre Ullern Terrasse 67, Oslo 3, Norway. *Office:* Psychiatric Department, Medical School, University of Oslo, Oslo 3, Norway.

CAREER: Hamar Hospital, Hamar, Norway, assistant, 1945-46; Ronvik Hospital, Ronvik, Norway, first assistant, 1946-48; Lovisenberg Hospital, Oslo, Norway, assistant, 1949; University of Oslo, Medical School, Oslo, professor of psychiatry and superintendent of department, 1949—. *Military:* Norwegian Armed Forces, chief psychiatric consultant, 1952—. *Member:* Norwegian Medical Association, Norwegian Psychiatric Association (president, 1963-67), Nordic Psychology Purkyne Medical Association (president), Australia and New Zealand Association for Forensic Psychiatry (honorary member), Norwegian Academy of Sciences, Norwegian Association of Medical Sciences (member of board), Danish Psychiatric Association, Israeli Medical Association, Nansen Committee. *Awards, honors:* King's Gold Medal; Brno University honorary medal; Bergen-Belsen International Award; Hebrew University of Jerusalem Remembrance Medal; Commander of Order of the Royal Norwegian St. Olav, 1978.

WRITINGS—In English: *Studies in Neuroses,* Munksgaard (Copenhagen), 1955; *Psykiatriske undersokelser bland flyktninger i Norge* (summary in English and Dutch), Universitetsforlaget (Oslo), 1958; *Concentration Camp Survivors in Norway and Israel,* Universitetsforlaget, 1964; (with Axel Strom) *Mortality and Morbidity After Excess Stress,* Humanities Press, 1973. Also author of *The Influence of Military Life on Young Norwegian Men's Mental Health,* 1954, *Psychiatric Investigations Among Refugees in Norway,* 1958, *The Origin of Neuroses,* 1962, and *Forensic Psychiatry,* 1971.

Other: (With Per Anchersen) *Nervoose lidelger og sinnets helse,* Aschehoug, 1955; (with Nils Retterstol) *Hvordan oppstar nevroser? Kortfattet oversikt over nevroseteorier,* Universitetsforlaget, 1962, new edition, 1967; (with Retterstol) *Nevroser* (textbook), Universitetsforlaget, 1970; (editor) *Alkoholism og narkomani i Norge,* Universitetsforlaget, 1970; (with Retterstol) *Rettspsykiatri,* Universitetsforlaget, 1971, new edition, 1976; *Sosial isolasjon i dagens samfunn,* Universitetsforlaget, 1972; (with Retterstol) *Psykoser,* Universitetsforlaget, 1973; *Glimt fra psykiatrisk forskning,* Universitetsforlaget, 1976; *Retten til a overleve,* Cappelen, 1976; (with Einer Kringlen) *Universitetets psykiatriske klinikk 1926-1976,* [Oslo], 1976.

* * *

ELIAS, Horace J(ay) 1910-

PERSONAL: Born March 22, 1910, in St. Louis, Mo.; son of Isaac (a department store buyer) and Marion (Sundheim) Elias; married Pauline Claire Engel (an editorial assistant), December 23, 1943; children: Elizabeth Elias Kaufman, John I. *Education:* Attended high school in Baltimore, Md. *Home and office:* 12 Stonehenge Circle, Apt. 7, Baltimore, Md. 21208.

CAREER: Owner of advertising agency in Baltimore, Md., 1950-78; writer, 1971—.

WRITINGS—All juvenile; published by Harper: *Fred and Barney Lay an Egg,* 1973; *Gentlemen Farmers,* 1974; *Fred, Mayor for a Day,* 1974; *The Computer That Went Bananas,* 1974; *Volunteer Fireman,* 1974; *How Does Your Garden Grow,* 1974; (author of adaptation) Robert Louis Stevenson, *Dr. Jekyll and Mr. Hyde,* 1976; *Flash Gordon in the Sand World of Mongo,* 1976; (author of adaptation) Frank L. Baum, *The Wizard of Oz,* 1976; *Tom and Jerry and the Real Gone Goose,* 1976.

Published by Grosset: *Pebbles and the Indignant Worm,* 1975; *The Hat,* 1975; *Fred and Barney Go Fishing,* 1975; *Boo Boo Wakes Up in the Winter,* 1975; *Yogi and the Snow Goose,* 1975; *Handy Hound,* 1975; *Wilma's Busy Day,* 1976; *The Fix-it Man,* 1976; *Surprising Corn,* 1976; *Everyone's Egg,* 1976; *Pebbles and Bamm Bamm Find Things to Do,* 1976; *Fred's Big Cleaning Day,* 1976; *Yogi and the Baby Skunk,* 1976; *Mosquito Flying Day,* 1976; *Playtime in Jellystone Park,* 1976; *The Big Blooming Rosebush,* 1976; *Magilla Gorilla and the Super Kite,* 1976; *The Jetson's Great Pizza Hunt,* 1976; (author of adaptation) *Mr. Magoo's "A Christmas Carol,"* 1977; *The Flintstone Story Book* (collection), 1978; *The Flintstones' Joke and Riddle Book,* 1978.

Published by Street and Smith (Bantam): *Doc Savage, Man of Bronze* (adaptation from original), 1979; (author of adaptation) Rod Serling, *Stories from the Twilight Zone,* 1979; (author of adaptation) Jim Kjelgaard, *Stormy,* 1979.

Published by Crown: *Collector's History of the Automobile* (adaptation of *A Pictorial History of the Motor Car*), 1978.

Published by Children's Press, all 1979: *The Illustrated Flintstone Dictionary; The Costume Party;* (author of adaptation) Glynis Holland, *Building a House;* (author of adaptation) Simon Goodenough, *Dinosaurs and Prehistoric Animals; Holly Hobbie's Time Book; Holly Hobbie's Alphabet Book.*

Published by Rand, McNally: *Holly Hobbie's Blue Sticker Fun Book,* 1977; *Holly Hobbie's Green Sticker Fun Book,* 1977; *Holly Hobbie's Yellow Sticker Fun Book,* 1977; *Holly Hobbie's Pink Sticker Fun Book,* 1977; *Holly Hobbie's Happy Day Book,* 1978; *Holly Hobbie's Around the House Book,* 1978; *Holly Hobbie's Book About Time,* 1978; *Holly Hobbie's Answer Book,* 1978; *Holly Hobbie's Book of ABC's,* 1978.

Also author of numerous adaptations of cartoons for Ottenheimer Publishers, World Distributors, and Modern Promotions.

WORK IN PROGRESS: Books for children.

SIDELIGHTS: Elias writes: "My literary output dates back to 1972. Prior to that, I had never written a line of fiction, except for advertising—which is, of course, pure fiction! A very good friend of mine, who was (and is) the president of Ottenheimer Publishers, said to me, 'I have just acquired the rights to all of the Hanna-Barbera material for children's books. Would you like to take a crack at it?' After some backing and filling, I managed to churn out one story. Ottenheimer's customer said okay. Then my friend said to me, 'Your first assignment—write seventeen more.' Since that first essay into writing for children I have amassed a total production which is staggering, at least to me!

"While the majority of the output has been based on the Hanna-Barbera characters, it has by no means been limited to them. My publisher happens to be a rather prolific rights-acquirer. Along the way, he has accumulated the publishing rights to the Peanuts comic strip characters for children's books, a number of Metro-Goldwyn-Mayer classic movies, and others. I've written adaptations, done revisions and editing—and wonder of wonders, my publisher is *still* a very good friend!

"Ottenheimer Publishers are, in the main, what I believe are called 'middleman publishers.' They acquire rights, then sell, and finally deliver a finished product to other publishers. My writing is strictly on assignment—I do no speculative writing at all. The publishers listed are those who purchased them through Ottenheimer. My only contact is with the latter.

"In the past few months, I have finally phased out the last vestiges of the advertising agency business, and now devote all of my working time to writing."

AVOCATIONAL INTERESTS: Golf, bridge, "a wild-eyed enthusiasm for baseball at the major league level."

* * *

ELIOT, Thomas H(opkinson) 1907-

PERSONAL: Born June 14, 1907, in Cambridge, Mass.; son of Samuel A. (a minister) and Frances (Hopkinson) Eliot; married Lois Jameson, October 10, 1936; children: Samuel A., Nancy F. Eliot Ulett. *Education:* Harvard University, A.B., 1928, LL.B., 1932; graduate study at Emmanuel College, Cambridge, 1928-29. *Religion:* Unitarian-Universalist. *Home:* 986 Memorial Dr., Cambridge, Mass. 02138.

CAREER: U.S. Social Security Board, Washington, D.C., general counsel, 1935-38; U.S. Department of Labor, Wage and Hour Division, regional director, 1938-41; U.S. Congress, Washington, D.C., Democratic member of House of Representatives, 1941-43; employed by Office of War Information, Office of Strategic Services, 1943-45; Foley, Hoag & Eliot, Boston, Mass., law partner, 1945-52; Washington University, St. Louis, Mo., professor of political science and constitutional law, 1952-62, chancellor of university, 1962-71; Salzburg Seminar, Salzburg, Austria, president, 1971-76; Buckingham Browne & Nichols School, Cambridge, Mass., teacher, 1977—. Member of board of overseers of Harvard University, 1964-70. *Member:* American Academy of Arts and Sciences. *Awards, honors:* Honorary degrees from Drury College, 1962, Hobart and William Smith Colleges, 1966, St. Louis University, 1969, Rockhurst College and Washington University, St. Louis, Mo., both 1971.

WRITINGS: *Basic Rules of Order,* Harcourt, 1952; (with William N. Chambers and Robert H. Salisbury) *American Government: Readings and Problems for Analysis,* Dodd, 1959, 2nd edition, 1965; *Governing America: The Politics of a Free People,* Dodd, Volume I: *National Government,* 1960, 2nd edition, 1964, Volume II: *National, State, and Local Government,* 1961, 2nd edition, 1964; (with Salisbury and Nicholas A. Masters) *State Politics and the Public Schools,* Knopf, 1964; *Public and Personal,* edited by Frank O'Brien, Washington University Press, 1971; (with Henry W. Bragdon) *The Bright Constellation,* Independent School Press, 1980. Contributor to political science journals and *Atlantic Monthly.*

WORK IN PROGRESS: Research for a history of Buckingham Browne & Nichols School, completion expected in 1983.

* * *

ELLIS, Jack C(lare) 1922-

PERSONAL: Born July 9, 1922, in Joliet, Ill.; son of Louis Nyle (a grocer and hardware executive) and Anna Louise (Cary) Ellis; married Shirley Krumbach in 1948; married second wife, Mary Kay Bent (a book editor), September 1, 1974; children: David Hodges, Cameron Cary. *Education:* Attended Wabash College, 1940-43; University of Chicago, M.A., 1948; Columbia University, Ed.D., 1955. *Home:* 2618 Grant St., Evanston, Ill. 60201. *Office:* Film Division, Northwestern University, 1905 Sheridan Rd., Evanston, Ill. 60201.

CAREER: Western Michigan University, Kalamazoo, instructor in English, 1948-50; Citizenship Education Project, New York, N.Y., audio-visual specialist, 1951-53; Northwestern University, Evanston, Ill., assistant professor, 1956-62, associate professor, 1962-67, professor of film, 1967—. Visiting assistant professor at University of California, Los Angeles, 1959-60; visiting associate professor at New York University, 1965-66; professor at University of Texas, 1972-73. U.S. delegate to United Nations Educational, Scientific and Cultural Organization's international meeting on teaching film and television appreciation, 1962; member of advisory committee of American Council on Education, 1964-66, advisory film panel of Illinois Arts Council, 1970-72, and film study panel of Committee on Institutional Cooperation, 1972—; consultant to Films, Inc. *Military service:* U.S. Army, 1943-46; became sergeant. *Member:* American Federation of Film Societies (president; chairperson of board of directors, 1955—), Society for Cinema Studies (president; member of council, 1959—).

WRITINGS: (Contributor) David C. Stewart, editor, *Film Study in Higher Education,* American Council on Education, 1966; (contributor) Seth Feldman and Joyce Nelson, editors, *Canadian Film Reader,* Peter Martin, 1977; (with Charles Derry and Sharon Kern) *The Film Book Bibliography, 1940-1975,* Scarecrow, 1979; *A History of Film,* Prentice-Hall, 1979. Contributor of about twenty-five articles and reviews to film, speech, drama, and education journals. Editor of *Cinema Journal,* 1976—.

WORK IN PROGRESS: *John Grierson: A Guide to References and Resources,* publication by G. K. Hall expected in 1982.

SIDELIGHTS: Ellis commented: "All my research and writing has grown out of my teaching. I am one of the pioneer teachers of film history and criticism; my doctoral dissertation, 'Approaches to Film as an Art Form,' was important in opening up the field for study.

"The history of the documentary film has become my academic specialty. For some time now I have been engaged in research on the career of John Grierson, pioneer and leader of the British documentary film movement and founding head of the National Film Board of Canada."

* * *

ELLISON, Glenn 1911-
(Glenn "Tiger" Ellison)

PERSONAL: Born February 7, 1911, in Pittsboro, Miss.; son of Samuel A. (in real estate) and Beadie (a teacher; maiden name, Payne) Ellison; married Elsie Mae Campbell (a teacher), July 6, 1938; children: Nita Lou Ellison McCoy, Barbara Ann Ellison Hartsook, Carolyn Joyce Ellison Buckley. *Education:* Denison University, A.B., 1933; Xavier University, Cincinnati, Ohio, M.A., 1957; further graduate study at Miami University, Oxford, Ohio, 1960-62. *Politics:* Republican. *Religion:* Baptist. *Home and office:* 15 Bellevue Dr., Treasure Island, Fla. 33706.

CAREER: Junior high school teacher of English, basketball, football, and track in Middletown, Ohio, 1933-35; high school teacher of English and history, and athletic coach in Middletown, Ohio, 1935-62; Ohio State University, Columbus, football coach and tutor in English, 1962-69; writer, 1963—.

MEMBER: National High School Athletic Association (vice-president, 1962), National Education Association, Ohio Football Coaches Association (life member; president, 1952, 1962), Ohio Education Association, Kentucky Colonels, Masons. *Awards, honors:* Valley Forge Medal from Ford Foundation, 1959; named Ohio coach of the year by sports writers of Ohio, 1961; coach of Ohio All-Star Football Team, 1950, 1952, 1956; member of Ohio High School Football Coaches Association's Coaches Hall of Fame.

WRITINGS—All under name Glenn "Tiger" Ellison: *Run-and-Shoot Football,* Prentice-Hall, 1965; *Persuasive Speaking for Coaches,* Prentice-Hall, 1966; *Power Speaking That Gets Results,* Prentice-Hall, 1974. Contributor to *Lincoln Library of Sports Champions.*

WORK IN PROGRESS: *The Son-of-a-Gun From Purple Ridge,* a novel about a confrontation between modern youth and an old-time football coach who stands for the "old-fashioned, competitive American Way," publication expected in 1980.

SIDELIGHTS: Ellison writes: "*Run-and-Shoot Football* is the only technical book by a football coach ever reviewed in the *New York Times.* The book described a new method of playing football that has become popular in every state in the country. *Persuasive Speaking for Coaches* became a popular textbook, not only for coaches, but also for ministers, teachers, and other professional people who faced the enervating task of standing up and facing a discerning audience. Its popularity led to *Power Speaking That Gets Results.*

"The novel in progress is a confrontation between an old-time football coach and modern youth. There's a great need today for more good stories that will keep us home in our libraries instead of out on the highways burning up the world's short supply of petroleum in our air-polluting gas buggies, stories written with so much impact that the reader becomes the character and life becomes more meaningful, more exciting, more fun, stories that will send us roaming while keeping us home reading—and saving energy."

* * *

ELLISON, Glenn "Tiger"
See ELLISON, Glenn

* * *

ELMANDJRA, Mahdi 1933-

PERSONAL: Born March 13, 1933, in Rabat, Morocco; son of M'hamed and Rabia (Elmrini) Elmandjra; married Amina Elmrini, August 25, 1956; children: Salima, Kenza (daughters). *Education:* Cornell University, B.A., 1954; graduate study at London School of Oriental and African Studies, 1954-55; London School of Economics and Political Science, Ph.D., 1957; postdoctoral study at University of Paris, 1961-63. *Religion:* Moslem. *Home:* B.P. 53, Rabat, Morocco; and 12 Rue Dufrenoy, 75016 Paris, France.

CAREER: University of Rabat, Rabat, Morocco, head of conferences in faculty of law, 1957-58; United Nations, New York, N.Y., chief adviser to Morocco's permanent mission to the United Nations, 1958-59; Radiodiffusion et Television Marocaine, Rabat, director-general, 1959-60; United Nations Educational, Scientific, and Cultural Organization (UNESCO), Paris, France, chief of African division in Office of Relations With Member States, 1961-63, director of cabinet, 1963-66, assistant director-general for social sciences, human sciences, and culture, 1966-69; University of London, Centre of International and Area Studies, London, England, professor of international studies and visiting fellow, 1970; UNESCO, assistant director-general in pre-programming, 1971-74, special counsel to director-general, 1975-76; University Mohammed V, Rabat, Morocco, professor of economics and international relations, 1976—. Member of council of Administration de Futuribles; member of steering committee of Pan-African Pugwash; member of board of directors of Bucharest's Centre International de Methodologies pour les Etudes sur le Futur et le developpement. Participant in symposia and conferences; consultant to the International Federation of Institutes for Advanced Study. *Member:* World Future Studies Federation (president), World Academy of Art and Science (fellow), Society for International Development, Informatics for the Third World, Association Maroc-Japon (vice-president). *Awards, honors:* Chevalier of French Order of Arts and Letters, 1970.

WRITINGS: (Contributor) *Nehru and the Modern World*, Indian National Commission for UNESCO, 1967; (contributor) *Economie et societe humanine* (title means "Economics and Society"), De Noel, 1972; *The United Nations System: An Analysis*, Archon Books, 1973; (contributor) College of Mexican Architects, editors, *Architecture and National Development*, International Union of Architects, 1978; (with James Botkin and Mincea Malitza) *No Limits to Human Learning*, Pergamon, 1979. Member of advisory editorial board of *Jeune Afrique* (weekly magazine).

WORK IN PROGRESS: Science and Technology and the Future; research on cooperation between developing countries; future studies in Africa.

SIDELIGHTS: Elmandjra has been published in Arabic, French, German, Spanish, Romanian, and Italian. He commented: "I was exposed to the United Nations at the age of sixteen, before the independence of my country. When I wrote my book on the United Nations system I had already worked for twelve years as an international civil servant with UNESCO. That work, my experience as a university professor, and my association with the World Future Studies Federation explain my keen interest in working on the 'learning report' of the Club of Rome which has just been published under the title *No Limits to Learning*."

AVOCATIONAL INTERESTS: Reading, skiing, music, swimming.

* * *

ELMEN, Paul H. 1913-

PERSONAL: Born June 4, 1913, in Lowell, Mass.; son of John (a minister) and Hannah (Johnson) Elmen; married Gretalyn Lund (a teacher), August 2, 1942; children: Elisabeth Elmen Levesque, John. *Education:* Northwestern University, B.A., 1934, M.A., 1936; Harvard University, Ph.D., 1946. *Religion:* Episcopal. *Home address:* Friar Hill, South Woodstock, Conn. 06267.

CAREER: Northwestern University, Evanston, Ill., instructor, 1948-52, assistant professor of English, 1952-58; Seabury-Western Theological Seminary, Evanston, assistant professor, 1958-60, associate professor, 1960-65, professor of English, 1965-78; writer and researcher, 1978—. President of Chicago Theological Institute, 1956-57, 1976-77. *Military service:* U.S. Army, Armor, chaplain; received Purple Heart, Bronze Star, and Silver Star. *Member:* American Society of Christian Ethics (president, 1966-67), Association of Chicago Theological Schools (vice-president, 1973-74), Swedish Pioneer Historical Society. *Awards, honors:* Ford Foundation grant, 1952-53; fellow of American Association of Theological Schools, 1966; Litt.D. from North Park College, 1974; gold medal from King of Sweden, 1978.

WRITINGS: Restoration of Meaning to Contemporary Life, Doubleday, 1958; *William Golding*, Eerdmans, 1967; *Wheat Flower Messiah: Eric Jansson of Bishop Hill*, University of Southern Illinois Press, 1977. Contributor to magazines, including *Christian Century*.

WORK IN PROGRESS: A book on Dag Hammerskjoeld; editing letters of Jeremy Taylor.

SIDELIGHTS: Elmen writes: "My two loves are theology and literature, and seventeenth-century Anglican writers. My book on Hammarskjoeld will study his movement from inner mysticism to practical statesmanship."

* * *

ELWIN, Malcolm 1903-1973

OBITUARY NOTICE: Born 1903 in West Bridgford, England; died December, 1973. Author, critic, and editor. Elwin co-founded and edited the magazine *West Country* and was also editor of *Macdonald Illustrated Classics*. An expert on nineteenth-century English literature, Elwin wrote a number of critical and biographical studies, including *Charles Reade: A Biography, Thackeray: A Personality, The First Romantics*, and *De Quincey's Confessions of an English Opium-Eater*. Obituaries and other sources: *Longman Companion to Twentieth Century Literature*, Longman, 1970; *The Author's and Writer's Who's Who*, 6th edition, Burke's Peerage, 1971.

ENGELMAN, Rose C. 1919(?)-1979

OBITUARY NOTICE: Born c. 1919 in Engelwood, N.J.; died of cancer, September 2, 1979, in Silver Spring, Md. Military historian and educator. Engelman was a faculty member at Hunter College before joining the Army Medical Department, where she became a chief historian. She was a principal architect of the department's multi-volume *Vietnam War History* and a co-author of *The Defense of the Americas in World War II, A Decade of Medical Progress,* and *Two Hundred Years of Military Medicine.* Obituaries and other sources: *Washington Post,* September 5, 1979.

* * *

EPPINGER, Josh 1940-

PERSONAL: Born March 5, 1940, in San Francisco, Calif.; son of Josh, Jr. and Helen (Kahn) Eppinger; married Sandra North, September 1, 1963; children: Nell. *Education:* University of California, Berkeley, B.A., 1962. *Office: Signature* Magazine, 260 Madison Ave., New York, N.Y. 10016.

CAREER/WRITINGS: Saturday Evening Post, New York City, associate editor, 1964-66; *Newsweek,* New York City, associate editor, 1966-71; *Parade,* New York City, associate managing editor, 1971-72; *Signature,* New York City, executive editor, 1973—.

* * *

EPSTEIN, Helen 1947-

PERSONAL: Born November 27, 1947, in Prague, Czechoslovakia; came to United States in 1948, naturalized in 1954; daughter of Kurt (an athlete) and Franci (a dressmaker; maiden name, Rabinek) Epstein. *Education:* Hebrew University, B.A., 1970; Columbia University, M.Sc., 1971. *Home:* 110 Bleecker St., New York, N.Y. 10012. *Agent:* Jim Brown, 25 West 43rd St., New York, N.Y. 10012. *Office:* Department of Journalism, New York University, New York, N.Y. 10003.

CAREER: Writer. New York University, New York, N.Y., assistant professor of journalism, 1974—, director of undergraduate program, 1979—.

WRITINGS: Children of the Holocaust, Putnam, 1979. Contributor to periodicals, including *New York Times, Village Voice, London Times, McCall's,* and *Jerusalem Post.*

WORK IN PROGRESS: Articles for *New York Times Magazine.*

SIDELIGHTS: In *Children of the Holocaust,* Epstein traces events and documents opinions expressed by children of the Holocaust survivors. Herself the offspring of two survivors, Epstein explained, "I wanted . . . to validate my own experience by getting stories from the others, to make sure it really happened, make sure there really was such a thing—I hadn't made it up."

One of the things Epstein discovered was that all the children of survivors had been named after people who had been murdered in the war. They shared common dreams and imagery. "First there are the shower heads," she related, "the kind you commonly see in school gyms or at children's camps in this country. Our association to them is the deadly 'shower heads' of Hitler's camps, that gave forth gas instead of water. The sight of smokestacks may recall the thought of crematoria. Trains become transports of Jews. Barbed wire means concentration camp."

In a review of the book, Jean Strouse wrote that Epstein "asks difficult questions not only of others but of herself. . . . With or without the Holocaust, that's brave." Strouse called *Children of the Holocaust* "an extraordinarily interesting study of intersecting pain and love, loyalty and anger, world events and private lives." James Atlas commented, "It is the author's own private drama that distinguishes 'Children of the Holocaust' and reminds us that what threatens to become an abstract, unfathomable event as it recedes into the past was a catastrophe that still reverberates in the lives of many who never knew it firsthand."

Epstein told *CA:* "I am primarily a university professor and a free-lance writer. As a teacher I am concerned with getting people anywhere from age seventeen to sixty to think more clearly and write better than they do. As a writer I am interested in social and cultural issues. I believe that social and cultural history is usually far more insightful than the usual political, economic, or military version of human life."

Epstein concluded: "I do not at this point intend to pursue the Holocaust as a subject. I am interested in medical, psychological and social topics, but have no immediate plans to write another book. I think far too many books are being published that are written by authors with nothing to say. I have said all that is on my mind in *Children of the Holocaust,* and I am going to wait a couple of years before I undertake another big writing project."

BIOGRAPHICAL/CRITICAL SOURCES: New York Times Book Review, April 29, 1979; *Chicago Tribune Arts & Fun/Books,* April 29, 1979; *New York Times,* May 4, 1979, June 8, 1979; *Washington Post Book World,* September 13, 1979; *Newsweek,* May 14, 1979; *Commentary,* June, 1979.

* * *

EPSTEIN, Melech (Michael) 1889(?)-1979

OBITUARY NOTICE: Born c. 1889; died in August, 1979. Journalist and author who in 1922 co-founded the Yiddish-language organ of the Communist party. When he felt the party's principles were betrayed by the Stalin-Hitler non-agression pact of 1939, he left the party and thereafter contributed articles to the *Jewish Daily Forward.* He was the author of numerous books, including *The Jew and Communism* and *Jewish Labor in U.S.A.* Obituaries and other sources: *Detroit Jewish News,* August 10, 1979.

* * *

ERBSEN, Claude E. 1938-

PERSONAL: Born March 10, 1938, in Trieste, Italy; came to the United States, 1951, naturalized citizen, 1956; son of Henry M. (a lawyer and businessman) and Laura (Treves) Erbsen; married Jill J. Prosky, 1959 (divorced, 1969); married Hedy M. Cohn, April 7, 1970; children: (first marriage) Diana; (second marriage) Allan H., Michael D. *Education:* Amherst College, B.A. (cum laude), 1959; graduate study at University of the Andes, Bogota, Colombia, 1960. *Home:* 27 Stratton Rd., Scarsdale, N.Y. 10583. *Office:* Associated Press, 50 Rockefeller Plaza, New York, N.Y. 10620.

CAREER/WRITINGS: Free-lance writer, Bogota, Colombia, 1960; Associated Press, reporter in New York, Key West, Fla., and Washington, D.C., 1960-61; chief of bureau in Rio de Janeiro, 1965-69; executive representative for Latin America, 1969; business manager and administrative director for Associated Press-Dow Jones in London, 1970-75; deputy director of World Service, 1975—. *Military service:* U.S. Naval Reserve, 1961-65; became lieutenant. *Member:* International Press Institute, Council on Foreign Relations. *Awards, honors:* Eduardo Santos Scholarship, Inter-American Press Association, 1960.

SIDELIGHTS: Erbsen commented: "The profession of journalism offers a ringside seat to the flow of history, and I thank my lucky stars that I have had the privilege of occupying such a seat."

* * *

ERICKSON, Arthur (Charles) 1924-

PERSONAL: Born June 14, 1924, in Vancouver, British Columbia, Canada; son of Oscar (an administration executive) and Myrtle Erickson. *Education:* Attended University of British Columbia, 1942-43; McGill University, B.Arch. (with honors), 1950. *Residence:* Vancouver, British Columbia, Canada. *Office:* Arthur Erickson Architects, 2412 Laurel St., Vancouver, British Columbia, Canada V5Z 3T2.

CAREER: University of Oregon, Eugene, assistant professor of architecture, 1955-56; University of British Columbia, Vancouver, instructor, 1956-58, assistant professor, 1958-60, associate professor of architecture, 1961; Erickson/Massey Architects, Vancouver, British Columbia, partner, 1963-72; Arthur Erickson Architects, Vancouver, British Columbia, owner, 1972—. Architectural designs include pavilions for Expo and International Trade Fair. Member of committee on urban development of Science Council of Canada, 1971; member of board of directors of Canadian Conference of the Arts, 1972; past member of Canadian Council on Urban Research; member of board of trustees of Institute for Research on Public Policy. *Military service:* Canadian Army, Intelligence Corps, 1943-45; served in India, Ceylon, and Malaya; became captain.

MEMBER: Royal Architectural Institute of Canada (fellow), Royal Canadian Academy of Arts (fellow), Institute for Research on Public Policy, Community Planning Association of Canada, Heritage Canada, Urban Land Institute, American Institute of Architects (fellow), American Society of Interior Designers, American Society of Planning Officials, Architectural Institute of British Columbia (honorary member), Planning Institute of British Columbia, Ordre des Architects de Quebec, Ontario Association of Architects, Museum of Modern Art, University of British Columbia Museum of Anthropology, Vancouver Art Gallery (life member), University Club of Vancouver. *Awards, honors:* McLennan fellowship for study in Egypt, Syria, Turkey, Greece, Italy, France, Spain, England, and Scandinavia, 1950-53; Canada Council fellowship for Japan, Cambodia, and Indonesia, 1961-62; Molson Prize from Canada Council, 1967; award from Royal Bank of Canada, 1971; D.Eng. from Nova Scotia Technical College, 1971; Tau Sigma Delta Gold Medal from American Institute of Architects, 1973; LL.D. from Simon Fraser University, 1973, McGill University, 1975, and University of Manitoba, 1978; officer of Order of Canada, 1973; Auguste Perret Award from International Union of Architects, 1974; more than thirty awards for architectural designs from organizations including Prestressed Concrete Institute, American Society of Landscape Architects, Canadian Housing Design Council, and National Society of Interior Designers.

WRITINGS: The Architecture of Arthur Erickson, Tundra Books, 1975; (contributor) *Towards a Quality of Life: The Role of Industrialization in the Architecture and Urban Planning of Developing Countries,* Hamdami Foundation, 1976; (contributor) William H. New, editor, *A Political Art,* University of British Columbia Press, 1978. Contributor to *Canadian Architect Yearbook* and *House Beautiful Building Manual.* Contributor of about a hundred articles to professional journals, popular magazines, and newspapers in Canada, the United States, and abroad, including *Time, Life, Canadian,* and *Arts Canada.*

WORK IN PROGRESS: A book of travel letters.

* * *

ERMINE, Will
See DRAGO, Harry Sinclair

* * *

EVANS, W(illiam) Glyn 1918-

PERSONAL: Born May 5, 1918, in Swansea, Wales; came to the United States in 1928, naturalized citizen, 1935; son of William John (a tin worker) and Edith (Miles) Evans; married Henrietta Wright Agnew, August 31, 1944; children: William Glyn, Jr., James Agnew, Nancy Miles. *Education:* Wheaton College, Wheaton, Ill., A.B., 1945, A.M., 1949; Northern Illinois University, A.M., 1969. *Residence:* Hingham, Mass. *Office:* South Shore Baptist Church, 578 Main St., Hingham, Mass. 02043.

CAREER: Licensed Baptist minister, 1937—; pastor of Bible churches in Michigan City, Ind., 1938-41, and LaGrange, Ill., 1941-45; Charles E. Fuller Evangelistic Foundation, Pasadena, Calif., evangelist, 1945-47; pastor of Baptist churches in Glen Ellyn, Ill., 1947-49, Cincinnati, Ohio, 1949-58, and Springfield, Ill., 1958-63; Wheaton College, Wheaton, Ill., assistant professor of practical theology, 1963-71; South Shore Baptist Church, Hingham, Mass., pastor, 1971—. Vice-president of Conservative Baptist Foreign Mission Society; director of Olive Branch, Inc.; member of board of directors of Cornerstone Books, Inc. Founder, past director and teacher at Bible Institute of Cincinnati. Minister to missionaries in Argentina. *Member:* Evangelical Theology Society, Conservative Baptist Ministers Association, Hingham Clergy Association.

WRITINGS: The Road to Power, Moody, 1961; *Studies in the Book of Job,* Scripture Press, 1969; (editor) *He Has Come,* Broadman, 1975; *Profiles of Revival Leaders,* Broadman, 1976; (editor) *Christ Is Victor,* Judson, 1977; *Daily With the King,* Moody, 1979. Also author of *The Second Coming Generation.* Author of adult church school lessons for Scripture Press.

SIDELIGHTS: Evans writes: "The pastor is like the coach of a team. His responsibility is to enable the team to function as a unit, moving unitedly forward to do the work of Christ in reaching the world for Him. All members of the team are necessary, each with his individual gift, to contribute to the benefit of the whole. There is no difference between missions and evangelism—it is our task to reach everyone (the man next door as well as the man farthest out) with the gospel of Christ's salvation for men.

"The function of the church is to kindle the fire, teach the newly born, encourage the use of gifts and talents, and send its members out to witness. Above all, it is to glorify God.

"I look upon all talent as God-given; hence my ability to write is a gift which I should use for God's glory and the uplifting of my fellowmen. I am an idealist. I do not think writing should be done primarily as a means of creating personal wealth, for in that case we authors would become commercializers who simply play up to the instincts of humanity."

AVOCATIONAL INTERESTS: Golf, mountain climbing, spectator sports (especially baseball), gardening, photography.

EVANS, Walker 1903-1975

OBITUARY NOTICE: Born November 3, 1903, in St. Louis, Mo; died April, 1975. Photographer, author, editor, and educator. Evans was an early innovator in the field of photography. His pictures, done mostly in black and white, have a factual exactness few of his contemporaries could achieve. During the Depression, Evans worked for the Farm Security Administration, documenting rural poverty with his camera. His photographs are featured in permanent collections in such museums as the Smithsonian Institute, the Metropolitan Museum of Modern Art, and the Art Institute of Chicago. Evans's pictures can also be seen in his books, including *American Photographs, Let Us Now Praise Famous Men,* and *Many Are Called.* In addition to his work in photojournalism, Evans was editor of both *Time* and *Fortune,* and professor in graphics at Yale University. Obituaries and other sources: *Current Biography,* Wilson, 1971; *Who's Who in the World,* 2nd edition, Marquis, 1973; *Who's Who in America,* 38th edition, Marquis, 1974; *Who Was Who in America,* 6th edition, Marquis, 1976.

* * *

EVERHART, James W(illiam), Jr. 1924-
(Jim Everhart)

PERSONAL: Born October 24, 1924, in Evanston, Ill.; son of James William (in oil business) and Sarah (de Beaubien) Everhart; married Martha Keith, 1949 (divorced, 1959); married Gail Mixon (a supervisor), July 8, 1960; children: James William III, Kim, Sara. *Education:* University of Illinois, A.B., 1950. *Home and office:* 1595 West Belt Dr. S., Houston, Tex. 77042.

CAREER: Denver Post, Denver, Colo., writer and in sales, 1950-53; in insurance sales in Golden, Colo., 1954-57; KHOU-TV, Houston, Tex., director of advertising, 1958-67; writer, 1968—. Actor for television, radio, and films; public speaker. *Military service:* U.S. Army Air Forces, 1943-45; became technical sergeant. *Member:* American Federation of Television and Radio Artists, Screen Actors Guild, Slippery Rock Boosters Club.

WRITINGS—All under name Jim Everhart: *The Illustrated Texas Dictionary of the English Language,* Cliff's Notes, Volume I, 1967, Volume II, 1968, Volume III, 1973, Volume IV, 1975, Volume V, 1979; *Forty Is . . . !?,* Cliff's Notes, 1969; *Up Your Bracket,* Shoal Creek Publishers, 1972; *CB Slanguage Illustrated,* Centennial Press, 1976; (editor) *A Nice Jewish Boy* (on Henry Kissinger), EPPS-Praxis Publishers, 1976; *Everything You Didn't Want to Know About Sex: But We're Going to Tell You Anyway,* Price, Stern, 1978. Also author of *Texas, More or Less* ("a gross exaggeration of what others think of Texas and Texans"), 1980, and *The Vacation,* 1980.

SIDELIGHTS: Everhart comments: "After hearing President Johnson start a television speech by saying 'Mah fellow Markins . . . ,' I realized Texans speak a language unique to the rest of the country, and the five volumes of the Texas dictionary are by far the most popular of my books, all of which are in photo-caption form. I have plans for many more photo-caption books to be published, since this is an area in publishing little explored by authors, particularly those shooting original photographs for each subject or book. Since all of my books are humorous (hopefully), I take great satisfaction in the fact that none of this humor is off-color or 'blue.' To me it is gratifying to make people laugh without resorting to material some people might find offensive."

BIOGRAPHICAL/CRITICAL SOURCES: New York Times, June 16, 1975.

* * *

EVERHART, Jim
See EVERHART, James W(illiam), Jr.

* * *

EWART, Gavin (Buchanan) 1916-

PERSONAL: Born in 1916, in London, England; son of George Arthur (a surgeon) and Dorothy (Turner) Ewart; married Margo Bennett (a school secretary), March 24, 1956; children: Jane Susan, Julian Robert. *Education:* Attended Christ's College, Cambridge, 1934-37. *Politics:* Labour. *Religion:* None. *Home:* 57 Kenilworth Court, Lower Richmond Rd., London S.W.15, England.

CAREER: Assistant in book review department, British Council, 1946-52; advertising copywriter, 1952-71; free-lance writer, 1971—. *Military service:* British Army, Royal Artillery, 1940-46; became captain. *Member:* Poetry Society (chairperson, 1978-79), Society of Authors, Performing Rights Society. *Awards, honors:* Cholmondeley Award, 1971, for achievement as a poet; travel scholarship from Royal Society of Literature, 1978.

WRITINGS—Poems: *Poems and Songs,* Fortune Press, 1939; (editor) *Forty Years On: An Anthology of School Songs,* Sidgwick & Jackson, 1964; *Londoners,* Heinemann, 1964; *Throwaway Lines,* Keepsake Press, 1964; *Two Children,* Keepsake Press, 1966; *Pleasures of the Flesh,* Alan Ross, 1966; *The Deceptive Grin of the Gravel Porters,* London Magazine Editions, 1968; *Twelve Apostles,* Ulsterman Publications, 1970; *The Gavin Ewart Show,* Trigram Press, 1971; *Venus,* Poem-of-the-Month Club, 1972; *The Select Party,* Keepsake Press, 1972; *Alphabet Soup,* Sycamore Press, 1972; *By My Guest!,* Trigram Press, 1975; *An Imaginary Love Affair,* Ulsterman Publications, 1975; *No Fool Like an Old Fool,* Gollancz, 1976; *Or Where a Young Penguin Lies Screaming,* Gollancz, 1977; *All My Little Ones,* Anvil Press, 1978; *The Collected Ewart, 1933-1980,* Hutchinson, 1980. Work represented in James Laughlin's *New Directions* anthologies.

WORK IN PROGRESS: A libretto for a full-length opera, with John Gardner; editing *The Penguin Book of Light Verse.*

SIDELIGHTS: Ewart writes that his interests are urban life, satire, and humor. He commented: "I am interested in all the forms available to the writer of verse in English. The poetry of W. H. Auden has had a great influence on my work—particularly the early work. Later influences have included John Betjeman and Peter Porter. I found it very hard to write during World War II, when I was on active service in North Africa and Italy. Alan Ross, editor of *London Magazine,* encouraged me to begin writing poetry again in 1959. Following the twenty-five-year intermission there have been twenty years of great activity."

* * *

EWING, Pebles
See KENNAWAY, James

* * *

EZERGAILIS, Andrew 1930-

PERSONAL: Born December 10, 1930, in Rite, Latvia; came to United States in 1949, naturalized in 1954; son of

Janis (a journalist) and Berta Ezergailis; married Inta Miske (a professor), July 27, 1957; children: Anna. *Education:* Michigan State University, B.A., 1956; New York University, M.A., 1960, Ph.D., 1968. *Home:* 1157 Danby Rd., Ithaca, N.Y. 14850. *Office:* Department of History, Ithaca College, Ithaca, N.Y. 14850.

CAREER: Ithaca College, Ithaca, N.Y., assistant professor, 1964-73, professor of history, 1973—. *Member:* American Historical Association, American Association for the Advancement of Slavic Studies, American Association of Baltic Studies.

WRITINGS: The 1917 Revolution in Latvia, Columbia University Press, 1974; *Russia in Our Stars* (essays), Echo Press, in press. Contributor to Slavic studies journals. Book review editor of *Nationality Papers.*

WORK IN PROGRESS: The Latvian Impact on the Bolshevik Revolution.

SIDELIGHTS: Ezergailis wrote: "My first book as well as the one that I am presently writing explores the Latvian relationship to the Russian Revolution in general and the Bolshevik Revolution in particular. During the years of revolution it was well known in the West that the Latvians, especially the Latvian *strelki,* had a great deal to do with bolstering the unstable ship of Lenin's state, but since those days Western historians have not given the Latvians their proper due. In my work my intention is to remedy that shortcoming. I think it can be reasonable argued that without the Latvian aid the Bolshevik Government would have collapsed within the first year of power. In addition to writing works of academic research, I write speculative essays in English and in Latvian on sundry historical and political problems."

* * *

EZORSKY, Gertrude

PERSONAL—Education: Brooklyn College (now of the City University of New York), B.A., 1947; New York University, M.A., 1955, Ph.D., 1961; Wolfson College, Oxford, M.A., 1969. *Office:* Graduate Center of the City University of New York, 33 West 42nd St., New York, N.Y. 10036.

CAREER: City University of New York, New York, N.Y., professor of philosophy at Brooklyn College and Graduate Center, 1961—, head of department, 1966, 1967. Member of visiting faculty at Brandeis University, Boston University, Columbia University, New York University, University of Pittsburgh, and Hunter College of the City University of New York; visiting scholar at Harvard University, 1972-73, 1973-74, and University of California, Berkeley, summers, 1976-77. *Member:* International Association of Philosophy of Law and Social Philosophy (member of American executive committee), American Philosophical Association (member of executive committee, 1976-79), Conference on Methods in Philosophy and the Sciences (head of executive committee, 1971-72), Philosophy and Public Affairs (member of executive committee, 1971-72, 1975-76). *Awards, honors:* Council for Philosophical Studies fellow, summers, 1966, 1968; American Council of Learned Societies fellow, 1973-74.

WRITINGS: (Editor and author of introduction) *Philosophical Perspectives on Punishment,* State University of New York Press, 1972.

Contributor: Amelia Rorty, editor, *Pragmatic Philosophy,* Doubleday, 1966; Sidney Hook, editor, *Dimensions of Mind,* New York University Press, 1969; *The Theory of Knowledge and Science,* University of Vienna, 1969; Hook, editor, *Language and Philosophy,* New York University Press, 1970; Milton Munitz and Howard Kiefer, editors, *Language, Belief, and Metaphysics,* Volume I: *Contemporary Philosophic Thought,* State University of New York Press, 1970; Milton Goldfinger, editor, *Contemporary Ethical Studies,* Volume V: *Punishment and Rights,* Schenkman, 1974; Elsie L. Bandman and Bertram Bandman, editors, *Bioethics and Human Rights,* Little, Brown, 1978; Jerome H. Skolnick and others, editors, *Crime and Justice in America,* Publishers, Inc., 1977. Contributor to *Philosophical Issues in Law* and *Encyclopedia of Philosophy.* Also contributor of more than twenty articles and reviews to newspapers and philosophy journals, including *Dissent.*

F

FAEGRE, Torvald 1941-

PERSONAL: Born April 12, 1941, in Maryland; son of David (a teacher) and Margaret (a teacher; maiden name, Barden) Faegre; married Sue Sommers (an artist). *Education:* Roosevelt University, B.A., 1965; attended Northwestern University, 1965-67. *Politics:* "Anarchist." *Home:* 1600 Ashland, Evanston, Ill. 60201.

CAREER: Self-employed carpenter and cabinetmaker, 1965—. Graphic artist and calligrapher.

WRITINGS: (Self-illustrated, with calligraphy) *Anarchist-Revolutionary Calendar,* Swallow, 1969-1972; (self-illustrated) *Tents: Architecture of the Nomads,* Anchor, 1979.

WORK IN PROGRESS: "Another book similar to *Tents*"; "examining another aspect of material culture around the world."

SIDELIGHTS: Faegre and his wife toured the area from Istanbul to Bombay, including one-month visits in Afghanistan and India. The trip resulted in an exhibition of their drawings and watercolors in Chicago, Ill. They are now planning a year of drawings, painting, and crafts studies in India and Nepal.

Faegre told *CA:* "I wrote *Tents: Architecture of the Nomads* because I found that Americans have a great interest in tents as temporary housing—particularly camping tents—but that they had little knowledge of tents used year around as housing. This led me to the life of the tent-dwellers, the nomads of the world, and the important part they have played in world history."

* * *

FAIR, Harold L(loyd) 1924-

PERSONAL: Born August 2, 1924, in Tyronza, Ark.; son of James A. (a rural mail carrier) and Clara (a teacher; maiden name, Williamson) Fair; married Wilma Alvis, May 27, 1951 (died March 5, 1955); married Agnes Hunt (a librarian), April 2, 1976; children: Kathryn, Robert. *Education:* Attended Millsaps College, 1949-50; University of Mississippi, B.A., 1952; Vanderbilt University, B.D., 1954, M.A., 1969, Ph.D., 1971. *Religion:* United Methodist. *Home:* 315 East Northfield, Murfreesboro, Tenn. 17130. *Office:* United Methodist Publishing House, 201 Eighth Ave. S., Nashville, Tenn. 37202.

CAREER: United Methodist Publishing House, Nashville, Tenn., associate editor, 1960-70, executive editor of youth publications, 1970-72, managing editor, 1972—. *Member:* American Society of Church History.

WRITINGS: (With Horace R. Weaver) *Key to Luke,* Graded Press, 1970; *Class Devotions: For Use With the 1975-76 International Lessons,* Abingdon, 1975; *Class Devotions: For Use With the 1976-77 International Lessons,* Abingdon, 1976; *Class Devotions: For Use With the 1977-78 International Lessons,* Abingdon, 1977; *Class Devotions: For Use with the 1978-79 International Lessons,* Abingdon, 1978.

WORK IN PROGRESS: Research on prohibition and religion in the South.

SIDELIGHTS: Fair told *CA:* "One of my avocations is blacksmithing, and I have a great interest in further research on the role of crafts among the plain people of the Old South. As I work in a local blacksmith shop, making fireplace tools and other utilitarian objects, I often ponder the roles of these artisans of the past. Often romanticized, they were nevertheless a part of the core of rural and frontier America. In our social history, they are still unsung—and I want to sing about them."

Fair also expressed an interest in biography: "After reading recently Vincent Cronin's *Napoleon Bonaparte,* I am interested in getting beyond the kind of writing I have been doing in the past and trying my hand at biography. Cronin's work succeeds in bringing Napoleon to life, and I would like to try this genre."

* * *

FAISON, S(amson) Lane, Jr. 1907-

PERSONAL: Born November 16, 1907, in Washington, D.C.; son of Samson Lane (an army general) and Eleanor (Sowers) Faison; married Virginia Weed, June 1, 1935; children: Gordon L., George W., Christopher M., Samson Lane III. *Education:* Williams College, B.A., 1929; Harvard University, M.A., 1930; Princeton University, M.F.A., 1932. *Politics:* Independent. *Home:* 145 Scott Hill Rd., Williamstown, Mass. 01267.

CAREER: Yale University, New Haven, Conn., began as instructor, became associate professor of art, 1932-36; Williams College, Williamstown, Mass., member of faculty, 1936-46, professor of art, 1946-76, professor emeritus, 1976—, head of department, 1940-69, director of Museum of Art, 1948-76. Director of U.S. State Department Central

Collecting Point in Munich, Germany, 1950-51. Visiting professor at University of Georgia, 1968; member of summer faculty at University of Pennsylvania, Columbia University, New York University, Harvard University (also executive secretary of committee on visual arts, 1954-55), and University of California, Berkeley; member of art advisory committee at Mt. Holyoke College and Wheaton College, Norton, Mass. Member of board of directors of Shaker Community, Hancock, Mass., and Park-McCullough House Association. *Military service:* U.S. Naval Reserve, active duty, 1942-46, with Office of Strategic Services, 1945-46; became lieutenant commander. *Member:* College Art Association of America (past president). *Awards, honors:* Chevalier of French Legion of Honor, 1952; Guggenheim fellow, 1960-61; D.Litt. from Williams College, 1971.

WRITINGS: Manet, H. N. Abrams, 1953; *Guide to the Art Museums of New England,* Harcourt, 1958; *Art Tours and Detours in New York State,* Random House, 1964; *Handbook to the Collection: The Williams College Museum of Art,* Stinehour Press, 1979. Contributor to professional journals and popular magazines, including *Saturday Review,* and newspapers. Art critic for *Nation,* 1950-53.

WORK IN PROGRESS: The Art Museums of New England, a revision of *Guide to the Art Museums of New England.*

SIDELIGHTS: Faison comments: "On the theory that scholarship need not be dull reading, I try to do something about avoiding that dread disease."

BIOGRAPHICAL/CRITICAL SOURCES: Harper's, August, 1958; *New York Times,* April 11, 1976.

* * *

FALCON
See NESTLE, John Francis

* * *

FALK, Robert 1914-

PERSONAL: Born February 28, 1914, in Milwaukee, Wis.; son of Harold Sands (an engineer) and Eugenia (Bechtner) Falk; married Jane Shepherd, January 11, 1936; children: Eugenia M. Falk Langford, Sara Jane Falk Guidotti. *Education:* Williams College, B.A., 1935; University of Wisconsin, Madison, Ph.D., 1941; University of Colorado, M.A., 1945. *Home:* 11209 Cashmere St., Los Angeles, Calif. 90049.

CAREER: Rutgers University, New Brunswick, N.J., assistant professor of English, 1947-50; University of California, Los Angeles, associate professor, 1951-60, professor of English, 1960-70. Exchange professor in Denmark, Germany, Poland, Italy, and Japan. *Military service:* U.S. Naval Reserve, active duty, 1942-46; became lieutenant junior grade.

WRITINGS: (Editor) *American Literature in Parody,* Twayne, 1955, reprinted as *The Antic Muse,* Grove, 1959; (contributor) Floyd Stovall, editor, *The Development of American Literary Criticism,* University of North Carolina Press, 1955; (editor with N. Foerster) *Eight American Authors,* Norton, 1963; (contributor) Wayne Morgan, editor, *The Gilded Age: A Reappraisal,* Syracuse University Press, 1963; *The Victorian Mode in American Fiction,* Michigan State University Press, 1965; (editor) *American Poetry and Prose,* two volumes, Houghton, 1965, 5th edition (with N. Foerster, N. S. Grabo, R. B. Nye, and E. F. Carlisle), 1965; (editor) *Literature and Ideals in America,* Ohio University Press, 1975. Contributor to language and literature journals.

SIDELIGHTS: Falk writes: "Writing and editing books and articles in the field of American literary history and American intellectual history was an outgrowth of my academic career (publish or perish!). My research in American literary history and scholarship led to writing and editing as a means of making myself a more effective teacher and obtaining a reputation in my field. Special interests of mine were nineteenth-century literary history, Henry James, literary realism in fiction during the post-Civil War years, and the American business ethic of that period. The latter interest led me into studying the 'rags to riches' philosophy as reflected in the boy-books of Horatio Alger, a kind of youthful barometer of the Protestant ethic in America.

"Henry James interested me most of the major writers of that time. Howells and Mark Twain were also subjects of study and writing. *The Victorian Mode in American Fiction* focused on those writers. James's 'international' novels and stories coincided with my own love of travel and interest in Europe generally."

* * *

FALLON, Padraic 1905-1974

OBITUARY NOTICE: Born January 3, 1905, in Athenry, Ireland; died October 9, 1974. Poet and author. Fallon wrote poetry, plays for the stage, television, and radio, and short stories. Some of his radio plays are written in verse. Fallon was a customs official for over forty years in Ireland. Some of his works are *Collected Poems, Lighting Up Time* (a collection of short stories), and the plays "The Seventh Step," "Sweet Love Till Morn," and "Deirdre's King." Obituaries and other sources: *Contemporary Poets,* 2nd edition, St. Martin's, 1975.

* * *

FANNING, Michael 1942-

PERSONAL: Born January 16, 1942, in Lubbock, Tex.; son of Tolbert C. (a teacher) and LaVona (Wilson) Fanning; married Lynda Earnest (a teacher), September 11, 1965; children: Rebekah, Brock, Rachel. *Education:* Abilene Christian College, B.A., 1963; University of Arkansas, M.A., 1965, Ph.D., 1971. *Home:* 1005 Easy St., Hammond, La. 70401.

CAREER: Leeward Community College, Pearl City, Hawaii, instructor, 1968-69; Southeastern Louisiana University, Hammond, La., associate professor, 1970—. Fulbright lecturer at Aristotelian University, 1978-79. *Awards, honors:* National Endowment for the Humanities grant, 1978.

WRITINGS: France and Sherwood Anderson: Paris Notebook, 1921, Louisiana State University Press, 1976. Contributor of stories, poems, and articles to journals, including *Black American Literature Forum, Carleton Miscellany,* and *Integrity.*

WORK IN PROGRESS: The Tao in Texas (tentative title), short stories; research comparing Dashiell Hammett and Andre Gide.

SIDELIGHTS: Fanning comments: "I am that common creature, a teacher-writer, and my teaching and writing show it. When I lecture, I tell stories; when I write literary criticism, it turns out like fiction; when I write fiction, it turns out like literary criticism. I cannot say where all this will lead. My other interests are French, Greek, and the 1920's. My home, body, and soul is really Texas, but travel includes France and Greece. I am a romantic; I keep thinking someplace else is better. My family, although uncomplaining, is doubtful."

AVOCATIONAL INTERESTS: Tennis.

FANON, Frantz 1925-1961

OBITUARY NOTICE: Born July 20, 1925, in Martinique, French Antilles; died December 6, 1961, of leukemia, in Washington D.C. Psychiatrist, philosopher of social revolution, and writer. Strongly influenced by Jean-Paul Sarte and Aime Cesaire, Fanon is a major contributor to the revolutionary philosophy of the Third World. Having lived in the West Indies and Algeria, both French colonies, Fanon began to hate colonialism and capitalism with its rampant materialism. As a psychiatrist, he studied the psychology of racism and oppression and concluded that society could not be improved by changing man, but rather society itself had to be changed, and then only by violence. Unlike Marx, Fanon believed the poorest of the poor would eventually revolt. They had nothing to lose and were so emasculated by the system that only violence could restore their self-respect. In this way, Fanon thought violence was a healing force. In 1956, he began working for the Algerian liberation movement. He was an editorial writer for its underground newspaper *El Moudjahid* and in 1960, was appointed ambassador to Ghana by the Algerian Provisional Government. His works include *Black Skin, White Masks; The Wretched of the Earth;* and *Studies in a Dying Colonialism.* Obituaries and other sources: *World Authors, 1950-1970,* Wilson, 1975.

* * *

FANTHORPE, Patricia Alice 1938-

PERSONAL: Born October 2, 1938, in Beetley, England; daughter of Arthur Richard (a lengthman roadworker) and Rosa Margaret (a dressmaker; maiden name, Roberts) Tooke; married Robert Lionel Fanthorpe (a high school headmaster and writer), September 7, 1957; children: Stephanie Dawn Patricia, Fiona Mary Patricia Alcibiadette. *Education:* Attended girls' secondary school in Dereham, England. *Politics:* "Somewhere in the middle." *Religion:* "Agnostic Humanist." *Home and office:* Minas Tirith, 30 Boverton St., Roath Park, Cardiff, Wales. *Agent:* Robert Reginald, P.O. Box 2845, San Bernardino, Calif. 92406.

CAREER: Drapery store assistant, 1953-56; in shoe manufacturing, 1956-57; writer, 1957-72; Bailey's Martham, England, horticulturist, 1972-73; International Telephone & Telegraph, Norwich, England, invoice clerk, 1976-79; writer, 1979—.

WRITINGS: (With husband, R. Lionel Fanthorpe) *Spencer's Metric Conversion Tables,* John Spencer, 1970; (with R. L. Fanthorpe) *Spencer's Decimal Payroll Tables,* John Spencer, 1971; (with R. L. Fanthorpe) *Metric and Decimal Companion,* John Spencer, 1971; (with R. L. Fanthorpe) *Office Guide,* John Spencer, 1971; *Racing Reckoner,* John Spencer, 1972. Contributor to *Sfear II.*

WORK IN PROGRESS: The Mysterious Treasure of Rennes le Chateau, with husband, R. Lionel Fanthorpe; *The Black Lion,* a "sword and sorcery novel," with R. L. Fanthorpe.

SIDELIGHTS: Patricia Fanthorpe writes: "I became a writer because Lionel was; if he'd been a plumber I'd have learnt to use a blowlamp instead. Collaboration on our books grew from my typing his manuscripts and discussing science fiction plots when his ideas weren't flowing. We got on to the office guides, decimalisation, and metrication books when the United Kingdom changed currency, weights, and measures in the early seventies. Because the compilation techniques were similar, I then did a racing guide on my own.

"Our home is a Victorian town house near Roath Park in Cardiff, crammed with books, board games, musical instruments, sports gear, and souvenirs. It looks 'lived-in' most of the week and tidy for about an hour each Sunday afternoon.

"Life with Lionel is tough, unpredictable, exciting, and adventurous. We get the scent of something—like the Rennes-le-Chateau mystery, stop what we're doing, pack a rucksack, catch the first boat to France, and spend the next day climbing the Pyrenees in a rainstorm. We cram thirty hours into the day and ten days into the week.

"We're not noticeably religious and we don't go overboard for any political theories. We care a lot about people, and we believe that they really matter *as individuals.* We're unashamed hedonists with the proviso that the deepest happiness comes from giving pleasure to people you love. Life is here to be lived: no excuses, no regrets, and no looking back—just get on with it and enjoy it!"

* * *

FARRELL, J(ames) G(ordon) 1935-1979

OBITUARY NOTICE—See index for *CA* sketch: Born January 23, 1935, in Liverpool, England; died by drowning, August 14, 1979, in Bantry Bay, Ireland. Author best known for his novels about the British Empire. His works include *Troubles, The Siege of Krishnapur,* and *The Singapore Grip.* Obituaries and other sources: *The Author's and Writer's Who's Who,* 6th edition, Burke's Peerage, 1971; *Contemporary Novelists,* 2nd edition, St. Martin's, 1976; *The Writer's Directory, 1980-82,* St. Martin's, 1979; *New York Times,* August 15, 1979; *Chicago Tribune,* August 15, 1979; *Publishers Weekly,* September 3, 1979; *AB Bookman's Weekly,* October 8, 1979.

* * *

FARRELL, James T(homas) 1904-1979
(Jonathan Titulcscu Fogarty, Esq.)

OBITUARY NOTICE—See index for *CA* sketch: Born February 27, 1904, in Chicago, Ill.; died August 22, 1979, in New York, N.Y. Author best known for his brutally realistic trilogy of novels involving Studs Lonigan, a youth growing up in Chicago from the 1900's to the Depression. Farrell wrote more than fifty other books, including numerous collections of short stories. He once defended his penchant for stark realism by intoning: "I am a second-generation Irish-American. The effects and scars of immigration are upon my life. The past was dragging through my boyhood and adolescence. Horatio Alger Jr. died only seven years before I was born. The 'climate of opinion' . . . was one of hope.But for an Irish boy born in Chicago in 1904, the past was a tragedy of his people." Obituaries and other sources: *Encyclopedia of World Literature in the Twentieth Century,* updated edition, Ungar, 1967; *Contemporary Novelists,* 2nd edition, St. Martin's, 1976; *Conversations With Writers,* Volume 2, Gale, 1978; *Who's Who,* 131st edition, St. Martin's, 1979; *The Writers Directory, 1980-82,* St. Martin's, 1979; *People,* March 12, 1979; *New York Times,* August 23, 1979; *Chicago Tribune,* August 23, 1979; *Washington Post,* August 23, 1979; *Detroit News,* August 26, 1979; *Time,* September 3, 1979; *AB Bookman's Weekly,* October 22, 1979.

* * *

FAWCETT, Roger Knowlton 1909-1979

OBITUARY NOTICE: Born December 3, 1909, in St. Paul, Minn.; died October 3, 1979, in New York, N.Y. Publisher, editor, and sprotsman who succeded his father as head of Fawcett Publications. He joined the family-owned company as an editor in 1930 and, during his presidency, Fawcett led the development of mass-market paperback publications with Crest, Gold Medal, and Popular Library. He was also the first to produce "novelizations" of popular movies. In addition to its many successful magazines, including *True Confessions, Mechanix Illustrated,* and *Women's Day,* the company realized handsome profits from the sale of numerous dieting books and a series of books by Charles Schulz based on his "Peanuts" comic strip. Partly because no other family member wished to succeed him, Fawcett sold the company to the Columbia Broadcasting System in 1977 for $50 million. An expert trapshooter, Fawcett twice won the Amateur Singles Championship of America. Obituaries and other sources: *Who's Who in America,* 38th edition, Marquis, 1974; *New York Times,* October 5, 1979.

* * *

FAY, S(amuel) P(rescott), Jr. 1926-

PERSONAL: Born October 12, 1926, in Boston, Mass.; son of Samuel P. (a financial adviser) and Hester (Davey) Fay; married Francoise Zighera (an artist), June 14, 1956; children: Marie-Denise, Jacqueline. *Education:* Bowdoin College, B.A., 1951. *Office:* Department of English, Anatolia College, Salonika, Greece.

CAREER/WRITINGS: Free-lance writer and photographer in Balkan countries, 1962—; English teacher in Istanbul, Turkey, 1972-73; Anatolia College, Salonika, Greece, English teacher, 1975—. Contributor of feature articles and photographs on Greece, Turkey, and Yugoslavia to newspapers and magazines, including *Life, Sports Illustrated, Saturday Review, Christian Science Monitor,* and *Baltimore Sun. Member:* Overseas Press Club of America. *Awards, honors:* First prize in *Saturday Review*'s World Travel Photographic Competition, 1968; first prize in BBC's World Service "Sound '71" Competition, 1971.

WORK IN PROGRESS: A collection of documentary photographs on life in Balkan countries during the post-World War II transitional years; a theatrical satire on modern technology and the energy crisis.

SIDELIGHTS: S. P. Fay, Jr. has a "general interest in preserving documents relating to cultural changes in Balkan countries since World War II," particularly "those aspects of cultural life which are disappearing."

Fay told *CA:* "A few years ago, perhaps in reaction to having spent over a decade in the Balkans, I found myself returning to my early love of classical jazz and theatre. I discovered a tremendous interest in jazz among young Greeks, and have enjoyed performing as a jazz pianist at local concerts. Also, I have written some jazz compositions which I have incorporated into a musical satire on the excesses of modern technology. So far no Balkan David Merrick has appeared to produce me. But trying one's hand at a new medium does add zest to life!"

BIOGRAPHICAL/CRITICAL SOURCES: Saturday Review, January 4, 1969.

* * *

FEDERICO, Ronald Charles 1941-

PERSONAL: Born January 9, 1941, in Bronx, N.Y.; son of Onofrio Frank (a building contractor) and Celeste (Icolari) Federico; married Jean Taylor, October 4, 1969 (divorced, 1974); children: Sylvia, Lydia. *Education:* Yale University, B.A. (magna cum laude), 1962; University of Michigan, M.S.W., 1965; Northwestern University, Ph.D., 1968. *Residence:* Cincinnati, Ohio. *Office:* University of Cincinnati, 411 French Hall, Cincinnati, Ohio 45221.

CAREER: University of Maryland, College Park, assistant professor, 1967-72, associate professor of sociology, 1972-73; University of North Carolina, Greensboro, associate professor of sociology and social work, 1973-78; University of Cincinnati, Cincinnati, Ohio, associate professor of social work, 1979—. *Member:* National Association of Social Workers, American Sociological Association, Council on Social Work Education (member of house of delegates, 1978—, and board of directors, 1979—), Association of Baccalaureate Program Directors, Yale Club, Phi Kappa Phi.

WRITINGS: The Social Welfare Institution, Heath, 1973, 3rd edition, in press; *Sociology,* Addison-Wesley, 1975, 2nd edition, 1979; (with Betty Baer) *Educating the Baccalaureate Social Worker,* Ballinger, Volume I, 1978, Volume II, 1979. Advisory editor for Longman Publishing.

WORK IN PROGRESS: A textbook on human behavior and the social environment, publication by Longman expected in 1981; a novel.

SIDELIGHTS: Federico comments: "I have worked as a curriculum consultant for schools and love the interchange with colleagues that results. My writing results from efforts to find better way to understand and teach. Trying to write a novel is a challenge for me—text writing is easier because it is structured.

"I also have a long-standing interest in the arts, especially ballet, and have been an amateur ballet-dancer for a number of years, performing with local groups."

* * *

FEDEROFF, Alexander 1927(?)-1979

OBITUARY NOTICE: Born c. 1927; died July 23, 1979. Novelist. Federoff was best known for his novels, *The Side of the Angels, Falling Through the Night,* and *Swords, Scepters, Coins, and Cups.* Obituaries and other sources: *AB Bookman's Weekly,* August 20, 1979.

* * *

FEINGOLD, Michael 1945-

PERSONAL: Born May 5, 1945, in Chicago, Ill.; son of Bernard C. (a tanner) and Elsie (Silver) Feingold. *Education:* Columbia University, B.A., 1966; Yale University, M.F.A., 1972. *Home:* 21 St. Charles Place, Highland Park, Ill. 60035. *Agent:* Peter L. Skolnik, Sanford J. Greenburger Associates, Inc., 825 Third Ave., New York, N.Y. 10022. *Office: Village Voice,* 80 University Place, New York, N.Y. 10003.

CAREER: Yale Repertory Theatre, New Haven, Conn., literary manager, 1969-76; Guthrie Theatre, Minneapolis, Minn., literary director, 1977—. Editor for Winter House Ltd., 1969-72. Member of National Endowment for the Arts theater advisory panel, 1972-76; member of board of directors of Theatre Communications Group, 1974-78. *Awards, honors:* Varsity show award from Broadcast Music, Inc., 1966; John Gassner Memorial Award from Yale University, 1972; Guggenheim fellow, 1978.

WRITINGS: (Contributor) *Collected Plays,* Volume II, Random House, 1977. Translator of plays by Brecht, Ibsen, Moliere, Offenbach, Donizetti, and Thomas Bernhard. Author of a theater review column in *Village Voice,* 1970—. Contributor to popular magazines, including *New Republic* and *Saturday Review,* and newspapers.

WORK IN PROGRESS: Translating Horvath's "Figaro

Laesst sich Scheiden" and several plays by Thomas Bernhard; studying American playwriting since 1945; musical theater projects.

* * *

FELDSTEIN, Paul J(oseph) 1933-

PERSONAL: Born October 4, 1933, in New York, N.Y.; son of Nathan and Sarah (Solomon) Feldstein; married Anna Martha Lee (a biostatistician), December 22, 1969; children: Julie, Jennifer. *Education:* City College (now of the City University of New York), B.A., 1955; University of Chicago, M.B.A., 1958, Ph.D., 1961. *Home:* 1130 Lincoln, Ann Arbor, Mich. 48104. *Office:* School of Public Health, University of Michigan, 1420 Washington Heights, Ann Arbor, Mich. 48105.

CAREER: American Hospital Association, Chicago, Ill., director of Division of Research, 1961-64; University of Michigan, Ann Arbor, assistant professor, 1964-67, associate professor, 1967-71, professor in School of Public Health and department of economics, 1971—. Fellow of Institute for European Health Services Research; member of U.S. House of Representatives advisory panel; member of National Institute of Mental Health manpower advisory committee, 1962-64; past member of board of directors of Michigan Delta Dental Plans; consultant to World Health Organization, U.S. Bureau of the Budget, and U.S. Social Security Administration. *Military service:* U.S. Army, 1955-57; became first lieutenant. *Member:* American Economic Association. *Awards, honors:* Grant from Robert W. Johnson Foundation, 1973-79.

WRITINGS: An Empirical Investigation of the Marginal Cost of Hospital Services, Graduate Program in Hospital Administration, University of Chicago, 1961; *Financing Dental Care: An Economic Analysis,* Heath, 1973; *Health Associations and the Demand for Legislation: The Political Economy of Health,* Ballinger, 1977; *Health Care Economics,* Wiley, 1979.

Contributor: Eugene M. Lerner, editor, *Readings in Financial Analysis and Investment Management,* Irwin, 1963; George Bugbee, editor, *Where Is Hospital Use Headed?,* Program in Hospital Administration, University of Chicago, 1964; George K. Chacko, editor, *The Recognition of Systems in Health Services,* Operations Research Society of America, 1969; Herbert Klarman, editor, *Empirical Studies in Health Economics,* Johns Hopkins Press, 1970; J. C. Morrealle, editor, *The Medical Care Industry: The Economist's Point of View,* Graduate School of Business Administration, University of Michigan, 1974; William E. Brown, editor, *Oral Health, Dentistry, and the American Public,* University of Oklahoma Press, 1974; John Rafferty, editor, *Health Manpower and Productivity,* Lexington Books, 1974; Michael Zubkoff, editor, *Health: A Victim and Cause of Inflation,* Milbank Memorial Fund, 1976; Howard Berman, editor, *Health Care in the American Economy: Issues and Forecasts,* Blue Cross Association, 1977. Contributor of more than a dozen articles and reviews to economic and health care journals. Member of editorial board of *Inquiry.*

WORK IN PROGRESS: Research on health economics, especially its political-economic aspects.

AVOCATIONAL INTERESTS: Sailing.

* * *

FELTON, John Richard 1917-

PERSONAL: Born March 25, 1917, in Toledo, Ohio; son of Elmer Franklin (an accountant) and Georgia Hazel (Templeton) Felton; married Katherine Adele Lofgren (a college instructor), January 25, 1947; children: James Lofgren, Joyce Adele. *Education:* University of California, Los Angeles, B.A., 1939, M.A., 1941, Ph.D., 1961. *Politics:* Democrat. *Religion:* Unitarian-Universalist. *Home:* 3481 Anaheim Dr., Lincoln, Neb. 68508. *Office:* Department of Economics, University of Nebraska, Lincoln, Neb. 68588.

CAREER: War Labor Board, San Francisco, Calif., head of food and distribution section, 1943-45; San Diego State University, San Diego, Calif., assistant professor of economics, 1948-51; Wage Stabilization Board, Washington, D.C., director of Los Angeles branch, 1951-53; U.S. Naval Weapons Center, China Lake, Calif., head of Systems and Procedures Division, 1953-55, education director, 1955-62; University of Nebraska, Lincoln, assistant professor, 1962-66, associate professor, 1966-68, professor of economics, 1968—. *Member:* American Economic Association, Association for Evolutionary Economics, Transportation Research Forum, Midwest Economics Association, Nebraska Economic and Business Association. *Awards, honors:* Meritorious civilian service award from U.S. Navy, 1962.

WRITINGS: (Contributor) J. R. Davidson and H. W. Ottoson, editors, *Transportation Problems and Policies in the Trans-Missouri West,* University of Nebraska Press, 1967; *The Economics of Freight Car Supply,* University of Nebraska Press, 1978. Contributor to economic journals.

WORK IN PROGRESS: The Impact of Highway Carrier Regulation Upon Transport Costs, publication by University of Nebraska Press expected in 1981.

SIDELIGHTS: Felton told *CA:* "My interest in transportation is a very practical one. Thus, my major efforts have been directed toward the identification and measurement, wherever possible, of the loss in economic welfare attributable to existing institutional arrangements in the transport industries. If the railroad industry were to inaugurate a system of freight car rental markets in lieu of the present inflexible car rental rates and arbitrary car allocation rules, it could effect savings of upwards of a billion dollars per year in 1972 prices. If the federal government were to cease its protection of established trucking companies and open the industry to the competition of all who wished to enter, the public would benefit to the extent of five billion dollars per year in 1976 prices. Even in an economy as large as the United States, these potential gains are not inconsiderable."

* * *

FENLON, Dick 1930-

PERSONAL: Born July 13, 1930, in Columbus, Ohio; son of Martin A. (an office manager) and Agnes L. Fenlon; married Roberta McLain, December 29, 1956; children: Judith, Richard, John, James. *Education:* Attended John Carroll University, 1948-49, and Ohio State University, 1949-52, 1955. *Religion:* Roman Catholic. *Home:* 3429 Eastside Dr., Louisville, Ky. 40220. *Office: Louisville Times,* 525 West Broadway, Louisville, Ky. 40202.

CAREER/WRITINGS: Findlay Republican-Courier, Findlay, Ohio, sports and general assignment reporter and editor, 1955-58; *Ohio State Journal,* Columbus, sports writer, 1958-59; *Cincinnati Enquirer,* Cincinnati, Ohio, sports writer, 1959-60; Nationwide Insurance Co., Columbus, press relations writer, 1960-62; *Louisville Times,* Louisville, Ky., sports editor and columnist, 1962—. Sports editor of *Louisville Courier-Journal,* 1962—. Contributor to magazines, including *Sports Illustrated, Big Ten Football,* and *Sporting*

News. Military service: U.S. Army, 1952-54; became corporal. *Awards, honors:* Award from Associated Press, 1977.

* * *

FENTON, Thomas Patrick 1943-

PERSONAL: Born February 15, 1943, in Jamaica, N.Y.; son of Thomas Joseph (a teacher) and Mary (Dempsey) Fenton; married Mary Jacqueline Heffron (an editor and publisher), June 16, 1973; children: Michael Heffron. *Education:* Maryknoll College, Glen Ellyn, Ill., B.A., 1964; Maryknoll School of Theology, Maryknoll, N.Y., M.Div., 1968, M.A., 1969. *Home and office:* Asia/North America Communications Center, 1110 Terrace Blvd., New Hyde Park, N.Y. 11040.

CAREER: Project Four: A Maryknoll Project for Justice and Peace, Hingham, Mass., co-director, 1969-73; communications consultant with NCC-USA China program, Hong Kong, 1973-75; Asia/North America Communications Center, co-director in Hong Kong, 1975-78, editor and publisher of *Asia Monitor,* 1975-78, co-director in New Hyde Park, N.Y., 1978—.

WRITINGS: (Editor with John Eagleson) *China Pac,* Orbis, 1971; *Coffee: The Rules of the Game and You,* Christophers, 1972; (editor) *Education for Justice,* Orbis, 1973; (editor with Mary Heffron) *A Bibliography of Education/Action Resources on Multinational Corporations,* Ateneo de Manila University, 1977; (with staff of Asia/North America Communications Center) *America in Asia,* Asia/North America Communications Center, Volume I: *Research Guides on U.S. Economic Activity in Pacific Asia,* 1979, Volume II: *A Handbook of Facts and Figures on U.S. Economic and Military Activity in Pacific Asia,* in press.

WORK IN PROGRESS: A reader's guide to multinational corporations, publication by Orbis expected in 1980; a collection of education/action resources on issues of international justice and peace, for publication in 1980; research and writing on political economy of the Third World and on America's activity in the Third World.

SIDELIGHTS: Fenton comments: "My writing has me involved with two quite different audiences. The first is those interested in the intricacies of United States political and economic involvement in the non-socialist Third World—particularly Asia; the second is those who have no such interest.

"Of the two, the latter is, in the end, the audience I want to reach. For I believe that the lives of working women and men in this country and in the Third World are profoundly affected by what may appear to them to be irrelevancies such as transnational corporations or the International Monetary Fund. I'm convinced that in this case what we don't know *will* hurt us. So, I've attempted to take issues of international investment, trade, and aid and translate them into terms that lay people can understand. I've done this in books, articles, education packets, and simulation games.

"The first audience mentioned above is of strategic importance to me. My writing for this audience has been more research-oriented. I've tried to collect, organize, and make easily retrievable, information on U.S. political and economic activity in the Third World. My aim in so doing is to provide other researchers and writers with tools that will make it possible for them to join me in reaching our lay audience. Much of my work with the Asia/North America Communications Center, both in Hongkong and New York, has been along these lines.

"Our quarterly magazine, *Asia Monitor,* is a synthesis and index of news of Asian-U.S. economic relations gathered from Asia's English-language newspapers and business magazines. The two volumes in our *America in Asia* series are primarily research and reference works, as is the bibliography we compiled on the subject of multinational corporations.

"The ultimate purpose of my research and writing is to widen the circle of those who are effectively critical of U.S. involvement overseas."

* * *

FERNSWORTH, Lawrence 1893(?)-1977(?)

OBITUARY NOTICE: Born c. 1893 in Beaverton, Ore.; died c. 1977 near Warner, N.H. Journalist and author. During the Spanish Civil War in the 1930's, Fernsworth was a correspondent for the *New York Times* and the *London Times.* His journalistic endeavors also included the operation of a weekly newspaper in Beaverton, Ore., plus positions with numerous other publications. Fernsworth disappeared while walking near his family farm on October 24, 1977. His remains were discovered on June 30, 1979, beside a stream near a road where he had been walking. Fernsworth wrote a book on the Spanish Civil War entitled *Spain's Struggle for Freedom.* Obituaries and other sources: *Washington Post,* July 20, 1979.

* * *

FERRARO, Gary P(aul) 1940-

PERSONAL: Born April 25, 1940, in New York, N.Y.; son of Charles A. (a civil engineer) and Ida (Sorgi) Ferraro; married Nancy Lee Berry (an administrator), May 8, 1977; children: John Carl Tyner (stepson), Kathryn Skye, Stefan Garret. *Education:* Hamilton College, B.A., 1962; Syracuse University, M.A., 1969, Ph.D., 1971. *Home:* 2018 Radcliffe Ave., Charlotte, N.C. 28207. *Office:* Department of Sociology, University of North Carolina, Charlotte, N.C. 28223.

CAREER: High school social studies teacher and assistant principal in Darien, Conn., 1963-65; University of North Carolina, Charlotte, assistant professor, 1971-76, associate professor of sociology, 1976—. *Member:* American Anthropological Association (fellow).

WRITINGS: (Contributor) Thomas K. Fitzgerald, editor, *Social and Cultural Identity: Problems of Persistence and Change,* University of Georgia Press, 1973; (with W. L. Hickman) *Society Says,* Macmillan, 1975; (with Brian Larkin) *The Invisible Castle,* Macmillan, 1975; (with Larkin) *The Worlds We Live In,* Macmillan, 1975; (contributor) William Arens, editor, *A Century of Change in East and Central Africa,* Mouton, 1976; *The Two Worlds of Kamau,* Inter-Culture Associates, 1978. Contributor to anthropology and sociology journals. Editor of *African Urban Studies,* winter, 1978-79.

WORK IN PROGRESS: Research on changing patterns of bridewealth among the Swazi while he is in Swaziland on a Fulbright fellowship.

* * *

FETTER, Richard (Leland) 1943-

PERSONAL: Born August 30, 1943, in Schenectady, N.Y.; son of Leland Louis and Rose (Epremian) Fetter; married Suzanne Clayton (a *Cordon Bleu* cook), December 28, 1968; children: Joel. *Education:* Hamilton College, A.B., 1965; University of Colorado, J.D., 1968. *Politics:* "Unaffiliated." *Religion:* Protestant. *Home and office:* 760 Racquet Lane, Boulder, Colo. 80303.

CAREER: Institut Le Rosey, Rolle, Switzerland, teacher and director of Moyen Section, 1969-74; Vranesh & Musick (water rights attorneys), Boulder, Colo., attorney, 1975-78; Colorado Municipal League, Wheat Ridge, Colo., staff attorney, 1978-79; free-lance writer, 1979—. *Member:* American Bar Association, Colorado Bar Association, Colorado Wildlife Federation (member of board of directors, 1978-80), Boulder Bar Association, Boulder Tennis Association (president, 1979), Phi Alpha Delta. *Awards, honors:* Certificate of appreciation from governor of Colorado, 1976.

WRITINGS: (With wife, Suzanne Fetter) *Telluride: From Pick to Powder,* Caxton, 1979. Also author of *The Complete Guide to Boulder Dining,* in press. Author of "Focus on Wine," a column in *Boulder Daily Camera.* Contributor to national and regional magazines, including *Colorado, Rocky Mountain,* and *Vintage.*

WORK IN PROGRESS: The Trace, a book about the Santa Fe Trail, publication expected in 1981.

SIDELIGHTS: Fetter wrote: "I have climbed Mt. Kilimanjaro, Mt. Blanc, and other peaks in the Swiss Alps on skis, and several fourteen-thousand-foot peaks in Colorado. I led a group up Mt. Bierstadt as part of Colorado's Centennial Fourteeners Climb Celebration in 1976, and have traveled throughout Europe, parts of Russia, East Africa, Morocco, and Egypt. I made a film in Kenya and Tanzania which I used to raise some money for the East African Wild Life Society.

"After law school I spent seven years working in Europe and traveling. Writing has become the only outlet I know for the stimulation provided by those years, as well as an effective means to act with regard to issues prevalent in this country. I returned to the United States to apply my law degree to the natural resources and energy issues that were developing in the seventies. Unfortunately, much seems to be tied up in court, government bureaucracy, and endless meetings.

"As time passed, I began to look at writing as a means to cut through the red tape and to effect change in people's minds, whether the topic be energy conservation, passive solar heating, or the conversion of methane gas from a hazard to an energy source. Writing permits this while allowing me to pursue other interests, however diversified and unrelated they may be (I also write on Western history, wine, travel, dining, and archaeology), and it offers the opportunity for me to work at my own hours.

"There is thus in essence a sense of the ancient Greek balance present in writing, both in the breadth of topics and interests that can be pursued and in the way one chooses to pursue them. In a world of specialization that is conducive to limited interests, writing provides a liberation and fulfillment not otherwise to be enjoyed.

"An influential book has been *The Ambassadors,* by James, which I never finished. There is one line, 'Live all you can while you can. It's a shame not to.' As much as anything, that sent me to Greece and Switzerland for seven years. If I become convinced that life here does not amount to a fulfillment of that philosophy, that line will provide the impetus to pull up roots once again."

AVOCATIONAL INTERESTS: Tennis, hiking, photography, powder skiing.

* * *

FIANDT, Mary K. 1914-

PERSONAL: Born July 1, 1914, in Superior, Wis.; daughter of James (a firefighter) and Theresa (Sutek) O'Brien; married William Fiandt, August 2, 1938 (died April 16, 1956); married Herbert Dann (a surveyor), September 2, 1965; children: Catherine, William, Michael, James. *Education:* St. Mary's School of Nursing, became R.N.; attended Wisconsin State College and University of Minnesota. *Home and office:* 1119 Hammond Ave., Superior, Wis. 54880. *Agent:* Joan Daves, 515 Madison Ave., New York, N.Y. 10022.

CAREER: Employed as supervisor in Superior, Wis., 1956-57; instructor in nursing in Superior, 1957-72; writer. *Member:* Authors Guild of Authors League of America.

WRITINGS: Willow Cabin, M. Evans, 1974. Contributor of stories to *Creative Wilderness.*

WORK IN PROGRESS: A contemporary novel.

* * *

FINE, Nathan 1893(?)-1979

OBITUARY NOTICE: Born c. 1893; died June 7, 1979, in Albany, Calif. Authority on U.S. labor movement and author. Fine's labor movement activities included work as a labor organizer in Cook County, Ill., in 1919, candidacy for the 1924 Farmer-Labor Party in New York's Sixth Assembly District, and governmental positions dealing with research on labor issues. He also managed Dudley Field Malone's New York gubernatorial campaign in 1920. Fine was affiliated with the Rand School of Social Science for ten years; during that time he wrote *Labor and Farmer Parties in the United States, 1828-1928.* Obituaries and other sources: *New York Times,* June 24, 1979.

* * *

FINKE, Jack A. 1918(?)-1979

OBITUARY NOTICE: Born c. 1918; died September 1, 1979, in New York, N.Y. Editor and author. In addition to serving as editor of *U & LC* ("Upper and Lower Case"), a national quarterly journal of the typographic craft, Finke wrote short stories and plays for radio and television. Obituaries and other sources: *New York Times,* September 5, 1979.

* * *

FINKELSTEIN, Milton 1920-

PERSONAL: Born May 30, 1920, in New York, N.Y.; son of Jacob (in business) and Esther (Sherr) Finkelstein; married Marilyn Bresenoff (an editor), October 12, 1947; children: Joan, David. *Education:* City College (now of the City University of New York), B.S.S., 1942; Columbia University, M.A., 1946; New York University, Ed.D., 1958. *Politics:* Independent. *Religion:* Jewish. *Home:* 33-60 21st St., Long Island City, N.Y. 11106.

CAREER: Board of Education, New York, N.Y., teacher of the homebound, 1943-45, teacher of history, 1945-56, school supervisor, 1956-75; full-time writer, 1975—. Lecturer at colleges. Past vice-president of U.S. Chess Federation; president of Intercollegiate Chess League. Consultant to King Features Syndicate. *Member:* National Council for the Social Studies, Association of Chess Journalists, Marshall Chess Club. *Awards, honors:* Special award for new curriculum from National Association of Temple Educators, 1957, for course of study for post-confirmants; Founders Day award from New York University, 1958, for *Contemporary World Problems.*

WRITINGS—Juveniles, except as indicated: (With John R. Frankson) *Mathematics 7,* Cambridge Book Co., 1960; (with

Jack Robbins) *Mathematics 9,* Cambridge Book Co., 1960; (with Lester Basch) *Spelling Self Taught,* Sterling, 1962; (with Harold H. Eibling, Fred M. King, and James Harlow) *The Story of America,* Laidlaw Brothers, 1964; (with Harold Hammond) *We Hold These Truths . . . ,* Cambridge Book Co., 1964, 2nd edition, 1969; (with Boyd C. Shafer, Everett Augspurger, and Richard A. McLemore) *A High School History of Modern America,* Laidlaw Brothers, 1966, new edition, 1976; (with Benjamin DaSilva and Arlene Loshin) *The African-American in United States History,* Globe Book Co., 1969; (with Jawn A. Sandifer and Elfreda S. Wright) *Minorities, U.S.A.,* Globe Book Co., 1971, new edition, 1977; (with Arthur Nitzburg) *Living in a Consumer's World,* Globe Book Co., 1974, 2nd edition, 1977; *The Substitute Teacher's Kit* (for adults), Globe Book Co., 1974; (with J. Norman Parmer and Robert M. Stephen) *People and Progress: A World History,* Laidlaw Brothers, 1978; (with James Flanagan) *World Geography and Cultures,* AMSCO School Publications, 1980; *The American Political System,* Random House, in press.

Chess books: (With George Koltanowski) *Practical Chess,* Kolty Publishing Co., 1947; (with Koltanowski) *Adventures of a Chessmaster,* McKay, 1965; *Self-Taught Chess,* Cambridge, 1962, revised edition, Doubleday, 1975; (with Koltanowski) *Checkmate!,* Doubleday, 1978.

WORK IN PROGRESS: War and Peace in Our World, with James Flanagan; *High Tide,* about the turning points of World War II; *The Metric Kit,* with Nathan L. Friedman.

SIDELIGHTS: Finkelstein writes: "Random House has dubbed me 'the Isaac Asimov of the textbook world' because of the large number of successful textbooks with which I have been associated. My doctorate was one of the few awarded whose thrust has been textbook construction. My books have always been directed to special audiences, with readability the key. I was associated with the first integrated high school text in American history. Renaissance interests and a chess player's memory have also led to texts in mathematics, science, and chess. My most important books have dealt with minority history. An introduction to one of my books calls me 'that rare author who is equally at home engaged in scholarly research or dealing with the needs of the disadvantaged student.'"

AVOCATIONAL INTERESTS: "My major interest outside of writing has been chess, with more than forty years of tournament play having resulted in a few major successes and a plethora of also-ran disappointments."

* * *

FIORI, Pamela A. 1944-

PERSONAL: Born February 26, 1944, in New Jersey; daughter of Edward A. (a florist) and Rita (a florist; maiden name, Rascate) Fiori. *Education:* Jersey City State College, B.A. (cum laude), 1966. *Office: Travel & Leisure* Magazine, 61 West 51st St., New York, N.Y. 10019.

CAREER/WRITINGS: High school English teacher in Berkeley, N.Y., 1966-67; *Holiday* (magazine), New York City, 1968-71, began as research assistant, became associate editor; *Travel & Leisure* (magazine), New York City, senior editor, 1971-75, editor, 1975—. Author of column, "Window Seat," in *Travel & Leisure.* Contributor to *Travel & Leisure* and *Holiday.* Has made public appearances on television and radio, and at conventions and seminars. *Member:* American Society of Magazine Editors, American Society of Travel Agents, Society of American Travel Writers (vice-president of North-East chapter), Discover America Travel Organization, New York Travel Writers.

SIDELIGHTS: Disenchanted with her teaching career, Fiori went to work for *Holiday* magazine as a research assistant. "I wasn't sure what a research assistant was, but I knew it had to better than teaching," she stated. Since joining the staff of *Travel & Leisure,* she has gained firm control of the magazine's overall development. "I'm trying," she remarked, "to convert, to *transform* the magazine from being merely a travel publication dealing, perhaps, with the more exotic places with some kind of dream element attached, to a magazine that's thoroughly realistic, with a more journalistic bent, with a somewhat less conventional approach, and with a philosophy that strives for excitement."

BIOGRAPHICAL/CRITICAL SOURCES: New York Times, August 27, 1975; *Folio,* June, 1976.

* * *

FISHER, Clay
See ALLEN, Henry Wilson

* * *

FISHER, Douglas Mason 1919-

PERSONAL: Born September 19, 1919, in Sioux Lookout, Ontario, Canada; son of Roy W. (a locomotive engineer) and Pearl (Mason) Fisher; married Barbara E. L. Lamont (a teacher of English), September 9, 1948; children: Mark, Matthew, Tobias, John, Luke. *Education:* University of Toronto, B.A. (with honors), 1949, B.L.S., 1950; studied at University of London, 1952. *Home:* 79 Pentland Place, Kanata, Ontario, Canada K2K 1V9. *Office:* Parliamentary Press Gallery, Ottawa, Ontario, Canada.

CAREER: Queen's University, Kingston, Ontario, government documents librarian, 1952-53; Forestry Library, Port Arthur, Ontario, founder, 1954-55; high school history teacher in Port Arthur, Ontario, 1955-57; Cooperative Commonwealth Federation-New Democratic party member of Parliament from Port Arthur, Ontario, 1957-65; *Toronto Telegram,* Toronto, Ontario, author of political column, "Inside Politics," 1963-71; *Toronto Sun,* Toronto, Ontario, author of syndicated political column, "Politics," 1971—. Political commentator and host of "Insight," on CJOH-TV, 1964—. Founding director and past chairperson of board of directors of Hockey Canada; member of Ontario Commission on the Legislature, 1972-75. Union nominee on conciliation and arbitration boards, especially for railway, airline, and grain trade local unions. *Military service:* Canadian Army, Manitoba Dragoons, 1941-45; served in Europe. *Member:* Coaching Association of Canada (founding director).

WRITINGS: (With S. F. Wise) *Canada's Sporting Heroes,* General Publishing, 1974. Contributor to magazines, including *Legion, Executive,* and *Motor Truck.*

WORK IN PROGRESS: Dictionary of Canadian Post-War Politics.

* * *

FISHER, James (Maxwell McConnell) 1912-1970

OBITUARY NOTICE: Born September 3, 1912, in Clifton, England; died September 29, 1970, in an automobile accident. Author, editor, conservationist, ornithologist, and broadcast personality. Fisher was an extremely popular figure in England, making over seven hundred radio broadcasts and two hundred television appearances. He was also editor at William Collins Sons & Co., Rathbone Books, and Aldus Books Ltd. Fisher wrote many books on birds, nature, and conservation, such as *Wildlife Crisis, The Migration of Birds, Zoos of the World,* and *The Wonderful World of the Sea.* Obituaries and other sources: *The Author's and Writer's Who's Who,* 6th edition, Burke's Peerage, 1971; *Who Was Who in America,* 5th edition, Marquis, 1973.

* * *

FITCH, James Marston 1909-

PERSONAL: Born May 8, 1909, in Washington; son of James Marston and Ellen Cromwell (Payne) Fitch; married Cleopatra Rickman, February 7, 1936. *Education:* Attended University of Alabama, 1925-26, Tulane University, 1927-28, and Columbia University, 1950-52. *Religion:* Episcopalian. *Home:* 232 East Fifth St., New York, N.Y. 10003; and Collaberg Rd., Stony Point, N.Y. 10980. *Office:* School of Architecture, Columbia University, New York, N.Y. 10027.

CAREER: Clarence Jones (architect), Chattanooga, Tenn., draftsman, 1928-30; Herbert Rodger (architect), Nashville, Tenn., chief designer, 1930-33; Tennessee State Planning Board, Nashville, in demographic research, 1934; Federal Housing Administration, Washington, D.C., housing analyst, 1935-36; associate editor of *Architectural Record,* 1936-41; technical editor of *Architectural Forum,* 1945-49; Columbia University, New York, N.Y., lecturer, 1949-53, associate professor, 1954-60, professor of architecture, 1960-77, professor emeritus, 1977—, director of graduate program in historic preservation. Visiting professor at Salzburg Seminars in American Culture, 1964, University of Urbino, 1968, University of Illinois at Chicago Circle, 1968 and 1972, Mid-East Technical University, 1972, International Council of Monuments and Sites Summer Traveling School for Preservationists (in France, Belgium, the Netherlands, and England), 1972, University of Sao Paulo, 1978, University of Pennsylvania, and Cornell University; visiting lecturer at York University, 1971, and University of Texas, 1978; distinguished visiting professor at University of Cincinnati, 1979; lecturer at other colleges and universities in the United States and Europe. President of Rockefeller Foundation, 1956-58. Director of preservation and rehabilitation for New York City's Central Park, 1974; member of U.S. delegation to historic preservation conference in the Soviet Union, 1975; member of panels, architectural awards juries, and international conferences; historic preservation consultant. *Military service:* U.S. Army Air Forces, meteorologist, 1942-45.

MEMBER: American Institute of Architects (associate member), Society of Architectural Historians (member of board of directors, 1970—), Architectural League, American Academy of Political and Social Science, American Association for the Advancement of Science, Victorian Society of America (member of board of directors), Association for Preservation Technology (founding member), Municipal Art Society (New York City; member of board of directors). *Awards, honors:* William K. Fellows scholarship, 1959, for Italy, Greece, and Turkey; Arnold W. Brunner scholarship from New York chapter of American Institute of Architects, 1974, medal, 1976; special achievement award from National Trust for Historic Preservation, 1974; Fulbright scholar in Peru and Guatemala, 1975; conservation service award from U.S. Department of the Interior, 1976; Guggenheim fellowship, certificate of appreciation from mayor of New York City, preservation award from Victorian Society of America, and certificate of merit from Municipal Art Society of New York City, all 1977.

WRITINGS: (With F. F. Rockwell) *A Treasury of American Gardens,* Harper, 1957; *Walter Gropius,* Braziller, 1960; *Architecture and the Esthetics of Plenty,* Columbia University Press, 1961; *Architecture, 1918-1928: From the Novembergruppe to the C.I.A.M.: Functionalism and Expressionism,* Department of Art History and Archaeology, Columbia University, 1962; *American Building,* Houghton, Volume I: *The Historical Forces That Shaped It,* revised edition, 1966, Volume II: *The Environmental Forces That Shape It,* 1972.

Contributor: *Building America,* McGraw, 1957; Walter MacQuade, editor, *Schoolhouse,* Simon & Schuster, 1958; *Four Great Makers of Modern Architecture: Gropius, Le Corbusier, Mies van der Rohe, Wright,* Da Capo Press, 1963; Kenneth S. Lynd, editor, *The Professions in America,* Houghton, 1965; *The Past as Prelude: New Orleans, 1728-1968,* Tulane University Press, 1968; *Light and Lasers,* Freeman & Co., 1969; Richard A. Miller, editor, *Four Great Makers of Modern Architecture,* Da Capo Press, 1970; Albert Fein, editor, *A Study of the Profession of Landscape Architecture: Technical Report,* American Society of Landscape Architecture Foundation, 1972; Robert Gutman, editor, *People and Buildings,* Basic Books, 1972; *Historic Fort Greene,* Fort Greene Landmarks Preservation Committee, 1973; (author of foreword) Harley J. McGhee, *Masonry,* National Trust for Historic Preservation, 1973; Don Yoder, editor, *American Folklore,* University of Texas Press, 1975; (author of foreword) M. David Egan, *Concepts in Thermal Comfort,* Prentice-Hall, 1975.

Contributor of nearly two hundred articles and reviews to art and architecture journals, popular magazines, and newspapers in the United States and abroad, including *Scientific American, American Heritage,* and *Horizon.* Architectural editor of *House Beautiful,* 1949-53.

SIDELIGHTS: Fitch's research on restoration and preservation of historic architecture has taken him to the Middle East, Africa, Scandinavia, the Soviet Union, Turkey, Greece, and other European countries. He has prepared historic preservation plans and programs for cities all over the United States, and for the historic core of Quito, Ecuador, and the Citadel in Cap Haitien, Haiti.

* * *

FITZPATRICK, Daniel Robert 1891-1969

OBITUARY NOTICE: Born March 5, 1891, in Superior, Wis.; died May 18, 1969. Editorial cartoonist. Fitzpatrick worked for the *Chicago Daily News* and the *St. Louis Post-Dispatch.* He won many awards for his cartoons, including the Pulitzer Prize in 1926 and 1954. Obituaries and other sources: *Current Biography,* Wilson, 1941; *Who Was Who in America,* 5th edition, Marquis, 1973.

* * *

FLAHERTY, Daniel Leo 1929-

PERSONAL: Born July 29, 1929, in Chicago, Ill.; son of Daniel Leo (a business executive) and Marguerite (Pauly) Flaherty. *Education:* Loyola University, Chicago, Ill., A.B., 1952, M.A., 1957; West Baden College, Ph.L., 1954, S.T.L., 1961; further graduate study at Northwestern University. *Home:* 201 Dempster St., Evanston, Ill. 60201. *Office:* Loyola University Press, 3441 North Ashland Ave., Chicago, Ill. 60657.

CAREER: Entered Society of Jesus (Jesuits), 1947, ordained Roman Catholic priest, 1960; America Press, Inc., New York, N.Y., book editor, 1962-65, executive editor, 1965-71, secretary, 1965-71, business manager, 1969-71, executive secretary of Catholic Book Club, 1967-71; Loyola University Press, Chicago, Ill., executive director, 1971-73; Society of Jesus, Chicago Province, Chicago, Ill., provincial, 1973-79; Loyola University Press, executive director, 1979—. Member of Appeal of Conscience Foundation, 1967—. Vice-chairperson of board of directors of Loyola University, 1971-73; head of board of directors of University of Detroit, 1972-73. *Member:* Catholic Press Association.

WRITINGS: (With W. D. Ciszek) *With God in Russia,* McGraw, 1964; (with Ciszek) *He Leadeth Me,* Doubleday, 1973. Contributor to magazines in the United States and abroad.

* * *

FLEMING, Irene 1923(?)-1979

OBITUARY NOTICE: Born c. 1923 in Cleveland, Ohio; died of leukemia, August 23, 1979, in Bethesda, Md. Journalist. Fleming was women's editor of the *Rome Daily American* for eight years and also wrote for the *International Daily News* in Rome. She contributed articles to newspapers, including the *New York Times,* and to magazines, including *Time.* Obituaries and other sources: *Washington Post,* August 30, 1979.

* * *

FLICK, Carlos Thomas 1927-

PERSONAL: Born November 10, 1927, in Roanoke, Va.; son of Fred J. (a factory worker) and Grace (a factory worker; maiden name, Thomas) Flick; married Marjorie Perry (a teacher), August 28, 1953 (divorced April, 1979); children: Amy, Stephen, Marc. *Education:* Wake Forest College (now University), B.A., 1953; graduate study at Southeastern Baptist Seminary, 1953-54; Duke University, M.A., 1957, Ph.D., 1960. *Office:* Department of History, Mercer University, Macon, Ga. 31207.

CAREER: Mercer University, Macon, Ga., assistant professor, 1958-63, associate professor, 1963-68, professor of history, 1968—. *Member:* Conference on British Studies.

WRITINGS: *The Birmingham Political Union and the Movements for Reform in Britain, 1830-1839,* Archon Books, 1978. Contributor to history journals.

* * *

FLIPPO, Chet 1943-

PERSONAL: Born October 21, 1943, in Ft. Worth, Tex.; son of Chet W. (a minister) and Johnnie July (in crafts; maiden name, Black) Flippo; married Martha Hume (a writer), July 10, 1971. *Education:* Sam Houston State University, B.S., 1965; Defense Language Institute, Washington, D.C., certificate, 1966; University of Texas, M.A., 1974. *Office: Rolling Stone* Magazine, 745 Fifth Ave., New York, N.Y. 10022.

CAREER/WRITINGS: Palestine Herald-Press, Palestine, Tex., reporter, 1965; *Rolling Stone,* New York, N.Y., associate editor, 1970—. Contributor of numerous articles to magazines, including *Texas Monthly, Texas Observer, Look,* and *Rolling Stone;* contributor to *American Mass Media,* edited by Robert Atwan, Barry Orton, and William Vesterman, Random House, 1978. Member of board of directors of Gibson Hall of Fame. *Military service:* U.S. Navy, 1966-69, served as intelligence analyst. *Member:* Sigma Delta Chi.

WORK IN PROGRESS: A biography of Hank Williams, publication by Simon & Schuster expected in 1980.

SIDELIGHTS: Flippo writes: "Chet Flippo became a magazine writer because newspapers wouldn't hire him. He is now grateful about that. *Rolling Stone,* a young magazine that the 'real world' of print media would not take seriously, offered for him, and indeed for a whole generation of young writers, a forum and a chance."

* * *

FLYNN, John Thomas 1882-1964

OBITUARY NOTICE: Born October 25, 1882, in Bladensburg, Md.; died April 14, 1964. Journalist, editor, and author. Flynn was city editor for the *New Haven Register* and the *New York Globe,* and editor of *Collier's.* He was also a columnist for the *New Republic* and commentator for the Mutual Broadcasting System (MBS). His works include *God's Gold: The Story of Rockefeller and His Times, Country Squire in the White House,* and *The Decline of the American Republic.* Obituaries and other sources: *Who Was Who in America,* 4th edition, Marquis, 1968; *American Authors and Books: 1640 to the Present Day,* Crown, 1972.

* * *

FOERSTER, Leona M(itchell) 1930-

PERSONAL: Born March 15, 1930, in Chicago, Ill.; daughter of Charles John (a contractor) and Helen (Linzer) Mitchell; married Eugene Paul Foerster, January 7, 1966 (divorced October 29, 1974). *Education:* Northwestern University, B.S.Ed. (summa cum laude), 1955; Texas Technological College (now Texas Tech University), M.Ed., 1964; University of Arizona, Ed.D., 1968. *Politics:* Republican. *Religion:* Presbyterian. *Home address:* Route 8, Box 14-H, Lubbock, Tex. 79407. *Office:* College of Education, Texas Tech University, Lubbock, Tex. 79409.

CAREER: Elementary school teacher in Reno, Nev., 1956, high school physical education and health teacher, 1956-57; high school physical education and dance teacher in Palm Springs, Calif., 1957; substitute teacher at U.S. Army dependents' schools in Frankfurt and Darmstadt, Germany, 1958, elementary school teacher at Army and Air Force dependents' schools in Darmstadt, 1958-59, and Rhein Main, Germany, 1959-60; elementary school teacher in Harlingen, Tex., 1960-62, Lubbock, Tex., 1962-65, Belleville, Ill., 1965, Somerton, Ariz., 1966-67, and Tucson, Ariz., 1968-69; Texas Tech University, Lubbock, assistant professor, 1969-72, associate professor, 1972-75, professor of education, 1975—, member of staff at Institute for Teachers and Aides of Migrant Children, 1969. Speaker and consultant.

MEMBER: National Education Association, National Council of Teachers of English, National Association for the Education of Young Children, Association for Supervision and Curriculum Development, Council on Anthropology and Education, Fund for the Animals, National Wildlife Federation, Texas Association for Supervision and Curriculum Development, Texas State Teachers Association, West Texas Museum Association, South Plains Archaeological Society, Lubbock Humane Society, Pi Lambda Theta, Phi Kappa Phi.

WRITINGS: (With Gene Rooze) *Teaching Elementary Social Studies: A New Perspective,* C. E. Merrill, 1972; *Post Office With a Punch: A Model for Teaching,* Croft Educational, 1973; *Body Language: A Model for Teaching,* Croft Educational, 1973; *Learning About Our Flag: A Model for Teaching,* Croft Educational, 1973; *Learning to Listen: A Model for Teaching,* Croft Educational, 1973; *Clothing a Lesson: A Model for Teaching,* Croft Educational, 1973;

Handbook for Communication, W. S. Benson, Books I-VI, 1975, revised editions, 1979, Book II—Transitional, 1979; *The First Americans: A Model for Teaching,* Croft Educational, 1976; *Exploring Transportation: A Model for Teaching,* Croft Educational, 1976; *Constantly Changing: A Model for Teaching,* Croft Educational, 1976; *Body Language: The Silent Communicator,* Croft Educational, 1976; *Specialization: A Model for Teaching,* Croft Educational, 1977; *What's All That Static?: A Model for Teaching,* Croft Educational, 1978; *Why Not Multicultural Education in Your Classroom?,* Croft Educational, 1978; (contributor) *Administration: Making Programs Work for Children and Families,* National Association for the Education of Young Children, 1979; (contributor) *Foundations of American Education: Readings,* 4th edition, Allyn & Bacon, 1979.

Editor of "Read-Along Woodland Fables," story cards for primary students, with sound tapes and teacher's manuals, Coronet Instructional Media, 1977. Editor of "Children's Page," a column in *Language Arts,* 1975-76. Contributor of more than fifty articles and reviews to education journals.

WORK IN PROGRESS: My Horse, of Course and *Kee Moves to the City,* children's books; *Song of the Ree,* the history of the Arikara tribe; "Multicultural Activity Box," for elementary school students; research on Native American history and culture.

SIDELIGHTS: Leona Foerster writes: "For quite some time, I have been interested in exploring the relationship between anthropology and education. I consider myself an educational anthropologist, and feel that this discipline can contribute substantially toward solving many educational problems, particularly in the areas of working with culturally diverse students and classroom organization and management.

"Although I can't claim Indian blood, I have been accepted by my Native American friends and feel a part of their culture. My goal in life at this time is to write children's books which will help young people understand more about America's first citizens and how they live here and now. I feel that the need for such understanding is critical."

* * *

FOGARTY, Jonathan Titulescu, Esq.
See FARRELL, James T(homas)

* * *

FOLEY, Leonard 1913-

PERSONAL: Born October 18, 1913, in Lafayette, Ind.; son of John Joseph and Frances (Schrader) Foley. *Education:* Duns Scotus College, B.A.; University of Detroit, M.A. (religious education); University of Cincinnati, M.A. (English). *Office: St. Anthony Messenger,* 1615 Republic, Cincinnati, Ohio 45210.

CAREER: Entered Ordo Fratrum Minorum (O.F.M.; Franciscans), ordained Roman Catholic priest; worked as seminary teacher in Cincinnati, Ohio, 1940-52; parish priest in Royal Oak, Mich., 1952-55; missionary, 1956-64; *St. Anthony Messenger,* Cincinnati, Ohio, editor, 1965-66; director and member of staff at Friarhurst Retreat House, 1966-74; *St. Anthony Messenger,* associate editor, 1977—.

WRITINGS: All published by St. Anthony Messenger Press: *What's Happening to Confession,* 1970; *Signs of Love,* 1971; (editor) *Saint of the Day,* Volume I, 1974, Volume II, 1975; *Your Confession, Using the New Ritual,* 1975; *Sincerely Yours, Paul,* 1977; *God Never Says Yes But,* 1979.

FORD, Edward (Charles) 1928-
(Whitey Ford)

PERSONAL: Born October 21, 1928, in New York, N.Y.; son of James (a bartender) and Edith Ford; married Joan Foran, April 14, 1951; children: Sally Ann, Eddie, Tommy. *Education:* Graduated from high school, 1946. *Residence:* Lake Success, N.Y. *Address:* % Shea Stadium, Roosevelt Ave. and 126th St., Flushing, N.Y. 11368.

CAREER: New York Yankees baseball team, New York City, pitcher, 1947-67, scout and minor league pitching coach, 1967, pitching coach with parent club, 1968; Fahnestock & Co. (brokerage firm), New York City, customer's man, 1968—. *Military service:* U.S. Army Signal Corps, 1951-53. *Awards, honors:* Named as pitcher on *Sporting News* All-Star major league teams, 1955 and 1956; named American League pitcher of the year by *Sporting News,* 1955, 1961 and 1963; named as pitcher on *Sporting News* American League All-Star teams, 1961 and 1963; voted most valuable player of World Series by *Sport* magazine, 1961; awarded Babe Ruth Trophy by baseball writers of New York City, 1961; won Cy Young Memorial Award, 1961; elected to baseball's Hall of Fame, 1974.

WRITINGS: (Under name Edward "Whitey" Ford; with Jack Lang) *The Fighting Southpaw,* Argonaut, 1962; (under name Whitey Ford; with Mickey Mantle and Joseph Durso) *Whitey and Mickey: A Joint Autobiography of the Yankee Years,* Viking, 1977.

SIDELIGHTS: In 1946, after pitching the Thirty-fourth Avenue Boys to a victory over the Bay Ridge Cubs, Whitey Ford attracted the attention of major league scouts. The New York Yankees, the Boston Red Sox, and the Brooklyn Dodgers all made a bid for the southpaw, who eventually signed with the Yankees for a $7,000 bonus. By the middle of the '47 season, the director of the Dodger farm system knew he'd made a mistake in failing to sign the young prospect. "Ford would have been a bargain at a bonus of fifty thousand," he admitted. "[He] has the guts of a burglar and the curve ball of a mature pro who had been pitching for ten years."

In 1950, Ford drew a rough introduction to major league competition, but finished his rookie season with an impressive record. The Yankees, locked in a pennant race with the Detroit Tigers, called on Ford for five innings of relief pitching against the Boston Red Sox. He gave up seven hits, six walks, and five runs. "I'm not worried," he remarked after the game. He then collected six straight victories. In the closing weeks of the pennant race, manager Casey Stengel picked Ford to pitch in a crucial game against the Tigers. Detroit held a half-game lead over the Yanks at game-time, but fell to second place when Ford hurled an 8-1 decision. The Yankees went on to win the American League pennant. For the season, Ford produced nine wins against one loss and won the fourth game of the World Series.

Ford spent the next two years with the U.S. Army Signal Corps. Though he continued to pitch on his own, he returned to the Yankees weighing 190 pounds and convinced that he wasn't half as effective as he was before entering the service. The next four seasons, however, proved to be triumphant ones: eighteen wins, six losses in 1953; sixteen wins, eight losses in 1954; eighteen wins, seven losses in 1955; nineteen wins, six losses in 1956.

Ford encountered a series of setbacks during the 1957 season. He was not only plagued with arm and shoulder troubles, but also was involved in the much publicized Copacabana incident. Throwing sliders in a jerky delivery had strained his arm muscles and, for a time, he thought his career had ended. Then, on May 16, he and five other Yankees—Mickey Mantle, Yogi Berra, Hank Bauer, Johnny Kucks, and Billy Martin—celebrated Martin's birthday at the Copacabana night club. That evening, another club patron claimed he was beaten by Hank Bauer. Because they had also broken training rules, the Yankee management fined each player $1,000 and later traded Billy Martin. Ford completed the season with only eleven wins and five losses, but found a smooth and long pitching motion alleviated his arm problem.

The 1961 and 1963 seasons were the Yankee pitcher's best years. Under new manager Ralph Houk in '61, Ford went to the mound every fourth day and by late July had accrued eighteen victories and two defeats. He had also tied a club record by winning fourteen consecutive games. He finished the year with twenty-five wins, four losses and won the Cy Young Memorial Award. His performance in '63 was equally as good, winning twenty-four games against seven defeats.

Ford never had a losing season until the end of his career. In 1966, he again experienced pain in his left shoulder and, in August, underwent an operation for circulatory blockage. He won only two games that year, losing five. The following year, he tested his arm until Memorial Day. In his seventh appearance of the year, May 30, 1967, he suddenly walked off the mound in a game with Detroit. When his teammates returned to the clubhouse he was gone, as were his clothes. Deciding not to struggle along as a mediocre pitcher, he had packed up his belongings, returned home, and retired at age thirty-eight. His pitching record showed two wins, four losses.

Ford established several major league records during his career, many of them coming in World Series play. In the 1960 series against the Pittsburgh Pirates, he tossed back-to-back shutouts. The next year, he blanked Cincinnati in the opening game of the World Series and was on his way to a fourth shutout when he was hit by a batted ball. Forced to leave the mound with a swollen foot after five innings, he had nevertheless broken the long-standing record for consecutive scoreless innings set by pitcher Babe Ruth. Ford extended his record streak of thirty-two scoreless innings to thirty-three-and-two-thirds innings in 1962. His other World Series records included most starts (twenty-two), most strikeouts (ninety-four), and most innings pitched (146).

In the book *Whitey and Mickey,* Ford and former teammate Mantle serve up "an ebullient, good-natured remembrance" of their careers with the Yankees. "What it does best is illustrate the camaraderie that professional athletes share with one another on and off the playing field and present a clubhouse view of two of the Yankees' greatest during some of their team's most memorable years," wrote Mel Watkins. A critic for *Saturday Review* called the reminiscence an "enchanting tale." He added: "Brawling, drinking, possibly womanizing wherever they happened to be, Mick and Slick, as their teammates called them, couldn't have composed a dull book, and with Mr. Durso's expert guidance they haven't."

BIOGRAPHICAL/CRITICAL SOURCES: Saturday Evening Post, May 12, 1956; *New York Post,* June 3, 1957, August 28, 1961; *New York Times,* October 13, 1960, May 20, 1962, June 18, 1977; *Sports Illustrated,* July 24, 1961; *Look,* June 5, 1962; *Dallas News,* January 16, 1974; *Newsweek,* January 28, 1974; *Biography News,* Gale, February, 1974; *New York Times Book Review,* May 1, 1977; *Saturday Review,* May 14, 1977.*

—*Sketch by B. Hal May*

* * *

FORD, Whitey
See FORD, Edward (Charles)

* * *

FORDE, Gerhard O(laf) 1927-

PERSONAL: Surname is pronounced *Fer*-dy; born September 10, 1927, in Starbuck, Minn.; son of Gerhard O. (a minister) and Hannah (a musician; maiden name, Halvorson) Forde; married Marianna Carlson (a professor), June 20, 1964; children: Timothy, Sarah, Geoffrey. *Education:* Luther College, Decorah, Iowa, B.A., 1950; graduate study at University of Wisconsin—Madison, 1950-51; Luther Theological Seminary, St. Paul, Minn., B.Th., 1955; Harvard University, Th.D., 1967. *Home:* 2245 Luther Place, St. Paul, Minn. 55108. *Office:* Luther-Northwestern Theological Seminaries, 2375 Como Ave., St. Paul, Minn. 55108.

CAREER: St. Olaf College, Northfield, Minn., instructor in religion, 1955-56; Luther College, Decorah, Iowa, assistant professor of religion, 1961-63; Luther-Northwestern Theological Seminaries, St. Paul, Minn., associate professor, 1964-71, professor of systematic theology, 1971—. Tutor at Mansfield College, Oxford, 1968-70. *Military service:* U.S. Army, 1946-47; became sergeant. *Member:* American Academy of Religion. *Awards, honors:* Fredrik A. Schoitz fellowship from Aid Association for Lutherans, 1972-73.

WRITINGS: The Law-Gospel Debate, Augsburg, 1969; *Where God Meets Man,* Augsburg, 1972; (with James Nestingen) *Free to Be,* Augsburg, 1975. Contributor to magazines. Member of editorial board of *Dialog.*

WORK IN PROGRESS: A book on the Luther-Erasmus debate.

SIDELIGHTS: Forde comments: "My specific interest is Lutheran theology. My first two books express the heart of my interests and point of view. My motivation is to express as clearly as possible the significance of Lutheran theology for the contemporary situation."

* * *

FORGIE, George B(arnard) 1941-

PERSONAL: Born May 31, 1941, in Philadelphia, Pa.; son of James William and Mary (Barnard) Forgie. *Education:* Amherst College, B.A., 1963; Stanford University, LL.B. and M.A., both 1967, Ph.D., 1972. *Home:* 3003 Bonnie Rd., Austin, Tex. 78703. *Office:* Department of History, University of Texas, Austin, Tex. 78712.

CAREER: Princeton University, Princeton, N.J., lecturer, 1969-72, assistant professor of history, 1972-74; University of Texas, Austin, assistant professor of history, 1974—. *Member:* American Historical Association, Organization of American Historians. *Awards, honors:* Allan Nevins Award from Society of American Historians, 1973, for "Father Past and Child Nation: The Romantic Imagination and the Origins of the Civil War"; Harry H. Ransom Award from University of Texas, 1979.

WRITINGS: Patricide in the House Divided: A Psychological Interpretation of Lincoln and His Age, Norton, 1979.

SIDELIGHTS: Forgie comments: "In *Patricide and the House Divided* I argue that the sectional crisis leading to the American Civil War was structured by one overbearing fact: the dominant figures in American politics and culture in the

1850's had been born in the early republic. They were reared to think of its founders as immortal fathers whom they must obey and imitate, themselves as brothers and sisters in a family, and the Union as an inherited house which they must preserve. These metaphors were far more than mere rhetorical decorations: they actually worked to transmit emotions and fantasies from the private realm to political conflicts—with fateful results.

"I show how the paradoxical imperative of imitating heroes in a post-heroic age deferring to the illustrious dead in a democracy puzzled and oppressed ambitious men—none more than Abraham Lincoln, who is the central figure in *Patricide*. He understood that fathers' achievements ruled out immortality for their successors, unless they should be summoned to save the fathers' institutions from patricidal destruction. Projecting his adverse feelings toward the fathers onto an imagined being, Lincoln first prophesied the emergence of a murderous son, and then found him in the representative figure of his great rival, Stephen A. Douglas, when the Little Giant engineered the passage of the Kansas-Nebraska bill in 1854. Lincoln hoped that isolating Douglas would peacefully resolve the crisis of the Union, save the fathers' house, and satisfy his own ambition. But the ironic—and direct—result of Lincoln's rise to prominence and power was the coming of the American Civil War, which separated Americans forever from the world of the fathers he had been struggling to restore."

* * *

FORREST, Leon 1937-

CAREER: Novelist, playwright, and poet.

WRITINGS: There Is a Tree More Ancient Than Eden (novel), introduction by Ralph Ellison, Random House, 1973; *The Bloodworth Orphans* (novel), Random House, 1977. Also author of poetry and plays.

SIDELIGHTS: At present Leon Forrest's works are few in number yet what he has written has been good, according to critics. His first novel, *There Is a Tree More Ancient Than Eden,* was widely reviewed.

Written in a stream-of-consciousness style, *There Is a Tree More Ancient Than Eden* is about the complex relationships between the illegitimate children of an old family who once owned slaves. The book "represents an awe-inspiring fusion of American cultural myth, Black American history, Black fundamentalist religion, the doctrine and dogma of Catholicism (stations of the Cross and the Precious Blood Cathedral), and an autobiographical recall of days of anxiety and confusion in the city," wrote Houston A. Baker, Jr., in *Black World.* Another *Black World* reviewer, Jack Gilbert, noted that "Forrest has woven an hypnotic fabric with words that are part jazz, part blues, part gospel," and likened the work to Ralph Ellison's *Invisible Man,* describing it as equally "moving and forceful in its poetic flow."

Because *There Is a Tree More Ancient Than Eden* is written in a stream-of-consciousness style and is shadowed by a feeling of doom, Forrest seems to think of himself as another William Faulkner, wrote L. J. Davis in *The New York Times Book Review.* But, Davis said, Forrest never explains why doom is being felt nor does he explain the mysterious symbolism he uses that cannot be interpreted by the reader. Joel Motley, who in the *Harvard Advocate* called the book "a powerful work of literature," noted that while Forrest does use a Faulknerian style, he makes it into his own to express the "urban black experience." Baker concluded that *A Tree More Ancient Than Eden* "contains insight, streaks of brilliance, and a finely-formed intelligence that promises further revelations."

BIOGRAPHICAL/CRITICAL SOURCES: Kirkus Reviews, March 15, 1973, March 1, 1977; *Publishers Weekly,* March 26, 1973, March 21, 1977; *New York Times,* June 8, 1973; *Booklist,* July 1, 1973, May 15, 1977; *New Leader,* July 9, 1973; *Choice,* October, 1973; *New York Times Book Review,* October 21, 1973, May 1, 1977; *Black World,* January, 1974; *Contemporary Literary Criticism,* Volume 4, Gale, 1975.*

* * *

FORSYTHE, Robert
See CRICHTON, Kyle Samuel

* * *

FORTY, George 1927-

PERSONAL: Born September 10, 1927, in London, England; son of Herbert James (a director) and Edith Forty; married Anne Wright (a writer), October 9, 1953; children: Simon, Jonathan, Adam, Jason. *Education:* Attended Queen's College, Oxford, 1945-46, Royal Military Academy, Sandhurst, 1947-48, and Staff College, Camberley, 1959. *Politics:* Conservative. *Religion:* Church of England. *Home:* 36 Heaton Grove, Bradford, West Yorkshire BD9 4DZ, England.

CAREER: Career officer in British Army, 1948-77, retired as lieutenant colonel; writer, 1977—. *Member:* Royal United Services Institution, Staff College Club, Royal Tank Regiment Association.

WRITINGS: Desert Rats at War, Ian Allan, Volume I: *North Africa,* 1975, Volume II: *Europe,* 1977; *Afrika Korps at War,* Volume I: *The Road to Alexandria,* Scribner, 1978, Volume II: *The Long Road Back,* Terminal House, 1978; *Patton's Third Army at War,* Ian Allen, 1978; (with wife, Anne Forty) *They Also Served,* Midas Books, 1979; *Modern Combat Vehicles: Chieftain,* Ian Allan, 1979; *U.S. Army Handbook of World War II,* Scribner, 1979; *The Fifth Army at War,* Scribner, 1980; (with A. Forty) *She-Warriors,* Midas Books, 1980; *Modern Combat Vehicles: Combat Vehicle Reconnaissance,* Ian Allan, 1980, *United Nations at War in Korea,* Ian Allan, 1981; *Called Up: A Pictorial History of National Service,* Ian Allan, in press. Also author of issue Number V of *Armed Forces* Magazine, distributed by Sky Books International, 1979. Contributor to *War Monthly, Model Soldier,* and *Military Modelling.*

* * *

FOSTER, Cedric 1900-1975

OBITUARY NOTICE: Born August 31, 1900, in West Hartford, Conn.; died March, 1975. Journalist and news commentator. Foster wrote for newspapers, including the *Hartford Courant* and the *San Francisco Associated Press.* He was also news commentator for the Mutual Broadcasting System (MBS) and a number of other radio stations in Hartford, Conn., and Denver, Colo. Foster received many awards for his work in broadcasting. Obituaries and other sources: *Who Was Who in America,* 6th edition, Marquis, 1976.

* * *

FOSTER, Genevieve Stump 1893-1979

OBITUARY NOTICE—See index for *CA* sketch: Born April 13, 1893, in Oswego, N.Y.; died August 30, 1979, in Westport, Conn. Commercial artist, illustrator, and author of children's books. Foster wrote nineteen children's books, and was best known for her technique of choosing historical figures and weaving a story around their perception of events around them. Her first book was *George Washington's World.* Obituaries and other sources: *Authors of Books for Young People,* 2nd edition, Scarecrow, 1971; *More Books by More People,* Citation, 1974; *The Writers Directory, 1980-82,* St. Martin's, 1979; *New York Times,* September 1, 1979; *Publishers Weekly,* September 17, 1979; *AB Bookman's Weekly,* October 8, 1979.

* * *

FOSTER, Herbert W. 1920(?)-1979

OBITUARY NOTICE: Born c. 1920 in Amarillo, Tex.; died September 16, 1979, in Cheverly, Md. Publicist and journalist. Since 1957 Foster had been associated with the National Coal Association, beginning as associate director of public relations and becoming vice-president for press relations in 1972. Before that time he had been a reporter with the United Press (now United Press International), working in the Atlanta, Ga., Raleigh, N.C., and Washington, D.C., bureaus. His assignments included coverage of two national political campaigns in the 1950's, and the vice-presidential campaign of Richard Nixon in 1956. Obituaries and other sources: *Washington Post,* September 18, 1979.

* * *

FOSTER, Margaret Lesser 1899(?)-1979

OBITUARY NOTICE: Born c. 1899 in Montana; died November 21, 1979, in New York, N.Y. Editor. Foster worked for a time on the *Seattle Post-Intelligencer* and the *Seattle Times,* but she is best known as editor of the children's book department for Doubleday, a position she held for thirty years. Obituaries and other sources: *New York Times,* November 23, 1979.

* * *

FOURNIER, Pierre 1916-
(Pierre Gascar)

PERSONAL: Born March 13, 1916, in Paris, France; son of Jean and Rachel (Bernardin) Fournier; married Jacqueline Salmon, July, 1946 (marriage ended); married Alice Simon, February 10, 1958; children: (first marriage) Jean-Pierre, Jacques. *Education:* Educated in France. *Address:* 13 boulevard du Montparnasse, 75006 Paris, France. *Agent:* Georges Borchardt, 14 West 55th St., New York, N.Y.

CAREER: France-Soir (newspaper), Paris, France, 1945-58, began as reporter, became literary critic; writer. Served as information officer for World Health Organization, 1956-57. Lecturer in several countries, 1958-65; visiting professor at University of Texas at Austin, 1969. *Awards, honors:* Prix des Critiques, 1953, for *Les Betes;* Prix Goncourt, 1953, for *Les Betes* [and] *Le Temps des morts;* grand prix de litterature, Academie francaise, 1969; chevalier de la Legion d'honneur. *Military service:* French Army, 1937-45.

WRITINGS—All under pseudonym Pierre Gascar; in English: *Les Betes* [and] *Le Temps des morts,* both selections also published separately (see below), Gallimard, 1953, translation by Jean Stewart published as *Beasts and Men,* Little, Brown, 1956, also published with *The Seed* (see below); *Les Betes* (short stories; contains "Les Chevaux," "La Vie eclarlate," "Les Betes," "Gaston," "Le Chat," and "Entre chiens et loups"), Gallimard, 1953, translation by Stewart published in *Beasts and Men* (see above); *Le Temps des morts,* Gallimard, 1955, translation by Stewart published in *Beasts and Men* (see above); *La Graine* (novel), Gallimard, 1955, translation by Merloyed published as *The Seed,* Little, Brown, 1956, also published with *Beasts and Men* (see below); *Les Femmes* (contains "Les Femmes," "L'Incendie," "L'Asile," and "La Mere"), Gallimard, 1955, translation published with *Soleils* in *Women and the Sun* (see below); *La Barre de corail* [and] *Les Aveugles de Saint-Xavier,* Gallimard, 1958, translation of *Barre de corail* published as *The Coral Barrier* (see below); *La Barre de corail,* Gallimard, 1959, translation by Lawrence published as *The Coral Barrier,* Little, Brown, 1961; *Beasts and Men* [and] *The Seed,* Meridan Books, 1960 (see above).

Soleils (contains "La Citerne," "Marbre," "Les Chasses d'Ethiope," and "La Petite Place"), Gallimard, 1960, translation published with *Les Femmes* in *Women and the Sun* (see below); *Le Fugitif,* Gallimard, 1961, translation by Lawrence published as *The Fugitive,* Little, Brown, 1964; *Chambord,* photographs by Andre Martin, Delpire, 1962, translation by Richard Howard published under same title, Macmillan, 1964; *Les Moutons de feu,* Gallimard, 1963, translation by Lawrence published as *Lambs of Fire,* Braziller, c. 1965; *Le Meilleur de la vie,* Gallimard, 1964, translation by Lawrence published as *The Best Years,* Braziller, 1967; *Women and the Sun* (contains translations of stories originally published in *Les Femmes* and *Soleils:* "The Cistern," "The Blind Men of St. Xavier," "Marble," "The Forest Fire," "The Asylum," "The Little Square," "Ethiopian Hunt," "The Watershed," and "The Women"; see above), Little, Brown, c. 1964.

In French: *Les Meubles* (novel), Gallimard, 1949; *Le Visage clos* (novel), Gallimard, 1951; *Aujourd'hui la Chine,* Clairefontaine, 1955; *Chine ouverte,* photographs by Erby Landau, Gallimard, 1955; *L'Herbe des rue* (novel), Gallimard, 1956; *Voyage chez les vivants,* Gallimard, 1958; *Le Pas perdus,* Gallimard, 1958.

Normandie, Arthaud, 1962; *Vertiges du present, ce difficile accord avec le monde,* Arthaud, 1962; *L'Expression des sentiments chez animaux,* Hachette, 1964; *Saint-Marc* (title means "San Marco"), photographs by Andre Matin, Delpire, 1964; *Les Charmes* (novel), Gallimard, 1965; *Histoire de la captivite de Francais en Allemagne,* Gallimard, 1967; *Auto,* Gallimard, 1967; *L'Or,* Delpire, 1968; *Les Chimeres,* Gallimard, 1969.

L'Arche, Gallimard, 1971; *Rimbaud et la commune,* Gallimard, 1971; *La Chine et les chinois,* photographs by Claude Arthaud and F. Herbert-Stevens, Arthaud, 1971; *Le Presage,* Gallimard, 1972; *Quartier latin,* Table, 1973; *L'Homme et l'animal,* A. Michel, 1974; *Les Sources,* Gallimard, c. 1975; *Dans la foret humaine,* Laffont, 1976; *Le Bal des ardents,* Gallimard, 1977; *Sur les routes de France,* Arthaud, 1978; *L'Ombre de Robespierre,* Gallimard, 1979; *Un jardin de cure,* Stock, 1979.

Plays: "Les Pas perdus", first produced in Paris, France, at Theatre Fontaine in 1957; "Les Murs", first aired on 1st Station, O.R.T.F.-TV, Paris, 1964; "La Nuit parle," first aired on 2nd Station, O.R.T.F.-TV, 1969. Contributor to *Le Figaro, Harper's, Mademoiselle, Evergreen, Atlantic,* and other periodicals.

WORK IN PROGRESS: Le Reve et la vie, a book about Paris during the romantic period.

SIDELIGHTS: Pierre Fournier, known primarily by his *nom de plume* Pierre Gascar, was taken prisoner by the Nazis during World War II. Twice he escaped, but was captured again and transported to a concentration camp in the

Ukraine. The profound effect that this experience had on Gascar prompted him to express his feelings in writing.

In *Beasts and Men,* a collection of six short stories and one novelette, Gascar symbolizes man's inhumanity to man by exploring the relationship between man and animals. The book won Gascar the Prix Goncourt in France and was also met with favorable reviews in the United States. A *New Yorker* critic noted: "Pierre Gascar's short stories in this collection, which all touch on accepted but extremely sinister relationships between men and animals are exceptionally fine, both in their writing and in their observation. But it is the short novel, 'The Season of the Dead,' that marks him as a writer of the first rank."

As in "The Season of the Dead," the prisoner of war theme is present in *The Fugitive.* The protagonist (Paul), like the author, has escaped from a German camp after having been captured during World War II. After the war he travels throughout Germany, in search of himself and a reason for being. Reviewers' opinions on the book conflicted. "The novel has moments of real visual power," observed a *Times Literary Supplement* critic, "but it is not well sustained and proves again that Pierre Gascar is much better when he sticks to shorter forms." Taking another stance, H. F. Peters expressed his view that Gascar's "evocative style," which "illuminates every page, transforms the most commonplace events, and produces an almost Rembrandtesque effect of chiaroscuro—haunting half-tones, somber and sonorous, the twilight of a soul in travail."

All of Gascar's works do not deal with the same theme, however. *The Seed,* for instance, considered by some critics as autobiographical, is written from the point of view of a small boy. The sensitive, unloved ten-year-old, living with an aunt and uncle in southern France, finds he must display cunning in order to survive. To help support himself he searches through garbage heaps for discarded peach seeds, begs, and builds a dam to trap fish, filching needed materials. The chance of rescue from such a stark existence arrives in the form of a scholarship. "It is a valuable social document as well as a book of genuine literary charm," observed Henri Peyre. Anthony West commented that it "is beyond question one of those imaginative and truthful novels that are destined to survive and be recognized as literature of value for a long time to come."

Writing to *CA,* Gascar called himself a literary *touche-a-tout,* or jack-of-all-trades. He has not only penned fictional works, but has also covered such diverse topics as politics, sociology, botany, ecology, animal psychology, history, and art in his writings. He grouped himself with the romantic age writers who, considering themselves educators, were well-versed in a variety of subjects. Voltaire could speak as well of history of religion as Newton's theories or the nature of fire, Gascar pointed out. And Jean Jacques Rouseau was able to write on botany, music, and the education of children. Gascar concluded that, as long as he can view each new topic with wonder, there is still a place for the jack-of-all-trades writer.

BIOGRAPHICAL/CRITICAL SOURCES: *New Yorker,* June 30, 1956, July 18, 1959; *New York Times,* May 31, 1959; *New York Times Book Review,* April 9, 1961, February 19, 1967; *Times Literary Supplement,* February 20, 1964; *Saturday Review,* April 11, 1964, March 13, 1965; *Books Abroad,* spring, 1965; *Christian Science Monitor,* April 8, 1965; *Book Week,* March 12, 1967; *Contemporary Literary Criticism,* Volume 11, Gale, 1979.

FOWLER, Eugene Devlan 1890-1960
(Gene Fowler)

OBITUARY NOTICE: Born March 8, 1890, in Denver, Colo.; died July 2, 1960. Editor, author, and one of the most important journalists of the twentieth century. After reporting for many newspapers, Fowler was editor of the *New York Daily Mirror,* the *New York American,* and the *New York Morning Telegraph.* He also wrote movie scripts for most of the major motion picture studios such as Twentieth Century-Fox, Paramount, Universal, and United Artists. Some of his more than twenty-five movie scripts are "Union Depot," "Call of the Wild," and "Jesse James." Fowler's works include *A Solo in Tom-Toms, Schnozzola: The Story of Jimmy Durante, Beau James,* and *Skyline.* Obituaries and other sources: *Current Biography,* Wilson, 1944, September, 1960; *Who Was Who in America,* 4th edition, Marquis, 1968.

* * *

FOWLER, Gene
See FOWLER, Eugene Devlan

* * *

FOX, Fontaine Talbot, Jr. 1884-1964

OBITUARY NOTICE: Born June 4, 1884, in Louisville, Ky.; died August 9, 1964, in Greenwich, Conn. Cartoonist and author. Creator of the cartoon strip "The Toonerville Trolley That Meets All the Trains," Fox was a cartoonist at the *Louisville Herald, Louisville Times,* and the *Chicago Evening Post.* His comic strips were featured by more than two hundred fifty newspapers. Fox's works include *Fontaine Fox's Funny Folks, Fontaine Fox's Cartoons,* and *The Toonerville Trolley.* Obituaries and other sources: *Who Was Who in America,* 4th edition, Marquis, 1968; *National Cyclopaedia of American Biography,* Volumes 1-51, reprinted edition, University Microfilms, 1971.

* * *

FOXX, Redd 1922-

PERSONAL: Birth-given name, John Elroy Sanford; born December 9, 1922, in St. Louis, Mo.; son of Fred (an electrician) Sanford; married Evelyn Killibrew (divorced, 1951); married Betty Jean Harris (a singer), 1955; children: Debraca. *Address:* c/o Bardu Ali, 1280 West 60th Place, Los Angeles, Calif. 90044.

CAREER: Comedian and actor. Performed as comedian in numerous nightclubs and on numerous recordings; performed with Slappy White, 1947-51; actor in television series "Sanford and Son," 1972-77, and "The Redd Foxx Show," 1977, and motion pictures, including "Cotton Comes to Harlem," 1970, and "Norman, Is That You?," 1976. Has appeared on numerous television shows, including "The Tonight Show," "The Today Show," "Time for Laughter," "Soul," and "The Flip Wilson Show." Associated with Dooto Records and Loma Records.

WRITINGS: (Co-editor with Norma Miller) *The Redd Foxx Encyclopedia of Black Humor,* Ritchie, 1977. Also author of more than forty recordings, including "Laff of the Party," 1956.

SIDELIGHTS: Foxx broke into show business at an early age when he ran away from home with two high-school chums. They headed for New York City where, after a brief encounter with the law, they began performing as the "Bon Bons." However, the act dissolved upon American involvement in World War II and Foxx took to working a variety of odd jobs, including a dishwashing position at Jimmy's Chicken Shack in Harlem where he worked alongside Malcolm X.

Employment for Foxx was infrequent throughout the early 1940's, and he was arrested several times for vagrancy and other violations. However, by 1945 things had improved: Foxx was working steadily in New York City as an entertainer when he met Slappy White, a vaudeville actor. Teaming up, the duo worked for a few years before an unsuccessful performance on Broadway ended the partnership.

Back on his own, Foxx began developing a following on the nightclub circuit in Los Angeles. In 1955, his career took another stride forward when he signed with Doota Records. His comedy recordings, laced with slang, scatalogical references, and risque material, were enormously successful and he became increasingly in demand at clubs. However, as a black performer, Foxx was not fully able to capitalize on his popularity; forced to play mostly in black nightclubs, Foxx was reaching only a portion of his potential audience.

Finally, in 1959, Foxx appeared before a primarily white audience and was a resounding success. He soon moved on to prestigious clubs in Los Angeles and San Francisco. Robert Kerwin chronicled Foxx's rising career in the 1960's: "Club bookings rolled in. Redd's weekly price rose from $1,250 to $4,000, and the Caesar's Palace people liked his Aladdin act so well they hired him in 1968 for their big room. That's all he needed: He had such impact on those Caesar's audiences that the Las Vegas Hilton International signed him in August 1970, for $930,000 for 32 weeks of work. Next it was NBC Hollywood for $960,000 a year, 40 million viewers weekly."

1970 was indeed a key year for Foxx: from the deal with Hilton International, it was also the year of his first film appearance in "Cotton Comes to Harlem." As Foxx recalled, "twenty-one years, no offers. And I was out looking hard. I did one film, 'Cotton Comes to Harlem,' and had to go to New York for that. Bit part—Uncle Bud, an old junk dealer—and it didn't pay anything."

But the "bit part" had been remembered by television executives; when it came time to cast a prospective series about a black junk dealer living with his son, Foxx got the job. The show, "Sanford and Son," quickly rose to the top of the network ratings and remained popular with audiences for five years before going into syndication.

Despite the predominantly black cast, Foxx felt that "Sanford and Son" had had little impact on Hollywood in terms of hiring practices. "The industry is about as segregated as it ever was," he said in 1974. "Some small changes, maybe. Four niggers don't make no big change. I guess everybody opens the door some. Even Stepinfetchit. He got in, opened it a little. But things the same now. A few black shows on the air, what's that? No change. Far as I can see, there's a long way to go."

Foxx is careful, however, to distinguish between his own beliefs and his act. He warned that "you gotta be careful and don't get into politics with your career, turn a lot of your audience against you.... My thinking about that goes like this: No way I'm gonna march and get hit in the head with a stick. I'll buy somebody the shoes—let him do the marching." He has his own way of dealing with racism, though. "Prejudice, I believe in fighting it my own way," he remarked. "People come and see my act, they may go out with a better attitude, I don't know. I hope so. I have faith in the power of humor. That's about it."

BIOGRAPHICAL/CRITICAL SOURCES: Ebony, April, 1967, July, 1972, June, 1974; *New York Times,* February 6, 1972; *Time,* April 17, 1972; *Houston Post,* December 16, 1973; *Biography News,* Gale, January, 1974.*

* * *

FRACCHIA, Charles A(nthony) 1937-

PERSONAL: Born August 10, 1937, in San Francisco, Calif.; son of Charles B. and Josephine (Giacosa) Fracchia; married Ann Escobosa Wharton, February 10, 1962 (divorced, 1971); children: Laura Elizabeth, Carla Alexandra, Charles A., Jr., Francesca Suzanne. *Education:* University of San Francisco, A.B., 1960; University of California, Berkeley, M.L.S., 1976; San Francisco State University, M.A., 1980. *Politics:* Democrat. *Religion:* Roman Catholic. *Residence:* San Francisco, Calif. *Office:* P.O. Box 569, San Francisco, Calif. 94101.

CAREER: Paine, Webber, Jackson & Curtis, San Francisco, Calif., stockbroker, 1961-65; J. Barth & Co., San Francisco, stockbroker and investment banker, 1965-70; Brennan Financial Co. (real estate syndicate), San Francisco, vice-president in marketing, 1970-71; Walker's Manual, Inc. (financial publishers), San Francisco, general manager, 1971-72; writer, 1972—. Member of faculty at San Francisco State University, Community College of San Francisco, and University of California Extension. Member of board of directors of *Rolling Stone,* 1968-70, Computer Synergy, 1968-70, and Firehouse Cantina, 1978—; consultant to Hibernia Bank. *Member:* California Historical Society (member of board of trustees, 1966-76).

WRITINGS: (With Jeremiah Bragstad) *Converted Into Houses,* Viking, 1976; (with Mark Kauffman) *So This Is Where You Work,* Viking, 1979; *Living Together Alone: The New American Monasticism,* Harper, 1979; *How to Be Single Creatively,* McGraw, 1979; *A Beginner's Guide to Junk Bonds,* McGraw, 1980; *The Last, Great Days of the U.S. Catholic Church,* Harper, 1980; *Golden Gate Park,* Harper, 1980.

WORK IN PROGRESS: Americans in Paris; a biography of John Henry Cardinal Newman.

SIDELIGHTS: Fracchia commented: "Establishing a new career after a decade in the investment business has been a demanding yet rewarding endeavor. My transition from investment banker to writer and teacher was accomplished by the intensive self-scrutiny that accompanied the collapse of the firm for whom I worked and my divorce in 1970. My interests were far-ranging, and I attempted to explore these interests in my books and articles, sharing them with readers."

* * *

FRANCA, Celia 1921-

PERSONAL: Born June 25, 1921, in London, England; daughter of Solomon Franks (a tailor); married James Morton (a musician), December 7, 1960. *Education:* Attended Guildhall School of Music, 1925, and Royal Academy of Dancing, 1932. *Residence:* Ottawa, Canada. *Agent:* David Haber Artists Management, Inc., 1235 Bay St., Suite 500, Toronto, Ontario, Canada M5R 3K4. *Office:* 250 Clemow Ave., Ottawa, Ontario, Canada K1S 2B6.

CAREER: Director, choreographer, dancer. Ballet Rambert, London, England, debut as dancer, 1936, soloist, 1936-38, leading dramatic dancer, 1938-39, guest artist, 1950; Ballet des Trois Arts, London, dancer, 1939; Arts Theatre Ballet,

London, dancer, 1940; International Ballet, London, dancer, 1941; Sadler's Wells Ballet (now Royal Ballet), London, leading dramatic dancer, 1941-46, choreographer and guest artist, 1946-47; Ballets Jooss, London, dancer and teacher, 1947; Metropolitan Ballet, London, soloist and ballet mistress, 1947-49; Ballet Workshop, London, dancer, 1949-51; National Ballet of Canada, Toronto, Ontario, founder and artistic director, 1951-74, dancer, 1951-59; National Ballet School, Toronto, co-founder, 1959—.

Principal roles include Operetta Star in "Offenbach in the Underworld," First Song in "Dark Elegies," Black Lady in "Winter Night," Bird in "Peter and the Wolf," Queen in "Hamlet," Prostitute in "Miracle in the Gorbals," Swanilda in "Coppelia," Young Girl in "Spector of the Rose," Woman in His Past in "Lilac Garden," and Black Queen in "Swan Lake." Choreographer of ballets, including "Midas," "Cancion," "Khadra," "Dance of Salome," "The Eve of St. Agnes," "Afternoon of a Faun," "Le Pommier," "Casse-Noisette," "Princess Aurora," "The Nutcracker," "Cinderella," and numerous others for Canadian Broadcasting Co. and Canadian Opera Co. Served on jury of Second International Ballet Competition, 1973, and Fifth International Ballet Competition, 1973. Producer of "Pineapple Poll" and "Offenbach in the Underworld," Joffrey Ballet; guest dancer with National Ballet of Canada (25th Anniversary season), 1976, 1977; guest teacher at Vancouver Ballet Association, Quinte Dance Centre, and The School of Dance, Ottawa; visiting teacher of classical ballet in China, 1978.

MEMBER: Association of Canadian Television and Radio Artists, Canadian Theatre Centre, Artists Equity Association. *Awards, honors:* Honorary doctorate degrees from Assumption University, 1959, Mount Allison University, 1966, Bishop's University, 1967, University of Toronto, 1974, Guelph University, Dalhousie University, and York University, 1976, and Trent University, 1977; civic award of merit from city of Toronto, 1963; Toronto Telegram award, 1965, for most outstanding contribution to the arts in Canada; Centennial Medal, 1967; officer of the Order of Canada, 1967; citation from National Academy of Television Arts and Sciences, 1970, for choreography of "Cinderella"; Molson Award, 1974; Canada Council Senior Grants award, 1975; award from International Society of Performing Arts Administrators, 1979.

WRITINGS: (With Ken Bell) *The National Ballet of Canada: A Celebration* (memoir-history), University of Toronto Press, 1978.

SIDELIGHTS: Franca began her ballet studies at the age of four. A student of some of the greatest figures in British ballet, including Stanislas Idzikowski, Judith Espinoza, Antony Tudor, and Marie Rambert, she made her professional debut at fifteen in Tudor's "The Planets." Writing of her later work with Sadler's Wells Ballet, Ninette de Valois commended Franca as "the finest dramatic dancer the Wells had ever had."

In February of 1951, Franca was engaged by a group of Toronto balletomanes who wanted to found a Canadian ballet company. In just ten-months time, she recruited and trained dancers, staged promenade concerts, organized a summer school, assembled an artistic staff, and brought the newly formed Canadian National Ballet to its November debut. She was also one of the company's principal dancers.

To build a repertoire, Franca emphasized the classics, drawing on the English tradition, works of contemporaries, and ballets of her own. Her "Cinderella" won an Emmy in 1970, and "The Nutcracker" remains a Christmas tradition. She has stressed throughout the importance of developing Canadian choreography, incorporating over thirty Canadian ballets into the repertoire. In addition, she started the Choreographic Workshops that have nurtured current choreographers Ditchburn, Kudelka, and Patsalas.

* * *

FRANCIS, Arlene 1912-

PERSONAL: Original name, Arline Francis Kazanjian; born October 20, 1912, in Boston, Mass.; daughter of Aram (a portrait photographer) and Leah (Davis) Kazanjian; married Neil Agnew (a movie executive), 1935 (divorced, 1945); married Martin Gabel (an actor, producer, and director), May 14, 1946; children: Peter Joseph. *Education:* Attended Finch College and Theatre Guild School. *Residence:* New York, N.Y. *Address:* 465 Park Ave., New York, N.Y. 10022; and c/o Actors Equity Association, 165 West 46th St., New York, N.Y. 10036.

CAREER: Actress in motion pictures, including "Murders in the Rue Morgue," 1932, "Stage Door Canteen," 1943, "All My Sons," 1948, "One, Two, Three," 1961, and "The Thrill of It All," 1963; has appeared in over thirty stage productions, including "One Good Year," 1936, "Horse Eats Hat," 1936, "The Women," 1936, "All That Glitters," 1938, "Danton's Death," 1938, "Journey to Jerusalem," 1940, "The Doughgirls," 1942, "The Overtons," 1945, "The French Touch," 1945, "Once More, With Feeling," 1958, "Old Acquaintance," 1961-62, "Tchin-Tchin," 1962, "Dinner at Eight," 1966, "Gigi," 1973, and "Don't Call Back," 1975; has appeared on radio programs, including "45 Minutes From Hollywood," "March of Time," "Cavalcade of America," "Amanda of Honeymoon Hill," "Mr. District Attorney," "What's My Name?," "Blind Date," "Arlene Francis at Sardi's," "Arlene Francis Show," "Monitor," "Emphasis," and "Home Show"; has appeared in several television programs, including "Blind Date," "The Arlene Francis Show," "Home," 1953-57, and "What's My Line?," 1950-67. Member of national advisory council of University of Utah. Member of boards of directors of Bonwit Teller, Ritz Associates, and Atrium Club. *Member:* American Federation of Television and Radio Artists, Actors Equity Association, Screen Actors Guild. *Awards, honors:* L.H.D., 1965, from American International College, and 1966, from Keuka College; elected to U.S. Hall of Fame, 1967.

WRITINGS: *That Certain Something: The Magic of Charm,* Messner, 1960; *No Time for Cooking: A New Kind of Cookbook,* Standard Packaging Corp., 1961; (with Florence Rome) *Arlene Francis: A Memoir,* Simon & Schuster, 1978. Contributor of articles to *Saturday Evening Post* and *McCall's.*

SIDELIGHTS: Arlene Francis was meant to be an actress, according to the nuns of her Catholic high school. Her parents, however, were less than enthusiastic about the idea and sent their daughter instead to Miss Finch's finishing school. Hoping to dissuade her from an acting career, her father even opened a Madison Avenue gift shop for her, but Francis soon demonstrated that a mistake had been made. Her business acumen was such that the shop folded after only eight months. She then changed her name and left for Hollywood.

Francis's first movie role, that of a demimondaine, came in 1932 with "Murders in the Rue Morgue." When it opened in New York, her father responded in a telegram: "HAVE

JUST SEEN YOU HALF NAKED ON BROADWAY. COME HOME." She complied. After the brief interruption, Francis resumed her show-business career in a bit part for radio. Her performance included seventy-two sound imitations, and were so well done that she next appeared on "45 Minutes From Hollywood" doing impressions of Greta Garbo and other film stars.

Until 1941, Francis's work in theatre and radio steadily increased, including her first major stage role in "All That Glitters" and appearances on the Jack Benny, Fred Allen, and Burns and Allen programs. During the war, she cut back her performance schedule to sell bonds, host benefit shows, and tour the country with her own radio program, "Blind Date." The show featured a competition among six servicemen for the chance to escort three girls on blind dinner dates.

In the 1950's, Francis participated in the growing popularity of a new entertainment medium, television. Her infectious laugh, poise, and spontaneous wit made her one of television's most sought after personalities. She excelled in the panelist situation, and when the "Home" show, a precursor of the "Today" show, conducted its search for a host, Francis was selected out of thirty other actresses for the editor-in-chief assignment. Described as an electronics magazine, the show featured how-to-do-it, cultural, and entertainment segments organized around home-making interests. She also appeared regularly on what became a Sunday night television tradition, "What's My Line?"

In 1954, *Look* magazine reported that Francis earned more than any other woman appearing on "live" television. But her fortunes have been mixed: in 1962 a dumbbell fell from her window and killed a man; a year later she was involved in an auto accident that killed a young woman. She once remarked, however, that she is not a "weeper," but one who maintains a defiant attitude toward hardship.

Francis's writings include *That Certain Something: The Magic of Charm* and *Arlene Francis: A Memoir.* In the first book, she discusses the genuine charm that emanates from a person when he is fully himself. A reviewer for the *Springfield Republican* commented: "The widely known actress, who is famous for her magnetic personality, writes a witty guide for people who want to be popular, and tells how to avoid the 'sandpaper personality' as she calls it, and the 'phony glamour of superciliousness,' and how, on the other hand, to develop true warm-hearted charm." In *Arlene Francis,* the author reminisces about the people she has known, her career, and her personal life. "She has produced a chatty, colloquial book that sounds as though it had been spoken at white heat into a tape recorder," wrote Doris Grumbach. "Almost everyone Arlene Francis knows arrives on the page accompanied by show-business superlatives. . . . Under all the gushing and the platitudes one does glimpse a generous-spirited woman who enjoys telling about her own 'four-star' double-entendre bloopers and malapropisms. She indulges in proud 'mom talk' about her son Peter and exults in her long, happy marriage to Martin Gabel. In both, she seems entirely genuine and likable."

AVOCATIONAL INTERESTS: Homemaking, cooking, horseback riding.

BIOGRAPHICAL/CRITICAL SOURCES: New York Post Magazine, May 15, 1943; *Cue,* April 17, 1954; *New York World-Telegram Magazine,* April 24, 1954; *Newsweek,* July 19, 1954; *American Magazine,* October, 1954; *Coronet,* February, 1956; *Springfield Republican,* May 22, 1960; *McCall's,* March, 1969; *Saturday Evening Post,* September, 1976; Arlene Francis and Florence Rome, *Arlene Francis: A Memoir,* Simon & Schuster, 1978; *New York Times Book Review,* March 26, 1978.*

* * *

FRANCIS, Michael J(ackson) 1938-

PERSONAL: Born March 24, 1938, in Oberlin, Kan.; son of Lowell Alexander (a coach) and Helen (a writer; maiden name, Dannefer) Francis; married Deanna Lockman (a reporter), June 19, 1960; children: Catherine Ann, Lowell Alexander II. *Education:* Attended National University of Mexico, 1960; Fort Hays State College, B.A., 1960; University of Virginia, Ph.D., 1963. *Religion:* Unitarian-Universalist. *Home:* 830 Park Ave., South Bend, Ind. 46616. *Office:* Department of Government, University of Notre Dame, Notre Dame, Ind. 46556.

CAREER: Texas A & M University, College Station, instructor in government, 1963-65; California State University, Fullerton, assistant professor of government, 1965-66; University of Notre Dame, Notre Dame, Ind., 1966—, began as assistant professor, currently professor of government and director of Institute for International Studies. *Member:* International Studies Association, American Political Science Association, Latin American Studies Association, American Association of University Professors, Common Cause (district officer).

WRITINGS: La Victoria de Allende, 1971, translation published as *The Allende Victory,* University of Arizona Press, 1973; *The Limits of Hegemony,* University of Notre Dame Press, 1977. Contributor to scholarly journals.

WORK IN PROGRESS: Research on U.S. foreign policy toward Latin America and politics of Chile.

* * *

FRANEY, Pierre 1921-

PERSONAL: Born January 13, 1921, in Tonnerre, France; came to the United States in 1939, naturalized citizen, 1942; son of Aristide and Charlotte (Grognet) Franey; married Elizabeth Chardenet, June 6, 1948; children: Claudia Franey Jensen, Diane Franey Schaldenko, Jacques Alain. *Education:* Attended high school in St. Vinnemer, France. *Home:* 210 Old Stone Highway, East Hampton, N.Y. 11937.

CAREER: La Pavillon Restaurant, New York, N.Y., began as member of kitchen staff, executive chef, 1953-60; Howard Johnson's, Queens Village, N.Y., consultant, 1960—. Worked at French Pavilion at the World's Fair, 1939 and 1940. *Military service:* U.S. Army, Infantry, 1942-45. *Member:* Vatel Club (president, 1955-60). *Awards, honors:* Merit agricole from government of France, 1965.

WRITINGS: (With Craig Claiborne) *Classic French Cooking,* Time-Life, 1970; (with Claiborne) *Craig Claiborne's Favorites From The New York Times,* New York Times Co., Volume I, 1975, Volume II, 1976, Volume III, 1977, Volume IV, 1978; (with Claiborne) *Veal Cookery,* Harper, 1978; *Sixty-Minute Gourmet,* New York Times Co., 1979. Author of "Kitchen Equipment," a column in *New York Times.*

WORK IN PROGRESS: Salt Free Cookbook, with Craig Claiborne, for New York Times Co.

SIDELIGHTS: Franey told *CA:* "I feel that my training in fine cooking in France, combined with my years of experience at the La Pavillion Restaurant in New York City (which was considered the country's finest restaurant), plus the experience gained through my association with a successful American restaurant chain, has given me a broad command of food preparation. In addition, it has been a pleasure to share my knowledge with the readers of the *New York Times* food page and to be able to lend my talents to the several cookbooks I have worked on in collaboration with Craig Claiborne. My new book, *The Sixty-Minute Gourmet,* should be of value to today's generation of cooks who want fine food but are limited in time. It shows that good cooking need not dominate one's time. The forthcoming *Salt Free Cookbook* should be a boon to the many today who must watch their salt intake—it proves that many tasty recipes can be made without salt."

* * *

FRANKEL, Charles 1917-1979

OBITUARY NOTICE—See index for *CA* sketch: Born December 13, 1917, in New York, N.Y.; died May 10, 1979, in Bedford Hills, N.Y. Educator, administrator, and author. For more than twenty-five years Frankel was a faculty member at Columbia University; he was Old Dominion Professor of Philosophy and Public Affairs from 1970 until the time of his death. From 1965 until he resigned in protest over the Vietnam War in 1967, Frankel was assistant secretary of state for educational and cultural affairs. His books include *The Faith of Reason, The Case for Modern Man, Religion—Within Reason,* and *The Democratic Prospect.* Obituaries and other sources: *Current Biography,* Wilson, 1966, July, 1979; *The Author's and Writer's Who's Who,* 6th edition, Burke's Peerage, 1971; *Who's Who in World Jewry,* Pitman, 1972; *Who's Who in America,* 40th edition, Marquis, 1978; *Directory of American Scholars,* Volume IV: *Philosophy, Religion, and Law,* 7th edition, Bowker, 1978; *New York Times,* May 11, 1979.

* * *

FRANKEL, Haskel 1926-

PERSONAL: Born February 11, 1926, in Brooklyn, N.Y.; son of Tobias (a storekeeper and realtor) and Sally (Edelblum) Frankel; married Marilyn Phylis Ellman (a writer), May 21, 1972; children: Elizabeth Emily. *Education:* St. Lawrence University, A.B., 1948; graduate study at Columbia University, 1948-49. *Residence:* Westbrook, Conn. *Agent:* Brandt & Brandt, 1501 Broadway, New York, N.Y. 10036.

CAREER: Saturday Evening Post, New York City, senior editor, 1965-67; *National Observer,* Silver Spring, Md., theatre critic, 1966-71; *New York Times,* New York City, theatre critic of Connecticut and Westchester Sunday sections, 1977—. *Military service:* U.S. Army, 1944-46.

WRITINGS: (With Uta Hagen) *Respect for Acting,* Macmillan, 1973; (with Milton Berle) *Milton Berle: An Autobiography,* Delacorte, 1974; (with Victoria Fydorova) *The Admiral's Daughter,* Delacorte, 1979; (with wife, Marilyn Frankel, and Louis Camuti) *All My Patients Are Under the Bed,* Simon & Schuster, 1980. Author of television plays, two for "The Phillip Morris Television Theater," WCBS-TV, 1953, and another, "The Perfect Wife," for "The Web" program, WCBS-TV, 1953. Author of column, "On the Fringe," in *Saturday Review,* until 1967.

WORK IN PROGRESS: Working with Joan Rivers on a literary project, publication by Delacorte expected in 1980.

SIDELIGHTS: Frankel told *CA:* "The theatre seems to be my major field of interest, though as time goes on, it fascinates me less as a writer (perhaps it is that my dramatic criticism takes care of it). As a writer, I seem to have found my stride expressing other people's lives for them, though whenever I get the chance, I try to work at a novel that has long interested me. To write for myself, rather than expressing myself through others, is still my main drive. I suspect that this is the case for all of us who write in collaboration with others."

* * *

FRANKLIN, Ben(jamin) A. 1927-

PERSONAL: Born November 12, 1927, in New York, N.Y.; son of Benjamin A. (a newspaper city editor) and Zilpha (a government official) Franklin; married Jane Burrage, June 10, 1950; children: Abigail J., Elizabeth A., Clare C. *Education:* University of Pennsylvania, A.B., 1948; Columbia University, M.S., 1950. *Politics:* Democrat. *Religion:* Episcopal. *Residence:* Garrett Park, Md. 20766. *Office: New York Times,* 1920 L St. N.W., Washington, D.C. 20036.

CAREER/WRITINGS: Evening Capital, Annapolis, Md., reporter, 1948-49; *Evening Star,* Washington, D.C., reporter, 1949-51, 1953-54; ABC-Radio, New York City, reporter for "Edward P. Morgan and the News," 1954-59; *New York Times,* New York City, regional correspondent (Middle Atlantic), 1959—. Contributor to *Saturday Evening Post, New Republic,* and *New York Times Magazine. Military service:* U.S. Coast Guard Reserve, 1951-55 (active duty, 1951-53); became lieutenant. *Awards, honors:* W. D. Weatherford Award from Berea College, 1971, for Appalachian reporting; Sigma Delta Chi Award, 1973, for Washington reporting on Spiro T. Agnew.

* * *

FRANKLYN, Robert Alan 1918-

PERSONAL: Born April 30, 1918; son of Joseph Franklyn; married Wilma Kemp; children: Apryl, Robyn. *Education:* New York University, A.B., 1937, M.D., 1941. *Office:* 8760 Sunset Blvd., Los Angeles, Calif.

CAREER: Currently a plastic surgeon in Los Angeles, Calif. Member of American Board of Cosmetic Surgery. Horse breeder. *Member:* International Academy of Cosmetic Surgery, American Aging Association.

WRITINGS: On Developing Bosom Beauty, Fell, 1959; (with Alyce Canfield) *Beauty Surgeon,* Whitehorn Publishing, 1960; (with Helen Gould) *The Art of Staying Young,* Fell, 1964; (with Marcia Borie) *Instant Beauty,* Fell, 1967; (with Borie) *A Doctor's Quick Way to Achieve Lasting Beauty: How to Play the Beauty Game,* Information, Inc., 1970; *Augmentation Mammoplasty,* International Academy of Cosmetic Surgery, 3rd edition, 1976; *Shi Atsu: Sixty Seconds to Facial Beauty,* Doctor Beauty Publications, 1976; *The Clinical Atlas of Cosmetic Plastic Surgery,* International Academy of Cosmetic Surgery, 1976; *Supercharge Yourself,* Information, Inc., 1979.

BIOGRAPHICAL/CRITICAL SOURCES: Sports Illustrated, September-August, 1970; Roger Rapoport, *Superdoctors,* Playboy Press, 1975.

* * *

FRANTZ, Ralph Jules 1902-1979

OBITUARY NOTICE—See index for *CA* sketch: Born November 1, 1902, in Springfield, Ohio; died of cancer, November 3, 1979, in Fair Lawn, N.J. Journalist, editor, and author. A co-founder of the Overseas Press Club, Frantz was associated with the *Paris Tribune,* the European edition of the *Chicago Tribune,* for nine years. In 1935 he joined the staff of the *New York Herald Tribune* as a copy editor, and was head of the Sunday Long Island section when he resigned in 1966. Until his retirement in 1971, Frantz was an editor of the *Bergen Record*. Obituaries and other sources: *New York Times*, November 4, 1979.

* * *

FRANZBLAU, Rose N(adler) 1905-1979

OBITUARY NOTICE—See index for *CA* sketch: Born January 1, 1905, in Vienna, Austria; died of cancer, September 3, 1979, in New York, N.Y. Psychologist, association executive, columnist, and author of eight books on psychological topics. During World War II, Franzblau was director of placement and training of overseas personnel for the United Nations Relief and Rehabilitation Administration. Later she worked for the United Nations again as associate director of UNESCO's international tensions research project. For twenty-five years, Franzblau was the author of a daily syndicated column which answered questions on sex, marriage, and parenthood. She was also host of the radio program "Dr. Franzblau's World of Children." Her books include *A Sane and Happy Life: A Family Guide*, *The Way It Is Under Twenty*, *The Middle Generation*, and *The Menopause Myth*. Obituaries and other sources: *Who's Who in World Jewry*, Pitman, 1972; *New York Times*, September 3, 1979; *AB Bookman's Weekly*, October 15, 1979.

* * *

FRASER DARLING, Frank 1903-1979

OBITUARY NOTICE—See index for *CA* sketch: Born June 23, 1903, in Scotland; died October 22, 1979, in Forres, Scotland. Ecologist and author of *A Herd of Red Deer*. Fraser Darling's expertise embraced biology, genetics, and agriculture. Obituaries and other sources: *The Author's and Writer's Who's Who*, 6th edition, Burke's Peerage, 1971; *The International Who's Who*, 43rd edition, Europa, 1979; *Who's Who*, 131st edition, St. Martin's, 1979; *New York Times*, October 26, 1979.

* * *

FREEMAN, Joseph 1897-1965

OBITUARY NOTICE: Born October 7, 1897, in the Ukraine, Russia (now U.S.S.R.); died August 9, 1965. Journalist, editor, poet, and author. Freeman was a correspondent for the *Chicago Tribune* in both Paris and London from 1920 to 1921, and worked on the editorial staff of the *Liberator* for three years. A socialist from the age of seventeen, Freeman joined the staff of the Soviet news agency Tass in 1925 and worked part-time with them until 1931. After co-founding *New Masses* in 1926, Freeman edited the journal during the thirties. In 1933, he published the first American anti-Nazi pamphlet and, later, helped found American anti-Nazi organizations. Freeman was co-founder and co-editor, from 1934 to 1936, of *Partisan Review*. He was the author of several volumes of poetry and numerous books on history, politics, and Marxist criticism, including *Voices of October*, a full-length study of Soviet art, literature, and film, and *Dollar Diplomacy: A Study of American Imperialism*. Obituaries and other sources: *The Oxford Companion to American Literature*, 4th edition, Oxford University Press, 1965; *Who Was Who in America*, 4th edition, Marquis, 1968; *Historian*, November, 1974.

* * *

FRENCH, Brandon 1944-

PERSONAL: Born January 3, 1944, in Chicago, Ill.; daughter of Benjamin (a singer) and Ruth (a dancer; maiden name, Hattis) Premack; children: Samantha Kaye. *Education:* University of California, Los Angeles, B.A., 1964; attended Actors Studio, New York, N.Y., 1967-69; University of California, Berkeley, Ph.D., 1973. *Politics:* "Liberal." *Religion:* None. *Home:* 11488 Huston St., North Hollywood, Calif. 91601. *Agent:* Stu Robinson, Robinson-Weintraub & Associates, 554 South San Vicente, Los Angeles, Calif. 90048. *Office:* Columbia Pictures—Television, Ventura Blvd., Sherman Oaks, Calif. 91403.

CAREER: Ogilvy & Mather, New York City, copywriter and producer, 1965-66; de Garmo, McCaffery, New York City, copywriter and producer, 1967-69; Image, New York City, free-lance copywriter, 1969-72; Yale University, New Haven, Conn., assistant professor of film and curator of Collection of Classic Films, 1973-78; Columbia Pictures—Television, Sherman Oaks, Calif., development executive, 1978—. Independent film producer, director, and scriptwriter, 1965—; director and editor for WSBE-TV, 1977.

MEMBER: Theater East. *Awards, honors:* Prize from California State Poetry Competition, 1960, for "Toreador"; prize from Lederer-Rader Poetry Contest, 1963, for "Caliban"; prize from Shrout Short Story Contest at University of California, Berkeley, 1970, for "And If You Know the Truth, Don't Tell Me"; "Penelope" was selected for grand tour by Ann Arbor Film Festival, 1970; "Brandy in the Wilderness" received grand prize from Ann Arbor Film Festival, 1969, first prizes from Kent State Film Festival, 1969, and Long Beach Film Festival, 1969, society of directors selection from Cannes Film Festival, 1969, and citation of merit from U.S.A. Film Festival, 1971; One Show/Merit Award from New York's Arts Directors Club and Copy Club of New York, 1974; certificate of excellence for communication graphics and print advertisements from American Institute of Graphic Arts, 1974.

WRITINGS: (Contributor) Ronald Gottesman and Harry Geduld, editors, *The Girl in the Hairy Paw*, Avon, 1976; (contributor) Gerald Peary and Roger Shatzkin, editors, *The Classic American Novel and the Movies*, Ungar, 1977; (contributor) Peary and Shatzkin, editors, *The Modern American Novel and the Movies*, Ungar, 1977; *On the Verge of Revolt: Women in American Films of the Fifties*, Ungar, 1978.

Films: "Penelope," 1969; (co-author) "In Pursuit of Treasure," 1970. Also co-author of unreleased film, "Brandy in the Wilderness." Contributor to magazines, including *New York*, *Yale Italian Studies*, and *Chrysalis*.

WORK IN PROGRESS: The Professors' Groupie, a novel; collaborating on feature-length filmscripts, "Running on Empty," "The Grand Master," "Families," and "The Second Hundred Years"; television films, "Andersen" and "Jason and Jasper"; "Nightmares," a play.

SIDELIGHTS: Brandon French comments: "My book allowed me to put together several of my primary interests: film as art, film as myth, film as a cultural reflector, as well as my experience of contemporary American life (since World War II). The book has also helped reopen the fifties to evaluation as a complex and important decade, a tidepool which clearly spawned the subsequent twenty years and which has heretofore been an unfairly neglected matriarch. *On the Verge of Revolt* has a feminist perspective tempered by a concern for both sexes and their effect upon one another. I would like to think that balanced concern is a feature of all my work."

FRENCH, Michael 1944-

PERSONAL: Born December 2, 1944, in Los Angeles, Calif.; son of Richard Louis (a surgeon) and Marjorie (Carson) French; married Patricia Goodkind, December 7, 1969; children: Timothy, Alison. *Education:* Stanford University, B.A., 1966; Northwestern University, M.S., 1967. *Home:* 951 Acequia Madre, Santa Fe, N.M. 87501. *Agent:* Jacques de Spoelberch, J. de S. Associates, Inc., One Point Rd., Wilson Point, South Norwalk, Conn. 06854.

CAREER: Hill and Knowlton (international public relations firm), New York City, financial writer, 1970-72; Wilson Brothers, New York City, assistant to president, 1972-74; founder and operator of day-care center, Brooklyn Heights, N.Y., 1974-78; full-time writer, 1978—.

WRITINGS: *Club Caribe* (novel), Fawcett, 1977; *Abingdon's* (novel), Doubleday, 1979; *The Throwing Season* (juvenile), Delacorte, 1980; *Rhythms* (novel), Doubleday, 1980.

WORK IN PROGRESS: *In Cold Pursuit,* a novel.

SIDELIGHTS: *Abingdon's* is a novel based on the world-famous Bloomingdale's department store in New York City. Despite the wide range of characters, such as "a foot fetishist, a pickpocket, a compulsive gambler, a mugger eating a Hostess Twinkie, a psychotically vengeful ex-wife, a live Prime Minister and a murderous male model," French manages to make the plot work "in an outrageous way," noted Nora Johnson. Leonore Fleischer complained that the book was sloppily edited and contained a "predictable, banal plot, and faceless sexless characters." Nevertheless, Johnson remarked that as long as the reader does not "take any of it too seriously" the book is "as enjoyable as a Saturday stroll through Bloomie's."

CA INTERVIEWS THE AUTHOR

CA interviewed Michael French by telephone May 30, 1979, at his home in Sante Fe, New Mexico.

CA: Does an agent have more contacts and ability to get things moving than an author working alone?

FRENCH: I think so. Publishers will pay more attention to what an agent says than an author because usually an agent is more objective about the work. He or she is also a screening mechanism, a critical set of eyes that publishers can trust. If he or she likes the book, then publishers will be inclined to read it with care.

CA: Speed is especially important with books you've been writing recently, such as Rhythms. *If the agent takes a long time to get the book placed, the topic may lose its timeliness.*

FRENCH: I feel that way. On the other hand, my editors at Doubleday tell me they're not worried about *Rhythms,* because even if disco dies suddenly, the novel—if it has merit—will stand on its own. This is partially true, yet a lot of readers will buy a novel about disco because they like the disco scene, the music. They may also buy the book for its plot and characters, but the whole disco theme is a fundamental lure. Fad or not, if my novel doesn't see publication soon, other writers will get their disco books out first. That has to hurt me a little.

CA: How did you do the research for Abingdon's?

FRENCH: I spent two or three months at it. I talked to a good many employees at Bloomingdale's—the rank and file mostly. I did not go to upper management and say, "Look, I'm doing a novel about your store. What can you tell me?" There was one major executive, a friend of a friend, who gave me a lot of information—off the record. But most people I spoke with—fashion coordinators, sales help, display artists—were candid with their opinions and anecdotes. They didn't care who found out what they said. For the nuts and bolts of store operations, I talked to security, the janitorial staff, maintenance people, stock room personnel. I also went to Abraham and Straus, which, like Bloomie's, is owned by Federated, and executives there were quite helpful, giving me the financial information about Bloomingdale's that I couldn't get from the horse's mouth. Having lived in New York for nine years and shopped at Bloomingdale's, I couldn't help transmitting my own feelings about the store and its customers to the novel. Bloomie's is quite a show. Its ambience played a large part in the tone of the novel and helped me decide what kind of characters I wanted to use. Once the book got started, I made additional trips to the store, looking for details.

CA: How much time did you spend at that?

FRENCH: I recall making several lengthy visits on Saturdays and on evenings, and around Christmas, just to see how much the store changed during these times. Department stores are kaleidoscopic. There are certain things you'll find one moment but not the next.

CA: What secondary sources did you use?

FRENCH: Bloomingdale's is a legend, an institution. It's chronicled in the society columns, in *New York Magazine,* in the *Times.* Secondary sources are ubiquitous.

CA: Jacques de Spoelberch, your agent, referred to Abingdon's *as a roman a clef. In your mind, what's the relationship between fiction and fact in the book?*

FRENCH: A couple of characters are based loosely on real people. But it's not a roman a clef as, say, Neal Travis's *Manhattan* was, which is the saga of Clay Felker and *New York Magazine.* Essentially I was trying to capture the flavor and mood of the store, of its people. Once when you begin writing, however, you realize you have certain fictional needs. The logic of your story requires that you handle characters and incidents in a certain way. If that seems contrary to what happens in real life at Bloomingdale's, you're not going to stick to the facts; you have to operate in the context of the novel, to be true to that art form.

CA: Where did you get the idea for Abingdon's?

FRENCH: Bloomingdale's is such an East Side mecca for the fashionable and chic that it seemed a natural for a novel. For characters and plot you have almost an infinite range of possibilities. The great thing about that store, which I tried to reflect in my narrative, is that things happen so rapidly and so many things happen simultaneously, the place is constantly jumping—particularly at holiday time like Christmas. It's another world.

CA: Have you been influenced by Arthur Hailey?

FRENCH: One weekend a couple of years ago I was despairing because I couldn't get any of my fiction published, and I started reading Hailey for the first time. I read *Airport, Hotel,* and *The Money-Changers.* I told myself I could do a pretty decent job in this genre. I didn't think it was beyond my capabilities, and it looked like a fair challenge, even fun. That was a definite motivation for *Club Caribe,* a book not dissimilar to *Hotel* and *Abingdon's.* Now I'm at the point where I'm not that interested in Mr. Hailey anymore, though

I still enjoy reading him. *Rhythms* is a departure from the Haileyesque genre. It's not the wildly episodic book that *Hotel* and *Abingdon's* are; it focuses on one main character, a complex and sympathetic woman who starts a disco against formidable odds. It's involved in more subtle themes and character interaction. Also, it's a much sexier book than I think Hailey would write.

CA: What's your feeling about having started as a writer of paperback originals?

FRENCH: It wasn't intentional. Fawcett was the only house that wanted *Club Caribe*. I signed a contract because, not having published up till then, I wanted to be in print.

CA: Had you been trying to publish hardback fiction?

FRENCH: Before *Club Caribe* I had written three novels. One, *The Throwing Season,* about corruption in high school athletics, will be published next spring by Delacorte/Dell as a juvenile title.

But this break didn't come until I'd sold *Abingdon's* to Doubleday. When I first sent *The Throwing Season* around, without an agent, no publisher wanted it. That's why I sat down in a mood of some discouragement and started reading Hailey, thinking if I set my sights on a particular genre, I'd have a better chance of getting published.

CA: You're extremely good at plot development. As you begin on a more ambitious work, do you intend to maintain plot as a dominant element, or are you going to begin emphasizing some of the more traditional trappings of serious art?

FRENCH: Plot is intriguing to me, and I think it's fun to work with, but the satisfaction I got from making the plot for *Abingdon's* isn't as strong a lure now. I get more of a challenge from creating a really three-dimensional character, which is what I'm doing in *Rhythms*. The plot is strong, and important to the novel, but I balance it with strong characterization. Ultimately, characterization is plot. In *Abingdon's,* who was going to do what next was the basis of the novel; in *Rhythms,* I hope to show some growth as a writer.

CA: You seem to set up challenges for yourself in writing. Is this deliberate?

FRENCH: Oh, yes; it's a conscious process. I think it's part of the growth cycle. You want to realize your potential. And you don't want to keep doing the same thing over and over; it would be boring, and it's not being true to yourself.

CA: So many writers fall into the trap of staying with the formula that works. It's very positive for a writer to assume he has things to learn.

FRENCH: I think one has to balance his financial needs against his artistic temperament and the demands he sets for himself for a serious work. I have a modest hang-up about money. I need to feel financially secure to try a literary novel—just in case it doesn't sell.

CA: How are you planning to do research on Priceless, *where obviously you can't wander in and spend hours in an auction house?*

FRENCH: It could be a problem. I went to New York last September, and I talked to people at Christie's and Sotheby Parke Bernet—public relations staff, middle-level executives. I was only after very general information to determine the broad outline of a novel. If I go ahead with the book, I'll have to think out my research approach carefully. The auction market, of course, is international—that's one of the glamorous things about it—and I would like to visit the auction houses in England, France, Monaco, even Hong Kong. That could be expensive. But it seems to me if I want to do a thorough job on this subject, it's going to require a lot of legwork and scrupulous reporting.

CA: When you're talking with these people at the lower levels, do you tell them what you're about?

FRENCH: I'm pretty direct. I say that I'm writing a novel, and that I'm not out to expose or discredit anyone, just to tell the reader what happens behind the scenes. Curiously, most people are eager to cooperate, even at the risk of painting unflattering portraits of themselves or their bosses or the organization they work for. I think that's human nature; if someone wants to write about you, you feel important, flattered. You feel compelled to be honest.

CA: Do you find that the further up the corporate ladder you go, the less willing people are to be so open?

FRENCH: Generally, that's to be expected. Higher-ups feel important when they're keeping secrets; that's in part how they justify their importance, by having secrets to keep. But on occasion you find someone who's totally honest and direct, and it makes your job that much easier.

CA: Have you had to do other work while you were getting established as a writer?

FRENCH: Always. I only started writing full-time last year. I was married in 1969; my wife and I moved from Los Angeles to New York City. I worked several years for an international public relations firm, later for a Fortune 500 company, and then my wife and I started a day-care center in Brooklyn Heights. We just sold that and are living happily in Santa Fe, New Mexico. But I do miss New York.

CA: What relationship do you see between that outside work and your writing? Was it creating problems for you?

FRENCH: Well, my corporate background—the ins and outs of financing, the politics, the conflicts—has been helpful in writing my novels. But outside work is a retardant in the sense of time and energy. When you spend eight hours doing someone else's work and you come home, the last thing you want to do is write. You want to read or watch television or just talk. It takes a good deal of discipline to keep writing—particularly when it isn't selling.

CA: When you were working full-time, did you have patterns such as writing at night or on weekends?

FRENCH: I would try to write at night *and* on weekends. And sometimes, if it was slow at the office, I would close my door and write there. It became an art—squeezing out times when you had the concentration to write intelligibly.

CA: What about goals in your writing?

FRENCH: I don't have specific ones. I have a general sense of self-improvement, the idea I'd like to see my writing get better. In terms of themes, I try to be aware of what's happening in this crazy world. In digesting the mess I decide if a particular theme or topic is worth a novel. But I don't see blueprinting a type of fiction. I don't feel committed to any genre. I'm probably more predisposed to certain kinds of fiction than others—historical romances and gothics don't engage me—but I wouldn't want to rule anything out.

CA: When did you start writing?

FRENCH: I started at Stanford, in the creative writing program, and pretty much kept with it afterwards.

CA: When you're putting a book together, do you do all the research first, or do you research and write alternately?

FRENCH: I try to research basics first. In fact, I over-research, gathering far more facts than I could ever use, because that's the only way I'll know which facts are worth using. Once the novel unfolds, inevitably there are certain gaps that I don't know how to fill, so I have to go back for more research.

CA: Do you do a lot of revision?

FRENCH: My goal is a thousand good words a day, and that usually involves two or three drafts. So I'm doing my revisions on a daily basis. Then when I finish about half the novel, I go back and do more revisions. I have a good idea what I want to do in a book before I type the first page, but as I go along I see changes have to be made. New ideas occur to me all the time. If they're good, they belong in the book.

CA: What percentage of your time goes to the original creation and what percentage to revision?

FRENCH: The most important time spent is in thinking out the book—planning the plot, characters, shaping the narrative, knowing the effects I want to create. The harmony, the resonance, has to feel right. The architecture has to be right. And when you've got that larger context down, you start working on the interior—first the chapters, then pages, paragraphs, sentences, working down to the smallest details, which can be the most crucial . . . the difference between a fair story and a good one.

CA: How detailed an outline do you work out before you start writing?

FRENCH: For pragmatic purposes—to get an advance from a publisher—I do fifty or sixty pages. That's usually a few chapters and an outline of the plot. Then I have my private notes—scribblings—which give body to the outline.

CA: Do you need the support of other writers around you when you're working?

FRENCH: I don't think so. There are a lot of writers where I live, but everybody goes his own way. Writing being a solitary pursuit, one is pretty much locked to a typewriter six or seven hours a day. When I have free time, I don't like to talk or think writing. And most writers I know, if they're not talking about their work, tend to be quiet and introverted. For company I prefer a little more stimulation. The best way to enjoy writers is through their books.

BIOGRAPHICAL/CRITICAL SOURCES: New York Times Book Review, March 4, 1979; *Washington Post Book World,* July 29, 1979.

—Interview by Richard E. Ziegfeld

* * *

FRENCH, Will 1890(?)-1979

OBITUARY NOTICE: Born c. 1890; died October 11, 1979, in Woodland, Calif. Educator and co-author of a high school administration textbook. French taught at Columbia University. Obituaries and other sources: *New York Times,* October 18, 1979.

FRENKEL, Jacob A(haron) 1943-

PERSONAL: Born February 8, 1943, in Tel Aviv, Israel; came to the United States in 1967; son of Kalman H. and Lea (Zweibaum) Frenkel; married Niza Yair (a professor of biology), September 3, 1968; children: Orli M., Tahl I. *Education:* Hebrew University of Jerusalem, B.A., 1966; University of Chicago, M.A., 1969, Ph.D., 1970. *Residence:* Chicago, Ill. *Office:* Department of Economics, University of Chicago, 1126 East 59th St., Chicago, Ill. 60637.

CAREER: M. Falk Institute for Economic Research in Israel, Jerusalem, research associate, 1967; Indiana University, Northwest Campus, Bloomington, instructor in money and banking, 1968-69; University of Chicago, Chicago, Ill., assistant professor of international economics and finance, 1970-71; Tel-Aviv University, Tel-Aviv, Israel, senior lecturer in economics, 1971-73; University of Chicago, assistant professor, 1973-74, associate professor, 1974-78, professor of economics, 1979—. Visiting assistant professor at University of Chicago, summer, 1972; adjunct senior lecturer at Hebrew University of Jerusalem, 1972-73. Member of Carnegie-Rochester Conference Series advisory council, 1977—. Research associate of National Bureau of Economic Research, 1978. *Member:* American Economic Association. *Awards, honors:* Lilly Honor fellowship, 1968-70; Ford Foundation grant, 1975-76; National Science Foundation grant, 1978-80; honorary research associate of Harvard University, 1978—.

WRITINGS: (With Nahum Libfeldt, Anna Trachtenbrodt, and Shmuel Greenspan) *Meshek Hadvdim* (title means "The Economics of the Sector Owned by Organized Labor"), Institute for Economic Research of the Histadrut, 1964; (editor with Amira Ofer) *Macro-Kalkala* (title means "Macroeconomics: Lecture Notes"), Tel-Aviv Branch, Mifal Hashichpul Hebrew University, 1965; (editor with H. G. Johnson, and contributor) *The Monetary Approach to the Balance of Payments,* University of Toronto Press, 1976; (editor with Johnson, and contributor) *The Economics of Exchange Rates: Selected Studies,* Addison-Wesley, 1978; (editor with Rudiger Dornbusch, and contributor) *International Economic Policy: Theory and Evidence,* Johns Hopkins Press, 1979.

Contributor: George Horwich and P. A. Samuelson, editors, *Trade, Stability, and Macroeconomics: Essays in Honor of L. A. Metzler,* Academic Press, 1974; R. Z. Aliber, editor, *National Monetary Policies and the International Financial System,* University of Chicago Press, 1974; D. I. Meiselman and A. B. Laffer, editors, *The Phenomenon of Worldwide Inflation,* American Enterprise Institute for Public Policy Research, 1975; Michael Parkin and George Zis, editors, *Inflation in the World Economy,* Manchester University Press, 1976; Emil Classen and Pascal Salin, editors, *Recent Issues in International Monetary Economics,* North-Holland Publishing, 1976; Ronald I. McKinnon, editor, *Money and Finance in Economic Growth and Development,* Dekker, 1976; Jan Herin, Assar Lindbeck, and Johan Myhrman, editors, *Flexible Exchange Rates and Stabilization Policy,* Westview, 1977.

Karl Brunner and A. H. Meltzer, editors, *Economic Policies in Open Economies,* North-Holland Publishing, 1978; Donald R. Lessard, editor, *Frontiers of International Financial Management,* Warren, Gorham & Lamont, 1979; Brunner and Manfred Neumann, editors, *Inflation, Unemployment and Monetary Control,* Drucker & Humboldt, 1979; *Managed Exchange-Rate Flexibility: The Recent Experience,* Federal Reserve Bank (Boston, Mass.), 1979; Giorgio Szego and Marshall Sarnat, editors, *International Finance and Trade,* Ballinger, 1979; David Bigham and Teizo Taya, editors, *The Functioning of Flexible Exchange Rates: Theory, Evidence, and Policy Implications,* Cambridge University Press, 1980; June Flanders and Assaf Razin, editors, *Development in an Inflationary World,* Academic Press, 1980.

Contributor to *International Encyclopedia of the Social Sciences.* Contributor of more than fifty articles to economics journals. Editor of *Journal of Political Economy,* 1975—; member of editorial board of *Journal of Monetary Economics,* 1978—.

WORK IN PROGRESS: A monograph on exchange rates, money, and prices in the 1920's and 1970's; editing, with David Laidler, the scientific writings of Harry G. Johnson, for M.I.T. Press.

BIOGRAPHICAL/CRITICAL SOURCES: Business Week, November 14, 1977; *Reports* (of University of Chicago), autumn, 1978.

* * *

FREY, John Andrew 1929-

PERSONAL: Born August 29, 1929, in Cincinnati, Ohio; son of George H. and Marie Elizabeth (Berter) Frey. *Education:* University of Cincinnati, A.B., 1951, M.A., 1952; Catholic University of America, Ph.D., 1957. *Religion:* Roman Catholic. *Home:* 225 Ninth St. S.E., Washington, D.C. 20003. *Office:* Department of Romance Languages and Literatures, George Washington University, Washington, D.C. 20052.

CAREER: St. Joseph's College, Philadelphia, Pa., instructor in French, 1958-60; George Washington University, Washington, D.C., assistant professor, 1960-64, associate professor, 1964-70, professor of French, 1970—. *Member:* American Association of Teachers of French.

WRITINGS: Motif Symbolism in the Disciples of Mallarme, Catholic University of America Press, 1957; *The Aesthetics of the Rougon-Macquart,* Porruas, 1978. Contributor of articles and reviews to literature journals. Member of advisory board of *Rendezvous.*

WORK IN PROGRESS: A book comparing nineteenth- and twentieth-century French poetry to painting and sculpture from Delacroix to Matisse.

SIDELIGHTS: Frey noted that his work "continues the stylistic method of the late Helmut A. Hatzfeld." In particular, *The Aesthetics of the Rougon-Macquart* "tries to broaden the scope of French Naturalism to show affinities with literary and painterly Impressionism and with French Symbolist poetry. My work in preparation relies little on existing labels—Romantic, Symbolist; rather a fundamental stylistic and structural unity is sought."

* * *

FREY, Richard L. 1905-

PERSONAL: Born February 12, 1905, in New York, N.Y.; son of Louis J. (a lawyer) and Bessie (a shop owner; maiden name, Butzel) Frey; married Mabel Planco (a poet), July 10, 1935; children: Steven L. (deceased), Stephanie Constance. *Education:* Attended Columbia University. *Home and office:* 235 East 87th St., New York, N.Y. 10028.

CAREER: Writer and cardplaying expert. Kern Playing Cards, Inc., New York City, sales manager, 1935-37; Morehead, Frey & Whitmen (advertising agency), New York City, president, 1936-38; free-lance writer of nonfiction, 1939-58; American Contract Bridge League, Memphis, Tenn., editor and director of public relations, 1958-70. Chairman of Charles Goren Editorial Board. *Member:* International Bridge Press Association (president), American Society of Journalists and Authors, American Bridge Teachers Association (honorary member), Cavendish Club.

WRITINGS: (Editor) *The New Complete Hoyle: An Encyclopedia of Rules, Procedure, Manners and Strategy of Games Played With Cards, Dice, Counters, Boards, Words, and Numbers,* McKay, 1947, revised edition (with Albert Hodges Morehead and Geoffrey Mott-Smith) published as *The New Complete Hoyle: The Official Rules of all Popular Games of Skill and Chance With the Most Authoritative Advice on Winning Play,* Garden City Books, 1956; *How to Play Canasta,* Diversey, 1949; *How to Play Samba, the Sensational New Three-Deck Canasta,* Avon, 1951; *How to Win at Contract Bridge, in Ten Easy Lessons,* Grosset, 1961; (editor) *The Official Encyclopedia of Bridge,* Crown, 1964, 3rd edition, 1976; (editor) *According to Hoyle. Rules of Games: Official Rules of More than 300 Popular Games of Skill and Chance, With Expert Advice on Winning Play,* Hawthorn, 1965, revised edition published as *According to Hoyle: Official Rules of More Than 200 Popular Games of Skill and Chance With Expert Advice on Winning Play,* Fawcett, 1970; (editor) Peggy Solomon and others, *Bridge for Women,* Doubleday, 1967; (editor) Morehead, *Morehead on Bidding,* Simon and Schuster, 1974. Contributor to *Encyclopaedia Britannica.* Editor of *Bridge World.* Author of syndicated column "Dealing With Bridge." Contributor to periodicals, including *Cosmopolitan, Coronet, Good Housekeeping, McCall's, Reader's Digest,* and *Sports Illustrated.*

WORK IN PROGRESS: An autobiography, *Those Were the Days.*

* * *

FRICK, Ford Christopher 1894-1978

OBITUARY NOTICE: Born December 19, 1894, in Wawaka, Ind.; died April 8, 1978, in Bronxville, N.Y. Baseball executive, journalist, and author. As commissioner of baseball during a "revolutionary era," Frick was credited with bringing "the game integrity, dedication and a happy tranquility." President of the National League for seventeen years, Frick held baseball's top executive position from 1951 to 1965. He was characterized as "unflappable," a reputation he had earned when he prevented a strike by St. Louis Cardinals players in 1947. The Cards had refused to play against the Brooklyn Dodgers and, specifically, against the first black player in the leagues, Jackie Robinson. Frick warned them, "You cannot do this because this is America." A journalist for over ten years, Frick was also a sportswriter for the *New York Journal* and then a sportscaster. A close friend of Babe Ruth, he often served as Ruth's ghostwriter for the newspaper columns that the Yankee slugger was often asked to write. In 1970, Frick was elected to Baseball's Hall of Fame. His autobiography is entitled *Memoirs of a Lucky Fan.* Obituaries and other sources: *Current Biography,* Wilson, 1945, June, 1978; *Who's Who in Professional Baseball,* Arlington House, 1973; *Who's Who in America,* 40th edition, Marquis, 1978; *New York Times,* April 10, 1978; *Newsweek,* April 17, 1978; *Time,* April 24, 1978.

* * *

FRIEDENBERG, Walter Drew 1928-

PERSONAL: Born December 22, 1928, in Meriden, Conn.; son of Gustav Edward and Adela (Drews) Friedenberg; married Ramona Avila, May 29, 1965; children: Christopher

Drew, Eric Avila, Karina. *Education:* Wake Forest College (now University), B.A., 1949; Harvard University, A.M., 1956; postgraduate study at University of Chicago, 1959. *Office: Cincinnati Post and Times-Star,* 800 Broadway, Cincinnati, Ohio 45202.

CAREER/WRITINGS: Pittsburgh Press, Pittsburgh, Pa., reporter, 1960-61; Scripps-Howard Newspaper Alliance, Washington, D.C., foreign correspondent in Europe, Asia, and Africa, 1961-68, editorial writer, 1966-69; *Cincinnati Post and Times-Star,* Cincinnati, Ohio, editor, 1969—. Institute of Current World Affairs fellow in Indian subcontinent, 1956-60. *Military service:* U.S. Army, 1951-52. *Member:* National Press Club, Phi Beta Kappa, Omicron Delta Kappa.

* * *

FRIEDENTHAL, Richard 1896-1979

OBITUARY NOTICE: Born June 9, 1896, in Munich, Germany (now West Germany); died of a pulmonary embolism, October 19, 1979, in Kiel, West Germany. Editor and author. Before his flight from Nazi Germany in 1938, Friedenthal was a reader and editor for Knaur Verlag and wrote what was considered to be the first compact, popular German-language encyclopedia. Except for a visit to West Germany at the time of his death, Friedenthal lived in London, where he continued to edit and write. His books include biographies of Martin Luther, G. F. Handel, Leonardo da Vinci, and Johann Wolfgang Goethe. Obituaries and other sources: *Who's Who in the World,* 2nd edition, Marquis, 1973; *The Oxford Companion to German Literature,* Clarendon Press, 1976; *The International Who's Who,* Europa, 1978; *Washington Post,* October 22, 1979; *New York Times,* October 22, 1979; *AB Bookman's Weekly,* November 5, 1979.

* * *

FRIEDGUT, Theodore H. 1931-

PERSONAL: Born February 1, 1931; son of Abraham Hirsh (an attorney) and Judith (Osovsky) Friedgut; married Rivkah Urovitz (a nutritionist), September 15, 1974; children: Tamar, Yonit, Ehud. *Education:* Attended University of Toronto, 1947-50; Hebrew University of Jerusalem, B.A., 1965, M.A., 1967; Columbia University, Ph.D., 1972. *Politics:* "Sobered Social Democrat." *Office:* Department of Russian Studies, Hebrew University of Jerusalem, Jerusalem, Israel.

CAREER: Columbia University, New York, N.Y., lecturer in political science, 1970-71; Hebrew University of Jerusalem, Jerusalem, Israel, professor of Russian studies, 1971—. Exchange student in Moscow, Soviet Union, 1969-70. *Military service:* Israel Defense Forces, reserve duty, 1959—, active duty, 1967, 1973. *Member:* Israel Association for the Advancement of Slavic Studies, American Association for the Advancement of Slavic Studies. *Awards, honors:* Woodrow Wilson fellow, 1970-71.

WRITINGS: Political Participation in the U.S.S.R., Princeton University Press, 1979. Also author of *Institutions in Soviet Society,* in press. Contributor to politics and Slavic studies journals.

WORK IN PROGRESS: Soviet Local Government Reforms, 1957-1980 publication expected in 1983; a biography of Nikita Khrushchev, publication expected in 1983.

FRIEDMAN, David 1945-

PERSONAL: Born February 12, 1945, in New York, N.Y.; son of Milton (an economist) and Rose (an economist; maiden name, Director) Friedman; married Diana Forwalter (marriage ended); children: Patri Aaron. *Education:* Harvard University, B.A., 1965; University of Chicago, earned M.S. and Ph.D. *Politics:* Libertarian. *Religion:* Agnostic. *Home:* 703 Hutcheson Dr., Blacksburg, Va. 24060. *Office:* Public Choice Center, Virginia Polytechnic Institute and State University, Blacksburg, Va. 24061.

CAREER: Columbia University, New York, N.Y., research associate in physics, 1971-73; University of Pennsylvania, Philadelphia, fellow and lecturer at Fels Center, 1973-76; Virginia Polytechnic Institute and State University, Blacksburg, Va., assistant professor of economics, 1976—. Member of board of directors of Holiday Universal, Inc. *Member:* Mont Pelerin Society, Philadelphia Society, Phi Beta Kappa.

WRITINGS: The Machinery of Freedom, Harper, 1971, 2nd edition, Arlington House, 1978; *Laissez-Faire in Population: The Least Bad Solution* (pamphlet), Population Council, 1972. Editor of *Ripon Quarterly.*

WORK IN PROGRESS: A medieval cookbook.

AVOCATIONAL INTERESTS: The Middle Ages (including cooking from period cookbooks and fighting with non-lethal replicas of medieval weapons), writing and reading poetry, medieval Iceland, the history of jewelry and jewelry-making techniques.

* * *

FRIEDMAN, Hal
See FRIEDMAN, Harold

* * *

FRIEDMAN, Harold 1942-
(Hal Friedman)

PERSONAL: Born May 24, 1942, in Bronx, N.Y.; son of Manuel M. and May (a secretary; maiden name, Weinreb) Friedman. *Education:* Rutgers University, B.A., 1964. *Home:* 41 West 10th St., New York, N.Y. 10011.

CAREER: Warren, Muller, Dolobowsky (advertising agency), New York City, vice-president and co-creative director, 1968-76; J. Walter Thompson (advertising agency), New York City, vice-president and associate creative director, 1977—. *Awards, honors:* Recipient of advertising awards.

WRITINGS—Under name Hal Friedman: *Tunnel: A Nightmare Come True,* Morrow, 1979.

WORK IN PROGRESS: A medical thriller.

* * *

FRIEDRICHS, Christopher R(ichard) 1947-

PERSONAL: Born March 19, 1947, in White Plains, N.Y.; son of Kurt Otto (a mathematician) and Nellie H. (a teacher; maiden name, Bruell) Friedrichs; married Rhoda Lange (a historian), June 28, 1970; children: Ellen, Jonathan. *Education:* Columbia University, B.A., 1968; Princeton University, Ph.D., 1973. *Home:* 54 West 23rd Ave., Vancouver, British Columbia, Canada V5Y 2G7. *Office:* Department of History, University of British Columbia, 2075 Westbrook Place, Vancouver, British Columbia, Canada V6T 1W5.

CAREER: Princeton University, Princeton, N.J., instructor in history, 1972-73; University of British Columbia, Vancouver, assistant professor, 1973-78, associate professor of history, 1978—. *Member:* Canadian Historical Association, American Historical Association, American Association for Reformation Research.

WRITINGS: Urban Society in an Age of War: Noerdlingen, 1580-1720, Princeton University Press, 1979. Contributor to history journals.

WORK IN PROGRESS: Research for *Citizens or Subjects?: Urban Revolutions in Early Modern Germany* (tentative title).

SIDELIGHTS: In *Urban Society in an Age of War,* Friedrichs wrote: "One sometimes encounters the attitude that local studies are, in some way, the second-class citizens of historical literature, useful only as building blocks upon which broad comparative studies or works of historical synthesis can be constructed. This is an attitude, however, which I firmly reject. No doubt there are some local studies, suffused with antiquarian detail or brimming over with statistical output, which take on meaning only when their findings are woven into some broader framework. But the best local studies can stand by themselves as contributions to our understanding of the past . . . [L]ocal history can illuminate some aspects of the past in ways that few works of broad historical synthesis can ever hope to equal."

BIOGRAPHICAL/CRITICAL SOURCES: Christopher R. Friedrichs, *Urban Society in an Age of War: Noerdlingen, 1580-1720,* Princeton University Press, 1979.

* * *

FRIES, James Franklin 1938-

PERSONAL: Born August 25, 1938, in Normal, Ill.; son of Albert Charles (a professor) and Orpha Lorene (a teacher; maiden name, Hair) Fries; married Sarah Elizabeth Tilton (an administrator), August 27, 1960; children: Elizabeth Ann, Gregory James. *Education:* Stanford University, A.B., 1960; Johns Hopkins University, M.D., 1964. *Home:* 160 North Balsamina Way, Menlo Park, Calif. 94025. *Office:* Department of Medicine, Hospital, Stanford University, Stanford, Calif. 94305.

CAREER: Johns Hopkins University, Baltimore, Md., intern, 1964-65, resident in internal medicine, 1965-68; Stanford University, Stanford, Calif., resident in internal medicine, 1968-69, instructor, 1969-71, assistant professor, 1971-77, associate professor of medicine, 1977—, director of Arthritis Clinic. Diplomate of American Board of Internal Medicine. *Member:* American Rheumatism Association (director of Medical Information System), American Federation for Clinical Research, Northern California Rheumatism Association. *Awards, honors:* Clinical scholar of Carnegie Foundation, 1969-71; fellow of Arthritis Foundation, 1970-73, clinical scholar, 1973-78; fellow, Center for Advanced Study in the Behavioral Sciences, 1978-79.

WRITINGS: (With H. R. Holman) *Systemic Lupus Erythematosus,* Saunders, 1975; (with Donald M. Vickery) *Take Care of Yourself,* Addison-Wesley, 1976; (with Vickery and Robert Pantell) *Taking Care of Your Child,* Addison-Wesley, 1977; (with Andrei Calin) *Ankylosing Spondylitis,* Medical Examination Publishing, 1978; *Arthritis: A Comprehensive Guide,* Addison-Wesley, 1979; *Prognosis: A Textbook of Medicine,* Charles Press, 1980.

WORK IN PROGRESS: A health education textbook, title not yet certain, to be published by Addison-Wesley, 1980.

SIDELIGHTS: Fries writes: "I write to effect social change. I am interested in medical decision-making, from the level of the patient to that of the sub-specialist. The best medical care is not complicated. The underlying premises of my writing include: the patient makes the most important decisions in medicine; health can be improved and costs reduced if patient decision-making is improved; patient behavior may be changed through education interventions; personal autonomy is an important goal and contributes independently to maintenance of youth; and United States medicine provides too many services of little or no value.

AVOCATIONAL INTERESTS: Marathon running, mountain climbing, "aging cowboy, *bon vivant.*"

* * *

FROMKIN, Victoria A(lexandria) 1923-

PERSONAL: Born May 16, 1923, in Passaic, N.J.; daughter of Henry (an artist) and Rose (Ravitz) Landish; married Jack Fromkin (a biomedical engineer and professor), October 24, 1948; children: Mark (deceased). *Education:* University of California, Berkeley, B.A., 1944; University of California, Los Angeles, M.A., 1963, Ph.D., 1965. *Residence:* Los Angeles, Calif. *Office:* Department of Linguistics, University of California, Los Angeles, Calif. 90024.

CAREER: University of California, Los Angeles, assistant professor, 1965-68, associate professor, 1968-71, professor of linguistics, 1971—, dean of graduate division and associate vice-chancellor of graduate affairs, 1979—. Member of executive board of Center for Applied Linguistics; member of linguistic delegation to China, 1974. *Member:* International Association of Phonetic Sciences, American Association for the Advancement of Science, American Association for Phonetic Sciences, Linguistic Society of America, Acoustical Society of America (fellow), Association for Computational Linguistics (vice-president, 1969).

WRITINGS: (With Robert Rodman) *Introduction to Language,* Holt, 1974, 2nd edition, 1978; (editor) *Speech Errors as Linguistic Evidence,* Mouton, 1974; (editor) *Tone: A Linguistic Survey,* Academic Press, 1978. Contributor to language and linguistic journals, and *Scientific American.* Member of editorial board of *Brain and Language, Studies in African Linguistics,* and *Journal of Applied Psycholinguistics.*

WORK IN PROGRESS: Research on language and the brain and on phonology.

* * *

FROST, Frank (Jasper) 1929-

PERSONAL: Born December 3, 1929, in Washington, D.C.; son of Frank J. (in business) and Eugenia (a teacher; maiden name, Morris) Frost; married Violet Nunez, July 27, 1953 (divorced, 1965); married Amanda Clark (an editor), October 31, 1976; children: Frank J., Esme E. (deceased), Victoria R. *Education:* University of California, Santa Barbara, A.B., 1955; University of California, Los Angeles, M.A., 1959, Ph.D., 1961. *Politics:* Democrat. *Religion:* None. *Home:* 2687 Puesta Del Sol, Santa Barbara, Calif. 93105. *Office:* Department of History, University of California, Santa Barbara, Calif. 93106.

CAREER: University of California, Riverside, assistant professor of classics, 1959-62; Hunter College of the City University of New York, New York, N.Y., assistant professor of history, 1962-64; University of California, Riverside, assistant professor of classics, 1964; University of California, Santa Barbara, assistant professor, 1965-69, associate professor, 1969-77, professor of history, 1977—. Professional jazz pianist. Santa Barbara county commissioner, 1972-76, chairperson of board of commissioners, 1976. *Military service:* U.S. Army, Combat Infantry, 1950-53; served in Korea; became sergeant. *Member:* American Philological Association, Archaeological Institute of America, Association of Ancient Historians, Hellenic Society, Classical Association, Society for Nautical Research.

WRITINGS: (Editor of revision) Adolf Bauer, *Plutarch's Themistokles fuer Quellenkritische Uebungen* (title means "Plutarch's Themistocles for Source Criticism"), Argonaut, 1967; (editor) *Democracy and the Athenians,* Wiley, 1969; *Greek Society,* Heath, 1971, 2nd edition, 1980; *Plutarch's Themistocles: A Historical Commentary,* Princeton University Press, 1980. Contributor of articles and reviews to scholarly journals.

WORK IN PROGRESS: Boat Move, a novel, publication expected in 1982.

SIDELIGHTS: Frost comments: "I love being an author, but hate writing. My unattained goal: solo circumnavigation in a sailboat." *Avocational interests:* Cooking, sailing, diving, rugby (referee), travel (especially Greece and France), good food and drink.

* * *

FROST, Robert (Lee) 1874-1963

PERSONAL: Born March 26, 1874, in San Francisco, Calif.; died January 29, 1963, in Boston, Mass.; son of William Prescott (a newspaper reporter and editor) and Isabel (a teacher; maiden name, Moodie) Frost; married Elinor Miriam White, December 28, 1895 (died, 1938); children: Eliot (deceased), Lesley (daughter), Carol (son; deceased), Irma, Marjorie (deceased), Elinor Bettina (deceased). *Education:* Attended Dartmouth College, 1892, and Harvard University, 1897-99.

CAREER: Poet. Held various jobs between college studies, including bobbin boy in a Massachusetts mill, cobbler, editor of a country newspaper, schoolteacher, and farmer. Lived in England, 1912-15. Tufts College, Medford, Mass., Phi Beta Kappa poet, 1915 and 1940; Amherst College, Amherst, Mass., professor of English and poet-in-residence, 1916-20, 1923-25, and 1926-28; Middlebury College, Middlebury, Vt., co-founder of the Bread-Loaf School and Conference of English, 1920, annual lecturer, beginning 1920; University of Michigan, Ann Arbor, professor and poet-in-residence, 1921-23, fellow in letters, 1925-26; Columbia University, New York City, Phi Beta Kappa poet, 1932; Yale University, New Haven, Conn., associate fellow, beginning 1933; Harvard University, Cambridge, Mass., Phi Beta Kappa Poet, 1916 and 1941, Charles Eliot Norton Professor of Poetry, 1936, board overseer, 1938-39, Ralph Waldo Emerson Fellow, 1939-41, honorary fellow, 1942-43; associate of Adams House; fellow in American civilization, 1941-42; Dartmouth College, Hanover, N.H., George Ticknor Fellow in Humanities, 1943-49, visiting lecturer. *Member:* International P.E.N., National Institute of Arts and Letters, American Academy of Arts and Letters, American Philosophical Society.

AWARDS, HONORS: Pulitzer Prize for poetry for *New Hampshire,* 1924, for *Collected Poems,* 1931, for *A Further Range,* 1937, and for *A Witness Tree,* 1943; Loines Prize for poetry, 1931; Mark Twain medal, 1937; Gold Medal of the National Institute of Arts and Letters, 1938; Silver Medal of the Poetry Society of America, 1941; Huntington Hartford Foundation award, 1958; unanimous resolution in his honor and gold medal from the U.S. Senate, March 24, 1950; participated in President John F. Kennedy's inauguration ceremonies, 1961, by reading his poems, "Dedication" and "The Gift Outright"; chosen poet laureate of Vermont by the State League of Women's Clubs; over forty honorary degrees from colleges and universities, including Oxford and Cambridge Universities, Amherst College, and the University of Michigan.

WRITINGS—Poetry: *Twilight,* [Lawrence, Mass.], 1894, reprinted, University of Virginia, 1966; *A Boy's Will,* D. Nutt, 1913, Holt, 1915; *North of Boston,* D. Nutt, 1914, Holt, 1915, reprinted, Dodd, 1977; *Mountain Interval,* Holt, 1916; *New Hampshire,* Holt, 1923, reprinted, New Dresden Press, 1955; *West-Running Brook,* Holt, 1928; *The Lone Striker,* Knopf, 1933; *Two Tramps in Mud-Time,* Holt, 1934; *The Gold Hesperidee,* Bibliophile Press, 1935; *Three Poems,* Baker Library Press, 1935; *A Further Range,* Holt, 1936; *From Snow to Snow,* Holt, 1936; *A Witness Tree,* Holt, 1942; *A Masque of Reason* (verse drama), Holt, 1942; *Steeple Bush,* Holt, 1947; *A Masque of Mercy* (verse drama), Holt, 1947; *Greece,* Black Rose Press, 1948; *Hard Not to Be King,* House of Books, 1951; *Aforesaid,* Holt, 1954; *The Gift Outright,* Holt, 1961; *"Dedication" and "The Gift Outright"* (poems read at the presidential inaugural, 1961; published with the inaugural address of J. F. Kennedy), Spiral Press, 1961; *In the Clearing,* Holt, 1962. Also author of *The Lovely Shall Be Choosers,* 1929, and *And All We Call American,* 1958.

Poems issued as Christmas greetings: *Christmas Trees,* Spiral Press, 1929; *Neither Out Far Nor In Deep,* Holt, 1935; *Everybody's Sanity,* [Los Angeles], 1936; *To a Young Wretch,* Spiral Press, 1937; *Triple Plate,* Spiral Press, 1939; *Our Hold on the Planet,* Holt, 1940; *An Unstamped Letter in Our Rural Letter Box,* Spiral Press, 1944; *On Making Certain Anything Has Happened,* Spiral Press, 1945; *One Step Backward Taken,* Spiral Press, 1947; *Closed for Good,* Spiral Press, 1948; *On a Tree Fallen Across the Road to Hear Us Talk,* Spiral Press, 1949; *Doom to Bloom,* Holt, 1950; *A Cabin in the Clearing,* Spiral Press, 1951; *Does No One but Me at All Ever Feel This Way in the Least,* Spiral Press, 1952; *One More Brevity,* Holt, 1953; *From a Milkweed Pod,* Holt, 1954; *Some Science Fiction,* Spiral Press, 1955; *Kitty Hawk, 1894,* Holt, 1956; *My Objection to Being Stepped On,* Holt, 1957; *Away,* Spiral Press, 1958; *A-Wishing Well,* Spiral Press, 1959; *Accidentally on Purpose,* Holt, 1960; *The Woodpile,* Spiral Press, 1961; *The Prophets Really Prophesy as Mystics, the Commentators Merely by Statistics,* Spiral Press, 1962; *The Constant Symbol,* [New York], 1962.

Collections: *Collected Poems of Robert Frost,* Holt, 1930, new edition, 1939; *Selected Poems,* Holt, 1934, reprinted, 1963; *Come In, and Other Poems,* edited by Louis Untermeyer, Holt, 1943, reprinted, F. Watts, 1967, enlarged edition published as *The Road Not Taken: An Introduction to Robert Frost,* reprinted as *The Pocket Book of Robert Frost's Poems,* Pocket Books, 1956; *The Poems of Robert Frost,* Modern Library, 1946; *You Come Too: Favorite Poems for Young Readers,* Holt, 1959, reprinted, 1967; *A Remembrance Collection of New Poems by Robert Frost,* Holt, 1959; *Poems,* Washington Square Press, 1961; *Longer Poems: The Death of the Hired Man,* Holt, 1966; *Selected Prose,* edited by Hyde Cox and Edward Connery Lathem, Holt, 1966, reprinted, Collier Books, 1968; *Complete Poems of Robert Frost,* Holt, 1968; *The Poetry of Robert Frost,* edited by Lathem, Holt, 1969; *Robert Frost: Poetry and Prose,* edited by Lawrence Thompson and Lathem, Holt, 1972; *Selected Poems,* edited by Ian Hamilton, Penguin, 1973.

Letters: *The Letters of Robert Frost to Louis Untermeyer,* Holt, 1963; *Selected Letters,* edited by Thompson, Holt,

1964; *Family Letters of Robert and Elinor Frost,* edited by Arnold Grade, State University of New York Press, 1972.

Other: *A Way Out* (one-act play), Harbor Press, 1929; *The Cow's in the Corn* (one-act play in rhyme), Slide Mountain Press, 1929; (contributor) John Holmes, editor, *Writing Poetry,* Writer, Inc., 1960; (contributor) Milton R. Konvitz and Stephen E. Whicher, editors, *Emerson,* Prentice-Hall, 1962; *Robert Frost on "Extravagance"* (the text of Frost's last college lecture, Dartmouth College, November 27, 1962), [Hanover, N.H.], 1963.

SIDELIGHTS: Robert Frost holds a unique and almost isolated position in American letters. "Though his career fully spans the modern period and though it is impossible to speak of him as anything other than a modern poet," writes James M. Cox, "it is difficult to place him in the main tradition of modern poetry." In a sense, Frost stands at the crossroads of nineteenth-century American poetry and modernism, for in his verse may be found the culmination of many nineteenth-century tendencies and traditions as well as parallels to the works of his twentieth-century contemporaries. Taking his symbols from the public domain, Frost developed, as many critics note, an original, modern idiom and a sense of directness and economy that reflect the imagism of Ezra Pound and Amy Lowell. On the other hand, as Leonard Unger and William Van O'Connor point out in *Poems for Study,* "Frost's poetry, unlike that of such contemporaries as Eliot, Stevens, and the later Yeats, shows no marked departure from the poetic practices of the nineteenth century." Although he avoids traditional verse forms and only uses rhyme erratically, Frost is not an innovator and his technique is never experimental.

Frost's theory of poetic composition ties him to both centuries. Like the nineteenth-century Romantics, he maintained that a poem is "never a put-up job. . . . It begins as a lump in the throat, a sense of wrong, a homesickness, a loneliness. It is never a thought to begin with. It is at its best when it is a tantalizing vagueness." Yet, "working out his own version of the 'impersonal' view of art," as Hyatt H. Waggoner observed, Frost also upheld T. S. Eliot's idea that the man who suffers and the artist who creates are totally separate. In a 1932 letter to Sydney Cox, Frost explained his conception of poetry: "The objective idea is all I ever cared about. Most of my ideas occur in verse. . . . To be too subjective with what an artist has managed to make objective is to come on him presumptuously and render ungraceful what he in pain of his life had faith he had made graceful."

To accomplish such objectivity and grace, Frost took up nineteenth-century tools and made them new. Lawrence Thompson has explained that, according to Frost, "the self-imposed restrictions of meter in form and of coherence in content" work to a poet's advantage; they liberate him from the experimentalist's burden—the perpetual search for new forms and alternative structures. Thus Frost, as he himself put it in "The Constant Symbol," wrote his verse regular; he never completely abandoned conventional metrical forms for free verse, as so many of his contemporaries were doing. At the same time, his adherence to meter, line length, and rhyme scheme was not an arbitrary choice. He maintained that "the freshness of a poem belongs absolutely to its not having been thought out and then set to verse as the verse in turn might be set to music." He believed, rather, that the poem's particular mood dictated or determined the poet's "first commitment to metre and length of line."

Critics frequently point out that Frost complicated his problem and enriched his style by setting traditional meters against the natural rhythms of speech. Drawing his language primarily from the vernacular, he avoided artificial poetic diction by employing the accent of a soft-spoken New Englander. In *The Function of Criticism,* Yvor Winters faulted Frost for his "endeavor to make his style approximate as closely as possible the style of conversation." But what Frost achieved in his poetry was much more complex than a mere imitation of the New England farmer idiom. He wanted to restore to literature the "sentence sounds that underlie the words," the "vocal gesture" that enhances meaning. That is, he felt the poet's ear must be sensitive to the voice in order to capture with the written word the significance of sound in the spoken word. "The Death of the Hired Man," for instance, consists almost entirely of dialogue between Mary and Warren, her farmer-husband, but critics have observed that in this poem Frost takes the prosaic patterns of their speech and makes them lyrical. To Ezra Pound "The Death of the Hired Man" represented Frost at his best—when he "dared to write . . . in the natural speech of New England; in natural spoken speech, which is very different from the 'natural' speech of the newspapers, and of many professors."

Frost's use of New England dialect is only one aspect of his often discussed regionalism. Within New England, his particular focus was on New Hampshire, which he called "one of the two best states in the Union," the other being Vermont. In an essay entitled "Robert Frost and New England: A Revaluation," W. G. O'Donnell noted how from the start, in *A Boy's Will,* "Frost had already decided to give his writing a local habitation and a New England name, to root his art in the soil that he had worked with his own hands." Reviewing *North of Boston* in the *New Republic,* Amy Lowell wrote, "Not only is his work New England in subject, it is so in technique. . . . Mr. Frost has reproduced both people and scenery with a vividness which is extraordinary." Many other critics have lauded Frost's ability to realistically evoke the New England landscape; they point out that one can visualize an orchard in "After Apple-Picking" or imagine spring in a farmyard in "Two Tramps in Mud Time." In this "ability to portray the local truth in nature," O'Donnell claims, Frost has no peer. The same ability prompted Pound to declare, "I know more of farm life than I did before I had read his poems. That means I know more of 'Life.'"

Frost's regionalism, critics remark, is in his realism, not in politics; he creates no picture of regional unity or sense of community. In *The Continuity of American Poetry,* Roy Harvey Pearce describes Frost's protagonists as individuals who are constantly forced to confront their individualism as such and to reject the modern world in order to retain their identity. Frost's use of nature is not only similar but closely tied to this regionalism. He stays as clear of religion and mysticism as he does of politics. What he finds in nature is sensuous pleasure; he is also sensitive to the earth's fertility and to man's relationship to the soil. To critic M. L. Rosenthal, Frost's pastoral quality, his "lyrical and realistic repossession of the rural and 'natural,'" is the staple of his reputation.

Yet, just as Frost is aware of the distances between one man and another, so he is also always aware of the distinction, the ultimate separateness, of nature and man. Marion Montgomery has explained, "His attitude toward nature is one of armed and amicable truce and mutual respect interspersed with crossings of the boundaries" between individual man and natural forces. Below the surface of Frost's poems are dreadful implications, what Rosenthal calls his "shocked sense of the helpless cruelty of things." This natural cruelty is at work in "Design" and in "Once by the Pacific." The ominous tone of these two poems prompted Rosenthal's further comment: "At his most powerful Frost is as staggered by 'the horror' as Eliot and approaches the hysterical edge of sensibility in a comparable way. . . . His is still the modern mind in search of its own meaning."

The austere and tragic view of life that emerges in so many of Frost's poems is modulated by his metaphysical use of detail. As Frost portrays him, man might be alone in an ultimately indifferent universe, but he may nevertheless look to the natural world for metaphors of his own condition. Thus, in his search for meaning in the modern world, Frost focuses on those moments when the seen and the unseen, the tangible and the spiritual intersect. John T. Napier calls this Frost's ability "to find the ordinary a matrix for the extraordinary." In this respect, he is often compared with Emily Dickinson and Ralph Waldo Emerson, in whose poetry, too, a simple fact, object, person, or event will be transfigured and take on greater mystery or significance. The poem "Birches" is an example: it contains the image of slender trees bent to the ground—temporarily by a boy's swinging on them or permanently by an ice-storm. But as the poem unfolds, it becomes clear that the speaker is concerned not only with child's play and natural phenomena, but also with the point at which physical and spiritual reality merge.

Such symbolic import of mundane facts informs many of Frost's poems, and in "Education by Poetry" he explained: "Poetry begins in trivial metaphors, pretty metaphors, 'grace' metaphors, and goes on to the profoundest thinking that we have. Poetry provides the one permissible way of saying one thing and meaning another. . . . Unless you are at home in the metaphor, unless you have had your proper poetical education in the metaphor, you are not safe anywhere."

Frost's own poetical education began in San Francisco where he was born in 1874, but he found his place of safety in New England when his family moved to Lawrence, Massachusetts, in 1884 following his father's death. The move was actually a return, for Frost's ancestors were originally New Englanders. The region must have been particularly conducive to the writing of poetry because within the next five years Frost had made up his mind to be a poet. In fact, he graduated from Lawrence High School, in 1892, as class poet (he also shared the honor of co-valedictorian with his wife-to-be Elinor White); and two years later, the *New York Independent* accepted his poem entitled "My Butterfly," launching his status as a professional poet with a check for $15.00.

To celebrate his first publication, Frost had a book of six poems privately printed; two copies of *Twilight* were made—one for himself and one for his fiancee. Over the next eight years, however, he succeeded in having only thirteen more poems published. During this time, Frost sporadically attended Dartmouth and Harvard and earned a living teaching school and, later, working a farm in Derby, New Hampshire. But in 1912, discouraged by American magazines' constant rejection of his work, he took his family to England, where he could "write and be poor without further scandal in the family." In England, Frost found the professional esteem denied him in his native country. Continuing to write about New England, he had two books published, *A Boy's Will* (1913) and *North of Boston* (1914), which established his reputation so that his return to the United States in 1915 was as a celebrated literary figure. Holt put out an American edition of *North of Boston* (1915), and periodicals that had once scorned his work now sought it.

Since 1915 Frost's position in American letters has been firmly rooted; in the years before his death he came to be considered the unofficial poet laureate of the United States. On his seventy-fifth birthday, the U.S. Senate passed a resolution in his honor which said, "His poems have helped to guide American thought and humor and wisdom, setting forth to our minds a reliable representation of ourselves and of all men." In 1955, the State of Vermont named a mountain after him in Ripton, the town of his legal residence; and at the Presidential Inauguration of John F. Kennedy in 1961, Frost was given the unprecedented honor of being asked to read a poem, "The Gift Outright," which he wrote for the occasion.

Though Frost allied himself with no literary school or movement, the imagists helped at the start to promote his American reputation. *Poetry: A Magazine of Verse* published his work before others began to clamor for it. It also published a review by Ezra Pound of the British edition of *A Boy's Will,* which Pound said "has the tang of the New Hampshire woods, and it has just this utter sincerity. It is not post-Miltonic or post-Swinburnian or post-Kiplonian. This man has the good sense to speak naturally and to paint the thing, the thing as he sees it." Amy Lowell reviewed *North of Boston* in the *New Republic,* and she, too, sang Frost's praises: "He writes in classic metres in a way to set the teeth of all the poets of the older schools on edge; and he writes in classic metres, and uses inversions and cliches whenever he pleases, those devices so abhorred by the newest generation. He goes his own way, regardless of anyone else's rules, and the result is a book of unusual power and sincerity." In these first two volumes, Frost introduced not only his affection for New England themes and his unique blend of traditional meters and colloquialism, but also his use of dramatic monologues and dialogues. "Mending Wall," the leading poem in *North of Boston,* describes the friendly argument between the speaker and his neighbor as they walk along their common wall replacing fallen stones; their differing attitudes toward "boundaries" offer symbolic significance typical of the poems in these early collections.

Mountain Interval (1916) marked Frost's turn to another kind of poem, a brief meditation sparked by an object, person or event. Like the monologues and dialogues, these short pieces have a dramatic quality. "Birches," discussed above, is an example, as is "The Road Not Taken," in which a fork in a woodland path transcends the specific. The distinction of this volume, *The Boston Transcript* said, "is that Mr. Frost takes the lyricism of 'A Boy's Will' and plays a deeper music and gives a more intricate variety of experience."

Several new qualities emerged in Frost's work with the appearance of *New Hampshire* (1923), particularly a new self-consciousness and willingness to speak of himself and his art. The volume, for which Frost won his first Pulitzer Prize, "pretends to be nothing but a long poem with notes and grace notes," as Louis Untermeyer described it. The title poem, approximately fourteen pages long, is a "rambling tribute" to Frost's favorite state and "is starred and dotted with scientific numerals in the manner of the most profound treatise." Thus, a footnote at the end of a line of poetry will refer the reader to another poem seemingly inserted to merely reinforce the text of "New Hampshire." Some of these poems are in the form of epigrams, which appear for the first time in Frost's work. "Fire and Ice," for example, one of the better known epigrams, speculates on the means by which the world will end. Frost's most famous and, according to J. McBride Dabbs, most perfect lyric, "Stopping by Woods on a Snowy Evening,'' is also included in this collection; conveying ''the insistent whisper of death at the heart of life,'' the poem portrays a speaker who stops his sleigh in the midst of a snowy woods only to be called from the inviting gloom by the recollection of practical duties. Frost himself said of this poem that it is the kind he'd like to print on one page followed with ''forty pages of footnotes.''

West-Running Brook (1928), Frost's fifth book of poems, is divided into six sections, one of which is taken up entirely by the title poem. This poem refers to a brook which perversely flows west instead of east to the Atlantic like all other brooks. A comparison is set up between the brook and the poem's speaker who trusts himself to go by ''contraries''; further rebellious elements exemplified by the brook give expression to an eccentric individualism, Frost's stoic theme of resistance and self-realization. Reviewing the collection in the *New York Herald Tribune,* Babette Deutsch wrote: ''The courage that is bred by a dark sense of Fate, the tenderness that broods over mankind in all its blindness and absurdity, the vision that comes to rest as fully on kitchen smoke and lapsing snow as on mountains and stars—these are his, and in his seemingly casual poetry, he quietly makes them ours.''

A Further Range (1936), which earned Frost another Pulitzer Prize and was a Book-of-the-Month Club selection, contains two groups of poems subtitled ''Taken Doubly'' and ''Taken Singly.'' In the first, and more interesting, of these groups, the poems are somewhat didactic, though there are humorous and satiric pieces as well. Included here is ''Two Tramps in Mud Time,'' which opens with the story of two itinerant lumbermen who offer to cut the speaker's wood for pay; the poem then develops into a sermon on the relationship between work and play, vocation and avocation, preaching the necessity to unite them. Of the entire volume, William Rose Benet wrote, ''It is better worth reading than nine-tenths of the books that will come your way this year. In a time when all kinds of insanity are assailing the nations it is good to listen to this quiet humor, even about a hen, a hornet, or Square Matthew. . . . And if anybody should ask me why I still believe in my land, I have only to put this book in his hand and answer, 'Well—here is a man of my country.' ''

Most critics acknowledge that Frost's poetry in the forties and fifties grew more and more abstract, cryptic, and even sententious, so it is generally on the basis of his earlier work that he is judged. His political conservatism and religious faith, hitherto informed by skepticism and local color, became more and more the guiding principles of his work. He had been, as Randall Jarrell points out, ''a very odd and very radical radical when young'' yet became ''sometimes callously and unimaginatively conservative'' in his old age. He had become a public figure, and in the years before his death, much of his poetry was written from this stance.

Reviewing *A Witness Tree* in *Books,* Wilbert Snow noted a few poems ''which have a right to stand with the best things he has written'': ''Come In,'' ''The Silken Tent,'' and ''Carpe Diem'' especially. Yet Snow went on: ''Some of the poems here are little more than rhymed fancies; others lack the bullet-like unity of structure to be found in 'North of Boston.' '' On the other hand, Stephen Vincent Benet felt that Frost had ''never written any better poems than some of those in this book.'' Similarly, critics were let down by *In the Clearing.* One wrote, ''Although this reviewer considers Robert Frost to be the foremost contemporary U.S. poet, he regretfully must state that most of the poems in this new volume are disappointing. . . . [They] often are closer to jingles than to the memorable poetry we associate with his name.'' Another maintained that ''the bulk of the book consists of poems of 'philosophic talk.' Whether you like them or not depends mostly on whether you share the 'philosophy.' ''

Indeed, many readers do share Frost's philosophy, and still others who do not nevertheless continue to find delight and significance in his large body of poetry. In October 1963, President John F. Kennedy delivered a speech at the dedication of the Robert Frost Library in Amherst, Massachusetts. ''In honoring Robert Frost,'' the President said, ''we therefore can pay honor to the deepest source of our national strength. That strength takes many forms and the most obvious forms are not always the most significant. . . . Our national strength matters; but the spirit which informs and controls our strength matters just as much. This was the special significance of Robert Frost.'' The poet would probably have been pleased by such recognition, for he had said once, in an interview with Harvey Breit: ''One thing I care about, and wish young people could care about, is taking poetry as the first form of understanding. If poetry isn't understanding all, the whole world, then it isn't worth anything.''

BIOGRAPHICAL/CRITICAL SOURCES—Selected Periodicals: *Poetry,* May, 1913; *New Republic,* February 20, 1915; *Boston Transcript,* December 2, 1916; *Bookman,* January, 1924; *New York Herald Tribune,* November 18, 1928; *Yale Review,* spring, 1934, summer, 1948; *Saturday Review of Literature,* May 30, 1936, April 25, 1942; *Books,* May 10, 1942; *American Literature,* January, 1948; *Virginia Quarterly Review,* summer, 1957; *South Atlantic Quarterly,* summer, 1958; *Wisconsin Library Bulletin,* July, 1962; *Commonweal,* May 4, 1962, April 1, 1977; *Atlantic Monthly,* February, 1964, November, 1966; *Times Literary Supplement,* December 14, 1967; *New York Times Magazine,* June 11, 1972, August 18, 1974; *America,* December 24, 1977.

Selected Books: Amy Lowell, *Tendencies in Modern American Poetry,* Macmillan, 1917; Gorham B. Munson, *Robert Frost: A Study in Sensibility and Good Sense,* G. H. Doran, 1927, reprinted, Haskell House, 1969; Lawrence Thompson, *Fire and Ice: The Art and Thought of Robert Frost,* Holt, 1942, reprinted, Russell, 1975; Marshall Louis Mertins and Esther Mertins, *Intervals of Robert Frost: A Critical Bibliography,* University of California Press, 1947, reprinted, Russell, 1975; Herbert Faulkner West, *Mind on the Wing,* Coward, 1947.

Leonard Unger and William Van O'Connor, *Poems for Study,* Holt, 1953; Ezra Pound, *The Literary Essays of Ezra Pound,* New Directions, 1954; Randall Jarrell, *Poetry and the Age,* Vintage, 1955; Louis Untermeyer, *Makers of the Modern World,* Simon & Schuster, 1955; Harvey Breit, *The Writer Observed,* World Publishing, 1956; Sidney Cox, *Swinger of Birches: A Portrait of Robert Frost,* New York University Press, 1957; Yvor Winters, *The Function of Criticism,* A. Swallow, 1957; Reginald L. Cook, *The Dimensions of Robert Frost,* Rinehart, 1958; Loring Holmes Dodd, *Celebrities at Our Hearthside,* Dresser, 1959; Louis Untermeyer, *Lives of the Poets,* Simon & Schuster, 1959; Thompson, *Robert Frost,* University of Minnesota Press, 1959.

Elizabeth Shepley, *Robert Frost: The Trial by Existence,* Holt, 1960; Roy Harvey Pearce, *The Continuity of American Poetry,* Princeton, 1961; James M. Cox, *Robert Frost: A Collection of Critical Essays,* Prentice-Hall, 1962; Emily Elizabeth Isaacs, *Introduction to Robert Frost,* A. Swallow, 1962, reprinted, Haskell House, 1972; Margaret Anderson, *Robert Frost and John Bartlett: The Record of a Friendship,* Holt, 1963; Edward C. Lathem and Thompson, editors, *Robert Frost: Farm-Poultryman,* Dartmouth Publishers, 1963; Untermeyer, *Robert Frost: A Backward Look,* U.S.

Government Printing Office, 1964; Franklin D. Reeve, *Robert Frost in Russia,* Little, Brown, 1964; Jean Gould, *Robert Frost: The Aim Was Song,* Dodd, 1964; Thompson, editor, *Selected Letters of Robert Frost,* Holt, 1964; Mertins, *Robert Frost: Life and Talks—Walking,* University of Oklahoma Press, 1965; John R. Doyle, Jr., *Poetry of Robert Frost: An Analysis,* Hafner, 1965; M. L. Rosenthal, *The Modern Poets,* Oxford University Press, 1965; Philip L. Gerber, *Robert Frost,* Twayne, 1966; Elizabeth Jennings, *Frost,* Barnes & Noble, 1966; Lathem, editor, *Interviews With Robert Frost,* Rinehart, 1966; Thompson, *Robert Frost: The Early Years, 1874-1915,* Holt, 1966; David A. Sohn and Richard Tyre, *Frost: The Poet and His Poetry,* Holt, 1967; Hyatt H. Waggoner, *American Poetry From the Puritans to the Present,* Houghton, 1968; Radcliffe Squires, *Major Themes of Robert Frost,* University of Michigan Press, 1969; Lesley Frost, *New Hampshire's Child: Derry Journals of Lesley Frost,* State University of New York Press, 1969.

Thompson, *Robert Frost: The Years of Triumph, 1915-1938,* Holt, 1970; Lathem, editor, *A Concordance to the Poetry of Robert Frost,* Holt Information Systems, 1971; Vrest Orton, *Vermont Afternoons With Robert Frost,* Tuttle, 1971; Robert Francis, recorder, *A Time to Talk: Conversations and Indiscretions,* University of Massachusetts Press, 1972; *Contemporary Literary Criticism,* Gale, Volume 1, 1973, Volume 3, 1975, Volume 4, 1975, Volume 9, 1978, Volume 10, 1979; Elaine Barry, compiler, *Robert Frost on Writing,* Rutgers University Press, 1973; Barry, *Robert Frost,* Ungar, 1973; Robert E. Spiller and others, *Literary History of the United States,* 4th revised edition, Macmillan, 1974; Donald J. Greiner and Charles Sanders, *Robert Frost: The Poet and His Critics,* American Library Association, 1974; Reginald L. Cook, *Robert Frost: A Living Voice,* University of Massachusetts Press, 1974; Peter Van Egmond, *The Critical Reception of Robert Frost,* G. K. Hall, 1974; Frank Lentriccia, *Robert Frost: Modern Poetics and the Landscapes of Self,* Duke University Press, 1975; Jac Tharpe, editor, *Frost: Centennial Essays II,* University Press of Mississippi, 1976; Robert Spangler Newdick, *Newdick's Season of Frost: An Interrupted Biography of Robert Frost,* edited by William A. Sutton, State University of New York Press, 1976; Thompson and R. H. Winnick, *Robert Frost: The Later Years, 1938-1963,* Holt, 1976; Donald Hall, *Remembering Poets,* Harper, 1977; Richard Poirier, *Robert Frost,* Oxford University Press, 1977; Linda Welshimer Wagner, editor, *Robert Frost: The Critical Reception,* B. Franklin, 1977.

OBITUARIES: New York Times, January 30, 1963; *Illustrated London News,* February 9, 1963; *Newsweek,* February 11, 1963; *Publishers Weekly,* February 11, 1963; *Current Biography,* March, 1963.*

—*Sketch by Andrea Geffner*

* * *

FUCILLA, Joseph G(uerin) 1897-

PERSONAL: Born December 14, 1897, in Chicago, Ill.; son of John (a factory worker) and Maria (De Marco) Fucilla; married Reba Ann South, May 9, 1925; children: Jasper S., Ivan S. *Education:* University of Wisconsin—Madison, B.A., 1921, M.A., 1922; University of Chicago, Ph.D., 1928. *Politics:* Independent. *Religion:* "Non-denominational." *Home:* 1862 Sherman Ave., Evanston, Ill. 60201. *Office:* Department of Spanish and Portuguese, Northwestern University, Evanston, Ill. 60201.

CAREER: Iowa State College (now University), Ames, instructor in romance languages, 1921-23; Butler College, Indianapolis, Ind., assistant professor of romance languages, 1923-28; Northwestern University, Evanston, Ill., assistant professor, 1928-32, associate professor, 1932-36, professor of romance languages, 1936-66, professor emeritus, 1966—. Visiting professor at University of Wisconsin, 1966-67, University of Colorado, 1967, and University of California, Santa Barbara, 1967-69. *Member:* National Federation of Modern Language Teachers Association, Modern Language Association of America, American Association of Teachers of Spanish and Portuguese, Renaissance Society of America, American Association of Teachers of Italian (honorary president, 1968—), American Name Society, Dante Society of America, Phi Beta Kappa, Phi Kappa Phi. *Awards, honors:* National Foreign Language Achievement award from National Federation of Modern Language Teachers Associations; distinguished achievement medal from Dante Society of America.

WRITINGS—In English: (with Joseph M. Carriere) *D'Annunzio Abroad: A Bibliographical Essay,* Columbia University, 1935; (with Carriere) *Italian Criticism of Russian Literature,* H. L. Hedrick, 1938; *Forgotten Danteiana: A Bibliographical Supplement,* Northwestern University, 1939, reprinted, Arno, 1970; (with Thomas Rossman and William Collar Holbrook) *A Bibliographical Guide to the Romance Languages and Literatures,* Chandler's, 1939, 7th edition, 1966; *Universal Author Repertoire of Italian Essay Literature,* S. F. Vanni, 1941; *The Follett Spanish Dictionary: Spanish-English and English-Spanish,* Follett, 1943, revised edition, 1964; *Our Italian Surnames,* Chandler's, 1949.

(Translator from the Italian) Pietro Antonio Domenico Buonaventura Mestastasio, *Dido Forsaken,* Valmartina, 1952; *Studies and Notes (Literary and Historical),* Istituto editoriale del Mezzogiorno, 1953; *The Teaching of Italian in the United States: A Documentary History,* American Association of Teachers of Italian, 1967.

Other: *Retrospettiva, pagine dementicate di bibliografia leopardiana,* G. Mauro, 1937; (editor) Carlo Goldini, *La locandiera,* Holt, 1939; *Relaciones hispanoitalianas,* [Madrid], 1953; *Saggistica letteraria italiana: Bibliografia per soggetti, 1938-1952,* Sansoni, 1956; (editor with Ferdinando Dante Maurino) *Cuentos hispano-americanos de ayer y de hoy,* Scribner, 1956; *Superbi colli e altri saggi,* Carruci, 1963; (editor with Alessandro Tortoreto) *Versi e prose ispirati al Tasso,* Centro di studi tassiani, 1966; (editor) Vicente Antonio Garcia de la Huerta, *Raquel: Tragedia espagnola tres jornadas,* Catedra, 1974.

Also author of *A Study of Petrarchism in Spain During the Sixteenth Century,* 1928. Editor of *Italica,* 1943-68.

* * *

FULFORD, Robert 1932-
(Marshall Delaney)

PERSONAL: Born February 13, 1932, in Ottawa, Ontario, Canada; son of Albert Edward (an editor) and Frances (Blount) Fulford; married Jocelyn Dingman, June 16, 1956 (deceased); married Geraldine Sherman (a broadcaster), November 28, 1970; children: James, Margaret, Rachel, Sarah. *Education:* Attended Malvern Collegiate Institute. *Home:* 153 Forest Hill Rd., Toronto, Ontario, Canada M5P 2N1. *Office: Saturday Night,* 69 Front St. E., Toronto, Ontario, Canada M5E 1R3.

CAREER: Toronto Globe & Mail, Toronto, Ontario, reporter, 1949-53; Maclean-Hunter Publishing Co., Toronto, Ontario, editor, 1953-55; *Toronto Globe & Mail,* reporter, 1956-

57; *Toronto Daily Star,* Toronto, Ontario, literary columnist, 1958-62, 1964-68; *Saturday Night,* Toronto, Ontario, editor, 1968—. Host of CBC-Radio program, "This Is Robert Fulford," and contributing broadcaster to CBC-TV programs, including "The Way It Is," "Man Alive," "Close-Up," "Background," and "Explorations," 1955—. *Awards, honors:* National Magazine award, 1977, for commentary.

WRITINGS: This Was Expo, McClelland & Stewart, 1968; *Crisis at the Victory Burlesk* (essays), Oxford University Press, 1968; (editor) *Harold Town Drawings,* McClelland & Stewart, 1969; (editor with David Godfrey and Abraham Rotstein) *Read Canadian,* James Lorimer Publishing, 1972; (under pseudonym Marshall Delaney) *Marshall Delaney at the Movies* (film reviews), Peter Martin Associates, 1974. Contributor to magazines, sometimes under pseudonym Marshall Delaney. Editor of magazines, including *Canadian Homes and Gardens,* 1955, *Mayfair,* 1956, and *Maclean's,* 1962-64.

SIDELIGHTS: Fulford comments: "At about age thirteen, in 1945, I began to think that I wanted to be a journalist, and at about age sixteen I began learning how to be a sportswriter. I left high school to cover sports for the *Toronto Globe* but soon realized my interests were in the arts and literature. Over the following quarter of a century I have written hundreds of articles and spoken (on television and radio) millions of words about books, painting, sculpture, and movies."

BIOGRAPHICAL/CRITICAL SOURCES: William Toye, editor, *Supplement to the Oxford Companion to Canadian History and Literature,* Oxford University Press, 1973.

* * *

FUNK, Wilfred (John) 1883-1965

OBITUARY NOTICE: Born March 20, 1883, in Brooklyn, N.Y.; died June 1, 1965. Publisher, editor, lexicographer, and author. Funk became secretary of the publishing firm Funk & Wagnalls in 1912 after the death of his father. He was vice-president from 1914 to 1925 and president from 1925 to 1940 when he resigned to form his own firm, Wilfred Funk, Inc. Funk was also a member of the editorial staff of *Literary Digest,* and later, editor-in-chief. As president and director of Kingsway Press, Yourself Publications, and Your Health Publications, Funk was also editorial director of such self-help magazines as *Your Life* and *Your Health.* He was consulting editor for the *Funk & Wagnalls Standard Dictionary,* and was the author of numerous books on word study and several volumes of poetry. Obituaries and other sources: *Current Biography,* Wilson, 1955, July, 1965; *New York Times,* June 2, 1965; *Who Was Who in America,* 4th edition, Marquis, 1968.

* * *

FUSON, Robert H(enderson) 1927-

PERSONAL: Born July 7, 1927, in Bloomington, Ind.; son of Ivan Raymond (an architect) and Daisy (Henderson) Fuson; married Amelia Fernandez, February 16, 1952; children: Karen Amelia, Robin Fernandez. *Education:* Indiana University, A.B., 1949; Florida State University, M.A., 1951; Louisiana State University, Ph.D., 1958. *Home:* 7910 Citrus Dr., Tampa, Fla. 33617. *Office:* Department of Geography, University of South Florida, Tampa, Fla. 33620.

CAREER: Aeronautical Chart & Information Service, Washington, D.C., geographer, 1952-54; Louisiana State University, Baton Rouge, instructor in geography, 1955-57; University of Miami, Coral Gables, Fla., instructor in geography, 1957-58; Louisiana State University, assistant professor of geography, 1958-60; University of South Florida, Tampa, assistant professor, 1960-61, associate professor, 1961-65, professor of geography, 1965—, head of department, 1960-65, 1967-72, and 1978—. *Military service:* U.S. Army Air Forces, 1944-45. U.S. Navy, 1945-46. U.S. Naval Reserve, 1946-51. U.S. Air Force Reserve, 1951-61; became first lieutenant. *Member:* Association of American Geographers, Royal Geographical Society (fellow), Authors Guild, Florida Society of Geographers (president, 1962-64), Phi Kappa Phi, Gamma Theta Upsilon, Alpha Phi Omega. *Awards, honors:* Outstanding service award from Florida Society of Geographers, 1969; outstanding contribution award from state of Florida, 1976.

WRITINGS: (With J. R. Ray, Jr.) *Problems in World Cultural Geography,* W. C. Brown, 1960, 2nd edition, 1967; (with Ray) *Resource Conservation in the United States,* W. C. Brown, 1961; *The Origin and Nature of American Savannas* (monograph), National Council for Geographic Education, 1963; *Fundamental Place-Name Geography,* W. C. Brown, 1966, 4th edition, 1978; *A Geography of Geography,* W. C. Brown, 1969; *Introduction to World Geography,* Kendall/Hunt, 1977.

Editor—All published by W. C. Brown: (With John F. Lounsbury) *Handbook for Weather and Climate,* 1968, 2nd edition, 1973; (with O. M. McMillon) *Geography of Middle America,* 1968; (with McMillon) *Geography of South America,* 1968; (with S. C. Rothwell) *A Geography of Earth Form,* 1968, 2nd edition, 1973; (with John Hidore) *Workbook of Weather Maps,* 1968, 2nd edition, 1971; (with A. H. Doerr) *An Introduction to Economic Geography,* 1969; (with W. H. Voskuil) *A Geography of Minerals,* 1969; (with Hidore) *A Geography of the Atmosphere,* 1969, 2nd edition, 1972; (with E. W. Miller) *A Geography of Industrial Location,* 1970; (with R. E. Olson) *A Geography of Water,* 1970; (with J. R. Anderson) *A Geography of Agriculture,* 1970; (with M. E. McGaugh) *A Geography of Population and Settlement,* 1970; (with D. J. DeLaubenfels) *A Geography of Plants and Animals,* 1970; (with J. E. Becht) *A Geography of Transportation and Business Logistics,* 1970; (with L. L. Haring and J. F. Lounsbury) *Introduction to Scientific Geographic Research,* 1971, 2nd edition, 1975; (with R. M. Basile) *A Geography of Soils,* 1971; (with J. H. Vann) *A Geography of Landforms,* 1971; (with J. R. McDonald) *A Geography of Relgions,* 1972; (with D. S. Rugg) *Spatial Foundations of Urbanism,* 1972, 2nd edition, 1979; (with W.A.D. Jackson and E. F. Bergman) *A Geography of Politics,* 1973; (with H. R. Wagstaff) *A Geography of Energy,* 1974; (with Bergman) *Modern Political Geography,* 1975.

Contributor: Martin H. Hall, *Sibley's New Mexico Campaign,* University of Texas Press, 1960; M. C. Boatwright, W. M. Hudson, and A. Maxwell, editors, *Singers and Storytellers,* Texas Folklore Society, 1961; L. F. Malpass, editor, *Human Behavior: A Programmed Textbook,* W. C. Brown, 1962. Contributor to *Encyclopaedia Britannica, Encyclopedia International,* and *Encyclopedia of Southern History.* Contributor to professional journals and popular periodicals, including *New York Times, TV Guide, Railroad, Cats, Quipu,* and *Ekistics.*

WORK IN PROGRESS: A definitive book on Christopher Columbus's first voyage, publication expected in 1982.

SIDELIGHTS: Fuson writes: "I am a professional educator who springs from a family that appears to contain a high percentage of writers. A number of Fusons are prominent in the newspaper field and we suspect a dominant gene within our breeding pool. While my writing has been largely related to geography, I fully intend to increase my nonfiction output on a free-lance basis.

"If one is willing to delay full-time creative writing until later in life, then geography would seem to be an excellent training ground. Professional geography has taken me all over the world and has led me into an examination of both the physical and cultural world. I have lived in Latin America and a number of my writings have been spinoffs of my work with the Maya Indians.

"My discovery that the ancient Mayas possessed a magnetic compass, and my pioneering work on magnetism, may lead, indirectly, to explaining the homing instincts in sea turtles and certain other animals. My work on Christopher Columbus should enable us to correct the historical record and, at long last, prove that East Caicos Island was the San Salvador of Columbus, not Watling Island, the choice of most historians.

"My future writing will follow those directions already charted: geographical and travel writing, voyages of discovery, sports (mostly baseball), radio, and subjects related to Florida and the Caribbean. Hopefully, any writing I do will have one purpose: to add to our existing knowledge.

"Had things taken a different turn some years back, I might have been a professional musician. In fact, I was at one time, and still consider myself to be reasonably proficient on the clarinet, saxophone, and oboe. Arranging for the big bands was a phase in my life, but now that they are virtually extinct I have to be content with playing clarinet in small groups where jazzmen gather."

AVOCATIONAL INTERESTS: Amateur radio operator (WA4DPV).

* * *

FYLER, John (Morgan) 1943-

PERSONAL: Born September 17, 1943, in Chicago, Ill.; son of Earl Harris (an executive) and Harriet (a college teacher; maiden name, Morgan) Fyler: married Julia A. Genster, August 5, 1978. *Education:* Dartmouth College, A.B., 1965; University of California, Berkeley, M.A., 1967, Ph.D., 1972. *Office:* Department of English, Tufts University, Medford, Mass. 02155.

CAREER: Tufts University, Medford, Mass., instructor, 1971-72, assistant professor, 1972-78, associate professor of English, 1978—. *Member:* Modern Language Association of America, Mediaeval Academy of America. *Awards, honors:* National Endowment for the Humanities grant, 1973; American Council of Learned Societies fellowship, 1975-76.

WRITINGS: Chaucer and Ovid, Yale University Press, 1979. Contributor to classical studies and language journals.

WORK IN PROGRESS: A monograph on the relation of *The Canterbury Tales* to medieval themes of language and signification.

G

GADDA, Carlo Emilio 1893-1973

PERSONAL: Born November 14, 1893, in Milan, Italy; died May 21, 1973, in Rome, Italy. *Education:* Attended Milan Polytechnic Institute. *Residence:* Rome, Italy.

CAREER: Engineer in Argentina, France, Germany, and Italy, 1920-35; essayist, novelist, and short story writer, 1935-73. *Military service:* Italian Army, served in World War I; prisoner of war, 1918. *Awards, honors:* Prix Formentar, 1957; International Library Prize, 1963, for *La cognizione del dolore*.

WRITINGS—In English: *Quer pasticciaccio brutto de via Merulana* (novel), Garzanti, 1957, translation by William Weaver published as *That Awful Mess on Via Merulana*, Braziller, 1965; *La cognizione del dolore* (novel), Einaudi, 1963, translation by Weaver published as *Acquainted With Grief*, Braziller, 1969.

Other: *Le meraviglie d'Italia*, Parenti, 1939, revised edition, Einaudi, 1964; *L'Adalgisa, disegni milanesi*, F. Le Monnier, 1945, reprinted, Einaudi, 1973; *Il primo libro delle favole*, N. Pozza, 1952; *Novelle del ducato in fiamme* (title means "Tales of Duchy in Flames"), [Firenze], 1953; *Giornale di guerra e di prigionia* (title means "Journal of War and Imprisonment"), Sansoni, 1955; *I viaggi la morte*, Garzanti, 1958; *Il castello di Udine* (title means "The Castle of Udine"), originally published in *Solaria*, 1934, Einaudi, 1961, new edition, 1973; *La madonna dei filosofi* (stories; title means "The Philosopher's Madonna"), originally published in *Solaria*, 1931, Einaudi, 1963; *I racconti accoppiamenti guidiziosi, 1924-1958*, Garzanti, 1963; *I Liugi di Francia*, Garzanti, 1964; *Eros e Priapo*, Garzanti, 1967; *Il guerriero, l'amazzone, lo spirito della poesia nel verso immortale del Foscolo*, Garzanti, 1967; *La meccanica* (novel), Garzanti, 1970; *Novella seconda* (includes "La Casa" and "Notte di luna"), Garzanti, 1971; *Meditazione milanese*, Einaudi, 1974.

SIDELIGHTS: Two of Gadda's early books, though not published until many years later, call on personal experience to demonstrate one of his major themes: human alienation. He recalled his World War I prisoner of war experiences in *Giornale di guerra e di prigionia* ("Journal of War and Imprisonment") and focused on his tormented family relationship in *La cognizione del dolore* ("Acquainted With Grief"). Loaded with satire, word tricks and puns, Gadda's works reveal a great passion for language and dialect. Erudite, allusive, and often difficult, he is generally classified among the moderns, being frequently compared to James Joyce.

The most distinguished element of Gadda's work is his use of language. According to Robert S. Dombrowski, Gadda believed "the writer must remain open to an infinite possibility of expression. And to do so . . . he must discipline himself in both past and present tongues and in the jargon of society's numerous institutions." Essentially, observed Joan McConnell-Mammarella, Gadda's use of language is eclectic: "it is a potpourri of archaic and learned words, dialects, highly specialized terminology and neologisms, all blended together in a framework of standard literary Italian." By critic Robert Bongiorno's count, Gadda employed fifteen separate languages or dialects in *Quer pasticciaccio brutto de via Merulana* ("That Awful Mess on Via Merulana"). In such a linguistically rich book, readers have found that the effects of Gadda's use of language can be varied. He "uses the juxtaposition of contrasting languages for comic effect and to underline the hopelessness of human dialogue," explained Bongiorno. And with his use of dialects in the same book, Gadda impressed McConnell-Mammarella: he "accentuates the social and economic division among his characters in a way that probably would have been impossible had he limited his vocabulary choice to standard Italian."

Gadda can be equally diverse in style as in language. "At times his style appears dry and reflects a desire for order and rational systemization, while at other times it is characterized by violent, uncontrolled expression and hyperbole," declared Dombrowski. Often compared to Joyce's prose style, Gadda's is "a highly allusive and literary style," revealed Robert Martin Adams, "full of buried and not-so-buried allusions to literary history, literary analogues, and literary predecessors." But, in William Weaver's view, Gadda's learning is no burden to his work. In *That Awful Mess*, for example, Gadda fused his knowledge of philosophy, physics, psychology, and engineering into "a single, difficult, rich, yet flowing style."

With language and style his primary concerns, Gadda's plots tend to suffer. But according to McConnell-Mammarella, Gadda really doesn't care: "Gadda never has true narrative interests in the situations he chooses for his novels, but rather uses them as a springboard for engaging in peripheral discussions which titillate his linguistic fantasy." (Some readers, however, find these "peripheral discussions" little more than frustrating digressions.) Similarly, Bongiorno believed Gadda succeeded in overcoming the limits of a barren plot in *That Awful Mess*. Given the story of a "philosopher-detective" who investigates two crimes committed in the same Rome apartment house—a robbery and the murder of a woman he loved—"Gadda takes this cliche structure and raises it to the level of the most profound art."

Gadda's outlook towards the world around him is characteristically bleak. His major theme, said Dombrowski, is human alienation. As a novelist he "likes to get close up to life," noted Robert Adams, "though he never forgets to remind us of how bad it smells." Gadda's characterization reinforces his view of human life. "The stupid ones contain no hidden wisdom, they are just stupid, and usually dirty and brutal as well," stated Adams. "The thoughtful are helpless in the torment of their own thought. Like Joyce, Gadda celebrates in the end a failure of mind—a failure of accommodation to the mess and inexactness of people and history." Several of his works typify his disenchantment. *Eros e Priapo* "is an exceptional enlargement of Gadda's perspective, of his polemic against the world and society," declared Gian-Paolo Biasin. And, in *That Awful Mess* "Gadda is self-indulgent, bitter, ironic, malicious, hateful, shrill, despairing and human," revealed Harold Brodkey. "Behind the language and the self-conscious posturing, the man is in agony." Perhaps the most agonizingly personal of Gadda's books, however, is *La cognizione del dolore*. Reflecting his own troubled relationship with his mother and his affection for his brother who died in World War I, *La cognizione* ends when the hero "not only causes his mother's death . . . but causes [her] to believe he is her assassin."

Gadda's works have been acclaimed most notably by a generation of experimental writers. "Gadda's followers," wrote Marc Slonim, "admire his subtle art, his satirical impact, his fantasy. Those who believe that the use of regional brogue and dialects would give a new dimension to Italian neo-realism, hail him as their master."

BIOGRAPHICAL/CRITICAL SOURCES: New York Times, September 29, 1963, May 22, 1973; *London Magazine*, October, 1963; *Books Abroad*, summer, 1965; Carlo Emilio Gadda, *That Awful Mess on Via Merulana*, translated by William Weaver, Braziller, 1965; *Saturday Review*, September 4, 1965, April 19, 1969; *New York Herald Tribune*, September 5, 1965; *Book Week*, September 5, 1965; *Newsweek*, September 6, 1965; *Christian Science Monitor*, September 9, 1965, March 4, 1969; *Times Literary Supplement*, September 30, 1965, May 26, 1966, May 22, 1969, September 25, 1969, April 27, 1973; *Nation*, November 1, 1965; *New Yorker*, December 25, 1965; *New York Review of Books*, January 20, 1966, July 23, 1970; *Virginia Quarterly Review*, winter, 1966; *Observer*, December 18, 1966; *Best Sellers*, March 15, 1969.

Joan Fisher and Paul A. Gaeng, editors, *Studies in Honor of Mario A. Pei*, University of North Carolina Press, 1972; *Rivista di Letterature Moderne e Comparate*, September, 1972; *Romance Notes*, autumn, 1972; Gian-Paolo Biasin, *Literary Diseases: Theme and Metaphor in the Italian Novel*, University of Texas Press, 1975; Robert Martin Adams, *After Joyce: Studies in Fiction After "Ulysses,"* Oxford University Press, 1977; *Contemporary Literary Criticism*, Volume 11, Gale, 1979.*

* * *

GAGARIN, Michael 1942-

PERSONAL: Born January 1, 1942, in New York, N.Y. Married Donna Dean Carter (an architect), May, 1974. *Education:* Stanford University, B.A., 1963; Harvard University, M.A., 1965; Yale University, Ph.D., 1968. *Office:* Department of Classics, University of Texas, Austin, Tex. 78712.

CAREER: Yale University, New Haven, Conn., instructor, 1968-69, assistant professor of classics, 1969-73; University of Texas, Austin, assistant professor of classics, 1973—. *Awards, honors:* Junior fellow at Center for Hellenic Studies, Washington, D.C., 1972-73.

WRITINGS: Aeschylean Drama, University of California Press, 1976.

WORK IN PROGRESS: Drakon and Early Athenian Homicide Law, publication expected in 1980; research on Greek law and ethics with plans to produce book on Greek procedural law and justice.

AVOCATIONAL INTERESTS: Nature (especially birdwatching).

* * *

GALLAGHER, Rachel (Kimbal Drake)

PERSONAL: Born in Brooklyn, N.Y.; daughter of John J. (a stockbroker) and Ethelyn (a real estate broker and caterer; maiden name, Tarzian) Gallagher. *Education:* Attended Roanoke College. *Home and office:* 65 Bank St., New York, N.Y. 10014.

CAREER: Esquire, New York City, editorial associate, 1965-69; Workman Publishing Co., Inc., New York City, acquisitions editor, 1969-70; writer, 1971—.

WRITINGS: (Under pseudonym Kimbal Drake; with Daphne Davis) *The New York In/Out Quiz Book*, Random House, 1966; (with Lorris Davis) *Letting Down My "Hair"* (nonfiction), Arthur Fields, 1973; *Games in the Street* (nonfiction), Four Winds Press, 1976. Contributor to magazines and newspapers, including *Esquire, Cue*, and *New York*. Editor of *Peter Max;* editor of "Open Forum Letters" in *Forum*.

WORK IN PROGRESS: A novel about Madame Magda Lupescu, mistress of King Carol II of Romania; a novel about a well-known rock star, completion expected in 1980.

SIDELIGHTS: Rachel Gallagher commented "Writing is a continual challenge and, once into it, I become energized by the very process of writing itself. That is, once into it. Getting into it is the key. I am a journalist who dreams of being a novelist. Two areas of interest to me personally and professionally are women (in the context of evolution or *evolving*) and consciousness (in all contexts, including men and women). These two areas motivate continual study and exploration, and what progress (or regress) I make can only be reflected by my work."

* * *

GALLAGHER, William M. 1923-1975

OBITUARY NOTICE: Born February 26, 1923, in Hiawatha, Kan.; died September 28, 1975. News photographer and winner of the Pulitzer Prize in 1953 for his picture of presidential candidate Adlai E. Stevenson with a hole in the bottom of his shoe. Gallagher was photographer for the *Flint Journal*. Obituaries and other sources: *Current Biography*, Wilson, 1953, November, 1975; *New York Times*, September 29, 1975.

* * *

GALLER, Meyer 1914-

PERSONAL: Born October 31, 1914, in Bialystok, Poland;

came to the United States in 1960, naturalized citizen, 1966; son of Ewel and Tamara (Porecki) Galler; married Esther Braer, May, 1940; children: Rimma. *Education:* Attended University of Warsaw, 1933-34, Agricultural University of Warsaw, 1935-39, and Lvov Polytechnic School, 1939-40; University of California, Berkeley, M.S., 1963, M.L.S., 1966. *Home:* 4045 Greenacre Rd., Castro Valley, Calif. 94546. *Office:* Library, California State University, Hayward, Calif. 94542.

CAREER: Technical manager of canneries in Lvov, Poland, 1940-41, and Alma Ata, Central Asia, 1941-42; Karaganda Food Processing Plant, Karaganda, Central Asia, chemist, 1958-59; Warsaw Agricultural Institute, Warsaw, Poland, researcher, 1960; J. W. Allen (food processing plant), Chicago, Ill., chemist, 1960-62; California State University, Hayward, librarian, 1966—. *Member:* American Association for the Advancement of Science, American Association for the Advancement of Slavic Studies.

WRITINGS: (With Harlan E. Marquess) *Soviet Prison Camp Speech: A Survivor's Glossary,* University of Wisconsin Press, 1972. Contributor of articles and stories to magazines.

WORK IN PROGRESS: Research on non-standard Russian speech, Soviet camp songs, and Soviet camp proverbs and expressions.

SIDELIGHTS: Galler writes: "In 1942 I was arrested by the MGB. I spent ten years in Soviet prisons and camps, from 1942 to 1952, and five years in exile in Siberia, from 1952 to 1957. In 1957 I was exonerated by Soviet authorities.

"Being one of the lucky persons, who managed to survive the Soviet inferno and escape to the West, I consider it my duty and obligation to call attention to the innocent victims of the Soviet prison camp system. I concentrate my efforts on camp speech, proverbs and sayings, and camp songs, because in this way I intend to pay tribute to those martyrs.

"Soviet prison camp speech is not a special language distinct from colloquial Russian. Basically it is the same language only adapted to a peculiar camp population, special camp conditions. The lingo of Russian professional criminals, expressions used by prisoners from non-Russian republics, and by prisoners from foreign countries, made a significant contribution to Soviet camp speech. It includes obscene and abusive language, a lot of expressions reflecting the inhuman treatment of prisoners by camp authorities, the prisoner's philosophy of life, his continuous struggle for survival, his frustrations and despair. Sometimes it is expressed with a curse, sometimes with a proverb, an expression borrowed from the criminal argot or by using gallows humor, or by humming a camp song."

* * *

GAMBRILL, Eileen 1934-

PERSONAL: Born December 11, 1934, in Philadelphia, Pa.; daughter of William and Irene (Williams) Gambrill. *Education:* University of Pennsylvania, B.A. (with honors), 1956; Bryn Mawr College, M.S.S., 1961; University of Michigan, M.A., 1963, Ph.D., 1965. *Home:* 427 Yale Ave., Kensington, Calif. 94708. *Office:* School of Social Welfare, University of California, 120 Haviland Hall, Berkeley, Calif. 94720.

CAREER: N. W. Ayer Advertising Co., Philadelphia, Pa., in advertising production, 1956-57; Municipal Court, Philadelphia, case investigator in Adoption Division, 1958-59; University of Wisconsin—Madison, assistant professor of social work and lecturer in psychology, 1966-67; University of Michigan, Ann Arbor, assistant professor, 1967-69, associate professor of social work, 1969-70; University of California, Berkeley, lecturer, 1970-76, associate professor, 1976-79, professor of social welfare, 1979—. Private practice in psychology. Visiting scholar at National Institute for Social Work, London. *Member:* American Psychological Association, Association for the Advancement of Behavior Therapy, Behavior Therapy and Research Society, Social Work Group for the Study of Behavioral Methods, Western Psychological Association. *Awards, honors:* Postdoctoral fellowship from National Institute for Mental Health for training in behavior therapy, 1965-66; grants from Office of Child Development, 1973-74, Community Services Administration Social and Rehabilitative Services, 1974-75, and U.S. Department of Health, Education and Welfare, 1975-76 and 1977-78.

WRITINGS: (Contributor) R. D. Rubin, Herbert Fensterheim, Cyril M. Franks, and A. A. Lazarus, editors, *Advances in Behavior Therapy, 1969,* Academic Press, 1971; (contributor) Edwin J. Thomas, editor, *Behavior Modification Procedure,* Aldine, 1974; (with Theodor J. Stein and Kermit T. Wiltse) *Foster Care,* Office of Child Development, U.S. Department of Health, Education and Welfare, 1975; (with Stein and Wiltse) *Decision Making in Foster Care: A Training Manual,* Extension Publications, University of California, Berkeley, 1976; (with Cheryl A. Richey) *It's Up to You: Developing Assertive Social Skills,* Les Femmes, 1976; *Behavior Modification: Handbook of Assessment, Intervention, and Evaluation,* Jossey-Bass, 1977; (with Stein and Wiltse) *Children in Foster Homes: Achieving Continuity in Care,* Praeger, 1978; (with Stein) *Supervision in Child Welfare: A Training Manual,* Extension Publications, University of California, Berkeley, 1978; (contributor) S. P. Shinke, editor, *Community Applications of Behavioral Methods: A Sourcebook for Social Workers,* Aldine, 1979; (contributor) C. L. Heckerman, editor, *The Evolving Female: Psychological Perspectives,* Human Sciences Press, 1979; (contributor) Neil Gilbert and Harry Specht, editors, *Handbook of the Social Sciences,* Prentice-Hall, 1980.

Author of videotape, "It's Up to You: Assertion Training for Women," 1975. Contributor of more than thirty articles and reviews to journals in the social and behavioral sciences. Editor of *AABT Newsletter* (of Association for the Advancement of Behavior Therapy), 1974-77; member of editorial board of *Behavior Therapy,* 1977-80, *Journal of Behavior Therapy and Experimental Psychiatry,* 1979-81, *Children and Youth Services,* and *Behavioral Counseling Quarterly.*

WORK IN PROGRESS: Casework: Offering Effective Service, publication by Prentice-Hall expected in 1981; research on administrative and educational practices of child welfare supervisors, ethical issues in social work practice, and designing effective decision making strategies for use in social work settings.

SIDELIGHTS: Gambrill told *CA:* "An important incentive in my own writing has been the importance of helping social workers to be aware of important empirical findings that can help them to help their clients. Toward this end, I have made a special effort to write clearly. This requires a constant vigilance against obscurity in writing. Certainly one of the great secrets of writing is skill in breaking down large tasks into ones that not only seem readily achievable but that actually lure one to the typewriter. Another is arranging one's life so that protected time is available for writing."

BIOGRAPHICAL/CRITICAL SOURCES: Social Service Review, March, 1978; *Contemporary Psychology,* November, 1978.

GANGEWERE, Robert J(ay) 1936-

PERSONAL: Born November 9, 1936, in Brooklyn, N.Y.; son of Jay H. (an engineer) and Carolyn June (Weiss) Gangewere; married Carol Kolb, June 13, 1959 (divorced, 1973); children: Jason Lee, Jessica. *Education:* Kutztown State College, B.S., 1958; University of Connecticut, M.A., 1963, Ph.D., 1966. *Home:* 508 Ivy St., Pittsburgh, Pa. 15232. *Office: Carnegie,* Carnegie Institute, 4400 Forbes Ave., Pittsburgh, Pa. 15213.

CAREER: American University in Cairo, Cairo, Egypt, assistant professor of English, 1963-65; Kutztown State College, Kutztown, Pa., assistant professor of English, 1965-67; Carnegie-Mellon University, Pittsburgh, Pa., assistant professor of English, 1967-73; Carnegie Institute, Pittsburgh, Pa., editor of *Carnegie,* 1973—. Part-time instructor of technical writing at Carnegie-Mellon University, 1973—.

WRITINGS: The Exploited Eden: Literature on the American Environment, Harper, 1972. Contributor to academic journals.

SIDELIGHTS: Gangewere writes: "The lesson of my own career is worth noting. After ten years as a professor, I became editor of a varied museum magazine and embarked upon a career of writing about natural history, fine art, literature, western Pennsylvania history, and so on. It is a unique job, and for a writer of my interests, ideal. This is either straight exposition or public relations journalism—not investigative or expose journalism. I consider myself very fortunate to be making a good living as a writer on subjects in both the arts and sciences, and I enjoy the recognition that comes with magazine journalism, but that escapes academic authors. Once contemptuous of the cliche, 'those that can, do, those that can't, teach,' I now respect it."

* * *

GANNETT, Lewis Stiles 1891-1966

OBITUARY NOTICE: Born October 3, 1891, in Rochester, N.Y.; died February 4, 1966. Journalist, book critic, and author. Gannett worked as a journalist for the *Manchester Guardian* and the *New York Herald-Tribune,* where he wrote the daily column "Books and Things." Gannett also wrote for *Nation.* His works include *Young China* and *Sweet Land.* Obituaries and other sources: *Current Biography,* Wilson, 1941, March, 1966; *New York Times,* February 4, 1966; *Who Was Who in America,* 4th edition, Marquis, 1968.

* * *

GARDNER, Richard N(ewton) 1927-

PERSONAL: Born July 9, 1927, in New York, N.Y.; son of Samuel I. and Ethel (Elias) Gardner; married Danielle Luzzatto, June 10, 1956; children: Nina Jessica, Anthony Laurence. *Education:* Harvard University, A. B. (magna cum laude), 1948; Yale University, LL.B., 1951; Oxford University, Ph.D. (in international economics), 1954. *Office:* American Embassy, 119 Via Veneto, Rome, Italy.

CAREER: Admitted to New York State Bar, 1952; Yale University, Law School, New Haven, Conn., teaching fellow, 1953-54; Coudert Bros. (law firm), New York City, attorney, 1954-57; Columbia University, New York City, associate professor, 1957-60, professor of law, 1960-61; U.S. Department of State, Washington, D.C., deputy assistant secretary of state for international organization affairs, 1961-65; Columbia University, professor of law and international relations, 1966, Henry L. Moses Professor of Law and International Organizations, 1967—; U.S. ambassador to Italy, 1977—. Visiting professor at University of Instanbul, 1958, and University of Rome, 1967-68. Deputy U.S. representative to U.N. Commission on Peaceful Uses of Outer Space, 1962-65; senior adviser to U.S. mission to the United Nations, 1965-67; member of the President's Commission on International Trade and Investment Policy, 1967-71; U.S. delegate to U.N. Conference on the Law of the Sea, 1972-76; consultant to U.S. secretary-general, U.N. Conference on Human Environment, 1972; rapporteur, U.N. committee of experts on economic trading, 1975; U.S. alternate delegate to 19th U.N. General Assembly, and senior adviser to U.S. delegates to 20th and 21st General Assemblies. Member of Trilateral Commission Council on Foreign Relations; member of board of directors of Atlantic Council, Atlantic Institute, Freedom House, United Nations Association, and International League for Human Rights. *Military service:* U.S. Army, 1945-46.

MEMBER: American Society of International Law (former vice-president), American Bar Association, American Economic Association, American Academy of Arts and Sciences, Royal Economic Society, Foreign Policy Association, New York State Bar Association, Association of the Bar of the City of New York, Order of the Coif, Phi Beta Kappa, Century Association (New York City), Metropolitan Club (Washington, D.C.). *Awards, honors:* Detur Prize for distinguished scholarship, 1948; Rhodes scholar, 1951-53; Arthur S. Flemming Award as one of ten outstanding young men in the Federal government, 1963.

WRITINGS: Sterling-Dollar Diplomacy: Anglo-American Collaboration in the Reconstruction of Multilateral Trade, Clarendon Press, 1956, revised and expanded edition published as *Sterling-Dollar Diplomacy: The Origins and the Prospects of Our International Economic Order,* McGraw, 1969; *New Directions in U.S. Foreign Economic Policy,* Foreign Policy Association, 1959; *In Pursuit of World Order: U.S. Foreign Policy and International Organizations,* Praeger, 1964, revised edition, 1966; (editor) *Blueprint for Peace: Being the Proposals of Prominent Americans to the White House Conference on International Cooperation,* McGraw, 1966; *International Law,* School of Law, Columbia University, 1969; *New Structures for Economic Interpendence,* Institute on Man and Science (Rensselaerville, N.Y.), 1975; *The World Food and Energy Crisis: The Role of International Organizations,* Institute on Man and Science, 1974; *Nuclear Energy and World Order: Implications for International Organizations,* Institute on Man and Science, 1976. Also author of published reports and addresses for national and international organizations. Note editor of *Yale Law Journal,* 1950-51.

SIDELIGHTS: According to Arnold Beichman, "One can say with only slight exaggeration that Professor Gardner invented the subject of international economic diplomacy, an amalgam of history, international relations, international law, and political science. Yet his book [*Sterling-Dollar Diplomacy*] is not a text on economic theory or statistical analysis. . . . Professor Gardner is a lawyer, a teacher at Columbia University, a political scientist, and an experienced diplomat. Such a background plus his skills as a writer make his book valuable to layman and specialist alike."

BIOGRAPHICAL/CRITICAL SOURCES: Christian Science Monitor, October 18, 1969.

* * *

GARLAND, Mary 1922-

PERSONAL: Born December 16, 1922, in Hamburg, Germany; married Henry B. Garland (a professor of German studies), 1949; children: two daughters. *Education:* Attended University of Hamburg, 1942-44; University of London, earned B.A. degree (first class honors), Ph.D., 1968. *Home:* 5 Rosebarn Ave., Exeter, Devonshire, England. *Office:* Department of German, University of Exeter, Queen's Dr., Exeter, Devonshire EX4 4QH, England.

CAREER: University of Exeter, Exeter, England, lecturer, 1950-69, senior lecturer, 1969-77, reader in German, 1977—. *Member:* International Vereinigung fuer Germanische Sprach-u. Literaturwissenschaft, Conference of Teachers in German at British and Irish Universitites, University Women's Club (London).

WRITINGS: Kleist's Prinz Friedrich von Homburg: An Interpretation Through Word Pattern, Mouton, 1968; *Hebbel's Prose Tragedies,* Cambridge University Press, 1972; (with husband, Henry Garland) *The Oxford Companion to German Literature,* Oxford University Press, 1976. Contributor to scholarly journals.

WORK IN PROGRESS: Research on German literature since the eighteenth century, especially the history of drama.

* * *

GASCAR, Pierre
See FOURNIER, Pierre

* * *

GATES, John D. 1939-

PERSONAL: Born January 22, 1939, in New York, N.Y.; son of John B. and Mildred (Davis) Gates; married Carroll M. Carpenter, September 16, 1961 (divorced, 1968); married Susan Stephenson (a needlepoint designer), April 4, 1970; children: Ashley, John D., Jr., Andrew, Susan Anna. *Education:* Yale University, B.A., 1962; Columbia University, M.S., 1963. *Home and office:* 3991-C Valley Court, Winston-Salem, N.C. 27106.

CAREER: Charlotte Observer, Charlotte, N.C., reporter, 1963-66; associated with Dean Witter-Reynolds (stockbrokers), Charlotte, N.C., 1966-68; *Wilmington News-Journal,* Wilmington, Del., editorial *factotum,* 1968-77; free-lance writer, 1977—. President of North Carolina School of the Arts Associates, 1978—. *Awards, honors:* First place award from Delaware, Maryland, and District of Columbia Press Association, 1969, for feature story about George Plimpton.

WRITINGS: The du Pont Family, Doubleday, 1979. Contributor to magazines.

WORK IN PROGRESS: A book on the Astor family, for Doubleday.

SIDELIGHTS: Gates comments: "I am, I hope, moving gradually (and financially precariously) toward fulfilling a more or less life-long ambition to write fiction about wealth, its advantages, and its disadvantages."

* * *

GAUDIOSE, Dorothy M(arie) 1920-

PERSONAL: Born November 27, 1920, in Crabtree, Pa.; daughter of Michael (a grocer) and Maria (Chill) Gaudiose. *Education:* Lock Haven State Teachers College, B.S., 1940; Pennsylvania State University, M.Ed., 1961; also attended Sorbonne, University of Paris. *Politics:* Republican. *Religion:* Roman Catholic. *Home:* 222 East Water St., Lock Haven, Pa. 17745.

CAREER: Keystone Central School District, Lock Haven, Pa., high school English teacher, 1943-74; teacher of religion in Eufaula, Ala., 1951; teacher of religion in Richmond, Va., 1956. Instructor at Pennsylvania State University, 1962-68. Assistant personnel director for General Armature Manufacturing Co. Engaged in volunteer activities. *Member:* National Education Association, Pennsylvania State Education Association (local president), Catholic Daughters of America.

WRITINGS: Prophet of the People: A Biography of Padre Pio, Alba, 1974. Contributor of travel articles to Roman Catholic magazines and local newspapers.

WORK IN PROGRESS: Mary Pyle: A Modern Saint Clare.

SIDELIGHTS: Dorothy Gaudiose wrote: "When I became a teacher, I traveled throughout the United States, Canada, Mexico, and then Europe, Asia, and northern Africa during the summer months. I studied Italian, Spanish, and French as languages to use in my travels.

"It was during my first visit to Europe in 1950 that I first met Padre Pio the stigmatist. I became so intrigued by his stigmata, unusual supernatural powers, and personality that I wanted to share his life and my experiences with the world, and that is why I wrote his story.

Since 1974 I have done lecture tours in the United States to promote my book, and have been on radio and television in Youngstown, Ohio, and Pittsburgh, Pa. I have donated one half of the profits from my book to benefit the hospital Padre Pio founded and named Home for the Relief of Suffering, in San Giovanni Rotondo, Foggia, Italy."

BIOGRAPHICAL/CRITICAL SOURCES: John Schug, *Padre Pio,* Our Sunday Visitor, 1976.

* * *

GAUMNITZ, Walter Herbert 1891-1979

OBITUARY NOTICE: Born October 10, 1891, in Rice, Minn.; died August 5, 1979, in Washington, D.C. Educator and author. An educator at several high schools and universities, Gaumnitz was best known for his expertise in the field of rural education. He served the U.S. Office of Education as principal specialist on rural school research and statistics. Gaumnitz wrote numerous articles, official reports, and books, including *Survey of Education in 1,200 Rural Counties,* published in 1959. Obituaries and other sources: *Who's Who in America,* 39th edition, Marquis, 1976; *Washington Post,* August 8, 1979.

* * *

GAY, Amelia
See HOGARTH, Grace (Weston Allen)

* * *

GAYE, Carol
See SHANN, Renee

* * *

GAYLORD, Edward King 1873-1974

OBITUARY NOTICE: Born March 5, 1873, in Muscotah, Kan.; died May 30, 1974, in Oklahoma City, Okla. Journalist, editor, and the first publisher to produce an entire newspaper edition with computerized typesetting in 1963. Gaylord was publisher and editor of the *Daily Oklahoman* and the *Oklahoma Times.* He also was an editorial writer for the *Colorado Springs Telegraph* and general manager of the *Oklahoma Farmer-Stockman.* Gaylord remained active as a publisher until his death at the age of 101. Obituaries and other sources: *Who's Who in the South and Southwest,* 13th edition, Marquis, 1973; *Who's Who in America,* 38th edition, Marquis, 1974; *Who Was Who in America,* 6th edition, Marquis, 1976.

* * *

GEHLEN, Reinhard 1902-1979

OBITUARY NOTICE: Born April 3, 1902, in Erfurt, Germany (now East Germany); died June 8, 1979, in Lake Starnberg, West Germany. Intelligence officer and author. The head of a German Army intelligence agency during World War II, Gehlen turned over copies of all his files to the Allies after surrendering to them near the end of the war. From 1955 to 1968, he headed the intelligence service in Bonn, West Germany. Thousands of agents operated in his spy network which, with financial backing from the United States, successfully uncovered much valuable information from East Berlin. Gehlen wrote a book of memoirs. Obituaries and other sources: Edward Spiro, *Gehlen: Spy of the Century,* Hodder & Stoughton, 1971; Heinz Hoehne and Hermann Zoling, *General Was a Spy: The Truth About General Gehlen and His Spy Ring,* Coward, 1972; *New York Times,* June 10, 1979.

* * *

GEIST, Roland C. 1896-

PERSONAL: Born in 1896 in Duluth, Minn. *Education:* City College (now of City University of New York), B.A., M.S.; Columbia University, M.A.; New York University, J.D.; Selwyn College, Cambridge, certificate; attended University of Vienna. *Residence:* New York, N.Y.

CAREER: Former instructor of business law; writer. Bicycling coach in New York City schools. Tour organizer in New England, Austria, New York City, and U.S. national parks. *Military service:* U.S. Army, Corps of Engineers. *Member:* Amateur Bicycle League of America, Unicycle Association of America, League of American Wheelmen, Wheelmen, Bicycle Touring League, Antique Bicycle Club, Middle Atlantic Skating Association, Century Road Club Association of New York (life member), Cyclists Touring Club of London (life member). *Awards, honors:* Founding member of Bicycle Hall of Fame.

WRITINGS: Bicycling as a Hobby, Harper, 1940; (contributor) *Outdoor Activities,* A. S. Barnes, 1947; *Cycling in the School Fitness Program,* edited by Paul D. White, National Education Association, 1963; *Bicycle Directory,* edited by Paul Auerbach, Bicycle Institute of America, 1967; *Bicycle People,* Acropolis Books, 1978. Also author of *Hiking, Camping, and Mountaineering: A Manual for the Beginner* and *The World of Ice Skating People.* Contributor to magazines.

SIDELIGHTS: Retired from teaching, Geist has, until recently, remained active in athletics. His bicycling career included army training for the U.S. Cycle Infantry, which never became a functioning part of the service, road and track racing in New York, and touring through several U.S. national parks and in England, France, Germany, Italy, and Austria.

But he has also participated in walking races and climbed about a dozen twelve-thousand-foot peaks in national parks. As an ice skater he raced and competed for a position on the U.S. Olympic team and the U.S. Speed Team; he also danced on ice in amateur productions in New York. In 1979 the active part of Geist's eighty-year career was ended when he was injured by a hit-and-run motorist while he was on tour.

* * *

GENT, Peter 1942-

PERSONAL: Surname is pronounced "Jent"; born August 23, 1942, in Bangor, Mich.; son of Charles Edward and Elizabeth Katherine (Davis) Gent; married Jo Ellen Walton, 1969; children: Holly, Carter. *Education:* Michigan State University, B.A. (with honors), 1964. *Residence:* Wimberley, Tex. 78676. *Agent:* The Sterling Lord Agency, Inc., 660 Madison Ave., New York, N.Y. 10021.

CAREER: Dallas Cowboys, Dallas, Tex., wide receiver, 1964-69; writer, 1969—. Film extra for "Kid Blue," 1971. *Member:* Authors Guild, Writers Guild.

WRITINGS: North Dallas Forty, Morrow, 1973; *Texas Celebrity Turkey Trot,* Morrow, 1978. Also author of screenplay, with Frank Yablans and Ted Kotcheff, "North Dallas Forty" (based on own novel), Paramount, 1979. Contributor of articles to periodicals, including *Sport.*

WORK IN PROGRESS: A screenplay on the life of Pancho Villa, with Edwin Shrake; a novel, *The Espantosa War.*

SIDELIGHTS: Peter Gent played football with the Dallas Cowboys for five years, but he is best known as author of *North Dallas Forty,* the novel based on his experiences in the National Football League. Joe Lapointe described the book as "a conscientious objector's opinion of professional football and how the businessmen who run it allegedly abuse their employes." The book contains stories of "a crazed, drunken hunting trip with three teammates, pre- and post-game drug and sex rituals, intimidation, sadism and exhibitionism on and off the field, and constant clashes with what Gent describes as a racist, sexist, dictatorial organization of businessmen devoted to winning football games at any cost," stated Charles Flowers.

Dick Schaap declared that Gent "proves his case without preaching, without sermonizing, almost without judging. He balances shock with humor, irony with warmth, detail with insight, and ends up with a book that easily transcends its subject matter." Describing *North Dallas Forty* as "a big, powerful, chaotic novel," Pete Axthelm noted that Gent's "unassuming bits of philosophy, complemented by some remarkable satire and self-mockery, produce the best moments in a book that has many good ones. There are also flaws, including endlessly repetitive medicine-cabinet drug listings and a wildly apocalyptic climax." Schaap, however, felt the end of the novel was "most powerful . . . and its impact is devastating. Reading the last few pages is like being kicked in the groin—or kneed by a linebacker."

In *North Dallas Forty* Gent described the sounds and feelings of excruciating injuries sustained on the football field. He told reporters that during his own years on the team he had cracked his vertebrae, broken the short ribs off his spine, broken his leg, dislocated his ankle, broken his nose "about a dozen times," and either dislocated or broken all of his fingers. Trainers helped the players endure the agony of their injuries by pumping them full of pain-killing drugs. "In all the years I played, the experiments performed on us taught them which drugs to use," Gent told Joe Lapointe. "To the teams, you are just equipment."

Another problem Gent found with the Dallas team was that the players were taught "pure self-interest. . . . If the team won and you didn't play well, you lost." Players were even pitted against each other in order to raise tempers for the games. As a result, there was little teamwork and much dissension among the players.

Despite the pain and dehumanizing treatment described in *North Dallas Forty,* Gent insists he is not bitter about professional football: he "only wrote about football because it was a subject he knew, and he wanted to write."

Gent told *CA:* "Man is the only animal in the universe who continually reorganizes time and space. I write out of that urge. There are no new things, only new relationships and different understandings of those relationships and each man's responsibility is to be true to his belief."

BIOGRAPHICAL/CRITICAL SOURCES: Newsweek, September 24, 1973; *New York Times Book Review,* October 28, 1973; *Detroit Free Press,* November 17, 1974, September 13, 1979; *Authors in the News,* Volume 1, Gale, 1976; *Sports Illustrated,* July 31, 1978; *New York Times,* July 29, 1979; *Washington Post,* September 16, 1979.

* * *

GERLACH, Russel L(ee) 1939-

PERSONAL: Born June 20, 1939, in Lincoln, Neb.; son of Alfred (a tavern owner) and Dorothy (Helzenreter) Gerlach; married Jean Miller (a postal personnel manager), June 3, 1961; children: John, Cindy, Andrew, James. *Education:* University of Nebraska, B.A., 1967, M.A., 1968, Ph.D., 1974. *Politics:* Democrat. *Religion:* United Church of Christ. *Home:* 707 East Delmar, Springfield, Mo. 65807. *Office:* Department of Geography and Geology, Southwest Missouri State University, Springfield, Mo. 65802.

CAREER: Southwest Missouri State University, Springfield, assistant professor, 1969-75, associate professor of geography, 1975-76; assistant master (Fulbright exchange professor) at secondary school in Repton, England, 1976-77; Southwest Missouri State University, associate professor, 1977-79, professor of geography, 1979—. Member of advisory board of Bittersweet, Inc. Director of National Science Foundation summer institute in geography, 1975. *Military service:* U.S. Army, 1961-64; served in Korea. *Member:* American Geographical Society, Association of American Geographers, National Council for Geographic Education, National Geographic Society, Association for Overseas Educators, Ozark States Folklore Society, Missouri Council for Geographic Education (president, 1972), Sigma Xi, Gamma Theta Upsilon. *Awards, honors:* National Science Foundation grant, 1975-76; author award from National Council for Geographic Education, 1977, for article "Our Cultural Roots: A Classroom Exercise in Historical Geography."

WRITINGS: (With Milton D. Rafferty and Dennis H. Hrebec) *Atlas of Missouri,* Aux-Arc Research Associates, 1970; *Immigrants in the Ozarks: A Study in Ethnic Geography,* University of Missouri Press, 1976; (contributor) Ellen Massey, editor, *Bittersweet Country,* Doubleday, 1978. Contributor of nearly twenty articles and reviews to geography and history journals. Editor of *Missouri Geographer,* 1973-76.

WORK IN PROGRESS: Entertainment in the Ozarks, 1885-1910, a monograph, with Robert K. Gilmore; research on illegal distilling in Arkansas and Missouri.

AVOCATIONAL INTERESTS: Bluegrass music, travel (Europe, Mexico, the Far East).

GERMAIN, Edward B. 1937-

PERSONAL: Born December 30, 1937, in Saginaw, Mich.; son of Edward (in sales) and Katherine (a teacher; maiden name, Barnard) Germain; married Sara Weeks (an arts administrator), February 24, 1960; children: Valerie. *Education:* Attended Northwestern University, 1956-58; University of Michigan, B.A., 1961, M.A., 1964, Ph.D., 1969. *Home address:* P.O. Box 278, Dublin, N.H. 03444. *Office:* Department of English, Phillips Academy, Andover, Mass. 01810.

CAREER: Eastern Michigan University, Ypsilanti, instructor in English, 1964-66; Pomona College, Claremont, Calif., assistant professor of English, 1969-76; Nathaniel Hawthorne College, Antrim, N.H., associate professor of English, 1976-79, head of cultural affairs committee, 1977; Phillips Academy, Andover, Mass., instructor in English, 1979—. Member of New Hampshire Citizens Committee on the Arts. Moderator of conferences; lecturer at colleges; guest on television and radio programs. *Military service:* U.S. Naval Reserve, in communications, 1960-65; became lieutenant. *Member:* Phi Kappa Phi. *Awards, honors:* Avery Hopwood Award from University of Michigan, 1968.

WRITINGS—Editor: *Flag of Ecstasy: Selected Poems of Charles Henri Ford,* Black Sparrow Press, 1972; *Shadows of the Sun: The Diaries of Harry Crosby,* Black Sparrow Press, 1978; *English and American Surrealist Poetry,* Penguin, 1978. Contributor of articles, poems, and stories to scholarly journals and literary magazines, including *Kayak, Spectator,* and *Gatherings.*

WORK IN PROGRESS: Stories; poems.

* * *

GEYL, Pieter (Catharinus Arie) 1887-1966

OBITUARY NOTICE: Born December 15, 1887, in Dordrecht, Netherlands; died December 31, 1966, in Utrecht, Netherlands. Historian, professor, and author. Geyl was professor of Dutch studies at the University of London and of modern history at the University of Utrecht. He was dedicated to replacing French with Flemish as the principal language of Flanders. Regarding the controversial split between Belgium and the Netherlands in the sixteenth century, Geyl theorized that simple geographical factors caused the separation, a theory that created heated historical debates. Geyl's works include *The Revolt of the Netherlands, 1555-1609; Orange and Stuart, 1641-1672;* and *Napoleon: For and Against.* Obituaries and other sources: *Who Was Who in America,* 4th edition, Marquis, 1968; *World Authors, 1950-1970,* Wilson, 1975.

* * *

GIBALDI, Joseph 1942-

PERSONAL: Born August 20, 1942, in Brooklyn, N.Y.; son of Ignatius and Angela (Peritore) Gibaldi; married Anita Newman (a teacher), August 15, 1962; children: Laura Anne, Joseph Milo. *Education:* City College of the City University of New York, B.A., 1965; City University of New York, M.A., 1967; New York University, Ph.D., 1973. *Office:* Modern Language Association of America, 62 Fifth Ave., New York, N.Y. 10011.

CAREER: High school English teacher in Brooklyn, N.Y., 1965-71; Brooklyn College of the City University of New York, Brooklyn, instructor in English education, 1972-73; University of Georgia, Athens, assistant professor of comparative literature, 1973-76; Modern Language Association of America, New York, N.Y., associate director of book publications and research programs, 1976—. *Member:* American Comparative Literature Association, Modern Language Association of America, Renaissance Society of America. *Awards, honors:* Fellow of Southeastern Institute of Medieval and Renaissance Studies, 1976.

WRITINGS: (With Robert J. Clements) *Anatomy of the Novella: The European Tale Collection From Boccaccio and Chaucer to Cervantes,* New York University Press, 1977; (with Clements) *MLA Handbook for Writers of Research Papers, Theses, and Dissertations,* Modern Language Association of America, 1977; (contributor) Aldo Scaglione, editor, *Ariosto 1974 in America,* Longo, 1977; (with Walter S. Achtert) *A Guide to Professional Organizations for Teachers of Language and Literature* (pamphlet), Modern Language Association of America, 1978; *Approaches to Teaching Chaucer's "Canterbury Tales,"* Modern Language Association of America, 1980; (editor) *Introduction to Scholarship in Modern Langauges and Literatures,* Modern Language Association of America, 1980. Contributor to literature and education journals.

WORK IN PROGRESS: Editing *Interrelations of Literature: Foundations, Dimensions, Perspectives,* with Jean-Pierre Barricelli, publication by Modern Language Association of America expected in 1981; editing *Renaissance Literature in England,* with A. Bartlett Giamatti, et al., Harcourt, 1981; *The Sondheim Musicals: West Side Story to Sweeney Todd.*

SIDELIGHTS: Gibaldi told *CA:* "I approach writing as a 'teacher,' in the very best sense of the word: one who explores the obscure as well as the familiar, the esoteric as well as the popular to seek out and share with others interesting and valuable information, observations, insights, and experiences in order to make the world more accessible, more comprehensible, and more pleasurable. In turn, I try to bring to my teaching the qualities I most identify with good writing: the ability to express the essential with economy, cogency, and originality."

* * *

GIBBONS, Maurice 1931-

PERSONAL: Born May 1, 1931, in Peterborough, Ontario, Canada; married; children: two. *Education:* University of British Columbia, B.A., 1956; University of Washington, Seattle, M.A., 1965; Harvard University, Ed.D., 1969. *Home:* 4140 Golf Dr., North Vancouver, British Columbia, Canada. *Office:* Faculty of Education, Simon Fraser University, Burnaby 2, British Columbia, Canada.

CAREER: Elementary school teacher in Vancouver, British Columbia, 1952-54, 1956-57; high school English teacher in Vancouver, British Columbia, 1957-60; English teacher at grammar school in Hatfield, England, 1960-61; high school English teacher and department head in Vancouver, British Columbia, 1961-63; University of British Columbia, Vancouver, lecturer and assistant professor of education, 1963-66; Simon Fraser University, Burnaby, British Columbia, professor of education, 1969—. Wood sculptor, with solo and group shows in Canada and Australia. Member of British Columbia Department of Education curriculum committees; public speaker and workshop participant in Canada, the United States, and Australia; program development consultant. *Member:* American Educational Research Association, National Council of Teachers of English, Phi Delta Kappa (head of task force on compulsory education and transition of youth, 1973-76). *Awards, honors:* Creative writing award from University of British Columbia, 1956; grant from Vancouver Foundation, 1971; distinguished achievement award from Educational Press Association, 1975, for article, "Walkabout: Searching for the Right Passage From Childhood and School."

WRITINGS: *The Predicaments of Eustace Prim* (stories), Musson, 1964; (with Alan Dawe) *The Accomplished Reader,* Bellhaven House, 1964; (editor) *A Catalogue of Fine Artists,* Simon Fraser University, 1971; *Individualized Instruction: An Analysis of the Programs,* Teachers College Press, 1971; (editor) *Contact: An Access Catalogue of Fine Artists for Schools,* Simon Fraser University, 1971; *The New Secondary Education: A Phi Delta Kappa Task Force Proposal,* Phi Delta Kappa, 1976; (editor with Gary Phillips and George Ivany) *Self-Education,* Phi Delta Kappa, in press; (with Phillips) *The Challenge Education Handbook,* Self-Education Press, in press.

Contributor: *Junior Secondary School English Curriculum Guide for British Columbia,* British Columbia Department of Education, 1964; *The Report on the Principal's Conference,* University of British Columbia Press, 1965; (author of introduction) *Man's Search for Values,* Gage, 1966; *Senior Secondary English Curriculum Guide for British Columbia,* British Columbia Department of Education, 1967; Geoffrey Mason, editor, *A Study of the Resource Course,* British Columbia Educational Research Council, 1969; I. G. Hendrick and L. Jones, editors, *Crisis: Student Dissent in the Public Schools,* Houghton, 1971; *The Teachers' Changing Role in the School of the Future,* World Confederation of Organizations of the Teaching Profession, 1971; T. Sawchuk and G. McIntosh, editors, *Revolution to Resolution: New Directions for the Seventies,* Council on School Administration, 1971.

Work represented in anthologies, including *Best Poems of 1966,* 1967.

Co-author of "Solo Flight: This Is the Poet Speaking" (multi-media resource package), Resources, Inc., 1971.

Scripts: "Profession: Teacher" (eight-part series), Canadian Broadcasting Corp. (CBC-TV), 1959; "Memories of a Sapling Logger," British Broadcasting Corp. (BBC-Radio), 1960; "Seeds of Fear and a Small Crop of Courage," BBC-Radio, 1960; "The Pacific National Exhibition, 1961," CBC-TV, 1961; "The Negotiated Learning Contract" (film), Simon Fraser University; "Becoming an Influential Parent" (film), Simon Fraser University. Author of about thirty segments for "Almanac," 1958-60.

Contributor of about seventy-five articles, poems, and stories to education journals, literary journals, and popular magazines, including *Fiddlehead, Prism International,* and *Canadian Forum.* Member of editorial board of *Harvard Educational Review,* 1968-69.

WORK IN PROGRESS: *The Curriculum Developer's Handbook.*

SIDELIGHTS: Gibbons is perhaps most widely recognized for his award-winning concept, "Walkabout," which has brought him requests for reprints from all over the world. More than forty "walkabouts" and similar programs have already been established in the United States and Canada, usually at the high school level, and he has other curriculum innovations and experimental programs in use, mainly in Canada.

His current research includes a project "designed to study the conditions, methods, and motives common among those who have learned effectively without formal training; to translate these findings and other knowledge about self-directed learning into a program for teaching students how to learn independently; and to develop this program through field testing, formative evaluation, and revision."

BIOGRAPHICAL/CRITICAL SOURCES: J. Parker, *The Hottest Seminar in Town,* Phi Delta Kappa, 1973.

* * *

GIBBS, Philip (Hamilton) 1877-1962

OBITUARY NOTICE: Born 1877; died in March, 1962. Author and editor. Gibbs was editor of the *Review of Reviews* and journalist on the *London Daily Mail.* Knighted for his work as a war correspondent in World War I, Gibbs was one of the most important front line correspondents of the war. His works include *Realities of War, The New Elizabethans,* and *The Riddle of a Changing World.* Obituaries and other sources: *The Reader's Encyclopedia,* 2nd edition, Crowell, 1965; *The New Century Handbook of English Literature,* revised edition, Appleton, 1967; *Who Was Who in America,* 4th edition, Marquis, 1968; *Twentieth Century Writing: A Reader's Guide to Contemporary Literature,* Transatlantic, 1969; *Longman Companion to Twentieth Century Literature,* Longman, 1970.

* * *

GICHON, Mordechai 1922-

PERSONAL: Original name, Mordechai Gichermann; name legally changed in 1948; born August 16, 1922, in Berlin, Germany; son of Nahum (a merchant) and Charlotte (Salomon) Gichermann; married Chava Renate Goldberg; children: Arion Ramit Shahaf, Eran Seev, Eyal Nahum. *Education:* Hebrew University of Jerusalem, M.A., 1956, Ph.D., 1967; Israel Defense Forces Command and Staff College, graduated, 1959. *Religion:* Jewish. *Home:* Assael St. 14, Zahala, Tel-Aviv, Israel. *Office:* Department of Classical Studies, Tel-Aviv University, Ramat-Aviv, Tel-Aviv, Israel.

CAREER: British Army, Palestine Regiment, 1942-46; Israel Defense Forces, 1949-62, assistant director of intelligence for research, 1949-55, director of School of Intelligence, 1957-59, left service as lieutenant colonel, 1962; Tel-Aviv University, Tel-Aviv, Israel, head of the chair of military history, 1961-63, and lecturer, 1963—, professor of Roman archaeology, 1970—, coordinator of Division of Archaeology. Conducted excavations at En Bogeg, 1968-70, Migdal Tsafit, 1971, Tamara, 1973-75, Emmaus, 1977-78, and Malatha, 1979. Guest on radio and television programs.

MEMBER: Israel Exploration Society (member of council, 1960—), Israel Oriental Society (founding member), Israel Military History Association (founding member; member of board of directors, 1974—), Israel Historical Association, Eranos-Israel Society of Classical Studies, Israel-Germany League (member of board of directors, 1978—), Deutsches Archaeologisches Institut (corresponding member), Rotary Club (president, 1970—). *Awards, honors:* Sukenik Prize for Archaeology from Hebrew University, 1958, for research in the Roman frontier defenses of Israel.

WRITINGS: Carta's Atlas of Palestine From Bethther to Tel Hai: Military History, Carta, 1970, 2nd edition, 1974; *Battles of the Bible,* Part I, Weidenfeld & Nicolson, 1978; *En Bogeg: Eine Ausgrabung am Toten Meer, 1968-70* (title means "En Bogeg: An Excavation on the Dead Sea Shore"), Philipp von Zabern, 1980. Also author of *Bar Kochba and His Time.* Contributor of about sixty-five articles to scientific journals, popular magazines, and newspapers.

WORK IN PROGRESS: Judea as a Roman Province, publication by Routledge & Kegan Paul expected in 1981.

SIDELIGHTS: Gichon comments: "Since archaeology is both work and hobby to me, the highlights of my career since leaving the regular army are my excavations: the oasis of En Bogeg, the Roman fortress of Tamara, the bathhouse at biblical Emmaus, and others in between. Excavating and doing historical work in Israel, by an Israeli, means searching for one's roots in this ancient-young country. This is especially exciting since many nations and cultures have left their marks upon the Holy Land.

"Historical writing and publications should contain the author's views upon the lessons to be drawn for present days. It should attempt at simplicity and, when not specifically aimed at the specialist, at readability and easy understanding for the non-specialist and layman. A comparative view is very important. Scholars and historical writers should be encouraged to gain proficiency (up to a point) in areas and periods outside their special fields of research. Originality, depth of thought, and research is more important than the 100 percent coverage of everything that has been published so far in the fields under consideration."

* * *

GILDER, Eric 1911-

PERSONAL: Born in 1911, in London, England; son of David Richard (an accountant) and Minnie (Walman) Gilder; married Jessica Clay (a secretary), December 23, 1939; children: Heather Melody, Paula June Gilder Day. *Education:* Attended Royal College of Music, London, 1936-39. *Politics:* None. *Religion:* None. *Home and office:* 48 Glade, Shirley, Croyden, Surrey, England. *Agent:* Ann Lee, 27 John Adam St., London W.C.2, England.

CAREER: Director of music at Cripplegate Institute, 1938-40; conductor of Ilford Girls Choir, 1950-53; director of Eric Gilder School of Music. Director of music at London County Council Literary Institute, 1938-40; worked for British Broadcasting Corp. (BBC). *Military service:* British Army, 1940-45; became sergeant. *Member:* Royal Musical Society, Composers Guild, Songwriters Guild.

WRITINGS: The Sleeping Beauty: A Pantomime (play), Evans Brothers, 1971; *Robinson Crusoe: A Pantomime* (play), Evans Brothers, 1974; *Potty Pantomime* (play), Evans Brothers, 1978; (with June G. Port) *Dictionary of Composers: Their Works,* Paddington Press, 1978.

Musical compositions include works for piano and orchestra, songs and choral works, both classical and for the theatre. Columnist for *Jazz News.*

WORK IN PROGRESS: A book of biographies of composers; a book of nonsense verse; a book of short stories.

AVOCATIONAL INTERESTS: Gardening.

* * *

GILDNER, Judith 1943-

PERSONAL: Born May 29, 1943, in Pontiac, Mich.; daughter of James H. (in business) and Olive L. (Reeh) McKibben; married Gary Gildner (a writer), January 5, 1963; children: Gretchen. *Education:* Attended Wayne State University, 1961-63, and Northern Michigan University, 1963-66; Drake University, B.A., 1969, M.A., 1972. *Home:* 2915 School, Des Moines, Iowa 50311. *Office: Annals of Iowa,* East 12th & Grand, Des Moines, Iowa 50319.

CAREER: High school science teacher in Des Moines, Iowa, 1971-72, *Annals of Iowa,* Des Moines, editor, 1972—. *Member:* Iowa Historical Materials Preservation Society.

WRITINGS: (Editor with husband, Gary Gildner) *Out of This World: Poems From the Hawkeye State,* Iowa State University Press, 1976. Contributor to magazines and newspapers, including *Old Northwest, Arizona and the West, Nebraska History,* and *Iowan.*

WORK IN PROGRESS: Iowans in the Arts, a series of interviews with Iowa artists and writers.

SIDELIGHTS: Judith Gildner writes: "The artist's affection for his origins, in particular the land, the place where he was nurtured, holds a fascination for me. Living in a prairie-agricultural region has increased my interest in finding out more about the artist's relationship to his surroundings. Through interviews I hope to compile a testimony on this subject."

BIOGRAPHICAL/CRITICAL SOURCES: Des Moines Register, August 14, 1977.

* * *

GITLOW, Benjamin 1891-1965

OBITUARY NOTICE: Born December 22, 1891, in Elizabethport, N.J.; died July 19, 1965. Author. Gitlow was very involved in Socialist and Communist activities. As leader of the Left Wing of the Socialist party and editor of its paper, Gitlow was arrested and imprisoned for three years. He ran twice for the vice-presidency of the United States on the Communist ticket. Gitlow renounced communism after he was expelled from the Party for criticizing Stalin. His works include *America for the People, I Confess: The Truth About American Communism,* and *The Whole of Their Lives.* Obituaries and other sources: *Who Was Who in America,* 4th edition, Marquis, 1968.

* * *

GIVNER, Abraham 1944-

PERSONAL: Born August 2, 1944, in New York; son of Solomon and Rose (Marcus) Givner; children: Jonathan. *Education:* Brooklyn College of the City University of New York, B.A., 1966; Yeshiva University, M.S., 1968, Ph.D., 1971. *Home:* 720 Greenwich St., New York, N.Y. 10014. *Office:* Department of Psychology, Yeshiva University, 55 Fifth Ave., New York, N.Y. 10003.

CAREER: Yeshiva University, New York, N.Y., associate professor of psychology, 1972—. Private practice of psychotherapy, 1974—. Member of School Psychology Educators Council of New York State. *Member:* American Psychological Association, New York State Psychological Association.

WRITINGS: (With Paul S. Graubard) *A Handbook of Behavior Modification in the Classroom,* Holt, 1974.

WORK IN PROGRESS: Behavior Therapy With Children; research on educational mainstreaming of special education students.

SIDELIGHTS: Givner writes: "I have worked extensively with children and adolescents with emotional and intellectual deficits and excesses. My book emanated from a two-year research grant to study emotionally disturbed children in New York City. A subsequent grant from the federal government was for investigating ways of returning disturbed children to normal settings."

Givner also spent one year living on a kibbutz in Israel.

* * *

GLICK, Ruth (Burtnick) 1942-

PERSONAL: Born April 27, 1942, in Lexington, Ky.; daughter of Lester Leon (a physician) and Beverly (a teacher; maiden name, Miller) Burtnick; married Norman Glick (a mathematician), June 30, 1963; children: Elissa, Ethan. *Education:* George Washington University, A.B., 1964; University of Maryland, M.A., 1967. *Politics:* Democrat. *Home and office:* 10594 Jason Court, Columbia, Md. 21044.

CAREER: Writer, 1972—. *Member:* Society of Children's Book Writers, Maryland Press Women, Washington Independent Writers.

WRITINGS: (With Nancy Baggett) *Dollhouse Furniture You Can Make,* A. S. Barnes, 1978; (with Baggett) *Dollhouse Lamps and Chandeliers,* Hobby House, 1979; *Dollhouse Kitchen and Diningroom Accessories,* Hobby House, 1979. Contributor to magazines, including *Good Health* and *Essence,* and to newspapers. Food editor of *Columbia Flier,* 1977—.

WORK IN PROGRESS: A guide to gourmet shopping in Washington, D.C., publication by Piper Publishing; two cookbooks; a science fiction novel for children.

SIDELIGHTS: Glick told *CA:* "I have found the new city of Columbia, Maryland, a very stimulating environment and an excellent place to launch a free-lance writing career. Because Columbia is located halfway between Washington, D.C., and Baltimore, I have had easy access to two large metropolitan markets.

"It was my then seven-year-old daughter's request for a dollhouse that prompted me to start designing dollhouse furniture and accessories five years ago. This lead to the writing of my first book and subsequent booklets and articles in that field.

"For me writing is a terrific career because it gives me the opportunity to learn about what interests me and get paid at the same time. Because crafts, food, nutrition, and health are primary interests for me, they have played a central part in my work."

BIOGRAPHICAL/CRITICAL SOURCES: Baltimore Sun, June 18, 1978.

* * *

GLOVER, Albert Gould 1942-

PERSONAL: Born November 19, 1942, in Boston, Mass. son of Frederic Lyon (in business) and Virginia (an artist; maiden name, Price) Glover; married Patricia Hall, March 3, 1962; children: Frederic Lyon, Manson Price, Charles Gooding. *Education:* McGill University, B.A., 1964; State University of New York at Buffalo, M.A., 1966, Ph.D., 1968. *Politics:* Independent. *Religion:* "Puritan." *Office:* Department of English, St. Lawrence University, Canton, N.Y. 13617.

CAREER: St. Lawrence University, Canton, N.Y., assistant professor, 1968-72, associate professor, 1972-78, professor of English, 1978—. Publisher of *Cirriculum of the Soul,* for Institute of Further Studies, 1971—.

WRITINGS: (With George F. Butterick) *A Bibliography of Works by Charles Olson,* Phoenix Bookshop (New York), 1967; (editor) *Charles Olson: Letters for Origin,* Cape, 1969; *A Trio in G* (poems), Frontier Press (West Newbury, Mass.), 1971; *The Mushroom* (verse and prose), Institute of Further Studies, 1972; *Paradise Valley* (poems), Bellevue Press, 1973. Editor of *Audit/Poetry,* 1965-67, *Magazine of Further Studies,* 1965-71, and *North Country Medicine,* 1971-72.

WORK IN PROGRESS: Back on Earth, poems from 1974-78; *The Rehearsal of Our Sympathy: A Book of Dreams; The*

Body of the Beloved: Marriage Within the Resurrection Body.

SIDELIGHTS: Glover writes: "I was brought up on Emily Dickinson and Robert Frost. Then, in Provincetown during my sixteenth summer, I met real beatniks and began reading Dylan Thomas and Jack Kerouac. In Buffalo I met Charles Olson and enrolled in his seminars, 'Myth and Literature' and 'Contemporary Poetry.' For ten years I studied archaic techniques of ecstasy.

"In 1971 my wife and I bought a dilapidated home on the Pleistocene Atlantic shoreline in northern New York. Since then we have been raising our family, restoring our home, and working in the garden. I have found husbandry a bridge between the shamanic tradition and the radical Puritan doctrine set forth in *Paradise Lost*. I aspire to be counted in Christ's Kingdom at the Day of Doom and seek company among the Sons of Light.

"My life has been constantly supported by St. Lawrence University, a community devoted to the search for truth in the best tradition of liberal education, for the past ten years."

* * *

GNAEGY, Charles 1938-
(Chris Grange, Chuck Gregory)

PERSONAL: Surname in pronounced *Nay*-gy; born November 15, 1938, in Paducah, Ky.; son of Ray A. (a florist) and Rena B. (a designer; maiden name, Vincent) Gnaegy; children: Laurette, Leslie. *Education:* American Academy of Art, Institute of Design, B.A. *Politics:* Independent. *Religion:* "Iconoclast." *Residence:* Miamarina, Miami, Fla. 33130. *Office address:* P.O. Box 430733, Miami, Fla. 33143.

CAREER: Mead Johnson & Co., Evansville, Ind., director of design, 1959-69; United Banking Group, Miami, Fla., director of public relations, 1969-71; Variety International, Miami, executive director, 1972-75; free-lance writer, 1975—. *Military service:* U.S. Army, Ranger Division. *Member:* American Society of Journalists and Authors, Outdoor Writers Association of America, Mensa. *Awards, honors:* First prize in fiction from Miami Writers Conference, 1971.

WRITINGS: Psycho-Reflex in Sports, PR Publishing, 1978; *Action!: Live Adventures With America's Heroes* (juvenile), Scholastic Book Services, 1979; *A Promise of Summer*, Manor, 1979. Contributor to magazines, under pseudonyms Chris Grange and Chuck Gregory. Editor for American College of Osteopathic Surgeons.

WORK IN PROGRESS: Four novels, *Nocturne, Alix, Orange Island Strike,* and *Grander.*

* * *

GODFREY, Jane
See BOWDEN, Joan Chase

* * *

GODLY, J. P.
See PLAWIN, Paul

* * *

GOLDBECK, Willis 1899(?)-1979

OBITUARY NOTICE: Born c. 1899 in New York, N.Y.; died September 17, 1979, in Southampton, N.Y. Motion-picture producer, director, and screenwriter. During a career that spanned from silents to sound movies, Goldbeck produced such films as "The Lone Ranger" and "I Died a Thousand Times," and directed eight others, including "Love Laughs at Andy Hardy" and "Ten Tall Men." Goldbeck wrote more than twenty screenplays, nine of which featured the popular character Dr. Kildare. His most recent screenplay was "The Man Who Shot Liberty Valance" (1962). Obituaries and other sources: *New York Times,* September 19, 1979.

* * *

GOLDMAN, Ralph M(orris) 1920-

PERSONAL: Born May 14, 1920, in Brooklyn, N.Y.; son of Benjamin (a pharmacist) and Rose (a sewing machine operator; maiden name, Smotroff) Goldman; married Joan Walsh (an art historian and curator), October 20, 1953; children: Peter T., Marjorie E. *Education:* New York University, B.A., 1947; University of Chicago, M.A. (with honors), 1948, Ph.D., 1951. *Politics:* Democrat. *Religion:* Agnostic. *Home:* 60 Amethyst Way, San Francisco, Calif. 94131. *Office:* Department of Political Science, San Francisco State University, San Francisco, Calif. 94132.

CAREER: Democratic National Committee, Washington, D.C., consultant in research division, 1952; American Political Science Association, Washington, D.C., staff associate, 1952-53; Brookings Institution, Washington, D.C., research associate, 1953-56; Michigan State University, East Lansing, assistant professor, 1956-57, associate professor of political science, 1957-62; San Francisco State University, San Francisco, Calif., professor of political science, 1962—, head of department, 1971-74, director of Institute for Research on International Behavior, 1964-67, associate dean for faculty research, 1965-67. Visiting instructor at American University, autumn, 1955; visiting professor at University of Chicago, 1961-62, and University of California, San Diego, winter and spring, 1979; visiting lecturer at University of California, Berkeley, spring, 1963; visiting professorial lecturer at Stanford University, spring, 1966. Political commentator for Radio-Keith-Orpheum, summer, 1964. Member of board of governors of Frederic Burk Foundation for Education, 1967-78, chairperson of board, 1968-69, 1970-71; member of Leonard D. White Memorial Fund Committee of University of Chicago. *Military service:* U.S. Army, 1942-46; served in the Philippines; became captain.

MEMBER: International Political Science Association, International Studies Association, International Education Association of the United States, American Political Science Association (life member), American Sociological Association, American Association of University Professors (chapter president, 1966-67), Western Political Science Association, United Professors of California, World Affairs Council of Northern California (member of board of directors), United Nations Association of San Francisco (member of board of directors). *Awards, honors:* Fellow of U.S. Air Force Office of Scientific Research, 1958; grants from U.S. Office of Naval Research, *San Francisco Examiner,* National Science Foundation, 1968, and Carnegie Corp.

WRITINGS: (With Bertram M. Gross) *The Legislative Struggle,* McGraw, 1953; (with Paul T. David and Malcolm Moos) *Presidential Nominating Politics in 1952,* five volumes, Johns Hopkins Press, 1954; (with David and Richard C. Bain) *The Politics of National Party Conventions,* Brookings Institution, 1960; *The Democratic Party in American Politics,* Macmillan, 1966.

Role Instruction for Social Studies and Occupational Devel-

opment (monograph), Center for Technological Education, San Francisco State University, 1970; *Contemporary Perspectives on Politics,* Van Nostrand, 1972; *The Future of Foundations,* Frederic Burk Foundation for Education, 1973; *Behavioral Perspectives on American Politics,* Dorsey, 1973; (with John H. Sloane and Paul Magnelia) *Simulation of Global Politics: Some Classroom Experiences in the California State University System,* School of Behavioral and Social Sciences, San Francisco State University, 1976; *Presidential Year 1976* (booklet), San Francisco State University, 1976; *The Political Science Concept Inventory,* ABC-Clio Books, 1979; *Search for Consensus: The Story of the Democratic Party,* Temple University Press, 1979.

Contributor: Alfred Junz, editor, *Present Trends in American National Government,* Hansard Society, 1960; Norman F. Washburne, editor, *Decision, Values, and Groups,* Volume II, Macmillan, 1962; Aaron Wildavsky, editor, *The Presidency,* Little, Brown, 1967; Julian Foster and Durward Long, editors, *Protest: Student Activism in America,* Morrow, 1970; Alfred deGrazia, R. Eric Weise, and John Appel, editors, *Old Government/New People,* Scott, Foresman, 1971; Louis Maisel and Joseph Cooper, editors, *Political Parties: Development and Decay,* Sage Publications, 1978.

Contributor to *Encyclopedia Americana, Arete Encyclopedia,* and *Encyclopaedia Britannica.* Contributor of more than thirty articles and reviews to scholarly journals, popular magazines, and newspapers, including *Vista, U.S. News and World Report,* and *New Republic.* Member of editorial committee of *Background,* 1963-66.

WORK IN PROGRESS: Feeling Safe in This World; The Arms Race, Peace Keeping, and Collective Security; The Arms Control Process; Conflict at the United Nations: A Casebook.

SIDELIGHTS: Goldman writes: "Four years of military service in World War II led me to the judgment that a good way to spend a life would be trying to figure out how political conflict could be carried on—but in a world without war. The answer seems to be: viable political party systems, particularly the development of a transnational party system."

BIOGRAPHICAL/CRITICAL SOURCES: Los Angeles Times Book Review, August 26, 1979.

* * *

GOLDSMITH
See MILLER, Lynne (Ellen)

* * *

GOODHART, Robert S(tanley) 1909-

PERSONAL: Born July 19, 1909, in Altoona, Pa.; son of R. Stanley (an optometrist) and Beatrice (Pape) Goodhart; married Sigrid Ericksen, November 20, 1935; children: Eric Neil, William Haldor. *Education:* Lafayette College, B.S., 1930; New York University, M.D., 1934, D.Med.Sci., 1940. *Home:* 67 Forest Rd., Tenafly, N.J. 07670.

CAREER: Brooklyn Hospital, Brooklyn, N.Y., intern, 1934-36; Bellevue Hospital, New York City, resident in psychiatry, 1936-38, assistant clinical visiting physician, 1938-41, assistant visiting physician, 1941-42; National Vitamin Foundation, Inc., New York City, scientific director, 1946-66, president, 1962-66; New York Academy of Medicine, New York City, executive secretary of committee on medical education, 1967-78, consultant, 1978—. Instructor at New York University, 1939-42, assistant professor, 1942-47, John Wyckoff Fellow in Medicine, 1939-41; lecturer at Columbia University, 1950-72; adjunct professor at Mount Sinai School of Medicine, 1969-73. Certified by American Board of Nutrition. Physician in charge of Washington Heights Nutrition Clinic, 1948-69; scientific director of Calorie Control Council, 1968-70. Chairperson of food committee of New York City's Welfare Emergency Division, 1950—; vice-chairperson of Nutrition Division of Health Council of Greater New York, 1951-52, chairperson of Nutrition Division of Welfare and Health Council of Greater New York, 1953-55, president of Food and Nutrition Council of Greater New York, 1958-60; chairperson of National Research Council, National Academy of Sciences, nutrition committee; member of scientific advisory committee of American Institute of Baking, 1961-66. *Wartime service:* U.S. Public Health Service, 1942-46, technical adviser on nutrition to Nutrition Division of Office of Defense, Health and Welfare Services, 1942-43, chief of Industrial Feeding Programs Division of War Food Administration, in U.S. Department of Agriculture, 1943-46.

MEMBER: American Institute of Nutrition, American Society for Clinical Investigation, American Society for Clinical Nutrition, Association of American Medical Colleges, Harvey Society, New York Academy of Medicine. *Awards, honors:* Rockefeller Foundation fellowship for Oxford University, 1938-39; Milbank Memorial Fund fellowship, 1941-42.

WRITINGS: The Nutrition Programme for Industry in the United States: Nutrition in Industry, International Labor Office (Montreal, Quebec), 1946; *Let's Keep the Industrial Feeding Program: Nutrition for Young and Old,* New York Joint Legislative Committee on Nutrition, 1946; (editor with Michael G. Wohl, and contributor) *Modern Nutrition in Health and Disease,* Lea & Febiger, 1955, 5th edition (with Maurice E. Shils), 1973, 6th edition, 1980; (with Shils) *The Flavonoids in Biology and Medicine,* National Vitamin Foundation, 1956; *Nutrition for You,* Dutton, 1958; (with Wohl) *Manual of Clinical Nutrition,* Lea & Febiger, 1964; *The Teen-Ager's Guide to Diet and Health,* Prentice-Hall, 1964.

Contributor: *Dietotherapy: Clinical Application of Modern Nutrition,* Saunders, 1945; Wohl, editor, *Nutrition and Diet in Health and Disease,* 5th edition (Goodhart was not included in earlier editions), Saunders, 1949, 6th edition, 1952; William J. Darby, editor, *Clinical Nutrition,* Paul B. Hoeber, 1950, 2nd edition, 1962; Norman Jolliffe, editor, *Long-Term Illness: Management of the Chronically Ill Patient,* Saunders, 1959. Editor of medical books for Communico, 1969-70. Editor of *Modern Drug Encyclopedia,* 1960-69. Contributor of about seventy-five articles to medical journals.

* * *

GOODMAN, Linda 1925-

PERSONAL: Born April 9, 1925, in Parkersburg, W. Va.; daughter of Robert Stratton and Mazie (McBee) Kemery; married William Herbert Snyder (a writer), April 29, 1949 (divorced); married Sam O. Goodman (a disc jockey), September 28, 1955 (separated); children: (first marriage) Melissa Anne, James, John Anthony, Sarah Elizabeth, William Dana; (second marriage) Jill Kemery, Michael Aaron. *Home:* 315 Carr Ave., Cripple Creek, Colo. 80813.

CAREER: Astrologer and author. WAMP-Radio, Pittsburgh, Pa., writer and broadcaster for "Letter From Linda" show, 1958-61; writer for radio shows, 1962-64; WHN-Radio New York, N.Y., continuity chief, 1964-66; speech writer for National Urban League, 1966-67. Member of Universal

Research Foundation, Sedona, Ariz., and Association for Research and Enlightenment, Virginia Beach, Va. *Member:* Authors League of America, American Federation of Television and Radio Artists, Writers Guild of New York. *Awards, honors:* Named Daughter of the Year by the West Virginia Society, Washington, D.C., 1971.

WRITINGS: Sun Signs (nonfiction), Taplinger, 1968, published as *Linda Goodman's Sun Signs,* Bantam, 1975; *Venus Trines at Midnight: Verses About Lions, Rams, Bulls, Twins, Archers, and Other Sun Signs and You* (poetry), Taplinger, 1970; *Linda Goodman's Love Signs: A New Approach to the Human Heart,* Harper, 1978. Contributor to popular magazines.

WORK IN PROGRESS: An "autobiographical account of reincarnation"; a book about Howard Hughes.

SIDELIGHTS: Due to the success of her first book, *Sun Signs,* Linda Goodman has become one of America's most influential and famous astrologers. Although Goodman claims to have been interested in astrology "since the time of Atlantis and before," according to her husband Sam and *People* magazine it was only after Sam brought home a copy of *The Coffee Table Book of Astrology* that she "stayed in a nightgown studying astrology 20 hours a day for a year."

Sun Signs has sold over four million copies to date and was, for a time, considered a "cult" book, read by all "hip" people, including Jane Fonda in the motion picture "Klute." *Love Signs,* already a best-seller, will probably follow its lead. Much of the success of these books is due to their readability; according to a *Newsweek* reviewer, "what seems to set [them] apart from other stargazing guides is their knowledgeable approach and comprehensive reach." For example, *Love Signs* covers "every possible pairing of signs—all 166 combinations—for romantic possibilities."

In addition to her career as an astrologer, Goodman has also founded a religion, "Mannitou," based on the teachings of St. Francis of Asissi and on American Indian beliefs. Over 49 percent of her income goes into the foundation for this new religion. Goodman is also a contributor to causes which she considers important: an environmental group, a plant-life experimenter, and a plastic surgeon whose "work she admires."

Even though she is wildly successful, Goodman has had her share of personal tragedy: the disappearance of a former lover and the alleged death of her twenty-one-year-old daughter. But she firmly believes that both will return to her soon.

Of her profession, Goodman once remarked, "I admit that to be an astrologer you live a great deal in the imagination." Her clients have often included Hollywood celebrities and members of the jet set.

BIOGRAPHICAL/CRITICAL SOURCES: Newsweek, December 18, 1978; *People,* May 14, 1979.*

* * *

GOOLAGONG, Evonne 1951-

PERSONAL: Born July 31, 1951, in Barellan, New South Wales, Australia; daughter of Kenneth (a sheep shearer) and Linda Goolagong; married Roger Cawley, June 19, 1975; children: Kelly. *Education:* Graduate of business college in Sydney, Australia. *Address:* c/o IMC, 1 Erieview Plaza, Cleveland, Ohio 44114.

CAREER: International tennis competitor, 1970—. *Awards, honors:* Australian hard court champion, 1970-72; winner of Wimbledon singles title, 1971; winner of championship titles, including French Open, 1971, South African Open, 1972, Italian Open, 1973, Australian Open, 1974-75, 1978, and Colgate Open, 1978; ranked number one in World Team Tennis on Pittsburgh Triangles, 1975; decorated Order of the British Empire.

WRITINGS: (With Bud Collins) *Evonne! On the Move,* Dutton, 1975.

SIDELIGHTS: That Evonne Goolagong has tennis in her blood was apparent even before she reached her first birthday, when she would squeeze a tennis ball in her hands. By the age of four she regularly swatted balls against a wall of her hometown's tennis club in Australia's Outback, using an old baseball bat. Five years later an aunt bought her a bona fide tennis racket. "I used to sleep with that racket," Goolagong reminisced.

The turning point in Goolagong's life came when she was discovered by a talent scout from Vic Edward's tennis school based in Sydney. As Edwards himself recalled, "Her most impressive quality was her grace around the court. And she could hit that ball really hard, right in the center of the bat. She had a homemade shot, a backhand volley, and it was a beauty." At this time, Goolagong had just turned ten.

Realizing that Goolagong's potential in tennis was likely to be squelched in the unambitious atmosphere of the Outback, Edwards became her legal guardian, taking her to live with his family in an affluent suburb of Sydney. With Edwards's encouragement, Goolagong attended finishing school in the evenings to learn elocution and poise. After high school, she enrolled at a business college for secretarial training, just in case she would ever need additional skills to fall back on. That never became necessary. In 1971, three years before Edwards predicted, Goolagong soundly defeated her former idol, first seeded Margaret Court, at Wimbledon. "The margin by which she destroyed her 28-year-old Australian opponent [6-4, 6-1], defies belief," declared Fred Tupper. Thus at nineteen Goolagong had become the world's top woman player of the year.

Still among the four best women players in the world today, Goolagong's deadly backhand underspin and tiring cross-court volley are her most formidable assets. Margaret Court commented on Goolagong's game, "she just won't play safe tennis and her shots are quite unpredictable." Even so, she is still graceful in competition. "Watching Evonne Goolagong play tennis is a little like looking at an Impressionist painting," observed Jane Leavy.

Two weaknesses in Goolagong's game most often cited are her forehand volley and the tendency for her mind to "walkabout," an Australian aboriginal term she uses for to "wander." She has also been faulted for lacking the killer instinct characteristic of many professionals, despite her fervor on the court. Virginia Wade reasoned that Goolagong is a "very modest, very gentle person," noting that her only display of emotion during a match is to walk very quickly when she is winning and to smile a little when she is not.

The press has often stressed Goolagong's aboriginal ancestry, a fact that she herself understates. She is not interested in the politics of being black, insisting on being viewed solely as a tennis professional.

In 1972 some controversy was stirred when Goolagong was permitted to play in a segregated South African tournament as an "honorary white." Black American tennis professional Arthur Ashe was forbidden to enter the country. Reacting to Goolagong's noncommittal attitude concerning race, Ashe said: "It's not a matter of personal preference. If you're born black you're committed in the race war." Goolagong replied, "Of course I'm proud of my race, but I don't want to be thinking about it all the time."

AVOCATIONAL INTERESTS: Golf, music.

BIOGRAPHICAL/CRITICAL SOURCES: *Sports Illustrated,* February 15, 1971, July 12, 1971, March 20, 1972, August 7, 1972, October 28, 1974, April 26, 1976, October 17, 1977, March 27, 1978; *Time,* March 1, 1971, July 17, 1972, June 30, 1975; *Newsweek,* July 5, 1971, July 17, 1972, March 19, 1973, June 30, 1975, April 26, 1976; *New York Times Biographical Edition,* July 8, 1971, August 31, 1971; *Life,* July 16, 1971; *New York Times Magazine,* August 29, 1971; *Seventeen,* August, 1972; George Sullivan, *Queens of the Court,* Dodd, 1974; Evonne Goolagong and Bud Collins, *Evonne! On the Move,* Dutton, 1975; *New York Times Book Review,* June 1, 1975; D.J. Huda, *Free Spirit: Evonne Goolagong,* photographs by Bruce Curtis and others, Raintree, 1976; *Ms.,* July, 1978.*

* * *

GORDON, Barbara 1913-

PERSONAL: Born in 1913, in Miami, Fla.; divorced. *Education:* Attended Vassar College and Barnard College.

CAREER: WCBS-TV, New York, N.Y., writer and producer of documentary films for "Eye On" series, including "Limbo People," "Super Land Lord—Who Owns This Town?," and "Reading, Writing and Recruiting." Has written and produced films for National Broadcasting Co. (NBC-TV) and Public Television, and contributed to television programs including "The Great American Dream Machine" and "NET Journal." Produced "Victor Marchetti vs. United States of America," a one-hour special film for "The Fifty-First State" series. Has produced films on Jane Fonda, Studs Terkel, Jason Robards, Earl Warren, Jose Quintero, Colleen Dewhurst, Dalton Trumbo, and many other celebrities. *Awards, honors:* Four Emmy awards from National Academy of Arts and Sciences; received a number of awards for films in WCBS-TV "Eye On" series.

WRITINGS: *I'm Dancing as Fast as I Can* (Literary Guild selection), Harper, 1979.

WORK IN PROGRESS: A film version of *I'm Dancing as Fast as I Can;* a novel.

SIDELIGHTS: Gordon had been a highly respected and successful television documentary producer who began taking Valium when going through a divorce. Ten years later, she was still being prescribed the sedative at a dose that over the years had increased from five to thirty milligrams a day. Although Gordon "had always been an independent, energetic, adventurous woman," by 1976 she "was experiencing uncontrollable panic at the mere thought of shopping in a busy department store or lunching in a crowded restaurant."

Finally, Gordon "had had enough." Wanting to face her anxiety without pills, she was advised by her psychiatrist "to go off Valium cold turkey." The resulting symptoms, including chronic insomnia, convulsions, and hallucinations, eventually required two hospitalizations over the course of a year.

After several months of hospital therapy, Barbara Gordon was released and "thought her former job at CBS . . . would be waiting for her. It wasn't." "There I was," she reflected, ". . . an ex-mental patient with no job. I didn't know what to do, so I sat down at the typewriter. I felt compelled to make myself understand who I was and where I had been."

I'm Dancing as Fast as I Can is Gordon's story of her recovery from Valium addiction. Her publisher describes the book as "a lucid account of psychiatric hospitalization. It is an inspiring story of conquering drug addiction. It is a powerful indictment of the blind use of Valium . . . a moving tribute to human survival." The book was published in May, 1979, but early sales figures "were not exciting." Gordon told Carol Lawson: "Whoever heard of Barbara Gordon? Harper & Row had the problem of how to market me. They advertised a lot, and I have been touring the country for two months." Gordon found the tour exhausting: "I had to relive my breakdown 10 times a day." The book later hit the best-seller lists.

When CBS offered Gordon her old job back, though, she turned it down. "I love writing, and have been afforded the luxury of changing careers at 43," she told Lawson. "I miss the camaraderie of television, though. The loneliness of the writer is still something I'm not used to. I did three freelance television projects when the book was nearing completion, but I won't go back to TV full time unless something marvelous comes up."

Apparently Gordon likes the challenge of writing a book. Her awards for her television documentaries were shared successes. The pleasure of winning them "wasn't as sweet as being on the best-seller list once," she declared. "This success is different. This is *mine.*"

Suzanne Fields, who reviewed Gordon's book for the *Washington Post,* admitted that "Gordon praises as she pans," writing humorously and vividly, but noted that "her powerful narrative suffers from her own limits of understanding." Fields pointed out that Gordon describes how her addiction is not surprising in view of the state of medical practice, but that Gordon "draws no distinctions in its use, its benefits and side effects, even as she insists that her book was written out of a concern for 'medical mismanagement.'" Fields declared: "[Gordon's] is the uncritical judgment of the new convert. . . . She still seeks a child's safe passage, and even if we don't learn why she wants to hold on to that long extension of the umbilical cord, we do get a vivid sense of her entanglement with it."

Paramount pictures has purchased the film rights to *I'm Dancing as Fast as I Can.*

BIOGRAPHICAL/CRITICAL SOURCES: Barbara Gordon, *I'm Dancing as Fast as I Can,* Harper, 1979; *Washington Post,* May 28, 1979; *People,* June 18, 1979; *New York Times Book Review,* July 1, 1979, August 5, 1979; *Detroit Free Press,* September 17, 1979.*

* * *

GORE, Robert Hayes 1886-1972

OBITUARY NOTICE: Born May 24, 1886, in Knottsville, Ky.; died December 26, 1972. Journalist, government worker, and inventor. During his association of sixty-four years with the *Fort Lauderdale News,* Gore presided over both R. H. Gore Co. and Gore Publishing. He was appointed governor of Puerto Rico by President Franklin Roosevelt in 1933. He also worked as scenarist for film studios during the silent era and is credited with the invention of an exercising bed. Obituaries and other sources: *Who's Who in the South and Southwest,* 13th edition, Marquis, 1973.

* * *

GOSSETT, Philip 1941-

PERSONAL: Born September 27, 1941, in New York; son of

Harold and Pearl (Lenkowsky) Gossett; married Suzanne Solomon (a college professor), August 15, 1963; children: David, Jeffrey. *Education:* Attended Columbia University, 1961-62; Amherst College, B.A. (summa cum laude), 1963; Princeton University, M.F.A., 1965, Ph.D., 1970. *Home:* 5509 South Kenwood Ave., Chicago, Ill. 60637. *Office:* Department of Music, University of Chicago, 5835 South University Ave., Chicago, Ill. 60637.

CAREER: University of Chicago, Chicago, Ill., assistant professor, 1968-73, associate professor, 1973-77, professor of music, 1977—, head of department, 1978—. Visiting associate professor at Columbia University, spring, 1975. *Member:* International Musicological Society, American Musicological Society (member of council, 1972-74; member of board of directors, 1974-76), American Institute of Verdi Studies (member of board of directors), Societa Italiana di Musicologia, Phi Beta Kappa. *Awards, honors:* Woodrow Wilson fellow, 1963-64, 1966-67; Fulbright scholar in Paris, France, 1965-66; Martha Baird Rockefeller fellow, 1967-68; Alfred Einstein Award from American Musicological Society, 1969, for "Rossini in Naples: Some Major Works Recovered"; Guggenheim fellow, 1971-72.

WRITINGS: (Translator and author of notes) Jean-Philippe Rameau, *Treatise on Harmony,* Dover, 1971; (contributor) *Studies in Renaissance and Baroque Music in Honor of Arthur Mendel,* Baerenreiter Verlag, 1974; *The Tragic Finale of Tancredi,* Fondazione Rossini, 1977. Contributor of articles and reviews to musicology journals.

Co-editor of "The Collected Works of Gioachino Rossini," Fondazione Rossini, and "Early Romantic Opera," Garland Publishing, 1978—; member of editorial board of "The Works of Giuseppe Verdi," University of Chicago Press. Member of editorial board of *Journal of the American Musicological Society,* 1972-78, *Critical Inquiry,* 1974—, and *Nineteenth-Century Music,* 1976—.

WORK IN PROGRESS: A critical edition of Gioachino Rossini's *Tancredi,* for Fondazione Rossini; a book on structural conventions in nineteenth-century Italian opera; cataloging the works of Rossini; studying Beethoven sketches and Verdi's operas; three articles, "A Critical Edition of Verdi's *Macbeth,*" for *A Macbeth Sourcebook* (Norton), "The Overtures of Rosini," for *19th-Century Music,* and "The Four Versions of Marzelline's Aria," for *Beethoven-Jahrbuch X.*

* * *

GOTTLIEB, Beatrice M. 1889(?)-1979

OBITUARY NOTICE: Born c. 1889; died July 14, 1979, in Manhattan, N.Y. Philanthropist, producer, and playwright. Gottlieb served on the boards of over twenty institutions, including the Children's Medical Relief International. She also produced several plays and was the co-author of "Brooklyn Biarritz," which was produced on Broadway during the 1930's. Obituaries and other sources: *New York Times,* July 16, 1979.

* * *

GOTTSCHALK, Shimon S. 1929-

PERSONAL: Born July 23, 1929, in Berlin, Germany; son of Arthur A. (an attorney) and Annemarie Gottschalk; children: Takana Ariella, Tikkun Samuel. *Education:* Brandeis University, B.A., 1954, Ph.D., 1972; Rutgers University, M.S.W., 1965. *Religion:* Jewish. *Home:* 1002 Waverly, Tallahassee, Fla. 32312. *Office:* School of Social Work, Florida State University, Tallahassee, Fla. 32306.

CAREER: The Temple, Atlanta, Ga., director of religious education, 1956-62; Bureau of Jewish Education, Atlanta, associate director, 1962-63; editor for Mobilization for Youth, New York City, 1964-65; Council of Community Services, Providence, R.I., planning director, 1965-68; Brandeis University, Waltham, Mass., lecturer in community organization at Florence Heller School and field instructor, 1969-70; International Independence Institute, Ashby, Mass., research director, 1971-72; Florida State University, Tallahassee, visiting associate professor, 1973, associate professor of social policy, 1973—. Field instructor at Boston College, 1965-68, visiting lecturer, 1972; participant in scholarly meetings; social planning consultant. Also worked as carpenter, dairy farmer, and cook. *Awards, honors:* Grants from National Institute of Mental Health, 1973, Florida Foundation for the Humanities, 1976, and Florida Hillel, 1977.

WRITINGS: (Contributor) Shirley Weiss, Edward Kaiser, and Raymond Barby, editors, *New Community Development,* University of North Carolina Press, 1971; *Rural New Towns: Toward a National Policy* (monograph), Center for Community Economic Development, Cambridge, Mass., 1971; (with Robert Swann, Edward Hansch, and Edward Webster) *The Community Land Trust,* International Independence Institute, 1972; *Communities and Alternatives: An Exploration of the Limits of Planning,* Wiley, 1975. Contributor of about a dozen articles to education and social science journals.

WORK IN PROGRESS: Research on "recycling the life cycle," with a book expected to result.

SIDELIGHTS: Gottschalk writes: "I have in recent years become the single parent father of two elementary school age children—a totally delightful experience. I have discovered how sadly deprived most men are in our society, in that they are not permitted to be (or they don't permit themselves to be) nurturing parents."

* * *

GOULD, Randall 1898(?)-1979

OBITUARY NOTICE: Born c. 1898 in Minnesota; died c. October 23, 1979, in Mill Valley, Calif. Journalist and author. Formerly a correspondent in Peking, China, Gould served as editor and publisher of the *Shanghai Evening Post and Mercury* from 1931 to 1949. As the only American-owned paper in Shanghai, it represented U.S. business interests there. Gould was forced to leave China after a dispute with Chinese Communist members of his staff. Back in the United States, he worked for the *San Rafael Independent-Journal* from 1959 to 1963. Apparently Gould died after killing his ailing wife and then shooting himself. He wrote *China in the Sun* in 1946. Obituaries and other sources: *New York Times,* October 26, 1979.

* * *

GOWERS, Ernest (Arthur) 1880-1966

OBITUARY NOTICE: Born June 2, 1880, in London, England; died of cancer, April 16, 1966. Rhetorician best known for his instructional books on the English language, including *The Complete Plain Words.* Gowers also wrote *A Life for a Life,* a book on capital punishment. He spent his final years revising H. W. Fowler's *Dictionary of Modern English.* Obituaries and other sources: *The New Century Handbook of English Literature,* revised edition, Appleton, 1967; *Longman Companion to Twentieth Century Literature,* Longman, 1970; *World Authors, 1950-70,* Wilson, 1975.

GRAE, Ida 1918-
(Ida Dean)

* * *

GRAHAM, Charlotte
See BOWDEN, Joan Chase

* * *

GRAHAM, Philip Leslie 1915-1963

OBITUARY NOTICE: Born July 18, 1915, in Terry, S.D.; died August 3, 1963. Lawyer and journalist. Graham published the *Washington Post* from 1946 to 1961. He served as president of that paper from 1961 until his death. Obituaries and other sources: *Current Biography,* Wilson, 1948, October, 1963; *New York Times,* August 4, 1963; *Who Was Who in America,* 4th edition, Marquis, 1968.

* * *

GRANGE, Chris
See GNAEGY, Charles

* * *

GRANIK, (S.) Theodore 1906-1970

OBITUARY NOTICE: Born in 1906 in Brooklyn, N.Y.; died September 21, 1970. Lawyer and moderator of television and radio shows. While working as an attorney, Granik hosted the radio and television program "American Forum of the Air." Among the many guests that appeared on the debate show were later-presidents Franklin Roosevelt and Harry Truman. Granik also created the television program, "Youth Wants to Know." Obituaries and other sources: *Current Biography,* Wilson, 1952, November, 1970; *New York Times,* September 23, 1970; *Who Was Who in America,* 5th edition, Marquis, 1973.

* * *

GRANT, H. Roger 1943-

PERSONAL: Born November 28, 1943, in Ottumwa, Iowa; son of H. R. (a produce wholesaler) and J. Marcella (a teacher; maiden name, Dinsmore) Grant; married Martha Farrington (a social worker), June 12, 1966; children: Julia Dinsmore. *Education:* Simpson College, B.A., 1966; University of Missouri, M.A., 1967, Ph.D., 1970. *Religion:* Unitarian-Universalist. *Home:* 737 Mentor Rd., Akron, Ohio 44303. *Office:* Department of History, University of Akron, Akron, Ohio 44325.

CAREER: University of Akron, Akron, Ohio, assistant professor, 1970-75, associate professor of history, 1975—. *Member:* American Historical Association, Organization of American Historians, Lexington Group, Southern Historical Association. *Awards, honors:* Woodrow Wilson fellow, 1966, 1969.

WRITINGS: (Editor) *An Icarian Communist in Nauvoo,* Illinois State Historical Society, 1971; (with L. Edward Purcell) *Years of Struggle: Farm Diary of Elmer G. Powers, 1931-1936,* Iowa State University Press, 1976; (with Charles W. Bohi) *The Country Railroad Station in America,* Pruett, 1978; *Insurance Reform: Consumer Action in the Progressive Era,* Iowa State University Press, 1979. Contributor to numerous history journals.

WORK IN PROGRESS: Self-help: America Confronts the Depression of the 1890's, publication expected in 1982; *The Chicago Great Western Railway,* publication expected in 1983.

GRANT, James G. 1926(?)-1979

OBITUARY NOTICE: Born c. 1926; died of a heart attack, September 15, 1979, in Westchester County, N.Y. Editor and author. An associate editor of *Time* magazine, Grant specialized in writing articles on business and economic affairs. Before joining *Time* in 1967, he had been a political reporter for the *Newburgh News* in New York and assistant managing editor of *Sales Management* magazine. Obituaries and other sources: *New York Times,* September 17, 1979.

* * *

GRAU, Shirley Ann 1929-

PERSONAL: Born July 8, 1929, in New Orleans, La.; daughter of Adolph Eugene and Katherine (Onions) Grau; married James Kern Feibleman (a professor at Tulane University), August 4, 1955; children: Ian James, Nora Miranda, William Leopold, Katherine Sara. *Education:* Tulane University, B.A. (honors in English), 1950. *Politics:* Democrat. *Religion:* Unitarian Universalist. *Residence:* New Orleans, La. *Agent:* Brandt & Brandt, 101 Park Ave., New York, N.Y. 10017.

CAREER: Novelist and short story writer. Board member, St. Martin's Episcopal School, New Orleans, La. *Member:* Phi Beta Kappa, Southern Yacht Club, Metaerie Country Club. *Awards, honors:* Pultizer Prize, 1965, for *The Keepers of the House.*

WRITINGS—All published by Knopf, except as noted: *The Black Prince and Other Stories,* 1955; *The Hard Blue Sky* (novel), 1958; *The House on Coliseum Street* (novel), 1961; (author of foreword) George Washington Cable, *Old Creole Days,* New American Library, 1961; *The Keepers of the House* (novel), 1964; *The Condor Passes* (novel), 1971; *The Wind Shifting West* (stories), 1973; *Evidence of Love* (novel), Random House, 1977. Contributor of stories and articles to journals and magazines, including *Atlantic, New Yorker,* and *Redbook.*

WORK IN PROGRESS: More fiction (novels and short stories).

SIDELIGHTS: Shirley Ann Grau made her entrance on the literary scene with considerable fanfare. *The Black Prince and Other Stories* was hailed as one of the most important books of 1955. Coleman Rosenberger declared, "We are in the presence of a literary event: the appearance of a new writer of unmistakable talent." A *Time* magazine reviewer called it "the most impressive U.S. short story debut between hard covers since J. D. Salinger's *Nine Stories.*"

In *The Black Prince,* Grau describes a primitive world and the conditions of survival for its white and black inhabitants. Set along the bayous of the Mississippi, her stories record "frustration and violence and death," but also "serenity, achievement, and life," stated William Peden. And though Grau usually limits herself to observable facts, noted Louise Y. Gossett, she occasionally introduces the supernatural, as in her title story. In "The Black Prince," violence erupts all around a black Lucifer-figure who mints coins from wax, seduces women with his wealth and power, and is finally dispatched with a magic silver bullet. In other stories, Gossett observed, "she sketches the primal roots of all human experience" and details the rudimentary conflict between man and nature, "depicting a direct relationship which has become increasingly rare in a mechanized world."

Grau has said that she rewrites everything at least three times, and several critics recognized in this early work the elements of her meticulous craftsmanship. Riley Hughes commented, "In all of these stories she has caught the authentic slur of speech, the slant of shadow on a blue night, and the random, spiraling movement of life." Likening Grau's initial success to that of Eudora Welty, John Nerber wrote in the *New York Times:* "Without being in the least like Miss Welty . . . , Miss Grau has the same unmistakable authority, the instinctive feeling for form and language, and that pervasive relish for the wonderful particularities of human nature that are part of the equipment of the born writer." William Peden added, "she is able, intelligent, and honest; her work is completely lacking in pretentiousness, bombast, or affectation." Other critics compared her lean prose to that of Hemingway, noting the simplicity and detachment of her characterization and her precise, impersonal treatment of nature.

Grau's first novel, *Hard Blue Sky,* returns to a primitive setting, the tiny Isle aux Chiens situated at the mouth of the Mississippi. In this isolated world live an inbred populace of French and Spanish descent who stoically confront the hazards of nature and their own volatile passions. Instead of a central plot, Grau uses interwoven episodes and flashbacks to dramatize a series of crises in the lives of individual islanders, while the community as a whole awaits the first hurricane of summer. In one episode Henry Livaudais vanishes into a swamp with a girl from a neighboring island. The incident sets off violent warfare between the two rival island groups, but it also leads Henry's mother to reaffirm her love for her husband by accepting his bastard son as her own. Another narrative strand focuses on the confusion and sexual anxieties of young Annie Landry, emphasizing "the psychological experiences that are typical of the adolescent in contemporary fiction," Gossett remarked.

The book met with good reviews. According to *Kirkus Reviews,* "This island world, alien and apart and tempered by the whims of the sea and the sky, has a somnolent fascination; the vitality and the violence of the lives it shapes are retained and reflected with a very realistic but unquestionable lyricism." In Gene Baro's view, "Grau has delineated her characters with firm individuality. . . . And, of course, she has rendered the physical world with distinction, sometimes with severe beauty, so that the island's summer heat, its salt-laden wind, blue sky, and cloudy water, its singing trees and clapboard houses are palpable to our senses." Added Elizabeth Bartelme: "You come off this island knowing the people intimately, the pattern and rhythm of their speech, the things that have shaped their lives, their fortitude, humor, simplicity."

Grau departs from the primitive with her second novel, *The House on Coliseum Street.* Dealing now with the complexities of life in New Orleans, Grau explores the heart and mind of a young woman, Joan Mitchell, whose affair with a man she does not love leads to an abortion and her obsessive need for revenge. After the abortion, Gossett observed, "she enacts in her life the death of her fetal child. She withdraws from reality and substitutes for it the sharp observation of scattered details. Miss Grau's skill in making hard and clear descriptions gives the dissociation of Joan the circumstantial vividness of a dream which cannot be forgotten." Commented *Kirkus Reviews,* "It is a sad, wistful, young, timeless story, graced by this writer's fine drawn perceptions of lives which are private but never ingrown, and by the still, soft enchantment of her prose."

In her Pulitzer Prize-winning *The Keepers of the House,* Grau chronicles three generations of the Howland family, set in the southern Delta country. After the death of his first wife and his daughter's marriage, plantation owner William Howland takes a black mistress, Margaret, into his home. He later gives shelter to his granddaughter, Abigail, after her mother's death, whom he and Margaret raise together with their three children. Margaret's children are eventually sent North to school, where they can "pass" for white and where they are expected to remain all their lives. Meanwhile, Abigail marries a segregationist politician who builds his career on the Howland name and the exploitation of racial prejudice. Their marriage collapses when, just before the gubernatorial primary, one of Margaret's children returns to provide proof that Will and Margaret were married. Abigail's husband deserts her and their children, angry whites attack the Howland plantation, and Abigail moves to defend her inheritance and to take revenge on the town. Wielding the wealth and power of the Howland estate, Abigail closes down the hotel, withholds her timber from market, and refuses to restock the slaughterhouse, dairy, and packing plant.

In his review of the book, Granville Hicks stated: "A novel of considerable dramatic force. Miss Grau makes her point—the absurdities as well as the cruelties to which prejudice leads—sharply enough, but this is a story, not a tract. The characters are striking, Margaret as well as William, and vigorously portrayed. . . . All the virtues of Miss Grau's earlier books are here, together with a new power." F. C. Crews contended that "her lucidity, her narrative directness, her reliance on the bare details of her plot instead of on ponderous philosophizing—all are non-Faulknerian traits, and in her hands they are agreeable virtues."

Critic Alwyn Berland concluded in 1963 that Grau's fiction lacked "the firm center, the center of a vision" and suggested that she was a "fictional anthropologist," one who records but does not interpret events. The author herself had a few years earlier announced that she has "no cause and no message." Accordingly, critics held that Grau remained a writer of great though unfulfilled promise; they awaited the appearance of some dominant, unifying theme or explicit philosophical view that would illuminate the purpose of her work.

One of those who attempted to resolve the nature of Grau's fictional world was Louise Gossett. In her 1965 study, *Violence in Recent Southern Fiction,* Gossett found that Grau "represents a new romanticism which cultivates the isolated and the out-of-the-way," whose bayou and island people are "new innocents in modern literature." Significantly, though, her primitives are not inspired with humanistic ideals or the beauty of nature; man is not "a free agent protected by his environment," but a stoic "reconciled to the terms of reality" and the "violence of nature which assails him." In the modern, urban setting, however, the experience of isolation is chiefly psychological. "Unrelated to their environment or to other persons," the characters are neurotic, rootless, and self-destructive, feeding on "sensations moment by moment without thinking them into meanings." The violence they exhibit "denotes anxiety, frustration, and insecurity. . . . If a simple equation were to be drawn it would link weakness with the city where man is anonymous and strength with the island where man perforce reckons with the natural world and where he trusts his community."

Muriel Haynes claimed that Grau's 1971 novel, *The Condor Passes,* psychologically ties the "obsession with money to the flight from death" and offers "an implicit argument for Dionysian man." Thomas Henry Oliver, referred to throughout the novel as the Old Man, has built a financial empire on a network of brothels and bootlegging operations in New Orleans. After three generations of wealth, power, and dominance over others, the Old Man lies at the point of death. The story of his corrupting influence and money is told from the multiple points-of-view of those who attend his bedside. Clearly, Grau has associated the ancient patriarch with the condor, drawing on the bird of Indian legend that carried messages to the other world, and with the natural, exotic world of his tropical greenhouse. Each successive generation of the family, however, demonstrates a moral, spiritual, even physical degeneracy that, as Ann Pearson observed, is "at least partially revealed in [the] rejection of nature."

According to Haynes, "[Grau] has centered her narrative on the deformations of sexuality, reflecting the split between body and mind, that are a particular disease of our acquisitive culture. From an inability to accept death—that is, to live freely in the body—there follows the paradoxical consequence of death in life. The money drive, Grau seems to be saying, is a morbid surrender of the body's creativity to the waste it must become, and we literally cannot 'come to our senses' until we acknowledge its neurotic impulse." In contrast to most of the other characters, Pearson noted, the Old Man's close identification with birds and exotic flowers integrates him with the forces of nature, granting him both strength and longevity. "It also reveals Grau's perception of nature as a vitalizing force as opposed to the indifference of the hard blue sky," she added.

Pearson is another critic who has tried to discover an overall purpose behind Grau's fiction. In her 1975 essay, "Shirley Ann Grau: Nature Is the Vision," she wrote: "A close examination of her work seems to yield only one plausible suggestion: she is portraying a world dominated by the seasons that only obliquely has meaning. Her only definable vision of the world lies in her perception of the ever present closeness of nature, that 'hard blue sky' which rules the lives of her characters. Thus, nature is her vision, the focal point of her best fiction." She also noted that Grau rarely integrates nature with the emotional life of her characters (the Old Man in *The Condor Passes* is one of the few exceptions). "Perhaps she is, then, the most pessimistic Southern contemporary, for her characters move, love, and die amid bright foliage, immense wealth, or grinding poverty, yet they rarely perceive a transcendent joy that reconciles them with the natural order."

A second collection of short stories, *The Wind Shifting West,* appeared in 1973. In Joan Joffe Hall's estimation, "the volume as a whole is satisfying because it consistently and without fanfare delivers [Grau's] vision of stoical endurance." Many of the stories illustrate a moment of self-realization, occasioned by the loneliness or isolation that follows "an intimate's death or departure, the approach of old age, or the emptiness of sex," noted Melody Hardy. Of particular concern here, Hall observed, is the response of women to these experiences. Unlike the self-destructive or emotionally violent women in the fiction of Joan Didion, Joy Williams, and Joyce Carol Oates, she contended, "Grau seldom strikes a self-pitying note. . . . One sees the strength that's gone into the rejection of passion and despair. For Grau's characters it's more important to cope with life than to fight against its conditions. Stoic endurance is a conventional female response, but Grau's best stories dramatize why it is better than emotionalism, passivity, or self-destruction."

In her fifth novel, *Evidence of Love,* Grau unfolds another family history that in some ways recalls *The Condor Passes.* Edward Milton Henley, like the Old Man, is a wealthy, self-indulgent patriarch whose extreme old age adds a mythic dimension to his character. As Mary Rohrberger observed, he takes on the role of Dionysus, buys a host of lovers, and "sublimates his real needs in sexual encounters," seeking all the while for some experience of the transcendent. Stephen, the son he begets by a woman he bought, rejects both his father and sexuality, becomes a Unitarian minister and classical scholar, and marries Lucy, who is also depleted of sexual desires. Throughout the novel, the modern search for love and meaning is attended by images, dreams, and fantasies of death, and love remains barely more than a shadowy possibility. Whereas Henley and Stephen vainly pursue some illusory, transcendent ideal, whether sexual or intellectual, only Lucy comes to terms with the natural cycle of birth and death, stoically resolved to face the isolation of a life without love.

Concluding her review of the book, Rohrberger declared that "*Evidence of Love* is a finely crafted, tightly woven, and powerful novel by a major American author whose works deserve far better treatment than they have received in myriad reviews. Shirley Ann Grau won't be confined, and as *Evidence of Love* indicates, her novels are the better for it."

CA INTERVIEWS THE AUTHOR

Shirley Ann Grau was interviewed by *CA* in February, 1979.

CA: You've created quite a range of characters from the primitives of the bayous in The Hard Blue Sky *to the complex figures in* Evidence of Love. *Do you base characters on people you've known?*

GRAU: Well, that's an extremely difficult question because there is no single answer to it. *The Keepers of the House* is based largely on family stories, but not with complete accuracy. In *The Condor Passes* the central character is based on two newspaper stories of men I've never met. I read their obituaries in the Chicago papers a very long time ago. The stories simply stuck and then eventually they came together and made one character. I combined this already combined character with some New Orleans stories I knew and put it together that way. I suppose the old man in *Evidence of Love* is as close to actual reporting as I've ever done; he is drawn more or less from life. But again you change things as you go along so it's really more misleading to say they are drawn from life than anything else. They may have started out as real people, but by the time you've changed them and heightened them. . . . Fictional characters have to be a little brighter colored than ordinary people to come through; they have to be bigger and brighter and more positive or negative in their actions just to make the dramatic point.

CA: You've been compared with several Southern writers. Do you feel that you've been strongly influenced by any one of them in particular?

GRAU: I don't think about myself very much—we'll start there. I suppose I've read just about all the Southern writers. I've read a bit of Faulkner and don't like him. I greatly admire Carson McCullers; I know I've read everything of hers, including the later work which is really not up to her level, but after all the poor woman was very ill. It seems to me that she has a vision and a strength in her writing that very few writers anywhere have. I also like Welty, though she annoys me because she is so deliberately small. It's perfectly beautiful; but it's always cameo, and I suppose I tend to like the bigger canvas. But she is an extraordinarily gifted writer. I haven't read her last book, but I'm chronically late in my reading. There are some few less well-known Southern writers that I like, too. I suppose it's inevitable that critics try to group writers regionally, but I don't think it's terribly helpful most times.

CA: Do you think that anyone who is within that region then is likely to be assessed from a regional point of view?

GRAU: Yes, oh, goodness yes. I suppose critics have to have a handle, or some way of classifying, but regional grouping seems to me not to make too much sense. Of course, the classification "woman writer" drives me absolutely mad. Isn't it awful? I mean, it's as if it were a special division, not quite up to—you know, there is a writer, then there is a woman writer, and one is sort of junior grade, like lieutenant junior grade in the Navy. It's very tiresome. And the patronizing that lurks behind it really is annoying. But I think perhaps the most harmful thing about the critical approach to Southern writing is that people have tended to value it in terms of its quaintness. You know, a little old darkie singing "Swanee River" or "Down by the Riverside" sort of thing. That isn't at all what's valuable or interesting. Truman Capote, for example, had to go to outlandish lengths to get rid of the label. I think *In Cold Blood* probably laid to rest his Southern label forever. By the way he's a remarkably fine writer. *Other Voices, Other Rooms* seems to me for its time—and it must be thirty years old now—a fantastic book. But anyway, we don't have Southern writing anymore. We have lots of writers in the South, but they tend to be writing without a strong regional background.

CA: In your last two books you moved away from the Southern setting. Was part of the reason behind that an attempt to avoid being categorized?

GRAU: I suppose that is what I did. I'm not sure that's what I set out to do. You begin with a story and some people, and they have a natural setting. I have rather left the primitives, I think—I hate to use that word for them—the French-speaking country folk of *Hard Blue Sky*. I have rather left them because that world has pretty much vanished. Civilization, if you care to call it that, has rather swept through. They're even teaching French in school. It's no longer a natural language; it's sort of been embalmed and put into the schools. So I have moved from that to—well, let me go back and say I think writing is a set of problems to be solved. In my first novels people were concerned with the immediate problems of survival. Now I've tried to move on to city—dwelling people who have solved the today problems and have other problems—problems of right and wrong, say. That's just a rough description. But their problems are far more complicated and more bound by tradition—what is done, what isn't done. In a way such people are much more difficult to do. But still I can only follow where my instinct leads me.

CA: There was a character from South Africa in Evidence of Love.

GRAU: For years my hobby has been reading South African and Indian diaries. There are quite a lot of diaries around, by the way—by people you've never heard of. They're published privately, usually by their sons and grandsons. I've been fascinated ever since I read Isak Dinesen's *Out of Africa* when I was in high school. I've read just about everything I can. So when I needed a setting for a character who had to be different, an outsider, I made her a white woman in Africa. It's to point up her differentness, aloneness, isolation. I had my hobby to draw on, and she fitted right into the landscape. She's a bit of a cross between all of the people in the various diaries, journals, and silly little books they wrote about Africa. None of them could write very well, but if you put them all together you get a very nice feel of a place. Their eyes were less complicated than ours are today, so it's in many ways a very childish picture, but very useful for somebody who's not been there.

CA: You've indicated that you chose writing as a career partly because you felt it would allow you to control your hours somewhat and to work at home. I believe I read that in an interview. And you've produced a steady flow of good work and raised a sizable family at the same time. How do you manage it?

GRAU: You start out with very healthy children. You know, nothing has ever really been wrong with them. I'm quite sure I could never have one of those nine-to-five jobs or ten-to-five. It's everything that I dislike. And I have never really liked working in a group. I think practically all writers are loners. That is why I've always avoided any sort of writing that put me in a group. I like to go in my little room and slam the door. I think freedom—personal freedom—is the most important thing in the world and this is a way of having it. No one bothers you; you can write or not write. It's just about the only job you can combine with a house and four children and something approaching a normal social life. I don't want to be isolated totally except during the day. I like crowds of people after five o'clock. It is absolutely heaven if you can do it. When the children were little I'll admit I was rather sleepy some days, but it can be done. I'm sure I could step up my writing pace now, because my children are no longer babies at home. It just seems to me that writing has to be part of a general approach to life, and though it's terribly important, it has to fit into your whole plan of things.

CA: In previous interviews you've expressed varying opinions about criticism and have indicated that your reactions to it have changed through the years. How do you feel now? Do you find any criticism intelligent and helpful?

GRAU: I'll start by saying there is nobody who can't stand improvement, and if criticism is helpful and specific that's great. Everyone needs a sort of second-eye view, an objective look. That sort of criticism is fine. And that is what you almost never get. What I have objected to, I think, is that criticism is done so carelessly. Not necessarily the critics' fault. They have to turn out so many reviews in such a short time that carelessness just is inevitable. I used to read them, and I used to be upset by them, and then I noticed that sometimes an error from an early review appeared in later reviews. The critics had not read the book, they had only read the earlier review. It's such careless quality of reviewing that bothers me. We don't really have a major book reviewer in this country. But then we don't really have a major book review either, do we? The sort of thing the English have with their *Books and Bookmen* and *British Book News*.

CA: How do you feel about the New York Times Book Review?

GRAU: It's constantly changing. The reviewers, with only one or two exceptions, constantly change. Some are marvelous, and some even fail to tell you what the book is about. I read reviews to see if I want to invest ten or twelve dollars in the book. I need a review to tell me what the book is, more than anything else. I would love to have a regular weekly critic, someone whose likes and dislikes, even if I didn't agree with them, were the prejudices of a civilized man. That's what we don't have, not really. It's a pity, because most people's only guide to books is an occasional review. Too bad. Some newspapers do excellent reviewing and some do miserably. So I don't quite know how you improve that except to pay more money to book reviewers, which no one is about to do.

CA: Your first published work was a short story, wasn't it?

GRAU: You mean my collection? Yes, I had a collection of short stories.

CA: What made you decide to do a novel? Was it part of your plan all along or was there some specific reason that you moved from short stories to novels?

GRAU: I don't really think that my plans were that specific. It just seemed to me that I had a story that needed the extra length of a novel, so I turned into a novelist. I haven't done short stories in, goodness, quite a few years now. I don't really know why.

CA: What about the essays? I read some of your travel essays, in Holiday *and* McCall's.

GRAU: I think that's all I've done.

CA: Did they fit into your work in a certain way at that time? Are you doing any more?

GRAU: Not really. I did them when I was first starting out and I simply had to build up experience. They're all travel pieces and though they were all in this general area, I don't think they specifically led into anything. They were great fun to do, a wonderful change of pace. It's a way of paying for a pleasant weekend.

CA: They created a nice mood.

GRAU: That's what they were supposed to do, to give the reader an idea of what the place was like rather than specific guidelines.

CA: Have you been approached to do any screenwriting?

GRAU: I suppose most writers get periodic offers, you know, but again it's always New York or the West Coast and I'm very happy here with a house and my garden and my three dogs and my one cat. As I said before, I don't really like to work with people. So I just stay here and, like Candide, tend my garden.

CA: Has there been any talk of adapting your novels for the movies?

GRAU: Oh, goodness, there is always movie talk. Most of it, though, has had the requirement that I do the screenplay. I don't go to the movies very much so I tend to be rather cavalier about the whole thing. I think the last movie I saw was "The Sting" and that does date me. I live sort of an isolated life, let's put it that way, and I just rattle around doing exactly what I please. I'm perfectly content doing it this way. A visualization would be nice, but only if someone else would do it. I am not a script writer. I am not a dramatist in that sense, and I'm sure I'd do it badly—that's the other reason. Purely practical. I don't think I could do a decent job. It's an entirely different discipline, I'm quite sure of that; and I suppose one could learn it, but it is something new that would have to be learned.

CA: How do you go about researching a book? Do you have any researchers to help you or do you just settle in at the library or go to whatever spot you need to find things out?

GRAU: I don't really consciously research. Over the years I've had certain hobbies or interests like the South African, Kenyan, life, but otherwise I only read newspapers, five or six a day, English and American. My mailman just hates me because there are so many. I rely on a very good memory, a lot of reading, newspapers and otherwise. I hate to travel, but I just adore reading travel books, and some places seem so fascinating that you want to stay there and learn a lot more about them. I suppose sooner or later those turn up in my writing. It's as simple as this! I have a lot of accumulated stories and I just pull them out when needed.

CA: Have you given any conscious thought to where you fit into fiction today? Do you have any goals?

GRAU: I'm not sure I can make out the shape of American fiction today. It seems to have so many directions that I don't know—I just can't think it out. As I said, the regional schools seem to be fairly well gone. We're going into a—what shall we call it—sort of an eternal landscape, people without any strong attachments to the scene they're in, like John Cheever's modern man, but he could be anywhere—that sort of thing. Lord knows where I fit in, because I find myself admiring all sorts of writers. For example, I like Louis Auchincloss very much, but I'm also fascinated by the writings of William Eastlake. Those two men have nothing in common, just nothing, but they both seem to say something to me. So Lord knows where I belong. I tend to avoid generalizations because they sound either trite or pompous. But it would seem to me that I have always wanted to put into words the enormous diversity of people, and if you like, the humor. Man is an amazing and, spectacular sight. I hope to write about him with affection and considerable admiration.

BIOGRAPHICAL/CRITICAL SOURCES: *New York Times,* January 16, 1955; *New York Herald Tribune Book Review,* January 16, 1955, June 22, 1958; *Time,* January 24, 1955, June 23, 1958, April 10, 1964, February 7, 1977; *Saturday Review,* January 29, 1955, March 21, 1964, September 18, 1971, February 19, 1977; *Catholic World,* March, 1955; *New York Times Book Review,* July 10, 1955, March 22, 1964, September 19, 1971, October 16, 1977; *Newsweek,* December 26, 1955; *Kirkus Reviews,* April 15, 1958, April 15, 1961; *Commonweal,* July 11, 1958; *Critique,* Volume 6, number 1, 1963, Volume 17, number 2, 1975; *Chicago Tribune Book Week,* March 22, 1964; *New Republic,* April 18, 1964, September 18, 1971, November 24, 1973; Louise Y. Gossett, *Violence in Recent Southern Fiction,* Duke University Press, 1965; *Washington Post Book World,* October 10, 1971, November 27, 1973; *New York Review of Books,* December 2, 1971; *Best Sellers,* January 1, 1974; *Sewanee Review,* fall, 1974; *Contemporary Literary Criticism,* Gale, Volume 4, 1975, Volume 9, 1978; *New Yorker,* March 21, 1977; *Hudson Review,* autumn, 1977; *New Statesman,* September 30, 1977; *Observer,* October 2, 1977; *Southern Review,* winter, 1978; *Dictionary of Literary Biography,* Volume 2, Gale, 1978.

—Interview by Jean W. Ross

—Sketch by B. Hal May

* * *

GRAY, Angela
See DANIELS, Dorothy

* * *

GRAY, Philip
See PERLMAN, Jess

* * *

GRAYSON, L(inda) M(ary) 1947-

PERSONAL: Born March 28, 1947, in Toronto, Ontario,

Canada; daughter of James Ambrose (a welder) and Mary (a civil servant; maiden name, O'Brien) Forrest; married J. Paul Grayson (a professor and writer), August 25, 1970; children: Kyle Andrew. *Education:* York University, B.A., 1969; University of Toronto, M.A., 1970, Ph.D., 1974. *Religion:* Agnostic. *Home:* 186 Bessborough Dr., Toronto, Ontario M4G 3J9, Canada. *Office:* Department of History, University of Toronto, Erindale College, Mississauga, Ontario L5L 1C6, Canada.

CAREER: University of Waterloo, St. Jerome's College, Waterloo, Ontario, assistant professor of history, 1973-75; University of Toronto, Erindale College, Toronto, Ontario, assistant professor of history, 1976—; writer. Part-time lecturer at York University, Atkinson College, Toronto, 1975-76. Member of Historical and Arts Board of East New York, 1979—. *Member:* Canadian Historical Association.

WRITINGS: (Co-editor with J. Michael Bliss) *The Wretched of Canada,* University of Toronto Press, 1971; (with husband, J. Paul Grayson) *Paddles and Wheels,* Oxford University Press, 1974; (co-editor with Samuel Clark and J. Grayson) *Prophecy and Protest: Social Movements in Twentieth-Century Canada,* Gage Educational Publishing, 1975. Contributor with J. Grayson to scholarly journals, including *Canadian Journal of Political Science, Canadian Review of Sociology and Anthropology, Canadian Forum,* and *Canadian Journal of Sociology.*

WORK IN PROGRESS: Work on Grace Anne Lockhart, "first woman granted a bachelor's degree (1875) by a university in the British Empire"; and "an analysis of significant social movements in twentieth-century Canada."

SIDELIGHTS: Grayson told *CA:* "*The Wretched of Canada* is still, for me, the most important contribution that I have made.

"For too long, the thirties in Canada were surrounded with myths—myths that obscured the real tragedies of the economic collapse. More importantly, the letters contained in the book clearly demonstrated the extent to which the 'false consciousness' of the victims had led them to believe that the fault for the calamity was their own.

"Since the publication of this first effort my interests have been moving in two separate, but related directions. The first is the unequal and disadvantaged position of the 'neglected majority'—women. The second is the examination of those (namely creative writers) who contribute much to the maintenance and development of a dominant ideology that justifies the unequal distribution of wealth, power, and opportunity in our society."

* * *

GREE, Alain 1936-

PERSONAL: Surname is pronounced "Gray"; born July 21, 1936, in Paris, France; son of Henri (in business) and Jeanne (Distinguin) Gree; married Monique Farge, February 24, 1960; children: Isabelle, Florence. *Education:* Ecole des Arts Appliques, Paris, diploma, 1955; attended Ecole des Beaux Arts, 1956-57. *Home and office:* 6 rue du Commandant Lareinty, St. Cloud 92, France.

CAREER: Writer and illustrator. *Military service:* French Army Reserve, 1959-67; became lieutenant.

WRITINGS—All for children, except as noted: (Self-illustrated) *Happy Morning* (translation from the original French edition), Ward, Lock, 1962; (self-illustrated) *Morning Noises* (translation from the original French edition), Wonder Books, 1962; (with Paul Guth) *Moustique dans la lune,* Casterman, 1963; (self-illustrated) *Home Sweet Home* (translation from the original French edition), Ward, Lock, 1964; *Les Ratons Laveurs dans la lune* (title means "The Racoons on the Moon"), Deux Coqs d'Ors, 1967; *Mini-Max,* Vilo, 1969; *Je sais tout* (title means "I Know Everything"), Hachette, 1969; *Let's Go to the Moon* (translation from the original French edition), Hamlyn, 1970; *Cesar le petit canard qui voulait faire le tour du monde* (title means "Cesar the Little Duck Who Wanted to Tour the World"), Casterman, 1972; *Mon premier alphabet* (title means "My First Alphabet"), Casterman, 1972; *The Home* (translation from the original French edition), Ward, Lock, 1972; *Beebo and the Funny Machine,* translated by Fix, J. Cape, 1975; *Beebo and the Fizzimen* (translation from the original French edition), J. Cape, 1975; (with Janine Ast) *The House That Beebo Built* (translation from the original French edition), J. Cape, 1975; *Voile-ecole* (for adults), Hachette, 1977, translation published as *Sailing: A Basic Guide,* Viking, 1979.

"Achille et Bergamote" series; all self-illustrated; all French editions published by Casterman; all English adaptations by Annemarie Ryba: *Achille et Bergamote en route,* 1963, adaptation published as *Keith and Sally Go Abroad,* Evans Brothers, 1965; *La Mer,* 1963, adaptation published as *Keith and Sally at the Seaside,* Evans Brothers, 1965; *La Ville* (title means "The City"), 1963; *La Foret,* 1964, adaptation published as *Sally and Billy in the Woods,* Hart, 1968; *Les Trains* (title means "Trains"), 1964; *Le Petrole,* 1965, adaptation published as *Keith and Sally Look for Oil,* 1967; *Les Navires,* adaptation published as *Sally and Billy Look at Ships,* Hart, 1965; *La Ferme,* 1965, adaptation published as *Sally and Billy on the Farm,* Hart, 1967, published as *The Farm,* Ward, Lock, 1972; *La Riviere,* 1966, adaptation published as *Keith and Sally by the River,* 1968; *La Montagne,* 1967, adaptation published as *The Mountains,* Ward, Lock, 1973; *La Television,* 1967, adaptation published as *Keith and Sally Look at Television,* Evans Brothers, 1969; *Sous l'-ocean* (title means "Under the Ocean"), 1967; *Au jardin,* 1968, adaptation published as *Keith and Sally in the Garden,* Evans Brothers, 1969; *L'Automobile* (title means "The Car"), 1968; *L'Electricite* (title means "Electricity"), 1969; *Petit Atlas* (title means "Little Atlas"), 1969; *Les Oiseaux,* 1970, adaptation published as *Keith and Sally's Bird Book,* Evans Brothers, 1972; *Les Plantes,* 1971, adaptation published as *Keith and Sally's Plant Book,* 1972; *Les Sports* (title means "Sports"), 1971; *L'Espace* (title means "Space"), 1972; *Les Insects* (title means "Insects"), 1974; *L'Energie* (title means "Energy"), 1976; *L'Eau* (title means "Water"), 1978.

"Romeo" series; all self-illustrated; all French editions published by Casterman: *Romeo cherche un emploi,* 1966, translation published as *Romeo Looks for a Job,* Lutterworth Press, 1968; *Romeo, champion de la neige* (title means "Romeo, Champion of the Snow"), 1967; *Romeo fait du cinema* (title means "Romeo Makes Movies"), 1968; *Romeo construit une fusee* (title means "Romeo Builds a Rocket"), 1968; *Romeo apprend la musique,* translation published as *Romeo Becomes a Musician,* Lutterworth Press, 1968; *Romeo pilote un avion,* 1967, translation published as *Romeo Flies a Plane,* Lutterworth Press, 1968; *Romeo veut faire fortune,* 1967, translation published as *Romeo Seeks a Fortune,* Lutterworth Press, 1968.

"I Know" series; all French editions published by Hachette, 1968; all English editions published by Methuen: *J'apprends a reconnaitre les fleurs,* translation published as *I Know About Flowers,* 1970; *J'apprends les autos,* translation published as *I Know About Cars,* 1970; *J'apprends a reconnaitre les couleurs,* translation published as *I Know About Colors,* 1970; *J'apprends a compter,* translation published as *I Know About Counting,* 1970; *J'apprends la geographie,* translation published as *I Know About Our World,* 1970; *J'apprends a reconnaitre les animaux,* translation published as *I Know About Animals,* 1971; *J'apprends a voyager.*

"Look" series; all French editions published by Hachette, 1968; all English editions published by Methuen, 1971; *Qu'est-ce qui tourne?,* translation published as *Look What Goes Round; Qu'est-ce qui fume?,* translation published as *Look What Smokes; Qu'est-ce qui vole?,* translation published as *Look What Flies.*

"Story" series; all French editions published by Hachette, 1968; all English editions published by Methuen: *Une Voiture m'a raconte,* translation published as *The Story of a Car,* 1971; *Un Voilier m'a raconte,* translation published as *The Story of a Ship,* 1971; *Un Wagon m'a raconte,* translation published as *The Story of a Train,* 1971; *Un Camion m'a raconte,* translation published as *The Story of a Truck,* 1972; *Une Fusee m'a raconte,* translation published as *The Story of a Rocket,* 1972; *Un Avion m'a raconte,* translation published as *The Story of an Aeroplane,* 1972; *Un Tracteur m'a raconte.*

"Find" series; all French editions published by Hachette, 1968; all English editions published by Methuen: *Il y a un petit poussin,* translation published as *Find the Yellow Chicken,* 1970; *Il y a un poisson rouge,* translation published as *Find the Goldfish,* 1970; *Il y a une petite abeille,* translation published as *Find the Bee,* 1971.

"Petit Tom" series; illustrated by Gerard Gree; all French editions published by Casterman: *Petit Tom decouvre les maisons* (title means "Little Tom Discovers Houses"), 1969; . . . *et son ami l'arbre* (title means ". . . and His Friend the Tree"), 1969; . . . *et les produits de la nature* (title means ". . . and the Products of Nature"), 1969; . . . *decouvre les formes* (title means ". . . Discovers the Forms"), 1970; . . . *et son amie l'abeille* (title means ". . . and His Friend the Bee"), 1971; *Un Journee de . . .* (title means "A Day of . . ."), 1971; . . . *et les instruments de musique* (title means ". . . and Musical Instruments"), 1972; . . . *veut tout mesurer,* adaptation by Alexandra Chapman published as *Tell Me About Measures,* Grosset, 1972; . . . *decouvre les couleurs,* adaption by Chapman published as *Tell Me About Color,* Grosset, 1972; . . . *et les animaux familiers,* 1972, adaptation by Lebreton published as *Little Tom and Some Animal Friends,* Harrap, 1978; . . . *sait lire l'heure,* adaptation by Lebreton published as *Tom Learns About Time,* Harrap, 1978; . . . *fait dix decouvertes,* adaptation by Lebreton published as *Little Tom Makes Ten Discoveries,* Harrap, 1978. Also author of . . . *decouvre les saisons* (title means ". . . Discovers the Seasons"), . . . *protege la nature* (title means ". . . Protects Nature"), . . . *et le code de la route* (title means ". . . and Road Signals"), . . . *et les secrets des bois* (title means ". . . and the Secrets of the Woods"), and . . . *et les malices de la nature* (title means ". . . and the Transformations of Nature").

"Les Farfeluches" series; all illustrated by Luis Camps; all published by Casterman: *Les Farfeluches a l'ecole* (title means "The Farfeluches at School"), 1973; . . . *au marche* (title means ". . . in the Market"), 1973; . . . *au bord de la mer* (title means ". . . at the Seashore"), 1973; . . . *a la maison* (title means ". . . at Home"), 1973; . . . *au cirque* (title means ". . . at the Circus"), 1973; . . . *prennent le train* (title means ". . . Take the Train"), 1973; . . . *au zoo* (title means ". . . at the Zoo"), 1975; . . . *en pleine action* (title means ". . . Moving"), 1976; *Vrai ou faux: les Farfeluches en vacances* (title means "True or False: The Farfeluches on Vacation"), 1976; . . . *font des achats* (title means ". . . in the Stores"), 1977; . . . *choisissent un metier,* 1978; . . . *aiment les animaux,* 1979. Also author of . . . *a la compagne* (title means ". . . in the Country") and . . . *sur la route* (title means ". . . on the Road").

"Le Liver-Jeu" series; all with games; all French editions published by Casterman: *Le Livre-Jeu de la foret* (title means "Books and Games of the Forest"), illustrated by Camps, 1970; . . . *du voyage* (title means ". . . of Travel"), illustrated by G. Gree, 1970; . . . *de la ferme,* illustrated by G. Gree, translation published as *The Farm,* Little, Brown, 1972; . . . *de la maison,* illustrated by Camps, 1971, translation published as *The Home,* 1972; . . . *de la montagne,* 1971; . . . *des voliers,* 1972, translation by Barbara Webb published as *Sailing,* Ward, Lock, 1974; . . . *des animaux,* illustrated by Camps, 1973, translation published as *The All-Color Activity Book of Animals,* Little, Brown, 1974; . . . *des metiers,* 1973; . . . *des saisons,* 1974; . . . *de l'aeroport* (title means ". . . of the Airport"), 1975; . . . *des quatre coins du monde,* 1978.

With records; all published by Casterman: *La Nature* (title means "Nature"), 1971; *Vitesse* (title means "Speed"), 1971; (illustrator) Francis Scaglia, *Popsy, la petite abeille qui allait plus vite que les autos* (title means "Popsy, the Little Bee Who Flies Faster Than Cars"), 1972; (illustrator) Scaglia, *Flap, le petit poisson qui voulait decouvrir l'ocean* (title means "Flap, the Little Fish Who Wanted to Discover the Ocean"), 1972; *Mille questions, mille responses* (title means "One Thousand Questions, One Thousand Answers"), 1974; *Pourquoi? Trente-huit questions de Petit Tom* (title means "Why? Little Tom's Thirty-Eight Questions"), 1975; *Quarante-cinq jeux pour tout seul* (title means "Forty-Five Games for Everyone"), 1975; *Quarante Jeux pour jouer a plusiers,* 1976.

Also author of activity books, *Acti-pile* and *Acti-boite.* Contributor of articles on ocean navigation to *Voiles et voiliers.*

WORK IN PROGRESS: An adult series of books on ocean navigation, publication by Gallimard.

SIDELIGHTS: Gree's books for children are both didactic and entertaining. Reviewing the "Achille et Bergamote" series, John Coleman noted that Gree's illustrations are also "beautifully clear and teaching."

A sailing enthusiast, Gree has cruised the Atlantic and the Caribbean. "I write on board," he says, "and it is a pleasure for me to join work and passion for the sea. When we help children to dream with books it is necessary to make dreams for ourselves."

Gree's books have been published in fifteen languages.

AVOCATIONAL INTERESTS: The sea, boating, travel (Tahiti, United States).

BIOGRAPHICAL/CRITICAL SOURCES: New Statesman, November 3, 1967.

* * *

GREEN, F(rederick) C(harles) 1891-1964

OBITUARY NOTICE: Born February 25, 1891, in Aberdeen, Scotland; died March 23, 1964. Educator and author of books on the French novel, including *Manners and Ideas: From the Renaissance to the Revolution* and *The Mind of Proust.* Green's criticism was rooted in Edwardianism. Among his other works are biographies of Rousseau and

Stendhal. Obituaries and other sources: *World Authors, 1950-1970,* Wilson, 1975.

* * *

GREENE, John C(olton) 1917-

PERSONAL: Born March 5, 1917, in Indianapolis, Ind.; son of Edward Martin (a professor) and Helen (Carter) Greene; married Ellen Wiemann, November, 1945; children: Ruth Greene Farooki, Edward, John David. *Education:* University of South Dakota, B.A., 1938; Harvard University, M.A., 1939, Ph.D., 1952. *Politics:* Independent. *Religion:* Protestant. *Home:* 10 Thompson Rd., Storrs, Conn. 06268. *Office:* Department of History, University of Connecticut, Storrs, Conn. 06268.

CAREER: University of Chicago, Chicago, Ill., instructor in history, 1948-52; University of Wisconsin, Madison, assistant professor of history, 1952-56; Iowa State University, Ames, associate professor, 1956-59, professor of history, 1959-62; University of California, Berkeley, visiting professor of history, 1962-63; University of Kansas, Lawrence, professor of history, 1963-67; University of Connecticut, Storrs, professor of history, 1967—. Visiting scholar at Corpus Christi College, Cambridge, 1974; visiting historian at Smithsonian Institution, 1978. *Military service:* U.S. Army, 1942-46; became captain; received Bronze Star. *Member:* International Academy of the History of Science (corresponding member), American Association of University Professors, History of Science Society (president, 1975-77), Midwest Junto of the History of Science (president, 1961), Society of Fellows of Harvard University, Phi Beta Kappa. *Awards, honors:* Guggenheim fellowship, 1966-67.

WRITINGS: The Death of Adam: Evolution and Its Impact on Western Thought, Iowa State University Press, 1959; *Darwin and the Modern World View,* Louisiana State University Press, 1961; (with John G. Burke) *The Science of Minerals in the Age of Jefferson,* American Philosophical Society, 1978. Contributor to learned journals.

WORK IN PROGRESS: American Science in the Age of Jefferson, publication by Harper expected in 1982; *From the Baconian Dream to the Orwellian Nightmare,* completion expected in 1985; a history of Darwinism, completion expected in 1987.

SIDELIGHTS: Greene writes: "I have two hats I wear: the history of evolutionary biology in the context of general intellectual history, and early American science. Starting out years ago with an interest in the relation between science and religion, I have been led on to a variety of studies of the influence and changing role of science in the Western world. More recently I have become interested in the historical relations of science, technology, society, and culture. Through these studies I hope to throw some light on the crisis of modern society and culture. I am a historian, not a scientist."

AVOCATIONAL INTERESTS: Music, tennis, travel.

* * *

GREENE, John William, Jr. 1946-
(Johnny Greene)

PERSONAL: Born July 24, 1946, in Demopolis, Ala.; son of John William (a farmer) and Frances Meador (Jones) Greene. *Education:* University of Alabama, B.A., 1971; Columbia University, M.F.A., 1973. *Religion:* Episcopalian. *Residence:* Tuscaloosa, Ala. *Agent:* Jack Drake, Drake & Pierce, Attorneys, 1509 University Blvd., Tuscaloosa, Ala. 35401. *Office:* c/o *Harper's* Magazine, 2 Park Ave., New York, N.Y. 10016.

CAREER/WRITINGS: Miller Lumber Co., Demopolis, Ala., lumberjack, 1963, 1964, 1966, 1967; free-lance writer, 1973—. Civil rights worker, Selma Project, 1970-71; placement officer for Vietnamese refugees, United Methodist Committee on Relief, summer, 1975. Notable assignments include coverage of the Tennessee-Tombigbee Waterway Project in Alabama and Mississippi, a profile of Pat Buchanan, an interview with Bryce Harlow, and a story about President Jimmy Carter called "The Dixie Smile."

Contributor of articles to newspapers and magazines, under name Johnny Greene, including *Los Angeles Times, New York Daily News Sunday Magazine, Detroit Free Press, New Times, Town & Country, Harper's, Christopher Street, Inquiry,* and *Quest. Awards, honors:* Several nonfiction writing awards from Birmingham (Ala.) Festival of Arts; two national awards for fiction writing.

WORK IN PROGRESS: Tombigbee Triumph (tentative title), a book about the Tombigbee River; works of fiction about the movement of drugs on the Tombigbee River and about dealing with the oil industry.

SIDELIGHTS: Greene told *CA:* "My major interest so far has been writing about the civil rights movement and the Tombigbee River. I was on a civil rights march in backwoods Alabama when I received my scholarship to go to Columbia. Then I got involved in my first Tombigbee River story for *Harper's,* which took about a year in all, from the 3:00 A.M. beer conversation at the Empire Diner in New York City, where it was conceived, to its publication in *Harper's.* The story was 15,000 words long and ran in April, 1977.

"I generally try to write about what I'm doing and experiencing, so I can get somewhere near the truth of the matter. That's why I like to report and write, or experience and write. I invest a great deal of time and energy in every story I write, whether it's for *Harper's* or the *Los Angeles Times.* And if that means re-writing paragraphs or entire sections thirty times to make them work, I do it.

"I figure I started free-lancing in 1973, while a student at Columbia Journalism. And they gave me, at *New Times,* some 'notable assignments.' *New Times* was brand new that fall, and I had two stories in its third issue and wrote about five or six more that year while a student. I went to the Nixon White House for *New Times* and wrote a profile of Pat Buchanan, for example, that often meant I would leave class at Columbia, hop a cab to LaGuardia, take a flight to D.C., conduct my interviews at the White House, and then hurry back to NYC and school. One of my professors at Columbia Journalism tried to can me because I cut his class in order to interview Bryce Harlow. He was mad because the subject of his seminar that day was 'How to Conduct an Interview.' And when the professor put the heat on—to the point of trying to have me booted from school—the editors of *New Times* had to call the dean of Columbia Journalism to see if they could 'get Johnny excused from class in order to conduct interviews at the White House.'"

BIOGRAPHICAL/CRITICAL SOURCES: New Times, April 19, 1974; *Harper's,* November, 1976.

* * *

GREENE, Johnny
See GREENE, John William, Jr.

* * *

GREENE, Stephen 1914-1979

OBITUARY NOTICE: Born December 18, 1914, in Boston,

Mass.; died May 25, 1979, in Chicago, Ill. Bookseller, publisher, journalist, and author. Greene was best known as the founder of Stephen Greene Press, which he owned for twenty-one years. He also operated a bookstore in Brattleboro, Vt., and was senior editor of *Vermont Life* magazine for nearly twenty years. Greene wrote *Kissing Bridges* and edited several books, including *Green Mountain Treasury* and *The Treasury of Vermont Life*. He died in what was considered to be the worst air disaster in U.S. history, the crash of an American Airlines DC-10 jet at Chicago's O'Hare International Airport. Obituaries and other sources: *Who's Who in America,* 40th edition, Marquis, 1978; *AB Bookman's Weekly,* July 30, 1979.

* * *

GREGOROWSKI, Christopher 1940-

PERSONAL: Born February 19, 1940, in Cape Town, South Africa; son of William Victor (an Anglican priest) and Doris (a teacher; maiden name, Skinner) Gregorowski; married Margaret Perold, June 20, 1964; children: Anna, Rachel, Rosalind. *Education:* University of Cape Town, B.A., 1960; graduate study at Cuddesdon College, Oxford, 1961-63; University of Birmingham, diploma, 1973. *Politics:* "Opposition." *Home and office:* St. Thomas Rectory, Rondebosch, Cape Town 7700, South Africa. *Agent:* Curtis Brown Ltd., 1 Craven Hill, London W2 3EP, England.

CAREER: Ordained Anglican priest, 1963; assistant curate at Anglican church in Cape Town, South Africa, 1963-66; parish priest in St. John's, Transkei, South Africa, 1966-74; St. Thomas Church, Cape Town, South Africa, parish priest, 1974—. *Member:* Institute of Race Relations, Celtic Harriers Athletic Club.

WRITINGS: Why a Donkey Was Chosen (juvenile), Doubleday, 1975. Contributor to *South African Outlook.*

WORK IN PROGRESS: Why the Donkey Has a Cross on His Back, a children's book; *The Revdoc: Six Short Stories.*

SIDELIGHTS: Gregorowski's first book has been translated into French, German, Norwegian, Swedish, Zulu, Xhosa, Tswana, North Sotho, and Afrikaans.

He commented: "My name is a Polish translation of MacGregor, and dates from the days when MacGregors were wanted men in Scotland and escaped to many parts of Europe. My family has been in South Africa since 1812. The first family member came with the Berlin Missionary Society. A non-ecclesiastical period followed until my father became an Anglican priest, as have two of his sons.

"My writing career really took off when my horse bit me on the elbow on one of my missionary treks. A letter to my goddaughter was so well-received that the donkey series followed. I spent eight years in the mission field in Transkei (I speak Afrikaans and Xhosa), and association with a saintly eccentric at the mission led to the 'Revdoc' stories and, hopefully, to his biography.

"In 1959-60 a friend and I hitchhiked from Cape Town through Africa to London, and in 1978 my wife and I visited Israel. The letters and diaries from these two trips give me great delight."

AVOCATIONAL INTERESTS: Travel (England, France, Italy, southern Africa), marathon running.

* * *

GREGORY, Chuck
See GNAEGY, Charles

GREGORY, Yvonne 1919(?)-1979

OBITUARY NOTICE: Born c. 1919 in Washington, D.C.; died of cancer, October 26, 1979, in New York, N.Y. Poet, editor, and author. Gregory's poetry appeared in many national black publications during the 1940's and 1950's, as well as in several poetry anthologies. She edited *We Charge Genocide: The Crime of Government Against the Negro People* and contributed articles to periodicals, including *Crisis, Our World,* and the *Philadelphia Afro-American.* Obituaries and other sources: *Washington Post,* October 28, 1979; *New York Times,* October 29, 1979.

* * *

GRENFELL, Joyce (Irene) 1910-1979

*OBITUARY NOTICE—*See index for *CA* sketch: Born February 2, 1910, in London, England; died of cancer, November 30, 1979, in London, England. Actress, entertainer, and author of such books as *This I Believe* and *Stately as a Galleon.* Grenfell performed in a variety of entertainment ventures, including talk shows, radio programs, wartime tours, and motion pictures. In 1954, Grenfell toured in a self-written, one-person stage show, "Joyce Grenfell Requests the Pleasure. . . ." She was especially lauded for her snob and spinster stage personas. Obituaries and other sources: *Current Biography,* Wilson, 1958; *The Biographical Encyclopaedia and Who's Who of the American Theatre,* James Heineman, 1966; *Who's Who in the Theatre,* 15th edition, Pitman, 1972; *Washington Post,* December 1, 1979; *Time,* December 10, 1979; *Newsweek,* December 10, 1979.

* * *

GRENIER, Judson A(chille) 1930-

PERSONAL: Born March 6, 1930, in Indianapolis, Ind.; son of Judson A. (a regional distributor) and Beatrice O. (a teacher) Grenier; married Nancy Hicks (an artist), August 9, 1954; children: Karen, Eric, Jonathan, Kathryn. *Education:* University of Minnesota, B.A., 1951; University of California, Berkeley, M.J., 1952; University of California, Los Angeles, Ph.D., 1965. *Home:* 587 33rd St., Manhattan Beach, Calif. 90266. *Office:* Department of History, California State University—Dominguez Hills, 1000 East Victoria St., Carson, Calif. 90747.

CAREER: Teacher in adult education program in San Francisco, Calif., 1951-52; El Camino College, Torrance, Calif., instructor, 1956-61, assistant professor of history, 1961-65; University of California, Los Angeles, visiting lecturer in history, 1965-66; California State University—Dominguez Hills, Carson, assistant professor, 1966-69, associate professor, 1969-73, professor of history, 1973—, head of department, 1967-70. Analyst for U.S. State Department's International Press Service, 1952. Research associate at Los Angeles County Museum of Natural History, 1977—; director of symposia. Member of Los Angeles Harbor Welfare Planning Commission, 1968-71, Manhattan Beach Historical Committee, 1972—, and History Committee for Los Angeles 200, 1978—. *Military service:* U.S. Army, Security Agency, 1952-55. *Member:* American Historical Association, Organization of American Historians, American Association of University Professors, History Guild of Southern California, Phi Alpha Theta, Phi Delta Kappa.

WRITINGS: Prairie Winds and Sea Winds, Pasadena City College, 1959; (editor with George Mowry) *Treason of the Senate,* Quadrangle, 1963; (editor with Robert Bersi) *Shaping Our Environment,* California State University—Dominguez Hills, 1967; (contributor) Royce Delmatier and others, editors, *The Rumble of California Politics,* Wiley, 1970; (with Mark Naidis) *Historical Writing,* Hawthorne, 1974; *Reminiscences of the Dominguez Ranch and Curson Family* (oral history), California State University—Dominguez Hills, 1976; (editor and contributor) *A Guide to Historic Places in Los Angeles County,* Kendall/Hunt, 1978. Reporter for *Los Angeles Mirror-News,* summers, 1948, 1958. Editor of "Manhattan Beach Historical Monograph Series," city of Manhattan Beach, California, 1973-78. Contributor of articles and reviews to history journals.

WORK IN PROGRESS: History of the California State University and Colleges.

SIDELIGHTS: Grenier writes: "My focus is upon the lives of typical, but enterprising, American men and women who have constructed new social, political, and economic institutions. I am especially interested in people who create revolutions without meaning to do so."

* * *

GRIFFIN, Edward M(ichael) 1937-

PERSONAL: Born September 25, 1937, in Pittsburgh, Pa.; son of Edward J. (a professor) and Margaret (a teacher; maiden name, Koessler) Griffin; married Jean Chisholm (a registered nurse), March 5, 1960; children: Patricia M., Theresa M., Joan M. *Education:* University of San Francisco, B.S., 1959; Stanford University, M.A., and Ph.D., both 1966. *Religion:* Roman Catholic. *Home:* 3125 Ridgewood Rd., St. Paul, Minn. 55112. *Office:* Department of English, University of Minnesota, 207 Church St. S.E., Minneapolis, Minn. 55455.

CAREER: University of Minnesota, Minneapolis, assistant professor, 1966-69, associate professor, 1969-79, professor of English, 1979—, director of graduate studies, 1972-75. Visiting lecturer at University of San Francisco, summer, 1963, 1964, visiting assistant professor, summer, 1968; visiting associate professor at Stanford University, 1971-72. *Military service:* U.S. Army, Field Artillery, 1959-62; served in Germany; became first lieutenant. *Member:* American Association of University Professors, Modern Language Association of America, Midwest Modern Language Association. *Awards, honors:* Grant from National Endowment for the Humanities, 1968.

WRITINGS: (Author of introduction) William Smith, *The College of Mirania,* Johnson Reprint Corporation, 1969; *Jonathan Edwards* (pamphlet), University of Minnesota Press, 1971; (contributor) Leonard Unger, editor, *American Writers: A Collection of Literary Biographies,* Scribner, 1974; *Old Brick: Charles Chauncy of Boston, 1705-1787* (monograph), University of Minnesota Press, 1979. Contributor of articles and reviews to scholarly journals. Assistant editor of American literature for *The Eighteenth Century: A Current Biography,* 1971—. Member of editorial board of *Early American Literature,* 1977—.

WORK IN PROGRESS: A series of essays on the uses made by John Berryman, John Barth, and Robert Lowell of seventeenth- and eighteenth-century American history; research on American Catholic literature since Vatican Council II.

SIDELIGHTS: Griffin wrote: "Some of the most interesting scholarly and critical work of the past ten or fifteen years has been done on early American subjects. The radical politics of the 1960's sent us back to the very radical politics of the 1620's and following years; the polemics of the Vietnam War illuminated the polemics of the Great Awakening of the 1740's, and vice versa; the bicentennial celebrations of the mid-1970's redirected our attention to the revolutionary days of the 1760's and 1770's. Through all this we began to discover the literary dimensions of 'extra-literary' works and the extra-literary dimensions of literary works. The whole colonial period is undergoing reassessment.

"I have been interested in two of the major figures of the American Great Awakening, Jonathan Edwards and his rival, Charles Chauncy. I am also interested in how the colonial period speaks to us today."

BIOGRAPHICAL/CRITICAL SOURCES: American Literary Scholarship: An Annual/1971; Early American Literature, number 6, 1971.

* * *

GRIFFIN, (Arthur) Gwyn 1922(?)-1967

OBITUARY NOTICE: Born c. 1922 in Egypt; died from a blood infection, October 12, 1967, in Introdacqua, Italy. Author of adventure novels, including *The Occupying Power* and *By the North Gate.* Griffin also wrote *Shipmaster,* the story of an officer faced with a rebellious crew and an impending cyclone after he assumes command from the ailing captain. The novel was later published in the United States as *Master of This Vessel.* Obituaries and other sources: *The Reader's Adviser: A Layman's Guide to Literature,* Volume I: *The Best in American and British Fiction, Poetry, Essays, Literary Biography, Bibliography, and Reference,* 12th edition, Bowker, 1974; *World Authors, 1950-1970,* Wilson, 1975.

* * *

GRIFFITH, Corinne 1898(?)-1979

OBITUARY NOTICE: Born c. 1898 in Texarkana, Ark.; died July 13, 1979, in Santa Monica, Calif. Actress and author. Known as the "Orchid of the Screen," Griffith starred in silent movies, including "Black Oxen," "Mademoiselle Modiste," and "Outcast." She retired from the screen after making one talking picture in 1931, but in 1958 appeared once more in "Paradise Alley." During her marriage to George Preston Marshall, owner of the Washington Redskins football team, Griffith wrote the lyrics for "Hail to the Redskins," designed the team's uniforms, and suggested that bands play before the games and at halftime. Her books included *My Life With the Redskins, Papa's Delicate Condition,* and *Truth Is Stranger.* Obituaries and other sources: *The ASCAP Biographical Dictionary of Composers, Authors, and Publishers,* American Society of Composers, Authors, and Publishers, 1966; Richard Lamparski, *Whatever Became of . . .?,* Crown, 1968; *Films in Review,* November, 1975; *Washington Post,* July 15, 1979.

* * *

GROPPER, William 1897-1977

OBITUARY NOTICE: Born December 3, 1897, in New York, N.Y.; died January 6, 1977. Artist and author. Gropper was best known for integrating his leftist politics into his political cartoons. He contributed to numerous political publications, including *New Masses* and *Sunday Worker.* In 1924, Gropper worked in Russia on the official Communist party paper, *Pravda.* His books include *The Golden Land, 56 Drawings of the U.S.S.R.,* and *The Lost Conscience.* Obituaries and other sources: *Current Biography,* Wilson, 1940, March, 1977; *A Dictionary of Contemporary American Artists,* 2nd edition, St. Martin's, 1971; *The Author's and*

Writer's Who's Who, 6th edition, Burke's Peerage, 1971; *Who's Who in World Jewry,* Pitman, 1972; *Who's Who in the World,* 2nd edition, Marquis, 1973; *Who's Who in American Art,* Bowker, 1973; *New York Times,* January 8, 1977.

* * *

GROSS, Alan 1947-

PERSONAL: Born June 29, 1947, in Chicago, Ill.; son of Melvin (a retailer) and Shirlee (Marks) Gross; married Norma Topa (an artist), June 26, 1978. *Education:* Attended University of Missouri, 1965-69. *Home and office:* Writer's Group, Inc., 1730 North Wells, Chicago, Ill. 60614. *Agent:* Samuel Liff, William Morris Agency, 1350 Avenue of the Americas, New York, N.Y. 10019.

CAREER: Writer, teacher, and actor. Worked as writer and creative director in advertising in Chicago, Ill., 1969-77; teacher for Chicago Public Library, Writer's Group, and Victory Gardens, all in Chicago, and Piven Theatre Workshop in Evanston, Ill., 1978-79; actor with "Second City" and theatres and workshops. *Member:* Dramatists Guild, Authors League. *Awards, honors:* Two Joseph Jefferson Awards, 1978, for "Lunching"; "Phone Room" was finalist in O'Neill Festival National Playwrights Conference, 1978.

WRITINGS—Juvenile: *Sometimes I Worry,* Children's Press, 1978; *What If the Teacher Calls On Me?,* Children's Press, 1979.

Plays: "Lunching" (two-act), first produced in Chicago, Ill., at The Body Politic, December, 1977, produced on Broadway October, 1979; "The Phone Room" (two-act), first produced in Chicago at Theatre Building, February, 1978; "The Man in 605" (two-act), first produced in Chicago at Theatre Building, June, 1979, produced on National Public Radio, fall, 1979.

Contributor to *Chicago* magazine.

WORK IN PROGRESS: How to Be a Native New Yorker, a satirical picture book; *The I Don't Want to Go to School Book,* for children; two plays, "Nora's Room" and "Soon to Be a Major Motion Picture"; and "film treatments."

SIDELIGHTS: "I want my life to be as simple and dull as possible," Gross told an interviewer, adding: "I spent years figuring creativity could wait until I got everything else straight, but as Abraham Maslow says, creativity is at the top of the hierarchy, and I realized you have to have it now, or it'll never happen. Making commercials is fine—I had a good living—but it'll never be literature. For years I wrote stories, which is the best preparation for a playwright. I want to be an old man who can look back on a string of plays and see my life in them and know it mattered."

"Lunching" has proven to be popular with Chicago audiences but Gross expressed dissatisfaction with the amount of laughter elicited by the play. He claimed that "it upsets me when people keep laughing through the whole show. They're waiting for the Profound Words. And there aren't any." Gross also dismissed critics who'd chosen to compare his work with Neil Simon's. "I think it's more of a write-off than a putdown," he observed.

BIOGRAPHICAL/CRITICAL SOURCES: Chicago Tribune, July 26, 1978.

* * *

GROSS, Ben 1891-1979

OBITUARY NOTICE: Born November 24, 1891, in Birmingham, Ala.; died of a heart attack, August 13, 1979, in New York, N.Y. Journalist, critic, and author. Gross spent forty-six years reporting on radio and television broadcasting for the *New York Daily News.* His book, *I Looked and Listened,* was about his coverage of early radio and television programs. Obituaries and other sources: *Who's Who in World Jewry,* Pitman, 1972; *Who's Who in America,* 40th edition, Marquis, 1978; *New York Times,* August 15, 1979.

* * *

GROVER, David S(teele) 1939-

PERSONAL: Born March 7, 1939, in Amberley, Gloucestershire, England; son of Richard S. (a piano manufacturer) and Amy (Silcock) Grover; married Jenny Johnson, June 11, 1966; children: Philip, Sarah. *Education:* Selwyn College, Cambridge, M.A., 1962. *Home:* Church House, Bell Lane, Minchinhampton, Gloucestershire GL6 9BP, England. *Office:* Bentley Piano Co. Ltd., Woodchester, Stroud, Gloucestershire GL5 5NW, England.

CAREER: Bentley Piano Co. Ltd., Stroud, England, 1962—, trainee in master piano makers course at Fachschule fuer Musikinstrumentenban, Ludwigsburg, Germany, 1962-63, director at Bentley, 1967-73, managing director, 1973—; Bentley Organ Co. Ltd., London, director, 1967—. Director of Stroud Festival, 1969-72. Freeman of City of London. *Member:* Confederation des Associations des Facteur des Instruments de Musique de la C.E.E. (European Economic Community; vice-president, 1979), Royal Society of Arts (fellow), Institute of Musical Instrument Technology (fellow; president, 1971-73), Piano Manufacturers Association (president, 1976-78), Worshipful Company of Musicians (freeman; liveryman).

WRITINGS: The Piano: Its Story From Zither to Grand, R. Hale, 1976, Scribner, 1978. Contributor to trade journals in England and Europe.

SIDELIGHTS: Grover writes: "After training in Germany, I thought I would 'keep my hand in' by writing articles. After some years the idea of writing a book was put to me. It was attractive, as it combined the three main areas of my activities—history, music, and piano-making (I am the fifth successive generation of piano-makers in my family).

"Piano-making is an intriguing combination of modern technology and traditional hand skills, of theoretical design and practical experience, of acoustics and music. It would take at least two lifetimes to learn everything about the piano, hence its lasting fascination as an instrument. Our firm, founded by my grandfather in 1906, has now made 150,000 pianos and exports Bentley pianos throughout the world. We are unusual among piano manufacturers as we make our own actions, hammers, and keyboards, usually supplied to piano-makers by specialist manufacturers. These many facets are reflected in *The Piano: Its Story From Zither to Grand,* which interlinks pianos and piano-making, past and present, with pianists and piano music, past and contemporary. It has appeal for all piano lovers, professional and amateur."

AVOCATIONAL INTERESTS: Playing piano and organ.

* * *

GUERNSEY, Otis L(ove), Jr. 1918-

PERSONAL: Born August 9, 1918, in New York, N.Y.; son of Otis Love and Margaret (Henderson) Guernsey; married Dorianne Downe, December 11, 1943. *Education:* Yale University, B.A., 1940. *Residence:* North Pomfret, Vt.

CAREER: New York Herald Tribune, New York, N.Y., 1941-60, began as copy boy, became reporter, associate film and drama critic, and film and drama critic, arts editor, 1955-60; free-lance writer, 1960—. Lecturer on modern theater; consultant. *Member:* American Theater Critics Association (charter member), Dramatists Guild, New York Newspaper Guild, New York Film Critics (past chairman), Phi Beta Kappa, Coffee House Club, Century Association.

WRITINGS—Editor: *The Best Plays of 1963-64 to 1964-65: The Burns Mantle Yearbook of the Theater,* two volumes (Volume I edited by H. Hewes), Dodd, 1965; *The Best Plays of 1965-66: The Burns Mantle Yearbook of the Theater,* Dodd, 1966, *1966-67,* 1967, *1967-68,* 1968, *1968-69,* 1969, *1969-70,* 1970, *1970-71,* 1971, *1971-72,* 1972, *1972-73,* 1973, *1973-74,* 1974, *1974-75,* 1975, *1975-76,* 1976, *1976-77,* 1977, *1977-78,* 1978; *Directory of the American Theater, 1894-1971,* Dodd, 1971; *Playwrights, Lyricists, and Composers on Theater,* Dodd, 1974.

Author of film stories. Contributor to professional journals. Drama critic and senior editor of *Show,* 1963-64; editor of *Dramatists Guild Quarterly,* 1964—; arts editor of *Diplomat,* 1965-67.

* * *

GUGGENHEIM, Harry Frank 1890-1971

OBITUARY NOTICE: Born August 23, 1890, in West End, N.J.; died January 22, 1971, in Long Island, N.Y. Businessman and journalist best known as co-founder of *Newsday* with wife Alicia Patterson. A millionnaire and staunch Republican, Guggenheim used his column in *Newsday* as a platform for his own views, though he insisted that the paper present an independent image. Guggenheim served as ambassador to Cuba in the early 1930's. He was also an avid horseman and his horse Dark Star topped the 1953 Kentucky Derby field. In later years, he was instrumental in the creation of the New York Racing Association. Obituaries and other sources: *Current Biography,* Wilson, 1956, March, 1971; *New York Times,* January 23, 1971.

* * *

GUILLEN, Jorge 1893-

PERSONAL: Surname pronounced with hard "G," Gee-*lyen;* born January 18, 1893, in Valladolid, Castile, Spain; came to United States in 1938; son of Julio Guillen Saenz and Esperanza Alvarez Guerra; married Germaine Cahen, October 17, 1921 (marriage ended); married Irene Sismondi, October 11, 1961; children: (first marriage) Teresa, Claudio. *Education:* Studied at Maison Perreyve of the French Fathers of the Oratory, Fribourg, Germany; attended University of Madrid and University of Granada. *Home:* 9 Windemere Park, Arlington, Mass. 02174.

CAREER: Sorbonne, University of Paris, Paris, France, lecturer, 1917-23; Oxford University, Oxford, England, lecturer, 1929-31; professor at University of Murcia, Murcia, Spain; University of Seville, Seville, Spain, professor of Spanish literature, 1931-38; professor at McGill University, Montreal, Quebec; Wellesley College, Wellesley, Mass., professor, 1940-57. Gave Charles Eliot Norton Lectures in Poetry at Harvard University, 1957, 1958. Visiting professor in other U.S. and Canadian colleges and universities, and in Mexico, Chile, and Puerto Rico.

WRITINGS—In English: *Cantico,* Revista, 1928, 2nd edition, Ediciones del Arbol, 1936, 3rd edition, published as *Cantico, fe de vida,* Litoral, 1945, 4th edition, Editorial Sudamericana, 1950, translation published as *Cantico: A Selection of Spanish Poems,* edited by Norman Thomas di Giovanni, Little, Brown, 1963; *Lenguaje y poesia,* Revista, 1961, translation published as *Language and Poetry: Some Poets of Spain,* Harvard University Press, 1961; *Affirmation: A Bilingual Anthology* (selections from *Aire nuestro;* see below), edited and translated from the Spanish by Julian Palley), University of Oklahoma Press, 1968; *Guillen on Guillen: Poetry and the Poet,* Princeton University Press, 1979.

In Spanish; poetry: *Tercer cantico,* limited edition, Ediciones "La Poesia Sorprendida," 1944; *El encanto de las serenas,* Grafica Panamericana, 1953; *Huerto de Melibea,* Insula, 1954; *Maremagnum* (also published in *Clamor* [see below]), Editorial Sudamericana, 1957; *Lugar de Lazaro,* limited edition, Daido, 1957; *Clamor* (contains *Maremagnum, Que van a dar en la mar,* and *A la altura de las circunstancias;* also published in *Aire nuestro* [see below]), Editorial Sudamericana, 1957; *Viviendo y otros poemas,* Editorial Seix Barral, 1958.

Poemas de Castilla (title means "Poems From Castille"), [Santiago, Chile], 1960; *Que van a dar en la mar* (also published in *Clamor* [see above]), Editorial Sudamericana, 1960; *Poesias* (title means "Poetry"), Ediciones Mito, 1960; *Versos* (title means "Poems"), edited by Miguel Pizarro, Ediciones Meridiano, 1961; *Las tentaciones de Antonio,* Santander Hermanos, 1962; *Segun las horas,* Editorial Universitaria,, 1962; *A la altura de las circunstances,* Editorial Sudamericana, 1963; *Treboles,* Publicationes la Isla de los Ratones, 1964; *Seleccion de poemas* (title means "Selection of Poems"), Gredos, 1965, enlarged edition, c. 1970; *Relatos,* Libreria Anticuaria el Guadalhorce, 1960; *Historia natural,* Ediciones de los Papeles de son Armedans, 1960; (author of poem) Francesco Sabadell Lopez, *Flores,* [Valladolid, Spain], 1961; *Clamor* [and] *A la altura de las circunstancias* (both also published separately; see above), Editorial Sudamericana, 1963.

Guirnalda civil, Halty Ferguson, 1970; *Antologia* (title means "Anthology"), edited by Jose Manuel Blecna, Anaya, 1970; *Obra poetica,* introduction by Joaquin Casalduero, Alianza, 1970; *Y otros poemas* (title means "And Other Poems"), Muchnik Editores, 1973; *Al margen,* Visor, 1974; *Convivencia,* introduction by Mario Hernandez, Turner, 1975; *Antologia: Aire nuestro* (contains *Cantico, Clamor,* and *Homenaje*), edited by Manuel Mantero, Plaza & Janes, 1975, published in two volumes, 1977; *Plaza major: Antologia civil,* introduction by Francisco Abad Nebot, Taurus, 1977.

Other: *Federico en persona: semblanza y epistolario,* Emece, 1959; *En torno a Gabriel Miro, breve epistolario* (contains "Gabriel Miro," "Amistad y correspondencia," and "Cartas"), Ediciones de Arte y Bibliofilia, c. 1969; *El argumento de la obra* (essays; contains "Una generacion," "El argumento de la obra," and "Poesia integral"), Libres de Sinera, 1969; (editor) Federico Garcia Lorca, *Obras completas* (title means "Complete Works"), Aguilar, 1969; *La Poetica de Becquer,* Hispanic Institute (New York, N.Y.), 1973. Also translator of *Le Cimetiere Marin* by Paul Valery.

SIDELIGHTS: Jorge Guillen is "beyond dispute the greatest living Spanish poet," Jorge Luis Borges has stated. Willis Barnstone went on to call him "one of the present masters of twentieth-century poetry, along with Elytis, Aleixandre, Borges, Voznesensky, Montate." But although Guillen has resided in the United States since the onset of the Spanish civil war, he is not yet widely known in the English-speaking world.

Unlike many contemporary Spanish poets who voice what

Miller Williams termed a "sweet pessimism," Guillen expresses an intense joie de vivre in his lyric poetry. In this regard, his style is reminiscent of classic poets of the sixteenth century: Luis de Leon, San Juan de la Cruz, and Luis de Gongora y Argote. His spontaneous enjoyment of each moment is expressed in the present tense, in short lines of nouns and verbs (with an emphasis on the former) ending in exclamation points.

Guillen devoted forty-seven years of work to *Anthologia: Aire neustro,* which combines in a single volume the previously published *Cantico, Clamor,* and *Homenaje*. In this collection Guillden not only emphasizes the joyful aspects of life, but also acknowledges the darker sides of existence. He writes of the personal pain caused by Spain's civil war and the discovery that violence is also present in the United States. Nevertheless, in all the poems, a *Times Literary Supplement* critic pointed out, Guillen's "language is purified to the point of being univocal."

To date only a small representation of Guillen's poetry has been translated into English. "The very purity and exactitude of Guillen's language makes him a difficult poet to translate," noted the *Times Literary Supplement*. But Barnstone remarked that, "despite other reviews to the contrary, Guillen's poetry translates admirably well into other languages."

BIOGRAPHICAL/CRITICAL SOURCES: Frances Avery Peak, *The Poetry of Jorge Guillen,* [Princeton, N.J.], 1942; J. B. Trend, *Jorge Guillen,* [Cambridge, Mass.], 1952; *Times Literary Supplement,* April 22, 1965, September 12, 1968; *New Statesman,* April 30, 1965; *New York Times Book Review,* June 20, 1965, August 18, 1968, September 12, 1968, July 3, 1977; *Virginia Quarterly Review,* Volume 41, autumn, 1965; *Hispania,* September, 1965; *Commonweal,* September 24, 1965; *Poetry,* October, 1967; *Books Abroad,* winter, 1968; *Modern Language Journal,* November, 1970; *New Republic,* April 9, 1977; Jorge Guillen, *Guillen on Guillen,* Princeton University Press, 1979; *Contemporary Literary Criticism,* Volume 11, Gale, 1979.*

* * *

GULLICK, Etta 1916-

PERSONAL: Born September 7, 1916, in Elstree, Hertfordshire, England; daughter of Lancelot Turtle and Frances Hedger (Duffus) Montgomery; married Charles Gullick (a university professor), December 7, 1938; children: Charles J.M.R. *Education:* St. Anne's College, Oxford, M.A., 1938. *Politics:* Liberal. *Religion:* Anglican. *Home:* Aniwa, Kirk Michael, Isle of Man, England.

CAREER: Oxford University, Oxford, England, tutor in historical geography at St. Edmund Hall, 1950-70, and St. Hugh's College, 1965-70, lecturer in spirituality at St. Stephen's House, 1965—. *Wartime service:* Worked for the Admiralty in naval intelligence in Norway, Italy, and other European countries, 1940-44.

WRITINGS—All published by Mayhew-McCrimmon, except as noted: (With Michael Hollings) *The One Who Listens,* Morehouse, 1971; (with Hollings) *It's Me, O Lord,* 1972, Doubleday, 1973; *The Shade of His Hand,* 1973; *You Must Be Joking, Lord,* 1975; *Prayers for the Sick,* 1976; *Night and Morning Prayers,* 1976; *Prayers of Love and Forgiveness,* 1976; (with Hollings) *Getting to Know You: Prayer and God,* 1976; *Prayers for Others,* 1977; *As Was His Custom,* 1979; *Benet of Canfield and the Rule of Perfection,* 1980. Contributor to *Admiralty Handbooks* and *Chamber's Encyclopaedia*. Contributor to theology journals.

SIDELIGHTS: Etta Gullick wrote: "My Scottish upbringing made me fascinated by theology. Also, the quest theme as found in the so-called fairy tales of Andrew Lang, who lived in my hometown of St. Andrews (his 'old grey city by the northern sea'), gave me an interest in other religions and encouraged me in my search for deeper knowledge of God.

"My study of theology at Oxford University made me realise how divorced modern theology can be from spirituality, and my discovery of the great spiritual writers of western Christianity made me aware of how the West was being deprived of a major part of its spiritual heritage. It was Bishop Christopher Butler, then abbot of Downside, who encouraged me to study Benet of Canfield (a sixteenth-century English Capuchin).

"I did a lot of work for ecumenism in Oxford and there met a Roman Catholic priest, Michael Hollings. We discovered a deep mutual interest in prayer and have combined to write together. I imagine we must have been the first Anglican-Roman team to write books of prayer together.

"I go about lecturing on prayer and trying to help people to pray in a simple wordless way."

AVOCATIONAL INTERESTS: Travel (Italy, Malta, France, Greece, Turkey, South Africa, West Indies, United States, Canada).

* * *

GUNNEWEG, Antonius H. J. 1922-

PERSONAL: Born May 17, 1922, in Rotterdam, Netherlands; son of Herman C. M. and C.M.A. (Lammerts) Gunneweg; married Jane Gasteyer, April 18, 1952. *Education:* Attended University of Utrecht and University of Marburg. *Home:* Raiffeisenstrasse 3, Bonn 1, West Germany. *Office:* Abterlung fuer Hermeneutik, Bonn 1, West Germany.

CAREER: Abterlung fuer Hermeneutik, Bonn, West Germany, professor of Old Testament, 1968—.

WRITINGS: Muendliche und schriftliche Tradition der vorexilischen Prophetenbuecher als Problem der neueren Prophetenforschung, Vandenhoeck & Ruprecht, 1959; *Leviten und Priester: Hauptlinien der Traditionsbildung und Geschichte des israelitsch-juedischen Kultpersonals,* Vandenhoeck & Ruprecht, 1965; *Der Gott, der mitgeht,* Guetersloher Verlagshaus G. Mohn, 1972; *Geschichte Israels bis Bar Kochba,* Kohlhammer, 1972, 3rd edition, 1979; *Vom Verstehen des Altes Testaments: ein Hermeneutik,* Vandenhoeck & Ruprecht, 1977, translation by John Bowden published as *Understanding the Old Testament,* Westminster, 1978.

WORK IN PROGRESS: Kommentar Ejir Nehemsa.

* * *

GUTTENBERG, Barnett

PERSONAL: Son of John (a violin maker) and Ida (Binder) Guttenberg; married Peggy Endel, June 24, 1967; children: Lisa. *Education:* Columbia University, B.A., 1959; Cornell University, M.A., 1966, Ph.D., 1971. *Home:* 4652 Southwest 14th St., Miami, Fla. 33134. *Office:* Department of English, University of Miami, Coral Gables, Fla. 33124.

CAREER: Vanderbilt University, Nashville, Tenn., instructor, 1967-70, assistant professor of English, 1970-74; University of Miami, Coral Gables, Fla., assistant professor, 1974-77, associate professor of English, 1977—. Participant in seminars. *Military service:* U.S. Army, 1960-63; became first lieutenant. *Member:* Modern Language Association of America.

WRITINGS: Web of Being: The Novels of Robert Penn Warren, Vanderbilt University Press, 1975. Contributor to *Sylvia Plath,* edited by Gary Lane, Johns Hopkins Press. Contributor of articles and reviews to literature journals. Editor of *Faulkner Studies,* 1979—.

WORK IN PROGRESS: The Fall in Southern Literature.

* * *

GWYNNE, Peter 1941-

PERSONAL: Born April 29, 1941, in Leeds, England; came to the United States; son of Edward and Kathleen (Goss) Gwynne; married Joanne Vasil; children: Shawn Michael, Gareth David, Patrick Andrew. *Education:* Balliol College, Oxford, M.A., 1964; also attended University of Sussex, 1964. *Religion:* Episcopalian. *Home:* 132 Westport Rd., Wilton, Conn. 06897. *Office: Newsweek,* 444 Madison Ave., New York, N.Y. 10022.

CAREER: Discovery, London, England, assistant editor, 1964-66; *Technology Review,* Cambridge, Mass., managing editor, 1966-68; *Boston Herald Traveler,* Boston, Mass., science editor, 1968-69; *Newsweek,* New York, N.Y., science editor, 1969—. *Member:* International Science Writers Association, National Association of Science Writers, Wilton Soccer Association (president, 1977-78). *Awards, honors:* Magazine prize from Aviation/Space Writers Association, 1974, for articles on "Skylab 1"; James Grady Award from American Chemical Society, 1979.

WRITINGS: (Editor with A. A. Loftas) *Advances in Material Science,* University of London Press, 1967; (with Henry O. Hooper) *Physics and the Physical Perspective,* Harper, 1977, 2nd edition, 1980. Contributor to scientific journals and a wide variety of popular magazines, including *National Wildlife, Science Digest,* and *Smithsonian.*

WORK IN PROGRESS: A physics textbook for non-science majors; research on general physics and astronomy; brain research.

SIDELIGHTS: Gwynne comments: "I believe science is a vital subject for daily life. Science writers fulfill the necessary task of informing the public of the meaning and implications of work by experts who are often unable to perform that service themselves."

H

HACKETT, Francis 1883-1962

OBITUARY NOTICE: Born January 21, 1883, in Kilkenny, Ireland; died April 25, 1962. Writer best known for his historical accounts, including *The Story of the Irish Nation* and *Henry the Eighth: A Personal History*. Hackett worked as associate editor of *New Republic* and book editor of *New York Times*. Obituaries and other sources: *The Oxford Companion to American Literature,* 4th edition, Oxford University Press, 1965; *Who Was Who in America,* 4th edition, Marquis, 1968; *Longman Companion to Twentieth Century Literature,* Longman, 1970.

* * *

HACKETT, John Winthrop 1910-

PERSONAL: Born November 5, 1910, in Perth, Australia; son of Sir John Winthrop and Deborah Vernon (Drake-Brockman) Hackett; married Margaret Frena, 1942; children: Bridget, Elizabeth, Susan. *Education:* New College, Oxford, B.A., 1933, B.Litt., 1936, M.A., 1945; postgraduate study at Imperial Defence College, 1951. *Home:* Coberly Mill, Cheltenham, Gloucestershire, England.

CAREER: British Army, career officer, 1931-68, commissioned to 8th King's Royal Irish Hussars, 1931-36, served in Palestine, 1936, with Transjordan Frontier Force, 1937-40, served in Syria, 1941, secretary of commission of control for Syria and Lebanon, 1941, general staff officer with 9th Army in Western Desert, 1942, and Raiding Forces Middle East Land Forces, 1942-43, commander of Fourth Parachute Brigade, 1943, served in Italy, 1943 and 1946, and Arnhem, 1944, head of British Intelligence Organization in Vienna, 1946, commander of Transjordan Frontier Force, 1947, deputy quartermaster-general of British Army of the Rhine, 1952, commander of Twentieth Armoured Brigade, 1954, general officer commanding Seventh Armoured Division, 1956-58, commandant of Royal Military College of Science, 1958-61, colonel-commandant of Royal Electrical and Mechanical Engineers, 1961-66, commander-in-chief of Northern Ireland Command, 1961-63, deputy chief of Imperial General Staff, 1963-64, deputy chief of general staff of Ministry of Defence, 1964-66, commander-in-chief of British Army of the Rhine and commander of Northern Army Group, 1966-68, retired as general; University of London, London, England, principal of King's College, 1968-75, fellow, 1968; writer, 1975—. Instructor at Royal Naval College, Greenwich, England, 1943-50; Lees Knowles Lecturer at Cambridge University, 1961; Kermit Roosevelt Lecturer in the United States, 1967; Harmon Memorial Lecturer at U.S. Air Force Academy, 1970; Basil Henriques Memorial Lecturer for National Association of Boys' Clubs, 1970; visiting professor in classics at Kings College, 1976-79.

MEMBER: Classical Association (president, 1970-71), English Association (president, 1973-74), Cavalry Club, Carlton Club, United Oxford and Cambridge University Club, White's Club. *Awards, honors*—Military: Distinguished Service Order and bar; Military Cross; honorary colonel of Tenth Battalion and Tenth Volunteer Battalion Parachute Regiment, Oxford University Officers Training Corps, and Queen's Royal Irish Hussars; mentioned four times in dispatches. Other: Member of Order of the British Empire, 1938, commander of order, 1953; companion of Order of Bath, 1962, knight commander, 1962, knight grand cross, 1967; LL.D. from Queen's University, Belfast, University of Western Australia, 1963, and University of Exeter; fellow of St. George's College, University of Western Australia, 1965, and New College, Oxford, 1973.

WRITINGS: The Profession of Arms, Times Publishing Co., 1963; *Reflections Upon Epic Warfare,* Classical Association, 1970; *Sweet Uses of Vicissitude,* United Kingdom English Association, 1972; *I Was a Stranger,* Chatto & Windus, 1977; (with Norman Macrae and others) *The Third World War: A Future History,* Sidgwick & Jackson, 1978, Macmillan, 1979. Contributor of articles and reviews to magazines.

WORK IN PROGRESS: Research in the medieval history of the eastern Mediterranean.

SIDELIGHTS: Hackett wrote: "I have been described as an academic who in a prolonged fit of absence of mind became a four-star general, and by someone else as an Indian at the White Man's camp fire. Perhaps there is an element of truth in both observations. Certainly the life I have led seems to have been marked by a restless quest for balance—between action and reflection, for instance, between form and content.

"I live here in an ancient mill-house in Gloucestershire. It is a place of almost paradisal beauty. I have watched visitors stand spellbound when they come for the first time up the stairs into the great oak-beamed drawing room, captured by the beauty of the room itself and enchanted by what can be seen through any of its many windows. The stream that feeds my mill-pond just outside, in which we fish for trout, is the nursling Thames. Mallards breed there, and moorhens, and the kingfisher flashes by. I never come into this room of a morning without a feeling of gratitude. It is important never to take anything for granted, to look at everything as though this were almost the first time you had seen it. 'A man, sir, should keep his friendship in constant repair,' said Doctor Johnson. Acquaintance with anyone or anything has always to be renewed. What is taken for granted tends to wilt and die.

"I do not think I take much for granted—certainly not the lovely place in which I live but there are also other places. London is only two hours away. And Oxford, with the college where I spent four of the very happiest years of my life as a young man, is less than half that distance from here. I love to go there too.

"My contemporaries and I graduated in the early thirties, when a war with Germany seemed to many of us certain. It was a war in which, of course, we should all get killed and it seemed to me tidier, on the whole, to be killed as a professional than as an amateur. And so, instead of becoming an academic straight away, I became a regular officer of the cavalry regiment in which my grandsire was commissioned on 11th August, 1783. All the same, following the principle that you must *always* have your cake and eat it too, if you possibly can, I went on with my academic pursuits and turned in some creditable work on the Third Crusade for which Oxford gave me a research degree. Contrast and variety is what makes life more enjoyable for me, perhaps, than anything else.

"I am basically a European and always was, even during my early youth, which was spent in Australia where I was born. There are many splendid places—like the United States, or Australia—in which to live. There are, in fact, far too many for comfort. But almost all of what I want is to be found in Europe and this is where I shall die—though not, of course, just yet. There is far too much to do and to enjoy to waste any time thinking about that.

"I read easily in six or seven languages and no day passes without my reading in some other than my own. But the more you read the more there still is to be read. That almost invites despair, or would do so if despair were permissable, which it isn't. This is just as well. The future of mankind in a world in which man has been too clever and not good enough is not too promising. We are all saying to each other more and more that this cannot go on. There has to be an end. I am in fact under heavy pressure just now to write a book about the end but I am no eschatologist and do not think I can.

"Meanwhile I shall go on living my own life, which is one of almost unbelievable complexity. Its main extravagances lie in salmon-fishing and drinking good wine, of which neither is an inexpensive pursuit. Life at Coberley Mill in Gloucestershire is an inexpensive pursuit. Life at Coberley Mill in Gloucestershire is in other respects by some standards lived on modest lines but I am sure I shall still have to set to now and then and earn an honest penny with my pen."

AVOCATIONAL INTERESTS: Travel, fishing, books, wine, music, medieval history.

BIOGRAPHICAL/CRITICAL SOURCES: New York Times Book Review, March 25, 1979; *Washington Post,* June 18, 1979.

* * *

HADLEY, Arthur T. 1924-

PERSONAL: Born June 24, 1924, in New York, N.Y.; son of Morris and Katherine (Blodgett) Hadley; married Jane Danish (a psychoanalyst), 1979; children: Arthur T. III, Kate H., George M., Nicholas J. *Education:* Yale University, B.A. (with honors), 1949. *Residence:* West Tisbury, Mass. 02575. *Office:* 155 East 42nd St., New York, N.Y. 10017.

CAREER: Free-lance writer. *Newsweek,* New York City, Department of Defense correspondent, 1949-53, White House correspondent, 1953-55, "Periscope" editor, 1955-56; *New York Herald Tribune,* New York City, assistant executive editor, 1957-60; *New Times,* New York City, Washington correspondent, 1974-78. Consultant on arms control to Stanford Research Institute, 1961-65, and on army training to Arthur D. Little, Inc., 1971—. Member-secretary of the U.S. Army Psychological Warfare Advisory Board, 1949-52. *Military service:* U.S. Army, 1942-46; became major; received Purple Heart and Silver Star. *Awards, honors:* Grants from American Academy of Arts and Sciences and 20th Century Fund, both 1960, both for "work in arms control"; received several other awards, including one from Sigma Delta Chi for reporting from Vietnam, 1971.

WRITINGS: Do I Make Myself Clear, Holt, 1956; *The Joy Wagon,* Viking, 1958; *The Nation's Safety and Arms Control* (Book-of-the-Month Club alternate), Viking, 1961; *Power's Human Face,* Morrow, 1966; (with James M. Gavin) *Crisis Now,* Random House, 1968; *A Life in Order,* Viking, 1970; *The Invisible Primary,* Prentice-Hall, 1976; *The Empty Polling Booth,* Prentice-Hall, 1978.

Plays: "Winterkill," first produced in Philadelphia, Pa., at The Playhouse in the Park, 1960; "The Four Minute Mile," first produced in New York City at Van Dam, 1961.

WORK IN PROGRESS: A novel.

SIDELIGHTS: Hadley's 1976 work, *The Invisible Primary,* was deemed "extremely well-written," by Brad Knickerbocker. The book deals with the years following a president's election up to the beginning of the next election's primaries. Knickerbocker also wrote that Hadley "very helpfully works in a history of the presidential selection process, also explaining well the intricacies and importance of recent 'reform' in the Democratic party and the complex and still-changing new campaign financing laws."

BIOGRAPHICAL/CRITICAL SOURCES: New York Times Book Review, March 28, 1976; *Christian Science Monitor,* April 13, 1976.

* * *

HALES, Loyde (Wesley) 1933-

PERSONAL: Born March 9, 1933, in Kansas City, Mo.; son of Thomas Wesley (a rural mail carrier) and Lola Alice (Bretches) Hales; married Annie King Loudon, March 21, 1960; children: Lavinia Anne, Loyde Wesley II, Lydia Elizabeth. *Education:* University of Kansas, B.S., 1956, M.S., 1960, Ed.D., 1964. *Home:* Regency Apartments, 1410 Southwest Broadway, Portland, Ore. 97201. *Office:* School of Education, Portland State University, Portland, Ore. 97207.

CAREER: Harvard University, Cambridge, Mass., research associate, 1964-66; Wichita State University, Wichita, Kan., assistant professor of educational psychology, 1966-67; Ohio University, Athens, assistant professor, 1967-70, associate professor, 1970-74, professor of education, 1974-78; Portland State University, Portland, Ore., professor of education, 1978—. Research and evaluation consultant to public schools, public agencies, and private companies. Lecturer on work values. *Military service:* U.S. Naval Reserve, active duty, 1956-59; became lieutenant, junior grade. *Mem-*

ber: American Educational Research Association, American Association of University Professors, American Personnel and Guidance Association, National Vocational Guidance Association, Association for Measurement and Evaluation in Guidance, Oregon Educational Research Association, Phi Delta Kappa. *Awards, honors:* Exchange scholar at University of Aberdeen, 1960-61; senior Fulbright scholar, 1974-75.

WRITINGS: (With Jon C. Marshall) *Classroom Test Construction,* Addison-Wesley, 1971; (with Bradford Fenner) *Ohio Work Values Inventory,* privately printed, 1971, 3rd edition, 1979; (with Marshall) *Essentials of Testing,* Addison-Wesley, 1972; (with Marshall) *Introduction to Educational Statistics,* Addison-Wesley, 1980. Contributor of about forty articles to professional journals and papers at professional meetings.

WORK IN PROGRESS: Research on work values.

SIDELIGHTS: Hales writes: "My major areas of vocational interest are test construction and evaluation, both normative and criterion-referenced, and the work values of adolescents and young adults. I have conducted extensive research in these areas, and am continuing my research efforts. My motivation in writing *Classroom Test Construction* was an awareness of the inadequacy of classroom teachers in the area of pupil evaluation based on teacher-constructed tests."

* * *

HALL, Josef Washington 1894-1960
(Upton Close)

OBITUARY NOTICE: Born February 27, 1894, in Kelso, Wash.; died in 1960. Lecturer, broadcaster, and author. Under the pseudonym Upton Close, Hall wrote numerous books celebrating the Oriental lifestyle, including *In the Land of the Laughing Buddha, Outline History of China,* and *The Challenge Behind the Face of Japan.* Hall was also an avid traveler and was involved in many excursions with the National Geographic Society. Obituaries and other sources: *Current Biography,* Wilson, 1944, January, 1961; *New York Times,* November 15, 1960.

* * *

HALSMAN, Philippe 1906-1979

OBITUARY NOTICE—See index for *CA* sketch: Born May 2, 1906,in Riga, Latvia; died June 25, 1979, in New York, N.Y. Photographer, lecturer, and author. Halsman was best known for his photographic portraits of such famous people as Sir Winston Churchill, Albert Einstein, Helen Hayes, Eleanor Roosevelt, and Dwight D. Eisenhower. His work, which included 101 covers for *Life* magazine, was exhibited in Paris, Tokyo, and New York. Halsman was a member of the guiding faculty of the Famous Photographers School and wrote about six books, including *Philippe Halsman on the Creation of Photographic Ideas, Halsman Sight and Insight,* and *Dali's Moustache.* Obituaries and other sources: *Current Biography,* Wilson, 1960, August, 1979; *The Author's and Writer's Who's Who,* 6th edition, Burke's Peerage, 1971; *Authors of Books for Young People,* 2nd edition, Scarecrow, 1971; *Who's Who in America,* 40th edition, Marquis, 1978; *New York Times,* June 26, 1979.

* * *

HAMILTON, Charles F(ranklin) 1915-

PERSONAL: Born August 31, 1915, in Wilkinsburg, Pa.; son of Charles S. (a personnel executive) and Elizabeth (McMasters) Hamilton; married Virginia L. Riley (a writer); children: Charles B., Grant M. *Education:* Attended University of Pittsburgh, 1934-35. *Politics:* Republican. *Religion:* Protestant. *Home:* 234 Union St., Dunedin, Fla. 33528.

CAREER: Associated with Keystone Adjusting Co., 1935-36; insurance adjuster at Lumbermens Mutual Casualty Co., 1936-41; assistant treasurer at Van der Voort & Co., Inc. (insurance agency), and secretary of corporation at Hostetter Corp. (medicine manufacturer), 1941-54; writer and producer of public service programs at KDKA-Radio and Television, 1954-57; Westinghouse Electric Corp., Buffalo, N.Y., manager of employee and community relations, 1957-75; free-lance writer and public relations consultant, 1975—. Past managing editor of *Planer Talk* (trade magazine). Lecturer on public relations and Elbert Hubbard and the Roycrafters movement, and at Medaille College. Member of communications advisory council at State University of New York at Buffalo. Past member of Buffalo board of directors of National Conference of Christians and Jews; past member of Elbert Hubbard Library-Museum Commission, East Aurora, N.Y., and Aurora City Council. *Military service:* U.S. Navy, 1945.

MEMBER: Public Relations Society of America (Niagara Frontier chapter; past president), Frontier Editors Association (past president), Public Relations Association of Western New York (honorary vice-president; past president), Aurora Historical Society (past president), Literary Clinic of the Niagara Frontier, Scriptores. *Awards, honors:* Public service and communications awards include Bishop Head Plaque from Diocese of Buffalo and its Labor Management College, 1973.

WRITINGS: Little Journeys to the Homes of Roycrofters, S-G Press, 1963; *As Bees in Honey Drown* (biography of Elbert Hubbard), A. S. Barnes, 1973; *Roycroft Collectibles,* A. S. Barnes, 1979. Contributor of several dozen articles to trade journals, history and communications journals, collectors' magazines, and newspapers. Past editor of *Planer Talk;* associate editor of *Wood Construction* and lumber trade magazines, 1954-57.

WORK IN PROGRESS: Research for books on politics, government, and women's liberation.

SIDELIGHTS: Hamilton writes: "I am motivated largely by a deep and abiding interest in history—past and in the making, American and world. My principal avocational interests are history-related: rare book and document collecting, antiques, memorabilia in general, and American memorabilia in particular."

AVOCATIONAL INTERESTS: Playing tennis, water skiing, fishing.

BIOGRAPHICAL/CRITICAL SOURCES: Sunshine, January, 1966.

* * *

HAMILTON, Mollie
See KAYE, M(ary) M(argaret)

* * *

HAMM, Michael Franklin 1943-

PERSONAL: Born August 29, 1943, in Ithaca, N.Y.; son of Franklin A. (a physicist) and Frances M. (Wertz) Hamm; married Jo Ann Wikoff (a teacher); children: Sarah, Jill. *Education:* Macalester College, B.A., 1965; Indiana University, M.A., 1967, Ph.D., 1971. *Religion:* Presbyterian. *Home:* 516 Seminole Trail, Danville, Ky. 40422. *Office:*

Department of History, Centre College, Danville, Ky. 40422.

CAREER: Centre College, Danville, Ky., assistant professor, 1970-76, associate professor of history, 1976—, director of programs in the Soviet Union and eastern Europe. *Member:* American Association for the Advancement of Slavic Studies, Middle East Institute. *Awards, honors:* Woodrow Wilson Dissertation fellowship, 1969-70; grants from U.S. Office of Education (for research in Yugoslavia), 1972, American Philosophical Society (for research in Finland), 1973, Centre College (for the Middle East), 1974, 1975, and International Research & Exchanges Board (for the Soviet Union), 1976-77; National Endowment for the Humanities fellowship, 1978.

WRITINGS: (Editor and contributor) *The City in Russian History,* University Press of Kentucky, 1976. Contributor to history and Slavic studies journals, including *Russian Review* and *Slavic Review.*

WORK IN PROGRESS: Research on conditions in pre-revolutionary Russian cities, folk architecture in eastern Europe, and the cities of Riga, Kiev, Kharkov, and Moldavia.

SIDELIGHTS: Hamm told *CA:* "My research is motivated by a desire to learn more about the nature of the Russian city between the revolutions of 1905 and 1917—about housing, ethnic interaction, municipal government, etc.—for a more sophisticated understanding of these matters can tell us a great deal about the collapse of the tsarist order and the vulnerability of various urban groups to revolutionary appeals."

AVOCATIONAL INTERESTS: Folk architecture in Eastern Europe, photography, tennis, basketball.

* * *

HANAMI, Tadashi (Akamatsu) 1930-

PERSONAL: Born February 15, 1930, in Tokyo, Japan; son of Katsujiro (a writer) and Shizuko Hanami; married Ryoko Akamatsu (a minister of Japanese permanent mission to the United Nations), 1953; children: Tadaaki. *Education:* University of Tokyo, LL.B., 1953, LL.D., 1962; graduate study at University of Cologne, 1959-61. *Home:* 2-7-1-207 Mita, Minato-ku, Tokyo, Japan. *Office:* Department of Law, Sophia University, 7 Kioicho, Chiyoda-ku, Tokyo, Japan.

CAREER: Japan Institute of Labor, Tokyo, research officer, 1956-66; Sophia University, Tokyo, Japan, professor of labor law, 1966—, dean of department of law, 1979—. Member of Tokyo Metropolitan Labor Relations Commission, 1968-79, and Bar Examination Commission, 1970—. *Member:* International Association of Social Security and Labor Law, International Industrial Relations Association, Japan Labor Law Association, Japan Association of Social Policy.

WRITINGS—In English: *Labor Relations in Japan Today,* Kodansha International, 1979; *Labor Law and Industrial Relations in Japan,* Kluwer-Deventer, 1979.

Other: *Roshi kan ni okeru chokaiken no kenkyu* (title means "Employer's Power to Discipline Workers"), Keiso Shobo, 1959; (with Kichiemon Ishikawa) *Nishi Doitsu no rodo saiban* (title means "Labor Court in West Germany"), Nihon Rodo Kyokai, 1962; (with Yoshio Keiya and Kiyohiko Hagisawa) *Rodoho kyoshitsu* (title means "Labor Law Class"), [Japan], 1964; (with Ishikawa) *Jishu rodoho sanjumon* (title means "Thirty Questions on Labor Law for Homework"), [Japan], 1966; (with Ken'ichi Jokao) *Kyozai rodoho nyumon* (title means "Cases and Materials: Introduction to Labor Law"), [Japan], 1967; (with Teruhisa Ishii) *Rodoho* (title means "Labor Law"), [Japan], 1968; (with Hagisawa) *Roshi Kankei no horitsu sodan* (title means "Legal Counsel for Labor Relations"), [Japan], 1969; *Rodo kihon ken* (title means "Fundamental Human Rights of Labor"), Chusksronsha, 1969; *Rodo sogi* (title means "Labor Dispute"), Nihon Keizai Shinbun Sha, 1973; (with Koichiro Yamaguchi) *Furekkusu taimu* (title means "Flex Time"), Diamond Publishing, 1975; (with Kishio Hobara) *Rosai hosho—anzen eisei gojukko* (title means "Fifty Lectures on Workmen's Compensation"), Yuhikaku, 1975.

WORK IN PROGRESS: Research on international comparison of dispute settlement in industrial relations and on the function of labor law in the development of society in developing countries.

SIDELIGHTS: Hanami writes: "Because of the remarkable success of the Japanese economy, the world's attention came to be focused on the characteristics of Japanese industrial relations. Westerners tend to consider the Japanese society a harmonious one and the employer-employee relationship amicable. This is partly true. But in actual industrial relations in Japan a lot of conflicts do exist and some of them would expand into very fierce confrontations. However, the uniqueness of Japanese industrial relations is found in the way of dispute settlement rather than in the non-existence of the dispute. The way of dispute settlement in Japan still holds the characteristics of the traditional way of conflict resolution. The judges and conciliators do not apply the universal norm but try to reestablish and recover the harmonious relationship between parties. They avoid giving clear-cut decisions but appeal to the sentiment and goodwill of the parties.

"Such a way of conflict resolution is more suitable to industrial relations which is in its substance more human and emotional than ordinary business transactions. Some of the difficulties of Western industrial relations systems today stem from the established formal system which has been very much suitable to the settlement of the problems of industrial society where the economic gain and achievements have been the most important. But as Western societies have reached the stage of postindustrialized society, the human and psychological problems of the workers are becoming more and more important while economic needs have been met in most of those so-called affluent societies. The temporary hypothesis of mine is rather inclined to see certain strong points in the Japanese way of the dispute settlement. This was the viewpoint which was advocated in my book, *Labor Relations in Japan Today.* The works which I am undertaking now will examine the merit of this hypothesis by the research of the more detailed actual situations of the different countries' industrial relations."

* * *

HANAU, Laia 1916-

PERSONAL: Born June 4, 1916, in Boston, Mass.; daughter of Samuel B. (a doctor and lawyer) and Lucy A. (a nurse and lawyer; maiden name, Greenwood) Pearlmutter; married Richard Hanau (a physicist), January 2, 1941; children: Loren Michael (Mrs. Richard H. Douglas). *Education:* Smith College, A.B., 1937; University of Rochester, M.A., 1960; graduate work at universities of Michigan, Kentucky, and Arizona. *Residence:* Lexington, Ky.

CAREER: Teacher and consultant in Hanau Method Study & Writing Techniques. *American Horseman,* Lexington, Ky., copy editor, 1947-49; University of Kentucky, Lexington, assistant editor of publications in department of public information, 1949-50, editorial assistant in department of animal pathology, 1950-52; Optical Society of America, Rochester, N.Y., editorial consultant, 1959; junior high school English teacher, 1960-61, senior high school English teacher, 1961-66, both in Lexington; University of Kentucky, instructor, 1967-69, assistant professor, 1970-73; consultant to more than fifteen professional and educational organizations, 1969—. Learning specialist, Sayre School, 1974-76. Participated in Breadloaf Writers' Conference, 1953. Editorial consultant to University of Kentucky College of Medicine, 1963-66. *Member:* Authors Guild. *Awards, honors:* Avery and Jule Hopwood Award in nonfiction, 1942, for fictionalized documentary, "Two Dollar House."

WRITINGS: The Study Game: How to Play and Win With "Statement-Pie", Barnes & Noble, 1974; *The Study Game Workbook: A Guide to Writing and Note Taking,* LMR Books, 1976; *The Study Game: How to Play and Win,* Harper, 1979.

WORK IN PROGRESS: A magazine article, "Causes of Study Problems."

SIDELIGHTS: With fitting irony, Hanau writes: "I grew up on a diet of the power of positive thinking and *Invictus:* I was the master of my Fate. I could intend, and plan, and it would be. Accordingly, I proceeded with my life, making my plans and mapping the strategies for implementing them.

"Nothing worked out. I planned three children, had one; educated myself to be an editor-writer, ended up a teacher—for which it embarrassingly turned out I had more talent than for any other role in my life (writer, wife, mother, friend, or dilettante *par excellence*).

"I recognized very early that I was an unadventurous hot house plant with a minimal interest in physical activity, and I planned my life to conform to my natural inclinations: residence in a warm climate, proper baths in modern houses, and the luxurious comfort of excellent medical care immediately at hand.

"I ended up living mostly in rigorous climates, buried inside layers of clothing for warmth, or shrouded in rubber and plastic against the rain. I struggle with the problems of semi-primitive housing. And I travel in lands where I suffer from cultural shock and medical anxiety.

"So now I have given up making plans or mapping strategies. Apparently someone or something else is in charge of my destiny, for I certainly am not. Now I sit quietly and wait for the next phone call or the next mail delivery—to find out what I'll be doing next.

"But there is one thing I planned that has worked out as I planned: that I would have a husband whom I loved (and vice-versa him-me) and we would be married to each other through our lifetimes. So far it's working, but I am suspicious of it. I don't know whether it's working because I am the master of my Fate or because he is master of his."

* * *

HANCOCK, Carla

PERSONAL: Daughter of Robert M. and Wilhelmina F. Hancock. *Education:* Oglethorpe University, B.A.; also attended Georgia State University. *Politics:* Republican. *Office:* c/o John Blair, 1406 Plaza Dr., S.W., Winston-Salem, N.C. 27103.

CAREER: Writer and investment manager. *Member:* National Alumni Association of Oglethorpe University (member of board of directors).

WRITINGS: Seven Founders of American Literature (juvenile), Blair, 1976. Contributor of articles and reviews to trade journals and newspapers.

SIDELIGHTS: Hancock told *CA:* "I am a firm anti-vivesectionist. I do not believe animals or people should be used for experimentation of any kind. I think business should be free to compete without governmental controls or intervention. I do not feel that the Equal Rights Amendment is necessary because anyone can attain any goal they may desire if they are willing to work hard enough to attain it; that is, make the sacrifices of self and time to reach that goal. There are numerous men and women in this nation who have proven this point. Quality is the important point, be it in business, government, or the arts; quantity is nothing without this element."

* * *

HANDMAN, Herbert Ira 1932-

PERSONAL: Born June 22, 1932, in New York, N.Y. son of Irving (a merchant) and Jean (Rappaport) Handman; married Elena Karena, June 30, 1969; children: Melissa Fanny, Justin I., Giorgio I. *Education:* New York University, B.A., 1953, LL.B., 1958. *Residence:* New York, N.Y. *Office:* 42 East 65th St., New York, N.Y. 10021.

CAREER: Worked as an attorney, 1958-68; realtor, 1968—. *Military service:* U.S. Army, 1953-55. *Member:* New York State Bar Association, Bar Association of the City of New York, Mensa.

WRITINGS: The Rights of Convicts, Oceania, 1975.

SIDELIGHTS: Handman comments: "As a former criminal lawyer I have a great interest in penology. It is possible I will write a book about that career. I am now active in the development of real estate, especially the renovation of city properties. The energy crisis and the expansion of cultural and leisure-time interests dictate a resurgence of city life. These developments may also inspire more writing."

* * *

HANSEN, Ron 1947-

PERSONAL: Born December 8, 1947, in Omaha, Neb.; son of Frank L. (an electrical engineer) and Marvyl (a stenographer; maiden name, Moore) Hansen. *Education:* Creighton University, B.A., 1970; University of Iowa, M.F.A., 1974; further graduate study at Stanford University, 1977-78. *Residence:* Menlo Park, Calif. *Agent:* Liz Darhansoff, 52 East 91st St., New York, N.Y. 10028. *Office:* Department of English, Stanford University, Stanford, Calif. 94305.

CAREER: Stanford University, Stanford, Calif., Jones Lecturer in Creative Writing, 1978—.

WRITINGS: Desperadoes, Knopf, 1979.

SIDELIGHTS: Hansen's first novel, *Desperadoes,* is the story of the Daltons, an outlaw gang that flourished in the West in the late 1800's. The story is told in 1937 by the last of the gang's survivors, Emmett Dalton. It is not only time that divides Dalton from his past: the former outlaw is now a "real-estate broker, a building contractor, a scriptwriter for Western movies; a church man, a Rotarian, a member of Moose Lodge 29."

Hansen generally impressed critics with *Desperadoes* though several flaws were cited in his work. Reviewer Henry McDonald felt the book was "overwritten" and objected to a style he found "inflated, pretentious, and generally painful to endure." Another critic, Anatole Broyard, took exception to Hansen's "interesting but slightly improbable fictional reconstruction of the exploits of the Dalton gang." Frederick Busch of the *Chicago Tribune,* on the other hand, found *Desperadoes* "the product of extensive research and plenty of talent." Though Busch viewed structure and point of view as "very seriously flawed elements in this novel," he admitted Hansen "already can sing a lovely song [and] is one day going to write a wholly good book, and probably soon." Jerome Charyn, too, was enthusiastic about Hansen's work: "The writing is so accomplished and the book has such an authoritative tone that one finds it difficult to think of this as a *first* novel."

BIOGRAPHICAL/CRITICAL SOURCES: Chicago Tribune, April 8, 1979; *Washington Post,* May 4, 1979; *New York Times Book Review,* June 3, 1979; *New York Times,* June 13, 1979.

* * *

HANSON, A(lbert) H(enry) 1913-1971

OBITUARY NOTICE—See index for *CA* sketch: Born April 20, 1913, in Swindon, Wiltshire, England; died April 27, 1971, in London, England. Educator and writer on history and politics. Hanson wrote a number of books on the nationalization of industry, including *Public Enterprise, Parliament and Public Ownership,* and *Managerial Problems in Public Enterprise.* Obituaries and other sources: *The Author's and Writer's Who's Who,* 6th edition, Burke's Peerage, 1971; *AB Bookman's Weekly,* June 7, 1971.

* * *

HARLOW, Joan Hiatt 1932-

PERSONAL: Born July 25, 1932, in Malden, Mass.; daughter of Albert E. (a singer) and Marguerite (a registered nurse; maiden name, Small) Hiatt; married Richard Lee Harlow (a banker and auditor), August 17, 1951; children: Deborah Balas, Lisa Bilodeau, Kristan Delphia, Scott, Jennifer. *Education:* Stenotype Institute of Boston, earned certificate, 1951. *Home:* 12 Horseshoe Rd., Chelmsford, Mass. 01824.

CAREER: Writer. Worked as administrative assistant for Redevelopment Authority in Wilmington, Mass., 1967-73; special-needs secretary of public schools in Littletown, Mass., 1977-78. *Member:* Society of Children's Book Writers, Westford Players (secretary and member of board of directors).

WRITINGS—Juvenile: (With daughter, Kristan Harlow) *Poems Are for Everything,* Christopher, 1973; *The Shadow Bear,* Doubleday, 1980. Contributor to periodicals, including *Child Life, Ranger Dick,* and *Young World.*

WORK IN PROGRESS: Sirius, the story of a Newfoundland dog.

SIDELIGHTS: Harlow confessed to an interviewer that writing children's books is "very easy, if you can think like a child." She also revealed that this thought process can overwhelm her adult behavior. "A while ago," she related, "I wrote a business letter and then realized it was all little short sentences. It read like 'Dick and Jane.' I had to redo the whole thing."

For Harlow, the pleasure of writing comes from "having somebody to share things with—somebody you don't know who's enjoying it, and maybe trying out something new." Harlow's enthusiasm for her subjects is so all-encompassing that even her family becomes involved in her interests. "The whole family gets excited because I write, eat, and sleep things," she noted, "I talk about them all the time and make loads of phone calls." Harlow's intense involvement has led to family vacations devoted to research for her topics. "It's difficult not to get carried away at times," she remarked.

AVOCATIONAL INTERESTS: Skiing, astronomy, photography, traveling.

BIOGRAPHICAL/CRITICAL SOURCES: Lowell Sun, June 10, 1979.

* * *

HARMIN, Merrill 1928-

PERSONAL: Born April 27, 1928, in Brooklyn, N.Y.; son of Henry (a workingman) and Blanche (Levy) Harmin; married Tomaji Komazaki (an artist), September 20, 1952; children: Andrea Ko, Jesse Ken. *Education:* Syracuse University, B.S., 1949; New York University, A.M., 1956, Ph.D., 1960. *Office:* School of Education, Southern Illinois University, Edwardsville, Ill. 62025.

CAREER: Goddard Neighborhood House, New York City, social group worker with delinquent youth, 1953-55; New School for Social Research, New York City, instructor in public planning, and associate director of Center for Community Participation, 1956-57; high school mathematics teacher in Long Beach, N.Y., 1957-60; Rutgers University, New Brunswick, N.J., assistant professor of education and workshop director, 1960-65; Southern Illinois University, Edwardsville, professor of education, 1965—. Social group worker for New York City Youth Board, 1953-55.

MEMBER: National Education Association, National Humanistic Education Center, American Association of University Professors, Association for Supervision and Curriculum Development, Association for Humanistic Psychology, Illinois Education Association. *Awards, honors:* Grants from Central Midwestern Regional Laboratory, 1966-67, and U.S. Office of Education, 1967-68.

WRITINGS: (With Louis E. Raths and Sidney B. Simon) *Values and Teaching,* C. E. Merrill, 1966, 2nd edition, 1977; (with Simon and Howard Kirschenbaum) *Clarifying Values Through Subject Matter,* Winston Press, 1973; (with Tom Gregory) *Teaching Is . . . ,* Science Research Associates, 1974; *How to Get Rid of Emotions That Give You a Pain in the Neck,* Argus Communications, 1976; *What I've Learned About Values Education,* Phi Delta Kappa, 1977; (with Saville Sax) *A Peacable Classroom: Activities to Calm and Free Student Energies,* Winston Press, 1977. Also author of *You're a Star, Not a Lump: Five Skills Make a Difference.*

Multi-media kits: "Making Sense of Our Lives," Argus Communications, 1973, 2nd edition, 1974; "People Projects," Sets A-C, Addison-Wesley, 1973; "I've Got to Be Me!" (for children), Argus Communications, 1976; "This Is Me!" (for children), Argus Communications, 1978.

Contributor: Donald Forgays, editor, *Critical Thinking,* New Jersey Secondary School Teachers Association, 1963; William Rogge and G. Edward Stormer, editors, *Inservice Training for Teachers of the Gifted,* Stipes, 1966; *Creative Developments in the Training of Educational Personnel,* U.S. Office of Education, 1969; *Teaching Mathematics in the Elementary School,* National Association of Elementary School Principals, 1970; Dwight Allen and Eli Seifman, editors, *Teacher's Handbook,* Scott, Foresman, 1971; Marshall Rosenberg, editor, *Educational Therapy,* Volume III, Special Child Publications, 1973; Saville Sax and Sandra Hollander, editors, *Kill the Dragon,* Reality Press, 1975; (author of introduction) Kenneth Morrison and Robert Havens, *Values Clarification in Counseling,* Educational Media Corp., 1976.

Author of "Values Clarification in the Classroom," Media Five Films, 1977. Contributor of more than forty articles to education journals.

SIDELIGHTS: Harmin writes: "For several years I carried on about how to clarify one's own values and live one's own life. Then I paused and immersed myself in metaphysics. When I returned I found both my students and I had changed. The students were much more ready to take charge of their lives; many *demanded* to do so. I was much more aware of what went into living a valued life; I even did better with *my* values. Working in this new space, I came to appreciate five skills that serve us particularly well nowadays and that are teachable at all age levels. Indeed, if there are basic skills for living in our seemingly nutty world, these five will beat the three R's any day of the week. I'd like to introduce the skill-development program that was assembled from this work and invite those interested to join this new humanistic education approach. To that end, I'm lately making speeches, writing bits and pieces, and preaching at my students about the importance of thinking for themselves."

* * *

HARMON, Nolan B(ailey) 1892-

PERSONAL: Born July 14, 1892, in Meridian, Miss.; son of Nolan Bailey, Sr. (a minister) and Juliet (Howe) Harmon; married Rebecca Barry Lamar, June 20, 1923; children: Nolan Bailey III, George Lamar. *Education:* Millsaps College, A.B., 1914; graduate study at Emory University, 1916-17; Princeton University, M.A., 1920. *Home and office:* 998 Springdale Rd. N.E., Atlanta, Ga. 30306.

CAREER: Ordained Methodist Episcopal minister, 1918; Walter Reed General Hospital, Washington, D.C., camp pastor, 1918-19; pastor of Methodist churches in Maryland and Virginia, 1920-23, and in Roanoke, Va., 1933-40; United Methodist Church, book editor, 1940-56; elected bishop, 1956; resident bishop of western North Carolina conference in Charlotte, 1956-60, South Carolina conference, 1956-60, Kentucky conference, 1960-61, and North Alabama conference, 1961-64; writer, 1964—. Editor of Abingdon Press, 1940-56. Visiting professor at Emory University, 1964—. Member of national church conferences and committees; member of national Methodist board for Christian colleges in China; member of executive committee of Federal Council of Churches, 1944-48; director of Save the Children Federation, 1940-48. Member of board of trustees of High Point College and Brevard College. *Military service:* U.S. Army, chaplain, 1918-23; became first lieutenant.

MEMBER: Kappa Sigma, Masons, University Club (New York). *Awards, honors:* D.D. from Millsaps College, 1929, Emory University, 1958, and Duke University, 1959; D.H.L. from Mount Union College, 1946; D.Litt. from American University, 1946, Western Maryland College, 1947, and Hamline University, 1947; LL.D. from Wofford College, 1961.

WRITINGS: The Famous Case of Myra Clark Gaines, Louisiana State University Press, 1946; *The Organization of the Methodist Church,* Methodist Publishing House, 1948, revised edition, 1962; *Ministerial Ethics and Etiquette,* c. 1950, revised edition, Abingdon-Cokesbury, 1958; *Understanding the Methodist Church,* Methodist Publishing House, 1955, revised edition, 1977. Also author of *The Rites and Ritual of Episcopal Methodism,* 1925, and *Is It Right or Wrong?,* 1938.

Editor: *Methodist Book of Discipline,* 1940; *The Interpreter's Bible,* Abingdon-Cokesbury, 1940-56; *Religion in Life,* 1940-56; *Encyclopedia of World Methodism,* 1964-74. Contributor to church periodicals.

* * *

HARMSWORTH, Esmond Cecil 1898-1978 (Viscount Rothermere)

OBITUARY NOTICE: Born May 29, 1898; died July 12, 1978, in London, England. Harmsworth is best known for his management of the British newspaper chain that includes the *London Evening News,* the *London Daily Mail,* and the *London Sunday Dispatch.* As Viscount Rothermere, Harmsworth also served in the House of Lords. Obituaries and other sources: *Current Biography,* Wilson, 1948, September, 1978; *Who's Who,* 126th edition, St. Martin's, 1976; *New York Times,* July 13, 1978.

* * *

HARPER, Harold W.

EDUCATION: Attended North Texas University, 1954-56; University of Texas, M.D., 1960; postdoctoral study at Nehan's Geriatrics Clinic, Institute of Geriatrics, Bucharest, Romania, Shimbushi Corrective Surgery Clinic, University of Tokyo, and Salvadore Mundy International Hospital. *Office:* Harper Metabology and Nutrition Medical Group, Bio-Med Medical Center, 11311 Camarillo St., Suite 103, North Hollywood, Calif. 91602.

CAREER: St. Joseph Hospital, Fort Worth, Tex., intern, 1960; American Institute of Hypnosis, Los Angeles, Calif., resident in hypnosis and hypnoanalysis, 1964-66; Harper Metabology and Nutrition Group, North Hollywood, Calif., founder and director, 1967—. Lecturer at national conferences.

MEMBER: International Society of General Semantics (member of local board of trustees, 1964; local president, 1965), International Academy of Preventive Medicine (fellow; member of board of trustees, 1972—; president, 1973-74), International Academy of Metabology (founding member), American Academy of Medical Preventics (fellow; founding president, 1973-76; head of board of directors, 1976—), American College of Endocrinology and Nutrition (fellow; member of board of trustees, 1968), American College of Medical Hypnotists (fellow; member of board of trustees, 1965), American Institute of Hypnosis (fellow), American Society of Bariatric Physicians (founding member), American Society of Geriatrics (fellow), California State Hypnosis Association (vice-president, 1969-70).

WRITINGS: (With Michael L. Culbert) *How You Can Beat the Killer Diseases,* Arlington House, 1978. Co-editor of "Reprints of Medical Literature on Chelation Therapy," 1975. Contributor to medical journals. Associate editor of *New Dynamics of Preventive Medicine,* 1974-77.

WORK IN PROGRESS: A book on early cancer and precancer detection.

* * *

HARRINGTON, Joseph Daniel 1923-

PERSONAL: Born September 29, 1923, in Boston, Mass.; son of James Patrick (a carpenter) and Anastatia (Lee) Harrington; married Bette Lou Allan, December 29, 1945 (divorced); married Virginia Clark, January 15, 1953 (divorced); married Carol Elizabeth Webster (a dining room manager), April 29, 1978; children: (second marriage) Sheila Frances, Polly Patricia, Matthew Joseph. *Education:* Attended high school in Boston, Mass. *Politics:* "Anarchist."

Home and office address: P.O. Box 1322, Hallandale, Fla. 33009.

CAREER: U.S. Navy, career enlisted man, 1942-63, retiring as chief petty officer; writer and editor for U.S. Government, 1963-64; Harrington Associates (national employment agency for military men entering private industry), Washington, D.C., president, 1964-71; carpenter, 1971-77; writer, 1977—. *Member:* Fleet Reserve Association. *Awards, honors:* Essay prizes from U.S. Naval Institute, 1952, for "Wanted—5000 Middlemen," 1953, for "Evaluating Enlisted Men's Performance," and 1955, for "Every Weapon to the Fray."

WRITINGS: Kaiten: The Story of Japan's Human Torpedos, Ballantine, 1962, reprinted as *Suicide Submarine,* 1979; *Rendezvous at Midway: The Story of the "U.S.S. Yorktown" and the Japanese Carrier Fleet,* John Day, 1968; *I-Boat Captain: The Story of Japan's Submarines at War* (Literary Guild's Military Book Club selection), Major Books, 1976; *Yankee Samurai: The Secret Role of Nisei in America's Pacific Victory* (Literary Guild's Military Book Club selection; first volume in trilogy), Pettigrew Enterprises, 1979; *The Bad, Bad Banzai Boys: The Story of the 442nd Regimental Combat Team* (second volume in trilogy), Pettigrew Enterprises, 1980.

WORK IN PROGRESS: The War That Won Their Battle, final volume of the trilogy, publication by Pettigrew Enterprises expected in 1982.

SIDELIGHTS: Harrington's interest in naval history began when he was working on a historical project for the Navy's public information department. His latest book, *Yankee Samurai,* involved interviews with some fifteen hundred Japanese-American veterans of World War II, fifteen thousand miles of travel, and extensive research in archives. It covers events and attitudes long kept secret by government officials and agencies: the prison camps and occupation, the discrimination and prejudice focused on these American citizens, and it covers what they are doing today.

Harrington comments: "The aim of my trilogy (and my life) is to demonstrate that hate, vindictiveness, prejudice, and discrimination are a WASTE, and that the civilized human being trying to lead a decent life just has no place for them in it. I have consistently (and successfully) challenged 'official' versions, and kind of wish that my fellow citizens would develop a general healthy skepticism."

BIOGRAPHICAL/CRITICAL SOURCES: Japan Times, November 19, 1978; *Miami Herald,* April 5, 1979.

* * *

HARRIS, Ben(jamin) Charles 1907-1978

OBITUARY NOTICE—See index for *CA* sketch: Born November 17, 1907, in Boston, Mass.; died February 9, 1978, in Miami, Fla. Pharmacist and author of eight books on herbs, including *Better Health With Culinary Herbs, Kitchen Tricks,* and *Make Use of Your Garden Plants.* Harris also wrote radio programs about herbs and moderated a television show on herbs and health. Obituaries and other sources: *Publishers Weekly,* February 27, 1978.

* * *

HARRIS, Daniel A(rthur) 1942-

PERSONAL: Born April 29, 1942, in New York, N.Y.; son of Howard M. (in real estate) and Constance (Wechsler Harris. *Education:* Yale University, B.A. (magna cum laude), 1964, M.A., 1966, Ph.D., 1968. *Office:* Department of English, Douglass College, Rutgers University, New Brunswick, N.J. 08903.

CAREER: University of Pennsylvania, Philadelphia, assistant professor of English, 1968-74; University of Florida, Gainesville, associate professor of English, 1974-75; University of Colorado, Boulder, associate professor of English, 1975-79; currently affiliated with Rutgers University, Douglass College, New Brunswick, N.J. Visiting professor at Swarthmore College, 1973-74. Workshop director; participant in conferences. *Member:* International Association for the study of Anglo-Irish Literature, Modern Language Association of America, Hopkins Society, Phi Beta Kappa. *Awards, honors:* Andrew Mellon fellowship, 1971-72; Florida State University System Humanities Council fellow, 1975; faculty book prize from University of Colorado, 1976, for *Yeats;* visiting fellow at Yale University, 1978-79; Guggenheim fellow, 1978-79; Newberry Library fellow, 1979-80.

WRITINGS: Yeats: Coole Park and Ballylee, Johns Hopkins Press, 1974. Contributor to *Women's Studies.* Member of editorial board of *English Language Notes.*

WORK IN PROGRESS: Inspirations Unbidden: The "Terrible Sonnets" of Gerard Manley Hopkins; Modernist Transformations of the Dramatic Monologue: Yeats, Eliot, Pound, Woolf, and Joyce; editing Yeats's *Prefaces and Introductions,* with Richard Finneran, for Macmillan; editing Yeats's *The Wind Among the Reeds,* for Cornell University Press.

SIDELIGHTS: Harris writes: "*Yeats: Coole Park and Ballylee* demonstrates Yeats's romantic transformations of the Jonsonian country house poem, provides a new interpretation of his debts to Castiglione, and offers detailed commentaries on all the poems he wrote about Coole Park and his own tower.

"In *Modernist Transformations of the Dramatic Monologue,* I will analyze the ways in which modern writers internalized the audience' typical of Browning and Tennyson (and thus approached interior monologue), altered the earlier conception of the hero, reformulated the function of historical or mythological displacement in dramatic monologue, and continued in wholly novel ways the experiments of their predecessors in playing with relations between space, action, and character.

"*Inspirations Unbidden* is based on a fresh examination of the manuscripts of Hopkins's 'terrible sonnets' and a new conception of the proper text. This book considers the relation between style and theology."

* * *

HARRIS, Jed
See HOROWITZ, Jacob

* * *

HARRIS, John (Wyndham Parkes Lucas) Beynon 1903-1969
(John Beynon, Lucas Parkes, John Wyndham)

OBITUARY NOTICE: Born July 10, 1903, in Knowle, Warwickshire, England; died March 11, 1969. Author. Harris wrote science fiction stories for twenty years before publishing his popular novel, *The Day of the Triffids.* Written under the pseudonym John Wyndham, the book tells of the anarchy and collapse of civilization that results when most of Earth's population is blinded by a huge explosion in space. His other books include *Midwich Cuckoos, Trouble With Lichen,* and *Chockey,* plus several collections of his science fiction short stories. Obituaries and other sources: *The Reader's Encyclopedia,* 2nd edition, Crowell, 1965; *World Authors, 1950-1970,* Wilson, 1975.

* * *

HART, Basil Henry Liddell
See LIDDELL HART, Basil Henry

* * *

HART, Moss 1904-1961

OBITUARY NOTICE: Born October 24, 1904, in New York, N.Y.; died December 20, 1961. Writer who teamed with George S. Kaufman to become one of America's favorite playwriting teams during the 1930's. Among the most popular Hart-Kaufman comedies are "Once in a Lifetime," "You Can't Take It With You," and "I'd Rather Be Right." Fearing that he'd be remembered only as half of a writing team, Hart split from Kaufman in 1940 after their play "George Washington Slept Here" was apathetically received by both critics and audiences. "Lady in the Dark," his first effort without Kaufman, featured music by Ira Gershwin. Hart ventured further from comedy in "Christopher Blake," his chronicle of a young boy's reaction to his parents' divorce. When his next drama, "The Climate of Eden," stumbled at the box-office, Hart abandoned playwriting in favor of writing his autobiography, *Act One.* A successful director as well as writer, Hart won a Tony Award in 1956 for his staging of "My Fair Lady." From 1932 to 1955, Hart also worked as a screenwriter; his career peaked in 1947 when "Gentlemen's Agreement," a film on anti-semitism which Hart wrote, received an Academy Award for best film. Obituaries and other sources: *Current Biography,* Wilson, 1940, 1960, February, 1962; *New York Times,* December 21, 1961; *Longman Companion to Twentieth Century Literature,* Longman, 1970; *McGraw-Hill Encyclopedia of World Drama,* McGraw, 1972; *Modern World Drama: An Encyclopedia,* Dutton, 1972; *Cassell's Encyclopaedia of World Literature,* revised edition, Morrow, 1973; *A Concise Encyclopedia of the Theatre,* Osprey, 1974.

* * *

HART, Winston Scott 1903(?)-1979

OBITUARY NOTICE: Born c. 1903 in Farmville, Va.; died of cancer, September 21, 1979, in Fairfax, Va. Journalist and author. Hart was a reporter for several newspapers in Virginia before joining the *Washington Post* as a columnist and feature writer from 1937 to 1943. He later worked as an editor of *Changing Times* magazine, as *Time* magazine correspondent in Washington, D.C., and as chief of the Washington bureau for *Coronet-Esquire* magazines. Hart wrote several books, including *The Moon Is Waning, Eight April Days, Route Obscure and Lonely,* and *Washington at War: 1941-1945.* Obituaries and other sources: *Washington Post,* September 22, 1979.

* * *

HARVEY, Kenneth 1919(?)-1979

OBITUARY NOTICE: Born c. 1919; died June 6, 1979, in Norwalk , Conn. Actor, director, and author. Harvey's acting career included seven years with the daytime television series "Search for Tomorrow," appearances on radio and early live television programs, roles in several touring company productions, and Broadway appearances in such plays as "Pipe Dream," "Calculated Risk," and "The Sound of Music." Harvey was a writer for the television series "All My Children." Obituaries and other sources: *New York Times,* June 8, 1979.

* * *

HARVEY, Marian 1927-

PERSONAL: Born January 31, 1927, in Chicago, Ill.; daughter of Thomas Francis, Jr. (a publisher) and Marian (an editor; maiden name, Dyer) Myers; married Kenneth H. Harvey (a musician), March 25, 1949; children: Minda Gene, Hiliry Gene. *Education:* Sacramento State University, B.A., 1954, received both elementary and secondary certification; Instituto Allende, M.A., 1970; also attended Mexico City College (now University of the Americas), and University of Mexico. *Home:* 246-4 Selby Ranch Rd., Sacramento, Calif. 95825.

CAREER: Lecturer at Sacramento State University and University of California, Davis, and on cruise ships. *Member:* Authors Guild, American Crafts Council, California Writers Club.

WRITINGS: Crafts of Mexico, photographs by husband, Kenneth Harvey, Macmillan, 1973.

Films—all released by Educational Filmstrips: "Color and Weaving in Mexico and Guatemala" (three parts); "Paper Flowers of Mexico" (two parts); "Festival Time in Mexico: San Miguel de Allende"; "Pinata"; "Amatl and the Bark Painting of Mexico." Contributor to magazines, including *Music Journal, Desert,* and *American Artist,* and newspapers.

WORK IN PROGRESS: A book and filmscripts on the crafts of Mexico.

SIDELIGHTS: Marian Harvey has lived in London and Rome and has visited many other parts of the world as well. She wrote: "My husband and I have researched and photographed some of the crafts of Italy, South America, and the South Pacific. This material still has to be organized and written.

"We spend several months of each year in Mexico. I lecture on the crafts of Mexico and other countires, and teach crafts on cruise ships. Because we will soon be leaving the teaching profession, we will be spending more time in Mexico and traveling.

"While doing research for my second book, we have traveled ten thousand miles in Mexico. We have ridden mules into some remote areas, and in two cases, walked. We have slept on *petates* on dirt floors and in hammocks in isolated mountain villages. We have now researched and photographed some fifty crafts in depth. The total, once written, would provide a compendium of Mexico's crafts which no one else has ever done. These include some pre-Conquest crafts, still being done today; some Spanish or colonial, little changed from those elegant days; other, post-Revolutionary and mestizo, are a mixture of Indian and Spanish.

"The craftspeople are both men and women, young and old, Indian and mestizo. Some are renowned in their fields, others anonymous, in the custom of the country. The crafts are found in the cities, towns, villages, on the ranches, and in remote and isolated regions. They range from the most primitive to the most sophisticated crafts to be found in the world today."

* * *

HASKELL, Douglas 1899-1979

OBITUARY NOTICE: Born June 27, 1899, in Monastir,

Turkey; died August 11, 1979, in Lake Placid, N.Y. Editor, critic, and author. Although not an architect, Haskell became deeply involved in architecture after college and specialized in the topic for over fifty years. From 1949 to 1964, he served as architectural editor, editorial chairman, and then editor of *Architectural Forum,* which was the leading architectural journal of the time. He wrote a monthly architectural column for the *Nation* for thirteen years, and contributed articles to journals, including *Architectural Record.* Haskell edited *Rehousing Urban America* and *Building U.S.A.* Obituaries and other sources: *Who's Who in American Art,* Bowker, 1973; *Who's Who in America,* 40th edition, Marquis, 1978; *New York Times,* August 14, 1979.

* * *

HASKINS, Barbara
See STONE, Barbara Haskins

* * *

HASSALL, Christopher (Vernon) 1912-1963

OBITUARY NOTICE: Born March 24, 1912, in London, England; died April 25, 1963. Writer who distinguished himself as poet, playwright, biographer, and librettist. Though he expressed an early interest in acting, Hassall turned to writing at the prompting of a fellow actor and playwright, Ivor Novello, for whom Hassall was understudy in a production of "Henry VIII." Hassall became the librettist for a number of Novello's musicals, including "The Dancing Years" and "King's Rhapsody." Among the collections of poetry for which he is admired are *The Slow Night* and *The Red Leaf.* As a biographer, Hassall is best known for *Edward Marsh: Patron of the Arts.* Obituaries and other sources: *The New Century Handbook of English Literature,* revised edition, Appleton, 1967; *Twentieth Century Writing: A Reader's Guide to Contemporary Literature,* Transatlantic, 1969; *Longman Companion to Twentieth Century Literature,* Longman, 1970; *World Authors, 1950-1970,* Wilson, 1975.

* * *

HATEM, Mohamed Abdel-Kader
See HATIM, Muhammad 'Abd al-Qadir

* * *

HATIM, Muhammad 'Abd al-Qadir 1918-
(Mohamed Abdel-Kader Hatem)

PERSONAL: Born in 1918, in Alexandria, Egypt. *Education:* Earned B.A., 1939; University of London, diploma (political economy), 1947; Staff College, M.A. (military science), 1952; Cairo University, M.A. (political science), 1952, Ph.D., 1957. *Address: Al-Ahram,* Gallaa St., Cairo, Egypt.

CAREER: Worked as Chief of Egyptian President Gamal Abdel Nasser's Press Office; director general of Egyptian Information Department; chairman of Information Committee of National Congress, began in 1957; member of People's Assembly for Abdin Constituency; counselor to President Nasser; minister of state, began in 1960; member of High Executive Committee of Arab Socialist Union, 1962-66; minister of information, culture, and tourism; deputy prime minister for information, culture, and tourism; deputy prime minister for information, 1971-74; acting prime minister, 1973-74; assistant to the President of the Republic and chairman of board of directors of *Al-Ahram,* 1974-75; supervisor general of Specialized National Councils, began in 1975; writer. *Military service:* Egyptian Armed Forces. *Member:* Political Science Society, Egyptian-Japanese Friendship Society, Egyptian-Spanish Friendship Society. *Awards, honors:* Order of Algamhouria (highest decoration in Egypt), 1964; honorary doctorates from University of Aix-en-Provence, 1967, and University of Seoul, 1973.

WRITINGS—In English: *Information and the Arab Cause* (textbook), Longman, 1974; *Life in Ancient Egypt,* Gateway Publishers, 1976; (under name Mohamed Abdel-Kader Hatem) *Land of the Arabs* (textbook), Longman, 1977. Also author of *History of the Egyptian Revolution.*

Other writings: *Al-Taqalid al-barlamaniyah* (title means "Parliamentary Traditions in the World"), two volumes, Kutub (Cairo), 1957; *Al-I'lam wa-al-di'ayah* (title means "Information and Propaganda"), [Cairo], 1960; *Rumil fi Siwah* (title means "Romel in Siwa"), Dar al-Najah (Beirut), 1971; *Al I'lam wa-al-di'ayah, nazariyat wa-tajarib* (title means "Propaganda: Theories and Experiences"), Maktabat al-Anglo al-Misriyah (Cairo), 1972; *Al-Ra'y al-amm* (title means "Public Opinion"), Maktabat al-Anglo al-Misriyah, 1972. Also author of numerous pamphlets on Egyptian government, culture, and tourism.

AVOCATIONAL INTERESTS: Plastic arts.

* * *

HAUTZIG, Deborah 1956-

PERSONAL: Born October 1, 1956, in New York, N.Y.; daughter of Walter (a musician) and Esther (a writer; maiden name, Rudomin) Hautzig. *Education:* Attended Carnegie-Mellon University, 1974-75; Sarah Lawrence College, B.A., 1978. *Politics:* "Anything reasonable." *Religion:* Jewish. *Residence:* New York, N.Y. *Office:* Random House, Inc., 201 East 50th St., New York, N.Y. 10022.

CAREER: Random House, Inc., New York, N.Y., promotion assistant in library marketing for Random House, Knopf, and Pantheon Books, 1978—. *Awards, honors: Hey, Dollface* was named best book for young adults by American Library Association, 1978.

WRITINGS—Children's books: *Hey, Dollface,* Greenwillow, 1978; *The Handsomest Father,* Greenwillow, 1979; *Rumpelstiltskin,* Random House, 1979.

WORK IN PROGRESS: Will the Real Leslie Hille Please Stand Up? (tentative title), a novel, for Greenwillow.

SIDELIGHTS: Deobrah Hautzig told *CA:* "I love to write more than anything in the world, and I can't help doing it. The one vital thing I tell myself about writing is: 'You're not out to teach; you're not out to preach. You're out to tell a story about real people, and anything else anyone derives from it is a fringe benefit.' I hope always to avoid didacticism. It's too easy to want to sound eloquent, wise, and witty, and use a book as a podium, rather than being true to its characters. You then dissipate and weaken your own book."

* * *

HAVENS, Shirley E(lise) 1925-

PERSONAL: Born November 19, 1925, in New York, N.Y.; daughter of A. Barton (a contractor) and Eva E. (Havens) Havens; *Education:* Hunter College (now of the City University of New York), B.A., 1947; Columbia University, graduate work, 1947-52. *Residence:* Flushing, N.Y. *Office:* R. R. Bowker Co., 1180 Avenue of the Americas, New York, N.Y. 10036.

CAREER/WRITINGS: Columbia University, New York

City, administrative assistant to bursar of Teachers College, 1947-52; Mental Health Film Board, New York City, executive secretary to secretary, 1952-54; Carnegie Endowment for International Peace, New York City, administrative secretary to librarian, 1954-57; R. R. Bowker Co., New York City, managing editor of *Library Journal,* 1959-66, associate editor, 1966-74, senior editor, 1975—. Contributor of articles, editorials, and book reviews to periodicals, including *Library Journal, School Library Journal,* and *Protestant Church Buildings & Equipment.* Editor of *Bulletin* of New York Library Club. Member of Library Committee of the President's Committee on Employment of the Handicapped. *Member:* American Library Association (member of Research and Publications Committee, member of awards committee of Intellectual Freedom Round Table), Phi Beta Kappa. *Awards, honors:* Commendation from President's Committee on Employment of the Handicapped, 1969.

SIDELIGHTS: Havens writes: "To me, writing is one of the most difficult, most disciplined, most agonizing of human pursuits; but there is perhaps no other endeavor which, when finally completed to one's satisfaction, results in such an enormous feeling of relief and accomplishment. Naturally, it is much easier to edit the labors of others, but nowhere nearly as satisfying in the end result."

AVOCATIONAL INTERESTS: "Coming from a long line of seafarers, I enjoy reading about, swimming in, and sailing on the sea."

* * *

HAYA de la TORRE, Victor Raul 1895-1979

OBITUARY NOTICE: Born February 22, 1895; died August 2, 1979. Writer and statesman who tried unsuccessfully for more than fifty years to obtain the presidency of Peru. Haya de la Torre spent much of his political life either in exile or in hiding, for Peru underwent many political changes during his lifetime. Though he failed in his efforts to win political office, Haya de la Torre was successful in uniting many Peruvian castes under a common front, the American Popular Revolutionary Alliance. Obituaries and other sources: *Current Biography,* Wilson, 1942, September, 1979; *Who's Who in the World,* 2nd edition, Marquis, 1973; *The International Who's Who,* 42nd edition, Europa, 1978; *New York Times,* August 14, 1979.

* * *

HAYDEN, Jay G. 1884-1971

OBITUARY NOTICE: Born December 8, 1884, in Cassopolis, Mich.; died October 24, 1971. Journalist best known for his political reporting for the *Detroit News* from 1915 to 1965. Hayden was one of only three reporters to witness the signing of the Treaty of Versailles that signified the end of World War I. Obituaries and other sources: *New York Times,* October 25, 1971; *Who Was Who in America,* 5th edition, Marquis, 1973.

* * *

HAYS, R. Vernon 1902-

PERSONAL: Born September 21, 1902, in Westerville, Neb.; son of Frank M. (a farmer) and Alice (Baker) Hays; married Wilma Pitchford, 1928; children: Grace Ann Hays Kone. *Education:* University of Nebraska, B.Sc., 1926, M.Ed., 1933; Harvard University, Ed.M., 1938. *Religion:* Congregational. *Home and office:* 1660 La Gorce Dr., Venice, Fla. 33595.

CAREER: Teacher of mathematics and science and boy's athletic coach at public school in Ansley, Neb., 1927-30, high school principal, 1930-32, school superintendent, 1933-36; principal of high schools in Wellfleet, Mass., 1937-38, and Mansfield, Mass., 1938-41; superintendent of schools in Danielson, Conn., 1941-53, and East Haven, Conn., 1954-62.

WRITINGS: Foods the Indians Gave Us, McKay, 1973; *Behind the Boondocks With Grandpa,* privately printed, 1977. Contributor to education journals.

WORK IN PROGRESS: "A family history for my three grandchildren."

SIDELIGHTS: Hays comments: "I grew up on a farm and was always interested in food, where it originated, how it has been improved. As a principal of high schools, I saw the need for a book written for junior and senior high school persons which was interesting and well researched so they would know about foods and, perhaps, would eat better and garden for themselves. *Foods the Indians Gave Us* has sold well for this group and older adults."

* * *

HEAD, Gwen 1940-

PERSONAL: Born April 21, 1940, in New Orleans, La.; daughter of Harry Gwen (a journalist) and Elsie (Scott) Head; married Allan Charles Schwartzman (an investor), May 23, 1963; children: Lee Tandy. *Education:* Attended Southern Methodist University, 1957, Trinity University, 1958-59, and St. Mary's University, 1962-63. *Home:* 907 East Howe, Seattle, Wash. 98102.*Office:* 914 East Miller, Seattle, Wash. 98102.

CAREER: Writer. Member of faculty at Aspen Writers' Conference, 1978. *Awards, honors:* Helen Bullis Prize from *Poetry Northwest,* 1968; Anne Sexton fellow at Bread Loaf Writers' Conference, 1975; fiction prize from Aspen Writers' Conference, 1979, for "Substantial Risk."

WRITINGS: Special Effects, University of Pittsburgh Press, 1975; *The Ten Thousandth Night,* University of Pittsburgh, Press, 1979.

WORK IN PROGRESS: A collection of short stories; a book of poems.

* * *

HEARNSHAW, Leslie Spencer 1907-

PERSONAL: Born December 9, 1907, in Southampton, England; son of F.J.C. (a professor of history) and Dorothea (a teacher; maiden name, Spencer) Hearnshaw; married Gweneth R. Dickins (a biologist), April 3, 1937; children: Alexandra Joy (Mrs. C.T.C. Wall), Carolyn Ann Woollard, Joanna Elizabeth Camus, John Bernard. *Education:* Christ Church, Oxford, B.A. (with first class honors), 1930; King's College, London, M.A. (first class honors), 1932. *Home:* 1 Devonshire Rd., West Kirby, Wirral L48 7HR, England.

CAREER: National Institute of Industrial Psychology, London, England, member of scientific staff, 1933-38; Victoria University of Wellington, Wellington, New Zealand, lecturer in psychology, 1938-47; University of Liverpool, Liverpool, England, professor of psychology, 1947-75, professor emeritus, 1975—. Director of Industrial Psychology Division of Department of Scientific and Industrial Research, Wellington, 1942-47; director of Medical Research Council unit for research on the occupational aspects of aging, 1955-57, 1963-70. Hobhouse Memorial Lecturer at University of London, 1966. *Member:* International Association of Applied Psychology (vice-president, 1964-74), British Psychological Society (member of council, 1949-57; head of industrial section, 1953-54; president, 1955-56).

WRITINGS: (With Ralph Winterbourn) *Human Welfare and Industrial Efficiency,* A. H. & A. W. Reed, 1945; *A Short History of British Psychology, 1840-1940,* Methuen, 1964; *The Comparative Psychology of Mental Development,* Athlone Press, 1966; *The Psychological and Occupational Aspects of Ageing,* Medical Research Council, 1971; *Cyril Burt, Psychologist,* Cornell University Press, 1979. Contributor to psychology journals. Editor of *Journal of the International Association of Applied Psychology,* 1964-74.

WORK IN PROGRESS: Studies in the history of psychology.

SIDELIGHTS: Hearnshaw comments: "In recent years I have been much influenced by the philosophical writings of Karl Popper. I have traveled in most European countries, and in North America, Asia, Australasia, the Pacific, and the Soviet Union. I have a reading knowledge of Latin, Greek, French, German, Russian, and Italian."

BIOGRAPHICAL/CRITICAL SOURCES: Revue de Psychologie Apliquee, Volume XVIII, number 2, 1968.

* * *

HEARST, George Randolph 1904-1972

OBITUARY NOTICE: Born April 23, 1904, in Washington; died January 26, 1972, in Los Angeles, Calif. Publishing executive and aviator. The eldest son of publisher William Randolph Hearst, George Hearst was publisher of the *San Francisco Examiner* and president of both the *New York American* and the *Los Angeles Examiner.* As a pilot, Hearst held the record for fastest flight in a monoplane from Oakland to Los Angeles. Obituaries and other sources: *New York Times,* January 27, 1972; *Who Was Who in America,* 5th edition, Marquis, 1973.

* * *

HEATTER, Gabriel 1890-1972

OBITUARY NOTICE: Born in 1890 in Manhattan, N.Y.; died March 30, 1972, in Miami, Fla. Radio journalist best known for his ad-lib coverage of the electrocution of kidnapper Bruno Hauptmann in 1936. Heatter delivered impassioned commentaries during World War II. During the 1950's and 1960's, he wrote a column for the *Miami Beach Sun.* Obituaries and other sources: *Current Biography,* Wilson, 1941, May, 1972; *New York Times,* March 31, 1972.

* * *

HEENEY, Brian 1933-

PERSONAL: Born January 17, 1933, in Montreal, Quebec, Canada; son of Arnold (a diplomat) and Margaret Heeney; married Goodith Feilding, June 2, 1956; children: Michael, Ann, Timothy, Matthew. *Education:* University of Toronto, B.A., 1954; graduate study at General Theological Seminary, New York, N.Y., 1954-56; Episcopal Theological School, Cambrige, Mass., B.D., 1957; Oxford University, D.Phil., 1962. *Home:* 550 Gilmour St., Peterborough, Ontario, Canada. *Office:* Library, Trent University, Peterborough, Ontario, Canada.

CAREER: Ordained Anglican minister, 1956; assistant curate of Anglican cathedral in Edmonton, Alberta, 1957-59; University of Alberta, Edmonton, Anglican chaplain, 1962-64, assistant professor, 1962-67, associate professor of history, 1967-71; Trent University, Peterborough, Ontario, professor of history, 1971—, master of Champlain College, 1971-77, director of library, 1977—. Visiting senior research fellow at Jesus College, Oxford, 1979-80. *Member:* Canadian Historical Association, Conference on British Studies.

WRITINGS: Mission to the Middle Classes: The Woodard Schools, 1848-1891. S.P.C.K., 1969; (editor) Arnold Heeney, *The Things That Are Caesar's,* University of Toronto Press, 1972; *A Different Kind of Gentleman: Parish Clergy as Professional Men in Early and Mid-Victorian England,* Archon Books, 1976.

WORK IN PROGRESS: Research on women's work in the Church of England, 1850-1920.

* * *

HEIM, Bruno Bernard 1911-

PERSONAL: Born March 5, 1911, in Olten, Switzerland; son of Bernhard (a teacher) and Elisabeth Heim-Studer. *Education:* St. Thomas University (Rome), Ph. Dr., 1934; University of Fribourg (Switzerland), B.D., 1937; Gregorian University (Rome), Dr. jur. can., 1946; Papal Ecclesiastical Academy, graduated, 1947. *Home:* 31 Zehnderweg, CH 4600 Olten, Switzerland; and 54 Park Tide, London SW19 5NF, England. *Office:* Apostolic Delegation, 54 Parkside, London SW19 5NF, England.

CAREER: Ordained Roman Catholic priest, 1938; vicar of parishes in Arbon and Basle, Switzerland, 1938-42; chief chaplain for Italian and Polish military internees in the Emmental, 1943-45; secretary at nunciature in Paris, France, first under Nuncio Roncalli, then under Pope John XXIII, 1947-51; auditor at nunciature in Vienna, Austria, 1952-54; councillor and charge d'affaires at nunciature in Bonn, West Germany, 1954-61; named archbishop of Xanthos, 1961; apostolic delegate to Scandinavia, based in Copenhagen, Denmark, 1961-69; pro-nuncio (ambassador) to Finland, 1966-69; pro-nuncio to Egypt and president of Caritas Egypt, Cairo, 1969-73; apostolic delegate to Great Britain, 1973—.

MEMBER: International Heraldic Academy (member of council), Swiss Heraldic Society (member of council), French Genealogical and Heraldic Society, Heraldic and Genealogical Society (Vienna), Societas Heraldica Scandinavica, Herold (Berlin; honorary). *Awards, honors:* Knight of the Roman Eagle, chaplain of Order of Malta, 1949; foreign member of Real Academia de la Historia (Madrid), 1950; laureate of Academie Francaise, 1950; officer of Palmes Academics, 1951; officer of Legion d'Honneur, 1951; grand officer of Order of the Holy Sepulcre, 1961; knight of Teutonic Order, 1961; Cross of Merit with star (West Germany), 1961; Grand Cross of Order of Malta, 1962; Golden Cross of Honor with star (Austria); grand officer of Order of Merit (Italy), 1965; Grand Cross of the Finnish Lion, 1969; Grand Cross of Order of St. Maurice and Lazarus, 1973; grand cordon first class, Order of the Republic (Egypt), 1974; received Silver Jubilee Medal of Queen Elizabeth II (Great Britain); Grand Cross of Order of St. John (Great Britain), 1979.

WRITINGS: Wappenbrauch und Wappenrecht in der Kirche (title means "Heraldic Customs and Law in the Catholic Church"), Walter-Verlag, 1947; *L'Oeuvre heraldique de Paul Boesch,* Zuercher Zug, 1974; (self-illustrated) *Heraldry in the Catholic Church: Its Origin, Customs, and Laws,* Humanities, 1978. Also author of *Die Freunschaft nach Thomas v. Aquin* (title means "Friendship in the Teaching of Thomas Aquinas"), 1934.

WORK IN PROGRESS: *Gold and Silver in Heraldry; Liber amicorum* (title means "The Book of Friends"), including signatures and coats of arms of friends and distinguished guests, publication expected in 1982.

SIDELIGHTS: Heim's work for the Roman Catholic church has taken him to many parts of the world; his languages subsequently include German, French, Italian, Spanish, Danish, Swedish, Norwegian, Dutch, Hungarian, Latin, and Greek. He has formulated a consistent set of rules to apply throughout the church in keeping with papal decrees and changes in church law, many of which occurred at his suggestion.

Heim is also at least equally recognized as a heraldic artist and expert on heraldry. He has designed coats of arms for Popes John XXIII, Paul VI, John Paul I, and John Paul II, as well as countless other church dignitaries. In addition, he writes for the newcomer to the field of heraldry, comparing heraldic laws and customs all over the world.

BIOGRAPHICAL/CRITICAL SOURCES: *Christian World,* January 18, 1979.

* * *

HEINDEL, Richard Heathcote 1912-1979

OBITUARY NOTICE: Born August 24, 1912, in Hanover, Pa.; died of cancer, July 31, 1979, in Harrisburg, Pa. Educator, scholar, and author. An expert on U.S. cultural programs, Heindel helped the government to reestablish educational and sociological bonds between the United States and former enemy countries. In the State Department he served as chief of the division of libraries and institutions for several years and was director of the department's UNESCO relations staff during the early 1950's. Heindel was also an administrator at University of Buffalo, Wagner College, Pratt Institute, and Pennsylvania State University at Middletown. He wrote *The American Impact on Great Britain.* Obituaries and other sources: *American Men and Women of Science: The Social and Behavioral Sciences,* 12th edition, Bowker, 1973; *Who's Who in America,* 40th edition, Marquis, 1978; *Washington Post,* August 3, 1979.

* * *

HEISE, David R(euben) 1937-

PERSONAL: Born March 15, 1937, in Evanston, Ill.; son of Frank Lewis (in business) and Bertha (a nurse; maiden name, Simms) Heise; married Marjorie Ochterbeck (divorced); married Elsa Lewis (a programmer); children: Stephen Saul. *Education:* Attended Illinois Institute of Technology, 1954-56; University of Missouri, B.J., 1958, A.B., 1959; University of Chicago, M.A., 1962, Ph.D., 1964. *Religion:* None. *Residence:* Chapel Hill, N.C. *Office:* Department of Sociology, University of North Carolina, Chapel Hill, N.C. 27514.

CAREER: University of Chicago, Chicago, Ill., technical writer and staff analyst at Laboratories for Applied Sciences, 1959-61; University of Wisconsin—Madison, instructor, 1963-64, assistant professor of sociology, 1965-69; Queens College of the City University of New York, Flushing, N.Y., associate professor of sociology, 1969-71; University of North Carolina, Chapel Hill, professor of sociology, 1971—, director of quantitative sociology and theory building training program, 1971-76. *Member:* American Sociological Association (chairperson of council of methodology section, 1975-76), American Psychological Association, Society of Experimental Social Psychology, Sociological Research Association, Southern Sociological Society. *Awards, honors:* Guggenheim fellowship, 1977; National Institute of Mental Health grant, 1977-79.

WRITINGS: (Contributor) Gene Summers, editor, *Attitude Measurement,* Rand McNally, 1970; (contributor) Edgar Borgatta, editor, *Sociological Methodology, 1970,* Jossey-Bass, 1970; (contributor) Herbert Costner, editor, *Sociological Methodology, 1973-1974,* Jossey-Bass, 1974; *Causal Analysis,* Wiley, 1975; (contributor) N. J. Demerath III, Otto Larsen, and K. F. Schuessler, editors, *Social Policy and Sociology,* Academic Press, 1975; *Computer-Assisted Analysis of Social Action: Use of Program INTERACT and SURVEY.UNC75,* Institute for Social Science Research, University of North Carolina, 1978; *Understanding Events: Affect and the Construction of Social Action,* Cambridge University Press, 1979. Contributor of about twenty articles to sociology and psychology journals. Associate editor of *Social Forces,* 1971—; member of board of editors of *Sociological Methods and Research,* 1971-79, and *Social Psychology Quarterly,* 1979-82; editor of *Sociological Methodology,* 1974-76, and *Sociological Methods and Research,* 1980—.

WORK IN PROGRESS: Research on affectual bases of social interaction.

SIDELIGHTS: Heise writes that the goal of his current research is to "define specific mechanisms relating values and attitudes to activity in social groups, thereby providing a theory of behavior having implications for socialization, rehabilitation, and psychotherapy. A computer model for generating sequences of behavioral dispositions from attitudes has been prepared, and experimental tests of the model have been positive. Overall, the evidence indicates that social interaction confirms people's basic feelings about themselves and about the behaviors they enact."

* * *

HEISKELL, John Netherland 1872-1972

OBITUARY NOTICE: Born November 2, 1872, in Rogersville, Tenn.; died December 8, 1972. Editor of the *Arkansas Gazette* from 1902 until his death, Heiskell received numerous awards for journalistic excellence. He served as U.S. senator from Arkansas for three weeks in 1913 by appointment of the governor. Obituaries and other sources: *Who Was Who in America,* 5th edition, Marquis, 1973; *New York Times,* April 23, 1971.

* * *

HELBING, Terry 1951-

PERSONAL: Born May 21, 1951, in Dubuque, Iowa; son of John B. (a banker) and Susan (Klaas) Helbing. *Education:* Attended Loras College and Clarke College, 1969-71; Emerson College, B.A. (with honors), 1973. *Home:* 90 Bank St., Apt. 5D, New York, N.Y. 10014. *Office: Drama Review,* 51 West Fourth St., Room 300, New York, N.Y. 10012.

CAREER/WRITINGS: East Cleveland Music Theatre, Cleveland, Ohio, business manager, 1973; Oxtoby-Smith, Inc., New York, N.Y., proofreader, 1974-75; *Drama Review,* New York, N.Y., assistant editor, 1975-77, managing editor, 1977—. Adjunct instructor at New York University, 1979—. Founder of JH Press, 1979. Author of column, "Off-Off Broadway," in *Omega One,* 1978—. Contributor to journals, including *Theatre Design and Technology, Villager, Body Politic,* and *Advocate.* Guest editor, *Christopher Street,* June, 1978; theatre editor, *Villager,* 1979. Pittsburgh Metro Theatre advisory board member; Glines Theatre Co. dramaturg and member of acting company. Literary agent for playwrights.

WORK IN PROGRESS: Research into theatre history of minority groups.

SIDELIGHTS: Helbing told *CA:* "I feel very fortunate to be in a position where everything I do relates to all of my other activities. I am, in order of income, an editor/writer/teacher/actor/agent, and I enjoy all of these activities immensely. I do not feel the need to distinguish between vocational and avocational interests, because writing and acting have been 'hobbies' of mine for years, and now they also happen to be my career. Everything I do is both 'work' and 'play' for me. Each part of my life feeds and energizes every other part—my writing relates to my acting, my acting to my teaching, my teaching to my editing (and vice versa), and so on. Of course, all of this keeps me very busy, but I enjoy it all so much. I feel vital and alive because of all the activity."

* * *

HENDERSHOT, Ralph 1896(?)-1979

OBITUARY NOTICE: Born c. 1896; died July 28, 1979, in Tequesta, Fla. Journalist. Hendershot became financial editor of the *New York Telegram* in 1927 and held that position for twenty-nine years, remaining with the paper through its mergers with the *New York World* and the *Sun*. His 1931 series of articles analyzing the Wall Street crash was credited with helping to establish the Securities and Exchange Commission in 1934. Obituaries and other sources: *New York Times,* August 2, 1979.

* * *

HENLEY, Gail 1952-

PERSONAL: Original surname, Olsheski; born December 6, 1952, in Barry's Bay, Ontario, Canada; daughter of Wilfred (a contractor) and Florence (a nurse; maiden name, Chippior) Olsheski. *Education:* McGill University, B.A., 1972; Jagiellonian University, Cracow, Poland, diploma, 1973; University of Toronto, M.A., 1974. *Politics:* "Humanist." *Religion:* "Polish Catholic." *Residence:* Toronto, Ontario, Canada. *Agent:* McClelland & Stewart, 25 Hollinger Rd., Toronto, Ontario, Canada.

CAREER: Henley Hygiene Ltd. (cosmetic hygiene firm), London, England, founder and president, 1975—. *Member:* Academy of Canadian Cinema, Association of Canadian Television and Radio Artists, British Actor's Equity Association.

WRITINGS: *Where the Cherries End Up* (novel), Little, Brown, 1978.

Author of "Odyssey of the Children," a film released by Film Consortium of Canada, 1980.

WORK IN PROGRESS: A novel, publication by Little, Brown expected in 1980; another film script.

SIDELIGHTS: Henley commented: "My life has been the theatre, films, and television. In England, after intensive training with the Royal Academy of Dramatic Art, I worked as an actress with Regional Repertory Theatres. I then moved into British television and appeared in numerous BBC and THAMES television series.

"In Canada I have appeared on numerous daytime television serials, but my most significant contribution to the CBC has been in the scriptwriting area. I was commissioned to write the screenplay for "Odyssey of the Children" which is both a theatrical and television release.

"Studying for a time in Poland has been one of my greatest joys. I explored acting technique with Jerzy Gotowski at his Theatre Lab in Wroclaw."

BIOGRAPHICAL/CRITICAL SOURCES: *Chicago Tribune,* June 17, 1979; *New York Times Book Review,* July 29, 1979.

* * *

HENRICHSEN, Walt(er Arlie), Jr. 1934-

PERSONAL: Born February 20, 1934, in Berkeley, Calif.; son of Walter Arlie and Dorothy (Davis) Henrichsen; married Leette Dillon, June 3, 1962; children: Deborah Lynn, Walter A. III, Jonathan Dillon, Janna Kay. *Education:* Modesto Junior College, A.A., 1954; Central College, B.A., 1956; Western Theological Seminary, Holland, Mich., M.Div., 1959. *Home and office:* 93 Raven Hills Court, Colorado Springs, Colo. 80919.

CAREER: Teacher of Bible studies at Christian high school in Bellflower, Calif., 1959-61; Wycliffe Bible Translators, Chiapas, Mexico, member of staff of navigators, 1961-62; Navigators, Pasadena, Calif., area director in Kalamazoo, Mich., 1962-67, regional director in Forth Worth, Tex., 1966-71, assistant to the president in Colorado Springs, Colo., 1971-72, international personnel director in Colorado Springs, 1972-75, deputy director in Christchurch, New Zealand, 1975-77; writer, lecturer, and consultant, 1977—.

WRITINGS: *Disciples Are Made Not Born,* Victor, 1974; *Understand,* Navpress, 1976; *A Layman's Guide to Interpreting the Bible,* Navpress, 1978; *After the Sacrifice* (commentary on Hebrews), Zondervan, 1979.

WORK IN PROGRESS: *Biblical Basis for the Layman's Ministry,* with William Garrison, publication expected in 1980.

SIDELIGHTS: Henrichsen comments: "Victor Books requested me to write the book on discipleship. Following this exercise I continued to write. *A Layman's Guide to Interpreting the Bible* came from a desire to make the subject of hermeneutics available to the layman. The commentary on Hebrews differs from other books of this nature in that it deals with a panoramic rather than a verse-by-verse exposition of the book. It is my conviction that from the Christian perspective this is the day of the laymen. The Living God is active in the lives of people in an unprecedented way and at the vanguard of this movement are business and professional men functioning in the market place. My writing is directed toward helping them in representing Jesus Christ more effectively in the context of their businesses and professions."

* * *

HENRY, Bill
See HENRY, William Mellors

* * *

HENRY, Will
See ALLEN, Henry Wilson

* * *

HENRY, William Mellors 1890-1970
(Bill Henry)

OBITUARY NOTICE: Born August 21, 1890, in San Francisco, Calif.; died April 13, 1970. Henry is best known for his broadcasts of news analysis. He was associated with the *Los Angeles Times* for more than fifty years. He wrote *An Approved History of the Olympic Games*. Obituaries and other sources: *Who Was Who in America,* 5th edition, Marquis, 1973.

HENSEY, Frederick G(erald) 1931-
(Fritz Hensey)

PERSONAL: Born October 30, 1931, in Albany, N.Y.; son of Gerald George and Borga Irene (Dwyer) Hensey; married Lilia Marban, October 15, 1955; children: Rosalinda (Mrs. Armand Lanier), Francisco. *Education:* Universidad de las Americas, B.A., 1956; graduate study at Universidad Autonoma de Mexico, 1960-62; University of Texas, Ph.D., 1967. *Home:* 1809 East 39th St., Austin, Tex. 78722. *Office:* Department of Spanish and Portuguese, University of Texas, Austin, Tex. 78701.

CAREER: Berlitz School, Mexico City, Mexico, teacher of English as a foreign language, 1956-62; University of Texas, Austin, instructor, 1965-67, assistant professor, 1968-71, associate professor of Spanish and Portuguese, 1971—. Visiting professor at Vanderbilt University, 1967, and Tulane University, 1968. Fulbright lecturer at Universidad de los Andes, 1977. Co-organizer of Texas Symposium on Romance Linguistics, 1974, and First Bogota Symposium on Dante and the Translation of Poetry, 1977. Consultant to United Nations Educational, Scientific, and Cultural Organization. *Military service:* U.S. Air Force, 1949-53. *Member:* American Association of Teachers of Spanish and Portuguese, Modern Language Association of America, American Council on Teaching of Foreign Languages, Associacion de Linguistica y Filologia de la America Latina, Fulbright Alumni Association. *Awards, honors:* Fulbright fellowship, 1964-65.

WRITINGS: (With F. P. Ellison and others) *Modern Portuguese,* with teacher's manual, Random House, 1970; *The Sociolinguistics of the Brazilian-Uruguayan Border,* Mouton, 1972; (under name Fritz Hensey; editor with Marta Lujan) *Current Studies in Romance Linguistics,* Georgetown University Press, 1976; (translator from the Catalan; with Burton Raffel and Thomas Glick) Salvador Espriu, *The Bull's Hide* (poetry), Writer's Workshop (Calcutta, India), 1977. Translations published in anthologies, including *The Newest Peruvian Poetry in Translation,* edited by Luis Ramos Garcia and Edgar O'Hara, Studia Hispanica, 1979. Contributor to scholarly journals in the United States, the Netherlands, Germany, and Brazil.

WORK IN PROGRESS: A beginner's textbook in Yiddish, publication by University of Texas Press expected in 1980 or 1981; translations of Brazilian poetry, to be included in the anthology *Tesserae;* research on the penetration of Portuguese into northern Uruguay; research on the sociolinguistic consequences of recent language policies in Spain (particularly Catalan), comparing two regional language situations (Cataluna and Asturias) with two non-European ones (French Canada, northern Uruguay).

SIDELIGHTS: Hensey writes: "My major vocational areas are sociolinguistics, Romance linguistics, applied linguistics, translation and poetry. My foreign languages are French, Spanish, Portuguese, Catalan, Italian, modern Greek, German, Yiddish, and Esperanto. My travels include residence in Mexico, Brazil, Uruguay, and Portugal.

"I like to consider myself a poet as well as a linguist. I think that linguists (and particularly sociolinguists) are in a position to make real contributions to peace through their work in the scientific study of language and culture contact. At the same time, I enjoy both the writing and the translation of poetry as an outlet for the sort of creative urge which scholarly research and writing does not always provide."

Hensey's poems, reviews, and translations have been published in Brazil, Uruguay, Mexico, and Germany.

HENSEY, Fritz
See HENSEY, Frederick G(erald)

* * *

HERBERT, Zbigniew 1924-

PERSONAL: Born October 29, 1924, in Lwow, Poland; son of Boleslaw (an attorney) and Maria (Kaniak) Herbert; married Katarzyna Dzieduszyska, April 30, 1968. *Education:* University of Krakow, M.A. (economics), 1947; Nicholas Copernicus University of Torun, M.A. (law), 1948; University of Warsaw, M.A. (philosophy), 1950. *Home:* Hewaldstrasse 5, 1 Berlin 62, West Germany.

CAREER: Poet, dramatist, and essayist. Also worked as a bank clerk, manual laborer, and journalist; did free-lance work for *Tworczosc* (literary review), 1955-76; co-editor of *Poezja* (poetry journal), 1965-68, resigned in protest of anti-semitic policies. Professor of modern European literature at California State College (now University), Los Angeles, 1970; professor at University of Gdansk, Gdansk, Poland, 1972. Has given poetry readings at universities and for national organizations throughout the United States, including the World Poetry Conference, State University of New York at Stony Brook, 1968, and Lincoln Center Festival, 1968. *Wartime service:* Member of Polish underground during World War II. *Member:* Polish Writers' Association (board member), P.E.N., Akademie der Kuenste, Bayerische Akademie der Schoenen Kuenste (corresponding member). *Awards, honors:* Millenium Prize, Polish Institute of Arts and Sciences (United States), 1964; Nicholas Lenau Prize (Austria), 1965, for his contribution to European literature; Knight's Cross, Order of Polonia Restituta, 1974 (refused to accept).

WRITINGS—In English: *Selected Poems,* translated from the original Polish by Czeslaw Milosz and Peter Dale Scott, Penguin, 1968; *Selected Poems* (includes selections from *Pan Cogito;* also see below), translated from the original Polish by John Carpenter and Bogdana Carpenter, Oxford University Press, 1977.

In Polish; all poems, except as noted: *Struna swiatla* (title means "A String of Light"), Czytelnik (Warsaw), 1956; *Hermes, pies i gwiazda* (title means "Hermes, a Dog and a Star"), Czytelnik, 1957; *Studium przedmiotu* (title means "The Study of an Object,"), Czytlenik, 1961; *Barbarzyna w ogrodzie* (essays; title means "A Barbarian in the Garden"), Czytelnik, 1962; *Dramaty* (plays; title means "Dramas"; includes "The Philosophers' Den" and "The Reconstruction of the Poet"), Panstwowy Instytut Wydawniczy (Warsaw), 1970; *Pan Cogito* (title means "Mr. Cogito"), Czytelnik, 1974. Author of *Napis* (title means "The Inscription"), 1969, and *Wiersze zebrane* (title means "Collected Verse"), 1971; also author of radio plays.

Work represented in anthologies, including: *The Broken Mirror,* edited by Pawel Mayewski, Random House (Toronto), 1958; *Introduction to Modern Polish Literature: An Anthology of Fiction and Poetry,* edited by Adam Gillon and Kudwik Krzyzanowski, Tawyne, 1964; and *Postwar Polish Poetry: An Anthology,* edited by Czeslaw Milosz, Doubleday, 1965.

SIDELIGHTS: Although Zbigniew Herbert's surname is English, he considers himself a Polish writer, "even an unfashionably patriotic one." In an interview with *New Leader,* Herbert discussed his diversified family background: "There is a legend in my family to the effect that one of my paternal forebearers left England during the 16th century at a time of religious controversy. One of my grandmothers was Armenian. I come of a family of military people, mostly, and lawyers."

Herbert began writing poetry when he was seventeen, but did not publish until 1956, "after fifteen years of writing for the drawer." Certainly one factor in the late publication of his work was the political climate in Poland during the forties and fifties: the suppression of all publishing during the Nazi occupation and the severe literary censorship of the repressive Stalinist regime. And as Czeslaw Milosz pointed out: "Before 1956 the price for being published was to renounce one's own taste and he [Herbert] did not wish to pay it." Herbert, however, is not bitter about the fifteen-year wait, on the contrary, he considers "a period of fasting" which gave him time to work on his attitudes without external pressures.

Described by Stephen Stepanchev as "a witness to his time," Herbert can be considered a political poet. But as Stephen Miller advised: "The word political may be misleading for it brings to mind the bad verse of the thirties, verse damaged by causes. . . . The political poet who deals directly with the events of contemporary history usually plays a losing game. His moral outrage will probably overwhelm his poetry, making it self-righteous, predictable, and shrill. . . . Although Herbert's poetry is preoccupied with the nightmares of recent history . . . it is not public speech. Subdued and casual, his poems shun both hysteria and apocalyptic intensity." According to A. Alvarez, Herbert "is political by virtue of being permanently and warily in opposition. . . . His opposition is not dogmatic: during the Nazi occupations he was not, to my knowledge, a Communist, nor during the Stalinist repression was he ever noticeably even Catholic or nationalist. Herbert's opposition is a party of one; he refuses to relinquish his own truth and his own standards in the face of any dogma."

Perhaps Herbert's "political" attitude can be found in his interpretation of the role of the poet. "In Poland," Herbert once stated, "we think of the poet as prophet; he is not merely a maker of verbal forms or an imitator of reality. The poet expresses the deepest feelings and the widest awareness of people. . . . The language of poetry differs from the language of politics. And, after all, poetry lives longer than any conceivable political crisis. The poet looks over a broad terrain and over vast stretches of time. He makes observations on the problems of his own time, to be sure, but he is a partisan only in the sense that he is a partisan of the truth. He arouses doubts and uncertainties and brings everything into question."

Although Herbert's purpose as a poet and the subjects of his poetry are serious, he mixes humor and satire effectively. "The most distinctive quality of Herbert's imagination," wrote Laurence Lieberman," is his power to invest impish fantasy, mischievously tender nonsense, with the highest seriousness. His humorous fantasy is the armor of a superlatively healthy mind staving off political oppression. Fantasy is an instrument of survival: it is the chief weapon in a poetry arsenal which serves as a caretaker for the individual identity, a bulwark against the mental slavery of the totalitarian church and state." Miller also saw Herbert's humor as "a way of resisting the dehumanizing and impersonal language of the state. . . . Keeping a sense of humor means keeping a private language and avoiding the total politicization of the self."

Herbert's poetry is also laced with biblical and Greek mythological allusions. Miller contended that "the lens of myth reduces the glare of contemporary experience, placing it in a perspective that enables [Herbert] to look at it without losing his sanity and sense of humor." He also pointed out that the use of myth "liberates [Herbert] from the confines of particular historical events. . . . At the same time the use of myth fleshes out the thin bones of the satire, making it sly and elegant, not obvious and heavy-handed." For example, a poem entitled "Preliminary Investigation of an Angel" offers a comparison between totalitarian regimes and biblical mythology: an "angel" of the state, a member of the hierarchy, is put on trial and judged to be guilty of crimes against the "heavenly" government. The poem is reminiscent of the Stalin purges when no "faithful" member of the party was free from suspicion. In another poem, "Why the Classics," Herbert contrasts Thucydides, the Greek historian who accepted the responsibility for the failure of his mission to capture Amphipolis, with the "generals of most recent wars" who wallow in their self-pity and state that everyone, and therefore no one, is responsible for *their* failures and actions.

Pan Cogito is Herbert's latest work and, according to Ruel K. Wilson, his most pessimistic. Wilson, who sees Herbert as "Poland's finest postwar poet," noted that his "concern [in *Pan Cogito*] . . . is for humanity rather than for ideologies, which so often betray those who naively embrace them." To Bogdana Carpenter and John Carpenter, Herbert's concern is self-identity: "If Herbert discovers in himself traces of others and feels menaced by biological and historical determinism, he has at the same time an acute awareness of his separation from other human beings. In his earlier books Herbert frequently used the pronoun 'we' with a feeling of great solidarity and compassion for others, while in his recent work he tends to use the first-person singular pronoun. This is surprising—the ability to identify with other people . . . is one of Herbert's most striking traits."

Mr. Cogito, the main character in the book, is a problem to many critics. Unable to determine satisfactorily the relationship between Herbert and Cogito, critics have labeled the character petty and mediocre. His concerns are practical and his life ordinary. Cogito enjoys reading sensationalist newspaper features, fails when he tries transcendental meditation, and "his stream of consciousness brings up detritus like a tin can." But both Wilson and the Carpenters have dismissed such criticisms by noting that Cogito is a very human and universal man. According to Wilson, Cogito is "a modern intellectual who reads the newspapers, recalls his childhood, his family; he also muses on pop-art, America, alienation, magic, an aging poet, the creative process." For the Carpenters Cogito "is a device allowing Herbert to admit this ordinariness we all share, to establish it and, once this is done, to build upon it. Herbert wants to underline ordinariness and imperfection because he wants to deal with practical, not transcendent, morality. The poems of *Pan Cogito* consistently apply ethics not only to action but to the possible, viable action of everyday life, taking human failings into account. The poems are tolerant and humane in their approach, and they are less categorical than the earlier poems, embracing a greater sense of contradictions." Wilson noted that "in the last analysis, Cogito's 'weaknesses'—his incapacity for abstract thought, his rejection of dogmaticism, his very human petty fears and anxieties, his feelings of inadequacy and the concomitant self-irony—become his greatest strengths and virtues." With regard to the role of characters in his work, Herbert once stated: "The speaker is my poems is a generalized figure who speaks not for himself or for me but for humanity. He is representative; he speaks for a generation, if you like; he makes historical and moral judgements."

BIOGRAPHICAL/CRITICAL SOURCES: A. Alvarez, *Under Pressure,* Penguin, 1965; *New Leader,* August 26, 1968; Alvarez, *Beyond All This Fiddle: Essays 1955-1967,* Random House, 1969; *Poetry,* April, 1969; *Mosaic,* fall, 1969; Alan Cheuse and Richard Koffler, editors, *The Rare Action: Essays in Honor of Francis Fergusson,* Rutgers University Press, 1970; *Books Abroad,* winter, 1972, spring, 1975; *World Literature Today,* spring, 1977, autumn, 1978; *Contemporary Literary Criticism,* Volume 9, Gale, 1978.

—*Sketch by Nancy M. Rusin*

* * *

HERMEREN, Goeren A. 1938-

PERSONAL: Born September 5, 1938, in Stockholm, Sweden; son of Harry A. W. and Margit V. (Paalsson) Hermeren; married Ingrid E. Neuman (a teacher), 1961; children: Karin, Anna. *Education:* University of Lund, Fil. kand., 1961, Fil. lic., 1964, Fil. dr., 1969. *Home:* Genarpsvaegen 31, 240 10 Dalby, Sweden. *Office:* Department of Philosophy, University of Lund, Kungshuset, Lundagaard, 223 50 Lund, Sweden.

CAREER: University of Lund, Lund, Sweden, docent in philosophy, 1969-70; University of Umeaa, Umeaa, Sweden, professor of philosophy, 1970-75; University of Lund, professor of philosophy, 1975—. Visiting fellow at Princeton University and University of Michigan, 1966, Temple University, 1972, and Trinity College, Dublin, 1974-75. *Member:* American Society for Aesthetics. *Awards, honors:* American Council of Learned Societies fellow, 1966-67; National Endowment for the Humanities fellow, 1972; Leverhulme scholar, 1974-75.

WRITINGS: Representation and Meaning in the Visual Arts: A Study in the Methodology of Iconography and Iconology, Laaromedelsforlaget, 1969; *Influence in Art and Literature,* Princeton University Press, 1975; Also editor with Lars Aagaard-Mogensen of *Contemporary Aesthetics in Scandinavia,* 1979.

In Swedish: *Oevningar i logik* (title means "Exercises in Logic"), two volumes, Studentlitteratur, 1968, revised edition, 1970; *Vaardering och objektivitet* (title means "Values and Objectivity"), Studentlitteratur, 1972; *Foersvarar vetenskapen det bestaaende?,* Prisma, 1975. Also author of *Naagra problem i de estetika vetenskapernas teori,* 1966. Editor with Lars Bejerholm of *Till Gunnar Aspelin,* 1963. Contributor to scholarly journals. Member of editorial board of *Journal of Aesthetics and Art Criticism.*

WORK IN PROGRESS: A book on objectivity, for Princeton University Press; research on the role and interplay of tradition and innovation in the arts, with a book expected to result.

AVOCATIONAL INTERESTS: Sailing, old books (seventeenth and eighteenth centuries), travel (Europe, United States, Israel).

* * *

HERNDON, James 1926-

PERSONAL: Born August 13, 1926, in Houston, Tex.; children: Jay, Jack. *Education:* Earned B.A. from University of California, Berkeley; earned M.A. from San Francisco State University. *Home:* 109 Clement, San Francisco, Calif. 94118.

CAREER: Junior high school teacher in California. *Member:* American Federation of Teachers (currently president of local branch).

WRITINGS—Nonfiction: *The Way It Spozed to Be,* Simon & Schuster, 1968; *How to Survive in Your Native Land,* Simon & Schuster, 1971; *Everything As Expected: A Remembrance of Jack Spicer,* Small Press Distribution, 1973.

WORK IN PROGRESS: Strawberries in the Snow, a memoir giving an account of growing up during World War II.

SIDELIGHTS: In his first book, *The Way It Spozed to Be,* Herndon recounted his experiences as a teacher in a poor, black junior high school in Oakland, California, in the early 1960's. Virtually every reviewer of the book called it the best of its type, including the author in a category with such popular and esteemed writers on education as John Holt, Herbert Kohl, and Jonathan Kozol. Martin Mayer's comment was typical: "This is the best book written of the decade's spate of battlefield reports from the classroom and perhaps the most honest."

"What Herndon has accomplished in his small, mordant book," Nat Hentoff wrote, "is the most accurate description so far in print of ghetto schoolchildren and the forces (teachers and administrators) lined up against them. Particularly the children—their speech, their fears, their prejudices, their strengths, and their very real knowledge of what the odds are."

When Herndon began teaching, he was unideological, unsentimental, and viewed teaching as just a job. This distance from his subjects enabled him to construct a work of "superb ethnography," Edgar Z. Friedenberg wrote, made more meaningful by the fact that Herndon did not approach his students "as either philanthropist or idealogue." Friedenberg continued, "But Mr. Herndon's book is much more than either the best reportage or the most constructive sociology could be. It is a cool crystalline account of the author's own gradual growth and commitment as a teacher and a man, while, with the subtlest irony, he slowly becomes aware that his own development makes him intolerable to the school and the system in which he must operate."

Mayer was one of the few reviewers who had reservations about the book. He commented: "But behind Herndon's reportage lies a profound lack of curiosity: he asks no questions at all." When one of his previously illiterate seventh graders suddenly began to read, Herndon offered no explanation and apparently, complained Mayer, looked for none. "Herndon, in short, is a *voyeur* of his students, sympathetic but despairing," Mayer wrote. "Like many engaged teachers, he likes children more than he likes grownups, and wants to believe that all childish activity not visibly harmful must be constructive. The notion that these children are going to be adults some day is not in his mind. . . . Mr. Herndon sees only instant behavior and its place in the social organism of the school."

"It is certainly the funniest book on the subject," John Holt declared. "Herndon is a gifted writer with a sharp eye and ear and the talent to make us see and hear what he has seen and heard. His descriptions are hilarious. . . . Yet Herndon does not use his school, or his pupils, or even his well-meaning and hopelessly incompetent principal as a mine for laughs. Like all true comic writers, he is deeply serious, and most funny when most serious."

In the course of teaching, Herndon became aware that the kind of order that other teachers struggled to impose on their students was not necessarily educationally efficacious. He decided to try a more free-form, non-authoritarian approach to learning in his classroom. Charles R. Moyer described the atmosphere in Herndon's classroom. "Mr. Herndon wanted his classes to find whatever order was necessary for them to do the things that they themselves had decided to do," Moyer wrote. "He certainly had to put up with a good deal of chaos and disorder before his classes finally did achieve a sense of solidarity and of common tasks which required a certain amount of self-discipline. These tasks may not have been quite the ones envisaged by the curriculum planners, since they most often involved group reading of plays and getting enough food into the classroom for Friday's 'Movie Day.' But Mr. Herndon is not at all sure that more real learning was not taking place amidst these unorthodox activities than ever occurred in the quieter classrooms of his fellow teachers."

At the end of the year Herndon's contract was not renewed: his principal disliked the noisy disorderliness of his classroom and labeled him unfit to teach. When Herndon argued that his students hadn't participated in the school's annual spring riots, the principal replied that that was proof Herndon was not imposing the order that would cause them to rebel.

Ten years later, Herndon was still a junior high school teacher, but in a predominately white, middle-class suburb of San Francisco. The problems he faced, as he related in his second book *How to Survive in Your Native Land,* were largely the same ones he wrote about in his first book. "His account of the experience," Ronald Gross wrote, "is crammed with all the goofiness and cruelty and confusion and hypocrisy and gentleness and ecstasy that crackle through the corridors and in the classrooms of any school. Like teachers forever, Herndon is saying, 'Pay attention!' But he means pay attention the way a novelist or poet pays attention—see, hear, feel the life throbbing through these youngsters as they build their monster kites, horse around, take photomat pictures of their private parts, and alternately hassle and comfort each other," Friedenberg declared, "[This] is also an extremely funny book in a wry, Vonnegutish way—the kind of writing that hurts only when you laugh. . . . The humor is inherent in the utter incongruity of the scenes and events."

At this school Herndon received support from some other teachers who decided that the competitive structure of education must be changed. They made attendance at classes voluntary, abolished grades, and gave the students the responsibility to decide and plan what they would study. But at the end of the non-directed year, the teachers decided that the "permissive" attitude was not the answer either. Herndon wrote of the failed experiment: "What we were doing was offering the kids an intolerable burden. We offered to make them decide what they would do. But they couldn't decide, because they had been in school for seven years and besides that knew from their lives-long all about the expectations of their parents and of the country of America. They were not free, no matter how often we said they were. No more were we." When the teachers decided to concentrate on teaching reading in a non-competitive atmosphere, they finally met with success. However, the school administration failed to recognize this and rejected their new curriculum proposals.

Herndon's conclusion in *How to Survive in Your Native Land* is that the future of education looks bleak. His own efforts at improvement found little approval and he felt that schools continued to damage students. One of the reasons for this, he explained, is that "an American public school must have winners and losers. . . . The school's purpose is not teaching. The school's purpose is to separate sheep from goats."

While the problems Herndon discussed have been identified by others, few writers have the qualities of "wholeness and genuineness" that Herndon possesses, Benjamin DeMott remarked. And DeMott wrote, "In the course of dealing with these familiar problems, Herndon doesn't simply choose up sides. He has the kind of teacherly mind that grasps simultaneously how life ought to go and how in fact it does go—a mind that links reality and hope, constantly requiring each to acknowledge the other. And the effect of these acknowledgments is to replace tough-mindedness, beamishness, and other common sins of experts with warm, complex good sense."

Critic Geoffrey Wolff called Herndon's work "a beautiful book, beautiful," and added that "Herndon's special, very special, genius is his novelist's feel for the gift of eccentricity, for the perishable quality of every child's singularity. He tells stories about children . . . that break my heart. Not because they are sad—though they are that too, sometimes—but because they must remind anyone who reads them that we have lost our capacity to distinguish between details and to read the meaning of distinctions. We believe—most of us—in grades, or pass-fail, or before and after. Herndon's on to something more interesting. Men like him may save us yet."

CA INTERVIEWS THE AUTHOR

James Herndon was interviewed by phone June 26, 1979, at his home in San Francisco.

CA: You seem to like kids. Is that what led you into teaching?

HERNDON: No. I discovered teaching by accident. I graduated from Berkeley, and I didn't know anything else to do, so I went to graduate school. I didn't really care for it; they wanted me to get serious, and I just wasn't serious. So I quit going to school and went to work in a machine shop down there in Berkeley. There I made some money, and with it I went off to Europe. I went to Germany, which is where I always wanted to go. It had nothing to do with the war or anything; it was more likely Grimm's fairy tales. I worked at various jobs there. I got to know a guy who was running the University of Maryland Overseas Division at Heidelberg. He'd also gone to Berkeley, but I hadn't known him before. In any case, he had a teacher of a history of arts course for American officers and civilians, and the teacher got sick and had to go home, and he asked me if I wanted to do it, and so I did it. I boned up on it and it was kind of fun. Then I got a job through him with the University of Maryland teaching high school GED-type courses to army guys who hadn't gone to high school. I did that for a little while. It was a good way to make money, and I didn't need much money. It was just part-time and kind of nice.

Later on—I was in Europe for about seven years—I was working in Paris and my job got canceled. I had gotten married. I needed a job, a real, actual job, not just some kind of part-time, fool-around job. So when I came back to the States, we came back here to San Francisco, and I went to SF State and UC and got a whole bunch of units and a part-time credential—I didn't have to have a real credential because there was a shortage of teachers—and that was that, and I liked it very much, oddly enough. My first job was in a high school up in the Sierras, and the second job was in a junior high back in town, which I wrote about in my first book.

As far as liking kids is concerned, I'm not so sure about liking them. Theoretically I like them, and from time to time I do like them. Let's put it this way: I don't mind spending my day with kids if it comes to it. But if I was a millionaire, I doubt if I would go to work every day in a school and do all that. But I'd had a lot of jobs in my life before I started teaching, and I couldn't stand any of them for more than six months; that was about the limit. The day would come when I would say "I just can't stand to go to work there, and I'm not going to go." But I never had a day like that teaching school. I always woke up and said, "Well, let's go." I would halfway look forward to it, you know. As a job, it suits me very well. Back to liking kids, well, I like them and I don't like them, but I must admit that I'm always terribly interested in them.

CA: You seem to have a genuine sympathy for them.

HERNDON: It's probably true to say that I have a very clear memory of myself as a kid. About twelve, thirteen, fourteen. It's a memory which I don't really mind; I kind of like it. And I don't think I've changed too much since then, which is probably not something one ought to say, but it's true.

CA: How were your own school years?

HERNDON: They were all right. I did well up until about the last year in high school, but those years were always clouded by the fact that my mother was terribly concerned about schooling and grades and all that. For me it was kind of an exercise in learning how to beat the system without ever giving in to it, I suppose. I didn't care for school particularly, but I managed to do well without giving in or losing anything of myself at it. For me that wasn't very hard. I was never particularly interested in college either. I was very happy to be at Berkeley at that time, which was a very exciting time, at least for me; but I didn't care much for the actual classroom part of it. Just enough to get along and stay in there.

CA: One of the criticisms you've made of schools is that they are based on a system that labels children and that in any given group of kids in a school there have to be losers and winners. Do you think it's possible to get away from that?

HERNDON: No, I guess not. Not as long as we have public schools as they are with a structure where so many kids are supposed to be doing so many things. All the time they are supposed to be doing something which is going to be *evaluated.* Some kids are always going to be better at it than others, and there doesn't seem to be any way out of that. Any given day when I'm working I'm kind of reconciled to that. I don't want to say it doesn't bother me, but I also believe it's not significantly different, or apart, from American life in general. So, given that the place is no good in many ways, I do just what I always have done—try to make my classroom a more decent place to be, if I possibly can. Sometimes I can't. I guess I look for kids who have always been on the losers' side and see how I can help them do a little winning for a change. That's about what I do. But as far as any way to get around that with the present structure—no, there ain't no way. It's built in.

CA: You said in How to Survive *that we might be better off if school attendance were made optional like church attendance. Do you still feel that way?*

HERNDON: Yes.

CA: You believe entirely too much time is spent on the teaching of things that don't really require much teaching?

HERNDON: Yes. Very little of it requires that much teaching. I didn't need to be taught about books by the school; I read them by the billions when I was a little kid. From time to time when something got tough, then a place like a school would be okay if you could find somebody who really knew something and say, "I read all this, but now what?" By and large most teachers don't know a hell of a lot anyway. Here, I don't mean teachers aren't intelligent. Just that, by and large, we ain't experts. Anyone who can stay alive with thirty or so kids in a small room is intelligent. I've taught science and I didn't know a damn thing about it. I can read a science book better than the kids can, that's about all. It ain't hard, and you've got all that authority anyway. I don't think of schools so much as places to learn academics, as places in which to learn what you're up against, and perhaps how to deal with that.

CA: Much of the news focuses on violence in the schools. You once wrote, "The violence of the school lies in the simple fact that it requires the child to deny what he knows of himself in favor of what the school knows about him." Do you feel the schools actually provoke violence in students?

HERNDON: Yeah, in the sense of what you just read. School is sort of like the army; it's requiring a person—in this case, a child—to do a whole lot of stuff that actually doesn't need to be done. It's only done so the person, whether he's a guy in the army or a kid in school, understands he's being required to do it. The school is requiring obedience. Lot of kids can do that. I could do it when I was in school, with a minimum of effort and no commitment whatever. There are still a lot of kids in school who can do that; I see them all the time. Those kids will be all right. But by and large most kids can't do it that easily, and they have to give up something, and they strike back.

Everybody says it's worse these days. I don't know if it's worse than when I was going to school or not, but in any case it's noticed more. One thing is that kids twelve, thirteen, fourteen do know a hell of a lot more about the world than they did when I was a kid. It may be that they take the school's promises—like "If you work hard, you'll be successful"—less seriously. When I was in school and didn't like it, I felt it was my fault. I was bored, exasperated, or whatever, and I was anxious to hide that. I felt I was some kind of freak. Everybody else was smiling and raising their hand, and it never occurred to me that maybe everybody else hated it also.

But today lots of kids don't seem to believe the school is right. No doubt that's progress. You tell them to do something, they say "What for?" I never have much of an answer. I say, "Because I said so." They say, "No kiddin'." I tell them, "Because you'll get an F in the class if you don't do it." They say, "I got an F before." You end up with kids who get mad and hit people and slash people's tires. They're angry, because they know they're doing all this stuff that's of no value. And they don't get paid. You get a Latino kid who works his ass off in an English class and gets a D. The teacher says, "You worked hard, but you're still no good." He gets angry.

Does the school provoke violence? I think so. But to add a bit, school's not the whole world. American society undoubtedly provokes a good deal of violence from a number of classes of people who understand at a very early age that they ain't going to make it, and they get mad. I think the school does its part; it's part of America, too.

CA: What's the best thing a teacher can do for a student?

HERNDON: Depends on the student. I don't really have any theory about what a kid or a student needs; I've never been able to develop any. If you're in a classroom with a number of kids, you soon find out which kids want to talk to you, so you talk to them. That's what they need. I suppose that's sympathy. You also find kids who really want you to help them learn to do something—read, for example—and are willing to trust you and willing to try once again to see if you and they will be able to do it. These are, of course, the really serious students, and that's another form of sympathy. Other kids just want you to give them an assignment, and they're used to doing it, and they want to get credit for putting their name in the right place and copying the encyclopedia and get out of there. That's okay with me, too. You find out who wants what and try to give it to them, without any theoretical notion that they'll grow up right or be successful or whatever.

I don't have any theoretical answer, and I don't think anybody in his right mind does. There's no theory of learning I've ever come across that makes any sense whatsoever. Fact is, nobody knows a damn thing about it. No one knows why a person can learn to read. But everybody can, unless something's gone wrong—that means, the person has been prevented from it.

CA: You've said you always hope to learn something through writing. How does that work for you?

HERNDON: I don't know how it works. I grew up—I mean my years at Berkeley—with people who were all writers and poets. I learned about writing from them, and they were all believers in magic and stuff like that, which I'm not. But the pleasure in writing, and the good part about it, seems to be that you're writing away with an idea in mind, and as you're doing it, something happens that you had never thought of before. That's all I meant. How it happens I really don't know and I don't care to know. But it does happen, and when it happens it's very exciting and a lot of fun and wonderful. It's always happened to me when I write. The simplest way to put it, outside of going into some kind of Coleridgean theory of association and so forth—all of which is interesting to think about, but that ain't the point now—is that one word leads to another. The words lead you on, not your own brain or mind. If it was just your own brain and you thought of it all beforehand and just wrote it down, it would be an incredible bore. I would never do it.

CA: You write because you enjoy doing it?

HERNDON: I have something in mind and I have some feeling that I'd like to see how it will come out. I enjoy it when I'm doing it, but there's long periods when I don't do anything at all. It's not really a big deal with me. I'm not a real writer in the sense of somebody who sits down every day and does a thousand words or whatever.

CA: What can parents do to help their kids learn without having the violence you've described done to their personalities?

HERNDON: The best thing, as far as I'm concerned, is don't treat the whole thing with such importance. Little kids have to go to school; most little kids want to go to school. All kinds of tragedies happen, and the parents should always stick up for the kid. (We're leaving out extremes now that have some really terrible psychopathology—I just mean regular little kids.) Always stick up for the kid and say, "You were right. It's all right." But don't place much importance on it. The worst thing is for somebody to say, "You've gotta do well in the first grade so you'll be good enough to go to second grade" and that sort of thing. Don't accept the school's description of what the kid or the world is about, and guard against the kid's doing so.

CA: Have you made enemies with the views you expressed in your books?

HERNDON: If I did, I never heard about it. There have been an awful lot of people writing me, from high school kids to grandmamas. I still get four or five letters a month. Used to get hundreds of them; it took all my time answering them. I never got any that were critical. Maybe people who didn't like it just said, "To hell with him; I ain't writin' him at all." There was one review that was nasty; it was in an air force magazine. But the air force reasoned that it didn't make much difference because after all it was all out in California, which was due to drop off into the Pacific Ocean any day now. But that's the only one I ever read that was actively saying, "This is no good." I don't think everyone shares my views about school, although I think more people do than one would suspect. They're just afraid, and they've got every right to be. It can do you some harm if you're a family and your kid's messing up in school. What I wanted to do in the books is to help people understand what it's about and to make them take it a little easier on themselves. Thus, it's interesting, maybe, but it ain't that important.

BIOGRAPHICAL/CRITICAL SOURCES: *Life,* March 22, 1968, April 23, 1971; *New Republic,* March 30, 1968; *Washington Post Book World,* April 14, 1968; *New York Review of Books,* May 23, 1968, December 13, 1973; *Carleton Miscellany,* Volume X, number 1, winter, 1969; *New York Times Book Review,* February 15, 1970, April 11, 1971, June 6, 1971, December 5, 1971; *Village Voice,* March 4, 1971; *Newsweek,* April 12, 1971; *Time,* May 31, 1971; *Antioch Review,* spring, 1971; *Saturday Review,* September 18, 1971.

—*Sketch by Barbara A. Welch*

—*Interview by Jean W. Ross*

* * *

HERR, Michael 1940(?)-

RESIDENCE: New York, N.Y. *Office:* c/o Alfred A. Knopf, Inc., 201 East 50th St., New York, N.Y. 10022.

CAREER: Writer.

WRITINGS: *Dispatches* (nonfiction), Knopf, 1977; (author of narration) Francis Coppola and John Milius, "Apocalypse Now" (screenplay), United Artists, 1979. Contributor of articles to *Rolling Stone, Esquire,* and *New American Review.*

SIDELIGHTS: In 1967 Herr arrived in Vietnam to cover the war there for *Esquire.* Ten years later, *Dispatches,* his impressions of that time, was hailed by literary critics as perhaps the finest documentation of what it was like in Vietnam during the late 1960's. *Dispatches* has been called "convulsively brilliant," "Nightmarish," and "awesome." C.D.B. Bryan called it "the best book to have been written about the Vietnam War."

Reporting the war was a difficult task. "I went to cover the war," Herr noted, "and the war covered me." Herr discovered that he actually enjoyed being there. As Paul Gray wrote, "Herr came to realize that Viet Nam was the most intense experience life was ever likely to offer him." Reveling in the danger of war, Herr wrote: "There were choices everywhere, but they were never choices that you could hope to make. There was even some small chance for personal style in your recognition of the one thing you feared more than any other. You could die in a sudden bloodburning crunch as your chopper hit the ground like dead weight, you could fly apart so that your pieces would never be gathered, you could take one neat round in the lung and go out hearing only the bubble of the last few breaths, you could die in the last stage of malaria with that faint tapping in your ears, and that could happen to you after months of firefights and rockets and machine guns.... You could be shot, mined, grenaded, rocketed, mortared, sniped at, blown up and away so that your leavings had to be dropped into a sagging poncho and carried to Graves Registration, that's all she wrote. It was almost marvelous."

As a correspondent, Herr was an oddity in Vietnam for he was there by choice. "A GI would walk clear across a firebase for a look at you if he'd never seen a correspondent before," wrote Herr, "because it was like going to see the Geek, and worth the walk." Another passage reflects the disbelief Herr encountered among soldiers:

"'Oh man, you *got* to be kidding me. You guys *asked* to come here?'

"'Sure.'

"'How long do you have to stay?' he asked.

"'As long as we want.'

"'Wish *I* could stay as long as *I* want,' the Marine called Love Child said. '*I'd* been home las' March.'

"'When did you get here?' I asked.

"'Las' March.'"

Although he romanticized many of his own experiences in Vietnam, Herr was still able to see the war as a "story that was as simple as it had always been, men hunting men, a hideous war and all kinds of victims." He wrote of one soldier who escaped death by hiding under the corpses of his fellow soldiers while the enemy went about bayoneting the dead. In another episode, American troops escaping by helicopter were forced to shoot their Vietnamese allies who'd jeopardized the take-off by also trying to jump aboard.

Herr's writing throughout is oddly detached yet subjective. "He preaches no sermons, draws no morals, enters no ideological disputes," declared Gray. "He simply suggests that some stories must be told—not because they will delight and instruct but because they happened." However, John Leonard called *Dispatches* "a certain kind of reporting come of age—that is, achieving literature. It is the reporting of the 1960's at last addressing itself to great human issues, subjective, painfully honest, scaled of abstractions down to the viscera, the violence and the sexuality understood and transcended." He concluded with one word: "Stunning."

Critics also praise Herr's ear for dialogue. Alfred Kazin wrote, "Herr caught better than anyone else the kooky, funny, inventively desperate code in which the men in the field showed that they were well and truly in shit." Another critic, Geoffrey Wolff, reported that Herr "had ears like no one else's ears over there, and he brought an entire language back alive." Typical of the dialogue in *Dispatches* is one GI's comment when he learns that another soldier will only be in Vietnam for four months. "'Four Months?'" comes the reply. "'Baby, four *seconds* in this whorehouse'll get you greased.'" Another soldier exclaims, "'A dead buddy is some tough shit, but bringing your own ass out alive can sure help you to get over it.'"

Kazin reserved his highest praise for the political aspects of *Dispatches*. Despite his enthusiasm for the language, Kazin claimed that Herr's "big effort is not literary but political. To his generation, Vietnam did come down to so much self-enclosed, almost self-deafened, despair. No one gets above that specific cruel environment." He cites one soldier's rationale for being in Vietnam, "'I mean, if we can't shoot these people, what . . . are we doing here?'" Explaining why he can't die in Vietnam, another soldier contends, "'Cause it don't exist.'" Herr contrasts his own position with that of a "young soldier speaking in all bloody innocence, saying, 'All that's just a *load,* man. We're here to kill gooks. Period.'" Herr amends the soldier's comment by insisting that that "wasn't at all true of me. I was there to watch."

Upon returning to America, Herr had to deal with his memories of the war. "Was it possible that they were there and not haunted?," he wondered of his friends from the war. "No, not possible, not a chance. I know I wasn't the only one. Where are they now? (Where am I now?) I stood as close to them as I could without actually being one of them, and then I stood as far back as I could without leaving the planet." While sharing departure with other correspondents, Herr observed: "A few extreme cases felt that the experience there had been a glorious one, while most of us felt that it had been merely wonderful. I think that Viet Nam was what we had instead of happy childhoods."

Gray concluded his review of *Dispatches* by noting, "Herr dared to travel to that irrational place and to come back with the worst imaginable news: war thrives because men still love it." But Bryan defended Herr's position: "To Michael Herr's credit he never ceased to feel deeply for the men with whom he served; he never became callous, always worried for them, agonized over them, on occasion even took up arms to defend them. His greatest service, I'm convinced, is this book."

BIOGRAPHICAL/CRITICAL SOURCES: Michael Herr, *Dispatches,* Knopf, 1977; *New York Times,* October 28, 1977; *Book World,* November 6, 1977; *Time,* November 7, 1977; *New Times,* November 11, 1977; *Newsweek,* November 14, 1977; *New York Times Book Review,* November 20, 1977; *New York Review of Books,* December 8, 1977; *Atlantic,* January, 1978; *Saturday Review,* January 7, 1978; *Esquire,* March 1, 1978.*

—Sketch by Les Stone

* * *

HERSHEY, Daniel 1931-

PERSONAL: Born February 12, 1931, in New York, N.Y.; son of Frank (a tailor) and Anna (a tailor; maiden name, Scharf) Hershey; married Barbara Drury (an art historian), September 5, 1965; children: Michael David, Andrea Lynn. *Education:* Cooper Union College, B.S., 1953; University of Tennessee, Ph.D., 1961. *Home:* 726 Lafayette Ave., Cincinnati, Ohio 45220. *Office:* Department of Chemical and Nuclear Engineering, University of Cincinnati, Cincinnati, Ohio 45221.

CAREER: University of Cincinnati, Cincinnati, Ohio, assistant professor, 1962-64, associate professor, 1964-69, professor of chemical engineering, 1969—. *Military service:* U.S. Army, 1954-56. *Member:* American Association of University Professors (president, 1971-72), American Institute of Chemical Engineers, American Association for Engineering Education, American Association for the Advancement of Science, Society for General Systems Research, American Aging Association, Gerontological Association, Sigma Xi (president, 1973-75). *Awards, honors:* Teaching awards from Tau Beta Pi, 1970, 1972; award from Cincinnati Editors Association, 1978, for public interest story, "In God We Trust."

WRITINGS: Chemical Engineering in Medicine and Biology, Plenum, 1967; *Blood Oxygenation,* Plenum, 1970; *Everyday Science,* Doubleday, 1971; *Transport Analysis,* Plenum, 1973; *Lifespan and Factors Affecting It,* C. C Thomas, 1974; *The University, My God,* Vantage, 1976; *A New Age-Scale for Humans,* Lexington Books, 1980. Contributor to *Cincinnati Post.*

WORK IN PROGRESS: Aging Systems.

SIDELIGHTS: Hershey writes: "My interest is in the aging theories of life, defining the meaning of life as applied to living and non-living systems, from humans to corporations to countries to civilizations. The book I am now writing, *Aging Systems,* deals with all aspects of longevity, in all systems.

"Aging is no disgrace; it is a natural process that happens to all of us. We should be allowed to age in dignity.

"Life is a series of events governed by the laws of probability. If we are wise, observant, and opportunistic, then we can discover the knack for improving our chances in life. Otherwise, we are carried along passively in the rapidly flowing stream of events."

* * *

HERZOG, Werner 1942-

PERSONAL: Birth-given name Werner H. Stipetic; adopted mother's maiden name; born September 5, 1942, in Munich, Germany; married wife, Martje (an actress), c. 1960; children: Rudolph Amos Achmed. *Education:* Attended University of Munich and University of Pittsburgh. *Residence:* Munich, West Germany. *Office:* c/o New Yorker Films, 43 West 61st St., New York, N.Y. 10023.

CAREER: Writer, producer, and director of motion pictures. Worked on docks in Manchester, England, and as factory worker, parking lot attendant, and rodeo hand in Pittsburgh, Pa. Founder of Werner Herzog Produktions. *Awards, honors:* Prize from Oberhausen Film Festival, 1967, for "Letze Worte"; Jury Prize from Cannes Film Festival, 1975, for "Jeder fuer Sich und Gott Gegen Alle.."

WRITINGS—Screenplays; all as director; all produced by Werner Herzog Film-produktion: "Lebenszeichen" (released in United States as "Signs of Life"; adapted from the story by Achim von Armin, "Der tolle Invalide auf dem Fort Ratonneau"), 1968; "Auch Zwerge Haben Klein Angefangen" (released in United States as "Even Dwarves Started Small"), 1970; "Behinderte Zukunft" (documentary; released in United States as "Frustrated Future"), 1970; "Fata Morgana," 1971; "Land des Schweigens und der Dunkelheit" (documentary; released in United States as "Land of Silence and Darkness"), 1972; "Aguirre, der Zorn Gottes" (released in United States as "Aguirre, Wrath of God"), 1973; "Jeder fuer Sich und Gott Gegen Alle" (released in United States as "Every Man for Himself and God Against All" and as "The Enigma of Kasper Hauser"), 1975; (with Herbert Achternbusch) "Herz aus Glas" (released in United States as "Heart of Glass"; adapted in part from the novel by Achternbusch, *Die Stunde des Todes*), 1976; "Stroszek," 1977.

Other; all as director: "Herakles" (short), 1962; "Spiel im Sand" (short; title means "Game in the Sand"), 1964; "Die Beispiellose Verteidigung der Festun Deutschkreutz" (short; title means "The Unprecedented Defense of Fortress Deutschkreuz"), 1966; "Letzte Worte" (short; released in United States as "Last Words"), 1967; "Massnahmen gegen Fanatiker" (short; title means "Precautions Against Fanatics"), 1969; "Die Fliegenden Aerzte von Ostafrika" (short documentary; title means "The Flying Doctors of East Africa"), 1969; "Die Grosse Ekstase des Bildschnitzers Steiner" (short documentary; released in United States as "The Great Ecstacy of the Sculptor Steiner"), 1975; "La Soufriere" (short documentary), 1976; "How Much Wood Would a Woodchuck Chuck?" (short documentary), 1977; "Nosferatu" (adapted from the film by F. W. Murnau), 1979; "Woyzeck" (adapted from the short story by Georg Buechner), 1979.

SIDELIGHTS: Herzog's films are considered by many critics to be among the most "intensely personal" of any filmmaker's. Eccentric in some of his actions, Herzog has cast one film with midgets, one with hypnotized actors, and another with a rooster in the lead role. His individuality and dedication to his own personal vision has often resulted in peril; he's been imprisoned, had his life threatened, and persevered under the threat of a volcano in order to achieve the desired effects. Herzog recalled a particularly bad experience during the filming of "Fata Morgana" when his cameraman was mistaken for a mercenary. "So we were captured at night and dragged into prison," recounted Herzog. "I had malaria and a very bad parasitic disease. . . . There was no light, no water, and people were tortured to death, two of them died. And we were very badly mistreated there. It went on like that, too. There was a warrant out for us all over the country. And either on purpose or out of slovenliness the officials forgot to destroy the warrant. So every time we passed through a town, we were arrested." But for Herzog, if the effort has often been painstaking, it has also been worth it. "I see something on the horizon that most people have not yet seen," he claimed. "I seek planets that do not exist and landscapes that have only been imagined."

At an early age Herzog showed an interest in films. "I never had a choice about becoming a director," he noted. "I wrote scripts at school and submitted them, but there was a long chain of humiliations and failures, so I decided to work at a steel factory at night to make money to produce my first short films."

One of Herzog's first films, "Game in the Sand," features a rooster. Fowl would later become a popular symbol in such films as "Signs of Life," in which a soldier shows another how to hypnotize a chicken, and "Stroszek," which ends with shots of a dancing rooster intercut with a circling truck and a ski-lift which carries the corpse of the lead character. "I *am* obsessed with chickens," Herzog confided to Jonathan Cott. "Take a close and very long look into the eye of a chicken and you'll see the most frightful kind of stupidity. Stupidity is always frightful. It's the devil: stupidity is the devil. Look in the eye of a chicken and then you'll know. It's the most horrifying, cannibalistic and nightmarish creature in this world."

Herzog's first full-length film, "Signs of Life," explored the dilemma of self-expression. It is the story of three soldiers stationed in Crete during World War II. One of the soldiers becomes insane after viewing a landscape filled with windmills. He chases the others off the island and turns to bombarding the mainland with fireworks. Herzog offered the following interpretation of the film: "In all of my films, in moments of utmost despair, there's silence and an exchange of signals—people exchange some kind of signals. You don't see the soldier anymore as a private person, as a psychological figure. You see him from a distance of 400 yards away, like an ant, as little as that. And he gives signals or signs—the same kind of signs of violence and despair that he himself received all the time. He wants to destroy the whole town with toy rockets. It's humiliating for him. It's such a humiliation that he only scorches a chair and he only manages to kill a donkey."

Herzog considered his second film, "Fata Morgana," too "frail" for general audiences. The film portrays the desert as a reflection of man's disregard for nature. Although numerous critics were baffled by its content, Colin L. Westerbeck, Jr., called "Fata Morgana" a "large, central and important" work. "A lot of that sense of comprehensiveness and incomprehensibility we get from Herzog's work is concentrated in 'Fata Morgana,'" Westerbeck wrote. "It is a bag of myths on which he can draw." Westerbeck also called it "Herzog's attempt to write his own Book of Genesis. Because it aims at accounting for all creation, like the Bible it cannot be too explicit. Its power comes from the quality of parable about it. It is imponderable, even mystical in a way, because it attempts to see life whole while at the same time respecting its mysteriousness."

After making "Frustrated Future" and "Land of Silence and Darkness," two documentaries about the handicapped, Herzog journeyed to the Amazon River for "Aguirre, Wrath of God," the film generally considered by critics as his first masterpiece. "It is the single unwavering movie continuity he has achieved," wrote Vernon Young: "inexorable in its progress, taciturn and deadly, hauntingly beautiful. . . ." Particularly memorable is the final scene in which Aguirre, an insane conquistador whose futile search for El Dorado has resulted in the elimination of his entire entourage, speaks of conquering his surroundings and marrying his daughter (who lies dead on a raft which floats downstream carrying only corpses, Aguirre, and countless water-monkeys). "'Aguirre,'" Young stated, "is among the outstanding film narratives ever."

Herzog followed "Aguirre" with "Kasper Hauser," perhaps his best known film. It is the story of a young man found in the middle of a small German town after spending most of his life in isolation. Hauser is eventually accommodated into society, after which he is abruptly murdered. The film proved immensely popular among college-student audiences impressed by Herzog's "visionary" style. When Cott mentioned the "extraordinary dreamlike quality," Herzog responded: "I'm looking for new images in film. . . . And somehow I have the positive knowledge of new images, like a far-distant strip of land on the horizon. . . . I'm trying to discover our innermost conditioning, it's a very deepdown brooding knowledge."

"Heart of Glass," Herzog's next film, was not met with the same critical enthusiasm as "Kasper Hauser." Herzog hypnotized the cast in this story of a community plunged into despair when the only possessor of the secret glass-coloring formula dies. Young remarked that "at the *simple*-story level, the film doesn't function; it's a looseleaf assembly of wondrous images, unclear hints and highlighted boors."

Despite critical reaction to "Heart of Glass," by 1976 Herzog was being hailed, along with Rainer Werner Fassbinder, Wim Wenders, and a half-dozen other German filmmakers, as the most refreshing thing in film since the French "new wave" of the late 1950's and early '60's. His films were receiving attention both in the United States, where he was quickly becoming a favorite among students, and in Europe, especially Paris where "Aguirre" played continuously for eighteen months. Oddly enough, Herzog's films were not particularly popular in his native Germany.

"Stroszek," released in 1977, has been called Herzog's most accessible film by many critics. As David Anson noted, Herzog "has moved closer to a normal range of experience. . . ." The film chronicles three Germans, a prostitute named Eva, Stroszek, a street-musician released from prison in the opening scenes, and an elderly man, who lives with Stroszek. After interfering between the prostitute and her two pimps, Stroszek and his elderly roommate become targets of the pimps' abuses. Eva, Stroszek, and his roommate eventually move to Wisconsin where they stay with a relative of the old man's. However, they soon find all their belongings repossessed by the bank. After Eva departs with a truck driver, Stroszek and the old man rob a bank; after the latter is arrested, a despairing Stroszek boards a ski-lift and shoots himself. Westerbeck called the final scene, which includes a dancing rooster and an ever-circling truck on fire, "a horrific image of the attempt to encompass somehow a void which we cannot know in any way."

In 1979 Herzog produced two more films, "Nosferatu" and "Woyzeck." The former is a remake of the 1922 film by German filmmaker F. W. Murnau who is greatly admired by Herzog. "Woyzeck" is an adaptation of the famous short story by Georg Buechner in which a persecuted soldier murders his girlfriend following her dalliance with a drum major.

In an interview with Cott, Herzog offered the following interpretation of his purpose as a filmmaker. "The appropriate time for me would be the Middle Ages," he related. "I feel close to the music and painting of that time. It would also fit the concept of my work. I don't feel like an artist, I feel like a craftsman. All the sculptors and painters of that period didn't regard themselves as artists, but rather as craftsmen. . . . That is exactly how I feel about my work as a filmmaker—as if I were anonymous, I couldn't even care."

BIOGRAPHICAL/CRITICAL SOURCES: Rolling Stone, November 18, 1976; *New York Times Magazine,* July 10, 1977; *New Yorker,* July 25, 1977; *Newsweek,* August 15, 1977; *Horizon,* September, 1977; *Commonweal,* September 16, 1977, September 30, 1977; *Hudson Review,* autumn, 1977; *Film Quarterly,* fall, 1977; *Time,* March 20, 1978.*

—Sketch by Les Stone

* * *

HEYDENBURG, Harry E. 1891(?)-1979

OBITUARY NOTICE: Born c. 1891; died June 11, 1979, in Chicago, Ill. Journalist. Beginning his career as a printing press operator at age eleven, Heydenburg worked for the *Chicago Journal* and the International News Service (now United Press International) before joining the *Chicago Herald and Examiner,* where he spent thirty-six years as a reporter on the Federal Building. Obituaries and other sources: *Chicago Tribune,* June 12, 1979.

* * *

HEYNE, Paul 1931-

PERSONAL: Surname is pronounced Hane; born November 2, 1931, in St. Louis, Mo.; son of Walter Martin (a Lutheran minister) and Ruth (Beiderwieden) Heyne; married Marjorie Fairchild, November 25, 1955 (divorced, 1965); married Juliana Becker (a painter), January 29, 1966; children: Eric, Margot, Brian, Michelle, Sarah. *Education:* Concordia Seminary, St. Louis, Mo., B.A., 1953, M.Div., 1956; Washington University, St. Louis, Mo., M.A., 1957; University of Chicago, Ph.D., 1963. *Home:* 103 17th Ave. E., Seattle, Wash. 98112. *Office:* Department of Economics, University of Washington, DK-30, Seattle, Wash. 98195.

CAREER: Valparaiso University, Valparaiso, Ind., instructor, 1957-59, assistant professor, 1959-63, associate professor of economics, 1963-65; Southern Methodist University, Dallas, Tex., associate professor, 1966-73, professor of economics, 1973-76; University of Washington, Seattle, lecturer in economics, 1976—.

WRITINGS: The World of Economics, Concordia, 1963; *Private Keepers of the Public Interest,* McGraw, 1968; *The Economic Way of Thinking,* SRA, 1973, 3rd edition, 1980; (with Thomas Johnson) *Toward Economic Understanding,* SRA, 1976.

WORK IN PROGRESS: The Moral Impulse and Economic Reform.

SIDELIGHTS: Heyne told *CA:* "It was an interest in ethics that first brought me to the study of economics. That interest hasn't wavered. But the longer I examine and reflect upon the relationship between economics and ethics, the more complex it becomes. Adam Smith correctly noted that 'moral sentiments' underlie the actions that produce the 'wealth of nations.' He knew what we are beginning to discover: that a functioning economic order is not compatible with just any system of functioning moral beliefs. My interests in recent years have focused on the role played by religious moralists in promoting economic reform, and the odd view of the economic universe that so often informs their proposals."

* * *

HEYWOOD, Rosalind 1895-

PERSONAL: Born February 2, 1895, in Gibraltar, England; daughter of Sir Coote (a military colonel) and Lady [Anna] Hedley; married Frank Heywood (a military colonel), March, 1921 (deceased); children: B. C., C. J. *Education:* Attended University of London. *Politics:* "Still trying to decide." *Religion:* "I wish I knew." *Home:* 3 The Drive, West Wimbledon, London S.W. 208T9, England.

CAREER: Psychic researcher, 1939—. Broadcaster. Worked as nurse in England and Macedonia during World War I. *Member:* Society for Psychical Research (vice-president; past member of council), Parapsychological Association, English-Speaking Union (past member of board of governors).

WRITINGS: (Translator) Gabriel Marcel, *Three Plays,* Secker & Warburg, 1952; *The Sixth Sense: An Inquiry Into Extra-Sensory Perception,* Chatto & Windus, 1959, revised edition, Pan Books, 1971, published in the United States as *Beyond the Reach of Sense: An Inquiry Into Extra-Sensory Perception,* Dutton, 1961; *ESP: A Personal Memoir,* Dutton, 1964 (published in England as *The Infinite Hive: A Personal Record of Extra-Sensory Experiences,* Chatto & Windus, 1964, revised edition, Penguin, 1978); (contributor) Arnold Toynbee, editor, *Man's Concern With Death,* Hodder & Stoughton, 1968; (contributor) J. R. Smythies, editor, *Science and E.S.P.,* Routledge & Kegan Paul, 1967; (contributor) *Life After Death,* Weidenfeld & Nicolson, 1976.

WORK IN PROGRESS: Parapsychology research.

SIDELIGHTS: Rosalind Heywood writes: "After my marriage I spent many years moving from country to country in the wake of my husband during his career as soldier, diplomat, businessman, and inventor. I have lived in India, Greece, Turkey, Belgium, Switzerland, Hungary, and the United States, and have travelled widely in Africa and elsewhere.

"It is only since I came to settle in England in 1939 that I have been able to pursue my main interest, psychical research. The study of the lesser-known faculties of the human being, from the strictly scientific standpoint, is one which appeals to me particularly, as I am to some extent a sensitive myself as well as an investigator, and I can be, in a sense, my own guinea pig."

Her books have been published in Sweden, Brazil, Argentina, and Japan.

* * *

HIGGINS, Ink
See WEISS, Morris S(amuel)

* * *

HIGH, Stanley (Hoflund) 1895-1961

OBITUARY NOTICE: Born December 30, 1895, in Chicago, Ill.; died February 3, 1961. Author of religion-oriented books, including *A Waking World* and *Billy Graham: The Personal Story of the Man, His Message, and His Mission.* High also worked for many years as senior editor of *Reader's Digest.* Obituaries and other sources: *Who Was Who in America,* 4th edition, Marquis, 1968.

* * *

HILARY, Christopher 1927(?)-1979

OBITUARY NOTICE: Born c. 1927 in Szopienice, Poland; died of a heart attack, September 30, 1979, in Fairfax, Va. Artist and author. Hilary's oil paintings, prints, and three-dimensional works have been exhibited in one-man shows in the Netherlands, West Germany, Switzerland, New Jersey, and Washington, D.C. His works are also displayed in several museums and private collections in Poland. Hilary was art editor of two major Polish periodicals during the 1950's and 1960's. Obituaries and other sources: *Washington Post,* October 5, 1979.

* * *

HILDRETH, Margaret Holbrook 1927-

PERSONAL: Born May 2, 1927, in Providence, R.I.; daughter of Herbert Rufus (an engineer) and Alfa (Christensen) Holbrook; married Richard Bentley Hildreth (a professor and radio-television producer), May 20, 1949; children: Martha Louise (Mrs. William P. Everts), Andrea Joyce (Mrs. R. Clay Jordan), Sara Margaret (Mrs. Leon T. Lewek), Laura Evangeline, Derek Richard. *Education:* Syracuse University, A.B., 1948; State University of New York College at Geneseo, M.L.S., 1970. *Religion:* Baha'i. *Home address:* R.R.1, Box 228-E, Carbondale, Ill. 62901. *Office:* Morris Library, Southern Illinois University, Carbondale, Ill. 62901.

CAREER: State University of New York College at Plattsburgh, library trainee, 1966-68; Southern Illinois University, Carbondale, library assistant, 1968-70, instructor, 1970-77, assistant professor of library science, 1977—. Has worked as cellist, radio and television news stringer, and newspaper teletypist. *Member:* American Library Association, Illinois Library Association.

WRITINGS: Harriet Beecher Stowe: A Bibliography, Archon Books, 1976.

WORK IN PROGRESS: Prairie Prophets: The Beechers in Illinois, publication expected in 1982.

SIDELIGHTS: Margaret Hildreth wrote: "My current research is an outgrowth of research done for the Stowe bibliography, in that other Beechers kept cropping up in newspaper files and the like, especially here in Illinois. At length curiosity got the better of me, and I began a preliminary genealogical search in 1976, which has grown to a full-scale operation.

"The nineteenth-century emigration from New York and New England through Ohio and Indiana brought many unacknowledged cousins of Lyman and his famous brood, some of whom became renowned, while others did not. Still curious, my research is discovering not only what these people did before they came here, but what their accomplishments were and are in the Prairie State. An emmigrant to Illinois myself, I empathize with them.

"When the current Beecher study is complete, and hopefully published, a new field of interest is awaiting my attention. The Hildreth grandame has suggested I 'do something about' Susan B. Anthony; it seems Anthony's sister married my husband's grandfather, and many of Anthony's letters and journals are languishing in a cousin's desk."

* * *

HILL, Daniel G., Jr. 1896(?)-1979

OBITUARY NOTICE: Born c. 1896 in Annapolis, Md.; died October 21, 1979, in Washington, D.C. Minister, educator, and author. Ordained a minister in the African Methodist Episcopal Church in 1921, Hill was a pastor at churches in Portland, Ore., Independence, Mo., and Denver, Colo. He was associated with the Howard University School of Religion for nearly twenty years as an instructor, dean of the Andrew Rankin Chapel, and dean of the school of religion. Hill wrote numerous articles on religion, sociology, and black history. Obituaries and other sources: *Washington Post,* October 24, 1979.

* * *

HILL, Ruth Beebe 1913-

PERSONAL: Born April, 1913, in Cleveland, Ohio; daughter of Hermann C. (an electrical engineer) and Flora M. Beebe; married Borroughs Reid Hill (a biochemist), 1940; children: Reid. *Education:* Western Reserve University (now Case Western Reserve University), B.A., 1935, graduate study, 1936-37; also studied at University of Colorado, 1939-40. *Residence:* San Juan Island, Wash. *Office:* Leigh Bureau (speaker's bureau), 9300 Wilshire Blvd., Beverly Hills, Calif. 91202.

CAREER: Books and Authors, Inc., Los Angeles, Calif., member of promotion department, 1949-55; *Newport-Balboa Press,* Newport Beach, Calif., news and feature writer, 1950-52; free-lance writer. Co-founder of Women's Auxiliary California Institute for Cancer Research. Speaker. *Member:* Daughters of the American Revolution (San Juan Islands chapter), Historical Society of Washington, Montana Historical Society. *Awards, honors:* Golden Plate Award from American Academy of Achievement, 1979.

WRITINGS: Hanta Yo (novel), Doubleday, 1979. Author of monthly column for *Western Life Magazine,* 1967-68.

WORK IN PROGRESS: Magazine articles on subjects taken from *Hanta Yo.*

SIDELIGHTS: As a young girl Ruth Beebe Hill was always interested in Indians. At Thanksgiving she would show more enthusiasm for learning about Indians than she did about the Pilgrims from whom she is directly descended. As the years went by, Hill's interest developed into a thirty-year project which resulted in the publication of *Hanta Yo.*

Hill began work on *Hanta Yo* in 1951 and spent the following three years doing research in local libraries. But library research was not enough for Hill and she soon left her home to visit Indian reservations where she talked with over a thousand Indians. In a *Smithsonian* article she discussed her experiences and warned: "If you go with camera and notebook, you might as well not go. You can count on being turned over—like inquiring anthropologists—to the biggest liar around. You want a legend? You'll get a legend. And it's all crap!"

During those years of research Hill was determined to experience the Indian way of life first hand. She spent summers "acquainting herself with the badger" and watching the beaver and buffalo. She is proud of her collection of feathers and moose, elk, and buffalo droppings. "Along the way," *Smithsonian* reported, "she trained her senses 'as the Indians do'.... As an exercise, she experienced a five-day starve—without eating, drinking, going to the bathroom."

Of the years she spent on *Hanta Yo,* the last fourteen were used in working with a bilingual Indian musician, Chunksa Yuha. After she had studied all the creatures of the woods and plains and "knew my trees, soils, waterways," Hill realized that something was missing. "I seemed to know everything," she told *CA,* "except the most important: the soul of the Indian. Who ever really knows the Indians through artifacts?"

Hill decided, then, that she should learn the ancient Indian language Dakotah, or, Lakotah. For this undertaking she needed the help of a bilingual Indian. After talking to numerous "Hollywood Indians" Hill met Yuha; or rather, he came to her door—word had gotten out that a white woman was looking for an Indian to work with her in the archaic Dakotah language. Hill answered the door and asked Yuha what was the Indian word for hail. Instead of the standard "frozen rain" interpretation, Yuha gave Hill three different words for hail: *wasu,* or seeds of snow, for hailstones about the size of marbles; *waheca,* for sleet "resembling birdshot"; and *magzu,* if the hail was mixed with rain. Hill opened the door and welcomed him, and they worked together continuously for over fifty hours.

Yuha is one of eight Santee Sioux who as young boys were "deliberately withheld from white schooling" in order to teach them the ancient Indian ways. He learned songs and ceremonies that had been supressed for two hundred years. Yuha is also a composer as well as a recorder of Indian music. Together he and Hill translated her manuscript into the Dakotah/Lakotah language, and then back again into the English of an 1806 Webster's dictionary. All this was done so that the book would be as close as possible to what Hill calls the Indian "altitude of mind." She is quick to point out the differences between "white man's words" and the Indian language. For example, the word "think" is conjugated properly only in the first person singular—"I think. No Indian presumes to say what another thinks." In addition, subjunctives are never used in the Indian language: "If you could or should, if you were an Indian, you acted." Other words which are not found in the Indian language include assume, believe, faith, forgive, and guilt.

The Indian language is also different in its expression of color and distance. For the Indian, there are only four colors: red, black, yellow, and white. Hill noted that green and blue are absent because "the Indians perceives blue as a darkened green or a green removed from light." Feet, inches, miles, all considered "white man's measurements," are missing and in their place, for example, is the distance "a fat man walks in a day."

Hanta Yo, which means "clear the way," is the story of how a small tribe of Teton Sioux existed and kept itself apart from white influence during the period of 1750 to 1834. Although considered fiction, *Hanta Yo* is, for Hill, "a documented novel." She notes that the names and deeds of the four heroes in the book are fictitious, but, otherwise, "everything really happened." "One of the different things about it," wrote Hill, "and this might be something to send people away, I suppose, is that it is a spiritual travelogue."

"*Hanta Yo* is infuriatingly portentous," noted Webster Scott, and "there's an uncharitable lack of irony or humor to relieve the strain," but it still "works." According to Scott, Hill "sets down layer upon layer of detail, peeking a facsimile of total experience, reaching for a portrait of an entire people. She gets it. The portrait is idealized and romanticized. It is more often informed by anthropology than psychology. The savages are always noble." To this Hill replied that "the humor is Indian, not white man's humor, and no savages exist in *Hanta Yo,* either noble or not noble."

Charles R. Larson called it "a celebration of the natural life, a paean to what was subsequently lost." He added, "There is little question that the visionary nature of Indian life has been treated by Ruth Hill with loving attention to detail." But Larson was "not convinced of the success of the such elaborate attempts to recapture Dakotah idioms or of the necessity for using that 1806 dictionary. The style throughout is regrettably lackluster." But N. Scott Momaday observed that in spite of the brittle texture, "it is not tedious and it never seems archaic. The reader is not, I think, moved to question whether or not the langauge is a true reflection of the Indian idiom." Although "characterization is at best a secondary quality," Momaday saw *Hanta Yo* as "a substantial novel, impressive in both conception and execution.... There is revealed a fascinating world. In one sense it is a small, nearly private world, a world so exclusive as to be available only in the pages of a book. But it is a whole world, too, full of good things and bad."

The rights to *Hanta Yo* have been bought by the Wolper Organization, Inc. for a "novel for television" series and by Warner Bros. for the screen.

BIOGRAPHICAL/CRITICAL SOURCES: Smithsonian, December, 1978; *Publishers Weekly,* January 8, 1979; *Washington Post Book World,* January 28, 1979; *Chicago Tribune,* February 11, 1979; *New York Times Book Review,* March 18, 1979, March 25, 1979; *Washington Post,* June 25, 1979; *People,* August 6, 1979.

* * *

HILLIX, W(illiam) A(llen) 1927-

PERSONAL: Born March 19, 1927, in Dearborn, Mo.; son of Allen Jasper (a farmer) and Anna Lee (Bywaters) Hillix; married Virginia Ray Gaines (divorced December, 1960); married Shirley Sue Sauer, December 28, 1960; children: (first marriage) Gaines Allen, Helen Ann, Lynn Dell, William Elliott, Elaine Marie and Louise Kathleen (twins), Cathleen Ann Cate; (second marriage) Allison Lea. *Education:* Attended University of Utah, 1945, Washburn Municipal University, 1945, and Oberlin College, 1945-46; University of Missouri, B.A., 1949, M.A., 1954, Ph.D., 1958. *Politics:* Democrat. *Religion:* "Panthcist." *Home:* 1861 El Pico Dr., El Cajon, Calif. 92020. *Office:* Department of Psychology, San Diego State University, San Diego, Calif. 92182.

CAREER: English teacher and principal of high school in Dearborn, Mo., 1949-52; University of Missouri, Columbia, instructor in psychology, 1952-58; U.S. Navy, Electronics Laboratory, San Diego, Calif., research psychologist, 1959-67; San Diego State College (now University), San Diego, assistant professor of psychology, 1963-67; University of Missouri, Kansas City, professor of psychology and head of department, 1967-69; San Diego State University, professor of psychology, 1969—. Exchange professor at University of Leiden, 1973. Participant in international meetings. Consultant to U.S. Navy Personnel Research & Development Laboratory. *Military service:* U.S. Army Reserve, 1944. *Member:* American Association for the Advancement of Science, Western Psychological Association (member of board of directors, 1978-80), Sigma Xi, Psi Chi. *Awards, honors:* U.S. Public Health Service fellowship, 1958-59; outstanding teacher award from Psi Chi, 1971-72.

WRITINGS: (With M. H. Marx) *Systems and Theories in Psychology,* McGraw, 1963, 3rd edition, 1979; (editor with Marx) *Systems and Theories in Psychology: A Reader,* West Publishing, 1974. Contributor to psychology journals, including *Psychology Today.*

WORK IN PROGRESS: Psychology: An Evolutionary Approach; a divorce manual.

SIDELIGHTS: Hillix wrote: "I initiated a series of academic exchanges between the University of Leiden and San Diego State University when I spent eleven months in the Netherlands as an exchange professor. I anticipate visiting Leipzig as one of ten Americans invited to participate in their Centennial Symposium for Wundt, founder of psychology.

"My house is a little bit like an international hotel. Most of the Dutch people who come from the University of Leiden to San Diego spend some time with my wife and me; so does my Yugoslavian friend, Vid Pecjak. I mention this because I think that ultimately the greatest significance of whatever I do may be helping to bring people from different countries into better relationships with each other.

"Most of my ideas for research or popular writing have come from incidents in my own life. One only has to keep one's mind open to everyday events in order to get ideas for a lifetime of research and writing."

Systems and Theories in Psychology has been published in Spanish and Portuguese language editions.

* * *

HILLMAN, James 1926-

PERSONAL: Born in 1926, in Atlantic City, N.J.; married Catharina Kempe, 1952 (marriage ended, 1974); married Patricia Berry, 1976; children: three daughters, one son. *Education:* Attended Georgetown University, 1943; Sorbonne, University of Paris, certificate, 1948; Trinity College, Dublin, M.A., 1950; University of Zurich, D. Phil., 1959. *Office:* Institute for Philosophic Studies, University of Dallas, Irvine, Tex. 75061.

CAREER: Worked as newswriter for American Forces Network, 1946-47; diplomate, analyst, and director of studies at C. G. Jung Institute, 1959-69; Spring Publications, New York, N.Y., editor, 1970-78, publisher, 1978—. Professor at University of Dallas, senior fellow of Institute for Philosophic Studies, and graduate dean, 1979—. *Military service:* U.S. Navy, 1944-46.

WRITINGS: Emotion, Routledge & Kegan Paul, 1960, Northwestern University Press, 1961, revised edition, 1963; *Suicide and the Soul,* Harper, 1964; (contributor) Gopi Krishna, *Kundalini: The Evolutionary Energy in Man,* Ramadhar & Hopman, 1967; *Insearch,* Scribner, 1967; *The*

Feeling Function, Spring Publications, 1971; *The Myth of Analysis,* Northwestern University Press, 1972; *Pan and the Nightmare,* Spring Publications, 1972; *Loose Ends,* Spring Publications, 1975; *Revisioning Psychology,* Harper, 1975; *The Dream and the Underworld,* Harper, 1979. Contributor of forty articles and translations to various publications, including *Eranos Jahrbuecher.*

Associate editor of *Envoy: An Irish Review of Literature and the Arts,* 1949-51; editor of *Studies in Jungian Thought* for Bucknell University Press.

SIDELIGHTS: In *The Dream and the Underworld,* Hillman reaches beyond dream theories of Freud and Jung in an attempt "to place dreams in the mainstream of myth, specifically the myth of the underworld," noted Edgar Levenson. Recommending the book highly, Levenson remarked that Hillman's theory, in which the "dream qua myth taps a rich underworld of imagery and experience" in the dreamer, is an "extraordinarily rich concept."

BIOGRAPHICAL/CRITICAL SOURCES: New York Times Book Review, August 26, 1979.

* * *

HILLYER, Robert (Silliman) 1895-1961

OBITUARY NOTICE: Born June 3, 1895, in East Orange, N.J.; died December 24, 1961. Educator and writer best known for his championing of the heroic couplet in works such as *Sonnets and Other Lyrics* and *In Pursuit of Poetry.* Hillyer received the Pulitzer Prize for *Collected Verse.* He also wrote novels, including *My Heart for Hostage* and *Riverhead.* Obituaries and other sources: *Current Biography,* Wilson, 1940, February, 1962; *New York Times,* December 25, 1961; *The Oxford Companion to American Literature,* 4th edition, Oxford University Press, 1965; *The Reader's Encyclopedia,* 2nd edition, Crowell, 1965; *The Penguin Companion to American Literature,* McGraw, 1971.

* * *

HINCKLE, Warren James III 1938-

PERSONAL: Born October 12, 1938, in San Francisco, Calif.; son of Warren James II and Angela (Devere) Hinckle; married Denise Libarle (a private school director), October 27, 1962; children: Pia Jeanne, Hilary Devere. *Education:* University of San Francisco, B.A., 1960. *Politics:* "Gadflyism." *Religion:* Catholic. *Home:* 263 Castro St., San Francisco, Calif. 94114. *Agent:* Barbara Lowenstein, 250 West 57th St., New York, N.Y. 10019. *Office: San Francisco Chronicle,* 901 Mission St., San Francisco, Calif. 94119.

CAREER: Writer. Hughes & Hinckle, San Francisco, Calif., in public relations, 1960-62; *San Francisco Chronicle,* San Francisco, reporter, 1962-64; *Ramparts,* San Francisco, editor, 1964-69, president, 1969; Scanlan's Literary House, San Francisco, vice-president, editor of *Scanlan's Monthly,* and member of board of directors, 1969-72; *City of San Francisco,* San Francisco, editor, 1975-76; *San Francisco Chronicle,* columnist, 1977—. Vice-president of Madison-Hobbs Co., 1973—; vice-president and director of Virginia City Restoration Co., 1977—; vice-president of Citizens Planning Committee of San Francisco. Adviser to San Francisco Youth Association. *Member:* San Francisco Press Club. *Awards, honors:* Tom Paine Award from Emergency Civil Liberties Committee, 1967, for "exposing CIA infiltration of American institutions."

WRITINGS: Guerrilla Warfare in the USA, Kritiese Biblioteek Van Gennep, 1971; (with Eliot Asinof and William Turner) *The Ten Second Jailbreak,* Holt, 1973; *If You Have a Lemon, Make Lemonade* (nonfiction), Putnam, 1974; (with Frederick Hobbs) *The Richest Place on Earth,* Houghton, 1978; (with Turner) *The Fish Is Red,* Times Books, 1980. Contributor to periodicals, including *Atlantic, Playboy, New West, Nation, Esquire,* and *New York Times.*

WORK IN PROGRESS: Smear: A Novel of California, about political generations from 1930's to 1950's.

SIDELIGHTS: Hinckle is best known for *If You Have a Lemon, Make Lemonade,* a series of reports of important stories published in *Ramparts* when he was the editor. Among the stories detailed are the Kennedy assassination conspiracy as investigated by James Garrison and a revelation concerning actual activities of military Special Forces in Vietnam. Marjorie Heins wrote, "The tales Hinckle has to tell are fascinating.... But the 'lunatic' brash and bawdy style detracts from the serious things which Hinckle has to say." A. M. Kaufman noted, "There is a lot of funny stuff here ... but it is no satire, it is Hinckle trying and, for the most part, succeeding at telling his story straight.... His sketches are excellent."

BIOGRAPHICAL/CRITICAL SOURCES: Christian Science Monitor, November 6, 1974; *New Republic,* February 15, 1975.

* * *

HINKLE, Gerald H(ahn) 1931-

PERSONAL: Born April 16, 1931, in Doylestown, Pa.; son of Arthur S. (a barber) and Etta F. (Hahn) Hinkle; married Anna Louise Eberts (a school teacher), 1953; children: H. Lucinda, A. Elizabeth. *Education:* Franklin and Marshall College, A.B. (magna cum laude), 1953; Lancaster Theological Seminary of the United Church of Christ, B.D., 1956; Yale University, M.A., 1962, Ph.D., 1964. *Home:* 301 West McGee St., Sherman, Tex. 75090. *Office:* Department of Philosophy, Austin College, Box 1550, Sherman, Tex. 75090.

CAREER: Ordained minister of United Church of Christ, 1956; pastor of United Church of Christ in Lancaster County, Pa., 1955-60, interim pastor in Middlebury, Conn., 1961-63; Ursinus College, Collegeville, Pa., assistant professor, 1963-64, associate professor of philosophy and head of department, 1965-68; Austin College, Sherman, Tex., associate professor, 1968-72, professor of philosophy, 1973—, head of department, 1968—. Coordinator of National Collegiate Honors Council small colleges exchange program. *Member:* American Philosophical Association, Phi Beta Kappa. *Awards, honors:* Fellow of Association for Innovation in Higher Education and Fund for the Improvement of Post-Secondary Education, 1977-78; Ford Foundation grant, 1979-80, for Project QUILL.

WRITINGS: Faith Among the Amorites: The Case for Critical Religious Humanism, Christopher, 1970; *Art as Event: An Aesthetic for the Performing Arts,* University Press of America, 1979.

Plays: "Three Men Writing" (three-act), first produced in Lancaster, Pa., November, 1958; "Without Desire" (three-act), first produced in Collegeville, Pa., at Ursinus College, April, 1966; "The Twenty-Fourth of February" (three-act), first produced in Sherman, Tex., at Austin College, December, 1976; "World of Snow" (two-act), first produced in Sherman at Austin College, January, 1978; "Feast of Ashes" (eleven-act), first produced in Sherman at Austin College, December, 1979. Also author of "Home Again, Home

Again, Jiggity-Jig,'' "a reverie and uninterrupted drama of interrelated 'scenes,' " first produced in 1980. Contributor of articles and reviews to theology and philosophy journals.

SIDELIGHTS: Hinkle writes: "Across a decade-and-a-half, on two campuses, I have worked with students in theater-related undertakings, all the while maintaining a quite amateur stance and interest in that regard, and allowing such efforts to serve the larger and more professional end of becoming a knowledgeable aesthetician; but I have found, especially in the last five or six years, that my 'avocation' has altered my vocation to the point where I feel myself ready to speak to issues in the philosophy of art from the very special vantage-point of involvement in one of the performing arts. Consequently, 'teaching philosophy' is less and less my 'business' (with playwriting and occasional directing my 'hobby'). I anticipate searching for still newer ways to underwrite what I have come to believe is an appropriate reflective view of the arts.

"I write plays for actors, not for audiences. So it is that, like my hero, Euripides, my scripts are long on characterization and inter-personal conflict and short on intricacy and interplay of plot. 'Feast of Ashes' takes its form from Elmer Rice and its theme from Euripides.

"I am deeply indebted to scores of undergraduates on two campuses who, by enrolling in my experimental courses and productions from time to time, either have risked philosophical enlightenment for the sake of a brief brush with drama, or have courted the bite of the theater bug for the sake of a modicum of reflective insight. What such students have done for those studies and stagings and what appears to have happened to them in the process, aesthetically and theatrically, has added immeasurably to my grasp of what I refer to as the 'event-full-ness' of art."

* * *

HINMAN, Charlton (Joseph Kadio) 1911-1977

OBITUARY NOTICE—See index for *CA* sketch: Born February 10, 1911, in Fort Collins, Colo.; died March 16, 1977, in Bethesda, Md. Bibliographer, educator, and author. To aid in comparing eighty different copies of Shakespeare's First Folio, Hinman invented the Hinman Collating Machine. The device is now in use at libraries and museums in the United States and England. The best pages from the eighty copies that Hinman compared were selected and published as *The Norton Facsimile: The First Folio of Shakespeare.* The results of his research on the First Folio are recorded in *The Printing and Proofreading of the First Folio of Shakespeare.* Hinman also edited some plays for the Shakespeare Quarto Facsimile series published by Oxford University Press. Obituaries and other sources: *Directory of American Scholars,* Volume II: *English, Speech, and Drama,* 6th edition, Bowker, 1974; *New York Times,* March 18, 1977; *Publishers Weekly,* March 28, 1977; *AB Bookman's Weekly,* July 25, 1977.

* * *

HIRSCH, Mark David 1910-

PERSONAL: Born July 7, 1910, in New York, N.Y.; son of Henry (a manufacturer's representative) and Mary (Wachskerz) Hirsch; married Cecelia Basin (a reading teacher), June 30, 1941; children: Gary Stephen, Andrea Gail. *Education:* City College (now of the City University of New York), B.S.S., 1931; Columbia University, M.A., 1932, Ph.D., 1948. *Home:* 15 Truesdale Place, Yonkers, N.Y. 10705.

CAREER: High school history teacher in New York City, 1939-59; professor at Long Island University, Brooklyn, N.Y.; Columbia University, New York City, lecturer, 1955-69; City College (now of the City University of New York), New York City, adjunct professor, 1955-60; Bronx Community College of the City University of New York, Bronx, N.Y., professor of history, 1959-75, head of department, 1959-75, professor emeritus, 1975—. Lecturer at Yale University, 1973. Panelist/Consultant to National Endowment for the Humanities, 1972-75. *Military service:* U.S. Army, 1943-45. *Member:* American Historical Association. *Awards, honors:* Social Science Research Council grant, 1951-54; grants from Columbia University, 1956-59, Institute of New York Area Studies, 1956-61, and State University of New York, 1971-73.

WRITINGS: William C. Whitney, Modern Warwick, Dodd, 1948, 2nd edition, 1961; (with Louis M. Hacker) *Proskauer: His Life and Times,* University of Alabama Press, 1978; (contributor) Irwin Yellowitz, editor, *Essays in the History of New York City: A Memorial to Sidney Pomerantz,* Kennikat, 1978. Contributor to history and political science journals. Member of board of editors of New York State Historical Association.

WORK IN PROGRESS: Research for a biography of Richard Croker.

SIDELIGHTS: Hirsch comments: "I am attracted to biography as a means of expressing my desire to do research and write, to learn, and to impart that information. My areas of interest are New York City, New York State, the 'Progressive Era,' and recent American history."

* * *

HOBBING, Enno 1920-

PERSONAL; Born July 12, 1920, in Berlin, Germany; came to the United States in 1927; naturalized citizen, 1937; son of Reimar Friedrich (a textile industry executive) and Hertha (Schlag) Hobbing; married Mary Bingham, July 4, 1941 (divorced, January 20, 1972); married Patricia Benton, April 1, 1972; children: Daniel, Jeffrey, Margaret, David. *Education:* Harvard University, B.S., 1940. *Religion:* Episcopalian. *Home:* 1667 35th St. N.W., Washington, D.C. 19802.

CAREER/WRITINGS: Die Neue Zeitung, Berlin, Germany, editor, 1946-49; *Time,* New York City, correspondent in Germany, France, and Washington, D.C., 1950-52; Central Intelligence Agency, Washington, D.C., official, 1953-54; *Life,* New York City, associate editor, 1954-61; Council of the Americas, New York City, vice-president, 1961-73; National Urban Coalition, Washington, D.C., assistant to president, 1974; associated with National Association of Securities Dealers, Inc., 1975—. Associate of Governor Nelson Rockefeller, 1960. Notable assignments include *Life*'s "black book" on the Hungarian Revolution and an issue on "Americans Abroad." Compiler of *Great Reading From Life,* Harper, 1962; author of *More Than Profits,* Council of the Americas, 1967. Contributor of articles to magazines, including *Time, Life, Reader's Digest, Esquire, Atlantic Monthly, Columbia Journal of World Business,* and *Business Society Review. Military service:* U.S. Army, 1942-46; received Bronze Star Medal. *Member:* George Town Club (Washington, D.C.). *Awards, honors:* Distinguished Intelligence Medal from Central Intelligence Agency.

* * *

HODGE, Alan 1915-1979

OBITUARY NOTICE: Born October 16, 1915, in Scarborough, England; died c. August, 1979, in London, England. Historian, journalist, and author. Hodge was joint editor of *History Today* since 1951. He was best known for two books written with Robert Graves, *The Long Weekend* and *The Reader Over Your Shoulder*, and for *The Past We Share*, written with Peter Quennell. Obituaries and other sources: *The Author's and Writer's Who's Who*, 6th edition, Burke's Peerage, 1971; *Who's Who*, 131st edition, St. Martin's, 1979; *AB Bookman's Weekly*, August 13, 1979.

* * *

HOFFMAN, Rosekrans 1926-

PERSONAL: Born January 7, 1926, in Nebraska; daughter of James Charles and Pearl (Hocking) Rosekrans; married Robert Hoffman (a product manager), 1955. *Education:* University of Nebraska, B.F.A., 1949. *Home and office:* 1 Campbell Ave., Apt. 66, West Haven, Conn. 06516. *Agent:* Helen Wohlberg, Kirchoff/Wohlberg, Inc., 433 East 51st St., New York, N.Y. 10022.

CAREER: Painter and illustrator.

WRITINGS: (Self-illustrated) *Anna Banana*, Knopf, 1974.

Illustrator: Alicen White, *Walter in Love*, Lothrop, 1973; Patty Wolcott, *Where Did That Naughty Hamster Go?*, Addison-Wesley, 1974; Dorothy Van Woerkom, *Alexandra the Rock Eater*, Knopf, 1978; Lee Bennett Hopkins, *Go to Bed* (poetry anthology), Knopf, 1979; Louise McClenathan, *My Mother Sends Her Wisdom*, Morrow, 1979; Hopkins, *In Ragwort Meadow* (poetry anthology), Knopf, 1980.

* * *

HOGARTH, Grace (Weston Allen) 1905-
(Amelia Gay; Allen Weston, joint pseudonym)

PERSONAL: Born November 5, 1905, in Newton, Mass.; daughter of John Weston (a lawyer) and Caroline (Hills) Allen; married William David Hogarth, August 22, 1936 (died September, 1965); married Philip Livermore Sayles, May 22, 1971 (divorced September, 1977); children: (first marriage) David Allen, Caroline Mary (Mrs. John Barron). *Education:* Attended University of California, Berkeley, 1924-25; Vassar College, A.B., 1927; graduate study at Massachusetts School of Art, 1927-28, and Yale University, 1928-29. *Religion:* Church of England. *Home:* 53 Ainger Rd., London NW3 3AH, England. *Agent:* Deborah Rogers Ltd., 5-11 Mortimer St., London W1N 7RH, England.

CAREER: Oxford University Press, 1929-38, worked in New York, N.Y., 1929-36, editor of children's books and staff artist in London, England, 1936-38; Chatto & Windus, London, editor of children's books, 1938-39; Houghton Mifflin Co., Boston, Mass., editor of children's books, 1940-43, scout in London, 1943-47; scout for publishers, 1947-56; Constable & Co. Ltd., London, editor of children's books, 1956-63, managing director of "Constable Young Books," 1963-68, chairperson, 1966-68; Longman, London, managing director of "Longman Young Books," 1968, director, 1968-73; William Collins, London, general editor of "Classics for Today" and "Lifetime Library," 1971—. Editor-in-chief of My Weekly Reader Family Book Service's "Lifetime Library," 1968-71. Member of board of governors of North London Collegiate School, 1965-71, and Camden School for Girls, 1965-71. *Member:* English-Speaking Union, Children's Book Circle (honorary member), Delta Gamma, Vassar Club (New York and London), College Club (Boston).

WRITINGS: *A Bible A.B.C.*, Lippincott, 1940; *Australia, the Island Continent* (juvenile), Houghton, 1943; *This to Be Love* (novel), J. Cape, 1949; *Lucy's League*, published in England under pseudonym Amelia Gay, Hodder & Stoughton, 1950, published in the United States under name Grace Hogarth, Harcourt, 1951; *John's Journey*, published in England under pseudonym Amelia Gay, Hodder & Stoughton, 1950, published in the United States under name Grace Hogarth, Harcourt, 1952; *The End of Summer* (novel), J. Cape, 1951; *Children of This World* (novel), J. Cape, 1953; (with Alice Mary Norton, under joint pseudonym Allen Weston) *Murders for Sale* (mystery), Hammond Hammond, 1954; *The Funny Guy*, Harcourt, 1955; *As a May Morning*, Harcourt, 1958; *Sister for Helen*, Deutsch, 1976.

Editor of *Illustrators of Children's Books*, 1967-76, and *Horn Book*, 1978.

WORK IN PROGRESS: Memoirs.

SIDELIGHTS: Grace Hogarth told *CA:* "I owe a great deal of success in life to Vassar College, not because I was a good student, but because Vassar gave me confidence. I wrote an article for the *Vassar Alumnae/i Quarterly*, 'Confession of a Liberated Woman,' which expresses my thoughts on this subject. In a letter to *Vassar Quarterly* I was attacked as 'neither a liberated woman nor a feminist' because I had 'come to accept as justified male condescension and discrimination against women.' I still feel this criticism to be untrue. Normal women who want home, family, and career, which I did, must have the cooperation and support of their husbands and children."

* * *

HOGE, James O(tey) 1944-

PERSONAL: Born August 2, 1944, in Roanoke, Va.; son of James Otey (a teacher) and Marian (Barrett) Hoge; married Carol Flynn. *Education:* Attended Davidson College, 1962-63; Virginia Polytechnic Institute and State University, B.A., 1966; Harvard University, M.A., 1967; University of Virginia, Ph.D., 1970. *Home address:* Route 3, Box 230, Blacksburg, Va. 24060. *Office:* Department of English, Virginia Polytechnic Institute and State University, Blacksburg, Va. 24061.

CAREER: University of Georgia, Athens, assistant professor of English, 1970-75; Virginia Polytechnic Institute and State University, Blacksburg, associate professor of English, 1975—. *Member:* Modern Language Association of America, Byron Society, Tennyson Society, South Atlantic Modern Language Association, Association for the Preservation of Virginia Antiquities (member of board of directors).

WRITINGS: *The Letters of Emily Lady Tennyson*, Pennsylvania State University Press, 1974; (editor with Clarke Olney) *The Letters of Caroline Norton to Lord Melbourne*, Ohio State University Press, 1974; (editor with Jane Marcus) *Selected Writings of Caroline Norton*, Scholar's Facsimiles and Reprints, 1978; *Lady Tennyson's Journal*, University Press of Virginia, 1980. Co-founder and co-editor of *Review* (annual), University Press of Virginia, 1979—; editor of newsletter of Association for the Preservation of Virginia Antiquities.

WORK IN PROGRESS: Second volume of *Review*.

SIDELIGHTS: Hoge told *CA:* "*Review* contains review-essays and reviews of scholarly work in English and American language and literature. It is also a major forum for discussion about the nature and purpose of scholarly reviewing."

HOLLAND, Louise Adams 1893-

PERSONAL: Born July 3, 1893, in Brooklyn, N.Y.; daughter of Charles F. (a lawyer) and Henrietta (Rozier) Adams; married Leicester B. Holland, December 27, 1923 (deceased); children: Barbara A., Marian R. Holland McAllister, Lawrence R. *Education:* Barnard College, A.B., 1914; Columbia University, M.A., 1915; Bryn Mawr College, Ph.D., 1920. *Home:* 415 West Price St., Philadelphia, Pa. 19144.

CAREER: Writer. Smith College, Northampton, Mass., instructor, 1917-22, assistant professor of Latin, 1923-24; Vassar College, Poughkeepsie, N.Y., assistant professor of Latin, 1925-27; Bryn Mawr College, Bryn Mawr, Pa., visiting professor of Latin, 1927-47; Miami University, Oxford, Ohio, professor of Latin, 1951-52; Smith College, Northampton, Mass., visiting professor of Latin, 1957-64. *Member:* American Philological Association, Archaeological Institute of America. *Awards, honors:* Fellowship from American Academy in Rome, 1922-23; annual award from American Philological Association, 1964, for *Janus and the Bridge;* Litt.D. from Smith College, 1965, and Columbia University, 1979.

WRITINGS: The Faliscans in Prehistoric Times (monograph), American Academy in Rome, 1925; *Janus and the Bridge,* American Academy in Rome, 1961; *Lucretius and the Transpadanes,* Princeton University Press, 1979. Also author of *A Study of the Commerce of Latium,* 1920. Contributor to philology and archaeology journals.

WORK IN PROGRESS: Studying "the origin of the Plebian order in ancient Rome."

* * *

HOLLOWAY, Marcella M(arie) 1913-

PERSONAL: Born December 1, 1913, in St. Louis, Mo.; daughter of John James (in insurance business) and Mary Maude (Kopp) Holloway. *Education:* University of Missouri, M.A., 1943; Catholic University of America, Ph.D., 1947; postdoctoral study at Oxford University. *Office:* Department of English, Fontbonne College, St. Louis, Mo. 63105.

CAREER: Roman Catholic nun of Sisters of St. Joseph of Carondelet (C.S.J.), 1932—; Avila College, Kansas City, Mo., professor of English and head of department, 1947-63; Fontbonne College, St. Louis, Mo., professor of English, 1963—. Member of summer faculty at Catholic University of America, 1948-70; speaker at scholarly meetings and workshops. Attended Yeats International Summer Workshop in Ireland, 1963, 1969, 1979; visiting scholar at Rockhurst College, 1978. Director of London Scene (student tour), 1972-73, 1975-76. Member of board of directors of St. Louis Poetry Center, 1978-81.

MEMBER: International Hopkins Association (senior scholar), National League of American Pen Women (historian, 1975-76), Modern Language Association of America, Hopkins Society (England), Missouri Philological Association, Missouri Writers Guild. *Awards, honors:* First prize for poetic drama from St. Louis Poetry Center, 1972, for "Talitha"; first prize from International Clover Poetry Contest, 1972, for "In Another Time"; first prize from Festival of Religious Arts, 1972, for play, "The Third Window"; National Endowment for the Humanities grants, 1973-77; award of excellence from Festival of Missouri Women in the Arts, 1974, for play, "St. Winifred's Well."

WRITINGS: The Prosodic Theory of G. M. Hopkins, Catholic University Press, 1948; (contributor) Peter Milward, S.J., and Raymond Schoder, S.J., editors, *Readings of "The Wreck",* Loyola University Press, 1976; *Should You Become a Sister?,* Liguorian Press, 1978.

Published plays: *The Last of the Leprechauns* (three-act; first produced in Kansas City, Mo., at College of St. Teresa, 1957), Samuel French, 1958; *The Little Juggler* (five-scene; first produced in St. Louis, Mo., at Fontbonne College, 1967), Samuel French, 1966; *A Christmas Carol* (two-act musical; first produced in St. Louis at Fontbonne College, 1972), Pioneer Drama Service, 1975; *Talitha* (one-act verse drama; first performed in St. Louis at Christ Church Cathedral, 1972), Ave Maria Press, 1976.

Unpublished plays: "Feathertop" (two-act musical; adapted from Nathaniel Hawthorne's tale of the same title); "Beyond the Mountain" (musical for children), first produced in Kansas City at Avila College; one volume of one-act liturgical dramas based on Old and New Testament stories.

Work represented in anthologies, including *International Anthology of Poetry,* England, 1973, and *The Clover Collection of Verse,* Volume V, edited by Evelyn Petry, Clover Publishing, 1971.

Contributor of stories, poems, and articles to scholarly journals and literary magazines, including *Downside Review, Catholic World, Sign, the Critic,* and *Studies in Philology.*

WORK IN PROGRESS: A personal account of the changes in religious life since the 1930's, tentatively titled *Life in the Convent Before and After Vatican II,* completion expected in 1980; a volume of one-act plays, tentatively titled *Plays of Mystery and Myth; And Still He Comes,* religious poems on Christ's life; *Moods of Many Colors,* children's poems; *Of Past and Present and Final Things,* poetry.

SIDELIGHTS: Holloway writes: "Since most of my years as a religious have been spent in the classroom, I think of myself primarily as a teacher and not a writer. The writing has been sandwiched in between my other work. One of my most rewarding and poignant memories is my teaching at Catholic University in Washington, D.C., the year I was completing my doctoral dissertation in 1946. My two classes in English composition consisted of boys who had just come back from World War II. I regret now that I did not keep their themes. They wrote honestly of their experiences and sat patiently in the classroom with the burden of those memories on their youthful shoulders.

"My own academic writing has largely centered around G. M. Hopkins. I first came in contact with his poetry in college and over these many years I have read, re-read, and memorized his poetry. I have visited his college, Balliol, Oxford, and his burial site at Glasnevin Cemetary in Dublin. I wrote both master's and doctor's theses on him, and have published six researched articles in literary magazines, plus a seventh based on the 'game-motif' in Hopkins's sonnets.

"I stumbled into creative writing about thirty years ago. Children's theatre was an important part of our program at St. Teresa's College and the drama director turned to me in desperation and asked, 'Why don't you write a play for us? So many I read are so stupid.' I wrote three that have been published. 'Beyond the Mountain' is as yet unpublished but has been produced many times. I know it works because I have sat in many audiences and watched the children's responses.

"For the past four years I have been an 'artist-in-the-schools' under a Missouri Arts Council program. This coming year I hope to conduct five-day sessions as a resource person, working with the students and the teachers in those schools who ask for this kind of service from the Council. In some ways the teaching of others to write and writing myself are two sides of the same golden coin. And gold is a precious commodity these days."

* * *

HOLMES, John Haynes 1879-1964

OBITUARY NOTICE: Born November 29, 1879, in Philadelphia, Pa.; died April 3, 1964. Clergyman, editor, and author of numerous books on religion, including *Religion for Today, Rethinking Religion,* and *The Sensible Man's View of Religion.* A modernist Unitarian, Holmes opposed denominationalism and firmly interwined his religious and political beliefs. Obituaries and other sources: *Current Biography,* Wilson, 1941, May, 1964; *New York Times,* April 4, 1964.

* * *

HOLMES, Robert Merrill 1925-

PERSONAL: Born May 4, 1925, in Mitchell, S.D.; son of Merrill Jacob (a minister and educator) and Carrie (McFadon) Holmes; married Polly Mudge (a state legislator), August 31, 1951; children: Stephen, Terrill, Krys. *Education:* Illinois Wesleyan University, B.A., 1948; Garrett Evangelical School of Theology, M.Div., 1951; Northwestern University, M.A., 1956; Pacific School of Religion, Th.D., 1965. *Politics:* Democrat. *Home:* 1620 Ave. F, Billings, Mont. 59102. *Office:* Department of Christian Thought, Rocky Mountain College, Billings, Mont. 59102.

CAREER: Ordained United Methodist minister, 1951; pastor of United Methodist church in Rapid City, S.D., 1953-61; University of the Pacific, Stockton, Calif., instructor in Bible, 1962-64; Rocky Mountain College, Billings, Mont., chaplain, 1965—, assistant professor, 1965-68, associate professor of Christian thought, 1968—.

WRITINGS: The Academic Mysteryhouse, Abingdon, 1970.

* * *

HOOD, Sarah
See KILLOUGH, (Karen) Lee

* * *

HOOPES, Clement R. 1906-1979

OBITUARY NOTICE—See index for *CA* sketch: Born October 28, 1906, in Philadelphia, Pa.; died August 14, 1979, in Chester, Pa. Advertising executive, administrator, and author. For fifteenyears Hoopes was a member of the advertising staffs of Harper & Brothers (now Harper & Row) and Time, Inc. He also served on the Marshall Plan mission to Dublin, Ireland, from 1950 to 1953, and was a writer with the U.S. Information Agency from 1954 to 1957. During the 1960's, Hoopes was director of national development for the American Shakespeare Festival Theater and Academy and organized the Shakespeare 400th birthday committee celebration. In addition to television scripts and magazine articles, he wrote three novels, including *Angry Dust.* Obituaries and other sources: *New York Times,* August 17, 1979; *AB Bookman's Weekly,* September 24, 1979.

* * *

HOOVER, Herbert (Clark) 1874-1964

OBITUARY NOTICE: Born August 10, 1874, in West Branch, Iowa; died October 20, 1964. Engineer, author, and politician. Hoover was the thirty-first president of the United States. During his tenure from 1929 to 1933, the country suffered an economic depression. Hoover made many attempts to overcome the crisis but most proved futile. In running for re-election in 1933, he was defeated by Franklin Roosevelt. Hoover then served on a committee to revise the government. Aside from his term as president, Hoover is best known for restructuring the Department of Commerce as secretary of that department during the presidency of Warren Harding. Among Hoover's numerous books on politics are *The Challenge to Liberty, The Problems of Lasting Peace,* and *The American Epic.* His memoirs are contained in three volumes. Obituaries and other sources: *Current Biography,* Wilson, 1963, January, 1965; *New York Times,* October 21, 1964; *The Oxford Companion to American Literature,* 4th edition, Oxford University Press, 1965; *The Reader's Encyclopedia,* 2nd edition, Crowell, 1965.

* * *

HOPKINS, Robert A. 1923-

PERSONAL: Born September 16, 1923, in Sandoval, Ill.; son of Arthur G. (a writer and merchant) and Bessie Mildred (in advertising; maiden name, Blacker) Hopkins; married Betty June Keller; children: Valerie Ann Hopkins Call, Vincent Robert, Laura June Hopkins Hess, Lowell Scot, Mark Stephen, Esther. *Education:* Attended Washington University, St. Louis, Mo., 1947, and St. Louis University, 1948-50; La Salle University, B.S., 1953. *Politics:* Independent. *Religion:* Church of Jesus Christ of Latter-day Saints (Mormons). *Home:* 135 Valley Vista Dr., Camarillo, Calif. 93010. *Office:* P.O. Box 847, Tarzana, Calif. 91356.

CAREER: Data Chart Corp., Canoga Park, Calif., vice-president and general manager, 1964-67; Data Graf Corp., Reseda, Calif., president, 1968-71; Slide Chart Corp., Van Nuys, Calif., president, 1970-72; Polymetric Services, Inc., Tarzana, Calif., president, 1972—. Editor and publisher at AMJ Publishing Co. Delegate to National Science Foundation's South Pacific conferences; speaker for U.S. Department of Commerce; lecturer at universities and colleges. *Military service:* U.S. Army, Artillery, 1942-45; served in European theater.

MEMBER: American Society for Testing and Materials, National Council of Teachers of Mathematics, American National Standards Institute, Society of Manufacturing Engineers, American National Metric Council, National Science Foundation. *Awards, honors:* Distinguished service award from American Society of Engineers; Metrication Achievement Award from Standards Engineers Society; awards from American Institute of Industrial Engineers and Fullerton College.

WRITINGS: ABC's of Measurement, Dell, 1972; *International (SI) Metric System and How It Works,* AMJ Publishing Co., 1973, revised edition, 1975; *Metric in a Nutshell,* AMJ Publishing Co., 1976; *Teaching Classroom Metric,* AMJ Publishing Co., 1977. Also author of *Tip the Scales in Your Favor,* 1965, and *Secrets of the Calculator,* 1971. Contributor to *Congressional Record.* Editor and publisher of *American Metric Journal.*

WORK IN PROGRESS: Survival in the Eighties, "on the economic disadvantages for John and Susie Q and how to cope with them, the disasters of modern financing with the credit card, ways to reduce costs of living and increase assets, and living without charge accounts."

SIDELIGHTS: Hopkins comments: "I have been exposed to life through advertising responsibilities for two multi-national corporations. I founded three California corporations and was chief operating officer. My interests have been in providing members of the community with accurate means of measurement and ways to control their economic lives and avoid the pitfalls and traps of the plastic cards and charge accounts."

* * *

HOPPER, Hedda 1890-1966

OBITUARY NOTICE: Born June 2, 1890, in Hollidaysburg, Pa.; died February 1, 1966. Actress and columnist best known for her gossip-style reporting on the motion picture industry. Together with fellow columnist Louella Parsons, Hopper wielded considerable influence over the careers of those in the film industry. Hopper was an actress on stage and in films, including "The Battle of Hearts," during the silent era. She wrote *From Under My Hat* and *The Whole Truth and Nothing But*. Obituaries and other sources: *Current Biography,* Wilson, 1942, March, 1966; *New York Times,* February 22, 1966; *Who Was Who in America,* 4th Edition, Marquis, 1968.

* * *

HOPSON, Janet L(ouise) 1950-
(Janet Hopson Weinberg)

PERSONAL: Born October 22, 1950, in St. Louis, Mo.; daughter of David Warren (an insurance company manager) and Ruth (Dierkes) Hopson; married Steven Weinberg (a professor of journalism), August, 1969 (divorced, December, 1975); married Michael Alan Rogers (a writer), October 23, 1976. *Education:* Southern Illinois University, B.A., 1972; University of Missouri, M.A., 1975. *Residence:* San Francisco, Calif. *Agent:* Elizabeth McKee, Harold Matson Co., Inc., 22 East 40th St., New York, N.Y. 10016.

CAREER: Science News, Washington, D.C., biology editor, 1974-76; *Outside,* San Francisco, Calif., contributing editor, 1976—. Member of founding advisory board of science magazine published by *Mother Jones*. Swimming and exercise instructor. *Member:* National Association of Science Writers, California Academy of Sciences, Media Alliance, Kappa Tau Alpha. *Awards, honors:* Science-writer-in-residence fellowship from National Institutes of Health, 1976.

WRITINGS: Scent Signals: The Silent Language of Sex, Morrow, 1979; (contributor) James K. Page, Jr. and Russell Bourne, editors, *Animals Alive,* Smithsonian Exposition Books, 1979. Author of "Natural Acts," a column in *Outside/Mariah,* 1976—. Contributor to *Encyclopedia Americana* and *Encyclopedia International*. Contributor to *Science News* magazine under name Janet Hopson Weinberg. Contributor to magazines, including *Smithsonian, Look, Cosmopolitan, Mademoiselle,* and *Rolling Stone,* and newspapers.

WORK IN PROGRESS: Research for a book on the human body's indigenous microbes, publication by Harcourt expected in 1981.

SIDELIGHTS: Hopson writes: "My primary interest is popular writing about nature, behavior, biology, and medicine for the general audience. The challenge—and a sizeable one—is to convince the reader that science can be fascinating." *Avocational interests:* Swimming, folkdancing, backpacking, weaving, tennis.

HORATIO, Algernon
(pseudonym)

PERSONAL: Born in New Rochelle, N.Y. *Education:* Doctorate from a university in the southwestern United States. *Politics:* Democrat. *Religion:* Unitarian-Universalist. *Agent:* Writers House, Inc., 21 West 26th St., New York, N.Y. 10010.

CAREER: Worked as plumber, museum curator, state civil servant, "federal bureaucrat," farmer, and manager of a cattle ranch; presently professor of economic philosophy at a university in the Midwest. *Member:* Explorers Club, American International Charolais Association, Trout Unlimited.

WRITINGS: The Penny Capitalist, Arlington House, 1979.

SIDELIGHTS: Horatio writes: "I am a taxpaid debtor, a veteran of the continuing war against high rates of taxation: no awards to date, and I have limited my losses.

"I write autobiographical material on how to invest when you don't have any money. My vocation developed out of my need to survive, raise a family, and simultaneously build a nest egg of invested capital for the future—an impossibility on a professor's salary ravaged by taxes and inflation."

* * *

HORN, Maurice 1931-
(Franck Sauvage)

PERSONAL: Born June 28, 1931, in Paris, France; came to the United States in 1959, naturalized citizen, 1965; son of Leon (in business) and Tauba (Koplowicz) Horn. *Education:* Sorbonne, University of Paris, B.Lett., 1951, graduate study, 1951-54. *Home:* 1 Fifth Ave., New York, N.Y. 10003.

CAREER: Mottier & Poulin, Paris, France, junior law partner, 1954-56; free-lance writer, editor, translator, interpreter, and lecturer, 1956—. Lecturer at schools in the United States and Europe, including Columbia University and Fairleigh Dickinson University. Co-organizer of comics exhibitions and the First International Comics Convention, 1968; member of board of directors of Academy of Comic Art. *Member:* Authors Guild of Authors League of America, American Society of Interpreters (vice-president, 1972-74; president, 1974-76). *Awards, honors:* Special award from International Comics Conference, 1969.

WRITINGS: Israel, Hachette, 1960; (with Pierre Couperie) *A History of the Comic Strip,* Crown, 1968; *Seventy-Five Years of the Comics,* Boston Book & Art, 1971; (editor) *The World Encyclopedia of Comics,* Chelsea House, 1976; *Comics of the American West,* Winchester Press, 1977; *Women in the Comics,* Chelsea House, 1977; (editor) *The World Encyclopedia of Cartoons,* Chelsea House, 1979, revised and enlarged edition, 1980.

Under pseudonym Franck Sauvage: *La mort au grand galop* (mystery; title means "Death at the Gallop"), L'Arabesque, 1958; *La mort et la belle* (mystery; title means "Death and the Beauty"), L'Arabesque, 1958; *L'homme de Hong-Kong* (spy novel; title means "The Man From Hong-Kong"), Editions Martel, 1959.

Author of introduction or preface: Burne Hogarth, *Tarzan: Seigneur de la Jungle,* Editions Azur, 1967; Alex Raymond, *Flash Gordon in the Ice Kingdom of Mongo,* Nostalgia Press, 1967; Robert Gigi and C. Moliterni, *Scarlett Dream,* Le Terrain Vague, 1967; Lee Falk and Ray Moore, *The Phantom,* Nostalgia Press, 1969; Falk and Phil Davis, *Mandrake in Hollywood,* Nostalgia Press, 1970; Milton Caniff, *Terry and the Pirates,* Nostalgia Press, 1970; Raymond,

Flash Gordon in the Water World of Mongo, Nostalgia Press, 1971; Hogarth, *Tarzan of the Apes,* Watson-Guptill, 1972; Lyman Young, *Cino e Franco,* Garzanti, 1973; Will Eisner, *The Spirit,* Number 1, Krupp Comics Works, 1973; Alfred Andriola, *Charlie Chan's Adventures,* Comics Stars in the World, 1976; Hogarth, *The Golden Age of Tarzan,* Chelsea House, 1977; Frank Godwin, *Connie,* Hyperion Press (Westport, Conn.), 1977; Lyonel Feininger, *The Kinder Kids,* Dover, 1979.

Author of radio and television plays, including scripts for "Allo Police" series on Radio-Tele-Luxembourg and "Les Auditeurs Menent l'Enquete" (title means "The Listeners Lead the Investigation") on Europe-1.

Author of recordings, including "Alerte a Cap Canaveral" (title means "Alert in Cape Canaveral"), Odeon, 1959; "Cris dans la Nuit" (title means "Screams in the Night"), RCA-France, 1959.

Editor of reprints of classic comics. Author of "The Comics: A Cultural History," a filmstrip series, Educational Audio Visuals, 1976. Contributor to *Collier's Encyclopedia.* Contributor of articles, stories, and poems to magazines in the United States and Europe, including *Marvel Preview, American Cartoonist,* and *Inside Comics.*

SIDELIGHTS: Horn's work as writer, lecturer, and interpreter has taken him to most countries of western Europe, Latin America, and the Middle East, and to Japan. He writes: "I have wanted to be a writer as far back as I can remember. My first writings (poems) were published in small magazines while I was still in high school. I have always loved the comics; in fact, the comics spurred my interest for reading and writing as a child. So, when the Club de Bandes Dessinees (Comic Strip Club) in Paris asked me in 1963 to become their representative in the United States, I accepted eagerly; and there we are. Few people, I believe, have had the privilege of combining both their hobby and their avocation into their main professional activity."

BIOGRAPHICAL/CRITICAL SOURCES: Midi Libre, January 17, 1974; *Le Parisien Libere,* July 20, 1978.

* * *

HORNBLOW, Arthur, Jr. 1893-1976

PERSONAL: Born March 15, 1893, in New York, N.Y.; died July 17, 1976; son of Arthur and Natalie (Lambert) Hornblow; married second wife, Leonora Schinasi, November 4, 1945; children: (first marriage) John Terry, (second marriage) Michael. *Education:* Attended Dartmouth College and New York Law School. *Home:* 45 Sutton Pl. S., New York, N.Y. 10022.

CAREER: Admitted to the Bar of New York State, 1917; writer and producer of plays, New York City, 1920-27; worked as assistant managing director for Charles Frohman Co.; Samuel Goldwyn Productions, Hollywood, Calif., supervisor, 1926, writer, 1927; motion picture producer for Paramount, 1933-42, and Metro-Goldwyn-Mayer, 1942-52; president of Arthur Hornblow Productions. Pictures produced include "Gaslight," 1947, "The Asphalt Jungle," 1950, "Oklahoma," 1955, and "Witness for the Prosecution," 1957. Chairman of the theatre advisory board, Dartmouth College. *Military service:* U.S. Army, Intelligence Corps, counter-espionage section, 1918-19; became first lieutenant; received Etoile Noire de la Legion d'Honneur (France) and U.S. Presidential Citation. *Member:* Dartmouth Club, Bucks Club.

WRITINGS—All with wife, Leonora Hornblow; all published by Random House: *Animals Do the Strangest Things,* 1964; *Birds Do the Strangest Things,* 1965; *Fish Do the Strangest Things,* 1966; *Insects Do the Strangest Things,* 1968; *Reptiles Do the Strangest Things,* 1970; *Prehistoric Monsters Did the Strangest Things,* 1974.

Also translator of several plays from the French, including Sacha Guitry's "Pasteur," 1925, and Edward Bourdet's "The Captive," 1926.

OBITUARIES: New York Times, July 18, 1976.*

* * *

HORNBY, Richard 1938-

PERSONAL: Born October 25, 1938, in Paterson, N.J.; son of Herbert (an accountant) and Roma (Berry) Hornby; married Faith Zager (a sales clerk), September 3, 1961; children: Sarah, Stephen. *Education:* Massachusetts Institute of Technology, B.S., 1962; Tulane University, M.A., 1965, Ph.D., 1966. *Home:* 4259 53rd St. N.W., Calgary, Alberta, Canada T3A 1V5. *Office:* Department of Drama, University of Calgary, Calgary, Alberta, Canada T2N 1N4.

CAREER: Bowdoin College, Brunswick, Maine, assistant professor of English and director of dramatics, 1966-70; University of British Columbia, Vancouver, assistant professor of theater, 1970-71; University of Calgary, Calgary, Alberta, associate professor, 1971-78, professor of drama, 1978—. Professional actor; visiting director of Harvard Summer Players, 1968. *Member:* Canadian Association of University Teachers, American Theatre Association (head of program in dramatic theory and criticism, 1974-78), Actors' Equity Association, Ibsen Society, Brecht Society, University and College Theater Association.

WRITINGS: Script Into Performance: A Structuralist View of Play Production, University of Texas Press, 1977. Contributor to education and theater journals.

WORK IN PROGRESS: Ibsen and Naturalism: A Structuralist Study.

* * *

HOROWITZ, David A. 1941-

PERSONAL: Born August 17, 1941, in Bronx, N.Y.; son of Nathan (a writer; in sales) and Dorothy (a guidance counselor, teacher, and writer; maiden name, Levine) Horowitz; married Charlene Lowry (a poet), December 18, 1977; children: Michael, Giovanni, Marnie (stepchildren). *Education:* Antioch College, B.A., 1964; University of Minnesota, Ph.D., 1971. *Home:* 8065 Southeast 16th Ave., Portland, Ore. 97202. *Office:* Department of History, Portland State University, Portland, Ore. 97207.

CAREER: Portland State University, Portland, Ore., instructor, 1968-69, assistant professor, 1969-79, associate professor of history, 1979—. Musical director of "Vaudeville II," at Portland's Storefront Actors Theater, summer, 1975.

WRITINGS: (With David W. Noble and Petter Carroll) *Twentieth Century Limited: A History of Recent America,* Houghton, 1980. Correspondent for *San Francisco Bay Guardian,* 1976. Author of a weekly column in *Vanguard,* 1972-75. Contributor to *Oregon Times.*

AVOCATIONAL INTERESTS: Playing piano.

* * *

HOROWITZ, David Charles 1937-

PERSONAL: Born June 30, 1937, in New York, N.Y.; son

of Max Leo and Dorothy (Lippman) Horowitz; married Suzanne E. McCambridge (a writer), 1972; children: two. *Education:* Bradley University, A.B., 1959; Northwestern University, M.S.J., 1961; post-graduate study at Columbia University, 1962-63. *Politics:* Independent. *Address:* P.O. Box 49740, Los Angeles, Calif. 90049. *Office:* NBC-TV, 3000 West Alameda Ave., Burbank, Calif. 91523.

CAREER: KRNT-Radio/TV, Des Moines, Iowa, newscaster, 1960-62; American Broadcasting Companies (ABC-Radio), New York City, newswriter and producer, 1963; National Broadcasting Corp. (NBC-TV), New York City, correspondent in Far East, 1963-64; WMCA-Radio, New York City, director of public affairs, 1964-66; NBC-TV, New York City, news correspondent, editor, and consumer ombudsman in Los Angeles, Calif., 1966—. Creator and host of syndicated television program, "David Horowitz Consumer Buyline"; lecturer. Director of National Broadcast Editorial Conference; member of board of advisers of Los Angeles County Heart Association, and of board of directors of American Cancer Society and Los Angeles Jewish Home for the Aged. *Military service:* U.S. Naval Reserve, 1954-62. *Member:* International Radio-Television Society, Academy of Television Arts and Sciences, International Platform Association, Radio-Television News Directors Association, National Education Writers Association, American Federation of Television and Radio Artists, Writers Guild of America, West, Overseas Press Club, Sigma Delta Chi, Kappa Delta Pi, Friars Club.

AWARDS, HONORS: All-American Writer of the Year Award from *Radio-TV Daily,* 1963; Golden Mike Award from San Fernando Valley State University, 1967; award from Veterans Administration, 1968, for outstanding service to veterans of America; John Swett Award from California Teachers Association, 1970 and 1972, for outstanding contribution to education; Distinguished Reporting Award from San Fernando Valley Press Club, 1971, for coverage of earthquake; named Newsman of the Year by American Cancer Society, 1973; Emmy Award from Academy of Television Arts and Sciences, 1973, for consumer reporting; Objective Newscasting Award from California Autobody Association, 1974 and 1975; proclamation from County of Los Angeles, 1974, for outstanding community service; Justice and Fair Play Award from Citizens Committee for Universal Justice Through Community Action, 1975; award from California Trial Lawyers Association, 1976, for excellence in consumer protection; Good Samaritan Award of the Mormon Church, 1976; Award of Excellence from Film Advisory Board, 1976, for hosting "David Horowitz Consumer Buyline"; Emmy Award, 1976, for consumer reporting; proclamation from County of San Bernardino, 1976, for outstanding service to consumers; Emmy Award, 1977, for consumer reporting; award from City of Simi Valley, Calif., 1977, for outstanding consumer service; Consumer Education Award from Daughters of the American Revolution, 1978; award from city council of City of Los Angeles, 1978, for civil service; Golden Pen Award from American Society of Travel Agents, 1979; Spirit of Light Award from City of Hope, 1979; Citation from State of California, 1979, for public service; and other awards and honors.

WRITINGS: Fight Back! And Don't Get Ripped Off, Harper, 1979. Contributor to periodicals, including *Family Circle, Playgirl,* and *Parade.*

SIDELIGHTS: Horowitz told *CA:* "My father came from France and mother made the trek from Eastern Europe. Both my parents were keenly aware that people tried to take advantage of them because of their language and educational problems. But if they were ripped off, they spoke up! They didn't just sit and take it. They were the original 'fight back duo' and much of that rubbed off on me. I learned early in life that when you come from such a background, survival is where it's at.

"As a kid-of-all-trades, I learned how ghetto-neighborhood cleaners, grocers and candy-store owners pulled scams on the unsuspecting public, a 'rip-off in reverse.' I may not, at that moment, have vowed to become a consumer crusader, but the experience made me wary—and being wary is a very important quality for an investigative reporter to have. I don't ever want anyone to take me for a sucker, and I don't like to see anyone else taken, either. A lot of things are unfair in life. It's tough, but that's the way it is. But, by heaven, if you can do something about it, do it!

"*Fight Back! And Don't Get Ripped Off* is not only the title of my book, it's my philosophy and course of action for consumer survival. For example: While pumping gas at a self-service station not long ago, I discovered that at least one pump started at three cents rather than at zero. I reported the station to the County Department of Weights and Measures. I found deceptive labeling while shopping in a local supermarket, and got the FDA involved. I got the City of Los Angeles to start an investigation into unsafe taxis when, while taking a cab to the airport, I found myself in a mechanically unsafe car. A discussion, prompted by the driver, led me to turn the matter over to the City. An investigation of the taxi company followed and nine of its cabs were pulled out of service and cited. People are always giving me ideas for our shows. They know I'm concerned and that I will try to help them.

"It was the runaway rating success of 'David Horowitz Consumer Buyline' in Los Angeles that led to national syndication of the program on NBC-TV's owned-and-operated stations and in many other markets nationally. The show is the highest rated prime-time access show in its time slot in southern California and in many other cities. Its popularity, and viewer's confidence in my purpose, bring approximately two thousand letters to my office each week from people all over the country.

"My ambition is to change the complexion of the country, make business more aware of what consumers want and do it honestly, with humor and entertainment. Why humor? The trouble with most of us is that we're scared by 'persons in power positions.' Let's stop being afraid. Let's have a sense of humor coupled with awareness and information—to enable us to Fight Back! and survive."

In an article in the *Los Angeles Times,* Horowitz described himself as "a sort of mister in-between." He added: "My wife . . . says I'm really an ombudsman, a person who hears and investigates complaints. I encourage consumers to sound off, but when they're wrong, I tell them, too."

AVOCATIONAL INTERESTS: Gardening.

BIOGRAPHICAL/CRITICAL SOURCES: Los Angeles Times, May 21, 1978; *Washington Post,* August 20, 1979.

* * *

HOROWITZ, Jacob 1900-1979
(Jed Harris)

OBITUARY NOTICE: Born February 25, 1900, in Vienna, Austria; died November 15, 1979, in New York, N.Y. Theatrical producer and author. Harris produced and directed a number of successful Broadway hits during the 1920's and 1930's, including "Broadway," "The Front Page," "Uncle

Vanya," and "A Doll's House." His reputation as a theatre genius drew such talented actors as Charles Boyer, Laurence Olivier, and Katharine Hepburn to appear in his productions. Harris wrote *A Dance on the High Wire* and was co-author of *Operation Mad Ball.* Obituaries and other sources: *The Biographical Encyclopaedia and Who's Who of the American Theatre,* James Heineman, 1966; *Who's Who in America,* 38th edition, Marquis, 1974; *New York Times,* November 16, 1979.

* * *

HORTON, Patricia Campbell 1943-

PERSONAL: Born September 8, 1943, in Glen Cove, N.Y.; daughter of Joseph B. and Eleanor M. Campbell; married Robert John Horton (employed in local clerk's office), August 1, 1965; children: Kevin Campbell. *Education:* Attended Adelphi College (now University), and Long Island University. *Home and office:* 170 Franklin Ave., Sea Cliff, N.Y. 11579. *Agent:* Valerie Berlitz, Old Estate Rd., Glen Cove, N.Y. 11542.

CAREER: Osrow Products, Glen Cove, N.Y., public relations editor, 1962-67; *Sea Cliff-Glen Head Times,* Sea Cliff, N.Y., publisher and editor, 1973-78; free-lance writer, 1978—. *Member:* Writer's Group of Long Island.

WRITINGS: Royal Mistress (historical novel), Avon, 1977; *Tender Fire* (historical novel), Bantam, 1978.

WORK IN PROGRESS: The Child Stands Alone, a novel of the occult; a contemporary novel; a historical novel.

SIDELIGHTS: Patricia Horton writes: "I'm a history buff. When my son was five years old, my husband and I took him to England where I did research, and he astounded people by confiding: 'My mother is looking all over England for King Charles II because she's in love with him, but I don't think she'll find him because he's been dead for three hundred years.' I write books that I would like to read myself, and love it when they demand travel for research. We would travel half the year if we had sufficient money."

* * *

HOSTOVSKY, Egon 1908-1973

OBITUARY NOTICE: Born April 23, 1908, in Hronov, Czechoslovakia; died May 6, 1973. Novelist best known for his books dealing with the anxieties of the exile, including *Letters From Exile* and *Seven Times the Leading Man.* A refugee himself, Hostovsky fled to the United States at the beginning of World War II. His later books are more concerned with suspenseful events, though he never abandoned his psychological bent. Obituaries and other sources: *Encyclopedia of World Literature in the Twentieth Century,* updated edition, Ungar, 1967; *Everyman's Dictionary of European Writers,* Dent & Sons, 1968; *The Penguin Companion to European Literature,* McGraw, 1969; *The Author's and Writer's Who's Who,* 6th edition, Burke's Peerage, 1971; *Cassell's Encyclopaedia of World Literature,* revised edition, Morrow, 1973; *World Authors, 1950-1970,* Wilson, 1975.

* * *

HOUSTON, Beverle (Ann) 1936-

PERSONAL: Born December 23, 1936, in Reading, Pa.; daughter of Sam and Jeanne (a secretary-treasurer; maiden name, Fishbein) Schwartzman; married David B. Houston (divorced). *Education:* University of Pennsylvania, B.A., 1957, M.A., 1961; University of California, Los Angeles, Ph.D., 1969. *Home:* 840 North Occidental Blvd., Los Angeles, Calif. 90026. *Office:* Scott 211, Pitzer College, Claremont, Calif. 91711.

CAREER: Pennsylvania State University, State College, instructor in English, 1965-66; San Fernando Valley State College (now California State University), Northridge, lecturer in English, 1967-69; high school English teacher in North Hollywood, Calif., 1969-70; Pitzer College, Claremont, Calif., assistant professor, 1970-74, associate professor, 1975-79, professor of English and film, 1979—, head of intercollegiate film studies field group, 1976-77. Visiting film critic at University of California, Los Angeles, 1976-77; participates in professional meetings; gives readings and lectures. Member of board of trustees of Oakwood Secondary School.

WRITINGS: (With Marsha Kinder) *Close-Up: A Critical Perspective on Film,* Harcourt, 1972; (with Kinder) *Self and Cinema: A Transformalist Perspective,* Redgrave Publishing, 1979. Contributor of about twenty articles and reviews to literature and film journals. Contributing editor of *Women and Film,* 1973-76; editor of *Quarterly Review of Film Studies,* winter, 1978-79, member of editorial board, 1978—.

WORK IN PROGRESS—Screenplays: "Mary Wollstonecraft" and "Tristram Shandy" (adaptation of Sterne's novel), both with Marsha Kinder; *Festival.*

SIDELIGHTS: Houston told *CA:* "Feminist film criticism and the integration of theory and practical criticism are of special interest to me. Screenwriting is a new direction. Learning to write in a new form has been exhilarating."

* * *

HOWAR, Barbara 1934-

PERSONAL: Born September 27, 1934, in Raleigh, N.C.; daughter of Charles Oscar and Mary Elizabeth (O'Connell) Dearing; married Ed Howar (divorced); children: Bader Elizabeth, Edmond Dearing. *Education:* Attended Holton-Arms Junior College. *Politics:* Democrat. *Home:* 1641 34th St., Washington, D.C., 20007. *Office:* Columbia Broadcasting System, Inc., 524 West 57th St., New York, N.Y. 10019.

CAREER: Columnist in *Washington Post* and *New Yorker;* television show hostess for "Panorama" and "Who's Who," 1976-1977; correspondent for Columbia Broadcasting System, Inc. (CBS-News). *Member:* International P.E.N., American Federation of Television and Radio Artists.

WRITINGS: Laughing All the Way, Stein & Day, 1973; *Making Ends Meet,* Random House, 1976.

SIDELIGHTS: As J. R. Coyne observed, "Mrs. Howar's career classification would in another capital in another age be 'lady-in-waiting,'" for she arrived as a Washington socialite during the Kennedy years and later served as a social aide to the Johnson family. *Laughing All the Way* recounts her experiences during both those administrations. Christopher Porterfield described the book as the story of "how a girl with looks, sass and plenty of hustle cultivates powerful people and becomes the next best thing to powerful—famous."

Howar herself seems to agree. In the book's introduction she says: "This story . . . is a report on a life lived in Washington; on a time, a town, and a heroine, all equally foolish. I came looking for glorious recognition, a seat in History. I was not equipped to play the power game. . . . I am not of the right sex to wield great political influence, but my gender has permitted me to consort with those who do."

In what the *New Yorker* called "remarkably goodnatured" gossip, Howar drops names: not only the various members of the Kennedy and Johnson clans, but such other notables as Henry Kissinger, Edmund Muskie, and an unidentified U.S. senator with whom she had an affair. The book made her many enemies, too, including David Suskind, Virginia Graham, and Clare Booth Luce.

R. Z. Sheppard noted that, like her first book, Howar's novel, *Making Ends Meet,* is "held together by a breezy cynicism . . . dispensed like hair spray." Its heroine is semi-autobiographical: Lilly Shawcross is a divorced, 40-year-old mother of two and the witty film critic for a Washington, D.C., television station. The plot, which unfolds to a large extent through flashback, traces Lilly's search for both love and independence. Yet the novel is not a feminist tract on a woman "finding herself." "Howar is at her best when she is giving a satiric thrust at her own kind," J. P. Lovering maintained, just as Sheppard felt that "her keenest instinct is for the spiky remark."

BIOGRAPHICAL/CRITICAL SOURCES: Life, July 29, 1966; *Newsweek,* April 12, 1971, February 23, 1976, January 24, 1977; *Esquire,* December, 1971, August, 1973; *Time,* March 26, 1973, June 4, 1973, May 3, 1976; *Salt Lake Tribune,* April 15, 1973; *Detroit Free Press,* May 6, 1973; *New York Times Book Review,* May 20, 1973, April 25, 1976; *Best Sellers,* June 1, 1973; *New Yorker,* July 16, 1973; *National Review,* July 20, 1973; *Commonweal,* October 26, 1973; *Book World,* June 16, 1974; *Village Voice,* March 29, 1976; *Washington Star,* April 18, 1976; *New York Times,* June 18, 1976; *Best Sellers,* August, 1976; *American Home,* October, 1976; *Washington Post Book World,* December 12, 1976, February 20, 1977; *Authors in the News,* Volumes 1 and 2, Gale, 1976.*

* * *

HOWARD, John Tasker 1890-1964

OBITUARY NOTICE: Born November 30, 1890, in Brooklyn, N.Y.; died November 20, 1964. Composer and author of books on music, including *A Short History of American Music.* Howard was music editor of *McCall's.* He also had his own radio show. Obituaries and other sources: *The ASCAP Biographical Dictionary of Composers, Authors, and Publishers,* American Society of Composers, Authors, and Publishers, 1966.

* * *

HOWARD, Roy Wilson 1883-1964

OBITUARY NOTICE: Born January 1, 1883, in Gano, Ohio; died November 20, 1964. Editor and publisher. Howard was president of United Press International (UPI) from 1912 until his death. He was appointed chairman of the board and business director of Newspaper Enterprise Association in 1921 by E. W. Scripps. The appointment afforded Howard considerable control of both the UPI Association and Scripps-McRae newspapers as well. By 1925, the latter was renamed Scripps-Howard, and Howard was named editorial director. In 1931, he organized the merger of the *New York World* and *New York Telegram.* Howard bought the *New York Sun* in 1950 and the three papers were later renamed the *New York World-Telegram & Sun.* Obituaries and other sources: *Current Biography,* Wilson, 1940, January, 1965; *New York Times,* November 21, 1964.

* * *

HOWE, Mark Anthony DeWolfe 1864-1960

OBITUARY NOTICE: Born August 28, 1864, in Bristol, R.I.; died December 6, 1960. Author of numerous biographies and nonfiction accounts, many of which are about the New England area, including *Boston Common: Scenes From Four Centuries* and *Bristol, R.I.: A Town Biography.* He received the Pulitzer Prize in 1924 for his biography, *Barrett Wendell and His Letters.* Obituaries and other sources: *The Reader's Encyclopedia,* 2nd edition, Crowell, 1965; *The Oxford Companion to American Literature,* 4th edition, Oxford University Press, 1965.

* * *

HOWES, Connie B. 1933-

PERSONAL: Born September 21, 1933, in Illinois; daughter of Kenneth Elmer and Marguerite (Hansen) Becker; married Allen Hudson Howes (an engineer), June 24, 1958; children: Bruce Becker, Marian Victoria. *Education:* Attended University of Colorado, 1950-52. *Home:* 765 East Morningside Dr., Lake Forest, Ill. 60045. *Office:* National Sporting Goods Association, 717 North Michigan Ave., Chicago, Ill. 60611.

CAREER/WRITINGS: Ski Week, Norwalk, Conn., midwest editor, 1967-68; *Chicago American/Today,* Chicago, Ill., ski editor, 1967-70; *Camping Industry,* Milwaukee, Wis., editor, 1965-68; *Selling Sporting Goods,* Chicago, Ill., associate editor, 1968—. Author of *Recreational Vehicle Handbook,* Rand McNally, 1974. Contributor of articles to magazines, including *Argosy, Lions, Better Homes and Gardens, Field & Stream, Camping Journal, Trailer Travel, Chicago Tribune Magazine,* and *Today's Health.*

MEMBER: American Society of Journalists and Authors, Outdoor Writers Association of America, American Business Press Editors, United States Ski Writers Association, Association of Great Lakes Outdoor Writers. *Awards, honors:* Magazine award from Recreational Vehicle Institute and Outdoor Writers Association of America, 1973; book award from Recreation Vehicle Industry Association, 1974, for *Recreational Vehicle Handbook;* honorable mention from Outdoor Writers Association of America, 1978, for black and white photographs.

* * *

HOYT, (Edwin) Palmer 1897-1979

OBITUARY NOTICE: Born March 10, 1897, in Roseville, Ill.; died June 25, 1979, in Denver, Colo. Editor and publisher. Beginning as a copy reader in 1926 for the *Portland Oregonian,* Hoyt worked his way through the ranks of reporter and editor to become publisher of the newspaper by 1938. He also was editor and publisher of the *Denver Post* for a time until his retirement in 1971. Obituaries and other sources: *Current Biography,* Wilson, 1943, August, 1979; *New York Times,* June 27, 1979; *Chicago Tribune,* July 1, 1979.

* * *

HUBBS, Carl Leavitt 1894-1979

OBITUARY NOTICE: Born October 18, 1894, in Williams, Ariz.; died of cancer, June 30, 1979, in La Jolla, Calif. Educator, marine biologist, and author. The founding director of Sea World in San Diego, Calif., Hubbs taught zoology at the University of Michigan for twenty-four years and had been professor of biology at University of California's Scripps Institute of Oceanography. He was co-author of *Fishes of the Great Lakes Region* and contributed more than seven hundred articles to scientific journals. Obituaries and other sources: *American Men and Women of Science: Physical and Biological Sciences,* 14th edition, Bowker, 1979; *Chicago Tribune,* July 8, 1979.

* * *

HUGHES, Daniel T(homas) 1930-

PERSONAL: Born February 7, 1930, in New York, N.Y.; married, 1969; children: one. *Education:* Bellarmine College, A.B., 1953, Ph.L., 1955, M.A., 1956; Woodstock College, Woodstock, Md., S.T.B., 1962; Catholic University of America, Ph.D., 1967. *Home:* 4322 Kenmont Place, Columbus, Ohio 43220. *Office:* Department of Anthropology, Ohio State University, Columbus, Ohio 43210.

CAREER: Ateneo de Manila University, Manila, Philippines, assistant professor of sociology and anthropology, 1967-69; Ohio State University, Columbus, assistant professor, 1970-72, associate professor, beginning 1972, currently professor of anthropology, head of department, 1976—. Research associate of Institute of Philippine Culture, 1967-68, National Research Council-National Academy of Sciences, 1969-70, and Bernice P. Bishop Museum. Conducted field studies in Micronesia, the Philippines, and the Caroline Islands. *Member:* American Anthropological Association (fellow), Current Anthropology (associate), Association for Social Anthropology in Oceania (fellow), Association for Anthropology in Micronesia, Pacific Asian Studies Association, Sigma Xi.

WRITINGS: *Political Conflict and Harmony on Ponape,* Human Relations Area File Press, 1970; (editor with S. Lingenfelter, and contributor) *Political Development in Micronesia,* Ohio State University Press, 1974; (contributor) F. King, editor, *Oceania and Beyond,* Greenwood Press, 1976; (editor with J. Boutilier and S. Tiffany, and contributor) *Church, Sect, and Mission in Oceania,* University Press of Hawaii, 1977. Contributor to anthropology and sociology journals.

WORK IN PROGRESS: Editing and writing a chapter for *Social Change and Cultural Continuity on Ponape,* with S. Riesenberg and J. Fischer.

* * *

HUGO, Herbert W. 1930(?)-1979

OBITUARY NOTICE: Born c. 1930; died c. July 16, 1979, near Maywood, Ill. Editor and author. Considered an authority on the world fuel situation, Hugo had been associated with the petroleum industry for nearly thirty years. He was senior editor of *Platts Oilgram.* Obituaries and other sources: *Chicago Tribune,* July 18, 1979.

* * *

HUNT, David C(urtis) 1935-

PERSONAL: Born December 7, 1935, in Oswego, Kan.; son of Burl H. and Julia (a piano teacher; maiden name, Long) Hunt; married Carol Beth Keene, February 2, 1969; children: Laura Allison, Anne Elizabeth. *Education:* University of Tulsa, B.A., 1958, M.A., 1968. *Politics:* Democrat. *Religion:* Roman Catholic. *Home:* 127 Saranac, Missoula, Mont. 59801. *Office:* Missoula Museum of the Arts, 335 North Pattee, Missoula, Mont. 59801.

CAREER: KTUL-TV, Tulsa, Okla., part-time production artist, 1956-58; KTSM-TV, El Paso, Tex., production artist, 1960-62; KOTV-TV, Tulsa, Okla., studio camera operator, 1962; Bendix Radio Corp., Kailua, Hawaii, illustrator in publications division, 1962-63; Douglas Aircraft (now McDonnell-Douglas Aircraft), Tulsa, Okla., illustrator and designer in publications division, 1963-65; Thomas Gilcrease Institute of American History and Art, Tulsa, Okla., exhibits specialist, 1965-67, curator of art, production manager, and associate editor of museum publications, 1967-72; Stark Foundation, Orange, Tex., curator at Stark Museum of Art, 1972-76; Missoula Museum of the Arts, Missoula, Mont., director, 1977—. Instructor at University of Tulsa, 1970-72. Artist (including commissioned murals). *Military service:* U.S. Army, technical illustrator for publications and training aids, 1958-60; served in Korea.

MEMBER: International Council of Industrial Editors, American Association of Museums, Montana Art Gallery Directors Association. *Awards, honors:* Art awards include Margaret C. Hewgley Award from Oklahoma Artists Annual, 1963; certificate of craftsmanship from Weyerhaeuser Paper Corp., 1966, for "Discovery in Meso America"; 3M printing job of the year awards, 1966, for "Naturalists in America," and 1968, for "W. R. Leigh: The Artist's Studio Collection"; award of excellence from Simpson Lee Paper Co., 1968, for work in *American Scene;* Wrangler Award from National Cowboy Hall of Fame and Western Heritage Center, 1969, for "W. R. Leigh: The Artist's Studio Collection," and 1972, for *The Art of the Old West;* certificates from Printing Industries of America graphic arts competition, both 1969, for "The Plains of Philippi" and "W. R. Leigh: The Artist's Studio Collection"; awards of excellence from International Council of Industrial Editors, both 1969, for *American Scene* and *The Gilcrease Institute: A National Treasury;* Mead Award from Mead Paper Corp., 1970, for "The Missouri River: Waterway West."

WRITINGS: (With Paul A. Rossi) *The Art of the Old West,* Knopf, 1971; *A Guide to Oklahoma Museums,* University of Oklahoma Press, 1979. Contributor to *The Reader's Encyclopedia of the American West.* Contributor to trade journals and *American History Illustrated.* Past associate editor of *American Scene.*

WORK IN PROGRESS: *A Portrait in Oil,* a biography of Frank Phillips, for University of Oklahoma Press.

SIDELIGHTS: Hunt writes: "I did not set out to be a writer. Writing and publishing both resulted from professional interests and activities associated with the occupation of a museum curator, but having gotten into the field, I now find that there are more and more subjects I'd like to research and write about. American art and history remain the chief areas of my interest.

"Growing up in the oilfields of northeastern Oklahoma, I was early exposed to public collections of fine art and western Americana assembled by oilmen such as Thomas Gilcrease, Waite Phillips, and Frank Phillips. My dad worked for Phillips Petroleum Company at the time, and we often visited the Phillips' ranch and museum at Woolaroc, west of Bartlesville. Later, I was employed at the Gilcrease Museum in Tulsa, where a professional interest in such collections developed.

"One of my duties at Gilcrease was that of production manager for the museum quarterly and related publications. I soon went from designing the quarterly to writing articles for same. Eventually, articles for other publications resulted. The highlight of my writing experience at Gilcrease was co-authoring *The Art of the Old West* for Alfred Knopf. Based entirely upon the resources of the vast Gilcrease collection, it has sold extremely well—'for an art book.' Nearly everything I have done since in the writing field has derived from that first success.

"Having taken only one class in journalism at the University of Tulsa as part of the general requirements for a commercial art degree, I necessarily developed subsequent writing skills on the job. I'm not sure what my 'philosophy' with respect to writing might be, other than to say that I try to write the way I like to read. Other than imparting information, a line or paragraph has to 'sound right' to me. A certain rhythm in phrasing and overall organization is important. Subject and emphasis should change at the right moment. It's not unlike writing music or dialogue for a play. I've done some of that, too.

"Natural history remains a secondary, non-professional interest of mine. As with writing, my introduction to nature and the wilderness ideal resulted from activities associated with the arts. I also admit to a lasting affection for the theatre and for amateur dramatics, in which I was once active."

* * *

HUNT, Herbert James 1899-1973

OBITUARY NOTICE: Born August 2, 1899, in Lichfield, England; died November 2, 1973. Educator and author of books on French literature of the nineteenth century, including *The Epic in Nineteenth Century France* and *Victor Hugo,* a biography. Hunt also edited and translated various writings of Balzac. He taught at the University of London. Obituaries and other sources: *Who's Who,* 126th edition, St. Martin's, 1974.

* * *

HUTCHINSON, Richard Wyatt 1894-1970

OBITUARY NOTICE—See index for *CA* sketch: Born December 22, 1894; died April 8, 1970, in England. Archaeologist, educator, and author. Hutchinson did field work in Crete, Mycenae, Lesbos, Nineveh, Macedonia, Poland, and Scotland. He wrote *A Century of Exploration at Nineveh* and *Prehistoric Crete.* Obituaries and other sources: *AB Bookman's Weekly,* May 4, 1970.

* * *

HUTSON, Joan 1929-

PERSONAL: Born March 10, 1929, in Wadena, Minn.; daughter of Anthony and Kathyrn (Pitzl) Ehlen; married Gerald Hutson, June 13, 1953; children: Mark, Mike, Mary Jo, Vicki, Greg, Jill, Jay. *Home:* R.R. 3, Wadena, Minn. 56482.

CAREER: Teacher.

WRITINGS: The Wind Has Many Faces: A Book of Minute Meditations, Abbey Press, 1974; *Heal My Heart O Lord,* Ave Maria Press, 1976; *An Instrument of Your Peace,* Doubleday, 1977; *A Hunger for Wholeness,* Ave Maria Press, 1978; *I Think I Know . . . ,* Ave Maria Press, 1979.

WORK IN PROGRESS: A sequel to *Heal My Heart O Lord;* a children's catechism; two children's books, *My Happy Ones* and *The Important Book,* for Daughters of St. Paul Publishing Co.

SIDELIGHTS: Hutson told *CA:* "All of my writing originates from a religious theme. My greatest joy is to understand God better and, through my writings, to help others understand Him better. My reader-response mail highly encourages me to stay in this realm of writing. I hardly need any other recompense! Praise God!"

AVOCATIONAL INTERESTS: Art, painting, liturgical music, playing the organ, piano, guitar, harp, and flute.

HUYCK, Dorothy Boyle 1925(?)-1979

OBITUARY NOTICE: Born c. 1925 in Madison, Wis.; died of cancer, August 24, 1979, in Washington, D.C. Author. Huyck contributed numerous articles on travel and conservation to magazines and newspapers, including *Christian Science Monitor, American Forests, New York Times,* and *Washington Post.* She also worked for several years for the State Department and the National Park Service. Obituaries and other sources: *Washington Post,* August 27, 1979.

* * *

HYLAND, Drew A(lan) 1939-

PERSONAL: Born February 9, 1939, in Wilkes-Barre, Pa.; son of G. Arthur (in engineering sales) and Catherine (Williams) Hyland; married Anne Sloat (a potter), October 3, 1964; children: Christopher, Craig. *Education:* Princeton University, A.B., 1961; Pennsylvania State University, M.A., 1963, Ph.D., 1965. *Home:* 21 Oak Knoll Rd., East Hampton, Conn. 06424. *Office:* Department of Philosophy, Trinity College, Hartford, Conn. 06106.

CAREER: University of Toronto, Toronto, Ontario, lecturer, then assistant professor of philosophy, 1964-67; Trinity College, Hartford, Conn., assistant professor, 1967-74, professor of philosophy, 1974—. *Member:* Society for Ancient Greek Philosophy, Society for Phenomenology and Existential Philosophy, Philosophic Society for the Study of Sport, Hegel Society, Heidegger Conference.

WRITINGS: (Contributor) E. Gerber, editor, *Sport and the Body,* Lea & Febiger, 1971; *The Origins of Philosophy,* Putnam, 1974. Contributor to philosophy and aesthetics journals.

WORK IN PROGRESS: A book on Plato's *Charmides.*

* * *

HYMAN, Paula 1946-

PERSONAL: Born September 30, 1946, in Boston, Mass.; daughter of Sydney M. (an accountant) and Ida (a bookkeeper; maiden name, Tatelman) Hyman; married Stanley Rosenbaum (a physician), June 7, 1969; children: Judith, Adina. *Education:* Hebrew College of Boston, B.J.Ed., 1966; Radcliffe College, B.A., 1968; Columbia University, M.A., 1970, Ph.D., 1975. *Religion:* Jewish. *Home:* 601 West 113th St., New York, N.Y. 10025. *Office:* Department of History, Columbia University, New York, N.Y. 10027.

CAREER: Columbia University, New York, N.Y., assistant professor of history, 1974—. Member of board of directors of Leo Baeck Institute, 1979—; member of American Jewish Congress Commission on Youth and Culture. *Member:* American Historical Association, Association for Jewish Studies (member of board of directors, 1978—), Coordinating Committee on Women in the Historical Profession. *Awards, honors:* National Endowment for the Humanities grant, 1977; American Council of Learned Societies fellowship, 1979.

WRITINGS: (With Charlotte Baum and Sonya Michel) *The Jewish Woman in America,* Dial, 1976; *From Dreyfus to Vichy,* Columbia University Press, 1979. Contributor to Jewish studies and feminist journals, including *Ms.*

WORK IN PROGRESS: The Case of Alsatian Jewry; editing an anthology on anti-Semitism; a monograph on emancipation and social change.

HYNDMAN, Jane Andrews Lee 1912-1978
(Lee Wyndham)

OBITUARY NOTICE—See index for *CA* sketch: Born December 16, 1912, in Russia; died March 18, 1978, in Morristown, N.J. Journalist, lecturer, and author of about thirty books, best known for her juvenile book, *Candy Stripers*. Hyndman was the author of a syndicated children's book column in five New Jersey newspapers. She was also children's book editor for the *Morristown Daily Record* and the *Philadelphia Inquirer*. Hyndman lectured on writing for children and teenagers to college audiences. She once stated, "Writing for young people is a great responsibility. An author can help mold character and even influence a young person's choice of and training for a career." An illustration of this is her book *Candy Stripers* which has inspired numerous teenage girls to become hospital volunteers. Obituaries and other sources: *Authors of Books for Young People*, 2nd edition, Scarecrow, 1971; *Who's Who in the East*, 14th edition, Marquis, 1973; *The Writers Directory, 1976-78*, St. Martin's, 1976; *Publishers Weekly*, April 10, 1978.

I

ICAZA CORONEL, Jorge 1906-1979

PERSONAL: Born July 10, 1906, in Quito, Ecuador; died May 26, 1979, in Quito; son of Jose Icaza Manso (a landed farmer) and Carmen Coronel; married Marina Moncayo (an actress), July 16, 1936; children: Cristina Icaza Prado, Fenia Icaza Moncayo. *Education:* Attended Universidad Central de Quito, 1924-27, and Conservatorio National, 1927-28. *Home:* Ave. Republica El Salvador #563, Quito, Ecuador.

CAREER: Playwright, 1929-36; writer, 1933-79. Actor in Compania Dramatica Nacional of Ecuador, 1928-31; Pagaduria General (government treasury), Pichincha, Ecuador, civil servant, 1932-37; bookstore proprietor, 1938-44; founder and titular member of Ecuadorian Cultural Council, 1944-63; National Library of Ecuador, Quito, director, 1963-73; ambassador to Soviet Union, 1973-77. Organizer of various acting companies, including "Campania de Variedades, 1931, and "Marina Moncayo," 1932 and 1946. Organizer and secretary-general of Union of Artists and Writers, beginning 1936. Professor at University of New Mexico, Quito, beginning 1969. Guest lecturer in Mexico and Costa Rica, 1940, New York, 1942, Venezuela and Cuba, 1948, Puerto Rico, 1949, Buenos Aires, Argentina, 1949, 1950, Bolivia, 1956, Lima, Peru, and University of San Marcos, 1957, People's Republic of China, 1960, Soviet Union, 1961, Cuba, 1962, Brazil, 1963, Mexico, 1967, and in thirty American universities, 1973. *Awards, honors:* Primer Premio de Novela Hispanoamericana, 1935, for *Huasipungo;* Primer Premio de Novela Nacional de Ecuador, 1935, for *En las calles;* gold medal from city of Guayaquil, 1958, for literary merit.

WRITINGS—In English: *Huasipungo* (novel), Talleres Graficos Nacionales, 1934, 9th edition, 1973, translation by Mervyn Savill published as *Huasipungo,* Dobson, 1962, authorized translation by Bernard M. Dulsey of expanded 1951 edition published as *The Villagers,* Southern Illinois University Press, 1973.

Other novels: *En las calles* (title means "In the Streets"), Talleres Graficos Nacionales, 1935, reprinted, Losada, 1964; *Cholos,* Editorial Sindicato de Escritores y Artistas, 1937; *Media vida deslumbrados,* Editorial Quito, 1942; *Huairapamushcas,* Editorial Casa de la Cultura Ecuatoriana, 1948, published as *Hijos del viento* (title means "Children of the Wind"), Plaza & Janes, 1973; *El Chulla Romero y Flores,* Editorial Casa de la Cultura Ecuatoriana, 1958; *Atrapados,* Losada, Volume I: *El Juramento* (title means "The Oath"), Volume II: *En la ficcion* (title means "In Fiction"), Volume III: *En la realidad* (title means "In Reality"), 1972.

Short stories: *Barro de la sierra,* Labor, 1933; *Viejos cuentos* (title means "Old Stories"), Editorial Casa de la Cultura Ecuatoriana, 1960; *Seis relatos* (title means "Six Tales"), Editorial Casa de la Cultura Ecuatoriana, 1962.

Plays: "El Intruso" (title means "The Intruder"), first produced in Quito, September 8, 1928; "La Comedia sin nombre" (three-act; title means "The Comedy Without a Name"), first produced in Quito, May 23, 1929; "Por el viejo" (title means "For the Old Man"), first produced in Quito, August 3, 1929; *Como ellos quieren* (contains "Cual es?," first produced in Quito, May 23, 1931, and "Como ellos quieren"), Labor, 1931; *Sin sentido* (title means "Without Meaning"), Labor, 1932; *Flagelo* (title means "The Scourge"), Imprenta Nacional, 1936.

Collection: *Obras escogidas,* Aguilar, 1961.

Editor of *SEA* (journal of Sindicato de Escritores y Artistas), 1938.

WORK IN PROGRESS: A novel, *Los Jauregui y la milagrosa;* a volume of plays.

SIDELIGHTS: Icaza Coronel is internationally renown for his realistic depictions of life in Ecuador. He began his career as a playwright, but when his version of Jules Romains's *Le Dictateur* was banned by the Ecuador government, he started writing novels instead.

Icaza Coronel's first novel, *Huasipungo* ("The Villagers"), was a tremendous success. It is his protest against the exploitation of Ecuadorian Indians by capitalists. Jose Yglesias observed that "the characters are sketchily drawn, the incidents rapidly developed; but the language of the Indians has an incantatory beauty, the horrors illustrate an undeniable logic, and its author's compassion and indignation are genuine."

Many of Icaza Coronel's books have been translated into Russian, French, and German.

BIOGRAPHICAL/CRITICAL SOURCES: America, April 11, 1964; *Nation,* April 13, 1964; *Book Week,* April 19, 1964; *Saturday Review,* May 30, 1964; *Christian Science Monitor,* December 29, 1964.

[Sketch verified by wife, Marina Moncayo Icaza]

IDDON, Don 1913(?)-1979

OBITUARY NOTICE: Born c. 1913; died of a heart attack, c. June , 1979, in New York, N.Y. Columnist. For twenty-two years, Iddon's *London Daily Mail* column provided British readers with humorous commentary on the American way of life. Obituaries and other sources: *New York Times,* June 19, 1979; *Time,* July 2, 1979.

* * *

IDRIESS, Ion L. 1891(?)-1979

OBITUARY NOTICE: Born c. 1891; died in 1979, in Sidney, Australia. Miner, drover, timber cutter, and author. Idriess's best known adventure books, often based on his own work experiences, include *Prospecting for Gold, The Cattle King,* and *Flynn of the Inland.* Obituaries and other sources: *Twentieth Century Writing: A Reader's Guide to Contemporary Literature,* Transatlantic, 1969; *AB Bookman's Weekly,* August 6, 1979.

* * *

ILARDO, Joseph A(nthony) 1944-

PERSONAL: Born October 2, 1944, in New York, N.Y.; son of Joseph A. and Christine (Torregrossa) Ilardo; married Roberta DiMattina (a reading consultant), October 9, 1965; children: Janine, Karen Leigh. *Education:* St. John's University, Jamaica, N.Y., B.A. (cum laude), 1965; Queens College of the City University of New York, M.A., 1966; University of Illinois, Ph.D., 1968; Adelphi University, M.S.W., 1980. *Home:* 8 Chestnut Hill Dr., New Fairfield, Conn. 06810. *Office:* Department of Speech and Theatre, Herbert H. Lehman College of the City University of New York, Bronx, N.Y. 10468.

CAREER: Herbert H. Lehman College of the City University of New York, Bronx, N.Y., assistant professor of communication, 1969—. Adjunct assistant professor at Western Connecticut State College, 1974—. Private practice of psychotherapy. Consultant to business and industry. *Member:* International Communication Association, National Association of Social Workers, Speech Communication Association of America, National Education Association, Eastern Communication Association.

WRITINGS: (With Abne M. Eisenberg) *Argument: A Guide to Formal and Informal Debate,* Prentice-Hall, 1972, 2nd edition, 1980; *The Risk Book,* Simon & Schuster, 1980; *Speaking Persuasively,* Macmillan, 1980. Contributor to speech and communication journals.

WORK IN PROGRESS: In Therapy: A Guide for Clients and People Who Love Them; Interviewing: Theory and Methods.

SIDELIGHTS: Ilardo writes: "Trained as a teacher of rhetoric and public speaking, I have moved far from these traditional roots. Study and teaching in the areas of interpersonal communication and small group communication have helped me discover my true love: helping people as a psychotherapist. I am now in the midst of a career expansion. I consider myself an educator/psychotherapist; like Paul Goodman, Peter Marin, and others, I think that there is no clear line of demarcation between the two professions. I have done therapy with college students, adults, children, couples, families, and prison inmates. We are all far more alike than we are different. Reaching people on a visceral level, touching them, is what interests me most.

"My work as an educator and psychotherapist has been influenced most strongly by the contributions of Carl Rogers, Rollo May, Erich Fromm, Fritz Perls, and Alan Watts. As a writer I also admire the work of E. Fuller Torrey, Alvin Toffler, and Peter Marin. My trade writing *(The Risk Book)* represented a synthesis of the views of these people, with an original slant.

"*The Risk Book* was written over a period of five years, without a contract. It was a labor of love. Encouragement from family and friends kept me going. The comment which had the most effect was, 'The book speaks to me.' I hope it speaks to many, many people. The reader-writer relationship is necessarily less personal than the therapist-client one or the teacher-student one. However, my hope is that in my writing I will be perceived as close to my reader psychologically—so that I may touch my readers as I do my clients and students."

* * *

IMBER, Gerald 1941-

PERSONAL: Born September 9, 1941, in New York, N.Y.; son of George Howard (an accountant) and Rose (Weiss) Imber; married Eileen Kass (a remedial reading specialist), June 28, 1964; children: Peter, Jason, Gregory. *Education:* Attended Brooklyn College of the City University of New York, 1961; State University of New York Downstate Medical Center, M.D., 1966. *Agent:* Arthur Pine Associates, Inc., 1784 Broadway, New York, N.Y. 10019. *Office:* 784 Park Ave., New York, N.Y. 10021.

CAREER: Intern at Long Island Jewish Hospital, N.Y., beginning 1966; Cornell University Medical College, New York City, resident in plastic surgery, 1972-74; plastic surgeon with private practice in New York City, 1974—. Diplomate of American Board of Plastic Surgery; member of faculty at The New York Hospital; instructor at Cornell University Medical College. Frequent guest on television programs. *Military service:* U.S. Air Force, 1968-70; became captain. *Member:* American Society of Plastic and Reconstructive Surgeons, New York State Medical Society, New York County Medical Society, New York Regional Society of Plastic Surgeons, Shinnelock Yacht Club, Harmonie Club.

WRITINGS: (With Kurt Wagner) *Beauty by Design,* McGraw, 1979. Contributor to plastic surgery journals.

WORK IN PROGRESS: "A biographical novel about medical figures at the turn of the century."

SIDELIGHTS: Imber is an avid spokesman for public information in medicine and for high standards of medical training and care. *Avocational interests:* Sports, art, food, wine collecting.

* * *

ISAACS, Susan 1943-

PERSONAL: Born in 1943 in Brooklyn, N.Y.; married Elkan Abramowitz (a trial lawyer); children: Andrew, Elizabeth. *Education:* Attended Queens College. *Agent:* Ana Borgersen, Jove/Harcourt Brace Jovanovich, 757 Third Ave., New York, N.Y. 10017.

CAREER: Writer. Worked as senior editor at *Seventeen* magazine.

WRITINGS: Compromising Positions (novel; Book-of-the-Month Club selection), Times Books, 1978.

WORK IN PROGRESS: A novel about New York state politics.

SIDELIGHTS: Compromising Positions is the story of Judith Singer, a frustrated Long Island housewife who turns detective in an effort to find the killer of local periodontist Dr. M. Bruce Fleckstein. Judith becomes interested in the case "when she discovers that no fewer than three of her friends have had encounters of something closer than the dental kind with M. Bruce, not to mention having had pictures taken of parts of their anatomy other than their bridgework," explained Carol Eisen Rinzler.

Isaacs's first novel received generally favorable reviews. A *New Yorker* critic commented that "Susan Isaacs has done for Shorehaven Acres, Long Island, what Cyra McFadden did for California's Marin County . . . and has concocted a fast-paced murder mystery to boot." Describing the author as "deft and clever, and even sometimes very funny," Rinzler said *Compromising Positions* "is a froth of a book, perfect for reading whilst aswing in a hammock. If the swing of the pendulum has put a feminist detective into the works, that seems less a reason for pontification than for pleasure." A *Newsweek* reviewer, however, was disappointed in the book: "One is left stranded between an insufficiently ingenious whodunit and an inadequately realized social comedy, hoping that Isaacs will get a good screenplay out of it and then sit down to write a second, better novel."

The film rights for *Compromising Positions* were purchased by Warner Brothers in 1978.

BIOGRAPHICAL/CRITICAL SOURCES: People, April 24, 1978; *New York Times Book Review,* April 30, 1978; *Newsweek,* May 1, 1978; *New Yorker,* May 15, 1978; *Times Literary Supplement,* November 3, 1978. *

* * *

IVEY, Donald 1918-

PERSONAL: Born August 10, 1918, in Easton, Pa.; son of Wesley R. (a bookkeeper) and Laura (Peltes) Ivey; married Helen Johnson, June 19, 1948; children: Elizabeth, Jonathan, Laura, Christopher. *Education:* University of Kentucky, B.Mus., 1951, M.Mus., 1955; University of Illinois, D.M.A., 1962. *Politics:* Independent. *Religion:* Presbyterian. *Home:* 109 Tartan Dr., Lexington, Ky. 40503. *Office:* School of Music, University of Kentucky, Lexington, Ky. 40506.

CAREER: Kentucky Wesleyan College, Owensboro, assistant professor, 1951-59, associate professor of music, 1959-61; University of Kentucky, Lexington, associate professor of music, 1961-74, professor of music, 1974—. Choir director; music festival adjudicator; vocal and choral clinician. *Military service:* U.S. Army, 1943-45; served in European theater. *Member:* Phi Kappa Phi. *Awards, honors:* National Foundation for the Humanities grant.

WRITINGS: Song: Anatomy, Imagery, and Styles, Free Press, 1970; *Sound Pleasure,* with set of record albums, Schirmer Books, 1977. Contributor to *Academic American Encyclopedia.* Contributor to music journals.

WORK IN PROGRESS: Appalachian Music, publication expected in 1981.

SIDELIGHTS: Ivey told *CA:* "The writing impulse is motivated strongly by the 'publish or perish' syndrome, still a strong force in academe. In spite of that pressure, writing gives me great pleasure. It is especially fun to try to avoid 'academese,' the professorial and unspeakably dull style so respected in my profession. Music is a very earthy, sensual kind of expression, nothing like the bloodless, almost ethereal enterprise it seems to be when scholars write about it. In my books, I try to bring that gutty quality alive. It may not always be successful, but I'm trying. As the jazz musicians say, 'Get up with it!'"

J

JACKSON, Bruce 1936-

PERSONAL: Born May 21, 1936, in Brooklyn, N.Y.; son of Irving and Julia (a nurse; maiden name, Pinsky) Jackson; married Diane Christian (a professor and film producer), September 22, 1973; children: Michael, Jessica, Rachel. *Education:* Rutgers University, B.A., 1960; Indiana University, M.A., 1962. *Agent:* A. L. Hart, Fox Chase Agency, Inc., 419 East 57th St., New York, N.Y. 10022. *Office:* Center for Studies in American Culture, Samuel Clemens 608, State University of New York at Buffalo, Buffalo, N.Y. 14260.

CAREER: Harvard University Society of Fellows, junior fellow, 1963-67; State University of New York at Buffalo, assistant professor, 1967, associate professor, 1968, professor of English and comparative literature, 1971—, adjunct professor of law and jurisprudence, 1974—, director of Center for Studies in American Culture, 1972—. Executive director of Documentary Research, Inc. Photographs have been exhibited in group and solo shows in the United States and Europe. Lecturer at colleges, universities, workshops, and conferences. Member or past member of advisory board or boards of directors of Newport Folk Foundation, Center for Southern Folklore, Fund for the Improvement of Post-Secondary Education, New York Commission on Correction, and Institute of the American West; consultant to President's Commission on Law Enforcement and Administration of Justice, Institute for Sex Research, and Smithsonian Institution.

AWARDS, HONORS: Nomination for Grammy Award from National Academy of Recording Arts and Sciences, 1975, for record album, "Wake Up Dead Man"; grants and fellowships from American Council of Learned Societies, American Film Institute, American Philosophical Society, National Endowment for the Humanities, New York Council for the Humanities, Playboy Foundation, Fund for Investigative Journalism, and Wenner-Gren Foundation; Guggenheim fellowship.

WRITINGS: (Editor) *Folklore and Society,* Folklore Associates, 1966; (editor) *The Negro and His Folklore in Nineteenth-Century Periodicals,* University of Texas Press, 1966; *A Thief's Primer,* Macmillan, 1969, reprinted as *Outside the Law: A Thief's Primer,* Dutton, 1972; *Wake Up Dead Man: Afro-American Worksongs From Texas Prisons,* Harvard University Press, 1972; *In the Life: Versions of the Criminal Experience,* Holt, 1972; *Get Your Ass in the Water and Swim Like Me: Narrative Poetry From Black Oral Tradition,* Harvard University Press, 1974; *Killing Time: Life in the Arkansas Penitentiary* (photographs), Cornell University Press, 1977; *The Programmer* (novel), Doubleday, 1979; *Criminal Justice,* Pantheon, 1980; (with wife, Diane Christian) *Death Row,* Beacon Press, 1980.

Films—Co-author: "Services Rendered," Documentary Research, 1979; "Death Row," Documentary Research, 1979.

Contributor to folklore and law journals, literary journals, popular magazines, and newspapers, including *Atlantic Monthly, Harper's, Nation, New Republic,* and *Rolling Stone.*

WORK IN PROGRESS: *Heroic Postures,* studies of *The Iliad,* western films, and Indian rituals; *The Right Thing,* a novel.

SIDELIGHTS: Jackson's books have been published in French and Portuguese. He has recorded and annotated documentary folk music albums: "Talkin' About My Time: Eugene Rhodes," Folk Legacy, 1963; "Behind These Walls: Hank Ferguson," Folk Legacy, 1963; "Negro Folklore From Texas State Prisons," Elektra, 1965; "Ever Since I Been a Man Full Grown: J. B. Smith," Takoma, 1966; "Wake Up Dead Man," Rounder, 1975; Get Your Ass in the Water & Swim Like Me," Rounder, 1976.

Jackson writes: "Lately, I've been doing a lot of film work. Diane Christian and I did two one-hour documentaries this year. 'Services Rendered' is about working people on Buffalo's west side, and 'Death Row' is about how people get by in the lonely years after a death sentence is uttered by a judge.

"I've been doing documentary work for years in print media, the most recent important item being the book of photographs from the Arkansas Penitentiary. I was interested in films for a long time, but avoided them because I couldn't see myself functioning well in the group context necessary to make films work. I'd grown used to setting my own pace and schedule.

"A few years ago we spent a week at a conference with a group of filmmakers who got us excited about making our own films—Henry King, King Vidor, Clint Eastwood, and Delmer Daves were on panels and in workshops with us, and we learned a lot from them.

"That was when I started writing fiction again—immediately afterward. I wrote three novels in the next year.

"I'll do occasional scholarly books in the future, but only when it's fun. Making movies and writing novels is always fun—except the waiting to see if someone will publish the novels and the hustle to make money to make the films."

* * *

JACKSON, Franklin Jefferson
See WATKINS, Mel

* * *

JACKSON, Martin A(lan) 1941-

PERSONAL: Born January 22, 1941, in New York, N.Y.; son of Gerald (a locksmith) and Beatrice (Katz) Jackson; married Joan H. Warren (a hospital administrator), June 6, 1964; children: Jonathan, Johanna. *Education:* City College of the City University of New York, B.A., 1962; New York University, M.A., 1965; City University of New York, Ph.D., 1970. *Home and office:* 257 West 19th St., New York, N.Y. 10011.

CAREER: Herbert H. Lehman College of the City University of New York, Bronx, N.Y., lecturer in history, 1967-70; New Jersey Institute of Technology, Newark, assistant professor of history, 1970-73; National Project Center for Film and the Humanities, New York City, associate director, 1973-76; State University of New York Maritime College, Bronx, assistant professor of humanities, 1976-79; writer, 1979—. Participant in seminars and conferences; film programming consultant. *Member:* Society for Cinema Studies, Conference on British Studies, Historians Film Committee (co-founder; chairperson, 1970—), Columbia University Film Seminar. *Awards, honors:* National Endowment for the Humanities grant, 1970.

WRITINGS: (Editor with John E. O'Connor) *American History/American Film,* Ungar, 1978; *A World in the Dark: A History of American Movies* (juvenile), Warne, 1980. Author of filmstrips for use in high schools, including "The American Court System" and "Liberalism Versus Conservatism." Feature writer and photograph editor for United Press International. Contributor of articles and reviews to history journals, popular magazines, and newspapers, including *New York Times.* Past film critic for *U.S.A. Today* and *Chelsea-Clinton News.* Co-editor of *Film and History.*

WORK IN PROGRESS: A study of the American image in British films.

SIDELIGHTS: Jackson told *CA:* "I completed a decade of academic life with the chilling knowledge that I was a stranger to the real world. The academic environment may have its good points but it keeps one in childhood, inexperienced and untested, and so I begin my writing career in competition with people ten years younger. The name of the game now is catch-up.

"What could I offer but my film experience? So I'm at work on a book for teen-age readers about American movies, a history of the Hollywood system. It's a big subject, of course, but useful to me for discipline; I need the daily stint at the typewriter to overcome the years of sloth. I find it feels good: up in the morning and over to the desk (after suitable delaying tactics, naturally). The pages roll out and the writing style gets more fluid. New ideas swoop down on me; I keep notes for future projects. An article assignment comes along with an impossible deadline but I accept anyway: somehow I'll fit it into the next month. I have an idea for a film script that I must put on paper, but there isn't time. Do all writers waste so much of their day? Does Philip Roth have to pick up the kids at school and take out the garbage?

"I'll deal with film and film history for awhile. Someday there'll be fiction too. The meaning of film for this century still hasn't been measured; it's all around us and has shaped our interior landscape. Now we need to understand what the movies have done to us. Some of that impact is good. A lot is unfortunate but it is never insignificant. I want to study British movies, in part because I like things British, in part because the British film industry is a hot-house flower that blooms slowly but beautifully. The next project (next year or next decade?) will be a look at Americans in British movies: how our cousins paint us on film. The material has been accumulating for years and soon it will turn into words. I want to understand how political events are turned into cinema, how the world outside gets into the films and movie houses. Or is it the other way around?

"I want to be labelled a writer. So far I haven't missed a deadline or given up an assignment. I'm a journeyman working toward master's rank. There is pride and satisfaction in seeing the work in print, and in joining an ancient craft."

AVOCATIONAL INTERESTS: Martial arts (ju-jitsu).

* * *

JACKSON, Neta 1944-

PERSONAL: Born October 26, 1944, in Winchester, Ky.; daughter of Isaac H. (a school administrator) and Margaret (a teacher; maiden name, Richards) Thiessen; married J. David Jackson (a writer and pastor), October 15, 1966; children: Julian David, Rachel Joy. *Education:* Wheaton College, Wheaton, Ill., B.A., 1966. *Religion:* Christian. *Home:* 810 Reba Place, Evanston, Ill. 60202.

CAREER: Pioneer Girls, Inc., Wheaton, Ill., staff writer and assistant editor of *Trails,* 1963-69; free-lance writer, 1969-73, 1978—. Member of board of directors of Ridgeville Neighborhood Association, 1973-75. *Awards, honors:* First place award from *Scholastic,* 1962, for story, "The Sacrifice."

WRITINGS: (With husband, David Jackson) *Living Together in a World Falling Apart: A Handbook on Christian Community,* Creation House, 1973.

Plays; all published by David C. Cook: "The Babe Gets Up From the Manger," (four-scene); "The Life of Solomon," (two-act); "Stranger in the Church," (dramatization of work by Carol Amen); "Don't Keep the Faith."

Author of church school curriculum material for David Cook. Contributor to magazines and newspapers, including *Eternity, Redbook, Campus Life,* and *Reflection.* Assistant editor of *Perspective;* contributing editor of *Other Side,* 1968-72.

WORK IN PROGRESS: Magazine writing.

SIDELIGHTS: Neta Jackson writes: "A lot of my motivation grows out of my Christian faith, and my continuing desire to learn how to apply the 'demands of Christ' to every area of life, large or small, global or personal. A lot of my writings are actually a sharing of my personal struggles, experiences, and growth.

"In the last ten years, a major focus for my husband and me has been a desire for a radical (meaning total) Christian life. For us this has meant discovering Christian church-community. The church, instead of being a building, is a living body of believers who share their everyday lives together in a total way, to give support to daily faithful discipleship. Our book grew out of this search.

"We made a personal decision to become part of Reba Place Fellowship, a Christian church-community in Evanston, Ill. Three hundred of us live close together within a four-block area for encouragement and support, sharing financially, committed to simple living, building one another up in the Christian faith. Our family of four lives is in an extended-family household of twelve persons. I am household manager and am also writing part-time. Our life together provides a wealth of experience in interpersonal relationships—and that is what I'm writing about now (hopefully for a general audience, not just those in the community)."

* * *

JACOBS, Jerome L. 1931-

PERSONAL: Born April 18, 1931, in New York, N.Y.; son of Sidney (a broker) and Estelle (Hyman) Jacobs; married Francine Kaufman (a writer), June 10, 1956; children: Laurie Gail, Larry Alan. *Education:* Queens College (now of the City University of New York), B.S., 1952; Cornell University, M.D., 1956. *Residence:* Mt. Kisco, N.Y.

CAREER: Clinical director of Division of Psychiatry at Grasslands Hospital; director of Division of Psychiatry at Northern Westchester Hospital. Diplomate of American Board of Psychiatry and Neurology. *Military service:* U.S. Army, neuropsychiatrist, 1958-60; became captain. *Member:* American Medical Association, American Psychiatric Association (fellow), American Association for the Advancement of Science.

WRITINGS: Interplay: A Psychiatrist Explains What He Does (and Does Not Do) and How and Why, McGraw, 1979; *Africa's Flamingo Lake* (photographs), Morrow, 1979.

AVOCATIONAL INTERESTS: Travel, photography, hiking, fishing, ski-touring.

* * *

JACOBS, Ruth Harriet 1924-
(Ruth Miller)

PERSONAL: Born November 15, 1924, in Boston, Mass.; daughter of Samuel J. and Jane (Gordon) Miller; married Neal Jacobs, July 18, 1948 (divorced); children: Eliha, Edith Jane, Aaron Joel (deceased). *Education:* Boston University, B.S., 1964, postdoctoral study, 1977-78; Brandeis University, M.A., 1966, Ph.D., 1969. *Religion:* Jewish. *Home:* 75 Highledge Ave., Wellesley, Mass. 02181. *Office:* Department of Sociology, Boston University, 100 Cummington St., Boston, Mass. 02215.

CAREER: Boston Herald-Traveler, Boston, Mass., reporter, 1943-49; Boston University, Boston, Mass., assistant professor, 1969-74, associate professor of sociology, 1974—. Consultant in gerontology. *Member:* American Sociological Association, Society for the Study of Social Problems, Gerontological Society, Clinical Sociology Association, Humanistic Sociology Association, Sociologists for Women in Society, Eastern Sociological Society, Massachusetts Sociological Association (vice-president, 1977-78), Boston Society for Gerontological Psychiatry. *Awards, honors:* American Association of University Women fellowship, 1972; grants from National Institute of Mental Health, 1972, 1975, and National Science Foundation, 1977.

WRITINGS: Life After Youth: Female, Forty, What Next?, Beacon Press, 1979; (with Barbara Vinick) *Re-Engagement in Later Life: Re-Employment and Re-Marriage,* Greylock, 1979. Contributor of about thirty articles to journals in sociology, anthropology, philosophy, psychology, history, and education. Also contributor of articles and poems under name Ruth Miller.

WORK IN PROGRESS: Ten Kinds of Women's Lives (poems), publication expected in 1980; a book on problems in higher education, for Beacon Press.

SIDELIGHTS: Ruth Jacobs writes: "Besides being a sociologist and poet, I am interested in a variety of other things. In 1977-78 I attended medical school to add to my gerontological expertise. I am especially interested in what happens to women when they age, and in *Life After Youth* I present a typology of role available for today's older women. I also utilize this typology in my forthcoming book of poetry, *Ten Kinds of Women's Lives.*

"What I think I am dealing with in all my work is the concept of expendability—that at various points in history or in various places, certain people are considered uneeded and allowed to be expendable in the name of the economic or national good, or just through inadvertence or callousness. I have been more fortunate than many women in re-engaging life after my child-rearing days were over. But I have a great deal of empathy and sympathy for women who are without meaningful roles in later life. *Life After Youth* is an attempt to help such women and the men in their lives, just as my writing on war or adolescence is aimed at helping other kinds of people. My writing stems from my social concern."

BIOGRAPHICAL/CRITICAL SOURCES: Change, July, 1977; *New Directions for Women,* summer, 1979.

* * *

JACOBS, T.C.H.
See PENDOWER, Jacques

* * *

JACOBSOHN, Gary J. 1946-

PERSONAL: Born March 29, 1946, in New York, N.Y.; son of Hans and Hilda (Loewenstein) Jacobsohn; married Janice Cook (an attorney), June 11, 1972; children: Vanessa Cook. *Education:* City College of the City University of New York, B.A., 1967; Cornell University, Ph.D., 1971. *Home address:* Shaffer Rd., Williamstown, Mass. 01267. *Office:* Department of Political Science, Williams College, Williamstown, Mass. 01267.

CAREER: Williams College, Williamstown, Mass., staff member in department of political science, 1971—, currently professor. *Member:* American Political Science Association. *Awards, honors:* National Endowment for the Humanities grant, 1979.

WRITINGS: Pragmatism, Statesmanship, and the Supreme Court, Cornell University Press, 1978. Contributor to political science and law journals.

WORK IN PROGRESS: Science and Constitutional Adjudication.

* * *

JACOBSON, Robert 1940-

PERSONAL: Born July 28, 1940, in Racine, Wis.; son of Joseph and Frances (Barr) Jacobson. *Education:* University of Wisconsin (now University of Wisconsin—Madison), B.A., 1962; graduate study at Columbia University, 1962-63. *Home:* 100 Hudson St., New York, N.Y. 10003. *Office: Opera News/Ballet News,* 1865 Broadway, New York, N.Y. 10023.

CAREER: Saturday Review, New York City, managing editor of Lincoln Center programs, 1965-73; *Opera News/Ballet News,* New York City, editor of *Opera News,* 1973-79, and *Ballet News,* 1979—. Music and dance critic for *Cue,* 1973-77.

WRITINGS: Reverberations: Interviews With the World's Leading Musicians, Morrow, 1974. Author of script for New York Philharmonic "Young People's Concert," aired by CBS-TV, 1978. Contributor to *New York Times Almanac.* Contributor to magazines and newspapers, including *High Fidelity, Dance,* and *Playbill.* Contributing editor to *After Dark,* 1970—, and *L'Officiel,* 1977—.

SIDELIGHTS: Jacobson prepared a sixteen-volume set of record albums of great symphonic music, for Funk.

He wrote: "I began writing at University of Wisconsin for the *Daily Cardinal,* having no journalism background, but an interest in the arts and a desire to write. Growing up not far from Chicago, I read the *Chicago Tribune* daily and was inspired by the writing and travels of its critic, Claudia Cassidy. I was also a regular reader of *Saturday Review* and its music critic, Irving Kolodin, whom I later had the pleasure of working for. The writers on the arts I have most admired have tried to uphold standards and keep the arts flourishing at the same time, and this is my goal as well. I travel a great deal to Europe and feel that submersing myself in various cultures helps my writing and understanding of the arts."

* * *

JACOBY, Neil H(erman) 1909-1979

OBITUARY NOTICE—See index for *CA* sketch: Born September 19, 1909, in Dundurn, Saskatchewan, Canada; died May 31, 1979, in Los Angeles, Calif. Economist, educator, administrator, executive, and author. Jacoby, who founded the University of California, Los Angeles, Graduate School of Management in 1948, was Arm and Hammer Professor Emeritus of Business Economics and Policy at the time of his death. He also served on the Council of Economic Advisers to President Eisenhower for two years, and acted as consultant to numerous firms, including the RAND Corp., the U.S. Treasury Department, and General Motors Corp. Jacoby wrote more than ten books on economics, including *Multinational Oil: A Study in Industrial Design* and *The Business-Government Relationship: A Reassessment.* Obituaries and other sources: *American Men and Women of Science: The Social and Behavioral Sciences,* 12th edition, Bowker, 1973; *Who's Who in Consulting,* 2nd edition, Gale, 1973; *New York Times,* June 1, 1979; *AB Bookman's Weekly,* August 6, 1979.

* * *

JACQUENEY, Theodore 1943(?)-1979

OBITUARY NOTICE: Born c. 1943 in New York, N.Y.; died October 31, 1979, in West New York, N.J. Editor and author. Jacqueney worked for the Agency for International Development as an adviser in Vietnam before resigning in 1971 to protest U.S. support of South Vietnamese President Thieu. After free-lancing for several years, he joined New Jersey's *Elizabeth Daily Journal.* Jacqueney had been associate editor of *Worldview* magazine since 1975. Obituaries and other sources: *New York Times,* November 3, 1979; *Washington Post,* November 3, 1979.

* * *

JAFFE, Dennis T(heodore) 1946-

PERSONAL: Born September 20, 1946, in New York, N.Y.; son of Sidney (a teacher) and Rhoda (a teacher; maiden name, Oltarsh) Jaffe; married Yvonne Durchfort (a family therapist), June 14, 1976; children: Oren, Kai. *Education:* Yale University, B.A., 1967, M.A., 1969, Ph.D., 1974. *Religion:* Jewish. *Home:* 4150 Rhodes Ave., Studio City, Calif. 91604. *Agent:* Mitchell J. Hamilburg Agency, 292 South La Cienega Blvd., Suite 212, Beverly Hills, Calif. 90211. *Office:* 1314 Westwood Blvd., Suite 107, Los Angeles, Calif. 90024.

CAREER: University of Southern California, Los Angeles, adjunct assistant professor of sociology and psychology, 1975-77; Learning for Health, Los Angeles, Calif., director of psychosomatic medicine clinic, 1977—. Associate in psychiatry, School of Medicine, University of California, Los Angeles, 1975—. Member of board of directors of Center for Integral Medicine. *Member:* American Psychological Association, Association for Humanistic Psychology.

WRITINGS: (With Ted Clark) *Worlds Apart: Young People and Drug Programs,* Vintage, 1974; (with Harold Bloomfield, Michael Cain, and Robert Kory) *TM: Discovering Inner Energy and Overcoming Stress,* Delacorte, 1975; (editor) *In Search of a Therapy,* Harper, 1975; (with Clark) *Number Nine: Autobiography of an Alternate Counseling Service,* Harper, 1976; (with Lawrence Allman) *Abnormal Psychology in the Life Cycle,* Harper, 1978; *Healing From Within,* Knopf, 1979; (editor with James S. Gordon and David Bresler) *Body, Mind, and Health: Toward an Integral Medicine* (monograph), National Institute of Mental Health, 1979.

WORK IN PROGRESS: A personal health self-help workbook; a book on families as living systems in which personal development takes place; several learning packages for health professionals on family therapy psychology, self-help, and health care, publication by UCLA Center for Integral Medicine.

SIDELIGHTS: "I became a writer almost by accident," Jaffe told *CA.* "In graduate school I became involved in a number of new mental health experiments, and I traveled to visit some around the world. I kept a journal, which I continued when I began my own street clinic in New Haven, Connecticut. I wrote some of my experiences and sent them to journals and magazines, without thinking, and they were published. Exciting events were set in motion, as I found that people contacted me and visited, sharing their experiences. I began to feel that the best service I could offer as a mental health practitioner was to help people, especially the recipients of services, to describe their needs and feelings to the public and professionals. I feel that such descriptions are an extension of my role as a service professional, therapist, and professor.

"My work has been concerned in many ways with self-help, with individual attempts to help one another. I have found that writing is a form of direct service. In my work I have tried to steer clear of promising incredible results, and of hucksterism, and to provide instead clear, simple, and useful accounts of self-help methods and projects. I have also worked with UCLA to create some self-learning packages for health professionals.

"I feel that therapists have increasingly chosen to be social prophets, guides, and public helpers, and that there is a need for a code of ethics, individual restraint, and professionalism in that area. My activity as a writer is to create a bridge between writing and other forms of professional activities.

"My purpose in writing is always to educate, and to serve the public. I write when I feel an issue is important, and I address my writing to a specific public, whether in a book, professional journal or popular magazine. I feel that all audiences can benefit from clear psychological information, and in the future I expect that more and more therapists will pursue this direction."

* * *

JAMES, Trevor
See CONSTABLE, Trevor James

* * *

JAMISON, A(lbert) Leland 1911-

PERSONAL: Born August 20, 1911, in Fulton, Mo.; son of Wayland H. (an electrician) and Pauline (Muir) Jamison; married Ruth Baker (a teacher), June 23, 1943; children: Ann Laura, Christopher W. *Education:* Westminster College, Fulton, Mo., A.B., 1933; Louisville Presbyterian Seminary, M.Div., 1936; University of Chicago, Ph.D., 1941. *Politics:* Independent. *Religion:* Presbyterian. *Home:* 826 Westcott, Syracuse, N.Y. 13210.

CAREER: Princeton University, Princeton, N.J., instructor, 1941-42, 1946-48, assistant professor of religion, 1948-54; Macalester College, St. Paul, Minn., professor of religion and head of department, 1954-57; Princeton University, research associate in religion, 1957-58; Macalester College, professor of religion and head of department, 1958-59; Syracuse University, Syracuse, N.Y., professor of religion and head of department, 1959-64, Willard Ives Professor of the English Bible, 1964-77, professor emeritus, 1977—. Jonathan Dickenson Bicentennial Preceptor at Princeton University. *Military service:* U.S. Army, chaplain, 1942-46; served in Iwo Jima; became major. *Member:* American Academy of Religion, American Jewish Historical Society, American Association of University Professors, Society for Values in Higher Education, Society of Biblical Literature.

WRITINGS: Light for the Gentiles: Paul and the Growing Church, Westminster, 1961; (editor with James Ward Smith) *The Shaping of American Religion,* Princeton University Press, 1961; (editor with Smith) *Religious Perspectives in American Culture,* Princeton University Press, 1961; (editor with Smith) *Religion in American Life,* Princeton University Press, 1961; (editor with Smith and N. R. Burr) *A Critical Bibliography of Religion in America,* Princeton University Press, 1961; (editor and author of introduction) *Tradition and Change in Jewish Experience,* Department of Religion, Syracuse University, 1978.

WORK IN PROGRESS: Judaism and Christian Origins.

SIDELIGHTS: Jamison comments: "My major field has been Biblical history and thought, with a secondary interest in Western religious history, particularly in America.

"The books on religion in American life grew from several seminars conducted by Professor J. W. Smith and me at Princeton University. *Tradition and Change* is a collection of lectures delivered by various scholars in an annual series of Judaic studies that I have directed since 1963."

Jamison's "travels include Great Britain, Italy, Greece, and the Near East." He has "modest competence in Latin, Greek, Hebrew, French, and German."

* * *

JANE, Nancy 1946-

PERSONAL: Born June 15, 1946, in Attleboro, Mass.; daughter of Robert A. and Margaret (a high school guidance counselor; maiden name, Ledbetter) Schultheiss; married Charles Morin (a physician), July 18, 1968 (divorced, 1975). *Education:* Lake Erie College, B.A. (magna cum laude), 1968; University of Massachusetts, B.S., 1978. *Politics:* "Avoided as much as possible." *Religion:* "Loyalty to the Earth." *Residence:* Jelm, Wyo. 82063.

CAREER: Writer. Child welfare worker in Los Angeles, Calif., 1968-71; St. Joseph's Hospital, Providence, R.I., child welfare worker, 1973-75; also worked for U.S. Forest Service in Minnesota, summer, 1977, and in Wyoming, summer, 1978, and as a substitute teacher and carpenter. *Member:* Laramie Cross-Country Ski Club.

WRITINGS: Bicycle Touring in the Pioneer Valley, University of Massachusetts Press, 1978.

WORK IN PROGRESS: Wildflowers of the Rocky Mountain Tundra; Outdoor Recreational Guide to the Medicine Bow National Forest.

SIDELIGHTS: Nancy Jane writes: "For some years, most intensively since I left behind marriage and a few other conventions, I have been on a quest, a search for self and homeland, both inextricably bound together and focused on environment, natural and unspoiled. I am outdoors and active as much as possible, pondering and exploring the wilderness and the wonders of the earth. I hope to share what I experience with others through writing."

AVOCATIONAL INTERESTS: Hiking, backpacking, cross-country skiing.

* * *

JANIK, Carolyn 1940-

PERSONAL: Born August 29, 1940, in New Britain, Conn.; daughter of Leon V. (a grocer) and Genevieve (a bookkeeper; maiden name, Pustelnik) Lech; married Joseph J. Janik (an electrical engineer), August 4, 1962; children: David, Laura, William. *Education:* Mount Holyoke College, A.B., 1962; Southern Connecticut State College, M.S., 1972. *Religion:* Roman Catholic. *Home and office:* 29 Old Coach Rd., Basking Ridge, N.J. 07920. *Agent:* Richard A. Balkin, Balkin Agency, 403 West 115th St., New York, N.Y. 10025.

CAREER: High school English teacher in Glastonbury, Conn., 1962-63; Allied Brokers, Branford, Conn., real estate agent, 1968-70; John P. Hurley, Realtor, Morris Plains, N.J., real estate agent, 1973—.

WRITINGS: The House Hunt Game, Macmillan, 1979; *Selling Your Home,* Macmillan, 1980.

WORK IN PROGRESS: Alexander Bear Sells His House, for pre-school age children, publication expected in 1981; a novel set in the suburban real estate world.

SIDELIGHTS: "Although still licensed as a real estate agent, I am no longer working actively in the field," Carolyn Janik told *CA*. "I am currently devoting full time to my novel. I also love to cook and fantasize about writing biographical novels of the world's greatest gourmets. I try always to write in a conversational, readable style, for I feel every book is a kind of conversation with the author (and always autobiographical)." *Avocational interests:* Music, playing piano, writing poetry, reading.

* * *

JAROCH, F(rancis) A(nthony) Randy 1947-
(Randy Jaroch)

PERSONAL: Surname is pronounced *Yar*-row; born December 24, 1947, in Chicago, Ill.; son of Stanley John (in sales) and Jayne Grace (a legal proofreader; maiden name, Wakely) Jaroch; married Jeanne D. Olson (a writer), January

2, 1971; children: Todd Christian, Noelle Christina. *Education:* Attended Bellevue College, 1968-70. *Home:* 531 South 52nd St., Omaha, Neb. 68106. *Office: Omaha World-Herald,* World-Herald Sq., Omaha, Neb. 68102.

CAREER: KLNG-Radio, Omaha, Neb., announcer and copywriter, 1970-71; *Omaha World-Herald,* Omaha, poetry editor and author of column, "Poetry Selected by Randy Jaroch," 1971—. Copywriter for Bozell & Jacobs, Inc., 1971-77. *Military service:* U.S. Air Force, 1966-70; became sergeant. *Member:* Joslyn Art Museum, Ak-Sar-Ben.

WRITINGS: The Ripening (poems), St. Mary's College Press, 1973.

Children's books; all with brothers, Timothy and Chipp Jaroch: *The Tornado,* Childrens Press, 1977; *The Ghost of Gleason Mansion,* Childrens Press, 1978; *Washout at Liberty Valley,* Childrens Press, 1978; *Rescue at Northbend Pass,* Childrens Press, 1979. Lyricist for local, regional, and national advertisers.

SIDELIGHTS: Jaroch comments: "'The Adventures of the Sneeky Sneekers' series is based on an actual club my brothers and I formed and enjoyed as children. Today, as adults, we are enjoying the way countless children are being entertained and influenced by our stories, each of which is designed, written, and illustrated to depict the closeness and excitement we experienced as youngsters growing up in Mundelein, Ill., with a heaping helping of fantasy added."

* * *

JAROCH, Randy
See JAROCH, F(rancis) A(nthony) Randy

* * *

JEANS, Marylu Terral 1914-

PERSONAL: Born January 15, 1914, in Hobart, Okla.; daughter of Thomas Ernest (in communications) and Anna Lee (Kennedy) Terral; married George Stephen Estabrook, June 8, 1934 (divorced, 1939); married Aubert N. Jeans, March 25, 1941; children: (first marriage) Richard Terral, (second marriage) Lawrence Neal. *Education:* Attended junior college in Long Beach, Calif. *Home:* 1731 Old Oregon Trail, Redding, Calif. 96001.

CAREER: Co-owner of store and post office in Ruth, Calif., 1941; writer, 1960—. *Member:* American Society of Composers, Authors, and Publishers, California Federation of Chaparral Poets. *Awards, honors:* First prize in Washington State Poetry Contest, 1962, for "The Poem Writes Itself"; grand prize from Ina Coolbrith Circle annual contest, 1973, for poem, "It Is Not Enough"; first prizes from Contra Costa Fair, 1976, for poem, "Tapestry," and 1976, for poem, "Signatures"; grand prize from California Federation of Chaparral Poets, 1979, for "High Country."

WRITINGS: Statue in the Stone (poems), Golden Quill, 1966; *Moonset* (poems), Golden Quill, 1971.

Work represented in anthologies, including *Gift of a Golden String,* edited by Benton, 1963; *A Door Ajar,* edited by Benton, 1965; *Clover Collection of Verse,* 1976.

Co-author of song lyrics, including "Driftsmoke," Southern Music, 1953; "A Stranger in My Arms," Chapell, 1957; "There Was No Snow in Bethlehem," Carmit, 1975. Contributor of articles and poems to magazines and newspapers, including *Good Housekeeping, Saturday Evening Post, Ladies' Home Journal, Writer's Digest,* and *Modern Maturity.*

WORK IN PROGRESS: The End of the Dream, a romantic novel; song lyrics for Christmas musical, "A World Without Children," music by Carmine Coppola, play by Jacquelyn Terral Andrews; a book of poetry, *A Seller of Purple.*

SIDELIGHTS: Marylu Jeans writes: "My work has opened wonderful doors for me, and I have enjoyed the public speaking it has brought about, to writers' groups, teachers, business groups, and classes.

"I believe every writer should have something definite to say, should learn the tools of the trade, and should say what he has to say as clearly and concisely as possible. I am unalterably opposed to pornography, sloppy writing, and 'phony' affectations. I firmly believe that our children are being raised with a 'taste for garbage' and I think it is time for all creative people to *think* about *self*-censorship—and *do* something about it.

"I write much free verse, but still prefer the traditional forms, especially the sonnet.

"I am not a *poet.* I write magazine verse for ordinary people like myself and though I am unlikely to survive in history, my poetry will (hopefully) survive in a few scrapbooks."

* * *

JELLINEK, George 1919-

PERSONAL: Born December 22, 1919, in Budapest, Hungary; son of Daniel (a restaurateur) and Jolan Jellinek; married Hedy D. (an economist and editor), July, 1942; children: Nancy Berezin. *Education:* Attended Pazmany Peter Tudomanyegyetem, 1938, and Lafayette College, 1943. *Home:* 565 Broadway, Hastings-on-Hudson, N.Y. 10706. *Office:* WQXR-Radio, 229 West 43rd St., New York, N.Y. 10036.

CAREER: SESAC, Inc., New York City, director of program services, 1955-64; Muzak, Inc., New York City, recording director, 1964-68; WQXR-Radio, New York City, music director, 1968—. Assistant adjunct professor at New York University, 1976—. Advisor to musical organizations. *Military service:* U.S. Army, 1942-46; became first lieutenant. *Member:* American Society of Composers, Authors, and Publishers, American Federation of Television and Radio Artists, Friends of Mozart, Inc. (member of board of directors). *Awards, honors:* Ohio State Award, 1978, for excellence in broadcasting; Major Armstrong Award from Columbia University, 1979; Oral Communications Award from Long Island University, 1979.

WRITINGS: Callas: Portrait of a Prima Donna, Ziff-Davis, 1960.

Operas; librettos: (Music by Eugene Zador) "The Magic Chair" (one-act), first produced in Baton Rouge, La., at Louisiana State University, May 14, 1966; (music by Zador) "The Scarlet Mill" (two-act), first produced in New York City at Brooklyn College Opera Theatre, October 26, 1968.

Contributing editor of *Stereo Review,* 1958—. Regular contributor to *Saturday Review,* 1953—, and *Opera News,* 1956—.

SIDELIGHTS: Jellinek told *CA:* "I studied the violin in early childhood, which explains my gravitational pull toward music. Music is my lifelong hobby and principal field of interest. Extensive reading motivated my interest in writing. I traveled extensively and speak several languages (German, Spanish, Italian, Hungarian). I am maintaining my proficiency by reading books and periodicals in all these languages. History and literature are my other specialties. I am an unscientific person, and seem to grow less and less interested in science as I grow older."

BIOGRAPHICAL/CRITICAL SOURCES: Cue, September 6, 1975; *Stereo Review,* January, 1976; *Opera News,* August, 1979.

* * *

JEMIE, Onwuchekwa 1940-

PERSONAL: Surname is pronounced Jay-me-yeh; born June 3, 1940, in Item, Imo, Nigeria; son of Jemie (a farmer) and Arunma (a farmer; maiden name, Ibekwe) Okereke; married Patricia Garland (a school teacher), June 13, 1964; children: Ada (daughter), Uchendu (son). *Education:* Columbia University, B.A., 1963, Ph.D., 1972; Harvard University, M.A., 1964. *Home:* Ebiabia Amokwe Item, Via Uzuakoli, Imo State, Nigeria. *Office:* Department of Mass Communication, Institute of Management and Technology, Enugu, Nigeria.

CAREER: Purdue University, Fort Wayne, Ind., instructor in English, 1964-66; Manhattan Community College of the City University of New York, New York, N.Y., 1967-73, began as instructor, became assistant professor, then associate professor of English and black studies; University of Minnesota, Minneapolis, associate professor of English and Afro-American studies, 1973-77; Institute of Management and Technology, Enugu, Nigeria, reader in mass communication and head of department, 1977—. Part-time lecturer at Columbia University, 1970-73, and Swarthmore College, 1972-73. *Awards, honors:* Danforth fellowship, 1963-64.

WRITINGS: Biafra: Requiem for the Dead in War, Papua Pocket Poets, 1970; *Voyage and Other Poems,* Pan-African Pocket Poets, 1971; *Langston Hughes: An Introduction to the Poetry,* Columbia University Press, 1976; (with Chinweizu and I. Madubuike) *Toward the Decolonization of African Literature,* Volume I: *African Fiction and Poetry and Their Critics,* Volume II: *An Anthology of Pan-African Literature,* Fourth Dimension Publishers, 1980.

WORK IN PROGRESS: The Signifying Monkey: A Collection of Afro-American Oral Literature, "toasts, jokes, boasts, threats, etc." gathered in New York City and Philadelphia, 1968-73; *Igbo Oral Poetry,* a bilingual collection.

SIDELIGHTS: Jemie writes: "My abiding interest is in the orature (oral literature), especially the poetry, of the world's peoples, particularly African peoples. My goal is to collect and make available the rich harvest of oral texts; to urge African writers to root themselves in those traditions, and point out to them examples of those in Africa and elsewhere who did; and to take inspiration from those traditions for my own writing."

* * *

JENKINS, Peter 1951-

PERSONAL: Born July 8, 1951, in Greenwich, Conn.; son of Frederick D. (an industrialist) and Mary (a nurse; maiden name, Robie) Jenkins; married second wife, Barbara Pennell (a writer), February 7, 1976. *Education:* State University of New York College of Ceramics, Alfred University, B.F.A., 1973. *Politics:* "Republican (usually), Independent." *Religion:* Christian (evangelical). *Home and office:* Gawain Apartments #23, 4452 Gawain Dr., New Orleans, La., 70127. *Agent:* Joan Stewart, William Morris Agency, New York, N.Y. 10019.

CAREER: Writer; free-lance photographer, 1973—. Walked across America, 1973-79.

WRITINGS: A Walk Across America, Morrow, 1979; *A Walk Across America, Part 2,* Morrow, 1980. Contributor of articles and photographs to *National Geographic.*

SIDELIGHTS: Jenkins told *CA:* "I never wanted to be a writer. Never wanted to be on the *New York Times* Best Seller List, etc. I just wanted to take a walk across America. I set out right out of college to see if America was as bad as I really thought it was. After walking 4,751 miles and living and working with the real people of this country I had to write about them. They inspired me and changed my outlook totally. That's my motivation."

Jenkins went through forty pairs of shoes and three tents and sleeping bags on the five-year odyssey. He left with little money and he and his wife Barbara (who joined him after they were married in 1976) stopped along the way to do odd jobs. People they met were often hospitable—Jenkins calls them "my American heroes"—and many flew to Oregon to join the couple as they walked the last few miles to the Pacific Ocean.

The first part of *A Walk Across America* chronicles Jenkin's trek from his college in New York to New Orleans; the second part covers the rest of the trip. Joyce Maynard found that part one contained "some very graceful writing." She concluded, "Sadly, though, this popular best-seller "does not convey the richness Mr. Jenkins must have experienced. Like those postcards that tell us only 'Having a wonderful time, wish you were here,' the book is mostly written in a kind of shorthand, full of generalities and exclamation points."

BIOGRAPHICAL/CRITICAL SOURCES: National Geographic, April, 1977, August, 1979; *Campus Life,* December, 1977, January, 1978; *New York Times Book Review,* February 25, 1979, April 8, 1979; *People,* March 19, 1979; *Moody Monthly,* April 19, 1979.

* * *

JENNER, Philip Norman 1921-

PERSONAL: Born October 16, 1921, in Seattle, Wash.; son of Charles Herbert and Ellen Marie (Stone) Jenner; married Miyo Marie Inouye (a registered nurse), September 6, 1947; children: Robert Kazuo, Barbara Tamako (Mrs. Albert J. Kramer). *Education:* Attended Whitman College, 1939-40; University of Washington, Seattle, B.A. (magna cum laude), 1946; University of Hawaii, Ph.D., 1969; also studied at University of Michigan, 1944-45, and University of Chicago, 1947-49. *Home:* 149 Laimi Rd., Honolulu, Hawaii 96817. *Office:* Department of Indo-Pacific Languages, University of Hawaii, 2540 Maile Way, Honolulu, Hawaii 96822.

CAREER: U.S. Army, civilian intelligence staff officer with Supreme Commander Allied Powers in Tokyo, Japan, 1949-58, and in Honolulu, Hawaii, 1958-64; University of Hawaii, Honolulu, instructor, 1964-69, assistant professor, 1969-74, associate professor of Cambodian and Southeast Asian literatures, 1974—. *Member:* Societe Asiatique, Phi Beta Kappa.

WRITINGS: A Preliminary Bibliography of Southeast Asian Literatures in Translation, University Press of Hawaii, 1973; (editor with Laurence C. Thompson and Stanley Starosta) *Austroasiatic Studies,* two volumes, University Press of Hawaii, 1976. Contributor of numerous papers on Mon-Khmer linguistics to various journals. Editor and director of "Mon-Khmer Studies," 1976—.

WORK IN PROGRESS: A Lexicon of Khmer Morphology; An Old Khmer Chrestomathy, nine volumes, publication of first three volumes expected by 1981; *An Old Khmer Dictionary.*

SIDELIGHTS: Jenner told *CA:* "My professional goals are to contribute to the development of Mon-Khmer and Austroasiatic linguistics, to establish Khmer studies as a minor but accepted field of academic endeavor, to show the relevance of Mon-Khmer linguistics and Khmer studies to world culture, and to help train a new generation of specialists."

* * *

JENNINGS, Dean Southern 1905-1969

OBITUARY NOTICE: Born June 30, 1905, in Rochester, N.Y.; died October 1, 1969. Author of *The Man Who Killed Hitler* and *We Only Kill Each Other.* Jennings worked as sports reporter for both the *San Francisco Herald* and the *San Francisco Examiner.* From 1951 to 1953, he was a columnist for the *San Francisco Chronicle.* Jennings co-wrote Jack L. Warner's memoirs, *My First 100 Years in Hollywood.* Obituaries and other sources: *American Authors and Books: 1640 to the Present Day,* 3rd revised edition, Crown, 1972; *Who Was Who in America,* 5th edition, Marquis, 1973.

* * *

JENS, Walter 1923-

PERSONAL: Born March 8, 1923, in Hamburg, Germany (now West Germany); son of Walter and Anna (Martens) Jens; married Inge Puttfarcken, February 10, 1951; children: Tilman, Christoph. *Education:* University of Hamburg, D.Phil., 1944; University of Freiburg, Ph.D., 1944. *Religion:* Evangelical Lutheran. *Home:* 5 Sonnenstrasse, Tuebingen, West Germany. *Office:* Neuphilologicum, Wilhelmstrasse 74, Tuebingen, West Germany.

CAREER: University of Tuebingen, Tuebingen, West Germany, docent, 1950-56, professor of classics and rhetoric, 1956—, head of Institute of Rhetoric, 1968—. *Member:* International P.E.N. (president of German section, 1970), German Academy of Language and Poetry, Berlin Academy of Art. *Awards, honors:* German-Swedish Culture Prize from City of Stockholm, Sweden, 1964; Lessing Prize from Hansestadt Hamburg, 1968; Ph.D. from University of Stockholm, 1969.

WRITINGS: In English: *Der Blinde,* 1951, Holt, 1959, translation by Michael Bullock published as *The Blind Man,* Macmillan, 1953 (also see below).

Other: *Vergessene Gesichter* (novel), Rowohlt, 1952 (also see below); *Der Mann der nicht alt werden wollte,* Rowohlt, 1955, revised edition, 1963; *Die Stichomythie in der fruehen griechischen Tragoedie,* C. H. Beck, 1955; *Hofmannsthal und die Griechen,* M. Niemeyer, 1955; *Das Testament des Odysseus,* G. Neske, 1957, 4th edition, 1968; *Statt einer Literaturgeschichte,* G. Neske, 1957, 6th edition, 1970; *Die Goetter sind sterblich,* G. Neske, 1959, revised edition, 1971.

(Editor) Eugen Gottlob Winkler, *Ausgewaehlt und eingeleitet,* Fischer-Buecherei, 1960; (editor) Thomas Mann, *Buddenbrooks,* Fischer-Buecherei, 1960; *Deutsche Literatur der Gegenwart: Themen, Stile, Tendenzen,* R. Piper, 1961, 4th edition, 1962; *Zueigningen: Elf literarische Portraets,* R. Piper, 1962; *Zueigningen: Zwoelf literarische Portraets,* R. Piper, 1962; *Herr Meister: Dialog ueber einen Roman,* R. Piper, 1963; (editor) Wolfdietrich Schnurre, *Kassiber,* Suhrkamp, 1964; (editor) *Hans Mayer zum 60. Geburtstag,* Rowohlt, 1967; *Der Besuch des Fremden* [and] *Vergessene Gesichter,* (contains "Der Besuch des Fremden," a radio play, and "Vergessene Gesichter," a play), edited by A. A. Wolf, St. Martin's, 1967; *Nein: Die Welt der Angeklagten* (novel), R. Piper, 1968; (editor) *Ilias und Odyssee,* O. Maier, 4th edition, 1968; *Inter Nationes,* 1968; *Von deutscher Rede,* R. Piper, 1969; *Die Verschwoerung* (play, aired on television by Fernsehstudios des Bayerischen Rundfunks, July, 1969), Norstar, 1969 (also see below).

(Editor) *Die Bauformen der griechischen Tragoedie,* W. Fink, 1971; *Am Anfang der Stall, am Ende der Galgen: Jesus von Nazareth,* Kreuz Verlag, 1972; (editor) *Der barmherzige Samariter,* Kreuz Verlag, 1973; *Fernsehen: Themen und Tabus—Momos, 1963-1973,* R. Piper, 1973; *Die Verschwoerung* [and] *Der toedliche Schlag: Zwei Fernsehspiele,* R. Piper, 1974; *Der Fall Judas,* Kreuz Verlag, 1975; *Republikanische Reden,* Kindler, 1976; *Vergessene Gesichter* [and] *Der Blinde,* R. Piper, 1976; *Eine deutsche Universitaet,* Kindler, 1977; *Um nichts als die Wahrheit,* R. Piper, 1978; *Assoziationen,* Radius-Verlag, 1978. Also author of *Zur Sudike,* 1978. Author of "Momos," a column in *Der Zeit,* 1964—.

WORK IN PROGRESS: A television play; translating the New Testament.

BIOGRAPHICAL/CRITICAL SOURCES: *Walter Jens: Eine Einfuehrung,* Piper, 1965; Herbert Kraft, *Das literarische Werk von Walter Jens,* Rotsch, 1974.

* * *

JESSEL, George (Albert) 1898-

PERSONAL: Born April 3, 1898, in New York, N.Y.; son of Joseph Aaron (a playwright) and Charlotte (Schwartz) Jessel; married Florence Courtney, 1919 (divorced, 1932); married Norma Talmadge (an actress), 1934 (divorced, 1939); married Katherine Lorraine Gourley (actress under pseudonym Lois Andrews), 1939 (divorced, 1941); children: Jerilynn. *Religion:* Jewish. *Address:* 10000 Pico Blvd., Los Angeles, Calif.

CAREER: Entertainer on vaudeville, Broadway, radio, motion pictures, and television; producer, songwriter, and writer. Worked in numerous vaudeville shows, including "The Imperial Trio," c. 1908, "Gus Edwards' School Boys and Girls," 1908-14, "Gaities," 1919, "The Troubles of 1920," 1920; actor in Broadway productions, including "The Jazz Singer," 1925, "The War Song," 1928, "Sweet and Low," 1930, "Show Time," 1942, and "Red, White, and Blue," 1950; appeared in radio productions, including "The Voice of Columbia Show," 1934, "Jessel's Jamboree," 1938-39, and "The George Jessel Show," 1958; actor in motion pictures, including "Widow at the Races," 1911, "Ginzberg the Great," 1928, "George Jessel and the Russian Choir," 1931, and "Can Heironymus Merkin Ever Forget Mercy Humppe and Find True Happiness?," 1969; appeared in television shows, including "Variety Show," 1953, and "George Jessel's Show Business," 1958. Producer of stage productions, including "The Troubles of 1920," 1920, "George Jessel's Troubles," 1922, and "Little Old New York," 1939-40, and motion pictures, including "The Broadway Kid," 1937, "The Dolly Sisters," 1945, "Golden Girl," 1951, and "Can Heironymus Merkin Ever Forget Mercy Humppe and Find True Happiness?," 1969. Associated with Twentieth Century-Fox, 1943-63. Chairman of board of Israel Hotel Co. *Member:* American Federation of Television and Radio Artists, American Guild of Variety Artists, Variety Clubs of America, National Vaudeville Artists (president), Jewish Theatrical Guild (vice-president), Screen Actors Guild, Writers Club, Friars. *Awards, honors:* Named Man of the Year by Beverly Hills chapter of B'nai Brith, 1952; honorary member of the U.S. Air Force.

WRITINGS: *So Help Me* (autobiography), Random House, 1943; *"Hello Mama": The Never to be Forgotten, Never to be Remembered Phone Conversations Between Georgie and*

His Momma; Also, Professor Labermacher, and Other Monologues and Essays, World Publishing, 1946; *This Way, Miss* (memoirs), Holt, 1955; *You Too Can Make a Speech,* Grayson Publishing, 1956; *Jessel, Anyone?,* Prentice-Hall, 1960; *Elegy in Manhattan,* Holt, 1961; *Halo Over Hollywood,* Toastmaster Publishing, 1963; *The Toastmaster General's Guide to Successful Public Speaking,* Hawthorn, 1969; *The Toastmaster General's Favorite Jokes; Openings and Closings for Speechmakers,* Hawthorn, 1973; (with John Austin) *The World I Lived In,* Regnery, 1975.

Plays: "George Jessel's Troubles," produced in New York City, 1922; "Box of Tricks," first produced in New York City at New Brighton Theatre, July 13, 1931; (with Bert Kalmar and Harry Ruby) "High Kickers," first produced on Broadway at Broadhurst Theatre, October 31, 1941.

Screenplays: (Author of dialogue) "Lucky Boy," Tiffany, 1929; (contributor of songs with Jack Meskill and Ted Shapiro) "Vivacious Lady," RKO, 1938; "Yesterday and Today," United Artists, 1953.

Also author of songs, including "If I Ever Lost You," "Julie," and "As Long As I Love."

SIDELIGHTS: Jessel is often referred to as "the toastmaster general of the United States," a title he received from President Franklin Roosevelt for serving in that capacity at more than three hundred banquets. As one of the most versatile and enduring entertainers of the twentieth century, Jessel has also enjoyed friendships with Presidents Truman, Kennedy, Johnson, and Nixon. While appearing at a function with the latter, Jessel related a couple of jokes involving Nixon, who found them so funny that he immediately made a gift of his cuff links to Jessel.

Jessel entered vaudeville at the age of ten, singing in a trio that included young Walter Winchell. Throughout the next fifteen years he played in numerous vaudeville productions and became quite popular. His big break, though, came when he appeared on Broadway in his first dramatic role as "The Jazz Singer." The play proved enormously successful and ran for more than one thousand performances. While appearing in the play, Jessel also served as toastmaster for the mayor of New York City, James Walker.

Jessel moved on to films and radio without deserting the stage. He was moderately successful on the screen in both two-reelers and feature films. Radio, however, was a less accommodating medium. Jessel reportedly felt uncomfortable with scripted material, and critics noted that his tendency to gear material to the New York audience diminished his chances for success in other cities.

By the late 1930's, Jessel was also involved in motion pictures as a producer. And his efforts as a producer for the stage were largely responsible for reviving vaudeville during World War II. In 1943 Jessel also wrote an autobiography, *So Help Me.* Dorothy Hillyer called it "as tawdry and glamorous, as brash and sentimental, as stupid and shrewd, as up and down as show business." Similarly, Jack Gould found it "both fascinating and irritating, not alone for what it tells of the show business but also for its revelations of one of the more complex publicized figures of today." Gould also noted that "Jessel almost has a fixation that his readers might not understand, that he has a way with the ladies."

Jessel continued to write, as well as perform, during the 1950's and 1960's. *This Way, Miss,* which contained memoirs and some of his more popular introductions as a toastmaster, was deemed "a hodgepodge of a book" by a critic for *Saturday Review.* Abel Green called it "shrill, staccato, sentimental, brittle, shrewd, ofttimes witty, betimes sage, on occasion unsubtle as he gives out with the back-of-me-hand to his personal Hate Parade." Green did concede, however, that "it's never dull."

A later volume, *Jessel, Anyone?,* was a collection of popular stories told by Jessel on the banquet circuit. "A funny story must be aged, and most of them are familiar," wrote William Leonard. "Nevertheless this is an amusing little book." A critic for the *Springfield Republican* declared that Jessel "writes as he talks—with a gifted sense of humor."

Jessel has continued performing throughout the 1970's. "At 75 his toupee and his hair are gray," observed Walter Evans. "But Jessel still cuts a fine figure and his eye is never still when there are women in the room." And Jessel still seems a bit preoccupied with his image as a womanizer. "They always made jokes about me and young girls," he acknowledged. "That wasn't true. I was married three times . . . and engaged a couple of times." He added, "But I don't have that eye for young girls they say I do."

AVOCATIONAL INTERESTS: Studying religion.

BIOGRAPHICAL/CRITICAL SOURCES: George Jessel, *So Help Me,* Random House, 1943; *Boston Globe,* May 19, 1943; *New York Times,* May 23, 1943, January 12, 1947; *Weekly Book Review,* June 13, 1943; Jessel, *This Way, Miss,* Holt, 1955; *Chicago Tribune,* April 17, 1955, September 25, 1960; *New York Herald Tribune Book Review,* May 8, 1955; *Saturday Review,* June 11, 1955; Jessel, *Jessel, Anyone?,* Prentice-Hall, 1960; *Springfield Republican,* May 29, 1960; *Time,* August 26, 1966; *Seattle Post-Intelligencer,* February 24, 1974; *Biography News,* Gale, April, 1974; Walter Wagner, *You Must Remember This,* Putnam, 1975; Jessel and John Austin, *The World I Lived In,* Regnery, 1975; Bill Smith, *Vaudevillians,* Macmillan, 1976.*

* * *

JESSUP, John Knox 1907-1979

OBITUARY NOTICE: Born March 5, 1907, in Rochester, N.Y.; died of a heart attack, October 26, 1979, in Wilton, Conn. Radio commentator, editor, and author. Jessup was associated with Time, Inc. for thirty-four years, writing for *Fortune* and *Time* before becoming the chief editorial writer for *Life* magazine in 1951. After retiring in 1969, Jessup hosted a daily radio commentary for CBS-Radio. He edited *The Ideas of Henry Luce,* a book about the founder of Time, Inc. Obituaries and other sources: *Who's Who in America,* 40th edition, Marquis, 1978; *New York Times,* October 27, 1979; *Newsweek,* November 5, 1979; *Time,* November 5, 1979.

* * *

JOBSON, Sandra
See DARROCH, Sandra Jobson

* * *

JOHNSON, Burges 1877-1963

OBITUARY NOTICE: Born November 9, 1877, in Rutland, Vt.; died in 1963. Educator and writer best known for his volumes of humor, including *Beastly Rhymes, Sonnets From the Pekinese,* and *The Lost Art of Profanity.* Obituaries and other sources: *American Authors and Books: 1640 to the Present Day,* 3rd revised edition, Crown, 1972.

JOHNSON, Claudia Alta (Taylor) 1912-
(Lady Bird Johnson)

PERSONAL: Born December 22, 1912, in Karnak, Tex.; daughter of Thomas Jefferson (a store owner) and Minnie Lee (Patillo) Taylor; married Lyndon Baines Johnson (former president of the United States), November 17, 1934 (died January 22, 1973); children: Lynda Bird (Mrs. Charles Robb), Lucy Baines (Mrs. Patrick Nugent). *Education:* University of Texas, B.A., 1933, B.J., 1934. *Religion:* Episcopalian. *Residence:* LBJ Ranch, Stonewall, Tex. 78671.

CAREER: Manager of Lyndon Johnson's congressional office, 1941-42; KTBC-Radio, Austin, Tex., station owner and manager, 1942-63; cattle rancher, 1942-73; Texas Broadcasting Co., Austin, Tex., owner and manager, 1963—. Participated actively in husband's campaigns for political office and acted as hostess to governmental and diplomatic leaders. Honorary chairwoman of National Headstart Program, 1963-68, board of trustees of John F. Kennedy Center for the Performing Arts, 1971—, Town Lake Beautification Project, and LBJ Memorial Grove; vice chairwoman of advisory board of National Parks, Historic Sites, Buildings, and Monuments, 1971-77; founder of Committee for a More Beautiful Capital, 1965; trustee of Jackson Hole Preserve; honorary trustee of Washington Gallery of Modern Art; member of University of Texas International Conference Steering Committee, 1969, board of regents of University of Texas, 1971—, and national committee of Helen Keller World Crusade for the Blind.

MEMBER: American Conservation Association, National Geographic Society, University of Texas Ex-Students Association. *Awards, honors:* Togetherness award, 1958; humanitarian award from B'nai B'rith, 1961; Crystal citation from Fashion Group of Philadelphia, 1961; businesswoman's award from Business and Professional Women's Club, 1961; Theta Sigma Phi citation, 1962; distinguished achievement award from Washington Heart Association, 1962; citation from National Association of Colored Women's Clubs, 1962; industry citation from American Women in Radio and Television, 1963; humanitarian citation from Volunteers of America, 1963; George Foster Peabody Award, 1966; Eleanor Roosevelt Golden Candlestick Award from Women's National Press Club, 1968; Damon Woods Memorial Award from Industrial Designers Society of America, 1972; Conservation Service Award from Department of the Interior, 1974; distinguished award from American Legion, 1975; named woman of the year by *Ladies' Home Journal,* 1975; Medal of Freedom, 1977. Also recipient of honorary degrees from University of Texas, Texas Woman's University, Middlebury College, Williams College, Southwestern University (Georgetown, Tex.), and University of Alabama.

WRITINGS: The Hill Country: Lyndon Johnson's Texas, National Broadcasting Co., c. 1966; *Report to the President From the First Lady's Committee for a More Beautiful Capital* (booklet), [Washington, D.C.], c. 1968; *The Vital Balance: Nature, Architecture, and Man* (booklet), [Washington, D.C.], 1968; (under name Lady Bird Johnson) *A White House Diary,* Holt, 1970. Contributor to *Reader's Digest, McCall's,* and *Redbook.*

SIDELIGHTS: A White House Diary is an account of Lady Bird Johnson's five years as First Lady of the United States. She began the diary on November 22, 1963, the day of John F. Kennedy's assassination, and continued it through January 20, 1969. The first diary to be published by a President's wife since Dolly Madison's, it is, according to Pauline J. Earl, "the story of how important the First Lady's job really is and how she must wear many hats simultaneously."

"It may not be literature, it certainly is not history—but it does have a human charm of its own," Anthony Howard has said of the book. Refraining from accounts of her husband's political activities, Lady Bird Johnson chronicles the daily life at the White House—from guest lists for State dinners to tree-planting stops on her beautification campaign. She offers insights into the personalities of public figures, including not only her husband's but those of the various Kennedy's as well. Yet the tumultuous events of the Johnson administration—assassinations, anti-war protests, urban riots—are reflected in her personal responses. In her entry for August 13, 1967, for example, she wrote: "I think the most frustrated I've been lately is reading a speech that Senator Fulbright made in which he indicated that the country is damned because we are spending so much in Vietnam instead of spending it here to take care of the poor and underprivileged—this from a man who has never voted for any civil rights measure and who even voted against Medicare in 1964. It will be sheer luxury someday to *talk* instead of to *act.*"

Critics diverged widely over the portrait of the lady that emerges from her diary. Christopher Lehmann-Haupt observed: "Mrs. Johnson comes across as a Bird in a gilded cage, worrying over her plumage and her offspring . . . always cut off from her partner by the burdens he bears, which she can never share." Pauline Earl, on the other hand, saw her as "a warm and wonderful woman with an amazing candor and ability to see things in honest perspective." While Anthony Howard reminded readers that, despite her folksy style, Lady Bird is a clever, formidable businesswoman, Dorothy Rabinowitz accepts her as "easily the most considerable and accomplished of the Ladies in the White House since Eleanor Roosevelt." Alison Plowden's conclusion embraced both sides: "She is a woman very properly concerned with such fundamental matters as her husband's health and well-being, her daughters' marriages and the birth of grandchildren, but here also is surely a woman of formidable capabilities—tough, shrewd, intelligent, observant and efficient."

BIOGRAPHICAL/CRITICAL SOURCES: Bill Adler, editor, *The Common Sense Wisdom of Three First Ladies,* Citadel, 1966; G. L. Hall, *Lady Bird and Her Daughters,* Macrae, 1967; Mary Brannum, *When I Was 16,* Platt, 1967; *New York Times Magazine,* September 10, 1967; *Sports Illustrated,* March 18, 1968; *Saturday Evening Post,* June 15, 1968; *McCall's,* December, 1968, July, 1973; *Newsweek,* December 9, 1968, November 2, 1970, September 10, 1973, April 18, 1977; *Good Housekeeping,* February, 1969, January, 1977; Sol Barzman, *First Ladies,* Cowles, 1970; Liz Carpenter, *Ruffles and Flourishes,* Doubleday, 1970; *New York Times Book Review,* October 25, 1970, December 6, 1970; *New York Times,* November 2, 1970; *Life,* November 6, 1970; *Saturday Review,* November 7, 1970, November 28, 1970; *Time,* November 9, 1970, May 21, 1973, October 30, 1978; *Observer Review,* November 29, 1970; *New York Review of Books,* December 3, 1970; *New Yorker,* December 26, 1970; *Books & Bookmen,* March, 1971; *Commentary,* June, 1971; *Vogue,* June, 1971; J. B. West, *Upstairs at the White House,* McCann, 1973; *U.S. News and World Report,* December 24, 1973, June 20, 1977; *Ladies' Home Journal,* October, 1974, May, 1975, July, 1978.

* * *

JOHNSON, Eleanor
See SEYMOUR, Dorothy Jane Z(ander)

JOHNSON, Joseph A., Jr. 1914(?)-1979

OBITUARY NOTICE: Born c. 1914 in Shreveport, La.; died September 25, 1979, in Shreveport. Clergyman, educator, and author. Johnson was the presiding bishop of the Christian Methodist Church of Mississippi and Louisiana. He taught religion at Fisk University, Phillips School of Theology, and the Inter-Denominational Theological Center in Atlanta, Ga. A noted New Testament scholar, his books include *Proclamation of Theology*. Obituaries and other sources: *New York Times*, September 28, 1979.

* * *

JOHNSON, Lady Bird
See JOHNSON, Claudia Alta (Taylor)

* * *

JOHNSON, Manly 1920-

PERSONAL: Born December 23, 1920, in Gardner, Kan.; son of Howard and Winnie (Moore) Johnson; married Mary Evans (a musician), February 14, 1944; children: Evan, Graham. *Education:* University of Michigan, B.A., 1946; graduate study at University of Washington, Seattle, 1946-47; Johns Hopkins University, M.A., 1950; further graduate study at Birkbeck College, London, 1953-54; University of Minnesota, Ph.D., 1957. *Politics:* Democrat. *Religion:* Unitarian-Universalist. *Home:* 4928 East 27th St., Tulsa, Okla. 74114. *Office:* Department of English, University of Tulsa, 600 South College, Tulsa, Okla. 74104.

CAREER: Johns Hopkins University, Baltimore, Md., junior instructor in writing, 1948-49, instructor in writing, 1950; Williams College, Williamstown, Mass., instructor in English, 1950-55; University of Michigan, Ann Arbor, instructor in English, 1957-58; University of Tulsa, Tulsa, Okla., assistant professor, 1958-62, associate professor, 1962-68, professor of English, 1968—, director of graduate program in English, 1965-70. Host and commentator on "Sunday Night at the Opera," on KWGS-FM radio station, 1974. Director of Language Arts for Living Arts of Tulsa, Inc., 1968-73; member of board of trustees for Janet Elson Scholarship Funds, 1971—, and Archaeological Associates, Inc., 1973-75, 1977—. *Military service:* U.S. Army, 1943-45.

MEMBER: Modern Language Association of America, American Association of University Professors (president elect of state conference, 1979-80), American Studies Association, Mid-Continent American Studies Association (member of executive committee, 1961-62), South Central Modern Language Association (president, 1976-77), Friends of Tulsa City-County Library (member of board of directors, 1965-71, 1973—), Darlington Park Homeowners Association (chairperson, 1977—). *Awards, honors:* Fulbright grant for England, 1953-54.

WRITINGS: (With Paul Alworth) *How to Gain a Year on College* (pamphlet), Random House, 1963; (with John Dratz and Terrence McCann) *Winning Wrestling,* Prentice-Hall, 1967; *Virginia Woolf,* Ungar, 1973; *Patrick White,* Ungar, 1980. Contributor to *Encyclopedia of World Literature in the Twentieth Century*. Contributor of articles and reviews to literature journals, and of poems to little magazines.

WORK IN PROGRESS: The journals of Ethan Allen Hitchcock.

SIDELIGHTS: Johnson told CA: "I am interested in applying theories of brain function to the analysis of literature—humanistically, not mechanistically. Literary criticism has gone about as far as specialization can take it. Critics must now discover ways to open their findings to a small but valuable public who want to know what is going on in literature and language."

* * *

JOHNSON, Sam Houston 1914(?)-1978

PERSONAL: Born c. 1914 in Texas; died December 11, 1978, in Austin, Tex.; son of Samuel Ealy and Rebekah (Baines) Johnson; twice divorced; children: (first marriage) one son, one daughter. *Education:* Received law degree from Cumberland University of Tennessee. *Residence:* Austin, Tex.

CAREER: Congressional and presidential aide to former President Lyndon Baines Johnson, 1937-67; author.

WRITINGS: My Brother Lyndon, Cowles, 1970.

SIDELIGHTS: "I know him a lot better than he knows me," Sam Houston Johnson often said of his brother, the late Lyndon Baines Johnson, "because he's been too damned busy with other matters to think about me, while I've had practically nothing to do except study him." *My Brother Lyndon* is the result of his close association and employment under Lyndon Baines Johnson, and, according to Gregory T. Wolf, does not "examine seriously the fascinating personality of Lyndon Johnson."

Rather than being a serious and critical study of the former president by one who should have known him well, *My Brother Lyndon* was described as a "lightweight performance of small talk, anecdotes and observations" by Ronnie Dugger of the *New York Times Book Review*. J. D. Lofton, Jr. of *National Review* agreed: "It is, from cover to cover, a sycophantic puff piece, oozing with nothing but adulation for the former President and caustic comments about those who differed with him. . . . Brother Sam pulls no punches because he throws none." Geoffrey Wolff called the book "interesting—I almost wrote valuable—as a work of crude homespun." He continued: "In this book a member of a much-celebrated majority breaks the much-discussed silence. Here is a full measure of simple loyalty leavened by bitterness and contempt from the kind of man who rarely—probably too rarely—feels the call to send a message to the world."

But *My Brother Lyndon* is more than just a biography, it is a no-holds-barred memoir of Sam Houston's relationship with his older and famous brother. Sam Houston, who described his occupation as "babysitter, chauffeur, political troubleshooter, administrative aide and general adviser," often compared his years of employment at the White House to serving time in a penitentiary and nicknamed his rooms "Cell 326." Among other things, Sam Houston related how a Secret Service agent was assigned to "keep him out of mischief, 'not that Mike Howard actually stopped me from drinking or wenching.'" He was also quick to point out that he wasn't "the only one in the family who takes a drink or three." With regard to LBJ as his employer, Sam Houston once stated that anyone who worked for Lyndon more than a month should receive a Purple Heart.

Often the butt of Lyndon's jokes and the recipient of his generosity, Sam Houston recalled in his book the incidents during his employment when he was asked to warm little Lynda's bed before she retired so that she could sleep well on cold nights. "That's what you get," he said, "when you've got a warm body; people seem to impose on you." Sam Houston also protested what he referred to as "an all-out snobbism against an accent, a mode of expression, a way of dressing, a way of eating—against a whole manner of living." According to Sam Houston, Lyndon Baines Johnson and his family were "ridiculed because they didn't have a fancy French chef in the White House kitchen, as if eating snails in garlic sauce will make you more civilized and human than eating plain meat and potatoes."

Although he maintained that the book did not alter his relationship with Lyndon, Sam Houston remained estranged from his older brother since 1970. In 1972, he stopped drinking and began attending services in a nearby Austin, Tex. church. When he filed for bankruptcy in 1973, Sam Houston listed assets of a government pension, social security benefits, and a $5,000 inheritance from his millionaire brother Lyndon.

BIOGRAPHICAL/CRITICAL SOURCES: Look, December 2, 1969, December 16, 1969; *Newsweek,* January 12, 1970; *Best Sellers,* February 1, 1970; *New York Times Book Review,* February 22, 1970; *National Review,* May 24, 1970. Obituaries: *Washington Post,* December 12, 1978; *Chicago Tribune,* December 12, 1978; *Time,* December 25, 1978.*

* * *

JOHNSON, Walter 1915-

PERSONAL: Born June 27, 1915, in Nahant, Mass.; son of F. Alfred (a shopkeeper) and Annie (a shopkeeper; maiden name, Hogan) Johnson; married Catherine Dunning, June 22, 1941 (divorced, 1955); married Bette Gifford, October 12, 1955; children: (second marriage) Deborah, Richard, Gifford. *Education:* Dartmouth College, B.A., 1937; University of Chicago, M.A., 1938, Ph.D., 1941. *Politics:* "Adlai Stevenson Democrat." *Home address:* Bass Lake, Route 1, Pentwater, Mich. 49449. *Agent:* Harold Ober Associates, Inc., 40 East 49th St., New York, N.Y. 10017. *Office:* Department of History, College of Arts and Sciences, Grand Valley State College, Allendale, Mich. 49401.

CAREER: University of Chicago, Chicago, Ill., instructor, 1940-43, assistant professor, 1943-49, associate professor, 1949-50, professor, 1950-66, Preston and Sterling Morton Professor of History, 1963-66, head of department, 1950-61; University of Hawaii, Honolulu, professor of history, 1966-80; Grand Valley State College, Allendale, Mich., visiting professor of history, 1980—. Harmsworth Professor of American History at Oxford University, 1957-58. Head of board of foreign scholarships of Fulbright Exchange Program, 1950-53; member of U.S. Department of State's Advisory Commission on International Educational and Cultural Affairs, 1961-66.

MEMBER: American Historical Association, Organization of American Historians, Society of American History, American Political Science Association, Southern Historical Association. *Awards, honors:* Fellow of Newberry Library, 1945; honorary degree from Hawaii Loa College, 1976.

WRITINGS: The Battle Against Isolation, University of Chicago Press, 1944; *William Allen White's America,* Holt, 1947; (editor) *Selected Letters of William Allen White,* Holt, 1947; (editor) *Roosevelt and the Russians,* Doubleday, 1949; *How We Drafted Adlai Stevenson,* Knopf, 1955; *1600 Pennsylvania Avenue: Presidents and the People, 1929-59,* Little, Brown, 1960; (with Francis J. Colligan) *The Fulbright Program: A History,* University of Chicago Press, 1965; (editor and contributor) *The Papers of Adlai Stevenson,* eight volumes, Little, Brown, 1972-79. Contributor to journals.

WORK IN PROGRESS: A book analyzing twentieth-century America.

JOHNSTON, George 1913-

PERSONAL: Born June 9, 1913, in Clydebank, Scotland; son of William George (a teacher) and Jenny (a teacher; maiden name, McKeown) Johnston; married Alexandra Gardner, August 6, 1941; children: Christine (Mrs. A. Griffin), Ronald, Janet (Mrs. J. Campbell). *Education:* University of Glasgow, M.A. (with honors), 1935, B.D. (with first class honors), 1938; attended University of Marburg, summer, 1938; Cambridge University, Ph.D., 1941. *Home:* 44 Academy, #8, Montreal, Quebec, Canada H3Z 1N6. *Office:* Faculty of Religious Studies, McGill University, 3520 University, Montreal, Quebec, Canada H3A 2A7.

CAREER: Ordained Christian minister, 1940; pastor of Church of Scotland in St. Andrews, 1940-47; Hartford Theological Sjminary, Hartford, Conn., associate professor of New Testament and church history, 1947-52; Emmanuel College, Toronto, Ontario, professor of New Testament, 1952-59, director of graduate studies, 1954-59; McGill University, Montreal, Quebec, professor of New Testament, 1959—, dean of faculty of religious studies, 1970-75, member of board of governors of university, 1971-75. Principal of United Theological College, Montreal, Quebec, 1959-70. Bruce Lecturer at Trinity College, Glasgow, 1943; Kellner Memorial Lecturer at Episcopal Theological School, Cambridge, Mass., 1951; lecturer at St. Mary's College, St. Andrews, Scotland, summers, 1951, 1956, St. Stephen's College, Edmonton, Alberta, winter, 1961, and United College, Winnipeg, Manitoba, winter, 1964. Member of executive committee of Humanities Research Council of Canada and head of its committee on aid to publication, 1974-75. Port Credit library commissioner. Participant in international ecumenical conferences; guest on radio and television programs, including "Man Alive." *Military service:* British Army, acting chaplain of Black Watch, 1945; served in Germany.

MEMBER: Canadian Society of Biblical Studies (president, 1963), Canadian Theological Society (president, 1966), Society of Biblical Literature (member of council, 1968-72, 1973-75). *Awards, honors:* D.D. from University of Glasgow, 1960, United Theological College, Montreal, Quebec, 1974, and Montreal Diocesan Theological College, 1975; Nuffield U.K. Award from Nuffield Foundation, 1956; fellowship from American Association of Theological Schools, 1967; LL.D. from Mount Allison University, 1974; Canada Council fellowship, 1975-76.

WRITINGS: The Doctrine of the Church in the New Testament, Cambridge University Press, 1943; *The Secrets of the Kingdom,* Westminster, 1954; *Ephesians, Philippians, Colossians, and Philemon,* Thomas Nelson, 1967; (editor with Wolfgang Roth, and contributor) *The Church in the Modern World: Essays in Honour of James Sutherland Thomson,* Ryerson, 1967; *The Spirit-Paraclete in the Gospel of John* (monograph), Cambridge University Press, 1970.

Contributor: Alan Richardson, editor, *A Theological Word Book of the Bible,* S.C.M. Press, 1950, Harper, 1951; William Neil, editor, *The Bible Companion,* Rainbird, McLean, 1959, McGraw, 1960; H. K. McArthur, editor, *New Testament Sidelights,* Hartford Seminary Foundation Press, 1960; S. J. Kitchen, editor, *Stewardship Sermons by Canadian Preachers,* Ryerson, 1963; Hugh Anderson and William Barclay, editors, *The New Testament in Historical and Contemporary Perspective: Essays in Memory of G.H.C. Macgregor,* Basil Blackwell, 1965; J. R. McKay and J. F. Miller, editors, *Biblical Studies: Essays in Honour of William Barclay,* Westminster, 1976.

Contributor to *Twentieth Century Encyclopedia of Religious Knowledge, Peake's Commentary on the Bible, The Interpreter's Dictionary of the Bible, Hastings' Dictionary of the Bible,* and *T. W. Manson's Companion to the Bible.* Contributor of more than forty articles and reviews to theology journals and popular magazines, including *Mid-Stream* and *Perspective.* Chairman of *Canadian Journal of Theology,* 1960-67.

WORK IN PROGRESS: Patterns of Christian Character: A Study in New Testament Ethics; a book on early Christian art, including Roman Britain; a book on Pictish and early Celtic Christian art in Scotland and Ireland.

SIDELIGHTS: Johnston writes: "I am chiefly an academic New Testament scholar and theologian, motivated by a powerful ecumenical concern and a passionate interest in social justice and the theological education of lay men and women in the churches. I have been a religious journalist, with published sermons, and try to avoid ivory tower isolation.

"For nearly twenty years I have educated myself in art history, which I find to be a liberating and enriching discipline. Since my M.A. specialized in classics and Roman history, my theology and my teaching have always included church history, and my ecumenical interests have taken me for long periods to Rome, I have naturally combined these in research and teaching early Christian art (pre-Constantine, Byzantine, and more recently, Celtic Ireland and Scotland up to the twelfth century).

"My writing has often been 'commissioned' stuff. It is an auxiliary to lecturing and teaching rather than 'creative literature.' But I try to cultivate good style, lucid syntax, and imaginative colour—as older rhetoricians did. *The Secrets of the Kingdom* is my most literary production, I suppose."

AVOCATIONAL INTERESTS: Travel (Jordan, Israel, India, Turkey, Italy, France, Germany).

* * *

JOHNSTON, John M. 1898(?)-1979

OBITUARY NOTICE: Born c. 1898; died August 1, 1979, in Santa Barbara, Calif. Journalist. Johnston was a columnist, associate editor, and editorial writer for the *Chicago Daily News* for more than twenty years. Before joining the *Daily News* in 1947, he worked as an associate editor at *Business Week.* Johnston is credited with establishing the McGraw-Hill News Bureau in Cleveland. Obituaries and other sources: *Chicago Tribune,* August 3, 1979.

* * *

JONAS, Steven 1936-

PERSONAL: Born November 22, 1936, in New York, N.Y.; son of Harold Jacob (a historian) and Florence (a translator; maiden name, Kyzor) Jonas; married Josephine Gear (an art historian), June 19, 1964 (divorced August 1, 1970); married Linda Friedman (a speech pathologist), November 23, 1971; children: Jacob Henry, Lillian Sara. *Education:* Columbia University, B.A., 1958; Harvard University, M.D., 1962; Yale University, M.P.H., 1967. *Politics:* "Progressive." *Religion:* Jewish. *Home:* 107 Randall Ave., Port Jefferson, N.Y. 11777. *Office:* Department of Community and Preventive Medicine, State University of New York at Stony Brook, Stony Brook, N.Y. 11794.

CAREER: Lenox Hill Hospital, New York City, intern, 1962-63; University of London, London, England, research fellow, 1963-65; Department of Health, New York City, resident in preventive medicine and public health, 1965-67, health officer, 1967-69; Morrisania City Hospital, Bronx, N.Y., chief of department of social medicine, 1969-71; State University of New York at Stony Brook, assistant professor, 1971-74, associate professor of community and preventive medicine, 1974—. Member of New York State Board for Medicine. *Member:* Association of Teachers of Preventive Medicine (president, 1977-78), American College of Preventive Medicine, American Hospital Association, American Public Health Association, Association of American Medical Colleges, Nassau Physicians Review Organization (member of board of directors, 1978—).

WRITINGS: Quality Control of Ambulatory Care, Springer Publishing, 1977; (editor and contributor) *Health Care Delivery in the United States,* Springer Publishing, 1977; *Medical Mystery: The Training of Doctors in the United States.* Norton, 1979. Chief editor of "Health Care and Society" and "Medical Education," series published by Springer Publishing. Contributor to health care journals.

WORK IN PROGRESS: Second edition of *Health Care Delivery in the United States,* publication by Springer Publishing expected in 1981.

SIDELIGHTS: Jonas comments: "Prevention is the key to health. The key to a prevention-oriented health care delivery system is prevention-oriented medical education. Working in a variety of ways to achieve this goal will provide the focus for my professional activities for the forseeable future.

"My book, *Medical Mystery,* holds that maintaining and promoting the health of the people is the principal responsibility of what we call the health care delivery system. Historically it has been shown that prevention is the key to health. The key to health care delivery system as it now operates is the medical profession, which has the most influence over the setting of priorities in the system. The profession has this power for three reasons: the licensing laws; the fact that it controls about 70 percent of the total expenditures made in the system; and its high level of training in the biomedical sciences. The medical profession is, by and large, disease-oriented rather than prevention-oriented. This is largely a result of the American system of medical education, which can be described as 'Disease-Oriented Physician Education,' DOPE for short. If the health care delivery system is become truly health-oriented, its physicians must become health-oriented themselves. To this end Medical Mystery proposes to replace DOPE with HOPE, 'Health-Oriented Physician Education.'"

* * *

JONES, A(rnold) H(ugh) M(artin) 1904-1970

OBITUARY NOTICE: Born in 1904 in Birkenhead, England; died April 7, 1970, in Cambridge, England. Educator and historian specializing in ancient civilizations. His books include *History of Abyssinia* and *The Decline of the Ancient World.* Obituaries and other sources: *AB Bookman's Weekly,* May 4, 1970; *The Author's and Writer's Who's Who,* 6th edition, Burke's Peerage, 1971.

* * *

JONES, Edgar A(llen), Jr. 1921-

PERSONAL: Born January 8, 1921, in Brooklyn, N.Y.; son of Edgar Allen (a railroad worker) and Isabel (Morris) Jones; married Helen Callaghan, September 14, 1945; children: Linda, Anne, Carol, Terry, Denis, Bob, Dave, Therese, Catherine, Nancy, Daniel. *Education:* Wesleyan University,

Middletown, Conn., B.A., 1942; University of Virginia, LL.B., 1950. *Home address:* P.O. Box 3453, W. Rogers Station, Santa Monica, Calif. 90403. *Office:* Law School, University of California, Los Angeles, Calif. 90024.

CAREER: University of California, Los Angeles, professor of law, 1951—. Director of Jimmy's Restaurant, Beverly Hills, Calif. Arbitrator of labor disputes. *Military service:* U.S. Marine Corps, 1942-45; became first lieutenant. *Member:* American Bar Association, National Academy of Arbitrators.

WRITINGS: (With Morris L. Meyers) *Arbitrability,* American Arbitration Association, 1974; *Lie Detectors in Labor Arbitration,* BNA, 1979. Co-author of audio cassettes on law subjects. Contributor to law journals.

WORK IN PROGRESS: A book on labor law and arbitration.

AVOCATIONAL INTERESTS: Pitching baseball.

* * *

JONES, Phillip L. 1928(?)-1979

OBITUARY NOTICE: Born c. 1928 in Crete, Neb.; died of cancer, August 16, 1979, in Harrisonburg, Va. Educator and author. Jones taught at the Montgomery Blair High School in Silver Spring, Md., for twenty-two years before his retirement in 1977. As an author, he wrote articles, short stories, and television scripts, including three episodes of NBC-TV's "Explorer" series. His autobiographical novel, *Searching for the Wind,* was privately printed. Obituaries and other sources: *Washington Post,* August 17, 1979.

* * *

JONES, Preston 1936-1979

OBITUARY NOTICE—See index for *CA* sketch: Born April 7, 1936, in Albuquerque, N.M.; died September 19, 1979, in Dallas, Tex. Actor, director, and playwright, best known for "A Texas Trilogy," his plays about the lives of ordinary citizens of the mythical Texas town of Bradleyville. From 1960 until the time of his death Jones was both actor and director with the Dallas Theatre Centre. He was also a member of the board of governors of the American Playwrights Theatre. Although his trilogy closed on Broadway after only sixty-three performances, it was extremely successful in both Dallas and Washington, D.C. Most critics praised "his gentle, realistic tales of small-town life," and felt that his work went beyond regional drama. Numbered among his other plays are "A Place on the Magdalena Flats" and "Santa Fe Sunshine." Obituaries and other sources: *Time,* September 27, 1976, October 1, 1979; *Current Biography,* Wilson, 1977, November, 1979; *New York Times,* September 20, 1979; *Washington Post,* September 21, 1979; *Detroit News,* September 23, 1979; *Newsweek,* October 1, 1979.

* * *

JONES, Ray O. 1930-

PERSONAL: Born April 19, 1930, in Selma, N.C.; son of Garland E. and Clara B. Jones; married wife, Miriam, November 11, 1950; children: Angela, Stephen, Anita, Gloria. *Education:* Tennessee Temple University, B.A., 1955; Temple Baptist Seminary, Th.G., 1957; University of Tennessee, M.S., 1971; Luther Rice Seminary, D.Min., 1976. *Home:* 3605 Sagewood Dr., Portsmouth, Va. 23703. *Office:* 3801 Turnpike Rd., Portsmouth, Va. 23701.

CAREER: Ordained Southern Baptist minister; pastor of Baptist churches in Camden, S.C., and Knoxville, Tenn.; Alexander Baptist Church, Portsmouth, Va., pastor. Vice-president of Tennessee Baptist Convention. Police chaplain of Portsmouth, Va. *Military service:* U.S. Air Force, chaplain; became lieutenant colonel.

WRITINGS: Top Sacred: Spiritual Ideas in Down-to-Earth Language, Broadman, 1972. Author of church school curriculum material. Contributor to magazines and newspapers, including *Upper Room* and *Open Windows.*

AVOCATIONAL INTERESTS: Weight lifting, karate (brown belt).

* * *

JONES, Russell 1918-1979

OBITUARY NOTICE: Born January 5, 1918, in Minneapolis, Minn.; died June 9, 1979, in Vienna, Austria. Journalist best known for his coverage of the 1956 Hungarian revolt. As a foreign correspondent for United Press International (UPI), Jones was one of the few journalists left in Budapest when Soviet troops stormed the city to quell the Hungarian uprising in November, 1956. For his reporting efforts, he won three of journalism's most prestigious awards: a Pulitzer Prize, a Sigma Delta Chi award, and the Overseas Press Club George Polk Memorial Award. Before joining UPI, Jones reported for *Stars and Stripes* during World War II and worked for the United Press in London. Beginning in 1957, he was a foreign correspondent and foreign bureau chief for American television networks. Obituaries and other sources: *Current Biography,* Wilson, 1957, August, 1979; *Who's Who in the World,* 2nd edition, Marquis, 1973; *Washington Post,* June 11, 1979; *New York Times,* June 11, 1979.

* * *

JORDAN, Borimir 1933-

PERSONAL: Born November 5, 1933, in Sofia, Bulgaria; son of Boris and Mira (Kowatschewa) Jordan; children: Jennifer, Angela, Nicole. *Education:* University of California, Berkeley, B.A., 1955, Ph.D., 1968; attended American School of Classical Studies in Athens, 1965-67. *Politics:* Republican. *Religion:* Roman Catholic. *Home:* 5513 Camino Cerralvo, Santa Barbara, Calif. 93111. *Office:* Department of Classics, University of California, Santa Barbara, Calif. 93106.

CAREER: University of Southern California, Los Angeles, assistant professor of classics, 1967-68; University of California, Santa Barbara, assistant professor, 1968-73, associate professor, 1973-78, professor of classics, 1978—. *Military service:* U.S. Navy, 1957-61; became lieutenant junior grade. *Member:* American Philological Association, Archaeological Institute of America, American Historical Association.

WRITINGS: The Athenian Navy in the Classical Period, University of California Press, 1975; *Servants of the Gods,* Vandenhoeck & Ruprecht, 1979. Contributor to scholarly journals.

WORK IN PROGRESS: Research on ancient history and literature and on the history of solar energy in antiquity.

BIOGRAPHICAL/CRITICAL SOURCES: Los Angeles Times, February 25, 1979; *New York Times,* April 24, 1979; *San Jose Mercury,* April 30, 1979.

* * *

JORDAN, Z(bigniew) A(ntoni) 1911-1977

OBITUARY NOTICE—See index for *CA* sketch: Born July

23, 1911, in Golaszyn, Poland; died in October, 1977, in Ottawa, Ontario, Canada. Journalist, educator, and writer on intellectual history, philosophy, and politics. At the time of his death Jordan was serving as professor of the philosophy of science at Carleton University. His publications include *Logical Determinism* and *The Sociology of Marx*. Obituaries and other sources: *American Men and Women of Science: The Social and Behavioral Sciences,* 12th edition, Bowker, 1973; *The Writers Directory, 1976-78,* St. Martin's, 1976; *The Author's and Writer's Who's Who,* 8th edition, Burke's Peerage, 1977; *AB Bookman's Weekly,* March 6, 1978.

* * *

JOURDAIN, Rose (Leonora) 1932-

PERSONAL: Born June 25, 1932, in Chicago, Ill.; daughter of Edwin B. (a political leader) and Emmaline (Hardwick) Jourdain; divorced; children: Jacqueline. *Education:* Lake Forest College, B.A., 1953; also attended Northwestern University. *Home:* 2032 Darrow, Evanston, Ill. 60201. *Agent:* William Morris Agency, 1350 Avenue of the Americas, New York, N.Y. 10019.

CAREER: Time, Inc., New York, N.Y., researcher, 1960-61; Scott, Foresman & Co., Glenview, Ill., social studies editor, 1971-72; Columbia College, Chicago, Ill., instructor in literature, 1975-78; Evanston Township High School, Evanston, Ill., teacher of history, 1975—. *Member:* International P.E.N. (American Center), Chicago Urban League (member of women's board), Glencoe Library (member of board).

WRITINGS: *Around You* (primary social studies text), Scott, Foresman, 1972; *Those the Sun Has Loved* (novel), Doubleday, 1978.

Author of several television plays.

WORK IN PROGRESS: Research for another historical novel.

SIDELIGHTS: Rose Jourdain comments: "I believe it is a primary responsibility of the novelist not only to entertain, but also to broaden and deepen the scope of our understanding of life. *Those the Sun Has Loved* covers seven generations of the free black tradition in America, a part of Americana that has been largely neglected by historians and novelists. Meticulously researched, it is the saga of a fictional black family which interacts with scores of black and white leaders from pre-Revolutionary War Boston, through the period of the firebrand abolitionists, the Civil War, and Reconstruction, on into the late twentieth century. It is a fresh view of black life; a view of achieving blacks who dared to overcome the odds and win places of honor in a nation where race has not been a ban to success, unless the race happened to be black."

* * *

JUDD, Harrison
See DANIELS, Norman

* * *

JUDSON, Horace Freeland 1931-

PERSONAL: Born April 21, 1931, in New York, N.Y.; son of Freeland (an economic statistician) and Harriet (Babcock) Judson; married second wife, Penelope Sylvia Jones, January 11, 1969; children: (first marriage) Grace Louise, Thomas Alexander; (second marriage) Olivia Phoebe, Nicholas Matthew Freeland. *Education:* University of Chicago, B.A., 1948, graduate study, 1949-51; further graduate study at Columbia University, 1962-63. *Religion:* Atheist. *Residence:* Cambridge, England. *Agent:* Michael Thomas, A.M. Heath & Co., 40-42 William IV St., London WC2N 4DD, England.

CAREER: Office of Military Government of the United States, Berlin, Germany, researcher, 1948-49; Reading Laboratory, New York City, writer, 1952-53; Harcourt, Brace & Co., New York City, editor, 1954-55; advertising copywriter in New York City, 1955-62; *Time,* New York City, staff writer, 1963-64, arts and sciences correspondent in London, England, 1965-69, and Paris, France, 1969-71, correspondent in New York City, 1972-73; free-lance writer, 1973—. Fellow of Center for Advanced Study in the Behavioral Sciences, 1980-81. *Awards, honors:* Prize from Overseas Press Club of America, 1974, for article "The British and Heroin,"; Medical Journalists Association award, 1975, for *Heroin Addiction in Britain;* Guggenheim fellowship, 1979-80.

WRITINGS: *The Techniques of Reading,* Harcourt, 1954, 3rd edition, 1972; *Heroin Addiction in Britain,* Harcourt, 1974; *The Eighth Day of Creation: Makers of the Revolution in Biology,* Simon & Schuster, 1979; *The Search for Solutions,* Holt, 1980. Contributor of articles and reviews to magazines, including *New Yorker, Harper's, Atlantic, Quest* and *Spectator*.

WORK IN PROGRESS: A book on the natural history of the wetlands, and wetland birds of Europe and North Africa, and the politics of their conservation, publication expected in 1982; a book on the sociobiology controversy, for publication by Simon & Schuster, 1981.

SIDELIGHTS: Judson writes: "By experience and preference I'm a critic of theater, books, and art. Almost by coincidence, I have found myself working in the history of science and along that contentious border where science marches with public policy. I have attempted to alloy the methods of the journalist with those of the historian—that is, to unite the oral record, brought out by intensive interviewing, with the written record in the correspondence, notebooks, memorandums, and published papers of the scientists and others whose work I'm writing about. This, in itself, doesn't strike me as especially original; and yet, in an era when more than half the scientists who have ever lived are still alive, I am repeatedly surprised to find that historians of science are reluctant to attempt interviews or to rely on them. I'm forced to suppose that I pursue the materials, both oral and written, more intensively than most.

"For *The Eighth Day of Creation,* which is a history of the chief discoveries of molecular biology and the circumstances—intellectual and social—in which they came to be made, I interviewed well over a hundred scientists, many of them more than once, several of them again and again, and collected, in all, more than a million words of interviews. For my next book, *The Search for Solutions,* which is a set of short, interlocking essays on the various ways that scientists approach the doing of science, I interviewed several dozen more.

"I work for the most part with a tape recorder—the latest and best is smaller than a paper-back detective story—and transcribe the interviews myself because nobody else can be as accurate as someone who took part in the original conversation. The crucial step is taken when I have completed an extended section of manuscript that puts the evidence from all sources into a single narrative. This I give to the principal figures, and when one of them has read it I interview him again, going over the text page by page, if necessary, with the tape recorder running. That's the occasion when the subject encounters his memories in relation to the rest of the evidence, and will ask, 'Did I really tell you that? Well, it wasn't *quite* like that—.' And then you get the gold."

BIOGRAPHICAL/CRITICAL SOURCES: New York Times Book Review, April 8, 1979; *Washington Post Book World,* April 15, 1979.

* * *

JUDY, Stephen N. 1942-

PERSONAL: Born January 31, 1942, in Naugatuck, Conn.; son of John Nelson (a chemist) and Anna L. (a consultant) Judy; married Susan Jane Schmidt (a college teacher), June 3, 1978; children: Stephen, Emily, Michael. *Education:* Hamilton College, B.A., 1963; Northwestern University, M.A., 1964, Ph.D., 1967. *Home:* 2011 Pawnee Trail, Okemos, Mich. 48864. *Office:* Department of English, Michigan State University, East Lansing, Mich. 48823.

CAREER: Northwestern University, Evanston, Ill., assistant professor of English and education, 1967-69; Michigan State University, East Lansing, assistant professor, 1969-71, associate professor, 1971-76, professor of English, 1976—. Guest instructor at University of British Columbia, 1975. *Member:* National Council of Teachers of English, Educational Press Association, Conference on College Composition and Communication, Conference on English Education, Michigan Council of Teachers of English. *Awards, honors:* Eight awards from Educational Press Association for excellence in educational journalism for *English Journal;* Charles Carpenter Fries Award from Michigan Council of Teachers of English, 1978, for distinguished service to the profession of English teaching.

WRITINGS: The Creative Word, Random House, 1973; *Explorations in the Teaching of English,* Harper, 1975; *Writing in Reality,* Harper, 1978; *The English Teacher's Handbook,* Winthrop Publishing, 1979; *The ABCs of Literacy,* Oxford University Press, 1979; *Teaching English: Reflections on the State of the Art,* Hayden, 1979; *Writing for Giving,* Scribner, 1980; *A Short Introduction to the Teaching of Writing,* Wiley, in press. Editor of *English Journal,* 1973—.

WORK IN PROGRESS: Exploring Language: From Wordplay to Correctness, publication by Winthrop Publishing expected in 1982; *Publishing in English Education,* expected in 1982.

SIDELIGHTS: Judy writes: "I am interested in the publication of young people's writing in all forms—from one-of-a-kind hand-bound books to authentic printed books. I teach and sponsor young writers' workshops with this in mind and take pride in helping unpublished writers get their work in print, particularly young writers who are normally excluded from participation in formal school publications."

K

KAHN, Albert E. 1912(?)-1979

OBITUARY NOTICE: Born c. 1912; died of a heart attack, September 15, 1979, near Glen Allen, Calif. Photographer, publisher, and author. Kahn was an outspoken critic of U.S. Government policy during the McCarthy era. Along with Angus Cameron he formed the Cameron & Kahn publishing firm so that writers blacklisted by the government could easily find an outlet for their works. One of the firm's publications, Harvey Matusow's *False Witness,* was described by John Steinbeck as "the straw that broke McCarthy's back." A self-described "radical in the tradition of Jack London," Kahn wrote several books on politics, including *Sabotage,* 1942, *The Great Conspiracy,* 1946, *High Treason,* 1950, and *The Unholy Hymnal,* 1971. He also wrote and contributed the photographs to a 1962 book, *Days With Ulanova,* a pictorial biography of Soviet ballerina Galina Ulanova. Obituaries and other sources: *New York Times,* September 19, 1979; *Washington Post,* September 20, 1979; *Publishers Weekly,* October 1, 1979.

* * *

KAHN, Sanders A(rthur) 1919-

PERSONAL: Born January 20, 1919, in New York, N.Y.; son of Robert and Hattie (Grossman) Kahn; married Miriam Lefkowitz, March 19, 1948; children: Leslie Arlene, Susan Betty, Richard Steven. *Education:* City College (now of the City University of New York), B.B.A., 1947; New York University, M.B.A., 1949, Ph.D., 1962. *Politics:* "Extreme moderate." *Home:* 428 Green Hill Rd., Kinnelon, N.J. 07405. *Office:* Sanders A. Kahn Associates, Inc., 341 Madison Ave., New York, N.Y. 10017.

CAREER: Associated with Adams & Co., Real Estate, Inc., 1939-42; vice-president of Walter Oertly Associates, Inc., 1946-48; associated with Dwight Helmsley, 1948-49; University of Florida, Gainesville, assistant professor of real estate, 1949-50; Port of New York Authority, New York City, manager of real estate planning, 1952-54; Sanders A. Kahn Associates, Inc. (real estate, housing, and land economics), New York City and Clifton, N.J., president, 1954—. Also worked concurrently as professor of land economics and real estate at City College (now of the City University of New York), and adjunct professor at Baruch College (now Bernard M. Baruch College of the City University of New York); currently adjunct professor of real estate at New York University. Member of planning association of North Jersey; director of Young Men's Christian Association (YMCA) of Passaic-Clifton-Garfield. *Military service:* U.S. Army Air Forces, 1942-45. *Member:* American Society of Real Estate Counselors, American Society of Appraisers (past president), American Society of Real Estate Professors, American Society of Planning Officials, Association of Federal Appraisers, Society of Real Estate Appraisers, Southern Economic Association, Mortgage Bankers Association of New York, Real Estate Board of New York.

WRITINGS: (With F. E. Case) *Real Estate Appraisal and Investment,* Ronald, 1963, 2nd edition, 1977; (co-author) *Principles of Right of Way Acquisition,* American Right of Way Association, 1972. Author of column, "Down to Earth." Contributor of articles and reviews to journals in his field.

SIDELIGHTS: Kahn writes: "I am an extreme moderate, which means to me that I try to fill a void so that we moderates can express ourselves strongly. We are the majority. More usually, we are the silent sheep surrounded by vocal extremists who only represent minority opinion. Moderate to me does not mean not being progressive. In considering a radical change, we should never take the first step on a stairway without understanding what is at the top of the first landing at least, preferably what is at the top of the entire stairwell. The words 'change' and 'progress' are not necessarily synonymous."

* * *

KAID, Lynda Lee 1948-

PERSONAL: Born August 22, 1948, in Harrisburg, Ill.; daughter of Billy Cameron (a farmer) and Leona (a secretary; maiden name, Oglesby) Kaid; married Clifford Alan Jones (an attorney), January 31, 1974. *Education:* Attended University of Illinois, 1966-68; Southern Illinois University, Carbondale, B.A., 1970, M.A., 1972, Ph.D., 1974. *Home:* 1114 Merrymen Green, Norman, Okla. 73069. *Office:* School of Journalism and Mass Communication, University of Oklahoma, Norman, Okla. 73019.

CAREER: Collins-Knaggs Associates (in political public relations), Austin, Tex., associate, 1971; University of Oklahoma, Norman, assistant professor of journalism and mass communication, 1974—. *Member:* International Communication Association, Center for the Study of the Presidency,

Southwestern Political Science Association, Central States Speech Association.

WRITINGS: The Judging of Debate: An Examination of the Critical Process Involved in Evaluating Oral Argument With Special Reference to Poverty in America, Springboards, 1973; (with Marvin Kleinau) *The Judging of Debate: Evaluating Oral Argument With Special Reference to Political Reform in America,* Springboards, 1974; (with Robert O. Hirsch and Keith Sanders) *Political Campaign Communication: A Bibliography and Guide to the Literature,* Scarecrow, 1974. Contributor to communication, speech, journalism, and political science journals.

WORK IN PROGRESS: Books on political campaign communication, including political advertising and political media.

* * *

KALICH, Jacob 1891-1975

OBITUARY NOTICE: Born November 18, 1891, in Rymanov, Poland; died March 16, 1975, in Lake Mahopac, N.Y. Screen, stage, and television actor, stage director and producer, and playwright. Beginning in 1910, Kalich worked in various capacities for the Yiddish Theatre. His directing efforts include the New York City productions of "Love Thief," 1931, "Here Runs the Bride," 1934, and "Take It Easy," 1950. He also wrote, directed, and appeared in his own plays, "Oy Is Dus a Leben," 1942, "Fablonjete Honeymoon," 1955, and "Kosher Widow," 1959. Kalich received a Humanitarian Award from the Yiddish Theatrical Alliance in 1958. Obituaries and other sources: *The Biographical Encyclopaedia and Who's Who of the American Theatre,* James Heineman, 1966; *New York Times,* March 17, 1975.

* * *

KANTER, Arnold 1945-

PERSONAL: Born February 27, 1945, in Chicago, Ill.; son of Norton W. (in business) and Mary (Stern) Kanter; married Anne Strassman, June 28, 1969; children: Clare, Noah. *Education:* University of Michigan, A.B. (with high honors), 1966; Yale University, M.Phil., 1969, Ph.D., 1975. *Home:* 1064 Carper St., McLean, Va. 22101. *Office:* Office of Systems Analysis, Bureau of Politico-Military Affairs, U.S. Department of State, Washington, D.C. 20520.

CAREER: Technology Planning Center, Ann Arbor, Mich., research associate, 1965-66; Brookings Institution, Washington, D.C., research assistant and fellow in foreign policy studies, 1969-71; Ohio State University, Columbus, instructor in political science, 1971-72; University of Michigan, Ann Arbor, instructor, 1972-75, assistant professor of political science, 1975-78, research associate at Institute of Public Policy Studies, 1972-75, assistant research scientist, 1975-78; U.S. Department of State, Washington, D.C., political-military affairs officer, 1977-78, deputy director of Office of Systems Analysis, 1978—. Guest lecturer at U.S. Air Force Air University, 1971, Naval War College, 1973, 1974, Air Command and Staff College, 1977, 1978, and Carnegie-Mellon University, 1978; guest on "Face to Face." Research associate at Vector Research, Inc., 1976-78. Business manager of *American Journal of Political Science,* 1973-76.

MEMBER: International Institute of Strategic Studies, American Political Science Association, Arms Control Association, Council on Foreign Relations, Midwest Political Science Association, Inter-University Seminar on the Armed Forces and Society, Phi Beta Kappa, Phi Kappa Phi, Pi Sigma Alpha. *Awards, honors:* Woodrow Wilson fellowship, 1966-67; international affairs fellowship from Council on Foreign Relations, 1977-78.

WRITINGS: (Editor with Morton H. Halperin, and contributor) *Readings in American Foreign Policy: A Bureaucratic Perspective,* Little, Brown, 1973; (contributor) Steven Rosen, editor, *Testing the Theory of the Military-Industrial Complex,* Heath, 1973; (with Halperin and Priscilla Clapp) *Bureaucratic Politics and Foreign Policy,* Brookings Institution, 1974; *Defense Politics: A Budgetary Perspective,* University of Chicago Press, 1979. Contributor to political science journals. Member of editorial board of *American Journal of Political Science,* 1973-76, and *Comparative Strategy,* 1977—.

WORK IN PROGRESS: A classified policy analysis for the U.S. State Department.

* * *

KANTOR-BERG, Friedrich 1908-1979 (Friedrich Torberg)

OBITUARY NOTICE: Born in 1908 in Vienna, Austria; died November 10, 1979, in Vienna, Austria. Poet, novelist, and translator. Kantor-Berg, best known by his pseudonym, was one of Austria's finest writers. He was the author of *The Student Gerber Has Graduated, Here I Am, Father,* and *Aunt Jollesch and Other Anecdotes,* and translated many of the works of Israeli humorist Ephraim Kishon. Obituaries and other sources: *The Oxford Companion to German Literature,* Clarendon Press, 1976; *Washington Post,* November 12, 1979.

* * *

KAPLAN, H. Roy 1944-

PERSONAL: Born March 10, 1944, in Newark, N.J.; married; children: two. *Education:* University of Bridgeport, B.A., 1966; University of Maine, M.A., 1968; University of Massachusetts, M.A., 1970, Ph.D., 1971. *Home:* 103 Berryman Dr., Snyder, N.Y. 14226. *Office:* Department of Sociology, State University of New York at Buffalo, Spaulding Quad, Amherst, N.Y. 14261.

CAREER: University of Maine, Orono, instructor in sociology, 1967-68; State University of New York at Buffalo, assistant professor, 1970-76, associate professor of sociology, 1976—. Visiting assistant professor at University of British Columbia, summer, 1974, and Pitzer College, 1976-77. Member of governor's casino gambling study panel; participant in professional meetings; consultant to Loto Canada. *Member:* Alpha Kappa Delta, Pi Gamma Mu, Delta Tau Kappa. *Awards, honors:* William E. Mosher Award from American Society for Public Administration, 1977, for article, "Humanism in Organizations: A Critical Approach."

WRITINGS: (Contributor) W. Warner Berke and Harvey A. Hornstein, editors, *The Social Technology of Organization Development,* NTL Learning Resources Corp., 1972; (contributor) Maurice Visscher, editor, *Humanistic Perspectives in Medical Ethics,* Prometheus Books, 1972; (editor and contributor) *American Minorities and Economic Opportunity,* F. E. Peacock, 1977; *Lottery Winners: How They Won and How Winning Changed Their Lives,* Harper, 1978; (contributor) Gordon Erikson, editor, *Social Problems,* Wadsworth, 1980. Contributor of about twenty-five articles and reviews to scholarly journals, including *Annals of the American Academy of Political and Social Science,* and to *McCall's.*

WORK IN PROGRESS: A book on the nature of work and

its relationship to the nature of life in our society, publication expected in 1981.

SIDELIGHTS: Kaplan writes: "I am primarily interested in the meaning of work and commitment to work in our society. My research on lottery winners started as a sociological study of people who have a choice between working and not working. As I began interviewing big money winners they related fascinating and totally unexpected experiences they had, and I decided to bring them together into a book.

Some of the unexpected material centered around religious and psychic experiences winners had which, they believe, influenced their winning. One third of all the winners I interviewed (33 of 100) related such experiences to me and firmly believed that God or supernatural forces had a hand in their winning. Contrary to most social science studies which indicate the commitment to work is strong and people would continue working if they had enough money to live comfortably without working, over eighty percent of the million dollar winners interviewed quit their jobs and many have been unemployed for a number of years. One might say that the moral of the research is that you can change a person's economic status overnight by giving them a great deal of money, but their social status changes much more slowly. Few people go to plays, the theatre, concerts, or other cultural activities and many stay at home watching television. But they still buy tickets hoping to win again and realize the American Dream that has eluded them."

* * *

KAPLER, Aleksei (Yaklovlevich) 1904(?)-1979

OBITUARY NOTICE: Born c. 1904 in Russia (now U.S.S.R.); died c. September, 1979, in Moscow, U.S.S.R. Screenwriter. Kapler first earned distinction as a filmmaker for his depictions of Lenin in the films "Lenin in October" and "Lenin in 1918." His career was halted in 1943, however, when the Stalin regime accused him of being a spy and exiled him for ten years. Stalin was also reportedly upset that Kapler, a Jew, had been seeing his daughter. Upon returning to civilian life, Kapler worked at Mosfilm Studios and taught at the Institute of Cinematography, both in Moscow. Among his other films are "Day After Day," "Behind the Show Window," and "No Ordinary Summer." Obituaries and other sources: *New York Times,* September 15, 1979.

* * *

KASZNER, Kurt
See SERWICHER, Kurt

* * *

KAUFFMAN, Milo (Franklin) 1898-

PERSONAL: Born February 13, 1898, near Harrisonville, Mo.; son of Levi Christopher and Rebecca E. (Sharp) Kauffman; married Clara E. Fricke, October 3, 1931; children: Marilyn Ferne Kauffman Miller, Loretta Joyce Kauffman Sears, Evelyn Kauffman Shellenberger, Gloria Kauffman Yoder, Milo Franklin, Jr., Bonnie Kauffman Sowers, Phyllis Kauffman Davis. *Education:* Hesston College, B.A., 1926; Northern Baptist Seminary, B.D., 1930; McCormick Theological Seminary, M.A., 1931. *Home:* 308 North Main, Hesston, Kan. 67062.

CAREER: Ordained Mennonite minister, 1924; pastor of Mennonite church near Peabody, Kan., 1924-25; assistant pastor of Mennonite church in Hesston, Kan., 1925-28; Hesston College, Hesston, president, 1932-51; part-time teacher, writer, and lecturer, 1951-54; Hesston College, preacher and faculty member in Bible, Greek, and Christian education, 1954-69, president emeritus, 1965—; interim pastor of Mennonite churches in Tiskilwa, Ill., 1969-70; Metamora, Ill., 1970-71, and Morton, Ill., 1973-74; writer, 1974—. Conducted teaching mission in India, Nepal, and Japan, 1962-63; assistant director of tours to Bible lands, 1972, 1974. Past member of state and national church boards and committees.

WRITINGS: Personal Work, Christian Light Publications, 1940, reprinted, 1970; *The Challenge of Christian Stewardship,* Herald Press, 1955; *Stewards of God,* Herald Press, 1975; *The Way of True Riches,* Herald Press, 1979. Contributor to church publications.

SIDELIGHTS: Kauffman told *CA:* "Since the publication of *The Challenge of Christian Stewardship* I have been asked to give stewardship messages in more than three hundred churches in the United States and Canada. I was also asked to visit our missions in India, Nepal, and Japan, giving Bible messages on the subject of stewardship. The messages were well received in these young churches.

"My latest book is *The Way to True Riches,* to be one in a series of seven entitled 'Mennonite Faith Series.' These are to be used as study books especially for young churches in various countries where the church is working. *The Way to True Riches* points the way to joy-filled giving.

"I believe man was created to share God's glory, love, peace, power, and wealth—in fact, to be filled with God. He wants us to be the channel through which His love, peace, power, and wealth flow. God's resources are sufficient to meet the needs of the world if only He had open channels through which these resources could flow."

* * *

KAUFFMANN, Samuel Hay 1898-1971

OBITUARY NOTICE: Born February 24, 1898, in Washington, D.C.; died January 12, 1971, in Washington, D.C. Newspaper executive. Kauffmann began his career at the District of Columbia's Evening Star Newspaper Co. in 1926, and served as president there from 1949 until retiring in 1963. Respected for his business acumen, he was credited with giving the *Star* a solid financial base despite the paper's former reputation for editorial blandness. Obituaries and other sources: *New York Times,* January 14, 1971; *Who Was Who in America,* 5th edition, Marquis, 1973.

* * *

KAUFMAN, Paul 1886-1979

OBITUARY NOTICE: Born July 29, 1886, in Providence, R.I.; died of heart failure, September 20, 1979, in Seattle, Wash. Educator and author. Kaufman taught at Yale, Harvard, and the University of Bordeaux before coming to the American University in 1920. An authority on Shakespeare and on the British Romantic period, he wrote several books, including *Outline Guide to Shakespeare* and *Heralds of Original Genius.* Kaufman edited the *Bulletin of the Shakespeare Association of America* from 1924 to 1933. Obituaries and other sources: *Directory of American Scholars,* Volume II: *English, Speech, and Drama,* 6th edition, Bowker, 1974; *Washington Post,* September 23, 1979.

* * *

KAVALER, Rebecca 1932-

PERSONAL: Born July 26, 1932, in Atlanta, Ga.; daughter of Emanuel and Mary (Yarwitz) Boorstein; married Frederic

Kavaler (a physiologist), 1955; children: Matthias, Joshua. *Education:* Attended Agnes Scott College, 1945; University of Georgia, B.A., 1949. *Home:* 425 Riverside Dr., New York, N.Y. 10025. *Agent:* Shirley Fisher, McIntosh & Otis, Inc., 475 Fifth Ave., New York, N.Y. 10017.

CAREER: Free-lance writer, 1948—; *Medical World News,* New York, N.Y., science writer, 1952-59; *Awards, honors:* Short fiction award from Associated Writing Programs, 1977, for *Further Adventures of Brunhild.*

WRITINGS: Further Adventures of Brunhild (stories), University of Missouri Press, 1978.

Work represented in anthologies, including *Best American Short Stories,* 1972, and *Best of Nimrod, 1957-1969.* Contributor to periodicals, including *Yale Review, Carolina Quarterly, Perspective, Phoenix,* and *Nimrod.*

WORK IN PROGRESS: A novel, *The Domestic Manners of Americans.*

SIDELIGHTS: In the introduction to *Further Adventures of Brunhild,* Wallace Stegner stated: "In Rebecca Kavaler's short stories we see, taken and vindicated, two famous pieces of literary advice. One is Henry James,s counsel that a writer should try to be one of those upon whom nothing is lost. The other is Robert Frost's corollary warning that he must be able to swing what he knows—swing both in the spirit of truth and in the spirit of a game, letting the reader in but not entirely in, surprising him, delighting him, or appalling him with the unexpected which, thought over, turns out to be the inevitable."

Reviewer Lynne Sharon Schwartz called Kavaler "a writer of extraordinary talent and vision." She wrote that her stories "forcefully stun us into recognition, fright, wry amusement, and most often, a profound sense of unease regarding the stability and benevolence of family, or more generally, human ties. In every highly charged situation she examines, Kavaler undercuts unquestioned assumptions and 'makes it new,' with a merciless eye and a wit that can peel hypocrisy bare in one ripping phrase."

Kavaler told *CA:* "Apparently I find the family a primordial 'soup'—like that which gave rise to life itself—from which all human passions are derived. The novel in progress distills from this brew the essence of marriage, concentrating on the 'shake-down' of a honeymoon spent in the bosom of an eccentric commune—a physical isolation from the outside world which is people by the familial past."

BIOGRAPHICAL/CRITICAL SOURCES: Further Adventures of Brunhild, introduction by Wallace Stegner, University of Missouri Press, 1978; *Saturday Review,* September 2, 1978.

* * *

KAVANAUGH, Cynthia
See DANIELS, Dorothy

* * *

KAYE, M(ary) M(argaret) 1909-
(Mollie Hamilton, Mollie Kaye)

PERSONAL: Born in 1909, in Simla, India; married Godfrey John Hamilton (an army officer); children: Carolyn. *Education:* Educated in England. *Address:* The Old House, Boreham St., Nr. Hailsham, Sussex, England.

CAREER: Writer; painter.

WRITINGS—All fiction: *Death Walked in Kashmir* (mystery), Staples Press, 1953; *Death Walked in Berlin* (mystery), Staples Press, 1955; *Death Walked in Cypress* (mystery), Staples Press, 1956; *Shadow of the Moon,* Messner, 1956, enlarged edition, St. Martin's, 1979; (under name Mollie Hamilton) *Later Than You Think,* Coward, 1958; *House of Shade,* Coward, 1959; *Trade Wind,* Coward, 1963; (self-illustrated) *The Animals' Vacation* (fable), New York Graphic Society, 1964; *The Far Pavilions* (historical novel), St. Martin's, 1978.

Also author of *Night of the Island,* Longmans, Green, *Six Bars at Seven,* Hutchinson, and *Strange Island,* Thacker.

For children; under name Mollie Kaye: *Potter Pinner Meadow,* decorations by Margaret Tempest, Collins, 1937. Also author of *Black Bramble Wood; Willow Witches Brook;* and *Gold Gorse Common,* Collins.

WORK IN PROGRESS: The *Far Pavilions Picture Book,* with original paintings, for Bantam.

SIDELIGHTS: Previously a successful author of children's books and mysteries, M. M. Kaye set these genres aside to concentrate on the historical novel *Far Pavilions.* After fourteen years and a grueling battle against cancer, Kaye finished the nearly one thousand-page work that has been compared to *Gone With the Wind* and Rudyard Kipling's *Kim.*

The bestselling *Far Pavilions* takes place in the mid-1800's. It chronicles "the India of the British Raj, the Bengal Mutiny and the Second Afghan War," telling of "Sahibs, murder, power and romance," described *Chapter One.* The late Paul Scott, author of *The Raj Quartet* and Kaye's editor and catalyst, remarked that "one might . . . think that M. M. Kaye had actually been present" during that era.

Kaye's sense of Indian history probably stems from the fact that she was born in India and was part of the third generation of British rule there. Brigitte Weeks pointed out Kaye's "tremendous affection, sensitivity and understanding of the Indian people, their culture, religion and traditions," as they struggled to live under British supremacy.

Another novel about India, *Shadow of the Moon,* was published in the United States in the 1950's, but not until it had been shaved of nearly sixty percent of the original manuscript. "It's about the Sepoy rebellion, and it came out when the Empire was going down the drain and feelings were very anti-colonial," Kaye explained. Then with the acclaim accorded *The Far Pavilions,* St. Martin's Press decided to republish the novel, this time in its entirety.

BIOGRAPHICAL/CRITICAL SOURCES: Washington Post, September 10, 1978, September 11, 1979; *Christian Science Monitor,* November 13, 1978; *People,* November 20, 1978; *New York Times Biographical Service,* December 3, 1978; *New York Times,* March 25, 1979; *Chapter One,* May-June, 1979; *Publishers Weekly,* June 25, 1979; *Detroit News,* October 7, 1979.*

* * *

KAYE, Mollie
See KAYE, M(ary) M(argaret)

* * *

KEACH, Richard L(eroy) 1919-

PERSONAL: Born February 8, 1919, in Norwich, Conn.; son of Edward L. (a banker) and Emma (a teacher; maiden name, Jordan) Keach; married Marjorie Walter (in real estate), January 31, 1946; children: Alison (Mrs. Robert D. Shenkus), David W., Kathlyn Keach McBride, Bruce. *Education:* Bates College, A.B., 1944; Andover Newton Theological School, B.D. (cum laude) and M.Div., both 1947, D.Min., 1977; attended Hahnemann Medical College, 1974. *Home:* 51 Randy Lane, Wethersfield, Conn. 06109. *Office:* Central Baptist Church, 457 Main St., Hartford, Conn. 06103.

CAREER: Ordained Baptist minister, 1947; Y.M.C.A. Camp Beckett, Beckett, Mass., counselor and religious education director, 1944-45; youth minister at Baptist churches in Lowell, Mass., 1945-46, and Newton Centre, Mass., 1946-47, assistant minister in Newton Centre, 1947-49; pastor of Baptist churches in Rock Springs, Wyo., 1949-52, Waterville, Maine, 1952-57, and Wayne, Pa., 1957-76; Central Baptist Church, Hartford, Conn., pastor, 1976—. New England representative to National Council of Churches, 1946-47. Member of board of directors of Center City Churches, 1976-79, and of Capital Region Conference of Churches, 1978-79. Chairman of long range planning commission of American Baptist Churches of Connecticut. Teacher at Ellen Cushing Junior College. Pastoral counselor. *Member:* Rotary International, Wethersfield Golf Club.

WRITINGS: The Purple Pulpit, Judson, 1971; *God's Spirit in the Church,* Judson, 1974. Author of church school curriculum material. Contributor of articles and reviews to church magazines.

WORK IN PROGRESS: A book on ministry in the 1980's.

SIDELIGHTS: Keach writes: "Preaching centered in the life of the people of God in the world and in the exposition of the Word of God in the Bible and the history of the church is powerful and helpful preaching. When the Spirit is present in a community, acts of love will be done. The preaching will help to interpret what God is doing through the community.

"Helping the members of a community become change agents in jobs and institutions, though risky and difficult, is essential. Worship which uses drama, visual, contemporary music and dance, as well as liturgy from the ages, which enlists persons to plan, lead, and share in the formation of the litany, will bring a community together and enable worship to become moving, meaningful, and exciting. By allowing and encouraging the community to assume responsibility for its worship life, educational life, and mission in the world, people become empowered and free to be involved."

AVOCATIONAL INTERESTS: Golf, skiing, carpentry, music, theater, reading.

* * *

KEE, (Alexander) Alistair 1937-

PERSONAL: Born April 17, 1937, in Alexandria, Scotland; son of Robert (a heavy plater) and Agnes Ballantyne (Stevenson) Kee. married Anne Mary Paterson (a secretary), 1961; children: Colin, Hilary. *Education:* University of Glasgow, M.A., 1955, B.D., 1961; Union Theological Seminary, New York, N.Y., S.T.M., 1962; Ph.D., 1964. *Religion:* Christian. *Office:* Department of Religious Studies, University of Glasgow, Glasgow, Scotland.

CAREER: Received licentiate from church of Scotland; assistant pastor of Govan Old Parish Church in Glasgow, Scotland, 1960-61; University of Rhodesia, Salisbury, lecturer in theology, 1965-67; University of Hull, Hull, England, lecturer in theology, 1967-76; University of Glasgow, Glasgow, senior lecturer and head of the department of religious studies, 1976—. Jaspers Lecturer at Ripon Hall, Oxford University, 1975. *Awards, honors:* Exchange scholar at University of Warsaw, 1979.

WRITINGS: The Way of Transcendence, Penguin, 1971; (editor) *Seeds of Liberation,* S.C.M. Press, 1973; *A Reader in Political Theology,* S.C.M. Press, 1974, revised edition, 1976; *The Scope of Political Theology,* S.C.M. Press, 1978; *Ideology, Utopia, and Religion,* S.C.M. Press, in press.

WORK IN PROGRESS: The Experience of Transcendence.

SIDELIGHTS: Kee writes: "My special interest is in the conscious or unconscious blurring of the distinction between religion and ideology. I have had practical experience in U.S. civil rights movements, and at political disturbances in Rhodesia at the time of the Unilateral Declaration of Independence (1965)."

* * *

KEEFE, Robert 1938-

PERSONAL: Born March 11, 1938, in Framingham, Mass.; son of Joseph R. and Ruth L. Keefe; married second wife, Janice A. VanderWal (a personnel officer), October 10, 1975; children: (first marriage) Heather C., Joel R. *Education:* Brandeis University, A.B., 1964; Princeton University, Ph.D., 1968. *Politics:* Democrat. *Religion:* United Church of Christ. *Home:* 24 Harlow Ave., Northampton, Mass. 01060. *Office:* Department of English, University of Massachusetts, Boston, Mass. 02108.

CAREER: University of Massachusetts, Amherst, assistant professor, 1967-77, associate professor of English, 1977—. Guest professor at University of Freiburg, 1972-73, 1977-78. Member of board of directors of Hampshire County Children's Aid and Family Service, 1979—; co-founder and member of board of directors of House, Inc. (halfway house for adolescents). *Military service:* U.S. Air Force, 1956-61. *Member:* Modern Language Association of America, Society for Religion in Higher Education. *Awards, honors:* Woodrow Wilson fellow, 1964-65.

WRITINGS: Charlotte Bronte's World of Death, University of Texas Press, 1979. Contributor to *Studies in the Novel* and *Gothic: Review of Supernatural and Horror Fiction.*

WORK IN PROGRESS: A book on Walter Pater, with wife, Janice Keefe; a biographical study of the Bronte family.

* * *

KEIFETZ, Norman 1932-

PERSONAL: Born March 21, 1932, in New York, N.Y.; son of Abraham and Edith (Berlin) Keifetz; married Joyce Engelson (an editor for a publishing company); children: Brom D., Amanda S. *Education:* New York University, B.A., 1954. *Home:* 1160 Fifth Ave., New York, N.Y. 10029. *Agent:* Philip G. Spitzer Literary Agency, 111-25 76th Ave., Forest Hills, N.Y. 11375. *Office:* 15 Park Row, New York, N.Y. 10038.

CAREER: Medical journalist and editor, 1956—. *Military service:* U.S. Navy, 1950-53. *Member:* American Academy of Sports Medicine.

WRITINGS: (With Charlotte Sheedy) *Cooking for Your Celiac Child,* Dial, 1972; *A Jack Is a King* (novel), Dial, 1962; *The Sensation* (novel), Atheneum, 1975; *Welcome Sundays* (novel), Putnam, 1979. Contributor to periodicals, including *Medical World News, Chicago Review, Quixote,* and *New York Times Magazine.*

WORK IN PROGRESS: Another novel.

SIDELIGHTS: Keifetz told *CA:* "I consider it pretentious, arrogant, and egomaniacal to set down my feelings about my work as a novelist. I hope that as I write my novels your readers will be kind enough to read me. And, in return, I hope I can provide them with some moments of enjoyment. All the rest is vanity, not worthy of sharing."

* * *

KEIL, Sally Van Wagenen 1946-

PERSONAL: Born July 10, 1946, in Glens Falls, N.Y.; daughter of Edward Richard (a conservationist) and Catherine (an early childhood education specialist; maiden name, Parker) Keil. *Education:* Vassar College, B.A., 1968; New York University, M.A., 1975. *Home:* 125 Riverside Dr., New York, N.Y. 10024.

CAREER: U.S. Congress, Washington, D.C., legislative assistant, 1968-69; New York Office of Community Affairs, New York City, writer, 1970-71; free-lance writer, 1971-75; Caribiner, Inc., New York City, writer, 1975-76; Robert Fearon Associates, New York City, part-time copywriter, 1977—.

WRITINGS: Those Wonderful Women in Their Flying Machines: The Unknown Heroines of World War II, Rawson, Wade, 1979. Contributor to magazines, including *New York, Money,* and *Viva.*

WORK IN PROGRESS: A biography of flier and businesswoman Jacqueline Cochran, publication expected in 1982.

SIDELIGHTS: Sally Keil writes: "I believe that social history, contemporary and from centuries past, can live on the page through its actors and, inevitably, one of the actors is the writer. It's the writer's responsibility—and joy—to live that history in the act of writing and to give of his or her ongoing emotional and intellectual life to a book. Nonfiction becomes novelistic, fiction resonates with reality.

"In writing about World War II's women pilots, of whom there were almost two thousand, totally ignored by the postwar generation, my five-year task was to uncover their astonishing story through interviews, research the context of their exploits, and portray them as human beings like you and me, suddenly finding the heroic in themselves.

"I had to learn to fly airplanes, as flying was the language in which these women expressed themselves. While writing, I had to live the terror of an engine fire and the grief of escorting a flying buddy's body home. Involvement in a subject can and must push the writer to broaden his or her experience and to learn ever new human languages.

"The fear, and challenge, in writing is that, as you put a story together from facts observed or details imagined, no one else can make judgments for you or even confirm that you are right. No one can tell you what to do, and no one can relieve you of that responsibility. It's a life of ultimate honesty—to yourself—and to an unremitting search to understand."

* * *

KELLAND, Clarence Budington 1881-1964

OBITUARY NOTICE: Born July 11, 1881, in Portland, Mich.; died February 18, 1964. Journalist, short story writer, novelist, and public relations worker. Early in his career Kelland was a reporter for the *Detroit News,* editor of *American Boy,* and lecturer at the University of Michigan. While at *American Boy,* he published the popular "Mark Tidd" series as well as several other juvenile writings. Kelland began writing fiction for adults in 1921 with perhaps his most popular work, *Scattergood Baines.* Among his numerous other books are *The Great Crooner,* 1933, *Valley of the Sun,* 1940, *Stolen Goods,* 1950, and *Mark of Treachery,* 1961. Obituaries and other sources: *The Oxford Companion to American Literature,* 4th edition, Oxford University Press, 1965; *The Reader's Encyclopedia,* 2nd edition, Crowell, 1965; *Who Was Who in America,* 4th edition, Marquis, 1968.

* * *

KELLER, Helen (Adams) 1880-1968

OBITUARY NOTICE: Born June 27, 1880, in Tuscumbia, Ala.; died June 1, 1968, in Westport, Conn. Author, worker on behalf of the blind and deaf, and counselor on international relations for American foundations for the blind. After an illness had left her blind and deaf at the age of nineteen months, Helen Keller rose to become a legend and inspiration for people throughout the world. With the ingenious aid of her teacher, Anne Sullivan, Keller was transformed from a wild and unruly seven-year-old to a young girl fascinated by learning. Taught to read with her fingertips, to speak by imitating the facial motions of those speaking, and to "hear" by feeling the lips and throats of others as they spoke, Keller made progress thought impossible in a time when most of the nation's deaf and blind were left in asylums. Her formal schooling began at fourteen; at twenty she had gained entrance to Radcliffe, where she graduated cum laude in 1904. Her first book, *The Story of Life,* was written during her college years, and was followed by several other books and inspirational articles. A growing awareness of social issues led Keller to join the Socialist party, but by 1921 she had decided she could serve humanity most effectively by working on behalf of the blind and deaf. Armed with her warm personality and her unrelenting spirit, she campaigned actively for the American Foundation for the Blind until 1962. For her work she received acclaim and awards internationally, including the Presidential Medal of Freedom from Lyndon Johnson in 1964. Among her other books are *My Religion,* 1927, *Helen Keller's Journal,* 1938, and the biography of Anne Sullivan, *Teacher,* 1955. Obituaries and other sources: *Current Biography,* Wilson, 1942, July, 1968; Van Wyck Brooks, *Helen Keller: Sketch for a Portrait,* Dutton, 1956; *The Oxford Companion to American Literature,* 4th edition, Oxford University Press, 1965; *The Reader's Encyclopedia,* 2nd edition, Crowell, 1965; *Faith of Helen Keller: The Life of a Great Woman,* edited by Jack Belck, Hallmark, 1967; *Helen Keller: Her Socialist Years* (writings and speeches), edited by Philip S. Foner, International Publications, 1967; *New York Times,* June 2, 1968; *Time,* June 7, 1968; *Newsweek,* June 10, 1968; Helen Keller, *Midstream: My Later Life,* Greenwood Press, 1968; Margery Weiner, *Helen Keller,* Heron Books, 1970; *Longman Companion to Twentieth Century Literature,* Longman, 1970; Keller, *My Religion,* Swedenborg Foundation, 1972; *Who Was Who in America,* 5th edition, Marquis, 1973; Keller, *Helen Keller's Journal,* Chivers, 1973; John William Tibble and Anne Tibble, *Helen Keller,* revised edition, Pan Books, 1973; Keller, *The Story of My Life,* Pendulum Press, 1974.

* * *

KELLEY, Win 1923-

PERSONAL: Born November 6, 1923, in Pryor, Okla.; son of William O. and Audrey (Bruce) Kelley; married Catherine Elizabeth Hann (a high school counselor), June 5, 1948; children: Klinda Kelley Sayers, Kasma, Kanda Kelley Whaley, Korwin. *Education:* Pacific University, B.A., 1950; University of Oregon, M.Ed., 1954; University of Southern California, Ed.D., 1962; graduate of Geller Theatre Workshop; also attended Pennsylvania State University, California State College, Long Beach, and California State College, Los

Angeles. *Politics:* Republican. *Religion:* United Methodist. *Home:* 1913 East Foothill Blvd., Glendora, Calif. 91740. *Office:* Department of Language Arts, Citrus College, Azusa, Calif. 91702.

CAREER: Professional actor in Hollywood and New York City, 1946-48; *New York Journal-American,* New York City, copy typist, 1948; high school English, speech, and drama teacher in Prospect, Coquille, and Coos Bay, Ore., 1950-56; Compton Community College, Compton, Calif., teacher and director of drama and speech, 1956-58; Citrus College, Azusa, Calif., speech-drama teacher and director of drama, 1958-64, director of forensics and speech, 1965—. Guest professor at University of Southern California, 1971-72. *Military service:* U.S. Army Air Forces, 1943-45; served in Pacific theater.

MEMBER: Speech Communication Association of America, American Forensics Association, National Education Association, American Association of University Professors, Western Speech Association, California Teachers Association, Faculty Association of California Community Colleges (member of council, 1965—), Inland Forensics Association (president, 1966-70), American Legion (commander, 1967-68). *Awards, honors:* Second place award from Portland Civic Theatre's national play contest, 1953, for "Wailatpu"; George Washington Honor Medal from Freedoms Foundation, 1972, for pageant, "America the Beautiful."

WRITINGS: Wailatpu; or, The Place of Rye Grass (three-act play; first produced in Coos Bay, Ore., at Little Theatre on the Bay, May 26, 1955), Pageant, 1952; *The Art of Public Address,* Brown Book, 1963; (with Leslie Wilbur) *Teaching in the Community Junior College,* Appleton, 1970; *Breaking the Barriers in Public Speaking,* Kendall/Hunt, 1978. Also author of unpublished plays, including "Death Takes a Hand," "The Road Beyond," and "America the Beautiful."

Author of "Tidbits From Broadway," drama column in *Talent Review,* 1947-48; "Kulture Korner," cultural arts column in *Coos Bay Times,* 1954-55; "Broadway Beat," drama column in *Coos Bay Times,* 1955-56. Contributor to speech and education journals. Member of editorial board of *Community Junior College Research Quarterly,* 1977-80.

WORK IN PROGRESS—Novels: *Orion Hill,* a fantasy; *Joshua Fit the Battle,* based on an event from Oregon history; *Snowball From Hell,* about an actor.

SIDELIGHTS: Kelley writes: "My work in education takes most of my time, but I'm very eager to get a novel into print. My motivation is my desire to express myself in writing and to share this with others. The process is challenging and stimulating; it's thrilling to know that one has contributed to the entertainment and/or instruction of the reader. It's one of the highest forms of art, and, as Henry James wrote, 'It is art that makes life, makes interest, makes importance, . . . and I know of no substitute whatever for the force and beauty of its process.'"

AVOCATIONAL INTERESTS: Oil painting, golf, travel.

*   *   *

KELLY, C(harles) Brian 1935-

PERSONAL: Born February 11, 1935, in New York, N.Y.; son of Lester J. (a businessman) and Claire (an entrepeneur; maiden name, Murray) Kelly; divorced; children: Katheryn, Charles, Jr., James, Elizabeth. *Education:* Yale University, B.A., 1957; also attended University of Virginia, Madison University, and Georgetown University. *Residence:* Charlottesville, Va.

CAREER/WRITINGS: Journalist, writer. *Richmond Times-Dispatch,* Richmond, Va., copy-desk trainee and stringer, 1958; *Harrisonburg Daily News-Record,* Harrisonburg, Va., staff writer, 1959-60; *Richmond News Leader,* Richmond, staff writer, 1960-61; *Washington Star,* Washington, D.C., staff writer, 1962-79. Notable assignments include coverage of murder of George Lincoln Rockwell and subsequent trial of accused murderer, political events in Virginia, and a seven-part series on seventeenth-century American rebel Nathaniel Bacon. Work anthologized in *True Stories of Great Escapes, Reader's Digest, 1977.* Contributor to periodicals, including *Reader's Digest, Catholic Digest, Fantasy and Science Fiction, West Indian Review, National Observer,* and *Friends. Military service:* Virginia Air National Guard; became first lieutenant. *Member:* National Press Club.

AWARDS, HONORS: First Prize from Washington Newspaper Guild, 1965, for local reporting; award for public affairs reporting from American Political Science Association, 1970, for political coverage in Virginia; fellowship from American Political Science Association, 1971-72; fourth-place for conservation reporting from Scripps-Howard Foundation, 1975; honorable mention from Washington Journalism Center, 1975 and 1976, for national conservation reporting; honorable mention from Washington-Baltimore Newspaper Guild, for public service reporting, 1976; Communicator of the Year Award from National Wildlife Federation, 1976, for coverage of Virginia's Kepone environmental disaster.

WORK IN PROGRESS: Two novels; a collection of stories, *Gentleman From Chuckatuck;* contributing chapter on Kepone contamination in Virginia for anthology being compiled by Ralph Nader.

SIDELIGHTS: Kelly told *CA:* "I simply enjoy telling a good story, fiction or non, but in transition from journalist to fiction writer I have noted a few differences along with the similarities. A number one is the new freedom—from fact. No need now to weigh each statement for factual accuracy or even for objectivity. In fiction, one is constrained only by the context of the work underway and the factual accuracy demanded by plausibility, i.e., cars bearing the hero will not go upsidedown. As one result, the new writing may seem like a breeze. But caution: too easily whipped off, the results may be utter garbage.

"Personally I find fiction more satisfying, because it offers more of an opportunity to develop the narrative story, my preference in either discipline. The fiction writer can find a journalistic background useful not only for its training, but also for the bits and pieces of plot situations that it serves up long after the fact.

"Naturally, one has more time in fiction writing to get the piece done, but the journalist-in-transition will find it a lonely adjustment. Beyond non-professional readers among family or friends, there is no 'desk' to react within hours—even minutes—to your most strenuous efforts. The cogent words of today will not appear in print today or even tomorrow. No strangers will call or write to agree or to argue. Assuming you can make that sale, it will be months before your material appears in print. And by then, you may be too wrapped up in a new project to pay that much attention anyway.

"In my own case, a career-long bent towards feature writing has been helpful. I find it agreeable to write a series of scenes—i.e., vignettes or features—carrying the story along. The key, however, is to approach the entire work, even the upcoming 'scene' with a basic story line in mind. The details seem to work themselves out. But all is lost if no plot soon appears.

"Whatever the form of my writing, the journalism of old or the new attempts at fiction, I believe my best preparation came in a single writing course at Yale University more than twenty years ago: 'Daily Themes.' While the lectures and individual conferences were helpful in that instance, the key was the requirement to turn in a short piece of writing every day, five days a week.

"I've been doing it ever since."

* * *

KELLY, Gary F(rank) 1943-

PERSONAL: Born November 24, 1943, in Canton, N.Y.; son of Homer T. (a bank president) and Eleanor (a dietitian; maiden name, Jamieson) Kelly; married Betsy Ann Leroux (a planned parenthood educator), May 31, 1975; children: Casey Delia. *Education:* St. Lawrence University, B.S. (cum laude), 1966, M.Ed., 1971. *Home address:* R.D. 1, Bagdad Rd., Potsdam, N.Y. 13676. *Agent:* Lorna Brown, Ned Brown, Inc., P.O. Box 2082, Grand Central Station, New York, N.Y. 10017. *Office:* Student Development Center, Clarkson College, Potsdam, N.Y. 13676.

CAREER: Teacher and counselor at public schools in Norwood, N.Y., 1967-73; Clarkson College, Potsdam, N.Y., director of Student Development Center, 1973—, and of student life and counseling for the Clarkson School program, 1978—. Adjunct assistant professor at St. Lawrence University, 1974—. Member of board of directors of Sex Information and Education Council of the United States, 1971-73, and Planned Parenthood of Northern New York, 1971-78.

MEMBER: American Association of Sex Educators, Counselors, and Therapists, American Personnel and Guidance Association, American College Personnel Association, Association of Specialists in Group Work, New York State Personnel and Guidance Association (northern region vice-president, 1979-80), Phi Beta Kappa, Beta Beta Beta, Psi Chi, Phi Delta Kappa. *Awards, honors:* Citations from Planned Parenthood and Sex Information and Education Council of the United States; *Learning About Sex* was listed among best books for young people by American Library Association, 1978.

WRITINGS: The Guidance Counselor as Sex Educator (monograph), Human Sciences Press, 1976; *Sex Education for Adolescents and Youth* (monograph), American Association of Sex Educators, Counselors, and Therapists, 1977; *Sex Counseling for Adolescents and Youth* (monograph), American Association of Sex Educators, Counselors, and Therapists, 1977; *Learning About Sex* (juvenile), Barron's, 1977; *Sexuality: The Human Perspective,* Barron's, 1979; *Good Sex: The Healthy Man's Guide to Sexual Fulfillment,* Harcourt, 1979. Guest editor of *Personnel and Guidance Journal,* 1976; media review editor of *Journal of Sex Education and Therapy.*

WORK IN PROGRESS: A book for parents, on teenagers; research on male sexuality and adolescent sexuality.

SIDELIGHTS: Kelly writes: "My involvement in the field of human sexuality has represented a workable blend of my undergraduate study in biology and my later career as a counselor and therapist. I am certified as a sex educator and sex therapist and feel that one of my main missions is to help people feel more comfortable with and accepting of their sexualities. It is an area that needs de-mystifying for the layperson, and current research provides interesting material for everyone interested in this vast and complex field.

"After three books, I feel that I have said about all I have to offer about sex for the time being. I am anxious to publish innovative ideas in other aspects of human relations and family life. It saddens me to see the dismal failures so common to contemporary marriages and family units, largely caused by the absence of help given to young people in understanding how to communicate and share emotions. Nowhere are people learning how much work and commitment must be a part of healthy, dynamic marital and family relationships. It is time institutions such as schools and churches woke up to the responsibilities they could be taking for improving the situation."

* * *

KEMAL, Yashar 1923-

PERSONAL: Original name, Yashar Kemal Gokceli; born in 1923, in Adana, South Anatolia, Turkey; son of Sadik and Nigar Gokceli; married Thilda Serrero, 1952; children: Rasit (son). *Education:* Attended elementary school and secondary schools in Turkey. *Home:* P K 14 Basinkoy, Istanbul, Turkey.

CAREER: Novelist and journalist. Prior to 1950 held a variety of jobs, including day laborer, watchman, and teacher; arrested in 1950 for alleged Communist propaganda, later acquitted; moved to Istanbul, Turkey, in 1951 and worked as a journalist, writing under the name of Yashar Kemal to escape further police harassment; reporter, then Anatolia bureau chief of *Cumhuriyet* (daily newspaper), Istanbul; member of Turkish Workers Party central committee, and political candidate in 1965; arrested and imprisoned in 1971 for political views, released, then later sentenced to eighteen months for Communist propaganda, sentence suspended under general amnesty. *Member:* Turkish Writers Union (president), Authors League of America. *Awards, honors:* Varlik Prize, 1956, for *Ince Memed;* Iskender Award for best play of 1965-66, for "Teneke"; first prize at Fourteenth International Theatre Festival, 1966, for "Yer demir, gok bakir"; Madarali Award for best Turkish novel, 1973, for *Demirciler carsisi cinayeti;* Prix du Meilleur Livre Etranger, 1978, for *Olmez otu.*

WRITINGS—In English; all novels, except as noted: *Ince Memed,* Remzi Kitabevi, 1955, translation of Part I by Edouard Roditi published as *Memed, My Hawk,* Pantheon Books, 1961, translation of Part II by Margaret E. Platon published as *They Burn the Thistles,* Collins, 1973, Morrow, 1977; *Ortadirek,* Remzi Kitabevi, 1960, translation by wife, Thilda Kemal, published as *The Wind From the Plain,* Collins, 1963, Dodd, 1969; *Yer demir, gok bakir,* Guven Yaginevi, 1963, translation by Thilda Kemal published as *Iron Earth, Copper Sky,* Collins, 1974, Morrow, 1979; *Butun hikayeler,* Ararat Yayinevi, 1967, translation by Thilda Kemal published as *Anatolian Tales* (short stories and a novella; contains "A Dirty Story," "The White Trousers," "The Drumming-Out," "On the Road," "The Baby," "Green Onions," and "The Shopkeeper"), Collins, 1968, Dodd, 1969; *Olmez otu,* Ant Yayinlari, 1968, translation by Thilda Kemal published as *The Undying Grass,* Collins, 1977, Morrow, 1978; *Agridagi efsanesi,* Cem Yayinevi, 1970, translation by Thilda Kemal published as *The Legend of Ararat,* Collins, 1975; *Binbogalar efsanesi,* Cem Yayinevi, 1971, translation by Thilda Kemal published as *The Legend of the Thousand Bulls,* Collins, 1976; *Demirciler carsisi cinayeti,* Cem Yayinevi, 1973, translation by Thilda Kemal published as *Murder in the Ironsmith's Market,* Collins, 1979.

In Turkish; nonfiction: *Yanan ormanlarda 50 gun* (reportages; title means "Fifty Days in the Burning Forests"), Turkiye Ormancilar Cemiyeti, 1955; *Cukurova yana yana* (reportages; title means "While the Chukurova Burns"), Yeditepe Yayinlari, 1955; *Peri bacalari* (reportages; title means "The Fairy Chimneys"), Varlik Yayinlari, 1957; *Tas catlasa* (essays; title means "The Stones Cry Out"), Atac Kitabevi, 1961; *Bu dijar bastan basa* (collected reportages; contains "Yanan ormanlarda 50 gun," "Cukurova yana yana," and "Peri bacalari"; also see above), Cem Yayinevi, 1972; *Bir bulut kayniyor* (collected reportages; title means "A Cloud Is Churning Up"), Cem Yayinevi, 1974; *Baldaki tuz* (essays and political writings; title means "Salt in the Honey"), Cem Yayinevi, 1974; *Allahin askerleri* (reportages; title means "God's Soldiers"), Milliyet Yayinlari, 1978.

Fiction: *Sari sicak* (short stories; title means "Yellow Heat"), Varlik Yayinlari, 1952; *Teneke* (novella), Varlik Yayinlari, 1955, English translation published in *Anatolian Tales* (also see above); *Uc anadolu efsanesi* (short stories; title means "Three Anatolian Legends"), Ararat Yayinevi, 1967; *Cakircali efe,* Ararat Yayinevi, 1972; *Yusufouk Yusuf* (novel; title means "Yusuf, Little Yusuf"), Cem Yayinevi, 1975; *Yilani oldurseler* (novel; title means "Kill the Serpent"), Cem Yayinevi, 1976; *Al gozum seyreyle salih* (novel; title means "Salih, the Gazer"), Cem Yayinevi, 1976; *Filler sultani ile kirmizki sakalli topal karinca* (novel for children; title means "The Sultan of the Elephants and the Red-Bearded Lame Ant"), Cem Yayinevi, 1977; *Kuslar da gitti* (novel; title means "The Birds Have Also Gone"), Milliyet Yayinlair, 1978; *Deniz kustu* (novel; title means "The Sea Is Sullen"), Milliyet Yayinlari, 1978.

Plays: "Teneke," first produced in Istanbul, 1965; "Yer demir, gok bakir," first produced in Nancy, France, at the Fourteenth International Theatre Festival, 1966, produced in Istanbul and Ankara, Turkey, 1967.

Also author of a folklore study in Turkish, published in 1943. Contributor of poetry, short stories, and folklore research to numerous Turkish periodicals.

WORK IN PROGRESS: Kimsecik, a novel in two volumes, title means "Little Nobody."

SIDELIGHTS: Descended from a family of feudal landowners on his father's side and a notorious group of bandits on his mother's, Yashar Kemal is a progressive and politically conscious writer who has been jailed repeatedly for his socialist convictions. Branded as a Communist early in his life, Kemal held over forty odd jobs before becoming a journalist and Turkey's most famous and "revered" novelist.

Kemal's early life almost seems to be a prelude to the lives of the characters in his best-selling novels. As a young boy of five he witnessed the murder of his father in a mosque; the tragic event left him with a severe stutter that lasted for several years. Determined to finish his education, and because there was no school in his village, the young Kemal went to live with relatives in the town of Kadirli and there completed his primary school education. He entered secondary school, but left after two years of study to work in the cotton fields and factories of Turkey.

Later, Kemal left the fields to earn his living as a public letter-writer. In 1950, he was arrested for spreading "Communist propaganda," but was acquitted after a trial. During his time in prison, however, an attempt was made on his life; he had made many enemies among the wealthy landowners who were often the targets of Kemal's letters. Even after his release the landowners sent the local police to his house two or three times a week to look for more propaganda. Kemal soon left his village for Istanbul and managed to get a job on the daily newspaper *Cumhuriyet*. Kemal's success, first as a journalist, and later as a novelist, provided him with protection against further harassment by the police, although he was imprisoned once more in 1971.

Kemal, as expected, has carried his political views into his work and, as Larry Rohter observed, "is set on portraying the essential decency of the peasant and the difficulty of his struggle for existence." For Kemal and other "proletarian writers," Rohter noted, "the novel exists primarily as a vehicle to examine social and political ills. . . . [But] Kemal feels so strongly about the issue of exploitation that it sometimes gets in the way of his writing. The episodes intended to show the evil nature of the landowners and their henchmen, for example, are social realism at its most melodramatic and clumsy."

In his first novel, *Ince Memed,* Kemal's hero is a kind of Turkish Robin Hood. Ince Memed, or "Slim Memed," leaves his village to fight against the agha (landowner) who has subjugated the villagers to a life of near starvation. Memed has been brutally beaten many times by the Agha Abdi. He sees fellow villagers toiling in the fields and then being forced to give half their grain to the agha. The contrast between the villagers and the agha is sharp: while the villagers are dressed in homespun, the agha parades around in an embroidered silk shirt, with a velvet cap perched on his head, and the large amber beads of a rosary in his hands.

Memed is determined to seek a better life for himself and leaves the village. His whereabouts are soon discovered and he is "returned" to the village. Upon his arrival Memed witnesses more of the viciousness of the agha: his mother is forced to pay in grain for the help she received in the fields during Memed's absence. The family will starve unless they are given food from other villagers, but the agha has forbidden it, threatening those who extend some help. The family is forced to sell their newly-born calf to the agha. Memed soon leaves the village again and becomes an "idealistic outlaw."

In English translation *Ince Memed* has appeared in two separate works, *Memed, My Hawk* and *They Burn the Thistles.* According to Paul Theroux, *They Burn the Thistles* "is a worthy successor to 'Memed, My Hawk' and ought to send readers swiftly to 'The Legend of the Thousand Bulls,' 'Anatolian Tales' or 'The Wind From the Plain.'" In this novel Memed once again rescues the villagers from an evil agha, but this time it is the "Tyrant Ali Safa Bey." For Theroux the plot of the novel is "like myth, but the mythic quality is given concreteness in the distinct personalities of the villagers; they are real people, not aspects of political argument."

Critics have agreed that Kemal is fair and realistic in the portrayal of the peasants he so loves. Rohter noted that Kemal "in his portrait of the common folk offers more detail and strikes a more balanced tone. Though he writes with great affection of their closeness to land and animals, their day-to-day routine, and their quiet faith—he criticizes their timorousness and lack of organization." Katha Politt agreed and added that Kemal's "villagers possess neither earthy wisdom nor natural piety—nor, one might add, class consciousness. They are gullible, cruel and calculating: their feuds and quarrels are so hotheaded as to seem positively whimsical." Phyllis Birnbaum found that Kemal "gives a sense of the villagers' despondency and of the soothing routine of their existence" in his writing. These villagers do not openly revolt against tyranny—in fact in most of the novels the hero is the only character who actively tries to change existing situations. As Birnbaum noted, "The villagers . . . feel no resentment toward the humans who keep them impoverished but rather curse the mosquitoes and the rains that may ruin the crop. They seek salvation not through organizing but through primitive religion."

Slim Memed is followed by another peasant hero, Long Ali, in *The Wind From the Plain* and *The Undying Grass*. According to Talat Sait Halman, *The Wind From the Plain* "lionizes the dauntless spirit of the peasant to survive": Long Ali, his wife, and his mother make a treacherous journey through the mountains to a cotton field where Ali hopes to get a job. In the sequel, *The Undying Grass,* Long Ali must again go to the cotton fields to find work, but this time only his wife accompanies him; his mother is left behind in the village because the journey proved to be too much for her last time and also because she slowed down her son so much that he missed the chance to pick cotton. Long Ali is on time for the season and is the fastest cotton picker, but he must deal with the antagonism of the other villagers who feel that he has surely committed his mother to death. Long Ali picks cotton at night so that he might sooner return to his village and his mother.

Halman called *The Wind From the Plain* "the Turkish village novel par excellence," because "it typifies the strongest features as well as some of the basic defects of this genre. The narration is fluent and forceful, dialogue crisp and colorful, and the plot engrossing. Its principal failing is also typical: The characters, while serving admirably as stock-types, are devoid of individual traits and lack psychological motivation except for the pressures of poverty."

Pollitt noted that *The Undying Grass* "is a bit slow-moving, but as a portrait of a people and a way of life it couldn't be better." Birnbaum, meanwhile, pointed out its essential pessimism: "If Kemal had written a manifesto, he might have allowed himself some optimism—for pure politics, unlike fiction, presumes change and hope. Yet a novel was the more difficult choice, and *The Undying Grass* proves that art can be as rousing as the soapbox. . . . This is how the villages continue and how they may remain forever. When the landlord arrives (with his paunch and the inevitable Mercedes) to dole out the meager wages, no guerrilla band swoops down from just over the hill. Such happy endings belong to the theorists. [This novel] is as chilling and realistic a portrayal of Third World village society as we are likely to get."

According to Theroux, "the author with whom Kemal feels a special kinship . . . is William Faulkner." But unlike Faulkner, Kemal has yet to win a Nobel Prize. Many critics pointed out that it is only a matter of time before Turkey's most famous novelist will be rightly recognized for his contributions to literature. "In the final analysis," Rohter noted, "it is probably because he deals so effectively with the theme of the soil that Kemal has become Turkey's first world-class novelist. To write simply and eloquently in a language whose modern mode is barely 50 years old—and in a form essentially foreign to the literary tradition of that language—is impressive enough. But to create a work that can be felt and understood by anyone with a yearning for justice and a love for humanity is even more so."

Most of Kemal's books have been published in foreign-language editions. *Ince Memed* alone was published in more than fifteen countries, including Sweden, Moldavia, Portugal, Hungary, and India. A play based on *The Wind From the Plain* was written by Alan Seymour and produced in Turku, Finland, in 1974. Ali Taygun wrote a play based on *The Legend of Ararat* that was produced in Istanbul, Turkey, on September 28, 1974.

BIOGRAPHICAL/CRITICAL SOURCES: Best Sellers, March 15, 1969; *Books Abroad,* winter, 1970; *Times Literary Supplement,* May 25, 1973, May 3, 1974; *New Statesman,* May 25, 1973, June 21, 1974; *Washington Post Book World,* July 3, 1977; *New York Times Book Review,* July 10, 1977, June 18, 1978, August 19, 1979; *World Literature Today,* autumn, 1977; *Saturday Review,* May 27, 1978.

—Sketch by Nancy M. Rusin

* * *

KEMENY, Peter 1938-1975

OBITUARY NOTICE—See index for *CA* sketch: Born December 24, 1938, in Chicago, Ill.; died December 11, 1975, in New York, N.Y. Editor, free-lance writer, and author of four books, including *The Way It Was: 1950-60*. Kemeny, who had been editor-in-chief of the scholarly reprint firm Garland Publishing, was also affiliated with George Braziller, Inc., Macmillan Publishing Co., and Viking Press. Obituaries and other sources: *New York Times,* December 16, 1975; *Publishers Weekly,* December 29, 1975.

* * *

KEMSLEY, Viscount
See BERRY, James Gomer

* * *

KENNAWAY, James 1928-1968
(Pebles Ewing)

OBITUARY NOTICE: Born in 1928 in Scotland; died in an automobile accident, December 21, 1968, near London, England. Kennaway left his publishing position with Longmans, Green in 1957, when the success of his first novel, *Tunes of Glory,* convinced him that he could make a living as a writer. The story of an ancient Scottish regiment, *Tunes of Glory* was adapted for the screen by Kennaway in 1960. As a novelist, Kennaway was respected for his intelligence and his versatility, as well as for his habit of probing for the realities beneath surface truths. Among his other works are the novels *The Mind Benders* and *Some Gorgeous Accident,* and the play, "Country Dance." Two other novels, *The Cost of Living Like This* and *Silence,* were published posthumously. Obituaries and other sources: *New York Times,* December 25, 1968; *Publishers Weekly,* January 20, 1969; *World Authors, 1950-1970,* Wilson, 1975.

* * *

KENNEDY, Eddie C. 1910-

PERSONAL: Born December 29, 1910, in Orton, W.Va.; son of Howard E. (a farmer) and Loretta (Lowther) Kennedy; married Marguerite Gerwig, May 13, 1927; children: Edward G., Helen K. Davies, Anita Lou, David L. *Education:* Glenville State College, A.B., 1947; George Peabody College for Teachers, A.M., 1948; Indiana University, Ed.D., 1951. *Home and office:* 3413 Collins Ferry Rd., Morgantown, W.Va. 26505.

CAREER: Public school teacher in Gilmer County, W.Va., 1932-42; Glenville State College, Glenville, W.Va., instructor and director of elementary student teaching, 1948-49; Indiana University, Bloomington, instructor, 1949-51; Glenville State College, department chairman of education and psychology, 1951-53; West Virginia University, Morgantown, director of elementary student teaching, 1953-55, department chairman of elementary education, 1955-58, acting dean of College of Education, 1958, Reading Center coordinator, 1959-72, professor of education, 1972-76, professor emeritus, 1976—. Private consultant in language arts, reading disabilities, and educational measurement. *Military service:* U.S. Army Air Forces, 1942-45; received Belgian Fourragere from Belgian Government and a Bronze Star, 1945.

WRITINGS: Reading for Classroom Teachers, College of Education, West Virginia University, 1957; *Handbook in Remedial Reading,* College of Education, West Virginia University, 1958, revised edition, 1970; *Language Arts for Classroom Teachers,* College of Education, West Virginia University, 1961; *Essentials in Teaching Reading,* McClain, 1966; *Classroom Approaches to Remedial Reading,* F. E. Peacock, 1971, 2nd edition, 1977; (with Ruth C. Lewis) *In-Service Training in Remedial Reading,* Paul S. Amidon & Associates, 1974; *Methods in Teaching Developmental Reading,* F. E. Peacock, 1979. Author of lecture series presented on Educational Television, 1965 and 1974. Contributor of articles to proceedings and to various journals in his field.

WORK IN PROGRESS: Secondary Reading Instruction; Reading for Slow Learners.

AVOCATIONAL INTERESTS: Refinishing antique furniture, constructing hand-made violins, guitars, mountain mandolins and dulcimers.

* * *

KENNY, Kathryn
See BOWDEN, Joan Chase

* * *

KENNY, Nicholas Napoleon 1895-1975
(Nick Kenny)

OBITUARY NOTICE: Born February 3, 1895, in Astoria, N.Y.; died December 1, 1975, in Sarasota, Fla. Newspaper columnist, poet, and songwriter. Kenny worked as a columnist, sports writer, and rewrite man for several eastern newspapers before joining the *New York Daily Mirror* in 1930. His syndicated column, "Nick Kenny Speaking," featured news about entertainment personalities as well as his own poetry, sentimental verse similar to that of Edgar A. Guest. Kenny also wrote popular songs, including "Love Letters in the Sand," "Little Old Cathedral in the Pines," and "There's a Gold Mine in the Sky." He was president of his Gold Mine in the Sky Publishing Co. from 1946 until 1975. Obituaries and other sources: *New York Times,* December 2, 1975; *Who Was Who in America,* 6th edition, Marquis, 1976.

* * *

KENNY, Nick
See KENNY, Nicholas Napoleon

* * *

KERR, Barbara 1913-

PERSONAL: Born September 21, 1913, in Chiswick, London, England; daughter of Arthur Francis (a botanist) and Daisy (Judd) Kerr. *Education:* Trinity College, Dublin, B.A., 1936; St. Anne's College, Oxford, B.Litt., 1939. *Politics:* Liberal. *Religion:* Church of England. *Home:* Grants Farm, Gallows Hill, Wareham, Dorsetshire BH20 6HH, England.

CAREER: War Cabinet Offices, London, England, assistant principal, 1942-44; United Nations Relief & Rehabilitation Administration, administrator in London, England, and Belgrade, Yugoslavia; soil sampler for Agricultural Executive Committee, England, 1950-53; tutor in London, England, 1954-56; writer. *Member:* Dorset Natural History and Archaeological Society. *Awards, honors:* Mansell-Pleydell Prize from Dorset Natural History and Archaeological Society, 1966.

WRITINGS: Bound to the Soil: A Social History of Dorset, 1750-1918, Humanities, 1968; *The Dispossessed: An Aspect of Victorian Social History,* John Baker, 1974. Contributor of more than a dozen articles to history journals and to *Lady.*

WORK IN PROGRESS: Research on eighteenth- and nineteenth-century agricultural history, with special reference to social problems in rural areas.

* * *

KESSEL, Joseph (Elie) 1898-1979

OBITUARY NOTICE: Born February 10, 1898, in Clara, Argentina; died July 23, 1979, near Paris, France. Journalist, novelist, and screenwriter. Kessel spent most of his early life in Russia and then in France, where he was educated and fought in World War I. He reflected his own passion for travel in his literary works, which earned a reputation for their action and adventure. After his involvement with the Resistance Movement in France during World War II, Kessel continued his work in journalism as well as his prolific output of novels. He wrote more than fifty in his career, including *L'Armee des ombres* ("Army of Shadows"), *Le Lion* ("The Lion"), *Belle du jour,* and *Les Cavaliers* ("The Horsemen"). Among his awards are the Grand Prix du Roman, 1927, the Prix des Ambassadeurs, 1958, and the Prix Rainier III, 1959. Obituaries and other sources: *The Reader's Encyclopedia,* 2nd edition, Crowell, 1965; *Encyclopedia of World Literature in the Twentieth Century,* updated edition, Ungar, 1967; *Cassell's Encyclopaedia of World Literature,* revised edition, Morrow, 1973; *Who's Who in the World,* 2nd edition, Marquis, 1973; *World Authors, 1950-1970,* Wilson, 1975; *The International Who's Who,* Europa, 1977; *New York Times,* July 25, 1979; *Chicago Tribune,* July 25, 1979; *Time,* August 6, 1979; *AB Bookman's Weekly,* August 20, 1979.

* * *

KESTNER, Joseph A(loysius) 1943-

PERSONAL: Born September 12, 1943, in Horton, Kan.; son of Joseph (an engineer) and Mary Jo (a music teacher; maiden name, Lindsay) Kestner. *Education:* State University of New York at Albany, B.A. (magna cum laude), 1965; Columbia University, M.A., 1966, Ph.D., 1969. *Residence:* New York, N.Y. *Office:* Graduate Faculty of Modern Letters, University of Tulsa, Tulsa, Okla. 74104.

CAREER: Princeton University, Princeton, N.J., assistant professor of English, 1969-73; Bernard M. Baruch College of the City University of New York, New York, N.Y., assistant professor of English, 1973-78; University of Tulsa, Tulsa, Okla., associate professor of modern letters, 1978—. *Member:* Jane Austen Society of North America, Modern Language Association of America, American Society for Aesthetics, Midwest Modern Language Association. *Awards, honors:* Woodrow Wilson fellowship, 1969.

WRITINGS: Jane Austen: Spatial Structure of Thematic Variations, University of Salzburg Press, 1974; *The Spatial-*

ity of the Novel, Wayne State University Press, 1978. Contributor to language and literature journals and *Opera News.*

WORK IN PROGRESS: A study of semiology of the novel; research on James Joyce's *Exiles.*

SIDELIGHTS: Kestner told *CA:* "The most stimulating kind of writing and scholarship links various fields rather than compartmentalizes; in *The Spatiality of the Novel* I used considerable theory from the plastic arts, music, and the physical sciences. In writing I tend to let an idea gestate for some time, taking notes when an impression or insight develops. After a draft is finished, I allow time before writing the final version.

"Since I teach nineteenth-century English and European literature, I feel my criticisms of contemporary literature are not flattering by comparison with the extraordinary achievements of the last century. The relationship between publishing and marketing is so pronounced in commercial publishing that I suspect many fine works never see the light. The vast part of contemporary fiction is distressing in its quite narrow scope, in its packaged format, in its insidious promotion. Fair or not, my standards originate with Jane Austen, Tolstoy, George Eliot, Stendhal, and Dostoyevsky.

"I am a voracious reader. In my opinion, only an extremely wide range of reading will generate new ideas and new approaches. It also supplies the stringent standards by which any honest writer must live."

* * *

KETCH, Jack
See TIBBETTS, John C(arter)

* * *

KETTNER, James H(arold) 1944-

PERSONAL: Born October 4, 1944, in Greenville, Ohio; son of E. Harold (a Lutheran minister) and Edna (Powell) Kettner. *Education:* Harvard University, A.B., 1966, Ph.D., 1978; University of Sussex, B.A., 1968. *Office:* Department of History, University of California, Berkeley, Calif. 94720.

CAREER: University of California, Berkeley, acting assistant professor, 1973-74, lecturer, 1974-77, assistant professor, 1977-79, associate professor of history, 1979—. *Member:* American Historical Associationiety for Legal History, Organization of American Historians, Association of Marshall Scholars and Alumni, Phi Beta Kappa. *Awards, honors:* Marshall scholarship for England, 1966-68; Jamestown Prize from Institute of Early American History and Culture, 1975, for *The Development of American Citizenship.*

WRITINGS: The Development of American Citizenship, 1608-1870, University of North Carolina Press, 1978. Contributor of articles and reviews to history and law journals.

WORK IN PROGRESS: Research on the late colonial and early national periods of American history and on the impact of the American Revolution on American law and constitutionalism.

SIDELIGHTS: A reviewer for *Choice* called *The Development of American Citizenship* "a truly great book . . . , the finest, freshest, and most significant book about any aspect of American history to have appeared in recent years." Beginning with the colonial period, Kettner traces the legal origins of American nationality through the post-Civil War era, illuminating, "as no work ever has, the history of naturalization in American jurisprudence." According to the *Choice* critic, he treats his subject "with stunning clarity" and produces a "whole new perspective of the meaning of citizenship."

BIOGRAPHICAL/CRITICAL SOURCES: Choice, April, 1979.

* * *

KEY, Alexander (Hill) 1904-1979

OBITUARY NOTICE—See index for *CA* sketch: Born September 21, 1904, in La Plata, Md.; died July 25, 1979, in Eufaula, Ala. Illustrator, free-lance writer, and author, best known for his children's book, *Escape to Witch Mountain.* Key, who illustrated his first book at the age of nineteen, taught art at Studio School of Art in Chicago. He was the author of a dozen children's books and two adult novels, *The Wrath and the Wind* and *Island Night.* Obituaries and other sources: *Authors of Books for Young People,* 2nd edition, Scarecrow, 1971; *The Writers Directory, 1980-82,* St. Martin's, 1979; *Publishers Weekly,* August 20, 1979.

* * *

KEYLOR, William R(obert) 1944-

PERSONAL: Born August 15, 1944, in Sacramento, Calif.; son of Robert and Thelma Keylor; married Rheta Grenoble (a clinical psychologist), December 28, 1968; children: Daniel Robert. *Education:* Stanford University, B.A., 1966; Columbia University, M.A., 1967, Ph.D., 1971. *Office:* Department of History, Boston University, Boston, Mass. 02215.

CAREER: Rutgers University, Newark, N.J., lecturer, 1968-69, instructor in history, 1970-72; Boston University, Boston, Mass., assistant professor, 1972-75, associate professor of history, 1975—. Guest on French television programs. *Member:* American Historical Association, Society for French Historical Studies, American Association of University Professors, Inter-University Center for European Studies. *Awards, honors:* Fulbright fellowship for University of Paris-Vincennes, 1969-70; Woodrow Wilson fellowship, 1970-71; Guggenheim fellowship, 1978.

WRITINGS: Academy and Community: The Foundation of the French Historical Profession, Harvard University Press, 1975; (editor with Dora B. Weiner, and contributor) *From Parnassus: Essays in Honor of Jacques Barzun,* Harper, 1976; *Jacques Bainville and the Renaissance of Royalist History in Twentieth-Century France,* Louisiana State University Press, 1979.

WORK IN PROGRESS: A History of International Relations Since 1914, publication by Oxford University Press expected in 1981; research on Franco-American relations, 1919-23.

SIDELIGHTS: Keylor writes: "My career as a student of modern French history began in the autumn of 1964. I had previously intended to specialize in American government and foreign policy, but my exposure to French society and culture, together with my high opinion of the European section of the Stanford University history department, diverted me from my chosen path.

"At Columbia University I found myself holding down three jobs simultaneously. While these obligations encroached upon my study time, each provided me with invaluable experience. In my capacity as an interviewer for the Oral History Research Office, I learned the art of coaxing autobiographical information out of the most reticent of interviewees. A year-long stint as a radio announcer for the French Government Radio Station in New York City (during which I conducted a program that was broadcast to France) enabled me to perfect my spoken French.

"In the spring of 1968 the entire university was disrupted by a student strike which proved to be the first in a series of campus disorders that engulfed the entire Western world. In the aftermath of these events, I was elected as a delegate to the student-faculty committee that was formed to recommend reforms of the history department. It was during this service that I first became interested in the issues that were later to serve as important themes in my first book: the nature of the historical profession, the relationship between scholarship and politics, and the role of the university in modern history.

"While my *scholarly* work has been in the field of modern French intellectual, political, and educational history, my *pedagogical* activities have centered on European-American international relations. During the past year and a half I have focused exclusively on that subject, conducting research in Washington, D.C., and in Paris."

BIOGRAPHICAL/CRITICAL SOURCES: Times Higher Education Supplement, October 24, 1975; *American Historical Review,* December, 1978.

* * *

KIESZAK, Kenneth 1939-

PERSONAL: Born March 31, 1939, in Brooklyn, N.Y.; son of Chester J. and Mary (Motyka) Kieszak; married Maria Janniello (a teacher), August 21, 1965; children: Stephanie, Christine, Denise. *Education:* Queens College of the City University of New York, B.A., 1961, M.S., 1965. *Religion:* Roman Catholic. *Home:* 2416 Ocean Ave., Brooklyn, N.Y. 11229. *Office:* John Ericsson Junior High School, 424 Leonard St., Brooklyn, N.Y. 11222.

CAREER: John Ericsson Junior High School, Brooklyn, N.Y., teacher of social studies, 1961—.

WRITINGS: They Showed the Way, Curriculum Research Press, 1970; *Turning Point: A Collection of Short Biographies,* Globe Book Co., 1973; *Puntos Criticos* (title means "Turning Point"), Globe Book Co., 1977; *Journeys to Fame: A Collection of Short Biographies,* Globe Book Co., 1978; *Information Please,* Globe Book Co., 1979.

WORK IN PROGRESS: Above the Crowd, a reading puzzle workbook, publication by Globe Book Co. expected in 1981; *Branching Out,* an interdisciplinary approach to biographical study for the gifted, Globe Book Co., 1982.

SIDELIGHTS: Kieszak writes: "From the age of twelve until I was twenty-one I worked as a dishwasher and waiter in the Catskills. After graduation, my future was unclear. I tried a number of jobs, but felt unhappy in what I was doing. I decided I would like to be a teacher and took the entrance examination for college. I failed. I was informed that I could attend college in the evening and when I could maintain a B average I would be accepted into the regular day college. I graduated from college in 1961.

"I returned to the place of my birth to teach. Besides my regular day school job, I worked for three years in the evenings teaching English to our foreign-born adults. I learned Japanese and became acquainted with teaching machines.

"My teaching career has been a very happy and rewarding experience. It has been my fortune to work with people in my profession who have stimulated me in finding new approaches to educating my students. One such approach was the Ethnic Culture Center that I initiated at my school. At present I am working as a member of a committee on the study of the gifted. I am exploring new avenues and hope to become involved in writing materials for the needs of these high-potential students."

AVOCATIONAL INTERESTS: Gardening, collecting material about Pope John Paul II.

* * *

KILDAHL, John P. 1927-

PERSONAL: Born December 24, 1927, in Owatonna, Minn.; son of Johan Lauritz and Edith (Glasoe) Kildahl; married Joyce Peterson. *Education:* St. Olaf College, B.A., 1949; Luther Theological Seminary, B.D., 1953; New York University, Ph.D., 1957. *Office:* 120 East 62nd St., New York, N.Y. 10021.

CAREER: Postgraduate Center for Mental Health, New York City, faculty member; New York Theological Seminary, New York City, professor of psychology and director of programs in pastoral psychology; Center for Personal Growth Programs, New York City, president; currently in private practice in psychotherapy and psychoanalysis. Consultant to agencies and institutions. *Military service:* U.S. Navy, 1945-46. *Member:* American Psychological Association, American Association of University Professors, New York State Psychological Association, Society of Clinical Psychologists, Society for the Scientific Study of Religion.

WRITINGS: (With Lewis R. Wolberg) *The Dynamics of Personality,* Grune, 1970; *The Psychology of Speaking in Tongues,* Harper, 1972.

WORK IN PROGRESS: A book on thinking.

* * *

KILGALLEN, Dorothy (Mae) 1913-1965

OBITUARY NOTICE: Born July 3, 1913, in Chicago, Ill.; died November 8, 1965. Journalist, columnist, and radio and television performer. With the *New York Evening Journal* Kilgallen first earned notoriety for her series of articles on her around-the-world flight in 1936. The articles, her comments from various stops on her twenty-four day trip, were published in book form as *Girl Around the World* in 1937. Kilgallen's attention switched to the entertainment industry in 1938 when she began her syndicated *Journal-American* column, "Voice of Broadway." She was also a film, television, and radio performer, appearing in the motion picture "Winner Take All," on the television program "What's My Line?," and with husband Dick Kollmar on the long-running radio program "Breakfast With Dorothy and Dick." Kilgallen, who was investigating the assassination of President John Kennedy at the time of her death, died of a lethal combination of drugs and alcohol. Obituaries and other sources: *Current Biography,* Wilson, 1952, January, 1966; *New York Times,* November 9, 1965; *Who Was Who in America,* 4th edition, Marquis, 1968; Lee Israel, *A Biography of Dorothy Kilgallen,* Delacorte, 1979.

* * *

KILLOUGH, (Karen) Lee 1942-
(Sarah Hood, Kathy Leigh)

PERSONAL: Born May 5, 1942, in Syracuse, N.Y.; daughter of Rex Ledonald (a teacher of Spanish) and Esther Margaret (in newspaper work; maiden name, Reed) Schwein; married Howard Patrick Killough, Jr. (an instructor in business law), August 27, 1966. *Education:* Attended Fort Hays State College, 1960-62, and Hadley Memorial Hospital

School of Radiologic Technology, 1962-64. *Politics:* Independent. *Religion:* Independent. *Home address:* P.O. Box 422, Manhattan, Kan. 66502. *Office:* Veterinary Hospital, Kansas State University, Manhattan, Kan. 66506.

CAREER: St. Joseph Hospital, Concordia, Kan., radiologic technician, 1964-65; St. Mary Hospital, Manhattan, Kan., radiologic technician, 1965-67; Morris Cafritz Memorial Hospital, Washington, D.C., radiologic technician, 1968-69; St. Mary Hospital, Manhattan, radiologic technician, 1969-71; Kansas State University, Veterinary Hospital, Manhattan, radiologic technician, 1971—. *Member:* World Science Fiction, Science Fiction Writers of America, Kansas Associated Writing Programs, Oklahoma Science Fiction Writers.

WRITINGS: A Voice Out of Ramah (science fiction novel), Del Rey Books, 1979; *The Doppelganger Gambit* (science fiction novel), Del Rey Books, 1979; *Ka'ch'ka* (science fiction adventure novel), Del Rey Books, 1980.

Work represented in anthologies, including *One Hundred Great Science Fiction Short Short Stories,* edited by Isaac Asimov, Martin H. Greenberg, and Joseph D. Olander, Doubleday, 1978. Contributor, sometimes under pseudonyms, of articles to technical journals and stories to magazines, including *Sol Plus, Fantasy and Science Fiction, Analog,* and *American Girl.*

WORK IN PROGRESS: Research for *Deadly Silence,* a science fiction mystery novel.

SIDELIGHTS: Lee Killough comments: "Mystery themes keep appearing in what I write. I was hooked on mysteries and science fiction in junior high school, and I suppose I've never outgrown the love of either. I seem to be able to combine the two in my writing.

"I find myself writing two different kinds of stories. Most of my short fiction is psychological or surrealistic, bordering on fantasy. For my novels, however, I work out extrapolations of today's softer sciences: sociology, anthropology, psychology.

"I take some pains to make the novels as realistic as I can, but without being too pessimistic. In spite of a somewhat cynical view of humanity as a whole, I tend to have faith in its individual members and I believe my general outlook is optimistic. If I didn't believe there was a future for Man, I don't believe I could write science fiction. But I do believe that some of Mankind will survive, perhaps be able to deal with the destructiveness and greed in our nature. I embrace science fiction as a delightful, hopeful genre and make full use of its open-end anything-is-possible outlook to play with ideas about the future and alternate realities."

* * *

KING, Alan 1927-

PERSONAL: Birth-given name, Irwin Alan Kniberg; born December 26, 1927, in New York, N.Y.; son of Bernard (a handbag cutter) and Minnie (Solomon) Kniberg; married Jeannette Sprung, February 1, 1947; children: Robert, Andrew, Elaine Ray. *Education:* Educated in Brooklyn, N.Y. *Religion:* Jewish. *Home:* 40 Shore Dr., Kings Point, Great Neck, N.Y. 11024. *Office:* 67 West 55th St., New York, N.Y. 10019.

CAREER: Comedian, Broadway producer, actor, and writer. Performed in nightclubs in United States and abroad; toured with Judy Garland during 1950's; appeared on television shows, including "The Ed Sullivan Show" and "The Garry Moore Show"; frequent guest-host on "The Tonight Show"; producer of Broadway productions, including "The Lion in Winter," 1965, and "Something Different," 1967; actor in stage productions, including "Guys and Dolls," 1965, and "The Impossible Years," 1965-66, and motion pictures, including "The Girl He Left Behind," 1956, "Miracle in the Rain," 1956, and "Bye, Bye Braverman," 1968. Founder of Alan King Diagnostic Medical Center in Israel. *Member:* Friars (New York City chapter).

WRITINGS—Humor: (With Kathryn Kyan) *Anybody Who Owns His Own Home Deserves It,* Dutton, 1962; (with Jack Shurman) *Help! I'm a Prisoner in a Chinese Bakery,* Dutton, 1964. Author of recordings, including "Alan King in Suburbia," Seeco Records, 1962. Contributor to periodicals, including *Show.*

SIDELIGHTS: After years of working as an opening act for such performers as Lena Horne and Billy Eckstein, King became a hit before an audience of Judy Garland's fans in 1956. His popularity increased greatly during a tour of Great Britain with Garland. When he returned to the United States King was a frequent guest on variety shows hosted by showbiz luminaries such as Ed Sullivan. King also began hosting his own specials but was turned down when he proposed his own weekly series.

During the 1960's, King's stage personality was that of the embittered "suburbs victim." He would lament about life outside the city with his wife as the primary nemesis. He told his audience that he once rose at 5 a.m. to go to the bathroom only to return and discover the bed already made. He later included this anecdote and many others in a collaborative effort, *Anyone Who Owns His Own Home Deserves It.* The book was essentially a compilation of King's tape-recorded comments on the suburbs as arranged by Kathryn Ryan. In a review of the book, Gene Graff wrote, "Rapid fire patter abounds, and virtually all home owners will agree King has captured the spirit of struggling along with crabgrass . . . and the inevitable cocktail and dinner parties." A critic for the *New York Herald-Tribune Books* was less impressed, noting that "all the jokes are about the same thing, a constant, monotonous threnody on the theme of 'What am I doing here?'"

King's second book, *Help! I'm a Prisoner in a Chinese Laundry,* was written in similar fashion and devoted to thirteen topics, including marriage, doctors, and pregnancy. A writer for *Best Sellers* found the witticisms "as funny to read as they are to hear straight from this master comedian's genial mouth." Obviously impressed, the same reviewer cautioned readers not to "send this to a friend hospitalized after abdominal surgery—he or she will bust stitches laughing."

King's humor grew increasingly political towards the end of the 1960's. He lashed out against Spiro Agnew and vowed that he wouldn't be intimidated by the Nixon administration. He also supported some politicians, including John Lindsay and Robert Kennedy. King's interest in family affairs became more pronounced, too. Faced with his son's drug addiction, King realized that he had slighted his family in favor of his career and various philanthropic activities. "It's not easy being a father," King related. "But I've been allowed a comeback. The greatest danger is that we see what is happening but we don't want to see it, we don't want to believe it." King's son is no longer a drug addict and the comedian reported a change in his family. "Now everyone kisses," he said. "We show our affections."

BIOGRAPHICAL/CRITICAL SOURCES: Chicago Tribune, May 13, 1962; *New York Herald-Tribune Books,* May 27, 1962; *Best Sellers,* October 15, 1964; *New York Post,* February 28, 1970; *New York Times,* July 31, 1972.*

KING, Frank O. 1883-1969

OBITUARY NOTICE: Born April 9, 1883, in Cashton, Wis.; died June 23, 1969. Artist and creator of cartoon strips. King drew for the *Minneapolis Times, Chicago Examiner,* the *Chicago Tribune,* and for the Chicago Tribune-New York News Syndicate. His "Bobby Make Believe" and "The Rectangle" comic strips appeared before he began his popular "Gasoline Alley" strip in 1918. Obituaries and other sources: *New York Times,* June 25, 1969; *Time,* July 4, 1969; *Newsweek,* July 7, 1969; *Who Was Who in America,* 5th edition, Marquis, 1973.

* * *

KING, Irving H(enry) 1935-

PERSONAL: Born May 31, 1935, in Milo, Maine; son of Cornelius Michael and Ina (Boyd) King; married Ann Bosland, August 26, 1961; children: Michael, Gregory, Elizabeth, Patrick. *Education:* University of Maine, B.A., 1959, M.A., 1962, Ph.D., 1968. *Politics:* Democrat. *Religion:* Roman Catholic. *Home:* 12 Erie Lane, Noank, Conn. 06340. *Office:* Department of Humanities, U.S. Coast Guard Academy, New London, Conn. 06320.

CAREER: King's College, Wilkes-Barre, Pa., assistant professor of history, 1963-66; U.S. Coast Guard Academy, New London, Conn., assistant professor, 1966-68, associate professor, 1968-72, professor of history, 1972—. Program evaluator for National Endowment for the Humanities. *Military service:* U.S. Army, 1954-56. *Member:* American Historical Association, New England Historical Association, Phi Mu Delta (past president), Phi Kappa Phi, Sigma Mu Sigma.

WRITINGS: George Washington's Coast Guard, U.S. Naval Institute Press, 1978. Contributor to history magazines.

WORK IN PROGRESS: A multi-volume history of the U.S. Coast Guard.

SIDELIGHTS: King writes: "Historians have paid surprisingly little attention to Coast Guard history, yet this service and its forerunners, the U.S. Revenue Cutter Service, the Lighthouse Service, and the Life-Saving Service, combine the fascinating story of national politics and the development of the maritime industry with the saga of sailing ships and the naval establishment. Not only was the Revenue Cutter Service the nineteenth-century ancestor of today's Coast Guard, but it later helped to build the U.S. Navy. My subsequent research continues to reveal equally fascinating and important new material about our nation's past."

* * *

KING, Ivan R(obert) 1927-

PERSONAL: Born June 25, 1927, in New York, N.Y.; son of Myram (an upholsterer) and Anne (Franzblau) King; married Alice Greene (an attorney), November 21, 1952; children: David, Lucy, Adam, Jane. *Education:* Hamilton College, A.B., 1946; Harvard University, A.M., 1947, Ph.D., 1952. *Residence:* Berkeley, Calif. *Office:* Department of Astronomy, University of California, Berkeley, Calif. 94720.

CAREER: Harvard University, Cambridge, Mass., instructor in astronomy, 1951-52; University of Illinois, Urbana-Champaign, assistant professor, 1956-61, associate professor of astronomy, 1961-64; University of California, Berkeley, associate professor, 1964-66, professor of astronomy, 1966—, head of department, 1967-70. Mathematician for Perkin-Elmer Corp., 1951-52. *Military service:* U.S. Naval Reserve, 1952-59, active duty, 1952-54; became lieutenant. *Member:* International Astronomical Union, American Astronomical Society (member of council, 1963-66; president, 1978-80), American Association for the Advancement of Science (head of Astronomy Section, 1973).

WRITINGS: The Universe Unfolding, W. H. Freeman, 1976. Contributor to scientific journals.

* * *

KING, James G. 1898(?)-1979

OBITUARY NOTICE: Born c. 1898; died September 22, 1979, in Cambridge, Mass. Historian and author. King taught American and British history at Black Mountain College, Boston University, and New York University. In addition to a co-authored biography of his great-great-grandfather, Federalist leader Rufus King, James King had also recently published two volumes of poetry. Obituaries and other sources: *New York Times,* September 25, 1979.

* * *

KING, Teri 1940-
(pseudonym)

PERSONAL: Born in 1940; daughter of Arthur William and Veronica Ratcliffe; married Kenneth Pickett (a songwriter); children: Deborah, Justin, Lindsay. *Education:* Attended grammar school in Battersea, London, England. *Politics:* "Open-minded." *Religion:* Church of England. *Home:* 6 Elm Grove Rd., Barnes, London S.W.13, England.

CAREER: Professional model, 1956-67; astrologer, 1971; free-lance writer, 1972; *Daily Scottish Record,* astrologer, 1973—.

WRITINGS: Love, Sex, and Astrology, Allison & Busby, 1972; *Business, Success, and Astrology,* Allison & Busby, 1974; *The Astrology Diet Book,* Allison & Busby, 1976; *A Deeper Understanding of Child and Baby Care,* Angus & Robertson, 1979. Contributor to magazines, including *Men Only* and *Successful Slimming,* and newspapers.

SIDELIGHTS: Teri King writes: "I became an astrologer in order to sort out my own life, then my friends' lives, and my children's. My first book was a worldwide success, then my husband began writing hit songs after taking my advice as an astrologer. Most recently I predicted the English Derby."

* * *

KING, William Donald Aelian 1910-

PERSONAL: Born June 23, 1910, in Surrey, England; married Anita Leslie (a writer); children: Tarka Dick, Leonie. *Education:* Attended Royal Naval College, 1923-27. *Home:* Oranmore Castle, Galway, Ireland.

CAREER: Writer. *Military service:* Royal Navy, submarine commander, 1939-45; became commander; received Distinguished Service Order with bar and Distinguished Service Cross. *Awards, honors:* Blue water trophy; Sir Francis Chichester Award.

WRITINGS: The Stick and the Stars, Hutchinson, 1967; *Capsize,* Nautical Publishing, 1969; *Adventure in Depth,* Putnam, 1975.

SIDELIGHTS: King writes: "I wrote my first book to describe what it was like to fight underwater for five years. I sailed around the world alone in the yacht *Galway Blaze,* and wrote the last book to explain how a five-month sail alone to Australia without touching land and a five-month sail home got the war out of my system."

KIPLINGER, Willard Monroe 1891-1967

OBITUARY NOTICE: Born January 8, 1891, in Bellefontaine, Ohio; died August 6, 1967. Journalist, publisher, and author. Kiplinger was best known for his publication, *The Kiplinger Washington Letter,* which he began in 1923. An opinionated assessment of Washington trends and events, the weekly letter sold throughout the nation to clients eager to know the nation's political and economic climate. Kiplinger's other publishing ventures included a book club, the *Kiplinger Foreign Trade Letter,* and the magazine, *Changing Times.* Among his books are *Washington Is Like That,* 1942, *Boom and Inflation Ahead,* 1958, and *Your Guide to a Higher Income,* 1959. Obituaries and other sources: *Current Biography,* Wilson, 1943, 1962, October, 1967; *New York Times,* August 7, 1967; *Time,* August 18, 1967; *Newsweek,* August 21, 1967; *Who Was Who in America,* 4th edition, Marquis, 1968.

* * *

KIPPHARDT, Heinar 1922-

PERSONAL: Born March 8, 1922, in Heidersdorf, Upper Silesia, Germany. *Education:* Attended Universities of Bonn, Koenigsberg, Breslau, and Wuerzburg; Medical Academy, Duesseldorf, received Doctor of Medicine. *Home:* Goteboldstrasse 54, D-8000 Munich, West Germany.

CAREER: Deutsches Theater, East Berlin, East Germany, literary adviser and chief dramatist, 1950-59; free-lance dramatist, short story writer, novelist, and poet, 1959-71; Kammerspiele (Intimate Theatre), Munich, West Germany, chief dramatist, 1971—. Assistant doctor at Charite Neurological Clinic, East Berlin, c. 1950-59. *Member:* German Academy of Representational Arts, West German P.E.N. Center. *Awards, honors:* East German National Prize, 1953; Schiller Memorial Prize, 1962; Gerhart Hauptmann Prize, 1964; Adolf Grimme Prize, 1965; television prize of the German Academy of Representational Arts, 1975; film prize of the Society of German Doctors, 1976; Prix Italia, 1976; Bremer Prize, 1977.

WRITINGS—Plays: *Shakespeare dringend gesucht: Ein satirisches Lustspiel in drei Akten* (title means "Shakespeare Urgently Sought: A Satirical Comedy in Three Acts"; first produced in West Germany, June, 1953), Henschelverlag, 1954; *Der Aufstieg des Alois Piontek: Eine tragikomische Farce* (title means "The Rise of Alois Piontek: A Tragicomic Farce"), Henschelverlag, 1956; "Die Stuehle des Herrn Szmil" (adapted from novel, *The Twelve Charis,* by Ilf and Petrov; title means "Mr. Szmil's Chairs"), first produced in Wuppertal, 1961; *Der Hund des Generals: Schauspiel* (title means "The General's Dog: Drama"; first produced in Munich, April, 1962), Suhrkamp, 1963; *In der Sache J. Robert Oppenheimer* (first produced in West Berlin at Freie Volksbuehne, 1964), Suhrkamp, 1966, translation by Ruth Speirs published as *In the Matter of J. Robert Oppenheimer* (produced in Los Angeles at Mark Taper Forum, June, 1968), Methuen, 1967, Hill & Wang, 1969; *Die Soldaten* (title means "The Soldiers"; adapted from play of the same title by Jacob Michael Reinhold Lenz), Suhrkamp, 1968; *Leben des schizophrenen Dichters, Alexander Maerz* (film scenario; title means "Life of the Schizophrenic Poet, Alexander Maerz"), Wagenbach, 1976; *Stuecke* (title means "Plays"), two volumes, Suhrkamp, 1973-74. Also author of: "Esel schreien im Dunkeln" (title means "Donkeys Bray in the Dark"), 1958; "Joel Brand: Die Geschichte eines Geschaefts" (title means "Joel Brand: The Story of a Deal"), 1963; "Der Nacht in der Chef geschlachtet wurde" (title means "The Night the Boss Was Slaughtered"), 1965.

Other works: *Die Ganovenfresse: Zwei Erzaehlungen* (title means "The Ganoven Mouth: Two Stories"; contains "Die Ganovenfresse" and "Der Hund des Generals"), Ruetten & Loening, 1964; *Maerz* (novel), Bertelsmann, 1976; *Der Mann des Tages und andere Erzaehlungen* (title means "The Man of the Day and Other Stories"; contains "Der Mann des Tages," "Der Hund des Generals," and "Der Deserteur"), Bertelsmann, 1977; *Angelsbrucker Notizen: Gedichte* (title means "Notes From Angelsbruck: Poems"), watercolors by Helmut Grieshaber, Bartelsmann, 1977.

SIDELIGHTS: Kipphardt's early life was deeply scarred by the horrors of the Nazi regime. He saw his father taken away to spend five years in Buchenwald. Later, his own medical studies were interrupted by his conscription into the Wehrmacht. He served with a panzer division on the Russian front until 1944, when he deserted. After the war, Kipphardt resumed his studies, qualifying as a neurologist. It was at this time that he began to write. Kipphardt worked for a time at the Charite Neurological Clinic in East Berlin, at the same time serving as literary adviser and chief dramatist at the Deutsches Theater in the same city. It was there that his first play was staged in June, 1953.

Kipphardt's first play, *Shakespeare dringend gesucht* ("Shakespeare Urgently Sought"), drew on his experience as a dramaturge to satirize postwar theatre in East Germany, where third-rate plays were being hailed as masterpieces if only they dealt earnestly enough with social problems. Two more satirical comedies followed, *Der Aufstieg des Alois Piontek* ("The Rise of Alois Piontek"), attacking East German bureaucracy, and "Esel schreien im Dunkeln" ("Donkeys Bray in the Dark"). Kipphardt resumed his attack on bureaucratic corruption and incompetence in *Die Stuehle des Herrn Szmil* ("Mr. Szmil's Chairs"), a dramatization of the famous Russian comic novel *The Twelve Chairs,* by Ilf and Petrov. The satire proved too sharp to be tolerated by the East German authorities and the play, due to open in 1959 at the Deutsches Theatre, was banned. The same year Kipphardt left East Berlin and moved to West Germany, settling first in Duesseldorf, later in Munich. *Die Stuehle des Herrn Szmil* was eventually staged in Wuppertal in 1961.

In the West, Kipphardt for a time abandoned satire and turned to the documentary mode that also produced Rolf Hochhuth's *The Deputy* and Peter Weiss's *The Investigation.* According to one critic, Kipphardt soon established himself as "West Germany's leading documentary dramatist. Schooled in the Brechtian tradition, Kipphardt works with spare language and hypotactic structures to reconsider the evidence of disputed political cases." His first experiment in this style dealt, in fact, with an imaginary case. *Der Hund des Generals* ("The General's Dog") puts on trial a German officer who had sent an entire regiment of soldiers to their death during the war because one of them had accidentally killed his dog. The play is both an investigation of the psychological roots of fascism and an indictment of postwar West Germany, where war criminals like Kipphardt's general live as free and respected citizens.

In the Matter of J. Robert Oppenheimer opened in 1964 at Erwin Piscator's famous West Berlin theatre, the Freie Volksbuehne. It was staged in Munich later the same year, and has since been seen all over Europe and in the United States. Oppenheimer was chairman of the General Advisory Committee of the United States Atomic Energy Commission, and was regarded as "the father of the atomic bomb." However, he was at one time an associate of communists and communist sympathizers, and he had puzzled some of his colleagues by his opposition to the crash program to develop the hydrogen bomb in 1949. In the McCarthyist America of 1954 this was enough to bring him before the Personnel Security Board of the AEC for an investigation into his loyalty. Kipphardt's play is based on the transcripts of the hearing, but does introduce some characters who were not in fact present at the hearing, and for dramatic and legal reasons takes certain other liberties with the facts. The play also makes use of such Brechtian "alienation effects" as newsreel clips, tape recordings, and newspaper headlines, all designed to prevent the audience from becoming so immersed in the human drama on stage that they forget the much larger tragedy of Hiroshima and the continuing threat of atomic war.

In the Matter of J. Robert Oppenheimer had its American premiere at the Mark Taper Forum in Los Angeles in June, 1968, and was revived in March, 1969, by the Repertory Theatre of Lincoln Center. The New York production, in particular, had an immensely controversial reception. Much of the debate centered on Kipphardt's decision "to subordinate word-for-word accuracy to accuracy of meaning." Oppenheimer himself objected to what he called "improvisations which were contrary to history and to the nature of the people involved." On the other hand, R. Hinton Thomas and Keith Bullivant in *Literature in Upheaval* pointed out that Kipphardt "is not attempting merely to recreate the trial but, without falsifying Oppenheimer's position, to use it as a means of making a more general statement—in this case about the relationship between the scientist and the politicians." It was this larger concern which reminded a number of critics of Brecht's *Galileo*.

There was also a mixed reaction to the play considered purely as a theatrical work. Eric Bentley, for example, thought it marred by an excess of themes, so that "there is no play-as-a-whole, there are at best energetic dialogues laid end to end," while the title character is too passive, is brought too little into dynamic relation with the other characters. He nevertheless found it "a lively, thought-provoking drama," and Clive Barnes enjoyed its "incidental humor, neat quirks of character, and sudden shifts of pace." Some critics took it much more seriously than this, and Catharine Hughes called it "easily one of the most significant American theatrical events of the late 1960's, even if it did again require a European to confront us with ourselves." Kipphardt himself has said that "if our theatre is not able to deal with the key political questions of our time, then one will no longer be able to take it seriously. Then it will sink to the level of other media for the manipulation of false sentiment."

A third documentary play followed, *"Joel Brand: Die Geschichte eines Geschaefts"* ("Joel Brand: The History of a Deal"). This is based on Adolf Eichmann's 1944 proposal that one million Hungarian Jews might be spared the death camps if the Allies would provide the Nazis with ten thousand trucks and trailers. It fell to Joel Brand, himself a Hungarian Jew, to try to negotiate this ghastly transaction. Kipphardt says that "the material and the main characters are historical. For the purpose of writing the drama the author took the liberty of concentrating the action around those major political points he thought important." As Thomas and Bullivant wrote in *Literature in Upheaval,* the extermination of the Jews was, for Eichmann and his colleagues, "simply a matter of doing a job. Their characteristic language was . . . [that] of the minor official under pressure, reducing human lives to mere statistics. . . . The horror of the situation is heightened by the ironic fact that those wishing to save the lives of the Jews are forced, because of the vastness of their undertaking and the nature of the negotiations, to talk the same language." Kipphardt illuminates the way people acted primarily through dialogue, using the language of what Theodor Adorno called the "verwaltete Welt"—a world dominated by the soulless problems of administration.

Kipphardt returned to the satirical mode in "Die Nacht, in der Chef geschlachtet wurde" ("The Night the Boss Was Slaughtered"), in which an average West German couple dream of escape from the confines of bourgeois life. Their dreams, conditioned by advertising, turn out to be nightmares of crass insensitivity and greed. *Die Soldaten* ("The Soldiers") is an adaptation of a play by an earlier German satirist, J.M.R. Lenz (1751-92), whose attack on eighteenth-century militarism and bourgeois complacency was, critics thought, much sharpened in Kipphardt's version. The author has also published poems and short stories and a prize-winning novel, *Maerz,* whose tormented hero is also the central figure in his film scenario, *Leben des schizophrenen Dichters, Alexander Maerz* ("Life of the Schizophrenic Poet, Alexander Maerz").

BIOGRAPHICAL/CRITICAL SOURCES: August Closs, *Twentieth Century German Literature,* Cresset Press, 1969; John Gassner and Edward Quinn, editors, *Reader's Encyclopedia of World Drama,* Crowell, 1969; Ronald Hayman, editor, *The German Theatre,* Barnes & Noble, 1971; Michael Anderson and others, *Crowell's Handbook of Contemporary Drama,* Crowell, 1971; Eric Bentley, *Theatre of War,* Viking, 1972; Catharine Hughes, *Plays, Politics, and Polemics,* Drama Book Specialists, 1973; R. Hinton Thomas and Keith Bullivant, *Literature in Upheaval: West German Writers and the Challenge of the 1960s,* Barnes & Noble, 1974; Henry and Mary Garland, *Oxford Companion to German Literature,* Clarendon Press, 1976.*

* * *

KIRKLAND, Wallace W. 1891(?)-1979

OBITUARY NOTICE: Born c. 1891 in Jamaica; died September 14, 1979, in Oak Park, Ill. Photographer and author. Kirkland directed a boy's club in Chicago before joining *Life* magazine as one of its first photographers. He became known for his work in photojournalism as well as his photographs of such dignitaries as Mohandas Gandhi and Franklin D. Roosevelt. His first book, *Recollections of a Life Photographer,* appeared in 1954; he was working on a second, *Jamaica Boy,* at the time of his death. Obituaries and other sources: *New York Times,* September 19, 1979.

* * *

KIRSCHENBAUM, Howard 1944-

PERSONAL: Born October 6, 1944, in New York, N.Y.; son of Abraham I. (an attorney) and Theone (Hamburger) Kirschenbaum; married Barbara Jean Glaser (an educator), March 2, 1973. *Education:* Attended Johns Hopkins University, 1962-64; New School for Social Research, A.B., 1966; Temple University, M.Ed. (with honors), 1968, Ed.D., 1975. *Religion:* Jewish. *Agent:* Donald R. Cutler, Sterling Lord Agency, Inc., 660 Madison Ave., New York, N.Y. 10021. *Office:* National Humanistic Education Center, 110 Spring St., Saratoga Springs, N.Y. 12866.

CAREER: High school English teacher in Abington, Pa., 1966-68; teacher of American studies at private school in New York, N.Y., 1968-69; Temple University, Philadelphia, Pa., instructor in educational psychology, 1969-71; National Humanistic Education Center, Saratoga Springs, N.Y., director, 1971—. Faculty member at Marywood College, University of Missouri, New School for Social Research, La Verne College, Goddard College, Campus Free College, and Michigan State University. Workshop participant and leader. Voter registration civil rights worker for Student Nonviolent Coordinating Committee (SNCC) in Mississippi, 1964; participant in folk music concerts; member of Philadelphia Street Players, 1967. Member of volunteer fire department of Upper Jay, N.Y.

WRITINGS: (With Rodney Napier and Sidney B. Simon) *WAD-JA-GET?: The Grading Game in American Education,* Hart Publishing, 1971; (with Simon and Leland Howe) *Values Clarification: A Handbook of Practical Strategies for Teachers and Students,* Hart Publishing, 1972; (with Simon and Merrill Harmin) *Clarifying Values Through Subject Matter,* Winston Press, 1973; (with James A. Bellanca) *A College Guide for Experimenting High Schools,* National Humanistic Education Center, 1973; (editor with Simon) *Readings in Values Clarification,* Winston Press, 1974; (with Rockwell Stensrud) *The Wedding Book: Alternative Ways to Celebrate Marriage,* Seabury, 1974; *Advanced Value Clarification,* University Associates, 1977; (with wife, Barbara Glaser) *Developing Support Groups: A Manual for Facilitators and Participants,* University Associates, 1978; (with Glaser) *Skills for Living,* Quest, Inc., 1978; *The Catalogue for Humanizing Education,* National Humanistic Education Center, 1978; *On Becoming Carl Rogers,* Delacorte, 1979.

Contributor: A. V. Repath, compiler, *And Who Are You?,* Longmans Canada, 1969; C. C. Collier and H. H. Lerch, editors, *Teaching Mathematics in the Elementary School: What's Needed? What's Happening?,* National Association of Elementary School Principals, 1970; James Bank and William Joyce, editors, *Teaching Social Studies to Culturally Different Children,* Addison-Wesley, 1970; *New Methods in the Teaching of English,* Allyn & Bacon, 1971; T. B. Roberts, editor, *Four Psychologies as Applied to Education,* Schenkman, 1974; A. Toffler, editor, *Learning for Tomorrow: The Role of the Future in Education,* Random House, 1974; V. Hash, editor, *Values: Awareness, Significance, and Action,* Kendall/Hunt, 1975; J. Meyer, B. Burnham, and J. Cholvat, editors, *Values Education: Theory, Practice, Problems, and Prospects,* Wilfrid Laurier University Press, 1975; Sidney B. Simon and James A. Bellanca, editors, *Degrading the Grading Myths: A Primer of Alternatives to Grades and Marks,* Association for Supervision and Curriculum Development, 1976; A. G. Craz, editor, *A Study of Non-Fiction,* McCormick-Mathers, 1976; *Moral Education in the Schools,* Association for Supervision and Curriculum Development, 1977.

Author of "Values and Career Education," a film released by Dave Bell Associates and Media Five. Contributor to *Collier's Encyclopedia.* Contributor of about twenty-five articles to education journals.

WORK IN PROGRESS: Research for a book on the value dilemmas inherent in financial and consumer decisions when one wants to develop a moral and ecological lifestyle, completion expected in 1983.

SIDELIGHTS: Kirschenbaum comments: "Stemming from my early involvement in the civil rights movement, I have considered myself a change agent. Therefore, the thrust of all my professional activities, including writing, is aimed at fostering change—changing individual behavior, schools, and society. My work is practical."

Kirschenbaum's most recent book, *On Becoming Carl Rogers,* is a biography of the well-known psychologist and author. In *New York Times Book Review* William Kessen noted that "Howard Kirschenbaum has written, with obvious enthusiasm, a kitschy story, a loosely strung assembly of admiring testimony, cute anecdotes and quoted jargon," and questioned the book's respresentation of Rogers's place in history. Christopher Lasch blamed the shortcomings of this "well-meaning but muddled account" on the fact that it was an official biography, completely overseen by Rogers. It was written "not to clarify issues but to create an agreeable sense of rapport between a speaker and his audience."

AVOCATIONAL INTERESTS: Marathon running.

BIOGRAPHICAL/CRITICAL SOURCES: New York Times Book Review, March 18, 1979; *New Republic,* March 31, 1979.

* * *

KIRTLAND, Helen Johns 1890(?)-1979

OBITUARY NOTICE: Born c. 1890; died September 29, 1979, in Bronxville, N.Y. Photographer and travel journalist. Following World War I, Kirtland was a European correspondent for *Leslie's Illustrated Weekly.* While in Europe she married explorer and author, Lucian Kirtland, whom she accompanied in travel, supplying the photographs for many of his articles. Obituaries and other sources: *New York Times,* October 3, 1979.

* * *

KLEILER, Frank Munro 1914-

PERSONAL: Born April 17, 1914, in Green Bay, Wis.; son of Frank Andrew (an engineer) and Addie (Munro) Kleiler; married Frances Pauline Brezon, April 10, 1939; children: David Allen, James Robert. *Education:* Antioch College, A.B., 1938; attended American University, 1937-38. *Home and office:* 9100 Warren St., Silver Spring, Md. 20910.

CAREER: Washington Evening Star, Washington, D.C., reporter, 1935-36; *Boston Herald,* Boston, Mass., reporter, 1936-37; National Mediation Board, Washington, D.C., clerk, 1937-39; National Labor Relations Board, Washington, D.C., assistant to member of board, 1939-41, field examiner in Cleveland, Indianapolis, and Chicago, 1941-44, regional director in Pittsburgh, 1944-47, executive secretary in Washington, 1947-51; Wage Stabilization Board, Washington, D.C., director of disputes, 1951-52, public member of review and appeals committee, 1952-53; National Labor Relations Board, executive secretary, 1953-60; U.S. Department of Labor, Washington, D.C., deputy commissioner of Bureau of Labor-Management Reports, 1960-62, director of Office of Welfare and Pension Plans, 1962-63, director of Office of Labor-Management and Welfare-Pension Reports, 1953-70, deputy assistant secretary of labor for planning and evaluation, at Labor Management Services Administration, 1970-73; Charles D. Spencer & Associates, Chicago, Ill., Washington correspondent and associate editor of *Employee Benefit Plan Review* and *EBPR Research Reports,* 1974—. *Member:* Industiral Relations Research Association (local president, 1966-67).

WRITINGS: Canadian Regulation of Pension Plans (monograph), U.S. Department of Labor, 1971; *European Regulation of Pension Plans* (monograph), U.S. Department of Labor, 1971; *Can We Afford Early Retirement?,* Johns Hopkins Press, 1978. Contributor to political science and labor relations journals.

KLEIN, Dave 1940-

PERSONAL: Born March 10, 1940, in Newark, N.J.; son of William H. (an editor) and Sandra (a teacher; maiden name, Tolchinsky) Klein; married Carole B. Chetkin, September 1, 1963; children: Aaron, Mindy. *Education:* Attended University of Oklahoma, 1958-60; Fairleigh Dickinson University, B.A., 1962. *Politics:* "Skeptic." *Religion:* Jewish. *Home:* 3 Indian Run, Scotch Plains, N.J. 07076. *Office: Star-Ledger,* Newark, N.J. 07101.

CAREER: Star-Ledger, Newark, N.J., daily sports columnist, 1961—. Assignments include Super Bowl, Olympics, professional football, and major boxing matches. Member of board of trustees of Valerie Fund.

WRITINGS: (Editor) *Cord Sportfacts College Basketball Guide,* Cord Communications Corp., 1970-79; *Great Moments in Baseball,* Cowles Book Co., 1971; *Great Moments in Golf,* Cowles Book Co., 1971; *Rookie: The World of the NBA,* Cowles Book Co., 1971; *The Vince Lombardi Story,* Lion Press, 1971; *Great Infielders of the Major Leagues,* Random House, 1972; *The New York Giants: Yesterday, Today, Tomorrow,* Regnery, 1973; *Playoff,* Stadia Sports Publishing, 1973; *Pro Basketball's Big Men,* Random House, 1973; *The Seventeenth Sunday!,* Stadia Sports Publishing, 1973; *Stars of the Major Leagues,* Random House, 1974; (with Joan Joyce) *Winning Softball,* Regnery, 1975; *The Game of Their Lives,* Random House, 1976; *On the Way Up: What It's Like in the Minor Leagues,* Messner, 1977; *The Pro Football Mystique,* New American Library, 1978; *A Thinking Person's Guide to Pro Basketball,* Grosset, 1978.

Author of "The Why of It," a daily column distributed by Newhouse Newspaper Chain. Contributor to *Best Sports Stories.* Contributor to sports magazines.

WORK IN PROGRESS: Another novel.

SIDELIGHTS: Klein comments: "I believe that sports, not in terms of scores but people, can provide some of the finest real drama in today's literature. I have tried to show this in my recent novel, and hope to continue doing so in the future."

* * *

KLEINKE, Chris (Lynn) 1944-

PERSONAL: Born January 13, 1944, in Chicago, Ill.; son of Hans R. and Hannah Kleinke. *Education:* Occidental College, A.B., 1965; Claremont Graduate School, M.A., 1967, Ph.D., 1972. *Office:* Department of Psychology, Wellesley College, Wellesley, Mass. 02181.

CAREER: Wheaton College, Norton, Mass., assistant professor of psychology, 1972-77; Wellesley College, Wellesley, Mass., assistant professor of psychology, 1977—. *Member:* Eastern Psychological Association, Western Psychological Association, New England Social Psychological Association.

WRITINGS: First Impressions: The Psychology of Encountering Others, Prentice-Hall, 1975; *Self-Perception: The Psychology of Personal Awareness,* W. H. Freeman, 1978. Contributor of more than thirty articles to professional journals.

WORK IN PROGRESS: Research on nonverbal communication, interpersonal attraction, first impressions, and self-perception.

* * *

KLEM, Kaye Wilson 1941-

PERSONAL: Born August 19, 1941, in Fairview, Okla.; daughter of Wesley Theron (a carpenter) and Fern Marie Wilson; married Thomas George Klem (in computer programming management), June 15, 1963; children: Thomas George, Jr. *Education:* Wichita State University, B.A. (magna cum laude), 1963. *Residence:* Englewood, Colo. *Agent:* James Seligmann Agency, 280 Madison Ave., New York, N.Y. 10016.

CAREER: Hartford Times, Hartford, Conn., reporter, 1968-69; free-lance writer, 1969—. Political campaign publicity director, 1970-72. *Member:* Colorado Authors League. *Awards, honors:* Best book award from Missouri Writers Guild, 1972, for *Touch the Sun;* award of honor from Alpha Phi, 1972.

WRITINGS—Novels: *Touch the Sun,* Doubleday, 1971; *Defiant Desire,* Fawcett, 1977; *Reckless Fires,* Fawcett, 1978; *East of Jamaica,* Fawcett, 1979.

WORK IN PROGRESS: A contemporary novel; research on ancient history.

SIDELIGHTS: Kaye Klem writes: "Character is central to the novel. The relationship between men and women is vital to most of our lives, and remains a valid question for the novelist. In a novel worthy of the name, human beings struggle with universal human dilemmas, with the question of individual morality in an imperfect world. Their struggle is to live with dignity in that world, to learn the difference between Sunday-school maxims and genuine humanity. A good novel must be entertaining if it is to reach more than a handful of readers, but it must be more, and in that lies the art of the novel.

"Though I am currently researching a twentieth-century novel, I have a lifelong interest in history and find historical research a pleasure. The commercial demands of today's fiction necessarily limit the amount of history visible in a finished manuscript, which makes my exhaustive research appear only as the tip of an iceberg, but I feel it is always worthwhile to the book and to me personally. History, simply stated, is people: who they were and what made them that way, and why they did the things they did, given the time in which they lived."

AVOCATIONAL INTERESTS: Horses, saddle seat and hunt seat equitation, aerobic dancing.

* * *

KLEMESRUD, Judy

PERSONAL: Born in Thompson, Iowa; daughter of Theodore S. (an editor and publisher) and Glee (Florence) Klemesrud. *Education:* University of Iowa, B.A., 1961; Columbia University, M.S. (journalism), 1962. *Politics:* Democrat. *Religion:* Methodist. *Home:* 340 East 57th St., New York, N.Y. 10022. *Agent:* Philip G. Spitzer Literary Agency, 111-25 76th Ave., Forest Hills, N.Y. 11375. *Office: New York Times,* 229 West 43rd St., New York, N.Y. 10036.

CAREER/WRITINGS: Chicago Daily News, Chicago, Ill., reporter, 1962-66; *New York Times,* New York, N.Y., reporter, 1966—. Notable assignments include coverage of the International Women's Year Conference in Mexico City, 1975, and the National Women's Conference in Houston, 1977. Contributor of articles to popular magazines, including *Esquire, Cosmopolitan, Glamour, Redbook,* and *New York* Magazine. *Member:* Newspaper Guild of New York, Zeta Tau Alpha, Mortar Board. *Awards, honors:* Penney-Missouri Award, 1975, for a story on coal miners' wives in Harlan County, Kentucky; Page One Award from Newspaper Guild of New York, 1973, for a story on the effects of the women's liberation movement in Hope, Indiana; Women In Communications Matrix Award, 1975, for general excellence in newspaper reporting.

SIDELIGHTS: Judy Klemesrud noted that part of the motivation in her journalism career stems from a prophecy in her high school yearbook which predicted that she would one day be the editor of the *New York Times*. She listed music as an interest: Klemesrud is an oboist with the *New York Times* Woodwind Quintette and a country and western singer. She also plays ping-pong and is a softball pitcher.

* * *

KLIMEK, David E(rnest) 1941-

PERSONAL: Born December 14, 1941, in Duluth, Minn.; son of August Frank (a contractor) and Lauretta (a teacher; maiden name, Talarico) Klimek; married Virginia Larson, December 18, 1965; children: Christopher, Jennifer. *Education:* Duluth Institute of Technology, A.A., 1962; University of Minnesota, B.S., 1966; University of Wisconsin—Madison, M.Ed., 1968; University of Wyoming, Ph.D., 1972. *Home:* 2364 Dundee Dr., Ann Arbor, Mich. 48103. *Office:* 1945 Pauline Blvd., Ann Arbor, Mich. 48103.

CAREER: Wichita Guidance Center, Wichita, Kan., clinical psychology intern, 1972-73; Sioux Trails Mental Health Center, New Ulm, Minn., clinical director, 1973-76; E. W. Cook Institute of Psychotherapy, Faribault, Minn., director, 1976-77; private practice in clinical psychology in Ann Arbor, Mich., 1977—. Adjunct professor at Mankato State College, 1973-77, and Antioch College, 1976-77; provost of Wilson Center for Education and Psychiatry, 1976-77. *Member:* American Psychological Association, National Register of Mental Health Providers, Michigan Psychological Association, Michigan Society for Consulting Psychologists, Michigan Association of Marriage Counselors, Michigan Society of Marriage and Family Counselors.

WRITINGS: Beneath Mate Selection and Marriage: The Unconscious Forces in Human Pairing, Van Nostrand, 1979.

WORK IN PROGRESS: Growing Up: Between Ages Twenty and Fifty, publication expected in 1980; *Parents Elite; Sixty Days and Sixty Nights.*

SIDELIGHTS: Klimek writes: "In my practice of clinical psychology I specialize in work with children, families, and young adults. I am very family oriented and enjoy being a husband and father. I enjoy life and try to see living as endless opportunity, even when I'm depressed.

"My writing has a 'tell-it-like-it-is' flair and precipitously walks a fine line between the being-dull style found in textbooks and journals, and the somewhat reckless and flamboyant style found in popular, contemporary writing. Because I tend to extract the commonality of the human heart and write about it, my writing tends to make people a little nervous, as they can usually identify with the examples, illustrations, and characters. Sometimes I make myself nervous by my writing!

"I have some rather unusual work habits when I write. First I become a compulsive neurotic. I sit at a hand-carved writing table that I made myself and get myself into a frame of mind where I feel like a king. I can write best in the early morning when the world is perfectly quiet—I then feel like a king who has the entire world to himself. In addition to my elegant writing table, I also always have a candle glowing in a crystal candle holder. Whenever possible, I also cut fresh flowers from my garden and place them on the table. Then, in my quiet, contemplative moments, I gaze at the candle, gaze at the flowers, and only when I feel 'like a king' and the master of myself can I produce good work. I need to get into a perfect feeling of love, unity, and peace of mind before I can create and 'give to the world.' Only when I am free of tension and feel harmony in myself can I flow with a clean, clear ebb of thought and creativity."

AVOCATIONAL INTERESTS: Designing, building, and remodeling houses, reading, camping, travel, skiing, backpacking, hunting, fishing, building fireplaces and furniture, rebuilding automobiles, gardening, athletics, bicycling, jogging, smoking a pipe in winter while sitting in front of a fireplace.

* * *

KLOPF, Donald W(illiam) 1923-

PERSONAL: Born January 22, 1923, in Milwaukee, Wis.; son of Milton H. and Lillian (Spiegler) Klopf; married Beverly Nakamura (a social worker), April 21, 1954; children: Donn R. *Education:* University of Hawaii, B.A., 1953, M.A., 1955; University of Washington, Seattle, Ph.D., 1958. *Home:* 516 Ulumu St., Kailua, Hawaii. *Office:* Department of Speech, University of Hawaii, Honolulu, Hawaii 96822.

CAREER: Bank teller in Milwaukee, Wis., 1941-43; Young Men's Christian Association, Milwaukee, Wis., branch executive, 1946-48; University of Hawaii, Honolulu, assistant professor, 1958-62, associate professor, 1962-70, professor of speech, 1970—. President of Hawaii Social and Religious Credit Union, 1953. *Military service:* U.S. Army Air Forces, 1943-46; became staff sergeant. *Member:* International Communication Association, Speech Communication Association of America, Communication Association of the Pacific (president, 1969-80).

WRITINGS: (With James McCroskey) *The Elements of Debate,* Arco, 1967; (with Carroll Lahman) *Coaching and Directing Forensics,* National Textbook Co., 1967; (with Stanley Rives) *Individual Speaking Contests: Preparation for Participation,* Burgess, 1967; *The Bases of Public Speaking,* Sansyusya Publishing, 1972; *Effective Academic Debate,* Gaku Shobo Publishing, 1973; *Winning Debates,* Gaku Shobo Publishing, 1974; *Debate: A Programmed Introduction,* J. Weston Walch, 1974; *The Bases of Debate,* Sansyusya Publishing, 1974; *Interacting in Groups: Discussion and Leadership,* Gaku Shobo Publishing, 1976; *Contest Speaking Manual,* Eichosha Publishing, 1977; *Judging Speech Contests,* Gaku Shobo Publishing, 1978; *Speech Tournament Management,* Gaku Shobo Publishing, 1978; (with Ronald Cambra) *Academic Debate: Practicing Argumentative Theory,* 2nd edition (Klopf was not associated with 1st edition), Morton Publishing, 1979. Editor of international series for Heim and speech series for Gaku Shobo Publishing and Sansyusya Publishing.

WORK IN PROGRESS: Research on communication apprehension; writing an introductory speech text.

SIDELIGHTS: Klopf told *CA:* "I like to think that I write, not to meet a 'publish or perish' need which academicians are constantly threatened by, but to share with others, students especially, what I found hard to acquire. As a consequence, my books tend to be less scholarly, yet more readable. While the reviews of all have been complimentary, the books weren't written for reviewers or faculty promotion and tenure committees. They were written for the users, the students. Too many textbooks are directed to the selectors, the faculty, or are written to get promoted or tenured. I would rather not write for those purposes."

KLOPFER, Walter G(eorge) 1923-

PERSONAL: Born December 14, 1923, in Frankfurt, Germany; came to the United States in 1934, naturalized citizen, 1940; son of Bruno (a psychologist) and Erna (a teacher; maiden name, Hene) Klopfer; married Ann Tillotson, December 31, 1942 (divorced, 1968); married Joan Quinn (a technical editor), October 4, 1968; children: Fred, Sylvia, Julie, Sally. *Education:* University of California, Berkeley, A.B., 1943, Ph.D., 1950; City College (now of the City University of New York), M.A., 1947. *Home:* 7840 Southwest 51st Ave., Portland, Ore. 97219. *Office:* Department of Psychology, Portland State University, Portland, Ore. 97207.

CAREER: Home for the Aged and Infirm, New York City, attending psychologist, 1946-47; University of California, Counseling Center, Berkeley, Calif. trainee, 1947-48; Oakland General Medical and Veterans Administration Hospital, Oakland, Calif., trainee, 1948-49; Veterans Administration Hospital, Palo Alto, Calif., trainee, 1949-50; Duke University, Durham, N.C., assistant professor of psychology, research associate, and senior clinical psychologist, 1950-52; University of Nebraska Medical College, Omaha, assistant professor of medical psychology, 1952-58; University of Portland, Portland, Ore., associate professor, 1958-61, professor of psychology and director of clinical training, 1961-65; Portland State University, Portland, professor of psychology, 1965—. Chief clinical psychologist at Norfolk State Hospital, 1952-58; school psychologist for public school system of Norfolk, Neb., 1952-58; staff member of Woodland Park Mental Health Center, 1976—. Member of board of directors of Oregon Graduate School of Professional Psychology, 1975—. Head of committee of visitors for Oregon Institutions for the Retarded, 1967-68; member of governor's committee on aging, 1967-68. *Military service:* U.S. Army, psychological assistant, 1944-46.

MEMBER: American Psychological Association (fellow), Society for Projective Techniques (president, 1963-64), American Association of University Professors, Oregon Academy of Professional Psychologists (president, 1974-75), New York Academy of Sciences, Portland Psychological Association (president, 1961-62), Sigma Xi, Psi Chi.

WRITINGS: (Editor) *Developments in the Rorschach Technique,* Volume I (with Bruno Klopfer, Mary D. Ainsworth, and Robert Holt; also contributor), World Book Co., 1954, Volume III (with Mortimer Meyer and Klopfer), Harcourt, 1970; *The Psychological Report: Use and Communication of Psychological Findings,* Grune, 1960; (editor with M. R. Reed) *Problems in Psychotherapy: An Eclectic Approach,* Wiley, 1974.

Contributor: *Developments in the Rorschach Technique,* Volume II, World Book Co., 1965; Benjamin Wolman, editor, *Handbook of Clinical Psychology,* McGraw, 1965; Robert Kastenbau and Ruth Aisenberg, editors, *Psychobiology of Aging,* Springer Publishing, 1966; *The Clinical Psychologist,* Aldine, 1967; Albert Rabin, editor, *Projective Techniques in Personality Assessment,* Springer Publishing, 1968; Paul McReynolds, editor, *Advances in Psychological Assessment,* Volume I, Science & Behavior Books, 1968. Contributor to *Psychology 73/74 Encyclopedia.* Contributor of about sixty articles and reviews to psychology journals. Editor of *Journal of Personality Assessment,* 1965—.

SIDELIGHTS: Klopfer writes: "I believe that the most important psychological issue is the development of androgyny as an alternative to the outworn gender stereotypes."

KNOLL, Erwin 1931-

PERSONAL: Born July 17, 1931, in Vienna, Austria; came to the United States in 1940, naturalized citizen, 1945; son of Carl (a printer) and Ida (Schaechter) Knoll; married Doris Ricksteen (a music teacher), March 1, 1954; children: David S., Jonathan R. *Education:* New York University, B.A., 1953; graduate study at George Washington University, 1958-60. *Home:* 6123 Johnson St., McFarland, Wis. 53558. *Office: Progressive,* 408 West Gorham St., Madison, Wis. 53703.

CAREER: Editor and Publisher, New York City, reporter, 1948-50, editor, 1950-56; *Better Schools,* New York City, associate editor, 1956-57; *Washington Post,* Washington, D.C., reporter, 1957-61, editor, 1961-62; Los Angeles Times-Washington Post News Service, Washington, D.C., Washington editor, 1962-63; Newhouse National News Service, Washington, D.C., White House correspondent, 1963-68; *Progressive,* Washington, D.C., Washington correspondent, 1968-73, editor in Madison, Wis., 1973—. *Military service:* U.S. Army, 1953-55.

WRITINGS: (With William McGaffin) *Anything But the Truth,* Putnam, 1968; (with McGaffin) *Scandal in the Pentagon,* Fawcett, 1969; (editor with Judith McFadden) *American Militarism 1970,* Viking, 1970; (editor with McFadden) *War Crimes and the American Conscience,* Viking, 1972. Contributor to magazines, including *Esquire, Commentary, Saturday Review, Washington Monthly,* and *Change.*

* * *

KNOWLAND, William Fife 1908-1974

OBITUARY NOTICE: Born June 26, 1908, in Alameda, Calif.; died of a self-inflicted gunshot wound, February 23, 1974, near Monte Rio, Calif. Newspaper editor, publisher, and U.S. senator. Introduced to politics at an early age, Knowland gained a spot on the California State Senate at the age of twenty-seven, chaired the executive committee of the Republican National Committee at thirty-two, and became a U.S. senator at thirty-seven. He was the Senate majority leader from 1953 to 1954, and minority leader from 1955 until 1958. While in the Senate he was vice-president and director of the Oakland Tribune Building Co.; he later became the *Oakland Tribune*'s editor and publisher. Obituaries and other sources: *Current Biography,* Wilson, 1947, April, 1974; *Who's Who,* 126th edition, St. Martin's, 1974; *New York Times,* February 24, 1974; *Time,* March 4, 1974; *Newsweek,* March 4, 1974; *Who Was Who in America,* 6th edition, Marquis, 1976.

* * *

KOFF, Richard Myram 1926-

PERSONAL: Born January 8, 1926, in New York, N.Y.; son of Harry and Riva (Mohi) Koff; married Mary Alice Coudreaut, May 3, 1958 (divorced, February, 1969); married Hunter Duncan Campbell (a business consultant), January 29, 1977; children: (first marriage) Christopher Stephen, Kathleen Janette. *Education:* New York University, B.M.E., 1948, M.M.E., 1950. *Home and office:* 1031 Sheridan Rd., Evanston, Ill. 60202. *Agent:* Curtis Brown Ltd., 575 Madison Ave., New York, N.Y. 10022.

CAREER: American Hydromath Corp., New York City, design engineer, 1949-55; McGraw-Hill Book Co., New York City, associate editor, 1955-58, senior associate editor, 1958-60, managing editor of *Product Engineering,* 1960-66; *Playboy,* Chicago, Ill., administrative editor, 1966-71, assistant publisher, 1972-77, manager of New Publications Division of Playboy Enterprises, 1971-74, director of new publications, 1974-76, vice-president, 1974-77, business manager, 1976-77; management consultant in Chicago, Ill., 1977—. Member of board of directors of Oasis, 1976—. *Military service:* U.S. Army Air Forces, 1944-45. *Member:* Institute of Electrical and Electronics Engineers (associate member), Society of Midland Authors (member of board of directors, 1979—). *Awards, honors:* Jesse H. Neal Editorial Achievement Award from American Business Press, 1959, for "Eight Steps to Better Writing," 1960, for "Design in Europe," and 1962, for "Design in Japan."

WRITINGS: (With John J. Pippinger) *Fluid-Power Controls,* McGraw, 1959; *How Does It Work?* (nonfiction), Doubleday, 1961; *Home Computers,* Harcourt, 1979; *The Home Electronics Catalog,* Contemporary Books, 1979; *The Hardware Catalog,* Doubleday, 1980. Contributor to *Cowles Complete Encyclopedia.* Contributor to magazines, including *Playboy, Nature and Science, Folio,* and *Product Engineering.*

WORK IN PROGRESS: A Dictionary of Corporate Behavior; Christopher, juvenile science fiction; research on choices in leisure entertainment.

SIDELIGHTS: Koff commented: "Electronics and computers are changing our physical environment. At the same time psychologists and philosophers are discovering powers of the mind that make the imagination reel. How can one help but be fascinated by what is being discovered? How can one help but join in the dance?"

* * *

KOHAN, Rhea

PERSONAL: Born in New York; daughter of Max S. (a principal) and Clair (Zbar) Arnold; married Buz Kohan (a writer, producer, and composer), July 17, 1962; children: Jono, David, Jenji. *Education:* Brooklyn College (now of the City University of New York), B.S. *Religion:* Jewish. *Home:* 2095 Loma Vista Dr., Beverly Hills, Calif. 90210.

CAREER: Free-lance television writer, 1975—. *Member:* Writers Guild of America (West).

WRITINGS: Save Me a Seat (novel), Harper, 1979. Also author of television scripts.

WORK IN PROGRESS: Another novel.

SIDELIGHTS: Rhea Kohan writes: "I like working alone, at home, with no impositions of discipline other than my own. I work obsessively rather than passionately; I begin projects reluctantly, since once begun I find I cannot stop until the project is completed. I am fascinated by the subconscious discoveries unearthed by the writing process, and am often amazed by what comes from my pencil."

* * *

KOLB, Carolyn 1942-

PERSONAL: Born June 29, 1942, in New Orleans, La.; daughter of J. Hugh Goldsby, Jr.; married Kenneth C. Kolb (an owner of an advertising agency), October 17, 1964; children: Pherabe, Kenneth. *Education:* Tulane University, B.A., 1963. *Politics:* Democrat. *Religion:* Episcopalian. *Office:* 126 Carondelet St., Suite 214, New Orleans, La. 70130.

CAREER: New Orleans Jazz Museum, New Orleans, La., director, 1967-68; writer.

WRITINGS: New Orleans: An Invitation to Discover One of America's Most Fascinating Cities, Doubleday, 1972. Contributor to local magazines.

KOLLMAR, Dick
See KOLLMAR, Richard Tompkins

* * *

KOLLMAR, Richard Tompkins 1910-1971
(Dick Kollmar)

OBITUARY NOTICE: Born December 31, 1910, in Ridgewood, N.J.; died January 7, 1971, in New York, N.Y. Actor, stage producer, and radio performer. Though both an actor and producer on Broadway, Kollmar was best known for his performances on the popular radio program, "Breakfast With Dorothy and Dick." Written and produced with his first wife, Dorothy Kilgallen, the show ran from 1945 until 1963. Obituaries and other sources: *Current Biography,* Wilson, 1952, February, 1971; *The Biographical Encyclopaedia and Who's Who of the American Theatre,* James Heineman, 1966; *New York Times,* January 9, 1971.

* * *

KOOIMAN, Gladys 1927-

PERSONAL: Surname is pronounced *Koy*-man; born August 24, 1927, in Waupun, Wis.; daughter of Otto (a farmer) and Janet (Redeker) Loomans; married Marvin Kooiman, June 20, 1950 (died, 1956); children: Linda, Emily, Mari, Judy, Howard, Merlin, David, Germaine. *Education:* Calvin College, B.S. *Home:* 502 McKinley St., Waupun, Wis. 53963.

CAREER: Waupun Christian School, Waupun, Wis., teacher, 1968—. *Member:* Widowed Unlimited (president, 1976-78), Penrock Writers Club (president, 1972-75).

WRITINGS: When Death Takes a Father, Baker Book, 1968; *After the Flowers Have Gone: Bea Decker-Kooiman,* Zondervan, 1973.

WORK IN PROGRESS: You Gotta Be Kidding, God, an inspirational book for teenagers, based on the Sermon on the Mount.

SIDELIGHTS: Gladys Kooiman writes: "I'm the mother of eight children, all young when their father died, I'm much in demand as a lecturer for single-parent groups and organizations for widowed people."

* * *

KOPF, David 1930-

PERSONAL: Born March 12, 1930, in Paterson, N.J. *Education:* New York University, B.A., 1951, M.A., 1956; University of Chicago, Ph.D., 1964. *Office:* Department of History, University of Minnesota, Minneapolis, Minn. 55455.

CAREER: University of Missouri, Columbia, assistant professor of history, 1964-67; University of Minnesota, Minneapolis, associate professor, 1967-73, professor of history, 1973—. Visiting professor at Rajshahi University and fellow of Institute of Bangladesh Studies, 1975-76. Chairperson of professional conferences. *Member:* International Society for the Comparative Study of Civilizations (member of executive council), American Historical Association, American Institute of Indian Studies (member of board of trustees, 1972-75). *Awards, honors:* Ford Foundation fellow in England and India, 1961-63, and in Bangladesh, 1975-76; senior fellow of American Institute of Indian Studies, Calcutta, 1969-71; Watumull Prize from American Historical Association, for mongraph; travel grant from University of Minnesota, 1972, for India, and 1975, for Bangladesh.

WRITINGS: British Orientalism and the Bengal Renais-

sance: The Dynamics of Indian Modernization, 1770-1835, University of California Press, 1969; *Classical Asian Civilizations,* Extension, University of Minnesota, 1976; *Medieval Asian Civilizations,* Extension, University of Minnesota, 1976; *Modern Asian Civilizations,* Extension, University of Minnesota, 1976; (with E. Farmer, G. Hambly, and others) *A Comparative History of Civilizations in Asia,* two volumes, Addison-Wesley, 1977; (with C. James Bishop) *Indian World,* Forum Press, 1978; *The Brahmo Samaj and the Shaping of the Modern Indian Mind,* Princeton University Press, 1979.

Contributor: E. Dimock, editor, *Bengal: Literature and History,* Michigan State University Press, 1967; R. Park, editor, *Urban Bengal,* Michigan State University Press, 1969; R. Crane, editor, *Transition in South Asia: Problems of Modernization,* Duke University Press, 1970; T. Metcalfe, editor, *Modern India: An Interpretative Anthology,* Macmillan, 1971; S. Lavan and B. Thomas, editors, *West Bengal and Bangladesh: Perspectives From 1972,* Michigan State University Press, 1973; *Contributions to Indian Sociology,* Institute of Economic Development (New Delhi, India), 1975; R.V.M. Baumer, editor, *Aspects of Bengali Society and Culture,* University Press of Hawaii, 1976; V. C. Joshi, editor, *Rammohun Roy and the Process of Modernization in India,* Vikas, 1976; J. McLane, editor, *Bengal in the Nineteenth and Twentieth Centuries,* Michigan State University Press, 1976; *Reflections on the Bengal Renaissance,* Institute of Bangladesh Studies, Rajshahi University, 1977. Contributor to professional journals. South Asia editor of *Newsletter of the Association for Asian Studies,* 1965-68.

* * *

KOPMAN, H(enri Marshall) 1918-

PERSONAL: Born March 17, 1918, in New Orleans, La.; son of Henry Hazlitt (a writer, government agent, and naturalist) and Laura Frances (Marshall) Kopman; married Jane Ellen Dewey (a stock manipulator), November 15, 1947; children: Catherine Ellen. *Education:* Tulane University, B.A., 1939; University of Paris, certificate, 1945; Middlebury College, M.A., 1949; University of Poitiers, diploma, 1952; New York University, Ph.D., 1959. *Politics:* "Left-wing Democrat." *Religion:* None. *Home:* 1611 Delano, Las Cruces, N.M. 88001. *Office:* Department of French, New Mexico State University, Las Cruces, N.M. 88003.

CAREER: English instructor at military academy in Delafield, Wis., 1943-44; Florida State University, Tallahassee, instructor in French, 1946-48; Birmingham-Southern College, Birmingham, Ala., assistant professor of French, 1948-51; Gadjah Mada University, Bulaksumur, Jogjakarta, Indonesia, director of phonetics at language institute, 1951-53; Assumption College, Worcester, Mass., assistant professor of French, 1953-56; Erskine College, Due West, S.C., professor of French and head of department, 1956-60; Western Maryland College, Westminster, professor of French and head of department of modern languages, 1960-65; New Mexico State University, Las Cruces, professor of French, 1965—. French interpreter for Foreign Tour Service of American Automobile Association, 1940—. *Military service:* U.S. Army, interpreter, 1944-45; served in France.

MEMBER: Modern Language Association of America, American Association of Teachers of French, Rocky Mountain Modern Language Association, Southwest Council on Foreign Languages. *Awards, honors:* Fulbright fellowship for France, summer, 1964.

WRITINGS: Phenomenon of Recontre in Le Temps Perdu, Xerox College Publishing, 1960; *L'Attrait et l'appel de la nature chez Proust* (booklet; title means "The Attraction and Call of Nature"), Presses Launay, 1969; *Recontres With the Inanimate in Proust's Recherche,* Mouton, 1972; *La nature a travers les siecles* (title means "Nature Throughout the Centuries"), Monograph Publishers, 1979.

Translator: *La culture des sangsues* (title means "The Culture of Leeches"), 1940; Gottfried Schuh, *Inseln der Goetter* (title means "Island of the Gods"), 1951; (contributor) *Le Monde malais* (title means "The Malayan World"), 1952; *Le Doping des chevaux de course* (title means "The Doping of Race Horses"), 1968; Raymond Barbeau, *La Cause du Cancer,* 1978; Barbeau, *La Cause inconnue des maladies* (title means "The Unknown Cause of Diseases"), 1978. Contributor of articles and reviews to French studies and nature journals. Editor of bulletin of Southwestern Conference for Languages, 1966.

WORK IN PROGRESS: Medical translation.

SIDELIGHTS: Kopman writes: "I have had rich experiences in nature, in upper Alberta, upper Quebec, tropical Latin America, France, Java, the Missouri Ozarks, and the Gila wilderness! I like to combine this interest with my lifelong knowledge of French language and literature. My specialties are the twentieth-century French novel and nature throughout French literature."

* * *

KOUFAX, Sandy
See KOUFAX, Sanford

* * *

KOUFAX, Sanford 1935-
(Sandy Koufax)

PERSONAL: Born December 30, 1935, in Brooklyn, N.Y.; son of Irving (a lawyer) and Evelyn Koufax; married Anne Heath Widmark, 1969. *Education:* Attended University of Cincinnati, 1953. *Religion:* Jewish. *Agent:* Ziegler-Ross Agency, 9255 Sunset Blvd., Los Angeles, Calif. 90069.

CAREER: Professional baseball pitcher for Brooklyn Dodgers, 1955-57, and Los Angeles Dodgers, 1958-66; sportscaster for National Broadcasting Co., 1966-73. *Awards, honors:* Named Major League player of the year, National League pitcher of the year, and selected to National League All-Star team, all from *Sporting News,* National League Most Valuable Player Award, and Cy Young Memorial Award for best Major League pitcher, all 1963; named National League pitcher of the year and selected to National League All-Star team, both from *Sporting News,* both 1964; named Major League player of the year, National League pitcher of the year, and selected to National League All-Star team, all from *Sporting News,* and Cy Young Memorial Award, all 1965; named National League pitcher of the year and selected to National League All-Star team, both from *Sporting News,* and Cy Young Memorial Award, all 1966; inducted into the Baseball Hall of Fame, 1971.

WRITINGS: (Under name Sandy Koufax; with Ed Linn) *Koufax* (autobiography), Viking, 1966.

SIDELIGHTS: From 1963 to 1966 Koufax was the premier pitcher in the National League. In that brief stretch he won almost one hundred games and was the league leader in strikeouts three out of four years. All four years he held the lowest earned run average. In 1963 and 1965 he helped pitch the Los Angeles Dodgers to the world championship, allowing only five runs in as many games in both of those World Series.

Koufax was a struggler in his early years as a major leaguer. Because his bonus was in excess of $6000, he had to be a member of the major league roster for two years before he could be sent to the minors. Some baseball experts later suggested that this rule robbed Koufax of valuable learning experience. In four appearances in 1955, Koufax won two games, including a two-hit shutout with fourteen strikeouts against the Cincinnati Reds and a five-hit shutout of the Pittsburgh Pirates, but he had also exhibited a great deal of wildness in his first year. This lack of control would plague Koufax throughout the next five years. In 1956, he averaged almost five walks per game; the following season was more of the same although he did strike out 122 batters in only 104 innings.

When the Dodgers moved from Brooklyn to Los Angeles, Koufax started pitching more regularly but he had yet to shake his inconsistency. In 1958, he finished the season with eleven victories and eleven defeats. The following season Koufax showed a slight improvement; his earned run average dropped, and in 153 innings he had 173 strike-outs, including sixteen in one game against the Philadelphia Phillies.

By the end of the 1960 season, the Dodgers organization had begun to lose patience with Koufax, though, for he had lost thirteen out of twenty-one decisions. He was still compiling strikeouts at an impressive rate (with eighteen in one game that season, he had tied the major league record for most strikeouts in a game), but he was also allowing too many walks.

The 1961 season was a turning point for Koufax. Acting on advice from catcher Norm Sherry, he reduced his speed in an effort to have more control. He also began working on other pitches besides his fastball. The changes proved surprisingly effective for Koufax. He won eighteen games and led the league in strikeouts. He continued to improve in 1962, although a finger injury ended his season prematurely. That year he led the league with an earned run average of 2.54 and he would not divest himself of leadership in that category until his retirement.

Koufax fully realized his potential in 1963 by winning twenty-five out of thirty decisions. The same year he struck out more than three hundred batters and pitched his team to the world championship with two post-season victories. In 1964, another season abbreviated by injury, Koufax led the league in winning percentage and pitched his third no-hitter.

Koufax's last two seasons were his most successful. In 1965, he struck out 382 batters en route to twenty-six wins. In the World Series that year, he won two games and allowed only two runs in twenty-four innings. The following season featured career highs for Koufax with twenty-seven victories and an earned run average of 1.73. However, an arthritic elbow finally forced his early retirement. In 1971, he became the youngest member of the Baseball Hall of Fame.

AVOCATIONAL INTERESTS: Reading, listening to music.

BIOGRAPHICAL/CRITICAL SOURCES: *Sports Illustrated,* January 4, 1966, April 4, 1966, November 28, 1966; *Newsweek,* March 28, 1966, August 8, 1966, November 28, 1966; *Life,* April 1, 1966; *Time,* September 9, 1966, November 25, 1966; Sandy Koufax and Ed Linn, *Koufax,* Viking, 1966; *Commentary,* February, 1967; Bob Broeg, *Super Stars of Baseball,* Sporting News, 1971.*

* * *

KRAFT, Betsy Harvey 1937-

PERSONAL: Born May 21, 1937, in Indianapolis, Ind.; daughter of Robert Sidney (a professor) and Helen (a librarian; maiden name, Porter) Harvey; married Michael Baker Kraft (a special projects director), November 28, 1970; children: Katherine Porter. *Education:* DePauw University, B.A., 1959; Brown University, M.A., 1961. *Residence:* Washington, D.C.

CAREER: Worked as children's book editor in New York, N.Y., for Macmillan, Bobbs-Merrill, and Dutton, 1962-68; writer. Director of education for energy trade association.

*WRITINGS—*Juvenile: *Coal,* F. Watts, 1976; *Careers in the Energy Industry,* F. Watts, 1977; *Oil and Natural Gas,* F. Watts, 1978.

WORK IN PROGRESS: Two picture books, one a juvenile nonfiction book; an adult novel.

SIDELIGHTS: Kraft told *CA:* "The children's books I have published are the result of my interest in the energy field. I also enjoy the world of children's fiction, especially picture books and stories for the seven to eleven-year-old age group. And, like every other author who has ever threaded paper into a typewriter, I am working on an adult novel—which happens to have one of the energy industries as a background."

* * *

KRASSER, Wilhelm 1925(?)-1979

OBITUARY NOTICE: Born c. 1925 in Brno, Czechoslovakia; died November 9, 1979, in Prague, Czechoslovakia. Journalist best known for breaking the story of the 1968 Soviet-led invasion of Czechoslovakia. He reported for the Vienna bureau of the *London Times* and covered the 1956 Hungarian revolt for the Rueter News Agency, before joining the West German news agency, DPA, in 1967. Obituaries and other sources: *Washington Post,* November 12, 1979.

* * *

KRAUS, Joe 1939-

PERSONAL: Born September 8, 1939, in Portland, Ore.; son of Joseph B. (an accountant) and Ethel (a secretary; maiden name, Riggs) Kraus; married Karren Kranwinkle (an elementary school teacher), April 8, 1968; children: Heidi Lorraine, Peter Brandon, Rebecca Elizabeth. *Education:* Attended Citrus College, 1963-67. *Politics:* Democrat. *Religion:* Church of Jesus Christ of Latter-day Saints (Mormon). *Home address:* P.O. Box 1148, Lancaster, Calif. 93534. *Office: Antelope Valley Daily Ledger-Gazette,* P.O. Box 4048, Lancaster, Calif. 93534.

CAREER: Prescott Evening Courier, Prescott, Ariz., managing editor, 1970-72; Palm Springs Convention and Visitors Bureau, Palm Springs, Calif., manager of news bureau, 1972-73; *Banning Record-Gazette,* Banning, Calif., managing editor, 1973-75; *Antelope Valley Daily Ledger-Gazette,* Lancaster, Calif., managing editor, 1975—. Co-founder and partner of Sun Country Associates (public relations firm), 1976—. *Military service:* U.S. Naval Reserve, active duty, 1961-63; served in Pacific. *Member:* Rotary International.

WRITINGS: Alive in the Desert, Paladin Press, 1979. Contributor of nearly one hundred-fifty articles to national magazines, including *Desert, National Wildlife, Lady's Circle, Young World,* and *Dynamic Years.*

WORK IN PROGRESS: A book on monarchies, *Children Who Ruled the World;* a book on Indian-white conflicts, *Battlefields of the Far West,* with photographs of present-day sites.

SIDELIGHTS: Kraus told *CA:* "I have always believed that the most important part of writing is the good idea. Without it you have nothing. With it you have the world. New writers presenting current work to publishers are not unlike aspiring actors waiting to be recognized. All too often, in both cases, there is little unique or different about them or their work. Writers willing to plow new ground, to strike upon topics untouched before, are those who will be remembered. The others, successful writers or not, will in the end only be followers."

Kraus commented on his 1979 book, *Alive in the Desert:* "There are several survival books around; most, however, work on the premise that a person is fairly well equipped and gets lost or stranded in wooded areas. Few, if any, concentrate on the desert area only, where most of the problems are. Few, if any, suppose that the person needing help is without supplies. *Alive in the Desert* is unique in this respect. It concentrates on the desert and it provides necessary information for those who have no supplies with them. The book not only tells the reader how to get out of his predicament but how to make or obtain what he needs from nature herself. The book is heavily illustrated and is filled with numerous case histories."

BIOGRAPHICAL/CRITICAL SOURCES: Fate, April, 1971; *Desert,* June, 1979; *Antelope Valley Daily Ledger-Gazette,* July 16, 1979.

* * *

KRETSCH, Robert W. 1913(?)-1979

OBITUARY NOTICE: Born c. 1913 in New York, N.Y.; died November 8, 1979, in New York, N.Y. Educator, scholar, and author. An authority on French and Spanish literature, Kretsch taught at the Polytechnic Institute of New York. He wrote a biography of the nineteenth-century French novelist and journalist, Alphonse Karr. Obituaries and other sources: *New York Times,* November 10, 1979.

* * *

KROEBER, Theodora (Kracaw) 1897-1979
(Theodora Kroeber-Quinn)

OBITUARY NOTICE—See index for *CA* sketch: Born March 24, 1897, in Denver, Colo.; died July 4, 1979, in Berkeley, Calif. Anthropologist and author, best known for her two works on North American Indians, *Ishi in Two Worlds* and *Ishi, Last of His Tribe.* Kroeber was also the author of a memoir about her life and work with her husband, Alfred Kroeber, also an anthropologist. Obituaries and other sources: *Chicago Tribune,* July 8, 1979; *Locus,* July-August, 1979.

* * *

KROEBER-QUINN, Theodora
See KROEBER, Theodora (Kracaw)

* * *

KROSBY, H(ans) Peter 1929-

PERSONAL: Born March 3, 1929, in Aas, Norway; immigrated to Canada, 1952; came to United States in 1958; Canadian citizen; son of Peter and Anna Elisabeth (Leganger) Krosby; married present wife, Vivien Mellon (a lecturer), November 25, 1971; children: Peter John, Anne Elizabeth, Kristin Marie, Karen Sidsel, Jane Ingrid; (present marriage) Erik Leganger and Garrett Lee (twins), Allison Reed, Meade Bicring. *Education:* University of British Columbia, B.A., 1955, M.A., 1958; Columbia University, Ph.D., 1967. *Home:* 10 Loudon Heights N., Loudonville, N.Y. 12211. *Office:* Department of History, State University of New York at Albany, 1400 Washington Ave., Albany, N.Y. 12222.

CAREER: University of British Columbia Alumni Association, Vancouver, assistant director, 1956-58; Fairleigh Dickinson University, Rutherford, N.J., instructor in history, 1959-62; University of Wisconsin, Madison, instructor, 1962-64, assistant professor, 1964-67, associate professor of history and Scandinavian studies, 1967-68, director of Scandinavian studies program, 1962-68; State University of New York at Albany, professor of history, 1968—, head of department, 1968-70. Instructor at Columbia University, summer, 1961; visiting lecturer at University of Maryland, summer, 1968; visiting professor at University of Minnesota, 1970-71, University of Helsinki, autumn, 1972, University of Turku, winter, 1973, and University of Joensuu, spring, 1973. American-Scandinavian Foundation, member, Lithgow Osborne Lecturer, 1966-67; member of U.S. Commission on Military History; participant in international symposia. *Military service:* Norwegian Army, Signals, 1948-49.

MEMBER: American Historical Association, Society for the Advancement of Scandinavian Study (member of executive council, 1968-72; president, 1973-75), Finnish Academy of Science and Letters (foreign member). *Awards, honors:* American-Scandinavian Foundation fellow in Finland, summer, 1962, 1972-73; University of Wisconsin travel grant for Finland, summer, 1967; State University of New York Research Foundation grants for Finland, summer, 1972, and for England, Denmark, and Canada, 1977-78; Finnish Ministry of Education grant, 1972-73; travel grant from Norwegian Foreign Ministry, summer, 1976; American Philosophical Society grant, 1977; American Council of Learned Societies grants, 1977, 1978.

WRITINGS: (Contributor) Harry T. Logan, editor, *Tuum Est: A History of the University of British Columbia,* University of British Columbia Press, 1958; *Nikkelidiplomatiaa Petsamossa, 1940-1941,* Kirjayhtymaa, 1966, revised edition of original English manuscript published as *Finland, Germany, and the Soviet Union, 1940-1941: The Petsamo Dispute,* University of Wisconsin Press, 1968; *Suomen valinta, 1941* (translated from the original English manuscript; title means "Finland's Choice, 1941"), Kirjayhtymaa, 1967; (editor with Harvey L. Dyck) *Empire and Nations: Essays in Honour of Frederic H. Soward,* University of Toronto Press, 1969; (contributor) Byron Dexter, editor, *The Foreign Affairs Fifty-Year Bibliography: New Evaluations of Significant Books on International Relations, 1920-1970,* Bowker, 1972; *Kekkosen linja* (translated from the original English manuscript; title means "The Kekkonen Line"), Kirjayhtymaa, 1978. Contributor to *Columbia Encyclopedia, World Book Encyclopedia,* and *Encyclopedia Americana.* Contributor of articles and reviews to scholarly journals, popular magazines, and newspapers in the United States, Canada, Finland, Germany, and Norway, including *McCall's.* Associate editor of *Scandinavian Studies,* 1971-73.

WORK IN PROGRESS: England and Finland, 1941: The Road to War; Modern Greenland: Emerging Nation in the Arctic; A Gateway to the Americas: Greenland in Allied Strategy, 1939-1945; Finland and the Soviet Union, 1944-1978.

* * *

KUH, Frederick Robert 1895-1978

OBITUARY NOTICE: Born October 29, 1895, in Chicago,

Ill.; died February 2, 1978, in Rockville, Md. Journalist. Kuh, who reported four days before the event that Italy would surrender to the Allies, was best known for his coverage of World War II. He worked for Chicago newspapers throughout his career, serving as London correspondent for the *Chicago Sun* from 1942 to 1947 and as London and then Washington correspondent of the *Chicago Sun-Times* from 1947 until 1963. Obituaries and other sources: *Who's Who in the South and Southwest,* 13th edition, Marquis, 1973; *New York Times,* February 4, 1978.

* * *

KUNZ, Marji 1939(?)-1979

OBITUARY NOTICE: Born c. 1939 in Detroit, Mich.; died August 28, 1979, in Southfield, Mich. Journalist and fashion reporter. Kunz wrote for *Glamour, Mademoiselle,* and the *Detroit Free Press* before joining the *Detroit News* in 1977. Known for her "educated" eye for fashion as well as her daring efforts to get behind a story (she once wrote a feature on wearing a seven-dollar gown to a formal ball), Kunz won two Penny-Missouri journalism awards. Obituaries and other sources: *Detroit Free Press,* August 29, 1979; *New York Times,* August 30, 1979.

* * *

KURALT, Charles Bishop 1934-

PERSONAL: Born September 10, 1934, in Wilmington, N.C.; son of Wallace Hamilton and Ina (Bishop) Kuralt; married Suzanna Folsom Baird, June 1, 1962; children: (from a previous marriage) Lisa Catherine, Susan Guthery. *Education:* Attended University of North Carolina. *Office:* CBS News, 524 West 57th St., New York, N.Y. 10019.

CAREER: Charlotte News, Charlotte, N.C., reporter and columnist, 1955-57; CBS-News, New York City, writer, 1957-59, correspondent, 1959—, feature reporter for "On the Road," 1967—. *Awards, honors:* Ernie Pyle Memorial Award from Scripps-Howard Foundation, 1959; Emmy Award from National Academy of Television Arts and Sciences, 1969; George Foster Peabody Broadcasting Awards from the University of Georgia, 1969 and 1976.

WRITINGS: To the Top of the World: The Adventures and Misadventures of the Plaisted Polar Expedition, March 28-May 4, 1967, Holt, 1968; *Dateline America,* Harcourt, 1979. Contributor to periodicals, including *Saturday Review, Field and Stream,* and *Readers Digest.*

SIDELIGHTS: Since 1967 Charles Kuralt has been combing the back roads of America in search of off-beat human interest stories for the CBS-News feature, "On the Road." Kuralt works at keeping the stories "unimportant and irrelevant and insignificant," and rejects any high-blown explanation of the purpose of his job. "We certainly didn't set out with any philosophy or to prove anything, but everybody has to justify what he does for a living," he told an interviewer. "It's so important on a national news show like Cronkite's to acknowledge that the whole world isn't in flames, that people go on living their lives in spite of big, black headlines." Although most of his features are on the light-side—Kuralt voted his story on a man who could hold about thirty eggs in one hand the most inconsequential—occasionally Kuralt broaches unpleasant topics, such as a feature on an unemployment line in Atlanta.

Kuralt and his three-man crew (a cameraman, sound man, and electrician) usually put about 50,000 miles a year on their van. They take turns driving, and luckily, Kuralt said, the other three men are good mechanics. When they first started out they criss-crossed the country stumbling unpredictably onto stories, but now they try to vaguely plan their destination. Most of the ideas for the three- or four-minute features come in the mail from viewers with suggestions, Kuralt explained, although the crew often stops when they find a story that seems promising.

While Kuralt doesn't claim to measure the mood of the nation, he did offer this observation in a recent interview: "There's a lot to be confident about. I've never heard calamity from the people. They seem to have a mystical confidence in themselves."

BIOGRAPHICAL/CRITICAL SOURCES: Newsweek, January 1, 1968; *Time,* January 19, 1968; *New York Times Book Review,* April 28, 1968; *Readers Digest,* December, 1968, March, 1973, December, 1978; *Times Literary Supplement,* July 3, 1969; *Courier Journal,* June 25, 1974; *Denver Post,* July 7, 1974; *Biography News,* Gale, August, 1974; *Seattle Post-Intelligencer,* October 29, 1974; *Authors in the News,* Volume 1, Gale, 1976; *Los Angeles Times Book Review,* September 2, 1979.*

* * *

KUZNETSOV, Anatoli 1929-1979
(A. Anatol)

OBITUARY NOTICE: Born in 1929 in Kiev, U.S.S.R.; died June 13, 1979, in London, England. Writer best known for *Babi Yar,* a documentation of the annihilation of Russian Jews by the Nazis. Once a staunch Communist who informed on his peers, Kuznetsov became disenchanted with Soviet censorship in the late 1960's, when he felt that he was being inaccurately depicted as an "ideological potboiler." He defected to England where he endured Soviet denunciations branding him a traitor. There he retaliated by accusing Soviet editors of censoring his writings "to the point of making them unrecognizable." The final months of his life were spent as a broadcaster for Radio Liberty. Obituaries and other sources: *New York Times,* June 14, 1979; *Washington Post,* June 15, 1979; *Chicago Tribune,* June 17, 1979; *Time,* June 25, 1979; *Newsweek,* June 25, 1979; *AB Bookman's Weekly,* July 9, 1979.

L

LACHENBRUCH, David 1921-

PERSONAL: Surname is pronounced *Lock*-en-brook; born February 11, 1921, in New Rochelle, N.Y.; son of Milton Cleveland (an accountant) and Leah Judith (a social worker; maiden name, Herold) Lachenbruch; married Gladys Kidwell, December 12, 1941; children: Ann Leah (Mrs. Daniel J. Zulawski). *Education:* University of Michigan, A.B., 1942. *Home:* 77 Seventh Ave., New York, N.Y. 10011. *Office: Television Digest,* 510 Madison Ave., New York, N.Y. 10022.

CAREER: Detroit Times, Detroit, Mich., correspondent, 1942-43; *York Gazette & Daily,* York, Pa., began as reporter and photographer, became assistant city editor and wire editor, 1946-50; Consumer Electronics, Washington, D.C., associate editor of *Television Digest,* 1950-58, managing editor, 1959-68, editorial director in New York, N.Y., 1968—, vice-president in Washington, D.C., 1962—. *Military service:* U.S. Army, 1942-45; became master sergeant. *Member:* Union International de la Presse Radiotechnique et Electronique, White House Correspondents Association.

WRITINGS: (Editor and contributor) *The New York Times Encyclopedia of Television,* Times Books, 1977; *Videocassette Recorders: The Complete Home Guide,* Everest House, 1979, revised edition, 1980; *Color Television, How It Works,* Raintree Press, 1980. Correspondent for *Variety,* 1942-43. Author of columns: "TV Q & A" and "What's New," in *TV Guide;* "Electronic Circuit," in *House and Garden;* "Videocassettes & Discs," in *Panorama;* "Looking Ahead," in *Radio-Electronics.* Contributor to magazines in the United States and Japan. Author and publisher of *Consumer Electronics Annual,* 1969-79.

WORK IN PROGRESS: A book on visual communications.

SIDELIGHTS: Lachenbruch told *CA:* "From the vantage point of longtime editorship of the leading weekly trade publication in television and video, I have the privilege of keeping in close touch with developments in these fields. My free-lance writing started as a by-product, an outlet for the information I had obtained but wasn't able to use in a tightly-written trade newsletter and as a way to put developments in perspective for myself as well as others. Over the years I have discovered there's great satisfaction in being able to put so-called 'technical' information in a manner which is understandable (and I hope, enjoyable) to non-technical people. Video communications increasingly will pervade our lives (whether we like it or not). Among the fields it will revolutionize is the one closest to me—publishing. The natural outgrowth of the videodisc and videocasette is a new area of publishing which will supplement, but not replace, the printed word. We hope soon to being issuing 'video editions' of *Television Digest* on those periodic occasions when action, color, and sound can tell a story better than print, or supplement it. One future personal project, now in the very early planning stages, is a text-and-video 'book,' or series of such books, the first perhaps being aimed at children (to use video as an aid to reading, not a substitute for it)."

* * *

LACK, David Lambert 1910-1973

OBITUARY NOTICE—See index for *CA* sketch: Born July 16, 1910, in London, England; died in 1973, in Oxford, England. Ornithologist, biologist, and author of books in his field. Lack was director of the Edward Grey Institute of Field Ornithology in Oxford, England for more than twenty-five years. During 1938 and 1939, he participated in a biological expedition to the Galapagos Islands. His books include *The Life of the Robin, Darwin's Finches,* and *Evolutionary Theory and Christian Belief.* Obituaries and other sources: *The Author's and Writer's Who's Who,* 6th edition, Burke's Peerage, 1971; *AB Bookman's Weekly,* July 30, 1973.

* * *

LAMB, Harold (Albert) 1892-1962

OBITUARY NOTICE: Born September 1, 1892, in Alpine, N.J.; died April 9, 1962. Historian and author. A diligent historian, Lamb spent many years studying Asian life in the Middle Ages. He also held a keen interest in Russia and its history, publishing both *The March of Muscovy* and *The City and the Tsar* in 1948. Among his other historical narratives and biographies are *Ghengis Khan, Hannibal, Omar Khayyam,* and *Theodora and the Emperor.* Obituaries and other sources: *The Oxford Companion to American Literature,* 4th edition, Oxford University Press, 1965; *The Reader's Encyclopedia,* 2nd edition, Crowell, 1965; *Who Was Who in America,* 4th edition, Marquis, 1968; *Authors of Books for Young People,* 2nd edition, Scarecrow, 1971.

* * *

LAMON, Lester C(rawford) 1942-

PERSONAL: Born October 12, 1942, in Maryville, Tenn.;

son of Howard F. (in business) and Ruth (Crawford) Lamon; married Sarah Elizabeth Luton, June 12, 1965; children: Ward Harper, Katherine Crawford. *Education:* Vanderbilt University, B.A., 1964, M.A.T., 1965; University of North Carolina, Ph.D., 1971. *Residence:* South Bend, Ind. *Office:* Department of History, Indiana University, South Bend, Ind. 46615.

CAREER: High school history teacher in Oak Ridge, Tenn., 1965-67; Indiana University, South Bend, assistant professor, 1971-75, associate professor of history, 1975—. *Member:* American Historical Association, Organization of American Historians, Southern Historical Association. *Awards, honors:* McClung Award from East Tennessee Historical Association, 1969, for "Tennessee Race Relations and the Knoxville Riot of 1919"; National Endowment for the Humanities grant, summer, 1972; American Philosophical Association grant, 1977-78; Leverhulme fellowship for New University of Ulster, 1978-79; American Council of Learned Societies grant, 1979-80.

WRITINGS: Black Tennesseans, 1900-1930, University of Tennessee Press, 1977; (contributor) Justin Wintle, editor, *Makers of Modern Culture,* Routledge & Kegan Paul, 1980. Contributor to *Encyclopedia of Black America* and *Dictionary of American Negro Biography.* Contributor of articles and reviews to history and social studies journals.

WORK IN PROGRESS: Integrated Higher Education in the South, 1865-1908; Ethnic Conflict in Comparison/Contrast: Northern Ireland and the United States.

* * *

LAMOTT, Kenneth (Church) 1923-1979

OBITUARY NOTICE—See index for *CA* sketch: Born April 8, 1923, in Tokyo, Japan; died of cancer, August 18, 1979, in Bolinas, Calif. Educator, administrator, and author. Lamott worked as an instructor at San Quentin Prison from 1952 to 1956, and in San Francisco public schools from 1956 to 1963. In 1963 he became director of research for the planning firm, Lester Gorskine Associates. Lamott wrote more than eight novels and nonfiction books, including *Chronicles of San Quentin, Anti-California,* and *Escape from Stress.* Obituaries and other sources: *Who's Who in the West,* 14th edition, Marquis, 1974; *The Writers Directory, 1980-82,* St. Martin's, 1979; *New York Times,* August 21, 1979; *Chicago Tribune,* August 26, 1979; *Time,* September 3, 1979.

* * *

LAMPHERE, Louise (Anne) 1940-

PERSONAL: Born October 4, 1940, in St. Louis, Mo.; daughter of P. Harold and Miriam (Bretschneider Johnson) Lamphere. *Education:* Stanford University, A.B. (with honors), 1962; Harvard University, M.A., 1966, Ph.D., 1968. *Office:* Department of Anthropology, Brown University, Providence, R.I. 02912.

CAREER: University of Rochester, Rochester, N.Y., visiting assistant professor of anthropology, 1967-68; Brown University, Providence, R.I., assistant professor of anthropology, 1968-75; University of New Mexico, Albuquerque, associate professor of anthropology, 1976-79; Brown University, associate professor of anthropology, 1979—. Research assistant at University of Colorado, summer, 1962; conducted fieldwork with Navajo Indians and field research in England; speaker at professional meetings; consultant to National Science Foundation. *Member:* American Anthropological Association (fellow), Current Anthropology (associate), Society for Applied Anthropology, American Ethnological Society, Royal Anthropological Institute of Great Britain and Ireland (fellow), Phi Beta Kappa. *Awards, honors:* National Science Foundation fellowship for London School of Economics and Political Science, 1971-72; Ford Foundation fellowship, 1975-76; National Institute of Mental Health grant, 1975-78.

WRITINGS: (Contributor) Keith Basso and Morris Opler, editors, *Apachean Culture History and Ethnology,* University of Arizona Press, 1971; (contributor) Walter W. Taylor, John L. Fischer, and Evon Z. Vogt, editors, *Culture and Life,* University of Southern Illinois Press, 1973; (editor with Michelle Zimbalist Rosaldo, and contributor) *Woman, Culture, and Society,* Stanford University Press, 1974; *To Run After Them: The Social and Cultural Bases of Cooperation in a Navajo Community,* University of Arizona Press, 1977; (contributor) George Foster, Elizabeth Colson, and other editors, *Long-Term Field Research in Social Anthropology,* Academic Press, 1978; (contributor) *The Educational and Occupational Needs of White Ethnic Women,* U.S. Government Printing Office, 1979; (contributor) Andrew Zimbalist, editor, *Case Studies in the Labor Process,* Monthly Review Press, 1979; (contributor) Roxanne Ortiz, editor, *Economic Development and Indian Reservations in New Mexico,* University of New Mexico Press, 1979. Contributor to *Handbook of North American Indians.* Contributor of about twenty articles and reviews to anthropology journals. Member of editorial board of *Signs: Journal of Women in Culture and Society,* 1975-79.

WORK IN PROGRESS: A book on women, work, and ethnicity in an urban setting; "Kin Networks and Strategies of Working Class Portuguese Families in a New England Town," to be included in *The Versatility of Kinship,* edited by Linda Cordell and Steve Beckerman.

* * *

LANDERS, Ann
See LEDERER, Esther Pauline

* * *

LANEGRAN, David A(ndrew) 1941-

PERSONAL: Born November 27, 1941, in St. Paul, Minn.; son of Walter B. and Lita E. (Wilson) Lanegran; married Karen Rae Nygren (in community education), September 11, 1964; children: Kimberley Rae, Elizabeth Ann, Erik David, Katherine Jane. *Education:* Macalester College, B.A., 1963; University of Minnesota, M.A., 1967, Ph.D., 1970. *Politics:* Democratic Farmer Labor party. *Religion:* Presbyterian. *Home:* 140 South Wheeler, St. Paul, Minn. 55105. *Office:* Department of Geography and Urban Studies, Macalester College, St. Paul, Minn. 55105.

CAREER: Macalester College, St. Paul, Minn., assistant professor, 1969-76, associate professor of geography, 1977—. Principal of Lanegran, Richter & Sandeen (consultants). Member of visiting faculty at University of Minnesota, University of California, Berkeley, and Pennsylvania State University. President of Minnesota Landmarks; member of board of directors of Old Town Restorations; past president of Minnesota Environmental Education Board; past member of board of directors of Grand Avenue Business Association. *Member:* Association of American Geographers. *Awards, honors:* Award of excellence from Minnesota Society of the American Institute of Architects, for contributions to "historical, architectural, and neighborhood awareness"; selected by *Change* magazine as one of the ten outstanding college teachers of geography in the United States.

WRITINGS: (With Risa Palm) *Invitation to Geography,* McGraw, 1973, revised edition, 1978; *Urban Dynamics in St. Paul,* Old Town Restoration Press, 1977; *The Lake District of Minneapolis,* Living Historical Museum Press, 1979; *St. Paul Omnibus: A Guide to Historic St. Paul,* Old Town Restoration Press, 1979.

WORK IN PROGRESS: A monograph on the neighborhoods of St. Paul, publication by Center for Urban and Regional Affairs, University of Minnesota expected in 1980.

SIDELIGHTS: Lanegran told *CA:* "I strive to increase the sense of place among the residents of the twin cities through publications and nonprofit renovation and restoration projects."

* * *

LANGE, Kelly

PERSONAL: Born in New York, N.Y.; daughter of Edmund V. (a pharmacist) and Alice (Reason) Scafard; divorced; children: Kelly Snyder. *Education:* Merrimack College, B.A. *Agent:* Norman Brokaw, William Morris Agency, 151 El Camino Dr., Beverly Hills, Calif. 90212. *Office:* NBC-TV News, 3000 West Alameda Ave., Burbank, Calif. 91503.

CAREER/WRITINGS: KABC radio and television, Los Angeles, Calif., radio talk show host, 1967-74, television reporter, 1969-70; KNBC-TV News, Burbank, Calif., newscaster and host of "Sunday Show," 1971—. Has hosted several programs on NBC-TV, including "Rose Parade," 1975-76, and "Take My Advice," 1976, has guest hosted the "Today Show" and the "Tomorrow Show," and has made guest appearances on several television shows. *Awards, honors:* Genii Award from American Women in Radio and Television, 1979, for contributions to the media and to the community; received several other awards.

WORK IN PROGRESS: A biography of Bob Brown, *Brownie,* the NBC cameraman who was killed in Guyana in November, 1978.

SIDELIGHTS: After her divorce in the early 1960's, Kelly Lange was left with "two things . . . a steam iron and a baby." Today she is an eminent television personality. Lange worked odd jobs as a model and as a cocktail waitress to support herself and her daughter before she landed a position as a radio station traffic reporter. Her jobs as a talk show host and newscaster soon followed, leading her to various other television appearances. Lange's success in the field was highlighted in 1979 when she received the Genii Award for successfully combining career, community, and home life. (One other candidate for the award was Barbara Walters; past recipients include Lucille Ball, Carol Burnett, Mary Tyler Moore, and Julie Andrews.)

As one who struggled to become a success in the male-dominated broadcasting industry, Lange sympathizes with women who are beginning to seek their own careers. She realizes that "everybody feels insecure, I do, you do," but insists "the doors are opening so now you [women] have to get the confidence and the skills, train yourselves and get those jobs."

Lange admits televison newscasting is largely only "headline reporting," but feels it is valuable nonetheless. "We hit on-the-spot news before it gets in the paper," she told one reporter. "The people can read the details, the whys behind the stories, in the paper the next morning." Her book on cameraman Bob Brown, meanwhile, has given her the opportunity to do some in-depth work of her own. A close personal friend, Brown was killed in Guyana in 1978. Lange overcame the shock of Brown's death "with the compulsion to write a book about the things he stood for, the integrity, what an unusual man he was."

BIOGRAPHICAL/CRITICAL SOURCES: Saturday Evening Post, September, 1978; *Valley,* May, 1979.

* * *

LANHAM, Edwin (Moultrie) 1904-1979

OBITUARY NOTICE—See index for *CA* sketch: Born October 11, 1904, in Weatherford, Tex.; died July 24, 1979, in Clinton, Conn. Journalist, free-lance writer, and author of more than twenty autobiographical and mystery novels. Lanham worked as a reporter for the *New York Evening Post* from 1930 to 1933 and for the New York City News Association from 1934 to 1939. After serving as a rewrite man for the *New York Herald Tribune* for five years, he became a free-lance writer. His books include *Banner at Daybreak, Sailors Don't Care,* and *The Wind Blew West.* Obituaries and other sources: *The Author's and Writer's Who's Who,* 6th edition, Burke's Peerage, 1971; *World Authors, 1950-1970,* Wilson, 1975; *New York Times,* July 25, 1979; *AB Bookman's Weekly,* August 20, 1979.

* * *

LAPRADE, William Thomas 1883-1975

OBITUARY NOTICE: Born December 27, 1883, in Franklin County, Va.; died May 14, 1975. Educator and author. Laprade taught history at Duke University (formerly Trinity College) from 1909 to 1953. His books include *England and the French Revolution,* 1909, *British History for American Students,* 1926, and *Public Opinion and Politics in Eighteenth Century England,* 1936. He also edited the *South Atlantic Quarterly* from 1944 to 1956. Obituaries and other sources: *South Atlantic Quarterly,* autumn, 1975; *American Historical Review,* February, 1976; *Who Was Who in America,* 6th edition, Marquis, 1976.

* * *

LARSEN, Roy E(dward) 1899-1979

OBITUARY NOTICE: Born April 20, 1899, in Boston, Mass.; died September 9, 1979, in Fairfield, Conn. Publishing executive. Larsen became *Time*'s circulation manager in 1922, months before the magazine was first published. Its phenomenal success led publisher Henry Luce to launch *Fortune, Life,* and several other magazines which established Time Inc. as the nation's most successful magazine publisher. After serving as vice-president for twelve years, Larsen took over the presidency of Time Inc. in 1939, a position he held for twenty-one years. When he retired in 1979, the company's publication list had expanded to include *Money, People,* and *Sports Illustrated.* Obituaries and other sources: *Current Biography,* Wilson, 1950; *Who's Who in America,* 39th edition, Marquis, 1976; *The International Who's Who,* Europa, 1977; *Who's Who,* 131st edition, St. Martin's, 1979; *New York Times,* September 10, 1979; *Washington Post,* September 10, 1979; *Chicago Tribune,* September 11, 1979.

* * *

LEAVELL, Landrum P(inson) II 1926-

PERSONAL: Born November 26, 1926, in Ripley, Tenn.; son of Leonard O. (a minister) and Annie (Elias) Leavell;

married Jo Ann Paris, July 28, 1953; children: Landrum P. III, Ann Paris, Roland Q. II, David E. *Education:* Mercer University, A.B., 1948; New Orleans Baptist Theological Seminary, B.D., 1951, Th.D., 1954. *Home:* 4111 Seminary Place, New Orleans, La. 70126. *Office:* 3939 Gentilly Blvd., New Orleans, La. 70126.

CAREER: Ordained Baptist minister, 1948; pastor of Baptist churches in Charleston, Miss., 1953-56, Gulfport, Miss., 1956-63, and Wichita Falls, Tex., 1963-74; New Orleans Baptist Theological Seminary, New Orleans, La., president, 1975—. First vice-president of Southern Baptist Convention, 1967-68; president of Baptist Sunday School Board, 1968-70, and Pastor's Conference, 1970-71, president of Baptist General Convention of Texas, 1971-73. Member of Wichita Falls Child Welfare Board and Citizen's Advisory Committee. *Member:* Rotary Club (past president). *Awards, honors:* George Washington Honor Medal from Freedoms Foundation, 1968, for sermon, "America at the Crossroads."

WRITINGS—All published by Broadman: *John's Letters: Light for Living,* 1970; *For Prodigals and Other Sinners,* 1973; *Angels, Angels, Angels,* 1973; *God's Spirit in You,* 1974; *Twelve Who Followed Jesus,* 1975; *Harvest of the Spirit,* 1976; *Sermons Worth Celebrating,* 1978; *Commission,* 1979; (editor with Harold T. Bryson of revised edition) Roland Q. Leavell, *Evangelism: Christ's Imperative,* 1979. Author of "On the Leavell," a column in *Vision.* Contributor to *One Volume Commentary.*

SIDELIGHTS: Leavell's most recent work is the revision of *Evangelism: Christ's Imperative,* written by his uncle, Roland Q. Leavell.

Leavell has traveled extensively in Europe and the Middle East.

* * *

LEAVITT, Richard Freeman 1929-

PERSONAL: Born March 30, 1929, in Colebrook, N.H.; son of Henry Walter (a semi-professional basketball player) and Marion R. (a civic worker; maiden name, Covell) Leavitt. *Education:* Attended University of New Hampshire, 1948, and University of Miami, Coral Gables, Fla., 1956. *Politics:* "Independent, usually liberal." *Home and office:* 4 Parsons St., Colebrook, N.H. 03576. *Agent:* Gloria Safier, Inc., 667 Madison Ave., New York, N.Y. 10021.

CAREER: TV Guide, Florida, advertising manager, 1956-58; sign painter in Colebrook, N.H., 1963-70; editor and publicist in New York, N.Y., 1970-73; writer. *Military service:* U.S. Navy, parachute rigger, for four years.

WRITINGS: (Editor) *The Colebrook Cookbook,* privately printed, 1970; *Yesterday's New Hampshire,* E. A. Seemann, 1975; *The World of Tennessee Williams,* Putnam, 1978. Also author of *Arlington: The Hallowed Ground* and *Colebrook: Yesterday.* Contributor to *Showbill.* Manuscript sales editor for Exposition Press.

WORK IN PROGRESS: The Witness Tree, a novel covering three generations of life in northern New England; research for *The World of Florenz Ziegfeld.*

SIDELIGHTS: Leavitt writes: "My interest centers around American roots: my own, my region's, and my state's. I am also interested in Arlington Cemetery and assorted show business people whose lives and work reflect the American scene. With me the past is prologue. I suffer from New England conscience; my writing stems from insatiable curiosity and love of the past."

AVOCATIONAL INTERESTS: Travel (including western Europe).

* * *

LEBREO, Steward
See WEINER, Stewart

* * *

LEBREO, Stewart
See WEINER, Stewart

* * *

LEDERER, Esther Pauline 1918-
(Ann Landers)

PERSONAL: Born July 4, 1918, in Sioux City, Iowa; daughter of Abraham B. (a motion picture exhibitor) and Rebecca (Rushall) Friedman; married Jules William Lederer (in business), July 2, 1939 (divorced, 1975); children: Margo Lederer Coleman. *Education:* Attended Morningside College, 1936-39, and Deree-Pierce Colleges, Athens, Greece, 1975. *Politics:* Democratic. *Religion:* Reformed Jewish. *Office: Chicago Sun-Times,* 401 North Wabash Ave., Chicago, Ill. 60611.

CAREER: Field Enterprises, Inc., Publishers-Hall Syndicate, syndicated human relations columnist, 1955—. Chair of Minnesota-Wisconsin council of the Anti-Defamation League, 1945-49; chair of Eau Claire, Wis., Gray-Lady Corps, American Red Cross, 1947-53; assistant Wisconsin chair of National Foundation for Infantile Paralysis, 1951-53; honorary national chair of National Tuberculosis Association Christmas Seal Campaign, 1963. Member of advisory committee of American Medical Association, 1968; member of board of sponsors of Mayo Clinic, 1970. County chair of Democratic Party of Eau Claire, Wis. Member of board of directors of Rehabilitation Institute of Chicago; member of national board of directors of American Cancer Society; member of visiting committee of board of overseers for Harvard Medical School. Trustee of Menninger Foundation, National Dermatology Foundation. *Awards, honors:* L.H.D., Morningside College, 1964; Hum.D., Wilberforce College (now University), 1972; L.H.D., University of Cincinnati, 1974.

WRITINGS—Under pseudonym Ann Landers: *Since You Ask Me,* Prentice-Hall, 1961; *Ann Landers Talks to Teenagers About Sex,* Prentice-Hall, 1963; *Ann Landers Says: Truth Is Stranger,* Prentice-Hall, 1968; *The Ann Landers Encyclopedia: Improve Your Life Emotionally, Medically, Sexually, Spiritually,* Doubleday, 1978; *Ann Landers Speaks Out,* Fawcett, 1978.

Author of booklets, including "Straight Dope on Drugs," "Teen Sex and 10 Ways to Cool It," "High School Sex and How to Deal With It: A Guide for Teens and Their Parents," and "Bugged By Parents? How to Get More Freedom."

Author of daily syndicated column.

SIDELIGHTS: In 1955, the *Chicago Sun-Times* was looking for a successor to Ruth Crowley, who had been writing a column under the name Ann Landers until her death in July, 1955. Esther Pauline Lederer was chosen over twenty-eight other women to fill the position, and she has since made Ann Landers a household word.

The "Ann Landers" column is one of the most widely read advice columns today, appearing in over nine hundred newspapers across the country. Every day Ann receives nearly one thousand letters asking for advice on every topic imaginable. She told Yolande Gwin, "When I first began, the letters were mostly for advice on marital problems. Oh, I still get them by the hundreds, but now the letter writers seek advice on sex, drugs, bi-racial marriages and living together-without-benefit-of-marriage."

Ann responds to her readers' problems with "a barrage of snappy patter, wisecracks, and sensible-shoes advice," observed Martin Kaplan. If she doesn't have the answer she calls on an expert to help her out. In her column and in *The Ann Landers Encyclopedia* she supplements her own advice with words of wisdom from such notables as Senator William Proxmire, Father Andrew Greeley, Eugene Kennedy, Erma Bombeck, Margaret Mead, and Dr. William Masters.

Kaplan described *The Ann Landers Encyclopedia* as "a compendium of sassy nostrums and no-nonsense guidance." It is an A to Z encyclopedia containing advice on acne, snoring, infidelity, freeloading in-laws, runaway children, birth control, and numerous other subjects. Though Candida Lund felt the book's subtitle, *Improve Your Life Emotionally, Medically, Sexually, Spiritually,* "seems a sweeping claim," she also praised the book, declaring "I know of no book today that mirrors more comprehensively our times—its problems, its challenges, its possibilities, and provides such phenomenal coverage."

One of Ann Landers's chief rivals in the advice business is Abigail Van Buren, or "Dear Abby," who is actually Ann's identical twin sister, Pauline Esther Friedman Phillips. Abby began writing her column in 1956, one year after Esther took over as Ann Landers.

Unfortunately, even Ann Landers doesn't have all the answers. In 1975 Ann announced to her readers that she and her husband were getting a divorce. The world was shocked that she was ending her marriage after thirty-six years when she had so often reminded readers that a successful marriage requires maintenance work. Ann did not give any explanation, noted *Newsweek,* "rejecting all inquiries with what amounted to an M.Y.O.B.B.—a favorite Landerism for 'Mind your own business, Buster.'"

BIOGRAPHICAL/CRITICAL SOURCES: Atlanta Journal, June 24, 1975; *Newsweek,* July 14, 1975; *Time,* July 14, 1975; *Biography News,* July/August, 1975; *Washington Post,* November 6, 1978; *Critic,* January 1, 1979; *New York Times Book Review,* February 25, 1979.*

* * *

LEE, Adrian Iselin, Jr. 1920-

PERSONAL: Born November 6, 1920, in Miami, Fla.; son of Adrian Iselin (a forester) and Adriana Lanier (Owen) Lee; married Marie Laine Santa Maria (a teaching supervisor); children: Adrian Iselin III, Catherine Taney, Thomas Sim, William Owen, Anne Marie, Louisa Carrell. *Education:* Spring Hill College, B.A., 1943. *Politics:* "Conservative Republican." *Religion:* Roman Catholic. *Home:* 119 West Springfield Ave., Philadelphia, Pa. 19118. *Office: The Bulletin,* 30th and Market Sts., Philadelphia, Pa. 19101.

CAREER/WRITINGS: Philadelphia Bulletin, Philadelphia, Pa., reporter, 1948—, columnist, 1970—. Notable assignments include Cuban missile crisis and United Nations debate, 1963, assassination of John F. Kennedy, 1963, Republican national conventions, 1964 and 1968, Vietnam War, 1966, Panamanian plebiscite on Canal treaty, 1977, and the conclave electing Pope John Paul II, 1978. *Military service:* U.S. Navy, 1943-46; became lieutenant; received unit commendation and four battle stars. U.S. Naval Reserves, 1943-46. *Member:* National Press Club, Philadelphia Press Association, Philadelphia Pen and Pencil Club. *Awards, honors:* Ten plaques and certificates for news, feature, and opinion-page writing, including Philadelphia Press Association award, 1965, for coverage of the John F. Kennedy assassination, and Sigma Delta Chi award, 1978, for column writing.

* * *

LEE, Henry F(oster) 1913-

PERSONAL: Born September 13, 1913, in Sargentville, Maine; son of Harry and Gertrude (Gay) Lee; married Margaret Pohl (an artist), April 15, 1939; children: Henry Gay, Cara. *Education:* Syracuse University, B.A., 1936, M.D., 1939. *Religion:* Unitarian-Universalist. *Home:* 8862 Norwood Ave., Philadelphia, Pa. 19118. *Office:* 8236 Germantown Ave., Philadelphia, Pa. 19118.

CAREER: Bryn Mawr Hospital, Bryn Mawr, Pa., intern, 1940-41; Children's Hospital of Philadelphia, Philadelphia, Pa., intern, 1941-42, assistant chief resident, 1942-43, chief resident, 1943-45, acting director, 1945-47; Lankenau Hospital, Philadelphia, acting chief of newborn department, 1947-48, chief of department, 1948-51, Pennsylvania Hospital, Philadelphia, chief of pediatrics for the newborn, 1953-64; Chestnut Hill Hospital, Philadelphia, director of department of pediatrics, 1963-78. Associate professor at University of Pennsylvania, 1968-80. Member of physicians review board of Philadelphia Blue Cross, 1966-70; past member of medical policy committee of Blue Shield of Pennsylvania; member of health insurance panels and committees. *Member:* American Medical Association, American Academy of Pediatrics, Pennsylvania Medical Association, Philadelphia County Medical Society (member of insurance mediation committee), Philadelphia Pediatric Society (president, 1966-67), Phi Beta Kappa, Alpha Omega Alpha.

WRITINGS: (With Violet Broadribb) *The Modern Parents Guide to Baby and Child Care,* Lippincott, 1973. Contributor of more than a dozen articles and reviews to medical journals and popular magazines, including *Aquarium, Down East,* and *Green Scene.*

SIDELIGHTS: Lee comments: "My motivation was to write a somewhat more sophisticated book than the usual 'baby book,' to answer those questions that twenty years' experience taught me parents ask about all the common ailments of babies and children."

AVOCATIONAL INTERESTS: Physiology, botany (desert plants), long distance sailing, building working models, botanical photography.

* * *

LEED, Eric J. 1942-

PERSONAL: Born December 11, 1942, in Missoula, Mont.; son of Bjarne Olaf (in merchant marine) and Alice (a laboratory technician; maiden name, Amundsen) Leed; married, February 11, 1968; wife's name, Lavina Jane (a musician); children: Andrea Ruth. *Education:* University of Oregon, B.A., 1964; University of Rochester, Ph.D., 1972. *Politics:* "Quixotic." *Religion:* "I have art and science." *Home:* 5836 Southwest 25th St., Miami, Fla. 33155. *Office:* Department of History, Florida International University, Miami, Fla. 33199.

CAREER: University of Rochester, Rochester, N.Y., instructor in history; University of British Columbia, Vancouver, lecturer in history, 1969-72; Florida International University, Miami, assistant professor, 1972-74, associate professor of history, 1974—. *Member:* American Historical Association, Greater Miami Black Music Association. *Awards, honors:* Fellow of National Humanities Institute, 1975-76; grant from National Endowment for the Humanities, 1979.

WRITINGS: No Man's Land: Combat and Identity in World War I, Cambridge University Press, 1979.

WORK IN PROGRESS: A History and Sociology of Travel, 1300-1900; A History of the Concept of Individualism in European Political Theory.

* * *

LEFFLER, Melvyn Paul 1945-

PERSONAL: Born May 31, 1945, in Brooklyn, N.Y.; son of Louis (in business) and Mollie (Fuchs) Leffler; married Phyllis Koran (a historian), September 1, 1968; children: Sarah Ann. *Education:* Cornell University, B.S., 1966; Ohio State University, Ph.D., 1972. *Home:* 1108 Sparta Rd., Nashville, Tenn. 37205. *Office:* Department of History, Vanderbilt University, Box 6130-B, Nashville, Tenn. 37235.

CAREER: Vanderbilt University, Nashville, Tenn., assistant professor, 1972-77, associate professor of history, 1977—. *Member:* American Historical Association, Organization of American Historians, Society for the History of American Foreign Relations, American Committee on the History of the Second World War. *Awards, honors:* American Council of Learned Societies grant, 1973; Gilbert Chinard Prize from Society for French Historical Studies and Institut Francais de Washington, 1975, for *The Struggle for Stability: American Toward France, 1921-33;* Fellow at Woodrow Wilson International Center, 1979-80, and Council on Foreign Relations, 1980-81.

WRITINGS: The Elusive Quest: America's Pursuit of European Stability and French Security, 1919-33, University of North Carolina Press, 1979. Contributor to history journals.

WORK IN PROGRESS: American Military Officials and National Security Policy, 1945-52.

* * *

LEIGH, Eugene
See SELTZER, Leon E(ugene)

* * *

LEIGH, Kathy
See KILLOUGH, (Karen) Lee

* * *

LELAND, Henry 1923-

PERSONAL: Born February 13, 1923, in New York, N.Y.; son of Ida (Miller) Leland; married Helen Faitas, August 13, 1948 (divorced, 1979); married Sherrie Ireland (a pre-school principal); children: Colombe, David Jean, Daniel Louis. *Education:* San Jose State College (now University), B.A., 1948; Sorbonne, University of Paris, D.U.P., 1952. *Politics:* Democrat. *Home:* 61 Glenmont Ave., Columbus, Ohio 43214. *Office:* Herschel W. Nisonger Center for Mental Retardation and Developmental Disabilities, Ohio State University, 1580 Cannon Dr., Columbus, Ohio 43210.

CAREER: New York State Mental Health Commission, Syracuse, senior clinical psychologist, 1952-54; Association for the Help of Retarded Children, Syracuse, N.Y., psychologist, 1954; Muscatatuck State School, Muscatatuck, Ind., clinical psychologist and director of department of psychological services, 1954-57; Parsons State Hospital and Training Center, Parsons, Kan., chief clinical psychologist, 1957-63, coordinator of professional training, education, and demonstration, 1963-70; Ohio State University, Columbus, associate professor, 1970-72, professor of psychology, 1972—, chief of psychology at Herschel W. Nisonger Center for Mental Retardation and Developmental Disabilities, 1970-72. Research associate at University of Kansas, 1963-70; associate professor at Kansas State College, 1958-60; distinguished visiting lecturer at University of Southern California, summer, 1969. Head of research committee for Kansas Mental Retardation Planning, 1964-68; head of Kansas State Board of Examiners of Psychologists, 1968-69. Member of board of directors of Arcraft, 1975—, head of board, 1978—. *Military service:* U.S. Army, 1942-45, served in Europe; became sergeant.

MEMBER: American Psychological Association (fellow; member of executive committee, 1969-74; president of executive committee, 1976; member of council, 1977-79), American Association on Mental Deficiency (fellow; member of council, 1964-68), American Association for the Advancement of Science (fellow), Ohio Psychological Association, Central Ohio Psychological Association, Psi Chi. *Awards, honors:* Grants from Vocational Rehabilitation Association, 1964-68, National Institute of Mental Health, 1964-70, and Ohio Department of Mental Health and Mental Retardation, 1972-75.

WRITINGS: (With Daniel E. Smith) *Play Therapy With Mentally Subnormal Children,* Grune, 1965, revised edition, Psychological Dimensions, 1980; (with Barbara Edmonson and E. M. Leach) *Social Perceptual Training Kit,* Educational Activities, Inc., 1968; (with Edmonson and Leach) *Social Inference Training of Retarded Adolescents at the Pre-Vocational Level,* Medical Center, University of Kansas, 1968; (with Kazoo Mihira, Ray M. Foster, and Max H. Shellhaas) *Adaptive Behavior Scales,* American Association on Mental Deficiency, 1969, revised edition, 1974; (with Edmonson, Leach, and J. B. deJung) *Test of Social Inference,* Educational Activities, Inc., 1974; (with D. E. Smith) *Mental Retardation: Current and Future Perspectives,* Charles A. Jones Publishing, 1974.

Contributor: *Brain Damage and Mental Retardation,* C. C Thomas, 1967, revised edition, 1971; Elias Katz, editor, *Mental Health Services for the Mentally Retarded,* C. C Thomas, 1972; George Tarjan, R. K. Eyman, and C. E. Meyers, editors, *Sociobehavioral Studies in Mental Retardation* (monograph), American Association on Mental Deficiency, 1973; Peter Mittler, editor, *Research to Practice in Mental Retardation Education and Training,* Volume II, University Park Press, 1977; Phyllis Magrab, editor, *Psychological Management of Pediatric Problems,* University Park Press, 1978. Contributor to *International Encyclopedia of Psychiatry, Psychology, Psychoanalysis, and Neurology.* Contributor of more than twenty articles to psychology and medical journals.

WORK IN PROGRESS: A book on adaptive behavior, publication by Psychological Dimensions expected in 1981; a children's adaptive behavior scale for publication by American Association on Mental Deficiency.

SIDELIGHTS: Leland writes: "The basis of all my writings is my belief that handicapped persons can be helped to live fruitful, contributing lives. A handicap does not have to become a disability.

"After twenty-five years work with handicapped and retarded persons, I have come to realize that all except the most profoundly retarded can benefit from the opportunity to live in a normal community with everyday types of experiences and can enjoy with us the freedom of an open society. When we institutionalize them we deny them their basic right to grow and mature, and, more important, we deny them the underlying human privilege of living with dignity through the taking of risks."

* * *

LENARD, Alexander 1910-1972

OBITUARY NOTICE—See index for *CA* sketch: Born March 9, 1910, in Budapest, Hungary; died April 14, 1972, in Brazil. Translator and author, best known for his Latin translation of *Winnie the Pooh,* entitled *Winni Ille Pu.* Lenard also translated Francoise Sagan's *Bonjour Tristesse* into Latin and wrote several volumes of poetry in both German and Italian. He contributed articles on medical subjects to numerous international publications. Obituaries and other sources: *New York Times,* May 3, 1972; *AB Bookman's Weekly,* May 15, 1972.

* * *

LENZ, Siegfried 1926-

PERSONAL: Born March 17, 1926, in Lyck, East Prussia, Germany (now Elk, Polish Masuria). *Education:* Attended University of Hamburg. *Religion:* None. *Politics:* German Social Democratic Party. *Home:* Obserstrasse 72, Hamburg 13, West Germany.

CAREER: Die Welt, feuilleton editor, 1949-51; free-lance novelist, short story writer, dramatist, travel writer, and critic, 1951—. *Member:* Free Academy of Arts, Hamburg. *Awards, honors:* Rene Schickele prize, 1952; Gerhart Hauptmann prize, 1961; Bremer prize, 1962; German Masonic literary prize, 1970.

WRITINGS—In English: *Das Feuerschiff* (stories), Hoffmann & Campe, 1960, translation of title novella by Michael Bullock published as *The Lightship,* Hill & Wang, 1962; *Stadtgespraeche,* Hoffmann & Campe, 1963, translation by Bullock published as *The Survivor,* Hill & Wang, 1965; *Deutschtunde,* Hoffmann & Campe, 1968, translation by Ernst Kaiser and Eithne Wilkins published as *The German Lesson,* Macdonald, 1971, Hill & Wang, 1972; *Myself for Example* (autobiographical essay) in *Motives,* edited by Richard Salis, Wolff, 1975; *Das Vorbild,* Hoffmann & Campe, 1973, translation by Douglas Parmee published as *An Exemplary Life,* Hill & Wang, 1976.

In German; fiction: *Es waren Habichte in der Luft* (novel; title means "There Were Hawks in the Air"), Hoffmann & Campe, 1951; *Duell mit dem Schatten* (novel; title means "Duel with the Shadow"), Hoffmann & Campe, 1953; *So zaertlich war Suleyken* (short stories; title means "How Sweet Was Suleyken"), Hoffmann & Campe, 1955; *Der Mann im Strom* (novel; title means "The Man in the Water"), Hoffmann & Campe, 1957; *Jaeger des Spotts: Geschichten aus dieser Zeit* (short stories; title means "Hunter of Mockery: Stories of Our Time"), Hoffmann & Campe, 1958; *Brot und Spiele* (novel; title means "Bread and Circuses"), Hoffmann & Campe, 1959; *Stimmungen der See* (short stories, with an autobiographical postscript; title means "Moods of the Sea"), Reclam, 1962; *Lehmanns Erzaehlungen; oder, So schoen war mein Markt: Aus den Bekenntnissen eines Schwarzhaendlers* (short stories; title means "Lehmann's Tales; or, Oh What a Lovely Market: From the Memoirs of a Black Marketeer"), Hoffmann & Campe, 1964; *Der Hafen ist voller Geheimnisse* (short stories; title means "The Harbor Is Full of Secrets"), Matthiesen, 1965; *Der Spielverderber* (short stories; title means "The Spoilsport"), Hoffmann & Campe, 1965; Colin Russ, editor, *Das Wrack* (short stories; title means "The Wreck"), Heinemann, 1967.

Gesammelte Erzaehlungen (title means "Collected Short Stories"), postscript by Russ, Hoffmann & Campe, 1970; Fritz Bachmann, compiler, *Das Wunder von Striegeldorf* (short stories; title means "The Miracle of Striegeldorf"), Hirschgraben, 1970; *So war es mit dem Zirkus: Fuenf Geschichten aus Suleyken* (stories for children; title means "That's How It Was With the Circus: Five Stories From Suleyken"), Hoffmann & Campe, 1971; *Einstein ueberquent die Elbe bei Hamburg* (short stories; title means "Einstein Crosses the Elbe at Hamburg"), Hoffmann & Campe, 1975; *Der Geist der Mirabelle: Geschichten aus Bollerup* (title means "Plum Brandy: Tales From Bollerup"), Hoffmann & Campe, 1975; *Die fruehen Romane* (title means "The Early Novels"; contains *Es waren Habichte in der Luft, Der Mann im Strom, Brot und Spiele,* and *Stadtgespraech*), postscript by Klaus Guenther Just, Hoffmann & Campe, 1976.

Plays: *Das schoenste Fest der Welt* (title means "The Greatest Celebration in the World"), Hans Bredow-Institut, 1956; *Zeit der Schuldlosen—Zeit der Schuldigen* (two radio plays; former first broadcast in 1960; titles mean "Time of the Innocents—Time of the Guilty"), Hans Bredow Institut, 1961, new edition edited by Albert R. Schmitt published under same title with English-German vocabulary and an introduction by the author, Appleton-Century-Crofts, 1967, stage adaptation as single play published as *Zeit der Schuldlosen* (first produced in 1961), Kiepenheuer & Witsch, 1962; *Das Gesicht: Komoedie* (title means "The Face: A Comedy"), Hoffmann & Campe, 1964; *Haussuchung: Hoerspiele* (title means "House to House Search: Radio Plays"; contains "Das schoenste Fest der Welt," "Die Enttauschung," "Das Labyrinth," "Haussuchung"), postscript by Heinz Schwitzke, Hoffmann & Campe, 1967; *Der Augenbinde* (title means "The Blindfold"), Rowohlt, 1969, also published with *Nicht alle Foerster sind froh: Ein Dialog* (title means "Not All Game-Keepers Are Happy: A Dialogue"), Rowohlt, 1970; *Der Amuesierdoktor* (title means "Ph.D. in Entertainment"), Eggebrecht, 1972.

Other works: *Das Kabinett der Konterbande* (appreciation of the publishing house of Hoffmann & Campe; title means "The Contraband Cabinet"), Hoffmann & Campe, 1956; (with Dieter Seelmann) *Flug ueber Land und Meer: Norder—Schleswig-Holstein—Ostsee* (title means "Flight Over Land and Sea: North Sea—Schleswig-Holstein—Baltic"), Westermann, 1967; *Lente von Hamburg* (title means "The People of Hamburg"), Hoffmann & Campe, 1969; *Beziehungen: Ansichten und Bekenntnisse zur Literatur* (essays; title means "Relationships: Opinions and Confessions About Literature"), Hoffmann & Campe, 1970; (with Seelmann) *Wo die Moewen schreien: Flug ueber Norddeutschlands Kuesten und Lander* (title means "Where the Seagulls Cry: Flight Over North Germany's Coasts and Countryside"), Christians, 1976.

SIDELIGHTS: Siegfried Lenz was drafted into the German navy in 1943, when he was seventeen. He ended the war in a British camp for prisoners of war, where he served for a time as an interpreter. Released in 1945, Lenz resumed his education at the University of Hamburg. In the chaos of postwar Germany, he was able to finance these studies only by selling his blood and dealing in the black market. Lenz had intended to become a teacher but while still a student in Hamburg began to contribute to the newspaper *Die Welt.* He enjoyed journalism and in 1949 left the university to join *Die Welt's* editorial staff. Lenz became a free-lance writer in 1951, when his first novel was published, and he has remained one, becoming one of the most popular and successful writers in West Germany.

Lenz himself says that his themes are "fall, flight, pursuit or persecution, indifference, revolt, lives founded on shaky principles." Brian Murdoch and Malcolm Read, in their book about Lenz, suggest that he is also concerned with the themes of duty and "the *Grenzsituation,* the borderline situation, requiring a decision that may well be a wrong one. He is concerned too, however, with perspective, with the impossibility of objective truth, something which he returns to time and again in his novels and short stories. . . . The notion of the witness and his responsibility recurs frequently in his work." Lenz has borrowed themes and habits of style from a variety of other writers who include Hemingway, Faulkner, Dostoevsky, and Camus as well as such German authors as Wolfgang Borchert and Heinrich Boell. Hemingway's influence, in particular, has been seen in Lenz's taut and anaphoric style, in his preoccupation with the testing "moment of truth," and in his fondness for the "loser," trapped by circumstances in a "borderline" situation where there is no right answer.

All of these elements were present in Lenz's first three novels, of which the most admired was *Der Mann im Strom* ("The Man in the Water"). It is about the deep-sea divers who operate out of Hamburg harbor, and centers on one diver who loses his job because he makes a mistake—a mistake that "consisted of growing old." Unlike Lenz's two earlier novels, which were marred by overblown descriptive writing and false aphorisms, *Der Mann im Strom* showed a new mastery of narrative method and characterization, and was praised for its tension, its "sober, unobtrusive quietness," and its "detailed, careful realism." The novel was filmed in 1958.

Meanwhile, Lenz's first collection of short stories had appeared in 1955 as *So zaertlich war Suleyken* ("How Sweet Was Suleyken"). He wrote these affectionate and humorous sketches of life in an imaginary Masurian village in order to provide his wife with a portrait of the world he grew up in. The Suleyken tales have been among the most popular of Lenz's writings, and have been adapted as films and reissued in illustrated gift editions. Later Lenz looked with a similarly indulgent eye at the inhabitants of "Bollerup," a town in North Germany. These unsentimental, sometimes ironical, but always sympathetic evocations of a vanishing way of life have little in common with Lenz's other short fiction, most of which resembles his novels in its grimly objective realism. Lenz's first volume of "stories for our time" was *Jaeger des Spotts,* containing fourteen short stories with a great variety of backgrounds—international athletics, Kenya at the time of Mau Mau, the Arctic, and Sardinia as well as modern Germany.

In an essay about Lenz's short stories, Colin Russ refers to the tale called "Stimmungen der See" ("Moods of the Sea"), the title story in a collection published in 1962. It deals with the clandestine attempt of three men to cross the Baltic but it is not easy, as Ross says, "to decide whether the action occurs during the war or afterwards, whether, in other words, the fugitives are trying to escape from the Nazi police state or from communist East Germany. Now what Lenz is doing in 'Stimmungen der See' is to concentrate on psychological tensions set against the background of the sea that he knows and describes better than any other German writer of our time. . . . The story's historical point of departure is, in the final analysis, irrelevant to its timeless themes: tension between the generations, the interplay of hope and fear, and man's cruelty to man." It seems to Russ that Lenz possesses in generous measure the writer's traditional skills—great narrative drive and readability, an ear for dialogue, and an eye for the detail which establishes character or atmosphere.

Buchner in Lenz's fourth novel, *Brot und Spiele* ("Bread and Circuses") is another loser—a fallen idol, who fails to survive the moment of truth. He is a famous long-distance runner, whose sometimes unscrupulous career is recalled by a life-long friend as Buchner runs his heroic last race. Like many of Lenz's stories, the novel is a parable, whose message according to Murdoch and Read is that "men are pursued by external forces that they do not have the wit to recognize as the furies, and everyone is a victim." *Stadtgespraeche* (translated as *The Survivor*) studies the complex tensions in a Norwegian town during the German occupation. Forty-four hostages are to be shot unless a young Resistance leader surrenders to the Nazis; he is ready to do so, but is assured that his importance as a symbol is worth more than the lives of the hostages. After the war, however, nothing looks quite the same. H. M. Waidson called this "a serious, subtle treatment of social relationships in a situation of anguished abnormality, presented in terms of understatement and open-minded concern."

The most admired and successful of Lenz's novels to date followed in 1968, *Deutschtunde* (translated as *The German Lesson*). Siggi Jepson, a youth in a German reform school, is told to write a short composition on "The Joys of Duty." He finds it almost impossible to begin, but when he does, the essay turns into a long reminiscence and meditation on the circumstances that turned him into a compulsive art thief. Siggi had grown up in a small community on the German-Danish border. His father had been the village policeman, the very embodiment of unthinking devotion to duty. A local artist is forbidden to paint because his Expressionist style displeases the Nazi authorities and the policeman, ignoring the claims of friendship, does his best to enforce this ruling. Siggi, who is drawn to and influenced by the artist, hides his paintings to protect them from his father. Later, in moral confusion and breakdown, he begins to steal and hide the work of other painters. In the end, having written all this down, Siggi has "only questions left, which no one can answer, not even the painter, not even him." There is a suggestion, nevertheless, that Siggi has taken a step forward—that when people are rigid and certain in their attitudes they are inevitably and dangerously in the wrong, and that Siggi's radical doubt and self-questioning is the highest freedom.

Lenz says that *Deutschtunde* presents a conflict between power and art. It does a number of other things as well, as Murdoch and Read point out: it is also "an investigation of the German past and its relationship to the present," revealing in the microcosm of a single quiet village the "social and mental attitudes upon which Nazi ideology was based and accepted." Hugely successful in Germany, where it was adapted as a memorable film, *Deutschtunde* was also warmly praised in its English translation. J. W. Charles wrote that its "bleak vision of how little has been learned in spite of World War II is intensified by Siggi's vivid descriptions of . . . the starkly beautiful North Sea coast. Mordantly witty, despairing, impassioned, this is one of the most deeply imagined and thought-provoking novels from Germany in years." Siggi rarely draws a moral or generalizes but when he does, Michael Hamburger said, "the effect within the context of this book whose ironies and satirical strands are as unobtrusive as its seriousness—is almost startling. . . . Lenz excels at the rendering of . . . family relations between people who are laconic, humorless, and trapped in a patriarchal order that it never occurs to them to question."

The tyranny of moral certainty is also an important theme in *Das Vorbild* (translated as *An Exemplary Life*). Three pedagogues meeting in Hamburg try to agree on a suitable biography for inclusion in a school reader. Each favors a different paragon, the choice reflecting the special circumstances of the educator's own life—his or her own prejudices and weaknesses. It had a relatively cool reception, reviewers finding it ambiguous, didactic, and ponderous.

Lenz has also had considerable success as a dramatist. *Zeit der Schuldlosen* ("Time of the Innocents"), broadcast as a radio play in 1960, illustrates Lenz's belief that there is no such thing as an "innocent bystander"—that those who fail to intervene against injustice share the guilt of the unjust. Nine men are rounded up at random and imprisoned together with a young revolutionary who has tried to assassinate the country's dictator. They will be freed only if they can learn the name of the revolutionary's accomplices, or persuade him to abandon his cause. The young man is eventually murdered, and the nine "innocent" men are released. A second radio play, *Zeit der Schuldigen* (1961), shows what happens after the revolution has succeeded, when the nine are arrested again and ordered, on pain of death, to identify the young man's murderer. In 1961 the two radio plays were combined as a stage play, *Zeit der Schuldlosen,* which has been very widely performed. Though some critics have found it excessively abstract and didactic, it has impressed others as what one writer called "the most brilliant and the most brutal treatment of the question of guilt which the postwar German theatre has produced." Lenz's later stage plays have been less successful, but his radio plays are generally admired and are said to have the virtues of his short stories, including narrative drive and a strong sense of character.

Lenz has also published literary criticism, travel books, and some interesting pen-portraits of the people of Hamburg. He was a member of the influential writers' association Group 47, and since the 1960's has been active as a political journalist and broadcaster, supporting the Social Democratic Party. Lenz's political views are not allowed to color his fiction and plays, however, and he has been attacked on this score by some activists. His literary non-engagement is conscious and deliberate; as Murdoch and Read have said, the key to his work is relativism—"he considers himself a witness to the world, and the German past, but never its judge."

BIOGRAPHICAL/CRITICAL SOURCES: Herbert Ahl, *Literarische Portraits,* Langen, 1962; H. F. Garten, *Modern German Drama,* Methuen, 1964; *Siegfried Lenz: Ein Prospekt,* Hoffmann & Campe, 1966; *German Life and Letters,* July, 1966, July, 1975; *New York Times Book Review,* February 23, 1969; Siegfried Lenz, *Beziehungen: Ansichten und Bekenntnisse zur Literatur* (includes autobiographical notes and interview), Hoffmann & Campe, 1970; Rudolph Ekkerhart, editor, *Protokoll zur Person,* List, 1971; H. M. Waidson, *The Modern German Novel,* University of Hull, 1971; Siegfreid Mandel, *Group 47,* Southern Illinois University Press, 1973; Trudis Reber, *Siegfried Lenz,* Colloquium Verlag, 1973; Colin Russ, editor, *Der Schriftsteller Siegfried Lenz,* Hoffmann & Campe, 1973; *Deutung und Bedeutung: Studies in German and Comparative Literature Presented to Karl-Werner Maurer,* Mouton, 1973; Ronald Hayman, editor, *The German Theatre,* Barnes & Noble, 1973; R. Hinton Thomas and Keith Bullivant, *Literature in Upheaval,* Manchester University Press, 1974; *Books Abroad,* summer 1974; Wilhelm Johannes Schwarz, *Der Erzaehler Siegfried Lenz,* Francke, 1974; Richard Salis, editor, *Motives,* Wolff, 1975; Hans Wagener, *Siegfried Lenz,* Beck, 1976; Heinz Ludwig Arnold, editor, *Siegfried Lenz,* Text & Kritik, 1976; Winfried Brassmann, *Siegfried Lenz,* Bouvier, 1976; *Times Literary Supplement,* April 29, 1977; Brian Murdoch and Malcolm Read, *Siegfried Lenz,* Wolff, 1978; *New York Times,* May 31, 1979.*

* * *

LESLIE, Seymour 1890(?)-1979

OBITUARY NOTICE: Born c. 1890; died in 1979 in England. Author. A cousin of Winston Churchill, Leslie did administrative work for the Chelsea Book Club and raised funds for hospitals during World War II. He wrote the book *Jerome Connexion.* Obituaries and other sources: *AB Bookman's Weekly,* September 3, 1979.

* * *

LESTER, James D. 1935-

PERSONAL: Born March 5, 1935, in Fort Smith, Ark.; son of Kenneth R. (a printer) and Fae Lester; married Martha Beaver, October 30, 1958; children: James D., Jr., Mark Alan. *Education:* East Central State College (now East Central University), B.A., 1957; Oklahoma State University, M.A., 1963; University of Tulsa, Ph.D., 1970. *Politics:* Democrat. *Religion:* Methodist. *Home:* 2316 Dogwood Lane, Clarksville, Tenn. 37040. *Office: Cumberland,* 128 Public Square, Clarksville, Tenn. 37040.

CAREER: Aide to U.S. Senator Robert Kerr, 1957-59; Fort Smith High School, Fort Smith, Ark., English teacher, 1959-63; Emporia State University, Emporia, Kan., assistant professor, 1963-67; University of Tulsa, Tulsa, Okla., graduate assistant, 1967-70; Austin Peay State University, Clarksville, Tenn., professor of English, 1970—. *Cumberland* (magazine), Clarksville, publisher and senior editor, 1977—. *Member:* Modern Language Association of America, National Association of Teachers of English, Conference on College Composition and Communication. *Awards, honors:* F. B. Parriott scholarship from University of Tulsa, 1969-70.

WRITINGS: Writing Research Papers, Scott, Foresman, 1967, 4th edition, 1980; *Patterns: Readings for Composition,* W. C. Brown, 1973.

WORK IN PROGRESS: Writing College Papers; a novel.

SIDELIGHTS: Lester told *CA:* "*Cumberland* is a regional magazine for Tennessee that has demanded more and more attention over recent months. As publisher, I am busy on all fronts. In particular, I write three to five articles for each issue of the magazine, which issues every other month, plus I work with advertising, sales, graphics, and production."

* * *

LEVANT, Howard 1929-

PERSONAL: Born in 1929, in Eveleth, Minn.; son of Harry A. (an insurance agent) and Sarah (Hironmous) Levant; married Virginia McMichael (an accountant and researcher), September 12, 1953; children: Jonathan, Moira. *Education:* University of Minnesota, B.A., 1950, M.A., 1954; Cornell University, Ph.D., 1961. *Home:* 3352 Morning Glory Drive, West Carrollton, Ohio 45449.

CAREER: University of Washington, Seattle, instructor in English, 1957-60; Morningside College, Sioux City, Iowa, assistant professor, 1960-63, associate professor of English,

1963-66; Muskingum College, New Concord, Ohio, associate professor of English and director of writing program, 1966-69; Hartwick College, Oneonta, N.Y., associate professor of English and head of department, 1969-73; Pepperdine University, Malibu, Calif., visiting research professor of humanities and director of Man Affirmative research project, 1973-79. Has given poetry readings at colleges and universities; speaker at professional meetings.

MEMBER: Modern Language Association of America (member of board of directors, 1961-65; head of film study advisers, 1965-68), Northeast Modern Language Association (head of modern literature section, 1971-72). *Awards, honors:* Fellow of writers' workshop at University of Iowa, 1953-54; grants from Ohio Arts Council, 1968-69, New York State Council on the Arts, 1971-72, and Scaife Family Charitable Trusts, 1973-79.

WRITINGS: (Contributor) Robert Murray Davis, editor, *Steinbeck: A Collection of Critical Essays,* Prentice-Hall, 1972; *The Novels of John Steinbeck,* University of Missouri Press, 1974; (editor and author of introduction) Douglas Shetler, *Perspectives: The Energy Issue,* Man Affirmative Editions, 1975; (editor and author of introduction) *The Writer and the World: Essays by Sidney Hook, Walter E. Williams, and A. Lawrence Chickering,* Man Affirmative Editions, 1976. Contributor of about twenty-five articles, poems, and reviews to journals, including *Choice, Modern Age, Poetry Now, Prairie Schooner,* and *Morningside Review.* Member of editorial advisory board of *Journal of Narrative Technique,* 1970—.

WORK IN PROGRESS: A book of poems; an analytical study of narrative technique, *Narrative in Fiction;* case studies of success and failure in the development and deployment of recent weapons systems.

SIDELIGHTS: Levant writes: "I endorse Melville's formula regarding the writer's expected conditions of work. What matters always is the finished work. The rest is commentary."

* * *

Le VAY, David 1915-

PERSONAL: Born May 14, 1915, in London, England; son of Monte (in business) and Eva (Goldstein) Le Vay; married Marjorie Cole (a physician), July 6, 1940 (marriage ended); married Sonja Hansen (a magistrate), May 17, 1957; children: Martin, Simon, Charles, Julian, Benedict, Lone-Beatrix, Jonathan, Lewis, David, Louise, Joshua. *Education:* University of London, M.B., B.S., 1937, M.R.C.S. and L.R.C.P., 1937, M.S. and F.R.C.S., 1940. *Politics:* Conservative. *Religion:* "Pantheist." *Home:* Old Buckhurst, Withyham, near Hartfield, Sussex, England. *Agent:* Curtis Brown Ltd., 1 Craven Hill, London W2 3EP, England.

CAREER: Surgeon, 1941-42; Southeast Metropolitan Regional Hospital Board, London, England, consultant orthopedic surgeon, 1946-77; writer, 1977—. Visiting professor at Pahlavi University, 1973. *Military service:* British Army, Royal Army Medical Corps, 1943-44; became captain. *Member:* Savage Club.

WRITINGS: A Guide to the National Health Service, Hamish Hamilton, 1946; *A Synopsis of Orthopedic Surgery,* H. K. Lewis, 1947; *Anatomy,* English Universities Press, 1948; *The Life of Hugh Owen Thomas,* E. & S. Livingstone, 1957; *Human Anatomy and Physiology,* English Universities Press, 1974; *Scenes From Surgical Life* (memoirs), P. Owen, 1976. Also author of *Physiology,* 1948, and co-editor of *Orthopedic Surgery and Traumatology,* 1973.

Translator: Colette, *Journey for Myself,* P. Owen, 1970; Colette, *Places,* P. Owen, 1970; Jean Giono, *Ennemonde,* P. Owen, 1970; Monique Wittig, *Les Guerilleres,* P. Owen, 1971; Wittig, *The Lesbian Body,* P. Owen, 1975; (with M. Crosland) Collette, *1001 Mornings,* P. Owen, 1975; Colette, *Looking Backwards,* P. Owen, 1975; Joseph Roth, *Flight Without End,* P. Owen, 1977; Roth, *The Silent Prophet,* P. Owen, 1979. Also translator of Colette, *Journal a rebours de ma fenetre,* 1974, and Valentin, *History of Orthopedics,* 1974.

WORK IN PROGRESS: Affectations and Impostures, memoirs.

SIDELIGHTS: Le Vay writes: "A consultant surgeon with life-long literary interests, I am now engaged mainly in creative writing, editorial work, and translations of novels and medical and other scientific material from German, French, and Spanish. I spent much of the last year working in Australia."

AVOCATIONAL INTERESTS: Music, polemics, growing roses.

* * *

LEVELL, Byrd 1911(?)-1979

OBITUARY NOTICE: Born c. 1911 in Washington, D.C.; died of a heart attack, November 5, 1979, in Charlottesville, Va. Hematologist, educator, and author. Levell taught for nearly fifty years at the University of Virginia Medical School, where he was chief of the hematology department from 1946 to 1971. He wrote more than fifty scientific articles in addition to a textbook on hematology. Obituaries and other sources: *Washington Post,* November 10, 1979.

* * *

LEVINE, Caroline Anne 1942-

PERSONAL: Born in 1942 in San Francisco, Calif.; daughter of Rudolph Braun and Marjorie (Melville) Hartmann; married Rodney Lee Levine (a neonatologist and biochemist), December 28, 1970; children: Sarah Lisa. *Education:* University of Santa Clara, B.A., 1965; University of Colorado, M.A., 1976. *Politics:* Democrat. *Religion:* Jewish. *Home:* 1502 Auburn Ave., Rockville, Md. 20850. *Office:* Montgomery County Schools, Rockville, Md. 20850.

CAREER: Teacher at public schools in Cupertino, Calif., 1967-73; reading specialist for public schools in Aurora, Colo., 1973-77; Montgomery County Schools, Rockville, Md., reading specialist, 1977—. *Member:* International Reading Association, Maryland State Teachers Association. *Awards, honors:* Helen Maehling fellowship from National Education Association, 1975, for England.

WRITINGS: Knockout Knock Knocks (juvenile), Dutton, 1978.

WORK IN PROGRESS: A novel for ten- to thirteen-year-old girls, in diary form, about a very small girl who is anxious about her size, publication expected in 1981.

SIDELIGHTS: Levine told *CA:* "As a reading specialist, I have been helping children with reading problems for six years now. I'm convinced that children learn to read better by reading a lot of what they want to read. They will read faster and with much more comprehension when they become engrossed in a book that really excites them. I want to be one of those authors who really excites young readers.

"The heroine in the novel I am presently working on is the eleven-year-old daughter of a pediatrician who specializes in newborns. Lisa's main problem is that she is one of the tiniest girls in middle school and she is very worried that there is something wrong with her. She sneaks into her father's study each night to look up facts about growth and development in adolescents. She keeps a diary of what happens to her during the first eight months of middle school and about her research in adolescent medical books.

"I love to read books written for boys and girls who are between nine and sixteen years old. I guess I read two or three novels a week. Some of my adult friends think I'm weird because I would rather read a young person's book than an adult bestseller.

"My favorite authors are Judy Blume, Norma Klein, Lee Bennett Hopkins, and Betsy Byars. I really enjoy the novels that these authors have written. They really know what kids are thinking.

"My goals in writing for children are to provide them with novels they will enjoy and to spread my basic love of reading to many, many children.

"I write in our 'office' at home. My two dogs, Godzilla and Buddha Bow-Wow, usually sit by my feet while I'm typing. Sometimes I let one of them sit on my lap when I'm writing a first draft. Now that I have a baby, the dogs always sit on the floor if the baby is awake and sitting in her papoose which is fastened to my chest."

* * *

LEVINE, Charles H(oward) 1939-

PERSONAL: Born July 13, 1939, in Hartford, Conn.; son of Benjamin (a businessman) and Elaine (a nurse; maiden name, Cohen) Levine; married Elaine Sandra Marcus (a teacher), September 11, 1966; children: Jordan Benjamin. *Education:* University of Connecticut, B.S. (with honors), 1964; Indiana University, M.B.A., 1966, M.P.A., 1968, Ph.D., 1971. *Home:* 3209 Rolling Rd., Chevy Chase, Md. 20015. *Office:* Institute for Urban Studies, University of Maryland, 2113 Woods Hall, College Park, Md. 20742.

CAREER: Time, Inc., New York, N.Y., library researcher, 1961; Nowland & Co., Greenwich, Conn., in marketing research, 1964; United Aircraft Corp., East Hartford, Conn., management intern, 1965; Indiana University, Bloomington, lecturer in business, 1966-68, survey researcher, 1968; Michigan State University, East Lansing, lecturer in public policy, 1969-71; University of Maryland, College Park, assistant professor of government and politics, 1971-73; Syracuse University, Syracuse, N.Y., assistant professor, 1973-75, associate professor of public administration, 1975-77; University of Maryland, associate professor of urban studies, 1977—, director of graduate studies, 1977-78, acting director of Institute for Urban Studies, 1979—, and Bureau of Governmental Research, 1979—. Research associate at National Academy of Public Administration, 1972. Adjunct professor at University of Southern California, 1973; visiting research professor at Cornell University, 1975-77. Participates in and directs conferences and panels. Consultant to U.S. Department of State, U.S. Agency for International Development, National Aeronautics and Space Administration, U.S. Department of Housing and Urban Development, and U.S. Department of Health, Education, and Welfare.

MEMBER: International City Managers Association, American Political Science Association, American Society for Public Administration, Academy of Management, National Association of Schools of Public Affairs and Administration, Policy Studies Organization, Southern Political Science Association, Pi Sigma Alpha. *Awards, honors:* Ford Foundation fellowship, 1970; William E. Mosher Prize from American Society for Public Administration, 1978, for article, "Organizational Decline and Cutback Management."

WRITINGS: Racial Conflict and the American Mayor: Power, Polarization, and Performance, Heath, 1974; (editor and contributor) *Managing Human Resources: A Challenge to Urban Governments,* Sage Publications, 1977; (editor with Harlan Hahn, and contributor) *Urban Politics: A Reader for the 1980's,* Longman, 1978; (contributor) Robert Agronoff and H. George Frederickson, editors, *Public Administration for Professionals,* F. E. Peacock, 1978; (contributor) Robert L. Lineberry, editor, *The Politics and Economics of Urban Services,* Sage Publications, 1978; (with Robert Backoff and William Siffin) *Understanding Public Management,* Winthrop Publishing, 1979; *Managing Fiscal Stress,* Chatham House, in press; *Fiscal Stress and Public Policy,* Sage Publications, in press.

Member of editorial board of "Sage Professional Papers in Administration and Policy Sciences," Sage Publications, 1974—; member of editorial advisory board of "Series in Political Science and Public Administration," Dekker, 1975—; editor of "Public Administration and Public Management," Winthrop Publishing, 1977—. Contributor of about thirty-five articles and reviews to political science and public administration journals. Founding co-editor of *Administration and Society,* 1973-76, member of editorial board, 1975—; member of editorial board of *Public Administration Review,* 1977—, editor, 1977-78; member of editorial board of *Urban Interest,* 1977—, and *International Journal of Public Administration,* 1978—.

WORK IN PROGRESS: Cutback Management: Administrating Sacrifice in the Public Sector.

SIDELIGHTS: Levine told *CA:* "Public management is a blend of politics and rational administrative practice. The difficulty of writing about public management lies in the gap between the normative images people hold about how government should conduct its affairs and the reality caused by the way people demand specific services from government. The irreconcilable gap between images of efficient practice and realities of political compromise befuddle and frustrate both citizens and bureaucrats alike and makes the study of public management confusing and its prescriptions often contradictory. To untangle this mess requires a writer to pick a point of entry that provides both theoretical leverage and concrete examples of the argument he/she wishes to make. I have chosen to build my bridge between political and administrative rationality on three clusters of policy activity: conflict resolution, information acquisition, and resource availability. By analysing these activities in government, I am able to argue that public management and business management are irreconcilably distinctive; that understanding public management requires an appreciaton for the uniqueness of public policy problems; and that there are analytic ways to unify political and administrative structures and dynamics into a common framework built on modern systems and organization theory."

* * *

LEVINE, Michael 1954-

PERSONAL: Born April 17, 1954, in New York, N.Y.; son of Arthur O. (in sales) and Virginia (Gaylor) Levine; married Darlene Mancuso (in advertising), January 14, 1977. *Education:* Attended Rutgers University, 1973. *Politics:* Democrat. *Religion:* "No formal religion." *Home:* 535 South Alexandria Ave., Los Angeles, Calif. 90005. *Office:* 256 South Robertson, Beverly Hills, Calif. 90211.

CAREER: *TV News* (magazine), Hollywood, Calif., president, 1977—. President of Sunset Merchandising (mail order business), 1978; public relations director for Deana Canova Enterprises. *Member:* ERAmerica, Hollywood Chamber of Commerce.

WRITINGS: *How to Reach Anyone Who's Anyone,* Price, 1979. Contributor to national magazines.

SIDELIGHTS: Levine writes: "Over four years ago I decided to put together a 'Guinness'-type book of addresses. *How to Reach Anyone Who's Anyone* is a combination recreational and reference book, listing addresses of every possible kind of notable person, including John Travolta, Charles Manson, Ronald McDonald, and Farrah Fawcett Majors. This book allows the average person to communicate with numerous world notables by providing an accurate, up-to-date address."

* * *

LEWIS, Fulton, Jr. 1903-1966

OBITUARY NOTICE: Born April 30, 1903, in Washington, D.C.; died August 20, 1966. Journalist and radio news broadcaster. Lewis began his career working in various capacities for the *Washington Herald* and the Universal News Service. He left in 1937 when he began his nightly news comments for his long-running Mutual network radio program. Noted for his right-wing politics, Lewis criticized the New Deal and supported Joseph McCarthy and Barry Goldwater. He also wrote the syndicated columns "The Washington Sideshow," 1933-36, "Fulton Lewis, Jr., Says," 1944-45, and "Washington Report." Obituaries and other sources: *Current Biography,* Wilson, 1942; *New York Times,* August 22, 1966; *Who Was Who in America,* 4th edition, Marquis, 1968; Irving E. Fang, *Those Radio Commentators,* Iowa State University Press, 1977.

* * *

LEWIS, Ralph F(erguson) 1918-1979

*OBITUARY NOTICE—*See index for *CA* sketch: Born January 21, 1918, in Dayton, Ohio; died June 7, 1979, in Paris, France. Businessman, editor, publisher, and author on business subjects. After holding a number of management positions, including posts with Time, Inc., *Fortune* magazine, and Arthur Young & Co., Lewis was named editor and publisher of the *Harvard Business Review.* He held that job from 1971 until his death. He was the author of *Management Uses of Accounting* and *Planning and Control for Profit.* Obituaries and other sources: *Who's Who in America,* 40th edition, Marquis, 1978; *The Writers Directory, 1980-82,* St. Martin's, 1979; *New York Times,* June 9, 1979.

* * *

LEWIS, Shari 1934-

PERSONAL: Born January 17, 1934, in New York, N.Y.; daughter of Abraham B. (an educator and magician) and Ann (a music coordinator; maiden name, Ritz) Hurwitz; married Jeremy Tarcher (a television producer), March 15, 1958; children: Mallory Jessica. *Education:* Attended Columbia University, 1951. *Office:* SLS Entertainment Enterprises, 6464 Sunset Blvd., Los Angeles, Calif. 90028.

CAREER: Ventriloquist and puppeteer. Star of television shows: "Facts 'n Fun," WRCA-TV, 1953; "Kartoon Klub," 1954; "Shari and Her Friends," 1955; "Shariland," 1956; "Hi, Mom," 1957; "The Shari Lewis Show," National Broadcasting Company (NBC-TV), 1960; "Shari at Six," British Broadcasting Corp. (BBC-TV), 1969-76; "The Shari Show," syndicated nationally and worldwide, 1976—; "Once Upon an Evening With Shari Lewis," Canadian Broadcasting Corp. (CBC-TV), 1978. Writer, producer, and star of television special "A Picture of Us," NBC-TV, 1973. *Awards, honors:* Emmy awards from National Academy of Television Arts and Sciences for best local program and outstanding female personality, 1957, for best children's show and outstanding female personality, 1958, 1959; Peabody award, 1960; Radio-Television Mirror award, 1960; Monte Carlo International Television award, 1961, for world's best variety show; Emmy award as outstanding children's entertainer, 1973-74.

WRITINGS: *The Shari Lewis Puppet Book,* Citadel, 1958; *Fun With the Kids,* Doubleday, 1960; (with Lillian Oppenheimer) *Folding Paper Puppets,* Stein & Day, 1962; (with Oppenheimer) *Folding Paper Toys,* Stein & Day, 1963; *Dear Shari,* Stein & Day, 1963; (with Oppenheimer) *Folding Paper Masks,* Dutton, 1965; *Making Easy Puppets,* Dutton, 1967; *The Tell It, Make It Book,* J. P. Tarcher, 1972; (with father, Abraham B. Hurwitz) *Magic for Non-Magicians,* J. P. Tarcher, 1975; *How Kids Can Really Make Money,* Holt, 1979; *Spooky Stuff,* Holt, 1979; *Impossible—Unless You Know How,* Holt, 1979; *Toy Store-in-a-Book,* Holt, 1979.

"Headstart" series; with Jacquelyn Reinach; published by McGraw: *The Headstart Book of Looking and Listening,* 1966; *The Headstart Book of Thinking & Imagining,* 1966; *The Headstart Book of Knowing & Naming,* 1966; *The Headstart Book of Be Nimble & Be Quick,* c. 1968.

"Kids-Only Club Book" series; published by J. P. Tarcher: *The Kids-Only Club Book,* 1976.

WORK IN PROGRESS: "Kids-Only Club Book" series.

SIDELIGHTS: Shari Lewis learned the basics of magic from her father when she was four years old. Five or six years later she learned puppetry, and at the age of seventeen added ventriloquism to her accomplishments. An appearance on "Arthur Godfrey's Talent Scouts" television program in 1953 helped launch her into radio and television work.

During this time Lewis's skill as a ventriloquist put her in high demand for making commercials. She could imitate myriad voices and sounds, so producers were able to save money by hiring one woman to perform many voices.

As the star of her own television programs, Lewis's best known co-star is Lamb Chop, a hand puppet which she manipulates and ventriloquially articulates. Her Las Vegas, Reno, and other night club appearances prove her versatility as an entertainer for adults as well as children. She has also conducted many of the major symphonies in the United States and Canada, including the Rochester Philharmonic, Denver Symphony, Minnesota Orchestra, and the Calgary Philharmonic.

The Kids-Only Club Book for children contains numerous details on how to form a club, run a carnival, construct games and costumes, and tackle other projects. Though critics considered the projects in some of Lewis's other books too difficult for children to perform alone, all the directions in this book are written so that children can handle them on their own without having to depend on adults for help. *Publishers Weekly* commented that "Lewis exhibits the imagination and zest in this how-to that have made her TV performances a hit with children."

Shari Lewis has recorded three albums: "Fun in Shariland," "Hi Kids," and "Shari in Storyland."

Lewis told *CA:* "I began my writing career when I married a publisher. During our honeymoon in Nassau my publisher husband, Jeremy Tarcher, would carry me off to our hotel room each day at 4:00 p.m. and lock me in alone, insisting that I meet my deadline on my first book, *The Shari Lewis Puppet Book.*

"I write because I enjoy sharing the know-how I have acquired during a lifetime as a television entertainer, scout leader, and mother.

"I write in bed for many reasons: (1) I've never found a desk as big as my king size bed, and I like to spread papers and collateral material around me as I work; (2) No desk chair could possibly support my body as well as my bed does, so I am able to write for many, many hours; (3) Since I'm a catnapper, I can simply put back my head and doze off at will.

"I wrote the first *Kids-Only Club Book* and am continuing to expand the 'Kids-Only Club Book' series because I am aware of the fact that, given the chance and the choice, kids know what they want to do in their spare time. They just don't always know how to do those things—and they certainly don't want to give up control of their spare time to adults, who have a way of taking over.

"In each book of the 'Kids-Only' series an area of great interest, excitement, and curiosity is vigorously and (I hope) clearly covered, step by step, so that the reader can succeed in exploring the activity.

"The books in the 'Headstart' series, which I wrote with Jackie Reinach, have been very successfully adapted as film strips by Miller-Brody. They had Rita Mareno record the material on one side in Spanish and I did the other side in English, and it has become a best-selling set of film strips in the field of early reading readiness."

BIOGRAPHICAL/CRITICAL SOURCES: Saturday Review, October 16, 1965; *Times Literary Supplement,* December 5, 1968; *Publishers Weekly,* December 11, 1967, March 13, 1978; *Observer,* November 23, 1969; *Booklist,* November 15, 1975.

* * *

LEWIS, Wilmarth Sheldon 1895-1979

OBITUARY NOTICE—See index for *CA* sketch: Born November 14, 1895, in Alameda, Calif.; died October 7, 1979, in Hartford, Conn. Book collector, editor, and author. While Lewis was en route to France to serve in World War I, he read a book about Horace Walpole and immediately became obsessed with that eighteenth-century writer. He devoted the rest of his life to assembling the single largest collection of works by and about Walpole. Most of his literary output is connected with this interest: Lewis wrote a biography of Walpole, compiled bibliographies about him, and edited many volumes of his correspondence. Obituaries and other sources: Wilmarth Sheldon Lewis, *One Man's Education,* Knopf, 1967; *Current Biography,* Wilson, 1973; *Time,* October 29, 1973; *Who's Who in America,* 40th edition, Marquis, 1978; *Who's Who,* 131st edition, St. Martin's, 1979; *Smithsonian,* May, 1979; *New York Times,* October 8, 1979; *AB Bookman's Weekly,* November 5, 1979.

* * *

LI, Shu Hua 1890(?)-1979

OBITUARY NOTICE: Born c. 1890 in Hopei Province, China; died of a heart attack, July 5, 1979, in New York, N.Y. Physicist, educator, and author. Li taught physics at the National University of Peking and served as acting president of the National Academy of Peking in 1929. He joined the staff at Columbia University in the 1950's. Among his writings on the history of science and on modern Chinese history are the books *Origin of Paper Making* and *Origin of Printing in China.* Obituaries and other sources: *New York Times,* July 8, 1979.

* * *

LIBERACE, Wladsiu Valentino 1919-

PERSONAL: Born May 16, 1919, in West Allis, Wis.; son of Salvatore (a musician) and Frances Liberace. *Education:* Attended Wisconsin College of Music. *Residence:* Las Vegas, Nev. *Office:* 4993 Wilbur St., Las Vegas, Nev. 89119.

CAREER: Pianist and composer. Performer with orchestras, including Chicago Symphony Orchestra, and as soloist, 1939—; featured entertainer on television program "The Liberace Show" during early 1950's; actor in motion pictures, including "Sincerely Yours," 1955, and "The Loved One," 1965. *Member:* American Society of Composers, Authors, and Publishers, National Academy of Recording Arts and Sciences. *Awards, honors:* Emmy awards for best entertainment program and outstanding male personality from Academy of Television Arts and Sciences, both 1952, both for "The Liberace Show."

WRITINGS: (With Carol Truax) *Liberace Cooks! Recipes From His Seven Dining Rooms,* Doubleday, 1970; *Liberace: An Autobiography,* Putnam, 1973; *The Things I Love,* edited by Tony Palmer, Grosset, 1976. Also composer of songs, including "Rhapsody by Candlelight," and "Boogie Woogie Variations."

SIDELIGHTS: Liberace is one of the most popular pianists performing today. Scorned by critics but a consistent favorite with the public, Liberace combines classical and pop melodies in his concerts. He plays uptempo arrangements of pieces by composers such as Beethoven and Chopin, as well as more current songs such as "I Don't Care" and "O Promise Me."

He began performing in 1939 with a local symphony in Wisconsin. Soon afterwards, the Chicago Symphony Orchestra came to town and, after auditioning for its conductor, Liberace played with them. It was as a local performer that Liberace began adding popular tunes to his concert repertoire. He also developed a stage banter that included humorous jokes and stories.

During the 1940's, tours and performances in New York City established him as a national favorite. He appeared in his own television show and still found time for concerts, including stints in Las Vegas. Always a flashy entertainer, Liberace sometimes punctuates his performances with costume changes, and plays elaborately designed pianos that always display his trademark, a candelabra.

In 1973, Liberace wrote his autobiography. P. J. Earle noted that Liberace "tells all with a sense of humor and a delightful lack of false modesty." He added that the book is "honest and pleasant."

AVOCATIONAL INTERESTS: Cooking, painting, collecting miniature pianos.

BIOGRAPHICAL/CRITICAL SOURCES: Wladsiu Valentino Liberace, *Liberace: An Autobiography,* Putnam, 1973; *Saturday Evening Post,* December, 1978.*

* * *

LIDDELL HART, Basil Henry 1895-1970

OBITUARY NOTICE: Born October 31, 1895, in Paris,

France; died January 29, 1970. Military strategist and author. After serving for Britain in World War I, Liddell Hart was a military correspondent for the *Daily Telegraph* and then a defense adviser for the *London Times*. A shaper of British military policy, he emphasized a strategy of defense over one of attack. In addition to his books on military technique, Liddell Hart wrote a number of military histories and biographies, including *Sherman: Soldier, Realist, American*, 1929, *Colonel Lawrence: The Man Behind the Legend*, 1934, and *A History of the Second World War*, 1962. Obituaries and other sources: *Current Biography*, Wilson, 1940, March, 1970; *The New Century Handbook of English Literature*, revised edition, Appleton, 1967; *Longman Companion to Twentieth Century Literature*, Longman, 1970; *New York Times*, January 30, 1970.

* * *

LIEBERMAN, Philip 1934-

PERSONAL: Born October 25, 1934, in Brooklyn, N.Y.; son of Harry Israel (a plumber) and Miriam (Mendelson) Lieberman; married Marcia Rubinstein (a writer), June 2, 1957; children: Benjamin, Daniel. *Education:* Massachusetts Institute of Technology, B.S.E.E., M.S.E.E., 1958, Ph.D. (linguistics), 1966. *Home:* 141 Elton St., Providence, R.I. 02906. *Office:* Brown University, Box E, Providence, R.I. 02912.

CAREER: Air Force Communication Research Laboratories, Bedford, Mass., research scientist, 1958-67; University of Connecticut, Storrs, associate professor of linguistics and electrical engineering, 1967-70, professor of linguistics, 1970-74; Brown University, Providence, R.I., professor of linguistics, 1978—. Member of research staff, Haskings Laboratories, 1967-74; guest instructor in linguistics, Massachusetts Institute of Technology, 1967-70. *Military service:* U.S. Air Force, 1958-62; became first lieutenant. *Member:* Modern Language Association of America, Linguistic Society of America, Acoustical Society of America, American Association of Physical Anthropology, American Anthropological Association, Swiss Alpine Club.

WRITINGS: Intonation, Perception, and Language, M.I.T. Press, 1967; *Speech Acoustics and Perception*, Bobbs-Merrill, 1970; *The Speech of Primates*, Mouton, 1972; *On the Origin of Languages: An Introduction to the Evolution of Human Language*, Macmillan, 1975; *Speech Physiology and Acoustic Phonetics*, Macmillan, 1977. Contributor of articles to journals, including *Language, Journal of the Acoustical Society of America, American Anthropologist, Brain and Language*, and *Linguistic Inquiry*.

WORK IN PROGRESS: Research into the development of speech in infants and children, "speech" communication in chimpanzees, and the evolution of language; analysis of speech pathologies and the acoustic detection of cancer and stress.

* * *

LIEBLING, A(bbott) J(oseph) 1904-1963

OBITUARY NOTICE: Born October 18, 1904, in New York, N.Y.; died December 28, 1963. A journalist and author, Liebling was a distinguished contributor to the *New Yorker* magazine, where he worked from 1935 until his death. Known as a brilliant reporter, his silent approach to interviewing could somehow coerce his subjects into revealing far more than they had ever intended. Liebling's criticism of America's news industry earned him the reputation as the gadfly of U.S. journalism—he once said that the Columbia School of Journalism "had all the intellectual status of a training school for future employees of the A. & P." Among his books are *Back Where I Came From*, 1938, *The Road Back to Paris*, 1944, and *The Wayward Pressman*, 1947. Liebling married his third wife, author Jean Stafford, in 1959. Obituaries and other sources: Roy Newquist, *Counterpoint*, Simon & Schuster, 1964; *The Oxford Companion to American Literature*, 4th edition, Oxford University Press, 1965; *Who Was Who in America*, 4th edition, Marquis, 1968; *The Penguin Companion to American Literature*, McGraw, 1971; *The Reader's Adviser: A Layman's Guide to Literature*, Volume 1: *The Best in American and British Fiction, Poetry, Essays, Literary Biography, Bibliography, and Reference*, 12th edition, Bowker, 1974; Edmund M. Midura, *A. J. Liebling: The Wayward Pressman as Critic*, Association for Education in Journalism, 1974.

* * *

LILLIE, Ralph D(ougall) 1896-1979

OBITUARY NOTICE: Born August 1, 1896, in Cucamonga, Calif.; died October 5, 1979, in New Orleans, La. Pathologist, educator, and author. Lillie spent forty years with the U.S. Public Health Service, including more than eleven years as chief of the pathology laboratory at the National Institute of Health. In 1947 he published *Histopathological Technic*, which was revised in 1965 as *Histopathological Technic and Practical Histochemistry*. He served as editor-in-chief of the *Journal of Histochemistry and Cytochemistry* from 1952 until 1964. Obituaries and other sources: *Who's Who in America*, 39th edition, Marquis, 1976; *American Men and Women of Science*, 13th edition, Bowker, 1976; *Washington Post*, October 6, 1979.

* * *

LIN, Yu-sheng 1934-

PERSONAL: Born August 7, 1934, in Mukden, China; came to the United States in 1960, naturalized citizen, 1973; son of Fu-chih and Yu-ing (Wu) Lin; married Tsu-gein Soong, January 20, 1966; children: Albert, Winifred. *Education:* National Taiwan University, A.B., 1958; University of Chicago, Ph.D., 1970. *Office:* Department of History, University of Wisconsin, Madison, Wis. 53706.

CAREER: University of Virginia, Charlottesville, visiting assistant professor, 1966-67, acting assistant professor of history, 1967-68; University of Oregon, Eugene, acting assistant professor of history, 1968-69; University of Wisconsin, Madison, assistant professor, 1970-75, associate professor of history and East Asian languages and literature, 1975—. *Member:* American Historical Association, Association for Asian Studies. *Awards, honors:* Social Science Research Council-American Council of Learned Societies grants, 1969-70, 1974-75.

WRITINGS: (Contributor) Benjamin I. Schwartz, editor, *Reflections on the May Fourth Movement*, Harvard University Press, 1972; (contributor) Charlotte Furth, editor, *The Limits of Change: Essays on the Conservative Alternatives in Republican China*, Harvard University Press, 1976; *The Crisis of Chinese Consciousness: Radical Antitraditionalism in the May Fourth Era*, University of Wisconsin Press, 1979. Contributor to scholarly journals.

WORK IN PROGRESS: The Emergence of Moral Consciousness in Ancient China.

LINDLEY, Ernest K(idder) 1899-1979

OBITUARY NOTICE: Born July 14, 1899, in Richmond, Ind.; died in 1979. Journalist. Lindley is credited with instituting the "Lindley rule" of journalism, whereby sources would agree to divulge information to reporters in exchange for their own anonymity. Reporting for the *New York World* and later the *New York Herald-Tribune,* Lindley followed closely the career of Franklin Roosevelt, writing three books on the former president, including *The Roosevelt Revolution,* 1933, and *Half Way With Roosevelt,* 1936. In 1937 Lindley began writing for *Newsweek,* where he became popular for his column, "Washington Tides." Obituaries and other sources: *Current Biography,* Wilson, 1943; *Directory of American Scholars,* Volume I: *History,* 6th edition, Bowker, 1974; *Who's Who in America,* 40th edition, Marquis, 1978; *Newsweek,* April 16, 1979.

* * *

LINET, Beverly 1929-

PERSONAL: Surname is accented on second syllable; born March 27, 1929, in Brooklyn, N.Y.; daughter of Joseph and Sally (Bobker) Linet. *Education:* Attended Brooklyn College (now of the City University of New York), 1945-46, and New School for Social Research, 1949-50. *Residence:* New York, N.Y. *Agent:* William Morris Agency, 1350 Avenue of the Americas, New York, N.Y. 10019.

CAREER: WHOM-Radio, Jersey City, N.J., news writer, 1948-49; *Show Business,* New York, N.Y., summer stage reviewer, 1949-50; free-lance writer and editor, 1950—. Advertising copy writer; public relations consultant. *Member:* Authors Guild of America.

WRITINGS: Kate and Spencer, Dell, 1972; *Ladd: The Life, the Legend, the Legacy of Alan Ladd,* Arbor House, 1979. Columns include "Information Desk" in *Modern Screen.*

Contributor of about one thousand articles to a wide variety of magazines, including *TV Guide, New York, This Month, Hair Do,* and *Ingenue.* Editor of *Who's Who in Hollywood,* 1956-67, *Who's Who in Television,* 1956-74, *Hollywood Yearbook,* 1963-73, *Hollywood Life Stories,* and *Screen Album,* 1956-72; film reviewer for *Modern Screen,* 1962-67; contributing editor of *Celebrity,* 1975-76.

WORK IN PROGRESS: A biography and a television pilot.

SIDELIGHTS: Beverly Linet began her career in film and television journalism at the age of fifteen. One of her first jobs involved answering thousands of questions a month about Hollywood films and film stars. She has written for nearly all the stage and Hollywood oriented magazines and interviewed hundreds of entertainers, including Judy Garland, Montgomery Clift, Maximilian Schell, and Anthony Quayle.

Linet's biography of Alan Ladd is based partially on her own acquaintance with the actor until his death in 1964. Seymour Peck praised *Ladd,* noting that "the complexities of Ladd's rise and fall, the contrasts between the public idol and the little-known private person, contain many surprises that Miss Linet has made an impressive effort to uncover. . . . By conscientious research and reasonably sober writing, Miss Linet has brought Ladd's story to light with dignity and sympathy."

BIOGRAPHICAL/CRITICAL SOURCES: Chicago Tribune, April 2, 1979; *New York Times Book Review,* April 8, 1979; *After Dark,* September, 1979.

LINTON, Robert R. 1909(?)-1979

OBITUARY NOTICE: Born c. 1909 in Scotland; died July 21, 1979, in West Newton, Mass. Vascular surgeon and author. At Massachusetts General Hospital Linton developed a number of methods for treating blood vessels, including the tourniquet clamp and the Linton balloon, a devise used to control bleeding in the neck. He wrote *The Atlas of Vascular Surgery* in 1973. Obituaries and other sources: *Washington Post,* July 23, 1979.

* * *

LISHKA, Gerald R 1949-

PERSONAL: Born June 8, 1949, in Bloomington, Ill.; son of Roy F. (a factory foreman) and Bernice (a secretary; maiden name, Danforth) Lishka; married a professional dancer (marriage ended). *Education:* University of Illinois, B.Mus., 1971, M.Mus. (with high honors), 1973; further graduate study at Indiana University, 1977. *Home:* 2601 LeBlanc Court, #6, Louisville, Ky. 40206. *Office:* Louisville Ballet, 200 East Oak, Louisville, Ky.

CAREER: Piano teacher, 1969-72; University of Illinois, Champaign-Urbana, accompanist and voice coach, 1972-74, instructor in studio piano, 1972-73; National Academy of Arts, Champaign, Ill., accompanist and piano instructor, 1973-76; Indiana University, Bloomington, head ballet accompanist, 1977; Hartford Ballet Company, Hartford, Conn., guest accompanist, 1977; Wayne State University, Detroit, Mich., dance accompanist and music consultant, 1977-78; Louisville Ballet, Louisville, Ky., accompanist, 1978—. Instructor for Van Tress Piano Studios, 1973-74; accompanist for Interlochen Arts Academy National Music Camp, summers, 1975-77, Oakland University, 1978, and American Dance Festival, 1978; accompanist for Severo School of Ballet, 1977, and Youth Performing Arts School, 1978—.

WRITINGS: A Handbook for the Ballet Accompanist, Indiana University Press, 1978.

WORK IN PROGRESS: An anthology of ballet music; a book on accompaniment for modern dance.

SIDELIGHTS: At the beginning of his career as a ballet accompanist, Lishka found himself with the difficult task of adapting and re-arranging nearly his entire repertoire for dancers who were demanding and critical, and quick to verbalize their criticism. Neither his graduate study in music nor his solo performances had prepared him for the world of dance, and he was surprised to discover that no pianist had written a book for the ballet accompanist. His own book covers not only the technical aspects of the accompanist's job, but the aesthetics of it and the development of rapport with the dancer, as well as other non-technical but crucial areas.

Lishka has made five recordings of piano solos to accompany ballet, published in three albums entitled "Ballet Music for Barre and Center Floor," for Roper Record Co. in 1978.

Lishka told *CA:* "I find professional dancers to be unique, complex, and exciting people. I am moved by their discipline and beauty, and am greatly inspired to work in an area where I can combine the visual art/discipline of dance with that of music. It has added a vast new dimension to my career and to my reservoir of perceptions in an esthetic and artistic sense.

"In writing about music and dance, I am seeking to bridge the communication gap between dancer and musician in order to create a more perfect art form. I feel that my book is an important step in realizing this goal."

BIOGRAPHICAL/CRITICAL SOURCES: Elmira Star-Gazette, August 3, 1978; *Corning Leader,* August 3, 1978.

* * *

LITVINOV, Pavel 1940-

PERSONAL: Born July 6, 1940, in Moscow, U.S.S.R.; came to the United States in 1974; son of Michael (an engineer and mathematician) and Flora (a biologist and researcher in physiology; maiden name, Yasinovsky) Litvinov; married Maya Kopelev (a teacher), 1968; children: Dimitri, Lara. *Education:* Moscow University, M.S., 1966. *Home and office:* 293 Benedict Ave., Tarrytown, N.Y. 10591.

CAREER: Moscow Chemical Institute, Moscow, U.S.S.R., lecturer in physics, 1966-68; Usugli Mines, Usugli, Siberia, U.S.S.R., electrician, 1969-72; Manhattanville College, Purchase, N.Y., lecturer in Russian literature and human rights in the U.S.S.R., 1974-75; Hackley School, Tarrytown, N.Y., instructor in physics and math, 1976—. Lecturer in political science at State University of New York at Purchase, 1975—. *Member:* International League for Human Rights (member of international advisory committee), Amnesty International, U.S. affiliate (member of board of directors), Democracy International (co-chairman).

WRITINGS: Delo o demonstratsii na Pushkinskoy ploshchadi 22 yanvary 1967 goda, Overseas Publication Interchange, 1968, translation by Manya Harari published as *The Demonstration in Pushkin Square: The Trial Records With Commentary and an Open Letter,* Gambit, 1969; (compiler and author of commentary) *The Trial of the Four: A Collection of Materials on the Case of Galanskov, Ginzburg, Dobrovolsky and Lashkova, 1967-68,* translated by Janis Sapiets, Hilary Sternberg, and Daniel Weissbort, Viking, 1972; (contributor) *Essays on Human Rights,* Jewish Publication Society of America, 1979. Contributor to *Index of Censorship,* 1975. Member of editorial board of Khronika Press.

WORK IN PROGRESS: "An autobiographical book mostly concerning my human rights activity in the U.S.S.R. and the history of dissent in the U.S.S.R.," publication by Knopf expected in 1980.

SIDELIGHTS: In 1966 two Soviet authors, Yuli Daniel and Andrei Sinyavsky, were accused and imprisoned for publishing in the West some offensive short stories and essays. Alexander Ginzburg protested the sentence with a letter to the Soviet government, but it was four of his associates who were arrested for challenging the government's decision. To argue this second arrest, a group of protesters staged a silent demonstration in Moscow's Pushkin Square. Carrying signs demanding the release of the four Ginzburg allies, the demonstrators were seized by Russian secret police. In the ensuing trial, two of the protestors were sentenced to three years of hard labor; three others were also formally charged with crimes. The incident would have gone largely unnoticed had it not been for Pavel Litvinov, who recorded the trial proceedings and, despite warnings from the KGB, smuggled the transcripts to the United States. His accounts of the trial were published in *The Demonstration in Pushkin Square*.

"The breach of peace was gross," accused the prosecutor, "gross because of its impudence—impudence as shown by the fact that they criticized existing laws and the activities of the secret services." Litvinov, in publishing his document, criticized Soviet law as well. "To publish the proceedings of a political trial in the Soviet Union, a state that functionally requires secrecy, is a most serious act of rebellion," revealed Lewis S. Feuer. "The Soviet regime and its apparatus of judges, prosecutors, secret police, and strong-arm men are loath to see their behavior made public, since the state itself is put on trial when people are informed of how it manages the 'trials' of individuals. . . . This remarkable document embodies, more than any study could, the spirit guiding the small, isolated circles of men and women who are the primary sources for Soviet freedom."

Litvinov himself was one of those sources. He outlined his Soviet experiences for *CA:* "While in high school and during my first university years, I was a devoted member of the Young Communist League. By the third year in the university, my Marxist views had finally collapsed after the clash with reality and my outlook became that of cynical indifference.

"The 1966 trial of Sinyavsky and Daniel made me return to social problems, probably due to my affection towards Russian literature, especially poetry. I began taking serious interest in history and philosophy, particularly the Russian philosophy of the beginning of this century, and also in problems of the defence of human rights. The arrest of two people I knew intimately, Galanskov and Ginzburg, in early 1967, finally determined my choice. Making photographed and typewritten copies of the Samizdat, arranging assistance to political prisoners and their families, producing protest letters and offering legal counseling—this is by far an incomplete list of my public activities at that time.

"In January, 1968, during the trial of Galanskov, Ginzburg, Dobrovolsky, and Lashkova, Larisa Bogoraz and I published in the Western press our 'Appeal to the World Public Opinion' which produced the explosion of the so-called 'letter-signing campaign' of protest letters. This subsequently transformed into a more-or-less steady turmoil among the intelligentsia, later named the 'Movement for Human Rights in the Soviet Union.' By that time I had already published in the Samizdat the collection of documents, *The Demonstration in Pushkin Square,* and had begun to prepare a new collection, *The Trial of the Four.* Both collections were later taken to the West and published.

"At the same time I was expelled from the Institute of Precision Chemical Technology where I had been teaching physics. On August 25, 1968, I participated in the peaceful demonstration in the Red Square protesting the invasion of Czechoslovakia by Soviet troops. Together with other participants, I was arrested there and spent five months in prison and four years of exile in eastern Siberia. In exile I worked as an electrician in a small mine. In December of 1972, I returned to Moscow, but for a long time I could not receive permission to live there. After several months, I was finally granted temporary permission to stay, but never found a job in my field. Then I was called in for the KGB interrogations during which I was offered to denounce my views and actions in exchange for a job and permission to stay in Moscow permanently.

"After I rejected the offer, it was indicated that the best thing for me to do would be to leave the country forever. In August, 1973, I resumed my activist work: I protested against the persecution of Andrei Amalrik and Andrei Sakharov and passed to the West information and documents concerning violations of human rights in the Soviet Union. On December 5, 1973, when I was on my way to the traditional annual demonstration in Pushkin Square, I was arrested by KGB agents and taken to a police station where I was bluntly told that if I did not leave the U.S.S.R. I would be sentenced to a long prison term. On March 18, 1974, I left the Soviet Union. At present I am living in the United States.

My plans are to teach physics, write, and continue my activities for the defense of human rights."

BIOGRAPHICAL/CRITICAL SOURCES: New Statesman, November 7, 1969; *Times Literary Supplement,* November 20, 1969; *Best Sellers,* January 1, 1970; *National Review,* January 13, 1970; *New Leader,* February 16, 1970; *Saturday Review,* February 28, 1970; *New York Review of Books,* April 23, 1970; *Books and Bookmen,* December, 1972.

* * *

LIU, Aimee 1953-

PERSONAL: Born April 19, 1953, in Connecticut; daughter of Maurice T. and Jane H. (Clark) Liu. *Education:* Yale University, B.A., 1975. *Residence:* New York, N.Y. *Agent:* Edward J. Acton, Inc., 17 Grove St., New York, N.Y. 10014.

CAREER: Wilhelmina Agency, New York City, fashion model, 1969-75; United Airlines, New York City, flight attendant, 1975-78; writer, 1978—.

WRITINGS: Solitaire, Harper, 1979.

Author of "Fisherman's Revenge" (one-act play), first produced in New York City at Fort Tryon Park, August 19, 1979.

WORK IN PROGRESS: Urban Affairs, a novel; *Childless Lives,* a sociological study; *On Foreign Soil,* a historical novel about the Liu family, completion expected in 1982.

SIDELIGHTS: Solitaire is the narrative of Aimee Liu's own affliction with and recovery from anorexia nervosa, a disorder that usually strikes young middle- to upper-class women between ages thirteen and thirty. Obsessed with fears of being overweight, they literally starve themselves by refusing to eat, taking excessive doses of laxatives, inducing vomiting, and exercising to the point of exhaustion. Still believing they are fat despite their emaciation, victims of the disease sometimes continue this behavior until hospitalization and death result.

"Miss Liu writes with a directness that is touching and, at times, profound," wrote Caroline Seebohm, noting the "gripping detail" with which Liu described "her neurotic attachment to the scale, her horrifying night binges, her endless self-castigation for not being thinner, better, more popular, more loved." Seebohm also agreed with other critics that Liu's sudden recovery at the end of *Solitaire* was not convincing, but added that "perhaps it is simply because there are no answers" to explain the development of this illness.

Aimee Liu told *CA:* "Many of my readers and friends have expressed amazement that I could have exposed such a personal side of my life as I did in *Solitaire*. Their reaction amazed me. The notion that I am so special, so precious that I must not open myself up for scrutiny irks me. We are all the same animal, we human beings. We all share the same feelings, appetites, needs. We differ in our modes of expression, in the traps we create for ourselves and the escape mechanisms we use to free ourselves, but basically we understand each other, or can when we learn the common language.

"To my mind, that's what writing is about: finding the language to demonstrate that we do all belong together. I have a horror of isolation. The paradox is that writing both separates me from and connects me with others, with life at large. There's an edge of schizophrenia to it that I don't enjoy. But the results, when they succeed, when they reach out and touch and bring people back to me, make the difficulty worthwhile.

"Recently I spent a month in China. The way I felt at home there was eerie, because I am only one-quarter Chinese, and was raised in a wholly Western context. But I would like to return, to learn more and write about China. Blending heritage, uniting fiction, or fantasy, with nonfiction, or truth: that's what excites me."

BIOGRAPHICAL/CRITICAL SOURCES: Washington Post, July 27, 1979, July 31, 1979; *New York Times Book Review,* July 29, 1979.

* * *

LIVERMORE, Jean
See SANVILLE, Jean

* * *

LLORENS, Vicente 1906-1979

OBITUARY NOTICE: Born January 10, 1906, in Valencia, Spain; died July 5, 1979, in Valencia. Educator and author. Llorens taught at several universities in Europe before joining the department of Romance languages at Princeton University in 1949. A specialist in Spanish literature, he wrote several volumes of critical and historical essays on Spanish and Spanish-American literature and culture. Obituaries and other sources: *Directory of American Scholars,* Volume III: *Foreign Languages, Linguistics, and Philology,* 6th edition, Bowker, 1974; *Washington Post,* July 7, 1979; *AB Bookman's Weekly,* August 6, 1979.

* * *

LLOYD, David 1946-

PERSONAL: Born December 30, 1946, in St. George, Utah; son of Sherman R. (a music teacher) and Carol (a music teacher; maiden name, Finlayson) Lloyd; married Janice Orr, May 27, 1967; children: David S., Wendy. *Education:* Dixie College, A.S., 1966; University of Utah, B.A., 1968, J.D., 1972. *Religion:* Church of Jesus Christ of Latter-day Saints (Mormons). *Home:* 5808 Fontaine Bleu, Salt Lake City, Utah 84121. *Office:* Watkins & Faber, 606 Newhouse Building, Salt Lake City, Utah 84111.

CAREER: Brigham Young University, Provo, Utah, assistant professor of law and law librarian, 1972-74; Watkins & Faber, Salt Lake City, Utah, attorney, 1974—. Member of Utah Department of Transportation's Environmental Council. *Military service:* U.S. Army, 1968-70. *Member:* American Bar Association, Utah Bar Association (vice-chairperson of Long Range Planning Commission, 1978-79), Coif.

WRITINGS: Understanding the Uniform Commercial Code, Oceana, 1973; *Finding the Law: A Guide to Legal Research,* Oceana, 1974. Contributor to law journals. Editor of *Workmen's Compensation Law Review,* 1974—.

WORK IN PROGRESS: Outline of Law of Evidence; a novel set in southern Utah, dealing with radiation problems from nuclear testing.

SIDELIGHTS: Lloyd writes: "As a child in Hurricane, Utah, we watched nuclear explosions in Nevada, and over the years friends and schoolmates have died of various cancers from that testing. Much of my practice of law is in trial work in areas of public interest."

* * *

LOCKHART, Robert (Hamilton) Bruce 1886-1970

OBITUARY NOTICE: Born September 2, 1886, in Anstruther, Fifeshire, Scotland; died February 27, 1970. Author, diplomat, and journalist. Lockhart served as British consul to Moscow before the Russian Revolution and later as unofficial British representative to the Bolshevik government. In 1918 he was accused of conspiring in the plot to kill Lenin and was condemned to die, but was later exchanged for a Russian prisoner in Britain. After working for eight years at the *London Evening Standard,* Lockhart returned to civil service as deputy undersecretary of the Foreign Office during World War II. Among his autobiographical books are *Memoirs of a British Agent,* 1932, *My Scottish Youth,* 1937, and *My Europe,* 1952. Lockhart also wrote a book on Czechoslovakian leader Jan Masaryk, as well as a history of Scotch whiskey. Obituaries and other sources: *New York Times,* February 28, 1970; *Publishers Weekly,* May 18, 1970; Robert Bruce Lockhart, *Memoirs of a British Agent,* Macmillan, 1974; Lockhart, *The Diaries of Sir Robert Bruce Lockhart,* Volume 1: *1915-38,* edited by Kenneth Young, St. Martin's, 1975.

* * *

LOEB, Catherine (Roberta) 1949-

PERSONAL: Born July 25, 1949, in Chicago, Ill.; daughter of Robert Myer (a hospital administrator) and Mary (a management consultant; maiden name, Toynton) Loeb; married David Scott Griffeath (a mathematics professor); children: Robin (son). *Education:* Attended University of California, Berkeley, 1967-69, and Dartmouth College, 1969-71; Cornell University, A.B. (with distinction), 1975, M.A., 1977. *Home:* 601 South Baldwin St., Apt. 1, Madison, Wis. 53703. *Office:* 112A Memorial Library, University of Wisconsin, 728 State St., Madison, Wis. 53706.

CAREER: University of Wisconsin—Madison, assistant to women's studies librarian-at-large, 1977—.

WRITINGS: (With Esther Stineman) *Women's Studies: A Recommended Core Bibliography,* Libraries Unlimited, 1979; (compiler with Linda Parker) *Women's Studies in Wisconsin: A Directory,* Memorial Library, University of Wisconsin—Madison, 1980. Editor, with Linda Parker, of *Feminist Collections: Library Resources in Women's Studies.*

WORK IN PROGRESS: Bibliographic research on such topics as feminist theory, sociobiology and women, and women and literature.

SIDELIGHTS: Loeb told *CA:* "Feminist theory and the oppression of women were the focus of much of my three years' graduate work at Cornell. My subsequent collaboration with Esther Stineman on the compiling and annotating of *Women's Studies* gave me the opportunity to pull together many of the threads of that work.

"The burgeoning field of women's studies is the child of the women's liberation movement. However, as women's studies programs become established, the authority of the women's movement tends to be supplanted by that of academia. This accounts, I would say, for the perennial tension in women's studies between impulses toward legitimation, on the one hand, and subversion, on the other. While the depoliticizing of women's studies does win favor from academic disciplines and administrations, it also forfeits the support of the movement which gave the field birth. In an era of retrenchment, such support should not be relinquished lightly.

"My own view is that women's studies must be critical, partisan, and political. It should look at women not simply out of intellectual curiosity, but out of a commitment to understand sexual oppression, its origins, its present forms, and possibilities for liberation. It needs to go beyond the narcissistic self-study of professional women to take the fate of all women as its focus. Women's studies must be more than an academic discipline; it must be a tool for change. In this it should establish a model for the emulation of all fields of inquiry."

* * *

LOESCH, Juli(anne) 1951-

PERSONAL: Surname is pronounced Lesh; born October 26, 1951, in Erie, Pa.; daughter of Edward (a laborer) and Wynne (Yochim) Loesch. *Education:* Attended Antioch College, 1969. *Politics:* "Catholic Worker Anarchism." *Religion:* "Catholic Worker Anarchism." *Home:* 345 East Ninth St., Erie, Pa. 16503.

CAREER: Writer, 1969—. Volunteer boycott organizer for United Farm Workers in Delano, Calif., 1969, Detroit, Mich., 1970, and Cleveland, Ohio, 1975; co-founder and member of Pax (Christian center for nonviolence), 1972—; co-founder of Pro-Lifers for Survival.

WRITINGS—Self-illustrated books of poems: *'Tis the Season to Be,* Know, Inc., 1971; *Little Tiny Radishes,* privately printed, 1971; *True Simplicity,* privately printed, 1972. Contributor of articles, poems, and illustrations to magazines and newspapers, including *America, New Human, Peacemaker, Catholic Family Farmer,* and *Woman Becoming.* Staff writer and editor of *Erie Christian Witness.*

WORK IN PROGRESS: Poems.

SIDELIGHTS: Juli Loesch writes: "I'm a pro/am religious person living in an empirical religious community. I don't care to die in a nuclear war, and am trying to turn the planet around.

"I am a moralist, a mammal, a cartoonist, and a crank. I'm the sort that feels uncomfortable in a crowd unless I have an armful of leaflets. I correspond intimately with rallies—thank God for the mimeo. I keep myself entertained by loving my enemies and exasperating my friends.

"My correspondence is like the experience of swimming upstream through an inhuman torrent of human utterance. I write entirely too many letters-to-the-editor and I have a fairly intense writing relationship with a whole bunch of fellow creatures whose ideas and sensibilities contrast and harmonize interestingly with my own. I find myself in a wilderness of paradox.

"If all this 'informal' writing of mine—these leaflets and letters-to-the-editor, this buzzing, bursting, clanging, and chiming personal correspondence could be collected—oh my, *there* would be a book for you. I'm a *potential* author, a nascent author. A pro-life feminist embryo. Maybe. A prayerful hell-raiser, certainly."

* * *

LOEWY, Ariel G(ideon) 1925-

PERSONAL: Born March 12, 1925, in Bucharest, Romania; came to the United States in 1946, naturalized citizen, 1965; son of Frederick (a manufacturer) and Eva (Ellman) Loewy; married Karin E. Rademacher, June, 1951 (divorced, 1971); married Martha Ridley Hurt (an attorney), March 12, 1977; children: Michael, Andreas F., Eva S., Daniel R., Martha R. *Education:* McGill University, B.S., 1945, M.S., 1946; University of Pennsylvania, Ph.D., 1950. *Politics:* "Radical." *Religion:* None. *Home:* 842 Buck Lane, Haverford, Pa. 19041. *Office:* Department of Biology, Haverford College, Haverford, Pa. 19041.

CAREER: Harvard University, Medical School, Boston, Mass., research associate, 1950-52; Cambridge University, Cambridge, England, research associate, 1952-53; Haverford College, Haverford, Pa., instructor, 1953-54, assistant professor, 1954-57, associate professor, 1957-63, professor of biology, 1963—. Consulting editor in the biological sciences, Holt, Rinehart & Winston, Inc., 1960-74. *Member:* American Society of Biological Chemists, American Society of Cell Biology, Sigma Xi. *Awards, honors:* Cardiovascular research award from James F. Mitchell Foundation, 1973.

WRITINGS: (With Philip Srekevitz) *Cell Structure and Function,* Holt, 1963, 2nd edition, 1969; (with James D. Ebert, Howard A. Schneiderman, and Richard S. Miller) *Biology,* Holt, 1973.

WORK IN PROGRESS: Research on protein structure and covalent interactions between protein molecules.

SIDELIGHTS: Loewy writes: "My two major contributions to science are the demonstrations in 1952 that cell motility is based on the same protein interactions as is muscle contraction, and in 1968 that the last step of blood clotting involves formation of chemical bonds between fibrin molecules. I now hope to relate these two discoveries to each other by showing that energy transformations by the proteins of the cell 'skeleton' involve the formation of certain chemical bonds between protein molecules.

"My other interest is to develop the kind of curriculum in the teaching of biology which will enable us to interpret to students the immense revolution in our recent understanding of molecular biology. Another concern is to help students develop an understanding of the precariousness of our social existence on this earth so that they might participate in the task of averting catastrophe."

* * *

LOFARO, Michael Anthony 1948-

PERSONAL: Born August 10, 1948, in Port Chester, N.Y.; son of Anthony L. and Helen (Wasson) Lofaro; married Nancy L. Durish, August 18, 1973. *Education:* Rensselaer Polytechnic Institute, B.S., 1970; University of Maryland, M.A., 1972, Ph.D., 1975. *Home:* 1115 Montview Dr., Knoxville, Tenn. 37914. *Office:* Department of English, University of Tennessee, Knoxville, Tenn. 37916.

CAREER: University of Maryland, College Park, instructor in English, 1971-72, 1973-75, director of independent study courses, 1972-73; University of Tennessee, Knoxville, assistant professor of English and co-chairperson of folklore colloquium, 1975—. Instructor for Veterans Administration, 1973-75. Participant and director of scholarly meetings; guest on radio program. *Member:* American Folklore Society, Modern Language Association of America, National Association for the Preservation and Perpetuation of Storytelling, Society for the Study of Southern Literature, South Atlantic Modern Language Association, Kentucky-Tennessee American Studies Association, Tennessee Folklore Society. *Awards, honors:* National Endowment for the Humanities grants, 1977—, 1978—; John C. Hodges grant from University of Tennessee; Richard H. Collins Award from Kentucky Historical Society.

WRITINGS: The Life and Adventures of Daniel Boone, University Press of Kentucky, 1978; (contributor) W. Hamilton Bryson, editor, *The Virginia Law Reporters Before 1880,* University Press of Virginia, 1978. Editor and author of introductions of *The Sermon in America, 1620-1800,* Scholars' Facsimiles & Reprints, Volume I and Volume II. Contributor of articles and reviews to folklore and history journals.

WORK IN PROGRESS: Editing *The Sermon in America, 1620-1800,* Volume III, with Richard Beale Davis, for Scholars' Facsimiles & Reprints; editing *Life of Boone,* by Lyman C. Draper; editing *Commonplace Book,* by William Byrd II; editing *The History of the Dividing Line,* by Byrd.

SIDELIGHTS: Lofaro told *CA:* "My interest in the study of early America has been directed toward making the period itself more accessible to the scholar and the general reader by working with, editing, and publishing various manuscript materials."

* * *

LOGAN, Joshua Lockwood 1908-

PERSONAL: Born October 5, 1908, in Texarkana, Tex.; son of Joshua Lockwood and Susan (Nabors) Logan; married Barbara O'Neill (an actress), 1940 (marriage dissolved, 1941); married Nedda Harrigan (an actress), 1945; children: Thomas Heggen, Susan Harrigan. *Education:* Princeton University, degree, 1931; further study at Moscow Art Theatre, 1931. *Office:* 435 East 52nd St., New York, N.Y. 10022.

CAREER: Director and producer of numerous plays and films, 1936—. Directed Broadway plays, including "On Borrowed Time," "I Married an Angel," "Knickerbocker Holiday," and "Stars in Your Eyes," all 1938; "Mornings at Seven," "Two for the Show," and "Higher and Higher," all 1939; "Charlie's Aunt," 1940; "By Jupiter" and "This Is the Army," both 1942; "Annie Get Your Gun" and "Happy Birthday," both 1945; "John Loves Mary," 1946; "Mister Roberts," 1948; "South Pacific," 1949; "The Wisteria Trees," 1950; "Wish You Were Here," 1952; "Picnic" and "Kind Sir," both 1953; "Fanny," 1954; "Middle of the Night," 1956; "Blue Denim" and "The World of Suzie Wong," both 1958; "There Was a Little Girl," 1960; "All American," 1961; "Mr. President" and "Tiger, Tiger, Burning Bright," both 1962; "Ready When You Are, C.B.," 1964; "Look to the Lillies," 1970; and "Miss Moffatt," 1974. Directed films, including "Garden of Allah," 1936; "I Met My Love Again," 1937; "Picnic," 1955; "Bus Stop," 1956; "Sayonara" and "South Pacific," both 1957; "Tall Story," 1959; "Fanny," 1960; "Ensign Pulver," 1963; "Camelot," 1966; and "Paint Your Wagon," 1968. Cofounder of University Players in Falmouth, Mass. *Military service:* U.S. Air Force, Combat Intelligence, 1942-45; became captain. *Awards, honors:* Pulitzer Prize for *South Pacific,* 1950; M.A. from Princeton University, 1953.

WRITINGS—Memoirs: *Josh: My Up and Down, In and Out Life,* Delacorte, 1976; *Movie Stars, Real People, and Me,* Delacorte, 1978.

Plays: (With Gladys Hurlbut) "Higher and Higher," first produced on Broadway at Shubert Theatre, April 4, 1940; (with Thomas Heggen) *Mister Roberts* (based on Heggen's novel; first produced on Broadway at Alvin Theatre, February 18, 1948), Random House, 1948; (with Oscar Hammerstein II) *South Pacific* (based on James A. Michener's stories, *Tales of the South Pacific;* first produced on Broadway at Majestic Theatre, April 7, 1949), Random House, 1949; *The Wisteria Trees* (based on Anton Chekhov's play, *The Cherry Orchard;* first produced on Broadway at Martin Beck Theatre, March 29, 1950), Random House, 1950; (with Arthur Kober) "Wish You Were Here," first produced on Broadway at Imperial Theatre, June 25, 1952; (with S. N. Behrman) *Fanny* (based on the play by Marcel Pagnol; first produced on Broadway at Majestic Theatre, November 4, 1954), Random House, 1955; (with Emlyn Williams) "Miss

Moffat," first produced in Philadelphia at Shubert Theatre, October 7, 1974; "Rip Van Winkle," first produced in Washington, D.C., at Kennedy Center, January 26, 1976. A play also represented in the anthology, *American Plays,* edited by Allan G. Halline, AMS Press, 1976.

Screenplays: (With Frank Nugent) "Mister Roberts," (based on the novel by Thomas Heggen and on the play by the author and Heggen), Warner Bros., 1955; (with Peter S. Feibleman) "Ensign Pulver" (based on the novel by Heggen), Warner Bros., 1964.

SIDELIGHTS: The venerable writer-director-producer Joshua Logan has had more Broadway hits than almost anyone else. In his first book of memoirs, *Josh: My Up and Down, In and Out Life,* Logan "re-creates an era that has almost entirely disappeared—a time when New York was the center of America's theatrical universe and a nude male torso on a Broadway stage was a subject of controversy," John Houseman commented.

In the book he discusses his associations with such theatrical giants as Margaret Sullavan, Henry Fonda, James Stewart, William Inge, David Merrick, Oscar Hammerstein, Richard Rodgers, Mary Martin, Helen Hayes, and Ethel Merman. Also included is a reminiscence of the great master of the theatre, Stanislavsky, under whom Logan studied in Russia after graduating from Princeton. Logan is also extremely candid in discussing the two nervous breakdowns that were linked to his career.

Movie Stars, Real People, and Me begins where the first book left off, and covers Logan's 1956 direction of the film, "Picnic," to the present, although not chronologically. Seymour Peck declared in his review of the book: "In many, short, fast, intense chapters, Mr. Logan plunges ahead, as if he were pacing one of his smash hits or urging an Ethel Merman to sing louder. Much of it is gossipy and inconsequential; much of it is funny and bawdy; much of it is impassioned and illuminating. Mr. Logan's emotions are usually at high pitch and catch the reader up. The pages whizz by."

CA INTERVIEWS THE AUTHOR

Joshua Logan was interviewed by phone at his home July 9, 1979, in New York City.

CA: Is directing an acquired skill, a talent one is born with, or a combination of the two?

LOGAN: There's no way you can go to school to be a director. I wasn't even going to be a director when I started; I was going to be an actor or a writer. I really wanted to write more than I wanted anything. By an accidental stroke, I was up on Cape Cod acting with the University Players with Fonda and Stewart, Mildred Natwick and Myron McCormick, and a lot of people who became very famous later. Charles Leatherbee and Bretaigne Windust were the directors of the company. Windust did most of the directing. I happened to come a little late one year, because I was nearly flunking out of Princeton, and I had to stay home to write some extra essays. So I got there two weeks later than the rest. I found that the company had split and was ready to move to different areas, and it was all on the subject of college. Because they called it the University Players, Windust felt they should only have university students. Leatherbee said they must have great people, no matter whether they went to a university or didn't. That was a big hassle. I came in and heard both of them, and I said, "I think you're both crazy. Why don't you combine them? Don't split the company, because it'll be no good then." And they were so grateful to have somebody help them, I think, that they made me a director to protect themselves. Three people would make decisions more quickly and definitely because two would always agree and that would prevail. Because of that, I was also invited to go with Charles Leatherbee on a scholarship to Russia the next winter to study with Constantin Stanislavsky. While I was watching him direct, I suddenly decided I wanted to be like him. I wanted to do everything he did—look like him, everything. That's what started me as a director. When I left, he wrote on his photograph, "To Joshua Logan. Love the art in yourself rather than yourself in the art."

I don't think directing can be learned. You've got to do it. It's just like swimming; you've got to get out in the water and swim. I think it helps to have been given a certain amount of training in being polite, tactful, and all that, because a director has to step into every kind of situation and, if possible, calm it down or stir it up, depending on what's needed. He is first of all an encourager—a cheerleader, a coach, a second in a boxing match, a preacher, a psychiatrist, and English teacher—he must assume any role that's needed. The main thing I did is when I was an actor, I made little notes saying, "I'll never do that," when a director would tell me something. For instance, I'd be doing a scene, and suddenly I'd pick up a cigarette and start to light it, without having anyone tell me to. Nothing was said about it, but when I got back to that scene, the director who was working for us said, "Oh, I think it's a good idea to pick up a cigarette there and light it." He stole the idea from me. I was so mad, I made a rule, "I will never steal from an actor." If someone gets a good idea, I say, "That's a marvelous idea. Do it again so you won't forget it." But I always give credit. That's one thing I think is very important.

I had a great cast for the Broadway production of "Picnic." I gave them so much freedom that it scared my producers. I felt they would find the way to rise and the moment to rise. Kim Stanley, Paul Newman, Janice Rule, Eileen Heckart, Ralph Meeker, Peggy Conklin, Reta Shaw, Elizabeth Wilson, Ruth McDevitt—they were great actors, all of them; all I did was create a comfortable atmosphere for them, so that they weren't afraid to do anything they wanted to. I think we got some things in it that way that would not have been done otherwise. But sometimes I find that actors want to be told exactly what to do. Then I get up and demonstrate, but only then.

CA: You've written about the necessity for firmness with certain performers. Is this a large part of successful directing?

LOGAN: It depends upon the performer. For instance, Arthur O'Connell, who is a marvelous actor but was unknown at that time, played the famous love scene in "Picnic" where the schoolteacher (Eileen Heckart) gets down on her knees and asks him to marry her. That scene was so touchy, so what the English call "close to the knuckle," that the audience would be apt to laugh. I said, "Arthur, you musn't look at the audience right after she says her lines; it's like Jack Benny. It's a perfect howl, but we don't want howls at that point." There was only one way I could threaten him. He wanted a run-of-the-play contract. He'd never had one. I said, "I know why. It's because you're always doing things that are a little bit off just to get a laugh. So I won't give you a run-of-the-play contract, but I will let you play it as long as you don't look at the audience in that scene." So he gave up the Jack Benny look. But he never got the run-of-the-play contract, because I didn't trust him.

But that's a rare exception, really. There are so few people who require that kind of treatment. I've worked with the very best artists in the world. Even though some people don't think Kim Novak is a good actress, I thought she *made* the movie "Picnic," because she was so nearly that character herself that she couldn't do anything wrong. I think she was the nearest thing to perfection in the whole movie.

CA: In Movie Stars, Real People, and Me *you wrote glowingly about an actress who was the despair of most directors—Marilyn Monroe. How did you create the atmosphere in which she could do her best work?*

LOGAN: Love. I loved her and I respected her; and I was sweet to her and never threatened her. I never did anything rough to her at all. To me she was a little woodland animal who had been frightened by the hunter—by many hunters. The only thing to do was coax her a bit and be gentle with her. And it paid off. I think she gave the best performance of her life in "Bus Stop." And it was an uplifting experience for me. I really think she was close to the most talented woman I ever worked with in my life. Maybe Kim Stanley was more talented; I'm not sure. But at any rate, Marilyn Monroe was not all a dumb blonde; she was a *brilliant* blonde. She knew everything there was to know, but she'd never had an education. So she was discovering Freud and other such people a little late and telling us all about them. Most people thought that was stupidity, but it wasn't; it was just endearing innocence. When I finished the show, the *New York Times* asked me to write an article for them: "Will Acting Spoil Marilyn Monroe" was the title they wanted. I wrote, "She's a combination of Greta Garbo and Charlie Chaplin. She is as beautiful as Garbo, and she has the ability in her acting to make you cry and laugh at the same time, which is what Chaplin has. And that's genius."

CA: Do you feel "Bus Stop" was your best movie?

LOGAN: I don't know whether "Camelot" or "Bus Stop" was my best picture; one of the two. I think both of them were better than "Picnic," although I think "Picnic" had great high spots. "Fanny" was another wonderful picture of mine, too, but I missed Harold Rome's songs. Jack Warner wouldn't let me have them, because he thought musicals were out.

CA: Would you comment further on your work with Stanislavsky?

LOGAN: Well, I certainly have never done what most of these opportunists did, which is call it the Method School of acting. There's no such thing. As Lynn Fontanne said, the Method is acting. It was something Stanislavsky had used at one time that was very helpful to young students who couldn't capture an emotion too quickly. He told them to recall and feel again some emotion from real life, such as the loss of a dog hit by traffic, a loved one's funeral, etc. And then, while the emotion was flowing through the body, transfer it to the playwright's scene—which might be a quarrel with a teacher or a wife. But then Stanislavsky said to me: "That is only used now when one is alone, preparing a part. That method is for the bathroom or the middle of a field or forest—never at a rehearsal when it would hold things up. It might be embarrassing. And remember, we have two years to rehearse and you have only four weeks. You haven't time for that sort of thing. Besides, it's only our cup of tea, not yours. You must develop your own methods, your own rules. And when you've made them, break them. Always break rules." And nobody knows how he felt about the Method but me, because he said it to me and Charles Letherbee, and Charles is dead. Stanislavsky was a great, marvelous man; but he was a director, and tough as nails. He would move in on someone with real fury when he thought that was necessary. He had so many graduates of music schools or music teachers, and they drove him up the wall. His students were surly to this great man because he was forcing them to do what their teachers told them not to do. They were taught to stand erect and sing with their hands clasped over their diaphragms. Stanislavsky said that might be very nice for singing, but what about the part you're acting? And he made them sing and move emotionally. His earlier dramatic students adored him. The whole Soviet Union adored him—so much they wouldn't let him leave the country, for fear he would become famous somewhere else.

CA: In 1961 you wrote in an article for Theatre Arts, *"There is no room in New York for the moderate success. . . . We must all produce hits or die." Do you think that situation led to the experimental theatre of Off-Off-Broadway later in the 1960's and early 1970's?*

LOGAN: If it didn't, it should have. By the time I made that statement, Broadway had priced itself right out of possibility. Everything had to be a big smash hit or close in three weeks. It was very hard to get a hit. I don't know what on earth happened to me that I was allowed to have so many, because very few other people had even one. I must have made the right choices or something. The theatre does not accept the words "mild" or "charming." If you say it's a charming play, nobody will go to see it. It's got to be "Don't ask questions—just *go*!"

CA: Do you think Off-Off-Broadway has had any effect on Broadway?

LOGAN: Of course it has. It's given jobs to kids who otherwise would be sitting at home waiting by the phone. I think it's marvelous what has happened to Broadway, Off-Broadway, and Off-Off-Broadway. It's just great. It reminds me of Paris when I was there during the war. They had little theatres all over the place. It's the same with us now. I think we're even beginning to have fine straight plays, and maybe we're even going to have some more great musicals. Who can tell? I think, unfortunately, shows like "Hair" and "Jesus Christ Superstar" were such a fad and so popular that producers decided not to dare risk anything else. That's not true anymore. They even took a chance on "Sweeney Todd," which is marvelous and beautifully done. It even suits Stephen Sondheim's strange and fearless talent.

CA: In a recent Saturday Review *column, Martin Gottfried called the past season [1978-79] "one of unparalleled disaster playing to no response," criticized the community for not caring when shows go down the drain, and concluded that "when theater becomes an impersonal marketing 'product,' it is dead." Would you comment?*

LOGAN: I don't know what he's talking about. The most beautiful shows are coming in, and they're lasting—the ones that should come in and should last. I don't think anything he says is accurate. He's writing for effect. He's following the Kenneth Tynan method of building his name as a critic. Only Kenneth Tynan does it better than anyone who tries to follow it, whether his name is Gottfried or Simon.

CA: What role do you think regional theatre should play in the cultural life of the country?

LOGAN: I think it should be given the most important place possible, because where are we going to find the actors or other theatrical artists except in regional theatre? They're all over this country—brilliant people—with no David Merricks or Robert Whiteheads or Hal Princes to see them. Of course I don't see why they want to leave once they're established in community theatre. They get beautiful parts. But I took a chance on four different places, and I was entranced by all of them. I directed three of them. Certainly the Firehouse Theatre in Omaha is a fine group of people with great actors to choose from. That is also true about the Fort Bragg Playhouse in Fayetteville, North Carolina, where I did "Bus Stop" as a musical. I found some brilliant people there. It's a shame we can't get anybody to put the money up to take it to Broadway.

It's hard directing regional theatre. You have to be more patient, and the actors don't appear for rehearsal as often as they should, because they've all got jobs. But otherwise I think it's the greatest training ground in the world, and I intend to continue my search for talent. We have no more stock companies. We don't even have summer stock, because they have these package shows that go touring around, and all they do now in these summer theatres is act as booking offices.

CA: You've described yourself as a workaholic. Do you have any advice for other workaholics?

LOGAN: Yes—keep at it. Hang on to your disease. I rather like being a workaholic. It's a little bit like being an alcoholic, but with more to show for it. I love work, and I fill my life with work so that when one project stops, I have something else to go on. It's like keeping irons in the fire. In the last two or three days I've canceled one show, I've finished the whole second act of another show, and I'm now ready to work on a third, which is going to go into rehearsal in September. It's a lot of work and just delightful.

BIOGRAPHICAL/CRITICAL SOURCES: Lucy Freeman, editor, *Celebrities on the Couch,* Price, Stern, 1970; Joshua Logan, *Josh: My Up and Down, In and Out Life,* Delacorte, 1976; *New York Times Book Review,* May 16, 1976, November 19, 1978; *Christian Science Monitor,* August 12, 1976; *Authors in the News,* Volume I, Gale, 1976; *Times Literary Supplement,* November 11, 1977; Logan, *Movie Stars, Real People, and Me,* Delacorte, 1978.

—*Interview by Jean W. Ross*

* * *

LOGUE, Jeanne 1921-

PERSONAL: Born May 2, 1921, in Brooklyn, N.Y.; daughter of William (in furniture business) and Carrie (Pfister) Neubecker; married Joseph Carl Logue (an electrical engineer), March 31, 1943; children: Raymond C., Marilyn Logue Bartlett, Paul J. *Education:* Attended Brooklyn College (now of the City University of New York), 1939-41; Cornell University, D.V.M., 1944. *Politics:* "Republican with Libertarian leanings." *Home:* 52 Boardman Rd., Poughkeepsie, N.Y. 12603.

CAREER: American Society for the Prevention of Cruelty to Animals Hospital, New York, N.Y., intern and staff doctor, 1946-47; private practice of large and small animal medicine and surgery in Kingston, N.Y., 1947-54; associate practice of small animal medicine and surgery in Wappingers Falls, N.Y., 1954-73; writer, 1973—. *Member:* American Veterinary Medical Association, New York Academy of Medicine (associate member), Poughkeepsie League of Women Voters (member of board of directors, 1955-57).

WRITINGS: The Wonder of It All (autobiography), Harper, 1979.

WORK IN PROGRESS: Three works about people who worked with animals; research on ancient India, ancient Greece, and turn-of-the-century South Africa.

SIDELIGHTS: Jeanne Logue comments: "At the age of five I decided to become an animal doctor. I never waffled or changed my mind about this decision and would make the same choice if I had to do it all over again.

"But I was also interested in English literature and world history, and had an urge to write. Since most people's first books seem to be invariably biographical, unintentional as it often is, I decided to really get this out of my system, and wrote an autobiography about my careers as wife, mother, and veterinarian. Future books will each be different from the other.

"Since retiring from active practice I have, in addition to writing, pursued activities I did not make time for during the busy years as a practicing veterinarian. At fifty-two I learned downhill skiing, and at fifty-four became a certified scuba diver. This last activity has opened another new world to me. I have met, face to face, more new animals in Bahamian waters in the last four years than I have on land in the last thirty. It is of great interest to me that the curricula of several veterinary colleges now include courses in the diseases of marine animals.

"Travel nowadays is quite limited to our home in the Bahamas, but research trips are scheduled for England and South Africa."

AVOCATIONAL INTERESTS: "I would be most interested to hear from anyone who can throw light on the deciphering of the Ancient Indus Valley Civilization script!"

* * *

LOMAX, Bliss
See DRAGO, Harry Sinclair

* * *

LONDON, Jack 1915-

PERSONAL: Born October 10, 1915, in Duluth, Minn.; son of Hyman (a merchant) and Dora (Sanders) London; married Ethel Robbins (a teacher and nurse), November 22, 1947; children: Robin London Forstein, Jack Murray, Daniel Gary. *Education:* Central YMCA College, Chicago, Ill., A.B., 1939; University of Chicago, Ph.D., 1952. *Home:* 2328 Derby St., Berkeley, Calif. 94705. *Office:* Department of Education, University of California, Berkeley, Calif. 94720.

CAREER: I. S. Berlin Co., Chicago, Ill., began as apprentice, became journeyman lithographer, 1931-39; worked as lithograph printer in Chicago, 1939-41; Buick Aviation Engine Plant, Melrose Park, Ill., metallurgical inspector, 1941-42; Veterans Administration, Chicago, training specialist for industry, 1946-48; University of Chicago, Chicago, assistant professor of industrial relations, 1948-53, research assistant at Industrial Relations Center, 1948-53, research associate, 1951-53; University of California, Berkeley, assistant professor, 1953-57, associate professor, 1957-64, professor of adult education, 1964—, assistant research sociologist, 1953-54, director of Nairobi Study Center, 1974-76. Part-time instructor at Roosevelt University, 1948-53; visiting lecturer at University of Ibadan, 1965; visiting professor at University of British Columbia, 1966, University of East Africa, 1969-70, and University of Toronto, 1971. Participant in international conferences. Member of executive board, board of directors, and advisory board of schools, education centers, and service organizations. Consultant to Malaysian Federation of Labor, United Nations Educational, Scientific, and Cultural Organization, and Volunteers in Service to America (VISTA). *Military service:* U.S. Army, 1942-45; served in Europe, Africa, and the Middle East.

MEMBER: Adult Education Association (member of executive board, 1955-58), American Sociological Association, Society for the Study of Social Problems, African Adult Education Association, Commission of Professors of Adult Education (chairman, 1960-62), Association for Humanistic Psychology. *Awards, honors:* Grant from U.S. Office of Education, 1960-63; award for distinguished service from Adult Education Association, 1978.

WRITINGS: (With Joel Seidman, Bernard Karsh, and D. L. Taglicozzo) *The Worker Views His Union,* University of Chicago Press, 1958; (with Robert Wenkert) *Some Reflections on Defining Adult Education* (monograph), Survey Research Center, University of California, Berkeley, 1963; (with Wenkert and Warren Hagstrom) *Adult Education and Social Class* (monograph), Survey Research Center, University of California, Berkeley, 1963.

Contributor: Malcolm Knowles, editor, *Handbook of Adult Education in the United States,* Adult Education Association, 1960; Sigmund Nosow and William H. Form, editors, *Man, Work, and Society,* Basic Books, 1962; Fred H. Goldman, editor, *Reorientation in Labor Education: A Symposium on Liberal Education for Labor in the University,* Center for the Study of Liberal Education for Adults, 1962; Arthur B. Shostak and William Gomberg, editors, *Blue-Collar World: Studies of the American Worker,* Prentice-Hall, 1964; Gale Jensen, A. A. Liveright, and Wilbur Hallenbeck, editors, *Adult Education: Outlines of an Emerging Field of University Study,* Adult Education Association, 1964; William A. Faunce, editor, *Readings in Industrial Sociology,* Appleton, 1967; Robert Smith, George Aker, and J. Roby Kidd, editors, *Handbook of Adult Education,* Macmillan, 1970; David W. Knight and Lora R. Friedman, editors, *Readings for Teachers of Reading in Adult Basic Education,* Mississippi State Department of Education, 1970; Stanley M. Grabowski, editor, *Paulo Freire: A Revolutionary Dilemma for the Adult Educator,* Publications in Continuing Education, 1972; *Adult Education Handbook,* Tanzania Publishing House, 1973; *Organization for Economic Co-Operation and Development,* Organization for Economic Co-Operation and Development, 1974; David W. Swift, editor, *American Education: A Sociological Perspective,* Houghton, 1976; Guy Benveniste and Charles S. Benson, editors, *From Mass to Universal Education,* Nijhoff, 1976.

Contributor of nearly a hundred articles and reviews to education and labor journals, and to *Annals of the American Academy of Political and Social Science.* Member of editorial advisory board of *Changing Education,* 1965-69.

WORK IN PROGRESS: A book on workers' education, publication expected in 1981.

SIDELIGHTS: London's studies of community development have taken him to Mexico, Nigeria, Ghana, Israel, Europe, Tanzania, Kenya, Uganda, India, Hong Kong, and Japan. His current research includes studies of workers' education in "third world" countries.

* * *

LONG, David E(dwin) 1937-

PERSONAL: Born November 21, 1937, in Washington, Ga.; son of Stewart H. (a Presbyterian minister) and Esther (Hansen) Long; married Barbara Baggett, 1962; children: Gordon, Geoffrey, Andrew. *Education:* Davidson College, A.B., 1959; University of North Carolina, M.A., 1961; Fletcher School of Law and Diplomacy, M.A., 1962; George Washington University, Ph.D., 1973. *Home:* 9728 Burke View Court, Burke, Va. 22015. *Office:* INR/RNA, U.S. Department of State, Washington, D.C. 20520.

CAREER: U.S. Department of State, Washington, D.C., foreign service officer in Khartown, Sudan, 1962-65, Tangier, Morocco, 1965-66, Jidda, Saudi Arabia, 1967-69, and Washington, D.C., 1970—. Professorial lecturer at Georgetown University (also senior fellow of Center for Strategic and International Studies, 1975-76, and executive director of Center for Contemporary Arab Studies), and Johns Hopkins School of Advanced International Studies; fellow of Council on Foreign Relations, 1974-75. *Member:* American Foreign Service Association, Middle East Studies Association of North America, Middle East Institute. *Awards, honors:* Averill Harriman Award from the American Foreign Service Association, 1972, for intellectual courage and creative dissent in the pursuit of professional duties.

WRITINGS: The Persian Gulf, Westview Press, 1976, revised edition, 1978; *Saudi Arabia,* Sage Publications, 1976; *The Hajj Today,* State University of New York Press, 1979.

Contributor of articles and reviews to history and foreign area studies journals, including *Middle East Journal* and *Wilson Review.*

WORK IN PROGRESS: Editing *Government and Politics of the Middle East,* with Bernard Reich, publication by Westview Press expected in 1980.

SIDELIGHTS: Long writes: "I lecture extensively in the United States and abroad both as a representative of the U.S. Department of State and as an academic Middle East specialist concentrating on the Arabian Peninsula and the Persian Gulf.

"My activities are a reflection of my belief that academia, business, and government have much to share and learn from each other in the field of foreign affairs and my concern that too great a communication gap exists among the three communities."

* * *

LONG, Esmond R(ay) 1890-1979

OBITUARY NOTICE: Born June 16, 1890, in Chicago, Ill.; died November 11, 1979, in Devon, Pa. Pathologist, educator, and author. A specialist in tuberculosis, Long spent most of his career at the University of Pennsylvania, where he taught from 1932 to 1950. He also directed the Henry Phipps Institute for the Study, Treatment, and Prevention of Tuberculosis. Among his books are *The Chemistry of Tuberculosis,* 1923, *History of the Therapy of Tuberculosis and the Case of Frederic Chopin,* 1955, and *A History of American Pathology,* 1962. Obituaries and other sources: *Who's Who in America,* Marquis, 1976; *American Men and Women of Science,* 13th edition, Bowker, 1976; *The International Who's Who,* Europa, 1979; *New York Times,* November 14, 1979.

* * *

LONGRIGG, Stephen Hemsley 1893-1979

OBITUARY NOTICE: Born August 7, 1893, in Sevenoaks, Kent, England; died in 1979 in Guildford, England. Oil executive and author. After serving in the Middle East in World War I, Brigadier Longrigg worked for the government of Iraq and for an Iraqi petroleum firm from 1918 to 1951. He wrote a number of books on the Middle East, including *Four Centuries of Modern Iraq, Oil in the Middle East,* and *The Middle East: A Social Geography.* Obituaries and other sources: *The Author's and Writer's Who's Who,* 6th edition, Burke's Peerage, 1971; *Who's Who,* 131st edition, St. Martin's, 1979; *AB Bookman's Weekly,* November 5, 1979.

* * *

LORDI, Robert J(oseph) 1923-

PERSONAL: Born October 18, 1923, in Rockland, Mass.; son of Nicola (a shoe laster) and Carmella (Beso) Lordi; married Dorothy Margaret Eckert (a teacher), February 5, 1955; children: Paul, Margaret. *Education:* College of the Holy Cross, A.B., 1950; graduate study at University of Wisconsin, Madison, 1951-52; Boston College, M.A., 1955; University of Illinois, Ph.D., 1958. *Politics:* Independent. *Home:* 52901 Winterberry Dr., South Bend, Ind. 46637. *Office:* Department of English, University of Notre Dame, Notre Dame, Ind. 46556.

CAREER: University of Notre Dame, Notre Dame, Ind., instructor, 1958-59, assistant professor, 1959-64, associate professor, 1964-70, professor of English, 1970—. Lecturer at University of Innsbruck, spring, 1966. *Military service:* U.S. Army Air Forces, bombardier, 1943-45; became flight officer. *Member:* Modern Language Association of America, Shakespeare Society of America, American Association of University Professors. *Awards, honors:* Fellow of Folger Shakespeare Library, summer, 1962; grants from American Philosophical Society, summers, 1963-64, 1971.

WRITINGS: (Editor) *Bussy D'Ambois,* University of Nebraska Press, 1964; (with James E. Robinson) *Richard III: A Scene-by-Scene Analysis With Critical Commentary,* American R.D.M. Corp., 1966; (contributor) John H. Dorenkamp, editor, *Professor Frank Drumm Memorial Volume,* College of the Holy Cross, 1973; (editor) *The Revenge of Bussy D'Ambois,* Institute fur Sprache und Literatur (Salzburg), 1977; (editor and translator) Thomas Legge, *Richardus Tertius: A Critical Edition With Translation,* Garland Publishing, 1979; (contributor) Allan Holaday, editor, *The Complete Dramatic Works of George Chapman,* Volume II, University of Illinois Press, in press. Contributor to *Reader's Encyclopedia of English Literature.* Contributor of more than twenty-five articles and reviews to literature journals. Associate editor of *Neo-Latin News,* 1961-65.

WORK IN PROGRESS: A study of the structural differences between the tragic hero and the comic hero, with special reference to Shakespeare.

SIDELIGHTS: Lordi comments: "Most of my research has centered on Renaissance drama, particularly Shakespeare and George Chapman. My editing of Chapman has led to teaching a course on analytical bibliography and textual criticism.

"It has led me also to two general convictions: (1) that sound critical evaluations cannot proceed successfully without dependable texts, i.e., texts that represent insofar as possible, the author's final intentions; and (2) that Chapman's plays have often been undervalued by critics due to unfair comparison to the plays of his greater contemporaries (Marlowe, Shakespeare, and Jonson), and due to the unfounded assumption that his 'genius was undramatic.'

"Writing in general has taught me that one seldom knows what he really knows or doesn't know until he attempts to formulate his thoughts in unforgiving prose, prose which neither 'all your Piety nor Wit / Shall lure . . . back to cancel half a Line.' Writing is a difficult, often onerous, task, one that brings little joy in the doing, but great joy in the research that precedes it, and in the sense of accomplishment when done. It is the teacher of teachers."

Lordi traveled extensively in Europe during his year at Innsbruck, where he lectured on Shakespeare.

AVOCATIONAL INTERESTS: Tennis, collecting antiques (American primitives, especially tools), spectator sports, travel, fishing, gardening.

* * *

LORRIMER, Claire (pseudonym)

CAREER: Writer.

WRITINGS—All novels: *A Voice in the Dark,* Souvenir Press, 1967; *The Shadow Falls,* Avon, 1974; *The Secret of Quarry House,* Avon, 1976; *Mavreen,* Arlington Books, 1976; *Tamarisk,* Arlington Books, 1978. Also author of nearly fifty other novels.

SIDELIGHTS: Lorrimer's *A Voice in the Dark* is the story of Laura, an English nurse who, while vacationing in Italy, lands a job as a "companion and musical entertainer" to a handsome but blind Italian, Domenico. The plot thickens when she discovers that Domenico is being hunted by murderers but can convince neither Domenico nor his family of the plot. Finally, after being dismissed from her job and surviving an attempt on her own life, Laura learns who the murderer is. "This brings her into immediate new peril and a race against death, both for herself and Domenico," summarized Judith Worthy of *Books & Bookmen.* Worthy classified *A Voice in the Dark* as "predictable romantic stuff with a dash of thriller to strengthen it and bright Italian skies to liven a drear winter's evening."

BIOGRAPHICAL/CRITICAL SOURCES: Books & Bookmen, February, 1968; *Best Sellers,* August 15, 1970; *West Coast Review of Books,* May, 1977.*

* * *

LOUW, Nicholaas Petrus Van Wyk 1906-1970

OBITUARY NOTICE: Born June 11, 1906, in Sutherland, South Africa; died June 18, 1970. Poet, playwright, critic, and professor. Louw was the leader of the Afrikaans poetry revival in the 1930's. Once a professor in Amsterdam and Johannesburg, he is considered the greatest poet in Afrikaans literature. His narrative poem, "Raka," is heralded as the best in the language, and his "Germanicus" is considered its finest play. Louw's numerous essays have had tremendous impact on South African thought, changing the course of Afrikaans literary criticism. His works include *Alleenspraak* (poems), *Swaarte en Ligpunte* (prose), and "Koning Eenoog" (a play). Obituaries and other sources: *The Penguin Companion to Classical, Oriental, and African Literature,* McGraw, 1969; *Cassell's Encyclopaedia of World Literature,* revised edition, Morrow, 1973; *Who's Who in Twentieth Century Literature,* Holt, 1976.

* * *

LOVEMAN, Brian E(lliot) 1944-

PERSONAL: Born in 1944 in Los Angeles, Calif.; son of Bernard J. and Rosalie Loveman; married Sharon Ann Siem. children: Taryn, Mara, Carly. *Education:* University of California, Berkeley, A.B., 1965; Indiana University, M.A., 1969, Ph.D., 1973. *Office:* Department of Political Science, San Diego State University, San Diego, Calif. 92182.

CAREER: U.S. Peace Corps, Washington, D.C., community development volunteer in southern Chile, 1965-67; San Diego State University, San Diego, Calif., assistant professor, 1973-76, associate professor, 1976-79, professor of Latin American politics, 1979—, head of Latin American studies program and co-director of Latin American Studies Center, both 1979—. Visiting assistant professor at University of California, San Diego, summer, 1974. Conducted field research in Mexico and Chile. Speaker at national seminars and meetings; consultant to U.S. Department of Agriculture's Economic Research Service. *Member:* Phi Beta Kappa, Phi Kappa Phi. *Awards, honors:* Woodrow Wilson fellow, 1965, 1971-72.

WRITINGS: El campesino Chileno le escribe a su Excelencia (title means "The Chilean Peasant Writes to 'His Excellency,'"), Instituto de Capacitacion e Investigacion en Reforma Agraria, 1971; *El mito de la marginalidad: Participacion y represion del campesinado Chileno* (title means "The Myth of Marginality: Participation and Repression of the Chilean Peasantry"), Instituto de Capacitacion e Investigacion en Reforma Agraria, 1971; *Antecedentes para el estudio del Movimiento Campesino Chileno: Pliegos de peticiones, huelgas y sindicatos agricolas, 1932-1966* (title means "Data for the Study of The Chilean Rural Labor Movement: Labor Petitions, Strikes, and Agricultural Unions"), two volumes, Instituto de Capacitacion e Investigacion en Reforma Agraria, 1971; *Struggle in the Countryside: Politics and Rural Labor in Chile, 1919-1973,* Indiana University Press, 1976; *Struggle in the Countryside: A Documentary Supplement,* International Development Research Center, Indiana University, 1976; (editor with Thomas M. Davies, Jr., and contributor) *The Politics of Antipolitics: The Military in Latin America,* University of Nebraska Press, 1978; *Chile: The Legacy of Hispanic Capitalism,* Oxford University Press, 1979.

Contributor: Arturo Valenzuela and J. Samuel Valenzuela, editors, *Chile: Politics and Society,* Transaction Books, 1976; *Foreign Investment in U.S. Real Estate,* Economic Research Service, U.S. Department of Agriculture, 1976; John Booth and Mitchell Seligson, editors, *Political Participation in Latin America,* Volume II, Holmes & Meier, 1979. Contributor to *Handbook of Contemporary Development in World Industrial Relations* and *Andean Research Guide.* Contributor of about fifteen articles and reviews to Latin American studies and history journals.

WORK IN PROGRESS: Editing *The Political Challenge of Urbanization in Latin America.*

SIDELIGHTS: Loveman's current research interests include recent military regimes, national development strategies, and local politics in Latin America, internal migration in Mexico, with special reference to Baja California, and the policy consequences of military rule in Latin America.

* * *

LOW, David (Alexander Cecil) 1891-1963

OBITUARY NOTICE: Born April 7, 1891, in Dunedin, New Zealand; died September 19, 1963. Cartoonist best known for his fictional character, Colonel Blimp, and for his satirical depictions of Hitler and the Nazis during the 1930's and 1940's. His books include *Low Again, Europe at War,* and *Low's Autobiography.* Obituaries and other sources: *Current Biography,* Wilson, 1940, November, 1963; *Who's Who in Graphic Art,* Amstutz & Herdeg Graphis, 1962; *New York Times,* September 21, 1963; *Longman Companion to Twentieth Century Literature,* Longman, 1970.

LUCE, Henry R(obinson) 1898-1967

OBITUARY NOTICE: Born April 3, 1898, in Tengchow, China; died February 28, 1967. Editor, publisher, co-founder of *Time,* and creator of *Fortune, Life,* and *Sports Illustrated.* Luce also acted as editor-in-chief of these magazines and two others owned by Time, Inc.: *Architectural Forum* and *House and Home.* Luce's magazine made significant advances in the field of weekly journalism. *Time* first introduced the concept of "group journalism," and *Life* was a landmark development in the field of photojournalism, helping to elevate the photograph as a major tool of the reporter. Luce received many awards for his work, including more than fifteen honorary degrees from universities and colleges. He was also honored by such countries as China, Greece, France, Germany, and the Netherlands. He was the husband of Clare Booth Luce, the well-known playwright, congresswoman, and ambassador to Italy. Obituaries and other sources: *Current Biography,* Wilson, 1941, 1961, April, 1967; *The Reader's Encyclopedia,* 2nd edition, Crowell, 1965; *Who Was Who in America,* 4th edition, Marquis, 1968; J. Kobler, *Luce: His Time, Life, and Fortune,* Doubleday, 1968; John Knox Jessup, editor, *The Ideas of Henry Luce,* Atheneum, 1969.

* * *

LUKE, Hugh J(ay) 1932-

PERSONAL: Born February 26, 1932, in Kilgore, Tex.; son of Hugh J. (a carpenter) and Stella (Hamon) Luke; married Joyce McCain, January 24, 1954 (divorced, 1968); married Virginia Pavelka (a religious education director), August 15, 1969; children: Richard Carlton, Katherine Pavelka. *Education:* Attended Baylor University, 1949-51; University of Texas, B.A., 1956, M.A., 1957, Ph.D., 1963. *Politics:* Liberal Democrat. *Religion:* Unitarian-Universalist. *Home:* 4640 Bryan Circle, Lincoln, Neb. 68506. *Office:* Department of English, University of Nebraska, Lincoln, Neb. 68588.

CAREER: Texas A&M College (now University), College Station, instructor, 1960-62, assistant professor of English, 1962-63; University of Nebraska, Lincoln, assistant professor, 1963-66, associate professor, 1966-71, professor of English, 1972—. *Military service:* U.S. Army, 1951-53; became sergeant. *Member:* American Association of University Professors. *Awards, honors:* Fellowships from University of Texas, 1958-59, 1959-60.

WRITINGS: (Editor and author of introduction) Mary Shelley, *The Last Man,* University of Nebraska Press, 1965; (editor and author of introduction) A. C. Swinburne, *William Blake: A Critical Essay,* University of Nebraska Press, 1971; (contributor) Greg Kuzma, editor, *A Book of Rereadings,* Best Cellar Press, 1979. Contributor to literature journals and literary magazines. Acting editor of *Prairie Schooner,* 1967-68, 1978-79, associate editor, 1968-80, editor, 1980—.

WORK IN PROGRESS: A collection of essays on contemporary American poets.

* * *

LUTIN, Michael 1940-

PERSONAL: Born September 1, 1940, in Hartford, Conn.; son of Felix J. (an automobile service manager) and Esther (a state employee; maiden name, Neporent) Lutin. *Education:* Attended Harvard University, summer, 1961; Trinity College, Hartford, Conn., B.A., 1962. *Home and office:* 800 Avenue of the Americas, New York, N.Y. 10001. *Agent:* Bill Berger Associates, Inc., 444 East 58th St., New York, N.Y. 10022.

CAREER: Junior high school teacher in West Hartford, Conn., 1963-64; oyster vendor in Paris, France, 1964; Ileana Sonnabend Gallery, Paris, France, manager, 1965-66; Western Publishing Co., Inc., New York, N.Y., writer of love comic books, 1966-67; writer and astrologer, 1977—. *Member:* Phi Beta Kappa.

WRITINGS: Mod Love, Western Publishing, 1967; *Your Two Year Horoscope,* twelve volumes, Grosset, 1975-76, 3rd edition, 1977-78; *Your Horoscope,* twelve volumes, Grosset, 1976-78, 4th edition, 1979; *Total Horoscope,* twelve volumes, Ace Books, 1978, 2nd edition, 1979; (editor) *Super Horoscope,* Grosset, 1976, 4th edition, 1979; (editor) *Astroanalysis,* Grosset, 1977, 2nd edition, 1978; *Saturn Signs,* Delacorte, 1979.

WORK IN PROGRESS: The Seventh House, publication expected in 1981; *Planetary Rhythm.*

SIDELIGHTS: Lutin told *CA:* "What does it mean to say that you are having your chart read? In my opinion it's a unique experience you will always be happy you had, because it's not only a glimpse into mysticism, but also a practical exercise as well. It's an amazingly precise and useful tool in business and personal relationships. I don't say it clears up your pimples or does wonders for your sex life, but then again, who knows?

"*Saturn Signs* combines a three-part system for turning anxieties into successes with a series of games and exercises intended to transform those ninety zillion squirming bits of panic and anxiety into confidence."

* * *

LUTZ, Jerry 1939-

PERSONAL: Born October 6, 1939, in Conesville, Iowa; son of Paul J. (in insurance sales) and Elizabeth (Hamilton) Lutz. *Education:* University of Iowa, B.A., 1961; Harvard University, Ph.D., 1965. *Home:* 31 Gray St., Cambridge, Mass. 02138. *Office:* Raytheon Service Co., Transportation Systems Center, Kendall Sq., Cambridge, Mass. 02142.

CAREER: University of California, Berkeley, assistant professor of English, 1965-68; University of Maryland, College Park, lecturer on English in Far East Division, 1968-69; University of Massachusetts, Boston, assistant professor of English, 1971—. Copy editor at U.S. Department of Transportation Reports, 1978-79; associated with Raytheon Service Co. *Member:* Phi Beta Kappa.

WRITINGS: Pitchman's Melody: Shaw About Pitchman's "Shakespear," Bucknell University Press, 1974.

* * *

LUTZE, Karl E(rnst) 1920-

PERSONAL: Born June 24, 1920, in Sheboygan, Wis.; son of Chas F. and Alma (Garbing) Lutze; married Esther Peters, May 12, 1945; children: Peter, Stephen, Thomas, Mark. *Education:* Attended Concordia College, 1934-40, and Concordia Seminary, 1940-45. *Home:* 4 Old Orchard Lane, Valparaiso, Ind. 46383. *Office:* Lutheran Human Relations Association of America, Valparaiso, Ind. 46383.

CAREER: Ordained Lutheran minister, 1945; pastor of Lutheran churches in Muskogee, Okla., 1945-52, and Tulsa, Okla., 1952-59; Lutheran Human Relations Association of America, Valparaiso, Ind., executive secretary, 1959—. Part-time instructor at Valparaiso University; guest instructor at Miles College; conducts and participates in human relations workshops and seminars. President and member of executive committee of Lutheran Church and Indian People; member of executive committee of National Indian Lutheran Board. *Member:* Lutheran Deaconess Association (member of board of directors and board of trustees).

WRITINGS: To Mend the Broken, Concordia, 1966; *Forgive Our Forgettings,* Concordia, 1972. Author of religious pamphlets. Editor of *Vanguard.*

SIDELIGHTS: Lutze began his career as a parish pastor in Muskogee's black community. His task in Tulsa was to establish a new church in the black community, which eventually served an integrated congregation. He was a charter member of the Tulsa Urban League and served as its president for two terms. His current teaching reflects his interest in the church as it confronts racial issues, and includes field trips to the South and to northern inner-city areas for research on community problems. He noted that current emphasis is on "congregations and day schools serving changing neighborhoods."

* * *

LYLE, Jerolyn R(oss) 1937-

PERSONAL: Born September 12, 1937, in Meridian, Miss.; daughter of Fred A. (an attorney) and Everette (Bynum) Ross; married Frank Allen Lyle (a business executive), June 21, 1958; children: Kathryn Everette, James Jeffrey. *Education:* Southern Methodist University, B.A., 1958; University of Maryland, M.A., 1966, Ph.D., 1970; attended Institute of Francisco Marroquin, 1975. *Religion:* Methodist. *Home:* 5512 Center St., Chevy Chase, Md. 20015.

CAREER: High school social science teacher in Dallas, Tex., 1958-59, Houston, Tex., 1959-61, and Arlington, Va., 1961-62; National Education Association, Washington, D.C., research associate, 1963; high school social science teacher in Arlington, Va., 1963-64, and Fairfax, Va., 1965; U.S. Office of Education, Washington, D.C., economist, 1966-68; U.S. Equal Employment Opportunity Commission, Washington, D.C., economist, 1968-70; American University, Washington, D.C., assistant professor of economics, 1971-75; U.S. Office of Management and Budget, Washington, D.C., economist, 1975-76; Federal Preparedness Agency, Washington, D.C., economist, 1976—. Lecturer at Smith College, spring, 1971, 1973-74, and Washington International Center, 1971-76. Economist with Inter-American Development Bank, 1974-75; participant in national and international meetings; consultant to Urban Institute. *Member:* American Economic Association, American Statistical Association, Society of Government Economists, Industrial Relations Research Association.

WRITINGS: (With Richard Zamoff) *Assessment of Day Care Services and Needs at the Community Level: Mt. Pleasant,* Urban Institute, 1971; (with Jane L. Ross) *Women's Role in Contemporary Society,* Avon, 1972; (with Ross) *Women in Industry: Employment Patterns of Women in Corporate America,* Lexington Books, 1973; (contributor) Dennis R. Young and Richard B. Nelson, editors, *Public Policy for Day Care of Young Children,* Lexington Books, 1973; (contributor) Robert Martinez, editor, *Readings in Hispanic Studies,* R. F. Publishing, 1974; (contributor) Bennet Harrison, George von Furstenberg, and Ann R. Horowitz, editors, *Patterns of Racial Discrimination,* Volume II: *Employment and Income,* Lexington Books, 1974; *The Dynamics of Recent Inflation in Latin America,* Inter-American Development Bank, 1975; *Estimating the Employment Impact of Trade Deficits for Input-Output Sectors of the U.S. Economy,* American Statistical Association, 1980. Contributor to scholarly journals.

SIDELIGHTS: Jerolyn Lyle comments: "I enjoy writing for technical audiences of economists and statisticians as well as for the general public. I consider it the responsibility of professional economists to contribute to the literature. My interests are policy-oriented and have evolved during my career as policy priorities have changed."

BIOGRAPHICAL/CRITICAL SOURCES: Span, June, 1978.

* * *

LYMAN, Lauren D(wight) 1891-1972

OBITUARY NOTICE: Born April 24, 1891, in Easthampton, Mass.; died July 11, 1972, in Bridgeport, Conn. Journalist and aircraft corporation executive. Lyman was considered one of the nation's foremost aviation journalists during his years at the *New York Times.* He left the *Times* in 1938 to join United Aircraft Corp., where he served from 1946 to 1959 as vice-president. Lyman won a Pulitzer Prize for reporting in 1936; his book, *The Wonder Book of the Air,* was published that same year. Obituaries and other sources: *New York Times,* July 12, 1972; *Who Was Who in America,* 5th edition, Marquis, 1973.

* * *

LYNCH, Hayden Wood 1927(?)-1979

OBITUARY NOTICE: Born c. 1927; died July 2, 1979, in Fort Lauderdale, Fla. Reporter and free-lance writer. Lynch reported for the *Chicago American* for seventeen years before working for the National Safety Council in Chicago. Obituaries and other sources: *Chicago Tribune,* July 12, 1979.

* * *

LYNCH, Henry T(homson) 1928-

PERSONAL: Born January 4, 1928, in Lawrence, Mass.; son of Henry Francis and Eleanore (Thomson) Lynch; married Jane Frances Smith (a registered nurse), November 9, 1951; children: Patrick, Kathleen, C. Ann. *Education:* University of Oklahoma, B.S., 1951; University of Denver, M.A., 1952; further graduate study at University of Texas, Austin, 1953-56; University of Texas, Galveston, M.D., 1960. *Office:* Department of Preventive Medicine and Public Health, School of Medicine, Creighton University, 2500 California St., Omaha, Neb. 68178.

CAREER: St. Mary's Hospital, Evansville, Ind., intern, 1961; University of Nebraska, Omaha, resident in internal medicine, 1961-64, senior clinical cancer trainee in clinical oncology at Eppley Institute for Research in Cancer and Allied Diseases, 1964-66; University of Texas, Houston, assistant professor of biology and assistant internist at M.D. Anderson Hospital and Tumor Institute, 1966-67; Creighton University, Omaha, Neb., assistant professor, 1967-68, associate professor, 1968-70, professor of preventive medicine and public health, 1970—, chairman of department, 1967—. Lecturer at University of Nebraska, Lincoln, 1962-65. Member of scientific advisory board of Council for Tobacco Research, 1973—; member of National Cancer Institute's virus cancer program scientific review committee, 1974—. *Military service:* U.S. Navy, 1944-46.

MEMBER: American Medical Association, American Society of Human Genetics, American Association for Cancer Education, American Association of Clinical Oncology, Nebraska State Medical Association, Omaha-Douglas County Medical Society, Sigma Xi, Psi Chi, Alpha Omega Alpha.

WRITINGS: Recent Results in Cancer Research, Volume XII: *Hereditary Factors in Carcinoma,* Springer-Verlag, 1967; (with Daniel Bergsma, A. J. Krush, and Edward Sharp) *International Directory of Genetic Services,* National Foundation on Birth Defects, 1968, 5th edition, 1977; *Dynamic Genetic Counseling for Clinicians,* C. C Thomas, 1969; *Cancer and You,* C. C Thomas, 1971; *Skin, Heredity, and Malignant Neoplasms,* Medical Examination Publishing, 1972; (editor) *Cancer Genetics,* C. C Thomas, 1976; *Cancer and Genodermatoses* (monograph), Van Nostrand, 1979; *Biomarkers and Cancer* (monograph), Van Nostrand, 1979; *Breast Cancer Genetics* (monograph), Van Nostrand, 1979; *Colon Cancer Genetics* (monograph), Van Nostrand, 1979.

Contributor: Jules H. Masserman, editor, *Current Psychiatric Therapies,* Volume XII, Grune, 1972; Arnold Sorsby, editor, *Clinical Genetics,* 2nd edition (Lynch was not included in 1st edition), Butterworth & Co., 1973; *The Etiology of Inherited Disorders,* Mss Information, 1974; J. J. Mulvihill, R. W. Miller, and J. F. Fraumeni, editors, *Genetics of Human Cancer: Progress in Cancer Research and Therapy,* Volume III, Raven Press, 1977; G. P. Murphy, editor, *Progress in Clinical and Biological Research,* Alan R. Liss, 1977; Martin Lipkin and R. A. Good, editors, *Gastrointestinal Tract Cancer,* Plenum, 1978; Seymour Kessler, editor, *Genetic Counselling: Psychological Dimensions,* Academic Press, 1979.

Author of film, "Heredity and Carcinoma: Guide to Early Diagnosis," 1967. Contributor of more than one hundred-fifty articles to medical journals in the United States and abroad, and popular magazines, including *Saturday Evening Post.*

* * *

LYNCH, Marilyn 1938-
(Melanie Ward)

PERSONAL: Born May 31, 1938, in Dos Palos, Calif.; daughter of John William (a farmer) and Ethel A. (Williams) Ward; married Ollie Monroe Lynch (an advertising director), September 6, 1957; children: Melanie Delores. *Education:* Attended University of Oklahoma.

CAREER: Writer.

WRITINGS—All novels; under pseudonym Melanie Ward: *Lady of Longing,* Pinnacle Books, 1973; *Where Love Was Lost,* Pinnacle Books, 1974; *The Sky Girls,* Ace Books, 1974; *Sky Girls, Part II,* Ace Books, 1975; *Dreams to Come,* Jove, 1978; *Casino,* Ace Books, 1979. Contributor of about five hundred articles and stories to magazines.

M

MACDONALD, Neil (William) 1936-

PERSONAL: Born August 21, 1936, in Calgary, Alberta, Canada; son of Charles A. (a businessman) and Violet (a painter; maiden name, Rogers) Macdonald; married Lea Margaret Pearson (a research director), August 18, 1960; children: Robert Loughlin, Diane Paige, Kenneth Scot. *Education:* University of British Columbia, B.A., 1958, M.A., 1960; University of Oregon, M.Sc., 1962; University of Minnesota, Ph.D., 1965. *Residence:* North Vancouver, British Columbia, Canada. *Office:* Department of Psychology, Vancouver Community College, 100 West 49th Ave., Vancouver, British Columbia V5Y 2Z6, Canada.

CAREER/WRITINGS: *Province* (newspaper), Vancouver, British Columbia, sportswriter, 1955-57; Canadian Press (wire service), Vancouver, reporter and deskman, 1958; *Province,* sportswriter, 1959-60; *Eugene Register-Guard* (newspaper), Eugene, Ore., sportswriter, 1960-62; British Columbia Institute of Technology, Burnaby, British Columbia, head of department of communications, 1967; Vancouver Community College, Vancouver, psychologist, 1968—, chairman of psychology department, 1971-72; psychologist in private practice, North Vancouver, 1979—; CKWX-Radio, Vancouver, writer and television critic for "On the Scene" radio show, 1979; Transworld News, Washington, D.C., author of syndicated column, "Psychology '79." Assistant professor of psychology at St. Francis Xavier University, 1965-66, University of New Brunswick, summer, 1966, Laurentian University, 1966-67, Manitoba Institute of Technology, summer, 1967, and University of Manitoba, summer, 1967. Has made guest appearances on radio and television programs. *Member:* British Columbia Psychology Association. *Awards, honors:* Award for best sportswriting in an alumni magazine from American Alumni Association, 1962, for writing in *Old Oregon.*

WORK IN PROGRESS: A novel on Jack the Ripper.

SIDELIGHTS: Macdonald has worked as an extra in several motion pictures, including "The Changeling," and on television shows, including "This Is Psychology." He worked as a partner in a comedy team, "Mac and Lamb," in the summer of 1979.

Macdonald told *CA:* "If it wasn't for golf, I'd be a better writer; and if it wasn't for writing, I'd be a better golfer."

MacFARLANE, Iris 1922-

PERSONAL: Born July 22, 1922, in Quetta, Pakistan; daughter of William Rhodes and Violet Juxon (Jones) James; married Donald MacFarlane, March 1, 1941; children: Alan Donald, Fiona Stirling (Mrs. John Pearson), Anne Elizabeth (Mrs. Erik Pearse). *Politics:* Socialist. *Home:* Sidinish, Isle of North Uist, Outer Hebrides.

CAREER: Writer.

WRITINGS: *Tales and Legends From India,* Chatto & Windus, 1965; *The Children of Bird God Hill,* Chatto & Windus, 1967, McGraw, 1968; *The Summer of the Lame Seagull,* Chatto & Windus, 1970; *The Mouth of the Night: Gaelic Stories Retold,* Chatto & Windus, 1973; *The Black Hole; or, The Making of a Legend,* Allen & Unwin, 1975. Author of stories for British Broadcasting Co. Regular contributor to *The Scotsman.*

WORK IN PROGRESS: Studying Gaelic; research with son into 17th-Century parish history.

SIDELIGHTS: *The Children of Bird God Hill* is about young people raised near a jungle. The children become interested in Krishna and eventually convert a temple into a haven for helpless animals. Jean MacGibbon called it a "humorous, sensitive record of childhood remembered. . . ." MacFarlane's *The Summer of the Lame Seagull* also received critical praise. Gladys Williams deemed the book "an imaginative and emotional story. . . ." However, Williams also noted that the book, which is about a polio-stricken girl and her struggles with love, religion, and growing up, "perhaps struggles a bit too hard to be realistic."

BIOGRAPHICAL/CRITICAL SOURCES: *New Statesman,* November 3, 1967; *Books and Bookmen,* April, 1971.*

* * *

MacFARLANE, Louise 1917(?)-1979

OBITUARY NOTICE: Born c. 1917; died of a heart attack, October 28, 1979, in Cedarcroft, Md. Public relations worker, correspondent, and free-lance journalist. MacFarlane, the first woman to serve as a White House correspondent, covered the Roosevelt, Truman, and Eisenhower administrations for the Mutual Broadcasting System. She also worked in public relations for the Holiday Inns, directed public relations for the Baltimore chapter of the American Cancer Society, and directed specialized media for a Baltimore advertising agency. Obituaries and other sources: *Chicago Tribune,* November 1, 1979.

* * *

MacMULLAN, Charles Walden Kirkpatrick 1889-1973 (C. K. Munro)

OBITUARY NOTICE: Born February 17, 1889, in Portrush, Antrim, Ireland; died July 20, 1973. Playwright under the pseudonym C. K. Munro. MacMullan began his career as a civil servant and rose to become under-secretary of the Ministry of Labour. He was created Commander of the Order of the British Empire in 1947. MacMullan's greatest success as a playwright was the boarding-house comedy, "At Mrs. Beam's." His other plays include "Wanderers" and "The Rumour." He is also author of a book of lectures, *Watching a Play,* and a book of essays, *The True Woman: A Handbook for Husbands.* Obituaries and other sources: *Longman Companion to Twentieth Century Literature,* Longman, 1970; *McGraw-Hill Encyclopedia of World Drama,* McGraw, 1972.

* * *

MADSEN, Roy Paul 1928-

PERSONAL: Born July 7, 1928, in Chicago, Ill.; son of Helmar Johan (in business) and Esther (Ellingssen) Madsen; married Barbara Tozier (an artist), September 6, 1953; children: Sally Dawn, Mark Hunter, Kristie Madsen Ross. *Education:* University of Illinois, B.F.A., 1951; University of Southern California, M.A., 1963, Ph.D., 1966. *Office:* Department of Telecommunications and Film, San Diego State University, San Diego, Calif. 92182.

CAREER: Chicago Museum of Natural History, Chicago, Ill., illustrator, 1950; Kling Studios, Chicago, artist and animator for industrial films and television commercials, 1951-52; Mango Metal Works, Chicago, industrial designer, 1952-54; professional artist (painter, illustrator, and animator), 1954-64; Syracuse University, Syracuse, N.Y., lecturer in education, director of animation, and writer, producer, director, and editor of documentary and educational films, 1963-66; San Diego State University, San Diego, Calif., assistant professor, 1966-69, associate professor, 1969-73, professor of film, 1973—. Lecturer at University of Southern California, 1961-63. Testified as communications expert at more than forty courtroom trials. International speaker for U.S. Information Agency, 1974-75; guest on foreign radio and television programs; public speaker in the United States and abroad; consultant to local and national government agencies and to business and industry.

MEMBER: International Association of Film Animators, World Affairs Council, American Film Institute, National Academy of Television Arts and Sciences, Society of Motion Picture and Television Engineers, National Wildlife Association, Audubon Society, National Geographic Society, Westerners, Zoological Society of San Diego. *Awards, honors:* Huntington Hartford Foundation fellowship, 1955-56, for painting; Stacey Prize from Stacey Foundation, 1962, for painting; Hollywood Screen Directors Guild fellowship, 1960; Jessie E. Lasky Prize from Screen Directors Guild, 1962.

WRITINGS: Animated Film: Concepts, Methods, Uses, Interland-Pitman, 1969; *The Impact of Film: How Ideas Are Communicated by Cinema and Television,* Macmillan, 1973; (editor) Frederic Whitaker, *The Crazy Art Business* (essays), North Light, 1979. Contributor to business, film, and photography journals.

WORK IN PROGRESS: Research for *The International Cinema: Forms, Themes, Concepts* and *International Propaganda.*

SIDELIGHTS: Madsen writes: "My interests are these: the communication of ideas through film and television, as expressed in my books; a love of wildlife, as expressed in my art; and a passion for public affairs, as reflected in my consulting work for local district attorneys' offices and federal agencies. My future writings will expand upon similar themes: books relating to media and their effects upon America; communications aspects of international affairs; propaganda; the 'new realism' in the art of America; the impact of Hispanic immigration on the demography of the Southwest, etc."

BIOGRAPHICAL/CRITICAL SOURCES: Thelma Newman, *Wax as Art Form,* A. S. Barnes, 1966; *American Artist,* May, 1971; *San Diego Union,* October, 1976.

* * *

MAEHL, William H(arvey) 1915-

PERSONAL: Born May 28, 1915, in Brooklyn, N.Y.; son of William Henry and Antoinette (Salamone) Maehl; married Josephine Scholl McAllister, December 29, 1941; children: Madeleine, Kathleen. *Education:* Northwestern University, B.Sc., 1937, M.A., 1939; University of Chicago, Ph.D., 1946. *Politics:* Independent. *Religion:* Roman Catholic. *Home:* 616 Green St., Auburn, Ala. 36830. *Office:* Department of History, A. & S. Haley Center, Auburn University, Auburn, Ala. 36830.

CAREER: St. Louis University, St. Louis, Mo., instructor in history, 1942-43; Centenary College, Shreveport, Ill., instructor in history, 1943-44; De Paul University, Chicago, Ill., assistant professor of European history, 1944-50; U.S. Army, military historian at European headquarters in Karlsruhe, Germany, 1951-52, chief civilian briefing officer at headquarters in Frankfurt, Germany, 1952-53, chief historian at Artillery School at Fort Sill, Okla., 1954-55; U.S. Air Force Headquarters, Burtonwood Lance, England, chief civilian war plans officer, 1955-56; Nebraska Wesleyan University, Lincoln, associate professor, 1956-58, professor of history, 1958-62; University of Auckland, Auckland, New Zealand, senior lecturer in European history, 1963-64; Nebraska Wesleyan University, professor of history, 1964-68; Auburn University, Auburn, Ala., professor of European history, 1968—. Overseas lecturer for University of Maryland, 1955; visiting professor at Midlands University and University of Nebraska; speaker to civic organizations.

MEMBER: International Institute of Arts and Letters (fellow), American Historical Association, Southern Historical Association, Alabama Academy of Science, Phi Kappa Phi, Phi Alpha Theta, Alma Mu Gamma, Phi Eta Sigma. *Awards, honors:* Danforth Foundation grant for the Soviet Union, 1961; grants from Auburn University, 1972-73, and 1973-74; American Philosophical Society grants, 1973-74, 1975; Deutscher Akademischer Austauschdienst grant for Germany, 1978.

WRITINGS: (Contributor) S. W. Halperin, editor, *Some Twentieth-Century Historians,* University of Chicago Press, 1961; *German Militarism and Socialism,* Nebraska Wesleyan University Press, 1968; *A World History Syllabus,* three volumes, Auburn University Press, 1971-73; (contributor) Hans Schmitt, editor, *Historians of Modern Europe,*

Louisiana State University Press, 1971; *Germany in Western Civilization,* University of Alabama Press, 1979; *August Bebel: Shadow Emperor of the German Workers,* American Philosophical Society, 1979. Contributor to political studies and history journals.

WORK IN PROGRESS: "German Social Democracy's Agrarian Policy Reconsidered," an article for *Central European History; The Social Democratic Party in the Weimar Republic, 1918-1933.*

SIDELIGHTS: Maehl writes: "I have been motivated from early youth by an interest in German history and a specific interest in European socialism. Under the influence of Bernadotte Schmitt, S. W. Halperin, and Hans Rothfels, I moved into my German diplomatic and political history specialty. My sympathy with the plight of the German working class in modern times has inspired most of my studies on German Social Democratic history. In a larger sense, my interest in German Social Democracy derives from my conviction that most of the gains of the working class in the modern world have resulted from the pressure that organizations of labor, and especially the Social Democrats (Socialists) parties, have exercised upon legislatures and public opinion."

* * *

MAGILL, Robert S(amuel) 1941-

PERSONAL: Born March 26, 1941, in Philadelphia, Pa.; son of Richard S. (in business) and Betty J. (Sickles) Magill; married Margaret Goldman, June 11, 1967; children: Andrew, Joanna. *Education:* Antioch University, B.A., 1964; Columbia University, M.S.W., 1966; University of Chicago, Ph.D., 1976. *Home:* 3263 North Marietta Ave., Milwaukee, Wis. 53211. *Office:* School of Social Welfare, University of Wisconsin, Milwaukee, Wis. 53201.

CAREER: Charlotte Area Fund, Charlotte, N.C., work supervisor, 1966-67; Health and Welfare Association of Allegheny County, Pittsburgh, Pa., planning assistant, 1967-69; University of Wisconsin—Milwaukee, assistant professor, 1970-77, associate professor of social welfare, 1977—. *Member:* International Sociological Association, National Association of Social Workers, Council on Social Work Education.

WRITINGS: Community Decision Making for Social Welfare: Federalism, City Government, and the Poor, Human Sciences Press, 1979. Contributor to social science journals.

WORK IN PROGRESS: Research for *Social Policy: An Introductory Textbook;* research on the work and training attitudes and experiences of the poor.

SIDELIGHTS: Magill told *CA:* "In recent years, there has been a growing antagonism toward government in general, and especially towards the federal government. Washington has become a dirty word, often associated with inefficiency, ineffectiveness and unresponsiveness. Political conservatives hail the anti-Washington attitudes as confirmation of their philosophy. Political liberals are in disarray. My purpose in writing *Community Decision Making for Social Welfare* was to analyze this trend and its effect on the provision of social services. After all, in Colonial America, services were almost totally provided by the local community. What would be the effect of a return to more community decision making for social welfare?

"The book is divided into three major sections. The first describes different conceptions of the role of the federal government in social welfare from a philosophical perspective. Section two analyzes the relationship between the federal government and the states and communities throughout American history. The final section contains an actual study of what happens to social welfare allocations under varying amounts of community control.

"I have tried to write a book which is readable and understandable. My hope is that it will be provocative and promote a more thoughtful consideration of the consequences of community decision making for social welfare."

* * *

MAGNUSON, Don(ald Hammer) 1911-1979

OBITUARY NOTICE: Born March 7, 1911, in Freeman, Wash.; died October 5, 1979, in Seattle, Wash. Member of the U.S. House of Representatives, reporter, and editor. Magnuson reported for the *Daily Olympian* and the *Seattle Times* before being elected to the U.S. House in 1952. He lost his bid for election to a sixth Congressional term in 1962, and later went on to write and edit for the U.S. Department of Labor. Among his several awards in journalism is the Heywood Broun Memorial Award from the American Newspaper Guild. Obituaries and other sources: *Who's Who in American Politics,* 7th edition, Bowker, 1979; *New York Times,* October 9, 1979.

* * *

MAGRID, Henry M. 1918(?)-1979

OBITUARY NOTICE: Born c. 1918 in New York N.Y.; died August 18, 1979, in New York, N.Y. Educator, lecturer, and author. Magrid was a professor of philosophy at the City College of the City University of New York before he retired because of illness in 1972. He also lectured on social philosophy for educational television in New York and appeared on the CBS television programs "Camera Three" and "It's Worth Knowing." Magrid wrote *English Pluralism* and edited John Stuart Mill's *The Logic of Moral Science.* Obituaries and other sources: *New York Times,* August 21, 1979; *AB Bookman's Weekly,* September 24, 1979.

* * *

MALLIN, Tom 1927(?)-1978

OBITUARY NOTICE: Born c. 1927; died in January, 1978, in Bury, St. Edmunds, England. Artist, playwright, and novelist. Mallin published his first novel, *Dodecahedron,* in 1970. In addition to the novels *Knut, Lobe,* and *Erowina,* he wrote a number of stage and radio plays, including "Curtains" and "The Novelist." Obituaries and other sources: *Contemporary Dramatists,* 2nd edition, St. Martin's, 1976; *AB Bookman's Weekly,* March 20, 1978.

* * *

MALLORY, Bob F(ranklin) 1932-

PERSONAL: Born June 11, 1932, in Blackwell, Okla.; son of Raymond Franklin (a railroad worker) and Violet Jane Mallory; married Juanita Katzer (a registered nurse), September 2, 1962; children: Paul, Stephanie, Patrick, Michael. *Education:* Attended Washburn University, 1951-53; University of Wichita (now Wichita State University), B.A., 1961; University of Missouri, Ph.D., 1968. *Home:* 611 West Third St., Maryville, Mo. 64468. *Office:* Department of Geology, Northwest Missouri State University, Maryville, Mo. 64468.

CAREER: Menninger Foundation, Topeka, Kan., recreational therapist, 1951-52; Kansas Historical Society Museum, Topeka, assistant to curator, 1952-53; Boeing Aircraft, Wichita, Kan., group leader in data processing, 1955-61; Tippet, Abbot, Meyers & Stratton, New York, N.Y., inspector of proposed missile sites, summer, 1961; Northwest Missouri State University, Maryville, assistant professor, 1968-75, associate professor, 1975-78, professor of earth science, 1978—, co-director of field trips. Guest on radio and television programs. *Military service:* U.S. Army, intelligence analyst, 1953-55; served in Germany.

WRITINGS: (With David N. Cargo) *Man and His Geologic Environment,* Addison-Wesley, 1974, 2nd edition, 1977; (with Cargo) *Physical Geology,* McGraw, 1979. Contributor to scientific journals and local newspapers.

WORK IN PROGRESS: An earth science textbook, publication by McGraw expected in 1983; a book on energy.

SIDELIGHTS: Mallory commented: "In my manuscript on energy I emphasize the geology of our energy resources (both fossil fuels and alternate sources), summarize the economics of each source and the problems and restraints associated with each."

* * *

MALONE, Kemp 1889-1971

OBITUARY NOTICE: Born March 14, 1889, in Minter, Miss.; died October 13, 1971, in Eastport, Me. Author, editor, educator, and philologist. A professor at Johns Hopkins University from 1926 to 1956, Malone wrote a number of books on English language and literature, including *The Literary History of Hamlet* and *Chapters on Chaucer.* He was also a co-founder of *American Speech* and a former president of the Modern Language Association of America and the Linguistic Society of America. Obituaries and other sources: *New York Times,* October 15, 1971; *English Studies,* February, 1972; *Speculum,* July, 1972.

* * *

MANK, Gregory William 1950-

PERSONAL: Born December 18, 1950, in Baltimore, Md.; son of William Charles (a refrigeration engineer) and Frances (Bowen) Mank; married Barbara Klein, October 14, 1972; children: Jessica. *Education:* Mount St. Mary's College, Emmitsburg, Md., B.A., 1972. *Home address:* R.D.2, Forge Hill, Delta, Pa. 17314.

CAREER: Free-lance writer, 1973—; Life-Like Products, Baltimore, Md., advertising copywriter, 1973-74; Baltimore Actors Theatre, Baltimore, instructor in creative writing and drama, 1974-76; Baltimore City Public Schools, Baltimore, teacher of English, 1975—. Actor with theatre companies, 1968—.

WRITINGS: (With James Robert Parish, L. DeCarl, and W. T. Leonard) *Hollywood Players: The Forties,* Arlington House, 1976; (with Parish and D. E. Stanke) *The Hollywood Beauties,* Arlington House, 1978; (with Parish and M. R. Pitts) *Hollywood on Hollywood,* Scarecrow, 1978; (with Parish, Leonard, and C. Hoyt) *The Funsters,* Arlington House, 1979; (contributor) Leonard Maltin, editor, *The Real Stars,* Popular Library, 1979; (contributor) Stephen Hanson and Patricia King Hanson, editors, *Masterpieces of Cinema,* Salem Press, 1979; (with Parish) *The Hollywood Reliables,* Arlington House, 1980; (with Parish) *The Best of MGM,* Arlington House, 1980; *Fifty Classic Horror Films,* Arlington House, in press.

Author of "Beasts and Other Talking Things" (one-act play for children), first produced in Baltimore, Md., at Baltimore Actors Theatre, August 1, 1974. Contributor to film magazines, including *Film Fan Monthly, Films in Review,* and *Cinefantastique.*

WORK IN PROGRESS: A monograph on the life and career of Greta Garbo; research for a book on the cinema saga of Frankenstein's monster, publication expected by A. S. Barnes.

SIDELIGHTS: Mank told *CA:* "The cinema has emerged as *the* dynamic art form of the twentieth century, producing a rich and fascinating history. Chronicling the artistry and energy of the cinema and its pioneers is necessary if the 'movies' are ever to gain the truly respectful recognition they demand and deserve."

* * *

MANKIEWICZ, Frank (Fabian) 1924-

PERSONAL: Born May 16, 1924, in New York, N.Y.; son of Herman J. (a screenwriter) and Sara (Aaronson) Mankiewicz; married Holly Jolley, April 23, 1952; children: Joshua, Benjamin. *Education:* University of California at Los Angeles, A.B., 1947; Columbia University, M.S., 1948; University of California at Berkeley, LL.B., 1955. *Home:* 5408 Duvall Dr., Bethesda, Md. 20014. *Office:* 2025 M St. N.W., Washington, D.C. 20036.

CAREER: Journalist in Washington, D.C., and Los Angeles, Calif., 1948-52; admitted to the Bar of California, 1955; practiced law in Beverly Hills, Calif., 1955-61; U.S. Peace Corps, Washington, D.C., director in Lima, Peru, 1962-64, Latin America regional director in Washington, D.C., 1964-66; press secretary for Senator Robert F. Kennedy, 1966-68; syndicated columnist and television news commentator, 1968-71; national presidential campaign director for Senator George McGovern, 1971-72; author and journalist, 1973—; National Public Radio, Washington, D.C., president, 1977—. Democratic candidate for California state legislature, 1950; Democratic candidate from Maryland for U.S. Congress, 1976. *Military service:* U.S. Army, infantry, 1943-46. *Member:* State Bar of California. *Awards, honors:* "Member of Nixon Enemies List, 1969-74."

WRITINGS: Perfectly Clear: Nixon From Whittier to Watergate, Quadrangle, 1973 (published in England as *Nixon's Road to Watergate,* Hutchinson, 1973); *U.S. v. Richard M. Nixon: The Final Crisis,* Quadrangle, 1975; (editor with Kirby Jones) *With Fidel: A Portrait of Castro and Cuba* (interviews), Playboy Press, 1975; (with Joel Swerdlow) *Remote Control: Television and the Manipulation of American Life,* Times Books, 1978. Author of syndicated column, with Tom Braden, 1968-71; columnist for the *Washington Post,* 1976-77. Contributor to newspapers and periodicals, including *Harper's* and *New York.*

SIDELIGHTS: After directing one of the most ill-fated presidential campaigns in U.S. history, Frank Mankiewicz has rebounded to become a major figure in American communications. In the meantime, he showed no reluctance to even the score after his and George McGovern's embarrassing 1972 defeat by publishing two books on the fallen president, Richard Nixon. "Would any of us, including Senator McGovern, change places with the 'winners'?" Mankiewicz asks. "We just lost an election; none of us went to jail and the Senator didn't need a pardon to stay out." His first book, *Perfectly Clear,* contended that Nixon's prevarications began long before Watergate—and he spared no bit of evidence in showing it. In his second book, *U.S. v. Richard M. Nixon,* he studied the political process that brought Nixon's career to an end. Content with America's disposal of the president, he then investigated the insidious U.S. television industry in *Remote Control: Television and the Manipulation of American Life*. Now president of National Public Radio (NPR), he is showing that at least some viewers have been lured away from the despicable tube: during the first two years of his leadership, the network nearly doubled its listening audience.

Mankiewicz knew Nixon long before leading McGovern's 1972 campaign against him. "A lifelong observer" of the president, in *Perfectly Clear* Mankiewicz revealed his knowledge of Nixon by telling the story of his political career from 1946 to the year of the book's publication, 1973. To reviewer Larry Adler, Mankiewicz's presentation was convincing. The "book is fascinating mainly for what it tells us, or reminds us, of the old Nixon," Adler said. "He was smearing, evading, lying in the 'forties." And, demonstrated Mankiewicz, in the fifties, sixties, and seventies, too. He detailed the circumstances surrounding Nixon's 1952 Checker's speech, his fraudulent 1962 California governorship campaign, and, of course, Nixon's handling of the Watergate affair. What was perfectly clear to Mankiewicz at the time was that Congress ought to impeach the president. *Perfectly Clear,* said S. R. Weisman, "is his brief on the matter."

Though Congress never impeached the president, Mankiewicz was altogether satisfied when Nixon resigned in August, 1974. In an interview with the *Philadelphia Bulletin,* Mankiewicz betrayed no sympathy for the deposed president: "I was delighted," he quipped. "I think we should celebrate August 9th as a day of national liberation every year. Every country celebrates the day the government got rid of its tyrants. We should too." In *U.S. v. Richard M. Nixon* Mankiewicz insisted that it was indeed the government—the judicial process—and not the press that had ended Nixon's presidency. As Guy Halverson of the *Christian Science Monitor* noted, "Mankiewicz has written a compelling and important study of how the very process of American justice—often ponderous and slow, but insistent and deliberate—served to bring the long months of Watergate to an end, and, as the tragic denoument, topple a president."

After his books on the presidency, Mankiewicz, along with Joel Swerdlow, tackled another major American institution in *Remote Control.* Television, they say, dominates our lives by continually propogating myths; it has created a phony reality. While TV crimes, for example, are solved within the hour, a majority of real crimes are either never solved or remain hopelessly tangled in litigation. In addition, "television gives us a totally unreal, almost lily-white crime world, except for the police," contend Mankiewicz and Swerdlow. Blacks are rarely depicted as the victims of crime and television neither shows the productivity of the black middle class nor the desolation of black slums. Advertisements, too, help to perpetuate this unreal world. While women have made gains in breaking out of stereotypical household roles, commercials still depict women as servants of their husbands and children. Even when some shows portray women in positive roles, their potential effect is ruined. "Mary Tyler Moore may be producing a news program and Bea Arthur (Maude) [may] be running for state office," the authors say, "but when the fadeout comes and it's time to sell things, the women are worried about ring around the collar, just as before."

The problem with *Remote Control,* several critics complained, was that it did not supply an effective antidote for the TV disease. "They have researched the outrage of television and cry out for the inevitable 'something' to be done," noted Coleman McCarthy. "In their conclusion they call for 'a more muscular Federal Communications Commission,' the flexing of which they dream will lead to television's being 'made more responsive to the public's needs.'" This solution, argued McCarthy, is "spineless." John J. Clarke agreed: "It disappoints by resolutely not attempting to chart what is most needed—a way out of the TV wasteland. Nothing is offered but a few vague, closing suggestions about community cable systems and a more muscular FCC."

Despite such dissatisfaction with the authors' conclusions, *Remote Control* still pleased readers with its thoroughly researched account of the problem. Mankiewicz's and Swerdlow's work involved conducting hundreds of interviews and reading thousands of articles—as evidenced by their fifteen-page bibliography. To one critic, Maya Pines, "its greatest contribution, however, is to open our eyes to an element so pervasive we have stopped seeing it. After reading this book, one can tell more clearly what events were made especially for television, and who benefits from them. One questions more sharply the messages that come through the screen. One thinks about possible remedies. And one quakes at the report—amply confirmed by observation—that when children aged four to six were asked, 'which do you like better, TV or Daddy?' 44 percent of them said they preferred TV."

Since August, 1977, when Mankiewicz took over the presidency of National Public Radio, he has set out to make radio a much more viable element in broadcasting. He has doubled the size of NPR's news department, has made network salaries comparable to journalists' pay, and has earned increased federal funding by promoting public radio in Congress. Part of the success, too, comes from a change in focus. "I think we're bolder now," Mankiewicz said. "Our response is more likely to be 'Let's do it' rather than 'Should we?' or 'We probably can't'." The results have been impressive. "Under his aggressive leadership," reported *Newsweek,* "NPR's audience has jumped from 3.1 million to at least 5 million a week, and the network has added nine new stations in the past year." It's most popular show, "All Things Considered," attracts between three and four million listeners itself.

BIOGRAPHICAL/CRITICAL SOURCES: Time, August 15, 1969; *Newsweek,* July 17, 1972, March 12, 1979; *New Yorker,* October 22, 1973, December 24, 1973; *Observer,* November 4, 1973; *Books and Bookmen,* December, 1973; *Spectator,* December 8, 1973; *New York Times Book Review,* December 23, 1973, February 19, 1978; *Best Sellers,* January 15, 1974, March 1, 1975, August, 1975, April, 1978; *Progressive,* February, 1974, April, 1975, February, 1978; *New Statesman,* February 22, 1974; *Commonweal,* December 6, 1974, August 18, 1978; *Christian Science Monitor,* February 28, 1975; *New York Times,* March 24, 1975; *Philadelphia Bulletin,* April 22, 1975; *Christian Century,* April 23, 1975; *Washington Post Book World,* May 18, 1975, July 13, 1975, February 12, 1978; *Biography News,* Gale, May/June, 1975; *Dissent,* summer, 1976; *National Review,* December 23, 1977; *Saturday Review,* April 1, 1978; *New York Review of Books,* April 6, 1978; *Nation,* June 17, 1978.

—*Sketch by David Versical*

* * *

MANN, (Robert Francis) Christopher Stephen 1917-

PERSONAL: Born March 7, 1917, in England; son of William Henry (in the military) and Elsie Emma (Brazier) Mann. *Education:* Attended Kelham Theological College, 1936-40; King's College, London, B.A., 1940, B.D., 1956, Ph.D., 1960; postdoctoral study at Johns Hopkins University, 1965-

68. *Home:* 107 East Chase St., Baltimore, Md. 21202. *Office:* Ecumenical Institute, St. Mary's Seminary and University, 5400 Roland Ave., Baltimore, Md. 21210.

CAREER: Ordained priest, 1941; pastor of churches in Middlesbrough, England, 1945-47, and Sheffield, England, 1947-53; lecturer in biblical studies at Nashdom Abbey, 1956-61; assistant master of school, 1961-65; lecturer at Maryland Diocesan School of Theology, 1966-67; St. Mary's Seminary and University, Baltimore, Md., adjunct member of faculty, 1967-68, associate dean of Ecumenical Institute, 1968-70, dean, 1970—. *Wartime service:* Royal Observer Corps, 1940-45. *Member:* Society for Biblical Literature (division vice-president, 1973; division president, 1974), Society for Old Testament Study, Catholic Biblical Association of America.

WRITINGS: The New English New Testament: An Introduction, Faith Press, 1961; (contributor) *Studia Evangelica III,* Akademie-Verlag, 1964; (contributor) *S.P.C.K. Theological Collections,* Number 6, S.P.C.K., 1965; (with W. F. Albright) *The Acts of the Apostles,* Doubleday, 1967; (contributor) M. Black, editor, *The Scrolls and Christianity,* S.P.C.K., 1969; (with Albright) *St. Matthew,* Doubleday, 1971; *The Man for All Time,* Morehouse, 1971; *The Message Delivered,* Morehouse, 1973. Contributor of about thirty articles and reviews to theology journals.

WORK IN PROGRESS: St. Mark, publication expected by Doubleday; *Do This,* publication expected by Morehouse.

SIDELIGHTS: Mann writes: "So far as my present career is concerned, the influence of one priest must be reckoned paramount—Robert Leighton Hodson, now deceased."

AVOCATIONAL INTERESTS: Railroads (discovering steam locomotives still in operation), exploring ghost towns in Nevada and Colorado, following the Oregon Trail in Wyoming.

* * *

MANTLE, Mickey (Charles) 1931-

PERSONAL: Born October 20, 1931, in Spavinaw, Okla.; son of Elvin Clark (a lead and zinc miner) and Lovell (Richardson) Mantle; married Merlyn Louise Johnson, December 23, 1951; children: Mickey Elvin, David Harold, Billy Giles, Danny. *Education:* Graduated from high school. *Business manager:* Roy J. True, 1515 Dallas Federal Savings Tower, Dallas, Tex. 75225.

CAREER: Baseball player. Signed with New York Yankees, 1949, played with Independence, Mo., team, 1949, Joplin, Mo., team, 1950, New York Yankees, firstbaseman and outfielder, 1951-68, spring training coach, 1969—; appeared in many World Series games; Reserve Life Insurance Co., Dallas, Tex., vice-president of special markets, 1973—. *Awards, honors:* Chosen Most Valuable Player in the American League, 1956, 1957, 1962; inducted into Baseball Hall of Fame, Cooperstown, N.Y., 1974.

WRITINGS: (With Ben Epstein) *The Mickey Mantle Story,* foreward by Casey Stengel, Holt, 1953; *The Quality of Courage* (juvenile), Doubleday, 1964; *The Education of a Baseball Player,* Simon & Schuster, 1967; (with Edward Ford and Joseph Durso) *Whitey and Mickey: A Joint Autobiography of the Yankee Years,* Viking, 1977.

SIDELIGHTS: During his years in professional baseball, Mickey Mantle became known as one of the greatest switch hitters in the game. He developed his talent as a youngster, learning to bat right-handed against his father's pitching and left-handed against his grandfather's pitching. Ten times during his career he hit both a right-handed and a left-handed home run in the same game.

Mantle seemed destined to be a baseball great, having been named after hall-of-famer Mickey Cochrane. Though his career was plagued by various health problems from knee and shoulder injuries to an abcessed hip and osteomyelitis, he nevertheless finished his career with impressive lifetime statistics, including 536 home runs, 1509 runs batted in, and ten seasons of batting .300 or better. He also earned the dubious honor of having the most strikeouts in baseball history, with 1,710.

Despite his obvious talents, "the Mick subscribes to the old adage that it's just as important to be lucky as it is to be good," according to Harless Wade. "'It was my pleasure to play in more World Series than any other outfielder in history,' he says, simply. 'Sure, an injury to my knee in my first World Series cut my career short, but I still say I was lucky.'" Mantle especially cherished his World Series records, hitting eighteen home runs in the sixty-five World Series games in which he appeared. He was also chosen the American League's Most Valuable Player in 1956, 1957, and 1962, and was only the seventeenth player in history to be voted unanimously into the Baseball Hall of Fame.

Though Mickey was a country boy he became great friends with urbanite pitcher Whitey Ford soon after joining the Yankees. They spent their baseball years together and both were elected into the Baseball Hall of Fame in 1974, much to Mantle's delight.

The two men related their account of life with the Yankees in *Whitey and Mickey,* described by Mel Watkins as "an ebullient, good-natured remembrance." Larry L. King complained that the book was too "mawkish and merry," with little mention of "Mantle's former surliness, when he cursed photographers and reporters," or of "all the hell-raising that Ford, Mantle and such saloon pals as Billy Martin accomplished." But Watkins noted: "After all, Ford and Mantle ended their playing careers before the current era of players' unions and free agents and the consequent management-player strife; moreover, during their 18-year tenure with the Yankees, the teams they played on won 13 pennants. Success, glamour, and, for that time, very high salaries marked their baseball careers, and they recount those days with obvious relish." Louis D. Rubin, Jr., commented that "there is comparatively little about baseball as such in this book" since they didn't "meditate on the game; they played it. . . . When not thus engaged, what they did most of the time was Live It Up, and this is the principal concern of their 'autobiography.'"

The Education of a Baseball Player is another Mantle autobiography, beginning with his rise from Joplin, Mo., to his career in the major leagues. Jim Brosnan was disappointed with the book, declaring it to be "mere legend," while revealing "little of Mantle's personality." E. G. Jacklin, however, observed that "Mickey recounts his story modestly and openly" and felt "this simple straightforward story will make enjoyable and instructive reading."

BIOGRAPHICAL/CRITICAL SOURCES: Mickey Mantle and Ben Epstein, *The Mickey Mantle Story,* foreword by Casey Stengel, Holt, 1953; *New York Times,* April 19, 1953, June 18, 1977; *New York Times Book Review,* October 1, 1967, May 1, 1977; *Best Sellers,* October 15, 1967; *Dallas News,* January 16, 1974, January 17, 1974; *Long Island Press,* January 17, 1974; *Newsweek,* January 28, 1974; *Biography News,* Gale, February, 1974; *Whitey and Mickey: A Joint Autobiography of the Yankee Years,* Viking, 1977; *Saturday Evening Post,* May, 1977; *Saturday Review,* May 14, 1977; *New Republic,* June 11, 1977.

MARCHETTI, Albert 1947-

PERSONAL: Born January 31, 1947, in Atlantic City, N.J.; son of Albert E. (a doctor) and Josephine (Collova) Marchetti. *Education:* Providence College, B.A., 1969; New Jersey College of Medicine, M.D., 1973. *Agent:* Peter Miller, 1021 Avenue of the Americas, New York, N.Y. 10018. *Office:* 11311 North 22nd St., Tampa, Fla. 33612.

CAREER: Tampa General Hospital, Tampa, Fla., 1973-77, began as intern, became resident; Pathology Associates Laboratory, Tampa, medical consultant, 1973—. Consultant to Southwest Florida Blood Bank, 1975-77, and to International Trading Company (ITC), 1979—. Clinical instructor at University of Southern Florida Medical School, 1973-77. Participant in international relief team bringing medical aid to Honduras after the 1974 Hurricane. *Member:* Writers Guild of America, American Medical Association, American Cancer Society (fellow), Chamber of Commerce (Tampa, Fla.).

WRITINGS: Common Cures for Common Ailments, Stein & Day, 1979; *Dr. Marchetti's Walking Program,* Stein & Day, 1979. Contributor of articles on popular medicine to periodicals, including *Cosmopolitan, Omni,* and *Parade.*

WORK IN PROGRESS: Articles on popular medicine; *Prescription for Murder,* a medical mystery novel; *Handbook on Childhood Poisoning.*

SIDELIGHTS: Marchetti writes: "A doctor has two major responsibilities to the general public; medical treatment and medical education. Most physicians focus on the treatment but few actively participate in educating their patients or the public at large. I enjoy teaching and want to help fill the void in current health educational programs by writing books and articles on popular medical topics."

Marchetti's first book, *Common Cures for Common Ailments,* evaluates over 1,500 non-prescription medications used to treat ailments from acne to warts. He lists the ingredients contained in each brand of drug and recommends specific products for their effectiveness. *Weekend Vistas* called the book "an indispensible reference book . . . [and] a survival guide of the most important kind, as it guides consumers through that most terrifying of labrynths—the drug store."

BIOGRAPHICAL/CRITICAL SOURCES: Journal Gazette (Fort Wayne, Ind.), March 4, 1979; *Nashville Banner,* March 17, 1979; *Chicago Sun-Times,* April 3, 1979; *Weekend Vistas,* April 27, 1979; *Seattle Post-Intelligencer,* April 15, 1979.

* * *

MARCOSSON, Isaac Frederick 1877-1961

OBITUARY NOTICE: Born September 13, 1877, in Louisville, Ky.; died March 14, 1961. Journalist, editor, biographer, and historian. Marcosson served on the staffs of the *Louisville Times, World's Work, Munsey's Magazine,* and *Saturday Evening Post.* An exponent of the free enterprise system, he frequently wrote about business, industry, and economics. Many of his articles have been collected into books. He also wrote biographies of Leonard Wood, David Graham Phillips, Henry Watterson, and Charles Frohman. Obituaries and other sources: Isaac Frederick Marcosson, *Before I Forget: A Pilgrimage to the Past,* Dodd, 1959; *Who Was Who in America,* 4th edition, Marquis, 1968; Martha Groves McKelvie, *Presidents, Politicians, and People I Have Known,* Franklin Publishing, 1971.

* * *

MARCUSE, Herbert 1898-1979

OBITUARY NOTICE: Born July 19, 1898, in Berlin, Germany; died of a stroke, July 29, 1979, in Starnberg, West Germany. Philosopher, educator, and author who was adopted by the New Left in the 1960's as a leader in the movement toward social change. A refugee from Nazi Germany, Marcuse began teaching at Columbia University in 1934 and subsequently held posts with the Office of Strategic Services and the Office of Intelligence Research. He joined the staff at Brandeis University in 1954 and, upon reaching mandatory retirement age, moved to the University of California at San Diego in 1965. Before the 1960's, Marcuse's books were virtually unknown outside academic circles. This obscurity was suddenly erased, however, when masses of students and other rebels embraced the ideas he set forth in this 1964 book, *One-Dimensional Man.* Marcuse argued that modern technological society had become enslaved to itself and that its own workers were in a "state of anesthesia," pacified by the products of their own labor. He argued that the only possibilities for changing this inherently repressive system, then, would come from those outside its borders—students, intellectuals, and minorities. With the decline of social unrest in the early 1970's, Marcuse's popularity faded, but he continued to write, publishing both *Counterrevolution and Revolt* and *Studies in Critical Philosophy* in 1972. Marcuse's other writings, often regarded as complex, discursive, but nonetheless stimulating, include *Reason and Revolution,* 1941, *Eros and Civilization,* 1955, and *Soviet Marxism,* 1958. Obituaries and other sources: *Current Biography,* Wilson, 1969, September, 1979; Alasdair C. MacIntyre, *Marcuse,* Fontana, 1970; Elisio Vivas, *Contra Marcuse,* Arlington House, 1971; *Atlantic,* June, 1971; Paul Mattick, *Critique of Marcuse,* Herder & Herder, 1972; *World Authors, 1950-1970,* Wilson, 1975; *Who's Who in America,* 40th edition, Marquis, 1978; *The International Who's Who,* Europa, 1979; *Who's Who,* 131st edition, St. Martin's, 1979; *New York Times,* July 31, 1979; *Washington Post,* July 31, 1979; *Time,* August 13, 1979; *Newsweek,* August 13, 1979.

* * *

MARSH, Henry
See SAKLATVALA, Beram

* * *

MARSHALL, John 1922-

PERSONAL: Born in 1922, in Nottingham, England; son of Thomas and Doris (Meyhew) Marshall; married Ann Simm, 1950; children: Simon, Andrew, Jennifer. *Education:* Attended secondary school in Loughborough, England. *Home:* 6 Shrewsbury Rd., Bolton BL1 4NW, England.

CAREER: Writer. Teacher in Bolton, England, until 1978. Lecturer at Victoria University of Manchester, 1970—. *Military service:* Royal Air Force, 1942-46. *Member:* Railway and Canal Historical Society, Stephenson Locomotive Society.

WRITINGS: The Lancashire and Yorkshire Railway, three volumes, David & Charles, 1969-72; *The Guinness Book of Rail Facts and Feats,* Guinness Superlatives, 1972, 3rd edition, 1979; *Metre Gauge Railways in South and East Switzerland,* David & Charles, 1974; *Rail Facts and Feats,* Two Continents Publishing, 1974; *Railway History in Pictures: Lancashire and Yorkshire Railway,* David & Charles, 1977; *A Biographical Dictionary of Railway Engineers,* David & Charles, 1978. Contributor to magazines, including *Railway* and *Railway World.*

WORK IN PROGRESS: Forgotten Railways in North West England; Great Northern Railway.

AVOCATIONAL INTERESTS: History of music, playing flute (amateur orchestra and chamber music groups), photography, travel, walking.

* * *

MARTIN, Benjamin F(ranklin, Jr.) 1947-

PERSONAL: Born May 3, 1947, in Winston-Salem, N.C.; son of Benjamin Franklin (a physician) and Harvey (Seward) Martin; married Judith Renaud (a librarian), May 20, 1972. *Education:* Davidson College, A.B., 1969; University of North Carolina, Ph.D., 1974. *Religion:* Episcopalian. *Residence:* Buckhannon, W.Va. *Office:* Department of History, West Virginia Wesleyan College, Buckhannon, W.Va. 26201.

CAREER: University of North Carolina, Chapel Hill, instructor in history, 1974-75; West Virginia Wesleyan College, Buckhannon, assistant professor, 1975-79, associate professor of history, 1979—. *Military service:* U.S. Army Reserve, 1969-77; became captain. *Member:* American Historical Association, Society for French Historical Studies, Western Society for French History, Phi Beta Kappa. *Awards, honors:* Woodrow Wilson fellowship, 1969; National Endowment for the Humanities fellowship, 1977.

WRITINGS: Count Albert de Mun: Paladin of the Third Republic, University of North Carolina Press, 1978. Contributor to history journals.

WORK IN PROGRESS: The Hypocrisy of Justice, on justice in Third Republic France.

* * *

MARTIN, David 1946-

PERSONAL: Born March 13, 1946, in Granite City, Ill.; son of Curtis C. (a steelworker) and Marjorie (Morris) Martin; married Gretchen Bayon (a teacher), June 15, 1968; children: Matthew David, Joshua Robert. *Education:* University of Illinois, B.S., 1969. *Home:* 6206 North 29th St., Arlington, Va. 22207. *Agent:* Ellen Levine, Curtis Brown Ltd., 575 Madison Ave., New York, N.Y. 10022. *Office:* 1055 Thomas Jefferson St. N.W., Washington, D.C. 20007.

CAREER: American School Board Journal, Evanston, Ill., managing editor, 1971-76; *Learning,* Palo Alto, Calif., managing editor, 1976-78; *American School Board Journal* and *Executive Educator,* Washington, D.C., editor and assistant publisher, 1978—. *Military service:* U.S. Air Force, 1969. *Awards, honors:* Eight All-America awards from Educational Press Association, including Laurence B. Johnson Award for Editorial Writing, 1975, for excellence in education journalism.

WRITINGS: Tethered (novel), Holt, 1979.

WORK IN PROGRESS: The Origin of Faith, a novel.

SIDELIGHTS: Martin told *CA:* "As a young man, my goal was to have a book published by the time I was thirty. Time passed. I got married, had children, and became involved in editing and writing for magazines. A few months before my thirtieth birthday, I recalled the goal and started the book. Although I missed the goal, seven years of editing and writing magazine articles did teach me the basics of the craft of writing—how to work words to build stories in the way a cabinet maker works wood to build cabinets. Writing in the evenings (typically between 10 P.M. and 2 A.M.) and on weekends, I built a presentable manuscript in approximately two years.

"No longer a young man, I no longer set goals that are linked to ages—a second novel by thirty-five, for example. I consider myself extremely fortunate even to have made an entry into this field of novel writing, but I do have this sense of having started late and being way back from where I should be. Which is why I run hard."

* * *

MARTIN, Gary M. 1936-

PERSONAL: Born July 24, 1936, in Manassa, Colo.; married Betty Jane Hanks, April 20, 1962; children: Karen, Alan, Amanda, Mark. *Education:* Adams State College, B.A., 1961, M.A., 1963; University of Oregon, Ph.D., 1965. *Religion:* Church of Jesus Christ of Latter-day Saints (Mormons). *Office:* School of Music, University of Oregon, Eugene, Ore. 97403.

CAREER: Band and choir director at parochial schools in San Luis, Colo., 1954; Mormon missionary in Switzerland and Austria, 1956-59; Adams State College, Alamosa, Colo., part-time piano teacher, 1959-61; vocal music teacher in public schools of Monte Vista, Colo., 1962-63; research assistant for Oregon State System of Higher Education, 1964-65; University of Oregon, Eugene, assistant professor, 1966-69, associate professor, 1969-74, professor of music, 1974—, head of department of music education, associate dean of School of Music, 1975, 1977, director of Eareley Musick Players (also performer). Gave private piano lessons, 1959-63. Visiting professor at University of Alaska, 1970; director of German Center for International Music Education, Stuttgart, 1970-71. Directs and participates in professional symposia and workshops.

MEMBER: Music Educators National Conference (head of Northwest region, 1968-70), Society for Research in Music Education (head of Northwest region, 1970-76; state chairperson, 1970-72), Pi Kappa Lambda (Beta Theta chapter), Phi Delta Kappa (Chi chapter).

WRITINGS: Basic Concepts in Music: A Programmed Textbook, Wadsworth, 1966, 2nd edition, 1980; *Musical Beginnings: For Teachers and Their Students,* Wadsworth, 1975. Contributor to music and education journals. Member of editorial board of *Journal of Research in Music Education,* 1978—.

* * *

MARTIN, Greg
See MILLER, George Louquet

* * *

MARTIN, Ovid A. 1904-1979

OBITUARY NOTICE: Born March 9, 1904, in Iberia, Mo.; died August 24, 1979, in McLean, Va. Journalist. Martin joined the Associated Press in Kansas City in 1933 and became the AP farm writer in Washington, D.C., in 1938. For the next thirty years he reported the events and changes in U.S. agriculture. He won a number of awards for his work, including outstanding service to American agriculture awards from the Midcontinent Farmers Association in 1966 and from the National Farmers Union in 1968. Obituaries and other sources: *Washington Post,* August 25, 1979; *Chicago Tribune,* August 26, 1979.

* * *

MARTIN, Peter W(illiam) 1939-

PERSONAL: Born April 11, 1939, in Cincinnati, Ohio; son

of Wilfred S. and Elizabeth (Myers) Martin; married Ann Wadsworth, 1964; children: Leah, Elliot, Isaac. *Education:* Cornell University, B.A. (with honors), 1961; Harvard University, J.D. (magna cum laude), 1964. *Home:* 608 East Seneca St., Ithaca, N.Y. 14850. *Office:* Law School, Cornell University, Myron Taylor Hall, Ithaca, N.Y. 14853.

CAREER: U.S. Air Force, attorney adviser in office of general counsel, 1964-67; University of Minnesota, Minneapolis, associate professor of law, 1967-71; Cornell University, Ithaca, N.Y., visiting associate professor, 1971-72, professor of law, 1972—. Visiting professor at University of Chicago, 1979-80. Chairman of Ithaca's Board of Zoning Appeals, 1974—; consultant to Administrative Conference of the United States.

WRITINGS: The Ill-Housed, Foundation Press, 1971; (with Robert J. Levy and Thomas P. Lewis) *Social Welfare and the Individual,* Foundation Press, 1971; (with Charles Donahue, Jr. and Thomas E. Kauper) *Property: An Introduction to the Concept and the Institution,* West Publishing, 1974, teacher's manual, 1975. Contributor to law journals and *Nation.*

WORK IN PROGRESS: The Art of Decoupling: The 1977 Social Security Amendments; Welfare Reform: The Demise of Cooperative Federalism?.

* * *

MASON, Edwin A. 1905-1979

OBITUARY NOTICE—See index for *CA* sketch: Born April 25, 1905, in Nottingham, England; died July 9, 1979, in West Hartford, Conn. Wildlife manager and author of two books for children, *Robins* and *Swans and Wild Geese.* In 1944 Mason founded Audubon's Arcadia Wildlife Sanctuary. He served as director of the sanctuary until 1962, when he was named director of the department of wildlife management for the Massachusetts Audubon Society. Obituaries and sources: *AB Bookman's Weekly,* August 20-27, 1979.

* * *

MASON, Frank Earl 1893-1979

OBITUARY NOTICE: Born February 8, 1893, in Milwaukee, Wis.; died June, 1979, in Leesburg, Va. Journalist and publisher. After serving as a European correspondent for the International News Service, Mason became president of that agency in 1928. From 1931 to 1945 he worked as a vice-president for National Broadcasting Company (NBC). He also served as a special assistant to the U.S. Secretary of the Navy from 1941 to 1944. Obituaries and other sources: *Who's Who in America,* 40th edition, Marquis, 1978; *New York Times,* June 19, 1979.

* * *

MASON, Gene (William) 1928-

PERSONAL: Born October 17, 1928, in Chicago, Ill.; son of Harold Abbott (an artist) and Alfrida (Johnson) Mason; married Lucille Winkler (a physician), February 19, 1954; children; Robert Scott, Jeff Richard, Linda Jean, Lori Ann. *Education:* Northwestern University, B.S., 1949; Chicago Medical School, B.Med., 1953, M.D., 1954. *Home:* 607 Shore Rd., Lake Stevens, Wash. 98258. *Office:* Medical Anesthesia Associates, 507 Medical-Dental Bldg., Everett, Wash, 98201.

CAREER: University of Washington, Seattle, resident in anesthesiology, 1956-58; Medical Anesthesia Associates, Inc., Everett, Wash., anesthesiologist, 1958—. Diplomate of National Board of Medical Examiners, 1953, and American Board of Anesthesiology, 1962. Clinical instructor at University of Washington, Seattle, 1960—; assistant professor at University of Dar es Salaam, 1972-74. President of Para-Medical Leasing Services, Inc. *Military service:* U.S. Air Force, flight surgeon, 1954-56; became captain.

MEMBER: International Anesthesia Research Society, American Medical Association, American College of Anesthesia (fellow), American Society of Anesthesiologists, Explorers Club, American Alpine Club, National Rifle Association of America, Washington State Medical Association, Washington State Society of Anesthesiologists (president, 1975-76), Washington State Federation of Anesthesiologists (president-elect, 1979), Snohomish County Medical Society, Seattle Rifle and Pistol Association, Elks, Everett Yacht Club. *Awards, honors:* Certificate from Mountain Rescue and Safety Council of Oregon, 1965; physicians recognition award from American Medical Association, 1969, 1974-77, 1978-81; certificate of recognition from Governor's Festival of the Arts, 1971, for *Minus Three.*

WRITINGS: Minus Three (nonfiction), Prentice-Hall, 1970; *Save Your License!: A Driver's Survival Guide,* Paladin Press, 1978. Author of "To the Summit of Kilimanjaro," a film released by KOMO Seattle, 1968. Contributor to medical journals, popular magazines, including *Summit, Woman's Day,* and *Washington Coach,* and newspapers.

WORK IN PROGRESS: A Cookbook for Lovers, "recipes with an aphrodisiac flair," with wife, Lucille Mason, publication expected in 1981; *A Cat Has Only Nine,* autobiographical adventures with high-risk sports.

SIDELIGHTS: Mason's mountain climbing expeditions include Century 21 Mount McKinley, 1962, American Aconcagua Expedition, 1965, American Kilimanjaro Expeditions, 1968, 1973, American Mount Elbrus Expedition, 1970, and Logan-Yukon Expedition, 1971.

Before that he raced sports cars in national competitions. He also lived in Africa for two years, where he engaged in big game hunting.

AVOCATIONAL INTERESTS: Scuba diving.

BIOGRAPHICAL/CRITICAL SOURCES: Seattle Post-Intelligencer, September 10, 1972.

* * *

MASON, R(onald) A(lison) K(ells) 1905-1971

OBITUARY NOTICE: Born January 10, 1905, in Penrose, New Zealand; died July 13, 1971. Poet, editor, dramatist, and trade union official. Known to have a tense, cynical, and pessimistic poetic style, his collected poems of 1934, *No New Thing,* was praised as "a landmark in the history of New Zealand verse." Mason was editor of the *Phoenix* magazine, a prolific contributor to left-wing political and critical journals, and a founder of the People's Theatre and the New Theatre Group in Auckland. Most of his best work is said to be found in *This Dark Will Lighten* (1941). Mason received an award from the New Zealand State Literary Fund in 1961, and held the Robert Burns Fellowship at the University of Otago in 1962. Obituaries and other sources: *Twentieth Century Writing: A Reader's Guide to Contemporary Literature,* Transatlantic, 1969; *Contemporary Poets,* St. Martin's, 1970; *Longman Companion to Twentieth Century Literature,* Longman, 1970;

* * *

MASSEY, Gerald J. 1934-

PERSONAL: Born February 11, 1934, in Wauseon, Ohio;

son of Charles Arnold and Ethel (Pry) Massey; married Ann Schultheis (a high school mathematics teacher), August 17, 1957; children: Charles, Mary, Stephane, Roberta. *Education:* University of Notre Dame, B.A. (maxima cum laude), 1956, M.A., 1960; attended University of Louvain, 1956-57; Princeton University, M.A., 1962, Ph.D., 1964. *Home:* 6035 Bunker Hill St., Pittsburgh, Pa. 15206. *Office:* Department of Philosophy, University of Pittsburgh, 724 Schenley Hall, Pittsburgh, Pa. 15260.

CAREER: Michigan State University, East Lansing, assistant professor, 1963-66, associate professor, 1966-68, professor of philosophy, 1968-70; University of Pittsburgh, Pittsburgh, Pa., professor of philosophy, 1970—, head of department, 1970-77. *Military service:* U.S. Marine Corps, 1958-61; became first lieutenant. *Member:* American Philosophical Association (member of board of officers), Association for Symbolic Logic. *Awards, honors:* Woodrow Wilson fellowship, 1956; Fulbright fellowship, 1956; Danforth fellowship, 1956; Mellon fellowship from University of Pittsburgh, 1969.

WRITINGS: Understanding Symbolic Logic, Harper, 1970.

WORK IN PROGRESS: Rules of the Mind (tentative title), on elementary logic.

* * *

MASSOW, Rosalind

PERSONAL: Born in New York, N.Y.; daughter of Morris S. (in manufacturing) and Ida (Kahn) Massow; married Norton M. Luger (a physician), January 31, 1959. *Education:* Hunter College (now of the City University of New York), B.A., 1945; also attended Columbia University. *Home and office:* 530 East 72nd St., New York, N.Y. 10021. *Agent:* Anita Diamant, Writer's Workshop, Inc., 51 East 42nd St., New York, N.Y. 10017.

CAREER: New York Journal American, New York City, reporter and feature writer, 1945-61; *Parade,* New York City, feature writer and women's editor, 1961-71; travel editor for *Medical/Mrs.,* Rye, N.Y.; free-lance writer, 1971—. President of Committee on the Status of Women and New York governor's advisory committee on minorities in the media. *Member:* Society of American Travel Writers, Overseas Press Club of America (member of board of directors, 1960—), Newswomen's Club of New York (president, 1964-66; past member of board of directors), New York Travel Writers, Sigma Delta Chi, Deadline Club. *Awards, honors:* Front Page Award from Newswomen's Club of New York, 1956, 1960,and 1966; Pegasus Award, 1967, for distinguished service.

WRITINGS: Now It's Your Turn to Travel, Macmillan, 1976. Contributor to magazines, including *Signature* and *Glamour,* and newspapers.

WORK IN PROGRESS: Revising *Now It's Your Turn to Travel,* publication by Macmillan; writing on medicine, travel and medicine, and travel and senior citizens.

* * *

MASTERS, Hardin (Wallace) 1899(?)-1979

OBITUARY NOTICE: Born c. 1899; died September 7, 1979, in Tucson, Ariz. Military officer, insurance executive, and author. Masters served in the U.S. Air Force until 1959, when he became vice-president and treasurer of an Oklahoma City insurance firm. He wrote *A Biographical Sketch* about his father, poet Edgar Lee Masters, the author of *Spoon River Anthology.* Obituaries and other sources: *Chicago Tribune,* September 12, 1979.

MATEK, Ord 1922-

PERSONAL: Born May 10, 1922, in Kamenetzpadolsk, U.S.S.R.; naturalized U.S. citizen; son of Samson (in sales) and Sonia (in sales; maiden name, Torgow) Matek; married Betsy Stein (a social worker), July 11, 1948; children: Beth Matek Weinstein, Debbie, Joel, Michael. *Education:* Roosevelt University, B.S., 1949; University of Chicago, M.S.W., 1951. *Religion:* Jewish. *Home:* 9000 Ewing, Evanston, Ill. 60203. *Office:* Jane Addams College of Social Work, University of Illinois at Chicago Circle, Chicago, Ill. 60680.

CAREER: Jewish Children's Bureau, Chicago, Ill., casework therapist and supervisor, 1951-56, director of residential treatment center for seriously emotionally disturbed adolescents, 1956-69; University of Illinois at Chicago Circle, Chicago, associate professor of social work, 1969—; lecturer at Illinois School of Professional Psychology, 1978—. Coordinator and dean of faculty for Summer Institute for Midwest Jewish Educators, 1960-67; lecturer at University of Illinois, 1964—; member of faculty at Allerton Summer Institute for Child Care, 1967-71, and field faculty at Goddard College, 1973-74; member of visiting faculty at Virginia Commonwealth University, 1973—, and University of North Carolina, summers, 1975-79. Private practice in clinical social work, 1957—; member of affiliate staff of Old Orchard Hospital. Conference chairperson in the United States and abroad; conducts workshops; member of task force on standards for licensed child caring institutions and maternity centers for State of Illinois, 1962-67. *Military service:* U.S. Army, 1943-46; served in Europe, Africa, and the Middle East.

MEMBER: American Association for Children's Residential Centers, National Association of Social Workers, Academy of Certified Social Workers, National Association of Temple Educators, American Association of Sex Educators, Counselors, and Therapists, Illinois Society for Clinical Social Work (vice-president, 1977), Illinois Child Care Society, Illinois Group Psychotherapy Society. *Awards, honors:* Curriculum award from National Association of Temple Educators, 1965, for "A Project in Interfaith Education"; first place award from National Association of Social Workers contest, 1972, for paper on sexual deviance; award from Ohio Conference on Youth Flight contest, 1974, for "Adolescent Flight: Three Basic Variations of Acting-Out."

WRITINGS: (Contributor) *From Chaos to Order: A Collective View of Residential Treatment of Children,* Child Welfare League of America, 1972; *The Bible Through Stamps,* Ktav, 1973; (contributor) Rocco D'Angelo, editor, *Confrontations With Youth,* Ohio State University Press, 1976; (contributor) Harvey Gochros and David Shore, editors, *Sexual Problems of Adolescents in Institutions,* C. C Thomas, 1979. Contributor to education, social work, and religious journals.

WORK IN PROGRESS: A Comparison of Models in the Management of Problem Behavior.

SIDELIGHTS: Matek's current research includes the use of painting as a tool in developing diagnostic skills and the use of fantasy as an enabling dimension in development throughout the life cycle. He also teaches volunteers for crisis telephone lines to respond therapeutically to callers with sex problems.

* * *

MATERER, Timothy (John) 1940-

PERSONAL: Born October 25, 1940, in Chicago, Ill.; son of

Ferdinand (a printer) and Anne (Sullivan) Materer; married Barbara Anne Leon, August 31, 1963; children: Nicholas, Andrew, Susan. *Education:* Loyola University, Chicago, Ill., B.S., 1962; Stanford University, M.A., 1966, Ph.D., 1968. *Politics:* Democrat. *Religion:* Roman Catholic. *Home:* 502 West Stewart Rd., Columbia, Mo. 65201. *Office:* Department of English, University of Missouri, Columbia, Mo. 65201.

CAREER: University of Pennsylvania, Philadelphia, assistant professor of English, 1967-73; University of Missouri, Columbia, associate professor of English, 1973—. *Awards, honors:* Grant from National Endowment for the Humanities, 1973.

WRITINGS: Wyndham Lewis, the Novelist, Wayne State University Press, 1976; *Vortex: Pound, Eliot, and Lewis,* Cornell University Press, 1979. Contributor to literature journals and *Commonweal.*

WORK IN PROGRESS: Editing the correspondence of Ezra Pound and Wyndham Lewis, for New Directions; a book on the poetry of W. H. Auden.

SIDELIGHTS: Materer writes: "I am particularly interested in the difficulty modern writers have in freeing themselves from political pressures, and in the relationship between the verbal and visual arts."

* * *

MATHE, Albert
See CAMUS, Albert

* * *

MATSUMOTO, Toru 1914(?)-1979

OBITUARY NOTICE: Born c. 1914; died of a heart ailment, July 1, 1979, in Kawasaki, Japan. Educator and author. For twenty-two years, Matsumoto's radio broadcasts taught English to the Japanese people. He also wrote several books on the English language. Obituaries and other sources: *Chicago Tribune,* July 8, 1979.

* * *

MATTESON, Michael T(ownsend) 1943-

PERSONAL: Born June 11, 1943, in Des Moines, Iowa. *Education:* Baylor University, B.A., 1965; University of Houston, M.A., 1968, Ph.D., 1969. *Home address:* Route 1, Box 689-B, Willis, Tex. 77378. *Office:* Center for Health Management, University of Houston, Houston, Tex. 77004.

CAREER: University of Houston, Houston, Tex., instructor, 1968-69, assistant professor, 1969-72, associate professor, 1972-77, professor of organizational behavior and management, 1977—, head of department, 1971-75, associate dean for academic affairs, 1976-79, director of Center for Health Management, 1979—. Conducts management training programs; speaker at scholarly meetings; consultant to Exxon Co., Shell Chemical Co., and Goodyear Tire & Rubber Co. *Member:* American Psychological Association, National Academy of Management, Southwestern Academy of Management, Texas Psychological Association, Sigma Xi, Sigma Iota Epsilon, Beta Gamma Sigma.

WRITINGS: (Contributor) J. Champagne, editor, *The Hardcore Low-Skilled Worker: A Collection of Papers,* Center for Human Resources, University of Houston, 1970; (editor) *Contemporary Personnel Management: A Reader on Human Resources,* Canfield Press, 1972; (editor and contributor) *The Individual and the Organization,* Harper, 1973; (contributor) M. Miner and J. Miner, editors, *Policy Issues in Contemporary Personnel and Industrial Relations,* Macmillan, 1977; *Management Classics,* Goodyear Publishing, 1977; *Work and Stress: A Managerial Perspective,* Scott, Foresman, 1980. Contributor to *American Petroleum Institute Validity Information Handbook.* Contributor of about twenty articles to business journals and journals in the behavioral and medical sciences.

* * *

MATTHEWS, Ellen 1950-

PERSONAL: Born May 2, 1950, in Greencastle, Ind.; daughter of Kendall Ray (an educator) and Murl (a secretary; maiden name, McGinnis) Keller; married Dwight Matthews (a medical researcher), August 12, 1972. *Education:* Butler University, B.S., 1972; Indiana University, M.S., 1975. *Religion:* Society of Friends (Quakers). *Home:* 809 Berick, University City, Mo. 63132. *Office:* New City School, 5209 Waterman, St. Louis, Mo. 63108.

CAREER: Elementary school teacher in Greencastle, Ind., 1972-73, and Brown County, Ind., 1973-77; New City School, St. Louis, Mo., elementary teacher, 1977—. *Member:* Society of Children's Book Writers, Missouri Press Women.

WRITINGS: Getting Rid of Roger (juvenile), Westminster, 1978; *The Trouble With Leslie* (juvenile), Westminster, 1979.

SIDELIGHTS: Ellen Matthews writes: "I enjoy working with children and helping them develop their reading interests and skills. My writing grew out of this, and I find that being a writer of children's books helps me understand their problems and interests better and also helps me create something enjoyable for the children in my classroom." *Avocational interests:* Running, bicycling, backpacking, photography, cooking, camping, outdoor activities.

* * *

MATUTE, Ana Maria 1925-

PERSONAL: Born July 26, 1925, in Barcelona, Spain; daughter of Facundo and Maria (Ausejo) Matute; married in 1952 (divorced in 1963); children: Juan-Pablo. *Education:* Attended Damas Negras French Nuns College. *Home:* 55 S/a Urgel, Barcelona 11, Spain.

CAREER: Writer. Visiting professor at Indiana University, Bloomington, 1965-66, and at University of Oklahoma, Norman, 1969. Writer-in-residence at University of Virginia, Charlottesville, 1978-79. *Member:* Hispanic Society of America, American Association of Teachers of Spanish and Portuguese (honorary fellow), Sigma Delta Pi (Hispanic chapter). *Awards, honors:* Runner-up for Premio Nadal, 1947, for *Los abel;* Cafe Gijon Prize, 1952, for *Fiesta al noroeste;* Planeta Prize, 1954, for *Pequeno teatro;* Critics Prize and Premio Nacional de Literature, 1958, for *Los hijos muertos;* Premio Miguel Cervantes, 1959, for *Los hijos muertos;* Premio Nadal, 1960, for *Primera memoria;* Lazarillo Prize, 1965, for *El polizon del "Ulises";* Fastenrath Prize, 1969, for *Los soldados lloran de noche.*

WRITINGS—In English: *Los hijos muertos,* Planeta, 1958, translation by Joan MacLean published as *The Lost Children,* Macmillan, 1965; *Primera memoria,* Destino, 1960, translation by Elaine Kerrigan published as *School of the Sun,* Pantheon, 1963 (translation by James Holman Mason published in England as *Awakening,* Hutchinson, 1963).

Other works: *Los abel* (title means "The Abels"), Destino, 1948; *Fiesta al noroeste, La ronda,* [and] *Los ninos buenos* (titles mean "Festival of the Northwest, The Round, [and] The Good Children"), A. Aguado, 1953; *Pequeno teatro* (title means "Little Theater"), Planeta, 1954; *En est tierra* (title means "On This Land"), Exito, 1955; *Los cuentos, vagabundos* (title means "The Stories, Vagabonds"), Ediciones G.P., 1956; *Los ninos tontos* (title means "The Foolish Children"), Arion, 1956; *El pais de la pizarra* (title means "The Country of the Blackboard"), Molino, 1957; *El tiempo* (title means "The Time"), Mateu, 1957; *Los mercaderes* (title means "The Merchants"), Destino, 1959.

Paulina, el mundo y las estrellas (title means "Pauline, the World and the Stars"), Garbo, 1960; *El saltamontes verde* [y] *El aprendiz* (titles mean "The Green Grasshopper [and] The Apprentice"), Lumen, 1960; *Tres y un sueno* (title means "Three and a Dream"), Destino, 1961; *A la mitad del camino* (title means "In the Middle of the Road"), Rocas, 1961; *Historias de la Artamila,* Destino, 1961, published as *Doce historias de la Artamila,* Harcourt, 1965; *El arrepentido* (title means "The Repentant One"), Rocas, 1961; *Libro de juegos para los ninos de los otros* (title means "Book of Games for the Children of Others"), Lumen, 1961; *Caballito loco* [y] *Carnivalito* (titles mean "Crazy Little Horse [and] Little Carnival"), Lumen, 1962; *El rio* (title means "The River"), Argos, 1963; *Los soldados lloran de noche* (title means "The Soldiers Weep at Night"), Destino, 1964; *El polizon del "Ulises"* (title means "The Draft of 'Ulysses'"), Lumen, 1965; *Algunos muchachos* (title means "Some Children"), Destino, 1968; *La trampa* (title means "The Trap"), Destino, 1969; *La torre vigia* (title means "The Watch Tower"), Lumen, 1971; *Olvidado rey Gudu* (title means "Forgotten King Gudu"), Lumen, 1980; *Diablo vuelve a casa* (title means "Devil, Come Back Home"), Destino, 1980. Also author of *La pequena vide* (title means "The Little Life"), Tecnos.

SIDELIGHTS: Ana Maria Matute was ten years old when the Spanish Civil War broke out; it disrupted her education and became a potent, permanent force in her life. As a child, she has said, she confronted the fact that the world is filled with much that is terrifying.

By the time she published her first story for Destino in 1942, Matute was using writing as a vehicle for expressing anger toward a cruel, unjust world. The civil war became a recurring theme in her work, sometimes merely as a backdrop (as in *Pequeno teatro*), but more often as her central concern. Nevertheless, unlike many post-war Spanish writers, Matute is not a political partisan: she conveys what Desmond MacNamara called "unpolitical Spanish pessimism," focusing not on party machinations but on the angst of her people, particularly the children.

Indeed, Matute "sees the world through the eyes of childhood [with a] quality of mystery, of magic, of fairy tale, combined in a unique mixture with the harsh and bitter realities of life," wrote George Wythe. Her children are introverted victims of an adult world whose cruelty they cannot understand; and they suffer the existential pains of alienation and despair one usually thinks of as reserved for adults.

Matute creates her hostile world by means of an imaginative, personal style characterized, J. Wesley Childers has noted, "by simile, metaphor, oxymoron, and the use of natural phenomena to reflect human frustrations." To Rafael Bosch, her language is "direct and wonderfully simple without ceasing to be tremendously creative and poetic."

Matute's manuscripts are housed at the Mugar Library of Boston University, which has organized the Ana Maria Matute Collection. Editions of her books have appeared in many languages, including Italian, French, German, Russian, Portuguese, Swedish, Polish, Japanese, Hebrew, Lithuanian, Bulgarian, and Esperanto.

BIOGRAPHICAL/CRITICAL SOURCES: New Leader, July, 1965; *Modern Language Journal,* November, 1966, December, 1971; *Books Abroad,* winter, 1966, winter, 1970, summer, 1972; *New Statesman,* October 27, 1967; *Times Literary Supplement,* December 28, 1967, October 8, 1971; Margaret E. W. Jones, *The Literary World of Ana Maria Matute,* University Press of Kentucky, 1970; Janet Diaz, *Ana Maria Matute,* Twayne, 1971; *Contemporary Literary Criticism,* Volume 11, Gale, 1979.

* * *

MAUDUDI, Maulana Abdul Ala 1903(?)-1979

OBITUARY NOTICE: Born c. 1903, in Aurangabad, India; died September 22, 1979, in Buffalo, N.Y. Scholar, party leader, and author. Maududi was a founder of Pakistan's Jamaat-i-Islami party, a fundamentalist Islamic group. He wrote a number of books on Islam and was the first recipient of the Faisal Award for Islamic literature. Obituaries and other sources: *New York Times,* September 23, 1979.

* * *

MAURIAC, Claude 1914-

PERSONAL: Born April 25, 1914, in Paris, France; son of Francois (a writer) and Jeanne (Lafon) Mauriac; married Marie-Claude Monte, July 11, 1951; children: Gerard, Nathalie, Gilles. *Education:* University of Paris, doctorate in law, 1943. *Home:* 24 Quai de Bethune, Paris 4e, France. *Office: Figaro,* Paris, France.

CAREER: Private secretary to General Charles de Gaulle, 1944-49; founder and director of *Liberte de l'Esprit* (magazine), 1949-53; literary critic for *Figaro* (newspaper), 1954—; film critic for *Figaro litteraire,* 1958—. *Member:* Societe Figaro-Edition (administrator, 1972—). *Awards, honors:* Chevalier de la Legion d'honneur; Prix Sainte Beuve, 1949, for *Andre Breton: Essai;* Prix Medicis, 1959, for *Le Diner en ville.*

WRITINGS—Novels: *Toutes les femmes sont fatales,* Michel, 1951, translation by Richard Howard published as *All Women Are Fatal,* Braziller, 1964; *Le Diner en ville,* Michel, 1959, translation by Merloyd Lawrence published as *The Dinner Party,* Braziller, 1960; *La Marquise sortit a cinq heures,* Michel, 1961, translation by Howard published as *The Marquise Went Out at Five,* Braziller, 1962; *L'Agrandissement* (title means "The Enlargement"), Michel, 1963; *L'Oubli* (title means "Oblivion"), Grasset, 1966.

Plays: *La Conversation* (also see below; first produced in Paris at Theatre de Lutece, January, 1966), Grasset, 1964; "Les Parisiens du dimanche" (also see below), first produced in Montreal at French Pavilion of World's Fair, June, 1967; *Theatre* (contains "La Conversation," "Ici, maintenant," "Le Cirque," "Les Parisiens du dimanche," and "Le Hun"), Grasset, 1968.

Criticism: *Introduction a une mystique de l'enfer* (title means "Introduction to a Mystique of Hell"), Grasset, 1938; *Aimer Balzac* (title means "To Love Balzac"), Soledi, 1945; *Jean Cocteau; ou, La Verite du mensonge* (title means "Jean Cocteau; or, The Truth of the Lie"), O. Lieutier, 1945; *Malreaux; ou, Le Mal du heros,* Grasset, 1946; *Andre Breton: Essai* (title means "Andre Breton: An Essay"), Editions de Flore, 1949; *Hommes et idees d'aujourd'hui* (title means "Men and Ideas of Today"), Michel, 1953; *L'Amour du cinema* (title means "Love of the Cinema"), Michel, 1954; (contributor) Jacques Hamelin, editor, *Process imaginaires: Affaires Colonel Shabert, Julien Sorel, Therese Desqueyroux,* Editions de Minuit, 1954; *Petite Litterature du cinema* (titile means "Handbook of the Cinema"), Editions du Cerf, 1957; *L'Alitterature contemporaine,* Michel, 1958, translation by Samuel I. Stone published as *The New Literature,* Braziller, 1959; *De la litterature a l'alitterature,* Grasset, 1969.

Other: *La Corporation dans l'etat* (title means "The Corporation in the State"), Imprimerie Briere, 1951; *Conversations avec Andre Gide: Extraits d'un journal,* Michel, 1951, translation by Michael Lebeck published as *Conversations With Andre Gide,* Braziller, 1965; (editor) *Proust,* Seuil, 1953, reprinted, 1977; *Le Temps immobile* (title means "Motionless Time"), Grasset, Volume I: *Une Amitie contrariee,* 1970, Volume II: *Les Espaces imaginaires,* 1975, Volume III: *Et comme l'esperance est violence,* 1976, Volume IV: *La Terrace de Malagar,* 1977; *Un Autre de Gaulle: Journal 1944-1954,* Hachette, 1971, translation by Moura Budberg and Gordon Latta published as *The Other de Gaulle: Diaries 1944-1954,* John Day, 1973.

Writer of weekly literary column, "La Vie des lettres," in *Figaro,* 1954—. Contributor to *L'Express,* 1972—.

SIDELIGHTS: Mauriac is best known for his suite of four novels, *The Interior Dialogue*. Principally, as Alice Mayhew observed, "they concern the mysterious and tricky technique of communication with others, and among one's selves." To illustrate this concern, Mauriac experiments with a complex presentation of simultaneous perceptions and points of view. A writer in the New Novelist tradition, he abandons conventional devices of fiction to seek greater effects of realism. Instead of traditional plots, narratives, and characters, his fiction consists of interior monologues and dialogues, the displacement of chronological time, and a minimum of narrative description.

The first volume, *All Women Are Fatal,* recounts four episodes in the life of Bertrand Carnejoux, the central character of the tetralogy and an aspiring novelist. Each chapter, presented as an interior monologue, introduces Carnejoux to the impossibility of love and the solitude of existence. Preoccupied with death and his own insignificance, Carnejoux seeks release from his isolation in a series of sexual encounters. Mayhew commented: "At the bottom of all this lies a personal obsession about the inevitability of solitude and the mystery of communion. One Mauriac personage affects another, if he does, principally by being a constant reminder that each is entirely replaceable for the other, that all men are interchangeable, all women are fatal, that each encounter is a reminder of our habitual aridity." V. R. Yantelli described the book as "a magnificent piece of rigorous writing, hard, spare, tightly interlocked, and, therefore, difficult to read." Cade Ware pointed out "the classic strength of [Mauriac's] style and the richness and value of his thought."

In *The Dinner Party,* his second novel, Mauriac develops an innovative "recording" technique for his realistic purposes. Focusing on a Parisian dinner party of eight people, "the book consists exclusively of a supposed transcription of the conversation and thoughts of those eight people seated around the table," reported Leon S. Roudiez. There is practically no description of the scene, however, beyond a diagram of the seating arrangements, and no narrator to identify the various characters. For the reader, the difficulties of the technique "require intense concentration," remarked Orville Prescott, but Henry Peyre felt that the book was "a virtuoso piece brilliantly carried off." Given the absence of plot and narrator, Roudiez observed, the effect Mauriac produces "affords a greater illusion of reality partly because of its newness, partly because the reader has been granted godlike powers to see (or hear) things 'as they really are.'" Whitney Balliett commented that on the strength of this approach, "Mauriac mercilessly and fruitfully examines the three great and simultaneous realities—the world outside us, the world inside us, and the interaction between the two. . . . He has created a super-reality pieced together out of his observations and his imagination." Though Richard McLaughlin thought that "Not everybody can be expected to go along with this technical experimenting, brilliant as it is," Balliett concluded: "This is a miraculous book, and not only for the reason that it will leave none of its readers unchanged."

With *The Marquise Went Out at Five,* Mauriac considers both his particular approach to fiction and the nature of time. The setting is a busy Paris intersection, the Carrefour de Buci, between the hours of five and six in the afternoon. Carnejoux spends the hour watching the street activity below his balcony and meditating about a novel he intends to write—the very novel, in fact, that Mauriac himself writes. "Once more there is no conventional narrator, only what appear to be transciptions of dialogues, interior dialogues, and interior monologues," Roudiez remarked. But as Mauriac's surrogate, he noted, Carnejoux's task throughout the tetralogy has been "to express himself on the techniques of fiction." In this novel, however, the distinction between author and character, Mauriac and Carnejoux, is very often dissolved. As Roudiez observed, "Mauriac seems to be sitting in an ideal hall of mirrors—observing himself watching himself writing a novel." This curious blurring of the difference between fiction and reality, Mayhew claimed, "is a major conception."

Another major feature of the novel is its consideration of time. In this book, Balliett remarked, "time is no longer an endless clicking by of present moments but past, present, and future forced into now." Through the Carrefour de Buci pass eight centuries of Parisian life. Roudiez explained: "Historical persons who have lived on the spot are followed by others who merely passed by. These are succeeded by fictional characters . . . and by real persons who simply might have passed by." Voltaire, Bonaparte, and Hugo all make an appearance. According to Robert Alter, "there is an acute perception of two concentric abysses beneath the artifice of the novel—history and death. *The Marquise Went Out* . . . attempts to exhaust the human experience intersecting [a] carefully delimited time and place." Roudiez concluded: "Broader in scope and more varied than his *The Dinner Party, The Marquise Went Out at Five* is an exciting accomplishment that keeps the reader constantly alert and challenged."

L'Agrandissement closes the series with a long interior monologue by Carnejoux. The entire novel, which expands upon a detail from *The Marquise Went Out,* attempts to reproduce Carnejou's thoughts in the two-minutes time it takes for a traffic light to change signals. He is still observing the Carrefour de Buci and ruminating on the techniques of his fiction, but for Mauriac "it marks a point beyond which the Carnejoux series could not logically be continued," Roudiez stated. Such a compression of time, he suggested, "might have permitted an enlargement encompassing the infinite depth of the human psyche." But as Alter observed, the attempt is "doomed to failure" because life and time are "surrounded, penetrated, absorbed . . . by the infinite pullulations of innumerable past moments." Nevertheless, Roudiez held that "the experiment was well worth undertaking."

In addition to his fiction, Mauriac has published several collections of critical essays, diaries, and journals. His essays in *The New Literature,* which examine the motivations behind much experimental fiction, cut "directly to the heart of his subject," wrote Kenneth Millar. "Because he himself is so familiar with the background of thought and experience in which this particular trend of literature has its source . . . , Mauriac is an excellent guide and initiator," Germaine Bree stated. His *The Other de Gaulle: Diaries 1944-1954,* which includes Mauriac's experience as a private secretary to the French leader, was described by J. A. Robbins as "far and away the most enlightening and valuable document on de Gaulle we have yet." *Le Temps immobile,* a series of journals covering the period between 1958 and 1975, largely concerns the influence of four men in Mauriac's life: General de Gaulle, Andre Malraux, Michel Foucault, and his novelist father, Francois. But it also describes Mauriac's active life in the politics of protest, as well as his preoccupation with the problem of time. Douglas Johnson thought that "this is a journal of particular interest and distinction."

BIOGRAPHICAL/CRITICAL SOURCES: Saturday Review, May 9, 1959, May 7, 1960, May 26, 1962, August 1, 1964; *San Francisco Chronicle,* May 31, 1959, May 10, 1960; *New York Times Book Review,* May 1, 1960, April 29, 1962, January 27, 1974; *New Yorker,* May 14, 1960, September 15, 1962; *Commonweal,* May 20, 1960, September 25, 1964; *New York Herald Tribune Book Review,* June 12, 1960, May 20, 1962; *Atlantic Monthly,* June, 1960; *Time,* April 27, 1962; *Newsweek,* August 10, 1964; *Best Sellers,* August 15, 1964; *Book Week,* August 16, 1964; *Nation,* February 1, 1965; Leon S. Roudiez, *French Fiction Today: A New Direction,* Rutgers University Press, 1972; *America,* March 9, 1974; *TriQuarterly 33,* spring, 1975; *Times Literary Supplement,* September 17, 1976; *Contemporary Literary Criticism,* Volume 9, Gale, 1978; *World Literature Today,* spring, 1979.*

—Sketch by B. Hal May

* * *

MAXWELL, Elsa 1883-1963

OBITUARY NOTICE: Born May 24, 1883, in Keokuk, Iowa; died November 1, 1963, in New York, N.Y. International society hostess, professional party giver, song writer, lecturer, author, and syndicated columnist. Maxwell's parties were the rage in continental Europe after World War I. In the United States during the 1940's, she reported the comings and goings of high society through her radio program, "Elsa Maxwell's Party Line," and a nationally syndicated gossip column (Press Alliance, Inc.). Maxwell appeared in "Stage Door Canteen" and other motion pictures, was the author of eighty published songs, and author of several books, including her autobiography, *My Last Fifty Years.* Obituaries and other sources: *Current Biography,* Wilson 1943, January, 1964; *The ASCAP Biographical Dictionary of Composers, Authors, and Publishers,* American Society of Composers, Authors and Publishers, 1966; *Who Was Who in America,* 4th edition, Marquis, 1968.

* * *

MAY, Herbert Gordon 1904-1977

OBITUARY NOTICE—See index for *CA* sketch: Born December 26, 1904, in Fair Haven, Vt.; died October 8, 1977, in Jacksonville, Fla. Educator, biblical scholar, editor, and author of books in his field. May was emeritus professor at Oberlin College where he had been professor of Old Testament language and literature since 1934. He was editor of the *Oxford Bible Atlas* and a member of the translation committee for the *Revised Standard Version Common Bible.* Obituaries and other sources: *Who's Who in the World,* 2nd edition, Marquis, 1973; *Directory of American Scholars,* Volume IV: *Philosophy, Religion, and Law,* 6th edition, Bowker, 1974; *New York Times,* October 11, 1977; *AB Bookman's Weekly,* February 6, 1978.

* * *

MAYER, Ellen Moers
See MOERS, Ellen

* * *

MAYER, Ralph 1895-1979

OBITUARY NOTICE—See index for *CA* sketch: Born August 11, 1895, in New York, N.Y.; died August 3, 1979, in New York, N.Y. Artist, educator, editor, and author. An expert on the technology of painting, Mayer was the author of the standard reference work, *The Artists Handbook of Materials and Techniques.* He also wrote *The Painter's Craft* and *A Dictionary of Art Terms and Techniques,* as well as serving as technical editor for *American Artist* magazine. Obituaries and other sources: *Who's Who in American Art,* Bowker, 1978; *New York Times,* August 4, 1979; *AB Bookman's Weekly,* October 8, 1979.

* * *

MAYO, Bernard 1902-1979

OBITUARY NOTICE: Born February 13, 1902, in Lewiston, Me.; died August 20, 1979, in Charlottesville, Va. Historian, educator, and author. Mayo taught for thirty-two years at the University of Virginia, where he retired as professor emeritus in 1972. He wrote a number of books, including *Henry Clay, Spokesman of the New West* and *Jefferson Himself: A Personal Narrative of a Many-Sided American.* Obituaries and other sources: *Who's Who in America,* 38th edition, Marquis, 1974; *Directory of American Scholars,* Volume I: *History,* 6th edition, Bowker, 1974; *Washington Post,* August 23, 1979.

* * *

MAZUR, Paul M(yer) 1892-1979

OBITUARY NOTICE: Born December 9, 1892, in Boston, Mass.; died July 30, 1979, in New York, N.Y. Investment banker and author. Mazur was a senior partner with Lehman Brothers, the New York City investment banking firm, where he began working in 1923. Called "the father of modern retailing" by an associate, he promoted installment buying and the five-day work week; later he complained that there was too much mathematics and not enough sociology in economics. Among his several books are *New Roads to Prosperity,* 1931, *The Dynamics of Economic Growth,* 1965, and *Unfinished Business: A Banker Looks at the Economy,* 1973. Obituaries and other sources: *Who's Who in America,* 40th edition, Marquis, 1978; *New York Times,* August 2, 1979.

* * *

McCABE, Charles B. 1899-1970

OBITUARY NOTICE: Born August 26, 1899, in Cleveland, Ill.; died May 29, 1970. Publisher of the *New York Daily Mirror* for twenty-eight years, executive with the Hearst Corporation from 1943-64, radio and television executive. McCabe directed the 1964-65 New York World's Fair, and served as consultant to many national and community organizations. Obituaries and other sources: *New York Times,* May 31, 1970; *Who Was Who in America,* 5th edition, Marquis, 1973.

* * *

McCALLUM, Ronald Buchanan 1898-1973

OBITUARY NOTICE—See index for *CA* sketch: Born August 28, 1898, in Scotland; died in 1973 in England. Educator, political scientist, historian, politician, and author of books in his field. McCallum, who was a lecturer in comparative politics at Oxford University, was best known for his initiation of the Nuffield series of studies on British general elections. He also coined the term psephology, the study of elections, which has been used by political scientists and educators around the world. McCallum served for many years on the city council of Oxford, England. Obituaries and other sources: *AB Bookman's Weekly,* July 30, 1973.

* * *

McCONNELL, Raymond A(rnott) 1915-1979

OBITUARY NOTICE: Born December 31, 1915, in North Ridgeville, Ohio; died October 22, 1979, in California. Journalist and author. McConnell was managing editor of the Journal Newspapers in Lincoln, Neb., from 1941 to 1957, and later became executive editor of the *Pasadena Star-News.* While in Lincoln he won a 1949 Pulitzer Prize for public service. His book, *Trampled Terraces,* appeared in 1950. Obituaries and other sources: *Who's Who in America,* 40th edition, Marquis, 1978; *New York Times,* October 25, 1979.

* * *

McCOWEN, George S(mith), Jr. 1935-

PERSONAL: Born January 22, 1935, in Macon, Ga.; son of George Smith (in business) and Doris (Horne) McCowen; married Gail Elizabeth Boden, June 23, 1962; children: Cecily Elizabeth, Duncan Green. *Education:* University of the South, B.A., 1957; Emory University, M.A., 1958, Ph.D., 1966. *Politics:* Independent. *Religion:* Episcopal. *Home:* 550 Hoyt St. S.E., Salem, Ore. 97302. *Office:* Department of History, Willamette University, Salem, Ore. 97301.

CAREER: Emory University, Atlanta, Ga., instructor in history, 1960-61; University of North Carolina, Greensboro, instructor in history, 1961-62; Wofford College, Spartanburg, S.C., assistant professor of history, 1962-67; Willamette University, Salem, Ore., associate professor, 1967-72, professor of history, 1972—, head of department, 1967-78. Member of advisory committee of Oregon Joint Committee for the Humanities, 1972-76. Conducted historical research in England, 1976. *Member:* American Historical Association, Organization of American Historians, American Association of University Professors, Oregon Historical Society, Phi Beta Kappa, Omicron Delta Kappa, Pi Gamma Mu. *Awards, honors:* Award from Daughters of the American Revolution, 1957; scholarship from Colonial Dames of America, 1959; grant from Shell Oil Company, 1968; Atkinson fellowship from Willamette University, 1973, 1979.

WRITINGS: The British Occupation of Charleston, 1780-1782, University of South Carolina Press, 1972.

SIDELIGHTS: McCowen noted that his research interests are "centered on the nature of political allegiance in the American Revolution and the sense of the past in Henry Adams and Henry James." He continued: "The line of demarcation between partiots and loyalists was often blurred as individuals switched sides, sometimes more than once. Ties of family and friendship often crossed political boundaries and created obligations in conflict with differences over political ideology. It is the impact of this on political allegiance during the Revolution that is the focus of my research into the history of the British-occupied cities.

"As a novelist James was intensely concerned with the sense of the past and its relation to the present. But James's concern with the past was essentially that of a precursor of the existentialist view of history, while Adams was positivistic in approach seeking to find the essential laws by which history operated. On the other hand, for James, the past was a reality in the present sometimes threatening, at other times inspiring, sensitive individuals. Essentially James sought to come to terms with the past by subtle, incisive delineation of feeling; Adams sought to master history by the power of analysis. Both men, in following two quite different paths sought a kind of personal affirmation, one might even say salvation, in their understanding of the past."

* * *

McCOWN, James H. 1911-

PERSONAL: Born February 24, 1911, in Mobile, Ala.; son of James Moore (in the oil industry) and Rosemary (Hart) McCown. *Education:* Spring Hill College, B.S., 1932; also attended St. Mary's School of Theology, St. Mary's, Kan. *Politics:* "Ardent Democrat." *Home and office:* 1321 El Paso St., San Antonio, Tex. 78207.

CAREER: Entered Society of Jesus (Jesuits), ordained Roman Catholic priest; high school teacher at Roman Catholic schools; high school counselor in Shreveport, La., 1950-51.

WRITINGS: Elephants Have the Right of Way: A Year of Content in East Africa, June 21, 1968-June 21, 1969 (travel book), Liguori Publications, 1974. Author of religious pamphlets.

WORK IN PROGRESS: Memories of a Catholic Boyhood (tentative title), an autobiography.

SIDELIGHTS: McCown writes: "I seem to have the ability to enjoy and appreciate foreign cultures and people, though this facility has developed in the past few years as a reaction to some unexpected, even unsought, traveling. I have been praised for being observant, warmly reactive to other cultures and peoples. My earlier writings were mostly dogmatic religious treatises and devotional tracts."

* * *

McDONALD, Stephen L(ee) 1924-

PERSONAL: Born August 8, 1924, in Arkadelphia, Ark.; son of Claud Bethel (in sales) and Ruth (Gresham) McDonald; married Elizabeth Brewer, August 14, 1945; children: Martha Elizabeth McDonald Worchel, Kathryn Ann McDonald McGlothlin. *Education:* Louisiana Polytechnic Institute (now Louisiana Tech University), B.A., 1947; University of Texas, M.A., 1948, Ph.D., 1951. *Home:* 4002 Sierra Dr., Austin, Tex. 78731. *Office:* Department of Economics, University of Texas, Austin, Tex. 78712.

CAREER: University of Texas, Austin, assistant professor of economics, 1950-56; Humble Oil & Refining Co., Houston, Tex., economist, 1956-57; Louisiana State University, Baton Rouge, associate professor, 1957-59, professor of finance and economics, 1959-61; University of Texas, professor of economics, 1961—, head of department, 1972-76,

1978-79. *Military service:* U.S. Navy, 1943-46; became lieutenant junior grade. *Member:* American Economic Association, Southern Economic Association, Southwestern Social Science Association.

WRITINGS: *Federal Tax Treatment of Income From Oil and Gas,* Brookings Institution, 1963; *Petroleum Conservation in the United States,* Johns Hopkins Press, 1971; *The Leasing of Federal Lands for Fossil Fuels Production,* Johns Hopkins Press, 1979. Member of board of editors of *Southern Economic Journal,* 1961-64.

WORK IN PROGRESS: A book on energy policy.

* * *

McFADDEN, Thomas M(ore) 1935-

PERSONAL: Born November 12, 1935, in Brooklyn, N.Y.; son of Thomas G. (in business) and Kathryn (Smith) McFadden; married Monica Dowdall (a social worker), August 16, 1967; children: Monica, David. *Education:* Cathedral College, B.A., 1957; Gregorian University, S.T.L., 1961; Catholic University of America, S.T.D., 1963. *Politics:* Democrat. *Home:* 1217 Larchmont Ave., Havertown, Pa. 19083. *Office:* Department of Theology, St. Joseph's University, Philadelphia, Pa. 19131.

CAREER: Ordained Roman Catholic priest, 1960; assistant at Roman Catholic churches in Brooklyn, N.Y., 1961-67; laicized, 1967; Corpus Instrumentorum, Inc., Washington, D.C., associate editor, 1968-70; St. Joseph's University, Philadelphia, Pa., assistant professor, 1970-73, associate professor, 1973-78, professor of theology, 1978—. Member of board of directors of Sane Education Fund, 1972—. Associate of Danforth Foundation, 1973—. *Member:* College Theology Society (head of publications committee, 1973-78; member of board of directors, 1976-78), American Association of University Professors (chapter president, 1976-78), Alpha Sigma Nu. *Awards, honors:* Grant from U.S. Department of Health, Education & Welfare, 1973, for study in India; Lindbach Award from Lindbach Foundation, 1978.

WRITINGS: (Editor) *Does Jesus Make a Difference?,* Seabury, 1974; (editor) *Liberation, Revolution, and Freedom,* Seabury, 1975; (editor) *America in Theological Perspective,* Seabury, 1976; (editor) *Theology Confronts a Changing World,* Twenty-Third Publications, 1977; (contributing editor) *Encyclopedic Dictionary of Religion,* three volumes, Corpus Publications, 1979. Area editor for *New Catholic Encyclopedia.*

WORK IN PROGRESS: Research on the relationship between economic structures and values systems, with emphasis on the distinction between capitalism and democratic socialism.

SIDELIGHTS: McFadden writes: "Over the past eight years, my editing and major professional involvements have been geared to the increased professionalization of religious studies on the undergraduate level. I now see that interest shifting to issues dealing with social change in the United States: the breakdown of society-centered culture to a more narcissistic one. The Puritan ethic which supported capitalism is abandoned, and a new set of values with great bearing upon economic and political choices will have to be forged. The definition of those values as generous and egalitarian or as narrow and exploitive should be a goal of academic humanists."

* * *

McGEE, (Doctor) Frank 1921-1974

OBITUARY NOTICE: Born September 12, 1921, in Monroe, La.; died April 17, 1974, in Scarsdale, N.Y. News commentator with National Broadcasting Co. (NBC) for fifteen years. Host of the NBC-TV morning show, "Today," and anchorman on the radio program, "Monitor," and the "NBC Evening News." During his years as a broadcaster, McGee covered presidential conventions and elections, space flights, and integration fights. Jack Gould of the *New York Times* commented that McGee had an "uncanny knack for flawless delivery under any circumstances." Some of McGee's best work was with documentaries, as demonstrated in the "instant specials" of the early 1960's, which were unscheduled news breaks documenting news events nearly as they happened. His three-hour documentary concerning the black struggle for civil rights, "The American Revolution of '63," earned McGee a Peabody Award in 1964. 'Same Mud, Same Blood," a one-hour documentary about the relations between black and white soldiers in the Vietnam War, was honored with a Brotherhood Award from the National Conference of Christians and Jews in 1967. CBS anchorman Walter Cronkite observed of McGee, "Behind Frank's soft-spoken, almost courtly manner, one sensed character and integrity of iron." Obituaries and other sources: *Current Biography,* Wilson, 1964; *Celebrity Register,* 3rd edition, Simon & Schuster, 1973; *New York Times,* April 16, 1974; *Who's Who in America,* 38th edition, Marquis, 1974.

* * *

McLAUGHLIN, Samuel Clarke 1924-

PERSONAL: Born October 6, 1924, in Greenwich, Conn.; son of Samuel Clarke and Mildred (Skibsted) McLaughlin; married Constance Barnard, January 26, 1945; children: Clarke, Marion McLaughlin DeJong. *Education:* Tufts College (now University), B.S., 1946, M.S., 1948; further graduate study at Harvard University, 1948-50. *Politics:* Democrat. *Religion:* Christian. *Home address:* R.F.D. 2, Limerick, Maine 04048.

CAREER: Kresge Eye Institute, Detroit, Mich., research associate, 1954-57; University of Michigan, Ann Arbor, instructor in ophthalmology, 1957-61; Tufts University, Medford, Mass., research associate, 1961-68, associate professor of psychology, 1968-76; independent researcher and writer, 1976—. *Military service:* U.S. Naval Reserve, active duty, 1943-46, 1951-54; became lieutenant commander.

WRITINGS: *On Feeling Good,* Autumn Press, 1978. Contributor of about twenty-five articles to scientific journals.

WORK IN PROGRESS: *The Geometry of Love* (tentative title).

SIDELIGHTS: McLaughlin writes: "The oldest and most persistent idea in the history of human thought is that there are higher levels of reality and existence than the world of matter and substance that are presented to us by our senses, and that human beings can somehow, by transcending sensory experience, attain those higher levels. This is the underlying theme and motivating principle of all great works of art. My purpose in writing is to express this ancient doctrine in the idiom of modern man—in the language of rational inquiry. I intend to bring that concept to center stage in Western culture, and to give it a prominent place among the ideas and symbols by which Western man, the rationalist and materialist, orders his existence and creates his reality.

"Looking back, it seems absurd that there could have been a time in my life when awareness of a higher level of being was not a central fact of my existence; but in fact I was forty-seven years old when I first became interested in the idea. In

1971, at the request of some of my students, I began teaching a course on 'altered states of consciousness,' a topic that was new to me. I discovered then that a sub-topic of 'altered states of consciousness' is 'higher states of consciousness,' and that the higher states of consciousness are states in which one becomes aware of higher levels of reality and existence. I began to envisage the possibility of using this concept to put the ancient teachings on a scientific footing. In 1976, I resigned my teaching position in order to devote full time to this task."

* * *

McLAUGHLIN, Virginia Yans
See YANS-McLAUGHLIN, Virginia

* * *

McMAHON, Ed(ward Leo Peter, Jr.) 1923-

PERSONAL: Born March 6, 1923, in Detroit, Mich.; son of Edward McMahon (a minstrel show interlocutor and fund raiser); married Alyce Ferrell, 1945 (divorced, February 1, 1976); married Victoria Valentine, March 6, 1976; children: Claudia, Michael, Linda, Jeffrey. *Education:* Catholic University of America, B.A., 1949; attended Boston College. *Residence:* Marina Del Ray, Calif.

CAREER: Television announcer, actor, and nightclub performer. Worked as "mike man" in calling bingo games on Northeast carnival circuit; worked at WLLH-Radio in Lowell, Mass.; WCAU-TV, Philadelphia, Pa., performer on television shows, including "The Take Ten Show," "Strictly for the Girls," and "McMahon and Company"; ABC-TV, New York City, announcer for "Who Do You Trust?," 1958-62; NBC-TV, New York City, announcer for "The Tonight Show Starring Johnny Carson," 1962—. Host of television game shows, including "Missing Links," 1963-64, "Snap Judgment," and "Whodunit?," 1979. Host of weekend "Monitor" spots on NBC-Radio, 1966. Performer on television specials, including "Timex Presents the All-Star Circus," "Kraft Music Hall," "Opening Night, U.S.A.," and "America's Junior Miss Pageant." Actor in stage productions, including "Guys and Dolls," "Annie Get Your Gun," and "The Impossible Years." Actor in motion pictures, including "The Incident," 1967, "Slaughter's Big Rip-Off," 1973, and "Fun With Dick and Jane," 1977. Performer in nightclubs, 1972—. Associated with Delphi Productions (talent management), Parthenon Productions, Inc. (real estate and entertainment), Lew Schwarz—Del Sol Productions, Inc. (film co.), and Unicorn Creations, Inc. (paper and novelty products). Member of board of governors of Bedside Network. *Military service:* U.S. Marine Corps; received six air medals. *Member:* Academy of Radio and Television Arts and Sciences (member of board), Alumni Association of Catholic University of America (president). *Awards, honors:* Nominated best new actor at Mar Del Plata Film Festival, 1967, for performance in "The Incident."

WRITINGS: Ed McMahon's Barside Companion, World Publishing, 1969; *Slimming Down,* Grosset, 1972; (with Carroll Carroll) *Here's Ed: Or, How to Be a Second Banana, From Midway to Midnight,* Putnam, 1976; (editor) *Grin and Beer It,* Pyramid Publications, 1976.

SIDELIGHTS: "A-n-n-d N-o-w H-e-e-e-r-r-e's Johnny!" is the nightly announcement of television's reigning second banana, Ed McMahon. Since 1962, the one-time carnival pitchman has heralded the start of "The Tonight Show Starring Johnny Carson" and played the loyal, though sarcastic, foil to the show's star. His preparation for the role included jobs as a pinball and bingo announcer in a traveling roadshow; as a hawker of vegetable slicers and juice makers on Atlantic City's Boardwalk; and as a clown on "The Big Top" television show that opened with a shot of McMahon's red nose lighting up and saying "Hello." A versatile entertainer who has recently added film and nightclub appearances to his career, McMahon found an early idol in Pittsburgh radio announcer Paul Douglas. "His was the voice of class," McMahon remarked. "And he made 'Pa.' sound like an abbreviation for Paradise. That is what I wanted to be able to do. He was what I wanted to be."

McMahon grew up in an atmosphere of show business. In *Here's Ed,* he recalled imitating favorite radio announcers with a flashlight for his microphone and his dog, Valiant Prince, for an audience. An even stronger performing influence was his father, who had been a minstrel show entertainer and later became a professional fund raiser at carnivals. As a boy, McMahon helped work the midway, selling bingo tickets for his father, "calling the ponies" in a pinball game that simulated a horse race, and eventually running his own bingo crew on the Northeast circuit. After a tour of duty in the Marine Corps and his graduation from college, he began his earliest television work at a Philadelphia station.

McMahon arrived at WCAU-Radio just as the station began its venture into television. He immediately went to work as the co-host and co-producer of "The Take Ten Show," a three-hour variety program. His other assignments included appearances on "Aunt Molly and Ed," a cooking show, and "Strictly for the Girls," a morning show that he wrote and produced. For another change of pace, he played a clown on "The Big Top," a circus show that would have been shown nationally by CBS but for McMahon's return to wartime service in Korea. At war's end, he resumed his television work at the same station, including a late-night talk show of his own, "McMahon and Company."

In 1956, McMahon used the money he had saved to launch "Operation Manhattan," a personal undertaking he hoped would lead to commercial work and a network show of his own. His plan involved commuting everyday to New York City, phoning sponsors, and arranging expensive lunches with promising contacts. But his real opportunity came unexpectedly at his own Philadelphia apartment building.

Living next door to the host of "American Bandstand," Dick Clark, McMahon attended a party given for Clark and the television crew of Edward R. Murrow's "Person to Person." He acted as the party's master of ceremonies and performed so well that he was brought to the attention of Al Stark, producer of ABC-TV's game show "Who Do You Trust?" As the show had just lost its announcer, he was invited for an interview with the star of the program, Johnny Carson. As McMahon related in his autobiography, "No matter how John and I met, we'd have developed a rapport, a sense of bonhomie and camaraderie." On October 13, 1958, he began appearing on "Who Do You Trust?" as Carson's announcer and sidekick.

Despite some NBC opposition, Carson brought McMahon with him when he took over as "The Tonight Show" host in 1962. It has been the flagship of talk-shows ever since, soundly defeating its ratings competitors year after year. As he did on "Who Do You Trust?," McMahon performs as the announcer and commercial promoter. But his duties also include acting as second banana, or straightman, to Carson in various comedy skits. When the opportunity arises, though, McMahon draws a laugh at the star's expense, usually with a sarcastic lampoon. "I poke fun at Johnny . . . , [but] the jibes are friendly," he stated. "They'd better be or I'll be looking for a job."

Over the years McMahon has developed interests in other areas of show business. In addition to his lucrative commercial work, he has appeared as a guest on several television specials and as the host of his own game shows. His work in films won him a Best New Actor nomination in 1967, and Vincent Canby called his performance "excellent" in "Fun With Dick and Jane." In 1972, he made his nightclub debut as a singer and comedian and has since added the college concert circuit to his schedule. According to McMahon, "Sinatra doesn't have a thing to worry about. I'm an acceptable whiskey baritone who tells jokes. I really began the whole idea as a favor to a friend who wanted me to open at the St. Regis in New York. I thought I'd agreed to something like being a toastmaster, but he finally convinced me to put an act together."

When McMahon is not otherwise performing, he's involved in several business or personal ventures. His concerns include a talent-management firm, two film companies, a paper and novelty manufacturer, and a real estate interest.

As an author, he has published four books, including an anecdotal barside companion and a guide to dieting. According to *Publishers Weekly,* McMahon's autobiography, *Here's Ed,* reveals his "Irish warmth, paired with an iron will" and is "sure-fire entertainment." The motivation behind all this activity, he once commented, is not entirely pecuniary. "I'm doing it because I like to see things done well—I like to be successful."

BIOGRAPHICAL/CRITICAL SOURCES: National Observer, December 25, 1967; *Newsweek,* January 29, 1968, September 1, 1969, March 22, 1976; *Time,* January 17, 1969, December 10, 1973; *Fort Lauderdale News,* May 19, 1974; *Biography News,* Gale, July, 1974; Ed McMahon and Carroll Carroll, *Here's Ed,* Putnam, 1976; *Publishers Weekly,* March 29, 1976; *New York Times,* February 10, 1977.*

—*Sketch by B. Hal May*

* * *

McMURTRY, Jo 1937-

PERSONAL: Born December 7, 1937, in Bristol, Va.; daughter of Claude H. (a public health officer) and Evelyn (a registered nurse; maiden name, Walker) Ballard; married Larry McMurtry, July 15, 1959 (divorced, 1966); children: James Lawrence. *Education:* Texas Woman's University, B.A., 1959; Rice University, Ph.D., 1969. *Office:* Department of English, University of Richmond, Richmond, Va. 23173.

CAREER: University of Richmond, Richmond, Va., assistant professor, 1969-74, associate professor of English, 1974—. *Member:* Modern Language Association of America, American Association of University Professors.

WRITINGS: Victorian Life and Victorian Fiction: A Companion for the American Reader, Shoe String, 1979.

WORK IN PROGRESS: The Victorians and English Studies: Furnivall, Collins, Masson, and Skeet, (tentative title), biographical perspectives on the development of English language and literature as an academic discipline.

SIDELIGHTS: Jo McMurtry comments: "Investigations of the Victorian period have suggested that we are still in it. Like the Victorians, we face problems related to population growth, urbanization, and the control of our expanding technology. New groups have appeared in both centuries to claim recognition as human beings, deserving of justice—slaves, factory workers, blacks, women. For these reasons, the study of even the seemingly remote and esoteric corners of Victoriana can become unexpectedly relevant to our own daily concerns."

* * *

McNAMARA, Michael M. 1940-1979

OBITUARY NOTICE: Born in 1940; died in an automobile accident, September 8, 1979, in Colorado. Educator and novelist. McNamara taught secondary school in Colorado and was a part-time lecturer at the University of Colorado and the University of Denver. He wrote three novels dealing with the problems in Ireland, *The Vision of Thady Quinlan,* 1974, *The Dancing Floor,* 1978, and *The Sovereign Solution,* 1979. Obituaries and other sources: *The Writer's Directory, 1980-82,* St. Martin's, 1979; *Publishers Weekly,* October 1, 1979.

* * *

McPHERSON, Holt 1907(?)-1979

OBITUARY NOTICE: Born c. 1907; died August 10, 1979, in High Point, N.C. Journalist. McPherson spent most of his career at the *High Point Enterprise,* where he retired as editor in 1972. He was also president of the journalism foundation at the University of North Carolina. Obituaries and other sources: *New York Times,* August 12, 1979.

* * *

McWHIRTER, Glenna S. 1929-
(Nickie McWhirter)

PERSONAL: Born June 28, 1929, in Peoria, Ill.; daughter of Alfred Leon (a bacteriologist) and Lorene Garnet (Short) Sotier; married Edward Ford McWhirter, May 16, 1952 (divorced, 1973); children: Suzanne Ford, Charles Edward and James Richard (twins). *Education:* University of Michigan, A.B., 1951, graduate study, 1958-59. *Residence:* St. Clair Shores, Mich. *Office:* Detroit Free Press, Inc., Detroit, Mich. 48231.

CAREER/WRITINGS: McGraw-Hill, New York, N.Y., assistant to the chief of news bureau in Detroit, Mich., 1951-54; *Detroit Free Press,* Detroit, 1963—, began as a feature writer in women's department, also worked as a newsroom features writer, general assignment and investigative reporter, special projects writer, business news writer, Sunday magazine contributor, assistant city editor, suburban editor, entertainment editor, and "Tipoff" editor, author of weekly advertising column, 1975-76, author of a syndicated four-time weekly column, under name Nickie McWhirter, 1977—. Writer of television and radio commercials for Campbell-Ewald Co., Detroit, 1965. On public relations committee for Michigan Heart Association, 1978-79. *Member:* Women in Communications, Detroit Press Club (member of board of governors). *Awards, honors:* Award from New York Film Critics, 1965, for best one-minute color spot, 1965; gold medallion from Detroit Press Club Foundation, 1965, for a series of articles on marriage counseling; Headliner Award from Women in Communications, 1978, for general excellence; first prize from Detroit Press Club Foundation, 1978, for commentary; first place from Associated Press, 1978, for commentary and opinion.

WORK IN PROGRESS: "I have promised to do a book—a fiction—sometime within the year. I have no idea what it will be called. It will be whatever it is."

SIDELIGHTS: McWhirter commented: "Motivation? To

earn my keep doing something I enjoy which I feel is valuable and appreciated by other human beings. To evolve and share the evolution. To think and share the thoughts. These are motivations to write which have operated in my life since about age five or six. My viewpoint shifts from a solid humanistic center, which holds. Does that make sense?

"I speak no language other than English; I read a little French. I have traveled in Europe variously, North Africa, Canada, and throughout the United States. I like kids, frogs and all beasties, trees and all vegetables. I am a Beethoven fan and in another life would be a physicist, mathematician, or J. S. Bach. I can't spell—our language is impossible. I like baseball; it is an intellectual game not haunted by time. Each play is one-to-one. Each player is a generalist and specialist both. All other games are too simple, except tennis. I play that."

* * *

McWHIRTER, Nickie
See McWHIRTER, Glenna S.

* * *

MEDEIROS, Earl Caton 1933-

PERSONAL: Born June 13, 1933, in Massachusetts; son of Manuel C. and Evangeline (Rapoza) Medeiros; married Konnie Rott, July 6, 1972; children: Earline Medeiros Watson, Laurie Ann, Monica Lynn. *Education:* Attended Boston College, 1951-55; St. Louis University, D.D.S., 1959. *Office:* 21 West Van Buren, Naperville, Ill. 60540.

CAREER: Dentist in Naperville, Ill. *Military service:* U.S. Navy, Dental Corps, 1959-63.

WRITINGS: Complete History and Philosophy of Kung Fu, Tuttle, 1975.

WORK IN PROGRESS: A book on the martial arts.

SIDELIGHTS: Medeiros has practiced kung-fu for eight years, and owned his own school for four years. He is a patented inventor in the field of martial arts. *Avocational interests:* Tennis, golf, skiing.

* * *

MEIR, Golda 1898-1978

PERSONAL: Hebraized name of Meyerson to Meir in 1956; born May 3, 1898, in Kiev, Russia (now U.S.S.R.); immigrated to United States in 1906; immigrated to Palestine (now Israel) in 1921; died December 8, 1978, in Jerusalem, Israel; daughter of Moshe Yitzhak (a cabinet maker) and Blume (Neiditz) Mabovitch; married Morris Meyerson (a sign painter), December 24, 1917 (separated, 1933); children: Menachem, Sarah. *Education:* Graduated from Milwaukee Teachers' Training College in 1917. *Address:* 8 Habaron Hirsch St., Ramat Aviv, Israel.

CAREER: Poalei Zion (Zionist Labor Organization), Milwaukee, Wis., staff member, c. 1917; member of Kibbutz Merhavia, Palestine, 1921-23; Histadrut (Israel labor organization), Tel Aviv, Palestine (now Israel), staff member of Office of Public Works, 1923-24, treasurer, 1924; Moetzet Hapoalot (women's labor council), Tel Aviv, secretary, 1928, representative to Histadrut executive committee, 1929-34; Pioneer Women's Organization, New York, N.Y., delegate, 1928-29, national secretary, 1932-34; Histadrut, head of mutual aid programs, 1936, head of political department, 1940, and chairman of board of directors of Kupat Holim (medical service organization); during World War II served on British War Economic Advisory Council; Jewish Agency for Palestine, Jerusalem, acting head of political department, 1946-48; signed declaration of independence of the State of Israel, May 14, 1948; Israeli minister to Soviet Union, 1948; elected to the Knesset (Israeli parliament) as a labor party candidate, 1949, member of parliament, 1949-74; minister of labor and social insurance, 1949-56; minister for foreign affairs, 1956-66; secretary-general of Israel Labor Party, 1966-68; prime minister of Israel, 1969-74; member of leadership forum and party executive of Israel Labor Party, 1976-78. Fundraiser for the World Zionist Organization and Jewish Agency for Palestine in the United States and Europe during the 1930's; speaker at numerous Zionist, socialist, and labor organization meetings. *Awards, honors:* Received honorary degrees from University of Wisconsin, Hebrew Union College, and University of Tel Aviv, 1971; Freedom of Jerusalem award, 1971; LL.D. from Brandeis University, 1973.

WRITINGS: This Is Our Strength; Selected Papers, edited by Henry M. Christman, foreword by Eleanor Roosevelt, Macmillan, 1962; *As Good as Golda: The Warmth and Wisdom of Israel's Prime Minister,* compiled and edited by Israel Shenker and Mary Shenker, McCall Publishing Co., 1970; *A Land of Our Own: An Oral Autobiography,* edited by Marie Syrkin, Putnam, 1973 (published in England as *Golda Meir Speaks Out,* Weidenfeld & Nicolson, 1973); *My Life* (memoirs), Putnam, 1975; (with Gemma Levine) *Israel: Faces and Places,* Putnam, 1978. Also author of published addresses, parliament reports, and essays in both English and Hebrew.

SIDELIGHTS: When she signed the proclamation of the independence of the State of Israel on May 14, 1948, Golda Meir wept. This had been her life's dream: a homeland for her people where Jews would be "masters, not victims, of their fate." Born in the Ukraine, Meir was a victim of the brutality of Russian anti-Semitism as a young child: her earliest memory was that of her father nailing boards across the family's front door upon word of an imminent pogrom. Meir often talked about that day and said that she recalled being frightened and angry, but "above all, I remember being aware that this was happening to me because I was Jewish."

In 1906, Meir left Russia with her mother and two sisters for Milwaukee, Wisconsin, where her father had been working for three years. Her memories of Milwaukee were often colored by poverty and an uncomfortable family life, but were absent of any anti-Semitism. As a young girl growing up in a different country Meir tried to reconcile the old ways with the new. Unfortunately, her parents did not follow her example: believing marriage to be the best thing for their daughter, the Mabovitchs were against Golda entering high school and tried to persuade her to take secretarial courses instead.

Fed up with working long hours at her mother's grocery store, being late for school, and her parents' unwillingness to let her continue her studies, Meir ran away to join her married sister, Sheyna, in Denver. It was there, in Sheyna's home, that Golda first learned about kibbutz life and Zionism. It was also in Denver that Golda met her future husband, Morris Meyerson, whom she admired for "his gentleness, his intelligence, and his wonderful sense of humor." Together they discussed poetry and went to concerts. Meyerson was part of the groups of Jewish immigrants that met at Sheyna's home to discuss and argue for hours on end about politics, the future of the Jewish people in Russia and elsewhere, and socialism and Zionism. Golda also learned about Yiddish literature and listened to discussions on Sholom Aleichem and I. L. Peretz.

But Golda soon found that her sister, Sheyna, had begun to treat her just as their mother had done, and "one day, after Sheyna had been particularly bossy, ordering me about and scolding me as though I were still a child, I decided that the time had come for me to try to live alone, without a mother hen and without being nagged all the time." So, at age sixteen, Golda left school and her sister's home to live on her own and work in a tailor's shop. About a year later Meir received a letter from her father asking that she return to Milwaukee because she was needed at home.

Meir resumed her interest in Zionism in Milwaukee and was often seen standing at street corners passing out leaflets about the need for a Jewish homeland and the pioneer spirit of the kibbutz settlers. She attended Milwaukee Teachers' Training College fully intending to become a schoolteacher, thus easing her parents' worry that she might not be able to support herself should she never marry. But Golda and Meyerson had been corresponding secretly and they finally decided to marry. Golda had wanted a civil ceremony, but acquiesed to the wishes of her mother who claimed that a civil ceremony would at once "kill" *her* and shame the entire Jewish community of Milwaukee.

Meir's dream to live in Palestine was finally realized in 1921 when she and Meyerson (whose name she hebraized at the request of Ben-Gurion in 1956) arrived in Tel Aviv. Meir later admitted that she was sure her husband would rather have married her without Palestine, but agreed to her nuptial stipulation that they try life on a kibbutz. They chose a kibbutz south of Nazareth, but were not accepted for membership at first because kibbutz leaders thought that "an 'American' girl either could or would not do the extremely tough physical work that was required." Once accepted at Kibbutz Merhavia ("God's wide spaces"), Meir raised chickens (of which she was never quite fond), picked almonds, planted trees, and took over management of the kibbutz kitchen, replacing chipped cups with glasses, serving oatmeal for breakfast instead of herring, and passing out cookies "twice a week instead of once."

Meyerson's health suffered at the severity of kibbutz life and, at the suggestion of his doctor, the couple moved to Tel Aviv and then to Jerusalem where their two children were born. Golda continued her activities with the Zionist labor movement and took a job with the Israel labor organization, the Histadrut. After the birth of her children, however, she quit working and took in laundry in order to subsidize the family's income. Later she looked upon that time as some of the roughest years of her life: "Was this what it was all about—poverty, drudgery and worry?"

In 1928, Golda returned to the Histadrut, this time as the secretary of the women's labor council. It was a difficult decision for her to make because, as she later wrote in her memoirs, *My Life,* "going back to work would spell the end to my attempts to devote myself entirely to the family." Golda also realized that she finally had to face the fact that her marriage was slowly disintegrating: "What I do regret—and bitterly so—is that although Morris and I remained married to each other and loving each other until the day he died . . . I was not able to make a success of our marriage after all." Returning to the Histadrut also meant relocation and so Golda left for Tel Aviv with her two children, while Morris remained in Jerusalem. Before his death in 1951, Morris Meyerson once remarked, "I came to Palestine for one reason only: to be with Goldie. But she was never there."

Meir was very candid in *My Life* when she discussed the problems of a working mother. On one hand she knew that her work for the labor movement fulfilled her and was an essential outgrowth of social and political beliefs, but she also felt terribly guilty about leaving her children with friends and relatives while she traveled all over the world for her job. "And still to this day," Meir wrote in 1975, "I am not sure that I didn't harm the children or neglect them, despite the efforts I made not to be away from them even an hour more than was strictly necessary." When Meir did stay home from the office because of a rare migraine headache, she said her children danced about the house and sang: "'Mommy's staying at home today! Mommy has a headache!'"

During the early thirties Meir traveled in the United States and spoke to Jewish organizations about the need to raise money for Palestine. When she returned from America, Meir served as chairman of the worker's sick fund of the Histadrut. By this time Arab hostility had burst into violence with daily riots in both Tel Aviv and Jerusalem. Meir, whose work involved travel between both cities, would kiss "the children good-bye in the morning knowing that I might well never come home again."

It was during this period of violence that Meir, along with other Jewish leaders, formulated their policy of *havlagah,* or, "self-restraint." Jews would fight to protect themselves but they would not retaliate with terrorist acts against either the British or the Arabs. This was one of the areas in which she differed from Menachem Begin, whose Irgun had once bombed a center for the British government, the King David Hotel. "I was and always have been," Meir stated, "unalterably opposed—both on moral grounds and tactically—to terror of any kind. . . . It was, and has remained, my firm conviction that although many individual members of these dissident groups were certainly extremely brave and extremely dedicated, they were wrong . . . from start to finish."

After the end of World War II, Meir, as a member of the Jewish Agency for Palestine, continued to work for the entry of Jewish refugees into Palestine. In 1939, the British government, under Arab pressure, had issued the notorious White Paper which limited Jewish immigration into Palestine. Even during the Nazi holocaust, when European Jews were being annihilated in the death camps, the British were unwilling to dispense with their quota system. An anguished Meir always believed that if the British had lifted their immigration restrictions, thousands of Jewish lives could have been saved. Now the refugees were in displaced persons' camps all over Europe and, in 1947, Meir visited one such camp on the island of Cyprus where she was told by medical personnel that the camp's children would not live through another winter. Meir then negotiated with a new official of the British government for a relaxation of the quota system with regard to children.

By this time the refugee problem had come to international attention and President Truman appealed to the British Government to allow one hundred thousand Jewish refugees from Germany and Austria to enter Palestine along with the usual monthly quota of fourteen hundred. The British remained adamant and turned away filled refugee ships. When the British even succeeded in pressuring the Italian Government into blocking passage of a Haganah ship, Meir joined with other members of the Jewish community in a hunger strike. According to Meir, the British policy only fueled the burning desire for statehood among the Palestinian Jews: "political independence was not something that we could go on regarding as a distant aim."

On November 29, 1947, the United Nations Special Committee on Palestine voted for partition. In January of 1948, Meir was sent by Ben-Gurion to the United States to raise funds for the upcoming struggle. At the end of her speaking tour Meir had received $50 million in pledges—more than double the amount that Ben-Gurion had hoped to raise. Upon her return to Palestine Meir was sent on another mission by Ben-Gurion, but this time she was to travel secretly to meet with King Abdullah of Transjordan. Abdullah, who was a moderate Arab leader, had met with Meir in 1947 at which time he promised that he would not join other Arab leaders in an attack upon Israel. Disguised as an Arab woman, Meir crossed the border and journeyed to Amman, only to discover that Abullah could no longer keep his promise and was bending under the pressure of the Arab League.

On May 15, 1948, one day after the declaration of statehood was signed, Israel was attacked by her Arab neighbors. Meir was sent to the United States again by Ben-Gurion to raise money, even though she desperately wanted to remain in Israel. While in America, Meir learned that the fighting had temporarily stopped and that she was to be the new minister to the Soviet Union.

In Moscow, Meir later remarked, she learned that the Soviet Union was not a classless society for she had seen rich women stepping out of cars in furs and high heels while poor women dug ditches in rags at temperatures below zero. On Rosh Hashanah (the Jewish New Year) Meir went to the local synagogue. The authorities had played down the visit and told Jews to stay away. But when she arrived, Meir was greeted by fifty thousand "good, brave Jews" who shouted and called her name. Meir was filled with strong emotions at this show of love and pride for the representative of the new state of Israel. Ten days later, on Yom Kippur, she visited the synagogue again and spent more time with the thousands of Russian Jews who had gathered in the streets. In retaliation for these demonstrations, Meir later learned, the Soviet authorities had closed the Yiddish theater in Moscow, the Yiddish publishing house Emes, and the newspaper *Enigkeit*.

Meir spent only seven months as minister to Moscow and, in 1949, she returned to Israel as minister of labor in Ben-Gurion's newly-formed cabinet. For seven years Meir strove to raise the standard of living in Israel, upgrade the living conditions of immigrants by building low-cost housing for them, and raise funds for the defense and education of all Israeli citizens. She co-founded the Bonds for Israel program in 1950, and presented Israel's first national insurance bill to the Knesset in 1952 when she firmly stated that "the State of Israel will not tolerate within it poverty that shames human life."

Throughout all of her career Meir experienced only one incident of sexism and that was during the 1955 elections. Meir had decided to run for mayor of Tel Aviv on the labor ballot, but her candidancy was voted down by members of the religious bloc of the Tel Aviv Council who were opposed to a woman in office. Meir was "enraged" at the action of the bloc "to exploit the fact that I was a woman, as if the women of Israel hadn't done their full share—and more—in the building of the Jewish state." She also noted that she had worked with men all of her life and had never asked for nor received preferential treatment from them. Meir was never ashamed of her sex, and when female kibbutzim shunned kitchen work for plowing and driving tractors, she gladly cooked because she enjoyed it. Ben-Gurion once called her "the only man in my cabinet"—to which Meir later remarked that she doubted if any man "would have been flattered if I had said about him that he was the only woman in the government!"

Meir was once again a member of Ben-Gurion's cabinet when he named her foreign minister in 1956. Her first assignment was to attend a secret meeting in France and negotiate with the French for arms for Israel's upcoming Sinai Campaign. Then in December, one month after the Sinai Campaign, Meir went to the United Nations to defend Israel's offensive against the Arab feyadeens who had terrorized Israeli settlements. Years later, Meir was onced again summoned by the U.N. Security Council to defend another Israeli action, the abduction of Nazi leader Adolf Eichmann from Argentina, and his subsequent trial, conviction, and execution. According to Meir, her speech to the Security Council left her drained and anxious because "I was speaking for the millions who could no longer speak for themselves and I wanted each word to have meaning."

As foreign minister, Meir met with U.S. Presidents Kennedy and Johnson. She credited Johnson in her memoirs with being the first president to sell fighter jets and deal openly in arms with Israel. Meir also noted that Johnson, who backed the Israelis when they refused to withdraw to pre-1967 borders after the Six-Day war, paved the way to U.S. support of Israel both morally and financially.

As foreign minister, Meir also expanded Israel's sphere of influence in Africa by sending specialists to train young Africans in agriculture and industry. Even though the independent African nations would later choose sides with the Arabs because of energy problems, Meir always felt that the experience was worthwhile and that it made new allies for Israel and new friends for her. Indeed, Meir was made a "paramount chief" of the tribe of Gola in northern Liberia. She regarded the honor, rarely given to women, as a coincidence because the Hebrew word for diaspora is *gola*.

At the age of seventy-one, Meir was nominated and then elected prime minister by the Knesset following Premeir Levi Eshkol's death in 1969. At first she protested, saying that she was too old, that she had given enough of her life to the country, and now she simply wanted to spend the remaining years of her life with her family and, most especially, her grandchildren. But Meir also knew that a decision between the two other choices, Moshe Dayan and Yigal Allon, might split the parliament and the nation. So Meir accepted and remained prime minister until her resignation in 1974.

As prime minister, Meir often worked a fifteen-hour day and ran her cabinet so tightly and so efficiently that she was *never* outvoted on major, let alone minor, issues. Not even the great statesman Ben-Gurion had accomplished such a feat. A former aide once remarked that nobody ever crossed Golda because she "never forgot a slight." She came on, according to one reporter, "as the classic Jewish mother: hectoring, fond, overwhelmingly concerned, vulnerable to slights, demanding affections." Diplomats would often emerge drained and "stunned" from meetings with her during which, they later revealed, she spoke about the fifty-year struggle for a Jewish state when they simply had wanted to discuss some minor customs regulation. Because of her manners and the fact that she regularly "lectured" Israeli citizens on what was good *for them,* Meir was often the victim of political satirists who portrayed her as being "schoolmarmish." Most Israelis, however, regarded her "as a kind of Mother Courage, radiating confidence and faith, the very personification of the Jews' will to survive as a people in the aftermath of the Nazi holocaust and in the face of repeated Arab attacks."

Under Golda's leadership the Israeli economy boomed, even though many critics complained that she did not spend enough time on domestic issues. Others have recently blamed the Palestinian problem on her by suggesting that her insistence on secure borders for Israel obscured her view of the growing Arab unrest in occupied territories. In fact, Meir once remarked in 1972 that "there is no such thing as the Palestinian people."

While many Americans lost faith in former president Richard M. Nixon, Meir claimed that, to Israel, he was a strong ally. "However history judges Richard Nixon," she once stated, "it must also be put on the record forever that he did not break a single one of the promises he made to us."

Golda Meir was fond of saying that her term of office began with one war and ended with another, and in between were such tragedies as the terrorist attack on Israeli atheletes at the 1972 Munich Olympics. Through it all Meir remained confident, firm, and headstrong about the survival of the Jewish homeland. Only the Yom Kippur War caused her to falter, to question her leadership abilities.

Although the war began on October 6, 1973, when Israel was attacked by both Egyptian and Syrian forces, Meir had been aware of a buildup of Arab troops near Israeli borders since early May. In September, intelligence reports indicated that Syrian troops had mobilized in the Golan Heights. On October 1, Meir met with Dayan, Allon, Galili, and the military chiefs of staff who once again assured her that war was not imminent. In spite of their protestations Meir had uneasy feelings about the reports and considered a call-up of reserve troops. Meir was ever more distressed to hear of the swift exit from Syria of the families of Russian advisers. All this reminded her of the situation before the Arab-Israeli war of 1967, but Meir hesitated and did nothing. The following day war broke out and, although they eventually won the Yom Kippur War, most Israelis blamed Golda for the deaths of their sons.

Meir resigned in the aftermath of that costly war, saying, "I can no longer bear the burden." Later, she soberly remarked that she would never again be the same person that she was before the war. Meir received numerous letters from parents specifically calling her the cause of their children's deaths. Yet she refused to pass on the blame to the advisers who had said that war could not occur. She simply stated that she was prime minister and that she had never hesitated to make a decision except on that day.

Even though she appeared tough in public and in parliament, Golda Meir often exuded a warmth characteristic of a typical "Jewish mother." There are legends about her brewing tea for her bodyguards on sleepless nights and holding those now famous cabinet meetings in her kitchen while serving chicken soup. A doting grandmother, Meir was often amused at the antics of her grandchildren who, she insisted, were more interested in what she had in her refrigerator than in whom she had in her living room.

In 1977, Meir was in New York City for the opening of "Golda," a play based on her memoirs, starring actress Anne Bancroft. She cut her trip short, however, in order to return to Jerusalem and greet Egyptain President Anwar el-Sadat on his visit to Israel. Meir met with her former enemy and later candidly remarked that "he's not as ugly as I thought." Of Camp David, Meir claimed that Israel had given away too much with the Sinai.

In retrospect, Golda Meir never really retired from politics; rather, she was like "a queen in exile," continuing to speak at Knesset meetings and often criticizing opposition leader Menachem Begin. When she died of complications from lymphoma, the disease which she had kept hidden for more than ten years, all the world mourned the loss. International leaders eulogized her; she was called a "stalwart lioness" and "the conscience of the Jewish people." But to the Israelis themselves, she was affectionately remembered as *Golda Shelanu*—"Our Golda."

BIOGRAPHICAL/CRITICAL SOURCES: Golda Meir, *My Life,* Putnam, 1975; *New Yorker,* November 10, 1975; *Saturday Review,* October 18, 1975; *New York Times Book Review,* November 30, 1975; *Los Angeles Times,* November 19, 1978.

OBITUARIES: New York Times, December 9, 1978; *Washington Post,* December 9, 1978; *Chicago Tribune,* December 10, 1978, December 13, 1978, December 14, 1978; *Newsweek,* December 18, 1978; *Time,* December 18, 1978; *New Republic,* December 23 and 30, 1978.*

—*Sketch by Nancy M. Rusin*

* * *

MELCHER, Frederic Gershom 1879-1963

OBITUARY NOTICE: Born April 12, 1879, in Malden, Mass.; died March 9, 1963. Publisher and editor for over half a century. A bookseller in Boston and Indianapolis for twenty-three years, Melcher became co-editor of *Publishers Weekly* in 1918, and chairman of R. R. Bowker & Co. in 1958. With Franklin K. Mathiews, the Boy Scouts' chief librarian, Melcher developed Children's Book Week in 1919, a week still observed by libraries, bookshops, and schools across the nation. He also established the John Newbery Medal in 1921, awarded annually for the most distinguished contribution to American literature for children, and in 1937, the Caldecott Medal, for the best American picture book for children. Obituaries and other sources: *Current Biography,* Wilson, 1945, April, 1963; *Who Was Who in America,* 4th edition, Marquis, 1968.

* * *

MELNICK, Jack 1929-

PERSONAL: Born July 23, 1929, in Philadelphia, Pa.; son of Milton M. (an accountant) and Hassie (Ostroff) Melnick; married Diana Rubens, October 6, 1955; children: Gail Robin Melnick Oring, Richard Harris. *Education:* University of Pennsylvania, B.S., 1951; also attended IBM Systems Research Institute, 1961. *Home:* 509 Whitingham Dr., Silver Spring, Md. 20904. *Office:* International Business Machines Corp., 10401 Fernwood Rd., Bethesda, Md. 20034.

CAREER: Daily Pennsylvanian, Philadelphia, Pa., feature editor, 1950-51; Penn Fruit Co., Philadelphia, management trainee, 1951; International Business Machines Corp., EDPM sales trainee in Philadelphia, 1955, field technical representative in Wilmington, Del., 1955, instructor in Harrisburg, Pa., 1955-56, advisory systems engineer and systems engineering manager in Trenton, N.J., 1956-63, manager of field techniques development projects in White Plains, N.Y., 1963-67, industry marketing manager and senior marketing support administrator in Bethesda, Md., 1967—. Instructor at Temple University, 1956-58. Owner of financial consulting business, 1976—. *Military service:* U.S. Navy, chief engineering officer on destroyer, 1951-55; served in Korea; became lieutenant senior grade. *Member:* International Platform Association, American Association of Motor Vehicle Administrators, University of Pennsylvania Alumni Association.

WRITINGS: A Unique Computable Name Code for Alphabetic Account Numbering, International Business Machines Corp., 1960, revised edition, 1966; *Motor Vehicle Data Processing Handbook,* International Business Machines Corp., 1966, new edition, 1979; *Identification Techniques,* International Business Machines Corp., 1969, 2nd edition, 1977; *Step-by-Step Guide to Your Retirement Security,* New York Times Co., 1978.

WORK IN PROGRESS: Revising *Step-by-Step Guide to Your Retirement Security,* publication by New York Times Co. expected in 1981 or 1982.

SIDELIGHTS: Melnick writes: "Trying to plan for early retirement at age fifty-five led to the creation of *Step-by-Step Guide to Your Retirement Security*. It was not possible to get an unbiased opinion on what financial solutions were needed to retire early. Everybody wanted to sell something—annuities, mutual funds, trusts. Nobody looked at the total picture. Research in this field led to my book and to my avocation as a financial consultant and planner, a field I plan to pursue after my own retirement. Everyone needs to retire *from* something, *to* something."

* * *

MENDEL, Arthur 1905-1979

OBITUARY NOTICE—See index for *CA* sketch: Born June 6, 1905, in Boston, Mass.; died Octobor 14, 1979, in Newark, N.J. Educator, conductor, editor, translator, and writer. Mendel combined his career as a professor of music at Princeton University with an equally illustrious career as the conductor of the Cantata Singers, a group specializing in the performance of seventeenth- and eighteenth-century music. An authority on Johann Sebastian Bach, Mendel edited *The Bach Reader* and served on the international editorial board of *Neue Bach Ausgabe,* a new critical edition of the collected works of Bach. Obituaries and other sources: *Who's Who in World Jewry,* Pitman, 1972; *Who's Who in America,* 39th edition, Marquis, 1974; *Directory of American Scholars,* 7th edition, Bowker, 1978; *New York Times,* October 18, 1979.

* * *

MERLEAU-PONTY, Maurice 1908-1961

OBITUARY NOTICE: Born March 14, 1908, in Rochefort-sur-Mer, France; died May 4, 1961. Psychologist, philosopher, and author of books on existentialism. Merleau-Ponty met Jean-Paul Sartre while both were students and later formed a strong personal and professional association with him. Together with Simone de Beauvoir, they founded the journal *Les Temps Modernes* in 1945. Merleau-Ponty served as political editor for the journal until his resignation seven years later. His resignation, resulting from strained relations with Sartre, represented a break which was, as Merleau-Ponty pointed out, a result of their basic differences in philosophy. As professor of philosophy, he served at the University of Lyon in 1945, the Sorbonne in 1949, and was named to the titular chair of philosophy at the College de France in 1952. His principal works include *The Structure of Behavior, Phenomenology of Perception, Humanism and Terror,* and *Sense and Not Sense*. Obituaries and other sources: *Who Was Who in America,* 4th edition, Marquis, 1968; *World Authors, 1950-1970,* Wilson, 1975.

* * *

MEROFF, Deborah 1948-

PERSONAL: Born September 3, 1948, in Bath, Me.; daughter of William and Lillian (Freeman) Meroff. *Education:* Bob Jones University, B.A., 1970; University of Maine, Orono, M.L.S., 1973. *Religion:* Protestant. *Home:* 129 Main St., Lisbon Falls, Me. 04252. *Office:* Lisbon Falls Community Library, 28 Main St., Lisbon Falls, Me. 04252.

CAREER: Auburn Public Library, Auburn, Me., head of circulation, 1973-76; librarian at Christian school in Derry, N.H., 1976-77; Lisbon Falls Community Library, Lisbon Falls, Me., head librarian, 1978—. *Member:* American Library Association, Maine Library Association.

WRITINGS: Coronation of Glory: The Story of Lady Jane Grey (novel), Zondervan, 1979.

WORK IN PROGRESS: A biographical novel.

SIDELIGHTS: Meroff told *CA:* "Biographical fiction provides the awesome medium of translating the dead to the living. Although the writer has a responsibility toward fact, he also has freedom to add color and dimension to cardboard characters. And with history so full of drama, the invention of persons and plot seems superfluous."

* * *

MERRILL, Robert 1944-

PERSONAL: Born December 3, 1944, in Miami, Fla.; son of Reed Miller (a professor) and Maurine (Wright) Merrill; married Dorothy Louise Coleman (a paralegalist), December 22, 1976. *Education:* University of Utah, B.A., 1966; University of Chicago, M.A., 1967, Ph.D., 1971. *Politics:* Democrat. *Home:* 837 Vine St., Reno, Nev. 89503. *Office:* Department of English, University of Nevada, Reno, Nev. 89557.

CAREER: University of Nevada, Reno, assistant professor, 1971-77, associate professor of English, 1977—. *Member:* Modern Language Association of America, Shakespeare Association of America.

WRITINGS: Norman Mailer, Twayne, 1978. Contributor to language, literature, and humanities journals.

WORK IN PROGRESS: A book on Ernest Hemingway and modern narrative tragedy; research on Vladimir Nabokov.

SIDELIGHTS: Merrill comments: "Mailer has been a major interest of mine from the age of twelve, so my book culminated a long-standing relationship with his work. My major areas of professional interest are American literature, especially modern fiction, and Shakespeare.

"I'm a sports fanatic, both as participant and spectator, and I like to gamble. Ending up in Reno was therefore peculiarly appropriate."

* * *

METCALF, Vicky 1901-

PERSONAL: Born December 14, 1901, in Belfast, Ireland; daughter of William John and Jane (Shaw) Waring; married George Metcalf (a business executive), July 20, 1927; children: George. *Religion:* Pentecostal. *Home:* 22 Rosemary Lane, Toronto, Ontario, Canada M5P 3E8.

CAREER: Writer, 1928—. Worked as machine operator, 1917-27, professional actress, 1920-27, and teacher of elocution, 1925-28. *Member:* Canadian Authors Society, Canadian Society of Children's Authors, Society of Children's Book Writers.

WRITINGS: Unwanted Legacy, Gospel Publishing, 1954, reprinted, Gospel Publishing, 1977; *Journey Fantastic,* Ryerson, 1970; *Catherine Schubert* (juvenile), Fitzhenry-Whiteside, 1978. Work represented in anthologies for children. Contributor of stories to children's magazines.

WORK IN PROGRESS: A story about elephants in the jungle.

SIDELIGHTS: Vicky Metcalf comments: "My becoming a writer was purely accidental. Six months after my marriage my husband's job took him to a radio station every night. I wondered what to do about the empty evenings. I began writing recitations for particular needs, sent them out, and sixty were accepted by Eldridge Entertainment Centre. Then I began to write children's stories, which also sold.

"I had never written any nonfiction, but on a trip out West, I saw an outdoor play about the first woman to cross the Rocky Mountains. I was fascinated by Catherine Schubert and, when I arrived in Victoria, I went to the museum there and was given five diaries of men who had been on the same trek. I then sought out her grandchildren. I went out West four times and to St. Paul, Minn., where I read old newspapers to find out her reasons for leaving St. Paul with her husband and friends to settle in Fort Garry.

"Fortunately for me I was able to proceed with my research in a very leisurely manner. I started in 1958; the book came out in 1970.

"Then Fitzhenry-Whiteside asked to add Catherine's story to their list for 'The Canadians,' a series for the schools. I got in touch with my cousin in Ireland, who went to Catherine's birthplace in Rathfriland, County Down, and obtained information on her life in Ireland before she left for work in Springfield, Mass. That book, *Catherine Schubert,* is now in the schools.

"*Unwanted Legacy* was printed in Braille for the blind and *Journey Fantastic* has been put on tape for the blind. I am more than happy about that."

* * *

MEYER, Doris 1942-

PERSONAL: Born January 2, 1942, in Summit, N.J.; daughter of Hans J. (an importer-exporter) and Maria L. (an editor and translator) Meyer. *Education:* Radcliffe College, B.A. (magna cum laude), 1963; University of Virginia, M.A., 1964, Ph.D., 1967. *Home:* 101 West 12th St., Apt. 19-F, New York, N.Y. 10011. *Agent:* Sanford J. Greenburger Associates, Inc., 825 Third Ave., New York, N.Y. 10022. *Office:* Department of Modern Languages, Brooklyn College of the City University of New York, Bedford Ave. and Ave. H, Brooklyn, N.Y. 11210.

CAREER: University of North Carolina, Wilmington, assistant professor of Spanish, 1967-69; Brooklyn College of the City University of New York, Brooklyn, N.Y., assistant professor, 1972-75, associate professor of Spanish, 1976—. *Member:* Modern Language Association of America, American Association of Teachers of Spanish and Portuguese, New Mexico Historical Society, Phi Beta Kappa. *Awards, honors:* Woodrow Wilson fellowship, 1964-66; American Philosophical Society grant, 1976; National Endowment for the Humanities fellowship, 1977-78.

WRITINGS: Traditionalism in the Works of Francisco de Quevedo, University of North Carolina Press, 1970; *Victoria Ocampo: Against the Wind and Tide,* Braziller, 1979. Contributor of articles and translations to history and Spanish studies journals and to *Nimrod.*

WORK IN PROGRESS: Translations and interviews with Latin American writers; continuing research on the life and works of Victoria Ocampo.

SIDELIGHTS: Doris Meyer writes: "I was motivated to write the book on Victoria Ocampo through a combination of an Argentine background on my mother's side and an intense concern with bringing to the attention of North American readers the remarkable contributions of a much-overlooked South American woman, a legend in her own country, a social rebel and a feminist. Other areas of interest are women's studies in general, and Mexican American literature."

Victoria Ocampo was praised by John Russell as a "decent, serious, well-researched survey, and it is graced by a discretion now rare among biographers." Doris Meyer knew Ocampo personally for nearly twenty years and was able to provide an "unremittingly earnest" view of her life. "Books and the men who wrote them were what she most cared for in life," Russell noted. "She had the looks, the means and the gall to chase the writers of her choice, and for much of her life she did just that." She greatly contributed to the literary life of South America by founding *Sur* magazine in 1931, a review of the best European and North American writings. She also ran a publishing company that provided Spanish translations of such literary giants as James Joyce, Andre Malraux, William Faulkner, and Vladimir Nabokov.

BIOGRAPHICAL/CRITICAL SOURCES: New York Times, August 9, 1979.

* * *

MIDGLEY, Mary 1919-

PERSONAL: Born September 13, 1919, in London, England; daughter of Tom Burton (a canon) and Evelyn Lesley (Hay) Scrutton; married Geoffrey Midgley (a university lecturer), December 18, 1950; children: Thomas, David, Martin. *Education:* Somerville College, Oxford, M.A. (with first class honors), 1942. *Office:* Department of Philosophy, University of Newcastle upon Tyne, Newcastle upon Tyne, England.

CAREER: Civil servant, 1942-43; high school teacher of classics in Berkshire, England, 1943-44, and in Bedford, England, 1944-45; University of Reading, Reading, England, lecturer in philosophy, 1949-50; University of Newcastle upon Tyne, Newcastle upon Tyne, England, part-time lecturer, 1965-70, full-time lecturer, 1970-75, senior lecturer in philosophy, 1975—. Broadcaster.

WRITINGS: Beast and Man: The Roots of Human Nature, Cornell University Press, 1978. Contributor of articles and reviews to philosophy journals and newspapers.

WORK IN PROGRESS: "Continuing research on human nature, with a view to using the wide range of animal comparisons to connect the constrictions and prejudices which have dogged enquiry into the psychology of motive and sterilized much English speaking moral philosophy in this century."

* * *

MIKDASHI, Zuhayr 1933-

PERSONAL: Born in Beirut, Lebanon; son of Ramez and Fatima (Tayara) Mikdashi; married Ghada el-Sayed in 1969; children: Bilal, Louay (both sons). *Education:* University of Lyon, certificat d'Etudes Litteraires Generales, 1953; American University of Beirut, M.A., 1954, B.A., 1956; Oxford University, B.Litt., 1958, D.Phil., 1971; Stanford University, diploma, 1963. *Home:* 12 ch. des Abeilles, CH-1010 Lausanne, Switzerland. *Office:* Batiment des Facultes des Sciences Humaines, University of Lausanne, Dorigny, CH-1015 Lausanne, Switzerland.

CAREER: Economist for Planning Board, government of Lebanon, 1955-56; American University of Beirut, Beirut, Lebanon, professor of business administration until 1976; University of Lausanne, Lausanne, Switzerland, professor of business administration, 1976—. Visiting lecturer at Arab Institute of Higher Studies and Research, 1966; visiting scholar at Institut Francais du Petrole, 1967, and Resources for the Future, 1971-72; associate visiting professor at Indiana University, 1970-71; guest lecturer at colleges, universities, and government agencies around the world; guest on television and radio programs; planner and director of seminars. Secretary-general of Arab-European Business Cooperation Committee; adviser to United Nations, Kuwait's minister of oil and finance, and United Arab Emirates; consultant to Organization of Petroleum Exporting Countries (OPEC), International Bank for Reconstruction and Development, and Organization for Economic Cooperation and Development. *Awards, honors:* British Council scholarship for Oxford University, 1956-58; Ford Foundation grant, 1970-73; Orden Francisco de Miranda from president of Venezuela, 1971; research fellow at Harvard University, 1971-72; visiting fellow at Japanese Institute of Developing Economies, 1972.

WRITINGS: A Financial Analysis of Middle East Oil Concessions, 1901-1965, Praeger, 1966; *Continuity and Change in the World Oil Industry,* Middle East Research and Publishing Center, 1970; *The Community of Oil Exporting Countries: A Study in Governmental Cooperation,* Cornell University Press, 1972; *Major Protagonists in Natural Resources and Their Views of Benefits* (monograph), Institute of Developing Economies (Tokyo, Japan), 1973; *An Analysis of World Energy Demand and Supply, 1974-1985* (monograph), Research Institute of Overseas Investment, Export-Import Bank of Japan, 1975; *The International Politics of Natural Resources,* Cornell University Press, 1976; (editor and contributor) *Partners in Development Through Resources and Technology,* Kommentator Verlag, 1978.

Contributor: *The Economic Development of Libya,* Johns Hopkins Press, 1960; *Middle East Economic Papers,* Johns Hopkins Press, 1969; M.A. Cook, editor, *Studies in the Economic History of the Middle East From the Rise of Islam to the Present Day,* Oxford University Press, 1970; Raymond Vernon, editor, *Enterprise and Government in Western Europe,* Harvard University Press, 1974; *Le Nouvel Ordre Petrolier: The New Petroleum Order,* Presses de l'Universite Laval, 1976; (author of foreword) Edmond Voelker, editor, *Euro-Arab Cooperation,* Sijthoff, 1976; N. Sherbiny and M. Tessler, editors, *Arab Oil: Impact on the Arab Countries and Global Implications,* Praeger, 1976; Vernon, editor, *The Oil Crisis,* Norton, 1976; *International Organizations in World Politics: Yearbook, 1975,* Croom Helm, 1976; A. Kapoor, editor, *Asian Business and Environment in Transition: Selected Readings and Essays,* Darwin Press, 1977. Contributor of more than thirty articles and reviews to professional journals.

SIDELIGHTS: With *The International Politics of Natural Resources,* Mikdash has achieved "an admirable blend of sympathetic understanding for the Third World's sense of injustice and inequity," commented critic Susan Strange.

BIOGRAPHICAL/CRITICAL SOURCES: International Affairs, October, 1977.

* * *

MILLER, George Louquet 1934-
(Greg Martin)

PERSONAL: Born October 23, 1934, in Artesia, Calif.; son of Roy Oakley (a police officer) and Edna (Louquet) Miller; married Marilyn Ann Rhoads (a registered nurse), December 26, 1959; children: Anne Louise, Andrew Louquet. *Education:* Los Angeles Valley Junior College, A.A., 1954; Occidental College, A.B., 1956; Princeton Theological Seminary, M.Div., 1960. *Home:* 1604 Crestview Dr., Cordell, Okla. 73632. *Agent:* Roland W. Tapp, Route 3, Box 92-D, Inverness, Fla. 32650. *Office:* P.O. Box 376, Cordell, Okla. 73632.

CAREER: Ordained United Presbyterian minister, 1960; pastor of Presbyterian churches in Sinclair, Wyo., 1960-62, and in Houston, Tex., and Post, Tex., 1964-74; united campus minister in Weatherford, Okla., and pastor in Cordell, Okla., 1975—. Pastor of Presbyterian church in Colony, Okla., 1975—. Volunteer member of local Community Action Board, Library Trustees Board, Juvenile Board, and the Red Cross.

WRITINGS: (Under pseudonym Greg Martin) *Spiritus Contra Spiritum* (title means "Spirit Against Spirits"), Westminster, 1977. Author of "Library Listening Post," a column in *Post Dispatch,* 1968-74, and a devotional column. Contributor to *Trends* and *Alive Now!.*

WORK IN PROGRESS: Under the Aspen, a novel.

* * *

MILLER, Gordon W(esley) 1918-

PERSONAL: Born November 3, 1918, in Quorn, Australia; son of George (a worker and evangelist) and Ada Eleanor (an evangelist; maiden name, Matters) Miller; married Enid McKinstry, March 27, 1943 (marriage ended, 1954); married Tamara Coates (a musician), December 20, 1954 (marriage ended, 1974); children: John Gordon, Sonya Joan, Paul Roger Albert. *Education:* University of Melbourne, diploma in music, 1950, B.A., 1962; London School of Economics and Political Science, London, Ph.D., 1967. *Politics:* "Freethinker and free voter." *Religion:* Christian. *Office:* Institute of Education, University of London, Bedford Way, London WC1H OAL, England.

CAREER: Melbourne Symphony Orchestra, Melbourne, Australia, French hornist, 1947-56; University of London, Institute of Education, London, England, in education and research, 1965—. Member of board of governors of Polytechnic of North London, 1975—. *Military service:* Royal Australian Air Force. *Member:* Royal Society of Arts (fellow), British Sociological Association, British Psychological Association, Society of Authors.

WRITINGS: Success, Failure, and Wastage in Higher Education, Harrap, 1970; *Higher Education Research in Australia and New Zealand,* Society for Research in Higher Education, 1970; *Educational Opportunity and the Home,* Longman, 1971; *Staff Development Programmes in British Universities and Polytechnics,* United Nations Educational, Scientific, and Cultural Organization, 1976; *The Interface Between Industry, Business, and Engineering Education,* National Foundation for Educational Research, 1979. Contributor to education and psychology journals in the United States, England, and Australia.

WORK IN PROGRESS: A novel.

SIDELIGHTS: Born into a working-class family of practicing evangelists, Miller read the entire Bible during his early teenage years, "an excellent moral and liberal education," and left school at the age of thirteen. He worked in factories, then went to sea, and did not enter the university until he had completed his military service.

Miller writes: "I am interested in improving my own and

others' life chances, partly through education and self-help. I am for freedom and independence, and against religious and political dogma from Right or Left."

AVOCATIONAL INTERESTS: Music, reading, yoga, travel, "idling," walking.

* * *

MILLER, Hugh 1897(?)-1979

OBITUARY NOTICE: Born c. 1897 in New York, N.Y.; died November 10, 1979, in Scottsdale, Ariz., from a circulatory ailment. Photojournalist. Miller covered all but one of the presidential inaugurations from 1921 to 1967. He retired in 1967 from his position as chief of the *Washington Post* photographic department. Obituaries and other sources: *Washington Post,* November 11, 1979.

* * *

MILLER, John C. 1916(?)-1979

OBITUARY NOTICE: Born c. 1916 in Escatawpa, Miss.; died of a heart attack, October 17, 1979, in Norfolk, Va. Educator and author. Miller had taught English at Old Dominion College since 1967. A specialist in early American literature, he wrote two books on Edgar Allan Poe, *Building Poe Biography* and *Poe's Helen Remembered.* In the former, Miller "depicted Poe not as a demented scoundrel, a popular view, but as an eccentric but stable man." Obituaries and other sources: *Washington Post,* October 19, 1979.

* * *

MILLER, June 1923-

PERSONAL: Born July 8, 1923, in Tennessee, daughter of William Right (a baker) and Mabel (Coffman) Stephens; married Hal M. Miller (a collector of fine arts and gems), September 8, 1941; children: Ray H., Mark S., Michael R., Joy Lynn Miller Engle, Jeffrey A. *Education:* Attended Moody Bible College and University of California. *Politics:* "Bipartisan." *Religion:* Baptist. *Home:* 59 El Arco, Santa Barbara, Calif. 93105. *Office:* Life Ministries International, P.O. Box 6068, Santa Barbara, Calif. 93111.

CAREER: Christian education consultant for publishers, 1964-66; director of Christian education and youth programs, 1966-69; television and radio broadcaster, lecturer, and writer, 1969—. Founder and president of Life Ministries International. Director of creative advertising and sales training programs. *Member:* International Platform Association, Zonta International, Smithsonian Institution, Museum of Natural History, Christian Women's Clubs.

WRITINGS: Why Sink When You can Swim?, Zondervan, 1973; *The God of the Impossible,* Zondervan, 1975; *Running Free,* Zondervan, 1977.

WORK IN PROGRESS: Three books.

SIDELIGHTS: June Miller commented: "My husband and I were actually married accidentally thirty-eight years ago! Since then we have discovered that God delights in using trauma to produce triumphant living. My books share humor and practical solutions for coping with stress, finances, children, and so on. I have proven my concepts through my battle with cancer, debilitating automobile accidents, and much more. I shall be speaking in major foreign countries, including India, the Far East, and the Middle East. After the round-the-world engagement tour I will return to Israel to speak in Jerusalem."

Miller's books have been translated into German and Spanish. She has also made a series of tape recordings, including "The Inner Person," "The Home," "The Physical Body," "Depression and Loneliness," "Outside Help for Inside Problems," "Somebody Left the Door Open," and "Beyond Tomorrow." They have been distributed to missionaries and Christian leaders in more than fifty countries.

* * *

MILLER, Lynne (Ellen) 1945-
(Goldsmith)

PERSONAL: Born August 6, 1945, in California; daughter of Eugene Maurice (a writer) and Nancy (a playwright and photographer; maiden name, Naumberg) Goldsmith; divorced. *Education:* Syracuse University, B.S., 1967; also attended New School for Social Research and School of Visual Arts. *Home:* 150 East 83rd St., New York, N.Y. 10028. *Agent:* Sarah Lee Freyman. *Office:* Thin Forever!, Inc., 12 East 46th St., New York, N.Y. 10017.

CAREER: Elementary school teacher in New York City, 1967-69; Scholastic Book Services, New York City, dividend editor for Arrow Book Club, 1969-74; Thin Forever!, Inc., New York City, founder and director, 1974—. Staff member at New School for Social Research; consultant to *Diet Times. Member:* American Women's Economic Development Corp., New York Women Business Owners, East Mid-Manhattan Chamber of Commerce.

WRITINGS: Short Span Activities, Scholastic Book Services, 1970; *A Christmas Carol* (juvenile dramatic adaptation), Scholastic Book Services, 1971; *Hans Brinker* (juvenile dramatic adapation), Scholastic Book Services, 1972; *Ten Tales of Christmas* (juvenile anthology), Scholastic Book Services, 1973; (under name Goldsmith) *Ready-Made Bulletin Boards* (juvenile), Scholastic Book Services, 1974; *Make Your Own Thing* (juvenile), Simon & Schuster, 1979.

WORK IN PROGRESS: Thin Forever Survival Kit, a booklet and tape recording.

SIDELIGHTS: Lynne Miller has created games, including "May the Best Knight Win," "Witch Way?," "The Museum Mystery Game," "The Bully Game," "Around the World Race," and "Arrow Authors Game," and teaching-activity kits, including "Charlotte's Web," "Stuart Little," "Sounder," "King of the Wind," "The Blind Colt," "Summer of the Swans," "A Wrinkle in Time," "Miss Hickory," "Island of the Blue Dolphins," "Call It Courage," and "My Dad Lives in a Downtown Hotel."

She writes: "As a child, I always felt like the underdog. I felt fat and ugly and never felt as though I belonged. I ran to Winnie the Pooh and Babar, my only friends. It has always been my fantasy to develop a book series revolving around the inferior child.

"In 1977 I founded Thin Forever! while writing *Make your Own Thing.* I am now interested in writing a book that will teach people how to custom-fit their own diets and how to lose weight and keep it off without feeling deprived. I have incorporated parts of this book in *Thin Forever Survival Kit.*

"I would also like to write of my joys, and the experiences and mistakes I made as a young woman—a former teacher going into business for herself without even having known how to balance her own checkbook, as well as a book on my own experience as an acute compulsive overeater, an 'I Hate to Cook Diet Cookbook,' and a satirical autobiography of a divorced Jewish princess (under a pseudonym)."

MILLER, Osborn (Maitland) 1896(?)-1979

OBITUARY NOTICE: Born c. 1896 in Perth, Scotland; died August 1, 1979, in New York, N.Y. Cartographer, photographer, and author. A former director of the American Geographical Society, Miller was best known for developing a number of mapmaking techniques. One of his projections, Miller's Cylindrical, revealed the entire globe, and his high oblique photography method enabled aerial photographs to be converted into maps. Miller co-authored *World Maps and Globes* in 1944 and contributed to other books as well, including *Problems of Polar Research* and *The Fjord Region of East Greenland.* Obituaries and other sources: *New York Times,* August 3, 1979.

* * *

MILLER, Ruth
See JACOBS, Ruth Harriet

* * *

MINOR, Audax
See RYALL, George

* * *

MINRATH, William R(ichard) 1900-1971

OBITUARY NOTICE—See index for *CA* sketch: Born June 14, 1900, in New York, N.Y.; died December 3, 1971, in Leesburg, Fla. Publishing executive, chemical engineer, and author of about seven books on chemistry, mathematics, and business. After working as a chemical engineer for several years, Minrath successfully blended his science background with a publishing career at Van Nostrand where he developed the Van Nostrand scientific encyclopedia and expanded the publication of books in the fields of chemistry, physics, and biology. Obituaries and other sources: *Publishers Weekly,* January 3, 1972.

* * *

MITCHELL, Burroughs 1914(?)-1979

OBITUARY NOTICE: Born c. 1914 in Glen Ridge, N.J.; died July 21, 1979, of heart failure, in New York, N.Y. Author and editor for over thirty years at Charles Scribner's Sons where he edited the works of such writers as C. P. Snow and James Jones. Mitchell eventually succeeded the legendary editor Maxwell Perkins as editor-in-chief of Scribner's. James Jones dedicated his well-known novel *From Here to Eternity* to Mitchell "for his sweating of it out over a period of almost three years without the slightest whimper and his fine editing." Mitchell's work includes *Education of an Editor.* Obituaries and other sources: *New York Times,* July 24, 1979; *AB Bookman's Weekly,* August 20, 1979.

* * *

MITCHELL, Leeds 1912-

PERSONAL: Born February 29, 1912, in Chicago, Ill.; son of Leeds (a stockbroker) and Dorothy (Day) Mitchell; married Martha Anne Flood, January 21, 1941 (divorced, 1965); married Margery Dyer, October 26, 1966; children: Leeanne Mitchell Thomas, Dorothy Mitchell Yoreo, Leeds III. *Education:* Attended Yale University and University of Chicago. *Home and office:* 371 Rumstick Point, Barrington, R.I. 02806.

CAREER: Fidelis Harrer, Inc. (color photographers), Chicago, Ill., sales manager, 1934-41; United Board & Carton Co., Warwick Neck, R.I., New England sales manager, 1946-56; employed by Gardner Board & Carton, Middletown, Ohio, 1956-59; employed by Pure Oil Co., Chicago, 1959-61; vice-president of North American Hydrofoils, Inc., 1960-62; president of Riverboat, Inc., 1962-66; writer, 1966—. President of General Hydrofoils, Motorless Flight Institute, and Bristol Sailing School. Harbormaster of Barrington, R.I. *Military service:* U.S. Army Air Forces, 1941-45. *Member:* Cruising Club of America, New York Yacht Club, Barrington Yacht Club. *Awards, honors:* Sailing trophies since 1919, including William S. Tripp Trophy and Merriman Trophy.

WRITINGS: Introduction to Sailing, Stackpole, 1972; *Protest Planner,* Yacht Racing, 1973. Contributor to sailing magazines.

SIDELIGHTS: Mitchell writes: "*Introduction to Sailing* was written when I was teaching novice adults to sail. I tried all available primers on them, and none seemed to be what was needed. One of my students suggested that I write my own."

AVOCATIONAL INTERESTS: Photography, sailing, flying, carpentry, gliders, hydrofoils.

* * *

MITCHELL, Leonel Lake 1930-

PERSONAL: Born July 23, 1930, in New York, N.Y.; son of Leonel E. W. (an Episcopal priest) and Doris (Lake) Mitchell; married Beverly Mills (a registered nurse), December 19, 1953; children: Anne V., David M. *Education:* Trinity College, Hartford, Conn., B.A., 1951; Berkeley Divinity School, S.T.B., 1954; General Theological Seminary, S.T.M., 1956, Th.D., 1964. *Home:* 649 Haven St., Evanston, Ill. 60201. *Office:* Seabury-Western Theological Seminary, 2122 Sheridan Rd., Evanston, Ill. 60201.

CAREER: Ordained Episcopal priest, 1954; rector of Episcopal churches in Copale Falls, N.Y., 1956-59, Warwick, N.Y., 1959-64, and Beacon, N.Y., 1964-71; University of Notre Dame, Notre Dame, Ind., assistant professor of theology, 1971-78; Seabury-Western Theological Seminary, Evanston, Ill., professor of liturgies, 1978—. *Member:* Societas Liturgica, North American Academy of Liturgy.

WRITINGS: Baptismal Anointing, S.P.C.K., 1966, University of Notre Dame Press, 1977; *Liturgical Change: How Much Do We Need?,* Seabury, 1975; *The Meaning of Ritual,* Paulist/Newman, 1977. Contributor to theology journals. Book editor of *Anglican.*

WORK IN PROGRESS: Studying sixteenth-century English primers and early Christian worship.

SIDELIGHTS: Mitchell told *CA:* "My principal concern is the worship of the Christian Church. My study, my teaching, and my writing are all geared to increasing the informed, active participation of Christians in their worship."

* * *

MOCHE, Dinah (Rachel) L(evine) 1936-

PERSONAL: Born October 24, 1936, in New York, N.Y.; daughter of Bertram A. (a lawyer) and Mollie (Last) Levine; married I. Robert Rozen, September 5, 1955 (died November 17, 1966); married Leonard H. Moche (a lawyer), August 24, 1969; children: (first marriage) Elizabeth Karen, Rebecca Ann. *Education:* Radcliffe College, B.A. (magna cum laude), 1958; Columbia University, M.A., 1961, Ph.D., 1976. *Residence:* Mamaroneck, N.Y. *Office:* Department of Physics, Queensborough Community College of the City University of New York, Bayside, N.Y. 11364.

CAREER: Columbia University, Radiation Laboratory, New York, N.Y., research assistant in physics, 1961-62; Bronx Community College of the City University of New York, Bronx, N.Y., instructor of physics, 1963-64; instructor of physics at Fashion Institute of Technology, 1964-65; Queensborough Community College of the City University of New York, Bayside, N.Y., lecturer, 1965-66, instructor, 1966-69, assistant professor, 1969-77, associate professor of physics, 1977—. Participant in (and sometimes director of) national meetings; guest on radio program, "Women Today." *Member:* American Physical Society, American Association of Physics Teachers, New York State Association of Two-Year College Physics Teachers, Phi Beta Kappa, Sigma Xi. *Awards, honors:* National Science Foundation grant, 1974-75, faculty fellowship, 1976, National Science Foundation grant, 1978-80.

WRITINGS—For children, unless otherwise indicated: *What's Up There?: Questions and Answers About Stars and Space,* Scholastic Book Services, 1975; *Magic Science Tricks,* Scholastic Book Services, 1977; *Astronomy* (adult), Wiley, 1978; *Mars,* F. Watts, 1978; *Search for Life Beyond Earth,* F. Watts, 1978; *The Astronauts,* Random House, 1979; *The Star Wars Question and Answer Book About Space,* Random House, 1979; *Radiation,* F. Watts, 1979; *Life in Space* (adult), Ridge Press, 1979; *More Magic Science Tricks,* Scholastic Book Services, 1980. Author of multi-media presentation, "Women in Science," American Association of Physics Teachers and National Science Teachers Association, 1975. Contributor of articles and reviews to professional journals and popular magazines. Contributing editor of *Science World,* 1976-77; member of editorial board of *Physics Teacher,* 1974-77, and of review board of *American Journal of Physics,* 1977—.

SIDELIGHTS: Moche told *CA:* "I aim to make science accessible, interesting, and exciting for people of all ages. I want my books to be accurate and enjoyable. To me, science and writing are fun."

BIOGRAPHICAL/CRITICAL SOURCES: Physics Teacher, September, 1976, February, 1979; *American Journal of Physics,* October, 1976.

* * *

MOERS, Ellen 1928-1979
(Ellen Moers Mayer)

OBITUARY NOTICE—See index for *CA* sketch: Born December 9, 1928, in New York, N.Y.; died of cancer, August 25, 1979, in New York, N.Y. Educator, literary critic, and author of scholarly works. An authority on nineteenth-century women writers, Moers wrote *The Dandy: Brummell to Beerbohm, Two Dreisers,* and *Literary Women.* Obituaries and other sources: *Foremost Women in Communications,* Bowker, 1970; *The Author's and Writer's Who's Who,* 6th edition, Burke's Peerage, 1971; *Who's Who in America,* 39th edition, Marquis, 1976; *Directory of American Scholars,* Volume II: *English, Speech, and Drama,* 7th edition, Bowker, 1978; *Publishers Weekly,* September 17, 1979; *AB Bookman's Weekly,* September 24, 1979.

* * *

MOGGACH, Deborah 1948-

PERSONAL: Born June 28, 1948, in London, England; daughter of Richard Alexander (a writer) and Charlotte (a writer and illustrator; maiden name, Woodyatt) Hough; married Anthony Austen Moggach (a publisher), November 21, 1971; children: Thomas Alexander, Charlotte Flora. *Education:* University of Bristol, B.A. (with honors), 1970. *Home:* 31 Jeffreys St., London NW1, England. *Agent:* Curtis Brown, Ltd., 1 Craven Hill, London W.2, England.

CAREER: Oxford University Press, London, England, librarian, 1970-72; free-lance journalist and teacher in Pakistan, 1972-74; free-lance journalist and author in London, 1978—. *Awards, honors:* Young Journalist award from Westminster Arts Council, 1975, for an article, "Karachi."

WRITINGS—All novels: *You Must Be Sisters,* Collins, 1978, St. Martin's, 1979; *Close to Home,* Collins, 1979; *A Quiet Drink,* Collins, 1980. Theatre critic for *Over 21* magazine; contributor to *Over 21, The Observer,* and other newspapers and periodicals.

WORK IN PROGRESS: A novel set in Pakistan, *Hot Water Man,* completion expected in 1980.

SIDELIGHTS: Deborah Moggach admitted that her hopes for having Collins publish the unsolicited manuscript of *You Must Be Sisters* were "highly romantic. . . . It's subject matter could hardly have been more predictable," she said. "First novel by middle-class girl charts the troubled adolescence of middle-class girl and her more sensible sister." Collins, apparently, was not quite so apprehensive: they published it.

Critics agreed that the plot had its limits, but also pointed to evidence of talent in Moggach's first work. Valentine Cunningham viewed *You Must Be Sisters* as a "noticeably first novel, negotiating well-trodden first novel ground." Nonetheless, Moggach's story catches "family life most achingly bared." Mary Hope echoed Cunningham's assessment, calling the novel "psychologically pedestrian but sharp and wry about the unliberated middle-class girl."

Moggach herself called the plot "familiar stuff," but explained, "I wanted to show the funnier and more embarrassing side of the struggle into adulthood. Too many novels, I felt, dealt with a woman's sexual awakening as something deft and in some way understood by her, whereas in reality one misjudges ones own emotions. In real life, too, one is so often embarrassed; I don't think that enough contemporary novels explore this commonest of complaints, preferring to remain stylish and cool. (This applies particularly to women novelists.) I also wanted to bridge the generation gap by showing sympathetically but ironically, the differing viewpoints of parents and children; I was tired of one-sided views and easy conclusions, especially about 'dull suburban lives.'

"When I was twenty-five I went to live in Pakistan for two years; my husband had a job there. This was when I started writing. I had the time; suddenly I was a leisured *memsahib* with a servant bringing me tea and doing the boring household chores. More importantly, everything I wrote for the local magazines was published simply because the standard was so low. This was marvellous; I had the rare opportunity of experimenting and developing *in print* rather than simply on the typewriter. This way one gains confidence, which is terribly important; confidence makes one write better. (Needless to say, none of this would have happened in England where one has to enter journalism the hard way.) I was also distanced, for the first time, from my background and so could see it and write about it with some detachment.

"By the time I was writing my second novel my life had changed. I was a London housewife with two babies, writing at the kitchen table when the children were asleep. Both my parents were professional authors working at home; with their example I could close the door on household chaos and write during my set hours. *Close to Home* was set in my area and was close to home in more senses than one, being about motherhood, neighbours and the suffocating, joyful, frustrating world of babyhood and its effects upon marriage."

Like *You Must Be Sisters,* Moggach's second novel, *Close to Home,* had problems with plot; still, it "is a funny, affectionate and unpretentious novel, cliched in places . . . but always a pleasure to read," declared Blake Morrison. Tired of "marital frustration in London NW3" as a literary genre, A. N. Wilson nevertheless rated the book "quite high" among "your Drabbles, Mortimers, Weldons, or Huths. . . . The book is a collection of hilarious incidents with which one intelligent woman might regale another when fetching time comes round at the local play-group." Moggach, too, had her own criticism of the book, calling its subject matter "hardly any great imaginative leap." To one critic's charges of the author's lack of ambition and underachievement she replied: "True, actually; though I'm incapable of setting a novel in, say fifteenth century Mongolia, one ought to extend one's range.

"So I wrote a third novel, *A Quiet Drink,* about a cosmeticsrep who travels the chemists shops promoting Liberesse beauty products (slogan: 'It's Not Just Yourself You'll be Changing'). I had a lot of fun with this book, making up advertising campaigns, using media images and exploring ironies about outer appearances and so on. It turned out to be a subject full of scope, particularly as my rep was married to a simple, very beautiful girl who was turning out to be disappointing beneath her perfect face. Woven in with this is the story of a strong, independent woman whose husband had left her for someone duller and more doting. A meeting takes place, at last, during the quiet drink of the title.

"For me this was a breakthrough. All novelists realize that they must step out of their own limiting experience, otherwise after a couple of autobiographical books they get into a repeating pattern or else dry up altogether. At the time I hadn't understood this. My fourth novel will be going one step further than the last; it will be set in Pakistan which sounds an unpromising place but is in fact a most intriguing combination of old Raj India and the materialistic Middle East."

BIOGRAPHICAL/CRITICAL SOURCES: Times Literary Supplement, February 17, 1978; *New Statesman,* February 17, 1978, March 30, 1979; *Spectator,* February 18, 1978; *Observer,* April 1, 1979; *Best Sellers,* May, 1979.

* * *

MOLER, Kenneth Lloyd 1938-

PERSONAL: Born March 24, 1938, in Baltimore, Md.; son of Kenneth Lloyd, Sr. and Mildred (McKewer) Moler; married Margaret Thomas, 1959 (divorced); children: Kathryn Griffing, March Cathcart. *Education:* Johns Hopkins University, B.A., 1958; Harvard University, M.A., 1960, Ph.D., 1964. *Home:* 1841 Pawnee St., Lincoln, Neb. 68502. *Office:* Department of English, University of Nebraska, Lincoln, Neb. 68583.

CAREER: University of Nebraska, Lincoln, assistant professor, 1964-67, associate professor, 1967-72, professor of English, 1972—. *Military service:* U.S. Army, Ordnance Corps, 1959. U.S. Army Reserve, 1959-67; became first lieutenant. *Member:* Modern Language Association of America.

WRITINGS: Jane Austen's Art of Allusion, University of Nebraska Press, 1968, 2nd edition, 1977; (contributor) John Halpern, editor, *Jane Austen: Bicentenary Essays,* Cambridge University Press, 1975. Contributor to literature journals.

MONTANA, Bob 1920-1975

OBITUARY NOTICE: Born October 23, 1920, in Stockton, Calif.; died January 4, 1975, in Meredith, N.H. Cartoonist who created the syndicated comic strip "Archie." Montana led his teenage character Archie, along with rival girlfriends Veronica and Betty and friend Jughead, through thirty years of humorous high school shenanigans by pitting them against each other and such establishment foils as Miss Grundy and Principal Weatherbee. Obituaries and other sources: *New York Times,* June 6, 1975; *Newsweek,* January 20, 1975, *Time,* January 20, 1975; *Who Was Who in America,* 6th edition, Marquis, 1976.

* * *

MOONEY, George A(ustin) 1911-1979

OBITUARY NOTICE: Born November 23, 1911, in New York, N.Y.; died September 3, 1979, after heart surgery, in New York, N.Y. Journalist and former New York State superintendent of banks. Mooney wrote for the *New York Times* for nearly thirty years, becoming its assistant business and financial news editor. In 1954, he was appointed superintendent of banks, and later held a number of positions in the financial world. Obituaries and other sources: *Who's Who in America,* 40th edition, Marquis, 1978; *New York Times,* September 4, 1979.

* * *

MOORE, Dorothy N(elson) 1915-

PERSONAL: Born October 30, 1915, in Bruce, S.D.; daughter of Nels T. (a building contractor) and Millie (a teacher; maiden name, Amundson) Nelson; married Raymond S. Moore (an educator and writer), June 12, 1938; children: Dennis R., D. Kathleen Moore Kordenbrock. *Education:* Attended Long Beach State College, University of California, Los Angeles, and University of Southern California; Pacific Union College, B.A., 1937; Andrews University, M.A. (with highest honors), 1959, further graduate study, 1976. *Home and office:* 553 Tudor Rd., Berrien Springs, Mich. 49103.

CAREER: Pacific Union College, Angwin, Calif., teacher of shorthand, 1935-37; elementary school teacher in South Whittier, Calif., 1937-41, and Artesia, Calif., 1943-44; preschool teacher in Angwin, 1947-51; teacher of English as a foreign language at elementary schools and preschools in Sodegaura-machi, Chiba-Ken, Japan, 1951-56; reading supervisor at school in Takoma Park, Md., 1957-60, 1964-67; Loma Linda University, Loma Linda, Calif., organizer and director of Cerebral Palsy Center, 1960-62; teacher of shorthand and typing in Keene, Tex., 1962-64; consultant in early childhood education in Hinsdale, Ill., 1967-70; Andrews University, Berrien Springs, Mich., part-time lecturer in remedial reading and early childhood education, 1970—. Lecturer at Indiana University. Seminar leader; consultant in the United States, Japan, and the Philippines.

WRITINGS: (With husband, Raymond S. Moore) *Better Late Than Early,* Reader's Digest Press, 1975; *Program Helps for Kindergarten,* Review & Herald, 1977; (with R. S. Moore) *School Can Wait,* Brigham Young University Press, 1979; (with R. S. Moore) *Exploring Early Childhood* (correspondence course), Home Study Institute, 1979; (with R. S. Moore) *While School Waits* (sequel to *School Can Wait*), Brigham Young University Press, 1980. Author of church school curriculum material. Author of "Understanding Young Children," a column in *Worker.* Contributor to education journals.

WORK IN PROGRESS: Articles on early childhood for periodicals.

SIDELIGHTS: Dorothy Moore told *CA:* "Early in my career as a remedial reading teacher, I became aware of the causes of reading failure and the ultimate damaging results if the student was not rehabilitated in time. The primary cause, it seemed, was the child's lack of maturity. I often lectured to groups on the value of delaying school entry. This included lecturing to parent groups on how best to help their children develop at home.

"*School Can Wait* is based on hundreds of significant studies and provides objective evidence that, wherever possible, children would benefit greatly from a reasonably warm, responsive home life until they are eight or ten years of age."

* * *

MOORE, Jack L(ynne) 1920-

PERSONAL: Born July 9, 1920, in DeKalb, Miss.; son of Lynne McNary (a restaurateur) and Lilla (Bishop) Moore; married Peggy Pankey, June 21, 1941; children: Peggy Ann (Mrs. Edward Barron), Michael, Judy, William, James, Suzi. *Education:* Attended Mississippi State University, 1937-41; University of Southern Mississippi, B.S., 1950; Austin Presbyterian Theological Seminary, M.Div., 1960. *Politics:* Independent. *Home and office:* 410 Tarrant, Port Arkansas, Mustang Island, Tex. 78373.

CAREER: Ordained Presbyterian minister, 1960; University of Southern Mississippi, Hattiesburg, director of public relations, 1949-57; pastor of Presbyterian church in Longview, Tex., 1960-62; Presbytery of Northeast Texas, Dallas, evangelist, 1962-66; associate pastor of Presbyterian church in Dallas, Tex., 1966-76; Community Presbyterian Church, Port Arkansas, Tex., pastor, 1976—. Executive director of ETS (a non-profit corporation to assist small churches), 1976—. Director of public information for Southern Bell Telephone Co. in Mississippi, 1951. Head of Port Arkansas Charter Commission. *Military service:* U.S. Marine Corps, 1942-46; became first lieutenant; received four battle stars. *Member:* Christian Writer's Association, Big Eight Writers (life member), Port Arkansas Tennis Association (vice-president), Coastal Bend Christian Service Association (member of board of directors).

WRITINGS: From a Listening Heart (nonfiction), Doubleday, 1975. Author of monthly column, "In a Mirror Dimly," in *Presbyterian Survey,* 1972—, and weekly column, "Jack L. Moore," in *South Jetty,* 1976—.

WORK IN PROGRESS: Chasing Sandpipers, a collection of vignettes; *The Last Ferry,* a novel on island life.

SIDELIGHTS: Moore writes: "The need to share personal feelings and my insights into personal relationships motivates my writing, which is closely tied to my vocation as a Christian minister. I moved to an island two-and-a-half years ago to write more, and have become so involved that I'm writing less. I would like to be contacted by interested agents. I am too far removed from publishing centers."

* * *

MOORE, Katharine 1898-

PERSONAL: Born in 1898, in Hampstead, England; daughter of Alfred William (an insurance manager) and Emily (Simpson) Yeo; married Harold Moore (a director of a research institute); children: two. *Education:* Lady Margaret Hall, Oxford, M.A. *Home:* Riverside House, Shoreham, Sevenoaks, Kent, England.

CAREER: Private coach, 1926-36; Walthamstow Hall (girls' school), Walthamstow, England, senior teacher of English, 1941-60; writer and lecturer, 1960—. *Member:* Cowdray Club.

WRITINGS: Moog (juvenile), St. Catherine Press, 1936; (co-author) *A Treasury of the Kingdom,* Oxford University Press, 1954; *The Spirit of Tolerance,* Gollancz, 1964; *Cordial Relations,* Heinemann, 1966; *Kipling and the White Man's Burden,* Faber, 1968; *Family Fortunes,* Faber, 1970; *Women,* Batsford, 1970; *Victorian Wives,* St. Martin's, 1974; *She for God,* Allison & Busby, 1978. Contributor to magazines, including *Blackwoods* and *Crucible.*

WORK IN PROGRESS: Writing and lecturing on English literature.

AVOCATIONAL INTERESTS: Music, travel, reading.

* * *

MOORE, Paul, Jr. 1919-

PERSONAL: Born November 15, 1919, in Morristown, N.J.; son of Paul and Fanny Weber (Hanna) Moore; married Jenny McKean, November 26, 1944 (deceased); married Brenda Hughes (a filmmaker), May 16, 1975; children: Honor, Paul III, Adelia, Rosemary, George Mead, Marian Shaw, Daniel Sargent, Susanna McKean, Patience. *Education:* Yale University, B.A., 1941; General Theological Seminary, New York, N.Y., S.T.B., 1949. *Home and office:* 1047 Amsterdam Ave., New York, N.Y. 10025. *Agent:* Monica McCall, 230 East 50th St., New York, N.Y. 10022.

CAREER: Ordained Episcopal priest, 1949; pastor of Episcopal church in New York City; member of team ministry at Episcopal church in Jersey City, N.J., 1949-57; dean of Episcopal cathedral in Indianapolis, Ind., 1957-70, elected suffragan bishop, 1963, consecrated bishop, 1964; Diocese of New York, New York City, bishop coadjutor, 1970-72, bishop, 1972—. Lecturer at St. Augustine's College, Canterbury, England, 1960. President of Episcopal Mission Society; honorary president of Seamen's Church Institute and Youth Consultation Service; past president of national Church and City Conference; head of Metropolitan Ecumenical Training Center and director of interfaith coalition for Operation Connection, both 1968; protector general of Society of St. Francis; bishop visitor of Order of the Holy Cross and Order of St. Helena. Head of peace mission to South Vietnam, 1970; member of national board of National Association for the Advancement of Colored People's Legal Defense Fund and head of its Committee of One Hundred. Member of Yale Corp.; member of boards of directors and trustees. *Military service:* U.S. Marine Corps Reserve, active duty as platoon leader, company commander, and operations officer, 1941-45; served in Guadalcanal and Guam; became captain; received Navy Cross, Silver Star, and Purple Heart.

MEMBER: Council on Foreign Relations, Ministerial Interfaith Association (member of board of directors), Urban League (member of board of directors), Century Club. *Awards, honors:* S.T.D. from General Theological Seminary, New York, N.Y., 1960; D.D. from Virginia Theological Seminary, 1964, and Berkeley Divinity School, 1971; award from New York City's Urban League.

WRITINGS: The Church Reclaims the City, Seabury, 1965, 2nd edition, 1970; *Take a Bishop Like Me,* Harper, 1979.

SIDELIGHTS: Moore is recognized for his views on homosexuality and women in the clergy. His second book, which is autobiographical, describes the crisis generated by his ordination of a professed lesbian. But he has also devoted much of his time to the plight of the cities and the people who live there. He has worked to enlarge the influence of the church in metropolitan areas, and involved himself in more secular concerns, such as black leadership and the white community, economic development in metropolitan areas, and the relationship of the ministry to psychiatry.

BIOGRAPHICAL/CRITICAL SOURCES: Library Journal, April 1, 1979; *New York Times,* August 16, 1979.

* * *

MOOSER, Stephen 1941-

PERSONAL: Born July 4, 1941, in Fresno, Calif.; son of Joseph Nathan (in business) and Lillian (a librarian; maiden name, Davidson) Mooser; married Etta Kralovec (a teacher), November 20, 1971; children: Chelsea. *Education:* University of California, Los Angeles, B.A., 1963, M.A., 1968. *Home and office:* 1310 Bluebird Canyon Rd., Laguna Beach, Calif. 92651. *Agent:* Marilyn Marlow, Curtis Brown Ltd., 575 Madison Ave., New York, N.Y. 10022.

CAREER: Photographer and producer of documentary films, Los Angeles, Calif., 1964-65; McGraw-Hill Book Co., Los Angeles, reporter, 1966-67; Southwest Regional Laboratory for Educational Research and Development, Los Angeles, story writer, 1969-74; free-lance writer, 1974—. *Member:* Society of Children's Book Writers (co-founder; president).

WRITINGS—Juveniles: (With Lin Oliver) *Bookmark Pre-Primer,* Harcourt, 1977; *101 Black Cats,* Scholastic Book Services, 1975; *The Ghost With the Halloween Hiccups,* F. Watts, 1977; *Monster Crafts,* Messner, 1979; *Into the Unknown: Nine Astounding Stories,* Lippincott, 1980.

WORK IN PROGRESS: Orphan Jeb and the Massacre Mine, a juvenile novel.

SIDELIGHTS: Mooser writes: "I have an on-going interest in treasure and have participated in a number of land and sea expeditions, ranging from the deserts of Utah to the jungles of Panama. I'm always open to a good treasure tale and, if the treasure isn't to be found at the end of the expedition, there's always a story to be told. Win or lose I'm always rewarded."

* * *

MORAY, Helga

PERSONAL: Born in Cape Town, South Africa; married Tay Garnett (a film director; marriage ended); married James Clayton (a research chemist; deceased); children: (first marriage) William. *Education:* Attended convent school in Cape Town, South Africa. *Religion:* Roman Catholic. *Home:* Eden Park, 35 Ave. Dr. Picaud, 06 400 Cannes, France. *Agent:* Lisa Collier, Collier Associates, 280 Madison Ave., New York, N.Y. 10016.

CAREER: Professional actress on stage, television, and films; writer.

WRITINGS—Historical novels: *Untamed,* Putnam, 1950; *Tisa,* McKay, 1952; *Carla,* Museum Press, 1954; *Dark Fury,* McKay, 1958; *Blood on the Wind,* R. Hale, 1973; *Clear to Sail,* R. Hale, 1974.

Also author of *Caviar or Crusts,* R. Hale; *Love the Hour,* Museum Press; *The Man Who Came Back,* R. Hale; *Not for a Day,* Museum Press; *Quest in the Sun,* R. Hale; *Francia; I, Roxana,* Playboy Press; *Roxana and Alexander,* Playboy Press,; *A Son for Alexander,* Playboy Press; *The Harvest Burns; The Savage Earth, Footsteps in the Night; To Make a Light; The Ruby Fleet;* and *Trenfell Castle.* Contributor of stories and articles to magazines.

WORK IN PROGRESS: Research on the French Revolution for another novel.

SIDELIGHTS: Helga Moray's books have been published in seventeen languages. *Untamed* was made into a feature film by Twentieth Century-Fox.

She writes: "I write mainly historical novels set in Turkey, Persia, India, and South Africa, and have traveled extensively for background material. I have visited fifty-six countries and sailed around the world on a yacht. The travel experiences motivated my writing. I wrote short stories, then articles, and worked up to novels."

AVOCATIONAL INTERESTS: Photography, archaeology.

* * *

MORETTI, Marino 1885(?)-1979

OBITUARY NOTICE: Born c. 1885; died July 6, 1979, in Cesenatico, Italy. Poet and member of the "crepuscular" school of poetry. Obituaries and other sources: *Chicago Tribune,* July 8, 1979.

* * *

MORGAN, Fred Troy 1926-
(Mordecia Bleeker)

PERSONAL: Born November 15, 1926, in Big Lick, N.C.; son of C. C. and Elizabeth (Springer) Morgan; married Isabelle Griffin, April 4, 1951; children: Rosemary Morgan Almond, Annette, Freddie. *Education:* Attended school in Stanly County, N.C. *Religion:* Baptist. *Home address:* Route 2, Box 112, Albemarle, N.C. 28001. *Agent:* Jay Garon-Brooke Associates, Inc., 415 Central Park W., New York, N.Y. 10025. *Office: Stanly News and Press,* Albemarle, N.C. 28001.

CAREER: North Carolina Highway Commission, truck driver, 1946-51; *Stanly News and Press,* Albemarle, N.C., feature editor and photographer, 1951—. Publicity writer for industry, including Ford Motor Co. Speaker to school children. Past member of board of directors of Stanly County Historical Properties Commission. Consultant to North Carolina Department of Juvenile Corrections. *Military service:* U.S. Navy, 1944-46. *Awards, honors:* National Endowment for the Arts fellowship, 1978.

WRITINGS: Ghost Tales of the Uwharries, Blair, 1968; *Uwharries,* Russwood, 1971; *Uwharrie Magic,* Moore Publishing, 1974. Contributor of several hundred articles and reviews to national magazines and newspapers, sometimes under the pseudonym Mordecia Bleeker.

WORK IN PROGRESS: Two adventure novels for young people.

SIDELIGHTS: Morgan writes: "My childhood fascination with folktales led to a special interest in ghosts as I grew up. This developed into a general interest in the supernatural, but right now I have more ideas than I can ever possibly develop. I find myself freewheeling with ideas more and somehow writing less. Is there a marketplace out there somewhere for original, creative, but undeveloped, ideas in a variety of areas? The Muse pulls me in this direction.

"For instance, why couldn't the creative and imaginative power of writers be harnessed, collectively, and focused on some of the tough problems facing our nation today? A think tank situation sort of. We've been through all the formalities of symposiums, workshops, seminars, alcoholic conventions, and assorted balderdash, most of which is hardly worth a burp in the basin. Surely there is a new and workable approach to this harnessing. New Motivation, new stimulation, new challenge, new vision. Yes, it will take almost superhuman leadership; perhaps an organizational effort of Herculean proportions; dedicated follow-through and distillation and all that; but if somehow and someway we can once strike that mystical chord and note that will impel Americans to shed this disastrous mantle of lethargy and greed, then get back to some genuine, grassroots individual and collective bootstrapping operations, we'll have renewed partriotism and confidence, which can do wonders for America. Writers can be the catalyst as well as any other group. Who'll volunteer some organizational effort?''

* * *

MORGAN, Patricia 1944-

PERSONAL: Born May 21, 1944, in London, England; daughter of Leonard (a plasterer) and Hilda (Mann) Morgan; married Stephen Williams (a government press officer), January 31, 1976. *Education:* West Ham College of Technology (now of University of London), B.Sc. (with honors), 1962. *Politics:* ''Moving rightward.'' *Religion:* Atheist. *Home:* 301 St. Margaret's Rd., Twickenham, Middlesex, England.

CAREER: Elementary school teacher, 1962-64; high school teacher of economics and social history, 1967-71; free-lance writer, 1971—.

WRITINGS: Child Care: Sense and Fable, Temple Smith, 1975; *Delinquent Fantasies,* Temple Smith, 1978. Also contributor to *Women and Their Role.* Contributor to magazines, including *New Society, Community Care,* and *Psychology Today,* and newspapers.

WORK IN PROGRESS: It's Up to You (tentative title), a book to combat delinquency; *The End of Upbringing?; The Labour Party and Crime.*

SIDELIGHTS: Patricia Morgan writes: ''I am an empiricist and a feminist—in that order. I am fascinated by the hold of ideas contrary to common sense and disproved daily by the most mundane facts.

''I have been particularly interested in and disturbed by child-centered psychological theory and the spread of child-rearing practices based upon it. This is largely scientifically groundless and frequently theoretically absurd. It has represented Man as profoundly non-cultural, even non-social. It has cast him as a creature of instinctual need and pre-programmed development, controlled by private, hidden emotional—or simply sensory—forces, rather than by what is learned, shared, and conscious. It has denied him the capacity to act with volition from any appreciation of alternatives—a process inherent in cultural status.

''If this 'ideology' has denied much of what is involved in being human it has, by the same token, denied the process of cultural transmission by which the child *becomes* human. The adult must no longer pass on the skills, traditions, norms, and values of his culture, but must take his cues from the child. The results of child-centeredness have been the growing rates of delinquency,disintegration to be found in Western societies. The child-centered focus logically implies not only the termination of society but the abandonment of the next generation—it is the end of upbringing and synonymous with neglect.

''Moreover, there is the widespread and often quite axiomatic assumption that our society is actually unworthy of being handed on. In Britain the perpetural focus on abnormalities, deviance, and problems, the disproportional attempts to placate actual or imagined injustices, and the continual criticism and condemnation of society has helped to create a cynical malaise amongst all sections of the population.

''The refusal to hand our society on to our children, the emphasis on its failings, and the denial of personal responsibility are together forming a threatening nihilism. I am now writing *The End of Upbringing?,* which traces the contraction in the child's adult environment—from nuclear family to mother alone to his abandonment to the peer-group, against the background of child-centered theory and recommendation. It raises the questions of whether or not the Western world—in giving up the task of cultural transmission—now has any use for children, or even likes the 'aliens' it has produced.''

* * *

MORGENSTERN, Julian 1881-1976

OBITUARY NOTICE—See index for *CA* sketch: Born March 18, 1881, in St. Francisville, Ill.; died December 4, 1976, in Macon, Ga. Rabbi, biblical scholar, educator, and author of more than ten books on ancient Semitic civilizations. Morgenstern, who received his rabbinical degree in 1902, was affiliated with Hebrew Union College—Jewish Institute of Religion for more than sixty years. In addition to his position as professor of Semitic languages, Morgenstern was president of the college from 1922 to 1947 when he became president emeritus. Obituaries and other sources: *New York Times,* December 7, 1976; *Who Was Who in America,* 6th edition, Marquis, 1976; *AB Bookman's Weekly,* January 31, 1977.

* * *

MORISEY, A. Alexander 1913-1979

OBITUARY NOTICE: Born December 3, 1913, in Smithfield, N.C.; died July 23, 1979, in New York, N.Y. Public relations practitioner and reporter. Morisey became one of the first black reporters for a white southern newspaper when hired by the North Carolina *Winston-Salem Journal* in 1949. He spent seven years at the *Journal* covering the black community and doing general assignment reporting before leaving to pursue a career in public relations. Morisey served as director of public relations for several organizations, including the American Friends Service Committee, Howard University, and the *New York Times.* At the *Times,* Morisey initiated a program to improve student newspapers in high schools and colleges whereby his office would supply resource materials and furnish speakers from the *Times* editorial staff. Obituaries and other sources: *Washington Post,* July 26, 1979; *Who's Who in Public Relations (International),* 4th edition, PR Publishing, 1972.

* * *

MORRIS, Edmund 1940-

PERSONAL: Born May 27, 1940, in Nairobi, Kenya; came to the United States in 1968, naturalized citizen, 1979; son of Eric Edmund (an airline pilot) and May (Dowling) Morris; married Sylvia Jukes (a writer), May 28, 1966. *Education:* Attended Rhodes University, 1959-60. *Home and office:* 240 Central Park S., New York, N.Y. 10019. *Agent:* Georges Borchardt, Inc., 136 East 57th St., New York, N.Y. 10022.

CAREER: Worked as advertising copywriter in London, England, 1964-68, and in New York, N.Y., 1968-71; writer, 1971—.

WRITINGS: The Rise of Theodore Roosevelt (Book-of-the-Month Club selection), Coward, 1979. Contributor to magazines. Contributing editor of *New York Times*, 1975-76.

WORK IN PROGRESS: Theodore Rex, Volume II, publication by Coward expected in 1982.

SIDELIGHTS: Morris writes: "I care very much for form and technique, and find that my imagination works best when shaped by the one and disciplined by the other. For example, *The Rise of Theodore Roosevelt* follows the symmetrical form of Bach's 'Goldberg Variations,' and the prologue is technically written in the second person, while seeming to be cast in the third. Of course readers should not be aware of such private contrivances; if they are, then one's art has not sufficiently concealed the art. I believe that literary talent, however slight, is a gift inscrutably bestowed, and that the recipient should pay for it by working very hard at the mechanics, which are, after all, ninety-nine per cent of any perfect manuscript."

The Rise of Theodore Roosevelt was highly praised by Christopher Lehmann-Haupt as a "stirring," "dramatic," "irrestible," and "wonderfully absorbing biography." He lauded Morris for presenting Roosevelt's dramatic activities and contradictory personality traits without technical explanations or analytical interpretations. The book is "a lot more than a string of dramatic anecdotes," noted Lehmann-Haupt, and "because Mr. Morris keeps his distances and submerges his picture of Roosevelt in carefully documented fact, his portrait remains alive and believable."

W. A. Swanberg was equally enthusiastic about Morris's "splendid, galloping narrative of the great galloper. The insights are keen. The pages turn quickly. . . . It is one of those rare works that is both definitive for the period it covers and fascinating to read for sheer entertainment. There should be a queue awaiting the next and concluding volume."

BIOGRAPHICAL/CRITICAL SOURCES: New York Times Book Review, March 25, 1979; *Book-of-the-Month Club News*, April, 1979; *New York Times*, May 21, 1979.

* * *

MORRIS, James M(atthew) 1935-

PERSONAL: Born July 13, 1935, in Reed City, Mich.; son of Fred M. (a laborer) and Florence (Weiland) Morris; married Nancy C. Becker, August 23, 1958; children: Patrick J., Anne C., Michael J., John E., Joseph A., Mary Jane. *Education:* Aquinas College, A.B., 1957; Central Michigan University, M.A., 1962; University of Cincinnati, Ph.D., 1969. *Religion:* Roman Catholic. *Home:* 364 Paulette Dr., Newport News, Va. 23602. *Office:* Department of History, Christopher Newport College, P.O. Box 6070, Newport News, Va. 23606.

CAREER: High school teacher of English and history in Muskegon, Mich., 1957-59, and Mt. Pleasant, Mich., 1959-62; College of Steubenville, Steubenville, Ohio, instructor in history, 1962-64; Providence College, Providence, R.I., assistant professor of history, 1967-71; Christopher Newport College, Newport News, Va., assistant professor, 1971-72, associate professor, 1972-77, professor of history, 1977—, head of department, 1972-74. Moderator of "Faculty Forum" on WVEC-Radio, 1977-78, and WGH-FM Radio, 1978—. Participant in international conferences. *Member:* North American Society for Oceanic History, American Historical Association, Organization of American Historians, U.S. Naval Institute.

WRITINGS: Our Maritime Heritage: Maritime Developments and Their Impact on American Life, University Press of America, 1979. Contributor to history journals.

WORK IN PROGRESS: Research on the decline of the American merchant marine in the nineteenth century.

SIDELIGHTS: Morris comments: "Basically I see my writing as an extension of my vocation as a college teacher. While my views on the importance of writing are hardly original, perhaps they bear repeating as a reaffirmation of the obligations of the journeyman teacher-scholar.

"First, serious writing allows the teacher to expand his audience. After he has studied a subject for a long time and has gained knowledge of it—and perhaps even a bit of wisdom—the exigencies of time and multiple classroom priorities war against full exposition on the subject, and, even at that, his academic audience is necessarily limited to those enrolled in his classes. Why not gain fuller exposition plus a wider audience for one facet of knowledge via the printed word? For me, that facet of knowledge is American maritime and naval history, a subject much neglected in American higher education.

"Second, serious writing forces the teacher to expand his knowledge and understanding. By doing so in a systematic way, he thereby becomes more effective. As there is no substitute for a dedication to truth, so there is no substitute for the discipline and mental expansiveness of research and writing.

"Thus, as I see it, writing is an invaluable aid to the teacher-scholar and a necessary part of his work."

* * *

MORRIS, Richard J(ules) 1942-

PERSONAL: Born February 19, 1942, in Chicago, Ill.; son of George A. and Pearl (Wohl) Morris; married Yvonne Goodman, June 3, 1967; children: Stephanie, Michael, Jacqueline. *Education:* University of Wisconsin (now University of Wisconsin—Madison), B.S., 1963; Roosevelt University, M.A., 1965; Arizona State University, Ph.D., 1970. *Office:* Department of Special Education, University of Arizona, Tucson, Ariz. 85721.

CAREER: Elgin State Hospital, Elgin, Ill., psychology intern, 1964-65, staff psychologist, summer, 1966; Good Samaritan Hospital, Phoenix, Ariz., psychology intern, 1967-68; Arizona State University, Tempe, clinical assistant at Clinical Psychology Center, 1968-69, assistant professor of psychology, spring, 1970; Syracuse University, Syracuse, N.Y., assistant professor, 1970-74, associate professor of psychology, 1974-78; University of Arizona, Tucson, associate professor of special education, 1978—. Clinical assistant professor at State University of New York Upstate Medical Center, 1974-78. Participant in professional gatherings in the United States and abroad; scientific consultant to Bavarian State Institute for Early Childhood Education and Child Study.

MEMBER: American Psychological Association, American Association on Mental Deficiency, American Association for the Advancement of Science, American Association of University Professors, Association for the Advancement of Behavior Therapy, Sigma Xi. *Awards, honors:* Grant from New York State Health Research Council, 1977-78.

WRITINGS: (Editor) *Perspectives in Abnormal Behavior*, Pergamon, 1974; *Behavior Modification With Children: A Systematic Guide*, Winthrop Publishing, 1976; (with J. R. O'Neill) *Verhaltensprobleme in Kinder: Ursprung und Behandlung* (title means "Behavior Disorders in Children: Etiology and Treatment"), in press.

Contributor: Gardner Lindzey, Calvin S. Hall, and Martin Manosevitz, editors, *Theories of Personality: Primary Sources and Research,* Wiley, 1973; J. R. Sutterer, editor, *Foundation of Human Behavior,* Syracuse University Press, 1973; Frederick Kanfer and A. P. Goldstein, editors, *Helping People Change,* Pergamon, 1975; Goldstein editor, *Prescriptions for Child Mental Health and Education,* Pergamon, 1978. Contributor to *Behavior Change Annual.* Contributor of about twenty articles and reviews to psychology journals.

WORK IN PROGRESS: A clinical methods textbook for teachers on teaching social and academic skills to severely handicapped children; a textbook on abnormal psychology; research on contact desensitization of fears in retarded persons, the use of the peer helper model to teach self-help skills to severely retarded children; a comparison of sign language training and verbal operant shaping in the development of language in autistic children; teaching problem-solving to parents of severely retarded children (along with behavior modification training).

SIDELIGHTS: Morris comments: "My major areas of interest include therapy research with autistic and other severely emotionally disturbed children, skill training in retarded children, and fear reduction research with phobic and anxious adults."

* * *

MORRIS, Robert 1910-

PERSONAL: Born November 21, 1910, in Akron, Ohio; son of Joseph (a grocer) and Katherine (Spielberger) Schmaltz; married Sara Myra Goldman, December, 1940. *Education:* University of Akron, A.B., 1931; Western Reserve University (now Case Western Reserve University), M.Sc., 1935; Columbia University, D.S.W., 1959. *Home:* 18 Battle Green Rd., Lexington, Mass. 02173.

CAREER: Jewish Family & Children's Bureau, Baltimore, Md., supervisor, 1936-39; Jewish Family Service, Cleveland, Ohio, supervisor, 1939-41; Workers Service Bureau, Cleveland, 1941-43; United Nations Relief & Rehabilitation Agency, principal welfare officer, 1945-46; regional director of social work service for Veterans Administration, 1947-49; National Council of Jewish Federations, New York City, planning consultant, 1949-59; Adelphi University, Garden City, N.Y., visiting lecturer in social work, 1952-55; Brandeis University, Florence Heller Graduate School for Advanced Studies in Social Welfare, Waltham, Mass., associate professor, 1959-61, professor of social planning, 1961-79, Kirstein Professor, 1965-79, professor emeritus, 1979—, director of Levinson Policy Institute, 1970-76, consultant, 1979—. Visiting lecturer at Columbia University, summer, 1961, University of California, Los Angeles, summer, 1967, University of Manitoba, 1967, Case Western Reserve University, spring, 1976, and University of Wisconsin—Madison, spring, 1977; lecturer at Harvard University, 1968—. Member of Veterans Administration special medical advisory board, 1967-71, behavioral science review board, 1971, and Federal Advisory Council for Geriatric Research, 1976-78; co-leader of American Foundation for the Blind task force on geriatric blindness, 1969-76; head of Conference Board of Associated Research Persons social welfare review committee, 1971—; participant in symposia and conferences. *Military service:* U.S. Army, 1943-45; psychiatric social worker.

MEMBER: American Public Health Association (fellow), Gerontological Society of America (fellow; president, 1966-67), National Association of Social Workers, Massachusetts Society for the Prevention of Blindness (member of board of directors, 1970-76), Easter Seal Society for Crippled Children and Adults of Massachusetts (member of board of directors and head of Center for Applied Studies, 1974-75). *Awards, honors:* Senior Fulbright awards for Italy, 1965-66, 1970; Ford Foundation research awards, 1969-70 (for England), 1974; National Science Foundation grant, 1976-78; Administration on Aging research grants, 1977-79.

WRITINGS: The Community Plans for Its Chronically Ill and Aged (monograph), Council of Jewish Federations and Welfare Funds, 1961; (editor) *Centrally Planned Change: Prospects and Concepts,* National Association of Social Workers, 1964; (with Robert Binstock and Martin Rein) *Feasible Planning for Social Change,* Columbia University Press, 1966; (editor with Michael Freund) *Trends and Issues in Jewish Social Welfare in the United States, 1899-1958,* Jewish Publication Society of America, 1966; (editor with Bernard Frieden) *Urban Planning and Social Policy,* Basic Books, 1968; *Toward a Caring Society,* School of Social Work, Columbia University, 1974; (with Robert Mayer and Robert Moroney) *Centrally Planned Change: A Re-Examination of Theories and Concepts,* University of Illinois Press, 1974; *Social Policies of the American Welfare State,* Harper, 1977.

Contributor: Arthur Dunham and Ernest Harper, editors, *Community Organization in Action,* Association Press, 1959; Herbert Millman, editor, *The Social Welfare Forum, 1961,* Columbia University Press, 1961; Thomas Sherrard, editor, *Community Organization, 1961,* Columbia University Press, 1961; *Public Health Concepts in Social Work Education,* Council on Social Work Education, 1962; James E. Birren, editor, *Relations of Development and Aging,* C. C Thomas, 1963; *Selected Biennial Round Table Conference Papers, 1963,* American Public Welfare Association, 1963; Elizabeth Meir, Cora Kasive, and Florence Ray, editors, *Social Work Practice, 1963,* Columbia University Press, 1963; *Research Utilization in Aging: An Exploration,* U.S. Government Printing Office, 1963; Morton Leeds and Herbert Shore, editors, *Geriatric Institutional Management,* Putnam, 1964; Matilda White Riley, editor, *Aging and Society,* Volume II, Russell Sage Foundation, 1966; Henry Maas, editor, *Five Fields of Social Service,* National Association of Social Workers, 1966; Lee J. Cary, editor, *Community Development as a Process,* University of Missouri Press, 1971; Daniel Bergsma and Anne Pulver, editors, *Developmental Disabilities,* Allen R. Liss, 1976; *Science and Technology in the Service of the Physically Handicapped,* National Research Council, 1976; Wayne Anderson, Bernard Frieden, and Michael Murphy, editors, *Managing Human Services,* International City Management Association, 1977.

Editor-in-chief of *Encyclopedia of Social Work,* 1970-72, editor, 1974-78. Contributor of more than a dozen articles and reviews to journals in the social sciences and to *Congressional Record.*

WORK IN PROGRESS: Research on psycho-social foundations for helping strangers "which underpin the historical evolution of philanthropy and the modern welfare state"; an evaluation of the feasibility of insurance or capitation methods for structuring longterm health and social care programs.

SIDELIGHTS: Morris writes: "I have long been interested in how humans organize their efforts (and try to improve them or to evade acting) to cope with recurring and predictable, but troubling, conditions such as illness, aging, psychological disorganization, physical disability, and unemployment. This interest has been pursued along with an unquenchable interest in all corners of the city, including the social and physical architecture of cities and the national designs of western and Mediterranean governments to undergird collective caring for vulnerable persons."

* * *

MORRIS, Suzanne 1944-

PERSONAL: Born January 27, 1944, in Houston, Tex.; daughter of Frank M. (a commercial artist) and Ruth (McMickle) Page; married J. C. Morris (a company president), August 17, 1963; children: Quentin Phillip. *Education:* Attended University of Houston, 1962-64. *Religion:* Episcopalian. *Address:* P.O. Box 722, Crosby, Tex.

CAREER: Writer. Worked as executive secretary, 1969-72. Member of board of directors of Space/Dance/Theater, 1978-79. *Member:* Authors Guild of Authors League of America, Association for Community Television, Citizens for Animal Protection, Animal Protection Institute, Friends of Houston Public Library. *Awards, honors:* First novel award from critic Evelyn Oppenheimer, 1976, for *Galveston.*

WRITINGS: Galveston (novel), Doubleday, 1976; *Keeping Secrets* (novel), Doubleday, 1979.

WORK IN PROGRESS: A novelette; research for a novel set in Texas, spanning about seventy years.

SIDELIGHTS: Morris told *CA:* "As a youngster I stood before the classroom and told mystery stories extemporaneously, my early beginning toward serious writing. I believe that the works of Daphne du Maurier further inspired me to become a writer, and certainly her work has had a strong influence on my own.

"Yet, dreaming of becoming a writer and then working to make the dream come true are not to be confused. My greatest motivation came from Rega McCarty, a creative writing teacher in Tacoma, Washington. I studied with her for a year, then continued to be guided by her via correspondence after returning to Texas in 1968.

"Another very important influence has been William Goyen, the renowned writer and playwright. He read *Galveston* in manuscript form and brought it to the attention of Doubleday. I credit him with launching my career in novel writing.

"Though I consider myself a storyteller, and enjoy all phases of researching and plotting, my approach to fiction is through character. It is the building of unique characters in depth that I strive for in any piece of fiction, and as these characters begin to take life, becoming more real for me than many people I know, I find myself from time to time accommodating the plot to suit them, and feel this is vital in keeping them real and believable.

"I hope never to be guilty of writing a story more than once."

* * *

MORRISON, Charles Clayton 1874-1966

OBITUARY NOTICE: Born December 4, 1874, in Harrison, Ohio; died March, 1966. Clergyman, editor, lecturer, and author of books on religious subjects. Ordained to the ministry of the Disciples of Christ Church in 1892, Morrison served as pastor to several Midwestern congregations before becoming editor of *Christian Century* in 1908, a post he held until 1947. In addition, Morrison was editor of the *Pulpit* from 1929 to 1956, and *Christendom* from 1935 to 1941. Morrison was lecturer at several seminaries and universities, and author of many books, including *The Meaning of Baptism* and *The Outlawry of War.* Obituaries and other sources: *Who Was Who in America,* 4th edition, Marquis, 1968.

* * *

MORSE, Theresa A. 1901-

PERSONAL: Born August 10, 1901, in Rochester, N.Y.; daughter of Isaac (a lawyer) and Cora (Barnet) Adler; married J. Warren Morse, April 22, 1920 (deceased); children: Jean Morse Joseph, Carol Morse Feiner. *Education:* Attended Smith College. *Politics:* Democrat. *Religion:* Jewish. *Residence:* Menemsha, Mass. 02552. *Agent:* Clara Claason, 20 Fifth Ave., New York, N.Y. 10011.

CAREER: Writer. Founder of Beach Plum Inn, Martha's Vineyard, Mass. Involved in civic activities. *Member:* National Association for the Advancement of Colored People.

WRITINGS: Future a la Carte (memoirs), McKay, 1955; *Never in the Kitchen When Company Arrives,* Doubleday, 1964; *The Best I Ever Tasted!,* Doubleday, 1969; *Life Is for Living: How You Can Make It Alone,* Doubleday, 1973; (with Fred Feiner) *The Beach Plum Inn Cookbook,* Doubleday, 1977.

WORK IN PROGRESS: An autobiography.

SIDELIGHTS: Theresa Morse writes: "I have been a fantastically happy mother and wife, active in fundraising events, and a supporter of the arts, particularly theater. I have had the luck to work with George Kaufman, Dorothy Parker, Robert Benchley, Marc Connelly, and others. My writing career was the outcome of an interesting life of work and travel."

* * *

MORTON, H(enry Canova) V(ollam) 1892-1979

OBITUARY NOTICE: Born in 1892 in Birmingham, England; died in 1979 near Cape Town, South Africa. Journalist and author of books on travel. H. V. Morton worked on many British newspapers during his career as a newsman, including the *London Daily Herald,* where he acted as special writer for eleven years. Best known for his best-selling travel books, Morton was considered the unchallenged expert on the British Isles. His travel books include *Ghosts of London, In Search of Scotland,* and *In Search of Ireland,* as well as works on the Middle East, South Africa, Spain, and other countries. A religious man, Morton wrote several books on Biblical personages and places. Impressed with South Africa during his travels, he eventually settled there and became a South African citizen. Morton's historical account, *The Atlantic Meeting,* came out of his being chosen to accompany Churchill and the Prince of Wales on the occasion of the establishment of the Atlantic Charter. Obituaries and other sources: *Twentieth Century Writing: A Reader's Guide to Contemporary Literature,* Transatlantic, 1969; *Longman Companion to Twentieth Century Literature,* Longman, 1970; *The Author's and Writer's Who's Who,* 6th edition, Burke's Peerage, 1971; *Who's Who,* 126th edition, St. Martin's, 1974; *The International Who's Who,* Europa, 1974; *AB Bookman's Weekly,* August 20, 1979.

* * *

MOSTEL, Samuel Joel 1915-1977
(Zero Mostel)

PERSONAL: Stage name, Zero Mostel; born February 28, 1915, in Brooklyn, N.Y.; died September 8, 1977, in Philadelphia, Pa.; son of Israel (a rabbi and vintner of sacramental wines) and Celia (Druchs) Mostel; married second wife, Kate Harkin (a dancer), July 2, 1944; children: Joshua, Tobias. *Education:* City College (now of the City University of New York), received degree, 1935; graduate study at New York University, 1935-36.

CAREER: Actor, comedian, painter. Painted and traveled in Louisiana and Mexico, 1936; factory worker, longshoreman, teacher and lecturer on art for Works Project Administration (WPA), and entertainer at neighborhood parties, 1937-42; comedian at Cafe Society Downtown, La Martinique, and other New York City night clubs, 1942. Appeared in plays, including "Keep 'Em Laughing," 1942, "Flight Into Egypt," 1952, "The Imaginary Invalid," 1952, "The Good Woman of Setzuan," 1956, "Ulysses in Nighttown," 1958 and 1974, "Rhinoceros," 1961, "A Funny Thing Happened on the Way to the Forum," 1962, "Fiddler on the Roof," 1964, "The Latent Heterosexual," 1968. Appeared in motion pictures, including "DuBarry Was a Lady," 1943, "The Guy Who Came Back," 1951, "Mr. Belvedere Rings the Bell," 1951, "The Model and the Marriage Broker," 1951, "A Funny Thing Happened on the Way to the Forum," 1966, "The Producers," 1967, "The Hot Rock," 1972, "Rhinoceros," 1974, "The Front," 1976. Appeared on radio shows, including "Chamber Music Society of Lower Basin Street"; appeared on television programs, including "Cavalcade," "The Ed Sullivan Show," "The World of Sholem Aleichem," 1960, "Waiting for Godot," 1961, a one-man show on "Festival of the Performing Arts," 1963, and "Gianni Schicchi" (opera), 1975. *Military service:* U.S. Army, Infantry, 1943.

MEMBER: Actors Studio. *Awards, honors:* Off-Broadway award from *Village Voice,* 1959, for his performance as Leopold Bloom in "Ulysses in Nighttown"; best actor, International Theatre Festival in Paris, 1959; Antoinette Perry Award for best actor, 1961, for his performance as John in "Rhinoceros"; entertainer of the year award from *Cue* magazine and Antoinette Perry Award for best actor, both 1962, both for his performance as Prologus in "A Funny Thing Happened on the Way to the Forum"; New York Drama Critics award, 1964-65, and Antoinette Perry Award for best actor, 1965, both for his performance as Tevye in "Fiddler on the Roof"; Einstein medal of art.

WRITINGS: (Contributor of partial text and drawings) Max Waldman, *Zero by Mostel,* photography by Waldman, Horizon Press, 1965; (with Israel Shenker) *Zero Mostel's Book of Villains,* Doubleday, 1976; (editor with Jack Gilford) Kate Mostel and Madeline L. Gilford, *One Hundred Seventy Years of Show Business,* Random House, 1978.

SIDELIGHTS: As his name suggests, Zero Mostel started his illustrious acting career from nothing. An artist by vocation, he began entertaining at neighborhood parties during his twenties in order to earn extra money for paints. A nightclub impresario discovered him in 1942 and booked him for his comedy debut at Cafe Society Downtown in New York City. Renamed Zero by his press agent, Mostel was an immediate hit and within a year had risen to phenomenal heights as star of stage and screen.

During his early years Mostel successfully played the role of villain in many plays and movies. Though popular at the time, movies such as "Mr. Belvedere Rings the Bell" and "The Model and the Marriage Broker" were not among his more brilliant works and are little remembered today.

Mostel's career ran into an unfortunate snag when he was blacklisted during the McCarthy era. Accused of attending a Communist meeting in Hollywood, Mostel invoked the Fifth Amendment when questioned by the House Un-American Activities Committee in October, 1955, and for several years was unable to obtain work. Ironically, in Zero Mostel's final movie appearance he starred in "The Front" as a blacklisted comic during the 1950's.

After this occupational lull Mostel triumphantly returned to play one of his greatest roles, that of Leopold Bloom in "Ulysses in Nighttown." Burgess Meredith aided Mostel's comeback by casting him in the lead of this 1958 Off-Broadway production. Jack Kroll noted that "the blacklist interrupted the string of negligible movies he was making, clearing the way for his new career as one of the world's major actors."

In 1961 Mostel stunned Broadway audiences with his fantastic interpretation of Ionesco's "Rhinoceros." "With no props or make-up but his own flexible flesh, he changed before your eyes from a man into a beast—a revelation about humanity that made you laugh with terror," declared Kroll.

Although his next role in "A Funny Thing Happened on the Way to the Forum" won him several awards, most critics agree with the *New York Times* that "it was as Tevye, the earthy Russian-Jewish dairyman in the Sholom Aleichem-based play 'Fiddler on the Roof,' that Mr. Mostel won his greatest acclaim." Mostel transformed the stage with his radiant portrayal of the dirt-poor milkman whose intimate dialogues with God "treated the Deity like a pinochle partner," reflected *Newsweek.* His wistful singing of Yiddish scat-syllables in "If I Were a Rich Man" was one highlight of his superb performance.

Despite his acting success, Zero Mostel always considered himself primarily an artist. He continued to paint during his acting days, once producing a limited-edition collotype of his impressions of Tevye and other Sholom Aleichem characters. The work, entitled "See You Again, Sholom Aleichem," sold for $325 per copy. Several of his sketches and washes were reproduced in *Zero by Mostel* and Haskel Frankel noted that they "suggest a smidge of Lautrec here, a dab of Picasso there, and a seriousness of purpose throughout."

Mostel served as co-editor of *One Hundred Seventy Years of Show Business,* but died before it was ready for publication. Nevertheless, Richard Shepard contended, it is "no lugubrious, tear-jerking memorial work." The book contains amiable reminiscences about the lives of Zero Mostel and Jack Gilford in times happy and sad. Zero's wife, Kate, and friend, Madeline Gilford, have together "written some kind of wonderful book," declared Howard Teichmann. "It is warm, touching and many, many times hilarious."

Though a master of pantomime, slapstick, and double-entendre, Mostel was not merely a comedian. He subtly fused the serious with the comic, triumphantly balancing the lightness and heaviness of existence with his zany wit and vibrant creativity. In every role, *Time* concluded, "Mostel was the master of paradoxes: a graceful fat man and a wise buffoon."

AVOCATIONAL INTERESTS: Collecting pre-Columbian, Peruvian, and Coptic art; modern art.

BIOGRAPHICAL/CRITICAL SOURCES: New York Times Book Review, January 9, 1966, May 21, 1978; *Saturday Review,* February 5, 1966; *New Yorker,* November 5, 1973; *Hartford Courant,* January 20, 1974; *Biography News,* Gale, March, 1974; *Newsweek,* September 22, 1975, November 17, 1975, September 19, 1977; *Time,* October 27, 1975, January 10, 1977; Kate Mostel and Madeline L. Gilford, *One Hundred Seventy Years of Show Business,* edited by Zero

Mostel and Jack Gilford, Random House, 1978; *New York Times,* May 26, 1978.

OBITUARIES: New York Times, September 9, 1977, September 10, 1977; *Time,* September 19, 1977; *Newsweek,* September 19, 1977.*

* * *

MOSTEL, Zero
See MOSTEL, Samuel Joel

* * *

MOULT, Thomas 1895-1974

OBITUARY NOTICE: Born in 1895 in Derbyshire, England; died in 1974. Journalist, poet, author, and editor of anthologies. Moult was music critic for the *Manchester Guardian,* art and dramatic critic for *Athenaeum* and the *English Review,* as well as sports writer for various English and Australian journals. In 1919 he founded *Voices,* an arts magazine, and he was chairman of the editorial board of the *Poetry Review* for ten years. Moult wrote novels, verse, biographical and critical studies, and books on sports. As an anthologist he is best known for his series of poetry collections, *The Best Poems.* Published annually for sixteen years, the collections served to introduce many promising poets of Moult's generation. Among his many works figure *Snow Over Eldon, Down Here the Hawthorn, Mary Webb,* and *Brown Earth.* Obituaries and other sources: *The New Century Handbook of English Literature,* revised edition, Appleton, 1967; *Longman Companion to Twentieth Century Literature,* Longman, 1970; *The Author's and Writer's Who's Who,* 6th edition, Burke's Peerage, 1971; *Who's Who,* 126th edition, St. Martin's, 1974.

* * *

MOUTOUX, John T. 1901(?)-1979

OBITUARY NOTICE: Born c. 1901 in Jasper, Ind.; died September 17, 1979, of a stroke, in Fairfax, Va. Reporter for the *Knoxville News,* United Press, and the Scripps-Howard newspapers, and news director of the U.S. Government Housing and Home Finance Agency. Moutoux was the reporter who broke the "Scopes Monkey Trial" story, the story about Dayton, Tenn., high school teacher John Thomas Scopes's arrest and subsequent trial for teaching Darwin's theory that man and ape could have evolved from a common ancestor, one of the biggest news makers of the 1920's. Moutoux also covered such stories as the establishment of the Tennessee Valley Authority (TVA) and the campaign for national parks. Obituaries and other sources: *Washington Post,* September 28, 1979; *Chicago Tribune,* September 30, 1979.

* * *

MUDGE, Lewis Seymour 1929-

PERSONAL: Born October 22, 1929, in Philadelphia, Pa.; son of Lewis Seymour (a minister) and Anne Evelyn (Bolton) Mudge; married Jean Bruce McClure (a writer and filmmaker), June 15, 1957; children: Robert Seymour, William McClure, Anne Evelyn. *Education:* Princeton University, B.A., 1951, Ph.D., 1961; Oxford University, B.A., 1954, M.A., 1958; Princeton Theological Seminary, B.D., 1955. *Politics:* "Democrat most of the time." *Home:* 1218 East Madison Park, Chicago, Ill. 60615. *Office:* McCormick Theological Seminary, 5555 South Woodlawn Ave., Chicago, Ill. 60637.

CAREER: Ordained Presbyterian minister, 1955; Princeton University, Princeton, N.J., Presbyterian university pastor, 1955-56; World Alliance of Reformed Churches, Geneva, Switzerland, secretary in department of theology, 1957-62; Amherst College, Amherst, Mass., assistant professor, 1962-65, associate professor, 1965-70, professor of religion and philosophy, 1970-75, head of department, 1969-70, 1974-75, college minister, 1962-68; McCormick Theological Seminary, Chicago, Ill., professor of theology and dean of seminary, 1975—. Member of World Council of Churches committees, 1958-62; committee member and study director for National Council of Churches, 1964-72; president of Westminster Foundation in New England, 1965-68; head of national committees of Presbyterian Church of the United States of America, 1965-72, head of board of directors of its Vocation Agency, 1972-73, member of executive committee, 1974-76; head of Theological Commission of Consultation on Church Union, 1977—. Lecturer at universities, ecumenical meetings, and lay gatherings. *Member:* Society of Biblical Literature, American Academy of Religion, Society for Values in Higher Education, Phi Beta Kappa. *Awards, honors:* Rhodes scholar at Oxford University.

WRITINGS: In His Service: The Servant Lord and His Servant People, Westminster, 1959; *One Church: Catholic and Reformed,* Westminster, 1963; *Is God Alive?,* United Church Press, 1963; (contributor) Keith R. Bridston and Walter Wagoner, editors, *Unity in Mid-Career,* Macmillan, 1963; *Why Is the Church in the World?,* Department of Church and Society, United Presbyterian Church of the United States of America, 1967; *The Crumbling Walls,* Westminster, 1970. Contributor of articles and reviews to theology journals.

WORK IN PROGRESS: Community and Reality: The Social Signification of the Gospel (tentative title); a critical introduction for an anthology of Paul Ricoeur's writings on biblical hermeneutics.

SIDELIGHTS: Mudge comments: "I am a theological educator, theologian, churchperson, ecumenist. My interests therefore turn on such issues as the role of theological reflection in the preparation of pastors, the relation between theology and the human sciences, and the question of the local and world-wide unity of the Church. As chairperson of the Theology Commission of the U.S. Consultation on Church Union, I am deeply involved in laying theological groundwork for current unity efforts."

BIOGRAPHICAL/CRITICAL SOURCES: New York Times, March 8, 1979, March 9, 1979; *Christian Century,* March 28, 1979.

* * *

MULHOLLAND, John 1898-1970

OBITUARY NOTICE—See index for *CA* sketch: Born June 9, 1898, in Chicago, Ill.; died February 25, 1970, in New York, N.Y. Magician, teacher, and author. Mulholland was considered by many to be a magician par excellence. In addition to performing, he gave lectures on magic around the world. Mulholland was editor of the magician's journal *Sphinx* for twenty-three years, and was the author of numerous books on magic, including *The Art of Illusion, Quicker Than the Eye,* and *The Story of Magic.* The Walter Hampden Memorial Library now holds his lifetime collection of memorabilia and books on magic. Obituaries and other sources: *New York Times,* February 26, 1970; *Newsweek,* March 9, 1970; *AB Bookman's Weekly,* March 16, 1970; *Who Was Who in America,* 5th edition, Marquis, 1973.

MULLIN, Robert N(orville) 1893-

PERSONAL: Born August 10, 1893, in Lincoln, Neb.; son of Joseph P. (a college professor) and Charlotte (a high school teacher; maiden name, Norville) Mullin; married Josephine Plumridge, November 21, 1916; children: Elizabeth Welch (deceased), Marjorie Mullin Jackson, Frances Mullin Daseler. *Education:* Attended high school in El Paso, Tex. *Politics:* Conservative Republican. *Religion:* Episcopal. *Residence:* South Laguna, Calif.

CAREER: Owner of bookstore in El Paso, Tex., 1912-15; Great Western Oil Co., Cleveland, Ohio, in sales in Texas, New Mexico, and Arizona, 1915; Calumet Oil Co. of Texas, president, 1917-27; Continental Oil Co., manager of Chicago division, 1917-30; Phillips Petroleum Co., manager of Chicago division, 1930-31; Gulf Refining Co., assistant manager of Toledo division, 1932; Gulf Oil Corp., manager of Chicago division, 1932-57. Consultant to Sumner Sollitt Engineering Co., 1957-60. Writer and researcher. Past member of El Paso City Council; past vice-president of El Paso Chamber of Commerce; director of various civic organizations. *Member:* Western Writers of America.

WRITINGS: Chronology of the Lincoln County War, Press of the Territorian, 1966; (with W. H. Hutchinson) *Whiskey Jim and a Kid Named Billie,* Clarendon Press, 1967; *The Boyhood of Billy the Kid,* Texas Western Press, 1967; (editor and contributor) Maurice Garland Fulton, *History of the Lincoln County War,* University of Arizona Press, 1968; *The Strange Story of Wayne Brazel,* introduction by J. Evetts Haley, Palo Duro Press, 1971; *An Item From Old Mesilla* (pamphlet), Carl Hertzog, 1971. Also author of *The Boyhood of Billy the Kid,* Texas Western Press. Contributor to regional history journals.

WORK IN PROGRESS: Research on pre-Civil War stage lines in the Southwest.

SIDELIGHTS: Mullin writes: "In 1915, I secured a position as a salesman for the Great Western Oil Co., selling lubricants to mines and manufacturing plants in west Texas, New Mexico, and Arizona, the principal interest being to examine courthouse records, old newspaper files, and interview early settlers in search of factual information concerning the Southwestern frontier.

"When Colonel Maurice Garland Fulton died in 1955, his wife found on his desk an unfinished letter. Fulton wrote that he had been searching for prime factual information concerning New Mexico's Lincoln County War for thirty years, and had completed about two-thirds of a manuscript draft. He doubted that he would live long enough to complete the work and knew of only two persons qualified to finish the book. Colonel Fulton had spent his earnings in excess of living expenses for his research work and was destitute when he died. His widow considered his uncompleted manuscript to be his one valuable asset and asked me to finish the book for publication. The result was *History of the Lincoln County War.*"

* * *

MULLIN, Willard 1902-1978

OBITUARY NOTICE: Born in Ohio in 1902; died December 21, 1978, in Corpus Christi, Tex. Sports cartoonist who created the Brooklyn Dodger Bum. Williams turned out six drawings a week for the *New York World-Telegram* from 1934 until the paper folded in 1966. Large cartoons, they often ran over four or five of the paper's six columns. A collection of three hundred of his drawings is housed in the Syracuse University Library, and one drawing hangs in the Metropolitan Museum of Art. Mullin was voted "sports cartoonist of the century" by the National Cartoonists Society in 1971, and received the "Reuben," the Oscar of cartooning, in 1955, as well as being voted best sports cartoonist of the year eight times by his peers. His illustrations appeared in hundreds of books and magazines, including the *Saturday Evening Post, Look, Newsweek, Esquire,* and the cover of *Time* magazine when the Mets won the pennant in 1969. Mullin, who had no formal art training, said at an exhibition of his works in 1971 that "there have been two schools of sports cartooning, the hip-hip-hooray school, and the look-askance school. I'm the hooray school." Obituaries and other sources: *New York Times,* January 10, 1971, December 22, 1978.

* * *

MUNGER, Hortense Roberta
See ROBERTS, Hortense Roberta

* * *

MUNRO, C. K.
See MacMULLAN, Charles Walden Kirkpatrick

* * *

MUNSON, Thurman (Lee) 1947-1979

OBITUARY NOTICE: Born June 7, 1947, in Akron, Ohio; died August 2, 1979, in a plane crash, in Akron, Ohio. Baseball catcher and team captain of the New York Yankees, Munson played on three Yankee pennant winners and two world championship teams. The first Yankee captain since Lou Gehrig, Munson played with New York for a decade, winning the Golden Glove Award in 1973, 1974, and 1975, and the American League Most Valuable Player Award in 1976. Munson's book, *Thurman Munson: An Autobiography,* was published in 1978. Obituaries and other sources: *Sports Illustrated,* September 13, 1976; *Current Biography,* Wilson, November, 1977, September, 1979; Bill Libby, *Thurman Munson, Pressure Player,* Putnam, 1978; *New York Times Biography Service,* May, 1978; *Sport,* June, 1978; *New York Times,* August 3, 1979.

* * *

MURDOCH, (Henry) Derrick 1909-

PERSONAL: Born December 7, 1909, in London, England; son of Henry Bedford (a businessman) and Alice Ada (an actress; maiden name, Skuse) Murdoch; married Felicite Kirby, December 28, 1939 (died June, 1975); children: Carole Sacripanti, Sarah Henry. *Education:* Attended public schools in Canterbury, England. *Home:* 485 Huron St., #101, Toronto, Ontario, Canada M5R 2R5.

CAREER: General Electric Company Ltd., London, England, sales executive, 1928-45; Truvox Ltd., London, general sales manager, 1945-50; Juno Company of Canada, Toronto, Ontario, president, 1950-62; full-time writer, 1963—. *Member:* Mystery Writers of America, Writers Union of Canada, Periodical Writers Association of Canada, Crime Writers Association, Bootmakers Of Toronto (first president, 1972).

WRITINGS: The Agatha Christie Mystery, Pagurian Press, 1976. Author of a crime fiction review column in the *Globe and Mail,* Toronto, 1964—. Contributor of articles to magazines, including *Maclean's, Books in Canada,* and *Pacific Quarterly.*

WORK IN PROGRESS: Disappeared (tentative title), "a book describing twenty or so disappearances, some famous and some little known, some solved and some still unsolved, of people in Canada in comparatively recent times."

SIDELIGHTS: Murdoch told *CA:* "Whenever anything I have written seems to convey all I hoped to say I realize my expectations were set too low."

AVOCATIONAL INTERESTS: Doing mathematical and word puzzles, music, food, wine, good liquor, reading light poetry.

* * *

MURPHY, Cornelius Francis, Jr. 1933-

PERSONAL: Born March 13, 1933, in Newport, R.I.; son of Cornelius Francis and Loretta (Nuss) Murphy; married Virginia McDonnell, July 2, 1957; children: Michael, Sean, Rachel, Neal. *Education:* College of the Holy Cross, B.S., 1954; Boston College, J.D., 1957; University of Virginia, LL.M., 1962. *Office:* Law School, Duquesne University, 600 Forbes Ave., Pittsburgh, Pa. 15219.

CAREER: Private practice of law in Newport, R.I., 1958-60; University of Maine, Portland, associate professor of law, 1962-64; Duquesne University, Pittsburgh, Pa., professor of law, 1966—. Visiting scholar at Harvard University, 1973-74. *Member:* International Society of Legal and Social Philosophy, American Society of International Law, United Nations Association of Pittsburgh (past president; member of board of directors).

WRITINGS: (Contributor) R. Falk, editor, *Vietnam and International Law,* Volume III, Princeton University Press, 1969; *Introduction to Law, Legal Process, Procedure,* West Publishing, 1977; *Modern Legal Philosophy,* Duquesne University Press, 1978. Contributor of articles and poems to law and public affairs journals and poetry magazines.

WORK IN PROGRESS: The Future of Canadian-American Relations; A Study of Liberalism.

SIDELIGHTS: Murphy told *CA:* "My work in legal philosophy and in international law has led to the conviction that an adequate understanding of law intrinsically depends upon political philosophy. This idea substantially influences the direction of my work, including the pending projects on Liberalism and the future of North America. In the former, an understanding of the relation between the individual and society depends in part upon an understanding of the nature of political life. Liberalism has generally ignored this dimension, relying instead upon ethical explanations of individual rights. In the study of Canadian-American relations I am exploring possibilities of a common life for citizens of both countries. The conception of public life which reflected the British conservative tradition once gave cohesion to English Canada. I believe that such a tradition could, in a new North American republic, balance the liberal individualism which now prevails in the United States.

"My poetic interests arise from my attraction to aesthetic modes of cognition. The intuitive truths of poetry also satisfy the desire for essential knowledge which are generally ignored in the anti-metaphysical temper of the modern world."

* * *

MURPHY, Fred P. 1889-1979

OBITUARY NOTICE: Born April 17, 1889, in Stamford, N.Y.; died October 27, 1979, in Stamford, N.Y. Publisher and president of Grolier, Inc. for over thirty years, Murphy elevated the company to its domination of the reference book field in the 1950's and 1960's. Murphy was credited with pushing Grolier's sales over the $181 million-a-year mark and capturing ninety-five percent of the market. Obituaries and other sources: *Who's Who in Finance and Industry,* 18th edition, Marquis, 1973; *New York Times,* October 29, 1979.

* * *

MURROW, Edward R(oscoe) 1908-1965

OBITUARY NOTICE: Born April 25, 1908, in Greensboro, N.C.; died April 27, 1965. Journalist, broadcaster, and author. One of the towering figures in American journalism, Murrow first came to prominence during World War II. Stationed in London as CBS's European correspondent, Murrow covered the war from start to finish, including such events as the Nazi invasion of Austria, Chamberlain's meeting with Hitler at Munich, the bombing of London, the campaign in North Africa, and V-E Day. "This Is London" was the phrase which began each of his broadcasts from that city, and those words became inseparably associated with his name. In 1941 some of his broadcasts were collected in a book called *This Is London.* After the war Murrow conducted two radio programs, "Hear It Now," a weekly survey of the news, and "This I Believe," a show in which people discussed their philosophies of life. With the advent of television, he turned to that medium, co-producing "See It Now," which received an Emmy Award. Murrow is credited with setting a new standard of journalistic excellence; he combined a newsman's love of accuracy and objectivity with his own humanitarian values and dramatic flair. From 1961 to 1963 he served as director of the United States Information Agency. Obituaries and other sources: *Current Biography,* Wilson, 1942, 1953, June, 1965; *New York Times,* April 28, 1965; Alexander Kendrick, *Prime Time: The Life of Edward R. Murrow,* Little, Brown, 1969; *Saturday Review,* May 31, 1975; *Atlantic,* January, 1976; Irving E. Fang, *Those Radio Commentators,* Iowa State University Press, 1977; Robert Franklin Smith, *Edward R. Murrow: The War Years,* New Issues Press, 1978.

N

NAGY, Ferenc 1903-1979

OBITUARY NOTICE: Born October 8, 1903, in Bisse, Hungary; died June 12, 1979, in Herndon, Va. Author, lecturer, and the last non-Communist prime minister of Hungary. Nagy was a leader of the democratic Smallholder's party in Soviet-occupied postwar Hungary. His party won the country's only free election after World War II, but little more than a year later, in 1947, the Hungarian Communist party took over the government with Russian aid. Nagy lived in the United States in exile and frequently lectured at colleges and universities about the political situation in Hungary. He was the author of *The Struggle Behind the Iron Curtain* and contributor of articles to newspapers and magazines. Obituaries and other sources: *Who's Who in the World,* 2nd edition, Marquis, 1973; *Washington Post,* June 13, 1979.

* * *

NALDER, Eric C(hristopher) 1946-

PERSONAL: Born March 2, 1946, in Coulee Dam, Washington; son of Phillip Richard (an engineer and foreign service administrator) and Mibs (Aardahl) Nalder; married Jan Christiansen, December 20, 1968; children: Britt Hillary. *Education:* University of Washington, B.A., 1968. *Office:* *Seattle Post-Intelligencer,* Sixth and Wall Sts., Seattle, Wash. 98121.

CAREER/WRITINGS: *Whidbey News-Times,* Oak Harbor, Wash., news editor, 1970-71; *Enterprise Newspaper,* Lynnwood, Wash., reporter, 1972; *Everett Herald-Western Sun,* Everett, Wash., reporter, 1972-75; *Seattle Post-Intelligencer,* Seattle, Wash., investigative reporter, 1975—. *Military service:* U.S. Army Signal Corps, 1969-70; became lieutenant.

MEMBER: Pacific Northwest Newspaper Guild (member of executive board), Washington Presswomen (second male member), Investigative Reporters and Editors, Inc. *Awards, honors:* First place award in business writing, Sigma Delta Chi (western Washington chapter), 1972; first place award for business writing and first place award for story with photo page, Sigma Delta Chi, 1973; national first place award for news writing, Washington Presswomen, 1974, for *Everett Herald* story about a family being evicted; first place in national Charles Stewart Mott Foundation competition, Education Writers Association, 1977, for ten stories regarding development and problems with Seattle's desegregation plan and racial segregation in Seattle schools; numerous other awards in several categories from Sigma Delta Chi and Washington Presswomen.

WORK IN PROGRESS: A fiction novel; nonfiction project about nuclear waste.

SIDELIGHTS: Nalder told *CA:* "My major interest in journalism is in stories that take time and digging to develop, which cannot be had in the normal day-to-day coverage of events. I recently covered a racketeering and political scandal in Pierce County, Wash., and a story on organized crime in King County, Wash. I was the education writer for one year while Seattle became the first city in the nation to decide to desegregate its schools by way of mandatory busing without being forced to do so by a federal court order."

In 1976 Nalder wrote a series on killer whales in Puget Sound. "The story ran one week before Seaworld captured six killer whales in Budd Inlet near the state capitol of Olympia, setting off a storm of protest. I followed that capture for a month until, with pressure from Senator Magnuson, the killer whales were released and Seaworld was never again allowed to capture whales in Puget Sound."

For another series Nalder went inside the Washington state prison at Walla Walla to study conditions there.

Nalder has lived in several countries, including France, Lebanon, where he attended high school, and Norway, where he and his wife lived and worked on a pig farm in 1970.

* * *

NAMATH, Joe
See NAMATH, Joseph William

* * *

NAMATH, Joseph William 1943-
(Joe Namath)

PERSONAL: Also known as Joe Willie Namath and "Broadway Joe"; born May 31, 1943, in Beaver Falls, Pa.; son of Frank Namath (a steel-mill worker) and Rose (Juhasz) Namath Szolnoki. *Education:* Received degree from University of Alabama, 1965. *Religion:* Roman Catholic. *Address:* c/o James C. Walsh, 450 Park Ave., Suite 1500, New York, N.Y. 10022.

CAREER: Professional football player; restauranteur; actor.

Quarterback with New York Jets, 1965-77, and Los Angeles Rams, 1977-78; actor in films "Norwood," 1969, "C.C. and Company," 1970, "The Last Rebel," 1971, and "Avalanche Express," 1979; also actor in television specials and series "The Waverly Wonders," 1978. Owner of restaurants in New York City, Tuscaloosa, Ala., and Fort Lauderdale, Fla. Frequent guest host of "The Tonight Show Starring Johnny Carson." Former chairman of Leukemia Society Coin Campaign; honorary chairman of American Hungarian Society. *Awards, honors:* Named American Football League (AFL) "Rookie of the Year," 1965; member of AFL All-Star teams, 1968, 1972; named "Most Valuable Player" of Super Bowl III, 1969; George Hala Most Courageous Athlete Award.

WRITINGS: (Under name Joe Willie Namath; with Dick Schaap) *I Can't Wait Until Tomorrow . . . 'Cause I Get Better-Looking Every Day* (autobiography), Random House, 1969; (under name Joe Namath; with Bob Oates, Jr.) *A Matter of Style,* Little, Brown, 1973.

SIDELIGHTS: During his thirteen years as a professional football player, Joe Namath captured the attention of the American public with his gutsy quarterbacking, his straightforward manners, and his glamorous and often robust lifestyle. He has been called everything from "an innocent, unsophisticated country lad" to "one of America's great, lovable, irresistable rogues." "Everyone has a favorite Joe Namath image," wrote *Esquire's* Mary Murphy, "[whether it's] of him with a dazzling smile, perhaps, or on a llama rug; of him in his mink coat or with his Johnnie Walker Red or his blondes." Then there's that Beauty Mist commercial with Joe in pantyhose, mocking the macho myth about football players, and the boyish enthusiasm exuded in the Faberge Brut endorsements.

Behind this "Broadway Joe" image, however, stands an athelete who continued to play professional football after four major knee operations, with his knees encased in steel braces, and in constant pain. Some of his greatest and worst memories are of the game: quarterbacking the underdog New York Jets to a 16-7 Super Bowl victory over the heavily favored Baltimore Colts; and the night of October 10, 1977, "when in front of the whole nation he was injured after throwing four interceptions on *Monday Night Football.*" For Namath, "football was an obsession. It works games on your head, mentally and physically. If you throw a bad pass and sixty thousand people boo you or talk about your mother or call you a bum or a rat, it's hell." He often felt that the fans expected too much from him and noted that when you're a superstar "you just don't go out and do the average guy's job."

His autobiography, *I Can't Wait Until Tomorrow,* and *A Matter of Style* both reflect Namath's views on the lifestyle professional atheletes can have and his feelings about the game. *Washington Post Book World* critic H. H. Brown stated: "Joe is certainly a refreshing change from the regiment of those who seem anxious that professional football shall . . . be considered a sort of school of citizenship or outdoor course in business administration. . . . Certainly in its celebration of Scotch and sex [*I Can't Wait Until Tomorrow*] is a big change from all those books that showed the way to the Higher Life as profitably lived by halfbacks, outfielders, pole vaulters and others. . . . There are little snapper jokes scattered through it which smack of the gagsters' conference, but a surprising amount of it sounds like Namath, sounds as fresh, as lively, as naive, as occasionally Byzantine, and as original, as I have found Namath to be when our paths have crossed." In *A Matter of Style* "just about every phase of quarterbacking is covered . . . by the most famous quarterback of the present time," wrote J. J. Fitzpatrick. "The first part focuses on Joe off the gridiron, his life-style, his personality, and how he keeps his cools."

Namath, who retired from football in 1978, has turned to a career in acting. He has also invested successfully in condominiums and restaurants. He would like to use his past glories to help him in business deals, but states that "living on the past is a trap. What you do is cherish the good things and don't allow yourself to think about the ugly memories. Look, one of the real rewards of achieving and succeeding as you move along in life is being able to remember. But living on the past is a way of life I would like to avoid."

AVOCATIONAL INTERESTS: Sailing, golf, reading (Richard Bach is a favorite author).

BIOGRAPHICAL/CRITICAL SOURCES: Sports Illustrated, October 17, 1966, August 17, 1970; *Esquire,* December, 1968, June 19, 1979; Joe Willie Namath and Dick Schaap, *I Can't Wait Until Tomorrow . . . 'Cause I Get Better-Looking Every Day,* Random House, 1969; *Look,* September 9, 1969; *Washington Post Book Review,* November 16, 1969; *Saturday Review,* November 29, 1969; *New York Times,* November 28, 1971, May 27, 1973; Joe Namath and Bob Oates, Jr., *A Matter of Style,* Little, Brown, 1973; *Best Sellers,* November 15, 1973; *Biography News,* Gale, December, 1974; *People,* September 25, 1978.*

* * *

NARAYAN, Jayaprakash 1902-1979

OBITUARY NOTICE: Born October 11, 1902, in Bihar, India; died October 8, 1979, of a heart ailment, in Patna, India. One of the last great followers of Mohandas Gandhi, Narayan worked with Gandhi and Nehru in their nonviolent campaign against the British occupation of India. Although Narayan never held public office, he had great influence over public opinion and led the fight against corruption in the government of prime minister Indira Gandhi. In 1977, he succeeded in ousting her. Narayan also worked to improve the lot of the Indian peasants by instituting a number of social reforms. His works include *Prison Diary,* written while jailed for criticizing the Gandhi administration. Obituaries and other sources: *Current Biography,* Wilson, 1958; *Who's Who in the World,* 2nd edition, Marquis, 1973; *The International Who's Who,* Europa, 1974; *New York Times Biography Service,* January, 1977; *Time,* March 7, 1977; *New York Times Magazine,* March 27, 1977; *Washington Post,* October 9, 1979.

* * *

NATELLA, Arthur A(ristides), Jr. 1941-

PERSONAL: Born November 8, 1941, in Yonkers, N.Y.; son of Arthur A. and Rose Natella. *Education:* Columbia University, B.A., 1963; Syracuse University, M.A., 1965, Ph.D., 1970. *Religion:* Roman Catholic. *Office:* Department of Modern Languages, Fordham University, Bronx, N.Y. 10458.

CAREER: Syracuse University, Syracuse, N.Y., instructor in Spanish, 1966-69; University of Maryland, College Park, assistant professor of Spanish and Portuguese, 1969-79; Fordham University, Bronx, N.Y., professor of Spanish, 1979—. *Member:* Modern Language Association of America, American Association of Teachers of Spanish and Portuguese, American Association of University Professors.

WRITINGS: The Spanish in America, 1513-1974, Oceana,

1974; (contributor) Gladys Zaldivar, editor, *Cinco aproximaciones a la narrativa hispanoamericana contemporanea* (title means "Five Critical Approaches to Contemporary Latin American Fiction"), Playor, 1976. Also author of a novel, *Guillaume*, 1980. Contributor to Latin American studies journals.

WORK IN PROGRESS: Systems in Your Life, nonfiction.

SIDELIGHTS: Natella writes: "I began my writing as a critic and scholar of Hispanic literature. Recently I have broadened my interest to include nonfiction dealing with the rootlessness of modern life (in the fullest sense) and with the effect of communication's technology on our lives. In fiction I am a neo-platonist, who tries to capture the essence of Oscar Wilde's comment: 'Far off, like a perfect pearl, one can see the City of God . . . it seems as if a child could reach it in a summer's day.'"

* * *

NATHANSON, Nathaniel L(ouis) 1908-

PERSONAL: Born December 21, 1908, in New Haven, Conn.; son of Samuel Jacob (a lawyer) and Lillian (Dante) Nathanson; married Leah Smirnow, June 22, 1941. *Education:* Yale University, B.A., 1929, LL.B., 1932; Harvard University, S.J.D., 1933. *Office:* 357 East Chicago Ave., Chicago, Ill. 60611.

CAREER: Admitted to bar in Massachusetts, 1933, U.S. Supreme Court bar, 1942, and Illinois bar, 1946; law clerk to Circuit Court Judge Julian Mack, 1933-34, and U.S. Supreme Court Justice Louis D. Brandeis, 1934-35; attorney for Security Exchange Commission, 1935-36; Northwestern University, Evanston, Ill., assistant professor, 1936-40, associate professor, 1940-45, professor of law, 1945-67, Frederic P. Vose Professor, 1967-77, professor emeritus, 1977—. Fulbright lecturer at Tokyo University, 1954-55; visiting distinguished professor at University of Washington, Seattle, 1968-69, and University of San Diego, 1977-78, 1979; visiting professor at Arizona State University, 1972, 1974, 1976. Visiting research scholar of Carnegie Endowment for International Peace, 1964-65. Associate general counsel for Office of Price Administration, 1941-45; member of council of Administrative Conference of the United States, 1961-62, public member of conference, 1968-70; hearing officer for U.S. Department of Justice, 1967; member of Special Utilities Commission of Illinois, 1951; consultant to U.S. Department of Justice and Indian Law Institute. *Member:* American Academy of Arts and Sciences, American Law Institute, Coif.

WRITINGS: (With Carl A. Auerbach) *Federal Regulation of Transportation,* West Publishing, 1954; (with Louis Leventhal Jaffe) *Administrative Law,* Little, Brown, 1960, 3rd edition, 1976. Editor-in-chief of *Yale Law Journal,* 1931-32. Contributor to law journals.

* * *

NAUMANN, Anthony Frank 1921-1971

OBITUARY NOTICE—See index for *CA* sketch: Born August 24, 1921, in London, England; died November 3, 1971, in England. Businessman, poet, and author. Although director of the firm Naumann, Gepp & Co. Ltd. since 1948, Naumann was best known for his poetry, and especially the volume *Flame in the Dark.* During World War II, Naumann saw active duty in Tunisia where he was blinded while on maneuvers. Obituaries and other sources: *AB Bookman's Weekly,* December 13, 1971.

NAUTICUS
See WALTARI, Mika (Toimi)

* * *

NELSON, Warren L. 1940-

PERSONAL: Born December 29, 1940, in Abington, Pa.; son of H. Lloyd (an executive) and Gertrude (a teacher; maiden name, Zaun) Nelson; married Susan Eberly (a journalist), July 1, 1972. *Education:* American University, B.A., 1962. *Politics:* Democrat. *Home:* 1609 North Fillmore St., Arlington, Va. 22201. *Office:* c/o Representative Les Aspin, House of Representatives, Washington, D.C. 20515.

CAREER: WBCB-Radio, Levittown, Pa., broadcaster and newsman, 1963; *Tehran Journal,* Tehran, Iran, editor, 1963-67; United Press International, New York, N.Y., international editor, 1967-69, Pentagon representative in Washington, D.C., 1970-75; legislative assistant to Representative Les Aspin in Washington, D.C., 1975—. Editor of English section of *Iran Times,* 1973—. Notable assignments include coverage of trial of Arthur Bremmer, jail riots in Washington, D.C., anti-war demonstrations in Washington, D.C., appeals for William Calley, return of United States prisoners-of-war from Vietnam, and numerous Pentagon-related events. Member of National Executive Committee of College of Young Democrats, 1961-62. *Member:* Wire Service Guild (chairman of United Press International unit in Washington, D.C.).

WORK IN PROGRESS: "Current work in military area emphasizes pamphleteering and articles about Pentagon waste and bureaucracy, burden of military pension system, and defense of the all-volunteer force."

* * *

NERBOVIG, Marcella H. 1919-

PERSONAL: Surname is accented on first syllable; born February 2, 1919, in Wisconsin. *Education:* Wisconsin State University (now University of Wisconsin), Whitewater, B.Ed., 1940; University of Wisconsin (now University of Wisconsin—Madison), M.S., 1953, Ph.D., 1956. *Religion:* Lutheran. *Home:* 220 East Hillcrest, #4210, DeKalb, Ill. 60115. *Office:* Department of Education, Northern Illinois University, Gabel 165-G, DeKalb, Ill. 60115.

CAREER: Northern Illinois University, DeKalb, professor of education, 1951—. *Military service:* U.S. Naval Reserve (Women's Reserve), 1945-46. *Member:* International Association for Supervision and Curriculum Development, International Education Association, Association for Supervision and Curriculum Development, National Education Association, National Society for the Study of Education, American Association of University Professors.

WRITINGS: (With Virgil E. Harrick) *Using Experience Charts With Children,* C. E. Merrill, 1964; (with Herbert J. Klausmeier) *Teaching in the Elementary School,* with instructor's manual, Harper, 3rd edition (Nerbovig was not associated with earlier editions), 1969, 4th edition, 1974; *Unite Teaching: A Model for Curriculum Development,* Charles A. Jones Publishing, 1970.

WORK IN PROGRESS: Research on educational alternatives and options.

* * *

NESTLE, John Francis 1912-
(Falcon)

PERSONAL: Born in 1912, in Winterbourne, Sutton, England; son of William David (in stock exchange) and Barbara Blair (a nurse; maiden name, Grierson) Nestle. *Education:* Attended Army College, Aldershot, England, 1931. *Politics:* Conservative. *Religion:* Church of England. *Home:* Blair House, P.O. Box 30, Kyrenia, Cyprus.

CAREER: Writer. Life governor of Royal Masonic Hospital. Freeman of City of London. *Military service:* British Army, Cavalry, 1932-38; served in India and Egypt; became lieutenant. *Member:* Harness Company, City Livery Club (life member).

WRITINGS: (With Phyllis Hinter) *Show Horses and Ponies: What Makes a Winner,* David & Charles, 1973.

Contributor to magazines and newspapers (sometimes under pseudonym Falcon), including *Horse and Hound* and *Horse World.*

WORK IN PROGRESS: Autobiographical research.

SIDELIGHTS: Nestle writes: "Living here in Cyprus I am naturally interested in world politics. America and England are interested in promoting world peace and Russia is doing her best to back the Arabs in preventing peaceful solutions."

* * *

NETO, Antonio Agostinho 1922-1979

OBITUARY NOTICE: Born in 1922 in Icolo-e-Bengo, Portuguese West Africa; died September 10, 1979, of cancer, in Moscow, U.S.S.R. Marxist poet and doctor, Neto was the first president of Angola. He led his popular Movement for the Liberation of Angola against Portuguese colonial rule, and in 1975, obtained Angola's freedom after a bloody civil war. Obituaries and other sources: *The Penguin Companion to Classical, Oriental, and African Literature,* McGraw, 1969; *African Authors: A Companion to Black African Writing,* Volume I: *1300-1973,* Black Orpheus Press, 1973; *The International Who's Who,* Europa, 1974; *Newsweek,* December 29, 1975, June 7, 1976, September 24, 1979; *New York Times,* September 12, 1979, September 18, 1979.

* * *

NEUBERGER, Richard Lewis 1912-1960

OBITUARY NOTICE: Born December 26, 1912, in Portland, Ore.; died March 9, 1960. U.S. senator, journalist, and author of six books. In addition to working as the *New York Times* correspondent in the Pacific Northwest, Neuberger wrote nearly three hundred articles for such national magazines as *New Republic, Harper's, Nation,* and *Reader's Digest.* Both he and his wife, Maurine, were active in Oregon politics, and at one time they served concurrently in the state legislature, he as a senator and she as a representative. They were the first such husband-and-wife team in American history. One of Neuberger's books, *Adventures in Politics: We Go to the Legislature,* describes the experiences he and his wife had in government. In 1955 Neuberger was elected U.S. senator from Oregon, a post he held until his death. Maurine Neuberger was selected to finish his term. Obituaries and other sources: Richard Lewis Neuberger, *Adventures in Politics: We Go to the Legislature,* Oxford University Press, 1954; *Current Biography,* Wilson, 1955, May, 1960; *New York Times,* March 10, 1960; *Political Profiles: The Eisenhower Years,* Facts on File, 1977.

* * *

NEUMANN, Robert 1897-1975

OBITUARY NOTICE: Born May 22, 1897, in Vienna, Austria; died January 3, 1975, in Munich, West Germany. Novelist, parodist, playwright, screenwriter, biographer, and autobiographer. A master of parody, Neumann wrote a number of humorous works, including *Mit fremden Federn, Unter falsche Flagge,* and *Vorsicht Buecher.* Most of his novels are concerned with the problems of wartime and postwar Europe. Although Neumann's early books were written in German, in 1943 he began writing in English as well. Some of his original English titles are *The Inquest, Insurrection in Poshansk,* and *The Dark Side of the Moon.* Neumann also was the author of several screenplays, the most recent of which was "Emigration." Obituaries and other sources: *Everyman's Dictionary of European Writers,* Dent & Sons, 1968; *Who's Who in World Jewry,* Pitman, 1972; *Who's Who in the World,* 2nd edition, Marquis, 1973; *Cassell's Encyclopaedia of World Literature,* revised edition, Morrow, 1973; *The International Who's Who,* Europa, 1974; *The Oxford Companion to German Literature,* Clarendon Press, 1976.

* * *

NEWBOLD, Robert T(homas, Jr.) 1920-

PERSONAL: Born February 26, 1920, in Miami, Fla.; son of Robert Thomas (a laborer) and Irene (Johnson) Newbold; married Ann Louise Worrell, August 1, 1944; children: Gregory. *Education:* Florida A. & M. University, A.B., 1942; Lincoln Theological Seminary, M.Div., 1945; McCormick Theological Seminary, M.A., 1946. *Home:* 936 Field Ave., Plainfield, N.J. 07060. *Office:* United Presbyterian Church of the United States of America, 475 Riverside Dr., Room 1201, New York, N.Y. 10027.

CAREER: Ordained Presbyterian minister; pastor of Presbyterian churches in Brunswick, Ga., 1944-46, Atlanta, Ga., 1946-53, and Baltimore, Md., 1953-68; United Presbyterian Church of the United States of America, New York, N.Y., associate executive secretary in department of ministerial relations in Columbus, Ohio, 1968-72, associate director of Council on Administrative Services in New York, 1973-75, associate stated clerk in New York, 1975—. Lecturer at Gammon Theological Seminary, New York Theological Seminary, New Brunswick Theological Seminary, and Johnson C. Smith Theological Seminary; visiting lecturer at Princeton Theological Seminary. *Awards, honors:* D.D. from Mary Holmes College, 1976.

WRITINGS: Black Preaching: Select Sermons in the Presbyterian Tradition, Geneva Press, 1977.

WORK IN PROGRESS: Preaching in the Black Idiom.

* * *

NEWHOUSE, Samuel I(rving) 1895-1979

OBITUARY NOTICE: Born May 24, 1895, in Bayonne, N.J.; died August 29, 1979, of a stroke, in New York, N.Y. Publisher and newspaper magnate, Newhouse owned thirty-one newspapers in twenty-two cities and several magazines, including *Vogue, Glamour, House & Garden,* and *Gentleman's Quarterly.* Newhouse reportedly paid the highest price ever in a newspaper transaction when he bought Booth Newspapers, Inc. for $305 million. Obituaries and other sources: *Current Biography,* Wilson, 1961; *Who's Who in America,* 38th edition, Marquis, 1974; *The International Who's Who,* Europa, 1974; *Business Week,* January 26, 1976; *Newsweek,* November 8, 1976; *New York Times,* August 30, 1979.

NEWMAN, Joseph 1912-

PERSONAL: Born December 11, 1912, in Pittsfield, Mass.; son of Jacob and Ida (Greenburg) Newman; married Lucia Meza Barros, 1949; children: Lucia, Jr., Consuelo, Pia, Joseph, Jr. *Education:* Williams College, B.A., 1935. *Home and office:* 3204 Highland Place N.W., Washington, D.C. 20008.

CAREER: New York Herald Tribune, New York City, bureau chief in Tokyo, Japan, 1940-41, general reporter in New York City, 1942-43, bureau chief in Latin America, based in Buenos Aires, Argentina, 1943-46, in Moscow, Soviet Union, 1947-49, in Berlin, Germany, 1949-50, in London, England, 1950-55, in Latin America, 1955-58, and at United Nations in New York, 1958-62, member of editorial board, 1962-66; *U.S. News & World Report,* Washington, D.C., assistant to publishing director, 1966-67, co-founder and directing editor of Book Division, 1967-79; free-lance writer, editor, and book producer, 1979—. Creator, producer, and moderator of "Editorial Page Conference," a weekly program on Radio-Keith-Orpheum television stations, and a daily radio news program; television producer and interviewer for special documentary programs aired by American Broadcasting Co., Metromedia, and Educational Television Network; radio correspondent in Buenos Aires, Argentina.

AWARDS, HONORS: Awards from Overseas Press Club, 1948-49, for correspondence from Moscow, from English-Speaking Union, 1953-54, for correspondence from London, and from Sigma Delta Chi, 1961, for series on Castro's Cuba; Guggenheim fellow, 1957.

WRITINGS: Goodbye, Japan, L. B. Fischer, 1942; *Cuba S.S.R.,* New York Herald Tribune, 1961; *A New Look at Red China,* U.S. News & World Report, 1971.

Editor; all published by U.S. News & World Report: *The United States on the Moon: What It Means to Us,* 1969; *Social Security and Medicare Simplified: What You Get for Your Money,* 1969; *Investments, Insurance, Wills Simplified: Planning for Your Family's Future,* 1969, 2nd edition, 1972; *Inflation Simplified: What It Means to You,* 1969; *Communism and the New Left: What They're Up to Now,* 1969.

What Everyone Needs to Know About Drugs, 1970; *Good Things About the United States Today,* 1970; *Our Poisoned Planet,* 1970; *How to Buy Real Estate: Profits and Pitfalls,* 1970; *U.S. News & World Report's Book on Income Taxes: How to Save Money and Avoid Trouble,* 1971 edition, 1970, 1972 edition, 1972; *U.S. Politics: Inside and Out,* 1970; *What Everyone Needs to Know About Law,* 1971; *Wiring the World,* 1971; *Guide to the '72 Elections,* 1972, juvenile supplement, 1972; *Our Country* (picture book), 1972; *Crime in America: Causes and Cures,* 1972; *Teach Your Wife How to Be a Widow,* 1973; *Two Hundred Years: A Bicentennial Illustrated History of the United States,* two volumes, 1973; *Stocks, Bonds, Mutual Funds,* 1973, revised edition, 1976; *A Bicentennial Portrait of the American People,* 1973; *Famous Soviet Spies: The Kremlin's Secret Weapon,* 1973; *How to Buy Insurance and Save Money,* 1974; *How to Live With Inflation: A Guide to Saving Money When Buying,* 1974; (with Eleanor Goldstein) *A Watch on World Affairs* (textbook), 1978; (with Goldstein) *A Watch on the Economy* (textbook), 1978; (with Goldstein) *A Watch on Government* (textbook), 1978.

SIDELIGHTS: Newman's assignments have included interviews with Fidel Castro, Juan Peron, Golda Meier, Madame Nhu, and Averell Harriman. In Buenos Aires he covered the rise and fall of Juan Peron; in Moscow, the cold war waged by Stalin; in Berlin, the Soviet attempt to expel the Western powers; in London, Winston Churchill's return to power; and at the United Nations, Khruschev's histrionics.

Newman told *CA:* "As an independent writer/editor/book producer I am presently preparing manuscripts for publication by various publishers. One of my projects is a new series of 'living textbooks' for high school and junior college students covering contemporary developments in major fields of science. My other work includes a manuscript on the battle to save the endangered species, with Paul Watson (hero of the ramming of the pirate whaler 'Sierra') and Warren Rogers, and a new educational program for the 1980's with former Commissioner of Education, Ernest L. Boyer."

* * *

NEWSOME, David Hay 1929-

PERSONAL: Born June 15, 1929, in Leamington Spa, England; married Joan Florence Trist, 1955; children: Clare, Janet, Louise, Cordelia. *Education:* Emmanuel College, Cambridge, B.A. and M.A. (first class honors), 1954, Litt.D., 1976. *Home:* The Retreat, Thornthwaite, Keswick, Cumbria, United Kingdom. *Office:* Christ's Hospital, Horsham, West Sussex, England.

CAREER: Assistant history master at private boys school in Wellington, England, 1954-59, head of department, 1956-59; Cambridge University, Cambridge, England, fellow of Emmanuel College, 1959-70, senior tutor, 1965-70, assistant lecturer, 1961-66, lecturer in ecclesiastical history, 1966-70, Bishop Westcott Memorial Lecturer, 1968; Christ's Hospital, Horsham, England, headmaster, 1970—. Gore Memorial Lecturer at Westminster Abbey, 1965; Birkbeck Lecturer at Cambridge University, 1972. *Military service:* Royal Army Education Corps, captain, 1948-50. *Member:* Royal Historical Society (fellow), Athenaeum Club, Marylebone Cricket Club.

WRITINGS: A History of Wellington College, 1859-1959, J. Murray, 1959; *Godliness and Good Learning: Four Studies in a Victorian Ideal,* J. Murray, 1961; *The Parting of Friends: A Study of the Wilberforces and Henry Manning,* J. Murray, 1966; *Two Classes of Men: Platonism and English Romantic Thought,* J. Murray, 1974; *On the Edge of Paradise: A. C. Benson, the Diarist,* J. Murray, 1979. Also author of *Bishop Westcott and the Platonic Tradition,* 1969. Contributor to history and theology journals.

WORK IN PROGRESS: More work on the diary collection of A. C. Benson.

AVOCATIONAL INTERESTS: Music, fell-walking.

* * *

NICHOLS, Dudley 1895-1960

OBITUARY NOTICE: Born April 6, 1895, in Wapakoneta, Ohio; died January 4, 1960. Motion picture producer, director, screenwriter, and journalist. After working for ten years on the staffs of the *New York Evening Post* and *New York World,* Nichols was lured to Hollywood to become a screenwriter. He wrote the scenarios for more than thirty movies, including "The Long Voyage Home," "For Whom the Bell Tolls," "Pinky," and "Stagecoach." In 1935, he was selected to receive an Academy Award for his work on "The Informer," but he declined it because of his opposition to the Academy of Motion Picture Arts and Sciences. Obituaries and other sources: *Current Biography,* Wilson, 1941, March, 1960; *New York Times,* January 6, 1960.

NICKLAUS, Jack (William) 1940-

PERSONAL: Born January 21, 1940, in Columbus, Ohio; son of Louis Charles, Jr. (a businessman) and Helen (Schoener) Nicklaus; married Barbara Bash, July 23, 1960; children: Jack William II, Steven Charles, Nancy Jean, Gary Thomas, Michael Scott. *Education:* Attended Ohio State University, 1957-62. *Home:* 11397 Old Harbour Rd., North Palm Beach, Fla. 33403. *Office:* 321 Northlake Blvd., North Palm Beach, Fla. 33403.

CAREER: Professional golfer. President of Golden Bear, Inc. *Member:* American Cancer Society (former chairman of Ohio division), National Easter Seal Society (former chairman of sports division), Ohio State University President's Club, Phi Gamma Delta. *Awards, honors:* Winner of U.S. Amateur Championship, 1959, 1961; winner of 83 professional tournaments worldwide (66 of them in the United States), including: U.S. Open, 1962, 1967, 1972, U.S. Masters, 1963, 1965, 1966, 1972, 1975, Professional Golfers Association (PGA) Championship, 1963, 1971, 1973, 1975, British Open, 1966, 1970, 1978, six Australian Opens, and three Tournament Players Championships; named PGA Player of the Year, 1967, 1972, 1973, 1975, 1976; member of five U.S. Ryder Cup teams, 1969-77; named Golf Writers Player of the Year, 1972, 1975, and 1976 (with Jerry Pate); Bobby Jones award for distinguished sportsmanship, 1975.

WRITINGS: Fifty-Five Ways to Lower Your Golf Score, illustrations by Francis Golden, Simon & Schuster, 1964; *Take a Tip From Me,* illustrations by Golden, Simon & Schuster, 1968; (with Herbert Warren Wind) *The Greatest Game of All: My Life in Golf* (autobiography), foreword by Robert Tyre Jones, Jr., Simon & Schuster, 1969; (with Ken Bowden) *Golf My Way,* illustrations by Jim McQueen, Simon & Schuster, 1974; *The Best Way to Better Golf,* Numbers 1-3, Fawcett, 1975; (with Bowden) *Jack Nicklaus' Lesson Tee,* illustrations by McQueen, Simon & Schuster, 1978; (with Bowden) *On and Off the Fairway* (pictoral autobiography), Simon & Schuster, 1979.

WORK IN PROGRESS: With Bowden, *Jack Nicklaus' Playing Lessons,* "dealing with strategy, tactics, and course management."

SIDELIGHTS: Jack Nicklaus, nicknamed the "Golden Bear" for his formerly large physique and platinum blonde hair, as well as his stature in the game, is regarded by many as the best golfer in the world. With the winning of his 14th major golf title in 1973, Nicklaus surpassed the previous record of 13 set by the famed Bobby Jones. Nicklaus now holds 17 of these titles. Moreover, he has earned more prize money than any other player in golf history: over three million dollars through 1978.

The Golden Bear was introduced to the game of golf by his father. The elder Nicklaus, having injured his ankle, did not want to slow down his regular partners' playing pace, so he asked his ten-year-old son Jack to accompany him in a round of golf. Jack took to the game so well that in just a few years he was capable of scoring in the high sixties.

In 1959 Nicklaus, still an amateur golfer, was one of nine to make the American Walker Cup team, a group selected to compete against a British team in Muirfield, Scotland. His spirits elevated by the coveted distinction, Nicklaus defeated his opponent in both of his matches, contributing toward the American team's final 9-3 triumph. Later that same year Nicklaus won an astounding twenty-nine matches out of thirty.

Two years later Nicklaus began to tour professionally. In 1962 he made a name for himself when he defeated Arnold Palmer by three strokes in an 18-hole playoff at that year's U.S. Open. Other major victories followed, but the newcomer's success did not endear him to "Arnie's Army," the name given to Arnold Palmer devotees. Eventually, however, "Nicklaus's power, growing finesse and positive attitude made him the automatic favorite in any tournament he chose to enter," wrote Thomas Rogers.

"The trouble is we're playing one game and Jack is playing another," Rogers quoted one lamenting golf professional as saying in 1965. Although he is a powerful player, Nicklaus's game is primarily one of intense concentration and precision. He is also gifted with what Alistair Cooke described as an "extraordinary self-discipline of . . . judgment, at the tensest times, of when to draw rein and when to cut loose." As to his basic philosophy, Nicklaus has stated: "The way seems to me, in golf you're always breaking a barrier. When you bust it, you set yourself a little higher barrier and try to break that one."

Nicklaus has also broken into the business world, and has become a renowned golf course architect, another area in which he excels. As president of the conglomerate, Golden Bear, Inc., Nicklaus has, among other things, designed golf courses in Hilton Head Island, S.C., Palm Beach, Fla., Cincinnati, Ohio, Columbus, Ohio, Japan, and Europe. Referring to Nicklaus's Muirfield Village course in Columbus (named after Muirfield in Scotland), Dan Jenkins noted that "it already deserves to be rated with the great layouts in this country, and it will prove as much in time."

Besides being involved in business ventures, designing golf courses, and touring the golf circuit, Nicklaus has written several books on basic golf techniques and strategy as well as autobiographical volumes. Alistair Cooke called Nicklaus "the most cerebral golfer since Ben Hogan."

AVOCATIONAL INTERESTS: Fishing, hunting, handball, basketball.

BIOGRAPHICAL/CRITICAL SOURCES—Books: Jack Nicklaus and Herbert Warren Wind, *The Greatest Game of All: My Life in Golf,* foreword by Robert Tyre Jones, Jr., Simon & Schuster, 1969; Rex Lardner, *Great Golfers,* Putnam, 1970; Michael McDonnell, *Golf: The Great Ones,* Drake, 1971; Nevin H. Gibson, *Great Moments in Golf,* Barnes, 1973; *Sports Immortals,* Prentice, 1974; *Business People in the News,* Volume I, Gale, 1976; Nicklaus and Ken Bowden, *On and Off the Fairway,* Simon & Schuster, 1979.

Articles: *Saturday Evening Post,* April 8, 1961; *New York Times,* June 18, 1962; *Sports Illustrated,* April 4, 1966, April 18, 1966, July 18, 1966, December 19, 1966, January 30, 1967, June 26, 1967, October 14, 1968, April 14, 1969, May 19, 1969, October 27, 1969, November 7, 1969, December 8, 1969, June 15, 1970, July 20, 1970, August 3, 1970, March 8, 1971, May 3, 1971, June 28, 1971, August 9, 1971, November 8, 1971, January 24, 1972, April 3, 1972, April 17, 1972, June 26, 1972, September 4, 1972, February 19, 1973, June 11, 1973, August 20, 1973, October 15, 1973, October 14, 1974, February 3, 1975, June 16, 1975, August 18, 1975, September 22, 1975, December 22, 1975, June 7, 1976, September 13, 1976, May 30, 1977, July 18, 1977, March 27, 1978, July 24, 1978, December 25, 1978.

Time, April 22, 1966, July 15, 1966, February 3, 1967, June 30, 1967, November 10, 1967, July 6, 1970, April 24, 1972; *Newsweek,* April 25, 1966, July 18, 1966, February 6, 1967, March 20, 1972, April 24, 1972, July 3, 1972, July 24, 1972, August 27, 1973, April 14, 1975, March 27, 1978, July 24,

1978; *New Yorker,* August 13, 1966, November 5, 1966, July 8, 1967, July 8, 1972; *Esquire,* April, 1968, April, 1973; *Look,* April 16, 1968; *New York Times Biographical Edition,* July, 1972, August, 1973; *New York Times Magazine,* July 9, 1972; *Readers Digest,* October, 1973; *Field & Stream,* April, 1974; *Biography News,* Gale, August, 1974; *Sport,* February, 1978.

[Sketch verified by Jean Bowden]

* * *

NIDETCH, Jean 1923-

PERSONAL: Born October 12, 1923, in Brooklyn, N.Y.; daughter of David (a cab driver) and Mae (a manicurist; maiden name, Fried) Slutsky; married Martin Nidetch, April 20, 1947 (divorced); children: David, Richard. *Education:* Attended City College of the City University of New York. *Office:* 10880 Wilshire Blvd., Los Angeles, Calif.

CAREER: Founder of Weight Watchers International, Inc., 1963, and president of Weight Watchers Foundation. Also worked for Internal Revenue Service, 1942-47, and as department store sales person, 1947. Consultant to New York State Assembly Mental Hygiene Commission, 1968; adviser to New York Joint Legislature Commission on Child Care Needs. Trustee of University of California at Los Angeles Foundation. Charity organizer. Lecturer. *Member:* American Federation of Television and Radio Artists, Professional Womens Club, Washington Square Business Club. *Awards, honors:* Woman of Achievement Award; speakers award from Sales Promotion Executives Association.

WRITINGS: Weight Watchers Cookbook, Hearthside Press, 1966; (with Joan Rattner Heilman) *The Story of Weight Watchers,* New American Library, 1970, revised edition, 1979; *Weight Watchers Program Cookbook,* Hearthside Press, 1973; *Ask Jean: Questions to Jean Nidetch, Founder of Weight Watchers,* New American Library, 1975; (author of introduction) *Weight Watchers International Cookbook,* New American Library, 1977. Author of a monthly column for *Weight Watchers Magazine.* Contributor of articles to popular magazines.

SIDELIGHTS: In 1973, Weight Watchers International celebrated its tenth anniversary—ten years of helping obese people lose weight and keep it off. President Jean Nidetch based Weight Watchers' technique on her own experience as a fat person trying to lose weight. A "professional dieter," Nidetch had tried numerous diets, over-the-counter appetite suppressants, and diet pills in order to lose weight, but found that she had a hard time maintaining any kind of weight loss. Often times, the weight she gained back would be more than she had lost.

Finally, in 1963, after attending sessions at the New York Department of Health Obesity Clinic, Nidetch decided that she needed support from her friends to help her through the program. A small group of fat friends would gather in Nidetch's living room to talk about their food addiction, while they followed the Clinic's diet. Soon the groups began to increase in number, and Nidetch was asked to speak to groups or individuals who could not attend her informal home meetings. Encouraged by one couple, Felice and Albert Lippert, Nidetch decided to make weight loss a business venture. Together the Lipperts and Nidetch formed Weight Watchers and operated out of a loft over a movie theater in Little Neck, Queens.

Today Weight Watchers is a multi-million dollar corporation which oversees franchises in the United States, Puerto Rico, Mexico, Canada, Great Britain, Ireland, Australia, and New Zealand. Although Weight Watchers is big business, the Nidetch touch is still evident in the supportive and informal weekly meetings.

BIOGRAPHICAL/CRITICAL SOURCES: Look, May 27, 1969; *McCall's,* May, 1970, October, 1973; Jean Nidetch and Joan Rattner Heilman, *The Story of Weight Watchers,* New American Library, 1970, revised edition, 1979; *Time,* February 21, 1972; *Newsweek,* September 10, 1973.*

* * *

NIEBUHR, Ursula 1907-

PERSONAL: Born August 3, 1907, in Southampton, Surrey, England; daughter of John Herbert (a physician) and Anne Sylvester (Webb) Keppel-Compton; married Reinhold Niebuhr (a clergyman and professor), December 22, 1931 (died June 1, 1971); children: Christopher, Elisabeth Niebuhr Sifton. *Education:* Attended University College (now Southampton University), 1924-26; St. Hugh's College, Oxford, B.A., 1930, M.A. (with honors), 1936; Union Theological Seminary, S.T.M., 1931. *Politics:* Democrat. *Religion:* Episcopal. *Home address:* Yale Hill, Stockbridge, Mass. 01262.

CAREER: Barnard College, New York City, lecturer, then assistant professor, 1941-46, associate professor of religion, 1946-61, head of department, 1946-61; Simon's Rock College, part-time teacher, 1966-68, trustee, 1969-75, member of Jerusalem Committee, 1973—. Scholar-in-residence at Ecumenical Institute for Advanced Theological Studies in Tantur, Israel, 1973; scholar-in-residence at Miskenot Sha'ananim in Jerusalem, Israel, 1975. Delegate to Democratic Charter Convention, May, 1979. *Member:* Guild of Scholars of the Protestant Episcopal Church (president, 1976). *Awards, honors:* Honorary fellow of Institute for Independent Study at Radcliffe College, 1961-62; D.D. from General Theological Seminary, 1976.

WRITINGS: (Editor) Reinhold Niebuhr, *Justice and Mercy,* Harper, 1974; (contributor) Stephen Spender, editor, *W. H. Auden: A Tribute,* Macmillan, 1975. Contributor of articles on religious topics to *Berkshire Eagle.*

* * *

NIELSEN, Veneta Leatham 1909-

PERSONAL: Born October 25, 1909, in Wellsville, Utah; daughter of Robert Painter (a teacher) and Alverta (Jensen) Leatham; married Harold M. Nielsen (a professor of biochemistry), 1926; children: Harold L., Helen Darielle Nielsen Wright. *Education:* Utah State University, B.S., 1940, M.S., 1950. *Politics:* "Nonpartisan." *Religion:* "Non-affiliate." *Home:* 535 East 5th N., Logan, Utah 84321.

CAREER: Utah State University, Logan, 1946-79, began as instructor, became professor of English, honor lecturer in fine arts, 1974, professor emeritus, 1979—. Creative writing teacher at Utah State Prison Women's Facility; workshop director. *Member:* American Association of University Women, Phi Kappa Phi. *Awards, honors:* National Endowment for the Humanities grants; National Poetry Prize from American Association of University Women; Utah Institute of Fine Arts Award, 1972.

WRITINGS: Under Sound: A Theory of Poetry With Some Original Poems (monograph), Utah State University Press, 1958; (with Carlton Culmsee) *Tree of Fire* (poems and essay), Utah State University Press, 1963; (with Culmsee) *Insurgent Form* (poems and essays), Utah State University

Press, 1966; *Familiar as a Sparrow* (poems), Brigham Young University Press, 1978.

*   *   *

NIXON, Hershell Howard 1923-

PERSONAL: Born August 4, 1923, in Duncan, Okla.; son of James Gilbert (a farmer) and Whirlie (Dickey) Nixon; married Joan Lowery (a writer), August 6, 1959; children: Kathleen Nixon Brush, Maureen, Joseph, Eileen. *Education:* University of Southern California, B.S., 1952. *Home:* 8602 Shadowcrest, Houston, Tex. 77074. *Agent:* Writers House, Inc., 21 West 26th St., New York, N.Y. 10010. *Office:* Strata Energy, Inc., 1 Allen Center, Suite 1555, Houston, Tex. 77002.

CAREER: Shell Oil Co., Billings, Mont., junior geologist, 1952-56; Getty Oil Co., geologist in Ventura, Los Angeles, and San Francisco, Calif., and Corpus Christi, Houston, and Midland, Tex.; Mitchell Energy Co., Houston, geologist, 1974-77; Strata Energy, Inc., Houston, geologist, 1977—. *Military service:* U.S. Navy, 1942-48; became quartermaster. *Member:* American Association of Petroleum Geologists, American Institute of Professional Geologists, West Texas Geological Society, Houston Geological Society, University of Southern California Alumni Association, Phi Sigma Kappa.

WRITINGS: (With wife, Joan Lowery Nixon) *Oil and Gas: From Fossils to Fuels,* Harcourt, 1977; *Volcanoes: Nature's Fireworks,* Dodd, 1978; *Glaciers,* Dodd, 1980.

SIDELIGHTS: Nixon writes: "My wife and I have traveled extensively in the United States and a little in other countries. I was motivated to write books on scientific topics by my children's questions about science. I have the background in science; my wife has the background in writing for young children. I appreciate the blend of the many cultures that make up America, the generosity, the humor of our people, and the way in which Americans face their problems and deal with them."

*   *   *

NOLAN, Madeena Spray 1943-

PERSONAL: Born May 1, 1943, in Arkansas City, Kan.; daughter of E. Lyman (in sales) and Virginia (a teacher; maiden name, Stubbs) Spray; married Michael Nolan (a comptroller), June 13, 1964; children: Andrew Shane, David Kelly. *Education:* Lindenwood College, B.A., 1965. *Politics:* "Liberal Democrat, moving left." *Religion:* Roman Catholic. *Home:* 1700 Ashwood Ave., Nashville, Tenn. 37212. *Agent:* Diane Cleaver, Sanford A. Greenburger Associates, Inc. 825 Third Ave., New York, N.Y., 10022.

CAREER: High school teacher of English in St. Charles, Mo., 1965-66; St. Louis State Hospital, St. Louis, Mo., editor of public relations magazine, 1967-69; free-lance author of humorous-political columns for *St. Louis Post-Dispatch,* 1970-72; free-lance writer, 1975—. Member of St. Charles County Democratic Committee; past president of Young Democrats. *Member:* National Organization for Women (past president), Women's Political Caucus (past member of state board of directors).

WRITINGS: My Daddy Don't Go to Work (juvenile), Carolrhoda, 1978. Also author of "The Other Side of the Wall" (one-act play).

WORK IN PROGRESS: The Gift, a novel; a novel on mothers and daughters.

SIDELIGHTS: Nolan comments: "Probably no writer knows with any certainty why she writes, but I am finding that my womanhood—how I fit as a female into the natural world, and into the society of today—is the basis of most of my work."

*   *   *

NORMAN, Don(ald) Cleveland 1909(?)-1979

OBITUARY NOTICE: Born c. 1909 in Georgia; died October 4, 1979, in Florence, Italy. Editor, biblical scholar, and author of the comprehensive study, *A Pictorial Census of the Gutenberg Bible.* Norman served in the ministry and edited a number of religious journals. He was also editor of the John A. Dickson Publishing Co. and Consolidated Book Publishers. His other works include *The Christian Book of Knowledge* and *Workbook for a Systematic Study of the New Analytical Bible.* Obituaries and other sources: *AB Bookman's Weekly,* November 26, 1979.

*   *   *

NOSSAL, Frederick (Christian) 1927-1979

OBITUARY NOTICE—See index for *CA* sketch: Born December 23, 1927, in Vienna, Austria; died September 29, 1979, in Belgrade, Yugoslavia. Official of the World Bank, journalist, and author of *Dateline Peking.* Among the newspapers Nossal worked for were the *Sydney Sun,* the *Melbourne Herald,* the *Toronto Globe and Mail,* and the *Toronto Telegram.* In 1959 he established a news bureau in Peking, China, for the *Toronto Globe and Mail.* It was the first Western news bureau to be opened after the Communist takeover, but Nossal was expelled from the country after working there only eight months. At the time of his death he was serving as an information officer for the World Bank. Obituaries and other sources: *The Author's and Writer's Who's Who,* 6th edition, Burke's Peerage, 1971; *Washington Post,* October 4, 1979.

O

O'CASEY, Sean 1880-1964 (Sean O'Cathasaigh)

PERSONAL: Birth-given name, John Casey; name Gaelicized to Sean O'Cathasaigh, c. 1909; surname Anglicized to O'Casey, 1923; born March 30, 1880, in Dublin, Ireland; self-exiled to England, 1926; died September 18, 1964, in Torquay, Devon, England; son of Michael (a clerk) and Susan (Archer) Casey; married Eileen Reynolds (an actress; stage name, Eileen Carey), 1928; children: two sons, Breon, Niall Ayamonn (died, 1956); one daughter, Shivaun. *Education:* Self-educated. *Religion:* Church of Ireland. *Residence:* Torquay, Devon, England.

CAREER: Playwright. Worked in ironmongery and hardware store, c. 1895-98; road worker, 1898-1910; laborer, 1910-23; secretary of Irish Citizen Army, 1913-14; full-time writer, 1924-64. *Member:* Gaelic League, St. Laurence O'Toole Pipers' Band (founding member). *Awards, honors:* Hawthornden Prize, 1926.

WRITINGS—Plays: "Cathleen Listens In" (one-act), first produced in Dublin, Ireland, at the Abbey Theatre, October 1, 1923; "Nannie's Night Out" (one-act), first produced in Dublin at the Abbey Theatre, September 29, 1924; *The Plough and the Stars* (four-act; first produced in Dublin at the Abbey Theatre, February 8, 1926), Macmillan, 1926; *The Silver Tassie* (four-act; first produced on the West End at Apollo Theatre, October 11, 1929), Macmillan (London), 1928.

The Shadow of a Gunman (two-act; first produced in Dublin at the Abbey Theatre, April 9, 1923), Samuel French, 1932; *Juno and the Paycock* (three-act; first produced in Dublin at the Abbey Theatre, March 3, 1924), Samuel French, 1932; *Within the Gates* (four-scene; first produced on the West End at Royalty Theatre, February 7, 1934), Macmillan (London), 1933; "A Pound on Demand" (one-act; first produced in New York City at American Repertory Theatre, January, 1947), published in *Five Irish Plays* (also see below), 1935; "The End of the Beginning" (one-act; first produced in Dublin at the Abbey Theatre, February 8, 1937), published in *Five Irish Plays* (also see below), 1935.

Purple Dust (three-act; first produced in Boston, Mass., at Boston Tributary Theatre, December 6, 1944), Macmillan (London), 1940, Dramatists Play Service, 1957; *The Star Turns Red* (one-act; first produced in London, England, at Unity Theatre, March 20, 1940), Macmillan (London), 1940; *Red Roses for Me* (four-act; first produced in Dublin at Olympia Theatre, April, 1943), Macmillan (London), 1942, Macmillan (New York), 1943; *Oak Leaves and Lavender; or, A World on Wallpaper* (first produced on the West End at Lyric Theatre, May 13, 1947), Macmillan (London), 1946, Macmillan (New York), 1947; *Cock-a-Doodle Dandy* (three-scene; first produced in Newcastle upon Tyne, England, at People's Theatre, December 11, 1949), Macmillan (London), 1949; "Hall of Healing, " "Bedtime Story," and "Time to Go" (one-act plays; all first produced in New York City at Yugoslav-American Hall, May 7, 1952), all published in *Collected Plays* (also see below), 1949-52.

The Bishop's Bonfire: A Sad Play Within the Tune of a Polka (first produced in Dublin at Gaeity Theatre, February 28, 1955), Macmillan, 1955; *The Drums of Father Ned* (first produced in Lafayette, Ind., 1959), St. Martin's, 1960; *Behind the Green Curtains* [and] *Figuro in the Night* [and] *The Moon Shines on Kylenamoe* (three plays; all first produced Off-Broadway at Theatre de Lys, 1962), St. Martin's, 1961.

Autobiographies: *I Knock at the Door: Swift Glances Back at Things That Made Me,* Macmillan, 1939, adaptation by Paul Shyre as two-act play published as *I Knock at the Door,* Dramatists Play Service, 1958, original edition reprinted, Pan Books, 1971; *Pictures in the Hallway,* Macmillan, 1942, adaptation by Shyre as two-act play published under same title, Samuel French, 1956 (first produced on Broadway at Playhouse Theatre, September 16, 1956), original edition reprinted, Pan Books, 1971; *Drums Under the Windows,* Macmillan (London), 1945, Macmillan (New York), 1946, adaptation by Shyre published under same title, A. Meyerson, 1960; *Inishfallen, Fare Thee Well,* Macmillan, 1949; *Rose and Crown,* Macmillan, 1952; *Sunset and Evening Star,* Macmillan, 1954; *Mirror in My House: The Autobiographies of Sean O'Casey,* two volumes, (Volume 1 contains *I Knock at the Door, Pictures in the Hallway,* and *Drums Under the Windows;* Volume 2 contains *Inishfallen, Fare Thee Well, Rose and Crown,* and *Sunset and Evening Star*), Macmillan, 1956 (published in England as *Autobiographies,* two volumes, Macmillan [London], 1963, published as *Autobiography,* Pan Books, 1971).

Other: (Under name Sean O'Cathasaigh) *Songs of the Wren,* [Dublin], 1918; (under name Sean O'Cathasaigh) *More Songs of the Wren,* [Dublin], 1918; (under name Sean O'-Cathasaigh) *The Story of Thomas Ashe,* Fergus O'Connor, 1918; (under name Sean O'Cathasaigh) *The Story of the Irish*

Citizen Army, Maunsel, 1919, reprinted, Talbot, 1971; *Windfalls: Stories, Poems, and Plays,* Macmillan, 1934; *The Flying Wasp,* Macmillan (London), 1937, reprinted, B. Blom, 1971; *The Green Crow,* Braziller, 1956; *Feathers From the Green Crow,* edited by Robert Hogan, University of Missouri Press, 1962; *Under a Colored Cap: Articles Merry and Mournful With Comments and a Song,* St. Martin's, 1963; *Blasts and Benedictions* (articles and stories), introduction by Ronald Ayling, St. Martin's, 1967; *The Sean O'Casey Reader: Plays, Autobiographies, Opinions,* edited with an introduction by Brooks Atkinson, St. Martin's, 1968; *The Sting and the Twinkle: Conversations With Sean O'-Casey,* compiled by H. H. Mikhail, Barnes & Noble, 1974; *The Letters of Sean O'Casey,* edited by David Krause, Macmillan, 1975.

Omnibus volumes: *Two Plays: Juno and the Paycock* [and] *The Shadow of a Gunman,* Macmillan, 1925; *Five Irish Plays* (contains "Juno and the Paycock," "The Shadow of a Gunman," "The Plough and the Stars," "The End of the Beginning," and "A Pound on Demand"), Macmillan, 1935; *Collected Plays,* four volumes, (contains "Juno and the Paycock," "The Shadow of a Gunman," "The Plough and the Stars," "The End of the Beginning," "A Pound on Demand," "The Silver Tassie," "Within the Gates," "The Star Turns Red," "Purple Dust," "Red Roses for Me," "Halls of Healing," "Oak Leaves and Lavender," "Cock-a-Doodle Dandy," "Bedtime Story," and "Time to Go"), Macmillian (London), 1949-52, St. Martin's, 1958.

Selected Plays, introduction by John Gassner, (contains "The Shadow of a Gunman," "Juno and the Paycock," "The Plough and the Stars," "The Silver Tassie," "Within the Gates," "Purple Dust," "Red Roses for Me," "Bedtime Story," and "Time to Go"), Braziller, 1954; *Juno and the Paycock* [and] *The Plough and the Stars,* Macmillan, 1957; *Three Plays: Juno and the Paycock, The Shadow of a Gunman, The Plough and the Stars,* Macmillan (London), 1957, St. Martin's, 1960; *Five One-Act Plays* (contains "The End of the Beginning," "A Pound on Demand," "Hall of Healing," "Bedtime Story," and "Time to Go"), St. Martin's, 1958; *Three More Plays,* introduction by J. C. Trewin (contains "The Silver Tassie," "Purple Dust," and "Red Roses for Me"), St. Martin's, 1965.

Work represented in anthologies, including *Six Great Modern Plays,* Dell, 1964, and *Masterpieces of Modern Irish Theatre,* Macmillan, 1967.

SIDELIGHTS: Sean O'Casey rose from the Dublin slums to become one of the most esteemed dramatists of the twentieth century. When he was six years old his father died, leaving a family of thirteen to fend for themselves in Dublin. Sean, the youngest child in the family, suffered from a chronic eye disease that threatened him with blindness throughout his life. Because of this he was seldom able to attend school, but taught himself to read and write by the time he was thirteen. He became a drama enthusaist, Shakespeare and Dion Boucicault being his favorite authors, and performed in local theatre groups.

During his early years O'Casey supported himself by working as a common laborer. He soon became involved with the Irish struggle for freedom. He joined the Gaelic league, learned to speak, read, and write fluent Gaelic, and Gaelicized his name from John Casey to Sean O'Cathasaigh, under which his writings of that time were published. He also learned to play bagpipes and helped found the St. Laurence O'Toole Pipers Band.

When he was thirty O'Casey began to devote his energies to the Irish labor movement headed by Jim Larkin, helping to fight the appalling living and working conditions of his fellow workers. He served under Larkin as the first secretary of the Irish Citizen Army, wrote articles for the labor union's newspaper, and helped organize a transport strike in 1913. He resigned his post, however, in 1914 when he was unable to prevent a rival group, the Irish Volunteers, from weakening the labor union.

In his mid-thirties O'Casey returned to his previous interest in drama and began to write plays. He used this medium to express his concern for the effects of the Irish rebellion on average Dubliners like himself. His first play to be produced was "The Shadow of a Gunman," followed by "Juno and the Paycock" and "The Plough and the Stars." Kevin Sullivan remarked that O'Casey's "reputation for genius begins, and I think ends," with these three plays. "That in any event is the commonly accepted critical judgment on O'Casey which only his most fervent admirers . . . would care to dispute." In Robert Hogan's view, the negative reception of O'Casey's later plays may be attributed to most critics' aversion to original thought and their unquestioning acceptance of the cliche that "when O'Casey left for England, he left his talent behind on the North Circular Road." Hogan himself believes "you can only prove the worth of a play by playing it," and having staged or performed in five of O'Casey's later plays he asserted that "most of O'Casey's late work is eminently, dazzlingly good."

O'Casey submitted several of his first playwriting attempts to the Abbey Theatre, which was run by William Butler Yeats and Lady Gregory. The Abbey finally accepted "The Shadow of a Gunman" for production in 1923. It was a tragedy of a poet and a peddler who become inadvertantly involved in the guerrilla warfare of the Irish Republican Army (IRA) and the British soldiers in Dublin during 1920. A peddler, Seumas Shields, allows Donal Davoren, a struggling poet, to stay in his tenement room. Donal is mistaken by the neighbors for a brave IRA fighter. One of them, Minnie Powell, falls in love with the image of Donal as a romantic poet-gunman. A real patriot hides explosives in Seumas's room, and when guards raid the tenement Minnie moves the bombs to her room in order to save Seumas and Donal. As a result Minnie is arrested and then accidentally killed in a cross-fire between Irish patriots and British guards.

Seumas's room is the setting for both acts of "The Shadow of a Gunman." It is cluttered with religious icons, pots and pans, a typewriter, flowers, and books. Bernice Schrank noted that "the setting creates an atmosphere of chaos congenial to the theme of breakdown which runs throughout the play." O'Casey's explicit stage directions call for a messy room to imply the confused psychological states of Donal and Seumas, as well as the confusion of the country.

O'Casey's second play, "Juno and the Paycock," was considered by T. E. Kalem to be "one of the granitic masterworks of modern dramatic art." This tragicomedy studies the effects of Dublin's post-war disturbances on a tenement family in 1922. The head of the family is "Captain" Jack Boyle, who struts about from pub to pub like a peacock (paycock) while his wife Juno struggles to make ends meet at home. The family has no income because the Captain is unemployed, his son Johnny has been injured in the fight for independence, and his daughter Mary has joined the workers strike.

The family rejoices when Mary's suitor, lawyer Charlie Bentham, informs the Boyles that they are to inherit half the property of a rich relative. They begin to buy lavishly on credit. The Captain even promises to give up drinking and get a job. When the interpretation of the will turns out to be erroneous, Bentham skips town, creditors repossess the new merchandise, and Mary discovers she is pregnant.

The family's reaction to these events provides "a continuous contrast between the masculine and the feminine personages, from which the women emerge as far superior to the men because of their capacity for love, altruism, and wisdom," noted William A. Armstrong. "The men in the play are all deluded, self-centered, and hypocritical." The Captain and Johnny turn viciously against Mary when they learn of her pregnancy, and Bentham and another boyfriend desert her as well. Juno, on the other hand, is supportive and gives Mary sensible advice in her time of need.

Among the play's most noteworthy aspects, according to Armstrong, are its "modulated movement from the apparently comic to the grievously catastrophic," and the paralleling of domestic and national themes as represented by the treachery, desertion, and dissolution occurring both among the Boyles and among the Irish people. Bernard Benstock also praised the characterization of the Captain as "probably O'Casey's finest achievement," and the first presentation of a character type that he used in many of his later plays: "the indolent, self-indulgent braggart whom he saw at the crux of the paralytic condition in Irish life, but whose boisterous wit and elan always brought him at least halfway back to redemption."

The final drama of O'Casey tragicomic trilogy was "The Plough and the Stars," whose title was taken from the symbols on the Irish Citizen Army flag. This play occurs in 1915 and 1916, before and during the Easter Rebellion. The plot revolves around Nora Clitheroe, a young bride who is expecting a baby. She unsuccessfully tries to prevent her husband, Jack, from leaving to become a troop commander in the IRA. In his absence chaos ensues. The tenement neighbors join in the looting of Dublin. Nora loses her baby and goes mad, so when word comes that Jack has died in the fighting she cannot even be told. The play closes as a neighbor is fatally shot trying to protect Nora from stray bullets, and Nora cries for Jack's help, still unaware of his heroic death.

During the fourth Abbey performance of this play a riot broke out in the audience. Benstock observed that "the same Dubliners who were being dissected and lampooned in . . . [O'Casey's first two] comic tragedies sat in the theatre and roared at themselves, until the full brunt of O'Casey's satire struck home in *The Plough and the Stars*." The blunt realism of O'Casey's depiction of sex and religion even offended some of the actors, and several refused to speak their lines.

Another reason for the uproar was that the people were accustomed to viewing Ireland as a fair land with the national fighters as hero-figures. But in "The Plough and the Stars" and his other plays the heroes are noncombatants, usually women who manage to survive the tragedies of war. "For O'Casey the essential reality of war, revolutionary or otherwise, no matter how splendid the principle for which it is fought, is pain, and pain dominates the last half of *The Plough and the Stars:* fear, madness, miscarriage, and death," noted Julius Novick. "No wonder the Nationalists rioted when the play was new; they did not want to see the seamy side of their glorious struggle."

Unhappy with the rioting, O'Casey moved to London in 1926. He continued to write, but his next play, "The Silver Tassie," was rejected by Yeats for production at the Abbey Theatre. Although most of the play was written in a naturalist style, in the second act O'Casey had used an expressionistic dream structure, a distorted setting, and stylized action. "Yeats told O'Casey that the play suffered from both inadequate technical prowess and imaginative unconvincingness," Richard Gilman related. O'Casey was bitter about the rejection and kept up a feud with Yeats for years because of it. He even published the correspondence concerning the rejection, claiming that Yeats had decided not to accept the play before he ever saw it. Denis Donoghue asserted: "Yeats made a critical error in rejecting the play, but the published correspondence shows that he was scrupulously honorable in reaching his decision. . . . The strongest argument against Yeats . . . is that *The Silver Tassie,* whatever its faults, was demonstrably superior to many of the plays that the Abbey had already accepted. But Yeats' critique of the play is formidable, and not all foolish or shallow."

After the rioting over "The Plough and the Stars" and Yeats's rejection of "The Silver Tassie," O'Casey was convinced that he could never achieve artistic freedom in Ireland. He remained in London, living "in stubborn exile a far remove from the people and places that fed his imagination and stirred his deepest feelings," reflected Kevin Sullivan. Although O'Casey never returned to Ireland, he and Yeats reconciled after several years, and his plays were once again produced at the Abbey Theatre.

When O'Casey began to write for the theatre he was a dedicated socialist, but Benstock said that despite this, "the early tenement plays are devoid of propagandistic evidence. He concentrated on real events, their complexities and their multiple effects on the people he knew, rarely showing his hand to his audience." William A. Armstrong noted that "the topical and the local elements in O'Casey's early plays are so strong that some critics belittled him as nothing more than a photographic realist who merely shuffled together for the stage familiar details of life in the Dublin slums during the time of the Troubles. This criticism is invalid, for O'Casey . . . has the myth-maker's great gift of discerning archetypal characters and situations, of distilling from everyday elements a quintessence of life far superior to the products of any documentary form of realism."

Even after his exile to England, O'Casey's "subject matter remained almost exclusively Irish, with only one or two exceptions, and for over thirty years he kept in touch with political and social changes in Ireland, mirroring them in his new plays and remaining a persistent critic of essential elements of Irish life under the Republic," Benstock noted. He continued to experiment with Expressionism in various themes from morality plays to comic fantasies. Although his use of stylization did not succeed in "The Silver Tassie," Joan Templeton declared that "the techniques of Expressionism . . . figure significantly in the success of the late comedies."

Among his more successful later plays were "Purple Dust" and "Cock-a-Doodle-Dandy." Most of these plays were comic pastorals containing the message that "merriment and joy are the primary virtues in a world that has denounced them too long," stated Joan Templeton. O'Casey often attempted to present a serious message through the comic mode, but this method did not always fare well. The "technique in these late comedies parallels that of the Dublin plays in their blend of the tragic and the pathetic with the wildly comic, but with strong elements of fantasy for leavening," Benstock noted. "Supernatural birds, superhuman heroes, mysterious priests who stir the youth to rebellion—all embodiments of the Life Force—take command in the more optimistic of the plays. . . . But in the more somber dramas, despite the many flashes of hilarity and song, the mood of bitterness predominates." Hogan said of the late plays that "by their verve, vitality, and brilliance, they and not the early masterpieces may ultimately prove to be O'Casey's great contribution to the theatre."

In 1939 O'Casey published the first book of his six-volume part-fictional autobiography. The autobiographies have many literary faults and have often been brushed aside as the work of an established writer's old age. But Gilman claimed that they were "perhaps the most durable of his contributions." In addition to providing valuable insight into O'-Casey's personality and writing methods, these volumes contain many fascinating passages about important figures such as Yeats, Lady Gregory, T. P. O'Connor, and Bernard Shaw, and serve as important social documents of the period.

The Letters of Sean O'Casey supplements the autobiographies with numerous letters to, from, and about Sean O'-Casey. Sullivan noted that the letters emphasize O'Casey's "generosity, his incredible energy and resilience," as well as his "perverse affection" for poverty "because it was *his* way of life," and his impatience "with any opinion that is not his own and, we suspect, precisely *because* it is not his own." Donoghue thought the letters presented O'Casey as "the most quarrelsome writer in Ireland, a notoriously quarrelsome country. . . . O'Casey brought his Ireland with him, and held on to its rancor wherever he happened to be; London, Devon, New York. He was always the man who was sacked from his first job." Nevertheless, a *New Yorker* critic concluded that "his grievances were, for the most part, real, and they are, even now, heartbreaking to read about."

Some critics have recently questioned O'Casey's place in literary history as one of the great modern playwrights. Richard Gilman contended that "O'Casey can't bear the weight of such an apotheosis. . . . There are too many bad and even deeply embarrassing plays in his *oeuvre* ('Within the Gates,' 'The Star Turns Red,' 'The Bishop's Bonfire,' et al.) and too many esthetic sins of naivete, rhetorical excess, sentimentality and tendentiousness in all but his very best work." Gilman suggested that O'Casey's reputation has less to do with his art than with other circumstances: "the sterility of the English-speaking theater in the twenties when he came to prominence with his 'Dublin' plays at the Abbey Theater; his ferocious battle with censorship; his own 'dramatic' story—slum childhood, self-education, lifelong nearblindness, self-exile."

Denis Donoghue declared that O'Casey's "career as an important dramatist came and went within five years. A man who writes *The Shadow of a Gunman* in 1923, *Juno and the Paycock* in 1924, *The Plough and the Stars* in 1926 and *The Silver Tassie* in 1928 should have the luck to continue writing good plays or the prudence to withdraw into dignity and silence. . . . But O'Casey lapsed into bad plays, hysterical essays, hectic reminiscences, blasts against the world, benedictions lavished upon communism, atheism, Welsh nationalism." Kevin Sullivan agreed, claiming that "the experimental plays . . . are interesting as experiments but hardly memorable as works of art. . . . Sean O'Casey was above all a passionate man and his genius, if granted, is concentrated in this quality of his life which only occasionally carried over into the work."

Despite this criticism, Irma S. Lustig reminds us that "it is unjust to obscure O'Casey's farsightedness . . . by recalling only the strident means by which he was driven to express his views." "Politically a realist as well as a humanitarian, he predicted the global successes of socialism, especially if there were repeated wars. He foresaw the consequences of dividing Ireland, and the impossibility of 'classless' nationalist struggle. He challenged the exaltation of reckless violence." In striving to express his views, O'Casey developed "a voice of his own, a style of his own, and a body of artistic work that reflected his personality and thinking with flair and color," Benstock declared. "Sean O'Casey stands as Irish drama almost by himself—and one of the best dramatists writing in the English language in his time in any country."

BIOGRAPHICAL/CRITICAL SOURCES: William A. Armstrong, *Sean O'Casey,* Longman, 1967; Bernard Benstock, *Sean O'Casey,* Bucknell University Press, 1970; *Modern Drama,* May, 1971, March, 1974; *New Yorker,* March 11, 1972, January 13, 1973, May 5, 1975; *Nation,* March 20, 1972, July 19, 1975; *Time,* March 27, 1972, November 18, 1974; *Contemporary Literary Criticism,* Gale, Volume 1, 1973, Volume 5, 1976, Volume 9, 1979, Volume 11, 1979; *Newsweek* January 15, 1973, March 31, 1975; Thomas Kilroy, editor, *Sean O'Casey: A Collection of Critical Essays,* Prentice-Hall, 1975; *New York Times Book Review,* March 16, 1975; *New Republic,* April 26, 1975; *Virginia Quarterly Review,* summer, 1975; *Times Literary Supplement,* January 2, 1976; *South Atlantic Quarterly,* summer, 1976; *Village Voice,* November 29, 1976; *MOSAIC,* fall, 1977.*

—*Sketch by Martha Winkel*

*　*　*

O'CATHASAIGH, Sean
See O'CASEY, Sean

*　*　*

O'CONNELL, Daniel Patrick 1924-1979

OBITUARY NOTICE—See index for *CA* sketch: Born July 7, 1924, in Auckland, New Zealand; died in 1979. Educator and author. O'Connell was a professor of international law and diplomacy at the University of Adelaide from 1953 to 1972. He helped draft the constitutions of many national and international bodies. Among his books are *The Law of State Succession, International Law,* and *The Influence of Laws on Seapower*. Obituaries and other sources: *Who's Who in the World,* 2nd edition, Marquis, 1973; *The Writers Directory, 1980-82,* St. Martin's, 1979; *Who's Who,* 131st edition, St. Martin's, 1979; *AB Bookman's Weekly,* July 30, 1979.

*　*　*

O'CONNOR, Garry 1938-

PERSONAL: Born January 31, 1938, in London, England; son of Cavan (a singer) and Rita (a singer; maiden name, Odoli-Tate) O'Connor; married Victoria Meredith-Owens, May 25, 1970; children: Tobias Cavan, Joseph Owen, Emily Margaret, Frederick Garry. *Education:* Attended King's College, Cambridge, B.A., 1961. *Religion:* Roman Catholic. *Residence:* Oxford, England. *Agent:* Deborah Rogers Ltd., 5-11 Mortimer St., London W.1, England.

CAREER: Royal Shakespeare Company, Stratford-upon-Avon, England, play director, 1963-66, director of Stratford Studio, 1963-64; Royal Court Theatre, London, England, director, 1965; Traverse, Edinburgh, Scotland, director, 1966; writer, 1968—. Drama teacher at London Drama Centre and Royal Academy of Dramatic Art, 1963-67. *Military service:* British Army, Educational Corps, 1956-58;

became sergeant. *Member:* Critics Circle. *Awards, honors:* Arts Council award, 1978.

WRITINGS: Le Theatre en Angleterre (title means "Theatre in England"; translated into French by Georgette Illes), French Information Service, 1968; *French Theatre Today,* Pitman, 1976; *The Pursuit of Perfection: A Life of Maggie Teyte,* Atheneum, 1979.

Plays: "The Musicians" (two-act), first produced in London, England, at Mercury Theatre, 1969; "I Learnt in Ipswich How to Poison Flowers" (two-act), first produced in Ipswich, England, at Arts Theatre, 1969; "Different Circumstances" (two-act), first produced in Oxford, England, at Newmans Rooms, 1974; "Semmelweis" (two-act), first produced in Edinburgh, Scotland, at Edinburgh Festival, St. Mary's Hall, 1975; "Dialogue Between Friends" (one-act), first produced in London at Open Space Theatre, 1976. Contributor to *Theatre Quarterly.* Television critic for *Queen,* 1965-66; theater critic for *Financial Times,* 1966—.

WORK IN PROGRESS: A novel about a musical family, publication expected in 1980.

SIDELIGHTS: O'Connor commented: "The plays, in various ways, explore the theme of the individual whose sense of, or discovery of, the truth puts him in conflict with other shaping forces in his society. The novel shows a father and son clash of temperaments over the years in the face of changing circumstances. The biography charts the struggle in a famous singer's life between her love of perfection and her human vulnerability which gradually brings about a hardening of her character."

BIOGRAPHICAL/CRITICAL SOURCES: New York Times Book Review, October 7, 1979.

* * *

O'DONNELL, James J(oseph, Jr.) 1950-

PERSONAL: Born February 26, 1950, in Giessen, Germany; American citizen born abroad; son of James Joseph (a civil servant) and Helen Theresa (Murphy) O'Donnell. *Education:* Princeton University, B.A., 1972; attended National University of Ireland University College in Dublin, 1972-73; Yale University, Ph.D., 1975. *Politics:* "Truculent." *Religion:* Roman Catholic. *Office:* Department of Classics, Cornell University, Ithaca, N.Y. 14853.

CAREER: Bryn Mawr College, Bryn Mawr, Pa., lecturer in Latin, 1975-76; Catholic University of America, Washington, D.C., assistant professor of Greek and Latin, 1976-77; Cornell University, Ithaca, N.Y., assistant professor of classics, 1977—, director of medieval studies program, 1979—. *Member:* North American Patristics Society, American Philological Association, Phi Beta Kappa.

WRITINGS: Cassiodorus, University of California Press, 1979. Contributor of more than a dozen articles and reviews to theology and classical studies journals.

WORK IN PROGRESS: A polemic outline of church history; research for a book on the life and times of Pope Gregory the Great; research for books on early Christianity and the fall of the Roman Empire.

SIDELIGHTS: O'Donnell writes: "If I have my way, I shall have already published my last book with a university press. Having gone through the mill to prove my academic credentials, I am more convinced than ever that scholars cannot go on chatting quietly with each other in the privacy of learned journals and technical monographs. I firmly believe in the importance—the necessity—of my scholarly work; and I believe I can and must make the effort to reach out to a wider audience to give my scholarship its full worth and impact. The challenge is to achieve vital readability while still living up to the highest standards of critical scholarship. My scholarship has met those standards and my teaching has shown that the most forbiddingly remote tracts of history can be brought roaringly to life.

"So the challenge and the resources to meet the challenge are there. In Gregory the Great I have the subject to galvanize an audience. Gregory is the spiritual linchpin between antiquity (pagan and Christian) and the modern world which Christianity built. He lived in a violent age of barbarian invasions in a Rome ravaged by plague, but in his writings and his deeds he established the moral basis of a new civilization which fought free of the smothering grasp of an increasingly totalitarian society, and succeeded in mastering a turbulent world with principles of the spirit, not manipulations of political power that deaden the spirit.

"Gregory's achievement is deadly important to recall—for it is the victory of authentic freedom against the stifling terrorism of Statism. The twentieth century congratulates itself for having shaken off what it thinks were the superstitious bonds of Christendom, only to find itself flirting with the oldest and most irrational of superstitions—that reasonable men acting with the best of intentions can enhance the happiness and prosperity of their fellows and themselves. Gregory, theologian of Murphy's Law, knew better and can show us the escape from the rat's maze we build for ourselves.

"My motto, from a contemporary of Gregory's, a wandering Irish monk named Columbanus, who settled in Italy, on fire with the same convictions that pilot my pen: '*Semper antiquior est veritas.*' "

* * *

OFSHE, Richard 1941-

PERSONAL: Born February 27, 1941, in New York, N.Y.; son of Jack (in sales) and Adele (Stoll) Ofshe; married Lynne Roberts, 1965 (divorced, 1970). *Education:* Queens College of the City University of New York, B.A., 1963, M.A., 1964; Stanford University, Ph.D., 1968. *Agent:* Virginia Barber Literary Agency, Inc., 44 Greenwich Ave., New York, N.Y. 10011. *Office:* Department of Sociology, University of California, Berkeley, Calif. 94705.

CAREER: University of California, Berkeley, assistant professor, 1967-71, associate professor of sociology, 1971—. *Member:* American Sociological Association, Pacific Sociological Association. *Awards, honors:* Guggenheim fellow, 1973-74.

WRITINGS: (With Lynne Ofshe) *Utility and Choice in Social Interaction,* Prentice-Hall, 1970; *The Sociology of the Possible,* Prentice-Hall, 1970, 2nd edition, 1977; *Interpersonal Behavior in Small Groups,* Prentice-Hall, 1973.

Contributor: Edgar Borgatta, editor, *Sociological Methodology,* Jossey-Bass, 1968; Charles Glock and Robert Bellah, editors, *New Religious consciousness,* University of California Press, 1976; Joseph Berger, Morris Zelditch, and Bo Anderson, editors, *Sociological Theories in Progress,* Houghton, 1972; Heinz Sauermann, editor, *Contributions to Experimental Economics,* J. C. B. Mohr, 1972; (with David and Kathy Mitchell) *Out of Control,* Ablex, in press; (with D. and K. Mitchell) *The Corporate Cult,* Seavue Press, in press. Contributor to sociology and planning journals. Associate editor of *American Sociological Review, American Journal of Sociology, Administrative Science Quarterly, Now Social Psychology,* and *Behavioral Science.*

WORK IN PROGRESS: Research on economic theory of consumer preference.

* * *

OHLIN, Bertil 1899(?)-1979

OBITUARY NOTICE: Born c. 1899 in Klippan, Sweden; died August 3, 1979, in Sweden. Educator, politician, author, and economist, Ohlin won the Nobel Prize in 1977 for his work in the field of international economics. Ohlin was credited with developing a model for explaining international trade patterns according to production factors in individual countries. He was a major figure in Swedish politics, heading the Liberal party and becoming minister of trade in 1944. Ohlin also taught at the University of Stockholm. His work includes *Interregional and International Trade,* and he contributed articles to the newspaper, *Dagens Nyheter*. Obituaries and other sources: *New York Times Biography Service,* October, 1977; *Economist,* October 22, 1977; *Newsweek,* October 24, 1977; *New York Times,* August 17, 1979; *Time,* August 27, 1979.

* * *

OLDFIELD, James E(dmund) 1921-

PERSONAL: Born August 30, 1921, in Victoria, British Columbia, Canada; came to the United States in 1949, naturalized citizen, 1965; son of H. Clarence (a farmer) and Doris Oldfield; married Mildred E. Atkinson, September 4, 1942; children: Nancy E. Oldfield McLaren, Kathleen E. Oldfield Sansone, David J., Jane E. Oldfield Imper, Richard A. *Education:* University of British Columbia, B.S.A., 1941, M.S.A., 1949; Oregon State University, Ph.D., 1951. *Home:* 1325 Northwest 15th St., Corvallis, Ore. 97330. *Office:* Department of Animal Science, Oregon State University, Corvallis, Ore. 97331.

CAREER: Oregon State University, Corvallis, assistant professor, 1951-56, associate professor, 1957-62, professor of animal science, 1963—, head of department, 1967—. *Military service:* Canadian Army, 1943-46; became captain; received Military Cross. *Member:* American Chemical Society, American Institute of Nutrition, American Society of Animal Science (president, 1967), Agricultural Institute of Canada, New York Academy of Sciences, Corvallis Kiwanis Club (president, 1964), Corvallis Toastmasters Club (president, 1960). *Awards, honors:* Morrison Award from American Society of Animal Science, 1972, for research in animal nutrition; Fulbright scholar in New Zealand, 1974.

WRITINGS: The Westminsters' War Diary, Mitchell Press, 1964; (editor) *Symposium: Selenium in Biomedicine,* Avi, 1966; (editor) *Sulphur in Nutrition,* Avi, 1970; *Nutrition Is Everybody's Business,* Massey University, 1974.

SIDELIGHTS: Oldfield writes: "My major interest is in animal nutrition, and specifically in the effects of soil-plant-animal relationships upon diet adequacy. This interest has focused most recently on the trace element selenium, and the effects that dietary deficiency in it cause in grazing livestock and also in humans. Travel has allowed first-hand observation of selenium-responsive disease conditions in New Zealand, China, Finland and Turkey. Recent articles have explored the continuing place of animal products (meat and milk) in the human food supply."

AVOCATIONAL INTERESTS: Travel (England, Europe, Scandinavia, New Zealand, Australia, Turkey, China).

OLIVER, Jane
See REES, Helen Christina Easson (Evans)

* * *

OLSHEN, Barry N(eil) 1944-

PERSONAL: Born April 12, 1944, in Brooklyn, N.Y.; son of Henry B. (an insurance broker) and Ethel (Horowitz) Olshen; married Toni A. Jacobs (a librarian), June 5, 1966; children: Jessica. *Education:* New York University, B.A., 1964, M.A., 1965; University of Toronto, Ph.D., 1972. *Office:* Department of English, Glendon College, York University, 2275 Bayview Ave., Toronto, Ontario, Canada M4N 3M6.

CAREER: York University, Glendon College, Toronto, Ontario, lecturer, 1969-71, assistant professor, 1971-74, associate professor of English, 1974—.

WRITINGS: John Fowles, Ungar, 1978; (with wife, Toni A. Olshen) *John Fowles Reference Guide,* G. K. Hall, 1980. Contributor to theatre, literature, and popular culture journals.

WORK IN PROGRESS: A children's Bible.

SIDELIGHTS: Olshen commented: "John Fowles is one of the most ambitious writers in English today. His aspirations seem almost as admirable as his accomplishments. Of special interest to me are the broad intellectual concerns of his work, his strong moral bent, and his successful use of a wide variety of styles and genres.

"Although I have published a number of articles on theatre and drama and two books on Fowles, my principal literary interest now is the Bible. I would like to produce an engaging and accurate children's Bible before my own daughter is too old to profit from it.

"In addition to teaching and writing, my other creative outlet lies in collage and assemblage. There has been one public showing of my work to date."

* * *

OLSON, Jane Virginia 1916-

PERSONAL: Born December 14, 1916, in Chicago, Ill.; daughter of Oscar Wilford and Mary (Bowles) Olson; married William M. Gooden, February 16, 1955 (divorced, 1957). *Education:* University of New Mexico, B.A., 1939. *Home:* 60 Ardmore St., Hamden, Conn. 06517. *Office: American Scientist,* 345 Whitney Ave., New Haven, Conn. 06511.

CAREER/WRITINGS: Vogue, New York, N.Y., copy editor, 1946-49; *Illinois Geological Survey,* Urbana, Ill., technical editor, 1949-55; Yale University Press, New Haven, Conn., science and social science editor, 1958-69; *American Scientist,* New Haven, editor, 1969—. *Member:* League of Women Voters, Scientific Research Society of North America, Inc., Sigma Xi.

* * *

OLSON, Richard G(eorge) 1940-

PERSONAL: Born November 4, 1940, in St. Paul, Minn.; married, 1962. *Education:* Harvey Mudd College, B.S., 1962; Harvard University, A.M., 1963, Ph.D., 1967. *Office:* Department of History, Harvey Mudd College, Claremont, Calif. 91711.

CAREER: Harvard University, Cambridge, Mass., tutor in history and science, 1964-66; Tufts University, Medford,

Mass., instructor in history, 1966-67; University of California, Santa Cruz, 1967-76, assistant professor, 1967-72, associate professor of history and head of history board of studies, 1972-74; Harvey Mudd College, Claremont, Calif., professor of history and Willard J. Keith Fellow in the Humanities, both 1976—. Directs and participates in scholarly meetings. *Member:* West Coast History of Science Society. *Awards, honors:* Woodrow Wilson fellowship, 1962; National Endowment for the Humanities younger humanist fellowship, 1971-72; grants from Lilly Foundation, 1977, 1978; Arnold L. and Lois S. Graves Award, from 1979-80.

WRITINGS: (Editor) *Science as Metaphor: The Historical Roles of Scientific Theories in Forming Western Culture,* Wadsworth, 1971; *Scottish Philosophy and British Physics, 1750-1850: Foundations of the Victorian Scientific Style,* Princeton University Press, 1975; (contributor) *Tradition and Transformation in the History of Science: Essays in Honor of I. Bernard Cohen,* Cambridge University Press, in press. Contributor of more than thirty articles and reviews to scientific journals.

WORK IN PROGRESS: Understanding and Undermining: An Interpretation of Scientism in Western Culture.

* * *

OLSON, Stanley 1948-

PERSONAL: Born June 8, 1948, in Akron, Ohio; son of Sidney (an executive) and Miriam (Klein) Olson. *Education:* Boston University, B.A., 1969; University of London, Ph.D., 1972. *Politics:* None. *Religion:* "Absolutely none." *Home:* 1-E Montagu Mews N., London W.1, England. *Agent:* Wallace & Sheil Agency, Inc., 118 East 61st St., New York, N.Y. 10021.

CAREER: Writer, 1974—. *Member:* International P.E.N., National Book League.

WRITINGS: Elinor Wylie: A Life Apart, Dial, 1979; (editor) *Letters and Diaries of the Honourable Harold Nicolson,* Collins, 1980. Contributor to magazines in England and the United States, including *Cosmopolitan* and *Saturday Review,* and newspapers.

SIDELIGHTS: Olson writes: "It is a popular myth that writers need inspiration. I have found this to be nonsense: there is nothing to make up for hard work and an iron-clad routine. I work amazingly slowly, hence the greater need for a routine. I also have considerable difficulty making up stories. Biography is my *metier.*"

AVOCATIONAL INTERESTS: "Food, wine, talking to my spaniel, and Wagner—all of which assume near-neurotic and obsessive proportions."

BIOGRAPHICAL/CRITICAL SOURCES: New York Times Book Review, February 11, 1979.

* * *

O'NEAL, Bill
See O'NEAL, John W(illiam)

* * *

O'NEAL, John W(illiam) 1942-
(Bill O'Neal)

PERSONAL: Born April 8, 1942, in Corsicana, Tex.; son of W. C. (employed by Texas A. & M. University Extension Service) and Jessie (Standard) O'Neal; married Faye Gipson, August 19, 1971; children: Lynn Katrice and Shellie Kaye (twins), Berri Joy. *Education:* Navarro Junior College, A.A., 1962; East Texas State University, B.A. (with high honors), 1964, M.A., 1969; attended University of Texas, summers, 1969, 1974, 1975, 1979. *Politics:* "Conservative, normally vote Republican." *Religion:* Southern Baptist. *Home:* 1002 West Holland, Carthage, Tex. 75633. *Office:* Panola Junior College, Carthage, Tex. 75633.

CAREER: Junior high school English teacher and football coach in Lampasas, Tex., 1964-67; high school English teacher, principal, and athletic coach in Anna, Tex., 1967-68; high school history teacher and head football coach in Waskom, Tex., 1969-70; Panola Junior College, Carthage, Tex., member of staff, history department, 1970—. Public speaker. *Member:* National Association for Outlaw and Lawman History, National Order of the Indian Wars, Texas Junior College Teachers Association, Texas State Historical Association, East Texas Historical Association.

WRITINGS—Under name Bill O'Neal: *Historical Survey of Panola County,* Panola Junior College, 1974; *History of Central Baptist Church, Carthage, Texas,* privately printed, 1976; *Encyclopedia of Western Gunfighters,* University of Oklahoma Press, 1979; *Henry Brown, Outlaw Marshal,* Creative Publishers, 1979. Contributor to athletic and history journals.

WORK IN PROGRESS: Encyclopedia of Western Indian Fighters, for publication by University of Oklahoma Press.

SIDELIGHTS: O'Neal told *CA:* "My first book was a biography of western gunman Henry Brown. Halfway through this work I realized that an encyclopedia of gunfighters was needed, and immediately launched the project. Only after completing the encyclopedia did I return to the biography of Brown.

"The concept for my encyclopedia was suggested by the 1955 *Encyclopedia of Baseball,* which is a favorite book of mine. As I worked on the Brown biography I saw the need for a book similar in concept about gunfighters. How many men did they actually shoot? How often were gunmen in shootouts? How long were they in the West? How many of them met violent ends? What were the most violent towns and states and years? I felt that accurate statistics should be compiled, and that there should be a single volume which would have the facts about all these fascinating characters.

"A delightful bonus occurred about two years into the project. While studying a range war in Lampasas County, Texas, I located a photo of eight participants, one of whom was named Jess Standard. My mother is from Lampasas and her maiden name was Jessie Standard. When asked, she told me that the man was her grandfather, and I was very pleased to be able to include my great-grandfather in the book and to dedicate it to: 'Jessie Standard O'Neal, mother of the author and granddaughter of a gunfighter.'

"My current project, *Encyclopedia of Western Indian Fighters,* will be a similar treatment of the frontiersmen who saw combat against hostiles."

* * *

O'NEIL, Daniel J. 1936-

PERSONAL: Born December 25, 1936, in New Orleans, La.; son of Daniel M. (in business) and Alma (Martinez) O'Neil. *Education:* Louisiana State University, B.A., 1959, M.A., 1961; University of Texas, Ph.D., 1966. *Home:* 128 South Fifth Ave., #6, Tucson, Ariz. 85701. *Office:* Department of Political Science, University of Arizona, Tucson, Ariz. 85721.

CAREER: University of Tennessee, Knoxville, assistant

professor of political science, 1965-66; University of Arizona, Tucson, assistant professor, 1966-72, associate professor of political science, 1972—. *Military service:* U.S. Air Force. *Member:* International Studies Association, American Political Science Association, Society for the Advancement of Scandinavian Study, Association for Canadian Studies in the United States, British Studies Conferences, Southern Political Science Association, Western Political Science Association, Arizona Political Science Association, Pi Sigma Alpha, Phi Kappa Phi.

WRITINGS: Church Lobbying in a Western State: A Case Study of Abortion Legislation, University of Arizona Press, 1970; *Three Perennial Themes of Anti-Colonialism: The Irish Case,* University of Denver Press, 1976. Contributor of more than a dozen articles to journals in the social sciences.

WORK IN PROGRESS: The Politics of Cultural Conflict.

SIDELIGHTS: O'Neil has traveled in England, Ireland, and Mexico. He comments: "Having an Irish father and Hispanic mother, and having been reared in the French country of Louisiana, my interests and research activities have moved into the area of cultural conflict. Can people of different cultures live together harmoniously?"

* * *

ORKENY, Istvan 1912-1979

OBITUARY NOTICE: Born April 5, 1912, in Budapest, Hungary; died June, 1979, in Budapest. Author and playwright of many successful plays, including "Catsplay," "The Tot Family," "The Silence of the Dead," and "Blood Relations." Orkeny also wrote such novels and short stories as *Consorts,* "The Lager People," "Fasting in Buda," and "Alien Earth." Obituaries and other sources: *Who's Who in the World,* 4th edition, Marquis, 1978; *The International Who's Who,* Europa, 1978; *New York Times,* July 29, 1979.

* * *

OSGOOD, David William 1940-

PERSONAL: Born May 19, 1940, in Grants Pass, Ore.; son of Samuel Baker (a physician) and Mary Elizabeth (a nurse; maiden name, Miller) Osgood; married Judith Stoddard (a free-lance writer), January 31, 1958; children: Kelley Sue, Eric Brett. *Education:* Portland State University, B.S., 1963; Duke University, M.A., 1965, Ph.D., 1968. *Home:* 337 Buckingham Dr., Indianapolis, Ind. 46208. *Office:* Department of Zoology, Butler University, Indianapolis, Ind. 46208.

CAREER: Duke University, Durham, N.C., temporary instructor in zoology, 1967-68; Butler University, Indianapolis, Ind., assistant professor, 1968-73, associate professor of zoology, 1973—. Visiting professor at Portland State University, summers, 1969, 1973, 1976. *Member:* American Association for the Advancement of Science, American Society of Ichthyologists and Herpetologists, American Society of Mammalogists, Herpetologists League, Sigma Xi, Phi Kappa Phi.

WRITINGS: (With J. W. Berry and P. A. St. John) *Chemical Villains: A Biology of Pollution,* Mosby, 1974. Contributor to scientific journals.

SIDELIGHTS: Osgood told *CA:* "My future writing will probably be limited to technical papers as one writer in the family seems like enough. The popularity of the study-tours that I have led to the Florida Keys, Andros Island (Bahamas), and Ecuador (Galapagos Islands, and the Amazonian Rain Forest) suggest a way that my free time might be spent in the future."

AVOCATIONAL INTERESTS: Sailing, skiing, mountain climbing.

* * *

OTERO, Blas de 1916-

PERSONAL: Born March 15, 1916, in Bilbao, Spain. *Education:* Attended University of Valladoid and University of Madrid. *Address:* c/o Alianza Editorial SA, Milan 38, Apdo 9107, Madrid 33, Spain.

CAREER: Poet. Teacher and lecturer in Madrid and Barcelona, Spain. *Awards, honors:* Received poetry prize, 1950, for *Angel fieramente humano.*

WRITINGS—In English: *Twenty Poems by Blas de Otero,* translation and introduction by Hardie St. Martin, Sixties Press, 1964. Also author, with Miguel Hernandez, of *Selected Poems: Miguel Hernandez and Blas de Otero,* edited by St. Martin and T. Baland, 1972.

Other: *Cantico espiritual* (title means "Spiritual Canticle"), Grafico-Editora, 1942; *Angel fieramente humano* (title means "Fiercely Human Angel"), Insula (Madrid), 1950; *Redoble de conciencia* (title means "Echo of Conscience"), Instituto de Estudios Hispanicos (Barcelona), 1951; *Pido la paz y la palabra* (title means "I Ask for Peace and the Word"), Cantalapiedra, 1955; *Ancia* (title means "Ancient"), [Barcelona], 1958.

Con la inmensa mayoria (title means "With the Immense Majority"), Losada (Buenos Aires), 1960; *En Castellano* (title means "In Castilian"), Universidad Nacional Autonoma de Mexico, 1960; *Hacia la inmensa mayoria* (title means "About the Immense Majority"), Losada, 1962; *Esto no es un libro* (title means "This Is Not a Book"), University of Puerto Rico Press, 1963; *Que trata de Espana* (title means "Dealing With Spain"), Puedo Iberico (Paris), 1964; *A modo de antologia (1941-1969)* (title means "In the Manner of an Anthology"), Alfaguara (Madrid), 1969.

Mientras (title means "In the Meantime"), Javalambre (Zaragoza), 1970; *Historias fingidas y verdaderas* (title means "False and True Stories"), Alfaguara, 1970; *Pais: Antologia 1955-1970* (title means "Homeland: Anthology 1955-1970"), Plaza y Janes, 1971; *Verso y prosa* (title means "Verse and Prose"), Catedra (Madrid), 1974; *Poesia con nombres* (title means "Poetry With Names"), Alianza (Madrid), 1977; *Todos mis sonetos* (title means "All of My Sonnets"), Turner (Madrid), 1977. Also author of *Poesias en Burgos* (title means "Poems in Burgos"), 1943, and *Expresion y reunion, 1941-1969* (title means "Expression and Reunion, 1941-1969"), 1969.

SIDELIGHTS: Two facts—that Otero studied with the Jesuits and that he fought on the republican side in the Spanish civil war—reflect the paradox of his poetry in which, according to J. M. Cohen, "social interests are bound up with religious." In the development of his work, from metaphysical quest to social commitment, he has been likened to a number of poets, including Miguel de Unamuno, William Blake, Arthur Rimbaud, and Robert Lowell.

Hardie St. Martin has written that in Otero's earlier work, "words exploded with savage passion in love poems to a withdrawn God." Such volumes as *Angel fieramente humano* and *Redoble de conciencia* evoke anguish and despair as the poet, seeking mystical revelation, attempts to communicate with God. Wrestling with his own spiritual convictions, he conveys a simultaneous faith and hopelessness.

Otero's later work, beginning with *Pido la paz y la palabra,* extends the poet's internal struggle outward. His solitary religious anguish is supplanted by the political suffering of a wider humanity. Richard Howard has described these poems "as chronicles of political injustice and the endurance of abused soil, as litanies of martial *anomie,* protests against the outrages of tyranny and the excesses of the Church Militant."

As his writing has evolved, Otero has combined politics, religion, and art into a single aesthetic in which poetry becomes both a weapon and a means to salvation. "Otero asserts the ethical or utilitarian function of literature," Geoffrey R. Barrow explained. By failing to choose between the poet as revolutionary or as visionary, his "belief in poetry as an instrument of knowledge and truth becomes a kind of religion."

BIOGRAPHICAL/CRITICAL SOURCES: Encounter, February, 1959; Charles D. Ley, *Spanish Poetry Since 1939,* Catholic University Press, 1962; Blas de Otero, *Twenty Poems by Blas de Otero,* translation and introduction by Hardie St. Martin, Sixties Press, 1964; Calvin Cannon, *Modern Spanish Poems,* Macmillan, 1965; *Times Literary Supplement,* June 24, 1965; *Hispania,* September, 1965; *Poetry,* February, 1966; *Hispanofila,* May, 1975; *Contemporary Literary Criticism,* Volume 11, Gale, 1979.*

* * *

OTTLEY, Roi (Vincent) 1906-1960

OBITUARY NOTICE: Born August 2, 1906, in New York, N.Y.; died October 1, 1960. Journalist and author of books about race relations and blacks in America. A columnist, reporter, and editor with the *Amsterdam News* from 1932 to 1938, Ottley became the first black war correspondent to work for a national publication when he accepted assignments with *PM* and *Liberty Magazine* in 1944. After the war, Ottley was a columnist with the *Chicago Tribune* until the time of his death. His first book, *New World A-Coming: Inside Black America,* about the people of Harlem and the leading citizens produced by the district, won the Houghton Life-in-America Award and a Rosenwald Fellowship. It also inspired a tone poem of the same name by Duke Ellington. His other books were *Black Odyssey: The Story of the Negro in America, No Green Pastures,* and *Lonely Warrior.* Ottley was also the winner of a Peabody Award in 1945. Obituaries and other sources: *Current Biography,* Wilson, 1943, December, 1960; *New York Times,* October 2, 1960; *Publishers Weekly,* October 17, 1960.

* * *

OUSBY, Ian (Vaughan Kenneth) 1947-

PERSONAL: Surname is pronounced *Ooz*-bee; born June 26, 1947, in Marlborough, Wiltshire, England; came to the United States in 1968; son of Arthur Valentine (a soldier) and Betty Lettice Grace (Green) Ousby. *Education:* Magdalene College, Cambridge, B.A., 1968, M.A., 1972; Harvard University, Ph.D., 1973. *Residence:* Washington, D.C. *Office:* Department of English, University of Maryland, College Park, Md. 20742.

CAREER: University of Durham, Durham, England, temporary lecturer in English, 1974-75; University of Maryland, College Park, assistant professor, 1975-78, associate professor of English, 1978—. Participant in scholarly meetings. Guest on Canadian radio program, "Ideas." *Awards, honors:* Fulbright grant, 1968-73.

WRITINGS: Bloodhounds of Heaven: The Detective in English Fiction From Godwin to Doyle, Harvard University Press, 1976; (contributor) George H. Ford and Sylvere Monod, editors, *Bleak House* (critical edition), Norton, 1977; *An Introduction to Fifty American Novels,* Barnes & Noble, 1979. Contributor to *Mystery Encyclopedia* and *Mystery and Detection Annual.* Contributor of about thirty articles and reviews to literature journals.

WORK IN PROGRESS: Editing *The Letters of John Ruskin to His Father, 1862,* with John L. Bradley.

* * *

OWEN, Douglas David Roy 1922-

PERSONAL: Born November 17, 1922, in Norton, Suffolk, England; married Berit Mariann Person, 1954; children: David Killian, John Adrian. *Education:* Attended University of Nottingham, 1942-43; Cambridge University, B.A., 1948, M.A., 1953, Ph.D., 1955. *Home:* 7 West Acres, St. Andrews, Fife, Scotland. *Office:* Department of French, University of St. Andrews, St. Andrews, Fife, Scotland.

CAREER: University of St. Andrews, St. Andrews, Scotland, lecturer, 1951-64, senior lecturer, 1964-71, reader, 1971-72, professor of French, 1972—. *Member:* International Arthurian Society, Society for French Studies, Modern Humanities Research Association, Cambridge Union Club.

WRITINGS: (Co-editor with Ronald Carlyle Johnston), *Fabliaux,* Basil Blackwell, 1957; *The Evolution of the Grail Legend,* Oliver & Boyd, 1968; (editor) *Arthurian Romance: Seven Essays,* Scottish Academic Press, 1970, Barnes & Noble, 1971; *The Vision of Hell: Infernal Journeys in Medieval French Literature,* Scottish Academic Press, 1970, Barnes & Noble, 1971; (editor with Johnston) *Two Old French Gauvain Romances,* Harper, 1972; (translator) *The Song of Roland: The Oxford Text,* Allen & Unwin, 1972; (editor) *Renaissance Studies: Six Essays,* Scottish Academic Press, 1972; *The Legend of Roland: A Pageant of the Middle Ages,* Phaidon, 1973; *Noble Lovers,* Phaidon, 1975. Contributor to language and literature journals. Editor of *Forum for Modern Language Studies,* 1965—.

WORK IN PROGRESS: Research on medieval literature, particularly the old French epic and Arthurian romance.

SIDELIGHTS: Owen told *CA:* "A particular interest is in the transmission and poet's refashioning of earlier historical and legendary material and in the medieval public's reception of their works." *Avocational interests:* Golf.

* * *

OWEN, (William) Harold 1897-1971

OBITUARY NOTICE—See index for *CA* sketch: Born September 5, 1897, in Shrewsbury, England; died November 26, 1971, in Oxfordshire, England. Painter, editor, and author of several volumes of memoirs. Owen's work was exhibited at the Claridge Galleris and the Royal Academy in London, England. He was editor of the *Collected Letters* of Wilfrid Owen. Obituaries and other sources: *AB Bookman's Weekly,* December 20, 1971.

P

PADDLEFORD, Clementine Haskin 1900-1967

OBITUARY NOTICE: Born September 27, 1900, in Stockdale, Kan.; died November 13, 1967, in New York. Described as the "best known food editor in the country" by *Time* magazine in 1953, Paddleford had an estimated weekly readership of twelve million readers. Her columns appeared in the *New York Herald Tribune* from 1936 until 1966, in the Sunday supplement *This Week* from 1940 to 1967, and in *Gourmet* magazine from 1941 to 1953. Honored on three separate occasions by the New York Newspaper Womens' Club, she was noted for her vivid descriptions of food. Paddleford was once known to write of a souffle as answering "with a rapturous, half-hushed sigh as it settled softly to melt and vanish in a moment like smoke or a dream." Obituaries and other sources: *Current Biography,* Wilson, 1958, January, 1968; *New York Times,* November 14, 1967; *Time,* November 24, 1967; *Newsweek,* November 27, 1967; *Publishers Weekly,* December 4, 1967.

* * *

PAGE, Vicki
See AVEY, Ruby

* * *

PAI, Anna C(hao) 1935-

PERSONAL: Born January 27, 1935, in Peking, China; daughter of Shih Hui and Huai Tung (Chang) Chao; married David H. C. Pai (a manager in engineering technology), August 29, 1959; children: Benjamin, Michael. *Education:* Sweet Briar College, B.A., 1957; Bryn Mawr College, M.A., 1959; Albert Einstein College of Medicine, Ph.D., 1964. *Office:* Department of Biology, Montclair State College, Normal Ave., Upper Montclair, N.J. 07043.

CAREER: High school teacher of mathematics and biology at religious girls' school in Bethlehem, Pa., 1959-60; Albert Einstein College of Medicine, New York, N.Y., instructor in genetics, 1964-65; Montclair State College, Upper Montclair, N.J., assistant professor, 1969-76, associate professor of biology, 1976—, head of department, 1979—. Visiting scientist at Roche Institute of Molecular Biology, 1978-79.

MEMBER: American Association for the Advancement of Science, American Association of University Women, National Association of Biology Teachers, American Society of Zoologists, Environmental Mutagen Society, Tissue Culture Association, Theobold Smith Society, American Bonsai Society, New York Academy of Sciences, Greater New York Bonsai Society, Phi Beta Kappa, Sigma Xi, New Jersey Alumni Association of Sweet Briar College (past president), West Essex Chinese Association (past vice-president).

WRITINGS: Foundations of Genetics: A Science for Society, McGraw, 1974; *Genetics: Concepts and Implications,* Prentice-Hall, 1980. Contributor to scientific journals.

SIDELIGHTS: Anna Pai comments: "I am very concerned that the public be informed of genetic concepts. Genetic research deals with phenomena which can directly affect all living organisms and society. I am concerned that the public learn genetic concepts to be able to evaluate exaggerated and sensationalist claims disseminated by the media. My first book is written for the non-scientist. The second is intended for the biology major."

* * *

PAIER, Robert (David) 1943-

PERSONAL: Born March 26, 1943, in New Haven, Conn.; children: Christina. *Education:* Columbia University, B.A., 1965; attended Price Technical School, 1978-79. *Agent:* Collier Associates, 280 Madison Ave., New York, N.Y. 10016.

CAREER: Writer. Worked various jobs, including lobster fisherman, desk clerk, and gas station attendant; probation officer in Stamford, Conn., 1970-75; Paie School of Art, Hamden, Conn., instructor in English, 1975-77. *Military service:* U.S. Army, Vietnamese linguist, 1965-69.

WRITINGS: The Pied Piper (novel), McGraw, 1979. Contributor to *Cavalier.*

WORK IN PROGRESS: Old Gray and the Kitten, with daughter, Christina Paier; "untitled novel describing a trip by a father and daughter away from the despair of contemporary life into the over-the-rainbow world of the Arizona desert where they meet a real practicing magician and man of power; *The Lefkedian Chronicle,* a novel about an American G.I. on R & R from Vietnam."

SIDELIGHTS: Paier comments: "With the most painful of the karma resulting from the writing and publication of *The Pied Piper* now just about expiated (but then, of course, one can never be completely sure in these matters), I, like other creatures subject to birth, sickness, old age, and death, find myself in a position of loneliness, confusion, and despair. I am trying like hell, through my writing and other means, to come to grips with this situation.

"*The Pied Piper* was a novel which both evoked and purged certain diabolical tendencies, a phenomenon which was not without profound effect on my non-literary life. It is now my goal to create something which may to some degree assuage, or at least come to some workable relationship with, human suffering. Quite simply, and in all humility, my goal now is Truth, at whatever cost, in both my literary and non-literary endeavors. It is my hope that I am allowed the time and strength necessary in achieving this end."

* * *

PALAZZESCHI, Aldo 1885-1974

PERSONAL: Birth-given name, Aldo Giurlani; known professionally as Aldo Palazzeschi; born February 2, 1885, in Florence, Italy; died August 17, 1974, in Rome, Italy.

CAREER: Poet, novelist, and memoirist. Briefly pursued an acting career in the company of Lyda Borelli. *Awards, honors:* Viarreggio Prize, 1949; Feltrinelli dei Lincei Accademia, 1957; honorary degree of letters from University of Padova, 1962; recipient of several other literary awards.

WRITINGS—In English; all fiction: *Il codice di Perela* (title means "The Code of Perela"), [Florence], 1920, adaptation by Peter M. Riccio published as *Perela, the Man of Smoke,* S. F. Vanni, 1936; *Sorelle Materassi,* Vallecchi, 1935, translation by Angus Davidson published as *The Sisters Materassi,* Doubleday, 1953; *Roma,* [Italy], 1953, Mondadori, 1960, translation by Mihaly Csikszentmihalyi published under same title, Regnery, 1965.

Other fiction: *Riflessi* (title means "Reflections"), [Florence], 1908, revised edition published as *Allegoria di novembre* (title means "Allegory of November"), 1944; *Il re bello* (title means "The Beautiful King"), [Florence], 1921; *La piramide: Scherzo di cattivo genere fuor di luogo* (title means "The Pyramid: Tricks of Out of Place and Wicked Sex"), [Florence], 1926; *Il palio dei buffi* (title means "The Prize of the Clowns"), Vallecchi, 1937; *Romanzi straordinari, 1907-1914* (title means "Extraordinary Novels"), Vallecchi, 1943; *Nell'aria di Parigi* (title means "In the Air of Paris"), Editrice cultura moderna, 1945; *I fratelli Cuccoli* (title means "The Brothers Cuccoli"), Vallecchi, 1948.

Viaggio sentimentale (title means "Sentimental Journey"), [Milan], 1955; *Scherzi di gioventu* (title means "Tricks of Youth"), R. Ricciardi, 1956; *Tutte le novelle* (title means "All the Novels"), Mondadori, 1957; *Opere giovanili* (title means "Juvenile Works"), Mondadori, 1958; *Vita militare* (title means "Military Life"), Rebellato, 1959; *I romanzi della maturita* (title means "The Novels of Maturity"), Mondadori, 1960; *Il piacere della memoria* (title means "The Pleasure of Memory"), Mondadori, 1964; *Il buffo integrale* (title means "The Whole Clown"), Mondadori, 1966; *Schizzi italograncesi* (title means "Franco-Italian Sketches"), All'insegna del pesce d'oro, 1966; *Il doge,* Mondadori, 1967; *Ieri oggi e . . . non domani* (title means "Yesterday Today and . . . No Tomorrow"), Vallecchi, 1967; *Stefanino,* Mondadori, 1969; *Storia di un'amicizio* (title means "Story of a Friendship"), Mondadori, 1971.

Poetry: *I cavalli bianchi* (title means "The White Knight"), [Florence], 1905; *Lanterna* (title means "Lantern"), [Florence], 1907; *Poemi* (title means "Poems"), [Florence], 1909; *L'Incendiario, 1905-1909* (title means "The Incendiary"), [Milan], 1913; *Poesie, 1904-1909* (title means "Poetry"), [Florence], 1925; *Poesie,* G. Preda, 1930; *Difetti* (title means "Defects"), [Milan], 1947; *Poesie, 1904-1914,* [Florence], 1949; *Cuor mio* (title means "My Heart"), Mondadori, 1968; *Via delle cento stelle, 1971-1972* (title means "The Way of a Hundred Stars"), Mondadori, 1972.

Other: *Due imperi . . . mancati* (title means "Two Emperors . . . Lost"), [Florence], 1920; *Stampe dell '800* (title means "The Influence of the 1800's"), Treves-Trecani-Tumminelli, 1932; *Tre imperi . . . mancati; cronaca, 1922-1945* (title means "Three Emperors . . . Lost; Chronicles, 1922-1945"), Vallecchi, 1945; *Bestie del '900,* [Florence], 1951; *Tutte le opere* (title means "All the Works"), Mondadori, 1957.

SIDELIGHTS: Palazzeschi once wrote: "Through laughter a man can dig himself out of pain and suffering, and the more he can do this the greater and more profound a man he is." He believed in the importance of a sense of humor as a means of dealing with the world's absurdity and of keeping one's sanity. He felt that, through the melancholy which results when one looks deeply into the world and oneself, must come a smile. Critics recognize his work as futuristic and avant-garde. In his poetry Palazzeschi makes use of a vivid fantasy to break through traditional verse; he also uses irony and the grotesque to point at the disorganization of society. He reduces things, moreover, to reasoned, intimate, private moments. "I'm not a literary man," Palazzeschi has written, "I'm a writer of instinct not of knowing."

When Alfred Kazin reviewed *Perelà: the Man of Smoke,* he described the author as "the impish Aldo Palazzeschi . . . a biting and intelligible satirist." Thomas G. Bergin noted "the spice and mischief" of *Stefanino,* "an exercise in playful and somewhat grotesque fantasy." Of *The Sisters Materassi,* critics have remarked such characteristics as its "shrewd observations and lively caricaturing," its "witty and evocative Italian text," and its "genial, mocking story."

BIOGRAPHICAL/CRITICAL SOURCES: New York Times, May 31, 1936, July 12, 1953, August 18, 1974; *Time,* June 15, 1936; *Manchester Guardian,* July 3, 1953; *Saturday Review,* July 18, 1953; *Nation,* July 18, 1953; *New Statesman and Nation,* July 25, 1953; *Chicago Sunday Tribune,* July 26, 1953; *Commonweal,* July 31, 1953; *Yale Review,* autumn, 1953; *Partisan Review,* November/December 1953; *Modern Language Notes,* January, 1964; *Times Literary Supplement,* April 30, 1970, August 27, 1971, December 22, 1972, February 20, 1976; *Books Abroad,* winter, 1971; *Washington Post,* August 18, 1974, August 19, 1974; *Contemporary Literary Criticism,* Volume 11, Gale, 1979.*

* * *

PALMER, Nicholas 1950-

PERSONAL: Born February 5, 1950, in London, England; son of Reginald (an editor) and Irene (a language teacher; maiden name, Markin) Palmer. *Education:* University of Copenhagen, M.Sc., 1972; University of London, Ph.D., 1975. *Home:* Riehenring 73, Basel, Switzerland. *Office:* Ciba-Geigy, Postfach, Basel, Switzerland.

CAREER: Ciba-Geigy, Basel, Switzerland, mathematician, 1977—. *Member:* National Games Club.

WRITINGS: The Comprehensive Guide to Board Wargaming (Military Book Club selection), Arthur Barker, 1977, McGraw, 1979, revised edition, Sphere, 1980; *Wargamers' Yearbook,* Arthur Barker, 1980. Wargames editor of *Games and Puzzles;* contributing editor of *Fire and Movement.*

SIDELIGHTS: Palmer writes: "Interest in wargaming has exploded over the twenty-five years since the first board wargame was published by a Baltimore company. There are now more than a hundred thousand active players and hundreds of games to choose from, ranging from grand strategic recreations of World War II to tactical gems dealing with the *minutiae* of ancient Hellenistic combat. Despite this, my book is the first to review the hobby.

"With annual sales of board wargames now running at nearly a million copies a year, one can foresee new books on specialised aspects of the hobby, just as chess gives rise to thousands of texts on opening and middle-game theory. For the present, the *Guide* remains alone in the field. I hope to see more newcomers into the hobby, so these extraordinarily challenging and intricate simulations of history can take a permanently established place beside chess, their long-standing parent, in the sympathies of people who like to think in their free time."

* * *

PANNWITZ, Rudolf 1881-1969

OBITUARY NOTICE: German philosopher, poet, and dramatist. Pannwitz was co-founder with Otto zur Linde of the periodical *Charon*. Chiefly concerned with civilization or culture, his philosophical works include *Die Krisis der europaischen Kulture, Deutschland und Europa,* and *Kosmos Atheos*. Pannwitz's other writings include the epic poem, *Konig Laurin,* and the dramatic work, *Dionysische Tragodien*. Obituaries and other sources: *The Oxford Companion to German Literature,* Clarendon Press, 1976.

* * *

PANOVA, Vera (Federovna) 1905-1973 (Vera Veltman)

OBITUARY NOTICE: Born March 20, 1905, in Rostov-on-Don, Russia (now U.S.S.R.); died March 4, 1973. Novelist, playwright, short story writer, and journalist. Panova began writing award-winning plays in the 1930's, but her favorite genre was the novel. Her experiences as a reporter in the northern Caucasus provided material for several of her books. *Sputniki,* a novel about the people working on an ambulance train during World War II, won a Stalin Prize, as did two of her subsequent novels, *Kruzhilika* and *Yasny bereg*. Panova's works are noted for their deftly drawn characterizations of ordinary people. Although most of her canon was in line with the official Soviet doctrine of social realism, *Vremena goda* was sharply criticized by some Soviet reviewers, and in 1954 she received a public reprimand. A collection of the plays Panova wrote in the 1960's was published in 1969 as *Pogovorim o stranostyakh lyubvi*. Obituaries and other sources: *The Reader's Encyclopedia,* 2nd edition, Crowell, 1965; *The Penguin Companion to European Literature,* McGraw, 1969; *Twentieth Century Writing: A Reader's Guide to Contemporary Literature,* Transatlantic, 1969; *Modern World Drama: An Encyclopedia,* Dutton, 1972; *Cassell's Encyclopaedia of World Literature,* revised edition, Morrow, 1973; *New York Times,* March 6, 1973; *World Authors, 1950-1970,* Wilson, 1975.

* * *

PAPACHRISTOU, Judy 1930-

PERSONAL: Born July 17, 1930, in New York; daughter of Max and Rose (Bradie) Reisner; married Tician Papachristou (an architect), June 11, 1951; children: Alexander, Nicholas. *Education:* Barnard College, B.A., 1952; University of Colorado, M.A., 1963, Ph.D., 1968. *Home:* 190 East 72nd St., New York, N.Y. 10021. *Office:* Department of History, York College of the City University of New York, 150 14 Jamaica Ave., Jamaica, N.Y. 11432.

CAREER: Educational Testing Service, Princeton, N.J., psychometrist, 1951-53; Western Interstate Commission on Higher Education, Boulder, Colo., writer and researcher, 1957-58; Hunter College of the City University of New York, New York City, lecturer in history, 1967-68; York College of the City University of New York, Jamaica, N.Y., associate professor of history, 1968—. *Member:* American Historical Association, Organization of American Historians, Institute for Research in History, New York Coordinating Committee on Women in the Historical Profession, City University of New York Women's Coalition, Phi Beta Kappa.

WRITINGS: (With Carol Wald) *Myth American,* Pantheon, 1975; *Women Together: A History in Documents of the Women's Movement in the United States,* Knopf, 1976. Contributor to scholarly journals.

WORK IN PROGRESS: A History of Abortion in Nineteenth-Century America.

* * *

PARENS, Henri 1928-

PERSONAL: Born December 18, 1928, in Lodz, Poland; came to the United States in 1942, naturalized citizen, 1949; married Rachel Anto (a writer), April 2, 1955; children: Erik F., Karl R., Joshua J. *Education:* Carnegie-Mellon University, B.F.A., 1952; Tulane University, M.D., 1959; postdoctoral study at Philadelphia Psychoanalytic Institute, 1965-70. *Office:* Eastern Pennsylvania Psychiatric Institute, Medical College of Pennsylvania, Henry Ave. at Abbottsford Rd., Philadelphia, Pa. 19129.

CAREER: Lankenau Hospital, Philadelphia, Pa., intern, 1959-60; University of Cincinnati, Cincinnati, Ohio, resident in psychiatry, 1960-62, fellow in child psychiatry, 1962-64; Irving Schwartz Institute, Philadelphia, Pa., staff child psychiatrist, 1964-66; University of Pennsylvania, Philadelphia, staff child psychiatrist at Philadelphia Child Guidance Clinic and research associate in psychiatry, 1966-69; Medical College of Pennsylvania, Philadelphia, clinical assistant professor, 1969-72, clinical associate professor, 1972-79, research professor of child psychiatry, 1979—, member of staff at Eastern Pennsylvania Psychiatric Institute and director of its early child development program, 1969—. Private practice of psychiatry and psychoanalysis of children and adults, 1964—. Instructor at Philadelphia Psychoanalytic Institute, 1972—, supervisor of child analysis, 1977—.

MEMBER: International Psychoanalytic Association, American Medical Association, American Psychoanalytic Association, Association for Child Psychoanalysis, American Academy of Child Psychiatry, Pennsylvania Psychiatric Association, Regional Council of Child Psychiatry, Philadelphia Psychiatric Association, Philadelphia Psychoanalytic Society, Sigma Xi, Alpha Omega Alpha.

WRITINGS: (With L. J. Saul) *Dependence in Man: A Psychoanalytic Study,* International Universities Press, 1971; (contributor) J. B. McDevitt and C. F. Settlage, editors, *Separation-Individuation: Essays in Honor of Margaret S. Mahler,* International Universities Press, 1971; (contributor) Stanley Greenspan and George Pollock, editors, *The Course of Life,* National Institute of Mental Health, 1979; *The Development of Aggression in Early Childhood,* Jason Aronson, 1979.

Co-author of films for Audio-Visual Media Section, Eastern Pennsylvania Psychiatric Institute: "Toward an Epigenesis of Aggression in Early Childhood," 1974; "Prevention: Early Intervention Mother-Infant Groups," 1974; "Toward an Epigenesis of Aggression in Early Childhood II: Aggression and Beginning Separation-Individuation," 1977; "The Child's Wish to Have a Baby," two parts, 1979.

Co-author of "Parenting: Love and Much More," a television series aired by WCAU-TV, June-July, 1979, and radio scripts on parenting. Contributor to *International Encyclopedia of Neurology, Psychiatry, Psychoanalysis, and Psychology*. Contributor to education and psychology journals.

WORK IN PROGRESS: "The development of a laboratory type curriculum on education for parenting for students in grades K through 12; further studies in aggression, gender formation, and human development."

SIDELIGHTS: In recent years Parens has directed his efforts toward training people for the important, but often neglected, job of parenting. He believes that even small children show a great interest in and ability to understand many of the concepts and problems related to the parenting education process, and feels that such a program should begin with first-grade students and continue throughout their school years. Such classes are now available at some Philadelphia-area Quaker schools, and Parens would like to see programs implemented in every school in the country.

BIOGRAPHICAL/CRITICAL SOURCES: Philadelphia Bulletin, December 26, 1976; *Houston Post,* October 23, 1977; *Philadelphia Inquirer,* February 4, 1979; *Studies in Education,* spring, 1979.

* * *

PARK, Joseph H. 1890(?)-1979

OBITUARY NOTICE: Born c. 1890 in Port Murray, N.J.; died October 6, 1979, in Morristown, N.J. Author, historian, and dean of New York University's Graduate School of Arts and Science. Park specialized in nineteenth-century British history and wrote such works as *The English Reform Bill of 1867* and *British Prime Ministers of the Nineteenth Century*. Park was also an authority on Wedgewood china and owned an extensive collection of it. Obituaries and other sources: *New York Times,* October 9, 1979; *AB Bookman's Weekly,* November 5, 1979.

* * *

PARK, Robert L. 1932-

PERSONAL: Born September 1, 1932, in Idaho Falls, Idaho; son of William D. (a farmer) and Ardella (a teacher; maiden name, Laird) Park; married Elaine Burke, May 24, 1962; children: Richard, Rhonda, Rita, Roxanne, Raquel. *Education:* Attended University of Idaho, 1950-53; Brigham Young University, B.S., 1956; Cornell University, Ph.D., 1962. *Religion:* Church of Jesus Christ of Latter-day Saints (Mormons). *Home:* 1218 North 1160 W., Provo, Utah 84601. *Office:* Department of Animal Science, Brigham Young University, Provo, Utah 84602.

CAREER: U.S. Department of Agriculture, Agricultural Research Service, Crops Research Division, Kingshill, St. Croix, Virgin Islands, agriculturalist, 1962-63, animal husbandman, 1963-65; Brigham Young University, Provo, Utah, assistant professor, 1965-68, associate professor, 1968-73, professor of animal science, 1973—. U.S. Virgin Islands representative to Caribbean Commission on Agriculture, 1962-64. *Military service:* U.S. Army, 1953-54. *Member:* American Dairy Science Association, American Society of Animal Science, Sigma Xi, Phi Kappa Phi, Alpha Zeta, Gamma Alpha.

WRITINGS: Agriculture: Food and Man, Brigham Young University Press, 1975. Contributor to scientific journals.

WORK IN PROGRESS: Research on dairy cattle selection and application of microcomputers to agriculture.

SIDELIGHTS: Park wrote: "It is extremely important for all people to know how the lack of food, or even the fear of a shortage of food, influences their lives."

* * *

PARKE, Margaret Bittner 1901-

PERSONAL: Born January 6, 1901, in Mauch Chunk, Pa.; daughter of Oscar H. and Laura (Rader) Bittner; married Roger I. Parke, December 24, 1937. *Education:* Attended Bloomsburg State Teachers College, 1923; Pennsylvania State College (now University), B.A., 1927; Columbia University, M.A., 1930, Ed.D., 1945. *Home:* 1655 Flatbush Ave., Brooklyn, N.Y. 11210.

CAREER: Elementary school teacher in Rockport, Pa., 1919-20, and Packerton, Pa., 1920-22; junior high school English teacher in Doylestown, Pa., 1923-26, Mount Vernon, N.Y., 1927-28, and Tuckahoe, N.Y., 1928-29 (guidance counselor and director of guidance and research, 1929-37); vocational counselor in public schools of New York, N.Y., 1937, junior research assistant with Bureau of Reference, Research, and Statistics, 1937-44, research associate at Bureau of Curriculum Research, 1944-51; Brooklyn College of the City University of New York, Brooklyn, N.Y., associate professor, 1951-58, professor of education, 1958-71. Assistant professor at Queens College of the City University of New York; lecturer at State University of New York College at Cortland, summers. Research assistant at Rockefeller Institute of Social and Religious Research; researcher for Center for Urban Education. In sales at Bookhouse for Children. Member of Citizens Union and Book Reading Council; participant in conferences.

MEMBER: Association of Teachers of Reading International, International Reading Association, National Education Association, National Conference on Research in English, National Council of Teachers of English, National Council of Administrative Women in Education, American Association of University Women, College English Educators (member of state executive board, 1967-71), PSC of College Teachers, Retired Teachers Association, American Association for the Advancement of Science (fellow), Common Cause, Daughters of the American Revolution, New York Academy of Public Education (member of board of directors, 1979), New York STA Women's Press Club of New York City (second vice-president, 1975-79), Pi Lambda Theta, Kappa Delta Pi. *Awards, honors:* Arts D. from Staley College, 1959; Fulbright award for University of Sydney, the Philippines, and Taiwan, 1960; certificate of merit from *International Biography,* 1969, for *Young Readers' Color-Picture Dictionary;* award from Library of Human Resources, of American Bicentennial Research Committee, 1974; citation from local chapter of International Reading Association, 1975; fellow of International Institute of Community Service, 1975.

WRITINGS: Young Readers' Dictionary: An Aid to Better Reading, Writing, and Spelling, Grosset, 1955; *My First Book to Read: For Three- to Five-Year-Olds,* Grosset, 1957; *My Second Book to Read: For Five- to Seven-Year-Olds,* Grosset, 1957; *Young Readers' Color-Picture Dictionary for Reading, Writing, and Spelling,* Grosset, 1958; (contributor) A. T. Burrows, editor, *Children's Writing: Research in Composition and Related Skills,* National Council of Teach ers of English, 1960; *The Practice Workbooks of Writing,* Books I-III, Grosset, 1967; *Picture Dictionary for Primary Grades,* Noble & Noble, 1960; *Getting to Know Australia,* Coward, 1962; (contributor) Helen Huus, editor, *Issues Here and Abroad,* University of Pennsylvania Press, 1963; *Young Readers' Dictionary Workbook,* Grosset, 1963; *You Can Teach Your Child to Read,* Grosset, 1968; *Vocabulary Workbook,* Grosset, 1970; *The Practice Workbook of Words,* Grosset, 1971.

Films: "A Third Grade at Work"; (co-author) "Helping First Grade Children to Learn." Writer for New York City's Board of Education. Contributor of more than thirty articles to education journals.

WORK IN PROGRESS: A bibliography of her childhood writings, for junior high school students.

SIDELIGHTS: Margaret Parke writes: "My writing has been directed toward helping parents of young children recognize the need for observing carefully whether or not their children were acquiring the basic skills in the early grades. Toward this end I wrote books for parents in the fifties, when many educators were saying, 'Parents, keep hands off. Let the schools teach.' Today there is a great awakening.

"I devoted much time and energy to selling the idea of dictionaries in our schools. I observed that some children who came from foreign countries brought bi-lingual dictionaries with them and were greatly helped. Schools have not yet caught up with the need for this procedure.

"Books labeled by grades, particularly workbooks, are not suited to all children in a given grade. With a picture dictionary, a child can be taught to speak about the pictures, match words and pictures, recognize words and read, detect sounds in words, learn to detect the various spellings for the sounds in our language, spell words as well as read them. Early America taught the language with one book. Rural schools thrived that way with heterogeneous classes. When we abandoned ability grouping in our schools, we set up the need for something other than graded textbooks. Publishers have been slow to see this and to buy the idea.

"We need a Department of Education in the federal government, divorced from health and welfare, to tackle the problem of education for a democracy. Published materials and new educational programs for teachers are badly needed, and should be financed with federal funds. Let's give teachers teachable classes and materials. Emphasize international phonetics as a basis for learning all languages. In our efforts to democratize education, we have failed to provide teachers with materials they need to meet the range of abilities in their classrooms."

AVOCATIONAL INTERESTS: Travel (all over the world).

* * *

PARKES, Lucas
See HARRIS, John (Wyndham Parkes Lucas) Beynon

* * *

PATRICK, John 1905-

PERSONAL: Birth-given name, John Patrick Goggan; name legally changed; born May 17, 1905, in Louisville, Ky.; son of John Francis and Myrtle (Osborn) Goggan. *Education:* Attended Holy Cross College, St. Edward's College, St. Mary's Seminary, Harvard University, and Columbia University. *Home address:* Box 2386, St. Thomas, Virgin Islands 00801. *Agent:* Jonathan Clowes, Ltd., 20 New Cavendish St., London W1A 3AH, England.

CAREER: Playwright and author of screenplays. Worked as writer for National Broadcasting Corp. (NBC-Radio), in San Francisco, Calif., 1933-36; free-lance writer in Hollywood, Calif., 1936-38. *Military service:* American Field Service, 1942-44; served as ambulance driver; became captain. *Member:* Dramatists Guild. *Awards, honors:* New York Drama Critics Circle Award for best American play of the year, Pulitzer Prize in drama, Antoinette Perry (Tony) Award from League of New York Theatres and Producers, Aegis Club Award, and Donaldson Award, all 1954, all for "The Teahouse of the August Moon"; Screenwriters Guild Award and Foreign Correspondents Award, both 1957, both for "Les Girls"; D.F.A. from Baldwin-Wallace College, 1972; honored with Patrick Film Festival, in Virgin Islands, 1979.

WRITINGS—Plays; all published by Dramatists Play Service, unless otherwise indicated: *The Willow and I* (three-act; first produced in Windsor, Ontario, December 10, 1942), 1943; *The Hasty Heart* (three-act; first produced Off-Broadway at Hudson Theatre, January 3, 1945), Random House, 1945; *The Story of Mary Surratt* (three-act; first produced on Broadway at Henry Miller's Theatre, February 8, 1947), 1947; *The Curious Savage* (three-act; first produced on Broadway at Martin Beck Theatre, October 24, 1950), 1951; *Lo and Behold!* (three-act; first produced on Broadway at Booth Theatre, December 12, 1951), Samuel French, 1952; *The Teahouse of the August Moon* (first produced on Broadway at Martin Beck Theatre, October 15, 1953; adapted from the novel by Verne J. Sneider), Putnam, 1954; *Everybody Loves Opal* (three-act; first produced on Broadway at Longacre Theatre, October 11, 1961), A. Meyerson, 1961.

Love Is a Time of Day (first produced on Broadway at Music Box, December 22, 1969), 1970; (with Stan Freeman) *Lovely Ladies, Kind Gentlemen* (first produced on Broadway at Majestic Theatre, December 28, 1970; adapted from the play by Patrick, "The Teahouse of the August Moon"), Samuel French, 1971; *A Barrel Full of Pennies* (two-act; first produced in Paramus, N.J., at Paramus Playhouse, May 12, 1970), 1971; *Opal Is a Diamond* (first produced in Flat Rock, N.C., at State Theatre of North Carolina, July 27, 1972), 1972; *Roman Conquest* (three-act; first produced in Berea, Ohio, at Baldwin-Wallace Summer Theatre, July 25, 1973), Samuel French, 1972; *Macbeth Did It* (three-act; first produced in Flat Rock at State Theatre of North Carolina, July, 1972), 1972; *The Savage Dilemma* (first produced in Long Beach, Calif., at Community Theatre, May 19, 1972), 1972; *Love Nest for Three,* Samuel French, 1973; *Sex on the Sixth Floor: Three One-Act Plays,* Samuel French, 1973; *Opal's Baby* (two-act; first produced in Flat Rock at State Theatre of North Carolina, June 26, 1973), 1974; *The Enigma* (first produced in Berea at Baldwin-Wallace Summer Theatre, June 12, 1972), 1974; *A Bad Year for Tomatoes* (first produced in North Royalton, Ohio, 1974), 1975; *Opal's Husband,* 1975; *Noah's Animals* (first produced in Berea, Ohio, 1975), 1976. Also author of *Scandal Point* (first produced in Paramus at the Paramus Playhouse, May 12, 1970), published by Dramatists Play Service.

Unpublished plays: "Hell Freezes Over," first produced in New York City at Ritz Theatre, December 28, 1935; "Good as Gold" (three-act; adapted from the novel by Alfred Toombs), first produced on Broadway at Belasco Theatre, March 7, 1957; "Juniper and the Pagans," first produced in Boston, Mass., at the Colonial, December 10, 1959; "Girls of the Garden Club," first produced in Berea, Ohio, at Berea Summer Theatre, July, 1979; "Opal's Million Dollar Duck," first produced in St. Thomas, Virgin Islands, at the School for Performing Arts, September, 1979.

Screenplays; all released by Twentieth Century-Fox, unless otherwise indicated: (With Lou Breslow and David Silverstein) "15 Maiden Lane," 1936; (with Breslow) "36 Hours to Kill," 1936; (with Breslow and Edward Eliscu) "High Tension," 1936; (with Katherine Kavanaugh and Edward T. Lowe) "Educating Father," 1936; (with Breslow) "International Settlement," 1936; (with Breslow) "The Holy Terror," 1937; (with Breslow, Helen Logan, and Robert Ellis) "Big Town Girl," 1937; (with Breslow) "Dangerously Yours," 1937; (with Breslow) "Look Out, Mr. Moto," 1937; (with Ellis and Logan) "Born Reckless," 1937; (with Breslow and Ben Markson) "Sing and Be Happy," 1937; (with Breslow) "One Mile From Heaven" (adapted from the short story by Judge Ben Lindsey, "Little Colored White Cloud"), 1937; (with Breslow) "Midnight Taxi" (adapted from the short story by Borden Chase), 1937; (with Breslow) "Time Out for Romance," 1937; (with Breslow) "Up the River," 1938; (with Breslow) "Five of a Kind," 1938; (with Breslow) "Battle of Broadway," 1938.

"Enchantment" (adapted from the novel by Rumer Godden, *A Fugue in Time),* RKO, 1948; "The President's Lady" (adapted from the novel by Irving Stone), 1953; "Three Coins in the Fountain" (adapted from the novel by John Secondari), 1954; "Love Is a Many Splendored Thing" (adapted from the novel by Han Suyin), 1955; "High Society" (adapted from the play by Philip Barry, "The Philadelphia Story"), 1956; "The Teahouse of the August Moon" (adapted from the play by Patrick), Metro-Goldwyn-Mayer (MGM), 1956; "Les Girls," MGM, 1957; "Some Came Running" (adapted from the novel by James Jones), MGM, 1958; "The World of Suzie Wong" (adapted from the play by Paul Osborne based on the novel by Richard Mason), Paramount, 1960; "Gigot," 1962; "The Main Attraction," MGM, 1963; (with James Kennaway) "The Shoes of the Fisherman" (adapted from the novel by Morris L. West), MGM, 1968.

Also author of teleplay, "The Small Miracle," NBC-TV, 1973. Author of more than eleven hundred radio plays. Scriptwriter for Helen Hayes's programs.

WORK IN PROGRESS: A game book of quotes.

SIDELIGHTS: Patrick's first two efforts as a playwright, "Hell Freezes Over" and "The Willow and I," were both box-office disappointments. After a stint with the American Field Service, Patrick wrote his first successful play, "The Hasty Heart." It was based in part on his experiences during World War II. Patrick's next two plays failed to duplicate the success of "The Hasty Heart." However, Patrick recouped his popularity in 1953 when he created his best known work, "The Teahouse of the August Moon." The play about the efforts of American soldiers to introduce American ways to Orientals was enormously successful and enjoyed a lengthy run on Broadway. Although he has written numerous other works, "The Teahouse of the August Moon" has remained Patrick's most popular play.

CA INTERVIEWS THE AUTHOR

John Patrick was interviewed by phone July 6, 1979, at his home, Fortuna Mill Estate, in the Virgin Islands.

CA: In doing adaptations for stage or movies, are there often conflicts with the author of the original work?

PATRICK: Always, in my case. Anything that I've adapted, the authors have hated me. Han Suyin, when I did "Love Is a Many-Splendored Thing," didn't even want to see me when I was in Hong Kong. When they offered me her next book to do, I refused to do it. Irving Stone was outraged at what I did to *The President's Lady.* I thought it was one of my better scripts. I wouldn't allow Vern Schneider in the theatre, because he published an article before we opened "Teahouse of the August Moon" in which he said that I had vulgarized his play. I thought that was terrible publicity for a play that hadn't even opened yet, so I gave orders he was not to be allowed in the theatre. I've never met him, and I've made half a million or so for him. I've never worked from anybody's book—Rumer Godden's or anybody's—who had a good word to say for me. There was one English novelist who said something very funny. I was sent a telegram to come to the Coast and do a book called *Les Girls.* So I flew out there and I said, "Where's the book." The producer said, "I don't want you to read it; I only bought the title." He gave me the general idea, and to this day I've never read the book on which the movie was based. And the author said, when it was chosen for the Command Performance in London, "I'm the highest-paid writer in the world; I got $85,000 for two words—*Les Girls.*"

CA: Did you go to the Command Performance?

PATRICK: Yes, I did. I couldn't tell them in advance whether I could come or not, so I didn't get on the presentation list. But it didn't make any difference. They treated me very well. They sent me four seats in the Queen's box.

CA: You've won the top awards. How do you feel about awards?

PATRICK: Well, from a commercial point of view, the Pulitzer is wonderful. Overnight it does not make you a better writer, but it does double your salary. I jumped from $80,000 to $150,000 per picture overnight. That's why I feel very warm about *that* prize. But I must say the way they give it to you is not very thrilling. They don't notify you. You read about it in the newspaper. I heard about it on the radio. I was on my farm, on my tractor, and I stopped to get some water and heard that I'd won the Pulitzer. They don't present it in a ceremony. Later on you get a check and the document in the mail—a very dull looking document.

CA: Were you on location for the filming of the movies you wrote?

PATRICK: Yes, throughout "Suzie Wong." I was a close friend of the producer, Ray Stark. Three of us—Ray Stark, Quentin Reynolds, and myself—went around the world looking for a girl. We held auditions everywhere—Japan, Honolulu, Hong Kong, Manila, and so on. We found Nancy Kwan in Hong Kong.

CA: Have technical changes in filming affected the screenwriter's job?

PATRICK: Yes, for the better. In the early days you had what we call the lap dissolve to go from one location to another. Now that's been eliminated. You cut directly from one scene to another. The montages are not used as much now. It's easier for the writer. When I first began writing for pictures, the producer called me in and said, "Look, you're wasting a lot of footage. You have everybody coming in through a door." I realized that in the theatre, that's the only way you can get people on stage. So the technical approach differs. I learned quickly.

CA: With television providing most at-home entertainment now, what do you think the future holds for radio?

PATRICK: Radio fills a need where you can't get television—in cars, small boats. There's a definite need for it. Again there's a great difference. I started out writing for radio. I wrote about eleven hundred scripts. In those days, you would have to say, "Hand me that *gun.*" You had to identify everything. The medium was auditory instead of visual.

CA: Do you foresee a resurgence of interest in radio drama?

PATRICK: I think there might be. Where one can only get radio, I think there's a need.

CA: It would be nice to hear "The Lone Ranger" again, wouldn't it?

PATRICK: I never heard it. I've always worked so hard that I've had very little time to see or hear everything I should. There are two or three movies I've written myself that I've never seen—"Some Came Running," "Shoes of the Fisherman." I get up at five o'clock every morning and get at my desk. I turn out three to six new plays a year for regional theatre.

CA: Would you comment on the role of regional theatre?

PATRICK: It seems to me there are two different theatre audiences—a sophisticated, jaded New York audience for whom a hit is the only thing, and regional theatre, where they are not as demanding, and emphasis is more on entertainment. By entertainment I don't mean to exclude intellectual stimulus. A great many places also support that. I visit regional theatre as often as possible. The people can be charming. But a lot of them don't even know what theatre is. People will come to the box office and say, "What time does the movie go on?" But they thoroughly enjoy themselves. These plays I turn out now—I know, I turn them out like sausages—but they are very satisfying to the average community theatre audience. I consider myself a craftsman—not an "artist."

CA: How do you feel about government subsidy for the arts?

PATRICK: I don't mind subsidy wherever it comes from. Amateur theatre is subsidy; the actors are giving their time. I don't care where the money comes from, so long as it pays actors and playwrights. Theatre needs support.

CA: Would you comment on the Off-Off-Broadway of the 1960's?

PATRICK: I really don't know much about it. My reason for not seeing Off-Broadway is not unique: it's where the theatres are located. I don't want to be mugged. So I can't have any valid opinion. I think it's fine as a showcase. Any theatre that puts on a play has my support whether I like the play or not.

CA: Have you directed or acted in any of your own scripts?

PATRICK: In radio I directed and acted in all of my own things. I started out at eighteen. I've directed Broadway and summer theatre. I don't like to direct. I only do it where no one else is available. In my opinion a director has to be—and *should* be—a mother, a lover, a psychiatrist, a brother, a sister, all these things, to the actors. I haven't the patience. Marlon Brando once was driving me to my hotel. An old man got in his way, and Marlon lost his temper and stopped and yelled at him. Later I said, "Marlon, you shouldn't do that." He said, "I know I shouldn't. But you've got to realize that whatever an actor has to give to his profession hangs by a thread and is easily broken." I've kept that in mind.

CA: Have you ever tried writing a novel?

PATRICK: I started one, and I got so bored. I thought, "All these words! Good God, I could write three, four, five plays in the time it took to put all these words on paper!" So I stopped and called a friend of mine, Robert Ludlum, who is on the best-seller list this week; and he took my idea and turned it into a novel. But he didn't do a very good job. I *am* doing a game book at the moment. It's a series of quotes, and one is given four guesses who said what. For instance, this morning I found a very good quote: "Every girl should use what Mother Nature gave her until Father Time takes it away." You have to guess whether Zsa Zsa Gabor said it, or President Kennedy, or who. It's just going to be an after-dinner or hospital fun game book. I'm doing a chapter on each of various subjects. I started naturally with sex, because that's where it *all* started. Then I have one on malice—all the horrible things people have said about each other. Then one on vanity, religion, twenty or twenty-five categories.

CA: Do you ever take a week or two off from writing?

PATRICK: Once in a while I'll go on a cruise with friends of mine down here to get away from Carnival. Everybody comes here for Carnival, and we get on a boat to get away from it. But a writer never stops working, really. He's always putting notes aside, stealing witty things from others.

CA: How did you happen to settle in the Virgin Islands?

PATRICK: I used to come down here every year for about eighteen years and rent a house. Then my taxes got so high in the States, I realized I'd have to be an Onassis or a Rockefeller to afford it, so I started searching for another place to live. I went to Greece, Italy, Venezuela, and every island on the chain, then here. I happened to find this place the day it went on sale and bought it before I even saw the inside. Because it was so theatrical. It has a 300-year-old sugarcane mill on the place, which is not an active mill, but the windmill is there. I use it for guests; it's been restored—very, very theatrical; I look down on the Atlantic on one side and the Caribbean on the other. Each room is built on the old slave quarters, and every room is a separate building. There are nine buildings.

When I came down here people said, "What will you do? Won't you be in an intellectual vacuum?" But I've had such friends come down to visit as Alan Alda, Burgess Meredith, Lillian Gish, Liv Ullman with José Quintero, Josh and Nedda Logan, Leslie Caron, Millie Natwick, and Eileen Heckart. A nice long list. Jimmie Kirkwood ("A Chorus Line") was so beguiled he bought an acre next to me.

CA: Movies have changed a great deal since you did the screenplays for some of the great movies of the 1950's. How do you feel about the trend to explicit sex and often gratuitous violence in the movies today?

PATRICK: I have no strong feelings about it, except the trend has made me passé.

CA: Your kind of movies may make a comeback.

PATRICK: We're all hopeful. It amazes me that wherever I go—and I dash around the country—I run into so much opinion that the pendulum will swing back and that people want it. They're tired of sex. They're weary. It became the sort of thing that I as a writer was not qualified to deal with. I cannot write a tender love story of incest. So I gave up Hollywood and it gave up me; it was mutual. Anything I've been offered since then I've turned down. In a way I should be grateful, because I have a far better life now. I write directly for regional theatre—neither Hollywood nor Broadway. And I don't have to contend with critics or unions or raising money. I just sit here on my hilltop estate, write plays when I feel like it, send them to the publishers, and enjoy a free and easy life.

—*Interview by Jean W. Ross*

* * *

PATRICK, Q.
See WHEELER, Hugh (Callingham)

* * *

PATTERSON, Alicia Brooks 1906-1963

OBITUARY NOTICE: Born October 15, 1906, in Chicago, Ill.; died July 12, 1963. Newspaper editor and publisher. A member of the famed Patterson-McCormick newspaper publishing dynasty, Alicia Patterson worked as a reporter, literary critic, and transport pilot before founding *Newsday* with her husband, Harry F. Guggenheim, in 1940. She served as editor and publisher of the daily until 1963. The Long Island tabloid won the Pulitzer Prize "for disinterested and meritorious public service" in 1954, after exposing corruption and graft at Long Island's trotting tracks, as well as several awards for excellence in typography. Patterson also held the woman's aviation record from New York to Philadelphia in 1931. Obituaries and other sources: *Current Biography,* Wilson, 1955, September, 1963; *New York Times,* July 3, 1963, July 4, 1963, July 6, 1963; *Time,* July 12, 1963; *Newsweek,* July 15, 1963.

* * *

PATTERSON, Janet McFadden 1915-

PERSONAL: Born April 3, 1915, in Nashville, Tenn.; daughter of Robert W. and Janet (Battle) McFadden; married Robert Clendening Patterson, Jr. (an obstetrician-gynecologist and writer), 1938; children: Robert Clendening III, Janet Patterson Gardner. *Education:* Attended Ward Belmont College, 1935; Vanderbilt University, B.A., 1937. *Politics:* Independent. *Religion:* "Non-denominational." *Home and office:* 1805 Otter Creek Rd., Nashville, Tenn. 37215.

CAREER: Writer, 1972—. *Member:* Kappa Alpha Theta, Belle Centennial Club, House and Garden Club (past president).

WRITINGS: A Pregnancy Primer, Aurora, 1972; *Doctor, I'm a Woman,* Thomas Nelson, 1974; *How to Live With a Pregnant Wife,* Thomas Nelson, 1975; *Abortion, the Trojan Horse,* Thomas Nelson, 1976; *A Pregnancy Calendar,* Aurora, 1976.

WORK IN PROGRESS: A book to be published in Taiwan; *Scripturally Speaking: Marriage;* research on China.

SIDELIGHTS: Patterson told *CA:* "Regarding books on pregnancy, I feel that emphasis on home deliveries set women's liberation back a hundred years. It also further stimulates husband or male abuse. A shocking number of husbands support home delivery for financial or sadistic reasons, rather than the sentimental ones of 'loving concern' and 'blessed sharing of an experience.' There is no sharing of an experience when one labors and the other sympathizes or empathizes.... Results of home deliveries are showing in female sexual frigidity and gynecological problems.

"On abortion: The law will not change and should not. There are'different strokes for different folks.' I personally feel that 'a baby is a baby is a baby' from conception but it is my faith that makes me feel this way. This is the 'land of the free' and the decision for or against abortion should be the woman's choice based on her own moral and mental judgment.

"On medical care: Preventive medicine is as important as curative medicine. Health is one of the most important features of life. Sophisticated medicine of today can be expensive but is as basic as food and shelter. The credentials of a doctor should be intelligently established. The 'marvelous doctor' of the next-door-neighbor may not be a marvelous doctor.

"I average only about 2½ full days of writing. I have never even opened a book after it is printed, nor do I have any interest in talking about same. . . ."

* * *

PAULEY, Barbara Anne 1925-

PERSONAL: Born January 12, 1925, in Nashville, Tenn.; daughter of William M. (a publisher) and Lucile (Dies) Cotton; married Robert Reinhold Pauley (an investment banker), June 22, 1946; children: Lucinda, Nicholas Andrew, Robert Reinhold, Jr., John. *Education:* Attended Wellesley College, 1942. *Politics:* Republican. *Religion:* Congregationalist. *Home:* 97 Larch Row, Wenham, Mass. 01984. *Agent:* Blassingame, McCauley & Wood, 60 East 42nd St., New York, N.Y. 10017.

CAREER: Editorial assistant, Ideal Publishing Corp.; free-lance writer. *Member:* Mystery Writers of America.

WRITINGS—Mystery novels: *Blood Kin,* Doubleday, 1972; *Voices Long Hushed,* Doubleday, 1976. Contributor of stories to romance magazines.

WORK IN PROGRESS: A romantic suspense novel; research for a historical family saga set in the age of Jackson.

SIDELIGHTS: Barbara Anne Pauley comments: "I have always loved a good story well-told and can't resist trying to do the same. I also enjoy editorial work and teach a group of aspiring novelists."

* * *

PEACE, Roger Craft 1899-1968

OBITUARY NOTICE: Born May 19, 1899, in Greenville, S.C.; died August 21, 1968. Publisher of the South Carolina *Greenville News.* Peace started with the paper in 1914, and later became sports editor, editor, and business manager before being named publisher in 1934, a post he held until 1966. In 1941 he was appointed U.S. senator from South Carolina to fill a vacancy left by James F. Byrnes. Obituaries and other sources: *Who Was Who in America,* 5th edition, Marquis, 1973.

* * *

PEACOCK, Wilbur Scott 1915(?)-1979

OBITUARY NOTICE: Born c. 1915 in Kansas; died July 7, 1979, of a cardiac arrest, in Los Angeles, Calif. Editor and writer of short stories and television scripts, Peacock was editor of *Planet Stories.* He was also creator of a number of television series such as "Sheena of the Jungle" and "Francois Villon." He contributed short stories to magazines, including *McCall's, Saturday Evening Post, Esquire,* and *Playboy.* Obituaries and other sources: *Locus,* July/August, 1979.

PECK, M(organ) Scott 1936-

PERSONAL: Born May 22, 1936, in New York, N.Y.; son of David W. (an attorney) and Elizabeth (Saville) Peck; married Lily Ho (a psychotherapist), December 27, 1959; children: Belinda, Julia, Christopher. *Education:* Attended Middlebury College, 1954-56; Harvard University, A.B., 1958; Case Western Reserve University, M.D., 1963. *Home and office:* Bliss Rd., New Preston, Conn. 06777.

CAREER: U.S. Army, 1963-72, intern at Tripler Medical Center, Honolulu, Hawaii, 1963-64, resident in psychiatry at Letterman General Hospital, San Francisco, Calif., 1967-70, chief of department of psychology at U.S. Army Medical Center, Okinawa, Japan, 1967-70, assistant chief of psychiatry and neurology at office of surgeon general, Washington, D.C., 1970-72, leaving service as lieutenant colonel; private practice of psychiatry in New Preston, Conn., 1972—. Medical director of New Milford Hospital Mental Health Clinic, Maramang Associates, and Interface; secretary and treasurer of Ouroborus, Inc. Consultant to U.S. surgeon general, 1970-72. *Awards, honors*—Military: Meritorious service medal with Oak Leaf Cluster.

WRITINGS: The Road Less Traveled: A New Psychology of Love, Traditional Values and Spiritual Growth, Simon & Schuster, 1978.

WORK IN PROGRESS: People of the Lie: Toward a Psychology of Evil, publication expected in 1981.

SIDELIGHTS: In *The Road Less Traveled,* M. Scott Peck begins with the premise: life is difficult. But as a psychiatrist he continually sees people who refuse to admit this, people broken by illusions of self sacrifice and by dreams of falling in love. Romantic love, he says, is a "dreadful lie. . . . I weep in my heart almost daily for the ghastly confusion that myth fosters." Instead, Peck believes, once an individual accepts the inherent difficulty in life, through self-discipline and love he can transfer weakness into strength. One aspect of this attitude is "real love," "an act of the will to extend oneself for the purpose of nurturing one's own or another's spiritual growth."

Peck moved critics by emitting a sense of his own sympathetic character throughout his book. Reviewer Robert Stensrud thought "Dr. Peck's incisiveness and breadth of understanding are impressive. . . . Of the self-help books I have read, this one impresses me most because the emphasis is more on accuracy and honesty than on titillating the reader." Phyliss Theroux of the *Washington Post* also compared Peck's book to other works on spiritual growth. "'The Road Less Traveled' is a clipper ship among Chris Crafts," she said. It is "a magnificent boat of a book, and it is so obviously written by a human being who, both in style and substance, leans toward the reader for the purposes of sharing something larger than himself, that one reads with the feeling that this is not just a book but a spontaneous act of generosity."

Currently, the principle area of interest and the focus of Peck's work "is the growing interface between religion and science."

BIOGRAPHICAL/CRITICAL SOURCES: Washington Post, September 29, 1978; *Best Sellers,* January, 1979.

* * *

PECKHAM, Lawton (Parker Greenman) 1904-1979

OBITUARY NOTICE: Born June 28, 1904, in Middletown, R.I.; died November 9, 1979, in Newport, R.I. Author and educator. A scholar of medieval French literature, Peckham was dean of the Graduate School of Arts and Sciences at Columbia University. He was decorated chevalier of the French Legion of Honor in 1959. Peckham's work includes *Prise Defur,* a volume of criticism. Obituaries and other sources: *Who's Who in America,* 38th edition, Marquis, 1974; *New York Times,* November 12, 1979.

* * *

PEGLER, (James) Westbrook 1894-1969

OBITUARY NOTICE: Born August 2, 1894, in Minneapolis, Minn.; died June 24, 1969, in Tucson, Ariz. Journalist. Pegler, who first gained national attention as a sports writer in the 1920's, began his famous nationally syndicated column, "Fair Enough," in 1933. The King Features column ran for nearly thirty years, during which time Pegler directed virulent, inflammatory statements at labor union officials, suspected Communist sympathizers, the "person, family, and associates" of President Roosevelt, Charlie Chaplin, Frank Sinatra, Walter Winchell, and a seemingly endless list of others. One such column, directed against magazine writer Quentin Reynolds, resulted in Pegler's involvement in a widely publicized libel suit. Reynolds won the case; Pegler and the Hearst Corp. (owners of King Features) were forced to pay the largest punitive award ever granted in a libel case. His association with the Hearst Corp. ended in 1962 when his contract was cancelled after attacks against members of the Hearst Corp., including William Randolph Hearst, Jr., were found in "Fair Enough." Pegler contributed articles to *American Opinion,* the monthly magazine published by the John Birch Society, until 1964. He was awarded the Pulitzer Prize (1941) for his exposure of labor union racketeering, was twice the winner of the National Headliners Club award, and received numerous other citations. He was the author of several books, including *George Spelvin, American,* and collections of his columns, such as *Tain't Right* and *Dissenting Opinions of Mister Westbrook Pegler.* Obituaries and other sources: *Current Biography,* Wilson, 1940, September, 1969; *The Oxford Companion to American Literature,* revised edition, Appleton, 1967; *Washington Post,* June 25, 1969; *Variety,* July 12, 1969; Oliver Ramsay Pilat, *Pegler: Angry Man of the Press,* Greenwood Press, 1973; Finis Farr, *Fair Enough: The Life of Westbrook Pegler,* Arlington House, 1975.

* * *

PENDER, Lex
See PENDOWER, Jacques

* * *

PENDER, Marilyn
See PENDOWER, Jacques

* * *

PENDOWER, Jacques 1899-1976
(Kathleen Carstairs, Tom Curtis, Penn Dower, T.C.H. Jacobs, Lex Pender, Marilyn Pender, Anne Penn)

OBITUARY NOTICE—See index for *CA* sketch: Born December 30, 1899, in Plymouth, Devonshire, England; died in 1976 in London, England. Author. Pendower wrote more than 180 mystery novels, westerns, and romances, under several different pseudonyms. He was the former chairman of the Crime Writers Association. Obituaries and other sources: *The Author's and Writer's Who's Who,* 6th edition,

Burke's Peerage, 1971; *AB Bookman's Weekly,* January 10, 1977.

* * *

PENGELLEY, Eric T. 1919-

PERSONAL: Born July 18, 1919, in Toronto, Ontario, Canada; naturalized U.S. citizen, 1948; children: two. *Education:* University of Toronto, diploma, 1949, B.A. (first class honors), 1954, Ph.D., 1959. *Office:* Department of Biology, University of California, Riverside, Calif. 92502.

CAREER: University of California, Davis, assistant professor of biology, 1959-60; University of California, Santa Barbara, assistant professor of biology, 1960-61; College of William and Mary, Williamsburg, Va., assistant professor of biology and research associate at Virginia Fisheries Research Laboratory, 1961-62; University of California, Riverside, assistant professor, 1962-67, associate professor, 1967-72, professor of biology, 1972—, past executive officer of College of Letters and Science. Lecturer at universities in the United States and Europe; participant (and sometimes organizer) in international symposia; scientific consultant. *Military service:* Royal Canadian Air Force, 1940-45.

MEMBER: California Heart Association (member of board of directors), Riverside County Heart Association (member of board of directors). *Awards, honors:* Grants from California Heart Association, 1970-74, and U.S. Heart and Lung Institute, 1975-77.

WRITINGS: (Editor with Frank E. South, John P. Hannon, and others, and contributor) *Hibernation and Hypothermia: Perspectives and Challenges,* North-Holland Publishing, 1972; *Sex and Human Life,* Addison-Wesley, 1974, 2nd edition, 1978; (editor and contributor) *Circannual Clocks: Annual Biological Rhythms,* Academic Press, 1974; (contributor) *Chemical Zoology,* Academic Press, 1979. Also *The Student's Guide to Education,* 1979. Contributor of more than fifty articles to scientific journals.

SIDELIGHTS: Eric Pengelley writes: "My primary interest is in the physiology of hibernation in mammals, biological rhythms, and cardiac physiology, but I have also worked on various aspects of marine organisms, and on the history of biology—particularly Darwiniana. I am a keen student of the historical aspects of Charles Darwin, and have collected all his works in first editions.

"At present I carry on an active program of research on hibernation in rodents, biological rhythms, and the cardiology of hibernating rodents."

* * *

PENN, Anne
See PENDOWER, Jacques

* * *

PENNEKAMP, John (David) 1897-1978

OBITUARY NOTICE: Born January 1, 1897, in Cincinnati, Ohio; died in 1978. Journalist. At the age of fourteen Pennekamp began as an office boy for the *Cincinnati Post,* where he worked for the famous editor and father of signed newspaper commentary, O. O. McIntyre. After becoming news editor at the Ohio paper, Pennekamp moved to the *Miami Herald* in 1925. Successively city editor, news editor, managing editor, and associate editor, Pennekamp was director of editorial policy and a daily columnist by the end of his fifty years with the *Herald.* An activist involved in community and environmental affairs, he helped to found the Orange Bowl in 1932 and was instrumental in acquiring the land and funds to establish the Everglades National Park. Pennekamp was honored by the National Audubon Society in 1954, U.S. Department of Interior in 1955, and the Sears Foundation in 1961. He was the subject of an important U.S. Supreme Court test case in 1944, *Pennekamp* v. *Florida,* which resulted in a major decision upholding freedom of the press. Pennekamp once said that the favorable decision of the court was one of the greatest things that ever happened to him. Obituaries and other sources: *Who's Who in the South and Southwest,* 13th edition, Marquis, 1973; *Authors in the News,* Volume 2, Gale, 1976.

* * *

PENTECOST, Hugh
See PHILIPS, Judson Pentecost

* * *

PERELMAN, S(idney) J(oseph) 1904-1979

OBITUARY NOTICE—See index for *CA* sketch: Born February 1, 1904, in Brooklyn, N.Y.; died October 17, 1979, in New York, N.Y. Humorist, screenwriter, dramatist, and cartoonist. Hailed as one of America's greatest humorists, Perelman was noted for his adept word play and zany imagination. Much of his work was in the form of short pieces for the *New Yorker* magazine. These essays have been collected in several books, including *Baby, It's Cold Inside; Rising Gorge;* and *Eastward Ha!* The stage and screen were also enlivened by Perelman's wit. Among his plays are "One Touch of Venus" and "Sweet Bye and Bye." He wrote the screenplays for two movies in which the Marx Brothers starred, "Monkey Business" and "Horse Feathers," and in 1956 received an Academy Award for the screenplay of "Around the World in Eighty Days." Obituaries and other sources: *Current Biography,* Wilson, 1971; *The Penguin Companion to American Literature,* McGraw, 1971; *Biography News,* Volume II, Gale, 1975; *Publishers Weekly,* May 19, 1975, November 5, 1979; *Authors in the News,* Gale, Volume I, 1976, Volume II, 1976; *Contemporary Dramatists,* 2nd edition, St. Martin's, 1977; *The Writers Directory, 1980-82,* St. Martin's, 1979; *Washington Post,* October 18, 1979; *Chicago Tribune,* October 18, 1979; *AB Bookman's Weekly,* November 5, 1979.

* * *

PERKINS, James S(cudday) 1899-

PERSONAL: Born June 29, 1899, in Patterson, La.; son of James S. (a merchant) and Minnie (Riggs) Perkins; married Kathrine Galbreath, December 29, 1924; children: Marian Torrance Perkins Taggart. *Education:* Attended University of Cincinnati, 1919-20, Art Academy, Cincinnati, Ohio, 1920-21, Art Students League, New York City, 1924, and Grand Central School of Art, New York City, 1929-30. *Home:* 29 Taormina Lane, Ojai, Calif. 93023.

CAREER: Commercial artist and illustrator, 1921-41; Theosophical Society, Wheaton, Ill., national vice-president, 1936-45, national president, 1945-60, Adyar, Madras, India, international vice-president, 1961-71; Manor Foundation, Sydney, Australia, administrative head, 1972-77; writer and lecturer, 1977—. Lecturer at Krotona Institute of Theosophy. *Military service:* U.S. Army, Corps of Engineers, 1918.

WRITINGS: *Through Death to Rebirth,* Theosophical Publishing House, 1961; *A Geometry of Space-Consciousness,* Theosophical Publishing House, 1964, 3rd edition, 1978; *Experiencing Reincarnation,* Theosophical Publishing

House, 1977, 2nd edition, 1979. Author of pamphlets. Contributor to periodicals. Editor of *American Theosophist*, 1945-61, and *Theosophist*, 1973.

SIDELIGHTS: Perkins wrote: "My sudden change from engineering to art was due solely to an extraordinary experience. Having completed the first year at University of Cincinnati, where a cooperative course in civil engineering was offered, alternating periods of work on outdoor industrial jobs with indoor attendance at classes, I happened to visit the Art Museum. The impact was immediate and sensational. The faint aroma of oil paints and general atmosphere aroused a queer sense of familiarity with this environment. I seemed to actually 'remember' that I had painted and created works in oil in some other time—certainly not in this life. I stood enthralled in the awareness that I had opened a fresh page in my life.

"Another page was turned when I came into contact with theosophical ideas. H. P. Blavatsky's *The Secret Doctrine* was responsible for a new turn in my career. The world horizons of the twentieth century had become too foreboding for me to spend my years in pursuit of an art career.

"I became involved in propagating the ideals and spreading the illuminative knowledge of theosophy. Administrative offices soon opened greater opportunities in their direction, leading to extensive travels and lecture tours throughout the United States and many other countries, both East and West, as well as 'down under,' in Australia and New Zealand.

"After forty-seven years of serving in administrative offices I have retired to Taormina, a theosophical community in Ojai, California—an environment suggestive of the Pythagorean outlook upon life.

"My wife and I venture upon occasional lecture jaunts and seminars on theosophical subjects. But my greater expectation is to produce a book that presents visually as well as verbally a modern version of theosophical ideas concerning the nature of Man and his relationship with the universe. And if that is accomplished, perhaps I will be able to return to my first love—painting—before dotage sets in and closes my book of life for this incarnation."

* * *

PERKINS, Lawrence A. 1917(?)-1979

OBITUARY NOTICE: Born c. 1917 in Jacksonville, Fla.; died August 4, 1979, of a pulmonary embolism, in Washington D.C. Educator, poet, author, and editor. Perkins wrote poetry and articles for Catholic publications and contributed science fiction to magazines, including the *Saturday Evening Post* and *Analog*. Obituaries and other sources: *Washington Post*, August 10, 1979.

* * *

PERLMAN, Bennard B(loch) 1928-

PERSONAL: Born June 19, 1928, in Baltimore, Md.; son of David Long (an electrical contractor) and Miriam (Bloch) Perlman; married Miriam Lois Walfish, August 20, 1950; children: Rosanne (Mrs. Barton Farris), Jonathan, Marjorie, Eileen. *Education:* Carnegie-Mellon University, B.F.A., 1949; University of Pittsburgh, M.A., 1950; also attended Johns Hopkins University, 1950-52. *Home:* 6603 Baythorne Rd., Baltimore, Md. 21209. *Office:* Department of Art, Community College of Baltimore, 2901 Liberty Heights, Baltimore, Md. 21215.

CAREER: Community College of Baltimore, Baltimore, Md., member of faculty, 1954-63, associate professor, 1963-65, professor of art and chairman of department, 1965—. Visiting instructor at Loyola College, Baltimore, Md., 1968, 1969, 1975, 1978, and Towson State University, 1971, 1972; visiting lecturer at Oxford University, autumn, 1975. Art critic for WBJC-FM Radio. Director of Art Consultants of Baltimore. Member of Maryland Arts Council, Baltimore's Civic Design Commission, and architectural advisory board for Baltimore's Committee for Downtown; member of Baltimore Museum of Arts artists committee; member of board of directors of Baltimore Heritage, Inc. *Member:* Artists Equity Association (national vice-president, 1977-79), Royal Society of Arts (fellow).

WRITINGS: The Immortal Eight: American Painting From Eakins to the Armory Show, 1870-1913, Exposition Press, 1962, revised edition, North Light, 1979; *One Percent Art in Civic Architecture,* R.T.K.L. Associates, 1973; *The Golden Age of American Illustration: F. R. Gruger and His Circle,* North Light, 1978. Contributor to *New Catholic Encyclopedia*. Contributor to magazines. Art critic for *Baltimore*.

WORK IN PROGRESS: The Art and Life of Robert Henri.

SIDELIGHTS: Perlman comments: "As an artist, teacher, and writer, I revel in the opportunity to perform creatively through the brush and the verbal and written word. For twenty-five years I have been penning prose on a free-lance basis for newspapers and magazines. Traveling abroad almost annually since 1966 has provided an additional foray into the realm of living a life through art. To paint, to teach others to do so, and to write about the notable artists of our recent past—these are more than mere vocations, they are aspects of an idyllic, dream-like existence."

* * *

PERLMAN, Jess 1891-
(Philip Gray)

PERSONAL: Born December 24, 1891, in New York, N.Y.; son of Abraham and Flora (Becker) Perlman; married wife, Rose; children: David. *Education:* City College (now of the City University of New York), B.A., 1911; Fordham University, LL.B., 1915, D.J., 1964. *Religion:* Jewish. *Home:* 150 West Waterview, Northport, N.Y. 11768.

CAREER: Teacher at public schools in New York City, 1911-15; Irene Kaufmann Settlement, Pittsburgh, Pa., executive director, 1915-16; Jewish Educational Alliance, Baltimore, Md., executive director, 1918-20; Jewish Philanthropies, Montreal, Quebec, executive director, 1920-22; Jewish Board of Guardians, New York City, executive director, 1922-27; Associated Guidance Bureau, New York City, executive director, 1927-34; Grove School (residential treatment center and high school for the emotionally disturbed), Madison, Conn., executive director, 1934-56; writer.

MEMBER: American Orthopsychiatric Association (fellow), Poetry Society of America. *Awards, honors:* Fiftieth Anniversary Award from *Lyric,* 1970; Stephen Vincent Benet Narrative Poem Award from *Poet Lore,* 1976.

WRITINGS—Poetry: *Looking Glasses,* Branden Press, 1967; *This World This Looking Glass,* South and West, 1970; *Bus to Chapingo,* Branden Press, 1970; *Poems Past Eighty,* Dragon's Teeth Press, 1979.

Translations are represented in numerous anthologies. Contributor of translations to magazines, sometimes under pseudonym Philip Gray.

SIDELIGHTS: Perlman has translated poetry from French, German, Spanish, Italian, Russian, Hebrew, Yiddish, Hindu, Urdu, modern Greek, Hungarian, and Romanian.

PERRY, Erma (Jackson McNeil)

PERSONAL: Born in Winthrop, Mass.; daughter of Martyn (in business) and Henrietta Dorothea (Jackson) McNeil; married Irving C. Perry (in insurance), April 29, 1939; children: Dorothy Gayle (Mrs. T. Jeffrey Toy), Irving C. III. *Education:* Boston University, B.S., 1936. *Politics:* Republican. *Religion:* Society of Friends (Quakers). *Home:* 134 Greenwood Ave., Jenkintown, Pa. 19046; and West Side Rd., North Conway, N.H. 03860.

CAREER/WRITINGS: Free-lance writer. Feature writer for Copley News Service, 1967—. Contributor to newspapers, including *Philadelphia Daily News, Philadelphia Inquirer,* and *Philadelphia Bulletin,* and magazines, including *Better Homes and Gardens, American Artist, Holiday, Family Circle,* and *Modern Maturity.* Member of women's committee of International House, 1951-56; member of Friends Social Order Committee, 1955-56, and Friends Prison Service Committee, 1965-67; member of board of trustees of Philadelphia Center for Older People, 1960-67, and board of directors of Quaker Women, 1964-69. *Member:* Society of American Travel Writers, American Society of Journalists and Authors, Bucks County Writers (president, 1970), Philadelphia Public Relations Association, North Conway Country Club. *Awards, honors:* Awards from *Writer's Digest,* 1971 and 1972; named honorary citizen of Texas, 1972.

* * *

PERRY, Margaret 1933-

PERSONAL: Born November 15, 1933, in Cincinnati, Ohio; daughter of R. Patterson (a college president and professor) and Elizabeth (Anthony) Perry. *Education:* Western Michigan University, A.B., 1954; University of Paris, certificate, 1956; further graduate study at City College (now of the City University of New York), 1957-58; Catholic University of America, M.S.L.S., 1959. *Politics:* Democrat. *Religion:* Roman Catholic. *Home:* 287 Melrose St., Rochester, N.Y. 14619. *Office:* Rush Rhees Library, University of Rochester, Rochester, N.Y. 14627.

CAREER: New York Public Library, New York, N.Y., young adult and reference librarian, 1954-55, 1957-58; U.S. Army, civilian librarian in Metz, Nancy, Toul, and Verdun, France, 1959-63, Orleans, France, 1964-65, and Hanau, Germany, 1965-67; U.S. Military Academy, West Point, N.Y., reference librarian, 1967-68, chief of circulation, 1968-70; University of Rochester, Rochester, N.Y., head of education library, 1970-75, assistant professor, 1973-75, associate professor of English, 1975—, assistant professor of education, 1974—, head of library's Reader Services Division, 1975-78, assistant director of libraries for reader services, 1978—, acting director of libraries, 1976-77. Speaker at professional meetings.

MEMBER: American Library Association (life member), College Language Association, Modern Language Association of America, Council for Basic Education, National Society of Literature and the Arts, American Civil Liberties Union, Urban League of Rochester (member of board of directors; second vice-president, 1978-80). *Awards, honors:* Scholarship from Salzburg Seminar in American Studies, for Schloss Leopoldskron, 1956; first prize from Armed Forces Writers League short story contest, 1966, for "Black Apostle"; second place from Frances Steloff Fiction Prize, 1969, for "Lions, Kings, and Dragons."

WRITINGS: A Bio-Bibliography of Countee P. Cullen, 1903-1946, Greenwood Press, 1971; (contributor) E. J. Josey, editor, *What Black Librarians Are Saying,* Scarecrow, 1973; *Silence to the Drums: A Survey of the Literature of the Harlem Renaissance,* Greenwood Press, 1976; *The Short Fiction of Rudolph Fisher,* Greenwood Press, 1977; *An Annotated Bibliography of the Harlem Renaissance,* Garland Publishing, in press. Contributor of articles, stories, and reviews to history and library journals, and to literary journals, including *Panache* and *Phylon.* Associate editor of *University of Rochester Library Bulletin,* 1970-73; contributing editor of *Afro-Americans in New York Life and History.*

WORK IN PROGRESS: One "serious" novel; one "not-so-serious" novel; short stories.

SIDELIGHTS: Margaret Perry writes: "Although the major portion of my published work is about Afro-American literature, I plan to devote more time to writing short stories. They are the poetry of fiction, and it's about time for me to give more time to them.

"I was always lucky to have encouragement from teachers and support from my parents. I sometimes think I had too easy a life; harder times may have given some bite to the fiction I write. But I must be content with my style and subjects, and try to make my stories an authentic expression of my artistry, however meager it may be."

AVOCATIONAL INTERESTS: Travel in France ("poking among the ruins"), collecting bookmarks and stamps (especially art stamps), playing violin (chamber music).

* * *

PETERSON, Esther (Allen) 1934-

PERSONAL: Born March 9, 1934, in Carson, N.D.; daughter of Samuel James (a Presbyterian minister) and Mildred (a secretary; maiden name, Justice) Allen; married Donald Frank Peterson (a Lutheran minister), June 14, 1952; children: Mary Peterson Olson, Donald Frank, Jr., Kirsten Peterson Olson, Deborah, Heidi Peterson Nordine, Paul. *Education:* Chicago City College, Wright Branch, A.A., 1973. *Religion:* Lutheran. *Home address:* P.O. Box 215, Karlstad, Minn. 56732.

CAREER: Church musician and piano teacher in Wisconsin, North Dakota, Illinois, and Minnesota, 1957-77; writer, 1977—. Personnel counselor in Chicago, Ill., 1970-72. Member of Kittson County Humanities Commission. *Member:* American Lutheran Church Women (president, 1974-75), Karlstad Mental Health Association (chairperson, 1977-78).

WRITINGS: Reach Out to Abused Children (pamphlet), Augsburg, 1976; *Reach Out to the Mentally Ill* (pamphlet), Augsburg, 1976; *Frederick's Alligator* (for children), Crown, 1979. Contributor to religious magazines, including *Scope* and *Lutheran Standard.*

WORK IN PROGRESS—For Children: *Herman Doesn't Have to Wash His Face Anymore,* for Crown; *Penelope Gets Wheels,* for Crown; *Fat Margaret; What Was Good About Our Fishing Trip?; Alexander and Benjamin and the Mountain Lion; Pickles for Breakfast.*

Other: *Do You Know About My Hurt, Lord?,* for Winston Press; *Something Happened on My Way to the Cross,* free-verse Lenten devotions; research for a novel on the settling of North Dakota.

SIDELIGHTS: Esther Peterson writes: "After I was thirty-five, I started college in Chicago and discovered I enjoyed writing even more than music. When we moved to northern Minnesota I had little opportunity in the music field, so I turned to writing. My first project was a book about our family's eight hundred-mile bicycle trip the previous summer. I did this for the family and it is not published, but doing it created a passion for putting words on paper.

"For me the main thing in writing children's books is to delight a child. Since children are put down so much by adults, I like to make them heroes in my books, mastering their own situations and solving their own problems. I want children to identify with my characters and feel good about themselves.

"In writing inspirational material I ponder my human condition, my struggle with myself, others, and God. Because I feel that we all experience similar joy, insecurities, pathos, desires, and dreams, I try to be starkly honest, and then maybe I will relate to the reader's life as he or she experiences it."

AVOCATIONAL INTERESTS: Golf, biking, playing bridge, travel (Germany, France, Austria, Switzerland, the Netherlands).

BIOGRAPHICAL/CRITICAL SOURCES: Grand Forks Herald, February 27, 1979; *North Star News,* May 3, 1979.

* * *

PETRIE, Charles (Alexander) 1895-1977

OBITUARY NOTICE—See index for *CA* sketch: Born September 28, 1895, in Liverpool, England; died December, 1977. Historian, biographer, editor, and author. Considered by many to be a preeminent historian, Petrie was editor of the *Household Brigade Magazine* of the Royal Horse Guards for more than thirty years. He also was affiliated with the *English Review, New English Review,* and the *Empire Review.* Petrie was the author of more than fifty biographies and books on history, including *The Victorians, Scenes of Edwardian Life, Wellington: A Reassessment,* and *A Historian Looks at His World.* Obituaries and other sources: *The Author's and Writer's Who's Who,* 6th edition, Burke's Peerage, 1971; *AB Bookman's Weekly,* March 6, 1978.

* * *

PEZZULO, Ted 1936(?)-1979

OBITUARY NOTICE: Born c. 1936 in Ticonderoga, N.Y.; died November 10, 1979, in New York, N.Y. Actor and playwright, Pezzulo wrote such plays as "A Song for the First of May," "The Wooing of Lady Sunday," and "Skaters." He also acted in his own plays and had minor roles in the motion pictures "Where Were You When the Lights Went Out?" and "The Night They Raided Minsky's." Obituaries and other sources: *New York Times,* November 12, 1979.

* * *

PFEIFER, Luanne

PERSONAL: Born in Tampa, Fla.; daughter of Willard George (in the military and Treasury Department) and Mary (Tierney) Malsie; married James Wayne Pfeifer (an engineer), August 13, 1955; children: Kathleen, Dianna, Michael. *Education:* University of Washington, Seattle, B.S., 1950. *Home:* 3224 Malibu Canyon Rd., Malibu, Calif. 90265.

CAREER: Santa Monica Evening Outlook, Santa Monica, Calif., author of column, "Down the Ski Trails," 1957-68; West Coast staff writer for *Ski,* 1968—. *Member:* American Society of Journalists and Authors, United States Ski Writers Association, Far West Ski Association, Ski Writers Association of Southern California (vice-president, 1966, 1967), Malibu Historical Society, Malibu Yacht Club. *Awards, honors:* William B. Berry Journalism Award from Far West Ski Association, 1967; United States Ski Writing Award from U.S. Ski Association, 1968, for excellence in ski journalism; honorable mention from Ski Industries America, 1974, for portrayal of the excitement of skiing; National Endowment for the Humanities journalism fellowship for Fletcher School of Law and Diplomacy, 1978.

WRITINGS: (Contributor) *Rand McNally Ski Guide,* Rand McNally, 1970; (contributor) *International Ski Trails,* Dell, 1973, new edition, 1974; (contributor) *Ski Guide,* Petersen, 1973; *Ski California,* with photographs by Paul Shaper, Praesidio Press, 1980. Los Angeles correspondent for Times-Mirror Magazines, 1969—. Author of "Skiing," a column in *Los Angeles Times,* 1968, 1969. Contributor to sport magazines and travel periodicals, including *Sports Illustrated, 'Teen, Ski,* and *Off Duty.* Senior editor of *World Travel,* 1972, 1973.

* * *

PHILIPS, Judson Pentecost 1903-
(Hugh Pentecost)

PERSONAL: Born in 1903, in Northfield, Mass.; son of Arthur (an opera singer) and Frederikco (an actress; maiden name, Pentecost) Philips; married second wife, Norma Burton (an actress), 1951; children: David, Caroline, John, Daniel. *Education:* Columbia University, B.A., 1925. *Home:* Emmons Lane, Canaan, Conn. 06018. *Agent:* Brandt & Brandt, 101 Park Ave., New York, N.Y. 10017. *Office:* 1501 Broadway, New York, N.Y. 10036.

CAREER: New York Tribune, New York, N.Y., high school sports reporter, beginning 1926; *Harlem Valley Times,* Amenia, N.Y., co-owner and editor, 1949-56; *Lakeville Journal,* Lakeville, Conn., political columnist and book reviewer, 1951—; Sharon Playhouse, Sharon, Conn., founder and director, 1951-72; WTOR-Radio, Torrington, Conn., talk-show host, 1970-76. *Member:* Mystery Writers of America (founding member and past president; Grand Master, 1973). *Awards, honors:* First prize in Dodd, Mead's mystery competition, 1939, for *Cancelled in Red.*

WRITINGS—All published by Dodd, except as noted: (With Robert W. Wood, Jr.) *Hold 'Em Girls! The Intelligent Woman's Guide to Men and Football,* Putnam, 1936; (with Thomas M. Johnson) *Red War,* Doubleday, 1936; *The Death Syndicate,* I. Washburn (New York), 1938; *Death Delivers a Postcard,* I. Washburn, 1939; *Murder in Marble; a Detective Story,* 1940; *Odds on the Hot Seat,* 1941; *The Fourteenth Trump,* 1942; *Killer on the Catwalk,* 1959.

Whisper Town, 1960; *Murder Clear, Track Fast,* 1961; *A Dead Ending,* 1962; *The Dead Can't Love,* 1963; *The Laughter Trap,* 1964; *The Black Glass City: A Peter Styles Mystery,* 1965; *The Twisted People: A Peter Styles Mystery,* 1965; *The Wings of Madness: A Peter Styles Mystery Novel,* 1966; *Thursday's Folly: A Peter Styles Mystery Novel,* 1967; *Hot Summer Killing: A Peter Styles Mystery Novel,* 1968.

Nightmare at Dawn: A Peter Styles Mystery Novel, 1970; *Escape a Killer,* 1971; *The Vanishing Senator,* 1972; *The Larkspur Conspiracy,* 1973; *The Power Killers,* 1974; *Walk a Crooked Mile,* 1975; *Five Roads to Death,* 1977; *Backlash,* Gollancz, 1977; *A Murder Arranged: A Peter Styles Murder Mystery,* 1978; *Why Murder?: A Peter Styles Murder Mystery,* 1979.

Under pseudonym Hugh Pentecost: *Cancelled in Red,* 1939; *The 24th Horse,* 1940; *I'll Sing at Your Funeral,* 1942; *The Brass Chills,* 1943; *Memory of Murder: Four Novelettes,*

Ziff-Davis, 1947; *Where the Snow Was Red,* 1949; *Shadow of Madness,* 1950; *Lieutenant Pascal's Tastes in Homicides,* 1954; *The Assassins,* 1955; *The Obituary Club,* 1958; *The Lonely Target,* 1959.

The Kingdom of Death, 1960; *Choice of Violence,* 1961; *The Deadly Friend,* 1961; *The Cannibal Who Overate,* 1962; (editor) *Cream of the Crime: The 15th Mystery Writers of America Anthology,* Holt, 1962; *The Tarnished Angel,* 1963; *The Shape of Fear,* T. V. Boardman, 1963, Dodd, 1964; *Only the Rich Die Young,* 1964; *Sniper,* 1965; *Hide Her From Every Eye: A John Jericho Mystery Novel,* 1966; *The Creeping Hour: A John Jericho Mystery Novel,* 1966; *The Evil That Men Do,* 1966; *The Golden Trap,* 1967; *Dead Woman of the Year: A John Jericho Mystery Novel,* 1967; *The Gilded Nightmare: A Pierre Chambrun Mystery Novel,* 1968; *Girl Watcher's Funeral: A Pierre Chambrun Mystery Novel,* 1969; *The Girl With Six Fingers: A John Jericho Mystery Novel,* 1969.

Around Dark Corners: A Collection of Mystery Stories, 1970; *A Plague of Violence,* 1970; *The Deadly Joke,* 1971; *Don't Drop Dead Tomorrow,* 1971; *Birthday, Deathday,* 1972; *The Champagne Killer,* 1972; *Walking Dead Man,* 1973; *The Beautiful Dead,* 1973; *Bargain With Death,* 1974; *The Judas Freak,* 1974; *Time of Terror,* 1975; *The Steel Palace,* 1977; *Murder as Usual,* 1977; *The Fourteen Dilemma,* 1977; *Deadly Trap,* 1978; *Death After Breakfast,* 1978; *Random Killer,* 1979.

Author of filmscripts, including "General Crack," Warner Bros., 1930.

Also author of television scripts, including "Studio One," "The U.S. Steel Hour," "Robert Montgomery Presents," and contributor of scripts to the series, "The Web." Author of radio scripts in the 1940's. Contributor of stories to periodicals, including *Saturday Evening Post, Liberty, Collier's, American, Ellery Queen's Mystery Magazine,* and *Cosmopolitan.*

WORK IN PROGRESS: Three books, publication by Dodd expected in 1980.

SIDELIGHTS: Judson Philips has been writing mystery and detective fiction for over fifty years; his output in that time has been prolific, amounting to nearly one hundred novels and countless short stories. He once told Tim Dumont of the *Hartford Courant,* "I never had any job in my life (except summer work) that didn't have to do with writing."

In a review of *Don't Drop Dead Tomorrow,* Newgate Callendar wrote that Philips's "name is a guarantee of smooth writing, an ingenuous story-line and convincing characterization." Similarly, Sergeant Cuff felt that *Nightmare at Dawn* contained "complications of the sort that only a top pro could handle with clarity and at a brisk pace. Judson Philips . . . is as pro as they come."

In part, such admiration derives from what Diana Leclercq has described as Philips's "talent for writing clean, hard prose." He is also admired for his series detectives, especially the bearded artist John Jericho, the public relations man Julian Quist, and the hotel manager Pierre Chambrun—all of whom were created under the pseudonym Hugh Pentecost.

The one detective Philips has written of under his own name is Peter Styles, a one-legged magazine columnist who has been characterized as a crusader for justice and the American way of life. Anthony Boucher has pointed out that the Styles novels display Philips's recent tendency "to explore the modern problem of meaningless violence." In *Wings of Madness* Styles combats a small-town, fascistic private army; in *Thursday's Folly* he faces a gang of young psychopaths; and in *Hot Summer Killing* he contends with a group of terrorists amidst an atmosphere of mounting racial tensions. Philips himself described his approach as an effort "to write stories that fit into the current climate."

BIOGRAPHICAL/CRITICAL SOURCES: Times Literary Supplement, December 2, 1965, February 23, 1967, January 25, 1968; *New York Times Book Review,* August 6, 1967, February 23, 1969, April 5, 1970; *Books and Bookmen,* February, 1968; *Punch,* March 5, 1969; *Saturday Review,* March 28, 1970, August 1, 1970, December 26, 1970; *Hartford Courant,* June 30, 1974; *Authors in the News,* Volume 1, Gale, 1976.

* * *

PHILLIPS, James E(merson, Jr.) 1912-1979

OBITUARY NOTICE: Born November 11, 1912, in Los Angeles, Calif.; died July 24, 1979, in Santa Monica, Calif. Educator and author. Phillips was a member of the faculty of the University of California at Los Angeles for nearly thirty years. His works include *The State in Shakespeare's Greek and Roman Plays* and *Images of a Queen: Mary Stuart in Sixteenth Century Literature.* Obituaries and other sources: *Directory of American Scholars,* Volume II: *English, Speech, and Drama,* 7th edition, Bowker, 1978; *Who's Who in America,* 40th edition, Marquis, 1978; *New York Times,* July 26, 1979; *AB Bookman's Weekly,* August 20, 1979.

* * *

PHILLIPS, O(wen) M(artin) 1930-

PERSONAL: Born December 30, 1930, in Parramatta, Australia; came to the United States in 1958; son of Richard Keith (an accountant) and Madeline (Lofts) Phillips; married Merle Winifred Simons, August 15, 1952; children: Lynette Michelle, Christopher Ian, Bronwyn Ann, Michael Stuart. *Education:* University of Sydney, B.Sc., 1952; Cambridge University, Ph.D., 1955. *Residence:* Baltimore, Md. *Agent:* John R. Riina, 5905 Meadowood Rd., Baltimore, Md. 21218. *Office:* Department of Earth and Planetary Sciences, Johns Hopkins University, Baltimore, Md. 21218.

CAREER: Cambridge University, Cambridge, England, fellow of Imperial Chemical Industries, 1955-57; Johns Hopkins University, Baltimore, Md., assistant professor, 1957-60, associate professor, 1960-63, professor of geophysics, 1963—, Decker Professor of Science and Engineering, 1976—, head of department of earth and planetary sciences, 1971-78. Fellow of St. John's College, Cambridge, 1957-60, assistant director of research, 1961-64. Member of council of National Center of Atmospheric Research, 1964—, and U.S. National Committee on Global Atmospheric Research project, 1968; member of board of trustees of Chesapeake Research Consortium, 1972-76, and Roland Park Country School; consultant to Westinghouse Electric Corp., Hydronautics, Inc., and Philadelphia Electric Co.

MEMBER: American Meteorological Society, American Geophysical Union, Royal Society (fellow), Maryland Academy of Sciences, Sigma Xi, Pi Tau Sigma. *Awards, honors:* Adams Prize from Cambridge University, 1964, for *Dynamics of the Upper Ocean;* Sverdrup Gold Medal from American Meteorological Society, 1973, for contributions to research.

WRITINGS: Dynamics of the Upper Ocean, Cambridge University Press, 1966, 2nd edition, 1977; *The Heart of the*

Earth, Freeman, Cooper, 1968; *The Last Chance Energy Book,* Johns Hopkins Press, 1979. Contributor of about sixty articles to scientific journals. Associate editor of *Journal of Fluid Mechanics,* 1964—.

WORK IN PROGRESS: Research on geophysics and oceanography, especially on U.S. national energy problems.

SIDELIGHTS: Phillips writes: "Most of my technical writing is done in Baltimore, the non-technical writing on Cape Cod. The aim of the latter is to communicate to a general audience, as simply, clearly, attractively, and accurately as possible, technical matters that impinge on our lives."

AVOCATIONAL INTERESTS: Sailing, working with his hands, travel (Europe, Asia, Australia).

* * *

PIDGEON, Mary E. 1890(?)-1979

OBITUARY NOTICE: Born c. 1890 in Winchester, Va.; died November 24, 1979, in Sandy Spring, Md. Author and former chief of the research division of the Women's Bureau at the Labor Department. Pidgeon wrote or contributed to all the major publications of the bureau, whose most important publication was the *Handbook of Women Workers,* a standard reference work. Pidgeon was an early suffragette and was involved with a number of women's organizations. Obituaries and other sources: *Washington Post,* December 1, 1979.

* * *

PIETROPINTO, Anthony 1938-

PERSONAL: Born July 10, 1938, in New York, N.Y.; son of Donato S. (a physician) and Anne (a registered nurse; maiden name, DeCarlo) Pietropinto; married Joy Ann Giusti (a business executive), June 25, 1966; children: Rita Diana, Laura Joy. *Education:* New York University, B.A., 1960; Columbia University, M.D., 1964. *Agent:* Jacqueline Simenauer, 22 Greenview Way, Upper Montclair, N.J. 07043. *Office:* 20 Fifth Ave., New York, N.Y. 10011.

CAREER: St. Vincent's Hospital, New York City, resident psychiatrist, 1965-68; Brooklyn-Cumberland Medical Center, New York City, director of geriatric psychiatry, 1970-71; private practice in psychiatry, New York City, 1970—; Lutheran Medical Center, New York City, medical director of Mental Health Center, 1972—. Associate attending psychiatrist at St. Vincent's Hospital, 1975. *Military service:* U.S. Army, 1968-70; received Bronze Star. *Member:* American Psychiatric Association, New York State Medical Society.

WRITINGS: (With Jacqueline Simenauer) *Beyond the Male Myth* (nonfiction), Times Books, 1977; (with Simenauer) *Husbands and Wives* (nonfiction), Times Books, 1979; (with Elaine Piller Congress) *The Clinic* (novel), Times Books, 1980.

Contributor: Jack J. Leedy, editor, *Poetry the Healer,* Lippincott, 1973; Jules H. Masserman, editor, *Current Psychiatric Therapies,* Volume XV, Grune, 1975; Silvano Arieti and Gerard Chrzanowski, editors, *New Dimensions in Psychiatry: A World View,* Volume II, Wiley, 1977.

Contributor of articles to *Gramercy Herald.*

WORK IN PROGRESS: Apollo's Children: An Introduction to Poetry Therapy (tentative title), publication by Nelson-Hall expected in 1981.

SIDELIGHTS: Pietropinto told *CA:* "My interest in writing dates back to my grammar school days, when I won praise for contributing poetry and essays to class newsletters. I was the first premedical student at New York University to serve as editor-in-chief of the tri-weekly newspaper, *Square Journal*. . . . I was able to find a link between creative writing and my profession as a psychiatrist by utilizing poetry therapy with patients.

"*Beyond the Male Myth* . . . was partly due to the success of the controversial *Hite Report,* whose findings were based on what was, in my opinion, very questionable research methods. *Beyond the Male Myth* was the first major scientific survey on sexuality to utilize a nationwide established marketing research firm, enabling me to poll a truly representative sample in a very short period of time. I find it discouraging, however, whenever people say 'the book is a survey'—actually, the book merely begins with a survey and, as a writer, I attempted to use it as a springboard for an exploration of the complex sphere of male sexuality, drawing on my clinical experience with patients, my personal experiences, and above all, the wisdom and wit of our classic and popular literature and culture, with contributions from W. C. Fields, Charlie Brown, the Greek philosophers, and especially my idol, George Bernard Shaw. Shaw's Don Juan in Hell drifts in and out of the book as an allegorical guide, much as Dante's Virgil guided him through the *Divine Comedy.* Just as the play, *Man and Superman,* of which Don Juan is protagonist, is a very puritanical work about a daring, wicked subject (sex), so too is *Beyond the Male Myth,* beneath its frank discussions of modern sexual practices, a harbinger of the conservative backlash to the sexual revolution. Unlike the entirely clinical works of Kinsey or Masters and Johnson, or the didactic self-help books of Dyer and Ringer, this book was designed to be provocative, unconventional, and a work that raised as many questions as it answered.

"*Husbands and Wives* followed the lead of its predecessor in starting with a nationwide survey (of current married couples). Here, even more liberties were taken than in the earlier work—there was less emphasis on concrete advice to the reader, more detailed case studies, and an overall view of marriage as an institution throughout the ages. Shaw's influence was even more pronounced than in *Beyond the Male Myth,* for the striking relevance of his turn-of-the-century play, *Getting Married,* sets the theme that the 'revolution' in our attitude towards marriage is more apparent than actual, since, before 1910, people were struggling with problems such as should private contracts replace state-controlled marriages, should women absorb their husband's identities, might not 'infidelity' help a marriage, should not society allow women to have children outside of marriage without stigma, etc.

"My collaborator, Jacqueline Simenauer, is a newspaperwoman and, in our work together, we have made a curious switch of roles. I, the 'scientist,' do the writing and she, the 'writer,' concentrates her efforts at organizing the research findings. While there are those heartening souls who tell me how much they enjoyed the books' whimsical and philosophical digressions, I am still somewhat distressed at the preponderance of reviewers who approach the books as surveys in the Kinsey mode and ignore the more unique aspects, however complimentary they may be to the books. Therefore, I hope to limit my next few efforts, at least, to more creative projects, unencumbered by statistics and other data.

"As a community psychiatrist, engaged in daily interaction with people with all types of problems, from all socio-economic strata of life, I have a wealth of material with which to fuel my literary flames. I hope to be able to take advantage of my unique position as director/therapist at Lutheran Medical Center to provide my readers with a diverse and fascinating view of the human psyche, as rich as that which I have been privileged to experience daily.

"As a writer who practices psychiatry to 'support my habit,' I get annoyed at people who ask if I have a ghost-writer and who point out that few psychiatrists or psychologists are able to write well. My personal opinion is that such therapists use the spoken word, use language as their prime healing instrument and should be expected to have an excellent range, understanding, and control of language, just as one would expect a surgeon to have better-than-average manual dexterity. I would view skill in lingusitic expression as paramount to the practice of psychoanalytically oriented or exploratory psychotherapy and would not expect anyone without exceptional facility in writing to be outstanding as a therapist."

AVOCATIONAL INTERESTS: "I collect unicorns and have a herd of more than twenty in my collection; my taste in reading centers around works of fantasy and humor."

BIOGRAPHICAL/CRITICAL SOURCES: Mademoiselle, November, 1977; *New York Times,* November 24, 1977; *Time,* December 12, 1977; *Us,* December 13, 1977; *New York Daily News,* February 9, 1977, February 10, 1977; *Gallery,* January, 1979.

* * *

PILCER, Sonia 1949-

PERSONAL: Born February 3, 1949, in Augsburg, Germany; came to United States, 1950; naturalized U.S. citizen, 1962; daughter of Benjamin and Lusia (Gradon) Pilcer. *Education:* City University of New York, B.A., 1970. *Residence:* New York, N.Y. *Agent:* Carl Brandt, Brandt & Brandt, 101 Park Ave., New York, N.Y. 10017.

CAREER: Ingenue, New York City, chief copywriter, 1970-71; *Movie Mirror,* managing editor, 1971-72; free-lance writer, 1972—. Adjunct professor of journalism at City College of the City University of New York; lecturer and reader. Associated with WNYC-Radio and WBAI-Radio. *Member:* Poets and Writers. *Awards, honors:* Fellowship from Yaddo and P.E.N., 1979.

WRITINGS: Teen Angel (novel), Coward, 1978. Work anthologized in *New Poems, New Poets,* Ann Arbor Review, 1976, and *Internal Weather,* edited by Fred Wolven. Staff writer for *Manhattan Park West,* 1975. Contributor to *Seventeen* and *Village Voice.*

WORK IN PROGRESS: A second novel, *Numero Uno* (tentative title).

SIDELIGHTS: Pilcer told *CA:* "I don't write for younger readers specifically, although I'm pleased that they do seem to respond to my work. What I do attempt to reach is the hard kernel of innocence, embarrassment, shame, joy, stirrings of the memory, and ideals in my readers which are often associated with youth. I see it as eternal in all who live and breathe."

* * *

PIMSLEUR, Meira Goldwater 1905(?)-1979

OBITUARY NOTICE—See index for *CA* sketch: Born c. 1905 in New York, N.Y.; died August 10, 1979, in New York, N.Y. Law librarian and editor of reference books. As the acquisitions librarian for Columbia University Law Library, Pimsleur was chiefly responsible for building that library's collection into the third largest in the United States. In 1971 she received the Joseph L. Andrews Bibliographical Award from the American Association of Law Libraries for her work, *Law Book for Libraries.* Obituaries and other sources: *A Biographical Directory of Librarians in the United States and Canada,* 5th edition, American Library Association, 1970; *New York Times,* August 16, 1979.

* * *

PINDYCK, Robert (Stephen) 1945-

PERSONAL: Born January 5, 1945, in New York, N.Y.; son of Charles and Marilyn Pindyck; married Nurit Eini (a systems analyst), September 25, 1977; children: Maya Ronit. *Education:* Massachusetts Institute of Technology, S.B., 1966, S.M., 1967, Ph.D., 1971. *Office:* Sloan School of Management, Massachusetts Institute of Technology, 50 Memorial Dr., Cambridge, Mass. 02139.

CAREER: Massachusetts Institute of Technology, Cambridge, assistant professor, 1971-76, associate professor, 1976-79, professor of applied economics, 1979—. Consultant to Federal Energy Administration and International Bank for Reconstruction and Development. *Member:* American Economic Association, Econometric Society.

WRITINGS: Optimal Planning for Economic Stabilization, North-Holland Publishing, 1973; *The Economics of the Natural Gas Shortage, 1960-1980,* North-Holland Publishing, 1975; *Price Controls and the Natural Gas Shortage,* American Enterprise Institute, 1975; *Econometric Models and Economic Forecasts,* McGraw, 1976; *The Structure of World Energy Demand,* M.I.T. Press, 1979; (editor) *Advances in the Economics of Energy and Resources,* JAI Press, 1979; (editor) *The Structure of Energy Markets,* Volume II: *The Production and Pricing of Energy Resources,* JAI Press, 1979.

* * *

PLAWIN, Paul 1938-
(J. P. Godly, Dirk Steele)

PERSONAL: Born April 26, 1938, in Norfolk, Va.; son of Paul Arthur (a minister) and Gladys (Bauman) Plawin; married Joan Irvin (in market research and sales), June 29, 1963; children: Jennifer Joan, Paul B. *Education:* Washington & Lee University, B.A., 1960. *Religion:* Christian. *Home:* 2329 North Oak St., Falls Church, Va. 22046. *Office: Changing Times,* 1729 H St. N.W., Washington, D.C. 20006.

CAREER: Free-lance writer. *Norfolk Ledger-Star,* Norfolk, Va., reporter and columnist, 1961-64; *Southern Living,* Birmingham, Ala., Southeast editor, 1964-67; *New Orleans,* New Orleans, La., managing editor, 1967; *Better Homes and Gardens,* Des Moines, Iowa, travel editor, 1967-70; *Changing Times,* Washington, D.C., associate editor, 1970—. Notable assignments include coverage of personalities in Southern cities, charities, and economic contributions of housewives. Member of board of directors and consultant with Inter-Media Reporting, Inc., 1978-79. *Military service:* U.S. Coast Guard Reserve, 1961-67; became lieutenant. *Member:* National Press Club, Society of American Travel Writers, Washington Press Club, Senate-House Periodical Gallery, W & L Colonnade Club. *Awards, honors:* Award from Virginia Press Association, 1962, for column "For Men Only."

WRITINGS: (Contributor) Dorothy Kendall Bracken, *SRS, Bracken's Specific Reading Skills,* Jones-Kenilworth, 1973. Author of articles on travel under pseudonyms J. P. Godly and Dirk Steele, 1970-77. Contributor to periodicals, including *Odyssey* and *Reader's Digest*.

WORK IN PROGRESS: "A novelty book called *Doggy Woof Woof,* another called *Tilt,* combining nonfiction and fiction accounts of offbeat and bizarre stories, completion expected in 1980 or 1981."

SIDELIGHTS: Plawin told *CA:* "I reported and wrote probably the first published article to establish a monetary value on the economic contributions of housewives. The article was later referred to as a standard by the *Wall Street Journal.* I developed and wrote one of the first ever reports rating American charities on a scale developed from ethical standards of the leading fundraising counsel and monitoring organizations. . . . Since the article was published, the National Information Bureau has begun making its reports on individual charities public and a number of consumer magazines have done similar reports.

"I did a series of cover stories for *Southern Living* in 1965 and 1966 on cities of the South which set the tone for the launch of the publication as 'the magazine of the new South.' The articles broke some new ground by 'discovering' new personalities in these Southern cities. For instance, my Miami piece uncovered the real estate developer who was even then quietly putting together the vast package of land for development of Walt Disney World; my Atlanta article gave extensive coverage to the work and ideas of local architect John Portman, who has since become internationally known for his atrium design towers which he was just beginning to develop in his plans for the Hyatt Regency Hotel in Atlanta at the time of the article.

"Among my travel writing, two projects of note were an innovative wrap-up I did of cruises available on inland U.S. waters for *Changing Times,* and a series of magazine features I developed for *Better Homes and Gardens* in which writers and photographers followed real couples and families on a series of trips to vacation destinations and reported first hand on their experiences and impressions.

"An area of continuing research: overlooked people, events and ideas that have had significant if unrecognized influence on the way we think. An outgrowth of this work is my interest and writing on leisure lifestyles, especially the impact of TV (still essentially leisure equipment) and pleasure travel on our lives."

BIOGRAPHICAL/CRITICAL SOURCES: Wall Street Journal, August 7, 1973.

* * *

PLUMB, Barbara Louise Brown 1934-

PERSONAL: Born April 22, 1934, in Pittsburgh, Pa.; daughter of Earle Alfred and Louise (Graham) Brown; married William Lansing Plumb, October 8, 1955 (divorced); children: Christian Chamberlain. *Education:* Attended Denison University, 1951-53; Cornell University, B.A., 1955. *Home:* 108 East 86th St., New York, N.Y. 10028. *Office:* 641 Lexington Ave., New York, N.Y. 10022.

CAREER: Woman's Day, editorial assistant, 1955; Eves Advertising Agency, copywriter, 1955; Walker Scott Department Store, copywriter, 1956-57; British School of Milan, Milan, Italy, teacher of English, 1957-59; *Interiors,* assistant editor, 1959-60, associate editor, 1961-62; *New York Times,* New York, N.Y., reporter, 1962-70; *American Home,* architecture and environment editor, 1970—. Editor for Charles Scribner's Sons, 1973—; senior editor at Pantheon Books, 1975—.

WRITINGS: Houses Architects Live In, Viking, 1977. Living editor of *Vogue,* 1975—.

* * *

POLLARD, James E(dward) 1894-1979

OBITUARY NOTICE—See index for *CA* sketch: Born October 25, 1894, in Chambersburg, Pa.; died October 13, 1979, in Columbus, Ohio. Journalist, educator, and author. Pollard was the head of the Ohio State University School of Journalism for almost twenty years. His books include *Principles of Newspaper Management, The Presidents and the Press,* and *William Oxley Thompson: Evangel of Education.* Obituaries and other sources: *Directory of American Scholars,* Volume I: *History,* 6th edition, Bowker, 1974; *Who's Who in America,* 40th edition, Marquis, 1978; *New York Times,* October 16, 1979.

* * *

POLLOCK, Harry 1920-

PERSONAL: Born May 31, 1920, in Opatow, Poland; son of Joseph and Bessie (Grosskopf) Pollock; married Vera Bacal, October 18, 1944; children: Allyn, Sharryn. *Education:* Attended University of Toronto, 1940, 1947-48; exchange student at University of Lodz and Catholic University of Lublin, summer, 1973. *Religion:* Jewish. *Home:* 68 Invermay Ave., Downsview, Ontario, Canada. *Office:* Stong College, York University, Toronto, Ontario, Canada.

CAREER: Free-lance writer, 1945-50; Grosberg, Pollock & Gwartzman Ltd. (advertising agency), Toronto, Ontario, partner, 1950-70; York University, Toronto, lecturer in modern literature and fellow at Stong College, York University, 1969—. Curator of Anglo-Irish collection at McMaster University, 1970-72; director of Hamilton School Theatre Company, 1972. Actor in Toronto; theatrical director; television producer. Gives readings in the United States and Canada; speaker at academic gatherings; consultant. *Member:* Writers Union of Canada, James Joyce Society of Canada (founding president, 1964—), Association of Canadian Television and Radio Artists, Polish Institute of Arts and Sciences in America. *Awards, honors:* Canada Council grants, 1967, 1968, 1969-71, 1976.

WRITINGS: (Editor with Ron Bates) *Litters From Aloft,* McMaster University Press, 1972; *Gabriel* (novel), McGraw, 1975.

Plays: "Yes I Will Yes" (one-act), first produced in Toronto at Central Library Theatre, January 30, 1967; "Night Boat From Dublin" (two-act), first produced in Dublin at Abbey Theatre, June 16, 1969; "The Lass of Aughrim" (one-act), first produced in Toronto at Central Library Theatre, January 20, 1969; "Naughtsy Calves" (one-act), first produced in Toronto at York University, February 12, 1970; "Jacomo de Trieste" (two-act), first produced in Tulsa, Okla., at University of Tulsa, February 26, 1971; "Up From the Pedestal" (two-act), first produced in Hamilton, Ontario, at Wentworth House, November 16, 1971.

Radio documentaries; all for Canadian Broadcasting Corp.: "Profile of James Joyce," aired June 15, 1969; "The Abbey Theatre," March 13, 1971.

Author of "The Penny Dreadful," a television script, produced by Toronto Learning Resources Centre, summer, 1970. Author of play adaptations from the works of James Joyce. Contributor of articles and reviews to magazines and newspapers, including *James Joyce Quarterly.*

WORK IN PROGRESS: A novel, *After the Funferall* (tentative title).

SIDELIGHTS: "A joyous Joycean celebration of style" permeates Pollock's novel, *Gabriel,* wrote Marq deVilliers. This is not surprising since Pollock is the founder and president of the Canadian James Joyce Society and guardian of the Anglo-Irish collection at McMaster University. There his internationally known "dramatizations of Joycean esoterica are still famous," noted de Villiers.

BIOGRAPHICAL/CRITICAL SOURCES: Toronto Globe, February 15, 1964, May 11, 1967, May 31, 1969, April 19, 1971, April 29, 1971, May 7, 1971, August 10, 1971, August 19, 1971, November 8, 1975; *Toronto Telegram,* February 18, 1964, June 12, 1964, November 20, 1964, October 7, 1965, June 24, 1966, November 28, 1966, January 6, 1968; *Toronto Star,* December 1, 1964, August 21, 1965, January 27, 1967, December 6, 1967, October 22, 1968, January 21, 1969, February 6, 1970, August 5, 1970, March 22, 1971, March 27, 1971, November 15, 1975; *Performing Arts in Canada,* spring, 1966; *London Daily Telegraph,* June 16, 1967; *Sunday Times,* June 18, 1967; *Toronto Life,* April, 1969; *Macleans,* June, 1969; Canadian Broadcasting Corporation (CBC) *Times,* June 14, 1969; *Tulsa World,* March 2, 1971; *Hamilton Spectator,* May 7, 1971, September 8, 1971, December 10, 1975; *Chicago Sun Times,* January, 1976; *Quill and Quire* (Canada), January, 1976; *Washington Star,* January 22, 1976.

* * *

PORSCHE, Ferdinand 1909-
(Ferry Porsche)

PERSONAL: Born September 19, 1909, in Wiener Neustadt, Austria; son of Ferdinand and Aloysia Johanna (Kaes) Porsche; married Dorothea Reitz, January 10, 1935; children: Ferdinand, Gerhard, Peter, Wolfgang. *Education:* Attended high school in Stuttgart, Germany (now West Germany). *Home:* 48 Feuerbacher Weg, Stuttgart 1, West Germany. *Office:* F. Porsche A. G., Porschestrasse 15-19, D-7140 Ludwigsburg, West Germany.

CAREER: Bosch (factory), Stuttgart, Germany, apprentice engineer, 1928-30; F. Porsche A.G., Stuttgart, 1930—, junior chief, 1930-34, head of research, 1934-38, assistant manager, 1938-49, managing director, 1949-72, president and head of board of directors, 1972—. *Awards, honors:* Order of Grosses Bundesverdienstkreuz, 1959; Doctor-Ingenieur from Technische Hochschule Vienna, 1965; Grosses Goldenes Ehrenzeichen of Austria, 1975.

WRITINGS: (Under name Ferry Porsche; with John Bentley) *We at Porsche,* Doubleday, 1976.

SIDELIGHTS: Porsche teamed with John Bentley and wrote *We at Porsche* after Bentley suggested Porsche's life story would interest the public.

BIOGRAPHICAL/CRITICAL SOURCES: New York Times Book Review, September 12, 1976.

* * *

PORSCHE, Ferry
See PORSCHE, Ferdinand

* * *

POST, Emily Price 1873-1960

OBITUARY NOTICE: Born October 3, 1873, in Baltimore, Md.; died September 25, 1960. Novelist, columnist, and author of books on etiquette. Post was social arbiter of the United States for nearly forty years. Born to wealth and social position, Post had penned several novels concerning elegant Americans living abroad before being persuaded by her publisher to write her best-known book, *Etiquette,* in 1922. The book sold half a million copies, went through numerous revisions, and established Post as an authority on manners and social customs. Post became a radio speaker and daily columnist, with her articles on good taste syndicated in nearly two hundred newspapers. Among her works are *The Flight of the Moth, Purple and Fine Linen, The Personality of a House,* and *Children Are People.* Obituaries and other sources: *Current Biography,* Wilson, 1941, November, 1960; *New York Times,* September 27, 1960; *Newsweek,* October 10, 1960; *Time,* October 10, 1960; *The Oxford Companion to American Literature,* 4th edition, Oxford University Press, 1965; *The Reader's Encyclopedia,* 2nd edition, Crowell, 1965.

* * *

POSTGATE, Raymond (William) 1896-1971

OBITUARY NOTICE—See index for *CA* sketch: Born November 6, 1896, in Cambridge, England; died March 25, 1971, in England. Journalist, civil servant, publisher, and author. Postgate, who had been editor of several left wing publications, founded the Good Food Club in 1950 and was the publisher of *The Good Food Guide to Britain.* He was credited with raising the standards of British restaurants. Postgate was the author of over forty books on British unions, history, and cuisine. Obituaries and other sources: *Twentieth Century Writing: A Reader's Guide to Contemporary Literature,* Transatlantic, 1969; *Longman Companion to Twentieth Century Literature,* Longman, 1970; *The Penguin Companion to English Literature,* McGraw, 1971; *AB Bookman's Weekly,* May 24, 1971; *The Author's and Writer's Who's Who,* 6th edition, Burke's Peerage, 1973; *Encyclopedia of Mystery and Detection,* McGraw, 1976.

* * *

POUND, Arthur 1884-1966

OBITUARY NOTICE: Born June 1, 1884, in Pontiac, Mich.; died January 14, 1966. Journalist, author, and historian. Contributor of the "Iron Man" papers to the *Atlantic Monthly,* Pound was later associate editor and then editor of that magazine. He also served as associate editor of the *Independent* and as editorial writer for the *New York Evening Post* and *New York Herald.* The official historian for the state of New York for four years, Pound was the founder and first president of the Society for Colonial History. His writings include *The Iron Man in Industry, Native Stock, Detroit: Dynamic City,* and *Lake Ontario.* Obituaries and other sources: *Who Was Who in America,* 4th edition, Marquis, 1968; *Americans Authors and Books: 1640 to the Present Day,* 3rd revised edition, Crown, 1972.

* * *

POWELL, (Drexel) Dwane (Jr.) 1944-

PERSONAL: Born November 7, 1944, in Lake Village, Ark.; son of Drexel Dwane (in business) and Minnie Louise (Ruth) Powell; married Janis Sue Lovell, April 10, 1971. *Education:* Arkansas A & M University (now University of Arkansas at Monticello), B.S.A., 1970. *Politics:* "Gadfly." *Home:* 2614 Wells Ave., Raleigh, N.C. 27608. *Office: Raleigh News and Observer,* Raleigh, N.C. 27602.

CAREER: Worked as reporter and cartoonist for Palmer News Media, *San Antonio Light,* and *Cincinnati Enquirer; Raleigh News and Observer,* Raleigh, N.C., editorial cartoonist, 1975—. Work exhibited at Southeastern Center for

Contemporary Art. *Military service:* National Guard, 1965-70. *Member:* Association of American Editorial Cartoonists. *Awards, honors:* Citation of excellence from Overseas Press Club of America, 1977; National Headliners Award from National Headline Club, 1977, for editorial cartoons.

WRITINGS: Is That All You Do? (cartoons), Book Division (Raleigh News and Observer), 1978. Editorial cartoons are distributed by Los Angeles Times Syndicate to newspapers all over the United States.

SIDELIGHTS: Powell's career as an editorial cartoonist began at the height of the "Watergate era," which proved to be a rich source of material for his work. But his cartoons are not limited to political figures alone; one depicts evangelist Billy Graham dialing a wall-safe mounted behind a picture of Jesus. *Avocational interests:* Playing guitar.

BIOGRAPHICAL/CRITICAL SOURCES: Cincinnati Enguirer, December 29, 1974; *Arkansas Gazette,* May 21, 1978; *Spectator* (Raleigh, N.C.), February 7, 1979.

* * *

POWNALL, David 1938-

RESIDENCE: South Africa.

CAREER: Novelist and playwright.

WRITINGS—All novels, except as noted: *The Raining Tree War,* Faber, 1974; *African Horse,* Faber, 1975; *The Dream of Chief Crazy Horse,* Faber, 1975; *My Organic Uncle, and Other Stories,* Faber, 1976; *God Perkins,* Faber, 1977; *Light on a Honeycomb,* Faber, 1978.

Plays: "All the World Should be Taxed", first produced in Lancaster, England, at The Duke's Playhouse, December 27, 1971; *Music to Murder by: A Play,* Faber, 1978.

SIDELIGHTS: Farce, satire, and comedy are the concerns of Pownall. According to Peter Ackroyd, *The Raining Tree War* "is a very funny first novel . . . which turned Africa's 'Liberation' into the material of farce at the same time as it brought the native breed into a new and sympathetic light." With characters like Maud Mamuntu, "six foot nine and a half inches of magnificant mammalian prophetess," Tarzan Cool-Guy the wrestler, and "Bwana Arse" the French aviator, Pownall "is not satirizing the black races themselves," Ackroyd remarked, "but rather the Western idea of them." And though the *Times Literary Supplement* recommended "greater technical sophistication," it found the book well stocked with "belly-laughs": "Mr. Pownall's sense of fun [is] obviously wide-ranging."

Another book, *African Horse,* "is Swiftian in its sharpness," observed H. B. Mallalieu. It describes, he thought, "the atmosphere in an emergent black nation as self-seeking, as ridiculous, as incompetent as its former rulers." Around the hero Hurl Halfcock's search for identity amid sexual, political, and alcoholic adventures, emerges a comic version of Africa. In its strong and humorous contradictions, "this 'Cradle of Man,' this 'Garden of Eden,' is both mother and spoiler, both violent and serene," Ackroyd noted. "In spite of the craziness, the goonery, the cruelty even," Mallalieu remarked, "a compassion comes through." Ackroyd concluded: "*African Horse* is the only novel to bring this puzzling life into the light without pomposity or the slow, grinding tedium of 'serious' novels."

With *God Perkins* the setting shifts to England in a "knockabout farce" of the theatre world. The story largely concerns the intrigues of those in a theatre company who contend for the influential manager's support. Ackroyd observed: "No comic novel is complete without its great set-scenes, when a whole dizzy edifice of coincidence and farce is suddenly made transparent—like water turning into ice, just for a second. Pownall contrives these moments with great care, skating easily over the fine boundary which divides old-fashioned English farce from old-fashioned English satire." A particularly effective scene, John Mellors reported, is the frustrated writer's attempt to commit suicide. "He climbs to a mountain tarn, puts on the leotard he had worn when 'forced to join the morning session of eurythmics and voice training,' and thrusts stones inside the garment until he bulges at every limb and looks like 'a human cairn.'" Wrote Peter Prince, "fans of freewheeling farce should certainly feel they have been taken a full fifteen rounds by *God Perkins.*"

As Eric Korn suggested, *Light on a Honeycomb* seems to proceed on the assumption that "all the world's mad except me and thee." The chief industry of Rougerossbergh is its insane asylum, where "doom-inspired Dr. Zander" encounters both the certified and uncertified mad. In the town reside Sir Alphonse Bourge who contrives plans for spray-on carpets and tidal power; the Class War Action Syndicate, composed of squatters, pot-heads, junior reporters, sociology students, and Marxist actors; a tycoon who, in love with the land, has sex with a trench; murderous bouncers from the Paradise Ballroom; and a yoga center operator who dreams of establishing a Western Europeanization Centre in Delhi. "Insanity impregnates the town like the smell from a brewery," Korn remarked. Only Kevin, a patient on leave from the asylum, and his friend Arnold are capable of challenging the town's lunacy. "Dr. Zander has told Kevin that a little bit of Creation will do him good," related Korn, "and literal-minded Kevin sets about replaying Genesis I with a tape-recorder. . . . It is not long before the creatures of Kevin's elaborate alternative universe come boiling up from the underground caverns where they have been thrust away for generations." "The result," as John Mellors remarked, "is fantasy run wild and a plot that defies precis." Korn concluded: "With a little assistance from the Class War Action Syndicate, a satisfactorily demented crescendo is achieved, a comic inferno of considerable unexpectedness and verve."

BIOGRAPHICAL/CRITICAL SOURCES: Observer, June 30, 1974, July 27, 1975, September 19, 1976, March 27, 1977, June 26, 1977, January 1, 1978; *Spectator,* July 6, 1974, July 26, 1975, October 2, 1976, March 12, 1977, June 17, 1978; *Times Literary Supplement,* August 2, 1974, July 25, 1975, September 24, 1976, March 11, 1977, June 30, 1978; *Listener,* March 17, 1977, June 15, 1978; *Contemporary Literary Criticism,* Volume 10, Gale, 1979.*

* * *

POYNTER, Dan(iel Frank) 1938-

PERSONAL: Born September 17, 1938, in New York, N.Y.; son of William Frank (a sales engineer) and Josephine (a newspaper columnist; maiden name, Thompson) Poynter. *Education:* Attended University of the Pacific, 1957-59; Chico State College, B.A., 1960; graduate study at San Francisco Law School, 1961-62. *Home address:* Route 1, Goleta, Calif. 93017. *Office address:* P.O. Box 4232, Santa Barbara, Calif. 93103.

CAREER: Paladin Sport Parachutes, Oakland, Calif., manager, 1962-64; Tri-State Parachute Company, Flemington, N.J., general manager, 1964-65; Parachutes Incorporated, Orange, Mass., sales manager, 1965-66; Strong Enterprises, Inc., North Quincy, Mass., parachute design specialist,

1967-73; Parachuting Publications, owner, North Quincy, 1969-74, Santa Barbara, Calif., 1974—; writer. *Military service:* U.S. Army Reserve, 1956-64. *Member:* American Institute of Aeronautics and Astronautics, National Aeronautics Association, National Pilots Association, United States Parachute Association (former secretary; member of board of directors, 1966—), United States Hang Glider Association, Aviation/Space Writers Association, Survival and Flight Equipment Association.

WRITINGS—All published by Parachuting Publications: *I-E Course: For Parachuting Instructor/Examiner Candidates,* 1971; *The Parachute Manual: A Technical Treatise on the Parachute,* 1972; *Hang Gliding: The Basic Handbook of Skysurfing,* 1974; *Manned Kiting: The Basic Handbook of Tow Launched Hang Gliding,* 1974; *Hang Gliding Manual and Log: A Basic Text for the Novice,* 1976; *Parachuting Manual and Log: A Text for the Novice,* 1976; *Parachute Rigging Course: A Course of Study for the FAA Rigger Certificate,* 1977; *Parachuting: The Skydivers' Handbook,* 1978; (with Mark Danna) *Frisbee Players' Handbook,* 1978; *The Self-Publishing Manual: How to Write, Print, and Sell Your Own Book,* 1979. Author of column, "Parachuting Poynters," in *Parachutist,* 1963—. Contributor of numerous aviation articles to periodicals, including *Skydiver, COSMEP Newsletter, Publishers Weekly,* and *Frisbee World.* Editor of *The Spotter,* 1965-74.

WORK IN PROGRESS: Aviation and publishing material.

SIDELIGHTS: An experienced parachutist with over twelve hundred jumps to his credit, Dan Poynter was a member of the U.S. Parachute Team delegation to Bulgaria in 1966, Germany in 1975, and Australia in 1977, has served as judge, equipment inspector, and jury president of the National Parachuting Championships since 1964, and has directed the Lake Placid Meet since 1967. He has earned the rating of instructor/examiner in the U.S. Parachute Association. In addition, Poynter has earned his Gold Wings as a pilot of both planes and gliders.

Poynter's books contain detailed information on numerous aspects of parachuting, hang gliding, and kiting. *Hang Gliding,* for example, covers such topics as ridge, wave, thermal, and dynamic soaring, launching, competition, accidents, public relations, group flights, legalities, construction details, plus a complete description of all materials needed for building a hang glider and a list of their sources. The book has been billed "the Bible of hang gliding."

Poynter told *CA:* "My writing career began with magazine articles. They helped me to develop an expertise as well as a writing style. The first book, *The Parachute Manual,* required eight years to research and draft. Since no publisher would be interested in such an obscure subject, it was self-published. This unique treatise sells at the rate of one thousand copies per year and has been revised. In 1973, the sport of hang gliding was being reborn. Unable to find a book on the subject, I wrote *Hang Gliding.* So far, it has been through the press nine times for 125,000 in print and there are two printings of a German edition. After that the book output accelerated to as many as two per year while all the other books were being revised as they came up for reprinting. All books were self-published except for the four translations. Noting my successes in publishing, many people asked for the secrets. To comply with their demands, I wrote *The Self-Publishing Manual* in 1979; it was self-published, of course.

"My publishing successes should be attributed to my marketing insight rather than to any literary ability. For years I wrote about aviation sports and served on the boards of the national and international sport aviation organizations. More recently, I've been applying all I have learned to the production and politics of publishing. Publishing is exciting and fun. Book marketing is stimulating—and easy if you don't do it the traditional New York way.

"I enjoy publishing and marketing my written wares. The information is useful and enjoyed by others while it provides a good living for me."

* * *

PRANCE, Claude A(nnett) 1906-

PERSONAL: Born June 28, 1906, in Portsmouth, England; son of Edgar Henry and Clara (Annett) Prance; married Patricia Dorothy Searle, March 29, 1932; children: Romaine Linnell Prance Temple, Jon. *Education:* Attended private schools in Southsea, England. *Home:* Il-Mejda Tal-Gordan, Wied Il-Ghasri, Gozo, Malta.

CAREER: Midland Bank Ltd., England and Wales, various positions in branch banking, including head of securities department and branch manager, 1923-41, 1946-50, manager's assistant in intelligence department, 1950-57, assistant manager in public relations department and bank advertising manager, both 1958-66; full-time writer, 1966—. *Military service:* Royal Air Force, 1941-46; served in England, North Africa, and the Middle East; became flight lieutenant. *Member:* Institute of Bankers (associate), Chartered Institute of Secretaries (associate), Charles Lamb Society, Private Libraries Association, Society for Theatre Research, National Book League, Selborne Society, Keats-Shelley Association of America.

WRITINGS: Peppercorn Papers (essays), Golden Head Press, 1965; *The Laughing Philosopher* (essays), Villiers, 1976; (with Frank P. Riga) *Index to the London Magazine,* Garland Publishing, 1978. Contributor to *Crowell's Reader's Encyclopaedia of English Literature.* Contributor to magazines.

WORK IN PROGRESS: A Companion to Charles Lamb, publication expected in 1980; *Who's Who in Peacock,* a guide to the novels of Thomas Love Peacock.

SIDELIGHTS: Prance's *Peppercorn Papers* and *The Laughing Philosopher* are collections of essays on such diverse subjects as eighteenth-century bookselling, books on cricket, and a host of minor poets and writers. Peter Stockham noted that the "pleasure of the book is its wide variety of essays, all having a gently civilized, nostalgic atmosphere, aimed at a bookish audience one is delighted to know still exists." A *Book Collector* critic recommended *The Laughing Philosopher* as a "bedside book, although the admirable index may keep you awake by leading you from one bit of Mr. Prance's well-stocked mind to another."

Prance wrote: "My life-long interest has been the study of English literature, particularly that of the early nineteenth century. Although for many years occupied in the world of finance, this love of literature instilled into me at school and at first a spare time, but absorbing, hobby, turned when opportunity permitted into a full time occupation. The desire and compulsion to write about books and things that interested me had always been great and this was further stimulated by the fortunate and life-long habit of frequenting antiquarian booksellers' shops and bookstalls where the material to fan this flame was found. Enthusiasm I consider one of the greatest inducements to work.

"The desire for self-expression is perhaps one of the strongest spurs to my work, which starting as a hobby, naturally took the subject which interested me most, and has led, I believe, to relative stability and contentment of mind.

"Although fashions in writing and style change from time to time, my own admiration is entirely for the writer whose style is simple and clear and whose meaning can in no way be misconstrued. Hard though it is to achieve such a style, it has been my aim, for I have no sympathy or understanding for the writer whose work is obscure, or who writes jargon, however erudite it may appear at first glance. After all the purpose of writing is generally communication to another and this is defeated if the reader is left in doubt as to the meaning.

"*Index to the London Magazine,* published in 1978 and which I wrote jointly with Dr. Frank P. Riga, was the result of ten years highly dedicated collaboration, and quite a few years of separate research before we found that we were both working on the same subject, one in Europe and the other in U.S.A. For me the subject followed naturally out of my interest in early nineteenth-century literature, a desire to fill a gap in it and to add to the existing knowledge of the authors of that period.

"I consider writing to be one of the greatest pleasures of my life."

AVOCATIONAL INTERESTS: World travel.

BIOGRAPHICAL/CRITICAL SOURCES: Book Collector, winter, 1977; *British Book News,* January, 1977.

* * *

PRATT, J(oseph) Gaither 1910-1979

OBITUARY NOTICE—See index for *CA* sketch: Born August 31, 1910, in Winston-Salem, N.C.; died November 3, 1979, in Virginia. Parapsychologist, educator, and author of books in his field. Pratt worked as a research associate at Duke University's Parapsychology Laboratory and at the University of Virginia, Charlottesville. One of the primary goals of his life was to dispel the skepticism and ignorance surrounding the study of extrasensory perception and psychokinesis. To this end, he published such books as *Handbook for Testing Extrasensory Perception, Parapsychology: Frontier Science of the Mind,* and *Parapsychology: An Insider's View of ESP.* Obituaries and other sources: *Current Biography,* Wilson, 1964; *Washington Post,* November 8, 1979.

* * *

PRESSMAN, David 1937-

PERSONAL: Born August 9, 1937, in Philadelphia, Pa.; son of Harry (a clothing manufacturer) and Mildred (a songwriter; maiden name, Goldberger) Pressman; married Roberta Briskin (a librarian), February 9, 1968. *Education:* Pennsylvania State University, B.S.E.E., 1959; George Washington University, J.D., 1963. *Office:* 1237 Chestnut St., San Francisco, Calif. 94109.

CAREER: U.S. Patent Office, Washington, D.C., patent examiner, 1961-63; Philco-Ford Corp., Philadelphia, Pa., senior patent attorney, 1963-70; Elco Corp., Willow Grove, Pa., patent counsel, 1970-73; Varian Associates, Inc., Palo Alto, Calif., senior patent attorney, 1973-76; private practice in patent and trademark law, San Francisco, Calif., 1976—. *Member:* International Society for General Semantics, American Natural Hygiene Association, Mensa, San Francisco Vegetarian Society (member of board of trustees), Eta Kappa Nu, Sigma Tau.

WRITINGS: Patent It Yourself!, McGraw, 1979.

SIDELIGHTS: Pressman writes that his book was intended "to help the individual inventor and demystify patent law."

* * *

PRICE, Robert W. 1925(?)-1979

OBITUARY NOTICE: Born c. 1925; died September 11, 1979, in River Vale, N.J. Author, editor, and financial public relations executive. Price was financial news editor of the *New York Herald Tribune.* Obituaries and other sources: *New York Times,* September 15, 1979.

* * *

PRICE, Vincent 1911-

PERSONAL: Born May 27, 1911, in St. Louis, Mo.; son of Vincent Leonard (president of a candy company) and Marguerite Cobb (Wilcox) Price; married Edith Barrett (an actress), 1938 (divorced, 1948); married Mary Grant (a designer), August 28, 1949 (divorced, 1972); married Coral Browne (an actress), 1974; children: (first marriage) Vincent B.; (second marriage) Mary Victoria. *Education:* Yale University, B.A., 1933; graduate study at University of London, 1934-35. *Home:* 580 North Beverly Glen, Los Angeles, Calif. 90024. *Office:* 315 South Beverly Dr., Beverly Hills, Calif. 90212.

CAREER: Actor in plays, including "Chicago," 1935, "Victoria Regina," 1935-37, "Outward Bound," 1939-40, "Angel Street," 1941-42, "Cocktail Party," 1951, "Don Juan in Hell," 1952, "The Lady's Not for Burning," 1952, "Darling of the Day," 1968, and "Oliver!," 1974; actor in over one hundred motion pictures, including "Service de Luxe," 1938, "The House of the Seven Gables," 1940, "The Song of Bernadette," 1943, "The Keys of the Kingdom," 1944, "Dragonwyck," 1946, "The Web," 1947, "The Three Musketeers," 1948, "Champagne for Caesar," 1950, "The House of Wax," 1953, "The Ten Commandments," 1956, "The Big Circus," 1959, "House of Usher," 1960, "The Pit and the Pendulum," 1961, "Masque of the Red Death," 1964, "The Abominable Dr. Phibes," 1971, and "Theatre of Blood," 1973. Appeared on radio programs, including "The Saint," 1947-50, and "Lux Radio Theatre"; appeared on over two thousand television shows, including "$64,000 Challenge," "The Man from U.N.C.L.E.," "Hollywood Squares," "Night Gallery," and "The Tonight Show." Lecturer on primitive and modern art and on the letters of Van Gogh at colleges and universities. Member of the board of Archives of American Artists; member of Whitney Museum Friends of American Artists; president of art council of University of California, Los Angeles; member of U.S. Indian Arts and Crafts Board; art consultant to Sears Roebuck & Co.; member of fine arts committee of the White House; member of board of directors of Center for Arts of Indian Affairs; member of advisory committee of Friends of Art, University of Southern California. Narrator of numerous sound recordings.

MEMBER: Royal Society of Art, Actors' Equity Association, Screen Actors Guild, Elizabethan Club, Yale Club. *Awards, honors:* Academy award for documentary from Academy of Motion Pictures Arts and Sciences, 1963.

WRITINGS: I Like What I Know (autobiography), Doubleday, 1959; *The Book of Joe: About a Dog and His Man,* Doubleday, 1961; (editor with Chandler Brossard) *Eighteen Best Stories by Edgar Allan Poe,* Dell, 1965; (with wife, Mary Price) *A Treasury of Great Recipes: Famous Special-*

ties of the World's Foremost Restaurants Adapted for the American Kitchen, Geis, 1965; (with Mary Price) *Mary and Vincent Price Present a National Treasury of Cookery,* compiled by Helen Duprey Bullock, Heirloom Publishing, 1967; (with Mary Price) *Mary and Vincent Price's Come Into the Kitchen Cook Book: A Collector's Treasury of America's Great Recipes,* Stravon, 1969; *Vincent Price: His Movies, His Plays, His Life,* Doubleday, 1978.

Art: (Author of introduction and catalogue notes) *Vincent Price Collects Drawings,* Oakland Art Museum, 1957; (author of introduction) *Drawings of Five Centuries,* Santa Barbara Museum of Art, 1959; (author of introduction) Eugene Delacroix, *Drawings,* Borden, 1966; *The Vincent Price Treasury of American Art,* Country Beautiful, 1972. Also author of introduction, Sears Vincent Price Gallery, *Nineteenth and Twentieth Century European Master Graphics,* [Chicago].

SIDELIGHTS: A star of stage and screen since the age of twenty-four, Vincent Price is now best known for his portrayal of nefarious roles in such horror classics as "House of Wax," "The Fly," and "The Abominable Dr. Phibes." He first entered this genre in 1941 when appearing on Broadway in "Angel Street." Reflecting on his role as a "villainous, smoking-jacketed smoothie," Price commented to Christopher Buckley: "'I came out for my curtain call . . . and the audience just *hissed.* I knew I'd found my niche.'"

Price proceeded to star in numerous films of the macabre. Among his most successful were a series of Edgar Allan Poe stories, including "The House of Usher" and "The Raven." A more recent example is "Theatre of Blood," in which he played a Shakespearean actor who murders drama critics for their harsh reviews and, as Buckley related, "avenges himself on Robert Morley by force-feeding him his two miniature poodles through a funnel."

Though the diabolical seems to be Price's forte, he actually began his early career playing such respectable characters as Prince Albert in "Victoria Regina" and the Reverend William Duke in "Outward Bound." Because of his careful diction he was often mistakenly labeled an Englishman. This plus his suave manner and royal bearing made him a popular and distinguished leading man during the 1940's. Among his more recent roles was that of Oscar Wilde in the one-man show, "Diversions and Delights," in 1978, which one critic called "Price's finest work."

The versatile actor has also starred in "clunkers" like "Abbott and Costello Meet Frankenstein" and "Dr. Goldfoot and the Bikini Machine." But Price does not apologize for these films, which, as he explained to Buckley, he did for "the money, chiefly; that, and a compulsive need to be busy."

In addition to his acting talents, Vincent Price is also considered an art expert. Since his youth, when he bought a Rembrandt etching for $34.50 on the installment plan, Price has added numerous works to his famous art collection and has lectured and written several books on art as well.

AVOCATIONAL INTERESTS: Gourmet cooking, swimming, hiking, collecting drawings and paintings.

BIOGRAPHICAL/CRITICAL SOURCES: Vincent Price, *I Like What I Know* (autobiography), Doubleday, 1959; *New York Times Book Review,* June 6, 1965; *Design,* January, 1966; *Newsweek,* June 14, 1971; Tony Thomas, *Cads & Cavaliers,* Barnes, 1973; *House Beautiful,* November, 1973; David Shipman, *Great Movie Stars,* A & W Visual Library, 1976; John Brosman, *Horror People,* St. Martins, 1976; Vincent Price, *Vincent Price: His Movies, His Plays, His Life,* Doubleday, 1978; *Esquire,* April 25, 1978.*

* * *

PRICHARD, Robert Williams 1923-

PERSONAL: Born May 30, 1923, in Jersey City, N.J.; son of George W. and Mathilde (Engelbrecht) Prichard; married Mary Hellen Blankley, April 6, 1946; children: Claudia Cadman (Mrs. Paul Shepard), Robert Williams, Jr. *Education:* George Washington University, M.D., 1947. *Religion:* Baptist. *Home:* 2751 Club Park Rd., Winston-Salem, N.C. 27104. *Office:* Bowman Gray School of Medicine, Winston-Salem, N.C. 27103.

CAREER: Gallinger Municipal Hospital (now District of Columbia General Hospital), Washington, D.C., rotating intern, 1947-48; Children's Hospital, Boston, Mass., fellow in pathology, 1948-49; New England Deaconess Hospital, Boston, assistant resident in pathology, 1949-50; Presbyterian Hospital, Philadelphia, Pa., resident in pathology, 1950-51; Bowman Gray School of Medicine, Winston-Salem, N.C., instructor, 1951-53, assistant professor, 1953-56, associate professor, 1956-61, professor of pathology, 1961—, head of department, 1973—, director of Clinical Microscopy Laboratory and Blood Bank, 1951-55, director of laboratories, 1957—. Fellow at Peter Bent Brigham Hospital, 1949; assistant instructor at University of Pennsylvania, 1950-51. Senior surgeon for U.S. Public Health Service in Thailand, 1955-57. Director of laboratories and associate pathologist (in surgical pathology) at North Carolina Baptist Hospital, 1957—. Member of board of directors of National Committee for Clinical Laboratory Standards; member of advisory committee of National Institutes of Health Primate Research Centers; consultant to Veterans Administration.

MEMBER: International Academy of Pathology, American Association of Blood Banks (head of ethics committee), American Association for the History of Medicine, American Association of Pathologists and Bacteriologists, American Heart Association, American Medical Association, American Society of Clinical Pathologists, American Society for Experimental Pathology, Council on Arteriosclerosis, North Carolina Literary and Historical Association, North Carolina Medical Society, North Carolina Society of Pathologists, Forsyth County Medical Society, Wachovia Historical Society, Sigma Xi, Alpha Omega Alpha.

WRITINGS: (Contributor) R. G. Siekert, editor, *Cerebrovascular Survey Report,* privately printed, 1970; (contributor) *Animal Models for Biomedical Research III: Proceedings of the National Academy of Sciences,* National Academy of Sciences, 1970; (with R. E. Robinson III) *Twenty Thousand Medical Words,* McGraw, 1972; (with A. Osol, G. Nellhaus, and others) *Blakiston's Gould Medical Dictionary,* 3rd edition (Prichard was not associated with earilier editions), McGraw, 1972. Contributor of more than four hundred articles and reviews to medical journals. Member of editorial board of *North Carolina Medical Journal.*

* * *

PRINCE, Gary Michael 1948-

PERSONAL: Born March 7, 1948, in New York, N.Y.; son of Joseph (a government inspector) and Sue (an office manager; maiden name, Dobson) Prince; married Adrienne Wolin (an elementary school teacher), June 6, 1976; children: Melissa Jo. *Education:* Brandeis University, B.A., 1969; State University of New York Downstate Medical Center, M.D., 1976. *Home and office:* 974 Walnut St., Newton, Mass. 02161.

CAREER: Tufts-New England Medical Center Hospital, Boston, Mass., intern in pediatrics, 1976-77, resident in adult psychiatry, 1977-79; McLean Hospital, Belmont, Mass., fellow in child psychiatry, 1979—.

WRITINGS: Vanya and the Clay Queen (juvenile), Carolrhoda, 1976.

WORK IN PROGRESS: A science fiction novella; short books for children; adapting Zen Buddhist tales to short story form.

SIDELIGHTS: Prince comments: "My interest is predominantly in children. Child psychiatry is my chosen profession."

* * *

PRITIKIN, Nathan 1915-

PERSONAL: Born August 29, 1915, in Chicago, Ill.; son of Jacob I. (in advertising) and Esther (Levitt) Pritikin; married Ilene Robbins (a nutritional consultant); children: Jack, Janet, Robert, Ralph, Kenneth. *Education:* Attended University of Chicago, 1933-35. *Office:* Longevity Research Institute, P.O. Box 5335, Santa Barbara, Calif. 93108.

CAREER: Self-employed in Chicago area, 1935-57, and in Santa Barbara area, 1957-76; Longevity Research Institute, Santa Barbara, Calif., director, 1976—. Director of Longevity Centers in Santa Barbara and Santa Monica, Calif., 1976—. Inventor, with U.S. and foreign patents in chemistry, physics, and electronics; researcher on nutrition, exercise, and degenerative disease.

WRITINGS: (With Jon Leonard and Jack Hofer) *Live Longer Now,* Grosset, 1974; (with Patrick McGrady, Jr.) *The Pritikin Program for Diet and Exercise,* Grosset, 1979; *The Complete Pritikin Program Cookbook,* Grosset, 1980; *The Complete Pritikin Exercise Program,* Grosset, 1980. Contributor to nutrition and medical communications journals.

WORK IN PROGRESS: Books on nutrition and preventive health for all ages; continuing research on nutritional relationships to disease and on nutrition and preventive health.

SIDELIGHTS: Pritikin writes: "The study of degenerative diseases has been my avocation, and since I have never had an employer to control my time, I have spent one quarter of all my working hours reading medical literature. The low incidence of atherosclerotic disease (such as cardiovascular disease, diabetes, hypertension, angina) in populations on low fat diets has been widely observed by many investigators. From this observation, I decided to see if putting people on a low fat, high complex carbohydrates diet would reverse these disease conditions.

"My first study of consequence, which I financed, was a twelve-month trial, very ambitious both in number of participants and in geographic extent. The study was done in 1974 with sixty physicians in twenty-two states and Canada who put two thousand patients on a diet that I designed. Later, I did a study in Long Beach, Calif., far more important because it was a controlled study. After a five-month trial, the results achieved on our diet were dramatic compared with the results on the American Heart Association diet. In addition to all the clinical improvements, the angiographic results indicated reversal of artery closure.

"I presented a paper at the 52nd Annual Session of the American Congress of Rehabilitation Medicine and the 37th Annual Assembly of the American Academy of Physical Medicine and Rehabilitation, in Atlanta, Ga., on November 19, 1975. Because of the very impressive results I reported, the local paper and the wire services gave it national coverage.

"In January, 1976, I opened the Longevity Center with nine patients and six spouses. Since then, because of our dramatic health improvements, such as saving people from bypass surgery, getting them back to health and taking them off medications, more and more patients over the months have come to the Center for our four-week therapy program of diet and exercise. By 1979, almost four thousand patients have been treated in our center, and the results continue to be better than any conventional medical therapy for degenerative diseases.

"In 1978, over six hundred physicians and health professionals attended our scientific meeting and were able to receive ten units of Class I Continuing Medical Education Credit, the same as a physician would receive if he attended an American Heart Association Conference.

"To widely disseminate our findings, I have spoken before many medical schools, hospital staffs, universities, the American Heart Association, and the American College of Cardiology. If I could have four hours of prime-time television, I could change the diet habits of half the people in the United States."

BIOGRAPHICAL/CRITICAL SOURCES: Us, June 28, 1977, May 15, 1979; *Executive,* June, 1979; *New York Times Book Review,* July 1, 1979.

* * *

PROUVOST, Jean 1885-1978

OBITUARY NOTICE: Born April 24, 1885, in Roubaix, France; died October 17, 1978, near Paris, France. Industrialist and newspaper publisher. A multimillionaire textile tycoon, Prouvost was one of France's most successful newspaper publishers for more than fifty years. His holdings included *Paris-Soir,* a paper which became France's most widley circulated daily, and the influential conservative daily, *Figaro.* As director, publisher, and chief editor of *Paris-Match,* he turned a onetime sports periodical into one of the world's finest photo-illustrated news magazines. Financial troubles forced Prouvost to sell his press holdings in 1975. Obituaries and other sources: *Who's Who in the World,* 2nd edition, Marquis, 1973; *The International Who's Who,* Europa, 1974; *New York Times,* November 6, 1978.

* * *

PULLIAM, Eugene C(ollins) 1889-1975

OBITUARY NOTICE: Born May 3, 1889, in Grant County, Kan.; died June 23, 1975, in Phoenix, Ariz. Journalist and newspaper publisher. Pulliam purchased his first newspaper, the *Atchison Champion* in Kansas, at the age of twenty-three. He owned and operated forty-six newspapers during his career, including the *Muncie Evening Press, Arizona Republic,* and *Phoenix Gazette.* A working newsman as well as a publisher, Pulliam's conservative editorials were reprinted extensively and his international reporting trips with his wife, Nina Pulliam, were the subject of a widely syndicated series. Elected to the board of directors of the Associated Press in 1961, Pulliam served the maximum three successive three-year terms. He was honored by an extensive list of prestigious awards, including the John Peter Zenger Award in 1966, an award for journalistic merit from the William Allen White Foundation, and selection to the Indiana Journalism Hall of Fame. He was also honored many times by Sigma Delta Chi, the journalism society he helped found in 1909. Obituaries and other sources: *The International Who's Who,* Europa, 1974; *Who's Who in America,* 38th edition, Marquis, 1974; *New York Times,* June 24, 1975; *Broadcasting,* June 30, 1975; *Time,* July 7, 1975; *Authors in the News,* Volume 2, Gale, 1976.

* * *

PURDY, Theodore Martindale 1903-1979

OBITUARY NOTICE: Born September 22, 1903, in Short Hills, N.J.; died July 12, 1979, in New Milford, Conn. Author, publisher, editor, and executive. Purdy was editor in chief of Appleton-Century-Crofts and G. P. Putnam's Sons. He was also president of Coward, McCann and founder of his own publishing company, Purdy, Carlisle Dodds, Inc. Purdy contributed articles to the *New York Times, Saturday Review,* and the *London Observer*. Obituaries and other sources: *Who's Who in America,* 40th edition, Marquis, 1978; *New York Times,* July 15, 1979; *AB Bookman's Weekly,* August 20, 1979.

Q

QUENTIN, Patrick
See WHEELER, Hugh (Callingham)

* * *

QUILLIGAN, Maureen 1944-

PERSONAL: Born August 16, 1944, in Ann Arbor, Mich.; daughter of J. J., Jr. (a physician) and Estelle (Klosky) Quilligan; married Michael Malone (a novelist), June 17, 1976; children: Margaret Elizabeth. *Education:* University of California, Berkeley, B.A., 1965, M.A., 1967; Harvard University, Ph.D., 1973. *Office:* Department of English, Yale University, New Haven, Conn. 06520.

CAREER: Yale University, New Haven, Conn., assistant professor, 1973-78, associate professor of English, 1978—.

WRITINGS: The Language of Allegory, Cornell University Press, 1979.

WORK IN PROGRESS: Milton's Spenser: The Rhetoric of Reading; a scholarly edition of *The Pylgremage of the Sowle,* a fifteenth-century allegorical dream vision, completion expected in 1985.

* * *

QUISPEL, Gilles 1916-

PERSONAL: Born May 30, 1916, in Rotterdam, Netherlands; son of Bartholomeus (a blacksmith) and Antonia Maria (a teacher; maiden name, Wagenaar) Quispel; married Lien de Langen, December 23, 1944; children: Christine Maria, Louise Henriette, Reinout, Caroline. *Education:* University of Leiden, doctorate in classical languages, 1940; University of Groningen, theology degree, 1942; University of Utrecht, Dr. Class. Litt., 1943. *Politics:* Christian Democrat. *Religion:* Dutch Reformed. *Home:* Noordhoudringelaan 32, Bilthoven, Netherlands. *Office:* Heidelberglaan 2, Utrecht, Netherlands.

CAREER: Teacher of Latin and Greek at secondary schools in Enschede, Netherlands, 1941-45, and Leiden, Netherlands, 1945-51; University of Utrecht, Utrecht, Netherlands, professor of church history, 1952—. Lecturer at Jung Institute, Zurich, 1951—; visiting professor at Harvard University, 1964-65; professor at Catholic University of Louvain, 1969—. *Awards, honors:* Knight of Order of the Netherlands.

WRITINGS: An Unknown Fragment of the Acts of Andrew, North-Holland Publishing, 1956; (with Henri Charles Puech and A. Guillanmont) *The Gospel According to Thomas,* Leiden, 1959; *Gnostic Studies,* Nederlands Historisch-Archaeologisch Institut in het Hebije Oosten, Volume I, 1972, Volume II, 1975; *Tatian and the Gospel of Thomas: Studies in the History of the Western Diatessaron,* E. J. Brill, 1975; *The Sacred Book of Revelation,* McGraw, 1979.

Other: *De bronnen van Tertullianus' Adversus Marcionem* (title means "The Sources of Tertullianus Against Marcion"), Burgersdijk & Niermans, 1943; *M. Minucii Felicis Octavius,* E. J. Brill, 1949, 2nd edition, 1973; (editor and translator) Ptolemaeus Gnosticus, *Lettre a Flora* (title means "Letter to Flora") Editions du Cerf, 1949, 2nd edition, 1966; *Gnosis als Weltreligion: Die Bedeutung der Gnosis in der Antike* (title means "Gnosis as a World Religion") Origo Verlag, 1951, 2nd edition, 1972; (with Henri Charles Puech) *Op zoek naar het Evangelie der waarheid* (title means "The Quest for the Gospel of Truth"), G. F. Callenbach, 1954; *Makarius, das Thomasevangelium und das Lied von der Perle* (title means "Macarius, the Gospel of Thomas and the Hymn of the Pearl"), E. J. Brill, 1967; *Het Evangelie van Thomas en de Nederlanden,* Elsevier, 1971; (contributor) *Jung een mens voor deze tijd* (title means "Jung: A Man of Our Time"), Lemniscaat, 1975; *Mystiek en bevinding* (title means "Mysticism and Experience"), Kok, 1977. Also author of *Tertulliani de testimonio animae: Addictis locis quisbusdam ad naturalem cognitionem pertinentibus in usum academicum* (title means "Passages in Tertullia Concerning the Soul's Knowledge of God"), 1952, and *Tractatus Tripartitus* (title means "The Threefold Treatise"), Volume I, 1973, Volume II, 1975; editor of *Evangelium Veritatis* (title means "The Gospel of Truth"), 1956, supplement, 1961. Contributor to journals.

WORK IN PROGRESS: A History of Early Christianity, publication by McGraw expected in 1983.

SIDELIGHTS: Quispel told *CA:* "It was gratifying to discover afterwards that my stress on the opposition of John the Apocalypticist against tyranny in his Book of Revelation provides a biblical foundation for Pope Wojtyla's action. The new Gnostic writings of Nag Hammadi allow us to give a new interpretation of John, Paul, and Jesus and so of the history of early Christianity. They help Western man to become Gnostic himself and so renounce dualism. They reveal that Judaism at the beginning of our era was much broader and livelier than subsequent rabbinical Judaism. If we want to remain Christians we need a new theology which must make clear that Jesus came to bring freedom to all mankind.''

R

RACHMAN, Stanley Jack 1934-
(Jack Durac)

PERSONAL: Born in 1934, in Johannesburg, South Africa; son of Harry (a violinist) and Tasha (a cellist; maiden name, Altuska) Rachman; married Clare Philips (a university lecturer), December 14, 1969; children: Carla, Gideon, Emily, Tom. *Education:* University of the Witwatersrand, B.A. (honors), 1954, M.A., 1955; University of London, Ph.D., 1961. *Office:* Department of Psychology, Institute of Psychiatry, University of London, De Crespigny Park, London SE5 8AF, England.

CAREER: University of London, Institute of Psychiatry, London, England, lecturer, 1961-67, senior lecturer, 1967-73, reader, 1973-76, professor of abnormal psychology, 1976—. Lecturer at University of the Witwatersrand, 1964-69. *Member:* British Psychological Society.

WRITINGS: (Editor) *Critical Essays on Psychoanalysis,* Pergamon, 1961; (with H. J. Eysenck) *Causes and Cures of Neurosis,* Routledge & Kegan Paul, 1965; *Phobias: Their Nature and Control,* C. C Thomas, 1968; (with John Teasdale) *Aversion Therapy and the Behaviour Disorders,* Routledge & Kegan Paul, 1969; (with Jaog Bergold) *Verhaltenstherapie bei Phobien* (title means "Behavioral Treatment of Phobias"), Urban & Schwarzenberg, 3rd edition, 1972; *The Meanings of Fear,* Penguin, 1974; (with wife, Clare Philips) *Psychology and Medicine,* Temple Smith, 1974; (editor) *Contributions to Medical Psychology,* Pergamon, Volume I, 1977, Volume II, 1980; *Fear and Courage,* W. H. Freeman, 1978; (with Philips) *Psychology and Behavioral Medicine,* Cambridge University Press, 1979; (with Raymond Hodgson) *Obsessions and Compulsions,* Prentice-Hall, 1979; (with G. T. Wilson) *The Effects of Psychological Therapy,* Pergamon, 1980.

Under pseudonym Jack Durac: *Wines,* Dutton, 1973; *The Art of Tasting,* Dutton, 1974; *A Matter of Taste,* Deutsch, 1974, new edition published as *A Matter of Taste and Tasting,* Magnum Books, 1979. Editor of *Behaviour Research and Therapy,* 1963—.

SIDELIGHTS: Rachman expressed a desire to eventually devote nearly as much time to writing about wines as he does about scientific matters.

RACKER, Efraim 1913-

PERSONAL: Born June 28, 1913, in Neu Sandez, Poland; came to the United States in 1941, naturalized citizen, 1974; married Franziska Weiss (a physician), August 24, 1945; children: Ann Racker Costello. *Education:* University of Vienna, M.D., 1938. *Home:* 305 Brookfield Rd., Ithaca, N.Y. 14850. *Office:* Section of Biochemistry, Molecular and Cell Biology, Wing Hall, Cornell University, Ithaca, N.Y. 14853.

CAREER: Cardiff Mental Hospital, Cardiff, Wales, research assistant in biochemistry, 1938-40; University of Minnesota, Minneapolis, research associate in physiology, 1941-42; Harlem Hospital, New York City, began as intern, became pneumonia resident and fellow, 1942-44; New York University, New York City, assistant professor of microbiology, 1944-52; Yale University, New Haven, Conn., associate professor of biochemistry, 1952-54; Public Health Research Institute of the City of New York, New York City, chief of Division of Nutrition and Physiology, 1954-66; Cornell University, Ithaca, N.Y., Albert Einstein Professor of Biochemistry, 1966—, head of section on biochemistry and molecular biology, 1966-70. Adjunct professor at New York University-Bellevue Medical Center, 1954-66; Robbins Lecturer at Pomona College, 1973; Christian A. Herter Lecturer at New York University Medical Center, 1975; Sir Frederick Gowland Hopkins Memorial Lecturer at University of Liverpool, 1975; Walker-Ames Lecturer at University of Washington, 1977. Head of board of scientific counselors at Cancer Institute, 1975-76.

MEMBER: American Society of Biological Chemists, American Academy of Arts and Sciences, American Association for the Advancement of Science, Harvey Society, British Biochemical Society. *Awards, honors:* Warren Triennial Prize from Massachusetts General Hospital, 1974, for contribution to knowledge of the mechanism of oxidative phosphorylation; National Medal of Science from President Jimmy Carter, 1976, for outstanding contributions in the biological sciences.

WRITINGS: (Editor) *Cellular Metabolism and Infections* (symposium), Academic Press, 1954; *Mechanisms in Bioenergetics,* Academic Press, 1965; (editor) *Membranes of Mitochondria and Chloroplasts,* Van Nostrand, 1970; (editor) *Energy Transducing Mechanisms,* University Park Press, 1975; *A New Look at Mechanisms in Bioenergetics,*

Academic Press, 1976; *Science and the Cure of Diseases: Letters to Members of Congress,* Princeton University Press, 1979. Member of editorial board of *Journal of Biological Chemistry,* 1959-72.

WORK IN PROGRESS: Bioenergetics, with G. Schatz, for Scientific American.

SIDELIGHTS: Racker's research interests are mechanism and reconstitution of oxidative phosphorylation and photophosphorylation, mechanism of action and reconstitution of ion pumps, and regulation of energy metabolism in normal and cancer cells.

* * *

RADELET, Louis A(ugust) 1917-

PERSONAL: Born December 10, 1917, in Green Bay, Wis.; son of John B. (a lumber dealer) and Alice C. (Bodart) Radelet; married Elizabeth Grace Delaney, June 20, 1942; children: John, Joseph, Ann, Michael, Timothy, David, Steven, Kevin. *Education:* Attended St. Norbert College, 1935-37; University of Notre Dame, A.B. (cum laude), 1939, M.A., 1947. *Residence:* East Lansing, Mich. *Office:* School of Criminal Justice, Michigan State University, East Lansing, Mich. 48824.

CAREER: University of Notre Dame, Notre Dame, Ind., instructor of sociology, 1946-51; National Conference of Christians and Jews, New York, N.Y., director of Indiana regional office in South Bend, 1948-51, educational director of East Central Division in Detroit, Mich., 1951-52, director of Commission on Community Organizations in New York City, 1952-54, director of national program operations, 1954-59, and national program development, 1959-62; Michigan State University, East Lansing, professor of criminal justice, 1963—. Administrative assistant for St. Joseph County Department of Public Welfare, 1946-48; founder and associate director of National Institute on Police and Community Relations, 1955-63, director, 1963-70; coordinator of National Center on Police and Community Relations, 1965-73; director of Michigan Institute on Community Relations and the Administration of Justice, 1970—. Past vice-president of Council of National Organizations for Adult Education; past member of executive committee of Council of National Organizations for Children and Youth; member of Michigan Commission on Crime, Delinquency, and Criminal Administration, 1966-68. Directs and participates in workshops in the United States and Canada; consultant to President's Commission on Law Enforcement and Administration of Justice and to National Advisory Commission on Civil Disorder. *Military service:* U.S. Army Air Forces, 1941-46; became second lieutenant.

MEMBER: International Association of Chiefs of Police, American Catholic Sociological Society, National Council of Catholic Men, American Association of University Professors, National Association of Intergroup Relations Officials (past vice-president), Adult Education Association, Academy of Criminal Justice Sciences, Society for Values in Higher Education (fellow), Michigan Association of Criminal Justice Educators, Phi Kappa Phi.

WRITINGS: (Editor with A. F. Brandstatter) *Police and Community Relations: A Sourcebook,* Glencoe Press, 1968; (with Hoyt Coe Reed) *The Police and the Community,* two volumes, Glencoe Press, 1973, 3rd edition, 1980. Contributor to criminal justice journals.

SIDELIGHTS: "Every serious issue in criminal justice involves community responsibility and the need for a community response," commented Radelet. "Communities have not yet made up their minds whether they want their police to be primarily crook-chasers or primarily peace officers using wide discretion in prevention of crime and disorder."

* * *

RADLEY, Gail 1951-

PERSONAL: Born May 21, 1951, in Boston, Mass.; daughter of Earl Adrian (a government employee) and Bernice (a social worker; maiden name, Howell) Radley; married Joseph Killeen (director of a community corrections center), July 23, 1975; children: Anthony, Jana. *Education:* Attended Boston University, 1970-72, Kent State University, 1973, and College of Notre Dame of Maryland, 1978—. *Politics:* "Not aligned." *Religion:* Baha'i. *Home and office:* 4905 Roller Rd., Millers, Md. 21107.

CAREER: Arlington Hospital, Arlington, Va., electrocardiograph technician, 1974-75; Great Oaks Center, Silver Spring, Md., health assistant, 1975; Springfield Hospital Center, Sykesville, Md., rehabilitation therapy associate, 1976; writer, 1976—.

WRITINGS: The Night Stella Hid the Stars (juvenile), Crown, 1979.

WORK IN PROGRESS—For children: *Carrie; Megan's Darkest Secret;* a third novel; "subjects explored in these books include the remarriage of a parent, the imprisonment of a parent, and the romantic involvement between a teacher and a student."

SIDELIGHTS: Gail Radley comments: "The single most profound influence on my life has been the Baha'i faith, which has brought me closer to the universe, to other people, and to myself. I have been a member since the age of fifteen.

"Present circumstances allow me to stay home and write, raise the kids, and take courses for a degree in photography.

"I'm currently interested in novels for older children which deal with the real and difficult issues they may face. Preteens are on the verge of a new awakening. They are trying to make sense of the world, to understand it, often while wading through some tough problems. They need to know that they are not alone, that there are answers."

BIOGRAPHICAL/CRITICAL SOURCES: Booklist, December 15, 1978; *Sykesville Herald Record,* December 27, 1978, May 30, 1979.

* * *

RAINEY, Bill G. 1926-
(Buck Rainey)

PERSONAL: Born July 18, 1926, in Oklahoma City, Okla.; son of Laurence G. (a plumber) and Violet (a social worker; maiden name, Burns) Rainey; married Rosalva Alvarez (a teacher), December 26, 1951; children: Rex Gordon, Tim Wayne, Ken Layne. *Education:* Southeastern Oklahoma State University, B.A., 1952, B.S., 1956; East Texas State University, M.E., 1955; North Texas State University, M.B.E., 1960; University of Oklahoma, Ed.D., 1964. *Politics:* "Registered Democrat—quite often vote Republican." *Religion:* Methodist. *Home and office:* 808 South Ohio, Tishomingo, Okla. 73460.

CAREER: High school business administration teacher in Broadus, Mont., 1952-54, and Cooper, Tex., 1954-55; Murray State College, Tishomingo, Okla., instructor and head of business department, 1955-65; East Central University, Ada,

Okla., associate professor, 1965-70, professor of business education, 1970—, head of department, 1965—. *Military service:* U.S. Navy, 1944-46; served in Pacific Theater. *Member:* National Education Association, National Business Education Association, Western Writers of America, National Cowboy Hall of Fame, Oklahoma Education Association. *Awards, honors:* Silver Beaver Award from Boy Scouts of America.

WRITINGS—All under name Buck Rainey: *The Saga of Buck Jones,* Western Film Collectors Press, 1975; *The Fabulous Holts,* Western Film Collectors Press, 1976; (editor with Charles W. Harris) *The Cowboy: Six-Shooters, Songs, and Sex,* University of Oklahoma Press, 1976; (with Les Adams) *Shoot-Em-Ups,* Arlington House, 1978; *Saddle Aces of the Cinema,* A. S. Barnes, 1979; (with Harris) *The Cowboys: Bunkhouses, Bordellos, and Big Tops,* University of Oklahoma Press, 1980; (with Adams) *Sweethearts of Sagebrush and Serial,* Arlington House, 1980. Contributor of dozens of articles to education journals and film magazines, including *Films in Review, Screen Thrills,* and *Western Film Collector.*

WORK IN PROGRESS: A book on western film stars, publication by Abrams; a book about western film star Buck Jones, with Adams, publication by Yesterday's Saturdays.

SIDELIGHTS: Rainey writes: "My motivation is to preserve the memory of the 'B' western and serial films of the period from 1910 to 1952. In those years thousands of boys grew up unashamed to have the movie cowboys as their heroes. That fabulous period of Hollywood history is worth cherishing and remembering forever. Through my research and the recollections of forty-five years spent in darkened theaters watching shoot-em-ups and cliffhangers, I'm trying to make a small contribution to the preservation of the memory of the Hollywood that was."

* * *

RAINEY, Buck
See RAINEY, Bill G.

* * *

RAM, Immanuel
See VELIKOVSKY, Immanuel

* * *

RAND, Austin Loomer 1905-

PERSONAL: Born December 16, 1905, in Kennville, Nova Scotia, Canada; son of Stanley Bayard and Carrie (Forsythe) Rand; married Rheua Medden, August 15, 1931; children: Austin Stanley, William Medden. *Education:* Acadia University, B.Sc., 1927; Cornell University, Ph.D., 1931. *Home address:* R.R.6, Box 447, Lake Placid, Fla. 33852. *Office:* Archbold Biological Station, Lake Placid, Fla. 33852.

CAREER: American Museum of Natural History, New York, N.Y., staff member, 1929-37, research associate, 1937-41; National Museums of Canada, Ottawa, Ontario, staff member, 1942-45, acting chief of Division of Biology, 1945-47; Field Museum of Natural History, Chicago, Ill., curator of birds, 1947-54, chief curator of zoology, 1955-70; Archbold Biological Station, Lake Placid, Fla., research associate, 1971—, vice-president of Archbold Expeditions, vice-president of board of directors, 1976—. Participated in expeditions to the Philippines, Madagascar, Dutch New Guinea, and Central America. *Member:* American Ornithologists Union (fellow; president, 1962-64), American Society of Mammalogists. *Awards, honors:* D.Sc. from Acadia University, 1961.

WRITINGS: (With Richard Archbold) *New Guinea Expedition: Fly River Area, 1936-1937,* first edition, 1940, reprinted, AMS Press, 1976; *List of Yukon Birds and Those of the Canol Road,* E. Cloutier, 1946; *Mammals of the Eastern Rockies and Western Plains of Canada,* E. Cloutier, 1948; *Birds of Southern Alberta,* E. Cloutier, 1948.

(With Rudyerd Boulton) *A Collection of Birds From Mount Cameroon,* Chicago Natural History Museum, 1952; (with Emmet R. Blake) *Birds the World Over, as Shown in Habitat Groups in Chicago Natural History Museum,* Chicago Natural History Museum, 1954; *Social Feeding Behavior of Birds,* Chicago Natural History Museum, 1954; *Stray Feathers From a Bird Man's Desk,* Doubleday, 1955; *American Water and Game Birds,* Dutton, 1956; (with Robert L. Fleming) *Birds From Nepal,* Chicago Natural History Museum, 1957.

(With Melvin Traylor) *Manuel de las aves de El Salvador* (title means "Manual of Birds of El Salvador"), Editorial Universitaria (San Salvador, El Salvador), 2nd edition, 1961; (with wife, Rheua M. Rand) *A Midwestern Almanac: Pageant of the Seasons,* Ronald, 1961; (contributor) Robert Leland Fleming, editor, *Notes on Nepal Birds,* Chicago Natural History Museum, 1961; *Birds in Summer* (juvenile), Encyclopaedia Britannica, 1962; (with E. Thomas Gilliard) *Handbook of New Guinea Birds,* Weidenfeld & Nicolson, 1967, Natural History Press, 1968; *Ornithology: An Introduction,* Norton, 1967; *Birds of North America,* Doubleday, 1971.

Also author of *Distribution and Habits of Madagascar Birds,* 1936; *Development and Enemy Recognition of the Curvebilled Thresher,* 1941; *Mammals of Yukon, Canada,* 1945.

Author of a weekly column, "Nature Notes," 1973—. Author of dozens of museum pamphlets. Contributor to professional journals. Ornithology editor of *Canadian Field Naturalist,* 1942-47.

SIDELIGHTS: Rand comments: "In my youth I was fascinated by birds and geography and wilderness areas, and with writing about them. With college came the study of ecology and taxonomy and behavior. Then came graduate school and finally a chance to go into the tropics for two years. The die was cast. Field work in tropical and rain forest and desert followed, alternated with museum study, then writing accounts of my observations and investigations, for fellow scientists and for the public."

* * *

RAPER, Arthur F(ranklin) 1899-1979

OBITUARY NOTICE—See index for *CA* sketch: Born November 8, 1899, near Lexington, N.C.; died August 10, 1979, in Virginia. Social scientist, government official, and author of books on race relations and rural development. Raper worked as a researcher for the Commission on Interracial Cooperation and the Carnegie-Myrdal Study of the American Negro before taking a post with the U.S. Department of Agriculture. He served as a consultant on agrarian reform to Japan, Southeast Asia, and Iran. Among his books are *The Tragedy of Lynching, Tenants of the Almighty,* and *The Japanese Village in Transition.* Obituaries and other sources: *American Men and Women of Science: The Social and Behavioral Sciences,* 12th edition, Bowker, 1973; *The Writers Directory, 1980-82,* St. Martin's, 1979; *Washington Post,* August 12, 1979.

RAPOPORT, Ron 1940-

PERSONAL: Born August 14, 1940, in Detroit, Mich.; son of Daniel B. (an engineer) and Shirley G. (a teacher) Rapoport; married Joan Zucker (a potter), September 2, 1968; children: Rebecca, Julie. *Education:* Stanford University, B.A., 1962; Columbia University, M.S., 1963. *Residence:* Evanston, Ill. *Office: Chicago Sun-Times,* 401 North Wabash Ave., Chicago, Ill. 60611.

CAREER: Minneapolis Star, Minneapolis, Minn., general assignment reporter, 1963-65; *Sport* (magazine), New York City, associate editor, 1965-66; Associated Press, sportswriter in New York City, 1966-68, and in San Francisco, Calif., 1968-70; *Los Angeles Times,* Los Angeles, Calif., sportswriter, 1970-77; *Chicago Sun-Times,* Chicago, Ill., author of sports column, 1977—. *Military service:* U.S. Army Reserve, 1963-69. *Awards, honors:* National award from Associated Press, 1978, for "Bill Bradley: The Fast-Break Candidate"; journalism awards include first-place award from Illinois Associated Press, 1979, for excellence in sports columns.

WRITINGS: (With Chip Oliver) *High for the Game,* Morrow, 1971; (with Stan Love) *Love in the NBA,* Dutton, 1975; (with Jim McGregor) *Called for Travelling,* Macmillan, 1978.

SIDELIGHTS: Rapoport writes: "Though daily newspaper journalism has changed quite a bit in the fifteen years I have been engaged in it (one big change is that it is now possible to make a reasonable living at it), some things remain the same. A curiosity about the actions and motivations of people and a fondness for sitting down at a typewriter (or these days a computer terminal) and explaining them are basic requirements. Sportswriting continues to intrigue me because the subjects are usually more interesting than city council meetings and less serious than foreign policy discussions. Thus, the stylistic freedom is greater."

* * *

RASOR, Eugene L(atimer) 1936-

PERSONAL: Born January 23, 1936, in Ware Shoals, S.C.; son of Paul W. (a store manager) and Annie (Riley) Rasor; married Claire Franklin (in public relations), December 23, 1957; children: Robin, Lynn, Laura. *Education:* Furman University, A.B., 1958; University of Virginia, M.A., 1965, Ph.D., 1972. *Religion:* Methodist. *Home address:* P. O. Box CC, Emory, Va. 24327. *Office:* Department of History, Emory and Henry College, Emory, Va. 24327.

CAREER: University of Virginia, Charlottesville, assistant professor of naval science, 1962-65; Emory and Henry College, Emory, Va., began as assistant professor, 1965, became associate professor of history, head of department, 1976—. Fellow of Institute of Historical Research, London, 1969-70, 1973; research associate at Indiana University, 1975. Participant in professional meetings. Head of board of directors of People, Inc., 1973-76; member of board of directors of Emory-Glade Community Center, 1969-76; member of Washington County Democratic Committee, 1975—. *Military service:* U.S. Naval Reserve, 1954-77, active duty on destroyers and submarines, 1958-65; became commander.

MEMBER: American Historical Association, Southern Historical Association, Southern Conference on British Studies, Carolinas Symposium on British Studies, Virginia Society of History Teachers, Virginia Consortium for Asian Studies, Rotary Club of Abingdon (president, 1978-79). *Awards, honors:* Grant from Virginia Foundation of Independent Colleges, 1974; McConnell fellowship, summer, 1975.

WRITINGS: Reform in the Royal Navy: A Social History of the Lower Deck, 1850-80, Shoe String, 1976. Also contributor to *New Sources and Changing Interpretations of Naval History.*

* * *

RATTRAY, Everett T. 1932-

PERSONAL: Born July 9, 1932, in Southampton, N.Y.; son of Arnold E. (in newspaper work) and Jeannette (in newspaper work; maiden name, Edwards) Rattray; married Helen Seldon (an editor), July 22, 1960; children: David, Daniel, Bess. *Education:* Dartmouth College, B.A., 1954; Columbia University, M.S., 1958. *Home:* 17 Edwards Lane, East Hampton, N.Y. 11937. *Agent:* Russell & Volkening, Inc., 551 Fifth Ave., New York, N.Y. 10017. *Office: East Hampton Star,* 153 Main St., East Hampton, N.Y. 11937.

CAREER: East Hampton Star, East Hampton, N.Y., editor, 1958-77, publisher, 1977—, author of column, "The Fifth Column." Member of board of directors of Graphics of Peconics, Inc. Member of Fire Island National Seashore Commission, 1964-68. *Military service:* U.S. Navy, 1954-57. *Member:* East Hampton Historical Society (member of board of directors).

WRITINGS: The South Fork: The Land and People of Eastern Long Island, Random House, 1979.

WORK IN PROGRESS: A book on small-town newspaper work, for Random House.

BIOGRAPHICAL/CRITICAL SOURCES: New York Times Book Review, March 18, 1979.

* * *

RAULSTON, J(ames) Leonard 1905-

PERSONAL: Born August 28, 1905, in Marion County, Tenn.; son of William Polk and Jeannette (Bible) Raulston; married Agnes Hicks, November 19, 1932; children: Leonard Polk, Michael McKeever. *Education:* University of Tennessee, B.S., 1930, also studied law; graduate study at Harvard University. *Politics:* Republican. *Religion:* Episcopalian. *Home:* 800 Holly Ave., South Pittsburg, Tenn. 37380; and 420 East Brow Rd., Lookout Mountain, Tenn. 37350.

CAREER: Admitted to the state bar of Tennessee, 1933; personnel director at University of Tennessee during the 1930's; vice-president, then general manager, and chairman of the board of U.S. Stove Co.; president of Orme Coal Co., 1945-78, and Raulston-Pryor Quarries, 1950-79. Member of South Pittsburg City Commission; vice-chairman of board of Blue Cross Blue Shield; director of First Bank of Marion County. Historian of Marion County. Former member of Quarterly Court of Marion County and county judge pro tempore. Member of board of trustees of University of Tennessee; trustee of American Institute of Appliance Manufacturers. Speaker. *Member:* Masons, Kappa Sigma, Omega Delta Kappa, Mountain City Club, Lookout Mountain Fairyland Club, Lookout Mountain Golf Club, Sequachee Valley Country Club. *Awards, honors:* Award of merit from American Association for State and Local History.

WRITINGS: The Raulstons and the Part They Played in American History, privately printed, 1970; (with James W. Livingood) *Sequatchee: A Story of the Southern Cumberlands,* University of Tennessee Press, 1974.

RAWSKI, Evelyn S(akakida) 1939-

PERSONAL: Born February 2, 1939, in Honolulu, Hawaii; daughter of Evan T. and Teruko (Watase) Sakakida; married Thomas George Rawski (an economist), December 16, 1967. *Education:* Cornell University, B.A. (with highest honors), 1961; Radcliffe College, M.A., 1962; Harvard University, Ph.D., 1968. *Office:* Department of History, University of Pittsburgh, Pittsburgh, Pa. 15260.

CAREER: University of Pittsburgh, Pittsburgh, Pa., assistant professor, 1967-73, associate professor of history, 1973—. *Member:* Association for Asian Studies (member of board of directors; member of China Inner Asia Council, 1976-79), Economic History Association. *Awards, honors:* Grant from American Council of Learned Societies, 1973-74; fellowship from National Endowment for the Humanities, 1979-80.

WRITINGS: Agricultural Change and the Peasant Economy of South China, Harvard University Press, 1972; *Education and Popular Literacy in Ch'ing China,* University of Michigan Press, 1979.

WORK IN PROGRESS: Research on China's rural elite, 1840-1957.

* * *

RAYMOND, Diana (Joan) 1916-

PERSONAL: Born April 25, 1916, in London, England; daughter of William Thomas and Hilda Joan (an artist; maiden name, Drummond-Black) Young; married Ernest Raymond (a writer), August, 1940 (died May 14, 1974); children: Peter John Francis. *Education:* Attended private girls' school in Cheltenham, England. *Religion:* Church of England. *Home:* 22 The Pryors, East Heath Rd., London NW3 1BS, England. *Agent:* A. P. Watt Ltd., 26/28 Bedford Row, London WC1R 4HL, England.

CAREER: Office of the Cabinet, London, England, personal assistant, 1937-39; Committee of Imperial Defence, London, personal assistant, 1937-39; Ministry of Food, London, personal assistant, 1939-40; writer, 1936—. *Member:* Society of Authors.

WRITINGS—All novels: *Joanna Linden,* Cassell, 1952; *The Small Rain* (Book Society selection), Cassell, 1954; *Between the Stirrup and the Ground,* Cassell, 1956; *Strangers' Gallery,* Cassell, 1958; *The Five Days,* Cassell, 1959; *Guest of Honour,* Cassell, 1960; *The Climb,* Cassell, 1962; *People in the House,* Cassell, 1964; *The Noonday Sword,* Cassell, 1965; *Front of the House,* Cassell, 1967; (editor) Pamela Frankau, *Colonel Blessington,* Bodley Head, 1968, Delacorte, 1968; *Are You Travelling Alone?,* Cassell, 1969; *The Best of the Day,* Cassell, 1972; *Incident on a Summer's Day,* Cassell, 1974; *Horseman Pass By,* Cassell, 1977; *The Dark Journey,* Cassell, 1978, Scribner, 1979; *Emma Pride,* Cassell, 1980.

SIDELIGHTS: Raymond told *CA:* "Writing is a lonely art. I do not think you choose it; it chooses you. I can not remember a time when I did not want to write. I wrote my first novel at seventeen; it was (mercifully) not published, but my second, written when I was nineteen, was published when I was twenty. Although I find writing hard and have (like many others) to fight the temptation to be distracted by other, less demanding jobs, I do not feel complete unless I *am* writing. I care deeply for words, and find it difficult to leave careless sentences to stand without correction.

"From the beginning I was close to the atmosphere of writing," Raymond recounted. "My cousin Pamela Frankau, a writer eight years older than myself, was a greatly loved and strong influence in my life. When she knew she was very ill, she asked me to help her finish her last novel, *Colonel Blessington.* After her death, which came all too soon, I completed it. And when I married, I married a writer, Ernest Raymond, many years older than myself, and long established as a novelist of high standing. From both Pamela and Ernest I learned a great deal about the novel; in my view there is no end to learning about the art.

"I would hope that what I write expresses for some people an aspect of their experiences, joys or griefs, that makes them say, 'Yes! *This* is what I felt but I could never get it into words.' I believe that emotion, vision, and ideas should be skillfully contained within a story that grips the attention, but still keeps within the bounds of reality.

"My latest book, *The Dark Journey,* deals with the experience of widowhood that I had undergone myself five years ago. I hoped that this book would be of help to those who had also known the experience, and be of interest to those who fortunately had not.

"Those reviews that have most pleased me have been of my book *People in the House.* Richard Church once wrote of the book in *Country Life:* 'The outstanding characteristic of Diana Raymond's work as a novelist is the sagacity with which she feels her way into the personality of her people. . . . Only a novelist of spiritual insight, with the aid of professional skill, could bring [this story] to a convincing resolution.' And Vernon Fane has commented in *Sphere,* '*People in the House* once and for all establishes this author in her right place among English novelists, as an immensely perceptive, sensitive and yet robust chronicler of some of the more familiar aspects of our island story.'

"To the aspiring writer I would say two things: read, read, and read, and learn from what you read, and then write, write, and write. Good or bad, do not stop. Remember Sinclair Lewis's comment: 'Inspiration is applying the seat of the pants to the seat of the chair.'

"The more one learns, the more difficult writing becomes. There is nothing easy about it; the returns depend much upon luck, or some sixth sense which enables you to write the right book at the right time. But luck or no, you must go on. There is much talent about, but less endurance. Both are essential."

Raymond concluded: "It has been said, 'You write what you are.' That is all you can do. As someone else has said, 'Do your best. Someone may like it.'

Raymond's books have been translated into French, Swedish, Spanish, German, Italian, and other languages.

AVOCATIONAL INTERESTS: Travel (Italy, Israel, United States, Spain, Switzerland).

* * *

RAYMOND, Ernest 1888-1974

OBITUARY NOTICE: Born December 31, 1888, in Argentieres, France; died May 14, 1974; buried in Hampstead Cemetery, London, England. Novelist, essayist, playwright, biographer, and author of his memoirs. Two facts about Raymond's early life illuminate the themes that later were examined in his fiction. First, as an illegitimate child who had to ferret out the truth about his own parentage, Raymond frequently wrote about the evil that may hide behind a facade of middle-class respectability. Second, he had been ordained as an Anglican priest and later resigned his holy orders, and thus his books were often concerned with the search for faith and fulfillment. Raymond's first and most popular novel, *Tell England,* was based on his experiences in school and in World War I. Subsequently he produced nearly fifty more books, including a long series of novels called "A London Gallery." Many critics consider *We the Accused,* the second book in that series, to be his finest work. He also wrote essays, biographies of Keats, Shelley, the Brontes, and St. Francis, and two plays, "The Berg" and "The Multabello Road." Obituaries and other sources: Ernest Raymond, *The Story of My Days: An Autobiography, 1888-1922,* Cassell, 1968; Raymond, *Please You, Draw Near: An Autobiography, 1922-1928,* Cassell, 1969; Raymond, *Good Morning, Good People: An Autobiography, Past and Present,* Cassell, 1970; *Contemporary Novelists,* St. Martin's, 1972; *Who's Who,* 126th edition, St. Martin's, 1974; *London Times,* May 16, 1974; *World Authors, 1950-1970,* Wilson, 1975.

* * *

RAYMOND, Janice G. 1943-

PERSONAL: Born January 24, 1943, in Pawtucket, R.I.; daughter of Earl G. (a cafeteria manager) and Alice M. (Hanley) Raymond. *Education:* Salve Regina College, B.A., 1965; Andover Newton Theological Seminary, M.A., 1971; Boston College, Ph.D., 1977. *Politics:* "Feminist." *Religion:* "Feminist." *Home address:* P.O. Box 123, Montague, Mass. 01351. *Office:* Women's Studies Program, University of Massachusetts, Amherst, Mass. 01003.

CAREER: Junior high school teacher in Rhode Island, 1965-69; New School for Social Research, New York, N.Y., lecturer, 1974-75; assistant professor at colleges in Amherst, Mass., 1975-78; University of Massachusetts, Hampshire College, Amherst, assistant professor of women's studies and medical ethics, 1978—. *Member:* American Academy of Religion, American Society of Christian Ethics, American Association for the Advancement of Science.

WRITINGS: The Transsexual Empire: The Making of the She-Male, Beacon Press, 1979. Contributor to magazines, including *Chrysalis, Quest,* and *Andover Newton Quarterly.*

WORK IN PROGRESS: Genetic Technology and the Future of Women; Essays in Women's Studies.

SIDELIGHTS: Raymond comments: "All of my work is informed by a feminist perspective."

BIOGRAPHICAL/CRITICAL SOURCES: New York Times Book Review, June, 10, 1979.

* * *

REED, Douglas 1895-1976

OBITUARY NOTICE: Born in 1895 in London, England; died in 1976. Foreign correspondent and writer. A correspondent for the *London Times,* Reed was stationed in Berlin from 1929 to 1935 and in Central Europe from 1935 to 1938. He worked as a war correspondent in Normandy in 1944 and was foreign editor for the Kemsley Newspapers in 1945. Reed traveled widely in Africa, South America, and North America as an independent writer from 1947 to 1973. He saw Communism and political Zionism as menaces to Christian society, and thought that "the grand design of the twentieth century" was the destruction of Christianity and the enslavement of the white races. He detailed his thoughts and suspicions in his many articles and books, including *The Burning of the Reichstag, Nemesis?, A Prophet at Home, All Our Tomorrows,* and his autobiography, *Insanity Fair.* Obituaries and other sources: *The New Century Handbook of English Literature,* revised edition, Appleton, 1967; *The Author's and Writer's Who's Who,* 6th edition, Burke's Peerage, 1971; *Who's Who,* 126th edition, St. Martin's, 1974.

* * *

REEDSTROM, Ernest Lisle 1928-

PERSONAL: Born December 8, 1928, in Chicago, Ill.; son of Ernest Earl (a farmer and mail clerk) and Helen (Kruslak) Reedstrom; married Shirley Ellen Plucinski, September 4, 1952; children: Karen Lee, Wesley Lisle. *Education:* Attended Academy of Fine Arts, Art Institute of Chicago, 1943-47, Arizona School of Art, 1951-52, and Arizona State University. *Politics:* None. *Religion:* Methodist. *Home and office:* 9907 West 109th Ave., Cedar Lake, Ind. 46303.

CAREER: Worked as gold and tungsten miner, laborer, sign painter, and artist, 1946-50; ghost artist of "Fan Fare" cartoon strip (syndicated), 1952-54; illustrator of *Arizona Wildlife,* 1953-56; creator of "Wildlife Wille" comic strip published in Arizona, 1954-55; art editor, Little Big Horn Associates, 1967—. Illustrator for PBI Books. Owner of Advance Advertising, Cedar Lake, Ind. Participant in group shows and solo exhibitions. Curator of John Dillinger Museum. *Military service:* U.S. Army, hospital corpsman, 1951-52; served in Korea. *Member:* Western Writers of America, Company of Military Historians, Westerners, Smithsonian Institution, Little Big Horn Association, Custer Battlefield. *Awards, honors:* Spur Award from Western Writers of America, 1978, for *Bugles, Banners, and War Bonnets.*

WRITINGS: (Self-illustrated) *Bugles, Banners, and War Bonnets,* Caxton, 1978.

Illustrator: *The Complete and Authentic Life of Jesse James,* Fell, 1953; *Out Where the Jest Begins,* Fell, 1956; *Empire on the Platte,* World, 1967; *The Double Yoke,* Citadel, 1968; *Saga of the Colt Six-Shooter,* Fell, 1969; *The Gunfighters,* Caxton, 1971; *Fife, Drum and Bugle,* Old Army Press, 1971; *Triggernometry,* Caxton, 1975; *General Custer's Libbie,* Superior, 1976; *People and the Way of Living in the New England Colonies,* Benefic, 1976; "Ranger Don" series, Benefic, 1978. Also illustrator of many other books. Contributor of more than twenty-five articles to gun magazines.

WORK IN PROGRESS: A book on the Apaches, publication by Caxton expected in 1981.

SIDELIGHTS: Reedstrom's subjects are the U.S. military, especially the cavalry, American Indians, and the Western. His paintings have appeared in books and on book covers. His work is drawn from his early experiences as a miner, prospector, and laborer in the western deserts and mountains, from his current travels to gather information and take photographs, and from meticulous research.

* * *

REES, Helen Christina Easson (Evans) 1903-1970 (Jane Oliver)

OBITUARY NOTICE—See index for *CA* sketch: Born October 12, 1903; died May 4, 1970, in Scotland. Social activist, secretary, and author. An ambulance driver during the London blitz, 1940 to 1943, Rees was active in the Red Cross throughout her lifetime. She also worked in a hospital and a bookshop before becoming a secretary for several authors. Rees wrote more than twenty-five historical novels under the pseudonym of Jane Oliver. Obituaries and other sources: *AB Bookman's Weekly,* June 15, 1970; *Authors of Books for Young People,* 2nd edition, Scarecrow, 1971.

REES, Richard (Lodowick Edward Montagu) 1900-1970

OBITUARY NOTICE—See index for *CA* sketch: Born April 4, 1900, in Oxford, England; died July 24, 1970, in London, England. Translator, publisher, editor, artist, and author. Rees, who was editor of *Adelphi* for six years, was considered to be an authority on Simone Weil and translated several of her works. During his association with *Adelphi,* he published the works of George Orwell and Dylan Thomas, among others. Rees was a part-time painter whose work was exhibited at the Royal Academy in London. Obituaries and other sources: *AB Bookman's Weekly,* August 21, 1970.

* * *

REEVES, Floyd (Wesley) 1890-1979

OBITUARY NOTICE: Born November 16, 1890, in Castalia, S.D.; died August 20, 1979, in East Lansing, Mich. Author, educational consultant, and professor at Michigan State University and the University of Chicago. Reeves served as consultant to the former president of Michigan State University, John Hannah. His works include *Personnel Administration in the Federal Service* and *The Liberal Arts College.* Obituaries and other sources: *American Men and Women of Science: The Social and Behavioral Sciences,* 12th edition, Bowker, 1973; *Adult Leadership,* September, 1976; *Who's Who in America,* 40th edition, Marquis, 1978; *New York Times,* August 31, 1979.

* * *

REEVES, Rosser 1910-

PERSONAL: Born September 10, 1910, in Danville, Va.; son of Thomas Rosser (a minister) and Mary Scott (Watkins) Reeves; married Elizabeth Lovejoy Street (a portrait painter), December 2, 1934; children: Rosser Scott III, Abbot Street, Elizabeth Lovejoy (Mrs. William Duryea, Jr.). *Education:* Attended University of Virginia, 1928-30. *Home:* 24 Gramercy Park S., New York, N.Y. 10003. *Office:* Rosser Reeves, Inc., 505 Park Ave., New York, N.Y. 10022.

CAREER: Richmond Times-Dispatch, Richmond, Va., police reporter, 1929; Bank of Virginia, Richmond, advertising manager, 1930-33; copywriter for advertising agencies in New York City, 1934-38; Blackett-Sample-Hummert, New York City, copy chief, 1938-39; associated with Benton & Bowles, New York City, 1939-40; Ted Bates & Co., Inc., New York City, co-founder, 1940, vice-president and copy chief, 1942-48, partner and head of creative department, 1949-55, head of executive committee, 1953, vice-chairperson of board of directors, 1955, chairperson of board of directors, 1955-66; Tiderock Corp., New York City, president, 1967-69; Rosser Reeves, Inc. (advertising agency), New York City, owner and chairman, 1976—. Limited partner of Oppenheimer & Co., 1966-67, and Bacon, Stevenson & Reeves, 1968-70. Created and directed Dwight Eisenhower's television presidential campaign, 1952; member of Foreign Operations Administration Marketing Commission to West Germany, 1953. Head of board of directors of American Chess Foundation, 1958-76. Member of board of trustees of Randolph-Macon Woman's College and St. John's College in Annapolis, Md. and Santa Fe, N.M.

MEMBER: New York Yacht Club, Racquet and Tennis Club, Manhattan Chess Club (president, 1971-72), Larchmont Yacht Club, Westchester Shore Chess Club, Miami Jockey Club. *Awards, honors:* Elected to Copywriters Hall of Fame, 1965; honorary fellow of Smithsonian Institution.

WRITINGS: Reality in Advertising, Knopf, 1961; (with Ray Martin) *The Ninety-Nine Critical Shots in Pool,* Times Publishing, 1977. Also author of *The 244 Major Mistakes in Backgammon* and *Popo,* both 1980. Contributor of articles, stories, and poems to magazines.

WORK IN PROGRESS: Adapting *Popo* for the stage.

SIDELIGHTS: Reeves writes: "*Reality in Advertising* was an important theoretical work in a business where there has been very little theory. The book stayed on the general best-seller lists for many weeks. It was widely reviewed and created a storm of controversy within the advertising business. It has since become required reading in most of the advertising courses in the world, as well as a great many business schools. It has been published in fourteen countries; it was pirated in Germany and Mexico, and excerpts have run in advertising magazines and such popular magazines as *Esquire.*

"*The Ninety-Nine Critical Shots in Pool,* written with world champion pool player, Ray Martin, is generally regarded as the most definitive book on the game."

* * *

REFF, Theodore Franklin 1930-

PERSONAL: Born August 18, 1930, in New York, N.Y.; son of Irving and Alice (Pinkowitz) Reff; married Arlene Gottesman, June 25, 1961; children: Lisa, Jonathan. *Education:* Columbia University, B.A., 1952; Harvard University, M.A., 1953, Ph.D., 1958. *Home:* 435 Riverside Dr., New York, N.Y. 10025. *Office:* Department of Art History, Columbia University, New York, N.Y. 10027.

CAREER: Columbia University, New York, N.Y., instructor, 1957-61, assistant professor, 1961-64, associate professor, 1964-67, professor of art history, 1967—. Visiting professor at Johns Hopkins University, 1970, City University of New York, 1971-72, and University of Michigan, summer, 1972. Director of seminar for college teachers, National Endowment for the Humanities, 1977-78, and summers, 1976, 1979. Member of Institute for Advanced Study, 1963. Organized exhibition on Edgar Degas at the Metropolitan Museum of Art. *Member:* College Art Association of America (head of Porter Prize selection committee, 1970-72; member of board of directors, 1977-80; director, 1978—). *Awards, honors:* Edward Bacon traveling fellowship from Harvard University, 1955-56; Guggenheim fellow, 1967-68, 1974-75; American Council of Learned Societies grant, 1963; American Philosophical Society grants, 1964, 1972.

WRITINGS: (Editor) *Cezanne Watercolors,* M. Knoedler, 1963; (editor) *Toulouse-Lautrec: Unpublished Correspondence,* Phaidon, 1969; *The Notebooks of Edgar Degas: A Catalogue of the Thirty-Eight Notebooks in the Bibliotheque National and Other Collections,* two volumes, Oxford University Press, 1976; *Degas: The Artist's Mind,* Harper, for the Metropolitan Museum of Art, 1976; *Art in Context* (edited by John Fleming and Hugh Honour), Viking, 1977. Contributor to art journals.

WORK IN PROGRESS: A book on essays on Cezanne, to be published by Harper.

SIDELIGHTS: Reff commented: "*Degas: The Artist's Mind* was published at the time that the Metropolitan Museum of Art was showing a large exhibition that I organized of all the works it owned by Degas, all 176 of them. The exhibition was called "Degas in the Metropolitan" and was seen by about half a million people, some of whom (not enough) also bought the book. At that time, too, I wrote an issue of the

Museum's *Bulletin* on the theme "Degas: A Master Among Masters," comparing Degas's works with those of artists he admired or influenced. And at about the same time *The Notebooks of Edgar Degas,* on which I had been working for about fourteen years, was at last published. John Russell had noted in the *New York Times* that 'few books in their field have been more eagerly awaited. . . . To those who think about Degas every day of their lives this edition of the notebooks will be "beyond price."' All in all, it was a great year for both Degas and myself."

* * *

REINITZ, Richard (Martin) 1934-

PERSONAL: Born February 22, 1934, in Brooklyn, N.Y.; son of Irving (a clerk) and Miriam (a secretary; maiden name, Grobgeld) Reinitz; married Janet Braun (an artist), April 24, 1960; children: Rachel, David, Ruth. *Education:* Queens College (now of the City University of New York), B.A., 1955; Hunter College (now of the City University of New York), M.A., 1961; University of Rochester, Ph.D., 1967. *Politics:* "Feminist Democratic Socialist." *Religion:* Jewish. *Residence:* Geneva, N.Y. *Office:* Department of History, Hobart and William Smith Colleges, Geneva, N.Y. 14456.

CAREER: Department of Welfare, New York City, social worker, 1955-58; State of New York, New York City, employment interviewer and counselor, 1958-61; University of London, London, England, assistant lecturer in history, 1963-64; Wayne State University, Detroit, Mich., instructor in history, 1964-67; Hobart and William Smith Colleges, Geneva, N.Y., assistant professor, 1967-71, associate professor, 1971-75, professor of history, 1975—, head of department, 1972-74. Visiting assistant professor at Brooklyn College of the City University of New York, 1974-75; Mary Ball Washington Professor of American History at National University of Ireland University College, Dublin, 1978-79. *Member:* American Historical Association, Organization of American Historians, Intellectual History Group. *Awards, honors:* Grants from National Endowment for the Humanities, 1968, 1977, 1979.

WRITINGS: *Tensions in American Puritanism,* Wiley, 1970; (contributor) Sacvan Bercovitch, editor, *Typology and Early American Literature,* University of Massachusetts Press, 1972; (contributor) Robert H. Canary and Henry Koxicki, editors, *The Writing of History: Literary Form and Historical Understanding,* University of Wisconsin Press, 1978; *Irony and Consciousness: American Historiography and Reinhold Niebuhr,* Bucknell University Press, 1979. Contributor of about fifteen articles and reviews to history and literature journals.

WORK IN PROGRESS: A book on Roger Williams; writing the section on nineteenth- and twentieth-century intellectual history of the United States and Canada, for *General History of the Americas,* edited by Guillermo Moron, with publication by Organization of American States.

SIDELIGHTS: Reinitz told *CA:* "I am interested in the use of irony as a form through which a general interpretation of American history can be developed. Some such generalizing structure is badly needed because of the disintegration caused by the intensive specialization in recent historical work. I am also interested in the relationship between form and interpretative substance in historical writing, in the application of ideas derived from certain kinds of structuralism to that writing, and in the tension between the view of a work of history as a linguistic construct and the more traditional view of it as a representation of 'reality.' My work on the history of American radicalism involves the attempt to demonstrate how the problems radicals have encountered in this country were anticipated by Roger Williams' relationship to the orthodox Puritans. This is concerned in part with the issues of American exceptionalism and the development of individualism."

* * *

REISING, Robert W(illiam) 1933-

PERSONAL: Surname is pronounced *Rize*-ing; born May 9, 1933, in New Haven, Conn.; son of Simon and Bessie (Geenty) Reising; married Flora Nell Sanderson (a secretary), October 2, 1965; children: Paula Simone, John Clark. *Education:* Michigan State University, B.A. (with honors in English), 1955; University of Connecticut, M.A., 1958; Duke University, Ed.D., 1969. *Home:* 402 Highland Ave., Lumberton, N.C. 28372. *Office:* Box 121, Pembroke State University, Pembroke, N.C. 28372.

CAREER: Baseball coach at Defiance College, Defiance, Ohio, 1960-62; faculty member at Tennessee Technological University, 1962-63, University of South Carolina, 1963-65, Fort Hays State College, Fort Hays, Kan., 1965-66, and Furman University, 1967-69; University of South Florida, Tampa, assistant professor of English education, 1969-70; Virginia Commonwealth University, Richmond, associate professor of education, 1970-71; Pembroke State University, Pembroke, N.C., associate professor, 1971-74, professor of communicative arts and American Indian studies, 1974—, director of English Education/Communications Center, 1971-74. Part-time faculty member at Robeson Technical Institute. Member of North Carolina Committee on Composition and Conference on English Education; workshop and conference director; participant in professional meetings; consultant. *Member:* National Council of Teachers of English, North Carolina English Teachers Association (president). *Awards, honors:* Grants from Duke University, 1972, Pembroke State University, 1976, and from National Endowment for the Humanities, 1978.

WRITINGS: *Jim Thorpe: The Story of an American Indian,* Dillon Press, 1974; *Jim Thorpe, Tar Heel,* Communique, 1974; (contributor) R. Baird Shuman, editor, *Creative Approaches to the Teaching of English: Secondary,* Peacock Publishers, 1974; (contributor) Shuman, editor, *Questions English Teachers Ask,* Hayden Book Co., 1977; (contributor) Denny T. Wolfe, editor, *Writing in the Wild Young Spring: Teaching Composition, 4-12,* North Carolina State Department of Public Instruction, 1978; (contributor) Edward F. J. Tucker, editor, *Culture and Literacy,* University of Michigan, 1979; (editor with Ralph Graber) *An Anthology of Poetry: Baseball,* Dillon Press, in press. Contributor of nearly fifty articles to education and English journals.

WORK IN PROGRESS: A high school textbook series for Macmillan; a junior high school textbook series for Harcourt.

SIDELIGHTS: Reising told *CA:* "Writing is for me, and for most people, hard work. Yet it is rewarding: it is a method of knowing, not merely a method of recording and communicating. Anyone who writes for reasons other than love of writing possesses questionable sanity. It is so taxing and frustrating that no amount of money can compensate. As an English teacher, I can only hope that my profession will teach writing not because of its practical, marketplace advantages but because of its humanistic ones."

REITSCH, Hanna 1912(?)-1979

OBITUARY NOTICE: Born c. 1912; died August 24, 1979, in Bonn, West Germany. Author and pilot. Reitsch was the first woman ever awarded the Iron Cross. A much-decorated favorite of Hitler, she flew the last plane out of Berlin hours before the city fell in 1945 and was one of the last persons to see the dictator alive. Reitsch was also the first person to fly over the Alps in a glider, the first female helicopter pilot, and the first German woman to win a captain's pilot license. She wrote an autobiography, *Flying Is My Life.* Obituaries and other sources: *New York Times,* August 31, 1979.

* * *

RENN, Ludwig
See VIETH von GOLSSENAU, Arnold Friedrich

* * *

RENNER, Al G. 1912-

PERSONAL: Born July 21, 1912, in Kremlin, Mont.; son of Gustave A. (a contractor) and Elsie (Hein) Renner; divorced. *Education:* University of Southern California, M.S., 1936. *Politics:* Republican. *Religion:* Protestant. *Home and office:* 860 Fairfield Circle, Pasadena, Calif. 91106.

CAREER: Pasadena Unified Schools, Pasadena, Calif., junior high school science teacher, 1936-72; writer, 1972—. Instructor at University of California, Los Angeles, 1962-72. *Military service:* U.S. Navy, 1942-46. *Awards, honors:* Ford Foundation fellowship, 1954-55.

WRITINGS: How to Make and Use a Microlab (juvenile), Putnam, 1971; *How to Make and Use Electric Motors* (juvenile), Putnam, 1974; *Lower Colorado River Guide,* Picacho Press, 1976; *How to Build a Better Mousetrap Car and Other Experimental Science Fun* (juvenile), Dodd, 1977; *Experimental Fun With the Yo-Yo,* Dodd, 1979.

WORK IN PROGRESS: Science Olympiad, for Dodd; research for a juvenile historical novel.

AVOCATIONAL INTERESTS: Backpacking in the Sierra Mountains, travel abroad.

* * *

RENSHAW, Domeena C(ynthia) 1929-

PERSONAL: Born July 20, 1929, in Douglas, South Africa; came to the United States, naturalized citizen, 1973; daughter of Alfred S. (in business) and Esme (in business; maiden name, Add) Joseph; married Robert Harris Renshaw (a professor of economics), June 13, 1965. *Education:* University of Cape Town, M.B., Ch.B., 1960. *Politics:* "Open-minded!" *Religion:* Roman Catholic. *Home:* 85 South Third Ave., Lombard, Ill. 60148. *Office:* Department of Psychiatry, Loyola Stritch School of Medicine, Loyola University, 2160 South First Ave., Maywood, Ill. 60153.

CAREER: Associated with Boston Children's Hospital, 1961-62; Loyola University, Loyola Stritch School of Medicine, Maywood, Ill., resident in psychiatry, 1965-68, professor of psychiatry, 1976—, director of Sexual Dysfunction Clinic, 1972—, assistant chair of department of psychiatry, 1965—, acting chair, 1979. Guest on television and radio programs. *Member:* American Board of Psychiatry and Neurology (fellow), American College of Psychiatry (fellow).

WRITINGS: The Hyperactive Child, Nelson-Hall, 1974. Contributor of more than a hundred-fifty articles to medical journals in the United States and Europe.

WORK IN PROGRESS: A book on incest and its treatment, publication by Little, Brown expected in 1980.

SIDELIGHTS: Domeena Renshaw comments: "I have a strong interest in helping others and in helping others to help others!"

* * *

REVERDY, Pierre 1889-1960

OBITUARY NOTICE: Born September 11, 1889, in Narbonne, France; died June 17, 1960. Poet best known for his contributions to the French surrealist movement. After the publication of a collection of his early poems, *Les Epaves du ciel,* in 1924, surrealists hailed Reverdy as the greatest living poet. He once described his poems as "crystals deposited after the effervescent contact of the spirit" with the absolute and the real. A collection of Reverdy's poetry. *Main d'ouvre,* was published in 1949, and his poetic theories are explained in his *Le Gant de crin,* published in 1926. Though few American poets have been influenced by Reverdy, according to poet John Ashbery, his work remains an important and influential force in France. Obituaries and other sources: *The Reader's Encyclopedia,* 2nd edition, Crowell, 1965; *The Oxford Companion to French Literature,* corrected edition, Oxford University Press, 1966; *The Penguin Companion to European Literature,* McGraw, 1969; *Cassell's Encyclopaedia of World Literature,* revised edition, Morrow, 1973; *Encyclopedia of World Literature in the Twentieth Century,* Volume IV supplement, Ungar, 1975; *World Authors, 1950-1970,* Wilson, 1975.

* * *

RHODES, James M. 1940-

PERSONAL: Born February 24, 1940, in Detroit, Mich.; son of James J. (an automobile dealer) and Marie (a bookkeeper; maiden name, Burghardt) Rhodes; married wife, Anne Marie, June 11, 1966; children: Jane, Maria. *Education:* University of Notre Dame, B.A., 1962, M.A., 1964, Ph.D., 1969. *Politics:* Independent. *Religion:* Roman Catholic. *Residence:* Milwaukee, Wis. *Office:* Department of Political Science, Marquette University, Milwaukee, Wis. 53233.

CAREER: Marquette University, Milwaukee, Wis., associate professor of political science, 1965—. *Awards, honors:* Grants from National Endowment for the Humanities, summers, 1970, 1978; fellow of Hoover Institution on War, Revolution, and Peace, 1971-72.

WRITINGS: The Hitler Movement, Hoover Institution, 1979. Contributor to *Modern Age, Interpretation,* and *Journal of Politics.*

WORK IN PROGRESS: Research on German democratic political theory and on the relationships between religion and politics.

SIDELIGHTS: Rhodes comments: "I lived in Germany in 1966 and 1967. *The Hitler Movement* argues that German National Socialism was a secular, millenarian (or apocalyptic) uprising. It precisely delineates the characteristics of the millenarian mentality as found in the Nazis and explains the historical, philosophical, social, and psychological causes of apocalyptic attitudes. It also explains the causes of the mass murder of the Jews."

* * *

RICE, Wayne 1945-

PERSONAL: Born November 6, 1945, in Clarksville, Tenn.; son of John F. (a building contractor) and Mary C. (Powers) Rice; married Marcella K. West, January 27, 1966; children: Nathan, Amber. *Education:* San Diego State University,

B.A., 1970. *Religion:* Protestant. *Home:* 10928 Vista Camino, Lakeside, Calif. 92040. *Office:* Youth Specialties, Inc., 861 Sixth Ave., San Diego, Calif. 92101.

CAREER: Youth Specialties, Inc. (publisher), San Diego, Calif., owner, 1969—. Musician and vocalist for Capitol Records, 1971-73; disc jockey for KSON-Radio, 1976—. *Member:* American Federation of Television and Radio Artists, Evangelical Press Association. *Awards, honors:* Award from Evangelical Press Association, 1976, for humorous article.

WRITINGS: *Way Out Ideas for Youth Groups,* Zondervan, 1974; *Far Out Ideas for Youth Groups,* Zondervan, 1975; *Fun 'n' Games,* Zondervan, 1977; *Junior High Ministry: A Guide for the Leading and Teaching of Early Adolescents,* Zondervan, 1978; *Super Ideas for Youth Groups,* Zondervan, 1979. Editor of *Wittenburg Door.*

SIDELIGHTS: Rice comments: "My primary interest is youth ministry, specializing in young adolescents, aged eleven to fourteen. I have been involved since 1963 as a youth director and camp director. My motivation is to reach young people for Christ and impart Christian values."

* * *

RICH, Edwin Ernest 1904-1979

OBITUARY NOTICE: Born August 4, 1904, in Brislington, England; died in 1979 in Cambridge, England. Educator and author. Rich was the Vere Harmsworth Professor of Naval and Imperial History at Cambridge University. His works include *Staple Courts of Bristol; The Hudson's Bay Company, 1670-1870;* and *Montreal and the Fur Trade.* Obituaries and other sources: *Who's Who,* 131st edition, St. Martin's, 1979; *AB Bookman's Weekly,* August 13, 1979.

* * *

RICHARDS, I(vor) A(rmstrong) 1893-1979

OBITUARY NOTICE—See index for *CA* sketch: Born February 26, 1893, in Sandbach, Cheshire, England; died September 7, 1979, in Cambridge, England. Literary critic, philosopher, educator, poet, and dramatist. One of the most influential literary critics of his time, Richards laid down the foundation for what came to be known as New Criticism in such books as *Principles of Literary Criticism* and *Practical Criticism.* In 1923 he published *The Meaning of Meaning,* a highly regarded study on the science of semantics. Richards was an advocate of Basic English, a stripped-down version of the language that he hoped would become a means of world communication. At age sixty, shortly before retiring from a long teaching career that had included posts at Cambridge, Harvard, and Quinghua University in Peking, Richards began to write poetry. Among his volumes of verse are *Goodbye Earth and Other Poems* and *The Screens and Other Poems.* Obituaries and other sources: *The Oxford Companion to American Literature,* 4th edition, Oxford University Press, 1965; *The Penguin Companion to English Literature,* McGraw, 1971; *The Reader's Adviser: A Layman's Guide to Literature,* Volume I: *The Best in American and British Fiction, Poetry, Essays, Literary Biography, Bibliography, and Reference,* 12th edition, Bowker, 1974; *Contemporary Poets,* 2nd edition, St. Martin's, 1975; *Encyclopedia of World Literature in the Twentieth Century,* Volume IV supplement, Ungar, 1975; *The Writers Directory, 1980-82,* St. Martin's, 1979; *New York Times,* September 8, 1979; *Washington Post,* September 8, 1979; *Publishers Weekly,* September 17, 1979; *Time,* September 17, 1979; *Newsweek,* September 17, 1979; *AB Bookman's Weekly,* October 22, 1979.

RICHARDSON, Anne
See ROIPHE, Anne Richardson

* * *

RICHMAN, Phyllis C. 1939-

PERSONAL: Born March 21, 1939, in Washington, D.C.; daughter of Abraham (a lawyer) and Helen (a realtor; maiden name, Lieberman) Chasanow; married Alvin Richman (a social science analyst), May 6, 1960; children: Joseph, Matthew, Libby. *Education:* Brandeis University, B.A., 1961; graduate study at University of Pennsylvania, 1961-62, and Purdue University, 1968-71. *Religion:* Jewish. *Home:* 5311 38th St. N.W., Washington, D.C. 20015. *Office: Washington Post,* 1150 15th St. N.W., Washington, D.C. 20071.

CAREER: City planner in Philadelphia, Pa., 1961-65; freelance writer, 1972-76; *Washington Post,* Washington, D.C., restaurant critic, 1976—. *Member:* Washington Independent Writers (member of board of directors, 1975-78).

WRITINGS: (With Charles F. Turgeon) *Dining Out in Washington,* Washington Books, 1975; (with Constance Stapleton) *Barter: How to Get Almost Anything Without Money,* Scribner, 1978.

* * *

RICKER, George Marvin 1922-

PERSONAL: Born September 12, 1922, in Boston, Mass.; son of Everett M. (a civil servant) and Elva (Betts) Ricker; married Frances Ryden, June 17, 1947; children: Lois, David, Philip. *Education:* Attended Cornell University, 1941; Southern Methodist University, B.A., 1949; Union Theological Seminary, New York, N.Y., M.Div., 1951. *Home:* 1406 Ethridge, Austin, Tex. 78703. *Office:* University United Methodist Church, 2409 Guadalupe, Austin, Tex. 78705.

CAREER: Ordained United Methodist minister, 1951; pastor of Methodist churches in Bertram, Tex., 1951-53, Fredericksburg, Tex., 1953-56, Columbus, Tex., 1956-59, San Angelo, Tex., 1959-67, Edinburg, Tex., 1967-70, and Corpus Christi, Tex., 1970-74; University United Methodist Church, Austin, Tex., pastor, 1974—. Senior instructor for Bi-Polar, Inc. Chairperson of United Methodist Southwest Texas Conference Commission on Higher Education and Board of Education. *Military service:* U.S. Army Air Forces, 1942-46; became captain.

WRITINGS: *New Creation* (leader's guide), Methodist Publishing House, 1969; *The Faith Once Given,* Westminster, 1978. Contributor to religious journals, including *Together* and *Pulpit Digest.*

WORK IN PROGRESS: *A New Look at the Old Commandments,* Westminster Press, 1981.

SIDELIGHTS: Ricker writes: "My pastoral ministry, which includes my writing, has been marked by the concern to interpret past writings from the Judeo-Christian tradition for today's enlightenment. I am convinced that when we really listen to the past, we get a word to build on in the present. My efforts are to maintain our roots while producing the fruit needed for today."

* * *

RIDER, (Arthur) Fremont 1885-1962

OBITUARY NOTICE: Born May 25, 1885, in Trenton, N.J.; died October 26, 1962. Rider edited several magazines, including *Delineator, Monthly Book Review, Publishers Weekly,* and *Library Journal,* before becoming librarian of Wesleyan University in 1933. He was the inventor of microcards, book trucks, and stack shelving, and the founder of Godfrey Memorial Library. His writings include *Songs of Syracuse,* 1905, *Are the Dead Alive?,* 1909, and *Between Seven and Eight,* 1910, as well as short stories and plays. He also edited several travel guides, including *Rider's New York City, Rider's Bermuda,* and *Rider's California*. Obituaries and other sources: *Who Was Who in America,* 4th edition, Marquis, 1968; *American Authors and Books: 1640 to the Present Day,* 3rd revised edition, Crown, 1972.

* * *

RIGA, Frank P(eter) 1936-

PERSONAL: Born January 1, 1936, in Buffalo, N.Y.; son of John (a custodian) and Marghretta (Cannito) Riga; married Mary Ann Crowley (a nurse), 1960; children: John, Mary, Joseph, Frank, Jeanne. *Education:* State University of New York at Buffalo, B.A., 1958, M.A., 1962, Ph.D., 1967. *Home:* 4297 Elmwood Ave., Blasdell, N.Y. 14219. *Office:* Department of English, Canisius College, Buffalo, N.Y. 14208.

CAREER: D'Youville College, Buffalo, N.Y., instructor in English, 1961-63; Canisius College, Buffalo, N.Y., assistant professor, 1964-68, associate professor, 1968-75, professor of English, 1975—, director of graduate studies, 1972-75. *Member:* Modern Language Association of America, Phi Beta Kappa. *Awards, honors:* National Endowment for the Humanities grant, summer, 1977.

WRITINGS: (With Claude A. Prance) *Index to the London Magazine,* Garland Publishing, 1978. Contributor to *Library Journal* and other periodicals.

WORK IN PROGRESS: Research on the English Romantic period, especially the works of John Keats, on modern drama, and on criticism, especially the work of C. S. Lewis.

SIDELIGHTS: Frank Riga told *CA:* "My love of Keats's work is continually sparked by the interest of my students. When we read the works of Keats together, my students begin to learn a good deal about poetry, and thus about human experience and aspiration, and I learn, largely by my students' development, that my preference for Keats is no mere prejudice, but a constantly fruitful engagement with human genius. At the moment I'm attempting to puzzle the connection of Keats's use of figurative language and the maturity of his imagination. We've known for a long time that figurative language generally is not pointless decoration, but a mode of perceptual rendition. My notion, simply, is that figurative language in Keats is not only perceptual rendition, but also perceptual exploration and expansion. I have a sense that it reveals a kind of dynamic epistemology.

"My work on *London Magazine* grew out of my interest in Keats and his circle. To complete my doctoral dissertation on the poetical works of John Hamilton Reynolds, the friend of Keats and parodist of Wordsworth, I had to explore Reynolds's connection with *London Magazine* and his admiration for Hazlitt (an admiration shared by Keats). One thing built upon another, especially with the encouraging example of Walter Houghton's *Wellesley Index to Victorian Periodicals,* and I decided an index to this great and important periodical would be of use to all kinds of scholars and students. At that point, via international post, I met Claude Prance. To this day we know each other only by mail, but the *Index to The London Magazine* is the result of that epistolary collaboration.

"Currently I'm also rereading the works of C. S. Lewis with care. Lewis is a kind of latter day romantic, and in his work I find much of my thinking on the 19th century romantics enhanced and enriched. In Lewis, for example, I gain a clearer understanding of what Keats meant when he said, 'what the imagination seizes as Beauty must be truth—whether it existed before or not.' And like Keats, Lewis educates our imaginations, both in his fictive and non-fictive work."

AVOCATIONAL INTERESTS: "I have an abiding interest in music, and I play saxophone or arrange band charts whenever I have time (and often when I don't)."

* * *

RIPPY, Frances (Marguerite) Mayhew 1929-

PERSONAL: Born September 16, 1929, in Fort Worth, Tex.; daughter of H. Grady (a tax accountant) and Marguerite Christine (O'Neill) Mayhew; married N. Merrill Rippy (a professor of history), August 29, 1955; children: Felix O'Neill, Conrad Mayhew, Marguerite Hailey. *Education:* Texas Christian University, B.A., 1949; Vanderbilt University, M.A., 1951, Ph.D., 1957; also attended Birkbeck College, London, 1952-53. *Politics:* Democrat. *Religion:* Episcopalian. *Home:* 4709 West Jackson, Muncie, Ind. 47304. *Office:* Department of English, Ball State University, Muncie, Ind. 47306.

CAREER: Texas Christian University, Fort Worth, instructor in English, 1953-55; Lamar State University, Beaumont, Tex., instructor, 1955-57, assistant professor of English, 1957-59; Ball State University, Muncie, Ind., assistant professor, 1959-65, associate professor, 1965-69, professor of English, 1969—. Visiting assistant professor at Sam Houston State University, summer, 1957; visiting lecturer at University of Puerto Rico, summer, 1959, 1960, visiting professor, summer, 1961.

MEMBER: Modern Language Association of America, National Council of Teachers of English, College English Association, American Society for Eighteenth-Century Studies, American Federation of Teachers, American Association of University Professors, Common Cause, Midwest Modern Language Association, Midwestern Society of Eighteenth-Century Studies, Johnson Society of the Central Region, Indiana College English Association, Indiana Council of Teachers of English, Friends of the Muncie Public Library (member of board of directors, 1976—). *Awards, honors:* Fulbright scholar, 1952-53; Danforth grant, summer, 1962, associate, 1966—; outstanding educator of America, 1973; Lilly Library small research grant from Indiana University, 1978.

WRITINGS: (Contributor) Geoffrey Tillotson, *Pope and Human Nature,* Clarendon Press, 1958; (contributor) Tillotson, *Augustan Studies,* Athlone Press, 1961; (contributor) B. F. Colquitt, editor, *Studies in Medieval, Renaissance, and American Literature: A Festschrift,* Texas Christian University Press, 1971; *Matthew Prior,* G. K. Hall, 1979. Contributor of nearly fifty articles and reviews to scholarly journals, *Writer,* and newspapers. Editor of *Ball State University Forum,* 1961—.

SIDELIGHTS: Frances Rippy comments: "My areas of special interest are Restoration and eighteenth-century British literature, literary criticism, James Joyce, course-related library instruction, and journal editing.

"I enjoy working on two areas of British literature as apparently different as Restoration eighteenth-century poetry (especially Prior and Pope) and twentieth-century British novel (especially Joyce) because I find their juxtaposition especially illuminating. On cursory examination, the two periods appear to be opposites. Prior and Pope prize in their art such virtues as discipline, order, hierarchy, clarity, balance, restraint; Joyce, in contrast, appears always to be pushing back the bounds of his medium, seeing how far he can bend the language and the form without shattering it entirely. Yet the artists have much in common: wit, a sharp sense of the genres and their limits, an acute awareness of the disparities between the Graeco-Roman cultural heritage and modern man. Prior, Pope, and Joyce (despite sharp dissimilarities among them) have in common the fact that each was at his best in domesticating the classical myth."

* * *

RITVALA, M.
See WALTARI, Mika (Toimi)

* * *

ROBBINS, Henry 1928(?)-1979

OBITUARY NOTICE: Born c. 1928, in Philadelphia, Pa.; died July 31, 1979, in New York, N.Y. Editor and publisher of such authors as John Irving, John Gregory Dunne, Wilfrid Sheed, and Fran Lebowitz. Robbins was editor in chief at E. P. Dutton and editor with several publishing companies, including Alfred A. Knopf and Simon & Schuster. Obituaries and other sources: *New York Times,* August 1, 1979; *Publishers Weekly,* August 6, 1979; *Time,* August 13, 1979; *AB Bookman's Weekly,* August 20, 1979.

* * *

ROBERTS, Hortense Roberta
(Hortense Roberta Munger)

PERSONAL: Born in Minneapolis, Minn.; daughter of Thomas Monfort (a merchant) and Grace (Fifield) Roberts; married Francis Munger (an entomologist). *Education:* University of Minnesota, B.A. *Politics:* Republican. *Religion:* Congregational. *Home:* 462 Poplar St., Laguna Beach, Calif. 92651.

CAREER: Writer. Speaker at colleges, high schools, and public gatherings. *Member:* American Association of University Women, Writers Club of Whittier (co-founder), Friends of the Library of Laguna Beach. *Awards, honors:* Literary prizes from poetry magazines.

WRITINGS—For children: *Insects Indoors and Out,* Melmont, 1957; *You Can Make an Insect Zoo,* Children's Press, 1974.

Work represented in more than fifteen anthologies, including *The Sound of a Few Leaves,* Rook Press, 1977; *Anthology of Magazine Verse and Yearbook of American Poetry,* Monitor, 1979; *A Windflower Almanac,* Windflower, 1980. Contributor of poems, articles (some under name Hortense Roberta Munger), and stories to more than one hundred fifty magazines for adults and children, including *Atlantic, Saturday Review, Ladies' Home Journal, Jack and Jill, Stone Country, Yankee,* and *Prairie Schooner.*

WORK IN PROGRESS: Sand Dollar (tentative title), poems, publication expected in 1980; a mystery novel.

SIDELIGHTS: Hortense Roberts writes: "Almost as soon as I could manage a pen and pencil I wrote, and began having my stories and poems accepted for publication when I was twelve.

"I lived in a fancy Minneapolis neighborhood in a big old house which would make a romantic setting for a mystery novel. Cedar Lake and Lake of the Isles were visible from our upstairs windows when the trees were bare. I could look down on the Mississippi River from the bridge near the University of Minnesota when I was a student there. Now I live in a little house on a hill from which, all year around, we can see the Pacific Ocean. I'm not happy living where there is no river, lake, or ocean, and many of my poems are about water.

"I first went abroad in 1960, and have traveled in Great Britain, France, Italy, the Greek Islands, Switzerland, Liechtenstein, Germany, the Netherlands, Norway, Sweden, and Denmark. Travel is a wonderful way to understand history, art, and literature. The scenery was unforgettable, but it was the people I enjoyed the most. I have gathered enough memories for a lifetime of writing, but it is no more valuable than what I saw and learned at home.

"In writing poetry and prose for both adults and children, I try for clarity and simplicity. On the other hand, I do not believe in omitting an unusual, long word because the reader might not know it. It is enriching to add new words to one's vocabulary, whether one is nine or ninety. I think that even coining a word is legitimate if it makes the writing come alive.

"Since it is both personal expression and an expression of the time in which one lives, poetry that sounds like the 1890's is not appropriate to the 1980's. I try to write the inner truth even though it is hard to come by."

* * *

ROBERTS, Jeanne Addison

PERSONAL: Born in Washington, D.C.; daughter of John West (a lawyer) and Sue Fisher (Nichols) Addison; married Harold Masengill, June 12, 1948 (divorced, 1960); married Markley Roberts (an economist), February 19, 1966; children: (first marriage) Addison Cary Steed, Ellen Carraway Masengill Coster. *Education:* Agnes Scott College, A.B., 1946; University of Pennsylvania, M.A., 1947; University of Virginia, Ph.D., 1964. *Politics:* Democrat. *Religion:* Episcopalian. *Home:* 4931 Albemarle St. N.W., Washington, D.C. 20016. *Office:* Department of Literature, American University, Washington, D.C. 20016.

CAREER: Science and English teacher at junior high school in Arlington, Va., summer, 1946; University of Virginia, Mary Washington College, Fredericksburg, instructor in English, 1947-48; Fairfax Hall Junior College, instructor of English and head of department, 1950-51; American University Association Language Center, Bangkok, Thailand, teacher of English, 1952-56; Beirut College for Women, Beirut, Lebanon, professor of English and head of department, 1957-60; American University, Washington, D.C., instructor, 1960-62, assistant professor, 1962-65, associate professor, 1965-68, professor of English, 1968—, distinguished faculty lecturer, 1975, dean of faculties, 1974. Lecturer for U.S. Information Service, 1952-56; teacher at Georgetown University, summers, 1961-62; lecturer at Howard University, 1971-72. Seminar leader.

MEMBER: Shakespeare Association of America (member of board of trustees), Modern Language Association of America (member of executive committee of Shakespeare Division), Phi Beta Kappa, Phi Kappa Phi, Mortarboard. *Awards, honors:* Danforth fellow, 1962-63; senior fellow at Folger Institute for Renaissance and Eighteenth-Century Studies, 1969-70.

WRITINGS: Radio English Lessons, U.S. Information Service, 1955; *Language Through Literature,* Khayat's, Volume I, 1959, Volume II, 1960; (editor with James G. McManaway) *A Selective Bibliography of Shakespeare,* University Press of Virginia, 1975; (contributor) Emilio C. Viano and Jeffrey H. Reiman, editors, *Police in Society,* Lexington Books, 1975; *Shakespeare's English Comedy: The Merry Wives of Windsor in Context,* University of Nebraska Press, 1979. Contributor of about twenty articles and reviews to language and literature journals. Member of editorial board of *Shakespeare Quarterly.*

WORK IN PROGRESS: A *varorium* edition of Shakespeare's *The Merry Wives of Windsor,* with Gerald Johnson, publication by Modern Language Association expected in 1983; an old spelling text of Shakespeare's *The Tempest,* for Burt Franklin.

* * *

ROBERTS, Roy Allison 1887-1967

OBITUARY NOTICE: Born November 25, 1887, in Muscotah, Kan.; died in February, 1967. Roberts worked as a city editor for the *Lawrence World* before joining the *Kansas City Star* in 1909. As managing editor, he was recognized for building the *Star* into a major daily newspaper. He later became the paper's president and general manager. Obituaries and other sources: *Who Was Who in America,* 4th edition, Marquis, 1968.

* * *

ROBERTS, Spencer Eugene 1920-

PERSONAL: Born April 17, 1920, in Catawissa, Pa.; son of Wilbur Henry and Sarah Elizabeth (Johnson) Roberts. *Education:* Bucknell University, A.B., 1942; Columbia University, M.A., 1953, Ph.D., 1961. *Religion:* Lutheran. *Office:* Department of Russian Language and Literature, Brooklyn College of the City University of New York, Bedford Ave. and Ave. H, Brooklyn, N.Y. 11210.

CAREER: U.S. Department of State, Washington, D.C., attache at embassies in Moscow, Soviet Union, 1948-50, and Vienna, Austria, 1950-52; Rutgers University, New Brunswick, N.J., assistant professor of Russian and head of Russian area program, 1957-61; Brooklyn College of the City University of New York, Brooklyn, N.Y., associate professor, 1961-71, professor of Russian language and literature, 1971—. Consultant to Standard Oil of New Jersey. *Military service:* U.S. Navy, 1942-46; became lieutenant. *Member:* Modern Language Association of America, American Association of Teachers of Slavic and East European Languages, Phi Beta Kappa. *Awards, honors:* Ford Foundation fellow in Eastern Europe, 1954, 1955.

WRITINGS: (Editor) *An Irkutsk Story* (textbook), Pitman, 1963; *A Workbook for Basic Russian,* Pitman, 1964; *Soviet Historical Drama: Its Role in the Development of a National Mythology,* Nijhoff, 1965; *Essays in Russian Literature: The Conservative View,* Ohio University Press, 1968; (translator with B. Martin) *Dostoevsky, Tolstoy, and Nietzsche,* Ohio University Press, 1969; (editor and translator) *Dostoevsky and the Legend of the Grand Inquisitor,* Cornell University Press, 1972; (contributor) *The Soviet System and Democratic Society,* Herder, 1972; *Four Faces of Rozanov: Christianity, Sex, Jews, and the Russian Revolution,* Philosophical Library, 1978. Contributor of articles and reviews to Slavic studies journals.

WORK IN PROGRESS: Nineteenth-Century Russian Writers Through the Eyes of Their Contemporaries.

AVOCATIONAL INTERESTS: Summer travel in Europe, playing piano and organ.

* * *

ROBSON, Marion M. 1908-

PERSONAL: Born June 15, 1908, in New York, N.Y.; daughter of Otto A. and Rebecca (Reutlinger) Mendelsohn; married Ernest M. Robson (a publisher), January 22, 1948; children: Robert O. *Education:* Attended New York Training School for Teachers. *Home and office address:* P.O. Box 105-A, Parker Ford, Pa. 19457.

CAREER: Board of Education, New York, N.Y., teacher, 1927-61; writer.

WRITINGS: I Only Work Here, Dufour, 1975.

WORK IN PROGRESS: Against Infinity: An Anthology of Contemporary Mathematical Poetry, with husband, Ernest M. Robson.

SIDELIGHTS: Marion Robson comments: "For the past fifteen years I have been an active amateur astronomer. I am also interested in all the physical sciences. Even though my present work, performing in the taping of our cassettes of sound poetry and in the live performances we give, is strictly 'avant-garde,' the lessons of my youth still give me several old-fashioned hobbies. I now do the calligraphy and orthography for our sound poems."

AVOCATIONAL INTERESTS: Artist (oils), cooking, needlework.

* * *

ROCKWELL, Norman (Percevel) 1894-1978

PERSONAL: Born February 3, 1894, in New York, N.Y.; died November 8, 1978, in Stockbridge, Mass.; son of J. Waring (a businessman) and Ann Mary (Hill) Rockwell; married Irene O'Connor (a teacher), 1916 (divorced, 1928); married Mary Rhodes (a teacher), April 17, 1930 (died, 1959); married Mary L. Punderson (a teacher), October 25, 1961; children: Jarvis Waring, Thomas Rhodes, Peter (second marriage). *Education:* Attended National Academy of Design, Chase Art School, and Art Students' League. *Residence:* Stockbridge, Mass. 01262.

CAREER: Free-lance book and magazine illustrator, 1911-78. Rockwell painted magazine covers and illustrated magazines, including *Saturday Evening Post, Ladies' Home Journal, Look, Boy's Life, American* magazine, *Woman's Home Companion,* and *McCall's.* He was art director for *Boy's Life* in the 1910's. His works are represented at the Metropolitan Museum of Art. *Military service:* Served in U.S. Navy during World War I. *Member:* Society of American Illustrators, Free Lance Artists American. *Awards, honors:* A.F.D. from University of Vermont, 1949, and University of Massachusetts, 1961; H.H.D. from Middlebury College, 1954; received Presidential Freedom Medal, 1977.

WRITINGS: My Adventures As an Illustrator as Told to Thomas Rockwell (memoirs), Doubleday, 1960; (with wife Molly Rockwell, and illustrator) *Willie Was Different: The Tale of an Ugly Thrushling* (for children), Funk, 1969; (author of introduction) J. C. Leyendecker, *The J. C. Leyendecker Poster Book,* Watson-Guptill, 1975.

Illustrator: Mark Twain, *Tom Sawyer,* Heritage Club, 1936; Twain, *The Adventures of Huckleberry Finn,* Heritage Club, 1936; *The Norman Rockwell Album,* Doubleday, 1961; Benjamin Franklin, *Poor Richard: The Almanacks for the Years 1733-1758,* Limited Editions Club, 1964, Heritage Press,

1965; Robert Coles, *Dead End School,* Little, Brown, 1968; Jan Wahl, *The Norman Rockwell Storybook,* Windmill Books, 1969; Thomas Rockwell, *Norman Rockwell's Hometown,* Windmill Books, 1970; Thomas S. Buechner, *Norman Rockwell: A Sixty Year Retrospective* (catalog), Abrams, 1972; (with George Mendoza) *Norman Rockwell's Americana ABC,* Dell, 1975; Michael Schau, editor, *The Norman Rockwell Poster Book,* Watson-Guptill, 1976; *The Second Norman Rockwell Poster Book* (introduction by Donald Holden), Watson-Guptill, 1977; Glorina Taborin, *Norman Rockwell's Counting Book,* Harmony Books, c. 1977; *Norman Rockwell's Christmas Book,* Abrams, c. 1977; William Hillcourt, *Norman Rockwell's World of Scouting,* Abrams, c. 1977.

SIDELIGHTS: Norman Rockwell has been America's most beloved artist for over half of a century. His illustrations of idealized, nostalgia-evoking American scenes have made him a tremendous popular success. It has been estimated that Rockwell's pictures have been seen by more people than have seen the combined works of Michelangelo, Rembrandt, and Picasso. But the always modest Rockwell considered himself to be an illustrator rather than an artist. "Some people have been kind enough to call me a fine artist," he once wrote. "I've always called myself an illustrator. I'm not sure what the difference is. All I know is that whatever type of work I do, I try to give it my very best. Art has been my life."

Rockwell's portrayal of America was described by one reviewer as "what middle-class America believed was the way it lived." Although he painted presidents from Roosevelt to Nixon (he painted the latter six times) and foreign heads of state, Rockwell's subjects were usually ordinary people doing everyday things: freckle-faced little boys going fishing; an old woman and a young boy saying grace over Thanksgiving dinner in a diner while truckers gawk; a kindly doctor putting a stethoscope to the heart of a little girl's doll; a young couple going to the soda fountain after the prom. Most of all, his paintings were evidence of the affection Rockwell felt for his subjects. "People somehow get out of your work just about what you put into it." Rockwell wrote, "and if you are interested in the characters that you draw, and understand them and love them, why, the person who sees them is bound to feel the same way."

Rockwell is most closely associated with the cover illustrations he did for the *Saturday Evening Post.* Between 1916 and 1963, he painted 317 covers for the magazine, averaging about one every seven weeks. A Rockwell cover during the magazine's heyday brought an extra 50,000 to 75,000 in newsstand sales, it was once estimated. Among Rockwell's best-loved creations was "Willie Gillis," a young solider who first appeared on the *Post's* cover in October, 1941, and appeared regularly throughout World War II. Probably the best known of Rockwell's work was the series of paintings he did depicting President Roosevelt's "Four Freedoms." Made into posters, the four paintings—"Freedom of Speech," "Freedom from Want," "Freedom from Fear," and "Freedom of Worship,"—were sent on tour to help sell war bonds. They sold almost $135 million worth of bonds nationwide.

Although considered to be the prototypical New Englander, Rockwell spent his youth in New York. His father had been an amateur painter and his maternal grandfather had been a professional artist—"an improverished painter of animals, potboilers and houses," as Rockwell described him. Rockwell remembered doing his first drawings of warships from the Spanish-American War when he was five. When he was a small boy his father liked to read aloud to the family, especially from works by Dickens, and Rockwell became accustomed to sketching characters as his father read.

Rockwell began his academic training while he was in high school, but left high school in his second year to pursue his art studies full-time. He was still a student at the Art Students' League when he landed his first job—illustrating the "Tell Me Why Stories," a series of children's books. Rockwell then began doing illustrations for *Boy's Life,* the magazine of the Boy Scouts. His association with that organization remained lifelong: from 1926 to 1976 Rockwell did the annual Boy Scout calendar every year but one.

In 1916 Rockwell decided the time was right to approach the editor of the *Saturday Evening Post,* the most prestigious magazine of that time, with two paintings and one sketch he had done for the cover. He traveled to Philadelphia in a new tweed suit and asked to be introduced to the editor. He didn't receive an audience, but his work was shown and immediately accepted. Rockwell's first cover, an illustration of a small boy pushing a baby carriage past a group of sneering boys dressed in baseball uniforms, appeared that year. Although when Rockwell was fifteen he had agreed with two fellow art students never to make more than fifty dollars a week and always to adhere to the highest artistic standards, he abandoned the first part of the pact rather early in his career. Before World War I he was making $40,000 a year and his salary never went below that even during the depression.

The painter was known for his photographic eye for detail and his accuracy. Even Rockwell detractors commended him for his fine technique. Rockwell always used models from the towns in which he lived (Stockbridge, Massachusetts from 1953 until his death), and owned an extensive and valuable collection of costumes and props. When he was hired to illustrate the Mark Twain books, *Tom Sawyer* and *Huckleberry Finn,* Rockwell realized that what was missing from previous illustrations was authenticity. So he traveled to Hannibal, Missouri, Twain's territory, made sketches on location, and brought back costumes from the area. His extra work proved successful because his illustrations of these books are regarded to be the best available. Beginning in 1936 Rockwell employed photography in his work, a practice which is almost universal among illustrators, although few admit it.

Despite his large popular following, art critics have generally ignored Rockwell's contributions or have derided him as the "Lawrence Welk of art." His one-man show at the prestigious Dannenberg Galleries in 1969 illustrated that clash of opinion between critics and the public. While the critical reception was lukewarm, the show was a huge popular success. "I could never be satisfied with just the approval of the critics, and, boy, I've certainly had to be satisfied without it," Rockwell commented.

Critics have accused Rockwell of portraying only the pleasant aspects of American life. He admitted that he viewed his subjects in an idealized fashion, and explained: "As I grew up and found that the world wasn't the perfectly pleasant place I had thought it to be, I unconsciously decided to compensate. So I painted only the ideal aspects of life—pictures in which there were no drunken slatterns or self-centered mothers, in which, on the contrary, foxy grandpas played baseball with the kids. . . . The people in my pictures aren't mentally ill or deformed. The situations they get into are commonplace, everyday situations, not the agonizing crises and tangles of life."

In the 1960's, however, after he had left the *Post* because of its new policy of "sophisticated muckraking," Rockwell began painting more realistic and timely scenes. As an on-the-scene illustrator for *Look* magazine, he painted a picture of a terrified black child being led to school by U.S. marshals and another of three civil rights workers who were murdered in the South. "For 47 years," he wrote, "I portrayed the best of all possible worlds—grandfathers, puppy dogs—things like that. That kind of stuff is dead now and I think it's about time."

Finally, Rockwell's major limitation as an artist was his lack of ideas. "My worst enemy is the world-shaking idea," he once said, "stretching my neck like a swan and forgetting that I'm a duck." Richard Reeves commented that Rockwell's ideas for paintings were seldom his own; he simply executed the suggestions of editors and others. "I found out that most of Norman Rockwell's work was other people's ideas," Reeves wrote,"—the man could have been a cobbler, a craftsman, although they'd be damn fine shoes—and that is his great and sad flaw." Thomas Buechner, however, defended Rockwell's work. "Millions of people have been moved by his picture stories," he commented. "To be popular with such an audience requires a very special kind of artist. He has to hide all personal opinions, causes and preferences that his readers might share."

John Russell remarked that Rockwell "was lucky enough to live at a time when the demand for what he could do had no limits. . . . He worked very hard, he took all the opportunities that came his way, and he happened to be around at a time when the cover of the *Saturday Evening Post* was an infallible index to popular feeling." Russell concluded: "Norman Rockwell will not live in the history of art; but as a witness to a certain view of what America should be, he was the right man in the right place at the right time."

BIOGRAPHICAL/CRITICAL SOURCES: Norman Rockwell, *My Adventures as an Illustrator as Told to Thomas Rockwell* (memoirs), Doubleday, 1960; Thomas S. Buechner, *Norman Rockwell: Artist and Illustrator,* Abrams, 1970; *New York Times Magazine,* February 28, 1971; *Look,* June 1, 1971; *Saturday Evening Post,* summer, 1971, September, 1973, March, 1974, May, 1976, July, 1976, July, 1977, January, 1978; *Forbes,* June 1, 1972; *Ladies Home Journal,* November, 1972; *Good Housekeeping,* April, 1976; *American Artist,* July, 1976; *Norman Rockwell and the Saturday Evening Post,* Rittenhouse, c. 1976; Donald Walton, *A Rockwell Portrait: An Intimate Biography,* Sheed Andrews & McMeel, 1978; *New York Times,* November 10, 1978; *Washington Post,* November 10, 1978.*

—*Sketch by Barbara A. Welch*

* * *

RODERUS, Frank 1942-

PERSONAL: Born September 21, 1942, in Pittsburgh, Pa.; son of Frank James (in sales) and Alice (Hollenshead) Roderus; married Kay Marsh, March 27, 1965 (divorced, August, 1977); married Betty Richardson, June 10, 1978; children: Melisse, Franklin, Stephen Quick, Amanda Quick. *Education:* Attended Emory-at-Oxford Junior College, 1958-60, and St. Petersburg Junior College, 1964-65. *Religion:* Associate Reformed Presbyterian. *Home:* 3310 Portal Dr., Colorado Springs, Colo. 80909.

CAREER: Free-lance writer, 1975—. *Military service:* U.S. Army, 1960-63. *Member:* Western Writers of America.

WRITINGS—Western novels: *The 33 Brand,* Doubleday, 1977; *Journey to Utah,* Doubleday, 1977; *Duster* (juvenile), Independence Press (Independence, Mo.), 1977; *Easy Money,* Doubleday, 1978; *The Keystone Kid,* Doubleday, 1978; *Home to Texas,* Ace Books, 1978; *Hell Creek Cabin,* Doubleday, 1979; *The Name Is Hart,* Ace Books, 1979; *Sheepherding Man,* Doubleday, 1980.

WORK IN PROGRESS: Another western novel, for Doubleday.

SIDELIGHTS: Roderus comments: "I wrote my first fiction (a western) at age five and never wanted to do anything else. I enjoy researching the American west as well as my travels in the area. My novels are built around my characters, who I like to think are representative of the people who still raise livestock in this great country."

* * *

RODGERS, Dorothy F(einer) 1909-

PERSONAL: Born May 4, 1909, in New York, N.Y.; daughter of Benjamin and May (Adelson) Feiner; married Richard Rodgers (a composer), May 5, 1930; children: Mary (Mrs. Henry Guettel), Linda (Mrs. Daniel Melnick). *Education:* Attended Wellesley College, 1926-28. *Residence:* Fairfield, Conn. 06430. *Office: McCall's,* 230 Park Ave., New York, N.Y. 10017.

CAREER: Repairs, Inc. (home refurbishing), New York City, president, 1935-41; *McCall's* magazine, New York City, co-author with daughter Mary of monthly column, "Of Two Minds," 1971—; appeared on nationally syndicated radio program, "A Word to the Wives," 1971-72. Sculptress; inventor of Jonny Mop and Basic Try-On Dress Patterns. Member of board of directors of New York chapter of American Red Cross, 1954-62; member of New York State Council on Arts; trustee at large, Federation of Jewish Philanthropies. *Member:* American Institute of Interior Designers, Cosmopolitan Club (New York City). *Awards, honors:* Named key woman of the year, Federation of Jewish Philanthropies, 1956.

WRITINGS: My Favorite Things: A Personal Guide to Decorating and Entertaining, Atheneum, 1964; *The House in My Head,* Atheneum, 1967; (with daughter, Mary Rodgers) *A Word to the Wives,* Knopf, 1970; *A Personal Book* (autobiography), Harper, 1977. Columnist. Inventor of Turn and Learn Storybooks, 1972.

SIDELIGHTS: Dorothy Rodgers is perhaps best known as the co-author with her daughter, Mary, of the *McCall's* column, "Of Two Minds." Each month readers pose several questions on such topics as marriage, weekend guests, careers, and in-laws to the mother/daughter team. Dorothy's advice appears in black ink; Mary's answers are in blue.

Word to the Wives, also co-authored by the Rodgers team, was written using the same format of different color type for each author. This book gives advice on coping with the problems of motherhood and housewifery in middle- to upper-class society. Judy Klemesrud describes the authors: Dorothy is "an elegant . . . former interior decorator whose friends rave about her taste and call her 'La Perfecta.' Mary Rodgers is a . . . composer and mother of five who likes to talk about her 'sloppy dinner parties' and 'frumpy clothes.'" The differences in age and preferred life styles of the women cause them to disagree on many topics, thus providing a wide range of opinions on each subject covered in the book. Dorothy Rodgers noted, however, that they both agree "the style in which you want to live is very much up to you."

In 1935 Rodgers began Repairs, Inc., a home refurbishing company. Later she became a professional interior decorator and wrote *The House in My Head,* "a step-by-step account of how she built her dream house." A *Time* reviewer remarked that the "story has an irresistable fairy-tale aura."

Rodgers's fourth book is an autobiography that includes stories of her courtship and marriage to renowned composer Richard Rodgers. A *Publishers Weekly* reviewer declared "when Mrs. Rodgers talks about her various careers it is obvious that this capable, creative woman was destined to emerge from the chrysalis of reflected fame."

BIOGRAPHICAL/CRITICAL SOURCES: New York Times Book Review, December 6, 1964; *Look,* October 31, 1967; *Time,* December 15, 1967; *Publishers Weekly,* September 21, 1970, February 21, 1977; *New York Times,* October 29, 1970, June 10, 1977; Dorothy Rogers, *A Personal Book* (autobiography), Harper, 1977; *Cue,* December 26, 1977.*

* * *

RODGERS, Richard (Charles) 1902-1979

PERSONAL: Born June 28, 1902, in New York, N.Y.; died December 30, 1979, in Manhattan, N.Y.; son of William Abraham (a physician) and Mamie (Levy) Rodgers; married Dorothy Feiner (an author and inventor), March 5, 1930; children: Mary (Mrs. Henry Guettel), Linda (Mrs. Daniel Melnick). *Education:* Attended Columbia University, 1919-21, and Institute of Musical Art of the Juilliard School of Music (now Juilliard School of Music), 1921-23. *Home:* 598 Madison Ave., New York, N.Y. 10022.

CAREER: Composer, producer, lyricist. Composer with lyricist Lorenz Hart of musical comedy scores, including "Garrick Gaieties," 1925, "Dearest Enemy," 1925, "A Connecticut Yankee," 1927, "On Your Toes," 1936, "Babes in Arms," 1937, and "Pal Joey," 1940; composer with lyricist Oscar Hammerstein II of scores, including "Oklahoma!," 1943, "State Fair" (film), 1945, "Carousel," 1945, "South Pacific," 1949, "The King and I," 1951, "Cinderella" (television), 1957, "Flower Drum Song," 1958, and "The Sound of Music," 1959; composer and lyricist of "No Strings," 1962, "The Valiant Years" (television), 1962, and "Androcles and the Lion" (television), 1970. Associated with Music Theatre of Lincoln Center, Barnard College, Actors Fund of America, and New York Philharmonic; former member of board of directors of Juilliard School of Music.

MEMBER: Authors League of America, National Institute of Arts and Letters, National Association of American Composers and Conductors, Dramatists Guild (past president). *Awards, honors:* Special Pulitzer award, 1945, for "Oklahoma!"; Donaldson award, 1945, for "Carousel" score; University Medal for Excellence, Columbia University, 1949; Donaldson award, 1949, Pulitzer Prize, 1950, and Antoinette Perry Award (Tony), 1950, all for "South Pacific"; Donaldson award, 1952, for "Pal Joey"; Antoinette Perry Award, 1952, and Christopher Award, 1956, both for "The King and I"; Columbia College award, 1952; U.S. Navy distinguished public service award, 1953; Alexander Hamilton Medal, Columbia College Alumni Association, 1956; Emmy Award from National Academy of Television Arts and Sciences, 1962, for "The Valiant Years"; Antoinette Perry Award, 1962, for "No Strings"; Creative Arts Award, Brandeis University, 1968. Academic: Honorary degrees from Drury College, 1949, Columbia University, 1954, University of Massachusetts, 1954, University of Bridgeport, 1962, University of Maryland, 1962, Hamilton College, 1965, Brandeis University, 1965, Fairfield University, 1968, New York University, 1971, New England Conservatory of Music, 1976.

WRITINGS: (Author of introduction and composer) *The Rodgers and Hart Song Book: The Words and Music of Forty-Seven of Their Songs From Twenty-Two Shows and Two Movies,* Simon & Schuster, 1951, reprinted, 1977; (with Oscar Hammerstein II) *Rodgers and Hammerstein Song Book,* Simon & Schuster, 1968; *One Hundred Best Songs From the Twenties and the Thirties,* Crown, 1973; (author of introduction) *The Best of Broadway,* Harmony, 1974; *Musical Stages* (autobiography), Random House, 1975. Coauthor of scripts for plays, including "By Jupiter," 1942.

SIDELIGHTS: Richard Rodgers demonstrated his musical talent at an early age. By the time he was four he had begun to pick out tunes from "The Merry Widow" on the piano and ten years later he wrote his first song, "My Auto Show Girl." Soon he began to compose songs for amateur productions. While attending Columbia College he was honored to be the first freshman ever to write the score for the annual varsity show.

At Columbia, Rodgers met Lorenz Hart and the two became collaborators for the next twenty years. The vastly different life styles and temperaments of the men made them seem unlikely associates, with the disciplined and meticulous Rodgers playing "Teacher to Hart's Errant Schoolboy," as Bobby Short described it. It was "a case of love at first sight," however, and the two formed a successful Broadway partnership until shortly before Hart's death in 1943. Some of their hit songs included "My Funny Valentine," "The Most Beautiful Girl in the World," "Manhattan," "Thou Swell," "Johnny One Note," "Blue Moon," "The Lady Is a Tramp," and "Bewitched, Bothered, and Bewildered."

In 1943, Rodgers teamed up with another Columbia friend, Oscar Hammerstein II, forming one of the best known songwriting teams in the history of the American musical. Their first collaboration was the Pulitzer Prize winning play, "Oklahoma!" This innovative play was the first ever to fully integrate the music and dance into the plot. Critics praised the songs for their appropriateness to the mood and character of the play. Several of the songs became popular hits, especially "Oh, What a Beautiful Mornin'" and "People Will Say We're in Love."

Rodgers and Hammerstein proceeded to produce a continuous stream of Broadway hits until Hammerstein's death in 1960. Many of the plays were adapted as motion pictures, the most profitable being "The Sound of Music." Some of their best-loved songs included: "June Is Bustin' Out All Over" and "If I Loved You" from "Carousel"; "I Enjoy Being a Girl" from "Flower Drum Song"; "Getting to Know You" from "The King and I"; "Some Enchanted Evening" and "I'm Gonna Wash That Man Right Outa My Hair" from "South Pacific"; and "My Favorite Things" and "Edelweiss" from "The Sound of Music."

Though now lacking a permanent lyricist, Rodgers has continued on his own, composing works for television and the stage. He served as his own lyricist for "No Strings" in 1962.

Commenting on his work, Rodgers told Mary Tanenbaum, "I guess I am proudest of 'Carousel,' because I like the score best and what the show has to say—based, of course, on the 'Liliom' of Molnar—about a man who really didn't know how to love his wife and child until too late. . . ."

Rodgers's autobiography, *Musical Stages,* contains anecdotes about the composer's experiences writing Broadway musicals. Margo Jefferson remarked that "in his implacably good-tempered, judiciously written autobiography, Richard Rodgers emerges as all of a piece: a man who knew what he wanted, who got it through a dedication to work that has been total but dispassionate, and one whose supreme gifts as a writer of popular songs remain a mystery—above all to himself." Mel Gussow reflected, "What makes this book a special pleasure are the reminiscences of those thriving days when songwriting seemed like the headiest occupation in the world."

BIOGRAPHICAL/CRITICAL SOURCES: Saturday Evening Post, January 28, 1967; *Cue,* December 26, 1970; Deems Taylor, *Some Enchanted Evenings: The Story of Rodgers and Hammerstein,* Greenwood Press, 1972; *Newsweek,* October 6, 1975; *New York Times Book Review,* October 12, 1975, November 21, 1976; *Christian Science Monitor,* November 5, 1975; Samuel Marx and Jan Clayton, *Rodgers & Hart,* Putnam, 1976; Dorothy Hart, *Thou Swell, Thou Witty,* Harper, 1976; *Choice,* February, 1976.

OBITUARIES: Chicago Tribune, January 1, 1980; *New York Times,* January 1, 1980; *Washington Post,* January 1, 1980.*

* * *

RODIN, Arnold W. 1917-

PERSONAL: Born March 31, 1917, in Bridgeport, Conn.; married wife, Sophie; children: Ellen, Richard. *Education:* City College (now of the City University of New York), B.A., 1939. *Home:* 1 East Schiller, Chicago, Ill. 60601. *Office:* Cox & Rodin, Inc., 230 North Michigan Ave., Chicago, Ill. 60601.

CAREER: Newark News, Newark, N.J., journalist, 1937-47; free-lance writer, 1947-53; public relations consultant, 1954-58; Imberman & DeForest, Chicago, Ill., executive vice-president, 1958-68; Cox & Rodin, Inc., Chicago, president, 1968—. Executive director of Home Ventilating Institute and Humidifier Institute; managing director of American Home Lighting Institute. *Member:* Public Relations Society of America.

WRITINGS: Woman Soldier, Fawcett, 1951, reprinted as *The Partisans,* Manor, 1973; *Moment of Truth,* Fawcett, 1953.

WORK IN PROGRESS: A novel.

* * *

ROGERS, Charles B. 1911-

PERSONAL: Born January 27, 1911, in Great Bend, Kan.; son of Walter and Sarah (Schoonover) Rogers; married Ruth Estella Walker; children: Robert Codey. *Education:* Attended National Academy of Design, 1935-36; Bethany College, Lindsborg, Kan., B.F.A., 1942; California College of Arts and Crafts, M.F.A., 1947. *Home:* 102 East Main St., Ellsworth, Kan. 67439. *Office:* Rogers House Museum-Gallery, Snake Row, Ellsworth, Kan. 67439.

CAREER: Bethany College, Lindsborg, Kan., head of School of Art, 1947-53; Huntington Hartford Foundation (art colony), Pacific Palisades, Calif., manager and assistant director, 1954-66; Kansas Wesleyan University, Salina, head of School of Art, 1966-67; Rogers House Museum-Gallery, Ellsworth, Kan., director, 1968—. Artist, with more than a hundred solo shows and two-hundred-fifty group shows in the United States, England, and Japan; work represented in permanent collections, including Library of Congress, Metropolitan Museum of Art, and Philadelphia Museum of Art; also worked as carpenter, sign painter, and artist's model. Member of faculty at California College of Arts and Crafts. *Military service:* U.S. Navy, printer, 1942-46.

MEMBER: Society of American Etchers, American Institute of Fine Arts (fellow), Society of American Graphic Artists, Kansas Federation of Art. *Awards, honors:* More than a hundred-thirty-five art awards, including Mikami Award, for Japanese brush painting; award from Metropolitan Museum of Art, for arms collection; purchase award from Library of Congress, for Pennell Collection; named Kansan of the year, 1969; honorary member of St. Mary's College of California; grants from Tiffany Foundation; Huntington Hartford Foundation fellowships.

WRITINGS—All self-illustrated: *Quill of the Kansan,* Rogers House, 1970; *The Great West,* Rogers House, 1973; *Images of the American West: Paintings and Haiku,* Celestial Arts, 1975; *Country Neighbor,* Rogers House, 1977; *Fine Points of Drawing and Sketching,* Rogers House, 1980. Contributor to art magazines.

WORK IN PROGRESS—Both self-illustrated: *Aphorisms on Art* and *The High Plains in Sumi Egg-Emulsion.*

SIDELIGHTS: Rogers built his first etching press at the age of seventeen, and became one of the youngest members of the Society of American Etchers. After a long career of teaching and exhibiting his work internationally, he returned to the high plains country and established Rogers House.

The museum and gallery was once a historic cowboy hotel in Ellsworth, the same Kansas town that hired Marshal Wild Bill Hickok. Now the hotel houses a wide variety of galleries comprising a tribute to the mountains, plains, and prairies.

Rogers comments: "My major interests are the variety of beauty in our land and the moods of nature. I wish to justify my time on earth by creating constructively, instead of being destructive, and I am responsible to myself in that endeavor. I am a loner, who finds it less than tolerable to suffer fools other than himself."

* * *

ROGERS, JoAnn V. 1940-

PERSONAL: Born July 28, 1940. *Home:* 620 Seattle Dr., Lexington, Ky. 40503. *Office:* College of Library Science, University of Kentucky, Lexington, Ky. 40506.

CAREER: Previously a high school teacher and high school library media specialist; University of Kentucky, Lexington, assistant professor of library science, 1974—.

WRITINGS: (Editor) *Libraries and Young Adults: Media, Services, and Librarianship,* Libraries Unlimited, 1979. Contributor to library journals.

* * *

ROGERS, Thomas Hunton 1927-

PERSONAL: Born June 23, 1927, in Chicago, Ill.; son of Thomas Hunton (a chemist) and Elizabeth (a chemist; maiden name, Vinsonhaler) Rogers; married Jacqueline Ragner, June 16, 1956; children: Rebecca, Susan. *Education:* Harvard University, B.A. (cum laude), 1950; University of Iowa, M.A., 1953, Ph.D., 1960. *Politics:* Democrat. *Religion:* Presbyterian. *Home:* 502 East Foster St., State College, Pa. 16801. *Agent:* Georges Borchardt, Inc., 136 East 57th St., New York, N.Y. 10022. *Office:* 131 South Burrows, University Park, Pa. 16801.

CAREER: University of Chicago, Chicago, Ill., instructor, 1955-58, assistant professor of English, 1958-61; Pennsylvania State University, University Park, Pa., assistant professor, 1961-68, associate professor, 1968-73, professor of English, 1973—. *Military service:* U.S. Army Air Forces, 1945-46. *Member:* P.E.N. *Awards, honors:* Guggenheim grant, 1969; Rosenthal Foundation Award, 1973, for *The Confession of a Child of the Century by Samuel Heather*; Friends of American Writers prize, 1973.

WRITINGS—Novels: *The Pursuit of Happiness,* New American Library, 1968; *The Confession of a Child of the Century by Samuel Heather,* Simon & Schuster, 1972; *Jerry in Love,* Simon & Schuster, 1980. Contributor of stories and reviews to various periodicals.

SIDELIGHTS: The Pursuit of Happiness, as the reviewer for *Newsweek* observed, is a decidedly pre-Vietnam novel about a young disenchanted couple. A National Book Award nominee, it is the story of William Popper and Jane Kaufman, graduate students at the University of Chicago and children of good families. When William faces a one-year prison sentence for killing an old woman in a car accident, they realize they cannot pursue happiness in the United States and exile themselves to Mexico.

Philip Roth dubbed the hero of this first novel "the WASP without a country, the wandering goy" and, indeed, many critics have zeroed in on the book's themes of alienation and distrust. Irving Howe wrote that "it seems so thoroughly to express the sentiments of a certain brand of campus radicalism—innocent, egocentric, middle-class, and apolitical—that younger readers will feel that here is a book which really speaks for them." On the other hand, John C. Devlin has pointed out the superficiality of Popper's non-conformity—his long hair, blue jeans, and lapsed driver's license—suggesting the satire in Rogers's portrait of an upper-class dropout.

Marian Engel noted some of the book's stylistic strengths: its flat, witty dialogue; its fidelity to speech patterns; its accurate rendering of human relationships. Similarly, Guy Davenport lauded Rogers's eye for detail and his ability to maintain an entertaining pace, while Richard Gilman, likening the book to Camus's *The Stranger,* praised its wry, deft humor and economy.

Rogers's second novel, *The Confession of a Child of the Century by Samuel Heather,* is a first-person narrative, told in the words of Samuel Heather. According to its "author," the book is a "comical historical pastoral" written in "a mixed style, both high and low, banal and eloquent, witty and sloppy." It begins in Kansas City in 1949, where Samuel, the son of the Episcopal bishop, is on vacation from Harvard. His story takes him from Boston to China by way of Korea, through a father-son struggle and love affairs with an Old Boston heiress and a Peking Maoist. After a stint with the CIA, he ends up writing successful spy novels.

Jonathan Yardley considered *Confession* a classic comedy, "fiction of great depth and distinction," and ranked Samuel as "one of the best realized characters of recent fiction, a 'mine of contradictions' who wrestles valiantly with the inanities, insanities and contradictions of the time." Roger Sale offered a dissenting opinion, describing Samuel as a "spoiled, educated, callow, aggressive young man"; yet Sale still found the book "an honorable failure."

The Pursuit of Happiness was adapted as a film in 1971.

CA INTERVIEWS THE AUTHOR

CA interviewed Thomas Rogers by phone October 25, 1979, at his office at Pennsylvania State University.

CA: You've written very sympathetically about young people at odds with the Establishment. Is your interest in young people as subjects of your novels related to your teaching?

ROGERS: In part it is, but preoccupation with adolescents and young people in their early twenties is fairly common among all novelists because the years from seventeen to twenty-five are when character takes shape. Fielding, Richardson, and Smollett were all middle-aged when they wrote about their young Toms and Clarissas and Humphreys. Dickens went on writing about young people when he was middle-aged. It's natural. A further reason why middle-aged novelists go on writing about young people is that if they are married and have children, they are seeing the whole process a second time through the lives of their children. This is certainly my case. I have been going through a second adolescence with my girls.

CA: One reviewer of The Pursuit of Happiness *complained that the 1960's young couple of that novel was more reminiscent of the 1950's. Although certain periods of rebelliousness stand out, such as the 1920's and the 1960's, don't you find aspects of youthful rebellion that are constant in almost every generation?*

ROGERS: I do. There is always the father problem, for instance. That reviewer was right, however, that Jane and William in *The Pursuit of Happiness* were originally conceived as young people of the 1950's or even late 1940's. Then, for reasons that no longer seem important, I put in a few references to The New Frontier at the beginning of the novel. When I was writing the book in the mid-1960's, the period 1948 to 1952 was not sufficiently far off to justify a "this-is-the-way-we-lived-then" novel, so I decided to pretend the action was happening in the early 1960's. I guess that reviewer picked it up.

It is not a serious flaw in the book—at least in my opinion—since my intentions were moral and comic rather than documentary. As I wrote the book I was thinking of a young man who had been an advisee of mine when I was teaching at Chicago in the late 1950's. He was thinking of not registering for the draft although he could easily have been exempted because he'd been brought up as a pacifist. Still, he felt he should not register at all, which would have meant a jail sentence. I tried to persuade him that he didn't *need* jail at his age. My novel was in part a carry-over from the arguments I had with that boy. I meant *The Pursuit of Happiness* to be an antiideological, anticonfrontational book.

CA: Have your teaching and writing complemented each other?

ROGERS: At times, as in the case I've just cited. Recently, though, I find that I cannot teach and write successfully at the same time, and there is less connection between what I am saying to my students and what I am writing at home. Also I have less energy now than I used to have, and I would really like to be able to stop teaching and devote my whole time to writing.

CA: Have you seen a change in educational standards during your teaching career?

ROGERS: It's hard to say, because I was educated at Chicago and at Harvard, but I don't teach there and don't know what undergraduates are like now at those places. At Penn State I get some quite good students who seem to me to be totally unprepared. They don't know anything, though they are very intelligent. Maybe at Harvard the undergraduates still arrive prepared for a college education. I hope so, though I have the feeling that standards of preparation have gone down everywhere. You just get fewer and fewer students who have done a substantial amount of reading when they turn up at college. Even the ones interested in writing and literature have read far less than was common when I was younger.

CA: Have you seen other notable changes in students?

ROGERS: I've been coming across a phenomenon that is curious. In many high schools students are encouraged to express their opinions about everything with the result that they do not learn how to listen. In my literature classes I will often introduce an author by giving a fair amount of biographical, historical, and cultural background. This seems to appall my students who don't know what to do with such material. Sometimes I'm asked at the end of class, "Do we have to know that?" My answer is, "I've told you, so now you do know it," but of course they don't. They are not receptive; facts do not seem to sink in. I don't know what really explains this, but few students seem to have the knack of simply absorbing things and remembering them. It's a pity, because memory is the mother of the muses.

CA: As a teacher of literature and writing, how do you feel a person can best help another person learn to write?

ROGERS: The best thing a teacher of writing can do is to help the student writer understand his own material. Often the student has characters he doesn't really understand and a plot whose full significance he hasn't seen. When I can show the student how much more there is in his story than he himself has seen, I feel I'm helping him. Teaching the so-called techniques of fiction (flashbacks, internal monologue, and so forth) is superficial, though one has to deal with such matters. The basic thing, however, is to help the student writer see what he is doing or trying to do. This takes a lot of time.

CA: The Confession of a Child of the Century *contains some very fine comedy: Jonathan Yardley in the* New York Times Book Review *called it "comedy in the classic sense." Are there writers whose work you admire specifically for comedy, irony, or satire?*

ROGERS: Quite a few. I love Dickens, George Bernard Shaw, Evelyn Waugh, Jane Austen, Mark Twain, Ring Lardner, H. L. Mencken, Robert Benchley. Benchley was one of my heroes when I was an adolescent. I still read him. I like Thurber, Salinger, A. J. Liebling, and Randall Jarrell. Jarrell wrote only one novel, but, boy, is it good.

CA: Has your humor been influenced by Fielding and Sterne?

ROGERS: I've not been able to read *Tristram Shandy*. I like the idea, and every now and then I open the book, but I don't get very far with it. It seems to me invertebrate. I do like Fielding, but I haven't read him for a long time. Back in eleventh grade *Tom Jones* was on our reading list, and I remember roaring with laughter, but I doubt that I have reread much of it since, though I remained fond of Fielding through college. I remember writing a senior paper about his minor works: *Jonathan Wild* and *A Journal of a Voyage to Lisbon*. But he's dropped out of the picture since, and Dickens and later writers are the ones I read most and find the funniest.

CA: Are there other writers that you enjoy reading now?

ROGERS: I read Trollope a great deal and Stendhal and Tolstoy and Colette, but since I am writing my own books and teaching, I don't have time to keep up with what's being written now. When I read for pleasure, I tend to go back to authors I'm already fond of, authors I cut my teeth on. I reread mainly.

CA: Was the past summer your first time at Yaddo?

ROGERS: I first went to Yaddo in 1968, and I've been there five or six times both in the winter and summer. It's always been a good experience except for one occasion. Yaddo has a peaceful, family kind of atmosphere, and I find it a quite noncompetitive, supportive place. At meals people sit around chatting pleasantly without trying to show off. I've gotten a lot done there. This summer was particularly productive. My one bad experience was in 1972 when I went up there to start a new novel. That was just a disaster. Maybe the atmosphere is not good for starting things, but it's certainly good for getting along with them.

CA: You won the Rosenthal Award for Confession. *How do you feel about awards?*

ROGERS: It's nice to win them. There's money involved, and some honor and glory. I enjoyed very much being a part of the National Institute ceremonial with a numbered chair on the seating plan. I wish there were more awards.

CA: Have you found any criticism helpful, any of the scholarly reviews or just plain book reviews?

ROGERS: There haven't been any scholarly reviews of my books. The scholarly and critical quarterlies ignore me. I'm well reviewed in the weeklies and in newspapers. I am quite impressed by the attention my books get in newspapers and by the sometimes felicitously worded and quite personal sounding columns that newspaper reviewers turn out. Of course reviews can't be helpful because the book is already finished by the time they are written. The helpful reactions come from my friends and from my editor, Ted Solotaroff. I read aloud from what I'm writing, and I find that helps a lot. People often make very useful and suggestive comments after a reading.

CA: Has your writing procedure changed with each novel?

ROGERS: I wish I had a procedure. I blunder my way through my novels. The first two began in the same way. I had an idea for the action, and I had certain characters I'd been thinking about, and suddenly the characters stepped into the action and the novels were born. With *The Pursuit of Happiness* and *The Confession of a Child of the Century*, the whole problem was to get my heroes from where they started to where they were supposed to end up. I had trouble with the middle part of both novels, and some of the flaws in those books stem from the fact that I never had a completed manuscript until the very end. There are first draft sections in both books. I kept trying to get it all perfect before I moved on to the next chapter, but the middles were so difficult for me that I skipped over and wrote the endings and then went back.

My current novel began very differently from either of my first books. It began as a long daydream with plot and characters united from the start. My writing "procedure" was similar in that I have blundered about a good deal, but a bit different in that I now have a completed manuscript and am trying to improve it. I believe now that the way to write novels is to bull along no matter how bad it sounds, and then revise.

CA: How much do you plan in your mind before you start the actual writing?

ROGERS: With my first two novels I knew the beginning and the ending, and I knew what the characters had to go through to get to the ending, but I didn't know exactly how they would make it through the middle.

CA: Does that unfold as you go?

ROGERS: Yes, if things are working well. With my current book, however, I am having a different problem. I did not know where the action really started, so I began writing in what has turned out to be the middle of the book. I had to work backwards, which is unusual for me.

CA: What is the new novel about?

ROGERS: It is about a person named Jerry Engels. As I originally conceived it, I was going to tell his story from his adolescence to his death in his thirties, but working on the book I discovered I had a whole novel just about his growing up and coming of age. As it now stands, the book is a coming-of-age story that ends when Jerry is still seventeen. I may write the sequel sometime, but not right away.

CA: Do you feel that age tends to help one's perspective as a novelist?

ROGERS: Yes. It has certainly helped my perspective, anyway. My novels deal with the Sturm and Drang of the college years or even earlier, and it takes a while to get some perspective on it all. That period can still be painful and threatening even in middle age. There are terrific pressures on young people at that age, and it is hard to deal with those pressures in a comic way that still does justice to them. I suppose if I had been able to write tragic or just serious novels, I might have been able to start publishing earlier than I did, but I've always wanted to be a comic writer. I didn't publish until I was thirty-nine. I think it takes that long before one can acquire a genuinely comic perspective on life, particularly adolescent life.

BIOGRAPHICAL/CRITICAL SOURCES: Harper's, May, 1968; *New York Times,* May 25, 1968; *Washington Post Book World,* June 9, 1968; *Life,* June 21, 1968; *National Review,* July 16, 1968; *Newsweek,* July 22, 1968, June 12, 1972; *Nation,* July 22, 1968; *New York Times Book Review,* July 28, 1968, June 11, 1972; *New York Review of Books,* August 1, 1968, June 29, 1972; *New Republic,* August 17, 1968; *New Yorker,* August 31, 1968; *Yale Review,* autumn, 1968; *Spectator,* April 18, 1969; *Books and Bookmen,* July, 1969; *Virginia Quarterly Review,* autumn, 1972.

—*Interview by Jean W. Ross*

* * *

ROIPHE, Anne Richardson 1935-
(Anne Richardson)

PERSONAL: Born December 25, 1935, in New York; daughter of Eugene (a lawyer) and Blanche (Phillips) Roth; married Jack Richardson, 1958 (divorced, 1963); married Herman Roiphe (a psychoanalyst), January 20, 1967; children: Emily, Kate, Becky; stepchildren: Margaret, Jean. *Education:* Sara Lawrence College, B.A., 1957. *Home:* 130 East 95th St., New York, N.Y. 10029. *Agent:* Carl Brandt, 101 Park Ave., New York, N.Y. 10028.

CAREER: Writer, 1966—.

WRITINGS—Novels: (Under name Anne Richardson) *Digging Out,* McGraw, 1967; *Up the Sandbox!,* Simon & Schuster, 1970; *Long Division,* Simon & Schuster, 1972; (under name Anne Richardson) *Torch Song,* Farrar, Straus, 1977.

SIDELIGHTS: Roiphe's novels, which largely explore a woman's search for identity, have been generally well received. Her first book, *Digging Out,* presents the personal reflections of Laura Smith as she attends the bedside of her dying mother. Laura recalls the history of her large and rich Jewish family, "from which she intends to secede at the first opportunity," interweaving its past with the details of her mother's illness. Stanley Kauffmann observed: "What the protagonist, Laura, is digging out is herself. . . . The relation with her dying mother is conveyed with heat, with a compressed, oblique anguish." Phoebe Adams found the book "energetic and intelligent, and [Roiphe] . . . has the storyteller's weapons of interest in people and an ability to order events for dramatic effect."

Roiphe's next book, *Up the Sandbox!,* "captures the minutiae of matrimony and maternity," according to I. P. Heldman, "evoking only too clearly the 'educated' woman's dilemma, torn between vulnerability for her children and her demands for self." The story alternates the inner musings of Margaret Reynolds, as a young Manhattan mother who ministers to the needs of her two small children, and the Margaret Reynolds who envisions wild dream adventures, such as blowing up the George Washington Bridge with a group of black militants. The novel, wrote Elizabeth Easton, "shows enormous insight into the problems that disturb women everywhere. A sensitive, perceptive, shrewd book—and often a very amusing one." Marilyn Bender commented: "Margaret operates on two levels: her real world of the submissive, discontented wife-mother and her surrealistic dream realm of the liberated woman she only half wishes to be. In representing the latter, Mrs. Roiphe displays considerable gifts as a satirist, black humorist and piercing analyst of fuzzy white liberalism."

Another novel, *Long Division,* looks at the problems faced by a wife and mother when her husband deserts her. "What I'm doing in this car flying down these screaming highways," says the protaganist Emily, "is getting my tail to Juarez so I can legally rid myself of the crummy son-of-a-bitch who promised me a tomorrow like a yummy fruitcake and delivered instead . . . a garbage of life." Emily's story, I. P. Heldman remarked, includes a rich "historical perspective on woman's lot" and the author's implicit conclusion that "Woman's Lib is viable for the few, not the many." "In probing the depths of one female's agonized psyche," Heldman continued, "Anne Roiphe has pursued an intensely personal vision and produced a piercing poignant portrayal of a modern woman."

Torch Song, Roiphe's fourth novel, is a story of a failed marriage. Marjorie Weiss, whose attraction to an aspiring artist eventually results in marriage, becomes the condoning, tolerant victim of her sexually sick, sadistic husband. Though motherhood, as Julian Moynahan noted, "helps to awaken her from this doze or daze of impotent resentment and suffering," she remains relatively un-enlightened by all that has happened to her. Even after she is abandoned by her husband, Moynahan added, the reader is struck by Marjorie's failure to understand her experience, persisting in the self-deception that she was naive and innocent. But the book, stated Valentine Cunningham, "is finally attractive because of the sense it gives of life being in fact inconclusive like this."

CA INTERVIEWS THE AUTHOR

CA interviewed Anne Roiphe by phone at home in Manhattan, April 2, 1979.

CA: Why did you decide to be a writer?

ROIPHE: I felt I could do it better than I could do anything else.

CA: Were you interested in writing at an early age, before college?

ROIPHE: Oh, yes.

CA: How did you get started?

ROIPHE: The first thing I wrote was a novel, *Digging Out*, which was published in 1967. The next novel was in 1970.

CA: You seem in your writing to be greatly concerned with the dilemma women face in wanting to be wife and mother but also a person apart from that. Do you think it's getting easier for women?

ROIPHE: Not only do I think it's easier, but even as you presented that to me, it sounded already like such a dated problem. I'm no longer interested in it, and I presume no one else is really anymore. That was very much the burden of those of us who grew up in the late 1950's, and I'd be very surprised if we see that problem in the new crop of novels by new young writers now. It was very much a problem of my particular time. But when I wrote *Up the Sandbox!*, I wasn't even conscious of it as a problem. There was no feminism. It was beginning, in places, but I didn't think of it; it wasn't everywhere. It was simply that the problem was coming directly out of my own life experience. Now I really think there are different problems.

CA: Does a writing career enable one to be a mother at the same time?

ROIPHE: That's a fairly ideal combination. It's easier than wanting to be the head of IT&T and a mother at the same time. You are in charge of your own time, so if you have a sick child you can still work. Clearly, in many ways, the solutions I've had to these problems have been easier because I've been a writer and not been a person who needed to go to an office. But I think that young people are finding solutions. I think there are solutions, and increasingly we are going to have to have the solution of the father sharing the burdens of the home and family. That is the ultimate weapon, and really the only one that's going to work over a long period of time. I think it's happening.

CA: You write also about anger and aggression, which you call "the dark part of ourselves" that we must learn to accept. Some of the women in your novels suppress the normal feelings to find identity only through their men. Did this sort of martyrdom, or inferiority complex, grow out of the 1950's and early 1960's?

ROIPHE: I think it's all part of what is now a familiar picture, where women were taught to survive on being liked and to maneuver rather than to confront; and to deny even within oneself one's own need for self assertion, for power, anger. The distortions that came out of that, of course, were very ugly and most of them, I think, backfired most painfully on men. But that also is something I see changing. It isn't that we've achieved everything, but the absolute, ridiculous extremes of distortion and hiding that women went to—some of that is gone.

CA: Would you like to comment on the Equal Rights Amendment?

ROIPHE: I desperately hope the ERA passes. I think we're seeing all kinds of positive changes. Even if they are not in the law, they are in the minds of the next generation, which is certainly free from some of the things that stopped us. What we now have to do is to make sure that the progress continues, and politically. I feel that very strongly. I'm not going to tell you anything that sixty thousand other far more political people won't say. I feel very identified with the movement, and I have all the same fears that everyone else does—that it may one day backslide, be reversed, and another generation will forget. That the job market, the economy, may make for a push against it. I think that's our concern. But I'm not panicked to the point of saying it's all lost; that I just don't think is true.

CA: In Long Division *there's a very funny chapter in which Emily Johnson's daughter is kidnapped by gypsies and Emily decides not to notify the authorities. Yet she's very happy when she's reunited with the child. Do you feel this kind of ambivalence is more prevalent in parent-child, especially mother-child, relationships, or is it a large part of all loving relationships?*

ROIPHE: According to Freud, there is no relationship without an ambivalence. It isn't that I think Freud is a bible, but I haven't yet found a relationship without ambivalence. I'm looking, but I haven't gotten it yet. I'm sure that if you're tied to someone by virtue of love, there have to emerge the pulling-away feelings which have to do with anger and hate. One needs to know only a little about adolescence to know precisely what that's all about. I think it's in every relationship, not just parent and child. In the early years of the parent-child relationship, the dependency is so great. One of the reasons I wrote about it is that it was one of those things we were not supposed to say, and I've always wanted to write about precisely the things that you're not supposed to say. A mother wasn't supposed to admit to anything but totally blissful feelings about a screaming baby that had kept it up for seven days straight. That's why I thought it was important to put the real feelings down where they could be seen and shared and recognized.

CA: Have you always lived in New York?

ROIPHE: Yes.

CA: Would it be difficult for you to move away?

ROIPHE: I think so. But I assume I could live anywhere. It just so happened that one thing led to another and I've never gotten very far away. But I don't have the sense that it's the pace of the city that keeps me alive. I somehow distrust all of that reliance on the external world, though I happen to like New York very much.

CA: Do you have favorite writers?

ROIPHE: At this very moment, my favorite writer is John Irving. But my longtime favorite? I don't know. It changes from month to month.

CA: Which writers have you been influenced by?

ROIPHE: Doris Lessing is my primary influence, in that what her books are about—what she's doing—is what I've always wanted to do. Other than that I'm influenced by, and hopefully absorb a little bit of, everything else decent that I read.

CA: Do you work closely with an editor?

ROIPHE: I've done it both ways. I like to work with an editor. I think it's a help to have another eye.

CA: Do you work toward specific goals?

ROIPHE: I work as best I can and sometimes there are bad years. My goal is that the work get deeper. I know that doesn't happen in a steady progression, each time getting a little better; it doesn't work that way. But I do hope I have some place to go still.

CA: Are you interested in any genre you haven't done?

ROIPHE: I'd like to do some book-length nonfiction. I consider the journalism as important to me as the fiction.

CA: How do you respond to criticism? Do you find any of it helpful?

ROIPHE: Well, I don't think it's meant to be helpful. That's not the purpose of it. It can be very hurtful, and it can certainly affect self-confidence. In that sense, I think all the writers I know have tried to devise some plan for self-protection, so that they can proceed. But it's a fact of professional life that you can spend three years on something and have everybody hate it. That is simply a fact not to be avoided or ignored. On the other hand, I don't assume the critics are wrong and I'm right. They may be absolutely right. The only criticism I won't accept is the one that says, "She should stop." Anything else—I hear it.

CA: Did you like Up the Sandbox! *as a movie?*

ROIPHE: You know, writers never do. It's never the way it was done in your head.

CA: Are there any more movies in the offing?

ROIPHE: Not at the moment.

CA: Have you ever done a screenplay or been approached to do one?

ROIPHE: I did one for *Long Division* that was never made into a movie. Sorry about that. It would have been terrific. But it's a very complicated business and sometimes you're terribly lucky and the right person wants to do it and the money comes and the whole thing works, and sometimes it just doesn't. I'd love it, because I'd love to make a lot of money and I would love it to happen again because it's fun, but it's on a level with my hoping that I'm going to walk along the street and a purse filled with gold is going to fall on my head. I suppose it could happen, but I'm not counting on it. I have contingency plans just in case.

BIOGRAPHICAL/CRITICAL SOURCES: Atlantic Monthly, February, 1967; *New Republic,* March 4, 1967; *New York Review of Books,* August 24, 1967, February 3, 1977; *Nation,* September 11, 1967; *New York Times Book Review,* January 17, 1971, November 5, 1972, January 9, 1977; *Time,* January 25, 1971, October 23, 1972; *Saturday Review,* February 6, 1971, October 14, 1972; *New Yorker,* April 17, 1971; *Book World,* April 18, 1971; *Contemporary Literary Criticism,* Gale, Volume 3, 1975, Volume 9, 1978; *Times Literary Supplement,* March 25, 1977.

—Interview by Jean W. Ross

* * *

ROLLS, Anthony
See VULLIAMY, Colwyn Edward

* * *

ROLT-WHEELER, Francis William 1876-1960

OBITUARY NOTICE: Born December 16, 1876, in London, England; died August 21, 1960. Rolt-Wheeler came to the United States in 1893, where he worked as an editor for several newspapers, including North Dakota's *Grand Forks Daily Plain Dealer,* the *Minneapolis Tribune,* and the *Chicago Daily Chronicle.* Ordained a priest in 1904, he augmented his pastoral work with positions as lecturer, editor of magazines, composer, and author. His writings include *The Boy With the United States Survey, The Polar Hunters, Heroes of the Ruins,* and *Colonial Ways and Wars.* Obituaries and other sources: *Who Was Who in America,* 4th edition, Marquis, 1968; *American Authors and Books: 1640 to the Present Day,* 3rd revised edition, Crown, 1972.

* * *

ROOSEVELT, (Anna) Eleanor 1884-1962

OBITUARY NOTICE: Born October 11, 1884, in New York, N.Y.; died November 7, 1962. Often described in her lifetime as the greatest president's wife since Dolly Madison, Eleanor Roosevelt was an especially active and visible First Lady who, it was claimed, did more to popularize the Franklin Roosevelt administration than any other person or factor. Her innumerable trips across the country and visits to workers and their families did much to promote her as one of the people, a democrat with a small "d." She was the first president's wife to hold White House press conferences, and millions of people read her syndicated column, "My Day," and listened to her fifteen-minute radio broadcasts. She was deeply committed to social service projects, particularly those ushered in by her husband's New Deal program, including the National Youth Administration, slum clearance, nursery schools, and playgrounds. During World War II, she traveled to Great Britain, Australia, the South Pacific, and army camps in the United States, boosting the morale and good will of the Allies and American servicemen. Her almost constant public exposure, however, left her vulnerable to criticism, and she was often the butt of "Eleanor" jokes in cartoons, the press, and on radio. She was especially criticized for her sponsorship of the American Youth Congress and her membership in the American Newspaper Guild: both, her critics charged, were dominated by Communists, but she steadfastly refused to end her association with those groups. After her husband's death in 1945, Eleanor Roosevelt was appointed by President Truman to the U.S. delegation to the United Nations. She was also elected chairman of the Commission on Human Rights. By 1949, she was being called the "First Lady of the World" and "Number One World Citizen." A *Woman's Home Companion* poll showed that she was the most popular living American of either sex, and in 1948, the American Institute of Public Opinion revealed that she was the "most admired woman living today in any part of the world." She was the recipient of numerous awards, including the first annual Franklin Delano Roosevelt Brotherhood Award in 1946, the Four Freedoms award, and the highest honor award of the National Society for Crippled Children and Adults. In addition to her syndicated column, she was a contributor of numerous articles to magazines and the author of several books, including *It's Up to Women, The Moral Basis of Democracy,* and *On My Own.* Obituaries and other sources: Eleanor Roosevelt, *This Is My Story,* Harper, 1937; *Current Biography,* Wilson, 1940, 1949, January, 1963; Roosevelt, *The Autobiography of Eleanor Roosevelt,* Harper, 1961; *The Oxford Companion to American Literature,* 4th edition, Oxford University Press, 1965; *The Reader's Encyclopedia,* 2nd edition, Crowell, 1965; *Longman Companion to Twentieth Century Literature,* Longman, 1970; *Biography News,* Volume 1, Gale, 1974.

ROSA, Joao Guimaraes 1908-1967

OBITUARY NOTICE: Born June 3, 1908, in Cordisburgo, Minas Gerais, Brazil; died November 19, 1967, in Rio de Janeiro, Brazil. Regarded as Brazil's greatest contemporary novelist, Rosa published nothing until his 1946 volume of short stories, *Sagarana.* Earlier, he had been a doctor in his native state of Minas Gerais, a participant in the Brazilian revolution and civil war of 1930-32, and a member of his country's diplomatic corps, retiring as the director of the Frontiers Service of the Ministry of Foreign Affairs in Rio de Janeiro. His experience of the *sertao,* Brazil's wilderness areas, became the source of his fictional landscapes, characters, language, myths, and legends, most fully developed in the novel *Grande sertao: Veredas.* Critical opinion holds that it is a masterpiece of form, style, and linguistic virtuosity unsurpassed by other novelists. His fiction is full of human and natural violence, the quest for identity, a poetic use of words and imagery, and the narrative techniques of Conrad, Faulkner, and Joyce. His other writings include a two-volume collection of novellas, *Corpo de baile,* and two more short story collections, *Primeiras estorias* and *Tutameia.* He was elected to the Brazilian Academy of Letters in 1963. Obituaries and other sources: *New York Times,* November 21, 1967; *Publishers Weekly,* December 11, 1967; *Time,* October 4, 1968; *Encyclopedia of World Literature in the Twentieth Century,* Volume IV supplement, Ungar, 1975; *World Authors, 1950-1970,* Wilson, 1975.

* * *

ROSALDO, Renato I(gnacio), Jr. 1941-

PERSONAL: Born April 15, 1941, in Champaign, Ill.; son of Renato Ignacio (a professor) and Mary Elizabeth (Potter) Rosaldo; married Michelle Zimbalist (a professor), June 12, 1966; children: Samuel Mario. *Education:* Harvard University, A.B., 1963, Ph.D., 1971. *Politics:* Socialist. *Home:* 235 Embarcadero Rd., Palo Alto, Calif. 94301. *Office:* Department of Anthropology, Stanford University, Stanford, Calif. 94305.

CAREER: Stanford University, Stanford, Calif., assistant professor, 1970-76, associate professor of anthropology, 1976—. Member of Institute for Advanced Study, Princeton, N.J. *Member:* American Anthropological Association, Phi Beta Kappa.

WRITINGS: Ilongot Headhunting, 1883-1974: A Study in Society and History, Stanford University Press, 1980.

* * *

ROSENBLATT, Joe
See ROSENBLATT, Joseph

* * *

ROSENBLATT, Jon M(ichael) 1947-

PERSONAL: Born January 7, 1947, in New York, N.Y.; son of Louis G. (a doctor) and Renee (Rosenfeld) Rosenblatt; married Carol Jean Simon (an artist), November 19, 1967; children: Joshua, Nina. *Education:* Harvard University, B.A., 1967; New York University, M.A., 1971; University of North Carolina, Ph.D., 1975. *Home:* 170 Brown St., Providence, R.I. 02906. *Office:* Rhode Island College, Providence, R.I. 02908.

CAREER: Rhode Island College, Providence, assistant professor, 1975—; writer, 1976—. *Member:* Modern Language Association of America.

WRITINGS: Sylvia Plath: The Poetry of Initiation, University of North Carolina Press, 1979.

WORK IN PROGRESS: Broken Bodies: Modern Poetry and the Body.

* * *

ROSENBLATT, Joseph 1933-
(Joe Rosenblatt)

PERSONAL: Born December 26, 1933, in Toronto, Ontario, Canada; son of Samuel (a house painter) and Bessie (Tee) Rosenblatt; married Faye Smith (a pianist), October 13, 1970; children: Eliot Howard. *Education:* Attended Toronto Central Technical School, 1954, and George Brown College, 1963. *Politics:* Canadian New Democratic Party. *Religion:* Pantheist. *Home:* 15 Greensides, Toronto, Ontario, Canada M6G 3P5. *Office: Jewish Dialogue,* #7-1498 Yonge St., Toronto, Ontario, Canada M6G 3P5.

CAREER: Poet. Worked variously as a laborer, factory worker, grave digger, plumber's mate, and civil servant, until 1958; Canadian Pacific Railway, Toronto, Ontario, railway worker, 1958-65; *Jewish Dialogue,* Toronto, editor, 1969—. Writer-in-residence at University of Western Ontario, London, 1979-80. *Member:* League of Canadian Poets. *Awards, honors:* Canada Council grants, 1966, 1968, and 1973; Ontario Arts Council poetry award, 1970; Governor General's Award for poetry, 1976.

WRITINGS—All poems, except as noted: *Voyage of the Mood,* Heinrich Heine Press, 1963; *The LSD Leacock,* Coach House Press, 1966.

Under name Joe Rosenblatt: *Winter of the Luna Moth,* House of Anansi, 1968; (contributor) John Robert Columbo, editor, *How Do I Love Thee: Sixty Poets of Canada (and Quebec) Select and Introduce Their Favourite Poems From Their Own Work,* M. G. Hurtwig, 1970; (and illustrator) *Greenbaum,* Coach House Press, 1971; (and illustrator) *The Bumblebee Dithyramb,* Press Porcepic, 1972; (and illustrator) *Blind Photographer,* Press Porcepic, 1972; *Dream Craters,* Press Porcepic, 1974; (and illustrator) *Virgins and Vampires,* McClelland & Stewart, 1975; *Top Soil,* Press Porcepic, 1976; *Loosely Tied Hands,* Black Moss, 1978; *Tommy and the Ant Colony* (short story), Black Moss, 1979; *Sleeping Lady* (sonnets), Exile Editions, 1979. Contributor to *Exile.*

Drawings: *Dr. Anaconda's Solar Fun Club,* Black Moss, 1978; *Snake Oil* (portfolio), Exile Editions, 1978.

SIDELIGHTS: While often focusing on the world of plants and animals, Joe Rosenblatt's poetry reflects his misanthropic view of the human race. His "bumblebees, bullfrogs, cats, rats and assorted other lower creatures are the pure metaphors for a modern-day Satyricon of human frailties," reported the *Quill & Quire.* Understandably, then, Rosenblatt feels closely allied with Jonathan Swift; he also holds a special reverence for Ambrose Bierce. His poetry itself, he says, is traditional and largely influenced by Hart Crane and Robert Frost.

Though he's known primarily as a small-press poet, Rosenblatt's reputation has steadily grown. He still, however, assumes a humble attitude toward his work: he refuses to write in the first person and claims he's not worried about becoming a popular poet because "no poems are meant to appeal to the masses."

AVOCATIONAL INTERESTS: Cats, hockey, basketball.

CA INTERVIEWS THE AUTHOR

During an interview at his home on May 25, 1979, Joseph Rosenblatt discussed his writing with Canadian poet Al

Purdy. Purdy, whose sketch can be found in *CA* 81-84, received the Governor General's award in poetry in 1966 for *The Cariboo Horses*. Purdy's *Being Alive: Poems 1958-78* was published in 1978 by McClelland & Stewart.

CA: We're sitting in Joe Rosenblatt's workroom; no books or doodads, spartan as hell. It's simply the place where he works. Do you write prose here or poems?

ROSENBLATT: Both, both.

CA: You once stated that your subject matter and method enabled you to probe below the surface of humanity, even though you were writing poems about butterflies or whatever. You also said you weren't much concerned with straight description.

ROSENBLATT: That's right, I'm not interested in the straight, outward social or political statement, or a definition of humanity, or what humanity should do. And I'm not interested in political systems as such, inasmuch as we are all victims of governments and bureaucracies. Essentially I write poetry to escape. I use poetry as somebody else would use opium. And that's my purpose.

CA: You mean you're high when you write poetry?

ROSENBLATT: I hide in my poetry, and I'm high when I write my poetry. I'm high and I hide, and basically I'm an escapist. This is why essentially I'm just a little bit on the periphery of society. I'm not really inputting to society at all. I think of poetry like films, for example: there was a tendency during the forties to get away mentally from the war. Comedies came in at that time, during the 1940's right? We had Laurel and Hardy; we had Abbott and Costello, the American comedians. And the reason we had comedies was because we wanted to blot out the war, the horrors of reality. And I think my poetry possibly—I say possibly—serves that kind of situation. I'm an escape artist.

CA: Don't you want to have "significance"?

ROSENBLATT: I don't care. Oh, well, I say the poems have their own significance. Inasmuch as Laurel and Hardy had their significance. Inasmuch as you would want to see the Three Stooges have significance, less than Laurel and Hardy, of course. I'm a comedian.

CA: You once said in a prose piece that you were getting under the surface; that this enabled you to say things about bugs that you can't say about humanity?

ROSENBLATT: Exactly. I use insects to talk about society. I use social insects. I want to make that clear. By social insects, I mean bees and so on.

CA: Which are the unsocial insects?

ROSENBLATT: Well, grasshoppers, they're not terribly social.

CA: Do you see yourself in any literary tradition? A tradition of other writers related to yourself? In fact, is there anyone writing right now you feel close to? Who works at all like you?

ROSENBLATT: That's a tough one. But no, there isn't anybody.

CA: Has there been, has there ever been? What about Edward Lear?

ROSENBLATT: He's dead.

CA: I'm serious. Isn't there anybody? Alive or dead?

ROSENBLATT: No. No, there isn't.

CA: You think you're unique?

ROSENBLATT: I'd have to. You know, I'm not a person who brags. I'd just say there isn't anbody who writes like me. And I'm not talking about Archy and Mehitabel either. But who gives a damn? Remember [in one of my poems], Archie the roach jumped on the typewriter keys! I believe Archie was the roach reincarnation of a poet.

CA: Let's talk about the past. As you grew up, went to high school and so on, when did you first start writing?

ROSENBLATT: In Grade 8. You must understand that essentially I was the offspring of immigrants, and my father could not speak English. My mother could. I'm going back over thirty years. My first language was Yiddish. In short, when I went to public school, it took some conditioning to even fit into the mold of the whole public school system. Because English wasn't my first language. That came when I was four or five. I was born here, but my parents were European—they arrived from Poland in the early 1930's—and very ghettoized. They liked to live completely within their own community.

CA: You didn't learn English until you were four or five?

ROSENBLATT: Absolutely none. That may sound incredible, but it's often true with the offspring of immigrants who arrive in a new country. So I was quite an alienated kid. I still am. A lot of my habits haven't changed. The biggest influence on me, of course, was man's inhumanity to man.

CA: That's because of later experience, isn't it?

ROSENBLATT: Also because of my paranoia, also because of my Jewish background, because of Hitler.

CA: I meant to get into that. What about that Jewish background?

ROSENBLATT: Well, Jewishness involves the Holocaust, and the fact that one is marked for death because one happens to be black or a Jew or Catholic or whatever he happens to be. Like being caught in the wrong bar at the wrong time. [laughs] Being gunned down in a gangster bar. You could be the victim, right? Nobody has to be Jewish, nobody has to be Catholic.

CA: Nobody has to be anything.

ROSENBLATT: But the very fact that one comes from some minority group means that nothing and nowhere on earth is terribly safe for you.

CA: Grade 8 and you started to write. Were you aware of your "Jewishness" at that time?

ROSENBLATT: In the background, and I was rebelling. It was about 1943 or 1944, the time of Adolf Hitler. I was protected from him, of course. I didn't learn about the full impact of the Holocaust until many years later.

CA: You were very affected by it, but you don't write about it now? Why not?

ROSENBLATT: I was affected by it, but it didn't affect me as a Jew; it affected me as a human being. Both Jew and human. I mean, I didn't see the Jewish question in terms of a

German versus Jew or a Jew versus Gentile. I looked on it as a whole condition, the human condition. I mean, what happened to the Jews also happened to the Irish and other races.

CA: But the Jews took it worse than most.

ROSENBLATT: Sure, they took it worse than most, but so did the blacks take it with slavery. So I had a pretty negative viewpoint of humanity, and I still have. Why I ever became a socialist is another question.

CA: All right. That leads into other things. Do you feel that any of us can ever escape this kind of oppression? For instance, can we, the mass of human beings, ever learn to love, as Auden in an early poem said we must, or die?

ROSENBLATT: No.

CA: Or trust? You don't think we can?

ROSENBLATT: I think that people can judge others as individuals. How many friends do we have on the face of the earth?

CA: Well, not many, obviously.

ROSENBLATT: And how many people are interested in our poems? There are more mobs interested in rock music than are interested in modern poetry.

Of course I'm a very negative person, but I want to tell you why I'm negative. Because I think that man is basically less than an animal. An animal kills only when he's hungry; man will kill for pleasure. Since 1900, since the first World War, with the wars in between, with famine and hunger, two hundred million people have vanished from the face of the earth. Two hundred million people who've been deliberately killed by other people. You name the reason. Because of their ethnic background, because of imperial designs. A lot of reasons—social reasons, savage reasons. That's why I'm negative.

CA: But I wanted to get at the Jewish aspect of your poems. I don't think they are specifically Jewish at all.

ROSENBLATT: No, they are not. I don't make a fetish or cause of Jewishness. Other poets do. They do. Irving Layton, Leonard Cohen. I don't. In other words, I'm not a Jewish chauvinist, I don't think being Jewish is everything. My poems are influenced by the human condition, not the Jewish one.

CA: In your human condition you once worked with your hands and body for a living. I notice plumber's mate and grave digger among your occupations. How come those jobs don't show up in what you write?

ROSENBLATT: Again, as I say, I hate reality. Being a wage earner, working on some mindless job from eight to five, that's as bad as being in a minority group.

CA: Were you writing when you were working at those jobs?

ROSENBLATT: No, I did most of my writing when I left the jobs. Then I lost my proletarian roots, my background.

CA: Perhaps we all do. Anyway, where do your poems come from? They have to come from somewhere; do you chase off into the country and watch butterflies and bugs?

ROSENBLATT: Well, everbody has bugs. Bugs are like demons in your head, and you need some kind of exorcism to get rid of those demons. You may write about various landscapes and people and politicians, and they're demons to you. But to me, the demons are people in insect form.

CA: Maybe the unconscious is where a large part of your writing comes from. If so, where are you going in your conscious mind? What are you consciously trying to say? Are there times when you know?

ROSENBLATT: I do get lines that come into my mind. They are like corpses with heads without any bodies. "The light grey man carries your luggage." It came bouncing in because I had a dream where I was in a long queue in a pharmacy and the pharmacist was passing out lanterns, and the lanterns were souls. There was a little flicker of illumination, and I thought, "Well, here is eternity. Buy eternity." I kept asking people in the lineup, "What does this mean, what does this mean?" And they would say, "Don't you know, don't you know?" Weeks and weeks later I said, "My God, those little flickering lanterns, they're souls, that's where you keep your soul. This is where you keep eternity."

CA: What about being Canadian? Robert Lowell, James Dickey and Robert Frost are or were American. It's sometimes possible to know the nationality of American and Canadian poets from the way they write, at least from the content of poems. But you're an exotic. Does being Canadian come into your poems?

ROSENBLATT: I can't answer that question. In my poetry I'm not a nationalist.

CA: I'm not talking about nationalism.

ROSENBLATT: Not in my poetry. Not because I want it to be absent. I think I'd be a lousy nationalist poet, no Rudyard Kipling.

CA: That isn't what I mean. Being born in Canada and unable to escape it and not wanting to—that's what I mean by nationalism. Not Kipling's jingoism. Does being Jewish connect with being Canadian?

ROSENBLATT: Indirectly.

CA: Karl Shapiro said in his book, To Abolish Children: *the one great innovator in American poetry is Walt Whitman. He was native, lived in North America, not Europe. And the western tradition continues in Europe, whereas many U.S. and Canadian poets feel they're cast off into outer darkness because of that, marooned on a strange continent without much past. Western tradition is Europe. Perhaps only Whitman was at home here. Are you and the American poets now at home on this strange continent?*

ROSENBLATT: Well, Whitman was the definite break with Europe. Before him all North American literature was influenced by Europe. One could say that Whitman was the first American chauvinist imperialist.

CA: The point Shapiro was getting at was: suddenly the old tradition was broken. Here we are on the edge of nowhere, a strange continent, the tradition belongs in Europe. We have to make a different tradition.

ROSENBLATT: Well, I think Whitman did make a different tradition.

CA: But who else?

ROSENBLATT: Well there was Melville, of course. And maybe William Faulkner.

CA: Okay, we don't really have anyone like that in Canada, and no audience large enough if we did. Don't you ever feel like we're writing the New Testament on the head of a pin?

ROSENBLATT: Let me speak as a Canadian chauvinist for a minute: Canada is going to be a great power.

CA: That's incredible, coming from Joe Rosenblatt.

ROSENBLATT: We have twenty-five million people here. For heaven's sake, we have to have a language, we have to have a culture, a mythology and an ethos and a vision to keep us going. And part of that vision is our playwrights and the poets who speak for Canada.

CA: But does Canada want to be a great power?

ROSENBLATT: Oh, I certainly want it to be a great power. I want to be an imperialist.

CA: You want imperialism, you want power? Look, the United States is a great power; how do you see them?

ROSENBLATT: They're a declining power.

CA: You mean Canada should replace the United States?

ROSENBLATT: Why not? What's wrong with that?

CA: Perhaps I'd better edit that part out.

ROSENBLATT: No, don't edit that. That's me.

CA: Okay. This is related, obliquely, to the idea of power. Tom Marshall says in a recent book that Canadian poets are obsessed with space, with enclosure and openness. He means, I think, something similiar to Dennis Lee who said Americans have a tendency to exploit their landscape, tailor it to fit themselves, whereas Canadians are awed and rather thunderstruck by the immense aspects of their own country.

ROSENBLATT: Of course. Americans don't realize that all the large Canadian cities are near the American border. You go up to Thunder Bay in northern Ontario, you can travel off the roads for hundreds of miles and see no people. Maybe an old trapper's hut in winter. That's all.

CA: It must be fifteen years ago now, but I remember you going down to Allen Gardens from your apartment in Toronto to break up some neo-Nazi public gathering. Remember that?

ROSENBLATT: Sure do. I went because they were Nazis, and I have the right to oppose them.

CA: But you didn't make it. In other words, there is no free speech for everyone?

ROSENBLATT: No, there isn't.

CA: Only poets?

ROSENBLATT: What's terribly wrong with that? That's the way all societies operate. Do you believe in the notion of democracy?

CA: Maybe that's more a North American tradition than a European one. Therefore, are U.S. writers as foreign to you as European ones?

ROSENBLATT: I'm evenly divided between some of the major American and British writers. In the United States, Louise Bogan—and a hundred years earlier, Emily Dickinson. She was incredible.

CA: I meant the question a little differently. You happen to be a Canadian and therefore North American. Consequently, while you may not feel as much liking for some U.S. writers as you do for some British, you are still closer to the United States.

ROSENBLATT: I don't like to say I'm North American.

CA: Why not?

ROSENBLATT: I don't feel that I'm in only one locale. I feel I'm in many locales. I mean, I read in Birmingham, Alabama, to a group of Southerners who had a study group on my poetry which they identified with. With them I could have been a southern writer, or a northern writer or a Canadian writer. There was immediate rapport with the audience. And I've read in New York City; the audience there was very cruel and standoffish, but nevertheless quite puzzled by my poems. I've read in upper New York State, and I might as well have been a Martian.

CA: You've said you have no ancestors in your writing; therefore, wouldn't you expect an audience to be a little puzzled when they have nothing to compare you with?

ROSENBLATT: Oh, absolutely. I might as well be a Martian with twenty thousand compound eyes and put on my boogie dancing shoes.

CA: Sure, an American audience is used to American writers. Just as a Canadian audience is more familiar with Canadian writers. Are you interested in them?

ROSENBLATT: Yes, I'm interested in Milton Acorn, Earle Birney, P. K. Page, Pat Lane. Some of them I might not even be in agreement with. For instance, I've never been in agreement with Pat Lane or Al Purdy, not political agreement, or social and visionary agreement. But I do admire them, admire them as individuals, and take their visions very seriously. But I may oppose them, I may fight them tooth and nail, but I regard them as serious people.

CA: And the younger Canadian poets, those who will replace the present generation?

ROSENBLATT: There isn't anybody.

CA: All right, then let's take Margaret Atwood as an example of the known writers. What do you think of her?

ROSENBLATT: Acorn, Birney, and others have said it better. I think Atwood is too cool, too reticent emotionally. She's too safe as a poet. And I think a lot of her poems are very similar.

CA: I have the feeling that some present-day poets are mapping the territory, the same territory that earlier writers filled with cliches. And there are people who live in these unmapped territories, who feel they are anonymous, without history or even objective existence as people. And some poet, writing about those remote places, suddenly makes those places come alive for them, their own personal and objective existence, makes them realize they are here, and it is important to be here. . . .

ROSENBLATT: The territory I'm mapping is cerebral territory, a metaphysical place. Not a land mass, not a province or state. I have to live here, but my thinking space is larger, maybe three thousand miles.

CA: That's what I'm talking about, not just physical space. A good poet does that. His purpose—

ROSENBLATT: Is to entertain; the essential motive force is that the poet should entertain, be a spokesman for his tribe when he can, expand the human consciousness.

CA: And yourself?

ROSENBLATT: I'm alone. When I die nobody will care. Perhaps someone will run across a dozen obscure or perhaps oblique poems. Maybe they won't be obscure then. Maybe I'll be discovered as some kind of cosmological nut. Perhaps they will all say, "There's the guy who came out for fresh air, God Bless, and we didn't even listen to him, but he's got dozens of poems about fresh air and bullfrogs." And suddenly I'll appear in all kinds of nature anthologies, and I wasn't even a nature poet.

CA: No, you were never that; you were a cerebral cartographer with a negative purpose, which you believe in.

ROSENBLATT: Of course. The essential motive force of the poet is that he should entertain, be the spokesman for the tribe when he can, to expand the human consciousness.

CA: Joe, that's not escapist any more. We've come full circle. And what will you be doing this next year [1979-80]?

ROSENBLATT: I'll be in London, Ontario, at the University of Western Ontario, talking to students about their poems. And writing a long poem.

CA: What's it about?

ROSENBLATT: Snakes.

BIOGRAPHICAL/CRITICAL SOURCES: Canadian Forum, June, 1975, June, 1977; *Quill & Quire,* December, 1975; *Authors in the News,* Volume 2, Gale, 1976.

—*Interview by Al Purdy*

* * *

ROSENFELD, Samuel 1896-1963
(Tristan Tzara)

OBITUARY NOTICE: Born April 4, 1896, in Moinesti, Rumania; died December 24, 1963, in Paris, France. Poet best known under pseudonym Tristan Tzara as founder of the Dada movement. In response to the meaninglessness of civilization demonstrated by World War I, Tristan Tzara, Hugo Ball, Hans Arp, and others formed the Dada movement in 1916. Calling for deliberate irrationality and the negation of all traditional artistic values, history, and religion, Dadaist theories spread quickly from their origin in Zurich, Switzerland, to the United States, France, and other countries. The purposely unproductive artists and writers left few permanent works when the movement disintegrated in 1923. Tzara's most prominent Dadaist play was "Le Coeur a gaz," translated in 1964 as "The Gas Heart." Other works include *L'Homme approximatif* ("Approximate Man"), *Grains et issues* ("Seeds and Outlets"), and *La Fuite* ("The Flight"). Obituaries and other sources: *The Reader's Encyclopedia,* 2nd edition, Crowell, 1965; Hans Richter, *Dada: Art and Anti-Art,* McGraw, 1966; *Encyclopedia of World Literature in the Twentieth Century,* updated edition, Ungar, 1967; Elmer Peterson, *Tristan Tzara,* Rutgers University Press, 1971; *World Authors, 1950-1970,* Wilson, 1975; *Who's Who in Twentieth Century Literature,* Holt, 1976.

* * *

ROSENTHAL, Andrew 1918(?)-1979

OBITUARY NOTICE: Born c. 1918; died November 11, 1979, in New York, N.Y. Playwright of such works as "Two of Everything," "Burning Deck," "Horses in Midstream," and "Third Person." Obituaries and other sources: *New York Times,* November 13, 1979.

* * *

ROSENTHAL, F(rank) F(ranz) 1911(?)-1979

OBITUARY NOTICE: Born c. 1911, in Beuthen, Germany (now Poland); died August 19, 1979, in Flossmoor, Ill. Rabbi, educator, and scholar. Rosenthal taught at Governors State University and Albion College, and lectured twice in West Germany as an official government guest. His scholarly work centered on Jewish history and philosophy. Obituaries and other sources: *Chicago Tribune,* August 21, 1979.

* * *

ROSMAN, Abraham 1930-

PERSONAL: Born September 8, 1930, in New York, N.Y.; son of Emanuel and Matilda (Maud) Rosman; married Paula G. Rubel (an anthropology professor and author); children: two. *Education:* City College (now of the City University of New York), B.A., 1952; Yale University, Ph.D., 1962. *Office:* Department of Anthropology, Barnard College, Columbia University, New York, N.Y. 10027.

CAREER: Vassar College, Poughkeepsie, N.Y., instructor in anthropology, 1958-60; Antioch College, Yellow Springs, Ohio, assistant professor of anthropology, 1960-61; Yale University, New Haven, Conn., instructor in anthropology, 1961-62; Columbia University, Barnard College, New York, N.Y., assistant professor, 1962-66, associate professor, 1966-72, professor of anthropology, 1972—. Fulbright lecturer in Pakistan and Israel, 1964-65. *Awards, honors:* Ford Foundation grant for Nigeria, 1956-57; Social Science Research Council grant, summer, 1968; National Science Foundation grants, 1969-70, 1971-72, 1974-75.

WRITINGS: (With wife, Paula G. Rubel) *Feasting With Mine Enemy: Rank and Exchange Among Northwest Coast Societies,* Columbia University Press, 1971; (with Rubel) *Your Own Pigs You May Not Eat,* University of Chicago Press, 1978; (contributor) George Dalton, editor, *Research in Economic Anthropology,* JAI Press, 1978; (with Rubel) *The Tapestry of Culture,* Scott, Foresman, in press. Contributor to *Encyclopaedia Britannica.* Contributor of about twenty articles to scholarly journals.

* * *

ROSS, Helaine
See DANIELS, Dorothy

* * *

ROSSI, Ino

PERSONAL: Born in Italy; son of Nicola and Edvige Rossi; married wife, Irene, 1969; children: Paul. *Education:* University of Chicago, M.A., 1966; New School for Social Research, Ph.D., 1969.

CAREER: Writer and educator.

WRITINGS: (Editor) *The Unconscious in Culture,* Dutton, 1974; *Anthropology Full Circle,* Praeger, 1977. Contributor to anthropology and sociology journals.

WORK IN PROGRESS: Editing a book on structural sociology; a book on recent trends in structural anthropology.

* * *

ROTHERMERE, Viscount
See HARMSWORTH, Esmond Cecil

ROUSE, John E(dward), Jr. 1942-

PERSONAL: Born July 23, 1942; son of John Edward and Zana (Wilson) Rouse. *Education:* Furman University, B.A., 1964; University of Maryland, M.A., 1967, Ph.D., 1974. *Politics:* Democrat. *Religion:* Baptist. *Home:* 204 North Martin St., Muncie, Ind. 47303. *Office:* Department of Political Science, Ball State University, Muncie, Ind. 47306.

CAREER: Ball State University, Muncie, Ind., assistant professor of political science, 1976—. Adjunct professor at George Washington University and University of Maryland. Consultant to U.S. Department of Health, Education and Welfare, Department of Housing and Urban Development, and D. A. Lewis Associates. Moderator for WBST-Radio show, "Public Affairs Roundtable." *Member:* American Society for Public Administration, American Political Science Association, Southern Political Science Association, Indiana Society for Public Administration.

WRITINGS: Urban Housing: Public and Private; A Guide to Information Sources, Gale, 1978; *Public Administration in American Society,* Gale, 1980.

SIDELIGHTS: Rouse's research interests include federal organization and structure, regional decentralization, and survey research.

* * *

ROVERE, Richard H(alworth) 1915-1979

OBITUARY NOTICE—See index for *CA* sketch: Born May 5, 1915, in Jersey City, N.J.; died of emphysema, November 23, 1979, in Poughkeepsie, N.Y. Editor, journalist, and author. Considered one of the most astute observers of the American political scene, Rovere contributed political columns to the *New Yorker* magazine for more than thirty years. Prior to joining the *New Yorker* staff, he had worked as an editor for *New Masses, Nation,* and *Common Sense.* In addition to his column, Rovere wrote a number of books on politics, including *Senator Joe McCarthy, The American Establishment,* and *The Goldwater Caper.* His memoirs were published in 1976 as *Arrivals and Departures: A Journalist's Memoirs.* Obituaries and other sources: *Oxford Companion to American Literature,* 4th edition, Oxford University Press, 1965; *Celebrity Register,* 3rd edition, Simon & Schuster, 1973; Richard H. Rovere, *Arrivals and Departures: A Journalist's Memoirs,* Macmillan, 1976; *Newsweek,* November 29, 1976, December 3, 1979; *Political Profiles: The Eisenhower Years,* Facts on File, 1977; *Who's Who in America,* 40th edition, Marquis, 1978; *New York Times,* November 24, 1979; *Washington Post,* November 25, 1979; *Time,* December 3, 1979.

* * *

ROWAN, Carl Thomas 1925-

PERSONAL: Born August 11, 1925, in Ravenscroft, Tenn.; son of Thomas David (a lumber stacker) and Johnnie (Bradford) Rowan; married Vivien Louise Murphy, August 2, 1950; children: Barbara, Carl Thomas, Jeffrey. *Education:* Attended Tennessee State University, 1942-43, and Washburn University, 1943-44; Oberlin College, A.B., 1947; University of Minnesota, M.A., 1948. *Home:* 3116 Fessenden St. N.W., Washington, D.C. 20008. *Office:* 1220 19th St. N.W., Washington, D.C. 20036.

CAREER: Minneapolis Tribune, Minneapolis, Minn., copywriter, 1948-50, staff writer, 1950-61; U.S. Department of State, Washington, D.C., deputy assistant secretary for public affairs, 1961-63; U.S. ambassador to Finland, based in Helsinki, 1963-64; director of United States Information Agency (USIA), 1964-65; *Chicago Sun-Times* (formerly *Chicago Daily News*), Chicago, Ill., columnist for Field Newpaper Syndicate (formerly Publishers Hall Syndicate), 1965—. National affairs commentator on "The Rowan Report," heard nationally on radio five days a week; political commentator for radio and television stations of Post-Newsweek Broadcasting Company; regular panelist on "Agronsky & Co.," a nationally syndicated public affairs television show; frequent panelist on "Meet the Press." Lecturer. Former member of U.S. delegation to the United Nations. *Military service:* Served in U.S. Navy.

AWARDS, HONORS: Sidney Hillman Award for best newspaper reporting, 1952; Sigma Delta Chi Awards, 1953, for coverage of school desegregation cases before the U.S. Supreme Court, 1954, for foreign correspondence from India, and 1955, for coverage of the conference in Bandung, Indonesia; distinguished achievement award from regents of University of Minnesota, 1961; communications award in human relations from Anti-Defamation League of B'nai B'rith, 1964; Contributions to American Democracy Award from Roosevelt University, 1964; Liberty Bell Award from Howard University, 1965; named Washington journalist of the year by Capital Press Club, 1978; American Black Achievement Award from *Ebony* magazine, 1978, for contributions to journalism and public communication. Recipient of twenty-nine honorary degrees from colleges and universities, including Oberlin College, Notre Dame University, Howard University, University of Massachusetts, Temple University, Atlanta University, and Clark University.

WRITINGS: South of Freedom, Knopf, 1952; *The Pitiful and the Proud,* Random House, 1956; *Go South to Sorrow,* Random House, 1957; *Wait Till Next Year: The Life Story of Jackie Robinson,* Random House, 1960; *Just Between Us Blacks,* Random House, 1974. Roving editor of *Reader's Digest.*

SIDELIGHTS: The *Washington Post* has called Rowan "the most visible black journalist in the country." Rowan is well known as the author of a syndicated column appearing three-times weekly nationwide, as well as a frequent commentator on public affairs radio and television programs. His other accomplishments have included government appointments in the Kennedy and Johnson administrations.

"First I see myself simply as a newspaper man and commentator," Rowan told interviewer Jacqueline Trescott. "I inform people and expose them to a point of view they wouldn't get. I work against the racial mind-set of most of the media."

BIOGRAPHICAL/CRITICAL SOURCES: Washington Post, October 28, 1978.

* * *

ROWLAND, Beryl

PERSONAL: Born in Tain, Scotland; married Edward Murray Rowland, September 3, 1948. *Education:* University of London, earned B.A. (with honors); University of Alberta, M.A., 1958; University of British Columbia, Ph.D., 1962. *Home:* 32 Valentine Dr., Don Mills, Ontario, Canada. *Office:* York University, Downsview, Ontario, Canada.

CAREER: University of British Columbia, Vancouver, lecturer in English, 1958-62; University of Toronto, Toronto, Ontario, lecturer in English, 1962-63; York University, Downsview, Ontario, assistant professor, 1963-67, associate professor, 1967-71, professor of English, 1971—. Visiting professor at University of California, Riverside, 1970. Speaker at professional meetings. *Member:* International Association of Professors of English (member of international advisory committee), English Association, Mediaeval Academy of America, Modern Language Association of America (head of Chaucer section, 1975), Association of Canadian University Teachers of English, Humanities Association, Melville Society. *Awards, honors:* Sir Sidney Lee Prize; Jubilee Drama Award from Government of Alberta for "Cressida in Alberta"; book award from Chicago University Presses, 1974; Huntington Library fellow, 1975.

WRITINGS: (Editor and contributor) *Companion to Chaucer Studies,* Oxford University Press, 1968; *Blind Beasts: Chaucer's Animal World,* Kent State University Press, 1971; *Animals With Human Faces,* University of Tennessee Press, 1974; (editor and contributor) *Chaucer and Middle English Studies in Honor of Rossell Hope Robbins,* Kent State University Press, 1974; *Birds With Human Souls,* University of Tennessee Press, 1978. Also author of *Medieval Woman's Guide to Health: The First Gynecological Treatise,* and *Women in Medieval Medicine,* B. Franklin.

Contributor: (Author of introduction) Bulfinch, *Mythology: The Age of Chivalry,* Ryerson, 1965; (author of preface) *Tom Jones,* Ryerson, 1966; (author of preface) William Shakespeare, *Much Ado About Nothing,* Ryerson, 1967; (author of preface) *Mark Twain,* Ryerson, 1967; (author of preface) Shakespeare, *All's Well That Ends Well,* Ryerson, 1967; (author of preface) Shakespeare, *King John,* Ryerson, 1967; (author of preface) Shakespeare, *Coriolanus,* Ryerson, 1967; (author of preface) Shakespeare, *Love's Labor's Lost,* Ryerson, 1969; (author of preface) Shakespeare, *Measure for Measure,* Ryerson, 1969; (author of preface) *Kenilworth,* Ryerson, 1969; (author of preface) Charles Dickens, *The Pickwick Papers,* Ryerson, 1969. Also contributor to *Studies in Honor of Tauno F. Mustanoja,* 1972, and *Chaucer at Albany,* B. Franklin, 1975.

Also author of a play, "Cressida in Alberta," and a radio play, "Behold a Pale Horse," aired by Canadian Broadcasting Corp. Contributor of more than fifty articles and reviews to literature and history journals. Member of editorial board of *Chaucer Review,* 1975—, and *Florilegium,* 1977.

WORK IN PROGRESS: Research on Chaucer, medieval medicine, and Herman Melville.

* * *

ROYKO, Mike 1932-

PERSONAL: Born September 19, 1932, in Chicago, Ill.; son of Michael (a saloon keeper) and Helen (a saloon keeper; maiden name Zak) Royko; married Carol Joyce Duckman, November 7, 1954; children: M. David, Robert F. *Education:* Attended Wright Junior College, 1951-52. *Home:* 6657 North Sioux Ave., Chicago, Ill. 60646. *Office: Chicago Sun-Times,* 401 North Wabash Ave., Chicago, Ill. 60611.

CAREER: Chicago North Side Newspapers, Chicago, Ill., reporter, 1956; Chicago City News Bureau, Chicago, reporter and assistant city editor, 1956-59; *Chicago Daily News,* Chicago, reporter and columnist, 1959-78, associate editor, 1977-78; *Chicago Sun-Times,* Chicago, columnist, 1978—. *Military service:* U.S. Air Force, 1952-56. *Member:* Chicago Newspaper Reporters Association. *Awards, honors:* Pulitzer Prize, 1972, for commentary.

WRITINGS: Up Against It (collection of columns), introduction by Bill Mauldin, Regnery, 1967; *I May Be Wrong, but I Doubt It* (collection of columns), Regnery, 1968; *Boss: Richard J. Daley of Chicago,* Dutton, 1971; *Slats Grobnik and Some Other Friends* (collection of columns), Dutton, 1973.

SIDELIGHTS: Columnist Royko, it has been said, "owns" the city of Chicago. His intimate knowledge of how the city runs and its people has made his column required reading for Chicagoans; he is attracting a national following as well. Royko grew up in a Polish neighborhood on the city's northwest side, the son of two saloon keepers. Raised on beer and barroom brawls, Royko was a tough street kid who quit school at the age of sixteen. After joining the Air Force he discovered his love of writing and wrote for the base newspaper. (He got the job by lying that he had been a writer for the *Chicago Daily News.*) Several years later the *Daily News* hired him for real and he wrote his five-times-weekly column until the paper folded in 1978. Now his column runs in the *Chicago Sun-Times.*

Royko is considered to be one of the few journalists with clout. William Brashler commented, "He wields enough power and influence to alter the course of major elections: the mayoralty of the city of Chicago, seats in the United States Senate, and some insist, the presidency." Brashler pointed to the recent victories of Senator Charles Percy and Chicago Mayor Jane Byrne as elections that Royko influenced. Although politicians are frequent targets of his mordant humor, Royko also writes about local people with hard luck stories to tell. Another favorite topic is his old neighborhood with its cast of characters including Slats Grobnik, Royko's alter ego.

Brashler wrote that much of the appeal of Royko's column is that it has "never suffered an identity crisis." As Brashler described Royko's work, "He seldom uses the column to pontificate. He prefers rather to let people tell their own stories and dig their own holes. He does not discuss weighty problems in the abstract nor draw ominous conclusions." Furthermore, Brashler stated, "he seldom praises anybody, even those who deserve it. It is easier to be funnier, more readable, and more effective when you are reaming someone instead of puffing for them. And Royko knows it."

Royko is probably best known for his scathing caricatures of Chicago's former mayor, Richard Daley. Although Chicago's motto was traditionally "the city that works," Royko called it the city of "Where's mine?" under Daley's rule. In 1971 he wrote a book about "duh boss" entitled *Boss: Richard J. Daley of Chicago.* Royko, Christopher Lehmann-Haupt wrote, "brings to his harpooning of Mayor Daley a caustic wit, an intimate knowledge of Chicago, and a deep and rich understanding of his subject's soft underbelly. And since no politician anywhere controls a city quite the way Mr. Daley controls Chicago, Mr. Royko's book is a pungent and precise portrait of how big-city machine politics work. And it is brisk and lively reading into the bargain." Dan Walker remarked: "*Boss* is a well-directed, devastating attack on the mayor and his machine. But the criticism is never overstated; instead, the evidence builds and builds.... By avoiding the sensationalizing of Chicago's problems, Royko has come up with a classic study of a big-city political machine and why we can do without it."

S. D. Alinsky concurred, calling *Boss,* a "primer in politics." He wrote: "Royko's facts are prodigious. To this reviewer, a native Chicagoan who assumed that he knew just about everything that went on, particularly with City Hall, page after page of *Boss* carried a fact that came as a shocker.... Once in a long while a book appears that leaves the reviewer fighting against the compulsion of quoting from it at length rather than watering it down by paraphrasing, summarizing and analyzing. Such a book is Royko's *Boss*. It is my nominee for the Pulitzer Prize in 1971."

Not all reviewers were as pleased. While Charles Monoghan judged the biography to be "neatly written, energetically paced, and full of marvelous stories sure to please lovers of urban politics," ultimately he found the book disappointing "because it doesn't tell us what makes Daley tick." He continued, "If a writer is going to devote a book to one man, he should try at some point to look at the world through his protagonist's eyes. Royko, however, has only a thorough, steely contempt for his subject—he doesn't want to spend a moment in Daley's mind. As a result, his mayor is a two-dimensional villain, a man of bad will, bad manners, bad grammar, and—one feels certain by the end—bad breath." Lehmann-Haupt concluded that despite its few flaws *Boss* was valuable reading. "One might wish that Mr. Royko's descriptions of Mayor Daley were a little less second-hand," he wrote. "One might wish that he had put matters in perspective with a more sympathetic treatment of the conditions that produced the Daleys. One might wish that he had written more about the Chicago that Norman Mailer has called 'perhaps the last of the great American cities.' One might wish, in sum, that Mr. Royko had written a book that one could read with emotions other than rage. But all in all, this is muckraking at its best, a remorseless book that bites and tears."

BIOGRAPHICAL/CRITICAL SOURCES: Washington Post Book World, March 28, 1971, September 19, 1971, February 3, 1974, May 26, 1974; *New York Times,* March 31, 1971; *Best Sellers,* April 1, 1971; *Life,* April 2, 1971; *New York Times Book Review,* April 4, 1971, June 6, 1971; *New Republic,* April 17, 1971; *Nation,* April 19, 1971; *Time,* April 19, 1971; *Saturday Review,* April 24, 1971, October 23, 1971; *Christian Science Monitor,* April 29, 1971; *National Review,* June 1, 1971; *Esquire,* July, 1971, March, 1972, May 8, 1979; *Commentary,* September, 1971; *McCall's,* February, 1972; *Village Voice,* January 10, 1974; *Detroit Free Press,* July 9, 1979.*

—*Sketch by Barbara A. Welch*

* * *

ROZIN, Skip 1941-

PERSONAL: Born October 3, 1941, in Cincinnati, Ohio; son of Arthur Edward (a manufacturer) and Freda (Sloan) Rozin. *Education:* University of Miami, Coral Gables, Fla., B.A., 1963. *Home address:* Loroco Lodge, Lancaster, Ohio. *Agent:* James Brown Associates, Inc., 25 West 43rd St., New York, N.Y. 10036. *Office:* 336 West 77th St., New York, N.Y. 10024.

CAREER: Miami Herald, Miami, Fla., general assignment reporter and sports writer, 1960-62; *Bethlehem Globe-Times,* Bethlehem, Pa., general assignment reporter and sports writer, 1965; *Mount Vernon Daily Argus,* Mount Vernon, N.Y., reporter and editor, 1966-67; free-lance indexer, 1968-71; free-lance writer, 1971—. *Military service:* U.S. Army Reserve, 1965-71.

WRITINGS: One Step From Glory, Simon & Schuster, 1979. Work represented in anthologies, including *The Essay, Structure and Purpose,* edited by Richard L. Cherry, Robert J. Conley, and Bernard A. Hirsch, Houghton, 1975, and *Put It in Writing,* edited by Arthur Daigon, Marion Levine, and Ruth Daigon, Harcourt, 1978. Contributor of stories and articles to magazines, including *Harper's, Oyez Review, Reader's Digest,* and *Audubon,* and newspapers, including *New York Times.*

WORK IN PROGRESS: Last Run of the Midnight Special, a novel.

SIDELIGHTS: Rozin writes: "I am a reporter, and have been since covering my first assignment for the University of Miami newspaper in 1959. Over the past ten years I have become fascinated with a single theme—people contending with stiff odds to preserve their chosen way of life. People, often ignoring the reality of their own limitations, in the pursuit of what they feel is their destiny. I have written about people struggling to survive in a tiny village on the Labrador coast, miners fighting for their land in the ruined hills of Appalachia, fishermen squeezing out an existence in the same waters they've fished for generations, waters that now happen to be the Everglades National Park. *One Step From Glory* follows the same theme. It is a book about professional athletes who are not stars, and therefore must fight for their jobs every day of their careers.

"My central effort in most of this work has been to report on a modern world which appears to be moving too fast to care for the rights and sensitivities of the individual. I have pursued these stories all over the United States, in South America, Canada, Greenland, and Western Europe. Along the way I've developed a great fondness for traveling, and for writing about it."

* * *

RUBEL, Paula G(licksman) 1933-

PERSONAL: Born March 13, 1933, in New York, N.Y.; daughter of Joseph and Frieda (Fromer) Rubel; married Abraham Rosman (an anthropology professor and author); children: two. *Education:* Hunter College (now of the City University of New York), A.B., 1953; Columbia University, Ph.D., 1963. *Office:* Department of Anthropology, Barnard College, Columbia University, New York, N.Y. 10027.

CAREER: Hunter College of the City University of New York, New York City, lecturer in anthropology, 1963-64; Columbia University, Barnard College, New York City, research associate, 1964-65, lecturer, 1965-66, assistant professor, 1966-70, associate professor, 1970-74, professor of anthropology, 1974—. Instructor at New York University, autumn, 1964. *Member:* American Anthropological Association (fellow), American Ethnological Society, Mongolia Society, Royal Anthropological Society (fellow). *Awards, honors:* National Institute of Mental Health grant for the Soviet Union, 1964-65; Social Science Research Council fellow, 1968; National Science Foundation fellow, 1969-70, 1971-72 (in Afghanistan), 1974-75.

WRITINGS: (Contributor) John Kreuger, editor, *Kalmyk Monograph Series,* Volume II, Indiana University Press, 1965; (with husband, Abraham Rosman) *Feasting With Mine Enemy: Rank and Exchange Among Northwest Coast Societies,* Columbia University Press, 1971; (contributor) Edward Allworth, editor, *Soviet Nationality Problems,* Columbia University Press, 1971; (contributor) Allworth, editor, *The Nationality Question in Soviet Central Asia,* Praeger, 1973; *The Kalmyk Mongols: A Study in Continuity and Change,* Indiana University Press, 1976; (contributor) George Dalton, editor, *Research in Economic Anthropology,* JAI Press, 1977; (with Rosman) *Your Own Pigs You May Not Eat,* University of Chicago Press, 1978; (with Rosman) *The Tapestry of Culture,* Scott, Foresman, in press. Contributor of articles and reviews to journals in the social sciences.

RUBENSTEIN, Roberta 1944-

PERSONAL: Born November 5, 1944, in Milford, Del.; daughter of Robert Jerome (in business) and Sarah (Taub) Rubenstein; married Charles R. Larson (a professor), May 2, 1971; children: Vanessa Hilary. *Education:* University of Colorado, B.A., 1966; University of London, Ph.D., 1969. *Home:* 3600 Underwood St., Chevy Chase, Md. 20015. *Office:* Department of Literature, American University, Washington, D.C. 20016.

CAREER: American University, Washington, D.C., instructor, 1969, assistant professor, 1969-74, associate professor of literature, 1974—, acting department head, 1976-77. *Member:* Phi Beta Kappa. *Awards, honors:* Woodrow Wilson fellow, 1966; Fulbright scholarship 1966-68.

WRITINGS: The Novelistic Vision of Doris Lessing: Breaking the Forms of Consciousness, University of Illinois Press, 1979. Contributor of articles, poems, and reviews to literature and film journals and popular magazines, including *Humanist, Modern Fiction Studies, Washingtonian, Contemporary Literature, Colorado Quarterly, Poem,* and *Progressive,* and newspapers.

WORK IN PROGRESS: An interdisciplinary study of women's images in fiction.

SIDELIGHTS: Rubenstein commented: "The two and a half years that I spent in England on a Fulbright grant provided a crucial catalyst in my life: crystallizing a career as a college professor in addition to broadening my cultural exposure and contributing to personal interests (travel, photography, music, theatre).

"In the course of writing a doctoral dissertation on Virginia Woolf, I was extremely fortunate to meet and converse with Leonard Woolf several times before his death in 1969. My research involved Woolf's interest in Russian literature (which she admired greatly, and which influenced her own efforts to develop a new form of fiction). However, my immersion in her work eventually led to my interest in psychology, unconventional and abnormal consciousness (including mysticism and madness), and other twentieth century women writers. I regard Woolf as one of the century's most original writers, whose gift, as a poet, of language has been confirmed again in her recently published diaries, letters, and autobiographical essays.

"My most recent work focuses on Doris Lessing, a writer whose range and evolution of provocative ideas have been maintained over a long (and still growing) canon. The two writers—Lessing and Woolf—have in common an urgent concern to fathom the subjective nature of consciousness, and to create psychic order through their literary art.

"I am also interested in myth and archetypal psychology, areas that contribute to my current interdisciplinary work on women writers."

AVOCATIONAL INTERESTS: Gardening, travel, photography, cuisine.

* * *

RUDKIN, (James) David 1936-

PERSONAL: Born June 29, 1936, in London, England; son of David Jonathan (a pastor) and Anne Alice (a teacher; maiden name, Martin) Rudkin; married Alexandra Margaret Thompson (an actress), May 3, 1967; children: Tom Joel, Jamie Samuel, Hannah Sophie, Jessica Anne. *Education:* St. Catherine's College, Oxford, M.A., 1961. *Agent:* Margaret Ramsay Ltd., 14A Goodwin's Ct., London WC2N 4LL, England.

CAREER: Playwright, translator, librettist, screenwriter, and film critic. Secondary school teacher of classics and music in Worcestershire, England, 1961-64. *Military service:* Royal Corps of Signals, 1955-57; became sergeant. *Member:* European Bridge Union, Institute of Hellenic Studies, Royal Anthropological Institute of Great Britain, Royal Society for the Protection of Birds, Havergal Brian Society. *Awards, honors:* Evening Standard Award for most promising playwright, 1962; John Whiting Award, 1974, for contribution to British Theatre.

WRITINGS: Afore Night Come (play; first produced in London at Arts Theatre Club, 1962; produced in New Haven, Conn., at Long Wharf Theatre, 1975), Grove, 1966 (also contained in *New English Dramatists, 7,* Penguin [Middlesex], 1965); (translator) Arnold Schoenberg, *Moses and Aaron* (libretto), Friends of Covent Garden, 1965; *The Grace of Todd* (libretto; first produced in Aldeburgh, England, 1969, produced in London, 1969), Oxford University Press, 1969; "The Filth Hunt" (one-act play), first produced in London at Ambiance Theatre, 1972; *Cries From Casement as His Bones Are Brought to Dublin* (stage adaptation of own radio play; first produced in London, 1973), British Broadcasting Corporation, 1974 (also see below); "No Title" (play; based on own television play, "House of Character"), first produced in Birmingham, England, 1974; *Penda's Fen* (television play), Poynter, 1975 (also see below); *Ashes* (play; first produced in Hamburg, Germany, at Malersaal, produced in London at Open Space Theatre, 1974, produced in New York City at Manhattan Theatre Club, 1976), Samuel French, 1976; "Burglars" (children's play; first produced in London, 1970), contained in *Prompt Two,* Hutchinson, 1976; "The Sons of Light" (play), first produced in Newcastle upon Tyne, England, March, 1976, produced in London, 1977; "Sovereignty Under Elizabeth" (one-act play), first produced in London at Ambiance Theatre, 1978; (translator) Euripides, "Hippolytus," first produced in Stratford, England, 1978, produced in London at Warehouse Theatre, 1979.

Television plays; all produced by British Broadcasting Corporation (BBC), except as noted: "The Stone Dance," Associated Television Ltd., 1963; "Children Playing," Associated Television Ltd., 1967; "House of Character," 1968; "Blodwen, Home From Rachel's Marriage," 1969; "Bypass," 1972; "Atrocity," 1973; "Penda's Fen," 1974; "Pritan" (part one of "Churchill's People" series), 1975; "The Coming of the Cross" (part three of "Churchill's People" series), 1975; "The Ash Tree" (based on the story by M. R. James), 1975; "The Living Grave," 1979. Also author of BBC radio plays "No Accounting for Taste," 1960, "The Persians" (translation of the play by Aeschylus), 1965, "Gear Change," 1967, "Cries From Casement as His Bones Are Brought to Dublin," 1973, and "Hecuba" (from the play by Euripides), 1975.

Author of ballet scenario, "Sun Into Darkness," 1966. Author of additional dialogue for screenplay by Francois Truffaut, "Fahrenheit 451," 1966. Also author of several unproduced stageplays, screenplays, librettos, and television plays.

WORK IN PROGRESS: "The Triumph of Death," "a play presenting man's quest for political and economic 'order' as an anti-life neurosis"; "The Mystery of Jesus," "a play seeking to uncover the historical events disguised and distorted by the later politically-motivated fabrications of the so-called 'Gospels'"; *Toward the Flame,* "a fusion of detective thriller and psycho-drama, set in Crete, concerning a lost fragment of an archaic religious inscription which becomes talisman to a terrible rebirth''; versions of Kleist's ''The Golem'' and ''The Pirate of Hamburg''; ''Magog,'' a large-scale horror film for television.

SIDELIGHTS: A member of a strict Evangelical Christian family, playwright David Rudkin was prohibited from seeing plays or movies when he was growing up. Despite this restriction, Rudkin claims that by the age of four he ''knew that he was a writer.'' After first experimenting with fiction and music writing, Rudkin turned to writing plays. His first play, ''Afore Night Come,'' met with some success while casting him as a proponent of the ''theatre of cruelty.'' Though Rudkin wrote in several varied media throughout the 1960's and early 1970's, his disappearance from the theatre forefront after ''Afore Night Come'' led some to dismiss him as a one-play playwright. Rudkin has countered that complaint more than a decade later with his most successful play to date, ''Ashes.''

''Afore Night Come'' enjoyed a brief but somewhat controversial 1962 premier by the Royal Shakespeare Company (RSC). Based on Rudkin's own experiences as a fruit picker in England, the play introduces a ''part tramp, part poet'' newcomer (Roche) to a group of fruit pickers. From this seemingly innocuous beginning, Roche becomes ''the focus of evil fears and desires and in the end their victim,'' wrote Frederick Lumley. Rudkin explained to Mel Gussow of the *New York Times* that when he worked in the orchards he found himself ''capable of a mute, irrational dislike'' for a new worker, a highly intelligent Irish laborer. ''It was a protective territorial thing,'' he continued. ''I thought, Christ, I'm murdering this man in my mind.'' In his play, Rudkin carried this situation to its extreme by having Roche assume a sacrificial role when he is brutally murdered by his co-workers.

The nightmarish aspects of the play enraged many members of the audience, who showed their disapproval by disrupting the performance or by leaving it entirely. When the RSC revived the play in 1974, Rudkin at first doubted the wisdom of the move: ''it would simply re-assert me as a one-play man.'' But to his surprise, ''England had caught up with the play. In 1962 it was Macmillan's England—amazingly innocent. In 1974 the play seemed bang in the world we lived in.'' Upon the play's 1974 American debut, however, patrons echoed the outrage of the original London audience.

During one such commotion in the London premier, one viewer reportedly ordered the audience to ''Shut up! Sit down and listen.'' Apparently, said Rudkin, the man was Harold Pinter, his ''godfather'' of playwriting. Four years earlier, seeing Pinter's ''The Birthday Party'' had affected Rudkin profoundly. ''The Birthday Party'' was ''like a grenade going off in my head,'' he later revealed. '''The Birthday Party' taught me how to listen. I was inhibited. I had a problem with language, with writing a language that had a presence on stage but that did not do violence to reality.''

After ''Afore Night Come'' Rudkin virtually disappeared from public attention while widening his range as an artist. He wrote ballet scenarios, wrote and translated opera librettos, and wrote numerous television and radio play scripts. Popular success never came, however, in part because Rudkin suffered from the stigma surrounding many television writers—few took them as seriously as they would have had they been writing for a different medium. In addition, reported Gerald Weales, his subject matter tended to be difficult and abrasive, thus further limiting his appeal. Ironically, a play turned down by BBC television, ''Ashes,'' provided Rudkin with the boost he needed to recapture public and critical attention.

''Ashes'' is the story of a childless couple, Colin and Anne Harding, and the struggles they face while attempting to have children. The advice of doctors, gynecologists, and seminologists does little more than increase their frustration and decrease their hopes for conception. As *Time*'s T. E. Kalem noted, ''The pair undergoes a series of fertility rituals, fecundity postures and time efficiency tests that are clinically presented and emotionally humiliating.'' Anne finally does become pregnant, but soon she miscarries and has to undergo a hysterectomy. The couple then decides to adopt children, only to learn later that the adoption agency has denied their request. The play takes on a broader dimension towards its close as Colin returns from his uncle's funeral in Northern Ireland, where he has seen the remains of relatives who were destroyed by Ulster's bombs. At this point, said Jack Kroll, Colin ''sees the destruction in Ireland as connected with the pain of two middle-class people who can never be parents: 'Self-certainty and acquiescence add up to a muckheap only violence will shift. We've known all along our old ways had to go. . . . Our only hope is to see what new people we have it in us to become.'''

Critics have noted that ''Ashes,'' most of all, is a play of losses. Colin had hoped to be a writer and Anne an actress; instead they are both teachers. After losing their career hopes, they lose the possibility of having children of their own, and then, any at all. Combined with these tangible losses is the loss of dignity, as Edith Oliver revealed: ''They are subjected to lectures from social workers and to more prying, humiliating interviews. At the end, there is a letter from the county: they have been turned down; no adoption, and no reason given.'' Furthermore, when Colin attends his uncle's funeral, ''his cousins refused to let him help carry his uncle's coffin because they said he was a runaway, not a true Ulsterman,'' Stanley Kauffmann pointed out. ''So Colin has had another loss: his country.''

Given the ashes of the Hardings' hopes, reviewers have interpreted the play on different levels. Some saw its many losses overcome by the spiritual bond created between Colin and Anne. As Gerald Weales stated, ''The play ends as Anne lifts Colin's head and looks into his face. . . . The shared final moment suggests that there are living coals in these ashes.'' In the same tone, Harold Clurman declared that ''for all its grimness, the play is not 'nihilistic.''' Clurman, too, referred to the final scene and perceived that ''a strange light like a spark of determination sharpens his [Colin's] gaze. They will face the future to wherever it may lead—regardless. That is the way of humankind, the way of life, that is all we can mean by hope.'' Oliver also felt ''Colin and Anne are unsinkable, endlessly resourceful, endlessly courageous. They will rise from the ashes.''

On a broader level, the plight of the couple has been interpreted as political metaphor. Kalem thought Rudkin failed in his intent. ''Where Playwright Rudkin eventually falters is in trying to make private grief a metaphor for public sorrow,'' the *Time* reviewer wrote. ''In a long and drenching monologue, he tries to link the childless couple's plight to the nightmare horrors of Northern Ireland.'' Clive Barnes, on the other hand, saw Rudkin ''marvelously'' change his focus from the personal to the political. ''Ashes'' ''talks about the necessary sterility of violence, and about a nation itself without birth,'' he said. ''Not everything with Mr. Rudkin is clear. The man flounders in floppy waves of genius. Yet you can perceive what he is saying to Western society. We have done angry things and in the silly violence, sterility may be our recompense. Northern Ireland is a country where no children can grow, and the whole world is poorer for it. . . .

Now the play, for me, takes on the image of a dying civilization."

In 1973 Rudkin wrote: "Ten years in the writing business, and I still have no outlet for the gifts I have." Since that time, "Afore Night Come" has enjoyed a successful revival, and a 1966 play, "The Sons of Light," has finally been produced. "Ashes," meanwhile, has secured Rudkin's position as a prominent British playwright. Now, with the outlet for his talents undoubtedly open, one can only wait and see what further gifts he will bring.

Rudkin told *CA:* "I think the less an author says outside of his work, the better."

AVOCATIONAL INTERESTS: Bridge ("as a trivial countertension"), music and musicology, languages (e.g., Hungarian, Russian, Modern Greek, the Celtic languages), philology, political philosophy, anthropology, botany, geomorphology, geology.

BIOGRAPHICAL/CRITICAL SOURCES: Frederick Lumley, *New Trends in 20th Century Drama: A Survey Since Ibsen and Shaw,* Oxford University Press, 1967; *New Yorker,* December 27, 1976; *Newsweek,* December 27, 1976; *Time,* January 3, 1977; *Nation,* January 8, 1977; *New York Times,* January 23, 1977, February 9, 1977, August 6, 1978; *New Republic,* February 19, 1977; *Saturday Review,* March 19, 1977; *Commonweal,* June 10, 1977.

—Sketch by David Versical

* * *

RUFFNER, Budge
See RUFFNER, Lester Ward

* * *

RUFFNER, Lester Ward 1918-
(Budge Ruffner)

PERSONAL: Born March 17, 1918, in Prescott, Ariz.; son of Lester Lee (in business) and Mary (a pianist; maiden name, Ward) Ruffner; married Elizabeth A. Friedrich (a historical preservation consultant), August 10, 1940; children: Melissa, Rebecca, George A. *Education:* Attended Loyola University, Los Angeles, Calif., 1938, 1939, and University of Virginia, 1940. *Politics:* Republican. *Religion:* Roman Catholic. *Home:* Barranca Dr., Prescott, Ariz. 86301. *Office:* P.O. Box 61, Prescott, Ariz. 86302.

CAREER: Ruffner-Cibola, Inc. (family real estate holdings), Prescott, Ariz., president, 1946—. Member of board of directors of Arizona Academy. *Military service:* U.S. Army Air Forces, gunner, 1942-45; became sergeant. *Member:* Western Writers of America, Arizona Historical Society (past president). *Awards, honors:* Al Merito Award from Arizona Historical Society, 1973, for significant contributions to the folklore and history of the American Southwest.

WRITINGS—Under name Budge Ruffner: *All Hell Needs Is Water* (nonfiction), University of Arizona Press, 1973, 2nd edition, 1976; *Shot in the Ass With Pesos* (nonfiction), Treasure Chest Press, 1979. Author of two weekly columns in *Prescott Evening Courier.* Contributor of stories and poems to *Arizona, New Mexico,* and *Arizona Highways.*

WORK IN PROGRESS: A film on the fur trade.

SIDELIGHTS: Ruffner writes: "The four-hundred-year history of the American Southwest offers a fertile field to the writer. As a native and constant traveler of the area, both inspiration and expertise are within me."

RUNNING, Leona Glidden 1916-

PERSONAL: Born August 24, 1916, in Mount Morris, Mich.; daughter of Charles Comstock (a design engineer) and Leona (a teacher; maiden name, Boat) Glidden; married Leif H. Running, May 17, 1942 (died August 20, 1946). *Education:* Emmanuel Missionary College (now Andrews University), B.A., 1937; Seventh-day Adventist Theological Seminary (now Andrews University), M.A., 1955; Johns Hopkins University, Ph.D., 1964. *Office:* Department of Old Testament, Seminary, Andrews University, Berrien Springs, Mich. 49104.

CAREER: Laurelwood Academy, Gaston, Ore., teacher of French and German, 1937-41; Voice of Prophecy, Inc., Glendale, Calif., foreign language secretary, 1944-48; *Ministry,* Takoma Park, Md., copy editor, 1950-54; Andrews University, Berrien Springs, Mich., instructor, 1955-60, assistant professor, 1960-64, associate professor, 1964-69, professor of biblical languages, 1969—. Research assistant to Professor William F. Albright, 1965-66. Secretary to conferences of Seventh-Day Adventists, 1942-44, and 1949-50. *Member:* Society of Biblical Literature, National Association of Professors of Hebrew, American Schools of Oriental Research, Chicago Society of Biblical Research.

WRITINGS: Thirty-Six Days and a Dream (on travel in Europe), Review & Herald, 1953; *From Thames to Tigris* (study tour), Washington College Press, 1958; (with David Noel Freedman) *William Foxwell Albright: A Twentieth-Century Genius,* Morgan Press, 1975. Contributor to theology journals.

WORK IN PROGRESS: Articles.

SIDELIGHTS: Leona Running writes: "After the death of biblical archaeologist, W. F. Albright, who was my teacher in his last year before retirement, my co-author and I spent three years gathering the material and writing his biography, a 'labor of love' for one whom we greatly respected and whose influence lives on in his many scholarly fields. Our aim was to interest the general reader who likes biography in the life of a great man and make his esoteric field understandable to the nonspecialist."

* * *

RUOTOLO, Andrew K. 1926(?)-1979

OBITUARY NOTICE: Born c. 1926; died August 8, 1979, of a heart attack while on vacation, in France. Psychoanalyst and author. Ruotolo maintained a private practice in psychiatry. He wrote *Once Upon a Murder,* a book based on interviews with eight alleged murderers. Obituaries and other sources: *New York Times,* August 16, 1979.

* * *

RYALL, George 1887(?)-1979
(Audax Minor)

OBITUARY NOTICE: Born c. 1887 in Toronto, Ontario, Canada; died October 8, 1979. Journalist best known for his coverage of horse racing. Under the pseudonym Audax Minor, he contributed to the *New Yorker* magazine for more than fifty years, writing profiles as well as racing features. Obituaries and other sources: *New York Times,* October 10, 1979; *Time,* October 22, 1979.

S

SACKETT, Theodore Alan 1940-

PERSONAL: Born March 24, 1940, in Los Angeles, Calif.; son of Alfred A. and Ruth S. Sackett; married Beverly Grace Artin (an executive secretary), June, 1964; children: Philip Joseph, Jason Alan. *Education:* University of California, Riverside, B.A., 1962; University of Arizona, M.A., 1965, Ph.D., 1966. *Home:* 10578 Cheviot Dr., Los Angeles, Calif. 90064. *Office:* Department of Spanish and Portuguese, University of Southern California, Los Angeles, Calif. 90007.

CAREER: Williams College, Williamstown, Mass., lecturer in Spanish and Portuguese, 1965-67; University of New Mexico, Albuquerque, assistant professor, 1967-70, associate professor of Spanish and Portuguese, 1970-71; University of Southern California, Los Angeles, associate professor of Spanish and Portuguese, 1971—, head of department, 1971-77. *Member:* Modern Language Association of America, American Association of Teachers of Spanish and Portuguese, American Association of University Professors, American Civil Liberties Union, Portuguese American Progressive Club. *Awards, honors:* National Defense Act Ph.D. fellowship, 1962-65; Del Amo fellowship from Del Amo Foundation of Los Angeles, 1975.

WRITINGS: Perez Galdos: An Annotated Bibliography, University of New Mexico Press, 1968; *El arte en la novelistica de Jorge Icaza* (title means "The Artistic Dimension in Icaza's Novels"), Casa de la Cultura Ecuatoriana, 1974. Contributor to language and Latin American studies journals. Assistant editor of *Berkshire Review,* 1966-67; hispanic book review editor of *Modern Language Journal,* 1978—.

WORK IN PROGRESS: Galdos y las mascaras: Historia teatral y bibliografia anotada (title means "Galdos and the Stage: Theatrical History and Annotated Bibliography"), publication expected in 1980; research on Galdos's *Electra* and Alfonso Sastre's *Prologo patetico.*

SIDELIGHTS: Sackett writes: "I am interested particularly in nineteenth-century Spanish fiction, drama, literary criticism, as well as Ecuadorian literature, twentieth-century Spanish drama, and hispanic bibliography."

* * *

SAETONE
See CAMUS, Albert

SAIDY, Anthony Fred 1937-

PERSONAL: Born May 16, 1937, in Los Angeles, Calif.; son of Fred Milhem (a playwright) and Marie Delores (Mallouk) Saidy. *Education:* Fordham University, B.S., 1958; Cornell University, M.D., 1962; University of California, Los Angeles, M.P.H., 1968. *Politics:* "Progressive." *Religion:* None. *Residence:* Los Angeles, Calif.

CAREER: Wadsworth Veterans Administration Hospital, Los Angeles, Calif., intern, 1962-63; Fort Miley Veterans Administration Hospital, San Francisco, Calif., resident in internal medicine, 1965-66; Los Angeles County Department of Health Services, Tuberculosis Control, Los Angeles, Calif., practice of preventive medicine, 1967—. Chess master, 1955—, international chess master, 1969—; captain of U.S. Women's Olympic Chess Team in Buenos Aires, Argentina, 1978. Diplomate of American Board of Preventive Medicine. *Military service:* U.S. Public Health Service, Peace Corps physician in Puerto Rico and Jamaica, 1963-65. *Member:* U.S. Chess Federation. *Awards, honors:* Chess awards include Canadian Open championship, 1960, and American Open championship, 1967.

WRITINGS: (With Norman Lessing) *The World of Chess,* Ridge Press, 1974; *The Battle of Chess Ideas,* Batsford, 1972, R.H.M. Press, 1975. Contributor to *Chess Life and Review.*

WORK IN PROGRESS: Research on history, psychology, and philosophy of chess, world affairs, history, the media, *belles lettres,* public health and preventive medicine, and comedy.

SIDELIGHTS: Saidy told *CA:* "The writer who most influenced me was my father, playwright Fred Saidy. Taking up pen had doubtless Freudian significance for the younger Saidy. My favorite American stylist is Mailer. My favorite neglected master: Zamyatin."

* * *

SAKLATVALA, Beram 1911-1976
(Henry Marsh)

PERSONAL: Born September 11, 1911, in Manchester, England; died September 27, 1976; son of Shapurji and Seri (Marsh) Saklatvala; married (separated). *Education:* Earned B.A. (with honors) from University College, London. *Home:* 52 Elm Grove, London S.E.15, England. *Office:* Tata Ltd., 18 Grosvenor Pl., London SW1X 7HS, England.

CAREER: Poet and writer. Working Men's College, London, England, dean of studies, 1952-61, vice-principal, 1961-66. Managing director of Tata Ltd.

WRITINGS: Devouring Zodiac: A Collection of Poems, Fortune Press, 1945; *Stubborn Heart* (poems) Tulip Press, 1945; *The Choice* (poems), Fortune Press, 1947; *Phoenix and Unicorn* (poems), Fortune Press, 1954; *Air Journey: A Sonnet Sequence,* Fortune Press, 1967; *Arthur: Roman Britain's Last Champion,* Taplinger, 1967; (translator) *The Complete Poems of Francois Villon,* Everyman's Library, 1968; *The Christian Island,* Dent, 1969, Fairleigh Dickinson University Press, 1970; *The Origins of the English People,* David & Charles, 1969, Taplinger, 1970; (with Krihna Kumar Khosla) *Jamsetji Tata,* Ministry of Information and Broadcasting, Government of India, 1970; *The Rebel Jew: The Story of St. Paul,* Fudge & Co., 1979.

Under pseudonym Henry Marsh: *Dark Age Britain: Some Sources of History,* Archon Books, 1970; (editor) *British Documents of Liberty: From Earliest Times to Universal Suffrage,* Fairleigh Dickinson University Press, 1971 (published in England as *Documents of Liberty: From Earliest Times to Universal Suffrage,* David & Charles, 1971); *The Caesars: The Roman Empire and Its Rulers,* St. Martin's, 1972; *Slavery and Race: A Story of Slavery and Its Legacy for Today,* St. Martin's, 1974; *The Rebel King: The Story of Christ as Seen Against the Historical Conflict Between the Roman Empire and Judaism,* Coward, 1975.

BIOGRAPHICAL/CRITICAL SOURCES: Times Literary Supplement, November 30, 1967; *Best Sellers,* August, 1975.

[Sketch verified by Yasmin Saklatvala]

* * *

SALAMON, Lester M(ilton) 1943-

PERSONAL: Born January 11, 1943, in Pittsburgh, Pa.; son of Victor William and Helen (Sanders) Salamon; married Lynda A. Brown, June 25, 1965; children: Noah Benjamin, Matthew William. *Education:* Princeton University, A.B., 1964; Harvard University, M.A., 1966, Ph.D., 1970. *Office:* Office of Management and Budget, Washington, D.C. 20503.

CAREER: Vanderbilt University, Nashville, Tenn., assistant professor of political science, 1970-73; Duke University, Durham, N.C., associate professor of political science, 1973-77; Office of Management and Budget, Washington, D.C., deputy associate director, 1977—. *Member:* American Political Science Association, Public Policy Association. *Awards, honors:* Woodrow Wilson fellow, 1964-65; Burchfield Award from American Society for Public Administration, 1977, for "Urban Policy: Case Studies and Political Theory."

WRITINGS: The Money Committees, Viking, 1975; *Land and Minority Enterprise,* U.S. Government Printing Office, 1976; *Welfare, the Elusive Consensus: Where We Are, How We Got There, and What's Ahead,* Praeger, 1978. Co-editor with J. F. Blumstein of special issue of *Law and Contemporary Problems,* 1979. Contributor to political science and public administration journals. Editor of *Administration and Society.*

* * *

SALEMME, Lucia (Autorino) 1919-

PERSONAL: Born September 23, 1919, in New York, N.Y.; daughter of Salvatore (a musician and painter) and Teresa (a singer; maiden name, Iovino) Autorino; married Attilio Salemme (an artist), September 26, 1943 (died, 1955); children: Vincent, Lawrence. *Education:* Attended Art Students League, 1932-34; also studied at National Academy of Design. *Religion:* Roman Catholic. *Office:* 112 West 21st St., New York, N.Y. 10011.

CAREER: Painter, with eleven solo exhibitions, group shows, and commissioned works; represented in public and private collections, including Whitney Museum of American Art and National Gallery of Art. Restorer of paintings for private art dealers and institutions. Instructor at Museum of Modern Art, 1958-68; associate professor at New York University, 1960-73, adjunct professor, 1970—. *Awards, honors:* Guggenheim fellow, 1941.

WRITINGS: Color Exercises for the Painter, Watson-Guptill, 1970; *Compositional Exercises for the Painter,* Watson-Guptill, 1973; *Painting Techniques,* Macmillan, 1979.

SIDELIGHTS: In 1965 Alexander Calder wrote: "A few years ago I told Lucia Salemme that she would have to choose between realism and fantasy in her painting. She feels she has gone toward fantasy, but I think that though her ideas may be fantastic, that her elements, i.e., the arts of her scenery, are very realistic, made of iron and concrete and very solid materials.

"Her colors are between primary and secondary, with pale blues and winery reds—imbued with mystic breezes and gusts of air. I'll admit that is rather eerie.

"But eerie or not, that is really not the question. I feel that she has stature as a professional painter. And she has nothing to do with pop-beats."

* * *

SALISBURY, Carola (Isobel Julien) 1943-

PERSONAL: Born January 11, 1943, in London, England; daughter of Jack Piers (a major in the Coldstream Guards) and Lady Anne (Herbert) Salisbury; married Michael James Rodd (a stockbroker), June 6, 1964 (divorced, 1969). *Education:* Attended high school in Bristol, England. *Agent:* Georges Borchardt, Inc., 136 East 57th St., New York, N.Y. 10022.

CAREER: Writer.

WRITINGS—All gothic novels: *Pride of the Trevallions,* Doubleday, 1974, published in England as *Mallion's Pride,* Collins, 1974; *Dark Inheritance,* Doubleday, 1975; *Dolphin Summer,* Doubleday, 1976; *The Winter Bride,* Doubleday, 1977.

WORK IN PROGRESS: Another gothic novel.

* * *

SANDERS, Donald 1915(?)-1979

OBITUARY NOTICE: Born c. 1915 in Selinsgrove, Pa.; died of cancer, November 22, 1979, in Alexandria, Va. Editor and journalist. Sanders worked for more than twenty years as supervisory editor of the Associated Press's Washington, D.C., bureau. He covered both art and politics. Obituaries and other sources: *New York Times,* November 23, 1979; *Washington Post,* November 24, 1979.

* * *

SANDY, Max
See SAUNDERS, Carl Maxon

* * *

SANGER, Margaret (Higgins) 1883-1966

OBITUARY NOTICE: Born September 14, 1883, in Corning,

N.Y.; died September 6, 1966. Leader of the birth control movement in the United States. In 1912, Margaret Sanger launched a long struggle against the ignorance, prejudice, religious tenets, and laws that prevented or opposed the practice of birth control. As a maternity nurse working in New York City's Lower East Side, she confronted the misery, helplessness, and oftentimes death that came to poverty-stricken, pregnant women. Disillusioned by the suffering she saw and her own inability to help and advise, she renounced her nursing career forever and resolved to campaign for the collection and dissemination of birth control literature and devices. In 1914 she founded the National Birth Control League and, under the slogan "No gods; no masters!," she published the *Woman Rebel* magazine and wrote of the need for contraceptive information. Her crusade, however, was met with persecution, court trials, and imprisonment: she was indicted in 1915 for sending pleas for birth control through the mails, and in 1916 she was arrested for operating a birth control clinic in Brooklyn, N.Y. While still in prison, she founded and edited the *Birth Control Review*. After organizing national and international conferences, founding the Birth Control Clinical Research Bureau, and writing and speaking on behalf of her cause, Sanger finally won the needed legislative changes that would allow doctors to prescribe contraceptives and educate the public. In 1942, the American Birth Control League merged with the Birth Control Clinical Research Bureau to form the Birth Control Federation of America, now known as the Planned Parenthood Federation of America. Sanger was the author of numerous books on birth control and sex education, including *What Every Girl Should Know; What Every Mother Should Know; The Case for Birth Control; Woman, Morality, and Birth Control; The Pivot of Civilization;* and *Motherhood in Bondage*. Obituaries and other sources: Margaret Sanger, *My Fight for Birth Control* (autobiography), Farrar & Rinehart, 1931; Sanger, *Margaret Sanger: An Autobiography,* Norton, 1938; *Current Biography,* Wilson, 1944, November, 1966; *The Oxford Companion to American Literature,* 4th edition, Oxford University Press, 1965; *New York Times,* September 7, 1966; *Who Was Who in America,* 4th edition, Marquis, 1968; *Longman Companion to Twentieth Century Literature,* Longman, 1970.

* * *

SANTOS, Eduardo 1888-1974

OBITUARY NOTICE: Born August 28, 1888, in Bogota, Colombia; died in March, 1974. Santos was elected president of Colombia in August, 1938, having previously served in the House of Representatives and the Senate. He was several times delegate to the League of Nations and Colombia's representative to the 1932 Disarmament Conference in Geneva. Considered the leading journalist of his country, Santos contributed to newspapers in Colombia and Madrid, Spain, the latter under pseudonyms, and was director of *El Tiempo Bogota* from 1912. Obituaries and other sources: *Who Was Who in America,* 4th edition, Marquis, 1968.

* * *

SANVILLE, Jean 1918-
(Jean Livermore)

PERSONAL: Born December 6, 1918, in Tionesta, Pa.; daughter of Forest Johnson (a physician) and Ruth (a school principal; maiden name, Dimond) Bovard; children: Joan Palmer, Peter Livermore. *Education:* University of Colorado, B.A., 1940; Smith College, M.S.S., 1942; further graduate study at University of Pittsburgh, 1942-43; International College, Los Angeles, Calif., Ph.D., 1978. *Home and office:* 1300 Tigertail Rd., Los Angeles, Calif. 90049. *Agent:* Neal Gantcher, Cohn, Glickstein, Lurie, Ostrin & Lubell, 1370 Avenue of the Americas, New York, N.Y. 10019.

CAREER: Caseworker for family service agencies in New York, N.Y., Pittsburgh, Pa., and Los Angeles, Calif., 1942-46; Veterans Administration, Psychiatric Clinic, Los Angeles, psychiatric social worker and supervisor, 1946-47; Hacker Psychiatric Clinic, Beverly Hills, Calif., psychotherapist, 1947-58; private practice in psychotherapy and psychoanalysis in Los Angeles, 1958—. Visiting associate professor at University of California, Los Angeles, 1948-53, lecturer, 1968-77; member of faculty at Los Angeles Institute for Psychoanalytic Studies. President of board of trustees of Institute for Clinical Social Work, 1974-76, dean of institute, 1977-79; mental health consultant to governments in Latin America, the Caribbean, and the Far East. *Member:* National Association of Social Workers (charter member), Association for Applied Psychoanalysis, American Orthopsychiatric Association (fellow; life member), Society for Clinical Social Work (president, 1974-76), Phi Beta Kappa.

WRITINGS: (Contributor) Charlotte Buehler, editor, *The Human Course of Life,* Springer Publishing, 1968; (with Joel Shor) *Illusion in Loving: A Psychoanalytic Approach to the Evolution of Intimacy and Autonomy,* International Universities Press, 1978; (contributor) E. James Anthony and Colette Chiland, editors, *The Vulnerable Child,* Wiley, 1978. Contributor to psychology journals, sometimes under name Jean Livermore. Member of editorial board of *Clinical Social Work Journal.*

WORK IN PROGRESS: A book to follow *Illusion in Loving,* treating the therapeutic implications of the first book, with Joel Shor.

SIDELIGHTS: Jean Sanville writes: "Changes in the social scene are making for changes in the nature of complaints with which patients come to psychotherapy. These necessitate a rethinking of old concepts, old approaches. Particularly important in our thinking is the dialectic between the two lines of development: that of the 'self' (autonomy) and that of the social (object relationships).

"I travel a great deal, and particularly enjoy travel which permits meaningful contact with local people in the lands we visit."

* * *

SARANT, P(eter) C. 1933(?)-1979

OBITUARY NOTICE: Born c. 1933 in Tamaqua, Pa.; died of cancer, October 6, 1979, in Olney, Ill. Government official in the field of accounting and author of *Government Payroll Record-Keeping and Procedures.* As an employee of the National Aeronautics and Space Administration, Sarant served as a contract auditor before becoming director of the Management Sciences Training Center. His book on zero-based budgeting was entitled *ZBB in the Public Sector.* Obituaries and other sources: *Washington Post,* October 9, 1979.

* * *

SARDUY, Severo 1937-

CAREER: Novelist, poet, essayist, and literary critic. Adviser to various French publishing houses. *Awards, honors:* Received Prix Medicis from France, for *Cobra.*

WRITINGS: Gestos, Editorial Seix Barral, 1963; *De Donde son los cantantes* (novella), Mortiz, 1967, translation by

Suzanne Jill Levine published in *Triple Cross* (contains "Holy Place" by Carlos Fuentes, "Hell Has No Limits" by Jose Donoso, and "From Cuba With a Song" by Sarduy), Dutton, 1972; *Escrito sobre un cuerpo: Ensayos de critica,* Editorial Sudamericana, 1969; *Flamenco,* Manus Presse, 1969; (contributor) H. M. Erhardt, *Mood Indigo,* Manus Presse, 1970; *Cobra* (novel), Editorial Sudamericana, 1972, translation by Levine published under same title, Dutton, 1975; *Overdose* (poetry), Las Palmas, Inventorios Provisionales, 1972; *Big Bang* (poetry), Fata Morgana, 1973; *Barroco,* Editorial Sudamericana, 1974. Editor of *Tel Quel.*

SIDELIGHTS: In his review of *Cobra,* Michael Wood commented: "We are invited into a magic space, into a tunnel of words, a place from which transformations sprout in all directions." Critics consistently note the transformations in Sarduy's work, especially as they seem to touch every aspect of his fiction. E. Rodriguez Monegal outlined these basic assumptions at work in Sarduy's novels: "Words are the only reality in fiction; the literary text does not refer to anything outside itself; the text of a book 'talks' only to itself." Thus, as Jerome Charyn stated, "language is everything in Sarduy's book." Everything from character to cosmos, Wood noted, is conditioned by language and its transformations: "Men become women and women become dwarfs; people die and do not die; Paris becomes Amsterdam, which in turn becomes Nepal." Or as Monegal said of "From Cuba With a Song," "fiction rules reality."

Roberto Gonzales Echevarria viewed Sarduy's first two novels as "rehearsals" for *Cobra.* In *Gestos,* the influence of the nouveau roman reveals itself in Sarduy's preoccupation with description. "An objective, unfastened, disinterested language dances before the eyes of the reader," remarked Echevarria. "Except that almost all the objects described in the novel are pictures. In other words, the novel does not produce an immediate reality but gives instead detailed descriptions of canvases by well-known painters and projects the action of the story upon them." At the bidding of words, reality again undergoes a series of metamorphoses in "From Cuba With a Song." In the last of three narratives, Monegal reported, "the moth-eaten image of Christ which two acolytes carry to Havana (they are also transvestites) gradually rots away in keeping with the metamorphosis of the Cuban landscape and the Spanish language. When they reach the tropical capital they find subways, kirsch factories, snow."

In his third novel, Sarduy concentrates on transformation as his theme. "*Cobra* is a book of changes," Wood commented. "And its title indicates not its meaning but the kind of activity it is engaged in." The book's narrative presents a hero-heroine named Cobra who begins life as a female wax doll, then undergoes a sex-change operation in a mysterious Tangier abortion clinic, joins a motorcycle gang in Amsterdam, who mutilates and destroys her/him in a kinky religious ceremony, and becomes, finally, an embodiment of the Hindu god of creation and destruction, Shiva. As Jerome Charyn remarked: "Sarduy disallows any satisfying permanence in his definition of humankind." But the snake-like shedding of personae and meaning "positively forbids us to read [the book] in depth," noted Robert Adams. "The book is primarily a stream of images, glittering, exotic, trite and disgusting, cosmic and squalid, grotesque and funny, strung on a set of generative puns." "If *Cobra* has a theme . . . ," Wood stated, "its theme is transformation." In fact, the real protagonist of the book, he suggested, may be the word cobra in all its possible references. At various times in the novel, cobra is the name of a snake, a motorcycle gang, a singer, a group of artists, a form of the Spanish verb *cobrar,* etc. "The references define the word cobra as a sort of crazy semantic crossroads, a linguistic point where unlikely meanings intersect, and it is the intersection that counts rather than the meanings themselves," Wood observed.

Cobra was well received by critics. Helene Cixous wrote: "*Cobra* is in a class of its own, unrelated to any 'serious' genre, whether encoded or codable, to any type except the one whose new genius it invents: a bizarre hybrid, a composite of snake, writings, rhythms, of a flight of luminous traces and a series of infinitesimal sparkling instants." A *New Yorker* critic remarked: "What is impressive is the rich vocabulary, the freewheeling imagination, and the utter cockiness. When, in a footnote, the author addresses us as 'moronic reader,' he has a certain charm." And though Adams received "a deep sense of astral chill" from the book, Wood concluded that *Cobra* remains a remarkable book, a nervous, flighty homage to the life of language."

BIOGRAPHICAL/CRITICAL SOURCES: New York Times Book Review, December 24, 1972, March 9, 1975; *Nation,* June 11, 1973; *Review 74,* winter, 1974; *New Yorker,* January 27, 1975; *New York Review of Books,* March 20, 1975; *Contemporary Literary Criticism,* Volume 6, Gale, 1976.*

* * *

SAUNDERS, Carl Maxon 1890-1974 (Max Sandy)

OBITUARY NOTICE: Born October 26, 1890, in Grand Rapids, Mich.; died October 2, 1974, in Grand Rapids, Mich. In 1949, Saunders won the Pulitzer Prize for his editorial "Prayer for Peace" in the *Jackson Citizen Patriot.* It was his contention that Memorial Day should be a national day of prayer. The U.S. Congress unanimously approved the proposal, and the prayer Saunders had written was used in Memorial Day services at Arlington National Cemetery. He was the editor of the *Jackson Citizen Patriot* from 1934 to 1960, having previously worked for the *Grand Rapids News, Kalamazoo Telegraph-Press, Detroit Free Press,* and *Grand Rapids Herald.* He was the author of *Booth of Michigan,* and a contributor, under the pseudonym Max Sandy, of magazine articles on the subject of conservation. Obituaries and other sources: *Current Biography,* Wilson, 1950, November, 1974; *Who Was Who in America,* 4th edition, Marquis, 1968; *New York Times,* October 4, 1974.

* * *

SAUVAGE, Franck

See HORN, Maurice

* * *

SAWATSKY, Harry Leonard 1931-

PERSONAL: Born February 10, 1931, in Canada; son of Johann Heinrich (a farmer) and Elisabeth (Penner) Sawatsky. *Education:* University of Manitoba, B.A., 1961; University of California, Berkeley, M.A., 1963, Ph.D., 1967. *Office:* Department of Geography, University of Manitoba, Winnipeg, Manitoba, Canada R3T 2N2.

CAREER: University of Manitoba, Winnipeg, professor of geography, 1966—. Alexander von Humboldt docent, 1971 and 1974. Farmer. Member of Northern Studies Committee and Natural Resource Institute. *Member:* Canadian Association of Geographers.

WRITINGS: They Sought a Country, University of California Press, 1971. Contributor to academic journals and *Mennonite Life.*

WORK IN PROGRESS: Research on arctic atmospheric optics, the role of background institutions in land-use decisions, and colonization by religious minorities in Latin America.

SIDELIGHTS: Sawatsky comments that his agrarian upbringing has influenced his interest in man-environment interrelationships and the role of culture and institutions. He maintains a three-hundred-seventy-five-acre commercial farm as a personal testing ground for his "concepts of improved resource-use without sacrifice of economic viability."

* * *

SAYER, Angela 1935-

PERSONAL: Born August 12, 1935, in Iver Heath, Buckinghamshire, England; daughter of Ronald and Dorothy (Rixon) Worrall-Bolton; married Michael John Sayer (a kennels proprietor), April 11, 1954; children: Jennifer Jane Sayer Hardman, Janet Angela Sayer Massey, Julia Michelle. *Education:* Open University, B.A., 1977. *Politics:* None. *Religion:* None. *Home and office:* Hunting Grove, Lowfield Heath, Crawley, Sussex RH11 OPY, England.

CAREER: Curlton Products Ltd., Iver, Buckinghamshire, England, director, 1958-62; Swift Post-Pax Ltd., East Grinstead, Sussex, England, director, 1962-66; Felcan Foods Ltd., Crawley, Sussex, England, director, 1972-76; Animal Graphics Ltd., Crawley, managing director, 1973—. *Member:* Royal Photographic Society, Fauna Preservation Society, National Trust, Racehorse Owners Association, Arab Horse Society, Rare Breeds Survival Trust, Cat Fancy (delegate to governing council), Oriental Tabby Cat Club (president), Cameo and Associated Varieties Cat Club (president).

WRITINGS: (And photographer) *Portrait of Cats,* Hamlyn, 1972; *Cats and Kittens in Colour,* Hamlyn, 1973, revised edition published as *Kittens and Cats,* 1975; *Beauty of Cats,* Hamlyn, 1974; (and photographer) *Love of Kittens,* Octopus, 1975; (and photographer) *Wonderful World of Horses,* Hamlyn, 1976; (with Grace Pond) *Cats,* Bartholomew, 1976; *World Encyclopaedia of Cats,* Octopus, 1977; (with Pond; also photographer) *The Intelligent Cat,* Davis-Poynter, 1977, Dial, 1978; (and photographer) *Wonderful World of Ponies,* Hamlyn, 1978; *The Encyclopaedia of the Cat,* Octopus, 1979; (and photographer) *Young Riders Handbook* (juvenile), Hamlyn, 1979; (and photographer) *The Family All-Colour Book of Dogs and Puppies,* Hamlyn, 1980; (and photographer) *The Family All-Colour Book of Cats and Kittens,* Hamlyn, 1980; (and photographer) *The Maltese Factor,* Heinemann, 1980.

Photographer: *Practical Guide to Cats,* Hamlyn, 1976; *Book of the Cat,* New Leaf, 1980; *Purnell's Encyclopedia of the Cat,* 1980. Contributor to animal encyclopedias. Contributor to natural history magazines.

WORK IN PROGRESS: Island Ponies, on segregation of gene pools on islands; *Kitchen Antiques,* on restoration and collecting; *Back Into Harness,* a manual on harness and driving.

SIDELIGHTS: Angela Sayer commented: "I am an animal person, keenly interested in the psychology and physiology of all animals. In 1976 I began to take my own pictures and have since started to indulge my love of travel, looking worldwide for material for meaningful and well-illustrated books. I specialise in cats, dogs, and horses, concentrating on behavioural pictures rather than posed portraits."

SAYLOR, David J(onathan) 1945-

PERSONAL: Born September 12, 1945, in Johnstown, Pa.; son of Tillman Kulp, Jr. (a lawyer) and Peggy (Berkebile) Saylor; married Virginia Lauer (an equal employment specialist), October 13, 1973; children: Elizabeth Tracy. *Education:* Williams College, A.B., 1967; Harvard University, J.D., 1970. *Home:* 4617 Reno Rd. N.W., Washington, D.C. 20008. *Office:* Federal Communications Commission, 1919 M St. N.W., #614, Washington, D.C. 20554.

CAREER: Hogan & Hartson, Washington, D.C., lawyer, 1972-75; Federal Trade Commission, Washington, D.C., assistant director, 1975-78; Federal Communications Commision, Washington, D.C., deputy general counsel, 1978—. Member of Federal Bar and U.S. Supreme Court Bar. Washington coordinator for Citizens for the Eastern Wilderness, 1973-74. *Member:* Hawaii Bar Association, District of Columbia Bar Association.

WRITINGS: Jackson Hole, Wyoming: In the Shadow of the Tetons, University of Oklahoma Press, 1970.

SIDELIGHTS: Saylor's interests include antitrust, communications, and energy law, environmental protection, wilderness preservation, and history, especially history of the early American West.

* * *

SAYRE, Joel 1900-1979

OBITUARY NOTICE: Born December 13, 1900, in Marion, Ind.; died of a heart attack, September 9, 1979, in Taftsville, Vt. Sayre, who looked like "a granite cottage wearing an old-Roman grin," was a reporter, war correspondent, screenwriter, and author of satirical novels. A man of imposing girth and exuberance, Sayre specialized in crime reporting for the *New York Herald Tribune,* and covered the career of gangster John Thomas "Legs" Diamond. During the thirties, he moved to Hollywood and worked as a screenwriter on such films as "Gunga Din," "Annie Oakley," and the "The Road to Glory." His own first novel, *Rackety Rax,* an "uproarious" satire about football and the Mob, was also made into a film. After covering America's Persian Gulf Command during World War II, he became a staff writer and correspondent for the *New Yorker* magazine. His story about a man who leaped to his death from a Gotham Hotel window ledge was produced as the motion picture "Fourteen Hours" in 1951. His other writings include *Persian Gulf Command* and *The House Without a Roof.* Obituaries and other sources: *New York Times,* September 14, 1979; *Time,* September 24, 1979.

* * *

SCHALK, David L(ouis) 1936-

PERSONAL: Born June 18, 1936, in Northampton, Mass.; son of Marshall (a professor) and Dorothy (an artist; maiden name, Stowell) Schalk; married Elisabeth Proske Barrett, February 1, 1964; children: Laura E., Peter Benjamin. *Education:* Wesleyan University, Middletown, Conn., A.B. (with high honors), 1958; Harvard University, M.A., 1959, Ph.D., 1964. *Office:* Department of History, Vassar College, Poughkeepsie, N.Y. 12601.

CAREER: Massachusetts Institute of Technology, Cambridge, instructor, 1963-64, assistant professor of humanities, 1964-68; Vassar College, Poughkeepsie, N.Y., associate professor, 1968-78, professor of history, 1978—, member of board of directors of Cooperative Bookshop, 1973-76, head of department, 1974-79. Participant in professional meetings; public lecturer. *Member:* American Association of University Professors (local president, 1970-72), Phi Beta Kappa. *Awards, honors:* Woodrow Wilson fellow, 1958-59; Harvard University traveling fellow in France, 1961-62; Old Dominion fellow in France, 1966; National Endowment for the Humanities grant, 1976.

WRITINGS: Roger Martin du Gard: The Novelist and History, Cornell University Press, 1967; *The Spectrum of Political Engagement: Mounier, Benda, Nizan, Brasillach, Sartre,* Princeton University Press, 1979. Contributor of about a dozen articles and reviews to scholarly journals.

WORK IN PROGRESS: "Additional study of the intellectual impact of the First World War, and further examination of the question of political involvement of the intellectual class, particularly in France during the period 1945-62."

* * *

SCHEFTER, Jim 1940-

PERSONAL: Born March 15, 1940, in Minnesota. *Education:* LaVerne College, B.A., 1975; University of Missouri at Kansas City, M.B.A., 1978. *Home and office:* 3722 Summershore Lane, Westlake Village, Calif. 91361.

CAREER/WRITINGS: Houston Chronicle, Houston, Tex., reporter, 1963-65; writer for *Time* and *Life* magazines in Houston, 1965-73; TRW, Inc., Redondo Beach, Calif., public relations employee, 1973-75; Midwest Research Institute, Kansas City, Mo., communications manager, 1976-78; *Popular Science,* Los Angeles, Calif., West Coast editor, 1978—. Communications consultant to Midwest Research Institute. Notable assignments include coverage of Gemini and Apollo programs for *Time* and *Life*. *Military service:* U.S. Army, 1960-63; became sergeant. *Member:* Aviation/Space Writers Association, National Association of Science Writers. *Awards, honors:* Regional and national writing awards from Aviation/Space Writers Association, 1976, 1977, 1978; science writing citation from New York Deadline Club, 1976.

Contributor of numerous articles to *Ambassador, Passages, Flightime, True, Family Weekly, Paris Match,* and other magazines.

WORK IN PROGRESS: "Ongoing coverage of all major aerospace missions, aviation, and related topics" for periodicals, including *Popular Science*.

SIDELIGHTS: "I am a firm believer in the need for, and benefits of, advanced technology," Schefter told *CA*. When asked what forces have motivated him in his career, he responded: "During a three-year period, from 1973-76, I reduced writing to one article per year and contemplated quitting entirely. One conversation with a Kansas resident rekindled my interest and I have been writing at a heavy pace since then. It helps to have someone ask questions like 'Why?'"

* * *

SCHEINFELD, Amram 1897-1979

OBITUARY NOTICE—See index for *CA* sketch: Born June 1, 1897, in Louisville, Ky.; died September 11, 1979, in New York, N.Y. Journalist, cartoonist, illustrator, novelist, and author of books on genetics. While working as a newspaperman and cartoonist in the 1920's and 1930's, Scheinfeld met such a wide variety of people that he began to wonder what made some people rise to the top and others remain at the bottom. His curiosity led him to study genetics and eventually to write on that topic. His books include *You and Heredity, The Human Heredity Handbook,* and *Why You Are You.* Shortly before he died he had completed another book, *The Human Sexes.* Obituaries and other sources: *The Authors and Writer's Who's Who,* 6th edition, Burke's Peerage, 1971; *Who's Who in World Jewry,* Pitman, 1972; *New York Times,* September 13, 1979; *AB Bookman's Weekly,* October 22, 1979.

* * *

SCHENCK, Anita A(llen) 1909-
(Anita Allen)

PERSONAL: Born August 24, 1909, in Knoxville, Tenn.; daughter of Fred Wood (in business) and Nellie (Ketchen) Allen; married Herbert H. Schenck, June 25, 1932 (divorced, 1947); children: William Allen, James Herbert. *Education:* Maryville College, Maryville, Tenn., B.A., 1929. *Politics:* Republican. *Religion:* Protestant. *Home:* 3415 Front St., San Diego, Calif. 92103. *Agent:* Larry Sternig Literary Agency, 742 Robertson Ave., Milwaukee, Wis. 53213.

CAREER: Piano teacher in Knoxville, Tenn., 1927-30; secretary for insurance companies in Knoxville, 1930-34, and St. Petersburg, Fla., 1946-49; secretary to Veterans Administration, 1949, and Naval Hospital, Bethesda, Md., 1950-51, administrative assistant at Navy Electronics Laboratory, San Diego, Calif., 1952-69; writer, 1969—. *Member:* National League of American Pen Women (local president, 1970-72). *Awards, honors:* Faith Baldwin Memorial Award from National League of American Pen Women, 1978, for *The Spell of Choti.*

WRITINGS—All novels; under name Anita Allen: *Thunder Rock,* Berkley Publishing, 1974; *The Spell of Choti,* Berkley Publishing, 1976; *The False Face of Death,* Doubleday, 1979. Contributor of articles and stories to local and national magazines.

WORK IN PROGRESS: The Golden Cowrie, a romantic suspense novel set in Micronesia, and using some Micronesian mystic beliefs.

SIDELIGHTS: Schenck told *CA:* "In writing *The Spell of Choti* and *The Golden Cowrie,* I used information collected during a visit to the Truk District, Micronesia, where my younger son and his family lived for four years. Much valuable data on the local beliefs and customs were supplied to me by my son and his wife, and I read everything I could get on all of Micronesia, then let my imagination do the rest.

"Fiction writing can convey emotions and point up truths much better than non-fiction. The reader identifies with a particular character, sees how the character solves problems that may be similar to the reader's, pointing the way. In suspense and mystery writing, the main purpose is a 'good read,' but often the characters involved in the story or novel give insights into emotions of people everywhere. Conversely, they can also help the reader to get away from problems for a while, so that when the reader must come back to the 'real' world, he finds a freshness of mind and spirit that helps in the solutions to his own problems. But I write for fun. There are enough books on the market telling everyone what to do, how to do it, and how to live in general. I want the reader to enjoy my novels and finish them with a sense of satisfaction.

"My advice to aspiring writers is to join writing classes, learn to accept criticism (both negative and positive), and write every day. Study the magazines for writers and any books on the subject, but get criticism—that's the most important tool they can have. Many other writers helped me by listening to my work and telling me what was good and what was bad about it. I'm afraid I'm not good at plotting beforehand so I usually have an idea, know where the story should start and end and then begin writing. The characters will soon take over and provide the action and the road to the end. It works for me although many writers make a complete outline of each chapter and each incident and scene."

* * *

SCHEPER, Nancy
See SCHEPER-HUGHES, Nancy

* * *

SCHEPER-HUGHES, Nancy 1944-
(Nancy Scheper)

PERSONAL: Born September 25, 1944, in New York, N.Y.; daughter of George Louis and Anne (Znojemsky) Scheper; married David Michael Hughes, December 21, 1971; children: Jennifer, Sarah, Nathanael. *Education:* University of California, Berkeley, B.A., 1970, Ph.D., 1976. *Politics:* Socialist. *Religion:* "Liberation Theology." *Office:* Anthropology Department, University of North Carolina, Chapel Hill, N.C. 27514.

CAREER: Co-director of Queens College Mexico Volunteers, Guerrero, Mexico, 1963; U.S. Peace Corps, Washington, D.C., volunteer in Pernambuco, Brazil, 1964-66, employed in Office of Recruitment, 1966-67; research assistant for anthropologist Hortense B. Powdermaker in Berkeley, Calif., 1969-70; University of California, Berkeley, teaching assistant and reader in social anthropology, 1971-76, consultant and instructor in Health Arts and Sciences program, 1976; Southern Methodist University, Dallas, Tex., assistant professor of anthropology, 1976-79, member of commission on the status of women, 1977, member of executive board of Women's Studies Council, 1977-79, associate program director of anthropology internship program, 1978-79, member of academic senate, 1979; University of North Carolina at Chapel Hill, assistant professor of anthropology, 1980—. Medical anthropology field school director at Fort Burgwin Research Center, Taos, New Mexico, summer, 1979.

MEMBER: American Anthropological Association (fellow), Society for Medical Anthropology, Society for Psychological Anthropology. *Awards, honors:* Wenner-Gren grant, 1970; National Institute of Health predoctoral training grant, 1971-76; Texas Department of Human Resources Title XX Formula grant and Department of Health Education and Welfare Office of Human Development Services program development grant, both 1978-79; National Institute of Mental Health postdoctoral grant, 1979-80, for study of family dynamics and mental health problems of Irish-Americans in South Boston, Mass.

WRITINGS: (Contributor under name Nancy Scheper) *Divided We Stand,* Canfield Press, 1970; *Saints, Scholars and Schizophrenics: Mental Illness in Rural Ireland,* University of California Press, 1979; (contributor) Margarita Kay, editor, *The Anthropology of Birth,* F. A. Davis, 1980. Contributor to periodicals and scholarly journals including *Ramparts, Popular Psychology, Marxist Perspectives, Medical Anthropology,* and *Journal of Comparative Family Studies.* Contributor under name Nancy Scheper to *Popular Psychology.*

WORK IN PROGRESS: Research on family dynamics and mental health among working-class Irish-Americans of South Boston, Mass.

SIDELIGHTS: To research her book, *Saints, Scholars, and Schizophrenics,* Nancy Scheper-Hughes and her family lived for more than a year in a tiny village in western Ireland. She knew of the pressures felt by the Irish people, on one hand pushed by a country trying to modernize, on the other hand held by centuries-old traditions that tie many Irish to living the same lonely and impoverished lives as did their forefathers. She was also well aware of the high rates of alcoholism and mental illness among Irish males, in addition to their reputation for having low self-esteem. In her book, Scheper-Hughes attempted to find explanations for some of these problems while describing the "cultural double binds" of the society and the ways its people deal with them.

Among her conclusions, said *Human Behavior,* is that the Irish male character has been influenced by "centuries of male dominance and matriarchal overprotection." Scheper-Hughes also cited religious doctrines and sexual asceticism as contributing factors in many cases of mental illness, noted Sidney Callahan. David Nowlan, critic for *The Irish Times,* found the book "a pleasing mixture of anecdote, sociological and psychological research and often elegant writing . . . [that] makes compelling, if vastly depressing, reading."

Scheper-Hughes outlined her philosophy of education for *CA:* "Insofar as I have anything which I can call a philosophy of education, it was formed during my years as a community organizer in Brazil where I tried to apply what I understood to be Paulo Freire's method of *conscientizacao,* which was passed on by word of mouth and through bits and pieces of his writings. As a community paramedic my thrust was largely educational—initially teaching the landless squatter peasants about the health hazards surrounding them: the microbes in the drinking water, the schistosomiasis in the local river, the worm eggs nesting in the warm, moist ground. My students in turn educated me: what use knowing about schistosomiasis in the river, when the river provides work for the many? What use knowing about round worm, hook worm, and other parasites when there was no money to buy shoes, water filters, or even the extra fuel needed to boil drinking water?

"The Nordestinos taught me about the themes and realities of their universe, and I tried to awaken them to the 'sociological imagination' so they might see themselves within social context and historical moment, and come to see their personal worries and troubles as social and historical issues. We raised each others consciousness in a continuing dialogue, first about the meaning of health and wholeness, later about the meaning of social justice, right(s), and might. The informal sessions in open air were transformed into literacy classes and peasant union meetings within the social center.

Workers brought the 'books' they had always wanted to read: the psalms, the bylaws of the banned peasant leagues, birth, marriage, death certificates, and letters yellowed with age, the ink barely legible. When we ran out of those we wrote our own 'books'—the constitution of the peasant union, the histories of local saints, outlaws and heroes. Those who graduated from the class went with me to the town jail where we used the method to teach the social and political outcasts as well as the half-witted and disoriented. Again we taught and learned with the words and the themes our students gave us: the violent as well as the gentle, the obscene as well as the naive. With words like knife, land, peasant, whore, home, and child we built phrases, sentences, paragraphs, literacy, and finally, a shared universe of meanings.

"Education is never a monologue. It is a continuing, critical dialogal encounter between consciousness and unconsciousness, reason and unreason, silence and words, between I and thou, self and others. Teacher and taught learn together. There is no neutral, passive education program, whether in adult literacy, in child care and pre-school, in grade and high school, or in college or graduate school. Education is either an instrument of conformity and adjustment or an instrument of criticism and change. If it is the latter, it may at times provoke tension and conflict; but it need not be a hostile or polemical argument. The educational dialogue can exist within an environment of respect and, yes, even love. As such it has the possibility of becoming what Freire would call 'the practice of freedom.'

"In Brazil I would ask my peasant 'students' to hang up their hats, knives, guns, and other tools of their trade at the front door of the social center so as to create a more open and relaxed environment for reflection and reaction. In Texas I would ask my socially prominent students to hang up their jogging shoes and pledge hats, their sun glasses and cultural blinders at the classroom door, so that the dialogue could begin."

BIOGRAPHICAL/CRITICAL SOURCES: Human Behavior, October, 1978; *Commonweal,* May 25, 1979; *Boston Globe,* May 31, 1979; *Irish Times,* August 4, 1979.

* * *

SCHIFF, Harold (Irvin) 1923-

PERSONAL: Born June 24, 1923, in Kitchener, Ontario, Canada; son of Jack and Lena (Bierstock) Schiff; married Daphne Line (a professor), December 30, 1948; children: Jack Michael, Sherry Line. *Education:* University of Toronto, B.A. (with honors), 1945, M.A., 1946, Ph.D., 1948. *Agent:* Paul R. Reynolds, Inc., 12 East 41st St., New York, N.Y. 10017. *Office:* Department of Chemistry, York University, Downsview, Ontario, Canada M3J 1P3.

CAREER: National Research Council, Ottawa, Ontario, fellow, 1948-50; McGill University, Montreal, Quebec, 1950-65, began as assistant professor, then associate professor, became professor of chemistry, director of Upper Atmosphere Chemistry Group, 1958-65; York University, Downsview, Ontario, professor of chemistry, 1965-66, 1968—, chairman of chemistry department, 1965-66, dean of faculty of science, 1965-66, 1968-72. Visiting Erskine Professor at University of Canterbury, 1974. Member of associate committee of National Research Council on Space Research; member of executive committee of International Conference on the Physics of Electronic and Atomic Collisions. *Member:* International Association of Geomagnetism and Aeronomy, American Meteorological Society. *Awards, honors:* Nuffield fellow at Cambridge University, 1959-60.

WRITINGS: The Ozone War, Doubleday, 1978.

* * *

SCHLEIER, Curt 1944-

PERSONAL: Born August 23, 1944, in Basel, Switzerland; came to the United States in 1947, naturalized citizen, 1952; son of Rudolph (a cutter) and Selma (Degen) Schleier; married Barbara Ann Weiss (a teacher), March 25, 1967; children: Michael Scott, Jennifer Loren. *Education:* Hunter College (now Herbert H. Lehman College of the City University of New York), B.A., 1965. *Politics:* "Middle of the road." *Religion:* Jewish. *Residence:* River Vale, N.J. *Office: Official Airline Guides,* 888 Seventh Ave., New York, N.Y. 10019.

CAREER: Herald Statesman, Yonkers, N.Y., reporter, 1964-66; *American Society of Travel Agents Travel News,* New York City, associate editor, 1966-68; *Official Airline Guides,* New York City, assistant publisher of travel magazines, 1967-72; *Drug Topics,* Oradell, N.J., senior editor, 1973-75; free-lance writer, 1975-77; *Official Airline Guides,* assistant publisher, 1977—. Member of River Vale Ambulance Corps.

WRITINGS: You'd Better Not Tell! (fiction), Westminster, 1979; *The Team Behind Your Airline Flight* (nonfiction), Westminster, 1980. Contributor to magazines.

WORK IN PROGRESS: Harold II (tentative title), a sequel to *You'd Better Not Tell!; The City Team* (tentative title).

SIDELIGHTS: Schleier told *CA:* "My immediate interest in terms of children's books is writing works that average kids can relate to. By average I mean normal children who are not on drugs, and who like baseball, Mom, and apple pie. Maybe that's corny, but I suspect that there are an awful lot of kids out there who still fantasize about the same things I did years ago and who like a good mystery/suspense/adventure yarn. They're the ones I write for. If I'm right and lucky, they'll find out about it."

* * *

SCHLESINGER, Marian Cannon 1912-

PERSONAL: Born September 13, 1912, in Franklin, N.H.; daughter of Walter B. (a physiologist) and Cornelia (a writer; maiden name, James) Cannon; married Arthur M. Schlesinger, Jr. (a writer; divorced November, 1970); children: Stephen Cannon, Katharine Bancroft Kinderman, Christina, Andrew Bancroft. *Education:* Radcliffe College, A.B., 1934. *Politics:* Democrat. *Religion:* Unitarian Universalist. *Home:* 109 Irving St., Cambridge, Mass. 02138.

CAREER: Free-lance artist, illustrator, and portrait painter, 1938—; writer, 1939—. Exhibitions held in Washington, D.C., Boston and Cambridge, Mass., and Paris, France; portraits in private collections in Washington, D.C., Chicago, Ill., New York, N.Y., Boston and Cambridge, London, England, and Geneva, Switzerland. *Member:* Nucleus, Cosmopolitan Club, Women's Travel Club.

WRITINGS: San Bao, Dutton, 1939; *Children of the Fiery Mountain,* Dutton, 1940; (with Wilma Cannon Fairbank) *Peter Is Sweeter,* Lothrop, 1942; *Twins at Our House,* Lothrop, 1945; *Snatched From Oblivion: A Cambridge Memoir,* Little, Brown, 1979. Contributor of articles and book reviews to publications, including *Washington Post, Boston Globe,* and *McCall's.*

* * *

SCHNEIDER, Leonard Alfred 1925-1966 (Lenny Bruce)

PERSONAL: Born October 13, 1925; died August 3, 1966, in Los Angeles, Calif.; son of Mickey (a podiatrist) and Sadie (an actress and dancer under pseudonym Sally Marr; maiden name, Kitchenberg) Schneider; married Harriet Lloyd (an actress and dancer under pseudonym Honey Harlow), June 15, 1951 (divorced); children: Kathleen. *Education:* Attended public schools in New York, N.Y. *Religion:* Jewish. *Residence:* Los Angeles, Calif.

CAREER: Comedian, actor, and writer. Performed in numerous nightclubs throughout the United States and England; appeared on television programs, including "Rocket to Stardom," "The Steve Allen Show," and "The Tonight Show"; actor in motion pictures, including "Dream Follies," "Dance Hall Racket," and "Leather Jacket."

WRITINGS—Under pseudonym Lenny Bruce: *How to Talk Dirty and Influence People: An Autobiography,* Playboy Press, 1965; *The Essential Lenny Bruce,* edited by John Cohen, Ballantine, 1967. Also author of *Stamp Help Out!,* 1964. Author of screenplays, including "Rocket Boy," "Dream Follies," "Dance Hall Racket," and "Leather Jacket." Author of television special, "The World of Lenny Bruce," and television pilot episode, "Fleetfoot." Also author of recordings, including "The Sick Humor of Lenny Bruce."

SIDELIGHTS: Bruce became popular during the late 1950's for his highly original brand of humor. Disdaining the standard joke-telling format, Bruce opted instead for a more intimate and direct attack: he launched tirades against the hypocrisy of morality, obscenity, and justice, punctuating his sketches with Yiddish phrases and street idiom. Of course, in attempting to question the values of accepted attitudes towards sex, politics, and religion, Bruce was destined to offend a great deal of society (which he did). Calling Bruce "a sad, sick, self-destructive genius of a dirty time," Jack Kroll wrote, "Like a child, Bruce found this dirt where it lay and held it up for inspection. Like a great comic . . . , he shaped the dirt into fantastic filth-castles, which at their best were triumphs of a cauterizing imagination and at their worst became the spattering tantrums of a spoiled brat."

He began as an emcee of strip shows, insulting the various dancers who were enjoying attention he felt rightly belonged to him. After numerous failed enterprises, including a joke-and-dance routine with his wife, stripper Honey Harlow, Bruce began making a name for himself as a "different" comedian. By the late 1950's he was in demand at college campuses throughout the country; his humor was considered so risque and avant-garde that television shows largely refused to feature him. On one show that took a chance with him, Bruce rushed up to a camera and shouted that Bobby Franks, the schoolboy murdered by Loeb and Leopold, was "a snotty brat."

Although he made few television appearances, Bruce had gained sufficient popularity by 1963 to do concert spots at such prestigious auditoriums as Carnegie Hall. In fact, one of Bruce's greatest nights as a performer occurred there in 1963 when a capacity crowd turned out despite a violent snowstorm.

With his unique assaults on sexual, religious, and moral attitudes, Bruce appealed primarily to college students, musicians, and other "hipsters." He would lecture audiences on the misfortune of being Jewish: "The Christian god, you're lucky in that way, because you've got Mary, a mother, a father, a beginning, five-and-ten little mangers—identity. Your god, the Christian god, is all over. He's on rocks, he saves you, he's dying on bank buildings—he's been in three films. He's on crucifixes all over. It's a story you can follow. The Jewish god—where's the Jewish god? He's on a little box nailed to the door jamb. In a *mezuzah.* There he is, in there. He's standing on a slant, god."

A favorite subject with Bruce was sexual morality. He claimed that children were "better off watching a stag movie than 'King of Kings.' Mine, anyway. Because I just don't want my kid to kill Christ when he comes back. And that's what's in 'King of Kings'—but tell me about a stag movie where someone got killed in the end, or slapped in the mouth, or heard any Communist propaganda. So the sense of values would be, the morals: 'Well, for kids to watch killing—Yes; but *schtupping*—No! Cause if they watch *schtup* pictures, they may do it some day.'"

Bruce experimented with various drugs up until his death. Because of his notoriety, he was considered a worthy "catch" by narcotics agents wherever he went. After several arrests, Bruce obtained some rare insight into the ways of law enforcement, especially narcotics control. In the following exchange between a junkie and an agent, Bruce parodies the dedicated agent:

AGENT: "You mean to tell me that you guys are gonna screw up our rehabilitation program? If *you're* not using any dope, you certainly *know* some people that need people."

JUNKIE: "We don't know anybody. We don't know *anybody. Please. I can't use any more dope.* I don't *like* it anymore."

AGENT: "Well, you really are selfish. You don't care about anybody but yourself. Do you know we have a center to rehabilitate people with fifteen hundred empty beds?"

JUNKIE: "I know, I'm shitty that way. I'll try."

Bruce was also arrested on numerous occasions for using obscenity in his act. "The first time I got arrested for obscenity was in San Francisco," Bruce recalled. "I used a ten-letter word onstage. Just a word in passing. . . . They said it was a favorite homosexual practice. Now that I found strange. I don't relate the word to a homosexual practice." Despite his flippant attitude ("I got arrested so many times this year—my fly is open, I'm on dope, *everything*"), the frequency of the arrests began to take a toll on Bruce's stamina. Typically, he began incorporating the subject into his act. He revealed to his audience: "The reason I got busted—arrested—is I picked on the wrong god. If I had picked on the god whose replica is in the whoopee cushion store—the Tiki god, the Hawaiian god, those idiots, their dumb god—I would've been cool. If I would've picked on the god whose belly is slashed—he's a bank. Chinese, those idiots, their yellow god. But I picked on the Western god—the cute god, the In-god, the Kennedy god—and that's where I screwed up."

He became obsessed with his trial proceedings and took to reading transcripts to the audiences. Frequently hiring and firing attorneys, and then acting as his own counsel, Bruce became, according to Kroll, a "frightening, law-obsessed paranoid." Misfortune soon set in on Bruce. An accidental fall from a window landed him in the hospital, his act became more and more burdened with legal jargon that bored audiences, and the court stipulations made it increasingly difficult for Bruce to get bookings. In response, he retreated to his constantly-revised home in California where he was attended by a group of close friends. He lived in semi-seclusion until his accidental drug overdose in 1966.

Perhaps Bruce foresaw his endless persecution when he commented on the convicted McCarthy-era screenwriters who were unable to get jobs when released from prison. Ridiculing the Christian ethic, he told his audience: "Now if you want to keep stringing them out and not forgive them, you're *pagans.* But if you *are* pagans, I don't care . . . but just be *consistent.* Say, 'We're *not* Christians, we're gonna persecute an ex-con, we're gonna lean on the flag and the Bible, we're gonna take those writers tomorrow and put them up against the wall and shoot them—'

"But Ronald Reagan has to pull the trigger. No one else, my friend.

"You believe in a law, solid. But once the cat pays his dues, that's enough. Let them alone. . . ."

BIOGRAPHICAL/CRITICAL SOURCES: Lenny Bruce, *How to Talk Dirty and Influence People: An Autobiography,*

Playboy Press, 1965; Bruce, *The Essential Lenny Bruce,* edited by John Cohen, Ballantine, 1967; Albert Goldman and Lawrence Schiller, *Ladies and Gentlemen Lenny Bruce!!,* Random House, 1974; *Newsweek,* June 24, 1974.*

—*Sketch by Les Stone*

* * *

SCHOENSTEIN, Paul 1902-1974

OBITUARY NOTICE: Born June 10, 1902, in New York, N.Y.; died April 14, 1974, in New York, N.Y. Pulitzer Prize-winning journalist who served as the last managing editor of the *New York Journal-American.* In 1944, when he was the city editor of the *Journal-American,* Schoenstein orchestrated a desperate search for then-rare penicillin, the only drug that could save the life of two-year-old Patricia Malone. Having been told that without the antibiotic the girl would die in seven hours, Schoenstein and a team of reporters successfully located a supply of the drug in New Brunswick, New Jersey, and arranged to have it flown to the hospital in time to save the child's life. They were awarded the Pulitzer Prize for their efforts. Schoenstein was also instrumental in the break-up of the German-American Bund and the capture of the Mad Bomber, who had terrorized New York City for sixteen years. Before joining the *Journal-American* in 1926, he had worked for the *Bronx Home News,* the *San Francisco Call-Bulletin,* and the *New York Herald Tribune.* After the *Journal-American* closed in 1966, he continued as the managing editor of its successor, the short-lived *New York World Journal Tribune,* and served as a consultant to the Hearst Corporation. Obituaries and other sources: *New York Times,* April 15, 1974; *Who's Who in America,* 38th edition, Marquis, 1974.

* * *

SCHOLL, Lisette 1945-

PERSONAL: Born September 5, 1945, in Los Angeles, Calif.; daughter of Jack Trevor (a songwriter) and Clio (Sangree) Scholl. *Education:* Whittier College, B.A., 1967, M.Ed., 1969. *Residence:* Morro Bay, Calif. *Agent:* Harvey Klinger, 250 West 57th St., New York, N.Y. 10019.

CAREER: High school English teacher in El Monte, Calif., 1968-72; teacher of adult education courses in writing, yoga, aerobics, and vision in Morro Bay, Calif.; free-lance writer. Member of San Luis Obispo Health Commission and head of its sub-commission on women's health issues.

WRITINGS: (With John Selby) *Visionetics: The Holistic Way to Better Eyesight,* Doubleday, 1978.

WORK IN PROGRESS: A novel; research on vision and on problems associated with menstruation.

SIDELIGHTS: Lisette Scholl writes: "My prime interests are the bond between physical and mental health (and how to achieve both) and living sanely within the environment. I am in the process of moving to the countryside, to see if a suburban woman, four house cats, and a spoiled German shepherd can adjust to 'real life.'

"I became interested in vision improvement due to my own frustration at my dependence on glasses. I discovered that what the eye doctors said was not so, and that vision could indeed be rehabilitated. It is my hope that my book will help people realize they can be responsible for their own visual health. In this way, we can avoid the situation most eye doctors predict by the turn of the century—that everyone will need glasses by the early grammar school years."

SCHOR, Naomi 1943-

PERSONAL: Born October 10, 1943, in New York, N.Y.; daughter of Ilya (an artist) and Resia (an artist; maiden name, Ajsztajn) Schor. *Education:* Barnard College, B.A., 1963; Yale University, Ph.D., 1969. *Home:* 26 President Ave., Providence, R.I. 02906. *Office:* Box E, Brown University, Providence, R.I. 12912.

CAREER: Columbia University, New York, N.Y., assistant professor of French, 1969-78; Brown University, Providence, R.I., associate professor of French, 1978—. *Member:* Modern Language Association of America, American Association of Teachers of French, Northeast Modern Language Association, Phi Beta Kappa . *Awards, honors:* Woodrow Wilson fellow, 1963-64; Fulbright fellow, 1965-67; American Council of Learned Societies fellow, 1976-77.

WRITINGS: Zola's Crowds, Johns Hopkins Press, 1978. Contributor to French studies and literature journals.

WORK IN PROGRESS: The Detail; Psychoanalysis and Feminism.

* * *

SCHRUTH, Peter Elliott 1917-1979

OBITUARY NOTICE: Born March 10, 1917, in Fargo, N.D.; died September 22, 1979, in Menlo Park, Calif. Publisher and broadcasting and advertising executive. Schruth was publisher of *Holiday.* He was also advertising director of the *Saturday Evening Post* and a vice-chairman of the Westinghouse Broadcasting Co. Obituaries and other sources: *Who's Who in Advertising,* 2nd edition, Redfield, 1972; *Who's Who in America,* 40th edition, Marquis, 1978; *New York Times,* September 23, 1979.

* * *

SCHULBERG, Stuart 1922-1979

OBITUARY NOTICE: Born November 17, 1922, in Los Angeles, Calif.; died June 28, 1979, in New York, N.Y. Producer, journalist, and writer. Schulberg produced the "Today" show and "David Brinkley's Journal" for the National Broadcasting Co. (NBC-TV). The executive producer of news documentaries at NBC-TV, he won four Emmy awards for his work. He was also a reporter for the *Washington Daily News.* Obituaries and other sources: *New York Times,* June 29, 1979; *Washington Post,* June 30, 1979.

* * *

SCHULMAN, J(oseph) Neil 1953-

PERSONAL: Born April 16, 1953, in Forest Hills, N.Y.; son of Julius (a violinist) and Betty (an artist; maiden name, Lindenbaum) Schulman. *Education:* Attended Borough of Manhattan Community College of City University of New York, 1971-72. *Politics:* "Revolutionary Propertarian Anarchist." *Address:* P.O. Box 94, Long Beach, Calif. 90801. *Agent:* Paul R. Reynolds, Inc., 12 East 41st St., New York, N.Y. 10017.

CAREER: New Libertarian Notes, New York City, executive editor, 1972-75; Libertarian Circle, New York City, director, 1974, director of Countercon Conferences, 1974 and 1975; *New Libertarian Weekly,* Long Beach, Calif., contributing editor, 1975-77; First Libertarian Church, Los Angeles, Calif., minister, 1976—. Writer, 1970—. Chairman of Committee to Eliminate the New Draft, Long Beach, 1977—. *Member:* Los Angeles Science Fantasy Society, C. S. Lewis Society.

WRITINGS: *Alongside Night* (novel), Crown, 1979. Contributor of articles and fiction to publications, including *Reason, New Banner, Anaheim Bulletin, Libertarian Forum, Libertarian Review,* and *New Libertarian Notes.*

Also author of unproduced screenplay, "Alongside Night" (adapted from own novel), 1977.

WORK IN PROGRESS: *The Carnal Commandment,* novel and screenplay to be completed in 1981; *Hello, Joe—Whadd'ya Know?,* novel and screenplay to be completed in 1982; "Poison Ivory," screenplay and teleplay to be completed in 1982.

SIDELIGHTS: Early in 1971, Schulman made a discovery that was to alter his life: libertarianism. In reading an article on the concept in a magazine, he learned this was what his lifetime belief system was called. He allied himself with the libertarian movement, subsequently forming two groups in New York and directing the Countercon Conferences on counter-economics in both 1974 and 1975. When asked the basic premise and immediate and future goals of libertarianism, Schulman replied: "In its distilled form, libertarianism is the belief in a person's right to self-determination and self-rule, and to be free in one's person and property from coercion by any other individual or group—especially the most vicious aggressor against human rights and freedom, the State. All libertarian goals ultimately boil down to demonstrating the morality and practicality of a society based on peaceful trade, voluntary association, and contractual relationships. Libertarians offer a number of strategies for achieving this kind of society, including the counter-economic approach dramatized in my first novel, *Alongside Night.*"

According to Schuman, *Alongside Night* combines several genres—"political thriller, coming-of-age novel, utopian and dystopian novel, and science fiction." He explained his approach to fiction in *Library Journal:* "I see it as the birthright of every storyteller to try saving the world. Each of us is in a messianic competition. While others can write either abstractedly or concretely about how things work—and why they often do not—only the fiction writer has the capability of using words to make abstract ideas concretely real, to give them mass and soul."

Alongside Night received some encouraging prepublication endorsements, including those from economist Milton Friedman, psychiatrist Thomas S. Szasz, and author Anthony Burgess.

BIOGRAPHICAL/CRITICAL SOURCES: *Library Journal,* June 15, 1979; *Kirkus Reviews,* August 1, 1979.

* * *

SCHULZ, James Henry 1936-

PERSONAL: Born July 20, 1936, in Abington, Pa.; son of Henry and Margaret (Stricker) Schulz; married December 31, 1958; children: three. *Education:* Miami University, Oxford, Ohio, B.A., 1958; Yale University, Ph.D., 1966. *Office:* Florence Heller Graduate School, Brandeis University, Waltham, Mass. 02154.

CAREER: University of New Hampshire, Durham, assistant professor, 1965-68, associate professor of economics, 1969-70; Brandeis University, Waltham, Mass., associate professor, 1971-75, professor of economics, 1976—. *Military service:* U.S. Navy, 1958-61; became lieutenant junior grade. *Member:* American Economic Association, Gerontological Society (fellow). *Awards, honors:* Woodrow Wilson fellow, 1961-62.

WRITINGS: *Providing Adequate Retirement Income: Pension Reform in the United States and Abroad,* University Press of New England, 1974; *The Economics of Aging,* Wadsworth, 1976, 2nd edition, 1979. Contributor to economic, gerontology, and pension journals.

WORK IN PROGRESS: Research on the economic impact of private pensions.

SIDELIGHTS: Schulz commented: "*The Economics of Aging* is the only book currently published that systematically surveys the diverse literature in this important area of aging research. The dramatic growth of information in this area presented a real challenge: to write a non-technical book for non-economists that was comprehensive but not encyclopedic."

* * *

SCHWARTZ, Audrey James 1928-

PERSONAL: Born April 6, 1928, in Camden, N.J.; daughter of Hyman (an engineer) and Sylvia (in public relations for radio and television; maiden name, Komito) James; married Murray L. Schwartz (a professor of law), February 12, 1950; children: Deborah, Jonathan, Daniel. *Education:* University of Pennsylvania, B.A., 1950, M.A., 1957; University of California, Los Angeles, Ed.D., 1968. *Office:* Department of Education, University of Southern California, Los Angeles, Calif. 90007.

CAREER: University of California, Los Angeles, lecturer in sociology of education, 1967-69; California State University, Northridge, assistant professor of sociology of education, 1969-70; University of Southern California, Los Angeles, assistant professor, 1970-74, associate professor, 1974-78, professor of sociology of education, 1978—. Consultant to American Civil Liberties Union. *Member:* American Sociological Association, American Educational Research Association, American Association of University Professors, Sociology of Education Association (president, 1973—).

WRITINGS: (With C. Wayne Gordon, David Nasitir, and Robert Wenkert) *Educational Achievement and Aspirations of Mexican-American Youth in a Metropolitan Context,* Center for Study and Evaluation, University of California, Los Angeles, 1968; *Comparative Values and Achievement of Mexican-American and Anglo Pupils,* Center for Study and Evaluation, University of California, Los Angeles, 1969; *Traditional Values and Contemporary Achievement of Japanese-American Pupils,* Center for Study and Evaluation, University of California, Los Angeles, 1970; (with K. Kaist and husband, Murray L. Schwartz) *The Evolution of Law in the Barrios of Caracas,* Latin American Center, University of California, Los Angeles, 1973; *The Schools and Socialization,* Harper, 1975. Contributor to sociology and education journals.

WORK IN PROGRESS: Analysis of data from panel of law students attempting to answer the question "What does law school do to law students?" with first article for publication in *Journal of Legal Education;* chapter on sociology of education for an introductory sociology text edited by D. Montero, for Houghton; survey research of American students of Chinese origin; observational study of a multi-racial school.

* * *

SCHWARZ-BART, Andre 1928-

PERSONAL: Born in 1928, in Metz, Lorraine, France; married wife, Simone (a writer), 1961. *Education:* Attended Sorbonne, University of Paris. *Residence:* Guadeloupe and Lausanne, France.

CAREER: Prisoner in German concentration camp during World War II; after the war, worked as a mechanic, salesman, miner, librarian, and foundry laborer; writer, 1959—. *Military service:* Served with French Resistance during World War II. *Awards, honors:* Prix Goncourt, 1959, for *Le Dernier des justes;* Jerusalem prize, 1967, for *Un Plat de porc aux bananes vertes.*

WRITINGS—All novels: *Le Dernier des justes,* Editions du Seuil, 1959, translation by Stephen Becker published as *The Last of the Just,* Bantam, 1961; (with wife, Simone Schwarz-Bart) *Un Plat de porc aux bananes vertes* (title means "A Plate of Pork With Green Bananas"), Editions du Seuil, 1967; (with S. Schwarz-Bart) *La Mulatresse Solitude,* Editions du Seuil, 1972, translation by Ralph Manheim published as *A Woman Named Solitude,* Atheneum, 1973.

SIDELIGHTS: In 1959, Schwarz-Bart quit his factory job to write fiction. He began with *The Last of the Just,* a novel of Jewish suffering and persecution that has been called "the most ambitious French-Jewish fictional effort of all times." It is also a book, reviewers noted, of special personal relevance to the author: his own parents, Polish Jews who had immigrated to France, died in a Nazi concentration camp. Beginning with the York massacre of 1185, the novel chronicles thirty-six subsequent generations of the Levy family, culminating in the Auschwitz death of Ernie Levy. Lothar Kahn observed that the author "regards suffering as the distinctive feature of Jewish destiny and the actions of the non-Jewish world as responsible for this suffering." Several critics remarked, however, that Schwarz-Bart's mood is never one of acrimony. Rather, it remains one of gentle grief measured by a language of restrained description. In John Mander's judgment, the book is "very nearly adequate—there is no higher praise—to its dreadful theme."

Seven years later in 1967, Schwarz-Bart collaborated with his wife Simone on *Un Plat de porc aux bananes vertes* ("A Plate of Pork With Green Bananas"). It is the first of seven volumes, reported Gloria Emerson, that will demonstrate what the authors feel "is the secret and desperate combat of most Negro women in Europe and the Americas today and will trace the lives of their characters' female ancestors in precolonial and colonial Africa." In this opening work, the story focuses on a crippled, half-blind woman from Martinique who is living out her last days. Confined to a French asylum for the aged, she evokes memories of her childhood and grandmother, and of the day she carried a plate of pork with green bananas to her mother's jailed lover. Marc Slonim asserted that *Un Plat de porc aux bananes vertes* is a novel of strong contrasts because the old woman with her exotic, colorful recollections of Martinique is forced to confront the "terrifying reality" of the institution. "The asylum resembles a concentration camp; it is the same world of misery, torture and death that reduces everybody to dust and nothingness," he stated. And, he concluded, it is Schwarz-Bart's "poetic, sophisticated diction, the intensity and unity of his language, the dismal incidents of his plot, that make his novel such an original, moving and at times stunning work of literature."

Schwarz-Bart next wrote *A Woman Named Solitude.* It is the tale of a mulatto slave from Guadeloupe who, transformed by the horrors of servitude, mounts an avenging campaign against the island's masters. Robert Alter wrote: "*A Woman Named Solitude* manages to be simultaneously one of the most exquisitely wrought lyric novels of recent years and an utterly convincing representation of the reality of historical suffering." The paradox, however, of distilling lyric beauty from bestiality received a mixed critical response. The horrors of slavery, contended one reviewer, "are recorded with so much finesse and tact that they seem more poetic and beautiful than disgusting." On the other hand, Alan Friedman perceived a "condition of passionate detachment that can, and does, make literature out of agony."

Furthermore, some critics wondered whether or not an imagination conditioned by Western culture can adequately express an essentially African experience. The novel's European and literary medium, Thomas R. Edwards suggested, reveals a "helplessness to penetrate and merge with an alien consciousness." Alter, however, marveled at "Schwarz-Bart's unfaltering ability to project himself into another race, another sex, another age." Evaluating *A Woman Named Solitude* and Schwarz-Bart's preceding work, Edward Weeks concluded: "His novels are like miniatures painted on ivory, and, perhaps because the author himself was a member of the Maquis who had been deported to an extermination camp and escaped, his stories are poignant with the cruelty which men inflict on one another."

BIOGRAPHICAL/CRITICAL SOURCES: New Statesman, February 10, 1961; *New York Times,* February 19, 1967; *New York Times Book Review,* April 16, 1967, February 11, 1973; Lothar Kahn, *Mirrors of the Jewish Mind: A Gallery of Portraits of European Jewish Writers of Our Time,* A. S. Barnes, 1968; *Time,* February 5, 1973; *National Review,* March 16, 1973; *New York Review of Books,* March 22, 1973; *Atlantic Monthly,* March, 1973; *Commentary,* May, 1973; *Contemporary Literary Criticism,* Gale, Volume 2, 1974, Volume 4, 1975.*

* * *

SCHWIEDER, Dorothy 1933-

PERSONAL: Born November 28, 1933, in Presho, S.D.; daughter of Walter (in business) and Emma (Anderson) Hubbard; married Elmer Schwieder (a university professor), March 20, 1955; children: Diane, David. *Education:* Dakota Wesleyan University, B.A., 1955; Iowa State University, M.S., 1968; University of Iowa, Ph.D., 1980. *Politics:* Democrat. *Religion:* Methodist. *Home:* 2218 Donald St., Ames, Iowa 50010. *Office:* Department of History, Iowa State University, 651 Ross Hall, Ames, Iowa 50010.

CAREER: Dakota Wesleyan University, Mitchell, S.D., instructor in history, 1960-62; Iowa State University, Ames, instructor in history, 1966—. *Member:* American Association of University Professors, American Association of University Women, Organization of American Historians, State Historical Society of Iowa.

WRITINGS: (Editor) *Patterns and Perspectives in Iowa History,* Iowa State University Press, 1973; (with husband, Elmer Schwieder) *A Peculiar People: Iowa's Old Order Amish,* Iowa State University Press, 1975. Contributor of more than a dozen articles to history and women's studies journals.

WORK IN PROGRESS: A history of coal mining in Iowa, publication expected in 1981; a history of rural women in the Midwest, completion expected in 1982.

SIDELIGHTS: Dorothy Schwieder comments: "I've become particularly interested in state and local history because I think it gives the historian an opportunity to get a much closer look at what I call 'people's history.' In limiting one's focus to a particular community or state, one can study individual families, individual ethnic settlements, and individual economic movements. Moreover, one can study change over time in greater detail, as well as the interaction of the various components of society. I have also done several extensive oral history projects and consider this a very exciting type of research. It adds a perspective that is just not present in history books and traditional sources."

* * *

SCOTT, Charles R(alph), Jr. 1914-

PERSONAL: Born April 3, 1914, in Westerleigh, N.Y.; son of Charles R. (in business) and Alice (Law) Scott; married Addie Millican, July 20, 1941; children: Cecilia R. Scott Smith, Charles E. *Education:* Cornell University, B.S., 1936, M.S., 1943. *Religion:* Methodist. *Home:* 5 Windsor Dr., Tuscaloosa, Ala. 35404. *Office:* University of Alabama, Box J, University, Ala. 35486.

CAREER: Carnegie Illinois Steel Co., Pittsburgh, Pa., special engineer, 1936-40; Cornell University, Ithaca, N.Y., assistant professor of administrative engineering, 1940-49; University of Alabama, University, associate professor, 1949-57, professor of industrial management, 1957—. Fulbright lecturer at Busan National University, 1970; exchange professor at University of Otago, 1978; participant in seminars in Europe and the United States. Budgetary specialist for Agency for International Development at Centro Nacional de Productividad in Lima, Peru, 1968. Research fellow at U.S. Steel Co., 1959.

MEMBER: Academy of Management (member of board of directors, 1964), American Institute of Industrial Engineering, American Association of University Professors (member of board of directors, 1964), Institute of Management Science, Southern Management Association (president, 1964), Southern Case Research Association, Alabama Academy of Science, Beta Gamma Sigma (president, 1967-68). *Awards, honors:* Outstanding service award from Southern Management Association, 1974.

WRITINGS: (With Alonzo J. Strickland III) *Tempomatic IV: A Management Simulation,* with manuals, Houghton, 1974, revised edition, 1980; (with Curtis E. Tate, Leon C. Megginson, and Lyle R. Trueblood) *Successful Small Business Management,* with teacher's manual, Business Publications, 1975, revised edition, 1978; (with Tate, Megginson, and Trueblood) *The Dow Jones-Irwin Business Papers,* Dow-Jones Irwin, 1977; (with Tate, Megginson, and Trueblood) *A Complete Guide to Your Own Business,* Dow Jones-Irwin, 1977; (with Tate, Megginson, and Trueblood) *Introduction to Business,* Business Publications, in press.

Contributor: Merwi M. Hargrove, Dennis M. Crites, and other editors, *Cases in Administrative Policies and Contemporary Issues,* D & A, Inc., 1973; Sexton Adams and Louis D. Ponthieu, editors, *Administrative Policy and Strategy,* Coral Industries, 1978; Arthur A. Thompson and Alonzo J. Strickland III, editors, *Strategy and Policy,* Coral Industries, 1978; Robert E. Schellenberger and F. Glenn Boseman, editors, *Policy Formulation and Strategy Management,* Reinhold Chemicals, 1978. Contributor to professional journals.

WORK IN PROGRESS: Simulation models of business organizations.

SIDELIGHTS: Scott comments: "My motivation is to write about business—particularly case studies about ongoing businesses. Writing cases keeps me in contact with the business world, contributes to teaching and records current business practices. My greatest joy is student plant visits, talks with management, and case writing by myself and by students. One particular case, of which I am proud, was written, under my supervision, by a student on his management of a base in Viet Nam. It has been used to teach the problems of managing where drugs, sex, pilferage, aliens, etc. were major factors. The case has been used for teaching military personnel.

"I am very interested in problems of increasing productivity—particularly in methods study. My stays abroad have impressed me with the United States' progressive heritage in this area and the attitudes of people who are brought up in this environment. In countries without this heritage, management appears to believe that buying a new machine is the only avenue to increased productivity. There is an attempt to skip over the development stage. However, today it appears many people in our country are forgetting our heritage, and we are losing our advantages.

"Today, we are using industrial management theory, methods and techniques in ever broadening areas of service industries—medical, universities, transportation, and others. These require more study of quantitative analysis to attack the variableness of their operations. Simulation of systems of production is one of the best tools for their study. The business management simulation has proved to be an excellent tool for teaching."

* * *

SCOTT, Donald F(letcher) 1930-

PERSONAL: Born November 29, 1930, in Norfolk, England; son of Alexander (a farmer) and Jean Scott; married Adrienne Mary Moffett (a psychologist), September 2, 1967; children: Caroline, James. *Education:* University of Edinburgh, M.B. 1957, M.R.C.P., 1959. *Home:* 25 Park Gate, Blackheath, London S.E.3, England. *Office:* London Hospital, Whitechapel, London E1 1BB, England.

CAREER: Maudsley Hospital, London, England, senior registrar, 1963-65; Mayo Clinic, Rochester, Minn., research assistant, 1965-66; London Hospital, London, England, consultant in charge of electroencephalography department, 1967—. *Member:* Royal College of Physicians (fellow), Electroencephalography Society, Electrophysiological Technologists Association, Association of British Neurologists, Association of British Clinical Neurophysiologists.

WRITINGS: (With Barbara Dodd) *Neurological and Neurosurgical Nursing: An Introduction,* Pergamon, 1966; *About Epilepsy,* International Universities Press, 1969, revised edition, 1973; *The Psychology of Work,* Duckworth, 1970; *The Psychology of Fire,* Scribner, 1974 (published in England as *Fire and Fire-Raisers,* Duckworth, 1974); *Understanding EEG: An Introduction to Electroencephalography,* Duckworth, 1975, Lippincott, 1976. Contributor to medical and scientific journals. Member of editorial board of British Epilepsy Association.

WORK IN PROGRESS: Research in clinical neurophysiology.

SIDELIGHTS: Scott writes: "I am interested in increasing the general public's awareness of the difficulties that people with epilepsy suffer, in an endeavour to help them individually and collectively, in terms of education of the general public and the caring professions."

* * *

SCOTT, Robert A. 1936-

PERSONAL: Born December 22, 1936, in Pennsylvania; son of Winfield W. (a laborer) and Edith (Harker) Scott; married

Nancy Jean Levinson (a writer and consultant); children: Michael, William, James, Sarah. *Education:* Pennsylvania State University, B.A., 1957; Stanford University, Ph.D., 1961. *Home:* 285 Western Way, Princeton, N.J. 08540. *Office:* Department of Sociology, Princeton University, Princeton, N.J. 08540.

CAREER: Russell Sage Foundation, New York, N.Y., research associate, 1962-66; Princeton University, Princeton, N.J., assistant professor, 1966-70, associate professor, 1971-78, professor of sociology, 1979—. *Member:* American Sociological Association, Society for the Study of the Social Problems, American Association for the Advancement of the Humanities, Eastern Sociological Association.

WRITINGS: *The Making of Blind Men,* Russell Sage, 1969; (editor with Jack D. Douglas) *Theoretical Perspectives on Deviance,* Basic Books, 1972; (with A. Shore) *Why Sociology Does Not Apply,* American Elsevier, 1979. Contributor to scholarly journals.

WORK IN PROGRESS: A study of madness in nineteenth-century English society; a study of a hospital for the criminally insane.

* * *

SCRIMSHAW, Nevin Stewart 1918-

PERSONAL: Born January 20, 1918, in Milwaukee, Wis.; son of Stewart (a professor of economics) and Harriet Fernwood (Smith) Scrimshaw; married Mary Ware Goodrich, 1941; children: Susan March, Norman Stewart, Nevin Baker, Steven Ware, Nathaniel Lewis. *Education:* Ohio Wesleyan University, B.A. (with honors), 1938; Harvard University, M.A., 1939, Ph.D., 1941, M.P.H. (with honors), 1959; University of Rochester, M.D. (with honors), 1945, postdoctoral study, 1947-49; studied at Marine Biological Laboratory, Woods Hole, Mass., summers, 1937, 1939. *Office:* Department of Nutrition and Food Science, Massachusetts Institute of Technology, Building 20A-201, Cambridge, Mass. 02139.

CAREER: Ohio Wesleyan University, Delaware, instructor in embryology and comparative anatomy, 1941-42; Gorgas Hospital, Canal Zone, Panama, intern, 1945-46; assistant resident in obstetrics and gynecology at Strong Memorial Hospital and Genessee Hospital, both in Rochester, N.Y., both 1948-49; Institute of Nutrition of Central America and Panama, Guatemala City, Guatemala, director, 1949-61, consulting director, 1961-65; Massachusetts Institute of Technology, Cambridge, professor of human nutrition, 1961-76, institute professor, 1976—, head of department of nutrition and food science, 1976-79, director of Clinical Research Center, 1962-66, 1979—, and international nutrition program, 1976—. Diplomate of National Board of Medical Examiners and American Board of Nutrition. Conducted field research in Canal Zone, 1940, and Panama, 1948. Adjunct professor at Columbia University, 1959-61, visiting lecturer, 1961-66; visiting lecturer at Harvard University, 1968—. Member of American Board of Nutrition, 1964—; member of scientific advisory committee of Nutrition Foundation, 1960—, board of directors of Agribusiness Council, 1967-72, and Center for Nutritional Research, 1977—, board of trustees of Rockefeller Foundation, 1971-80, and Neurosciences Research Foundation; member of White House Conference on Food, Nutrition, and Health, and international committee of Nutrition Foundation of Italy, 1977—; member and chairperson of advisory committees of National Institutes of Health, U.S. Department of Agriculture, National Academy of Sciences-National Research Council, and United Nations; consultant to World Health Organization. *Military service:* U.S. Army, Medical Administrative Corps, 1942-45.

MEMBER: International Epidemiological Association, International Union of Nutritional Sciences (committee chairperson, 1967-69; vice-president, 1972-78; president, 1978-81), American Institute of Nutrition (member of council, 1964-68), American Society for Clinical Nutrition, American Physiological Society, American Chemical Society, American Society for Tropical Medicine and Hygiene, American Public Health Association (fellow; member of governing council, 1966-69, 1970-74; vice-president, 1975-76; head of food and nutrition section, 1963, and task force on nutrition, 1970), American College of Preventive Medicine, American Association for the Advancement of Science, American Epidemiological Society, American Dietetic Association (honorary member), American Academy of Arts and Sciences (fellow), Genetic Society of America, Biometric Society, Institute of Food Technologists, Harvey Society (honorary member), Group of European Nutritionists (corresponding member), Royal Society of Health (England; fellow), Royal Society of Sciences (Sweden), Czechoslovak Society for Gastroenterology (corresponding member), Asociacion Medica Nacional de Panama (honorary member), Asociacion Pediatrica de Guatemala (honorary member), Asociacion de Nutricionistas y Dietistas de Centro America y Panama (honorary member), Asociacion Argentina de Nutricion y Dietologia (honorary member), Sociedad Argentina de Pediatria (honorary member), Sociedad Latinoamericana de Nutricion, New England Public Health Association, Pan American Society of New England (member of board of directors, 1962-70), Massachusetts Public Health Association, Massachusetts Medical Society (fellow; head of nutrition committee, 1975), Middlesex South District Medical Society, Phi Beta Kappa, Sigma Xi, Phi Tau Sigma. *Awards, honors:* Mead-Johnson Prize from Rochester Academy of Medicine, 1947; Osborne-Mendel Award from American Institute of Nutrition, 1960; Order of Rodolfo Robles from Government of Guatemala, 1961; D.Public Service from Ohio Wesleyan University, 1961; international award from Institute of Food Technologists, 1969; Joseph Goldberger Award in Clinical Nutrition from American Medical Association, 1969; award for excellence from American Public Health Association, 1974; D.Sc. from University of Rochester, 1974; McCollom Award from American Society for Clinical Nutrition, 1975; Conrad A. Elvehjem Award from American Institute of Nutrition, 1976; Bolton L. Corson Medal from Franklin Institute, 1976; medal of honor from Fundacion F. Cuenca Villoro, 1978; Ph.D. from University of Tokushima, 1979.

WRITINGS: (With Carl E. Taylor and John E. Gordon) *Interactions of Nutrition and Infection* (monograph), World Health Organization, 1968; (editor with Gordon) *Proceedings of the International Conference on Malnutrition, Learning, and Behavior,* M.I.T. Press, 1968; (editor with Aaron M. Altschul) *Amino Acid Fortification of Protein Foods,* M.I.T. Press, 1971; (editor with Alan Berg and David L. Call) *Nutrition, National Development, and Planning,* M.I.T. Press, 1973; (editor with Steven R. Tannenbaum and Bruce R. Stillings) *The Economics, Marketing, and Technology of Fish Protein Concentrate,* M.I.T. Press, 1974; (editor with Moises Behar) *Nutrition and Agricultural Development: Significance and Potential for the Tropics,* Plenum, 1976. Contributor of more than four hundred articles to scientific, medical, and health care journals. Member of editorial board of *American Journal of Physiology,* 1973-76,

Journal of Applied Physiology, 1973-76, and *Proceedings of the National Academy of Sciences*, 1979-81.

* * *

SCRUTON, Roger 1944-

PERSONAL: Born February 27, 1944, in Buslingthorpe, England; son of John and Beryl C. (Haynes) Scruton. *Education:* Jesus College, Cambridge, B.A., 1965, M.A., 1967. *Home:* 6 Linden Gardens, London W.2, England.

CAREER: Called to the bar at Inner Temple, 1978; Cambridge University, Cambridge, England, fellow of Peterhouse, 1969-71; University of London, Birkbeck College, London, England, lecturer in philosophy, 1971—.

WRITINGS: (Contributor) John Casey, editor, *Morality and Moral Reasoning*, Methuen, 1971; *Art and Imagination: A Study in the Philosophy of Mind*, Harper, 1974; *The Aesthetics of Architecture*, Princeton University Press, 1979; *The Meaning of Conservatism*, Penguin, 1980. Contributor to scholarly journals and literary magazines.

WORK IN PROGRESS: A Short History of Modern Philosophy, publication by Routledge & Kegan Paul expected in 1981.

SIDELIGHTS: Scruton writes: "*Art and Imagination* is a study in the philosophy of mind, designed to give a general theory of aesthetic value. *The Aesthetics of Architecture* is a systematic statement of principles, beginning from the philosophical basis of aesthetics, and attempting to provide a foundation for criticism. It develops a critique of the modern movement in architecture, and a defence of classicism. *The Meaning of Conservatism* is a statement of position, designed to show that the conservative attitude in politics is systematic and reasonable, and that it is rendered feeble and confused by the attempt to dilute it with the doctrines of American liberalism. It also argues for a separation of conservative politics from adherence to a free market economy.

"My training is in analytical philosophy, but my principal interests have always included the arts and politics. I do not think that philosophy can be a valuable enterprise until connected to critical intelligence in the fields of human value, and this, combined with a deeply felt allegiance to conservative ways of thought, has led me to attempt to apply my philosophical training in describing subjects which have been bewildered by the impetuous pursuit of fashion, and rendered vulnerable to the opinions of people unable or unwilling to enquire after truth."

* * *

SEAMAN, John E(ugene) 1932-

PERSONAL: Born March 23, 1932, in Denver, Colo.; son of J. Edwin and Olive (Andrews) Seaman; married Nancy Ross (a senior social worker), September 11, 1953; children: Roger McDonald, Mark Campbell, Martha Lynn, Anne Caroline. *Education:* Princeton University, A.B., 1954; Stanford University, M.A., 1960, Ph.D., 1962. *Home:* 3728 North Monitor Circle, Stockton, Calif. 95209. *Office:* Department of English, University of the Pacific, Stockton, Calif. 95211.

CAREER: University of the Pacific, Stockton, Calif., professor of English and department chairman, 1969—. *Military service:* U.S. Army, Security Agency, 1954-56. *Member:* Modern Language Association of America, Commonwealth Club of California.

WRITINGS: The Moral Paradox of "Paradise Lost," Mouton, 1972. Contributor to professional journals.

WORK IN PROGRESS: A study devoted to grammar, rhetoric, and style.

* * *

SEATON, Frederick Andrew 1909-1974

OBITUARY NOTICE: Born December 11, 1909, in Washington, D.C.; died January 17, 1974, in Hastings, Neb. Publisher, communications executive, and politician. Seaton was the president of several businesses, including the Seaton Publishing Co., the Winfield Publishing Co., the Western Farm Life Publishing Co., Sheridan Newspapers, the Manhattan Broadcasting Co. in Kansas, and KHAS-TV in Hastings, Neb. Seaton was made assistant secretary of defense in 1953 and was the recipient of the Medal of Freedom. Obituaries and other sources: *Who's Who in Government*, Marquis, 1972; *Who's Who in American Politics*, 4th edition, Bowker, 1974.

* * *

SEATON, George 1911-1979

OBITUARY NOTICE: Born in 1911 in South Bend, Ind.; died of cancer, July 28, 1979, in Beverly Hills, Calif. Screenwriter, producer, and director of motion pictures. Seaton received Academy Awards for the screenplays "Miracle on 34th Street" and "The Country Girl." In 1969, he wrote and directed "Airport," which became Universal's biggest moneymaker to date. Among his many other screenwriting credits is the Marx Brothers' film, "A Day at the Races." Obituaries and other sources: *New York Times*, July 29, 1979; *Washington Post*, July 30, 1979; *Time*, August 13, 1979.

* * *

SEBERG, Jean 1938-1979

OBITUARY NOTICE: Born November 13, 1938, in Marshalltown, Iowa; died in August or September, 1979, of a barbiturate overdose, in Paris, France. Actress and author. Seberg is best known for her roles in the motion pictures "Bonjour Tristesse," "Breathless," "Lilith," "Paint Your Wagon," and "Airport." Seberg catapulted to fame when, at the age of seventeen, she was selected by producer and director Otto Preminger from among thousands of contestants to play Joan of Arc in the motion picture "Saint Joan." During her career, the politically liberal actress was embroiled in controversy for staunchly supporting the Black Panthers. When Seberg was pregnant in 1970, a rumor allegedly circulated from Central Intelligence Agency (CIA) sources maintained that it was the child of a black militant. The shock caused by the false story induced a premature birth and the child died. The actress never recovered psychologically and reportedly attempted suicide each year on the anniversary of the event. Seberg wrote a book about her psychiatric treatment called *Blue Jeans*. Obituaries and other sources: *Current Biography*, Wilson, 1966; *Who's Who in the World*, 2nd edition, Marquis, 1973; *Who's Who of American Women*, 8th edition, Marquis, 1973; *Biography News*, Volume I, number 6, Gale, 1974; *International Motion Picture Almanac*, Quigley, 1975; *Washington Post*, September 9, 1979; *Chicago Tribune*, September 10, 1979.

* * *

SECOR, Robert 1939-

PERSONAL: Born June 29, 1939, in Brooklyn, N.Y.; son of Harry Aaron (a sales manager) and Jean (Kregstein) Secor; married Marie Jennette (a professor of English), October 22,

1965; children: Anna, Laura. *Education:* Syracuse University, B.A., 1960; Brown University, M.A., 1963, Ph.D., 1969. *Politics:* Democrat. *Religion:* Jewish. *Home:* 525 West Prospect Ave., State College, Pa. 16801. *Office:* Department of English, Pennsylvania State University, University Park, Pa. 16802.

CAREER: Northwestern University, Evanston, Ill., instructor in American literature and creative writing, 1966-69; Pennsylvania State University, University Park, professor of American and British literature and American studies, 1969—, currently director of graduate studies for English department. *Member:* Modern Language Association of America.

WRITINGS: *The Rhetoric of Shifting Perspectives,* Pennsylvania State University Press, 1971; *American Literature I: The Colonial Period, 1792 to 1890,* Simon & Schuster, 1972; (editor and contributor) *Pennsylvania 1776,* Pennsylvania State University Press, 1975. Contributor of more than twenty articles and reviews to magazines, including *Explicator, Mad River Review, Studies in American Fiction, Women and Literature,* and *Modern Fiction Studies.*

WORK IN PROGRESS: A critical biography of Violet Hunt.

SIDELIGHTS: Secor commented: "My current project is a critical biography of Violet Hunt and her family. Her father, Alfred Hunt, was a landscape painter and her mother, Margaret, a novelist like herself. The book will tell of the family's relationships with famous men and women for over a hundred years, from William Wordsworth to Rebecca West."

* * *

SEDGEWICK, Ellery 1872-1960

OBITUARY NOTICE: Born February 27, 1872, in New York, N.Y.; died April 21, 1960. Editor and writer who began his career as an assistant editor of *Youth's Companion* in 1896. Sedgewick later became the highly respected editor of the *Atlantic Monthly* magazine. He was the author of a biography, *Thomas Paine,* and his own memoirs, *The Happy Profession,* in which he recalled meetings with famous persons. He also served as the editor of *Atlantic Harvest.* Obituaries and other sources: *American Authors and Books: 1640 to the Present Day,* 3rd revised edition, Crown, 1972.

* * *

SEDGWICK, Michael Carl 1926-

PERSONAL: Born March 20, 1926, in Maidenhead, Berkshire, England; son of John Barcham (a paper manufacturer) and Lorna (Green) Sedgwick. *Education:* Corpus Christi College, Oxford, M.A. (second class honors), 1947. *Politics:* "Moderate right, no party affiliations." *Religion:* Church of England. *Home and office:* Paddock View, Easebourne Rd., Midhurst, Sussex GU29 9AY, England.

CAREER: Christopher Johnson Ltd., London, England, 1947-54, began as trainee, became production manager; teacher at preparatory school in England, 1955-57; free-lance writer, 1957-58; Montagu National Motor Museum, Beaulieu, England, curator, 1958-66; free-lance writer, 1966—. British research associate for *Automobile Quarterly,* 1963—. Member of advisory council of National Motor Museum; consultant to Christies International. *Member:* Veteran Car Club of Great Britain, Vintage Sports Car Club, Guild of Motoring Writers, Society of Automotive Historians. *Awards, honors:* Montagu Trophy from Guild of Motoring Writers, 1974, for *Fiat: A History.*

WRITINGS: *Early Cars,* Weidenfeld & Nicolson, 1961; *Cars in Colour,* Batsford, 1968; *Cars of the 1930's,* Batsford, 1970; *Veteran and Vintage Cars in Colour,* Batsford, 1971; *Cavalcade of Cars,* Macmillan, 1973; *Fiat: A History,* Batsford, 1974; *Passenger Cars, 1924-1942,* Blandford, 1975; *Klassische Wagen III* (title means "Classic Cars"; translated from the original English manuscript by Ferdinand Hediger), Hallweg, 1979; *The Motor Car, 1946-56,* Batsford, 1979. Contributor to automobile magazines in England, Europe, Australia, and the United States. Assistant editor of *Veteran and Vintage,* 1959—.

WORK IN PROGRESS: Research on automotive history, 1930-60; two short books on vintage cars.

SIDELIGHTS: Sedgwick wrote: "I have always been international in my outlook and have tried to build perspective into my work, explaining my subject against the background of external events against which they occurred. I regard automotive history—like all hobby subjects—as one that breaks down barriers rather than creating them. I maintain a correspondence with fellow enthusiasts and writers from all countries—and of a diversity of race and creed.

"I began a writing career largely because I had always felt the urge to write and felt frustrated by an education that was exclusively and traditionally classical. As a full-time professional automotive historian and writer, writing is part of the job, but the only part of it that is done outside office hours, so to speak. My work covers jobs like consultancy, answering international historical queries, valuing antique cars, and acting as a consultant to antique car auctions."

AVOCATIONAL INTERESTS: Gardening, meeting people, travel.

* * *

SEED, Sheila Turner 1937(?)-1979
(Sheila R. Turner)

OBITUARY NOTICE: Born c. 1937; died June 22, 1979, of a brain aneurysm, in Evanston, Ill. Editor, writer, and photographer. Seed was an editor at Scholastic magazines, a director of Scholastic's Youth News Service, and a contributor to the travel section of the *New York Times.* Obituaries and other sources: *New York Times,* June 23, 1979.

* * *

SEESE, Ethel Gray 1903-

PERSONAL: Born September 13, 1903, in Brandenburg, Ky.; daughter of David Clarence (a farmer) and Mary Emily (Bruner) Gray; married Charles S. Roberts, March 3, 1923 (divorced, 1937); married Raymond P. Seese, June 10, 1938 (divorced, 1946); children: (first marriage) Charles S., Jr., David H.; (second marriage) Perry Gray, Carol N. Seese Parker. *Education:* Attended Wayne State University. *Politics:* Independent. *Religion:* Baptist. *Home address:* P.O. Box 90, Lake Ann, Mich. 49650.

CAREER: Teacher in one-room school, 1923; worked for doctors, 1935-36; Wyandotte General Hospital, Wyandotte, Mich., 1937; worked for a doctor, 1937-41; Bohn Brass & Aluminum Co., 1942; Herman Kiefer Hospital, Detroit, Mich., and Maybury Sanitarium, Northville, Mich., 1943-69; writer, c. 1960—. Attended conferences in London and Taiwan. Volunteer worker in probate court. *Member:* Internationally Yours, World Congress of Poets for Peace, Kentucky Poetry Society, Poetry Society of Michigan, Detroit Women Writers, Lansing Poetry Club. *Awards, honors:* Plaque from World Congress of Poets for Peace, 1976; three awards from Poetry Society of Michigan; first prize from Kentucky state poetry contest, 1978, for *Psychic Hinge*.

WRITINGS: Psychic Hinge (poems), Golden Quill, 1974.

WORK IN PROGRESS: A book of *haiku;* another book of poems; children's poems.

SIDELIGHTS: Ethel Seese writes: "When I was a child, my grandmother recited poetry from Byron, Burns, Shakespeare, and Tennyson; I learned to read it at an early age. It sang in my head, but I was in my fifties before I realized I could put anything on paper.

"I have just returned from England, where I attended a conference and toured Scotland. In 1970 I toured Europe, the Greek isles, and Israel. In 1973, I attended a world congress in Taiwan, then went with missionaries into the mountains—a wonderful experience."

* * *

SEIDENSTICKER, Edward G. 1921-

PERSONAL: Born February 21, 1921, in Castle Rock, Colo.; son of Edward G. (a rancher) and Mary D. Seidensticker. *Education:* University of Colorado, B.A., 1942; Columbia University, M.A., 1947; graduate study at Harvard University, 1947-48, and Tokyo University, 1950-54. *Office:* Department of East Asian Languages and Cultures, Columbia University, New York, N.Y. 10027.

CAREER: Stanford University, Stanford, Calif., professor of Japanese, 1962-66; University of Michigan, Ann Arbor, professor of Japanese, 1966-77; Columbia University, New York,N.Y., professor of Japanese, 1977—. *Awards, honors:* National Book Award, 1970, for translation *The Sound of the Mountain.*

WRITINGS: (With others) *Japan,* Time-Life, 1961; *Kafu the Scribbler: The Life and Writings of Nagai Kafu, 1879-1959,* Stanford University Press, 1965; *Genji Days,* Kodansha, 1977; (editor with Hyoe Murakami) *Guide to Japanese Culture,* Japan Publications, 1977; *This Country Japan,* Kodansha, 1979.

In Japanese: *Nihongo rashii hyogen kara Eigo rashii hyogen e* [Tokyo], 1962; *Gendal Nihon sakka ron* (title means "Modern Japanese writers"), [Tokyo], 1964; *Yushima no yado ni te* (title means "At Home in Yushima"), [Tokyo], 1976.

Translator: Fujiwara Michitsuna no haha, *The Kagero Nikki: Journal of a Tenth Century Noblewoman,* [Tokyo], 1955; Komiya Toyotaka, editor, *Japanese Music and Drama in the Meiji Era,* Obunsha, 1956; (with Donald Keene) Yasunari Kawabata, *The Izu Dancer,* Harashobo, 1964; Fujiwara Michitsuna, *The Gossamer Years: The Diary of a Noblewoman of Heian Japan,* Tuttle, 1964; Kawabata, *Japan the Beautiful and Myself,* Kodansha, 1968; Kawabata, *House of the Sleeping Beauties,* Kodansha, 1969; Kawabata, *The Sound of the Mountain,* Knopf, 1970; (with Glenn William Shaw) Masuji Ibuse, *Honjitsu kyushin: No Consultation Today* (bilingual edition), Hava Shoko, 1971; Murasaki Shikibu, *The Tale of Genji,* Knopf, 1976; (with Thomas J. Harper) Junichiro Tanizaki, *In Praise of Shadows,* Leetes, 1977.

* * *

SEITLIN, Charlotte 1907(?)-1979

OBITUARY NOTICE: Born c. 1907; died in 1979 in New York, N.Y. Seitlin was an editor with Simon & Schuster for over forty years, working with such writers as Janet Flanner, Beatrice Trum Hunter, Gypsy Rose Lee, and Jimmy Savo. Obituaries and other sources: *New York Times,* June 21, 1979; *AB Bookman's Weekly,* August 6, 1979.

* * *

SELBOURNE, David 1937-

PERSONAL: Born June 4, 1937, in London, England; son of Henri Armand Hugh (a physician) and Sulamith (Amiel) Selbourne. *Education:* Balliol College, Oxford, B.A. (with honors), 1958. *Agent:* Unna & Durbridge Ltd., 1 Beaumont Mews, Marylebone High St., London W.1, England. *Office:* Ruskin College, Oxford OX1 2HE, England.

CAREER: Called to the Bar at Inner Temple, 1959; University of Aston, Gosta Green, Birmingham, England, lecturer, 1959-65; Ruskin College, Oxford, England, tutor in social and political theory, 1965—. *Awards, honors:* Aneurin Bevan memorial fellowship from government of India, 1975; Southern Arts Commission playwrights award, 1978.

WRITINGS—Plays: *The Play of William Cooper and Edmund Dew-Nevett* (three-act; first produced in Exeter, England, at Northcott Theatre, January 25, 1968), Methuen, 1968; *The Two-Backed Beast* (two-act; first produced in Liverpool, England, at Everyman Theatre, December 4, 1968), Methuen, 1969; *Dorabella* (fourteen scenes; first produced in Edinburgh, Scotland, at Traverse Theatre, October 28, 1969), Methuen, 1970; *Samson* (first produced in London at Soho Theatre, December, 1971), Calder & Boyars, 1970; *Alison Mary Fagan* (first produced in Auckland, New Zealand, at Downstate Theatre, in 1972), Calder & Boyars, 1972; *The Damned* (first produced as Bengali opera in Calcutta, India, December, 1979), Methuen, 1972; "Three Class Plays" (juvenile; includes three one-act plays), first produced in London at Roundhouse Theatre, December, 1973; *Class Play* (one-act; first produced in London at Roundhouse Theatre, December, 1973), Hutchinson, 1975; *Two Plays for Children* (includes "What Acting?" and "Think of a Story, Quickly!," both one-act; first produced in London at Cockpit Theatre, September, 1977), Edward Arnold, 1977.

Unpublished and unproduced plays: "The Tragedy of Miss Rosie Rose," 1975; "Gehenna," 1977; "Sunday Times," 1978.

Nonfiction: *An Eye to China,* Black Liberator Press, 1975, 2nd edition, Orient Longman, 1978; *An Eye to India,* Penguin, 1977.

Author of a column on political affairs in *India Today,* 1978, and a political affairs column in *Sunday,* 1979. Contributor to journals in India, England, and the United States, including *Harper's, New Statesman, New Internationalist, Guardian, Tribune,* and *Mainstream.*

WORK IN PROGRESS: Passages from a Northern Childhood; Actuality and Observation: Essays in Theory and in Practice.

SIDELIGHTS: The dialogues of many of Selbourne's intellectual plays are in verse.

BIOGRAPHICAL/CRITICAL SOURCES: Stage, June 11, 1970.

* * *

SELL, Henry Blackman 1889-1974

OBITUARY NOTICE: Born November 14, 1889, in Whitewater, Wis.; died of a heart attack, October 23, 1974, in New York, N.Y. Editor, advertiser, and developer of specialty foods who began his career as the literary editor of the *Chi-*

cago Daily News. In 1920, William Randolph Hearst hired him as editor-in-chief of *Harper's Bazaar*, where he discovered writer Anita Loos and published chapters of her then uncompleted book, *Gentlemen Prefer Blondes*. He became president of the Blaker Advertising Agency in 1926 and developed Sell's Specialties and Sell's Liver Pate, but returned to the Hearst organization in 1949 as editor of *Town and Country*. A kinsman of William "Buffalo Bill" Cody, Sell was the co-author of *Buffalo Bill and the Wild West*. Obituaries and other sources: *New York Times*, October 25, 1974; *Who Was Who in America*, 6th edition, Marquis, 1976.

* * *

SELLERS, Robert Victor 1894-1973

OBITUARY NOTICE—See index for *CA* sketch: Born October 18, 1894, in Scholes, Cleckheaton, Yorkshire, England; died January 21, 1973. Educator, minister, biblical scholar, and author of books in his field. Sellers, who was ordained a minister in the Church of England in 1920, was chancellor and canon at Wells Cathedral in England. He was also associated with the University of London as both a professor and fellow in theology. Obituaries and other sources: *The Author's and Writer's Who's Who*, 6th edition, Burke's Peerage, 1971; *AB Bookman's Weekly*, March 26, 1973.

* * *

SELTZER, Daniel 1933-

PERSONAL: Born February 13, 1933, in Passaic, N.J.; son of William and Rose (a teacher; maiden name, Magill) Seltzer. *Education:* Princeton University, B.A. (summa cum laude), 1954; graduate study at Oxford University, 1954-55; Harvard University, Ph.D., 1959. *Office:* Department of English, Princeton University, Princeton, N.J. 08540.

CAREER: Harvard University, Cambridge, Mass., instructor, 1959-61, assistant professor, 1961-64, associate professor, 1964-69, professor of English, 1969-70, Loeb Drama Center acting director, 1963-64, associate director, 1964-70; Princeton University, Princeton, N.J., professor of English, 1970—, president and board chairman of McCarter Theatre Company, 1971-75, director of theatre and dance program, 1974—. Edgar Stone Lecturer at University of Toronto, 1965; lecturer in Shakespeare at numerous institutions, including Stratford (Ontario) Shakespeare Seminar, 1973, Shakespeare Association of America, 1973, International Shakespeare Conference at University of Birmingham, 1976, and Royal Shakespeare Company at Stratford-upon-Avon, 1976. Actor in plays, including "Man for All Seasons," "Antigone," and "Knock Knock." *Member:* Modern Language Association of America, Shakespeare Association of America, Malone Society (Oxford), Phi Beta Kappa. *Awards, honors:* Guggenheim research fellowship, 1964-65; nominated for Antoinette Perry Award and *Theatre World* award, both 1975-76, both for performance in "Knock Knock."

WRITINGS—Editor: John Pickeryng, *Horestes: The Interlude of Vice*, Clarendon Press, 1962; William Shakespeare, *Troilus and Cressida*, New American Library, 1963; Robert Greene, *Friar Bacon and Friar Bungay*, University of Nebraska Press, 1963; *The Modern Theater: Readings and Documents* (anthology), Little, Brown, 1967.

Contributor: Norman Rabkin, editor, *English Institute Essays*, Columbia University Press, 1969; Samuel Schoenbaum, editor, *A New Companion to Shakespeare*, Cambridge University Press, 1972; W. K. Wimsatt, editor, *Literary Criticism: Idea and Act*, University of California Press, 1974; *Studies on Hamlet*, Bucknell University Press, 1975. Contributor of articles to journals, including *Journal of English and Germanic Philology*, *Modern Language Review*, *Shakespeare Quarterly*, *Stratford-Upon-Avon Studies*, and *Harvard Review*.

WORK IN PROGRESS: *The Shape of Nature*, a book-length study of Shakespearean and modern acting styles and methods, and on the phenomenology of acting in general.

* * *

SELTZER, Leon E(ugene) 1918-
(Eugene Leigh)

PERSONAL: Born August 14, 1918, in Auburn, Maine; son of Samuel (a shoe factory foreman) and Sadye (Shapiro) Seltzer; married Lenore Chafetz (a professor of psychology), March 14, 1948; children: Deborah Seltzer Griffen, Janet, Marcia. *Education:* Columbia University, B.A., 1940; Stanford University, J.D., 1974. *Politics:* Democrat. *Religion:* Jewish. *Home:* 459 Traverso Ave., Los Altos, Calif. 94022. *Office:* Stanford University Press, Stanford, Calif. 94305.

CAREER: Columbia University Press, New York, N.Y., editor, 1940-41, 1946-52, sales promotion manager, 1952-56; Stanford University Press, Stanford, Calif., director, 1956—. Admitted to California bar, 1974. Scholar-in-residence at Center for Advanced Study in the Behavioral Sciences, 1975-76. *Military service:* U.S. Army, Corps of Engineers, 1941-46; became major. *Member:* American Bar Association, Association of American University Presses (president, 1968-69). *Awards, honors:* Guggenheim fellow, 1975-76.

WRITINGS: (Editor) *The Columbia Lippincott Gazetteer of the World*, Columbia University Press, 1950; *Exemptions and Fair Use in Copyright: The Exclusive Rights Tensions in the Copyright Act of 1976*, Harvard University Press, 1978. Assistant editor of *Columbia Encyclopedia*, 1946-52. Contributor of stories, essays, and verse, sometimes under pseudonym Eugene Leigh, to magazines, including *New Yorker* and *Woman's Home Companion*.

* * *

SERWICHER, Kurt 1912-1979
(Kurt Kasznar)

OBITUARY NOTICE: Born August 12, 1913, in Vienna, Austria; died of cancer, August 6, 1979, in Santa Monica, Calif. Stage, screen, and television actor, and author, Kasznar was best known for his Broadway roles in "The Sound of Music," "Waiting for Godot," and "Barefoot in the Park." A durable performer, he was the only actor to appear in each of the first one thousand performances of "The Sound of Music," and also played in a number of motion pictures, including "Kiss Me Kate," "Casino Royale," and "A Farewell to Arms." During World War II Kasznar wrote a one-act play, "First Cousins," which won a soldiers-playwrights contest and was later performed as part of a Broadway benefit. Obituaries and other sources: *The Biographical Encyclopaedia and Who's Who of the American Theatre*, James Heineman, 1966; *Who's Who in the Theatre*, 16th edition, Pitman, 1977; *Who's Who in America*, 40th edition, Marquis, 1978; *International Motion Picture Almanac*, Quigley, 1979; *New York Times*, August 8, 1979.

* * *

SESKIN, Eugene P(aul) 1948-

PERSONAL: Born July 16, 1948, in Cleveland, Ohio; son of

Sam (in mail order business) and Elka (a hospital administrator; maiden name, Bass) Seskin; married Nancy M. Gordon (an economist), December 25, 1974. *Education:* Carnegie-Mellon University, B.S., 1972, M.S., 1972, Ph.D., 1973. *Home:* 2801 New Mexico Ave. N.W., #310, Washington, D.C. 20007. *Office:* Bureau of Economic Analysis, U.S. Department of Commerce, 1522 K St. N.W., Washington, D.C. 20230.

CAREER: Carnegie-Mellon University, Pittsburgh, Pa., assistant professor of economics, 1973; Urban Institute, Washington, D.C., research associate, 1973-74; National Bureau of Economic Research, Washington, D.C., research associate, 1974-76; Resources for the Future, Washington, D.C., research associate, 1975-76, senior research associate, 1976-79; U.S. Department of Commerce, Bureau of Economic Analysis, Washington, D.C., special assistant to the chief of the environmental and nonmarket economics division, 1979—. Member of National Academy of Sciences committee on prototype explicit analyses for pesticides. *Member:* American Economic Association.

WRITINGS: (With Henry M. Peskin) *Cost-Benefit Analysis and Water Pollution Policy,* Urban Institute (Washington, D.C.), 1975; (with Lester B. Lave) *Air Pollution and Human Health,* Johns Hopkins Press, 1977.

WORK IN PROGRESS: Theoretical and empirical studies in economics, econometrics, and urban problems.

SIDELIGHTS: Seskin wrote: "In our book, *Air Pollution and Human Health,* Lester Lave and I explore the association between air pollution and human health. Specifically, we investigate the quantitative relationship between human mortality and certain air pollutants to gain more precise measures of the benefits and costs associated with implementing the national air quality standards. Our primary focus is on two types of pollutants (sulfates and particulates) from so-called 'stationary sources' such as solid waste disposal plants, electric power plants, and factories.

"Using carefully controlled statistical analyses of both cross sectional and time series data for a large number of U.S. metropolitan areas, we conclude that the benefits associated with a substantial abatement of air pollution from stationary sources are greater than the costs of such abatement. In contrast, the situation for 'mobile sources'—chiefly cars and trucks—is less clear cut. That is, we conclude that the costs of implementing currently mandated standards for automobile emissions probably exceed their potential health benefits."

* * *

SETTLE, Mary Lee 1918-

PERSONAL: Born July 29, 1918, in Charleston, W. Va.; daughter of Joseph Edward (a civil engineer) and Rachel (Tompkins) Settle; married Rodney Weathersbee (divorced); married Douglas Newton (a journalist; divorced); married William Littleton Tazewell (a writer), 1978; children: Christopher Weathersbee. *Education:* Attended Sweet Briar College, 1936-38. *Politics:* Democrat. *Religion:* Episcopalian. *Home:* 544 Pembroke Ave., Norfolk, Va. *Agent:* Roberta Pryor, International Creative Management, 40 West 57th St., New York, N.Y. 10019.

CAREER: Writer. Worked as editor of *Harper's Bazaar,* 1945; English correspondent for *Flair,* 1950-51. *Military service:* Women's Auxiliary Air Force, 1942-44; associated with Office of War Information in England, 1944-45. *Awards, honors:* Guggenheim fellowships, 1957-58, 1959-60; award from Merrill Foundation, 1975; National Book Award, 1978, for *Blood Tie.*

WRITINGS—Novels, unless otherwise indicated: *The Love Eaters,* Harper, 1954; *The Kiss of Kin,* Harper, 1955; *Oh Beulah Land,* Viking, 1956; *Know Nothing,* Viking, 1960, published as *Pride's Promise,* Pinnacle Books, 1976; *Fight Night on a Sweet Saturday,* Viking, 1964; *All the Brave Promises: Memories of Aircraft Woman 2nd Class 2146391* (autobiographical nonfiction), Delacorte, 1966; *The Story of Flight* (juvenile nonfiction), Random House, 1967; *The Clam Shell,* Delacorte, 1971; *The Scopes Trial: The State of Tennessee vs. John Thomas Scopes* (nonfiction), F. Watts, 1972; *Prisons,* Putnam, 1973 (published in England as *The Long Road to Paradise,* Constable, 1974); *Blood Tie,* Houghton, 1977. Also author of play "Juana La Loca," produced in New York City at American Place Theatre, 1965. Contributor of short stories to periodicals, including *Harper's, Paris Review,* and *Argosy.*

WORK IN PROGRESS: A continuation of the saga begun with *Prisons* and continuing with *O Beulah Land* and *Know Nothing.*

SIDELIGHTS: Although Settle is best known for her novels, she also impressed critics with her autobiographical account of her life in the WAAF in World War II entitled *All the Brave Promises.* James Drawbell wrote that "Settle has the bright, perceptive eye, the sensitive ear and the depth of understanding that enabled her to live, and now relive, the whole variety of experiences in all their intensity." A writer for *Times Literary Supplement* concurred, noting, "This is experience not transmuted but filtered and refined by memory." Alan Pryce-Jones wrote: "Miss Settle's victory is to show that a nasty experience was not entirely pain; her book, for all its rawness, is the book of a sympathetic and understanding woman. It is also relived with stereoscopic sharpness of outline. I hope it has . . . the success it deserves, among the few really good books to come out of the World War II."

Settle received the National Book Award for her most recent novel, *Blood Tie.* The story of expatriates living in Turkey, *Blood Tie* was especially effective in depicting the culture of the small group. Anatole Broyard described the characters as "the culture dropouts of the 70's, someone who puts an ocean between himself and his past, who visits a foreign country and as a crasher enters a party." He noted of Settle, "Even for an experienced novelist, even for a good writer, she has done a remarkable job of capturing the culture that is, in a sense, the most important character in her book."

CA INTERVIEWS THE AUTHOR

Mary Lee Settle was interviewed by *CA* on June 6, 1979.

Mary Lee Settle, who only makes rare visits to New York from her home in Virginia, was interviewed in New York City in the lounge of the Algonquin Hotel. The occasion that brought her to the city was the 1979 National Book Awards (NBA) ceremony. She had been a winner in 1978 for *Blood Tie* and had therefore been placed on the jury for the 1979 award for fiction. She and fellow jurors Wallace Stegner and Alison Lurie chose Tim O'Brien's *Going After Cacciato,* a choice with which she was much delighted; she said there was little question in the minds of the three jurors that it would be the winner after each of them had read it.

Settle is a downright person. Her opinions are firmly held, with the sort of aristocratic, no-nonsense forthrightness normally associated with members of the British social or intellectual elite. In fact, she spent a number of formative years as a writer in England after journeying there quixotically early in World War II, fresh out of Sweetbriar College, to enlist in the women's air force (WAAF) of Britain. She wrote about this experience, a difficult one, in *All the Brave Promises,* hailed by some critics as one of the more remarkable war memoirs.

Settle recalled how the English novelist Rosamond Lehmann had once commented about the time Settle was working in the British Office of War Information (where she'd been moved when her presence in the WAAF was discovered), "How dreadful, that you had to do journalism!" "Not at all," snorts Settle. "It's the best training in the world. During that time I learned how to meet deadlines, I grew up as a get-it-on-the-page journalist who could research enough to write 5,000 lively words about anything in a few days."

She is inclined to be short with the idea of writing as sacred calling. "I never recall wanting consciously to be a writer," she claimed, "though I did write some poetry, which didn't deserve to survive. I don't believe in people who say they always wanted to be writers—it's usually something else they really wanted. If you're a writer you just do it."

When Settle actually began writing seriously—she stayed on in England after the war, married, and became a magazine journalist, writing for *Harper's Bazaar* and *Flair*—she wrote six plays before even trying a novel. "But the trouble with plays is that you keep getting taken to lunch by people who say, 'Darling, it's a work of genius,' then you never hear from them again," she said. "I wrote my first novel because I decided that was the only way I could do the whole thing myself—be my own actors, set designer, producer, everything."

Her first published novel, *The Love Eaters,* was actually the second she had written. She sent it and the first book she had written, *The Kiss of Kin,* to all the big American publishers and both were turned down universally. Then Heinemann (in England) accepted the second book, *The Love Eaters,* and her career was launched. "It got marvelous reviews," Settle exclaimed. "It was one of those magical times when they all seemed to be published at once, right on time, and they were all good. After that, I had cables from five American publishers, all of whom had turned the book down at reader level—though of course I didn't mention that to any of them."

Kiss of Kin quickly found publishers on both sides of the Atlantic. "I remember the reviewers saying how good it was not to have a second novel be a disappointment after the first one. What they didn't realize, of course, was that I'd actually written it first."

After that she started research in the British Museum on what was to be her *magnum opus* to date, the five novels referred to collectively as *O Beulah Land* (also the title of the second volume), a complex study of American political and cultural development over many generations. "I knew when I began that it would be more than one book," Settle noted, "but I didn't expect that it would keep me busy for 25 years." She thought of calling the series a "quincunx," from Lawrence Durrell, "but that sounds dirty, so I think I'll call it a 'quintessence.'" Her idea was to set forth "the sort of social and political impulses that formed America—the reasons many of our forebears came here." Out of any given 100,000 settlers who came to Virginia from 1675 to 1775, she noted with a glint, 80,000 would probably be felons. "It's extraordinary that no Virginian ever seems to have been descended from any of them—they must all have been sterile."

"In my historical writing," Settle declared, "I am concerned with what people thought was happening during the times they lived in, rather than what historians tell us was really happening. I never read a single secondary source, or any book published after 1649, when I was working on that first volume. What I looked for mostly in the second volume was popular books of the time by people who had been captured by Indians, then escaped back to England—that sort of thing."

Settle labored at her researches and writing in the British Museum every day for eight years. "I got my historical education there," she said. "And of course it was heated, and in London in those days that was very important too."

Asked how the concept of taking the narrative from the time of Cromwell's England to the late twentieth century came to her, Settle replied: "I had a picture of one man hitting another in a West Virginia drunk tank one Saturday night, and the idea was to go all the way back to see what lay behind that blow. At first I went back all the way to 1755, then I realized that wasn't far enough, and I went back further still, to Cromwell's England, in *Prisons,* to trace the idea of liberty from which so much of the American experience sprang."

Is there a key scene in the saga—something everything focuses on? "Paul Goodman said you never write your key scene—and there always is one of course—until you absolutely have to. You're sort of afraid of it. In my series, the key scene is the discovery of coal in West Virginia. That changed the entire lives of everyone living there; it became a feudal coal culture, as it were."

Settle seems always to have been writing about places from afar: she wrote of West Virginia while in London and Turkey, Britain while in America, and Turkey while in West Virginia. "It's difficult to write a book in the place where it's set." she explained. "You have to have relief from the pitch of concentration involved in the writing. If when you get up from your desk you simply go out into the same scenes you're writing about, it's too much. I wrote *Prisons* in Turkey. I went there simply because I wanted somewhere warm and cheap to write. Then while I was there I gradually became aware of the outsiders living there, and the effect they had on the natives. That gave me the idea for *Blood Tie.* I didn't write the book in Turkey, of course, but after I came back to Charlottesville. I don't think any writer except E. M. Forster has really tried to empathize with the hosts of the transplanted foreigners he writes about, and I wanted to do that. This need to get away from the scene you're writing about is probably why there are still so many expatriate American writers. They have to have a rest from the place—it's still a country in the making after all."

Does she think of herself as predominantly a historical or a contemporary novelist? "I don't like the mental division people are inclined to make between those categories," she frowned. "As far as I'm concerned, anything that takes place before the moment at which you are reading or writing is already history. The NBA-winning book, *Going After Cacciato,* for instance, is already a historical novel."

Why did Settle often wait so long before committing a subject to paper, as in the nearly twenty-year lapse between the wartime experiences in *All The Bright Promises* and the appearance of the book itself? "So many young writers start out by writing thinly disguised autobiography. I think you should end up with it, not begin with it," she said. "A writer should start out by discovering what he *doesn't* know rather than depend so heavily on what he does—that's too easy."

Working now on what she confidently expects will be the

last volume of the "Beulah Land" series, Settle added with a grin, "When I'm through I'll probably do a rewrite of *Rebecca of Sunnybrook Farm*—something cheerful at any rate. I'm tired of coal mines and death."

BIOGRAPHICAL/CRITICAL SOURCES: Commonweal, March, 1967; *Times Literary Supplement,* April 20, 1967; *Books and Bookmen,* June, 1967; *New York Times,* August 18, 1977.

—*Interview by John F. Baker*

* * *

SEVERS, Vesta-Nadine 1935-

PERSONAL: Born May 28, 1935, in Racine, Mo.; daughter of Delmer William (a contractor) and Anna Marie (Hiebert) Severs; married, 1960 (divorced, March, 1974); children: Jonathan, Felicia, Nathan, Stanley, Diana. *Education:* Draughon's School of Business, graduated, 1954; attended Oklahoma University, Norman. *Home:* 109 West Larry Rd., Shawnee, Okla. 74801.

CAREER: Earl L. Hogard & Co., Tulsa, Okla., secretary and bookkeeper, 1954-56; North American Aviation, Inc., Neosho, Mo., cryptograph operator, 1956-60; Barton Construction Co., Tulsa, Okla., secretary and bookkeeper, 1967-68; writer, 1968—. *Member:* National Writers Club, Society of Children's Book Writers, Oklahoma Writers Federation, Shawnee Writers. *Awards, honors:* Ten art and writing awards include a tie for first place in contest sponsored by Ozark Writers-Artists Guild, 1970, for article, "Art: Shadow of the Divine Perfection"; second place from Oklahoma Writers Federation contest, 1975, for *Lucinda*.

WRITINGS: Lucinda (juvenile historical novel), Concordia, 1978. Contributor of articles, stories, and artwork to magazines and newspapers, including *Southwest Art, Orbit, Lutheran Journal, Mid-America Reporter,* and *Oklahoma Woman*.

WORK IN PROGRESS: Cry of the Killdeer, a juvenile historical novel; research for a three-volume family saga, the first volume on gambling and steamboats, the second on counterfeiting, the third an explanation of mysterious questions raised in the first two.

SIDELIGHTS: Severs commented: "Writers are always cautioned to 'write what you know' and I followed this advice in writing *Lucinda*. I know German family life so I decided Lucinda's family would be German. I also knew about the Civil War battles included in the book because they happened within thirteen miles of my home town, Neosho, which was also involved in several skirmishes in which the Court House was burned by the Indian cavalry unit commanded by General Stand Waite. I knew the book would be a winner because only one other book written of this era for young people had a female protagonist. One young boy (and it wasn't one of my children) said he had read *Lucinda* four times and 'it's better each time.'

"At the age of fifteen I wanted to write and illustrate children's books. But our small town didn't offer many opportunities for such ambitions and my parents were unable to afford an art career for me. Instead I went into the business world as a secretary in Tulsa.

"Finally I saw an article about a local children's author, Bessie Holland Heck. I contacted her and went on from there. At first I apprenticed myself to writing feature articles for newspapers and regional magazines, then after taking an Oklahoma University novel writing class taught by Jack Bickham I decided to launch out into fiction. So far everything fiction I've written has been historical, partly because I love history and partly because the contemporary scene frightens me.

"Recently I decided to try something contemporary as my son wanted a certain type of book written and I half-way promised it to him. Then before I got started a friend told me the history of a family house. It was so fascinating that as she talked ideas for three books popped into my mind. And so I'm off again on historical novels.

"My artwork is quite limited at this time. Maybe once my children leave home I'll be able to pursue this avocation further. But at the present I feel like using all my available time at the typewriter."

* * *

SEWTER, Albert Charles 1912-

PERSONAL: Born November 29, 1912, in Beckenham, Kent, England; married Annie Beatrice Dixon (died, 1941); married Margarita Masters (divorced, 1964); children: two sons. *Education:* London School of Economics and Political Science, London, B.Sc., 1933; Courtauld Institute of Art, London, M.A., 1935. *Home:* The Cottage, Altrincham, Cheshire, England. *Office:* Victoria University of Manchester, Oxford Rd., Manchester M13 9PL, England.

CAREER: Editor of *Burlington,* 1939-40; University of Birmingham, Birmingham, England, assistant director of Barber Institute, 1940-49; Victoria University of Manchester, Manchester, England, reader in art history, 1973—; writer. Assistant at Leicester City Museum and Art Gallery. *Member:* Museums Association (fellow), Royal Society of Arts (fellow).

WRITINGS: Glyn Philpot, Batsford, 1949; (with D. Maxwell White) *I Disegni di G. B. Piazzetta nella Biblioteca Reale di Torino,* Istituto Poligrafico dello Stato, 1969; *The Stained Glass of William Morris and His Circle,* Yale University Press, Volume I, 1974, Volume II, 1975. Editor of *The Art of Fresco Painting,* Tiranti. Contributor to art magazines, including *Apollo* and *Connoisseur*.

* * *

SEYMOUR, Dorothy Jane Z(ander) 1928-
(Eleanor Johnson)

PERSONAL: Born July 5, 1928, in Cleveland, Ohio; daughter of Henry (a printer) and Katherine (Reinert) Zander; married Harold Seymour (a historian), May 21, 1949. *Education:* Attended Cleveland State University, 1946-49; Case Western Reserve University, B.S., 1950, M.S., 1952. *Home:* 647 Commonwealth Ave., Newton Centre, Mass. 02159. *Office:* Ginn & Co., 191 Spring St., Lexington, Mass. 02173.

CAREER: Elementary school teacher in Cleveland, Ohio, 1950-53, and Parma Heights, Ohio, 1953-56; nursery school teacher in Buffalo, N.Y., 1957; elementary school teacher in Pelham, N.Y., 1957-63, and Warwick, N.Y., 1963-66; Xerox Education Publications, Middletown, Conn., contributing editor, 1966-67; Ginn & Co., Boston, Mass., editor, 1967-68, senior editor, 1968-69, editorial specialist for linguistics, 1969-73; free-lance writer and editor, 1973-79; Ginn & Co., Lexington, Mass., senior editor and intermediate level manager, 1979—. *Member:* International Reading Association, National Retired Teachers Association.

WRITINGS—Children's books: *The Tent,* Pitman, 1965; *Big Beds and Little Beds,* Pitman, 1965; *The Rabbit,* Pitman, 1965; *Bullerina Bess,* Pitman, 1965; *The Pond,* Pitman, 1965; *On the Ranch,* Pitman, 1965; *Stop Pretending,* Pitman, 1965;

Bill and the Fish, Pitman, 1965; *Ann Likes Red,* Pitman, 1965; *The Sandwich,* Pitman, 1965; *Brad and Nell,* Pitman, 1965; *The Crate Train,* Grosset, 1966; *The Pine Park Team,* Ginn, 1974.

Author of workbook revisions: *Phonics and Word Order,* three volumes, Xerox Education Publications, 1976; *Inside Out,* Ginn, 1976; *One to Grow on,* Ginn, 1979.

Contributor: J. R. Block, editor, *i.t.a. as a Language Arts Medium,* Pitman, 1968; Mildred A. Dawson, editor, *Teaching Word Recognition Skills,* International Reading Association, 1971; Roger Shuy, editor, *Language Differences: Do They Interfere?,* International Reading Association, 1973.

Work represented in anthologies, including *With Skies and Wings,* Ginn, 1969. Author of column, under pseudonym Eleanor Johnson, in *My Weekly Reader,* Teachers' Edition, 1967. Author of "I.T.A. Antics," a children's comic strip in *Warwick Dispatch,* 1965-66, and *Playmate,* 1967-68. Contributor to *Beginning Dictionary.* Contributor of articles, poems, and children's stories to professional journals and popular magazines, including *Commonweal, Discovery,* and *Western People.* Contributing editor of *My Weekly Reader,* Teachers' Edition.

WORK IN PROGRESS: Two books.

SIDELIGHTS: Seymour commented: "Although my writing career began with professional articles, more people know me through my Wonder Books for Grosset. These are preschool readers with minimal vocabularies which began as stories for my own first-grade class. I am much interested in the beginning reader, who needs the encouragement and confidence to be gained through success with a short but interesting book written with words of linguistically-common form and elements.

"Of all my writing I think I am most satisfied, however, with my professional articles. I write on contemporary educational issues about which I feel strongly and in which I have sufficient background. In this aspect of my writing I have been influenced by my husband, a historian, who inspired my interest in research and scholarship. I enjoy being a member of a two-person writing family; each of us can try out ideas on the other. Although I have long been an editor as well as a writer and like to edit my husband's work, I appreciate the fact that he has learned to edit my work, too, with keen interest and effectiveness.

"Our two and a half years of retreat in Ireland, although not idyllic (grey weather was a psychological strain) was a fascinating experience. We bought a stone cottage in County Mayo—in the west of Ireland, the least developed area—and lived among the farmers about four miles from an old market town. Reading the local and national literature and mythology, talking to local people for flavor and understanding, and taking long walks and bus rides gave us an appreciation for a kind of life different from any we had known. But more important, we gained a new perspective on America and the assumptions of Americans about life and how to lead it."

* * *

SHACHTMAN, Tom 1942-

PERSONAL: Born February 15, 1942, in New York, N.Y. *Education:* Tufts University, B.S., 1963; Carnegie-Mellon University, M.F.A., 1966. *Residence:* New York, N.Y. *Agent:* Mel Berger, William Morris Agency, 1350 Avenue of the Americas, New York, N.Y. 10019.

CAREER: Free-lance writer, producer, and director for television, 1966—. Assistant chief of the television division, National Geographic Society, 1969-70. *Member:* Writers Guild of America, East. *Awards, honors:* Shubert fellowship, 1965-66; gold award from Atlanta Film Festival, award from New York International Film Festival, and Golden Gate award from San Francisco Film Festival, all 1972, all for "Children of Poverty"; gold award from Virgin Islands Film Festival, and award from New York International Film Festival, both 1973, both for "Children of Trouble"; gold award from Virgin Islands Film Festival, award from New York International Film Festival, and local Emmy awards, all 1975, all for "Children of Violence"; local Emmy award for "Winning Isn't Everything," 1977, and for other works.

WRITINGS: Beginnings (nonfiction), photographs by Donn Renn, Macmillan, 1961; "The Coming Forth by Day of Osiris Jones" (adapted from poem by Conrad Aiken), first produced in New York City at Actors Experimental Theater, 1971; (author of dialogue) Werner Herzog, "Nosferatu" (screenplay; adapted from novel by Bram Stoker, *Dracula*), released by Twentieth-Century Fox, 1979; *The Day America Crashed,* Putnam, 1979; *Edith and Woodrow* (nonfiction), Putnam, 1980. Also author of one-act plays.

Television scripts: "The Twenty-First Century," Columbia Broadcasting System, Inc. (CBS-TV), 1966-69; "Discovery," American Broadcasting Companies, Inc. (ABC-TV), 1970-71; "NBC Reports," National Broadcasting Company, Inc. (NBC-TV), 1971; "Children of Poverty" (trilogy; includes "Children of Poverty," "Children of Trouble," and "Children of Violence"), 1972-75; "Broken Treaty at Battle Mountain," Public Broadcasting Service (PBS-TV), 1973; "The Masks We Wear," ABC-TV, 1973; "Rainbow Sundae," ABC-TV, 1973-75; "Sixty Minutes," CBS-TV, 1974; "Decades of Decision," PBS-TV, 1976.Contributor of articles to magazines.

SIDELIGHTS: Shachtman commented: "A style and feeling for audience given me by a dozen years' work in documentaries for television has been carried over into my nonfiction books." One of his books, *The Day America Crashed,* reconstructs events across America on October 24, 1929, the day of the first large stock market crash.

By looking at the day's range of activity in such detail, "Mr. Shachtman is able to convey the profound and extensive sense of shock that altered the prevailing psychology of the times, which in turn may have contributed as much to the coming of the Depression as actual economic conditions did," critic Christopher Lehmann-Haupt wrote.

BIOGRAPHICAL/CRITICAL SOURCES: New York Times, March 26, 1979; *Dallas Morning News,* May 6, 1979; *Los Angeles Times,* May 17, 1979.

* * *

SHAHN, Ben(jamin) 1898-1969

OBITUARY NOTICE: Born September 12, 1898, in Kaunas, Russia; died March 14, 1969. Painter, educator, writer, and illustrator of numerous books. Shahn, who immigrated with his family to the United States in 1906, first received fame for his 1932 satirical paintings about the Sacco and Vanzetti murder trial. The murals, posters, and drawings that followed continued along the lines of social import, and earned Shahn his reputation as one of the most powerful of American humanists. Of all his work, the artist thought that his murals for the Social Security building in Washington, D.C., provided him his most exhilarating experience. As an educator, he taught and lectured at museums, galleries, and colleges, and was appointed Charles Eliot Norton Professor at Harvard University in 1956. His paintings were exhibited in museums and one-man shows throughout the United States and abroad, and were selected to represent contemporary America at the 1954 Venice Biennale Exhibition of International Art. His writings include *Shape of Content, The Alphabet of Creation: An Ancient Legend From the Zohar,* and *Love and Joy About Letters.* Obituaries and other sources: *Current Biography,* Wilson, 1954, May, 1969; *Who's Who in Graphic Art,* Amstutz & Herdeg Graphis, 1962; *The Oxford Companion to American Literature,* 4th edition, Oxford University Press, 1965; *New York Times,* March 15, 1969; *A Dictionary of Contemporary American Artists,* 2nd edition, St. Martin's, 1971; *Atlantic Brief Lives: A Biographical Companion to the Arts,* Little, Brown, 1971.

* * *

SHALE, Richard 1947-

PERSONAL: Born January 9, 1947, in Youngstown, Ohio; son of Don and Virginia (Williams) Shale. *Education:* Ohio Wesleyan University, B.A., 1969; University of Michigan, M.A., 1972, Ph.D., 1976. *Home:* 12 Southwoods Ave., #10, Youngstown, Ohio 44512. *Office:* Department of English, Youngstown State University, Youngstown, Ohio 44555.

CAREER: Youngstown State University, Youngstown, Ohio, instructor in English, 1976—. *Military service:* U.S. Army Reserve, 1970-76. *Member:* American Film Institute, National Parks and Conservation Association, Popular Culture Association, Sierra Club, Phi Beta Kappa.

WRITINGS: Academy Awards: An Ungar Reference Index (Movie Entertainment Book Club selection), Ungar, 1978. Contributor to magazines, including *Motion, Cinegram,* and *Funnyworld.*

WORK IN PROGRESS: Revision of Ph.D. dissertation, "Donald Duck Joins Up: The Walt Disney Studio During World War II"; an index to the Emmy Awards.

SIDELIGHTS: Shale writes: "I decided to compile an index to the Academy Awards because I couldn't find quick answers to simple questions about the Oscars. Despite a number of books already published, I found few sources which listed nominees as well as winners, and none which thoroughly indexed all awards. The line between serious historical questions and trivia can be an exceedingly fine one; I was interested in writing a book which would satisfy both the buff and the scholar."

* * *

SHANN, Renee 1907(?)-1979
(Carol Gaye)

OBITUARY NOTICE: Born c. 1907; died in 1979 in London, England. Novelist. Shann was a very prolific writer, authoring almost two hundred romance novels. Her titles include *Pound Foolish, Some Day You'll Know,* and *Tread Softly in Love.* Obituaries and other sources: *The Writers Directory, 1980-82,* St. Martin's, 1979; *AB Bookman's Weekly,* November 5, 1979.

* * *

SHARIF, Omar
See CHALHOUB, Michael

* * *

SHEEN, Fulton J(ohn) 1895-1979

OBITUARY NOTICE—See index for *CA* sketch: Born May 8, 1895, in El Paso, Ill.; died December 9, 1979, in New York, N.Y. Roman Catholic archbishop, broadcaster, educator, and author. Sheen's long career as a radio and television evangelist made him one of the best-known Roman Catholic clergymen in the United States. He began his broadcast career in 1930 as a regular speaker on NBC-Radio's "Catholic Hour," and in later years appeared in three popular television series. One of them, Life Is Worth Living," received an Emmy Award in 1952. Among his converts to Catholicism were such people as Henry Ford II, Clare Boothe Luce, and Heywood Broun. Sheen, who taught philosophy for twenty-four years at Catholic University, turned out more than fifty books and pamphlets. These titles include *Philosophies at War, Peace of Soul, The Ideological Fallacies of Communism,* and *The Quotable Fulton J. Sheen.* Obituaries and other sources: *Current Biography,* Wilson, 1951; *Celebrity Register,* 3rd edition, Simon & Schuster, 1973; *Political Profiles: The Eisenhower Years,* Facts on File, 1977; *Who's Who in America,* 40th edition, Marquis, 1978; *The International Who's Who,* Europa, 1979; *Who's Who,* 131st edition, St. Martin's, 1979; *New York Times,* December 10, 1979; *Chicago Tribune,* December 11, 1979; *Newsweek,* December 24, 1979.

* * *

SHEINESS, Marsha 1940-

PERSONAL: Surname is pronounced *Shy*-ness; born November 20, 1940, in Corpus Christi, Tex.; daughter of Lewis (a merchant) and Sylvia (Krasner) Sheiness. *Education:* Attended Baylor University, 1958-59, and Los Angeles City College, 1960-61; Los Angeles State College of Applied Arts and Sciences (now California State University, Los Angeles), B.A., 1963. *Politics:* "Liberal-Progressive." *Home and office:* 315 West 19th St., New York, N.Y. 10011. *Agent:* Bret Adams Ltd., 36 East 61st St., New York, N.Y. 10021.

CAREER: Worked as typist; computer typesetter, 1972-79; writer. Consultant to Creative Artists Public Service Program. *Member:* Actors' Equity Association, Screen Actors Guild, Dramatists Guild, Writers Guild of America, East. *Awards, honors:* Exxon Award, 1974, for "Monkey Monkey Bottle of Beer, How Many Monkeys Have We Here?"; award from *Dramatics,* 1974, for "Professor George."

WRITINGS: Two Swallows in No Time, Chelsea House, 1970.

Plays: *Monkey Monkey Bottle of Beer, How Many Monkeys Have We Here?* (two-act; first produced in New York City at New Theater, 1971), Samuel French, 1975; *Professor George* (one-act; first produced in Waterford, Conn., at O'Neil National Playwright's Conference, 1972), Samuel French, 1975; *The Spelling Bee* (two-act; first produced in Waterford at O'Neil National Playwright's Conference, August, 1975), Samuel French, 1976.

Unpublished plays: "Pancho Pancho" (one-act), first produced in New York City at Little Room Theatre, 1970; "Clair and the Chair" (one-act), first produced in New York City at Playwright Horizons, fall, 1971; "Stop the Parade" (two-act), first produced in New York City at Playwright Horizons, 1972. Also author of "Dealer's Choice," a two-act play, first produced at Playwright Horizons, and a screenplay, "Have a Nice Weekend."

WORK IN PROGRESS: "Floaters," a two-act play.

* * *

SHERRY, John E(rnest) H(orwath) 1932-

PERSONAL: Born March 17, 1932, in New York, N.Y.; son

of John H. (a professor of law and attorney) and Margaret (Horwath) Sherry; married Margaret Louise Singer, September 16, 1961; children: John II, Suzanne Conver, Douglas Marshall. *Education:* Yale University, B.A., 1954; Columbia University, J.D., 1959; New York University, LL.M., 1968. *Politics:* Independent. *Religion:* Protestant. *Home:* 1026 Hanshaw Rd., Ithaca, N.Y. 14850. *Office:* School of Hotel Administration, Cornell University, Ithaca, N.Y. 14853.

CAREER: Admitted to the Bar of New York State, 1962, and U.S. Supreme Court and State of Ohio, both 1967. Clerk to U.S. District Court judge, New York City, 1959-60; Baker, Nelson, Williams & Mitchell (law firm), New York City, associate, 1960-61; attorney at law, New York City, 1962—; confidential clerk to judge in New York State Court of Claims, 1963-65; John H. Sherry (law firm), New York City, associate, 1965-67; University of Akron, Akron, Ohio, assistant professor of law and director of clinical programs, 1967-70; California State University, San Diego (now University of San Diego), associate professor of law, 1970-72; Cornell University, Ithaca, N.Y., associate professor of law, 1972—. U.S. Department of State, member of Advisory Committee on Hotelkeepers' Liability, 1973—, diplomatic representative, 1979; consultant to Sales Managers Association, 1974-75, and American Hotel and Motel Association. *Military service:* U.S. Army, 1955-57, served in Korea; became first lieutenant. U.S. Army, 1961-62, Fort Bragg, N.C.; became captain, 1965.

WRITINGS: (With father, John H. Sherry) *The Laws of Innkeepers,* Cornell University Press, 1972, second edition, 1980; *Hotel and Motel Law: Instructors Guide and Student Manual,* Educational Institute of the American Hotel and Motel Association, 1976. Author of column, "The Innside of the Law," in *Cornell Hotel and Restaurant Administration Quarterly*. Contributor to various law reviews.

WORK IN PROGRESS: Legal Aspects of Tourism and Travel Abroad, for Cornell University Press, completion expected in 1982.

SIDELIGHTS: Sherry told *CA:* "Since graduation from law school, I have practiced in the hospitality field with my father when not engaged in teaching activities. My father and uncles have made their careers in this industry, particularly in the areas of hotel accounting and law, and this provided me with strong motivation and interest in developing legal texts as industry guides and as research vehicles for future scholarship. My current work with the State Department has reinforced this objective, and I have had the opportunity to meet with government and industry representatives throughout the world toward that end. My overall aim is to provide both the travel consumer and the industry executive with a balanced, objective view of the current state of the law and to point up future problem areas, with the ultimate objective of establishing a uniform international set of rules for innkeepers akin to the Warsaw Convention for air carriers."

* * *

SHIPPEY, (Henry) Lee 1884-1969

OBITUARY NOTICE: Born February 26, 1884, in Memphis, Tenn.; died in December, 1969. Shippey was a columnist, feature writer, and foreign correspondent for the *Kansas City Star* before joining the *Los Angeles Times* in 1927. He edited his "Lee Side o' Los Angeles" column until 1950, and wrote numerous books, including *The Testing Crowd, Where Nothing Ever Happens, The Girl Who Wanted Experience, The Great American Family, It's an Old California Custom, The Los Angeles Book,* and his autobiography, *The Luckiest Man Alive.* Obituaries and other sources: *Publishers Weekly,* February 9, 1970; *Who Was Who in America,* 5th edition, Marquis, 1973.

* * *

SHIRLEY, Glenn 1916-

PERSONAL: Born December 9, 1916, in Payne County, Okla.; son of Ellis Dean (a farmer and rancher) and Effie (Knorr) Shirley; married Carrie M. Jacob (a deputy court clerk), 1946; children: Glenda Lea Shirley Womack, Kenneth Ellis. *Education:* Institute of Applied Science, School of Criminology, diploma, 1937; Chicago School of Law, LL.B., 1940; New York Institute of Photography, diploma, 1941; International Criminologist School, diploma, 1948; Delehanty Institute, diploma, 1949; Oklahoma A & M College, diploma, 1950. *Home and office address:* P.O. Box 824, Stillwater, Okla. 74074.

CAREER: Police Department, Stillwater, Okla., sergeant, 1936-43, captain and assistant police chief, 1946-57; Sheriff's Office, Payne County, Okla., criminal deputy and identification officer, 1957-59; Oklahoma State University, Stillwater, assistant chief of security, 1959-69; Oklahoma State University Press, Stillwater, assistant to director, 1969—. Lecturer at University of Oklahoma and Oklahoma State University, 1950, at history seminars, and at workshops on professional writing. *Military service:* U.S. Army, 1943-46; served in East Africa and the Middle East. National Association and Center for Outlaw and Lawman History, Western Writers of America, Western History Association, Oklahoma Writers Federation (life member; past president), Oklahoma Historical Society, Kansas Historical Society, Montana Historical Society, Westerners (past president of Indian Territory posse).

WRITINGS—All nonfiction: *Toughest of Them All,* University of New Mexico Press, 1953; *Six-Gun and Silver Star,* University of New Mexico Press, 1955; *Law West of Fort Smith: A History of Frontier Justice in the Indian Territory, 1834-1896,* Holt, 1957, reprinted, University of Nebraska Press, 1978; *Pawnee Bill: A Biography of Gordon W. Lillie,* University of New Mexico Press, 1958; *Buckskin and Spurs: A Gallery of Frontier Rogues and Heroes,* Hastings House, 1958.

Outlaw Queen, Monarch, 1960; *Heck Thomas, Frontier Marshal,* Chilton, 1962; *Born to Kill,* Monarch, 1963; *Henry Starr: Last of the Real Badmen,* McKay, 1965, reprinted as *Last of the Real Badmen,* University of Nebraska Press, 1976; *Buckskin Joe: The Unique and Vivid Memoirs of Edward Jonathan Hoyt, Hunter-Trapper, Scout, Soldier, Showman, Frontiersman, and Friend of the Indians, 1840-1918,* University of Nebraska Press, 1966.

Shotgun for Hire: The Story of "Deacon" Jim Miller, Killer of Pat Garrett, University of Oklahoma Press, 1970; *The Life of Texas Jack: Eight Years a Criminal, Forty-One Years Trusting in God,* Nortex, 1973; *Red Yesterdays,* Nortex, 1977; *West of Hell's Fringe: Crime, Criminals, and the Federal Peace Officer in Oklahoma Territory, 1889-1907,* University of Oklahoma Press, 1978; *Temple Houston: Lawyer With a Gun,* University of Oklahoma Press, 1979.

Contributor: Joe Austell Smith, editor, *The Best of True West,* Messner, 1964; Tom W. Blackburn, editor, *They Opened the West,* Doubleday, 1967; Phil Hirsch, editor, *Great True Stories of the Wild West,* Pyramid Publications, 1971; (author of foreword) Ellsworth Collings and Alma Miller England, *The 101 Ranch,* University of Oklahoma Press, 1971; *The Gunfighters,* Time-Life, 1974; Robert Elman, *Badmen of the West,* Ridge Press, 1974. Contributor of nearly eight hundred articles and stories (some under pseudonyms) to western, detective, and men's magazines, and to popular journals.

WORK IN PROGRESS: Belle Starr and Her Times; three untitled non-fiction books.

AVOCATIONAL INTERESTS: Collecting Western Americana.

* * *

SHOLINSKY, Jane 1943-

PERSONAL: Born August 30, 1943, in Wilmington, Del.; daughter of Milton H. (a physician) and Tessa (a college registrar; maiden name, Protaz) Redish; married Stephen Sholinsky (an artist and printmaker), February 19, 1967; children: Marc Adam. *Education:* Curry College, B.S., 1965. *Home:* 515 East 89th St., New York, N.Y. 10028.

CAREER: Kindergarten teacher in Ridgefield Park, N.J., 1965-67; Scholastic Magazines, Inc., New York, N.Y., writer for weekly and summer elementary school magazines, 1968-69, associate editor of primary magazines, 1969-71, editor of elementary skills book program, 1971-76; writer, 1976—.

WRITINGS: Dinosaur Bones: A Creative Expression Book for Children, Scholastic Book Services, 1973; *Map Skills Series: Three Books That Help Build Skills in Reading and Understanding Maps,* Scholastic Book Services, 1974; *Word Mastery With Puzzles and Games,* Scholastic Book Services, 1975; *Dictionary Skills Series: Three Books That Acquaint Students With the Kinds of Information Found in a Dictionary,* Scholastic Book Services, 1976; *Getting to Know the Library: A Three-Book Series on How to Use the Library,* Scholastic Book Services, 1976.

Children's books: *Growing Plants From Fruits and Vegetables,* Scholastic Book Services, 1974; *The Challenge of Skiing: A Book for Young Skiing Enthusiasts,* F. Watts, 1974; *In the Saddle: A Book for Young Equestrians,* Messner, 1977; *Peanut Parade: A Book of Peanut Craft,* Messner, 1979. Contributor of stories and poems to children's magazines, including *Golden, Search,* and *News Ranger.*

WORK IN PROGRESS: A historical novel for adults, set in the Hudson River Valley, 1795-1800.

SIDELIGHTS: Jane Sholinsky writes: "I am an avid equestrian, skier, and horticulturist, and my children's books reflect those interests. I am also the mother of a five-year-old son, whose interests led me to write the peanut craft book. I have always been fascinated with the eighteenth century and that, coupled with my love for horseback riding, is paramount in my latest venture. My historical novel deals with horse racing in the northern states after the Revolutionary War."

* * *

SHOR, Joel 1919-

PERSONAL: Born July 11, 1919, in New York, N.Y.; son of Abraham and Fanny (Garfinkle) Shor; children: Heidi Shor Ruthchild, Robert Bartley Shor. *Education:* City College (now of the City University of New York), B.S.S. (cum laude), 1939, M.S.E., 1943; New York University, Ph.D., 1948; also attended New School for Social Research, 1939-42. *Home and office:* 1300 Tigertail Rd., Los Angeles, Calif. 90049. *Agent:* Neal Gantcher, 1370 Avenue of the Americas, New York, N.Y. 10019.

CAREER: City College (now of the City University of New York), New York City, clinical assistant at Psycho-Educational Clinic, 1935-39, staff psychologist, 1939-41, instructor in mental hygiene and psychology, 1939-41, 1946-47; private practice of psychoanalysis and psychoanalytic therapy in New York City, 1949-60, London, England, 1961-63, and Los Angeles, Calif., 1964—. Diplomate and senior examiner of American Boards in Professional Psychology. Instructor and therapist at Yale University, 1946-48; lecturer at New York University, 1948-51; professor at Sarah Lawrence College, 1948-52; lecturer in psychoanalysis for National Psychological Association, 1949-55; visiting professor at University of Southern California Law Center, 1968-70; department coordinator at California School for Professional Psychology, 1971-73; lecturer in University of California, Los Angeles, Program in Medicine, 1979—. Research associate and senior psychologist at Tavistock Clinic, 1961-63; research psychologist for California Department of Mental Health, 1963-64; research director for Wells Foundation and Medical Group, 1964-66; research psychoanalyst at Hacker Clinic, 1966-69. Participant in national and international congresses. *Military service:* U.S. Army, clinical psychologist in psychiatric hospitals, 1942-46; became lieutenant.

MEMBER: International Council of Psychology, American Psychological Association, American Academy of Psychotherapy, Association for Applied Psychoanalysis, British Psychological Society (Medical Section), Los Angeles County Psychological Association, Los Angeles Institute for Psychoanalytic Studies (member of institute faculty; training analyst).

WRITINGS: (With Jean Sanville) *Illusion in Loving: A Psychoanalytic Approach to the Evolution of Intimacy and Autonomy,* International Universities Press, 1978. Contributor of about twenty articles and reviews to professional journals.

WORK IN PROGRESS: Illusion in Psychoanalytic Therapy, with Jean Sanville, for Berkeley Press.

SIDELIGHTS: Shor wrote that his "prime interest is to redefine and update the major concepts, methods, and principles of psychoanalysis." This has already been of "great value to me personally as well as to the humanities and human sciences," he commented.

* * *

SHOWALTER, Dennis 1942-

PERSONAL: Born February 12, 1942, in Delano, Minn.; son of Edwin Thomas (in sales) and Ann (Jaunich) Showalter; married Clara Anne McKenna (a writer), November 27, 1965; children: Clara Kathleen, John. *Education:* St. John's University, B.A., 1963; University of Minnesota, M.A., 1965, Ph.D., 1969. *Home:* 2110 Essex Lane, Colorado Springs, Colo. 80909. *Office:* Department of History, Colorado College, Colorado Springs, Colo. 80903.

CAREER: University of Minnesota, Minneapolis, instructor in history, 1968-69; Colorado College, Colorado Springs, assistant professor, 1969-77, associate professor of history, 1977—. Guest lecturer at National War College and Marine Corps Command and Staff College, 1976; speaker at professional meetings. *Member:* American Historical Association, American Military Institute, Western Association for German Studies. *Awards, honors:* Woodrow Wilson fellow, 1963-64; Fulbright fellow at University of Freiburg, 1966-67; Ford Foundation grants, 1970, 1971, 1972; National Endowment for the Humanities grant, 1973.

WRITINGS: Railroads and Rifles: Soldiers, Technology,

and the Unification of Germany, Shoe String, 1975; (contributor) Michael Adelstein and Jean Pival, editors, *The Reading Commitment,* Harcourt, 1978. Associate editor of "Doctoral Dissertations in Military Affairs," a series, *Military Affairs,* 1977—. Contributor of about forty articles and reviews to history and military journals. Member of editorial advisory board of *Military Affairs,* 1975-78, 1979-80.

WORK IN PROGRESS: Little Man, What Now? Julius Streicher's "Der Stuermer" as an Instrument of Popular Culture and Propaganda in the Weimar Republic; German Military History Since 1648: A Critical Bibliography, Garland Publishing; editing Arthur G. Pettit's *Greaser and Gringo: Images of the Mexican in English-Language Popular Fiction.*

SIDELIGHTS: Showalter writes: "My first book was a revision of my doctoral dissertation. I began *Little Man, What Now?* when I realized that Streicher's *Der Stuermer* was discussed or mentioned in a wide variety of works on Nazi Germany, but the newspaper itself was so noxious that few scholars seemed to have been able to stomach more than samples of it. I decided that a journal of that type would be an excellent focal point for a study of popular antisemitism, Nazi politics, and the problems of press freedom in the Weimar Republic. In 1976 a close friend died, leaving an incomplete manuscript, *Greaser and Gringo,* which I have revised and edited for publication. My articles are a similarly mixed bag, ranging from a study of patterns of authority in the medieval Dominican order to one on Archie Bunker, Lenny Bruce and Ben Cartwright: 'Taboo-Breaking and Character Identification in "All in the Family."'

"I regard versatility as extremely important for the academic writer. Too often professors limit themselves to such limited fields that their own students have difficulty reading the results of their research. As for the often-mentioned dichotomy between research and teaching, this is nothing but an intellectual red herring. Ten years of teaching in a liberal arts college stressing classroom interaction have convinced me that the professor who hopes to remain an effective instructor *must* also maintain himself as a productive scholar. Otherwise he risks finding himself in the position of either repeating the same ideas year after year, or far worse, of becoming a local 'expert,' garnering cheap triumphs in an environment which is too accustomed to his presence, or just too polite, to subject his work to rigorous intellectual criticism. Particularly with the virtual end of job mobility in the academic community, writing for publication keeps the professor in contact with the intellectual world beyond his own campus. And I know of nothing like a stack of rejection slips to contribute to a sense of identity with the freshman struggling with his first college term paper!"

* * *

SHULMAN, Max 1919-

PERSONAL: Born March 14, 1919, in St. Paul, Minn.; son of Abraham (a house painter) and Bessie (Karchmer) Schulman; married Carol Rees, December 21, 1941 (died, May 17, 1963); married Mary Gordon, June 14, 1964; children: Daniel, Max, Jr., Peter, Martha. *Education:* University of Minnesota, B.A., 1942. *Residence:* Los Angeles, Calif. *Agent:* Harold Matson, 22 East 40th St., New York, N.Y. 10016.

CAREER: Writer. *Military service:* U.S. Army Air Force, 1942-45. *Member:* Authors Guild, Dramatists Guild, Writers Guild of America, West.

WRITINGS: Barefoot Boy With Cheek (novel), Doubleday, 1943 (also see below); *Feather Merchants* (novel), Doubleday, 1944; *Sleep Till Noon* (novel), Doubleday, 1950; *The Many Loves of Dobie Gillis,* Doubleday, 1953 (also see below); *Max Shulman's Guided Tour of Campus Humor* (anthology), Doubleday, 1955; *Rally Round the Flag, Boys* (novel), Doubleday, 1957; *I Was a Teen-Age Dwarf,* Random House, 1959; *Anyone Got a Match,* Harper, 1964; *Max Schulman's Large Economy Size* (anthology), Doubleday, 1965; *Potatoes Are Cheaper* (novel), Doubleday, 1971. Also author of *Zebra Derby,* 1946.

Plays: "Barefoot Boy With Cheek" (musical comedy; adapted from own novel with George Abbott), first produced on Broadway at Martin Beck Theatre, April 3, 1947; (with Robert Paul Smith) "The Tender Trap" (comedy), first produced on Broadway at Longacre Theatre, October 13, 1954; *How Now, Dow Jones* (musical comedy; first produced on Broadway at Lunt-Fontanne Theatre, December 7, 1967), Samuel French, 1968.

Screenplays: "A Steak for Connie"; (with Herman Wouk) "Confidentially Connie," Metro-Goldwyn-Mayer, 1952; "Affairs of Dobie Gillis," Metro-Goldwyn-Mayer, 1953; "Half a Hero," Metro-Goldwyn-Mayer, 1953; (with Julius J. Epstein) "House Calls," 1978.

Creator and author of scripts for the television series, "The Many Loves of Dobie Gillis," CBS, 1959-62.

Author of syndicated weekly column, "On Campus," 1954-70. Contributor of short stories to periodicals, including *Saturday Evening Post, Good Housekeeping, Esquire,* and *Mademoiselle.*

SIDELIGHTS: Shulman was discovered by an editor at Doubleday when he was a college undergraduate writing for the campus humor magazine. The editor was so impressed with the "Shulmanisms" he heard that he encouraged him to write his first novel, *Barefoot Boy With Cheek,* now recognized as a classic of campus humor. Shulman has been a successful humor writer ever since and has garnered such accolades as Al Morgan's description of him as "the master of undergraduate humor, the outrageous pun, and the verbal caricature." Others have compared him to the master of American comedy, S. J. Perelman. Once, Shulman related, he was even accused of copying Perelman and was quite upset until he discussed the situation with Perelman. Perelman told him, "Forget it, I used to be accused of imitating Ring Lardner."

Shulman takes his comedy writing quite seriously. He impressed on interviewer Glen Evans the need for extensive research when writing comedy. "Facts are essential to comedy. Recognizable facts and verifiable details give the appearance of reality you need to make comedy stand up." He also told Evans: "I don't think there's any kind of writing more serious than funny writing—nor more difficult or demanding of more dedication and work hours. It's tough to do (and I know I'll be accused of special pleading here). Just remember, you've got all the rules of fiction to follow in humor writing—plus you've got to make somebody laugh, too."

One of Shulman's most popular works has been the long-running television series "Dobie Gillis." Shulman's novel, *Rally Round the Flag,* was adapted as a popular film starring Paul Newman and Joanne Woodward.

BIOGRAPHICAL/CRITICAL SOURCES: Time: April 10, 1950; *New York Herald Tribune,* August 11, 1957, March 22, 1959; *Nation:* January 1, 1968; *Writer's Digest,* March, 1972.

SIEBENSCHUH, William R(obert) 1942-

PERSONAL: Born August 27, 1942, in Chicago, Ill.; son of Robert William (a professor of political science) and Twila (a teacher and administrator; maiden name, Mouck) Siebenschuh; married Sandra Kent (a production editor), August 21, 1965; children: Ellen Anne, Robert William. *Education:* Grinnell College, B.A., 1964; University of California, Berkeley, M.A., 1966, Ph.D., 1970. *Religion:* Presbyterian. *Home:* 2637 Dartmoor Rd., Cleveland Heights, Ohio 44118. *Office:* Department of English, Case Western Reserve University, Cleveland, Ohio 44106.

CAREER: Fordham University, Bronx, N.Y., assistant professor of English, 1970-78; Case Western Reserve University, Cleveland, Ohio, assistant professor of English and director of composition at the Writers Center, 1978—. *Member:* Modern Language Association of America, National Council of Teachers of English, American Society for Eighteenth Century Studies, Augustan Reprint Society.

WRITINGS: Form and Purpose in Boswell's Biographical Works, University of California Press, 1971; (with Robert T. Mundhenk) *Contact: A Guide to Writing Skills,* Houghton, 1978.

WORK IN PROGRESS: A critical book on the role of fiction methods in factual works; a remedial writing text.

* * *

SIEGLE, Bernard A(ndrew) 1914-

PERSONAL: Born February 25, 1914, in Wilkes-Barre, Pa.; son of Paul and Anna (Evans) Siegle. *Education:* Catholic University of America, B.A., 1941, J.C.B., 1946; St. Thomas Pontifical International University, J.C.L. (cum laude), 1948, J.C.D., 1952. *Office:* St. Francis Seminary, Loretto, Pa. 15940.

CAREER: Entered Third Order Regular of St. Francis (T.O.R.; Franciscans), 1935, ordained Roman Catholic priest, 1944; St. Francis Seminary, Loretto, Pa., assistant cleric master and faculty member, 1944-45; College of St. Teresa, Winona, Minn., chaplain and professor of religion and church history, 1946-47; St. Francis Seminary, professor of canon law and pastoral theology, 1949-51, 1952—, vice-rector and dean, 1953-68, member of board of trustees of Southern Alleghenys Museum of Art, 1976—. Professor at Saints Cyril and Methodius Byzantine Catholic Seminary, 1960-74. Member of Pontifical Commission for the Revision of the Universal Laws of the Catholic Church (Oriental Catholic Church). Member of Provincial Curia of Sacred Heart Province and board of directors of Colleges of the Province, 1966-69. *Officialis* of Metropolitan (Byzantine) Archdiocese of Pittsburgh, Pa., 1969, and chief judge of its Tribunal. Participant in conferences throughout the world. *Member:* International Canon Law Society for Eastern (oriental) Churches both Catholic and Orthodox, Canon Law Society of America (vice-president, 1967-68), Catholic Education Association of America. *Awards, honors:* M.Th. from Pope John Paul II, 1979.

WRITINGS: Marriage Today, Alba, 1966, 3rd edition, 1979. Author of "Canon Law Forum," a weekly column in *Byzantine Catholic World.* Contributor to *New Catholic Encyclopedia* and *Eastern Catholic Life.* Contributor to theology and canon law journals and religious newspapers.

SIDELIGHTS: Siegle writes: "After Vatican Council II, I presented *Marriage Today* for publication. The board at Alba House were very reluctant to publish because they said, 'The Council is finished, new laws will be published soon by the Vatican.' The editor overruled their decision and published it in 1966. Laws are still being revised and formulated to this very year (1979). Nothing was published, as such, namely, a Code of Canon Law by the Vatican. Therefore, *Marriage Today,* was the only book on marriage and was selling world wide.

"It was so popular that in 1972 a 2nd edition was published, updating the 'peacemeal' laws as they were issued by the Vatican. Since 1972 to 1979, many important laws and documents were issued periodically by the Vatican, but as yet, no new Code of Canon Law was published because of conflicts and discussions among the codifiers. In the meantime, I have been gathering these various documents, and various decrees and decisions of the Holy See, especially of the Roman Rota (supreme court) of the Catholic Church, whose jurisprudence in settling marriage cases world wide set the pace for tribunals throughout the world to act accordingly, despite the fact we did not have a Code of Canon Law. In other words, this jurisprudence was to be followed immediately. This we have been doing throughout the world, and especially in the United States. Unfortunately, all this material is not readily available to all people, especially priests, and some bishops and Catholic people because one must acquire these from many sources.

"Since 1972, the time of the 2nd edition publication, I have researched all these with my Canon Law classes and have compiled the material for the 1979 edition in one volume. The Code of Canon Law is not yet published and may not be published for several years. Therefore, *Marriage Today* is the *life-line* of law on marriage in the Catholic Church until a new Code of Canon Law is published by the Vatican. The book contains all the important and essential documents promulgated by the Holy See for today's world.

"Now that I am retired from teaching, I intend to write articles, perhaps some books on such subjects as: 'What would you do in the next ten years to activate in a better way the momentum in the Catholic Church?' I would: (1) Divide archdioceses in the world into smaller dioceses, so bishops would know their priests and people. It is a great honor for an archbishop or a cardinal to govern his people, but 'honor' as such is 'static' and 'passive,' and does not advance the Church's mission. Something should be done about it. (2) Today, people are exposed to good English, to good speaking, to intellectual media through the radio and television, yet the calibre of the Sunday sermons are low grade and inferior in most instances. To advance the cause of the Church, I believe each diocese should have someone appointed in each parish to tape every sermon preached and then have the tape sent to a central office to be examined and graded by experts for diction, content, etc., and reported accordingly. According to one knowledgeable bishop who gave the commencement address at Boston College, some bishops and priests have not read a book in forty years. Hence, I say, the well is dry; so how can we give drink to the thirsty in such a situation?

"These and many other ideas I hope to put into writing."

AVOCATIONAL INTERESTS: Languages (Latin, Italian, French, Russian, Slovak, Polish, Old Slavonic), swimming, skiing, tennis, chess, painting, classical music.

BIOGRAPHICAL/CRITICAL SOURCES: Wilkes-Barre Evening News, June 28, 1966; *Byzantine Catholic World,* November 14, 1971.

SIEVERS, Allen M. 1918-

PERSONAL: Born October 15, 1918, in Boston, Mass.; son of Maurice Jerome (a social worker) and Esther (Bloom) Sievers; married Anita Ress (an educator); children: Marc Jonathan. *Education:* University of Chicago, A.B., 1939; Columbia University, M.A., 1941, Ph.D., 1948. *Home:* 701 I St., Salt Lake City, Utah 84103. *Office:* Department of Economics, University of Utah, Bu0328, Salt Lake City, Utah 84112.

CAREER: University of North Carolina, Greensboro, assistant professor of economics, 1945-48; Tufts University, Medford, Mass., associate professor of economics, 1948-49; University of Massachusetts, Amherst, associate professor of economics, 1949-51; U.S. Department of Commerce, Washington, D.C., chief of economic analysis section in Bureau of Foreign Commerce, 1952-53; University of Florida, Gainesville, professor of economics, 1954-68; University of Utah, Salt Lake City, professor of economics, 1968—, head of department, 1968-71. Member of U.S. delegation to United Nations Economic and Social Council, 1952, 1953; consultant to governments of Korea, Indonesia, and Thailand. *Military service:* U.S. Army Air Forces, 1942-45; became captain. *Member:* American Economic Association.

WRITINGS: Has Market Capitalism Collapsed?: A Critique of Karl Polanyi's New Economics, Columbia University Press, 1948; *General Economics,* Lippincott, 1952; *Revolution, Evolution, and the Economic Order,* Prentice-Hall, 1962; *The Mystical World of Indonesia: Culture and Economic Development in Conflict,* Johns Hopkins Press, 1975.

* * *

SILLS, Beverly 1929-

PERSONAL: Birth-given name, Belle Miriam Silverman; born May 25, 1929, in Brooklyn, N.Y.; daughter of Morris (an insurance broker) and Shirley (Bahn) Silverman; married Peter Bulkeley Greenough (a newspaper editor), November 17, 1956; children: Meredith (Muffy), Peter, Jr. (Bucky); stepchildren: Lindley, Nancy, Diana. *Education:* Graduate of New York City public schools; studied singing with Estelle Liebling. *Agent:* Edgar Vincent Associates., 156 East 52nd St., New York, N.Y. 10022. *Office:* New York City Opera Company, Lincoln Center, New York, N.Y. 10023.

CAREER: Made radio debut as "Bubbles Silverman" on "Uncle Bob's Rainbow House," 1931; appeared on "Major Bowes Capitol Family Hour," 1934-41; made operatic debut as Micaela in "Carmen," 1941; toured with Shubert Tours of Charles Wagner Opera Company, 1950-51; New York City Opera Company, New York City, coloratura soprano, 1955-80, director, 1980—. Made debut with San Francisco Opera as Helen of Troy in "Mefistofele," 1953; with New York City Opera as Rosalinda in "Die Fledermaus," 1955; with Vienna State Opera as Queen of the Night in "Die Zauberflote," 1967; at La Scala in "The Siege of Corinth," 1969; at Royal Opera House, Covent Garden, in the title role of "Lucia di Lammermoor," 1970; with Metropolitan Opera as Pamira in "The Siege of Corinth," 1975. Has appeared at most of the major opera houses in Europe, Latin America, and the United States, and has given recitals throughout the United States. Has made recordings for Columbia, RCA, Angel, and ABC-Audio Treasure. Member of council of National Endowment for the Arts, 1970-76; member of Carnegie Commission on Future of Public Broadcasting; honorary national chairman of March of Dimes Mothers March on Birth Defects, 1972—; chairman of National Opera Institute; member of board of directors of National Foundation for the Arts, Bagby Foundation, and Circle-in-the-Square Theatre. *Awards, honors:* Mus.D. from Temple University, 1972, New York University, 1973; New England Conservatory, 1973, and Harvard University, 1974; Edison Award, 1972, for recording of "Manon."

WRITINGS: Bubbles: A Self-Portrait, Bobbs-Merrill, 1976.

SIDELIGHTS: Beverly Sills is the premier American operatic soprano. Her delightful coloratura voice, superb acting skills, warm personality, and beauty have won her the highest praise from critics in this country and abroad. Sills has appeared in every major opera house in the United States and Europe and has played at many of the lesser-known houses (including an engagement at the Cincinnati Zoo Opera). With her repertoire of almost ninety roles she has won accolades for her performances in numerous operas. She is tremendously popular with American audiences, some of whom know her only from her television appearances on talk and variety shows.

Born Belle Silverman in Brooklyn, New York, Sills began her career at the age of three on a popular children's radio show called "Uncle Bob's Rainbow House." Appearing as "Bubbles," the precocious tot was a regular on the show for four years, and by the age of seven had graduated to regular performances on "Major Bowes Capitol Family Hour." On that program she charmed listeners by tap dancing, chatting with the host, and singing selections from the twenty-two operatic arias she had learned phonetically from the Galli-Curci recordings her mother played at home. She appeared on several radio shows and in films during this time, and also sang the original "Rinso White" commercial jingle, one of the first of its kind.

Sills "retired" from show business at the age of twelve when her parents decided that she should devote more time to her studies. She continued to take singing lessons with Estelle Liebling and piano lessons with Paolo Gallico. Sills began taking voice with Liebling, the voice coach of Amelita Galli-Curci, when she was only seven years old. (Liebling was the only voice teacher Sills ever had.) Liebling and Sills shared a warm personal relationship as well, and the young Sills was often invited to attend musical evenings at Liebling's studio, where she met many musical greats.

After graduation from high school, Sills was taken under the wing of the theatrical impressario J. J. Shubert and toured the country with his Gilbert and Sullivan Opera Company, singing seven different leading roles. She made her operatic debut at the age of seventeen when she sang Micaela in the Philadelphia Civic Opera's production of "Carmen." Following that success, Sills toured with the Charles Wagner Opera Company for two seasons and sang more than forty Violettas and sixty-three Michaelas.

Sills's singing career was accelerating. In 1953 she was invited to San Francisco to sing Helen of Troy in "Mefistofele." From 1952 to 1955 she sang eight auditions for the New York City Opera. Finally she was accepted into the company and made her debut there in October, 1955, as Rosalinda in "Die Fledermaus." Three years later she scored a triumph as Baby Doe in Douglas Moore's opera "The Ballad of Baby Doe"; today she is still regarded as the creator of that role. "Baby became an integral part of my operatic experience," Sills related in her autobiography, *Bubbles: A Self Portrait.* "It was difficult to shake her off even after I left the opera house. If I have ever achieved definitive performances during my career thus far, Baby Doe is one of them."

While on tour with the New York City Opera in Cleveland,

Sills met Peter Greenough, then associate editor of the *Cleveland Plain Dealer,* which was owned by his family. They were married in 1956 in Liebling's studio and Sills became the stepmother of Greenough's three daughters by a previous marriage. A few years later Sills interrupted her career when she and her husband started a family of their own. The Greenoughs' seemingly ideal life was shattered when their two-year-old daughter Muffy was discovered to have a profound hearing loss and two months later their infant son Bucky was diagnosed as severely retarded. The experiences with her children matured and strengthened Sills. "In a strange way," she wrote, "my children had brought me an inner peace. The first question I had asked when I learned of their tragedies was a self-pitying 'Why *me*?' Then gradually it changed to a much more important 'Why *them*?' Despite their handicaps they were showing enormous strength in continuing to live as normal and constructive lives as possible. How could Peter and I show any less strength? After all that had happened, I felt that we could survive anything." Sills has since been very active in helping handicapped children and has served as the honorary chairman of the March of Dimes Mothers March on Birth Defects.

When Sills returned to opera a few years later she related that her career "seemed to be moving along at a faster clip." She was singing in several cities and she returned to the New York City Opera with a portrayal of all the female leads in Offenbach's "Tales of Hoffman," a daring venture that proved to be most successful.

The turning point of Sills's career, though, was her performance as Cleopatra in Handel's "Julius Caesar," which was staged for the official opening of the New York City Opera's new home in the Lincoln Center. Sills herself considers it one of her most memorable performances: "It was—and I don't mean to be immodest, but after all these years I *am* a pretty good judge of performances—one of the great performances of all time in any opera house." Sills received raves from music critics and the public; her reputation as America's leading soprano was secured.

Sills attributed part of the new dimension in her singing to her family problems. She explained that she had learned that it was more important for her to love others than it was for them to love her. "Feeling that way turns your whole life around: living becomes the act of giving. When I do a performance now, I still need and like the adulation of an audience, of course, but my *real* satisfaction comes from what I have given of myself, from the joyful act of singing."

Sills was now in top vocal form and was greatly in demand by American opera companies. She appeared in a number of productions for Sarah Caldwell's opera company in Boston. Another success was her performance in the title role of "Manon" in 1968 and 1969. *New Yorker* critic Winthrop Sergeant was typically appreciative: "If I were recommending the wonders of New York City to a tourist, I should place Beverly Sills as Manon at the top of the list—way ahead of such things as the Statue of Liberty and the Empire State Building."

Despite her status America's most accomplished, celebrated singer, Sills had never sung either in Europe or at the Metropolitan Opera. Sills was one of the few well-known singers who had been trained exclusively in the United States. Until recently American singers were discriminated against by many of the major companies. Sills commented recently that twenty years ago, "if the name was unpronounceable it was automatically a great singer." American singers have finally been recognized in this country and around the world, and Sills was instrumental. Now, she remarked, "American opera stars with perfectly pronounceable names are doing very well. You can't dismiss Price and Horne and Verrett and Arroyo and Milnes and I may immodestly include myself. We're holding our own extremely well. We have arrived. The day of European supremacy, for my taste, is over. We're one of the great art forces—instead of armed forces—of the world."

Rudolf Bing, the general manager of the Metropolitan Opera until 1972, was one of the major detractors of American talent, according to Sills. In her memoirs she stated, "Mr. Bing had a thing about American singers, especially those who had not been trained abroad: he did not think very much of them as singers or of their ability to 'draw' at his opera house."

Sills proved Bing wrong. After her debut at Milan's La Scala in 1969 she was catapulted to international stardom and has since appeared at all the major houses in Europe. In 1975 she was finally invited to make her debut with the Metropolitan Opera. The excitement and intensity surrounding the long-awaited debut was phenomenal. A sixty dollar ticket to her performance as Pamira in Russini's "Siege of Corinth" was the hottest ticket in town. Sills did not disappoint her fans: the performance won rave reviews. A *Newsweek* critic wrote: "Beverly Sills's greatness did not need certification by the Met. With her vocal beauty and a new dimension in acting, she has revolutionized the operatic hierarchy. She is the only American to make a great international career without either singing in Europe first or going to the Met. What the fuss was really about was not her debut with the Met but the Met's debut with Beverly Sills." Sills commented after her performance: "I guess every American singer wants the Met in her obituary. It's nice for my mother, a dream come true. And I'll never have to answer that question again about why I'm not singing at the Met. I was raised believing big-league ball players played for the Yankees and big-league singers sang at the Met. But I'm here to tell you there are great ball players on the Mets and great singers at the New York City Opera."

In 1976 Sills wrote her autobiography, *Bubbles: A Self Portrait,* which further delighted her fans. Peter Allen, a colleague of Sills, remarked, "Miss Sills has no pretensions to literary elegance: She tells her story simply, with remarkable candor, in a straightforward, almost naive style utterly removed from the emotional power and finesse she displays on stage." The critic for the *New York Times Book Review,* Donal Henahan, stated: "She seems unsinkable, and her smiling good nature radiates through her writing just as it does through her singing. This is not deeply introspective or especially revealing writing: Her book sounds as if it were talked at full speed by a totally likable woman who, as she says in connection with her singing career, has never been able to say no."

In January, 1978, Sills announced that she would retire from singing in the fall of 1980: her last performances will be with the San Diego Opera in October. At the same time it was announced that Sills will be the director of the New York City Opera, the company she has been associated with since 1955. She explained: "In 1980, I will be 51. I have no operas left that I want to sing in, and by the time the next year or so is over, I will have recorded everything I ever dreamed of. My voice has served me very well, and I would like to be able to put it to bed, so that it can go quietly and with pride."

There is speculation that Sills's skills as an administrator and fund raiser will be greatly beneficial to the financially ailing New York City Opera. In a recent press conference Sills announced the kick-off of a $12 million fund drive and a $10 thousand competition for a one-act opera written by an American. She has begun to schedule operas for her tenure, and in keeping with her sympathies, the company will remain ninety-five percent American.

BIOGRAPHICAL/CRITICAL SOURCES: Newsweek, October 10, 1966, October 2, 1967, April 8, 1968, October 26, 1970, March 20, 1972, April 21, 1975, July 4, 1976; *Opera News,* February 11, 1967, September 19, 1970, April 19, 1975, February 14, 1976, April 7, 1979; *New York Times* magazine, October 1, 1967; *Esquire,* February, 1968, September, 1974; *Time,* June 7, 1968, October 17, 1969, November 22, 1971, March 4, 1974, April 7, 1975, April 21, 1975, January 23, 1978, December 25, 1978; *Life,* January 17, 1969; *New Yorker,* March 1, 1969, March 6, 1971, October 8, 1973, January 26, 1976; *Saturday Review,* February 28, 1970, April 24, 1971, April 1, 1972; *New York Times,* October 24, 1971, February 11, 1977; Beverly Sills, *Bubbles: A Self Portrait,* Bobbs-Merrill, 1976; *Good Housekeeping,* August, 1976; *Christian Science Monitor,* January 24, 1977; *New York Times Book Review,* March 6, 1977.*

—Sketch by Barbara A. Welch

* * *

SILVER, Gary (Thomas) 1944-

PERSONAL: Born September 6, 1944, in Minneapolis, Minn.; son of Morris Z. (a retail executive) and Bea (a banker; maiden name, Bix) Silver. *Education:* University of California, Berkeley, B.S., 1966. *Office:* Yellow Press, Box 14141, San Francisco, Calif. 94114.

CAREER: Houston Chemical Co., San Francisco, Calif., chemist, 1966-70; free-lance designer, 1970-72; Yellow Press (antiquarian newspaper clipping service), San Francisco, Calif., head of company, 1972—.

WRITINGS: The Dope Chronicles, 1850-1950, Harper, 1979. Contributor to magazines.

WORK IN PROGRESS: A book of press clippings about feminism and images of women, publication by Harper expected in 1980.

SIDELIGHTS: In the early 1970's, Silver began collecting tons of old newspapers and periodicals that were being discarded by libraries. With an accumulation of approximately ten million pages, he founded his antiquarian newspaper clipping service, Yellow Press, and started sorting, categorizing, trading, selling, and collating his archives. He has since organized the massive amount of data into more than one thousand general and specific topics, ranging from natural disasters to political cartoons and chess, many of which he then sold to other collectors, researchers, and institutions. "I kept twenty portfolios of topics to republish myself," Silver told *CA,* "topics which would have a tremendous impact in light of contemporary perspectives on each issue."

Silver's first book, *The Dope Chronicles: 1850-1950,* is an assemblage of clippings from newspapers, magazines, and books that show how the American press treated "the dope menace." The book devotes chapters to Opium, The Drug Crusades, Celebrities and Drugs, The Jazz Age, Marijuana, and other related themes. Silver commented: "I thought the best way to present the material was to collage and juxtapose thousands of anti-dope, scare images into a work which showed that the politics of prohibition were to be feared much more than that which was to be prohibited. Ultimately, it's the collage that's important. It helps to see the different articles side-by-side, juxtaposed, turned inside out, distorted, duplicated. The gestalt, or overall image—the collage—is more important than the content." A reviewer for *HiLife* observed: "In all, this adds up to a fascinating survey of the drug scene in America. . . . No one interested in the subject of the American drug experience can fail to be amused, amazed, and enlightened by this book."

AVOCATIONAL INTERESTS: Backgammon, animation, "the art of assemblage."

BIOGRAPHICAL/CRITICAL SOURCES: San Francisco Bay Guardian, August 11, 1977; *HiLife,* June, 1979.

* * *

SILVER, Roy R. 1918-1979

OBITUARY NOTICE: Born September 27, 1918, in Brooklyn, N.Y.; died September 24, 1979, in Rhinebeck, N.Y. Journalist. Silver was a reporter for the *New York Times* for over thirty-five years, and had become known as the "dean" of the press corps at New York's supreme court. During World War II he served in Europe as a public relations specialist and received a Bronze Star medal and six battle stars. Obituaries and other sources: *New York Times,* September 25, 1979.

* * *

SILVERTHORNE, Elizabeth 1930-

PERSONAL: Born July 18, 1930, in Hot Springs, Ark.; daughter of Joel William (a physician) and Ivy (a teacher; maiden name, Fletcher) MacDonald; married M. Clark Silverthorne (a physician), June 10, 1950 (deceased); children: Carol Ann, Stephen Clark (deceased). *Education:* Attended Rice University, 1946-47, University of Mexico, 1948, and Queens College (now of City University of New York), 1952-53; Texas Woman's University, B.A. (with honors), 1960; North Texas State University, M.A. (with honors), 1961. *Religion:* Episcopalian. *Home:* 4209 Eagle Rd., Temple, Tex. 76501.

CAREER: Secretary in Houston, Tex.; airline stewardess and purser; North Texas State University, Denton, instructor in English, 1962-66; Temple Junior College, Temple, Tex., instructor in English, 1966—, head of department, 1969-79, director of Division of Communications and Modern Languages, 1972-79. Conducted writing workshops; judge of writing competitions. *Member:* National Council of Teachers of English, National Writer's Club, Society of Children's Book Writers, Conference of College Teachers of English, Texas Junior College Teachers' Association, Texas Poetry Society (local charter member), Sigma Tau Delta, Friends of Temple Public Library. *Awards, honors:* Literary awards include first prize from Louzelle Rose Barclay Literature Contest, 1973.

WRITINGS: The Ghost of Padre Island (juvenile), Abingdon, 1975; *First Ladies of Texas,* Stillhouse Hollow Press, 1976; *I, Heracles* (juvenile), Abingdon, 1978. Contributor of articles and stories to magazines, including *Oceans, Images, Mature Years, Young Miss,* and *Lookout.*

WORK IN PROGRESS: Research for a biography of Ashbel Smith, nineteenth-century leader of Texas; "fantasy for middle grades."

SIDELIGHTS: Elizabeth Silverthorne comments: "My favorite recreation is travel, and I do so at every opportunity. This activity has provided settings and inspiration for several of my stories and articles. My interest in history and mythology have also supplied me with ideas and subject matter. The best reward I have received for my writing efforts has been the warm, refreshingly honest, and totally unpredictable response from children."

* * *

SIMMONS, Charles (Paul) 1924-

PERSONAL: Born August 17, 1924, in New York, N.Y.; son of Charles S. (a salesman) and Mary (Landrigan) Simmons; married Helen Elizabeth Fitzgerald, February 8, 1947 (divorced); married Nancy Nicholas, September 17, 1977; children: Deidre, Maud. *Education:* Columbia University, A.B., 1948. *Home:* 221 West 82nd St., New York, N.Y. 10024. *Office:* 229 West 43rd St., New York, N.Y. 10036.

CAREER: Unicorn Press, New York City, picture editor, 1948-51; *New York Times,* New York City, member of staff, 1951-63, assistant editor of *New York Times Book Review,* 1963—. *Military service:* U.S. Army, 1943-46. *Member:* P.E.N. *Awards, honors:* William Faulkner Award for notable first novel, 1964, for *Powdered Eggs.*

WRITINGS: Plots That Sell to Top-Pay Magazines, Funk, 1952; (editor with Nona Balakian) *The Creative Present: Notes on Contemporary American Fiction,* Doubleday, 1963; *Powdered Eggs* (novel), Dutton, 1964; *An Old-Fashioned Darling* (novel), Coward, 1971; *Wrinkles* (novel), Farrar, Straus, 1978.

Contributor of stories, articles, and literary criticism to periodicals, including *Esquire, Saturday Review, New York Times Book Review,* and *New York Times Magazine.*

WORK IN PROGRESS: Planning a novel.

SIDELIGHTS: Simmons's third novel, *Wrinkles,* has been enormously successful with critics. In forty-four short, self-contained chapters he broached a variety of subjects from the perspectives of the past (the narrator's childhood), present (his middle age), and future (his projected old age). "I have never read anything like it," reviewer David Evanier proclaimed. "*Wrinkles* has far more humor and concreteness than Sherwood Anderson, more believability, vulnerability, and real sexuality than Hemingway. Yet it has things in common with both of them: crystalline prose, sharp compression, a strong tactile sense, and, most importantly, a new and probably unduplicable prose form."

The original form of the novel was highly praised. Tony Schwartz likened the technique to "the way Seurat painted: hundreds of tiny strokes, nearly indistinguishable up close, accrete at a distance." Doris Grumbach explained that Simmons "tells a story by fragmenting it by showing the interrelation of its parts out of their proper order." She also noted, "As a result of this careful organization the effect is more like a poem than a piece of prose, and the whole is a serene, passionless but wholly absorbing narrative."

Simmons's subjects are not obscure or intellectualized. His concerns are universal: regrets, birthdays, children, love, anger, authority, animosity, charity, appearances, companionship, duties, gratifications, and fear of death, among other topics, are considered. "In 'Wrinkles,'" Anatole Broyard commented, "Charles Simmons continually discovers what I think of as the poignancy of the unspectacular. He makes me feel the tragicomedy of scale, the fact that we are moved by such small events. The epic implications of being human end in no more than this. We start our lives as if they were momentous stories, with a beginning, a middle and an appropriate end, only to find that they are mostly middles." Robert Towers remarked: "Charles Simmons insists upon an unsparing recognition of our lesser selves, of whatever is mean-spirited, treacherous, ignobly lustful, and generally disreputable in our nature. In Simmons the other elements—the decencies, the tolerances, and the capacity for love—are there too, but they are scarcely emphasized.... Art based upon such lucidity can be bracing rather than depressing—especially when it is shaped with an elegance that transforms the ordinary human muck from which it is lifted."

Reviewer Thomas R. Edwards admired "Mr. Simmons's understanding that, even for intelligent and thoughtful people, experience seldom leads to more than a limited wisdom. Each section of the book ends with a kind of aphorism.... These are good enough to be interesting, but they reassuringly confess that the years haven't brought him much more of the philosophic mind than they've brought the rest of us."

"The novel moves swiftly," a reviewer for *New Republic* wrote, "and yet arrives nowhere, except back in childhood ready to set out on another strand of life; we glimpse the graphic details of a man's life, but never really feel intimate with him. Rather than suspense and strong emotion, there is a steady clarity throughout the book which reveals a flawed and undramatic life emerging from the collage of partial accounts." Earl Shorris commented: "Were it not for the timelessness of form, *Wrinkles* would be unbearably mortal; art demands that the contemplation of death be tempered with births. Simmons has kept his direction in the novel, driving the horses of form and content with balance, composing a novel as clear as ancient music, and playing it remarkably well."

"Self-knowledge—not happiness—is the issue here," Schwartz concluded, "and the hero's pursuit of it is uplifting. At one point, Simmons writes: 'Eventually he will understand that most people have as hard a time in life as he. He will try to make literature from this understanding, but he will not be able to.' Simmons can, however. By celebrating life's wrinkles, he has made marvelous literature."

CA INTERVIEWS THE AUTHOR

CA talked to Charles Simmons in the cafeteria of the *New York Times* one muggy afternoon in early spring, 1979. Simmons has worked on the *New York Times Book Review* as an editor for sixteen years, and seems by now like a fixture around the newspaper. He is a quiet, extremely unassuming person, who nevertheless seems to enjoy talking to an interviewer. In the end the interview takes longer than expected, with both parties lingering over their cups of cafeteria coffee, and with Simmons confiding a number of his hopes and fears about publishing, which, he says, "are not for publication."

Simmons began, after his graduation from Columbia, trying to write short stories that would sell to popular magazines. "I had no success to speak of, though I did sell a couple of early ones to *Esquire.*" Then when he was about thirty-three years old, he began to write what he calls more ambitious stories—"not serious, but at least ambitious." And success struck decisively. "I wrote ten and I sold ten." This early work was published in a number of magazines—*Esquire* again, *Nugget, Noble Savage,* and *Town* magazine in England.

He recalls with a wry grin that some editor once thought of collecting these early stories in book form. "She said they all seemed to be about marital discord, though they were supposed to be comic as far as I was concerned. She also said she thought they probably read better one at a time than as a collection. I think she was quite right." In any case, the collection was never published.

Simmons had been trying to write novels during this period, but without success. "I couldn't seem to get interested enough to get very far." (The matter of pleasing himself in his writing recurs throughout the conversation.) At one point, however, he found that one kind of writing he was doing interested him a great deal and gave him considerable satisfaction: "It was a series of letters I was writing to a friend on the West Coast, describing my life in New York. I was confident that he'd understand my frame of reference, so I could write them in a kind of shorthand, which gave them great immediacy." Simmons decided that he had accidentally hit upon the right tone for a novel, and began to work on what turned out to be his first published novel, *Powdered Eggs*. "It turned out to be a one-way epistolary novel—I stopped writing to my friend while I was working on the book, incidentally." Simmons says he worried about the exposition in the book, feeling that it might be a problem for the reader to get his bearings at first. "I think a reader might wonder after the first section: 'What the hell's going on?' but after that all would become clear."

As in *Wrinkles,* which he published fourteen years later, the book contained a careful mixture of present and past narrative, and Simmons says he was able to write in a free-association sort of way. "The hero in the book was writing about an invisible man—I had had a go at that myself—and the invisible man became a fictional analog for anxiety." The book also contained a series of fables within the main narrative called Very Tales. "I invented these," says Simmons, "though I ascribed them to a character other than the hero."

"There are many generalizations made about a second novel," mused Simmons. "In my case part of the problem was that the first had taken me so long that I wanted to get out quickly with the second. Still, it came very hard." It took seven years and was "a much more traditional comic novel" called *An Old-Fashioned Darling*.

Before *Old-Fashioned Darling* was finished Simmon's long-term marriage broke up, and in the shock, he recalls, "I couldn't seem to concentrate on narrative anymore, so I just did very short essays on basic subjects to keep busy: clothes, food, sex, and so on." Also at this time, he recalls, "I was forty-two years old and beginning for perhaps the first time to think seriously about the future—the fact that my life was finite, and what was going to happen to me?" Years later these preoccupations led to *Wrinkles* taking the form it did: a series of brief exercises, in past, present, and future tenses, examining, almost aphoristically, the various aspects of a man's life.

Simmons concedes that two of his three novels have been essentially experimental in approach. "Sure," he says, "I'd like to be able to write more traditional novels, maybe publish one a year, regularly, and get well paid for it. But the trouble is, I get terribly bored with straight, conventional writing. I guess you could call boredom unexamined anxiety. I'm probably in a perpetual state of anxiety, so I suppose somehow I feel that if I'm doing something that's special to me, that interests me, I have more right to it. In a way, it's coming to terms with the editor inside of me."

Simmons insists that the editor in him is an essential part of him. "I've been an editor at the *New York Times Book Review* for over fifteen years. I like editing, tinkering with language, and that's mostly what I do there." He doesn't actually do much reviewing, by choice, preferring to read for pleasure. As for his own writing, "I find I place my words very carefully, the result of my editing experience. I find words come easily, ideas not so easily. I revise a great deal, trying to get things just right. I probably do ten times as many drafts as most writers, doing each chapter over constantly until I feel it has reached its final form. Sometimes it never does, then eventually I give up and throw it away." There are forty-four chapters in *Wrinkles* and Simmons guesses he gave up and threw away five.

If he did more reviewing, what areas would he be particularly interested in? "Well, it wouldn't be fiction. Actually, I'm passionately interested in photography. I could even imagine writing a book about that, certainly reviewing books in the field. I love reading about it, thinking about it, looking at photographs—I like all those things much more than actually taking pictures myself."

Simmons is sternly self-critical. "If I wrote a book I didn't like, I certainly wouldn't publish it. Money is good, and I want to be paid, and paid well, for what I do, but it really isn't everything."

His favorite writers? Like many writers, particularly critics, Simmons hesitates to offer a list for fear of leaving out someone he cares for but temporarily has forgotten. As a short list, however, he offers for a start John Updike, Philip Roth, early Evan Connell, Muriel Spark, Bernard Malamud, and Richard Yates.

Simmons is working at present on a new novel, "but it's not yet at any kind of stage where I want to talk about it."

BIOGRAPHICAL/CRITICAL SOURCES: Nation, September 30, 1978; *Chicago Tribune,* November 5, 1978; *New York Times Book Review,* November 12, 1978; *New York Times,* November 16, 1978; *New Republic,* November 18, 1978; *Newsweek,* January 1, 1979; *National Review,* January 19, 1979; *New York Review of Books,* January 25, 1979.

—Interview by John F. Baker

* * *

SIMMONS, Edwin Howard 1921-

PERSONAL: Born August 25, 1921, in Paulsboro, N.J.; son of Edwin Lonsdale and Nettie Emma (Vankirk) Simmons; married Frances Bliss, April 25, 1962; children: Edwin Howard, Clarke Vankirk, Bliss, Courtney. *Education:* Lehigh University, B.A., 1942; Ohio State University, M.A., 1955; further graduate study at National War College, 1966-67. *Home:* 9020 Charles Augustine Dr., Alexandria, Va. 22308. *Agent:* Blanche C. Gregory, Inc., 2 Tudor Place, New York, N.Y. 10017. *Office:* Headquarters, U.S. Marine Corps, Washington, D.C. 20380.

CAREER: U.S. Marine Corps, career officer, 1942-78; federal employee, 1978—. Served in the Pacific Theatre, 1943-46, managing editor of *Marine Corps Gazette,* 1946-49, company commander in Korean War, 1950-51, assistant professor at Ohio State University, 1952-55, logistics planner at headquarters in Washington, D.C., 1955-59, naval attache in the Dominican Republic, 1959-60, senior editor for Marine Corps Schools, 1960-62, strategic planner at headquarters, 1962-65, operation and commanding officer in Vietnam, 1965-66, deputy fiscal director in Washington, 1967-70, assistant division commander in Vietnam, 1970-71, director of Marine Corps history and museums in Arlington, Va., 1971—, retiring rank, brigadier general. Member of U.S. Commission on Military History.

MEMBER: American Society of Military Comptrollers (national vice-president, 1967-69; president, 1969-70), American

Military Institute (president, 1979—), Company of Military Historians (fellow), Inter-University Seminar on the Armed Forces (fellow), National War College Alumni Association (vice-president, 1969-70, 1974-75), Marine Corps Association (governor, 1976—), Marine Corps Historical Foundation (founder and vice-president, 1979—), Phi Beta Kappa, Omicron Delta Kappa, Phi Sigma Kappa. *Awards, honors*—Military: Distinguished Service Medal, Silver Star, Legion of Merit with gold star, Bronze Star with gold star, Meritorious Service Medal, and Purple Heart; knight of National Order of Vietnam; Vietnamese Cross of Gallantry with two palms and silver star. Other: Centennial Distinguished Graduate Medallion, 1970, from Ohio State University.

WRITINGS: The United States Marines, Leo Cooper, 1974; *The United States Marines: The First Two Hundred Years, 1775-1975,* Viking, 1976.

Contributor: *The Secret War,* Orbis, 1975; *History of the Second World War,* Cavendish, 1975.

Contributor to encyclopedias, including *Encyclopaedia Brittannica, Dictionary of American History,* and *Academic American Encyclopedia.* Contributor to magazines and annuals.

WORK IN PROGRESS: A military history of Vietnam, completion expected in 1981, publication by Dutton expected in 1982.

SIDELIGHTS: Simmons comments: "When I was very young I was undecided as to whether I wanted to be a soldier, a writer, or a teacher of history. The Marine Corps has given me the opportunity to be all three, particularly for these past seven years that I have been director of Marine Corps history and museums. I am in the fortunate position of being able to combine my avocation with my vocation. I am reminded of Samuel Eliot Morison's advice to young writers: 'Dream your dreams. Aye, and write them too. But live them first.'"

* * *

SIMON, Claude 1913-

PERSONAL: Surname is pronounced See-*moan*; born October 10, 1913, in Tananarive, Madagascar; French citizen by birth; son of Louis (a career officer) and Suzanne (Denamiel) Simon; married Yvonne Ducing, 1951 (marriage ended); married Rhea Karavas, May 29, 1978. *Education:* Educated in France. *Home:* 3 Place Monge, 75005 Paris, France. *Office:* Editions de Minuit, 7 rue Bernard-Palissy, 75006 Paris, France.

CAREER: Writer. *Military service:* French Cavalry, 1939-40; became brigadier. *Awards, honors:* Prix de l'Express, 1960, for *La Route des Flandres;* Prix Medicis, 1967, for *Histoire.*

WRITINGS—Novels in English: *Le Vent,* Editions de Minuit, 1957, translation by Richard Howard published as *The Wind,* Braziller, 1959; *L'Herbe,* Editions de Minuit, 1958, translation by Howard published as *The Grass,* Braziller, 1960; *La Route des Flandres,* Editions de Minuit, 1960, translation by Howard published as *The Flanders Road,* Braziller, 1961; *La Palace,* Editions de Minuit, 1962, translation by Howard published as *The Palace,* Braziller, 1963; *Histoire,* Editions de Minuit, 1967, translation by Howard published under same title, Braziller, 1968; *La Bataille de Pharsale,* Editions de Minuit, 1969, translation by Howard published as *The Battle of Pharsalus,* Braziller, 1971; *Les Corps conducteurs,* Editions de Minuit, 1971, translation by Helen Lane published as *Conducting Bodies,* Viking, 1974; *Triptyque,* Editions de Minuit, 1973, translation by Lane published as *Triptych,* Viking, 1976.

Other novels: *Le Tricheur* (title means "The Cheat"), Sagittaire, 1945; *La Corde Raide* (title means "The Taut Rope"), Editions de Minuit, 1947; *Gulliver,* Calmann-Levy, 1952; *Le Sacre du printemps* (title means "The Crowning of Spring"), Calmann-Levy, 1954; *Orion aveugle* (title means "Blind Orion"), Skira, 1970; *Lecon de choses* (title means "Object Lesson"), Editions de Minuit, 1975.

WORK IN PROGRESS: A novel.

SIDELIGHTS: Though considered one of the most important New Novelists in France, Claude Simon has been slow to gain recognition in the United States. Because at first glance Simon's writing "seems incoherent, merely a series of disconnected fragments, a lyrical but meaningless collection of images," observed Morton P. Levitt, "even a reasonably conscientious reader is apt to be confused by what appears to be, in the worst modern tradition, a narrative experiment without meaning or substance. These impressions are misleading, however, for Simon is one of the finest living novelists."

Four of Simon's novels, *The Grass, The Flanders Road, The Palace,* and *Histoire,* form part of a single work connected by various recurring characters and incidents. The best known of the four is *Histoire,* which won the Prix Medicis in 1967.

Superficially, *Histoire* is "the history of the narrator's story of his family as it is captured on the page by reminiscences of intimately evocative material possessions: the ancestral home, bits of furniture, family portraits, faded album photos and postal cards," stated the *Virginia Quarterly Review.* But Georges Schlocker noted that "the essence of the book lies in the confrontation of its characters with passing time and in the states of mind resulting therefrom." The book attempts to recall and recreate reality, which to Simon is "made up of occurrences scattered in time and space, yet belonging to the same emotional or spiritual experience." As a result, all the characters and events are jumbled together. "The past often invades the present without the usual typographical warnings of a new sentence or paragraph," Leo Bersani observed, "and the mixture is made even more confusing by the fact that the whole novel is written in past tenses. The 'he' referred to in one line may not be the same person as the 'he' mentioned in the next line."

Some critics were put off by the vagaries of the text. For example, the book jacket explains that one of the central occurences in *Histoire* is the "suicide of a cousin adored but somehow betrayed by the narrator." Hugh Kenner complained: "At the publishing house they will have given 'Histoire' more than one reading, and 'somehow' was still the best they could do. ('Hey, George, how the heck shall I say he betrayed her?' 'Somehow.')" But Levitt defended the novel: "If it is incomplete, it is only because the narrator refuses to fill in all the gaps; if it seems disordered, it is because it is the product of a disordered point of view. The narrator fails in his effort to know himself, and, because form and function are here indistinguishable, we can know him only if we can understand the method of his narrative." A *Time* reviewer explained it this way: "Simon is at ease with uncertainties and loose ends. In fact, loose ends are his antennae. How he uses them to convey his own private perceptions is his mystery and his art."

In the tradition of other New Novelists such as Sarraute, Robbe-Grillet, and Butor, Simon attempts to create an awesome awareness of reality through experimentation with different points of view. But Simon transcends the New Novel by exploring the possibilities of language and by sympathetically presenting each of his characters as "a kind of everyman who suffers for all men," noted Levitt. The *Virginia Quarterly Review* contended that "what distinguished 'Histoire' from so many dreary and boring *nouveau roman* attempts at capturing the truths of reality is that Claude Simon structures his remembrances around crucial centripetal happenings that manage to sustain the reader's interest."

Numerous critics have pointed out the influence of Faulkner and Proust on Simon's writing. The *Tri-Quarterly* noted that "a Simon novel translated by an American reads so like a Faulkner novel" because of the long, convoluted sentences, lack of punctuation, abrupt transitions, and confused chronology. Simon himself once commented that *The Sound and the Fury* "truly revealed to me what writing could be. But what I prefer in Faulkner is his Joycean and Proustian side." In a similar vein, Hugh Kenner remarked that "Simon is investing his Proustian material with Faulknerian mechanisms and mannerisms."

BIOGRAPHICAL/CRITICAL SOURCES: Tri-Quarterly, winter, 1967; *Times Literary Supplement,* June 8, 1967, December 24, 1971, July 11, 1975; *New York Times,* November 28, 1967; *New York Times Book Review,* January 21, 1968, July 14, 1968, September 15, 1974; *Time,* March 29, 1968; *Books Abroad,* spring, 1968; *New Republic,* June 8, 1968; *Virginia Quarterly Review,* autumn, 1968, summer, 1971; *Kenyon Review,* Issue 1, 1967; *Spectator,* April 18, 1969, July 19, 1969; *Critique,* Volume XII, Number 1, 1970; *Best Sellers,* April 15, 1971; *Saturday Review,* April 17, 1971; *Contemporary Literary Criticism,* Gale, Volume 4, 1975, Volume 9, 1978; *Washington Post Book World,* August 15, 1976.

* * *

SIMON, Howard 1903-1979

OBITUARY NOTICE—See index for *CA* sketch: Born July 22, 1903, in New York, N.Y.; died October 15, 1979, in White Plains, N.Y. Artist, illustrator, book designer, educator, and author. Simon illustrated more than fifty books, including a number of children's books written by his second wife, Mina Lewiton. He collaborated with Lewiton on *If You Were an Eel, How Would You Feel?* and *Who Knows Where Winter Goes?*. Among the other books he wrote were *500 Years of Art and Illustration, From Albrecht Duerer to Rockwell Kent; Primer of Drawing for Adults;* and *Cabin on a Ridge*. At the time of his death Simon was artist-in-residence at the Barlow School. Obituaries and other sources: *Illustrators of Books for Young People,* 2nd edition, Scarecrow, 1975; *Who's Who in American Art,* Bowker, 1978; *New York Times,* October 17, 1979.

* * *

SIMONOV, Konstantin (Kirill) Mikhailovich 1915-1979

OBITUARY NOTICE: Born November 28, 1915, in Petrograd (now Leningrad), Russia; died August 28, 1979, in U.S.S.R. Poet, novelist, playwright, and journalist. Simonov first distinguished himself as a war correspondent for the Russian *Red Star*. His most famous work, translated as *Days and Nights,* was a direct result of his wartime experiences. The novel, which chronicles the siege and defense of Stalingrad during World War II, was praised for its truthful and non-biased portrayal of the times. Also well-known were the verses dedicated to his wife, translated as *With Her and Without Her*. and a play glorifying the courage of his country-men and women during World War II translated as *The Russian People*. Simonov received a total of five Stalin Prizes, three Orders of Stalin, the Order of the Red Banner, and numerous other honors for his writings. Obituaries and other sources: *Encyclopedia of World Literature in the Twentieth Century,* updated edition, Ungar, 1967; *McGraw-Hill Encyclopedia of World Drama,* McGraw, 1972; *Modern World Drama: An Encyclopedia,* Dutton, 1972; *New York Times,* August 29, 1979; *Washington Post,* August 30, 1979; *AB Bookman's Weekly,* October 8, 1979.

* * *

SIMPSON, Joan Murray 1918-1977

OBITUARY NOTICE: Born December 16, 1918, in London, England; died December 31, 1977, in England. Poet and historical novelist widely known in England for her public poetry readings and recordings. She wrote the novels *Picaflor and the Viceroy* and *A Bracelet of Bright Hair,* as well as three books of verse, including *High Places*. Obituaries and other sources: *Contemporary Poets,* St. Martin's, 1970; *AB Bookman's Weekly,* February 6, 1978.

* * *

SIMPSON, Michael Andrew 1944-

PERSONAL: Born September 7, 1944, in Pretoria, South Africa; came to the United States in 1979; son of Errol F. (a company director) and Margaret Joyce (a company director; maiden name, McIntosh) Simpson. *Education:* Guy's Hospital Medical School, London, M.B., B.S., 1968; University of London, D.P.M., 1972, M.R.C.Psych., 1973. *Office:* Health Sciences Center, Temple University, 3401 North Broad St., Philadelphia, Pa. 19140.

CAREER: Worked as intern; University of London, Guy's Hospital Medical School, London, England, psychiatrist, 1970-73; McMaster University, Hamilton, Ontario, assistant professor of psychiatry, 1973-76; University of London, Royal Free Hospital Medical School, senior lecturer in psychiatry and medicine and senior research fellow in education, both 1976-79; Temple University, associate professor of psychiatry, family practice, and community health, 1979—. Consultant in education, medical education, thanatology, and terminal care. *Member:* International Work Group on Death, Dying, and Bereavement, Royal College of Surgeons, Royal College of Psychiatrists (member of board of examiners). *Awards, honors:* Grande chevalier of Ordre d'Astragale.

WRITINGS: Medical Education, British Medical Association House, 1968; *Medical Education: A Critical Approach,* Butterworth & Co., 1972; *Dying, Death, and Grief,* Plenum, 1979; *The Facts of Death,* Prentice-Hall, 1979; *Clinical Psycholinguistics,* Wiley, 1979; *Psychiatry Self-Tutor,* Heinemann, 1980.

Contributor: Ronald W. Raven, editor, *The Dying Patient,* Pitman, 1975; E. S. Shreidman, editor, *Suicidology: Contemporary Developments,* Grune, 1976; Herman Feifel, editor, *New Meanings of Death,* McGraw, 1977; Horst Noak, editor, *Primary Care and Medical Education,* Croom Helm, 1979; Norman Farberow, editor, *The Many Faces of Suicide,* McGraw, 1979; Hannelore Wass, editor, *Dying: Facing the Facts,* Hemisphere, 1979.

Author of "Simpson Agonistes," a column in *Stress Today,* and "Simpson Speaks," a column in *Pharmedia*. Co-editor of reprint series on death and dying, Arno, 1977. Contributor to medical journals. Senior editor of *Medical Teacher;* member of editorial board of *Death Education, Sexuality and Disability,* and *Essence;* past editor of *Pulse* and *Intermedica.*

WORK IN PROGRESS: The Munchausen Syndrome; Talking With Patients: A Textbook of Clinical Communication Skills; a textbook on terminal care; a textbook on consultation-liaison psychiatry.

SIDELIGHTS: Simpson writes: "I believe that there is no need for an academic book to be dull, or for a popular book to be ignorant. I have generally written books which needed to be written, to draw attention to areas needing action. . . . I cannot write in the morning; I work best at night and in bed, when I can spread my notes about me and write undisturbed. Then I write fast, perhaps completing a book in eight to ten weeks, and in one draft.

"Yet I don't enjoy writing at all. I find some enjoyment in *having written,* but not much. After swiftly examining the first copy of the book, like a mother inspecting her newborn to insure there are only two hands with five fingers on each, that fades. There is satisfaction in the . . . evidence that one's book executes, annoys, moves, and stimulates others. It is *intending to write* that I enjoy most of all, that delicious stage when the ideas and concepts gel. Maybe that's why I keep on writing, because it is only by completing *this* book or article that I can enjoy planning the next one. Once it becomes an actual work physically in progress, there must be another next book to enjoy intending."

* * *

SINGER, Burns
See SINGER, James Hyman

* * *

SINGER, James Hyman 1928-1964
(Burns Singer)

OBITUARY NOTICE: Born April 29, 1928, in New York; died of heart disease in 1964 in Plymouth, England. Poet, translator, critic, and marine biologist who began to write at age six and resolved at seventeen to revolutionize English poetry. After an unhappy, impoverished childhood in Glasgow, Scotland, he traveled to London, Paris, Germany, and Holland and earned his living by teaching, interpreting, and translating. Having once studied zoology at Glasgow University, he worked for a period of four years at the Marine Laboratory in Aberdeen, spending much of that time at sea and writing poetry. He won a reputation as a rising young man of letters for his poems, broadcasts, and contributions to the *Times Literary Supplement,* the *Listener,* and *Encounter* during the 1950's and published *Still and All* in 1957, his only book of poems to appear in his lifetime. Singer's other writings include an account of the Scottish fishing industry, *Living Silver,* the documentary film "Between the Tides," *Five Centuries of Polish Poetry,* and *Collected Poems.* Obituaries and other sources: *Contemporary Poets,* 2nd edition, St. Martin's, 1975; *World Authors, 1950-1970,* Wilson, 1975.

* * *

SINGER, Richard G. 1943-

PERSONAL: Born August 20, 1943, in New York; married Anne Rosenzweig (an attorney), August 13, 1966; children: Laurel, Karyn. *Education:* Amherst College, B.A., 1963; University of Chicago, J.D., 1966; Columbia University, LL.M., 1971, J.S.D., 1978. *Home:* 272 James St., Morristown, N.J. 07960. *Office:* Law School, Rutgers University, 15 Washington St., Newark, N.J. 07102.

CAREER: University of Alabama, Tuscaloosa, assistant professor of law, 1967-69; University of Cincinnati, Cincinnati, Ohio, associate professor of law, 1970-72; American Bar Association, Washington, D.C., director of Resource Center on Correctional Law, 1972-73; Rutgers University, Newark, N.J., professor of law, 1973—.

WRITINGS: (With W. P. Statsky) *Rights of the Imprisoned,* Bobbs-Merrill, 1974; *Just Deserts: Sentencing Based on Equity and Desert,* Ballinger, 1979.

* * *

SINGLETON, Frederick Bernard 1926-

PERSONAL: Born October 13, 1926, in Hull, Yorkshire, England; son of Bernard Nelson (a clerk) and Ethel Ada (Puckering) Singleton; married Elizabeth Anne Croft Andrew (a library assistant), February 23, 1957; children: Elizabeth Anne, Catherine Mary, Andrew Frederick, James Peter. *Education:* University of Leeds, B.A., (with honors), 1950, M.A., 1952. *Home:* 21 Eaton Rd., Ilkey, Yorkshire, England. *Office:* Postgraduate school of Yugoslav Studies, University of Bradford, Bradford BD7 1DP, England.

CAREER: Teacher at grammar school in Bradford, England, 1952-55; Workers Educational Association, organizing tutor for North Yorkshire District, 1955-62; University of Bradford, Bradford, England, lecturer, 1962-68, senior lecturer in geography, 1968—, reader in Yugoslav studies, 1977—, head of Postgraduate School of Yugoslav Studies, 1973—. Television and radio broadcaster. *Military service:* Royal Navy, radar, 1944-47. *Member:* Royal Geographical Society (fellow), Royal Institute of International Studies, British Yugoslav Society, British Association for Soviet and East European Studies (chairperson, 1976-79).

WRITINGS: (With William Edward Tate) *A History of Yorkshire,* Darwen Finlayson, 1960, revised edition, Phillimore Press, 1975; (with M. Heppell) *Yugoslavia,* Benn, 1961, revised edition, 1965; (with Anthony J. Topham) *Workers' Control in Yugoslavia,* Fabian Society, 1963; *Background to Eastern Europe,* Pergamon, 1965, revised edition, 1969; *Industrial Revolution in Yorkshire,* Dalesman, 1970; *Yugoslavia: The Country and Its People,* Queen Anne Press, 1970; *Twentieth-Century Yugoslavia,* Columbia University Press, 1976; (editor) *Environmental Misuse in the Soviet Union,* Praeger, 1976; (editor with Ken Coates) *The Just Society,* Spokesman Books, 1977. Contributor to scholarly journals.

WORK IN PROGRESS: Research on environmental problems; studying the role of the neutral and non-aligned nations in international affairs.

SIDELIGHTS: Singleton comments: "I am interested in contemporary political problems, especially international relations." *Avocational interests:* travel, fell walking.

* * *

SIRROM, Wes
See WEISS, Morris S(amuel)

* * *

SKINNER, Cornelia Otis 1901-1979

*OBITUARY NOTICE—*See index for *CA* sketch: Born May 30, 1901, in Chicago, Ill.; died July 9, 1979, in New York, N.Y. Actress, monologuist, playwright, humorist, and biographer. The theatre was in Skinner's blood: her father, Otis

Skinner, was a matinee idol and her mother, Maude Durbin, was an actress. In 1921 Skinner made her Broadway debut as a member of her father's company in "Blood and Sand." Thereafter she appeared in a number of plays, including "Lady Windermere's Fan," "Major Barbara," "The Searching Wind," and "Candida." Because producers had trouble finding suitable roles for her, Skinner began writing, producing, and starring in her own monodramas. Among them are "The Wives of Henry VIII," "The Loves of Charles II," and "The Empress Eugenie." Renowned for her wit, Skinner turned out a number of humorous books about her life, of which the most famous is *Our Hearts Were Young and Gay*. In her later years she tried her hand at biography, writing about Sarah Bernhardt in *Madame Sarah* and about Howard Lindsay and Russell Crouse in *Life With Lindsay and Crouse*. Obituaries and other sources: *Current Biography,* Wilson, 1964, September, 1979; *The Oxford Companion to American Literature,* 4th edition, Oxford University Press, 1965; *Twentieth Century Writing: A Reader's Guide to Contemporary Literature,* Transatlantic, 1969; *Longman Companion to Twentieth Century Literature,* Longman, 1970; *The Penguin Companion to American Literature,* McGraw, 1971; *Who's Who in the Theatre,* 16th edition, Marquis, 1978; *The Writers Directory, 1980-82,* St. Martin's, 1979; *Washington Post,* July 10, 1979; *Chicago Tribune,* July 10, 1979; *Time,* July 23, 1979; *Newsweek,* July 23, 1979; *AB Bookman's Weekly,* July 30, 1979.

* * *

SKIRPA, Kazys 1895(?)-1979

OBITUARY NOTICE: Born c. 1895 in Lithuania; died August 18, 1979, in Bethesda, Md. Skirpa was at one time prime minister of Lithuania for six weeks before the German forces invaded Russia and deposed the existing government. He moved to the United States after the war and became affiliated with the Library of Congress for over fifteen years, achieving the post of senior librarian. Skirpa was the author of *Uprising for the Restoration of Lithuania's Sovereignty*. Obituaries and other sources: *Chicago Tribune,* August 22, 1979.

* * *

SLADE, Afton 1919-

PERSONAL: Born March 2, 1919, in Salt Lake City, Utah; daughter of Frank Arthur (a lawyer) and Edna (a musician; maiden name, Evans) Johnson; married Sherman Slade (in advertising), September 7, 1940 (divorced); children: Jeffrey Christopher, Steven Richard, Sharon Ann, Mark Douglas. *Education:* University of Utah, B.A. (magna cum laude), 1938. *Politics:* Independent Democrat. *Religion:* Society of Friends (Quakers). *Home and office:* 2456 Azure Coast Dr., La Jolla, Calif. 92037. *Agent:* Roslyn Targ Literary Agency, Inc., 250 West 57th St., Suite 1932, New York, N.Y. 10019.

CAREER: Worked as social secretary, 1941-43, and personal assistant, 1947-49, in Beverly Hills, Calif.; writer, 1950—. Church soloist, 1965-70. President of Stamp Out Smog (member of board of directors, 1958-73) and Footlighters, 1969-70; air pollution consultant.

WRITINGS: (Contributor) Nathaniel Lande, editor, *Mindstyles/Lifestyles,* Price, Stern, 1976; *Stages: Understanding How You Make Moral Decisions,* Harper, 1979. Author of "Outlook From Oak Pass," a column in *Canyon Crier*. Contributor to *Harper's Bazaar*.

WORK IN PROGRESS: A biography of her parents.

SIDELIGHTS: Afton Slade writes: "My interest in yoga and other Eastern disciplines led me into some fascinating research projects. In 1973 I went to India with Dr. Barbara Brown on a funded research trip to study Yoga centers and some of the leading swamis. Excellent work was being done by the Indian government in an effort to find scientific, medical explanations for benefits derived from the five-thousand-year-old system of exercise and meditation—the ancient asanas. With rather primitive equipment, but a lot of ingenious ideas, they were indeed providing a scientific rationale for the yogic practices. I stayed at the Sivananda ashram at Rishikesh, on the headwaters of the Ganges, in very primitive accommodations, and found it a remarkable experience. Rishikesh has been a center of meditation and spiritual life for many generations, and I had an almost palpable feeling of peace and harmony as I looked out over the wide green river. I never found any real magic in meditation, just relaxation; but I do the asanas faithfully and am sure they'll keep me supple on into senility.

"In preparing material for *Mindstyles/Lifestyles* I became involved with Re-evaluation Counseling, a kind of simplistic one-on-one therapy with echoes of Janov's Primal Scream. The idea is to cry and laugh and bring up all the negative emotion you have suppressed since birth in the company of a sympathetic and attentive listener. By this 'discharge' you gain relief and emotional health. Then, in turn, you listen for the same length of time to your partner—the therapist becomes the patient. I felt that the process did really work, to a degree, and certainly was quicker and less expensive than the usual psychiatric treatment. I also joined in the Synanon 'game,' an abusive, verbal battle with people sitting around in a circle yelling four-letter words at each other. It was not for the faint of heart—people screaming what an ass-hole you were to try to challenge your ideas and your picture of yourself. (It made a startling contrast with the dear hearts and gentle people in Re-evaluation Counseling). I believe the Synanon game played a great part in their early success with alcoholics and drug addicts, the power of the group to abuse you, shake you up, and then enfold you in its warmth. Unfortunately, this group power can lead to very negative things as well, as indicated by some of the recent activities described in the press (which I didn't personally experience).

"I was impressed with Dr. Lawrence Kohlberg's theories of moral development, which I studied in preparing for *Stages*. I agree with many of his ideas and think they are a helpful basis for moral education—debate and stimulation of new thinking, rather than indoctrination and preaching. However, I don't think people always reason at the same moral level, but think and act on many different levels as they move through the various areas of their lives. It was interesting to relate thinking typical of groups such as Synanon and others as they fit on Dr. Kohlberg's scale of moral development.

"This smorgasbord of therapies and ideas—all interesting, nearly all helpful—had a major problem. Each group or discipline thought they had a monopoly on the truth—True Believers, doctrinaire, clinging to orthodoxy, refusing to permit any questioning of their basic corpus of belief. In this respect, they were too much like religions, and far too narrow. I'm still sampling the smorgasbord and taking nourishment from each separate dish."

* * *

SLADE, Joseph W(arren) 1941-

PERSONAL: Born August 20, 1941, in Columbus, Ga.; son

of Joseph Warren (in sales) and Nell (Huffman) Slade; married Catherine Anderson, June 23, 1962 (divorced, 1978); married Judith A. Yaross Lee (a professor), December 16, 1978. *Education:* Attended University of Texas, 1960-61; Southern Methodist University, B.A., 1963, M.A., 1964; further graduate study at Rutgers University, 1964-65; New York University, Ph.D (with distinction), 1971. *Politics:* None. *Religion:* None. *Home:* 215 West 101st St., #9-B, New York, N.Y. 10025. *Office:* Communications Center, Brooklyn Center, Long Island University, University Plaza, Brooklyn, N.Y. 11201.

CAREER: Dallas Public Library, Dallas, Tex., bookmobile librarian, 1963-64; New York Public Library, New York, N.Y., librarian, 1964-65; Long Island University, Brooklyn Center, Brooklyn, N.Y., instructor, 1965-70, assistant professor, 1971-74, associate professor, 1974-78, professor of English, 1979—, director of Communications Center, 1977—, and media arts program, 1977—. Adjunct associate professor at New York University, 1970—. Fellow of National Humanities Institute at University of Chicago, 1976-77. *Member:* Modern Language Association of America, Committee of Small Magazine Editors and Publishers, Council of Editors of Learned Journals, Phi Beta Kappa.

WRITINGS: Thomas Pynchon, Warner Paperback, 1974; (contributor) Ray C. Rist, editor, *The Pornography Controversy,* Rutgers University Press, 1975; (contributor) Edward Mendelson, editor, *Thomas Pynchon,* Prentice-Hall, 1978; (contributor) Gerald Nemanic, editor, *Bibliographic Guide to Midwestern Literature,* University of Iowa Press, 1980. Contributor of about fifteen articles to academic journals. Editor of *Markham Review,* 1968—.

WORK IN PROGRESS: A monograph on the history of stag films, publication expected in 1980.

SIDELIGHTS: Slade's interests include technology and literature, technology and culture, pornography, film, and television. He commented: "My writing stresses the impact of technology on American culture in particular, and on the humanities in general."

* * *

SLESSOR, Kenneth 1901-1971

OBITUARY NOTICE: Born March 27, 1901, in Orange, New South Wales, Australia; died June 29, 1971. Journalist, editor, and poet best known for his contribution to the development of modern Australian poetry. He worked for Australian newspapers all his life, principally as an editor, special writer, book reviewer, and leader writer, and became literary editor for the *Sydney Sun* in 1944. His earliest poetry appeared in the influential *Vision* magazine, and demonstrated a Nietzschean exuberance for "Beauty" and "Life." Under the influence of Pound, Eliot, and the Sitwells, however, his poetry focused on technical innovation and rhythmic experiments, and he emerged during the 1930's as one of the two leading voices in Australian letters. His "Captain Dobbin" has been called the Australian "Prufrock," and the elegaic *Five Bells* is considered his best-known and most important work. Slessor's other writings include *Thief of the Moon, Earth Visitors,* and *Cuckoo Contrey*. Obituaries and other sources: *Twentieth Century Writing: A Reader's Guide to Contemporary Literature,* Transatlantic, 1969; *Contemporary Poets,* St. Martin's, 1970; *Longman Companion to Twentieth Century Literature,* Longman, 1970; *The Penquin Companion to English Literature,* McGraw, 1971; *Cassell's Encyclopaedia of World Literature,* revised edition, Morrow, 1973; *World Authors, 1950-1970,* Wilson, 1975.

SLIMMING, John 1927-1979

OBITUARY NOTICE—See index for *CA* sketch: Born March 20, 1927, in London, England; died in 1979 in Hong Kong. Civil servant, novelist, and author of books on the Orient. Slimming held various government jobs in Malaya and Burma before joining the staff of the Hong Kong Information Services. Among his books are *Temiar Jungle: A Malayan Journey, Green Plums and a Bamboo Horse,* and *The Pepper Garden*. Obituaries and other sources: *AB Bookman's Weekly,* August 20, 1979.

* * *

SLONE, Verna Mae 1914-

PERSONAL: Born October 9, 1914, in Caney, Ky.; daughter of Isom B. (a farmer) and Sarah Jane (Owens) Slone; married Willie S. Slone, May 17, 1936; children: Milburn David, Orben Blondel, Losus Agnell, Willie Vernon, Marcel Len. *Education:* Attended high school in Knott County, Ky. *Politics:* Democrat. *Religion:* Baptist. *Home address:* P.O. Box 32, Pippa Passes, Ky. 41844.

CAREER: Owner of gasoline station and grocery store in Pippa Passes, Ken., 1950-72; writer, 1974—.

WRITINGS: In Remembrance, Pippa Valley Printing, 1974; *Common Folks,* Photo Comp, 1978; *What My Heart Wants to Tell,* New Republic, 1979.

WORK IN PROGRESS: Sarah Ellen, a novel based on her own life in the Kentucky mountains; a glossary of "hillbilly" words, expressions, recipes, and short stories.

SIDELIGHTS: Verna Slone told *CA:* "I never wrote anything until I was past sixty. I want to show the other side of mountain life, to dispel some of the myths and misunderstandings. Someone said I was poor and proud of it. Not so. I am poor and not ashamed of it. I would love to prove to others that a person can be happy without all the things most other people count as riches."

Writing in the *New York Times Book Review,* critic Doris Grumbach declared that *What My Heart Wants to Tell* "has some anthropological value." She wrote that "every page of Verna Mae Slone's recollections made me see for the first time beyond the cliches of mountain life." She also summed up the book as a "direct, simply written account of the lives of a family of Kentucky mountain people, the Slones."

BIOGRAPHICAL/CRITICAL SOURCES: New York Times Book Review, May 13, 1979; *Winston-Salem Journal,* May 20, 1979; *Book World,* June 3, 1979.

* * *

SMITH, C. Willard 1899(?)-1979

OBITUARY NOTICE: Born c. 1899 in Pottstown, Pa.; died October 22, 1979, in Lewisburg, Pa. Educator and author. Smith was associated with Bucknell University for over forty years, as professor, chairman of the English department, and secretary of the faculty. He was the author of *Browning's Star Imagery*. Obituaries and other sources: *New York Times,* October 24, 1979; *AB Bookman's Weekly,* November 26, 1979.

* * *

SMITH, Edna Hopkins 1932(?)-1979

OBITUARY NOTICE: Born c. 1932 in Washington, D.C.; died June 25, 1979, in Washington, D.C. Librarian and author. Smith joined the Department of Health, Education and Welfare in 1961, holding such positions as librarian, staff assistant, and program analyst. She wrote publications for both HEW and OEO (Office of Economic Opportunity), and was the co-author of *D.C. Handbook for Lawyers.* Obituaries and other sources: *Washington Post,* June 28, 1979.

* * *

SMITH, Frank Seymour 1898-1972

OBITUARY NOTICE—See index for *CA* sketch: Born November 22, 1898, in London, England; died April 1, 1972, in Sussex, England. Bibliographer, librarian, broadcaster, and author of books on library science and book collecting. Smith was affiliated with W. H.Smith & Son Ltd. as an editor and bibliographer since 1950. He also hosted a radio series of book talks for British Services Abroad for ten years. Smith is best known, however, for *An English Library,* presently in its fifth edition. He was also the author of *The Writer in the Market Place, Build Your Own Library,* and *Bibliography in the Bookshop.* Obituaries and other sources: *The Author's and Writer's Who's Who,* 6th edition, Burke's Peerage, 1971; *AB Bookman's Weekly,* May 15, 1972.

* * *

SMITH, Jessie Carney 1930-

PERSONAL: Born September 24, 1930, in Greensboro, N.C.; daughter of James and Vesona (Bigelow) Carney; married Frederick Douglas Smith, December 2, 1950 (divorced); children: Frederick Douglas, Jr. *Education:* North Carolina Agricultural and Technological State University, B.S., 1950; Michigan State University, M.A., 1956; George Peabody College for Teachers, A.M.L.S., 1957; University of Illinois, Ph.D., 1964. *Politics:* Democrat. *Religion:* Methodist. *Home:* 5039 Hillsboro Rd., #146, Nashville, Tenn. 37215. *Office:* University Library, Fisk University, 17th Ave. N., Nashville, Tenn. 37203.

CAREER: Tennessee State University, Nashville, instructor and head cataloger at library, 1957-60, assistant professor of library science and coordinator of library service, 1963-65; Fisk University, Nashville, Tenn., professor of library science and university librarian, 1965—, director of library training institutes, 1970-75, 1978. Lecturer at George Peabody College for Teachers, 1969—, Alabama A&M University, 1971, and University of Tennessee, 1973. Member of Biomedical Library Review Committee, 1972-76. Member of board of directors of Bethlehem Center, 1965-68. Consultant to U.S. Office for Civil Rights. *Member:* American Medical Library Association (member of council, 1969-71), Association of College and Research Libraries, American Association of University Professors, Links, Southeastern Medical Library Association, Tennessee Medical Library Association (head of college and university section, 1969-70), Beta Phi Mu (president, 1976-77), Pi Gamma Mu, Alpha Kappa Alpha. *Awards, honors:* Fellow of Council on Library Resources, 1969; certificate of achievement from Alpha Kappa Alpha, 1977, for outstanding work in the community and in the library profession.

WRITINGS: Black Academic Libraries and Research Collections: An Historical Survey, Greenwood Press, 1977; (editor) *Directory of Significant Twentieth-Century Minority Women in America,* Gaylord, 1979. Contributor to professional journals. Member of editorial board of *Choice,* 1969-74.

WORK IN PROGRESS: Ethnic Genealogy, publication expected in 1980.

SIDELIGHTS: Jessie Smith writes: "While most of my research and publications have been on black themes, none has been more fascinating or heartwarming than the compilation of the directory of minority women—my most recent book. My research initiated a friendship with more than seven hundred minority women in America. As I prepared their biographies, I have come to know these women well and to understand the sufferings which each endured as a minority and as a woman. The same double bind which they have known I have also endured."

BIOGRAPHICAL/CRITICAL SOURCES: College and Research Libraries, summer, 1965; *Ebony,* June, 1967.

* * *

SMITH, Paul H(ubert) 1931-

PERSONAL: Born June 21, 1931, in East Sparta, Ohio; son of J. Hubert (a minister) and Floy (a teacher; maiden name, Ulm) Smith; married Kathleen Burkley, September 3, 1954 (divorced, 1978); married Virginia Brown (a grant administrator), February 14, 1979; children: Leslie Sue, Spencer A. *Education:* Bowling Green State University, B.S., 1954, M.A., 1955; University of Michigan, Ph.D., 1961. *Religion:* Protestant. *Home:* 8201 16th St., Silver Spring, Md. 20910. *Office:* Library of Congress, Washington, D.C. 20540.

CAREER: Memphis State University, Memphis, Tenn., assistant professor of history, 1960-62; University of Nevada, Reno, assistant professor, 1962-65, associate professor of history, 1965-66, head of department, 1965-66; University of Florida, Gainesville, associate professor of history, 1966-69; Library of Congress, Washington, D.C., historical specialist, 1969-71, editor of *Letters to Delegates of Congress, 1774-1789,* 1971—. *Military service:* U.S. Army, in personnel management, 1952-54. *Member:* American Historical Association, Organization of American Historians, Association of Documentary Editors, Institute of Early American History.

WRITINGS: Loyalists and Redcoats, University of North Carolina Press, 1964; *English Defenders of American Freedoms, 1774-78,* U.S. Government Printing Office, 1972; *Manuscript Sources for the Study of the American Revolution,* U.S. Government Printing Office, 1975; (editor) *Letters to Delegates of Congress, 1774-1789,* U.S. Government Printing Office, Volume I, 1976, Volume II, 1977, Volume III, 1978, Volume IV, 1979.

WORK IN PROGRESS: Editing *Letters to Delegates of Congress, 1774-1789,* Volumes V-XXV, completion expected in 1995; *Congress During the American Revolution,* publication expected "upon retirement in about 1996."

SIDELIGHTS: Smith writes: "I abandoned the academic scene in 1969 because of my disillusionment with students' interest in education, the depersonalized and bureaucratic environment in universities (including large lecture classes and committee and curricular disputes), and the trivialization of my discipline, fueled by professional specialization, overemphasis on research and publication, and narrow concern with peer approval rather than humanistic values. I also wanted the opportunity to work in a great environment with access to primary documents pertaining to the American Revolution."

AVOCATIONAL INTERESTS: Loyalists in the American Revolution.

* * *

SMITH, Robert Ellis 1940-

PERSONAL: Born in East Providence, R.I.; married wife,

Terry (a political consultant), 1966; children: two sons. *Education:* Harvard University, B.A., 1962; Georgetown University, J.D., 1975. *Politics:* Democrat. *Religion:* Protestant. *Office address:* P.O. Box 8844, Washington, D.C. 20003.

CAREER: *Detroit Free Press*, Detroit, Mich., reporter, 1962-63, 1966; *Newsday*, Garden City, N.Y., reporter, 1967-70; Department of Health, Education and Welfare, Washington, D.C., public affairs officer for civil rights, 1970-73; attorney in Washington, D.C., 1975—. Editor and publisher of monthly newsletters, *Privacy Journal*, 1974—, and *Americans Abroad*, 1977-78. Consultant and lecturer on privacy. *Military service:* U.S. Army, 1963-65. *Member:* Newsletter Association of America, Washington Independent Writers.

WRITINGS: (Contributor) Alfred Balk and James Boylan, editors, *Our Troubled Press*, Little, Brown, 1971; (contributor) Grant S. Wilson, editor, *The Right to Privacy*, Wilson, 1976; *Privacy: How to Protect What's Left of It*, Anchor Press/Doubleday, 1979.

Also author and publisher of *Compilation of State and Federal Privacy Laws*, 1975, 1976, 1978. Contributor of articles to periodicals, including *Ms.*, *Washington Post*, *Computer Decisions*, *Family Circle*, and *Los Angeles Times*.

WORK IN PROGRESS: Regular research and writing on "individual privacy and the impact of technology on individuals—specifically computer data banks, lie detectors, wire-taps, and other surveillance devices."

SIDELIGHTS: Smith is an activist journalist who frequently testifies before Congress and other legislative bodies and who argues the case for the consumer in government agencies and business groups. He has been called "the Ralph Nader of privacy." Robert Sherrill called his book *Privacy* "an absolutely essential book for our time." A reviewer for *Business Week* wrote: "The real value of the book is not as a warning of what can go wrong, but as a detailed, amazingly dispassionate, outline of just where intrusions on one's privacy can take place and—the keystone of the enterprise—of what one can do about it. The advice is good and immediately useful."

Smith has published the consumer-oriented monthly newsletter, *Privacy Journal*, since 1974. It reports on new laws, new technology, and new public attitudes affecting the confidentiality of personal information. The *New Yorker* called it "the most interesting publication to come out of the capital since I. F. Stone's walloping *Weekly*."

Smith writes that he also has "an interest in left-handedness—its causes and its impact on people."

BIOGRAPHICAL/CRITICAL SOURCES: *New Yorker*, May 30, 1977; *Washington Post*, June 28, 1977; *New York Times*, October 12, 1977; *New York Times Book Review*, February 18, 1979; *Business Week*, March 5, 1979; *Chicago Tribune*, June 7, 1979.

* * *

SMITH BRINDLE, Reginald 1917-

PERSONAL: Born January 5, 1917, in Bamber Ridge, England; son of Robert and Jane Anne (Staziker) Smith Brindle; married Giulia Laura Maria Borsi (a teacher), April 7, 1947; children: Diana, Olivia, Cloud, Alban. *Education:* University College of North Wales, Bangor, B.Mus., 1949, D.Mus., 1959; Academia de S. Cecilia, diploma, 1952. *Religion:* Roman Catholic. *Home:* Turnpike Cottage, Milford, Godalming Surrey, England. *Office:* Department of Music, University of Surrey, Guildford, England.

CAREER: University of Wales, University College of North Wales, Bangor, lecturer, 1957-62, senior lecturer, 1962-64, reader, 1964-67, professor of music, 1967-70; University of Surrey, Guildford, England, professor of music, 1970—; writer. Broadcaster for Radio Italiana, British Broadcasting Corp., and Canadian Broadcasting Corp. *Military service:* British Army, Royal Engineers, 1940-46, became captain.

WRITINGS: *The Music of Henry Purcell* (in Italian), Radio Italiana, 1960; *La tecnica corale di Luigi Dallapiccola in L'Opera di Luigi Dallapiccola* (title means "The Choral Technique of Luigi Dallapiccola in 'The Work of Luigi Dallapiccola'"), Einaudi, 1965; *Serial Composition*, Oxford University Press, 1966; (editor and translator) Bruno Bartolozzi, *New Sounds for Woodwind*, Oxford University Press, 1967; *Contemporary Percussion*, Oxford University Press, 1969; (editor) Bartolozzi, *Neue Klange fuer Holzblasinstrumente* (title means "New Sonnet for Woodwind"), Mainz, 1971; *The New Music: The Avant-Garde Since 1945*, Oxford University Press, 1975.

Contributor: Howard Hartog, editor, *European Music in the Twentieth Century*, Routledge & Kegan Paul, 1957, revised edition, Penguin, 1961; Malcolm Sargent and Martin Cooper, editors, *The Outline of Music*, George Newnes, 1963; Colin Mason, editor, *The New Music*, Oxford University Press, 1964; F. W. Sternfeld, editor, *A History of Music*, five volumes, Weidenfeld & Nicolson, 1971.

Musical compositions; all published by C. F. Peters: *Sinfonia for Orchestra*, 1954; *Variations on a Theme by Dallapiccola for Orchestra*, 1955; *El Polifemo de Ora for Guitar*, 1956; *Symphonic Variations for Orchestra*, 1957; *String Quartet Music*, 1958; *Homage to H. G. Wells for Orchestra*, 1960; *Genesis Dream for Female Voice and Chamber Orchestra*, 1962; *Creation Epic: A Choreographic Suite for Orchestra*, 1964; *Segments and Variations for Wind Quintet*, 1965; *Orion M.42 for Solo Percussion*, 1967; *Antigone: A Chamber Opera for Narrator, Mezzo-Soprano, Bass, and Chamber Orchestra*, 1969; *Apocalypse for Orchestra*, 1970; *Worlds Without End for Female and Male Reciters, Chorus, Orchestra, and Electronic Tapes*, 1973.

Contributor to *Encyclopaedia Britannica*, *Enciclopedia dello spettacolo*, and *Encyclopedie de musiques sacres*. Contributor of more than a hundred articles and reviews to music journals and newspapers, including *Musical America*.

WORK IN PROGRESS: *Musical Composition*, publication by Oxford University Press expected in 1983.

SIDELIGHTS: Smith Brindle told *CA*: "My writings are almost exclusively in the field of contemporary music, and aim at illuminating and educating students with an enthusiasm for new music. This is not done because I think the music of today is better than that of the past—far from it! But I do believe it is not easy to understand and needs some explanation. Only then can it be a fully rewarding experience and reveal its true value. Nevertheless, I believe that, like music of the past, only a small fraction of present-day music will endure and have permanent value."

* * *

SOCKMAN, Ralph W(ashington) 1889-1970

OBITUARY NOTICE—See index for *CA* sketch: Born October 1, 1889, in Mount Vernon, Ohio; died August 29, 1970, in New York, N.Y. Clergyman, theologian, educator, broadcaster, and author of about twenty inspirational books. Sockman was minister of Christ Church in New York City for over forty years, and became minister emeritus in 1961.

He was chaplain at New York University and associate professor at Union Theological Seminary. Sockman was best known for his participation in the program, "National Radio Pulpit." Obituaries and other sources: *New York Times,* August 30, 1970; *Christian Century,* September 9, 1970; *Newsweek,* September 14, 1970; *Time,* September 14, 1970; *AB Bookman's Weekly,* September 21, 1970; *Current Biography,* Wilson, November, 1970; *Who Was Who in America,* 5th edition, Marquis, 1973.

* * *

SOKOLOFF, Boris Theodore 1889-

PERSONAL: Born November 12, 1889, in St. Petersburg, Russia (now U.S.S.R.); came to United States, 1929; naturalized U.S. citizen, 1933; son of Theodore (a lawyer) and Maria (Verchovtzev) Sokoloff; married Alice Hunt (a writer and composer), June 2, 1912; children: Boris Theodore, Kiril. *Education:* University of St. Petersburg, Ph.D., 1913; Charles University (Prague), Sc.D., 1916; Second Medical School (Petrograd), M.D., 1917. *Home:* 825 Vistabula St., Lakeland, Fla. 33801. *Office:* Southern Bio-Research Institute, Florida Southern College, Lakeland, Fla. 33802.

CAREER: National Institute of Science, St. Petersburg, Russia, head of experimental medicine, 1918-20; University of Brussels, Brussels, Belgium, research fellow, 1923-24; Pasteur Institute, Paris, France, research fellow, 1925-26; University of Prague, Prague, Czechoslovakia, research fellow, 1927; Rockefeller Institute, New York City, medical researcher, 1929-30; Columbia University Cancer Institute, New York City, medical researcher, 1930-31; Washington University Medical School, St. Louis, Mo., resident fellow in pathology department, 1931-35; Columbia University Cancer Institute, resident fellow in physiology and chemistry, 1935-42; Southern Bio-Research Institute, Florida Southern College, Lakeland, Fla., director, 1947—. Managing editor of *Growth,* 1963—. Elected member of All-Russian Constituent Assembly, 1917; secretary of education in North Russian democratic government. *Military service:* Russian Army, 1917-18; became captain; received Order of St. Vladimir. *Member:* American Cancer Research Association, American Chemical Society, American Society of Biology Editors, American Academy of Arts and Sciences, Royal Society of Medicine, Royal Society of Arts and Letters, New York Academy of Sciences.

WRITINGS—In English: *Prestuplenie doktora Garina,* Povolozky, 1927, translation by Sokoloff published as *The Crime of Dr. Garine,* introduction by Theodore Dreiser, Covici-Friede, 1928; *Bio-Dynamics: The Battle for Youth,* Covici-Friede, 1930; *Death of Simon,* Logos Publishing, 1931; *Vitality,* Dutton, 1934; *The Achievement of Happiness,* Simon & Schuster, 1935; *Napoleon, a Doctor's Biography,* Prentice-Hall, 1937, (published in England as *Napoleon: A Medical Approach,* Selwyn & Blount, 1938); *Middle Age Is What You Make It,* Greystone Press, 1938.

Unconquered Enemy, Greystone Press, 1940; *The Civilized Diseases: You Can Cure Them,* Howell, Soskin, 1944; *The Story of Penicillin,* Ziff Davis, 1945 (published in England as *Penicillin: A Dramatic Story,* Allen & Unwin, 1946); *Jealousy: A Psychiatric Study,* Howell, Soskin, 1947 (published in England as *Jealousy: A Psychological Study,* Corroll & Nicholson, 1948); *The Miracle Drugs,* Ziff-Davis, 1949, 3rd edition, Prentice-Hall, 1954; *Science and the Purpose of Life,* Creative Age Press, 1950; *Cancer: New Approaches, New Hope,* Devin-Adair, 1952; *The White Nights: Pages From a Russian Doctor's Notebook,* Devin-Adair, 1956. *Doctor Strand,* Vantage, 1960; *The Mad Philosopher, Auguste Comte,* Vantage, 1961, reprinted, Greenwood Press, 1975; *Chapel of St. Christophe,* Vantage, 1962; *Martha,* Vantage, 1963; *Three Sisters,* Stockwell, 1967; *The Spring in Paris,* Stockwell, 1968; *Carcinoid and Serotonin,* Springer Verlag, 1968; *The Permissive Society,* Arlington House, 1971; *On the Banks of the River Neva,* Stockwell, 1973.

Other: *Na povorotie,* Povolozky (Paris), 1919; *Nauka v Sovietskoi Rossii,* Russkoe universal'noe izd-vo, 1921; *Padenic Sievernoi oblasti,* Slovo (Berlin), 1923, reprinted, Mouton (The Hague), 1970; *Edvard Benesh,* Povolozky, 1926. Also author of *Bolsheviki o bolshevikakh,* 1919, *Spasite dietei,* 1921, *Palach,* 1922, and *Gibel Simona,* 1930.

SIDELIGHTS: As an anti-Communist and a member of the Social-Revolutionary Party, Boris Sokoloff fought Lenin and his Communist party in 1917. In later years he was twice condemned to death as an arch enemy of Communism, but he finally managed to escape to Estonia. With his newly gained freedom Sokoloff continued the scientific studies he had begun at college, most notably, his passionate concern for the cancer problem.

Sokoloff writes: "I am a son of St. Petersburg. Our present is interwoven with our past and future. This bond cannot be destroyed by any circumstances of environment, nor by desire to cut short and to forget our past. Long ago I left Russia. Yet in my dreams, I often see the magnificent whiteness of the snow-covered Neva and I hear the ringing of the church bells and the creaking of the sleighs.

"From my early youth I had a passion for solitary walks. As a boy of ten I would sneak out of our home, often late at night, saying nothing to my parents, and would wander slowly along the banks of the river Neva. I paid no attention to the weather, indifferent to the icy cold, when deep snow covered the streets, or to heat in the summer. Old St. Petersburg was in my bones. It still is, after so many years far from my beloved city.

"To the men born there, this unique city was enchanting. It was created on a whim of Peter the Great, the drunkard, the dreamer, the violent-tempered fighter, the visionary of restrained audacity. To the newcomer, to a stranger, the coldness, the placidity, the abstractedness, the emotionlessness of the city was oppressive, if not hostile. For it was a city of introversion, of split personalities, of the underlying messianic feeling of passion deeply hidden under a reserved and detached behavior. Only a native could love it with tender passion, could feel acutely its soul, its mystical entity, and accept it without reservation as a part of himself. Only the true children of this city could enjoy the silent gloomy nights, the muddy autumns, the dirty canals and rivers. Only they would be enchanted by the snow and savage ice of the winters, the ice breakers of the Neva in the spring, the unsmiling passersby, the small poorly lighted bars where endless talks about the futility of life went on night after night. Only they would accept the beggars, the drunkards, who would engage you on the streets in a conversation about immortality of the soul, the majestic churches and sobors where numerous men and women prayed before the image of Christ.

"Yes, it was a city of ideas, exuberant and vibrant, fermenting in an extreme individualism, conflicting, inspiring, hopelessly foreign to the realities of man's existence.

"Walking in the streets late at night I would stop for many long minutes before the lighted basement windows and watch a group of men and women sitting around a table, drinking interminable cups of tea from a boiling samovar, eating black bread with bologna, smoking endless cigarettes, engaged in philosophical discussion about life and death. I tried, young as I was, to understand their inner life and thoughts, moved deeply by my compassionate proximity to these unknown yet near-to-me humans.

"I belong to the Russian intelligentsia. St. Petersburg was the center of a peculiar multi-million tribe known as the intelligentsia. Nothing comparable to the intelligentsia could have existed in any other country. There is nothing in common between what we in America or Europe call intellectuals, and the Russian intelligentsia of the past. The intelligentsia was inspired and inflamed by compassion, often vague and exaggerated, towards the human race in general and Mother Russia in particular. They believed in democracy, not so much as a political system but as a way of living. They lacked all traces of materialistic tendencies. They lived modestly, if not actually in near poverty. The professional men—physicians, lawyers, engineers, and government clerks, the majority of them belonging to the low or middle class, never looked for, demanded, or even dreamed of improving their economic position. Physicians would never send bills to their patients and if paid by them felt somewhat confused for they believed in the Hippocratic ethics that a physician should devote his life to suffering mankind. Educators and teachers would refuse a better-paid position to take one in some small village where their work was paid occasionally by food stuffs brought by the parents of their students. There is no doubt that they were socialistically minded, but their socialistic beliefs were not formulated in any specific philosophical system. It was much more a Christian attitude than an actual socialistic credo. They were not realistic—they were full of illusions about man and human behavior. They were highly educated on a broad basis, and many of them were highly specialized physicians, scientists of all kinds, and educators.

"Hundreds of books were written about pre-Soviet and Soviet Russia, but a very few, if any in fact, were devoted to describing Russians as individuals. There certainly were no books published about St. Petersburgians as such. Among Russian writers perhaps only Dostoevski, himself a St. Petersburgian, has presented a powerful psychological picture of those who lived and suffered in this city. As a high school student, I was completely obsessed by the writings of Dostoevski. I read again and again, every line he had written. His writings inspired me to follow his steps as a writer."

* * *

SOKOLOWSKI, Robert (Stanley) 1934-

PERSONAL: Born May 3, 1934, in New Britain, Conn.; son of Stanley A. (an aircraft machinist and foreman) and Maryann C. (Drag) Sokolowski. *Education:* Catholic University of America, B.A., 1956, M.A., 1957; University of Louvain, S.T.B., 1961, Ph.D., 1963. *Home:* 620 Michigan Ave., Washington, D.C. 20017. *Office:* School of Philosophy, Catholic University of America, Washington, D.C. 20064.

CAREER: Ordained Roman Catholic priest, 1961; Catholic University of America, Washington, D.C., instructor, 1963-65, assistant professor, 1965-67, associate professor, 1967-71, professor of philosophy, 1971—. Visiting associate professor at New School for Social Research, 1969-70; visiting professor at University of Texas, 1978. *Member:* American Philosophical Association (member of executive committee of Eastern Division, 1978-81), American Catholic Philosophical Association, Metaphysical Society of America, Society for Phenomenology and Existential Philosophy, Deutsche Gesellschaft fuer phaenomenologische Forschung. *Awards, honors:* Younger humanist fellowship from National Endowment for the Humanities, 1971-72.

WRITINGS: The Formation of Husserl's Concept of Constitution, Nijhoff, 1963; (contributor) Lester Embree, editor, *Life-World and Consciousness,* Northwestern University Press, 1972; *Husserlian Meditations: How Words Present Things,* Northwestern University Press, 1974; *Presence and Absence: A Philosophical Investigation of Language and Being,* Indiana University Press, 1978. Contributor to philosophy journals, including *Review of Metaphysics.*

WORK IN PROGRESS: Research on the relation between philosophy and Christian theology; studies in phenomenology.

* * *

SOKOLSKY, George Ephraim 1893-1962

OBITUARY NOTICE: Born September 5, 1893, in Utica, N.Y.; died December 12, 1962. Columnist, author, lecturer, and industrial consultant. Though an eager supporter of the 1917 Russian Revolution, Sokolsky was so disillusioned by the Kerensky and early Lenin regimes that he became an ardent promoter of capitalism and the "American way" of life. He was the editor for two years of the *Russian Daily News* in Petrograd before being deported to China in 1918, where he worked as a reporter, editor, and correspondent for numerous publications, including the *North China Star,* the *Shanghai Gazette,* the *Philadelphia Public Ledger,* the *New York Evening Post,* and the *London Daily Express.* After fourteen years in the Orient, he returned to the United States to write columns for the *New York Herald Tribune* and editorials for the *New York Sun.* He also made weekly radio broadcasts for the National Association of Manufacturers, served as an industrial consultant, and contributed numerous articles to *Liberty* magazine. Sokolsky wrote *Outlines of Universal History, The Tinder Box of Asia, Labor's Fight for Power, We Jews,* and *The American Way of Life.* Obituaries and other sources: *Current Biography,* Wilson, 1941, January, 1963; *New York Times,* April 1, 1963; *Who Was Who in America,* 4th edition, Marquis, 1968.

* * *

SOMERS, Suzanne
See DANIELS, Dorothy

* * *

SOWERS, Miriam R. 1922-

PERSONAL: Born October 4, 1922, in Bluffton, Ohio; daughter of Paul S. (in business and teaching) and Edith (Triplehorn) Hochstettler; married H. Frank Sowers (a furniture designer and sculptor), April 15, 1944; children: Craig V., Keith A. *Education:* Attended Miami University, Oxford, Ohio, 1940-44, Art Institute of Chicago, 1944-46, and University of New Mexico, 1957. *Religion:* Christian Scientist. *Home:* 3020 Glenwood Dr. N.W., Albuquerque, N.M. 87104. *Office:* Symbol Gallery of Art, 2049 South Plaza N.W., Albuquerque, N.M. 87104.

CAREER: Painter, 1944—. Owner of Symbol Gallery of Art, 1961—. Has had group and solo exhibitions; several thousand paintings are represented in galleries and private collections in the United States and Europe, including National Archives and United Nations Gallery. *Member:* Delta Phi Delta (past president), Phi Delta Theta. *Awards, honors:* Prizes from Toledo Museum of Art, 1951, for "Mothers

Jewels," New Mexico State Fair, 1967, for "Goodbyes Are Never"; and Ourax, Colorado National Exhibit, for "Mysterio #2."

WRITINGS: (And illustrator) *Parables From Paradise* (poems), Branden Press, 1976. Contributor to *Albuquerque Tribune.*

WORK IN PROGRESS: Suns of Man, a self-illustrated book of poems about the "sermon on the Mount"; a catalog of "symbolic portraits, magic moral miniatures, and philosophical celebrations."

SIDELIGHTS: Miriam Sowers's specialty as a painter is oils on gold leaf, symbolizing man and nature.

She has written: "Painting comes first. As a poet I am mainly a painter, and as a painter mainly a poet. I title my paintings symbolically because man blended with nature inspires morality and morale.

"In my book [*Parables From Paradise*] I suggest that the creation is Today, and that Nature speaks the Ten Commandments. My drawings of the American southwest, with half-hidden birds, hands, faces, and figures, symbolize morality and hopeful morale, winging from each of us to the other."

AVOCATIONAL INTERESTS: Gardening, swimming, hiking.

BIOGRAPHICAL/CRITICAL SOURCES: Western Review, winter, 1967; *Albuquerque Club Woman,* March, 1969; *New Mexico Cultural News,* May, 1969; *Southwest Art,* April, 1973; *Santa Fe New Mexican,* January 9, 1977.

* * *

SPALDING, Graydon (Edward) 1911-

PERSONAL: Born July 4, 1911, in Windsor, Vt.; son of Charles Daniel (a carpenter and toolmaker) and Gertrude (Hanaford) Spalding. *Education:* Attended Pasadena City College, 1930-31. *Politics:* Independent. *Religion:* Protestant. *Home:* 3151 College St., Costa Mesa, Calif. 92626.

CAREER: Pasadena Playhouse, Pasadena, Calif., actor, 1928-68; Henry E. Huntington Library, Art and Botanical Gardens, San Marino, Calif., supervisor of rare book vaults, 1945-75; writer, 1945—. Actor with Eighteen Actors, Inc., 1951-53, Little Rep, Inc. (also member of board of directors), 1956-59, and with Spectrum Productions, 1971-74. *Military service:* U.S. Army, 1942-45. *Member:* Alumni and Associates of Pasadena Playhouse, Fine Arts Club of Pasadena (vice-president), Rounce and Coffin Club (co-chairperson of Western Books Show, 1953; emeritus member, 1975—).

WRITINGS: How the Grouch Spell Left Mirthwell (juvenile), Harper, 1979.

Author of three-act plays "Kenilworth," "Quentin Durwood," "Never the Morrow," "Requiem for a Genius," "Barcarole," "Framed in Celluloid," "Chivalry Deferred," and "There's a Spot in My Heart." Also author of one-act plays "Seeing Nellie Home," "Murder Will Out," "His Lordship Trumps," and "That Critic."

Contributor to newspapers, *New England Galaxy, Westways,* and to library journals in Glasgow, Scotland.

WORK IN PROGRESS: Bachelor Without Buttons, a biography; *Husband Optional,* a novel based on his theatrical experiences.

SIDELIGHTS: Spalding comments: "Writing plays has been easy. I lived next door to the Townhall in Windsor, Vt., and that brought me in contact with theatrical road companies at an early age—they borrowed 'props' and gave passes to my folks. The chautauqua was another incentive: there, under their tent, I saw Frederick Warde, who had acted in Edwin Booth's Shakespearean company. I was in my twenties when I toured the Avon trail to the literary clubs of Los Angeles with such Shakespearean stalwarts as William Farnum, Richard Vroom, Eric Main, and Fritz Leiber.

"My early student years in Pasadena were given over to printing with moveable type as a possible future occupation. I did compositing and press work from junior high school through city college. At the Huntington Library I ran a Chandler-Price job press for twenty years, in addition to my supervising duties in the rare book vaults. Another privilege there was the use of a flatbed proof press once used at the Kelmscott Press in Hammersmith by William Morris—poet, artist, printer, designer, and typographer.

"The nearness of scholars and writers of national note in my library years did not go unappreciated, but I believe my letters to friends and my journals over the years have been a means of ordering and making my writing alive and enjoyable to others, and my travels to various places in the world have added their gloss (or patina) to my characters and reasoning."

* * *

SPARGO, John 1876-1966

OBITUARY NOTICE: Born January 31, 1876, in Stithians, Cornwall, England; died August 17, 1966. Writer and museum curator who actively worked for the socialist cause in England before coming to the United States in 1901. He wrote and lectured on behalf of the American Socialist Party until 1917, when he left the party because of its opposition to World War I. That same year, he helped Samuel Gompers found the American Alliance for Labor and Democracy and the Nationalist Party. Spargo became the director and curator of the Bennington Historical Museum and Art Gallery in the twenties, a position he held until 1954. He was the author of numerous books about socialism, labor relations, historical matters, and masonry, including *The Bitter Cry of the Children, The Common Sense of Socialism, Karl Marx, Ethan Allen at Ticonderoga, The Consecrated Century,* and *Covered Bridges of Bennington and Vicinity.* Obituaries and other sources: *The Reader's Encyclopedia of American Literature,* Crowell, 1962; *Who Was Who in America,* 4th edition, Marquis, 1968.

* * *

SPARKMAN, G(rady) Temp 1932-

PERSONAL: Born March 25, 1932, in Quebeck, Tenn.; son of James Cooper and Emma Sparkman; married Faye Roy (a child care director and teacher), December 5, 1958; children: Teresa Elizabeth, Laura Suzanna (deceased), Jennifer Lynn. *Education:* Belmont College, A.A., 1953, B.S., 1955; Southern Baptist Theological Seminary, M.R.E., 1957; doctoral study at University of Kansas. *Politics:* Democrat. *Home:* 4954 North College, Kansas City, Mo. 64119. *Office:* Department of Religious Education, Midwestern Baptist Theological Seminary, 5001 North Oak, Kansas City, Mo. 64118.

CAREER: Minister of education at Baptist churches in Paragould, Ark., 1957-59, Pensacola, Fla., 1960-65, Bowling Green, Ky., 1965-68, and Louisville, Ky. 1968-72; Midwestern Baptist Theological Seminary, Kansas City, Mo., associate professor of religious education, 1972—. *Member:* Religious Education Association of the United States and Canada, Association of Professors and Researchers in Religious Education, National Society for the Study of Education, Midwest Religious Education Association (president, 1976-77), Kansas City Society for Theological Studies. *Awards, honors:* First place award from Baptist Sunday School Board, 1968, for hymn text, "Where's the Promise of the City?"; F. Glenn Austin Memorial Award from University of Kansas, 1979-80.

WRITINGS: Leadership Roles for Youth, Convention Press, 1970; *Being Disciple,* Broadman, 1972; (editor and contributor) *Knowing and Helping Youth,* Broadman, 1977; (contributor) Lloyd Householder and John Hendrix, editors, *The Equipping of Disciples,* Broadman, 1977; *Writing Your Own Worship Materials,* Judson, 1979. Work represented in anthologies. Contributor of poems to education journals and denominational magazines.

WORK IN PROGRESS: From the Central Deep, poems; *Time and Event,* inspirational articles; *The Awakening to Faith* (tentative title), a theory of religious education; *Existence and Faith,* completion expected in 1984.

SIDELIGHTS: Sparkman comments: "My poetry and inspirational articles come from being an observer of life and sensitive to people's actions, words, and feelings. I have a strong inner compulsion to interpret in poetry and prose whatever I experience."

He adds: "I am now researching the application of different schools of learning theory (Skinner, Piaget, humanistic, psychoanalytic) to the teaching-learning situation, as these schools influence our understanding of content, methodology, the teacher, pupil, and learning outcomes. I have my own formula for the teaching-learning situation.

"Within the next ten years I want to do limited research on religious thinking and moral reasoning, focusing primarily on the ten-to-fifteen-year-old group, perhaps comparing findings from religious and non-religious settings."

AVOCATIONAL INTERESTS: Painting with oils (semi-professionally), pen sketches, playing (and making) the dulcimer, swimming, basketball, handball.

* * *

SPEETH, Kathleen Riordan 1937-

PERSONAL: Born February 12, 1937, in New York, N.Y.; daughter of John (a mathematician) and Mavis (a literary agent; maiden name, McIntosh) Riordan; married Thomas Charles O'Keefe, Jr., 1954 (divorced, 1957); married Sheridan D. Speeth, 1961 (divorced, 1964); children: (first marriage) Deborah; (second marriage) Lauren. *Education:* Barnard College, B.A., 1959; Columbia University, M.A., 1963, Ph.D., 1967. *Home:* 1196 Curtis St., Albany, Calif. 94706. *Office:* California Institute of Transpersonal Psychology, 250 Oak Grove Ave., Menlo Park, Calif. 94025.

CAREER: Basic Systems, Inc., New York City, senior systems analyst, 1963-66; Xerox Education Group, New York City, educational psychologist, 1966-68; Individual Learning Systems, San Rafael, Calif., materials manager, 1970-71, vice-president, 1971-72; Nymgma Institute, Berkeley, Calif., member of faculty, 1973-77; California Institute of Transpersonal Psychology, Menlo Park, professor of psychology, 1977—. Psychotherapist in private practice, 1978—. Faculty member at Indian Valley College and College of Marin, both 1971-72; instructor at SAT Institute, 1972-76. Consultant to government agencies and educational research companies. *Member:* American Psychological Association, Association for Transpersonal Psychology, Authors Guild, Authors League of America, Sigma Xi.

WRITINGS: (Editor with Philburn Ratoosh) *Introductory Psychology,* Individual Learning Systems, 1971; (contributor) Charles Tart, editor, *Transpersonal Psychologies,* Harper, 1974; *The Gurdjieff Work,* And-Or Press, 1976; (with Ira Friedlander) *Gurdjieff: Seeker of the Truth,* Harper, 1979; (editor with Daniel Goleman) *A Primer of Psychotherapy,* New American Library, 1980.

SIDELIGHTS: Kathleen Speeth writes: "I teach graduate students how to use their attention in a meditative way, in psychotherapeutic interaction. I am deeply interested in the practical help hidden within the sacred traditions of the world."

AVOCATIONAL INTERESTS: Rose gardening, baroque music.

* * *

SPENCER, Zane A(nn) 1935-

PERSONAL: Born May 21, 1935, in Murray, Ky.; daughter of James H. and Patsy Lee (Jones) Story; married Robert J. Spencer (an educator and school principal), August 7, 1954; children: Mark, Michael, Matthew, Leeann. *Education:* Eastern Michigan University, B.A., 1970, M.A., 1975. *Home:* 2173 West Reid Rd., Flint, Mich. 48507.

CAREER: Elementary school teacher in Flint, Mich., 1954-73; Mott Community College, Flint, Mich., instructor in creative writing, 1970-79. Curriculum writer for Kennedy Center, Flint, Mich.; conducts teacher workshops and speaks to school children in association with Michigan Council for the Arts. *Member:* National Writers Club, Flint Writers Club (president, 1968-69).

WRITINGS: Writing Enrichment for Elementary Grades, Mott Publishers, 1969; *Flair* (on creative writing for elementary school students), Educational Service, 1972; *Prevent* (on safety for elementary school students), Educational Service, 1975; *150 Plus* (preschool and kindergarten sourcebook), Fearon, Pittman, 1976; *Writing With Sound and Fun,* Media Materials, 1977; *Following Directions: First Things First,* Media Materials, 1977.

For children: (With Jay Leech) *Cry of the Wolf* (novel), Westminster, 1977; (with Leech) *Bright Fawn and Me,* Crowell, 1979; (with Leech) *Branded Runaway,* Westminster, 1980; (with Leech) *Moon of the Big Dog,* Crowell, 1980. Also author of unpublished book, *Body in Elevator M,* 1974.

WORK IN PROGRESS: Flair II, publication by Educational Service expected in 1981; *Luther Lone Tree,* publication by Crowell expected in 1981.

SIDELIGHTS: Zane Spencer writes: "Writing for teachers and children seemed a natural progression from lesson plans, journals, and diaries when my own four children came along and my teaching career had to be interrupted. After I was free to return to the classroom, I discovered writing was something I could not give up. I loved it. It was part of me and the more I thought about it, the more I sincerely believed I could touch more children through writing than I could through teaching.

"I freely admit that my educational books and speeches are written from a personal soap box. I'm convinced writing is the neglected middle child of the three R's and that this neglect causes many of our problems in education today. Children who are encouraged to think and then express their thoughts on paper clearly, correctly, and creatively develop stronger self concepts. This alone can have a great impact on learning and living.

"Enhancement of the self concept is also the underlying theme of the fiction I have written with my co-author, Jay Leech. Through our writing, we hope to dapple the bumpy road of life with a few coins of moving sunlight.

"Of course, every writer has hopes and dreams for the future. I do too. I have a great idea for an adult novel, and the advice I give myself daily is the same advice I would give to all aspiring writers: *You must believe your ideas are great, but always remember they won't work unless you do.*"

* * *

SPRAGUE, Arthur Colby 1895-

PERSONAL: Born April 16, 1895, in Boston, Mass.; son of Philo Woodruff (a minister) and Harriette Appleton (Woods) Sprague; married Rosamond Kent (a professor), August 3, 1946. *Education:* Harvard University, A.B., 1919, M.A., 1922, Ph.D., 1925. *Politics:* Republican. *Religion:* Anglican Catholic. *Home:* 829 Barnwell St., Columbia, S.C. 29201.

CAREER: Harvard University, Cambridge, Mass., instructor, 1925-30, assistant professor of English, 1930-36; Bryn Mawr College, Bryn Mawr, Pa., associate professor, 1936-50, professor of English, 1950-63, Mary E. Garrett Foundation Professor, 1957-63, professor emeritus, 1963—. Fulbright lecturer at Cambridge University and Royal University of Malta, 1951-52; visiting professor at University of Basel, 1966, and Voorhees College, 1968-70; member of Jesus College, Cambridge. *Military service:* U.S. Army, American Field Service, 1917-19. *Member:* Stratford-on-Avon Shakespeare Society (president, 1973), Philadelphia Shakespeare Society, Players Club. *Awards, honors:* Fellow of Shakespeare Institute, Stratford-on-Avon, England, 1963-65.

WRITINGS: *Beaumont and Fletcher on the Restoration Stage,* Harvard University Press, 1926, reprinted, Benjamin Blom, 1965; *Shakespeare and the Audience: A Study in the Technique of Exposition,* Harvard University Press, 1935, reprinted, Russell, 1966; *Shakespeare and the Actors: The Stage Business in His Plays, 1660-1905,* Harvard University Press, 1944; *Shakespearian Players and Performers,* Harvard University Press, 1953; *The Stage Business in Shakespeare's Plays: A Postscript* (pamphlet), Society for Theatre Research, 1954, Folcroft, 1969; *Shakespeare's Histories: Plays for the Stage,* Society for Theatre Research, 1964; (editor) Samuel Daniel, *Poems and a Defence of Rhyme,* University of Chicago Press, 1965; (with John C. Trewin) *Shakespeare's Plays Today: Some Customs and Conventions of the Stage,* Sidgwick & Jackson, 1970, University of South Carolina Press, 1971. Contributor to literature and theatre journals.

SIDELIGHTS: Sprague writes: "My special subject is Shakespeare on stage and I now spend half my time in England to see the plays."

BIOGRAPHICAL/CRITICAL SOURCES: Joseph Price, *The Triple Bond,* University of Pennsylvania Press, 1975.

* * *

SPRAGUE, Charles Arthur 1887-1969

OBITUARY NOTICE: Born November 12, 1887, in Lawrence, Kan.; died March 13, 1969. Publisher and newspaper editor who became the governor of Oregon in 1939. Sprague was the editor and publisher of the *Ritzville Journal-Times,* the business manager of the *Corvallis Gazette Times,* and the editor and manager of the *Oregon Statesman* before taking political office. When his term of office expired in 1943, he returned to editing and publishing the *Oregon Statesman.* Obituaries and other sources: *Who Was Who in America,* 5th edition, Marquis, 1973.

* * *

SPYRIDAKIS, Stylianos 1937-

PERSONAL: Born January 27, 1937, in Crete, Greece; son of Vasilios (a farmer) and Eleutheria Spyridakis. *Education:* Attended University of Athens, 1955-56; University of California, Los Angeles, B.A., 1960, Ph.D., 1966; graduate study at University of Heidelberg, 1963-64. *Office:* Department of History, University of California, Davis, Calif. 95616.

CAREER: University of Nebraska, Lincoln, assistant professor of history, 1966-67; University of California, Davis, assistant professor, 1967-70, associate professor, 1970-79, professor of history, 1979—. Visiting professor at University of Crete, 1979-80. *Member:* American Hellenic Educational Progressive Association, Pan-Cretan Association of America, American-Hellenic Professional Society of Northern California.

WRITINGS: *Ptolemaic Itanos and Hellenistic Crete,* University of California Press, 1970. Contributor to classical studies journals.

WORK IN PROGRESS: Research on prosopography of ancient Crete, culture of the Aegean, and ancient paganism.

SIDELIGHTS: Spyridakis comments: "I am interested primarily in the history and culture of post-Minoan Crete."

* * *

STAGGE, Jonathan
See WHEELER, Hugh (Callingham)

* * *

STAHLMAN, James Geddes 1893-1976

OBITUARY NOTICE: Born February 28, 1893, in Nashville, Tenn.; died in 1976. Stahlman was the president and publisher of the *Nashville Banner* from 1930 to 1972, and the chairman of the board of the Newspaper Printing Corp. Obituaries and other sources: *The International Who's Who,* Europa, 1974; *Who's Who in America,* 38th edition, Marquis, 1974; *New York Times,* May 3, 1976.

* * *

STALLINGS, Laurence 1894-1968

OBITUARY NOTICE: Born November 25, 1894, in Macon, Ga.; died February 28, 1968. Playwright, screenwriter, editor, and novelist best known for the play he wrote with Maxwell Anderson, "What Price Glory?," which he later adapted for the screen. He was also the editor of the best-selling *The First World War,* told through a collection of photographs and an anti-war perspective. Early in his career, he worked as a reporter for the *Atlanta Journal* and edited a literary column, "The First Reader," for the *New York World.* His other writings include the novel *Plumes,* the operas "Deep River" and "Rainbow," a dramatic version of Ernest Hemingway's *A Farewell to Arms,* and several other screenplays. Obituaries and other sources: *The Oxford Companion to American Literature,* 4th edition, Oxford University Press, 1965; *The Reader's Encyclopedia,* 2nd edition, Crowell, 1965; *The Biographical Encyclopaedia and Who's Who of the American Theatre,* James Heineman, 1966; *The Penguin Companion to American Literature,* McGraw, 1971;

McGraw-Hill Encyclopedia of World Drama, McGraw, 1972; *Modern World Drama: An Encyclopedia,* Dutton, 1972.

* * *

STAMBAUGH, Joan 1932-

PERSONAL: Born June 10, 1932, in Pittsburgh, Pa.; daughter of H. F. (a lawyer) and Elizabeth (a registered nurse; maiden name, Collin) Stambaugh. *Education:* Vassar College, B.A., 1953; Columbia University, M.A., 1955; University of Freiburg, Ph.D., 1958. *Residence:* New York, N.Y. *Office:* Department of Philosophy, Hunter College of the City University of New York, 695 Park Ave., New York, N.Y. 10021.

CAREER: University of Freiburg, Freiburg, Germany, lecturer in English, 1962-63; Vassar College, Poughkeepsie, N.Y., assistant professor of philosophy, 1964-69; Hunter College of the City University of New York, New York, N.Y., began as associate professor, became professor of philosophy, 1969—. Lecturer at Dutchess Community College, 1966-68.

WRITINGS: Untersuchungen zum Problem der Zeit bei Nietzsche (title means "The Problem of Time in Nietzsche"), Nijhoff, 1959; (author of introduction) G. S. Dickinson, *Handbook of Style in Music,* Da Capo Press, 1969; *Nietzsche's Thought of Eternal Return,* Johns Hopkins Press, 1972; *Nietzsche Today,* Syracuse University Press, 1974.

Translator: Ulrich Schneider, *On the Buddhist Origin of the Christian Legend of Placidus,* J.A.S., 1962; (also author of introduction) Martin Heidegger, *Identity and Difference,* Harper, 1969; (also author of introduction) Heidegger, *On Time and Being,* Harper, 1972; (also author of introduction) Heidegger, *The End of Philosophy,* Harper, 1973; (also author of introduction), Heidegger, *Selected Writings,* Harper, 1976; Heidegger, *Being and Time,* Harper, 1980. Also translator of Heidegger's *Schelling on Human Freedom.* Co-editor of "Heidegger Translation Projects," Harper. Contributor of articles and reviews to philosophy journals.

WORK IN PROGRESS: The Real Is Not the Rational.

SIDELIGHTS: Joan Stambaugh's language competence includes French, German, Latin, Greek, Sanskrit, and Swedish. She writes that she has a "strong interest in Buddhism, particularly the work of Japanese twelfth-century thinker, Dogen." *Avocational interests:* Classical piano.

* * *

STANFORD, Melvin Joseph 1932-

PERSONAL: Born June 13, 1932, in Logan, Utah; son of Joseph S. (a professor) and Pearl (Ivie) Stanford; married Linda Barney, September 2, 1960; children: Connie Stanford Tendick, Cheryl Stanford Gordon, Joseph, Theodore, Emily, Charlotte, Charles, Sarah. *Education:* Utah State University, B.S., 1957; Harvard University, M.B.A., 1963; University of Illinois, Ph.D., 1968. *Politics:* Republican. *Religion:* Church of Jesus Christ of Latter-day Saints (Mormons). *Home:* 1163 East 820 N., Provo, Utah 84601. *Office:* Brigham Young University, 203 JKB, Provo, Utah 84602.

CAREER: Arabian American Oil Co., Dhahran, Saudi Arabia, accounting staff analyst, 1963-66; Brigham Young University, Provo, Utah, assistant professor, 1968-69, associate professor, 1969-74, professor of business management, 1974—. Management consultant, 1968—. Visiting professor at Boston University (in Europe), 1975-76. *Military service:* U.S. Air Force, 1951-55, U.S. Army Reserve, 1956—; became lieutenant colonel. *Member:* Academy of Management, American Institute for Decision Sciences, Alpha Kappa Psi, Sons of the American Revolution (state president, 1978-79; member of national board of trustees).

WRITINGS: New Enterprise Management, Brigham Young University Press, 1975; *Management Policy,* Prentice-Hall, 1979. Contributor of more than seventy articles to management journals.

WORK IN PROGESS: Revising *New Enterprise Management;* a book on strategic planning; cases on corporate strategy.

SIDELIGHTS: Stanford writes: "My consulting activity is in business development and new technology. My point of view is that of the general management of the firm and the integration of various business functions in strategic responsibilities. I have lived in the Middle East and in Europe and have traveled widely throughout the world.

"Management cases, which are my particular area of interest in writing, are a unique literary form. I think it is important to portray a professional (as compared to theoretical) viewpoint, by structuring a decision situation as well as conveying background information."

AVOCATIONAL INTERESTS: Skiing, hiking, camping.

* * *

STANTON, Edward F(eagler) 1942-

PERSONAL: Born October 29, 1942, in Colorado Springs, Colo.; son of Edward F., Jr. (self-employed) and Rose (Sunseri) Stanton; married Raquel Diaz, June 16, 1970; children: Daniel E. *Education:* University of California, Los Angeles, B.A., 1964, M.A., 1969, Ph.D., 1972. *Office:* Department of Spanish and Italian, University of Kentucky, Lexington, Ky. 40506.

CAREER: University of Kentucky, Lexington, assistant professor, 1972-78, associate professor of Spanish and Italian, 1978—. *Member:* Modern Language Association of America, Phi Beta Kappa.

WRITINGS: The Tragic Myth, University Press of Kentucky, 1978. Contributor of articles, poems, tranlations, and reviews to literary journals in the United States and abroad, including *Antioch Review, Epoch,* and *New River Review.*

WORK IN PROGRESS: A study of Ernest Hemingway and Spain; editing *Jose Basilio da Gama's "Uruguay"* with Frederick C. H. Garcia; *Rages and Ennuis* (poems).

* * *

STANTON, Maura 1946-

PERSONAL: Born September 9, 1946, in Evanston, Ill.; daughter of Joseph (a salesman) and Wanda (a nurse; maiden name, Haggard) Stanton; married Richard Cecil, 1972. *Education:* University of Minnesota, B.A., 1969; University of Iowa, M.F.A., 1972. *Residence:* Tucson, Ariz. *Office:* Department of English, University of Arizona, Tucson, Ariz. 85721.

CAREER: Poet and novelist. Associated with State University of New York at Cortland, 1972-73, University of Richmond, 1973-77, Humboldt State University, 1977-78, and University of Arizona, 1978—. *Awards, honors:* Yale Younger Poets Prize, 1974; National Endowment for the Arts grant, 1974; Frances Steloff Fiction Award, 1975.

WRITINGS: Snow on Snow (poems), foreword by Stanley Kunitz, Yale University Press, 1975; *Molly Companion* (novel), Bobbs-Merrill, 1977. Contributor of poetry to *American Review* and *Poetry*.

SIDELIGHTS: Stanton's poetry is known for its bitter irony and unusual metaphors and themes. Terry Eagleton commented: "Maura Stanton's *Snow on Snow* is a strikingly mature first work, full of eloquent, spontaneously lyrical pieces which combine bizarre Freudian fantasy with a sharply realistic intelligence. The complex and inventive imagery flows too fast to cloy, and though the craftsmanship isn't obvious, most of the poems are unobtrusively shaped and controlled beneath their apparently random surfaces."

Reviewers have compared Stanton's poetry to that of Sylvia Plath. Vernon Young remarked: "A comparison with Sylvia Plath may be alarming yet it is, I think, inevitable: [in *Snow on Snow* there] is the same imperilled hermeticism, the same wizard capacity for transmuting an inner nightmare (of frigidity, metamorphosis, explosion) in a coherent but exotic complex of images, often under the aspect of the mythopoeic memory. At incandescent junctures, the always beautifully integrated poem threatens to consume itself in its own tranquil fury; it never does: the crisis, dire and insupportable, finds its agonized, mollifying musical resolution."

J. D. McClatchy also likened Stanton to Plath "with a flat, midwestern accent." He continued: "[She] has layered her confessional excerpts with effective dramatic monologues—both imaginative and allusive—that vary the volume's tonality. Both sustain a similar thematic concern: the inability to sort motives from consequences. We are not lost *in* experience, but *from* experience. . . . Stanton is strongest when she combines her fabular instinct with her persistent anxiety." Lorrie Goldensohn also admired Stanton's use of myth. She wrote: "The complex changes rung on her basic counters—brain, whiteness, stone, skin, water and air—create a literally fluid balance of tone. It seems in keeping, then, that so many of the voices of the poems are also fluid, or ambiguously split in point of view. Irony may be comfortable to this poet because it can straddle value possibilities; because it supports a boundary-sitting consciousness always testing the thought of crossing over. Stanton's most successful poems are frequently revisions of myth, ambiguously poised black comedy where the bite of the retelling is downward and satirical."

A section of the poetry collection was called "Extracts from the Journal of Elisa Lynch," and was written in the voice of the Irish mistress of the nineteenth-century dictator of Paraguay. Stanton received a grant to do research in Paraguay and developed the poems into a novel, *Molly Companion*. Stanton wrote: "I was more interested in the rumor and legend surrounding the war than in actual fact, so that Molly Companion, while utilizing real historical characters and events, is more mythical than historical. At the same time, I think it accurately depicts the terror of a country, like modern day Uganda, in the grip of an insane dictator."

Stanton disagreed with her critics, telling *CA*, "The poems in *Snow on Snow* are really not 'confessional.' I have read Sylvia Plath, of course, but I don't think of her as an influence." She also told *CA* that "Henry James is the writer most important to my work."

BIOGRAPHICAL/CRITICAL SOURCES: Saturday Review, April 19, 1975; *Yale Review,* autumn, 1975; *Village Voice,* December 15, 1975; *Hudson Review,* winter, 1975-76; *Stand,* Volume 17, number 1, 1975-76; *Parnassus: Poetry in Review,* spring-summer, 1976; *Library Journal,* October 1, 1977; *Contemporary Literary Criticism,* Volume 9, Gale, 1978.

STAPLETON, Richard John 1940-

PERSONAL: Born November 3, 1940, in Corpus Christie, Tex.; son of Richard Gathwright (in business) and Ida Belle (an accountant; maiden name, Coston) Stapleton; married Virginia Marie Luchsinger (a music teacher), April 1, 1969; children: Jonathan Richard. *Education:* Texas Tech University, B.S., 1962, M.B.A., 1966, D.B.A., 1969. *Home:* 111 Holly Dr., Statesboro, Ga. 30458. *Office:* Department of Management, Georgia Southern College, Statesboro, Ga. 30458.

CAREER: Wolfforth-Frenship Gazette, Wolfforth, Tex., founder and publisher, 1962-65; Texas Tech University, Lubbock, instructor in economics, 1966-69; University of Southwest Louisiana, Lafayette, associate professor of management, 1969-70; Georgia Southern College, Statesboro, associate professor, 1970-77, professor of management, 1977—. *Member:* International Transactional Analysis Association, International Entrepreneur's Association, Independent Consultants of America, Southern Management Association.

WRITINGS: Managing Creatively: Action Learning in Action, University Press of America, 1976; *De-Gaming Teaching and Learning: How to Motivate Learners and Invite OKness,* Effective Learning Publications, 1979; *How to Learn How to Succeed,* Effective Learning Publications, 1980. Contributor to education, economic, and management journals. Associate editor of *Southern Business Review*.

SIDELIGHTS: Stapleton commented: "In high school I decided I wanted to be a writer. In college I decided to become a businessman. As it has turned out, both writing and making money have been avocations. My career has been devoted largely to teaching business, but I still haven't give up on really making it as a writer and businessman."

* * *

STARK, George Washington 1884-1966

OBITUARY NOTICE: Born February 22, 1884, in Detroit, Mich.; died January 29, 1966. Journalist and broadcaster whose daily feature column in the *Detroit News* and weekly radio program sought to recapture the atmosphere of a bygone Detroit. He was instrumental in the campaign to erect the Detroit Historical Museum, and was appointed city historiographer of Detroit. Stark was the author of *In Old Detroit* and *City of Destiny,* and co-author with his wife, poet Anne Campbell, of *Two Heads Are Better.* Obituaries and other sources: *Who Was Who in America,* 4th edition, Marquis, 1968; William W. Lutz, *The News of Detroit,* Little, Brown, 1973.

* * *

STEBBINS, Theodore Ellis, Jr. 1938-

PERSONAL: Born August 11, 1938, in New York, N.Y. *Education:* Yale University, B.A., 1960; Harvard University, J.D. (with honors), 1964, M.A., 1966, Ph.D., 1971. *Home:* 57 Hedge Rd., Brookline, Mass. 02146. *Office:* Museum of Fine Arts, Boston, Mass.

CAREER: Smith College, Northampton, Mass., instructor in art history, 1967-68; Yale University, New Haven, Conn., lecturer, 1968-71, assistant professor, 1971-75, associate professor of art history and American studies, 1975-77, associate curator of "Garvan Collections of American Art," 1968-77, curator of American painting and sculpture, 1971-77, acting director of art gallery, 1975; Museum of Fine Arts, Boston, Mass., curator of American painting, 1977—. Visiting professor at Boston University, 1978; lecturer at museums, galleries, and scholarly meetings. Member of board of trustees of Wyeth Endowment for the American Arts and American Federation of the Arts. *Member:* Friends of American Art at Yale (chairperson).

WRITINGS: (Editor and contributor) *Martin Johnson Head,* Museum of Fine Arts (Boston, Mass.), 1969; *The Life and Works of Martin Johnson Heade* (monograph and catalog), Yale University Press, 1975; (with John Caldwell and Carol Troyen) *American Master Drawings and Watercolors: A History of Works on Paper From Colonial Times to the Present,* Harper, 1976; (author of introduction) *Dennis Miller Bunker Rediscovered,* New Britain Museum of American Art, 1978; *Close Observation: Selected Oil Sketches by Frederic Edwin Church,* Museum of Fine Arts (Boston, Mass.), 1978. Author of exhibition catalogs. Contributor to *Art Works: Law, Policy, Practice,* edited by Stephen Weil and Franklin Feldman, 1974, and *The Hudson River School: Nineteenth-Century American Landscapes in the Wadsworth Atheneum,* Wadsworth Atheneum, 1976. Contributor to *Britannica Encyclopedia of American Art.* Contributor of articles and reviews to art and art history journals. Member of editorial board of *American Art Journal.*

* * *

STEEL, Anthony Bedford 1900-1973

OBITUARY NOTICE—See index for *CA* sketch: Born February 24, 1900, in Dehra Dun, India; died October 3, 1973, in England. Educator, administrator, historian, and author. Steel was a life fellow in history at Christ's College, Cambridge University. He was also vice-chancellor of the University of Wales for several years, and principal of University College. Steel was the author of several books on history and a contributor to the *Cambridge History of the British Empire.* Obituaries and other sources: *AB Bookman's Weekly,* December 3, 1973.

* * *

STEEL, Eric M. 1904-

PERSONAL: Born Feburary 11, 1904, in Paisley, Scotland; came to United States, 1938; naturalized U.S. citizen, 1945; son of William Henry and Elizabeth (Elder) Steel; married Madeleine Chevrot, May 15, 1937; children: Diana Steel Rarig. *Education:* University of Caen, Licence-es-lettres, 1924; Glasgow University, M.A., 1925; Columbia University, Ph.D., 1941. *Home:* 44 West Ave., Brockport, N.Y. 14420.

CAREER: Writer. Antioch College Preparatory School, Yellow Springs, Ohio, teacher and director of glee club, 1926-28; Chateau de Bures School, Paris, France, teacher, 1928-30, headmaster, 1930-37; Brooklyn Polytechnic Institute, Brooklyn, N.Y., instructor in English, 1938-42; State University of New York College at Brockport, Brockport, N.Y., professor of French and English, 1942-62, director of dramatics, 1942-48, tennis coach, 1948-63, chairman of modern languages department, 1962-69, member of faculty, 1969-74. *Member:* Amnesty International, American Humanistic Society, Modern Languages Association, Americans United for the Separation of Church and State (president of Rochester, N.Y., chapter). *Awards, honors:* Chevalier des Palmes Academiques from Societe des Palmes Academiques, New York, 1972(?).

WRITINGS: Diderot's Imagery: A Study of a Literary Personality, Corporate Press, 1941; *Readable Writing,* Macmillan, 1950; *Cyrano de Bergerac* (five-act; adapted from the play by Edmond Rostand), Barron's Educational Series, 1970; *Polyeucte* (five-act; adapted from the play by Corneille), Barron's Educational Series, 1970.

Plays: "Joseph the Dreamer" (three-act), first produced in France, 1932; "A Good Man's Love" (two act), first produced in Brockport, N.Y., 1945; "And I Will Be Heard" (one-act), first produced in Rochester, N.Y., 1948;"Don Quixote de la Mancha" (four-act; adapted from the novel by Cervantes, *Don Quixote),* first produced in 1950; "Epilogue to Moliere's Imaginary Invalid," first produced in Brockport, 1960.

Verse adaptions: "Tartuffe" (five-act; adapted from the play by Moliere), first produced in Brockport, 1961; "School for Wives" (five-act; adapted from the play by Moliere), first produced in 1964.

Contributor of articles to newspapers and periodicals, including *Romanic Review, Rochester Times-Union,* and *Brockport Republican-Democrat.*

WORK IN PROGRESS: "Short easy pieces."

SIDELIGHTS: Steel told *CA*: "I retired at seventy and though not old (I hope that a man is not old until he spends more money on pills than he does on liquor), I have had to give up tennis. . . . I am still active in Amnesty International and Americans United for the Separation of Church and State, but not as active as I would like to be. And I still walk my poodle, of whose quasi-divine nature I am daily more convinced."

AVOCATIONAL INTERESTS: Golf, gardening.

* * *

STEELE, Dirk
See PLAWIN, Paul

* * *

STEFFEK, Edwin F(rancis) 1912-

PERSONAL: Born August 1, 1912, in New York, N.Y.; son of Frank and Pauline (Dolezal) Steffek; married Elizabeth Esdale, February 14, 1941; children: Edwin Francis, Jr., Janice E. Steffek Jeneral, Deborah M. Steffek Romig. *Education:* University of Massachusetts, B.S., 1934. *Home and office:* 10 Cedar Hill Rd., Dover, Mass. 02030.

CAREER: Massachusetts Horticultural Society, Boston, assistant editor of *Horticulture,* 1937-49; *House Beautiful,* New York City, staff horticulturist, 1949-50; *Popular Gardening,* New York City, horticultural editor, 1950-63; Massachusetts Horticultural Society, editor of *Horticulture,* 1963-75, editor emeritus, 1975—. Public lecturer; also worked in advertising and public relations. Charter delegate to Massachusetts Conservation Council; member of Massachusetts Roadside Council. Member of Dover Republican Town Committee. Founder and first executive director of Open Space Action Committee; past commissioner of parks and recreation in Darien, Conn.; past member of Darien special commission on conservation; founder and past member of board of trustees of Darien Parkland Association. *Military service:* U.S. Army Air Forces, Air Transport Command, 1942-46.

MEMBER: American Horticultural Society, Men's Garden Clubs of America (member of national board of directors), American Rose Society, American Rock Garden Society (New England chairperson and treasurer), Garden Writer's Association of America, New England Wild Flower Society (member of board of trustees), New England Rose Society,

Massachusetts Horticultural Society, Horticultural Club of Boston, Gardener's and Florist's Club of Boston. *Awards, honors:* Citation from American Horticultural Society, 1976.

WRITINGS: Wild Flowers and How to Grow Them, Crown, 1954; *Pruning Made Easy,* Holt, 1958, revised edition published as *The Pruning Manual,* Van Nostrand, 1969; *Gardening the Easy Way: The Homeowner's Complete Guide to Gardening,* Holt, 1961; *The Gardener's Almanac,* Massachusetts Horticultural Society, 1967; (with G. Jay Gogue) *Tree Repair,* National Park Service, U.S. Department of the Interior, 1975.

Editor: *Rock Gardens and What to Grow in Them,* Hale, Cushman & Flint, 1937; *Herbs: How to Grow Them and How to Use Them,* Hale, Cushman & Flint, 1939; *The Vegetable Garden,* Hale, Cushman & Flint, 1939; *Begonias and How to Grow Them,* Hale, Cushman & Flint, 1940; *The Lawn: How to Make It and How to Maintain It,* Hale, Cushman & Flint, 1940; *The Gardener's Travel Book,* Oxford University Press, 1949; *Plant Buyer's Guide of Seed and Plant Materials in the Trade,* Massachusetts Horticultural Society, 1949; *The Marshall Cavendish Illustrated Encyclopedia of Gardening,* Marshall Cavendish Corp., 1971; *Home Growing: Your Complete Guide to Growing Vegetables, Fruit, and Herbs,* St. Martin's, 1977; *The Weekend Gardener,* Butterick, 1978.

Contributor: *House Plants: A Complete Book on Plant Care,* Banner, 1975; *An Illustrated History of Gardening,* Paddington, 1978.

Also consulting editor and general editor of botanical guides.

SIDELIGHTS: Steffek told *CA:* "It is my belief that books in specialized fields such as gardening and the outdoors should make a distinct contribution; the author should contribute something to the store of knowledge that has not been there heretofore. Also, it has been my hope, during these past many years of writing, editing books and magazines, and lecturing, to increase the pleasures people receive through gardening and related fields by helping them to be more successful and to encourage others to share in these pleasures and satisfactions."

* * *

STEINBERG, Saul 1914-

PERSONAL: Born June 15, 1914, in Romanic-Sarat, Romania; came to United States, 1942; naturalized U.S. citizen, 1943; son of Maurice (a box manufacturer) and Rosa (a cakemaker; maiden name, Jacobson) Steinberg; married Hedda Lindenberg Sterne (a painter), October 11, 1943. *Education:* Attended University of Bucharest, 1932; Reggio Politecnico (Milan), Dottore Architettura, 1940. *Home:* 3 Washington Sq., New York, N.Y. 10012. *Office:* c/o *New Yorker,* 25 West 43rd St., New York, N.Y. 10036.

CAREER: Artist. Worked as cartoonist in Milan, Italy, for *Bertoldo,* 1936-39; practicing architect in Milan, 1939-41; free-lance cartoonist and illustrator, 1941—; writer, 1949—. Artist-in-residence at Smithsonian Institution, 1967. Has held numerous one-man exhibitions, including Museum of Modern Art, 1946, Galerie Mai, Paris, 1953, and Sidney Janis Gallery, 1973. *Military service:* U.S. Naval Reserves, 1943-46; became lieutenant. *Awards, honors:* Gold Medal from American Academy of Arts and Letters, 1974.

WRITINGS—All self-illustrated: *All in Line,* Duell, Sloan & Pearce, 1945; *The Art of Living,* Harper, 1949; *The Passport,* Harper, 1954, reprinted, Random House, 1979; *The Labyrinth,* Harper, 1960; *The Catalogue: A Selection of Drawings Reprinted From The Art of Living, The Passport, and The Labyrinth,* World Publishing, 1962; *The New World,* Harper, 1965; *The Inspector,* Viking, 1973. Artwork represented in numerous collections, including *Drawings,* R. Piper [Munich], 1958, and *Saul Steinberg: Zeichnungen, Aquarelle, Collagen, Gemaelde, Reliefs, 1963-1974,* Koelnischer Kunstverein, 1974. Contributor of writings and artwork to periodicals, including *Harper's Bazaar, Life,* and *New Yorker.*

SIDELIGHTS: "The life of the creative man is led, directed and controlled by boredom," said Steinberg. "Avoiding boredom is one of our most important purposes. It is also one of the most difficult, because the amusement always has to be newer and on a higher level." Perhaps this explains both Steinberg's creative expansion and his increasing recognition as an artist. He has long been revered for his cartoons and his cover-art for *New Yorker.* But in the 1970's he has been acknowledged as an equally creative painter with both oils and water colors, and his incorporation of random items such as sales receipts and bags have been hailed for inventiveness and charm. "I want the minimum of performance in my work," declared Steinberg. "Performance bores me. What interests me is the invention. I like to make a parody of bravura. You have to think of a lot of my work as some sort of parody of talent."

Steinberg's art mimics numerous styles: cubism, pointalism, constructivism, children's art, and others. Reiterating Steinberg's notion of art as parody, Donald Goddard wrote: "To doubt the work's validity as art plays into the esthetic confusion Steinberg himself sets up through constant references to other styles. . . . Yet the nagging thought remains that the pictures are not art but conglomerations of conventions into which a momentary, cartoony life has been pumped by an excess of cleverness. This is the ultimate paradox; the imitation of art produces an esthetic reality, defined as fake." Goddard then reported that Steinberg's manipulation of art "is compounded in the still-life tables of 1971-73, in which even the pencils, pens, and brushes, rulers and other tools used to make art are faked, whittled in wood."

Steinberg's artistic roots are in cartooning and it is for this work that he is best known. "As a cartoonist," observed Walter Robinson, "Steinberg has access to a sensibility somehow outside both figurative and abstract 20th-century traditions." Indeed, Steinberg often refers to his cartoons as "writings." Art critics are quick to cite him as one of those rare artists capable of combining form, style, and humor. As Robinson noted, "Steinberg is one of the few whose work shows how the pragmatically human side of art finds its home in the artist's compulsive love of form." This is exemplified in numerous works of Steinberg's, beginning with "Self Portrait" in 1945, which show an artist creating himself. "The drawing which makes itself has become a Steinberg trademark," noted Robinson, "and he uses variations of it often in his cartoons and drawings to remind us of his own presence as artist."

Because Steinberg employs such a variety of styles, he defies categorization. "Steinberg's work does not have much bearing on the rest of postwar art history," wrote Mark Stevens. "He is too ironic and detached to be linked closely to the abstract expressionists, and he is much too much the wordly philosopher to be linked to pop art." Instead of adapting his art to new concepts, Steinberg adapts the concepts to his art. "His work is a powerful fusion of past and present in which he is the main protagonist," wrote Goddard.

During the 1970's, Steinberg viewed his recognition as a "serious" artist as "one of the biggest satisfactions of my life." But it is doubtful whether the newfound popularity will influence him. "I think of myself as being a professional," he told Robert Hughes. "My strength comes out of doing work which is liked for itself, and is successful by itself, even though it is not always perfectly accessible. I have never depended on art historians or the benedictions of museums and critics. That came later. Besides I like work to be on the page. I never like to sell the object."

BIOGRAPHICAL/CRITICAL SOURCES: Nation, December 19, 1966; *Art in America,* November 1970, September/October, 1978; *New Yorker,* December 26, 1970; *Horizon,* April, 1978; *New York Times Magazine,* April 16, 1978; *Newsweek,* April 17, 1978; *Time,* April 17, 1978; *Vogue,* May, 1978; *People,* May 29, 1978; *National Review,* July 7, 1978; *ARTnews,* summer, 1978; *Forbes,* December 25, 1978.*

* * *

STENHOUSE, David 1932-

PERSONAL: Born May 23, 1932, in Surrey, England; son of Jack F. M. (a psychiatrist) and May McLeod (a nurse; maiden name, MacNeill) Stenhouse; married Kathleen Kane, 1956 (divorced, 1978); children: May, John, David J., Andrew, Douglas, Alan. *Education:* University of Saskatchewan, A.A., 1950; University of Otago, B.A., 1955, M.A. (honors), 1958, B.Sc., 1958. *Politics:* Independent. *Religion:* Christian. *Residence:* Palmerston North, New Zealand. *Agent:* Bionui Enterprises Ltd., 2 Karaka St., Palmerston North, New Zealand. *Office:* Department of Education, Massey University, Palmerston North, New Zealand.

CAREER: New Zealand Marine Department, Dunedin, fisheries officer, 1955-57; University of Otago, Dunedin, New Zealand, lecturer in zoology, 1957; University of New Zealand, Lincoln College, Canterbury, lecturer in zoology, 1958-59; University of Queensland, Brisbane, Australia, lecturer in zoology and psychology, 1960-65; Massey University, Palmerston North, New Zealand, senior lecturer in education, 1966—. Member of corporate boards of directors. *Military service:* Royal New Zealand Naval Volunteer Reserve, 1951-53. *Member:* International P.E.N., Institute of Biology (London), Academy of Zoology, Association for the Study of Animal Behaviour, Educational Standards Association.

WRITINGS: Crisis in Abundance, Heinemann, 1966; (editor and contributor) *Unstated Assumptions in Education: A Cross-Cultural Investigation,* Hicks, Smith, 1972; *The Evolution of Intelligence: A General Theory and Some of Its Implications,* Barnes & Noble, 1974; *Active Philosophy in Education and Science,* Allen & Unwin, 1979; *Towards the Pacific Civilization: Critical Issues in Polynesian Education in New Zealand,* Sweet & Maxwell, 1980; (contributor) Zvi Lamm, editor, *New Trends in Education,* Yachav Publishing, 1980. Contributor of articles to professional journals and popular magazines, including *Nature, Interchange,* and *British Journal of Education Studies.*

WORK IN PROGRESS: The "Ethnology-and-Intelligence" Paradigm in the Behavioural and Social Sciences; Evaluation of Pupils, Teachers, Exams, and Education Systems; Instinct and Intelligence in History: A Re-Interpretation of Toynbee's Thesis; Neglected Problems in Human Evolution.

SIDELIGHTS: Stenhouse commented: "I am deeply concerned about the world crisis of population versus resources and the need to re-adapt, on a world scale, involving all our social, political, economic, and educational systems. Our human intelligence has created our problems but also provides the only means of dealing with them. I want to understand better the nature of intelligence and how it can be made more effective in society. This must involve changes in education and social thinking. I'm endeavoring to play a part, further to what has already been done, in some of the crucial theoretical areas, specifically in the improvement of education so that it will enhance both individual and societal adaptability."

* * *

STEPHENS, Reed

See DONALDSON, Stephen R.

* * *

STERN, Bill 1907-1971

OBITUARY NOTICE: Born July 1, 1907, in Rochester, N.Y.; died of a heart attack, November 19, 1971, in Rye, N.Y. From 1939 to 1971, Stern was annually named the most popular sports announcer in the United States by the Nation's Radio Editors. A regular member of the NBC Special Events staff since 1937, his play-by-play accounts were peppered with colorful, flamboyant anecdotes about the sports world that won him both millions of listeners and a few sports-page critics. According to Stern, Thomas A. Edison went deaf when, as a boy, he was hit in the head by a ball while batting in a baseball game; the pitcher, he contended, was Jesse James. He also once stated that President Abraham Lincoln's dying words inspired Colonel Abner Doubleday to invent the game of baseball. Stern was familiar to movie-goers as the voice behind MGM's "News of the Day," and he worked in his later years for the Mutual Broadcasting System. Obituaries and other sources: *Current Biography,* Wilson, 1941, January, 1972; *New York Times,* November 20, 1971; *Who Was Who in America,* 5th edition, Marquis, 1973.

* * *

STERN, Laurence (Marcus) 1929-1979

OBITUARY NOTICE—See index for *CA* sketch: Born June 16, 1929, in New York, N.Y.; died August 11, 1979, in Martha's Vineyard, Mass. Journalist and author. After working briefly for the U.S. Information Agency, Stern landed a job with the *Washington Post.* While serving as a member of the *Post* staff, he covered Vietnam, Cambodia, Laos, Cyprus, the Middle East, London, Paris, and Greece. Among the honors he received for his work in journalism were the George Polk Memorial Award, the Headliners Club Award, and the Newspaper Guild Award. Stern was the author of the highly praised book, *The Wrong Horse,* on U.S. interventionist policies in Cyprus. In 1978 he assisted Charles Krause and Richard Harwood in the five-day marathon writing of *The Guyana Massacre.* Obituaries and other sources: *Washington Post,* August 13, 1979.

* * *

STERN, Simon 1943-

PERSONAL: Born September 12, 1943, in London, England; son of Peter Francis and Honour (Sayer) Stern; married Sylvia Caveney (an author and teacher), 1972; children: Suzannah. *Education:* Attended London College of Printing & Graphic Arts, 1960. *Home:* 19 Corringham Rd., London N.W.11, England.

CAREER: Worked for various publishers in production and design; free-lance book illustrator, 1969—. *Member:* National Union of Journalists, Association of Illustrators, Society of Authors.

WRITINGS—All self-illustrated; all juvenile: (Editor) *The Life and Fables of Aesop,* Taplinger, 1970; *The Hobyahs,* Prentice-Hall, 1977; *Mrs. Vinegar,* Prentice-Hall, 1979.

"Astonishing Adventures of Captain Ketchup" series: *Neptune's Treasure,* Methuen, 1972; *Moon Trip,* Methuen, 1973; *Jungle Journey,* Methuen, 1974; *Kidnapped,* Methuen, 1976.

WORK IN PROGRESS: Researching, reading, and illustrating folk tales, "in particular a ludicrously ambitious set of illustrations to a Russian folk tale called 'Marko the Rich' which is going so slowly it may never see the light of day."

SIDELIGHTS: Stern told *CA:* "When I was about ten years old I was given two huge books of fairy tales. One was a complete Grimm; the other a book of Russian tales. Fairy tales have fascinated me ever since, and when I decided to be an illustrator, it was these stories that I most wanted to illustrate.

"I do my own adaptations because no one else has offered to do it, and because that way I get the whole royalty."

* * *

STEVENS, Harold 1917-

PERSONAL: Born June 7, 1917, in Philadelphia, Pa.; son of Louis and Lillian Stevens; married wife, Estelle (a biochemist), August 13, 1940. *Education:* Temple University, B.S., 1940, B.F.A., 1940, M.F.A., 1947; also City College of New York (now of the City University of New York). *Office:* Department of Art, C. W. Post Center, Long Island University, Greenvale, N.Y., 11548.

CAREER: Instructor in art at Pratt Institute, New York Institute of Technology, and other institutions of learning; Long Island University, C. W. Post Center, Greenvale, N.Y., associate professor of art, 1968—. Artist (painter). *Military service:* U.S. Army Air Forces, 1942-46; became first lieutenant.

WRITINGS: Ways With Art: Fifty Techniques for Teaching Children, Reinhold, 1963; *Art in the Round: Elements and Materials of Three-Dimensional Design,* Reinhold, 1965; *Design in Photo-Collage,* Reinhold, 1968; *Transfer: Designs, Textures, and Images,* Davis Publications, 1975, reprinted as *Relief and Design Transfer: Creating a Three-Dimensional Illusion on a Flat Surface,* Hawthorn, 1975. Contributor of science fiction to *Fantastic.*

WORK IN PROGRESS: "I am organizing material for a book on stereography which will deal with various ways of achieving spatial illusion with stereo graphic painting, drawing, design, and photography."

SIDELIGHTS: Stevens told *CA:* "Although I am primarily a painter, I enjoy writing because it involves similar artistic problems. Organizing words and ideas into a coherent, self-contained structure is much like arranging colors and shapes into a unified, expressive composition.

"Art, of course, is a language in its own right. A painting need not—and cannot—be translated into words. It can be explained technically, and described physically, but its intrinsic meaning must partly remain a mystery. For this reason I confine my writing to the objective and technical side of art. I am certain that if I tried to write about the subjective art experience, I would feel that I am imposing cold-blooded rationality and order upon something that should be emotionally direct, intuitive, and spontaneous. An artist should be careful never to invade the privacy of his own mind."

* * *

STEVENS, Harvey A(lonzo) 1913-

PERSONAL: Born October 20, 1913, in West Allis, Wis.; son of Daniel Augusta (a construction contractor) and Genevieve Alice (Kingston) Stevens; married Irene Josephine Borkowski, June 22, 1940; children: Patricia Ann Stevens Kasten. *Education:* University of Wisconsin, Milwaukee, B.S., 1939; graduate study at University of Wisconsin, Madison, 1946-48. *Home:* 606 Morningstar Lane, Madison, Wis. 53704. *Office:* Waisman Center on Mental Retardation and Human Development, University of Wisconsin, 1500 Highland Ave., Madison, Wis. 53706.

CAREER: High school teacher of mentally retarded children in South Milwaukee, Wis., 1939-43; Northern Wisconsin Colony and Training School (now Northern Wisconsin Center for the Developmentally Disabled), Chippewa Falls, principal, 1944-46; Wisconsin Department of Public Instruction, Bureau of Handicapped Children, Madison, state supervisor of classes for the mentally retarded, 1946-48; Southern Wisconsin Colony and Training School (now Southern Wisconsin Center for the Developmentally Disabled), Union Grove, superintendent, 1948-55; Edward R. Johnstone Training and Research Center, Bordentown, N.J., superintendent, 1955-58; Central Wisconsin Colony and Training School (now Central Wisconsin Center for the Developmentally Disabled), Madison, superintendent, 1958-69; Wisconsin Department of Health and Social Services, Madison, director of Wisconsin Bureau of Mental Retardation, 1969-72; University of Wisconsin, Madison, program administrator at Waisman Center on Mental Retardation and Human Development, 1972-79; emeritus program administrator, 1979—. Lecturer at University of Wisconsin, Madison, 1966-69. Cochairperson of International London Conference for the Scientific Study of Mental Deficiency, 1960; member of White House Conference on Mental Retardation, 1963; member of joint U.S.-Canadian Committee on Manpower and Training, 1971; member of Federal Hospital Council of U.S. Department of Health, Education & Welfare, 1972-76; head of mental retardation planning and implementation committee of Wisconsin Department of Health and Social Services, 1967-68. Participant in international and national forums and conferences; consultant to U.S. Public Health Service. *Military service:* U.S. Army, supervised training of illiterate soliders, 1943-44.

MEMBER: International Association for the Scientific Study of Mental Deficiency (first president, 1964-67; member of council, 1967-73; honorary vice-president, 1973-79; honorary president, 1979—), Council for Exceptional Children (past member of board of governors), American Association on Mental Deficiency (life member; member of council, 1954-55; president, 1964-65; head of planning board, 1969-70), American Association of University Affiliated Programs (member of council, 1973-79; vice-president, 1973-74; president, 1974-75), Mexican Association for the Scientific Study of Mental Deficiency (honorary president, 1967), Venezuelan Association for the Scientific Study of Mental Deficiency (honorary president, 1967), Brazilian Association for the Scientific Study of Mental Deficiency (honorary president, 1967), Wisconsin Association for Retarded Citizens (founding member; member of Mental Retardation Research Institute, 1972—), Wisconsin Conference on the Retarded (founding member). *Awards, honors:* Distinguished service award from Wisconsin Association for Retarded Citizens,

1963; Joseph P. Kennedy International Award for Leadership in the Field of Mental Retardation from Joseph P. Kennedy Foundation, 1968; distinguished service citation from Wisconsin Academy of Sciences, Arts, and Letters, 1969; leadership award from American Association on Mental Deficiency, 1973.

WRITINGS: (Editor with Rick Heber, and contributor) *Mental Retardation: A Review of Research,* University of Chicago Press, 1964; (with Julian W. Clark) *Understanding and Helping the Mentally Retarded,* Division of Mental Hygiene, Wisconsin Department of Public Welfare, 1965; (with James Jerome McCarthy) *Program Development for Severely Retarded, Institutionalized Children,* University of Wisconsin, Madison, 1969; (with Earl Edward Balthazar) *Managing the Mentally Retarded Through Interdisciplinary Action* (monograph), Research Department, Central Wisconsin Center for Developmentally Disabled, 1971; (with Balthazar) *The Emotionally Disturbed, Mentally Retarded,* Prentice-Hall, 1975; (with William Sloan) *A Century of Concern: A History of the American Association on Mental Deficiency, 1876-1976,* American Association on Mental Deficiency, 1976.

Contributor: Maria E. Frampton and Elena C. Gall, editors, *Special Education for the Exceptional Child,* Volume III, Sargent, 1956; M. Michael Klaber, editor, *Conference on Residential Care,* University of Hartford, 1968; David Gibson and R. I. Brown, editors, *Managing the Severely Retarded: A Sampler,* C. C Thomas, 1976; Peter Mittler, editor, *Research to Practice in Mental Retardation,* Volume I: *Care and Intervention,* University of Park Press, 1977. Contributor to *International Encyclopedia of Neurology, Psychiatry, Psychoanalysis, and Psychology.* Contributor of more than forty articles to scholarly journals.

WORK IN PROGRESS: Revising *Mental Retardation: A Review of Research,* with Rick Heber, publication by University of Chicago Press expected in 1981; research on ethical issues in mental retardation, alternatives to residential living, the effectiveness of group homes for the retarded, and the protection of human subjects for research.

SIDELIGHTS: Stevens comments: "Most of my writing has been directed toward various aspects of the care, treatment, and training of mentally retarded individuals. In addition, I have attempted to express my deep concern for the rights of the mentally retarded, and have commented on administrative aspects of programs serving the mentally retarded on local, state, and national levels. In my work and writings I describe new patterns and directions for residential and community programs. I have expressed caution and concern for programs that are based upon emotional concerns rather than research findings.

"My writings will continue to emphasize that the mentally retarded still tend to be isolated and rejected by the community. Public attitudes toward them have basically remained the same over the past fifty years. Achieving social acceptance, economic independence, and integration into all aspects of community living is still to be achieved. Many of the profound and severely mentally retarded still require continuous twenty-four-hour supervision, care, and treatment for their survival, and many more are dependent upon society to improve their quality of life. In my writings I will continue to inform the public and legislatures about proven ways to improve the quality of life of these individuals."

* * *

STEVENSON, Burton Egbert 1872-1962

OBITUARY NOTICE: Born November 9, 1872, in Chillicothe, Ohio; died May 13, 1962. Journalist, librarian, author, and editor best known for his anthologies, including *The Home Book of Verse; The Home Book of Modern Verse; The Home Book of Quotations; The Home Book of Proverbs, Maxims, and Familiar Phrases;* and *The Standard Book of Shakespeare Quotations.* He began his career as the city editor of the *Chillicothe Daily News* and the *Daily Advertiser,* but left journalism to become a librarian at the Chillicothe Public Library in 1899. He later founded the American Public Library in Paris, France. Stevenson's writings include some forty novels, mystery stories, books for children, and the play "A King in Babylon." Obituaries and other sources: *The Reader's Encyclopedia,* 2nd edition, Crowell, 1965; *Who Was Who in America,* 4th edition, Marquis, 1968.

* * *

STEVENSON, John Albert 1890(?)-1979

OBITUARY NOTICE: Born c. 1890 in Woonsocket, S.D.; died October 29, 1979, in Washington, D.C. Scientist and author. Stevenson was head of the Agriculture Department's division of mycology and disease survey. He was the author of numerous articles and two technical books. Stevenson received many awards, including the Agriculture Department's superior service award. Obituaries and other sources: *Washington Post,* November 3, 1979.

* * *

STEWART, Bill 1942(?)-1979

OBITUARY NOTICE: Born c. 1942; died June 20, 1979, in Managua, Nicaragua. Journalist. Stewart was an ABC-News correspondent in Nicaragua at the time of his death, reporting on the fighting between the Sandanista rebels and the National Guard of President Anastasio Somoza. He had been stopped at a roadblock by the guardsmen, ordered out of his van, told to lie face down on the ground, and shot. Stewart's killing was described as an execution by press colleagues who witnessed the shooting. In protest, many of the U.S. journalists left Nicaragua after the incident. Obituaries and other sources: *Detroit Free Press,* June 21, 1979; *New York Times,* June 30, 1979; *Newsweek,* July 16, 1979.

* * *

STEWART, Lawrence D(elbert) 1926-

PERSONAL: Born November 7, 1926, in Champaign, Ill.; son of Delbert A. (an artist) and Lucile (Boyer) Stewart. *Education:* Attended St. Norbert College, 1944, and University of West Virginia, 1945; Northwestern University, B.Sc., 1948, M.A., 1949, Ph.D., 1952. *Religion:* Congregationalist. *Home:* 356 South Clark Dr., Beverly Hills, Calif. 90211. *Office:* Department of English, California State University, Northridge, Calif. 91330.

CAREER: University of California, Los Angeles, instructor, 1952-54, assistant professor of English, 1954-55; archivist for Ira Gershwin in Beverly Hills, Calif., 1955-68; California State University, Northridge, assistant professor, 1969-73, associate professor, 1973-77, professor of English, 1977—. Fulbright lecturer in Isfahan, Iran, 1977-79, and in Hyderabad, India, 1979. American Studies Research Center, Hyderabad, India. *Military service:* U.S. Army, Signal Corps, 1944-46. *Member:* Modern Language Association of America, Friends of the Princeton University Library, Friends of the University of Texas Library, Phi Beta Kappa.

WRITINGS: *John Scott of Amwell,* University of California Press, 1956; (with Edward Jablonski) *The Gershwin Years,*

Doubleday, 1958, revised edition, 1973; *The Gershwins: Words Upon Music,* Verve, 1959; (editor with Jablonski) *The Gershwin Years in Song,* New York Times Co., 1973; *Paul Bowles: The Illumination of North Africa,* Southern Illinois University Press, 1974. Associate editor of *Mystery and Detection Annual,* 1972—.

WORK IN PROGRESS: A critical bibliography of the "lost generation," publication by American Studies Research Center.

SIDELIGHTS: Stewart commented: "I have always been particularly interested in writers' journals, and in my own work (which is generally biographical in its approach) I have relied heavily on my own journals. My attitudes toward the relationship between life-as-lived and life-as-literature have undoubtedly been highly influenced by my association with Ira Gershwin, S. N. Behrman, and Alice B. Toklas, each of whom I considered as a singular talent."

* * *

STEWART, Mark Armstrong 1929-

PERSONAL: Born July 23, 1929, in Yeovil, England; came to the United States in 1957, naturalized citizen, 1962; son of Francis Hugh (a physician) and Violet (Knight) Stewart; married Pamela Mary Finlow (a nurse practitioner), March 19, 1955; children: Sarah, Anne, Duncan. *Education:* Cambridge University, B.A., 1953; St. Thomas' Hospital Medical School, London, M.D., 1956. *Politics:* Independent. *Religion:* Society of Friends (Quakers). *Home address:* R.R.1, Box 52-C, Oxford, Iowa 52322. *Agent:* Julian Bach Literary Agency, Inc., 3 East 48th St., New York, N.Y. 10017. *Office:* 500 Newton Rd., Iowa City, Iowa 52242.

CAREER: Washington University, St. Louis, Mo., resident in psychiatry, 1957-61, assistant professor, 1961-63, associate professor, 1963-69, professor of psychiatry, 1969-72; University of Iowa, Iowa City, Ida P. Haller Professor of Child Psychiatry, 1972—. *Military service:* British Army, 1947-49. *Member:* American Psychiatric Association (fellow), American Academy for Child Psychiatry, American Medical Association, American Society for Biological Chemistry, Psychiatric Research Society, Society for Research in Child Development, Association for Child Psychology and Psychiatry. *Awards, honors:* National Institute of Mental Health grant, 1961-71; media award from Family Services Association of the United States, 1974.

WRITINGS: (With Sally W. Olds) *Raising a Hyperactive Child,* Harper, 1973; (with Ann Gath) *Psychological Disorders of Children,* Williams & Wilkins, 1978.

Contributor: J. P. Brady and K. H. Brodie, editors, *Controversy in Psychiatry,* Saunders, 1978; H. Rie and E. Rie, editors, *Handbook of Minimal Brain Dysfunctions,* Wiley, in press; S. Gabel and M. T. Erickson, editors, *Child Development and Developmental Disabilities,* Little, Brown, in press. Also contributor of about seventy articles to medical journals.

WORK IN PROGRESS: Research on the origins and course of antisocial behavior in children.

SIDELIGHTS: Stewart writes: "I think of myself as a scientist first, clinician second, and writer third. I believe I am a fairly original researcher and usually find myself taking stands that are unpopular with the establishment. An example was *Raising a Hyperactive Child,* which took a skeptical line on treating children with drugs. This raised the hackles of many of my physician colleagues. I think of myself as a good clinician with a fairly wide knowledge of basic research in child development, brain chemistry, and genetics. I am a reasonably good writer. I like to illustrate my work with vignettes from novelists, poets, and other writers, believing that these people have penetrating insights into the kinds of people upon whom I do my research. I wish that I could write poetry and fiction myself but I seem to be too much of a rationalist.

"In my clinical work I assume that children's psychologic problems most often result from the interaction of genetic and social influences. I believe strongly in the adage 'The fruit does not fall far from the tree' and believe that many of my patients are born with difficult temperaments which are determined by multiple genes. These influences are not sufficient, but social factors tend to enhance difficult tempermental traits such as irritability and impulsivity. In treatment I lean heavily on social learning approaches for parents and training in social skills, self regulation, and self awareness for children. These ideas have become clearer in my mind over the past few years and I have expressed them more confidently in my books and in chapters that I am asked to write on the diagnosis and treatment of childrens' problems."

* * *

STEWART, William Stanley 1938-

PERSONAL: Born August 16, 1938, in Los Angeles, Calif.; son of John H. F. (an inventor and hydraulic engineer) and Elizabeth (Turner) Stewart; married Elizabeth Anne Culver (a librarian), June 24, 1964; children: Emily Culver and John Melross (twins). *Education:* Pomona College, B.A. (cum laude), 1960; graduate study at Princeton University, 1960; Indiana University, M.A., 1967; University of North Carolina, Ph.D., 1972. *Home:* 1805 Broadway, Chico, Calif. 95926. *Office:* Department of Political Science, California State University, Chico, Calif. 95929.

CAREER: U.S. Peace Corps, Washington, D.C., volunteer, 1962-63, professor of English as a foreign language at Universidad de Oriente in Cumana, Venezuela, 1963-64; assistant English master at high school in Raglan, New Zealand, 1965-66; Fauquier Community Action Committee, Warrenton, Va., area development supervisor, 1967-68; North Carolina Committee on Law and Order, Raleigh, investigator and field research supervisor, summers, 1969-70; Emory and Henry College, Emory, Va., assistant professor of political science, 1972-75; California State University, Chico, assistant professor, 1975, associate professor of political science, 1979—, director of Morelia program, 1978-79. U.S. Marine Corps, 1961-62. *Member:* Latin American Studies Association, American Political Science Association, Pacific Coast Council on Latin American Studies. *Awards, honors:* Woodrow Wilson fellow, 1960.

WRITINGS: (Contributor) John Martz and David Meyers, editors, *Venezuela: The Democratic Experience,* Praeger, 1977; *Change and Bureaucracy: Public Administration in Venezuela,* University of North Carolina Press, 1978.

WORK IN PROGRESS: Innovation, Efficiency, and Strategies of Administrative Reform, to be published by the Organization of American States.

SIDELIGHTS: Stewart told *CA:* "Latin America is the future of the United States, not its past. Resource-poor countries maintain cultures consistent with scarcity, usually one of both internal and external exploitation. As the United States develops its own scarcities, we will most probably develop (or perhaps simply extend) a similar culture. Only if we know what is happening in Latin America do we have a chance to avoid it."

STOKES, Adrian Durham 1902-1972

OBITUARY NOTICE—See index for *CA* sketch: Born October 27, 1902, in London, England; died in 1972 in London, England. Author of about twenty books on art, dance, and culture. His works include *Tonight the Ballet, Colour and Form, Practical Landscape Painting, Greek Culture and the Ego,* and *Reflections on the Nude.* Obituaries and other sources: *Art News,* October, 1972; *The Author's and Writer's Who's Who,* 6th edition, Burke's Peerage, 1973; *AB Bookman's Weekly,* February 5, 1973.

* * *

STOKES, Bob
See WILKENING, Howard (Everett)

* * *

STOKES, Robert
See WILKENING, Howard (Everett)

* * *

STOLTENBERG, Donald Hugo 1927-

PERSONAL: Born October 15, 1927, in Milwaukee, Wis.; son of Hugo and Leora (Belitz) Stoltenberg. *Education:* Illinois Institute of Technology, B.S., 1953. *Home address:* Satucket Rd., Brewster, Mass. 02631.

CAREER: Painter and printmaker, with exhibits at institutions and galleries, including Pratt Graphics Center, Boston's Museum of Fine Arts, Art Institute of Chicago, and Corcoran Gallery. Instructor at De Cordova Museum School, 1956-74; visiting critic at Rhode Island School of Design, 1962-63. *Member:* Boston Printmakers (member of board of directors, 1971—), Boston Watercolor Society. *Awards, honors:* First purchase prize from Portland Museum Arts Festival, 1957; grand prize from Boston Arts Festival, 1957, first prize in painting, 1959; first prize from Boston Watercolor Society, 1974; second prize in printmaking from Worcester Art Museum, 1977.

WRITINGS: Collagraph Printmaking, Davis Publications, 1975; *The Artist and the Built Environment,* Davis, in press. Contributor to *School Arts.*

SIDELIGHTS: Stoltenberg wrote: "Visual images rather than words are my vocabulary of communication, but years of teaching have taught me the importance of sometimes augmenting the former with the latter.

"Collagraph printmaking is a recent technique which allows the artist to build up his image in an additive way, collage fashion, on a plate from which it will be inked and printed. In helping to expand and teach this technique, I felt that it should be documented as an aid for artist, students and teachers who might be more comfortable with this method than the more traditional substractive ones (such as intaglio).

"*The Artist and the Built Environment* reflects my own lifelong interests in drawing, painting and printmaking the architectural, transportation and engineering works around us. It reproduces work by artists of the past with captions to augment and give background and it shows how some artists, currently active, approach and interpret this subject matter. It is my feeling that how the environment is seen and evaluated is in large measure due to how artists have interpreted it and that as our surroundings become ever more urbanized, the built environment is an increasingly important subject for the visual artist."

STONE, Barbara Haskins 1924(?)-1979
(Barbara Haskins)

OBITUARY NOTICE: Born c. 1924, in Plymouth, England; died November 8, 1979, in Washington, D.C. Stone served as editor for many organizations, including the World Confederation of Organizations of the Teaching Profession, the National Education Association, and the Brookings Institution. She established a prize-winning journal for students, *Impact,* during the 1960's. Obituaries and other sources: *Washington Post,* November 11, 1979.

* * *

STONE, Elaine Murray 1922-

PERSONAL: Born January 22, 1922, in New York, N.Y.; son of Herman (a banker and diplomat) and Catherine (Fairbanks) Murray-Jacoby; married Frederic Courtney Stone (an electrical engineer), May 30, 1944; children: Catherine (Mrs. Robert Rayburn), Pamela (Mrs. Don E. Webb), Victoria. *Education:* Attended Julliard School of Music, 1939-41; New York College of Music, diploma, 1942; Trinity College of Music, licentiate, 1947. *Religion:* Episcopal. *Home:* 13660 Montfort Dr., Dallas, Tex. 75248. *Agent:* Theron Raines, 475 Fifth Ave., New York, N.Y. 10017. *Office:* KXTX-TV, 3900 Harry Hines Blvd., Dallas, Tex. 75219.

CAREER: Musician, composer, and writer. Accompanist with Strawbridge Ballet, 1944-45; Cass, Inc., Melbourne, Fla., editor-in-chief of educational tape cassettes, 1970-71; WTAI-Radio, Melbourne, director of continuity, 1971-74; Engle Realty, Inc., Indialantic, Fla., realtor associate, 1975-78; KXTX-TV, Dallas, Tex., writer and producer of juvenile news program, "Countdown," 1978—. Organist for churches in New York, New Jersey, and Florida; piano teacher. Member of board of promotion of Diocese of Southern Florida, 1960. *Member:* American Society of Composers, Authors, and Publishers, National League of American Penwomen, Women in Communications, Space Pioneers, Daughters of the American Revolution (state chairman of music in Florida, 1964). *Awards, honors:* Won South Carolina music contest, 1939; first prize in photojournalism contest in Florida, 1966, and second place in letters contest in Dallas, 1979, both from National League of American Penwomen.

WRITINGS: Love One Another, Holy Cross Press, 1948; *The Taming of the Tongue,* Holy Cross Press, 1954; *Pedro Menendez de Aviles and the Founding of St. Augustine,* Kenedy, 1969; *The Melbourne Bicentennial Book,* 1976; *Uganda: Fire and Blood,* Logos, 1977. Author of play "The Examination," produced in Melbourne, Fla., 1962. Author of more than two-hundred scripts for television series "Countdown," 1978—. Associate editor of *Goodtime Gazette,* 1978-79. Contributor to periodicals, including *Charleston News, Christian Life, Holy Cross,* and *Indian River.*

WORK IN PROGRESS: Tekla and the Lion; Saints and Martyrs of Today; Submission; The Judas Touch; Ten Thousand Years.

SIDELIGHTS: Stone told *CA:* "I spent the first half of my life on Fifth Avenue in New York as the child of a very successful banker and diplomat. My father was chairman of the board of North American Waterworks, in addition to being president of his own banking concern on Wall Street. He was appointed by Herbert Hoover to represent the U.S.A. at the coronation of Haile Selassie in 1930. My parents entertained many of the greats of this century at our home. I attended private schools and in 1939 won the South Carolina state music contest in piano. I then applied to enter the Juilliard School of Music which I attended from 1939-41. Due to poor health, repeated pneumonia, etc., I changed to the New York College of Music from which I graduated in 1942. I have composed music since I was nine and have had my works performed all over the United States. After leading such a social life the first half of my existence, my husband and two daughters moved to Florida for my health in 1950 and lived in the shadow of Cape Canaveral until last year.

"My interests are very broad and wide. This is fortunate, because the television show I write and produce covers every subject imaginable. I adore research, and enjoy tracking down impossible bits of information no one can find.

"As the space correspondent for Religious News Service, I covered every manned space launch in U.S. history. I was also at the Kennedy Space Center for many other important launches all through the sixties and seventies and hobnobbed with the great newscasters and journalists from every country on earth. I was also in a documentary called 'In the Shadow of the Moon.' I have been interviewed on many television and radio stations about my book, *Uganda: Fire and Blood*. I have a huge scrapbook just filled with ads, reviews, and other mementos about that book.

"I guess I've enjoyed being a television producer about as much as anything I've ever done in my life. I had no training in it, and learned on the job after I was hired to write the scripts. 'Countdown' is aired thirty times per week on the entire CBN network. 'Countdown' is a sixty second news show for children shown during the cartooning periods to educate children. We go on location and have guests come to the studio, but mostly we use films and slides to illustrate the story.

"My father, the United States ambassador to Ethiopia, made many trips to Africa. This sparked my interest in the 'Dark Continent' at an early age. This resulted in a book on Uganda and one on Ethiopia. I have traveled extensively myself since I was a small child. I speak French and Spanish. I became unusually devout during my teens, which resulted in the reading of most of the great saints and mystics. Out of this grew over half of my books and all of my published articles. Even though all of my education was in music, I have yet to write on this subject!"

AVOCATIONAL INTERESTS: "My favorite occupations are travel, sailing, swimming, diving, television, Greek, reading, visiting my grandchildren, conversation, movies, theatre, attending concerts, eating; my favorite composer is Bach, my favorite writer is C. S. Lewis; I enjoy needlepoint and embroidery."

* * *

STONE, John H(enry) 1936-

PERSONAL: Born February 7, 1936, in Jackson, Miss.; son of John Henry (a production head at a glass plant) and Pauline (a teacher of the deaf; maiden name, Marler) Stone; married Lu Crymes (a teacher), August 16, 1954; children: John, James. *Education:* Millsaps College, B.A., 1958; Washington University, St. Louis, Mo., M.D., 1962; postdoctoral study at University of Rochester, 1962-64, and Emory University, 1966-1969. *Home:* 3983 Northlake Creek Court, Tucker, Ga. 30084. *Office:* 80 Butler St., Atlanta, Ga. 30303.

CAREER: Emory University, Atlanta, Ga., assistant professor, 1969-72, associate professor, 1972-77, professor of cardiology, 1977—, lecturer in English, 1979, director of emergency medicine residency at Grady Hospital, 1975—, also assistant dean for emergency medicine. *Military service:* U.S. Public Health Service, 1964-66; became lieutenant commander. *Member:* American College of Emergency Physicians, American Heart Association, Alpha Omega Alpha (member of faculty council, 1979—). *Awards, honors:* Literary achievement award for poetry from Georgia Writer's Association, 1972, for *The Smell of Matches*.

WRITINGS: The Smell of Matches (poems), Rutgers University Press, 1972; (editor with George R. Schwartz, Peter Safar, and others) *Principles and Practice of Emergency Medicine,* Saunders, 1978, *In All This Rain* (poems), Louisiana State University Press, 1980.

WORK IN PROGRESS: Another book of poems.

SIDELIGHTS: Stone comments: "The marriage of writing and the practice of medicine is a natural one, though it may not appear to be. The practice of medicine requires that one get to know people—and for me that's where the poetry comes from. And the practice of poetry had definite beneficial effects on the practice of medicine."

BIOGRAPHICAL/CRITICAL SOURCES: Dannie Abse, editor, *My Medical School,* Robson Books, 1978.

* * *

STONE, Reynolds 1909-1979

OBITUARY NOTICE: Born in 1909 in England; died in 1979 in England. Engraver, illustrator, and writer. Stone illustrated books, designed various banknotes for the Bank of England, created the Peace Stamp of Britain in the 1940's, and cut memorials to Winston Churchill, T. S. Eliot, Stanley Morison, and Lord Britten. He was the editor of two books of engraving and the contributor of numerous articles on printing and engraving to periodicals. Many of his illustrations were reproduced in *Reynolds Stone: Engravings*. Obituaries and other sources: *AB Bookman's Weekly,* September 10, 1979.

* * *

STONUM, Gary Lee 1947-

PERSONAL: Born July 10, 1947, in Sacramento, Calif.; son of Donald W. and Gwen (Caffey) Stonum; married Marilyn Shea (an attorney), August 22, 1970. *Education:* Reed College, B.A., 1969; Johns Hopkins University, M.A., 1971, Ph.D., 1973. *Office:* Department of English, Case Western Reserve University, Cleveland, Ohio 44106.

CAREER: Case Western Reserve University, Cleveland, Ohio, assistant professor, 1973-78, associate professor of English, 1979—. Member of board of directors of Circle Press.

WRITINGS: Faulkner's Career, Cornell University Press, 1979. Editor of *Pieces: A Journal of Short Fiction*.

WORK IN PROGRESS: "A book on power in nineteenth-century American literature."

* * *

STOREY, Edward J. 1901-

PERSONAL: Born May 10, 1901, in Somerville, Mass.; son of William J. (a grocer) and Josie Belle (Glidden) Storey; married Helen E. Farley (a volunteer worker), June 18, 1932; children: Edward J., Jr., Amy Storey Rokoszak. *Education:* University of New Hampshire, B.S., 1922; graduate study at Temple University, 1925, and Columbia University, 1926-28; New York University, M.S., 1929, Ed.D., 1941; further study at Peoples College, Austria, 1936. *Religion:* Protestant. *Home and office:* 4519 West Tradewinds Ave., Lauderdale by the Sea, Fla. 33308.

CAREER: Worked as cable engineer in Newfoundland, and as chicken farmer, insurance salesman, football player, and administrator; teacher of science, mathematics, and athletics in Duxbury, Mass., 1922-23; high school teacher of mathematics, chemistry, biology, and shop (and athletic coach) in Shippensburg, Pa., 1923-24, and Collingdale, Pa., 1924-25; Mamaroneck Public Schools, Mamaroneck, N.Y., psychology teacher and director of health and physical education, 1925-61; writer and consultant, 1961—. Owner and director of Camp Half Moon for Boys, 1944-69. Member of National Football Foundation and President's Physical Fitness Committee; lecturer at football clinics. *Military service:* U.S. military reserve, 1922-37; became first lieutenant. *Member:* Sword and Scabbard. *Awards, honors:* Achievement award from Brian Piccolo chapter of National Football Foundation, 1978.

WRITINGS: Secrets of Kicking the Football, Putnam, 1971. Contributor to education journals, newspapers, and popular magazines, including *World Digest* and *You and Your Child.*

WORK IN PROGRESS: Research on the use of both Viseo Motor Rehearsals and hypnosis in teaching athletic skills.

SIDELIGHTS: Storey comments: "I have always been a very curious individual, and after determining the needs have tried to find means of satisfying them. Early in athletics I was aware of the need for small footballs for small hands and feet. I designed them. In 1932 I designed the tee used by the Little League for teaching batting. I designed athletic equipment with indications of how to use it on the equipment or the packing box.

"A future goal is to write *I Can Always Get a Job* to foster positive attitudes toward work experiences and career development. I found out I didn't like it as a cable engineer in Newfoundland, came back to Boston, and in four days landed a job as a teacher. The main idea as far as I am concerned, at this stage of my life, is to be doing things for people and not carrying all my knowledge to the grave. It has taken me a long time to get it."

* * *

STORKE, Thomas More 1876-1971

OBITUARY NOTICE: Born November 23, 1876, in Santa Barbara, Calif.; died of a stroke, October 12, 1971, in Santa Barbara, Calif. Publisher, editor, and Pulitzer Prize-winner who acquired Santa Barbara's three newspapers and merged them under the *Santa Barbara News-Press* masthead. In 1961, Storke launched an expose of the John Birch Society, which had branded many citizens in the Santa Barbara area as Communists. His editorial attacks condemned the society as totalitarian and challenged its members to "come up from underground." For his crusade, Storke won the 1961 Lauterbach Award for "outstanding work in defense of civil liberties," a 1962 Pulitzer Prize for editorial writing, and the 1962 Elijah Lovejoy Award for courageous journalism. He also served out the remainder of California Senator William McAdoo's term of office when McAdoo resigned in 1938. His reminiscences are recalled in *California Editor* and *I Write for Freedom.* Obituaries and other sources: Thomas More Storke, *California Editor,* Westernlore, 1958; Storke, *I Write for Freedom,* McNally & Loftin, 1962; *Current Biography,* Wilson, 1963; *New York Times,* October 13, 1971; *Who Was Who in America,* 5th edition, Marquis, 1973.

STORM, Lesley
See COWIE, Margaret

* * *

STOUT, Wesley Winans 1889-1971

OBITUARY NOTICE: Born January 26, 1889, in Junction City, Kan.; died November 15, 1971, in Louisville, Ky. Journalist and editor who worked for several newspapers before joining the *Saturday Evening Post* in 1922. Under the tutelage of *Post* editor George Horace Lorimer, Stout wrote and ghostwrote innumerable articles for the magazine and became its editor in 1937. He introduced readers to the magazine's first photographic covers, to the work of 15 new artists, and the work of 147 new authors. When he resigned his position in 1942 because of a disagreement on policy, Stout went to work for the Chrysler Corp. in Detroit. He later wrote a column for the *Fort Lauderdale Daily News.* Obituaries and other sources: *Current Biography,* Wilson, 1941; *New York Times,* November 16, 1971; *Who Was Who in America,* 5th edition, Marquis, 1973.

* * *

STOWE, James L(ewis) 1950-

PERSONAL: Born August 25, 1950, in El Paso, Tex.; son of Jesson L. (a physician) and Bernice (Hulen) Stowe; married Debra Reese, October 17, 1973 (divorced June, 1977). *Education:* University of Texas, El Paso, B.A., 1973, M.A., 1978. *Home:* 624 East University Ave., El Paso, Tex. 79902. *Agent:* Paul R. Reynolds, Inc., 12 East 41st St., New York, N.Y. 10017.

CAREER: KVIA-TV, El Paso, Tex., in television production, 1969-71; University of Texas, El Paso, instructor of creative writing, 1978-79; writer, 1979—.

WRITINGS: Winter Stalk (suspense novel), Simon & Schuster, 1979.

Co-author of screenplays "The Game of Troy" and "The Garden Game," both adaptations of novels.

WORK IN PROGRESS: Another suspense novel.

SIDELIGHTS: Stowe writes: "I grew up on a steady diet of film and television, but unlike a lot of kids growing up today, I also read a great deal. Film has helped me develop a good visual sense which I try to give my writing. Basically, I wish to entertain a reader—to elicit an emotional response, usually fear and apprehension in a suspense novel. I want the reader to keep turning the pages, to care about the characters. Reading and studying good contemporary fiction is a never-ending education."

The film rights for *Winter Stalk* were purchased by Universal Pictures.

* * *

STRANDBERG, Victor H(ugo) 1935-

PERSONAL: Born May 16, 1935, in Deerfield, N.H.; son of Arne E. (a contractor) and Agnes K. (Hammarstrom) Strandberg; married Penelope Hamilton (a computer programmer), January 28, 1961; children: Anne C., Susan E. *Education:* Clark University, A.B., 1957; Brown University, M.A., 1959, Ph.D., 1962. *Politics:* "Without hope." *Religion:* Christian. *Home:* 2709 Augusta Dr., Durham, N.C. 27707. *Office:* Department of English, Duke University, Durham, N.C. 27706.

CAREER: University of Vermont, Burlington, instructor, 1962, assistant professor of English, 1963-66; Duke University, Durham, N.C., assistant professor, 1966-69, associate professor of English, 1969—. Fulbright lecturer at University of Uppsala, 1973, and Catholic University of Louvain, 1980. *Member:* Modern Language Association of America, American Association of University Professors, Smithsonian Institution, South Atlantic Modern Language Association, Phi Beta Kappa.

WRITINGS: A Colder Fire: The Poetry of Robert Penn Warren, University Press of Kentucky, 1965; *The Poetic Vision of Robert Penn Warren,* University Press of Kentucky, 1977. Contributor of about twenty-five articles to literature journals.

WORK IN PROGRESS: Religious Psychology in American Literature: A Study in the Relevance of William James; Faulkner's Debts and Affinities, a comparison to other artists and thinkers.

SIDELIGHTS: Strandberg comments: "I like to focus on the broad design of a writer's work: the 'vision' that makes up the 'figure in the carpet' that Henry James talked about. My approach attempts to be analytical, correlating the inner workings of a writer's art with disclosures afforded by interviews, letters, biographies, and affinities with other artists and thinkers, so that in the end we might better understand both the artist and his work. My criticism as a whole has a religious-psychological coloration."

* * *

STRANGE, Maureen 1948-

PERSONAL: Born May 20, 1948, in Brooklyn, N.Y.; daughter of Julius and Sylvia (an interior decorator; maiden name, Montagne) Koch. *Education:* Harpur College of the State University of New York at Binghampton, B.A., 1969.

CAREER: Novelist.

WRITINGS: Beginners (novel), Doubleday, 1979.

WORK IN PROGRESS: A second novel.

SIDELIGHTS: Maureen Strange's first novel, *Beginners,* is "a novel with the volume turned up full blast," remarked Linda Osborne. The story deals with twenty years in the life of the Becker family and their adventures in such activities as house-hunting, infidelity, sibling rivalry, and school problems. The plentiful supply of loud arguments, moaning, and lack of affection between family members "is not inaccurate; not unlike the Archie Bunkers', who also have something to tell about the way things really are," noted Osborne. But it could have been improved upon by going "beyond familiar jokes about the working class and the suburbs, beyond constant nagging and moaning, into the hearts of the characters, their failures, their gentleness, their dreams." Sheryl Fitzgerald, on the other hand, thought "reading about Chickie and Rudy Becker is like listening to a good stand-up comedian. The patter comes so quickly and is so speckled with witticisms that you have to listen hard to catch the good ones."

Strange reflected on her writing habits: "I have a story in mind, but when I sit down to write each day I can't be sure of what my characters will do or say. One of the important things, I think, is to learn to not let your advance notions about story and characters get in the way of the life they assume on their own. Have you ever played with a Ouija board? That's what writing is like. You have to apply just enough pressure to achieve motion, but not so much as to inhibit or change the direction the piece wants to take on its own. It's a delicate balance. You may plan for a character to have a certain trait, but when it comes down to it they'll go their own way. From time to time I can hear them calling out to me to get off their backs, let them call their own shots.

"We all ask ourselves, 'what am I doing here?' Well, writing is what I'm doing here until I figure out what it is I'm doing here; which may turn out to be, quite simply, *writing.*

"Although I like the idea of reaching people through writing, of moving them the way the work of other authors has moved me, I would be lying if I said that that is the reason I write. I write because I love to. I write because I have to."

AVOCATIONAL INTERESTS: "I am a vegetarian and animal lover, interested in nature, nutrition, historical geology, and speculation about life beyond life as we know it. I enjoy concerts; many different kinds of music from New Wave to classical and Tom Waits. I like going to museums and art galleries. And I love the work of J. D. Salinger and Donald Barthelme. The company and closeness of friends are important to me."

BIOGRAPHICAL/CRITICAL SOURCES: Washington Post, January 4, 1979; *Newsday,* March 11, 1979.

* * *

STRAUS, Nathan 1889-1961

OBITUARY NOTICE: Born May 27, 1889, in New York, N.Y.; died September 12, 1961. State senator, radio station executive, journalist, editor, publisher, and author. One of Straus's first journalistic endeavors was the purchase of *Puck,* a humor weekly that he edited and published from 1914 to 1917. He also served as a New York State senator during the 1920's and as the first administrator of the U.S. Housing Authority. Straus was also president and chairman of radio station WMCA for eighteen years. His writings include *Seven Myths of Housing* and *Two Thirds of a Nation: A Housing Program.* Obituaries and other sources: *Current Biography,* Wilson, 1944, November, 1961; *Who Was Who in America,* 4th edition, Marquis, 1968.

* * *

STRAUSS, David 1937-

PERSONAL: Born July 19, 1937, in St. Louis, Mo.; son of Leonard and Jenny (Nathan) Strauss; married Anne Beilby (in antique business), January 30, 1965; children: Benjamin David, Jesse, Anne Benedict. *Education:* Amherst College, B.A. (cum laude), 1959; Columbia University, M.A., 1963, Ph.D., 1968. *Home:* 158 Bulkley, Kalamazoo, Mich. 49007. *Office:* Department of History, Kalamazoo College, Kalamazoo, Mich. 49007.

CAREER: Brooklyn College of the City University of New York, Brooklyn, N.Y., lecturer in European history, 1966-67; Colgate University, Hamilton, N.Y., assistant professor of American history, 1967-74; Kalamazoo College, Kalamazoo, Mich., associate professor of American history, 1974—, director of American studies program, 1975—. Fulbright professor at University of Lyon, 1970-71. Program officer for National Endowment for the Humanities, 1977-78; speaker at professional meetings. *Member:* American Historical Association, Organization of American Historians, American Studies Association. *Awards, honors:* Grant from French Government, 1959-60; Fulbright fellow at University of Clermont-Ferrand, 1960-61.

WRITINGS: Menace in the West: The Rise of French Anti-Americanism in Modern Times, Greenwood Press, 1978. Contributor to American studies and popular culture journals.

WORK IN PROGRESS: "I am currently at work on an interpretive history of American culture in the 1920's which will describe the nation's 'coming of age.' For the first time, in this decade, America becomes a civilization. The dimensions of this enterprise including corporate capitalism, a mass economy, ethnic diversity, and the acute conflicts of a generational, racial, and sexual nature are essentially unique. The book will explain the complex relationship between these elements."

SIDELIGHTS: Strauss writes: "I was originally drawn to the subject of French anti-Americanism by what seemed to me the gross distortions of the realities of American life in the works of contemporary French intellectuals. I was intrigued as well by the surprisingly derivative quality of many French books in the 1950's and 1960's dealing with the United States. Their frequent references to earlier French and American writers of the 1920's pointed me toward that decade as a formative moment in the history of modern Franco-American relations. While the focus of my work has been on what Frenchmen said about American culture—particularly their comments on American values and institutions—I became increasingly interested in how their views of the culture might be shaped by the political and economic context in which they were writing. In fact, French remarks on the assembly line, films, American ethnic groups, jazz, skyscrapers, and the family were frequently accompanied by hostile comments on such American policies as disarmament, the war debts, and the investments of American multinational corporations in Europe. These policies provided the narrow context in which judgments about American culture were made, but French intellectuals were also aware of larger developments, particularly the decline of their own country and continent as centers of power and culture in the world. This awareness also influenced their remarks on the United States.

"Once the environment of the critics became clear, my own emphasis shifted from calculating distortions in French views to understanding the relationship of the French image of America to the circumstances of Franco-American relations. French intellectuals' vision of American reality was refracted through their special concerns for the future of France and the community of French intellectuals as these were affected by American civilization in the 1920's.

"In the light of these findings, the derivative quality of current French writing on America could be explained. In effect, French intellectuals had identified in the United States of the 1920's a phenomenon which we now call 'mass society.' They had also expressed in unmistakable terms their hostility to this new society. Since developments during the Depression and World War II did not alter the basic structure of American society nor bring France back to a position of primacy in world affairs, it is not surprising that French intellectuals continued to criticize the American system. In this sense, Charles de Gaulle may be understood as the heir of a well-established anti-American tradition in modern France."

* * *

STRAUSS, Victor 1907(?)-1979

OBITUARY NOTICE: Born c. 1907; died in 1979 in Vienna, Austria. Author. Strauss centered his work and writings around the graphic arts. His *The Printing Industry,* a sort of encyclopedia, was his most famous work. Some of his other writings include *Lithographer's Manual* and *Graphic Arts Management.* Strauss was the founder of a screen process printing company, the recipient of frequent awards. Obituaries and other sources: *AB Bookman's Weekly,* August 20, 1979.

* * *

SUCHER, Harry V(ictor) 1915-

PERSONAL: Surname is pronounced *Soo*-ker; born October 18, 1915, in Santa Rosa, Calif.; son of Victor Emmanual (a farmer) and Clara Gunn (Van Wormer) Sucher; married Lois Jean Welch, June 6, 1940 (divorced, August, 1960); married Margery Alberta Tuck (an executive secretary), May 27, 1961; children: Harry V., Jr., Cynthia Christine Sucher Lehman, Vincent Howard. *Education:* Washington State University, B.S., 1938, D.V.M., 1940. *Politics:* Conservative. *Religion:* Protestant. *Home:* 9652 Joyzelle Dr., Garden Grove, Calif. 92641. *Office:* 8841 Garden Grove Blvd., Garden Grove, Calif. 92641.

CAREER: Veterinarian with small animal practice in Sacramento, Calif., 1942-53, and Garden Grove, Calif., 1953—. Owner of commercial real estate investment and holding company. *Member:* American Veterinary Medical Association, California Veterinary Medical Association, Southern California Veterinary Medical Association.

WRITINGS: Simplified Boat Building, Volume I: *The Flat Bottom Boat,* Volume II: *The V Bottom Boat,* Norton, 1974; *The Iron Redskin: The Story of the Indian Motorcycle,* J. H. Haynes, 1978; *Harley-Davidson: The Milwaukee Marvel,* J. H. Haynes, 1980. Editor of television and radio scripts; writer of nightclub acts. Ghostwriter of articles for medical journals. Contributor to magazines, including *Yachting, Motorboating, Sea,* and *Sport Aviation.*

WORK IN PROGRESS: History of Harley-Davidson Motor Co.

SIDELIGHTS: Sucher writes: "My rural background and interest in animals inspired my entrance into the field of veterinary medicine, but I also grew up with a lifelong interest in boating, motorcycling, and aviation.

"I spent much time on the California coast examining the classic Monterey power boats used by the local fishermen. I had been studying naval architecture and small boat design, and during 1963-66 had a series of my low-cost boat designs published in *National Fisherman.* I was greatly influenced by Howard I. Chapelle, the acknowledged dean of American marine historians whose friendship I enjoyed for many years, and I hope to do for traditional American power boats what he did for sailing craft.

"I was also greatly interested as a boy in the motorcycling activities of a cousin who had an adventurous journey across the continent on a 1914 Harley-Davidson. Then I was taken for rides on a 1921 Indian Powerplus machine by a neighbor, and I witnessed board track motorcycle racing on a mile-and-a-quarter oval track.

"I also developed a continuing interest in aviation, and wrote a number of articles on aircraft design.

"As this type of writing is not particularly lucrative, I have always practiced veterinary medicine on a full-time basis, and continued my lifelong activities in the real estate investment field. I saw no point in being a derelict writer."

* * *

SULLIVAN, Ed(ward Vincent) 1902(?)-1974

OBITUARY NOTICE: Born September 28, 1902(?), in New York, N.Y.; died October 13, 1974, in New York, N.Y.

Television emcee, newspaper columnist, and author. Sullivan was best known as master of ceremonies for the popular television variety program, "The Ed Sullivan Show." Each Sunday night for twenty-three years his "rilly big shew" provided Americans with a large array of entertainment and featured the television debuts of such greats as Jackie Gleason, Elvis Presley, Rudolf Nureyev, and the Beatles. Before embarking on his television career, Sullivan had already earned fame as a syndicated gossip columnist for the *New York Daily News,* a position he held from 1932 to 1974. Sullivan was the author of *Mister Lee: The Story of the Shuberts,* as well as several television biographies and screenplays. Obituaries and other sources: *Current Biography,* Wilson, 1952; *Who's Who in America,* 38th edition, Marquis, 1974; *New York Times,* October 14, 1974.

* * *

SULZBERGER, Arthur Hays 1891-1968

OBITUARY NOTICE: Born September 12, 1891, in New York, N.Y.; died December 11, 1968. Newspaper publisher and journalist. Sulzberger worked in the newspaper business for seventeen years before succeeding his father-in-law, Adolph S. Ochs, as publisher of the *New York Times* upon Ochs's death in 1935. Sulzberger also served as director and chairman of the board of the New York Times Co. until 1968. During these years he was an important factor in the growth of the paper's influence and circulation. Obituaries and other sources: *Current Biography,* Wilson, 1943, February, 1969; *Who Was Who in America,* 5th edition, Marquis, 1973.

* * *

SUMMERFIELD, Margie 1949-

PERSONAL: Born May 22, 1949, in the Midwest. *Education:* "Attended a variety of schools but I've been 'educated' on the streets of life and in the bars on the Russian River." *Residence:* Sebastopol, Calif. *Agent:* Andy Ross, 2454 Telegraph, Berkeley, Calif. 94704.

CAREER: X-ray technician, 1967-71; housekeeper and maid, 1971-74; Wisteria (antique clothing shop), Forestville, Calif., co-owner, 1974-77; owner of Cheek to Cheek (mail order underwear business), 1977—. Shiatszu masseuse, 1975-77.

WRITINGS: Compression Tested (novel), McGraw, 1978.

WORK IN PROGRESS: Solutions, a science fiction novel dealing with individual sexual identity and the "gay liberation" movement; a novel dealing with the "born-again" movement's anti-feminist effects on a woman; two books of poems.

SIDELIGHTS: Summerfield comments: "God gave me a sense of humor and a love for words and told me to write about what I knew, so I did and I still am. My characters are struggling with more primitive problems (heat, shelter, food), more of the basic human needs, than many of the current personalities of women's fiction. Poverty can provide a lot of good material. My current favorite writers are Erma Bombeck, Kurt Vonnegut, and Ann Landers. I'll take on any subject matter—the war between the sexes, gay identity crises, amputations, frigidity, religion, herpes, the right to suicide, et al. But from an overall view I am expressing my love for women and their sanity-saving humor. I'd like to create literary respect for female characters, but more than anything I want to make people laugh. *Compression Tested* is the funny bitter story of Nordis Knight, a Russian River resident torn between suicidal futility and a hormonal desire for orgasms. I write because God told me it would keep me from going insane and maybe earn me some money."

* * *

SUTTON, Jane 1950-

PERSONAL: Born May 11, 1950, in New York, N.Y.; daughter of Milton (a creative director for an advertising agency) and Freema (Balloff) Sutton; married Alan G. Ticotsky (an elementary school teacher), August 10, 1975. *Education:* Brandeis University, B.A. (magna cum laude), 1972. *Residence:* Lexington, Mass. *Office:* Instrumentation Laboratory, Inc., 113 Hartwell Ave., Lexington, Mass. 02173.

CAREER: Harlem Valley State Hospital, Wingdale, N.Y., mental health worker with retarded adults, 1972-74; *Mid-Hudson Leisure,* Poughkeepsie, N.Y., staff writer, 1974-75; Instrumentation Laboratory, Inc. (manufacturers of medical and analytical instruments), Lexington, Mass., in public relations, 1975—. Member of Lexington FISH and Citizens for Lexington Conservation. *Member:* Phi Beta Kappa.

WRITINGS: What Should a Hippo Wear? (juvenile), Houghton, 1979.

Work represented in anthologies, including *Contained Reading Comprehension and Fluency Development,* Level E, edited by Dorothy M. Bogart, A/V Concepts Corp., 1976, and *In View Of,* co-edited by John Molloy and Robert Ward, Joist Productions, 1976.

WORK IN PROGRESS: Two picture books for children; short stories for adults; "humorous nonfiction for adults."

SIDELIGHTS: Sutton told *CA:* "In *What Should a Hippo Wear?,* I have tried to capture the sense of awkwardness both children and adults experience when they feel they don't fit in, that they have to look or act a certain way in order to be accepted. Bertha the hippo learns that she is much better off being herself, that her true friends like her for what she is. This is a happy lesson that many of us, including myself, need to be reminded of once in a while.

"I enjoy writing for children. It's satisfying to me to invent situations they can identify with and to share what little knowledge I have gained of the world. Also, in children's works I can express a strong moral message . . . without having to couch it in cautiously subtle language so that the modern reader can feel that he or she has read between the lines.

"My short stories for adults are very important to me also. But as I write this, it occurs to me that there is less game playing in writing for children."

BIOGRAPHICAL/CRITICAL SOURCES: Lexington Minute-Man, May 17, 1979.

* * *

SUVIN, Darko (Ronald) 1930-

PERSONAL: Born July 19, 1930, in Zagreb, Yugoslavia; son of Miroslav (a physician and professor) and Gertrude (Weiser) Suvin; married Nevenka Eric (a teacher), 1961. *Education:* University of Zagreb, M.Sc., 1954, B.A., 1956, Ph.D., 1970; also attended University of Bristol, Sorbonne, University of Paris, and Yale University. *Politics:* Socialist. *Office:* Department of English, McGill University, 853 Sherbrooke W., Montreal, Quebec, Canada H3A 2T6.

CAREER: Free-lance translator and critic, 1954-59; University of Zagreb, Zagreb, Yugoslavia, assistant lecturer in theatre arts and comparative literature, 1959-67; University of Massachusetts, Amherst, visiting lecturer in English,

1967-68; Indiana University, Bloomington, visiting associate professor of comparative literature, summer, 1968; McGill University, Montreal, Quebec, assistant professor, 1968-70, associate professor, 1970-76, professor of English and comparative literature, 1976—. Member of Croat National Theatre Board, 1962-64, and National Library Board, 1963-65; director of national and international colloquia on science fiction, drama, and social theory of literature. *Member:* Union Internationale des Theatres Universitaires (vice-president, 1962-65), International P.E.N., Canadian Comparative Literature Association, Modern Language Association of America, Brecht Society, Science Fiction Research Association (member of executive committee, 1970-73; vice-president, 1977-78). *Awards, honors:* Ford Foundation fellowship, 1965-66; Canada Council grants, 1969, 1972, 1973-74, 1975, 1976, 1977-78, 1979; grant from government of Quebec, 1975-77; Pilgrim Award from Science Fiction Research Association, 1979, for distinguished contributions to the study of science fiction.

WRITINGS: Other Worlds, Other Seas: Science-Fiction Stories From Socialist Countries, Random House, 1970; (editor with M. D. Bristol, and contributor) *A Production Notebook to Brecht's "St. Joan of the Stockyards,"* McGill University, 1973; *Russian Science Fiction, 1956-1974: A Bibliography,* Dragon, 1976; (editor with R. D. Mullen, and contributor) *Science-Fiction Studies: Selected Articles on Science Fiction, 1973-1975,* Gregg-Hall, 1976, Second Series: *Selected Articles on Science Fiction, 1976-1977,* 1978; (editor with R. M. Philmus, and contributor) *H. G. Wells and Modern Science Fiction,* Bucknell University Press, 1977; *Metamorphoses of Science Fiction,* Yale University Press, 1979.

Other: *Dva vida dramaturgije* (title means "Two Aspects of Dramaturgy"), Razlog, 1965; *Od Lukijana do Lunjika* (title means "From Lucian to the Lunik"), Epoha, 1965; (editor, translator, and contributor) Bertolt Brecht, *Dijalektika u teatru* (title means "Dialectics in the Theater"), Nolit, 1966; *Uvod u Brechta* (title means "Introduction to Brecht"), Skolska knjiga, 1970; *Pour une poetique de la science-fiction* (title means "For a Poetics of Science Fiction"), Presses de l'Universite du Quebec, 1977; *Dubrovacke kronike i ljepota smrti: Geneza i struktura dramaturskog modela Vojnovica* (title means "The Chronicles of Dubrovnik and the Beauty of Death: Vojnovic's Dramaturgic Model, Its Genesis and Structure"), Liber, 1979; *Poetik der SF* (title means "Poetics of Science Fiction"), Suhrkamp, 1979.

Contributor: Ruby Cohn, editor, *Casebook on "Waiting for Godot,"* Grove, 1967; James Blish, editor, *Nebula Award Stories Five,* Doubleday, 1970; Stanislaw Lem, *Solaris,* Walker & Co., 1970; Erika Munk, editor, *Brecht,* Bantam, 1972; C. S. Mews and H. Knust, editors, *Essays on Brecht,* University of North Carolina Press, 1974; N. Rudich, editor, *Weapons of Criticism,* Ramparts, 1976. Contributor of about three hundred articles and reviews to literary magazines and theatre journals. Co-editor of *Science Fiction Studies,* 1973—, publisher, 1979—; advisory editor of *Wellsian.*

WORK IN PROGRESS: Research on science fiction, modern drama, and literary and cultural theory.

SIDELIGHTS: Suvin wrote: "As a critic, I try to contest both the Platonic notion that works of literature and art are a transparency 'expressing' something else (myth, ideology, truth, reality, or what have you), and the notion that they are isolated from social history which, in fact, informs them most intimately. I am equally interested in so-called 'high' and 'low' culture, and consequently in theory-*cum*-history."

BIOGRAPHICAL/CRITICAL SOURCES: Andromeda SF 2, Bigz, 1977.

* * *

SWAN, Jon 1929-

PERSONAL: Born in 1929, in Iowa; married Marianne Hamaker, March 3, 1962; children: Claudia, Izette, Anna. *Education:* Oberlin College, B.A., 1950; Boston University, M.A., 1954. *Home address:* P.O. Box 107, Rural Free Delivery, Canaan, Conn. 06018.

CAREER: Poet.

WRITINGS: Journeys and Return (poems), Scribner, 1960; *Three Plays* (includes "Football," "Short Sacred Rite of Search and Destruction," and "Fireworks for a Hot Fourth"), Grove, 1969; *A Door to the Forest* (poems), Random House, 1979.

Work represented in anthologies, including *Poems and Poets,* McGraw, 1965.

Contributor to magazines, including *American Scholar, Antaeus, London, New Yorker,* and *Prairie Schooner.*

* * *

SWEENEY, Karen O'Connor 1938-

PERSONAL: Born April 8, 1938, in Chicago, Ill.; daughter of Philip K. (a business broker) and Eva (Ennis) O'Connor; married John E. Sweeney (an attorney), June 11, 1960 (divorced, July, 1979); children: Julie, James, Erin. *Education:* Clarke College, B.A., 1960. *Home:* 4738 Park Granada, #243, Calabasas Park, Calif. 91302.

CAREER: Elementary school teacher in North Hollywood, Calif., 1960-61; tutor, 1972-76; teacher in Los Angeles Valley College Outreach Program, 1976—. Advertising writer for Mellinger Co., Wilshire Book Co., and Almquist Manufacturing Ltd. *Member:* American Society of Journalists and Authors (local president), Society of Children's Book Writers, Women's National Book Association (past member of board of directors). *Awards, honors:* Award from Chicago International Film Festival, 1975, for "A Visit With 'Don Juan in Hell.'"

WRITINGS: Everywoman's Guide to Family Finances, Major Books, 1976; *Improve Your Love Life,* Major Books, 1976; *How to Make Money,* F. Watts, 1977; *Entertaining,* F. Watts, 1978; *I Am a Compleat Woman: An Adventure in Self-Discovery,* Wilshire, 1978; *Illustrated Tennis Dictionary for Young People,* Harvey House, 1979; *Nature Runs Wild,* F. Watts, 1979; *Special Effects,* F. Watts, 1980. Also author of *Working With Horses: A Round-Up of Careers* (juvenile), Dodd.

Films: "Gold: The First Metal," North American Film Co., 1978. Also author of "A Visit With 'Don Juan in Hell,'" released by North American Film Co.

Work represented in anthologies, including *Look Who's Here* and *Metrovoices.* Author of "Women Who Win" and "Everywoman's Guide to Money Matters," columns in *Money-Making Opportunities.* Contributor of more than two hundred articles to magazines for adults and children.

WORK IN PROGRESS: A book on holistic health for teenagers; a book on women adventurers.

SIDELIGHTS: Karen Sweeney writes: "With my background in teaching, scout leadership, and volunteer library activities, I've always worked with children and young adults. I feel I have a real affinity with their needs, desires, aspirations, and interests. I love writing for them.

"I also enjoy expressing my talent in advertising promotion. The contrast to my other work provides challenge, variety, and a new and stimulating pace. There isn't any area of nonfiction writing that I don't enjoy. I've tried most and will continue to expand in every way I can."

AVOCATIONAL INTERESTS: Horses, tennis, natural foods, running, the oceans and mountains, travel (England, France, Tahiti, Mexico), the western United States and its heritage and culture.

* * *

SWEETS, John Frank 1945-

PERSONAL: Born July 18, 1945, in Knoxville, Tenn.; son of John R., Jr. (an electrical engineer) and Evelyn (Irby) Sweets; married Judith Metcalf (a lacemaker), August 24, 1967; children: Craig William. *Education:* Florida State University, B.A., 1967; Duke University, M.A., 1969, Ph.D., 1972; attended Sorbonne, University of Paris, 1966. *Office:* Department of History, University of Kansas, Lawrence, Kan. 66045.

CAREER: University of Kansas, Lawrence, assistant professor, 1972-76, associate professor of history, 1977—. Visiting professor at National University of Ireland, University College, Dublin, 1978. *Member:* American Historical Association, Society for French Historical Studies, Western Society for French History (member of council). *Awards, honors:* Woodrow Wilson fellowship, 1967; Danforth fellowship, 1969-71; National Endowment for the Humanities fellowship, 1978-79.

WRITINGS: The Politics of Resistance in France, Northern Illinois University Press, 1976. Contributor of articles and reviews to journals.

WORK IN PROGRESS: Clermont-Ferrand During the Second World War, completion expected in 1980.

* * *

SWICK, Clarence 1883(?)-1979

OBITUARY NOTICE: Born c. 1883 in Niagara County, N.J.; died December 4, 1979, in Arlington, Va. Mathematician and author. Swick was associated with the U.S. Coast and Geodetic Survey for over thirty-five years. His major field, that of geodesy, is a mathematical science concerned with measurement of the earth. Swick was the author of *Modern Methods of Measuring the Intensity of Gravity,* in addition to many papers on different aspects of geodesy. Obituaries and other sources: *Washington Post,* December 6, 1979.

* * *

SWING, Raymond Gram 1887-1968

OBITUARY NOTICE: Born March 25, 1887, in Cortland, N.Y.; died December 22, 1968, in Washington, D.C. Broadcaster, foreign correspondent, and author. Swing was best known for his commentaries on American affairs. During World War II, he worked as an announcer and commentator for the British Broadcasting Co. He also worked for both American Broadcasting Co. and Columbia Broadcasting System. His books include *How War Came, In the Name of Sanity,* and *Good Evening: A Professional Memoir.* Obituaries and other sources: *Current Biography,* Wilson, 1940, February, 1969; *Longman Companion to Twentieth Century Literature,* Longman, 1970.

SZABO, Denis 1929-

PERSONAL: Born June 4, 1929, in Budapest, Hungary; came to Canada, 1958, Canadian citizen, 1963; son of Denis and Catherine (Zsiga) Szabo; married Sylvie Grotard (a psychologist), June, 1956; children: Catherine, Marianne. *Education:* University of Louvain, Ph.D., 1956; Sorbonne, University of Paris, diploma, 1958. *Home:* 4742 Roslyn, Montreal, Quebec, Canada H3W 2L2. *Office:* International Centre for Comparative Criminology, University of Montreal, P.O. Box 6128, Montreal, Quebec, Canada H3C 3J7.

CAREER: Lecturer in sociology, University of Paris, Paris, France, and University of Lyon, Lyon, France, 1956-58; University of Montreal, Montreal, Quebec, assistant professor, 1958, associate professor, 1959, founder and director of department of criminology, 1960-70, professor of sociology, 1966—, founder and director of International Centre for Comparative Criminology, 1969—. Visiting professor and lecturer at numerous universities in United States, Europe, Africa, and Asia. Committee member of public institutions, including President's Committee on Law Enforcement and Administration of Criminal Justice, and Joint Committee on Correctional Manpower Training. *Member:* Societe internationale de criminologie (member of scientific commission, 1961-75; member of board of directors, 1966; vice-president, 1975-78; president), Societe internationale de defense sociale (Canadian scientific representative), Association internationale de sociologie, American Society of Criminology, American Sociological Society (fellow), National Council on Crime and Delinquency (Canadian correspondent), Royal Society of Canada (fellow), Societe canadienne de criminologie (vice-president, 1962-64), Societe canadienne de sociologie et d'anthropologie, Association canadienne des anthropologues, Psychologues sociaux et sociologues de langue francaise, Canadian Association of University Teachers, Association des sociologues de langue francaise, Societe de criminologie du Quebec (secretary-general, 1960-70). *Awards, honors:* Sutherland Award of American Society of Criminology, 1968; Beccaria Medal of Societe Allemande de Criminologie, 1970; officer of National Order of the Ivory Coast, 1972; Presidential Citation for distinguished contributions to Canadian criminology, 1975.

WRITINGS: Ordre et changement (title means "Social Order and Social Change"), Les Presses de l'Universite de Montreal, 1959; *Contribution a l'etude de la delinquance sexuelle: Les Delits sexuels des adolescents a Montreal* (title means "Contribution to the Study of Sexual Delinquency: Sexual Offences Among Adolescents in Montreal"), University of Montreal, 1960; *Crimes et villes: Etude statistique de la criminalite urbaine et rurale en France et en Belgique* (title means "Crime and the City: Statistical Study of Urban and Rural Crime in France and Belgium"), Cujas, 1960; *Delinquance sexuelle des adolescents a Montreal* (title means "Sexual Delinquency Among Adolescents in Montreal"), University of Montreal, 1960; *Delinquance juvenile: Etiologie et prophylaxie* (title means "Juvenile Delinquency: Etiology and Treatment"), North Holland Publishing Co., 1963; *Criminologie* (title means "Criminology"), Presses de l'Universite de Montreal, 1965; *Criminalite et deviance* (title means "Criminality and Deviance"), Colin, 1970; (with J. L. Beaudouin and J. Fortin) *Le Terrorisme et la justice* (title means "Terrorism and Justice"), Montreal Editions de Jour, 1971; (with D. Gagne and A. Parizeau) *L'Adolescent et la societe* (title means "The Adolescent and Society"), Dessart, 1972.

L'Afrique occidental: Development et societe (title means

"West Africa: Development and Society"), University of Montreal, 1972; (with M. Molins-Ysal and Parizeau) *La Theorie de la defense sociale et ses implications empiriqued* (title means "The Theory of Social Defence and Its Empiric Implications"), [Quebec], 1972; *Criminalite, planification de la prevention du crime et services de traitement des delinquants: La Cas de l'Afrique de l'Ouest* (title means "Criminality, Planning for the Prevention of Crime and Services for the Treatment of Delinquents: The Case of West Africa"), [Quebec], 1973; *La Criminologie: Theorie et Praxis* (title means "Criminology: Theory and Practice"), University of Montreal, 1974; (with Brillon, Tounissoux, and Normandeau) *Attitudes et opinion du public canadien envers l'administration de la justice* (title means "Attitudes and Opinions of the Canadian Public Regarding the Administration of Justice"), International Centre for Comparative Criminology, 1976; (with Parizeau) *Le Traitement de la criminalite au Canada,* Presses de l'Universite de Montreal, 1977, published as *The Canadian Criminal Justice System,* Lexington Books, 1978; (with R. D. Crelinsten) *Terrorism and Criminal Justice: An International Perspective,* Lexington Books, 1978; *Criminologie et politique criminelle* (title means "Criminology and Crime Policy"), Vrin, 1978; (with Crelinsten) *Hostage Taking,* Lexington Books, 1979.

Editor: J. M. Rico and G. Tardif, *Enquete d'opinion publique sur la police au Quebec* (title means "Public Opinion Survey on the Quebec Police"), R. Lefebvre, 1969; Rico and Tardif, *Enquete d'opinion aupres de cinq services de police du Quebec* (title means "Opinion Survey Among Five of the Quebec Police Services"), R. Lefebvre, 1969; E. A. Fattah and A. Normandeau, *Sondage d'opinion publique sur la justice criminelle au Quebec* (title means "Public Opinion Survey on Criminal Justice in Quebec"), R. Lefebvre, 1970; J. L. Beaudouin and J. Fortin, *Sondage aupres des criminalistes de Montreal sur la justice criminelle au Quebec* (title means "Survey Among Criminal Lawyers on Criminal Justice in Quebec"), R. Lefebvre, 1970; Fattah and Rico, *Le Role de l'enseignement et de la recherche criminologique dans l'administration de la justice* (title means "The Role of Criminological Education and Research in the Administration of Justice"), R. Lefebvre, 1970; Fattah, R. Tremblay and C. Toutant, *L'Alcool chez les jeunes Quebecois* (title means "Alcohol and the Youth of Quebec"), Les Presses de l'Universite Laval, 1970; P. Dubois, J. Archambault, and R. Boissonneault, *La Satisfaction au travail des policiers municipaux du Quebec* (title means "Work Satisfaction Among Quebec Municipal Policemen"), R. Lefebvre, 1970.

(With G. Canepa) *Traitement des criminels et proces penal* (title means "The Treatment of Criminals and the Criminal Trial"), [Quebec], 1972; *La Criminalite urbaine et la crise de l'administration de la justice* (title means "Urban Crime and the Crisis in the Administration of Justice"), Les Presses de l'Universite de Montreal, 1973; *Police, culture et societe* (title means "The Policy, Culture and Society"), Les Presses de l'Universite de Montreal, 1973; (with Canepa) *Therapeuthique et recherche* (title means "Therapeutics and Research"), [Quebec], 1973; (with Canepa) *Diagnostic et pronostic differentiels de l'etat dangereux et traitement de ladelinquance juvenile* (title means "Differential Diagnosis and Prognosis on the State of Dangerousness and Treatment of Juvenile Delinquency"), [Quebec], 1974; (with Canepa) *Homocide, controle et autorite en institution* (title means "Homocide, Institutional Control and Authority"), [Quebec], 1975; (with S. Katzenelson) *Offenders and Corrections,* Praeger, 1978. Canadian correspondent, *Revue de droit penal et de criminologie.* Contributor of articles to publications, including *Criminal Law Quarterly, British Journal of Criminology,* and *Journal of Criminal Law and Criminology. Criminology* (formerly *Acta Criminologica*), founder, editor, 1968-75, now director; founding member, *Reseau;* member of editorial committees, *Criminologica* and *Bulletin de medecine legale et de toxicologie.*

SIDELIGHTS: Szabo told *CA:* "Variations and permanent features in deviant and criminal activities of men is a basic fact of the history of mankind. Relations between those features and civilizations of diverse types constitutes my basic interest.

"The history of mankind goes in cycles. To judge whether it is up or down depends on the criteria we use. Progress for some may be regression for others. As far as I am concerned, I feel that humanity is undergoing a deep crisis which originates mainly in the confusion between the philosophy of skepticism and relativism, proper to scientific endeavour, but unacceptable as a philosophy of life. It requires a commitment to specific values. You can equate two values as a social analyst; you cannot as a man, as a citizen. You must choose—you have to have options. You cannot accept paralyzing compromises."

T

TAFEL, Edgar Allen 1912-

PERSONAL: Born March 4, 1912, in New York, N.Y.; son of Samuel and Rose (Chary) Tafel. *Education:* Attended New York University, 1930-32, and Frank Lloyd Wright's Taliesin Fellowship, Wisconsin and Arizona, 1932-41. *Home:* 14 East 11th St., New York, N.Y. 10003.

CAREER: Architect and consultant in New York, N.Y., 1946—. Adjunct professor at New School for Social Research. Lecturer at Smithsonian Institution, Metropolitan Meseum of Art, and schools, including Princeton University, Yale University, New York University, and Columbia University; lecturer for U.S. Information Service in India, Israel, England, and the Netherlands. Architectural designs include places of worship, college facilities, museums, and homes. *Military service:* U.S. Army, 1944-46; served in China-Burma-India theater; became staff sergeant.

MEMBER: American Institute of Architects (member of local executive committee), National Academy of Design, Guild of Religious Architecture, New York Society of Architects, New York City Mission Society (member of board of directors), Washington Square Association (president). *Awards, honors:* Award of merit from Fifth Avenue Association, 1960, for design of Presbyterian church; service citation from State University of New York College at Geneseo, 1970.

WRITINGS: Apprentice to Genius: Years With Frank Lloyd Wright, McGraw, 1979. Contributor to architecture journals. Contributing editor of *Your Church,* 1965—.

SIDELIGHTS: Tafel's architectural designs include a Protestant chapel, the fine arts building at State College in Geneseo, N.Y., and over ninety residences. He also has worked on the restoration of Frank Lloyd Wright's D. D. Martin house in Buffalo, N.Y., and on the Tafel-designed Allentown (Pa.) Art Museum. He instigated the saving of Wright's Little House in Minneapolis, Minn., for installation at the Metropolitan Museum of Art in New York City.

* * *

TAICHERT, Louise C(ecile) 1925-

PERSONAL: Born May 16, 1925, in Las Vegas, N.M.; daughter of Joseph A. (a wool merchant) and Annie (Stein) Taichert; married Sanford E. Feldman (a surgeon and research scientist); children: John Taichert. *Education:* University of California, Berkeley, B.A., 1947; University of Denver, M.S., 1949; University of Colorado, M.D., 1954; postdoctoral study at University of California, San Francisco, 1966-67. *Residence:* Mill Valley, Calif. *Office:* 3600 California St., San Francisco, Calif. 94118.

CAREER: Mt. Zion Hospital, San Francisco, Calif., intern, 1954-55; Children's Hospital, Oakland, Calif., resident in pediatrics, 1955-56; Children's Hospital, San Francisco, Calif., resident in pediatrics, 1956-57; St. Mary's Hospital, San Francisco, Calif., resident in pediatrics, 1959-60; private practice of pediatrics, 1961-66, and management of children's learning and behavior problems and family therapy, 1967—. Diplomate of American Board of Pediatrics; physician at Mt. Zion Hospital's Pediatric Outpatient Clinic, 1961-66. Assistant clinical professor at University of California, San Francisco, 1967—. President of board of directors of Sterne School (private school for the educationally handicapped). *Member:* American Psychiatric Association, American Academy of Child Psychiatry, American Academy of Pediatrics (fellow), California Medical Association, San Francisco Medical Society.

WRITINGS: Childhood Learning, Behavior, and the Family, Behavioral Publications, 1973; (contributor) Glen Austin, editor, *The Parent's Guide to Child Raising,* Prentice-Hall, 1978. Contributor to medical and health journals.

SIDELIGHTS: Louise Taichert comments: "I recognize and write about the importance of the child's inherent learning and language ability, the effects of family dynamics on the emotional and personality development of the child, and the need to take a *neuro-developmental-family approach* in the evaluation and treatment of children with emotional and behavioral problems."

AVOCATIONAL INTERESTS: Music, tennis, the Southwest (is a New Mexico landscape artist).

* * *

TAPSCOTT, Stephen 1948-

PERSONAL: Born November 5, 1948, in Des Moines, Iowa; son of Leo J. (a farmer) and Mary Jean (a journalist; maiden name, Nesbitt) Tapscott; married Susan N. Tarrant, June 10, 1972. *Education:* University of Notre Dame, B.A., 1970; Cornell University, Ph.D., 1975. *Home:* 50 Old County Rd., Hudson, Mass. 01249. *Office:* Department of Humanities, Massachusetts Institute of Technology, Cambridge, Mass. 02139.

CAREER: University of Kent at Canterbury, Canterbury, England, lecturer in English, 1976-77; Massachusetts Institute of Technology, Cambridge, assistant professor of English, 1977—. Member of faculty at Goddard College, 1976—.

WRITINGS: *Mesopotamia* (poems), Wesleyan University Press, 1975.

WORK IN PROGRESS: A volume of poetry, *Letter to an Immigrant.*

* * *

TARNOWER, Herman 1910-

PERSONAL: Born March 18, 1910, in New York, N.Y. *Education:* Syracuse University, M.D., 1933; post-graduate study in cardiology at London Hospital, London, England, and in internal medicine at Wilhelmona Gasthuis, Amsterdam, Holland, 1936-37. *Office:* 259 Heathcote Rd., Scarsdale, N.Y. 10583.

CAREER: Bellevue Hospital, New York, N.Y., intern, 1933-35, resident, 1935-36; White Plains Hospital, White Plains, N.Y., attending cardiologist, 1939—; Grasslands Hospital, director of cardiology, 1946-75; consulting cardiologist at St. Agnes Hospital, 1973—, and at Westchester County Medical Center, 1975—. Presbyterian Hospital, New York City, assistant physician, 1939-50; Columbia College of Physicians and Surgeons, New York City, assistant in medicine, 1939-50; New York University, New York City, associate professor, 1958-65; New York Medical College, New York City, clinical professor of medicine, 1975—. Scarsdale Medical Center, Scarsdale, N.Y., founder and senior staff member. *Military service:* U.S. Army, Medical Corps, 1942-46; chief of service at station hospitals; member of Atomic Bomb Casualty Survey Commission at Nagasaki and Hiroshima. *Member:* American College of Physicians (fellow), American Medical Association, American Heart Association, Westchester Heart Association (president, 1950-55; chairman of the board of directors, 1955—).

WRITINGS: (With Samm Sinclair Baker) *The Complete Scarsdale Medical Diet,* Rawson, Wade, 1979.

SIDELIGHTS: Dr. Tarnower has been a practicing internist and cardiologist for over forty years. A firm believer in good nutrition, he often counsels his heart patients about losing weight. The Scarsdale Diet started in Dr. Tarnower's office: he made a list of good foods to eat and the foods to resist, and then mimeographed copies for his patients. But the diet that became so successful for his patients was passed on by word of mouth to other overweight people and Dr. Tarnower was soon besieged by thousands of requests for his diet.

Tarnower is pleased by the success of his weight-reduction plan, especially since he is not a "diet doctor." In *The Complete Scarsdale Medical Diet* he discusses the background for the diet, answers questions concerning the foods listed on the diet, and describes, in addition to the core diet, other variations such as a vegetarian diet and an international diet. Tarnower also includes his weight maintenance program for preventing future weight gain.

The Scarsdale Diet is successful because weight is lost quickly. Tarnower reported: "Studying other diets and their faults and flaws, I came to the conclusion that they were too complicated to too slow, overly demanding, or had other defects that turned people away." The maximum weight loss per each two week period on the core diet is twenty pounds, according to Tarnower, and in the book he includes quotes from those who have lost weight on the diet to substantiate his claims.

In the book Tarnower reveals an understanding of the mind of the obese person who is desperately trying to lose weight. For instance, he notes: "The more you worry about food, the more you even think about it while you're on a diet, the more difficult and tiresome the whole process can become." Tarnower has planned the diet around the problems and anxieties of the overweight person and has been successful where other basic twelve-hundred calorie diets have failed. His knowledge and understanding, gained through years of clinical practice, are a boon to those persons who are struggling with the problems of the overweight.

BIOGRAPHICAL/CRITICAL SOURCES: Herman Tarnower and Samm Sinclair Baker, *The Complete Scarsdale Medical Diet,* Rawson, Wade, 1979.

* * *

TASCA, Henry J. 1912-1979

OBITUARY NOTICE: Born August 23, 1912, in Providence, R.I.; died August 22, 1979, in Lausanne, Switzerland. Diplomat and author. Tasca served as the U.S. ambassador to both Morocco and Greece. In addition he was associated with, among others, the U.S. Operations Mission in Italy, the Marshall Plan, the Treasury Department, and the National Defense Committee in various economic and political positions. He was awarded the Medal of Freedom, the Korean distinguished service award, and the Grand Cordon of the Ouissam Alaouite from Morocco. Tasca was the author of several books, including *World Trading Systems: A Study of American and British Commercial Policies* and *The Reciprocal Trade Policy of the U.S.: A Study in Trade Philosophy.* Obituaries and other sources: *Newsweek,* August 12, 1974; *Who's Who in American Politics,* 6th edition, Bowker, 1977; *Who's Who in the World,* 4th edition, Marquis, 1978; *The International Who's Who,* Europa, 1979; *New York Times,* August 25, 1979; *Washington Post,* August 25, 1979.

* * *

TAUBER, Gerald E(rich) 1922-

PERSONAL: Born October 31, 1922, in Vienna, Austria; son of Friedrich and Helen (Kreidl) Tauber; married Lydia Rudoler, October 21, 1956; children: Peter M., Robert B., Chanan D. *Education:* University of Toronto, B.A. (with honors), 1946; University of Minnesota, M.A., 1947, Ph.D., 1951. *Home:* 93 Hauniversita, Tel Aviv, Israel. *Office:* Department of Physics, Tel Aviv University, Tel Aviv, Israel.

CAREER: McMaster University, Hamilton, Ontario, lecturer in physics, 1950-52; Western Reserve University (now Case Western Reserve University), Cleveland, Ohio, assistant professor, 1954-57, associate professor, 1957-61, professor of physics, 1961-66; Tel Aviv University, Tel Aviv, Israel, professor of physics, 1966—. Consultant to Franklin Institute. *Member:* American Physical Society, Religious Zionists of America (chairperson of B'nai Akiba, 1946-50), Israel Physical Society, Canadian Association of Physicists. *Awards, honors:* National Research Council fellow, 1952-54.

WRITINGS: *Internal State of Gravitating Gas,* American Physical Society, 1961; *Man's View of the Universe: A Pictorial History,* Crown, 1979; *Albert Einstein's General Theory of Relativity,* Crown, 1979; *Einstein on Zionism, Palestine, and Arabs,* Tel Aviv University, 1979. Contributor of about fifty articles to scientific journals.

WORK IN PROGRESS: *Source and Notebook on Cosmology,* publication expected in 1980; *Mathematical Methods of Physics; Unified Field Theories;* research on cosmology, general relativity, and relativistic astrophysics.

SIDELIGHTS: Tauber told *CA:* "I had started a slide collection on the history of astronomy for a course I was intending to give when it occurred to me that this could form the basis for a book on the subject. Herbert Michelman, president of Crown Publishers, was interested, but thought that more than just pictures was needed. Also, he wanted about nine hundred pictures, which was twice the amount I had gathered. I began to work in earnest, seeking illustrations from observatories, publishers, and everyone who had some connection with the subjects I wanted to cover. All that took a lot of time, and money as well, because I had neglected to ask for a special grant in my contract. But it was worthwhile.

"*Man's View of the Universe* tells the whole story from earliest times until the present, in words and pictures. It is written in nontechnical language, but is scientifically correct. A lot of the so-called popular expositions are either too technical or oversimplify matters and tell only part of the story. I have always believed that it is important to popularize science for the general reader, but at the same time to tell all the facts and not try to gloss over more difficult points.

"Einstein's 100th birthday was celebrated in March of 1979. Since my own field of research was general relativity, I was familiar with his work and had even had the privilege of meeting Einstein in 1952 and discussing my Ph.D. thesis with him. I convinced Herbert Michelman, who had also known Einstein, that we could pay tribute to the memory of Einstein by publishing his more popular writings along with short articles by well known scientists to bring the book up to date. That's how *Albert Einstein's General Theory of Relativity* was born. Despite its imposing title it contains mostly nontechnical articles.

"Now that my appetite has been whetted I want to continue writing books. I have also designed several educational games for math and physics, again out of the desire to make learning palatable to the average student."

* * *

TAYLOR, Albert E(dward) 1908-

PERSONAL: Born March 9, 1908, in Kilgore, Idaho; son of Peter E. (a farmer) and Esther (a school matron; maiden name, Schofield) Taylor; married Ruby Colony (a librarian), September 16, 1931; children: Arlen E., Carla Taylor Ellis, Glamae Taylor Brigham. *Education:* Attended Idaho Technical Institute (now Idaho State University), 1926-27; University of Idaho, Southern Branch (now Idaho State University), A.S., 1929; University of Kansas, B.A., 1930, M.A., 1934; University of Michigan, Ph.D., 1945. *Home:* 805 South 19th Ave., Pocatello, Idaho 83201.

CAREER: Idaho State University, Pocatello, instructor, 1930-38, assistant professor, 1938-46, associate professor, 1946-57, professor of chemistry, 1957-73, dean of graduate school, 1957-73, assistant dean of liberal arts division, 1965-67; writer, 1973—. Member of board of directors of Idaho State Civic Symphony and Tendoy Girls' Camp (head of board, 1974—). *Member:* American Chemical Society, American Association for the Advancement of Science, Idaho Academy of Science (president, 1960-61), Sigma Xi (president, 1959-60).

WRITINGS: (With William E. Davis) *It's a Long Way to Camas Meadows,* Idaho State University Press, 1976. Contributor to scientific journals.

SIDELIGHTS: Taylor told *CA:* "I had two older brothers who flew fighter planes with the Royal Air Force in World War I. One returned after thirteen months in a German prison camp. The other was missing in action on August 24, 1918, and never found, but during his service and training he wrote over one hundred letters home. Those letters are the basis of the publication *It's a Long Way to Camas Meadows.* I was hopeful that the League of Nations would pave the way to lasting peace among nations, but unfortunately that was not the case. We have a second chance now with the United Nations, and I hope that this time we are successful."

AVOCATIONAL INTERESTS: Hunting, fishing, cross-country skiing, hiking.

* * *

TAYLOR, (Joseph) Deems 1885-1966

OBITUARY NOTICE: Born December 22, 1885, in New York, N.Y.; died July 3, 1966. Composer, critic, editor, translator, and writer. Taylor attracted a large and diverse following because his compositions, writings, and radio presentations were intended for people of all types of musical taste. In addition to his positions as music critic for the *New York World* and music editor for *Encyclopaedia Britannica,* Taylor was also commentator for the New York Philharmonic Sunday broadcasts from 1936 to 1943. He revised and published these broadcasts as *Of Men and Music.* Among his musical compositions are the operas "The King's Henchman" and "Peter Ibbetson," both of which were performed at the Metropolitan Opera House. In 1967 the American Society of Composers, Authors and Publishers (ASCAP) established the annual ASCAP-Deems Taylor Award for outstanding books and articles about music, musicians, or composers. Obituaries and other sources: *Current Biography,* Wilson, 1940, November, 1966; *The Oxford Companion to American Literature,* 4th edition, Oxford University Press, 1965; *The ASCAP Biographical Dictionary of Composers, Authors, and Publishers,* American Society of Composers, Authors and Publishers, 1966; *Who Was Who in America,* 4th edition, Marquis, 1968.

* * *

TAYLOR, Margaret Stewart (Margaret Collier)

PERSONAL: Born in Coventry, England; daughter of Stewart (a headmaster) and Florence (Bolderston) Taylor. *Education:* St. Hilda's College, Oxford, M.A. *Home:* St. Tydfil's Court, Flat 36, Caedraw Rd., Merthyr Tydfil, Glamorganshire, Wales.

CAREER: Coventry Public Libraries, Coventry, England, c. 1934; University of London, London, England, lecturer in library science, 1935-46; Merthyr Tydfil Corp., Merthyr Tydfil, Wales, chief librarian, 1947-67; free-lance writer, 1967—. *Member:* Library Association (fellow), Soroptimist International (president of Wales Division, 1963-64).

WRITINGS—Nonfiction: *A Handbook of Classification and Cataloguing for School and College Librarians,* Allen & Unwin, 1939; *Fundamentals of Practical Cataloguing,* Allen & Unwin, 1947; *County Borough of Merthyr Tydfil, 1905-1955: Fifty Years of Municipal Progress Following the Grant of a Charter of Incorporation,* privately printed, 1956; *The Crawshays of Cyfarthfa Castle: A Family History,* R. Hale, 1967; *St. Helena: Ocean Roadhouse* (travel book), R. Hale, 1969; *Wht's Yr Nm* (juvenile), Harcourt, 1970; *Basic Reference Sources: A Self-Study Manual,* Scarecrow, 1971, new edition, 1973; *Focus on the Falkland Islands* (travel book), R. Hale, 1971; *Caravan* (poems), privately printed, 1973; (with Rochelle Holt) *Yellow Pears, Smooth as Silk,* Ragnarok, 1975.

Historical novels: *Another Door Opened,* R. Hale, 1963; *The Link Was Strong,* R. Hale, 1964; *Marian's Daughter,* R. Hale, 1967; *The Nymphet,* New English Library, 1970; *Napoleon's Captor,* R. Hale, 1971; *Pursuit of a Heart,* R. Hale, 1972; *Marriage of Convenience,* R. Hale, 1973; *The Wayward Jilt,* R. Hale, 1974; *Because of a Duel,* R. Hale, 1975; *The Missing Heirloom,* R. Hale, 1976; *A Dream Reborn,* R. Hale, 1977; (under pseudonym Margaret Collier) *The Mangrove Swamp,* R. Hale, 1978; *The Bell Stone,* R. Hale, 1979. Contributor to magazines and newspapers, including *Glamorgan Historian* and *Country Quest.*

WORK IN PROGRESS: Research for a historical novel about the S.S. *Great Britain.*

SIDELIGHTS: Margaret Taylor writes: "I use my own name for historical novels of the eighteenth century, and the pseudonym Margaret Collier for novels of the early nineteenth century. I do a great deal of research through travel (Europe, Iceland, the United States, including Alaska, Mexico, Guatemala, Belize, the Falklands, St. Helena, India, Iran, and Anatolia) and extensive use of books and manuscripts in libraries."

* * *

TAYLOR, Phoebe Jean 1921(?)-1979

OBITUARY NOTICE: Born c. 1921 in New York, N.Y.; died November 12, 1979, in Washington, D.C. Counselor, lecturer, and author. Taylor was affiliated with several personnel firms before beginning her own consulting service in career counseling. She was a frequent lecturer and authored the book *How to Succeed in the Business of Finding a Job.* Obituaries and other sources: *Washington Post,* November 15, 1979.

* * *

TELL, Jack 1909(?)-1979

OBITUARY NOTICE: Born c. 1909; died August 26, 1979, in Las Vegas, Nev. Tell was well known as the founder and editor of a weekly Jewish newspaper, the *Las Vegas Israelite.* He worked for *Billboard* magazine before moving to the *New York Times* for ten years as assistant to the picture editor. At one time he organized a group to purchase the *Territorial Enterprise,* a newspaper originally belonging to Mark Twain. Obituaries and other sources: *New York Times,* September 8, 1979.

* * *

TEMPLE, Robert Kyle Grenville 1945-

PERSONAL: Born January 25, 1945; married Olivia Moyra Nockolds (an artist), December 30, 1972. *Education:* University of Pennsylvania, B.A., 1965; graduate study, 1965-67; University of Warwick, Ph.D., 1980. *Agent:* David Higham Associates Ltd., 5-8 Lower John St., Golden Sq., London WIR 3PE, England.

CAREER: Writer. Director of Foundation for the Study of Intelligent Life in the Universe, 1979—. *Member:* British Astronomical Association, British Interplanetary Society (fellow), Royal Astronomical Society (fellow), Royal United Services Institute for Defence Studies, American Association for the Advancement of Science, P.E.N., Egypt Exploration Society, Foreign Press Association of London, English-Speaking Union (and Club), L-5 Society (for space colonization).

WRITINGS: The Sirius Mystery, Sidgwick & Jackson, 1976; *Foreshadows,* Sidgwick & Jackson, 1980. Contributor to *Second Look* and *Biographical Dictionary of Seventeenth Century Radicals.* Senior editor of *Second Look,* 1978.

WORK IN PROGRESS: A book dealing with the execution of King Charles I and the founding of the Republic, entitled *The Men Who Killed the King;* a novel about alchemy.

SIDELIGHTS: Temple told *CA:* "It is essential that we prepare for the greatest trauma in the history of mankind since the discovery of fire: contact with intelligent life elsewhere in the universe. My writing and editing has been primarily devoted to this subject. Only by comparison with other intelligent beings can we hope to arrive at a realistic appraisal of our selves and our status as a species. This in turn will enable us to view many of our serious problems in a more helpful perspective, but whether we can deal with these problems will inevitably depend on our own strength of will and character. Thus it is necessary to have always in mind the desperate need for a continual elevation of our culture, an exhorting towards ethical aims, and a building of true civilization. Our writing should always touch upon the eternal verities, and never descend to wallowing self-indulgence."

BIOGRAPHICAL/CRITICAL SOURCES: Observatory, April, 1975; *Washington Star,* September 1, 1975; *London Sunday Express,* January 25, 1976; *London Times,* February 26, 1976, February 27, 1976, February 29, 1976; *London Daily Telegraph,* February 26, 1976; *Manchester Guardian,* February 27, 1976; *London Observer,* March 7, 1976; *Nature,* June 17, 1976.

* * *

THAMM, Robert 1933-

PERSONAL: Born June 7, 1933, in Oak Park, Ill.; son of Les W. (a bus driver) and Violet (Baethke) Thamm. *Education:* Drake University, B.S., 1955; Northern Illinois University, M.S., 1957, C.A.S., 1959; Michigan State University, Ph.D., 1968. *Politics:* "Liberal-Radical." *Religion:* Agnostic. *Home:* 361 West Rincon, Campbell, Calif. 95008. *Office:* Department of Sociology, San Jose State University, San Jose, Calif. 95192.

CAREER: San Jose State University, San Jose, Calif., associate professor of sociology, 1969—. *Military service:* U.S. Air Force, 1957; became second lieutenant. *Member:* National Council on Family Relations.

WRITINGS: Beyond Marriage and the Nuclear Family, Canfield Press, 1979. Contributor to *Transactional Analysis Journal.*

WORK IN PROGRESS: The Sociology of Emotions: Towards a General Systematic Theory.

SIDELIGHTS: Thamm writes: "My interest is in alternative life styles: I have lived in a communal family for the past six years. I am also interested in open mate relationships as opposed to the traditional monogamy and superficial single life." *Avocational interests:* Architecture, construction.

* * *

THAYER, Geraldine
See DANIELS, Dorothy

* * *

THAYER, V(ivian) T(row) 1886-1979

OBITUARY NOTICE—See index for *CA* sketch: Born October 13, 1886, in Tomora, Neb.; died July 19, 1979, in Winter Haven, Fla. Educator and author. A leader in progressive education, Thayer served as the director of the Ethical Culture Schools in New York City from 1928 to 1948. His interest in the philosophy of John Dewey led him to write *John Dewey: Middle Works, 1899-1924,* and he wrote a number of other books as well, including *American Education Under Fire, The Role of the School in American Society,* and *Formative Ideas in American Education.* Obituaries and other sources: *Who's Who in America,* 39th edition, Marquis, 1976; *New York Times,* July 22, 1979.

* * *

THE GALLERITE
See BASON, Frederick (Thomas)

* * *

THOMAS, R(onald) S(tuart) 1913-

PERSONAL: Born in 1913 in Cardiff, Wales; married Mildred Eldridge (a painter); children: one son. *Education:* University of Wales, B.A., 1935; attended St. Michael's College, Llandaff. *Home:* Aberdaron, Pwllheli, Caernarvon, Wales.

CAREER: Ordained a deacon of the Anglican Church, 1936, priest, 1937; curate of Chirk, 1936-40; curate of Hanmer, 1940-42; rector of Manafon, Montgomeryshire, 1942-54; vicar of St. Michaels's, Eglwysfach, Cardiganshire, 1954-67; vicar of St. Hywyn, Aberdaron, with St. Mary, Bodferin, 1967—. *Awards, honors:* Heinemann Award, 1955, for *Song at the Year's Turning;* Queen's Gold Medal for Poetry, 1964; Welsh Arts Council Award, 1968.

WRITINGS—Poetry: *The Stones of the Field,* Druid Press, 1946; *An Acre of Land,* Montgomeryshire Printing Company, 1952; *The Minister,* Montgomeryshire Printing Company, 1953; *Song at the Year's Turning: Poems 1942-1954,* Hart-Davis, 1955; *Poetry for Supper,* Hart-Davis, 1958, Dufour, 1961; *Judgment Day,* Poetry Book Society, 1960; *Tares,* Dufour, 1961; (with Lawrence Durrell and Elizabeth Jennings) *Penguin Modern Poets,* Volume 1, Penguin (London), 1962; *The Bread of Truth,* Dufour, 1963; *Pieta,* Hart-Davis, 1966; *Not That He Brought Flowers,* Hart-Davis, 1968; (with Roy Fuller) *Pergamon Poets,* Volume 1, edited by Evan Owen, Pergamon, 1968; *Postcard: Song,* Fishpaste Postcard Series, 1968; *The Mountains,* Chilmark Press, 1963; *H'm: Poems,* St. Martin's, 1972; *Young and Old,* Chatto & Windus, 1972; *Selected Poems 1946-1968,* Hart-Davis MacGibbon, 1973, St. Martin's, 1974; *What Is a Welshman?,* Christopher Davies, 1974; *Laboratories of the Spirit,* Macmillan (London), 1975, Godine, 1976.

Prose: *Words and the Poet,* University of Wales Press, 1964.

Editor: *The Batsford Book of Country Verse,* Batsford, 1961; *The Penguin Book of Religious Verse,* Penguin (London), 1963; Edward Thomas, *Selected Poems,* Faber, 1964; *A Choice of George Herbert's Verse,* Faber, 1967; *A Choice of Wordsworth's Verse,* Faber, 1971.

SIDELIGHTS: "Harsh" is a word that recurs in discussions of R. S. Thomas's poetry, and it applies to his style as well as to the Welsh hills that provide the grim setting for his verse. From the appearance of his first volume, *The Stones of the Field,* in 1946, he has concerned himself with the hard realities of the human condition, offering what James F. Knapp described as "an unsparingly bleak view of man" in poems that are austere and unadorned.

Thomas explained his point of view in an essay, "A Frame for Poetry," which appeared in the *Times Literary Supplement* in 1966. "We are told with increasing vehemence that this is a scientific age", he wrote, "that science is transforming the world, but is it not also a mechanized and impersonal age, an analytic and clinical one; an age in which under the hard gloss of affluence there can be detected the murmuring of the starved heart and the uneasy spirit?"

Thomas's struggle, Alan Brownjohn believes, "is to make sense of the relationship between his world, his poetry, and his religion." The barren fields of the Welsh countryside and the cold machines of modern urban centers figure equally as he wrestles with simultaneous scorn and sympathy for those who share his surroundings. Aware of the merciless nature of things, he wrestles, too, with God and with "the failure of words, in poetry as in prayer."

The unrelenting harshness of the lives he portrays is carried over into Thomas's style. His language is simple, with no obvious devices—what Ian Hamilton has called "the plain, sombre style" and Russell Davies has called "the peculiarly straight-talking private idiom of North Wales." Peripherally associated with the Movement in Britain, those post-World War II poets who combined a devotion to the "plain style" with a sense of social responsibility, Thomas's work is still praised for such qualities as clarity, economy, and purity. Brownjohn explains: "Innovation is unimportant. . . . The only point is the exactest possible application of word to bitter experience." Julian Symons has defined the resultant poems as "finely wrought" while Peter Porter found them "seamless."

Although R. S. Thomas is considered the most famous Welsh poet after Dylan Thomas, his work is not widely known in the United States, a fact bemoaned by many critics. In a review of *Laboratories of the Spirit, Choice* concluded: "Thomas has a very solid talent for poetry and deserves to gain here the reputation he enjoys at home." And Peter Porter, who actually didn't enjoy *Not That He Brought Flowers,* believed nevertheless that "Reverend Thomas is a master, without doubt."

BIOGRAPHICAL/CRITICAL SOURCES: Times Literary Supplement, March 3, 1966; *Punch,* November 13, 1968; *New Statesman,* December 13, 1968, September 29, 1972, October 24, 1975; *Observer Review,* December 15, 1968; *London Magazine,* March, 1969; *Twentieth Century Literature,* January, 1971; *Choice,* July/August, 1976; *Contemporary Literary Criticism,* Volume 6, Gale, 1976.*

* * *

THOMAS, Stephen N(aylor) 1942-

PERSONAL: Born February 17, 1942, in Lewiston, Idaho; son of Donald Albert (a writer) and Marian Elaine Thomas. *Education:* Harvard University, A.B., 1964; Massachusetts Institute of Technology, Ph.D., 1968. *Home and office:* 2809 Boyer Ave. E., Seattle, Wash. 98102.

CAREER: Massachusetts Institute of Technology, Cambridge, instructor in philosophy, 1968-69; University of Washington, Seattle, assistant professor, 1969-77; author and philosopher, 1977—. *Member:* American Philosophical Association, Phi Beta Kappa.

WRITINGS: Practical Reasoning in Natural Language, Prentice-Hall, 1977, 2nd edition, 1981; *The Formal Mechanics of Mind,* Cornell University Press, 1978.

SIDELIGHTS: Thomas writes: "My books follow the precept that philosophy fundamentally should involve the construction and remodeling of *conceptualizing structures* for dealing with ourselves, with others, and with the realities of our external surroundings. My first book provides a workable new model of the nature of reasoning in natural languages, and utilizes this model to show readers effectively how to analyze and evaluate reasoning and arguments in general. My second book offers a revolutionary, modern, scientific model of the psychophysical relationship that solves many long-standing philosophical problems about the mind-body relationship."

* * *

THOMPSON, Dorothy 1894-1961

OBITUARY NOTICE: Born July 9, 1894, in Lancaster, N.Y.; died January 30, 1961. Journalist and author. An outspoken foreign correspondent and political columnist, Thompson's numerous crusades included the New York women's suffrage campaign. She wrote for the *New York Herald Tribune,* the *New York Post,* and the *Ladies' Home Journal.* Her books include *The Courage to Be Happy, I Saw Hitler!,* and *Let the Record Speak.* Obituaries and other sources: *Current Biography,* Wilson, 1940, March, 1961; *The Oxford Companion to American Literature,* 4th edition, Oxford University Press, 1965; *The Reader's Encyclopedia,* 2nd edition, Crowell, 1965; *Who Was Who in America,* 4th edition, Marquis, 1968.

* * *

THOMPSON, Era Bell 1905-

PERSONAL: Born August 10, 1905, in Des Moines, Iowa; daughter of Stewart C. and Mary (Logan) Thompson. *Education:* Attended University of North Dakota, 1929-31; Morningside College, B.A., 1933, LL.D., 1965; also attended Northwestern University, 1938, 1940. *Religion:* Presbyterian. *Home:* 2851 Martin Luther King Dr., Apt. 1910, Chicago, Ill. 60616. *Office: Ebony,* 820 South Michigan Ave., Chicago, Ill. 60605.

CAREER: Senior interviewer, U.S. Employment service, 1942-46, and Illinois Employment Service, Chicago, 1946-47; Johnson Publishing Co., Inc., Chicago, associate editor, 1947-51; *Ebony,* Chicago, co-managing editor, 1951-64, international editor, 1964—. Member of North Central Region Manpower Advisory Committee, 1965-67; public member of U.S. Information Agency foreign service selection boards, 1976—. Member of board of trustees of Hull House, 1960-64. *Member:* Association for the Study of Afro-American Life and History, National Association for the Advancement of Colored People, Society of Midland Authors (member of board of directors, 1961-75), Urban League (Chicago), Friends of Chicago Public Library (member of board of directors, 1959-60), Iota Phi Lambda, Sigma Gamma Rho. *Awards, honors:* Fellow of Bread Loaf Writers Conference, 1949; Rockefeller fellowship, 1953; named woman of the year by Iota Phi Lambda, 1965; LL.D. from Morningside College, 1965; Patron Saints Award from Society of Midland Authors, 1968, for *American Daughter;* L.H.D. from University of North Dakota, 1969; Theodore Roosevelt Roughrider Award from state of North Dakota, 1976, for bringing credit to the state; cultural center at the University of North Dakota was named in honor of Era Thompson, 1979.

WRITINGS: American Daughter, University of Chicago Press, 1946, revised edition, 1974; *Africa: Land of My Fathers,* Doubleday, 1954; (editor with Herbert Nipson) *White on Black,* Johnson Publishing Co., 1963. Contributor to magazines.

SIDELIGHTS: Era Thompson comments: "For twenty-five years I have traveled all over the world, writing stories for *Ebony* on such diverse subjects as the racial situation in Australia, the independence of Nauru, and an interview with Rhodesia's Ian Smith. My chief interest, however, lies in the continent of Africa and its people."

* * *

THOMPSON, Fred P(riestly), Jr. 1917-

PERSONAL: Born November 15, 1917, in Lawton, Kan.; son of Fred P. (in law enforcement) and Mattie (Leonard) Thompson; married Dorothy Williams, September 30, 1940; children: Janet Thompson McClain, David, Donald, Dennis. *Education:* Pacific Christian College, B.A., 1939; Pepperdine University, B.A., 1948, M.A., 1950; Christian Theological Seminary, Indianapolis, Ind., B.D., 1952; postgraduate work at Garrett Theological Seminary, Evanston, Ill., 1959-64, and University of Chicago, 1965-66. *Politics:* Republican. *Home:* 1906 Eastwood Dr., Johnson City, Tenn. 37601. *Office:* Emmanuel School of Religion, Johnson City, Tenn. 37601.

CAREER: Ordained minister of Christian Church, 1938; pastor of Christian churches in Los Angeles, Calif., 1940-50, Greenwood, Ind., 1950-53, and Chicago, Ill., 1953-68; Emmanuel School of Religion, Johnson City, Tenn., president and professor of Christian doctrine, 1969—. *Member:* American Academy of Religion, Karl Barth Society, Theta Phi, Eta Beta Rho.

WRITINGS: Bible Prophecies, Standard Publishing, 1966; *The Holy Spirit,* Scripture Press, 1978; (contributor) William J. Richardson, editor, *Studies in Christian Doctrine,* Standard Publishing, 1980. Author of "At Issue," a column in *Action,* and "Reflecting on the News," a column in *Christian Standard.*

WORK IN PROGRESS: The Biblical Doctrines of Heaven and Hell, publication by College Press expected in 1981; a book on the Bible, *The Nature of Scripture* (tentative), publication expected in 1981.

SIDELIGHTS: Thompson writes: "I have been especially influenced by the works of P. T. Forsyth, C. S. Lewis, and Karl Barth. Issues of present concern are the relation of Revelation to scripture, the relation of the church to culture, and the nature of human nature. For instance, I regard it as crucial for the church to come to terms with the question of its proper response to the growing secularism of society. How can the church be rescued from becoming completely domesticated by the social order?

"I am also deeply concerned about environmental pollution as a result of the rape of nature by modern technology. Can the human race survive on this planet if technological sophistication is allowed to proceed without being made answerable to ethicists and theologians, or at least to ethical and theological judgments of value?"

* * *

THOMPSON, Ralph 1904-1979

OBITUARY NOTICE: Born November 11, 1904, in West Orange, N.J.; died November 12, 1979, in New York, N.Y. Critic, book club executive, educator, and author. Thompson was a book critic and columnist for the *New York Times* in the 1930's and 1940's, before he moved to *Time* magazine as contributing editor. He joined the Book-of-the-Month Club in 1951 as a secretary and rose in rank to editor and executive. He remained there until his death. He was the author of *American Literary Annuals and Gift Books,* and translator of *Uhde: Five Primitive Masters.* Obituaries and other sources: *New York Times,* November 13, 1979; *Washington Post,* November 15, 1979; *Chicago Tribune,* November 18, 1979; *AB Bookman's Weekly,* November 26, 1979; *Time,* November 26, 1979.

* * *

THORSELL, Richard Lawrence 1938-

PERSONAL: Born December 29, 1938, in Hartford, Conn.; son of Edward Perkins and Margaret (Johnson) Thorsell; married Carolyn Mayo, September 14, 1968 (divorced, 1976). *Education:* Attended Massachusetts Institute of Technology, 1956-58; University of Connecticut, B.A., 1962; Harvard University, M.B.A., 1964; doctoral study at Institute of Advanced Psychological Studies, Adelphi University, 1979—. *Office:* 30 Fifth Ave., New York, N.Y. 10011.

CAREER: Wells Fargo Bank, San Francisco, Calif., analyst, 1964-65; J. Barth & Co., San Francisco, senior analyst, 1965-68; Shareholders Management Co., Los Angeles, Calif., portfolio manager, 1968-72; Fidelity Management & Research, Boston, Mass., portfolio manager, 1972-74; Paine Webber, New York, N.Y., research director and chairman of investment committee, 1974-76; writer, 1976—. Member of Joint Council for Mental Health Services, and National Accreditation Association and American Examining Board of Psychoanalysis. Chairman of board of directors of Adams House (publisher); past member of corporate boards of directors. *Member:* National Psychological Association for Psychoanalysis (member-in-training, 1976—), Financial Analysts Federation (fellow), New York Society of Security Analysts, Phi Beta Kappa.

WRITINGS: The I.R.S. Audit Guide, Tax Rights, 1974, 3rd edition, Adams House, 1980; *The Independent Investor,* Adams House, 1977; *Investing on Your Own,* McGraw, 1979.

WORK IN PROGRESS: Revising *The Independent Investor,* publication by Adams House expected in 1981; a psychology book; a science fiction novel.

SIDELIGHTS: Thorsell comments: "I retired from the investment business at the age of thirty-seven, and wrote *Investing on Your Own* as a farewell gesture, to give others access to ideas which worked well for me. I am now working toward a doctorate in clinical psychology and certification in psychoanalysis. Future writing will reflect this complete change in career and a mid-life broadening of interests."

* * *

THRONEBERRY, Jimmy B. 1933-

PERSONAL: Born December 3, 1933, in Huntsville, Ala.; son of Oscar Lee and Florence (Timmons) Throneberry; married Barbara Miller (an elementary school teacher), September 12, 1954; children: James Barton, Christopher Lee. *Education:* David Lipscomb College, B.A., 1954; George Peabody College for Teachers, M.A., 1956; Michigan State University, Ph.D., 1962. *Politics:* Independent. *Religion:* Independent. *Home:* 714 Farris Rd., Conway, Ark. 72032. *Office:* Department of Biology, University of Central Arkansas, Conway, Ark. 72032.

CAREER: Abilene Christian College, Abilene, Tex., instructor, 1956-58, assistant professor, 1958-59, associate professor of biology, 1962-65; University of Central Arkansas, Conway, associate professor of biology, 1965-67; Arkansas State University, Jonesboro, professor of biology and head of department, 1968; University of Central Arkansas, began as associate professor, became professor of biology, 1969—. *Member:* American Institute of Biological Sciences, American Society of Zoologists, American Association of University Professors (state president, 1970; local president, 1971), Sigma Xi.

WRITINGS: (With N. D. Buffaloe) *Principles of Biology,* Prentice-Hall, 1967; (with Buffaloe and Collins) *Laboratory Manual for General Biology,* Prentice-Hall, 1967; (with Buffaloe) *Concepts of Biology,* Prentice-Hall, 1973.

WORK IN PROGRESS: Revising *Principles of Biology;* research on developmental biology.

SIDELIGHTS: Throneberry writes: "My interests are primarily in teaching and secondarily in research. I find the teaching of general biology to general education students quite challenging. I suppose this was my motivation for writing the textbooks. My specific research interest is cell and tissue differentiation."

AVOCATIONAL INTERESTS: Tennis, racquetball, fishing.

* * *

THURMOND, (J.) Strom 1902-

PERSONAL: Born December 5, 1902, in Edgefield, S.C.; son of John William and Eleanor Gertrude (Strom) Thurmond; married Jean Crouch, November 7, 1947 (died January, 1960); married Nancy Moore, December 22, 1968; children: (second marriage) Nancy Moore, J. Strom, Jr., Juliana Gertrude, Paul Reynolds. *Education:* Clemson College (now University), B.S., 1923. *Politics:* Republican. *Religion.* Baptist. *Residence:* McLean, Va. *Office:* Senate Office Bldg., Washington, D.C. 20510.

CAREER: Originally worked as a farmer; teacher and athletic coach in schools in South Carolina, 1923-29; admitted to the Bar of South Carolina, 1930; city attorney, county attorney, and superintendent of education in Edgefield County, S.C., 1929-33; South Carolina state senator, 1933-38; circuit judge in South Carolina, 1938-46; governor of South Carolina, 1947-51; Thurmond, Lybrand & Simons, Aiken, S.C., partner, 1951-55; U.S. senator from South Carolina, 1955—, serving on Armed Services Committee, ranking representative on Judiciary and Veteran Affairs Committees. States Rights candidate for U.S. president, 1948. Delegate at national Democratic conventions, 1932, 1936, 1948 (chairman of South Carolina delegation and national committeeman), 1952, 1956, and 1960; delegate at national Republican conventions, 1968 (chairman of South Carolina delegation), 1972, and 1976. Chairman of Southern Governors Conference, 1950. Admitted to practice in all Federal courts, including U.S. Supreme Court. Past trustee of Winthrop College; member of board of directors of Georgia-Carolina council of Boy Scouts of America. *Military service:* U.S. Army, 1942-46, served in European and Pacific theaters; became major general; received Legion of Merit with Oak Leaf Cluster, Bronze Star, Purple Heart, Croix de Guerre (France), Cross of Order of Crown (Belgium), Presidential Unit Citation, and numerous other medals and awards.

MEMBER: American Bar Association, American Legion (member of national defense committee), Military Government Association (past national president), Reserve Officers Association (past national president), South Carolina Bar Association (past vice-president), South Carolina Farm Bureau, Clemson College Alumni Association (past president), Lions International (past president), Woodmen of the World, Loyal Order of Moose, Masons, Phi Alpha Delta. *Awards, honors:* LL.D. from Bob Jones University, 1948, Presbyterian College, 1960, Clemson College, 1961, Lander College, 1963, and Yonsei University (Korea), 1974; Dr. Mil. Sci. from The Citadel, 1961; L.H.D. from Trinity College,

1965, and Allen University, 1974; Litt. D. from California Graduate School of Theology, 1970; Minuteman of the Year award from Reserve Officers Association, 1971; Patriots Award from Congressional Medal of Honor Society, 1974; distinguished public service award from American Legion and D.C.L. from Limestone College, both 1975.

WRITINGS: The Faith We Have Not Kept, Viewpoint Books, 1968; (with David Cortright) *Unions in the Military?: Pro, David Cortright; Con, Strom Thurmond,* American Enterprise Institute for Public Policy Research, 1977.

SIDELIGHTS: Long known as a vigorous but conservative politician, Strom Thurmond has been a fixture in the U.S. Senate for more than twenty-five years. Though most of his work has been in politics, he originally planned for a career in law by taking a nighttime correspondence class in the 1920's. Years later, backed with his experience as a judge and as a state senator, Thurmond defeated ten other candidates to win the 1947 South Carolina governorship and gained a U.S. Senate seat in 1954 through a write-in election (the first senator in history to do so). Serving his fifth term in the Senate, Thurmond is approaching his eightieth birthday as a continuing legend in South Carolina and the upper house of Congress.

Never known to back off a stand, Thurmond has spattered his career with evidence of his pungent politics. At the 1948 national Democratic convention he protested the party's civil rights platform by running for president himself—as a Dixiecrat. Later, he set a Senate filibuster record—twenty-four hours, eighteen minutes—while protesting a piece of civil rights legislation. In 1964, an angered Thurmond wrestled a fellow senator outside a Senate committee room; also in that year, he bolted from the Democratic party and joined the Republicans and Barry Goldwater in their States Rights-oriented campaign.

Aside from his political escapades, Thurmond has aroused many with his stances on certain issues. He has favored capital punishment and private ownership of handguns, and has opposed integration and the Panama Canal treaty. "He has been called a hawk, a reactionary and a racist by his critics," reported *Newsweek.* Nonetheless, Thurmond has earned the reputation of a winning politician: "He's absolutely the best politician I've ever run into, bar none," revealed Donald Fowler. Former Thurmond aide, Harry Dent, echoed this praise. "Strom is like a cat with nine lives," he said. "You could throw him off the Empire State Building and he'd land on his feet every time."

In recent years, Thurmond has acted to dispel the racist label often hurled at him. He has hired black staff members and has channeled federal dollars into South Carolina's predominantly black schools. Franklin Ashley cited a typical appeal to blacks during Thurmond's 1978 Senate campaign: "We admit Thurmond has made mistakes in the past, but the past is over. There is no doubt that Thurmond brings home the bacon and the fact is, he's going to be reelected, so why not get behind him?" Evidently, the pitch succeeded: ten of South Carolina's eleven black mayors endorsed him in the election. And while Thurmond could not carry these entire towns, the mayors' support "did make it difficult to organize the black vote against him," noted the *Nation.*

Despite his advancing age, Thurmond continues to serve actively in the Senate. In 1972, however, critics cited age as a factor in his campaign for reelection. Another term later, in 1978, Thurmond campaigned with the reputation as a physical fitness buff and with a campaign crew including his thirty-two-year-old wife and his four young children; few bothered to question the vitality of the indefatigable senator.

BIOGRAPHICAL/CRITICAL SOURCES: Nation, April 29, 1968, December 1, 1969, January 6, 1979; *Newsweek,* August 19, 1968, August 3, 1970, September 13, 1971, January 14, 1974, September 5, 1977, October 16, 1978; *New Republic,* August 24, 1968, August 31, 1968, November 4, 1978; *New York Times Magazine,* October 6, 1968; *Time,* August 3, 1970, October 16, 1978; *Atlantic,* May, 1972; George Douth, *Leaders in Profile: The U.S. Senate,* Speer & Douth, 1975; *Biography News,* Gale, November/December, 1975; *Economist,* September 10, 1977; *U.S. News and World Report,* October 16, 1978; *Politics Today,* November, 1978; *Macleans,* November 6, 1978; *People,* November 27, 1978.*

* * *

THURSTON, Elliott Ladd 1895-1975

OBITUARY NOTICE: Born October 1, 1895, in Fall River, Mass.; died September 2, 1975. Journalist. Thurston worked as reporter and Washington correspondent for newspapers, including the *Providence Journal, New York Sun, Philadelphia Record,* and *New York World.* For the latter he was chief of the Washington bureau from 1929 to 1931. Thurston was also an assistant to the board of governors of the Federal Reserve System for twenty-five years. Obituaries and other sources: *Who's Who in America,* 38th edition, Marquis, 1974.

* * *

TIBBETTS, John C(arter) 1946-
(Jack Ketch)

PERSONAL: Born October 6, 1946, in Leavenworth, Kan.; son of James C. (a printer) and Dorothy G. Tibbetts. *Education:* University of Kansas, B.A., 1969, M.A., 1975, Ph.D., 1979. *Home:* 1138 Indiana St., #1, Lawrence, Kan. 66044. *Office:* National Film Society, Shawnee Mission, Kan. 66204.

CAREER: KANU-FM Radio, Lawrence, Kan., announcer, 1966-70; University of Kansas, Lawrence, instructor in film, 1973-78; Avila College, Kansas City, Mo., instructor in film, 1977—. Free-lance commercial artist. *Military service:* U.S. Army, Security Agency, German linguist, 1970-73. *Member:* Society of Cinema Studies, American Film Institute, National Film Society (member of board of governors).

WRITINGS: (With James Welsh; self-illustrated) *His Majesty the American: The Cinema of Douglas Fairbanks, Sr.,* A. S. Barnes, 1977; (editor) *Introduction to the Photoplay,* Academy of Motion Picture Arts and Sciences, 1978. Contributor of artwork and articles to film and literature journals. Editor (and contributor, sometimes under pseudonym Jack Ketch) of *American Classic Screen,* 1977—.

WORK IN PROGRESS: Research on the film/theater interaction, 1896-1930; an authorized biography of film music composer Max Steiner.

SIDELIGHTS: Tibbetts wrote: "Studying the rise of mass culture in the last century affords a fascinating glimpse into the ways people entertain themselves. Entertainment and art have so coalesced that they are at times quite indistinguishable, which challenges our own deeply rooted concepts of the nature of the art image as opposed to the mere transmission of information. The motion picture has always been for me an art form that pinwheels the observer off onto other tracks, historical, sociological, cultural, political, etc. It becomes *the* challenge to those aforementioned definitions of art and information. Thus it often confounds us to the extent that we are compelled to go further than the mere visual perception of a film; it becomes necessary to contemplate a different kind of literacy of the future—that of the image as well as the word.

"My own viewing experiences constitute a series of blinding encounters over the years, primarily with those events of *movement* and grand gesture, whether they be in my early years of viewing the films of Douglas Fairbanks and Buster Keaton, or, later, with the operatic works of Visconti and Ken Russell. These experiences have not been so very different from my other encounters with the important *writers* of my life—artists who also seemed to specialize in the leaping gesture, the vibrant prose, and the imaginative vision. And I'm talking about the works of Charles Dickens, Ray Bradbury, G. K. Chesterton. Or take some of the composers who also are singularly self-propelled: Robert Schumann, Hector Berlioz, Carl Nielsen. Whether it's a film like Keaton's 'Seven Chances,' Fairbanks's 'The Gaucho,' or a book like Chesterton's *The Napoleon of Notting Hill,* or a composition like Schumann's 'Davidsbundler Dances,' they all reveal the essentially modern predilection with flux and change, speed and device. These are art images that, as Strindberg noted in his preface to *A Dream Play,* constantly change, divide, and multiply.

"To enjoy and write about such things is to be caught up in this bewildering sense of constant shift. Each time I attempt to grapple with the aesthetic implications of the modern cultural image, it is like staking out a claim, albeit provisional, on an uncharted territory. Prospector-like, you work the territory, sifting and looking for the sensible and the significant. At times this is not easy, since our society is so flooded with mass-produced images to the extent that we are benumbed and desensitized. It is perhaps not so daring to write a book on mass marketers such as Doug Fairbanks and Max Steiner; it is not even so daring to attempt to delineate the social and cultural significances of such work; but it is a challenge to scan their work with a pretension toward calling it art. Indeed, it can be the height of pretention to apply aesthetic criteria toward it at all (and if so, whose criteria?).

In the classes I have taught, I have found that the search for significance is itself problematic. Posit an interior meaning to "Hamlet" and no one can object to that act, but examine the films of Buster Keaton with an eye toward the twentieth century's preoccupation with man and machine, and eyes begin looking askance. We have refused to seriously examine our modern images for fear their entertainment values will diminish. My collaborator James Welsh and I tried to meet those fears with our book on Fairbanks. In a word, we both exerted the modern tendency to keep the bread buttered on both sides: to reveal an image's cultural and artistic significance, while firmly maintaining that image's role as entertainer.

"For me one of the nicest aspects of the above is that it enables one to creatively interpret modern images, whether they be visual, aural, or musical. There was once a time when the tenets of art seemed securely defined, as with the *Discourses* of Sir Joshua Reynolds late in the eighteenth century. Now we perhaps rarely admit of such definitions. Like the art images themselves, they are constantly subjected to fresh buffets, ongoing revisions, and new provisional definitions. To write about popular culture is, I think, to participate in this continual re-creation.

"So, while I continue to be entertained and delighted by the acrobatics of Fairbanks, the inner musings of Robert Schumann, the word-play of Chesterton, the baroque line of Visconti, etc., I am compelled at the same time to not let matters rest there. These things and others demand my own participation. So I write and will continue to write about that perplexing world of popular images all around me. And they are not images tucked away in a museum; they are clustered around us all, jostling for attention. What kind of attention, and whether it will be an essentially enlightened attention, we give them is a troubling issue. To feel that I am even on the road toward such resolution is enough justification for me.

"Perhaps it is more revealing than I care to admit to parenthetically note that my middle name is Carter. 'John Carter' was a fictional character from the wild imagination of Edgar Rice Burroughs. Carter was an earthling, a Confederate captain, who is miraculously transported to Mars. Through a series of books, he swashes and buckles away across the exotic landscapes, leaping with thirty-foot strides in the lesser gravity, on his way toward yet another rescue of his beloved princess, Deja Thoris. I grew up on these wonderful books, always conscious that my name had been given to me by Mr. Burroughs himself (and I have a letter from him to prove it). Perhaps that accounts for my seemingly innate tendencies to jump off roofs, over walls, and across streams whenever the chance affords itself. Maybe it even justifies the sense I often have of living in an exotic landscape peopled with creatures about whom I am constantly watchful. Certainly to wander among the popular images described above is in itself a visit to a strange planet that is curiously familiar but ultimately strange in its aspect."

AVOCATIONAL INTERESTS: Classical piano, collecting record albums and books (especially those by G. K. Chesterton and Robert Schumann), silent film (primarily those featuring Buster Keaton and Douglas Fairbanks, Sr.), illustrating for fantasy publications, American illustrators (Brandywine and Ash-Can schools), photography.

* * *

TITON, Jeff Todd 1943-

PERSONAL: Born December 8, 1943, in Jersey City, N.J.; son of Milton and Edith Titon; married Paula Protze, July 16, 1966; children: Emily. *Education:* Amherst College, B.A., 1965; University of Minnesota, M.A., 1967, Ph.D., 1971. *Home:* 109 Grove St., Wellesley, Mass. 02181. *Office:* Department of English, and Department of Music, Tufts University, Medford, Mass. 02155.

CAREER: Lazy Bill Lucas Blues Band, Minneapolis, Minn., guitarist, 1969-71; Tufts University, Medford, Mass., assistant professor, 1971-77, associate professor of English and associate professor of music, 1977—. Visiting assistant professor of folklore at Indiana University, 1977. *Member:* American Studies Association, American Folklore Society, Society for Ethnomusicology (member of council, 1977—). *Awards, honors:* National Endowment for the Humanities fellowship, 1977-78; Deems Taylor Award from American Society of Composers, Authors, and Publishers, 1977, for *Early Downhome Blues.*

WRITINGS: Early Downhome Blues: A Musical and Cultural Analysis, University of Illinois Press, 1977. Contributor to folklore and ethnomusicology journals. Contributing editor of *Alcheringa: Ethnopoetics.*

WORK IN PROGRESS: Sacred Speech, Chant, and Song in an Appalachian Baptist Church, publication by University of Texas Press expected in early 1980's.

TODMAN, Bill
See TODMAN, William S.

* * *

TODMAN, William S. 1916-1979
(Bill Todman)

OBITUARY NOTICE: Born July 31, 1916, in New York, N.Y.; died July 29, 1979, in New York, N.Y. Radio and television writer, director, and producer. Todman is best-remembered as the latter half of the Goodson-Todman partnership that brought to the screen quiz and game shows such as "What's My Line?," "I've Got a Secret," "To Tell the Truth," "Password," and "Match Game." Although known principally for these productions, the team also produced dramatic shows, including "The Rebel," "Philip Marlowe," and "Branded." Goodson and Todman eventually formed Capital City Publishing, an enterprise that at one time owned seventeen newspapers and a radio station. Before teaming with Goodson, Todman wrote and directed, among others, the "Connie Boswell Show," "Anita Ellis Sings," and "Treasury Salute Dramas." Obituaries and other sources: *New York Times,* July 31, 1979.

* * *

TOLSON, M(elvin) B(eaunorus) 1900-1966

OBITUARY NOTICE: Born February 6, 1900, in Moberly, Mo.; died August 29, 1966. Educator, poet, and dramatist. In addition to teaching at several universities, Tolson was mayor of Langston, Okla., and a columnist for the *Washington Tribune.* Tolson was chosen Poet Laureate of Liberia in 1947, and received much critical acclaim for his *Libretto for the Republic of Liberia,* written for the country's centennial. His plays include "The Moses of Beale Street" and "The Fire in the Flint," and his poetry has been included in numerous anthologies. Obituaries and other sources: *The Penguin Companion to American Literature,* McGraw, 1971; *Webster's New World Companion to English and American Literature,* World Publishing, 1973; *Black American Writers Past and Present: A Biographical and Bibliographical Dictionary,* Scarecrow, 1975; *World Authors, 1950-1970,* Wilson, 1975.

* * *

TOLSTOY, Alexandra L(vovna) 1884-1979

OBITUARY NOTICE—See index for *CA* sketch: Born July 1, 1884, in Yasnaya Polyana, Russia; died September 26, 1979, in Valley Cottage, N.Y. Political and social activist, practical nurse, lecturer, and author. The daughter of Russian novelist Leo Tolstoy, Alexandra Tolstoy spent her early life in service to her father and her later life in service to mankind. When she was only seventeen, she became her father's secretary. After he died she served as executor of his will and prepared the definitive edition of his works. Three of the books she wrote concern her father: *The Tragedy of Tolstoy, Tolstoy: A Life of My Father,* and *The Real Tolstoy: A Critique and Commentary.* Because Alexandra shared Tolstoy's belief in nonviolence and the rights of the poor, she devoted much of her time to welfare work. She worked as a nurse behind the front lines in World War I. After the war, in her capacity as curator of the Leo Tolstoy Museum and Educational Center, she founded schools and medical facilities in the Soviet Union. Because Alexandra objected to Communist antireligious propaganda, she was forced to leave her native land in 1929. Eventually she came to the United States, where she founded the Tolstoy Foundation, an organization that lends assistance to refugees from Communist bloc nations. Obituaries and other sources: Alexandra L. Tolstoy, *The Tragedy of Tolstoy,* Yale University Press, 1933; A. Tolstoy, *I Worked for the Soviets,* Yale University Press, 1934; *New Yorker,* March 22, 1952; *Current Biography,* Wilson, 1953, November, 1979; *New York Times,* July 2, 1974; *Who's Who,* 131st edition, St. Martin's, 1978; *Washington Post,* September 27, 1979; *Chicago Tribune,* September 28, 1979; *Newsweek,* October 8, 1979; *Time,* October 8, 1979; *AB Bookman's Weekly,* October 22, 1979.

* * *

TOMALIN, Claire 1933-

PERSONAL: Born June 20, 1933, in London, England; daughter of Emile (a scholar) and Muriel (a songwriter; maiden name, Herbert) Delavenay; married Nicholas Tomalin, September 17, 1955 (died October, 1973); children: Josephine, Susanna, Emily, Thomas. *Education:* Newnham College, Cambridge, M.A., 1954. *Religion:* None. *Home:* 57 Gloucester Cres., London N.W.1, England. *Agent:* Deborah Rogers, 5-11 Mortimer St., London W.1, England. *Office: Sunday Times,* Gray's Inn Rd., London W.C.1, England.

CAREER: New Statesman, London, England, literary editor, 1974-77; *Sunday Times,* London, reviewer, 1977—. *Member:* Royal Society of Literature (fellow). *Awards, honors:* Whitbread Award, 1974, for *The Life and Death of Mary Wollstonecraft.*

WRITINGS: The Life and Death of Mary Wollstonecraft, Weidenfeld & Nicolson, 1974, Harcourt, 1975; *Shelley and His World,* Thames & Hudson, 1979; *Katherine Mansfield,* Knopf, in press. Contributor to *Punch* among other English periodicals.

WORK IN PROGRESS: A study of English feminism.

SIDELIGHTS: Tomalin writes that she is interested in the Enlightenment, history of feminism, and nineteenth-century literature and ideas.

* * *

TONKS, Rosemary (D. Boswell)

PERSONAL: Born in London, England. *Home:* 46 Downshire Hill, London N.W.3, England.

CAREER: Poet, novelist, illustrator, and writer of children's fiction. Poetry reviewer for British Broadcasting Corp. (BBC) European Service.

WRITINGS: On Wooden Wings: The Adventures of Webster (juvenile), Murray, 1948; *The Wild Sea Goose* (juvenile), Murray, 1951; *Notes on Cafes and Bedrooms* (poetry), Putnam, 1963; *Opium Fogs* (novel), Putnam, 1963; *Emir* (novel), Adam Books, 1963; *Iliad of Broken Sentences* (poetry), Bodley Head, 1967; *The Bloater* (novel), Bodley Head, 1968; *Businessmen as Lovers* (novel), Bodley Head, 1969, published as *Love Among the Operators,* Gambit, 1970; *The Way Out of Berkeley Square* (novel), Bodley Head, 1970, Gambit, 1971; *The Halt During the Chase* (novel), Bodley Head, 1972, Harper, 1973. Contributor of short stories to *Accent, Queen, Encounter,* and other publications.

SIDELIGHTS: Rosemary Tonks avoids the mundane and the ordinary by creating unusual wordings and punctuations in her poetry. Criticism of her *Iliad of Broken Sentences* characterizes the wide range of response her style has evoked. John Thompson defined the work as "a collection of poems that presents a genuine personality, even a character, and a whole way of life." He added: "[Tonks] can handle the least kind of thing her craft demands, that is, a simple description. Sometimes it is the sort of description, hovering on the edge of preciousness, which we wouldn't like much in a male poet. . . . The poems do not have the obvious elements of song—rhyme, or regularly repeated rhymes, or refrains—but with a kind of cumulating repetition of words and phrases she creates a movement of melody. The speech is direct, scrappy, and reckless . . . alive, and even, if you will pardon the expression, charming." Brian Jones dissented, declaring: "Miss Tonks is all gesture and assertiveness, full of willed decadence, willed despair, willed world-weariness. Her poems read like translations of some nineteenth-century French poet who never quite existed."

One of Tonks's most original poetic techniques is a fairly new innovation—the use of electronic accompaniment with poetry readings. *Observer Review* noted that the idea, which first came to the poet about 1965, is seen by Tonks as "a way of livening up poetry readings." The poet's goal, in her own words, is "to bring poetry into its own dramatically."

BIOGRAPHICAL/CRITICAL SOURCES: Listener, October 19, 1967, August 22, 1968; *Punch,* October 25, 1967, September 4, 1968, October 1, 1969; *Times Literary Supplement,* November 9, 1967, November 13, 1970, April 28, 1972; *London Magazine,* March, 1968; *Books and Bookmen,* August, 1968; *New York Review of Books,* August 1, 1968; *Observer Review,* September 1, 1968; *New York Times Book Review,* March 28, 1971; *Best Sellers,* April 1, 1971; *Christian Science Monitor,* August 29, 1973.*

* * *

TOOHEY, Robert E(ugene) 1935-

PERSONAL: Born December 28, 1935, in Paris, Ky.; son of Robert E., Sr. (a laborer) and Mabel (a nurse's aide; maiden name, Smart) Toohey. *Education:* Georgetown College, Georgetown, Ky., B.A., 1958; University of Kentucky, M.A., 1961, Ph.D., 1975. *Religion:* Southern Baptist. *Home address:* P.O. Box 251, Paris, Ky. 40361. *Office:* Department of History, Elizabethtown Community College, Elizabethtown, Ky. 42701.

CAREER: High school history teacher in Paris, Ky., 1959-64; Brenau College, Gainesville, Ga., assistant professor of history, 1964-66; Elizabethtown Community College, Elizabethtown, Ky., associate professor of history, 1966—. Teacher of adult education courses. *Member:* American Historical Association, American Association of University Professors, Southern Historical Association.

WRITINGS: Liberty and Empire, University Press of Kentucky, 1978.

WORK IN PROGRESS: Research on late eighteenth-century English radical political thought and its connections with contemporary thinking on parliamentary reform and the constitutional problems raised by difficulties within the British Empire.

SIDELIGHTS: Robert Toohey wrote: "My first obligation is to acknowledge God and do His will as I understand it in order to serve my fellow man as a historian and teacher. It is important that the historian, in his study of the past, pursues and finds the simple truths about human nature and the plight of man, and discerns between the actual truth and the mythologies which men of each generation tend to accept for explaining the mysteries and complexities of life. My main interest is the study of British civilization with special attention to modern English history.

"I have lived most of my life in the beautiful 'blue grass country' and am deeply attached to it. Its very rural and natural qualities tempered by the beauty of the great horse farms lend some degree of stability and continuity in a world which has become much urbanized, mobile, and insecure."

AVOCATIONAL INTERESTS: Reading, music, drama, baseball, travel.

* * *

TORBERG, Friedrich
See KANTOR-BERG, Friedrich

* * *

TRACHTE, Don(ald) 1915-

PERSONAL: Surname is pronounced "Trockty"; born May 21, 1915, in Madison, Wis.; son of Arthur F. (an inventor) and Meta (Woerpel) Trachte; married Elizabeth Torgeson, 1941 (divorced, 1973); children: Marjorie Trachte Linkletter, Donald, David, Jon. *Education:* Attended University of Wisconsin, 1933-35, 1940-41. *Office:* King Features Syndicate, 235 East 45th St., New York, N.Y. 10017.

CAREER/WRITINGS: Cartoonist, artist, and actor. King Features Syndicate, cartoonist for "Henry" comic page, 1942—. Actor in local theatre groups and summer stock. *Military service:* U. S. Army, 1941-45; became lieutenant. *Member:* National Cartoonist Society, Southern Vermont Artists Association. *Awards, honors:* Received an award for his role in "Johnny Belinda."

SIDELIGHTS: Trachte told *CA:* "As a pre-schooler I literally learned to read by looking at the comics. The fascination has stayed with me all my life. I sat in on the birth of 'Henry' with old friend and neighbor Carl Anderson, who was freelancing for *Saturday Evening Post* in 1931." The King Features syndicate purchased the rights to "Henry" in 1934 and made it into a daily strip. When Anderson was forced by illness to retire in 1942, Trachte took over the drawing of the "Henry" Sunday comics and John Liney drew the dailies. "Henry" is one of the few pantomime comic strips to remain popular in recent years.

Trachte described his other enterprises: "I pursue painting, piano, and acting almost as seriously as cartooning. I moved to Vermont many years ago to be inspired by friends Mead Schaeffer and Norman Rockwell, whose works I so admire.

"I won't be a 'professional' artist until I'm at least as good as Rembrandt and that will take another forty years if I keep at it. I have exhibited in Southern Vermont member shows and had two exhibitions of a Norwegian series in Minneapolis the year of King Olaf's visit to that city."

In his acting career, Trachte has worked under three Broadway directors. His major roles in theatre groups and summer stock include the part of Jonathan Brewster in "Arsenic and Old Lace," Jim Lucas in "Dream Girl," Fred in "John Loves Mary," Paul Sycamore in "You Can't Take It With You," and Black McDonald in "Johnny Belinda." He won a critics' award for the latter.

Commenting on his diverse interests, Trachte said: "I discovered long ago that the seemingly disparate professions of medicine, drama, and graphic art have a common bond of interest. Some psychologists, working with statistical findings from interest, personality, and aptitude tests, have indicated that there may be indeed more than a random bond of interest among this group."

TRACY, Robert E. 1928-

PERSONAL: Born November 23, 1928, in Woburn, Mass.; son of Hubert (in sales) and Vera (Hurley) Tracy; married Rebecca Garrison (a teacher), August 26, 1956; children: Jessica, Hugh, Dominick. *Education:* Boston College, A.B., 1950; Harvard University, M.A., 1954, Ph.D., 1960. *Home:* 2611 Derby, Berkeley, Calif. 94705. *Office:* Department of English, University of California, Berkeley, Calif. 94720.

CAREER: Harvard University, Cambridge, Mass., assistant librarian, 1950-54, teaching fellow in general education, history, and literature, 1954-58; Carleton College, Northfield, Minn., instructor in English, 1958-60; University of California, Berkeley, assistant professor, 1960-66, associate professor of English, 1966—. Kathryn W. Davis Professor of Slavic Studies at Wellesley College, autumn, 1979. *Member:* Modern Language Association of America, American Society for Theatre Research, Philological Association of the Pacific Coast. *Awards, honors:* Bruern fellow at University of Leeds, 1965-66; Leverhulme fellow at Trinity College, Dublin, 1971-72.

WRITINGS: (Editor) John M. Synge, *The Aran Islands and Other Writings,* Vintage, 1962; (editor) Anthony Trollope, *The Way We Live Now,* Bobbs-Merrill, 1974; *Trollope's Later Novels,* University of California Press, 1978; (translator) Osip Mandelstam, *Stone,* Princeton University Press, in press. Contributor of translation to *Penguin Anthology of Women Poets,* 1978. Contributor to *Oxford Companion to the Theatre.*

WORK IN PROGRESS: Research on Samuel Lover and William Butler Yeats.

SIDELIGHTS: Tracy writes: "I am interested in verbal precision, the effort to fix reality in words. This links apparently disparate interests (Trollope, Mandelstam); in working with Yeats I am studying his efforts to realize his poetry on stage in the verse he wrote for the Abbey."

* * *

TRADER VIC
See BERGERON, Victor (Jules, Jr.)

* * *

TREMBLAY, Bill
See TREMBLAY, William Andrew

* * *

TREMBLAY, William Andrew 1940-
(Bill Tremblay)

PERSONAL: Born June 9, 1940, in Southbridge, Mass.; son of Arthur Achilles (a truck driver) and Irene (a lens grinder; maiden name, Fontaine) Tremblay; married Cynthia Ann Crooks (a radio producer), September 28, 1962; children: William Crooks, Benjamin Phillip, John Fontaine. *Education:* Attended Columbia University, 1957-58; Clark University, A.B., 1962, M.A., 1969; University of Massachusetts, M.F.A., 1972. *Home:* 3412 Lancaster Dr., Fort Collins, Colo. 80525. *Office:* Department of English, Colorado State University, Fort Collins, Colo. 80523.

CAREER: Leicester Junior College, Leicester, Mass., assistant professor of English, 1967-70; Springfield College, Springfield, Mass., instructor in English, 1972-73; Colorado State University, Fort Collins, assistant professor, 1973-78, associate professor, 1978-79, professor of creative writing, 1979—. *Member:* American Academy of Poetry, Associated Writing Programs, Rocky Mountain Modern Language Association. *Awards, honors:* Hoyt Poetry Prize from Clark University, 1961 and 1962; Fulbright fellow in Portugal, 1979.

WRITINGS—Under name Bill Tremblay; all poetry: *A Time for Breaking,* Yellow Bus Press, 1970; *Crying in the Cheap Seats,* University of Massachusetts Press, 1971; *The Anarchist Heart,* New Rivers Press, 1977; *Home Front,* Lynx House Press, 1978; *The Peaceable Kingdom,* Four Zoas Press, 1979.

Author of "The Next Level" (three-act play). Author of scripts for radio and educational television. Contributor of poems to literary journals, including *Chicago Review, Three Rivers Poetry Journal, Zahir,* and *Midwest Quarterly.* Poetry editor of *Colorado State Review* and Colorado State Review Press.

WORK IN PROGRESS: Ao Deus Desconhecido (tentative title; title means "To the God Unknown"), a book of poems.

SIDELIGHTS: Tremblay writes: "My recent stay in Portugal was important: I slowly acquired the language in buses, trains, *supermercados;* nonverbal images of the sea, birds, palm trees were also important, and out-of-country perspectives on the United States. It was an awakening—the earth resurrects us every moment. I have always preferred content in literary art to abstractions; I agree with Levertov, 'the world is not with us enough.'"

* * *

TREVELYAN, George Macaulay 1876-1962

PERSONAL: Born February 16, 1876, in Stratford-on-Avon, England; died July, 1962, in Cambridge, England; son of George Otto (a historian) and Caroline (Philips) Trevelyan; married Janet Penrose Ward (a writer and social worker), 1904; children: one son, one daughter. *Education:* Attended Trinity College, Cambridge.

CAREER: Historian and author. Cambridge University, Cambridge, England, Regius Professor of Modern History, 1927-40, Master of Divinity of Trinity College, 1940-51. Chancellor of Durham University, 1951-58; trustee of British Museum and National Portrait Gallery; chairman of estates committee of the National Trust; president of Youth Hostels Association. *Military service:* British Ambulance Unit, World War I, served in Italy; received Italian medal for valor. *Member:* British Academy (fellow); Athenaeum National Liberal Club. *Awards, honors:* Commander of the Order of the British Empire, 1920; Order of Merit, 1930; made chevalier of the Order of St. Maurice and St. Lazarus; honorary member of Massachusetts Historical Society; honorary fellow of Oriel College, Cambridge; Hon. D.C.L. from Oxford University, St. Andrews University, University of Edinburgh, Cambridge University, University of London, Manchester University, Durham University, Yale University, and Harvard University.

WRITINGS: England in the Age of Wycliffe, Longmans, Green, 1899, 3rd edition, 1900, reprinted, AMS Press, 1975; *England Under the Stuarts,* Methuen, 1904, 21st edition, 1949, Barnes & Noble, 1965; *The Poetry and Philosophy of George Meredith,* A. Constable, 1906, Russell, 1966; *Garibaldi's Defence of the Roman Republic,* Longmans, Green, 1907, new edition, 1908, reprinted, Greenwood Press, 1971 (also see below); *Garibaldi and the Thousand,* Longmans, Green, 1909 (also see below).

Garibaldi and the Making of Italy, Longmans, Green, 1911 (also see below); (editor) *English Songs of Italian Freedom,*

Longmans, Green, 1911; *The Life of John Bright,* Houghton, 1913, reprinted, Greenwood Press, 1971; *Clio, a Muse, and Other Essays Literary and Pedestrian,* Longmans, Green, 1913, 2nd edition published as *The Recreations of a Historian,* T. Nelson, 1919, new edition published under original title, 1930, reprinted, Books for Libraries, 1968; *Scenes From Italy's War,* Houghton, 1919.

Lord Grey of the Reform Bill, Being the Life of Charles Second Earl Grey, Longmans, Green, 1920, reprinted, Greenwood Press, 1970; *British History in the Nineteenth Century (1782-1901),* Longmans, Green, 1922, 2nd edition published as *British History in the Nineteenth Century and After (1782-1919),* Longmans, Green, 1937, reprinted, Harper, 1966; *Manin and the Venetian Revolution of 1848,* Longmans, Green, 1923, reprinted, Fertig, 1974; *History of England,* Longmans, Green, 1926, 3rd edition, Doubleday, 1953, illustrated edition published as *Illustrated History of England,* McKay, 1962; *Walking,* Mitchell, 1928; (editor) *Select Documents for Queen Anne's Reign Down to the Union With Scotland, 1702-07,* Cambridge University Press, 1929, reprinted, Scholarly Resources, 1973; *Must England's Beauty Perish? A Plea on Behalf of the National Trust for Places of Historic Interest or Natural Beauty,* Faber & Gwyer, 1929.

England Under Queen Anne, Longmans, Green, Volume I: *Blenheim,* Volume II: *Ramillies and the Union With Scotland* Volume III: *The Peace and the Protestant Succession,* 1930-34; *The England of Queen Anne* (contains portions of Volume I of *England Under Queen Anne*), Longmans, Green, 1932, reprinted, 1959; *Sir George Otto Trevelyan: A Memoir,* Longmans, Green, 1932; *Garibaldi: Being "Garibaldi's Defence of the Roman Republic," "Garibaldi and the Thousand,"* [and] *"Garibaldi and the Making of Italy,"* Longmans, Green, 1933; *Grey of Fallodon: The Life and Letters of Sir Edward Grey, Afterwards Viscount Grey of Fallodon,* Houghton, 1937; *The English Revolution, 1688-1689,* Butterworth, 1938, Holt, 1939, reprinted, Oxford University Press, 1965.

English Social History: A Survey of Six Centuries, Chaucer to Queen Victoria, Longmans, Green, 1942, third edition, McKay, 1965, illustrated edition published as *Illustrated English Social History,* four volumes, Longmans, Green, 1949-52, McKay, 1969; *A Shortened History of England,* Longmans, Green, 1942; *Trinity College; An Historical Sketch,* Cambridge University Press, 1948; *An Autobiography and Other Essays,* Longmans, Green, 1949, Books for Libraries, 1971; *A Layman's Love of Letters,* Longmans, Green, 1954.

SIDELIGHTS: G. M. Trevelyan gained eminence in his field for more than his sweeping histories of England. While his essays, his biographies, and his chronicles of English history are characterized by their objectivity and thorough research, Trevelyan spiced his writing with an outstanding ability to retell history dramatically. His books have been valuable to scholars and have fascinated general audiences as well, remaining popular years after their publication. More than thirty of Trevelyan's books are still in print.

Trevelyan's appeal rests largely in his distinction as an unbiased historian. In *England Under the Stuarts,* for example, he praised the English by demonstrating "the significance of the Stuart epoch lies in the fact that whereas the continental people of Europe attained nationality only through military despotism," summarized an *Outlook* reviewer, "the English people under the Stuarts solved the same problem unconsciously through a free constitution, manifesting and vindicating itself in the face of monarchial despotism." Nonetheless, Trevelyan presented his complimentary picture of the English with "fairness and breadth of view," said *Outlook.* An *Athenaeum* critic, too, praised Trevelyan's "impartial" commentary. Trevelyan strengthened his reputation for objectivity years later in *British History in the Nineteenth Century,* where he "writes like a judge and not like an advocate," declared J. St. Loe Strachey. The same book's revised edition prompted a *Christian Science Monitor* critic to call Trevelyan a "strikingly unprejudiced arbiter" of the "different groups and personalities within the political game in England." But, this same critic noted, "his deeper assumptions he has never examined. He is so English that it has never even occurred to him to view history from a universal angle."

Trevelyan broadened his focus to the whole of England in his 1926 work, *History of England.* Immediately, critics recognized its importance. F. G. Marcham declared "Trevelyan has written by far the best history of England for the experienced reader," and the *Springfield Republican* reported that "among the comprehensive one-volume histories lately appearing, this is one of the most alert, most vivid and most brilliant." Trevelyan's treatment included coverage of Scottish, Irish, and Welsh issues as well as some discussion of overseas imperialism. The *Boston Transcript* thought Americans especially would appreciate Trevelyan's analysis of pertinent international issues: "No part of the discussion will appeal more strongly to Americans in its keenness of analysis than the friendly and judicious opinions respecting relations of England with the U.S. during the days of the war."

Years after *History of England* Trevelyan published his *English Social History,* which he labeled "the history of a people with the politics left out. . . . Its scope may be defined as the daily life of the inhabitants of the land in past ages." Preston Slosson acknowledged the difficulty of the author's task: "In English social history, more perhaps than in any other branch of history anywhere, changes are both perpetual and gradual; the stream is never twice the same, and yet at no time altogether altered. Mr. Trevelyan's book gives us a perfect impression of this tenacious and yet involving life of the British people." *English Social History* was reprinted in a four-volume illustrated edition in 1950.

Aside from his histories of England, Trevelyan devoted most of his writing attention to Italy. In 1911 he edited *English Songs of Italian Freedom.* Along with his introduction giving a "brief account of English sympathy with Italian aspirations to freedom," Trevelyan offered representative writings of Percy Shelly, George Byron, George Meredith, and others. Earlier, Trevelyan had detailed the life of Italian Patriot Giuseppe Garibaldi in a three-volume series. Later, in 1919, he called on his experience in the British Red Cross Unit during the Italian campaign to help him write *Scenes From Italy's War.* Reviewing this book, the *Spectator* examined Trevelyan's temperament as a writer on Italy: "Trevelyan has not turned his opportunities to sensational use. He writes not to inflame but to enlighten, and he comes to his task with the triple equipment of an historian, a lover of Italy, and the master of a fascinating style." Trevelyan's last book on Italy, *Manin and the Venetian Revolution of 1848,* appeared in 1923.

Trevelyan's histories are reinforced by his method as a historian. The first volume of *England Under Queen Anne,* for example, represented "the achievements of ripe scholarship, meticulous research, and sound judgment," commented C. E. Fayle. Similarly, the *New York Times* praised *Garibaldi and the Thousand* because "Trevelyan writes history with his eyes glued to the authorities and skillfully extracts the meat from personal impression as well as from scientific judgment." Perhaps Trevelyan's most important asset as a historian, however, was his devotion to living history, not just studying it. David Knowles explained: "Behind the trilogy of Garibaldi and the volumes of Queen Anne lie years of travel in Italy, years of work in libraries and the British Museum, and a formidable bibliography; behind the *Social History* is a lifetime of reading, reflection and experience. Of this the reader sees nothing. He remembers only a hundred pictures." And the reader remembers these pictures for one main reason: Trevelyan's extraordinary ability in painting life into his writing.

"The art of history," Trevelyan once wrote, "remains always the art of narrative. That is the bed-rock." Trevelyan succeeded in unveiling more than the facts behind history: he brought his history to life. The *Boston Tribune* cited *Clio, a Muse* as evidence that "he possesses . . . such an imaginative and allusive style that he may be read with a constant pleasure." Likewise, the *Spectator* announced "he infects the reader with his zest and compels him to keep pace with him." Other various critics have commended Trevelyan's "enthusiasm," his "vivid style," and his "clear and picturesque narrative." "He is the poet of English history," wrote biographer John H. Plumb. In essence, Trevelyan's histories, once praised as more interesting than a romantic novel, erased the conception that history must be dull.

BIOGRAPHICAL/CRITICAL SOURCES: Athenaeum, February 4, 1905, July 13, 1907; *Outlook,* February 11, 1905, December 9, 1911; *Nation,* November 2, 1905, June 20, 1907, July 31, 1913, March 13, 1943; *New York Times,* June 9, 1906, December 11, 1909, October 29, 1911, July 14, 1912, July 20, 1913, January 11, 1914, September 28, 1919, June 27, 1920, December 30, 1923, September 19, 1926, May 29, 1932, April 29, 1934, March 7, 1937, November 28, 1943, November 20, 1949, May 16, 1954; *Saturday Review,* June 16, 1906, November 18, 1911, June 28, 1913, April 12, 1919, March 27, 1920, July 31, 1926, October 4, 1930, December 3, 1932, March 6, 1937, February 20, 1943, March 25, 1950; *Spectator,* April 20, 1907, October 16, 1909, October 14, 1911, January 27, 1912, May 31, 1913, June 7, 1913, November 29, 1913, March 22, 1919, March 27, 1920, July 1, 1922, July 8, 1922, December 8, 1923, March 26, 1932, October 15, 1932, May 19, 1934, March 5, 1937, October 14, 1938, May 27, 1949, March 12, 1954, February 17, 1956; *Academy,* May 11, 1907.

Boston Transcript, November 26, 1913, September 11, 1926; *New Republic,* September 8, 1920, August 23, 1922, June 16, 1937; *Times Literary Supplement,* March 25, 1920, May 25, 1922, October 11, 1923, July 1, 1926, June 26, 1930, September 25, 1930, March 10, 1932, October 6, 1932, March 15, 1934, March 6, 1937, January 22, 1938, October 15, 1938, October 16, 1943, August 5, 1949, March 5, 1954; *New Statesman,* August 5, 1922, November 10, 1923, August 7, 1926, September 27, 1930; *Springfield Republican,* November 7, 1926; *New York Herald Tribune,* February 6, 1927.

Nation and Athenaeum, October 11, 1930; *Christian Science Monitor,* April 14, 1934, March 31, 1937, March 29, 1938, January 26, 1940, September 1, 1949, March 4, 1950, December 31, 1952; *American Historical Review,* October, 1934, October, 1937, July, 1943, February, 1976; *English Historical Review,* January, 1935; *Atlantic,* May, 1937, March, 1943.

George Macaulay Trevelyan, *English Social History: A Survey of Six Centuries, Chaucer to Queen Victoria,* Longmans, Green, 1942, third edition, McKay, 1965; *Yale Review,* summer, 1943; *Annals of the American Academy of Political and Social Science,* July, 1943; John H. Plum, *G. M. Trevelyan,* Longmans, Green, 1951; *Contemporary Review,* May-August, 1974; *Midwest Quarterly,* October, 1976.*

* * *

TROEGER, Thomas H(enry) 1945-

PERSONAL: Born January 30, 1945, in Suffern, N.Y.; son of Henry (an engineer) and Lorena (a teacher; maiden name, McDonald) Troeger; married Merle Marie Butler (a lawyer), June 25, 1967. *Education:* Yale University, B.A. (cum laude), 1967; Colgate-Rochester Divinity School, B.Div., 1970. *Residence:* Rochester, N.Y. *Office:* Rochester Center for Theological Studies, 1100 South Goodman, Rochester, N.Y. 14620.

CAREER: Ordained Presbyterian minister, 1970; associate minister of Presbyterian church in New Hartford, N.Y., 1970-77; Rochester Center for Theological Studies, Rochester, N.Y., assistant professor of preaching and parish, 1977—. *Member:* Academy of Homiletics.

WRITINGS: Meditation: Escape to Reality, Westminster, 1977; *Rage! Reflect. Rejoice!,* Westminster, 1977; *Are You Saved? Answers to the Awkward Question,* Westminster, 1979.

WORK IN PROGRESS: A novel; a collection of short stories.

SIDELIGHTS: Troeger writes: "I try to interpret the Christian faith in contemporary terms so that it can make sense to secular society. My writing is aimed at the seeking and the skeptical, individuals who find Billy Graham too simplistic and Paul Tillich too abstruse. I am turning to fiction because the narrative style is more faithful to the dynamics of biblical literature than rational discourse. I have played and taught flute in the past, and music is providing me with many of the materials and metaphors for my work."

* * *

TROIDEN, Richard (Russell) 1946-

PERSONAL: Born November 13, 1946, in Minneapolis, Minn.; son of Russell A. (a lithographer) and Muriel (a telegrapher; maiden name, Pomasel) Troiden. *Education:* University of Minnesota, B.A. (magna cum laude), 1969; State University of New York at Stony Brook, M.A., 1971, Ph.D., 1978. *Office:* Department of Sociology and Anthropology, Miami University, 344 Hoyt Library, Oxford, Ohio 45056.

CAREER: Miami University, Oxford, Ohio, instructor in sociology, 1975-77, assistant professor, 1978-79, associate professor of sociology, 1980—. *Member:* American Sociological Association, Society for the Study of Social Problems, National Gay Task Force, Association for Humanistic Sociology, Marijuana Task Force.

WRITINGS: (Editor with Erich Goode) *Sexual Deviance and Sexual Deviants,* Morrow, 1974. Contributor to psychiatry and social science journals.

WORK IN PROGRESS: Becoming Homosexual, "a book which details the process by which men arrive at the decision that they are homosexual."

SIDELIGHTS: Troiden writes: "My introduction to the sociological perspective as an undergraduate was a turning point in my career. An understanding of the sociological dialogue led me to reason that this approach was more meaningful, both professionally and personally, than the psychological perspective I had held previously."

TROY, William 1903-1961

OBITUARY NOTICE: Born July 11, 1903, in Chicago, Ill.; died May 26, 1961. Educator, critic, and author. Troy was noted for his superb lecturing and his critiques of works by such literary figures as James Joyce, Henry James, Gertrude Stein, D. H. Lawrence, and Shakespeare. Often considered one of the most neglected critics of his generation, Troy won the most recognition for his *Selected Essays,* a collection that was published posthumously. Obituaries and other sources: *New York Times,* May 27, 1961; *Nation,* June 12, 1967; *Poetry,* May, 1968; *Commonweal,* May 10, 1968; *World Authors, 1950-1970,* Wilson, 1975.

* * *

TRUNK, Isaiah Elezer 1905-

PERSONAL: Born July 21, 1905, in Kutno, Poland; came to United States in 1954, naturalized citizen, 1962; son of Itzhak Yehuda (a rabbi and founder of the Mizrachi movement in Poland) and Frymet (Bornstein) Trunk; married Celia Baar (a secretary), September 26, 1948; children: Gabriel. *Education:* University of Warsaw, M.A., 1929; Jewish Teachers Seminary of America, D.J.L., 1969. *Religion:* Jewish. *Home:* 144-39 37th Ave., Flushing, N.Y. 11354. *Office:* Yivo Institute for Jewish Research, 1048 Fifth Ave., New York, N.Y. 10028.

CAREER: Historian. Member of editorial staff of *Journal* of Historical Institute, Warsaw, Poland, and Beth Lohamei Hagetaot, Israel, 1951-53; Yivo Institute for Jewish Research and Max Weinreich Center for Advanced Jewish Studies, New York, N.Y., chief archivist, chairman of the commission for training and research, and professor of Jewish history, 1954—. *Member:* Historical Society of Israel, Workmen's Circle (New York). *Awards, honors:* Awards from Diana Blumenfeld Foundation, 1965, and Jewish Book Council of America, 1967; National Book Award in history, 1973, and Leon Jolson Award from Jewish Book Council of the National Jewish Welfare Board, 1975, both for *Judenrat.*

WRITINGS: Di geshikte fun Yidn in Plotzk (title means "History of the Jews in Plotzk"), [Warsaw], 1939; *Gesntaltn un gesheenishn* (title means "Personalities and Events"), [Buenos Aires], 1962; *Lodzsher geto* (title means "Ghetto Lodz"), with English introduction and index, Yad Vashem Martyrs' and Heroes' Memorial Authority and Yivo Institute for Jewish Research, 1962; *Shtudies in Yidisher geshikte in Poyln* (title means "Studies in Jewish History in Poland"), [Buenos Aires], 1963; *Judenrat: The Jewish Councils in Eastern Europe Under Nazi Occupation,* introduction by Jacob Robinson, Macmillan, 1972; *Jewish Responses to Nazi Persecution,* Stein & Day, 1978. Also author, in Yiddish, of *History of the Jews in Kutno,* 1934, and of other histories of Jewish Communities. Contributor of articles to history journals.

SIDELIGHTS: Trunk's *Judenrat* is a comprehensive study of the Nazi-ordered Jewish councils in Eastern European ghettos and the winner of the National Book Award in history for 1973. According to a *New York Times Book Review* critic, Trunk "has done much new research in a subject that has not exactly been ignored. Unlike some scholars, he does not utterly condemn the councils but finds that they were subjected to unbearable pressures by sadistic Nazi overlords."

The subject of the ghetto councils is, to say the least, controversial, and not all Jewish historians are able to absolve the councils of guilt in the deaths of other Jews at the hands of the Nazis. Neal Ascherson, however, has observed a new trend in understanding the councils: "[The] great dispute has blown itself out at last. Nobody now is going to fall upon Trunk for saying in his preface that 'it was not my intention to pronounce judgment either way on these institutions' . . . and reproach him for lack of moral courage. It is possible for the facts about the Councils to be collected and deployed and, at least, heard out with respect."

While most critics have agreed that the book is an exhaustive analysis of the councils, including sketches about the council leaders and questionnaire results from former members, they also have pointed out flaws in Trunk's conclusions. I. L. Horowitz stated: "As a work of social analysis, replete with the accoutrements of survey questionnaires of Council members and ghetto police, and tabular materials on the fiscal and demographic characteristics of ghetto life, the book succeeds admirably. As a work of history, it is less successful, not really putting into adequate perspective the indifference and ennui of Christian Europe to the plight of the Jews."

A *Times Literary Supplement* critic praised Trunk for his "compassionate and humane scholarship" and noted that the "greatest virtue of this important book based upon half a decade of research and sound scholarship is that it is not an objective study. Objectivity would be indecent here."

CA INTERVIEWS THE AUTHOR

Isaiah Trunk was interviewed by phone July 6, 1979, at the Yivo Institute in New York City.

CA: How would you explain the renewed general interest in the Holocaust?

TRUNK: I think the decline of moral values and the constant turmoil—both social and political—of our times have stimulated people to reflect and search for causes. Among other things the Holocaust is often considered one of the causes. Also, it became the catchword and the horrible symbol of the moral and social decline of our times. In addition, I regard the renewed interest in the Holocaust as a hidden subconscious feeling of guilt on the part of the most sensitive segment of the population, especially of the Church in the Western countries. The Holocaust has become a universal problem of mankind and stopped being only a Jewish problem, as it was in years before.

CA: Do you feel the National Book Award in 1973 for Judenrat *indicated the renewed interest and perhaps also an increasing respect for scholarship on the subject?*

TRUNK: Yes. The National Book Award with which I was honored is indicative of the growing interest in our learned society in the historical problems of the Holocaust and its implication for our times.

CA: You listed diaries and underground papers as secondary sources of reference for Judenrat. *How were these preserved, and how difficult was it to gain access to them?*

TRUNK: First of all I will answer about the climate in which these documents were created. The horrible experiences of the Jews under Nazi rule evoked an urge to record them for posterity. Many people in the ghettos and in hiding kept diaries or other literary forms in which they put down their experiences. The majority of them were destroyed together with their authors. However, a certain number, hidden in the clandestine ghetto archives or by non-Jewish friends in the so-called Aryan side, survived, were discovered, and some of them published after the war. An exception is the archives in the U.S.S.R., to which there is almost no access. I have easy access to the archival material everywhere except Poland, which refused me a visa in 1967.

CA: One reviewer of Judenrat *commented that "a distance of thirty years is obviously not quite enough to achieve scholarly objectivity." Do you agree?*

TRUNK: Maybe I am subjective, but he is not correct, because I regard the tempo and changes of our time making the distance of thirty years—this is a whole generation—relatively quite a long period. Besides, after the disappearance of my generation, which lived through the Holocaust, its understanding became more difficult due to the uniqueness of the Nazi era, which has no parallel in the history of mankind. So one cannot use the same approach in examining the Holocaust that you would in searching other chapters of Jewish history. People who lived in this climate can impart the exact and adequate feeling and understanding of what really happened.

CA: Was there much sympathy among the ghetto communities for the council members or the ghetto police?

TRUNK: First I think we have to differentiate between the council and the ghetto police and deal with the two subjects separately. In many ghettos, especially in the small, provincial ones, the councils, the chairmen, and individual members enjoyed the esteem and even sympathy of the ghetto inmates. I will give you one example. According to a poll conducted in the United States and Israel in 1971 and 1972, sixty-two percent of those polled evaluated more or less positively the ethical attitudes and activities of the councils. In contrast, the overwhelming majority polled condemned the role played by the ghetto police. No wonder, in my opinion. The ghetto police were the instrument which enforced the Nazi decrees against the Jewish population—to the bitter end, to the deportation. They were feared, hated, and despised. I think that, as a rule, the police in general—even in normal times—enjoy no popularity with the population at large, and especially in such times as the Holocaust. Of course there were also in the ghetto exceptions to this rule, and I dealt at length in *Judenrat* with the difficult problems of the ghetto police.

CA: You've written in Judenrat *about the continuation of theatrical and musical activities during the Holocaust years. Were these very significant in keeping up morale?*

TRUNK: Positively so. In general, I think the cultural life in the ghettos was a reaction to the Nazi methods of human and national degradation. And the cultural life therefore played an important role. On one hand, the cultural activities were an attempt to immunize—with more or less success—the more pensive and sensitive segment of the ghetto inmates, especially the youth, against the demoralization of ghetto life. There was a demoralization in the ghetto, this is without doubt, and the conditions were prone to create such results. It created a spiritual support in the climate of naked, often brutal, selfishness and materialism. On the other hand, the cultural activities strengthened the ghetto Jew in his sense of self-esteem and human dignity. This effort bore the clear stamp of spiritual and intellectual resistance.

CA: Is there any historical reason Hitler made a particular target of the Jewish communities of Eastern Europe?

TRUNK: I think it was for very sound reasons that the Nazis pinpointed first of all the Eastern European Jewish communities for total destruction. The Nazis were well aware of the central role played by the Jewish communities in Eastern Europe for the whole diaspora. Eastern European Jewry was the reservoir of national and cultural energy and the rejuvenating lifeblood for the Western Jewry in the diaspora. This awareness is evident in the motivation of Himmler's decree of October, 1940, forbidding emigration of the Jews from Eastern Europe to the West. And there is a very clear reason why. Because they would not allow the Jews of Eastern Europe, who played such an important role, to emigrate and strengthen the Jewish communities elsewhere.

CA: In what ways does the Yivo Institute encourage research?

TRUNK: Yivo was founded in Vilna in 1925 and was there until its headquarters were transferred to New York in 1940. Because Vilna was under Soviet occupation and later under Nazi occupation, it was clear that the Institute very soon would not exist in its established form; there was a danger of the destruction of the Institute, of taking out holdings. We had a branch here in the United States, and this branch decided in 1940 to transfer the headquarters here. From this time on, Yivo was the first research institution in the United States that started to gather material and publish documentation on the Holocaust. Yivo holds the richest archival material, especially with regard to Eastern Europe and the Holocaust. Some materials unearthed after the war were hidden by Yivo followers in Vilna in the cellars, and so on, or smuggled out from the Institute there, and hidden within or outside the ghetto. The same is true of our library, which is the richest United States library on the Holocaust. Together with the Yad Vashem Memorial Authority in Jerusalem, Yivo published fourteen bibliographical volumes on the Holocaust literature in many languages and a number of monographs, diaries, and anthologies. Our Center for Advanced Jewish Studies has been for almost ten years systematically conducting courses on the destruction of European Jewry. Yivo has stimulated through its correspondents in the Jewish communities the world over the gathering of documentation (for instance, eyewitness accounts) and research.

CA: Does the Institute play a social role as well?

TRUNK: Yes. In the United States, although there *are* other academic institutions, Yivo is the best known address for anyone doing research work on the Holocaust and Eastern European Jewry, its language and culture, because Yivo is known to have the richest and the greatest holdings on these topics. Many monographs, theses, and dissertations were prepared on the basis of our archival material.

CA: What does your own work there mainly consist of?

TRUNK: I am the chief archivist and chairman of the commission for training and research.

CA: Your major works are in the field of Jewish history, aren't they? Do you have a secondary field of historical interest?

TRUNK: I started as a young historian of Polish Jewry in Warsaw fifty years ago. This field of historical research, going back into the Middle Ages, is my secondary field of interest.

CA: Would you comment on the recent [1978] *television production of "Holocaust"—its authenticity, its timeliness, your own response to it?*

TRUNK: I know the Holocaust film is controversial, but in spite of its flaws and errors, I regard the showing of the film to millions of people, the majority of whom had probably not the slightest knowledge or even notion of the Holocaust, a good thing. I can recall that the statistical figures of the impact of the show in Germany alone—where it was very important, as well as in this country—support my conviction. Almost forty-seven percent of those polled in Germany said that the show made a strong impact on them, and they started to understand what the Nazis did.

CA: As a historian, how do you feel about the new peace treaty between Israel and Egypt and the stance of the other Arab nations on the treaty? Can you foresee a real peace in the future?

TRUNK: I'm embarrassed at this question, because as a historian I am not inclined to reply to hypothetical questions. However, history taught me that there were not and will not be eternal conflicts among people. Sooner or later they end, by agreements or simply by their losing their actual relevance. We had in the Middle Ages a war between Great Britain and France that lasted a hundred years, a war in Germany and the Netherland countries and France in the seventeenth century that lasted thirty, and now we see that they are only subjects of historical research. So although it is very difficult to foresee the time, I am quite sure that the Israeli-Arab conflict will end somehow sooner or later, maybe even in our generation.

BIOGRAPHICAL/CRITICAL SOURCES: New York Times Book Review, December 10, 1972; *Commonweal*, April 13, 1973; *New York Review of Books,* June 14, 1973; *Times Literary Supplement,* April 5, 1974.

—*Interview by Jean W. Ross*

* * *

TRUSCOTT, Lucian K(ing) IV 1947-

PERSONAL: Born April 11, 1947, in Japan; son of Lucian K. III (an Army colonel) and Anne (a medical secretary; maiden name, Harloe) Truscott; married Carol Troy (a journalist and writer), March 17, 1979. *Education:* Graduated from United States Military Academy, West Point, 1969. *Residence:* New York, N.Y.; and Sag Harbor, Long Island, N.Y. *Address:* c/o Betty A. Prashker, Doubleday & Co., 245 Park Ave., New York, N.Y. 10017.

CAREER: U.S. Army, commissioned infantry lieutenant stationed in Ft. Carson, Colo., 1969-70, resigned commission, 1970; *Village Voice,* New York, N.Y., staff writer, 1970-75; writer, 1975—.

WRITINGS: The Complete Van Book, Harmony, 1976; *Dress Gray* (novel; Literary Guild selection), Doubleday, 1979. Contributor to periodicals, including *Village Voice, New York Times, Esquire, Saturday Review, Harper's, Nation, New Yorker, Playboy,* and *Penthouse.*

WORK IN PROGRESS: A novel about a businesswoman, publication by Doubleday expected in 1981.

SIDELIGHTS: Reviews of *Dress Gray,* the best-selling novel about scandal at West Point, have invariably referred to the author's military background. Lucian K. Truscott IV was born into an Army family: his grandfather was a four-star general who commanded the Allied invasion at Italy's Anzio Beach during World War II, and his father was also a career army officer. "I grew up liking army officers," Truscott told an interviewer. "I bagged their groceries, I washed their cars, I mowed their lawns."

From the time he was a small boy, Truscott wanted to attend the United States Military Academy at West Point. When the opportunity finally came, however, he soon grew disillusioned with the rigidity of the academy, which was then beset by problems caused by public opposition to the Vietnam War. As a cadet, Truscott was involved in several controversies. He challenged the academy's rule of compulsory attendance at chapel—a challenge that was later upheld by the U.S. Supreme Court.

In another incident, Truscott received thirty demerits for charging long distance calls to a telephone credit card number that supposedly belonged to the Students for a Democratic Society (SDS). He claimed that he wasn't calling radicals; he was calling friends and relatives. "I didn't see anything wrong in having the SDS pay for my long distance calls," he explained.

Truscott's writing career got its start at West Point. A prolific letter writer, he besieged the *Village Voice* with missives written from a conservative point of view. Soon the newspaper began running his letters on a regular basis. Truscott continued writing after he graduated from West Point in 1969 and was sent to Ft. Carson, Colorado. At Ft. Carson his proclivity for getting into trouble again manifested itself. He wrote an article about heroin addiction among enlisted men at Ft. Carson and then further enraged the brass by refusing to serve on courts-martial. These actions eventually led to his resigning with a general discharge, known as a "bad discharge."

His career in the military over, Truscott packed his bags and headed for New York City, where he wrote free-lance articles for magazines and worked as a staff writer on the *Village Voice.* Soon his literary ambitions extended beyond writing for newspapers and magazines. He conceived the idea of writing a nonfiction book about his West Point class but ran into legal problems. The indemnity clause in book contracts holds the author largely responsible for any lawsuits that may ensue from a book, and Truscott wished to avoid such entanglements. Instead of writing a factual book about West Point, he decided to write a novel—*Dress Gray.*

Rysam P. Slaight III, a junior cadet at West Point, is the hero of *Dress Gray.* When the body of a first-year cadet is found floating on a lake, Slaight suspects foul play. He convinces the doctor who performed the autopsy to reveal the findings: the cadet was murdered shortly after engaging in homosexual intercourse. The superintendent of the academy, for complex reasons of his own, has had the affair hushed up. Slaight's struggles to discover the murderer and expose the cover-up occupy most of the book.

Although most critics considered *Dress Gray* to be an important book, they found numerous flaws in the novel. A frequent complaint was that the characters were flat. Christopher Lehmann-Haupt described the generals in *Dress Gray* as "blundering caricatures," while Tony Schwartz observed that "what finally sinks this first novel is the absence of any characters to make you care about the outcome." Other reviewers faulted Truscott's style; they felt the book was too wordy and that Truscott had a tendency to overexplain. James Webb objected to the intrusion of Truscott's own views in the narrative. "Truscott ceases to show the academy through his characters, and settles on lengthy diatribes that ring not with humanistic truth but with his own biases," he contended.

Outweighing these flaws, however, was Truscott's vivid depiction of military life during the social unrest of the late 1960's. Gene Lyons wrote that *Dress Gray* was "as compelling and important a popular novel as has emerged or is likely to emerge from the Vietnam era. If he is not quite the Stendhal, Lucian K. Truscott IV clearly would like to be the

Mario Puzo of West Point." Many commentators applauded the authenticity of the novel. "There are stretches of drabness in *Dress Gray,* but these are more than made up for with details about West Point life and mores, how it works and what it thinks of itself," Eliot Fremont-Smith wrote. A similar opinion was voiced by Webb, who reflected that "Truscott has a feel for the innuendo, the paradoxes of the service academy existence, and the book deserves to be read for these observations." Lehmann-Haupt found *Dress Gray* praiseworthy on three counts: its "compelling portrait" of life at West Point, its dramatization of the social upheaval in the 1960's, and its "interesting use" of the homosexual theme.

Although Truscott reveals many sordid facts about West Point in *Dress Gray,* it was not his intention to denigrate that institution, but rather to reform it. When asked by an interviewer if his grandfather would have liked *Dress Gray,* Truscott replied, "Like my father, who enjoyed the book, he might have been disturbed by some parts of it, but he would have recognized my aim. "Dress Gray" isn't an attack on West Point but an attempt to make it a better place."

The financial and popular success of *Dress Gray*—it was a Literary Guild selection and on the best seller list for many weeks—turned Truscott into a rich man and thrust him into the limelight. According to Judy Klemesrud, he and his wife, writer Carol Troy, have become "New York City's newest literary darlings," and their extravagant way of life has led some to compare them to Scott and Zelda Fitzgerald. But Truscott has no intention of letting his wealth and social position interfere with his writing. He is already at work on his next novel, which will be about a courageous businesswoman.

Truscott told *CA:* "I enjoy writing novels. I would recommend it as an occupation to those who call themselves critics. The pay is sure as hell better."

The motion picture rights for *Dress Gray* have been sold to Paramount. Gore Vidal has written the screenplay, and Truscott reports that the movie will be produced by Richard Roth and directed by Herbert Ross.

BIOGRAPHICAL/CRITICAL SOURCES: New York Times Book Review, January 7, 1979, April 1, 1979; *New York,* January 8, 1979; *New York Times,* January 15, 1979; *Village Voice,* January 22, 1979; *Washington Post,* January 23, 1979; *New Yorker,* January 29, 1979; *Chicago Tribune,* February 4, 1979; *Newsweek,* February 5, 1979; *Time,* February 19, 1979; *Interview,* March, 1979; *Best Sellers,* March, 1979; *Harper's,* March, 1979; *National Review,* March 30, 1979; *People,* June 4, 1979.

—Sketch by Ann F. Ponikvar

* * *

TRUSSELL, C(harles) P(rescott) 1892-1968

OBITUARY NOTICE: Born August 3, 1892, in Chicago, Ill.; died October 2, 1968. Journalist. For over thirty years Trussell worked as a Washington correspondent, first for the *Baltimore Sun* and then for the *New York Times.* He was awarded a Pultizer Prize in 1949 for distinguished reporting on national affairs for the *New York Times.* In addition to his newswriting, Trussell contributed articles to periodicals, including *Nation's Business.* Obituaries and other sources: *Current Biography,* Wilson, 1949, December, 1968.

* * *

TUGENDHAT, Christopher Samuel 1937-

PERSONAL: Born February 23, 1937, in London, England; son of Georg and Marie (Littledale) Tugendhat; married Julia Dobson, April 8, 1967; children: James Walter, Angus George. *Education:* Cambridge University, M.A. (with honors), 1960. *Office:* Commission of the European Communities, 200 rue de la Loi, 1049 Brussels, Belgium.

CAREER: Financial Times, London, England, editorial writer, 1960-70; British Parliament, London, member for cities of London and Westminster, 1970-76; Commission of the European Communities, Brussels, Belgium, member of commission, 1977—. Member of board of directors of Sunningdale Oils Ltd., 1971-76, and Phillips Petroleum International Ltd., 1972-76. *Military service:* British Army, 1955-57. *Member:* Carlton Club. *Awards, honors:* Management research award from McKinsey Foundation, 1971, for *The Multinationals.*

WRITINGS: Oil: The Biggest Business, Putnam, 1968, new and revised edition, Eyre Methuen, 1975; *The Multinationals,* Eyre & Spottiswoode, 1971, Random House, 1972; *Britain, Europe, and the Third World,* Conservative Political Centre, 1976; *Conservatives in Europe* (pamphlet), Conservative Political Centre, 1979.

SIDELIGHTS: Tugendhat writes: "My sole regret about being a European Commissioner, which I find an interesting, enjoyable, and challenging job, is that it gives me no time to write."

* * *

TUGWELL, Rexford Guy 1891-1979

OBITUARY NOTICE—See index for *CA* sketch: Born July 10, 1891, in Sinclairville, N.Y.; died of cancer, July 21, 1979, in Santa Barbara, Calif. Economist, political theorist, educator, and author. One of the original members of President Franklin D. Roosevelt's "Brains Trust," Tugwell served as under secretary of agriculture and headed the Rural Resettlement Administration in the 1930's. He drew upon his memories of these years in writing several of his books, including *The Brains Trust* and *Roosevelt's Revolution.* Fearing that his reputation as "Rex the Red" would harm Roosevelt's bid for re-election, Tugwell resigned his government posts in 1936 and thereafter held a variety of jobs. The time he spent as governor of Puerto Rico is discussed in such books as *The Stricken Years* and *The Place of Planning in Society.* In 1964 Tugwell joined the staff of the Center for Study of Democratic Institutions, where he supervised the drafting of a model new constitution for the United States, one version of which was published in 1970. Obituaries and other sources: *Current Biography,* Wilson, 1963, September, 1979; *American Men and Women of Science: The Social and Behavioral Sciences,* 13th edition, Bowker, 1973; *Who's Who in America,* 40th edition, Marquis, 1978; *The International Who's Who,* Europa, 1979; *The Writers Directory, 1980-82,* St. Martin's, 1979; *New York Times,* July 24, 1979; *Washington Post,* July 25, 1979; *Chicago Tribune,* July 25, 1979; *Newsweek,* August 6, 1979; *Time,* August 6, 1979.

* * *

TURNER, Sheila R.
See SEED, Sheila Turner

* * *

TWEETEN, Luther 1931-

PERSONAL: Born December 4, 1931, in Las Vegas, N.M.; son of Gilbert B. (a farmer) and Mae (Dahlby) Tweeten; married Eloyce Hugelen, June 6, 1960; children: Brent, Lon,

Deonne, Karyn. *Education:* Attended Waldorf College, 1950-52; Iowa State University, B.S., 1954, Ph.D., 1962; Oklahoma State University, M.S., 1958. *Office:* Department of Agricultural Economics, Oklahoma State University, Stillwater, Okla. 74074.

CAREER: Oklahoma State University, Stillwater, assistant professor, 1962-63, associate professor, 1963-65, professor, 1965-72, Regents Professor of Agricultural Economics, 1972—. Visiting professor at Stanford University, 1966-67, and University of Wisconsin—Madison. *Military service:* U.S. Army, Counter Intelligence Corps, 1954-56. *Member:* American Economic Association, American Agricultural Economics Association (president, 1980), Southern Agricultural Economics Association, Western Agricultural Economics Association, Sigma Xi, Phi Kappa Phi, Phi Theta Kappa. *Awards, honors:* Awards from Western Agricultural Economics Association, 1972, for article "An Economic Analysis of Carry-Love Policies for United States Wheat Industry."

WRITINGS: Resource Demand and the Structure of the Agricultural Industry, Iowa State University Press, 1963; *Roots of the Farm Problem,* Iowa State University Press, 1965; *Foundations of Farm Policy,* University of Nebraska Press, 1970, 2nd edition, 1979; *Micropolitan Development,* Iowa State University Press, 1976. Contributor of more than two hundred articles to scholarly journals.

WORK IN PROGRESS: The Economic Structure of Agriculture; Rural Development; Human Resource Development.

* * *

TZARA, Tristan
See ROSENFELD, Samuel

U

ULMAN, William A. 1908(?)-1979

OBITUARY NOTICE: Born c. 1908 in New York, N.Y.; died August 21, 1979, in Chevy Chase, Md. Government official and author. During the 1950's, Ulman served as assistant administrator for the Housing and Home Finance Agency, a forerunner to the Department of Housing and Urban Development. He later moved to the Department of Health, Education, and Welfare as congressional liaison officer. Ulman received a Bronze Star with two Oak Leaf clusters and the Legion of Merit during World War II. He was created a Commander of the Order of the British Empire. Ulman also wrote articles for *Saturday Evening Post, Collier's, Esquire,* and *New Yorker,* and co-authored several books of a political nature. Obituaries and other sources: *Washington Post,* August 24, 1979.

* * *

URDANG, Laurence 1927-

PERSONAL: Born March 21, 1927, in New York, N.Y.; son of Harry (a teacher) and Annabel (a teacher; maiden name, Schafran) Urdang; married Irena Ehrlich vel Sluszny (an antiques dealer), May 23, 1952; children: Nicole Severyna, Alexandra Stefanie. *Education:* Columbia University, B.S., 1954. *Residence:* Essex, Conn. *Office:* Laurence Urdang, Inc., P.O. Box 668, Essex, Conn. 06426.

CAREER: Funk & Wagnalls Co., New York City, editor, 1955-57; Random House, Inc., New York City, director of reference department, 1957-69; Laurence Urdang, Inc. (preparer of reference books), Essex, Conn., president, 1969—. Head of Laurence Urdang Associates, Ltd., Aylesbury, England, 1970—. *Military service:* U.S. Naval Reserve, active duty, 1944-45. *Member:* International Linguistic Association, Dictionary Society of North America, American Dialectic Society, American Name Society, Association for Computational Linguistics, Association for Computing Machinery, Association for Literary and Linguistic Computing, Linguistic Society of America, Popular Culture Association, American Association for Applied Linguistics, American Society of Indexers, Name Society (England), British Association for Applied Linguistics, New York Academy of Sciences, Linguistic Club of Yale University.

WRITINGS—Editor: *The Random House Vest Pocket Dictionary of Synonyms and Antonyms,* Random House, 1960; *The Random House Dictionary of the English Language,* college edition, Random House, 1968; *The Random House College Dictionary,* Random House, 1968; *The New York Times Everyday Reader's Dictionary of Misunderstood, Misused, Mispronounced Words,* Quadrangle, 1972 (published in England as *A Dictionary of Misunderstood, Misused, Mispronounced Words,* Thomas Nelson, 1972); *Dictionary of Advertising Terms,* Tatham-Laird & Kudner, 1977; *Verbatim: Volumes I and II,* Stein & Day, 1978; *Roget's Thesaurus,* Dale Books, 1978; *Webster's Dictionary,* Dale Books, 1978; *The Basic Book of Synonyms and Antonyms,* New American Library, 1978; *A Basic Dictionary of Synonyms and Antonyms,* Thomas Nelson, 1979; *Private Lives of English Words,* Chelsea House, 1979; *Word for Word,* Verbatim, 1979; *British English: A to Zed,* Verbatim, 1979; *Dictionary of Allusions,* Gale, 1980; *Dictionary of Suffixes in English,* Gale, 1980; *Treasury of Picturesque Expressions,* Gale, 1980. Editor and publisher of *verbatim: Language Quarterly,* 1974—.

V

VACCARO, Ernest B. 1905(?)-1979
(Tony Vaccaro)

OBITUARY NOTICE: Born c. 1905 in Memphis, Tenn.; died November 11, 1979, in Memphis. Journalist. Vaccaro first joined the Associated Press staff in 1924. He soon became the Washington correspondent, a position he held for more than thirty years. Vaccaro won national acclaim for an interview with President Harry S Truman, subsequently becoming his regular traveling companion. Vaccaro was elected to the Society of Professional Journalists Hall of Fame in 1973. Obituaries and other sources: *Washington Post,* November 13, 1979; *New York Times,* November 14, 1979; *Chicago Tribune,* November 18, 1979.

* * *

VACCARO, Tony
See VACCARO, Ernest B.

* * *

VAILLAND, Roger (Francois) 1907-1965

OBITUARY NOTICE: Born October 16, 1907, in Acy-en-Multien, France; died May 11, 1965. Novelist, journalist, essayist, and dramatist. Vailland earned international recognition for the crisp dialogue, economical prose style, and dry, ironic humor of his writings. His first novel, *Drole de jeu,* which was translated as *Playing for Keeps,* won the Prix-Interallie in 1945. Formerly a foreign correspondent, Vailland became a full-time writer after World War II. He wrote numerous novels, including *Les Mauvais Coups (Turn of the Wheel), La Loi, La Truite,* and *Bon Pied, bon oeil,* as well as several plays. Obituaries and other sources: *New York Times,* September 28, 1958, May 13, 1965; *Times Literary Supplement,* September 28, 1967; *World Authors, 1950-1970,* Wilson, 1975.

* * *

VALASKAKIS, Kimon Plato 1941-

PERSONAL: Born September 29, 1941; son of Platon and Marie-Claire (Zalzal) Valaskakis; divorced; children: two. *Education:* University of Lyons, B.en Droit, 1959; American University, B.A., 1961; Cornell University, Ph.D., 1967. *Office:* Gamma Institute and Department of Economics, University of Montreal, Montreal 101, Quebec, Canada.

CAREER: University of Montreal, Montreal, Quebec, Canada, assistant professor, 1967-72, associate professor, 1972-78, professor of economics, 1978—, associate director of Research Center for Economic Development, 1970-72, director of Gamma Institute of Montreal, 1978—. Assistant professor at Sir George Williams University, 1968-70. Director of Niger-Nigeria integration project for Canadian International Development Agency, 1971-73; project director for Niger Research Center for Economic Development, 1972-73. *Member:* Canadian Economic Association, Canadian Peace Research and Education Association, American Economic Association.

WRITINGS: Interpretations du developpement economique occidental, 1750-2000, University of Montreal Press, 1970; (co-author) *Le Quebec qui se fait,* HMH, 1971; *Economic Nationalism and French Trade, 1870-1914,* Editions Scientifiques Le Caire, 1971; (contributor) *Futures,* International Publishing Corp., 1975; (contributor) *The Future as an Academic Discipline,* Elsevier, 1975; (with P. S. Sindell, J. G. Smith, and I. E. Martin) *La Societe de Conservation,* Editions Quinze, 1978, translation published as *The Conserver Society,* Harper, 1979.

WORK IN PROGRESS: The Information Society, publication expected in 1980; *International Development.*

SIDELIGHTS: Valaskakis told *CA:* "My principal field of interest is future studies, which unifies the various disciplines of law, economics, history, philosophy, and the theatre. Within future studies three areas are of particular concern and are likely to be the subject of forthcoming books: energy futures, socio-economic impacts of the information revolution, and geopolitics."

* * *

Van BUITENEN, Johannes Adrian Bernard 1928(?)-1979

OBITUARY NOTICE: Born c. 1928 in the Netherlands; died September 21, 1979, in Champaign, Ill. Educator, editor, and translator. Van Buitenen joined the staff of the University of Chicago in 1959 as associate professor of Sanskrit and Indic studies. He later became professor of linguistics and chairman of the South Asian languages and civilizations department. His books include *Rumanuja on the Bhagavadgita, Tales of Ancient India,* and *Maitrayaniya Upanishad.* He edited a Sanskrit dictionary and the Hindu epic, *The Mahab-*

harata, which he also translated. Obituaries and other sources: *New York Times,* September 22, 1979.

* * *

VANDERBILT, Gloria (Laura Morgan) 1924-

PERSONAL: Born February 20, 1924, in New York, N.Y.; son of Reginald (a financier) and Gloria (Morgan) Vanderbilt; married Pat Di Cicco (an actor's agent), 1941 (divorced, 1944); married Leopold Stokowski (a conductor), April 21, 1945 (divorced, 1955); married Wyatt Cooper (a writer), December 24, 1963; children: (second marriage) Stan, Christopher; (third marriage) Carter V., Anderson H. *Education:* Attended Neighborhood Playhouse School of the Theatre, New York, N.Y., 1955-58.

CAREER: Actress, painter, author, and textile and fashion designer. Acted with numerous stock company productions during the 1950's, including productions in "The Swan," at Pocono (Pa.) Playhouse, August, 1954, and in "Peter Pan," at Andover (Mass.) Playhouse, August, 1958; has also appeared on television programs, including "Kraft Theater" (NBC), "Studio One" (CBS), and "U.S. Steel Hour" (CBS). Painter, with exhibitions in several one-man shows, including Rabun Studio, New York City, 1948, Bertha Schaeffer Gallery, New York City, 1954, Cord Gallery, New York City, 1966, and Neiman-Marcus, Dallas, Tex., 1968; has also had exhibits in group shows in Washington, D.C., and San Francisco, Calif.

Riegel Textile Corp., New York City, director of design, beginning 1970; designer of fabrics for Bloomcraft Co.; designer of stationery and greeting cards for Hallmark Co. Chairman of board of Gloria Vanderbilt, Ltd., 1976—. *Member:* American Federation of Television and Radio Artists, American Federation of Arts, Authors League of America, Actors Equity Association, Screen Actors Guild. *Awards, honors:* Sylvania Award, 1959; Neiman-Marcus Fashion Award, 1969; Fashion Hall of Fame Award, 1970; Fashion Home Sewing Award, 1973; Frederick Atkins certificate, 1974; San Francisco beautiful citation, 1975; American Mart pace-setter award, 1976; gold medal from National Society of Arts and Letters, 1976; Euster Award, 1977.

WRITINGS: Love Poems, World Publishing, 1955; (with Alfred Allen Lewis) *Gloria Vanderbilt's Book of Collage,* Gallahad, 1970; *Woman to Woman,* Doubleday, 1979. Also author of plays "Three by Two: A Play Taking Place at the Perdita Hotel," 1961, and "Cinamee." Contributor of poems, short stories, book reviews, and articles to newspapers and periodicals, including *McCall's, Ladies' Home Journal, Vogue, Cosmopolitan, New York Time,* and *Saturday Review.*

SIDELIGHTS: Great-great-granddaughter of Cornelius Vanderbilt, the financier, Gloria Vanderbilt received notoriety at an early age as the subject of a custody dispute involving her mother and an aunt. Since then her name and photograph have constantly appeared in society columns, for she is a prominent socialite/hostess and fashion trendsetter. She is often on the list of best-dressed women, and she now heads a ready-to-wear company bearing her name. At times she has tried to dodge publicity, particularly in an effort to separate her artistic work from her name. But about her own publications she has said: "Writing seems to have no reality unless somebody is reading it."

Her first book was a collection of poetry, *Love Poems,* illustrated by her friend Ann Bridges Groth. Drawn from a "diary of feelings" she kept as a young girl, the twenty-seven poems convey her search for love and happiness.

The Gloria Vanderbilt Book of Collage is an attempt to share the joy and pleasure she finds in visual arts and encourages her readers to make collages out of scraps and mementos. Her most recent book, *Woman to Woman,* extends this sharing to her flair for living in general. It suggests that women actively mold and decorate their environments, an idea that Caroline Seebohm considered fluff for rich children. Yet Seebohm did find valuable support for women in the fact "that Gloria Vanderbilt only began to feel all right as a person when she started earning money on her own, and that was quite late in life." *Woman to Woman* traces her evolution as an individual and as an artist. As Wyatt Cooper says of his wife in the introduction to the *Book of Collage:* "If she has not yet made of herself a living work of art, she's come damned close."

BIOGRAPHICAL/CRITICAL SOURCES: New York Herald Tribune Book Review, August 14, 1955; *Life,* October 4, 1968; *Harper's Bazaar,* February, 1970, August, 1973; *House and Garden,* April, 1971, July, 1976; *Vogue,* June, 1972, June, 1975; *Time,* July 28, 1975; *House Beautiful,* February, 1977; Phyllis Hingston Roderick, *Gloria Vanderbilt Designs for Your Home,* Simon and Schuster, 1977; *New York Times Book Review,* March 11, 1979.*

* * *

VANDERGRIFF, (Lola) Aola 1920-

PERSONAL: Born May 7, 1920, in LeMars, Iowa; daughter of Cecil Reno and Lola Hazel (Dannelley) Seery; married William Palmer Vandergriff (a civil servant), July 11, 1942; children: Jacquelyn (Mrs. Vance H. Yount), William Ladd, Rebecca L. (Mrs. Charles L. Williams), Jamie D. (daughter), Michael, Patrick. *Education:* Attended American River College, 1971-72. *Politics:* Republican. *Religion:* Protestant. *Home address:* P.O. Box 176, La Luz, N.M. 88337. *Agent:* Henriette Neatrour, 444 East 58th St., New York, N.Y. 10022.

CAREER: Worked at KTOK-Radio, Oklahoma City, Okla., 1937-38; *Minuteman Messenger,* Grand Forks, N.D., columnist, 1964-65; free-lance writer, 1966—. Member of faculty at American River College, 1973-74; public lecturer. *Member:* International Platform Society, National League of American Pen Women, National Press Women. *Awards, honors:* First prize from *Writer's Digest,* 1968, for short story; ZIA Award, 1976; recipient of several other awards.

WRITINGS—All novels; all published by Warner Paperback: *Sisters of Sorrow,* 1974; *House of the Dancing Dead,* 1974; *Wyndspelle,* 1975; *Belltower of Wyndspelle,* 1976; *Wyndspelle's Child,* 1976; *Daughters of the Southwind,* 1978; *Daughters of the Wild Country,* 1978; *Daughters of the Far Islands,* 1979. Also author of *Golden Harvest* (poems), 1936. Contributor of more than twenty-five hundred stories to magazines, including *True Story.* Associate editor of *Writer's Digest,* 1975—.

WORK IN PROGRESS: Daughters of the Opal Skies (tentative title), a novel; *Iron Lace* (tentative title), on the Battle of New Orleans.

SIDELIGHTS: Aola Vandergriff writes: "I live in a haunted canyon, eight miles from the nearest village, in the high desert of New Mexico, in an adobe house we built ourselves. This has accounted for more than a few adobe-tinted manuscript pages.

"I do personal research for each book. I have journeyed to Alaska and British Columbia, Hawaii and Hong Kong. I have just returned from Fiji, New Zealand, and Australia, and will go to England, Ireland, Scotland, and Wales. I try to keep my historical data and background as authentic as possible. The Australian Embassy set up a tour into aborigine country, where I felt for myself the discomfort of heat and flies. There will be camels in my present book, so I rode a camel.

"Does all this time and effort mean that my books are examples of great literature? Indeed not. But a book that sells is a book that fills a *need*.

"I have invented an imaginary reader. In our two-paycheck economy, many wives must work. My reader probably has two children. She also has a yearning for something more than an eight-hour day at work, four or five more at home, and the lethargy that comes from exhaustion. She *needs* romance. She *needs* to travel to faraway places with strange-sounding names. She *needs* a few moments of escape.

"Oddly enough, I've picked up a large number of male fans. I don't know whether they are turning to escape reading, or if it's due to the authenticity of historical data and background."

AVOCATIONAL INTERESTS: "I average reading a book a day. I love to travel. Like Michener, I have a passion for islands. I am intrigued by water: the gray-tan tint of Alaskan waters, the churning tawny Frazer River in British Columbia, the white-laced blue off the Hawaiian islands, the green China Sea—the green of a Seven-Up bottle. And the even greener green of Sydney Harbor."

BIOGRAPHICAL/CRITICAL SOURCES: Alamogordo Daily News, May 11, 1978.

* * *

Van DOREN, Irita 1891-1966

OBITUARY NOTICE: Born March 16, 1891, in Birmingham, Ala.; died December 18, 1966. Journalist. Van Doren was the literary editor of the *Books* section of the *New York Herald Tribune* for nearly forty years. She also worked for a time as advertising manager and associate editor of *Nation,* as well as editorial consultant to William Morrow & Co. publishers. An annual Irita Van Doren Book Award was established in 1960 to honor long and meritorious service to book publishing. Obituaries and other sources: *Current Biography,* Wilson, 1941, February, 1967; *Who Was Who in America,* 4th edition, Marquis, 1968.

* * *

Van HOOSE, William H. 1927-

PERSONAL: Born September 20, 1927, in Louisa, Ky.; son of Millard (a farmer) and Elizabeth Van Hoose; married Hazel Smith, September 5, 1955; children: Frederick W., Pamela S. *Education:* Morehead State University, A.B., 1950; Indiana University, M.S., 1957; Ohio State University, Ph.D., 1965. *Politics:* Democrat. *Religion:* Presbyterian. *Home:* 3404 Indian Springs Rd., Charlottesville, Va. 22901. *Office:* Department of Counselor Education, University of Virginia, Charlottesville, Va. 22903.

CAREER: Worked as a counselor, school psychologist, counselor for juvenile offenders, and as a supervisor of child study and guidance; lecturer in education at College of William and Mary, Williamsburg, Va.; University of Michigan, Ann Arbor, assistant professor of educational psychology, 1963-65; Wayne State University, Detroit, Mich., professor of counseling, 1965-72, head of department of counseling and guidance; University of Virginia, Charlottesville, professor of counselor education, 1972—, head of department. Past chairperson of state and national professional committees. *Member:* Association for Counselor Education and Supervision (national chairperson of Commission on Standards Implementation).

WRITINGS: (With Herman Jacob Peters) *Guidance in Elementary Schools,* Rand McNally, 1965; (with Mildred Peters and George E. Leonard) *The Elementary School Counselor,* Wayne State University Press, 1967, 2nd edition, 1970; *Counseling in the Elementary School,* F. E. Peacock, 1968; (editor with John J. Pietrofesa) *Counseling and Guidance in the Twentieth Century: Reflections and Reformulations,* Houghton, 1970; (with Pietrofesa) *The Authentic Counselor,* Rand McNally, 1971; (editor with Pietrofesa and Jon Carlson) *Elementary School Guidance and Counseling: A Composite View,* Houghton, 1973; (with Jeffrey A. Kottler) *Ethical and Legal Issues in Counseling and Psychotherapy,* Jossey-Bass, 1977. Contributor of more than thirty articles to education and counseling journals.

WORK IN PROGRESS: Adulthood in the Life Cycle, for Brooks/Cole; *Ethics in Counseling,* for Carroll Press.

SIDELIGHTS: Van Hoose's current interests are ethics, adult development, guidance for elementary school children, and professionalization of counseling.

* * *

Van SCHAICK, Frances L. 1912(?)-1979

OBITUARY NOTICE: Born c. 1912 in Rochester, N.Y.; died October 26, 1979, in Washington, D.C. Researcher, editor, and writer. Van Schaick worked as a researcher for author Walter Lippmann, in addition to writing and editing on her own. She edited an autobiography of Thomas W. Lamont, the noted bank executive, and wrote for Editorial Research Reports for almost ten years. Obituaries and other sources: *Washington Post,* October 27, 1979.

* * *

Van SCYOC, Sydney J(oyce) 1939-

PERSONAL: Born July 27, 1939, in Mt. Vernon, Ind.; daughter of John W. (a postal employee) and Geneva (Curry) Brown; married Jim R. Van Scyoc (an engineer), June 23, 1957; children: Sandra K., John Scott. *Education:* Attended University of Hawaii, 1964-65. *Politics:* "Liberally oriented." *Religion:* Unitarian-Universalist. *Home:* 2636 East Ave., Hayward, Calif. 94541. *Agent:* Adrienne Martine, 5228 Miles, Oakland, Calif. 94618.

CAREER: Science fiction writer, 1959—. *Member:* Science Fiction Writers of America, Alameda County Association for the Retarded.

WRITINGS—Science fiction novels: *Saltflower,* Avon, 1971; *Assignment, Nor'Dyren,* Avon, 1973; *Starmother,* Berkley Publishing, 1976; *Cloudcry,* Berkley Publishing, 1977; *Sunwaif,* Berkley Publishing, 1980.

Work represented in numerous anthologies, including: *World's Best Science Fiction: 1969,* edited by Donald Wollheim and Terry Carr, Ace Books, 1969; *Two Views of Wonder,* edited by Tom Scortia and Chelsea Quinn Yarbro, Ballantine, 1974; *Valence and Vision: A Reader in Psychology,* edited by Rich Jones and Richard L. Roe, 1974; and *Social Problems Through Science Fiction,* edited by Joseph Olander, St. Martin's Press, 1975. Contributor to science fiction magazines.

WORK IN PROGRESS: Darkchild, a science fiction novel; research on the Marquesa Islands.

SIDELIGHTS: Van Scyoc writes: "I began writing science fiction in 1959. My early short fiction dealt primarily with individuals struggling against an increasingly dehumanizing technological society. In the late 1960's my focus shifted to short fiction set on other planets and dealt primarily with communities struggling against inexplicable alien environments. I am increasingly intrigued by the genetic and social changes which I believe will overtake us when we begin to colonize other planets. I prefer not to deal in much detail with technology. Instead, I like to set my fiction on isolated worlds inhabited by a relatively small human population. My personal orientation is increasingly pantheistic and in my longer fiction I am attempting to deal with the spiritual relationship of human to environment."

AVOCATIONAL INTERESTS: Gardening, philately, cats, swimming.

* * *

Van SLYKE, Helen (Lenore) 1919-1979

OBITUARY NOTICE—See index for *CA* sketch: Born July 9, 1919, in Washington, D.C.; died July 3, 1979, in New York, N.Y. Business executive, editor, and novelist. At age fifty, Van Slyke abandoned a highly successful business career to write best-selling novels about middle-aged women. Her first career had begun at age eighteen, when she was named fashion editor of the *Washington Star*. Later she held key executive positions for *Glamour* magazine, Henri Bendel's department store, and Norman, Craig & Kummel advertising agency. In 1963 she was named president of the House of Fragrance, and in 1968 she became vice-president of creative activities at Helena Rubinstein. After breaking into print with *The Rich and the Righteous,* Van Slyke turned to writing full time, producing such romantic novels as *The Heart Listens, A Necessary Woman,* and *The Best Place to Be,* which served as the basis of an NBC-TV mini-series. Shortly before she died, she completed another novel, *No Love Lost*. Obituaries and other sources: *Who's Who of American Women,* 9th edition, Marquis, 1975; *Publishers Weekly,* January 31, 1977, July 16, 1979; *The Writers Directory, 1980-82,* St. Martin's, 1979; *New York Times,* July 5, 1979; *Washington Post,* July 5, 1979; *Detroit News,* July 5, 1979; *Chicago Tribune,* July 6, 1979; *Detroit Free Press,* July 6, 1979; *Newsweek,* July 16, 1979; *Time,* July 16, 1979; *AB Bookman's Weekly,* August 6, 1979.

* * *

Van VALKENBURGH, Paul 1941-

PERSONAL: Born April 8, 1941, in Marysville, Kan.; son of Garner (a lawyer) and Lida (Bahr) Van Valkenburgh; married Mary Kay Scallon (a family counselor), September 29, 1973; children: John Paul. *Education:* Attended University of Kansas, 1960-63, and University of California, Los Angeles, 1971; California State University, Long Beach, B.A., 1974, M.A., 1976. *Home:* 6903 Anaheim, Long Beach, Calif. 90815.

CAREER: Douglas Space Systems, Huntington Beach, Calif., draftsman, 1963-65; Chevrolet Engineering, Warren, Mich., research engineer, 1965-69; Peterson Publishing, Los Angeles, Calif., editor, 1969-70; free-lance writer, 1971-77; Systems Technology, Hawthorne, Calif., research engineer, 1977—. Editor for Benziger, Bruce & Glencoe, Inc. *Military service:* U.S. Marine Corps, 1959-65.

WRITINGS: Chevrolet Racing, Haessner, 1973; (with Mark Donohue) *The Unfair Advantage,* Dodd, 1975; *Race Car Engineering,* Dodd, 1976. Contributor to *Encyclopaedia Britannica Yearbook*. Contributor of more than two hundred articles to journals. Founding editor of *Human Power*.

WORK IN PROGRESS: Research for *Behavioral and Social Systems Analysis,* publication expected in 1981; a screenplay.

SIDELIGHTS: Van Valkenburgh writes: "I have been making a gradual transition over the past twenty years: from engineering machines to writing about machines, to writing about people, to finding engineering systems answers to people's problems. My major goal is to develop systematic methods of finding solutions to large-scale societal problems."

* * *

Van VECHTEN, Carl 1880-1964

OBITUARY NOTICE: Born June 17, 1880, in Cedar Rapids, Iowa; died December 21, 1964. Photographer, critic, translator, editor, and author. Van Vechten was author of several sophisticated satires about New Yorkers during the 1920's. His *Nigger Heaven* was among the first novels written about Harlem, and is still considered one of the best. Other novels include *Peter Whiffle, The Blind Bow-Boy,* and *Parties*. In addition, Van Vechten wrote five books of music criticism and an autobiography entitled *Sacred and Profane Memories*. Obituaries and other sources: *The Reader's Encyclopedia,* 2nd edition, Crowell, 1965; *Who Was Who in America,* 4th edition, Marquis, 1968.

* * *

VARNEY, Carleton B(ates) 1937-

PERSONAL: Born January 23, 1937, in Lynn, Mass.; son of Carleton Bates and Julia (Raczkowskos) Varney; married Suzanne Maria Lickdyke (a creative director of a fabric and wallcovering company), December 25, 1969; children: Nicholas, Seamus, Sebastian. *Education:* University of Madrid, M.A., 1957; Oberlin College, B.A., 1958; also attended New York University, 1960. *Religion:* Episcopalian. *Home:* 45 East 66th St., New York, N.Y. 10021. *Agent:* Rosalind Cole, Waldorf Towers, Park Ave. at 50th St., New York, N.Y. 10022. *Office:* Dorothy Draper & Co., Inc., 60 East 56th St., New York, N.Y. 10022.

CAREER: Dorothy Draper & Co., Inc., New York, N.Y., assistant to the president, 1959-63, executive vice-president, 1963-66, president, 1966—. School teacher in New Rochelle, N.Y., 1959-63. *Member:* International Society of Industrial Designers, National Society of Industrial Designers, New York Athletic Club, Millbrook Golf and Tennis Club, Shannon Rowing Club (Ireland). *Awards, honors:* Design achievement award from Shelby Williams, 1972.

WRITINGS: You and Your Apartment, Bobbs-Merrill, 1967; *The Family Decorates a Home,* Bobbs-Merrill, 1968; *Carleton Varney's Book of Decorating Ideas,* Bobbs-Merrill, 1970; *Decorating With Color,* Meredith Corp., 1971; *Decorating for Fun,* Bobbs-Merrill, 1972; *Carleton Varney Decorates Windows,* Meredith Corp., 1975; *Carleton Varney Decorates From A to Z,* Bobbs-Merrill, 1977; *Be Your Own Decorator,* Playboy Press, 1978; *Confessions of a Decorator,* Bobbs-Merrill, 1980. Author of "Your Family Decorator," a column distributed by Field Syndicate, 1968—. Contributor to *Architectural Digest, House Beautiful,* and *Family Circle*.

BIOGRAPHICAL/CRITICAL SOURCES: Architectural Digest, November, 1977, July-August, 1979; *Lodging Hospitality,* January, 1979.

VELIKOVSKY, Immanuel 1895-1979
(Immanuel Ram)

OBITUARY NOTICE—See index for *CA* sketch: Born June 10, 1895, in Vitebsk, Russia; died in 1979 in Princeton, N.J. Physician, psychologist, and author. In *Worlds in Collision,* Velikovsky set forth his theory of cosmic catastrophism. He argued that about 1500 b.c. the earth was struck twice in a period of some fifty years by a fragment from the planet Jupiter. According to Velikovsky, these collisions account for some of the miraculous events recorded in the Old Testament. Although reviewers admired Velikovsky's erudition and the lucidity of his prose, few scientists lent any credence to his theory. His subsequent works also generated considerable controversy. Among them are *Ages in Chaos, Earth in Upheaval,* and *Peoples of the Sea.* Obituaries and other sources: *Current Biography,* Wilson, 1957; *The Author's and Writer's Who's Who,* 6th edition, Burke's Peerage, 1971; *Newsweek,* February 25, 1974; *Who's Who in America,* 39th edition, Marquis, 1976; Alfred De Grazia and others, *Velikovsky Affair: Scientism versus Science,* Sphere, 1978; *Time,* December 3, 1979.

* * *

VELTHUIJS, Max 1923-

PERSONAL: Born May 22, 1923, in The Hague, Netherlands. *Politics:* "Left-thinking." *Religion:* None. *Home and office:* Veenkade 98, The Hague, Netherlands.

CAREER: Teacher of graphic art in The Hague, Netherlands; free-lance designer. *Awards, honors:* Received gold medal award and graphic arts award.

WRITINGS—For children: *Der Junge und der Fisch,* Nord-Sued Verlag, 1969, translation published as *The Little Boy and the Big Fish,* Platt & Munk, 1969; *Der arme Holzhacker und die Taube,* Nord-Sued Verlag, 1970, translation published as *The Poor Woodcutter and the Dove,* Delacorte, 1970; *Der Maler und der Vogel,* 1971, translation by Ray Broekel published as *The Painter and the Bird,* Addison-Wesley, 1975.

Other: *Tobias und das Schloss der Taube,* O. Maier, 1970; *Das gutherzige Ungeheuer* (self-illustrated), Nord-Sued Verlag, 1973; *Das gutherzige Ungeheuer und die Raeuber,* Nord-Sued Verlag, 1976.

Illustrator: Mischa Damjan (pseudonym), *Der Wolf und das Zicklein,* Nord-Sued Verlag, 1968, translation published as *The Wolf and the Kid,* McGraw, 1968 (published in England as *The Wolf and the Little Goat,* Abelard, 1968).

SIDELIGHTS: Velthuijs comments: "I started to work out my own ideas as a graphic artist, and I had to write."

* * *

VELTMAN, Vera
See PANOVA, Vera (Federovna)

* * *

VESEY, Godfrey (Norman Agmondisham) 1923-

PERSONAL: Born June 22, 1923, in Harrogate, England; son of Norman Agmondisham (a minister) and Violet (Taylor) Vesey; married Doreen Hayes Brown (in Women's Royal Volunteer Service), August 9, 1949; children: Joanna Elizabeth Mary, Rachel Louise. *Education:* Cambridge University, B.A., 1949, M.A., 1952, M.Litt., 1958. *Home:* 73 Bushmead Ave., Bedford MK40 3QW, England. *Agent:* Curtis Brown Academic Ltd., 1 Craven Hill, London W2 3EP, England. *Office:* Faculty of Arts, Open University, Milton Keynes MK7 6AA, England.

CAREER: University of London, King's College, London, England, assistant lecturer, 1952-53, lecturer, 1953-65, reader in philosophy, 1965-69; Open University, Milton Keynes, England, professor of philosophy, 1969—. *Military service:* British Army, 1942-47. *Member:* Royal Institute of Philosophy (honorary director, 1966-79; fellow, 1979), Mind Association, Aristotelian Society.

WRITINGS: Embodied Mind, Humanities, 1965; *Perception,* Doubleday, 1971; *Personal Identity,* Cornell University Press, 1974.

Editor: *Body and Mind,* Humanities, 1964; *The Human Agent,* St. Martin's 1968; *Talk of God,* St. Martin's, 1969; *Knowledge and Necessity,* St. Martin's, 1970; *The Proper Study,* St. Martin's, 1971; *Reason and Reality,* St. Martin's, 1972; *Philosophy and the Arts,* St. Martin's, 1973; *Understanding Wittgenstein,* Cornell University Press, 1974; *Philosophy in the Open,* Open University Press, 1974; *Impressions of Empiricism,* St. Martin's, 1976; *Communication and Understanding,* Humanities, 1977; *Human Values,* Humanities, 1978; *Idealism, Past and Present,* Harvester Press, 1980. Assistant editor of *Philosophy,* 1965-69.

WORK IN PROGRESS: Dictionary of Philosophy, publication by Penguin expected in 1984.

SIDELIGHTS: Vesey told *CA:* "My two major motivations are to make worthwhile contributions in the general area of history of philosophy and the special area of philosophy of mind, and to make good philosophy accessible to a wider public. The second motivation explains my thirteen years as honorary director of the Royal Institute of Philosophy and my ten years as professor of philosophy at Britain's Open University. Some of the Open University's philosophy teaching is broadcast on BBC radio and television, and there are scripts of it in *Philosophy in the Open.*"

* * *

VESS, David M(arshall) 1925-

PERSONAL: Born November 4, 1925, in Birmingham, Ala.; son of David W. and Eulalia (Kerby) Vess; married Jean Buchanan, December 30, 1948; children: John Buchanan. *Education:* Howard College (now Samford University), A.B., 1948; Vanderbilt University, M.A., 1950; further graduate study at Harvard University, 1950-52; University of Alabama, Ph.D., 1965. *Religion:* Baptist. *Office:* Department of History and Political Science, Samford University, Birmingham, Ala. 35209.

CAREER: Howard College (now Samford University), Birmingham, Ala., instructor in history and political science, 1949-50; American Legion, Montgomery, Ala., director of youth programs, 1952-57; Samford University, instructor, 1957-58, assistant professor, 1958-65, associate professor, 1965-69, professor of history and political science, 1969—, head of department, 1970—, co-director of Institute of Genealogical and Historical Research, 1960—. President of Alabama State Council for the Social Studies, 1972-73; member of Consortium on Revolutionary Europe. *Military service:* U.S. Navy, aviation electronics technician, 1943-46; served in Pacific theater.

MEMBER: American Historical Association, French Colonial Historical Society, Southern Historical Association, Southern Baptist Historical Association, Association of Alabama Historians (member of board of directors, 1974), Alabama Baptist Historical Society, Pi Gamma Mu (member of state board of governors, 1975—; sponsor for Alabama Gamma chapter), Phi Alpha Theta, Omicron Delta Kappa, Alpha Epsilon Delta.

WRITINGS: The Medical Revolution in France, 1789-1795, University of Florida Press, 1975. Editor-in-chief of home study courses for American Association of Ophthalmology, 1968—. Contributor to history, education, and scientific journals.

WORK IN PROGRESS: A history of medicine.

SIDELIGHTS: Vess writes: "My interest in the history of medicine began in 1965 during doctoral dissertation research into a relatively undeveloped area, the impact of the French Revolution upon the French medical profession. The unexpected opportunity that followed to explore the military medical archives of the Val-de-Grace in Paris broadened into a full-length study, published in 1975. Another unforeseen opportunity came in 1968, when asked to help develop a two-year correspondence course for the American Association of Ophthalmology for training ophthalmic assistants. Then, in 1971, with the sudden death of a colleague, I took over the course in the history of medicine, which now serves the School of Nursing, the School of Pharmacy, and the pre-medical and pre-dental students at Samford University. The process of changing from a humanistic layman to someone adequately familiar with the specialty of medicine has demanded much research and publication effort to establish credibility in a very demanding area of history. It has also demonstrated that valuable insights into "traditional" history from this perspective enrich one's grasp and understanding of mankind. The long struggle of men to overcome ignorance and error can be seen nowhere more clearly or dramatically than in his progress in the development of modern medicine."

* * *

VESTAL, David 1924-

PERSONAL—Education: Attended Art Institute of Chicago, 1941-44; studied photography with Sid Grossman. *Residence:* Bethlehem, Conn. *Agent:* Frances Collin, 156 East 52nd St., New York, N.Y. 10022. *Office: Popular Photography,* 1 Park Ave., New York, N.Y. 10016.

CAREER: Photographer and writer. *Awards, honors:* Guggenheim fellow, 1966, 1973-74.

WRITINGS: The Craft of Photography, Harper, 1975, updated edition, 1978. Author of column in *Popular Photography,* "As I See It," 1977—. Contributor to photography magazines. Contributing editor, *Popular Photography,* 1977—.

SIDELIGHTS: Vestal wrote: "I have photographs in museums, but can't make a living from that. Fortunately people pay me to write, teach, and edit in photography."

* * *

VESTDIJK, Simon 1898-1971

OBITUARY NOTICE: Born October 17, 1898, in Harlingen, Netherlands; died March 23, 1971. Physician, novelist, poet, short story writer, and essayist. After graduating from medical school and working as a physician for five years, Vestdijk determined to become a full-time writer in 1933. For several years he was also literary editor for *Forum.* He was known for the analytic but objective insight and the vitality of his writings. Vestdijk was such a prolific writer that after 1955 he was able to live on the royalties from his books. *Rumeiland (Rum Island)* was one of his nearly forty novels. He also wrote thirty books of essays and criticism, twenty books of poetry, and ten collections of short stories. Obituaries and other sources: *Cassell's Encyclopaedia of World Literature,* revised edition, Morrow, 1973; *World Authors, 1950-1970,* Wilson, 1975; *Who's Who in Twentieth Century Literature,* Holt, 1976.

* * *

VESTERMAN, William 1942-

PERSONAL: Born February 8, 1942, in East Orange, N.J.; son of William Francis and Evelyn (Van Sant) Vesterman; married Susan Lange, August 29, 1964; children: three. *Education:* Amherst College, B.A. (cum laude), 1964; Rutgers University, Ph.D., 1971. *Home:* 29 Mitchell Ave., Piscataway, N.J. 08854. *Office:* Department of English, Livingston College, Rutgers University, New Brunswick, N.J. 08903.

CAREER: Little, Brown & Co., Boston, Mass., 1968-69; Rutgers University, Livingston College, New Brunswick, N.J., instructor, 1969-70, assistant professor, 1970-75, associate professor of literature, 1975—. Consultant to Bell Laboratories.

WRITINGS: (Contributor) Leverenz and Levine, editors, *Mindful Pleasures,* Little, Brown, 1976; *The Stylistic Life of Samuel Johnson,* Rutgers University Press, 1977; *American Media: Industries and Issues,* Random House, 1978. Contributor to literature journals.

WORK IN PROGRESS: Computerized analysis of prose style.

* * *

VIETH von GOLSSENAU, Arnold Friedrich 1889-1979 (Ludwig Renn)

PERSONAL: Born April 22, 1889, in Dresden, Germany (now East Germany); died July, 1979. *Education:* Attended University of Goettingen and University of Munich, 1920-23; attended University of Vienna, 1926. *Politics:* Socialist. *Home:* Am Kornfeld 78, 1138 Berlin Kaulsdorf, German Democratic Republic.

CAREER: Novelist and author. Worked as officer with German security police, 1920, and as art society secretary, 1922-24; secretary and editor of Confederation of Proletarian-Revolutionary Writers journal, *Linkskurve,* 1928-32; teacher of history of war at Marxist Worker's School in Berlin, Germany, 1931-32; imprisoned for literary treason by National Socialist regime, 1933-35; participated in Spanish Civil War as commander of Thaelmann Battalion, 1936, as chief of staff of Eleventh International Brigade, 1937, and as director of Republican People's Army Officer's School, 1938; University of Morelia, Michoacan, Mexico, professor of modern history, 1940-41; Free German Movement, Mexico City, Mexico, president, 1940-47; Institute of the History of Civilization, Dresden, East Germany, director, 1947-51; Dresden Technische Hochschule, Dresden, professor of anthropology, 1947-51. *Military service:* German Army, 1911-20; served as officer in Saxon Guards. *Member:* East German P.E.N. Center (honorary president, beginning 1971), East Berlin Academy of Arts (honorary president, beginning 1969). *Awards, honors:* Honorary doctorate from Dresden Technishe Hochschule, 1949; Children's Book Prize, 1954, 1955, 1956, 1958, and 1961; East German National Prize, 1955 and 1961.

WRITINGS—All under pseudonym Ludwig Renn; in English: *Krieg,* Frankfurter Societaets Druckerei, 1928, Aufbau, 1948, translation by Willa Muir and Edwin Muir published as *War,* Secker & Warburg, 1929, Fertig, 1978; *Nachkrieg,* Agis Verlag, 1930, translation by W. Muir and E. Muir published as *After War,* Dodd, 1931; *Vor grossen Wandlungen,* Oprecht, 1936, translation published as *Death Without Battle,* Dodd, 1937; *Kriegfuehrung und Propaganda,* 1939, translation by Edward Fitzgerald published as *Warfare: The Relation of War to Society,* Oxford University Press, 1939, reprinted, Books for Libraries Press, 1971.

Other: *Russlandfahrten* (title means "Travels in Russia"), Lasso Verlag, 1932; *Adel im Untergang* (novel; title means "Aristocracy in Decay"), Editorial El Libro libre (Mexico), 1944; *Morelia: Eine Universitaetsstadt in Mexico* (title means "Morelia: A University Town in Mexico"), Aufbau, 1950; (editor) *Zwoelf Holzschnitte aus Volkschina* (title means "Twelve Chinese Wood-Engravings"), Thueringer Volksverlag, 1951; *Vom alten und neuen Rumaenien* (title means "Of Romania Old and New"), Aufbau, 1952; *Der Spanische Krieg* (title means "The Spanish War"), Aufbau, 1955, published as *Im Spanischen Krieg* (title means "In the Spanish War"), 1959; *Meine Kindheit und Jugend* (title means "My Childhood and Youth"), Aufbau, 1957; *Krieg ohne Schlacht* (novel, title means "War Without Battle"), Aufbau, 1957; *Auf den Truemmern des Kaiserreichs* (novel; title means "On the Ruins of the Empire"), Aufbau, 1961; *Inflation* (novel), Aufbau, 1963; *Gesammelte Werke* (title means "Complete Works"), ten volumes, Aufbau, 1964-70; *Zu Fuss zum Orient* (title means "On Foot in the East"), Aufbau, 1966; *Ausweg* (title means "Way Out"), Aufbau, 1967.

Juvenile: *Trini: Die Geschichte eines Indianerjungen* (title means "Trini: The Story of a Young Indian"), Kinderbuchverlag, 1954; *Der Neger Nobi* (title means "The Negro Nobi"), Kinderbuchverlag, 1955, published as *Nobi,* 1966; *Herniu under der blinde Asni* (title means "Herniu and Blind Asni"), Kinderbuchverlag, 1956; *Herniu und Armin* (title means "Herniu and Armin"), Kinderbuchverlag, 1958; *Herniu,* Aufbau, 1959; *Camilo: Eine ungewoehnliche Gedichte aus Kuba, von einem tapferen kleinen Jungen und seinem Grossvater* (title means "Camilo: An Unusual Story From Cuba, of a Brave Little Boy and His Grandfather"), Kinderbuchverlag, 1963.

SIDELIGHTS: Arnold Vieth von Golssenau began his crowded and adventurous life in Dresden. His father, a member of an aristocratic Saxon family, was a landowner and soldier with some Irish blood who left the army for an academic career; his mother was of Russian-German ancestry. As a child, Vieth von Golssenau suffered from anemia and was sent for treatment and a healthier climate to Switzerland and Italy. His health began to improve when he was about sixteen, and he developed an intense interest in painting and architecture. At the age of twenty, nevertheless, in accordance with family tradition, he entered the German Army as an officer cadet. From 1911 to 1914 he attended all the functions of the Saxon royal court, becoming a personal friend of the Crown Prince of Saxony, whom his father tutored. In 1914 he visited Scandinavia and was greatly impressed by the democratic spirit he encountered there.

His experiences during World War I as an officer in the Saxon Guards completely destroyed his already uncertain allegiance to the Prussian military tradition. He was almost continuously at the front, as a company commander and later as adjutant of his regiment, and was twice wounded.

Leaving the army, Vieth von Golssenau served for a time in the security police. He then resumed his education until inflation made his inheritance almost worthless. After working for two years as secretary of a commercial art society, he settled down to finish his first book, *War,* but could find no publisher. A prolonged hiking trip followed, which took him and an Italian friend—a multilingual shoemaker—all over Italy and to Greece, Turkey, and Egypt. What he saw in Italy of the rise of Fascism made him a passionate opponent of that ideology. Further study followed at the University of Vienna, where his reading completed his political conversion. He joined the Communist party in 1928. His novel *War* was published the same year.

Vieth von Golssenau had begun to write during the war, developing a stark, bare, and rigorously objective style which, he said, was influenced by the travel books of Sven Hardin. His first novel is a fictionalized but extremely detailed, exact, and realistic account of World War I as seen by a German private soldier (later sergeant) in a small infantry unit. The authorship of the novel is ascribed to the narrator, Sergeant Ludwig Renn, and Vieth von Golssenau used this pseudonym in all his subsequent writings. The book had a tremendous impact in Germany in 1928, when antiwar feeling was at its peak, but was somewhat eclipsed by the even greater popularity of Erich Remarque's 1929 book, *All Quiet on the Western Front.* This was reflected in some reviews of the English translation of *War.* J. B. Wharton, for example, wrote that "*War* lacks the philosophic perspective of Remarque's *All Quiet on the Western Front.* It is perhaps not so great a book," though "Renn's descriptions of actual combat, and the front, are truer, more real and accurate."

This reaction was by no means universal, however. A critic in the *Times Literary Supplement* said that Vieth von Golssenau "records his impressions with the extreme simplicity which is one of the highest forms of literary art." Herschel Brickell called *War* "a remarkable document, and a contribution to the real history of the World War of prime importance."

In 1929 and 1930 Vieth von Golssenau traveled in Russia and the Caucasus, returning for the publication of his second novel, *After War,* which, like its predecessor, closely reflected the author's own experiences. Sergeant Renn, unable to find a civilian job after the war, enlists in the army of the Social Democratic state and finds himself unwillingly involved in political intrigue. Things are no better when he joins the security police and in the end Renn decides to try Communism. V. S. Pritchett wrote: "For its laconic, objective, plain statement in which the fatal corruption of the revolution of the soldiers and populace against the officer class is depicted, Herr Renn's book is excellent. Herr Renn himself emerges simple, scrupulous, honest, unimaginative—a man who has felt more powerfully than he will say." However, though Lambert Davis admired the book as "an honest and detailed report of one man's experience in the incredible turmoil of post-war Germany," he concluded that it lacked "the imagination to capture the sweep of revolutionary forces in action or the introspective power to fathom the individual's deeper emotions in such a crisis." Other reviewers found the novel dull, and most thought it inferior to *War.*

Russlandfahrten (1932), the author's account of his Russian travels, was, he said, "suppressed by a boycott under Prussian nationalistic leadership." Meanwhile, he was engaged in an intense study of military science, at the same time teaching war history in the Marxist Workers' School in Berlin. This brought him a brief period of imprisonment in 1932, and in 1933, on the night of the Reichstag fire, he was arrested again and jailed for two and a half years. Released, he escaped in 1936 to Switzerland, where he wrote *Death With-*

out Battle. Set in the Germany he had so recently fled, the novel describes with brutal directness Hitler's rise to power, the Reichstag fire, the assassination of Dollfuss, and the other horrors and outrages of the time.

Later in 1936, Vieth von Golssenau went to Spain, where he served as a senior officer with the Loyalist forces. In 1937 he toured North America, lecturing on the war and raising funds. With the defeat of the Republicans in 1939, he escaped to France, where he was detained for a time in a French prison camp. Released, he lived illegally in Paris, writing the book published as *Warfare: The Relation of War to Society.* Reviewers noted that his approach was historical rather than theoretical, describing the evolution of warfare and of armies, and showing how the latter have been modified in their nature and techniques by different forms of government and by social and economic change. Critics found the book a little disjointed, and over-simplified in its argument, but one concluded that "nothing that is said in this cogent, lucid, economical book is unimportant."

Leaving France, Vieth von Golssenau went to England and then to Mexico, where he taught at the University of Morelia and wrote a book about the university and its town. In 1941 he was called to Mexico City to become president of the Free German Movement there. During the war years he studied anthropology and archaeology and wrote *Adel im Untergang,* an autobiographical novel about his experiences as a young officer. He went home to Dresden in 1947 and taught there until 1951, when he settled in East Berlin as a much honored elder statesman of the literary establishment. Until the time of his death, he published books about the Spanish Civil War, Romania, and his own childhood. *Krieg Ohne Schlacht* and *Auf den Trummern des Kaiserreichs* are novels dealing respectively with World War II and the German revolution of 1918. Vieth von Golssenau has also written several prize-winning stories for children. None of his later books has been translated into English, and in the United States and Britain his reputation rests most solidly on his first novel, *War,* which Wilhelm K. Pfeiler once described as "one of the few great books that came out of the First World War."

AVOCATIONAL INTERESTS: Anthropology, history of art, prehistory, war history.

BIOGRAPHICAL/CRITICAL SOURCES: Wilhelm Karl Pfeiler, *War and the German Mind,* Columbia University Press, 1941; *Ludwig Renn: Hilfsmaterial fuer den Literaturunterricht,* Volk & Wissen Volkseigener, 1956; Ludwig Renn, *Der Spanische Krieg,* Aufbau, 1956; Renn, *Meine Kindheit und Jugend,* Aufbau, 1957; *Ludwig Renn zum 70. Geburtstag,* Aufbau, 1959.*

* * *

VINAL, Harold 1891-1965

OBITUARY NOTICE: Born October 17, 1891, in Vinalhaven, Me.; died March 9, 1965. Editor, publisher, critic, essayist, and poet. Founder and editor of *Voices,* a quarterly poetry magazine, Vinal also worked as a free-lance writer for over forty years. Maine's beautiful scenery was often the subject of his poems. His poetry collections include *A Stranger in Heaven, Hymn to Chaos,* and *Hurricane.* Obituaries and other sources: *The Reader's Encyclopedia of American Literature,* Crowell, 1962; *Who Was Who in America,* 4th edition, Marquis, 1968.

VINCITORIO, Gaetano L(eonard) 1921-

PERSONAL: Born September 11, 1921, in Brooklyn, N.Y. *Education:* St. John's University, Brooklyn (now St. John's University), B.S. (summa cum laude), 1942; Fordham University, M.A., 1943, Ph.D., 1950; also attended Columbia University, 1946. *Office:* Department of History, St. John's University, Jamaica, N.Y. 11439.

CAREER: High school teacher of history in public schools in New York; Pace College (now University), New York, N.Y., instructor in political and social sciences, 1946-48; St. John's University, Jamaica, N. Y., instructor, 1948-50, assistant professor, 1950-54, associate professor, 1954-57, professor of history, 1957—, head of department, 1977—, head of Humanities Research Advisory Board. *Member:* American Historical Association, American Catholic Historical Association, Conference on British Studies, Modern Language Association of America, U.S. Catholic Historical Society (member of executive board), Historical Association (England), Long Island British Studies Group (past executive secretary), American Legion. *Awards, honors:* Grant from Relm Foundation.

WRITINGS: (With J. S. Hoffman and Morrison Swift) *Man and His History: World History and Western Civilization,* Doubleday, 1958, revised edition, 1963; (with Thomas J. Murphy) *Testing Program for "Conceived in Liberty,"* Doubleday, 1959; (with Murphy) *Testing Program for "The Common Good,"* Doubleday, 1959; (editor) *Studies in Modern History,* St. John's University Press, 1968; (editor and contributor) *Crisis in the "Great Republic,"* Fordham University Press, 1969; *The Record of 1969,* Scribner, 1971; *The Record of 1970-71,* Scribner, 1974; *The Record of 1972-73,* Scribner, 1975. Also author of *The Record of 1976,* Scribner. Contributor to *Catholic Encyclopedia for Home and School* and *New Catholic Encyclopedia.* Contributor of articles and reviews to history and humanities journals. Member of editorial board of *Review of National Literatures.*

* * *

VINSON, J(ohn) William 1916-1979

OBITUARY NOTICE: Born April 15, 1916, in Tampa, Fla.; died September 7, 1979, in Manchester, Mass. Educator and poet. Vinson was affiliated with Harvard University for more than twenty years. He became an associate professor of microbiology and established himself as an authority on tropical and venereal diseases. Vinson received the Hans Zinsser Memorial Award in 1964. Obituaries and other sources: *American Men and Women of Science: The Physical and Biological Sciences,* 12th edition, Bowker, 1971-73; *New York Times,* September 16, 1979.

* * *

VITA-FINZI, Claudio 1936-

PERSONAL: Born November 21, 1936, in Sydney, Australia; son of Paolo E. G. A. (a writer) and Nadia (Touchmalova) Vita-Finzi; married Penelope Angus (a scholar), May 1, 1969; children: Leo. *Education:* Cambridge University, B.A. (with honors), 1958, Ph.D., 1962. *Religion:* None. *Home:* 22 South Hill Park, London N.W.3, England. *Agent:* A. D. Peters, 10 Buckingham St., London WC2N 6BU, England. *Office:* University College, University of London, Gower St., London WC1E 6BT, England.

CAREER: Cambridge University, Cambridge, England, fellow of St. John's College, 1961-64; University of London, London, England, lecturer in geography, 1964—.

WRITINGS: (With J.J.E. Aarons) *The Useless Land,* R. Hale, 1959; *The Mediterranean Valleys,* Cambridge University Press, 1969; *Recent Earth History,* Macmillan, 1973; *Archaeological Sites in Their Setting,* Thames & Hudson, 1978.

WORK IN PROGRESS: Research on recent crustal movements in the Near East.

SIDELIGHTS: Vita-Finzi wrote: "A thread running through my books and research papers is the chronicling of time. *Recent Earth History* dealt with this explicity; the rest do so by seeking to trace some kind of change (e.g. the evolution of a landscape) in order to see how it relates to some concurrent sequence (e.g. human settlement of that landscape). The next stage is to use time to find an explanation; my current work on earth movements is designed to discover how fast and how regularly the crust shifts in different areas in the hope that the findings will help us understand why. In such an enterprise it is wise to avoid reading books on the philosophy of time because, if you do, you will soon become convinced that you are—wasting your time."

* * *

VOGT, Bill
See VOGT, William McKinley

* * *

VOGT, William McKinley 1935-
(Bill Vogt)

PERSONAL: Born July 3, 1935, in Fremont, Neb.; son of William F. C. and Marjorie M. Vogt; married Lorraine Dolinsky (a home economist), July 15, 1967; children: Arthur, Alton. *Education:* Attended Doane College, 1953-55, and Iowa State University, 1955-58; University of Nebraska, Omaha, B.S., 1962; University of Wisconsin—Madison, M.S., 1972. *Politics:* Democrat. *Religion:* Methodist. *Home:* 1105 East Racine Ave., Waukesha, Wis. 53186. *Office: National Wildlife,* 225 East Michigan, Milwaukee, Wis. 53202.

CAREER: WOW-TV, Omaha, Neb., newscast writer, 1962-66; Virginia Polytechnic Institute and State University, Blacksburg, director of publications, 1966-70; Wisconsin Department of Natural Resources, Madison, acting press officer, 1970-71; *Outdoor Life,* New York, N.Y., senior editor, 1971-76; *National Wildlife,* Milwaukee, Wis., senior editor, 1976—. *Military service:* U.S. Army, in artillery fire direction, 1958-60; served in Korea. *Member:* Outdoor Writers of America.

WRITINGS—Under name Bill Vogt: *How to Build a Better Outdoors,* McKay, 1978. Author of "Conservation Trails," a monthly column in *Outdoor Life.* Contributor to *Encyclopedia Americana* yearbook, *National Wildlife,* and *International Wildlife.* Editor of newsletter of Conservation Education Association.

WORK IN PROGRESS: Research for a book on nature activities; maintaining extensive files on natural history and conservation.

SIDELIGHTS: Vogt told *CA:* "My major field is conservation, which to me implies the wise use of natural resources. By 'wise use' I mean the setting of environmental *and* economic goals that are compatible. Sound objectives of both kinds may appear to be poles apart in the short term, but in the long run they are inseparable. An unhealthy environment cannot nurture a healthy economy. By the same token, the world's economy must be strong in order to pay the costs of cleaning up the environment. Obviously, some short-term tradeoffs must be made so that, in the long run, we will be able to enjoy both prosperity and a livable environment.

"Wild animals and native plants are the first organisms to be affected by pollution and other forms of environmental degradation. Therefore, these organisms provide vital advance information about the quality of the air, water, and soil—and consequently about the quality of human life itself. In my opinion, the importance of the world's fauna and flora as environmental indicators far outweighs even their esthetic value, and is the best social and economic argument for wildlife conservation.

"I am a journalist who is trying to strengthen communications between the scientific community and the public, and though my academic and professional background includes the biological sciences, I write as a layman. If I am writing about a controversial issue, I try to see both sides with compassion."

Jack Lorenz, executive director of the Izaak Walton League of America, called Vogt's book, *How to Build a Better Outdoors,* "a major new work offering concerned citizens a workable formula for meaningful conservation action." In the book's foreword, Lynn A. Greenwalt, director of the U.S. Fish and Wildlife Service, said: "Bill Vogt helps to bridge the gap between novice and veteran conservationists by providing a clear and readable response to that recurrent question: 'What can I do to help?' His book is, in the finest sense, a primer. It helps the reader take the first steps in finding his or her niche in the realm of helping the natural world."

AVOCATIONAL INTERESTS: Folk music, antique fishing equipment, fishing, camping.

BIOGRAPHICAL/CRITICAL SOURCES: Outdoor America, November/December, 1978; Bill Vogt, *How to Build a Better Outdoors,* McKay, 1978.

* * *

von MISES, Margit 1896-

PERSONAL: Born July 3, 1896, in Hamburg, Germany (now West Germany); came to the United States, 1940; daughter of Albert (a dentist) and Selica (Fontheim) Herzfeld; married G. F. Sereny (a businessman), February, 1917 (died, 1923); married Ludwig von Mises (an economist), July 6, 1938 (died October 10, 1973); children: (first marriage) Guido F., Gitta Sereny (Mrs. Don Honeyman). *Education:* Educated in Hamburg, Germany. *Home:* 777 West End Ave., New York, N.Y. 10025.

CAREER: Actress in Bremerhaven, Lubeck, and Hamburg, Germany, and Vienna, Austria, 1913-23; translator and adapter of French and English plays for the German and Austrian stage, 1923-38.

WRITINGS: My Years With Ludwig von Mises, Arlington House, 1976; (author of foreword) Ludwig von Mises, *Notes and Recollections,* Gateway, 1979; (author of foreword) L. von Mises, *Economic Policy: Thoughts for Today and Tomorrow,* Gateway, 1979. Translator of numerous plays from French and English into German, including: Van Druten, "Distaff Side"; Maxwell Anderson, "Mary of Scotland"; Donald Ogden Stewart, "Rebound"; and Denis Amiel, "Liberty."

WORK IN PROGRESS: Revision and enlargement of *My Years With Ludwig von Mises* in German.

SIDELIGHTS: Margit von Mises told *CA:* "My life was so closely connected with that of my late husband, Ludwig von

Mises, that whatever I have to say about myself will always be in relation to him." She described her life up to the time she met von Mises: "I was born in Hamburg, Germany, but when I was one year old my parents went to America, where my father continued his study of dentistry at the University of Chicago. After more than five years we returned to Hamburg.

"My parents took care that I got a good education. My father wanted me to study medicine, but against his will I insisted on becoming an actress. I had a promising career, and played leading parts in Bremerhaven, Hamburg, and Vienna. Here, during the first World War, I married G. F. Sereny, a Hungarian businessman. He died of cancer when I was still in my twenties and I was left alone with two small children —alone, and almost without any money in the worst runaway inflation of all time.

"I had to go to work immediately, but I was too shaken to continue acting. Thanks to my knowledge of the theatre and my bilingual education I could take up translating and adapting French and English plays for the German stage, working in Vienna for George Marton, the literary agent."

Margit met Ludwig von Mises at a party in 1925. The famous Austrian economist had already become known for his brilliant, original theories, his inflexible honesty and patriotism, and an unfaltering pursuit of his own ideas. He was extremely dedicated to his work and had organized his life into an efficient routine.

Von Mises fell in love with Margit "almost upon their first meeting," Richard M. Ebeling related, "but he seemed unable to make the commitment that would involve a radical change in his life and activities." They became engaged after a year, but Margit wrote that soon "he grew afraid of marriage, the bond it would mean, the change that children would bring to a quiet home, and the responsibilities that might detract him from his work." Finally after thirteen years they were married.

During their thirty-five year marriage Margit dedicated her life to Ludwig's work and has continued to do so even after his death at the age of ninety-two. She has spread her husband's "ideas about individual liberty and the free market, and his fight against inflation and communism." She had eight of his books published posthumously, including a book of his Argentine lectures.

Though Ludwig von Mises was described by Milton Friedman as "one of the great men of our time," John Chamberlain noted that "when he died in 1973 there were innumerable tributes to his work, but nothing much about him as a human being." *My Years With Ludwig von Mises* was the first book to remedy that situation by recalling the warmth and humor of the man. In addition, the book describes historical events in Europe during the inter-war period and World War II that affected von Mises's economic theories. Many prominent figures are featured, such as Paul Mantoux, Wilhelm Roepke, Hans Kelsen, Henry Hazlitt, Albert Hahn, and Friedrich von Hayek.

Friedman declared that *My Years With Ludwig von Mises* "gives a rare and unusual insight into the personality and character of this man who has done more than perhaps any other person to keep shining during dark days a beacon showing the road to a free society. It is also, quite unintentionally, a tribute to a remarkable woman who was able to perceive this greatness and tend it with loving care and complete selflessness." Chamberlain remarked that although von Mises "protests that she is an amateur writer . . . she is actually as skilled as any professional. Those years when she was translating plays for the Vienna theatre have paid off."

BIOGRAPHICAL/CRITICAL SOURCES: Freeman, February, 1977; *Libertarian Forum,* January, 1977; *New American Review,* November, 1977.

* * *

von RIEKHOFF, Harald 1937-

PERSONAL: Born December 27, 1937, in Reval, Estonia; son of Johannes (a landowner) and Gisela (Baroness von Maydell) von Riekhoff; married Anita, Baroness von Koskull, August 8, 1971; children: Andre Christopher. *Education:* University of Western Ontario, B.A., 1960; Yale University, M.A., 1961, Ph.D., 1965. *Religion:* Lutheran. *Home:* 19 Marlborough Ave., Ottawa, Ontario, Canada K1N 8E6. *Office:* Department of Political Science, Carleton University, Ottawa, Ontario, Canada K1S 5B6.

CAREER: Carleton University, Ottawa, Ontario, assistant professor, 1965-68, associate professor, 1968-74, professor of political science, 1974—. Visiting scholar at University of Michigan, 1971-72. Member of policy analysis group of Canadian Department of External Affairs, 1973-74. *Military service:* Royal Canadian Navy (Reserve), 1956-62; became lieutenant. *Member:* International Institute of Strategic Studies, Canadian Institute of International Affairs, American Political Science Association. *Awards, honors:* Defense fellow of Canadian Institute of International Affairs, 1964-65.

WRITINGS: NATO: Issues and Prospects, Canadian Institute of International Affairs, 1967; *The Communist States and the West,* Praeger, 1968; *German-Polish Relations, 1918-1933,* Johns Hopkins Press, 1971. Contributor to political science journals.

WORK IN PROGRESS: Research on U.S.-Canadian relations, foreign policy in asymmetric dyads, and domestic instability and foreign policy crises in Germany, 1904-14, 1929-39.

* * *

VOZNESENSKY, Andrei 1933-

PERSONAL: Born May 12, 1933, in Moscow, U.S.S.R.; son of Andrei (an engineer and professor) and Antonina (a teacher; maiden name, Pastuschichina) Voznesensky; married Zoya Boguslavskaya (an author and literary critic); children: Leonid. *Education:* Received degree from Institute of Architecture (Moscow), 1957. *Home:* Kotelnicheskaya, nab. 1/15, Block W, Apt. 62, Moscow, U.S.S.R. *Agent:* c/o U.S.S.R. Union of Writers, Ulitsa Vorovskogo, 52, Moscow, U.S.S.R.

CAREER: Poet. *Member:* Union of Soviet Writers, American Academy of Arts and Letters, Bayerischen Kunst Acad., French Academy Merime. *Awards, honors:* Nomination for Lenin Prize in literature, 1966, for *Antimiry* ("Antiworlds"); nomination for Books Abroad/Neustadt International Prize for literature, 1975; State Literature Prize, 1978, for *Vitrazhnykh del master;* International award for distinguished achievement in poetry, 1978, for *Nostalgia for the Present.*

WRITINGS—All poems; in English: *Selected Poems,* translated and introduction by Anselm Hollo, Grove, 1964; *Antimiry,* [Moscow], 1964, translation by W. H. Auden, Richard Wilbur, Stanley Kunitz, William Jay Smith, and others published as *Antiworlds,* Basic Books, 1966, enlarged edition published as *Antiworlds, and the Fifth Ace,* text in English and Russian, 1967; *Voznesensky: Selected Poems,* translation and introduction by Herbert Marshall, Hill & Wang,

1966 (published in England as *Selected Poems,* Methuen, 1966); *Dogalypse* (translations from San Francisco poetry reading), City Lights, 1972; *Little Woods: Recent Poems by Andrei Voznesensky* (includes poems from *Ten'zvuka;* also see below), translated by Geoffrey Dutton and Igor Mezbakov-Koriakin, introduction by Yevgeny Yevtushenko translated by Eleanor Jacka, Sun Books (Melbourne), 1972; *Avos,* translation by Kunitz and others published as *Story Under Full Sail,* Doubleday, 1974; *Nostalgia for the Present,* translated by Wilbur, Smith, Lawrence Ferlinghetti, Robert Bly, Allen Ginsburg, and others, forewords by Edward Kennedy and Arthur Miller, Doubleday, 1978.

Other: *Mozaika* (title means "Mosaic"), [Vladimir], 1960; *Parabola,* [Moscow], 1960; *Pishetsya kak lyubitsya* (title means "I Write as I Love"), text in Russian and Italian, Feltrinelli (Milan), 1962; *Treugol'naya grusha* (title means "The Triangular Pear"), [Moscow], 1962; *Menya pugayut formalizmom,* Flegon Press, 1963; *Akhillesovo serdtse* (title means "An Achilles Heart"), [Moscow], 1966; *Moi lybovnyi dnevnik* (title means "My Diary of Love"), Flegon Press, 1966; *Stikhi,* [Moscow], 1967; *Ten' zvuka* (title means "The Shadow of Sound"), [Moscow], 1970; *Vzglyad* (title means "The Glance"), [Moscow], 1972; *Vypusti ptitsu!* (title means "Let the Bird Free"), [Moscow], 1974; *Dubovyi list violonchel'nyi* (title means "Violoncello Oak Leaf"),[Moscow], 1975; *Vitrazhnykh del master* (title means "The Stained-Glass Panel Master"), [Moscow], 1976; *Soblazn* (title means "Temptation"), [Moscow], 1978.

SIDELIGHTS: "The name of Voznesensky in Soviet poetry often becomes the centre of heated discussion," observed Vladimir Ognev. "The young poet leaves nobody indifferent. Widely differing estimations are given to his poetry—some call him a daring innovator, others a cold rhymester." Regardless of the more critical views of his work, Voznesensky warmed the hearts of his followers—and heated the tempers of Soviet officials—during his rise to international prominence in the 1960's. His swift, uncluttered, and often bold verse differed radically from the restricted poetry the Soviet Union had known in the Stalin years; and Russian audiences responded enthusiastically to the young poet's work. Though often compared to the verse of Yevgeny Yevtushenko, Voznesensky's poetry is considered more complex and more intellectual than that of his peer. The public acclaim he enjoyed early in the 1960's dwindled considerably at the end of the decade, largely because of recurrent Soviet crack-downs on authors who failed to promote the country's cause. But Voznesensky continues to write, maintaining the respect of American audiences and a core of American writers in the meantime. His latest book, *Nostalgia for the Present,* marked his first major English publication in more than ten years.

As a child, Voznesensky was introduced to Russia's great literary tradition by his mother, who surrounded him with books by great authors—Blok, Dostoevsky, Pasternak—and read poetry to him as well. Voznesensky experimented a bit with writing when he was young, but devoted himself mainly to painting and drawing. After receiving his degree from the Moscow Architectural Institute, however, his interest in architecture dropped. "Architecture was burned out in me," he recollected. "I became a poet." Some of his poems appeared in magazines at that time and two years later, in 1960, he published his first book, *Mosaika.*

Despite having a tremendously rich Russian poetic tradition to follow, "the only poet who influenced me," Voznesensky once declared, "was Pasternak, who was my god, my father, and for a long time, my university." Strangely, however, Voznesensky feels no similarity between his own poetry and that of his mentor. As a teenager he had sent some of his poems to Pasternak, who consequently invited Vosnesensky to visit. The poems were obvious Pasternak imitations. Later, though, Voznesensky sent some of his post-graduate poems to Pasternak, revealing an entirely different poet. "Yes, this is no longer Pasternak," an admiring Pasternak reportedly said. "This is Voznesensky, a poet in his own right." The compliment encouraged Voznesensky: "I felt I had finally made it."

Several factors contributed to Voznesensky's "meteoric" rise from a developing poet to one of the Soviet Union's most prominent literary figures. To begin with, poetry is Russia's "national art," contends Voznesensky. This natural interest in poetry combined with a Soviet generation which had "finally achieved sufficient material well-being to afford an interest in spiritual and philosophical matters," reported Peter Young. Thus, when artists like Yevtushenko and Voznesensky began giving poetry readings, these "semipolitical acts," wrote *Newsweek,* "gave voice to the dissatisfaction and exuberance of Soviet youth and created a huge audience" for poetry. By American standards, the audiences were stupendous. Typical crowds for readings by Yevtushenko and Voznesensky numbered more than fourteen thousand. Enthusiasm for the printed word matched the enthusiasm for the spoken. Voznesensky's *Akhillesovo serdtse* ("An Achilles Heart"), for example, had a printing of 100,000 to meet public demand for more than a half-million orders. Such statistics alone support Stanley Kunitz's contention that "the Russian appetite for poetry is simply enormous." Even today, reports say, Voznesensky's new books sell out within hours of publication.

The popularity of Yevtushenko and Vosnesensky brought inevitable comparisons between the two. As Olga Carlisle pointed out, while "Voznesensky's popularity among young Russians is second only to Yevtushenko's . . . he often rates first with the connoisseurs. His verse is full of youthfulness and talent—youth is his main theme as it is Yevtushenko's; in Voznesensky, however, it is never coquettish." David Burg offered another comparison between the two poets: "Voznesensky, a friend and initially a protege of Yevtushenko's, is a poet of an entirely different type. Being more bookish and more clearly conscious of his literary forbears, Voznesensky perpetuates (probably consciously) one specific trend in Russian poetry—the school of futurism, represented by Khlebnikov and Mayakovsky, Tsvetayeva, and Pasternak." According to Robin Milner-Gulland, however, their shared significance overshadows their differences: "Yevtushenko and Voznesensky: their work is certainly different enough," he declared. "The one rhetorical, the other cerebral; but their melodious names are inseparable, used (not only in the West but in their own country) to typify modern Russian poetry."

For a poet with such a popular audience, Voznesensky can be surprisingly complex; but he has continually defended himself against those who feel he is unnecessarily oblique. "The poet is not the one to supply the answers for mankind," he once contended. "All he can do is pose the questions. And if the poems are complicated, why then so is life. The problem of the poet as a human being is not to become standardized, [but] to be individual, and in this effort the poet provides the reader with the material and way of thinking to achieve it."

To Soviet government officials and heads of the Soviet Writers Union, Voznesensky has been somewhat more of an individual than they would like: many times during his career he has been at the center of controversy. Charges of obscurantism were among the several hurled at Voznesensky in the early 1960's. One especially noteworthy denunciation took place in 1963, when Nikita Khrushchev reprimanded Voznesensky and other Western-oriented intellectuals, accusing them of straying from the paths of "Soviet realism." Attacks continued in 1965 when the government-controlled Communist youth newspaper accused him of obscurity of content and experimenting with complicated poetic forms. Three years later the Soviet press again stood against him, including Voznesensky in a group of "so-called intellectuals [who] continue to display ideological immaturity," reported the *Washington Post*. By 1969, government suppression had erased Voznesensky's name from Soviet literary journals. And, early in 1979, Voznesensky and several other writers were chastised for their roles in the publication of *Metropol*, a new literary magazine which challenged the government's strict control of the arts.

One much publicized incident involving Soviet restrictions occurred in 1967, when a New York City reading had to be canceled. Two days before the scheduled reading, rumors that Voznesensky had been the target of attempts to contain him were confirmed when he wired an uncharacteristically terse message, "Can't come." The powerful and conservative Soviet Writers Union apparently objected to Voznesensky's pro-American attitudes and his refusal to propogate Soviet politics during a previous American tour. (Voznesensky has always avoided political discussions on his U.S. visits.) At first, messages from Moscow said Vosnesensky was sick; later reports revealed that his passport had been sent to the U.S. Embassy with a request for a visa. But renewed hope for Voznesensky's appearance faded when the poet himself phoned New York and canceled his visit. One of the program's participants, Stanley Kunitz, remained unconvinced by the Writers Union's apparent change of heart. "This was a ruse to get off the hook," he charged. "It's very clear what they did. We are not fooled by the last minute reversal [by the Soviet authorities]." Voznesensky himself attacked the Writers Union in a letter addressed to the Communist party newspaper, *Pravda*. "Clearly," he wrote, "the leadership of the union does not regard writers as human beings. This lying, prevarication and knocking people's heads together is standard practice." *Pravda* refused to publish the letter; weeks later it appeared in the *New York Times*.

Despite his conflicts with Soviet authorities, Voznesensky maintains an intense love for his own country. In one poem, for example, "he exalted the ancient idea that it is Russia's mission to save the world from darkness," reported the *New York Times*. He simply believes that artists should enjoy a far more relaxed atmosphere than they do now. Voznesensky has also admired the United States and, particularly, Robert Kennedy. The poet and the senator met together in 1967 and discussed, among other topics, the youth of their respective countries. After Kennedy's death, Voznesensky published a poem paying tribute to his assassinated friend.

Besides earning the attention of U.S. audiences, Voznesensky has become a favorite of several distinguished U.S. literary figures. Among the poets who have translated his work into English are Kunitz, Richard Wilbur, William Jay Smith, Robert Bly, W. H. Auden, Allen Ginsburg, and Lawrence Ferlinghetti. In his introduction to *Nostalgia for the Present*, playwright Arthur Miller assessed Voznesensky's efforts: "He has tried to speak, in these poems, as though he alone had a tongue, as though he alone had learned the news of today and tomorrow, as though the space taken up by his poem were precious and must not be used by counterfeit words." Another Voznesensky admirer, Auden, once gave these reasons for appreciating the poet: "As a fellow maker, I am struck first and foremost by his craftmanship. . . . Obvious, too, at a glance is the wide range of subject matter by which Mr. Voznesensky is imaginatively excited . . . and the variety of tones, elegiac, rebellious, etc., he can command. Lastly, every word he writes, even when he is criticizing, reveals a profound love for his native land and its traditions."

One particular theme in Voznesensky's work is that of the individual lost in a technological society. In his review of *Antiworlds*, Graham Martin noted "Voznesensky's main bogy is 'the cyclotron,' symbol of all the dehumanising pressures in the modern world, and in 'Oza,' a long difficult poem, he deploys all his satiric force against 'the scientist,' damn his eyes." Similarly, M. L. Rosenthal found in Vosnesensky "a satirist . . . who is against the computerization of the soul." As Auden pointed out, however, Voznesensky's focus can vary considerably. Miller Williams explained: "Voznesensky is an exciting writer who bangs and tumbles through his poems, knocking over icons and knocking down walls, talking with curiosity, anguish, and joy—in sharp and startling metaphor—about love and technology, science and art, the self and the soul and Andrei Voznesensky and people." Another admirer, A. Alvarez, praised Voznesensky too, for "whatever direct, passionate thrust launches them [his poems in *Antiworlds*], they curve obliquely and brilliantly through layer after layer of experience before they land again." "They also burst effortlessly through conventions: he mixes slang with formal diction, anger with tenderness, the comic with the serious, and uses every trick of assonance and stress in the book; 'his metrical effects,' W. H. Auden writes, 'must make any translator despair.'"

Translations have been a difficulty with reviewers of Voznesensky's work, especially in some of the earlier volumes. Anselm Hollo's translations in *Selected Poems* (1964), for example, disappointed Gibbons Ruark. Voznesensky's "work is clearly superior to Yevtushenko's," Ruark wrote in comparing the two poets. "Unfortunately, his excellence seldom shows through Anselm Hollo's translations." Critics agreed that Herbert Marshall's translations in *Voznesensky: Selected Poems* surpassed Hollo's. "The volume of selections by Herbert Marshall is, on the whole, an improvement over Anselm Hollo," wrote the *Hudson Review*. "But it is still an awkward and in places a careless performance." Other translations of Voznesensky's work have received considerably more praise. M. L. Rosenthal compared the translations in *Antiworlds* to those of Marshall and concluded "We are better off with the seven translators of . . . [*Antiworlds*]. They adapt themselves, often superbly, to his temperament. They help us, through purely poetic means as well as through their attempt to render his sense both literally and connotatively, to feel his compassion, his pain, his hilarity, his buffoonery, his delicacy and calculated coarseness." Meanwhile, Alvarez offered this unequivocal praise for *Antiworlds*: "The translations . . . are immaculate; they simply couldn't have been better done." *Nostalgia for the Present* also featured seven translators, but according to Stefan Kanfer "they are not of equal worth. . . . The best work is the least obtrusive: working with Voznesensky's supple and difficult lines, Max Hayward, Vera Durham and William Jay Smith have given the Russian, both man and language, a new voice."

Voznesensky himself has spoken with a new voice in his more recent poetry. He has become more introspective; his poems more complex. He explained some changes to William Jay Smith while on his 1977 U.S. reading tour: "When I came before, I was like a rock and roll star. I read poems like 'Goya' and 'Moscow Bells' that were perhaps more dramatic than my recent work. My new poems are more delicate maybe, but I was happy that my audiences liked them too." Voznesensky also detected a change in U.S. audiences, finding them more serious and more conservative than in the past, prompting Smith to wonder if "the poet himself was more mature, probing farther beneath the surface in his search for reality. If so, he had in the process of maturing lost none of the exuberance, humor, and vitality that make him one of the world's finest poets as well as one of the most enjoyable."

BIOGRAPHICAL/CRITICAL SOURCES: Olga Carlisle, *Voices in the Snow,* Random, 1962; *Problems of Communism,* September-October, 1962; *New York Times,* August 23, 1965, August 29, 1965; March 24, 1966, March 26, 1966, June 19, 1966, April 1, 1967, April 22, 1967, May 6, 1967, June 19, 1967, June 20, 1967, June 21, 1967, June 22, 1967, August 3, 1967, August 11, 1967, September 7, 1967, June 17, 1968, June 20, 1968, May 27, 1969, May 22, 1978; *Life,* April 1, 1966; *Christian Science Monitor,* April 7, 1966, June 30, 1967, November 13, 1978; *New York Review of Books,* April 14, 1966; *Atlantic,* July, 1966; *Spectator,* July 5, 1966; *Hudson Review,* spring, 1967, autumn, 1968; *Poetry,* April, 1967, November, 1967; *New York Times Book Review,* May 14, 1967, April 16, 1972, December 17, 1978, July 8, 1979; *Newsweek,* May 15, 1967, July 3, 1967, August 21, 1967; *London Magazine,* June, 1967; *New Republic,* July 1, 1967, November 18, 1972; *Observer Review,* July 9, 1967; *Time,* August 16, 1967, March 9, 1970, May 18, 1970, January 15, 1979; *New York Times Magazine,* August 20, 1967; *New Yorker,* August 26, 1967; *Listener,* September 7, 1967; *Times Literary Supplement,* November 2, 1967, November 27, 1970, October 11, 1974.

Shenandoah, winter, 1968; *Partisan Review,* winter, 1968; *Washington Post,* June 15, 1968, February 4, 1979; *Encounter,* July, 1968; *Nation,* November 11, 1968; Carlisle, *Poets on Street Corners,* Random, 1969; *New York Times Biographical Edition,* October 21, 1971; *Vogue,* February 1, 1972; *Saturday Review,* February 4, 1978; Andrei Voznesensky, *Nostalgia for the Present,* Doubleday, 1978.

—Sketch by David Versical

* * *

VULLIAMY, Colwyn Edward 1886-1971
(Anthony Rolls)

OBITUARY NOTICE: Born June 20, 1886; died September 4, 1971, in England. Author. Although Vulliamy studied art and was actively involved in field archaeology for some time, he is best known for his many novels and biographies of the Johnsonian era. His most controversial biography was *James Boswell,* which revealed Boswell as an opportunist in his friendship with Samuel Johnson. Vulliamy also wrote biographies on Voltaire, Rousseau, John Wesley, and Byron, and contributed articles to *Spectator* and other periodicals. He also wrote under the pseudonym Anthony Rolls. Obituaries and other sources: *Encyclopedia of Mystery and Detection,* McGraw, 1976.

* * *

VYN, Kathleen 1949-

PERSONAL: Born August 25, 1949, in Toledo, Ohio; daughter of John C. (a history teacher) and Patricia (an instructional materials center director; maiden name, Hammontree) Vyn. *Education:* Northern Illinois University, B.A., 1972; San Francisco State University, M.A., 1979. *Politics:* Democrat. *Religion:* Presbyterian. *Home and Office:* 150 Coronado, Daly City, Calif. 94015. *Agent:* Hy Cohen Literary Agency Ltd., 111 West 57th St., New York, N.Y. 10019.

CAREER: High school teacher of English and French in Crystal River, Fla., 1973-74; Lake Country Forest Preserve District, Libertyville, Ill., writer and naturalist, 1975-76; Singer Publications, Highland Park, Ill., reporter, 1976; free-lance writer, 1976—. Writer for KGO-TV, 1978—. *Member:* Sierra Club, California Writers Club, Writers Workshop (Highland Park, Ill.), Sigma Tau Delta.

WRITINGS: The Prairie Community, Messner, 1978; *Springtime in the Mountains*, Messner, 1980.

WORK IN PROGRESS: The Complete California Earthquake Book; *Conversations With the Muse,* interviews with women writers; *The Werewolf Chronicles,* an adult horror novel; three children's books, two about Native Americans, and one about exotic plants; a made-for-television film about terrorist activities.

SIDELIGHTS: Kathleen Vyn told *CA:* "I feel that writing for children is more difficult than writing for adults, though all writing is difficult and requires a lot of persistence and hard work. In order to write for children, particularly nonfiction, one must change one's perceptions, try to think in simple terms, and uncomplicate a complicated world.

"I choose to write about ecological subjects because I believe that children should understand the importance of preserving our few remaining natural places. They are, after all, the only ones who can do it.

"I want to convey through my writing the thrill I have when I look at the cliffs of a mountain or the rolling grasses of a prairie. If they feel the way I do about nature, perhaps when they grow up they will stop indiscriminate building. Perhaps they will understand that nature is not something you can measure in dollars or by profits."

W

WACHTEL, Isidore H. 1909(?)-1979

OBITUARY NOTICE: Born c. 1909 in New York, N.Y.; died September 14, 1979, in Washington, D.C. Lawyer and author. Wachtel was associated with the New York Housing Authority, the Office of Price Administration, and the Reconstruction Finance Corp. in the late 1930's and 1940's. He founded the firm of Wachtel, Ross & Matzkin in 1947, and remained senior partner until his death. Wachtel co-authored *Government Contracts,* long regarded as an authoritative source in federal courts. Obituaries and other sources: *Washington Post,* September 20, 1979.

* * *

WADE, Harry Vincent 1894-1973

OBITUARY NOTICE: Born March 26, 1894, in Boston, Mass.; died in September, 1973. Journalist and editor. In addition to editorial writing, Wade's fifty-one years with the *Detroit News* included two years as associate editor and six years as editor during the 1950's. After that time he continued to serve as consultant to the publisher. Wade created a daily feature, "Senator Soaper Says," that was syndicated from 1930 to 1953. Obituaries and other sources: *Who Was Who in America,* 6th edition, Marquis, 1976.

* * *

WALCOTT, Derek (Alton) 1930-

PERSONAL: Born January 23, 1930, in Castries, St. Lucia, West Indies; son of Warwick (a civil servant) and Alix (a teacher) Walcott; married Fay Moston, 1954 (divorced, 1959); married Margaret Ruth Maillard, 1962; children: three. *Education:* St. Mary's College, St. Lucia, B.A., 1953; attended University of the West Indies, Kingston, Jamaica. *Home:* 165 Duke of Edinburgh Ave., Diego Martin, Trinidad. *Agent:* Bridget Aschenberg, International Famous Agency, 1301 Avenue of the Americas, New York, N.Y. 10019.

CAREER: Poet and playwright. Teacher at St. Mary's College, St. Lucia, at Boys' Secondary School, Grenada, and at Kingston College, Jamaica. Feature writer for *Public Opinion,* Kingston, Jamaica. Art critic and book reviewer for *Trinidad Guardian,* Port-of-Spain, Trinidad. Former director of Little Carib Theatre Workshop, Trinidad; founding director of Trinidad Theatre Workshop, 1959—. *Awards, honors:* Rockefeller fellowship, 1957; Jamaica Drama Festival prize, 1958, for "Drums and Colours"; Guinness Award, 1961; Royal Society of Literature Award, 1964; Heinemann Award for verse, 1966; Cholmondeley Award, 1969, for *The Gulf;* Eugene O'Neill Foundation-Wesleyan University fellowship, 1969; Order of the Humming Bird, Trinidad and Tobago, 1969; Obie Award, 1971, for "The Dream on Monkey Mountain"; Jock Campbell Award, 1974.

WRITINGS—Plays: *Henri Christophe: A Chronicle* (seven-scene; first produced in St. Lucia, West Indies, 1950, produced in London, England, 1951), Barbados Advocate (Bridgetown), 1950; *Henri Dernier: A Play for Radio Production,* Barbados Advocate, 1951; *Sea at Dauphin* (one-act; first produced in Trinidad, 1954, produced in London, 1960), Extra-Mural Department, University College of the West Indies, 1954 (also see below); *Ione: A Play With Music* (first produced in Trinidad, 1957), Extra-Mural Department, University College of the West Indies, 1954; "Ti-Jean and His Brothers," first produced in Port-of-Spain, Trinidad, 1958, produced Off-Broadway at Delacorte Theatre, July 20, 1972 (also see below); "Malcochon" (one-act), first produced in St. Lucia, 1959, produced in London under title "Six in the Rain," 1960, produced Off-Broadway at St. Mark's Playhouse, March 25, 1969 (also see below).

"Drums and Colours" (first produced in Trinidad, 1958), published in *Caribbean Quarterly,* Volume 7, numbers 1 and 2, 1961; "In a Fine Castle," first produced in Jamaica, 1970, produced in Los Angeles, Calif., 1972; *The Dream on Monkey Mountain and Other Plays* (contains "The Dream on Monkey Mountain," first produced in Toronto, Ontario, 1967, produced Off-Broadway at St. Mark's Playhouse, March 9, 1971; also contains plays "Sea at Dauphin," "Malcochon," and "Ti-Jean and His Brothers," and essay "What the Twilight Says"), Farrar, Strauss, 1971; "The Charlatan," first produced in Los Angeles, 1974; *The Joker of Seville and O Babylon!,* Farrar, Strauss, 1978; "Remembrance," produced Off-Broadway at The Other Stage, May 9, 1979.

Poetry: *Twenty-Five Poems,* Guardian Commercial Printery, 1948; *Epitaph for the Young,* Barbados Advocate, 1949; *Poems,* City Printery, 1953; *In a Green Night: Poems 1948-1960,* J. Cape, 1962; *Selected Poems,* Farrar, Straus, 1964; *The Castaway and Other Poems,* J. Cape, 1965; *The Gulf and Other Poems,* J. Cape, 1969, published as *The Gulf,* Farrar, Straus, 1970; *Another Life,* Farrar, Straus, 1973; *Sea*

Grapes, Farrar, Straus, 1976; *Selected Verse,* Heinemann, 1976; *The Star Apple Kingdom,* Farrar, Straus, 1979.

SIDELIGHTS: In both his poetry and plays, Walcott strives toward a unified whole—a synthesis of Caribbean culture and English literature, of the black world and the white.

The language of Walcott's poems provides the basis of this union. Robert Graves once said that Walcott "handles English with a closer understanding of its inner magic than most (if not any) of his English-born contemporaries." With "a Miltonic command of the full power of the English language," wrote critic Chad Walsh, Walcott celebrates the natural beauties of the Caribbean in verse that has been compared to that of such poets as Wordsworth, Hart Crane, and T. S. Eliot. He communicates "the moral significance of place and landscape" in "packed, complex, profusely metaphorical verse," a *Times Literary Supplement* reviewer observed. Within controlled patterns of metrics and imagery, he conveys not only the lushness of his native island, but its people and dialects, its poverty and passion, its delights and despair. To accomplish this, critics often note, Walcott relies heavily on metaphor, "the artery along which the blood of his poems courses," as J. T. Demos explained.

Focusing on revolutionary themes in his latest collection of poetry, *The Star-Apple Kingdom,* Walcott touches on the political struggle between world powers and the underdeveloped countries. In one particular poem, entitled "Egypt, Tobago," Walcott has achieved "an experience of heroic suspension, an interval during which exploitive power is immobilized by a perception of its own emptiness and by an intimation of a new way of inhabiting the world and time," noted Benjamin DeMott. The entire collection, DeMott concluded, brings about "the headiest and rarest kinds of poetic experience—fruitful to people who practice the art and to all the rest of us, too."

But Walcott's poetry has also been criticized for being redundant and ostentatious. "The writing is prosy in verse and prosaic in prose," commented John Simon. "No symbol goes unexplained, or, indeed, unre-explained." And in Denis Donoghue's opinion, "Mr. Walcott's language does not give enough allowance to mystery or silence."

In his plays, many of which are verse dramas, Walcott takes his poetic theme of cultural ambiguity further, dealing more explicitly with racial tension and violence. Yet verbally he continues to balance such elements as Creole songs and island fables within his English text. The most broadly admired of his plays to date has been *The Dream on Monkey Mountain,* which not only won an Obie Award when it was staged in New York, but was also produced in a widely hailed television adaptation. Kimmis Hendrick described the work as "a Caribbean play . . . [that] proceeds as though it were a black man's dream of Africa." On the other hand, Clive Barnes found in it "hints of 'Don Quixote,' 'Waiting for Godot,' the Bible and a heritageful of Elizabethan and Jacobean playwrights." Yet these divergent elements cohere, as Clayton Riley observed: "The play is rich and complex . . . [and] achieves a lush depiction of the many moods implicit in the ritual and realistic aspects of Caribbean black life."

In still another way, Walcott has helped to join the two poles of his cultural heritage. For two years, on a Rockefeller Fellowship, he studied theater under Jose Quintero at the Circle in the Square and under Stuart Vaughan at the Phoenix Theater. Then, in 1959, he founded the Trinidad Theatre Workshop, a group of approximately twenty actors who, following eight years of preparation, began to offer throughout the Caribbean a repertoire of classical, modern, and West Indian drama. In 1969 they presented *The Dream on Monkey Mountain* at the Eugene O'Neill Memorial Theatre Foundation's Playwrights' Conference in Waterford, Conn., after which NBC-TV filmed a documentary of the troupe at home and at work. With their fees for this project, the group built a permanent home for their productions and retained Walcott as their director.

BIOGRAPHICAL/CRITICAL SOURCES: London Magazine, November, 1969; *Times Literary Supplement,* December 25, 1969; *Christian Science Monitor,* September 9, 1970; *Book World,* December 13, 1970; *New York Times,* March 15, 1971, April 4, 1971, March 21, 1979, August 21, 1979; *New Yorker,* March 27, 1971; *New York Review of Books,* May 6, 1971, June 13, 1974; *New York Magazine,* August 14, 1972; *New York Times Book Review,* May 6, 1973, May 13, 1979; *Contemporary Literary Criticism,* Gale, Volume 2, 1974, Volume 4, 1975, Volume 9, 1978; *Virginia Quarterly Review,* winter, 1974; *Village Voice,* April 11, 1974; *World Literature Today,* spring, 1977.*

* * *

WALDHEIM, Kurt 1918-

PERSONAL: Born December 21, 1918, in Sankt Andrae-Woerdern, Austria; son of Walter (a civil servant) and Josefine (Petrasch) Waldheim; married Elisabeth Ritschel, August 19, 1944; children: Liselotte, Gerhardt, Christa. *Education:* University of Vienna, J.D., 1944. *Office:* Secretariat, United Nations, New York, N.Y. 10017.

CAREER: Austrian Diplomatic Service, Vienna, member of Austrian delegation to Paris, London, and Moscow for negotiations of Austrian State Treaty, 1945-47, first secretary of Austrian embassy in Paris, 1948-51, head of personnel division for Ministry of Foreign Affairs, Vienna, 1951-55, permanent Austrian observer to United Nations in New York City, 1955-56, envoy to Canada in Ottawa, 1956-58, ambassador to Canada in Ottawa, 1958-60, director-general for political affairs for Ministry of Foreign Affairs, Vienna, 1960-64, permanent Austrian representative to United Nations, 1964-68, federal minister for foreign affairs in Vienna, 1968-70, permanent Austrian representative to United Nations, 1970-71; secretary-general of United Nations, 1972—. Chairman of United Nations Committee on Peaceful Uses of Outer Space, 1965-68, 1970-72; chairman of United Nations Special Committee on the Definition of Aggression, 1967; president of United Nations Conference on the Exploration and Peaceful Uses of Outer Space, 1968; chairman of safeguards committee of International Atomic Energy Agency, 1970; Conservative People's Party candidate for presidency of Austria, 1971. *Military service:* Austrian Army, 1937-38; became corporal. German Army, 1939-43; drafted as lieutenant.

AWARDS, HONORS: Grand Badge of Honor in Gold (Republic of Austria); Grand Cross Order of St. Michael and St. George (Great Britain); Grand Cross Order of Merit (Germany); Commander, Order of Dannebrog (Denmark); Grand Officer, Order of St. John of Jerusalem; Grand Officer, Order of Orange-Nassau (Netherlands); Commander, Legion of Honor (France); Commander, Order of Oak Crown (Luxembourg); Commander, Order of the Polar Star (Sweden); Kr. Karl Renner Prize (Vienna). LL.D. from Fordham University, Carleton University, University of Chile, and Rutgers University, all 1972, Jawarharlal Nehru University, University of Bucharest, and Wagner College, all 1973, Catholic University of America and Wilfred Laurier University, both 1974, Catholic University of Leuven, Charles

University, and Hamilton College, all 1975, University of Denver and University of the Philippines, both 1976, American University, Kent State University, University of Warsaw, Moscow State University, and Mongolian State University, Ulan Bator, all 1977.

WRITINGS: *Der oesterreichische Weg,* Molden, 1971, translation by Ewald Osers published as *The Austrian Example,* Macmillan, 1973; *Uses of the Sea,* United Nations, 1972; *Human Rights and Scientific and Technological Developments,* United Nations, 1974. Also author of *Un metier unique au monde,* 1977.

SIDELIGHTS: Since the end of World War II, Waldheim has been involved in international politics. His first two years in politics were spent representing Austria in the Austrian State Treaty negotiations. After brief tenures in Paris and Vienna, Waldheim accepted a position as Austria's permanent observer in the United Nations. The appointment took place in 1955, the same year Austria was admitted into the United Nations. Aside from his post as permanent observer, Waldheim was also chosen to represent Austria in the United Nations.

In 1956, Waldheim began the first of four years involvement with Canada on behalf of his native Austria. He served as an envoy and an ambassador. He followed his stint in Canada with four more years of service in Austria in such capacities as director general of political affairs.

Waldheim returned to the United Nations in 1965 as chairman of its Committee on Peaceful Uses of Outer Space. In his role as chairman, Waldheim contributed to the formation of a treaty which prohibited the use of planets and other space bodies for military purposes. But in 1968 Waldheim was needed again in Austria, and he returned there to fill the position of minister of foreign affairs. In that capacity, Waldheim attempted unsuccessfully to bring peace in Vietnam by insisting that the warring factions adhere to the Geneva Convention held fourteen years earlier.

A change of leadership in Austria in 1970 led to Waldheim's dismissal from the defense post. He returned to his work with the United Nations, though, and commenced chairing a faction of the International Atomic Energy Agency. In 1971, he attempted to re-enter politics on his homefront by making a bid for leadership there. Waldheim was unsuccessful, but he did manage to receive more than forty percent of the popular vote. The election had been a close one.

Waldheim was appointed secretary-general of the United Nations in 1972. Since assuming this position, he has dealt with international problems ranging from civil rights to territorial disputes. He also helped thwart the United Nations' once-impending bankruptcy by meeting with world leaders for assurance that the organization was a necessary one.

AVOCATIONAL INTERESTS: Skiing, swimming, fishing, boating, walking, music, gardening, collecting antique glass.

BIOGRAPHICAL/CRITICAL SOURCES: *Time,* November 29, 1971; *Newsweek,* March 20, 1972, November 15, 1976; *Saturday Review,* September 23, 1972; *New Yorker,* September 30, 1972; *Nation,* October 2, 1972; *Saturday Review/World,* March 23, 1974, August 24, 1974; *UN Monthly Chronicle,* May, 1974, August, 1974; *UN Chronicle,* February, 1975, August, 1975, November, 1975, January, 1976, February, 1976, May, 1976, August, 1976, October, 1976, January, 1977, March, 1977, April, 1977, July, 1977, August, 1977, October, 1977.*

WALKER, Joseph A. 1935-

PERSONAL: Born February 23, 1935, in Washington, D.C.; son of Joseph (a house painter) and Florine Walker; married Barbara Brown (divorced, 1965); married Dorothy A. Dinroe, 1970. *Education:* Howard University, B.A.; Catholic University of America, M.F.A., 1970; New York University, Ph.D. *Residence:* New York, N.Y. *Office:* Department of Speech and Theatre, City College of the City University of New York, New York, N.Y. 10031.

CAREER: Educator, actor, director, playwright. Worked as taxi driver, shoe and cosmetics salesman, and postal clerk; English teacher at junior high and high schools in Washington, D.C. and New York City; actor, set designer, and playwright, in New York City, began in 1967; Negro Ensemble Co., New York City, playwright, director and choreographer, began in 1969; Yale University, New Haven, Conn., playwright-in-residence, 1970; City College of the City University of New York, New York City, currently instructor; Howard University, Washington, D.C., currently instructor of advanced acting and playwrighting. Actor in stage productions, including "The Believers," 1967, and "Cities of Beziques," 1969, in motion pictures, including "April Fools," 1969, and "Bananas," 1971, and in television program "N.Y.P.D." (ABC-TV); narrator of "In Black America" (CBS-TV). Co-founder and artistic director of The Demi-Gods (dance-music theatre repertory co.) *Military service:* U.S. Air Force; became second lieutenant. *Awards, honors:* Obie Award, 1973, for "The River Niger".

WRITINGS—Plays: (With Josephine Jackson) *The Believers* (first produced in New York at Garrick Theatre, May 9, 1968), published in *The Best Plays of 1967-1968,* edited by Otis L. Guernsey, Dodd, 1968; "The Harrangues" (two one-act plays), first produced in New York at St. Mark's Playhouse, December 30, 1969; *Ododo* (title means "The Truth"; first produced in New York at St. Mark's Playhouse, November 24, 1970), published in *Black Drama Anthology,* edited by Woodie King and Ron Milner, Columbia University Press, 1972; *The River Niger* (three-act; first produced in New York at St. Mark's Playhouse, December 5, 1972), Hill & Wang, 1973; "Yin Yang," first produced in New York at St. Mark's Playhouse, May 30, 1973; "Antigone Africanus," first produced in New York, 1975. Also author of "Themes of the Black Struggle" and "The Hiss."

SIDELIGHTS: When Joseph A. Walker's first solo effort, "The Harangues," was produced by the Negro Ensemble Company in 1970, Walter Kerr wrote: "The company has come upon a playwright whose theatrical instincts are strong even when he is letting them gallop along a little bit ahead of him; that is better than playing it shy, or tentative, or safe."

Certainly, Walker does not play it safe. Alan Bunce described "The Harangues" as "an unabashed polemic whose impact on the stage is ultimately stirring." The play consists of two main segments sandwiched between a tribal prologue and interlude. In the first main act, a black man, engaged to a pregnant white woman, intends to murder his fiancee's millionaire father; the other of the two long segments concerns another pregnant white woman, her "liberal" brother, and her black fiance, all of whom are confronted by a gun-wielding black intruder who talks them into confessing their true racial attitudes. Likening the entire performance to the films of Luis Bunuel, Martin Washburn wrote: "Walker's play is strong because he has the courage to speak directly from his tradition instead of disguising it."

After seeing "Ododo," Clive Barnes was prompted to observe that the Negro Ensemble Company seemed to have become more "separatist, militant and black" than it had previously been. The play is a musical, tracing the background and history of the North American black from the African jungle through slave ships, American slavery, Lincoln, and reconstruction to the ghetto and contemporary black consciousness. While John Simon dismissed "Ododo" as "a black supremist, racist show," Barnes conceded that, though propaganda, it is "beautifully-written propaganda" nevertheless.

With *The River Niger* Walker achieved his first true critical success. Mel Gussow said that Walker "has a distinct voice and his own sensitive awareness of what makes people different. The play is rich with character, atmosphere, and nuance." Walter Kerr described the dialogue as "exemplary, knife sharp when adrenalin is meant to flow and gently rhetorical whenever the father of a Harlem family remembers that he meant to be a poet." Dedicated "to my mother and father and to highly underrated Black daddies everywhere," the play is semi-autobiographical and centers on the father's struggle and sacrifice for his family amidst the violent world they live in. Reviewing the play in the *Washington Post,* Anthony Astrachan said, "It is unquestionable black theater: Its characters could only be black. But it is also universal theater: It speaks to audiences of all colors."

BIOGRAPHICAL/CRITICAL SOURCES: New York Times, May 10, 1968, January 14, 1970, January 25, 1970, November 25, 1970, December 6, 1970, December 14, 1970, December 6, 1972, December 17, 1972, May 31, 1973; *Village Voice,* January 22, 1970; *Christian Science Monitor,* January 23, 1970; *New Yorker,* January 24, 1970; *Show Business,* November 28, 1970; *Cue,* December 5, 1970; *Variety,* December 9, 1970; *New York,* December 14, 1970; *Time,* January 1, 1973; *Washington Post,* April 13, 1973.*

* * *

WALLACE, Henry Agard 1888-1965

OBITUARY NOTICE: Born October 7, 1888, in Adair County, Iowa; died November 18, 1965. Plant breeder, government official, editor, and author. An experienced farmer, Wallace developed a strain of high-yielding corn and discovered a method for forecasting corn yields. For fourteen years he preached his farming policies as editor of *Wallace's Farmer,* and in 1933 was assigned by President F. D. Roosevelt to be his Secretary of Agriculture. During the next few years Wallace put into effect the controversial Agricultural Adjustment Act. This act promoted crop control by plowing under corn and cotton crops and killing pigs, both in an attempt to raise plummeting farm prices. Although the act was deemed unconstitutional, a revised form of it remained in use to stabilize farm incomes. Wallace served as vice-president of the United States under Roosevelt from 1941 to 1945 and as Secretary of Commerce from 1945 to 1946. He ran unsuccessfully as progressive party candidate for U.S. president in 1948. Considered one of the most widely read politicians of the time, Wallace's best known books were *Sixty Million Jobs* and *America Must Choose.* He was also editor of the *New Republic* for several years. Obituaries and other sources: *Current Biography,* Wilson, 1947, January, 1966; *Who Was Who in America,* 4th edition, Marquis, 1968.

* * *

WALLACH, Sidney 1905-1979

OBITUARY NOTICE: Born July 4, 1905, in Horochow, Poland; died June 24, 1979, in New York, N.Y. Public affairs consultant, editor, and author. Wallach served first as educational director, then as executive director of the American Jewish Committee, and founded their *Current Jewish Record,* later re-titled *Commentary* magazine. He subsequently formed a consulting firm for organizations, associations, and individuals. Wallach authored *Hitler: Menace to Mankind,* and co-authored *Justice, Justice, Shalt Thou Pursue.* Obituaries and other sources: *Who's Who in World Jewry,* Pitman, 1972; *Who's Who in America,* 40th edition, Marquis, 1978; *New York Times,* June 29, 1979.

* * *

WALN, Nora 1895-1964

OBITUARY NOTICE: Born June 4, 1895, in Grampian Hills, Pa.; died February 27, 1964. Journalist and author. During World War I, Nora Waln wrote a column entitled "Woman's Work in the War." In the following years she wrote books and articles about her worldwide travels, including *House of Exile,* about her years in China, and *Reaching for the Stars,* an anti-Nazi but pro-German view of her stay in Germany. Obituaries and other sources: *Current Biography,* Wilson, 1940, November, 1964; *Who Was Who in America,* 4th edition, Marquis, 1968.

* * *

WALTARI, Mika (Toimi) 1908-1979 (Nauticus, M. Ritvala)

OBITUARY NOTICE—See index for *CA* sketch: Born September 19, 1908, in Helsinki, Finland; died August 26, 1979, in Helsinki. Writer of poetry, detective stories, short stories, plays, criticism, screenplays, and novels. Waltari's forte was the long historical novel. He achieved his greatest success with *Sinuhe egyptilaeinen,* translated into English as *The Egyptian,* which sold a million copies in Europe and was on the bestseller lists in the United States for almost a year. *The Egyptian* was made into a lavish motion picture by Twentieth Century-Fox. Several of Waltari's other books were translated into English, including *The Adventurer, The Wanderer, A Nail Merchant at Midnight,* and *The Roman.* Obituaries and other sources: *Current Biography,* Wilson, 1950; *Encyclopedia of World Literature in the Twentieth Century,* updated edition, Ungar, 1967; *The Penguin Companion to European Literature,* McGraw, 1969; *Cassell's Encyclopaedia of World Literature,* revised edition, Morrow, 1973; *Who's Who,* 131st edition, St. Martin's, 1979; *New York Times,* August 28, 1979; *Publishers Weekly,* September 17, 1979; *AB Bookman's Weekly,* September 24, 1979.

* * *

WALTER, Hartmut 1940-

PERSONAL: Born July 13, 1940, in Stettin, Germany; came to the United States in 1972; son of Heinz L. W. (a civil servant) and Gertrud (a teacher; maiden name, Frischer) Walter; married Geraldine Ann Gargola; children: Hanspeter. *Education:* University of Bonn, D.Sc., 1967. *Residence:* West Los Angeles, Calif. *Office:* Department of Geography, University of California, Los Angeles, Calif. 90024.

CAREER: University of Chicago, Chicago, Ill., research fellow, 1968; University of California, Berkeley, lecturer in geography, 1969; United Nations Educational, Scientific, and Cultural Organization, Paris, France, regional associate expert on ecology and conservation in Africa, 1970-71; University of California, Los Angeles, assistant professor, 1972-75, associate professor of geography, 1975—. Co-founder of Institute of Mediterranean Thought.

MEMBER: American Ornithologists' Union, Cooper Ornithological Society, Ecological Society of America, Association of American Geographers, British Ecological Society, Deutsche Ornithologen-Gesellschaft. *Awards, honors:* Heinrich-Hoerlin Prize from German Biological Society, 1960; foreign exchange fellowship from University of Bonn, 1961-62; Harkness fellow at University of California, Berkeley, 1967-69.

WRITINGS: Eleonora's Falcon: Adaptations to Prey and Habitat in a Social Raptor, University of Chicago Press, 1979.

WORK IN PROGRESS: A textbook on zoogeography, publication by Allen & Unwin expected in 1982; a book on man-nature-energy relationships; a book on California birds; research on "sociable raptors."

SIDELIGHTS: Walter writes: "My father has been active in the German nature conservation movement since 1920. He taught me about birds and the value of the unspoiled outdoors. I'm an avid photographer of birds and landscapes. I have been all over Europe and in many parts of Africa and the Middle East. I especially love Italy.

"I am very concerned about the increasing danger of poisonous chemicals in most sectors of our industrial societies: our food, our water, our farms, and our forests are contaminated. I am appalled at the lack of ecological land-use planning in the U.S. If we want to conserve Africa's wildlife, we have to assist the African countries with expertise and money!"

AVOCATIONAL INTERESTS: Photography, birdwatching, track, soccer, gymnastics.

* * *

WALTERS, Basil L(eon) 1896-1975

OBITUARY NOTICE: Born May 3, 1896, in Frankfort, Ind.; died August 29, 1975. Educator, journalist, editor. After serving as editor for the *Des Moines Register and Tribune* and the *Minneapolis Star-Journal and Tribune,* Walters became executive editor and director of Knight Newspapers, Inc. After fifteen years in this position he worked as editor of *Chicago Daily News,* then a Knight publication, for several years before taking over as president of Newspaper Research Associates. Obituaries and other sources: *The International Who's Who,* Europa, 1974; *Who's Who in America,* 38th edition, Marquis, 1974.

* * *

WALTON, John 1937-

PERSONAL: Born September 22, 1937, in Los Angeles, Calif.; son of Delvy T. (an attorney) and Florence H. (a literary critic) Walton; married wife, Priscilla Helen (a teacher), September 8, 1963; children: Casey Helen. *Education:* San Fernando Valley State College, B.A., 1960, M.A., 1962; University of California, Santa Barbara, Ph.D., 1966. *Home:* 4338 San Marino, Davis, Calif. 95616. *Office:* Department of Sociology, University of California, Davis, Calif. 95616.

CAREER: San Fernando Valley State College, San Fernando, Calif., instructor in sociology, 1961-62; Probation Department of Los Angeles County, Los Angeles, Calif., probation counselor, summers, 1963-64; Northwestern University, Evanston, Ill., assistant professor, 1966-71, associate professor, 1971-75, professor of sociology and urban affairs, 1975-78; University of California, Davis, professor of sociology, 1978—. Visiting associate professor at University of Hawaii, summer, 1971, and University of Texas, 1971-72; participant in international seminars. *Member:* International Sociological Association, International Studies Association (vice-chairperson of Urban Internet, 1976-79), American Sociological Association (chairperson of committee on current research, 1973-74), Society for the Study of Social Problems (chairperson of Community Research and Development Division, 1972-73), Midwest Sociological Society, Southwestern Social Science Association. *Awards, honors:* Grants from American Sociological Association, 1966, and Ford Foundation, 1967-69.

WRITINGS: (Editor with Donald Carns, and contributor) *Cities in Change: Studies on the Urban Condition,* Allyn & Bacon, 1973, 2nd edition, 1976; (with Alejandro Portes) *Urban Latin America: The Political Condition From Above and Below,* University of Texas Press, 1976; (editor with Louis H. Masotti, and contributor) *The City in Comparative Perspective: Cross National Research and New Directions in Theory,* Sage Publications, 1976; *Elites and Economic Development: Comparative Studies on the Political Economy of Latin American Cities,* University of Texas Press, 1977; (with Luis M. Salces) *The Political Organization of Chicago's Latino Communities* (monograph), Center for Urban Affairs, Northwestern University, 1977.

Contributor: Terry N. Clark, editor, *Community Structure and Decision Making: Comparative Approaches,* Chandler Publishing, 1968; Hawley and Frederick M. Wirt, editors, *The Search for Power in American Communities,* Prentice-Hall, 1969; Aiken and Mott, editors, *The Structure of Community Power,* Random House, 1970; Wirt, editor, *Future Directions in the Study of Community Power,* Institute of Governmental Affairs (Berkeley, Calif.), 1971; Michael Armer and Allan Grimshaw, editors, *Comparative Social Research: Methodological Problems and Strategies,* Wiley, 1973; Andrew Effrat and Marcia Effrat, editors, *The Community: Approaches and Applications,* Bobbs-Merrill, 1974; Robert B. Williamson, William P. Glade, and Karl M. Schmitt, editors, *Latin American-U.S. Economic Interactions: Conflict, Accommodation, and Policies for the Future,* American Enterprise Institute for Public Policy Research, 1974; Wayne A. Cornelius and Felicity M. Trueblood, editors, *Latin American Urban Research,* Volume V: *Urbanization and Inequality: The Political Economy of Urban and Rural Development in Latin America,* Sage Publications, 1975; Harley L. Browning and Alejandro Portes, editors, *Future Directions of Urban Research in Latin America,* University of Texas Press, 1976; Hans Haacke, editor, *Framing and Being Framed: Seven Works, 1970-75,* New York University Press, 1976; Roland C. Warren, editor, *Perspectives on the American Community,* 3rd edition (Walton was not included in earlier editions), Rand McNally, 1977; Cornelius and Robert V. Kemper, editors, *Latin American Urban Research,* Volume VI: *Metropolitan Problems and Governmental Response in Latin America,* Sage Publications, 1978.

Contributor to *Americana Annual/Encyclopedia Yearbook.* Contributor of about fifty articles and reviews to journals in the social sciences. Advisory editor of *Social Science Quarterly,* 1971—; associate editor of *Journal of Political and Military Sociology,* 1973—; member of editorial board of *Urban Affairs Quarterly,* 1974—, *African Journal of Behavioral Sciences,* 1978—, *American Sociologist,* 1979-81, and *Latin American Research Review,* 1979—.

SIDELIGHTS: Walton's research interests include political sociology, sociology of economic development, urban sociology, comparative sociology, theory and theory construction, social class and inequality, and world systems.

WANIEK, Marilyn Nelson 1946-

PERSONAL: Surname is pronounced *Von*-yek; born April 26, 1946, in Cleveland, Ohio; daughter of Melvin M. (in U.S. Air Force) and Johnnie (a teacher; maiden name, Mitchell) Nelson. *Education:* University of California, Davis, B.A., 1968; University of Pennsylvania, M.A., 1970; University of Minnesota, Ph.D., 1979. *Politics:* "Yes." *Religion:* "Yes." *Office:* Department of English, University of Connecticut, Storrs, Conn. 06268.

CAREER: National Lutheran Campus Ministry, Ithaca, N.Y., lay associate, 1969-70; Lane Community College, Eugene, Ore., assistant professor of English, 1970-72; Norre Nissum Seminariam, Norre Nissum, Denmark, teacher of English, 1972-73; St. Olaf College, Northfield, Minn., instructor in English, 1973-78; University of Connecticut, Storrs, assistant professor of English, 1978—. *Member:* Modern Language Association of America, Society for the Study of Multi-Ethnic Literature of the United States, Society for Values in Higher Education.

WRITINGS: For the Body, Louisiana State University Press, 1978.

WORK IN PROGRESS: Poems for children; studying Rilke.

* * *

WANTLING, William 1933-1974

OBITUARY NOTICE: Born November 7, 1933, in Peoria, Ill.; died May 4, 1974. Poet and novelist. Wantling's poetry is based on personal experiences, such as his addiction to heroin during the Korean War and his five-and-a-half year term in San Quentin prison for forgery and narcotics convictions. Although not well known in the United States, Wantling attracted a large following in England. He wrote two novels, *Young and Tender* and *Sick Fly,* plus many books of poetry, including *Heroin Haikus; Down, Off, and Out; The Awakening;* and *10,000 RPM and Diggin It, Yeah.* Obituaries and other sources: *Contemporary Poets,* St. Martin's, 1970, 2nd edition, 1975.

* * *

WARBURTON, Clark (Abram) 1896-1979

OBITUARY NOTICE—See index for *CA* sketch: Born January 27, 1896, in Shady Grove, N.Y.; died September 18, 1979, in Fairfax, Va. Economist, educator, and author. Renowned for his scholarly work on the relation of banking and monetary policy to business fluctuation, Warburton worked for the Federal Deposit Insurance Corporation (FDIC) from 1934 until 1965. He was the author of *The Economic Results of Prohibition; America's Capacity to Consume;* and *Depression, Inflation, and Monetary Policy.* Obituaries and other sources: *Washington Post,* September 22, 1979.

* * *

WARD, Allen M(ason) 1942-

PERSONAL: Born April 18, 1942, in Lawrence, Mass.; son of Allen Mason, Sr. (a metal fabricator) and June T. (a nurse; maiden name, Taylor) Ward; married Catherine M. Reardon, June 5, 1965 (divorced, 1975); married Ellen Evans Whiting (in paralegal work), May 14, 1977; children: Ellen Barrett, Alexander David. *Education:* Brown University, B.A., 1964; Princeton University, M.A., 1966, Ph.D., 1968. *Politics:* Independent. *Religion:* "No formal ties." *Office:* Department of History, University of Connecticut, Box U-103, Storrs, Conn. 06268.

CAREER: Columbia University, New York, N.Y., assistant professor of Greek and Latin, 1967-69; University of Connecticut, Storrs, assistant professor, 1969-72, associate professor, 1972-79, professor of history, 1979—. Associate of Columbia University's seminar on classical civilization, 1970—. *Member:* American Historical Association, American Philological Association, Association of Ancient Historians, Friends of Ancient History, Classical Association of New England (president of Connecticut section, 1976-77). *Awards, honors:* Woodrow Wilson fellow, 1964-65, 1966-67; National Endowment for the Humanities grant, 1973.

WRITINGS: Marcus Crassus and the Late Roman Republic, University of Missouri Press, 1977. Contributor to scholarly journals.

WORK IN PROGRESS: Antigonus Gonatas and the Hellenistic World, completion expected in 1985; research on the Conference of Luca.

SIDELIGHTS: Ward comments: "Being raised by grandparents in an old New England town gave me a great love of and feeling for old things and the past. I went to college with the goal of becoming a classicist. Interested and dedicated teachers at all levels gave me the skills and inspiration to realize my goal. By my research and writing, I hope that I can repay my family and teachers for the time and effort spent on me, and give future generations a clearer understanding, not only of what happened in antiquity, but why it happened. History does not repeat iself and the past is often very different from the present, but where valid parallels and links do exist, it can help us to understand and deal with contemporary problems."

AVOCATIONAL INTERESTS: Woodworking, growing and preserving his own food.

* * *

WARD, Melanie
See LYNCH, Marilyn

* * *

WARHOL, Andy

PERSONAL—Education: Attended Carnegie Institute of Technology (now Carnegie-Mellon University). *Residence:* New York, N.Y. *Office:* Andy Warhol Enterprises, 860 Broadway, New York, N.Y. 10003.

CAREER: Artist and writer. Has held numerous one-man exhibitions throughout world since early 1960's. Director and photographer of motion pictures, including "Eat," 1963, "Harlot," 1964, "My Hustler," 1965, "Lonesome Cowboys," 1968, and "Imitation of Christ," 1969. Producer of recording "The Velvet Underground," 1966. Publisher and co-founder of *Andy Warhol's Interview. Awards, honors:* Art Director's Club medal from Art Director's Club, 1957, for creation of giant shoe; Independent Film Award from *Film Culture,* 1964, for "Eat," "Haircut," "Sleep," "Kiss," and "Empire"; award from Los Angeles Film Festival, 1964.

WRITINGS: (With Gerard Malanga) *Screen Test: A Diary* (poems and drawings), Kulchur Press, 1967; (with Stephen Shore, David Paul, and others) *Andy Warhol's Index (Book),* Random House, 1967; *a: A Novel,* Grove, 1968; *Blue Movie: A Film* (screenplay), Grove, 1970; *The Philosophy of Andy Warhol: From A to B and Back Again,* Harcourt, 1975; *Andy Warhol's Exposures,* (photographs), Grosset & Dunlop, 1979.

Plays: "Pork" (two-act comedy), first produced in London at the Roundhouse, August 2, 1971.

Screenplays; all as director: "Harlot," 1964; "My Hustler," 1965; "The Chelsea Girls," 1966; "Nude Restaurant," 1967; "Four Stars," 1967; "I, a Man," 1967; "Bike Boy," 1967; "Blue Movie; Or, F—," 1969; "Andy Warhol's Lonesome Cowboys," 1969; "Imitation of Christ" (suggested from writings of Thomas a Kempis), 1970. Also creator of motion pictures, including "Eat," 1963, "Sleep," 1963, "Kiss," 1963, "Haircut," 1963, "Empire," 1964, and "More Milk," "Yvette," "Vibrations," "Blow Job," "Wee Love of Life," "13 Most Beautiful Girls," and "Poor Little Rich Girl."

Art work represented in collections, including *Raid the Icebox With Andy Warhol: An Exhibition Selected From the Vaults of the Museum of Art, Rhode Island School of Design,* [Providence, R.I.], 1969, *Andy Warhol,* Buechergilde Gutenberg, 1971, and *Ladies and Gentlemen/Andy Warhol: Presentazione di Janus,* G. Mazzotta, 1975.

Contributor to *Andy Warhol's Interview.*

SIDELIGHTS: Warhol broke into the art scene in the early 1960's when he became a forerunner of pop art. His early work was based on exact duplication and, sometimes, tedious repetition. Among his best known works from his early period are a large portrait of comic-strip character Dick Tracy and a painting showing endless rows of Campbell's soup cans. Repetition and commercial subjects, including boxes of Brillo Pads and silk screens of photographs of Marilyn Monroe and Elizabeth Taylor, became his specialty. By the mid-1960's, he'd abandoned painting in favor of photography and silk screening.

This shifting of means proved commercially successful for Warhol, since he could reproduce large quantities of silk screens and photographs much quicker than he could paint. Warhol even organized a factory for processing his works and shrugged off observations that he was not a "creator" but a "recreator." He described his art as "liking things" and accomodated himself to the concept of banality. "The acquisition of my tape recorder really finished whatever emotional life I might have had," he confessed, "but I was glad to see it go."

Some critics believe Warhol's bland personality has outlasted his art. A. T. Baker reported that Warhol's "banality endowed him with an air of mystery, since few people could bring themselves to believe that any artist could possibly be so banal." In contrast, Baker found Warhol's art "somehow stranded." He noted, "Incessant exposure has dulled their impact, and what one sees is the brisk, elegant and paper-thin sensibility of a commercial—illustrator—designed-in rawness, hand-rubbed indifference. Similarly, Jack Kroll wrote that Warhol "uses the most 'banal' of mechanical means to body forth . . . his compassion. He has sinned; he has created chic icons for empty people to decorate their emptiness."

Warhol also began using film during the mid-1960's and he soon distinguished himself as a premier underground filmmaker. His approach was simple. In films such as "Haircut" and "Sleep," he merely aimed the camera at the action and photographed. "Sleep" is a six hour film of a sleeping man's face in which there is no cutting or movement of the camera. Similarly, "Empire" is an eight hour shot of the Empire State Building. Later Warhol films featured sound and color film but these also show a disdain for cinematic technique. "Blue Movie," one of Warhol's most controversial films, is 140 minutes of philosophical and trivial discussions between two people who then make love before the cameras for approximately ten minutes.

Most of Warhol's acting entourage consisted of non-professionals, a distinction which many critics noted as being too clearly evident in the films. In a review of "Andy Warhol's Lonesome Cowboys," Andrew Sarris wrote that the actors "seem unable to decide whether they are improvising fictions and fantasies or confessing facts and fancies." Paul Morrissey, director of such Warhol productions as "Trash" and "Flesh," outlined the duties of an actor in a Warhol production. "You really don't have time to think about how you feel when you act, since there is no script at all," he said. "You just have to keep talking, and even if there are people around, you don't even know they are around."

Warhol has also applied his banal quality to writing, most notably in *a* and *Andy Warhol's Philosophy. A* is 451 pages of transcribed interview with a friend of Warhol named Ondine. Throughout most of the interview Ondine is under the influence of amphetamines. Sally Beauman called most of the novel "incomprehensible snippets and gobbets of talk." She also called it "cheapjack, shoddy, derivative $10's worth of incomprehensible yelpings and yowlings." Howard Junker adivsed readers that *a* "is something to be dipped into, not read straight."

A *New Yorker* critic found *Andy Warhol's Philosophy* uninformative. "Possibly intentionally," the critic conceded, "there is absolutely nothing of interest here except for the uncharacteristically self-mocking portrait that the author paints." Barbara Goldsmith contended that Warhol was intentionally elusive in the book. "Our expectation is that at last Warhol will interpret himself to us," she wrote. "And he does this—by not doing it. Warhol's basic philosophical premise is 'nothing.'"

BIOGRAPHICAL/CRITICAL SOURCES: Village Voice, February 21, 1967, June 6, 1968, January 16, 1969, February 20, 1969, May 8, 1969, July 2, 1970; *National Observer,* October 28, 1968; *Newsweek,* December 2, 1968, September 15, 1975; *New York Times Book Review,* January 12, 1969, October 7, 1973, September 14, 1975; *New York Review,* April 24, 1969; *New Republic,* April 26, 1969; *New York Times,* May 18, 1969, September 17, 1969, November 9, 1969; *Life,* June 13, 1969; *Time,* September 17, 1969, August 4, 1975; *Saturday Night,* February, 1970; *Vogue,* March 1, 1970; *Cue,* November 14, 1970; *Esquire,* March, 1974; *New Yorker,* October 27, 1975.*

* * *

WARNER, Rex (Ernest) 1905-

PERSONAL: Born March 9, 1905, in Birmingham, England; came to the United States, 1961; son of Frederick Ernest (a clergyman) and Kathleen (Luce) Warner; married Frances Chamier Grove, 1929 (divorced); married Barbara Rothschild, 1949 (marriage ended); remarried Frances Clamier Grove, 1966; children: two sons; two daughters. *Education:* Wadham College, Oxford, B.A. (with honors), 1928. *Home:* Horse Barn Hill Lane, Storrs, Conn. 06268. *Office:* Department of English, University of Connecticut, Storrs, Conn. 06268.

CAREER: Writer. Worked as teacher in England and Egypt, 1928-45; associated with control commission in Berlin, Germany, 1945; director of British Institute in Athens, Greece, 1945-48; Bowdoin College, Brunswick, Me., Tallman Professor of Classics, 1961-62; University of Connecticut, Storrs, professor of English, 1962—. *Military service:* British Home Guard, 1942-45. *Member:* New England Classical Association, Savile Club. *Awards, honors:* Honorary fellow of Wadham College, Oxford; Black Memorial Prize, 1961; decorated commander of the Royal Order of the Phoenix (Greece), 1963; D.Litt. from Rider College, 1968.

WRITINGS—Novels: *The Wild Goose Chase,* Boriswood, 1937, Knopf, 1938; *The Professor,* Boriswood, 1938, Knopf, 1939; *The Aerodrome: A Love Story,* John Lane, 1941, Lippincott, 1946; *Why Was I Killed?: A Dramatic Dialogue,* John Lane, 1943, published as *Return of the Traveller,* Lippincott, 1944; *Men and Stones: A Melodrama,* John Lane, 1949, Lippincott, 1950; *Escapade: A Tale of Avenge,* John Lane, 1953; *The Young Caesar,* Little, Brown, 1958; *Imperial Caesar,* Little, Brown, 1960 (published in England as *Julius Caesar,* Collins, 1967); *Pericles the Athenian,* Little, Brown, 1963; *The Converts: A Historical Novel,* Little, Brown, 1967 (published in England as *The Converts: A Novel of Early Christianity,* Bodley Head, 1967).

Other: *The Kite,* Basil Blackwell, 1936, revised edition, Hamish Hamilton, 1963; *Poems,* Boriswood, 1937, Knopf, 1938 (revised edition published in England as *Poems and Contradictions,* John Lane, 1945); *The English Public Schools,* Collins, 1945; *The Cult of Power: Essays,* John Lane, 1946, Lippincott, 1947; *John Milton,* Parrish, 1949, Chanticleer, 1950, reprinted, Haskell House, 1975; *Views of Attica and Its Surroundings,* Lehmann, 1950; *La liberta e la creazione letteraria e artistica* (originally published in England as the article "Freedom in Literary and Artistic Creation"), Edizioni di Communita, 1950; *Men and Gods* (also see below), MacGibbon & Kee, 1950, Farrar, Straus, 1951; (with Lyle Blair) *Ashes to Ashes: A Post-Mortem on the 1950-51 Tests,* MacGibbon & Kee, 1951; (with M. Hurlimann) *Eternal Greece,* MacGibbon & Kee, 1951, Studio Publications, 1953, revised edition, Viking, 1962; *Greeks and Trojans* (also see below), MacGibbon & Kee, 1951, Michigan State College Press, 1953; (co-editor) *New Poems, 1954: A P.E.N. Anthology,* M. Joseph, 1954; *The Vengeance of the Gods* (also see below), MacGibbon & Kee, 1954, Michigan State College Press, 1955; *Athens,* Thames & Judson, 1956, Studio Publications, 1957; *The Greek Philosophers,* New American Liberary, 1958; (contributor) Bernard Blackstone, editor, *Virginia Woolf,* University of Nebraska Press, 1964; *The Stories of the Greeks* (contains *Men and Gods, Greeks and Trojans,* and *The Vengeance of the Gods;* also see above), MacGibbon & Kee, 1967; *Athens at War: Retold From the History of the Peloponnesian War of Thucydides,* Bodley Head, 1970, Dutton, 1971; *Men of Athens: The Story of Fifth Century Athens,* Viking, 1972.

Translator: *The Medea of Euripides,* John Lane, 1944, Chanticleer, 1949; Aeschylus, *Prometheus Bound,* Bodley Head, 1947, Chanticleer, 1949; Xenophon, *The Persian Expedition,* Penguin, 1949; Euripides, *Hippolytus,* Chanticleer, 1950; *The Helen of Euripides,* Bodley Head, 1951; Thucydides, *The History of the Peloponnesian War,* Penguin, 1954, revised edition, 1972; Plutarch, *The Fall of the Republic: Marius, Sulla, Crassus, Pompey, Caesar, Cicero, Six Lives,* Penguin, 1958, revised edition, 1972; Julius Caesar, *War Commentaries of Caesar,* New American Library, 1960; Georgios Sepheriades, *Poems,* Little, Brown, 1960; Aurelius Augustinus, *Confessions,* New American Library, 1963; (and author of preface) Aeschylus, *Prometheus Bound* (also contains *Prometheus Unbound* by Percy Bysshe Shelley), J. Enschede, 1965, Heritage Press, 1966; (with T. D. Frangopoulos; and author of introduction) Sepheriades, *On the Greek Style: Selected Essays in Poetry and Hellenism,* Little, Brown, 1966; (and editor) Xenophon, *History of My Times: Hellenica,* Little, Brown, 1966; (and editor and author of introduction) Plutarch, *Moral Essays,* Penguin, 1971.

Contributor to *Freedom and Culture.* Contributor to periodicals, including *London Mercury, New Statesman,* and *Saturday Review.*

SIDELIGHTS: Warner's early novels were considerably influenced by the writings of Franz Kafka. *The Wild Goose Chase* is concerned with three brothers in an unnamed country who search for the wild goose, which represents the hope of mankind. Thomas Churchill wrote that "*The Wild Goose Chase* . . . describes a quest motivated by aims certainly as high as those that spurred on the prosaic seekers after the holy grail. . . . The novel . . . is a case study of the good-Many against the totalitarian state, established on power, violence, and fear."

The Aerodrome is similar to *The Wild Goose Chase* in theme and setting. "*The Aerodrome* and *The Wild Goose Chase* are given meaning by the 'great' wars that loomed at the writer's back and all around him," wrote Churchill, "and in them the concept of blood finds an important place. Brothers are protagonists and antagonists, fathers fall upon sons, and lovers shoot mistresses only to be killed by the offspring of those loves." Churchill also noted that "in each novel the hero is most threatened when he forgets or somehow loses contact with the earth itself."

Warner pursued moral and political issues in his next three novels, but in them there is also evidence of a greater concern for structure. But by the 1940's Warner had also established himself as a translator of Greek classics. The synthesis of his interest in classical literature and his abilities as a novelist were historical novels such as *Julius Caesar* and *Pericles the Athenian.*

One of Warner's best known historical novels is *The Converts,* which features St. Augustine as its protagonist. "By evoking the total environment—including intellectual ferment, social change, and political activity of the age—Rex Warner makes ancient history come alive," declared Clara M. Siggins. She summed up *The Converts* as a "beautifully written book." Philip Toynbee called it "a decent, good and skillful novel throughout, and it rises to genuine and persuasive passion at the point where this was needed."

BIOGRAPHICAL/CRITICAL SOURCES: Observer Review, May 21, 1967; *Times Literary Supplement,* May 25, 1967, April 16, 1970; *Punch,* June 6, 1967; *Best Sellers,* June 15, 1967; *New York Times Book Review,* July 30, 1967; *London Magazine,* August, 1967; *Commonweal,* October 6, 1967; *Virginia Quarterly Review,* winter, 1968; *Critique,* Volume X, No. 1, 1968; *Spectator,* May 9, 1970.*

* * *

WARTSKI, Maureen (Ann Crane) 1940-
(M. A. Crane)

PERSONAL: Born January 25, 1940, in Ashiya, Japan; naturalized U.S. citizen, 1962; daughter of Albert Edwin (in business) Josephine (a teacher; maiden name, Wagen) Crane; married Maximilian Wartski (in business), June 1, 1962; children: Bert, Mark. *Education:* Attended University of Redlands, 1958-59; Sophia University, B.A., 1962. *Home:* 15 Francis Rd., Sharon, Mass. 02067.

CAREER: Free-lance writer. *English Mainichi,* Kobe, Japan, reporter, 1957-58; teacher at public schools in Sharon, Mass., 1968-69; high school history teacher in Sharon, Mass., 1978-79.

WRITINGS: My Brother Is Special (juvenile), Westminster, 1979; *A Boat to Nowhere,* Westminster, 1980. Also author of juvenile plays. Contributor of articles, stories, and plays (sometimes under name M. A. Crane) to magazines, including *Highlights, Scholastic, Catholic Digest,* and *American Girl.*

WORK IN PROGRESS: Short stories.

SIDELIGHTS: Maureen Wartski writes: "All I ever wanted to do was write. My career seemed assured when I sold my first story at age fourteen, but then there were several years before I published anything else!

"*My Brother Is Special* was my first try at a young-adults book. I wanted, at first, to write about the Special Olympics. The story did not come together until my husband rescued a crippled black duck and brought it home for our sons to nurse back to health. I feel that it is a worthwhile story. I have known and loved special children and have always felt that each of us has our own race to run, our own problems to overcome. Too often, young people (and older ones for that matter) feel that courage is shown by winners, by people who are physically strong, or who get there first. I wanted to show that true courage means a great deal more.

"My second book is about Vietnamese boat people who escape the war-torn country and head out into nowhere. The fact that our family had lived in Bangkok, 1962-66, was helpful as background, and I had also visited Vietnam around that time."

* * *

WATKINS, Mel 1940-
(Franklin Jefferson Jackson)

PERSONAL: Born March 8, 1940, in Memphis, Tenn.; son of Pittman (a laborer) and Katie Watkins; married Patricia M. Marsh, June 27, 1963 (divorced); children: Kim Danielle. *Education:* Colgate University, B.A., 1962. *Home:* 23 East 10th St., New York, N.Y. 10003. *Agent:* Roslyn Targ Literary Agency, Inc., 250 West 57th St., Suite 1932, New York, N.Y. 10019. *Office: New York Times,* 229 West 43rd St., New York, N.Y. 10036.

CAREER: Federal Social Security Department, New York City, claims examiner, 1962-64; *New York Times,* New York City, staff writer and editor, 1964—. *Member:* International P.E.N., National Book Critics Circle. *Awards, honors:* Grant from Alicia Patterson Foundation, 1979-80.

WRITINGS: (With Jay David) *To Be a Black Woman: Portraits in Fact and Fiction,* Morrow, 1971; (editor) *Black Review #1,* Morrow, 1971; *Black Review #2, Morrow,* 1972; *Race and Suburbia* (juvenile), Harper, 1973; (author of introduction) Joe Okpaku, *Superfight #2,* Third Press, 1974.

Under name Franklin Jefferson Jackson: Contributor of stories to *Black Review #1* and of stories and essays to *Nickel Review.*

WORK IN PROGRESS: A book on African art, for young people, for publication by Rockefeller Publishing; a novel; research for a book on black humor, 1930-79.

SIDELIGHTS: Watkins comments: "My two major interests in writing are fiction and the nonfictional documentation of the often-slighted influence of black culture and style on the larger American culture. The book I'm researching, on black humor, reflects the latter interest."

* * *

WATSON, Jean 1936-

PERSONAL: Born March 18, 1936, in Tachu, Szechuan, China; daughter of William Hugh C. (a minister and missionary) and Lilian Alice (a missionary; maiden name, Wilden) Simmonds; married Michael John MacLaren Watson (in sales and engineering), June 8, 1963; children: Malcolm MacLaren, Rachel Joy, Esther Jean. *Education:* London University, B.A., 1957; University of Birmingham, certificate in education, 1958. *Religion:* Church of England. *Home and office:* 33 Braeside Ave., Sevenoaks, Kent TN13 2JJ, England.

CAREER: High school teacher of English and history in Wolverhampton, England, 1958-61; Cassell & Co., London, England, educational editor, 1961-63; teacher at primary school in Kent, England, 1963-64; River Green Playgroup (for pre-schoolers), Kent, England, supervisor, 1967-75; tutor and writer, 1965—. *Member:* Waterloo Arts Centre Group.

WRITINGS: The Pilgrim's Progress: Retold in Modern English From the Original Story by John Bunyan, Scripture Union, 1978; *See All the Things We Share* (juvenile), Lion Publishing, 1979.

"In Times of . . . " series; all published by Scripture Union, 1979: *In Times of Success; In Times of Sorrow; In Times of Need; In Times of Joy; In Times of Growth; In Times of Doubt; In Times of Courage; In Times of Change.*

Also author of *The Kingdom That God Builds.* Scriptwriter for British Broadcasting Corp. juvenile and religious programs, 1967—.

WORK IN PROGRESS: Abridged editions of children's classics.

SIDELIGHTS: Jean Watson comments: "I want to write more children's books, the texts for picture books, and longer books for older children, perhaps allegorical in style. But I would not wish to trivialise important matters, or to deny the worth of every human being. Probably everything I write will have some bearing on the great question, 'What is man?' Words have great power and writers are responsible for the ways they use that power. Beauty and truth are inseparable; so are the medium and the message."

* * *

WATSON, Mark Skinner 1887-1966

OBITUARY NOTICE: Born June 24, 1887, in Plattsburg, N.Y.; died March 25, 1966. Journalist. Watson worked for over forty-five years with the *Baltimore Sun* as assistant managing editor, Sunday editor, and war correspondent. His first-hand accounts of World War II battles earned him a Pulitzer Prize in 1945 for distinguished telegraphic reporting of international events. Obituaries and other sources: *Current Biography,* Wilson, 1946, April, 1966; *Who Was Who in America,* 4th edition, Marquis, 1968.

* * *

WATTS, Franklin (Mowry) 1904-1978

OBITUARY NOTICE—See index for *CA* sketch: Born June 11, 1904, in Sioux City, Iowa; died May 21, 1978, in New York, N.Y. Publisher, bookseller, and author. Watts was founder and president of Franklin Watts, Inc., a firm which specialized in books for children and young people. He was also affiliated with Vanguard Press, Julian Messner, and Heritage Press. In addition to his work as publisher, Watts was the author of a number of children's books and several books for adults. Obituaries and other sources: *The Author's and Writer's Who's Who,* 6th edition, Burke's Peerage, 1973; *New York Times,* May 23, 1978; *Publishers Weekly,* June 5, 1978.

WAUGH, Linda R(uth) 1942-

PERSONAL: Born November 2, 1942, in Boston, Mass.; daughter of David F. (a professor) and Molly J. (Jauncey) Waugh. *Education:* Tufts University, B.A. (magna cum laude), 1964; Stanford University, M.A., 1965, Ph.D., 1970. *Home:* 215 Bryant Ave., Ithaca, N.Y. 14850. *Office:* Department of Modern Languages, Cornell University, Ithaca, N.Y. 14850.

CAREER: Cornell University, Ithaca, N.Y., assistant professor, 1971-76, associate professor of linguistics, 1976—, member of executive board of women's studies program, 1977—, Society for the Humanities fellow, 1979-80; Linguistic Society of America, faculty member of summer linguistic institute, 1976. Visiting associate professor at Yale University, spring, 1978. Member of New York State Council on Linguistics (president, 1976-77). Participant in Ossabaw Island Project, Ossabaw Island, Ga., 1977—. *Member:* American Association of Teachers of French, Linguistic Society of America, Semiotic Society of America, Linguistic Association of Canada and the United States, Modern Language Association. *Awards, honors:* Ford Foundation grant, 1977; National Endowment for the Humanities grant, 1979-80.

WRITINGS: Roman Jakobson's Science of Language, de Ridder, 1976; *A Semitic Analysis of Word Order,* E. J. Brill, 1977; (with Roman Jakobson) *The Sound Shape of Language,* Indiana University Press, 1979; (editor) *Contributions to Grammatical Studies: Semantics and Syntax,* E. J. Brill, 1979; *The Melody of Language,* University Park Press, 1979; *Contributions to Historical Studies: Issues and Materials,* E. J. Brill, 1980. Contributor to language journals.

WORK IN PROGRESS: A project on "the semantics of language and of other semiotic systems"; a project on "metaphor and metonymy in linguistic semantic structure and cognate patterns in culture and poetry."

SIDELIGHTS: Waugh told *CA:* "I have always had a great interest in language and in the scientific study of language, for language is one of those attributes which separate human beings from animals. To know about language is to know about human nature in some of its most fundamental aspects. It is for this reason that in my work I explore anthropology, psychology, and the study of literature, for languge is an important part of all of these disciplines.

"My primary interest in all of this is the study of meaning—how and what things mean, why things mean what they mean, and how certain kinds of meaning are most important for language and other human systems. It is for this reason that the new, developing system of semiotics is so important, for semiotics is the study of all human meaning systems, especially those which are symbolic in nature, including language.

"Some of the most important research impinging upon linguistics is that done on the brain and on the difference between the left and right hemispheres with respect to how language is handled by each half of the brain. Some of the conclusions which linguists have come to strictly on the basis of linguistic material are now being tested by these neurological studies and other studies of the brain.

"Women's liberation and especially feminism have been most important for me in my intellectual development. Being involved in education has also been valuable because it has given me the freedom to grow intellectually, to think in new ways, to avoid stagnation, and to constantly be open to new ideas and new perspectives. In this sense, my teaching, my research, and my writing are all ways of maintaining and fostering that growth."

The Sound Stage of Language has been translated into French, Italian, and Japanese.

* * *

WAYRE, Philip 1921-

PERSONAL: Born May 26, 1921, in Surbiton, Surrey, England; son of Frederick Oliver (a company director) and Hester Evelyn (Spill) Wayre; married Ann Hanson, January, 1949 (divorced, 1956); married Jeanne Helen Franklin, January, 1975; children: Sonia Anne, Claire Hanson. *Education:* Attended private school in Dorset, England. *Home:* River Farm, Earsham, near Bungay, Suffolk, England. *Agent:* Joan Ling, English Theatre Guild Ltd., 5-A South Side, London SW4 7AA, England.

CAREER: Farmer, 1945-61; Norfolk Wildlife Park, Great Witchingham, Norwich, England, founder and director, 1961—. Founder and honorary director of Pheasant Trust, 1959—, and Otter Trust, 1975—; head of Eastern Regional Council for Sport and Recreation, 1976. Naturalist and television broadcaster; producer and director of television films, including "Wind in the Reeds," released by Anglia Television, 1962; "A Wind in the Heath," released by Anglia Television, 1966; "Pheasants to Formosa," British Broadcasting Corporation (BBC-TV), 1967; "Twilight of the Tiger," BBC-TV, 1972; "Otters," BBC-TV, 1976; "The Vanishing Otter," Anglia Television, 1978. Quiz master of "Nature Trail," 1965-67, and "The Survival Game," 1969-70, both television series for children. Member of wildlife filming expeditions to India, 1967, 1970, and Taiwan, 1967; conservation consultant to foreign governments. *Military service:* Royal Naval (Volunteer) Reserve, Coastal Forces, 1940-45; became lieutenant.

MEMBER: International Council for Bird Preservation (head of publicity committee), International Union for Conservation of Nature and Natural Resources (member of Survival Service Commission), Federation of Zoological Gardens of Great Britain and Ireland (head of breeding and conservation committee), Linnaean Society (fellow), Zoological Society (fellow), Avicultural Society, Fauna Preservation Society (member of council), British Ornithologists Club, Norfolk Naturalists Trust (head of conservation committee).

WRITINGS: Wind in the Reeds, Collins, 1964; *A Guide to the Pheasants of the World,* Hamlyn, 1970; *The River People,* Collins, 1976; *Lutra: The Story of an Otter,* Collins, 1979; *The Private Life of the Otter,* Batsford, 1979. Contributor to *International Zoo Yearbook.* Contributor to ornithological journals.

SIDELIGHTS: A naturalist, Wayre breeds rare species of deer and waterfowl on his land, where he lives in a sixteenth-century Suffolk farmhouse. His home is adjacent to an otter trust, founded by him, which has become "a tremendous success and recognized as the leading authority on otter conservation in Europe," Wayre reported. In 1959 Wayre also founded a pheasant trust that is "still the leading authority in the world."

The Norfolk Wildlife Park, another project initiated by Wayre, is comprised of "the world's largest collection of mammals and birds under almost natural conditions. The park's breeding successes with these species have never been equalled by any other collection anywhere in the world as far as is known," Wayre told *CA.* Wayre has also been responsible for "re-introducing endangered species to the wild."

AVOCATIONAL INTERESTS: Fishing, skindiving.

WEAVER, Warren 1894-1978

PERSONAL: Born July 17, 1894, in Reedsburg, Wis.; died November 24, 1978, in New Milford, Conn.; son of Isaiah (a druggist) and Kittie Belle (Stupfell) Weaver; married Mary Hemenway (a teacher), September 4, 1919; children: Warren, Jr., Helen Hemenway. *Education:* University of Wisconsin (now University of Wisconsin—Madison), B.S., 1916, C.E., 1917, Ph.D., 1921. *Residence:* New Milford, Conn.

CAREER: Throop College, Pasadena, Calif., assistant professor of mathematics, 1917-18; California Institute of Technology, Pasadena, assistant professor of mathematics, 1919-20; University of Wisconsin—Madison, assistant professor, 1920-25, associate professor, 1925-28, professor of mathematics and chairman of department, 1928-32; Rockefeller Foundation, New York, N.Y., director of natural sciences, 1932-55, vice-president for natural and medical sciences, 1955-59; trustee and member of executive committee of Alfred P. Sloan Foundation, 1956-67, vice-president, 1959-64, consultant on scientific affairs, 1964-78, honorary trustee, 1967-78. Lecturer at University of Chicago, 1928. Director of division of natural sciences of General Education Board, 1932-37; member of physical sciences division of National Research Council, 1936-39, 1944-47, appointed to committee on computing machines in mathematics division, 1951; chief of applied mathematics panel of Office of Scientific Research and Development, 1943-46. Member of board of scientific consultants to Sloan-Kettering Institute of Cancer Research, 1951-54, trustee, 1954-67, chairman of committee on scientific policy, 1955-59, member of executive committee, 1956-67, vice-president, 1958-59, chairman of board and chairman of committee on scientific policy of Memorial Sloan-Kettering Cancer Center, 1960-67. Member of governing council of Courant Institute of Mathematical Sciences, 1962-72; member of board of directors of Scientists' Institute for Public Information, 1963-67.

Chairman of Section D-2 (fire control division) of National Defense Research Committee of Office of Scientific Research and Development, 1940-42, chief of applied mathematics panel of National Defense Research Committee, 1943-46; chairman of Naval Research and Advisory Committee and member of research advisory panel of War Department, 1946-47; chairman of basic research group of research and development board, Department of Defense, 1952-53, Member of natural science board of National Science Foundation, 1956-60; member of national advisory council of U.S. Public Health Service, 1957-60; member, vice-chairman, and member of executive committee of Health Research Council, New York City, 1958-60; member of board of managers of Memorial Center for Cancer and Allied Diseases, 1958-60; member of board of trustees of Academy of Religion and Mental Health, 1959-63, vice-president, 1961-63, honorary vice-president, 1963-78; member of executive committee and board of directors of Memorial Hospital for Cancer, 1960-67; director and president of Public Health Research Institute of City of New York, 1961-63; member of Governor Rockefeller's committee on hospital costs, New York State, 1964-65. Member of board of directors of Council on Library Resources, 1956-60. Trustee of University of Pennsylvania, 1959-63; trustee, chairman of board, and non-resident fellow of Salk Institute of Biological Studies, 1962-78; trustee of Eastman Fund. *Military service:* U.S. Army Air Service, 1917-19; became second lieutenant.

MEMBER: American Academy of Arts and Sciences (fellow), National Academy of Sciences (past president and chairman of board), American Association for the Advancement of Science (fellow and member of executive committee), American Physical Society, American Mathematical Society, Mathematical Association of America, American Philosophy Society (councillor, 1957-60), American Society of Naturalists, American Society for Symbolic Logic, Christian Michelsens Institute (Norway; corresponding member), Candlewood Lake Club (Brookfield, Conn.), Cosmos Club (Washington, D.C.), Century Club (New York City), Town Club (Scarsdale, N.Y.), Phi Kappa Sigma, Tau Beta Pi, Sigma Xi. *Awards, honors:* Medal for Merit, 1948; King's Medal for Service in the Cause of Freedom (Great Britain), 1948; LL.D. from University of Wisconsin, 1948; Sc.D. from University of Sao Paulo (Brazil), 1949, Drexel Institute of Technology, 1961, and from University of Pittsburgh, 1964; French Legion of Honor (officer), 1951; public welfare medal from National Academy of Science, 1957; D.E. from Rensselaer Polytechnic Institute, 1962; L.H.D. from University of Rochester, 1963; Kalinga Prize from UNESCO, 1964; Arches of Science Award from Pacific Science Center, 1964.

WRITINGS: (With Max Mason) *The Electromagnetic Field,* Dover, 1929; (editor) *The Scientists Speak* (radio talks), Boni & Gaer, 1947; (with Claude E. Shannon) *The Mathematical Theory of Communication,* University of Illinois Press, 1949; *Lady Luck: The Theory of Probability,* Anchor Books, 1963; *Alice in Many Tongues: The Translations of Alice in Wonderland,* University of Wisconsin Press, 1964; *U.S. Philanthropic Foundations: Their History, Structure, Management, and Record,* Harper, 1967; *Science and Imagination: Selected Papers,* Basic Books, 1967; *Scene of Change: A Lifetime in American Science* (autobiography), Scribner, 1970. Contributor of articles to periodicals including *Scientific American* and *Scientific Monthly*.

SIDELIGHTS: As an administrator of the Rockefeller Foundation, Warren Weaver devoted his life to improving society by promoting scientific research. After beginning his career in the academic world, Weaver switched his focus when he became director for the natural sciences at the Rockefeller Foundation. During his twenty-four years there he promoted research in experimental biology and agricultural science, with an emphasis on improving human nutrition. Behind Weaver, the Rockefeller Foundation's natural science division contributed funds towards the construction of California's two hundred-inch Mt. Palomar telescope and helped finance Howard W. Florey's research which led to the discovery of penicillin. Weaver called on his experience with the Rockefeller Foundation in writing his 1967 book, *U.S. Philanthropic Foundations*. Among his other books are several on science-related subjects and one on his special love: Lewis Carroll's *Alice in Wonderland*.

Weaver's *U.S Philanthropic Foundations* attempted "to bring dependable information to bear on the question of the continuing existence of foundations as tax-free institutions," wrote the author in his preface. Divided into two sections, the book first provides Weaver's explanation of the history, philosophy, management, and policies of philanthropic foundations; the second part features contributor's analyses of the effects of foundations on society. The book "is a primer on foundations written by a man who is clearly convinced of their social value and of the essential merits of their philanthropic influence," summarized Peter Schragg. While Schragg did note Weaver's suggestion that foundations will play an increasingly important role in financing experiments and innovations, he also felt that "the lack of extended analysis of the contemporary and future role of the foundations . . . sometimes gives this book the tone of a memorial."

Aside from his professional activities, Weaver was a passionate admirer of the works of Lewis Carroll. He reportedly held the largest collection of Carroll's writings, a collection now owned by the University of Texas. Weaver's book, *Alice in Many Tongues,* "is a fascinating chronicle of Alice's many appearances on the national and the international scene," commented E. L. Bassett. Another reviewer, Leon Carnovsky, voiced additional praise for *Alice*. The book "takes us on a delightful excursion into the wonderland of translation," Carnovsky said. "One ends the journey with a renewed affection for the original and an appreciation of the difficulties of transferring its flavor into another vernacular."

Weaver summarized his professional career in his autobiography, *Scene of Change: A Lifetime in American Science.* According to W. R. Gruner, the book "should be considered a professional autobiography, with a personal overture and a philosophical finale." Critic Dael Wolfle felt *Scene of Change* is "of value not solely as the story of an unusually effective man, but also because of what he can tell us of . . . midcareer changes and of the life of a science administrator." Wolfle added that Weaver's autobiography "is an illuminating and graceful introduction to a man who has earned" the satisfaction of "enjoying one's work and knowing it has been good."

BIOGRAPHICAL/CRITICAL SOURCES: Book Week, August 2, 1964; *Library Quarterly,* January, 1966; *Modern Philology,* November, 1965; Warren Weaver, *U.S. Philanthropic Foundations: Their History, Structure, Management, and Record,* Harper, 1967; *New York Times Book Review,* October 22, 1967; *Science,* April 12, 1968, February 6, 1970; *Bulletin of the Atomic Scientists,* September, 1970; *New York Times,* November 25, 1978.*

* * *

WEBBER, Gordon 1912-

PERSONAL: Born October 25, 1912, in Linden, Mich.; son of Roy Eugene and Dorothea (Boyd) Webber; married Jeanne Carol Curtis, June 29, 1940 (died, December, 1971); children: Jacqueline, Dorothea, Laura. *Education:* Jamestown College, A.B., 1933; University of Michigan, M.A., 1936. *Home:* 7 East 86th St., New York, N.Y. 10028; and Cleveland Dr., Montauk, N.Y. 11954. *Agent:* Harold Matson Co., Inc., 22 East 40th St., New York, N.Y. 10016.

CAREER: Writer. National Broadcasting Co., New York City, writer and editor in news department, 1938-48; Benton & Bowles, Inc., New York City, worked as copywriter, head of creative group, and associate creative director, 1948-69, senior vice-president, 1969-75, manager of creative department, 1970-75; Parsons School of Design, New York City, instructor in writing, 1975-76; writer, 1976—. Executive producer of film, "The Endless War," 1970; producer of national campaign, "Unsell the War," 1971; producer-director of "The Jogger." Co-chairperson of Rye council on Human Rights, 1963-64. *Military service:* U.S. Naval Reserve, active duty, 1942-45; became lieutenant senior grade.

MEMBER: International P.E.N., Writers Guild of America, Alpha Epsilon Rho, Classic Car Club of America (founding president). *Awards, honors:* Citations from Friends of American Writers, 1954, for *The Far Shore,* and Jamestown College, 1959, for *What End But Love*; award from Michigan Historical Society, 1959, for *What End But Love*; Cine Gold Eagle from Edinburgh Film Festival, 1971, for "The Jogger."

WRITINGS: Years of Eden (novel), Little, Brown, 1950; *The Far Shore* (novel), Little, Brown, 1954; *What End But Love* (novel), Little, Brown, 1960; *The Great Buffalo Hotel* (novel), Little, Brown, 1979; *Our Kind of People* (history of Benton & Bowles), Riverside Press, 1979. Writer for television series, "I Remember Mama," 1950-55. Contributor of stories to magazines.

SIDELIGHTS: Webber told *CA:* "'Writing,' as E. B. White once said, 'is an act of faith.' For me, it is the only faith I have, which means, among other things, that one's salvation lies, not in the stars, but in one's own hands. Writing is the hardest work in the world—and when it works—the best. Nothing can match a well-made sentence or paragraph for sheer satisfaction. And when the sentences and the paragraphs finally, after months or years, add up to a book, that is the greatest satisfaction of all. . . . How do you learn to write? Two ways: by reading the writing of others (being careful to choose good models), and by writing. Every day and every day. Writing courses may help by providing discipline, by setting tasks and making you meet a deadline. But, finally, all writers are self-taught. . . . Writing is something like being in love: an aura of wonder and magic surrounds the act of creation, just as it does the act of love."

* * *

WEBBER, Robert (Eugene) 1933-

PERSONAL: Born November 27, 1933, in Stouchburg, Pa.; married Joanne Lindsell; children: John, Alexandra, Stefany, Jeremy. *Education:* Bob Jones University, B.A., 1956; Reformed Episcopal Seminary, B.D., 1959; Covenant Theological Seminary, Th.M., 1960; Concordia Theological Seminary, Th.D., 1969. *Religion:* Episcopal. *Office:* Wheaton College, Wheaton, Ill. 60187.

CAREER: Wheaton College, Wheaton, Ill., associate professor of theology, 1968—.

WRITINGS: Common Roots: A Call to Evangelical Maturity, Zondervan, 1978; (editor with Donald Bloesch) *The Orthodox Evangelicals,* Thomas Nelson, 1978; *The Secular Saint: A Case for Evangelical Social Responsibility,* Zondervan, 1979; *God Still Speaks: Communications in Biblical Perspective,* Thomas Nelson, 1980; *Worship: A Call to Evangelical Renewal,* Zondervan, 1980.

* * *

WEBER, David R(yder) 1943-

PERSONAL: Born June 25, 1943, in New York, N.Y.; son of Louis A. (in sales) and Dorothy D. (a counselor; maiden name, Kyder) Weber; married Ilona Wagner, June 19, 1965; children: Anya Ryder. *Education:* Dartmouth College, A.B., 1965; Columbia University, M.A., 1967; further graduate study at Cornell University, 1967-70. *Home:* 33 Main St., Exeter, N.H. 03833. *Office:* Phillips Exeter Academy, Exeter, N.H. 03833.

CAREER: Phillips Exeter Academy, Exeter, N.H., instructor in English, 1970—. Member of board of trustees of Dartmouth College, 1971-80. *Awards, honors:* A.M. from Dartmouth College, 1971.

WRITINGS: (Editor) *Civil Disobedience in America: A Documentary History,* Cornell University Press, 1978. Contributor of poems, articles, and reviews to education journals and newspapers.

WORK IN PROGRESS: A Dog's Life and Others: Leaves From a Father's Journal.

SIDELIGHTS: Weber writes: "I am interested in nonfiction

writing and in the governance of private colleges and secondary schools."

* * *

WEIDENFELD, Sheila Rabb 1943-

PERSONAL: Born September 7, 1943, in Cambridge, Mass.; daughter of Maxwell M. (an attorney) and Ruth (Cryden) Rabb; married Edward L. Weidenfeld (an attorney), August 11, 1968. *Education:* Brandeis University, B.A., 1965. *Home:* 2903 Q St. N.W., Washington, D.C. 20007. *Agent:* Edward Weidenfeld, 1750 K St. N.W., Washington, D.C. 20006.

CAREER: WNEW-TV, New York City, associate producer, 1965-68; NBC-TV, New York City, talent coordinator, 1968-69, coordinator of game shows, 1969-71; WTTG-TV, Washington, D.C., producer of "Panorama" and documentary programs, 1971-73; WRC-TV, Washington, D.C., creator and producer of "Take It From Here," 1973-74; special assistant to President Gerald Ford and press secretary to Mrs. Betty Ford, 1974-77; WRC-TV, creator, producer, and moderator of "On the Record," 1977-78; writer, 1978—. Member of President's Advisory Council on Historic Preservation, 1977—; member of board of directors of Wolftrap Foundation for the Performing Arts, 1977—; consultant to U.S. Department of State.

MEMBER: National Academy of Television Arts and Sciences, American Women in Radio and Television, American Newspaper Women's Club, American Federation of Television and Radio Artists, Washington Press Club, Sigma Delta Chi. *Awards, honors:* Emmy Award from National Academy of Television Arts and Sciences, 1972; achievement awards from American Association of University Women, 1973 and 1974.

WRITINGS: First Lady's Lady, Putnam, 1979.

WORK IN PROGRESS: The Media and Politics.

BIOGRAPHICAL/CRITICAL SOURCES: Washingtonian, May, 1973; *Los Angeles Times,* October 14, 1974, February 7, 1979; *Boston Globe,* November, 1974; *Parade,* April 25, 1976.

* * *

WEINBERG, David Henry 1945-

PERSONAL: Born February 1, 1945, in New York, N.Y.; son of Louis and Ann (Kesselman) Weinberg; married Judith Goldfarb, June 30, 1968; children: Joshua Marc, Rachel Beth. *Education:* City College of the City University of New York, B.A. (cum laude), 1966; University of Wisconsin, Madison, M.A., 1968, Ph.D., 1971; also attended Jewish Theological Seminary of America, 1960-66. *Home:* 3436 Goddard Rd., Toledo, Ohio 43606. *Office:* Department of History, Bowling Green State University, Bowling Green, Ohio 43403.

CAREER: Bowling Green State University, Bowling Green, Ohio, assistant professor, 1971-76, associate professor of history, 1976—. Lecturer at Toledo College of Jewish Studies, 1971—; associate professor at Spertus College of Judaica, summer, 1978. Member of academic advisory committee to Bund Jewish Labor Archives; member of executive committee of National Holocaust Resource Center; participant in symposia and conferences; consultant to National Endowment for the Humanities. *Member:* American Historical Association, Association for Jewish Studies. *Awards, honors:* Ford Foundation fellow, 1969-70; grants from National Foundation for Jewish Culture, 1969-70, and Memorial Foundation for Jewish Culture, 1969-70; publication award from Ohio Academy of History, 1978, for *A Community on Trial: The Jews of Paris in the 1930's.*

WRITINGS: (Contributor) Jeffrey Orenstein and Louis Patsouras, editors, *The Politics of Community: New Aspects of Socialist Theory and Practice,* Kendall/Hunt, 1973; *Les Juifs a Paris de 1933 a 1939: Une communaute a l'epreuve* (title means "A Community on Trial: The Jews of Paris from 1933 to 1939"), Calmann Levy, 1974; *A Community on Trial: The Jews of Paris in the 1930's,* University of Chicago Press, 1977; (contributor) Byron Sherwin, editor, *Encountering the Holocaust,* Hebrew Publishing Company, 1979; *The Challenge of Modern Jewish Emancipation,* Forum Press, 1979. Contributor of articles and reviews to history journals.

WORK IN PROGRESS: Research on Eastern European Jewish acculturation in Paris and London, 1880-1939; essay on the reconstruction of the French Jewish community after World War II; edited volume on the reconstruction of European Jewish communities after World War II.

SIDELIGHTS: Weinberg's research interests are European Jewry in the interwar period (especially French Jewry), European working-class culture in the early twentieth century, immigrant acculturation in France in the nineteenth and twentieth centuries, and the use of films in the teaching and study of history.

* * *

WEINBERG, Gerald M(arvin) 1933-

PERSONAL: Born October 27, 1933, in Chicago, Ill.; married Daniela Libon (a professor), 1961. *Education:* University of Nebraska, B.Sc., 1955; University of California, Berkeley, M.A., 1956; University of Michigan, Ph.D., 1965. *Home address:* R.R. 2, Lincoln, Neb. 68505. *Office:* Ethnotech, Inc., P.O. Box 6627, Lincoln, Neb. 68506.

CAREER: International Business Machines Corp., San Francisco and Los Angeles, Calif., applied science representative, 1956-58, manager of supervisory programming for "Project Mercury" in Washington, D.C., 1958-60, senior staff member at Systems Research Institute in New York, N.Y., 1960-67, senior research associate in Yorktown Heights, N.Y., 1966-69, senior staff member and manager of data processing in Geneva, Switzerland, 1967-69; State University of New York at Binghamton, professor of advanced technology, 1969-75; Ethnotech, Inc., Lincoln, Neb., chief scientist, 1972—. Adjunct professor at Columbia University, 1965-67; visiting professor at University of Oslo, 1974.

MEMBER: Society of General Systems Research (member of board of advisers, 1976—), Association for Computing Machinery (national lecturer, 1970-72), Authors Guild of Authors League of America, Phi Beta Kappa, Sigma Xi, Pi Mu Epsilon. *Awards, honors:* Bronze award from New York Television and Film Festival, 1975, for film, "Top-Down Programming."

WRITINGS: (With H. D. Leeds) *Computer Programming Fundamentals,* McGraw, 1961, 2nd edition, 1966; *PL/1 Programmer Primer,* McGraw, 1966; (contributor) Sadovski and Yodin, editors, *Research in General Systems Theory,* Progress (Moscow, Soviet Union), 1969.

(With H. D. Leeds) *Computer Programming Fundamentals: Based on the I.B.M. System 360,* McGraw, 1970; *PL/1 Programming: A Manual of Style,* McGraw, 1970; *The Psychology of Computer Programming,* Van Nostrand, 1971; (contributor) George Klir, editor, *Trends in General Systems Theory,* Wiley, 1972; (with N. F. Yasakawa and Robert

Marcus) *Structured Programming in PL/C,* with teacher's guide, Wiley, 1973; *Introduction to General Systems Thinking,* Wiley, 1975; (with Tom Gilb) *Humanized Input,* Winthrop Publishing, 1976; (with Steve Wright, Richard Kauffman, and Marty Goetz) *High-Level COBOL Programming,* Winthrop Publishing, 1977; (with Daniel P. Freedman) *EthnoTECHnical Review Handbook,* Ethnotech, 1977, 2nd edition, 1979; (with Donald C. Gause) *Are Your Lights On?: A Treatise on the Definition of Diverse Problems,* Ethnotech, 1978; (with wife, Daniela Weinberg) *Principles of the Design of Stable Systems,* Wiley, 1979; *The Programming Problem,* Ethnotech, 1979.

Co-author of films, with workbooks: "Critical Program Reading I and II," Edutronics, 1975; "Top-Down Programming: Development by Refinement I and II," Edutronics, 1975; "Control Structures I and II," Edutronics, 1975; "Principles of Specifications Design," Robert J. Brady, 1979. Author of "Errurs" a column in *SIGDOC,* 1978, and "Stateside," in *Datalink,* 1978. Editor of "Winthrop Computer Systems Series," Winthrop Publishing, 1975—, and "Brady Computer Systems Series," Robert J. Brady, 1976—. Contributor to *General Systems Yearbook, Encyclopedia Americana,* and *Encyclopedia of Philosophy.* Contributor of about forty articles to technical journals and popular magazines, including *Human Factors, Think,* and *National Parks and Conservation.* Editor of *Pragmatic Programming and Sensible Software,* 1978; member of editorial board of *Transactions of Software Engineering,* of Institute of Electrical and Electronics Engineers, 1976—.

SIDELIGHTS: Weinberg told *CA:* "My writing and research interests have always been the same—how to improve the quality of human life through improvement of the quality of human thought. All my publications share that common thread, though they range over many subjects. I believe the problem of human happiness is extremely deep and difficult, so that any method that works to increase our understanding is legitimate. I also believe deeply in the power of each human being, given a chance, to learn with or without the aid of institutions. That's why I write. It allows me to reach many more people more easily and more directly than I ever could, for instance, teaching in a university. Of course, writing is a lonely business. My two greatest joys are co-authoring a piece and receiving letters from my readers.

"Naturally, I also enjoy generous reviews of my works, as when *Datamation* said of *The Psychology of Computer Programming,* 'This is certainly the best book about programming yet to be published.' Sometimes, when the difficulties, delays, and loneliness of writing get me down, I leaf through the hundreds of reviews and letters I've received. Don't ever believe that authors are immune to praise!"

Weinberg's books have been published in Japanese, French, Spanish, German, Hungarian, and Russian.

* * *

WEINBERG, Janet Hopson
See HOPSON, Janet L(ouise)

* * *

WEINER, Richard 1927-

PERSONAL: Born May 10, 1927, in Brooklyn, N.Y.; son of George M. (a printer) and Sally (Kosower) Weiner; married Florence Chaiken (an author), December 9, 1956; children: Jessica, Stephanie. *Education:* University of Wisconsin, B.S., 1949, M.S., 1950. *Office:* Richard Weiner, Inc., 888-7 Seventh Ave., New York, N.Y. 10019.

CAREER: Creative Radio Associates, Madison, Wis., president, 1951; associated with Weiner-Morton & Associates, Madison, 1951-53; Ruder & Finn, Inc., New York City, senior vice president, 1953-68; Richard Weiner, Inc. (public relations), New York City, president, 1968—. *Member:* American Medical Writers Association, Public Relations Society of America, Publicity Club of New York, Sigma Xi. *Awards, honors:* Silver Anvil award from Public Relations Society of America, 1965.

WRITINGS: Professional's Guide to Public Relations Services, Prentice-Hall, 1968, third edition, Weiner, 1975; (editor) *News Bureaus in the U.S.,* Weiner, 1969, fifth edition, 1979; *Professional's Guide to Publicity* (textbook), Weiner, 1975, second edition, Weiner, 1978; *Syndicated Columnists,* Weiner, 1975, third edition, 1979; *Military Publications,* Weiner, 1979.

SIDELIGHTS: Richard Weiner's *Syndicated Columnists* contains biographical information and commentary on several hundred past and current newspaper columnists, as well as discussions of the current trends in journalism and column syndication. The largely expanded third edition features such notable columnists as Ann Landers, Abigail Van Buren, Walter Winchell, "Mr. Dooley," William Safire, Dr. Morris Fishbein, and Dr. Joyce Brothers. The book is considered to be the most extensive book solely devoted to newspaper columnists.

BIOGRAPHICAL/CRITICAL SOURCES: Booklist, March 1, 1978.

* * *

WEINER, Skip
See WEINER, Stewart

* * *

WEINER, Stewart 1945-
(Skip Weiner; Steward Lebreo, Stewart Lebreo, pseudonyms)

PERSONAL: Surname pronounced *Wine*-er; born September 11, 1945, in Cincinnati, Ohio; son of Alfred Lawrence (a physician) and Janet (an artist; maiden name, Lackner) Weiner. *Education:* University of Missouri, B.J., 1967. *Home:* 8939 Keith Ave., West Hollywood, Calif. 90069. *Office: OUI* Magazine, 8560 Sunset Blvd., Los Angeles, Calif. 90069.

CAREER/WRITINGS: J. Walter Thompson Company, New York City, copywriter, 1967-69; Bailey, Erskine, Roberts (advertising agency), Cincinnati, Ohio, owner, 1969-73; *Writer's Digest,* Cincinnati, editor-in-chief, 1973-76; *Provincetown Poets,* Provincetown, Mass., senior editor, 1977-78; Playboy Enterprises, Los Angeles, Calif., senior editor of *OUI* magazine, 1978—. Contributor of articles to periodicals under name skip Weiner and pseudonyms Steward Lebreo and Stewart Lebreo.

WORK IN PROGRESS: Whisky Tango Foxtrot: A Fantasy, publication expected in 1982; *Southern California Lecture Series,* publication expected in 1983.

SIDELIGHTS: Weiner told *CA:* "The same lazy instincts that led me into advertising copywriting jelled when I discovered that magazine editors got to play with copy that was already written. How much easier than having to think up all this stuff yourself!"

Of his duties as senior editor of *OUI* magazine, Weiner commented: "Just my luck, I'm responsible for most of the words in a picture magazine. It's like being responsible for the photos in *Foreign Policy*." Weiner was editor-in-chief of *Writer's Digest* for three years, and noted that there is "no difference except *Writer's Digest* may have been sexier."

* * *

WEININGER, Richard 1887(?)-1979

OBITUARY NOTICE: Born c. 1887 in Baden, Austria; died October 15, 1979, in Mount Kisco, N.Y. Financier, industrialist, and author. Weininger was chairman of the board of several firms, including the Martin Parry Company, Ward Industries, and the New York and Cuba Mail Steamship Companies. He later became president of the Premier Investing Corporation. Weininger wrote an autobiography, *Exciting Years*, when he was ninety years of age. Obituaries and other sources: *New York Times*, October 16, 1979.

* * *

WEISGAL, Meyer W(olf) 1894-1977

OBITUARY NOTICE: Born November 10, 1894, in Kikl, Poland; died September 29, 1977, in Rehovot, Israel. Zionist leader, theatrical producer, and editor. As a member of the Zionist Organization of America, Weisgal worked on the editorial board of its publications, *The Maccabean* and *The New Maccabean*. He was a delegate to the annual World Zionist Congresses beginning in 1924, a personal representative of Chaim Weizmann in the United States for six years, and president and chancellor of the Chaim Weizmann Institute of Science in Rehovot, Israel. In addition, Weisgal produced several plays, including "The Eternal Road," a musical drama of Jewish history. His books include an autobiography, *. . . So Far*. Obituaries and other sources: Meyer Weisgal, . . . So Far, *Random House, 1971;* Current Biography, *Wilson, 1972, 1977;* Who's Who in the World, *2nd edition, Marquis, 1973.*

* * *

WEISS, Morris S(amuel) 1915-
(Ink Higgins, Wes Sirrom)

PERSONAL: Born August 11, 1915, in Philadelphia, Pa.; son of Jacob (a tie weaver) and Dora (Rosenblum) Weiss; married Blanch Diton, May 30, 1944; children: Wendy Carol, Jacob, Jerome, David. *Education:* Attended Art Students League. *Home and office:* 1180 Northeast 128th St., North Miami, Fla. 33161. *Agent:* McNaught Syndicate, Inc., 60 East 42nd St., New York, N.Y. 10017.

CAREER/WRITINGS: Worked as first assistant to H. H. Knerr on comic strip, "Katzenjammer Kids," 1935; assistant author and illustrator to Lank Leonard on syndicated comic strip, "Mickey Finn," 1936-71, author and illustrator of "Mickey Finn," 1971-77. Creator of cartoon panel, "It Never Fails," c. 1940; illustrator of daily comic stirp, "Joe Jinks," 1942-43; creator of comic book, *Wendy Parker*, 1947; author and illustrator of numerous comic books, some under pseudonym Ink Higgins, including *Tessie the Typist, Margie, Miss America, Boxie Weaver, Worthless Wiggins, Go-Ahead Gallagher, Ruffy Ropes*, and *Pinky Lee*. Also author and illustrator of comics under pseudonym Wes Sirrom. Speaker on subject of American illustrators at Ft. Lauderdale Museum of the Arts, 1977, and at Daytona Beach Museum of Arts and Sciences, 1977. Founder and first president of Miami Society for Autistic Children (now South Florida Society for Autistic Children), 1968. *Military service:* U.S. Army, 1944-45. *Member:* National Cartoonists Society, National Society for Autistic Children (past board member), Miami Touchdown Club. *Awards, honors:* First place award from *Newport News* (Va.), 1945, for graphic rendering.

SIDELIGHTS: Weiss told *CA* that he has "devoted my life to writing and drawing comics," but has also become active in "providing education and training for autistic children." A collector of original illustrations since 1934, Weiss held an exhibition of his extensive collection, entitled "Great American Illustrators," at both the Ft. Lauderdale Museum of the Arts and the Daytona Beach Museum of Arts and Sciences. His private collection of eighty-five paintings include works by Norman Rockwell, N. C. Wyeth, James Bama, J. C. Leyendecker, E. A. Abbey, Gordon Grant, and many others.

* * *

WELKER, Robert Henry 1917-

PERSONAL: Born July 5, 1917, in Altoona, Pa.; son of Melvin George (a chemist) and Bertha (a teacher; maiden name, Lingenfelter) Welker; married Cynthia Templeton (a teacher), December 27, 1958. *Education:* Franklin and Marshall College, B.A., 1940; Harvard University, Ph.D., 1953. *Politics:* "Thoreauvian." *Home:* 940 Woodview Rd., Cleveland Heights, Ohio 44121. *Office:* Department of American Studies, Mather House, Case Western Reserve University, Cleveland, Ohio 44106.

CAREER: Hamilton College, Clinton, N.Y., instructor in English, 1946-47; currently associated with Case Western Reserve University, Cleveland, Ohio. *Military service:* U.S. Army, 1942-46; served in Africa and Italy; became first lieutenant; received Bronze Star. *Member:* American Association of University Professors, American Civil Liberties Union, Massachusetts Audubon Society, Burroughs Nature Club, Hawk Mountain Sanctuary Association, Clergy and Laity Concerned, War Resistors League, Phi Beta Kappa.

WRITINGS: *Birds and Men*, Harvard University Press, 1955, revised edition, Atheneum, 1966; *A Different Drummer*, Beacon Press, 1958; *Natural Man: The Life of William Beebe*, Indiana University Press, 1975. Contributor to magazines, including *Saturday Review of Literature, American Scholar, Nation*, and *Variety*.

WORK IN PROGRESS: Editing a series of his letters to friends overseas, 1960-77, as contemporary records of "engagement and response to civil rights, the antiwar movement, the counterculture generally, and through Watergate to Jimmy Carter."

SIDELIGHTS: Welker writes: "Recently we bought a house that was a quarter of a century old when I was born. Some day we'll get all the repairs done, and may resume our camping trips, see Europe again, and take up where we left off, reading and reflecting and working, and hoping for times more benign."

* * *

WELLERSHOFF, Dieter 1925-

PERSONAL: Born November 3, 1925, in Neuss, Germany; son of Walter and Claere (Weber) Wellershoff; married Maria von Thadden, May 16, 1952; children: Irene, Gerald, Marianne. *Education:* Gymnasium Grevenbroich, diploma, 1946; University of Bonn, Dr. Phil., 1952. *Home:* Mainzer Strasse 45, Cologne, West Germany 5000. *Office:* Verlag Kiepenheuer & Witsch, Rondorfer Strasse 5, Cologne, West Germany 5000.

CAREER: Deutsche Studentenzeitung, Bonn, West Germany, editor, 1953-56; Verlag Kiepenheuer & Witsch (publisher), Cologne, West Germany, reader, 1959—. *Military service:* German Army, 1943-45. *Member:* International

P.E.N., Academy of Science and Literature, German Writers' Association. *Awards, honors:* Hoerspielpreis der Kriegsblinden, 1961; Kritikerpreis, 1971.

WRITINGS—In English: *Ein schoener Tag* (novel), Rowohlt Verlag, 1969, translation by Dorothea Oppenheimer published as *A Beautiful Day,* Harper, 1971.

Other writings: *Gottfried Benn: Phaenotyp dieser Stunde* (title means "Gottfried Benn: Phenotype of This Hour"), Kiepenheuer & Witsch, 1958; (editor) Gottfried Benn, *Gesammelte Werke* (title means "Collected Works"), four volumes, Limes, 1958-62; *Am ungenauen Ort* (two radio plays; title means "At an Uncertain Place"), Limes, 1960; *Anni Nabels Boxschau* (title means "Anni Nabels' Box-Show"), Kiepenheuer & Witsch, 1962; *Ein Tag in der Stadt: Sechs Autoren variieren ein Thema* (title means "A Day in Town: Variations on a Theme by Six Authors"), Kiepenheuer & Witsch, 1962; *Der Gleichgueltige: Versuche ueber Hemingway, Camus, Benn, und Beckett* (literary criticism; title means "The Indifferent: Essays on Hemingway, Camus, Benn, and Beckett"), Kiepenheuer & Witsch, 1963; *Wochenende: Sechs Autoren variieren ein Thema* (title means "Weekend: Variations on a Theme by Six Authors"), Kiepenheuer & Witsch, 1967; *Die Bittgaenger [und] Die Schatten* (two radio plays; title means "The Supple Cat [and] Shadows"), Reclam, 1968; *Die Schattengrenze* (novel; title means "The Edge of the Shadow"), Kiepenheuer & Witsch, 1969; *Literatur und Veraenderung: Versuche zu einer Metakritik der Literatur* (title means "Literature and Change: Essays on a Metacritic of Literature"), Kiepenheuer und Witsch, 1969.

Das Schreien der Katze im Sack (radio plays; title means "Cry of the Cat in the Bag"), Kiepenheuer & Witsch, 1970; *Einladung an alle* (novel; title means "Invitation to Everyone"), Kiepenheuer & Witsch, 1972; *Literatur und Lustprinzip* (essays; title means "Literature and Lustprinzip"), Kiepenheuer & Witsch, 1973; *Doppelt belichtetes Seestueck und andere Texte* (title means "Double Exposed Seascape and Other Texts"), Kiepenheuer & Witsch, 1974; *Die Auflosesung des Kunstbegriffs* (title means "The Dissolution of the Art Concept"), Suhrkamp, 1976; *Die Schoenheit des Schimpansen* (novel; title means "The Beauty Lie of the Chimpanzee"), Kipenheuer und Witsch, 1977.

Television plays: "Eskalation" (title means "Escalation"), 1976; "Gluecksucher" (title means "Happiness Hunter"), 1977; "Freiheiten der Langeweile" (title means "Freedom and Boredom"), 1978; "Phantasten," 1979. Also author of movie script for "Gluecksucher," 1979.

WORK IN PROGRESS: Narratives, essays, television motion pictures.

SIDELIGHTS: Affiliated with a major German publishing house, Wellershoff is credited with bringing together German "new novelists" to form the Koelner Schule. In addition, he has won renown as a radio playwright and as a new novelist himself.

A Beautiful Day was praised by Hans-Bernhard Moeller as a "new-novel view of a neurotic family which, at times, approached the power of Sartre's *No Exit.*" However, reviewing *Die Schattengrenze,* Moeller judged that "even sympathizers of the nouveau roman who are accustomed to absence of characterization, of symbols, and of edification, would find this outside view of a private pathology episodic and monotonous."

In *Literatur und Veraenderung,* Wellershoff exhibits what he terms a "new realism." That is, he eschews any form of order or particular pattern, claiming that reality is actually made up of a continual series of risks. "Wellershoff sees the function of the writer as a constant breaking of categories," observed Rainer Schulte. "In such moments new possibilities for ritual and mystery are being created. He rejects established patterns and hopes to lead through his writing to the excitement of an unpredictable future."

Wellershoff commented: "For me to write means to renew the perception of life, to free it from prejudice and conformist and schematic points of view. That is why crisis experiences and light as well as violent emotions in a usual situation especially attract me. In periods of instability, in the situation of loss of orientation are the chances of renewal. My books reckon with curious and fearless readers, who are interested in the human being and are ready to follow extreme developments to their end.

"I would describe myself as a realist. Reality, however, is never a durable possession. It escapes, it must always be explored and be questioned again. This is an endless task. And, in contrast with science, literature does not impart knowledge, but experiences. Experiences are ardent knowledge. They encroach upon existence and set themselves in motion."

BIOGRAPHICAL/CRITICAL SOURCES: Books Abroad, spring, 1970, autumn, 1970.

* * *

WELLMAN, Alice 1900-

PERSONAL: Born May 11, 1900, in Salt Lake City, Utah; daughter of Frederick Creighton (a physician) and Lydia (a teacher; maiden name, Isely) Wellman; married Carl S. Flanders, March 15, 1932 (died November, 1936); married I. Harry Harris, April 12, 1939 (died August, 1974); children: (first marriage) Alison Elise Flanders Webster; (second marriage) Jeffrey Dewey Harris. *Education:* Pomona College, B.A., 1922; Wichita State University, B.S., 1923. *Politics:* Independent. *Religion:* Protestant. *Home and office:* 3151 College St., Costa Mesa, Calif. 92626. *Agent:* Larry Sternig Literary Agency, 742 Robertson St., Milwaukee, Wis. 53210.

CAREER: Actress and singer in Warner Bros. films and on stage in New York, N.Y., and Boston, Mass., including performances in light operas and performances with John Murray Anderson's "Revues," 1926-49; performed in European concerts, on Broadway, and on tour; manager and director of summer sessions at Yardley Theater, Bucks County, Pa., and Berwyn Theater, Philadelphia, Pa.; casting director for Howard Film Productions. Writer, 1965—. Lecturer at San Diego State College, Long Beach City College, University of California, Los Angeles, University of California, Irvine, and University of North Carolina; private writing teacher, adviser, and editor. *Member:* International P.E.N., California Writers Guild, Southern California Authors League, Southern California Council on Literature for Children and Young People, Quill-Pen Club, Newport Writers Group (founding member; chairperson), Fine Arts Club of Pasadena (honorary member), Friends of Newport Library; Friends of University of California, Irvine, Library. *Awards, honors:* Received three awards for children's books.

WRITINGS—Juvenile: *Tammy: Adventure in Hollywood,* Whitman Publishing, 1964; *Time of Fearful Night,* Putnam, 1970; *Tatu and the Honey Bird,* Putnam, 1972; *Small-Boy Chiku,* Houghton, 1973; *The Baby Elephant's Day,* Putnam, 1973; *The Wilderness Has Ears,* Harcourt, 1975; *White Sorceress,* Putnam, 1976.

Other: (Contributor) *A Treasury of Success Unlimited,* Hawthorn Books, 1966; (editor) *Rawhide and Orange Blossoms,* Pioneer Press, 1967; *Spirit Magic,* Berkly Medallion, 1973; *Africa's Animals,* Putnam, 1973.

Ghost writer of portions of Michael Evlanoff's and Marjorie Fluor's *Alfred Nobel, the Loneliest Millionaire,* Ward Ritchie, 1969. Contributor of articles and stories to various adult and children's magazines. Writer and script editor for Hollywood television stations; contributing writer for Loretta Young television series.

WORK IN PROGRESS: Noted Women of Africa's Past, for Harcourt; *Baboons are People,* for Putnam.

SIDELIGHTS: Wellman told *CA:* I grew up in Angola, Portuguese West Africa, where my parents worked as missionaries. During my tenth to twelfth years I would accompany my father on his professional visits to London, Lisbon, Funchal and the West African cities of Bailundu and Chiyaka. Becoming thirteen was a memorable time—my first return to the States and Washington, D.C., and my father's visit to Teddy Roosevelt at Oyster Bay to confer on the planning of TR's coming safari in Africa. The ex-president didn't neglect me. He declared me to be a lovely little girl (John Murray Anderson was later to bill me in his Broadway 'Revues' as the 'Toy Soprano'), presented me with a fatherly kiss and held me on his knee while we talked about what I liked about America. Of course, my writing career started late because of my musical involvement; but I watched with admiration and sisterly pride the rise of my three writing brothers: author-historian Paul I., author Manly Wade, and the scientific plant researcher and professor emeritus Frederick L.

"My career as an actress-prima donna singer took me to Paris and London, and on tour to all major cities of the United States, Canada and the islands of the Caribbean. My books, from the vivid impressions on an active mind and later meticulous research and reading, have been written with the thought that my early associations and growing up among the highland natives should be visualized in words as I remembered them—the native huts we lived in, my pet savannah monkey, my playmates, the sick and the lame whom my father nursed, especially Wandenjoi my constant guard on medical research safaris, the honeybirds, my mother's ministrations, and the Chiyakan villagers who gifted me with love and taught me the way of the wild things. All in all, the essence of a life that is fast disappearing in Africa.

"I believe I have left some of me in my books."

* * *

WELSH, Susan
See COLLINS, Margaret (Brandon James)

* * *

WERNER, Alfred 1911-1979

OBITUARY NOTICE: Born March 30, 1911, in Vienna, Austria; died July 14, 1979, in New York, N.Y. Art critic, poet, and author. Werner came to the United States in 1940, after having been imprisoned in the Dachau concentration camp for almost one year. He wrote on a free-lance basis, contributing articles to the *New York Times, Kenyon Review,* and *Commentary,* among others. He authored many biographies, including ones on Modigliani, Barlach, Chagall, Munch, Utrillo, and other famous artists. Werner later became a frequent lecturer at universities and other organizations. He edited various publications, including *Die Stimme* and *Universal Jewish Encyclopedia.* Obituaries and other sources: *Who's Who in World Jewry,* Pitman, 1972; *Who's Who in America,* 40th edition, Marquis, 1978; *New York Times,* July 16, 1979; *AB Bookman's Weekly,* September 10, 1979.

* * *

WERTHMAN, Michael S(cott) 1939-

PERSONAL: Born July 6, 1939, in Gloversville, N.Y.; son of Ben (an executive) and Lorrayne (Hand) Werthman; married Deven Zweigman (a company director), July 4, 1967. *Education:* Columbia University, A.B. (summa cum laude), 1962, graduate study, 1962-63; further graduate study at San Diego State University, 1965-66. *Office:* 4598 39th St., #7, San Diego, Calif. 92116.

CAREER: Free-lance writer. Prentice-Hall, Inc., Englewood Cliffs, N.J., editor, 1963-64; Brand Rating Research Corp., New York, N.Y., assistant to president, 1964; CRM Books, Del Mar, Calif., staff writer, 1969-70; Psychology Today Books, Del Mar, Calif., editor, 1973. *Member:* Phi Beta Kappa, Phi Alpha Theta. *Awards, honors:* Woodrow Wilson fellowship, 1962; merit award from Communicating Arts Group of San Diego, 1973, for *Civilization,* a brochure.

WRITINGS: (Editor with N. F. Cantor, and contributor) *The English Tradition,* Macmillan, 1967; (editor with Cantor) *The Structure of European History,* Crowell, 1967, 2nd edition, 1972; (editor with Cantor, and contributor) *The History of Popular Culture,* Macmillan, 1968; (editor with Michael Dalby) *Bureaucracy in Historical Perspective,* Scott, Foresman, 1971; (editor with Jon Sutherland) *Comparative Concepts of Law and Order,* Scott, Foresman, 1971; (editor with Sutherland and Robert Detweiler) *Environmental Decay in Its Historical Context,* Scott, Foresman, 1973; *Struggle for Change,* Scott, Foresman, 1974; *The Psychology Primer,* Publisher's, Inc., 1978, 2nd edition, 1979; *Self-Psyching,* J. P. Tarcher, 1978.

WORK IN PROGRESS: Self-Psyching for Teenagers; The Mad God (tentative title), a partly autobiographical novel.

SIDELIGHTS: Werthman writes: "My writing career began while I was still in college, when I did most of the writing and all the editing of a medieval history textbook that became the best-seller in its field during the sixties. Thus I had a career thrust upon me, getting successive writing and editing assignments over the following twenty years. Though I have concentrated on nonfiction—history, psychology, sociology, anthropology, and other social science fields, I have written children's books and am now undertaking fiction.

"I continue to write to make a living and to make sense, to make sense to those who read what I write and to bring sufficient order to the ideas with which I deal that they make sense to me. Writing is a wonderful thing to have done; it is a dreadful task to contemplate; and I usually wish I were doing something else when actually writing. Nothing makes me feel better—or worse. Nothing takes more out of me yet gives me more. I value writing because it has the power to counter chaos and entropy, to exalt life and humanity over life-ignoring mechanicalism. Everyone should write more—though a few might do well to write less—to add their minds and spirits to the totality of ordered thought and honest feeling."

* * *

WESSEL, Milton R(alph) 1923-

PERSONAL: Born August 19, 1923, in New York, N.Y.; son of Harry Nathan (a lawyer) and Elsie (Strettner) Wessel;

married Joan L. Strauss; children: Douglas C., Kenneth L., Michael R. *Education:* Yale University, A.B., 1946; Harvard University, LL.B. (cum laude), 1948. *Religion:* Jewish. *Home:* 1 Tall Tree Lane, Pleasantville, N.Y. 10570.

CAREER: Associate of Cahill, Gordon & Reindel, 1948-53; assistant U.S. Attorney in southern district of New York City, 1953-55; associate of Cahill, Gordon & Reindel, 1955-58; special assistant to U.S. attorney-general in Washington, D.C., and chief of Special Group on Organized Crime in the United States, 1958-60; Kaye, Scholer, Fierman, Hays & Handler, New York City, partner, 1960-73; Chemistry Industry Institute of Toxicology, Research Triangle Park, N.C., general counsel, 1974—. Visiting professor of law at Columbia University, 1972-77, 1979—, and New York University, 1975-78; acting professor at Stanford University, 1978. Member of bar of New York State and U.S. Supreme Court; general counsel for Association of Data Processing Service Organizations, 1966—, and American Federation of Information Processing Societies, 1968-75; special litigation counsel for Dow Chemical Co., 1974-78. Member and administrator of workshops and panels. President and member of board of trustees of Henry Kaufmann Campgrounds, 1956-73. *Military service:* U.S. Army, 1942-45; served in European theater. *Member:* American Bar Association, New York State Bar Association, Association of the Bar of the City of New York.

WRITINGS: Federal Pretrial and Jury Trial Procedure, Practicing Law Institute, 1955; (with Bruce Gilchrist) *Government Regulation of the Computer Industry,* American Federation of Information Processing Societies, 1972; *Materials and Cases on Computers and Law,* privately printed, 1974, 5th edition, 1978; *Freedom's Edge: The Computer Threat to Society,* Addison-Wesley, 1974; *Materials on Socio-Scientific Dispute Resolution,* privately printed, 1976, 4th edition, 1979; *The Rule of Reason: A New Approach to Corporate Litigation,* Addison-Wesley, 1976; *Science, Society, and Sense,* Columbia University Press, 1980.

Author of "On the Legal Side," a column in *Computer Services Journal,* 1969-72. Contributor to *Encyclopedia of Computer Science.* Contributor of about thirty-five articles to journals in law, medicine, and computer sciences, and to popular magazines and newspapers, including *Nation, New York,* and *Saturday Evening Post.* Member of editorial board of *Datamation,* 1971-75.

* * *

WEST, Mae 1893-

PERSONAL: Born August 17, 1893, in Brooklyn, N.Y.; daughter of John Patrick (a livery stable owner) and Matilda (a fashion model; maiden name, Delker-Doelger) West; married Frank Wallace, 1911 (divorced, 1943). *Education:* Privately educated. *Home:* 514 Pacific Coast Highway, Santa Monica, Calif. *Agent:* William Morris Agency, 151 El Camino Dr., Beverly Hills, Calif. 90212.

CAREER: Actress, singer, songwriter, and writer. Appeared in stage productions, including "Little Nell the Marchioness," 1897, "Vera Violetta," 1911, "Such Is Life," 1913, "Sex," 1926, "The Wicked Age," 1927, "Diamond Lil," 1928, "The Constant Sinner," 1931, "Catherine Was Great," 1944, "Come On Up . . . Ring Twice," 1952, and "Sextet," 1961, in motion pictures, including "Night After Night," 1932, "She Done Him Wrong," 1933, "I'm No Angel," 1933, "Bell of the Nighties," 1934, "Go West Young Man," 1936, "My Little Chickadee," 1940, "Myra Breckenridge," 1969, and "Sextette," 1979, and in television shows, including "The Red Skelton Show," 1960, and "Mister Ed," 1964; toured in plays and as nightclub performer. Associated with Paramount Pictures during 1930's.

WRITINGS: Babe Gordon (novel), Macaulay, 1930; *Diamond Lil* (novel), Macaulay, 1932; *Goodness Had Nothing to Do With It* (autobiography), Prentice-Hall, 1959, revised edition, Macfadden-Bartell, 1970; *The Wit and Wisdom of Mae West,* edited by Joseph Weintraub, Putnam, 1967; *Mae West on Sex, Health, and ESP,* W. H. Allen, 1975; *Pleasure Man; or, Virtue Had Nothing to Do With It,* Dell, 1975.

Plays: "Sex," first produced in New York City at Daly's Theater, April 26, 1926; "The Drag," first produced in Paterson, N.J., 1926; "The Wicked Age," first produced in New York City at Daly's Theater, November 4, 1927; "Diamond Lil," first produced in New York City at Teller's Shubert Theater, April, 1928, first produced on Broadway at Royale Theater, April 9, 1928; "The Pleasure Man," produced on Broadway at Biltmore Theater, 1928; "Catherine Was Great," first produced on Broadway at Shubert Theater, August 2, 1944; "Ring Twice Tonight," produced in Los Angeles, Calif., May, 1948, later produced as "Come On Up"; "Sextet," produced in 1961.

Screenplays: "I'm No Angel," Paramount, 1933; "She Done Him Wrong" (adapted from the play by West, "Diamond Lil"), Paramount, 1933; "Klondike Annie," Paramount, 1935; (with W. C. Fields) "My Little Chickadee," 1940.

Author of recording "The Fabulous Mae West," Decca, 1955.

WORK IN PROGRESS: Adapting the play "The Drag" as a motion picture.

SIDELIGHTS: "Sixty years ago," wrote Gerald Clarke, "Mae West looked in the mirror and ordered the clock stopped. So far as she is concerned, it has never dared to start again." Indeed, countless celebrity chroniclers have noted that West has appeared virtually without change for more than sixty years. "If I argue, I get nasty," she revealed, "so I don't have anyone around who argues with me. I also don't smoke and I don't drink. I think drinking puts spots on your hands. I always drink bottled water. Water with minerals in it clogs your arteries, and I want to keep my insides clean."

The Mae West "personality"—suggestive and worldly—was created by West in her 1928 play, "Diamond Lil." Playing the title role of the saloon singer, West uttered the immortal line to a captain, "Come on up and see me sometime." In another scene, a doting admirer murmurs "your lips, your hair, your magnificent shoulders" to West, who replies impatiently, "What're you doin', honey? Makin' love or takin' inventory?"

The huge success of "Diamond Lil" capped West's rather controversial career on Broadway. Her first writing effort, "Sex," was a tremendous hit in New York City but charges of moral corruption were leveled against West because of the suggestive nature of her presence and the subject matter. Later, the successful "Wicked Age" was prematurely closed when a conflict between West and the lead male could not be resolved.

West toured the United States in productions of "Sex" and "Diamond Lil" during the late 1920's and early 1930's and then headed for Hollywood, whereupon she signed an agreement with Paramount Pictures that netted her $5000 per week. In her first film, "Night After Night," West appeared with George Raft, who later acknowledged her commanding screen presence. Her next two films solidified her reputation as the cinema's suggestive sultress. "She Done Him Wrong," an adaptation of "Diamond Lil," also starred Cary Grant and became one of the most successful films of its time. In "I'm No Angel," West actually climbed into a lion cage to realize one of her childhood ambitions. The same film also featured her memorable line, "Beulah, peel me a grape." Later films contained such immortal comments by West as "When I'm good, I'm very good, but when I'm bad I'm better," and "Is that a gun in your pocket, or are you just glad to see me?"

By 1936, West was being paid $300,000 per acting performance and $100,000 per screenplay. But her notorious characterizations and steamy double entendres had become the target of the Hays Commission, an organization designated to "clean up" films and eliminate excess violence and sex. West was a major victim of the commission since most of her films relied heavily on her worldly character and suggestive innuendos. Her later films, such as "Go West Young Man" and "Everyday's a Holiday," were still popular with audiences but West was reduced to portraying a less provocative caricature of her former screen-self. After teaming up with W. C. Fields, another victim of the Hays Commission, in the disappointing "My Little Chickadee," West made one more film, "The Heat's On," before returning to the stage in "Catherine Was Great."

West toured the United States during the 1950's with a nightclub act featuring numerous men clad in loincloths. She also revived "Diamond Lil" in London and New York City. In 1955 she recorded many of her most popular songs for "The Fabulous Mae West" and followed that with two more albums in 1966: "Way Out West," which contained renditions of songs by, among others, Lennon and McCartney and Bob Dylan, and "Wild Christmas," which featured "Put the Loot in the Boot, Santa."

Published in 1959, West's autobiography, *Goodness Had Nothing to Do With It,* received mixed reviews. A. H. Weiler called it "a theatre-wise, basically clean, sometimes corny, often entertaining yarn." Maurice Richardson exclaimed: "I was surprised to find how much of an author she is. . . . She tells some quite good stories of vaudeville and Hollywood." William Leonard declared: "This is a book about a gal in show business, but it contains precious little about show business as such. This is Mae West talking about Mae West—humorously and light heartedly and with a philosophy as shallow as a pie pan."

West has appeared in two films since 1943, "Myra Breckenridge" and "Sextette." The former is considered by many film reviewers to be among the worst films ever made, although West herself is one of the few principals featured to escape the critics' wrath. In 1979 she appeared in "Sextette," which Clarke called "one of those movies rarely seen these days, a work so bad, so ferally innocent, that it is good, an instant classic to be treasured by connoisseurs of the genre everywhere."

Despite more than fifty years in the entertainment business, West still maintains her youthful appearance. "I've never had any face lifts," she told an interviewer. "You can tell by my hands and wrists. They can't operate on your hands. I've never had anything done, and I look the way I did when I was 22."

AVOCATIONAL INTERESTS: Weightlifting.

BIOGRAPHICAL/CRITICAL SOURCES: Mae West, *Goodness Had Nothing to Do With It,* Prentice-Hall, 1959, revised edition, Macfadden-Bartell, 1970; *Saturday Evening Post,* November 14, 1964; *Esquire,* July, 1967; West, *The Wit and Wisdom of Mae West,* edited by Joseph Weintraub, Putnam, 1967; *Vogue,* June 1, 1970; Jon Tuska, *The Films of Mae West,* Citadel, 1973; Michael Bayer, *Mae West,* Harcourt, 1975; *Time,* March 15, 1976, May 22, 1978; Tristram Potter Coffin, *The Female Hero in Folklore and Legend,* Seabury, 1977; Leonard Martin, *Great Movie Comedians,* Crown, 1978; Lowell Swortzell, *Here Come the Clowns,* Viking, 1978; *Working Woman,* February, 1979.*

—Sketch by Les Stone

* * *

WEST, Robert C(raig) 1947-

PERSONAL: Born July 15, 1947, in Joplin, Mo.; son of Harold Robert (in real estate) and Mary Jean (a librarian; maiden name, Windler) West; married Susan Hauck (an educator), August 16, 1969; children: Robert, Jocelyn, Christine. *Education:* University of Missouri, A.B., 1969; Northwestern University, Ph.D., 1974. *Politics:* "Eclectic." *Religion:* Protestant. *Office:* Department of Economics, Drake University, Des Moines, Iowa 50311.

CAREER: University of Maryland, College Park, assistant professor of economics, 1973-78; Drake University, Des Moines, Iowa, associate professor of economics, 1978—. Associate of Mitchell & Mitchell (economists). *Member:* American Economic Association, Economic History Association, History of Economics Society.

WRITINGS: Banking Reform and the Federal Reserve, 1863-1923, Cornell University Press, 1977. Contributor to economic and history journals.

WORK IN PROGRESS: An economic history of nineteenth-century India.

* * *

WESTON, Allen
See HOGARTH, Grace (Weston Allen)

* * *

WESTON, Helen Gray
See DANIELS, Dorothy

* * *

WEYBRIGHT, Victor 1903-1978

OBITUARY NOTICE: Born March 16, 1903, in Keymar, Md.; died in 1978. Author and editor. Weybright was the editor-in-chief of the New American Library of World Literature, Inc., the publisher of Mentor and Signet paperback books. Weybright's works include *Spangled Banner, Buffalo Bill and the Wild West,* and *Making of a Publisher.* Obituaries and other sources: *The Author's and Writer's Who's Who,* 6th edition, Burke's Peerage, 1971; *Who's Who in America,* 38th edition, Marquis, 1974; *The Writers Directory, 1976-78,* St. Martin's, 1976.

* * *

WHALEN, George J. 1939-

PERSONAL: Born September 2, 1939, in New York, N.Y.; son of George C. (a textile executive) and Veronica R. (Southwick) Whalen; married Joyce A. George, July 31, 1966; children: David Scott, Russell Craig. *Education:* Attended Polytechnic Institute of Brooklyn, 1962-65; Hofstra University, B.A., 1965. *Home:* 59 Lambert Lane, New Rochelle, N.Y. 10804. *Office:* Graf-Whalen Corp., 111 Van Etten Blvd., New Rochelle, N.Y. 10804.

CAREER: Assistant publications manager, Safe Flight Instrument Corp., 1966-1970; Electronics for Medicine, Inc., marketing communications manager, 1970—. Holds several patents in electronics and thermodynamics. *Member:* National Association of Home and Workshop Writers, Institute of Electrical and Electronic Engineers.

WRITINGS—All with Rudolf F. Graf: *Automotive Electronics,* Sams, 1970; *The Manual of Car Electronics,* Foulsham, 1971; *Twenty-Five Solid-State Projects,* Hayden, 1970; *How It Works: Illustrated,* Harper, 1974; *Solid-State Ignition Systems,* Sams, 1974; *The Electronics Quiz Book,* Sams, 1975; *The Build-It Book of Fun Electronics,* Sams, 1975; *The Build-It Book of Car Electronics,* Sams, 1976; *The Build-It Book of Home Electronics,* Sams, 1976; *The Build-It Book of Security Electronics,* Sams, 1976; *The Reston Encyclopedia of Biomedical Engineering Terms,* Reston, 1977; *Van Nostrand Reinhold Illustrated Guide to Power Tools,* Van Nostrand, 1978; *Home Wiring: It's a Cinch,* Prentice-Hall, 1979.

Contributor to *Popular Science Homeowner's Encyclopedia,* Fuller & Dees, 1974. Contributor of articles to periodicals, including *Popular Science Monthly, Popular Mechanics, Family Handyman,* and *Journal of American Hospital Association.*

WORK IN PROGRESS: Van Nostrand Reinhold Guide to Hand Tools, publication by Van Nostrand.

SIDELIGHTS: Whalen told *CA:* "Samuel Johnson said: 'No man but a blockhead ever wrote except for money.' For motivation, I would have to agree that Dr. Johnson's argument is powerful and, in my case, true. That aside, however, writing *is* a peculiarly satisfying craft. Especially when practiced in the how-to field. Surprisingly, this includes almost every phase of human existence and endeavor. We must all learn 'how-to,' from the moment of birth. Learning pervades our lives. I enjoy learning, digesting, researching and then, milling, refining and expressing information in print, to help others see the simplicity of things and processes, which seem at first, complex. Technology and investigative efforts dump so many devices and techniques at the thresholds of our minds. Yet, each must be shaped to pass through the 'doorway' of our perception, experience, and understanding, before we can acquire it as useful knowledge. That, to me, is the writer's job.

"I've grappled with the exquisite subtleties of cardiac catheterization, the mysteries of flight, the intricacies of automotives, and the 'electronification' of automobiles, the inner workings of our bodies and our mechanisms—always, the veil of uncertainty that clouds each subject and makes it seem complicated, lifts suddenly, exposing the true simplicity of the subject and the 'way to go' in expressing it to my readers.

"This grappling, this struggle, is the hand-over-hand, knee-banging, and muscle-wrenching toil that makes writing so much like mountain-climbing. But in the exhiliration of the view from the peak, with all about me in order and beauty, what matter how great the struggle? There is always another subject . . . waiting, like a mountain. And, I am eager to climb."

* * *

WHEELER, Hugh (Callingham) 1912-
(Q. Patrick, Patrick Quentin, Jonathan Stagge)

PERSONAL: Born March 19, 1912, in London, England; naturalized U.S. citizen; son of Harold (a civil servant) and Florence (Scammell) Wheeler. *Education:* University of London, B.A., 1932. *Home:* Twin Hills Farm, Monterey, Mass. 02145. *Agent:* William Morris, 1350 Avenue of the Americas, New York, N.Y. 10019.

CAREER: Novelist; playwright. *Military service:* Served in U.S. Army Medical Corps. *Member:* Dramatists Guild. *Awards, honors:* Edgar Allen Poe award, 1963, 1973; Antoinette Perry award, 1973, for "A Little Night Music," 1974, for "Candide," and 1979, for "Sweeney Todd"; Drama Critics Circle award, 1973, for "A Little Night Music," 1974, for "Candide," 1975, for "Pacific Overtures" (with Hohn Weidmann), and 1979, for "Sweeney Todd"; Drama Desk award, 1973, for "A Little Night Music," 1974, for "Candide," and 1979, for "Sweeney Todd"; Outer Critics Award, 1979, for "Sweeney Todd."

WRITINGS—Plays: *Big Fish, Little Fish* (first produced in New York City at the ANTA Theatre, March 15, 1961), Random House, 1961, also published in *Broadway's Beautiful Losers,* edited by Marilyn Stasio, Delacorte, 1972; *Look: We've Come Through!* (first produced in New York City at the Hudson Theatre on October 25, 1961), Dramatists Play Service, 1963, sound recording of Chicago Radio Theatre's production, All-Media Dramatic Workshop, 1976; "Rich Little Rich Girl" (adaptation of a play by Miguel Mihura and Alvaro deLaiglesia), first produced in Philadelphia at the Walnut Street Theatre on November 14, 1964; *We Have Always Lived in the Castle* (adaptation of the novel by Shirley Jackson; first produced in New York at the Ethel Barrymore Theatre on October 19, 1966), Dramatists Play Service, 1967.

Musicals: *A Little Night Music* (adaptation of a film by Ingmar Bergman, with music and lyrics by Stephen Sondheim; first produced in New York City at the Shubert Theatre on February 25, 1973), Dodd, Mead, 1974; (with Joseph Stein) "Irene" (adaptation of the play by James Montgomery, with music by Harry Tierney, lyrics by Joseph McCarthy, adaptation by Harry Rigby), first produced in New York City at the Minskoff Theatre, on March 13, 1973; "Candide" (adaptation of the novel by Voltaire, with music by Leonard Bernstein, lyrics by Richard Wilbur), first produced in New York City at Brooklyn Academy of Music, on December 20, 1973; (with John Weidmann) "Pacific Overtures" (with music and lyrics by Sondheim), first produced in New York City at the Winter Garden Theatre on January 11, 1976; "Sweeney Todd" (adaptation of play by Christopher Bond; music and lyrics by Sondheim), first produced on Broadway at Uris Theatre, March 1, 1979.

Screenplays: (With Peter Viertel) "Five Miles to Midnight," United Artists, 1962; "Something for Everyone," National General, 1970; (with Jay Presson Allen) "Cabaret," Allied Artists, 1972; (with Allen) "Travels With My Aunt," Metro-Goldwyn-Mayer (MGM), 1972. Also author of "A Little Night Music," an adaptation of the original musical, 1977, and "Nijinski," to be released.

Novels: *The Crippled Muse,* Hart Davis, 1951, Rinehart, 1952.

Under pseudonym Q. Patrick, with Richard Wilson Webb: *Death Goes to School,* Smith & Haas, 1936; *Death for Dear Clara,* Simon & Schuster, 1937; *File on Fenton and Farr,* Morrow, 1937; *File on Claudia Cragge,* Morrow, 1938; *Death and the Maiden,* Simon & Schuster, 1939; *Return to the Scene,* Simon & Schuster, 1941 (published in England as *Death in Bermuda,* Cassell, 1941); *Danger Next Door,* Cassell, 1951; *The Girl on the Gallows,* Fawcett, 1954. Also co-author of *The Grindle Nightmare,* 1935, and *Famous Trials.*

Under pseudonym Patrick Quentin; all mystery novels: *A*

Puzzle for Fools, Simon & Schuster, 1936; *Puzzle for Players,* Simon & Schuster, 1938; *Puzzle for Puppets,* Simon & Schuster, 1944; *Puzzle for Wantons,* Simon & Schuster, 1945; *Puzzle for Fiends,* Simon & Schuster, 1946; *Puzzle for Pilgrims,* Simon & Schuster, 1947; *Run to Death,* Simon & Schuster, 1948; *The Followers,* Simon & Schuster, 1950; *Black Widow,* Simon & Schuster, 1952 (published in England as *Fatal Woman,* Gollancz, 1953); *My Son, the Murderer,* Simon & Schuster, 1954 (published in England as *The Wife of Ronald Sheldon,* Gollancz, 1954); *The Man With Two Wives,* Simon & Schuster, 1955; *The Man in the Net,* Simon & Schuster, 1956; *Suspicious Circumstances,* Simon & Schuster, 1957; *Shadow of Guilt,* Simon & Schuster, 1958; *The Green-Eyed Monster,* Simon & Schuster, 1960; *The Ordeal of Mrs. Snow,* Random House, 1962; *Family Skeletons,* Random House, 1964.

Under pseudonym Jonathan Stagge, some written jointly with Richard Wilson Webb, some written solely by Wheeler: *Murder Gone to Earth,* Joseph, 1936, published as *The Dogs Do Bark,* Doubleday, 1937; *Murder or Mercy,* Joseph, 1937, published as *Murder by Prescription,* Doubleday, 1938; *The Stars Spell Death,* Doubleday, 1939 (published in England as *Murder in the Stars,* Joseph, 1940); *Turn of the Table,* Doubleday, 1940 (published in England as *Funeral for Five*), Joseph, 1940; *The Yellow Taxi,* Doubleday, 1942 (published in England as *Call a Hearse,* Joseph, 1942); *The Scarlet Circle,* Doubleday, 1943 (published in England as *Light From a Lantern,* Joseph, 1943); *Death, My Darling Daughters,* Doubleday, 1945 (published in England as *Death and the Dear Girls,* Joseph, 1946); *Death's Old Sweet Song,* Doubleday, 1946; *The Three Fears,* Doubleday, 1949.

Short stories; all under pseudonym Patrick Quentin: *The Ordeal of Mrs. Snow and Other Stories,* Gollancz, 1961, Random House, 1962; *Family Skeletons,* Random House, 1965.

Contributor of short stories and novelettes to national magazines under all three pseudonyms.

SIDELIGHTS: Until 1961, Hugh Wheeler wrote detective novels, published under three different pseudonyms; until about 1950, these were collaborative efforts, written with Richard Wilson Webb. So successful was the Wheeler/Webb partnership that Wheeler has always been able to support himself by writing and has been able to live in a variety of places—including France, Italy, North Africa, Mexico, Brazil, and the West Indies, as well as Massachusetts, where he now resides.

Reaction to *The Crippled Muse,* the one novel published under his own name, clarifies Wheeler's popular appeal. The *New York Herald Tribune Book Review* said: "He writes about people with maturity and he shows a particular understanding of the creative person. This, plus an amiable sort of humor, make his novel genuinely enjoyable despite its hackneyed structure." Similarly, Walter Havighurst wrote in the *Saturday Review* that "the meaning of 'The Crippled Muse' is all but crowded out by its plot, but no one is likely to put this novel down"; and in the *New Statesman and Nation,* Jocelyn Brooke wrote that the book was, "for all its faults, intelligently written and easy to read."

In 1961, Wheeler turned to writing for the legitimate theatre and was rewarded with Broadway productions of his first two plays. Not only did "Big Fish, Little Fish" star Jason Robards, Jr., but it was staged by Sir John Gielgud. Howard Taubman, who reviewed the play for the *New York Times,* found flaws—an occasional false ring in characterization, gratuitous wisecracking—but he also found "a current of honest feeling and human warmth" and felt that Wheeler had written with "beguiling integrity." "Look: We've Come Through" was staged by Jose Quintero and featured Burt Reynolds in a supporting role, and like "Big Fish, Little Fish," it got mixed reviews. Howard Taubman, again in the *New York Times,* said that "the writing has the accuracy and unexpectedness of a thoughtful mind and appreciative ear" but concluded that "the play has not been shaped into a dramatic sum that matches individual sections."

Wheeler's first hit came in 1973 with "A Little Night Music," which was based on an old Ingmar Bergman film, "Smiles of a Summer Night." Marilyn Stasio thought Wheeler's adaptation "elegant," while Clive Barnes considered it "uncommonly urbane and witty." "Sweeney Todd" is Wheeler's latest work for the stage. "As theatre, 'Sweeney Todd' is fascinating but also elitist in the extreme," Sylvia Drake commented in *Los Angeles Times.* Richard Eder compared it to Brecht-Weill's "Three-Penny Opera." "There is more of artistic energy, creative personality and plain excitement in 'Sweeney Todd' . . . than in a dozen average musicals," he remarked.

CA INTERVIEWS THE AUTHOR

Hugh Wheeler was interviewed by phone June 26, 1979, at his home in Monterey, Massachusetts.

CA: You've written stories, novels, plays, and screenplays. Do you think of yourself now as primarily one kind of writer?

WHEELER: Well, one of my rather ridiculous efforts was to try to write in every medium, which I've somewhat self-consciously done. But of course now I see that theatre is by far the most important. I suppose it's because I'm so happy with my collaborators that I think of the musical theatre as number one on my list. And I don't think I would be interested in writing novels anymore. Then again I do write movies and will continue to do that. Just recently I'm going into the opera field with Hal Prince. We have discovered a Kurt Weill opera called "Silverlake" ("Silbeisee") which had only one performance in Germany, first, because Hitler threw it out, and second, because it had about a three-hour-long, very metaphysical Georg Kaiser sort of expressionist play with it that nobody could understand anyway. So we hope that we are rescuing the music from that. We have already done it, and although the plot is more or less the same, I've written an entirely new book, which Hal will direct at New York City Opera next April [1980]. There's a new chamber opera house opening in Kennedy Center in Washington, and we are opening it with a thing we've put together out of Mozart's "Impresario" and the Karl Maria von Weber "Abu Hassan," which is a one-act Arabian Nights sort of thing. There again, like the Kurt Weill, the Mozart "Impresario" has four marvelous arias, and in 1812 it was put together with a long and impossible play, and nobody's ever known quite what to do with it. So now I've written about a forty-minute libretto, which will involve the Mozart opera, about a company who are rehearsing to put on the second opera, which is "Abu Hassan." The first act is with the Mozart arias, all the catastrophies impinging on trying to get the opera on that night, and the second act is the von Weber opera. I don't know how that's going to come out, but that's my second opera, and we open on July 10th [1979] at Kennedy Center. So much for my versatility.

CA: You've written under three pseudonyms that I know of, and maybe there are more.

WHEELER: There are not. That is rather complicated, and

certainly boring, but when I was very young there was a pseudonym called Q. Patrick, and that one was used by a man called Richard Webb and somebody else, a girl. Together they had written about four mysteries. And then the girl went away and got married, leaving Webb as half a mystery-story writer. That was my first job. He hired me to take her place, so the Q. Patricks, of which I did about five, were in collaboration with him. Then that partnership dissolved, but because it was fairly well-known, I switched the name around into Patrick Quentin. I then continued as Patrick Quentin on my own. Now the Jonathan Stagge is the third one. That again is rather a bastard, because the first Jonathan Stagges were written with that same Mr. Webb. About half-way through the Jonathan Stagges he went away, and the last Jonathan Stagges were by me alone. I've written one novel—*The Crippled Muse*—under my own name, which I just wrote because I felt like it.

CA: But aside from that, you preferred to use the pseudonyms?

WHEELER: No I didn't. I was very young when I got into them, and nobody told me I wasn't meant to be a mystery-story writer. So I just went on doing it until I wrote a play called "Big Fish, Little Fish"—just because it came out. I wrote it in about six days, and there it was, and I was very lucky because the first people who saw it put it on. Then I thought, why do I have to be a mystery writer just because somebody said I should? So I switched from that.

CA: Did you ever find yourself working on a novel and a play at the same time?

WHEELER: There was an overlapping period indeed when I wrote "Big Fish, Little Fish" in a brief period of time. I was halfway through one of the Patrick Quentins. So I finished that. You can call that an overlap.

CA: Did that present any problems?

WHEELER: No, I don't think so. I'm quite good at doing several things at once. Now I'm getting a play ready for Broadway, and I'm doing a movie at the same time. That doesn't confuse me.

CA: Did you want to write plays long before you actually started writing them?

WHEELER: It really began suddenly, but it seemed by accident that practically all my friends for the ten years before I went into the theatre were theatrical people. It never occurred to me to join them, but I lived in a world of theatrical people, so that obviously had something to do with it.

CA: Has your screenwriting taken you to Hollywood?

WHEELER: I've been in Hollywood many times for those ghastly conferences and what have you, but I can't work in California at all. I don't know why. It's absolutely impossible for me. I go there to have meetings, and then I come back here and write movies. I'm one of those people who can't work in California. I've been fairly shrewd, because all the movies I've done have been in Europe. They've been American movies, but they've been on location in Europe, which I'm very happy about. There's one called "Something for Everyone," which is a sort of cult movie now. I did that with Hal Prince and Angela Lansbury in Austria and Bavaria. Then I did a movie called "Travels With My Aunt," which was just sort of any old movie. And then I worked with Bob Fosse on "Cabaret," a major movie, in Germany. But there was this tremendously elaborate Writers Guild thing about credit. I didn't get the writer's credit, and everybody was so cross that they gave me my own credit, equally large and very mysterious because my name appears on the screen with nothing by it, no indication of why I should be there at all. But, in fact, I went right through it with Bob Fosse, and we worked together very well. Then I did a rather ill-fated movie of "A Little Night Music" last year with Hal Prince, again in Austria. I think it's very good, but there was some terrible, mysterious backbiting, so it practically never got released. I've just done with Herb Ross a movie called "Nijinsky," about Nijinsky and Diaghilev, with Alan Bates. And that has been finished now. I haven't seen a rough draft yet, but it is finished. I'm quite happy about the script, and Herb Ross seems to be, too. People have been trying to do it for years, but it never worked. And now, for better or worse, we've done it. I feel Alan Bates will be splendid.

CA: You've won several awards. Is there one that you are proudest of?

WHEELER: Maybe I shouldn't talk about awards. I think they are lovely to get, but just because that means you haven't *not* got them. I've had three Tony awards, but "Sweeney Todd" is the one, all things considered, we're all proudest of. Of course, it's nice getting the New York Drama Critics Circle Award, which I've gotten four times. You can only believe that they must think you're all right if they keep on giving you awards. I've got others, too, but we won't drag them in. I am against awards in that I think if five totally different things have been nominated, it's awfully unfair to decide one is the best when the others are not trying to be what it is. So I don't really approve of them, but so long as they are around, I love to win them.

CA: What are your work habits?

WHEELER: I get up very early in the morning. I work in the country or I go to an obscure island in the Caribbean in the winter, and I get up around six and work until about eleven, and that's my work day. Unless I'm in rehearsal. In rehearsal you never know when you've got to be rewriting or what hours of the night or in what town.

CA: Do you write with specific goals?

WHEELER: No. I just sit down and hope that something will come out, but I am very rigorous about going to my desk at the set time. Occasionally, of course, something takes longer, and that's too bad. So in that case I go on longer.

CA: How does one happen to write the book for a play like "A Little Night Music"? Are you asked by someone to do it?

WHEELER: Well, in that case Steve [Stephen Sondheim] and Hal thought it would be nice to do a waltz musical and called me in and said would I like to do a waltz musical, and I said fine. So we looked at a lot of properties like Renoir films and then decided that the one we could jump off from was Bergman's thing, "Smiles of a Summer Night." In such a collaboration we have a few conferences and I go up and write it as if it were a play. That's the first draft. I bring it back and give it to Steve, with, of course, Hal's supervision, and Steve finds what aspects of it he would like to musicalize. I don't instruct him to put in a song here and put in a song there. I just present it exactly as a play. Then he, as it were, cannibalizes it as he needs it. He decides a certain scene is going to be a song, and therefore it's no longer a scene, it's a song. But it's always that way, particularly with us. Again with "Candide" it was Hal Prince who suggested doing it and I said okay.

CA: You have some assurance then that a play is going to be produced when you start writing it?

WHEELER: That's always been true in my case. I've been very lucky.

CA: Do you get involved with the actual stage production?

WHEELER: Absolutely. I'm there every day from the first day of rehearsal. Every now and then I go away for a couple of days, but I am there all the time. And I'm constantly there for Hal. If either one of us gets an idea, we bend and adapt as we sit in rehearsal. Not so much true with Steve, of course, because it's far more difficult and complicated to change music. You've got to get new music, and it's got to be arranged and printed. Hal and I can change a scene in five minutes, but changing a song is far more cumbersome.

CA: How do you approach the writing of a mystery novel? Do you have the plot outlined completely before you start writing?

WHEELER: They all come in very different ways. Sometimes one thinks of a situation. Somebody will get killed because of the tensions involved in the situation. And then sometimes you don't really know how you're going to end it. You get it started, and you know how people feel about each other and what they might do as you are going. It resolves itself. It isn't terribly rigid; I never wrote that way. Quite often whatever the gimmicks were and who did it gets changed in my mind when I'm about two-thirds of the way through. It's really a situation that one looks for to start with.

CA: Do you ever take a vacation from writing?

WHEELER: I don't know that I ever have. I feel I can do the two things at once, you see. I work only part of the day, and the rest of the day I'm relaxing. I go to the Caribbean every winter for two or three months and work in the morning, and what is more relaxing than just lying around on beaches? And I do so much of the movies abroad, and then we go over and put on a musical in London, or go to Vienna to put on "Candide." So I get all sorts of holidays disguised as business.

CA: How did you become a United States citizen?

WHEELER: It never for a moment occurred to me I would live anywhere else. But I was in the American army in World War II, and by some sort of confusion people in the company told me to report to Barracks Y at 10 a.m. one day. Apparently because I was in the army, I was eligible for citizenship. It happened like that. My intention would have been the same, but it just happened that way.

CA: Have you always done a lot of traveling?

WHEELER: I've done a terrible lot of traveling. I did one book a year, by and large, when I was on detective stories; that meant six months of writing, which I would do here or wherever, and I would travel for the other six months. So for a long period of time I went everywhere. Now that I'm in the theatre, it's not so easy to delegate time, because I never know when I'm wanted where.

CA: Your life seems to be alternately hectic and peaceful.

WHEELER: Very much so. I treasure this place, which is a thousand miles from anywhere. And my focus is where I want to be. Here is where I work, and then I go off and do all these other things. I know I can always come back here.

CA: Did you do any other jobs before you became a successful writer?

WHEELER: No, I've never done a day's other work. I've never been hired by anybody.

CA: What are your current writing plans?

WHEELER: In theory I would like to do a movie and either a musical or a play a year, but plays are so difficult these days. Nobody knows how to write an American play, including me. Even with musicals now, the costs are so staggering that the gamble is absolutely insane. I can't imagine that people will be willing much longer to give us any money to do it. A musical costs over a million dollars to put on and you have to have another two or three hundred thousand dollars for advertising and promotion after it is open. And then with the stagehands and orchestral musicians always wanting bigger and bigger wages, and indeed with equity with actors—it's almost reached the point where success is no longer feasible. We're doing very well with "Sweeney Todd," but it's not going to be tomorrow that the investors are going to get their money back. It costs a fortune just to keep it running. Thank heavens it's a success.

CA: Do you plan to try anything that you've never attempted at all before?

WHEELER: I want to. Theoretically that's what I'd like to do, but I can't think what it would be.

CA: Maybe a short poem?

WHEELER: I'll think about that. Actually, I did one when I was five, if that's valid. I remember it:

Oriana, oh my love,
Canst thou hear the cooing dove?

BIOGRAPHICAL/CRITICAL SOURCES: New Statesman and Nation, November 10, 1951; *New York Herald Tribune Book Review,* March 23, 1952; *Saturday Review,* April 26, 1952; *New York Times,* March 16, 1961, October 26, 1961, February 26, 1973, May 17, 1979; *Cue,* March 3, 1973; March 2, 1979; *Los Angeles Times,* March 2, 1979.

—Interview by Jean W. Ross

* * *

WHITEHOUSE, Arch
See WHITEHOUSE, Arthur George Joseph

* * *

WHITEHOUSE, Arthur George Joseph 1895-1979 (Arch Whitehouse)

OBITUARY NOTICE—See index for *CA* sketch: Born December 11, 1895, in Northampton, England; died November 15, 1979, in Lincoln Park, N.J. Author, cartoonist, screenwriter, and journalist. Whitehouse drew upon his experiences as an aerial gunner in World War I and as a correspondent in World War II to write more than forty books on warfare and aviation. Among the books he produced are *Hell in the Heavens, Bombers in the Sky, Squadron 44,* and *Wings for the Chariots.* Before he began writing about the military, Whitehouse had worked as a sports writer and cartoonist on the *Passaic Daily News* and *Elizabeth Daily Journal.* Obituaries and other sources: Arch Whitehouse, *The Fledgling,* Duell, Sloan & Pearce, 1965; *Authors of Books for Young People,* 2nd edition, Scarecrow, 1971; *New York Times,* November 16, 1979.

WHITING, John (Robert) 1917-1963

OBITUARY NOTICE: Born November 15, 1917, in Salisbury, England; died June 16, 1963, of cancer. Playwright and critic. Whiting was a forerunner of the "new wave" in English theatre. His style is infused with an air of hopelessness and is characterized by the use of obscure imagery with heavy philosophical and religious overtones. Whiting's innovative plays, severely criticized in his lifetime, include "Saint's Day," "A Penny for a Song," and "The Devils." He also wrote criticism such as *John Whiting on Theatre* and *The Art of the Dramatist.* Obituaries and other sources: *The New Century Handbook of English Literature,* revised edition, Appleton, 1967; *Longman Companion to Twentieth Century Literature,* Longman, 1970; *The Penguin Companion to English Literature,* McGraw, 1971; *Modern World Drama: An Encyclopedia,* Dutton, 1972; *A Concise Encyclopedia of the Theatre,* Osprey, 1974; *World Authors, 1950-1970,* Wilson, 1975.

* * *

WHITTON, Charlotte (Elizabeth) 1896-1975

OBITUARY NOTICE: Born March 8, 1896, in Renfrew, Ontario, Canada; died January 25, 1975, in Ottawa, Ontario, Canada. Politician, feminist, social worker, journalist, and author of studies of welfare conditions. Whitton was the first woman mayor of Ottawa, a post she held from 1951 to 1956 and from 1960 to 1964. Before her entry into public life, she had worked for a number of social agencies, including a fifteen-year stint as the executive director of the Canadian Welfare Council. Most of her writings are connected with her interest in social work. She produced many pamphlets on that topic and edited the journal *Canadian Welfare.* She also contributed to magazines and wrote a column for several Canadian newspapers, including the *Ottawa Citizen* and *Halifax Herald Chronicle.* Among her books are *A Hundred Years A-Fellin'* and *The Dawn of Ampler Life.* Obituaries and other sources: *Current Biography,* Wilson, 1953, March, 1975; *Who's Who in Canada,* International Press, 1973; *Who's Who,* 126th edition, St. Martin's, 1974; *New York Times,* January 26, 1975.

* * *

WHYBRAY, Roger Norman 1923-

PERSONAL: Born July 26, 1923, in East Molesey, Surrey, England; son of Walter Wilfred (a schoolmaster) and Carrie Evelyn Whybray; married Helene Francoise Weill (died April 24, 1978); married Mary Elizabeth Dudman Carmack (an adviser on remedial education), May 5, 1979; children: (first marriage) Peter Basil. *Education:* Keble College, Oxford, B.A., 1944, M.A., 1947, D.Phil., 1962. *Home:* 4 Chestnut Ave., Hessle, North Humberside HU13 ORH, England. *Office:* Department of Theology, University of Hull, Hull HU6 7RX, England.

CAREER: Ordained priest, 1947; assistant curate of Church of England in Basingstoke, England, 1946-48; General Theological Seminary, New York, N.Y., fellow and instructor in biblical Hebrew and the Old Testament, 1948-50; curator of Church of England at Marbourne and part-time lecturer in the Old Testament at Queen's College, Birmingham, England, 1950-52; Central Theological College, Tokyo, Japan, professor of Old Testament, 1952-65; University of Hull, Hull, England, lecturer, 1965-69, reader, 1969-78, professor of Hebrew and Old Testament studies, 1978—. *Member:* Society for Old Testament Study, United Society for the Propagation of the Gospel (former head of overseas committee; member of council; head of personnel group), Society of Biblical Literature, Carlton Club. *Awards, honors:* Award from Japan Foundation.

WRITINGS: Aendai no Kyukaku Seisho Kenkyu Aaikan (title means "A Survey of Modern Study of the Old Testament"), Kyobunkwan, 1961; *Wisdom in Proverbs,* S.C.M. Press, 1965; *The Succession Narrative,* S.C.M. Press, 1968; *The Heavenly Counsellor in Isaiah XI 13-14,* Cambridge University Press, 1971; *The Book of Proverbs,* Cambridge University Press, 1972; *The Intellectual Tradition in the Old Testament,* De Gruyter, 1974; *Isaiah 40-66,* editors, *New Century Bible,* Oliphants, 1975; *Thanksgiving for a Liberated Prophet,* University of Sheffield Press, 1978. Contributor of articles and reviews to theology journals. Editor of *Book List* for Society for Old Testament Study, 1973—.

WORK IN PROGRESS: Research on Isaiah, with a book expected to result; research on Ecclesiastes and on Old Testament wisdom literature in general.

SIDELIGHTS: Whybray comments: "My career is concerned with Old Testament research and Biblical Hebrew. I am competent in French, German, and Japanese, in which, although not entirely competent in the written language, I lectured for thirteen years. Apart from competence in ancient Hebrew, I am familiar with Aramaic, Syriac, Akkadian, Ugaritic, Latin, and Greek."

* * *

WIECKERT, Jeanne E. (Lentz) 1939-

PERSONAL: Born February 1, 1939, in Chicago, Ill.; daughter of Stanley and Augusta (Borne) Lentz; married Warren G. Wieckart, 1959; children: Kim, William. *Education:* University of Northern Illinois, B.S., 1960; University of Northern Colorado, M.S., 1974. *Home:* 4338 North 109th St., Lafayette, Colo. 80026. *Office:* Denver Public Schools, 2475 West 29th St., Denver, Colo. 80211.

CAREER: Chicago Public Schools, Chicago, Ill., teacher, 1962-69; Denver Public Schools, Denver, Colo., media specialist, 1969—. *Member:* American Library Association.

WRITINGS: (With Irene Wood Bell) *Basic Media Skills Through Games,* Libraries Unlimited, 1979.

WORK IN PROGRESS: Related Media Skills Through Games.

SIDELIGHTS: Wieckert commented: "*Basic Media Skills Through Games* has evolved through a process of attempting to 'reach' inner city students. Conventional approaches to teaching skills fail to motivate students, resulting in little retention or facts and concepts. The successful game approach provides positive experiences and hopefully, makes teaching and learning more enjoyable."

* * *

WIEHL, Andrew (M.) 1904-

PERSONAL: Born March 23, 1904, in Passau, Germany; came to the United States in 1923, naturalized citizen, 1960; son of Andrew (a butcher) and Anna (Greimel) Wiehl; married Mildred Waranka, May 12, 1931; children: Vernoghn Wiehl Haradon, Maryann Wiehl Thurlow. *Education:* Attended high school in Nuremberg, Germany. *Home:* 920 Southeast 33rd Ave., Portland, Ore. 97214.

CAREER: In electronics, 1930-71; owner of West Slope Radio & T.V., 1971—; writer and inventor, 1971—. Director of activities for senior citizens and the handicapped, 1975—. Past president of West Slope Boosters Club. *Member:* Oregon Electronics and Television Association, German Aid Society.

WRITINGS: Creative Visualization: How to Unlock the Secret Powers of Mind and Body for Full Self-Realization and Happiness, Greenwich Press, 1958, reprinted, Llewellyn, 1973; *Develop Your Psychic Gift in Three Months* (home study course), privately printed, 1971. Contributor to newspapers.

WORK IN PROGRESS: Another book.

SIDELIGHTS: Wiehl has been practicing creative visualization, or constructive thinking, since his youth, and it is to this that he attributes his success in business and as a writer and inventor. In his book he has set down the rules for constructive thinking and has provided exercises to practice. He also discusses the relationships between good and evil, death and reincarnation, hope and fear, and the conscious and unconscious mind.

Wiehl told CA: "In 1946, after reading *The Message of a Master* by John McDonald, I realized that I had been using that system of which Mr. McDonald wrote ever since I was nine years old without understanding its value and importance. It was 'Visualization' (only he didn't call it that). Now I understand the reason 'WHY' in 1923 I was able to leave Germany, where my chances were one in a million. Unemployment was at its record high and so was inflation. I was broke but had a will, determination, and a goal to go to America.

"One day while at work I was suddenly startled by a voice saying, 'Andrew get your ship now or never.' Who spoke to me? There was no one within fifteen feet? I left work immediately and got me a ship. . . . I signed a contract with the captain [that] read from Germany to the far East and back to Germany. Before sailing to the far East we stopped in Newport News, Va. Some of our crew left ship and signed on [with] some other ship. Here was my chance. I asked the captain to change my contract, which he was unwilling to do, but finally gave in. The contract read from U.S.A. to the far East and back to the U.S.A. I also received double pay.

"That book was an eye opener. I went to work and devised my own system. . . . To test everything out I served as my own guinea pig. I wrote that book in order to pass on the information for the younger generation."

* * *

WIELAND, George F(red) 1936-

PERSONAL: Born July 14, 1936, in New York, N.Y.; son of Gottlieb and Martha Wieland; married Sharon Kane, February 2, 1959; children: Susan, Sandra, Michael, Patience. *Education:* Stanford University, A.B., 1958; University of Michigan, Ph.D., 1965. *Home:* 820 Granger Ave., Ann Arbor, Mich. 48104.

CAREER: University of Michigan, Ann Arbor, assistant study director at Institute for Social Research, 1961-65, study director, 1965-66, 1968-69; Guy's Hospital Medical School, London, England, research associate, 1966-69; Vanderbilt University, Nashville, Tenn., assistant professor, 1969-73, associate professor of management, 1973-74; University of Michigan, associate research scientist in public health, 1974-76; independent consultant and free-lance writer, 1976—. *Member:* American Psychological Association, American Sociological Association, Academy of Management, Authors Guild.

WRITINGS: (Editor with Hilary Leigh) *Changing Hospitals,* Tavistock Publications, 1971; (with Robert A. Ullrich) *Organizations: Behavior, Design, and Change,* Irwin, 1976, revised edition, Irwin, 1980.

WORK IN PROGRESS: Two books on management in health care organizations.

SIDELIGHTS: Wieland writes: "My general interests are in the social-psychological study of individuals in organizations, and individuals assimilating or adapting to modern society. What are the human costs of living in an organizational society? How are integrity, morality, and social responsibility affected by using people as means toward organizational ends? Is the attempt to humanize the work place an answer, or part of the problem?"

BIOGRAPHICAL/CRITICAL SOURCES: Academy of Management Review, January, 1976.

* * *

WILDER, Billy
See WILDER, Samuel

* * *

WILDER, Samuel 1906-
(Billy Wilder)

PERSONAL: Professionally known as Billy Wilder; born June 22, 1906, in Sucha, Austria (now part of Poland); came to the United States in 1934, naturalized citizen, 1939; son of Max (a businessman) and Eugenie (Dittler) Wilder; married Judith Coppicus, December 20, 1936 (divorced, 1947); married Audrey Young, June 30, 1949; children: Victoria. *Education:* Attended University of Vienna, 1924. *Politics:* Democrat. *Religion:* Jewish. *Residence:* Los Angeles, Calif. *Agent:* Paul Kohner, Paul Kohner-Michael Levy Agency, 9169 West Sunset Blvd., Los Angeles, Calif. 90069.

CAREER: Journalist, screenwriter, producer, and director of motion pictures. *Die Stunde* (newspaper), Vienna, Austria, reporter and feature writer, 1925-26; free-lance writer and contributor of articles to German publications, including *Berliner Zeitung am Mittag, Die Nachtausgabe, Tempo,* and *Boersenkurier,* Berlin, Germany, 1927-29; UFA (motion picture co.), Berlin, screenwriter, 1928-33; immigrated to Paris, France, 1933; wrote and co-directed French motion picture "Mauvaise Graine," 1933; immigrated to United States, 1934; Paramount Pictures, Hollywood, Calif., screenwriter and director, 1936-54; screenwriter, director, and producer of motion pictures, 1954—. Director of motion pictures, including "The Major and the Minor," 1942, "Double Indemnity," 1944, "The Lost Weekend," 1945, "Sunset Boulevard," 1950, "Ace in the Hole," 1951, "Stalag 17," 1953, "Some Like It Hot," 1959, "The Apartment," 1960, "Irma La Douce," 1963, "Avanti!," 1972, and "Fedora," 1978. *Military service:* U.S. Army, 1945; served as head of film section of Psychological Warfare Division in American Zone in Germany; became colonel.

AWARDS, HONORS: Received Academy Award nominations from Academy of Motion Picture Arts and Sciences, 1939, for "Ninotchka"; 1941, for "Hold Back the Dawn"; 1944, for "Double Indemnity"; 1948, for "A Foreign Affair"; 1951, for "Ace in the Hole"; 1954, for "Sabrina"; 1959, for "Some Like It Hot"; and 1966, for "The Fortune Cookie"; received Academy Awards from Academy of Motion Picture Arts and Sciences, 1945, for best screenplay and best director for "The Lost Weekend"; 1950, for best story and screenplay for "Sunset Boulevard"; and 1960, for best screenplay, best director, and producer of best picture for "The Apartment"; Writers Guild awards from Writers Guild of America, 1957, for "Love in the Afternoon," 1959, for "Some Like It Hot," and 1960, for "The Apartment"; New York Film Critics award, 1960, for "The Apartment."

WRITINGS—Published screenplays; all with I.A.L. Diamond, unless otherwise noted: *Love in the Afternoon,* Enterprise Printers & Stationers, 1957; *Some Like It Hot,* New American Library, 1959; *Irma La Douce: A Screenplay,* Tower, 1963; *The Apartment and The Fortune Cookie: Two Screenplays,* Praeger, 1971; (with Charles Brackett and Walter Reisch) *Ninotchka,* Viking, 1972.

Screenplays: "Der Teufelsreporter" (title means "The Devil's Reporter"), Universal (Germany), 1929; "Menschen am Sonntag" (title means "People on Sunday"), Filmstudio Germania, 1929; (with Ludwig Hirschfeld and Kurt Siodmak) "Der Mann, der seinen Moerder sucht" (title means "The Man Who Looked for His Murderer"; adapted from the play by Ernst Neubach), UFA, 1931; (with Paul Franck and Robert Liebmann) "Ihre Hoheit Befiehlt" (title means "Her Highness's Command"), UFA, 1931; (with Franck) "Der falsche Ehemann" (title means "The Wrong Husband"), UFA, 1931; "Emil und die Detektive" (title means "Emil and the Detectives"; adapted from the story by Erich Kastner), UFA, 1931; "Es War Einmal ein Walzer" (title means "Once There Was a Waltz"), Aafa-Film AG, 1932; (with Walter Reisch) "Ein blonder Traum" (title means "A Fairer Dream"), UFA, 1932; (with Max Kolpe) "Das Blaue vom Himmel" (title means "The Blue From the Sky"), Aafa-Film AG, 1932; (with Kolpe) "Madame Wuenscht Keine Kinder" (title means "Madame Wants No Children"; adapted from the novel by Clement Vautel), Lothar-Stark-Film, 1933; (with Franz Schulz) "Was Frauen Traumen" (title means "A Woman's Dreams"; adapted from the novel by Emil Hosler), Superfilm-Hayman, 1933; (with Alexander Esway and H. G. Lustig; also co-director) "Mauvaise Graine" (title means "The Bad Seed"), Compagnie Nouvelle Cinematographique, 1933.

(With Howard I. Young) "Music in the Air" (adapted from the play by Oscar Hammerstein II), Fox, 1934; (with Schulz) "Lottery Lover" (adapted from the story by Siegried M. Lorzig and Maurice Hanline), Fox, 1935; (co-author of screen story) "Champagne Waltz," Paramount, 1936; (with Charles Brackett) "Bluebeard's Eighth Wife" (adapted from the play by Alfred Savoir), Paramount, 1938; (with Brackett) "Midnight," Paramount, 1939; (with Brackett) "What a Life" (adapted from the play by Clifford Goldsmith), Paramount, 1939; (with Brackett and Walter Reisch) "Ninotchka," Metro-Goldwyn-Mayer, 1939.

(Co-author of screen story) "Rhythm on the River," Paramount, 1940; (with Brackett) "Arise, My Love," Paramount, 1940; (with Brackett) "Hold Back the Dawn" (adapted from the novel by Ketti Frings), Paramount, 1941; (co-author of screen story) "Ball of Fire," RKO, 1941; (with Brackett; and director) "The Major and the Minor" (adapted from the play by Edward Chiles Carpenter, "Connie Comes Home," and the short story by Fannie Killbourne, "Sunny Goes Home"), Paramount, 1942; (with Brackett; and director) "Five Graves to Cairo" (adapted from the play by Lajos Biro, "Hotel Imperial"), Paramount, 1943; (with Raymond Chandler; and director) "Double Indemnity" (adapted from the novel by James M. Cain), Paramount, 1944; (with Brackett; and director) "The Lost Weekend" (adapted from the novel by Charles R. Jackson), Paramount, 1945; (with Brackett; and director) "The Emperor Waltz," Paramount, 1948; (with Brackett and Richard L. Breen; and director) "A Foreign Affair," Paramount, 1948.

Also as director: (With Brackett and D. M. Marshman, Jr.) "Sunset Boulevard," Paramount, 1950; (with Lesser Samuels and Walter Newman) "Ace in the Hole" (also released as "The Big Carnival"), Paramount, 1951; (with Edwin Blum) "Stalag 17" (adapted from the play by Donald Bevin and Edmund Trzcinski), Paramount, 1953; (with Samuel Taylor and Ernest Layman) "Sabrina" (adapted from the play by Taylor, "Sabrina Fair"), Paramount, 1954; (with George Axelrod) "The Seven Year Itch" (adapted from the play by Axelrod), Fox, 1955; (with Wendell Mayes) "The Spirit of St. Louis" (adapted from the book by Charles A. Lindbergh), Warner Bros., 1957; (with I.A.L. Diamond) "Love in the Afternoon" (adapted from the novel by Claude Anet, *Ariane*), Allied Artists, 1957; (with Harry Kurnitz) "Witness for the Prosecution" (adapted from the play by Agatha Christie), United Artists, 1957; (with Diamond) "Some Like It Hot" (adapted from the film by Robert Thoeren and M. Logan, "Fanfaren der Liebe" ["Fanfares of Love"]), United Artists, 1959.

Co-author with Diamond; all as director: "The Apartment," United Artists, 1960; "One, Two, Three" (adapted from the play by Ferenc Molnar), United Artists, 1961; "Irma La Douce" (adapted from the musical play by Alexandre Breffort), United Artists, 1963; "Kiss Me, Stupid" (adapted from the play by Anna Bonacci, "L'Ora della Fantasia"), Lopert, 1964; "The Fortune Cookie," United Artists, 1966; "The Private Life of Sherlock Holmes" (based on characters created by Sir Arthur Conan Doyle), United Artists, 1970; "Avanti!" (adapted from the play by Samuel Taylor), United Artists, 1972; "The Front Page" (adapted from the play by Ben Hecht and Charles MacArthur), Universal, 1974; "Fedora" (adapted from the novella by Thomas Tryon, "Fedora," contained in *Crowned Heads*), United Artists, 1978. Contributor to "Under Pressure," 1935.

WORK IN PROGRESS: Two more screenplays.

SIDELIGHTS: According to Maurice Zolotow, Billy Wilder had an unlikely introduction to the film business. During the 1920's, Wilder worked as a journalist and free-lance writer in Berlin, and like every other reporter of the time, he was trying to write scenarios and break into the movie business. One night he inadvertently sold his first screenplay when he agreed to help his landlady's daughter, Lulu, out of an awkward situation. Lulu, who occasionally worked as a prostitute, was similarly engaged for the evening when her jealous boyfriend, Heinz, arrived in a rage. Hoping to work a deception, she urgently transferred her customer to Wilder's room before allowing Heinz into the apartment building, whereupon she proclaimed her innocence. To Wilder's delight, he recognized his naked guest as Galitzenstein, the president of Maxim Films. Wilder at once presented himself as a writer with several scripts to sell, and though the astonished Galitzenstein balked at first, both men overheard Heinz say that he would cut the throat of any man he caught with Lulu. "Here," Wilder directed, "read one of them—now." Weighing the script in his hand, Galitzenstein answered, "I'll buy it. It feels like a good story. Is five hundred marks suitable?" Though the script was apparently never produced, Wilder soon after began writing scenarios for UFA, Germany's front rank movie company.

The German archives credit Wilder with only twelve screenplays, but Wilder claims to have worked on at least fifty scenarios during his five years at UFA. He worked mostly as a ghostwriter for other scenarists who, to meet their monthly quotas, commonly employed a staff of apprentice writers. Wilder's earliest film of record, "Der Teufelsreporter" ("The Devil's Reporter," 1929), is one he chooses to dismiss as "absolute bullshit." Instead, he regards "Menschen am Sonntag" ("People on Sunday," 1929) as his first picture, a film about how two young couples spend a typical Sunday in Berlin. Directed by Robert Siodmak, it was hailed in the German press and made Wilder famous overnight. Wilder recalled: "It was sort of a Rossellini picture, kind of *cinema verite,* for a very good reason: We didn't have the money to have actors, so we had to take people *verite.* And we had to shoot in real backgrounds." Wilder's screenwriting career flourished until 1933, when Adolf Hitler rose to power. After the Reichstag fire in February, Wilder, a Jew, packed all he could into one suitcase and fled to Paris.

Wilder made one film, "Mauvaise Graine" ("Bad Seed"), during his ten-month stay in France. The movie featured Danielle Darrieux in a story about a gang of young automobile thieves in Paris. Limited to a shoestring budget, Wilder worked as both writer and co-director. "We didn't use a single sound stage, most of the interiors were shot in a converted garage, and even the living-room scenes were shot in it," he revealed. Afterwards, he wrote "Pam-Pam," a script designed to draw Hollywood's attention. Columbia Pictures bought the story and hired him to write the screenplay.

Wilder arrived in Hollywood in 1934. When he completed the screenplay six months later, his contract with Columbia expired. He then weathered two years of unemployment. His limited English, culled from American song lyrics, novels, and phrase books, complicated his situation. "I kind of starved for a little bit," he admitted. "I shared a room with Peter Lorre, and we lived on a can of soup a day." At one point, he was reduced to living in the ladies' room of the Chateau Marmont for several weeks. He once managed to sell two synopses to a Paramount producer (in a men's room), but most of his writing assignments fell through. Then, in 1936, he landed a job at Paramount, and on the whim of a producer, he was teamed with Charles Brackett, a novelist and former drama critic for the *New Yorker.*

Wilder and Brackett became Hollywood's most famous writing team. Together they wrote fourteen consecutive hits, including "Ninotchka," "The Lost Weekend," and "Sunset Boulevard." Though *Life* magazine once described them as the "happiest couple in Hollywood," Wilder and Brackett were temperamental opposites who often clashed violently. Wilder, owning a short-fused temper, frequently goaded his partner until Brackett, normally reserved and well-mannered, exploded with anger. "After Charlie had used up his curses he would throw objects—heavy objects—telephone books and inkstands and wastebaskets," wrote Zolotow. "Charlie would try to hit Billy in the head; and he was serious. Behind closed doors, [secretary] Helen Hernandez would tremble, as she listened to them screaming and then the sounds of breaking ashtrays and falling lamps."

During the 1930's, Wilder and Brackett produced some of the best comedies of the decade. After their initial success with "Bluebeard's Eighth Wife," a modern variant on "The Taming of the Shrew," the two screenwriters won additional applause for "Midnight." The movie concerns an American chorus-girl, broke in Paris, who agrees to act as lecherous John Barrymore's companion in his ploy to win back his wife's affections. Commented Charles Higham: "Splendidly upholstered in the best Paramount-Hans Dreier tradition, it gives a stylized but penetrating exposition of an upper class that vanished almost immediately after the film was completed, with the outbreak of World War Two. . . . This film remains one of the peaks of Wilder's career."

In 1939 Wilder and Brackett combined forces with Walter Reisch and director Ernst Lubitsch on a film many describe as a classic, "Ninotchka." An MGM project, the movie was originally conceived as a comic vehicle for Greta Garbo; just as "Anna Christie" had earlier been promoted with the slogan "Garbo Talks," the studio next wanted a picture for the slogan "Garbo Laughs." Melchior Lengyel suggested the story: "Russian girl saturated with Bolshevist ideals goes to fearful, capitalistic, monopolistic Paris. She meets romance and has an uproarious good time. Capitalism not so bad, after all." After an assortment of writers, including Lengyel, failed at the screenplay, Wilder and Brackett joined the staff. They all envisioned a film of typical Lubitsch fare, a sophisticated comedy-romance, but soon recognized that politics lay at the core of "Ninotchka."

Much of "Ninotchka"'s immediate impact stemmed from the social and political realities of the time. The intelligentsia in Hollywood lent at least their sympathetic allegiance to the Communist experiment in Russia, and any criticism of a nation hostile to Hitler's Germany was considered to be in bad taste. On the strength of the character created for Garbo, though, Wilder and the others knew that they would have to confront the Moscow trials, the purges, Five-Year-Plans, and forced collectivization. Until the third act, Lubitsch had remained faithful to the film's comic intentions. But Ninotchka had all along been presented as a woman of conscience and strong ideals who, though in love with a Parisian, would have to give up her lover and return to Moscow. At this point, the movie turns away from romantic comedy and takes the route of political satire. As it was, the indignation "Ninotchka" might have caused all but vanished when Russia signed a friendship treaty with Germany just weeks before the film's premiere. The movie "was praised to the skies," reported Zolotow, and proved to be "the most sublime and passionate political picture ever made in Hollywood."

Frustrated with the treatment some of his scripts received from other directors, Wilder assumed the duty himself in 1942. In an interview with Charles Higham, Wilder revealed: "I had made myself rather unpopular as a writer at Paramount because I would come on the set and they would chase me off it. I was always trying to put them right on misinterpretations. I was known as The Terror: they would say, 'Keep Wilder away from us, he's always raising hell, he wants everything done his way.'" Though Paramount eventually agreed to let him sink or swim as the director of "The Major and the Minor," Wilder knew the studio expected him to fail and thereafter behave himself. "But I was careful," he remarked. "I didn't go out to make a so-called 'artistic success,' I went out to make a commercial picture I wouldn't be ashamed of." Wilder has directed his pictures ever since.

For some critics, the 1944 film "Double Indemnity" is the first of Wilder's major works. "Between 1943 and 1951—the years on which Wilder's critical reputation chiefly rests—his vision grows increasingly more distinct," Higham observed. "The world is ugly and vicious, selfishness and cruelty are dominant in men's lives. Greed is the central impetus of the main characters." In "Double Indemnity," Fred MacMurray plays a corrupt insurance salesman in love with a vicious, sex-driven Barbara Stanwyck. Together they murder Stanwyck's husband for a large insurance settlement, learning afterwards that they cannot collect the money. The film ends with a climactic showdown between the two lovers: Stanwyck shoots MacMurray but doesn't have the heart to finish him off; when she lets the gun drop to the floor, MacMurray guns her down, returns to his office, and bleeds to death as he dictates the story into a machine. "Perhaps the purest, the least compromised and sensationalised of all Wilder's films, *Double Indemnity* retains an undiminished power," asserted Higham. "Aided by John F. Seitz's harsh photography, Wilder liverishly explores a world shorn of beauty and decency."

The making of "Double Indemnity" brought Wilder several unpleasant experiences. After a heated argument with Brackett, Wilder sought out mystery writer Raymond Chandler's assistance. Their sole collaboration dragged on for six months in a plague of arguments, apologies, and tantrums. Then, for aesthetic reasons, Wilder felt he had to scrap the film's original ending, a sequence of scenes he considers one of the two best he ever directed: "We shot the execution of Fred MacMurray, a complete duplication of a gas chamber scene in San Quentin running a reel, the pellets dropping, the whole thing done with the utmost care." Nominated for best screenplay and best director that year, Wilder's final disappointment came when Leo McCarey's "Going My Way" swept the Academy Awards. When McCarey won for best director, Wilder was in such bad humor that "as McCarey strode down to get his statuette, Wilder . . . stuck out his foot and tripped up his colleague, who fell flat on his face," reported Zolotow.

The next Wilder-Brackett venture, "The Lost Weekend," turned out one of the most powerful films ever made on the subject of alcoholism. Its study of four agonizing days in the life of a frustrated, alcoholic writer blazed the way for more American movies about social problems. Wilder again employed the expressionistic talents of cinematographer John Seitz and strived for a stark realism: he used the exterior of New York's Bellevue Hospital, the elevated train clanging across Third Avenue, the litter-strewn streets, and detailed replicas of P. J. Clark's and Bellevue's alcoholic ward. "But the long episodes in which [the writer] Birnam is alone obviously fascinate Wilder the most," Higham noted, "and these are observed with cold detachment: the famous sequence of Birnam's D.T.'s, seeing a bat pounce on a mouse, the blood trickling down the wall, is ferociously directed; a hangover is masterfully conveyed in a single giant close-up of one of his eyes."

Wilder and Brackett finished the film believing they had done their finest work. At a sneak preview in Santa Barbara, however, the audience reacted to the movie with derisive laughter, and some simply walked out of the theatre in disgust. A host of Paramount executives panicked and decided to shelve the film indefinitely. Humiliated by the experience and anxious to get out of Hollywood, Wilder accepted an invitation to join the Psychological Warfare Division of the U.S. Army in Germany.

Wilder left for Germany in May, 1945. Given the rank of colonel, he was to assist in the postwar reconstruction of the German film industry and take responsibility for all theatres and radio stations. His duties also included screening out former Nazis. It was during this time that he learned his mother, grandmother, and stepfather had all been gassed to death in Auschwitz. "After the war," Wilder recalled, "some Germans wanted to put on a passion play, and a carpenter wrote me asking permission to play Jesus. After we screened them we found out that six of the Apostles were Gestapo men and the carpenter was a stormtrooper. I said, 'Yes, as long as the nails are real.'"

When Wilder returned to New York in September, 1945, he found that Paramount had reversed itself and decided to release "The Lost Weekend," after all. The picture not only opened to good reviews but also brought Wilder Academy Award nominations for best screenplay and best director. Among his competition that year was David O. Selznick's "Spellbound" which, in its advertising campaign, featured Gregory Peck and Ingrid Bergman locked in an embrace, with Peck holding a straight-edged razor behind her back. Warner Bros., on the other hand, promoted its pictures under the banner "Good Citizenship With Fine Motion Picture Making." Wilder decided to lampoon them both in an ad that showed he and Brackett embracing, each with a knife at the other's back, and the slogan "Combining Good Citizenship With Good Cutlery." Wilder won his first two Oscars, and "The Lost Weekend" won for best picture.

Wilder immediately exercised his newly-gained power at Paramount. As a tribute to his old mentor, Ernst Lubitsch, he set out to duplicate the famous "Lubitsch touch" for subtlety and delicacy, for sophisticated comedy and romance. He called his musical comedy "The Emperor Waltz," a spare-no-expense movie about the love between an American phonograph salesman and an Austrian countess. Filming on location in the Canadian Rockies of Jasper National Park, he had miles of roadway painted ochre because they photographed "either too darkly or too palely"; for a particular dance number, he imported four thousand daisies and had them all painted cobalt blue because "white photographs too glaringly"; when he wanted a background of magnificent pine trees, he again found nature lacking and imported dozens of California pines at a cost of $20,000; finally, for the sake of a "love scene" between two dogs, he directed his engineers to build a $90,000 island in Lake Leach, complete with earth, rocks, flowers, and trees. Even so, the movie made millions of dollars for Paramount.

"A Foreign Affair" followed "The Emperor Waltz." Both pictures appeared in 1948, but "A Foreign Affair" offended so many people that Paramount quietly withdrew it from circulation. The story concerns an American denazification officer who, while consorting with the former mistress of a Nazi, pretends to court an investigating congresswoman and thereby divert attention from his girlfriend. The movie presented such an unflattering view of the American occupation of Berlin that it was denounced on the floor of the House of Representatives. Paramount came under fire from several quarters, including the Department of Defense which issued a statement condemning the film and extolling the nobility of the American Army. "Looking back from the perspective of almost thirty years, it is evident that *Foreign Affair* was one of the first realistic and honest post-war films," Zolotow commented. "It cut deep and meanly and it told the truth."

Wilder and Brackett's last collaboration was "Sunset Boulevard," a film Mark Spiller called "a magnificent, gloomy cinematic experience." It is the most revered of Wilder's films and has often been described as the best movie ever made about Hollywood. The story tells of an aging, once-popular star of silent movies, Norma Desmond (Gloria Swanson), whose desperate dream of a come-back is lived out in a somber, rundown mansion on Sunset Boulevard. To sustain her delusions of undiminished youth and fame, she becomes the consort of a young gigolo screenwriter, Joe Gillis (William Holden), and faithfully reads the fan mail that, unbeknownst to her, is written by her own butler. When Gillis attempts to leave his benefactress, she shoots him in the back, and he falls dead in her swimming pool. The movie ends with a totally insane Desmond greeting a rush of newsreel cameramen, whom she mistakes for cinematographers. "The film succeeds entirely through the application of a mannered, stylized technique so brilliantly manipulated that disbelief is totally suspended," Higham stated. "*Sunset*

Boulevard is consciously a Big Show; and as such it is never less than dazzling."

"Sunset Boulevard" is replete with celebrated scenes. The movie opens with a riveting shot of Gillis's corpse floating face down in the pool, the camera looking up through the water at the distorted faces of policemen and photographers. As successful as the scene is, Wilder still regrets having to cut out the original beginning, a sequence that, like the gas-chamber scene in "Double Indemnity," was never seen by the general public. The earlier version had Gillis arriving at the Los Angeles morgue where, in the company of eight other bodies, he listens to the corpses tell each other how they died. Then Gillis recounts the story of "Sunset Boulevard," but as Wilder explained, "when we previewed the picture in Chicago and the suburbs of New York people just screamed with laughter." Other famous scenes include the "waxworks" card game, played by silent screen stars Anna Q. Nilsson, Buster Keaton, H. B. Warner, and Gloria Swanson, and a garden funeral staged for Desmond's dead chimpanzee.

The premiere of "Sunset Boulevard" caused a stir in Hollywood, just as Wilder knew it would. In fact, he had taken extraordinary measures to keep the movie a secret; fearing that Paramount would kill the project if they knew about its real subject matter, he sent the studio executives weekly progress reports on a nonexistent film entitled "A Can of Beans." When the picture was completed, Paramount invited the elite of Hollywood to a preview showing in its largest theatre. Related Wilder: "I've never seen so many prominent people at once—the word was out that this was a stunner, you see. After the picture ended there were violent reactions, from excitement to pure horror." Barbara Stanwyck was so moved by the picture that she tearfully fell to her knees in front of Gloria Swanson and kissed the hem of her gown. Louis B. Mayer, however, stormed out of the theatre cursing Paramount, shaking his fist and shouting, "We should horsewhip this Wilder, we should throw him out of this town, he has brought disgrace on the town that is feeding him!" But beyond the bounds of Hollywood, the picture won worldwide acclaim: it was featured on the cover of *Newsweek* and spawned laudatory essays in *Cahiers du Cinema* and *Sight and Sound;* later, it brought Academy Awards to Wilder, Brackett, and D. M. Marshman, Jr. for best original story and screenplay.

One year later, Wilder again shocked his audience with "Ace in the Hole," a film he describes as "the runt of my litter" and "the best picture I ever made." Though it did well in Europe, the movie was such a commercial flop in the United States that Paramount retitled it "The Big Carnival." In this film, according to George Morris, "Wilder goes about as far as he can go without actually embracing nihilism." Kirk Douglas portrays a vicious, cynical reporter, Chuck Tatum, who finds himself banished to a small newspaper in Albuquerque, New Mexico. When he discovers a man trapped inside a cave, he attempts to rebuild his ruined career on the interment story. To keep the story alive, he bribes the sheriff and deliberately delays the rescue operation for a week: a carnival arrives, hot dogs are sold, and songs are composed about the trapped man's ordeal. Then, after the cave-in victim develops pneumonia, Tatum has a change of heart and earnestly tries to free the man. But Tatum's efforts prove futile, the man dies, and his widow stabs Tatum to death with a pair of scissors.

Wilder has pointed out that he based the movie on the facts of the Floyd Collins case in the 1920's: "When we showed the carnival moving in and the songs being composed, and the hot dogs being sold, it was all factual. . . . But people just don't want to see this in a film, the way we really are." Since its release in 1951, "Ace in the Hole" has been rediscovered by several critics and recognized as one of Wilder's strongest achievements. Together Joseph McBride and Michael Wilmington observed: "The narrative has the purity of a mathematical formula, abetted by the almost documentary veracity of the physical details and the characters' behavior. . . . If Wilder does not reach greatness with *Ace in the Hole,* he comes close enough to justify the comparison with [Erich von Stroheim's] *Greed.*" Charles Higham concluded that "as a statement against life, as destructive criticism of human beings, *Ace in the Hole* has rarely been matched in the history of commercial cinema." And Maurice Zolotow noted, "It was a totally uncompromising film at a time when the movies were said to be totally compromised."

After the financial disaster of "Ace in the Hole," Paramount warned Wilder that his next picture would have to make enough money to pay for both films. Wilder came back strong with "Stalag 17," the biggest grossing picture he ever made at Paramount, earning more than $10 million in its first year of release. The picture's success surprised even its star, William Holden, who had predicted the film would fail and damage his own career. Playing the part of Sefton, a conniving, wicked, and sneering hustler in a German prisoner-of-war camp, Holden urged Wilder to at least soften the anti-American, antiwar sentiments of his character. But Wilder, who never alters a single word of his screenplays, counseled faith and patience. Holden won the Academy Award for best actor, beating out Burt Lancaster, Marlon Brando, Richard Burton, and Montgomery Clift.

Wilder made his last Paramount picture, "Sabrina," in 1954. A romantic comedy, the movie was such a hit in Europe that Paramount, hoping to capitalize on Wilder's popularity, wanted to make a special dubbed version of "Stalag 17" for German release. But when the studio suggested that Wilder change a character in the story (the executive in charge of worldwide distribution wanted the Nazi spy role to be a Polish prisoner-of-war who has sold out to the Nazis), he reacted with outrage. Wilder, who was proud of the Jewish resistance in Warsaw during World War II, refused to make any such change and threatened to quit unless he received an apology. No apology arrived, and Wilder left Paramount for good.

After three more successful pictures—"The Seven Year Itch," "Love in the Afternoon," "Witness for the Prosecution"—Wilder found a new collaborator, I.A.L. Diamond, and made what some call his masterpiece, "Some Like It Hot." Despite cost overruns, production delays, and a disastrous preview, the movie rang up the biggest gross ($14 million) ever achieved by a Hollywood comedy up to that time. Still, it disappointed box-office expectations, according to Wilder, because 1959-America was not quite ready for a film that featured two men dressed in women's clothing.

The plot concerns two broke musicians, Joe and Jerry, who accidentally witness the St. Valentine's Day Massacre of 1929, whereupon gangster Spats Colombo orders them killed. To effect their getaway, Joe and Jerry don female garb, pass themselves off as Josephine and Daphne, and join an all-girl band bound for a Miami hotel. At the resort, gorgeous band vocalist Sugar Kane is out to catch a millionaire, Joe and Jerry are after Sugar, and millionaire Osgood Fielding III is wooing "Daphne." Having redisguised himself as a millionaire, Joe eventually wins Sugar's love, whereas Jerry finds himself engaged to Osgood. After accidentally witnessing another gangland murder, Joe and Jerry make a second escape, this time in the company of Sugar and Osgood. As all four speed off in a motorboat, the movie ends with Osgood still planning marriage to Jerry, who finally tears off his wig and declares he's a man. Replies the unswervable Osgood, "Nobody's perfect!"

Several elements contributed to the success of "Some Like It Hot." The acting performances turned in by Jack Lemmon, Tony Curtis, and Marilyn Monroe are among their best. Though Wilder struggled mightily with the temperamental Monroe ("It behooves the Screen Directors Guild to award me a Purple Heart"), he tolerated the thirty, forty, fifty takes she often needed because there is no one "as utterly fabulous on the screen, and that includes Garbo." Fearing that a picture in Technicolor might encourage the charge of transvestism, Wilder shot the film in black and white. "The masquerade comedy comes, not from swishing about, but from the very maleness of two young men in a harem situation and unable to do anything about it," observed Stanley Kauffmann.

The movie also contains several playful references to other films. In his guise as millionaire, Tony Curtis (Joe) mimics the suave Cary Grant of "Monkey Business" and "Bringing Up Baby." When Edward G. Robinson, Jr. is seen flipping a coin *a la* George Raft in "Scarface," Raft himself, in the role of Spats, snatches the coin away and says, "Where did you pick up that cheap trick?" At a gangster banquet, Spats angrily picks up a grapefruit, as if to push it into another hood's face, recalling what Jimmy Cagney did to Mae Clarke in "The Public Enemy." Commented Kauffmann: "The particular grace of these references is that they are inessential but enriching. If you don't understand them, you are not left out. If you do understand them, you sense how the history of film is being used in irreverent affection."

"The Apartment" followed "Some Like It Hot," giving Wilder back-to-back hits: "trenchant" . . . "sardonic" . . . "tumbling with wit" . . . "the most sophisticated movie I have ever seen," ran the reviews. In the movie, Jack Lemmon advances his career by letting his bosses use his apartment for their adulterous affairs; when the Shirley MacLaine-Fred MacMurray liaison crumbles, MacLaine attempts suicide, Lemmon nurses her back to health, and they begin a romance of their own. Wilder enjoyed his best evening ever at the Academy Awards' ceremony, winning three Oscars for writing, directing, and producing, the first time anyone had won those three major awards in one night.

With the success of "The Apartment," Wilder's career had reached its zenith. As Pauline Kael noted in 1961, "In Hollywood, it is now common to hear Billy Wilder called the world's greatest movie director." But it was Kael and critics like Andrew Sarris, Dwight Macdonald, and John Simon who attacked Wilder's cynicism and sentimentality: he is "a film-maker with false or no morality," charged Simon; "His eye is on the dollar," contended Kael; "Billy Wilder is too cynical to believe even his own cynicism," Sarris declared.

At various times, Wilder has answered his critics by saying, "I am a dedicated man, not after the fast buck. But if there is one thing I loathe more than not to be taken seriously, it's to be taken too seriously." "I want to be truthful, but if I have to choose between truth and entertainment, I will always choose entertainment." "I have been criticized for happy endings. The easiest ending is the unhappy ending—that you can write anytime. . . . The question is whether you have a right to get people into the theater, and they expect a cocktail and they get a shot of acid. People don't want to hear that they stink." "I wanted to say [in 'The Apartment']: 'How corrupt we are, how money mad we are. . . .' I guess that's the theme of all my pictures. Maybe my philosophy is cynical, but I have to be true to what I feel." "I am not going to reform the audience. I am not going to better the audience. I just want to force the audience to drop the popcorn and listen. I have a vast and terrible desire never to bore an audience."

After "One, Two, Three," a satirical farce set in West Berlin, Wilder scored his biggest box-office success with "Irma La Douce," a picture that earned $11,910,000 in rentals and grossed $25 million at the box office. Jack Lemmon plays a pimp who disguises himself as an English lord so that Shirley MacLaine will have no other customers except him. According to McBride and Wilmington, the comic, "'pastel' flavor of the prostitution in *Irma La Douce* was no doubt intended as a reaction against heavily emotional treatments of the subject." This, however, is precisely what many reviewers found so objectionable. While crowds were flocking to the movie all around the world, Wilder's chief critical detractors "loathed him as an immoral beast," reported Zolotow, "for glamorizing pimps and prostitutes."

"Kiss Me, Stupid" in 1964 evinced pure critical venom and nearly marked the end of Wilder's career. The picture was called "coarse and smutty," "squalid," "sleazy," and "the slimiest movie of the year" by the New York critics. The Catholic church's Legion of Decency gave it a C (Condemned) rating and decried its "condonation of immorality." An Indiana minister denounced the movie over the NBC network, and Thomas Thompson, author of *Blood and Money,* wrote an article for *Life* magazine calling for Wilder's deportation. Wilder, who thought he had made a film about human dignity (and still does), fled to Europe in suicidal despair: "I thought of killing myself. I thought I would never make another movie. I did not know what to do with my life. I did not want to live."

"The pursuit of sex and money is always a major impulse in Wilder's movies, but here it has become all-consuming," observed George Morris. The movie, set in the bleak town of Climax, Nevada, focuses on Orville J. Spooner, a piano teacher and amateur songwriter who dreams of breaking into the big-time. When Dino, a Las Vegas singer, is trapped overnight in the town, Spooner lures the entertainer into his home and stages a desperate audition of his songs. To ensure success, Spooner has also substituted his wife with the town whore, Polly, who is expected to satisfy Dino's daily dose of sex. During the night of deception, however, both Spooner and Polly awaken to their humanity and give up the charade. After throwing Dino out of his house for making advances toward his "wife," Spooner turns out the lights and disappears with Polly into the bedroom.

One of the few critics in 1964 to recognize the film's value was the reviewer for *Vogue* magazine, Joan Didion: "*Kiss Me, Stupid* shows Wilder doing exactly what only he can do. It is a profoundly affecting film, as witnessed by the number of people who walk out on it. . . . The Wilder world is one seen at dawn through a hangover, a world of cheap *double entendres* and stale smoke, and drinks in which the ice has melted: the true country of despair." Added George Morris, "Wilder risks offending us initially in order to strengthen the emotional reversals that deepen the second half of the film. . . . Although it portrays a sordid world of topsy-turvy morality and transient relationships, *Kiss Me, Stupid* ultimately, if ironically, reaffirms the values it so gleefully annihilates."

After the debacle of "Kiss Me, Stupid," the popular critical view held that Wilder was an artist in decline. In 1963 Charles Higham had already suggested that the filmmaker had exhausted his talents: "Certainly, his work raises the old question of whether an artist can be against life and still create successfully; and it may well be that, having set out to destroy our last illusions, Wilder has destroyed his own power." As if to confirm Higham's judgment, no Wilder film after "Irma La Douce" has been a critical or financial success. But the late seventies have seen a resurgence of interest in Wilder's work and a new critical appreciation for his accomplishments.

In 1964 the film curator of New York's Museum of Modern Art, Richard Griffith, had introduced a retrospective of Wilder's films by calling him "the most precise, indeed relentless, chronicler of the postwar American, in shade as well as light, that the motion picture has produced." Fifteen years and six films later, Joseph McBride and Todd McCarthy pointed out that Wilder's traditionally "precise social criticism and examination of contemporary American life" had been displaced by "more openly romantic" films. Earlier, in 1977, Maurice Zolotow concluded that Wilder's constant struggle with the relationship between love and money, men and women, is finally resolved in the later works; he successfully breaks out of the "disillusioned romanticism" of the earlier films, "freeing love from all thoughts of money and all stereotyped feminine poses."

In response to a query from *CA,* Joseph McBride addressed the issue of Wilder's evolving art: "The question of Billy Wilder's supposed 'cynicism' is the key to understanding the evolution of his entire career. Critics who have hailed his earlier work as 'cynical,' 'heartless,' 'a statement against life,' are not only exposing their own misanthropic bias in so doing, but they are also seriously misrepresenting Wilder's considerably more complex point of view. Wilder himself rejects the label of cynic, describing himself as 'an old-fashioned romantic.' Both labels are misleading.

"From his earliest work, Wilder exhibited the scars of a wounded idealism, the disillusioned romanticism of a modernist who was both outraged and amused by the world's corruption. He assailed that corruption in his films, and also took a kind of perverse joy in it; from this came his twofold reputation as a satirist and a cynic. From the 1940's through the early 1960's—Wilder's most successful period commercially as well as with the mainstream of American critical opinion—Wilder was in a class by himself among Hollywood directors in viewing human corruption with a clear and unblinking eye. It is understandable that his reputation was made on those grounds, while the more romantic side of his work—always a large and equally important aspect of it—was less celebrated.

"A cynic is a person who does not believe in anything, and this certainly never was an accurate description of Wilder; he could more accurately be described as a skeptic. Wilder has always centered his attention on the interplay between idealism and corruption in his characters; his protagonists have sometimes been jaded, corrupt people, and sometimes they have been innocents experiencing their first bittersweet taste of corruption. Often these two poles have co-existed in a single film, but even at his 'blackest' never has Wilder failed to express his deepfelt regret at the inevitable corruption of innocence by experience. In his later work, this regret has been heightened perhaps by his advancing age (in the time of Andy Hardy, Wilder seemed to be a cynic; in the time of 'Deep Throat' he appears to be an old-fashioned romantic) and by his disillusionment with so much of what he sees in contemporary society, but also because the movies have learned so much from him.

"Where once he was virtually alone in confronting corruption, today that is the normal subject of American films. In such a climate as today's, his tender concern with lost innocence makes him seem anachronistic, and his intransigent individualism spurs him to emphasize that side of his nature all the more strongly. Wilder has changed, certainly; he has mellowed to some degree; but the Billy Wilder of the later films has the same concerns, angers, and affections of the earlier films. His work exhibits a remarkable degree of artistic integrity, though critics who don't analyze it with enough clarity may not realize how consistent his view of the world really is."

Another critic, George Morris, evaluated the importance of the films following "Irma La Douce." "These last six films of Wilder's seem to me among the profound achievements of his career. In them he extends his cinematic vocabulary to penetrate, and confront with astonishing directness, his deepest, most personal feelings about life, love, and filmmaking. The commercial failure of these movies during the late Sixties and Seventies is a depressing reminder that the New Hollywood and its audiences are totally uninterested in the mature reflections of a man who has finally come to terms with himself and the world around him."

Wilder's most personal film, and his most romantic, "The Private Life of Sherlock Holmes," managed a run of only a few weeks in the United States. Again, the disfavor of audiences and critics alike dealt a devastating blow to Wilder, who had cherished and worked on the screenplay for fifteen years. He had also been forced to cut the film's length of three hours, twenty minutes by one hour. "And after the changes—ah, the reasons why I wanted to make this picture so much, they are hardly to be seen after the cuts," he lamented.

Both Zolotow and Morris contended that the film is Wilder's most autobiographical, embodying "all of his own contradictions as a man and artist" in the character of Holmes. Wilder conceives his detective as a witty, detached, and cynical man who lives solely by his reason. In isolated close-ups and one-shots, though, the cool aloofness of his public image is time and again shown to be a facade that veils his human vulnerability and loneliness. When in the course of his investigations he is drawn into a romance with the beautiful Ilse von Hoffmanstal, the feelings of tenderness and love he had suppressed for so many years are finally released. Though Holmes discovers that the woman he loves is actually a German spy, he chooses to affirm love rather than duty and secures her freedom. The emergence of his emotional life, however, has sufficiently unsettled his reasoning powers that he fails to solve the mystery of Herr von Hoffmanstal's disappearance. "Sherlock Holmes has failed to be Sherlock Holmes precisely because he has fallen in love, and yet he is a better human being than he was ever before," Wilder explained.

Two years later, in 1972, Wilder again portrayed the emotional and spiritual rebirth of a man whose business life and values have left him stiff, detached, and cynical. Like "Sherlock Holmes," "Avanti!" is bathed in soft pastel colors, and the beautiful Italian island of Ischia is the setting for romance. Wendell Armbruster, Jr. arrives on the island to claim the body of his father who has died in a car wreck. There he meets an English woman, Pamela Piggott, who has also come to claim her mother's body. Gradually, Armbruster learns what Pamela always knew: their parents had been lovers for the past ten years. Patiently, tenderly, Pamela defends their parents' love to the morally-shocked Armbruster, who undergoes a painful reevaluation of his own life and values.

The resolution of "Avanti!" echoes that of "Sherlock Holmes." In both films women who are as loving as they are intelligent release a new self-awareness in emotionally crippled men. The personal crisis Armbruster faces is complicated when Pamela extends her love to him. "As Wendell gradually accepts and reciprocates the love of Pamela," Morris observed, "he seems reconciled at last to the possibility that a woman's love is not always measured in terms of money." In the end, Pamela and Wendell relive the relationship of their parents. Morris concluded: "In *Avanti!* Wilder accepts with equanimity the approach of age and the potential for happiness between a man and a woman. It is his most affirmative, hopeful film."

Wilder has often remarked on the problems he faces in the "New Hollywood." "Today we are dealing with an audience that is primarily under 25 and divorced from any literary tradition. They prefer mindless violence to solid plotting; four-letter words to intelligent dialogue; pectoral development to character development." "I'm the only man in town not thinking in terms of Dracula pictures, disco pictures, another Viet Nam picture, or a monster extravaganza with gorgons made out of gorgonzola." "I get to see those lunatic kinds of pictures that obviously have been compiled . . . [according to] what works, what doesn't work. . . . It's just like when they ran to the computer and asked what would be the most successful picture, and it came out a Biblical Western, called *The Pistol-Packing Apostle.*" As a result, he has found it increasingly difficult to make the kind of pictures he wants to make.

The biggest problem Wilder now faces is the exhausting process of financing a film project. "As George Axelrod said, very rightly, 'Before, you were confronted with an illiterate, finagling, tyrannical guy who was very difficult to converse with, to convince, but once you did that job, that was it, you went ahead. But now there are *twenty* of those guys.' You haven't got the strength to weed them out, you know. And then you find out after a year and a half that you have been kissing the wrong ass all along. . . . It's Kafka."

For his 1978 film, "Fedora," Wilder was forced to seek tax shelter financing in Germany. "Look, I can't lose," he said, "because if this picture is a big hit, it's my revenge on Hollywood. If it is a total financial disaster, it's my revenge for Auschwitz." The movie, about an actress who remains forever young, "has the resonance of an epitaph," wrote Janet Maslin. "'Fedora' is old-fashioned with a vengeance, a proud, passionate remembrance of the way movies used to be, and a bitter smile at what they have become."

Fedora is a legendary, reclusive movie actress who appears to the world as if she had not aged in fifty years. William Holden, as a Hollywood producer fallen on hard times, travels to her island hideaway in Greece, hoping she can be persuaded to end her retirement and star in his version of "Anna Karenina." There he learns the bizarre secret of Fedora's miraculous youth and beauty: to perpetuate her own legend, Fedora had trained her daughter, Antonia, to take her place both on- and off-camera. The film's tragic denoument comes about when Antonia, in love with one of her co-stars but imprisoned by the masquerade she cannot escape, throws herself under the wheels of a train. "Rich, majestic, very close to ridiculous, and also a little bit mad . . . , [it is] a Hollywood reckoning of the price of art, the sacrifice worth making for the sake of a grand illusion," Maslin stated.

"Fedora" is a picture that intentionally recalls "Sunset Boulevard." The presence of Holden is meant to serve as a link between the two films, and he again acts as the narrator of an unfolding drama. Like the earlier film, this one too explores the themes of self-delusion, fraud, masquerade, and mad, cunning schemes of fame and immortality. The two films are even structurally similar: "Fedora" opens with a crowd of mourners gathered around Antonia's coffin, modeling the scene of the dead Joe Gillis in "Sunset"; and the story, as before, is a recollection of events, this time presented in a sequence of flashbacks. In their assessment of the film, McBride and McCarthy found that Wilder creates a "meditation on mortality . . . with a grace and elegance that is becoming increasingly rare in world cinema."

Wilder admits to a certain nostalgia for a bygone Hollywood, "when we made movies and didn't call it 'Cinema,'" but he also resists living in the past. "I do not have in my cellar prints of my old movies. . . . All I think is, 'What are we gonna do right now? What are we gonna do later like nothing had happened before?' Never do I dwell in the past." He jokes about leaving "The Bermuda Triangle" of Universal, Columbia, and Warner Bros. to join a Japanese baseball team, but quickly adds that movies are all he knows: "I'll go to bat here again if they let me."

Meanwhile, Wilder finds himself currently out of fashion in the new corporate Hollywood, struggling against "all those vice presidents . . . , all those worldly wise young men who ask for their quiche Lorraine al dente and have 'The World According to Garp' on their coffee tables." He describes it as a "catch-22" situation, with one camp of executives asking only for a Billy Wilder comedy and another calling for one more "Sunset Boulevard" or "Double Indemnity." The trouble is, he noted, "I always have been all over the place, with an appetite for trying every species of picture. . . . It would be very boring for me to make always the same species. I make pictures of various moods. . . . I cannot always wear the same suit and the same tie."

AVOCATIONAL INTERESTS: Classical music; gourmet cooking; watching professional sports; playing chess, bridge, and gin rummy; collecting art works, early American toys, and Japanese dwarf trees; collecting and flying kites.

BIOGRAPHICAL/CRITICAL SOURCES: Life, December 11, 1944; *Quarterly of Film, Radio and Television,* fall, 1952, summer, 1953; *Films and Filming,* February, 1957, January, 1960; *New York Times Magazine,* January 24, 1960; *Time,* June 27, 1960, January 5, 1970; *Theatre Arts,* July, 1962; *Sight and Sound,* spring, 1963, winter, 1967/68, autumn, 1974; *Playboy,* June, 1963; *Vogue,* March 1, 1965; *Saturday Review,* September 24, 1966; *Saturday Evening Post,* December 17, 1966; *London Magazine,* June, 1968; Andrew Sarris, *The American Cinema,* Dutton, 1968; *Cinema,* October, 1969; Axel Madsen, *Billy Wilder,* Indiana University Press, 1969; Charles Higham and Joel Greenberg, *Celluloid Muse,* Regnery, 1969; *Film Quarterly,* summer, 1970, spring, 1971; *Action,* November-December, 1970; Tom Wood, *The Bright Side of Billy Wilder, Primarily,* Doubleday, 1970; *Esquire,* April, 1972; *Film Heritage,* summer, 1973; Higham, *The Art of the American Film,* Anchor Press-Doubleday, 1973; *Horizon,* winter, 1973; *Newark Star-Ledger,* July 21, 1974; *The Real Paper* (Boston), July 31, 1974; *Biography News,* Gale, September, 1974; *New York,* November 14, 1975; Richard Koszarski, *Hollywood Directors, 1941-1976,* Oxford University Press, 1977; Maurice Zolotow, *Billy Wil-*

der in Hollywood, Putnam, 1977; Steve Seidman, *The Film Career of Billy Wilder,* G. K. Hall, 1977; *Film Comment,* January-February, 1979; *New York Times,* April 15, 1979, June 29, 1979.

—*Sketch by B. Hal May*

* * *

WILEY, John P., Jr. 1936-

PERSONAL: Born May 22, 1936, in Rahway, N.J.; son of John P (an engineer) and Arabella (Bassett) Wiley; married Barbara Hick (a teacher), August 5, 1961; children: John, Peter, Catherine, James. *Education:* Fordham University, B.S., 1958; studied writing at Columbia University, 1966-67. *Home:* 12601 Running Brook Dr., Clarksburg, Md. 20734. *Office: Smithsonian Magazine,* 900 Jefferson, Washington, D.C. 20560.

CAREER/WRITINGS: Associated with United Press International, New York City, 1967-68; *Physics Today,* New York City, associate editor, 1968-69; *Natural History* Magazine, New York City, senior editor, 1969-72; *Smithsonian Magazine,* Washington, D.C., member of editorial board, 1973—. Author of "Sky Reporter" column in *Natural History,* 1967-72. Member of Westchester County (N.Y.) democratic committee, 1970-72. *Military service:* U.S. Naval Reserve, 1954-62; became quartermaster. *Member:* National Association of Science Writers.

* * *

WILKENING, Howard (Everett) 1909-
(Bob Stokes, Robert Stokes)

PERSONAL: Born December 10, 1909, in New York, N.Y.; son of George Henry and Mary (Pyatt) Wilkening; married Mary Louise Kohler, December 26, 1936; children: Barbara Hope (Mrs. Norman Ahern), Gregory Pyatt, Peter Kohler, Carol Virginia (Mrs. William Vilas). *Education:* New York University, B.S., 1933, Ph.D., 1941; University of Colorado, M.A., 1934; also attended Purdue University, 1938-41, and Columbia University. *Home:* 3532 Greenfield Ave., Los Angeles, Calif. 90034.

CAREER: Domestic Relations Court, New York City, psychiatric interviewer, 1933-34; City of New York, N.Y., special assistant to Mayor La Guardia and Legal Division, 1934-36; Department of Social Welfare, New York City, social worker and psychologist, 1936; Dependent Children's Agency, New York City, social worker and psychologist, 1936-38; Purdue University, West Lafayette, Ind., assistant professor of psychology and track coach, 1938-43; Vallejo Housing Authority, Vallejo, Calif., area director, 1943-44; U.S. Army Air Forces, Washington, D.C., civilian operations analyst and director of research, 1944-46; University of Southern California, Los Angeles, associate professor of psychology, 1947-48; California State University, Los Angeles, professor of psychology, 1948—, head of department, 1948-61. Vocational counselor, chief psychologist at Marion Davies Clinic, and lecturer at University of California, Los Angeles, 1946-48. Public relations coordinator for Lockheed Aircraft, 1945-46. Clinical psychologist and head of department of mental hygiene at Los Angeles Orthopaedic Hospital, 1946-48; chief psychologist and head of department of psychology at Los Angeles Child Guidance Clinic, 1948-65, member of board of directors, 1962-65; president and director of Richard Neutra Foundation, 1964-67. President of Scanstyles, Inc. and Denlon International Corp.; member of boards of directors of American and foreign industries; consultant to National Cash Register Co., American Potash & Chemical Corp., and Bobrick Washroom Equipment. *Member:* American Psychological Association (fellow). *Awards, honors:* Citation from War Department, 1946.

WRITINGS: Student's Handbook of Psychology, Dryden, 1959; *Bufano: An Intimate Biography,* Howell-North Books, 1972; *The Psychology Almanac,* Brooks/Cole, 1973. Contributor of stories to magazines, sometimes under pseudonyms Bob Stokes and Robert Stokes. Editor of Scanstyles journal; associate editor of *Journal of Marriage and Family Living* and publications of National Board of Review of Motion Pictures.

WORK IN PROGRESS: Double Vision (tentative title), a novel covering a single family, 1840-1980, in New Orleans, Paris, Athens, Istanbul, Brussels, and New York City.

SIDELIGHTS: Wilkening writes: "At New York University I studied under Thomas Wolfe, where I learned to emulate his indefatigable drive to devour experiences by writing a novel, longer and more sprawling than any of his own, but I had no Maxwell Perkins, so my story suffered suffocation by the morning-glory syndrome; that is, death through overgrowth. Perkins, by the way, did attend Wolfe's class occasionally (when Wolfe was indisposed), and once recommended that writers not try to emulate Wolfe, since he suffered from logorrhea. 'It might be best for some writers,' he said, 'to write a one-word title, and no more. That, in itself, is a story.'

"During the Depression years, I became a movie critic, cub reporter, and reader for film companies. I appeared with Katharine Hepburn in 'The Warrior's Husband,' playing the part of an off-stage warrior (or so it seemed to me). I also played in 'The Lord Blesses the Bishop,' but the Lord neglected to bless either me or the play, since it closed before He even touched the holy water font. Then I sprouted off to become a radio commentator in New York, then sports announcer, movie reviewer, games programmer and developer, and introduced such programs as 'Information Please' (which had been based on one of my games) and 'Battle Between the Cities.' I went to Hollywood and did an outstanding job holding a spear in Garbo's 'Queen Christina.' I continued on my rapid descent into anonymity by finding it necessary to seek and obtain a job as a plumber's assistant, all my previous work bearing heavily on my acceptance for such an elevating job. I tried to hitchhike back to New York, but got stranded in Denver, and appeared at Elitche's Gardens there.

"All the while, I was trying to write. I finished one novel and hitched through South America with it. Everything I owned was stolen at Tierra del Fuego. When I got back to Los Angeles, I started rewriting my stolen novel. Five years later, almost finished, everything was swept off my desk and out of my cabinets in another burglary. I began to learn from experience. I thought of Thomas Wolfe, and I wrote and wrote and wrote, and lo—I have fifteen hundred pages. No burglar would try to lift the stuff, hoping to find cash cached between the pages, or, not finding any, throw the whole manuscript into a trash barrel. After becoming somewhat happily schizoid and paranoid after such rude interruptions, I now have copies distributed in various parts of the world, and I won't even dare mention what countries they're in. There's nothing wrong with my mind. I'm just cautious. But I still think that writing is the most damnably great fun one can ever experience!"

* * *

WILLARD, Nancy 1936-

PERSONAL: Born June 26, 1936, in Ann Arbor, Mich. *Edu-*

cation: University of Michigan, B.A., 1958, Ph.D., 1963; Stanford University, M.A., 1960. *Home:* 133 College Ave., Poughkeepsie, N.Y. 12603. *Office:* Department of English, Vassar College, Poughkeepsie, N.Y.

CAREER: Writer. Lecturer in English at Vassar College, Poughkeepsie, N.Y. *Awards, honors:* Hopwood Award, 1958; Woodrow Wilson fellowship, 1960; Devins Memorial Award, 1967, for *Skin of Grace;* O. Henry Award for best short story, 1970.

WRITINGS: In His Country: Poems, Generation (Ann Arbor, Mich.), 1966; *Skin of Grace* (poetry), University of Missouri Press, 1967; *A New Herball: Poems,* Ferdinand-Roter Gallerias, 1968; *The Lively Anatomy of God* (short stories), Eakins, 1968; *Testimony of the Invisible Man: William Carlos Williams, Francis Ponge, Rainer Maria Rilke, Pablo Neruda,* University of Missouri Press, 1970; *Nineteen Masks for the Naked Poet: Poems,* Kayak, 1971; *Childhood of the Magician,* Liveright, 1973; *The Carpenter of the Sun: Poems,* Liveright, 1974; *The Merry History of a Christmas Pie: With a Delicious Description of a Christmas Soup* (juvenile), Putnam, 1974; *Sailing to Cythera and Other Anatole Stories* (juvenile), Harcourt, 1974; *All on a May Morning* (juvenile), Putnam, 1975; *The Snow Rabbit* (juvenile), Putnam, 1975; *Shoes Without Leather* (juvenile), Putnam, 1976; *The Well-Mannered Balloon* (juvenile), Harcourt, 1976; *Simple Pictures Are Best* (juvenile), Harcourt, 1977; *Strangers' Bread* (juvenile), Harcourt, 1977; *The Highest Hit* (juvenile), Harcourt, 1978.

SIDELIGHTS: Although her most recent work has been aimed at juvenile readers, Willard began her career with poetry. Hayden Carruth observed in Willard's collection *Skin of Grace,* "fake sentiment" but acknowledged that there was "good writing as well, intelligent and never only facile or correct." Many critics have noted Willard's optimism in her poetry. John N. Morris wrote that *Carpenter of the Sun* is "a book full of poems about flowers and vegetables and animals and her son . . . and with not a single hard word to say about her husband and the difficulty of being a poet and a wife. . . ." Stanley Poss confessed that he admired her "because her poems are poised, assured, calm, they bid us not to be too hard on ourselves. . . . She's deft, laconic, not merely gemuetlich, undaunted and undaunting, accessible, witty, fanciful—and happy." However, he also acknowledged that Willard "writes gently surrealist and grotesque poems, as in . . . *19 Masks for a Naked Poet.*"

Other critics have also responded enthusiastically to Willard's good-natured poetry. "Nancy Willard's best poems—and her best are as good as they come—illuminate local, humble subjects: flowers, moss, children, the patterns of domestic life," declared Jonathan Holden in a review of *Carpenter of the Sun.* He wrote that the poems "are filled with a shy wonderment, a tenderness toward Creation that is rare in contemporary poetry." Hilda Gregory noted, "Willard can work magic," and called her "a teacher, a storyteller."

Willard has also received praise for her collections of short stories. Joseph M. Flora called *Childhood of the Magician* "an immensely satisfying book. . . ." He added: "There is an abundance of good humor in these stories. At the same time, Nancy Willard excellently evokes the pathos of life. Her children play and ponder and amuse us, but we also recognize the truth of life in the several old people in the stories." In summation, he declared, "Nancy Willard gives us something closer to blessing and benediction." In a review of the same collection, Doris Grumbach wrote, "Everything in these charming stories points to a genuine talent. It would be patronizing to say that I look forward to their flowering in a novel . . . ; they are in many ways a flowering in themselves."

Willard's works for children are also frequently cited for their charm. A reviewer for the *New York Times Book Review* called *Simple Pictures Are Best* a "frolicsome . . . account of a shoemaker and his wife having their anniversary picture taken." Natalie Babbitt had similar praise for *Stranger's Bread.* "This is a good-natured little story full of mostly unimporant inconsistencies."

BIOGRAPHICAL/CRITICAL SOURCES: New Republic, May 25, 1974, January 4, 1975, Januray 11, 1975; *Hudson Review,* autumn, 1975; *Western Humanities Review,* autumn, 1975; *Open Places,* fall/winter, 1975-76; *Michigan Quarterly Review,* winter, 1975; *Prairie Schooner,* summer, 1976; *Contemporary Literary Criticism,* Volume 7, Gale, 1977.*

* * *

WILLIAMS, William Carlos 1883-1963

PERSONAL: Born September 17, 1883, in Rutherford, N.J.; died March 4, 1963, in Rutherford; son of William George (in business) and Raquel Helene (Hoheb) Williams; married Florence Herman, December 12, 1912; children: William Eric, Paul Herman. *Education:* University of Pennsylvania, M.D., 1906; postgraduate study at University of Leipzig, 1909-10. *Home:* 9 Ridge Rd., Rutherford, N.J. 07070.

CAREER: Poet, playwright, novelist, essayist, and physician. French Hospital and Nursery and Child's Hospital, New York, N.Y., intern, 1906-09; private medical practice in Rutherford, N.J., 1910-51. Visiting professor of English at University of Washington, Seattle, 1948. *Member:* American Academy of Arts and Letters, National Institute of Arts and Letters, Academy of American Poets, Bergen County (N.J.) Medical Association. *Awards, honors: Dial* Award, 1926, for distinguished service to American literature; Guarantors Prize from *Poetry,* 1931; LL.D. from University of Buffalo, 1946, and Fairleigh Dickinson University, 1959; Russell Loines Memorial Award for poetry from National Institute of Arts and Letters, 1948; Litt.D. from Rutgers University, 1948, Bard College, 1948, and University of Pennsylvania, 1952; appointed to chair of poetry at Library of Congress, 1949 (appointment withdrawn, but subsequently renewed); National Book Award for poetry, 1950, for *Selected Poems* and *Paterson,* Book III; Bollingen Prize in poetry from Yale University Library, 1952; Levinson Prize, 1954, and Oscar Blumenthal Prize, 1955, both for poems published in *Poetry;* Academy of American Poets fellowship, 1956; Brandeis University creative arts medal in poetry-fiction-nonfiction, 1957-58, in recognition of a lifetime of distinguished achievement; Pulitzer Prize in poetry for *Pictures From Brueghel* and American Academy of Arts and Letters gold medal for poetry from National Institute of Arts and Letters, both 1963.

WRITINGS—Poems: (Under name William C. Williams) *Poems,* privately printed, 1909; *The Tempers,* Elkin Mathews, 1913; *Al Que Quiere!,* Four Seas, 1917; *Kora in Hell: Improvisations,* Four Seas, 1920, reprinted, Kraus Reprint, 1973 (also see below); *Sour Grapes,* Four Seas, 1921; *Go Go,* Monroe Wheeler, 1923; *Spring and All,* Contact Publishing, 1923, reprinted, Frontier Press, 1970 (also see below); *The Cod Head,* Harvest Press, 1932; *Collected Poems, 1921-31,* preface by Wallace Stevens, Objectivist Press, 1934; *An Early Martyr and Other Poems,* Alcestis Press, 1935; *Adam*

& Eve & The City, Alcestis Press, 1936; *The Complete Collected Poems of William Carlos Williams, 1906-1938,* New Directions, 1938.

The Broken Span, New Directions, 1941; *The Wedge,* Cummington Press (Cummington, Mass.), 1944; *Paterson,* New Directions, Book I, 1946, Book II, 1948, Book III, 1949, Book IV, 1951, Book V, 1958, Books I-V published in one volume, 1963; *The Clouds,* Wells College Press and Cummington Press, 1948; *Selected Poems,* introduction by Randall Jarrell, New Directions, 1949, revised edition, 1968; *The Pink Church,* Golden Goose Press, 1949.

The Collected Later Poems, New Directions, 1950, revised edition, 1963; *Collected Earlier Poems,* New Directions, 1951, revised edition, 1966; *The Desert Music and Other Poems,* Random House, 1954 (also see below); *Journey to Love,* Random House, 1955 (also see below); "The Lost Poems of William Carlos Williams or The Past Recaptured," collected by John C. Thirlwall, published in *New Directions 16,* New Directions, 1957; *Pictures From Brueghel and Other Poems* (includes "The Desert Music" and "Journey to Love"), New Directions, 1962; *Selected Poems,* introduction by Charles Tomlinson, Penguin, 1976.

Other: *The Great American Novel,* Three Mountains Press, 1923, reprinted, Folcroft, 1973 (also see below); *In the American Grain* (essays), A. & C. Boni, 1925, reprinted, introduction by Horace Gregory, New Directions, 1967; *A Voyage to Pagany* (novel), Macaulay, 1928, reprinted, New Directions, 1970; (translator) Philippe Soupault, *Last Nights of Paris,* Macaulay, 1929; *The Knife of the Times and Other Stories* (short stories), Dragon Press, 1932, reprinted, Folcroft, 1974; *A Novelette and Other Prose,* TO Publishers, 1932 (also see below); "The First President" (three-act libretto for an opera), published in *American Caravan,* 1936; *White Mule* (novel; part I of trilogy), New Directions, 1937, reprinted, 1967; *Life Along the Passaic River* (short stories), New Directions, 1938.

In the Money (novel; part II of *White Mule* trilogy), New Directions, 1940, reprinted, 1967; *A Dream of Love* (three-act play), New Directions, 1948; *A Beginning on the Short Story: Notes,* Alicat Bookshop Press, 1950, reprinted, Norwood, 1978; *Make Light of It: Collected Stories,* Random House, 1950; *Autobiography,* Random House, 1951, published as *The Autobiography of William Carlos Williams,* New Directions, 1967; *The Build-Up* (novel; part III of *White Mule* trilogy), Random House, 1952; (translator with mother, Raquel Helene Williams) Pedro Espinosa, *A Dog and the Fever* (novella), Shoe String Press, 1954; *Selected Essays,* Random House, 1954; *The Selected Letters of William Carlos Williams,* edited by John C. Thirlwall, McDowell, Obolensky, 1957; *I Wanted to Write a Poem: The Autobiography of the Works of a Poet,* edited by Edith Heal, Beacon Press, 1958; *Yes, Mrs. Williams: A Personal Record of My Mother,* McDowell, Obolensky, 1959.

Many Loves and Other Plays: The Collected Plays of William Carlos Williams, New Directions, 1961; *The Farmers' Daughters: Collected Stories,* introduction by Van Wyck Brooks, New Directions, 1961; *The William Carlos Williams Reader,* edited and introduced by M. L. Rosenthal, New Directions, 1966; *Imaginations* (contains "Kora in Hell," "Spring and All," "The Great American Novel," "The Descent of Winter," and "A Novelette and Other Prose"), edited by Webster Schott, New Directions, 1970; *The Embodiment of Knowledge* (philosophy), edited by Ron Loewinsohn, New Directions, 1974; *Interviews With William Carlos Williams: "Speaking Straight Ahead,"* edited and introduced by Linda Welshimer Wagner, New Directions, 1976; *A Recognizable Image: William Carlos Williams on Art and Artists,* edited by Bram Dijkstra, New Directions, 1978.

Contributor to numerous literary magazines and journals, including *Poetry, The Dial, Origin, Blast, Pagany, Little Review, New Masses, Partisan Review,* and *Glebe.* Contributing editor of literary magazines and journals, including *Contact I,* 1920-23, and *Contact II,* 1932.

SIDELIGHTS: William Carlos Williams has always been known as an experimenter, an innovator, a revolutionary figure in American poetry. Yet in comparison to artists of his own time who sought a new environment for creativity as expatriates in Europe, Williams lived a remarkably conventional life. A doctor for more than forty years serving the New Jersey town of Rutherford, he relied on his patients, the America around him, and his own ebullient imagination to create a distinctively American verse. Often domestic in focus and "remarkable for its empathy, sympathy, its muscular and emotional identification with its subjects," Williams's poetry is also characteristically honest: "There is no optimistic blindness in Williams," wrote Randall Jarrell, "though there is a fresh gaiety, a stubborn or invincible joyousness."

Born the first of two sons of an English father and a Puerto Rican mother of French, Dutch, Spanish, and Jewish ancestry, Williams grew up in Rutherford, where his family provided him with a fertile background in art and literature. His father's mother, coincidentally named Emily Dickinson, was a lover of theatre, and his own mother painted. Williams's father introduced his favorite, Shakespeare, to his sons and read Dante and the Bible to them as well; but Williams had other interests in study. His enthusiastic pursuit of math and science at New York City's Horace Mann High School "showed how little writing entered into any of my calculations." Later in high school, though, Williams took an interest in languages and felt for the first time the excitement of great books. He recalled his first poem, also written during that time, giving him a feeling of joy.

Aside from an emerging writing consciousness, Williams's early life was "sweet and sour," reported Reed Whittemore; Williams himself wrote that "terror dominated my youth, not fear." Part of this terror, speculated James Breslin, came "from the rigid idealism and moral perfectionism his parents tried to instill in him." Williams's letters written while a student at the University of Pennsylvania to his mother exemplify some of the expectations he carried: "I never did and never will do a premeditated bad deed in my life," he wrote in 1904. "Also . . . I have never had and never will have anything but the purest and highest and best thoughts about you and papa." It was largely parental influence that sent him directly from high school to Pennsylvania in the first place—to study medicine. But as Breslin noted, Williams used his college experiences as a means to creativity, instead of, as his parents might have wished, as a means to success.

The conflict Williams felt between his parents' hopes for their son's success in medicine and his own less conventional impulses is mirrored in his poetic heroes of the time—John Keats and Walt Whitman. Keats's traditionally rhymed and metered verse impressed the young poet tremendously. "Keats was my God," Williams later revealed; and his first major poetic work was a model of Keats's "Endymion." In contrast, Whitman's free verse offered "an impulse toward freedom and release of the self," said Donald Barlow Stauffer. Williams explained how he came to associate Whitman with this impulse toward freedom when he said, "I reserved my 'Whitmanesque' thoughts, a sort of purgation and confessional, to clear my head and heart from turgid obsessions." Yet, by his first year at Pennsylvania Williams had found a considerably more vivid mentor than Whitman in a friend, Ezra Pound.

Williams's friendship with Pound marked a watershed in the young poet's life: he later insisted, "before meeting Pound is like B.C. and A.D." "Under Pound's influence and other stimuli," reported John Malcom Brinnin, "Williams was soon ready to close the door on the 'studied elegance of Keats on one hand and the raw vigor of Whitman on the other.'" Aside from the poetic influences, Pound introduced Williams to a group of friends, including poet Hilda Doolittle (H.D.) and painter Charles Demuth, "who shared the kinds of feelings that in Rutherford had made him frightened and isolated," Breslin declared. H.D., for example, with her arty dress and her peculiarities—sometimes she'd splash ink onto her clothes "to give her a feeling of freedom and indifference towards the mere means of writing"—fascinated Williams with a "provocative indifference to rule and order which I liked."

In a similar way, it was a reaction against the rigid and ordered poetry of the time that led Williams to join Pound, H.D., and others as the core of what became known as the Imagist movement. While correlative revolutionary movements had begun in painting (Cezanne), music (Stravinsky), and fiction (Stein), poetry was still bogged down by "the inversions and redundancies imposed by the effort 'to fill out a standard form,'" explained David Perkins. The Imagists broke from this formulaic poetry by stressing a verse of "swift, uncluttered, functional phrasing." Williams's first book, *Poems* (1909), a "conventional" work, "correct in sentiment and diction," preceded the Imagist influence. But in *The Tempers* (1913), as Bernard Duffey realized, Williams's "style was directed by an Imagist feeling, though it still depended on romantic and poeticized allusiveness." And while Pound drifted towards increased allusiveness in his work, Williams stuck with Pound's tenet to "make it new." By 1917 and the publication of his third book, *Al Que Quiere!,* "Williams began to apply the Imagist principle of 'direct treatment of the thing' fairly rigorously," declared James Guimond. Also at this time, as Perkins demonstrated, Williams was "beginning to stress that poetry must find its 'primary impetus' . . . in 'local conditions.'" "I was determined to use the material I knew," Williams later reflected; and as a doctor, Williams knew intimately the people of Rutherford.

Beginning with his internship in the decrepit "Hell's Kitchen" area of New York City and throughout his forty years of private practice in Rutherford, Williams heard the "inarticulate poems" of his patients. As a doctor, his "medical badge," as he called it, permitted him "to follow the poor defeated body into those gulfs and grottos . . . , to be present at deaths and births, at the tormented battles between daughter and diabolic mother." From these moments, poetry developed: "it has fluttered before me for a moment, a phrase which I quickly write down on anything at hand, any piece of paper I can grab." Some of his poems were born on prescription blanks, others typed in a few spare minutes between patient visits. Williams's work, however, did more than fuel his poetry: it allowed him "to write what he chose, free from any kind of financial or political pressure. From the beginning," disclosed Linda Wagner, "he understood the trade-offs: he would have less time to write; he would need more physical stamina than people with only one occupation. . . . [He] was willing to live the kind of rushed existence that would be necessary, crowding two full lifetimes into one, . . . learning from the first and then understanding through the second." There is little doubt that he succeeded in both: Richard Ellman and Robert O'Clair called him "the most important literary doctor since Chekov."

Williams's deep sense of humanity pervaded both his work in medicine and his writings. "He loved being a doctor, making house calls, and talking to people," his wife, Flossie, fondly recollected. Perhaps a less subjective appraisal came from Webster Schott, who defined Williams as "an immensely complicated man: energetic, compassionate, socially conscious, depressive, urbane, provincial, tough, fastidious, capricious, independent, dedicated, completely responsive. . . . He was the complete human being, and all of the qualities of his personality were fused in his writings." And, as Randall Jarrell pointed out, it is precisely in his written work where Williams demonstrates that "he *feels,* not just says, that the differences between men are less important than their similarities—that he and you and I, together, are the Little Men."

Corresponding with Williams's attraction to the local was his lifelong quest to have poetry mirror the speech of the American people. Williams had no interest, he said, in the "speech of the English country people, which would have something artificial about it"; instead he sought a "language modified by our environment, the American environment." Marc Hofstadter explained: "Thinking of himself as a local poet who possessed neither the high culture nor the old-world manners of an Eliot or Pound, he sought to express his democracy through his way of speaking. . . . His point was to speak on an equal level with the reader, and to use the language and thought materials of America in expressing his point of view."

While Williams continued with his innovations in the American idiom and his experiments in form, he fell out of favor with some of his own contemporaries. *Kora in Hell: Improvisations,* for example, suffered some stinging attacks. For a year Williams had made a habit of recording something—anything—in his notebooks every night, and followed these jottings with a comment. One of "Williams's own favorite books . . . , the prose poetry of *Kora* is an extraordinary combination of aphorism, romanticism, philosophizing, obscurity, obsession, exhortation, reverie, beautiful lines and scary paragraphs," wrote Webster Schott. Yet, as Hugh Fox reported, few peers shared Williams's enthusiasm for the book. Pound called it "incoherent" and "un-American"; H.D. objected to its "flippancies," its "self-mockery," its "un-seriousness"; and Wallace Stevens complained about Williams's "tantrums." Fox defended the avant-garde Williams against his critics by saying, "Anything hitherto *undone* is tantrums, flippancy, opacity . . . they don't see (as Williams does) that they are confronting a new language and they have to learn how to decipher it before they can savor it."

Surrounded by criticism, Williams became increasingly defensive during this time. His prologue to *Kora* came from his need "to give some indication of myself to the people I knew; sound off, tell the world—especially my intimate friends—how I felt about them." With or without allies, Williams was determined to continue the advances he felt he had made in American poetry.

What Williams did not foresee, however, was the "atom bomb" on modern poetry—T. S. Eliot's *The Waste Land.* Williams had no quarrel with Eliot's genius—he said Eliot was writing poems as good as Keats's "Ode to a Nightingale"—but, simply, "we were breaking the rules, whereas he was conforming to the excellencies of classroom English." As he explained in his *Autobiography,* "I felt at once that it had set me back twenty years and I'm sure it did. Critically, Eliot returned us to the classroom just at the moment when I felt we were on a point to escape to matters much closer to the essence of a new art form itself—rooted in the locality which should give it fruit." Not only did Williams feel threatened by Eliot's success, but also by the attention *The Waste Land* received. As Karl Shapiro pointed out, "he was left high and dry: Pound, who was virtually the co-author of Eliot's poems, and Marianne Moore were now polarized to Eliot. Williams felt this and would feel it for another twenty years. His own poetry would have to progress against the growing orthodoxy of Eliot criticism." But while the Eliot wave undoubtedly sunk his spirits, at the same time it buoyed his determination: "It was a shock to me that he was so tremendously successful," Williams admitted. "My contemporaries flocked to him—away from what I wanted. It forced me to be successful."

According to Bresslin, *The Waste Land* was one of the "major influence[s] on that remarkable volume," Williams's next book, *Spring and All.* The last in a decade of experimental poetry, *Spring and All* viewed the same American landscape as did Eliot but interpreted it differently. Williams "saw his poetic task was to affirm the self-reliant, sympathetic consciousness of Whitman in a broken industrialized world," Stauffer noted. "But unlike Eliot, who responded negatively to the harsh realities of this world, Williams saw his task as breaking through restrictions and generating new growth."

Fox explained how Williams used the imagination to do just that: "Williams . . . sees the real function of the imagination as breaking through the alienation of the near at hand and reviving its wonder." Williams himself explained in one of *Spring and All*'s prose passages that "imagination is not to avoid reality, nor is it a description nor an evocation of objects or situations, it is to say that poetry does not tamper with the world but moves it—It affirms reality most powerfully and therefore, since reality needs no personal support but exists free from human action, as proven by science in the indestructibility of matter and of force, it creates a new object, a play, a dance which is not a mirror up to nature but—."

Just as meeting Pound had measurably affected Williams's early life, the appearance of Eliot's *The Waste Land* marked important changes in his mid-career. Though some of Williams's finest poetry appeared in the 1923 *Spring and All,* he did not release another book of poems for nearly ten years. "One reason," speculated Rod Townley, "was probably Eliot's success. Another may have been his own success, known only to a few, in *Spring and All.* For decades thereafter he could not outdo himself; some think he never did." Instead, Williams wrote prose. And in it he concentrated on one subject in particular: America.

Williams explained his attraction towards America in a 1939 letter to Horace Gregory: "Of mixed ancestry I felt from earliest childhood that America was the only home I could ever possibly call my own. I felt that it was expressedly founded for me, personally, and that it must be my first business in life to possess it." He later echoed this sentiment in his preface to *Selected Essays.* "I loved my father but never forgave him for remaining, in spite of everything, a British subject," Williams admitted. "It had much to do with my sometimes violent partisanship towards America." As a result of such feelings, reasoned Vivienne Koch, "the logic of Williams' allegiance to the quest for a knowledge of localism, for a defining of the American grain, has compelled in his fiction a restriction to American materials."

So, in *In the American Grain,* Williams tried "to find out for myself what the land of my more or less accidental birth might signify" by examining the "original records" of "some of the American founders." In its treatment of the makers of American history, ranging from Columbus to Lincoln, *In the American Grain* has impressed many as Williams's most succinct definition of America and its people. D. H. Lawrence, for example, learned from Williams that "there are two ways of being American, and the chief . . . is by recoiling into individual smallness and insentience, and gutting the great continent in frenzies of mean fear. It is the Puritan way. The other is by *touch;* touch America as she is; dare to touch her! And this is the heroic way." Another prose book of the period, *Voyage to Pagany,* was a type of travel book based on the author's 1924 trip to Europe. "While its subject matter is essentially Europe," informed Koch, "it is, in reality, an assessment of that world through the eyes of America too." Williams focused directly on America and the Depression in his aptly titled short story collection, *The Knife of the Times.* In these stories and in other similar works of the thirties, "Williams blamed the inadequacies of American culture for both the emotional and economic plight of many of his subjects," declared James Guimond.

Williams's novel trilogy, *White Mule, In the Money,* and *The Build-Up,* also focused on America, and on one family in particular—his wife's. He first conceived the idea for *White Mule* because he wanted to write about a baby—he delivered more than two thousand in his career—and had heard stories of Floss's babyhood. But beyond the story of the infant Floss Stecher is the story of her infant American family, immigrants growing toward success in America. Philip Rahv gave this description of Joe and Gurlie Stecher: "Gurlie is so rife with the natural humors of a wife that she emerges as a veritable goddess of the home, but since it is an American home she is constantly urging her husband to get into the game, beat the other fellow, and make money. Joe's principal motivation, however, is his pride of workmanship; he is the pure artisan, the man who has not yet been alienated from the product of his labor and who thinks of money as the reward of labor and nothing else." In *In the Money* Williams follows Joe as he establishes his own printing business and moves to the suburbs, making way for the picture of middle-class life he presents in *The Build-Up.* W. T. Schott gave these examples of Williams's focus: "The stolid admirable Joe, the arrogant Gurlie on her upward march in society, a neighbor woman ranting her spitefulness, . . . Flossie and her sister at their little-girl wrangling over bathroom privileges." Reed Whittemore felt that such moments reveal Williams's fond tolerance of middle-class life. The *Build-Up* does have its "tough sections," Whittemore admitted, but "its placidness is striking for a book written by a long-time literary dissenter. What it is is a book of complacent reflection written from inside apple-pie America. It has not the flavor of the letters of the real young doctor-poet sitting in his emptiness forty years earlier in Leipzig. . . . Between 1909, then, and the time of the writing of *The Build-Up* WCW was *taken* inside, and found that with reservations he liked it there."

One reservation Williams may have had about middle-class America—and Rutherford in particular—was its reception of him as a poet. Few in Rutherford had any awareness of who Williams-the-poet was and beyond Rutherford his reputation fared no better: even after he had been writing for nearly thirty years, he was still virtually an unknown literary figure. Rod Townley reported a typical public response to his early works: "The world received his sixth and seventh books as it had the five before them, in silence." At times, Williams took a resilient view of his own obscurity. In a 1938 letter to Alva Turner (one of the many amateur poets with whom he frequently corresponded), Williams assessed the profits of the pen: "Meanwhile I receive in royalties for my last two books the munificent sum of one hundred and thirty dollars—covering the work of a ten or fifteen year period, about twelve dollars a year. One must be a hard worker to be able to stand up under the luxury of those proportions. Nothing but the best for me!" Beneath the shell of this attitude, though, lay a much angrier Williams. Obviously bitter about the success of Eliot and the attention Eliot stole from him and others, Williams wrote, "Our poems constantly, continuously and stupidly were rejected by all the pay magazines except *Poetry* and *The Dial*." As a result, Williams founded and edited several magazines of his own throughout the lean years. Until the 1940's and after, when his work finally received some popular and critical attention, the magazines provided a small but important readership.

While the many years of writing may have gone largely unnoticed, they were hardly spent in vain: Breslin revealed that "Williams spent some thirty years of living and writing in preparation for *Paterson*." And though some dismiss the "epic" label often attached to the five-book poem, Williams's intentions were certainly beyond the ordinary. His devotion to understanding his country, its people, its language—"the whole knowable world about me"—found expression in the poem's central image, defined by Whittemore as "the image of the city as a man, a man lying on his side peopling the place with his thoughts." With roots in his 1926 poem, "Paterson," Williams took the city as "my 'case' to work up. It called for a poetry such as I did not know, it was my duty to discover or make such a context on the 'thought.'"

In his prefatory notes to the original four-book *Paterson,* Williams explained "that a man himself is a city, beginning, seeking, achieving and concluding his life in ways which the various aspects of a city may embody—if imaginatively conceived—any city, all the details of which may be made to voice his most intimate convictions." A. M. Sullivan outlined why Williams chose Paterson, New Jersey: It was once "the prototype of the American industrial community . . . the self-sustaining city of skills with the competitive energy and moral stamina to lift the burdens of the citizen and raise the livelihood with social and cultural benefits." One hundred years later, continued Sullivan, "Williams saw the Hamilton concept [of 'The Society of Useful Manufacturers'] realized, but with mixed results of success and misery. The poet of Paterson understood the validity of the hopes of Hamilton but also recognized that the city slum could be the price of progress in a mechanized society." The world Williams chose to explore in this poem about "the myth of American power," added James Guimond, was one where "this power is almost entirely evil, the destructive producer of an America grown pathetic and tragic, brutalized by inequality, disorganized by industrial chaos, and faced with annihilation."

Williams revealed "the elemental character of the place" in Book I. The time is spring, the season of creativity, and Paterson is struck by the desire to express his "immediate locality" clearly, observed Guimond. The process is a struggle: to know the world about him Paterson must face both the beauty of the Passaic Falls and the poverty of the region. In Book II, said Williams, Paterson moves from a description of "the elemental character" of the city to its "modern replicas." Or, as Guimond pointed out, from the "aesthetic world" to the "real material world where he must accomplish the poet's task as defined in Book I—the invention of a language for his locality. . . . The breakdown of the poet's communication with his world is a disaster," both for himself and for others. Williams himself, on the other hand, made his own advance in communication in Book II, a "milestone" in his development as a poet. A passage in Section 3, beginning "The descent beckons . . . ," "brought about—without realizing it at the time—my final conception of what my own poetry should be." The segment is one of the earliest examples of Williams's innovative method of line division, the "variable foot."

To invent the new language, Paterson must first "descend from the erudition and fastidiousness that made him impotent in Book II," summarized Guimond. As Paterson reads—and reflects—in a library, he accepts the destruction in Book II, rejects his learning, and realizes "a winter of 'death' must come before spring." Williams believed that "if you are going to write realistically of the concept of filth in the world it can't be pretty." And so, Book IV is the dead season, symbolized by the "river below the falls," the polluted Passaic. But in this destruction, the poet plants some seeds of renewal: a young virtuous nurse; a Paterson poet, Allen Ginsburg, who has promised to give the local new meaning; Madame Curie, "divorced from neither the male nor knowledge." At the conclusion of Book IV, a man, after a long swim, dresses on shore and heads inland—"toward Camden," Williams said, "where Walt Whitman, much traduced, lived the later years of his life and died." These seeds of hope led Breslin to perceive the basic difference between *Paterson* and Williams's long-time nemesis, Eliot's *Waste Land*. "'The Waste Land' is a kind of anti-epic," Breslin said, "a poem in which the quest for meaning is entirely thwarted and we are left, at the end, waiting for the collapse of western civilization. *Paterson* is a pre-epic, showing that the process of disintegration releases forces that can build a new world. It confronts, again and again, the savagery of contemporary society, but still affirms a creative seed. Eliot's end is Williams's beginning."

Williams scrapped his plans for a four-book *Paterson* when he recognized not only the changes in the world, but "that there can be no end to such a story I have envisioned with the terms which I have laid down for myself." To Babette Deutsch, Book V "is clearly not something added on, like a new wing built to extend a house, but something that grew, as naturally as a green branch stemming from a sturdy ole tree. . . . This is inevitably a work that reviews the past, but it is also one that stands firmly in the present and looks toward the future. . . . 'Paterson Five' is eloquent of a vitality that old age cannot quench. Its finest passages communicate Dr. Williams's perennial delight in walking in the world." Book VI was in the planning stages at the time of Williams's death.

While Williams himself declared that he had received some "gratifying" compliments about *Paterson,* Breslin reported "reception of the poem never exactly realized his hopes for it." *Paterson*'s mosaic structure, its subject matter, and its alternating passages of poetry and prose helped fuel criticism about its difficulty and its looseness of organization. In the process of calling *Paterson* an "'Ars Poetica' for contemporary America," Dudley Fitts complained, "it is a pity that those who might benefit most from it will inevitably be put off by its obscurities and difficulties." Breslin, meanwhile, accounted for the poem's obliqueness by saying, "*Paterson* has a thickness of texture, a multi-dimensional quality that makes reading it a difficult but intense experience."

Paterson did help bring Willams some of the attention he had been missing for many years. One honor came in 1949 when he was invited to become consultant to the Library of Congress. Whittemore reported that Williams first refused the appointment because of poor health, but decided in 1952 that he was ready to assume the post. Unfortunately for Williams, the editor and publisher of the poetry magazine, *Lyric,* got word of Williams's appointment and subsequently announced Williams's "Communist" affiliations. Williams's poem "Russia," she insisted, spoke in "the very voice of Communism." Though few newspapers brought the charges to light, the Library of Congress suddenly backed off from the appointment. After several excuses and postponements, some made, ostensibly, out of a concern for Williams's health, Librarian Luther Evans wrote, "I accordingly hereby revoke the offer of appointment heretofore made to you." A few months before the term was to have ended, Williams learned that the appointment had been renewed. The Library of Congress, however, made no offer to extend the appointment through the following year.

While Williams may have felt abandoned when few came to his defense during the Library of Congress incident, little could have bolstered him the way the cult of third generation poets did when they adopted him as their father in poetry. "*Paterson* is our *Leaves of Grass,*" announced Robert Lowell. "The times have changed." And indeed they had. The dominant school of poetry, the academic school of Eliot and Allen Tate, was giving way to what Whittemore called the fifties' "Revolution of the Word." Such poets as Lowell, Allen Ginsburg, Charles Olson, Denise Levertov, Robert Creely, and Cid Corman found in Williams an alternative to the academics. As Bruce Cook explained, Williams "withstood the influence of Eliot, ignored the New Critics and the academic poets who followed their lead, and simply went his own way, his lines growing shorter, more austere, more pointed with each poem." With this style, reported James Dickey, he appealed to many aspiring writers who looked at his work and said, "Well if *that's* poetry, I believe I might be able to write it too!" But while the younger poets, including the Beats, found a prophet, a father, and a personal friend in Williams, the old master was no easy critic. "It was Williams who told Ginsberg that 'Howl' needed cutting by half," disclosed Linda Wagner. "It was Williams who argued with Denise Levertov about her sometimes too-poetic diction."

According to Williams himself, his own special gift to the new poets was his "variable foot—the division of the line according to a new method that would be satisfactory to an American." He revealed his enthusiasm over the variable foot in a 1955 letter to John Thirlwall: "As far as I know, as my forthcoming book [*Journey to Love*] makes clear, I shall use no other form for the rest of my life, for it represents the culmination of all my striving after an escape from the restrictions of all the verse of the past." Breslin, meanwhile, downplayed Williams's exuberance: "A reader coming to these poems [in *The Desert Music and Other Poems*] across the whole course of Williams's development will recognize that the new line is simply one manifestation of a pervasive shift of style and point of view." Whittemore, too, while heralding Williams as a prophet in the "Revolution of the Word," de-emphasized the role of the variable foot: "In other words the variable foot represented a change in mood more than measure."

Williams's health accounts for a major change in mood. In the late 1940's he suffered the first of several heart attacks and strokes which would plague him for the rest of his life. And though Williams later complained of the effects of a particularly serious stroke (1952)—"That was the end. I was through with life"—his devotion to poetry did not suffer. Breslin reported that after retiring from medicine in 1951, and after recuperating from a stroke, Williams spoke "optimistically of the 'opportunity for thought' and reading afforded by his new idleness." Hofstadter pointed out that "death was a major focus of this reflectiveness," and explained how Williams reflected his concerns in his poetry: "In the face of death what Williams seeks is *renewal*—not a liberation toward another world but an intensified return to this one. Revitalization both of one's inner energies and of one's contact with the outside world, renewal is the product of two forces: love and the imagination. . . . Love and imagination are the essence of life. He who loses them is as good as dead."

Williams explored the theme of renewed love in two particular later works, the play, "A Dream of Love," and the poem, "Asphodel, That Greeny Flower." In "A Dream of Love" the protagonist has an affair with his secretary and confesses to his wife that he did it only to "renew our love." The explanation fails to convince her. Thus, Williams dramatizes his belief in the "conflict between the male's need for emotional renewal in love and the female's need for constancy in love," explained Guimond. According to Thomas Whitaker, "'A Dream of Love' points to an actuality that Williams at this time could not fully face but that he would learn to face—most noticeably in 'Asphodel, That Greeny Flower.'" In this "elegiac epithalamian," Williams confesses his infidelities to his wife and asks for her forgiveness; "he seeks new life on the very edge of death," said Whitaker. While Williams proclaimed his life as a husband in his love poem, his strength as a poet was evident, too: "Asphodel" received some very complimentary reviews, including W. H. Auden's praise as "one of the most beautiful poems in the language."

"Asphodel" was among several of Williams's highly esteemed later works. Prior to his 1952 stroke he had been under a taxing three-book contract at Random House, a contract he fulfilled with *The Build-Up, Autobiography,* and *Make Light of It.* The hurried writing of the *Autobiography,* evidenced by its many factual mistakes, as well as the worry over the Library of Congress debacle, have both been cited as contributing factors in his declining health.

But Williams's weakened physical powers, apparently, strengthened his creative ones. "I think he did much better work after the stroke slowed him down," reflected Flossie. Stanley Koehler agreed. *The Desert Music* and *Journey to Love,* he said, "were written in an unusual period of recovery of creative power after Dr. Williams's first serious illness in 1952." Aside from featuring the variable foot and such outstanding poems as "Asphodel," these two books impressed readers as the mature work of a poet very much in control of his life and craft. *Desert Music* reviewer Kenneth Rexroth called the title poem "an explicit statement of the irreducible humaneness of the human being." The book's ideas are simple, indisputable, presented with calm maturity," continued Rexroth. "I prophesy that from now on, as Williams grows older, he will rise as far above his contemporaries as Yeats did in his later years." The love poems of *Journey to Love* were no less impressive to Babette Deutsch. "The poet gives us vignettes of the daily scene, notations on the arts, affirmations of a faith no less sublime for being secular, in the language, the rhythms. that he has made his own," reported Deutsch. "The pages bear the indelible signature of his honesty, his compassion, his courage." Finally, to highlight a decade of productivity, Williams's last book, *Pictures From Brueghel,* won a Pulitzer Prize in 1963.

Despite his failing health, Williams lived as productively as possible throughout his later years. He traveled, gave lectures, and entertained writers in the same home that had been visited by members of the Imagist movement more than forty years earlier. Williams wrote, too—poetry, of course, as well as essays and short stories. He continued to cooperate with writers interested in him and his work: John Thirlwall worked with him in the publication of *Selected Letters* and a series of discussions with Edith Heal became the "autobiography" of his works, *I Wanted to Write a Poem.* A partially paralyzing stroke in 1958 and a 1959 cancer operation, however, stole much of his remaining energy and capabilities. No longer able to read, by the end of the decade he depended on Floss to read to him, often as long as four hours a day. A particularly painful view of the aging Williams appeared in his 1962 interview with Stanley Koehler for the *Paris Review.* "The effort it took the poet to find and pronounce words can hardly be indicated here," reported Koehler. Continued failing health further slowed Williams until, on March 4, 1963, he died in his sleep.

BIOGRAPHICAL/CRITICAL SOURCES—Books: Vivienne Koch, *William Carlos Williams,* New Directions, 1950; Babette Deutsch, *Poetry in Our Time,* Holt, 1952; Randall Jarrell, *Poetry and the Age,* Knopf-Vintage, 1953; William Carlos Williams, *Selected Essays,* Random, 1954; Williams, *Selected Letters,* edited by John C. Thirlwall, McDowell, Obolensky, 1957.

Karl Shapiro, *In Defense of Ignorance,* Random House, 1960; M. L. Rosenthal, *The Modern Poets: A Critical Introduction,* Oxford University Press, 1960; John Malcolm Brinnin, *William Carlos Williams,* University of Minnesota Press, 1963; Williams, *Paterson,* Books I-V, New Directions, 1963; Linda Welshimer Wagner, *The Poems of William Carlos Williams,* Wesleyan University Press, 1964.

Alan Ostrom, *The Poetic World of William Carlos Williams,* Southern Illinois University Press, 1966; J. Hillis Miller, editor, *William Carlos Williams: A Collection of Critical Essays,* Prentice-Hall, 1966; A. Kingsley Weatherhead, *The Edge of the Image: Marianne Moore, William Carlos Williams, and Some Other Poets,* University of Washington Press, 1967; Leonard Ungar, editor, *Seven Modern American Poets: An Introduction,* University of Minnesota Press, 1967; Walter S. Peterson, *An Approach to "Paterson,"* Yale University Press, 1967; Williams, *The Autobiography of William Carlos Williams,* New Directions, 1967; *Writers at Work: The Paris Review Interviews,* third series, introduction by Alfred Kazin, Viking, 1967; Thomas R. Whitaker, *William Carlos Williams,* Twayne, 1968; James Guimond, *The Art of William Carlos Williams: A Discovery and Possession of America,* University of Illinois Press, 1968; Sherman Paul, *The Music of Survival: A Biography of a Poem by William Carlos Williams,* University of Illinois Press, 1968; James Dickey, *Babel to Byzantium,* Farrar, Strauss, 1968; Dennis Donoghue, *The Ordinary Universe,* Macmillan, 1968; Hyatt H. Waggoner, *American Poetry From the Puritans to the Present,* Houghton, 1968; Bram Dijkstra, *The Hieroglyphics of a New Speech: Cubism, Stieglitz, and the Early Poetry of William Carlos Williams,* Princeton University Press, 1969; Jarrell, *The Third Book of Criticism,* Farrar, Strauss, 1969; Bernard Dekle, *Profiles of Modern American Authors,* Tuttle, 1969; John Engels, *Guide to William Carlos Williams,* Merrill, 1969.

Wagner, *The Prose of William Carlos Williams,* Wesleyan University Press, 1970; Joel Conarroe, *"Paterson": Language and Landscape,* University of Pennsylvania Press, 1970; James E. Breslin, *William Carlos Williams: An American Artist,* Oxford University Press, 1970; Williams, *Imaginations,* edited by Webster Schott, New Directions, 1970; Bruce Cook, *The Best Generation,* Scribner's, 1971; Kenneth Rexroth, *American Poetry in the Twentieth Century,* Herder, 1971; Mike Weaver, *William Carlos Williams: The American Background,* Cambridge University Press, 1971; Guy Owen, editor, *Modern American Poetry: Essays in Criticism,* Everett/Edwards, 1972; Richard Ellman and Robert O'Clair, editors, *The Norton Anthology of Modern Poetry,* Norton, 1973; Jerome Mazzaro, *William Carlos Williams: The Later Poems,* Cornell University Press, 1973; Walter Sutton, *American Free Verse: The Modern Revolution in Poetry,* New Directions, 1973; *Contemporary Literary Criticism,* Gale, Volume 1, 1973, Volume 2, 1974, Volume 5, 1976, Volume 9, 1978; Donald Barlow Stauffer, *A Short History of American Poetry,* Dutton, 1974; Charles Angoff, editor, *William Carlos Williams,* (papers by four critics), Fairleigh Dickinson University Press, 1974; Joseph N. Riddel, *The Inverted Bell: Modernism and the Counterpoetics of William Carlos Williams,* Louisiana State University Press, 1974.

Reed Whittemore, *William Carlos Williams: Poet From New Jersey,* Houghton, 1975; Robert Coles, *William Carlos Williams: The Knack of Survival in America,* Rutgers University Press, 1975; Paul L. Mariani, *William Carlos Williams: The Poet and His Critics,* American Library Association, 1975; Rod Townley, *The Early Poetry of William Carlos Williams,* Cornell University Press, 1975; Louis Simpson, *Three on the Tower: The Lives and Works of Ezra Pound, T. S. Eliot and William Carlos Williams,* Morrow, 1975; David Perkins, *A History of Modern Poetry: From the 1890's to the High Modernist Mode,* Harvard University Press, 1976; Wagner, editor, *Interviews With William Carlos Williams: "Speaking Straight Ahead,"* New Directions, 1976; Karl Malkoff, *Escape From the Self: A Study in Contemporary Poetry and Poetics,* Columbia University Press, 1977; Bernard Duffy, *Poetry in America: Expression and Its Values in the Times of Bryant, Whitman, and Pound,* Duke University Press, 1978; Wagner, *William Carlos Williams: A Reference Guide,* G. K. Hall, 1978.

Periodicals: *Saturday Review,* December 19, 1925, May 7, 1932, June 26, 1937, March 19, 1938, February 11, 1939, November 9, 1940, September 25, 1948, October 9, 1948, August 20, 1949, May 20, 1950, December 9, 1950, September 21, 1951, October 20, 1951, March 15, 1952, October 18, 1952, June 5, 1954, November 20, 1954, February 18, 1956, September 7, 1957, October 11, 1958, July 11, 1959, August 1, 1970, November 14, 1970; *New York Times,* February 7, 1926, September 30, 1928, February 18, 1934, November 15, 1936, June 20, 1937, July 23, 1939, November 7, 1954, December 18, 1955, September 1, 1957, April 13, 1958, September 14, 1958, October 25, 1966; *New Republic,* March 24, 1926, April 18, 1934, July 15, 1936, July 7, 1937, December 21, 1938, November 18, 1940, February 12, 1945, February 24, 1951, August 27, 1951, February 7, 1955, November 13, 1961, December 20, 1970; *Nation,* April 4, 1926, March 28, 1934, June 26, 1937, November 19, 1938, November 23, 1940, April 14, 1945, August 24, 1946, June 19, 1948, July 9, 1949, April 8, 1950, March 3, 1951, August 25, 1951, November 8, 1952, April 24, 1954, January 22, 1955, October 5,

1957, May 31, 1958, November 23, 1970, December 14, 1970, December 11, 1976; *Times Literary Supplement,* November 29, 1928, March 23, 1951, February 1, 1952, January 29, 1954, July 29, 1965, February 10, 1966, April 13, 1967, June 22, 1967.

Poetry, May, 1934, May, 1936, November, 1936, September, 1939, April, 1945, February, 1947, April, 1949, May, 1952, April, 1954, March, 1955, March, 1956, June, 1958, May, 1959, February, 1964, October, 1967; *Yale Review,* spring, 1939, autumn, 1948, spring, 1950, autumn, 1951, winter, 1952, winter, 1955, December, 1957, December, 1958, May, 1959, December, 1961, June, 1970; *Commonweal,* October 4, 1946, November 7, 1952, December 10, 1954; *Briarcliff Quarterly,* October, 1946; *New York Herald Tribune Book Review,* June 27, 1948, March 5, 1950, December 3, 1950, December 17, 1950, July 1, 1951, September 16, 1951, November 2, 1952, March 28, 1954, November 7, 1954, November 13, 1955, September 1, 1957, July 6, 1958, September 28, 1958, June 21, 1959.

Time, December 4, 1950, March 15, 1963, September 21, 1970; *Atlantic,* October, 1951, September, 1957, May, 1958, July, 1959; *Partisan Review,* November-December, 1951; *Kenyon Review,* summer, 1952, spring, 1959; *Western Review,* summer, 1953; *Perspective,* autumn-winter, 1953; *Christian Science Monitor,* April 10, 1958, November 14, 1970; *New York Times Book Review,* June 28, 1959, December 26, 1971, October 5, 1975.

Hudson Review, winter, 1961-62; *Massachusetts Review,* winter, 1962; *Newsweek,* March 16, 1963; *Illustrated London News,* March 16, 1963; *National Review,* March 26, 1963; *Modern Poetry Studies,* Volume 1, number 6, 1970; *Encounter,* December, 1971; *Criticism,* winter, 1972; *London Magazine,* June/July, 1974; *Southwest Review,* summer, 1974; *The New Leader,* June 9, 1975; *Twentieth Century Literature,* October, 1975; *New York Review of Books,* November 13, 1975; *Journal of Modern Literature,* September, 1976; *The Explicator,* fall, 1976; *Twentieth Century Literature,* December, 1977.*

—*Sketch by David Versical*

* * *

WILLIAMSON, John Butler 1943-

PERSONAL: Born March 18, 1943, in Gloversville, N.Y.; son of John W. and Nancy Butler Chambers. *Education:* Massachusetts Institute of Technology, B.S., 1964; Harvard University, Ph.D., 1969. *Home:* 50 Paul St., Newton, Mass. 02159. *Office:* Department of Sociology, Boston College, Chestnut Hill, Mass. 02167.

CAREER: Boston College, Chestnut Hill, Mass., assistant professor, 1969-75, associate professor of sociology, 1975—. Consultant to National Consumer Law Center and Joint Center for Urban Studies (of Massachusetts Institute of Technology and Harvard University). *Member:* American Sociological Association, Society for the Study of Social Problems.

WRITINGS: (With J. F. Boren, F. J. Mifflen, N. A. Cooney, and others) *Strategies Against Poverty in America,* Halsted, 1975; *Social Problems: The Contemporary Debates,* Little, Brown, 1974, 2nd edition, 1977; *The Research Craft,* Little, Brown, 1977; *Growing Old: The Social Problems of Aging,* Holt, 1980; *Aging and Society,* Holt, 1980. Contributor to sociology journals.

WORK IN PROGRESS: Research on adult life stages and the politics of aging.

WILLIAMSON, Lamar, Jr. 1926-

PERSONAL: Born July 24, 1926, in Monticello, Ark.; son of Lamar and Lillian (Phillips) Williamson; married Ruthmary Bliss, September 1, 1949; children: Fred T., Martha (Mrs. Michael Williamson), Ruth, Allen L. *Education:* Davidson College, A.B., 1947; Union Theological Seminary, Richmond, Va., B.D., 1951; Faculte de Theologie Protestante, Montpellier, France, B.Th., 1952; Yale University, Ph.D., 1962. *Home:* 3406 Gloucester Rd., Richmond, Va. 23227. *Office:* Presbyterian School of Christian Education, 1205 Palmyra Ave., Richmond, Va. 23227.

CAREER: Ordained Presbyterian minister, 1951; pastor of Presbyterian church in Hazard, Ky., 1952-56; Ecole Unie de Theologie, Kananga, Zaire, missionary and professor of New Testament and related fields, 1956-66; Union Theological Seminary, Richmond, Va., visiting professor of New Testament, 1966-68; Presbyterian School of Christian Education, Richmond, Va., professor of Biblical studies, 1968—. *Military service:* U.S. Army Air Force, 1945. *Member:* Society of Biblical Literature.

WRITINGS: God's Work of Art, John Knox, 1971; (with Madeline H. Beck) *Mastering New Testament Facts,* John Knox, 1973; (with Beck) *Mastering Old Testament Facts,* John Knox, 1978.

WORK IN PROGRESS: The Gospel of Mark, publication by John Knox expected in 1981.

SIDELIGHTS: Williamson writes: "All of my published writing is in the field of the Bible. *God's Work of Art* is a church school curriculum piece for adults. In *Mastering New Testament Facts,* I teamed up with Dr. Beck, a specialist in education, to produce a four-volume programmed reading guide for those who want to know the content of the New Testament without paying much attention to criticism or interpretation. This proved useful enough to call for the four-volume *Mastering Old Testament Facts. The Gospel of Mark* will be a more substantive book, which seeks to combine historical exegesis and theological reflection in a way which will be helpful to those whose vocations involve them in Biblical interpretation."

* * *

WILMORE, Sylvia (Joan) Bruce 1914-

PERSONAL: Born April 19, 1914, in Guildford, Surrey, England; daughter of Albert Ernest (a traveler) and Eliza (Bruce) Dann; married Kenneth Alexander Wilmore (an accountant), August 2, 1942; children: Ian Bruce, Malcolm Alexander. *Education:* Attended convent boarding school in Ramsgate, England. *Politics:* "Right-wing socialist." *Religion:* Roman Catholic. *Home:* 12 Brook Lane, Bexley, Kent DA5 1DW, England. *Agent:* Laurence Pollinger Ltd., 18 Maddox St., Mayfair, London W1R 0EV, England.

CAREER: Secretary in Canterbury, England, 1932; worked as hotel receptionist, 1933, 1935, and as secretary, 1935-48; writer, 1962—. *Member:* Society of Women Writers and Journalists, Wildfowl Trust (fellow), British Trust for Ornithology, Royal Society for the Prevention of Cruelty to Animals, Crusade Against All Cruelty to Animals. *Awards, honors:* Writing awards include: prize from *The Writer,* 1966, for short story "Crime in the Crypt"; prizes for poetry from the *Reading Mercury,* 1966 (two), 1968, and 1970; prize for poetry from the *Cork Weekly Examiner,* 1969.

WRITINGS: Swans of the World, Taplinger, 1974; *Crows, Jays, Ravens, and Their Relatives,* Paul Eriksson, 1977. Author of radio scripts for British Broadcasting Corp. Contributor of more than one hundred stories, articles, and poems to magazines, including *Lady, Popular Gardening, Life and Countryside, Modern Caravan,* and *Illustrated London News.*

WORK IN PROGRESS: The Life of the Swan.

SIDELIGHTS: Sylvia Wilmore writes: "When I moved to Bexley, I became acquainted with the swans on our lake, and was inspired to write about them. My articles are mostly on animals and nature, particularly swans, dogs, and birds. My short stories have included mystery. Now they are mostly of the dramatic confessional type, dealing with young people. I am interested in conservation, ecology, and preservation of the animal kingdom."

* * *

WILSON, Arthur M(cCandless) 1902-1979

OBITUARY NOTICE—See index for *CA* sketch: Born July 29, 1902, in Sherrard, Ill.; died June 12, 1979, in Hanover, N.H. Educator and author. A professor of biography at Dartmouth College for more than thirty years, Wilson devoted most of his life to writing a two-volume biography of Diderot that received the National Book Award in 1973. Wilson was also the author of *French Foreign Policy Under the Administration of Cardinal Fleury, 1726-1743.* Obituaries and other sources: *Directory of American Scholars,* Volume I: *History,* 6th edition, Bowker, 1974; *Who's Who in America,* 40th edition, Marquis, 1978; *The Writers Directory, 1980-82,* St. Martin's, 1979; *Chicago Tribune,* June 17, 1979; *AB Bookman's Weekly,* September 10, 1979.

* * *

WILSON, Carroll L(ouis) 1910-

PERSONAL: Born September 21, 1910, in Rochester, N.Y.; son of Louis William and Edna (Carroll) Wilson; married Mary Alice Bischoff, April 1, 1937; children: Diana (Mrs. Paul B. Hoven), Paul, Rosemary, Barbara. *Education:* Massachusetts Institute of Technology, B.S., 1932. *Home:* 130 Jacob St., Seekonk, Mass. 02771. *Office:* World Coal Study, Massachusetts Institute of Technology, Room 1-143, Cambridge, Mass. 02139.

CAREER: Massachusetts Institute of Technology, Cambridge, Mass., assistant to president, 1932-36, adviser to administration, 1936-37; Research Corporation of New York, Boston, Mass., manager of university patents, 1937-40; Office of Scientific Research and Development, Washington, D.C., executive assistant to director, 1940-46; National Research Corp., Boston, vice-president, 1946-47; U.S. Atomic Energy Commission, Washington, D.C., general manager, 1947-51; president and director of industrial development, Climax Molybdenum Co., 1951-54; Metals and Controls Corp., Attleboro, Mass., vice-president, 1954-56, general manager, 1954-58, president, 1956-58; Massachusetts Institute of Technology, Seman Lecturer, 1959-60, professor of management, 1959-77, professor of engineering, 1977—, Mitsui Professor of Problems of Contemporary Technology, 1974-76, Mitsui Professor Emeritus, 1976—, director of workshop on alternative energy strategies, 1974-77, and world coal study, 1977—, director of fellows in Africa and Latin America.

President of Climax Uranium Co., 1951-54; member of board of directors of Millipore Corp., Hitchener Manufacturing Corp., and Procor, Inc. Director of studies on critical global environmental problems, 1970, and man's impact on the climate, 1971. Chairman of governing board of International Centre for Insect Physiology and Ecology, Nairobi, 1969-74; member of board of trustees and head of World Peace Foundation; member of board of trustees of International Federation of Institutes of Advanced Study, Stockholm; member of Trilateral Commission and Committee on Critical Choices for Americans; honorary member of board of directors and trustees of Rhode Island Hospital and Rhode Island Hospital Trust. U.S. chairman of Organization for Economic Co-operation and Development committee on scientific research, 1961-70, and Economic and Social Council of the United Nations advisory committee on applications of science and technology to development, 1964-70; senior adviser to United Nations Conference on Human Environment; consultant to Woods Hole Oceanographic Institution.

MEMBER: American Academy of Arts and Sciences, Council on Foreign Relations (member of board of directors; vice-chairperson), Royal Swedish Academy of Engineering Sciences. *Awards, honors:* Sc.D. from Williams College, 1947; Eng.D. from Worcester Polytechnic Institute, 1976; officer of Order of the British Empire.

WRITINGS—Contributor: *Man's Impact on the Global Environment: Assessment and Recommendations for Action,* M.I.T. Press, 1970; *Inadvertent Climate Modification,* M.I.T. Press, 1971; Paul S. Basile, editor, *Energy Demand Studies: Major Consuming Countries,* M.I.T. Press, 1976; *Energy: Global Prospects, 1985-2000,* McGraw, 1977; William F. Martin, editor, *Energy Supply to the Year 2000: Global and National Studies,* M.I.T. Press, 1977; Basile, editor, *Energy Supply-Demand Integrations to the Year 2000: Global and National Studies,* M.I.T. Press, 1977. Also contributor to *World Energy Prospects to the Year 2000,* 1978. Contributor to *Foreign Affairs, Bulletin of Atomic Scientists,* and *Washington Post.*

WORK IN PROGRESS: World Coal Study.

* * *

WILSON, Elena 1907(?)-1979

OBITUARY NOTICE: Born c. 1907 in Paris, France; died July 27, 1979, in Cape Cod, Mass. Editor. Wilson worked for *Town and Country* magazine as proofreader and assistant to the editor in chief. After her husband, Edmund Wilson, died, she published a collection of his correspondence under the title *Letters on Literature and Politics, 1912-1972,* a two volume series. The second volume is expected to be published in 1980. Obituaries and other sources: *New York Times,* July 29, 1979; *AB Bookman's Weekly,* August 20, 1979.

* * *

WILSON, Katharine M(argaret) 1895-

PERSONAL: Born March 29, 1895, in Rhynie, Aberdeenshire, Scotland; daughter of Hugh (a farmer) and Florence Eva (Blackett) Wilson. *Education:* University of Aberdeen, M.A. (with first class honors), 1917; Newnham College, Cambridge, Ph.D., 1924. *Religion:* Society of Friends (Quakers). *Home:* 3 Wythfield Rd., London SE9 5TG, England.

CAREER: Writer, 1920—.

WRITINGS: Mint Sauce (essays), P. Davies, 1927; *The Real Rhythm in English Poetry,* University of Aberdeen Press, 1929, Folcroft, 1972; *Sound and Meaning in English Poetry,* J. Cape, 1930, Kennikat, 1970; *Thought and Imagination in Art and Life,* Allen & Unwin, 1936; *Caw-Taw: The Story of a Rook* (juvenile), Hutchinson, 1950; *The Nightingale and the Hawk: A Psychological Study of Keats' Ode,* Allen & Unwin, 1964, Barnes & Noble, 1965; *Shakespeare's Sugared Sonnets,* Barnes & Noble, 1974.

Poetry represented in anthologies, including *Verses From New Kings,* edited by A. A. Jack, Wyllie, 1938, and *Vintage Voices,* edited by Charles Kohler, Quaker Fellowship of the Arts, 1977. Contributor of articles and poems to magazines, including *London Mercury, Contemporary Review, Faith and Freedom,* and *Friend.* Founding editor of *Reynard,* 1955-63; editor of journal of Seeker Association, 1962-69.

SIDELIGHTS: Wilson told *CA:* "Writing has been the one absorbing activity of my life; I am not really happy unless I have something on hand. Most of my published books resulted from some specific curiosity. The two books on rhythm and sound and meaning in English poetry explore the nature of what constitutes a sense of the 'music' we are aware of when reading poetry." Wilson's books on Keats and Shakespeare were written to help her discover if her impressions of certain works by each poet were justified, she said.

Wilson also noted that besides poetry she is interested in "the intersection between religion and philosophy." She has "contributed relevant articles to, I believe, all the main liberal, non-conformist religion quarterlies in the England of our age. Luckily, the only one that still survives the increasing economic pressures, *Faith and Freedom,* has taken all I have offered, the last being a detailed comparison of Jung's psychology and the mystical 'way' of St. John of the Cross."

* * *

WINKLER, Erhard M(ario) 1921-

PERSONAL: Born January 8, 1921, in Vienna, Austria; came to the United States in 1948, naturalized citizen, 1953; son of Wilhelm (a professor) and Clara (Deutsch) Winkler; married Isolde Koenig (a real estate broker), December 21, 1953; children: Gabriela, Manfred. *Education:* University of Vienna, Ph.D., 1945. *Home:* 17635 Juday Lake Dr. S., South Bend, Ind. 46635. *Office:* Department of Earth Sciences, University of Notre Dame, Notre Dame, Ind. 46556.

CAREER: Vienna Technical University, Vienna, Austria, first assistant in geology, 1946-48; University of Notre Dame, Notre Dame, Ind., instructor, 1948-50, assistant professor, 1950-56, associate professor, 1957-73, professor of geology, 1974—. *Member:* Geological Society of America (fellow), Association of Engineering Geologists, American Association for the Advancement of Science (fellow), American Society for Testing and Materials, National Association of Geology Teachers, Sigma Xi. *Awards, honors:* E. B. Burwell Award from Engineering Geology Division of Geological Society of America, 1975, for *Stone: Properties, Durability in Man's Environment.*

WRITINGS: Stone: Properties, Durability in Man's Environment, Springer-Verlag, 1973, revised edition, 1975; (editor) *Engineering Geology Case Histories: Decay and Preservation of Stone,* Geological Society of America, 1978.

WORK IN PROGRESS: Stone Decay and Stone Preservation; "research on urban stone decay, honeycomb weathering, rate of surface reduction."

* * *

WINOKUR, Stephen 1941-

PERSONAL: Born June 16, 1941, in New York, N.Y.; son of Morris (a professor) and Muriel Winokur; married Saundra Copeland (a psychologist), December 18, 1970. *Education:* City College of the City University of New York, B.A., 1962; University of Minnesota, Ph.D., 1967. *Office:* Department of Psychology, Texas Christian University, Fort Worth, Tex. 76129.

CAREER: University of Minnesota, Minneapolis, instructor, 1964-66, assistant professor of psychology, 1967-68, research associate, 1964, research fellow at Center for Research in Human Learning, 1965-67; Texas Christian University, Fort Worth, assistant professor, 1968-71, associate professor, 1971-79, professor of psychology, 1979—. Visiting associate professor at University of Minnesota, 1971-72, and California State University, Hayward, 1972-73, 1974, 1975, 1977. Management intern with San Jose police department, 1975; research associate at Minnesota Center for Philosophy and Science, 1970-73. Public speaker; consultant to police departments and the military.

MEMBER: American Association for the Advancement of Science (fellow), American Psychological Association, Association for Behavior Analysis, Psychonomic Society, New York Academy of Sciences, Sigma Xi (vice-president).

WRITINGS: (Editor with Michael Radner) *Analyses of Theories and Methods of Physics and Psychology,* University of Minnesota Press, 1970; *A Primer of Verbal Behavior: An Operant View,* Prentice-Hall, 1976. Contributor of about fifty articles and reviews to journals in the behavioral sciences.

WORK IN PROGRESS: Article on development of "verbal imitation in children"; research on "interaction of Pavlovian and instrumentally conditioned behaviors."

SIDELIGHTS: Winokur writes: "My research program for the last twelve years has emphasized studies with animal subjects in the fields of conditioned reinforcement. In the past few years I have also attempted to extend my work into the applications of the analysis of behavior (with probation and police personnel), but I have decided to abandon that area. For the past three years I have also been developing a research program in the operant conditioning analysis of verbal behavior; this has been successful and is being continued."

* * *

WINSLOW, Thyra Samter 1893-1961

OBITUARY NOTICE: Born March 15, 1893, in Fort Smith, Ark.; died December 2, 1961. Short story writer, novelist, critic, journalist, screenwriter, television writer, and author of books on weight reduction. Most of Winslow's stories and novels are set in Arkansas, where she grew up, or in the New York City theatre world, where she worked as a drama critic for the *Gotham Guide.* Her short stories are collected in several books, among them *Picture Frames, My Own, My Native Land,* and *The Sex Without Sentiment.* For a time she was employed as a screenwriter by Columbia, RKO, and Warner Bros.; later she wrote television plays for the National Broadcasting Company (NBC). She contributed to such magazines as *New Yorker, Good Housekeeping, Cosmopolitan, Town and Country,* and *Saturday Evening Post.* Obituaries and other sources: *The Oxford Companion to American Literature,* 4th edition, Oxford University Press, 1965.

* * *

WINTON, Chester Allen 1941-

PERSONAL: Born April 4, 1941, in Rockville Centre, N.Y.; son of Harry and Cecile (Emanuel) Winton; married Susan Meyers, August 27, 1967 (divorced, February, 1978); children: Michelle Suzanne, Jeffrey Harris. *Education:* University of California, Riverside, B.A. (with honors), 1962; University of California, Berkeley, M.A., 1965, Ph.D., 1970. *Religion:* Jewish. *Home:* 3238 Kimber Court, #118, San Jose, Calif. 95124. *Office:* 125 South Seventh St., San Jose, Calif. 95192.

CAREER: San Jose State University, San Jose, Calif., assistant professor, 1967-70, associate professor, 1970-76, professor of sociology, 1976—, associate dean of graduate studies, 1972-73, assistant academic vice-president, 1974-76, coordinator of marriage and family counseling program, 1975—. Lecturer in sociology at United College, Chinese University of Hong Kong, 1973-74; visiting scientist at Tavistock Institute of Human Relations, 1978. Adult probation officer in San Mateo County, Calif., summers, 1970-71; member of Santa Clara County Alcoholism Council; president of board of directors, San Jose Parental Stress Hotline, 1979—. Public lecturer; participant in workshops; consultant to Hong Kong Marriage Guidance Council. *Member:* California Association of Marriage and Family Counselors.

WRITINGS: *Theory and Measurement in Sociology,* Schenkman, 1974; *The Dynamics of Family Life,* Benjamin/Cummings, 1980. Contributor to research journals.

SIDELIGHTS: Winton writes: "At Tavistock Institute of Human Relations and Tavistock Clinic's department of children and parents, in London, England, I learned the principles and techniques of Structural Family Therapy. Much of my current writing is in this area, using this approach, which involves family therapy with families having problems with children and adolescents."

* * *

WINWAR, Frances 1900-

PERSONAL: Birth-given name, Francesca Vinciguerra; born May 3, 1900, in Taormina, Sicily; came to the United States, 1907, naturalized citizen, 1929; daughter of Domenico (a singer) and Giovanna (Sciglio) Vinciguerra; married Bernard D. N. Grebanier, September 22, 1925 (divorced); married Richard Wilson Webb, 1943 (divorced); married F. D. Lazenby, 1949; children: (first marriage) Francis (son). *Education:* Attended Hunter College (now of the City University of New York) and Columbia University. *Politics:* Democrat. *Address:* P.O. Box 1267, Jensen Beach, Fla. 33457. *Office:* Harper & Row, 10 East 53rd St., New York, N.Y. 10022.

CAREER: Biographer, novelist, critic, and translator. Visiting professor at University of Kansas City, 1942; lecturer at various universities and women's clubs. Leonardo da Vinci Art School, co-founder, 1923, executive secretary, 1923-30. *Member:* Poetry Society of America. *Awards, honors:* $5,000 nonfiction prize from *Atlantic Monthly,* 1933, for *Poor Splendid Wings.*

WRITINGS: *The Ardent Flame* (novel), Century, 1927; *The Golden Round* (novel), Century, 1928; *Pagan Interval,* Bobbs-Merrill, 1929; *Poor Splendid Wings: The Rossettis and Their Circle,* Little, Brown, 1933; *The Romantic Rebels,* Little, Brown, 1935; *Gallows Hill* (novel), Holt, 1937; *Farewell the Banner: "Three Persons and One Soul"—Coleridge, Wordsworth and Dorothy,* Doubleday, 1938; *Puritan City: The Story of Salem,* R. M. McBride, 1938.

Oscar Wilde and the Yellow 'Nineties, Harper, 1940; *American Giant: Walt Whitman and His Times,* Harper, 1941; *The Sentimentalist* (novel), Harper, 1943; *The Life of the Heart: George Sand and Her Times,* Harper, 1945; *The Saint and the Devil: A Biographical Study of Joan of Arc and Gilles de Rais,* Harper, 1948; *Joan of Arc,* Bantam, 1948.

The Immortal Lovers: Elizabeth Barrett and Robert Browning, Harper, 1950; *Napoleon and the Battle of Waterloo* (juvenile), Random House, 1953; *The Eagle and the Rock* (novel), Harper, 1953; *The Last Love of Camille* (novel), Harper, 1954; *Queen Elizabeth and the Spanish Armada* (juvenile), Random House, 1954; (translator) Giovanni Boccaccio, *The Decameron,* Modern Library, 1955; *Wingless Victory: A Biography of Gabriele d'Annunzio and Eleonora Duse,* Harper, 1956 (published in England as *Wings of Fire,* Redman, 1957); *Elizabeth: The Romantic Story of Elizabeth Barrett Browning* (juvenile), World, 1957; *The Monument in Staten Island: Meucci, Garibaldi and the Telephone,* E. Clemente, 1957; *Italy and Her People,* Lutterworth, 1957; *The Haunted Palace: A Life of Edgar Allan Poe,* Harper, 1959; *Cupid: The God of Love* (juvenile), Random House, 1959.

The Land of the Italian People (juvenile), Lippincott, 1961, revised edition published as *The Land and People of Italy,* 1972; *Jean-Jacques Rousseau: Conscience of an Era,* Random House, 1961; *All About Napoleon Bonaparte,* W. H. Allen, 1967.

Also translator of libretti for the Metropolitan Opera Association. Contributor to magazines, including *Freeman, New York Times Book Review, Saturday Review, Tomorrow,* and *English Journal.*

SIDELIGHTS: Winwar began her career by writing historical romances. Her first, *Ardent Flame,* is a novelized version of a story told by both Dante and D'Annunzio of two ill-fated thirteenth-century lovers; this was followed by *Golden Round,* also set in the thirteenth century. Both novels won her many admirers and praise for her sensuous power and poetic expression. She has set other novels in contemporary Sicily and seventeenth-century Salem, and based one on the life of Napoleon and another on the life of Franz Liszt, all of which continued her mode of impassioned romanticism.

Yet Winwar is chiefly known for her sentimentalized but historically accurate biographies of famous people. The first of these, *Poor Splendid Wings,* is about the pre-Raphaelite Brotherhood, the artistic movement of the late 1800's that centered around such figures as Dante Gabriel Rossetti and Algernon Swinburne. In this book she introduced her method of applying to biography the novelistic techniques of her historical romances. This method prompted C. G. Stillman to write: "It reads like a novel, but it is not fictionalized biography. Wide reading, thoughtful analysis, a sense of drama and character and a modern psychological approach without psychological verbiage are the components of this study." Similarly, the reviewer for the *Boston Transcript* observed: "Frances Winwar makes lavish use of her facts and she does the same with her imagination. Neither hampers the other."

S. C. Chew called her next work, *The Romantic Rebels,* "dove-tailed biography" because it interweaves the life stories of Byron, Shelley, and Keats. Critics generally admired her ability to organize her material into interesting narrative "while regretting," as did H. A. Perry, that "more homage was not paid to the poetry." *Farewell the Banner,* a composite biography of William and Dorothy Wordsworth and Samuel Taylor Coleridge, was also praised as an entertaining yet "valuable fund of information." Of this book Percy Hutchison wrote: "With the instinct and the art of one who has done fiction, she has held strictly to biographical and historical truth in a narrative that often reads like fiction."

Winwar's subsequent biographies—of Oscar Wilde, Walt Whitman, George Sand, Joan of Arc, Elizabeth Barrett and Robert Browning, Gabriele D'Annunzio, Edgar Allan Poe, and Jean-Jacques Rousseau—continued to reap critical acclaim. The last of these, *All About Napoleon Bonaparte,* was acknowledged by the *Times Literary Supplement* as likely "to arouse the important initial interest in Napoleon's undoubted achievements" by means of its abundant details, graphic sentences, and bold outline of the period.

BIOGRAPHICAL/CRITICAL SOURCES: New York Herald Tribune Books, April 3, 1927, October 28, 1928, June 16, 1929, September 24, 1933, November 10, 1935, December 11, 1938; *Boston Transcript,* June 15, 1927, October 6, 1928, September 23, 1933, December 28, 1935, March 20, 1937, October 1, 1938; *New York Times,* July 17, 1927, October 7, 1928, September 24, 1933, November 17, 1935, March 21, 1937, September 25, 1938, November 16, 1941, November 7, 1943, June 4, 1950, May 3, 1953, April 18, 1954, November 14, 1954, August 18, 1957, January 18, 1959; *Saturday Review of Literature,* October 5, 1929, October 7, 1933, January 20, 1934, November 9, 1935, March 20, 1937, September 17, 1938, December 13, 1941, January 1, 1944; *Christian Science Monitor,* September 23, 1933, December 11, 1935, March 31, 1937; *Nation,* October 18, 1933; *New Republic,* December 6, 1933, December 18, 1935, October 12, 1938; *Commonweal,* December 15, 1933, February 20, 1948; *Catholic World,* December 1938, July 1953; *Time,* March 25, 1940, October 29, 1945; *Atlantic,* May, 1940; *Times Literary Supplement,* May 25, 1967.*

* * *

WISE, Terence 1935-

PERSONAL: Born May 13, 1935, in London, England; son of Frederick Joseph (a carpenter) and Margaret Louise (Marsh) Wise; married Shirley Orton (a librarian), April 5, 1969; children: Edward, Rachel. *Home:* 20 St. Marys Rd., Doncaster, South Yorkshire DN1 2NP, England.

CAREER: Free-lance writer, 1967—. Also worked on whaling ships and as a bookshop manager. *Military service:* British Army, 1953-56; served in Germany. *Member:* Flag Institute (librarian), Military Heraldry Society (librarian), Victorian Military Society, Solo Wargames Association, Society of Ancients, Napoleonic Association.

WRITINGS: Guide to Military Museums, Model & Allied, 1969; *Introduction to Wargaming,* Model & Allied, 1969; *To Catch a Whale* (autobiography), Bles, 1970; *Military Vehicle Markings,* Model & Allied, Part I, 1972, Part II, 1973; *American Camouflage and Markings,* Almark, 1973; *Forts and Castles,* Almark, 1973; *European Edged Weapons,* Almark, 1974; *Polar Exploration,* Almark, 1974; *Medieval European Armies,* Osprey, 1975; *Medieval Warfare,* Osprey, 1976; *Airfix Guide to A.C.W. Wargaming,* Patrick Stephens, 1977; *Military Flags of the World,* Blandford, 1978; *Wars of the Crusades,* Osprey, 1978; *Armies of the Crusades,* Osprey, 1978; *Napoleonic Flags,* two volumes, Osprey, 1978; *D-Day to Berlin,* Arms & Armour Press, 1979; *1066, Year of Crisis,* Osprey, 1979, schools edition, Wayland Publishing, 1979; *Saxon Viking Norman,* Osprey, 1979; *Napoleonic Artillery Equipments,* Osprey, 1979; *Medieval Heraldry,* two volumes, Osprey, 1980; *The Conquistadores,* Osprey, 1980; *Armour Markings of the World, 1939-1945,* Patrick Stephens, 1980.

Author of "Battles for Wargames," a series of six booklets, Model & Allied, 1972-74; editor of series on campaigns, 1979—. Author of "Observation Post," a monthly column in *Military Modelling.*

SIDELIGHTS: Wise comments: "I write because I have always wanted to, because the lonely life suits my nature, and because I am pig-headed and stupid. After eleven years of professional full-time writing I can advise all would-be authors that all they need to qualify is persistence, persistence, and persistence. I write military history, covering the more neglected subjects, because I like to eat and to pass on knowledge which is inaccessible to most, but inside me there struggles a novelist, and somewhere in this mare's nest of an office I still have five (or is it seven?) unpublished novels. One day I may get out from under the bread-earning workload and write more fiction."

* * *

WISEMAN, Donald John 1918-

PERSONAL: Born October 25, 1918, in Emsworth, England; son of Percy John (a Royal Air Force officer) and G. M. (Savage) Wiseman; married Mary Catherine Ruoff, September 18, 1948; children: Gillian Wiseman Manifold, Mary Wiseman Young, Catherine Jane. *Education:* King's College, London, B.A., 1939; Wadham College, Oxford, M.A., 1952; School of Oriental and African Studies, London, D.Litt., 1969. *Religion:* Christian. *Home:* Low Barn, 26 Downs Way, Tadworth, Surrey KT20 5DZ, England. *Office:* School of Oriental and African Studies, University of London, London WC1E 7HP, England.

CAREER: British Museum, London, England, assistant keeper of Egyptian and Assyrian antiquities, 1948-55, assistant keeper of western Asiatic antiquities, 1955-61; University of London, School of Oriental and African Studies, London, England, professor of Assyriology, 1961—. Joint director of British School of Archaeology in Iraq, 1961-65, chairman, 1970—. Epigraphist for archaeological excavations. *Military service:* Royal Air Force Volunteer Reserve, chief intelligence officer for Mediterranean Allied Tactical Air Forces, 1939-45; became group captain; received Bronze Star. *Member:* British Academy (fellow), Society of Antiquaries (fellow), German Archaeological Institute (corresponding member). *Awards, honors:* Officer of Order of the British Empire, 1943.

WRITINGS: The Alalakh Tablets, British Institute of Archaeology at Ankara, 1953; *Chronicles of Chaldean Kings,* British Museum, 1956; *Cuneiform Texts From Cappadocian Tablets in the British Museum,* Volume V, British Museum, 1956; *Vassal-Treaties of Esarhaddon,* British School of Archaeology in Iraq, 1958; *Illustrations From Biblical Archaeology,* Inter-Varsity Press, 1959, revised edition, 1962; *Cylinder Seals of Western Asia,* Batchworth Press, 1959; *Catalogue of Western Asiatic Seals I,* British Museum, 1960; *The Expansion of Assyrian Studies,* University of London Press, 1962; *Assyria and Babylonia Circa 1200-1000 B.C.,* Cambridge University Press, 1965.

Editor and contributor: *The New Bible Dictionary,* Inter-Varsity Press, 1962, revised edition, 1980; *The New Bible Commentary Revised,* Inter-Varsity Press, 1970; *Notes on Some Problems of the Book of Daniel,* Tyndale House, 1965; *Peoples of Old Testament Times,* Oxford University Press, 1973; (with Edwin Yamauchi) *Archaeology and the Bible: An Introductory Study,* Zondervan, 1979.

General editor of "Tyndale Old Testament Commentaries," Inter-Varsity Press, 1964—. Contributor to *Encyclopaedia Britannica.* Contributor of more than a hundred articles to academic journals. Editor of *Iraq,* 1953-78; co-editor of *Reallexion der Assyriologie,* 1959—.

WORK IN PROGRESS: The Nabu Temple Texts, series of

cuneiform texts from Nimrud, publication by British School of Archaeology (Iraq), expected in 1981.

* * *

WITMER, Helen L(eland) 1898-1979

OBITUARY NOTICE—See index for *CA* sketch: Born July 17, 1898, in Lansford, Pa.; died November 20, 1979, in Arlington, Virginia. Sociologist, educator, and author of books in her field. Witmer was the director of research at Smith College School of Social Work from 1929 to 1949 and at the Children's Bureau of the Department of Health, Education, and Welfare from 1952 to 1965. Her publications include *The Field of Parent Education, Personality in the Making,* and *On Rearing Infants and Young Children in Institutions.* Obituaries and other sources: *American Men and Women of Science: The Social and Behavioral Sciences,* 12th edition, Bowker, 1973; *Washington Post,* November 22, 1979.

* * *

WITT, James F. 1937-

PERSONAL: Born May 16, 1937, in Brooklyn, N.Y.; son of Frederick (a printer) and Marie (Wunderlin) Witt; married Nancy Mueller (a pupil personnel director); children: Thomas, Karen, Faith. *Education:* Adelphi University, B.A., 1959; Queens College of the City University of New York, B.S., 1962. *Home address:* Mill St., Putnam Valley, N.Y. 10579. *Office:* Fleetweather, Inc., Orbit Lane, Hopewell, N.Y.

CAREER: Science teacher at Lakeland schools in Shrub Oak, N.Y., 1959-77, head of department, 1968-77; weather consultant, 1970—. Vice-president of Fleetweather, Inc. Owner of Pre Serv-A-Shine. *Member:* Beta Beta Beta.

WRITINGS: Traveling Weatherwise, U.S.A., Dodd, 1975.

WORK IN PROGRESS: Understanding and Forecasting Weather.

SIDELIGHTS: "Ninety percent of my time is currently being devoted to long-range research in the field of weather," Witt told *CA*.

* * *

WOLTMAN, Frederick (Enos) 1905-1970

OBITUARY NOTICE: Born March 16, 1905, in York, Pa.; died March 5, 1970. Journalist. An investigative reporter for the *New York World-Telegram,* Woltman was best known for his exposes of Communist activities. His series on the real estate mortgage bond racket, written with Joseph Lilly, earned the *World-Telegram* a Pulitzer Prize in 1933 for the most disinterested and meritorious public service for the year. Woltman also earned a Pulitzer Prize for distinguished reporting in 1947. Obituaries and other sources: *Current Biography,* Wilson, 1947, April, 1970; *Who Was Who in America,* 5th edition, Marquis, 1973.

* * *

WOMBLE, Vernon G. 1942(?)-1979

OBITUARY NOTICE: Born c. 1942 in New York, N.Y.; died August 24, 1979, in Washington, D.C. Reporter and television field producer. Womble worked for WRC-TV, an affiliate of NBC-TV, for over ten years before he joined the NBC news bureau in 1970. He began as news editor and was promoted to the post of field producer. Womble was associated with the *Boston Globe* and the Pennsylvania *York Gazette* prior to his affiliation with NBC-TV. Obituaries and other sources: *Washington Post,* August 25, 1979.

WOODIWISS, Kathleen E.

PERSONAL: Born in Alexandria, La.; married Ross Woodiwiss (an officer in U.S. Air Force); children: three sons. *Education:* Attended schools in Alexandria, La. *Residence:* Princeton, Minn. *Address:* c/o Avon Books, Hearst Corporation, 959 Eighth Ave., New York, N.Y. 10019.

CAREER: Writer.

WRITINGS—All published by Avon: *The Flame and the Flower,* 1972; *The Wolf and the Dove,* 1974; *Shanna,* 1977; *Ashes in the Wind,* 1979.

SIDELIGHTS: When Avon published Kathleen Woodiwiss's first book, *The Flame and the Flower,* it began a new tradition in paperback book publishing, namely that of the "erotic historical romance." Woodiwiss was the first writer in this tradition. Following her lead have been such romance writers as Rosemary Rogers, Laura McBain, and Joyce Verette. The historical romances that Woodiwiss and her colleagues write are stories that often stretch beyond their four-hundred-page minimum length and are filled with scenes of sexual tension between the heroine and the men in her highly adventurous life. The setting is usually exotic and constantly changing from continent to continent. Often "innocent," the heroine is usually introduced to love by a dashing and handsome man with whom she instantly falls in love, only to be parted from him. The book invariably ends with the heroine being reunited with her first and true love.

Woodiwiss is disturbed by commentators who label her books as "erotic." "I'm insulted when my books are called erotic," she told an interviewer. "I don't think people who say that have read my books. I believe I write love stories. With a little spice. Some of the other current romances are a bit savage, though. They make sex dirty. It's embarrassing to read them. But women are searching for the love story. I get a lot of fan mail, and they tell me that. After all, we should be glad to be women. I am. I find it satisfying. And I plan to go on writing about romance."

BIOGRAPHICAL/CRITICAL SOURCES: Publishers Weekly, January 31, 1977, May 30, 1977; *Cosmopolitan,* February, 1978.*

* * *

WORCHEL, Stephen 1946-

PERSONAL: Born February 27, 1946, in Washington, D.C.; son of Philip (a professor) and Libby (Goldberg) Worchel; married Frances Ferris; children: Leah Marie. *Education:* University of Texas, B.A. (with honors), 1967; Duke University, Ph.D., 1971. *Residence:* Ruckersville, Va. *Office:* Department of Psychology, University of Virginia, Charlottesville, Va. 22901.

CAREER: Duke University, Durham, N.C., instructor in psychology, 1969-71; University of North Carolina, Chapel Hill, assistant professor of psychology, 1971-74; University of Virginia, Charlottesville, associate professor, 1974-78, professor of psychology, 1978—. Summer lecturer at Chulalongkorhn University, 1969; visiting assistant professor at North Carolina Central University, spring, 1971; visiting lecturer at Fort Bragg, 1971-73. Research assistant for Stimulmatics, Inc., 1967; trainee with U.S. Public Health Service, 1967-68; research associate at Institute of Research in Social Science. Chairperson of professional meetings. *Member:* American Psychological Association, Society of Experimental Social Psychology, Eastern Psychological Association, Southeastern Psychological Association, Sigma Xi, Psi Chi. *Awards, honors:* National Science Foundation grants, 1973-

75, 1977-80; Wilson Gee Foundation grant, 1976; Fulbright fellowship for Greece, 1979-80.

WRITINGS: (With Joel Cooper) *Understanding Social Psychology,* Dorsey, 1976, revised edition, 1979; (editor with W. G. Austin, and contributor) *The Social Psychology of Intergroup Relations,* Brooks/Cole, 1979; (with Peter Sheras) *Clinical Psychology: A Social Psychological Approach,* Van Nostrand, 1979; (with George Goethals) *The Psychology of Individual Adjustment,* Random House, in press.

Contributor: Lawrence Wrightsman and J. C. Brighan, editors, *Contemporary Issues in Social Psychology,* Brooks/Cole, 1973; Samuel Himmelfarb and A. H. Eagly, editors, *Readings in Attitude Change,* Wiley, 1974; J. H. Harvey, W. J. Ikes, and R. F. Kidd, editors, *New Directions in Attribution Research,* Erlbaum Associates, 1977; Andrew Baum and Yakov Epstein, editors, *Human Response to Crowding,* Erlbaum Associates, 1978.

Author of scripts for training films for Virginia prison personnel. Editor of psychology series for Van Nostrand, 1977-78. Contributor of about forty articles to psychology journals. Associate editor of *Personality and Social Psychology Bulletin,* 1977—; member of editorial board of *Environmental Psychology and Nonverbal Behavior,* 1976—.

WORK IN PROGRESS: An Introduction to Psychology, with Wayne Shebilski, publication by Prentice-Hall expected in 1982.

SIDELIGHTS: Worchel writes: "My major interest is in writing psychology books that illustrate the relevance of the field to the readers. As the world becomes increasingly complex, individuals experience greater difficulties in developing meaningful interpersonal relationships. The psychological study of human relations should provide some useful guidelines. In addition to writing, my academic interests include research and teaching in social and environmental psychology."

AVOCATIONAL INTERESTS: Farming (raising livestock and horses), international travel (Greece, Southeast Asia, Mexico).

* * *

WRENN, Tony P(entecost) 1938-

PERSONAL: Born May 11, 1938, in Roxboro, N.C.: son of Joseph Cleveland (a farmer) and Lottie Mae Tillman (a gardener; maiden name, Pentecost) Wrenn. *Education:* Wake Forest University, B.A., 1955; Universitaet Wien, diploma (with honors), 1959. *Politics:* Democrat. *Residence:* Fredericksburg, Va. *Office:* P.O. Box 233, Fredericksburg, Va. 22401.

CAREER: Berlitz School of Languages, Nuernberg, West Germany, teacher of English, 1959; Gesellschaft fuer Konsumforschung, Nuernberg, West Germany, writer and researcher, 1959; farm worker in North Carolina, 1960; National Archives, Washington, D.C., archivist in documentary publications, 1960-61; National Trust for Historic Preservation, Washington, D.C., archivist, 1962-66; writer, researcher, and historic preservation consultant, 1966—. Worked at archaeological excavations. Work is represented in photography exhibitions. *Military service:* U.S. Army, Military Intelligence, 1955-59. *Member:* National Trust for Historic Preservation, Pioneer Society America (member of board of directors), Kenmore Association, Society for the Prevention of Cruelty to Animals, Audobon Society, Society for the Preservation of Virginia Antiques. *Awards, honors:* Grant from National Trust for Historic Preservation, 1970.

WRITINGS: (With Robert L. Montague III) *Planning for Preservation,* American Society of Planning Officials, 1964; (contributor and photographer) H. H. Harwood, Jr., editor, *Rails to the Blue Ridge,* Pioneer Society America, 1969; (editor and photographer) Mollie Somerville, *Washington Walked Here,* Acropolis Books, 1970; (contributor and photographer) Robert G. Ferris, editor, *Signers of the Declaration,* U.S. Government Printing Office, 1973; *Woodbury, Connecticut: A New England Townscape* (self-illustrated), National Trust for Historic Preservation, 1975; *Washington, D.C. Walking Tours,* Preservation Press, 1975; (contributor) Nancy Love, editor, *Washington: The Official Bicentennial Guidebook,* Washingtonian Books, 1975, reprinted as *The Best of Washingtonian: The Washingtonian Magazine's Guide to Life in the Nation's Capital,* 1977; (with Elizabeth D. Mulloy) *America's Forgotten Architecture,* (with own photographs; selection of Book-of-the-Month Club and others) Pantheon, 1976; (photographer) Moussa M. Domit, editor, *Two Hundred Years of the Visual Arts in North Carolina,* North Carolina Museum of Art, 1976; (photographer) David C. Driskell, *Two Centuries of Black American Art,* Knopf, 1976; *Wilmington, North Carolina: An Historical and Architectural Portrait,* University Press of Virginia, 1980.

Created and contributed photographs to *A Northern Virginia Calendar,* Pioneer Society America, 1969. Contributor of articles and photographs to professional journals, popular magazines, and newspapers, including *Preservation News* and *Echoes of History.* Past editor of *Pioneer America.*

WORK IN PROGRESS: An American Architectural Dictionary and Building Watcher's Guide, publication expected in 1981; *Tom Day, Cabinetmaker,* on a free black artisan in pre-Civil War North Carolina; research on the architecture of Baptist churches and on the artisans of Fredericksburg, Va.

SIDELIGHTS: Wrenn writes: "My major interests are building watching and gardening. I walk whenever possible, shunpike when I cannot walk, and do both slowly to learn as much as possible about both the built and natural environment. My mother's advice on gardening was to look at the garden as frequently as possible. That also works with buildings and landscapes for different seasons, weather, light, surroundings, even our own moods, affect not only what we see but how we perceive it. Constant looking is necessary for understanding, even between old friends."

AVOCATIONAL INTERESTS: Herb gardening, book collecting.

* * *

WRENN, Winnie Holden 1886(?)-1979

OBITUARY NOTICE: Born c. 1886 in Centreville, Va.; died August 5, 1979, in Alexandria, Va. Columnist. Wrenn authored a weekly news column in the *Loudon Times-Mirror* and other newspapers for over thirty years. Obituaries and other sources: *Washington Post,* August 11, 1979.

* * *

WRIGHT, Gavin Peter 1943-

PERSONAL: Given name is pronounced Gay-vin; born September 30, 1943, in New Haven, Conn.; son of Charles F. (a government employee) and Agnita Greisen (a director in education) Wright; married Cathe Winn (an actress), 1965; children: Anders Frank, Nicholas Charles. *Religion:* Society of Friends (Quaker). *Education:* Swarthmore College, B.A., 1965; Yale University, M.A., 1966, Ph.D., 1969. *Office:*

Department of Economics, University of Michigan, Ann Arbor, Mich. 48104.

CAREER: Yale University, New Haven, Conn., assistant professor of economics, 1969-72; University of Michigan, Ann Arbor, assistant professor, 1972-73, associate professor, 1973-77, professor of economics, 1977—. *Member:* American Economic Association, Economic History Association, Agricultural History Society. *Awards, honors:* National Science Foundation fellow, 1971-72; Cole Prize for best article from *Journal of Economic History,* 1974; grant, 1977-79.

WRITINGS: Reckoning With Slavery, Oxford University Press, 1976; *The Political Economy of the Cotton South,* Norton, 1978. Contributor to economic journals.

WORK IN PROGRESS: Comparative studies in labor supply and early industrialization, with Gary Saxonhouse; a history of the economy of the South since the Civil War.

SIDELIGHTS: "New Economic History, the self-conscious application of economic analysis and econometric techniques to historical subjects," Wright remarked in the preface to his book, *The Political Economy of the Cotton South,* "[has] frequently been valuable and stimulating, but I now believe that it is a mistake for economic history to define itself merely as economics applied to old data. Instead, economic history offers a distinctive intellectual approach to the study of economics, a view of the economic world in which historical time plays a fundamental role. Resource allocation is affected not just by the interaction of tastes and technology at time *t,* but also by the experience and endowment of the past. Initial conditions do matter, and the historical order of events does matter; a given stimulus may evoke radically different responses at different historical times."

In reviewing Wright's book, Roger L. Ransom commented that a "feature of this book, which particularly appealed to me, was Wright's admonition that the economist-historian must be careful about indiscriminate use of economic theories whose assumptions 'are fundamentally inappropriate to antebellum America'.... Wright's analysis deals with nineteenth-century farms . . . and he questions whether conventional theory can deal with this situation. He develops his own economic model that stresses the importance the farm operator placed on ownership of the farm, the need to rely on family labor, and the problem of risk. It is refreshing to come across a cliometrician who recognizes the limits of economic theory in historical investigation." In sum, Ransom declared: "This is excellent economic history. Some years ago Lance Davis entitled a critique of cliometrics: 'And It Will Never be Literature'.... He may have been right, but in *The Political Economy of the Cotton South,* Gavin Wright proves that we have made considerable progress in the last decade. Literature or not, this is historical political economy at its best."

BIOGRAPHICAL/CRITICAL SOURCES: Journal of Economic History, December, 1978.

* * *

WRIGHT, Richard J. 1935-

PERSONAL: Born April 19, 1935, in Akron, Ohio; married in 1959; children: three. *Education:* University of Akron, B.S., 1957, M.A., 1963; Kent State University, Ph.D., 1968. *Office:* Center for Archival Collections, Bowling Green State University, Bowling Green, Ohio 43403.

CAREER: High school social studies teacher in Akron, Ohio, 1957-65; Bowling Green State University, Bowling Green, Ohio, assistant professor, 1968-74, associate professor of history, 1974—, director of Center for Archival Collections, 1968—. Member of National Archives Regional Advisory Council, 1969-73, White House Public Forum on Domestic Policy, 1975, and U.S. Commission of Maritime History. Member of regional advisory council of National Historical Publications and Records Commission. Participant in conferences.

MEMBER: World Ship Society, International Shipmasters' Association, North American Society of Oceanic History, American Historical Association, Organization of American Historians, Society of American Archivists, Steamship Historical Society of America, U.S. Navy Institute, Belgian Nautical Research Association, Great Lakes Historical Society, Great Lakes Maritime Institute, Ohio Academy of History, Ohio Historical Society, Society of Ohio Archivists, Wisconsin Marine Historical Society, Wood County Historical Society, Toronto Marine Historical Society, Marine Historical Society of Detroit, Maritime Historical Society of Detroit (member of advisory committee, 1972—). *Awards, honors:* Named Great Lakes historian of the year by Marine Historical Society of Detroit, 1978.

WRITINGS: Freshwater Whales: A History of the American Ship Building Company and Its Predecessors, Kent State University Press, 1969; (contributor) *Ahoy and Farewell,* Marine Historical Society of Detroit, 1970; *The John Hunt Memoirs: Early Years of the Maumee Basin, 1812-1835,* Maumee Valley Historical Society, 1978. Contributor of articles and reviews to professional and popular magazines and newspapers, including *Skin Diver* and *Telescope.* Editor of *Northwest Ohio Quarterly,* 1975—.

* * *

WYETH, Betsy James 1921-

PERSONAL: Born September 26, 1921, in East Aurora, N.Y.; daughter of Merle Davis (a newspaper editor) and Amy Elizabeth (Browning) James; married Andrew Wyeth (an artist), May 15, 1940; children: Nicholas, James Browning. *Education:* Attended Colby Junior College. *Religion:* Protestant. *Home and office address:* Chadds Ford, Pa. 19317. *Agent:* Robert Lescher, 155 East 71st St., New York, N.Y. 10021.

WRITINGS: (Editor) *The Wyeths: The Intimate Correspondence of N. C. Wyeth, 1901-1945,* Gambit, 1971; *Wyeth at Kuerners,* Houghton, 1976; *The Stray* (juvenile), Farrar, Straus, 1979; *The Art of Jamie Wyeth,* Houghton, 1980.

SIDELIGHTS: Betsy James Wyeth's first book, *The Wyeths: The Intimate Correspondence of N. C. Wyeth, 1901-1945,* is a collection of letters written by her father-in-law, Newell Convers Wyeth, an American illustrator and mural painter best known for his illustrations of such novels as *Treasure Island, Kidnapped,* and *Robin Hood.* The letters, written to various family members, are "rich with color, informal, affectionate, and as observant as Thoreau, whom he admired greatly," noted Edward Weeks. Lincoln Kirstein commented that "these letters, devotedly assembled, accompanied by too many snapshots and too few of [Wyeth's] own paintings, might have enjoyed sharper editing."

In her second publication Wyeth concentrated on the art of her husband, Andrew Wyeth, renowned for his detailed landscapes and interiors. *Wyeth at Kuerners* was lauded by the *Washington Post Book World:* "This is not only an extraordinarily beautiful book, but one that gives a unique view of the artist at work—the things he observes and his way of looking at them, the changes he makes in the natural landscape to suit his purpose, his selection and elimination of details as he moves toward the finished artistic whole." The book contains a selection of the meticulous preliminary sketches and studies of Wyeth's paintings of the Kuerner farm in Pennsylvania. John Richardson claimed that "the good things are swamped by an embarrassment of sketches. Mrs. Wyeth should have left most of these vignettes in the drawers to which her husband wisely relegated them, for they make one wonder whether all that painstaking brushwork, which passes in some circles for genius, is not an attempt to camouflage the triteness of the original conception." On the contrary, *Washington Post Book World* said "she has written a simple commentary and sensitively grouped the sketches and paintings." P. L. Adams also contended that Betsy James Wyeth "has succeeded admirably in showing how Wyeth's eye and mind work in the creation of a painting."

BIOGRAPHICAL/CRITICAL SOURCES: Atlantic, December, 1971, December, 1976; *Saturday Review,* December 11, 1971; *Nation,* January 24, 1972; *New York Review of Books,* December 9, 1976; *Washington Post Book World,* December 12, 1976.

* * *

WYLER, Brenda (Florence) 1951-

PERSONAL: Born August 8, 1951, in Cleaver's Port, N.J.; daughter of Walter (a conservationist and brewer) and Gladys K. (a pianist and brewer; maiden name, Coburn) Sekay; married Harry Mumstone (a logger), 1971 (divorced); married Parnell Wyler (a pharmacist), 1979; children: Clive, Satch. *Education:* Attended Mumstone School for Arts and Crafts, 1974-76. *Politics:* "Animals don't vote—why should people?" *Religion:* "Earth is enough heaven and hell for me!" *Office:* c/o Great Lakes Writers Cooperative, 221 Lewiston Rd., Grosse Pointe Farms, Mich. 48236.

CAREER: Writer. Worked as yeast specialist in breweries in Mumstone, Wyo., 1971-75; free-lance nature consultant, 1975—. Served on Mumstone Committe to Save the Beavers, 1974, Mumstone Committee to Eliminate Harmful Pestilence, 1975, and Mumstone Committee to Save the Bogs, 1976. *Member:* Nature's Children. *Awards, honors:* Silver Sixpack Award from Association of Wyoming Beer Manufacturers, 1977, for *Bless the Beasts and the Yeasts;* special citation from Mumstone Anti-Pollution Society, 1978, for *He Who Litters Kills the Critters.*

WRITINGS: Beavers of Wyoming, Tusk Books, 1972; *A Tourist's Guide to Mumstone, Wyoming,* Mumstone Special Libraries Publications, 1972; *Bless the Beasts and the Yeasts* (verse), Tusk Books, 1977; *Salt Lick!* (novel), Discreet Highways Press, 1977; *He Who Litters Kills the Critters* (verse), Tusk Books, 1978; (with sister P. Sekay) *Walter Drunk the River* (Mumstone folktales), Poem Salvager's Press, 1979.

WORK IN PROGRESS: The Wanton Huntress, a gothic; *The Husky Maiden,* a modern romance.

SIDELIGHTS: Wyler told *CA:* "I owe most of my career as a writer to my first husband, Harry Mumstone. I met him at a carnival that was set up in one of the parking lots near where I was living in New Jersey. It was love at first sight when I saw the way he could bowl those cement milk bottles over. I guess I was pretty impressionable in my early adulthood. So he whisked me off to Mumstone, a town in Wyoming named after his great-grandfather Arthur Mumstone, the founder of Mumstone Malt Fermenters. Well, I fell in love with the wilderness there and was especially interested in the beavers. I would often camp aside the river for weeks on end for just a glimpse of the proud beast. The culmination of this interest was *Beavers of Wyoming,* in which I give brief descriptions of the activities of the many beavers I encountered.

"Unfortunately, I became so preoccupied with beaver-life that I neglected my marriage. After Harry divorced me, I became despondent, drank heavily, and tried unsuccessfully to forget about the beavers. I drifted for a while and wrote a pair of introspective works, *Bless the Beasts and the Yeasts* and *Salt Lick!* The former was well received by critics who seemed familiar with my sense of symbolism and verse structure. However, *Salt Lick!,* my only novel, was roundly criticized by the same reviewers who were unable to accept my depiction of the salt lick as a metaphor for life. In the book, which is virtually unheard of outside Wyoming, a Vietnam vet returns to his hometown only to find it overtaken by beavers. Ignorant of their ways, the vet plants salt licks about the village with the intention of killing the beavers when they approach them. However, the beavers express no interest in the salt licks. When the vet, in a fit of hysterical frustration, assaults one of the blocks, he accidently knocks himself unconscious. He awakes to find himself taken captive by the beavers. They teach him their ways and by novel's end, the veteran is cheerily working alongside the beavers as they construct a dam. I had hoped that this novel would reflect an appreciable attitude regarding Man's ignorance of nature. Sadly, I now feel that it is my greatest failure as an artist.

"Things perked up when I moved to Michigan, though, for I managed to meet several other writers who shared my eccentric approach to the craft. Together we formed a cooperative workshop. Since 1978, this workshop has provided much-needed counseling and assistance to prospective writers who share our 'off-center' approach to writing. Also, the workshop has proved invaluable to me. My verse epic, *He Who Litters Kills the Critters,* was spawned from many hours of discussion with my fellow writers. It depicts life in a rural village in which accidental spillage from a brewery results in alcoholic wildlife. Since my family background is entrenched in the beer industry, I consider this a better-than-usual book on the subject."

* * *

WYLIE, Ruth C(arol) 1920-

PERSONAL: Born January 24, 1920, in Beaver Falls, Pa.; daughter of Harry N. (a professor) and Georgiana (a professor; maiden name, Roney) Wylie. *Education:* Geneva College, B.S. (with highest honors), 1939; University of Pittsburgh, M.A., 1940, Ph.D., 1943. *Residence:* Baltimore, Md. *Office:* Department of Psychology, Goucher College, Dulaney Valley Rd., Towson, Md. 21204.

CAREER: Stephens College, Columbia, Mo., teacher of psychology, 1943-45; Connecticut College, New London, began as instructor, became assistant professor of psychology, 1942-52; Lackland Air Force Base, San Antonio, Tex., researcher at Human Resources Research Center, summer, 1952; Sarah Lawrence College, Bronxville, N.Y., member of psychology faculty, 1952-62; Goucher College, Towson, Md., professor of psychology, 1962—, head of department, 1962-70, 1975—. Visiting lecturer at Northwestern University, 1961-62.

MEMBER: American Psychological Association (fellow), American Association for the Advancement of Science (fellow), Psychonomic Society, American Association of University Professors, Sigma Xi. *Awards, honors:* Grants from American Philosophical Society, 1955, National Science Foundation, 1961-62, and National Institutes of Health.

WRITINGS: The Self Concept: A Critical Survey of Pertinent Research Literature, University of Nebraska Press, 1961, revised edition published as *The Self Concept,* Volume I: *A Review of Methodological Considerations and Measuring Instruments,* 1974, Volume II: *Theory and Research on Selected Topics,* 1979; (contributor) E. F. Borgatta and W. W. Lambert, editors, *Handbook of Personality Theory and Research,* Rand McNally, 1968. Contributor of more than a dozen articles to psychology journals.

WORK IN PROGRESS: Continuing research on self-concept variables.

* * *

WYNDHAM, John
See HARRIS, John (Wyndham Parkes Lucas) Beynon

* * *

WYNDHAM, Lee
See HYNDMAN, Jane Andrews Lee

* * *

WYSCHOGROD, Michael 1928-

PERSONAL: Born September 28, 1928, in Berlin, Germany; came to United States in 1939, naturalized citizen, 1945; son of Paul (a chess master) and Margaret Wyschogrod; married Edith Shurer (a professor) in 1955; children: Daniel, Tamar. *Education:* City College (now of the City University of New York), B.S.S., 1949; Columbia University, Ph.D., 1953. *Home:* 151 West 86th St., New York, N.Y. 10024. *Office:* Department of Philosophy, Bernard M. Baruch College of the City University of New York, 17 Lexington Ave., New York, N.Y. 10010.

CAREER: Hunter College (now of the City University of New York), New York City, lecturer in philosophy, 1953-57; Bar-Ilan University, Ramat-Gan, Israel, assistant professor of philosophy, 1957-58; Hunter College, lecturer, 1958-59, assistant professor of philosophy, 1960-63; Bernard M. Baruch College of the City University of New York, New York City, assistant professor, 1963-66, associate professor, 1966-71, professor of philosophy, 1971—, head of department, 1974—. Assistant professor at New School for Social Research, summers, 1962, 1964, visiting professor, 1977-78; visiting lecturer at Jewish Theological Seminary of America, 1967-68; visiting associate professor at Dropsie College (now University), 1968-69, visiting professor, 1969-70. Associate of Columbia University seminar on religion, 1960—; consultant to Synagogue Council of America. *Awards, honors:* Research grants from Memorial Foundation for Jewish Culture, 1963, 1966.

WRITINGS: Kierkegaard and Heidegger: The Ontology of Existence, Routledge & Kegan Paul, 1954; (contributor) Marc H. Tannenbaum, Marvin R. Wilson, and A. James Rudin, editors, *Evangelicals and Jews in Conversation,* Baker Book, 1978; (with David Berger) *Jews and "Jewish Christianity",* Ktav, 1978. Contributor to *Encyclopedia Americana* and *Encyclopedia of Philsophy.* Contributor of about fifty articles and reviews to a wide variety of scholarly journals and popular magazines, including *Man and World, Kenyon Review, Humanist,* and *Commentary.* Member of editorial board of *Tradition,* 1960—, *Judaism,* 1965—, and *Journal of the American Academy of Religion,* 1978—.

WORK IN PROGRESS: A study of Jewish philosophical theology.

SIDELIGHTS: Wyschogrod wrote: "From the beginning, I have had two basic interests: Judaism and philosophy. In philosophy it was phenomenology and existentialism that attracted me because they dealt with ethico-religious questions. I studied Judaism under Rabbi Joseph Soloveitchik at Yeshiva University. In recent years, I have become particularly interested in the relationship between Judaism and Christianity, and especially the work of Karl Barth.

"I hope to write about Judaism's meaning for the contemporary world. Jewish theology needs deepening because Jews need to know who they are and what their history means."

Y

YAGGY, Elinor 1907-

PERSONAL: Born April 18, 1907, in Waterloo, Iowa; daughter of Samuel Edward (a minister) and Mabel (Felmley) Yaggy. *Education:* University of Idaho, B.A., 1924, M.A., 1939; University of Washington, Seattle, Ph.D., 1946. *Residence:* Seattle, Wash. *Office:* Department of English, University of Washington, Seattle, Wash. 98195.

CAREER: High school teacher of English in southern Idaho, 1929-39; University of Washington, Seattle, 1940-77, began as associate professor, became professor of English; writer, 1977—. *Member:* Modern Language Association of America, American Association of University Professors, Philological Association of the Pacific Coast (PAPC), Melville Society.

WRITINGS: (With Glenn Leggett) *Writing a Paper,* Ronald, 1955; *How to Write Your Term Paper,* Chandler Publishing, 1958, 4th edition, Harper, 1980. Contributor to literature journals.

WORK IN PROGRESS: A textbook on writing short stories; popular fiction.

SIDELIGHTS: Elinor Yaggy writes: "In 1958 I was teaching freshman English and was asked to write a book on research. Seeing the need for it, I wrote one which has been, fortunately, very well received. Any other writing I have done has been the result of a sudden interest in the particular subject I wrote about."

* * *

YAKOBSON, Sergius O. 1901-1979

OBITUARY NOTICE: Born May 9, 1901, in Moscow, Russia; died November 13, 1979, in Washington, D.C. Foreign affairs specialist and author. Yakobson was a Russian affairs specialist for the Library of Congress since 1941, and was named director of the Slavic and Central European division when it was established in 1951. Yakobson received an award from the American Association for the Advancement of Slavic Studies in 1972 for distinguished services in his field. He was a frequent contributor to journals, and authored *Conflict and Change in Soviet Historical Scholarship.* Obituaries and other sources: *American Men and Women of Science: The Social and Behavioral Sciences,* 12th edition, Bowker, 1973; *Washington Post,* November 15, 1979.

YANS-McLAUGHLIN, Virginia 1943-

PERSONAL: Born February 12, 1943, in Portchester, N.Y.; daughter of Frank (a building contractor) and Isabella (an assistant dress designer; maiden name, Ginocchi) Yans; divorced. *Education:* Skidmore College, B.A., 1964; State University of New York at Buffalo, M.A., 1966, Ph.D., 1970. *Office:* Department of History and Women's Studies, Douglass College, Rutgers University, New Brunswick, N.J. 08903.

CAREER: John Jay College of Criminal Justice of the City University of New York, New York City, instructor in history, 1970-71; Princeton University, Princeton, N.J., assistant professor of history, 1971-73; City College of the City University of New York, New York City, assistant professor of history, 1973-76; Sarah Lawrence College, Bronxville, N.Y., professor of history, 1977-78; Rutgers University, Douglass College, New Brunswick, N.J., associate professor of history and director of women's studies, 1978—. *Member:* American Historical Association, Organization of American Historians, Italian-American Historical Association. *Awards, honors:* National Endowment for the Humanities grant, 1976; Rockefeller Foundation fellowship, 1977-78; Howard Marraro Prize from American Historical Association, 1978, for *Family and Community.*

WRITINGS: *Immigration and the New Order,* Dushkin, 1973; (contributor) *Family and Community: Italian Immigrants in Buffalo, 1880-1930,* Cornell University Press, 1977; (contributor) M. Cantor and B. Laurie, editors, *Class, Sex, and the Woman Worker,* Greenwood Press, 1977. Contributor to history and social studies journals.

WORK IN PROGRESS: Research on Margaret Mead and on American ethnic groups.

SIDELIGHTS: Yans-McLaughlin told *CA:* "Although I am trained as a professional academic historian my writings are concerned with addressing one issue: How did ordinary men and women create their lives and their culture? My interest in Margaret Mead is not unrelated to humanistic concerns. What does a woman have to compromise, how must she design her life, what conflicts must she endure in order to achieve power and fame?"

* * *

YARDLEY, Richard Q(uincy) 1903-1979

OBITUARY NOTICE: Born March 11, 1903, in Baltimore,

Md.; died November 24, 1979, in Baltimore, Md. Cartoonist. Yardley was an editorial and political cartoonist for various newspapers, including the *Baltimore Evening Sun, Morning Sun,* and *Baltimore Sun.* He was associated with the latter of these for more than twenty years. Yardley created the syndicated comic strip, "Our Ancestors," and contributed cartoons to *New Yorker* and *Reporter.* Obituaries and other sources: *Who's Who in America,* 40th edition, Marquis, 1978; *New York Times,* November 25, 1979.

* * *

YATES, Gerard Francis 1907-1979

OBITUARY NOTICE: Born April 1, 1907, in Staten Island, N.Y.; died September 13, 1979, in Auriesville, N.Y. Jesuit priest, educator, editor, and writer. Yates was affiliated with Georgetown University for more than thirty years. Beginning as an instructor, he held many positions, including professor emeritus, dean of the graduate school, and director of international student programs. Yates was ordained a priest in 1936. He was the editor of *Papal Thought on the State,* and was a frequent contributor to Catholic publications. Yates was honored in 1979 by Georgetown University when their new field house was named after him. Obituaries and other sources: *American Men and Women of Science: The Social and Behavioral Sciences,* 12th edition, Bowker, 1973; *Who's Who in America,* 40th edition, Marquis, 1978; *Washington Post,* September 14, 1979.

* * *

YESHAYAHU, Yisrael 1910-1979

OBITUARY NOTICE: Born April 14, 1910, in Sana, Yemen; died June 20, 1979. Yeshayahu served as a speaker of the Israeli Parliament for five years before his political party was replaced by that of Prime Minster Menachem Begin in 1977. He was a minister of posts during the late 1960's, and was named secretary general of his Labor party in 1970. He was considered one of the foremost authorities on the Yemenite Jews, and authored books and articles on the subject. Obituaries and other sources: *New York Times,* June 21, 1979.

* * *

YEZIERSKA, Anzia 1885-1970

OBITUARY NOTICE: Born in 1885 in Russia; died November 21, 1970, in Ontario, Calif. Author. Yezierska is best known for her sympathetic stories about Jewish immigrants living on the lower east side of New York City in the 1920's. Her works include *Hungry Hearts, Bread Givers,* and *Children of Loneliness.* Obituaries and other sources: *The Oxford Companion to American Literature,* 4th edition, Oxford University Press, 1965.

* * *

YINGER, J(ohn) Milton 1916-

PERSONAL: Born July 25, 1916, in Quincy, Mich.; son of George D. (a minister) and Emma (a writer and speaker; maiden name, Bancroft) Yinger; married Winnie McHenry (a volunteer worker), July 20, 1941; children: Susan, John, Nancy. *Education:* DePauw University, B.A., 1937; Louisiana State University, M.A., 1939; University of Wisconsin—Madison, Ph.D., 1942. *Politics:* Democrat. *Religion:* Congregational. *Home:* 272 Oak St., Oberlin, Ohio 44074. *Office:* Department of Sociology-Anthropology, Oberlin College, King Building, Oberlin, Ohio 44074.

CAREER: Ohio Wesleyan University, Delaware, instructor, 1941-43, assistant professor, 1943-46, associate professor of sociology and anthropology, 1946-47; Oberlin College, Oberlin, Ohio, associate professor, 1947-52, professor of sociology and anthropology, 1952—, head of department, 1969-75. Visiting professor at University of Michigan, spring, 1958, University of Washington, Seattle, summer, 1959, University of Hawaii, spring and summer, 1961, summer, 1965, and Wayne State University, winter, 1971; senior specialist at East-West Center, Honolulu, 1968-69. *Member:* American Sociological Association (member of council and executive committee, 1965-68; president, 1976-77), American Anthropological Association (fellow), Society for the Scientific Study of Religion, Sigma Xi. *Awards, honors:* Shared in Anisfield-Wolf Award in Race Relations from *Saturday Review,* 1958, for *Racial and Cultural Minorities: An Analysis of Prejudice and Discrimination;* grant from U.S. Office of Education, 1965-70; Guggenheim fellowship, 1968-69; fellowship from National Endowment for the Humanities, 1976-77; visiting fellow of Clare College, Cambridge, 1976.

WRITINGS: Religion in the Struggle for Power: A Study in the Sociology of Religion, Duke University Press, 1946; (with George E. Simpson) *Racial and Cultural Minorities: An Analysis of Prejudice and Discrimination,* Harper, 1953, 4th edition, 1972; *Religion, Society, and the Individual,* Macmillan, 1957; *Sociology Looks at Religion,* Macmillan, 1963; *A Minority Group in American Society,* McGraw, 1965; *Toward a Field Theory of Behavior,* McGraw, 1965; *The Scientific Study of Religion,* Macmillan, 1970; (with Kiyoshi Ikeda, Frank Laycock, and Stephen Cutler) *Middle Start: An Experimental Study of Educational Enrichment in Early Adolescence,* Cambridge University Press, 1977; (editor with Cutler) *Major Social Issues: A Multidisciplinary View,* Free Press, 1978.

Contributor: H. E. Barnes, editor, *An Introduction to the History of Sociology,* University of Chicago Press, 1948; Robin M. Williams and Margaret W. Ryan, editors, *Schools in Transition,* University of North Carolina Press, 1954; Robert Merton, Leonard Broom, and Leonard Cottrell, editors, *Sociology Today,* Basic Books, 1959; R. W. Kernodle, editor, *Unsolved Issues in American Society,* College of William and Mary, 1960; Willem Veenhoven, editor, *Case Studies on Human Rights and Fundamental Freedoms,* Volume I, Nijhoff, 1975; Lewis Coser and Otto Larsen, editors, *The Uses of Controversy in Sociology,* Free Press, 1976; Gordon J. DiRenzo, editor, *We, the People: American Character and Social Change,* Greenwood Press, 1977.

Contributor to *International Encyclopedia of the Social Sciences, Handbook of Political Psychology,* and *Encyclopaedia Britannica.* Contributor of about thirty-five articles to scholarly journals, including *Urban Review, American Sociological Review, American Journal of Sociology, Daedalus, Antioch Review, Common Ground,* and *American Anthropologist.* Co-editor of *Annals of the American Academy of Political and Social Science,* 1957, 1978; associate editor of *Social Problems,* 1957-60, *American Sociological Review,* 1959-62, and *Journal of Conflict Resolution,* 1964-70.

WORK IN PROGRESS: Countercultures: Their Origins and Influences; Ethnicity in the Modern World.

SIDELIGHTS: Yinger's books have been translated into Italian, French, Spanish, Oriya, and Portuguese. He writes: "My aim as a writer has been to leap over boundaries, to try to bring some wholeness into the study of society and human behavior. In methodology I am an eclectic, with work in the humanistic tradition and in the empirical, quantitative tradition. In connection with my writing, and as an avocation, I have traveled extensively in Europe and Asia, seeking for a more comparative view of the human situation.

"The subjects of greatest interest to me now are ethnicity—its influence on social integration, justice, and social change in multi-ethnic societies around the world, and the cultural crisis of our time seen comparatively—the conditions that foster the malaise now so widely felt and the influence of the oppositional culture that spring from that malaise."

BIOGRAPHICAL/CRITICAL SOURCES: Journal for the Scientific Study of Religion, Volume XVII, number 3, 1978.

* * *

YOUNG, Alan R(oger) 1941-

PERSONAL: Born January 25, 1941, in Chelmsford, England; son of Robert Alec and Phyllis (Siggers) Young; married Margaret Haines, September 4, 1966 (separated, 1979); children: Eleanor May, Julian Blair. *Education:* University of Bristol, B.A. (with honors), 1963; University of East Africa, diploma in education, 1964; University of East Anglia, M.A., 1967; University of Alberta, Ph.D., 1970. *Residence:* Wolfville, Nova Scotia, Canada. *Office:* Department of English, Acadia University, Wolfville, Nova Scotia, Canada B0P 1X0.

CAREER: Government of Kenya, Kapsabet, education officer, 1964-66; Simon Fraser University, Burnaby, British Columbia, instructor in English, 1967-68; University of Alberta, Edmonton, lecturer in linguistics, 1969; Acadia University, Wolfville, Nova Scotia, assistant professor, 1970-75, associate professor of English, 1975—. Longman visiting fellow at University of Leeds, 1976-77. *Member:* Association of Canadian University Teachers of English, Shakespeare Association of America, Renaissance Society of America.

WRITINGS: (Author of introduction) Ernest Buckler, *Ox Bells and Fireflies,* McClelland & Stewart, 1974; *Ernest Buckler,* McClelland & Stewart, 1976; (author of introduction) Henry Peacham, *Emblemata Varia,* Scolar Press, 1976; (author of introduction) Buckler, *The Cruelest Month,* McClelland & Stewart, 1977; *Henry Peacham,* Twayne, 1979; *The English Prodigal Son Plays,* University of Salzburg, 1980. Contributor to history and literature journals.

WORK IN PROGRESS: A study of Thomas H. Raddall.

SIDELIGHTS: Young writes: "I am primarily concerned with the study of Canadian literature and English Renaissance literature. My writing reflects my research interests and indeed is the means by which I communicate the products of my academic studies. I like to think of myself as both critic and researcher. My goal might best be expressed in the words of Howard Mumford Jones: 'Our business, as I understand it, is to find out in a humble spirit of inquiry what literary masterpieces really say.'"

* * *

YOUNG, Stark 1881-1963

OBITUARY NOTICE: Born October 11, 1881, in Como, Miss.; died January 6, 1963. Educator, critic, poet, dramatist, essayist, editor, and novelist. Young retired from a teaching career in 1921 to become a full-time writer. Of his many plays, essays, and novels, *So Red the Rose* received the most acclaim. During the 1920's, Young was an important drama critic for the *New York Times, Theatre Arts Monthly,* and *New Republic.* Obituaries and other sources: *Who Was Who in America,* 4th edition, Marquis, 1968; *Longman Companion to Twentieth Century Literature,* Longman, 1970.

* * *

YOUNGER, Edward Eugene 1909-1979

OBITUARY NOTICE: Born June 29, 1909, in Pindall, Ark.; died June 23, 1979, in Charlottesville, Va. Educator and author. Younger first became associated with the University of Virginia in 1946, and remained there until his retirement in May, 1979. In addition to the post of professor of history, Younger served as chairman of the history department and, for three years, acted as dean of the graduate school of arts and letters. He was a Fulbright professor at the University of Allahabad from 1957-58, and an Ernest J. King visiting professor at the Naval War College from 1960-61. Younger authored *John A. Kasson: Diplomacy and Politics From Lincoln to McKinley,* a winner of the Phi Beta Kappa Prize in 1955, *Inside the Confederate Government: Diary of R.G.H. Kean,* a Civil War Book Club selection, and was editing a book of essays at the time of his death, entitled *Governors of Virginia Since 1860.* Obituaries and other sources: *Directory of American Scholars,* Volume I: *History,* 6th edition, Bowker, 1974; *Who's Who in America,* 40th edition, Marquis, 1978; *Washington Post,* June 26, 1979.

Z

ZELMER, A(dam) C(harles) Lynn 1943-

PERSONAL: Born March 19, 1943, in Calgary, Alberta, Canada; son of Hubert A. and Winona (May) Zelmer; married Amy Elliott (a university professor), December 16, 1969; children: Jennifer. *Education:* University of Alberta at Calgary, B.Ed., 1965; Stout State University, M.S., 1969; further graduate study at State University of New York at Buffalo, 1969-70. *Home and office address:* P.O. Box 8268, Station F, Edmonton, Alberta, Canada T6H 4P1.

CAREER: Public school teacher in Calgary, Alberta, 1964-68; University of Alberta, Edmonton, assistant professor of educational media, 1968-73; International Communications Institute, Edmonton, Alberta, consultant (with clients in India, Sri Lanka, the Maldives, and Malaysia), 1973—.

WRITINGS: *Community Media Handbook,* Scarecrow, 1973, 2nd edition, 1979; *Pretesting of Text and Visuals in Sri Lanka,* UNICEF, 1978; *Pretesting of Visuals in the Maldives,* UNICEF, 1978. Author of multi-media programs.

WORK IN PROGRESS: Simulations and learning games for education of health professionals.

SIDELIGHTS: Zelmer describes his primary interests as "development education, appropriate use of technology, and non-formal education."

ZOSKY, Brenda 1942-

PERSONAL: Born January 24, 1942, in Toronto, Ontario, Canada; daughter of Barry Edward (a real estate broker) and Katherine (a real estate agent; maiden name, Rosen) Perlman; married Jack Gerald Zosky (an oral surgeon), June 12, 1962 (separated, April, 1978); children: Dana, Jennifer and Stacy (twins). *Education:* University of Toronto, B.A., 1972; attended Ryerson Polytechnical School, 1973-74. *Residence:* Balmoral Ave., Toronto, Ontario, Canada. *Office:* *Toronto Star,* 1 Yonge St., Toronto, Ontario, Canada.

CAREER/WRITINGS: *Toronto Star,* Toronto, Ontario, reporter, 1974—. Notable assignments include the Deborah Ellis child abuse case, a series on involuntary committal to mental hospitals, and a study of the wealthy but unhappy work force. *Awards, honors:* National newspaper award for feature writing in Canada, 1977.

WORK IN PROGRESS: A collection of short stories about middle class marriage.

SIDELIGHTS: Zosky told *CA:* "I began as a journalist at the age of 32 after almost a ten-year hiatus at home raising three children and getting my university education part time. Now I specialize in writing about social and legal issues for the *Toronto Star.*"